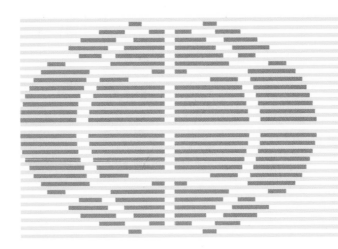

The World Book Atlas

Published by
World Book Encyclopedia, Inc.

A subsidiary of World Book–Childcraft International, Inc.
Chicago London Sydney Tokyo Toronto

The World Book Atlas

Copyright © 1980, 1979 by Rand McNally & Company

Our Planet Earth section, pages 1A-73A inclusive,
Copyright © by Mitchell Beazley Publishers Limited 1973
as The Good Earth. Fully revised 1976

Printed in the United States of America

Library of Congress Card Number 80-51751
ISBN 0-7166-3108-3

1981 Printing

Preface

The World Book Atlas serves both the specific needs of students and the general needs of the office and home. It is an atlas designed to meet the educational needs of those in school, and also to provide an opportunity for browsing and informal study.

The use of maps is essential to a thorough understanding of the world in which we live. The World Book Atlas brings together different kinds of maps, demonstrating meaningful relationships that make it possible for a user to study a particular area of the Earth and compare it with other areas. The World Book Atlas is also designed to be an effective reference tool that answers specific questions about the land forms, weather, and climate of the Earth, and about the location of countries, cities, rivers, mountains, and other geographic features.

The World Book Atlas combines thematic and general reference maps with charts, tables, and special illustrative material to tell the story of our Earth. Special emphasis has been given to world metropolitan areas, which have become vital in today's increasingly urbanized environment.

The World Book Atlas is divided into six major sections. It opens with the exciting story of Our Planet Earth, told with fascinating illustrations and informative text. This section deals with subjects ranging from the solar system to the control of pollution. Next, a comprehensive section of World Thematic Maps uses maps and other graphics to present information on the world distribution of major geographic, social, and economic elements. The third section is devoted to maps of 62 of the world's Major Cities. The main section of the Atlas is devoted to Country and Regional Maps of the world arranged continent by continent. Appropriate thematic maps are also included in this section. The final map section—Ocean Floor Maps—provides the reader with a view of one of the Earth's last great frontiers, the ocean floors. Handy reference tables and indexes—including up-to-date population tables, a glossary of foreign geographical terms, a separate index for the major city maps, and a pronouncing index for the reference maps—complete the Atlas.

Each section of the Atlas has a separate introduction. Appropriate legends for the maps in the major city, country, and regional sections appear there.

The World Book Atlas represents the combined efforts of the cartographic and research staff of Rand McNally and Company and the editors, designers, and researchers of The World Book Encyclopedia.

The world thematic maps and country and regional maps originally appeared in the well-known Goode's School Atlas, first published more than 50 years ago.

Cartographic Editors

Edward B. Espenshade, Jr., Ph.D.
Professor of Geography at Northwestern University. Dr. Espenshade has served as President of the Association of American Geographers; Chairman of the Earth-Science Division of the National Academy of Sciences—National Research Council; and Chairman of the Commission on College Geography of the Association of American Geographers.

Joel L. Morrison, Ph.D.
Associate Professor of Geography and Director of the Cartographic Laboratory of the University of Wisconsin at Madison. Dr. Morrison's specialties include cartographic communication and automation in map-making.

Contents

Scale and Projection

Map Scale. A map can only show a reduced representation of the Earth's surface or any part of it. Therefore, the reader has to answer the question: What is the relationship between the size of the map and the actual size of the portion of the Earth it depicts? This proportional relationship is the *scale* of a map. To help the reader, most maps in this Atlas give the scale in three ways—as a ratio, in written form, and graphically.

As a *ratio*, the scale of a map is expressed as, for example, 1:4,000,000. This means one inch on the map represents four million inches on the Earth. In *written form*, this ratio is expressed as: "one inch to sixty-four miles." This means one inch on the map represents sixty-four miles on the Earth. *Graphically*, scale is shown with a bar scale, on which distance calculations may be made directly.

Map Projections. There is no way to represent the curved surface of the globe on the flat surface of a map without some distortion of distance, direction, shape, or area. Only a globe can show the Earth without distortion. On large-scale maps that cover only a few square miles, this distortion is negligible. However, on maps that represent large areas, such as a large country, a continent, or the whole world, the distortion is considerable. Unless understood, distortion may result in serious misconceptions on the part of the reader.

A *map projection* is a way to transfer locations on the Earth to locations on a map. The number of possible projections is unlimited and several hundred of them are used by cartographers. None avoids some distortion of the spatial relationships that only a globe can show truthfully. No single flat map can accurately show area, shape, angle, and scale. However, a cartographer can select a projection that will accurately depict a particular property, such as shape. It is also possible to compromise by limiting the distortion of one or more properties at the expense of the others.

Most of the maps used in this Atlas are drawn on projections that give equality of area, good land and ocean shapes, and parallels of latitude that are parallel. However, the maps do have distortions and the reader should make allowances for them. One of the best ways to understand the nature of a map's distortion is to compare the latitude and longitude grid lines of the flat map with the grid of the globe. To do this, the reader should understand the basic characteristics of a globe grid:

1. All meridians of longitude are equal in length and meet at the poles.

2. All parallels of latitude are parallel.

3. The length, or circumference, of the parallels decreases from the equator to the poles. At 60° latitude, the circumference of the parallel is half the circumference of the equator.

4. Distances along the meridians between any two parallels are equal.

5. All parallels and meridians meet at right angles.

For example, the map on page 47 uses a projection that produces meridians and parallels that are straight lines which meet at right angles. But all the parallels are the same length, which is not true on a globe. This results in considerable exaggeration of areas in the higher latitudes, near the poles. For example, northern Canada looks much larger in proportion to the rest of the world than it really is. In the projection used on pages 4-5, parallels and meridians meet at oblique angles in higher latitudes, which distorts land shapes in such areas as Alaska and Greenland. Their areas, however, are accurately portrayed in relation to each other.

Some of the more commonly used projections and an indication of their properties are shown on the following pages.

PROJECTIONS

A map projection is merely an orderly system of parallels and meridians on which a flat map can be drawn. There are hundreds of projections, but no one represents the earth's spherical surface without some distortion. The distortion is relatively small for most practical purposes when a small part of the sphere is projected. For larger areas, a sacrifice of some property is necessary.

Most projections are designed to preserve on the flat map some particular property of the sphere. By varying the systematic arrangement or spacing of the latitude and longitude lines, a projection may be made either equal-area or conformal. Although most projections are derived from mathematical formulas, some are easier to visualize if thought of as projected upon a plane, or upon a cone or cylinder which is then unrolled into a plane surface. Thus, many projections are classified as plane (azimuthal), conic, or cylindrical.

For a fuller discussion of map projections, see Preface. Figures with asterisks indicate projections used in this atlas.

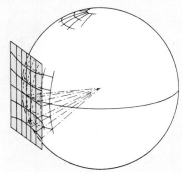

(A) GNOMONIC PROJECTION

A geometric or perspective projection on a tangent plane with the origin point at the center of the globe. Shapes and distances rapidly become increasingly distorted away from the center of the projection. Important in navigation, because all straight lines are great circles.

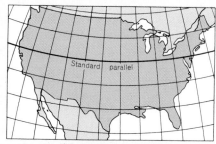

(B) LAMBERT EQUAL AREA PROJECTION*

A mathematically designed azimuthal equal-area projection. Excellent for continental areas. For larger areas away from the center, distortion of distances and shapes is appreciable.

FIGURE 1.–TYPICAL PLANE PROJECTIONS

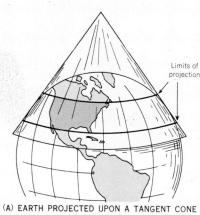

(A) EARTH PROJECTED UPON A TANGENT CONE

(B) CONE CUT FROM BASE TO APEX

A perspective projection on a tangent cone with the origin point at the center of the globe. At the parallel of tangency, all elements of the map are

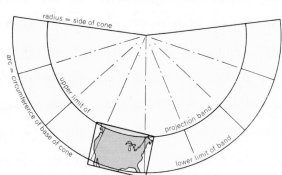

(C) CONE DEVELOPED INTO A PLANE SURFACE

true- angles, distances, shapes, areas. Away from the tangent parallel, distances increase rapidly, giving bad distortion of shapes and areas.

FIGURE 2.–SIMPLE CONIC PROJECTIONS

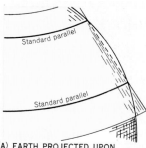

(A) EARTH PROJECTED UPON AN INTERSECTING CONE

This modification of the conic has two standard parallels, or lines of intersection. It is not an equal-area projection, the space being reduced in size between the standard parallels and

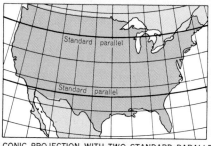

(B) CONIC PROJECTION WITH TWO STANDARD PARALLELS*

progressively enlarged beyond the standard parallels. Careful selection of the standard parallels provides, however, good representation for areas of limited latitudinal extent.

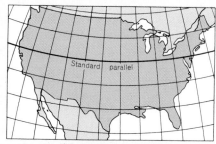

(C) BONNE PROJECTION*

An equal-area modification of the conic principle. Distances are true along all parallels and the central meridian; but away from it, increasing obliqueness of intersections and longitudinal distances, with their attendant distortion of shapes, limits the satisfactory area.

FIGURE 3.–MODIFIED CONIC PROJECTIONS

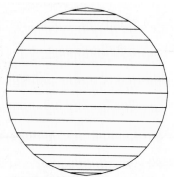

(A) EARTH CONSIDERED AS FORMED BY BASES OF CONES

This variation is not equal-area. Parallels are non-concentric circles truly divided. Distances along the straight central meridian are also true, but

(B) DEVELOPMENT OF THE CONICAL BASES

along the curving meridians are increasingly exaggerated. Representation is good near the central meridian, but away from it there is marked distortion.

(C) POLYCONIC PROJECTION*

FIGURE 4.–POLYCONIC PROJECTION

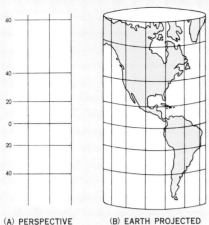

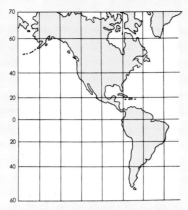

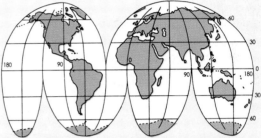

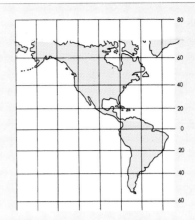

(A) PERSPECTIVE PROJECTION

A perspective projection on a tangent cylinder. Because of rapidly increasing distortion away from the line of tangency and the lack of any special advantage, it is rarely used.

(B) EARTH PROJECTED UPON A CYLINDER

(C) MERCATOR CONFORMAL PROJECTION

Mercator's modification increases the latitudinal distances in the same proportion as longitudinal distances are increased. Thus, at any point shapes are true, but areas become increasingly exaggerated. Of value in navigation, because a line connecting any two points gives the true direction between them.

(D) MILLER PROJECTION*

This recent modification is neither conformal nor equal-area. Whereas shapes are less accurate than on the Mercator, the exaggeration of areas has been reduced somewhat.

FIGURE 5.—CYLINDRICAL PROJECTIONS

(A) MOLLWEIDE'S HOMOLOGRAPHIC PROJECTION

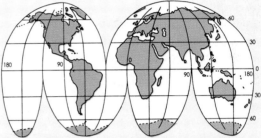

(B) GOODE'S INTERRUPTED HOMOLOGRAPHIC PROJECTION

(C) SINUSOIDAL PROJECTION*

(D) GOODE'S INTERRUPTED HOMOLOSINE PROJECTION*

Although each of these projections is equal-area, differences in the spacing and arrangement of latitude and longitude lines result in differences in the distribution and relative degree of the shape and distance distortion within each grid. On the homolographic, there is no uniformity in scale. It is different on each parallel and each meridian. On the sinusoidal, only distances along all latitudes and the central meridian are true. The homolosine combines the homolographic, for areas poleward of 40°, with the sinusoidal. The principle of interruption permits each continent in turn the advantage of being in the center of the projection, resulting in better shapes.

FIGURE 6.—EQUAL AREA PROJECTIONS OF THE WORLD

A conformal projection in which a selected great circle of the globe is considered as the "equator" of the ordinary Mercator projection, with the cylinder tangent along the great circle. It is used chiefly for charts of great-circle air routes between distant cities.

FIGURE 7.—TRANSVERSE MERCATOR PROJECTION

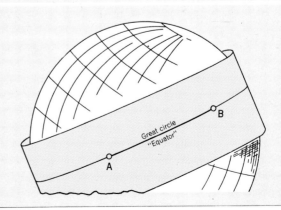

Our Planet Earth

Our home is the Earth, a small planet that revolves around the Sun. The Sun is a star, but only one of the hundred thousand million which exist in the local system of stars, or galaxy, of which we are a part. Our own galaxy, we now know, is just one of millions of other galaxies in the universe.

Scientists generally believe that the Earth was formed about 4.5 billion years ago. Since that time the planet's surface has been ceaselessly altered and its present physical features are the result of numerous processes that interact with each other, usually very slowly, but sometimes very violently. The land is eroded by the wind and rain, washed away by the rivers and seas, and reduced to sediment that builds up elsewhere. Other changes are created by more spectacular events, such as explosive volcanic eruptions and vast out-pourings of molten lava. The records of these processes can be seen in the rocks themselves.

There are various theories about the exact origin of life on Earth. But one thing is certain, the planet upon which life came into being was very different from the world we know now. With agonizing slowness, through hundreds of millions of years, life gradually changed with the environment. The struggle to stay alive produced new plants and animals of millions of varieties, from tiny bugs to giant whales and from speck-like algae to towering trees. These formed a thin frosting of life over the surface of the planet. It was into this world that human beings eventually emerged.

Because of the vast size of the Earth, people long believed that its natural resources could never be exhausted. However, the dramatic growth in population and industrial and agricultural demands has made it obvious that our planet has limits, and in some instances these limits are being fast approached. Of course some new sources remain to be discovered and others will be replaced by man-made material, but we no longer can afford to waste our heritage.

The Sun is the controlling body of the solar system and is far more massive than all its planets combined. Even Jupiter, much the largest of the planets, has a diameter only about one-tenth that of the Sun. The solar system is divided into two main parts. The inner region includes four relatively small, solid planets: Mercury, Venus, the Earth and Mars. Beyond the orbit of Mars comes a wide gap in which move many thousands of small minor planets or asteroids, some of which are little more than rocks. Further out come the four giants: Jupiter, Saturn, Uranus and Neptune. Pluto, on the fringe of the system, is a curious little planet; it appears to be in a class of its own, but at present very little is known about it and even its size is a matter for conjecture. Maps of the solar system can be misleading in that they tend to give a false idea about distance. The outer planets are very widely separated. For example, Saturn is further away from Uranus than it is from the Earth.

The contrasting planets

The inner, or terrestrial, planets have some points in common, but a greater number of differences. Mercury, the planet closest to the Sun, has almost no atmosphere and that of Mars is very thin; but Venus, strikingly similar to the Earth in size and mass, has a dense atmosphere made up chiefly of carbon dioxide, and a surface temperature of over 400°C. The giant planets are entirely different. At least in their outer layers they are made up of gas, like a star; but, unlike a star, they have no light of their own and shine only by reflecting the light of their star, the Sun. Several of the planets have moons. The Earth has one (or it may be our partner in a binary system), Jupiter has at least 13, Saturn 10 (discounting its rings), Uranus five and Neptune two. Mars also has two satellites but these are less than 15 mi (24 km) in diameter and of a different type from the Earth's Moon. The Earth is unique in the solar system in having oceans on its surface and an atmosphere made up chiefly of nitrogen and oxygen. It is the only planet suited to life of terrestrial type. It is not now believed that highly evolved life can exist on any other planet in the Sun's family, though it is still possible that some primitive life forms may exist on Mars.

Observing the planets

Five of the planets, Mercury, Venus, Mars, Jupiter and Saturn, were known to the inhabitants of the Earth in very ancient times. They are starlike in aspect but easy to distinguish because, unlike the stars, they seem to wander slowly about the sky whereas the true stars appear to hold their position for century after century. The so-called proper motions of the stars are too slight to be noticed by the naked eye, but they can be measured by modern techniques. Mercury and Venus always appear to be in the same part of the sky as the Sun. Mercury is never prominent but Venus is dazzlingly bright, partly because its upper clouds are highly reflective and partly because it is close; it can come within 25,000,000 mi (40,000,000 km), only about 100 times as far as the Moon. Jupiter is generally very bright, as is Mars when it is well placed. Saturn is also conspicuous to the naked eye, but Uranus is only just visible and Neptune and Pluto are much fainter.

The Sun's active surface *right*

The structure of a star, such as the Sun, is immensely complex. The very concept of its surface is hard to define, and the size of the Sun depends on the wavelength of the light with which it is viewed. Using the 'hydrogen alpha' wavelength the bright surface of the Sun, known as the photosphere, appears as shown right, above. The surface, at about 5500 °C, is dotted with light and dark patches as a result of the violent upcurrents of hotter gas and cooler areas between them. Larger, darker regions are sunspots (right), temporary but very large disturbances.

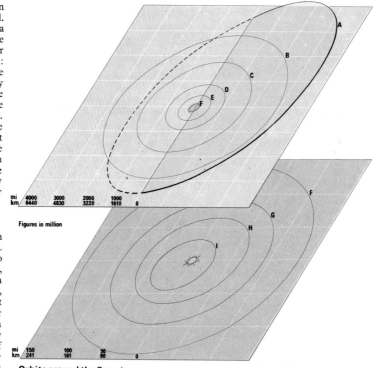

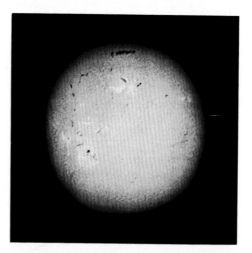

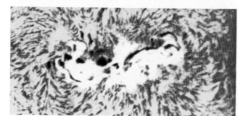

Orbits around the Sun *above*
The Sun's nine known planets, and the asteroids, describe heliocentric orbits in the same direction. But some planetary orbits are highly eccentric, while some asteroids are both eccentric and steeply inclined. The outermost planet, Pluto, passes within the orbit of Neptune, while one asteroid reaches almost to the radius of Saturn. Over 350 years ago Johannes Kepler showed that the planets do not move in perfect circles, and found that the line joining each planet to the Sun sweeps out a constant area in a given time. so that speed is greatest close to the Sun.

A	Pluto
B	Neptune
C	Uranus
D	Saturn
E	Jupiter
F	Mars
G	Earth
H	Venus
I	Mercury

mi / km scale: 4000/6440 3000/4830 2000/3220 1000/1610 0
Figures in million

mi / km scale: 150/241 100/161 50/80 0

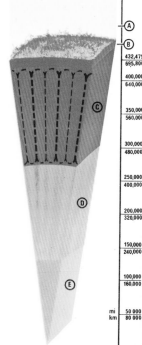

The Sun's structure *right*

The Sun is made up of highly dissimilar regions. This narrow sector includes the inner part of the corona (A) which, though very diffuse, has a temperature of some 1,000,000 °C. Into it leap solar prominences, 'flames' thousands of miles long which arch along the local magnetic field from the chromosphere (B), the outer layer of the Sun proper, which covers the visible photosphere with a layer of variable, highly mobile and rarefied gas about 6000 mi (10000 km) thick. Inside the Sun the outer layer (C) of gas is in constant movement and transfers heat from the interior. Inner region D is thought to transfer energy mainly by radiation. The innermost zone of all (E), the conditions of which can only be surmised but are thought to include a temperature of some 15,000,000 °C, sustains the energy of the Sun (and its planets) by continuous fusion of hydrogen into helium.

mi / km:
1,250,000 / 2,000,000
432,475 / 695,800
400,000 / 640,000
350,000 / 560,000
300,000 / 480,000
250,000 / 400,000
200,000 / 320,000
150,000 / 240,000
100,000 / 160,000
50,000 / 80,000

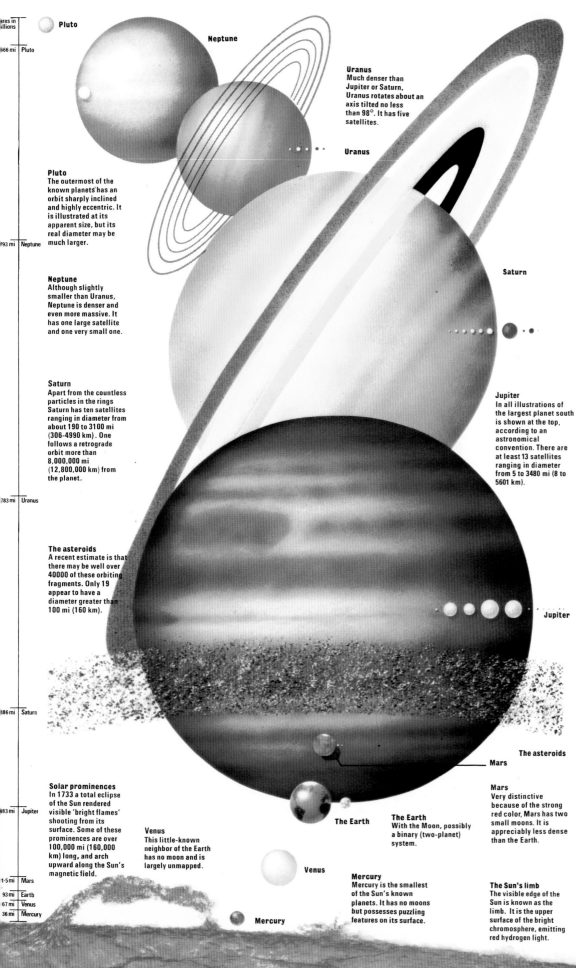

Pluto

Neptune

Uranus
Much denser than
Jupiter or Saturn,
Uranus rotates about an
axis tilted no less
than 98°. It has five
satellites.

Uranus

Pluto
The outermost of the
known planets has an
orbit sharply inclined
and highly eccentric. It
is illustrated at its
apparent size, but its
real diameter may be
much larger.

Saturn

Neptune
Although slightly
smaller than Uranus,
Neptune is denser and
even more massive. It
has one large satellite
and one very small one.

Saturn
Apart from the countless
particles in the rings
Saturn has ten satellites
ranging in diameter from
about 190 to 3100 mi
(306-4990 km). One
follows a retrograde
orbit more than
8,000,000 mi
(12,800,000 km) from
the planet.

Jupiter
In all illustrations of
the largest planet south
is shown at the top,
according to an
astronomical
convention. There are
at least 13 satellites
ranging in diameter
from 5 to 3480 mi (8 to
5601 km).

The asteroids
A recent estimate is that
there may be well over
40000 of these orbiting
fragments. Only 19
appear to have a
diameter greater than
100 mi (160 km).

Jupiter

The asteroids

Mars

Mars
Very distinctive
because of the strong
red color, Mars has two
small moons. It is
appreciably less dense
than the Earth.

Solar prominences
In 1733 a total eclipse
of the Sun rendered
visible 'bright flames'
shooting from its
surface. Some of these
prominences are over
100,000 mi (160,000
km) long, and arch
upward along the Sun's
magnetic field.

Venus
This little-known
neighbor of the Earth
has no moon and is
largely unmapped.

The Earth

The Earth
With the Moon, possibly
a binary (two-planet)
system.

Venus

Mercury
Mercury is the smallest
of the Sun's known
planets. It has no moons
but possesses puzzling
features on its surface.

The Sun's limb
The visible edge of the
Sun is known as the
limb. It is the upper
surface of the bright
chromosphere, emitting
red hydrogen light.

Mercury

The solar system *left*
The Sun is the major body in the solar system. It lies 30000 light-years from the center of our galaxy and takes about 200 million years to complete one journey around it. There are nine planets and their satellites in the system, as well as comets and various minor bodies such as meteoroids. The diagram on the left shows the upper limb of the Sun (bottom) and the main constituent members of the solar system very greatly condensed into a smaller space. To indicate the amount of the radial compression, the limb of the Sun is drawn for a near-sphere of 5 ft (1.52 m) diameter. On this scale the Earth would be about 420 ft (127 m) away and the outermost planet Pluto, no less than 3 mi (4.9 km) distant.

Pluto, discovered in 1930, has a very eccentric orbit, with a radius varying between 2766 and 4566 million mi (4500 and 7400 million kilometers). Being so far from the Sun, it is extremely cold, and probably has no atmosphere.

Neptune, discovered in 1846, has a diameter of 30760 mi (49500 km) and is made up of gas, although little is known of its interior. It orbits the Sun once in 164¾ years. Seen through binoculars it is a small bluish disk.

Uranus, discovered in 1781, is apparently similar to Neptune, but less massive. Although faintly visible to the naked eye, even large telescopes show little detail upon its greenish surface.

Saturn is the second largest planet, its equatorial diameter being 75100 mi (120,900 km). Visually it is unlike any other heavenly body, because of its equatorial system of rings made up of particles of various sizes. The planet itself is less dense than water and at least its outer layers are gaseous.

Jupiter, the largest planet, has an equatorial diameter of 88700 mi (142,700 km), but its rapid spin, once every 9¾ hours, makes it very flattened at the poles. It appears to have cloud belts, possibly of liquid ammonia, and various spots, of which the great red spot seems to be permanent.

The asteroids, a mass of apparent planetary material ranging in size from dust up to one lump about as large as the British Isles, orbit mainly between Mars and Jupiter, though some have eccentric orbits which approach the Earth.

Mars is about 4200 mi (6760 km) in diameter. It has a thin atmosphere, mainly of carbon dioxide, and its surface is pitted with Moon-like craters. It is not thought today that the planet contains any life.

The Earth/Moon system is today regarded as a double planet rather than a planet and satellite. The Moon has an average distance from Earth of 238,857 mi (384,403 km) and it is now known that it has never contained life.

Venus is almost the twin of the Earth in size and mass. It is too hot to contain life, and its very dense atmosphere is mainly carbon dioxide. It has a year of 224¾ Earth days, and it spins on its axis once every 243 Earth days.

Mercury, the innermost planet, is only about 3100 mi (5000 km) in diameter, and has lost almost all of its atmosphere. Like Venus it shows phases, but it is always close to the Sun when viewed from the Earth and cannot be seen clearly.

Earth's Companion: The Moon

The Moon is our companion in space. Its mean distance from the Earth is less than a quarter of a million miles – it varies between 221,460 miles (356,410 km) and 252,700 miles (406,685 km) – and it was the first world other than our Earth to come within the range of man's space probes. At first mere masses, these then became instrument packages and finally spacecraft carrying men. With their aid our knowledge of the Moon has been vastly increased in the past decade. Astronauts Neil Armstrong and Edwin Aldrin made the first human journey to the lunar surface in July 1969, and the Moon has since been subjected to detailed and direct investigation.

The mean diameter of the Moon is 2158 miles (3473 km), and its mass is 1/81st as much as that of the Earth. Despite this wide difference the ratio is much less than that between other planets and their moons, and the Earth/Moon system is now widely regarded as a double planet rather than as a planet and satellite. The Moon's mean density is less than that of the Earth, and it may lack a comparable heavy core. Escape velocity from the lunar surface is only 1.5 mi/sec (2.4 km/sec), and this is so low that the Moon has lost any atmosphere it may once have had. To Earth life it is therefore an extremely hostile world. Analysis of lunar rock brought back to Earth laboratories and investigated by Soviet probes on the Moon has so far revealed no trace of any life. The Moon appears to have always been sterile.

Much of the surface of the Moon comprises large grey plains, mis-called 'maria'(seas), but most of it is extremely rough. There are great ranges of mountains, isolated peaks and countless craters which range from tiny pits up to vast enclosures more than 150 miles (240 km) in diameter. Many of the craters have central mountains or mountain-groups. Some of the larger craters show signs of having been produced by volcanic action, while others appear to have resulted from the impacts of meteorites.

The Moon rotates slowly, performing one complete turn on its axis every 27 days, 7 hours, 43 minutes. It always presents the same face to the Earth. But in October 1959 the Soviet probe *Lunik 3* photographed the hidden rear hemisphere and it has since been mapped in detail. It contains no large 'seas'. The appearance of the lunar surface depends strongly on the angle at which it is viewed and the direction of solar illumination. In the photograph on the right, taken from a height of about 70 miles (115 km) with the Earth having once more come into full view ahead, the lunar surface looks deceptively smooth; in fact, there is practically no level ground anywhere in the field of vision. The lunar horizon is always sharply defined, because there is no atmosphere to cause blurring or distortion. For the same reason, the sky seen from the Moon is always jet black.

Full Moon *below*
This striking photograph was taken by the *Apollo 11* astronauts in July 1969. It shows parts of both the Earth-turned and far hemispheres. The dark plain near the center is the Mare Crisium.

Earthrise *above*
This view of the Earth rising was visible to the crew of
Apollo 10 in May 1969 as they orbited the Moon 70 miles
(112 km) above the surface. They had just come round
from the Moon's rear hemisphere.

Eclipses

Once regarded as terrifying actions of angry gods,
eclipses are today merely useful. They provide a
different view of the Sun and Moon that opens up
fresh information. In a lunar eclipse the Earth passes
directly between the Sun and Moon; in a solar eclipse
the Moon passes between Sun and Earth. Both the
Earth and Moon constantly cast a shadow comprising
a dark inner cone surrounded by a region to which
part of the sunlight penetrates. A body passing
through the outer shadow experiences a partial
eclipse, while the inner cone causes a total eclipse in
which all direct sunlight is cut off.

A total solar eclipse is magnificent. The bright star
is blocked out by a black Moon, but around it the
Sun's atmosphere flashes into view. The pearly
corona of thin gas can be seen extending a million
miles from the Sun. Closer to the surface huge
'prominences' of red hydrogen leap into space and
curve back along the solar magnetic field. In a partial
solar eclipse these things cannot be seen, while in a
total eclipse caused by the Moon at its greatest
distance from Earth a ring of the Sun is left visible.
As the Moon's orbit is not in the same plane as the
Earth's, total solar eclipses occur very rarely, on
occasions when the tip of the Moon's dark shadow
crosses the Earth as a spot 169 miles (272 km) wide.

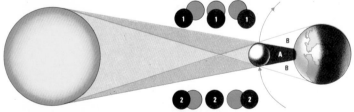

Eclipses *left and below*
When the Moon passes in
front of the Sun as in
sequence 1 its shadow B
causes a partial solar
eclipse (below, left, taken
21 November 1966).
But in the case of sequence
2, shadow cone A gives a
total eclipse (below, right,
15 February 1961).

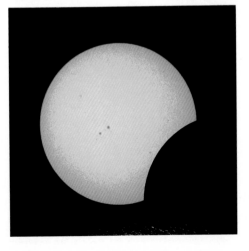

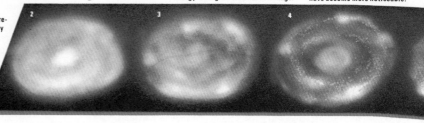

1 According to the most widely accepted theory, (the 'accretion' theory) the solar system originally consisted only of a mass of tenuous gas, and dust. There was no true Sun, and there was no production of nuclear energy. The gas was made up chiefly of hydrogen, with occasional random condensations.

2 Gravitational forces now cause the cloud to shrink and assume a more regular shape. Its density and mass near the center increase, but there are still no nuclear processes.

3 The gas cloud begins to assume the form of a regular disk. The infant Sun begins to shine - by the energy from gravitational shrinkage.

4 Material is thrown off from the Sun to join that already in the solar cloud, whose condensations have become more noticeable.

How did the Earth come into existence? This question has intrigued mankind for centuries, but it was not until the start of true science that plausible theories were advanced. Although some theories held sway for many years, they were eventually deposed by the discovery of some fatal flaw. Even today, it is impossible to be sure that the main problem has been solved, but at least some concrete facts exist as a guide. It is now reasonably certain that the age of the Earth is of the order of 4550-4700 million years. The other planets are presumably about the same age, since they were probably formed by the same process in the same epoch.

Several centuries ago Archbishop Ussher of Armagh maintained that the world had come into being at a definite moment in the year 4004 BC. This estimate was made on purely religious grounds, and it soon became clear that the Earth is much older. In 1796 the French astronomer Laplace put forward the famous Nebular Hypothesis, according to which the Sun and the planets were formed from a rotating cloud of gas which shrank under the influence of gravitation. As it shrank, the cloud shed gaseous rings, each of which condensed into a planet. This would mean that the outer planets were older than those closer to the Sun which itself would represent the remaining part of the gas cloud.

The Nebular Hypothesis was accepted for many years, but eventually serious mathematical weaknesses were found in it. Next came a number of tidal theories according to which the Earth and other planets were formed from a cigar-shaped tongue of matter torn from the Sun by the gravitational pull of a passing star. The first plausible theory of this kind came from the English astronomer Sir James Jeans, but this too was found to be mathematically untenable and the idea had to be given up.

Most modern theories assume that the planets were formed by accretion from a rotating solar cloud of gas and finely-dispersed dust. If the Sun were originally attended by such a cloud, this cloud would, over a sufficiently long period of time, become a flat disk.

If random concentration had become sufficiently massive, it would draw in extra material by virtue of its gravitational attraction, forming 'proto-planets'. When the Sun began to radiate strongly, part of the mass of each proto-planet would be driven off due to the high temperatures, leaving a solar system of the kind that exists today.

The fact that such an evolutionary sequence can be traced emphasizes that in talking about the origin of the Earth we are considering only a small part of a continuous story. What will become of the Earth in the far future? The Sun is radiating energy because of the nuclear process within it: hydrogen is being converted into helium causing mass to be lost with a resulting release of energy. However, when the supply of hydrogen begins to run low, the Sun must change radically. It will move towards a red giant stage swelling and engulfing the Earth. Fortunately, this will not happen for at least another 6000 million years, but eventually the Sun which sustains our planet will finally destroy it.

Alternative theories

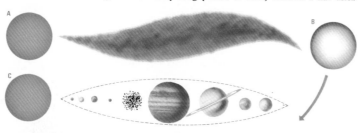

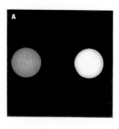

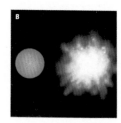

Contracting nebula *above* Laplace suggested that a contracting nebula might shed gas which then condensed.

Tidal theories *above* In 1917 Sir James Jeans postulated that Sun A was attracted to another star B which passed at close range. A cloud of matter was drawn off by their gravitational attraction. Star B moved on while the cloud condensed to form planets circling our Sun at C.

A violent beginning *above* One of the theories of how the solar system came to be formed assumes that the Sun once had a binary companion star. This exploded as a supernova (above) and was blown off as a white dwarf

16 As the 'fuel' runs out, the radiation pressure falls, and under internal gravity the Sun will collapse inwards changing in only 50000 years from a red giant into a super-dense white dwarf.

17 As a white dwarf, the Sun will continue to radiate feebly for an immense period. At last all radiation must cease, and the Sun will remain as a dead, dark globe - a black dwarf.

15 By now all the inner planets will have long since been destroyed. The Sun will become unstable, reaching the most violent stage of its career as a red giant, with a vast, relatively cool surface and an intensely hot, dense core.

14 When the center of the Sun has reached another critical temperature, the helium will begin to 'burn' giving the so-called 'helium flash'. After a temporary contraction the Sun will then swell out to a diameter 400 times that at present.

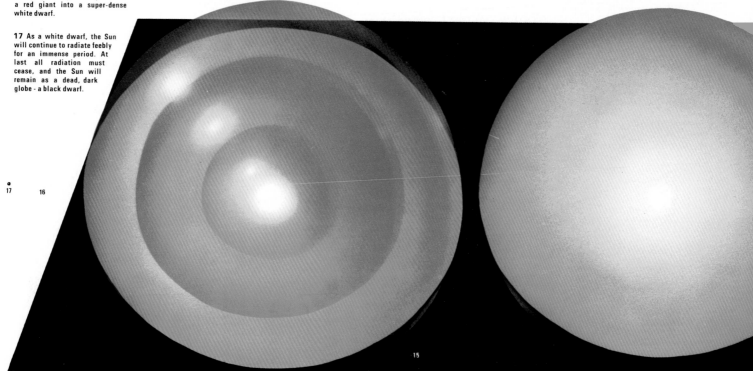

5 The Sun, still contracting, continues to radiate because of gravitational effects. More and more of the solar cloud collects into the condensations.

6 The Sun, surrounded by a system of regularly-shaped proto-planets, shrinks to about its present size, though its surface is only half as bright.

7 By now the solar system becomes recognizable, though the Sun is still orange and slowly contracting. Much of the material in the solar cloud has been absorbed.

8 The core of the Sun reaches the critical temperature to start the nuclear reaction that converts hydrogen into helium. There are relatively few proto-planets left.

9 As the Sun settles down to a period of stable radiation, the proto-planets assume a spherical shape. The four largest, Jupiter, Saturn, Uranus and Neptune, are over 400 million miles from the Sun.

The lifespan of the Earth

The Earth was produced from the solar cloud (1-6 on main diagram). It had no regular form, but, as more and more material was drawn in, it began to assume a spherical shape (7-8)

When it had reached its present size (9), the Earth had a dense atmosphere; not the original hydrogen atmosphere but one produced by gas from the interior. Life had not started.

The Earth today (10), moving in a stable orbit, has an equable temperature and oxygen-rich atmosphere, so that it alone of all the planets in the solar system is suitable for life.

When the Sun nears the red giant stage (11-13), the Earth will be heated to an intolerable degree. The atmosphere will be driven off, the oceans will boil and life must come to an end.

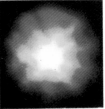

As the Sun reaches the peak of its violence (14-15) it will swell out until the Earth is engulfed. Its natural life is probably no more than 8000 million years: its end is certain

Birth of the solar system

60000 million years
Sun as a black dwarf

Outer planets

4500 million years
Conditions on Earth favourable to life

Sun consumes inner planets

Sun as white dwarf

Timescale of the solar system *above*
Taking the vertical 12 o'clock position as the time when the Sun and solar system were created (illustration 1 in the main sequence, above left) the present time appears at about the 1 o'clock position. By half-past two the Sun will flare up and consume its inner planets, thereafter dying a slow death.

10 The solar system today is made up of the Sun (which is the central remnant of the original cloud), the nine principal planets, of which four are giants, and various smaller bodies. The Sun's rate of rotation has been considerably reduced, and the interplanetary material is largely restricted to the main plane of the system.

star (above), leaving behind a cloud of fragments. These then coalesced into the planets as we know

them today, having organized themselves into heliocentric orbits (above). Few subscribe to this theory now.

13 The expansion of the Sun will continue, with the hydrogen-burning region approaching the surface. After another 600 million years, the Sun will be fifty times its present diameter. It will have become a red giant, engulfing the inner planets, including Earth.

11 When the supply of hydrogen at the Sun's core runs low, as will happen in perhaps 6000 million years, the region of the hydrogen-burning will move out towards the surface. The Sun will become larger, with a lower surface temperature but greater output.

12 The change in the Sun will continue as the hydrogen-burning region inside its globe moves farther and farther away from the core. The overall increase in energy output will raise the temperatures of the planets considerably, and the inner planets will become intolerably hot.

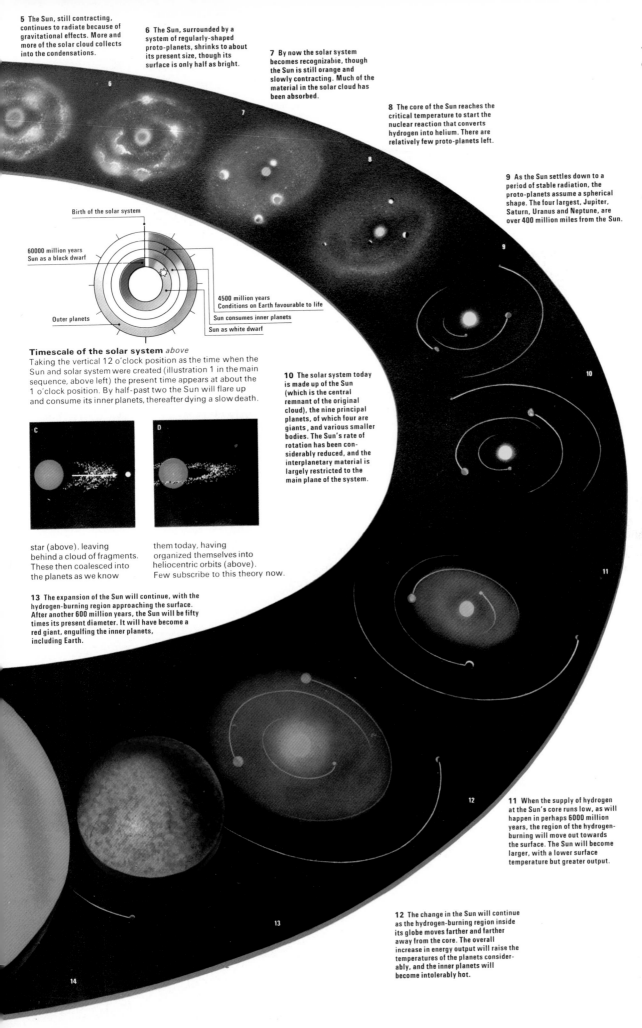

8A The Active Earth

Man's most powerful nuclear weapons pale into insignificance beside the violence of an earthquake or the destructive and indiscriminate force of a volcano. These cataclysmic phenomena frequently occur along the same belts of instability in the Earth's crust and are often only different manifestations of the same fundamental processes. About 800 volcanoes are known to have been active in historical times, and many are extremely active today. All the mid-ocean ridges are volcanic in origin, and many underwater eruptions occur along these submarine mountain ranges. Spectacular volcanic eruptions sometimes break the ocean surface, such as during the formation in 1963 of the island of Surtsey, south of Iceland (photograph, right). Some islands, such as Iceland itself, are the products of continued outpourings of lava along the crest of the mid-ocean ridge.

Oceanic earthquakes caused by sudden sea-floor displacements may result in tsunamis or giant sea waves. About 80 per cent of the shallow earthquakes and almost all deep ones take place along the belt around the Pacific. Clear evidence of the large scale movements of the mantle are provided by the zones within which earthquake shocks are generated along some Pacific island arc systems. These zones plunge down from sea-floor level to depths as great as 400 miles (640 km) beneath the adjacent continents and mark the positions of downward flow of the mantle convection currents (page 11A). The corresponding upwelling regions lie along the mid-ocean ridges, where new basic volcanic material is continually being added to the ocean crust as outward movement takes place away from the ridges.

These sea-floor spreading movements act as 'conveyor belts' for the continents, and constitute the basic mechanism for the large displacements involved in continental drifting. Geological data confirm the former close fits of the margins of the reassembled continental jig-saw puzzle, and also corroborate the detailed paleomagnetic evidence visible in today's rocks of the movements of the continents relative to the geographic poles.

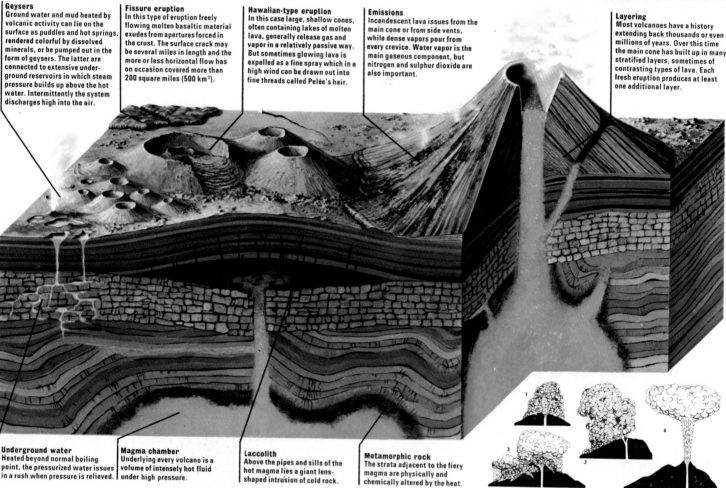

Geysers
Ground water and mud heated by volcanic activity can lie on the surface as puddles and hot springs, rendered colorful by dissolved minerals, or be pumped out in the form of geysers. The latter are connected to extensive underground reservoirs in which steam pressure builds up above the hot water. Intermittently the system discharges high into the air.

Fissure eruption
In this type of eruption freely flowing molten basaltic material exudes from apertures forced in the crust. The surface crack may be several miles in length and the more or less horizontal flow has on occasion covered more than 200 square miles (500 km²).

Hawaiian-type eruption
In this case large, shallow cones, often containing lakes of molten lava, generally release gas and vapor in a relatively passive way. But sometimes glowing lava is expelled as a fine spray which in a high wind can be drawn out into fine threads called Pelée's hair.

Emissions
Incandescent lava issues from the main cone or from side vents, while dense vapors pour from every crevice. Water vapor is the main gaseous component, but nitrogen and sulphur dioxide are also important.

Layering
Most volcanoes have a history extending back thousands or even millions of years. Over this time the main cone has built up in many stratified layers, sometimes of contrasting types of lava. Each fresh eruption produces at least one additional layer.

Underground water
Heated beyond normal boiling point, the pressurized water issues in a rush when pressure is relieved.

Magma chamber
Underlying every volcano is a volume of intensely hot fluid under high pressure.

Laccolith
Above the pipes and sills of the hot magma lies a giant lens-shaped intrusion of cold rock.

Metamorphic rock
The strata adjacent to the fiery magma are physically and chemically altered by the heat.

Where the Earth seems active *right*
Although we live on a white-hot globe with a thin cool crust, the fierce heat and energy of the interior is manifest only along fairly clearly defined belts. Around the Pacific, volcanoes and earthquakes are frequent. Another belt traverses the mountains from southeast Asia through the Middle East to the Mediterranean. Every site is an external expression of activity within the crust and upper mantle. The underlying cause is a slow flowing of the rocks of the mantle in response to changes in temperature and density.

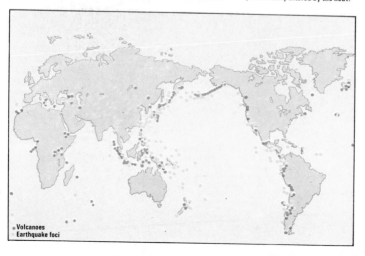

• Volcanoes
• Earthquake foci

Types of eruption *above*
Volcanic cones differ in both shape and activity. The Strombolian (1) erupts every few minutes or hours; the Peléan form (2) gives a hot avalanche; the Vesuvian (3) is a fierce upward expulsion, while the Plinian (4) is the extreme form.

A caldera *left*
Expulsion of lava (A) from the magma chamber (B) may leave the central core (C) without support. A collapse results in a large, steep-sided caldera (D). The magma chamber may cool and solidify (E), and water may collect inside the caldera (F).

Earthquake *right*
Along lines of potential movement, such as fault planes, stresses may build up over many years until the breaking strength of some part of the rock is exceeded (A). A sudden break occurs and the two sides of the fault line move, generating shock-waves which travel outward in all directions from the focus at the point of rupture (B). The point on the surface directly above the focus is the epicenter (C). While the fault movement reaches its fullest extent, the shockwaves reach the surface (D). Far right the aftermath of an earthquake.

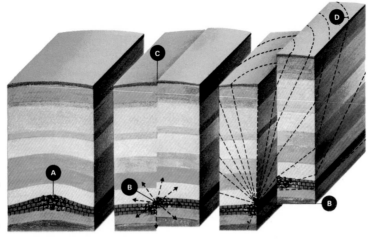

Destructive waves *right*
The Japanese, who have suffered severely from them, have given the name tsunami to the terrifying waves which follow earthquakes. Their character depends on the cause. In the case of a sudden rift and slump in the ocean bed (A) the wave at the surface is initially a trough, which travels away to both sides followed by a crest and subsequent smaller waves (B). A fault causing a sudden changed level of sea bed (C) can generate a tsunami that starts with a crest (D). Travelling at 400 miles (650 km) per hour or more the tsunami arrives at a beach as a series of waves up to 200 feet (60 m) high (E), the 'trough first' variety being heralded by a sudden withdrawal of the ocean from the shore. Warning stations ring the Pacific (far right) and the concentric rings show tsunami travel time from an earthquake site to Hawaii at the center.

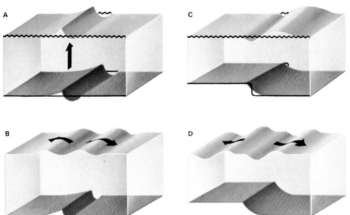

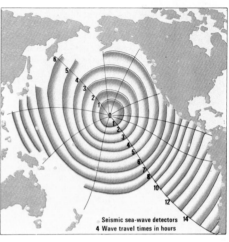

Tsunami warning *above*
Numerous seismographic warning stations around the earthquake belt of the Pacific Ocean maintain a continuous alert for earthquake shocks and for the tsunami waves that may follow it. Possible recipients of such waves plot a series of concentric rings, such as these centered on the Hawaiian Islands, which show the time in hours that would be taken for a tsunami to travel from any earthquake epicenter. Aircraft and satellites are increasingly helping to create a globally integrated life-saving system.

Seismic waves *right*
An earthquake caused by a sudden movement in the crust at the focus (A) sends out a pattern of shock waves radiating like ripples in a pond. These waves are of three kinds. Primary (P) waves (full lines) vibrate in the direction of propagation, and thus are a rapid succession of high and low pressures. Secondary (S) waves (broken lines), which travel only 60 per cent as fast, shake from side to side. Long waves (L) travel round the crust. In a belt around the world only waves of the L-type occur, giving rise to the concept of a shadow zone (B and shaded belt in inset at lower right). But intermittent records of P waves in this zone led seismologists to the belief that the Earth must have a very dense fluid core (D, lower drawing) capable of strongly refracting P waves like a lens. Seismic waves are almost man's only source of knowledge about the Earth's interior.

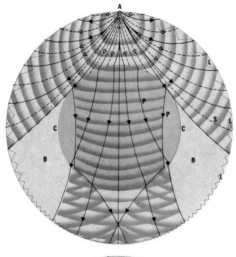

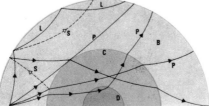

Seismology *right*
Seismic waves of all three types (P, S and L) are detected and recorded by seismographs. Usually these contain a sprung mass which, when an earthquake shock passes, stays still while the rest of the instrument moves. Some seismographs detect horizontal waves (A) while others detect vertical ones (B). The pen in the instrument leaves a distinctive trace (P-S-L). P (primary) waves are a succession of rarefactions and compressions, denoted by the packing of the dots; S (secondary) waves are a sideways shaking, shown here in plan view.

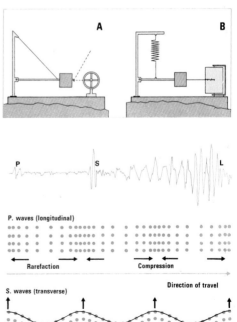

A fundamental mystery that still confronts science even today is the detailed internal structure of the planet on which we live. Although Jules Verne's intrepid 'Professor Otto Lindenbrock was able to journey to the center of the Earth, this is one scientific fantasy that will never be achieved. The deepest boreholes and mines do little more than scratch the surface and so, deprived of direct observation, the geologist is forced to rely almost entirely on indirect evidence to construct his picture of the Earth's anatomy. In spite of these drawbacks, he can outline with some confidence the story of the planet's development from the time of its formation as a separate body in space some 4550 million years ago.

Since that time the Earth has been continuously evolving. The crust, mantle and inner core developed during its first 1000 million years, but there is only scant evidence of how they did so. Probably the original homogenous mass then partly or completely melted, whereupon gravitational attraction caused the densest material to form a part-liquid, part-solid central core overlaid by the less dense mantle. The extremely thin outermost layer of 'scum' began to form at an early stage and as long ago as 3500 million years parts of it had reached almost their present state. But most of the crust evolved in a complex way through long-term cyclic changes spanning immense periods of time. The evidence of today's rocks can be interpreted in different ways; for example, the core, mantle and crust could have separated out quickly at an early stage or gradually over a longer period.

Today's restless Earth

Many of the changes which have taken place in the Earth's structure and form have been very gradual. For example, although it may well be that our planet has been getting larger (as illustrated below), the rate of increase in radius has been no more rapid than $2\frac{1}{2}$ inches (65 mm) per century. But this does not alter the fact that the Earth is very far from being a mere inert sphere of matter. Although it is not possible faithfully to portray it, almost the whole globe is at brilliant white heat. If the main drawing were true to life it would contain no color except for a thin band, about as thick as cardboard, around the outer crust in which the color would change from white through yellow and orange to red. With such high temperatures the interior of the Earth is able to flow under the influence of relatively small differences in density and stress. The result is to set up convection currents which are now believed to be the main driving force behind the formation of mountain ranges and the drifting apart of continents. But the fact remains that our knowledge of the interior of our planet is derived almost entirely from indirect evidence, such as the passage of earthquake shock waves through the mantle (page 13A). Direct exploration is confined to the surface and to boreholes which so far have never penetrated more than five miles (8 km) into the crust. It is difficult to imagine how man could ever devise experiments that would greatly enhance and refine his knowledge of the Earth's interior. Indeed, he knows as much about the Moon and other much more distant heavenly bodies as he does about the Earth below a depth of a mere 20 miles (32 km).

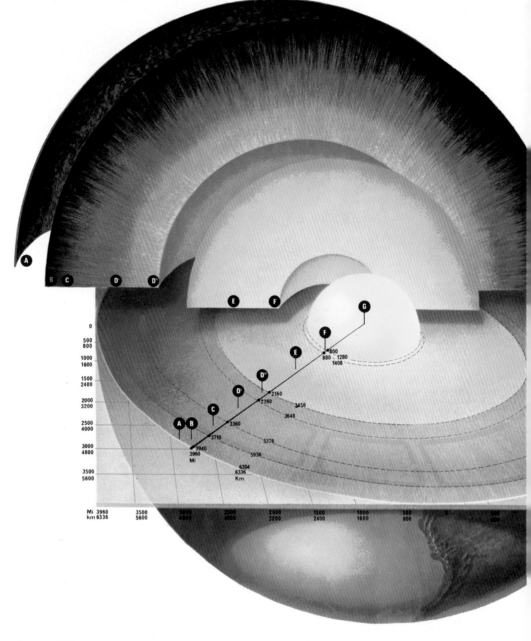

The crust (A)
This varies in thickness from 20 miles (32 km) in continental regions, where it is largely granitic, to 5 miles (8 km) under the oceans, where it is basaltic.

The upper mantle (B, C)
From the crust down to 375 miles (600 km), this layer is divided into upper and lower zones with differing P wave speeds (see page 39).

The lower mantle (D¹, D²)
Made of peridotite, as is the upper mantle, this zone extends down to a depth of 1800 miles (2900 km). P wave speeds increase still further.

The outer core (E, F)
Largely iron and nickel, this molten zone reaches to 3200 miles (5120 km). Dynamo action of convection currents may cause the Earth's magnetic field.

Not a true sphere *below*
The Earth's shape is controlled by equilibrium between inward gravitational attraction and outward centrifugal force. This results in the average radius at the equator of 3963 miles (6378 km) slightly exceeding that at the poles of 3950 miles (6356 km).

An expanding Earth?
During its history the Earth may have gradually expanded. Some 4500 million years ago it may have been wholly covered with crust equal in area to today's continents. An intermediate stage with a radius of 2735 miles is suggested by the worn-down stumps of ancient mountain folds, while the symmetry of younger fold-mountains indicates that the radius when they were formed was approximately 3730 miles. If the shapes of the modern continents are preserved as nearly as possible they would fit a globe about 2600 miles in radius, which may be the size at which the crust was formed.

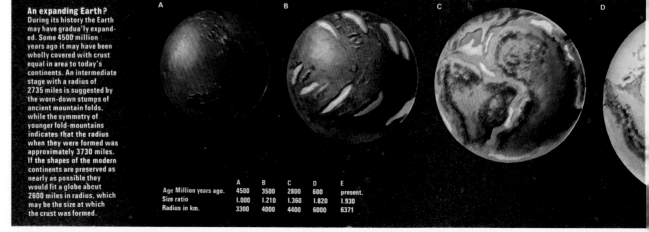

	A	B	C	D	E
Age Million years ago.	4500	3500	2800	600	present.
Size ratio	1.000	1.210	1.360	1.820	1.930
Radius in km.	3300	4000	4400	6000	6371

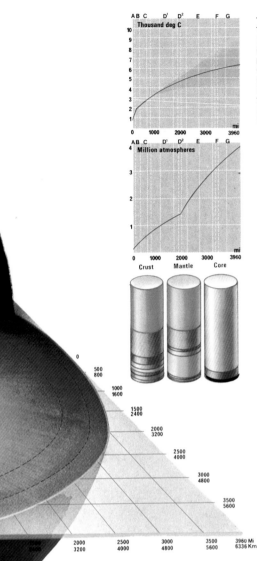

Temperature *left*
Temperature inside the Earth increases with depth, initially at a rate of 48°C per mile (30°C/km) so that 60 miles (100 km) down it is white hot. The rate of increase then falls, and the shaded area indicates how uncertain is man's knowledge of great depths.

Pressure *left*
This likewise increases with depth. Only 200 miles (320 km) down it reaches 100,000 atmospheres, 1200 times the pressure at the deepest point in the ocean. A change of state at the discontinuity between the mantle and core shows as a kink on the graph.

Crust   Mantle   Core

O₂	OXYGEN
Si	SILICON
Al	ALUMINUM
Fe	IRON
Ni	NICKEL
Co	COBALT
Mg	MAGNESIUM
Ca	CALCIUM
Na	SODIUM
K	POTASSIUM

Chemical composition *above*
The crust is made of mainly light elements and has relatively low density. Towards the base of the crust the composition is probably richer in iron and magnesium. The mantle is composed of heavier elements and the core is probably of iron and nickel.

X Core
Y Mantle
Z Crust

Density *left*
Virtually all man's knowledge of the interior of the Earth stems from measuring the transit of earthquake waves. The resulting data indicate sharp increases in density at the boundaries of both the outer core and the 'solid' inner core, with several intermediate zones.

The inner core (G)
The pressure of 3½ million atmospheres (35000 kg/mm²) keeps this a solid ball of 800 miles (1300 km) radius. Its density varies from 14 to about 16.

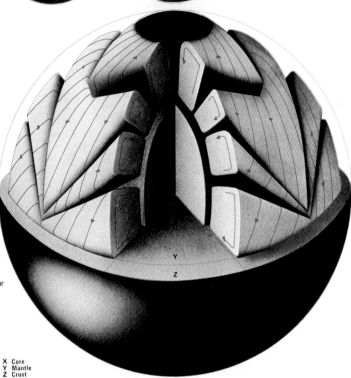

Convection currents
The fundamental pattern of movement in the mantle (A) is modified by the Earth's rotation (B) and also by friction between adjacent cells as shown in the main figure, below, in which core (X) and mantle (Y) are shown but crust (Z) is removed.

Convection theory
Geologists and geophysicists are not unanimous on the question of whether there are convection currents present in the Earth's mantle or not, nor on the part these could play in providing the driving mechanism for major movements of the continents. Slow movement of 'solid' rocks can occur over long periods of time when the temperature is high and only relatively small density differences would be required to trigger them. Another matter for debate is whether convection is confined to the upper mantle or is continuous throughout the whole. It is not certain whether changes of physical state at different levels would constitute barriers to mantle-wide convection. The convection cells above are highly schematic but could largely explain the formation of some of the major geosynclinal fold mountains in the crust over the past thousand million years. Large-scale convection current systems in the mantle could also be the driving force for sea floor spreading and the associated continental drift.

The watery Earth *below*
Almost three-quarters of the Earth is covered by water. Basically the continents are rafts of relatively light crust 'floating' on generally denser oceanic crust. They comprise not only the visible land but also the adjacent continental shelves covered by shallow water. Oceanic crust underlies the deep sea platforms and ocean trenches. The areas of the major lands and seas (below, left) do not take into account the continental shelves but are the gross areas reckoned in terms of the land and water distribution at mean sea level. Extra area due to terrain is not included.

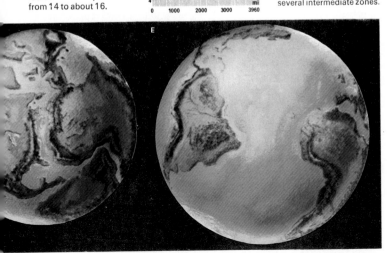

The watery Earth *right*
Key to numbered areas.

Oceans	Area (x 1000) Sq mi	km²
1 Arctic	5541	14350
2 Pacific	63,800,000	165,200,000
3 Atlantic	31530	81660
4 Indian	28,356,000	73,441,700

Continents		
5 Americas	16,301,000	42,219,000
6 Europe (excluding USSR)	1903	4929
7 Asia (excluding USSR)	10661	27611
8 USSR	8649	22402
9 Africa	11,707,000	30,320,000
10 Oceania	3286	8510
11 Antarctica	5 100,000	13,209,000

Measured against the time standards of everyday life, the major forces that shape the face of the Earth seem to act almost unbelievably slowly. But in geological terms the erosion of rock formations by river, marine or ice action is in fact rather rapid. Indeed, in isolated locations, on coasts or below waterfalls, visible erosion can take place in a period of months or even days.

Over large regions of the Earth the rates of river erosion, expressed as the mass of material removed from each unit of land area in a given time, range between 34 and 6720 short tons per square mile per year (12–2354 metric tons/km²/year). The main factor determining the rate at any place is the climate. The average rate of erosion for Eurasia, Africa, the Americas and Australia, a land area of some 50 million sq. mi. (130 million km²), has been calculated to be about 392 short tons per sq. mi. per year (137 metric tons/km²/year). This corresponds to a general lowering of the surface of the land by about 40 inches (one meter) every 22000 years. At this rate these continents would be worn down to sea level in less than 20 million years, which in geological terms is a fairly short span of time.

In practice, the surface of the land would be most unlikely to suffer such a fate. Although isolated areas could be worn away, worldwide erosion on this scale and at a steady rate would be balanced or prevented by a number of factors, one of which is the continuing large-scale uplift of the land in other regions. Nevertheless long-term estimates do emphasize the cumulative effects of the apparently slow processes of erosion. Even man's own structures wear away. Already the portland stone of St. Paul's cathedral in London has lost half an inch (13 mm) overall in 250 years, aided by the additional force of atmospheric pollution.

Where do all the products of this erosion go? By far the largest accumulations of sediments occur in river deltas, and at many periods in the geological past great thicknesses of such deposits have been laid down in extensive subsiding troughs called geosynclines. A rate of deposition of 1/250 inch (0.1 millimeter) per year is enough to lay down 12 miles (20 km) of strata in 200 million years.

The cycle of rock change

The agents of weathering
Gross break-up of the Earth's surface rocks is caused by earthquakes, the ceaseless cycle of diurnal and annual heating and cooling, and by the freezing of water trapped in fissures and crevices. The water of the seas, rivers and rain dissolves some rocks and in others leaches out particular minerals. Water is especially powerful as a weathering agent when it contains dissolved acidic chemicals. Today's main sources are plants and animals (1), but in the primeval world such chemicals were evolved mainly by volcanoes (2).

Erosion of the land

Only the material exposed at the surface of the Earth by volcanic action (2) or uplift (3) is subjected to erosion, but this material is constantly changing. Chemical erosion is an extension of the weathering process, converting the surface material into different and usually physically degraded substances. Physical erosion (4) is effected by running water and the wind (in both cases accelerated by the presence of an abrasive load) and by ice action and frost shattering.

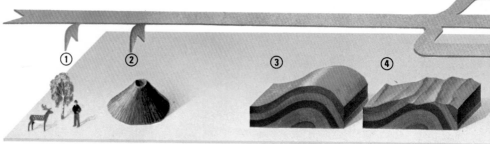

Extrusions
Most lavas are at a temperature of 900-1200°C. Acidic (granitic) lava is fairly viscous, but basic (basalt) lava flows relatively freely and when extruded from surface fissures or volcanoes can cover large areas (15). Lavas which have originated from partial melting of crustal rocks can also be erupted.

Basic magmas
Basic magma generated by partial melting in the mantle (14) may rise into and through the crust to be extruded from surface volcanoes. Basic magmas are the hottest, as well as the most freely flowing, and are often generated at very considerable depth. In their ascent they can intrude large areas of the crust and finally extrude through fissures in the surface.

Intrusions
Contact metamorphism is a form of baking and re-crystallization caused by the intrusion of hot magma into existing strata (13).

Granitic magmas
Partial melting deep in the crust generates new granitic magma—hot, rather viscous molten rock of an acidic nature which is able to migrate both upwards and laterally (12). This may inject and mix with the surrounding rocks to form a migmatite complex.

Slow uplift
Strata can be slowly uplifted (11) until they once more appear at the surface; continued or violent uplift results in mountain-building. In either case, erosion begins afresh.

Deep metamorphism
If the strata are depressed far down, to depths up to about 25 miles (40 km), deep metamorphism at high pressures and high temperatures (10) results in complete re-crystallization. This gradually converts the original sediments into a complex of new rock types.

Erosion

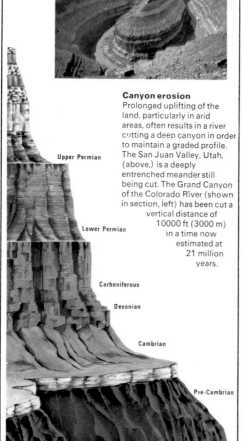

Canyon erosion
Prolonged uplifting of the land, particularly in arid areas, often results in a river cutting a deep canyon in order to maintain a graded profile. The San Juan Valley, Utah, (above,) is a deeply entrenched meander still being cut. The Grand Canyon of the Colorado River (shown in section, left) has been cut a vertical distance of 10000 ft (3000 m) in a time now estimated at 21 million years.

Upper Permian

Lower Permian

Carboniferous

Devonian

Cambrian

Pre-Cambrian

Wind erosion
Laden with grains of sand and other air-transportable debris, the wind exerts a powerful sculpturing effect. Rate of erosion varies with rock hardness, giving rise to odd effects (Mushroom Rock, Death Valley, California, left). Desert sand forms 'barchan' dunes (right), which slowly travel points-first.

Sculpture by the sea
The ocean shapes the land by the pounding of the waves, scouring by the currents, chemical solution and deposition of debris. Around the Atlantic coast of the Portuguese Algarve are particularly fine wave-eroded rocks (at Piedade, left) while some of the principle mechanisms and coastal features are seen at right (key, far right).

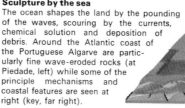

River development
The youthful river flows fast, eroding a narrow channel in an otherwise unchanged landscape. In maturity the channel is wider; flow is slower and some transported debris is deposited. The old river meanders across a broad flood plain (River Wye near Goodrich, left), some meanders becoming cut off as ox-bow lakes.

Glacial action
Briksdal Glacier, Norway (left), is a remnant of the Ice Ages, carving U-shaped valleys (2) in the pre-glacial rock (1). The bergschrund (3) forms close to the back wall, while other crevasses (4) form at gradient changes. Eroded rocks form a longitudinal moraine (5).

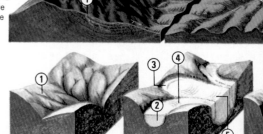

Transportation

As material is worn away from the surface rocks it is carried away by various processes. The most important transport system is flowing water (5), which can move sediments in suspension, in solution or carried along the beds of river channels. In open country, and especially over deserts, much solid debris is blown by the wind (6). Even slow-moving glaciers (7) perform a significant erosion and transport role by bearing heavy burdens of rock debris.

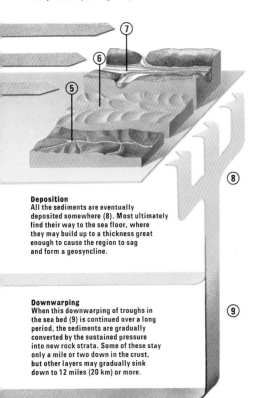

Deposition

All the sediments are eventually deposited somewhere (8). Most ultimately find their way to the sea floor, where they may build up to a thickness great enough to cause the region to sag and form a geosyncline.

Downwarping

When this downwarping of troughs in the sea bed (9) is continued over a long period, the sediments are gradually converted by the sustained pressure into new rock strata. Some of these stay only a mile or two down in the crust, but other layers may gradually sink down to 12 miles (20 km) or more.

250 million years ago

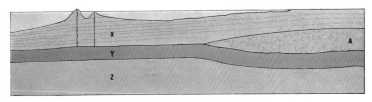

180 million years ago

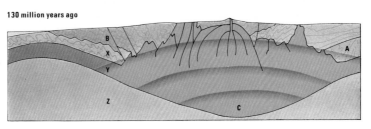

130 million years ago

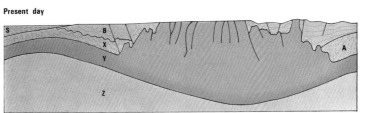

Present day

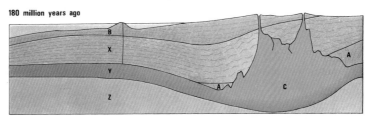

Late Paleozoic *left*

The formation of a geosyncline begins with the laying down of heavy sediments. In the creation of the Sierra Nevada range sediments X were deposited by the primeval ocean on top of Precambrian rock A, basalt crust Y and peridotite mantle Z.

Jurassic *left*

Downwarping of the crust causes the deposition of Mesozoic sediments B and carries the lower basalt crust and sediments into the zone of the mantle's influence. The bottom of the bulge is gradually converted into hot, fluid magma C.

Cretaceous *left*

In this period the geosynclinal process is in a mature stage. The inner rocks reach their maximum downward penetration into the mantle and are metamorphosed by high temperature and pressure. The deep metamorphism spreads (curved shading).

Present day *left*

Uplift and cooling opens the way to a new cycle of formation. The metamorphic rocks are exposed at the surface and subsequently eroded to yield today's complex landscape structure. Final withdrawal of the sea exposes marine sediments S.

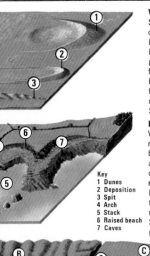

Wind-blown sand *left*

Sand deserts exhibit dunes of various forms. Unlike a barchan the parabolic blowout (1) travels with points trailing. In elongated form this becomes a parabolic hairpin (2), and a third form is the longitudinal ridge (3), known in the Sahara as a seif dune.

Emerging coastline *right*

Where the shoreline is rising, the continental shelf becomes exposed. River silt accumulates and forms an offshore bar, pierced by the river flow. Eventually infilling forms a tidal salt marsh through which the braided river reaches a new shore. Spain (far right) and Italy provide good examples.

Key
1 Dunes
2 Deposition
3 Spit
4 Arch
5 Stack
6 Raised beach
7 Caves

Key
A Youthful stage
B Mature stage
C Old Age stage
1 Pothole
2 Ox-bow
3 Meander

Glaciated landscape *left*

The landscape shows evidence of former ice coverage. Broken rock debris forms valley-floor moraines (6), the peaks are sharp and knife-edged (7), and hanging valleys (8) mark the entry of the glacier's tributaries. Terminal moraines (9) are a characteristic feature.

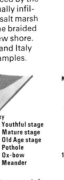

Key
A Initial stage
B Late youth
C Early maturity
1 Cut-off
2 Spit
3 4 Bars
5 Lagoon

Key
A Initial stage
B Bar development
C Emergence complete

Key
1 Esker
2 Recessional moraine
3 Drumlin
4 Lake
5 Terminal moraine
6 Outwash delta
7 Lake deposits
8 Kettle lake
9 Outwash plain
10 Kettle hole

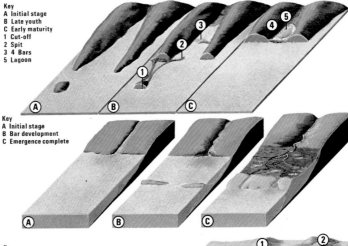

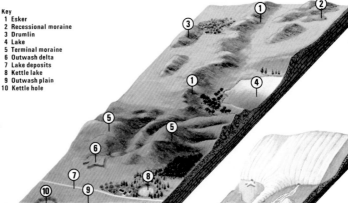

Subsiding coastline *left*

Most coastal regions undergoing submergence are highly irregular. Drowned hills are eroded by the waves to form cliff headlands, or cut-offs; spits and bars cross the submerged valleys, enclose them and form lagoons. Finally all these features wear back to a new shoreline.

Area previously sea

Mediterranean Sea

Neapolis

SPAIN

Glaciated landforms *left*

Throughout a vast area of the temperate lands evidence of past glacial action is abundant. A geomorphologist, studying the landscape shown in the larger illustration, would deduce the former glacial situation depicted in the inset. Weight and sculpture by the ice carved out characteristic depressions, some later filled with water. Subglacial streams left alluvial deposits in the form of eskers and an outwash fan or delta, while the limit of the glacier is suggested by rocks deposited as a terminal moraine. Kettle holes result from the melting of ice within moraine debris.

The Active Oceans

The surface of the oceans presents an infinite variety of contrasts ranging from glassy calm to terrifying storms with towering waves and wind-whipped wraiths of spray. But no part of the oceans is ever really still. Together the oceans comprise 300 million cubic miles (1250 million km³) of ever-active water. The whole mass ebbs and flows on a global scale with the tides. The surface is disturbed by winds into great patterns of waves which eventually break on the shores of the land. And the largest and most far-reaching movements of all are the ocean currents, some on or near the surface and others at great depths, which profoundly alter not only the oceans but also the weather.

Best known of all these currents is the Gulf Stream, which was discovered in late medieval times when early navigators found that their ships were consistently not in the place predicted by their calculations of course and estimated speed. Some 500 years ago it had become customary for Spanish captains voyaging to the New World to keep well south of the Gulf Stream on their outward journey and then use its swift four or five knot (8–9 km/hr) current to help them along on the return. The Gulf Stream brings mild weather to northwest Europe, and a corresponding role is played on the other side of the globe by the Kuroshio, a warm current which flows northeastward off Japan. Conversely, in the southeastern Pacific the Peru Current brings cold water from the sub-Antarctic region northward towards the equator. The surface flow is accompanied during most months of the year by an 'upwelling' of water rich in nutrients along the coast of Chile and Peru, and this, like many other cold currents elsewhere, supports great fisheries.

In coastal seas the water movements are often dominated by the currents that accompany the rise and fall of the tide. Because of the friction of the tides, the Moon is moving slowly further from the Earth.

Wave generation *right*
Waves are generated on the surface by the wind. Once a slight undulation has been formed it will react on the air flow so that an eddying motion, with a reduced pressure, is produced on the lee side (A) of each crest. Combined with the wind pressure on the windward side (B), this causes the waves to grow in height. The wave travels forward in the direction of the wind, but the individual water particles (X) move in almost closed orbits (C).

Internal motion *right*
On the surface of deep water these orbits are almost circular. Below the surface the radii of the orbits decrease with depth and become very small at a depth equal to half a wavelength. In shallow water the orbits are ellipses, becoming flatter towards the bottom.

Shore and rip currents *below*
In addition to its circular movement, each water particle slowly moves in the direction of propagation. When waves approach a coast water tends to pile up at the shoreline. This leads to a return flow seaward (X) which is concentrated in narrow, fast-flowing rip currents (Y). Beyond the breaker zone these spread out into a head and gradually disperse (Z).

Ocean currents *left*
Beyond the continental shelf (A) and continental slope (B) lies an ocean bewildering in its complexity. Far from being homogenous, the marked contrasts in ocean temperature, density and salinity even within short geographical distances or narrow ranges of depth almost defy description ,and measurement. For example, off the east coast of the United States a cold current (D) moves southward below the Gulf Stream (C), a warm surface current that flows northeast towards Western Europe. Near its source the Gulf Stream borders the western edge of the Sargasso Sea (E).

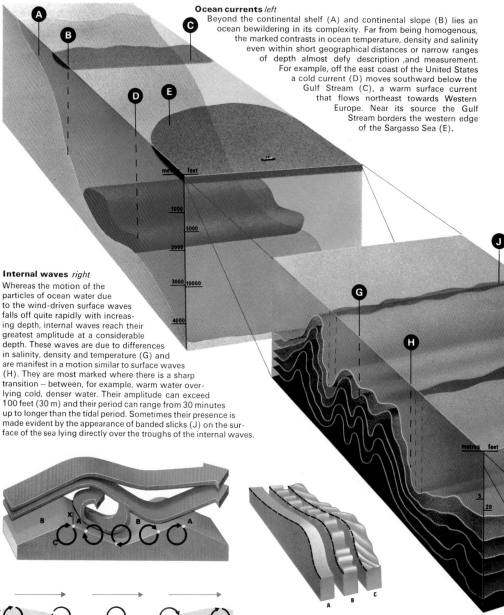

Internal waves *right*
Whereas the motion of the particles of ocean water due to the wind-driven surface waves falls off quite rapidly with increasing depth, internal waves reach their greatest amplitude at a considerable depth. These waves are due to differences in salinity, density and temperature (G) and are manifest in a motion similar to surface waves (H). They are most marked where there is a sharp transition – between, for example, warm water overlying cold, denser water. Their amplitude can exceed 100 feet (30 m) and their period can range from 30 minutes up to longer than the tidal period. Sometimes their presence is made evident by the appearance of banded slicks (J) on the surface of the sea lying directly over the troughs of the internal waves.

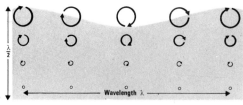

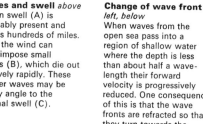

Waves and swell *above*
Ocean swell (A) is invariably present and travels hundreds of miles. On it the wind can superimpose small waves (B), which die out relatively rapidly. These smaller waves may be at any angle to the original swell (C).

Change of wave front
left, below
When waves from the open sea pass into a region of shallow water where the depth is less than about half a wavelength their forward velocity is progressively reduced. One consequence of this is that the wave fronts are refracted so that they turn towards the shallower water, and the wave crests tend to line up parallel to the shore. In the diagram X-X is the original frontal axis of the waves coming in from the ocean. When the depth of water varies along a coast, waves tend to become focused on the shallower areas (Y) and to diverge from the deeper ones such as the head of a submarine valley or canyon (Z). For the same reason large waves can often be seen breaking on a headland while the breakers in an area of originally deeper water, leading to a bay, are relatively much smaller.

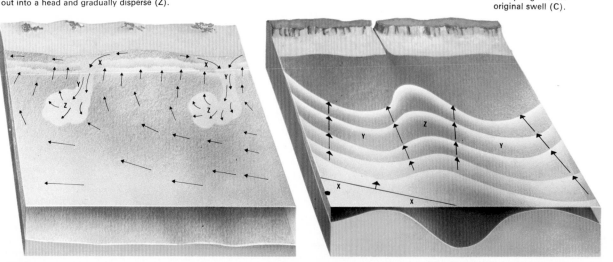

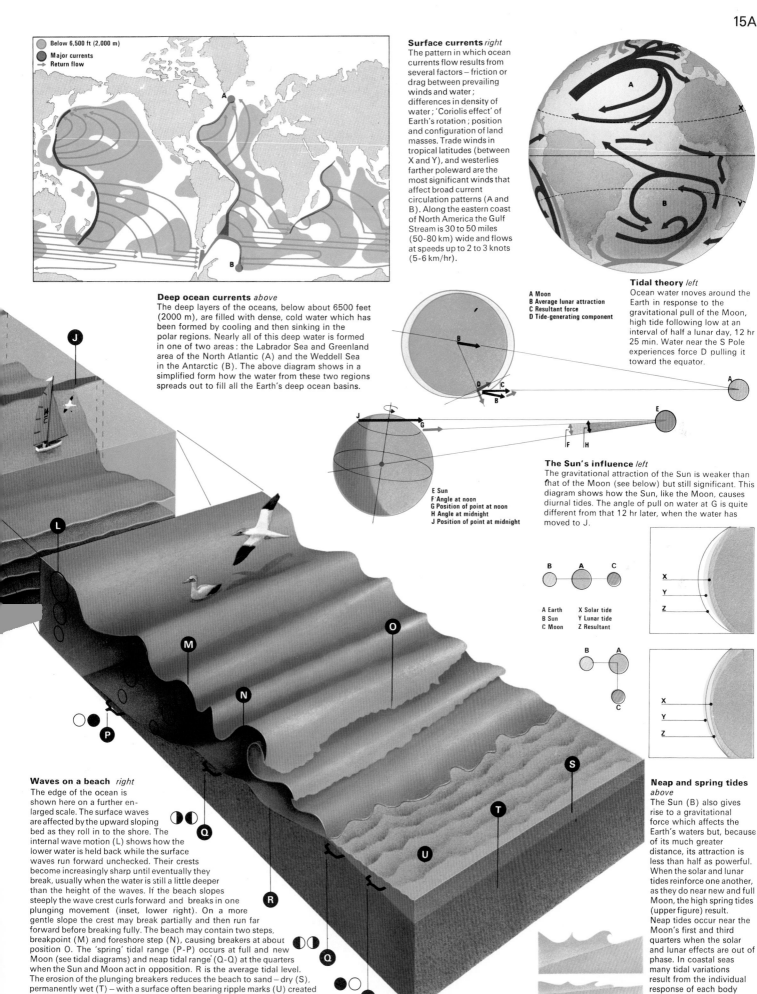

Below 6,500 ft (2,000 m)
Major currents
Return flow

Surface currents *right*
The pattern in which ocean currents flow results from several factors – friction or drag between prevailing winds and water; differences in density of water; 'Coriolis effect' of Earth's rotation; position and configuration of land masses. Trade winds in tropical latitudes (between X and Y), and westerlies farther poleward are the most significant winds that affect broad current circulation patterns (A and B). Along the eastern coast of North America the Gulf Stream is 30 to 50 miles (50-80 km) wide and flows at speeds up to 2 to 3 knots (5-6 km/hr).

Deep ocean currents *above*
The deep layers of the oceans, below about 6500 feet (2000 m), are filled with dense, cold water which has been formed by cooling and then sinking in the polar regions. Nearly all of this deep water is formed in one of two areas: the Labrador Sea and Greenland area of the North Atlantic (A) and the Weddell Sea in the Antarctic (B). The above diagram shows in a simplified form how the water from these two regions spreads out to fill all the Earth's deep ocean basins.

A Moon
B Average lunar attraction
C Resultant force
D Tide-generating component

Tidal theory *left*
Ocean water moves around the Earth in response to the gravitational pull of the Moon, high tide following low at an interval of half a lunar day, 12 hr 25 min. Water near the S Pole experiences force D pulling it toward the equator.

E Sun
F Angle at noon
G Position of point at noon
H Angle at midnight
J Position of point at midnight

The Sun's influence *left*
The gravitational attraction of the Sun is weaker than that of the Moon (see below) but still significant. This diagram shows how the Sun, like the Moon, causes diurnal tides. The angle of pull on water at G is quite different from that 12 hr later, when the water has moved to J.

A Earth   X Solar tide
B Sun   Y Lunar tide
C Moon   Z Resultant

Waves on a beach *right*
The edge of the ocean is shown here on a further en-larged scale. The surface waves are affected by the upward sloping bed as they roll in to the shore. The internal wave motion (L) shows how the lower water is held back while the surface waves run forward unchecked. Their crests become increasingly sharp until eventually they break, usually when the water is still a little deeper than the height of the waves. If the beach slopes steeply the wave crest curls forward and breaks in one plunging movement (inset, lower right). On a more gentle slope the crest may break partially and then run far forward before breaking fully. The beach may contain two steps, breakpoint (M) and foreshore step (N), causing breakers at about position O. The 'spring' tidal range (P-P) occurs at full and new Moon (see tidal diagrams) and neap tidal range (Q-Q) at the quarters when the Sun and Moon act in opposition. R is the average tidal level. The erosion of the plunging breakers reduces the beach to sand – dry (S), permanently wet (T) – with a surface often bearing ripple marks (U) created by the turbulence and undercutting by the receding water after each wave.

Neap and spring tides *above*
The Sun (B) also gives rise to a gravitational force which affects the Earth's waters but, because of its much greater distance, its attraction is less than half as powerful. When the solar and lunar tides reinforce one another, as they do near new and full Moon, the high spring tides (upper figure) result. Neap tides occur near the Moon's first and third quarters when the solar and lunar effects are out of phase. In coastal seas many tidal variations result from the individual response of each body of water.

The Earth Under the Sea

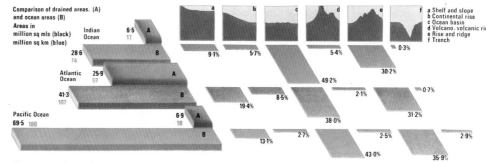

Comparison of drained areas. (A) and ocean areas (B)
Areas in
million sq mls (black)
million sq km (blue)

Indian Ocean	6·5 / 17	A
	28·6 / 74	B
Atlantic Ocean	25·9 / 67	A
	41·3 / 107	B
Pacific Ocean	6·9 / 18	A
69·5 / 180		B

a Shelf and slope
b Continental rise
c Ocean basin
d Volcano. volcanic ridge
e Rise and ridge
f Trench

9·1%   5·7%   5·4%   0·3%

30·2%   49·2%

19·4%   8·5%   2·1%   0·7%

38·0%   31·2%

13·1%   2·7%   2·5%   2·9%

43·0%   35·9%

The water planet *left*
From directly over Tahiti the Earth appears to be covered by water. The Pacific averages 2.5 miles (4 km) deep, with great mountains and trenches.

Ocean drainage *above*
The ratio between the areas of the oceans and the land they drain varies greatly. Many large rivers feed the Atlantic but few discharge into the Pacific.

Ocean proportions *above*
The major oceans show a similarity in the proportions of their submarine topography. By far the greatest areas contain deep plains with rises and ridges. More prominent features, the mid-ocean volcanic ridges and trenches, occupy much smaller areas. About one tenth of each ocean is continental shelf.

At present the sea covers about 71 per cent of the Earth's surface. But if the continents could be sliced away and put into the deep oceans to make a perfectly uniform sphere the sea would have an average depth of about 8000 feet (2500 m) over the whole planet. In the distant past the level of the sea has fluctuated violently. The main cause has been the comings and goings of the ice ages. Glaciers and ice-caps lock up enormous volumes of water and the advance and recession of ice has alternately covered the continental shelves with shallow seas and revealed them as dry land. If the Earth's present polar ice-caps and glaciers were to melt, the mean sea level would rise by about 200 feet (60 m), which would submerge half the world's population. Average depth of the sea is more than 12000 feet (3600 m), five times the average height of the land above sea level.

The deep oceans

Below the level of the continental shelf lies the deep ocean floor with great topographical contrasts ranging from abyssal plains at a depth of about 13000 feet (4 km) to towering submarine mountain ranges of the mid-ocean ridges which reach far up toward the surface. Great advances have recently been made in exploring the ocean floors which were previously unknown. Most of the ocean area is abyssal plain which extends over about 78 million square miles (200 million km²). But a more remarkable feature of the deep ocean is the almost continuous mid-ocean mountain range which sweeps 40000 miles (64000 km) around the globe and occasionally – as at Iceland – is seen above sea level in the form of isolated volcanic islands. The basic symmetry of the oceans is the central ridge flanked by abyssal plain sloping up to the continental shelves. On the deep floor sediments accumulate at a rate of 30–35 feet (10 m) per million years; they also build up more slowly at the central ridges. No ocean sediments have been found older than 150 million years, which suggests that the material which now makes up the floors of the deep oceans was formed comparatively recently. Exploration and detailed mapping of the ocean bed is still in its infancy.

Submarine landscape

Principal features of the bed of the oceans can be grouped into a much smaller space than they would actually occupy. Although each ocean differs in detail, all tend to conform to the general layout of a central volcanic ridge (which can break the surface in places), broad abyssal plains with occasional deep trenches and shallow slopes and shelves bordering the continents.

Submarine relief *below*
The bottom of the sea is very far from being flat. If the ocean waters were removed a new landscape would become visible, with immense relief features.

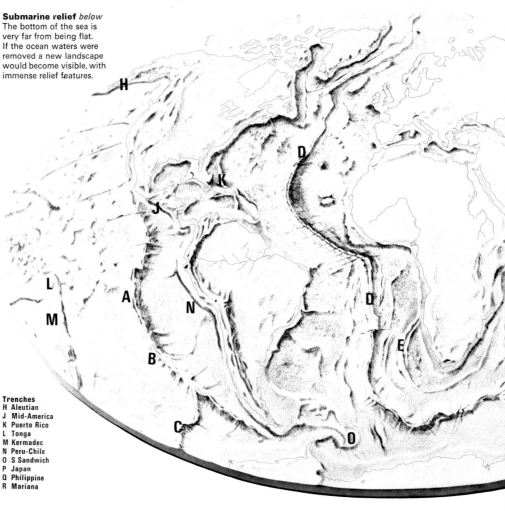

Trenches
H Aleutian
J Mid-America
K Puerto Rico
L Tonga
M Kermadec
N Peru-Chile
O S Sandwich
P Japan
Q Philippine
R Mariana

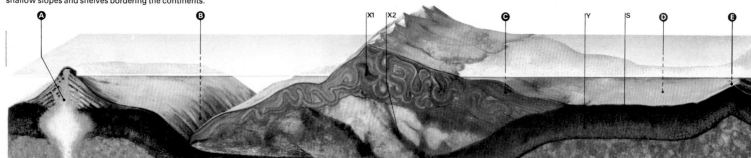

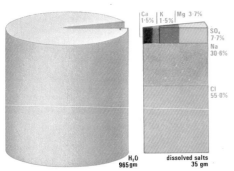

Composition of sea-water *above*
The water of the Earth's oceans is an exceedingly complex solution of many organic and inorganic salts, together with suspended solid matter. In a typical kilogram of sea-water there are 35 grams of chlorine, sodium, sulphates, magnesium, potassium and calcium.

Ca 1·5% | K 1·5% | Mg 3·7%
SO₄ 7·7%
Na 30·6%
Cl 55·0%
H₂O 965gm
dissolved salts 35 gm

Continental shelf *left*
The submerged continental fringes lie at depths to about 450 feet (135 m) and have a total area of some 11 million square miles (28 million km²). The surface of the land is eroded and carried by rivers to form sedimentary deposits on the shelf. At its outer margin it slopes down to the abyssal plains of the deep ocean at about 2½ miles (4 km) below sea level.

A Scree fan
B Gully opposite river
C River delta
D Slump (turbidite) mass
E Scar left by (D)
F Continental slope
X Granite
Y Basalt

Mid-ocean ridge *left*
Well-marked ridges are found along the centers of the major oceans and form an extensive worldwide system. The central part of the ridge may have a double crest with an intervening deep trough forming a rift valley, or there may be several ridges. They are volcanic in nature and along them is generated new basaltic ocean crust. The volcanoes become progressively younger as the mid-ocean ridge is approached.

A Mid-ocean ridge
B Abyssal plain
S Ocean floor sediments
Y Basalt crust
Z Mantle

Oceanic trench *left*
These long and relatively narrow depressions are the deepest portions of the oceans, averaging over 30,000 feet (10 km) below sea level. Around the Pacific they lie close to the continental margins and in the western Pacific are often associated with chains of volcanic islands. Some trenches are slowly becoming narrower as the ocean floor plates on either side converge.

A Trench wall
B Canyon
C Island arc
D Trench
S Sediment
Y Basalt
Z Mantle

Rises and Ridges
A E Pacific
B SE Pacific
C Pacific-Antarctic
D Mid-Atlantic
E Walvis
F Indian Ocean
G SE Indian

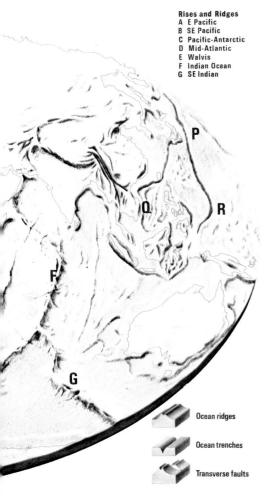

Ocean ridges
Ocean trenches
Transverse faults

A Volcano in mid-ocean ridge
B Deep oceanic trench and sediments
C Continental shelf
D Abyssal plain
E Mid-ocean ridge
F Guyots
G Oceanic islands
X1 Upper granitic crust
X2 Lower granitic crust
Y Basaltic crust
Z Mantle

A sinking island *below*
A pre-requisite to the formation of a coral atoll is an island that is becoming submerged by the sea. Such islands are formed by the peaks of the volcanic mountains which are found on the flanks of the great mid-oceanic ridges.

Coral grows *below*
Millions of polyps, small marine animals, secrete a substance which forms the hard and often beautiful coral. The structure grows round the island in shallow water and extends above the sinking island to form an enclosed and shallow salt-water lagoon.

The mature atoll *below*
Continued submergence of the volcano results in the disappearance of the original island, but the upward growth of the coral continues unabated. The reef is then worn away by the sea and the coral debris fills in the central part of the lagoon.

A guyot *below*
Eventually the coral atoll itself begins to sink beneath the ocean surface. By this time the lagoon is likely to have become completely filled in by debris eroded from the reef, and the result is a submerged flat island, known as a guyot.

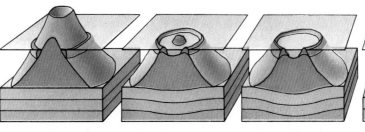
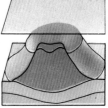

The Evolution of Land and Sea

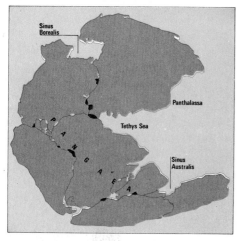

Pangaea *above*
About 200 million years ago there was only a single land mass on Earth, named Pangaea. The map shows how today's continents can be fitted together, with the aid of a computer, at the edge of the continental shelf at a depth of 1000 fathoms (6000 ft, 1830 m).

Although land and water first appeared on the Earth's surface several thousand million years before anyone could be there to watch, modern man has a very good idea of how it came about. The Earth's gravitational field caused the lighter, more volatile elements gradually to move outwards through the mantle and form a solid crust on the surface. By far the largest proportion of material newly added to the crust is basaltic volcanic rock derived from partial melting of the mantle beneath; in fact the oceanic crust which underlies the Earth's great water areas is made of almost nothing else. So the earliest crust to form was probably volcanic and of basaltic composition.

Air and water appear
The earliest records of the existence of an atmosphere of air and a hydrosphere of water are to be found in sediments laid down some 3300 million years ago from the residue of erosion of previously existing rocks. These sediments could not have been formed without atmospheric weathering, water transport and water deposition. The atmosphere was probably originally similar to the fumes which today issue from volcanoes and hot springs and which are about three-quarters water vapor. Once formed, the primitive atmosphere and oceans could erode the crust to produce vast layers of sediments of new chemical compositions. Gradually the oceans deepened and the land took on a more varied form. Convection in the mantle produced mountain ranges which in turn eroded to generate new sedimentary rocks. The ceaseless cycles of growth and decay had started, causing continually changing patterns of seas, mountains and plains. And in the past few years man has discovered how the continents and oceans have developed over the most recent 200 million years of geological time. The results of this research are to be seen in the maps on this page.

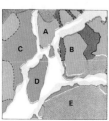

Another arrangement *left*
India (A) may have been separated by Australia (B) from East Antarctica (E) more than 200 million years ago on the evidence of today's geological deposition zones. Africa (C) and Madagascar (D) complete this convincing fit.

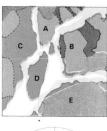

Migrant Australia *left*
By measuring the direction of magnetization of old Australian rocks it is possible to trace successive positions of that continent with respect to the Earth's magnetic pole. It appears to have moved across the world and back during the past 1000 million years.

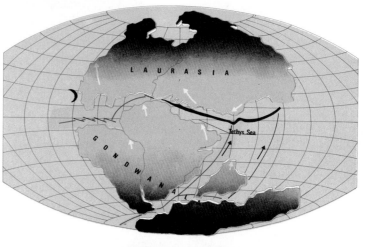

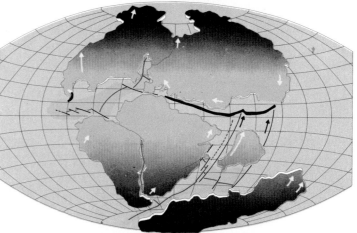

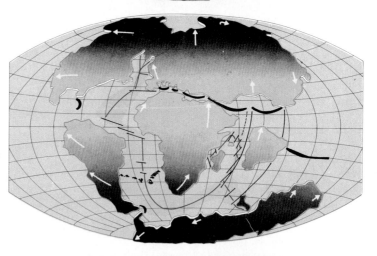

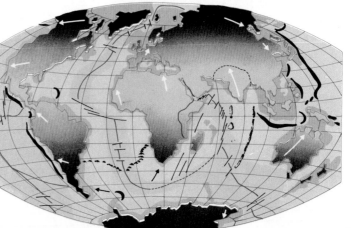

180 million years ago
At this time the original Pangaea land mass had just begun to break up. The continents first split along the lines of the North Atlantic and Indian Oceans. North America separated from Africa and so did India and Antarctica. The Tethys Sea, between Africa and Asia, closed somewhat, and the super continents of Laurasia to the north and Gondwanaland to the south became almost completely separated. In effect the Earth possessed three super landmasses, plus an India that had already begun to move strongly northward.

135 million years ago
After a further 45 million years of drifting, the world map had still not taken on a form that looks familiar today. But the two original splits, the North Atlantic and the Indian Ocean, have continued to open out. The North Atlantic is now about 600–650 miles (1000 km) wide. Rifting is extending towards the split which opened up the Labrador Sea and this will eventually separate Greenland from North America. India has firmly launched itself on its collision course with the southern coast of Asia, which is still 2000 miles (3200 km) away.

65 million years ago
Some 135 million years after the start of the drifting process the continents have begun to assume their present configuration. South America has at last separated from Africa and in Gondwanaland only Australia and Antarctica have yet to move apart. A continuation of the North Atlantic rifting will shortly bring about another big separation in Laurasia. Greenland will move apart from Europe and eventually North America will separate completely from the Eurasian landmass. The pink area (below) shows the extent of the crustal movements.

Today's positions
The Atlantic is now a wide ocean from Arctic to Antarctic, the Americas have joined and Australia has separated from Antarctica and moved far to the north. India has likewise moved northwards and its collision with Asia and continued movement has given rise to the extensive uplift of the Himalayas. All the continents which formerly made up the great land mass of Pangaea are now separated by wide oceans. Comparison of areas shows how much of India has been submerged by sliding underneath the crust of Asia (see facing page, far right).

Plate tectonics

This theory has revolutionized the way the Earth's crust – continents and oceans – is interpreted on a global scale. The crust is regarded as being made up of huge plates which converge or diverge along margins marked by earthquakes, volcanoes and other seismic activity. Major divergent margins are the mid-ocean ridges where molten lava forces its way upward and escapes. This causes vast regions of crust to move apart at a rate of an inch or two (some centimeters) per year. When sustained for up to 200 million years this means movements of thousands of miles or kilometers. The process can be seen in operation today in and around Iceland. Oceanic trenches are margins where the plates are moving together and the crust is consumed downward. The overall result is for the crustal plates to move as relatively rigid entities, carrying the continents along with them as if they were on a giant conveyor belt. Over further considerable periods of geologic time this will markedly change today's maps.

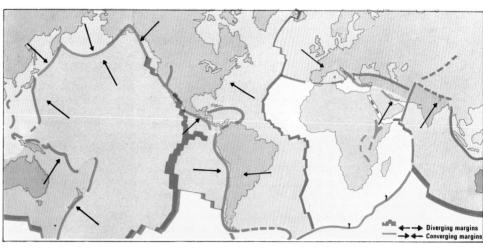

Diverging margins
Converging margins

Sea-floor spreading *left*
Arrows show how the lava flows on the ocean bed spread out on each side of a mid-ocean ridge. Evidence for such movement is provided by the fact the rock is alternately magnetized in opposing directions (coloured stripes).

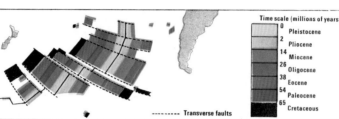

Time scale (millions of years)

0	Pleistocene
2	Pliocene
14	Miocene
26	Oligocene
38	Eocene
54	Paleocene
65	Cretaceous

-------- Transverse faults

Plate movements
above and left
The Earth's crust is a series of large plates 'floating' on the fluid mantle. At their edges the plates are either growing or disappearing. Magnetic measurements in the S. Pacific (left) show rock ages on each side of the mid-ocean ridges.

Plate movements in cross-section *above*
The basic mechanism of plate movements is illustrated above in simplified form with the vertical scale greatly exaggerated. This figure is explained in detail in both of the captions below.

Crustal divergence
above and right
The Earth's crust (1) behaves as a series of rigid plates which move on top of the fluid mantle (2). At their mating edges some of these plates are moving apart (3). This was the mechanism that separated North America (A) from Europe (B). The plates moved to the north and also away from each other under the influence of convection currents in the mantle (C). Between the land areas appeared an oceanic gap with a mid-ocean ridge (D) and lateral ridges (E). The movements continued for some 200 million years, fresh volcanoes being generated by igneous material escaping through the plate joint (F) to add to the lateral ridges which today cross the Atlantic (G). The volcanoes closest to the median line in mid-Atlantic are still young and active — whereas those nearer to the continents are old and extinct.

Crustal convergence
above and right
Diverging plate margins occur only in the centers of the major oceans (see map above) but plates are converging on both sea and land. Where an oceanic plate (4, above) is under-riding a continental plate (5) a deep ocean trench is the result (6). Such trenches extend around much of the Pacific; those around the northwest Pacific include the deepest on Earth where the sea bed is almost seven miles below the ocean surface. The continental margin is squeezed upward to form mountains such as the Andes or Rockies (7). If continental masses converge, such as India (A, right) and Asia (B), the convection in the mantle (C) pulls the plates together so hard that the upper crust crumples (D). Sedimentary deposits between the plates (E) are crushed and squeezed out upward (F), while the mantle on each side is turned downward, one side being forced under the other (G). Continued movement causes gross deformation at the point of collision. The static or slow-moving crust is crushed and tilted, and giant young mountains (the Himalayas, H) are thrust upward along the collision just behind the edge of the crumpled plate.

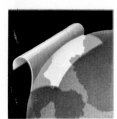

A thin coating *left*
The protective atmospheric shell around the Earth is proportionally no thicker than the skin of an apple. Gravity compresses the air so that half its mass lies within 3.5 miles (5.5 km) of the surface and all the weather within an average depth of 12 miles (20 km).

Space exploration has enabled man to stand back and take a fresh look at his Earth. Even though we, like all Earth life, have evolved to suit the Earth environment, we can see today as never before how miraculous that environment is. And by far the most important single factor in determining that environment is the atmosphere.

The Earth orbits round the Sun in a near-total vacuum. So rarefied is the interplanetary medium that it contains little heat energy, but the gas molecules that are present are vibrating so violently that their individual temperature is over 2000°C. And the surface of the Sun, at some 6000°C, would · melt almost everything on the surface of the Earth, while the tenuous chromosphere around the Sun is as hot as 1,000,000°C. From the chromosphere, and from millions of other stars and heavenly objects, come radio waves. Various places in the universe, most of them far beyond the solar system, send us a penetrating kind of radiation known as cosmic rays. The Earth also receives gamma rays, X-rays and ultraviolet radiation, and from the asteroid belt in the solar system (see page 3A) comes a stream of solid material. Most of these are small micrometeorites, no more than flying specks, but the Earth also receives meteors and meteorites.

A meteorite is a substantial mass that strikes the Earth; fortunately, none has yet hit in a populous area. Apart from these extremely rare objects, every other influence from the environment that would be dangerous to life is filtered out by the atmosphere. Meteors burn up through friction as they plunge into the upper parts of the atmosphere. To avoid burning up in the same way, spacecraft designed to return to the Earth from lunar or interplanetary flight require a special re-entry shield.

Much of the ultraviolet radiation is arrested many miles above the Earth and creates ionized layers known as the ionosphere which man uses to reflect radio waves. Much of the infra-red (heat) radiation is likewise absorbed, lower down in the atmosphere, and most of the cosmic radiation is broken up by collisions far above the ground into such particles as 'mu-mesons'. Only a few cosmic rays, harmless radio waves and visible light penetrate the blanket of air to reach the planetary surface and its teeming life.

Credit for our vital atmosphere rests with the Earth's gravitational attraction, which both prevents the molecules and atoms in the atmosphere from escaping into space and also pulls them down tightly against the Earth. As a result nearly all the atmosphere's mass is concentrated in a very thin layer; three-quarters of it lies below 29000 feet (8840 m), the height of Mount Everest. The highest-flying aircraft, 22 miles (35 km) up, are above 90 per cent of the atmosphere. The total weight of the atmosphere is of the order of 5000 million million tons. In the lower parts are some 17 million million tons of water vapour.

The water vapor plays a great part in determining the weather on Earth, the only way in which the atmosphere consciously affects daily human life. All the weather is confined to the lower parts of the atmosphere below the tropopause. In this region, called the troposphere, temperature falls away sharply with increasing altitude. The Sun heats up the Earth's surface, water is evaporated from the surface of the oceans and an immensely complicated pattern of global and local weather systems is set up. Every part of the air in the troposphere is in motion. Sometimes the motion is so slow as to be barely perceptible, while on other occasions, or at the same time in other places, the air roars over the surface with terrifying force at speeds of 200 miles (320 km) per hour or more. It erodes the land, lashes the surface with rain and clogs cold regions with snow. Yet it is man's shield against dangers, an ocean of air without which we could not exist.

Characteristics of the atmosphere *right*
Basically the Earth's atmosphere consists of a layer of mixed gases covering the surface of the globe which, as a result of the Earth's gravitational attraction, increases in density as the surface is approached. But there is very much more to it than this. Temperature, composition and physical properties vary greatly through the depth of the atmosphere. The Earth's surface is assumed to lie along the bottom of the illustration, and the various major regions of the atmosphere—which imperceptibly merge into each other—are indicated by the numbers on the vertical scale on the facing page.
Thermosphere (1)
The thermosphere is the top layer of the Earth's atmosphere. It is made up of an upper and extremely rarefied region, called the *exosphere*, and a lower region called the *ionosphere*. The exosphere is taken to start at a height of some 400 miles (650 km) and to merge above into the interplanetary medium. Atomic oxygen exists up to 600 mi (1000 km); from there up to about 1500 mi (2400 km), helium and hydrogen are approximately equally abundant. The ionosphere contains electrically conducting layers capable of reflecting radio waves and thus of enabling radio signals to be received over great distances across the Earth. The major reflecting layers, designated D, E, F1 and F2, are at the approximate heights shown. Meteors burn up brightly at heights of around 100 mi (160 km).
Mesosphere (2)
The mesosphere lies between the thermosphere and the stratosphere. It extends from a distance of about 30 mi (48 km) to about 50 mi (80 km) above the Earth's surface. In the upper levels of this region the trails left by meteors become visible. The upper layer of the mesosphere is called the *mesopause*, and that is where the lowest temperatures in the atmosphere occur, dropping to about −135°F (−93°C).
Stratosphere (3)
This lies above the tropopause which varies in altitude from about 10 mi (16 km) over the equator to just below 7 mi (11 km) in temperate latitudes. The lower stratosphere has a constant temperature of -56°C up to 19 mi (30 km); higher still the 'mesosphere' becomes warmer again. One of the vital properties of the stratosphere is its minute ozone content which shields the Earth life from some harmful short-wave radiations which, before the Earth's atmosphere had developed, penetrated to the surface.
Troposphere (4)
Within this relatively very shallow layer is concentrated about 80 per cent of the total mass of the atmosphere, as well as all the weather and all the Earth's life. The upper boundary of the troposphere is the tropopause, which is about 36000 ft (11000 m) above the surface in temperate latitudes; over the tropics it is higher, and therefore colder, while it is at a lower altitude over the poles. Air temperature falls uniformly with increasing height until the tropopause is reached; thereafter it remains constant in the stratosphere. Composition of the troposphere is essentially constant, apart from the vital factor of clouds and humidity.

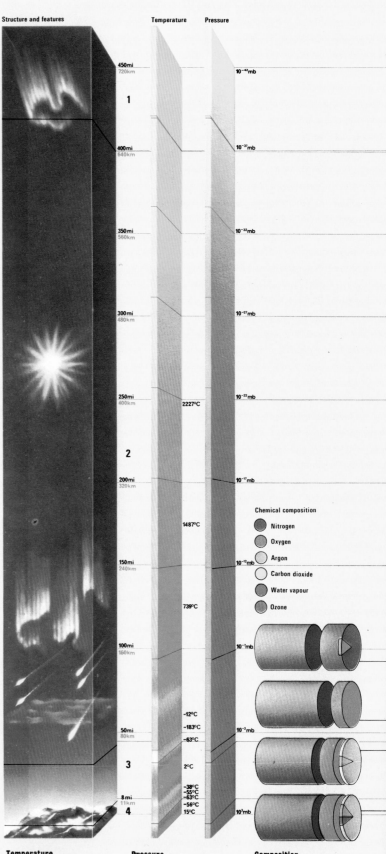

Structure and features

Temperature   Pressure

450mi
720km
1

400mi
640km

350mi
560km

300mi
480km

250mi
400km   2227°C

2

200mi
320km

1487°C

150mi
240km

739°C

100mi
160km

-12°C

50mi
80km   -183°C
               -63°C

2°C

8mi   -38°C
11km   -55°C
4   -63°C
             -56°C
             15°C

10⁻⁴²mb

10⁻³⁷mb

10⁻³²mb

10⁻²⁷mb

10⁻²²mb

10⁻¹⁷mb

10⁻¹⁰mb

10⁻⁶mb

10⁻³mb

10³mb

Chemical composition

- Nitrogen
- Oxygen
- Argon
- Carbon dioxide
- Water vapour
- Ozone

Temperature
The mean temperature at the Earth's surface is about 15°C. As height is gained the temperature falls swiftly, to −56°C at the tropopause. It remains at this value to 19 miles (30 km), becomes warmer again, and then falls to a very low value around 60 miles (100 km). It rises once again in space.

Pressure
At sea level the pressure is some 1000 millibars, or about 14.7 pounds per square inch. The total force acting on the surface of an adult human body is thus of the order of 20 tons. But only 10 miles (16 km) above the Earth the pressure, and the atmospheric density, have both fallen by some 90 per cent.

Composition
Chemical composition of the atmosphere varies considerably with altitude. In the troposphere the mixture of nitrogen, oxygen and other gases is supplemented by water vapor, which exerts a profound influence on the weather. Ozone in the stratosphere shields life from harmful ultraviolet rays.

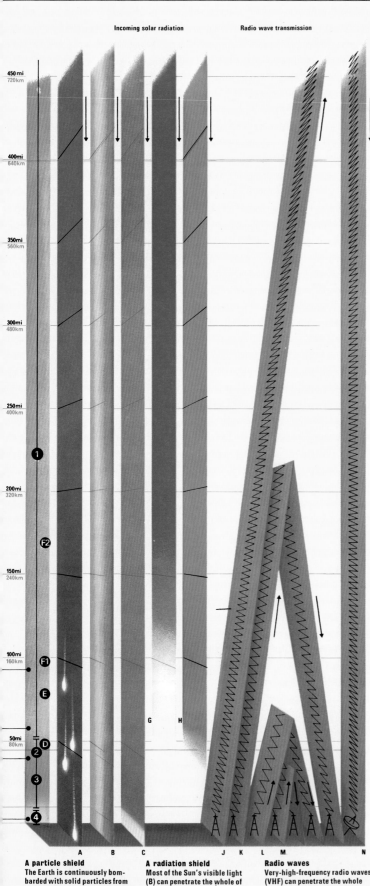

Incoming solar radiation — Radio wave transmission

450 mi / 720 km	
400 mi / 640 km	
350 mi / 560 km	
300 mi / 480 km	
250 mi / 400 km	
200 mi / 320 km	
150 mi / 240 km	
100 mi / 160 km	
50 mi / 80 km	

A particle shield
The Earth is continuously bombarded with solid particles from elsewhere in the solar system and possibly from more distant parts of the universe. Only the largest meteors (A) reach the surface. Small meteorites generally burn up through friction caused by passage through the thin air more than 40 miles (65 km) up.

A radiation shield
Most of the Sun's visible light (B) can penetrate the whole of the atmosphere right down to the Earth's surface, except where cloud intervenes. But only some of the infra-red radiation gets through (C); the rest (G) is cut off, along with the harmful ultraviolet radiation (H), by atmospheric gases.

Radio waves
Very-high-frequency radio waves (VHF) can penetrate the whole depth of the atmosphere (J), but short-wave transmissions are reflected by the Appleton F2 layer (K). Medium (L) and long waves (M) are reflected at lower levels by the D, E or F1 layers. Yet radio waves from distant stellar sources can be received (N).

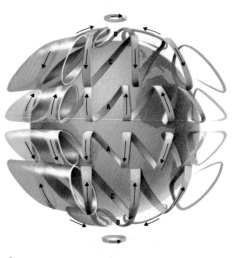

The circulation of the atmosphere *left*
The atmosphere maintains its equilibrium by transferring heat, moisture and momentum from low levels at low latitudes to high levels at high latitudes where the heat is radiated to space. This circulation appears to comprise three distinct 'cells' in each hemisphere. In the tropical (A) and polar (B) cells the circulations are thermally direct – warm air rises and cold air sinks – but the mid-latitude circulation, the Ferrel cell (C), is distorted by the polar front as shown in greater detail below.

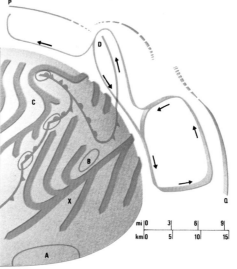

Frontal systems *left*
Although the figure above shows a true general picture, the actual circulation is more complicated. A portion of the Earth on a larger scale shows how frontal systems develop between the polar and tropical air masses. The tropopause, the demarcation between the troposphere in which temperature falls with height, and the stratosphere above, is much higher in the tropics than in the polar cell. Between the cells the polar front causes constant successions of warm and cold fronts and changeable weather. Surface winds are shown, together with areas of low pressure and high pressure. The scale along the bottom, although exaggerated, indicates the greater height of the tropical tropopause compared with that in polar regions. Conventional symbols indicate warm and cold fronts.

Warm front / Cold front

A Area of low pressure
B Area of high pressure
C Area of low pressure
D Polar front
P Polar cell tropopause
Q Tropical tropopause

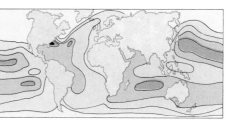

Precipitation *left*
This map shows the mean annual rain, hail and snow over the Earth.

Cm per year: 0 / 25 / 50 / 100 / 200

Evaporation *left*
Accurate estimates of evaporation can be made only over the oceans.

Cm per year: 0 / 60 / 100 / 150 / 200 / 250

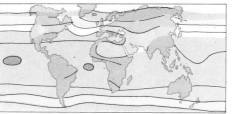

Surface radiation *left*
Variations in heat output over the Earth's surface affect air and ocean circulations.

K/cal per cm² per year: 60 / 40 / 20 / 0 / −20 / −40 / −60

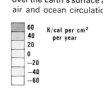

The Structure of Weather Systems

Until recently there were few scientists in the tropics or the polar regions, and the science of meteorology therefore evolved in the mid-latitudes. Likewise, the early concepts of meteorology were all based on observations of the mid-latitude atmosphere. Originally only two types of air mass were recognized: polar and tropical. Today a distinct equatorial air mass has been identified, as well as Arctic and Antarctic masses at latitudes even higher than the original polar ones. The concept of a 'front' between dissimilar air masses dates from as recently as 1919, and three years later the development of a cyclone – a large system of air rotating around an area of low pressure– was first described. Today satellite photographs have confirmed the validity of these early studies and enable the whole Earth's weather to be watched on daily computer processed photo-charts as it develops.

Why the weather varies

Anywhere in the Earth's mid-latitudes the climate is determined mainly by the frequency and intensity of the cyclones, with their frontal systems and contrasting air masses, which unceasingly alter the local temperature, wind velocity, air pressure and humidity. In turn, the frequency of the cyclonic visits is governed principally by the behavior of the long waves in the upper westerlies. When these waves change their shape and position the cyclonic depressions follow different paths. The major changes are seasonal, but significant variations also occur on a cycle of 5-6 weeks. It is still proving difficult to investigate the long wave variations. As a front passes, a fairly definite sequence of cloud, wind, humidity, temperature, precipitation and visibility can be seen. The most obvious change is the type of cloud, of which nine are shown opposite. Each cyclone contains numerous cloud types in its structure. Within these clouds several forms of precipitation can form; raindrops are the most common, but ice precipitation also forms, with snow in winter and hail in the summer when intense atmospheric instability produces towering cumulonimbus clouds topped by an 'anvil' of ice crystals.

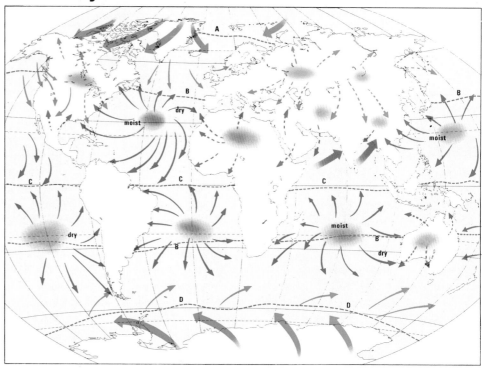

Air masses and convergences *above*
An air mass is an extensive portion of the atmosphere in which, at any given altitude, the moisture and temperature are almost uniform. Such a mass generally arises when the air rests for a time on a large area of land or water which has uniform surface conditions. There are some 20 source regions throughout the world. A second pre-requisite is large-scale subsidence and divergence over the source region. The boundary between air masses is a convergence or front. (A Arctic, B Polar, C Equatorial, D Antarctic.) The polar front is particularly important in governing much of the weather in mid-latitudes. The pattern depicted provides a raw framework for the world's weather. It is considerably modified by the air's vertical motion, by surface friction, land topography, the Earth's rotation and other factors.

Arctic	Equatorial
Polar maritime	Tropical maritime
Polar continental	Tropical continental
Cold air masses	Warm air masses

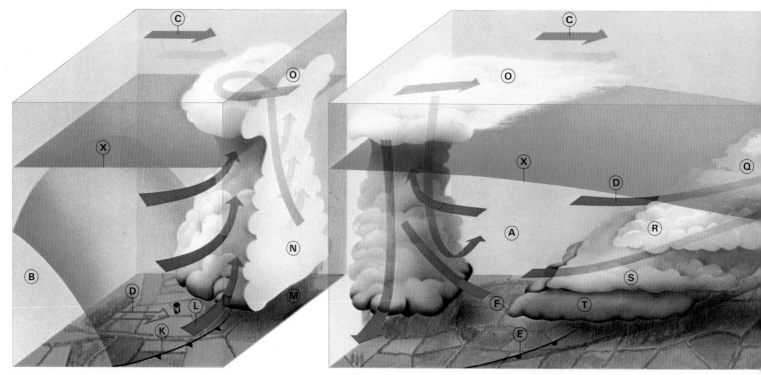

Anatomy of a depression

Seen in cross section, a mature mid-latitude cyclone forms a large system which always follows basically the same pattern. Essentially it comprises a wedge of warm air (A) riding over, and being undercut by; cold air masses (B). (Page 23A shows full development.) The entire cyclone is moving from left to right, and this is also the basic direction of the winds (C) and (D). To an observer on the ground the warm front (E) may take 12-24 hours to pass, followed by the warm sector (F) perhaps 180 miles (300 km) wide.

The cold front (K)

As this frontal zone, about one mile (1-2 km) wide, passes overhead the direction of the wind alters (L) and precipitation (M) pours from cumuliform clouds (N). If the air above the frontal surface is moving upwards then giant cumulonimbus (O) may grow, with heavy rain or hail. Cirrus clouds then form in air above the freezing level (X). Sometimes the front is weak with subsidence of air predominant on both sides of it. In this case there is little cloud development and near-zero surface precipitation.

The warm front (E)

The front is first heralded by cirrus clouds (P), followed by cirrostratus (Q), altocumulus (R), stratus (S) and finally nimbostratus (T). The descending layers are due partly to humidity distribution and partly to the warm air rising over the sloping frontal surface. Precipitation may be steady and last for hours. Alternatively some warm fronts have a predominantly subsident air motion, with the result that there is only a little thin cloud and negligible precipitation. Air temperature increases as the front passes.

Development of a depression *right*

Most mid-latitude depressions (cyclones) develop on the polar front (map above). An initial disturbance along this front causes a fall in pressure and a confluence at the surface, deforming the front into a wave (1, right). The confluence and thermal structure accelerate the cyclonic spin into a fully developed depression (2). The depression comprises a warm sector bounded by a sharp cold front (A) and warm front (B). The fast-moving cold front overtakes the warm front and eventually the warm sector is lifted completely clear of the ground resulting in an occlusion (3). The continued overlapping of the two wedges of cold air eventually fills up the depression and causes it to weaken and disperse (4). By the time this occurs the warm sector has been lifted high in the atmosphere. In this way, depressions fulfil an essential role in transferring heat from low to high levels and from low to high latitudes.

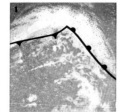
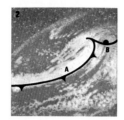

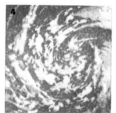

Examples of the three major cloud groups

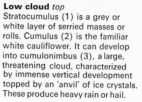

Low cloud *top*
Stratocumulus (1) is a grey or white layer of serried masses or rolls. Cumulus (2) is the familiar white cauliflower. It can develop into cumulonimbus (3), a large, threatening cloud, characterized by immense vertical development topped by an 'anvil' of ice crystals. These produce heavy rain or hail.

Medium cloud *left*
Nimbostratus (4) is a ragged grey layer producing drizzle or snow. Altocumulus (5) comprises rows of 'blobs' of ice and water forming a sheet at a height of 1.5-4.5 miles (2-7 km). Altostratus (6) occurs at similar heights but is a water/ice sheet either uniform, striated or fibrous in appearance.

High cloud *right*
Cirrus (7) is the highest cloud and appears as fine white ice filaments at 8-10 miles (13-16 km), often hair-like or silky. Cirro-cumulus (8) forms into thin white layers made up of very numerous icy globules or ripples. Cirrostratus (9) is a high-level veil of ice crystals often forming a halo round the Sun.

Plan view *left*
A developing cyclone will appear this way on the 'synoptic' weather chart. Lines of equal pressure (isobars) are nearly straight within the warm sector but curve sharply in the cold sector to enclose the low pressure focus of the system.

Rain limits

Four kinds of precipitation

Rain
Most rain results from the coalescence of microscopic droplets (1) which are condensed from vapor onto nuclei in the atmosphere. The repeated merging of small droplets eventually forms water droplets (2) which are too large to be kept up by the air currents. Rain drops may also form from melting of ice crystals in the atmosphere.

Sleet
In completely undisturbed air it is possible for water to remain liquid even at temperatures well below freezing point. So air above the freezing level (X) may contain large quantities of this 'supercooled water'. This can fall as rain and freeze on impact with objects, coating them with ice.

Dry snow
The origin of snow differs from that of rain in that the vapor droplets (1) settle on microscopic crystals of ice and freeze. The result is the growth of a white or translucent ice crystal having a basically hexagonal form (photomicrograph below). The crystals then agglomerate into flakes (2).

Hail
In cumulonimbus clouds raindrops (formed at 1,2) may encounter up-currents strong enough to lift them repeatedly back through a freezing level (X). On each pass (3) a fresh layer of ice is collected. The hailstone builds up like an onion until it is so heavy (4) that it falls to the ground.

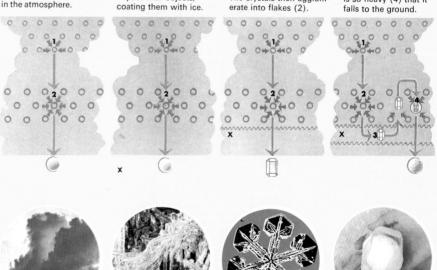

Tropical weather, between the Tropic of Cancer at 23½°N and the Tropic of Capricorn at 23½°S, differs fundamentally from that at higher latitudes. Overall there is a considerable surplus of heat, giving high mean temperatures; and the 'Coriolis force' due to the Earth's rotation, which deflects air currents to the right in the northern hemisphere and to the left in the southern, is almost non-existent. As a result, tropical weather hardly ever contains distinct air masses, fronts and cyclones. Instead the region is occupied mainly by the tradewinds, which are laden with moisture and potentially unstable. Thunderstorms are frequent, especially over land, and the pattern of land and sea leads to local anomalies, such as the monsoon of southeast Asia. This particular anomaly, too big to be called local, changes the prevailing wind over a vast area. It is superimposed on the apparently simple global circulation near the Equator.

Polar weather

At very high latitudes the atmosphere radiates heat to space. The Arctic is essentially an ocean surrounded by land, whereas the Antarctic is land surrounded by ocean. The land around the Arctic quickly takes up solar heat but the southern oceans transfer heat to deeper water to make the Antarctic the coldest region on Earth. Because the air is so intensely cold it can hold very little moisture, so the south polar region is a freezing desert with exceptionally clean air.

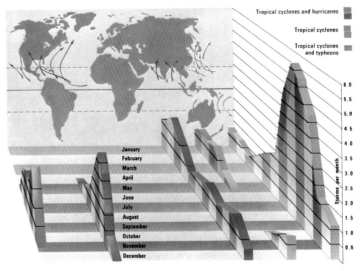

Tropical cyclones and hurricanes

Tropical cyclones

Tropical cyclones and typhoons

The afflicted areas *above*
Tropical cyclones build up over the warm oceans, and many of them—about half over the Caribbean and

four-fifths over the western Pacific—develop into hurricanes. Precisely how a hurricane is triggered is still not fully known, but there is

no doubt it is a thermodynamic engine on a giant scale which either misfires completely or runs with catastrophic effect.

Hurricanes *left*
These violent storms form over ocean warm enough (27°C) to maintain strong vertical circulation, except for the belt closest to the equator where lack of a Coriolis force prevents cyclonic spin from building up. Condensation of the moisture taken up from the ocean surface releases latent heat and thus provides energy to drive the storm. The daily energy can be equivalent to that released by several hundred H bombs. Despite their formidable power hurricanes are penetrated by specially equipped aircraft whose mission is both to provide early warning and to gather data enabling the storm's mechanism to be better understood.

Hurricane structure
A Spiral rainbands.
B High-altitude winds.
C Easterly tradewinds.

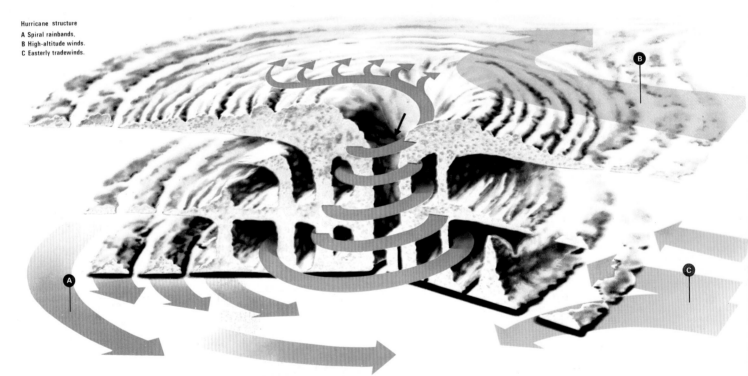

Structure of a hurricane *above*
A hurricane consists of a huge swirl of clouds rotating around a calm center known as the eye. This cyclonic circulation may be as much as 250 miles (400 km) in diameter, and it extends right through the troposphere which is about 9-12 miles (15-20 km) thick. The clouds, nearly all of the cumulonimbus type, are arranged in bands around the eye. The largest form the wall of the eye and it is here that precipitation is heaviest. The whole system is usually capped by streamers of cirrus. Wind speeds range from about 110 mph (180 kmh) at 20–25 miles (30–40 km) from the eye wall down to about 45 mph (72 kmh) at a distance of 90 miles (140 km). Warm, calm air in the eye is sucked downwards.

Hurricane development *below*

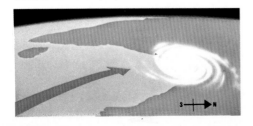

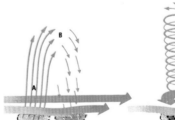

Nature's giant energy *left and above*
A hurricane such as that which killed over half a million people in Bangladesh in November 1970 (left) dissipates thousands of millions of horsepower. The spiral structure is clearly visible from a satellite (above).

Birth of a storm.
Hurricanes usually have their origin in a low-pressure disturbance directing part of an easterly wind (A) to the north. The air rises to some 40,000 ft (12 km) where it releases heat and moisture (B) before descending.

The young hurricane
The Earth's rotation imparts a twist to the rising column which becomes a cylinder (C) spiralling round a relatively still core (D). Warm, moist air off the sea picks up speed and feeds energy at a very high rate to intensify the rising column.

Dying of starvation
The hurricane does not begin to die until it moves over colder water or over land (E). Then, cut off from its supply of energy, the speed of the spiralling winds falls away. The eye begins to fill with clouds, the hurricane expands (F) and dissipates.

The monsoon *right*
In principle the processes which give rise to the monsoon are the same as those causing a sea breeze but on a vastly larger scale in space and time. In southeast Asia each May and June warm, moist air streams in from the south causing heavy rain and occasional violent storms. In winter the circulation is reversed and winds come mainly from high pressure over Siberia. In detail the monsoon is considerably modified by the Himalayas and the positions of the waves in the westerlies in the atmosphere's upper levels, but its mechanism is not fully known.

Duststorm *right*
In arid regions strong wind circulations can become filled with dust and extend over considerable areas. The storm typically arrives in the form of an advancing wall of dust possibly five miles (8 km) long and 1000 ft (300 m) high. The haboobs of the Sudan, a recurrent series of storms, are most frequent from May to September and can approach from almost any direction. They usually occur, after a few days of rising temperature and falling pressure, where the soil is very dry. Dust-devils, small local whirlwinds forming pillars of sand, can dot the land.

Nacreous cloud *right*
At high latitudes, when the Sun is below the horizon, these clouds sometimes come into view as fine filmy areas containing regions of bright spectral color. They look rather like a form of cirrus, but are far higher. Nacreous cloud in the Antarctic—such as that in the photograph, taken in Grahamland—has been measured at heights from 8.5 to 19 miles (13.5-30 km), and Scandinavian observations lie in the 20-30 km range. Despite their great altitude, nacreous clouds are undoubtedly formed as a result of air being lifted by passage across high mountains.

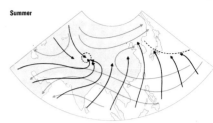
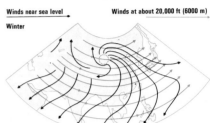

The monsoon seasons *below*
In summer an intense low-pressure area over northwest India overcomes the equatorial low pressure region. In winter an intense high over central Asia blows cold, dry air in the reverse direction.

Summer

Winter

Winds near sea level → → →   Winds at about 20,000 ft (6000 m) →

Flash flood *below*
In historic times floods have drowned millions. Even in a modern advanced country a major flood is a national disaster. The scene below is a flooded crossing on the road from Lake Grace to Dumbleyung, W Australia. It is a 'flash flood', caused by heavy rain and poor drainage.

After the hurricane *left*
Whereas a tornado can cause buildings to explode, as a result of the sudden violent difference in pressure between inside and outside, a hurricane just blows. But the wind can demolish sound houses, such as this residence in Biloxi, Mississippi.

Blown snow *above*
When the wind blows in polar regions it soon begins to lift dry powdery snow and ice granules from the surface. As the wind increases in strength this drifting snow forms a thicker layer, as at this British base in Antarctica. When the entrained material reaches eye level it is known as blown snow. Any further rise in wind velocity swiftly increases the concentration of particulate matter, causing the visibility rapidly to fall to zero. When this is the case the term blizzard is appropriate, as it also is when high winds are combined with a heavy snowfall.

The Record in the Rocks

All the past history of the Earth since the original formation of the crust is there to be discovered in the rocks existing today if only the appropriate techniques are used to find it. Sedimentary, igneous and metamorphic – the three basic types of rock – all have an enormous amount of information stored within them on such diverse aspects of the Earth's history as, for example, the variations of past climates in space and in time, the incidence of ice ages and the positions of former mountain ranges. The migrations of the ancient geo-magnetic poles at different periods of time can be discovered by studying some sedimentary and igneous rocks, while other types can yield their ages of formation or metamorphism – their changed character over long periods. The prevailing wind directions over certain regions, the direction of stream flow in river deltas that have long since vanished, or the ways in which the ice flowed in some past ice age are all there to be discovered. So are the past distributions of land and sea, areas of deposition, periods of uplift and the raising of great mountain chains (see pages 12–13A and 18–19A). Even lightning strikes millions of years old can be clearly seen.

The first task of the geologist is to make a map showing the positions and relative ages of the various rock types in a region. It is around this basic information incorporated into the geological map that all else is built, whether it is to be studies of the geological history and evolution of the region, or detailed investigations of the flora and fauna, or any of many other lines of research – such as the disentangling of various periods of deformation which have affected the region during which the rocks may have been folded or faulted (foot of this page) or eroded down to sea level. Two of the most important methods of dating, by which the age of rock is determined, are the study of fossils and the use of radiometric methods in which age is calculated by analyzing radioactive minerals having a known half-life (opposite page). Using a combination of 'correlation' techniques and either method of dating it is possible for a skilled geologist to compare the relative time sequences of geological events in any regions in the world.

A geological map below
A geological map records the outcrop pattern and the structural features of each region as they are today, corresponding with the final stage of the reconstruction—right.

How the story unfolds
right
The complex 3500 million year story of the rocks is very far from being superficially obvious. Even a skilled geologist can do no more than study the land as it is today, plot a geological map and then try to think backward over periods of millions of years in an endeavor to determine the sequences which produced the present terrain. On the right is depicted such a sequence, which might reasonably be arrived at after studying the map below, left.
The history begins (A) with the landmass rising and the sea retreating, leaving behind 'off-lap' sediments. The landmass continues to rise and is folded by compressive forces, the fold tops then being eroded (B). Over a long period the landmass then subsides and tilts; the sea once more advances, laying down 'on-lap' sediments (C). Then a great upheaval causes the sea to retreat completely.
The landmass is strongly uplifted and faulted, and the higher mass is at once attacked by erosion (D). Continued erosion gradually reduces the region to a more or less common level. Rivers, formed at stage C, carry eroded materials away and deposit them at lower levels (left side of E). Finally, the northeast part of the region is invaded by an extrusive mass of volcanic material. Of course, the processes of change would continue even now.

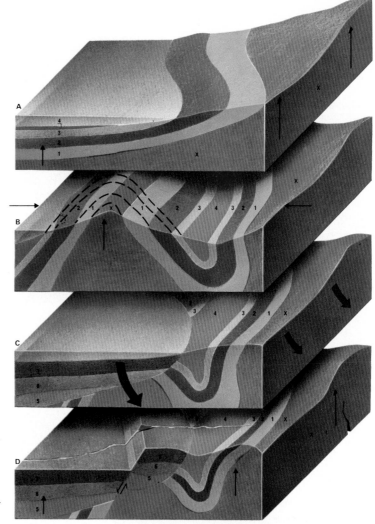

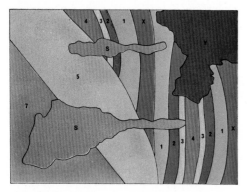

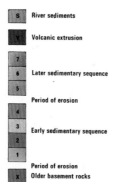

S	River sediments
V	Volcanic extrusion
7	
6	Later sedimentary sequence
5	
4	Period of erosion
3	
2	Early sedimentary sequence
1	
	Period of erosion
X	Older basement rocks

The language of geology
Plane of movement of a normal fault (1) displacing strata to right (downthrow side) relative to left (upthrow side).

Block of strata (2) dropped between two tensional faults forming a rift valley. Other strata are compressional.

Normal anticline (3) and syncline (4) with symmetrically dipping limbs on either side of the axial plane of the strata.

Positions of the axial planes (5, 6) passing through an asymmetrical anticline (5) and an asymmetrical syncline (6).

Compressional reversed fault (7). In this case the left side of the fault is over-riding basically horizontal strata on the right.

Monoclinal fold (8), with a relatively steep limb separating basically horizontal areas of strata at two levels.

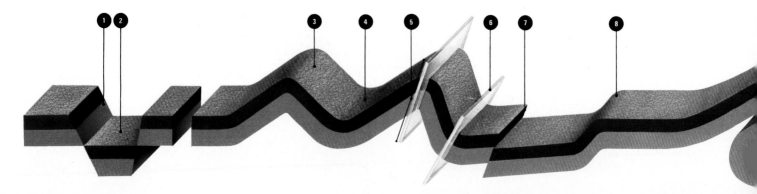

Geological dating

The relative dating of geological strata is found from the sequence in which the layers were deposited, the oldest being at the base of a local sequence and the youngest at the top. On this basis, together with correlations over wide areas based on the fossil evidence of the forms of life at different stages of the 'geological column', the main periods and sub-divisions can be worked out.

Prior to the Cambrian, the oldest epoch of the Paleozoic era (see scale at right), evidence of life is seldom found in the rocks. The extremely primitive earliest forms of life have generally not been preserved in the form of fossils, and so correlations by palaeontological methods cannot be applied to the Precambrian.

In recent years the progressive evolution of radio-carbon dating has enabled geologists to assign actual dates to the relative sequences of strata. This is done by measuring the amount of radioactive decay of an isotope of carbon, carbon-14, or C^{14}. This radio-isotope decays to form nitrogen, its half-life being about 5,730 years. After the death of a living organism, it no longer takes carbon dioxide into its body, so that the amount of carbon-14 that body contains is fixed as a known quantity in relation to its total weight. As time goes by, this amount lessens in accordance with radioactive decay. The precise amount that remains is determined by refined physical and chemical analysis. In this way the age of a specimen can be approximately determined, for even after millions of years no radioactive isotope is ever quite used up.

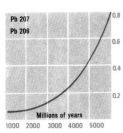

Pb 207
Pb 206
Millions of years
1000 2000 3000 4000 5000

0.8
0.6
0.4
0.2

Half-life *left*
Radioactive materials decay according to a law. Each isotope has a characteristic half-life, the time required for the number of radioactive atoms to decay to half the original number. The half-life for each element is unalterable.

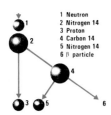

| U 238 | U 235 | Th 232 | Rb 87 | K 40 |

| 8 He 4 | 7 He 4 | 6 He 4 | | |

Million years: 4498 | 713 | 13900 | 50000 | 11850 | 1470

| Pb 206 | Pb 207 | Pb 208 | Sr 87 | A 40 | Ca 40 |

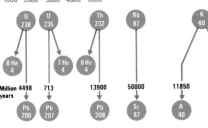

1 Neutron
2 Nitrogen 14
3 Proton
4 Carbon 14
5 Nitrogen 14
6 β particle

Degeneration
above and left
Some of the isotopes, shown above with their half-lives and end-products can be used for dating over the whole age of the Earth. For more recent dating, radio-carbon with a half-life of 5570 years is used (left).

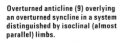

Overturned anticline (9) overlying an overturned syncline in a system distinguished by isoclinal (almost parallel) limbs.

Plane of thrusting (10) causes the overturned anticline (11) to ride over lower strata in form of a horizontally displaced 'nappe'.

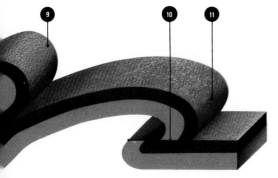

Period scale column

Million years	Major periods
	Cenozoic
	Mesozoic
500	Palaeozoic
	Upper Proterozoic
1000	Lower Proterozoic
1500	
2000	Archaean
2500	
3000	Katarchaean
3500	Oldest known crust
4000	formation of the earth
4500	

Period scale (Million years): 65, 100, 136, 190, 200, 225, 280, 300, 345, 395, 400, 430, 500, 570, 600

Quaternary
This most recent period of geological history leads up to the appearance of man and the present day. Changes of climates took place which brought on the great ice ages with glacial periods alternating with warmer sequences between them. And, of course, the period is still in progress.

Tertiary
A complex history of changes took place, each epoch of the Tertiary period from Paleocene to Pliocene showing a diverse sequence of volcanism and mountain-building in different regions. Shallow seas alternated with sub-tropical delta flats harboring the precursors of today's life.

Cretaceous
The Tethys Sea spread over large areas of the adjacent continents. Fossil evidence reveals a diverse flora and fauna. The South Atlantic reached a width of some 1900 miles (3000 km) and only Antarctica and Australia and the northern lands of the North Atlantic remained unseparated.

Jurassic
The North Atlantic had opened to a width of some 600 miles (1000 km). Sedimentary deposits formed marginal belts around the continents which had separated, and deeper-water sediments were deposited in the Tethys Sea. Extensive eruption of basalts accompanied the rifting of the South Atlantic.

Triassic
This was the period in which the continental drift began. The progressive opening of the North Atlantic was accompanied by rift-valley faulting and large outpourings of basalt along the eastern seaboard of what is today North America. Gondwanaland in the south began to break up.

Permian
Many areas were characterized by arid or semi-arid climates, with frequent salt lakes giving rise to evaporite deposits and red desert sandstones. Much volcanic activity took place on a local scale. This was the last period in which Pangaea remained a single continental mass. New flora were abundant.

Carboniferous
Extensive forest and deltaic swamp conditions led to the eventual formation of coal basins in North America and Europe. Phases of folding and mountain formation occurred in many places. In Gondwanaland widespread glaciation occurred, with glaciers radiating from a great central ice-cap.

Devonian
Large areas of arid continental and sandstone deposits formed, partly as the products of erosion of the mountains formed previously. Intervening basins of shallow sea or lagoonal deposits occurred, with abundant fossil fish. Distinct faunal provinces have been recognized from this period.

Silurian
In this period further widespread basins of thick sedimentary deposits were laid down. Many of these are characterized by the abundance of marine fossils, including corals. The Caledonian mountains were formed in Laurasia in which enormous volumes of granitic rocks were later emplaced.

Ordovician
Graptolites and trilobites continued to be important forms of marine life. Thick marine sediments continued to be laid down, and there were extensive and widespread outbursts of volcanic activity. In some regions deformation and uplift of the rocks created major mountain ranges.

Cambrian
Rocks of this period contain the earliest fossilized remnants of more complex forms of life such as graptolites, brachiopods, trilobites and gastropods. In many regions the Cambrian period was characterized by the deposition of thick sequences of sedimentary rocks, usually on an eroded basement.

Precambrian
By far the longest period of geological time is included in the Precambrian. This encompasses a complex history of sedimentation, mountain-building, volcanism, and granitic intrusions. Precambrian rocks form basements of many sedimentary deposits, and make up the nuclei of continents.

In 1833 Charles Lyell courageously proposed that the fragments of bones of animals and men that persistently cropped up in deep geological strata could mean only one thing: that the Earth had been created long before the date of 4004 BC accepted by Christianity. Since then practically the whole of our knowledge of man's early development has come from systematic digging. At first a lone archaeologist could do the whole job, but today digging for early man involves a team of specialized archaeologists, geologists, technologists and laboratory workers. They hope to identify everything significant, study it in relation to its resting place, the history of the region and nearby finds, and also subject chosen items to detailed laboratory tests – such as accurate age determination by the potassium/argon method (p.27A). A major dig needs experts on rocks, on soils and on plant pollen.

Although there are remarkable instances of well-preserved human bodies being found (for example, in peat bogs) and of woolly mammoths whose flesh could be eaten after a million years in frozen Siberia, almost all archaeology rests on bones and on man's artifacts. Gradually, from small fragments of jaw, teeth, skull and other bones, it has been possible to piece together what appears to be a fairly complete history of human evolution. The artist can then cover a deduced skeleton with tissue, as has been done in these pages. But pigmentation of skin and degree of hairiness is still a matter for conjecture.

Among the significant factors studied in early man are his brain size, jaw structure, posture and loco-motion. Today's great apes have a stooping, occasionally four-legged posture. So did early man from 20 million down to five million years ago; then, gradually, the hominid line learned to walk upright. Its members also learned to use tools, and to make them progressively better. Even later, true men began to leave behind evidence of their growing culture in their burials, their artifacts and their art. All these things can be studied in bone caves, such as the imaginary one illustrated on the right, and in excavation sites.

The cave in use
The cave is modeled after European examples of the Upper Paleolithic period of the order of 25000 years ago. It was at about this time that cave paintings appear to have become widespread. The river was then close to its present level, but the rock falls and piles of debris were still to come.

A bone cave *above and right*
From about 100,000 years ago caves provided many types of early men with a ready-made refuge. Probably most of these caves still exist. Although many are buried under later strata, and virtually all are greatly changed by subsequent developments, it is still possible with experience to read the message contained in them.

A burrow in the cave
Here a small animal has burrowed into the floor. It was deflected sideways by the hard flowstone until it could continue down, throwing fossil bones up on to the floor above. Finally it died at the end of its burrow.

A buzzard's nest?
Just inside the lip of the cave mouth a bird of prey built its nest. Directly beneath it on the slope of the rock debris are scattered small rodent bones.

River level
In general, the lowest geological sediments are the oldest, but it is unwise to jump to this con-clusion. In this hypothetical cave the earliest of all the deposits is a river terrace A above the cave on the hillside, indicating that the whole cave was originally submerged. At about this period insoluble limestone residue was settling on the cave floor at B. As the river cut its valley its level fell to C, leaving silt bed D. Continued deepening of the valley brought the river to its present level, leaving the cave dry and eroding the thick layer of silt at the mouth of the cave.

An obstructed mouth
Early man sheltered in the mouth of the cave and lit fires there for warmth and to cook food. The ashes of these fires gradually accumulated in three main layers, each denoting a long period of use. The 'contemporary' inset illustrates the third of these periods. Later the cave was abandoned by man and the mouth gradually became blocked by a pile of rock debris.

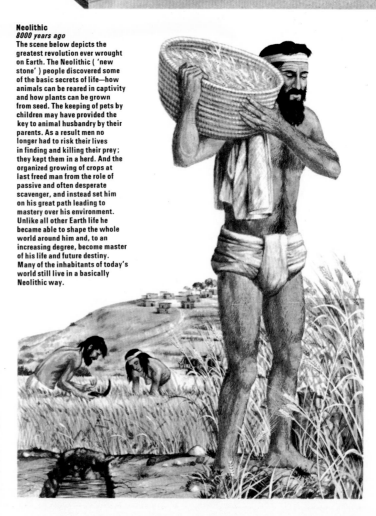

Mesolithic
About 10,000 years ago
About 20000 years ago the great ice sheets began slowly to recede, a process that is still continuing. As the climate grew warmer the Late Paleolithic people gave way to the Mesolithic (transitional) about the year 8000 BC. Milder conditions allowed man to exploit the rivers and seas, using fishing nets and even elaborate barricades and weirs made of woven saplings. The family had by now become a firm social unit, while people also explored the territory of their neighbors. For the first time there is evidence of large groups combining in habitation, hunting, art and making useful articles. Although farming of crops and animals had yet to come, the Mesolithic period saw a great enrichment of life and—probably— the development of a social conscience.

Neolithic
8000 years ago
The scene below depicts the greatest revolution ever wrought on Earth. The Neolithic ('new stone') people discovered some of the basic secrets of life—how animals can be reared in captivity and how plants can be grown from seed. The keeping of pets by children may have provided the key to animal husbandry by their parents. As a result men no longer had to risk their lives in finding and killing their prey; they kept them in a herd. And the organized growing of crops at last freed man from the role of passive and often desperate scavenger, and instead set him on his great path leading to mastery over his environment. Unlike all other Earth life he became able to shape the whole world around him and, to an increasing degree, become master of his life and future destiny. Many of the inhabitants of today's world still live in a basically Neolithic way.

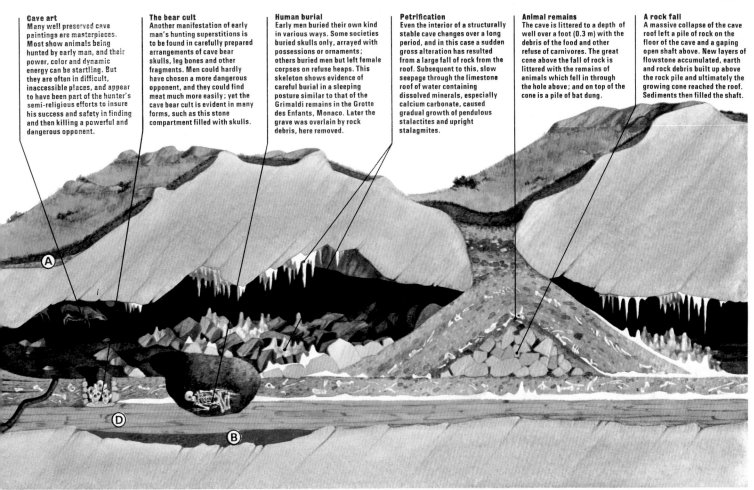

Cave art
Many well preserved cave paintings are masterpieces. Most show animals being hunted by early man, and their power, color and dynamic energy can be startling. But they are often in difficult, inaccessible places, and appear to have been part of the hunter's semi-religious efforts to insure his success and safety in finding and then killing a powerful and dangerous opponent.

The bear cult
Another manifestation of early man's hunting superstitions is to be found in carefully prepared arrangements of cave bear skulls, leg bones and other fragments. Men could hardly have chosen a more dangerous opponent, and they could find meat much more easily; yet the cave bear cult is evident in many forms, such as this stone compartment filled with skulls.

Human burial
Early men buried their own kind in various ways. Some societies buried skulls only, arrayed with possessions or ornaments; others buried men but left female corpses on refuse heaps. This skeleton shows evidence of careful burial in a sleeping posture similar to that of the Grimaldi remains in the Grotte des Enfants, Monaco. Later the grave was overlain by rock debris, here removed.

Petrification
Even the interior of a structurally stable cave changes over a long period, and in this case a sudden gross alteration has resulted from a large fall of rock from the roof. Subsequent to this, slow seepage through the limestone roof of water containing dissolved minerals, especially calcium carbonate, caused gradual growth of pendulous stalactites and upright stalagmites.

Animal remains
The cave is littered to a depth of well over a foot (0.3 m) with the debris of the food and other refuse of carnivores. The great cone above the fall of rock is littered with the remains of animals which fell in through the hole above; and on top of the cone is a pile of bat dung.

A rock fall
A massive collapse of the cave roof left a pile of rock on the floor of the cave and a gaping open shaft above. New layers of flowstone accumulated, earth and rock debris built up above the growing cone reached the roof. Sediments then filled the shaft.

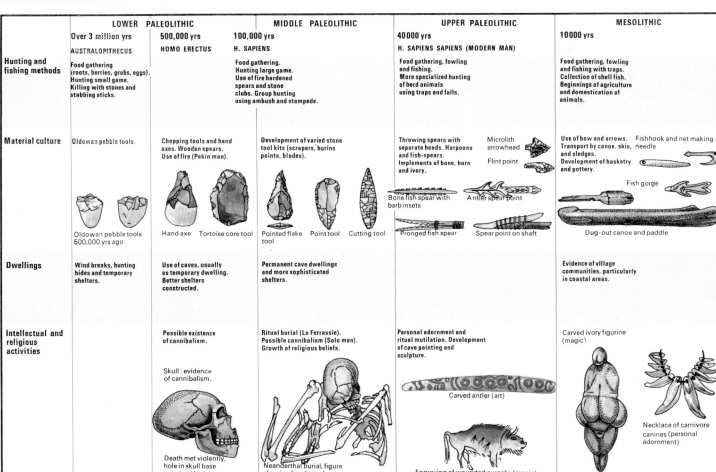

	LOWER PALEOLITHIC		MIDDLE PALEOLITHIC		UPPER PALEOLITHIC	MESOLITHIC
	Over 3 million yrs AUSTRALOPITHECUS	500,000 yrs HOMO ERECTUS	100,000 yrs H. SAPIENS		40000 yrs H. SAPIENS SAPIENS (MODERN MAN)	10000 yrs
Hunting and fishing methods	Food gathering (roots, berries, grubs, eggs). Hunting small game. Killing with stones and stabbing sticks.		Food gathering. Hunting large game. Use of fire hardened spears and stone clubs. Group hunting using ambush and stampede.		Food gathering, fowling and fishing. More specialized hunting of herd animals using traps and falls.	Food gathering, fowling and fishing with traps. Collection of shell fish. Beginnings of agriculture and domestication of animals.
Material culture	Oldowan pebble tools. Oldowan pebble tools 500,000 yrs ago	Chopping tools and hand axes. Wooden spears. Use of fire (Pekin man). Hand axe Tortoise core tool	Development of varied stone tool kits (scrapers, burins points, blades). Pointed flake tool Point tool Cutting tool		Throwing spears with separate heads. Harpoons and fish-spears. Implements of bone, horn and ivory. Bone fish spear with barb insets Pronged fish spear Microlith arrowhead Flint point Antler spear point Spear point on shaft	Use of bow and arrows. Fishhook and net making Transport by canoe, skis, needle and sledges. Development of basketry and pottery. Fish gorge Dug-out canoe and paddle
Dwellings	Wind breaks, hunting hides and temporary shelters.	Use of caves, usually as temporary dwelling. Better shelters constructed.	Permanent cave dwellings and more sophisticated shelters.			Evidence of village communities, particularly in coastal areas.
Intellectual and religious activities		Possible existence of cannibalism. Skull: evidence of cannibalism. Death met violently, hole in skull base to extract brain.	Ritual burial (La Ferrassie). Possible cannibalism (Solo man). Growth of religious beliefs. Neanderthal burial, figure clasping boar's jawbone.		Personal adornment and ritual mutilation. Development of cave painting and sculpture. Carved antler (art) Engraving of wounded aurochs (magic)	Carved ivory figurine (magic) Necklace of carnivore canines (personal adornment)

Treasures of the Earth

One of the wonders of the Earth must be the subtle interplay between light and structure that transforms common minerals into precious jewels. In most cases man's hand can be detected in their creation, but even in the natural state many minerals have a range of color, shape, texture and form that makes them the treasures of the Earth.

By popular definition, anything that is mined is called a mineral and on this basis coal and oil are the most important minerals (pages 34–35A). However, geologists reserve the term for naturally occurring materials which have an unvarying chemical composition and crystalline structure. The basic structural elements are arranged in a rigid pattern within three-dimensional crystal matrices.

Each crystal grows from a nucleus by adding atoms layer by layer. A freely growing crystal assumes one of seven basic forms, depending on the relative angles of its faces and the distances between opposite parallel pairs. But in practice the shape of naturally occurring crystals is generally influenced by the space in which it is constrained to grow. Thus in nature crystals develop characteristic habits or over-all shapes. The faces may be all of the same size or unequal. They may occur in narrow layers or grow like a bunch of grapes.

Minerals can be identified by their structure, habit, hardness, density, and the ease with which they can be cleaved along particular planes. Hardness, for example, is normally measured against a scale of increasing hardness from talc to diamond, devised in 1822 by the German mineralogist, F. Mohs. Color is frequently the result of minute proportions of impurities. These often result in minerals of such startling beauty that they are coveted by man as gemstones. The brilliance of transparent gems is due to the way light is reflected inside the stone, and man has learned how to cut gems to enhance their optical properties. The stone is cut or ground to a precise external form with face angles arranged to insure the maximum brilliance based on the refractive index of the material. Rocks (below) are composed of different combinations of a limited number of minerals

Basic igneous rock
Dolerite, a basic igneous rock, is composed of laths of plagioclase (grey and black), pyroxene (yellow and orange) and oxides of iron and titanium (blackish regions).

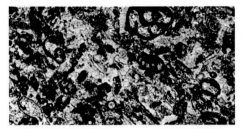

Sedimentary rock *above*
Limestone is composed of finely crystalline calcite. It shows the fossilized remains of foraminifera.

Acid igneous rock *below*
Granite is a hard igneous rock made up of quartz, potassium feldspar and red-brown crystals of biotite.

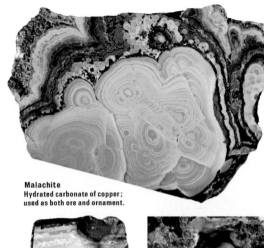

Azurite
Carbonate of copper, possibly the first metal used by man.

Opal
Amorphous silicon dioxide with a variable content of water.

Malachite
Hydrated carbonate of copper; used as both ore and ornament.

Hemimorphite
A zinc silicate, botryoidal crystal found with other zinc deposits.

Cerussite
Very clearly defined crystals of lead carbonate.

Pyromorphite
A bed of fine hexagonal columns of lead chlorophosphate.

Sphene
Silicates are abundant; sphene is calcium titanium silicate.

Crystal size
Although crystal shapes are governed by internal structure, individual sizes are controlled only by conditions of growth. For example, plates of mica— seen as minute biotite flakes in granite sections (lower left)— have reached 33ft (10m) by 14ft (4.3m) wide as in one 90-ton example discovered in Canada.

Quartz
Columnar crystals of silicon dioxide.

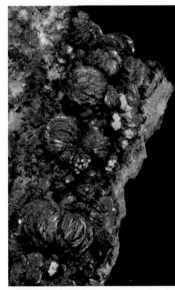
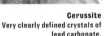

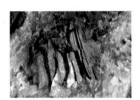

Torbernite
Hydrous copper uranium
phosphate; a uranium source.

Beryl
Beryllium aluminium silicate is
known in crystals of 25 tons.

Pyrite on calcite
Crystals of iron disulphide,
on calcium carbonate.

Cassiterite
Tin was one of man's earliest
metals; this is the dioxide ore.

Wavelite
Crystals of hydrous basic
aluminium phosphate.

Calcite
Often occurs as stalactites and
stalagmites.

Citrine
The yellowish variety of quartz
(silicon dioxide).

Diamonds in kimberlite
Native diamonds (crystalline
carbon) in their original rock.

Ruby in host rock
The deep red variety of
corundum (aluminium oxide).

Polished diamond
For use as a gemstone the
diamond is skilfully cut.

Polished ruby
Large rubies are among the most
precious of all gemstones.

Sulfur
Crystalline sulphur (brimstone)
occurs in nature.

Fluorite
Calcium fluoride occurs in various
colorful forms.

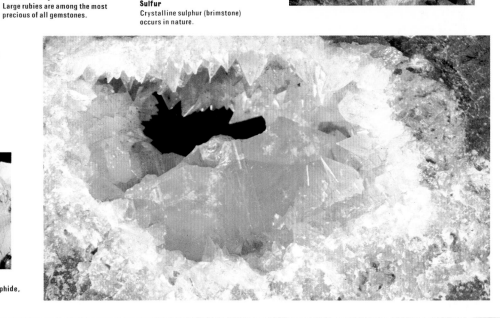

Galena
Cubic crystals of lead sulphide,
a major ore of lead.

Minerals Under the Land

Of about 2000 minerals in the Earth's crust only 100 or so are of economic importance. These are distributed very irregularly, so that no country today can boast all the minerals it needs. As a result minerals are a source of great national wealth, exploitation and even of rivalry. And the strife is likely to intensify as man's demands grow, because the total of the Earth's minerals is limited.

Against this background of uneven distribution, economic warfare and sharply increasing demand, man's use of minerals constantly changes. Coal, in 1920 the most important mineral in the world on a tonnage basis, is today unable to compete in several of its former markets because of the high cost of transporting it, and its use is increasingly changing from that of a fuel to that of a raw material for plastics and chemicals. Nitrates for fertilizers and explosives sustained the economy of Chile until 1914, when Germany found a way to 'fix' nitrogen from the atmosphere. Aluminum, one the most abundant minerals, was costly and little used until a large-scale refining process was discovered which made use of cheap hydroelectricity.

Taking the broad view, the Earth's minerals are seen as a stern test of man's ability to make proper use of the resources available to him. Already some nations have amassed enormous stockpiles of what are today considered to be strategically important minerals. Nickel is one such metal, and the bulk of the world's supply comes from Canada. Another is manganese, and in this case the dominant supplier is the Soviet Union; but manganese is one of the many minerals which might be dredged from the sea bed.

Uneven distribution of minerals is paralleled by uneven consumption. Paradoxically, the industrialized countries which owed their original development to the presence of mineral resources, particularly iron and coal, now rely for their continued prosperity on developing nations. If the latter were to develop a similar demand for materials a mineral famine would ensue which would have repercussions throughout the world.

World output *right*
The most important commercial minerals and main producers. At the foot of each column is annual world output in millions of long tons. Precious mineral outputs (asterisked) are: gold 52 million fine troy ounces; silver 240 m.f.t.o.; platinum 3.4 m.f.t.o.; diamonds 30 million metric carats.

Key to mineral producers

1 Soviet Union	15 Zambia
2 USA	16 Australia
3 France	17 Spain
4 S Africa	18 Italy
5 Philippines	19 Malaysia
6 Zaire	20 United Kingdom
7 Canada	21 Thailand
8 Morocco	22 Argentina
9 Brazil	23 Uganda
10 Chile	24 India
11 New Caledonia	25 Mexico
12 SW Africa	26 Peru
13 Finland	27 Congolese Rep.
14 China (People's Rep.)	28 Ghana

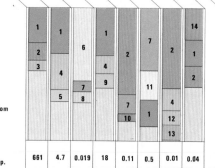

Ferro-alloy metals								Non-ferrous metals					Light metals	Nuclear fuels			Precious metals			
Iron ore	Chromite	Cobalt	Manganese	Molybdenum	Nickel	Vanadium	Tungsten	Copper	Lead	Mercury	Tin	Asbestos	Aluminium	Beryllium	Uranium	Thorium	Gold	Silver	Platinum	Diamonds
	1	1		1	1		14	2	2	17			7	2	22	2	24		7	27
	2		6			7		1	1	16	19				23			4	25	1
	3	4		2	4		2	15		18					9				26	
		5	7		9	11				20	1			1		7	19			4
			8		7	1	4	2		21			9			9		1	4	28
					10		12					4					7		7	
							13													
661	4.7	0.019	18	0.11	0.5	0.01	0.04	5.3	2.9	0.01	0.21		3.47	7.7	0.003		0.024	0.0006	*	*	*	*

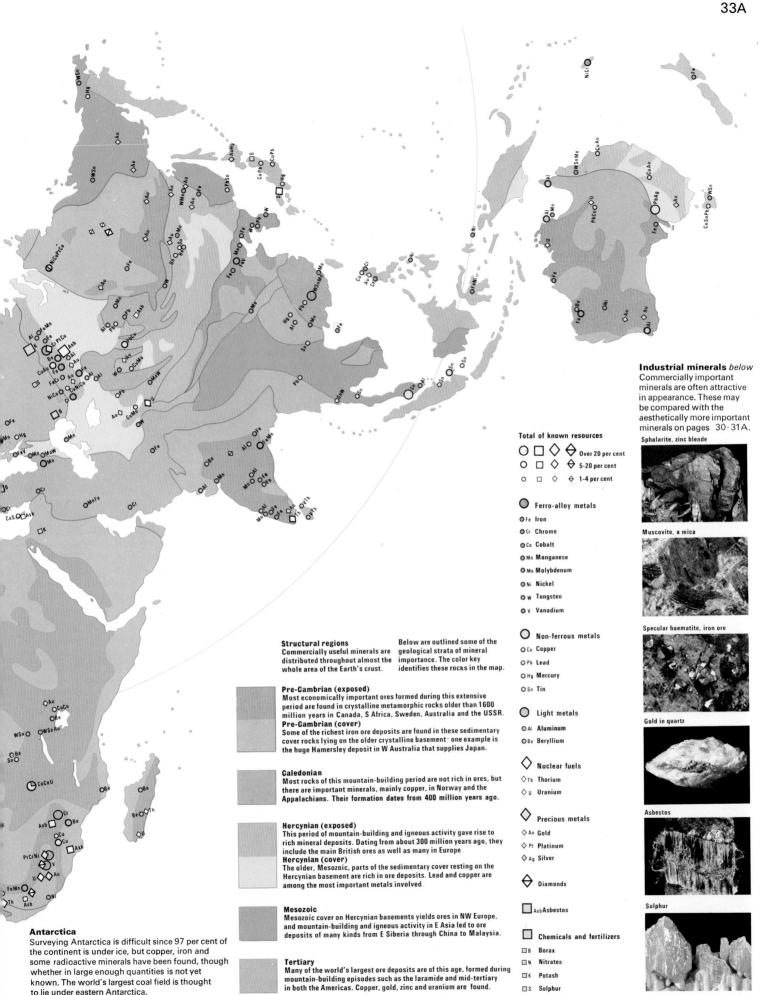

Industrial minerals *below*
Commercially important minerals are often attractive in appearance. These may be compared with the aesthetically more important minerals on pages 30-31A.

Sphalarite, zinc blende

Muscovite, a mica

Specular haematite, iron ore

Gold in quartz

Asbestos

Sulphur

Total of known resources

⭕	⬜	◇	⬦	Over 20 per cent
○	▫	◇	⬦	5-20 per cent
∘	▫	⋄	⬦	1-4 per cent

Ferro-alloy metals
- Fe Iron
- Cr Chrome
- Co Cobalt
- Mn Manganese
- Mo Molybdenum
- Ni Nickel
- W Tungsten
- V Vanadium

Non-ferrous metals
- Cu Copper
- Pb Lead
- Hg Mercury
- Sn Tin

Light metals
- Al Aluminum
- Be Beryllium

Nuclear fuels
- Th Thorium
- U Uranium

Precious metals
- Au Gold
- Pt Platinum
- Ag Silver

Diamonds

Asb Asbestos

Chemicals and fertilizers
- B Borax
- N Nitrates
- K Potash
- S Sulphur

Structural regions
Commercially useful minerals are distributed throughout almost the whole area of the Earth's crust.

Below are outlined some of the geological strata of mineral importance. The color key identifies these rocks in the map.

Pre-Cambrian (exposed)
Most economically important ores formed during this extensive period are found in crystalline metamorphic rocks older than 1600 million years in Canada, S Africa, Sweden, Australia and the USSR.
Pre-Cambrian (cover)
Some of the richest iron ore deposits are found in these sedimentary cover rocks lying on the older crystalline basement: one example is the huge Hamersley deposit in W Australia that supplies Japan.

Caledonian
Most rocks of this mountain-building period are not rich in ores, but there are important minerals, mainly copper, in Norway and the Appalachians. Their formation dates from 400 million years ago.

Hercynian (exposed)
This period of mountain-building and igneous activity gave rise to rich mineral deposits. Dating from about 300 million years ago, they include the main British ores as well as many in Europe.
Hercynian (cover)
The older, Mesozoic, parts of the sedimentary cover resting on the Hercynian basement are rich in ore deposits. Lead and copper are among the most important metals involved.

Mesozoic
Mesozoic cover on Hercynian basements yields ores in NW Europe, and mountain-building and igneous activity in E Asia led to ore deposits of many kinds from E Siberia through China to Malaysia.

Tertiary
Many of the world's largest ore deposits are of this age, formed during mountain-building episodes such as the laramide and mid-tertiary in both the Americas. Copper, gold, zinc and uranium are found.

Antarctica
Surveying Antarctica is difficult since 97 per cent of the continent is under ice, but copper, iron and some radioactive minerals have been found, though whether in large enough quantities is not yet known. The world's largest coal field is thought to lie under eastern Antarctica.

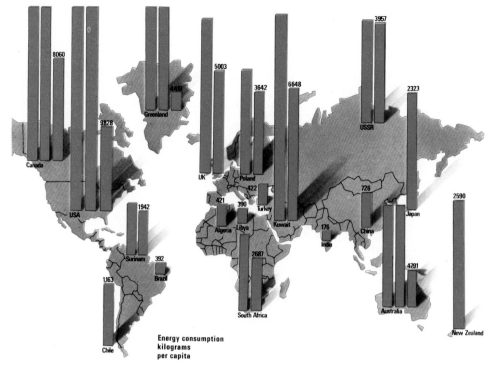

**Energy consumption
kilograms
per capita**

The concept of energy arose only very recently in the period of man's life on Earth, but already it dominates the whole quality of this life. Early man had no mechanical energy but that of his muscles. By about 2500 years ago he had learned to harness draft animals, such as the ox and horse, and to devise crude water wheels to harness part of the energy of the flow of water in a river. Soon afterwards he added sails to make the fickle wind propel his ships, and by 1000 years ago had started to dot his landscape with windmills. By this time he was adept at burning combustible materials, and during the past 500 years his energy has been increasingly based upon fire, first using wood, and subsequently coal, gas made from coal, petroleum, and natural gas.

All these energy sources, including animal muscle and the wind, are based on the energy radiated by the Sun. Although modern man has begun to use this energy directly in a few trivial installations in hot countries, almost all his energy is derived from solar heat locked up in fossil fuels. The known reserves of these fuels are tending to increase, as a result of prospecting, even faster than man is burning them up. But if no more were discovered most of man's world would come to a halt inside 20 years.

But there should be no energy gap. The promise of nuclear energy is such that, by using fast reactors that breed more fuel than they consume, energy should become one of the very few really plentiful and cheap commodities in man's world of the future. The challenges reside in extracting the fuels and using them effectively.

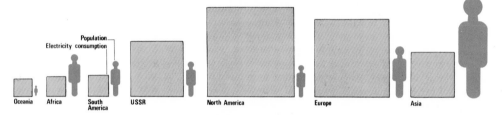

Power and people *above*
World consumption of energy is very uneven. One way of measuring it is to reduce all forms of energy to an equivalent weight of coal burned. The columns on the world map are proportional to the 'coal equivalent' of selected national consumptions expressed in kilograms per head. Electricity consumption is even more disproportionate, as witness the square areas and figure heights immediately above.

Fuels and energy *right*
The caloric value of a fuel is the quantity of heat generated by burning a unit mass. Figures are in British Thermal Units per pound. The surrounding curve shows the increase in the rate at which man is consuming energy; one joule (j) per second is equal to one watt.

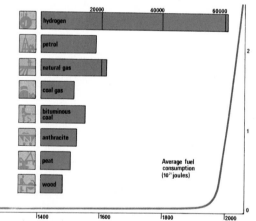

Average fuel consumption (10²⁰ joules)

Sources of power *below*
For many centuries the only alternative sources of power to muscles were wood fires, waterwheels and windmills — and the latter had too slight an effect to be shown on the figure below. The left portion shows the way in which, since 1850, the United States has enjoyed successive new sources of energy. In 1920 the US economy was not untypical in being based on coal, but since then more energetic, cleaner and more efficiently used fuels have dominated the picture. In the future, nuclear power, shown in the right-hand figure, promises to make good shortages of fossil fuels.

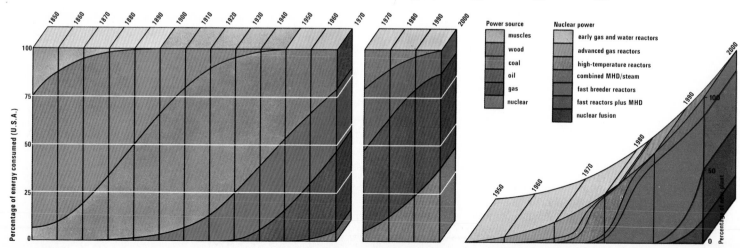

Power source
- muscles
- wood
- coal
- oil
- gas
- nuclear

Nuclear power
- early gas and water reactors
- advanced gas reactors
- high-temperature reactors
- combined MHD/steam
- fast breeder reactors
- fast reactors plus MHD
- nuclear fusion

Coal into electricity
To reduce costs modern coal-fired generating stations are sited on coalfields ; Lea Hall colliery feeds Rugeley power station (background).

Coal

For three centuries the most important of the fossil fuels, coal is the result of some 300 million years of subterranean decay of vegetation. Many thousands of generations of the Carboniferous trees have become compressed and hardened, first into peat, then into lignite, then into bituminous coal and finally into anthracite. Until this century coal was used inefficiently as a source of heat. Today it is becoming equally important as a raw material producing plastics, heavy chemicals, insecticides, perfumes, antiseptics, road surfaces and many other products. Great advances have been made in automating the mining of coal, but it remains a laborious task and is therefore becoming increasingly expensive. However, coal mining remains a worldwide industry that passes on to modern man the products of the solar energy captured by a younger Earth.

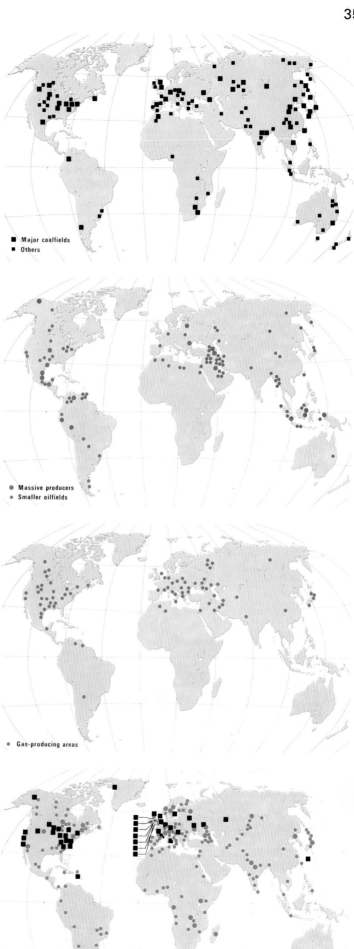

■ Major coalfields
■ Others

Flare in the desert
Once oil has been struck, harmful gases are burned off in the atmosphere. Similar 'flares' are a prominent feature of petroleum refineries.

Petroleum

Like coal, oil is a mixture of fossil remains, but yields few clues as to its origin. Crude oil, from the locations shown on the map at right, is carried by tanker ships to refineries in the user countries. Here it is heated in pipe stills until the various constituent 'fractions' are boiled off. The result is a wide range of products from gasoline through kerosene and gas oil to heavy fuel oils, lubricants and vaseline, with a wide range of other by-products used in many thousands of chemicals and plastics materials. Petroleum fuels are replacing coal in heating and transport applications, partly owing to their easier handling and partly to reduce air pollution by sulphurous compounds. LPG, liquefied pertroleum gas, is even cleaner burning and may become more important than gasoline and kerosene in road vehicles and aircraft over the next 25 years.

● Massive producers
● Smaller oilfields

Drilling for gas
To reach natural gas trapped in submarine strata a drill rig is used to bore a hole at a location determined by the prospectors

Gas

In 1807 a London street was lit by town gas, a mixture of hydrogen (about 50%), methane, carbon monoxide and dioxide and other gases, formed by cooking coal at high temperature in a retort. By 1950 this manufactured gas was an important fuel, but in many advanced countries its place is now being taken by natural gas, a primary fuel consisting mainly of methane piped straight from deposits sometimes conveniently sited from the user's point of view (right). Intensive prospecting is discovering natural gas faster than it is being used, and during the past 20 years natural gas has become man's largest single source of energy. In refrigerated form, as a compact liquid, it promises to become an attractive fuel for transport vehicles. A major benefit is that the exhaust from such a vehicle would contain less pollutants than from those using gasoline.

● Gas-producing areas

Nuclear power station
Nearly all today's nuclear energy is used to generate electricity. One of the largest stations is Wylfa, Wales, rated at 1180 million watts.

Nuclear energy

In 1956 Britain opened the world's first electricity generating station using the heat of nuclear fission. It was fuelled with rods of natural uranium, a heavy silvery metal containing a small proportion of atoms capable of spontaneous fission when struck by a free neutron. Fission releases further neutrons capable of sustaining a continuous chain reaction. Such a reaction generates heat which is used to provide steam for turbines. The prime advantage of nuclear power is that the fuel is used extremely slowly. Now the fast reactor, which uses raw 'fast' neutrons instead of ones artificially slowed down, has been developed. Not only can the fast reactor generate great energy from a small bulk but it creates fresh fuel faster than the original (plutonium) fuel is consumed. Fast reactors, using uranium from granite, could provide limitless cheap energy.

■ Nuclear power stations
● Large hydro-electric plant
● Smaller hydro schemes

Without water there would be no life as we know it on the Earth. Life began in the oceans and the life of the land, both plant and animal, still remains utterly dependent on water for its survival. The atmosphere plays a vital role in the terrestrial water system. Spurred by the energy of the Sun, the moist layer surrounding the globe forms a vast heat engine, operating at a rate of billions of horsepower. All the exposed water surface is constantly being converted into vapor. Eventually the air holding the vapor cools, and the vapor condenses as rain, hail or snow. Most of this precipitation falls into the sea, but nearly a quarter of it falls on the land. Altogether about two-thirds of it evaporates back into the air, or is transpired by plants; the rest runs off in rivers, or filters through the ground to the water table beneath.

Satisfying the collective thirst of man and his industry grows daily more difficult. Almost always the demand is for fresh water; but the proportion of the Earth's water in rivers and streams is less than one part in a million. If the Antarctic ice cap were to melt, it would feed all the rivers for 800 years. Although schemes have been suggested for towing giant freshwater icebergs from Antarctica to the Californian coast, man is unlikely to make extensive use of the ice cap. Far more promising is the large supply of subterranean water. At the same time great strides are being made in desalination of sea water, using a variety of methods. Management of the Earth's water resources is seen ever more clearly as a technical challenge of the greatest magnitude.

Distribution of the world's water resources
- The atmosphere
- Lakes, rivers and streams
- Ground—water and soil
- Ice caps and glaciers
- Oceans, saline lakes and inland seas

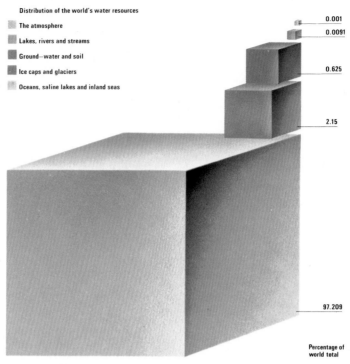

0.001
0.0091
0.625
2.15
97.209

Percentage of world total

The world's water *left*
The total volume of the Earth's water is about 326 million cubic miles (1400 million km³). Practically all of it is in the oceans, in a form rich in dissolved salts. Solar heating is constantly evaporating this mass, converting it ultimately into precipitation of fresh water which falls back to the surface. Run-off from the surface in rivers and streams is one of the forms of terrestrial water most visible to man, but it accounts for a negligible fraction of the total. Some 80 times as much water lies in salt lakes and inland seas, 90 times as much in freshwater lakes, more than 6000 times as much in ground water beneath the land surface, and almost a quarter-million times as much in ice caps and glaciers. So far man has made little attempt to use these sources of fresh water. Instead he interrupts the hydrologic cycle in the easy places: the rivers and lakes, where, because of the small volumes and flows available, he causes significant pollution.

A valued resource *above*
Shiupur head, the headwaters of the Gang canal in Rajasthan province, India. This and other canal systems are gradually bringing to this arid province an assured supply of irrigation water from the Himalayas.

Annual precipitation 100%

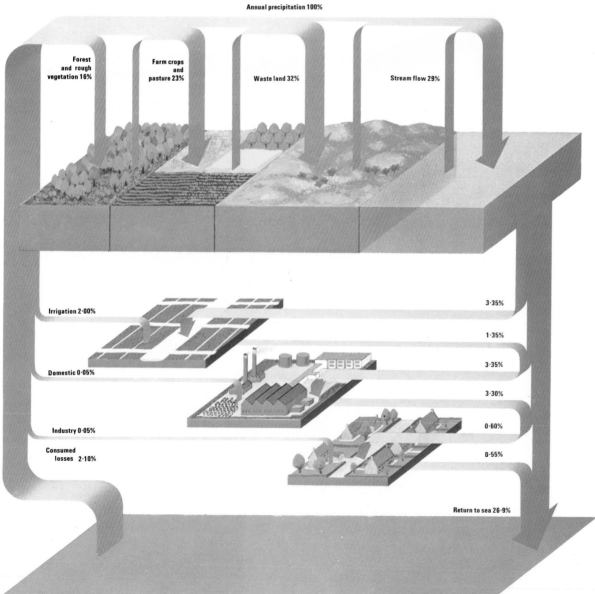

Forest and rough vegetation 16%

Farm crops and pasture 23%

Waste land 32%

Stream flow 29%

Irrigation 2·00%

3·35%

1·35%

3·35%

3·30%

Domestic 0·05%

Industry 0·05%

0·60%

Consumed losses 2·10%

0·55%

Return to sea 26·9%

The hydrologic cycle *left*
This diagram is drawn for United States, but the basic features of the cycle are common to most of the Earth's land. Just over three-quarters of the rain snow and hail falls on the oceans. The usual measure for water in huge quantities is the acre-foot (one acre of water, one foot deep). Each year about 300 thousand million acre-feet of water falls on the oceans and 80 thousand million on the land. In the diagram all the figures are percentages. In the US, which is not unusual in its proportion of farmland, less than one-quarter of the water falling on the land falls directly on crops or pasture. A greater amount falls into rivers and streams, from which man takes varying small fractions for his own purposes. It can be seen that, even in the US, the total quantity of water withdrawn for use is only 7.3 per cent of the fraction of water falling on the land. Yet, to attain even this performance, Americans spend more than $10000 million each year on improving their water supplies.

Domestic use of water

In some countries the total consumption of water is less than one gallon per head, but in the United States more than 70 US gallons are consumed by each person daily, on average, in domestic use alone. The way this consumption is split up varies greatly, but these percentages, for 'an average home in Akron, Ohio' are typical for modern urban areas having piped water to flush toilets. Total domestic water consumption in the industrially advanced countries is usually between five and 30 per cent of the national total.

Flushing toilet 41%

Washing and bathing 37%

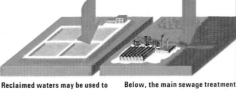

Kitchen use 6%

Drinking 5%

Laundry 4%

Household cleaning 3%

Garden 3%

Cleaning car 1%

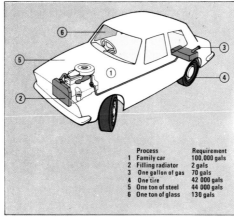

	Process	Requirement
1	Family car	100,000 gals
2	Filling radiator	2 gals
3	One gallon of gas	70 gals
4	One tire	42 000 gals
5	One ton of steel	44 000 gals
6	One ton of glass	130 gals

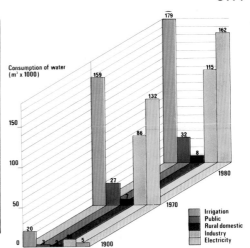

Consumption of water (m³ x 1000)

Rising demand *above*
Civilized man needs more water every year. Plotted graphically, the rising demand for water in the United States is startling ; the rate of increase is about three times the rate of population growth. Rural domestic supplies are from wells ; others are piped.

Irrigation
Public
Rural domestic
Industry
Electricity

Irrigation *below*
Irrigation of land by man is at least 7000 years old, yet still in its infancy. The grey areas on the world map are virtually without irrigation. The last column of data shows the percentage of each continent irrigated. Only Japan and the UAR exceed 50 per cent.

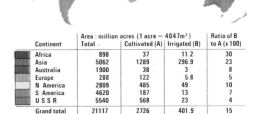

Continent	Area : million acres (1 acre = 4047m²)			Ratio of B to A (x 100)
	Total	Cultivated (A)	Irrigated (B)	
Africa	898	37	11.2	30
Asia	5062	1289	296.9	23
Australia	1900	38	3	8
Europe	288	122	5.8	5
N America	2809	485	49	10
S America	4620	187	13	7
U S S R	5540	568	23	4
Grand total	21117	2726	401.9	15

Most liquid wastes are generated by mixed human concentrations–including habitations, businesses and industry. Before reclamation, any wastes having excessive or toxic mineral content must be segregated from the main flow.

Liquid wastes from residential and business areas normally comprise sewage suitable for reclamation without pre-treatment or segregation.

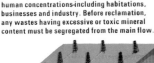

Oilfields on the land invariably generate large and varied liquid wastes, particularly including concentrated brines, which must be excluded from conventional reclamation processes.

This water reclamation plant supplies water to the city (above) and to agriculture and industry (below, right). Sludge and grease are returned to the sewer (route, far right).

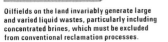

This water reclamation plant accepts mainly residential effluent. Water reclaimed is returned for re-use, while sludge and grease are returned to the sewer and piped to the main sewage treatment plant. A proportion of the output is supplied to spreading grounds at the coast (below) to replenish the ground water table.

Reclaimed waters may be used to maintain underground supplies by spreading them on percolation beds (above), where the water filters down to the storage basin.

Below, the main sewage treatment plant can operate by a variety of methods, including long-term open storage, aeration, mechanical filtration and softening.

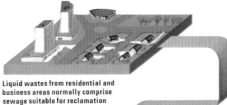

Reclaiming used water

In almost every country the quality of the water pumped into domestic supplies is subject to precise controls, and the proportion of some substances may not exceed one or two parts per million. National water systems make maximum use of water reclaimed close to the point of consumption by plant which returns the heavy sludges and greases to the sewer for treatment at a large sewage works. This facilitates effluent quality control and also provides an emergency outlet for a temporarily overloaded or faulty reclamation plant. In the example here the main treatment plant discharges wastes into an ocean outfall (left), while the fresh water spreading grounds just inshore replenish the water table and thus prevent infiltration by the ocean water.

Desalination

Man's growing demand for fresh water cannot readily be met without an enormous increase in his capacity to desalinate salt water. A choice between several ways of doing this is invariably made on economic grounds. Nearly all the large installations in use are multi-stage flash evaporators in which some form of heat – if possible, heat otherwise wasted - is used to convert sea water to steam which is condensed by the incoming salt water. But in some circumstances more economic results can be obtained by freezing, reverse osmosis or other methods.

GROWTH OF DESALTING CAPACITY 1961 TO 1968

Year Ending	Municipal water use M gal per day	Industrial/other uses M gal per day	Total
1961	17.6	42.2	59.8
1962	20.9	45.5	66.4
1963	28.4	50.4	78.8
1964	32.5	53.5	86.0
1965	39.3	58.9	98.2
1966	52.6	101.6	154.2
1967	102.2	115.3	217.5
1968	121.4	125.8	247.2
Historical annual growth %	32	17	23
Projection to 1975	835	415	1250
Projected annual growth %	32	19	26

SIZE RANGES OF THE WORLD'S DESALTING PLANTS

Size range M gal per day	Number of Plants	Total capacity M gal per day
0.025–0.1	351	17.8
0.1–0.3	218	35.3
0.3–0.5	34	13.0
0.5–1.0	31	21.3
1.0–5.0	46	95.4
5.0–7.5	3	17.5
over 7.5	3	46.9
TOTAL	686	247.2

The Oceans' Mineral Resources

A submerged land almost equal to the area of the Moon is being urgently explored for its store of minerals. The continental shelf around the Earth's land has the proportions of a seventh continent; around Britain or Japan its area is several times larger than that of the land itself. The shelf is rich in minerals, some of which are accumulating faster than man can at present use them.

By far the most important resources of the shallow seas are the deposits of oil and gas locked in the strata below the bed. Hundreds of drilling rigs are constantly probing for new deposits. Great Britain, for instance, located oil in the 1970s from a number of fields under the North Sea, and in 1980 was able to announce to the world that she had become self-sufficient in oil from that source. Next to oil and gas the most important marine mineral is lowly sand and gravel. It is becoming increasingly difficult and costly to win these from the land, and marine deposits are fast becoming of great commercial importance. Often their extraction is combined with land reclamation. The Dutch, for example, have devised several systems that help to create new land and, as at Europoort, deep-water channels.

Last in importance, but very high in speculative interest, come the heavy minerals. Some, such as gravels rich in ilmenite, rutile and zircon, have been concentrated by the sorting action of the waves. Others, including tin, gold and diamonds, have been derived from igneous deposits. But in most cases these minerals can still be obtained more cheaply on land, except in one or two freak instances where concentrated deposits can be easily reached.

Exploiting the shallow sea

One of the most important recent discoveries of oil and natural gas has occurred in the North Sea, on the very doorstep of industrial Western Europe. The North Sea gas is found mainly in layers of a porous sandstone deposited under desert conditions. Since both natural gas and oil are thought to have originated from the compressed remains of animals and plants that swarmed in the warm seas of the Carboniferous period, the gas could not have formed in the rocks where it is now found.

Immediately below the sandstone lie thick coal measures, and the gas appears to have risen from these into the porous sandstone until halted by a thick layer of salt and limestone. Where the limestone is broken and porous, the gas has risen into it and become trapped under salt domes. In the Gulf of Mexico these domes have themselves become a source of minerals. While drilling down to a promising dome an oil company came across the third largest sulphur deposit in the United States.

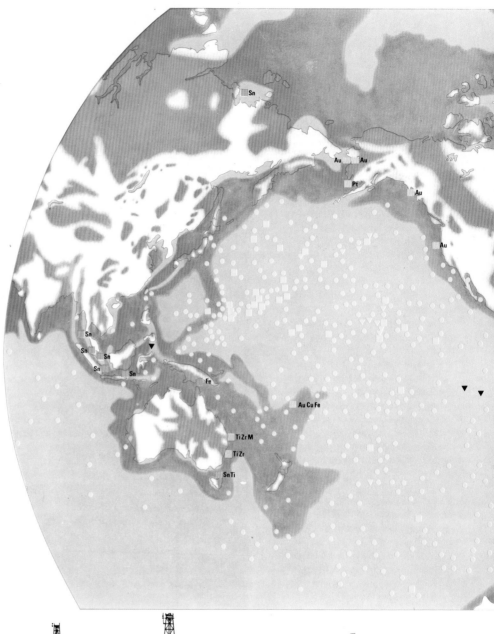

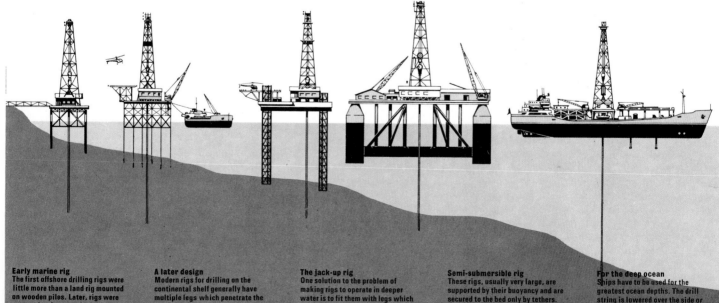

Early marine rig
The first offshore drilling rigs were little more than a land rig mounted on wooden piles. Later, rigs were mounted on barges which were floated to the site and then sunk to rest on the seabed. But neither of these systems was adequate for efficient sea drilling.

A later design
Modern rigs for drilling on the continental shelf generally have multiple legs which penetrate the sea floor. Such a rig can be moved to a fresh site, a major factor in reducing prospecting costs. Helicopters and ships bring crews and the drill strings.

The jack-up rig
One solution to the problem of making rigs to operate in deeper water is to fit them with legs which can be extended until they meet the bottom. Such rigs often have 350 foot (105 m) legs and can operate in a depth of 170 feet (50 m), but may capsize in storms.

Semi-submersible rig
These rigs, usually very large, are supported by their buoyancy and are secured to the bed only by tethers. Rough seas pass through the structure; the rig above rode 50 foot (15 m) waves in a hurricane, although another was lost in a North Sea storm.

For the deep ocean
Ships have to be used for the greatest ocean depths. The drill string is lowered over the side or through a hole in the hull. One deep-ocean drilling ship, *Glomar Challenger* (above), discovered oil in rocks of the abyssal plain under 10000 feet (3000 m) of water.

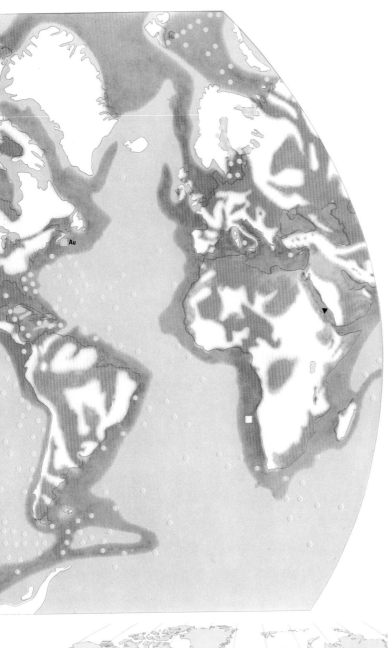

Undersea resources *left*

Deep ocean basins

Sedimentary basins locally favourable for petroleum

Au: gold

Sn: tin

Fe: iron

Ti: titanium

D: diamonds

Mn sampled

Mn photo 25+ per cent.

Mn photo 25— per cent.

Metal-bearing muds

The large map gives a broad general picture of the distribution of petroleum resources, shown as favorable sedimentary basins, and of major subsea mineral deposits, but does not attempt to indicate commercial value or even which regions are worth exploiting. These are multi-billion dollar questions which are taxing mining companies in many countries. The manganese oxide deposits are shown only where they have been sampled or photographed (with symbols to indicate whether the nodules cover more or less than one-quarter of the sea floor). The metal-bearing muds are a recent exciting discovery. Deep down in the Red Sea, off Indonesia and elsewhere, prospectors have discovered concentrated brines rich in valuable industrial metals.

Mining the oceans *below*

For 20 years industry has been tantalized by the prospect of literally sucking or sweeping valuable minerals off the ocean floor. But the most widespread loose nodules (see photograph below) have a composition ill-matched to world demand (foot of page), and even the mining system sketched below, in which ships operate what is in effect a giant vacuum cleaner, has yet to be used on a commercial scale. The technical, economic and political problems associated with such ventures are immense: but the potential rewards are great enough to sustain interest.

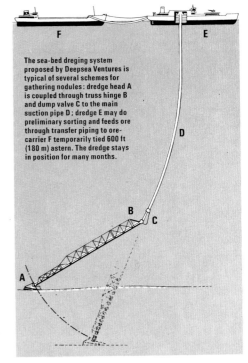

The sea-bed dreging system proposed by Deepsea Ventures is typical of several schemes for gathering nodules: dredge head A is coupled through truss hinge B and dump valve C to the main suction pipe D; dredge E may do preliminary sorting and feeds ore through transfer piping to ore-carrier F temporarily tied 600 ft (180 m) astern. The dredge stays in position for many months.

Manganese nodules

One of the most tempting concepts is to scoop minerals off the bed of the ocean. One of the few products which could thus be harvested is manganese, which is found in the form of potato-sized nodules scattered on the ocean floor.
Unfortunately not only are there technical difficulties standing in the way of such an operation but production would be out of step with world needs. The undersea production of the world's needs of manganese, equivalent to more than 18.6 million tons of ore, would lead to a 453 per cent glut of cobalt. Similarly, if all the world demand for copper were met from the same source, the glut of cobalt would be no less than 11335 per cent (right).

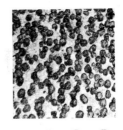

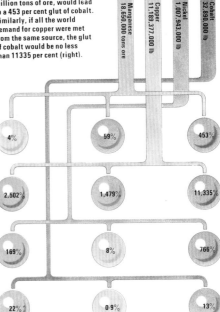

Manganese 18,650,000 tons ore — 4%

Copper 11,189,377,000 lb — 59%

Nickel 1,007,943,000 lb — 453%

Cobalt 32,890,000 lb

2,502% | 1,479% | 11,335%

169% | 8% | 766%

22% | 0.9% | 13%

oil

gas

tin

iron

coal

salt

heavy minerals

sulphur

diamonds

magnesium

fresh water

other minerals

oil and gas exploration

Undersea production

Man's commercial use of the ocean minerals is so far confined almost entirely to the continental shelves around the land.

The Oceans' Living Resources

Fish and shellfish were probably the first marine resources to be exploited by man. Many of his early settlements in coastal and estuarine areas bear witness to this with their ancient mounds of oyster and mussel shells. Even now, coastal fisheries remain a vital source of high quality protein for numerous primitive communities. And yet, in spite of this long history of coastal fishing, the commercial fisheries have been dominated by a mere handful of nations until recent times. Three-quarters of the world fish catch is still accounted for by only 14 countries.

The world fish catch is the only source of food that has managed to increase dramatically since the end of World War II. In the decade from 1958-68 alone, it rose from below 34 million tons to 64 million tons. Although the catch fell by two per cent in 1969, it is expected to continue to improve and may even top the 120 million ton mark by the mid-1980s.

The steady growth of the commercial fisheries since the war has relied on improvements in technology and boats, and the spread of these modern techniques from traditional northern fisheries to newer ones being developed in the southern oceans. Peru, for example, now has the world's largest single species fishery, catching some 10 million tons of anchoveta a year: in 1958 the catch was only 960,000 tons. However, the time is fast approaching when few fish stocks will remain unexploited.

Already many established fisheries are beginning to suffer from the effects of over-fishing with too many boats pursuing too few fish, leading to the capture of younger, smaller fish and a decline in the fish stocks and the fisheries that they support. Only the briefest respite may be needed for the fish to recover: a single female fish can lay thousands of eggs in a single season. Over-exploitation of the whales and turtles is a much more serious matter. Already several species of whale are on the verge of extinction and, with one young born to a female every two years, the prospects for their recovery are poor.

The living resources of the oceans must be conserved and managed if they are to continue to provide mankind with food. It is now clear that the world fish catch has a finite limit, possibly about 200 million tons. With adequate international agreement and controls, this limit might one day be approached. The productivity of the oceans could be increased further only by harvesting animals lower than fish in the marine food chain or by artificially fertilizing and farming the seas. Some of the first steps in this direction are now in progress. Perhaps in the future a new pattern of exploitation will emerge, with fleets harvesting the oceanic fish while other fish, shellfish and crustaceans such as lobster and prawn are farmed in the shallow coastal waters.

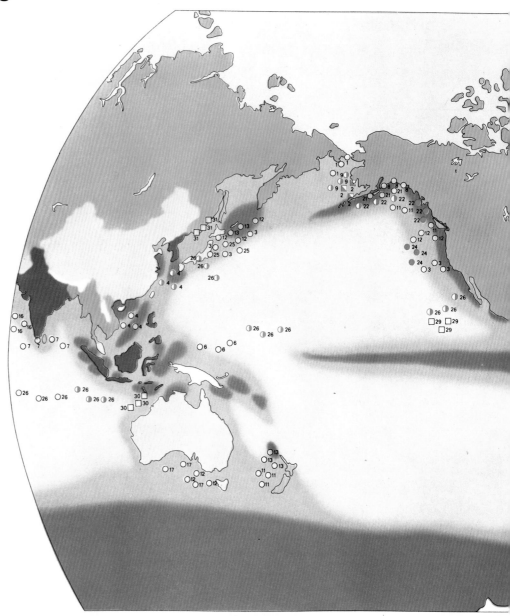

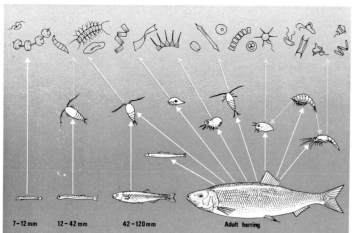

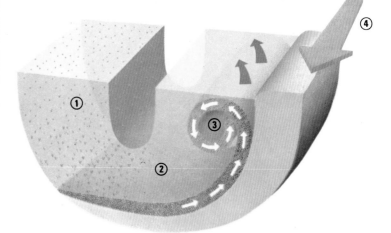

Marine food web *above*
The path leading to food fish such as the herring involves a succession of feeding and energy levels. The plants drifting in the plankton first convert the Sun's energy into a usable form through the process of photosynthesis (top band). The plants are then eaten by small planktonic animals (middle band). These in turn are eaten by the fish during its growth (bottom band). However, as the arrows indicate, the path from plant to fish is far from simple. At each point in the web, energy is exchanged and lost so that the adult fish receives less than a thousandth of the original energy captured in photosynthesis. This loss of energy has prompted suggestions for short-circuiting the process by harvesting members of the plankton itself – either the plants or the small crustaceans and other animals that feed on them.

Upwelling *above*
Most of the world's great fisheries occur in regions of upwelling where nutrient-rich water rises to the surface and supports prolific marine life. Deep ocean waters accumulate the remains of dead and decaying organisms (1) that rain down from the surface. When this nutrient-rich water (2) rises to the surface (3) it contains all the minerals and salts necessary for plant growth in approximately the ratio best suited to stimulate maximum growth. The actual mechanism which causes the water to rise to the surface can vary, but a common source is the interaction between surface winds and ocean currents running along the edge of continents. The wind (4) causes the surface water to move away from the coast, enabling the deep water to swirl up to the surface where it renews the supplies of plant nutrients.

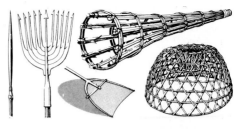

World fisheries *left*

With more nations claiming a share of the oceans' living resources few productive regions remain unexplored by fishing fleets. Already many fisheries show signs of over-exploitation and some coastal states are demanding exclusive rights to very large areas of sea, e.g. Iceland's demand for a 50 mile limit.

Biological productivity

▨ Very favorable conditions for the growth of marine life

▨ Moderately favorable conditions for the growth of marine life

Exploitation of fish stocks

● Over-exploited by 1949

◗ Over-exploited by 1968

○ Under-exploited

Exploitation of crustaceans

◣ Over-exploited by 1968

□ Under-exploited

Key to numbers

1	Alaska pollack	17	Pilchard
2	Anchoveta	18	Plaice
3	Anchovy	19	Pamfret
4	Demersal fish	20	Red fish
5	Capelin	21	Rock fish
6	Carangidae	22	Salmon
7	Clupeidae	23	Sand eel
8	Cod	24	Sardine
9	Flat fish	25	Saury
10	Haddock	26	Tuna
11	Hake	27	King crab
12	Herring	28	Krill
13	Jack mackerel	29	Red crab
14	Mackerel	30	Shrimp
15	Menhaden	31	Squid
16	Pelagic		

Fishing limits

▢ Nations claiming a 3 mile exclusive zone

▨ Nations claiming a 6 mile exclusive zone

▨ Nations claiming a 12 mile exclusive zone

▨ Nations claiming more than 12 miles

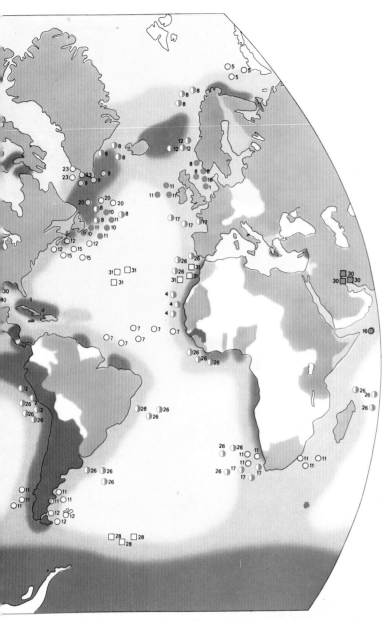

Fishing gear

Primitive fisheries use a wide range of techniques (above) including spears, nets and basket traps.

Mainstays of the modern commercial fisheries (below) are the gill net (top), the seine net and the otter trawl (bottom).

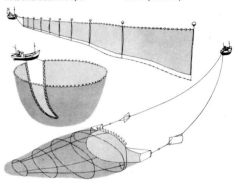

Commercial fish

Although the oceans contain many thousands of different fish species, very few of these support large commercial fisheries. The anchoveta supplies the largest single species fishery in the world with an annual catch of about 10 million tons. This is slightly greater than the total catch of the other species illustrated here.

Anchoveta — 5 in, 13 cm; 2–3 oz, 85 g
Herring — 12 in, 30 cm; 8 oz, 227 g
Cod — 72 in, 182 cm; 200 lbs, 91 kg
Haddock — 44 in, 112 cm; 36 lbs, 16 kg
SA Pilchard — 7 in, 18 cm; 4–5 oz, 140 g

The first marine farms, *right*

An early use of marine stockades was to keep alive fish caught at sea until they were needed for eating (A). An advance on this is to catch young fish and then fatten them in fertile coastal waters (B). But marine farming really begins with the production of 'seed fish' which can be reared until they are large enough to survive at sea (C). Such a scheme was proposed in the early 1900s as a means of increasing the productivity of the North Sea fisheries. The proposal was rejected, although marine fish hatcheries existed at the time. These hatcheries, however, were unable to feed their young fish once the yolk sacs had become exhausted. Success became possible with the discovery that brine shrimps, hatched in large numbers, could be used as fish food and that antibiotics would prevent marine bacteria from coating the eggs and killing or weakening the fish embryos inside. The point has now been reached at which fish farming is possible, although fish reared in this way are still too expensive to compete with those caught at sea. In one scheme, eggs collected from adult fish kept in ponds are hatched and the young fed on diatoms and brine shrimps until large enough to be put into marine enclosures (D).

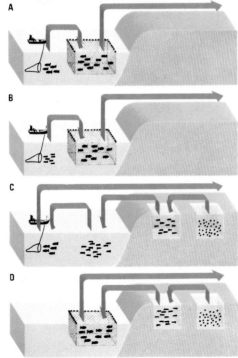

A

B

C

D

Enriching the sea *right, below*

Some marine farms in the future will exploit the store of nutrients that lie in the cold, deep ocean water. The value of this marine 'fertilizer' is clearly seen in areas where deep water rises to the surface. One project to create an artificial upwelling was started in the Virgin Islands in 1970. When completed it could include both a marine farm and provide fresh water supplies. In this system the cold nutrient-rich water (1) would be raised to the surface by a pump (2) driven by the warm, humid, prevailing winds (3). The cold water would then pass through a condenser (4) where it would be used to cool the wind and release its store of fresh water (5). Finally, the water, now warmed to the temperature of the surface waters, would be used to promote the growth of marine plants and animals such as shellfish, prawn and valuable food fish within net enclosures in the lagoon (6). Deep ocean water may also be used to combat thermal pollution, particularly in tropical areas where marine organisms live close to their upper temperature limit. The cold water would cool down the warm effluent discharged from power stations as well as provide valuable nutrients for marine aquiculture.

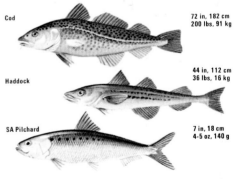

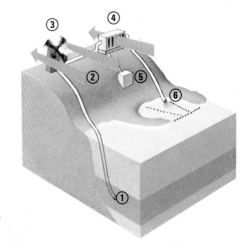

Combine harvester discharging wheat into trailer

Agriculture has always been a cornerstone of human civilization. Until man was able to give up the life of a nomadic hunter he could not be called civilized, and it was the settled life based on the land which enabled progress toward modern society to begin. Today agriculture is the occupation of more people than all other industries, but the pattern of their work varies greatly. In poor or developing lands as many as 90 per cent of the population live directly off the land, whereas in the most industrialized countries the proportion can be as low as three per cent.

The underlying purpose of farming is to convert the energy of sunlight into a form in which it can be assimilated by humans. Initially this can be done only by photosynthesis in green plants, and here the efficiency of the conversion process – expressed in terms of assimilable food energy obtained from a given amount of sunlight – varies from about two per cent down to less than one part in 1000. Further stages involve the consumption of plants by livestock to provide meat and other food for man, or the direct consumption of fruit, vegetables and cereals by man himself. Each additional step in this food chain involves large losses in energy, lowering the overall 'efficiency' of the process.

For many years research has led to improved methods of producing crops, by developing new plant strains with a higher edible yield or greater resistance to disease, by increasing both the area of land under cultivation and the nutritional value of the soil, by devising swifter and surer techniques of cultivation and by reducing the labor effort needed. Improved methods are especially needed in regions of poor farming. The 'Green Revolution' of SE Asia has already shown how yields can be increased dramatically, although at a greater cost in terms of agricultural chemicals and water supplies. Another promising way of increasing food supplies is to extract protein from plants such as soybean and even grass, and to convert them into forms that have the texture and taste of meat. For the more distant future there are prospects of growing single-cell protein and other revolutionary foods which in theory could at least double the Earth's ability to produce food.

World crop production and trade *right above*
In the large map, symbols and shading indicate the pattern of distribution of a selection of the most important crops used for human food The distribution shown is that of growing area. This is often far removed from the plant's original center, and today the world crop pattern is being subjected to dramatic changes. For example, enormous increases have taken place in Italy's yield of maize (corn) and the United States' production of rice. Pie diagrams are used to show world crop trade, the pie area giving output and the color segments the products (key, far right).

Some important crops *right*
Eight of the world's chief human food crops are described individually at right. The figure below the name is the aggregate world production expressed in metric tons (1m. ton is 0.984 British ton and 1.12 US tons). The pie diagrams in the form of segmented drums show the percentage of the world total raised by the three largest producing countries (in each case China is the People's Republic). The sketches illustrate the mature plant and its fruit, a form often unfamiliar to consumers. Similar panels on the next two pages deal with livestock, fish and oils.

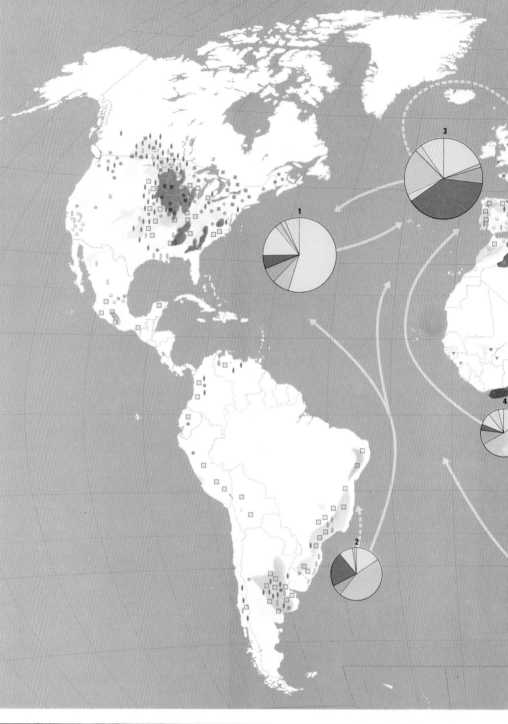

Millet and sorghum
107.4

India 15.9 | USA 17.5 | China 20.8

Several species of plant of the millet family form staple food crops throughout the Earth's warmer countries. The main genuses are *Panicum, Pennisetum,* and *Sorghum* or African millet. Chief growing regions are tropical and warm temperate Asia and Africa.

Potatoes
352.0

China (M) 10.4 | Poland 14.4 | USSR 29.0

Maize (corn)
284.0

Brazil 4.5 | China 11.6 | USA 39.3

Maize was originally brought from America by Columbus. Although it needs a growing period of 140 days in a soil rich in nitrogen, it can be made into bread and is the subsistence diet of much of Asia and Africa and is important in North America and Britain.

Grapes
53.7

USSR 8.4 | France 18.4 | Italy 19.2

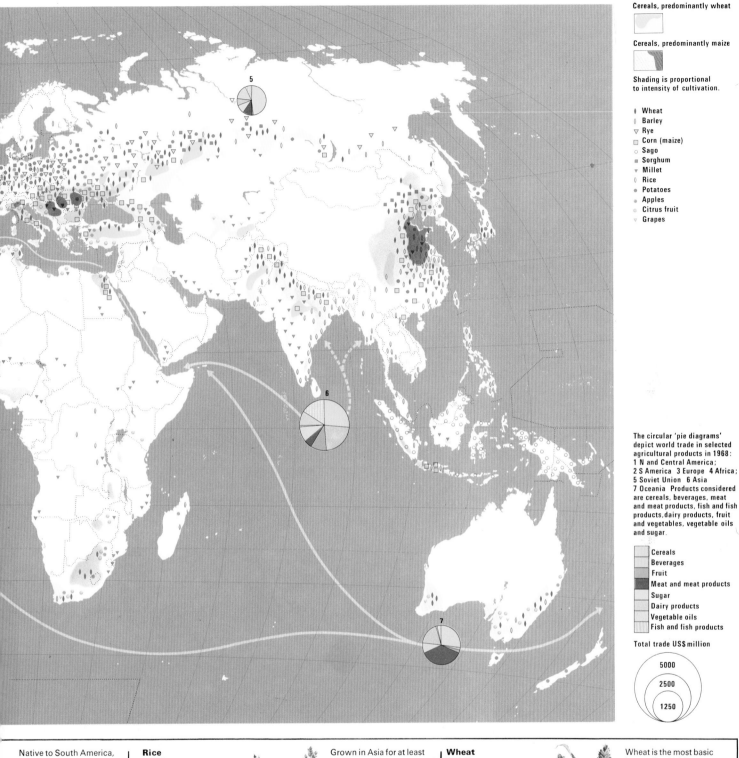

Cereals, predominantly wheat

Cereals, predominantly maize

Shading is proportional
to intensity of cultivation.

⧫ Wheat
◊ Barley
▽ Rye
□ Corn (maize)
○ Sago
■ Sorghum
▼ Millet
◊ Rice
● Potatoes
● Apples
○ Citrus fruit
▽ Grapes

The circular 'pie diagrams'
depict world trade in selected
agricultural products in 1968:
1 N and Central America;
2 S America 3 Europe 4 Africa;
5 Soviet Union 6 Asia
7 Oceania Products considered
are cereals, beverages, meat
and meat products, fish and fish
products, dairy products, fruit
and vegetables, vegetable oils
and sugar.

Cereals
Beverages
Fruit
Meat and meat products
Sugar
Dairy products
Vegetable oils
Fish and fish products

Total trade US$ million

5000

2500

1250

Native to South America,
the potato was introduced
by Spanish explorers to an
intrigued Europe about
1572. Although it needs a
long, cool growing season,
and a high nutrient level. it
yields more food per area of
land than cereals. It is a
source of alcohol.

The vine thrives in warm,
temperate areas, although
the quality of its rootstock
is critical to its nutrient
demand and its resistance
to disease and drought.
About 80 per cent of the
world crop is made into
wine, but large quantities
are dried for raisins.

**Rice
284.2**

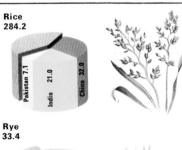

Pakistan 7.1 | India 21.0 | China 32.0

**Rye
33.4**

W Germany 9.5 | Poland 25.5 | USSR 42.2

Grown in Asia for at least
5000 years, rice was
introduced into Europe by
the Arabs. Irrigation or a
very heavy rainfall is
essential for growing rice,
with the fields being flooded
for most of the season. The
main source of vitamins, the
husk, is removed in milling.

Gradually giving way to
other cereals, rye is
important where soils are
sandy and acid and the
winters long and harsh.
From Britain deep into
Siberia it remains a staple
foodstuff used for animal
feeds, for various forms of
bread and for whisky.

**Wheat
332.5**

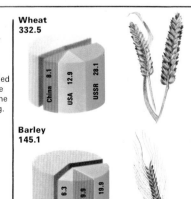

China 8.1 | USA 12.9 | USSR 28.1

**Barley
145.1**

USA 6.3 | China 9.9 | USSR 19.9

Wheat is the most basic
human food of the
temperate zone. It flourishes
in well-drained, fertile
conditions, but can rapidly
exhaust the soil. New breeds
have been genetically
tailored to improve yield
and resistance to disease

Barley has a very short
growing season and so can
be produced further north
and at a higher altitude than
any other cereal. It needs
good drainage and non-
acid soil. More than half the
world crop is eaten by
livestock, and 12 per cent
goes into making beer.

Unloading frozen lamb carcasses.

Beverages
Coffee, cocoa and tea are grown in the tropics for export to economically advanced countries where their chief role is to add flavor rather than to provide nutrition. Tea is the cheapest at present.

● Coffee
● Cocoa
● Tea

Spices
Invariably these are pungent, aromatic vegetable products. They have been important European imports since pre-Roman times, and a major source today is Indonesia. Spices are extracted from buds, bark and pods.

■ Pimento
▲ Ginger
◆ Nutmeg
● Mace
■ Pepper
◆ Cloves
● Cinnamon
■ Cassia
▲ Vanilla

Alcohol and tobacco
Originally native to South America, tobacco was brought to Europe by the Spanish 400 years ago. Today, it is grown all over the world in various climates and soils. The US is the biggest producer.

■ Beer
● Wine
▲ Spirits
□ Tobacco

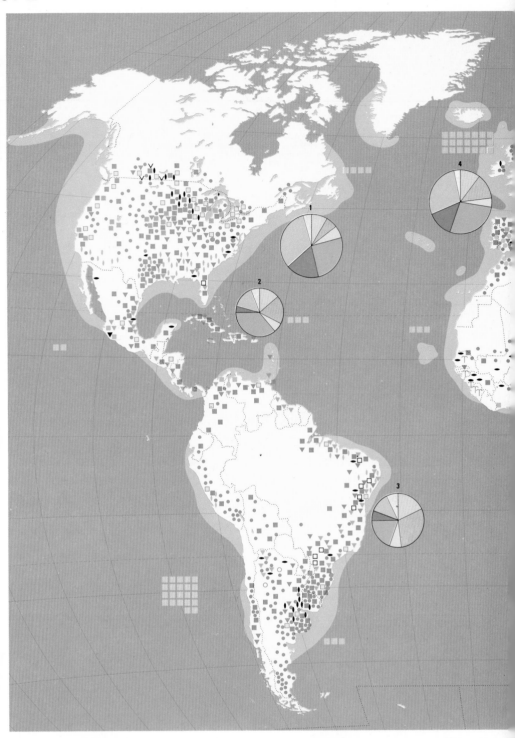

**Beef cattle
Beef 29.7**

The two principal types of domestic cattle, the European and the tropical Zebu or humped type, are found all over the world in every type of climate. There is an urgent need in the developing countries for better breeding, disease control and management.

Argentina 8.6 | USSR 18.5 | USA 33.0

**Dairy cattle
415.8**

Specialized dairy farming takes place mainly near densely populated urban areas with a high standard of living, though there is an increasing trend towards combined milk/meat herds. Various forms of processing, such as canning and freezing, extend product life.

France 8.1 | USA 13.8 | USSR 20.3

**Sheep
Mutton 4.5**

Sheep are kept mainly for meat and wool, although in southern Europe they may be milked and in the tropics the hides are the most important product. Sheep do not lend themselves readily to 'factory farming' and are raised on marginal land only.

India 8.2 | Australia 15.0 | USSR 22.3

**Pigs
Pork 24.5**

Because they are often kept indoors, the distribution of pigs depends more on food supply than on the climate. They are often found on mixed farms where they are fed on by-products such as skim milk. Their breeding cycle is complete in about six months.

China 11.0 | USSR 16.7 | USA 24.1

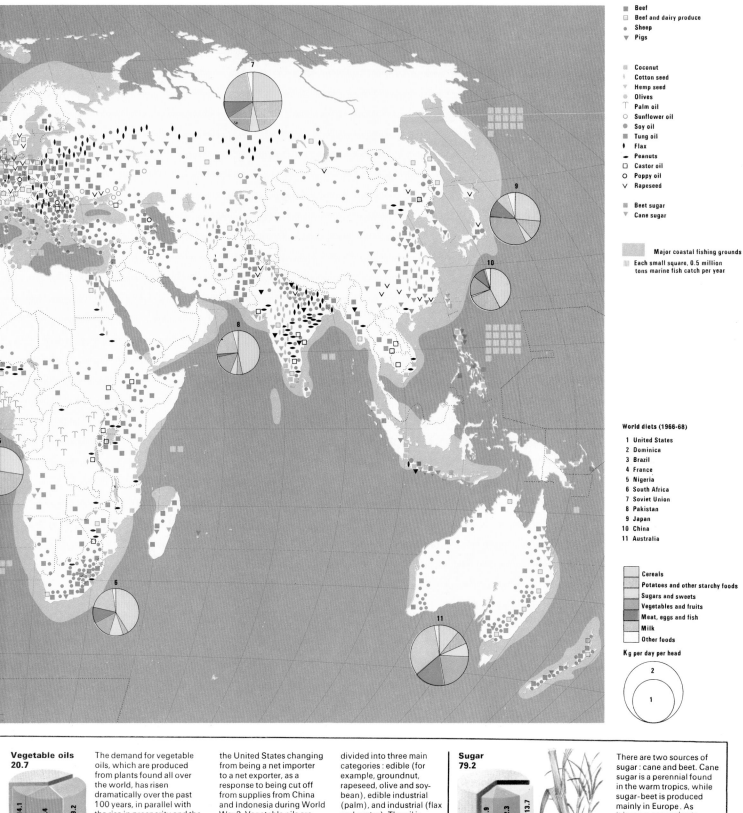

Beef
Beef and dairy produce
Sheep
Pigs

Coconut
Cotton seed
Hemp seed
Olives
Palm oil
Sunflower oil
Soy oil
Tung oil
Flax
Peanuts
Castor oil
Poppy oil
Rapeseed

Beet sugar
Cane sugar

Major coastal fishing grounds

Each small square, 0.5 million
tons marine fish catch per year

World diets (1966-68)

1 United States
2 Dominica
3 Brazil
4 France
5 Nigeria
6 South Africa
7 Soviet Union
8 Pakistan
9 Japan
10 China
11 Australia

Cereals
Potatoes and other starchy foods
Sugars and sweets
Vegetables and fruits
Meat, eggs and fish
Milk
Other foods

Kg per day per head

2

1

**Vegetable oils
20.7**

Russia 14.1 · China 17.4 · USA 29.2

The demand for vegetable oils, which are produced from plants found all over the world, has risen dramatically over the past 100 years, in parallel with the rise in prosperity and the discovery of new uses. The pattern of production has also altered markedly, with the United States changing from being a net importer to a net exporter, as a response to being cut off from supplies from China and Indonesia during World War 2. Vegetable oils are used in the manufacture of such products as margarine, soap and paint. They can be divided into three main categories : edible (for example, groundnut, rapeseed, olive and soy-bean), edible industrial (palm), and industrial (flax and castor). The oil is produced by crushing the seeds, and the residue often makes good cattle feed.

Groundnut
Soya bean
Olive
Flax
Sesame
Palm nut
Sunflower
Cotton
Castor
Not to scale

**Sugar
79.2**

Cuba 5.9 · USSR 12.3 · India 13.7

**Fish
64.0**

China 11.8 · Japan 13.5 · Peru 16.4

There are two sources of sugar : cane and beet. Cane sugar is a perennial found in the warm tropics, while sugar-beet is produced mainly in Europe. As it is more expensive to produce than cane its production is often protected by tariffs.

Fish are a valuable source of protein. As they putrify so easily and thus are subject to distribution problems, an increasing amount of the world catch is converted into meal for use in animal feeds. Most fish are caught near the coasts over the continental shelves.

Earth's Diverse Environments

To survive, animals must be adapted to their environment. They must be able to resist cold if they live in polar regions, drought if they live in deserts. They must find food, escape from predators and reproduce. Their offspring must mature and reproduce in turn. Adaptations of anatomy, physiology and behavior have evolved, so that today animals are found in all the Earth's diverse environments.

Ecologists divide the Earth into natural zones or 'biomes', each with its own highly adapted and integrated animal and plant communities. Inside each broad climatic zone animals have become adapted to various local environments or habitats. In tropical forests, for example, there are several layers of vegetation from the ground up to the tallest trees, and different animals with contrasting ways of life live in different layers. One species eats leaves and another eats berries, and so they avoid competition. Indeed the animals and plants of a community are interdependent. Herbivores eat plants, and carnivores eat herbivores. Food chains and the whole balance of a natural community can be altered by destroying one part of it. Thus, insecticides kill insects but also poison other animals in the area and the predators which prey on them.

Today's animals and plants are those whose ancestors survived immense changes. Continents drifted apart and moved together, seas rose and fell, mountains erupted and were levelled by erosion, glaciers advanced and retreated. Life evolved. Some animals became extinct; others adapted to the changes and spread to new areas. Sometimes they met impassable oceans, mountains and deserts. Groups of animals then became isolated and continued to evolve independently. Marsupials, mammals with pouches, were isolated in Australia before placental mammals, whose young are nourished for a long time in the mother's uterus, evolved in Europe and Asia. Placental mammals then supplanted marsupials everywhere but in Australia. Scientists divide the world into six zoogeographical realms each containing animals not found elsewhere. Some animals mix in transitional zones such as the Sahara Desert and the Himalayas.

Environmental factors

Climate is determined by the Sun's radiation on the Earth's atmosphere, oceans and continents. It varies with the time of day and season. Winds generated by the solar heating carry moisture inland, and heat away from the tropics. Ocean currents affect the prevailing temperature over large regions. Solar radiation, winds and ocean currents, together with latitude, altitude and the form of the land, combine to produce each local climate.

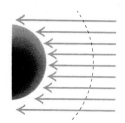

Solar heating *left*
The tropics are hotter than the poles because the Sun's rays pass almost vertically through a shallower depth of atmosphere and so are less attenuated. The Sun's vertical rays shift seasonally between the Tropics of Cancer and Capricorn, altering the length of daylight.

Wind and weather *left*
Hot air at the equator rises and moves north and south to higher latitudes. It subsides, producing trade winds, deflected by the rotation of the Earth, back again to the tropics. Westerly winds blow from the sub-tropics highs poleward toward the sub-polar lows.

Oceans *left*
Surface currents created by prevailing winds and variations in the density of the water are deflected by landmasses and the Coriolis effect' of rotation. Onshore winds across ocean currents are a major climatic control.

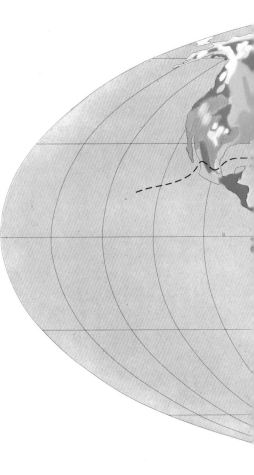

The zoogeographical classification of environments

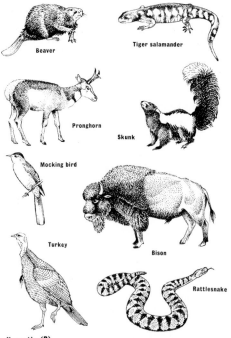

Roe deer · Flycatcher · Warbler · Dunnock · Wild ass · Hedgehog · Edible dormouse · Wild Sheep

Beaver · Tiger salamander · Pronghorn · Skunk · Mocking bird · Turkey · Bison · Rattlesnake

Orangutan · Tree shrew · Gibbon · Fairy bluebird · Tiger · Peacock · Indian elephant

Palearctic (A)
This zoogeographical realm, the extent of which is shown on the map at right, is often grouped with the Nearctic to form the so-called Holarctic region. Roe deer, hedgehogs, dormice and the Asian wild ass are all unique here. Ancestors of modern horses crossed into it from North America during an ice age when the continents were bridged with ice.

Nearctic (B)
Covering the whole of North America from Greenland to the high plateau of Mexico, this realm contains beavers, elk and caribou. The prairie buffalo, which were slaughtered in their millions by 19th century man, have been saved from total extinction. And the American wild turkey has now been very successfully domesticated.

Oriental (C)
Comprising the southern part of Asia, Indonesia and the Philippines, this realm is largely isolated from the Palearctic realm to the north by the great folded barrier of the Himalayas, thrown up when the Indian subcontinent collided with Asia. Indigenous animals include tree shrews, tarsiers, gibbons, orangutans and the Indian elephant.

The ecological classification of environments *left*
The living world of the Earth can be divided into at least nine broad ecological zones or biomes (key, below) each distinguished by its climate, vegetation and other environmental factors. In the following pages it is this system of classification that is followed. The letters indicate the zoogeographical regions shown in detail below.

Key to zones

	Permanent ice
	Tundra
	Mountains
	Coniferous forest
	Temperate forest
	Grasslands
	Tropical forest
	Thorn scrub and semi-desert
	Desert

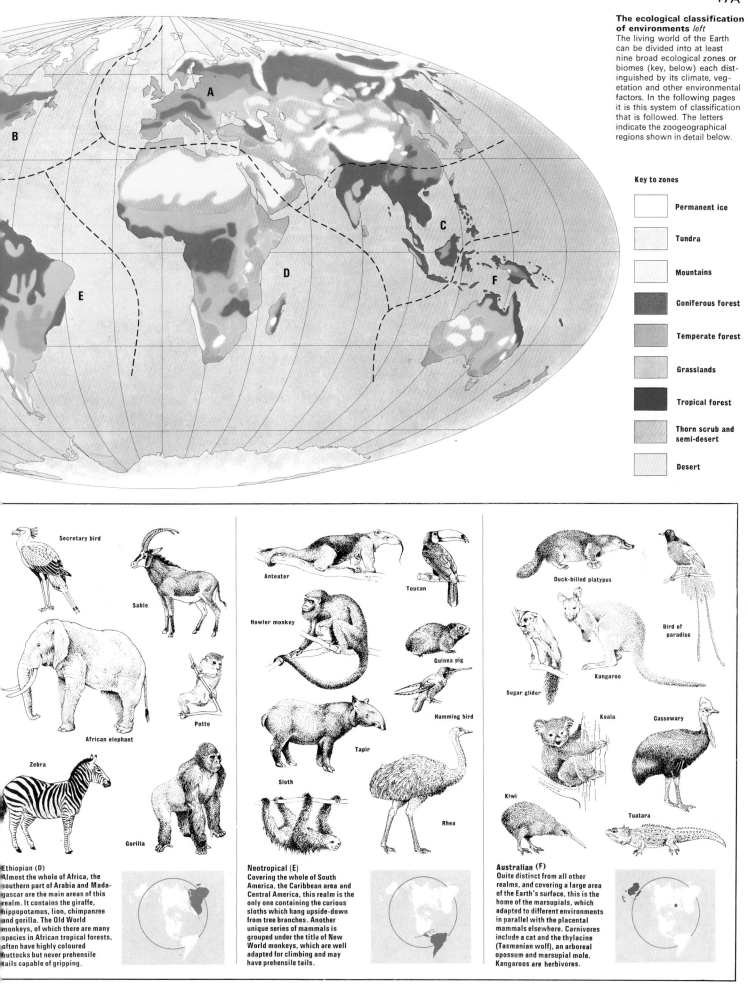

Ethiopian (D)
Almost the whole of Africa, the southern part of Arabia and Madagascar are the main areas of this realm. It contains the giraffe, hippopotamus, lion, chimpanzee and gorilla. The Old World monkeys, of which there are many species in African tropical forests, often have highly coloured buttocks but never prehensile tails capable of gripping.

Secretary bird
Sable
African elephant
Potto
Zebra
Gorilla

Neotropical (E)
Covering the whole of South America, the Caribbean area and Central America, this realm is the only one containing the curious sloths which hang upside-down from tree branches. Another unique series of mammals is grouped under the title of New World monkeys, which are well adapted for climbing and may have prehensile tails.

Anteater
Toucan
Howler monkey
Guinea pig
Humming bird
Tapir
Sloth
Rhea

Australian (F)
Quite distinct from all other realms, and covering a large area of the Earth's surface, this is the home of the marsupials, which adapted to different environments in parallel with the placental mammals elsewhere. Carnivores include a cat and the thylacine (Tasmanian wolf), an arboreal opossum and marsupial mole. Kangaroos are herbivores.

Duck-billed platypus
Bird of paradise
Kangaroo
Sugar glider
Koala
Cassowary
Kiwi
Tuatara

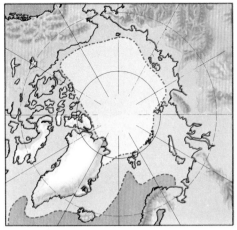

..... Pack ice limit   ---- Drifting ice limit

The Arctic ice cap is the opposite of Antarctica in much more than mere location. It is principally an area of permanently frozen sea ice, although it also includes part of Greenland. It has an indigenous human population, despite the average annual temperature of −24°F on the Greenland ice cap, who have managed to adapt themselves to a ferocious environment by copying the animals around them. Just as the seals and polar bears shelter under the snow, bearing their cubs in dens, the Eskimos developed the igloo built from blocks of wind-packed snow. These ice homes are windproof and the temperature inside can rise to 59°F.

Fur and feathers are good heat insulators because each hair or feather is surrounded by air, which conducts heat poorly and thus lessens the amount of body heat escaping. Polar animals have very thick fur. Eskimos wear two layers of skins, one fur side in and the other fur side out. But fur is less efficient if it is wet, so seals and walruses have a thick layer of fatty blubber under the skin. Fat, like air, is a poor heat

conductor. Circulation can be restricted so that some animals maintain two body temperatures: one normally warm-blooded inside the body and one as cold as the environment in the feet, flippers and nostrils, which must be free of fur or blubber to function. Extremities from which heat is easily lost, such as ears, are small in polar bears and absent in seals. Heat lost through radiation is proportional to the body's surface. Relative to its volume, a large animal has less surface area than a small one. So a large animal will lose heat more slowly. Polar bears, for instance, are bigger than bears in more temperate regions.

Few eskimos are still hunters of seals, walruses and whales. There has been mass slaughter of seals for their skins, and the population has rapidly declined. Life in the Arctic is changing. Uranium, titanium and other minerals have been discovered. In Alaska oil is bringing prosperity and industrialization. Much of the energy devoted to opening up these great 'lands of tomorrow' has been triggered by military needs. Now the main spur is becoming an economic one.

Polar bears
Bigger animals have less surface area for each unit of body weight than small animals, and thus lose heat less rapidly. Polar bears are among the largest bears. The adult male (top right) can be 11 feet (3.4 m) long, compared with the 9-10 ft (2.7-3 m) of the brown grizzly (center right) and 4-4.5 ft (1.2-1.4 m) of the sun bear (bottom right). Most polar bears winter in a den roughly eight feet (2.4 m) long, but two-room dens have been found.

Vulnerable *right*
On land the polar bear is supreme, even on slippery ice. But if a bear is forced to enter deep water it becomes much more vulnerable and can be harried even by young seals. A big bull walrus, illustrated, can kill it swiftly.

Walrus bulls *below*
Weighing up to 3000 pounds. the 12 foot (3.7 m) bull walrus uses its tusks for digging out shellfish, breaking air-holes in the ice and fighting. One-third of its weight is blubber, in a 2½ inch (63.5 mm) thick layer under the skin (right).

Dermis
Follicle
Gland
Fat projections

Blubber with blood vessels

Muscle

Pack ice *above*
Open pack ice, stretching as far as the eye can see, reflects the pink rays of the low Sun. Such ice is seldom more than one year old and usually gets crushed or melted in a shorter time. Unlike the dangerous bergs, it is no hazard to navigation.

Seal and tern *below*
The shores of the Irish Sea are among the wide areas of rocky coast on both sides of the North Atlantic inhabited by the grey seal (female illustrated: the male is larger) and sandwich tern (once common at Sandwich in Kent).

Arctic tern *below*
Distinguished from other terns by its vivid beak and feet, the Arctic tern migrates down the coasts of Europe and Africa to the Antarctic before returning to the Arctic to nest. The round trip (left) can be a remarkable 22000 miles (35000 km).

Sandwich tern

Female grey seal

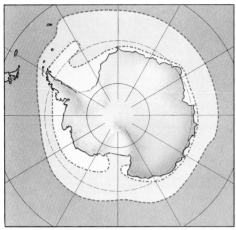

..... Pack ice limit (March)   ____ Pack ice limit (September)

In complete contrast to the North Polar region, the Antarctic is a frozen continent encircled by ocean. Mountains surround low-lying land covered with ice so thick that it forms a high plateau. It is the coldest region on Earth. Throughout almost all of Antarctica no monthly average temperature exceeds 0°C, and the average annual temperature at the South Pole is –60°C. Blizzards blow when a shallow layer of colder air over the ice-sheet flows downslope, and the snow is packed into a hard pavement.

Around the continental edges, icebergs up to 1000 feet (300 m) thick break off the ice caps or valley glaciers and fall into the sea. The ice, formed of compacted and recrystallized snow, is only slightly less dense than sea-water, so icebergs float low in the ocean with five-sixths to eight-ninths of their bulk below the surface. The Antarctic icebergs are tabular, with flat tops and cliff-like sides; Arctic bergs from the Greenland ice cap are peaked and rarely break off in the sizes common in Antarctica, where the floating ice islands can be as much as ten miles (16 km) long.

Until 450 million years ago the Earth had no ice caps. In the Antarctic, ice formed in the center of the continent and moved out towards the sea. Cooling at the North Pole probably occurred later.

In summer, when the ice breaks up and the amount of daylight increases, there is a rapid growth of tiny floating plants called phytoplankton. These plants provide 'grazing' for the zooplankton, small animals of which the shrimp-like krill are the most numerous, which in turn are eaten by the larger animals, among them seals and whalebone whales. One of these whales, the blue whale, is the largest animal ever to inhabit the Earth. A variety of birds live in the Antarctic, including penguins and the skuas which prey on them, snow petrels and albatrosses. These warm-blooded animals all have to keep their body temperature well above that of the environment. Many birds avoid the polar winter by migrating to temperate lands. But emperor penguins stay, and in an Antarctic blizzard colonies of them huddle tightly together to reduce the exposed surface area of their bodies.

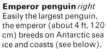

Adélie penguins *above*
They make devoted parents and may, as shown here, produce two chicks at different times in one season.

Emperor penguin *right*
Easily the largest penguin, the emperor (about 4 ft, 120 cm) breeds on Antarctic sea ice and coasts (see below).

Seals *left and below*
Seals abound in the Antarctic. The crab-eater (left) bears the scars of an encounter with a killer whale. The Weddell seal (below left) is guarding its three-week pup. South Georgia elephant seals (below) are wallowing among tussock grass.

Fjord *above*
A scene of rare beauty north of Marguerite Bay in the Antarctic Peninsula (Grahamland). Here the rock of the continent is visible, with a glacier at the right and brash ice at the left floating on water ruffled only by the gentle passage of the ship.

Incubating *above*
The male emperor hatches the eggs, which rest on the feet beneath a warm brood flap of fatty skin.

Macaroni *left*
There are several species of crested penguins. Tallest is the macaroni, here seated on its nest. (18 in, 45 cm)

Great skua *right*
Skuas are scavengers. They steal penguins' food and eggs, kill young chicks and prey on weak adults.

Lichen *below*
The red lichen on this rock could be 1000 years old. Its slow metabolism survives the cold.

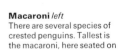

The cold lands *above*
In the northern hemisphere there are vast areas of land at latitudes higher than 60°. The warmer parts of these regions are colonized by immense numbers of conifers (facing page) which extend right across the Earth's widest land mass. Where the climate is too severe for trees, the forest gives way to tundra.

Permanent residents of the tundra

Life is hard in the Arctic tundra, but a great variety of animal life is adapted to it. Grass and other plant food grows for no more than two out of each 12 months, but many animals live off it all the year round and even eat the roots while the surface is covered with snow. Carnivores depend to a great degree on the population of lemmings (below) which reaches a peak about every third year. In spring the land becomes ablaze with flowers, and birds abound.

Lemmings
These small rodents are about five inches (125 mm) long. They have short tails, and ears hidden by thick fur. Every three or four years a population explosion triggers a mass migration in which thousands of lemmings die.

Seasonal plumage
Many of the Arctic birds and animals change their appearance to blend into the contrasting summer and winter backgrounds. For example, the rock ptarmigan is mottled brown in July (left) but white in winter until May (below). Both hunted animals, such as

Surrounding the Arctic Ocean are the Arctic tundra and, farther south, coniferous forest. There is very little land at such latitudes (60°-70°) in the southern hemisphere. Seasonal changes are extreme. The Sun may shine continuously in summer and not at all in mid-winter. Winter cold and summer heat are greatest in the continental interiors, where it is also drier than around the coasts. Interaction between polar and tropical air masses causes storms.

In the treeless tundra the average temperature of the warmest month is below 10°C (50°F). The land is forested where the average for at least one month is above that temperature. In some places the tundra and forest are divided by a distinct tree-line; in other regions the true coniferous forest is preceded by grasses, sedges and lichens. The soils are affected by 'permafrost' and are almost permanently frozen. In summer the surface becomes waterlogged and often flooded, but the seasonal thaw reaches a depth of only 4-24 inches (100-600 mm). Soil water under the plants melts, and a thick mud forms which may

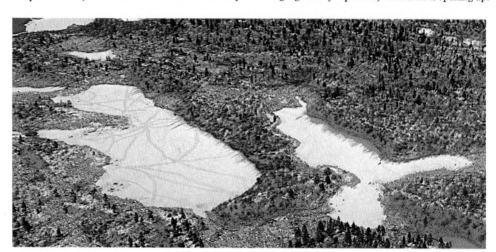

the Arctic hare, and their predators change their color. The Arctic fox, which preys on the rock ptarmigan, is white or very pale in winter (above) but changes into a summer coat which is usually brown but in the so-called "blue-foxes" is deep blue-grey (right).

flow downslope making bulging terraces. Because of recent glaciation there are many lakes and swamps, called muskeg in Canada.

Lemmings feed on the vegetation of the tundra. In winter they dig for roots in an underground network of tunnels where it is about 10°C (18°F) warmer than on the surface. If their population increases so much that there is competition for space, masses of lemmings move into the forest and cross streams, lakes and rivers as they go. Many drown.

Herds of American caribou and closely related European reindeer migrate up to several hundred miles from their summer pasture on the tundra to find winter food on the forest fringes. Nomadic Lapps follow the reindeer and use them for transport, food and clothing. They milk them and make cheese. In contrast, the caribou have never been domesticated: the Indians of northern Canada were hunters. Their skill as trappers was exploited by the European fur trade. And in the Siberian tundra every resource is being vigorously exploited; a new land is opening up.

Winter and summer
above and left
In winter the cold lands are dull and seemingly barren, although at the edges of the tundra stunted conifers are dotted among the lakes. But in summer the plant life flourishes. Reindeer graze among flowers from Norway to the Pacific.

Arctic color *below*
Tundra is not always dull. In the Alaskan September plant life is in full bloom.

Early blooms *above*
The Pasque flower is in evidence throughout Alaska as early as May.

The Coniferous Forests

Except for the Siberian larch, which sheds its needles in winter, the trees of the coniferous forest are evergreen. Spruce, fir, pine and hemlock (associated near water with mountain ash, poplar, balsam, willow and birch) are widespread through Eurasia and North America. The similarity between the distribution of plants and animals is the result of frequent freezing of the Bering Strait which allowed migration between the continents.

The forest animals depend on the trees for food. Beavers eat bark, and squirrels and birds eat buds and seeds. In summer, when there is more food, multitudes of birds migrate to the forest to nest.

The cold forests are of enormous extent. Lumbering is a major industry, and the numerous rivers are used to transport the logs to the sawmills. Great volumes of softwoods are consumed every year, mainly in the building industry and for papermaking. Minerals are now being mined in the cold lands. Iron ore is mined in Labrador and Quebec, and Alaska's gold, copper, iron, oil and gas are being exploited.

The beaver's handiwork
Throughout northern America, and in northern Europe and Asia, the beaver gnaws through trees to secure the soft inner bark from the upper branches. It stores these in a still pool formed by damming a river, and nearby constructs a remarkable lodge with as many as eight underwater entrances.

Ventilation shaft
Beaver lodge
Dam
Raised water level
Food store
Entrances

Tree types *above*
Temperate broad-leaved trees could not survive the northern winter. Most cold forest trees are conifers, with needle-like leaves. From the left : scots pine ; larch, which sheds its leaves ; Norway spruce ; Douglas fir.

Burrowers *right and below*
The woodchuck (right) is one of the cold forest dwellers that hibernates. Its winter metabolism falls almost to a standstill ; then it awakens in March and is busy until fall. The European polecat (below) sometimes kills marmots and uses their burrows.

Grizzlies *above*
Although a carnivore, the giant brown bear often digs for roots, as here.

Ground squirrel *below*
The striped ground squirrel does not climb trees but eats roots, leaves and insects.

Contrasting diets
above and right
Despite its formidable appearance the moose lives on small plants, berries and tree shoots. Only the male has antlers. But the lynx (right) is a carnivore, whose population follows that of its principal prey, the hare.

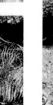

The Temperate Forests

South of the coniferous forest is extensive deciduous woodland of oak, beech and chestnut which flourishes wherever there is an annual rainfall of 30-60 inches (750-1500mm) distributed throughout the year. Woodland once covered large areas of the northern hemisphere, but most has now been cleared for agriculture. There are different mid-latitude climates on the east and west sides of continents: east coast climates are continental, with hot summers and cold winters, while winds blowing off the ocean bring rain to the more equable west coasts.

In winter the deciduous trees shed their broad leaves which would be vulnerable to frost. The leaves slowly rot to a rich humus, and in boggy places peat forms. Nutrients circulate by water draining through the soil and then being drawn up by evaporation and transpiration through the leaves.

Tree types
In North America and Asia the oak, beech, hickory and maple dominate; in Europe the oak, ash, linden and chestnut, with beech in cool moist areas. On damp ground near rivers willow, alder, ash and elm are found. Conifers grow faster so that they often supplant deciduous trees in managed forests. They form the natural forest on the west coast of North America, where some of the largest trees are found.

Near the tropics are the broadleaf evergreen forests. In Japan and the southeast of the United States there are evergreen oaks, laurel and magnolia, with palms, bays and ferns in the swamps of the Mississippi delta. The warm wet forest of New Zealand's South Island contains conifers, podocarp and evergreen beeches, with tree ferns, palms and bamboos. In a Mediterranean type of climate the summers are hot and dry. Cork oaks have hard, leathery leaves covered with a thick cuticle to minimize water loss. The Mediterranean forest is now only a narrow coastal belt. Tree felling and frequent summer fires have left scrub known as the maquis. The chaparral of California and Mexico is similar.

Redwoods *above*
Along the west coast of the United States is a foggy coastal belt where the redwood forests flourish. The giant redwoods and sequoias may be several thousand years old and up to 400 feet (120 m) high. They are among the Earth's oldest living things.

Beechwoods *left*
Typical of the cool northern deciduous forest, Burnham Beeches, near London, generates millions of beech leaves each year. Littering the ground, they decompose into a rich humus which overlies the soil and supports plant life, worms and a variety of insects.

Little owl *above*
Predator of woodland animals, its forward-facing eyes give good binocular vision for judging distance in dim light.

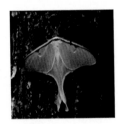

Luna moth *above*
Found in American deciduous forest, the moth prefers a diet of rhododendrons. India has a tropical variety.

Animal variety
above and left
Woodland inhabitants of the New England states are the box turtle and wood frog (above). The Yugoslavian four-lined snake (left) has the slender body and angled scales common to snakes which need to obtain purchase on bark.

Forest birds
The crossbill (left) can pry open tough pine cones; the pheasant (below,) of which there are 49 species, is concealed on the ground by its camouflage.

The ecology of an oak
Oaks of various sub-species are among the most important trees in the northern deciduous forests, and they play a major role in local wildlife. Oaks have a history dating back over 50 million years, and 7000 years ago covered vast tracts of temperate land. Throughout recorded history man has prized the oak for its hard, durable wood, which has been favored above all others for making houses, ships, furniture and other artifacts. The oak population has thus dwindled, and in modern managed forests the faster-growing conifers are preferred. But each remaining oak is a microcosm of nature. The autumn leaf-fall returns valuable nutrients to the soil, providing a source of humus. In the spring up to a quarter of a million new leaves grow, providing an area for photosynthesis as great as 10000 sq ft (930 m²). Small streamers of flowers are pollinated by wind-borne pollen, leading in midsummer to the crop of acorns which are stored by grey squirrels, badgers and many other animals for the coming winter. As many as 200 species of insect can feed on one tree. Largest is the leaf-eating stag beetle, and the most prominent the gall wasp whose marble gall houses the larva. The damage insects inflict often results in the tree producing a second crop of midsummer leaves. The serotine bat and tawny owl are the main nocturnal predators of the oak forest. The former takes winged insects in flight, while small rodents form the staple diet of the owl.

Marble gall showing larva of gall wasp

Serotine bat

Tawny owl

Grey squirrel

Stag beetle

Badger

The mature oak *right*
The extensive buttressed roots of an old oak can provide the portal through which a fox (1) tunnels to its lair. Low on the trunk a beefsteak fungus (2) may grow, providing fruiting bodies upon which feed many kinds of animals and insects. The trunk often decays locally (3), providing a home for both bats and owls. The fallow deer (female, 4) and jay (5) collect acorns, while in the branches a clump of mistletoe (6) grows, nurtured by the tree on which it is a parasite.

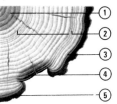

Record in the rings *above*
In deciduous trees each year's growth adds a ring of new tissue to the trunk, as shown by this section segment from an oak with an age of 24 years. Within the first five years is the dark heartwood (1). Between years 7-10 growth was slowed (2), possibly by drought or the crowding of other trees. Growth was also slow in years 19-22, and in the 21st year part of the tree was burned, leaving a scar (4) which gradually heals with further growth. Present growth takes place in the cambium (3) just inside the bark (5).

Paper wasp
The queen starts the football-like nest, which is made of chewed wood and has a paper-like consistency. Her subjects enlarge it.

Mole
Moles live in burrows excavated underground by their strong front claw-feet. Emerging into the open, their eyes see poorly.

Dormouse
Most of the forest rodents store food for the winter, but the dormouse hibernates, at a reduced body temperature.

Dormouse nest
Although the dormouse lives deep in the undergrowth, it is very agile, and builds a spherical nest above ground level.

Sparrowhawk
Like many birds of prey the sparrowhawk makes a substantial nest of twigs and forest debris high in a tree, where its young are safe.

Blue tit
A favorite choice of home for the blue tit is a hole in a tree. Inside the cavity it constructs a nest of moss and soft debris.

Common oak
Widespread and important to commerce and forest life, the oak grows slowly and is yielding to other species.

Silver birch
Mature at 50, the silver-barked birch is found in all temperate forest and extends far into the tundra.

Beech
Big and densely packed, the beech is very beneficial. Essentially a forest tree, it prefers drained chalky soil.

Ash
Although it exhausts soil, the ash produces tough wood. Its multi-leaflet leaves are one foot (0.25 m) long.

Sweet chestnut
Originally from Asia Minor, the sweet chestnut fruit is a preferred food of many forest animals.

Sycamore
One of the maple family, the sycamore prefers exposed positions where its seeds can travel on the wind.

Alder
The inconspicuous alder prefers marshy ground and river banks. Although not a conifer, it bears cone fruit.

The Tropical Forests

The hot, humid conditions in equatorial rainforests which encourage a profusion of life, change very little over the year, daily variations being greater than seasonal ones. The average temperature is about 27°C, while the rainfall, which is as high as 80-160 inches (2000-4000 mm) a year, falls regularly in heavy thunderstorms.

Tropical forests are the highest, densest and most varied on Earth, in spite of having infertile soil. This is because nutrients are contained in the plants which grow, flower and fruit throughout the year. As leaves and fruits fall to the ground and decay, the minerals are rapidly taken up again by the roots of the growing shrubs and trees. The crowns of the tall, broad-leaved trees form a canopy of foliage. Underneath, it is shady and the tree trunks are smooth and unbranched, while lianas and creepers thrust upwards to the light.

Forest animals find a variety of habitats in the different layers. Monkeys, apes, sloths, lizards and frogs are adapted to climbing or swinging through trees. Multitudes of birds feed on nectar, insects or fruit. Many animals browse on the forest floor, and a vast number of animal and plant species co-exist.

Lianas *below*
Long rope-like stems loop from tree to tree, ever climbing toward the light that pierces the canopy.

Deep rainforest *right*
The hot, humid atmosphere of tropical rainforest encourages most luxuriant plant growth.

Flowers *right and below*
Tropical blooms are famed for their size and beauty. The very small seasonal variation in climate means plants can germinate, grow and flower without interruption throughout the year. Right, blossoms of Royal Poinciana; below, Strelitzia, native to Africa.

Contrasting predators
right and below
Tropical forests are the home of the largest spiders and largest snakes. But, whereas the monkey spider of Trinidad (right) kills its prey by a venomous bite, the 30 foot (10 m) royal python (below) crushes and suffocates its victim.

Butterflies
right and below
There are more butterflies and moths in the rainforest than in all the rest of the Earth; typical species are the Ulysses butterfly (right), *Precis almana* (below right) and Rajah Brooke's bird-wing *Trogonoptera brookiana* (below).

Hovering jewel *right*
Hummingbirds, such as Pucheran's emerald variety illustrated here, are found only in the Americas. Their wings, which beat about 100 times a second and allow them to hover while drinking nectar, are covered with iridescent feathers of brilliant hues.

Forest reptile and amphibian *above and right*
As large as a man, the iguana (above) has feet with long digits provided with hard scales and curved claws adapted to tree-climbing. Another climber is the African grey tree frog (right) whose nest of foam overhangs the water.

Spinetail swift
White rumped swift
Indian crested swift
Harpy eagle

The emergents
Some trees break through the canopy formed by the main tree population. Many of these emergent.trees reach to 150 ft (46 m), although all tree heights are reduced with increasing altitude or distance from the equator. Life at this topmost level is almost wholly insects and birds. The swifts, which fly above the forest at over 100 mph (160 kmh), catch insects on the wing. The harpy eagle preys on animals in the upper branches.

100 feet
30 m

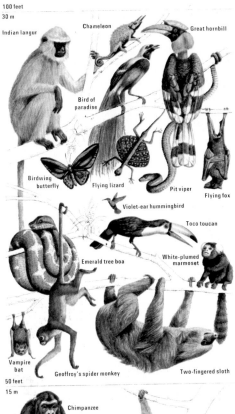

Indian langur
Chameleon
Bird of paradise
Great hornbill
Birdwing butterfly
Flying lizard
Pit viper
Flying fox
Violet-ear hummingbird
Toco toucan
Emerald tree boa
White-plumed marmoset
Vampire bat
Geoffroy's spider monkey
Two-fingered sloth

The canopy
This is one of the major life zones of the tropical forest, and it exerts a powerful effect on all the lower levels. Most of the forest trees grow to 100-120 ft (30-37 m) and form an almost continuous layer of leafy vegetation at this height, cutting off direct sunlight from below and markedly altering the climate inside' the forest to a shady coolness. Most of the trees of tropical forests have straight stems which do not branch until quite close to the canopy; emergent tree (1) passes straight through without branching. Many tropical trees are cauliflorous—they produce flowers which grow directly out of the trunks and branches and frequently dot the canopy with color (2). Inside the forest is a tangle of creepers and climbers which tend to bind the branches of the canopy into a tight mass. The fauna of the canopy is adapted to specialized feeding from particular flowers, fruit or other food. Winged insects and animals range readily through the whole stratum. Many of the birds (for example, the great hornbill and toucan) have long bills with which they can reach food through the mat of vegetation. The non-flying animals are invariably adapted to running along branches, swinging from one branch to another and even leaping 50 ft (15 m) or more.

50 feet
15 m

Chimpanzee
Leopard
White handed gibbon
Ocelot

The middle layer
There may be no sharp division between this layer and the canopy, but in general the middle is made up of smaller trees whose crowns do not form a continuous mat. In this layer are found nest epiphytes (3), non-parasitic plants growing in sunlight on trees where they seed in cracks in the bark. Some store water while others absorb it through hanging roots (4). Cauliflorous growths (5) hang from some trees, while many trunks are covered in vines and lianas (6). The trees are sturdy enough to bear heavy animals. Whereas many inhabitants of the canopy seldom if ever come down to ground level, a considerable proportion of the middle-level animals spend part of their life on the forest floor.

25 feet
7.5 m

Mandrill
Tiger
Bay duiker
Red jungle fowl
Giant armadillo
Jaguar
Red rumped agouti

The lower levels
The bottom strata of the humid tropical forest can be divided into a shrub layer below 15 ft (4.5 m), a herb layer below 3 ft (1 m) and a fungus layer on the surface. The fallen tree (7) may have died from strangulation by parasitic vegetation. At the right air roots (8) pick up moisture, while a trunk (9) is almost hidden by two types of epiphyte. Fungi (10) cover the ground near a massive buttressed tree root (11), while in the rear is a stilt root (12) of a kind common in swamp forest. The ground here is covered in sparse vegetation (13) typical of the shady floor. The features illustrated are typical of hot rain forest throughout the tropics, but the elephant (14) is Indian.

The Grasslands

Flat or rolling grasslands lie between the forests and deserts in the dry interiors of all the continents, in the transitional zones where dry and moist climates merge into each other. There are two major types of grassland, the temperate which is hot in summer and cold in winter and the tropical which has a fairly uniform high temperature all the year round.

The height of the grass is dependent upon the annual rainfall. There are few trees on these wide plains to break the wind or provide shelter. In spring or summer there is a short rainy season when the grasses and shrubs flourish and there is rich grazing; then the long dry season comes and growth halts as a severe drought develops. The grasslands may result from frequent fires during this period, which kill the trees and shrubs leaving grass-roots unharmed. An extreme example of severe drought occurred during the late 1960s and early 1970s in the Sahel region of Africa, on the southern fringe of the Sahara. It completely devastated the area's agricultural economy.

Animal life
Throughout most of the tropical grasslands the climate is semi-arid, the soil poor, yet their meager grazing supports a rich and varied assortment of animals. In most grassland regions the fauna has been used by man with care for the future, but in the biggest savanna of all, that of Africa, man has done little but misuse and destroy the grassland animals. To a considerable degree this has been the result of emphasis by both Africans and white ranchers, on domestic cattle. Such beasts graze only on certain species of grass, and have been bred principally for the temperate regions of Europe. In contrast, the natural fauna makes full use of the whole spectrum of vegetation, grazing selectively at different levels and in different places. As a result there is no deterioration of the environment despite the large numbers of animals supported by each area of land. Moreover, the wild animals need not be fed or sheltered, nor inoculated against the sleeping sickness carried by the tsetse fly which ravages cattle. Now that game can be seen to have a distinct commercial value the grassland animals, particularly easily domesticated species such as the eland, are at last being more generally preserved so that controlled game-cropping can provide an additional source of high quality protein.

The dust bowls
Man has often interfered in the grassland environment sometimes with disastrous consequences. The American grassland soil is rich and farmers have turned the wetter tall-grass prairie into the corn belt and the short-grass prairie into the wheat belt. Further west is the cattle country. But in years of drought crops fail and the valuable topsoil, lacking the protective cover of grass, blows away in great dust clouds, leaving behind large areas of barren land.

Venomous snakes *left*
Grasslands in every continent harbor dangerous snakes. The Egyptian cobra (far left) is the largest cobra in Africa. The prairie rattlesnake (near left) is the most common venomous snake in the United States and causes many deaths each year.

African savanna *above*
The Serengeti plains of Tanzania are among the most beautiful areas of big game country in the world. Here animals of a great range of species graze on fine grassland amongst the kopjes — rocky outcrops which are characteristic of central Africa.

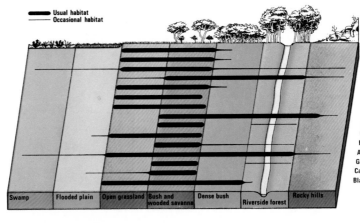

Lion
Spotted hyena
Griffon vulture
Anubis (olive) baboon
Grant's zebra
Brindled gnu (wildebeest)
White rhinoceros
Impala
Giraffe
Cape eland
Kirk's long-snouted dik-dik
African elephant
Gerenuk
Cape buffalo
Black rhinoceros

Ecological co-existence *above*
The African savanna supports a very large and varied animal population. Most of the animals are herbivores which have each adapted to a particular habitat and a particular section of the available food. These sections are divided geographically, as shown here, and also into different feeding levels above the ground.

Lion Spotted hyena Griffon vulture Anubis baboon Grant's zebra Brindled gnu (wildebeest) White rhinoceros

Buffalo *above*
African buffalo at Manyara, Tanzania. Buffalo live in herds of up to 100 or more males and females of all ages, with a firm hierarchy among the males. They use their horns and horn-bosses in pushing contests that help to decide their ranks.

Impala *below*
African grassland has 72 species of antelope, weighing from a few pounds to 1800 lb (800 kg).

7ft, 213cm

Tick bird *left*
The yellow-billed oxpecker rides on the backs of rhinos and other large animals and eats ticks and flies living in or on the hide. Sometimes the birds swoop off their perch to take large insects which have been disturbed by the animal.

Leopard *right*
Stealthy and athletic, the leopard is found through most of Africa and southern Asia. It often rests in trees, and this fine specimen has pulled its prey, a reedbuck, onto a high branch.

Giraffes *left*
Tallest of all land animals, the giraffe eats acacia leaves and other greenery high above the ground (see large illustration below). Here a group gallops past zebras across a bare patch of ground.

Griffon vulture *left*
Vultures soar at high altitudes on their large wings while searching to the horizon for carrion.

Jackrabbit *above*
Big ears are not only for keen hearing : they help radiate heat and control body temperature.

Ostrich *below*
The tall ostrich can see for miles across the African plains and run swiftly from danger.

8ft, 240cm

Feeding habits
The great grasslands of Africa, and to a lesser degree those of other continents, teem with wild life of remarkable variety. In this wide open environment conceal-ment is difficult and the majority of animals survive by having good long-distance vision and by being fleet of foot. Some of the smaller plant eaters escape their preda-tors by burrowing. The key to the co-existence of the herbivores is that they tend to feed at different levels. The elephant can reach up to 15 feet (4·5 m) above the ground to tear at broad-leafed trees, while the giraffe can feed on its favored acacias at even higher levels. The rhino, buffalo, gerenuk and eland eat not only low shrubs and trees but also grass. Only the gnus, zebras and some rhinos com-pete for the same areas, but these areas are so large that there is little fear of over-grazing. The baboon delves for roots and what-ever it can find, while the carni-vores include the carrion-eating hyenas and vultures and the pre-datory lion, cheetah and leopard. Left to themselves, the wild animals of the savanna do little harm to their habitat, but the growing herds of domesticated cattle and goats pose a threat. Whereas the native fauna leaves living shoots which can sprout into a fresh plant, the cattle and goats eat the whole of the grass and tree shoots so that the vegetation is soon eradicated. Over-grazing and poor range management are encouraged by the fact that some African tribes still regard cattle as symbols of wealth. The value of the indigen-ous savanna animals has been forcefully demonstrated in parts of South Africa and Rhodesia where ranges run down by domestic cattle have been restored by grazing 10 to 12 varieties of antelope in their place.

Impala   Giraffe   Cape eland   Kirk's dik-dik   African elephant   Gerenuk   Cape buffalo   Black rhinoceros

The Deserts

The desert is a harsh, arid and inhospitable environment of great variety where the average rainfall for a year is less than five inches (125 mm) and in some years there is none at all. The cloudless sky allows the Earth's surface to heat up to 40°C (104°F) by day and cool near to freezing at night. Relative humidity is low. On the basis of temperature arid lands are divided into low-latitude hot deserts and mid-latitude deserts. The latter, in central Asia and the Great Basin of the United States, are bitterly cold in winter. In the coastal deserts of Peru and Chile the cold offshore current flowing northward from the Antarctic Ocean cools the moist air producing a swirling sea fog.

Landscapes are rocky, and weathered to strange shapes by the winds and sudden rains (pp. 12-13A). Sand dunes shifted and shaped by the wind are common in Saudi Arabia and the Sahara. The dunes are almost sterile, but most deserts have some sparse plant cover. Stems and leaves are hard, to prevent loss of water and protect the plant from sand erosion. Succulent cacti and euphorbias store water in fleshy stems or leaves, and have widespread shallow roots to absorb the dew. Sahara oases were probably cultivated 7000 years ago, producing grain, olives, wine, figs and dates. The Egyptians channelled the waters of the flooding Nile to irrigate the land, and today the Imperial Valley of California's Colorado desert and the Arizona desert near Phoenix are highly productive agricultural land.

Water in the desert
Most of the world's deserts are neither billowing sand dunes (such as that on the opposite page) nor totally devoid of water. But in all deserts water, especially fresh water, is a precious commodity. In the great stony deserts brief rains allow stunted vegetation to provide a basis for animal life. The neighborhood of Monument Valley, Utah (above) is surprisingly full of life which has adapted to arid conditions. Some life is also found in the Sahara, where sudden torrential rains cause flash flood erosion (south of Ouargla, left) leaving smooth ridges and deep gullies Sometimes

the water table is at the surface. The water may be brackish and undrinkable, as in Cyrenaica west of the Siwa Oasis (below), but the true oasis contains fresh water at which a camel can drink copiously (right). Even the meager dew is stored by plants — nothing is wasted.

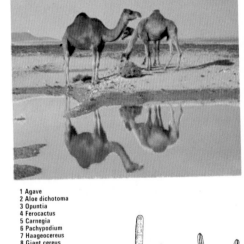

Desert plants *right*
Deserts test the ability of plants to adapt to a near absence of water. Plants survive by throwing out large catchment areas for dew at night, minimizing water loss by evaporation during the day, growing deep roots to find water far below the surface, storing what water they find, and in extreme cases by lying dormant during dry years and springing to life as soon as it rains.

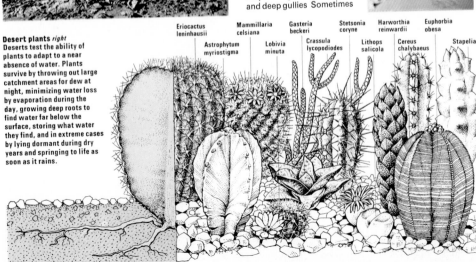

Eriocactus leninhausii
Mammillaria celsiana
Astrophytum myriostigma
Gasteria beckeri
Lobivia minuta
Crassula lycopodiodes
Stetsonia coryne
Harworthia reinwardii
Lithops salicola
Euphorbia obesa
Cereus chalybaeus
Stapelia

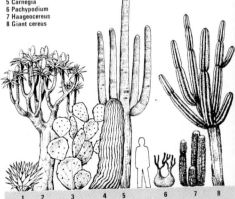

1 Agave
2 Aloe dichotoma
3 Opuntia
4 Ferocactus
5 Carnegia
6 Pachypodium
7 Haageocereus
8 Giant cereus

Desert animals

Many animals are so well adapted to retain water that they survive on the moisture in their food. Some, such as the armadillo lizard, scorpions, insects and spiders, have hard, impenetrable skins to reduce water loss. The urine of camels and gazelles is very concentrated to minimize excretion of water. Arabian camels can lose 30 per cent of their body weight (which would be lethal for a man) without distress, and then regain it by drinking up to 27 gallons (120 liters) at a time. This does not dilute their blood dangerously. A camel does not sweat until its body temperature reaches 40°C, and it loses heat easily during the cold night because it stores its fat in the hump and not as a layer under the skin. Its fur insulates against the heat, as do the loose clothes of the people. Snakes hide in crevices, and sand-swimming lizards burrow to avoid extreme temperatures. Jerboas and kangaroo rats hop along, and some lizards run on their hind legs to keep their bellies off the ground. As soon as it rains, swarms of dormant life surge into activity.

Desert Burrowers

White-footed mouse · Burrow taken over by horned lizard · Horned lizard · American badger · Pocket mouse · Kit fox · Kangaroo rat in nest · Food store · Green-collared lizard · Kangaroo rat

Ant lions *right and below*
Some types of ant lion catch their prey — mainly ants — by digging a smooth conical pit and waiting at the bottom ; others bury themselves in the sand with only eyes and jaws protruding. The larval stage (right) precedes the winged adult (below).

Sand desert *above*
Only one-seventh of the Sahara looks like this Hollywood-style vista of giant dunes in Algeria.

Dung beetles *left*
These female scarabs are rolling a pellet of animal dung into a ball containing an egg.

Painted lady *above*
N African desert thistles provide nectar for their migration through Europe as far as Iceland.

Gila monster *right*
This venomous N American lizard tracks its prey with the aid of a sensor in its mouth (right, lower).

20in, 51cm

Nasal cavity · External nostril · Sensory part of Jacobsons organ · Duct · Internal nostril

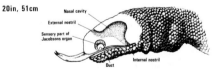

8in, 21cm

Scorpion and snake
When scorpions mate, the male deposits a patch of sperm on the ground and then contrives to maneuver a female over it in what looks like a square dance (above, left). The dangerous rattlesnake (above) senses the heat radiated by its prey using organs on its face.

Plants and predator
The leopard tortoise (left) enjoys a meal of cactus, a plant which stores water and minimizes evaporation (Ferocactus of Arizona, right). Other desert blooms include Echinopsis rhodatricia and Chamacerus silvestri (far right, upper and lower).

The Mountains

The mountain environment varies enormously with height and the direction of the prevailing wind. Temperature falls about 2°C (3.4°F) for each 1000 feet (300 m) increase in altitude. Barometric pressure also falls until lack of oxygen makes any human exertion cause shortness of breath. Before people adjust to the conditions they often suffer from mountain sickness —headache, weakness and nausea.

Sun temperature may be 28°C (83°F) hotter than in the shade or at night, and the slope of a mountain facing the equator is warmer than the other sides. Mountains force rain-bearing winds to rise, so that they cool and have to release moisture. Clouds form, and rain falls on the windward slope; on the opposite slope the descending winds are drying.

High-altitude life

Altitude has the same effect on vegetation as latitude. At about 5000 feet (1500 m) tropical rainforest changes to montane forest resembling a temperate rainforest. At twice this height the broad-leaved trees disappear but there are conifers and shrubs such as laurel. Above the treeline, where the average monthly temperature never exceeds 10°C, is alpine tundra or heath. The snowline at the equator is at about 15000 feet (4500 m). In Peru irrigated sugar and cacao cover the lower slopes, and above the timberline corn grows at 11000 feet, wheat at 12000, barley at 13000 and potatoes up to 14000 feet. The Incas had terraced the Andes and had an efficient agricultural system by 1000 AD.

The mountain life zone which is unique is that above the treeline. The animal communities are isolated, since mountains act as a barrier to migration. Most plants and insects on mountain tops can withstand freezing. Some animals burrow or shelter under rocks where temperature variations are smaller. Ibexes, yaks, deer and sheep all have thick coats but move down the mountain-side in winter. Mountain animals have enlarged hearts and lungs and extra oxygen-carrying red blood corpuscles to make the most of the thin air. The vicuna, for example, has nearly three times the number of red corpuscles per cubic millimeter of blood as man.

Near Murren *above right*
The environment on a high mountain is essentially polar, even in a tropical country. Above the timberline ice and snow replace animals and plants, and the conditions are further modified by intense solar radiation and low atmospheric pressure.

Lichens *above and right*
Lichens comprise a fungus and an alga in close association. The alga govern the color (page 49A for red lichen). The metabolism of lichens is exceedingly slow; barely alive, they can subsist on mountain rock in harsh conditions for hundreds of years.

Altitude and latitude *right*
At extreme latitudes – for example, in the Antarctic – the climate is so severe at sea level that no very pronounced change takes place even as one climbs a mountain, although the mountain's presence can strongly modify the local weather. In contrast, mountains near the equator rise from hot, steamy forests into freezing, arid peaks, with almost every kind of Earth environment in between. To most kinds of terrestrial life large mountains are barriers. As altitude increases, plants and animals become adapted to the environment and then peter out entirely.

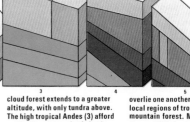

Tundra	Coniferous/deciduous forest	Temperate evergreen
Alpine	Mixed temperate	Mountain forest
Boreal	Cloud forest	Tropical rainforest

21000 ft / 6400 m
18000 ft / 5500 m
15000 ft / 4570 m
12000 ft / 3650 m
9000 ft / 2750 m
6000 ft / 1830 m
3000 ft / 910 m
0

1 2 3 4 5

Mountain zones *above*
At high latitudes a mountain offers fewer contrasts; much of New Zealand (1) has cool, humid cloud forest, topped by alpine heath and tundra. In SE Australia, SE Africa and S Brazil (2) the cloud forest extends to a greater altitude, with only tundra above. The high tropical Andes (3) afford contrasts surpassed only by the mountainous regions of the eastern Himalayas and SE Asia (4), where six distinct regions overlie one another, with very local regions of tropical mountain forest. Mountains of Europe (5) lie in regions where there are already great contrasts in climate at sea level. Boreal is a north-facing mountain region.

Tortoise *above*
The margined tortoise is native to mountainous regions in Greece and the Balkans.

Plants *left*
Purple gentian and (upper) auricula are typical of mountain dwarf perennials; some can resist freezing.

Butterflies
Mountains are often rich in insects. The six-spot burnet (mating, left) is common. Some Apollo butterflies (below) are found above 17000 feet (5200 m) in the Himalayas. Erebia (right) is carrying an orange mite, a parasite which can survive freezing. Mountain insects rely for much of their food on pollen, seeds and even insects swept up in the frequent updraft of winds from the warm lowlands.

4in, 8cm

African birds of prey
Small mountain rodents
make a tasty meal for the
jackal buzzard (left), a bird
with exceedingly acute
vision. The black eagle (with
three-week chick, right)
lives on rats and lizards but
can tackle animals as large
as the 7 lb (3.2 kg) rock
hyrax. It nests in July.

Rodents
Whereas the alpine marmot
(below) hibernates in
winter, the pika of Tibet
(in group, below right)
stores its supplies. The
chinchilla and cavy both
come from South America.
Above 10000 ft (3000 m)
rodents outnumber all
other animals.

Salamander *right*
This Pyrenean salamander
is climbing out of a cool
mountain stream, but the
true alpine salamander has
had to become adapted to
an arid habitat. Much darker
than the lowland varieties,
it does not lay its eggs in
water but bears its young
alive. It remains amphibious.

American cougar *left*
Also known as the puma or
mountain lion, the cougar
hunts by day above the
timberline. When it makes a
large kill it is able to store the
carcass for weeks at sub-
zero temperature. Most of
these beasts range over a
fixed area, although some
wander down to lower levels.

Yak *right*
Domesticated in its native
Tibet, the shaggy yak is still
found in local wild herds in
central Asia. It is a hardy
animal, adapted to eating
snow in the absence of
water, and moss and lichens
when no better vegetation
is available. It is found up to
20000 ft (6000 m).

Grazers
Sure-footed, the mountain
goat (left) inhabits the
northern Rockies.
The chamoix (above) is
scattered through moun-
tain regions of southern
Europe, while ibexes (right)
are a very widespread
family. Specialized sheep
also graze at high altitudes.

Freshwater environments range from puddles to lakes which cover thousands of square miles, from small streams to rivers that stretch hundreds of miles from mountain source to the ocean. Together, they provide a diversity of habitats that supports a wide range of plant and animal life.

In rivers the type and variety of life is controlled by the depth and speed of water. Fast mountain streams have few plants and the fish are either fast swimmers or shelter among stones. The slower, wider lowland rivers are rich in vegetation and many of the fish have mouths adapted to sucking food from the rich silt of the river bed. In the brackish waters of the estuary few freshwater animals can survive because of the increasing salinity. But migratory fish, such as eels and Atlantic salmon, adapt to fresh and salt water at different stages of their life cycles.

In standing water the surface is often much warmer than the depths. This produces layers which are so distinct that separate habitats are created. The deeper waters may be completely devoid of oxygen because they do not mix with the well-aerated surface layers. Lakes go through three stages of development: oligotrophic with barren sides and clear water; eutrophic when the lake has begun to silt up and is rich in life; and, finally, dystrophic with decayed organic matter developing into swamp or peat bog. This natural process of eutrophication normally takes thousands of years, but man can, by his indiscriminate pollution and over-enrichment of some lakes condense this process dangerously into a few decades.

Near its source a river is cold, clear and well oxygenated, and flows swiftly.

In the middle reaches the river runs deep, but is still clear and fast-flowing.

A mature river is broad and sluggish; it may be clouded and polluted.

Fish of the river *below*
In the swift-flowing upper reaches only the powerful swimming fish can survive, although small fish nestle near the bottom. The water is well oxygenated, and remains so into the less tumultuous middle reaches. The sluggish lowland river contains deep-bodied fish.

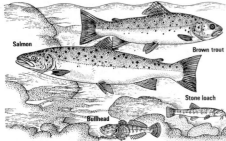

Trout stream

Salmon
Brown trout
Stone loach
Bullhead

Minnow reach

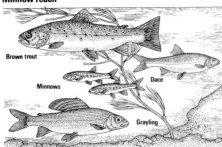

Brown trout
Minnows
Dace
Grayling

Lowland river

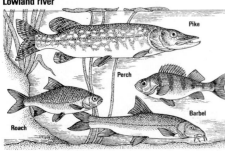

Pike
Perch
Barbel
Roach

Salmon leaping *above*
Mature salmon return from the ocean to the rivers in which they hatched. Swimming against the current, and leaping up rapids and waterfalls, they finally gain the upper reaches where they spawn. After 1-3 years, the next generation migrates to the sea.

Kingfisher *above*
These colorful birds are by far the most numerous of the many species that take fish while on the wing. Plunging across the surface in a shallow dive, they seize in their long beaks prey they had spotted while on the branch of a tree. Average size 7 in (18 cm).

Teeming with life *left*
Most lakes begin life in the oligotrophic stage, barren of life and with clear, bright waters. After a time the water is colonized, and gradually a community rich in plant and animal species occupies the freshwater habitat. Such a lake is eutrophic.

A swamp *left*
The Indian name of Lake Okeefenokee, Georgia, means 'land of trembling earth'. Measuring some 30 miles by 40 (48 by 64 km), it is a region of perfect mirror-like reflections and teeming wild life.

Swamp butterfly *above*
There are many sub-species of swallowtail; this is the eastern tiger swallowtail from the marshes of Georgia. Average size 4 in (10 cm).

Tree frog *above*
Devouring flies and gnats by the million, green tree frogs breed in the warm swamp waters. Average size is 2½in (6 cm).

Lubber grasshopper *left*
Bigger even than the majority of desert locusts, it makes a tasty meal for birds and young alligators.

Alligator *above*
Generally not aggressive, they keep open the channels in American swamps. Average size is 10 ft (3 m).

Terrapin *above*
The Suwannee river terrapin is sometimes found in the Gulf of Mexico. Average size is 7 in (18 cm).

Swamp turtle *above*
The soft-shelled turtles have a leathery skin without an outer covering of horny plates. Size 14 in (36 cm).

The pond environment *left*
1 Common frog (male, ×0.5)
2 Starwort (×0.5)
3 Water crowfoot (×0.25)
4 Aplecta hypnorum (×2)
5 Wandering snail (×0.75)
6 Keeled ramshorn snail (×0.5)
7 Curled pondweed (×0.25)
8 Bithynia (×1)
9 Ramshorn snail (×0.3)
10 Water lily root (×0.25)
11 Great pond snail (×0.8)

Near the surface
12 Pond skater (×0.5)
13 Whirligig beetle (×0.25)
14 Water boatman (×1)
15 Non-biting midge (×5)
16 Mosquito pupa (×5)
17 Dragonfly (male, ×0.65)
18 China-marks moth (×0.75)
19 Mayfly (female, ×0.2)

Middle depths
20 Water flea (Daphnia, ×2.5)
21 Smooth newt (male, ×0.5)
22 Cyclops (typical of species, ×8)
23 Flagellate (×650)
24 Great diving beetle (male, ×1)
25 Hydra (×4)
26 Stickleback (male, ×0.5)
27 Common frog tadpole (×1.5)
28 Flagellate (Euglena, ×180)
29 Water mite (×5)

The bottom
30 Caddis-fly larva in case
31 Chaetonotus (×150)
32 Horny-orb shell (×1)
33 Tubifex worms (×0.2)
34 Midge larva (×3.5)
35 Pond sponge (×0.2)
36 Leech (Helobdella sp., ×4)
37 Water hog-louse (×2.5)
38 Flatworm (×2)

Pond life *below*
The essential characteristic of pond life is adaptation to a fresh-water environment without a flowing current. As in almost every other habitat on Earth the life is divided into distinct zones —atmosphere, surface film, middle depths and bed—although many species cross from one zone to another. The newt, for example, is active everywhere from the bed of a pond to dry land. Throughout the ecology of freshwater life all food is manufactured by green plants. First-order animals, such as zooplankton and many fish and insects, feed directly on the plants; everything else feeds on predators lower in the food chain or web. The water itself is very far from being a pure compound of hydrogen and oxygen. It contains dissolved oxygen and nitrogen salts and much organic material. The life of the pond establishes ecological cycles which constantly balance inputs and outputs between water, air, and life. For example, the supply of nitrates washed in from the land is augmented by the decomposition of dead organisms in the water itself

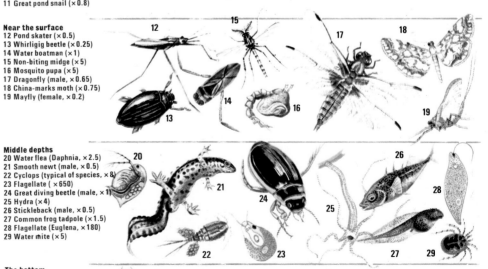

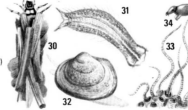

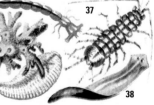

The oceans are a continuous mass of 5000 million million tons of water; but variations in light, pressure, salinity, temperature, currents, waves, and tides interact to create numerous regions each with its own typical forms of life.

Plants are the basis of ocean food chains, just as they are on land. Since all plants need sunlight they are found only in the upper layer of the sea. Myriads of tiny marine plants called phytoplankton are eaten by the small floating zooplankton and by tiny fish, which in turn support a succession of predators. Deep-water animals are adapted to great pressure and to darkness. Most are predators but some of them are scavengers which depend on a rain of food debris from above.

Some ocean islands are coral, built by millions of polyps resembling sea anemones which produce a hard stony skeleton (p. 17A). But most are thrust up by volcanic eruptions. They are completely isolated and were never joined to a continent. Such islands are usually wet and windswept.

Island plant and animal communities evolved from the few original forms which crossed the ocean and colonized. Island colonization is difficult, and is seldom accomplished by land mammals apart from bats, nor even by amphibians. Land and freshwater animals may have evolved from sea-dwelling ancestors. Once a species has colonized an island it interbreeds, because of its isolation, and adapts to its new conditions and competitors. Often new endemic species evolve.

The first colonizers are usually sea birds. They bring nutrients, so seeds and the spores of mosses, lichens and ferns carried by the wind can take root. The wind also brings insects, spiders and bats, and occasionally land birds in storms, but such birds rarely establish themselves. Reptiles and some land animals may cross the sea on driftwood rafts. Many island reptiles, perhaps because of the lack of mammals, have become unusually large. Examples include such creatures as the Komodo dragon and the giant tortoises of the Galapagos.

The ocean layers

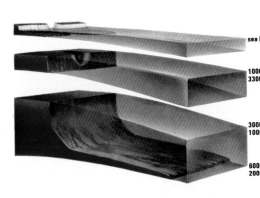

sea level
1000 m
3300 ft
3000 m
10000 ft
6000 m
20000 ft

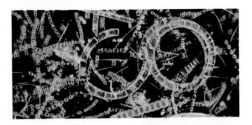

Phytoplankton *above*
All marine life depends ultimately on microscopic plant plankton, which is mostly single-celled. (x 20)

Tiger cowrie *right*
Cowries are tropical marine snails. This spotted example is feeding, with its mantle extended below.

Zooplankton *above*
These microscopic animals feed on the phytoplankton and on each other. In turn they support fish. (x 8)

Leopard coral *right*
The derivation of the name of this hard coral is obvious. Each 'spot' is an individual in the colony.

Soft coral *above*
Photographed in Mauritius, a bluish coral has almost finished reproducing by splitting into two.

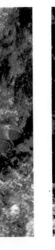

Sea urchin *below*
This 'slate pencil' variety from Mozambique coral reefs contrasts with spiny types. Size 10 in (25 cm).

Sea slug *above*
Many of these marine relatives of land slugs are colorful. This one from the Indian Ocean is 4 in (10 cm).

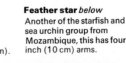

Feather star *below*
Another of the starfish and sea urchin group from Mozambique, this has four inch (10 cm) arms.

Air and surface life
The seabirds (right) are typical of a range of species, some of them exceptionally large birds, which navigate unerringly over thousands of miles of ocean. Most have wide wingspans and use favourable airflow over the waves to soar apparently without effort. Sunlight penetrates the warm upper layers of the ocean to provide energy for photosynthesis, permitting the prolific growth of the phytoplankton (plant life). This is the starting point for the whole complex web of marine life which leads ultimately to large predatory fish such as the tuna and marlin, and to human foods.

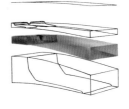

Near the surface
above and right
Seabirds generally keep below 1000 ft (300 m) but can be found much higher. The upper layer of ocean is taken to extend down to 3300 ft (1000 m). Water temperature is about 10°C and sunlight may reach to 650 ft (200 m).

Middle dwellers
In this range of depths, most of which (down to 6000 ft) is known as the bathyal or bathypelagic zone, the water cools to 4°C, the temperature at which the density of water reaches its peak. Little or no light penetrates, and the life is made up of free-swimming fish, crustaceans and cephalopods (squids, for example) possessing body fluids at the same hydrostatic pressure as the environment and having approximately the same degree of salinity. At night some middle dwellers migrate to the surface to feed on other animals which in turn congregate to 'graze' on the plankton.

Middle depths
above and right
The horizontal 'slice' of ocean water in which live the middle-depth species illustrated opposite is taken to extend from 3300 down to 10000 ft (1000-3000 m). Here the temperature falls from 10°C down to below 4°C at the lower level.

Bottom dwellers
Below 3000 meters the life comprises a range of animals, most of them very small, adapted to living in near-freezing water at extremely high pressures. The only light in this region comes from the curious luminescent organs common to many deep-sea creatures. Although the deep waters contain abundant salts and nutrient minerals, these are useless without the energy of sunlight. Every abyssal organism is therefore either a scavenger, depending for its supply of food on a rain of debris from above, or a predator. Yet the abyssal zone supports a surprising variety of life.

The abyss
above and right
The bottom layer of the ocean is here taken to extend down to about 20000 ft (6000 m). Temperature is always below 4°C, hydrostatic pressure is enormous and the environment is perpetually devoid of sunlight.

sea level

Great Shearwater
span 8½ in 0.2 m

Wandering albatross
span 11 ft 3.35 m

Red-billed tropic bird
span 1 ft 0.3 m

Magnificent frigate bird
span 8 ft 2.45 m

Portuguese man o' war
11 in 0.28 m
(tentacles 100 ft 30 m)

Flying fish
9 in 0.23 m

Marlin
10 ft 3 m

Ocean sunfish
10 ft 3 m

Anchovies
6 in 0.15 m

Basking shark
40 ft 12 m

Ocean bonito
2 ft 0.6 m

Dolphin fish
4 ft 1.2 m

Squid
1 ft 0.3 m

Bluefin tuna
7 ft 2 m

Mackerel shark
12 ft 3.6 m

Lantern fish
3 in 0.075 m

Diretmus argentus
2 in 0.05 m

Photostomias guerni
7 in 0.18 m

1000 m
3300 ft

Giant squid
55 ft 17 m

Hatchet fish
1 in 0.025 m

Oarfish
20 ft 6 m

Ghost shark
4 ft 1.2 m

Chiasmodus niger
3 in 0.075 m

Gulper eel
4 ft 6 in 1.4 m

3000 m
10000 ft

Angler fish
3 in 0.075 m

Deep sea swimming cucumber
4 in 0.1 m

Prawn
4 in 0.1 m

Viper fish
1 ft 0.3 m

Angler fish
2 in 0.05 m

Pelican eel
10 in 0.25 m

Deep sea jellyfish
3 in 0.075 m

Rat tail
18 in 0.45 m

Tripod fish
10 in 0.25 m

Abyssal octopus
4 in 0.1 m

Brotulid
6 in 0.15 m

Abyssal sea cucumber
¾ in 0.02 m

Sea snail
9 in 0.23 m

Brittle star 3 in 0.075 m

From Landscape to Townscape

The story of man's use of the land is one of increasing diversity and complexity. Preagricultural man developed perhaps six land uses; hunting, trapping, fishing, gathering wild fruits, fashioning tools and sheltering in caves. Modern man has developed several thousand forms, and frequently concentrates hundreds within a single square mile. For most of them he has created distinctive environments; one can tell at a glance whether the land is being used to grow carrots, make cement, repair ships, treat sewage, sell antiques, mine coal or educate children.

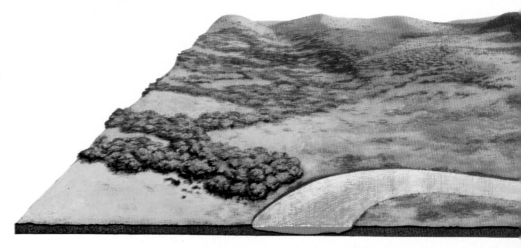

Although every place is unique in the ways its land uses intermingle, we can nevertheless recognize five major land-use patterns. Each has sprung into prominence at some major crossroads in human history. The first of the five is wildscape, which man uses so lightly and so rarely that nature is still in chief control. Some of it is still almost wholly natural, as in the remote parts of the Antarctic icecap. Other areas have been quite profoundly changed, as on the Pennine moorlands where generations of sheep have nibbled away tree seedlings and prevented the regeneration of forest, or where polluted air is now preventing the growth of sphagnum moss. But these areas are still wildscape. Man uses their resources but he leaves nature to replenish them.

The rural landscape evolves

Farmscape dates from man's first great technical advance, the Neolithic agricultural revolution of about 8000 years ago. For the first time he began to alter the landscape and live with the results instead of moving on; he ploughed and harvested, enclosed fields and diverted water for irrigation. During subsequent millennia this more controlled form of land-use spread over enormous areas of every continent, with a cumulative stream of diversifications as man applied his ingenuity to it in different environments. The rural landscape was now distinctively divided into the wild and the cultivated.

Townscape also existed from an early date, but had to await man's second great technical advance before it could develop at all extensively. Not until the twin agrarian and industrial revolutions of the 18th century did agriculture develop sufficiently to support a vastly greater population than its own labor force, or industry develop sufficiently to be able to employ a vast non-agricultural population. Once this possibility was established as a world trend, townscape began to develop rapidly.

Conflicts in land use

There are now three 'scapes' of increasing artificiality and complexity, respectively dominated by nature, the individual farmer and the public authority. So different are these three 'scapes' that problems tend to arise where they confront and interact with each other. Unfortunately such fringes of conflict have been intensified as side effects of two otherwise beneficial transport revolutions.

The first, or long-distance, transport revolution began with the steamship and the train in the 19th century. It opened up competition in foodstuffs on a global scale: the benefit was cheaper food from more favored areas, and the cost was the decline of less-favored areas. Some farmscape reverted to wildscape, resolving the problem. Elsewhere, the land remained good enough to reclaim in times of booming prices but too poor to be profitable in times of recession. The result in such areas is recurrent farm poverty.

The long-distance transport revolution also had a similar effect upon less competitive mining areas which tended to become derelict as a result, forming rurban (rural-urban) fringe. The main growth of rurban fringe, however, was stimulated by the second, or personal, transport revolution, in which the car gave city workers the opportunity to live in the country and commute daily to a neighboring city. The result was an unprecedented intermingling of urban areas and farmland, and an unprecedented degree of conflict between the two. Farmland became fragmented and subjected to many kinds of urban pressures so that much of it became uneconomic to farm. The urban area, on the other hand, experienced many difficulties in service facilities, because its sprawling layout multiplied distances and costs. Thus both marginal fringe and rurban fringe have become areas of patchy, conflicting landuses.

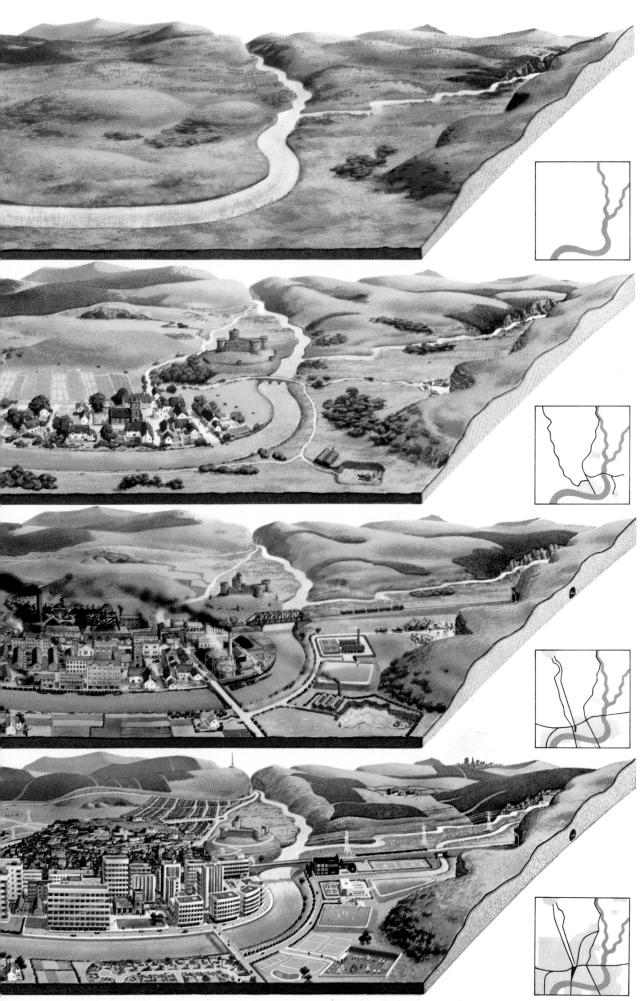

Prehistoric landscape

The natural prehistoric landscape consisted of a series of wildscape ecosystems wherein all forms of life interacted in a stable balance of nature. The land falls from distant hills to a coastal plain where the river widens into a broad estuary. Woodlands partially cover the plains, thinning into scrub on the hills. Stone age man used this wildscape in diffuse and restricted ways. He roamed the forest and heath hunting game but, apart from a cave shelter or toolmaking floor, rarely set aside land for a particular use. He exerted no perceptible influence upon the landscape apart from the fact that grazing animals gradually retarded the regeneration of the forest and led to a more open vegetation. But the presence of flat land, water, coal, stone and good access were ideal for later man.

Medieval

After he had developed agriculture man was able to use the land in more ways. It is possible by this time to detect at least a dozen types of stable land use. This was basically an age of slowly developing farmscape, when wildscape was reclaimed for food production and most settlement was designed to serve agricultural communities. Villagers are cultivating open strip fields in rotation for winter corn, spring corn and fallowing, surrounded by common grazing lands. The improved standard of shelter is reflected in clearance of forest to obtain timber, and the land is quarried for clay (near left), stone (left) and iron ore (background). With such burdens man has improved his transport methods. And the river is now becoming polluted.

19th Century

The industrial revolution was a marked change in man's use of land. Coal was deep-mined as a source of unprecedented power which led to the concentration of crafts in large factories. Gasworks, flour mills and textile mills were basic industries, in turn leading to an industrial townscape. Different types of land use can be measured by the score. Building stone and brick-making continue to flourish, but imports have replaced the old ironworkings. Agriculture plays its part by more efficient production from larger fields to support the growing population. Greatly improved communications are evident. But there is marked pollution of both the river and the atmosphere, and filter beds and clean-water reservoirs are necessary.

Modern

Land uses are now so differentiated as to be countless. Many hundreds of new uses are service functions, ranging from financial institutions to children's playgrounds (the former brick pit) and hairdressers. Dwellings abound in great variety, many of them made of new materials by new methods. Electricity has wrought a revolution that extends to virtually every human construction, and the urgent demand for better transport has led to a complete transformation of the scene on this ground alone. A more subtle effect of better transport is that uneconomic local farming has given way to imported food, and much of the land is being reforested. Perhaps most important of all is the fact that man has become concerned about his environment.

Pollution is harmful waste. All living creatures produce waste, often with marked effects on the environment. Pine leaves blanket out the flowers which would otherwise grow on the forest floor; the droppings of seabirds can cover nesting islands meters deep in guano. Plants as well as road vehicles give off carbon dioxide; volcanoes as well as power stations emit sulphur dioxide.

What turns man's waste into pollution? First, we produce too much waste: only man lives in such vast communities that his excreta de-oxygenates whole rivers. Secondly, the unwanted by-products of man's industrial metabolism change so rapidly that the environment has little hope of accommodating it. African grassland has evolved over millions of years to accept piles of elephant dung, with many species of animals specially adapted to living inside dungheaps and helping to decompose them. But the ecosystem is often unable to cope with our latest pollutants: few bacteria are able to digest plastics. Thirdly, man's waste is often extremely persistent: DDT may remain unchanged for decades, passing from one animal to another, poisoning and weakening them all.

Pollution may harm man directly: smoke causes bronchitis, and fouled drinking water can spread typhoid. Pollution may harm us indirectly, reducing the capacity of the land, rivers and seas to supply us with food. But perhaps the most insidious effects are the least obvious. Small doses of separate pollutants, each harmless by itself, may together weaken wild populations of animals so that they cannot recover from natural disasters. Acute pollution kills tens of thousands of animals; chronic pollution gradually reduces the quality of the entire human environment.

Pollution is wasteful. Too often modern technology painstakingly extracts a metal from the crust, uses it once and then discards it. For example, once unwanted chromium or mercury is released into the seas it will be diluted many millions of times and is unlikely ever to be recoverable except at prohibitive expense. If man is not to face raw material famines in the foreseeable future, he must learn to recycle everything from air and water to the rarer elements.

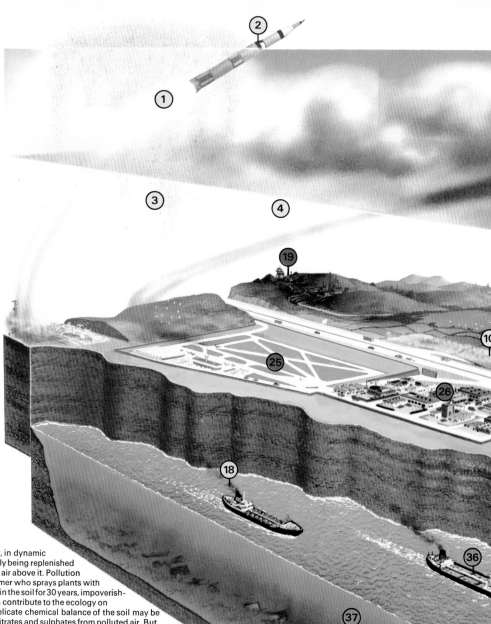

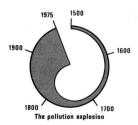

The pollution explosion

Pollution of the land
The soil is a living organic layer, in dynamic equilibrium with, and continually being replenished by, the rocks beneath it and the air above it. Pollution affects it in many ways. The farmer who sprays plants with insecticides may leave residues in the soil for 30 years, impoverishing the micro-organisms which contribute to the ecology on which his crops depend. The delicate chemical balance of the soil may be disrupted by rain loaded with nitrates and sulphates from polluted air. But the land is also a de-pollutant. Some substances can be buried in the knowledge that before they can re-appear they will have been oxidized to harmless compounds.

⬤ **Pollution of the air**

1 Rocket exhaust contains a variety of combustion products.

2 Space launchings leave jettisoned propellants and other debris orbiting above the atmosphere.

3 Nuclear weapon testing can leave fall-out on a global scale.

4 Increased air traffic creates noise pollution over wide areas.

5 Jet efflux contains kerosene combustion products, unburned fuel and particles of soot.

6 Nuclear weapons can cause radioactive contamination; together with chemical and biological devices they could eradicate all life on Earth.

7 Jet aircraft cause intense local noise, and supersonic aircraft create a shock-wave boom.

8 Large-scale aerial transport of pollutants distributes particles and gaseous matter.

9 Carbon dioxide build-up and 'greenhouse effect' traps solar heat within the atmosphere.

10 Pesticide spraying can cause widespread contamination, and organochlorine residues (such as DDT) can build up in animals and disrupt natural food chains.

11 Nuclear power station is potential source of escaping radioactive or liquid coolant.

12 Thermal (coal or oil fired) power station causes thermal and chemical pollution from exhaust stacks.

13 Power station cooling towers transfer waste heat to the air.

14 Sulphur dioxide from high roof-level chimneys falls into 'canyon streets' causing irritation to eyes and lungs.

15 Refinery waste gases burned in the air cause heavy pollution unless the flame is extremely hot.

16 Road vehicle exhausts and crankcase gases contain lead, unburned hydrocarbons, carbon monoxide and oxides of nitrogen, and can cause widespread pollution; action of sunlight on nitrogen oxides causes smog.

17 Most domestic fuels are very inefficiently burned, causing smoke and chemical pollution.

18 Steam boilers or diesel smoke can cause persistent trails of gaseous and particulate matter.

⬤ **Pollution of the land**

19 Coal mining leaves unsightly and potentially dangerous tips.

20 Electricity transmission pylons are a classic of visual pollution.

21 Powerful air-conditioning cools buildings in summer by heating the immediate surroundings.

22 Visual pollution of highways is accentuated by billboards.

23 Unreclaimed wastes are often dumped and not recycled.

24 Quarrying leaves unsightly scars.

25 Growth of air traffic is reflected in increasing size and number of airports which occupy otherwise valuable land.

26 Even modern industrial estates invariably cause chemical and thermal pollution, and pose waste-disposal problems.

27 Limited access highways, especially intersections, occupy large areas of land.

28 Campgrounds may cause severe local chemical, as well as visual, pollution.

29 Modern litter includes high proportion of non-biodegradable plastics materials.

⬤ **Pollution of the water**

30 Nuclear power station discharges waste heat into river and can cause radioactive contamination.

31 Industrial wastes are often poured into rivers without treatment.

32 Cooling water from thermal power stations can cause very large-scale heating of rivers, changing or destroying the natural fauna and flora.

33 Refinery and other chemical plants generate waste heat and liquid refuse which may be discharged directly into the river.

34 Oil storage installation can cause intermittent pollution.

35 When it reaches the sea the river is heavily polluted by nitrates and phosphates from fertilizers and treated sewage, as well as by heavy toxic metals.

36 Tanker too close inshore risks severe beach pollution from accidental release of cargo.

37 Radioactive and corrosive wastes often dumped without enough knowledge of local conditions to insure that the containers will not leak before contents have decomposed; nothing should be dumped on continental shelf and adequate dilution is essential.

38 The main influx of pollutants into the sea is via rivers; typical categories include agricultural and industrial chemicals, waste heat, treated and untreated sewage and solid matter.

39 Excess nutrients from untreated sewage, agricultural chemicals and nuclear wastes can lead to 'blooms' of toxic marine plankton or, through their oxidation and decay, to severely reduced oxygen levels in the water.

40 Sewage sludge dumped at sea contains persistent chemicals such as PCB (polychlorinated biophenyl) compounds, toxic heavy metals and nutrients.

41 Large oil slicks are released by tanker accidents or deliberate washing at sea, and by oil-rig blow-outs.

42 Sediments stirred by mineral exploitation, dumped from ships or carried by rivers may form thick layers on the ocean floor which suffocate the organisms living there.

43 Clouds of particulate matter, both organic and inorganic wastes, reduce the penetration of sunlight and sharply curtail marine productivity.

44 Oil rigs suffer explosive blow-outs, a serious problem off the California coast.

45 In some waters wrecks, many of them uncharted, pose hazards to shipping which may lead to further pollution.

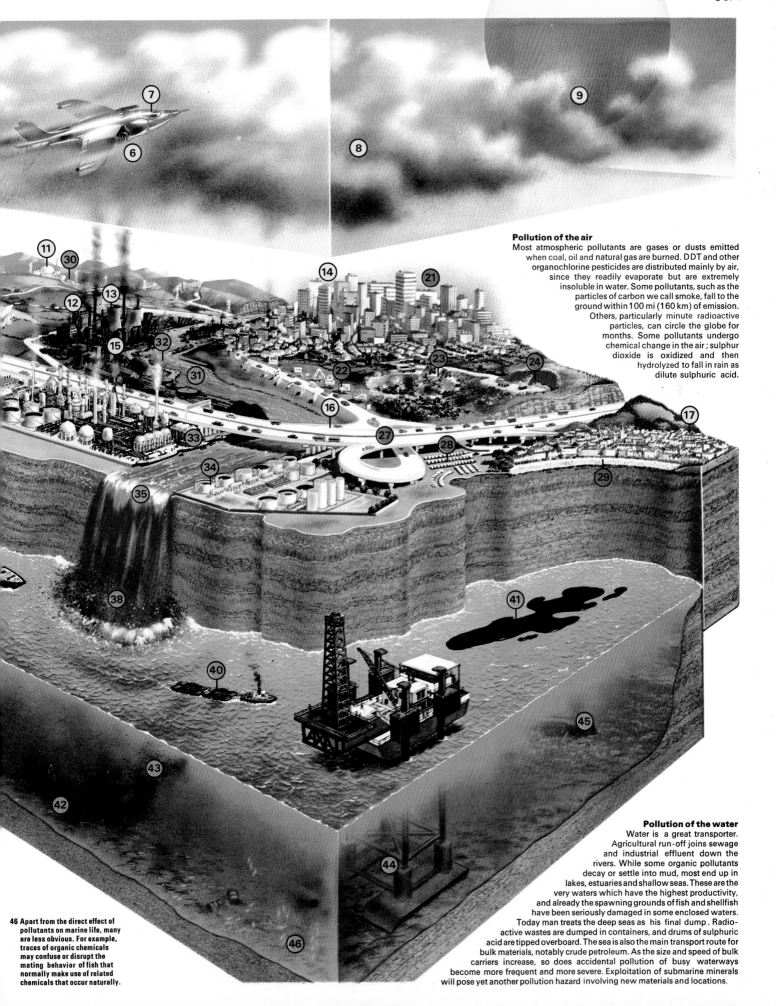

Pollution of the air
Most atmospheric pollutants are gases or dusts emitted when coal, oil and natural gas are burned. DDT and other organochlorine pesticides are distributed mainly by air, since they readily evaporate but are extremely insoluble in water. Some pollutants, such as the particles of carbon we call smoke, fall to the ground within 100 mi (160 km) of emission. Others, particularly minute radioactive particles, can circle the globe for months. Some pollutants undergo chemical change in the air; sulphur dioxide is oxidized and then hydrolyzed to fall in rain as dilute sulphuric acid.

Pollution of the water
Water is a great transporter. Agricultural run-off joins sewage and industrial effluent down the rivers. While some organic pollutants decay or settle into mud, most end up in lakes, estuaries and shallow seas. These are the very waters which have the highest productivity, and already the spawning grounds of fish and shellfish have been seriously damaged in some enclosed waters. Today man treats the deep seas as his final dump. Radio-active wastes are dumped in containers, and drums of sulphuric acid are tipped overboard. The sea is also the main transport route for bulk materials, notably crude petroleum. As the size and speed of bulk carriers increase, so does accidental pollution of busy waterways become more frequent and more severe. Exploitation of submarine minerals will pose yet another pollution hazard involving new materials and locations.

46 Apart from the direct effect of pollutants on marine life, many are less obvious. For example, traces of organic chemicals may confuse or disrupt the mating behavior of fish that normally make use of related chemicals that occur naturally.

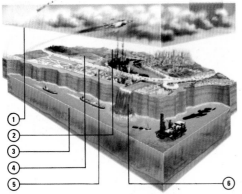

① ② ③ ④ ⑤ ⑥

Pollution often travels along strange pathways, and these must be unravelled if the menace is to be controlled and its effects predicted. It is unwise ever to assume the obvious. DDT was found in the soil of apple orchards in Kent months after spraying, and it was also detected in local rivers. The obvious conclusion was that it was leaching down through the soil into the groundwater. But analysis of the springs and wells showed no DDT at all. In fact the insecticide was leaving the surface by evaporation and falling again as rain.

Pollution can be distributed over vast distances. The insecticide BHC is carried by the prevailing westerly winds from the Soviet Union across China and N America and to Europe. Water likewise carries contaminants down rivers to oceans. But the most important pathway is the food chain. A pollutant is released into the air, soil or sea. It is absorbed by plants. These are eaten by a herbivore, which in its turn is eaten by a carnivore which is itself eaten by a predator. The chain may have many links or only a few, but at every stage the pollutant is more concentrated. If a hawk eats 100 birds which each ate 100 insects it may die from pollution 10000 times the strength met by the insect.

Pollution and health

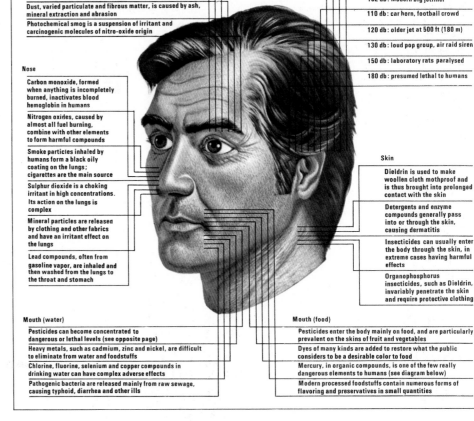

Eyes

Ozone from various industrial processes is extremely toxic and irritates the eyes

Sulphur dioxide is generated by burning all sulphurous fuels: coal, oil and gas

Smoke is mainly particulate carbon plus mixed carbohydrate molecules, some of them carcinogenic

Dust, varied particulate and fibrous matter, is caused by ash, mineral extraction and abrasion

Photochemical smog is a suspension of irritant and carcinogenic molecules of nitro-oxide origin

Nose

Carbon monoxide, formed when anything is incompletely burned, inactivates blood hemoglobin in humans

Nitrogen oxides, caused by almost all fuel burning, combine with other elements to form harmful compounds

Smoke particles inhaled by humans form a black oily coating on the lungs; cigarettes are the main source

Sulphur dioxide is a choking irritant in high concentrations. Its action on the lungs is complex

Mineral particles are released by clothing and other fabrics and have an irritant effect on the lungs

Lead compounds, often from gasoline vapor, are inhaled and then washed from the lungs to the throat and stomach

Ears

30 decibels: watch ticking

60 db: normal conversation

90 db: close heavy truck

102 db: modern big jetliner

110 db: car horn, football crowd

120 db: older jet at 500 ft (180 m)

130 db: loud pop group, air raid siren

150 db: laboratory rats paralysed

180 db: presumed lethal to humans

Skin

Dieldrin is used to make woollen cloth mothproof and is thus brought into prolonged contact with the skin

Detergents and enzyme compounds generally pass into or through the skin, causing dermatitis

Insecticides can usually enter the body through the skin, in extreme cases having harmful effects

Organophosphorus insecticides, such as Dieldrin, invariably penetrate the skin and require protective clothing

Mouth (water)

Pesticides can become concentrated to dangerous or lethal levels (see opposite page)

Heavy metals, such as cadmium, zinc and nickel, are difficult to eliminate from water and foodstuffs

Chlorine, fluorine, selenium and copper compounds in drinking water can have complex adverse effects

Pathogenic bacteria are released mainly from raw sewage, causing typhoid, diarrhea and other ills

Mouth (food)

Pesticides enter the body mainly on food, and are particularly prevalent on the skins of fruit and vegetables

Dyes of many kinds are added to restore what the public considers to be a desirable color to food

Mercury, in organic compounds, is one of the few really dangerous elements to humans (see diagram below)

Modern processed foodstuffs contain numerous forms of flavoring and preservatives in small quantities

---

① **Radiation** *right*
No pollutant has been so continuously monitored as nuclear radiation. But it is not a problem created solely by modern man. In the modern world nearly all the radioactivity issues from the rocks, and, as far as humans are concerned, from the body.

Rocks	50 %
Cosmic	25 %
Body	23¼ %
Tests	1½ %
Waste	¼ %

② **Radiation and life** *right*
Living cells concentrate radiation. In an above-ground nuclear-weapon test all heavy radioactive particles drop within hours in a narrow region down-wind of the explosion. Their residence time in the atmosphere varies from four weeks in the troposphere to ten years in the mesosphere. One such product, strontium 90, is taken up from the soil by plants. Eaten by cattle and released in their milk, it ends up in human bone where it is only slowly liquidated. As it decays it can destroy the marrow which produces red blood cells, in extreme cases causing death through pentaemia. Radiation pollution can also arise from power reactors or nuclear waste. Plankton can concentrate radioactivity a thousandfold. Fish eat plankton, and on migration can disperse the radiation far from its source. In the 1950s this mechanism caused radiation sickness in Japanese fishermen hundreds of miles from US test sites in the Pacific.

Concentration of atomic waste (phosphorus 32) in animal food chains

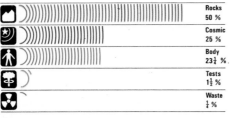

Water 1

Aquatic invertebrates 35

Ducks 7500

Duck eggs 200,000

Egg yolks 2,000,000

③ **Deadly mercury** *right*
Compounds of mercury have for 1000 years been known to be highly toxic. An industrial plant often discharges such compounds, but it was thought these rested at the sea bed. Man has now learned that bacteria can convert inorganic mercury compounds to deadly methyl mercury, which can then be successively concentrated in marine food chains. Shell-fish are particularly good concentrators of methyl mercury. When eaten by humans they cause severe disabling of the central nervous system, and in extreme cases cause death (below).

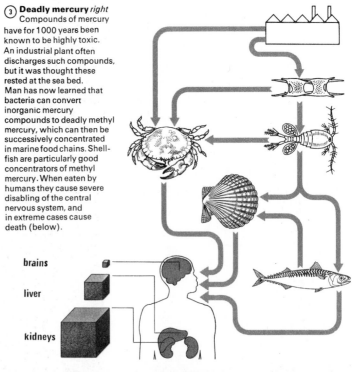

brains

liver

kidneys

Minimata tragedy *right*
In 1953 people living in this Japanese city became ill. Ultimately over 120 were afflicted, and 43 (black) died. The cause was methyl mercury concentrated in sea-foods. Some acet-aldehyde plants still emit methyl mercury.

4 **The DDT menace** *right*
Introduced during World War 2, DDT appeared to be ideal. It would kill lice on soldiers weeks after the treatment of their clothes. Houses sprayed against malaria remained lethal to mosquitoes long after the health teams had departed. But the persistence brought its own problems. DDT and other organochlorine pesticides, such as BHC, Dieldrin, Endosulfan and Heptachlor, are only slightly broken down by animal metabolism. An insect receiving a non-lethal dose of DDT retains it in its body and passes it on up the food chain. Animals at the head of the chain often build up large residues in their fatty tissues. Under stress these residues can be released and fatally damage the liver, kidney and brain. DDT can evaporate from soil, travelling round the globe, before being adsorbed on to dust and falling as rain. The organochlorines soon penetrate every corner of an ecosystem.

DIELDRIN

 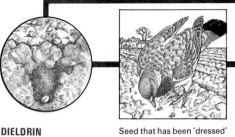   

Seed that has been 'dressed' is eaten by a wood pigeon. The bird finds the seeds palatable, and may eat dozens to hundreds in a day.

The pigeon is devoured by a badger (or a cat, fox, hawk or other predator). The badger may build up poison from eating many pigeons.

In this case the pesticide-soaked grain is attractive to a yellowhammer, typical of many small birds which pick seeds off the land.

The yellowhammer has fallen prey to a sparrowhawk. In a few weeks dieldrin may build up causing death or inability to breed.

DDT

Sap-sucking insects, such as aphids, feed on sprayed wheat and build up a DDT concentration not sufficiently high to kill them.

A predator ladybird climbs wheat grain devouring aphids in large numbers. It soon builds up a very large residue of DDT in its body.

On a nettle at the edge of the field the ladybird is in turn eaten by a whitethroat, spotted flycatcher or other insect-eating bird.

Finally the bird suffering from severe DDT toxicity, is devoured by a hawk. In many countries birds of prey have almost vanished.

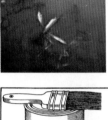

6 **Misuse of a river by overloading** *above and left*
In moderation, man can safely pour his effluents into the rivers. A farmhouse beside a river (above) causes a little local pollution which is soon oxidized; the fish population does not suffer. A village causes no lasting pollution but merely a depression of the dissolved oxygen in the water for

a mile or two downstream. But a large city pours out so much effluent that the river is completely de-oxygenated. All the fish and plants are killed and the river becomes foul in an irreversible way (left). Whereas a river may be capable of processing pollutants from 50000 people, pollutants from 100000 may destroy the ecological cycle.

PCB uses *left*
Polychlorinated biphenyls have numerous uses in modern industry. They serve as plasticizers in paints, as fillers in plastics and in electrical capacitors.

5 **The PCB problem**
PCBs (polychlorinated biphenyls) are persistent and can be scattered in smoke from burning or washed down a drain adsorbed on dust particles. Virtually all these molecules end up in the sea in the form of non-biodegradable particles which can be intensely concentrated as they move within the marine food chain. Their lethal effect was first driven home when the population of Irish sea birds, especially guillemots, crashed in 1969. Almost all the corpses were found to have liver and kidney lesions characteristic of PCB poisoning. Fat, healthy birds can carry a large PCB load safely, but the Irish birds were starving and had drawn on their fatty reserves, where the PCB was stored. Passing into the circulation, the chemical accumulated in the birds' organs in lethal amounts.

Guillemots *right*
These sea birds live on fish and thus form the end link in a marine food chain.

0·01 seawater

30 zooplankton

100 mussels

100 lobster

200 shrimps

2000 herring

1000 sprat

1000 sand-eel

3400 guillemot

Thin guillemot *below*
When a guillemot with 3400 ppb of PCB in its body becomes emaciated it draws on its reserves of fat. The chemical becomes concentrated in its organs, reaching a lethal level of 60000 ppb.

brain

up to 60000 in liver

liver

kidneys

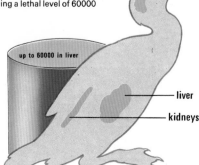

Fat guillemot *left*
Healthy guillemots (feeding at sea, far left) can have 3400 parts per billion (ppb) of PCBs in the body but only 400 in the liver.

Pollution is a global problem. It affects the land, the sea and the atmosphere in an inter-related way that is incredibly complex and often very subtle. At least in the industrially developed countries man has learned that he must do better than merely bury his unwanted materials in the ground, pour them into the rivers or burn them to pollute the air. But learning the best ways of disposing of them – or, preferably, of storing them until they can be used again – is a difficult, long-term process; and time is not on man's side.

Once pollutants are dispersed, controlling them becomes extremely costly or even impossible. The answer is to prevent their release, wherever possible, into the arterial pathways of water and air. The growing awareness of this is reflected in the legislation of many countries. It is seen in the Clean Air Act of Great Britain, the German convention banning harmful detergents, the tight California restrictions on car exhaust gases, and so on. But this is only the start of the movement to clean-up the environment and conserve its resources.

Much of the action against pollution has been piecemeal in nature, often in response to particular disasters. Now comes the promise, in no small part due to the public mood, for more widespread action against pollutants that are already known to be harmful to the environment and man. For example, public health authorities in most countries are alive to the hazard of mercury contamination in fish and other foods. At the international level, the convention on oil pollution is being strengthened and the permissible levels of radioactive discharges reviewed. At the same time, industry is slowly becoming persuaded that waste should be regarded as a valued resource which is often capable of being recycled over and over again instead of discarded.

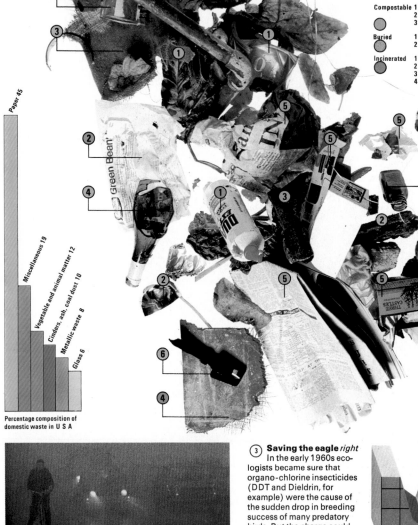

② Domestic waste
Man's garbage has never ceased to grow in volume and to change in character. In the past much of it, such as wood, cloth and paper, was biodegradable – exposure to micro-organisms and the weather slowly rotted them away. Even iron slowly oxidized. But today's refuse contains increasing amounts of materials which do not decay. These new materials demand new or improved methods of disposal, which with the growing recognition of the problem are now being adopted in many places.

Recyclable
1 Ferrous metals
2 Non-ferrous metals
3 Rubber
4 Glass
5 Paper and cardboard
6 Cloth

Compostable
1 Vegetable matter
2 Animal matter
3 Cloth

Buried
1 Mineral dust
2 Brick, stone

Incinerated
1 Plastics
2 Polythene
3 Polystyrene
4 Linoleum

Percentage composition of domestic waste in U S A

- Paper 45
- Miscellaneous 19
- Vegetable and animal matter 12
- Cinders, ash, coal dust 10
- Metallic waste 8
- Glass 6

① Air pollution in cities
Smoke is one of the commonest, most dangerous and most visible of all air pollutants. It is the direct cause of bronchitis and other respiratory diseases. But many nations are cleaning their urban atmosphere by introducing smokeless zones. Since 1956 winter sunshine in British city centers has increased by over 50 per cent. Smoke from railways (violet segment, right) has dwindled as steam traction has been superseded. Industrial smoke has likewise been reduced, although iron oxide dust from steelworks (above) remains a problem as do domestic coal fires.

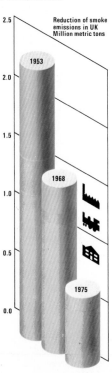

Reduction of smoke emissions in UK Million metric tons
- 1953
- 1968
- 1975

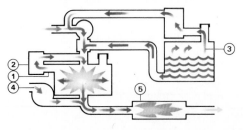

The menace of the car *below*
Dramatic reductions in air pollution will result as soon as simple alterations are universally adopted. One of the worst sources, the crankcase breather (1), is not opened to the air but piped through a vacuum-sensing valve (2) back to the intake. Fuel-tank vapor (3) is filtered and similarly dealt with. The exhaust is made oxygen-rich with extra fresh air (4) to burn up all but a few combustion products; the residue is oxidized to harmless compounds by passage through a high temperature furnace (5) in the presence of a chemical catalyst which promotes the desired reactions.

③ Saving the eagle *right*
In the early 1960s ecologists became sure that organo-chlorine insecticides (DDT and Dieldrin, for example) were the cause of the sudden drop in breeding success of many predatory birds. But the charge could not be proved, and in most countries the use of these pesticides continued. One bird affected was the golden eagle. Scottish highland sheep were dipped in Dieldrin to kill ticks. The chemical became dissolved in the mutton fat, and this eagle lives largely on sheep carrion. In one area the proportion of eagle eyries producing young fell from 72 to 29 per cent, following the introduction of Dieldrin sheep dips in 1960. Scotland's 300 pairs of eagles seemed doomed. But in 1966 Britain banned Dieldrin sheep-dips. By the early 1970s more than enough young survived to maintain the eagle population.

1960 1963 1966 1969
Golden eagle: percentage breeding successes

④ Oil pollution

Every year millions of tons of oil enter the oceans either directly through spills, accidents and deliberate discharge or indirectly via air and water from the land. Hardly any part of the ocean remains free from contamination. Some oil pollution is the disturbing result of industrial society's dependence on an oil-based technology. Equally, there is no doubt that much oil pollution is unnecessary and can be controlled or prevented. One of the earliest attempts to do this occurred in 1926 when the United States tried to obtain international agreement to limit the discharge of oil. This and later attempts by the United Kingdom failed and it was not until 1958 that the International Convention for the Prevention of Pollution of the Sea by Oil came into force – four years after it was agreed. Even then, the Convention did not ban completely the release of oil into the sea. This must be the ultimate goal. However, even if this is achieved, the problem will persist – oil pollution from sources on land is more than double that occurring directly at sea. One of the chief offenders are gasoline and diesel engines. The crankcases of such engines contribute at least 2.8 million metric tons of oil to the sea every year. A serious waste of a vital resource, steps are at last being taken in some countries to curb it.

The Torrey Canyon disaster
In 1967 the sea had its first major case of oil pollution when the Torrey Canyon ran aground off the Cornish coast (above left). Within a few days the first oil began to sweep onto the beaches. To disperse it, large quantities of detergent were sprayed both from boats (above) and on the shore, turning the sea creamy white with a froth of oily emulsion (center left). Unfortunately the use of these detergents probably caused more damage to marine life than did the oil – except for the early kill of seabirds (bottom left). The oil also drifted across to France coating the shore with congealed oil (right).

Oil movements *left*
Increased transport is reflected in the percentage growth of the world tanker fleet (below).

Thousand million tons

2			
1			
0	1963	1965	1967

Major oil routes

Oil entering the oceans   Million metric tons

Industrial machine waste	1.3
Motor vehicle waste	1.8
Refineries	0.3
Accidental spillage	0.2
Offshore drilling	0.1
Tanker operations	0.53
Other ships	0.5

Sources of oil pollution *left*
Although the spectacular incidents such as tanker collisions and drilling rig accidents receive most publicity, they release little oil compared with motor vehicles and industrial machines.

Oil tankers' new load-on-top system *below*
Before the introduction of this system, ballast water and tank washings, along with a hundred or so tons of oil which had originally stuck to the internal steelwork, were discharged into the sea before taking on a new cargo. In the load-on-top system, one cargo compartment (A) is used as a 'slop tank'. Water in a ballast tank (B) is run off until only oil and oily water remains (C). The residue together with washings from the tanks are collected in the slop tank (D). Here the mixture is finally separated before running clean water off (E). The load goes on top of the remaining oil.

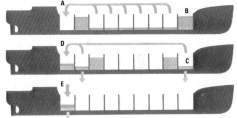

⑤ Thermal pollution *above and below*

Man throws away a great deal of unwanted heat into rivers. This is done on the largest scale by electricity generating stations whose condensers cycle cooling water in vast quantities. In Britain the hot effluent is spread as a thin film on an otherwise cool river, causing visible steam (above, River Trent) but minimal disturbance to river life. The problem is accentuated by the spread of very large nuclear stations (in the US, below), which for safety reasons have so far generally been sited miles from urban areas on rivers which previously were quite unpolluted. In Britian all such stations are on the sea shore or wide estuaries.

Nuclear power stations

○ Operating

○ Under construction

⑥ Lake pollution

Lakes pass through a sequence of physical and chemical states from youth to maturity (p66A). Man's sewage and industrial effluents accelerate the intake of nutrient salts — such as the phosphates and nitrates shown in the bar chart above the map — which feed the natural population of algae. Combined with sunny weather the result can be an algal 'bloom'. Billions of algae use up the water's dissolved oxygen, killing fish and other life. The aerobic (oxygen-breathing) bacteria needed to degrade sewage and other organic matter are replaced by anaerobic forms which decompose the refuse not to carbon dioxide and water but to foul gases and black slimes. Eventually the bloom is replaced by an algal 'crash' and the countless bodies, often visible as a colored tide, evolve toxic decomposition products which, concentrated in food chains, can prove lethal to sea birds and even humans. The answer is better water treatment plants, possibly combined with new forms of fertilizers, detergents and other products of modern civilization which contain smaller quantities of nutrient salts.

Main pollutants : percentages

Phosphate	20	43	37
Nitrate	9	17	74

☐ Lakeshore sewage
▨ Sewage from tributaries
■ Natural inflow from rivers

Ludwigshafen
Überlingen
Radolfzell
Konstanz
Friedrichshafen
Steckborn
Kreuzlingen
Lindau
Romanshorn
Rorschach
Bregenz

1
2
3
4
5
6
7   Numbers indicate increasing pollution

Reviving a dying lake *above*
One of the largest European freshwater lakes, Lake Constance (Bodensee), is a prime example of how the increasing load of industrial and domestic effluent causes serious pollution. The aim now is to install treatment plant at source rather than use the lake as a liquid refuse dump.

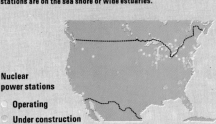

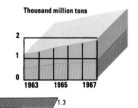

World Thematic Maps

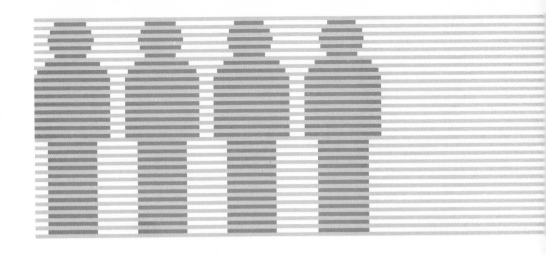

This section contains more than 50 thematic maps that present world patterns and distributions in visual form. Together with accompanying graphs, these maps communicate basic information on mineral resources, agricultural products, trade, transportation, and other selected aspects of the natural and human environment.

The thematic map uses symbols to communicate information. Generally, each map tells about only one class of geographical information, such as climate or population. This "theme" of a thematic map is placed over a map that gives basic geographic information, such as coastlines, country boundaries, rivers, and oceans. A thematic map's primary purpose is to give the reader a general idea of the subject. For example, the map on page 37 shows the distribution of cattle by the use of dot symbols. From this, the reader can learn that cattle are distributed much more uniformly throughout the United States than in China. The reader can also see that America has more cattle than China. But there is no way to tell the exact number in each country.

This is true of most thematic maps. They are not intended to provide exact statistical information. A reader who wants precise statistics should consult the bar graphs that appear with the thematic maps in this Atlas or other sources, such as encyclopedias or almanacs.

Thematic maps use point, line, and area symbols, singly and in combination. These can show both *qualitative differences* (differences in kind) and *quantitative differences* (differences in amount). For example, the Natural Vegetation map (page 16) uses color and pattern symbols to show the kind of vegetation that grows naturally in various parts of the world. This is qualitative information. Quantitative information is shown on the Annual Precipitation map (page 14). By means of lines that connect points of equal rainfall, the reader can tell, in general, how much rain an area receives in a year. Color is used to show the area between the lines. Thus, the thematic maps communicate general information far better than could volumes of words and tables.

One of the most important uses of the thematic maps section is to show comparisons and relationships. For example, a reader can compare the relationship of population density (page 20) with agriculture (page 28) and annual precipitation (page 14).

The maps and graphs in this section also give an idea of the relative importance of countries in the distributions mapped. The maps are based on recent statistics gathered by the United Nations and various governmental and nongovernmental sources. However, no single year affords a realistic base for production, trade, and certain economic and demographic statistics; averages of data for three or four years are used.

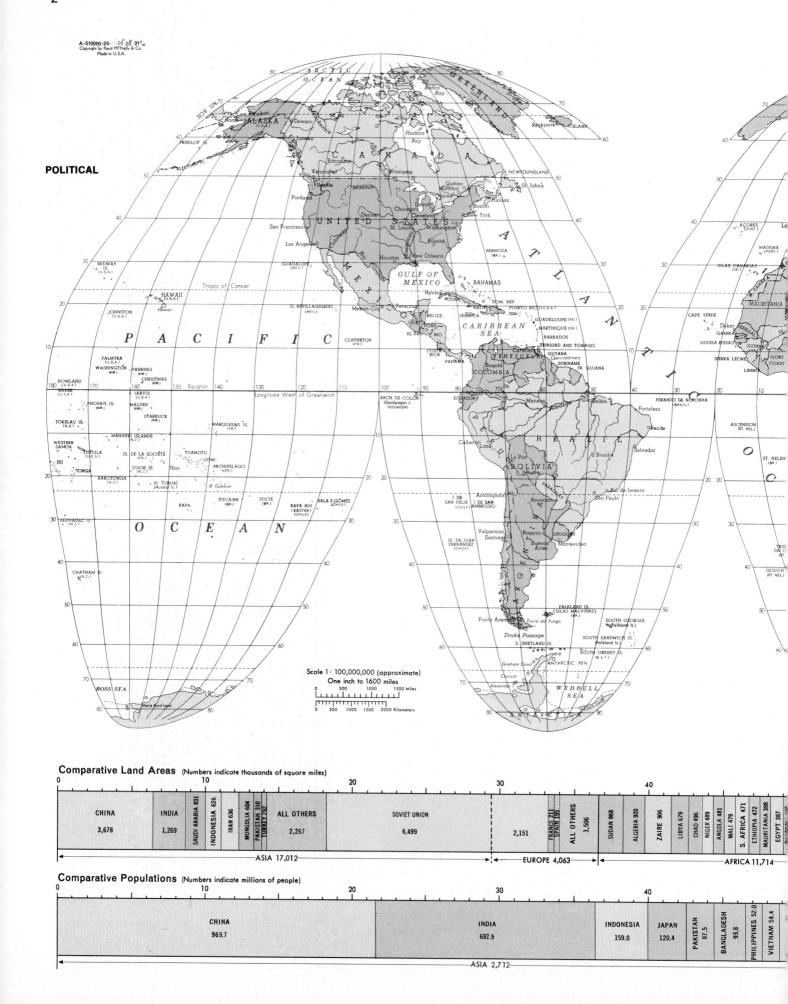

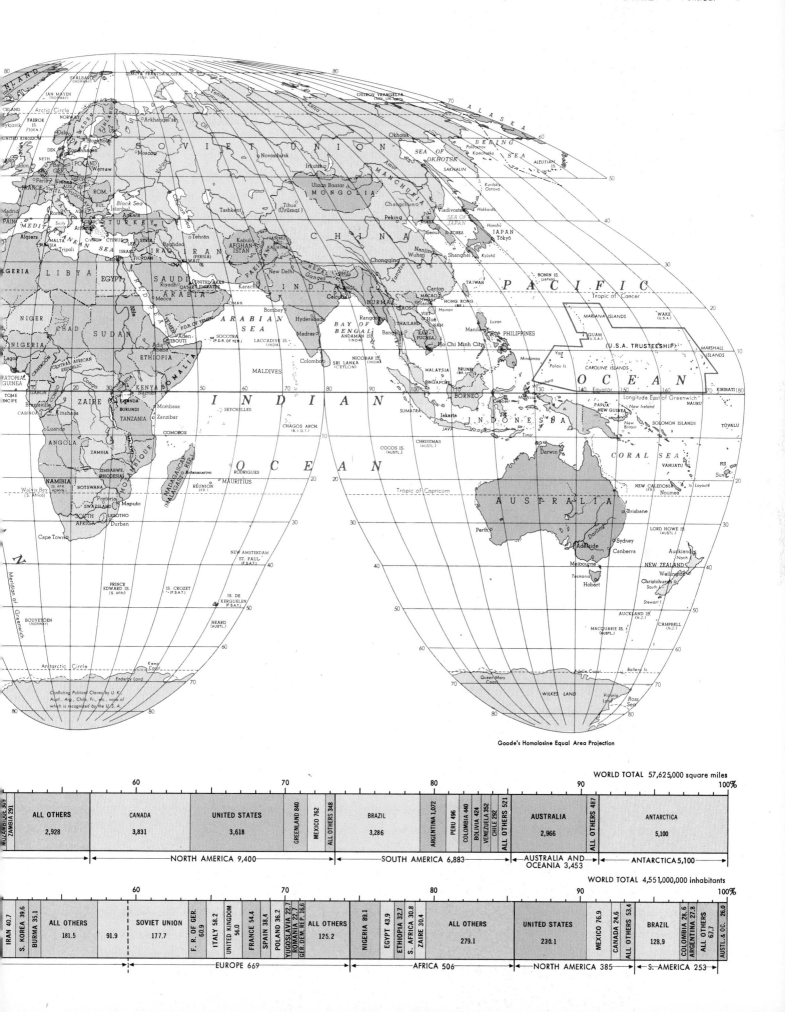

Goode's Homolosine Equal Area Projection

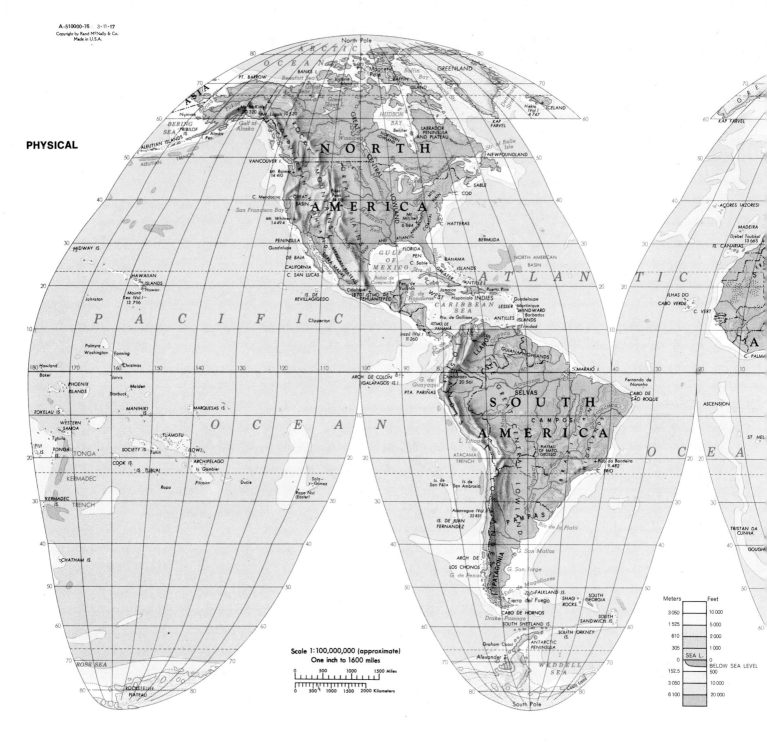
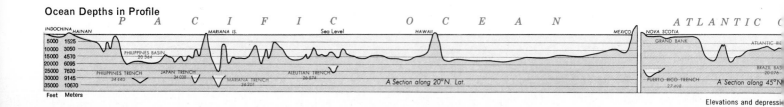

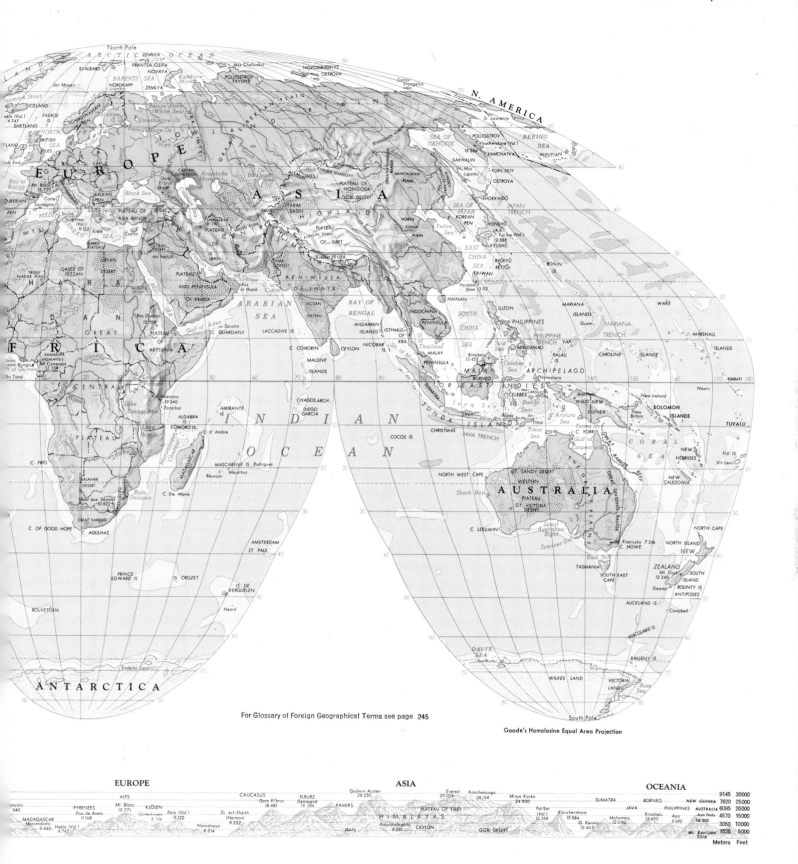

For Glossary of Foreign Geographical Terms see page 245

Goode's Homolosine Equal Area Projection

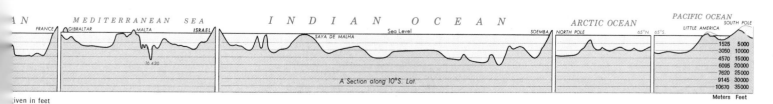

A Section along 10°S. Lat.

6

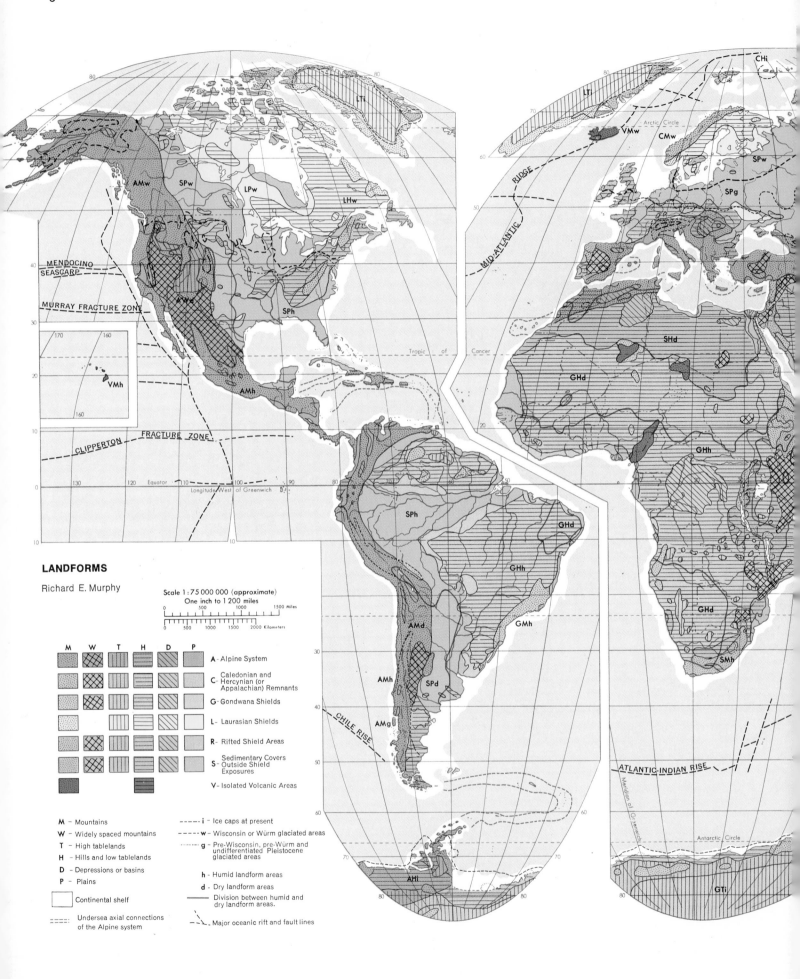

LANDFORMS

Richard E. Murphy

Scale 1 : 75 000 000 (approximate)
One inch to 1 200 miles

M	W	T	H	D	P	

A - Alpine System

C - Caledonian and Hercynian (or Appalachian) Remnants

G - Gondwana Shields

L - Laurasian Shields

R - Rifted Shield Areas

S - Sedimentary Covers Outside Shield Exposures

V - Isolated Volcanic Areas

M - Mountains
W - Widely spaced mountains
T - High tablelands
H - Hills and low tablelands
D - Depressions or basins
P - Plains

Continental shelf

Undersea axial connections of the Alpine system

i - Ice caps at present

w - Wisconsin or Würm glaciated areas

g - Pre-Wisconsin, pre-Würm and undifferentiated Pleistocene glaciated areas

h - Humid landform areas

d - Dry landform areas

Division between humid and dry landform areas.

Major oceanic rift and fault lines

MENDOCINO SEASCARP

MURRAY FRACTURE ZONE

CLIPPERTON FRACTURE ZONE

Equator

Longitude West of Greenwich

Tropic of Cancer

MID-ATLANTIC RIDGE

Arctic Circle

CHILE RISE

ATLANTIC-INDIAN RISE

Meridian of Greenwich

Antarctic Circle

8

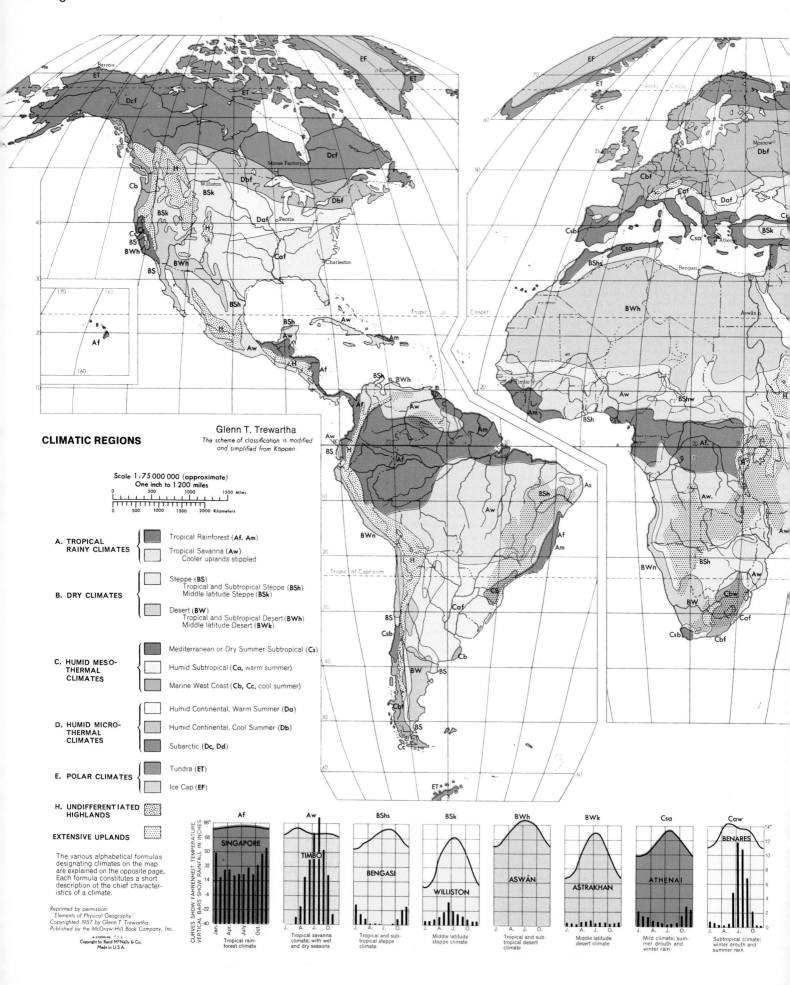

CLIMATIC REGIONS

Glenn T. Trewartha
*The scheme of classification is modified
and simplified from Köppen.*

Scale 1:75 000 000 (approximate)
One inch to 1 200 miles

0   500   1000   1500 Miles

0   500   1000   1500   2000 Kilometers

A. TROPICAL
RAINY CLIMATES
- Tropical Rainforest (**Af. Am**)
- Tropical Savanna (**Aw**)
  Cooler uplands stippled

B. DRY CLIMATES
- Steppe (**BS**)
  Tropical and Subtropical Steppe (**BSh**)
  Middle latitude Steppe (**BSk**)
- Desert (**BW**)
  Tropical and Subtropical Desert (**BWh**)
  Middle latitude Desert (**BWk**)

C. HUMID MESO-
THERMAL
CLIMATES
- Mediterranean or Dry Summer Subtropical (**Cs**)
- Humid Subtropical (**Ca**, warm summer)
- Marine West Coast (**Cb, Cc,** cool summer)

D. HUMID MICRO-
THERMAL
CLIMATES
- Humid Continental, Warm Summer (**Da**)
- Humid Continental, Cool Summer (**Db**)
- Subarctic (**Dc, Dd**)

E. POLAR CLIMATES
- Tundra (**ET**)
- Ice Cap (**EF**)

H. UNDIFFERENTIATED
HIGHLANDS

EXTENSIVE UPLANDS

The various alphabetical formulas
designating climates on the map
are explained on the opposite page.
Each formula constitutes a short
description ot the chief characteristics of a climate.

*Reprinted by permission.
"Elements of Physical Geography".
Copyrighted 1957 by Glenn T. Trewartha.
Published by the McGraw-Hill Book Company, Inc.*

A-510000-68
Copyright by Rand McNally & Co.
Made in U.S.A.

CURVES SHOW FAHRENHEIT TEMPERATURE
VERTICAL BARS SHOW RAINFALL IN INCHES

Af	Aw	BShs	BSk	BWh	BWk	Csa	Caw
SINGAPORE	TIMBO	BENGASI	WILLISTON	ASWÂN	ASTRAKHAN	ATHENAI	BENARES
Tropical rain-forest climate	Tropical savanna climate; with wet and dry seasons	Tropical and subtropical steppe climate	Middle latitude steppe climate	Tropical and subtropical desert climate	Middle latitude desert climate	Mild climate; summer drouth and winter rain	Subtropical climate; winter drouth and summer rain

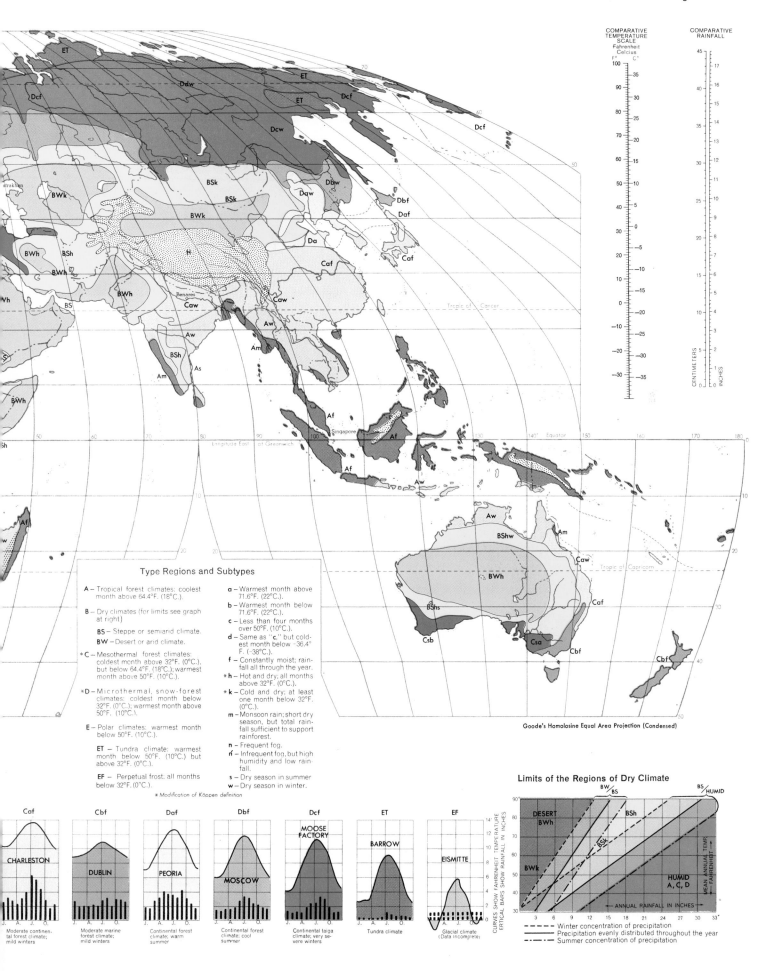

COMPARATIVE
TEMPERATURE
SCALE
Fahrenheit
Celcius

COMPARATIVE
RAINFALL

Goode's Homolosine Equal Area Projection (Condensed)

Type Regions and Subtypes

A – Tropical forest climates: coolest
month above 64.4°F. (18°C.).

B – Dry climates (for limits see graph
at right)

BS – Steppe or semiarid climate.
BW – Desert or arid climate.

*C – Mesothermal forest climates:
coldest month above 32°F. (0°C.).
but below 64.4°F. (18°C.); warmest
month above 50°F. (10°C.).

*D – Microthermal, snow-forest
climates: coldest month below
32°F. (0°C.); warmest month above
50°F. (10°C.).

E – Polar climates: warmest month
below 50°F. (10°C.).

ET – Tundra climate: warmest
month below 50°F. (10°C.) but
above 32°F. (0°C.).

EF – Perpetual frost: all months
below 32°F. (0°C.).

a – Warmest month above
71.6°F. (22°C.).
b – Warmest month below
71.6°F. (22°C.).
c – Less than four months
over 50°F. (10°C.).
d – Same as "c," but coldest month below -36.4°
F. (-38°C.).
f – Constantly moist; rainfall all through the year.
*h – Hot and dry; all months
above 32°F. (0°C.).
*k – Cold and dry; at least
one month below 32°F.
(0°C.).
m – Monsoon rain; short dry
season, but total rain-
fall sufficient to support
rainforest.
n – Frequent fog.
ñ – Infrequent fog, but high
humidity and low rain-
fall.
s – Dry season in summer
w – Dry season in winter.

* Modification of Köppen definition

Limits of the Regions of Dry Climate

Caf
CHARLESTON
Moderate continen-
tal forest climate;
mild winters

Cbf
DUBLIN
Moderate marine
forest climate;
mild winters

Daf
PEORIA
Continental forest
climate; warm
summer

Dbf
MOSCOW
Continental forest
climate; cool
summer

Dcf
MOOSE
FACTORY
Continental taiga
climate; very se-
vere winters

ET
BARROW
Tundra climate

EF
EISMITTE
Glacial climate
(Data incomplete)

CURVES SHOW FAHRENHEIT TEMPERATURE
ERTICAL BARS SHOW RAINFALL IN INCHES

DESERT
BWh

BSh

BWk

BSk

HUMID
A, C, D

MEAN ANNUAL TEMP.
FAHRENHBT

BW/BS   BS/HUMID

ANNUAL RAINFALL IN INCHES

- - - - Winter concentration of precipitation
———— Precipitation evenly distributed throughout the year
– · – · – Summer concentration of precipitation

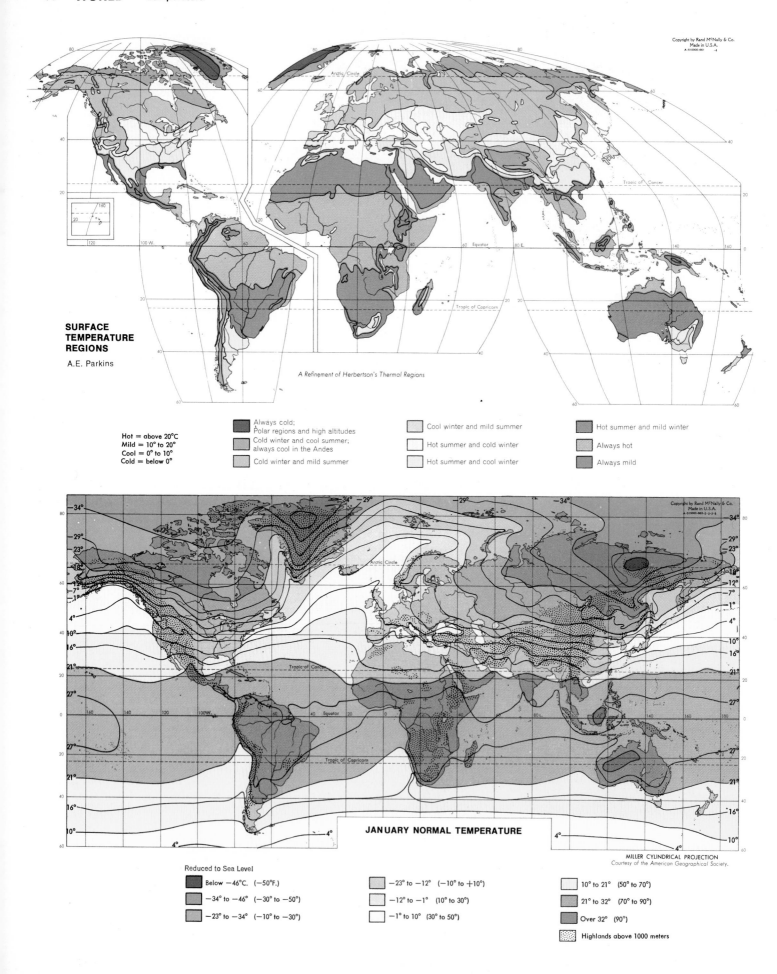

Copyright by Rand McNally & Co.
Made in U.S.A.
A-510000-661

SURFACE TEMPERATURE REGIONS

A.E. Parkins

A Refinement of Herbertson's Thermal Regions

Hot = above 20°C
Mild = 10° to 20°
Cool = 0° to 10°
Cold = below 0°

- Always cold; Polar regions and high altitudes
- Cold winter and cool summer; always cool in the Andes
- Cold winter and mild summer
- Cool winter and mild summer
- Hot summer and cold winter
- Hot summer and cool winter
- Hot summer and mild winter
- Always hot
- Always mild

JANUARY NORMAL TEMPERATURE

Copyright by Rand McNally & Co.
Made in U.S.A.
A-510000-663-2-2-3-5

MILLER CYLINDRICAL PROJECTION
Courtesy of the American Geographical Society.

Reduced to Sea Level

- Below −46°C. (−50°F.)
- −34° to −46° (−30° to −50°)
- −23° to −34° (−10° to −30°)
- −23° to −12° (−10° to +10°)
- −12° to −1° (10° to 30°)
- −1° to 10° (30° to 50°)
- 10° to 21° (50° to 70°)
- 21° to 32° (70° to 90°)
- Over 32° (90°)
- Highlands above 1000 meters

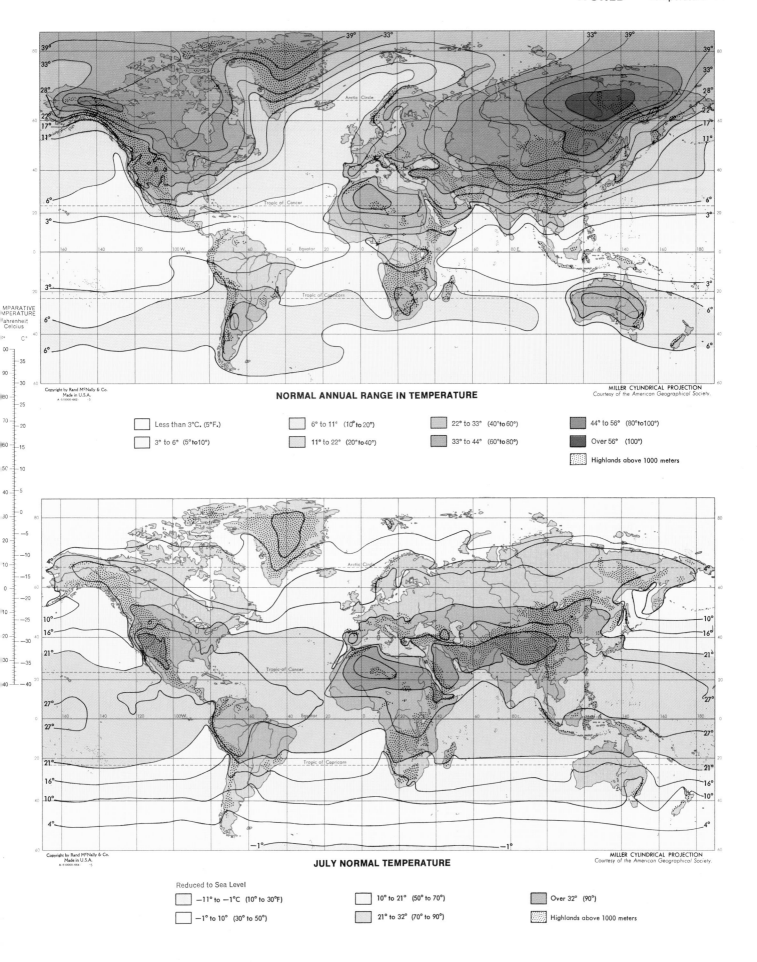

NORMAL ANNUAL RANGE IN TEMPERATURE

MILLER CYLINDRICAL PROJECTION
Courtesy of the American Geographical Society.

Copyright by Rand McNally & Co.
Made in U.S.A.

☐ Less than 3°C. (5°F.)

☐ 3° to 6° (5°to10°)

☐ 6° to 11° (10°to 20°)

☐ 11° to 22° (20°to40°)

☐ 22° to 33° (40°to60°)

☐ 33° to 44° (60°to80°)

☐ 44° to 56° (80°to100°)

☐ Over 56° (100°)

☐ Highlands above 1000 meters

JULY NORMAL TEMPERATURE

MILLER CYLINDRICAL PROJECTION
Courtesy of the American Geographical Society.

Copyright by Rand McNally & Co.
Made in U.S.A.

Reduced to Sea Level

☐ −11° to −1°C (10° to 30°F)

☐ −1° to 10° (30° to 50°)

☐ 10° to 21° (50° to 70°)

☐ 21° to 32° (70° to 90°)

☐ Over 32° (90°)

☐ Highlands above 1000 meters

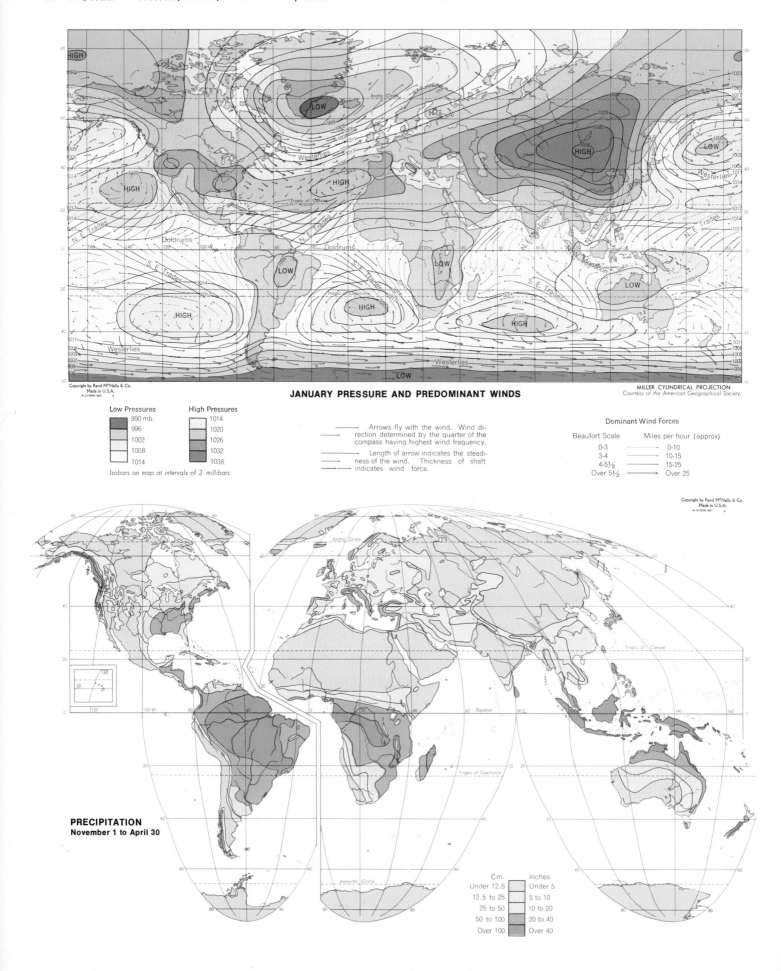

JANUARY PRESSURE AND PREDOMINANT WINDS

MILLER CYLINDRICAL PROJECTION
Courtesy of the American Geographical Society.

Copyright by Rand McNally & Co.
Made in U.S.A.
A-510000-865 4

Low Pressures
990 mb.
996
1002
1008
1014

High Pressures
1014
1020
1026
1032
1038

Isobars on map at intervals of 3 millibars

Arrows fly with the wind. Wind direction determined by the quarter of the compass having highest wind frequency.

Length of arrow indicates the steadiness of the wind. Thickness of shaft indicates wind force.

Dominant Wind Forces

Beaufort Scale	Miles per hour (approx)
0-3	0-10
3-4	10-15
4-5½	15-25
Over 5½	Over 25

Copyright by Rand McNally & Co.
Made in U.S.A.
A-510000-667 4

PRECIPITATION
November 1 to April 30

Cm.	Inches
Under 12.5	Under 5
12.5 to 25	5 to 10
25 to 50	10 to 20
50 to 100	20 to 40
Over 100	Over 40

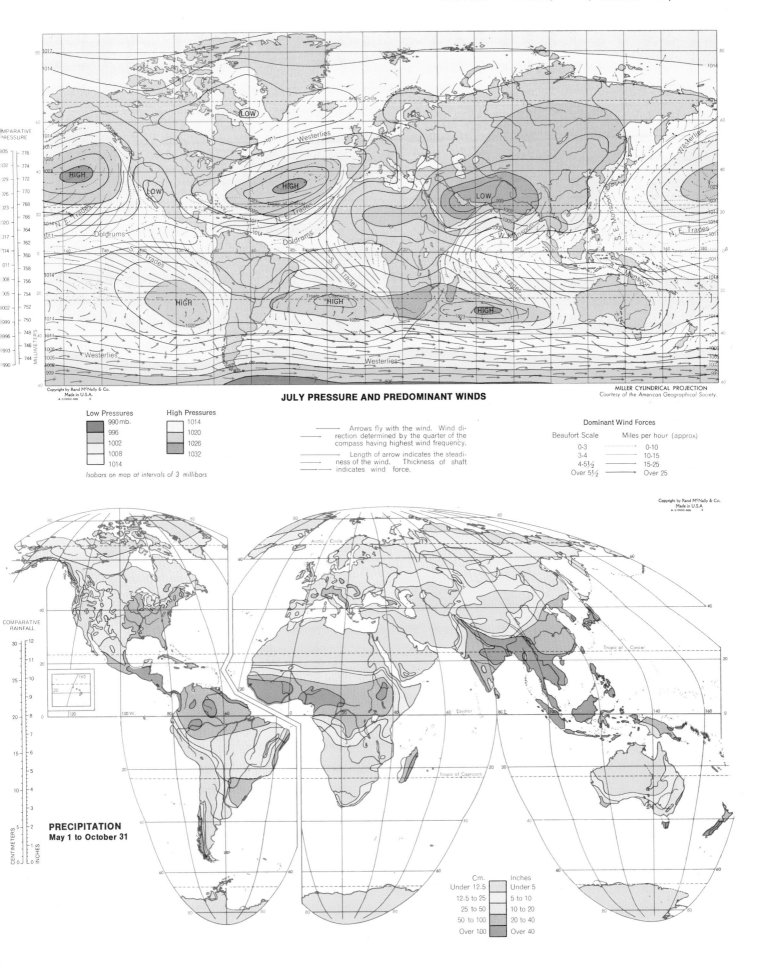

JULY PRESSURE AND PREDOMINANT WINDS

MILLER CYLINDRICAL PROJECTION
Courtesy of the American Geographical Society.

Copyright by Rand M°Nally & Co.
Made in U.S.A.
A-510000-888   4

Low Pressures
990 mb.
996
1002
1008
1014

High Pressures
1014
1020
1026
1032

Isobars on map at intervals of 3 millibars

→ Arrows fly with the wind. Wind direction determined by the quarter of the compass having highest wind frequency.

→ Length of arrow indicates the steadiness of the wind. Thickness of shaft indicates wind force.

Dominant Wind Forces

Beaufort Scale	Miles per hour (approx)
0-3	0-10
3-4	10-15
4-5½	15-25
Over 5½	Over 25

Copyright by Rand M°Nally & Co.
Made in U.S.A.
A-510000-888   4

PRECIPITATION
May 1 to October 31

Cm.	Inches
Under 12.5	Under 5
12.5 to 25	5 to 10
25 to 50	10 to 20
50 to 100	20 to 40
Over 100	Over 40

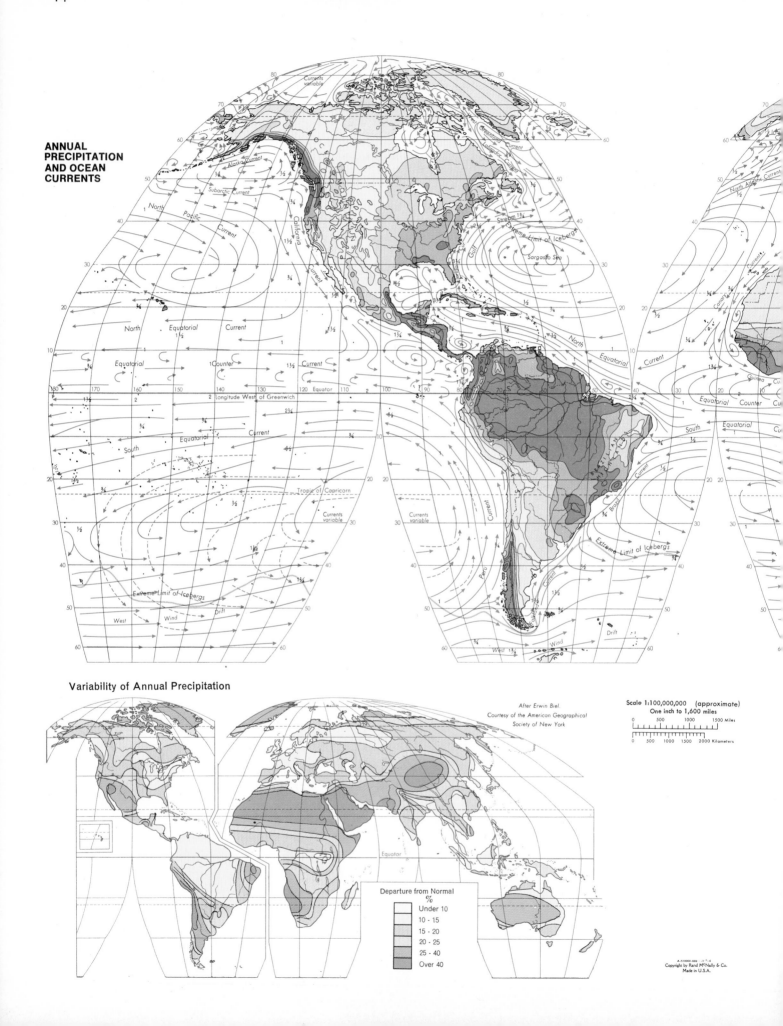

14

ANNUAL
PRECIPITATION
AND OCEAN
CURRENTS

Variability of Annual Precipitation

After Erwin Biel.
Courtesy of the American Geographical
Society of New York

Scale 1:100,000,000 (approximate)
One inch to 1,600 miles

Departure from Normal
%
Under 10
10 - 15
15 - 20
20 - 25
25 - 40
Over 40

Copyright by Rand McNally & Co.
Made in U.S.A.

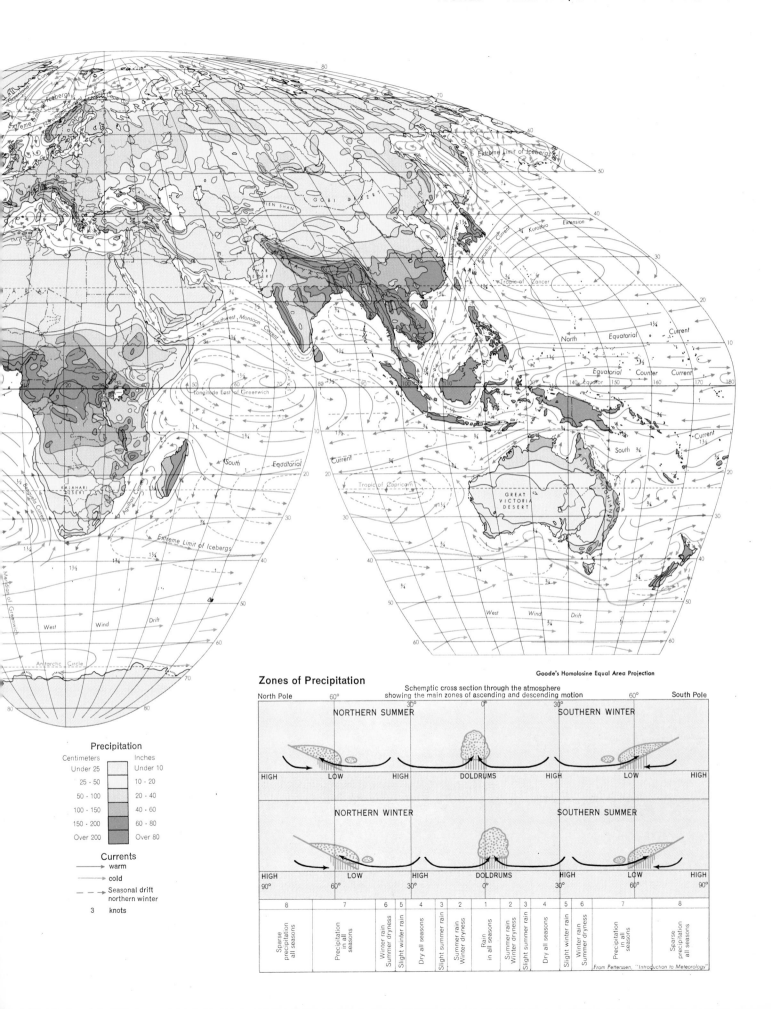

Goode's Homolosine Equal Area Projection

Precipitation

Centimeters		Inches
Under 25		Under 10
25 - 50		10 - 20
50 - 100		20 - 40
100 - 150		40 - 60
150 - 200		60 - 80
Over 200		Over 80

Currents

→ warm
- - - cold
– – – Seasonal drift northern winter

3   knots

Zones of Precipitation

Schematic cross section through the atmosphere
showing the main zones of ascending and descending motion

North Pole   60°   30°   0°   30°   60°   South Pole

NORTHERN SUMMER   SOUTHERN WINTER

| HIGH | LOW | HIGH | DOLDRUMS | HIGH | LOW | HIGH |

NORTHERN WINTER   SOUTHERN SUMMER

| HIGH | LOW | HIGH | DOLDRUMS | HIGH | LOW | HIGH |
| 90° | 60° | 30° | 0° | 30° | 60° | 90° |

8	7	6	5	4	3	2	1	2	3	4	5	6	7	8
Sparse precipitation all seasons	Precipitation in all seasons	Winter rain Summer dryness	Slight winter rain	Dry all seasons	Slight summer rain	Summer rain Winter dryness	Rain in all seasons	Summer rain Winter dryness	Slight summer rain	Dry all seasons	Slight winter rain	Winter rain Summer dryness	Precipitation in all seasons	Sparse precipitation all seasons

From Petterssen, "Introduction to Meteorology"

16

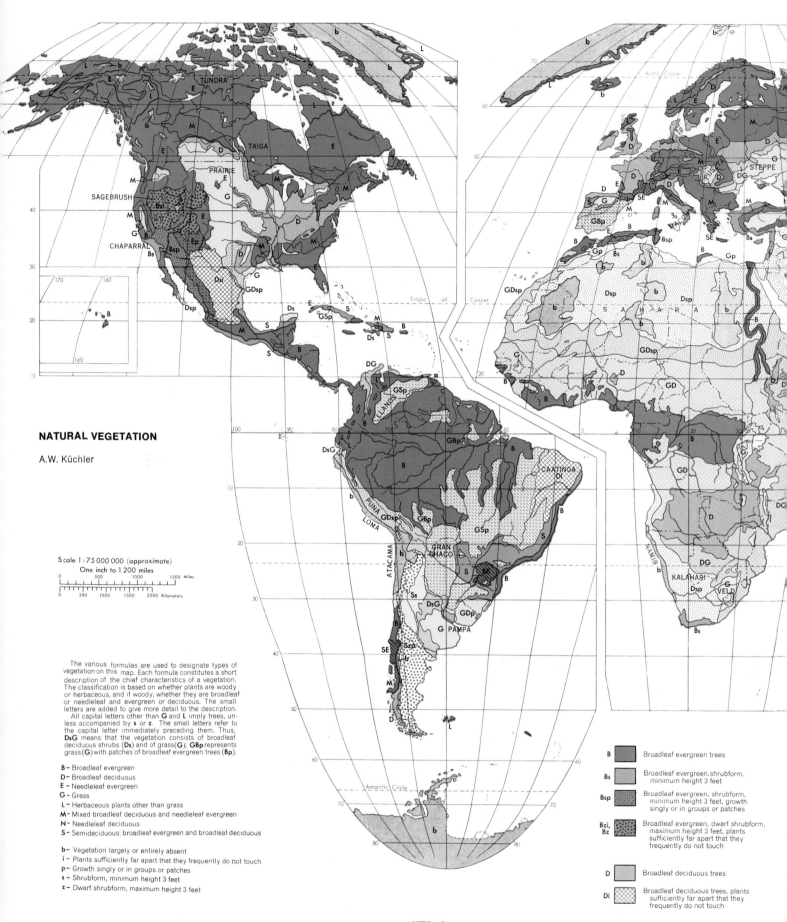

NATURAL VEGETATION

A.W. Küchler

Scale 1:75 000 000 (approximate)
One inch to 1 200 miles

0   500   1000   1500 Miles

0   500   1000   1500   2000 Kilometers

The various formulas are used to designate types of
vegetation on this map. Each formula constitutes a short
description of the chief characteristics of a vegetation.
The classification is based on whether plants are woody
or herbaceous, and if woody, whether they are broadleaf
or needleleaf and evergreen or deciduous. The small
letters are added to give more detail to the description.
All capital letters other than **G** and **L** imply trees, unless accompanied by **s** or **z**. The small letters refer to
the capital letter immediately preceding them. Thus,
DsG means that the vegetation consists of broadleaf
deciduous shrubs (**Ds**) and of grass (**G**); **GBp** represents
grass (**G**) with patches of broadleaf evergreen trees (**Bp**).

B – Broadleaf evergreen
D – Broadleaf deciduous
E – Needleleaf evergreen
G – Grass
L – Herbaceous plants other than grass
M – Mixed broadleaf deciduous and needleleaf evergreen
N – Needleleaf deciduous
S – Semideciduous: broadleaf evergreen and broadleaf deciduous

b – Vegetation largely or entirely absent
i – Plants sufficiently far apart that they frequently do not touch
p – Growth singly or in groups or patches
s – Shrubform, minimum height 3 feet
z – Dwarf shrubform, maximum height 3 feet

B	Broadleaf evergreen trees
Bs	Broadleaf evergreen, shrubform, minimum height 3 feet
Bsp	Broadleaf evergreen, shrubform, minimum height 3 feet, growth singly or in groups or patches
Bzi, Bz	Broadleaf evergreen, dwarf shrubform, maximum height 3 feet, plants sufficiently far apart that they frequently do not touch
D	Broadleaf deciduous trees
Di	Broadleaf deciduous trees, plants sufficiently far apart that they frequently do not touch

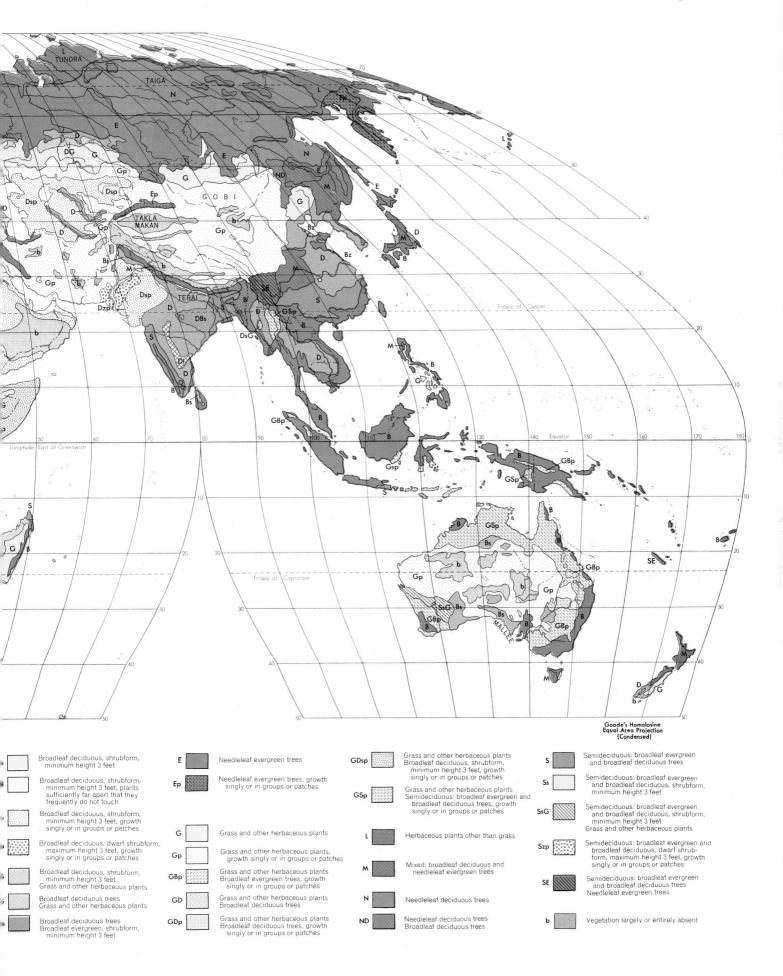

Goode's Homolosine
Equal Area Projection
(Condensed)

		Broadleaf deciduous, shrubform, minimum height 3 feet
		Broadleaf deciduous, shrubform, minimum height 3 feet, plants sufficiently far apart that they frequently do not touch
		Broadleaf deciduous, shrubform, minimum height 3 feet, growth singly or in groups or patches
		Broadleaf deciduous, dwarf shrubform, maximum height 3 feet, growth singly or in groups or patches
		Broadleaf deciduous, shrubform, minimum height 3 feet Grass and other herbaceous plants
		Broadleaf deciduous trees Grass and other herbaceous plants
		Broadleaf deciduous trees Broadleaf evergreen, shrubform, minimum height 3 feet

E		Needleleaf evergreen trees
Ep		Needleleaf evergreen trees, growth singly or in groups or patches
G		Grass and other herbaceous plants
Gp		Grass and other herbaceous plants, growth singly or in groups or patches
GBp		Grass and other herbaceous plants Broadleaf evergreen trees, growth singly or in groups or patches
GD		Grass and other herbaceous plants Broadleaf deciduous trees
GDp		Grass and other herbaceous plants Broadleaf deciduous trees, growth singly or in groups or patches

GDsp		Grass and other herbaceous plants Broadleaf deciduous, shrubform, minimum height 3 feet, growth singly or in groups or patches
GSp		Grass and other herbaceous plants Semideciduous: broadleaf evergreen and broadleaf deciduous trees, growth singly or in groups or patches
L		Herbaceous plants other than grass
M		Mixed: broadleaf deciduous and needleleaf evergreen trees
N		Needleleaf deciduous trees
ND		Needleleaf deciduous trees Broadleaf deciduous trees

S		Semideciduous: broadleaf evergreen and broadleaf deciduous trees
Ss		Semideciduous: broadleaf evergreen and broadleaf deciduous, shrubform, minimum height 3 feet
SsG		Semideciduous: broadleaf evergreen and broadleaf deciduous, shrubform, minimum height 3 feet Grass and other herbaceous plants
Szp		Semideciduous: broadleaf evergreen and broadleaf deciduous, dwarf shrubform, maximum height 3 feet, growth singly or in groups or patches
SE		Semideciduous: broadleaf evergreen and broadleaf deciduous trees Needleleaf evergreen trees
b		Vegetation largely or entirely absent

18

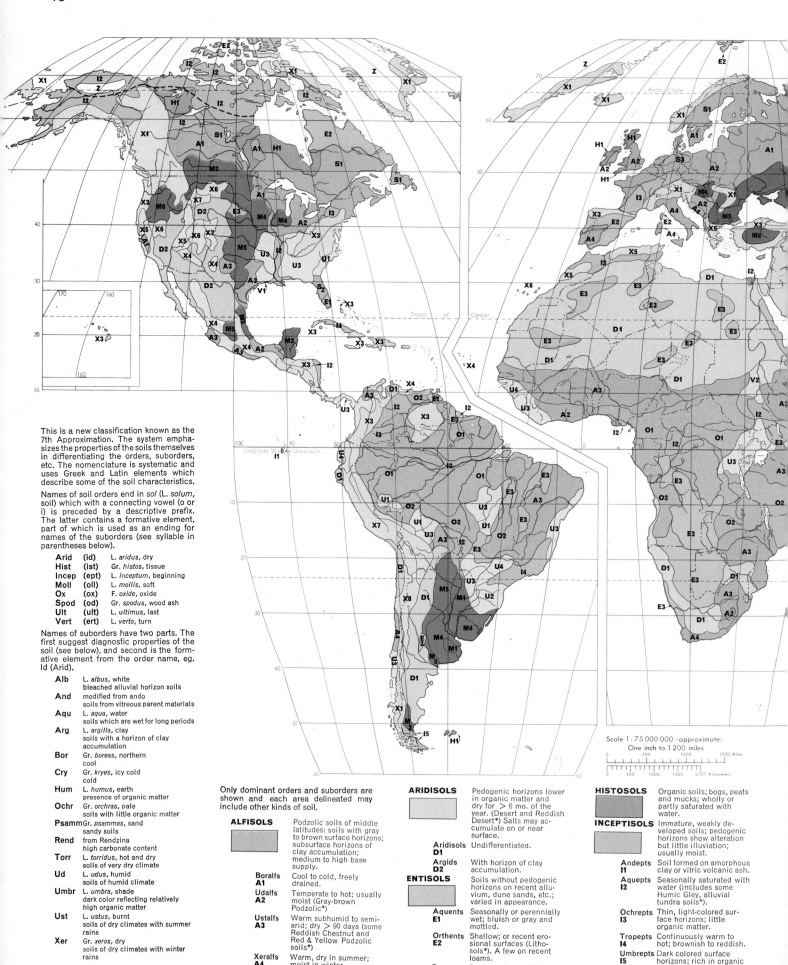

This is a new classification known as the 7th Approximation. The system emphasizes the properties of the soils themselves in differentiating the orders, suborders, etc. The nomenclature is systematic and uses Greek and Latin elements which describe some of the soil characteristics.

Names of soil orders end in *sol* (L. *solum*, soil) which with a connecting vowel (o or i) is preceded by a descriptive prefix. The latter contains a formative element, part of which is used as an ending for names of the suborders (see syllable in parentheses below).

Arid	(id)	L. *aridus*, dry
Hist	(ist)	Gr. *histos*, tissue
Incep	(ept)	L. *inceptum*, beginning
Moll	(oll)	L. *mollis*, soft
Ox	(ox)	F. *oxide*, oxide
Spod	(od)	Gr. *spodus*, wood ash
Ult	(ult)	L. *ultimus*, last
Vert	(ert)	L. *verto*, turn

Names of suborders have two parts. The first suggest diagnostic properties of the soil (see below), and second is the formative element from the order name, eg. Id (Arid).

Alb	L. *albus*, white	bleached alluvial horizon soils
And	modified from ando	soils from vitreous parent materials
Aqu	L. *aqua*, water	soils which are wet for long periods
Arg	L. *argilla*, clay	soils with a horizon of clay accumulation
Bor	Gr. *boreas*, northern	cool
Cry	Gr. *kryes*, icy cold	cold
Hum	L. *humus*, earth	presence of organic matter
Ochr	Gr. *orchras*, pale	soils with little organic matter
Psamm	Gr. *psammas*, sand	sandy soils
Rend	from Rendzina	high carbonate content
Torr	L. *torridus*, hot and dry	soils of very dry climate
Ud	L. *udus*, humid	soils of humid climate
Umbr	L. *umbra*, shade	dark color reflecting relatively high organic matter
Ust	L. *ustus*, burnt	soils of dry climates with summer rains
Xer	Gr. *xeros*, dry	soils of dry climates with winter rains

Only dominant orders and suborders are shown and each area delineated may include other kinds of soil.

ALFISOLS — Podzolic soils of middle latitudes: soils with gray to brown surface horizons; subsurface horizons of clay accumulation; medium to high base supply.

Boralfs **A1** — Cool to cold; freely drained.

Udalfs **A2** — Temperate to hot; usually moist (Gray-brown Podzolic*).

Ustalfs **A3** — Warm subhumid to semi-arid; dry > 90 days (some Reddish Chestnut and Red & Yellow Podzolic soils*)

Xeralfs **A4** — Warm, dry in summer; moist in winter.

ARIDISOLS — Pedogenic horizons lower in organic matter and dry for > 6 mo. of the year. (Desert and Reddish Desert*) Salts may accumulate on or near surface.

Aridisols **D1** — Undifferentiated.

Argids **D2** — With horizon of clay accumulation.

ENTISOLS — Soils without pedogenic horizons on recent alluvium, dune sands, etc.; varied in appearance.

Aquents **E1** — Seasonally or perennially wet; bluish or gray and mottled.

Orthents **E2** — Shallow; or recent erosional surfaces (Lithosols*). A few on recent loams.

Psamments **E3** — Sandy soils on shifting and stabilized sands.

HISTOSOLS — Organic soils; bogs, peats and mucks; wholly or partly saturated with water.

INCEPTISOLS — Immature, weakly developed soils; pedogenic horizons show alteration but little illuviation; usually moist.

Andepts **I1** — Soil formed on amorphous clay or vitric volcanic ash.

Aquepts **I2** — Seasonally saturated with water (includes some Humic Gley, alluvial tundra soils*).

Ochrepts **I3** — Thin, light-colored surface horizons; little organic matter.

Tropepts **I4** — Continuously warm to hot; brownish to reddish.

Umbrepts **I5** — Dark colored surface horizons; rich in organic matter; medium to low base supply.

Scale 1 : 75 000 000 (approximate)
One inch to 1 200 miles

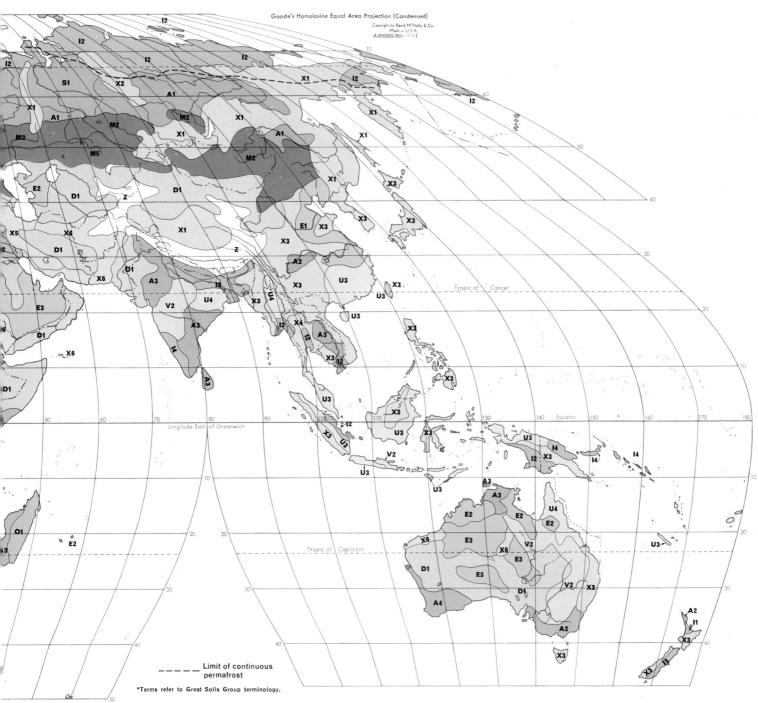

Goode's Homolosine Equal Area Projection (Condensed)

Copyright by Rand M°Nally & Co.
Made in U.S.A.
A-510000-761- -1-1-1

_ _ _ _ _ Limit of continuous
permafrost

*Terms refer to Great Soils Group terminology.

MOLLISOLS

Soils of the steppe (incl. Chernozem and Chestnut soils*). Thick, black organic rich surface horizons and high base supply.

Albolls M1	Seasonally saturated with water; light gray sub-surface horizon.
Borolls M2	Cool or cold (incl. some Chernozem, Chestnut and Brown soils*).
Rendolls M3	Formed on highly calcareous parent materials (Rendzina*).
Udolls M4	Temperate to warm; usually moist (Prairie scils*).
Ustolls M5	Temperate to hot; dry for > 90 days (incl. some Chestnut and Brown soils*).
Xerolls M6	Cool to warm; dry in summer; moist in winter.

OXISOLS

Deeply weathered tropical and subtropical soils (Laterites*); rich in sesquioxides of iron and aluminum; low in nutrients; limited productivity without fertilizer.

Orthox O1	Hot and nearly always moist.
Ustox O2	Warm or hot; dry for long periods but moist > 90 consecutive days.

SPODOSOLS

Soils with a subsurface accumulation of amorphous materials overlaid by a light colored, leached sandy horizon.

Spodo-sols S1	Undifferentiated (mostly high latitudes).
Aquods S2	Seasonally saturated with water; sandy parent materials.
Humods S3	Considerable accumulations of organic matter in subsurface horizon.
Orthods S4	With subsurface accumulations of iron, aluminum and organic matter (Podzols*).

ULTISOLS

Soils with some subsurface clay accumulation; low base supply; usually moist and low inorganic matter; usually moist and low in organic matter; can be productive with fertilization.

Aquults U1	Seasonally saturated with water; subsurface gray or mottled horizon.
Humults U2	High in organic matter; dark colored; moist, warm to temperate all year.
Udults U3	Low in organic matter; moist, temperate to hot (Red-Yellow Podzolic; some Reddish-Brown Lateritic soils*).
Ustults U4	Warm to hot; dry > 90 days.

VERTISOLS

Soils with high content of swelling clays; deep, wide cracks in dry periods dark colored.

Uderts V1	Usually moist; cracks open < 90 days.
Usterts V2	Cracks open > 90 days; difficult to till (Black tropical soils*).

MOUNTAIN SOILS

Soils with various moisture and temperature regimes; steep slopes and variable relief and elevation; soils vary greatly within short distance.

X1 Cryic great groups of Entisols, Inceptisols and Spodosols.

X2 Boralfs and Cryic groups of Entisols and Inceptisols.

X3 Udic great groups of Alfisols, Entisols and Ultisols; Inceptisols.

X4 Ustic great groups of Alfisols, Entisols, Inceptisols, Mollisols and Ultisols.

X5 Xeric great groups of Alfisols, Entisols, Inceptisols, Mollisols and Ultisols.

X6 Torric great groups of Entisols; Aridisols.

X7 Ustic and cryic great groups of Alfisols, Entisols; Inceptisols and Mollisols; ustic great groups of Ultisols; cryic great groups of Spodosols.

X8 Aridisols; torric and cryic great groups of Entisols, and cryic great groups of Spodosols and Inceptisols.

z Areas with little or no soil; icefields, and rugged mountain.

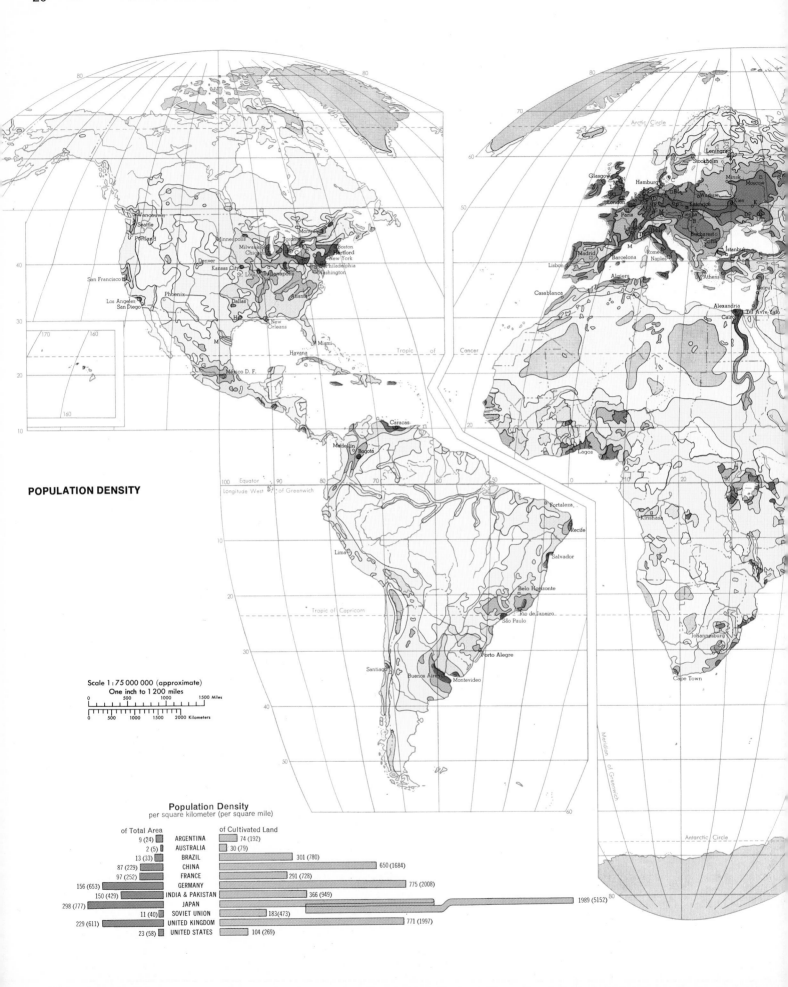

20

POPULATION DENSITY

Scale 1 : 75 000 000 (approximate)
One inch to 1 200 miles

0   500   1000   1500 Miles

0   500   1000   1500   2000 Kilometers

Population Density
per square kilometer (per square mile)

	of Total Area	of Cultivated Land
ARGENTINA	9 (24)	74 (192)
AUSTRALIA	2 (5)	30 (79)
BRAZIL	13 (33)	301 (780)
CHINA	87 (229)	650 (1684)
FRANCE	97 (252)	291 (728)
GERMANY	252 (653)	775 (2008)
INDIA & PAKISTAN	150 (429)	366 (949)
JAPAN	298 (777)	1989 (5152)
SOVIET UNION	11 (40)	183 (473)
UNITED KINGDOM	229 (611)	771 (1997)
UNITED STATES	23 (58)	104 (269)

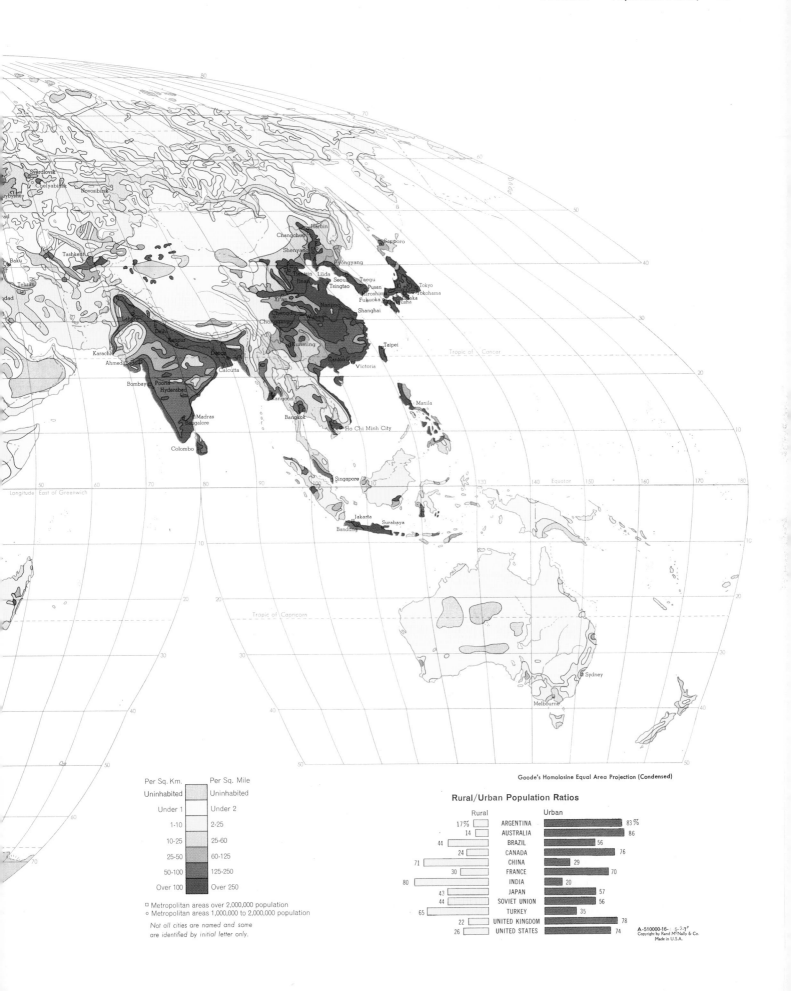

Per Sq. Km.	Per Sq. Mile
Uninhabited	Uninhabited
Under 1	Under 2
1-10	2-25
10-25	25-60
25-50	60-125
50-100	125-250
Over 100	Over 250

□ Metropolitan areas over 2,000,000 population
○ Metropolitan areas 1,000,000 to 2,000,000 population

*Not all cities are named and some
are identified by initial letter only.*

Goode's Homolosine Equal Area Projection (Condensed)

Rural/Urban Population Ratios

Rural		Urban	
17%	ARGENTINA		83%
14	AUSTRALIA		86
44	BRAZIL		56
24	CANADA		76
71	CHINA		29
30	FRANCE		70
80	INDIA		20
43	JAPAN		57
44	SOVIET UNION		56
65	TURKEY		35
22	UNITED KINGDOM		78
26	UNITED STATES		74

A-510000-16- 5-2-7ᴾ
Copyright by Rand McNally & Co.
Made in U.S.A.

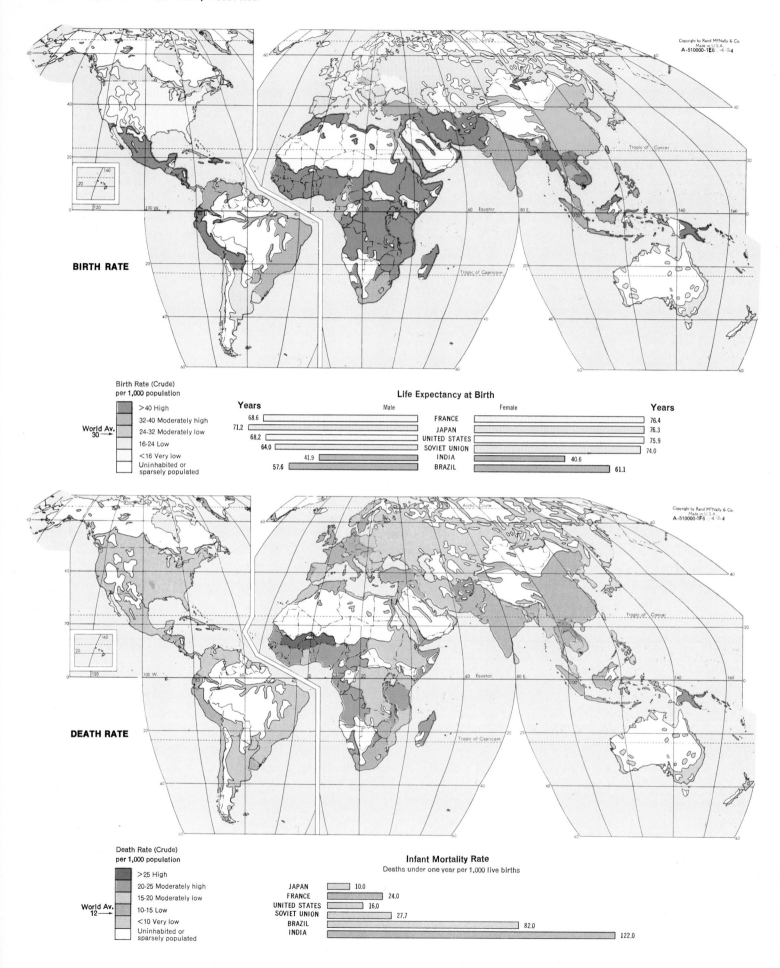

BIRTH RATE

Birth Rate (Crude)
per 1,000 population

- >40 High
- 32-40 Moderately high
- 24-32 Moderately low
- 16-24 Low
- <16 Very low
- Uninhabited or sparsely populated

World Av. 30 →

Life Expectancy at Birth

Years	Male		Female	Years
68.6		FRANCE		76.4
71.2		JAPAN		76.3
68.2		UNITED STATES		75.9
64.0		SOVIET UNION		74.0
41.9		INDIA		40.6
57.6		BRAZIL		61.1

DEATH RATE

Death Rate (Crude)
per 1,000 population

- >25 High
- 20-25 Moderately high
- 15-20 Moderately low
- 10-15 Low
- <10 Very low
- Uninhabited or sparsely populated

World Av. 12 →

Infant Mortality Rate

Deaths under one year per 1,000 live births

JAPAN	10.0
FRANCE	24.0
UNITED STATES	16.0
SOVIET UNION	27.7
BRAZIL	82.0
INDIA	122.0

Copyright by Rand M°Nally & Co.
Made in U.S.A.
A-510000-1E6

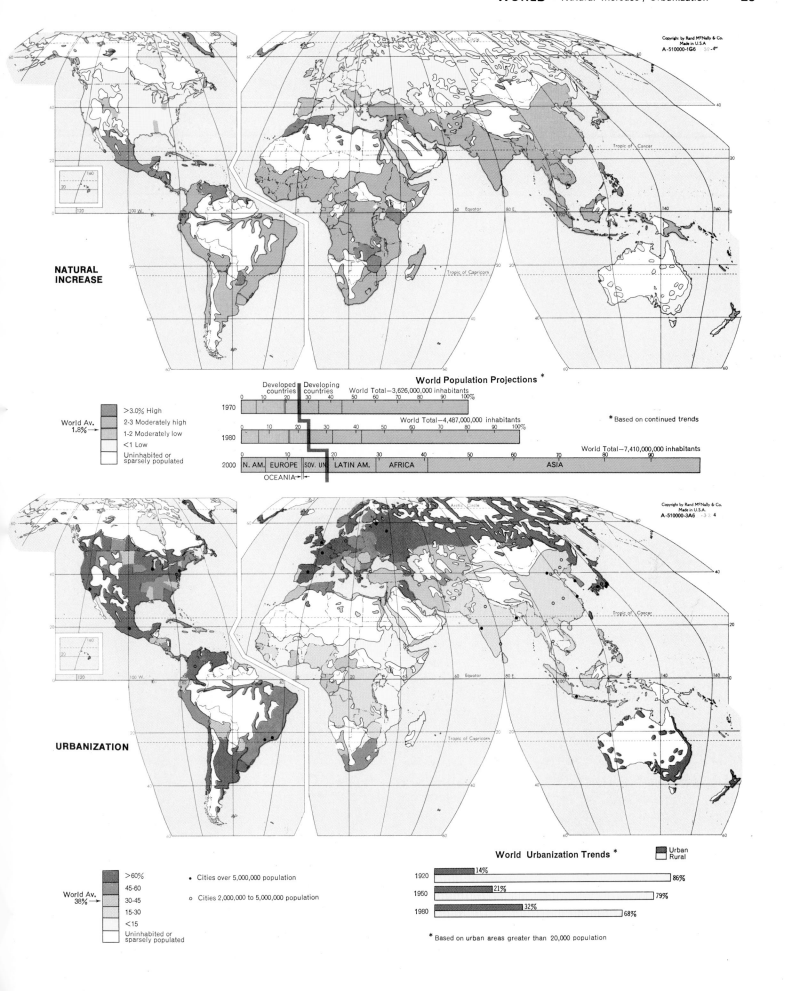

NATURAL INCREASE

World Av.
1.8%

- \>3.0% High
- 2-3 Moderately high
- 1-2 Moderately low
- <1 Low
- Uninhabited or sparsely populated

World Population Projections *

Developed countries   Developing countries

1970   World Total—3,626,000,000 inhabitants
0   10   20   30   40   50   60   70   80   90   100%

1980   World Total—4,487,000,000 inhabitants
0   10   20   30   40   50   60   70   80   90   100%

2000   World Total—7,410,000,000 inhabitants
0   10   20   30   40   50   60   70   80   90
N. AM.   EUROPE   SOV. UN.   LATIN AM.   AFRICA   ASIA
OCEANIA

* Based on continued trends

URBANIZATION

World Av.
38%

- \>60%
- 45-60
- 30-45
- 15-30
- <15
- Uninhabited or sparsely populated

- • Cities over 5,000,000 population
- ○ Cities 2,000,000 to 5,000,000 population

World Urbanization Trends *

■ Urban
□ Rural

1920   14%   86%
1950   21%   79%
1980   32%   68%

* Based on urban areas greater than 20,000 population

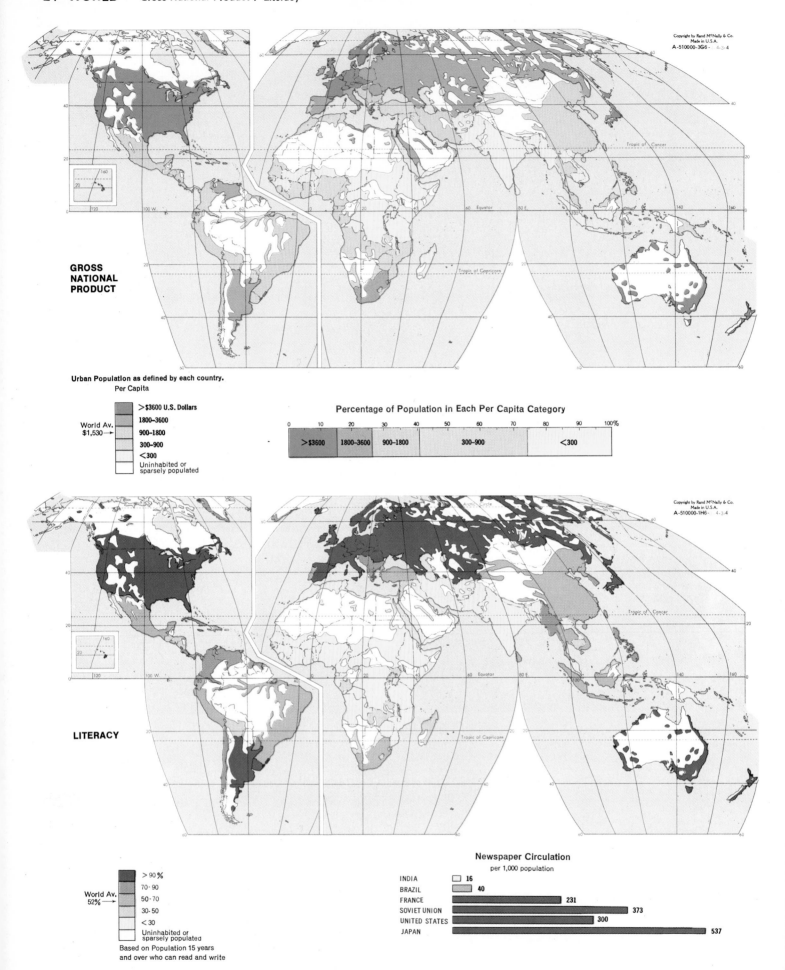

GROSS NATIONAL PRODUCT

Urban Population as defined by each country.

Per Capita

World Av. $1,530 →

> $3600 U.S. Dollars
1800–3600
900–1800
300–900
< 300
Uninhabited or sparsely populated

Percentage of Population in Each Per Capita Category

0 10 20 30 40 50 60 70 80 90 100%

| > $3600 | 1800–3600 | 900–1800 | 300–900 | < 300 |

LITERACY

World Av. 52% →

> 90 %
70 - 90
50 - 70
30 - 50
< 30
Uninhabited or sparsely populated

Based on Population 15 years and over who can read and write

Newspaper Circulation
per 1,000 population

INDIA	16
BRAZIL	40
FRANCE	231
SOVIET UNION	373
UNITED STATES	300
JAPAN	537

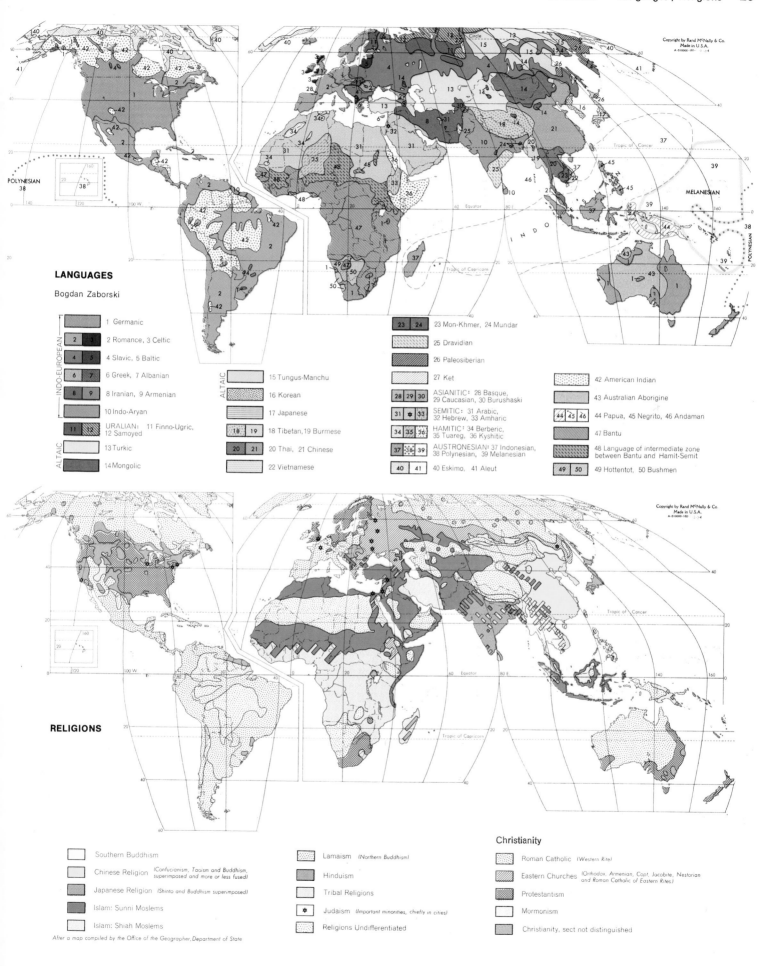

LANGUAGES

Bogdan Zaborski

INDO-EUROPEAN
- 1 Germanic
- 2 Romance, 3 Celtic
- 4 Slavic, 5 Baltic
- 6 Greek, 7 Albanian
- 8 Iranian, 9 Armenian
- 10 Indo-Aryan

URALIAN: 11 Finno-Ugric, 12 Samoyed

ALTAIC
- 13 Turkic
- 14 Mongolic
- 15 Tungus-Manchu
- 16 Korean
- 17 Japanese
- 18 Tibetan, 19 Burmese
- 20 Thai, 21 Chinese
- 22 Vietnamese

- 23 Mon-Khmer, 24 Mundar
- 25 Dravidian
- 26 Paleosiberian
- 27 Ket
- **ASIANITIC:** 28 Basque, 29 Caucasian, 30 Burushaski
- **SEMITIC:** 31 Arabic, 32 Hebrew, 33 Amharic
- **HAMITIC:** 34 Berberic, 35 Tuareg, 36 Kyshitic
- **AUSTRONESIAN:** 37 Indonesian, 38 Polynesian, 39 Melanesian
- 40 Eskimo, 41 Aleut
- 42 American Indian
- 43 Australian Aborigine
- 44 Papua, 45 Negrito, 46 Andaman
- 47 Bantu
- 48 Language of intermediate zone between Bantu and Hamit-Semit
- 49 Hottentot, 50 Bushmen

POLYNESIAN 38

MELANESIAN

RELIGIONS

- Southern Buddhism
- Chinese Religion (Confucianism, Taoism and Buddhism, superimposed and more or less fused)
- Japanese Religion (Shinto and Buddhism superimposed)
- Islam: Sunni Moslems
- Islam: Shiah Moslems
- Lamaism (Northern Buddhism)
- Hinduism
- Tribal Religions
- ✡ Judaism (Important minorities, chiefly in cities)
- Religions Undifferentiated

Christianity
- Roman Catholic (Western Rite)
- Eastern Churches (Orthodox, Armenian, Copt, Jacobite, Nestorian and Roman Catholic of Eastern Rites.)
- Protestantism
- Mormonism
- Christianity, sect not distinguished

After a map compiled by the Office of the Geographer, Department of State

Copyright by Rand McNally & Co.
Made in U.S.A.

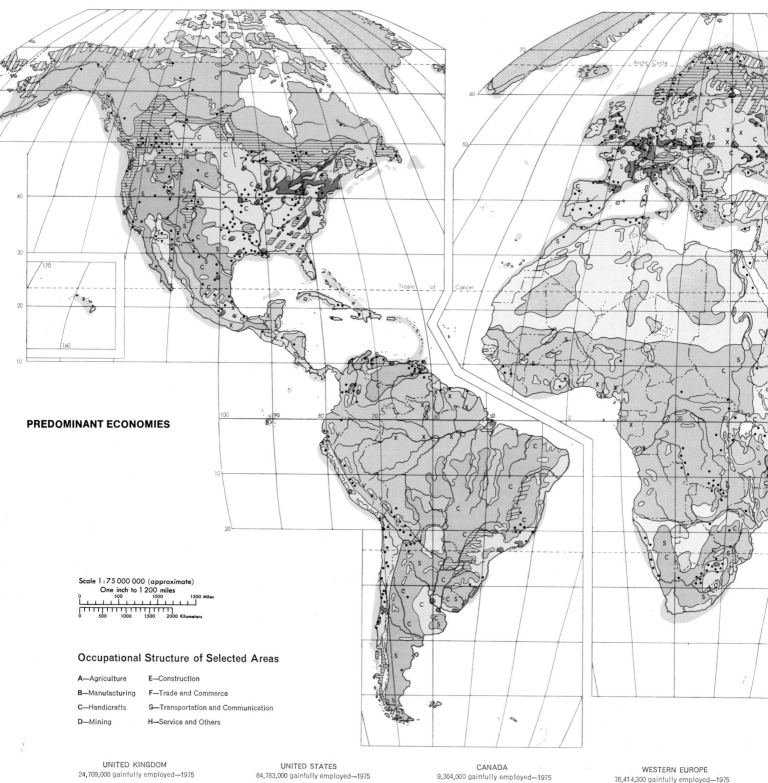

PREDOMINANT ECONOMIES

Scale 1 : 75 000 000 (approximate)
One inch to 1 200 miles

0   500   1000   1500 Miles

0   500   1000   1500   2000 Kilometers

Occupational Structure of Selected Areas

A—Agriculture   E—Construction

B—Manufacturing   F—Trade and Commerce

C—Handicrafts   G—Transportation and Communication

D—Mining   H—Service and Others

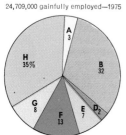

UNITED KINGDOM
24,709,000 gainfully employed—1975

A 3, B 32, D 2, E 7, F 13, G 8, H 35%

UNITED STATES
84,783,000 gainfully employed—1975

A 4, B 23, D 1, E 4, F 38%, G 6, H 24

CANADA
9,364,000 gainfully employed—1975

A 6, B 20, D 2, E 6, F 23, G 8, H 35%

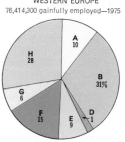

WESTERN EUROPE
76,414,300 gainfully employed—1975

A 10, B 31%, D 1, E 9, F 15, G 6, H 28

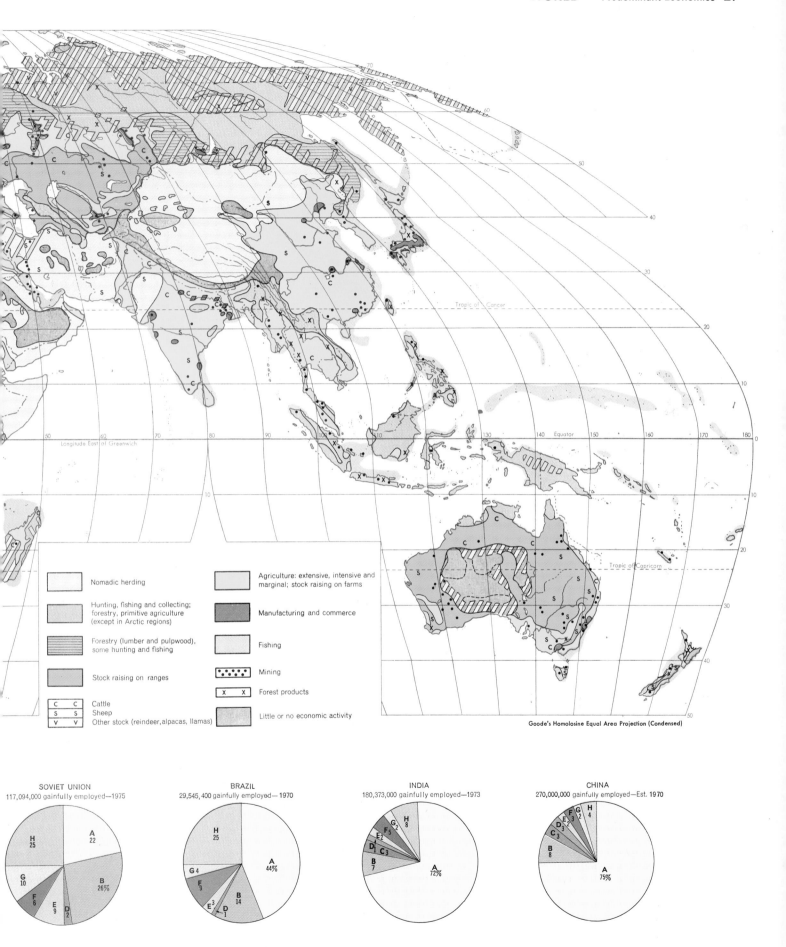

Nomadic herding

Hunting, fishing and collecting; forestry, primitive agriculture (except in Arctic regions)

Forestry (lumber and pulpwood), some hunting and fishing

Stock raising on ranges

C	C	Cattle
S	S	Sheep
V	V	Other stock (reindeer, alpacas, llamas)

Agriculture: extensive, intensive and marginal; stock raising on farms

Manufacturing and commerce

Fishing

| • • • • • | Mining |

| X   X | Forest products |

Little or no economic activity

Tropic of Cancer

Equator

Tropic of Capricorn

Longitude East of Greenwich

Goode's Homolosine Equal Area Projection (Condensed)

SOVIET UNION
117,094,000 gainfully employed—1975

A 22
B 26%
D 2
E 9
F 6
G 10
H 25

BRAZIL
29,545,400 gainfully employed—1970

A 44%
B 14
D 1
E 3
F 9
G 4
H 25

INDIA
180,373,000 gainfully employed—1973

A 72%
B 7
C 3
D
E 2
F 5
G 2
H 8

CHINA
270,000,000 gainfully employed—Est. 1970

A 75%
B 8
C 3
D 3
E 2
F
G 2
H 4

28

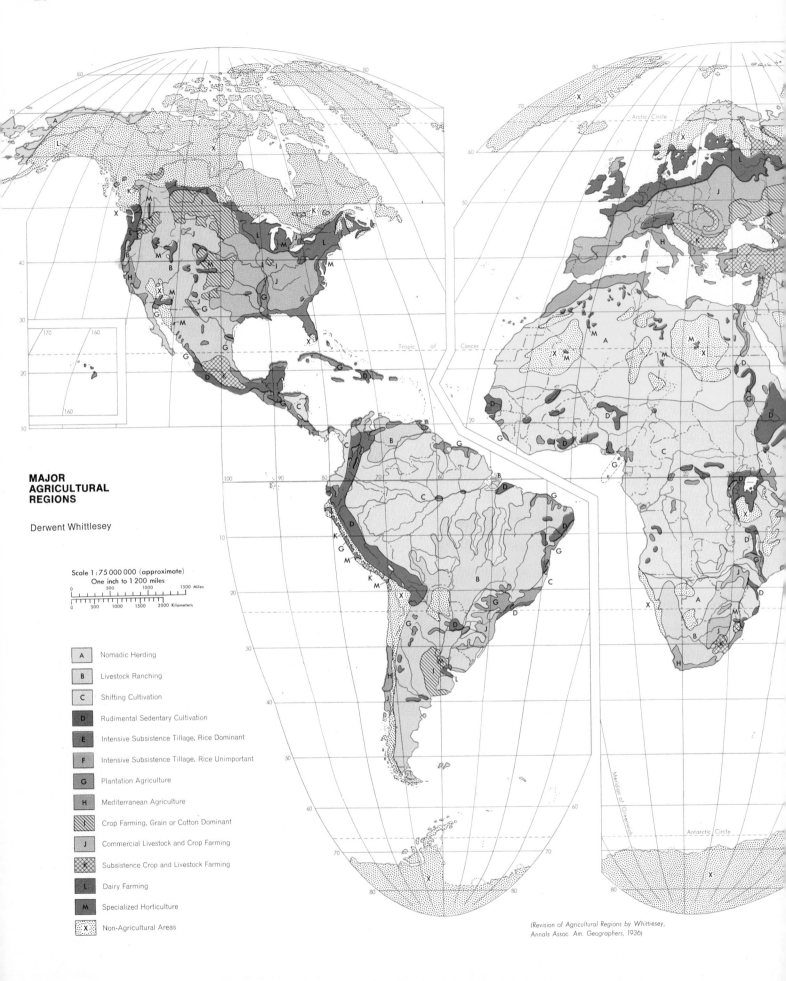

**MAJOR
AGRICULTURAL
REGIONS**

Derwent Whittlesey

Scale 1 : 75 000 000 (approximate)
One inch to 1 200 miles

A	Nomadic Herding
B	Livestock Ranching
C	Shifting Cultivation
D	Rudimental Sedentary Cultivation
E	Intensive Subsistence Tillage, Rice Dominant
F	Intensive Subsistence Tillage, Rice Unimportant
G	Plantation Agriculture
H	Mediterranean Agriculture
I	Crop Farming, Grain or Cotton Dominant
J	Commercial Livestock and Crop Farming
K	Subsistence Crop and Livestock Farming
L	Dairy Farming
M	Specialized Horticulture
X	Non-Agricultural Areas

(Revision of Agricultural Regions by Whittlesey,
Annals Assoc. Am. Geographers, 1936)

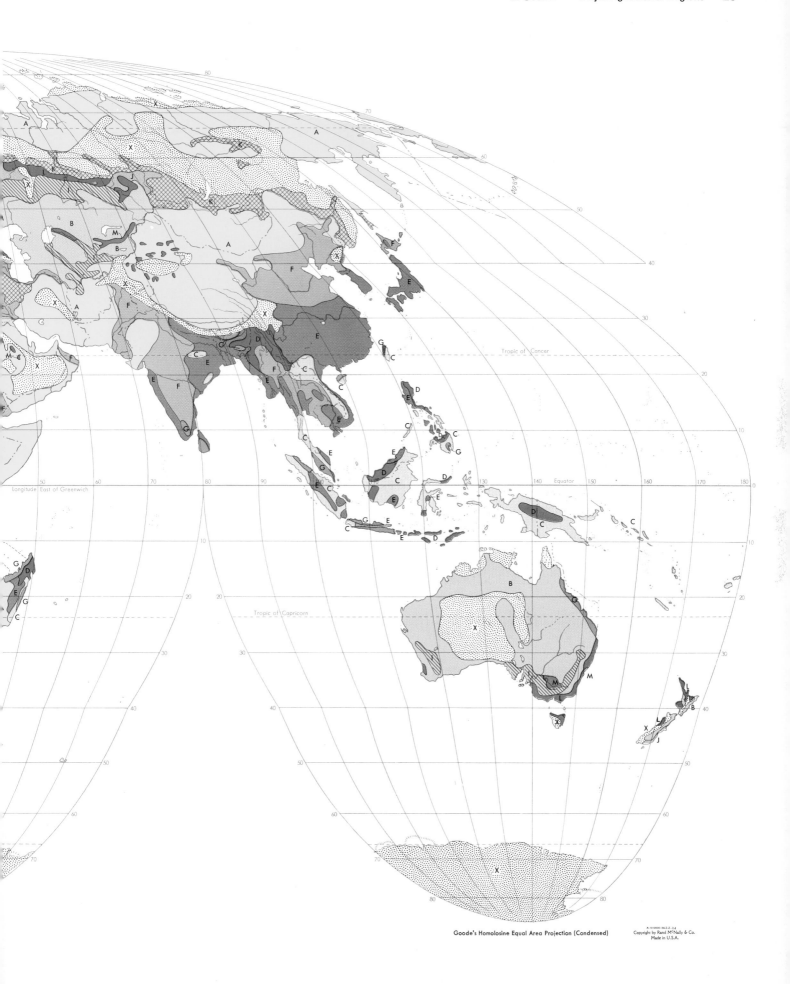

Goode's Homolosine Equal Area Projection (Condensed)

A-510000-362-2-3.4
Copyright by Rand McNally & Co.
Made in U.S.A.

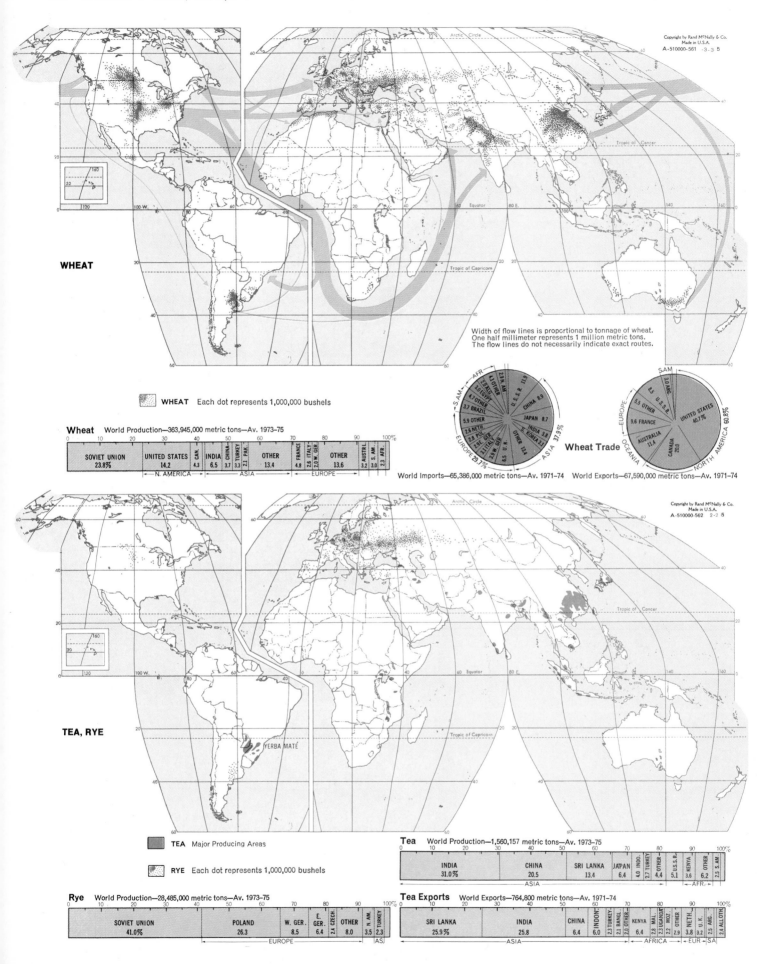

WHEAT

Copyright by Rand McNally & Co.
Made in U.S.A.
A-510000-561 -3-3 5

Width of flow lines is proportional to tonnage of wheat.
One half millimeter represents 1 million metric tons.
The flow lines do not necessarily indicate exact routes.

WHEAT   Each dot represents 1,000,000 bushels

Wheat   World Production—363,945,000 metric tons—Av. 1973–75

0	10	20	30	40	50	60	70	80	90	100%
SOVIET UNION 23.8%		UNITED STATES 14.2	CAN. 4.3	INDIA 6.5	CHINA 3.7	TURKEY 3.3	2.1 PAK.	OTHER 13.4	FRANCE 4.8	2.6 ITALY	2.9 W. GER.	OTHER 13.6	AUSTRL. 3.2	S. AM. 3.0	AFR. 2.3

N. AMERICA — ASIA — EUROPE

Wheat Trade

World Imports—65,386,000 metric tons—Av. 1971–74   World Exports—67,590,000 metric tons—Av. 1971–74

TEA, RYE

Copyright by Rand McNally & Co.
Made in U.S.A.
A-510000-562 2-2 5

YERBA MATÉ

TEA   Major Producing Areas

RYE   Each dot represents 1,000,000 bushels

Tea   World Production—1,560,157 metric tons—Av. 1973–75

0	10	20	30	40	50	60	70	80	90	100%
INDIA 31.0%		CHINA 20.5	SRI LANKA 13.4	JAPAN 6.4	4.0 INDO.	2.7 TURKEY	OTHER 4.4	5.1 U.S.S.R.	KENYA 3.6	OTHER 6.2	2.5 S. AM.

ASIA — AFR.

Rye   World Production—28,485,000 metric tons—Av. 1973–75

0	10	20	30	40	50	60	70	80	90	100%
SOVIET UNION 41.0%			POLAND 26.3	W. GER. 8.5	E. GER. 6.4	2.4 CZECH.	OTHER 8.0	N. AM. 3.5	TURKEY 2.3

EUROPE — AS.

Tea Exports   World Exports—764,800 metric tons—Av. 1971–74

0	10	20	30	40	50	60	70	80	90	100%
SRI LANKA 25.9%		INDIA 25.8	CHINA 6.4	INDON. 6.0	2.3 TURKEY	2.0 BANGL.	OTHER	KENYA 6.4	2.8 MAL.	2.3 UGANDA	MOZ.	OTHER 2.9	NETH. 3.8	U. K. 3.2	2.5 ARG.	2.4 ALL OTH.

ASIA — AFRICA — EUR. — SA

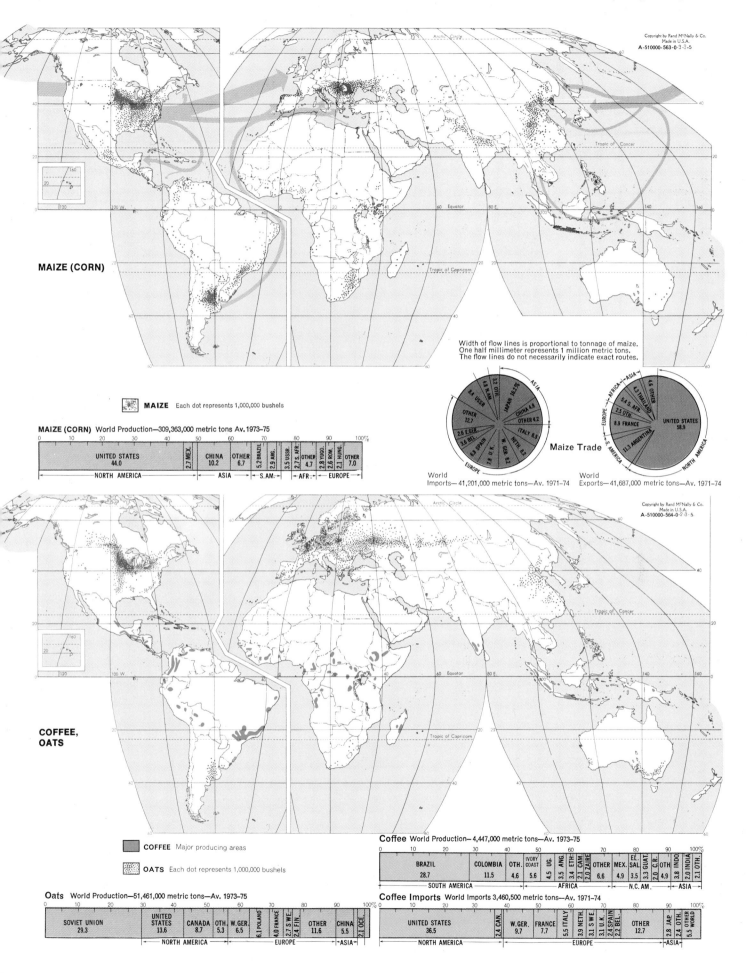

MAIZE (CORN)

MAIZE Each dot represents 1,000,000 bushels

MAIZE (CORN) World Production—309,363,000 metric tons Av. 1973–75

UNITED STATES 44.0	2.7 MEX.	CHINA 10.2	OTHER 6.7	5.2 BRAZIL	2.9 ARG.	3.5 U.S.S.R.	2.7 S. AFR.	OTHER 4.7	2.8 YUGO.	2.6 ROM.	2.1 HUNG.	OTHER 7.0
◄———————— NORTH AMERICA ————————►		◄—— ASIA ——►		◄— S.AM. —►		◄— AFR. —►		◄———— EUROPE ————►				

Width of flow lines is proportional to tonnage of maize.
One half millimeter represents 1 million metric tons.
The flow lines do not necessarily indicate exact routes.

Maize Trade

World Imports—41,201,000 metric tons—Av. 1971–74

World Exports—41,687,000 metric tons—Av. 1971–74

COFFEE, OATS

COFFEE Major producing areas

OATS Each dot represents 1,000,000 bushels

Coffee World Production—4,447,000 metric tons—Av. 1973–75

BRAZIL 28.7	COLOMBIA 11.5	OTH. 4.6	IVORY COAST 5.6	4.5 UG.	3.5 ANG.	3.4 ETH.	2.1 CAM.	2.0 ZAIRE	OTHER 6.6	MEX. 4.9	EL. SAL 3.5	3.3 GUAT.	2.0 C.R.	OTH 4.9	3.8 INDO.	2.0 INDIA	2.1 OTH.
◄———— SOUTH AMERICA ————►			◄———————————— AFRICA ————————————►							◄———— N.C. AM. ————►					◄——— ASIA ———►		

Oats World Production—51,461,000 metric tons—Av. 1973–75

SOVIET UNION 29.3	UNITED STATES 13.6	CANADA 8.7	OTH. 5.3	W. GER. 6.5	6.1 POLAND	4.0 FRANCE	2.7 S WE.	2.4 FIN.	OTHER 11.6	CHINA 5.5	2.1 OCE.
	◄—— NORTH AMERICA ——►			◄——————— EUROPE ———————►						◄— ASIA —►	

Coffee Imports World Imports 3,460,500 metric tons—Av. 1971–74

UNITED STATES 36.5	2.4 CAN.	W.GER. 9.7	FRANCE 7.7	5.5 ITALY	3.9 NETH.	3.1 S WE	3.1 U.K.	2.4 SPAIN	2.2 BEL.	OTHER 12.7	2.8 JAP.	2.4 OTH.	OTHER WORLD 5.5
◄———— NORTH AMERICA ————►		◄———————————— EUROPE ————————————►									◄—— ASIA ——►	

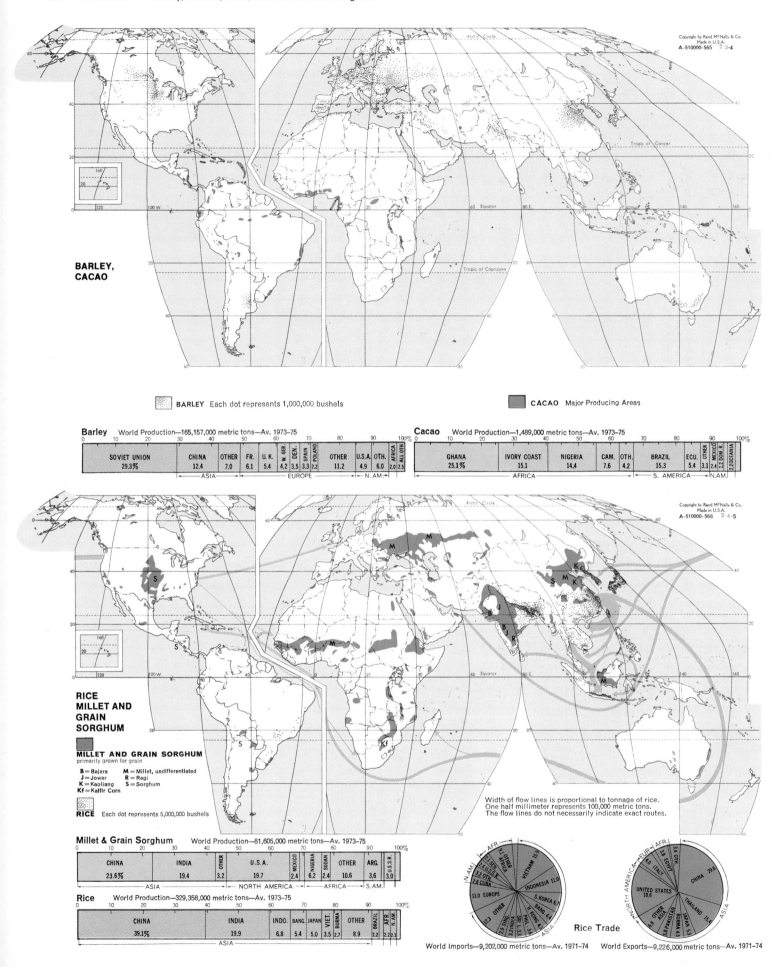

Copyright by Rand McNally & Co.
Made in U.S.A.
A-510000-565 2 3-4

**BARLEY,
CACAO**

BARLEY Each dot represents 1,000,000 bushels

CACAO Major Producing Areas

Barley World Production—165,157,000 metric tons—Av. 1973–75

	0	10	20	30	40	50	60	70	80	90	100%

SOVIET UNION 29.3%	CHINA 12.4	OTHER 7.0	FR. 6.1	U.K. 5.4	W. GER. 4.2	DEN. 3.5	SPAIN 3.3	POLAND 2.2	OTHER 11.2	U.S.A. 4.9	OTH. 6.0	AFRICA 2.0	ALL OTH 2.5

ASIA — EUROPE — N. AM.

Cacao World Production—1,489,000 metric tons—Av. 1973–75

	0	10	20	30	40	50	60	70	80	90	100%

GHANA 25.1%	IVORY COAST 15.1	NIGERIA 14.4	CAM. 7.6	OTH. 4.2	BRAZIL 15.3	ECU. 5.4	OTHER 3.1	MEXICO 2.4	DOM. R. 2.2	OCEANIA 2.2

AFRICA — S. AMERICA — N.AM.

Copyright by Rand McNally & Co.
Made in U.S.A.
A-510000-566 3·4·5

**RICE
MILLET AND
GRAIN
SORGHUM**

▨ **MILLET AND GRAIN SORGHUM**
primarily grown for grain

B = Bajara   M = Millet, undifferentiated
J = Jowar   R = Ragi
K = Kaoliang   S = Sorghum
Kf = Kaffir Corn

▨ **RICE** Each dot represents 5,000,000 bushels

Width of flow lines is proportional to tonnage of rice.
One half millimeter represents 100,000 metric tons.
The flow lines do not necessarily indicate exact routes.

Millet & Grain Sorghum World Production—81,605,000 metric tons—Av. 1973–75

	0	10	20	30	40	50	60	70	80	90	100%

CHINA 23.6%	INDIA 19.4	OTHER 3.2	U.S.A. 19.7	MEXICO 2.4	NIGERIA 6.2	SUDAN 2.4	OTHER 10.6	ARG. 3.6	U.S.S.R. 3.0

ASIA — NORTH AMERICA — AFRICA — S. AM.

Rice World Production—329,358,000 metric tons—Av. 1973–75

	0	10	20	30	40	50	60	70	80	90	100%

CHINA 39.1%	INDIA 19.9	INDO. 6.8	BANG. 5.4	JAPAN 5.0	VIET. 3.5	BURMA 2.7	OTHER 8.9	BRAZIL 2.2	AFR. 2.2	N. AM. 2.1

ASIA

Rice Trade

World Imports—9,202,000 metric tons—Av. 1971–74

World Exports—9,226,000 metric tons—Av. 1971–74

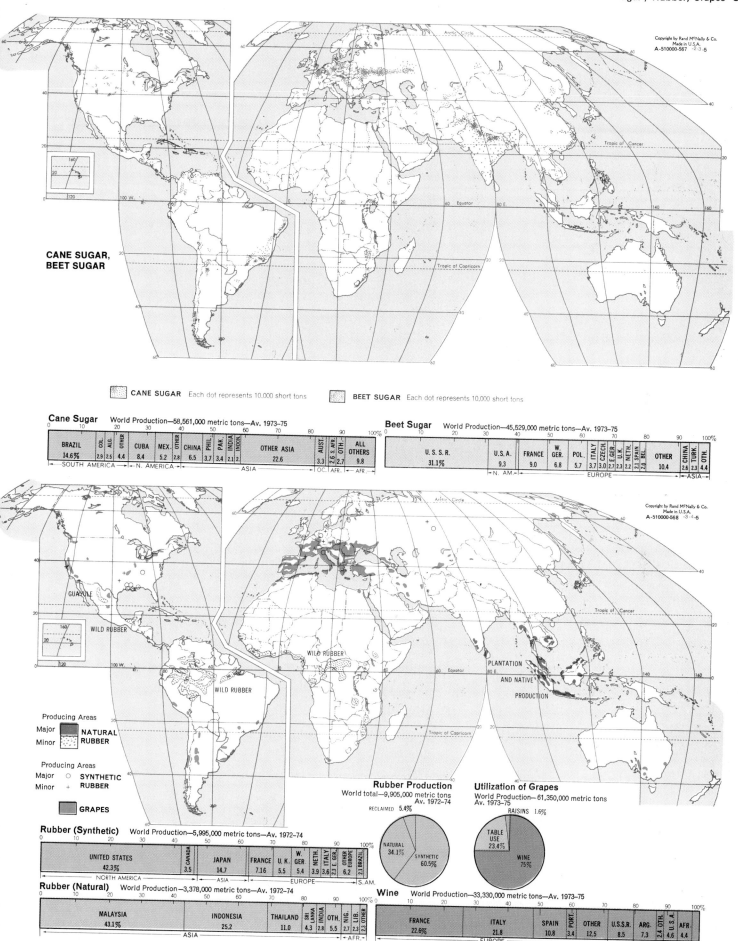

CANE SUGAR, BEET SUGAR

CANE SUGAR Each dot represents 10,000 short tons   BEET SUGAR Each dot represents 10,000 short tons

Cane Sugar World Production—58,561,000 metric tons—Av. 1973–75

BRAZIL 14.6%	COL. 2.9	ALG. 2.5	OTHER 4.4	CUBA 8.4	MEX. 5.2	OTHER 2.8	CHINA 6.5	PHIL. 3.7	PAK. 2.1	INDIA 2.1	INDON. 2	OTHER ASIA 22.6	AUST. 3.3	S. AFR. 2.6	OTH. 2.7	ALL OTHERS 9.8

SOUTH AMERICA — N. AMERICA — ASIA — OC. AFR. — AFR.

Beet Sugar World Production—45,529,000 metric tons—Av. 1973–75

U.S.S.R. 31.1%	U.S.A. 9.3	FRANCE 9.0	W. GER. 6.8	POL. 5.7	ITALY 3.7	CZECH. 3.0	E. GER. 2.7	U.K. 2.6	NETH. 2.2	SPAIN 2.1	BEL. 2.0	OTHER 10.4	CHINA 2.6	TURK. 2.3	OTH. 4.4

N. AM. — EUROPE — ASIA

GUAYULE

WILD RUBBER

WILD RUBBER

WILD RUBBER

PLANTATION AND NATIVE PRODUCTION

Producing Areas
Major ■ NATURAL
Minor ░ RUBBER

Producing Areas
Major ○ SYNTHETIC
Minor + RUBBER

■ GRAPES

Rubber Production
World total—9,905,000 metric tons
Av. 1972–74

RECLAIMED 5.4%
NATURAL 34.1%
SYNTHETIC 60.5%

Utilization of Grapes
World Production—61,350,000 metric tons
Av. 1973–75

RAISINS 1.6%
TABLE USE 23.4%
WINE 75%

Rubber (Synthetic) World Production—5,995,000 metric tons—Av. 1972–74

UNITED STATES 42.3%	CANADA 3.5	JAPAN 14.7	FRANCE 7.16	U.K. 5.5	W. GER. 5.4	NETH. 3.9	ITALY 3.6	E. GER. 2.3	OTHER EUROPE 6.2	BRAZIL 2.1

NORTH AMERICA — ASIA — EUROPE — S. AM.

Rubber (Natural) World Production—3,378,000 metric tons—Av. 1972–74

MALAYSIA 43.1%	INDONESIA 25.2	THAILAND 11.0	SRI LANKA 4.3	INDIA 2.8	OTH. 5.5	NIG. 2.7	LIB. 2.3	OTHER 2.3

ASIA — AFR.

Wine World Production—33,330,000 metric tons—Av. 1973–75

FRANCE 22.6%	ITALY 21.8	SPAIN 10.8	PORT. 3.4	OTHER 12.5	U.S.S.R. 8.5	ARG. 7.3	OTH. 2.4	U.S.A. 4.6	AFR. 4.4

EUROPE — S. AM.

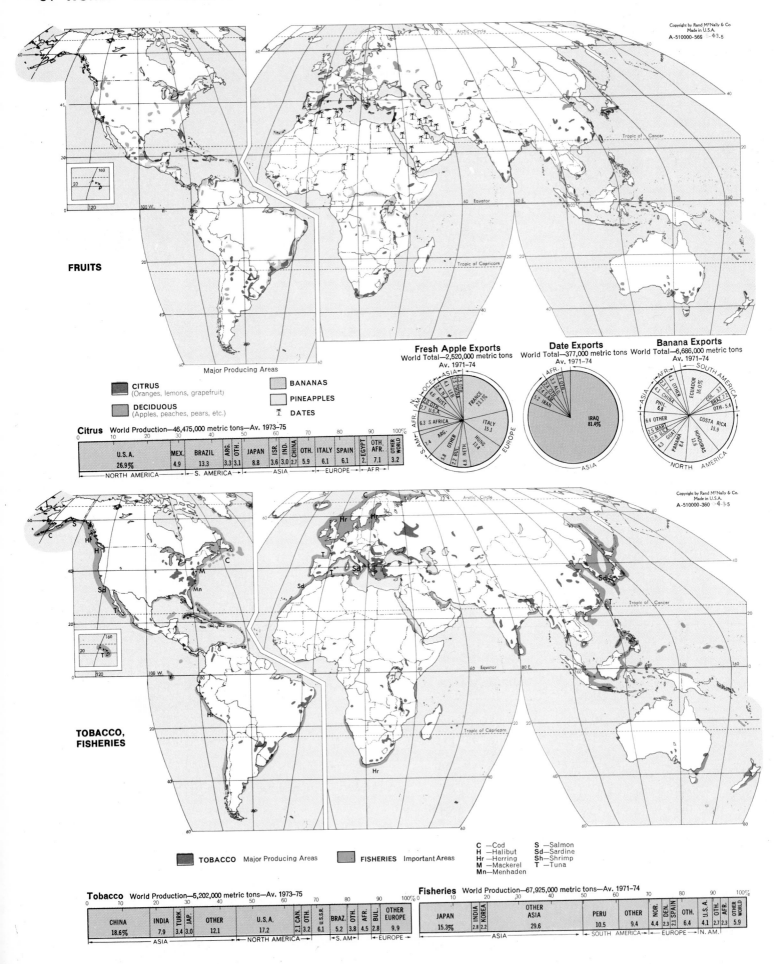

FRUITS

Major Producing Areas

CITRUS
(Oranges, lemons, grapefruit)

DECIDUOUS
(Apples, peaches, pears, etc.)

BANANAS

PINEAPPLES

DATES

Fresh Apple Exports
World Total—2,520,000 metric tons
Av. 1971–74

Date Exports
World Total—377,000 metric tons
Av. 1971–74

Banana Exports
World Total—6,686,000 metric tons
Av. 1971–74

Citrus World Production—46,475,000 metric tons—Av. 1973–75

U.S.A. 26.9%	MEX. 4.9	BRAZIL 13.3	ARG. 3.3	OTH. 3.1	JAPAN 8.8	ISR. 3.6	IND. 3.0	CHINA 2.7	OTH. 5.9	ITALY 6.1	SPAIN 6.1	EGYPT 2.	OTH. AFR. 7.1	OTHER WORLD 3.2

NORTH AMERICA — S. AMERICA — ASIA — EUROPE — AFR.

TOBACCO, FISHERIES

TOBACCO Major Producing Areas

FISHERIES Important Areas

C —Cod
H —Halibut
Hr —Herring
M —Mackerel
Mn—Menhaden

S —Salmon
Sd—Sardine
Sh—Shrimp
T —Tuna

Tobacco World Production—5,202,000 metric tons—Av. 1973–75

CHINA 18.6%	INDIA 7.9	TURK. 3.4	JAP. 3.0	OTHER 12.1	U.S.A. 17.2	CAN. 2.1	OTH. 3.2	BRAZ. 6.1	OTH. 5.2	AFR. 3.8	BUL. 4.5	OTHER EUROPE 9.9

ASIA — NORTH AMERICA — S. AM — EUROPE

Fisheries World Production—67,925,000 metric tons—Av. 1971–74

JAPAN 15.3%	INDIA 2.8	KOREA 2.2	OTHER ASIA 29.6	PERU 10.5	OTHER 9.4	NOR. 4.4	DEN. 2.3	SPAIN 2.1	OTH. 6.4	U.S.A. 4.1	OTH. 2.7	AFR. 2.3	OTHER WORLD 5.9

ASIA — SOUTH AMERICA — EUROPE — N. AM.

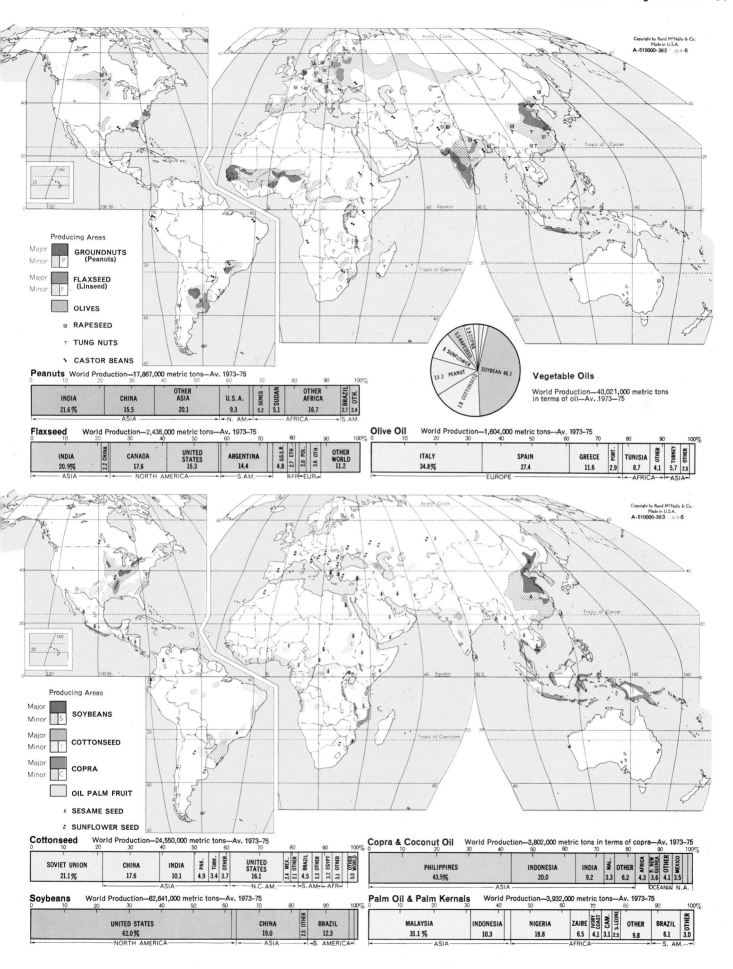

Producing Areas

Major / Minor P	**GROUNDNUTS** (Peanuts)
Major / Minor F	**FLAXSEED** (Linseed)
	OLIVES
ш	**RAPESEED**
т	**TUNG NUTS**
↓	**CASTOR BEANS**

Vegetable Oils

World Production—40,021,000 metric tons
in terms of oil—Av. 1973–75

Pie chart: SOYBEAN 46.1, PEANUT 13.2, COTTONSEED 18, SUNFLOWER 8, RAPESEED 5.5, COPRA 2.8

Peanuts   World Production—17,867,000 metric tons—Av. 1973–75

INDIA 21.6%	CHINA 15.5	OTHER ASIA 20.1	U.S.A. 9.3	SENEG. 5.2	SUDAN 5.1	OTHER AFRICA 16.7	BRAZIL 2.7	OTH. 2.4

ASIA ← | → N. AM. ← | → AFRICA ← | → S. AM.

Flaxseed   World Production—2,438,000 metric tons—Av. 1973–75

INDIA 20.9%	CHINA 2.2	CANADA 17.6	UNITED STATES 15.3	ARGENTINA 14.4	U.S.S.R. 4.8	ETH. 2.7	POL. 2.0	OTH. 3.6	OTHER WORLD 11.2

ASIA ← | → NORTH AMERICA ← | → S. AM. ← | → AFR.–EUR.

Olive Oil   World Production—1,604,000 metric tons—Av. 1973–75

ITALY 34.8%	SPAIN 27.4	GREECE 11.6	PORT. 2.9	TUNISIA 8.7	OTHER 4.1	TURKEY 5.7	OTHER 2.5

EUROPE ← | → AFRICA ← | → ASIA

Producing Areas

Major / Minor S	**SOYBEANS**
Major / Minor	**COTTONSEED**
Major / Minor C	**COPRA**
	OIL PALM FRUIT
↓	**SESAME SEED**
↺	**SUNFLOWER SEED**

Cottonseed   World Production—24,550,000 metric tons—Av. 1973–75

SOVIET UNION 21.1%	CHINA 17.6	INDIA 10.1	PAK. 4.9	TURK. 3.4	OTHER 3.7	UNITED STATES 16.1	MEX. 2.4	OTHER 2.1	BRAZIL 4.5	OTHER 3.3	EGYPT 3.2	OTHER 3.1	OTHER WORLD 3.0

ASIA ← | → N.C. AM. ← | → S. AM. ← | → AFR.

Copra & Coconut Oil   World Production—3,802,000 metric tons in terms of copra—Av. 1973–75

PHILIPPINES 43.5%	INDONESIA 20.0	INDIA 9.2	MAL. 3.3	OTHER 6.2	AFRICA 4.3	P. NEW GUINEA 3.6	OTHER 4.1	MEXICO 3.5

ASIA ← | → OCEANIA ← | → N.A.

Soybeans   World Production—62,641,000 metric tons—Av. 1973–75

UNITED STATES 62.0%	CHINA 19.0	OTHER 2.5	BRAZIL 12.3

NORTH AMERICA ← | → ASIA ← | → S. AMERICA

Palm Oil & Palm Kernals   World Production—3,932,000 metric tons—Av. 1973–75

MALAYSIA 31.1%	INDONESIA 10.3	NIGERIA 18.8	ZAIRE 6.5	IVORY COAST 4.1	CAM. 3.1	S. LEONE 2.5	OTHER 9.8	BRAZIL 6.1	OTHER 3.0

ASIA ← | → AFRICA ← | → S. AM.

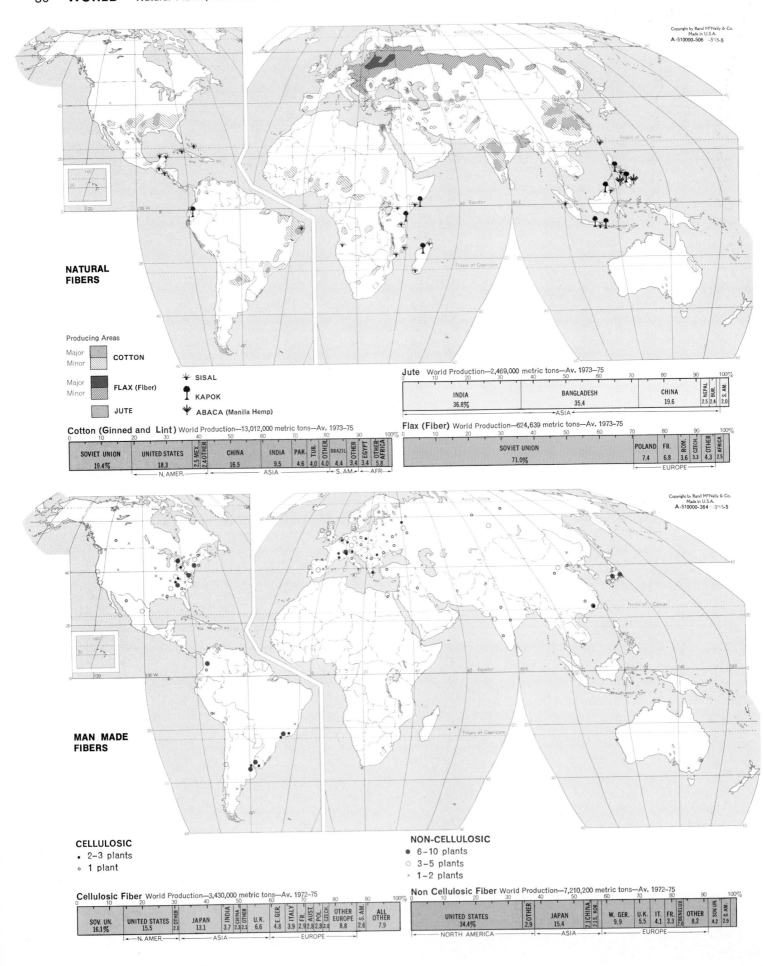

NATURAL FIBERS

Producing Areas

Major / Minor	COTTON
Major / Minor	FLAX (Fiber)
	JUTE

✶ SISAL

♣ KAPOK

✺ ABACA (Manila Hemp)

Jute World Production—2,469,000 metric tons—Av. 1973-75

INDIA 36.8%	BANGLADESH 35.4	CHINA 19.6	NEPAL 2.5	BUR. 2.4	S. AM. 2.0

←——————————————————— ASIA ———————————————————→

Cotton (Ginned and Lint) World Production—13,012,000 metric tons—Av. 1973-75

SOVIET UNION 19.4%	UNITED STATES 18.3	MEX. 2.5	OTHER 2.4	CHINA 16.5	INDIA 9.5	PAK. 4.6	TUR. 4.0	OTHER 4.0	BRAZIL 4.4	OTHER 3.4	EGYPT 3.4	OTHER AFRICA 5.8

←— N. AMER. —→ ←——————————— ASIA ———————————→ ←— S. AM. —→ ←— AFR. —→

Flax (Fiber) World Production—624,639 metric tons—Av. 1973-75

SOVIET UNION 71.0%	POLAND 7.4	FR. 6.8	ROM. 3.6	CZECH. 3.3	OTHER 4.3	AFRICA 2.5

←————————————————————————— EUROPE —————————————————————————→

MAN MADE FIBERS

CELLULOSIC
- • 2-3 plants
- ○ 1 plant

NON-CELLULOSIC
- ● 6-10 plants
- ○ 3-5 plants
- × 1-2 plants

Cellulosic Fiber World Production—3,430,000 metric tons—Av. 1972-75

SOV. UN. 16.1%	UNITED STATES 15.5	OTHER 2.1	JAPAN 13.1	INDIA 3.7	CHINA 2.3	U.K. 6.6	E. GER. 4.8	ITALY 3.9	FR. 2.9	AUST. 2.8	POL. 2.8	CZECH. 2.0	OTHER EUROPE 8.8	S. AM. 2.6	ALL OTHER 7.9

←— N. AMER. —→ ←——————— ASIA ———————→ ←——————————— EUROPE ———————————→

Non Cellulosic Fiber World Production—7,210,200 metric tons—Av. 1972-75

UNITED STATES 34.4%	OTHER 2.9	JAPAN 15.4	CHINA 2.1	S. KOR. 2.1	W. GER. 9.9	U.K. 5.5	IT. 4.1	FR. 3.3	BENELUX 2.0	OTHER 8.2	SOV. UN. 4.2	S. AM. 2.9

←———— NORTH AMERICA ————→ ←——————— ASIA ———————→ ←———————— EUROPE ————————→

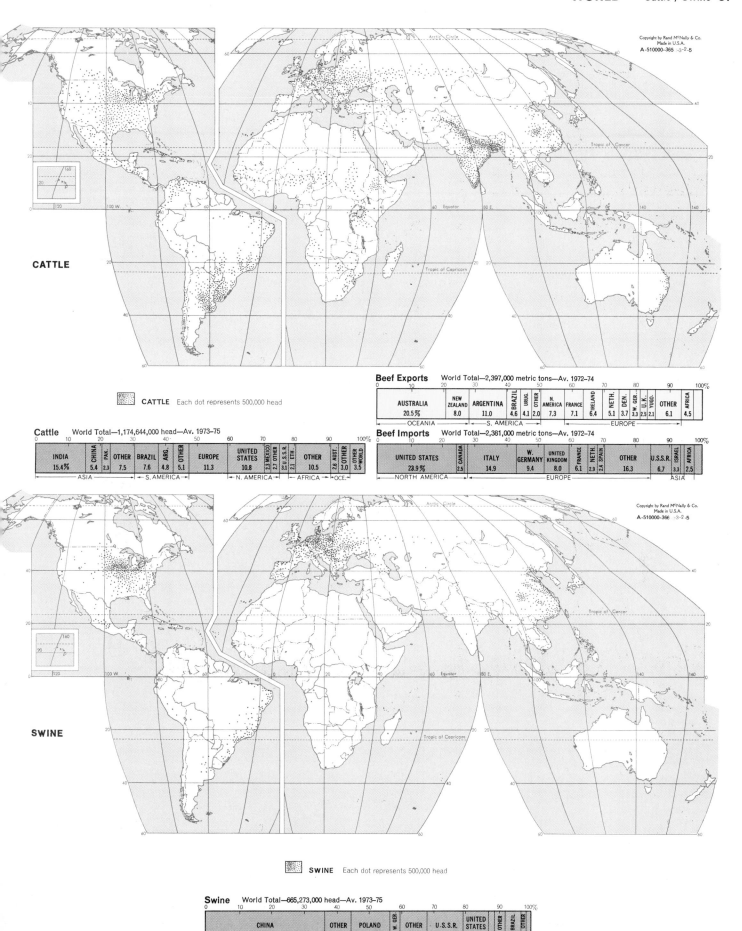

CATTLE

CATTLE Each dot represents 500,000 head

Cattle World Total—1,174,644,000 head—Av. 1973–75

INDIA 15.4%	CHINA 5.4	PAK. 2.3	OTHER 7.5	BRAZIL 7.6	ARG. 4.8	OTHER 5.1	EUROPE 11.3	UNITED STATES 10.8	MEXICO 2.3	OTHER 2.7	U.S.S.R. 3.1	ETH. 2.1	OTHER 10.5	AUST. 2.6	OTHER 3.0	OTHER WORLD 3.5
←——— ASIA ———→				←— S. AMERICA —→				←— N. AMERICA —→				←—— AFRICA ——→		OCE.	

Beef Exports World Total—2,397,000 metric tons—Av. 1972–74

AUSTRALIA 20.5%	NEW ZEALAND 8.0	ARGENTINA 11.0	BRAZIL 4.6	URUG. 4.1	OTHER 2.0	N. AMERICA 7.3	FRANCE 7.1	IRELAND 6.4	NETH. 5.1	DEN. 3.7	W. GER. 3.3	U.K. 2.5	YUGO. 2.1	OTHER 6.1	AFRICA 4.5
OCEANIA		←——— S. AMERICA ———→				←——————— EUROPE ———————→									

Beef Imports World Total—2,381,000 metric tons—Av. 1972–74

UNITED STATES 23.9%	CANADA 2.5	ITALY 14.9	W. GERMANY 9.4	UNITED KINGDOM 8.0	FRANCE 6.1	NETH. 2.9	SPAIN 2.4	OTHER 16.3	U.S.S.R. 6.7	ISRAEL 3.3	AFRICA 2.5
←——— NORTH AMERICA ———→		←——————————— EUROPE ———————————→							←—— ASIA ——→		

SWINE

SWINE Each dot represents 500,000 head

Swine World Total—665,273,000 head—Av. 1973–75

CHINA 35.9%	OTHER 8.5	POLAND 11.8	W. GER. 3.0	OTHER 8.4	U.S.S.R. 10.5	UNITED STATES 8.8	OTHER 2.1	BRAZIL 5.1	OTHER 2.4
←——— ASIA ———→		←————— EUROPE —————→				←— N. AM. —→		←S. AM.→

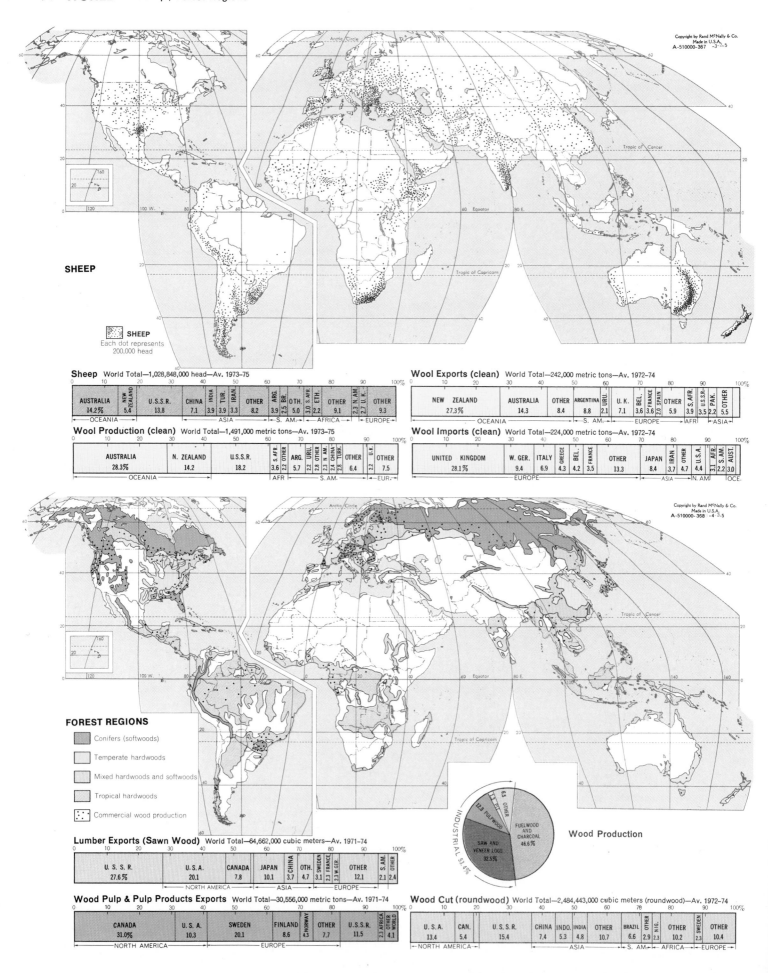

Copyright by Rand McNally & Co.
Made in U.S.A.
A-510000-367 -3-2-5

SHEEP

SHEEP
Each dot represents
200,000 head

Sheep World Total—1,028,848,000 head—Av. 1973–75

AUSTRALIA 14.2%	NEW ZEALAND 5.4	U.S.S.R. 13.8	CHINA 7.1	INDIA 3.9	TUR. 3.9	IRAN 3.3	OTHER 8.2	ARG. 3.9	BR. 2.5	OTH. 5.0	S.AFR. 3.0	ETH. 2.2	OTHER 9.1	N.AM. 2.3	U.K. 2.7	OTHER 9.3

OCEANIA — ASIA — S. AM. — AFRICA — EUROPE

Wool Exports (clean) World Total—242,000 metric tons—Av. 1972–74

NEW ZEALAND 27.3%	AUSTRALIA 14.3	OTHER 8.4	ARGENTINA 8.8	URU. 2.1	U.K. 7.1	BEL. 3.6	FRANCE 3.6	SPAIN 2.0	OTHER 5.9	S.AFR. 3.9	U.S.S.R. 3.5	PAK. 2.2	OTHER 5.5

OCEANIA — S. AM. — EUROPE — AFR. — ASIA

Wool Production (clean) World Total—1,491,000 metric tons—Av. 1973–75

AUSTRALIA 28.3%	N. ZEALAND 14.2	U.S.S.R. 18.2	S.AFR. 3.6	OTHER 2.2	ARG. 5.7	URU. 2.2	N.AM. 2.3	CHINA 2.4	TURK. 2.8	OTHER 6.4	U.K. 2.2	OTHER 7.5

OCEANIA — AFR. — S. AM. — EUR.

Wool Imports (clean) World Total—224,000 metric tons—Av. 1972–74

UNITED KINGDOM 28.1%	W. GER. 9.4	ITALY 6.9	GREECE 4.3	BEL. 4.2	FRANCE 3.5	OTHER 13.3	JAPAN 8.4	IRAN 3.7	OTHER 4.7	U.S.A. 4.4	S.AM. 2.2	AUST. 3.0

EUROPE — ASIA — N. AM. — OCE.

Copyright by Rand McNally & Co.
Made in U.S.A.
A-510000-368 -4-3-5

FOREST REGIONS

Conifers (softwoods)

Temperate hardwoods

Mixed hardwoods and softwoods

Tropical hardwoods

Commercial wood production

Lumber Exports (Sawn Wood) World Total—64,662,000 cubic meters—Av. 1971–74

U.S.S.R. 27.6%	U.S.A. 20.1	CANADA 7.8	JAPAN 10.1	CHINA 3.7	OTH. 4.7	SWEDEN 3.1	FRANCE 2.3	W.GER. 2.3	OTHER 12.1	S.AM. 2.1	OTHER 2.4

NORTH AMERICA — ASIA — EUROPE

Wood Production

Pie chart: INDUSTRIAL 53.4% (SAW AND VENEER LOGS 32.5%, PULPWOOD 12.8, OTHER 1.7, 6.5 OTHER), FUELWOOD AND CHARCOAL 46.6%

Wood Pulp & Pulp Products Exports World Total—30,556,000 metric tons—Av. 1971–74

CANADA 31.0%	U.S.A. 10.3	SWEDEN 20.1	FINLAND 8.6	NORWAY 4.3	OTHER 7.7	U.S.S.R. 11.5	AFRICA 2.3	OTHER WORLD 4.1

NORTH AMERICA — EUROPE

Wood Cut (roundwood) World Total—2,484,443,000 cubic meters (roundwood)—Av. 1972–74

U.S.A. 13.4	CAN. 5.4	U.S.S.R. 15.4	CHINA 7.4	INDO. 5.3	INDIA 4.8	OTHER 10.7	BRAZIL 6.6	NIG. 2.9	OTHER 10.2	SWEDEN 2.3	OTHER 10.4

NORTH AMERICA — ASIA — S. AM. — AFRICA — EUROPE

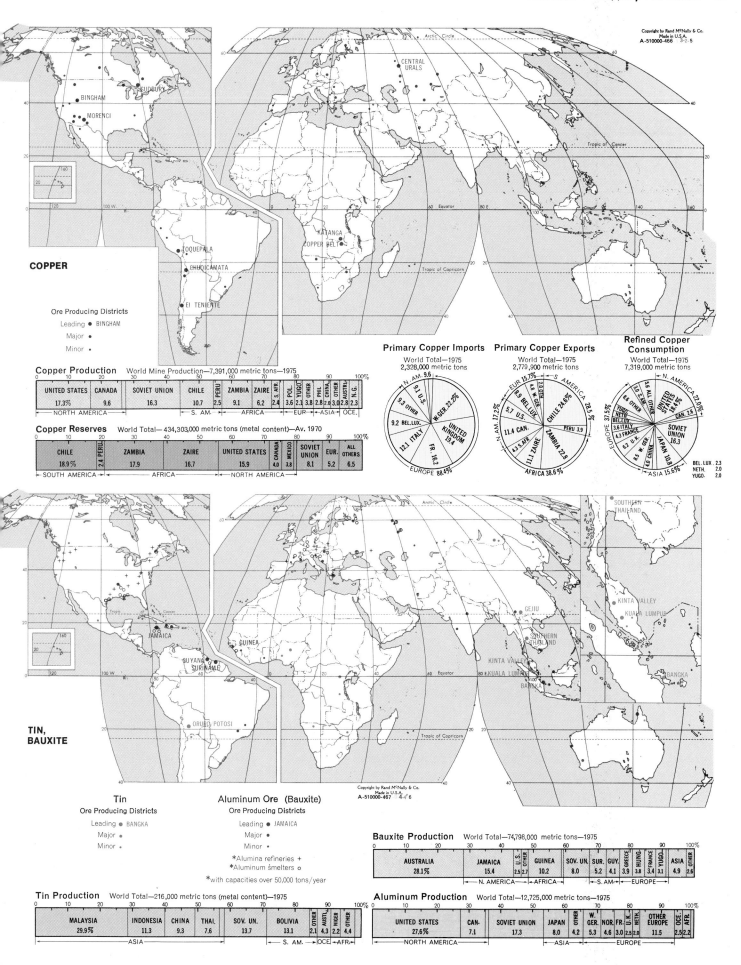

CENTRAL URALS

SUDBURY

BINGHAM

MORENCI

KATANGA

COPPER BELT

TOQUEPALA

CHUQICAMATA

EL TENIENTE

COPPER

Ore Producing Districts

Leading ● BINGHAM

Major ●

Minor ●

Copper Production   World Mine Production—7,391,000 metric tons—1975

| 0 | 10 | 20 | 30 | 40 | 50 | 60 | 70 | 80 | 90 | 100% |

| UNITED STATES 17.3% | CANADA 9.6 | SOVIET UNION 16.3 | CHILE 10.7 | PERU 2.5 | ZAMBIA 9.1 | ZAIRE 6.2 | S. AFR. 2.4 | POL. 3.6 | YUGO 2.1 | OTHER 3.8 | PHIL. 2.8 | CHINA 2.0 | OTHER 3.0 | AUSTRL. 2.8 | N.G. 2.3 |

NORTH AMERICA ─ S. AM. ─ AFRICA ─ EUR. ─ ASIA ─ OCE.

Copper Reserves   World Total—434,303,000 metric tons (metal content)—Av. 1970

| 0 | 10 | 20 | 30 | 40 | 50 | 60 | 70 | 80 | 90 | 100% |

| CHILE 18.9% | PERU 2.4 | ZAMBIA 17.9 | ZAIRE 16.7 | UNITED STATES 15.9 | CANADA 4.0 | MEXICO 3.8 | SOVIET UNION 8.1 | EUR. 5.2 | ALL OTHERS 6.5 |

SOUTH AMERICA ─ AFRICA ─ NORTH AMERICA

Primary Copper Imports
World Total—1975
2,328,000 metric tons

N. AM. 9.6
9.1 U.S.
9.3 Other
9.2 BEL.LUX.
12.1 ITALY
W.GER. 22.8%
UNITED KINGDOM 19.4
FR. 16.2
EUROPE 88.4%

Primary Copper Exports
World Total—1975
2,779,900 metric tons

EUR. 15.7%
10.1% W. GER
8.9 BEL.LUX.
5.7 U.S.
11.4 CAN.
N. AM. 17.2%
4.3 S.AFR.
11.1 ZAIRE
AFRICA 38.6%
22.8 ZAMBIA
CHILE 24.6%
PERU 3.9
S. AMERICA 28.5%
4.8 W. GER

Refined Copper Consumption
World Total—1975
7,319,000 metric tons

5.5 ALL OTHER
6.6 OTHER
YUGO
NETH.
BEL.LUX.
3.6 ITALY
4.3 FRANCE
6.2 U.K.
8.5 W. GER
4.0 CHINA
EUROPE 37.5%
UNITED STATES 18.4%
CAN. 2.6
N. AMERICA 22.0%
SOVIET UNION 16.3
JAPAN 10.8
ASIA 15.6%

BEL.LUX. 2.3
NETH. 2.0
YUGO. 2.0

SOUTHERN THAILAND

GEJIU

KINTA VALLEY

KUALA LUMPUR

SOUTHERN THAILAND

KINTA VALLEY

KUALA LUMPUR

BANGKA

JAMAICA

GUINEA

GUYANA

SURINAME

ORURO POTOSI

TIN, BAUXITE

Tin
Ore Producing Districts

Leading ● BANGKA

Major ●

Minor ●

Aluminum Ore (Bauxite)
Ore Producing Districts

Leading ● JAMAICA

Major ●

Minor ●

*Alumina refineries +
*Aluminum smelters o

*with capacities over 50,000 tons/year

Bauxite Production   World Total—74,798,000 metric tons—1975

| 0 | 10 | 20 | 30 | 40 | 50 | 60 | 70 | 80 | 90 | 100% |

| AUSTRALIA 28.1% | JAMAICA 15.4 | U.S. 2.5 | OTHER 2.7 | GUINEA 10.2 | SOV. UN. 8.0 | SUR. 5.2 | GUY. 4.1 | GREECE 3.9 | HUNG. 3.8 | FRANCE 3.4 | YUGO. 3.1 | ASIA 4.9 | OTHER 2.6 |

N. AMERICA ─ AFRICA ─ S. AM. ─ EUROPE

Tin Production   World Total—216,000 metric tons (metal content)—1975

| 0 | 10 | 20 | 30 | 40 | 50 | 60 | 70 | 80 | 90 | 100% |

| MALAYSIA 29.9% | INDONESIA 11.3 | CHINA 9.3 | THAI. 7.6 | SOV. UN. 13.7 | BOLIVIA 13.1 | OTHER 2.1 | AUSTL 4.3 | NIGER 2.2 | OTHER 4.4 |

ASIA ─ S. AM. ─ OCE ─ AFR.

Aluminum Production   World Total—12,725,000 metric tons—1975

| 0 | 10 | 20 | 30 | 40 | 50 | 60 | 70 | 80 | 90 | 100% |

| UNITED STATES 27.6% | CAN. 7.1 | SOVIET UNION 17.3 | JAPAN 8.0 | OTHER 4.2 | W. GER. 5.3 | NOR. 4.6 | FR. 3.0 | U.K. 2.5 | NETH. 2.0 | OTHER EUROPE 11.5 | OCE. 2.5 | AFR. 2.2 |

NORTH AMERICA ─ ASIA ─ EUROPE

IRON ORE AND FERROALLOYS

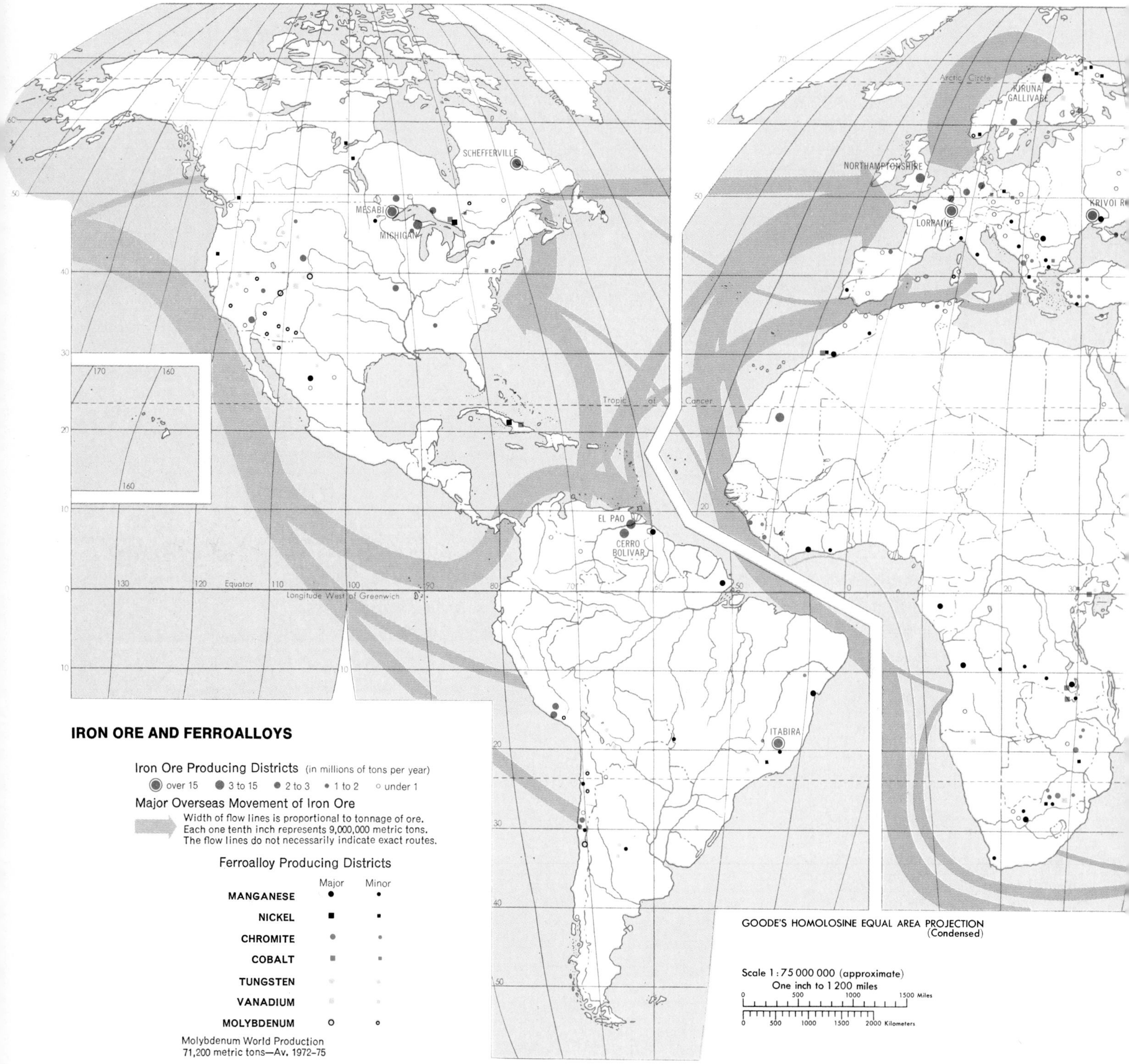
Iron Ore Producing Districts (in millions of tons per year)
over 15 · 3 to 15 · 2 to 3 · 1 to 2 · under 1
Major Overseas Movement of Iron Ore
Width of flow lines is proportional to tonnage of ore. Each one tenth inch represents 9,000,000 metric tons. The flow lines do not necessarily indicate exact routes.
Ferroalloy Producing Districts
Major Minor
MANGANESE
NICKEL
CHROMITE
COBALT
TUNGSTEN
VANADIUM
MOLYBDENUM
Molybdenum World Production 71,200 metric tons—Av. 1972–75
SCHEFFERVILLE
MESABI
MICHIGAN
KIRUNA
GALLIVARE
NORTHAMPTONSHIRE
LORRAINE
KRIVOI R
EL PAO
CERRO BOLIVAR
ITABIRA
Arctic Circle
Tropic of Cancer
Equator
Longitude West of Greenwich
GOODE'S HOMOLOSINE EQUAL AREA PROJECTION (Condensed)
Scale 1:75 000 000 (approximate)
One inch to 1 200 miles
0 500 1000 1500 Miles
0 500 1000 1500 2000 Kilometers

Manganese World Production—22,834,000 metric tons (metal content)—1974

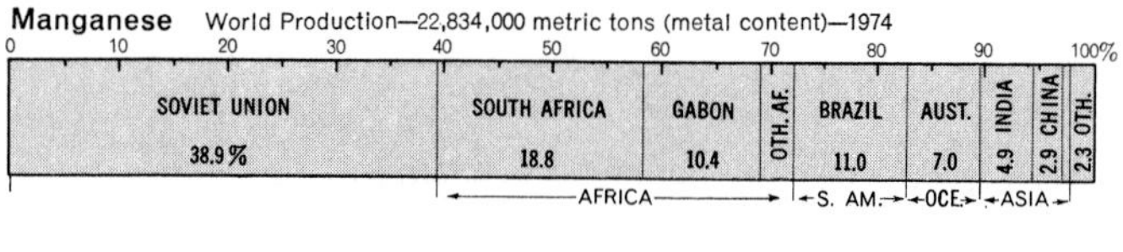
0 10 20 30 40 50 60 70 80 90 100%
SOVIET UNION 38.9%
SOUTH AFRICA 18.8
GABON 10.4
OTH. AF.
BRAZIL 11.0
AUST. 7.0
4.9 INDIA
2.9 CHINA
2.3 OTH.
AFRICA
S. AM.
OCE.
ASIA

Tungsten World Production—36,200 metric tons (60% WO_3)—1974

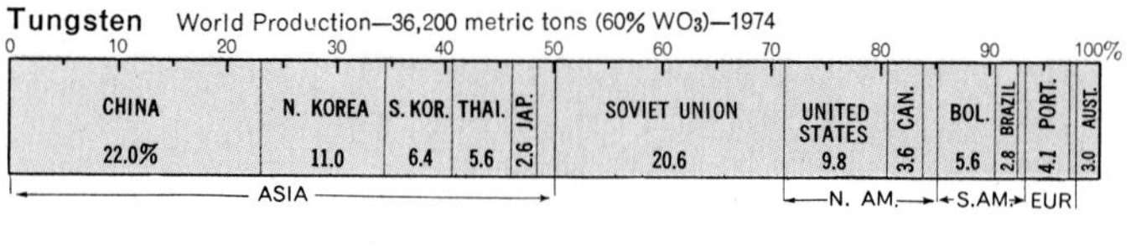
0 10 20 30 40 50 60 70 80 90 100%
CHINA 22.0%
N. KOREA 11.0
S. KOR. 6.4
THAI. 5.6
2.6 JAP.
SOVIET UNION 20.6
UNITED STATES 9.8
3.6 CAN.
BOL. 5.6
2.8 BRAZIL
4.1 PORT.
3.0 AUST.
ASIA
N. AM.
S. AM.
EUR

Nickel World Production—723,000 metric tons (metal content)—1975

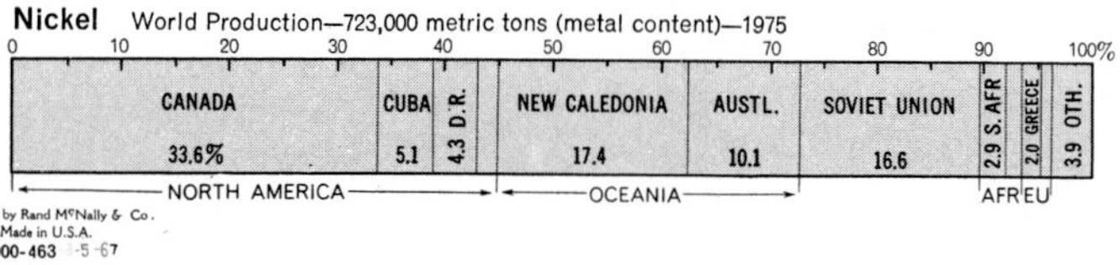
0 10 20 30 40 50 60 70 80 90 100%
CANADA 33.6%
CUBA 5.1
4.3 D.R.
NEW CALEDONIA 17.4
AUSTL. 10.1
SOVIET UNION 16.6
2.9 S. AFR
2.0 GREECE
3.9 OTH.
NORTH AMERICA
OCEANIA
AFR EU

Vanadium World Production—19,700 metric tons—1974

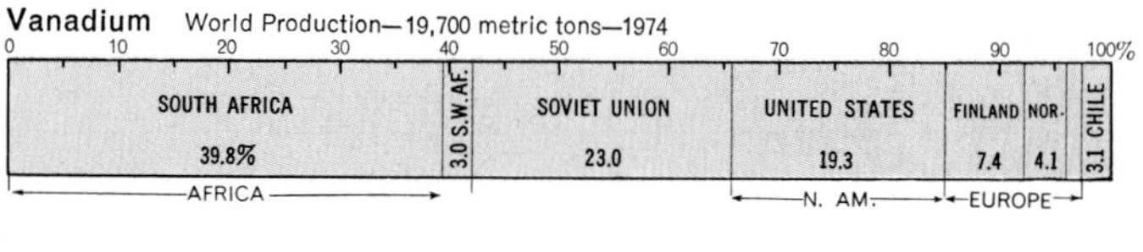
0 10 20 30 40 50 60 70 80 90 100%
SOUTH AFRICA 39.8%
3.0 S.W. AF.
SOVIET UNION 23.0
UNITED STATES 19.3
FINLAND 7.4
NOR. 4.1
3.1 CHILE
AFRICA
N. AM.
EUROPE

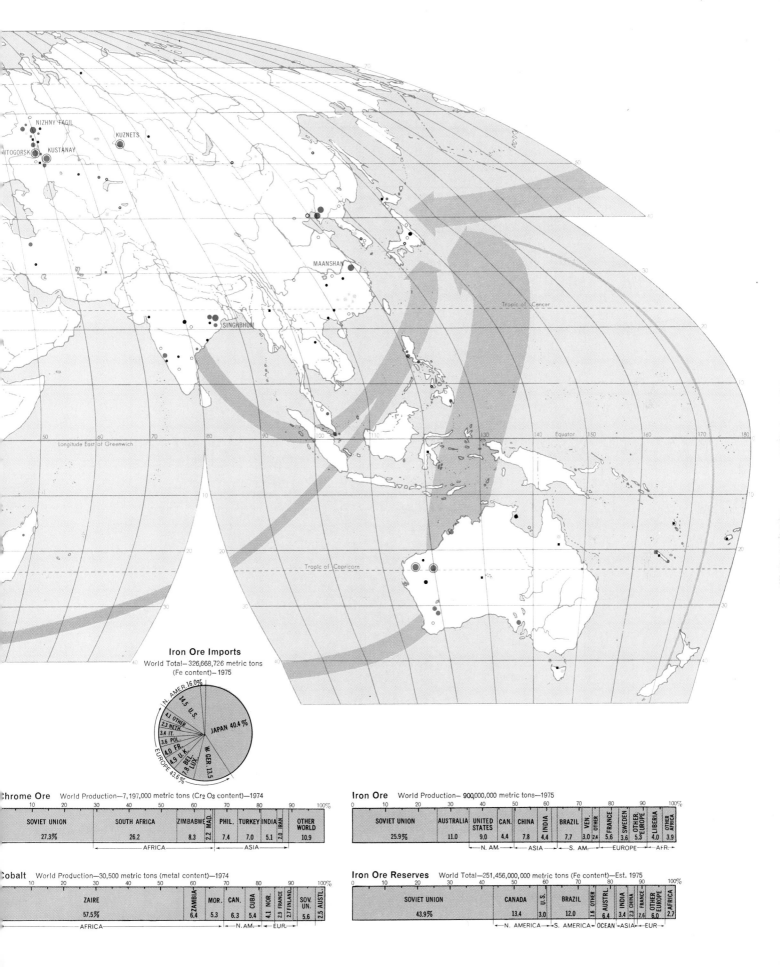

NIZHNY TAGIL
KUZNETS
KUSTANAY
ITOGORSK
MAANSHAN
SINGHBHUM

Iron Ore Imports
World Total—326,668,726 metric tons
(Fe content)—1975

N. AMER. 16.0%
14.5 U.S.
4.1 OTHER
2.3 NETH.
3.4 IT.
3.6 POL.
4.0 U.K.
4.9 FR.
7.8 BEL. LUX.
EUROPE 43.6%
W. GER. 13.5
JAPAN 40.4%

Chrome Ore   World Production—7,197,000 metric tons (Cr$_2$O$_3$ content)—1974

	10	20	30	40	50	60	70	80	90	100%
SOVIET UNION 27.3%			SOUTH AFRICA 26.2			ZIMBABWE 8.3	MAD. 2.2	PHIL. 7.4	TURKEY 7.0	INDIA 5.1	IRAN 2.0	OTHER WORLD 10.9

AFRICA ————— ASIA

Cobalt   World Production—30,500 metric tons (metal content)—1974

	10	20	30	40	50	60	70	80	90	100%
ZAIRE 57.5%					ZAMBIA 6.4	MOR. 5.3	CAN. 6.3	CUBA 5.4	NOR. 4.1	FRANCE 2.9	FINLAND 2.7	SOV. UN. 5.6	AUSTL. 2.5

AFRICA ————— N. AM. — EUR.

Iron Ore   World Production— 900,000,000 metric tons—1975

0	10	20	30	40	50	60	70	80	90	100%
SOVIET UNION 25.9%			AUSTRALIA 11.0	UNITED STATES 9.0	CAN. 4.4	CHINA 7.8	INDIA 4.4	BRAZIL 7.7	VEN. 3.0	OTHER 2.4	FRANCE 5.6	SWEDEN 3.6	OTHER EUROPE 5.3	LIBERIA 4.0	OTHER AFRICA 3.9

N. AM. — ASIA — S. AM. — EUROPE — AFR.

Iron Ore Reserves   World Total—251,456,000,000 metric tons (Fe content)—Est. 1975

0	10	20	30	40	50	60	70	80	90	100%
SOVIET UNION 43.9%				CANADA 13.4	U.S. 3.0	BRAZIL 12.0	OTHER 1.6	AUSTRL. 6.4	INDIA 3.4	CHINA 2.3	FRANCE 2.6	OTHER EUROPE 6.0	AFRICA 2.7

N. AMERICA — S. AMERICA — OCEAN — ASIA — EUR.

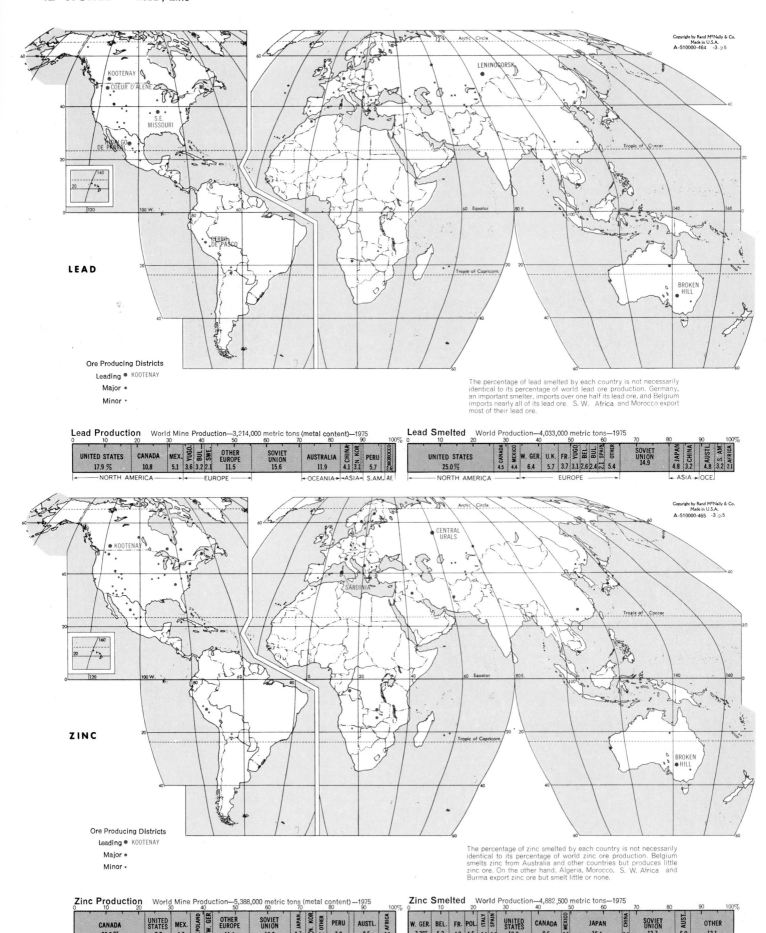

LEAD

Ore Producing Districts

Leading ● KOOTENAY

Major ●

Minor ·

The percentage of lead smelted by each country is not necessarily identical to its percentage of world lead ore production. Germany, an important smelter, imports over one half its lead ore, and Belgium imports nearly all of its lead ore. S. W. Africa and Morocco export most of their lead ore.

Lead Production World Mine Production—3,214,000 metric tons (metal content)—1975

UNITED STATES 17.9 %	CANADA 10.8	MEX. 5.1	YUGO. 3.6	BUL. 3.2	SWE. 2.1	OTHER EUROPE 11.5	SOVIET UNION 15.6	AUSTRALIA 11.9	CHINA 4.1	N. KOR. 3.1	PERU 5.7	MOROCCO 2.6
← NORTH AMERICA →			← EUROPE →					← OCEANIA →	← ASIA →		S.AM.	AF.

Lead Smelted World Production—4,033,000 metric tons—1975

UNITED STATES 25.0 %	CANADA 4.5	MEXICO 4.4	W. GER. 6.4	U.K. 5.7	FR. 3.7	YUGO 3.1	BEL. 2.6	BUL. 2.4	SPAIN 2.1	OTHER 5.4	SOVIET UNION 14.9	JAPAN 4.8	CHINA 3.2	AUST. 4.8	S.AM. 3.2	AFRICA 2.1
← NORTH AMERICA →			← EUROPE →									← ASIA →		OCE.		

ZINC

Ore Producing Districts

Leading ● KOOTENAY

Major ●

Minor ·

The percentage of zinc smelted by each country is not necessarily identical to its percentage of world zinc ore production. Belgium smelts zinc from Australia and other countries but produces little zinc ore. On the other hand, Algeria, Morocco, S. W. Africa and Burma export zinc ore but smelt little or none.

Zinc Production World Mine Production—5,388,000 metric tons (metal content)—1975

CANADA 22.8 %	UNITED STATES 8.7	MEX. 4.7	POLAND 4.2	W. GER.	OTHER EUROPE 11.4	SOVIET UNION 12.6	JAPAN 4.7	N. KOR. 3.0	OTHER 2.8	PERU 7.2	AUSTL. 8.5	AFRICA 5.2
← NORTH AMERICA →			← EUROPE →				← ASIA →			S.AM.	← OCE. →	

Zinc Smelted World Production—4,882,500 metric tons—1975

W. GER. 7.3%	BEL. 5.3	FR. 4.8	POL. 4.6	ITALY 3.5	SPAIN 2.5	UNITED STATES 10.0	CANADA 9.5	MEXICO 2.3	JAPAN 16.4	CHINA 2.0	SOVIET UNION 13.7	AUST. 5.0	OTHER 13.1
← EUROPE →						← NORTH AMERICA →			← ASIA →			OCE.	

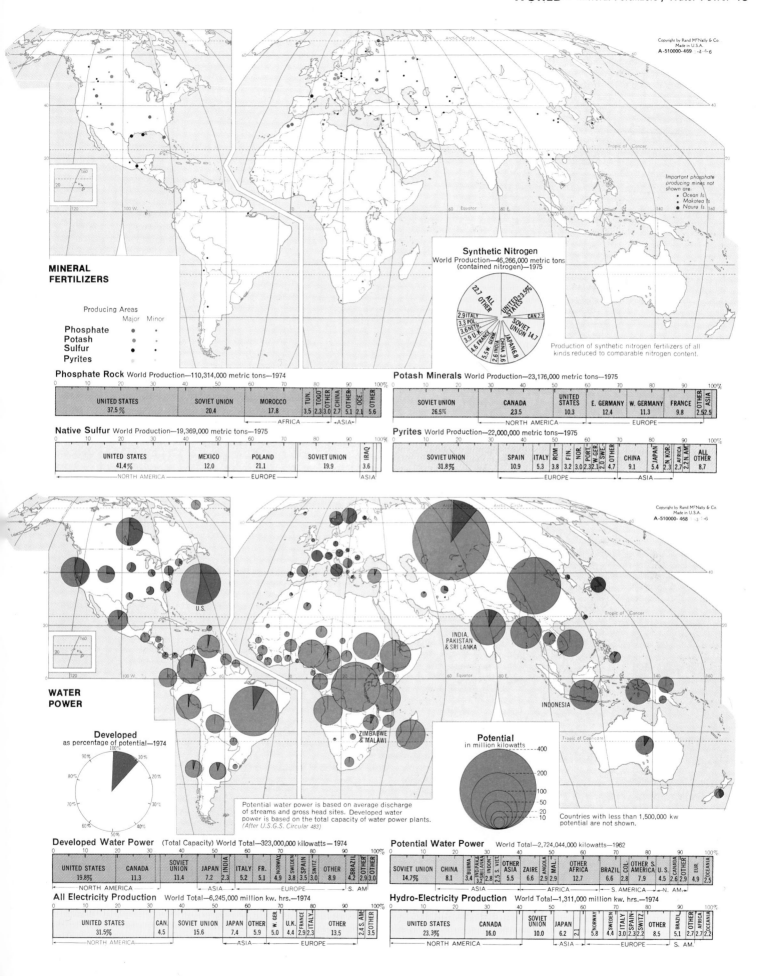

Important phosphate
producing mines not
shown are:
● Ocean Is.
▲ Makatea Is.
● Nauru Is.

MINERAL FERTILIZERS

Producing Areas

	Major	Minor
Phosphate	●	·
Potash	●	·
Sulfur	●	·
Pyrites	●	·

Synthetic Nitrogen
World Production—46,266,000 metric tons
(contained nitrogen)—1975

UNITED STATES 23.5%
CAN.2.3
SOVIET UNION 14.7
JAPAN 6.8
CHINA 3.6
2.6 INDIA
3.5 W. GER.
4.6 FRANCE
3.9 U.K.
3.6 NETH.
3.3 POL.
2.9 ITALY
22.7 ALL OTHER

Production of synthetic nitrogen fertilizers of all
kinds reduced to comparable nitrogen content.

Phosphate Rock World Production—110,314,000 metric tons—1974

0	10	20	30	40	50	60	70	80	90	100%

UNITED STATES 37.5%	SOVIET UNION 20.4	MOROCCO 17.8	TUN. 3.5	TOGO 2.3	OTHER 3.0	CHINA 2.7	OCE. 5.1	2.1	OTHER 5.6

AFRICA — ASIA

Native Sulfur World Production—19,369,000 metric tons—1975

0	10	20	30	40	50	60	70	80	90	100%

UNITED STATES 41.4%	MEXICO 12.0	POLAND 21.1	SOVIET UNION 19.9	IRAQ 3.6

NORTH AMERICA — EUROPE — ASIA

Potash Minerals World Production—23,176,000 metric tons—1975

0	10	20	30	40	50	60	70	80	90	100%

SOVIET UNION 26.5%	CANADA 23.5	UNITED STATES 10.3	E. GERMANY 12.4	W. GERMANY 11.3	FRANCE 9.8	OTHER 2.5	ASIA 2.5

NORTH AMERICA — EUROPE

Pyrites World Production—22,000,000 metric tons—1975

0	10	20	30	40	50	60	70	80	90	100%

SOVIET UNION 31.8%	SPAIN 10.9	ITALY 5.3	ROM. 3.8	FIN. 3.2	NOR. 3.0	PORT. 2.3	W. GER. 2.1	SWE. 2.0	OTHER 4.7	CHINA 9.1	JAPAN 5.4	N.KOR.	AFRICA 2.2	N. AM.	ALL OTHER 8.7

EUROPE — ASIA

WATER POWER

U.S.

INDIA, PAKISTAN & SRI LANKA

INDONESIA

ZIMBABWE & MALAWI

Developed
as percentage of potential—1974

100% 10%
90% 20%
80% 30%
70% 40%
60% 50%

Potential water power is based on average discharge
of streams and gross head sites. Developed water
power is based on the total capacity of water power plants.
(After U.S.G.S. Circular 483)

Potential
in million kilowatts

— 400
— 200
— 100
— 50
— 20
— 10

Countries with less than 1,500,000 kw
potential are not shown.

Developed Water Power (Total Capacity) World Total—323,000,000 kilowatts—1974

0	10	20	30	40	50	60	70	80	90	100%

UNITED STATES 19.8%	CANADA 11.3	SOVIET UNION 11.4	JAPAN 7.2	INDIA 2.3	ITALY 5.2	FR. 5.1	NORWAY 4.9	SWEDEN 3.8	SPAIN 3.5	SWITZ. 3.0	OTHER 8.9	BRAZIL 4.2	OTHER 2.9 3.0

NORTH AMERICA — ASIA — EUROPE — S. AM.

Potential Water Power World Total—2,724,044,000 kilowatts—1962

0	10	20	30	40	50	60	70	80	90	100%

SOVIET UNION 14.7%	CHINA 8.1	BURMA 3.4	INDIA PAKISTAN & SRI LANKA 3.2	INDON. 2.8	S. VIET 2.1	OTHER ASIA 5.5	ZAIRE 6.6	ANGOLA 2.9	MAL. 2.9	OTHER AFRICA 12.7	BRAZIL 6.6	COL. 2.8	OTHER S. AMERICA 7.9	U.S. 4.5	CANADA 2.6	OTHER 2.9	AFRICA 2.7	EUR. 4.9	OCEANIA 2.5

ASIA — AFRICA — S. AMERICA — N. AM.

All Electricity Production World Total—6,245,000 million kw. hrs.—1974

0	10	20	30	40	50	60	70	80	90	100%

UNITED STATES 31.5%	CAN. 4.5	SOVIET UNION 15.6	JAPAN 7.4	OTHER 5.9	W. GER. 5.0	U.K. 4.4	FRANCE 2.9	ITALY 2.3	OTHER 13.5	S. AM. 2.4	OTHER 3.5

NORTH AMERICA — ASIA — EUROPE

Hydro-Electricity Production World Total—1,311,000 million kw. hrs.—1974

0	10	20	30	40	50	60	70	80	90	100%

UNITED STATES 23.3%	CANADA 16.0	SOVIET UNION 10.0	JAPAN 6.2	2.1	NORWAY 5.8	SWEDEN 4.4	ITALY 3.0	SPAIN 2.7	SWITZ.	OTHER 8.5	BRAZIL 5.1	OTHER 2.7	AFRICA 2.7	OCEANIA 2.2

NORTH AMERICA — ASIA — EUROPE — S. AM.

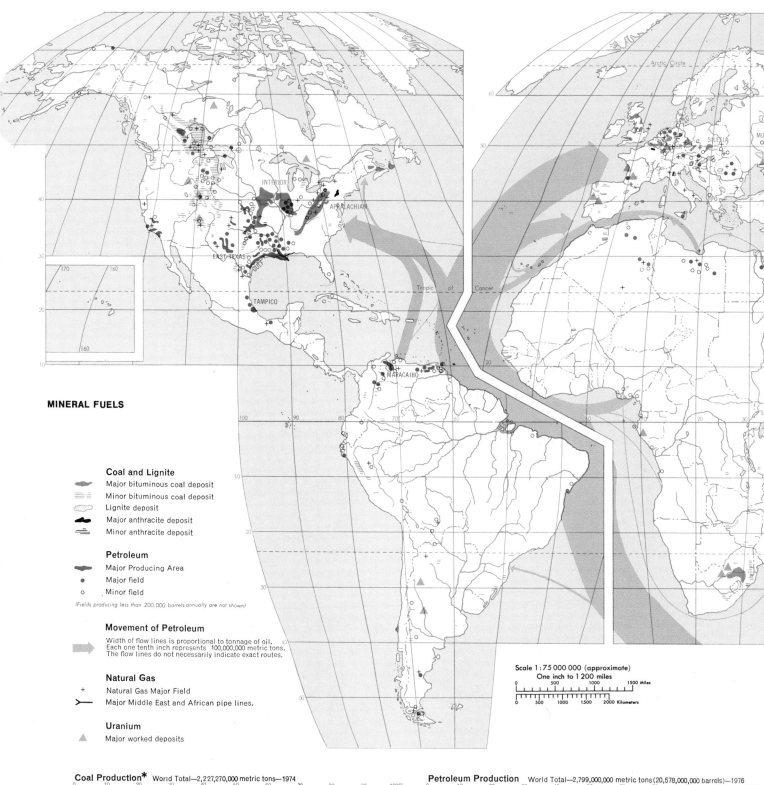

MINERAL FUELS

Coal and Lignite
- Major bituminous coal deposit
- Minor bituminous coal deposit
- Lignite deposit
- Major anthracite deposit
- Minor anthracite deposit

Petroleum
- Major Producing Area
- Major field
- Minor field

(Fields producing less than 200,000 barrels annually are not shown)

Movement of Petroleum

Width of flow lines is proportional to tonnage of oil.
Each one tenth inch represents 100,000,000 metric tons.
The flow lines do not necessarily indicate exact routes.

Natural Gas
- + Natural Gas Major Field
- Major Middle East and African pipe lines.

Uranium
- Major worked deposits

Scale 1 : 75 000 000 (approximate)
One inch to 1 200 miles

0   500   1000   1500 Miles

0   500   1000   1500   2000 Kilometers

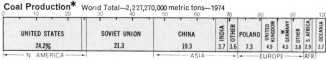

Coal Production* World Total—2,227,270,000 metric tons—1974

UNITED STATES 24.2%	SOVIET UNION 21.3	CHINA 19.3	INDIA 3.7	OTHER 3.6	POLAND 7.3	UNITED KINGDOM 4.9	W. GERMANY 4.5	E. GER. 3.8	S. AFRICA 2.9	OCEANIA 2.7
← N. AMERICA →		← ASIA →			← EUROPE →				AFR.	

*Bituminous and Anthracite Lignite World Total—749,975,000 metric tons, 19% of which was produced in the Soviet Union.

Coal Reserves** World Total—1,417,048,000,000 metric tons—1975

UNITED STATES 25.6%	CHINA 21.1	OTHER 2.8	SOVIET UNION 19.3	W. GER. 7.1	UNITED KINGDOM 7.0	POLAND 2.7	E. GER. 2.1	OTHER 3.5	AUSTRALIA 5.2	AFRICA 2.1
← N. AMERICA →	← ASIA →			← EUROPE →					OCE.	

Petroleum Production World Total—2,799,000,000 metric tons (20,578,000,000 barrels)—1976

SOVIET UNION 18.2%	SAUDI ARABIA 14.7	IRAN 10.5	IRAQ 3.7	KUWAIT 3.0	U.A.E. 2.4	INDONESIA 2.4	CHINA 2.7	OTHER 3.8	UNITED STATES 14.4	VENEZUELA 4.7	CANADA 2.3	OTHER 3.5	NIG. 3.6	LIBYA 3.4	OTHER 3.1	EUROPE 2.3
	← ASIA →								← W. HEMISPHERE →				← AFRICA →			

Petroleum Reserves World Total—75,530,000 metric tons (555,368,000,000 barrels)—Av. 1974

SAUDI ARABIA 19.6%	KUWAIT 13.7	IRAN 12.3	IRAQ 6.2	U.A.E. 4.6	CHINA 2.8	INDO. 2.1	SOVIET UNION 8.7	UNITED STATES 6.1	VEN. 2.8	OTHER 3.2	NIG. 3.5	OTHER 6.7	U.K. 2.2
← ASIA →								← W.HEMIS. →		← AFRICA →			EUR.

**Including lignite and coke

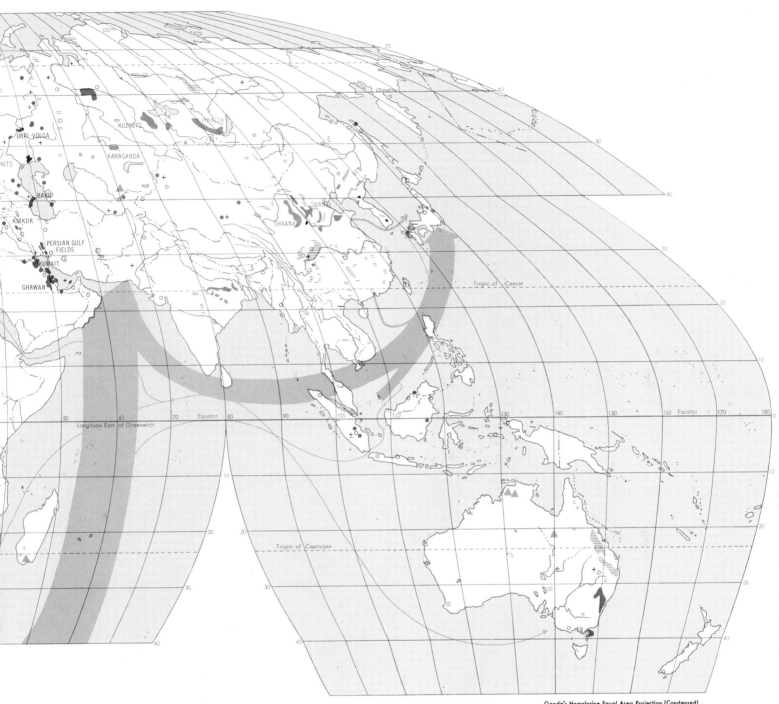

URAL-VOLGA

KUZNETS

IRKUTSK

KARAGANDA

NETS

BAKU

KIRKUK

PERSIAN GULF
FIELDS

KUWAIT

GHAWAR

SHANXI

SHAANXI

Tropic of Cancer

Equator

Longitude East of Greenwich

Tropic of Capricorn

Equator

Goode's Homolosine Equal Area Projection (Condensed)

Natural Gas Production. World Total—1,423,371,000,000 cubic meters—1976

10	20	30	40	50	60	70	80	90	100%		

| UNITED STATES 39.7% | CAN. 6.2 | OTHER 4.1 | SOVIET UNION 22.5 | NETH. 7.1 | U.K. 2.3 | OTHER 4.7 | IRAN 3.4 | CHINA 2.8 | OTHER 2.0 | AFRICA 3.2 | ALL OTHER 2.0 |

W. HEMISPHERE — EUROPE — ASIA

Natural Gas Reserves World Total—59,195,000,000,000 cubic meters—1974

10	20	30	40	50	60	70	80	90	100%		

| SOVIET UNION 33.5% | IRAN 17.9 | SAUDI ARABIA 2.9 | OTHER 8.5 | UNITED STATES 11.3 | CAN. 2.7 | VEN. 2.1 | OTHER 3.7 | ALGERIA 4.7 | NIG. 2.4 | OTHER 2.2 | NETH. 3.7 | OTHER 4.4 |

ASIA — W. HEMIS. — AFRICA EUROPE

Uranium Production World total— 27,800 metric tons—1976

0	10	20	30	40	50	60	70	80	90	100%

| UNITED STATES 44.0% | CANADA 24.8 | SOUTH AFRICA 10.5 | NIGER 6.5 | GABON 3.9 | FRANCE 7.2 | OTHER 3.1 |

NORTH AMERICA — AFRICA — EUR.

Uranium Reserves World Total—1,080,000 metric tons—1975

0	10	20	30	40	50	60	70	80	90	100%

| UNITED STATES 29.6% | CANADA 13.3 | AUSTRALIA 22.5 | SOUTH AFRICA 17.2 | NIGER 3.7 | ALGERIA 2.6 | OTHER 2.8 | FRANCE 3.4 | OTHER 2.0 | ALL OTHER 2.9 |

N. AMERICA — AFRICA — EUR.

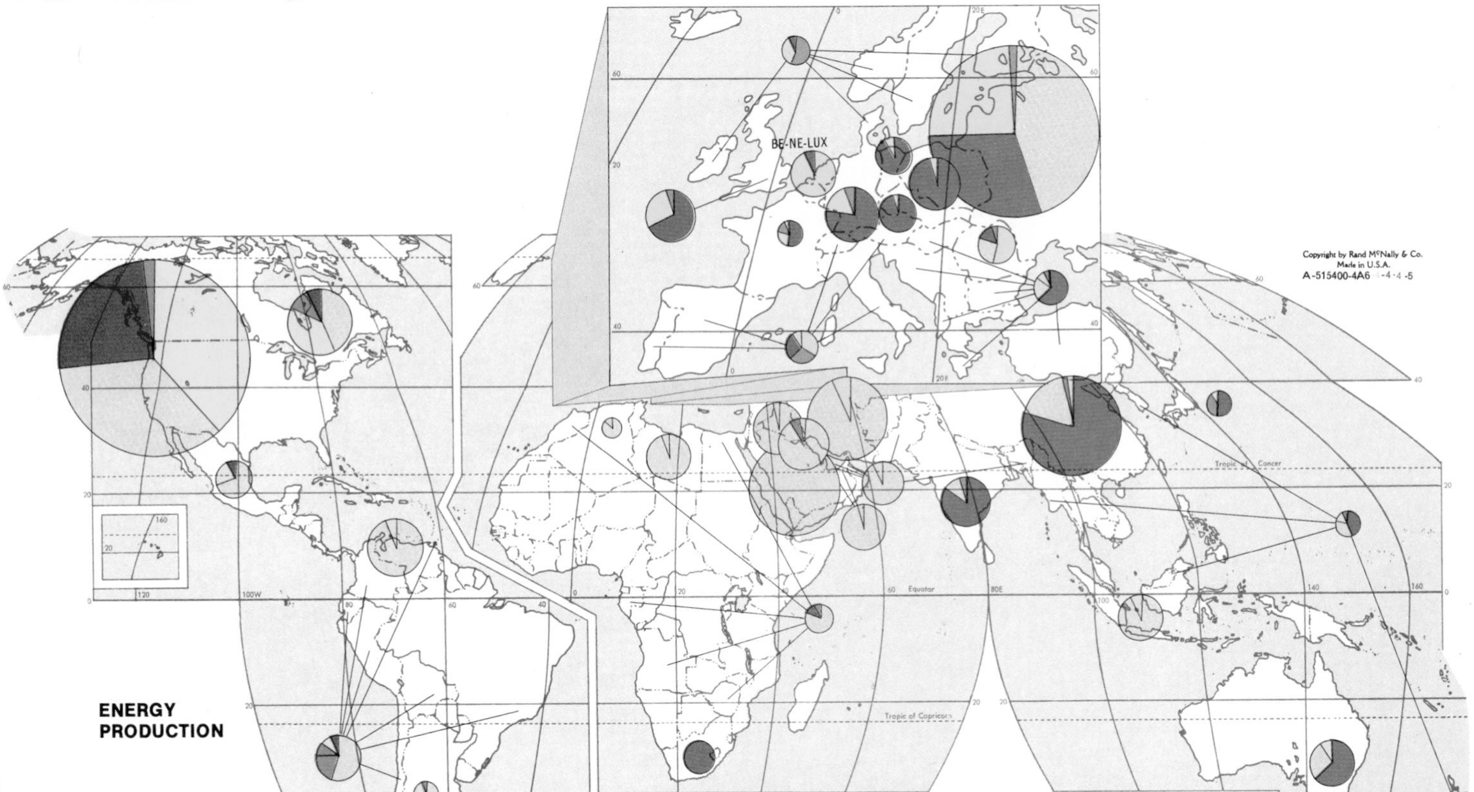

**ENERGY
PRODUCTION**

Energy Production World Total—8,554,765,000 metric tons (coal equivalent)—1975

0	10	20	30	40	50	60	70	80	90	100%

UNITED STATES	CAN.	SOVIET UNION	CHINA	SAUDI ARABIA	IRAN	KUWAIT	OTHER	VEN.	POLAND	U.K.	W. GER.	OTHER	AFRICA
23.8%	3.1	19.3	7.0	6.2	5.0	2.0	8.7	2.4	2.2	2.1	2.0	8.1	5.3

— NORTH AMERICA —   — ASIA —   — S.A — EUROPE —

Volume of Energy
in millions of metric tons
(Coal equivalent)

- - - - 2,500
— 1,000
— 500
— 250
— 100
— 0–4

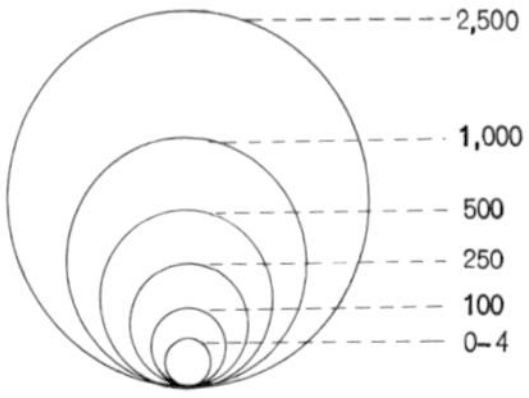

All countries with less than 0.5 million metric tons
(Coal Equivalent) are not shown.

Composition of Energy
(Data based on 1975)

Solid fuels	Liquid fuels	Natural and imported gas	Hydro, nuclear & imported electricity	All other

Per Capita Consumption
(Kg. per capita—1974)

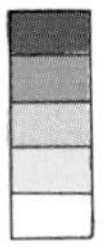

- 3,600-10,800 kg.*
- 1,200-3,600
- 400-1,200
- < 400
- Uninhabited or sparsely populated

* Netherland Antilles and Kuwait exceed this level.

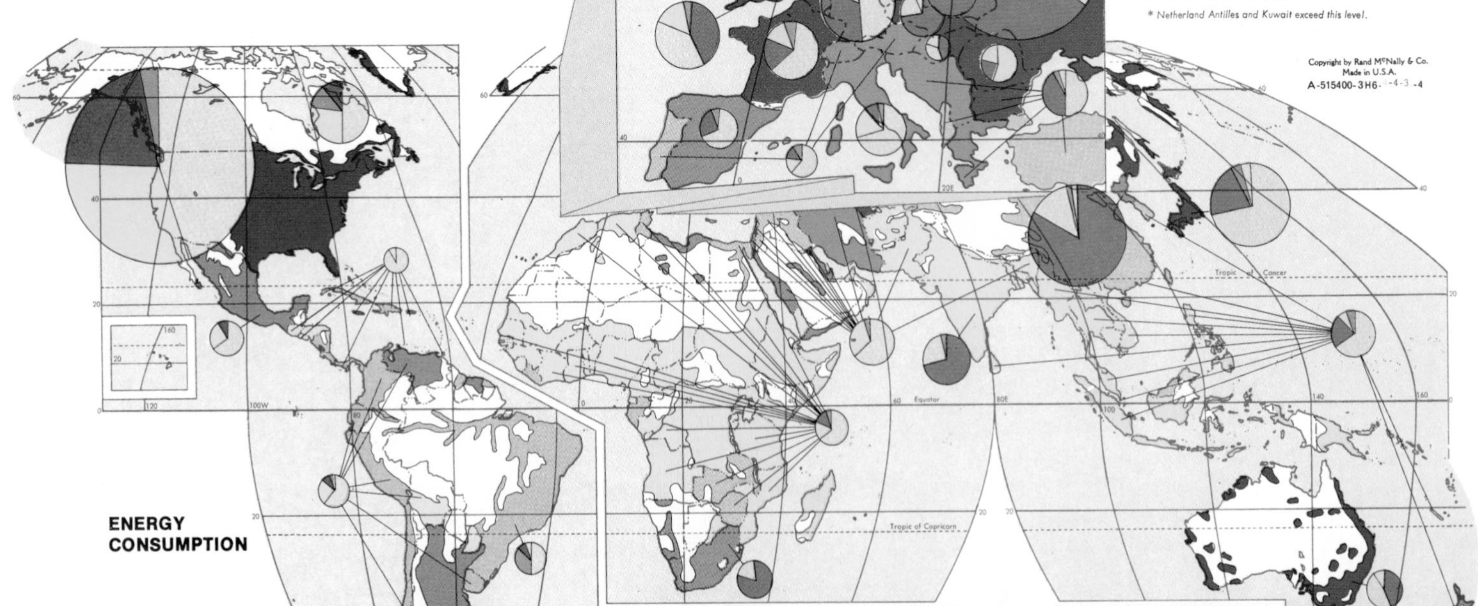

**ENERGY
CONSUMPTION**

Energy Consumption World Total—8,291,379,000 metric tons (coal equivalent)—1975

0	10	20	30	40	50	60	70	80	90	100%

UNITED STATES	CAN.	SOVIET UNION	CHINA	JAPAN	OTHER	W. GER.	FR.	U.K.	ITALY	OTHER	S. AM.	AFRICA
28.3%	2.7	17.0	6.9	4.8	5.4	3.5	2.5	2.0	2.0	15.8	2.4	2.0

— N. AMERICA —   — ASIA —   — EUROPE —

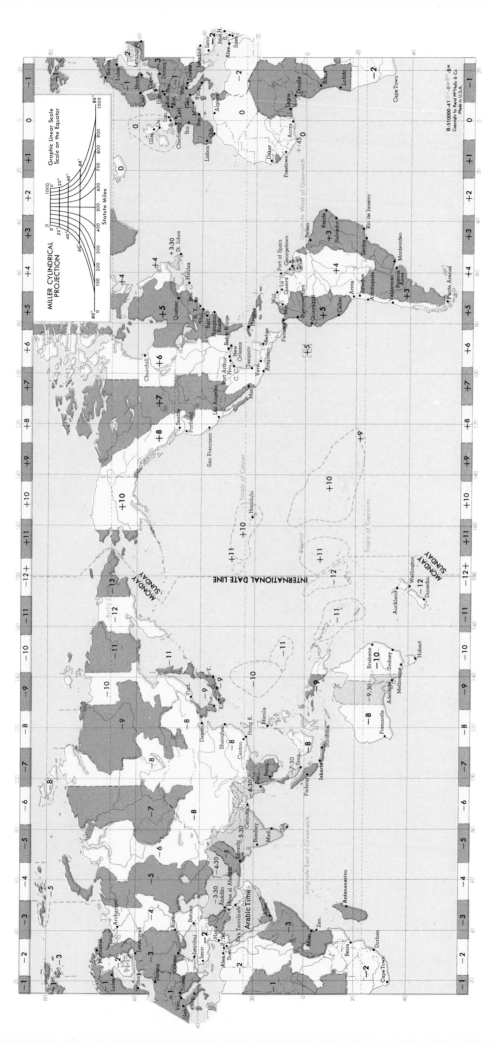

Time Zones

The surface of the earth is divided into 24 time zones. Each zone represents 15° of longitude or one hour of time. The time of the initial, or zero, zone is based on the central meridian of Greenwich and is adopted eastward and westward for a distance of 7½° of longitude. Each of the zones in turn is designated by a number representing the hours (+ or —) by which its standard time differs from

Greenwich mean time. These standard time zones are shown by bands of brown and yellow. Orange indicates areas which have a fractional deviation from standard time. The irregularities in the zones and the fractional deviations are due to political and economic factors.

(Revised to 1973. After U.S. Oceanographic Office)

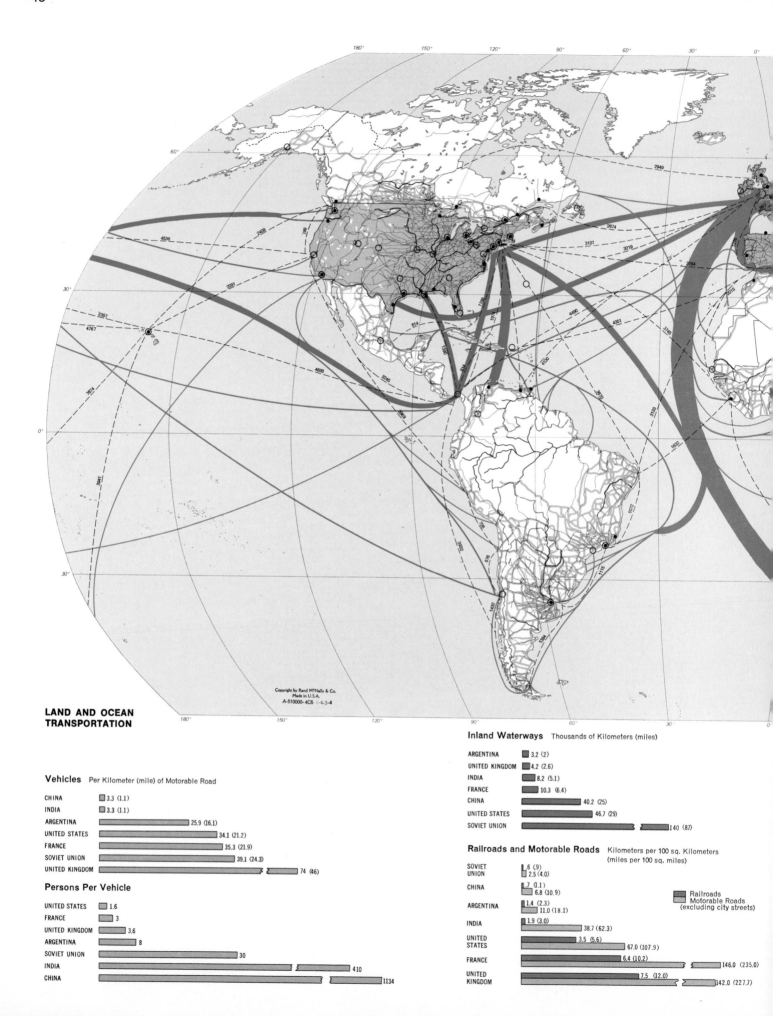

48

LAND AND OCEAN TRANSPORTATION

Vehicles Per Kilometer (mile) of Motorable Road

CHINA	3.3 (1.1)
INDIA	3.3 (1.1)
ARGENTINA	25.9 (16.1)
UNITED STATES	34.1 (21.2)
FRANCE	35.3 (21.9)
SOVIET UNION	39.1 (24.3)
UNITED KINGDOM	74 (46)

Persons Per Vehicle

UNITED STATES	1.6
FRANCE	3
UNITED KINGDOM	3.6
ARGENTINA	8
SOVIET UNION	30
INDIA	410
CHINA	1134

Inland Waterways Thousands of Kilometers (miles)

ARGENTINA	3.2 (2)
UNITED KINGDOM	4.2 (2.6)
INDIA	8.2 (5.1)
FRANCE	10.3 (6.4)
CHINA	40.2 (25)
UNITED STATES	46.7 (29)
SOVIET UNION	140 (87)

Railroads and Motorable Roads Kilometers per 100 sq. Kilometers (miles per 100 sq. miles)

SOVIET UNION	.6 (9)
	2.5 (4.0)
CHINA	.7 (1.1)
	6.8 (10.9)
ARGENTINA	1.4 (2.3)
	11.0 (18.1)
INDIA	1.9 (3.0)
	38.7 (62.3)
UNITED STATES	3.5 (5.6)
	67.0 (107.9)
FRANCE	6.4 (10.2)
	146.0 (235.0)
UNITED KINGDOM	7.5 (12.0)
	142.0 (227.7)

Railroads
Motorable Roads (excluding city streets)

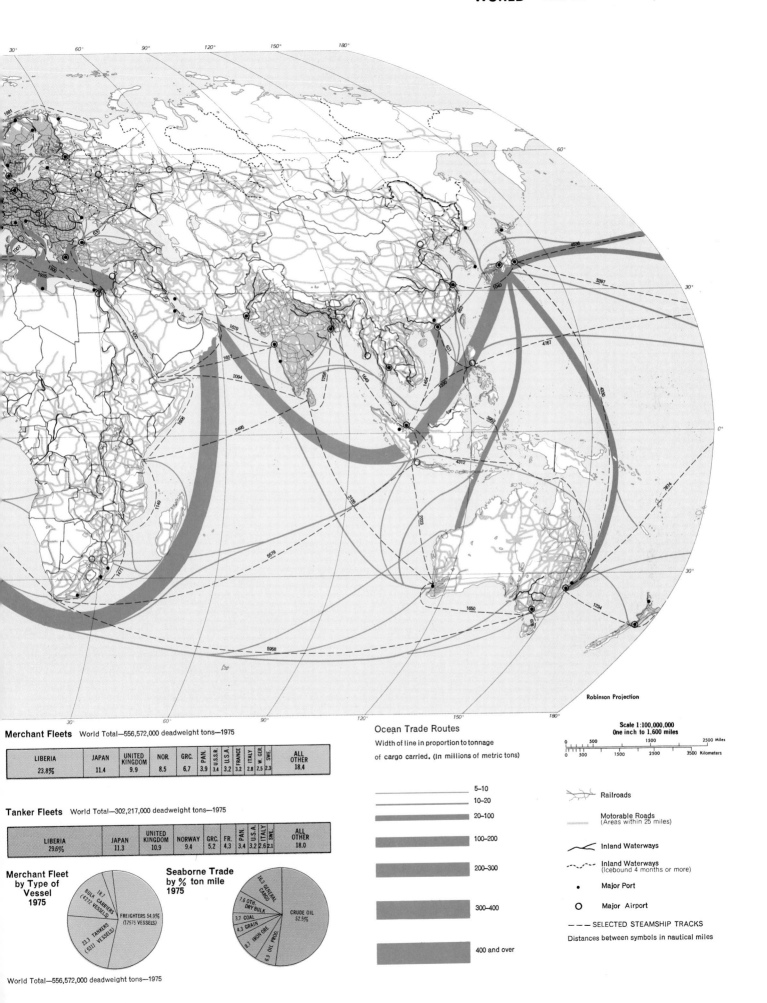

Ocean Trade Routes

Width of line in proportion to tonnage
of cargo carried. (In millions of metric tons)

Robinson Projection

Merchant Fleets World Total—556,572,000 deadweight tons—1975

LIBERIA 23.8%	JAPAN 11.4	UNITED KINGDOM 9.9	NOR. 8.5	GRC. 6.7	PAN. 3.9	U.S.S.R. 3.4	U.S.A. 3.2	FRANCE 2.8	ITALY 2.5	W. GER. 2.3	SWE. 2.3	ALL OTHER 18.4

Tanker Fleets World Total—302,217,000 deadweight tons—1975

LIBERIA 29.6%	JAPAN 11.3	UNITED KINGDOM 10.9	NORWAY 9.4	GRC. 5.2	FR. 4.3	PAN. 3.4	U.S.A. 3.2	ITALY 2.6	SWE. 2.1	ALL OTHER 18.0

Merchant Fleet by Type of Vessel 1975

BULK CARRIERS 18.7 (4272 VESSELS)
TANKERS 23.3 (3531 VESSELS)
FREIGHTERS 54.9% (12575 VESSELS)

World Total—556,572,000 deadweight tons—1975

Seaborne Trade by % ton mile 1975

16.3 GENERAL CARGO
7.6 OTH. DRY BULK
3.7 COAL
4.3 GRAIN
8.7 IRON ORE
6.3 OIL PROD.
CRUDE OIL 52.5%

Scale 1:100,000,000
One inch to 1,600 miles

0   500   1500   2500 Miles
0   500 1500 2500 3500 Kilometers

Railroads

Motorable Roads
(Areas within 25 miles)

Inland Waterways

Inland Waterways
(Icebound 4 months or more)

• Major Port

○ Major Airport

– – – SELECTED STEAMSHIP TRACKS

Distances between symbols in nautical miles

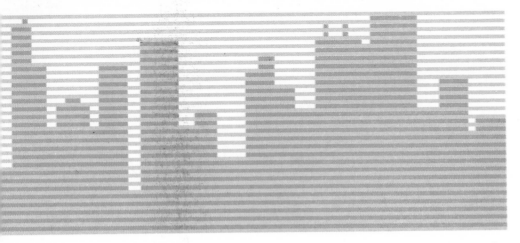

Major Cities

This section consists of 62 maps of the world's most populous metropolitan areas. In order to make comparisons easier, all the metropolitan areas are shown at the same scale, 1:300,000. An index to the places shown on the maps in this section can be found on page 232. The names of many large settlements, towns, suburbs, and neighborhoods can be located in these large-scale maps. For the symbols used on the maps, see the legend on the facing page.

The world is becoming increasingly urbanized as people move from country areas to city areas. This makes the study of metropolitan areas more important than ever before. The maps in this section enable the reader to study and compare urban extent, major industrial areas, parks, public land, wooded areas, airports, shopping centers, streets, and railroads. A special effort has been made to portray the various metropolitan areas in a manner as standard and comparable as possible.

Notable differences occur in the way cities are laid out. In most of North America, cities developed from a rectangular pattern of streets, with well-defined residential, commercial, and industrial zones. Most European cities are different and more complex. They have irregular street patterns and less well-defined land-use zones. In Asia, Africa, and South America the form tends to be even more irregular and complex, partly due to widespread dispersion of craft and trade activities. Some cities have no identifiable city centers, and some cities have both old and modern city centers.

Major City Map Legend

Inhabited Localities

The symbol represents the number of inhabitants within the locality

- • 0—10,000
- ○ 10,000—25,000
- ◉ 25,000—100,000
- ▣ 100,000—250,000
- ▤ 250,000—1,000,000
- ■ >1,000,000

The size of type indicates the relative economic and political importance of the locality

Écommoy	
Trouville	St.-Denis
Lisieux	PARIS

Hollywood ▪   Section of a City,
Westminster   Neighborhood
Northland ▪
Center   Major Shopping Center

 Urban Area (area of continuous industrial, commercial, and residential development)

 Major Industrial Area

 Wooded Area

Political Boundaries

International (First-order political unit)

▬▬▬▬ Demarcated, Undemarcated, and Administrative

▬ ▬ ▬ Demarcation Line

Internal

▬▬▬ State, Province, etc. (Second-order political unit)

▬▬▬ County, Oblast, etc. (Third-order political unit)

▬ ▬ ▬ Okrug, Kreis, etc. (Fourth-order political unit)

▬ ▬ ▬ City or Municipality (may appear in combination with another boundary symbol)

Capitals of Political Units

BUDAPEST   Independent Nation

Recife   State, Province, etc.

White Plains   County, Oblast, etc.

Iserlohn   Okrug, Kreis, etc.

Transportation

Road

Primary

Secondary

Tertiary

Railway

┼─CANADIAN NATIONAL─┼ Primary

┼──┼──┼ Secondary

────── Rapid Transit

Airport

 LONDON (HEATHROW) AIRPORT

Rail or Air Terminal

■ SÜD BAHNHOF

)(REICHS-BRÜCKE   Bridge

)(GREAT ST. BERNARD TUNNEL   Tunnel

Houston Ship Channel   Shipping Channel

Canal du Midi   Navigable Canal

TO MALMÖ   Ferry

Hydrographic Features

〜〜〜 Shoreline

- - - Undefined or Fluctuating Shoreline

Amur   River, Stream

- - - Intermittent Stream

≪≪≪   Rapids, Falls
SALTO ANGEL

Canal du Midi   Navigable Canal

▭   Irrigation or Drainage Canal

Los Angeles Aqueduct   Aqueduct

┼─────┼ Pier, Breakwater

〜〜〜 Reef
GREAT BARRIER REEF

L. Victoria   Lake, Reservoir

- - - Intermittent Lake

The Everglades   Swamp

Miscellaneous Cultural Features

PARQUE NACIONAL LANÍN
▲   National or State Park or Monument

FORT DIX
▪   Military Installation

GREENWOOD CEMETERY   Cemetery

▲
SORBONNE   Point of Interest (Battlefield, museum, temple, university, etc.)

⚲
STEPHANSDOM   Church, Monastery

∴
UXMAL   Ruins

Ψ
WINDSOR CASTLE   Castle

ℐ   Lighthouse

ASWĀN DAM \   Dam

<>   Lock

○
Crib   Water Intake Crib

▒   Quarry or Surface Mine

⋈   Subsurface Mine

Topographic Features

Mt. Kenya
5199 △   Elevation Above Sea Level

Elevations are given in meters

★   Rock

A N D E S   Mountain Range, Plateau,
KUNLUNSHANMAI   Valley, etc.

BAFFIN ISLAND   Island

POLUOSTROV
KAMČATKA   Peninsula, Cape, Point, etc.
CABO DE HORNOS

a

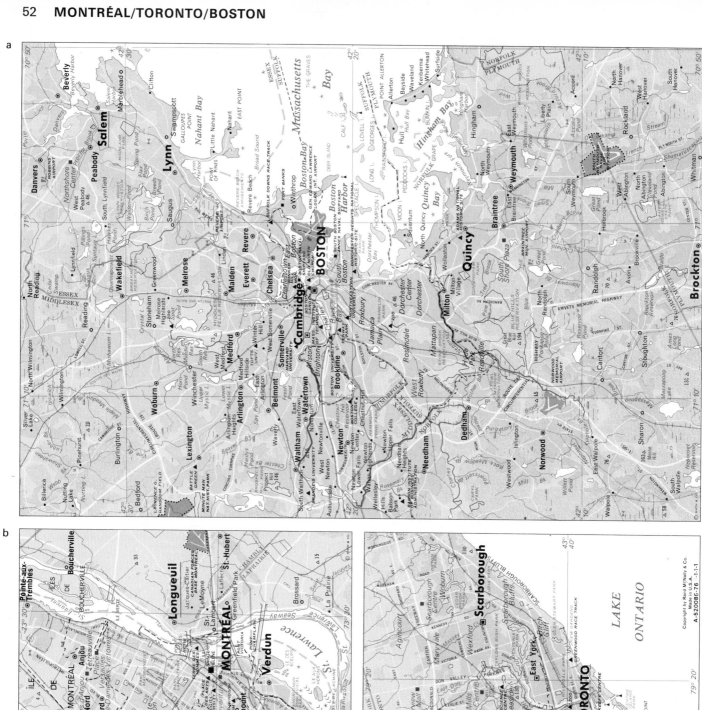

b

c

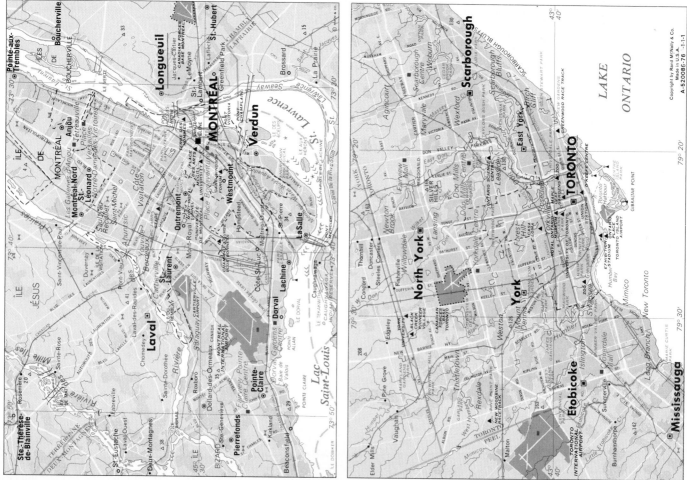

0   5   10 Miles

0   5   10 Kilometers

Scale 1:300,000; one inch to 4.7 miles.

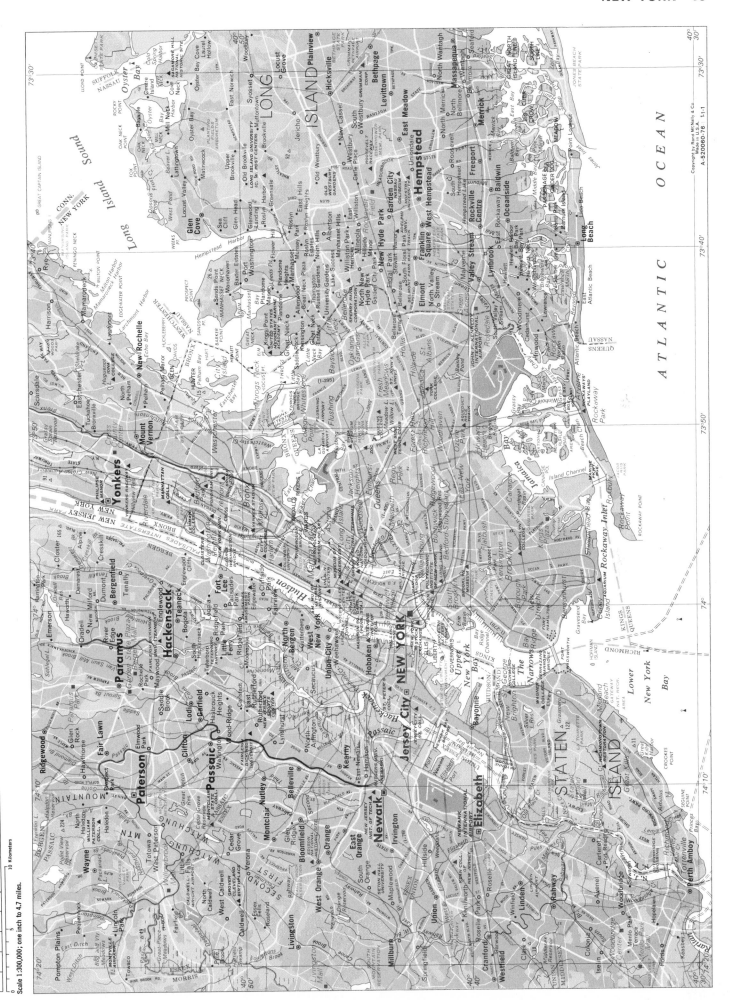

Scale 1:300,000; one inch to 4.7 miles.

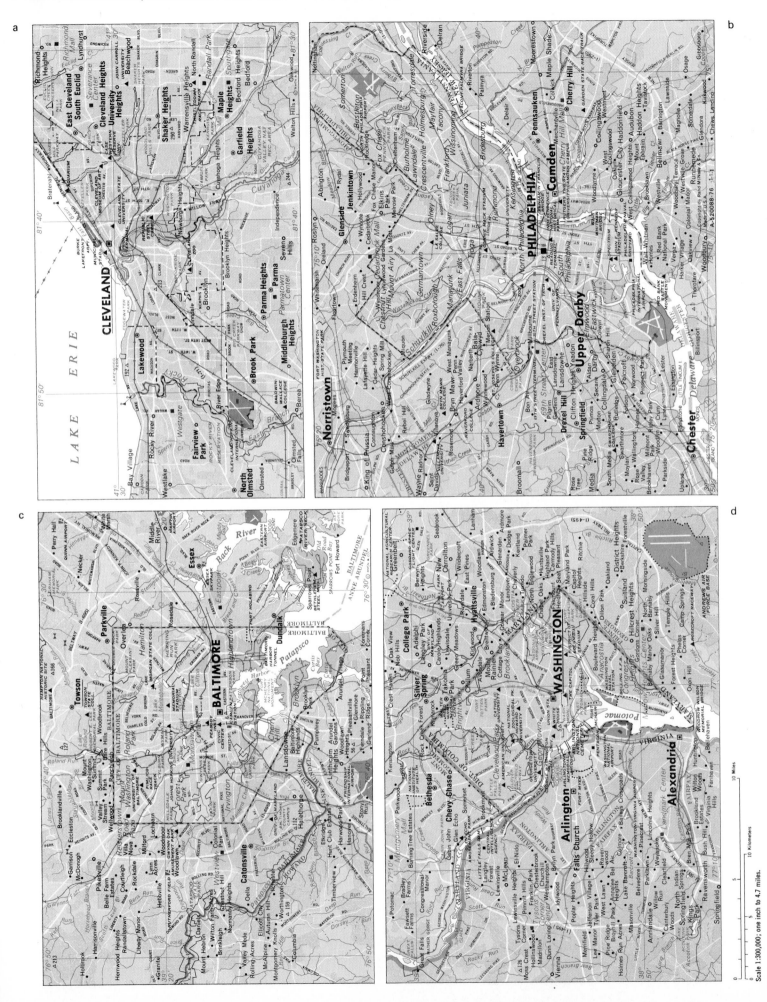

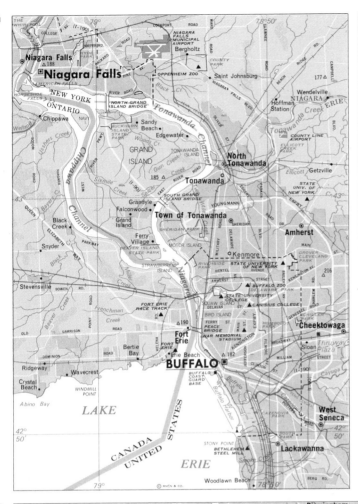

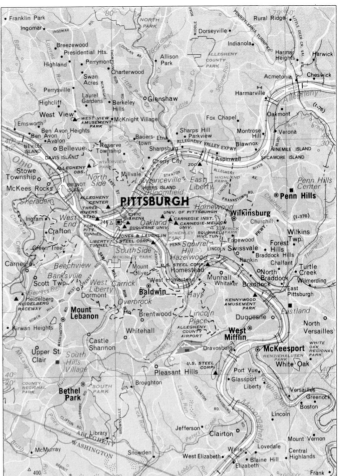

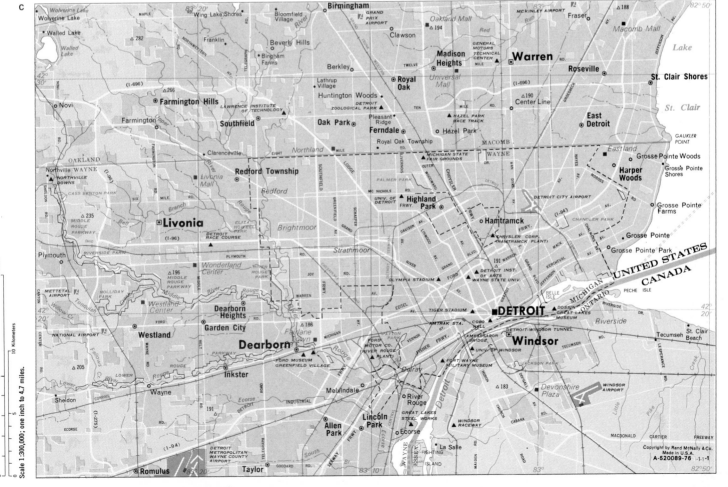

a

b

Scale 1:300,000; one inch to 4.7 miles.

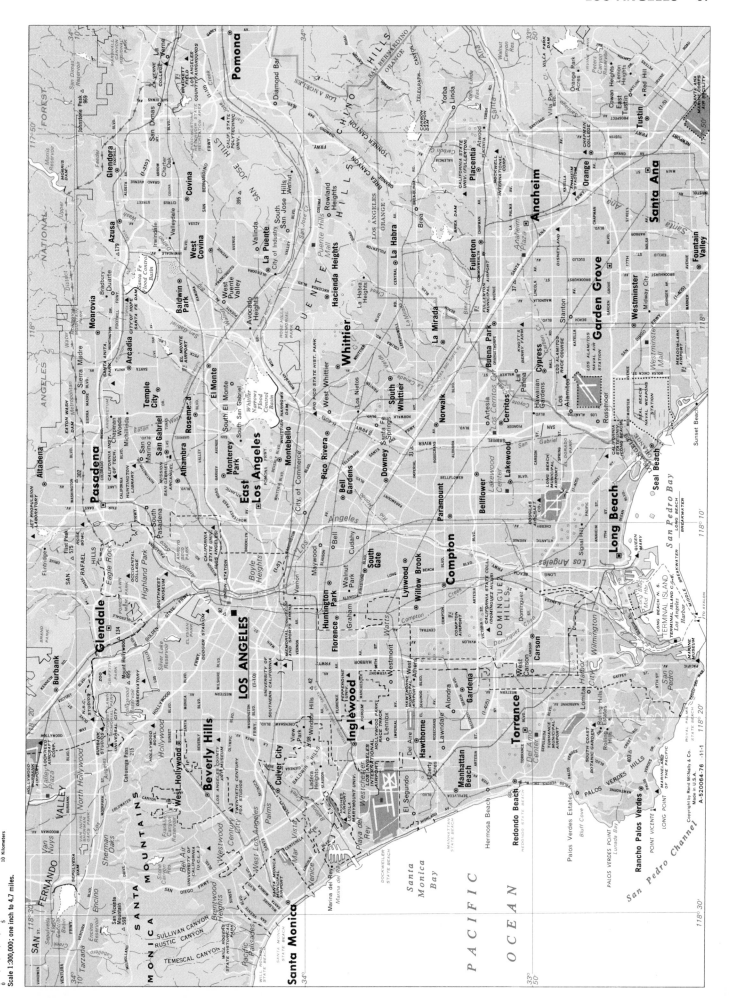

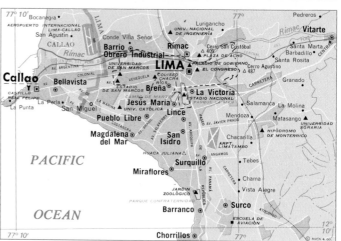

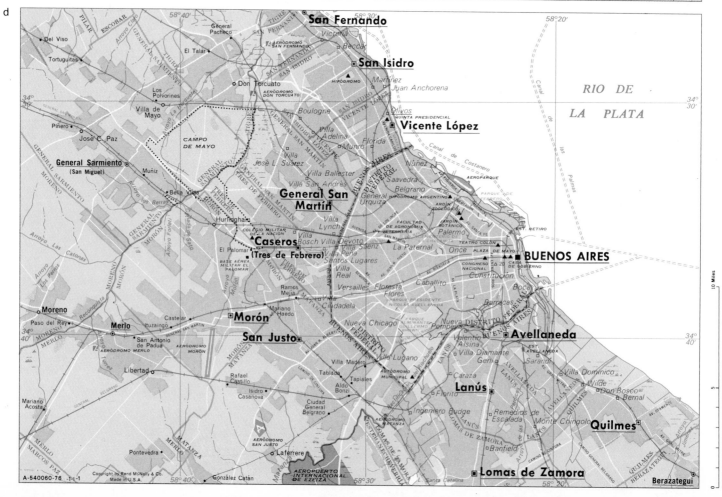

Scale 1:300,000; one inch to 4.7 miles.

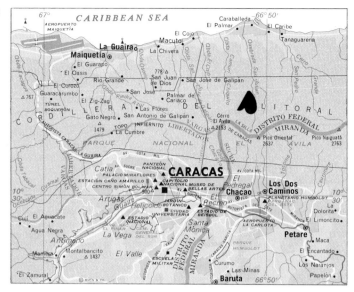

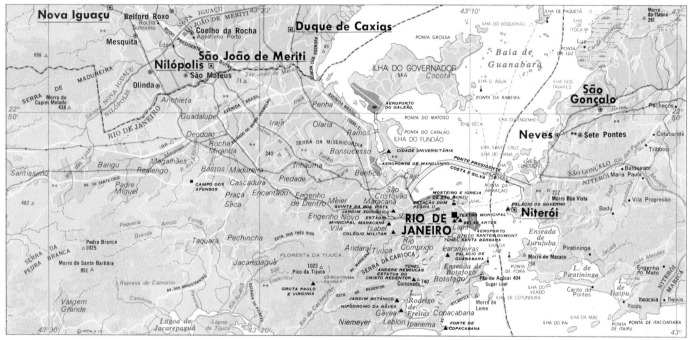
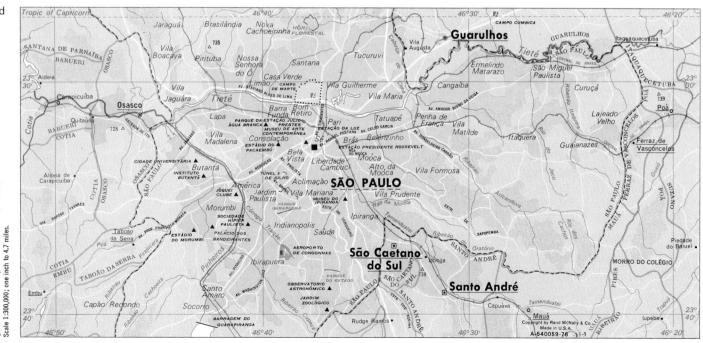

LONDON

Chelmsford

Basildon

Brentwood

Tilbury

Grays

Gravesend

Dartford

Sevenoaks

Saint Albans

Hemel Hempstead

Berkhamsted

Watford

Cheshunt

Loughton

Chigwell

Enfield

Barnet

Harrow on the Hill

Rickmansworth

Slough

Windsor

Woking

Weybridge

Walton

Leatherhead

Epsom

Ewell

Caterham

EPPING FOREST

GREATER LONDON

HERTFORDSHIRE

ESSEX

KENT

SURREY

BUCKINGHAMSHIRE

BERKSHIRE

Scale 1:300,000; one inch to 4.7 miles.

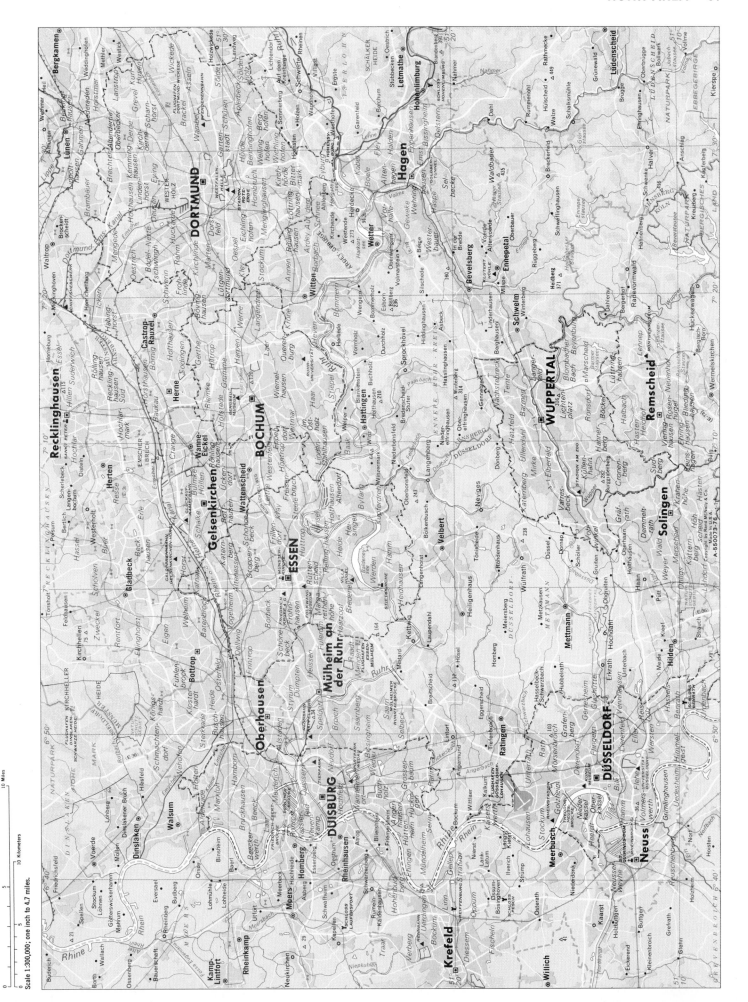

Scale 1:300,000; one inch to 4.7 miles.

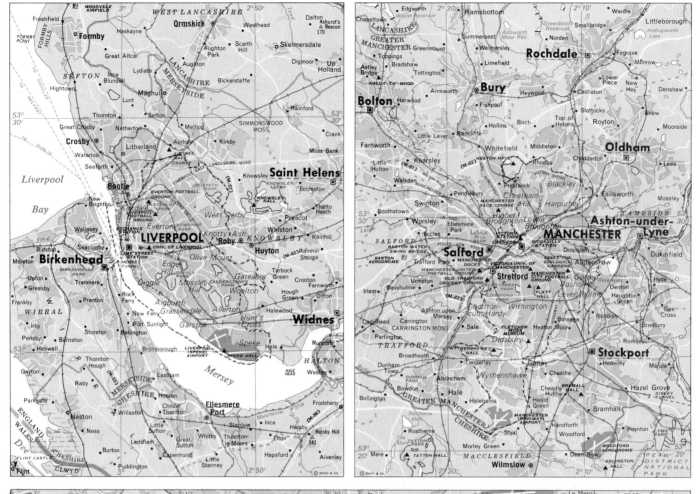

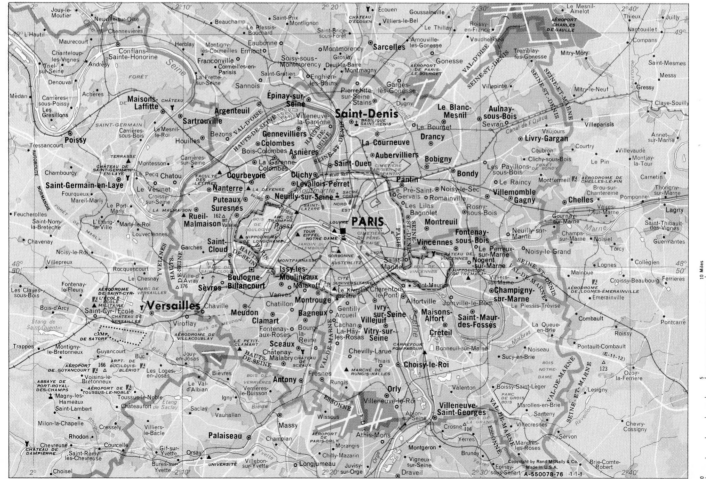

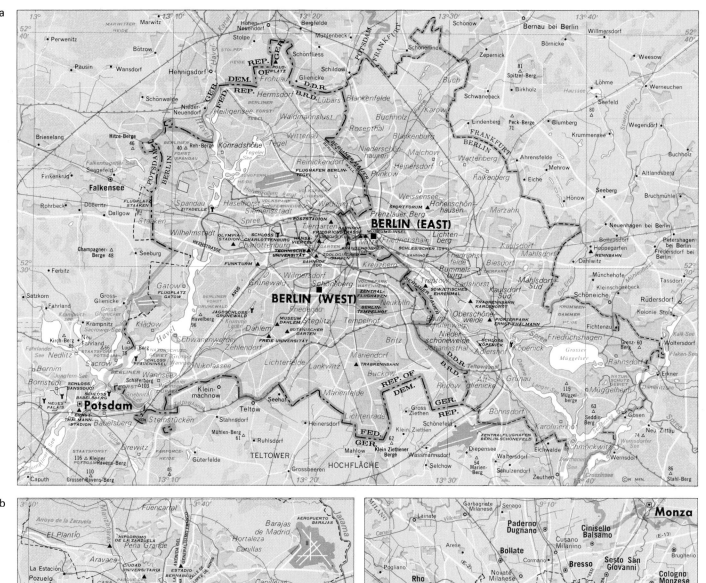

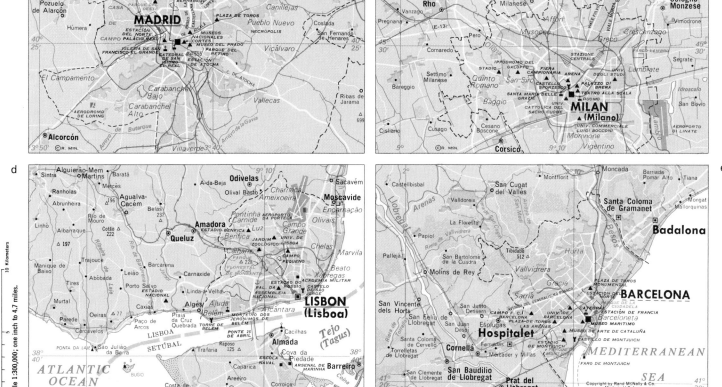

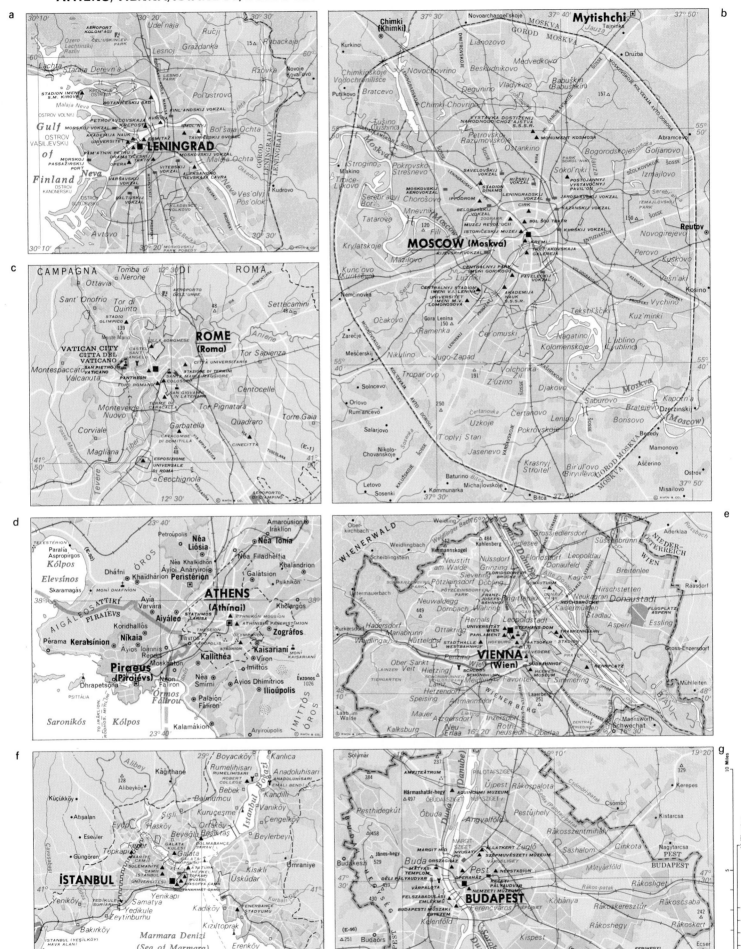

Copyright by Rand McNally & Co.
Made in U.S.A.

A-550080-76 -1-1-1

Scale 1:300,000; one inch to 4.7 miles.

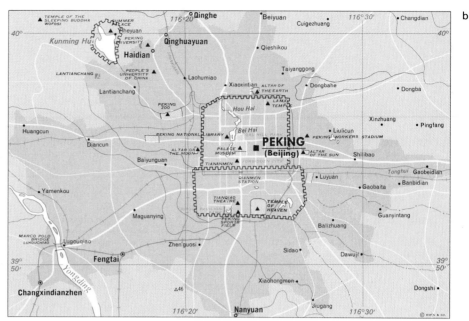

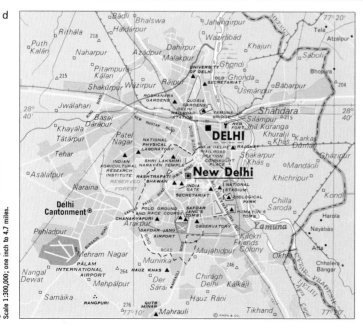

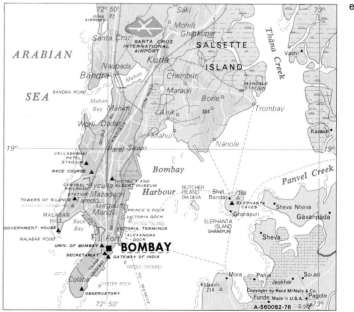

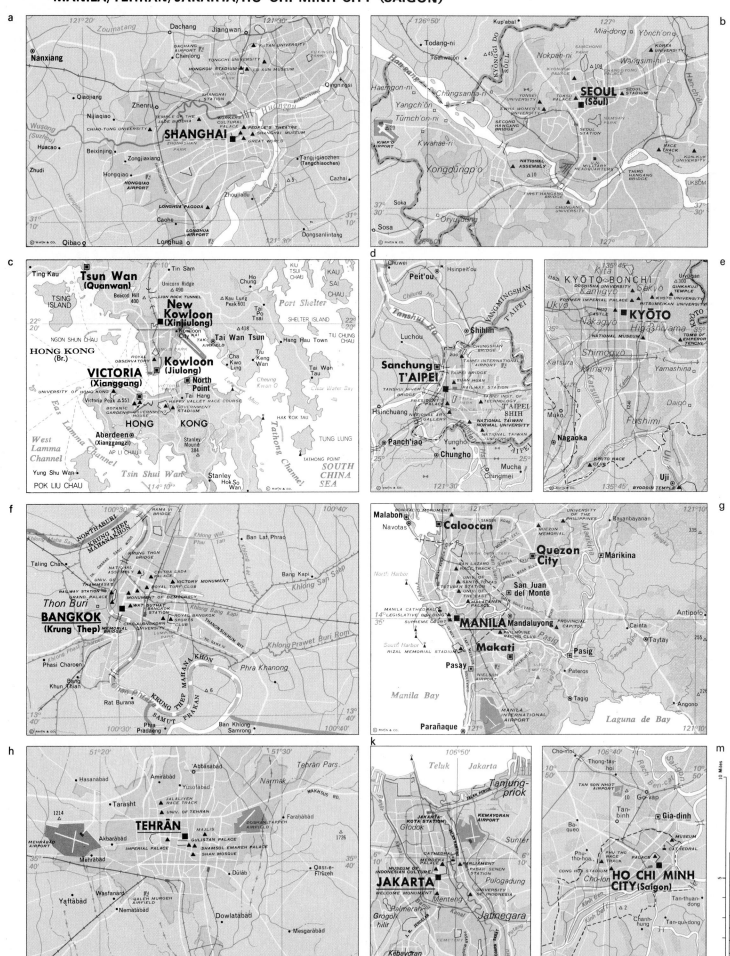

Scale 1:300,000; one inch to 4.7 miles.

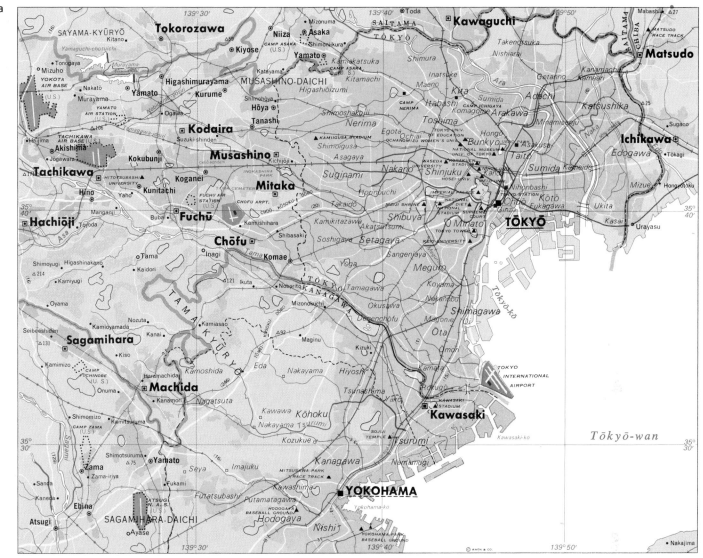

a
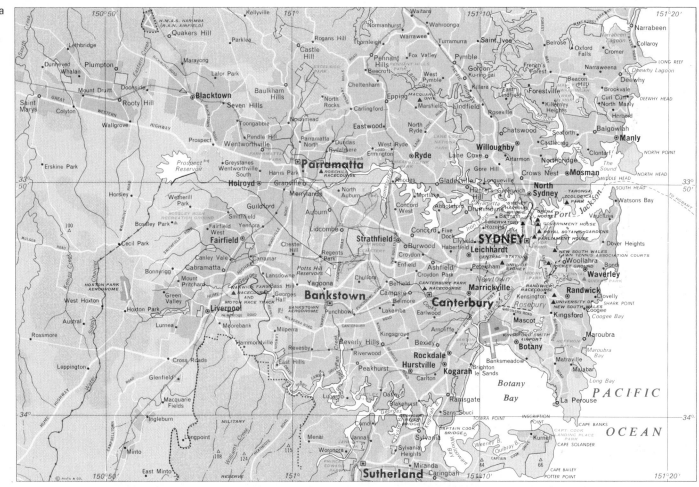

b

Scale 1:300,000; one inch to 4.7 miles.

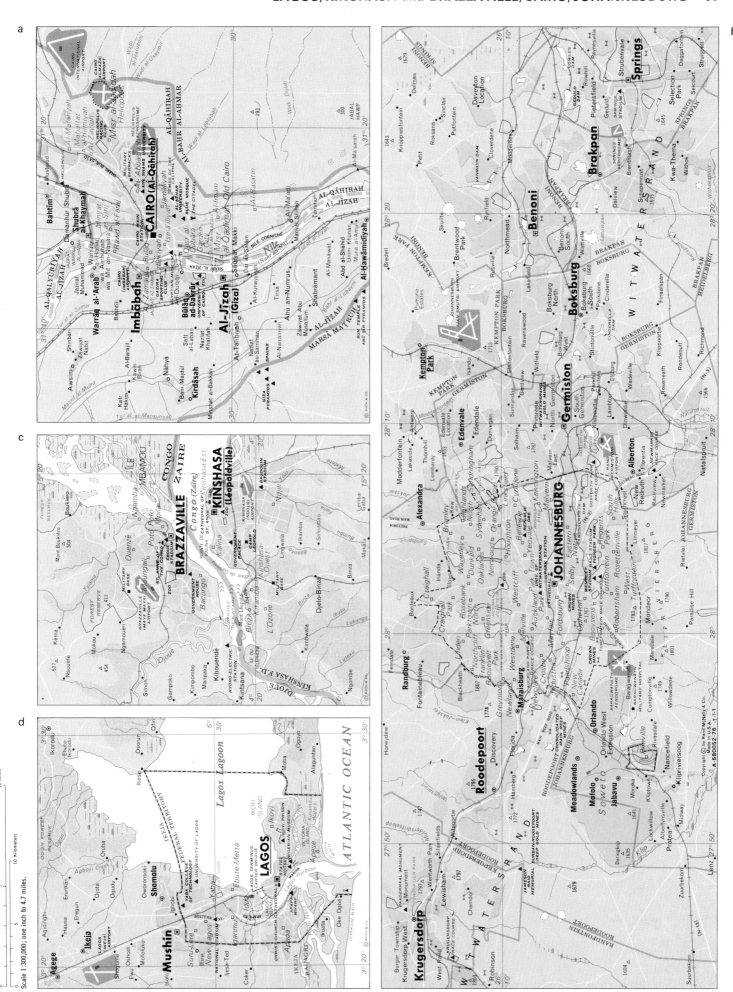

Scale 1:300,000; one inch to 4.7 miles.

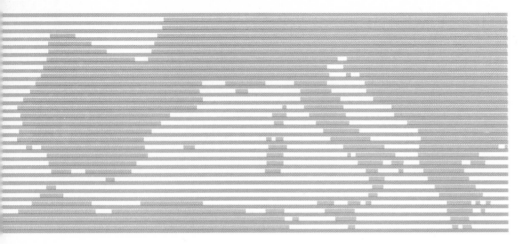

Country
and
Regional
Maps

This section provides the reader with basic continental, regional, and country reference maps of the world's land areas. The maps are arranged by continents: North America, South America, Europe, Asia, Australia, and Africa. Each section begins with a series of basic thematic maps dealing with the environment, culture, and economy of each continent. Place names on the reference maps are listed in the unique pronouncing index, the last section of the Atlas. A complete legend on the facing page provides a key to the symbols on the reference maps in this section.

To aid the reader in making comparisons, uniform scales for comparable areas were used whenever possible. All continental maps are at the same scale, 1:40,000,000. In addition, most of the world is covered by a series of regional maps at scales of 1:16,000,000 and 1:12,000,000.

Maps at 1:10,000,000 provide even greater detail for parts of Europe, Africa, and Southeast Asia. The United States, parts of Canada, and much of Europe and the Soviet Union are mapped at 1:4,000,000. Seventy-six urbanized areas are shown at 1:1,000,000.

The reference maps use different colors (layer tints) to show general elevation above and below sea level. A legend on each map provides a key to the colors used for elevation.

The maps also provide the reader with a three-dimensional impression of the way the land looks. This terrain representation, superimposed on the layer tints, provides a realistic and readily visualized impression of the surface.

This Atlas generally uses a *local name* policy for naming cities and towns and local land and water features. However, for a few major cities the Anglicized name is preferred and the local name given in parentheses, for instance, Moscow (Moskva), Vienna (Wien), Cologne (Köln). Names in Chinese, Japanese, and other nonalphabetic languages are transliterated into the Roman alphabet. In countries where more than one official language is used, the name is in the dominant local language. The generic parts of local names for land and water features are usually self-explanatory. A complete glossary of foreign geographical terms is given on page 245.

Country and Regional Map Legend

Cultural Features

Political Boundaries

━━ ─ ─ ─ (over water)   International
(Demarcated, Undemarcated, and Administrative)

━━ ─ ━ ─ ━ Disputed de facto

─ ─ ─ ─ ─ Disputed de jure

▬▬ ▬▬ ▬▬ ▬▬ Indefinite or Undefined

━━━ ─ ─ (over water)   Secondary, State, Provincial, etc.

◻ Parks, Indian Reservations

City Limits   Built-up Areas

Cities, Towns and Villages

🌳
PARIS   1,000,000 and over
(Metropolitan Area Population)

◎ 🏭
Ufa   500,000 to 1,000,000
(Metropolitan Area Population)

⊙
Győr   50,000 to 500,000

○
Agadir   25,000 to 50,000

○
Moreno   0 to 25,000

TŌKYŌ   National Capitals

Boise   Secondary Capitals

Note: On maps at 1:20,000,000 and smaller, and on maps at 1:1,000,000, the type size indicates the relative importance of cities, not the specific population classification shown above.

Transportation

─────   Railroads

────   Railroads
On 1:1,000,000 scale maps

─ ─ ─ ─   Railroad Ferries

Roads

Major
────   On 1:1,000,000 scale maps
Other

Major
────   On 1:4,000,000 scale maps
Other

────   On other scale maps

· · · · · · ·   Caravan Routes

✈   Airports

Other Cultural Features

〰╲   Dams

•─•─•─•   Pipelines

▲   Pyramids

∴   Ruins

Land Features

△   Peaks, Spot Heights

=   Passes

▨   Sand

⬭   Contours

Water Features

Lakes and Reservoirs

⬭   Fresh Water

⬭   Fresh Water: Intermittent

⬭   Salt Water

⬭   Salt Water: Intermittent

Other Water Features

⬭   Salt Basins, Flats

〰   Swamps

〰   Ice Caps and Glaciers

〰   Rivers

〰   Intermittent Rivers

┈┈┈   Aqueducts and Canals

════   Ship Channels

〰   Falls

┼┼┼   Rapids

♪   Springs

△   Water Depths

▨   Fishing Banks

▨   Sand Bars

〰〰   Reefs

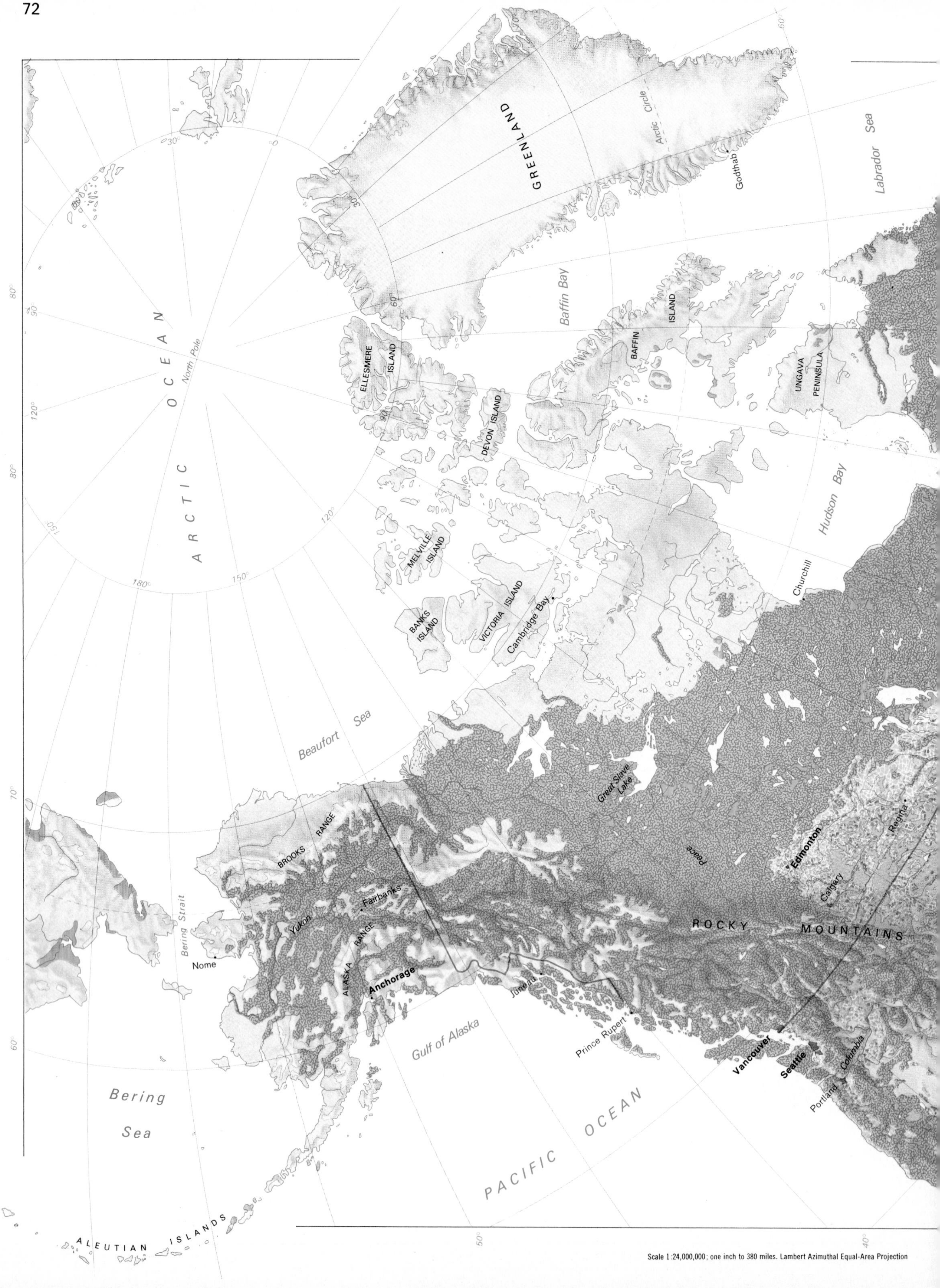

GREENLAND

Arctic Circle

Godthåb

Labrador Sea

Baffin Bay

ELLESMERE ISLAND

BAFFIN ISLAND

UNGAVA PENINSULA

A R C T I C   O C E A N

North Pole

DEVON ISLAND

Hudson Bay

MELVILLE ISLAND

Churchill

VICTORIA ISLAND

BANKS ISLAND

Cambridge Bay

Beaufort Sea

Great Slave Lake

Edmonton

Regina

Peace

Calgary

BROOKS RANGE

Fairbanks

R O C K Y   M O U N T A I N S

Yukon

Bering Strait

ALASKA RANGE

Nome

Anchorage

Juneau

Gulf of Alaska

Prince Rupert

Columbia

Vancouver

Seattle

Portland

Bering Sea

P A C I F I C   O C E A N

A L E U T I A N   I S L A N D S

Scale 1:24,000,000; one inch to 380 miles. Lambert Azimuthal Equal-Area Projection

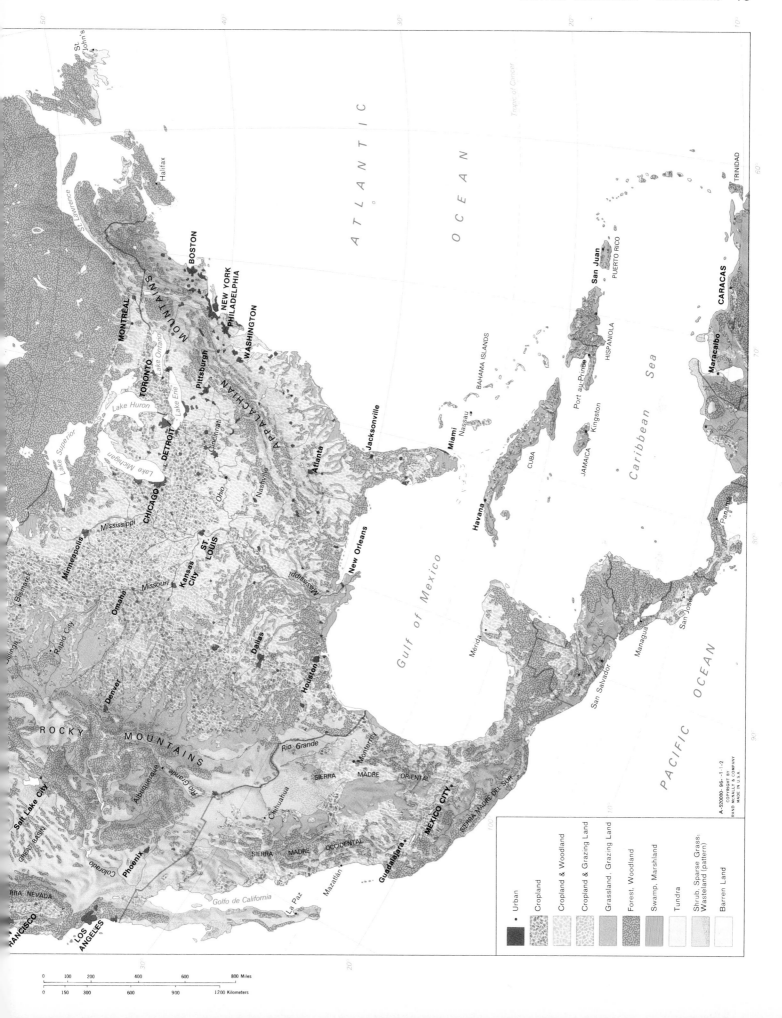

ATLANTIC OCEAN

PACIFIC OCEAN

St. John's

Halifax

BOSTON
NEW YORK
PHILADELPHIA
WASHINGTON
MONTRÉAL
TORONTO
Pittsburgh
DETROIT
Cincinnati
Nashville
Atlanta
Jacksonville
CHICAGO
ST. LOUIS
Kansas City
Minneapolis
Bismarck
Rapid City
Omaha
Denver
Dallas
Houston
New Orleans
Miami
Havana
Nassau
Kingston
Port au Prince
San Juan
CARACAS
Maracaibo
Mérida
Managua
San José
San Salvador
Panama
MEXICO CITY
Guadalajara
Monterrey
Chihuahua
Albuquerque
Phoenix
Salt Lake City
LOS ANGELES
SAN FRANCISCO
La Paz
Mazatlán

APPALACHIAN MOUNTAINS
ROCKY MOUNTAINS
SIERRA NEVADA
GREAT BASIN
SIERRA MADRE OCCIDENTAL
SIERRA MADRE ORIENTAL
SIERRA MADRE DEL SUR

Lake Superior
Lake Huron
Lake Michigan
Lake Erie
Lake Ontario
St. Lawrence
Mississippi
Missouri
Ohio
Rio Grande
Colorado
Golfo de California

BAHAMA ISLANDS
CUBA
JAMAICA
HISPANIOLA
PUERTO RICO
TRINIDAD
Caribbean Sea
Gulf of Mexico
Tropic of Cancer

Legend:
- Urban
- Cropland
- Cropland & Woodland
- Cropland & Grazing Land
- Grassland, Grazing Land
- Forest, Woodland
- Swamp, Marshland
- Tundra
- Shrub, Sparse Grass, Wasteland (pattern)
- Barren Land

A-520000.96—1 1-2
COPYRIGHT BY
RAND MCNALLY & COMPANY
MADE IN U.S.A.

0 100 200 400 600 800 Miles
0 150 300 600 900 1200 Kilometers

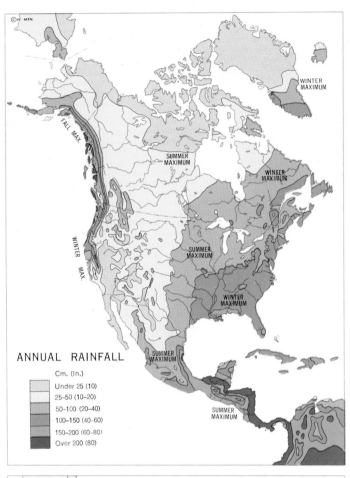

ANNUAL RAINFALL

Cm. (In.)

- Under 25 (10)
- 25–50 (10–20)
- 50–100 (20–40)
- 100–150 (40–60)
- 150–200 (60–80)
- Over 200 (80)

FALL MAX.
WINTER MAX.
WINTER MAX.
SUMMER MAXIMUM
WINTER MAXIMUM
SUMMER MAXIMUM
WINTER MAXIMUM
SUMMER MAXIMUM
SUMMER MAXIMUM

TUNDRA
TAIGA
PRAIRIE
CHAPARRAL

VEGETATION

G	Tall grass
L	Tundra
Ep.E.N	Coniferous forest
B	Tropical rain forest
S	Semideciduous forest
D	Deciduous forest
B.Bs	Mediterranean vegetation
M	Mixed forest: coniferous-deciduous
GDsp	Low grass savanna
Bsp	Desert shrub
Dxi	Xerophytic open forest
b	Little or no vegetation

For explanation of letters in boxes,
see Natural Vegetation Map by A. W Kuchler, **p. 16**

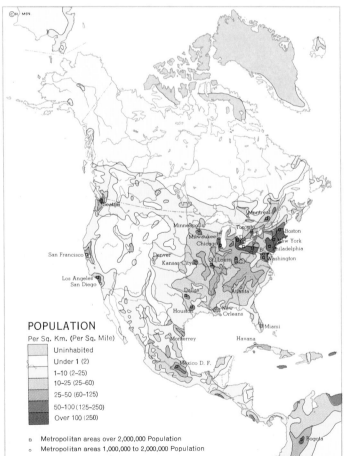

Seattle
Montreal
Minneapolis
Toronto
Milwaukee
Boston
Chicago
New York
San Francisco
Detroit
Philadelphia
Denver
Washington
Kansas City
St. Louis
Los Angeles
San Diego
Dallas
Atlanta
Houston
New Orleans
Miami
Monterrey
Havana
Mexico D. F.
Bogota

POPULATION

Per Sq. Km. (Per Sq. Mile)

- Uninhabited
- Under 1 (2)
- 1–10 (2–25)
- 10–25 (25–60)
- 25–50 (60–125)
- 50–100 (125–250)
- Over 100 (250)

□ Metropolitan areas over 2,000,000 Population
○ Metropolitan areas 1,000,000 to 2,000,000 Population

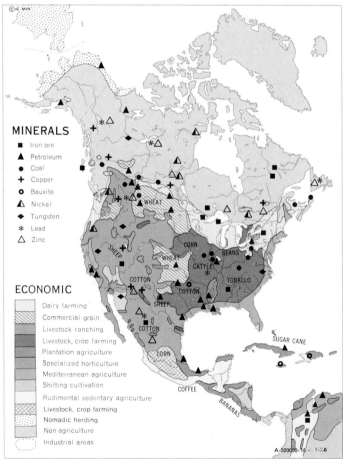

MINERALS

- ■ Iron ore
- ▲ Petroleum
- ● Coal
- + Copper
- ○ Bauxite
- △ Nickel
- ◆ Tungsten
- ✳ Lead
- △ Zinc

WHEAT
WHEAT
SHEEP
CORN
BEANS
CATTLE
COTTON
TOBACCO
COTTON
COTTON
SHEEP
CORN
COTTON
SUGAR CANE
COFFEE
BANANAS

ECONOMIC

- Dairy farming
- Commercial grain
- Livestock ranching
- Livestock, crop farming
- Plantation agriculture
- Specialized horticulture
- Mediterranean agriculture
- Shifting cultivation
- Rudimental sedentary agriculture
- Livestock, crop farming
- Nomadic herding
- Non agriculture
- Industrial areas

A-520000-16 - 1-2-6

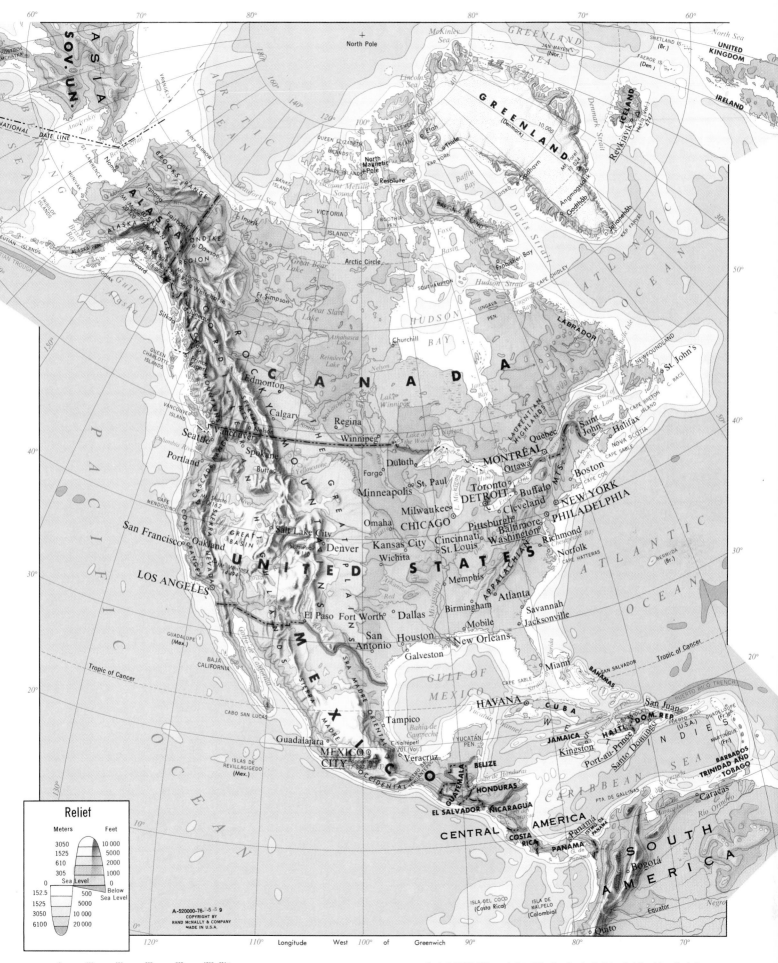

Relief

Meters	Feet
3050	10 000
1525	5000
610	2000
305	1000
0	Sea Level 0
	Below
152.5	500 Sea Level
1525	5000
3050	10 000
6100	20 000

A-520000-76- -5 -5 9
COPYRIGHT BY
RAND McNALLY & COMPANY
MADE IN U.S.A.

| 0 | 200 | 400 | 600 | 800 | 1000 | Miles |
| 0 | 400 | 800 | 1200 | 1600 | Kilometers |

Scale 1:40 000 000; one inch to 630 miles. Lambert's Azimuthal Equal Area Projection
Elevations and depressions are given in feet

Longitude   West   100°   of   Greenwich

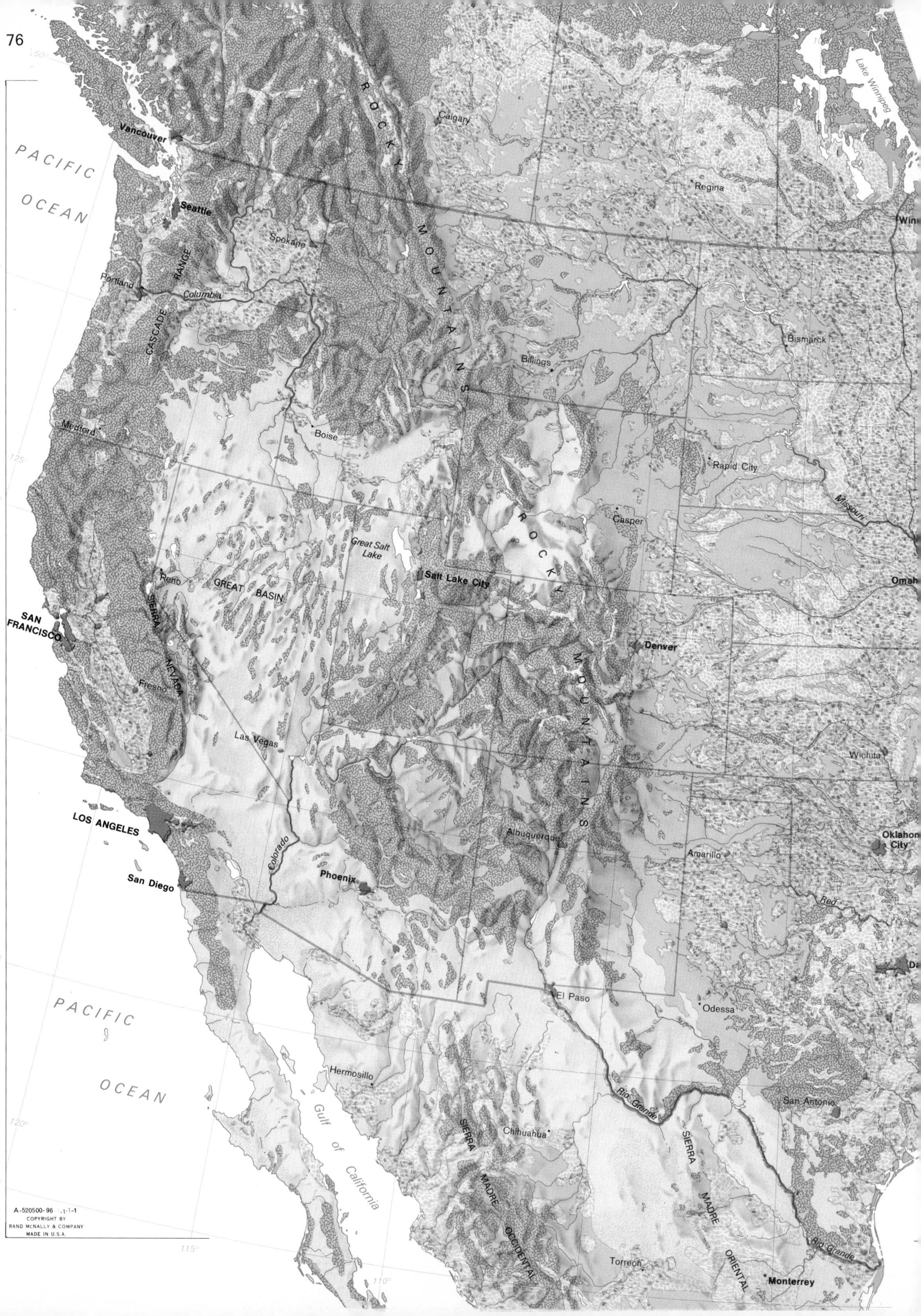

PACIFIC

OCEAN

Vancouver

Seattle

Spokane

Portland

Columbia

CASCADE RANGE

Medford

Boise

ROCKY MOUNTAINS

Calgary

Regina

Billings

Bismarck

Rapid City

Casper

Missouri

Great Salt Lake

Salt Lake City

GREAT BASIN

Reno

SIERRA NEVADA

SAN FRANCISCO

Fresno

Las Vegas

ROCKY MOUNTAINS

Denver

Omah

LOS ANGELES

Colorado

Albuquerque

San Diego

Phoenix

Amarillo

Wichita

Oklahoma City

Red

El Paso

Odessa

Da

PACIFIC

OCEAN

Hermosillo

Gulf of California

Rio Grande

San Antonio

SIERRA MADRE OCCIDENTAL

Chihuahua

SIERRA MADRE ORIENTAL

Rio Grande

Torreon

Monterrey

Lake Winnipeg

Win

50°

45°

125°

40°

35°

30°

25°

120°

115°

110°

Scale 1:12,000,000; one inch to 190 miles. Polyconic Projection

0	50	100	200	300	400 Miles	

0	75	150	300	450	600 Kilometers

Legend:
- Urban
- Cropland
- Cropland & Woodland
- Cropland & Grazing Land
- Grassland, Grazing Land
- Forest, Woodland
- Swamp, Marshland
- Shrub, Sparse Grass, Wasteland (pattern)
- Barren Land

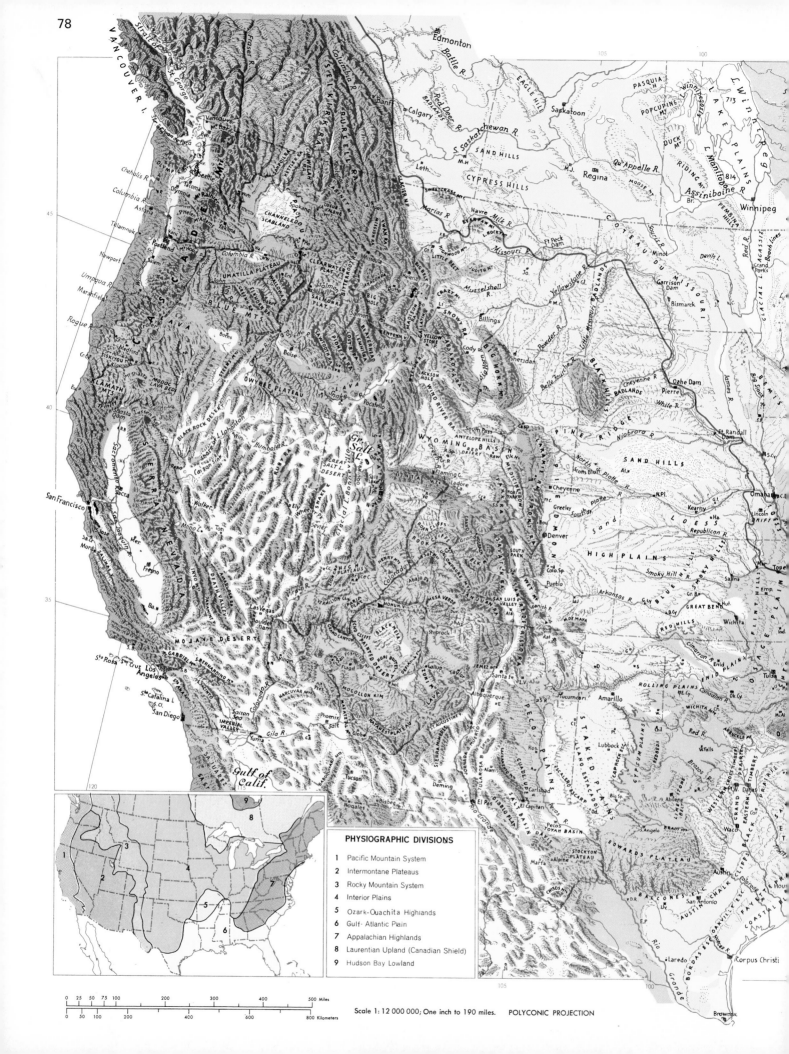

PHYSIOGRAPHIC DIVISIONS

1　Pacific Mountain System
2　Intermontane Plateaus
3　Rocky Mountain System
4　Interior Plains
5　Ozark-Ouachita Highlands
6　Gulf-Atlantic Plain
7　Appalachian Highlands
8　Laurentian Upland (Canadian Shield)
9　Hudson Bay Lowland

0 25 50 75 100　200　300　400　500 Miles

0　50　100　200　400　600　800 Kilometers

Scale 1: 12 000 000; One inch to 190 miles.　POLYCONIC PROJECTION

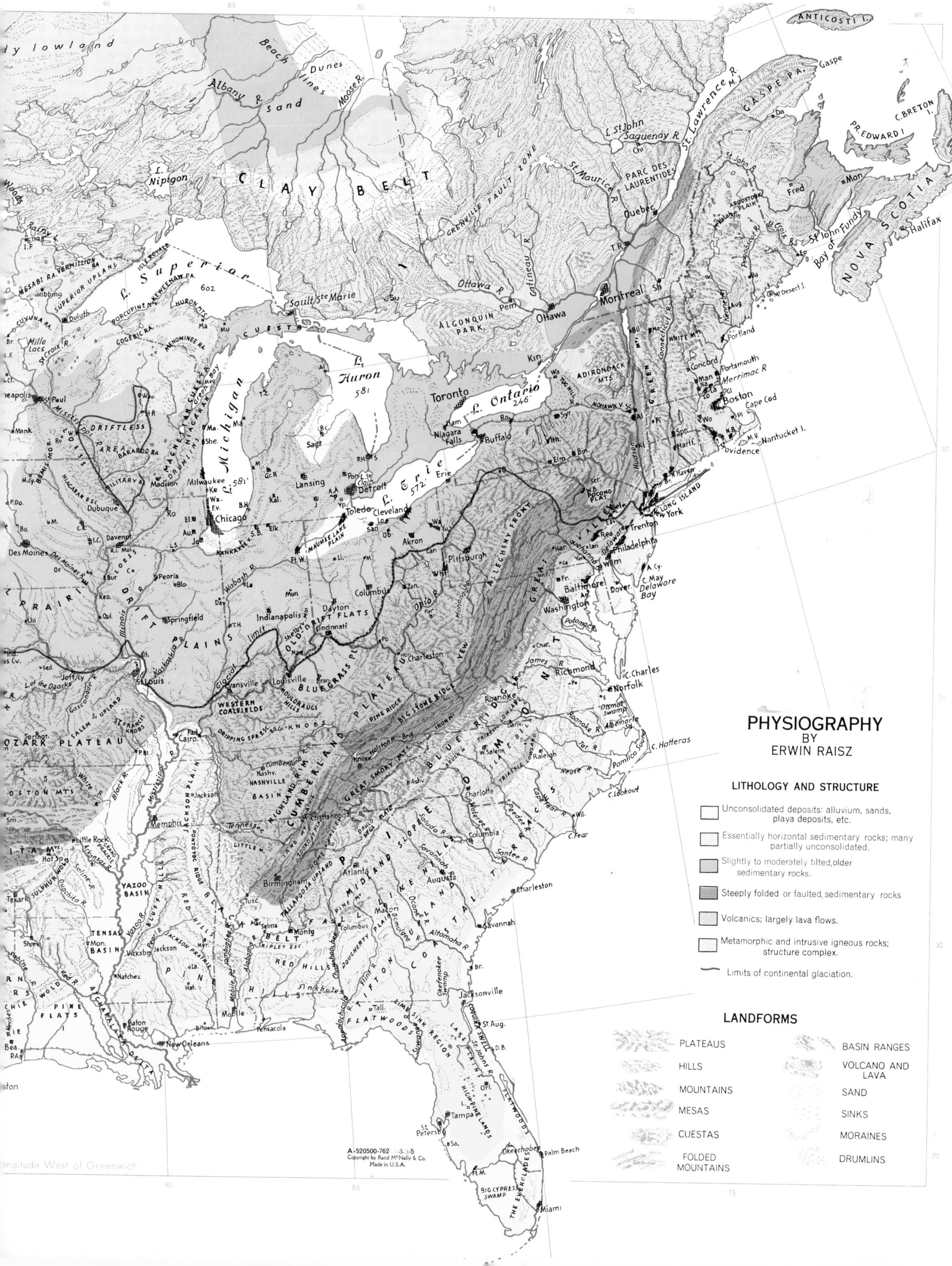

PHYSIOGRAPHY
BY
ERWIN RAISZ

LITHOLOGY AND STRUCTURE

- Unconsolidated deposits: alluvium, sands, playa deposits, etc.
- Essentially horizontal sedimentary rocks; many partially unconsolidated.
- Slightly to moderately tilted, older sedimentary rocks.
- Steeply folded or faulted, sedimentary rocks.
- Volcanics; largely lava flows.
- Metamorphic and intrusive igneous rocks; structure complex.
- — Limits of continental glaciation.

LANDFORMS

PLATEAUS	BASIN RANGES
HILLS	VOLCANO AND LAVA
MOUNTAINS	SAND
MESAS	SINKS
CUESTAS	MORAINES
FOLDED MOUNTAINS	DRUMLINS

ANTICOSTI I.

GASPE PA. Gaspe

C. BRETON I.

PR. EDWARD I.

NOVA SCOTIA Halifax

Bay of Fundy

St. John R.

GRENVILLE FAULT ZONE

PARC DES LAURENTIDES

L. St. John Saguenay R.

St. Maurice R.

Quebec

St. Lawrence R.

Montreal

Ottawa R. Gatineau R.

ALGONQUIN PARK

Ottawa

WHITE MTS. Portland

Concord Portsmouth

Merrimac R. Boston

Cape Cod

Nantucket I.

Providence

M.V.

Long Island

New York

Trenton

Philadelphia

Wilm.

Baltimore Dover

Delaware Bay

Washington

Potomac R.

C. May

GREEN MTS.

ADIRONDACK MTS.

MOHAWK V.

Hudson R.

POCONO PLAT.

ALLEGHENY FRONT

Pittsburgh

Buffalo

Niagara Falls

Toronto

L. Ontario 246

L. Erie 572

Erie

Cleveland

Detroit

Toledo

Akron

Columbus

Dayton Cincinnati

Indianapolis

Springfield

Chicago

Lansing

Milwaukee

Madison

L. Michigan 581

L. Huron 581

L. Superior

NIAGARA CUESTA

DRIFTLESS AREA

BARABOO

LOESS

St. Paul

Minneapolis

Dubuque

Davenport

Des Moines

Peoria

St. Louis

OLD DRIFT FLATS

BLUE GRASS PL.

Louisville

Evansville

KNOBS

WESTERN COALFIELDS

CUMBERLAND PLATEAU

Nashville

NASHVILLE BASIN

HIGHLAND RIM

GREAT SMOKY MTS.

BLUE RIDGE

PIEDMONT

Richmond

Norfolk

C. Hatteras

C. Lookout

Raleigh

Charlotte

Columbia

Charleston

Savannah

Augusta

Macon

Atlanta

Birmingham

Montg.

BLACK BELT

RED HILLS

PINE HILLS

New Orleans

Baton Rouge

Mobile

Pensacola

YAZOO BASIN

Memphis

Little Rock

Hot Springs

OZARK PLATEAU

BOSTON MTS.

OUACHITA MTS.

Shreveport

Jackson

Vicksburg

Natchez

JACKSON PLAIN

COASTAL PLAIN

PINE FLATS

FLATWOODS

LIME SINK REGION

BIG CYPRESS SWAMP

THE EVERGLADES

Miami

Palm Beach

Okeechobee

Tampa

St. Petersburg

Jacksonville

St. Aug.

Okefenokee Swamp

Dismal Swamp

James R.

Roanoke R.

Neuse R.

Cape Fear R.

Santee R.

Savannah R.

Altamaha R.

CLAY BELT

Albany R. Moose R.

Beach lines sand Dunes

L. Nipigon

MESABI RA.

SUPERIOR UPLAND

Duluth

Rainy L.

L. of the Woods

Hibbing

PORCUPINE MTS. KEWEENAW PA.

GOGEBIC RA.

MENOMINEE RA.

Sault Ste. Marie

ISLE ROYALE

602

PRAIRIE PLAINS

DRIFT PLAINS

Mille Lacs

A-520500-762
Copyright by Rand McNally & Co.
Made in U.S.A.

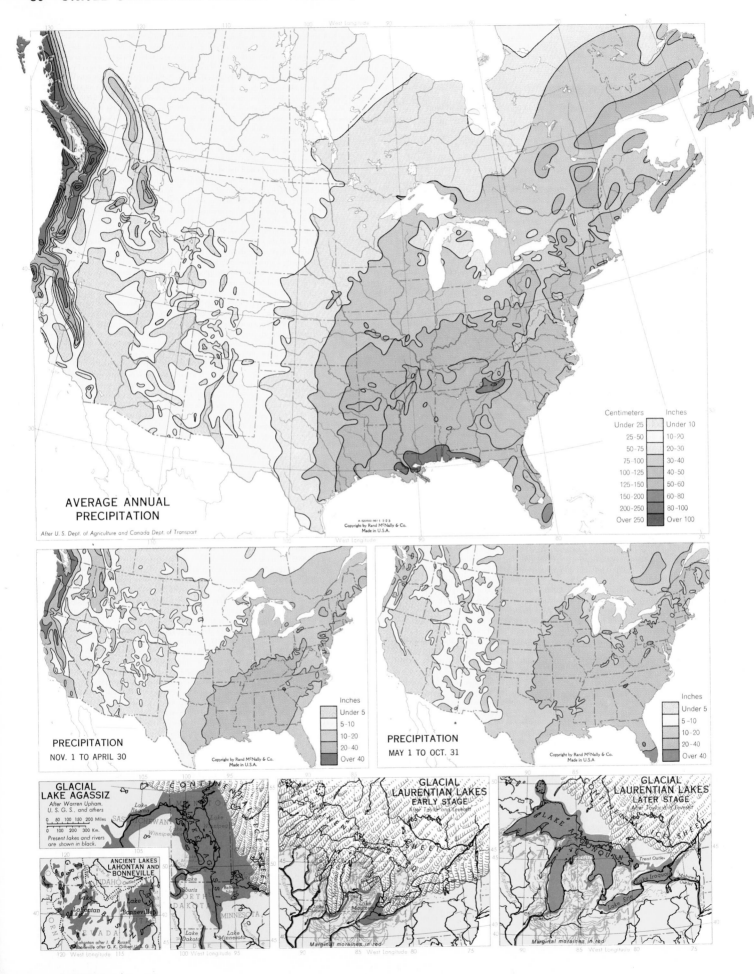

AVERAGE ANNUAL PRECIPITATION

After U. S. Dept. of Agriculture and Canada Dept. of Transport

A-520500-961 1-2-2-3
Copyright by Rand McNally & Co.
Made in U.S.A.

Centimeters	Inches
Under 25	Under 10
25-50	10-20
50-75	20-30
75-100	30-40
100-125	40-50
125-150	50-60
150-200	60-80
200-250	80-100
Over 250	Over 100

PRECIPITATION
NOV. 1 TO APRIL 30

Copyright by Rand McNally & Co.
Made in U.S.A.

Inches
Under 5
5-10
10-20
20-40
Over 40

PRECIPITATION
MAY 1 TO OCT. 31

Copyright by Rand McNally & Co.
Made in U.S.A

Inches
Under 5
5-10
10-20
20-40
Over 40

GLACIAL LAKE AGASSIZ
After Warren Upham,
U. S. G. S. and others

0 50 100 150 200 Miles
0 100 200 300 Km.

Present lakes and rivers
are shown in black.

ANCIENT LAKES LAHONTAN AND BONNEVILLE

Lahontan after I. Russell
Bonneville after G. K. Gilbert U. S. G. S.

GLACIAL LAURENTIAN LAKES
EARLY STAGE
After Taylor and Leverett

Marginal moraines in red

GLACIAL LAURENTIAN LAKES
LATER STAGE
After Taylor and Leverett

Marginal moraines in red

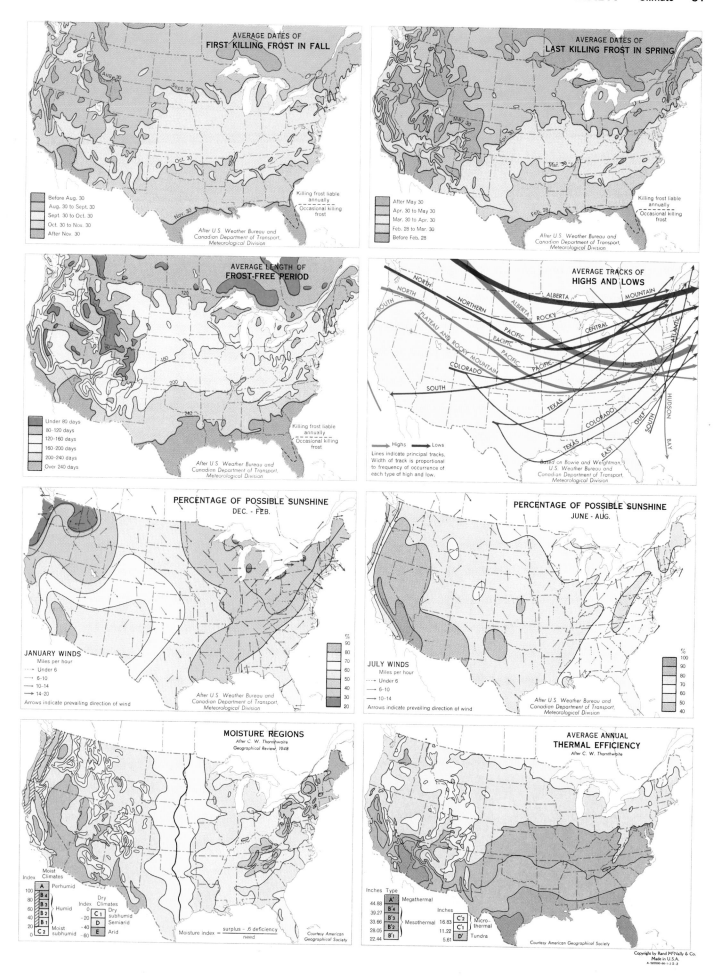

AVERAGE DATES OF
FIRST KILLING FROST IN FALL

Before Aug. 30
Aug. 30 to Sept. 30
Sept. 30 to Oct. 30
Oct. 30 to Nov. 30
After Nov. 30

Killing frost liable annually
Occasional killing frost

After U.S. Weather Bureau and Canadian Department of Transport, Meteorological Division

AVERAGE DATES OF
LAST KILLING FROST IN SPRING

After May 30
Apr. 30 to May 30
Mar. 30 to Apr. 30
Feb. 28 to Mar. 30
Before Feb. 28

Killing frost liable annually
Occasional killing frost

After U.S. Weather Bureau and Canadian Department of Transport, Meteorological Division

AVERAGE LENGTH OF
FROST-FREE PERIOD

Under 80 days
80-120 days
120-160 days
160-200 days
200-240 days
Over 240 days

Killing frost liable annually
Occasional killing frost

After U.S. Weather Bureau and Canadian Department of Transport, Meteorological Division

AVERAGE TRACKS OF
HIGHS AND LOWS

Highs   Lows

Lines indicate principal tracks. Width of track is proportional to frequency of occurrence of each type of high and low.

Based on Bowie and Weightman, U.S. Weather Bureau and Canadian Department of Transport, Meteorological Division

PERCENTAGE OF POSSIBLE SUNSHINE
DEC. - FEB.

JANUARY WINDS
Miles per hour
Under 6
6-10
10-14
14-20
Arrows indicate prevailing direction of wind

%
90
80
70
60
50
40
30
20

After U.S. Weather Bureau and Canadian Department of Transport, Meteorological Division

PERCENTAGE OF POSSIBLE SUNSHINE
JUNE - AUG.

JULY WINDS
Miles per hour
Under 6
6-10
10-14
Arrows indicate prevailing direction of wind

%
100
90
80
70
60
50
40

After U.S. Weather Bureau and Canadian Department of Transport, Meteorological Division

MOISTURE REGIONS
After C. W. Thornthwaite
Geographical Review, 1948

Index	Moist Climates		Index	Dry Climates	
100	A	Perhumid	0	C1	Dry subhumid
80	B4		-20	D	Semiarid
60	B3	Humid	-40	E	Arid
40	B2		-60		
20	B1	Moist subhumid			
0	C2				

Moisture index = surplus - .6 deficiency / need

Courtesy American Geographical Society

AVERAGE ANNUAL
THERMAL EFFICIENCY
After C. W. Thornthwaite

Inches	Type		Inches		
44.88	A'	Megathermal			
39.27	B'4		16.83	C'2	Micro-thermal
33.66	B'3	Mesothermal	11.22	C'1	
28.05	B'2		5.61	D'	Tundra
22.44	B'1				

Courtesy American Geographical Society

82

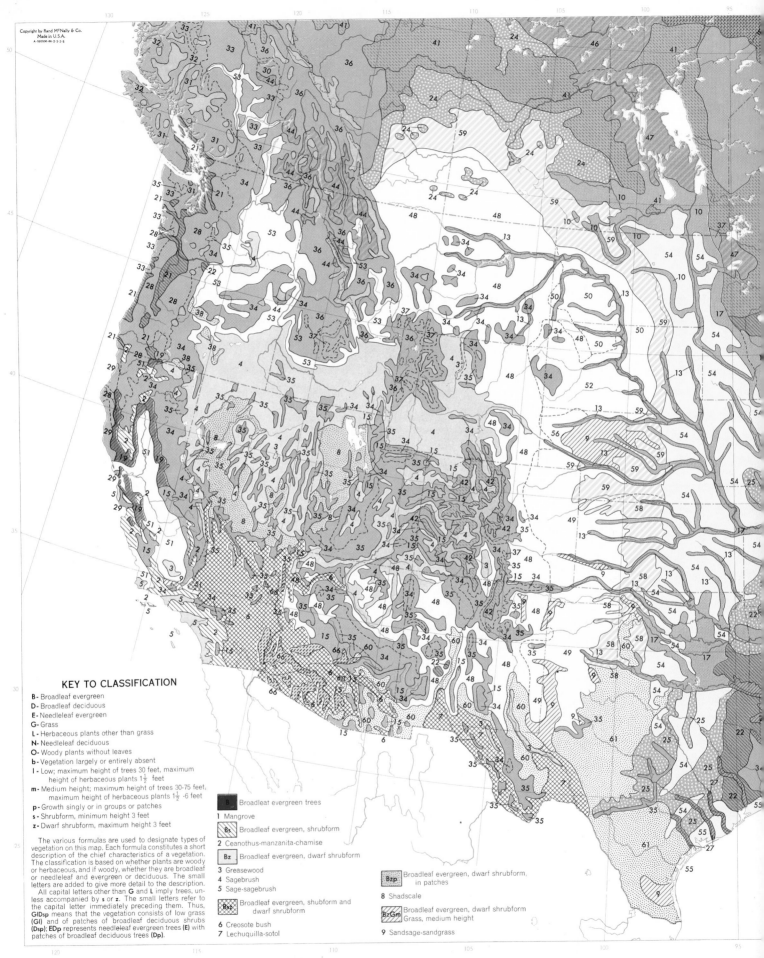

Copyright by Rand McNally & Co.
Made in U.S.A.
A-520500-86-2-2-2-2

KEY TO CLASSIFICATION

B- Broadleaf evergreen
D- Broadleaf deciduous
E- Needleleaf evergreen
G- Grass
L- Herbaceous plants other than grass
N- Needleleaf deciduous
O- Woody plants without leaves
b- Vegetation largely or entirely absent
l- Low; maximum height of trees 30 feet, maximum
      height of herbaceous plants $1\frac{1}{2}$ feet
m- Medium height; maximum height of trees 30-75 feet,
      maximum height of herbaceous plants $1\frac{1}{2}$ -6 feet
p- Growth singly or in groups or patches
s- Shrubform, minimum height 3 feet
z- Dwarf shrubform, maximum height 3 feet

The various formulas are used to designate types of
vegetation on this map. Each formula constitutes a short
description of the chief characteristics of a vegetation.
The classification is based on whether plants are woody
or herbaceous, and if woody, whether they are broadleaf
or needleleaf and evergreen or deciduous. The small
letters are added to give more detail to the description.
All capital letters other than **G** and **L** imply trees, unless accompanied by **s** or **z**. The small letters refer to
the capital letter immediately preceding them. Thus,
GlDsp means that the vegetation consists of low grass
(**Gl**) and of patches of broadleaf deciduous shrubs
(**Dsp**); **EDp** represents needleleaf evergreen trees (**E**) with
patches of broadleaf deciduous trees (**Dp**).

B Broadleaf evergreen trees

1 Mangrove

Bs Broadleaf evergreen, shrubform

2 Ceanothus-manzanita-chamise

Bz Broadleaf evergreen, dwarf shrubform

3 Greasewood
4 Sagebrush
5 Sage-sagebrush

Bsz Broadleaf evergreen, shubform and
      dwarf shrubform

6 Creosote bush
7 Lechuguilla-sotol

Bzp Broadleaf evergreen, dwarf shrubform,
      in patches

8 Shadscale

BzGm Broadleaf evergreen, dwarf shrubform
      Grass, medium height

9 Sandsage-sandgrass

0 25 50 75 100   200   300   400   500 Miles

0 50 100   200   400   600   800 Kilometers

Scale 1:14 000 000; One inch to 220 mile

NATURAL VEGETATION
BY A. W. KÜCHLER

Based on "A Physiognomic Classification of Vegetation"
Annals of the Assoc. of American Geographers, Vol. 39, September, 1949

D Broadleaf deciduous trees

10 Aspen-oak
11 Beech-maple
12 Beech-tulip tree-maple-basswood
13 Cottonwood-willow
14 Maple-basswood
15 Oak
16 Oak-ash-maple
17 Oak-hickory
18 Oak-tulip tree

DB Broadleaf deciduous trees
Broadleaf evergreen trees

19 Oak-madrone

DE Broadleaf deciduous trees
Needleleaf evergreen trees

20 Maple-yellow birch-hemlock-pine
21 Oak-Douglas fir
22 Oak-pine
23 Maple-beech-hemlock

D
Gmp Broadleaf deciduous trees
Grass, medium height, in patches

24 Aspen-needle grass-wheat grass
25 Oak-hickory-bluestem

DN Broadleaf deciduous trees
Needleleaf deciduous trees

26 Bay trees-bald cypress
27 Tupelo-gum-bald cypress

E Needleleaf evergreen trees

28 Douglas fir
29 Douglas fir-redwood
30 Hemlock-arbor vitae
31 Hemlock-arbor vitae-Douglas fir
32 Hemlock-arbor vitae-fir
33 Hemlock-spruce
34 Pine
35 Pine-juniper
36 Pine-spruce
37 Spruce-fir

Esp Needleleaf evergreen, shrubform,
in patches

38 Juniper

EDp Needleleaf evergreen trees
Broadleaf deciduous trees, in patches

39 Douglas fir-pine-aspen
40 Pine-spruce-birch
41 Spruce-aspen
42 Spruce-fir-aspen
43 Spruce-poplar-birch

EN Needleleaf evergreen trees
Needleleaf deciduous trees

44 Hemlock-arbor vitae-Douglas fir-larch
45 Pine-bald cypress
46 Pine-spruce-larch
47 Spruce-larch

Gl Grass, low

48 Grama grass
49 Grama grass-buffalo grass
50 Grama grass-needle grass
51 Needle grass-blue grass
52 Wheat grass
53 Wheat grass-blue grass

Gm Grass, medium height

54 Bluestem
55 Broom grass-water grass
56 Marsh grass
57 Saw grass

Gml Grass, medium and low height

58 Bluestem-bunch grass
59 Needle grass-wheat grass

Gl
Dsp Grass, low
Broadleaf deciduous, shrubform, in patches
60 Bunch grass-oak

Gm
Dsp Grass, medium height
Broadleaf deciduous, shrubform, in patches
61 Mesquite grass-mesquite

L Herbaceous plants other than grass

62 Lichens, etc.

LEp Herbaceous plants other than grass
Needleleaf evergreen trees, in patches
63 Lichens-spruce

LEp
Np Herbaceous plants other than grass
Needleleaf evergreen trees, in patches
Needleleaf deciduous trees, in patches
64 Lichens-spruce-larch

N Needleleaf deciduous trees

65 Bald cypress

Op Woody plants without leaves, in patches

66 Palo verde-cacti-ocotillo

b Vegetation largely or entirely absent

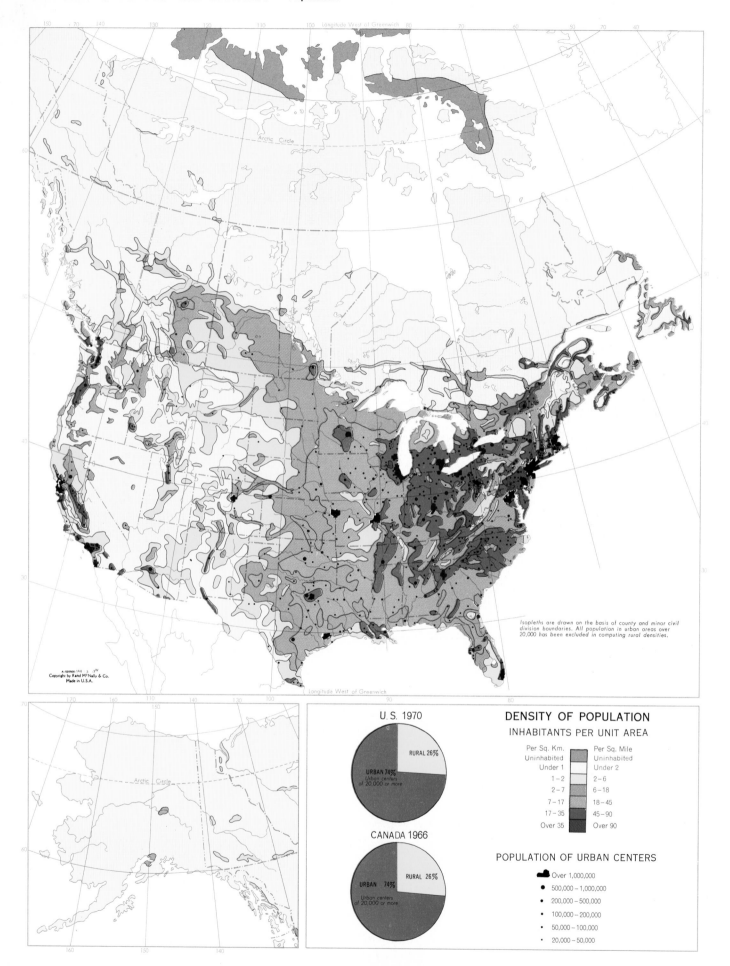

Isopleths are drawn on the basis of county and minor civil division boundaries. All population in urban areas over 20,000 has been excluded in computing rural densities.

Copyright by Rand McNally & Co.
Made in U.S.A.

U.S. 1970

RURAL 26%

URBAN 74%
Urban centers of 20,000 or more

CANADA 1966

RURAL 26%

URBAN 74%
Urban centers of 20,000 or more

DENSITY OF POPULATION
INHABITANTS PER UNIT AREA

Per Sq. Km.	Per Sq. Mile
Uninhabited	Uninhabited
Under 1	Under 2
1 – 2	2 – 6
2 – 7	6 – 18
7 – 17	18 – 45
17 – 35	45 – 90
Over 35	Over 90

POPULATION OF URBAN CENTERS

- Over 1,000,000
- 500,000 – 1,000,000
- 200,000 – 500,000
- 100,000 – 200,000
- 50,000 – 100,000
- 20,000 – 50,000

Scale 1: 32 000 000; One inch to 500 miles.   LAMBERT CONFORMAL CONIC PROJECTION

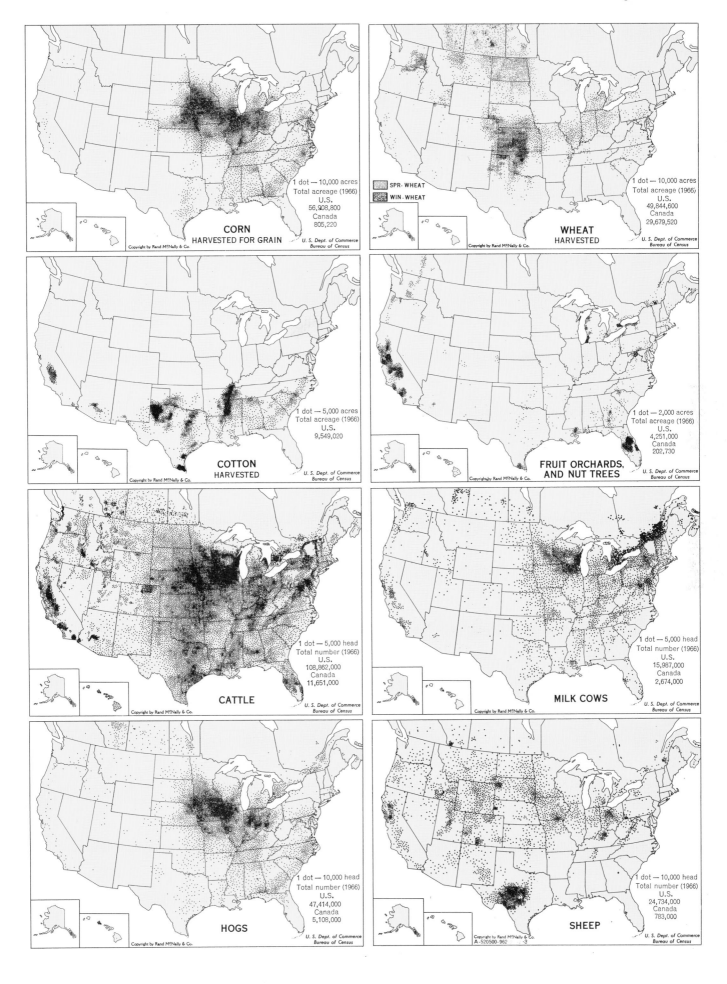

CORN
HARVESTED FOR GRAIN

1 dot — 10,000 acres
Total acreage (1966)
U.S.
56,908,800
Canada
805,220

U. S. Dept. of Commerce
Bureau of Census

Copyright by Rand McNally & Co.

SPR. WHEAT
WIN. WHEAT

WHEAT
HARVESTED

1 dot — 10,000 acres
Total acreage (1966)
U.S.
49,844,600
Canada
29,679,520

U. S. Dept. of Commerce
Bureau of Census

Copyright by Rand McNally & Co.

COTTON
HARVESTED

1 dot — 5,000 acres
Total acreage (1966)
U.S.
9,549,020

U. S. Dept. of Commerce
Bureau of Census

Copyright by Rand McNally & Co.

FRUIT ORCHARDS,
AND NUT TREES

1 dot — 2,000 acres
Total acreage (1966)
U.S.
4,251,000
Canada
202,730

U. S. Dept. of Commerce
Bureau of Census

Copyright by Rand McNally & Co.

CATTLE

1 dot — 5,000 head
Total number (1966)
U.S.
108,862,000
Canada
11,651,000

U. S. Dept. of Commerce
Bureau of Census

Copyright by Rand McNally & Co.

MILK COWS

1 dot — 5,000 head
Total number (1966)
U.S.
15,987,000
Canada
2,674,000

U. S. Dept. of Commerce
Bureau of Census

Copyright by Rand McNally & Co.

HOGS

1 dot — 10,000 head
Total number (1966)
U.S.
47,414,000
Canada
5,108,000

U. S. Dept. of Commerce
Bureau of Census

Copyright by Rand McNally & Co.

SHEEP

1 dot — 10,000 head
Total number (1966)
U.S.
24,734,000
Canada
783,000

U. S. Dept. of Commerce
Bureau of Census

Copyright by Rand McNally & Co.
A-520500-962   -3

LEGEND

General farming
Feed grains and livestock
Wheat and small grains
Cotton
Tobacco and general farming
Special crops and general farming
Irrigated ⎱ Fruit, truck and
Non-irrigated ⎰ mixed farming
Dairy
Year-long grazing ⎱ Range
Seasonal grazing ⎰ livestock
Non-farming
Self-sufficing and part-time agriculture

GENERALIZED TYPES OF FARMING

After U.S. Dept. of Agriculture
and Canada Dept. of Agriculture

A-520500-56 -3-3-5
Copyright by Rand McNally & Co.
Made in U.S.A.

CANADA

Graphs show percentages
of total value added
by manufacture.

28%

A-520500-369 -3-3-5

U.S.

33%

TYPES OF MANUFACTURING

Machinery, metal goods
Textiles, clothing
Food, tobacco
Chemicals, fuels, rubber products
Paper, wood products, furniture
Transportation equipment
Printing, publishing
Miscellaneous

VALUE ADDED BY MANUFACTURE

IN MILLIONS OF DOLLARS

Cities		SMSA or CMA	
Over 150		Over 5000	
75–150		1000–5000	
Less than 75		500–1000	
		Less than 500	

Value added is determined by subtracting cost of materials, fuel, electricity, etc., from the gross value of the products.

Total value added, 1972: In United States $353,973,400,000; 1974 in Canada $35,084,752,000

Note: Value Added symbols were plotted by computer.

Only cities with a population of more than 10,000 are shown.

After Census of Manufacturers, 1972 U.S. Dept. of Commerce,

Manufacturers of Canada, 1974 Statistics Canada.

Scale twice that of main map.

Scale 1: 28 000 000; One inch to 440 miles.   LAMBERT CONFORMAL CONIC PROJECTION

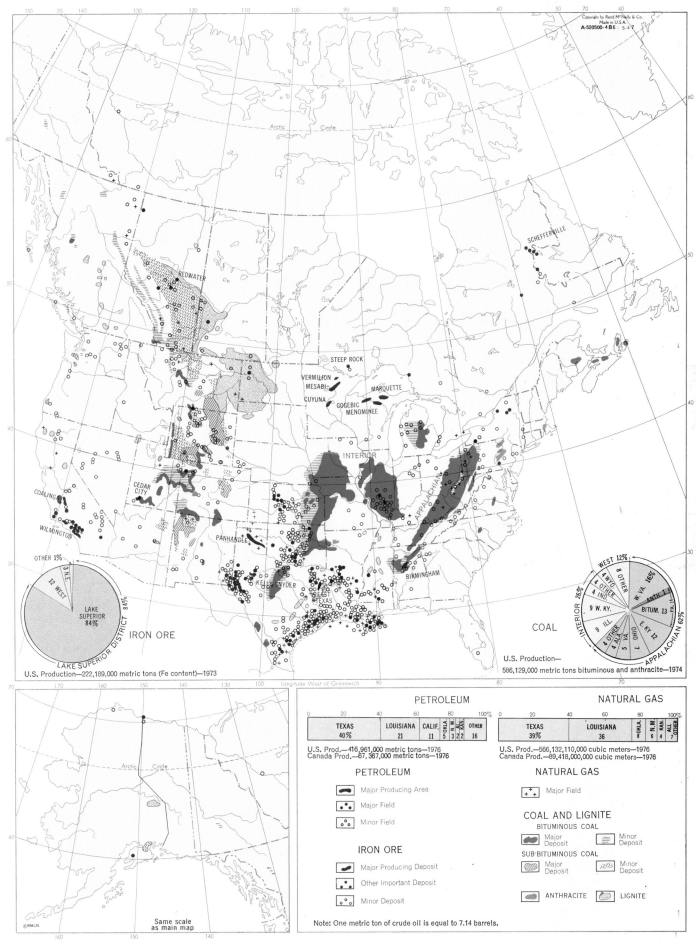

Copyright by Rand McNally & Co.
Made in U.S.A.
A-520500-4 B6   5-4-7

REDWATER

SCHEFFERVILLE

STEEP ROCK

VERMILION
MESABI
CUYUNA
GOGEBIC
MENOMINEE
MARQUETTE

INTERIOR

CEDAR
CITY

COALING

WILMINGTON

PANHANDLE

KELLY-SNYDER

EAST
TEXAS

APPALACHIAN

BIRMINGHAM

IRON ORE

OTHER 1%
3 N.E.
12 WEST
LAKE
SUPERIOR
84%
LAKE SUPERIOR DISTRICT 84%

U.S. Production—222,189,000 metric tons (Fe content)—1973

COAL

WEST 12%
8 OTHER
4 WYO.
4 OTHER
4 IND.
9 W. KY.
INTERIOR 26%
9 ILL.
4 OTHER
4 ALA.
5 VA.
OHIO
7
E. KY. 12
W. VA. 16%
ANTH. 1
BITUM. 13
PA.
APPALACHIAN 62%

U.S. Production—
586,129,000 metric tons bituminous and anthracite—1974

Arctic Circle

Same scale
as main map

©RMCN.

PETROLEUM

TEXAS 40%	LOUISIANA 21	CALIF. 11	OKLA. 5	N.M. 3	ALA. 2	KAN. 2	OTHER 16

0   20   40   60   80   100%

U.S. Prod.—416,961,000 metric tons—1976
Canada Prod.—67,367,000 metric tons—1976

NATURAL GAS

TEXAS 39%	LOUISIANA 36	OKLA. 8	N.M. 6	KAN. 4	ALL OTHER 7

0   20   40   60   80   100%

U.S. Prod.—566,132,110,000 cubic meters—1976
Canada Prod.—89,418,000,000 cubic meters—1976

PETROLEUM

◖ Major Producing Area

⬚ Major Field

⬚ Minor Field

IRON ORE

◗ Major Producing Deposit

⬚ Other Important Deposit

⬚ Minor Deposit

NATURAL GAS

⬚ Major Field

COAL AND LIGNITE

BITUMINOUS COAL

◖ Major Deposit   ▤ Minor Deposit

SUB-BITUMINOUS COAL

▨ Major Deposit   ▨ Minor Deposit

◼ ANTHRACITE   ▢ LIGNITE

Note: One metric ton of crude oil is equal to 7.14 barrels.

Scale 1: 32 000 000; One inch to 500 miles.   LAMBERT CONFORMAL CONIC PROJECTION

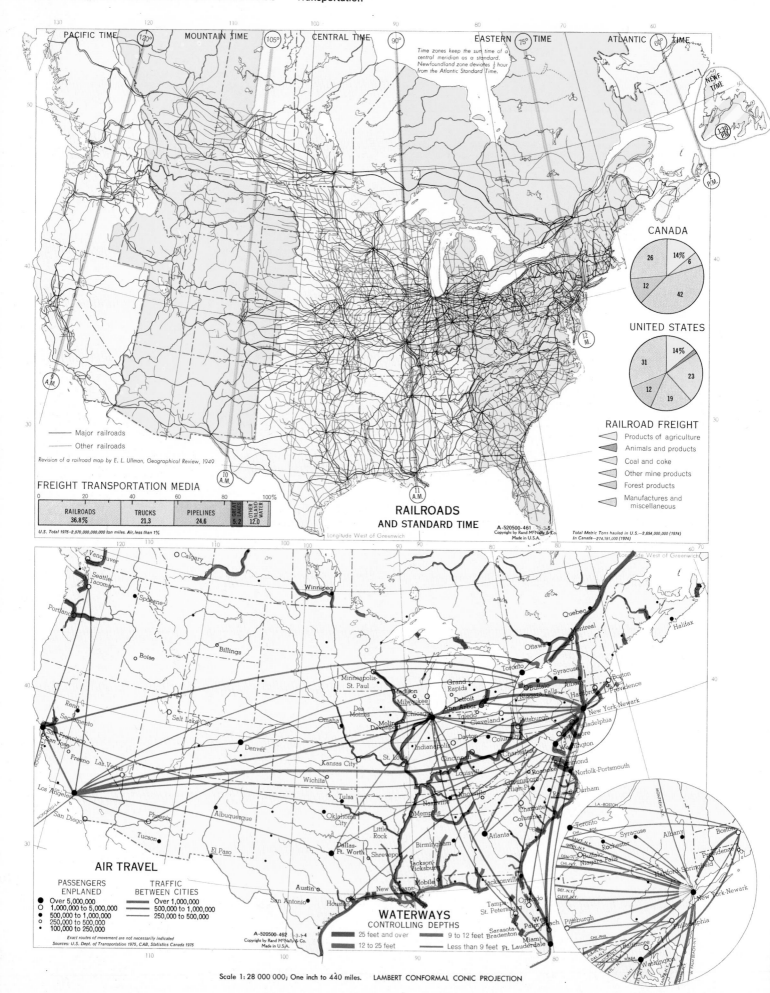

PACIFIC TIME   MOUNTAIN TIME   CENTRAL TIME   EASTERN TIME   ATLANTIC TIME

Time zones keep the sun time of a central meridian as a standard. Newfoundland zone deviates ½ hour from the Atlantic Standard Time.

NEWF. TIME

CANADA

| 26 | 14% | 6 |
| 12 | 42 | |

UNITED STATES

| 31 | 14% | 23 |
| 12 | 19 | |

RAILROAD FREIGHT

- Products of agriculture
- Animals and products
- Coal and coke
- Other mine products
- Forest products
- Manufactures and miscellaneous

— Major railroads
— Other railroads

Revision of a railroad map by E. L. Ullman, Geographical Review, 1949

FREIGHT TRANSPORTATION MEDIA

| 0 | 20 | 40 | 60 | 80 | 100% |

| RAILROADS 36.8% | TRUCKS 21.3 | PIPELINES 24.6 | GREAT LAKES 5.2 | OTHER INLAND WATER 12.0 |

U.S. Total 1975–2,070,000,000,000 ton miles. Air, less than 1%

RAILROADS
AND STANDARD TIME

A-520500-461
Copyright by Rand McNally & Co.
Made in U.S.A.

Total Metric Tons hauled in U.S.–2,654,000,000 (1974)
In Canada–274,391,000 (1974)

Longitude West of Greenwich

Vancouver
Seattle-Tacoma
Portland
Calgary
Spokane
Winnipeg
Quebec
Montreal
Halifax
Billings
Boise
Ottawa
Toronto
Syracuse
Boston
Buffalo
Niagara Falls
Hartford
Providence
Reno
Sacramento
Minneapolis-St. Paul
Madison
Milwaukee
Grand Rapids
Detroit
Ann Arbor
Albany
New York-Newark
San Francisco
San Jose
Salt Lake City
Des Moines
Moline
Davenport
Chicago
Toledo
Cleveland
Pittsburgh
Philadelphia
Fresno
Omaha
Baltimore
Washington
Las Vegas
Denver
Dayton
Columbus
Richmond
Los Angeles
Kansas City
St. Louis
Indianapolis
Cincinnati
Charleston
Norfolk-Portsmouth
Honolulu
San Diego
Wichita
Louisville
Roanoke
Greensboro
High Pt.
Raleigh
Durham
Phoenix
Albuquerque
Tulsa
Nashville
Knoxville
Charlotte
Columbia
Tucson
Oklahoma City
Memphis
El Paso
Little Rock
Birmingham
Atlanta
Dallas-Ft. Worth
Shreveport
Jackson-Vicksburg
Jacksonville
Austin
Mobile
New Orleans
San Antonio
Houston
Tampa
St. Petersburg
Orlando
Sarasota-Bradenton
West Palm Beach
Miami
Ft. Lauderdale

AIR TRAVEL

PASSENGERS ENPLANED
- ● Over 5,000,000
- ◉ 1,000,000 to 5,000,000
- ● 500,000 to 1,000,000
- • 250,000 to 500,000
- · 100,000 to 250,000

TRAFFIC BETWEEN CITIES
- Over 1,000,000
- 500,000 to 1,000,000
- 250,000 to 500,000

Exact routes of movement are not necessarily indicated
Sources: U.S. Dept. of Transportation 1975, CAB, Statistics Canada 1975

A-520500-462
Copyright by Rand McNally & Co.
Made in U.S.A.

WATERWAYS
CONTROLLING DEPTHS
- 25 feet and over
- 12 to 25 feet
- 9 to 12 feet
- Less than 9 feet

MONTREAL-N.Y.
LA.-BOSTON
Toronto
Syracuse
Albany
Rochester
Boston
Buffalo
Niagara Falls
Providence
Hartford-Springfield
New York-Newark
Pittsburgh
Philadelphia
Baltimore
Washington

Scale 1: 28 000 000; One inch to 440 miles.   LAMBERT CONFORMAL CONIC PROJECTION

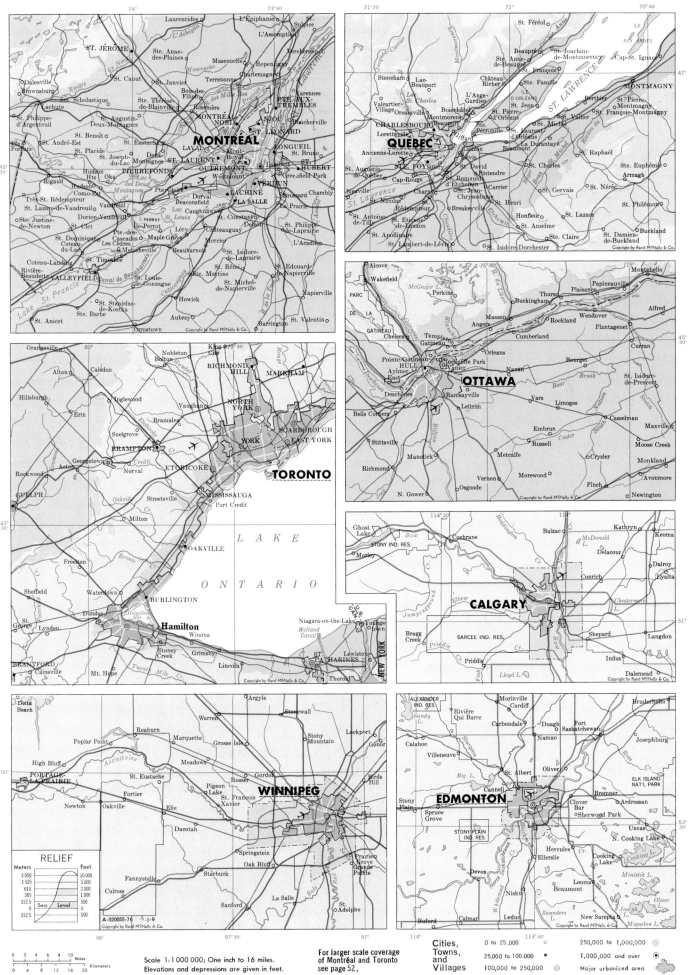

RELIEF

Meters		Feet
3 050		10 000
1 525		5 000
610		2 000
305		1 000
152.5		500
0	Sea Level	0
152.5		500

A-520055-76 -5 -5-9

0 2 4 6 8 10 Miles
0 4 8 12 16 20 Kilometers

Scale 1:1 000 000; One inch to 16 miles.
Elevations and depressions are given in feet.

For larger scale coverage
of Montréal and Toronto
see page 52.

Cities,
Towns,
and
Villages

	0 to 25,000		250,000 to 1,000,000
	25,000 to 100,000		1,000,000 and over
	100,000 to 250,000		Major urbanized area

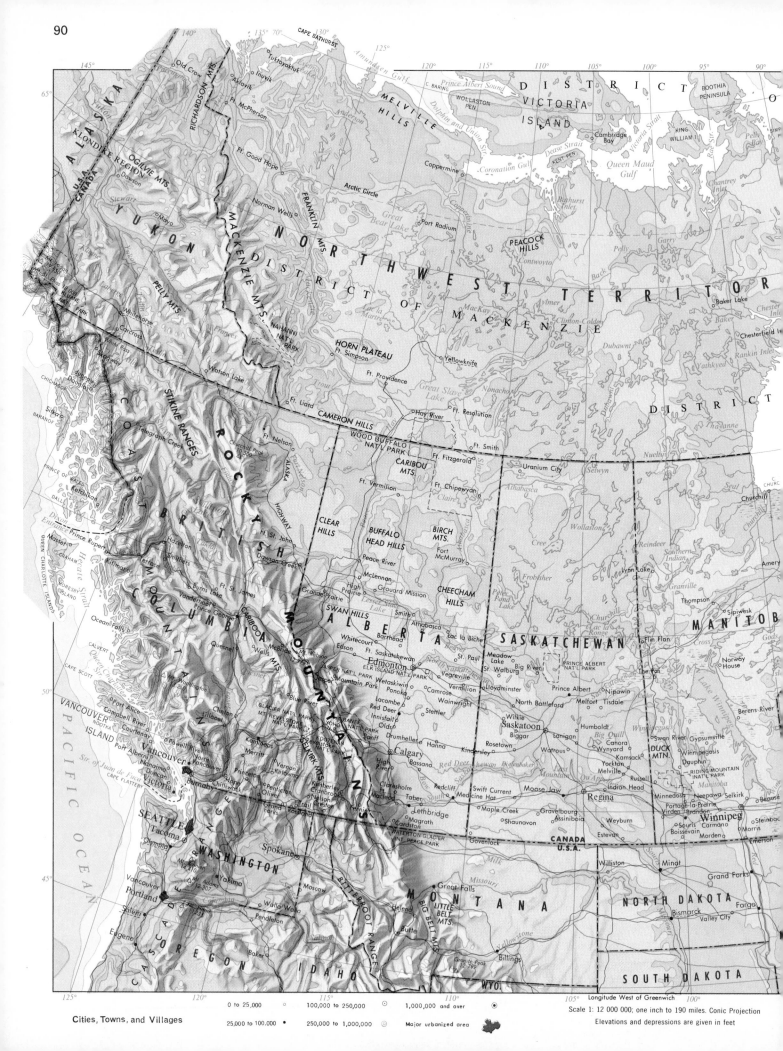

90

Relief

Meters	Feet
3050	10 000
1525	5000
610	2000
305	1000
152.5	500
Sea Level	0
0	
152.5	500
1525	5000

A-520220-76-4-4-5
COPYRIGHT BY
RAND McNALLY & COMPANY
MADE IN U.S.A.

Continued on pages 110-111

Longitude West of Greenwich

Scale 1:4 000 000; one inch to 64 miles. Conic Projection

Elevations and depressions are given in feet.

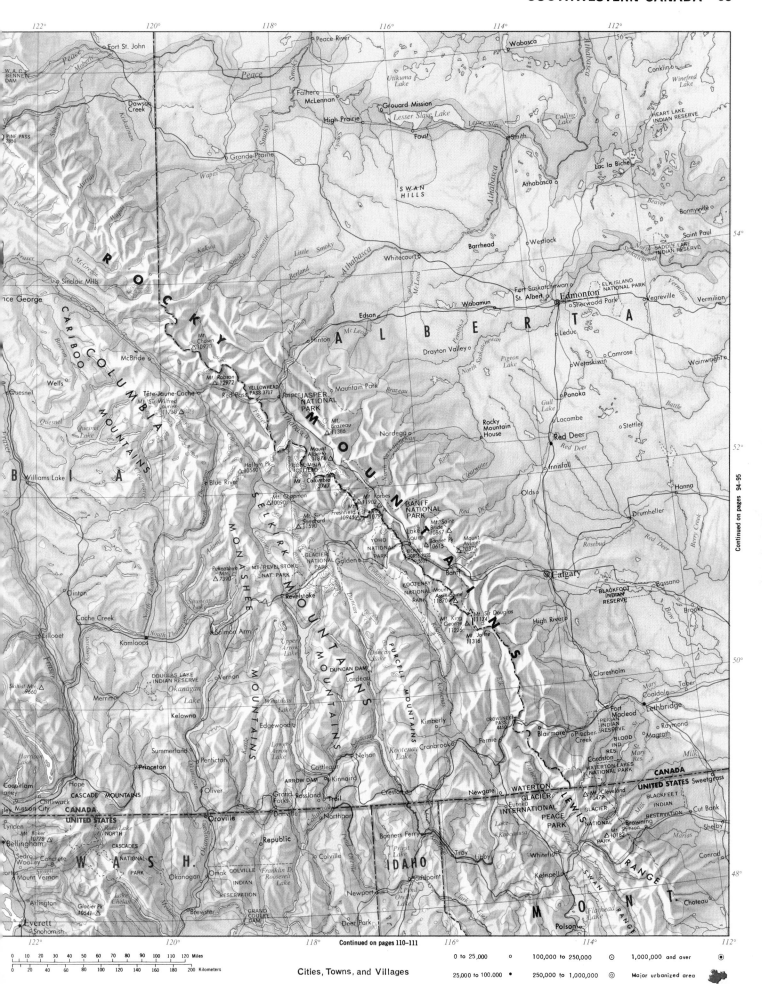

Cities, Towns, and Villages

0 to 25,000	○	100,000 to 250,000	⊙	1,000,000 and over	◉
25,000 to 100,000	●	250,000 to 1,000,000	◎	Major urbanized area	

Continued on pages 94-95

Continued on pages 110-111

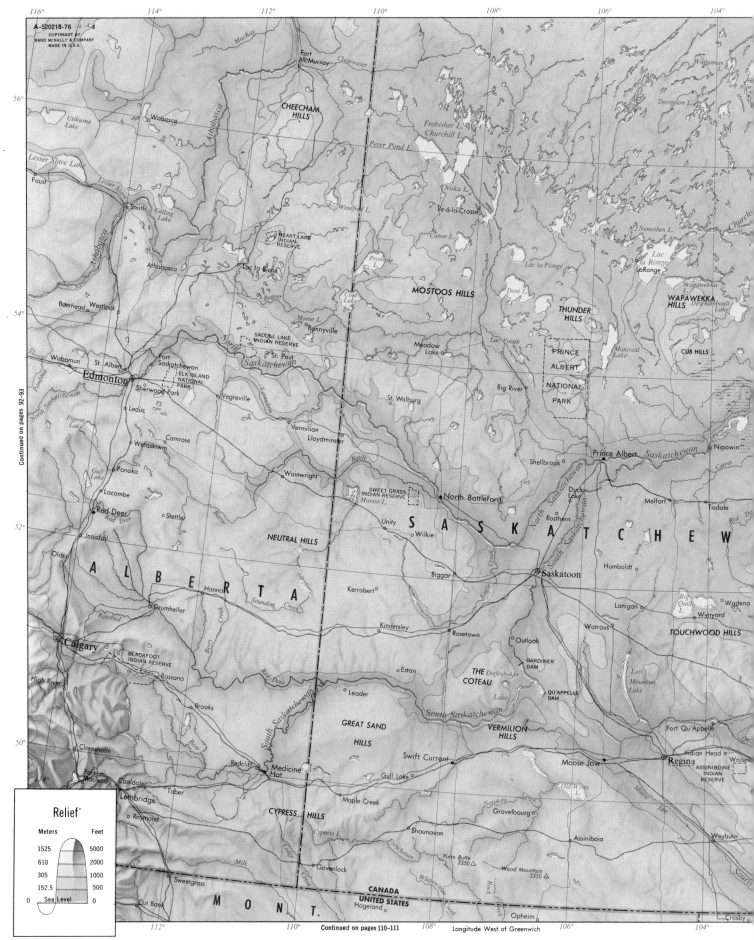

Continued on pages 92–93

Continued on pages 110–111

Longitude West of Greenwich

Scale 1:4 000 000; one inch to 64 miles. Conic Projection

Elevations and depressions are given in feet.

Relief

Meters		Feet
1525		5000
610		2000
305		1000
152.5		500
0	Sea Level	0

A-520218-76

COPYRIGHT BY
RAND McNALLY & COMPANY
MADE IN U.S.A.

HUDSON   BAY

92°   90°

York
Factory

Port Nelson

Thibaudeau

Amery

Reindeer L.

Lynn Lake

Southern
Indian

South Indian Lake

Baldock L.

Churchill

Waskaiowaka L.

Nelson

Split

56°

Russell
Lake

Suwannee L.

Churchill

Thompson

Pikwitonei

Sipiwesk

Utik L.

Kettle

Sherridon

Flin Flon

Reed L.

Wabowden

Cross L.

Walker L.

Oxford

Bear L.

Hayes

Gods L.

Red Sucker L.

Little Sachigo L.

54°

M   A   N   I   T   O   B   A

Snow Lake

Cormorant L.

Moose L.

The Pas

Moose Lake

ROSS
ISLAND

Kiskitto L.

Kiskittogisu L.

Playgreen L.

Echimamish

Molson L.

Limestone
Bay

Norway House

Gunisao

Island L.

Opasquia

Sandy

Sachigo L.

Sakwaso L.

Dyment

Cedar

BIG MOSSY POINT

Grand Rapids

LAKE

LONG POINT

Mukutawa

WINNIPEG

Deer
L.

MacDowell
L.

Weagamow L.

52°

Lake

Winnipegosis

BIRCH
I.

Dawson
Bay

Pelican
Bay

Swan

REINDEER ISLAND

BERENS
ISLAND

Berens River

Berens

Moar L.

Fishing L.

Berens

O   N   T   A   R   I   O

HUDSON
Hudson
Bay

PORCUPINE
HILLS

Hart Mountain
2700

Baldy
Mountain
2727

Swan
River

Sturgeon
Bay

Anama Bay

Lake
St. Martin

MOOSE I.

Fisher
Bay

Red Lake

Trout
L.

Sioux Lookout

Minnitaki

50°

Canora

Kamsack

Winnipegosis

Gypsumville

PEGUIS
INDIAN
RESERVE

BLACK I.

HECLA
I.

Lake
Winnipeg

ELK
ISLAND

FORT ALEXANDER
INDIAN RESERVE

Pine Falls

Bissett

English

Lac
Seul

Yorkton

Roblin

Dauphin L.

Dauphin

RIDING

RIDING MOUNTAIN

NATIONAL

PARK

Gimli

Sioux

Melville

Russell

Esterhazy

Lake
Manitoba

Kenora

Dryden

Moosomin

Minnedosa

Neepawa

Portage-la-Prairie

Selkirk

Beauséjour

Winnipeg

Kenora

AULNEAU
PENINSULA

Mtn.
2730

WHITE BEAR
INDIAN RESERVE

Virden

Brandon

Souris

Wawanesa

Carman

Steinbach

Morris

Whitemouth

Lake
of the
Woods

BIG
ISLAND

Manor

Oxbow

Melita

Whitewater L.

Boissevain

Morden

Winkler
Altona

Emerson
Pembina

Rainy
River

Rainy L.

Fort Frances
International Falls
VOYAGEURS NAT'L PARK

CANADA
UNITED STATES

N. DAK.   MINNESOTA

Hannah

Badger

102°   100°   98°   96°   94°

0 10 20 30 40 50 60 70 80 90 100 110 120 Miles
0 20 40 60 80 100 120 140 160 180 200 Kilometers

Cities, Towns, and Villages

0 to 25,000   100,000 to 250,000   1,000,000 and over

25,000 to 100,000   250,000 to 1,000,000   Major urbanized area

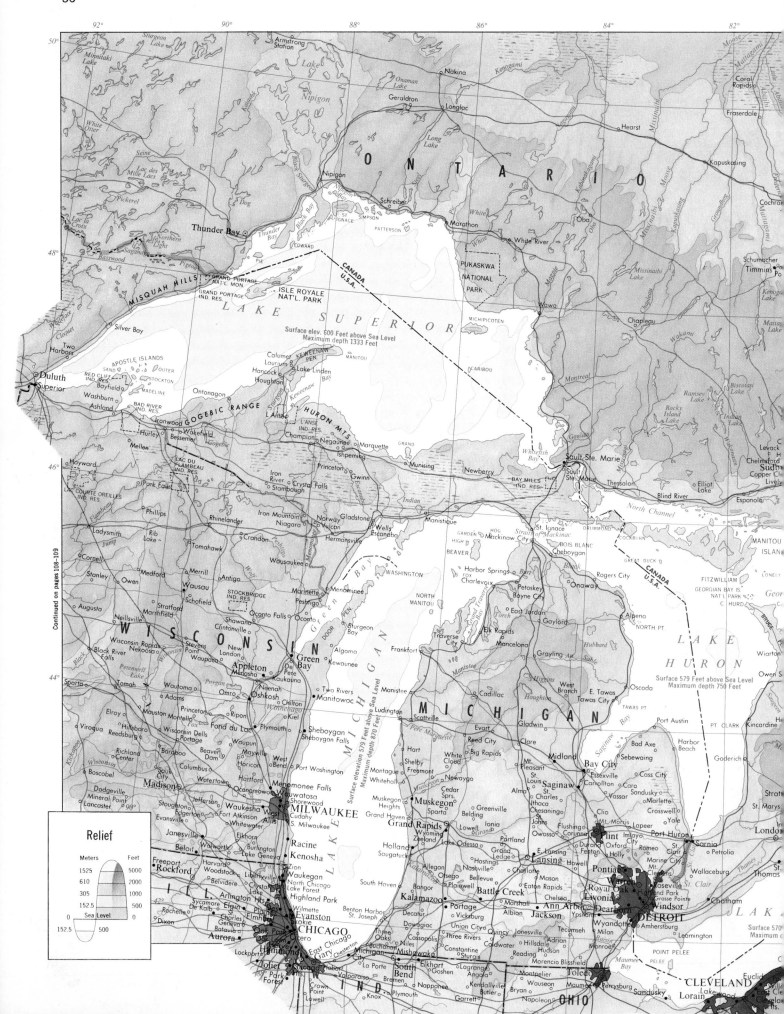

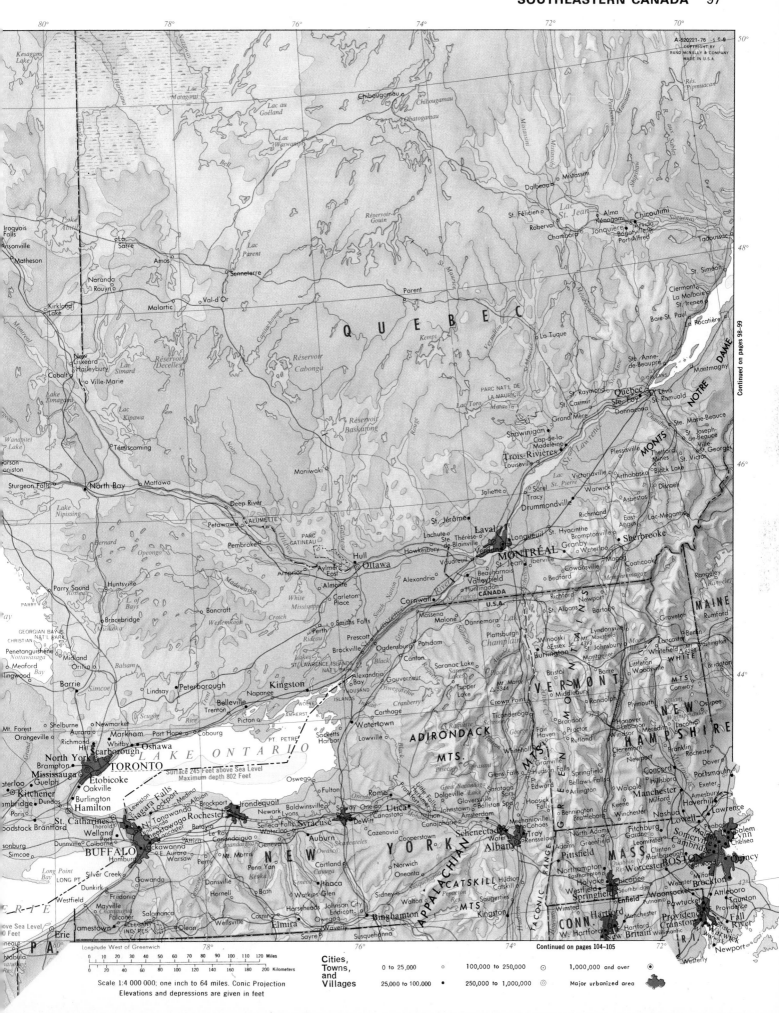

Continued on pages 98-99

Continued on pages 104-105

Cities,
Towns,
and
Villages

0 to 25,000 ○   100,000 to 250,000 ⊙   1,000,000 and over ◉

25,000 to 100,000 •   250,000 to 1,000,000 ◎   Major urbanized area

Scale 1:4 000 000; one inch to 64 miles. Conic Projection
Elevations and depressions are given in feet

Longitude West of Greenwich

0 10 20 30 40 50 60 70 80 90 100 110 120 Miles

0 20 40 60 80 100 120 140 160 180 200 Kilometers

98

Continued on pages 104-105

Scale 1:4 000 000; one inch to 64 miles. Conic Projection
Elevations and depressions are given in feet.

Longitude West of Greenwich

0 10 20 30 40 50 60 70 80 90 100 110 120 Miles
0 20 40 60 80 100 120 140 160 180 200 Kilometers

Relief

Meters		Feet
1525		5000
610		2000
305		1000
152.5		500
0	Sea Level	0
152.5		500
1525		5000

LABRADOR (Nfld.)

St. Anthony
Hare Bay
C. BAULD

GROAIS
BELL

LABRADOR SEA

Notre Dame Bay
Twillingate
Fogo
C. FREELS

NEWFOUNDLAND

LONG RANGE MTS.
ANNIEOPSQUOTCH MTS.

Corner Brook
Deer Lake
Grand Falls
Gander
TERRA NOVA NAT'L PARK

Bonavista Bay
Bonavista
Trinity

GULF OF ST. LAWRENCE

ÎLE D'ANTICOSTI (Que.)

PTE HEATH

BRION
ÎLES DE LA MADELEINE (Que.)
Grindstone Island

Cabot Strait

CAPE NORTH
Aspy Bay

CAPE BRETON HIGHLANDS NAT'L PARK

PRINCE EDWARD ISLAND

NOVA SCOTIA

Sydney
Glace Bay
Louisburg
CAPE BRETON ISLAND

CAPE CANSO

ATLANTIC OCEAN

SABLE (N.S.)

St. John's
C. SPEAR
AVALON PEN.
Placentia
Ferryland
Trepassey
C. RACE

ST. PIERRE & MIQUELON (Fr.)
St. Pierre

Scale 1:1 000 000

MASSACHUSETTS BAY

BOSTON

Worcester

Brockton

Quincy

A-510705-76 -5-6-10
COPYRIGHT BY
RAND McNALLY & COMPANY
MADE IN U.S.A.

Cities, Towns, and Villages

| 0 to 25,000 | 100,000 to 250,000 | 1,000,000 and over |
| 25,000 to 100,000 | 250,000 to 1,000,000 | Major urbanized area |

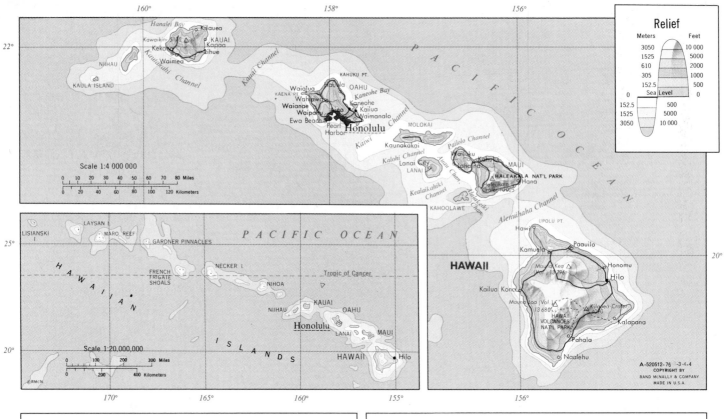

Relief

Meters	Feet
3050	10 000
1525	5000
610	2000
305	1000
152.5	500
Sea Level	0
152.5	500
1525	5000
3050	10 000

Scale 1:4 000 000

0 10 20 30 40 50 60 70 80 Miles
0 20 40 60 80 100 120 Kilometers

PACIFIC OCEAN

HAWAIIAN ISLANDS

Scale 1:20,000,000

0 100 200 300 Miles
0 200 400 Kilometers

Tropic of Cancer

A-520512-76   -3-4-4
COPYRIGHT BY
RAND McNALLY & COMPANY
MADE IN U.S.A.

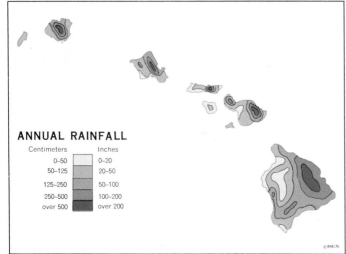

ANNUAL RAINFALL

Centimeters	Inches
0–50	0–20
50–125	20–50
125–250	50–100
250–500	100–200
over 500	over 200

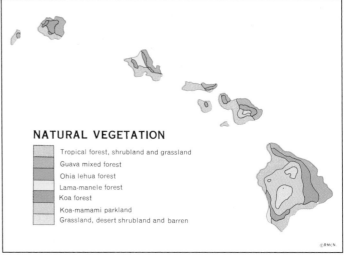

NATURAL VEGETATION

- Tropical forest, shrubland and grassland
- Guava mixed forest
- Ohia lehua forest
- Lama-manele forest
- Koa forest
- Koa-mamami parkland
- Grassland, desert shrubland and barren

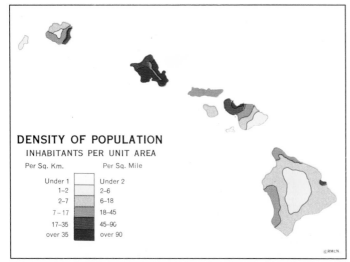

DENSITY OF POPULATION
INHABITANTS PER UNIT AREA

Per Sq. Km.	Per Sq. Mile
Under 1	Under 2
1–2	2–6
2–7	6–18
7–17	18–45
17–35	45–90
over 35	over 90

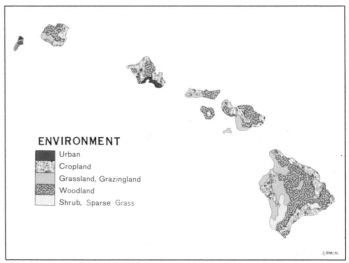

ENVIRONMENT

- Urban
- Cropland
- Grassland, Grazingland
- Woodland
- Shrub, Sparse Grass

Cities, Towns, and Villages

| 0 to 25,000 | ∘ | 100,000 to 250,000 | ⊙ | 1,000,000 and over | ⊚ |
| 25,000 to 100,000 | • | 250,000 to 1,000,000 | ◎ | Major urbanized area | |

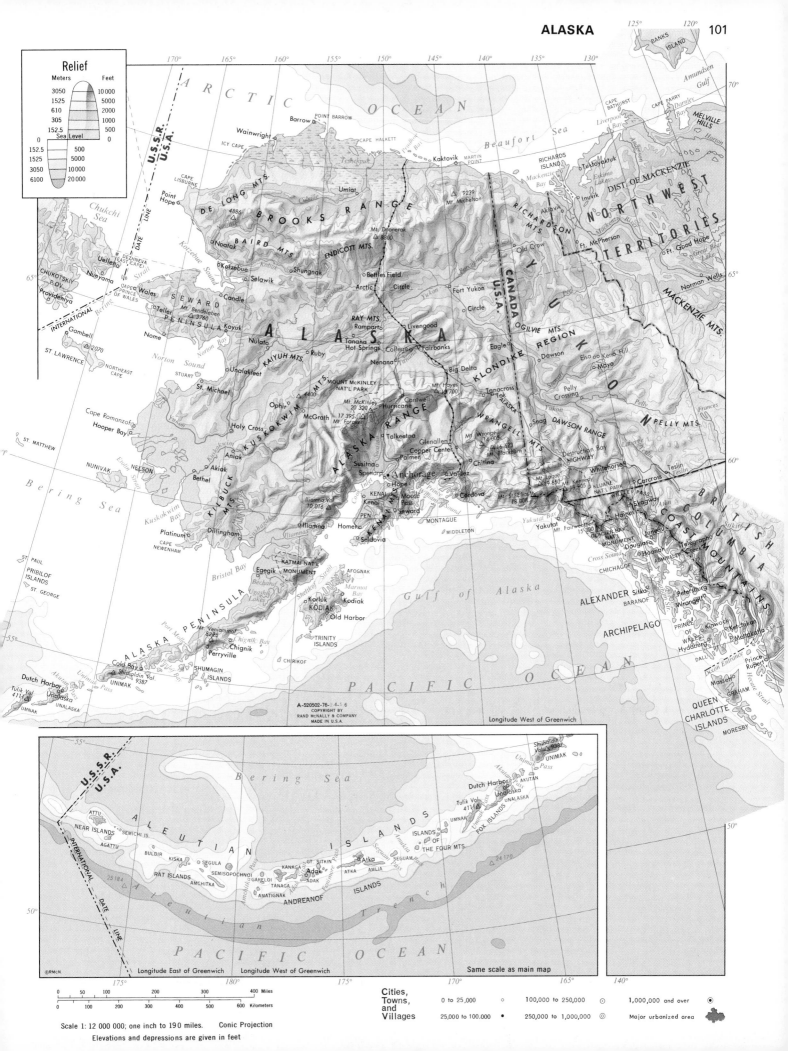

Relief

Meters	Feet
3050	10 000
1525	5000
610	2000
305	1000
152.5	500
Sea Level	
0	0

152.5	500
1525	5000
3050	10 000
6100	20 000

ARCTIC OCEAN

Amundsen Gulf

BANKS ISLAND

CAPE BATHURST
CAPE PARRY
Darnley Bay
Liverpool Bay
MELVILLE HILLS
Horton

Barrow
POINT BARROW
CAPE HALKETT
Wainwright
ICY CAPE
Beaufort Sea
Kaktovik
MARTIN POINT
RICHARDS ISLAND
Tuktoyaktuk
Eskimo Lakes
DIST. OF MACKENZIE
Inuvik

CAPE LISBURNE
DE LONG MTS.
△4884 Noatak
Umiat
Mt. Michelson △9239
Akiavik
Old Crow
Ft. McPherson
NORTHWEST TERRITORIES
Ft. Good Hope

Point Hope
BROOKS RANGE
BAIRD MTS.
Mt. Doonerak △8800
ENDICOTT MTS.
RICHARDSON MTS.
Great Bear Lake

Chukchi Sea
CAPE DEZHNEVA EAST CAPE
Ulelen
Noatak
Kotzebue
Shungnak
Bettles Field
Norman Wells
MACKENZIE MTS.

CHUKOTSKIY P.OV.
Providentiya
CAPE PRINCE OF WALES
Wales
Teller
Selawik
Arctic Circle
Fort Yukon
Circle
YUKON
OGILVIE MTS.
Elsa oo Keno Hill

Gambell
△2070
ST. LAWRENCE
NORTHEAST CAPE
Nome
Candle
RAY MTS.
Ramparto
Livengood
Eagle
Dawson
Mayo

Nunyama
Mt. Bendeleben △3760
Koyuk
ALASKA
Nulato
Tanana
Hot Springs
College Fairbanks
KLONDIKE REGION
Pelly Crossing

Norton Sound
KAIYUH MTS.
Ruby
Nenana
Big Delta
Mt. Hayes △700
Tanacross Tok
ALASKA
Shag
DAWSON RANGE
PELLY MTS.
Frances

ST. MATTHEW
Unalakleet
St. Michael
MOUNT McKINLEY NAT'L PARK
Cantwell
WRANGELL MTS.
Mt. Wrangell △14,005
Destruction Bay

Cape Romanzof
Hooper Bay
Ophir
McGrath
Mt. McKinley 20,320 △
Hurricane
Mt. Foraker 17,395
Glennallen
Copper Center
Mt. Blackburn △16,523
ALASKA HIGHWAY
Whitehorse
Teslin

NUNIVAK
NELSON
Aniak
Bethel
Holy Cross
KUSKOKWIM MTS.
ALASKA RANGE
Talkeetna
Palmer
Chitina
Mt. Lorare △19,850
Mt. Kennedy △13,905
KLUANE NAT'L PARK
Carcross
Atlin
BRITISH COLUMBIA

Bering Sea
Kuskokwim Bay
KILBUCK MTS.
Iliamna Vol. 10,016
Susitna
Spenard
Anchorage
Hope
Valdez
Cordova
Mt. St. Elias 18,008
Yakutat
Skagway
Haines
COAST MOUNTAINS

Platinum
Dillingham
Iliamna
Kenai
Moose Pass
Seward
MONTAGUE
MIDDLETON
Mt. Fairweather 15,300
GLACIER BAY NAT'L MONUMENT
Juneau
Telegraph Creek

CAPE NEWENHAM
Homer
Seldovia
KENAI PEN.
Gulf of Alaska
Yakutat Bay
Cross Sound
CHICHAGOF
Douglas
Hoonah
ADMIRALTY
Stikine

ST. PAUL
PRIBILOF ISLANDS
ST. GEORGE
KATMAI NAT'L MONUMENT
Egegik
Becharof
Ugashik Lakes
AFOGNAK
Marmot Bay
ALEXANDER
BARANOF
Sitka
Petersburg
Wrangell
Klawock

Bristol Bay
ALASKA PENINSULA
Korluk
KODIAK
Kodiak
Old Harbor
ARCHIPELAGO
PRINCE OF WALES
Hydaburg
Ketchikan
Metlakatla
DALL

Mt. Veniaminof 8225
Chignik Bay
Chignik
Perryville
TRINITY ISLANDS
CHIRIKOF
QUEEN CHARLOTTE ISLANDS
Masset
Prince Rupert
GRAHAM

Cold Bay
Shishaldin Vol. 9387
SHUMAGIN ISLANDS
PACIFIC OCEAN
MORESBY
Dixon Entrance
Hecate Strait

Dutch Harbor
Tulik Vol. 4111 △
UNIMAK
Unimak Pass
Akutan Pass
UNALASKA
UMNAK

A-520502-76- /4-5 6
COPYRIGHT BY
RAND McNALLY & COMPANY
MADE IN U.S.A.

Longitude West of Greenwich

U.S.S.R. U.S.A.
DATE LINE
INTERNATIONAL
Bering Strait

Bering Sea

ATTU
NEAR ISLANDS
SEMICHI IS.
AGATTU
BULDIR
KISKA
SEGULA
RAT ISLANDS
SEMISOPOCHNOI
AMCHITKA
ALEUTIAN ISLANDS
GT. SITKIN
KANAGA
Adak
GARELOI
TANAGA
AMATIGNAK
ANDREANOF
ATKA
AMLIA
ISLANDS OF THE FOUR MTS.
Shishaldin Vol. 9387
UNIMAK
Unimak Pass
Akutan Pass
AKUTAN
Dutch Harbor
Unalaska
Tulik Vol. 4111 △
UMNAK
FOX ISLANDS
UNALASKA
Seguam Pass

25 184
Aleutian Trench
24 170

PACIFIC OCEAN

U.S.S.R. U.S.A.
INTERNATIONAL DATE LINE

Longitude East of Greenwich
Longitude West of Greenwich
Same scale as main map

0 50 100 200 300 400 Miles
0 100 200 400 600 Kilometers

Scale 1: 12 000 000; one inch to 190 miles.   Conic Projection
Elevations and depressions are given in feet

Cities, Towns, and Villages	0 to 25,000 ○	100,000 to 250,000 ⊙	1,000,000 and over ◉
	25,000 to 100,000 ●	250,000 to 1,000,000 ⊚	Major urbanized area

©RMCN

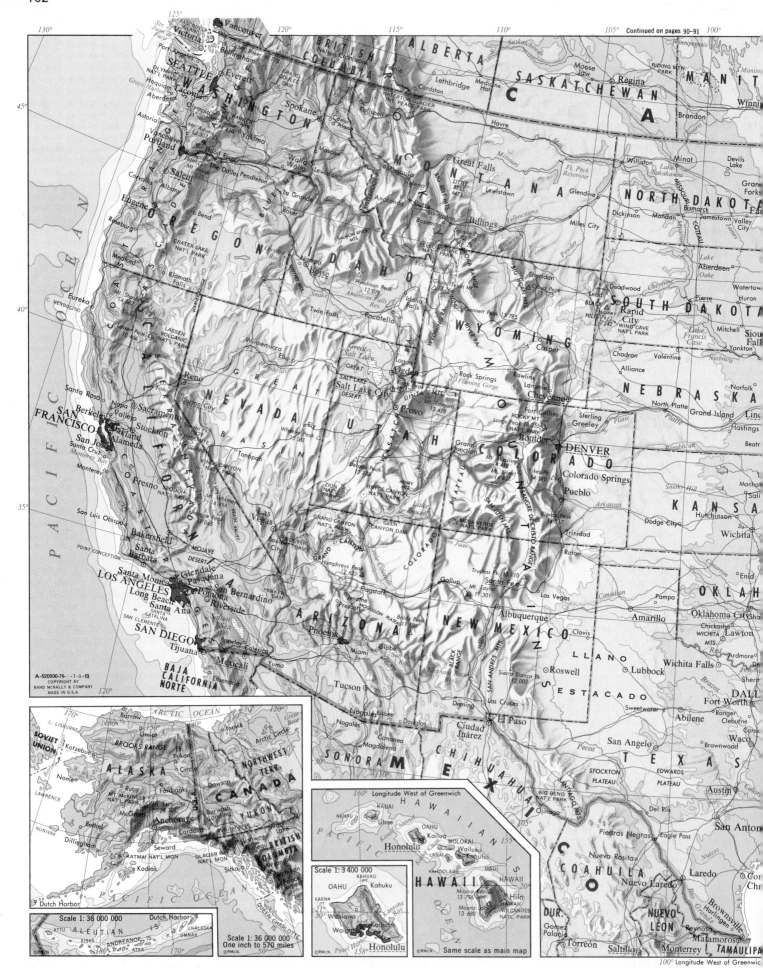

Continued on pages 90-91

Scale 1: 36 000 000

Scale 1: 36 000 000
One inch to 570 miles
©RMCN.

Scale 1: 3 400 000
©RMCN.

Same scale as main map
©RMCN.

100° Longitude West of Greenwic

Scale 1:12 000 000; one inch to 190 miles. Polyconic Projection
Elevations and depressions are given in feet

Sault Ste. Marie

North Channel

MANITOULIN ISLAND

Georgian Bay

LAKE HURON
Surface 579 Feet above Sea Level
maximum depth 750 Feet

W I S C O N S I N

MICHIGAN
Surface 579 Feet above Sea Level
maximum depth 870 Feet

M I C H I G A N

Green Bay

MILWAUKEE

Madison

Rockford

CHICAGO

I L L I N O I S

DETROIT

Windsor

LAKE E—

Surface 570 Feet above Sea Level
maximum depth 210 Feet

CLEVELAND

Youngstown

Akron

Canton

O H I O

Springfield

Columbus

I N D I A N A

Indianapolis

Dayton

Cincinnati

ST. LOUIS

Louisville

Lexington

W E S T
VA.

Charleston

Huntington

K E N T U C K Y

Scale 1:4 000 000; one inch to 64 miles.   Conic Projection
Elevations and depressions are given in feet

Longitude West of Greenwich

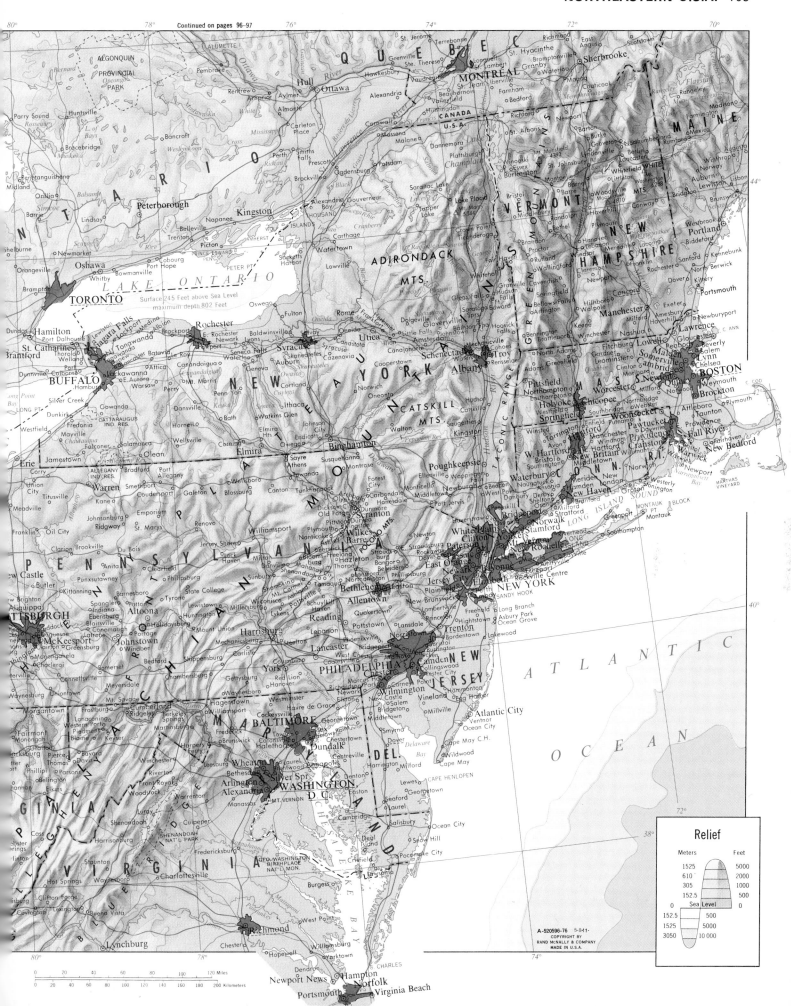

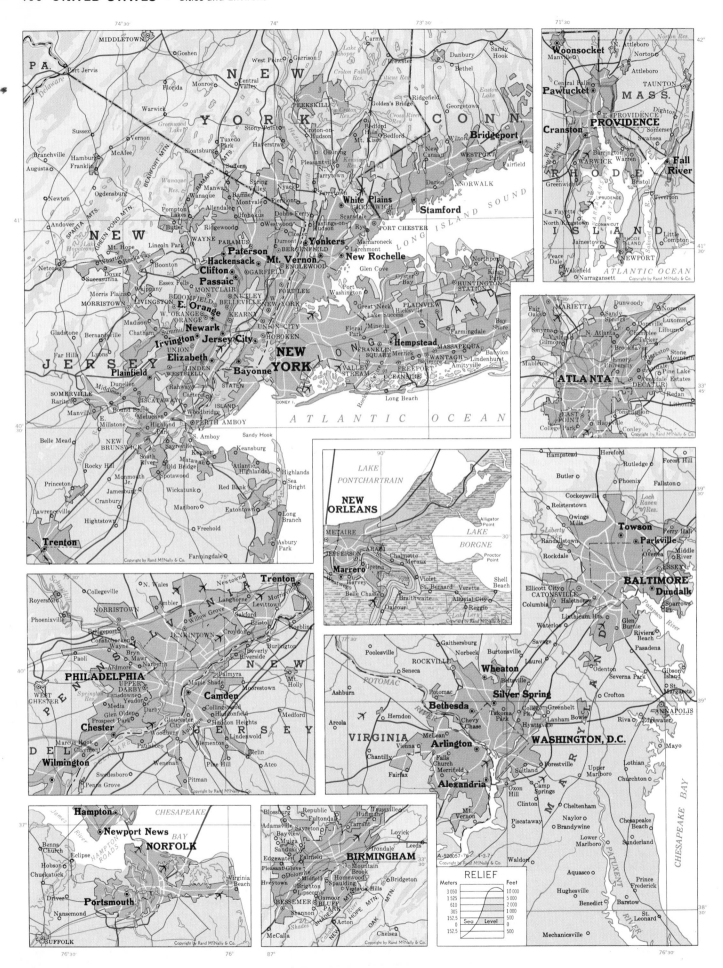

Scale 1:1 000 000; One inch to 16 miles.
Elevations and depressions are given in feet.

For larger scale coverage of New York, Baltimore, Washington, D. C. and Philadelphia see pages 53 and 54.

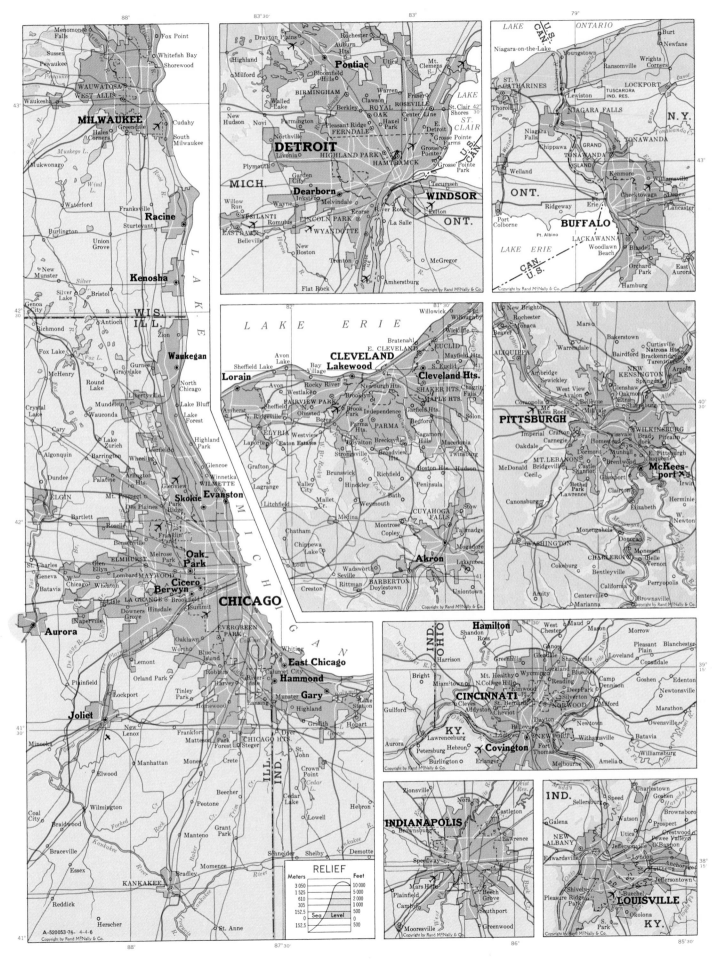

RELIEF

Meters		Feet
3 050		10 000
1 525		5 000
610		2 000
305		1 000
152.5		500
0	Sea Level	0
152.5		500

Scale 1:1 000 000; One inch to 16 miles.
Elevations and depressions are given in feet.

For larger scale coverage
of Chicago see page 56.

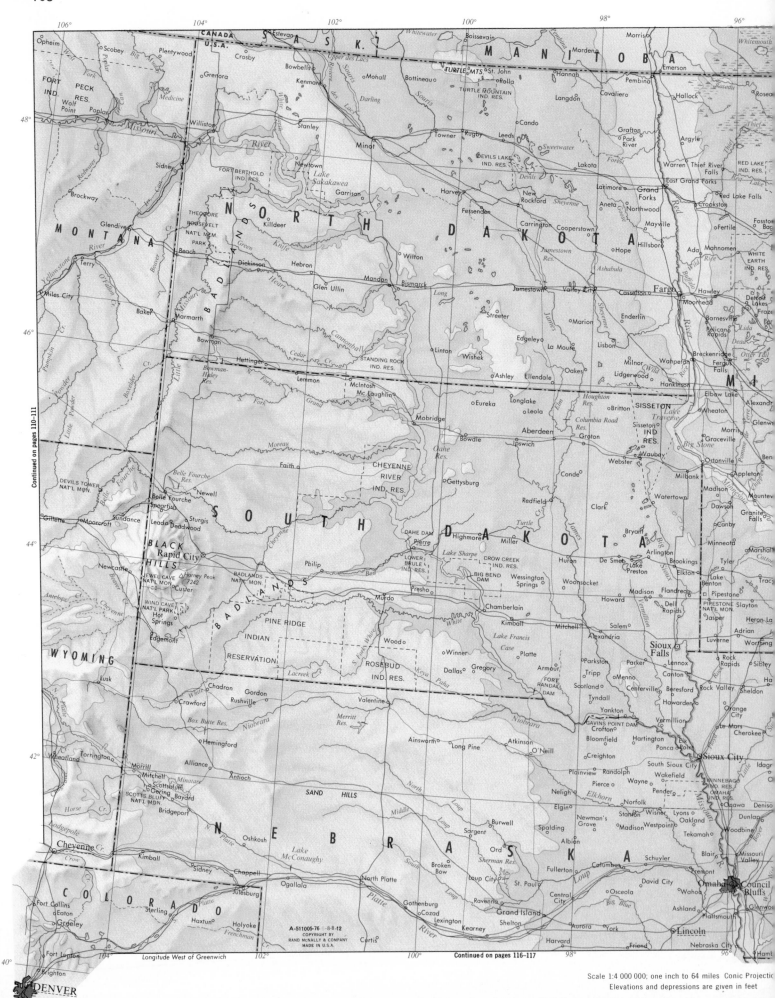

DENVER

Scale 1:4 000 000; one inch to 64 miles Conic Projectic
Elevations and depressions are given in feet

Continued on pages 110–111

Continued on pages 116–117

A-511005-76 8-8-12
COPYRIGHT BY
RAND McNALLY & COMPANY
MADE IN U.S.A.

Longitude West of Greenwich

Continued on pages 104–105

Continued on pages 116–117

Relief

Meters	Feet
1525	5000
610	2000
305	1000
152.5	500
0 Sea Level	0
152.5	500

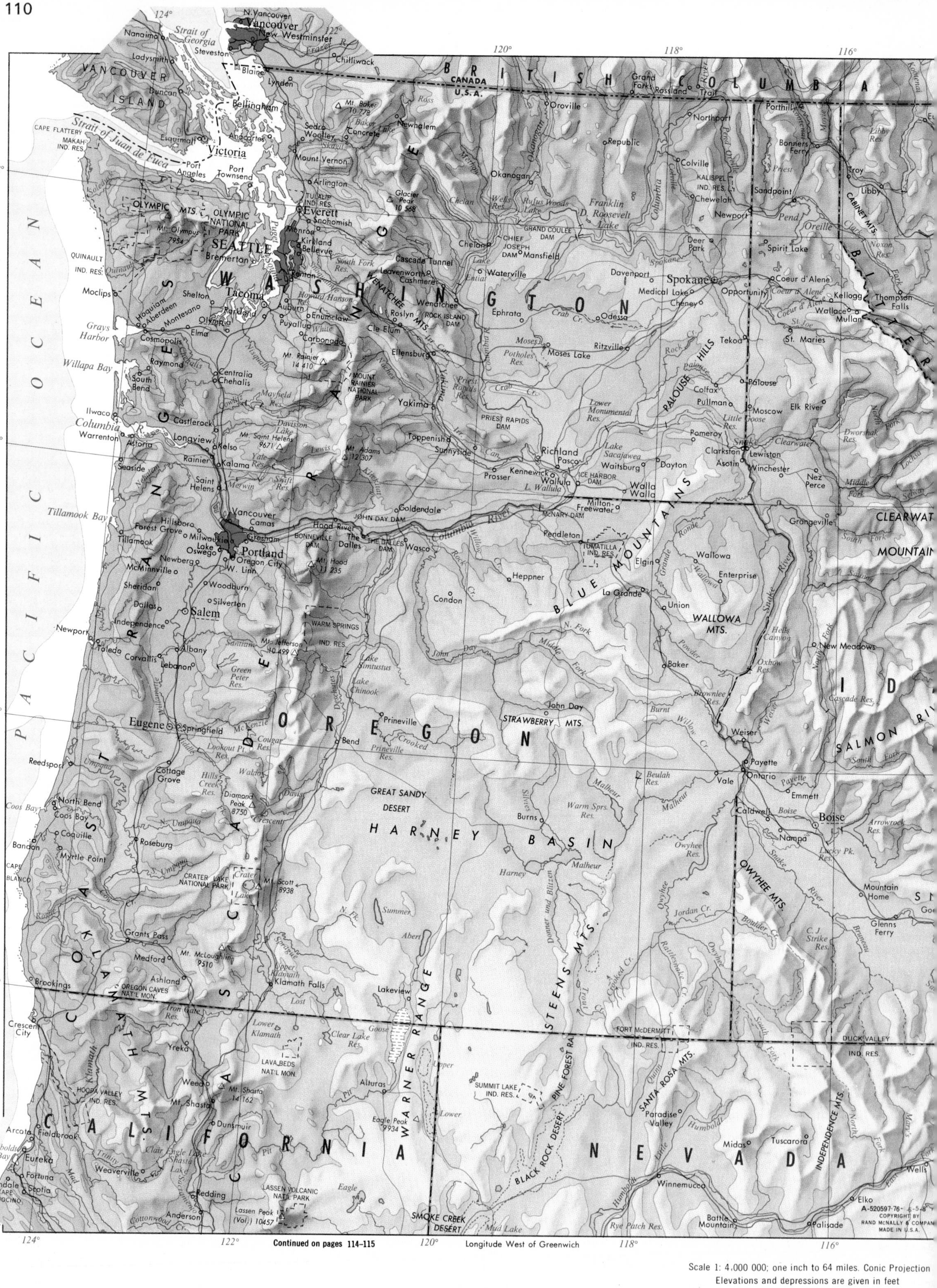

BRITISH COLUMBIA

CANADA
U.S.A.

PACIFIC OCEAN

VANCOUVER ISLAND

Strait of Georgia

Strait of Juan de Fuca

CAPE FLATTERY
MAKAH IND. RES.

Nanaimo
Ladysmith
Duncan
Esquimalt
Victoria
Steveston
New Westminster
N. Vancouver
Vancouver
Blaine
Lynden
Chilliwack
Sumas
Ross

Mt. Baker 10,778
Baker L.
Newhalem
Concrete
Glacier Peak 10,568
Oroville
Grand Forks
Rossland
Trail
Porthill
Northport
Bonners Ferry
Libby Res.
Troy
Libby
CABINET MTS.

Bellingham
Sedro Woolley
Mount Vernon
Anacortes
Port Angeles
Port Townsend

Okanogan
Republic
Colville
Chewelah
Sandpoint
Newport
Deer Park
Spirit Lake
Priest
Pend Oreille
Voxon Res.

WASHINGTON

OLYMPIC MTS.
OLYMPIC NATIONAL PARK
Mt. Olympus 7954

QUINAULT IND. RES.

Moclips
Hoquiam
Aberdeen
Montesano
Elma
Cosmopolis
Olympia
Shelton

Everett
Snohomish
Monroe
Kirkland
Bellevue
SEATTLE
Bremerton
Tacoma
Renton
Auburn
Puyallup
Enumclaw
Carbonado

Chelan
Wells Res.
Rufus Woods Lake
GRAND COULEE DAM
CHIEF JOSEPH DAM
Mansfield
Franklin D. Roosevelt Lake
KALISPEL IND. RES.
Colville

Spokane
Medical Lake
Cheney
Opportunity
Coeur d'Alene
Kellogg
Wallace
Mullan
THOMPSON FALLS
St. Maries

Cascade Tunnel
Leavenworth
Cashmere
Wenatchee
Waterville
Davenport
Crab Cr.
Odessa

Roslyn
Cle Elum
Ellensburg
ROCK ISLAND DAM

CASCADE
RANGE
WENATCHEE MTS.

Moses Lake
Ritzville
Tekoa
PALOUSE HILLS
Rock L.
Colfax
Palouse
Moscow
Elk River
DWORSHAK Res.

Grays Harbor
Willapa Bay
South Bend
Raymond
Centralia
Chehalis

Mt. Rainier 14,410
MOUNT RAINIER NATIONAL PARK
Mayfield Res.

Yakima
Toppenish
Sunnyside
Potholes Res.
Priest Rapids Res.
PRIEST RAPIDS DAM
Lower Monumental Res.
Pullman
Pomeroy
LITTLE GOOSE Res.
Little Goose
Clarkston
Lewiston
Nez Perce

Columbia R.
Willapa Bay
Castlerock
Longview
Kelso
Rainier
Kalama
Woodland

Mt. Saint Helens 9671
Yale Res.
Swift Res.
Merwin
Lewis R.
Mt. Adams 12,307

Goldendale
Richland
Pasco
Kennewick
Wallula
L. Wallula
ICE HARBOR DAM
Walla Walla
Milton-Freewater
Waitsburg
Dayton
Winchester
Asotin
Clearwater

Astoria
Warrenton
Seaside
Ilwaco

Vancouver
Camas
JOHN DAY DAM
Hood River
The Dalles
BONNEVILLE DAM
THE DALLES DAM
Wasco
McNARY DAM
Pendleton
UMATILLA IND. RES.
Elgin
BLUE MOUNTAINS
Wallowa
Grangeville
CLEARWATER MOUNTAINS

Tillamook Bay
Tillamook

Hillsboro
Forest Grove
Milwaukie
Lake Oswego
PORTLAND
Gresham
Oregon City
W. Linn
Newberg
Sheridan
McMinnville
Dallas

Heppner
Condon
Enterprise
Union
WALLOWA MTS.
Hells Canyon
New Meadows

Salem
Silverton
Woodburn
Independence
Albany
Lebanon
Corvallis
Toledo
Newport

WARM SPRINGS IND. RES.
Mt. Jefferson 10,499
Green Peter Res.
Santiam R.
Lake Simtustus
Lake Chinook
John Day R.
Oxbow Res.
Baker
Brownlee Res.

OREGON

COAST RANGE

Eugene
Springfield
Reedsport
Cottage Grove
Hills Creek Res.
Lookout Pt. Res.
McKenzie R.
Cougar Res.
Waldo L.
Diamond Peak 8750
Davis L.
Crescent

Prineville
Bend
Crooked R.
Prineville Res.
STRAWBERRY MTS.
John Day
Burnt R.
Willow Cr.
Weiser
Payette
SALMON RIVER

North Bend
Coos Bay
Coquille
Roseburg
Myrtle Point
Bandon
CAPE BLANCO

N. Umpqua R.
Umpqua R.

GREAT SANDY DESERT
HARNEY BASIN
Burns
Warm Sprs. Res.
Malheur
Vale
Ontario
Emmett
Caldwell
Nampa
Boise
Arrowrock Res.

CASCADE RANGE

Grants Pass
Medford
Ashland
CRATER LAKE NATIONAL PARK
Crater L.
Mt. Scott 8938
Mt. McLoughlin 9510
Upper Klamath Lake
Klamath Falls
Summer L.
Abert L.
Harney L.
Malheur L.
Owyhee Res.
Jordan Cr.
OWYHEE MTS.
Mountain Home
Glenns Ferry
C. J. STRIKE Res.

KLAMATH MTS.
OREGON CAVES NAT'L MON.
Brookings
Iron Gate Res.
Lower Klamath
Clear Lake Res.
Lakeview
WARNER RANGE
STEENS MTS.
Donner und Blitzen R.
FORT McDERMITT IND. RES.
DUCK VALLEY IND. RES.

Crescent City
Yreka
Weed
Mt. Shasta 14,162
Dunsmuir
LAVA BEDS NAT'L MON.
Weed
Alturas
Pit R.
Goose L.
Upper L.
Lower L.
Eagle Peak 9934
SUMMIT LAKE IND. RES.
PINE FOREST RA.
SANTA ROSA MTS.
Paradise Valley
BLACK ROCK DESERT
INDEPENDENCE MTS.

CALIFORNIA

Arcata
Fieldbrook
Eureka
Fortuna
Ferndale
Scotia
CAPE MENDOCINO
Humboldt Bay
HOOPA VALLEY IND. RES.
TRINITY MTS.
Weaverville
Clair Engle Lake
CLAIR ENGLE Res.
Redding
Anderson
Cottonwood
LASSEN VOLCANIC NAT'L PARK
Lassen Peak (Vol.) 10,457
Eagle L.

NEVADA

SMOKE CREEK DESERT
Mud Lake
Rye Patch Res.
Winnemucca
Battle Mountain
Palisade
Elko
Wells
Midas
Tuscarora
Humboldt R.

IDAHO

Longitude West of Greenwich

Scale 1: 4,000,000; one inch to 64 miles. Conic Projection
Elevations and depressions are given in feet

A-520597-76
COPYRIGHT BY
RAND McNALLY & COMPANY
MADE IN U.S.A.

ALBERTA
CANADA
U.S.A.
SASKATCHEWAN

Milk

WATERTON-GLACIER INTERNATIONAL PEACE PARK

BLACKFOOT IND. RES.

Sunburst
Cut Bank
Shelby
Browning
Whitefish
Kalispell
Hungry Horse Res.
SWAN RANGE
Valier
Conrad
Choteau

Morgan
Opheim
West Fork
Plentywood
Scobey
Grenora

Hogeland
Chinook
Harlem
Havre
Malta

FORT PECK IND. RES.

Medicine

Williston

N. DAK.

48°

Glasgow
Wolf Point
Poplar
Missouri River
Sidney

Fresno Res.
Lodge Cr.

Big Sandy
Marias
Tiber Res.

ROCKY BOYS IND. RES.

Ft. Peck
Fort Peck Res.

Brockway
Glendive
Beach

Milk River

Ronan
NATIONAL BISON RANGE
Missoula
Lolo
Stevensville
Hamilton

ROCKY

LEWIS RANGE

Helena
East Helena
Townsend

BIG BELT MTS.

Fort Benton
Great Falls
Belt

LITTLE BELT MTS.
Neihart

White Sulphur Spgs.

Winifred
Lewistown
Winnett

MONTANA

Terry
Glendive

Miles City
Baker
Marmarth

Missoula
Philipsburg
Anaconda
Walkerville
Butte
Three Forks

BIG HOLE NAT'L BATTLEFIELD
PIONEER MTS.
Twin Bridges
Dillon

Deer Lodge
Bozeman
Livingston
Columbus
Laurel

Harlowton
Roundup

CRAZY MTS.
Bigtimber

Billings
Hardin

CUSTER BATTLEFIELD NAT'L MON.
NORTHERN CHEYENNE IND. RES.
Lame Deer

Colstrip

Forsyth

Araxa Mt. 10 900
Madison Res.
Electric Peak 10 715
Gardiner

Red Lodge
Granite Peak 12 799
Bear Creek

Crow Agency
CROW IND. RES.

104°

Sheridan

BIGHORN MOUNTAINS

DEVILS TOWER NAT'L MON.
Sundance

Gillette
Moorcroft

HOLE
MTS.
LEMHI RANGE
BEAVERHEAD MTS.
Salmon
Borah Pk. 12 662
Mackay
Boulder Peak 10 966
Hyndman Peak 12 078
Arco

Hap Hawkins Lake
Lima Res.

Mammoth Hot Springs
Mt. Washburn 10 317
YELLOWSTONE NATIONAL PARK
7731 ft. above sea level

ABSAROKA RANGE

Lovell
Powell
Greybull
Basin
Cloud Peak 13 175
Buffalo

44°

St. Anthony
Ashton

Cody

Shoshone

Ten Sleep
Worland
Gebo
Thermopolis

Kaycee

Midwest
Antelope

RIVER PLAINS
SNAKE

Idaho Falls
Rexburg
Rigby

Jackson Lake
GRAND TETON NAT'L PARK
Grand Teton Mt. 13 766
Gros Ventre

Gooseberry Cr.
Owl Cr.

WIND RIVER
Shoshoni
Powder River
Glenrock

CRATERS OF THE MOON NAT'L MON.

Shelley
Blackfoot
FORT HALL
Pocatello

WIND RIVER RANGE
Gannett Peak 13 785
Fremont Peak 13 730
WIND RIVER IND. RES.

Riverton
Lander

Douglas
Casper
Orin

American Falls Res.
Snake
American Falls
Rupert
Burley

Grays L.
Blackfoot River Res.

WYOMING RANGE

Green
Wind

Alcova Res.

WYOMING

Shoshone
Twin Falls
Oakley

Lava Hot-Sprs.
Soda Springs
Meade Peak 9353
Afton
Montpelier

Fontenelle Res.
Sandy

Pathfinder Res.

Seminoe Res.

Wheatland

42°

Malad
Preston
Lewiston
Richmond
Smithfield
Logan
Providence
Wellsville
Brigham

BEAR RIVER RANGE
Bear

Kemmerer
Green River
Rock Springs

Superior
Rawlins

GREAT DIVIDE BASIN

Hanna

FRONT RANGE

Medicine Bow

Wheatland Res.

Lucin
GREAT SALT LAKE DESERT

Surface elev. approx. 4200 ft. above sea level
Great Salt Lake

Huntsville
Ogden
Morgan
Farmington

Flaming Gorge Res.

Craig
Steamboat Sprs.

TOANA RANGE
Wendover

Bountiful
Salt Lake City
Bingham Canyon
Tooele
Midvale
Heber

UTAH

UINTA MTS.
Wilson Peak 12 095
Park City
Kings Peak 13 528
Mt. Emmons 13 428

DINOSAUR NAT'L MON.

Vernal

PARK RANGE

COLO.

Oak Creek

108°

Continued on pages 108-109
Continued on pages 114-115

Relief

Meters		Feet
3050		10000
1525		5000
610		2000
305		1000
152.5		500
Sea Level		0
1525		500

0 20 40 60 80 100 120 Miles
0 20 40 60 80 100 120 140 160 180 200 Kilometers

114°   112°   110°   108°   106°

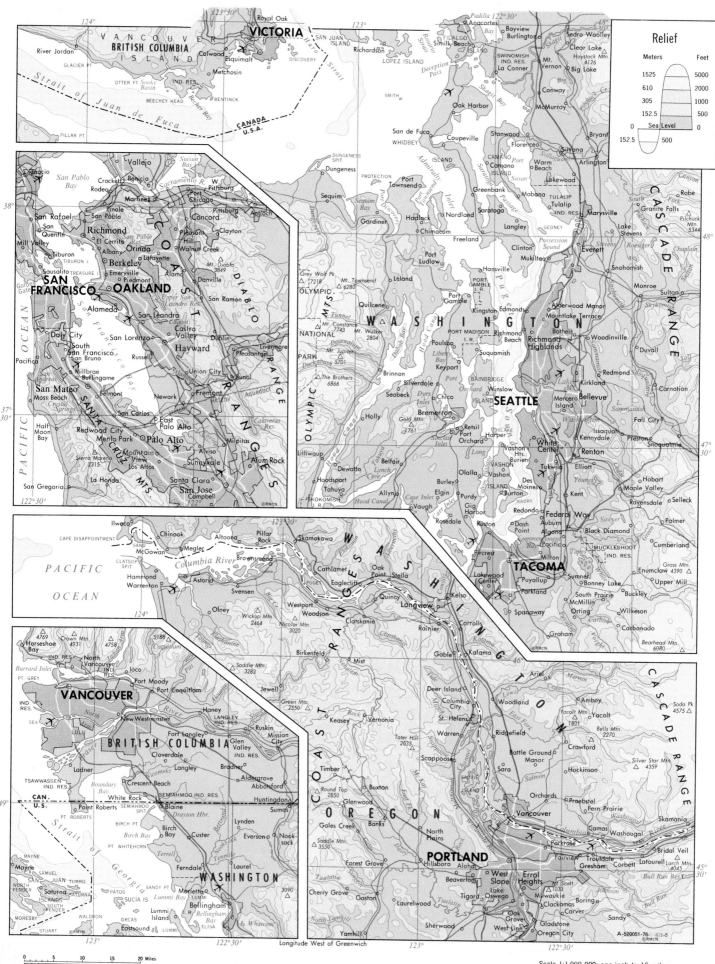

Relief

Meters		Feet
1525		5000
610		2000
305		1000
152.5		500
0	Sea Level	0
152.5		500

Scale 1:1 000 000; one inch to 16 miles.
Elevations and depressions are given in feet.

Longitude West of Greenwich

0 5 10 15 20 Miles
0 4 8 12 16 20 24 28 32 Kilometers

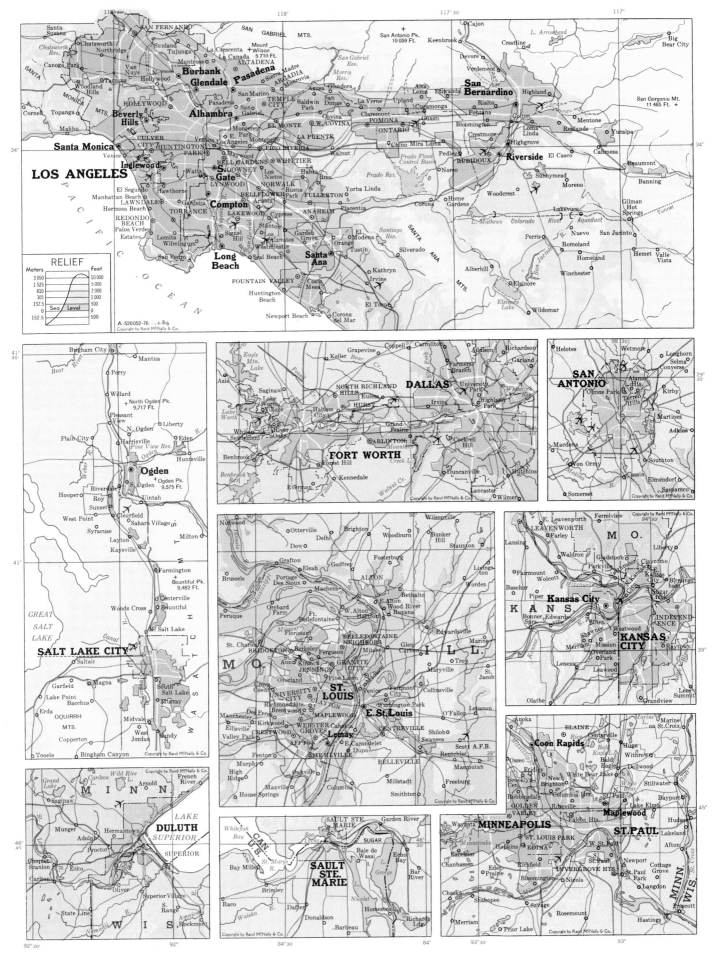

Scale 1:1 000 000; One inch to 16 miles.
Elevations and depressions are given in feet.

For larger scale coverage
of Los Angeles see page 57.

Relief

Meters		Feet
3050		10000
1525		5000
610		2000
305		1000
152.5		500
0	Sea Level	0
		Below
152.5		500 Sea Level
1525		5000
3050		10000

Continued on pages 110-111

SAN DIEGO

Scale 1:1 000 000

0   5   10 Miles
0   4   8   12   16 Kilometers

©RMcN.

A-520599-76 ~6~7-10
COPYRIGHT BY
RAND McNALLY & COMPANY
MADE IN U.S.A.

Scale 1:4 000 000; one inch to 64 miles. Conic Projection
Elevations and depressions are given in feet

Longitude West of Greenwich

0   20   40   60   80   100   120 Miles
0   20   40   60   80   100   120   140   160   180   200 Kilometers

Continued on pages 116-117

Continued on pages 118-119

116

Continued on pages 108–109

106°   104°   102°   100°   98°

Continued on pages 114–115

W Y O

Cheyenne

Oshkosh   Lake McConaughy   Ord   Sherman   A Loup

Kimball   Sidney   Chappell   Ogallata   North Platte   Broken Bow   Loup City   St. Paul   Fullerton

Julesburg   Gothenburg   Cozad   Lexington   Grand Island   Shelton   Aurora

Sterling   Haxtun   Holyoke   Curtis   Mc Cook   Minden   Hastings   Harvard

N E B R A S

Fort Collins   Windsor   Eaton   Greeley

Boulder   Fort Lupton   Brush   Akron   Yuma   Wray   Benkelman   Beaver City   Alma   Franklin   Red Cloud   Superior

Golden   DENVER   Brighton   Fort Morgan   Holdrege

R O C K Y   C O L O R A D O

K A N S A S

N E W   M E X I C O   M O U N T A I N S

O K L A

T E X A S

L L A N O   E S T A C A D O

Continued on pages 118–119

Longitude West of Greenwich

Scale 1:4 000 000; one inch to 64 miles. Conic Projection
Elevations and depressions are given in feet

A-511006-76-6-7 9
COPYRIGHT BY
RAND McNALLY & COMPANY
MADE IN U.S.A.

Relief

Meters		Feet
3050		10 000
1525		5000
610		2000
305		1000
152.5		500
0	Sea Level	0

Continued on pages 108–109

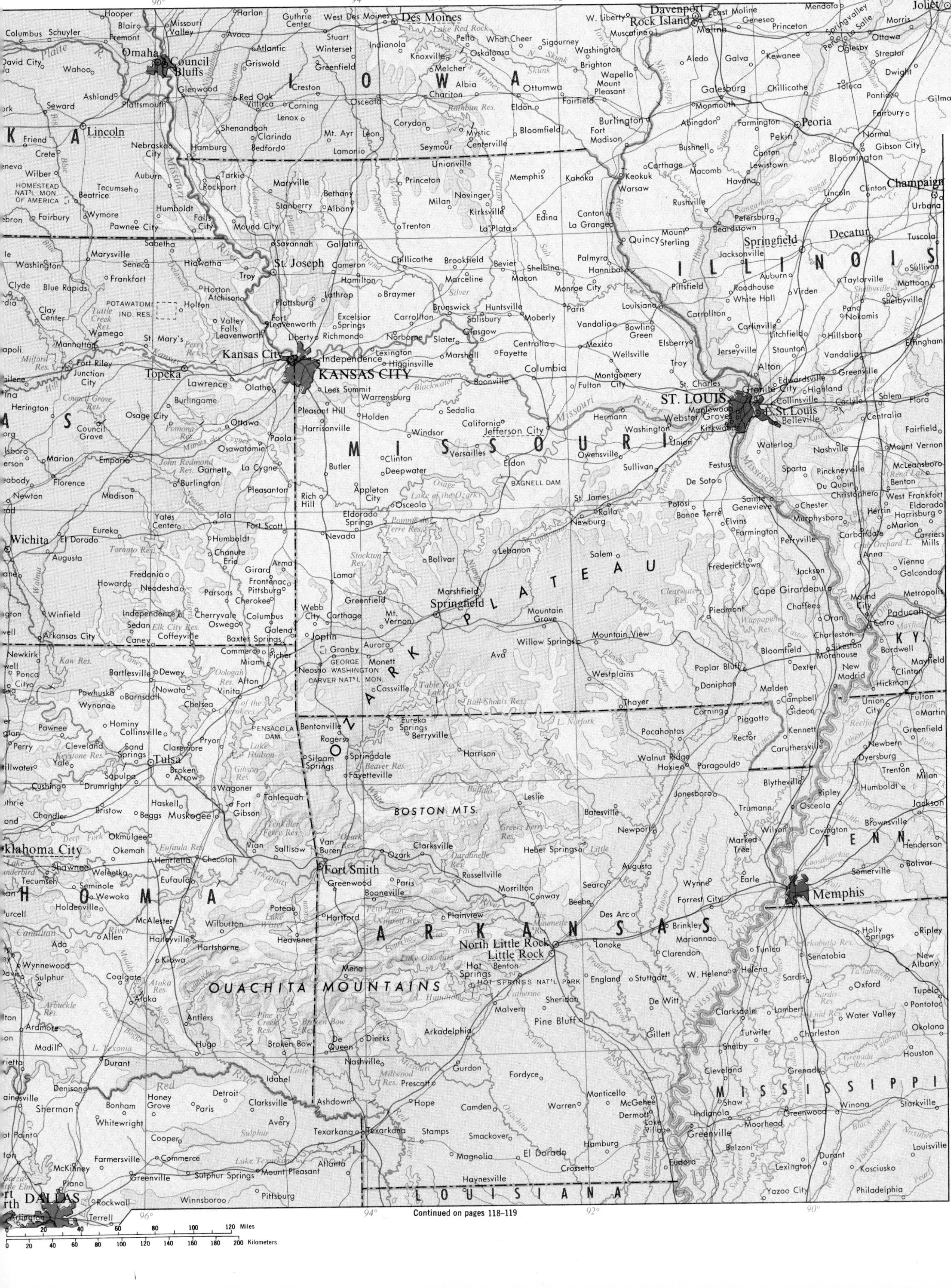

Continued on pages 104–105

Continued on pages 120–121

Continued on pages 118–119

CHICAGO

IOWA

ILLINOIS

MISSOURI

KANSAS

OKLAHOMA

ARKANSAS

TENN.

MISSISSIPPI

LOUISIANA

KY.

OZARK PLATEAU

BOSTON MTS.

OUACHITA MOUNTAINS

Omaha
Council Bluffs
Lincoln
Des Moines
Kansas City
KANSAS CITY
Topeka
St. Joseph
St. Louis
E. St. Louis
Springfield
Peoria
Champaign
Decatur
Tulsa
Oklahoma City
Fort Smith
Little Rock
North Little Rock
Hot Springs
Memphis
DALLAS
Wichita

100   120 Miles
200 Kilometers

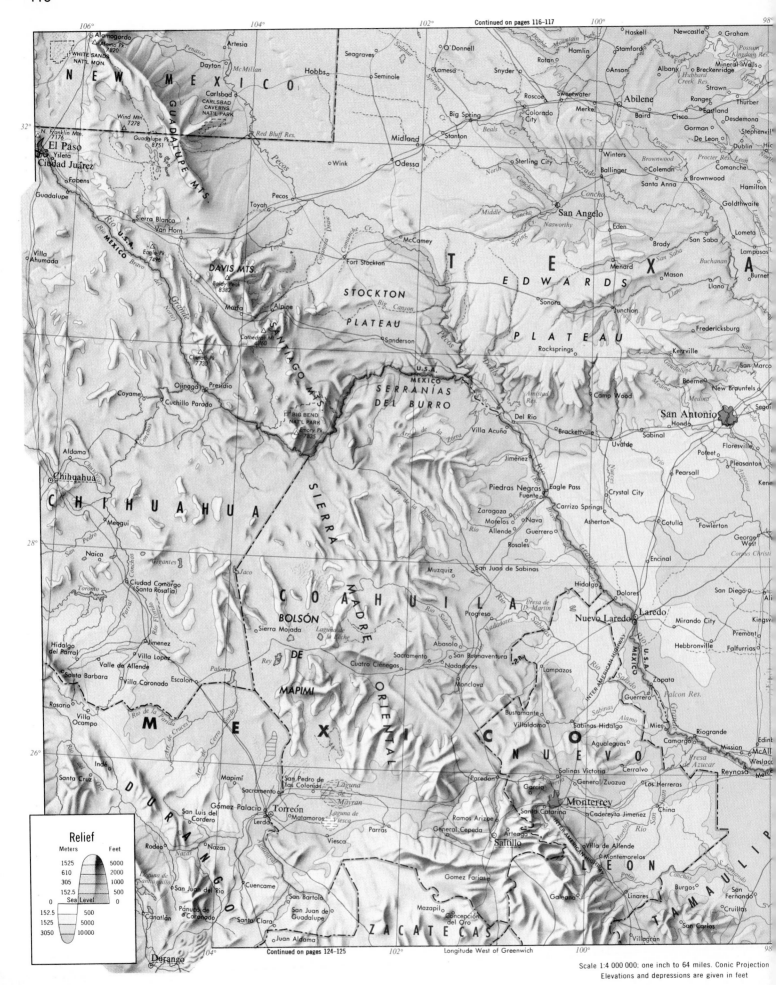

Continued on pages 116–117

NEW MEXICO

Alamogordo
Alamo Pk.
7820
WHITE SANDS
NAT'L MON.

Artesia

Dayton
McMillan

Seagraves

O'Donnell

Haskell   Newcastle   Graham

Hobbs   Lamesa   Hamlin
                                    Stamford
Carlsbad   Seminole   Snyder Rotan   Albany
CARLSBAD   Roscoe Sweetwater   Mineral Wells
CAVERNS   Colorado   Breckenridge
NAT'L PARK   City   Ranger
Wind Mtn.   Merkel Abilene   Eastland Thurber
7278   Big Spring   Baird   Cisca   Desdemona
                                      Colorado   Gorman Dublin
N. Franklin Mtn. Guadalupe Pk.   Stanton City Winters   De Leon
7176   8751   Midland   Ballinger Coleman Brownwood
El Paso   Sterling City   Comanche
Ysleta   Red Bluff Res.   Odessa   Santa Anna Hamilton
Ciudad Juárez   Wink   North Concho   Goldthwaite
Fabens   San Angelo Eden   San Saba
Guadalupe   Pecos Toyah   Brady   Lometa
                    Sierra Blanca   Middle Concho   Menard Lampasas
Villa   Van Horn   McCamey   Sonora Junction
Ahumada   Fort Stockton   Mason   Burnet
            Eagle Pk. DAVIS MTS.   Rocksprings Llano Fredericksburg
            7496   Baldy Peak   EDWARDS PLATEAU   Kerrville
                    8382   Alpine   STOCKTON
                    Marfa   PLATEAU   San Marco
            Cathedral Mt.   Sanderson   Boerne New Braunfels
Coyame   Chinati Pk. Santiago MTS. U.S.A.   San Antonio
Cuchillo Parado 7730 Ojinaga Presidio MEXICO Camp Wood   Hondo Floresville
                    BIG BEND SERRANIAS Del Rio   Uvalde Poteet
Aldama   NAT'L PARK DEL BURRO Villa Acuña Brackettville Sabinal Pleasanton
            Emory Pk.   Jiménez Eagle Pass   Pearsall Kene
Chihuahua   7835   Piedras Negras Crystal City
                                         Fuente   Carrizo Springs Cotulla Fowlerton
Meoqui   CHIHUAHUA SIERRA   Zaragoza Nava Asherton   George
                                         Morelos Allende   West
Naica   MADRE   Rosales Guerrero   Encinal Corpus Christi
            Gigantes Jaco   Muzquiz San Juan de Sabinas
Ciudad Camargo   DE   Hidalgo Dolores   San Diego Ali
(Santa Rosalia)   COAHUILA ORIENTAL   Progreso Nuevo Laredo Laredo Mirando City Premont
Hidalgo   BOLSÓN   Abasolo Nadadores   Hebbronville Falfurrias
del Parral Jimenez Sierra Mojada   Sacramento San Buenaventura
            Villa Lopez Laguna de   Cuatro Cienegas Lampazos Zapata
Valle de Allende la Leche   Monclova   Mier Riogrande
Santa Barbara Rey   Bustamante Sabinas Hidalgo Camargo Edint
Rosario   Escalon MAPIMI   Villaldama Aguleguas Mission McAll
Villa   NUEVO Cerralvo Presa Weslac
Ocampo MEXICO   Salinas Victoria de Azucar Reynosa Mc
Indé   Paredon General Zuazua Los Herreras
Santa Cruz   DURANGO Mapimí   Garcia Monterrey
            Sacramento San Pedro   Santa Catarina Cadereyta Jimenez China
Gomez Palacio de las Colonias Laguna Ramos Arizpe   TAMAULIP
San Luis del Torreón de Mayran   General Cepeda Arteaga Villa de Alfende
Cordero Lerdo Matamoros Laguna de   Saltillo Montemorelos
San Juan del Rio Viesca Parras   LEON
Rodeo Nazas   Gomez Farias   Potosi
Cuencame   Mazapil Concepcion Galeana Linares San
San Juan del Rio   del Oro   Burgos Fernando
Pánuco de   ZACATECAS   Cruillas San Carlos
Coronado Santa Clara San Juan de
Canatlán San Bartolo Guadalupe
Durango   Juan Aldama

Continued on pages 124–125

Longitude West of Greenwich

Relief

Meters	Feet
1525	5000
610	2000
305	1000
152.5	500
0 Sea Level	0
152.5	500
1525	5000
3050	10000

Scale 1:4 000 000; one inch to 64 miles. Conic Projection
Elevations and depressions are given in feet

Continued on pages 116–117

Continued on pages 120 121

ARK.

MISSISSIPPI

LOUISIANA

GULF OF MEXICO

HOUSTON

GALVESTON BAY

EAST BAY

BOLIVAR PENINSULA

GALVESTON ISLAND

WEST BAY

GULF OF MEXICO

Scale 1:1 000 000

0   5   10 Miles

0   4   8   12   16 Kilometers

A-511007-76- 5- 6-
COPYRIGHT BY
RAND McNALLY & COMPANY
MADE IN U.S.A.

0   20   40   60   80   100   120 Miles

0   20   40   60   80   100   120   140   160   180   200 Kilometers

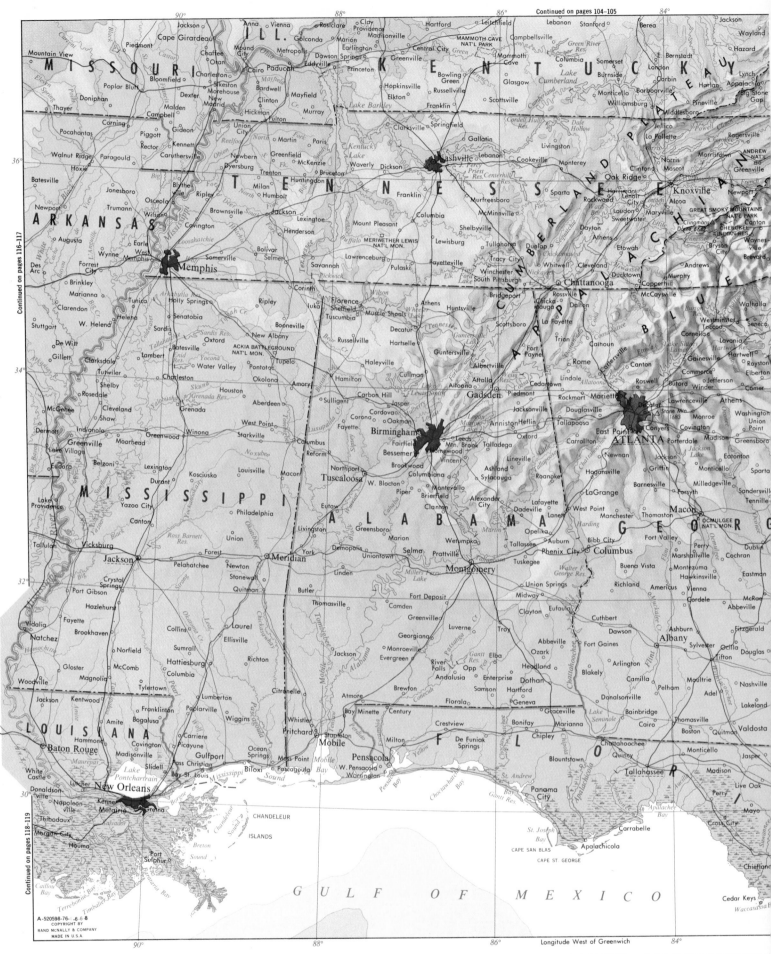

120

Continued on pages 104–105

Continued on pages 116-117

Continued on pages 118-119

MISSOURI

ILL.

KENTUCKY

TENNESSEE

ARKANSAS

CUMBERLAND PLATEAU

APPALACHIAN

BLUE

MISSISSIPPI

ALABAMA

GEORGIA

LOUISIANA

FLO

Memphis

Nashville

Knoxville

Chattanooga

Birmingham

Atlanta

Macon

Montgomery

Columbus

Jackson

Meridian

Baton Rouge

New Orleans

Mobile

Pensacola

Albany

Tallahassee

GREAT SMOKY MOUNTAINS NAT'L PARK

MAMMOTH CAVE NAT'L PARK

CHANDELEUR ISLANDS

Lake Pontchartrain

G U L F   O F   M E X I C O

A-520598-76- 6-6-8
COPYRIGHT BY
RAND McNALLY & COMPANY
MADE IN U.S.A.

Longitude West of Greenwich

Scale 1:4 000 000; one inch to 64 miles. Conic Projection
Elevations and depressions are given in feet

Relief

Meters	Feet
1525	5000
610	2000
305	1000
152.5	500
0 Sea Level	0
152.5	500
1525	5000

Same scale as main map

W.VA.

VIRGINIA

Richmond
Petersburg
Newport News
Norfolk
Portsmouth
Virginia Beach
Hampton

NORTH CAROLINA

Winston-Salem
Greensboro
Durham
Raleigh
Charlotte

SOUTH CAROLINA

Columbia
Charleston

GEORGIA

Augusta
Savannah

ATLANTIC OCEAN

GULF OF MEXICO

FLORIDA

Jacksonville
Tampa
St. Petersburg
Orlando
MIAMI
Miami Beach
Fort Lauderdale
W. Palm Beach

FLORIDA KEYS

Key West

Scale 1:16 000 000; one inch to 250 miles. Polyconic Projection
Elevations and depressions are given in feet

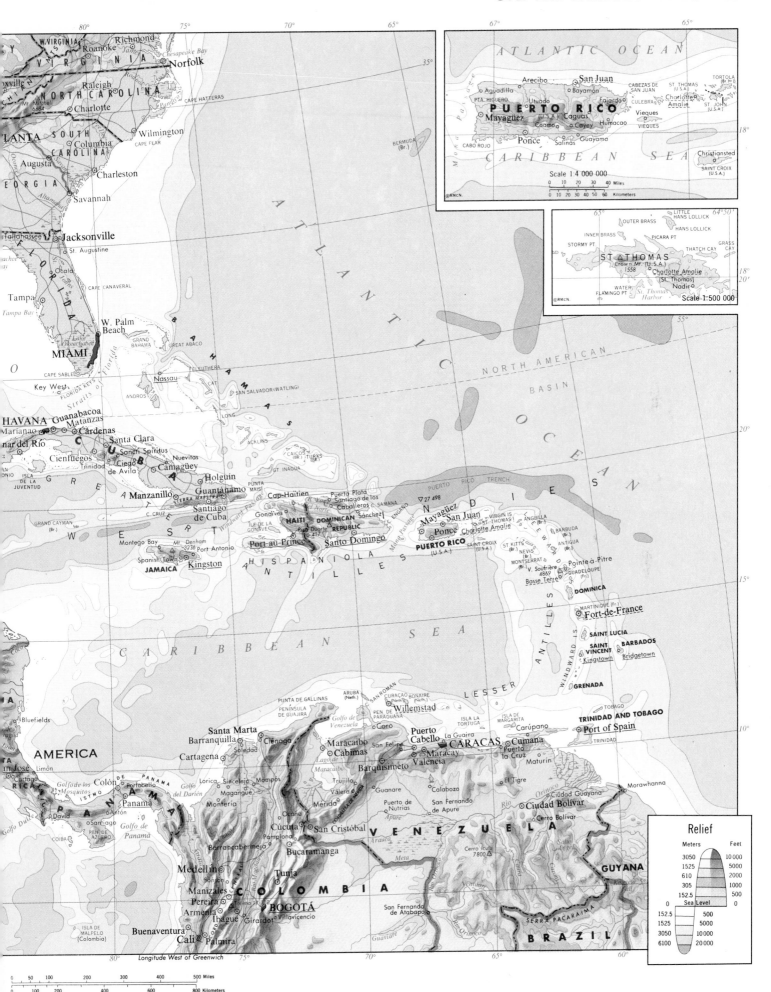

124

Continued on pages 118-119

PACIFIC

OCEAN

Relief

Meters		Feet
3050		10 000
1525		5000
610		2000
305		1000
152.5		500
Sea Level		0
152.5		500
1525		5000
3050		10 000

A-531695-76- 5 5-10
COPYRIGHT BY
RAND McNALLY & COMPANY
MADE IN U.S.A.

Longitude West of Greenwich

Scale 1:4 000 000; one inch to 64 miles. Conic Projection
Elevations and depressions are given in feet

GULF OF MEXICO

BAHÍA DE CAMPECHE

Tropic of Cancer

Laguna Almagre

Laguna de San Andres

PTA. JEREZ

CABO ROJO
ARRECIFE BLANQUILLA
ISLA DE LOBOS

Laguna Tamiahua

ARRECIFE TANQUIJO
ARRECIFE TÚXPAN

Altamira
Ciudad Madero
Tampico
Villa Cuauhtémoc
Tampico Alto

Ozuluama
Tancoco
Alamo
Tamiahua
Túxpan

Tihuatlán
Poza Rica
Gutiérrez Zamora
Furbero
Coyutla
Tecolutla
Nautla

Cuetzalan del Progreso
Tlapacoyan
Misantla
Vega de Alatorre

Teziutlán
Atempan
Jalacingo
Altotonga
Naolinco

Las Vigas
Perote
PUNTA ZEMPOALA
Nauchampatepetl

Jalapa Enriquez
Coatepec
Antigua Veracruz

Teocelo
Huatusco
Coscomatepec

Veracruz
ARRECIFE CABEZA

Orizaba
Córdoba
Medellín

Nogales
Maltrata
Omealca
Cotaxtla

Tlacotepec

Tlalixcoyan
Alvarado

Tierra Blanca

San Martín (Vol.)
Santiago Tuxtla
San Andrés Tuxtla
Catemaco

PTA. ZAPOTLÁN

Tlacotalpan

Cosamaloápan
Chacaltianguis

Soteapan
Pajápan

Coatzacoalcos
(Puerto México)

San Pedro

ISLA DEL CARMEN

Laguna de Términos

Ciudad del Carmen

PUNTA FONTERA

Frontera

Paraíso
Allende

Comalcalco
Jalpa

Cárdenas
Cunduacán

Villahermosa

Huimanguillo

San Carlos

Tacotalpa
Teapa

Palizada

Candelaria

Balancán
Emiliano Zapata

Palenque

MEXICO
GUATEMALA

Tenosique

Continued on pages 126-127

YUCATÁN

Sisal
Hunucmá
Maxcanú
Halachó
Calkini
Dzitbalché
Hecelchakán

CAMPECHE

Lerma
Campeche
Seybaplaya
Champotón
Pustunich
Sabancuy
Chicbul
Mamantel

MESETA DE AGUA ESCONDIDA

OAXACA / ISTMO DE TEHUANTEPEC / CHIAPAS / GUATEMALA

Tehuacan
Ajalpan
Zoquitlán

Coxquihui
Zozocolco

Huajuapan de León
Coixtlahuaca

Oaxaca de Juárez

Tuxtla Gutiérrez

Las Casas
Ciudad de las Casas

Comitán

SIERRA MADRE DE CHIAPAS

Golfo de Tehuantepec

GUATEMALA

For larger scale coverage of Mexico City see page 58.

Mexico City inset

MÉXICO
HIDALGO
TLAXCALA
PUEBLA
MORELOS
DISTRITO FEDERAL

Morelos
Nicolás Romero
Cuautitlán
Tutitlán
Tecamac
Teotihuacán
Acolman
Chiconautla
Tepexpan
Otumba
Apan

Cahuacán
Coacalco
Pyramids of Teotihuacán
Calpulalpan

San Bartolo
Ixtlahuaca
Cerro La Catedral 13 000
Atizapán
Tlalnepantla
Mazatla
Tlalnepantla
Tepetlaoxtoc
Texcoco
San Jerónimo
Nanacamilpa

Jiquipilco
Temoaya
Atzcapotzalco
Naucalpan
Gustavo A. Madero
Lago de Texcoco (Dry Lake)
Coatlinchán
Chicoloapan

Mimiapan
Chimalpa
MEXICO CITY
Ixtacalco
Los Reyes
Río Frío
HY

Huixquilucan
Cuajimalpa
Villa Obregón
Contreras
Ixtapalapa
Ayotla
Iztapaluca
INTER-AMERICAN
Texmelucan

Toluca
Lerma
San Andrés
Tláhuac
Tlalpan
Xochimilco
Coyoacán
Chalco
Tecómitl

Capultitlán
Metepec
Mexicalcingo
Cerro Muneco 12 655
Ajusco
Cerro Ajusco 12 850
Topilejo
Oxtotepec
Milpa Alta
Tlalmanalco
Iztaccíhuatl 17 343

Almoloya
Coatepec
Tenango
Amecameca

Nevado de Toluca 14 409
Tenango
Tres Cumbres
Volcán Popocatépetl 17 887

Huitzilac
Tepoztlán
Tlalnepantla
Ozumba

Cuernavaca
Tlayacapan

Scale 1:1 000 000

© RMcN.

20

40

60

80

100

120 Miles

200 Kilometers

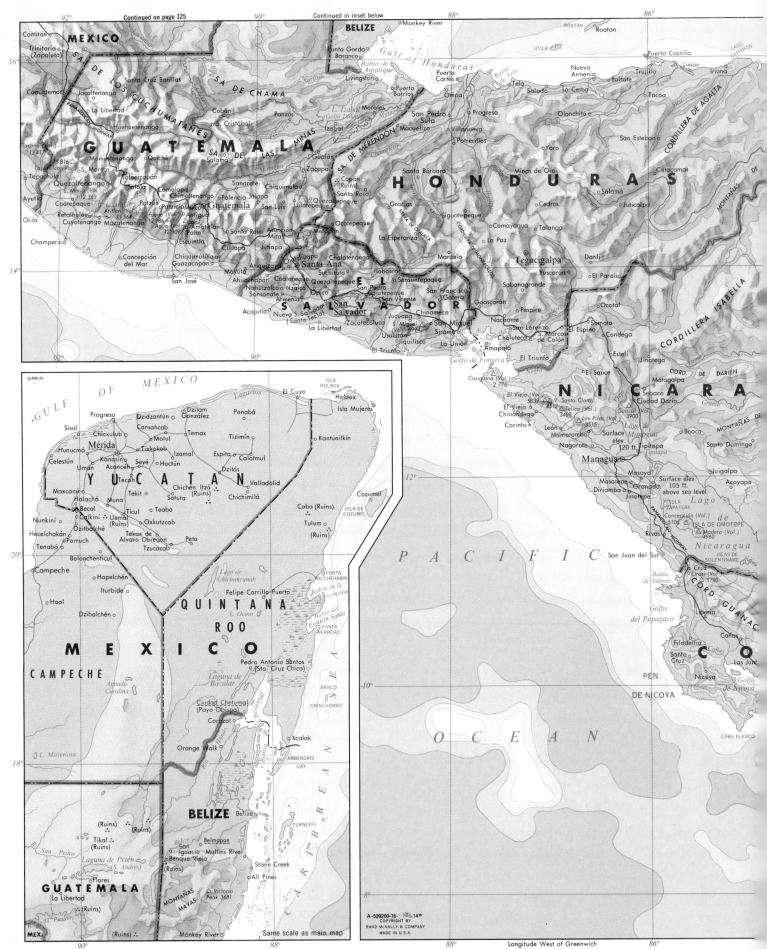

Continued on page 125
Continued in inset below

MEXICO

GUATEMALA

BELIZE

HONDURAS

EL SALVADOR

NICARA

Tegucigalpa

San Salvador

Golfo de Fonseca

PACIFIC

OCEAN

GULF OF MEXICO

YUCATAN

Mérida

QUINTANA ROO

MEXICO

CAMPECHE

BELIZE

Belmopan

GUATEMALA

CARIBBEAN SEA

Lago de Managua

Managua

Lago de Nicaragua

CORD. GUANAC

PEN. DE NICOYA

Longitude West of Greenwich

Scale 1:4 000 000; one inch to 64 miles. Sinusoidal Projection

Elevations and depressions are given in feet

A-539200-76
COPYRIGHT BY
RAND McNALLY & COMPANY
MADE IN U.S.A.

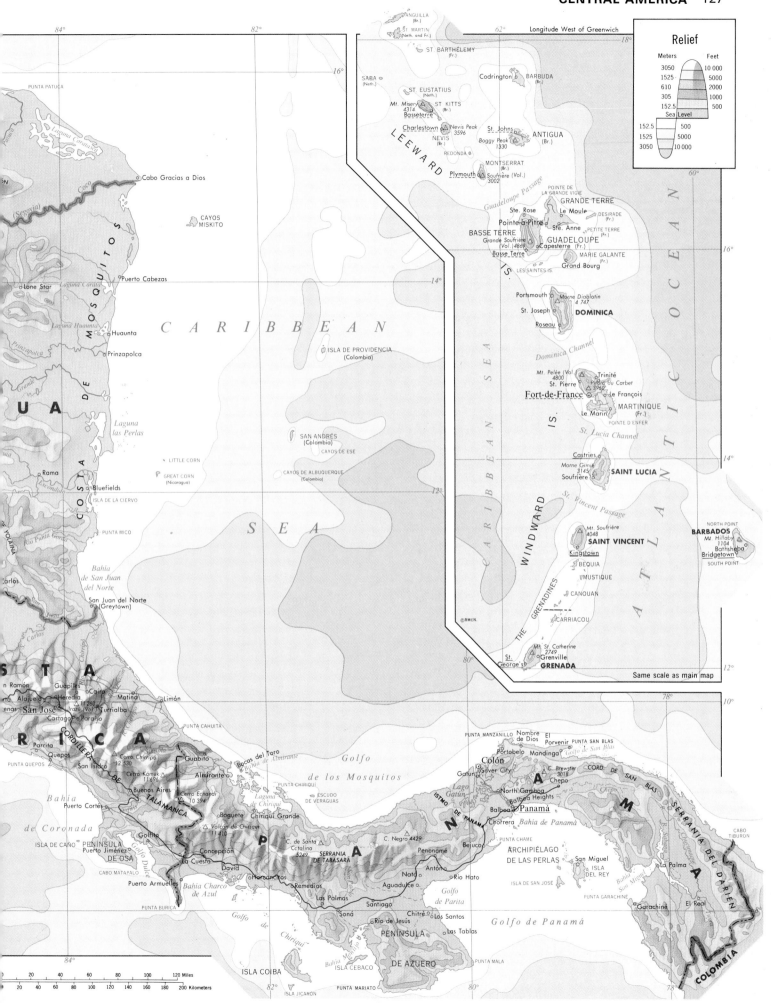

GULF

OF

MEXICO

FLORIDA

Naples
Big Cypress Swamp
Everglades
EVERGLADES
EVERGLADES NATIONAL PARK
SEMINOLE IND. RES.
Orange
MIAMI
Homestead
Delray Beach
Fort Lauderdale
Dania
Miami Beach
Biscayne Bay
CAPE ROMANO
TEN THOUSAND ISLANDS
CAPE SABLE
Whitewater Bay
Florida Bay
KEY LARGO
Pine Is.
Key West
DRY TORTUGAS
MARQUESAS KEYS
FLORIDA KEYS
Straits of Florida
Tropic of Cancer

LITTLE BAHAMA BANK
SETTLEMENT PT.
LITTLE ABACO
West End
Freeport
GRAND BAHAMA
PINDER POINT
Northwest Providence Channel
GREAT ISAAC
BROTHERS
LITTLE ISAAC
NORTH BIMINI
SOUTH BIMINI
Barnett Harbor
N. CAT CAY
Dollar Harbor
RIDING ROCKS
ORANGE CAY
NORTH ELBOW CAYS
DOG ROCKS
CAY SAL
CAY SAL BANK
DAMAS CAYS
ANGUILLA CAYS
Santaren Channel
Nicholas Channel
HURRICANE FLATS

Whale Cay Channels
GREAT ABACO
Marsh Harbour
GREAT GUANA CAY
ELBOW CAY
Pelican Harbor
Cherokee Sound
GORDA CAY
Cross Harbor
Cornwall
SOUTHWEST PT.
GREAT HARBOR CAY
BERRY ISLANDS
FRAZIERS HOG CAY
WHALE CAY
BONDS CAY
ROYAL
SHIP CHANNEL CAY
HIGHBORNE CAY
Nassau
NEW PROVIDENCE
PARADISE
SIMMS PT.
Nicolls Town
Staniard Creek
WILLIAMS
JOULTER'S CAYS
SALVADOR PT.
North Bight
Middle Bight
South Bight
Turner Sound
ANDROS ISLAND
GREEN CAY
BOOBY ROCKS
SNAP PT.
CURLY CUT CAYS
TONGUE OF THE OCEAN
Northeast Providence Channel
BRIDGE
CURREN

Santa Lucia
ARCHIPIELAGO DE LOS COLORADOS
Bahia Honda
CIUDAD DE LA HABANA
HAVANA
Marianao
Guanabacoa
Regla
Guanajay
San Antonio de los Baños
Artemisa
Bejucal
Güines
HABANA
Güira de Melena
Batabanó
Unión de Reyes
Jovellanos
Alacranes
Matanzas
Cárdenas
Corratillo
Martí
Quemado de Güines
CAYO BLANCOS
Bahia de Matanzas
Bahia de Cárdenas
Bahia de Santa Clara
ARCHIPIELAGO DE SABANA
Sagua la Grande
CAYO FRAGOSO
CAYO SANTA MARIA
CAYO

Pan de Guajaibon
2532
Candelaria
Los Palacios
PINAR
DEL RIO
SIERRA
Consolación del Sur
VUELTA ABAJO
Pinar del Río
San Juan y Martínez
Guane
PEN. DE GUANAHACABIBES
CABO FRANCES
CABO CORRIENTES
Mantua
Bahia de Guadiana
Ensenada de Cortés
PORGANOS
PUNTA GORDA
Ensenada de la Broa
GOLFO DE BATABANO
CAYOS LAGUNA
ISLAS DE MANGLES
CAYO DE DIOS
CAYOS DE SAN FELIPE
Nueva Gerona
ISLA DE LA JUVENTUD
Santa Fé
CAYOS DE LOS INDIOS
ARCHIPIELAGO DE LOS CANARREOS
CAYOS INGLES
Ensenada de la Siguanea
PTA. FRANCES
CABO PEPE
BANCO JARDINES
CAYO ROSARIO
CAYO CANTILES
CAYO LARGO
BANCO XAGUA
Pedro Betancourt
Navajas
Jagüey Grande
Colón
Santo Domingo
Lajas
Esperanza
Cruces
Rodas
Aguada
Palmira
CIENFUEGOS
Cienfuegos
Bahia Cienfuegos
Pico San Juan
Ensenada de Cochinos
Bahia Cochinos
Golfo de Cazones
VILLA CLARA
Santo
Santa Clara
Remedios
Caibarién
Camajuaní
Zulueta
Yaguajay
Florida
SANCTI SPIRITUS
Sancti Spiritus
SIERRA DE TRINIDAD
Trinidad
Casilda
Tunas de Zaza
Jatibonico
Morón
CIEGO DE AVILA
Ciego de Avila
Júcaro
Fomento
Minas
CAMAGÜEY
Camagüey
Santa Lucia
CAYOS ANA MARIA
CAYOS CINCO BALAS
CAYOS DE LAS DOCE LEGUAS
Canal de Caballones
LABERINTO DE LAS DOCE LEGUAS
Santa Cruz del Sur
Guayabal
GOLFO DE GUACANAYABO
Campechuela
Niquero
Manzanillo
SIERRA
GRANMA
Pico Ojo del Toro
1748
CABO CRUZ
CAYO COCO
CAYO SANTA MARIA
CAYO GUILLERMO
Bahia Buena Vista
CAYO ROMANO
CAYO CRUZ
CAYO SABINAL
Bahia de Nuevitas
Nuevitas
Puerto Padre
LAS TUNAS
Victoria de las Tunas
Bahia Turiguano
Laguna de Leche
Old Bahama Channel
CAYO LOBOS
CAYO PAREDON GRANDE

CARIBBEAN SEA

CAYMAN ISLANDS (Br.)
LITTLE CAYMAN
CAYMAN BRAC
Georgetown
GRAND CAYMAN

Montego Bay
Lucea
SOUTH NEGRIL PT.
Savanna la Mar
Black River
Falmouth
St. Ann's Bay
Annotto Bay
JAMAICA
Mr. Denham
3236
Bull Head
2798
Spanish Town
Kingston
May Pen
GT. PEDRO BLUFF
PORTLAND PT.
Portland Bight

A-533200-76
COPYRIGHT BY
RAND McNALLY & COMPANY
MADE IN U.S.A.

Longitude West of Greenwich

Scale 1:4 000 000; one inch to 64 miles. Conic Projection
Elevations and depressions are given in feet.

Havana Inset

Scale 1:1 000 000
0 5 10 Miles
0 8 16 Kilometers

GULF OF MEXICO

HAVANA
(La Habana)

Playa de Guanabo
Cojimar
Guanabacoa
Regla
Campo Florido
Playa de Santa Fé
Marianao
Baracoa
San Francisco de Paula
Arroya Arena
Cotorro
Quatro Caminos
Calabazar
Rancho Boyeros
Bauta
Santiago de las Vegas
Managua
San José de las Lajas
Caimito del Guayabal
Bejucal
La Sabina
L. de Ariguanabo
Buenaventura
△ 950
Ceiba del Agua
San Antonio de los Baños
San Antonio de las Vegas
23°
©RMcN.
82°30'   82°15'

Main Map

76°   74°   72°   70°   26°   24°   22°   20°

A T L A N T I C   O C E A N

Tropic of Cancer

JAMES PT.
Governor's Harbour
PALMETTO PT.
ELEUTHERA
rpum Bay
ELL
Rock Sound
EUTHERA PT.
LITTLE SAN SALVADOR
xuma Sound
CAT
Arthur's Town
NORTHEAST PT.
Old Bight
GREAT GUANA CAY
HAWKS NEST PT.
COLUMBUS PT.
SAN SALVADOR (WATLING)
(Columbus, Oct. 12, 1492)
SOUTHWEST PT.
CONCEPTION
LEE STOCKING
Rolleville
CAPE STA. MARIA
RUM CAY
ARBY
GREAT EXUMA
George Town
HOG CAY
LITTLE EXUMA
LONG
JUMENTO CAYS
WATER CAY
Clarence Town
SAMANA OR ATWOOD CAY
FLAMINGO CAY
BIRD ROCK
CROOKED
NORTHEAST PT.
Man of War Channel
JAMAICA CAY
CAP VERDE
FORTUNE
PLANA OR FLAT CAYS
SEAL CAYS
DIANA BANK
FISH CAY
The Bight of Acklins
ACKLINS
Abraham's Bay
OCHINOS BANKS
NURSE CAY
RACCOON CAY
SALINA PT.
MAYAGUANA
GREAT RAGGED
CASTLE
COLUMBUS BANK
MIRA POR VOS ISLETS
MIRA POR VOS PASS
CAY VERDE
Crooked Island Passage
Mayaguana Passage
CAICOS PASSAGE
CAY STA. DOMINGO
PROVIDENCIALES
NORTH CAICOS
GRAND CAICOS
HOGSTY REEF
WEST CAICOS
CAICOS IS. (Br.)
CAPE COMETE
EAST CAICOS
BROWN BANK
LITTLE INAGUA
C A I C O S   B A N K
SOUTH CAICOS
GRAND TURK
NORTHEAST PT.
WEST SAND SPIT
AMBERGRIS CAYS
Grand Turk
TURKS IS. (Br.)
SALT CAY
PALMETTO PT.
Ocean Bight
SEAL CAYS
Turks I. Passage
Mouchoir Passage
MOUCHOIR BANK
Man of War Bay
The Lake
GREAT INAGUA
Matthew Town
South Bay
Ocean Bight
S I L V E R   B A N K
Silver Bank Passage
NAVIDAD BANK

Gibara
CABO LUCRECIA
Banes
Antilla
Bahía de Nipe
Holguin
OLGUIN
Mayari
Sagua de Tánamo
CUCHILLA DE TOA
SA. DE NIPE
Baracoa
STRA
SANTIAGO DE CUBA
△3100
SA. DE PURIAL
Soriano
Alto Songo
GUANTANAMO
PUNTA MAISI
Canex
San Luis
401
Guantánamo
Bahía de Ovando
Santiago de Cuba
Caimanera
Yateras
Naval Station (U.S.A.)
Bahía de Guantánamo
W i n d w a r d   P a s s a g e
ÎLE DE LA TORTUE
CABO ISABELA
CAP ST. NICOLAS
Port de Paix
Le Borgne
Cap-Haïtien
Monte Cristi
Puerto Plata
CABO FRANCES VIEJO
Le Môle
Limbé
Guayubin
CORDILLERA SEPTENTRIONAL
Pico Diego Ocampo
4009
PTE. PLATEFORME
Fort Liberté
Dajabón
Gaspar Hernández
Grande Rivière du Nord
Santiago Rodriguez
Bahia Escocesa
Ouanaminthe
Moca
Salcedo
Nagua
Gonaïves
Valliere
Santiago de los Cabelleros
CABO SAMANA
GOLFE DES GONAÏVES
St. Michel-de-l'Atalaye
La Vega
Riva
Sabana de la Mar
Bahia de Samaná
CABO SAN RAFAEL
EA
Hinche
DOMINICAN
Jarabacoa
Cotui
Miches
St. Marc
Pic Bonhomme
△5883
Mte. Mira 7434
Pico Duarte △ 10,417
CORDILLERA ORIENTAL
Canal de Saint-Marc
CORDILLERA CENTRAL
Hato Mayor
POINT OUEST
ÎLE DE LA GONÂVE
2548
H A I T I
Bánica
San Juan
Azua
Bayaguana
Los Llanos
Seibo
Jérémie
ÎLE GRANDE CAYEMITE
Mirebalais
Lascahobas
Mte. Tina △9285
R E P U B L I C
FORMIGAS BANK
CAP DAME MARIE
Anse d'Hainault
Baie des Baradères
Anse à Veau
Léogane
Petionville
SIERRA DE NEIBA
San Cristóbal
Pedro de Macoris
La Romana
CAP DES IROIS
Rico de Macaya △ 7920
Port-au-Prince
Étang Saumâtre
Lago Enriquillo
Neiba
San
MASSIF DE LA HOTTE
Miragoâne
Petit-Goâve
MASSIF DE LA SELLE
8793
CUL DE SAC
Duverge
Barahona
Bani
NAVASSA (U.S.A.)
Tiburon
Coteaux
Aquin
Jacmel
Belle-Anse
Limón
SIERRA DE BAHORUCO
Bahia de Ocoa
SANTO DOMINGO
Santo Domingo
ort Antonio
Roche à Bateau
Les Cayes
ÎLE À VACHE
H I S P A N I O L A
Enriquillo
PTA. PALENQUE
SAONA
CATALINA
POINTE À GRAVOIS
Oviedo
L. Trujin
MORANT PT.
BEATA
CABO BEATA
CABO FALSO
△ ALTO VELO

Scale Bar

0 10 20 30 40 50 60 70 80 90 100 110 120 Miles
0 20 40 60 80 100 120 140 160 180 200 Kilometers

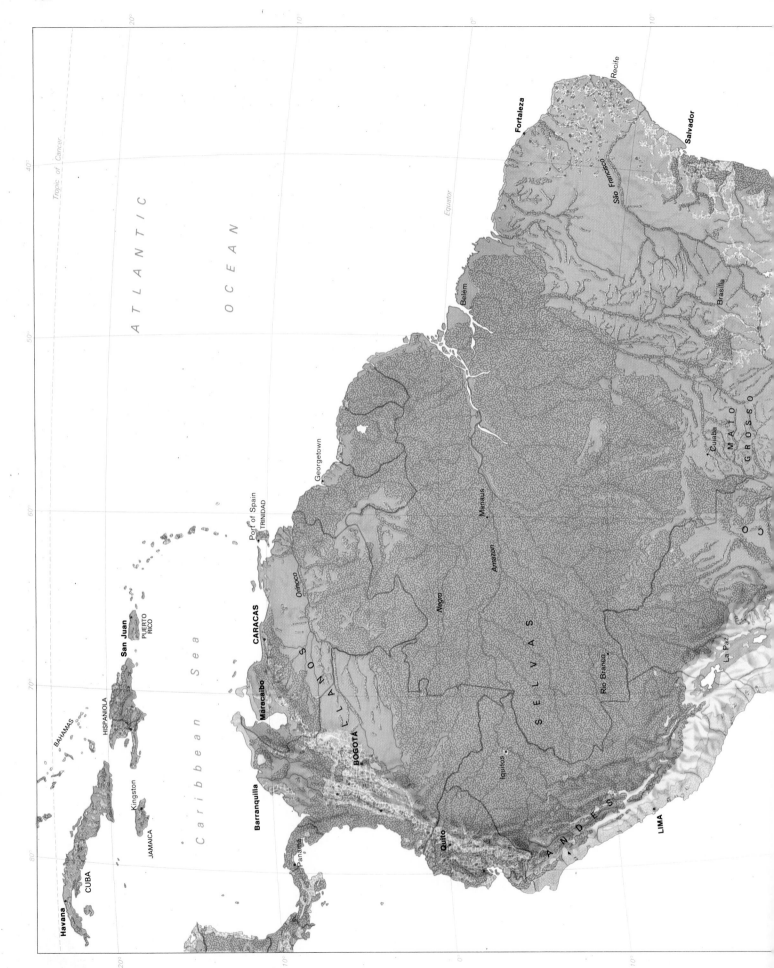

Scale 1:24,000,000; one inch to 380 miles. Lambert Azimuthal Equal-Area Projection

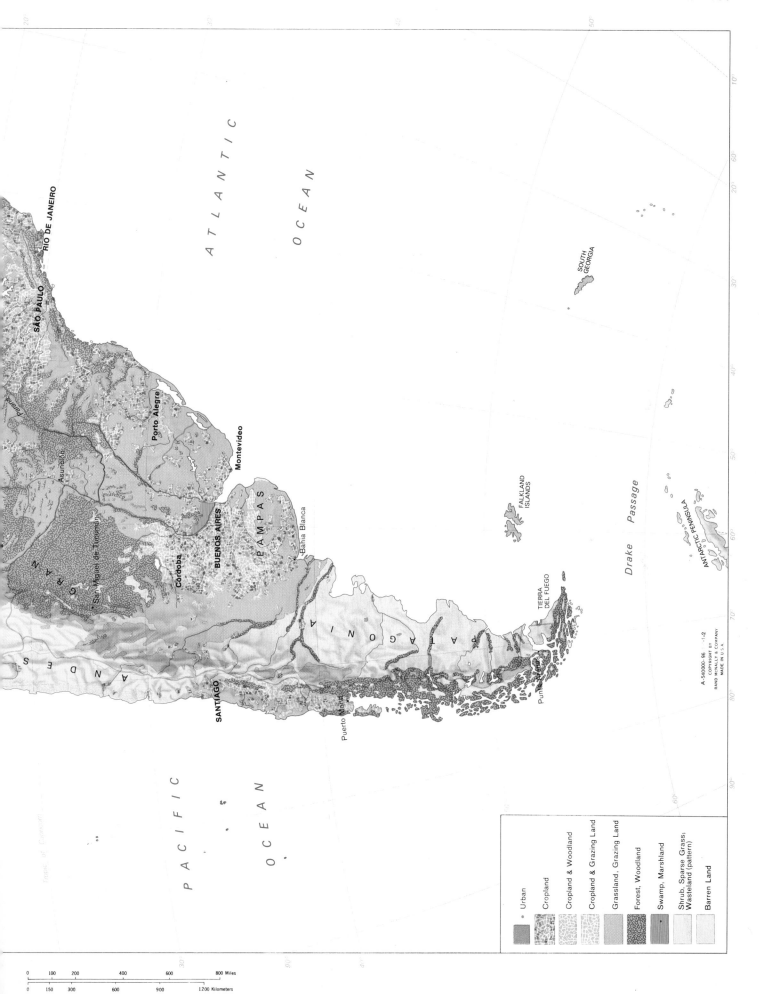

SOUTH
GEORGIA

FALKLAND
ISLANDS

Drake Passage

ANTARCTIC PENINSULA

TIERRA
DEL FUEGO

PATAGONIA

SANTIAGO

Puerto Montt

Punta

ANDES

ANDES

GRAN

San Miguel de Tucumán

Córdoba

BUENOS AIRES

P A M P A S

Bahía Blanca

Asunción

Paraná

Montevideo

Porto Alegre

SÃO PAULO

RIO DE JANEIRO

A T L A N T I C

O C E A N

P A C I F I C

O C E A N

Tropic of Capricorn

A-540000-96   -1-2
COPYRIGHT BY
RAND McNALLY & COMPANY
MADE IN U.S.A.

Urban	
Cropland	
Cropland & Woodland	
Cropland & Grazing Land	
Grassland, Grazing Land	
Forest, Woodland	
Swamp, Marshland	
Shrub, Sparse Grass; Wasteland (pattern)	
Barren Land	

0   100   200   400   600   800 Miles
0   150   300   600   900   1200 Kilometers

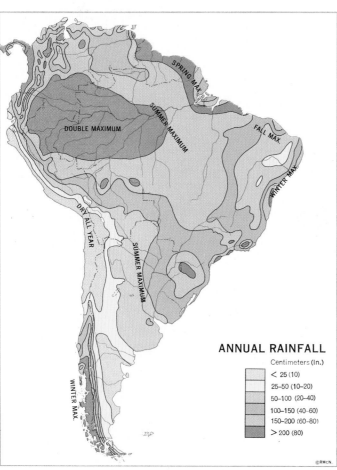

ANNUAL RAINFALL

Centimeters (In.)

- < 25 (10)
- 25–50 (10–20)
- 50–100 (20–40)
- 100–150 (40–60)
- 150–200 (60–80)
- > 200 (80)

©RMCN.

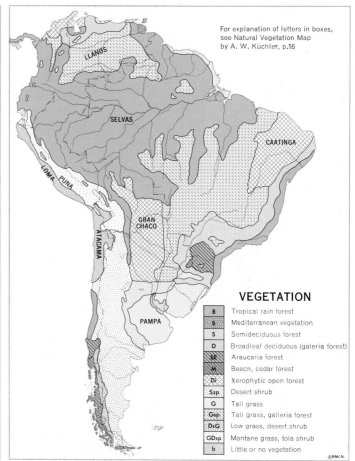

For explanation of letters in boxes, see Natural Vegetation Map by A. W. Küchler, p.16

VEGETATION

B	Tropical rain forest
B	Mediterranean vegetation
S	Semideciduous forest
D	Broadleaf deciduous (galeria forest)
SE	Araucaria forest
M	Beech, cedar forest
Di	Xerophytic open forest
Szp	Desert shrub
G	Tall grass
Gsp	Tall grass, galleria forest
DsG	Low grass, desert shrub
GDsp	Montane grass, tola shrub
b	Little or no vegetation

©RMCN.

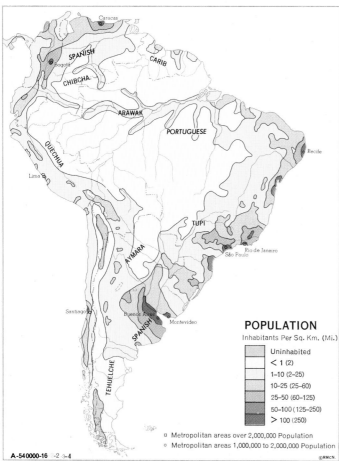

POPULATION

Inhabitants Per Sq. Km. (Mi.)

- Uninhabited
- < 1 (2)
- 1–10 (2–25)
- 10–25 (25–60)
- 25–50 (60–125)
- 50–100 (125–250)
- > 100 (250)

□ Metropolitan areas over 2,000,000 Population
○ Metropolitan areas 1,000,000 to 2,000,000 Population

A-540000-16 -2 -3-4

©RMCN.

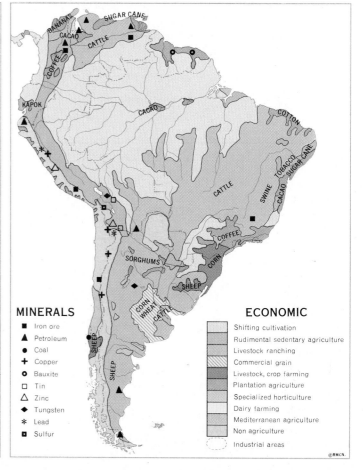

MINERALS

- ■ Iron ore
- ▲ Petroleum
- ● Coal
- + Copper
- ◉ Bauxite
- □ Tin
- △ Zinc
- ◆ Tungsten
- ∗ Lead
- ▪ Sulfur

ECONOMIC

- Shifting cultivation
- Rudimental sedentary agriculture
- Livestock ranching
- Commercial grain
- Livestock, crop farming
- Plantation agriculture
- Specialized horticulture
- Dairy farming
- Mediterranean agriculture
- Non agriculture
- Industrial areas

©RMCN.

ATLANTIC OCEAN

PACIFIC OCEAN

CENTRAL AMERICA

HAVANA

CARIBBEAN SEA

WEST INDIES

NORTH AMERICAN BASIN

Tropic of Cancer

San Juan

PUERTO RICO (U.S.A.)

BARBADOS

TRINIDAD AND TOBAGO
Port of Spain

Barranquilla
Cartagena
Panamá
Maracaibo
La Guaira
Valencia CARACAS
Mérida
Ciudad Bolívar
VENEZUELA
Georgetown
Paramaribo
Cayenne
GUYANA
SURINAME FR. GUIANA

Medellín
BOGOTÁ
COLOMBIA
Boa Vista do Rio Branco
GUIANA HIGHLANDS

Nevado del Tolima 17 110

Quito
Cotopaxi 19 347
ECUADOR
Guayaquil Chimborazo 20 561
Iquitos
Leticia
Manaus (Manáos)
Rio Negro
Rio Amazonas
Belém (Pará)
São Luís (Maranhão)
Equator
ROCEDOS SÃO PEDRO E SÃO PAULO (Brazil)

ARCHIPIÉLAGO DE COLÓN (GALÁPAGOS ISLANDS) (Ec.)

Chiclayo
Trujillo
PERU
LIMA
Rio Solimões (Amazonas)
Rio Madeira
Pôrto Velho
Rio Branco
BRAZIL
Fortaleza (Ceará)
Teresina
Natal
João Pessoa (Paraíba)
RECIFE (Pernambuco)
Maceió

Nevs. Huascarán 22 205

Callao Cuzco
ANDES MTS.
CHAPADA DE MATO GROSSO
Cuiabá
Brasília
Salvador (Bahia)

Volcán Misti 19 098
Arequipa
La Paz
BOLIVIA
Sucre
Potosí
Diamantina
Belo Horizonte
Pico da Bandeira 9 482
Vitória

Mollendo
Iquique
GRAN CHACO
PARAGUAY
Asunción
SÃO PAULO
Santos
RIO DE JANEIRO
CABO FRIO

Antofagasta
Salta
ARGENTINA
Tucumán
Corrientes
Iguassú Falls

Tropic of Capricorn

ISLA DE SAN FÉLIX (Chile)
ISLA DE SAN AMBROSIO (Chile)
Copiapó
Coquimbo
Santa Fe
Salto
URUGUAY
Rio Grande
Pôrto Alegre
Florianópolis

Valparaíso
Córdoba
Rosario
SANTIAGO
Mendoza
BUENOS AIRES
La Plata
MONTEVIDEO

ISLAS DE JUAN FERNÁNDEZ (Chile)

Concepción
PAMPAS
Rio de la Plata

Valdivia
Bahía Blanca

Puerto Montt
Viedma
Golfo San Matías

ISLA DE CHILOÉ

ARCHIPIÉLAGO DE LOS CHONOS

Comodoro Rivadavia
Golfo San Jorge

Monte Valentín 13 314

WELLINGTON
Río Gallegos
Stanley
SOUTH GEORGIA (Falkland Is.)

HANOVER
Estrecho de Magallanes
TIERRA DEL FUEGO
ISLA DE LOS ESTADOS

Punta Arenas
DESOLACIÓN
Mt. Sarmiento 8100
CABO DE HORNOS (CAPE HORN)

SOUTH SHETLAND ISLANDS (B.A.T.)
SOUTH ORKNEY IS. (B.A.T.)
SOUTH SANDWICH ISLANDS

Drake Passage

JOINVILLE
JAMES ROSS
Antarctic Circle

Longitude West of Greenwich

A-540000-76 2-3-5-11
COPYRIGHT BY
RAND McNALLY & COMPANY
MADE IN U.S.A.

Relief		
Meters		Feet
3050		10 000
1525		5000
610		2000
305		1000
0	Sea Level	0
152.5		500
1525		5000
3050		10 000
6100		20 000

			Miles
0 200 400 600 800 1000			
0 400 800 1200 1600			Kilometers

Scale 1:40 000 000; one inch to 630 miles. Lambert's Azimuthal, Equal Area Projection
Elevations and depressions are given in feet

Scale 1:16 000 000; one inch to 250 miles. Sinusoidal Projection
Elevations and depressions are given in feet

Port of Spain
TRINIDAD AND TOBAGO
TRINIDAD

Boca Grande
Morawhanna
Georgetown

Bartica Rosignol New
Amsterdam
Wismar
Rockstone
Skeldon
Totness
Nieuw
Nickerie Paranam
Sinnamary
ILE DU DIABLE
(DEVIL'S I.)
Maengo
St.
Albina Laurent
Paramaribo

SURINAME
FRENCH
GUIANA

Cayenne

Saint-Georges
CABO ORANGE

Amapá

AMAPÁ
(TER.)

Macapá

Mazagão
ILHA CAVIANA

Equator   0°

ATLANTIC OCEAN

ILHA
DE
MARAJO

Araraí

Breves
Rio
Da

Belém (Pará)

Bragança

Manaus
(Manáos)

Itacoatiara
ILHA
TUPINAMBARANAS
Maués
Santarém
Óbidos
Alenquer
Faro
Parintins

Mgrapanim

Abaetetuba

São Luís
(Maranhão)

Cametá

Cururupu

Alcântara

Tutóia
Camocim
Acaraú

FORTALEZA (Ceará)   5°

Borba
Altamira
Brasília Legal
(Fordlândia)

Itaituba

Tucuruí

PARÁ

Viana
Itapecuru-
Mirim
Rosário
Parnaíba
Marangaupe
Baturité
Ipu
Sobral

ARQUIPÉLAGO
FERNANDO DE
NORONHA
(Brazil)

Pedreiras

Codó
Caxias
Campo
Maior
Teresina
Quixadá
Russas
Aracati
Areia Branca
CABO DE SÃO ROQUE
ATOL
DAS ROCAS
(Brazil)

MARANHÃO

CEARÁ

Macau
RIO GRANDE
DO NORTE
Ceará-Mirim

BRAZIL

Tocantinópolis

São João
do Araguaia
Araguatins

Grajaú
Barra do Corda

Miradoro
Loreto

Balsas
Floriano
Oeiras

Amarante
Picos

Senador
Pompeu
Iguatu
Icó
Crateús
Pedro II

Currais Novos
Nova
Cruz
Natal
João Pessoa
(Paraíba)
Nazaré da Mata
Olinda
RECIFE
(Pernambuco)

Juazeiro
do Norte
Crato
Flores

Patos
Campina
Grande

Carolina

Riachão

Santa
Filomena

São Raimundo
Nonato

Paulistana

Granito
Sertânia
Jaboatão

Cabrobó
Caruaru

PERNAMBUCO
PLANALTO
DA BORBOREMA

Pôrto
Nacional

Natividade

Parnaguá

Juàzeiro
Petrolina

Garanhuns
Palmares
Pôrto de Pedras

Barreiras

Barra

Morro do Chapéu

Jacobina

Jeremoabo
Senhor do Bonfim
Palmeira
dos Índios
los indios

Maceió
ALAGÔAS
Propriá
Penedo
Coruripe

SERGIPE
Aracaju

GOIÁS

Cavalcante

Correntina

Carinhanha

Caetité

Mucugê

Itabaiana

Serrinha

Inhambupe

Feira de Santana
Lençóis
Cachoeiro
Nazaré
Santo Amaro

São Cristóvão
Estância

BAHIA

Alagoinhas
Catu

SALVADOR (Bahia)

Aratuípe

Valença

Barra do
Méndes

Pilar de
Goiás
Goiás

Januária

Rio Pardo de Minas

Jequié
Condeúba
Vitória da
Conquista
Itabuna
Ilhéus

Canavieiras

Formosa
DF
Brasília
São Francisco
Pedra Azul

Belmonte
Pôrto Seguro

Goiânia
Luziânia
Silvânia

Paracatu

Piraporá

Montes
Claros

Grão
Mogol

Araçuaí

Caravelas

ARQUIPÉLAGO
DOS ABROLHOS

Bela Vista de Goiás

Rio
Verde

Morrinhos

Ipameri

Catalão

Araguari

Patos
de Minas

Diamantina
Teófilo
Otoni

São Mateus

MINAS
SA. DOS
AIMORÉS

Uberlândia
Uberaba

Araxá

Corinto
Curvelo

Gov.
Valadares
Colatina

Aracruz

GERAIS

ESPÍRITO
Sete
Lagoas

BELO
HORIZONTE

STA. Bárbara
Ponte Nova
Vitória
Guarapari
Cachoeiro de Itapemirim

Formiga
Divinópolis

Campo
Grande

São José
do Rio Prêto
Franca
Barretos

Ribeirão Prêto

Passos
Poços de Caldas

Conselheiro
Lafaiete
Barbacena
Barra
Mansa

Itaperuna

Campos

Araçatuba

Tupã

Araraquara
São Carlos

Lins

Rio Claro

Marília

Bauru

Piracicaba

Jundiaí

SÃO PAULO

Itajubá
Volta
Redonda
Caxambu
Pouso Alegre
Taubaté

Juiz de Fora
Nova Friburgo
Petrópolis

Niterói
RIO DE JANEIRO

Campinas

PARAGUAY

Londrina

Jacarèzinho

Sorocaba

Mogi das Cruzes
RIO DE JANEIRO

Tropic of Capricorn

SÃO PAULO
São
Vicente

Santos

PARANÁ

Ponta Grossa

Curitiba

Continued on page **136**

Relief

Meters		Feet
3050		10 000
1525		5000
610		2000
305		1000
152.5		500
0	Sea Level	0
152.5		500
1525		5000
3050		10 000
6100		20 000

CARIBBEAN SEA

CARACAS

Maracay
Valencia

Scale 1:4 000 000

DISTRITO FEDERAL
MIRANDA
CARABOBO
COJEDES
GUÁRICO
ANZOÁTEGUI
SUCRE
NUEVA ESPARTA

ISLA DE MARGARITA

Cumaná

Continued on pages 134–135

Relief

Meters	Feet
3050	10 000
1525	5000
610	2000
305	1000
152.5	500
0 Sea Level	0
152.5	500
1525	5000 Below
3050	10 000 Sea Level
6100	20 000

Scale 1:16 000 000; one inch to 250 miles. Sinusoidal Projection
Elevations and depressions are given in feet

Longitude West of Greenwich

COPYRIGHT BY
RAND McNALLY & COMPANY
MADE IN U.S.A.
A-549200-76-107-9

0 50 100 200 300 400 500 Miles
0 100 200 400 600 800 Kilometers

BUENOS AIRES
Scale 1:1 000 000
0 5 10 Miles
0 4 8 16 Kilometers

RIO DE JANEIRO
Scale 1:1 000 000
0 4 8 16 Kilometers

For larger scale coverage of Buenos Aires,
Rio de Janeiro, and São Paulo see pages 58 and 59

ATLANTIC OCEAN

PACIFIC OCEAN

CHILE
ARGENTINA
BOLIVIA
PARAGUAY
URUGUAY
BRAZIL

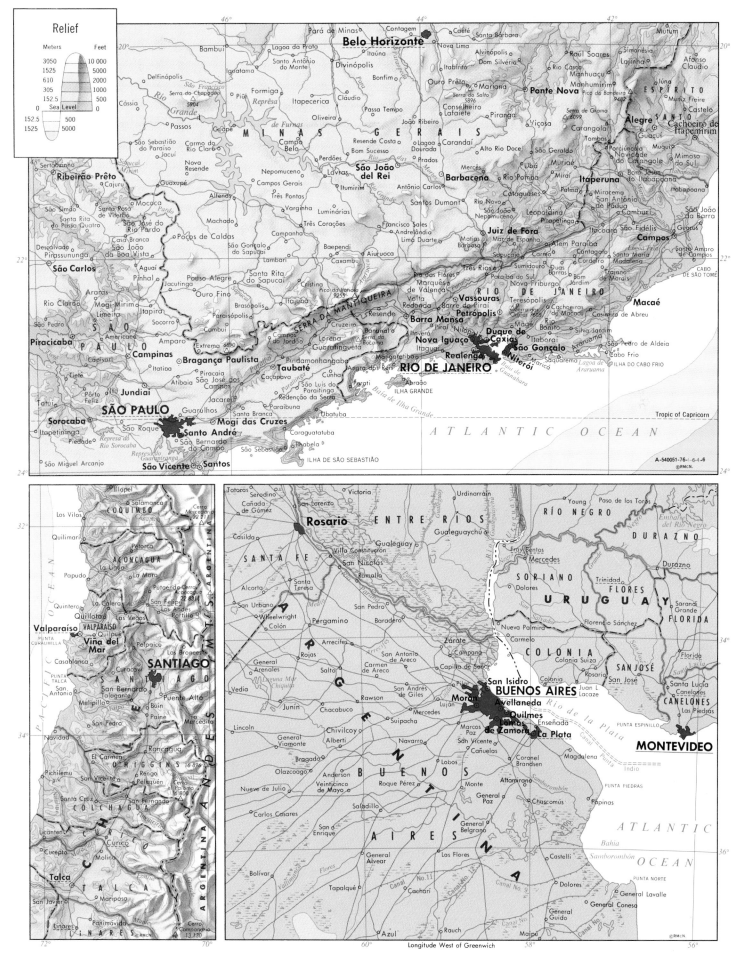

Relief

Meters		Feet
3050		10 000
1525		5000
610		2000
305		1000
152.5		500
0	Sea Level	0
152.5		500
1525		5000

Belo Horizonte

Pará de Minas · Contagem
Caeté · Santa Bárbara

Ribeirão Prêto

MINAS GERAIS

Ponte Nova

ESPÍRITO SANTO

Alegre · Cachoeiro de Itapemirim

São João del Rei

Barbacena

Itaperuna

Campos

Juiz de Fora

São Carlos

Piracicaba

Campinas

Bragança Paulista

SÃO PAULO

Taubaté

SERRA DA MANTIQUEIRA

Vassouras
Petrópolis
Barra Mansa
Nova Iguaçu
Realengo

RIO DE JANEIRO

Duque de Caxias
São Gonçalo
Niterói

RIO DE JANEIRO

Macaé

SÃO PAULO

Sorocaba

Mogi das Cruzes
Santo André
São Bernardo do Campo

São Vicente · Santos

ILHA DE SÃO SEBASTIÃO

Tropic of Capricorn

ATLANTIC OCEAN

A-540051-76-1-6-4-6
©RMcN

COQUIMBO

Rosario

ENTRE RÍOS

RÍO NEGRO

DURAZNO

SANTA FE

URUGUAY

ACONCAGUA

FLORES

FLORIDA

Valparaíso
VALPARAÍSO
Viña del Mar

SANTIAGO

SORIANO

COLONIA

SAN JOSÉ

SANTIAGO

San Isidro
BUENOS AIRES
Morón
Avellaneda
Quilmes
Lomas de Zamora
La Plata

CANELONES

MONTEVIDEO

O'HIGGINS

COLCHAGUA

BUENOS

AIRES

ANDES MTS.

ARGENTINA

CURICÓ

ATLANTIC

OCEAN

TALCA

Talca

LINARES

Longitude West of Greenwich

Scale 1:4 000 000; one inch to 64 miles.

Elevations and depressions are given in feet.

0 10 20 30 40 50 60 70 80 90 100 110 120 Miles
0 20 40 60 80 100 120 140 160 180 200 Kilometers

Urban

Cropland

Cropland & Woodland

Cropland & Grazing Land

Grassland, Grazing Land

Forest, Woodland

Swamp, Marshland

Tundra

Shrub, Sparse Grass,
Wasteland (pattern)

Barren Land

• Oasis

Reykjavik

Narvik

Muri

Une

Trondheim

Gulf of Bothnia

Bergen

Oslo

Helsinki

LENINGRAD

Tallinn

Stockholm

Göteborg

Riga

Glasgow

North
Sea

Copenhagen

Baltic Sea

Belfast

MANCHESTER

Kaliningrad

Minsk

Dublin

Hamburg

Amsterdam

Elbe

BERLIN

Oder

Warsaw

Pripy

LONDON

Antwerp

Essen

Leipzig

Brest

Frankfurt

Prague

Kraków

L'vov

PARIS

Seine

Strasbourg

Danube

CARPATHIANS

Loire

Rhine

Munich

VIENNA

Tisza

La Coruña

Bay of Biscay

Bordeaux

Zürich

BUDAPEST

ATLANTIC

Garonne

Lyon

A L P S

Save

OCEAN

Bilbao

Rhône

MILAN

Zagreb

Belgrade

Douro

PYRENEES

Venice

Bucharest

Ebro

MADRID

Marseille

Genoa

Adriatic

Danube

Lisbon

BARCELONA

CORSICA

ROME

Sofia

Sevilla

SARDINIA

Tirane

Tanger

ISLAS BALEARES

Naples

Aegean

Algiers

Mediterranean

Tyrrhenian Sea

Athens

Oran

Palermo

Casablanca

ATLAS
MOUNTAINS

Tunis

SICILY

Sea

MALTA

CRETE

Longitude West of Greenwich   0°   Longitude East of Greenwich

Scale 1: 16,000,000; one inch to 250 miles. Conic Projection

0 50 100   200   300   400   500 Miles

0   100   200   400   600   800 Kilometers

40°   50°

Nar'yan-Mar

Pechora

White Sea

Arkhangelsk

U   R   A   L   S

Vologda

Kirov

Perm'

SVERDLOVSK

Volga

Kazan'

Kama

Ufa

Gorki

Magnitogorsk

MOSCOW

Kuybyshev

Orsk

Tula

Volga

Saratov

Ural

DEPRESSION

CASPIAN

Khar'kov

Don

VOLGOGRAD

Kiev

Volga

Dnepropetrovsk   Donetsk

Astrakhan'

Dnepr

MANYCH   DEPRESSION

Odessa

Krasnodar

C A U C A S U S   M T S.

Black   Sea

TBILISI   BAKU

Yerevan

İSTANBUL

ELBURZ   MTS.

Ankara

TEHRAN

DASH-E-KAVIR

TOROS   AĞRI

Nicosia

CYPRUS

Tigris

ZAGROS

Euphrates   Baghdād

MOUNTAINS

Beirut

Kerman

Abādān

60°   70°

Ob

Irtysh

Omsk

Novosibirsk

Ob

Karaganda

Balkhash

Kzyl-Orda

Syr-Dar'ya

Aral'skoye
More
(Aral Sea)

PESKI
KYZYLKUM

Amu Dar'ya

PESKI KARAKUMY

Ashkhabad

C a s p i a n   S e a

50°

40°

30°

A-550000-96 1-1-3
COPYRIGHT BY
RAND McNALLY & COMPANY
MADE IN U.S.A.

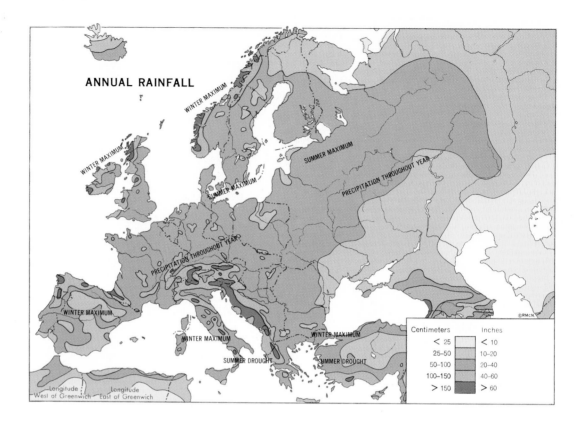

ANNUAL RAINFALL

Centimeters		Inches
< 25		< 10
25–50		10–20
50–100		20–40
100–150		40–60
> 150		> 60

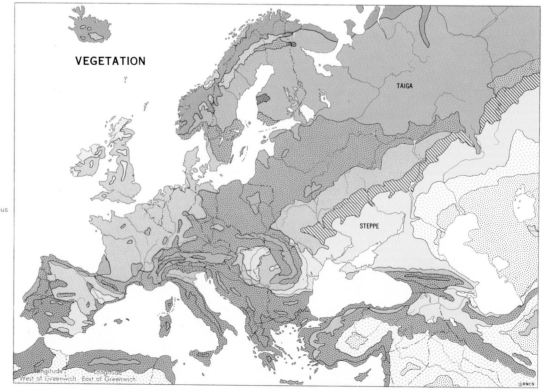

VEGETATION

VEGETATION

E	Coniferous forest
B,Bs	Mediterranean vegetation
M	Mixed forest: coniferous-deciduous
S	Semi-deciduous forest
D	Deciduous forest
DG	Wooded steppe
G	Grass (steppe)
Gp	Short grass
Dsp	Desert shrub
L	Heath and moor
L	Alpine vegetation tundra
b	Little or no vegetation

For explanation of letters in boxes,
see Natural Vegetation Map
by A. W. Kuchler, **p. 16**

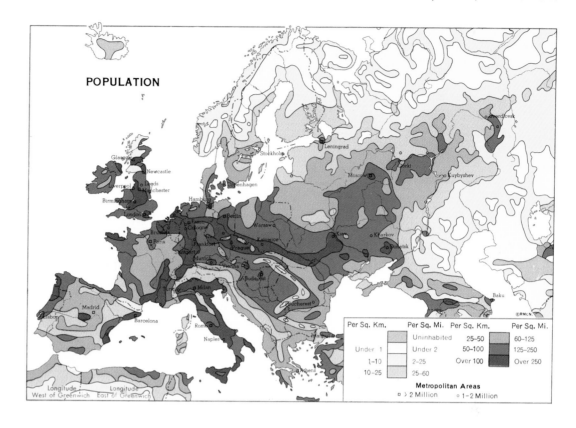

POPULATION

Per Sq. Km.	Per Sq. Mi.	Per Sq. Km.	Per Sq. Mi.
Uninhabited	Uninhabited	25–50	60–125
Under 1	Under 2	50–100	125–250
1–10	2–25	Over 100	Over 250
10–25	25–60		

Metropolitan Areas
▫ > 2 Million   ○ 1–2 Million

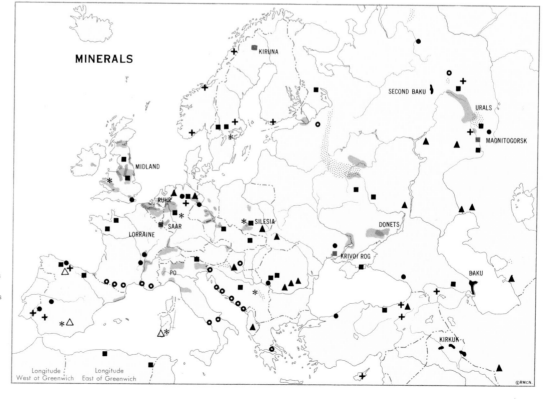

MINERALS

MINERALS

Industrial areas
Major coal deposits
Major petroleum deposits
Lignite deposits
▲ Minor petroleum deposits
● Minor coal deposits
■ Major iron ore
■ Minor iron ore
✳ Lead
○ Bauxite
△ Zinc
✛ Copper

Longitude West of Greenwich   Longitude East of Greenwich

Scale 1:16 000 000; one inch to 250 miles. Conic Projection
Elevations and depressions are given in feet.

PHYSIOGRAPHIC PROVINCES

Western Uplands (Mostly old rocks)   Great European Plain   Central Uplands   Alpine System

EUROPE DURING THE ICE AGE

Tundra   Forest   Steppe

PHYSIOGRAPHY
BY
ERWIN RAISZ

LITHOLOGY AND STRUCTURE

Unconsolidated deposits: alluvium, sands, bottom lands.

Essentially horizontal sediments, also uplands and terraces in the plains.

Moderately folded sedimentary rocks.

Strongly folded and faulted rocks. The "Younger Series" in Norway.

Metamorphic and intrusive igneous rocks.

volcanics, lava flows, basalts, etc.

LANDFORMS

PLATEAUS   CUESTAS   SAND

HILLS   FOLDED MOUNTAINS   SINKS

MOUNTAINS   BASIN RANGES   MORAINES

MESAS   VOLCANO AND LAVA   DRUMLINS

EUROPE LANGUAGES
BY
BOGDAN ZABORSKI

Scale 1:16,500,000; one inch to 260 miles Conic Projection

Longitude West of Greenwich Longitude East of Greenwich

Arctic Circle

0	100	200	300	400	500	600 Miles

0	200	400	600	800	1000 Kilometers

B-550000-1C8-1-1-51
COPYRIGHT BY
RAND McNALLY & COMPANY
MADE IN U.S.A.

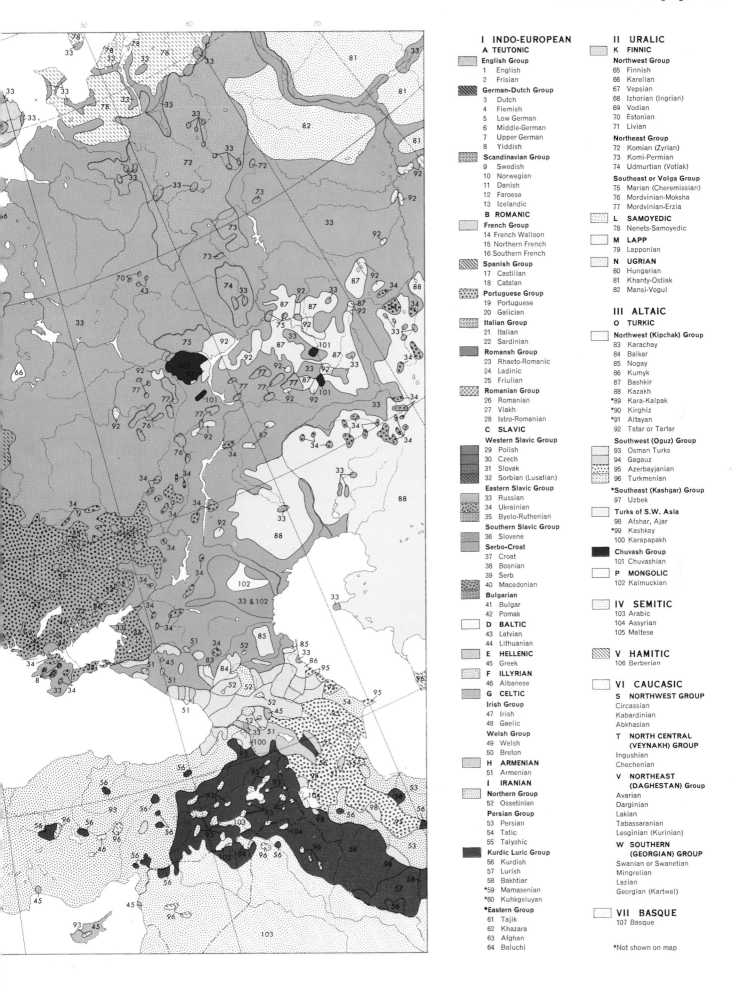

I INDO-EUROPEAN
A TEUTONIC
English Group
1 English
2 Frisian
German-Dutch Group
3 Dutch
4 Flemish
5 Low German
6 Middle-German
7 Upper German
8 Yiddish
Scandinavian Group
9 Swedish
10 Norwegian
11 Danish
12 Faroese
13 Icelandic
B ROMANIC
French Group
14 French Walloon
15 Northern French
16 Southern French
Spanish Group
17 Castilian
18 Catalan
Portuguese Group
19 Portuguese
20 Galician
Italian Group
21 Italian
22 Sardinian
Romansh Group
23 Rhaeto-Romanic
24 Ladinic
25 Friulian
Romanian Group
26 Romanian
27 Vlakh
28 Istro-Romanian
C SLAVIC
Western Slavic Group
29 Polish
30 Czech
31 Slovak
32 Sorbian (Lusatian)
Eastern Slavic Group
33 Russian
34 Ukrainian
35 Byelo-Ruthenian
Southern Slavic Group
36 Slovene
Serbo-Croat
37 Croat
38 Bosnian
39 Serb
40 Macedonian
Bulgarian
41 Bulgar
42 Pomak
D BALTIC
43 Latvian
44 Lithuanian
E HELLENIC
45 Greek
F ILLYRIAN
46 Albanese
G CELTIC
Irish Group
47 Irish
48 Gaelic
Welsh Group
49 Welsh
50 Breton
H ARMENIAN
51 Armenian
I IRANIAN
Northern Group
52 Ossetinian
Persian Group
53 Persian
54 Tatic
55 Talyshic
Kurdic Luric Group
56 Kurdish
57 Lurish
58 Bakhtiar
*59 Mamasenian
*60 Kuhkgeluyan
*Eastern Group
61 Tajik
62 Khazara
63 Afghan
64 Baluchi

II URALIC
K FINNIC
Northwest Group
65 Finnish
66 Karelian
67 Vepsian
68 Izhorian (Ingrian)
69 Vodian
70 Estonian
71 Livian
Northeast Group
72 Komian (Zyrian)
73 Komi-Permian
74 Udmurtian (Votiak)
Southeast or Volga Group
75 Marian (Cheremissian)
76 Mordvinian-Moksha
77 Mordvinian-Erzia
L SAMOYEDIC
78 Nenets-Samoyedic
M LAPP
79 Lapponian
N UGRIAN
80 Hungarian
81 Khanty-Ostiak
82 Mansi-Vogul

III ALTAIC
O TURKIC
Northwest (Kipchak) Group
83 Karachay
84 Balkar
85 Nogay
86 Kumyk
87 Bashkir
88 Kazakh
*89 Kara-Kalpak
*90 Kirghiz
*91 Altayan
92 Tatar or Tartar
Southwest (Oguz) Group
93 Osman Turks
94 Gagauz
95 Azerbayjanian
96 Turkmenian
*Southeast (Kashgar) Group
97 Uzbek
Turks of S.W. Asia
98 Afshar, Ajar
*99 Kashkay
100 Karapapakh
Chuvash Group
101 Chuvashian
P MONGOLIC
102 Kalmuckian

IV SEMITIC
103 Arabic
104 Assyrian
105 Maltese

V HAMITIC
106 Berberian

VI CAUCASIC
S NORTHWEST GROUP
Circassian
Kabardinian
Abkhasian
T NORTH CENTRAL
(VEYNAKH) GROUP
Ingushian
Chechenian
V NORTHEAST
(DAGHESTAN) Group
Avarian
Darginian
Lakian
Tabassaranian
Lesginian (Kurinian)
W SOUTHERN
(GEORGIAN) GROUP
Swanian or Swanetian
Mingrelian
Lazian
Georgian (Kartwel)

VII BASQUE
107 Basque

*Not shown on map

Relief

Meters		Feet
3050		10 000
1525		5000
610		2000
305		1000
152.5		500
0	Sea Level	0
152.5	Below	500
	Sea Level	
1525		5000
3050		10 000

Scale 1: 16 000 000; one inch to 250 miles. Conic Projection
Elevations and depressions are given in feet

Continued on pages 210–211

Longitude West of Greenwich   Longitude East of Greenwich

| 0 | 50 | 100 | 200 | 300 | 400 | 500 Miles |
| 0 | 100 | 200 | 400 | 600 | 800 Kilometers |

Continued on pages 172-173

Continued on pages 186-187

A-519697-76
COPYRIGHT BY
RAND McNALLY & COMPANY
MADE IN U.S.A.

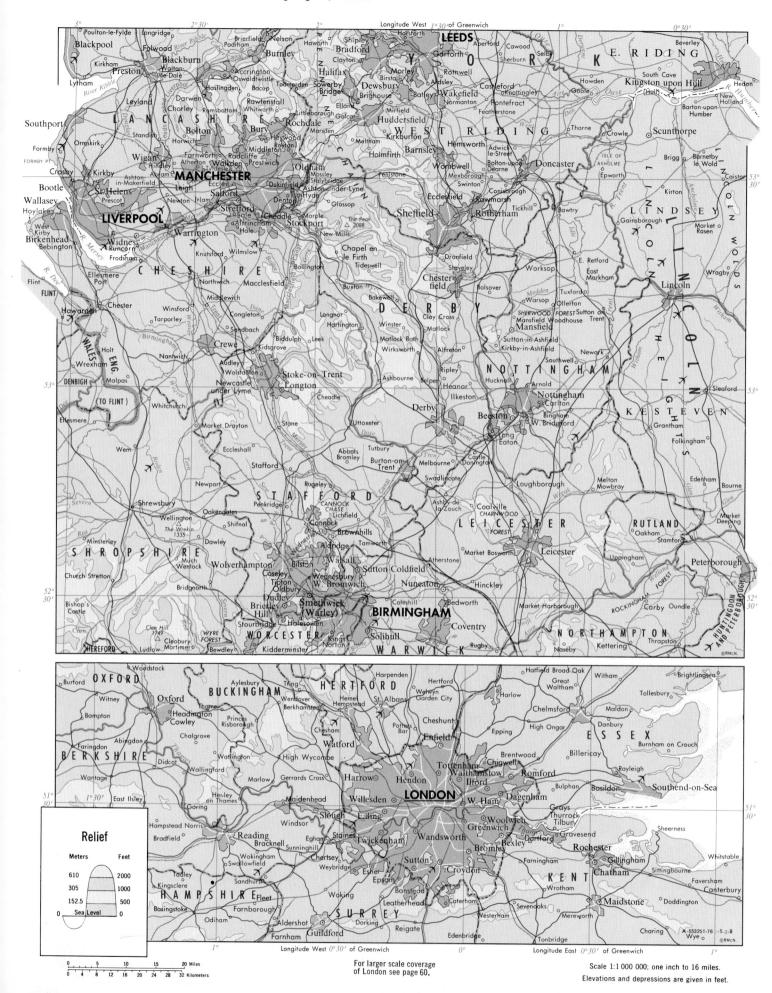

For larger scale coverage
of London see page 60.

Scale 1:1 000 000; one inch to 16 miles.
Elevations and depressions are given in feet.

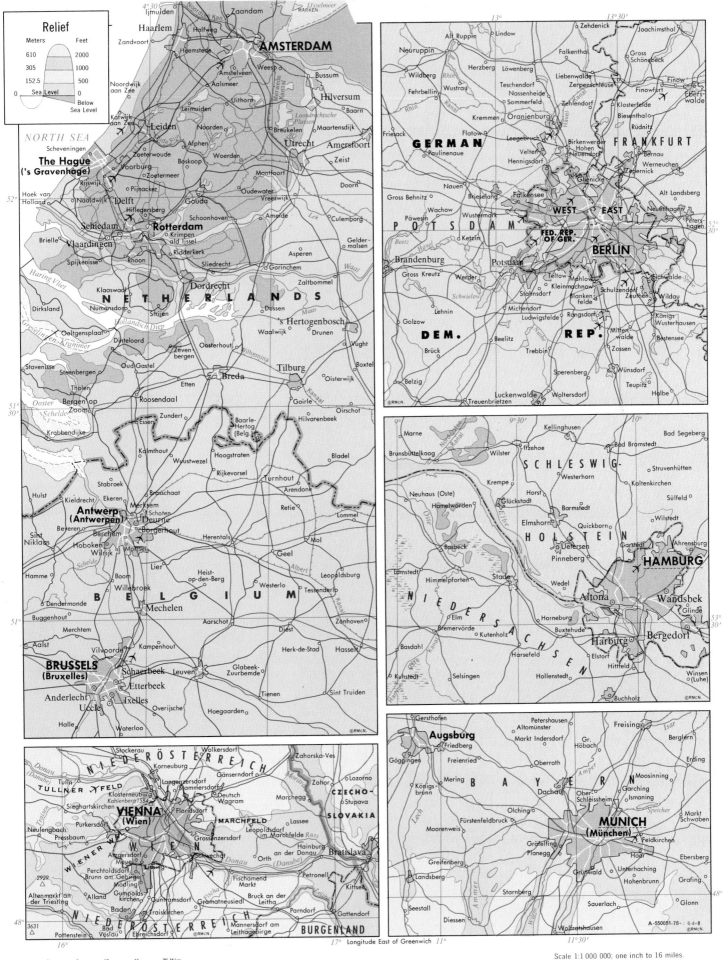

Relief

Meters	Feet
610	2000
305	1000
152.5	500
0 Sea Level	0 Below Sea Level

NORTH SEA

IJmuiden Zaandam Noordzee Kan. IJsselmeer MARKEN

Haarlem Halfweg
Zandvoort Heemstede **AMSTERDAM**
Amstelveen Weesp Bussum
Aalsmeer Uithoorn **Hilversum**
Noordwijk aan Zee Leiden Noorden Maartensdijk Baarn
Katwijk aan Zee Alphen Breukelen Utrecht Amersfoort
Scheveningen Zoeterwoude Woerden Zeist
The Hague ('s Gravenhage) Voorburg Boskoop Montfoort Doorn
Rijswijk Zoetermeer Gouda Oudewater Vreeswijk
Hoek van Holland Naaldwijk Pijnacker Hillegersberg Schoonhoven Ameide Culemborg Gelder-malsen
Delft Lek Asperen
Schiedam **Rotterdam** Krimpen ald IJssel Gorinchem Waal
Brielle Vlaardingen Ridderkerk Sliedrecht Zaltbommel
Spijkenisse Rhoon Maas 's Hertogenbosch
Haring Vliet Klaaswaal **NETHERLANDS** Dussen
Dirksland Numansdorp Strijen Waalwijk Drunen Vught
Graellingen-Krammer Oud Gastel Dinteloord Zeven-bergen Oosterhout Wilhemina Kanaal Boxtel
Stavenisse Steenbergen Tilburg Oisterwijk
Ooltgensplaat Tholen Bergen op Zoom Breda Etten Goirle Oirschot
Krabbendijke Roosendaal Zundert Hilvarenbeek
Ooster Schelde Essen Kalmthout Baarle-Hertog (Belg.) Bladel
Hulst Wuustwezel Hoogstraten Turnhout
Sint Niklaas Stabroek Rijkevorsel Arendonk Retie Lommel
Beveren Kieldrecht Ekeren Merksem Schoten **Antwerp (Antwerpen)** Deurne Borgerhout Retie Mol
Hoboken Berchem Herentals Geel
Wilrijk Mortsel Lier **BELGIUM** Leopoldsburg
Hamme Boom Heist-op-den-Berg Westerlo Tessenderlo
Dendermonde Willebroek Mechelen Albert Kanaal
Buggenhout Aarschot Diest Zonhoven
Merchtem Kampenhout Herk-de-Stad Hasselt
Aalst Vilvoorde Glabbeek-Zuurbemde Leuven Sint Truiden
BRUSSELS (Bruxelles) Schaerbeek Tienen
Anderlecht Etterbeek Overijsche Hoegaarden
Uccle Ixelles
Halle Waterloo

Stockerau Wolkersdorf **NIEDERÖSTERREICH** Zahorska-Ves
Donau (Danube) Korneuburg Gänserndorf Lozorno
Tulln TULLNER FELD Langenzersdorf Stammersdorf Deutsch Wagram Marchegg CZECHO-SLOVAKIA
Klosterneuburg Kahlenberg 1584 Floridsdorf Lassee Stupava
Sieghartskirchen **VIENNA (Wien)** MARCHFELD
Neulengbach Purkersdorf Grossenzersdorf Leopoldsdorf im Marchfelde Russ
Pressbaum WIEN Hainburg an der Donau **Bratislava**
WIENER WALD Mauer Schwechat Orth Petronell
2929 Perchtoldsdorf Liesing Fischamend Kittsee
Altenmarkt an der Triesting Brunn am Gebirge Mödling Markt
Alland Gumpoldskirchen Bruck an der Leitha
3631 Baden Guntramsdorf Leitha Parndorf Gattendorf
Pottenstein Bad Vöslau Ebreichsdorf Traiskirchen Mannersdorf am Leithagebirge **BURGENLAND**
NIEDERÖSTERREICH

16°

Alt Ruppin Lindow Zehdenick Joachimsthal
Neuruppin Herzberg Löwenberg Falkenthal Gross Schönebeck Finow
Wildberg Wustrau Teschendorf Liebenwalde Finowfurt Eberswalde
Fehrbellin Nassenheide Zehlendorf Klosterfelde Biesenthal Rüdnitz
Friesack Flatow Kremmen Oranienburg Sommerfeld **FRANKFURT**
GERMAN Leegebruch Birkenwerder Hohen Neuendorf Bernau Werneuchen
Paulinenaue Velten Hennigsdorf Glienicke Zepernick
Gross Behnitz Nauen Brieselang Falkensee **WEST** **EAST** Alt Landsberg Neuenhagen
Wachow Wustermark **POTSDAM** **FED. REP. OF GER.** Petershagen
Päwesin Ketzin **BERLIN** Eichwalde
Brandenburg Gross Kreutz Werder Potsdam Teltow Mahlow Schulzendorf Zeuthen Wildau
Gross Kreutz Schwielow Kleinmachnow Blankenfelde Königs Wusterhausen
Golzow Lehnin Michendorf Rangsdorf Mitten-walde Bestensee
DEM. Beelitz Ludwigsfelde **REP.**
Brück Trebbin Zossen
Belzig Treuenbrietzen Luckenwalde Woltersdorf Sperenberg Wünsdorf Teupitz Halbe

13° 13°30'

Marne Kellinghusen Bad Segeberg
Brunsbüttelkoog Wilster Itzehoe Bad Bramstedt
SCHLESWIG- Westerhorn Struvenhütten Kaltenkirchen
Neuhaus (Oste) Krempe Horst Barmstedt Sülfeld
Hamelwörden Glückstadt Elmshorn Quickborn Wilstedt
HOLSTEIN Garstedt Ahrensburg
Basbeck Uetersen **HAMBURG**
Lamstedt Elbe Pinneberg Wandsbek
Himmelpforten Stade Wedel Altona Glinde
Elm Horneburg Harburg Bergedorf
Bremervörde Buxtehude **53°30'**
Basdahl Kutenholz Harburg
Bremervörde Harsefeld Hittfeld Winsen (Luhe)
Kuhstedt Selsingen Hollenstedt Buchholz

9° 9°30' 10°

Gersthofen Petershausen Freising
Augsburg Altomünster Markt Indersdorf
Göggingen Friedberg Freinried Oberroth Berglern
Königs-brunn Mering Dachau Ober-Schleissheim Moosinning Garching Ismaning Erding
BAYERN Olching Isar
Moorenweis Fürstenfeldbruck **MUNICH (München)** Haar Markt Schwaben
Gröfelfing Feldkirchen
Greifenberg Planegg Unterhaching Ebersberg
Landsberg Grünwald Hohenbrunn Grafing
Starnberg Sauerlach Glonn
Seestall Diessen Wolfratshausen

11° 11°30' 12°

17° Longitude East of Greenwich 11°

Scale 1:1 000 000; one inch to 16 miles.
Elevations and depressions are given in feet.

A-550051-76 6-4-8

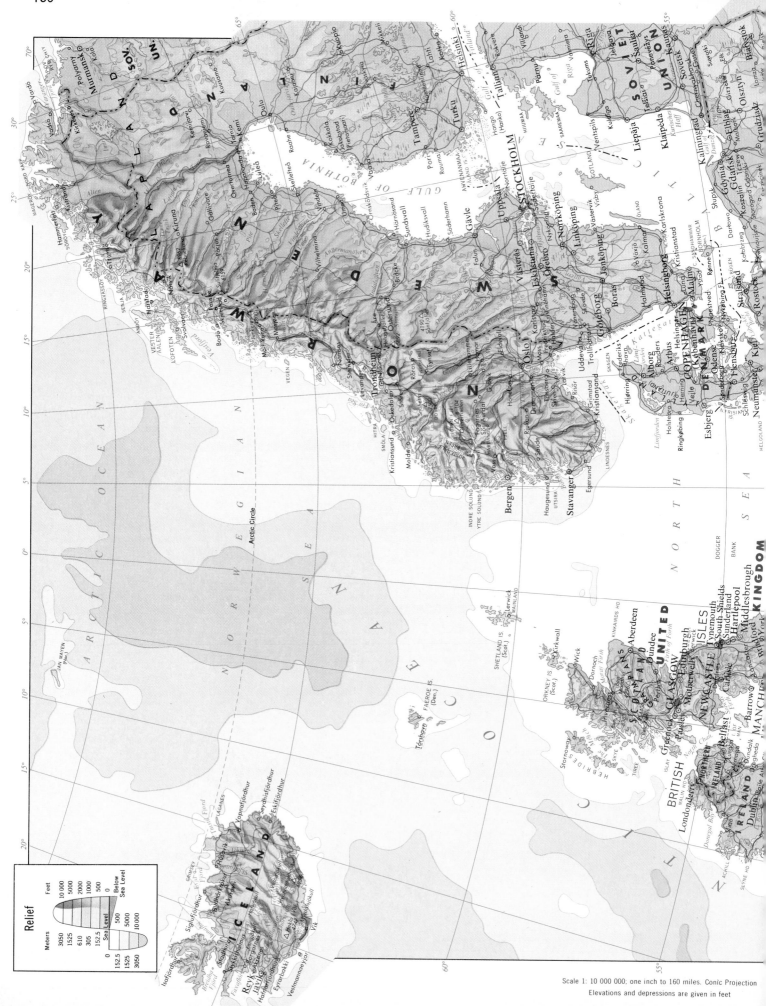

Scale 1: 10 000 000; one inch to 160 miles. Conic Projection
Elevations and depressions are given in feet

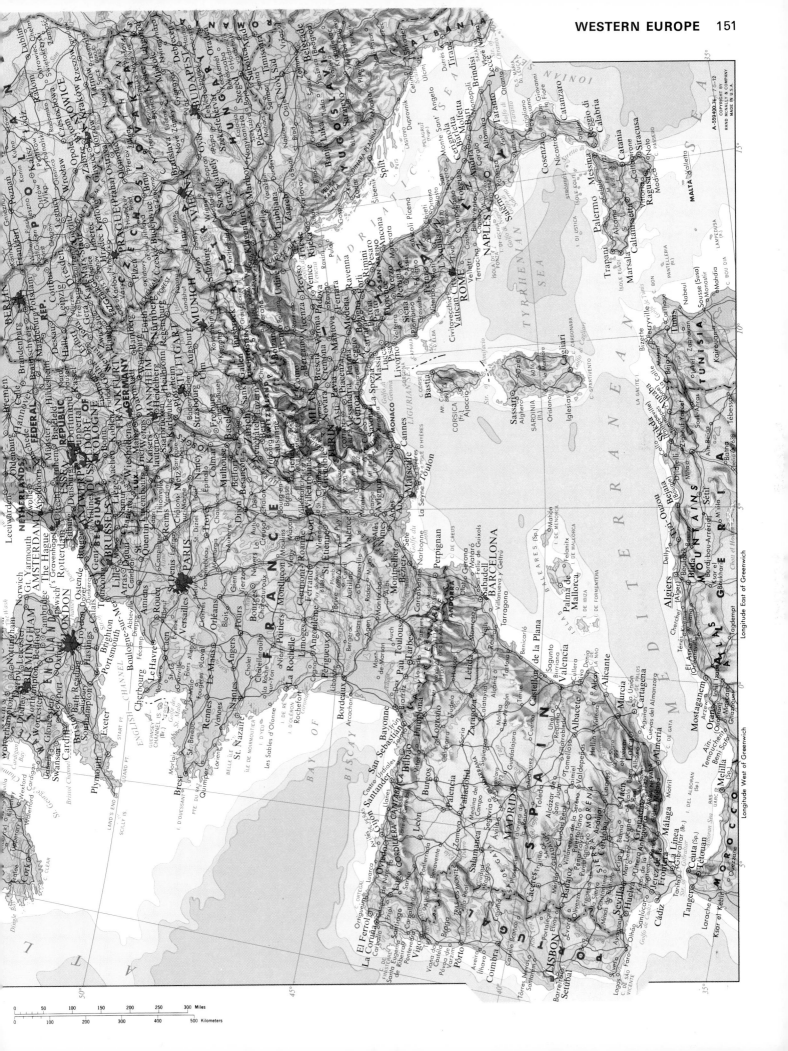

ATLANTIC
OCEAN

BAY
OF
BISCAY

FRANCE

SPAIN

PORTUGAL

LISBON

MADRID

BARCELONA

MEDITERRANEAN

LIGURIAN SEA

CORSICA
(Fr.)

SARDINIA
(It.)

TYRRHENIAN
SEA

ITALY

ROME

VATICAN CITY

NAPLES

SICILY

MALTA

MOROCCO

ALGERIA

TUNISIA

TARABULUS
(TRIPOLITANIA)

GRAND ERG OCCIDENTAL

GRAND ERG ORIENTAL

HAMMĀDAH AL HAMRĀ

SAHARAN ATLAS

HAUT ATLAS

MOYEN ATLAS

Relief

Meters		Feet
3050		10000
1525		5000
610		2000
305		1000
152.5		500
0	Sea Level	0
152.5		500 Below
1525		5000 Sea Level
3050		10000

A-558300-76- 10-6-17
COPYRIGHT BY
RAND McNALLY & COMPANY
MADE IN U.S.A.

Longitude West of Greenwich   0°   Longitude East of Greenwich

Scale 1: 10 000 000; one inch to 160 miles. Bonne's Projection
Elevations and depressions are given in feet

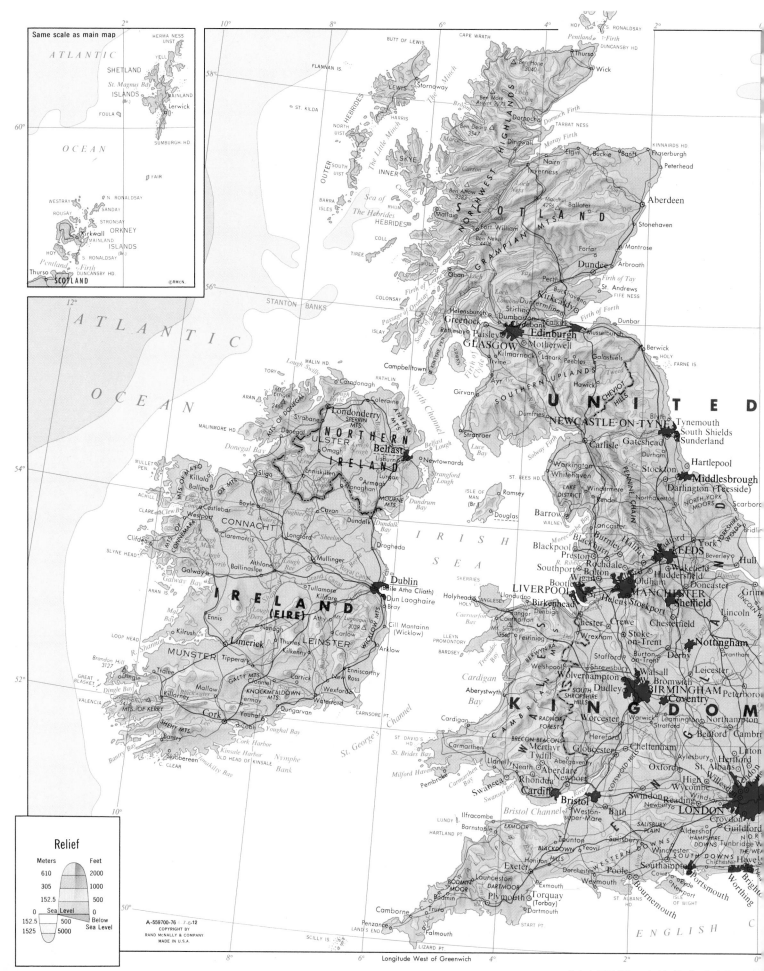

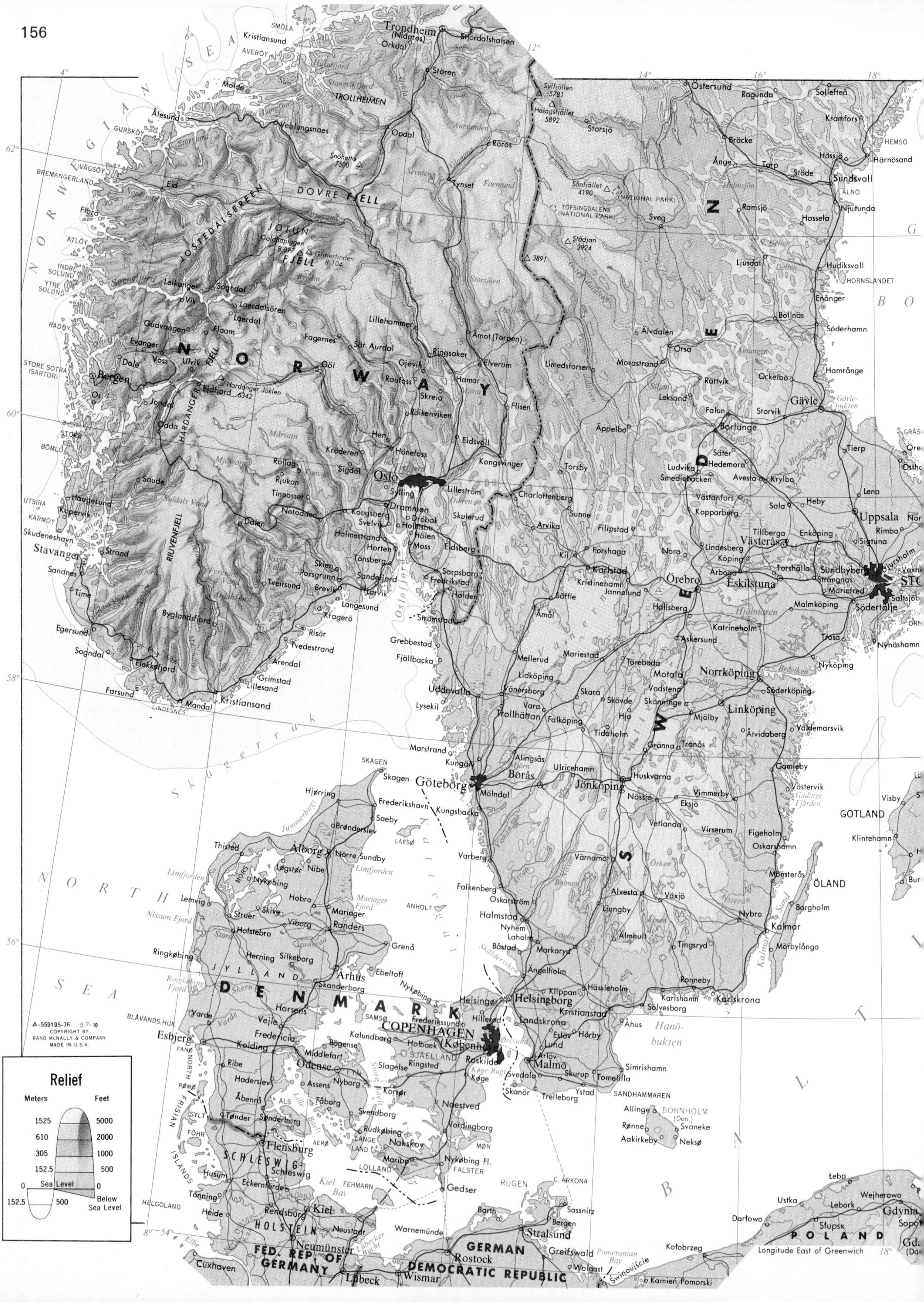

NORWEGIAN SEA

SMØLA
Kristiansund
AVERØY
Molde
Veblungsnaes
Ålesund
VÅGSØY
GURSKØY
ATLØY
FLORØ
INDRE SOLUND
YTRE SOLUND
RADØY
STORE SOTRA (SARTOR)
BØMLO
UTSIRA
KARMØY
Kopervik
Skudeneshavn
Haugesund
Stavanger
Sandnes
Time
Egersund
Sogndal
Farsund

Trondheim (Nidaros)
Stjørdalshalsen
Orkdal
Støren
Opdal
HALTDALEN
TROLLHEIMEN
Snøhetta 7500
DOVRE FJELL
Tynset
Røros
JOTUN FJELL
Galdhøpiggen 8097
Glittertinden 8104
Leikanger
Sogndal
Vik
Gudvangen
Lærdalsøren
Lærdal
Flåm
Evanger
Dale
Voss
Ulvik
JOSTEDALSBREEN
HARDANGER FJELL
Bergen
Os
Jondal
Odda
Saude
Hardanger Jøkelen
Eidfjord 6342
Lillehammer
Fagernes
Sør Aurdal
Gjøvik
Raufoss
Skreia
Hen
Hønefoss
Ringsaker
Hamar
RIUVENFJELL
Rollag
Kroderen
Sigdal
Notodden
Kongsberg
Svelvik
Dalen
Tinnosset
Rjukan
Skien
Porsgrunn
Brevik
Tveitsund
Byglandsfjord
Risør
Tvedestrand
Arendal
Grimstad
Lillesand
Flekkefjord
Mandal
Kristiansand
LINDESNES

NORWAY

Åmot (Torpen)
Elverum
Flisen
Eidsvoll
Kongsvinger
Oslo
Sylling
Lillestrøm
Drammen
Drøbak
Hølen
Holmsbu
Holmestrand
Horten
Moss
Tønsberg
Sandefjord
Larvik
Eidsberg
Sarpsborg
Fredrikstad
Halden
Strømstad
Grebbestad
Fjällbacka
Uddevalla
Lysekil
Marstrand
Kungälv

Skien
Åmot
Hølen

Östersund
Ragunda
Sollefteå
HEMSÖ
Sylfjällen 5781
Storsjön
Bräcke
Kramfors
Härnösand
Ånge
Tarp
Stöde
Sundsvall
Hässlö
ALNÖ
Sånfjället 4190
(NATIONAL PARK)
TÖFSINGDALENS (NATIONAL PARK)
Sveg
Ramsjö
Hassela
Njurunda
Städjan 3924
3891
Ljusdal
Orsa
Dellen
Hudiksvall
HORNSLANDET
Enånger
Älvdalen
Morastrand
Bollnäs
Söderhamn
Rättvik
Ockelbo
Hamränge
Leksand
Falun
Storvik
Gävle
Gävle-bukten
Borlänge
Säter
Hedemora
Avesta
Krylbo
Ludvika
Smedjebacken
Västanfors
Sala
Heby
Lena
Kopparberg
Tierp
Nora
Lindesberg
Köping
Tillberga
Enköping
Sigtuna
Uppsala
Rimbo
Västerås
Örebro
Arboga
Torshälla
Eskilstuna
Strängnäs
Sundbyberg
STOCKHOLM
Mariefred
Södertälje
Saltsjö
Hallsberg
Malmköping
Askersund
Katrineholm
Mariestad
Töreboda
Motala
Vadstena
Skänninge
Norrköping
Söderköping
Tranås
Mjölby
Linköping
Åtvidaberg
Valdemarsvik
Nyköping
Nynäshamn
Trosa
Bråviken

SWEDEN

Charlottenberg
Arvika
Sunne
Filipstad
Forshaga
Kil
Karlstad
Kristinehamn
Jannelund
Säffle
Åmål
Mellerud
Lidköping
Vänersborg
Skara
Skövde
Hjo
Tidaholm
Falköping
Vara
Trollhättan
Gränna
Tranås
Huskvarna
Jönköping
Nässjö
Vetlanda
Virserum
Eksjö
Vimmerby
Gamleby
Västervik
Figeholm
Oskarshamn
Mönsterås

NORTH SEA
Thisted
MORS
Nykøbing
Løgstør
Nibe
Ålborg
Nørre Sundby
Limfjorden
Hobro
Lemvig
Struer
Skive
Viborg
Mariager
Randers
Holstebro
Ringkøbing
Herning
Silkeborg
Grenå
Ebeltoft
Århus
Skanderborg
Horsens
Vejle
Varde
Esbjerg
Fredericia
Kolding
Middelfart
Odense
Assens
Nyborg
Korsør
Fåborg
Svendborg
Rudkøbing
Nakskov

DENMARK

SKAGEN
Skagen
Hjørring
Frederikshavn
Sæby
LÆSØ
Brønderslev
Kungsbacka
Varberg
Falkenberg
Oskarström
Halmstad
Nyhem
Laholm
Båstad
Markaryd
Ängelholm
Göteborg
Mölndal
Borås
Ulricehamn
Värnamo
Alvesta
Ljungby
Växjö
Älmhult
Nybro
Tingsryd
Ronneby
Karlshamn
Sölvesborg
Åhus
Kristianstad
Hässleholm
Klippan
Eslöv
Hörby
Helsingborg
Landskrona
Lund
Malmö
Arlöv
Skurup
Tomelilla
Simrishamn
Ystad
Trelleborg
Skanör
Svedala
SANDHAMMAREN
Hanö-bukten
Allinge
BORNHOLM (Den.)
Rønne
Svaneke
Aakirkeby
Neksø

GOTLAND
Visby
Klintehamn
ÖLAND
Borgholm
Kalmar
Mörbylånga

Frederikssund
Hillerød
COPENHAGEN
København
Roskilde
Køge Bugt
Køge
Næstved
Vordingborg
Nykøbing Fl.
FALSTER
MØN
Gedser
Bøgebjerg
Kalundborg
Holbæk
Slagelse
Ringsted
SJÆLLAND
LOLLAND
Maribo
SAMSØ
Helsingør
Helsingborg

ANHOLT
LÆSØ
Kattegat

Relief

Meters		Feet
1525		5000
610		2000
305		1000
152.5		500
0	Sea Level	0
152.5		Below Sea Level 500

A-559195-76 8-7-10
COPYRIGHT BY
RAND McNALLY & COMPANY
MADE IN U.S.A.

BLÅVANDS HUK
NORTH FRISIAN ISLANDS
RØMØ
SYLT
FØHR
HELGOLAND
Husum
Eckernförde
Tønning
Heide
SCHLESWIG
Flensburg
Schleswig
Kiel Bay
Rendsburg
Neumünster
HOLSTEIN
FED. REP. OF GERMANY
Neustadt
Lübeck
Cuxhaven
Elbe
Haderslev
Åbenrå
ALS
Sønderborg
Tønder
AERØ
LANGELAND
FEHMARN

Rügen
C. ARKONA
Sassnitz
Bergen
Stralsund
Greifswald
Wolgast
Barth
Warnemünde
Rostock
Wismar
GERMAN DEMOCRATIC REPUBLIC
Pomeranian Bay
Świnoujście
Kamień Pomorski
Kołobrzeg

POLAND
Łeba
Ustka
Wejherowo
Lębork
Darłowo
Słupsk
Gdynia
Sopot
Gdańsk
Longitude East of Greenwich

BALTIC SEA

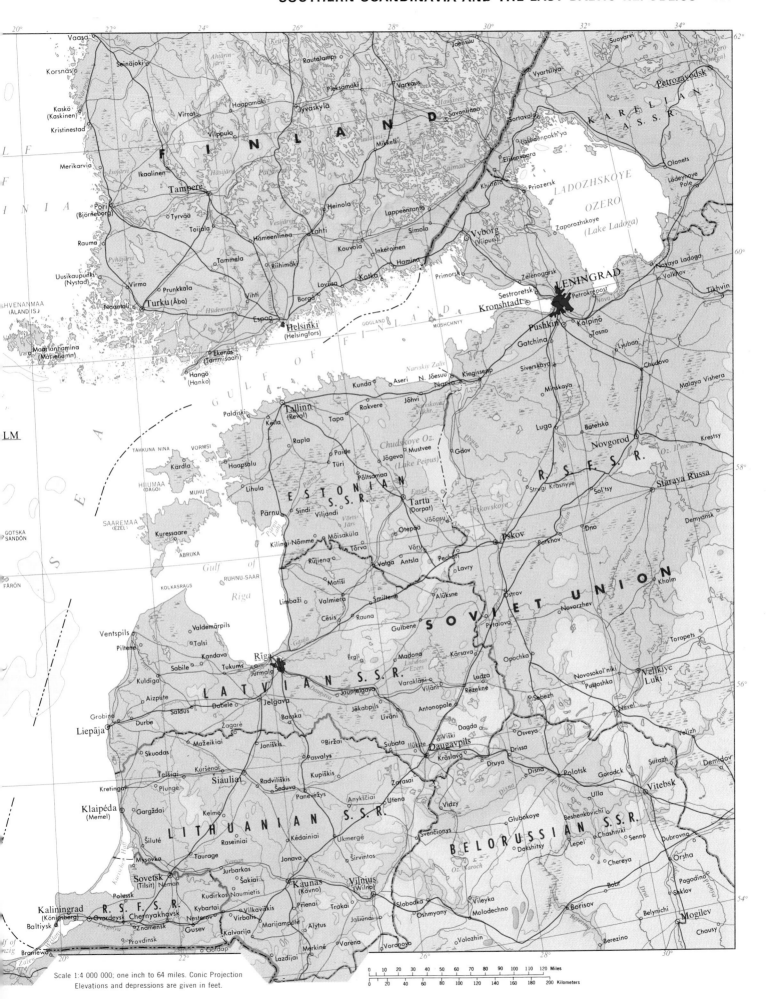

NORTH SEA

DENMARK

Flensburg · Schleswig · Rendsburg · Kiel · Neumünster · Neustadt · Eckernförde · Husum · Heide · Itzehoe · Bad Oldesloe · Elmshorn

Sønderborg · Rudkøbing · Nakskov · Maribo · Nykøbing Fl. · FALSTER · Gedser · MØN · LOLLAND

BALTIC

RÜGEN · Sassnitz · Bergen · Stralsund · Greifswald · Swinoujście · Kolobrzeg · Koszalin

FRISIAN ISLANDS · Norderney · Wangeroog · Cuxhaven · Borkum · Norden

HAMBURG · Lübeck · Wismar · Rostock · Schwerin · Güstrow · Demmin · Anklam · Uckermünde · Szczecin (Stettin) · POMERANIA

NETHERLANDS · AMSTERDAM · Den Helder · Alkmaar · Leeuwarden · Groningen · Emden · Wilhelmshaven · Bremerhaven · Stade · Lüneburg · Ludwigslust · Parchim · Neubrandenburg · Waren · Pasewalk · Neustrelitz

Zwolle · Almelo · Oldenburg · Delmenhorst · Bremen · LÜNEBURGER HEIDE · Soltau · Celle · Stendal · Perleberg · Wittenberge · Neu Ruppin · Oranienburg · Eberswalde · Bad Freienwalde · Gorzów Wlkp.

Arnhem · Nijmegen · Kleve · Münster · Osnabrück · Minden · Hannover · Braunschweig · Wolfsburg · Helmstedt · Magdeburg · Brandenburg · Potsdam · BERLIN · (East) · Frankfurt · Poznań

FEDERAL REPUBLIC · NIEDERSACHSEN · Bielefeld · Herford · Detmold · Paderborn · Hameln · Hildesheim · GERMAN DEMOCRATIC REPUBLIC · MECKLENBURG

DÜSSELDORF · ESSEN · Dortmund · Bochum · Wuppertal · Hagen · Solingen · Kassel · Göttingen · Nordhausen · HARZ · Halberstadt · Quedlinburg · Dessau · Wittenberg · Lübben · Cottbus · Zielona Góra

COLOGNE (Köln) · Bonn · Aachen · Siegen · Marburg · Gießen · Fulda · THÜRINGEN · Eisenach · Gotha · Erfurt · Weimar · Jena · Gera · Leipzig · Dresden · Görlitz · Legnica

NORDRHEIN · WESTFALEN · WESTERWALD · Koblenz · Limburg · GERMANY · FRANKFURT AM MAIN · Wiesbaden · Offenbach · Hanau · Schweinfurt · ERZGEBIRGE · Karl-Marx-Stadt · Zwickau · Plauen · Hof · Most · Chomutov · Jelenia Góra · Wałbrzych

LUXEMBOURG · Trier · RHEINLAND-PFALZ · Mainz · Darmstadt · Mannheim · Heidelberg · Würzburg · Bamberg · Bayreuth · Weiden · BOHEMIAN FOREST · Plzeň · PRAGUE (Praha) · ČESKÉ · BOHEMIA · Hradec Králové

FRANCE · Metz · Saarbrücken · Kaiserslautern · Karlsruhe · Pforzheim · STUTTGART · Heilbronn · Ansbach · Nürnberg · Fürth · Erlangen · Regensburg · České Budějovice

Strasbourg · BADEN · Tübingen · Reutlingen · Ulm · Heidenheim · Augsburg · Ingolstadt · Landshut · Passau · Linz

Freiburg · SCHWÄBISCHE · Biberach · Memmingen · Kempten · MUNICH (München) · Rosenbach · Salzburg · VIENNA (Wien)

Basel · SWITZERLAND · Zürich · St. Gallen · VORARLBERG · LIECHTENSTEIN · Innsbruck · HOHE TAUERN · OBERÖSTERREICH · Wels · Steyr

Bern · Lausanne · Geneva (Genève) · BERNER ALPEN · BRENNER PASS · TAUERN · KÄRNTEN · Villach · Klagenfurt · Graz

ITALY · Bolzano · Trento · DOLOMITES · CARNIC ALPS · KARAWANKEN · Udine · YUGOSLAVIA · Maribor

Continued on pages 160-161
Continued on pages 164-165
Longitude East of Greenwich

Scale 1:4 000 000; one inch to 64 miles. Conic Projection
Elevations and depressions are given in feet.

Relief

Meters		Feet
3050		10 000
1525		5000
610		2000
305		1000
152.5		500
Sea Level		0
152.5		500
1525		5000

A-550900-76- 6-4 9
COPYRIGHT BY
RAND McNALLY & COMPANY
MADE IN U.S.A.

Scale 1:1 000 000

0   5   10 Miles
0 4 8 12 16 Kilometers

©RMcN.

Scale 1:4 000 000; one inch to 64 miles. Conic Projection
Elevations and depressions are given in feet

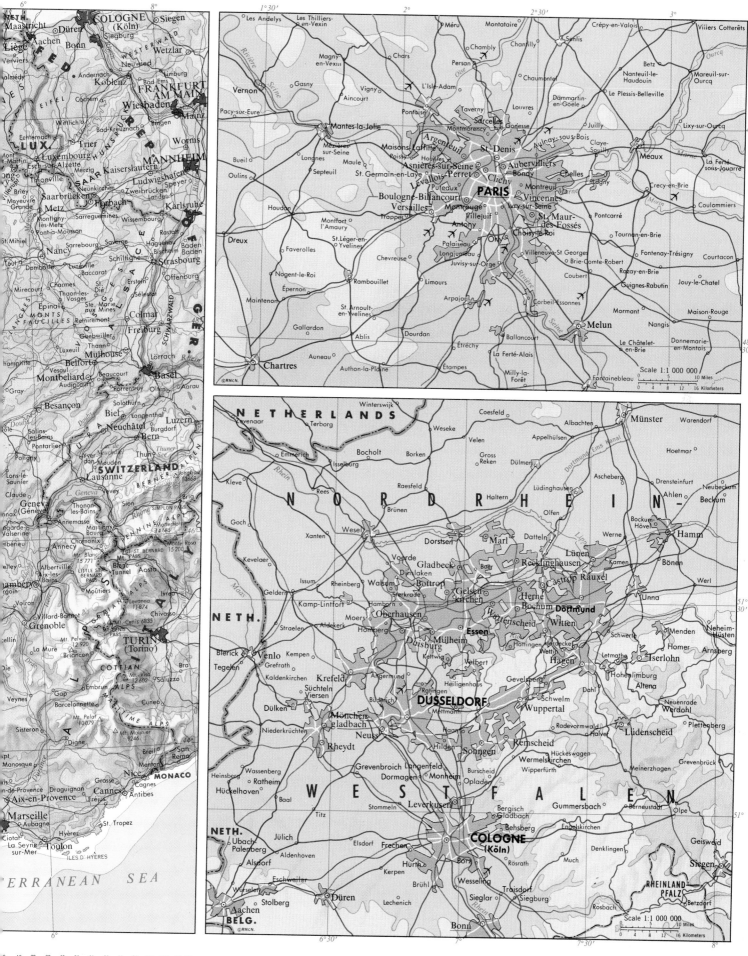

NETH.
Maastricht • Düren COLOGNE (Köln) • Siegen
Liège Aachen Siegburg
Verviers Bonn
W E S T E R W A L D Wetzlar
Andernach Neuwied
E I F E L Koblenz Limburg
Wittlich Cochem Bad Ems
Echternach Trier Bingen FRANKFURT AM MAIN
LUX. Wiesbaden Mainz
Luxembourg Esch-sur-Alzette Merzig Bad Kreuznach Worms
Thionville Saarbrücken Kaiserslautern MANNHEIM
Briey Forbach Ludwigshafen Speyer
Metz Sarreguemines Neunkirchen Zweibrücken Landau
Montigny-lès-Metz Saarbourg Wissembourg Karlsruhe
Pont-à-Mousson Savgrne Rastatt
St. Mihiel Nancy Sarrebourg Haguenau Baden Baden
Lunéville Bischheim
Toul Charmes Baccarat Schiltigheim Strasbourg
Dombasle St. Dié Ste. Marie aux Mines Offenburg
Mirecourt Thaon-les-Vosges Sélestat
Épinal Remiremont Colmar Freiburg
MONTS FAUCILLES Guebwiller
Luxeuil Thann Lörrach
Vesoul Belfort Mulhouse
Gray Montbéliard Audincourt Beaucourt Basel
Besançon Porrentruy Olten Aarau

Les Andelys • Les Thilliers-en-Vexin
Vernon Magny-en-Vexin Chars Méru Montataire Chantilly Crépy-en-Valois Villers Cotterêts
Gasny Vigny L'Isle-Adam Persan Chaumontel Senlis Nanteuil-le-Haudouin Betz Mareuil-sur-Ourcq
Pacy-sur-Eure Aincourt Pontoise Taverny Sarcelles Gonesse Juilly Lixy-sur-Ourcq
Mantes-la-Jolie Montmorency Aulnay-sous-Bois Claye-Souilly Meaux La Ferté-sous-Jouarre
Bueil Mézières-sur-Seine Maisons-Laffitte Argenteuil St.-Denis Bondy Chelles Crécy-en-Brie
Longnes Houilles Asnières-sur-Seine Aubervilliers Coulommiers
Oulins Septeuil Maule St. Germain-en-Laye Levallois-Perret Clichy Montreuil
Houdan Puteaux PARIS Vincennes Pontcarré
Dreux Versailles Boulogne-Billancourt Montrouge Ivry-sur-Seine St. Maur-des-Fossés Tournan-en-Brie
Montfort l'Amaury Trappes Antony Villejuif Choisy-le-Roi Rozay-en-Brie
Faverolles St. Léger-en-Yvelines Palaiseau Orly Villeneuve-St Georges Brie-Comte-Robert Fontenay-Trésigny Courtacon
Nogent-le-Roi Chevreuse Longjumeau Juvisy-sur-Orge Coubert Guignes-Rabutin Jouy-le-Chatel
Maintenon Rambouillet Limours Arpajon Corbeil-Essonnes Mormant Maison-Rouge
Épernon St. Arnoult-en-Yvelines Melun Nangis
Gallardon Dourdan Ballancourt Le Châtelet-en-Brie Donnemarie-en-Montois
Ablis Auneau Étréchy La Ferté-Alais Étampes
Chartres Authon-la-Plaine Milly-la-Forêt Fontainebleau
Scale 1:1 000 000

NETHERLANDS Winterswijk Coesfeld Münster Warendorf
Zevenaar Terborg Weseke Albachten Hoetmar Beckum
Emmerich Isselburg Borken Gross Reken Dülmen Lüdinghausen Ascheberg Drensteinfurt Ahlen Neubeckum
Kleve Bocholt Velen Appelhülsen Olfen Bockum-Höövel
Goch Rees Raesfeld Haltern Werne Hamm Bönen
Xanten Brünen Dorsten Marl Datteln Lünen Werl
Kevelaer Wesel Voerde Gladbeck Recklinghausen Castrop-Rauxel Kamen Unna
Geldern Issum Dinslaken Bottrop Gelsen-kirchen Herne Bochum Dortmund Menden
NETH. Kamp-Lintfort Walsum Sterkrade Wattenscheid Witten Neheim-Hüsten
Straelen Rheinberg Hamborn Oberhausen Essen Hattingen Hagen Schwerte
Blerick Venlo Kempen Aldekerk Moers Homberg Duisburg Mülheim Hattingen Hagen Letmathe Iserlohn Arnsberg
Tegelen Grefrath Kaldenkirchen Velbert Gevelsberg Hohenlimburg Altena
Krefeld Angermund Kettwig Heiligenhaus Homer
Dülken Süchteln Viersen Ratingen Schwelm Dahl Neuenrade Werdohl
Niederkrüchten Büderich DÜSSELDORF Mettmann Wuppertal Plettenberg
Mönchen-gladbach Neuss Haan Radevormwald Halver Lüdenscheid
Rheydt Hilden Solingen Remscheid Hückeswagen Meinerzhagen Grevenbrück
Wassenberg Grevenbroich Langenfeld Burscheid Wermelskirchen Wipperfürth
Heinsberg Ratheim Dormagen Monheim Opladen
Hückelhoven Baal Stommeln Leverkusen Bergisch Gladbach Gummersbach Berneustadt Olpe
NETH. Titz Bensberg Behsberg Engelskirchen
Ubach-Palenberg Jülich Elsdorf Frechen COLOGNE (Köln) Denklingen
Alsdorf Aldenhoven Hürth Rösrath Much Geisweid
Würselen Stolberg Düren Kerpen Porz Siegen
Aachen Eschweiler Brühl Wesseling Troisdorf
BELG. Lechenich Sieglar Siegburg RHEINLAND-PFALZ
Bonn Rosbach Betzdorf
Scale 1:1 000 000

SWITZERLAND
BERNER ALPEN
Lausanne Thuner See SIMPLON PASS
Geneva (Genève) Brig
Thonon-les-Bains Sion
Annemasse Martigny A. P. Matterhorn GT. ST. BERNARD PASS Monte Rosa 15 200
Chamonix Mt. Blanc 15 771 Aosta
Albertville LITTLE ST. BERNARD PASS
Aix-les-Bains Mt. Cenis 6835
Chambéry Mt. Cenis Lanzo
Voiron Mt. Pelvoux 12 920 Susa Chivasso
Grenoble Mt. Visa 12 602 TURIN (Torino)
La Mure Briançon COTTIAN ALPS Saluzzo
Veynes Gap Embrun Cuneo
Barcelonnette
Sisteron Digne Mt. Pelat 10 079 MARITIME ALPS
Mt. Mounier 9246
Manosque Breil San Remo
Grasse Draguignan Nice MONACO
Aix-en-Provence Cannes Antibes
Marseille Fréjus
Aubagne St. Tropez
La Seyne sur-Mer Toulon Hyères ÎLES D. HYÈRES

MEDITERRANEAN SEA

0 10 20 30 40 50 60 70 80 90 100 110 120 Miles
0 20 40 60 80 100 120 140 160 180 200 Kilometers

Scale 1:4 000 000, one inch to 64 miles. Conic Projection
Elevations and depressions are given in feet

Longitude West of Greenwich

Scale 1:4 000 000; one inch to 64 miles. Conic Projection
Elevations and depressions are given in feet

Continued on pages 158–159

Continued on pages 160–161

Relief

Meters	Feet
3050	10 000
1525	5000
610	2000
305	1000
152.5	500
Sea Level	0
152.5	500
1525	5000
3050	10 000

A-558396-76-2-6-9
COPYRIGHT BY
RAND McNALLY & COMPANY
MADE IN U.S.A.

Longitude East of Greenwich

0 10 20 30 40 50 60 70 80 90 100 110 120 Miles

0 20 40 60 80 100 120 140 160 180 200 Kilometers

Scale 1:4 000 000; one inch to 64 miles. Conic Projection
Elevations and depressions are given in feet

ATLANTIC OCEAN

ARCTIC

BARENTS SEA

KARSKOYE (Kara Sea)

SVALBARD (SPITSBERGEN) (Nor.)

ZEMLYA FRANTSA IOSIFA (FRANZ JOSEF LAND)

M. ZHELANIYA

NOVAYA ZEMLYA

M. Matochkin

Matochkin Shar

BELYY

P-OV YAMAL

P-OV GYDANSKIY

NORTH SEA

BALTIC SEA

GULF of Bothnia

WHITE SEA

UNITED KINGDOM

Glasgow, Edinburgh, Aberdeen, Newcastle

NORWAY, SWEDEN, FINLAND

Oslo, Bergen, Trondheim, Hammerfest, Vardö, Nordkapp

STOCKHOLM, Göteborg, Norrköping, Malmö, Åbo, Turku, Vaasa, Luleå, Kemi

Helsinki, Tampere, Viborg

DENMARK, COPENHAGEN, Kiel, Ålborg

GER. DEM. REP., HAMBURG, BERLIN

POLAND, WARSAW, Gdańsk, Poznań, Łódź, Kraków, Ostrava, Wrocław

LENINGRAD, Pskov, Tallinn, Tartu, Riga, Kaunas, Vilnius, Kaliningrad

ESTONIAN S.S.R., LATVIAN S.S.R., LITHUANIAN S.S.R.

BELORUSSIAN S.S.R., Minsk, Mogilev, Vitebsk, Baranovichi, Brest, Gomel', Pinsk

Murmansk, Kirovsk, KOLA PEN., Polyarnyy, Kandalaksha, KOL. ZAL.

KARELIAN A.S.S.R., Petrozavodsk, ONEGA

Arkhangel'sk (Archangel), Mezen', Pinega, Onega

KOMI A.S.S.R., Syktyvkar, Ust'-Kulom, Pechora, Troitsko-Pechorsk

PECHORA BASIN, Nar'yan-Mar, Vorkuta, Khal'mer-Yu, Ust'-Tsil'ma

Novyy Port, Salekhard, Berezovo, Tazovskoye

MOSCOW (Moskva), Kalinin, Yaroslavl', Ivanovo, Vladimir, Serpukhov, Kaluga, Orekhovo-Zuyevo, Shuya

Smolensk, Bryansk, Orël, Kursk, Yelets, Lipetsk, Voronezh, Tambov, Ryazan, Saransk, Penza

Novomoskovsk, Velikiye Luki, Vyshniy Volochëk, Cherepovets, Vologda, Kostroma, Kirov

GORKI, Murom, Alatyr', Syzran', Saratov, Borisoglebsk

KIEV, KHAR'KOV, DNEPROPETROVSK, DONETSK, Sumy, Poltava, Zaporozh'ye, Voroshilovgrad, Shakhty

UKRAINIAN S.S.R., MOLDAVIAN S.S.R., Zhitomir, Vinnitsa, Chernovtsy, Chernigov, Krivoy Rog, Nikolayev, Kishinëv

Odessa, Simferopol', Sevastopol', Kerch', Novorossiysk, Krasnodar

L'vov, Iaşi

BLACK SEA, Sochi, Sukhumi, Batumi, Sinop, Samsun, Trabzon

CAUCASUS, GEORGIAN S.S.R., Tbilisi, Yerevan, ARMENIAN S.S.R., AZERBAYDZHAN S.S.R., BAKU, Kirovabad, Grozny, Stavropol', Armavir, Maykop

CASPIAN SEA, Astrakhan, Gur'yev, CASPIAN DEPRESSION, Surface 92 feet below Sea Level

Makhachkala, Krasnovodsk, Lenkoran'

KUYBYSHEV, Ul'yanovsk, Kazan', Izhevsk, Chistopol', Ufa, Buzuluk, Sterlitamak, Orenburg, Magnitogorsk

PERM', SVERDLOVSK, Chusovoy, Gubakha, Krasnotur'insk, Nizhniy Tagil, Zlatoust, Chelyabinsk, Kurgan

Glazov, Slobodskoy, Kirov, Yaransk, Kotel'nich

Kungur, Krasnoufimsk, Nev'yansk, Irbit, Kamyshlov, Shadrinsk

URAL MTS.

Orsk, Aktyubinsk, Ural'sk, Sol'-Iletsk, Mednogorsk, Kustanay

KAZAKH S.S.R., KIRGIZ STEPPE, TURGAY, Tselinograd (Akmolinsk), Atbasar, Temir Tau, Karaganda, Balkhash, Ozero Balkhash

Omsk, Petropavlovsk, Tatarsk, Tara, Tyumen', Ishim, Tyukalinsk

WESTERN SIBERIAN LOWLAND, Khanty-Mansiysk, Surgut, Narym, Kolpashevo, Tomsk

NOVOSIBIRSK, Barnaul, Rubtsovsk, Kemerovo, Anzhero-Sudzhensk, Kiselëvsk, Novokuznetsk, Kamen'-na-Obi

Kargat, Cherlak, Pavlodar, Semipalatinsk, Semiyarskoye, Bayan-Aul, Zyryanovsk, Zaysan, Ayaguz, Urdzhar, Leninogorsk

ARAL'SKOYE MORE (Aral Sea), Surface elev. 174 ft. above sea level, Aral'sk, Novo-Kazalinsk, Tyura-Tam, Kzyl-Orda, Chelkar, Baykonur

PLATO UST'-URT

UZBEK S.S.R., TASHKENT, Samarkand, Bukhara, Chardzhou, Chimkent, Dzhambul, Turkestan, Arys

TURKMEN S.S.R., Ashkhabad, Mary, Chardzhou, PESKI KARAKUMY (DESERT), PESKI KYZYL KUM (DESERT)

PESKI MUYUN-KUM

TADZHIK S.S.R., Dushanbe, Leninabad, Dzhalal-Abad, Andizhan, Fergana, Kokand

KIRGIZ S.S.R., Frunze, Przheval'sk, Alma-Ata, Tokmak, Panfilov

TIEN SHAN, Kashgar, Ürümqi

TURKEY, Erzurum, Erzincan, Kars, Sivas, Tokat, Malatya, Diyarbakir, Siverek, Sizre

IRAQ, Baghdad, Mosul (Al Mawsil), Kirkuk, Hit, Tikrit

IRAN, TEHRĀN, Tabrīz, Zanjān, Rasht, Hamadān, Kermānshāh, Kāshān, Qom, Mashhad, Shahrūd

ZAGROS MTS., ELBURZ MTS., KOPET MTS.

GR. SALT DESERT

AFGHANISTAN

Relief

Meters		Feet
3050		10 000
1525		5000
610		2000
305		1000
152.5		500
0	Sea Level	0
152.5		500
1525		5000 Below
3050		10 000 Sea Level

ARCTIC OCEAN

VRANGELYA (WRANGEL)

CHUKOTSKIY P-OV

LAPTEV SEA

EAST SIBERIAN SEA

DE LONGA

NOVOSIBIRSKIYE O-VA (NEW SIBERIAN ISLANDS)

MALYY LYAKHOVSKIY

SEVERNAYA ZEMLYA (NORTHERN LAND)

M. CHELYUSKIN

TAYMYR GORY BYRRANGA

BOL'SHOY BEGICHEV

P-OV GORY

CHUKOTSKOYE NAGOR'YE

M. SHELAGSKIY

Amguema

Arctic Circle

Markovo

Anadyr'

Anadyrskiy Zaliv

M. OLYUTORSKIY

KORYAKSKIY KHREBET

Nordvik

Ust'-Olenek

Khatanga

Bulun

Tiksi

M. SVYATOY NOS

KOTEL'NYY

M. BUOR KHAYA

Kazach'ye

Allaikha

Nizhne-Kolymsk

Sredne-Kolymsk

Gizhiga

Penzhino

KHREBET GYDAN (KOLYMSKIY)

KARAGIN

Noril'sk

GORY PUTORANA

Turukhansk

Khatanga

Tura

Nizhnyaya Tunguska

G. Pektan 3543

Yartsevo

Yeniseysk

Podkamennaya Tunguska

Baykit

arka

Zhigansk

Vilyuysk

Suntar

Olekminsk

Mukhtuya

Peleduy Vitim

G. Golets Purpula 3277

PATOM PLATEAU

Bodaybo

Golets-Skalistyy 9186

Kirensk

KHREBET CHERSKOGO

A.S.S.R.

Verkhoyansk

Goye Chen

Abryy

Zashiversk

Zyryanka

VERKHOYANSKIY KHREBET

YAKUT

Yakutsk

Aldanskoye

Amga

Ust'-Maya

Omyakon

Nel'kan

Okhotsk

Magadan

M. TAYGONOS

M. ALEVINA

Shelekhova Guba

M. ALEVINA

KAMCHATKA

Klyuchevskiy (Vol.) 15 584

Verkhne-Kamchatsk

Petropavlovsk-Kamchatskiy

Ust'-Bol'sheretsk

SOCIALIST REPUBLIC

Aldan

Tommot

DZHUGDZHUR KHREBET

Ayan

Chumikan

Udskaya Guba

SHANTAR

M. YELIZAVETY

Okha

SAKHALIN (Sov. Union)

Aleksandrovsk

Poronaysk

Uglegorsk

M. TERPENIYA

SEA OF OKHOTSK

Ilimsk

Nizhne-Angarsk

BURYAT

Baykal (Lake Baikal)

Barguzin

Surface 1535 ft.

Nizhneudinsk

Zhigalovo

Kachuga

STANOVOY KHREBET

Tyndinskiy

Skovorodino

Zeya

Svobodnyy

Belogorsk

Ust'-Tyrma

Bureya

Nikolayevsk-na-Amure

Komsomol'sk na-Amure

Sovetskaya Gavan

Malmyzh

KHREBET BUREINSKIY

SIKHOTE ALIN

Kholmsk

Korsakov

Yuzhno-Sakhalinsk

Wakkanai

Esashi

HOKKAIDŌ

Otaru Sapporo

Krasnoyarsk

Bogotol

Balakhta

Kansk

Tayshet

Bratsk

Bratskoye

Tulun

Minusinsk

Abakan

Piramida 10801

Cheremkhovo

Angarsk

Irkutsk

Kotulika

Munku Sardyk 11457

KHREBET

SAYAN

TANNU-OLA

Kyzyl

Kyren

Ulan-Ude

Petrovsk-Zabaykal'skiy

Gorodok

Kyakhta

Nyal

Hara Usa

Jibhalanta

Jirgalanta

HANGAYN NURUU

HANGAIN KHANGAI MTS.

Bogdo Ula 13865

MONGOLIA

Sayr Usa

GOBI OR SHAMO (DESERT)

Hami

BAYKAL'SKIY KHREBET

YABLONOVYY KHREBET

Bargu

Aginskoye

Chita

Nerchinsk

Sretensk

Nerchinskiy Zavod

NERCHINSKIY KHREBET

Borzya

Aksha

Onon

Kerulen

Öndör Haan

Ulaan Baatar

Selenge Gol

A.S.S.R.

Ulan-Ude

KHINGAN RANGE

Blagoveshchensk

Amur

Birobidzhan

Khabarovsk

Dal'nerechensk

Spassk-Dal'niy

Ussuriysk

Artëm

Partizansk

Nakhodka

Vladivostok

Ol'ga

KHREBET

Najin

Chŏngjin

SEA OF JAPAN

Wenquan

GREATER KHINGAN

Nenjiang

Goukou

Tsitsihar (Qiqihar)

Hailun

Suihua

Boli

Mudanjiang

HARBIN

Jilin

Dunhua

Hunchun

Tao'an

Jarud Qi

Fuyu

Shuangliao

CHANGCHUN

MANCHURIA

LESSER KHINGAN RANGE

HONSHŪ

Kanazawa

Kanazawa

Tottori

Matsue

Okayama

Kyoto

KOBE

OSAKA

Kōchi

Hiroshima

JAPAN

Sanin Kaigan

KOREA

P'yŏngyang

SEOUL

Kaesŏng

Andong

Taegu

PUSAN

Korea Bay

Kanazawa

Chifeng

Weichang

Chengde

SHENYANG FUSHUN

Kalgan

Fengzhen

Baoding

PEKING (Beijing)

TIENTSIN (Tianjin)

Lüshun

Lüda

CHINA

Bo Hai

SHANDONG BANDAO

YELLOW SEA

Longitude East of Greenwich

100 200 300 400 500 600 Miles

200 400 600 800 1000 Kilometers

A-570000-76 8°-14°

COPYRIGHT BY
RAND McNALLY & COMPANY
MADE IN U.S.A.

170

Continued on pages 150–151

Scale 1:10 000 000; one inch to 160 miles. Conic Projection

Elevations and depressions are given in feet.

Continued on pages 152–153

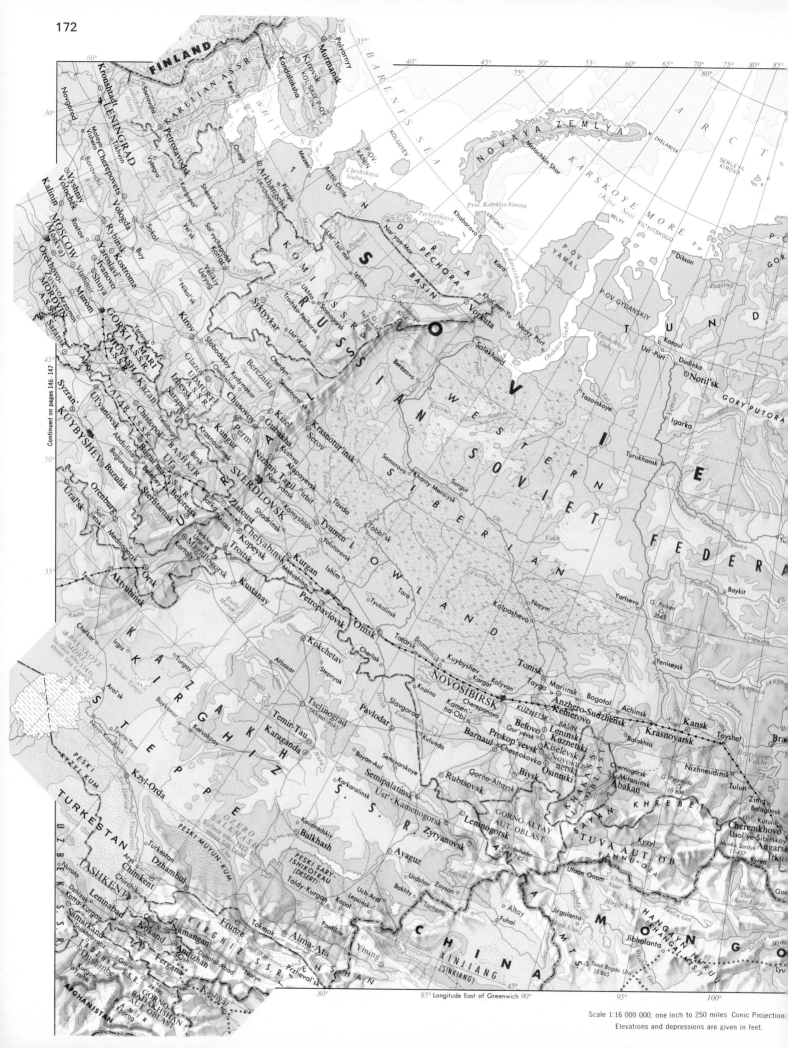

Continued on pages 188–189

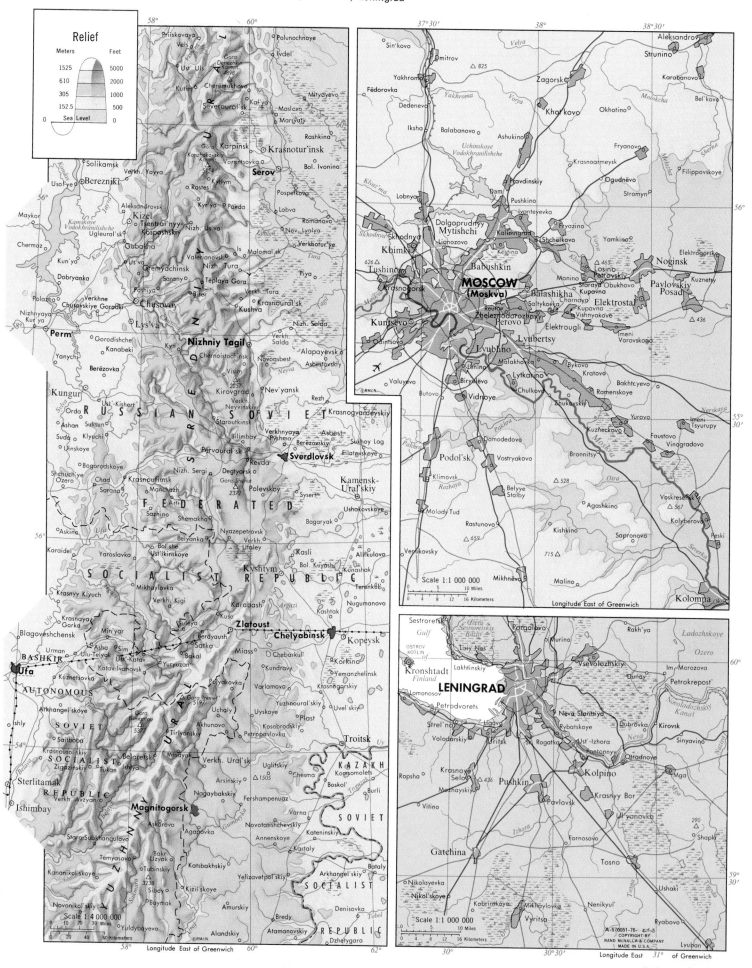

Relief

Meters		Feet
1525		5000
610		2000
305		1000
152.5		500
0	Sea Level	0

Scale 1:4 000 000

Scale 1:1 000 000

Scale 1:1 000 000

Longitude East of Greenwich

Longitude East of Greenwich

Longitude East of Greenwich

A-570051-76-
COPYRIGHT BY
RAND McNALLY & COMPANY
MADE IN U.S.A.

For larger scale coverage
of Moscow see page 64.

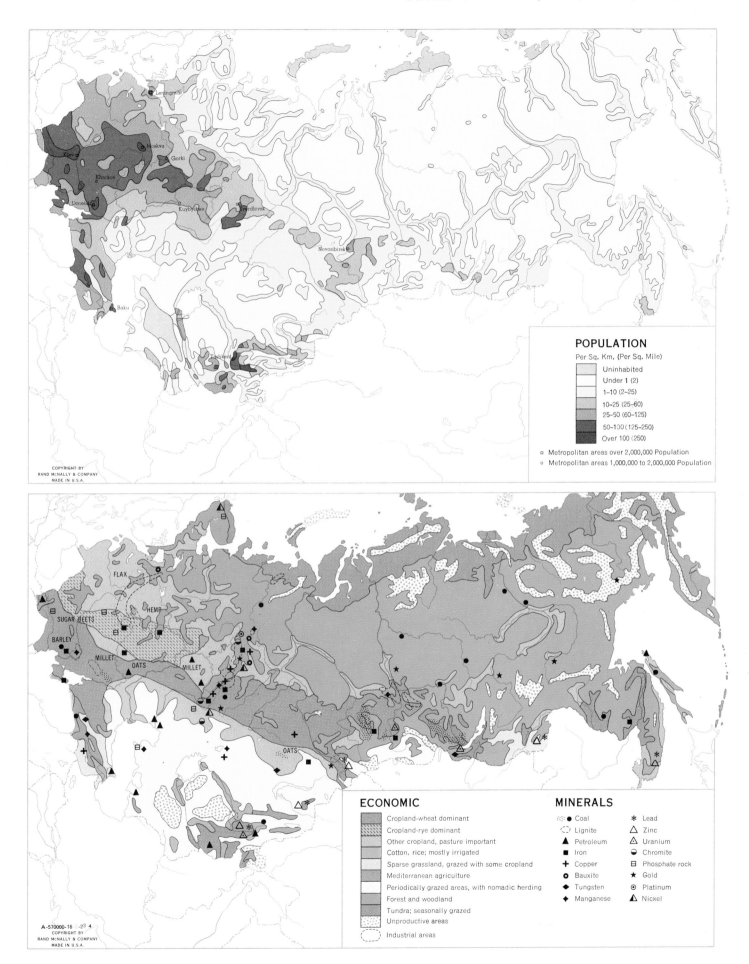

POPULATION

Per Sq. Km. (Per Sq. Mile)

	Uninhabited
	Under 1 (2)
	1–10 (2–25)
	10–25 (25–60)
	25–50 (60–125)
	50–100 (125–250)
	Over 100 (250)

▫ Metropolitan areas over 2,000,000 Population

◦ Metropolitan areas 1,000,000 to 2,000,000 Population

ECONOMIC

- Cropland-wheat dominant
- Cropland-rye dominant
- Other cropland, pasture important
- Cotton, rice; mostly irrigated
- Sparse grassland, grazed with some cropland
- Mediterranean agriculture
- Periodically grazed areas, with nomadic herding
- Forest and woodland
- Tundra; seasonally grazed
- Unproductive areas
- Industrial areas

MINERALS

●	Coal	✳	Lead
◌	Lignite	△	Zinc
▲	Petroleum	△	Uranium
■	Iron	◠	Chromite
✛	Copper	⊟	Phosphate rock
◉	Bauxite	★	Gold
◆	Tungsten	⊙	Platinum
◆	Manganese	△	Nickel

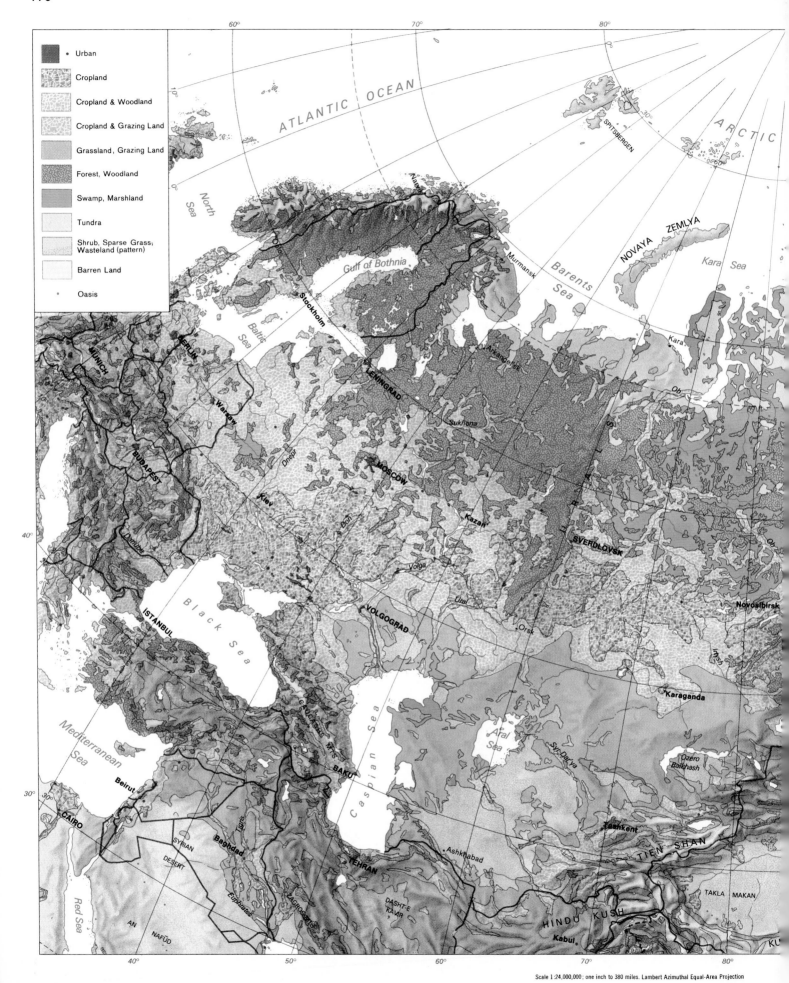

Urban
Cropland
Cropland & Woodland
Cropland & Grazing Land
Grassland, Grazing Land
Forest, Woodland
Swamp, Marshland
Tundra
Shrub, Sparse Grass;
Wasteland (pattern)
Barren Land
Oasis

Scale 1:24,000,000; one inch to 380 miles. Lambert Azimuthal Equal-Area Projection

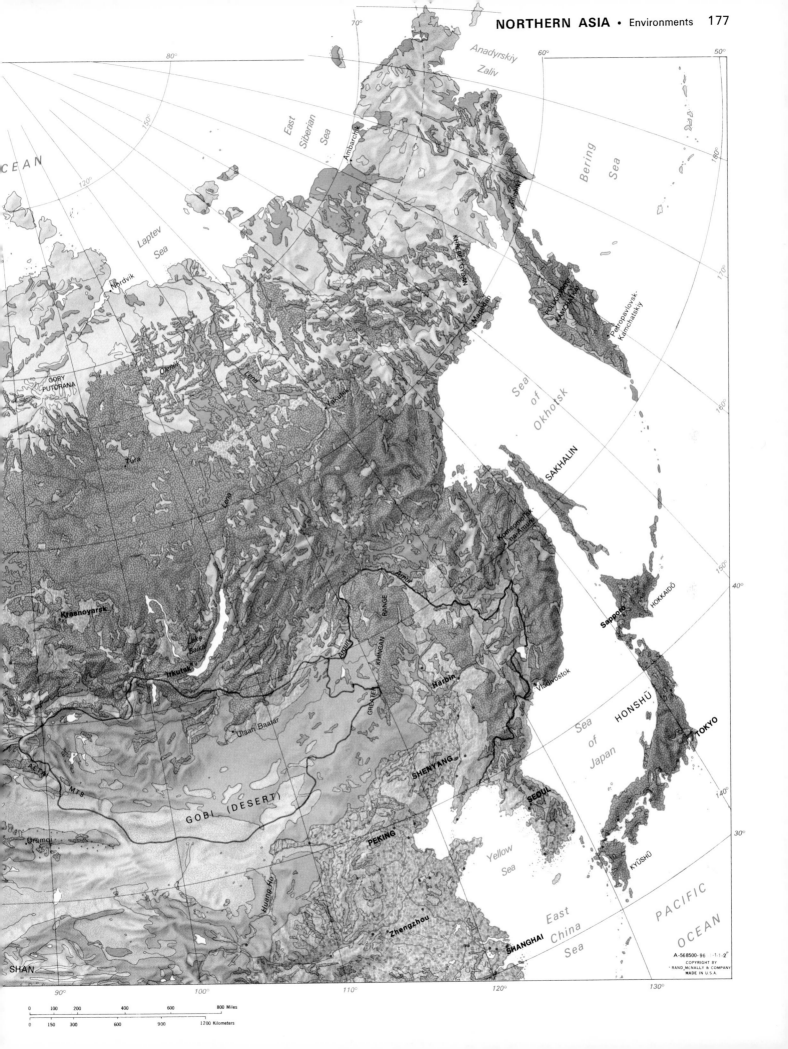

70°

80°

Anadyrskiy Zaliv

60°

50°

180°

East Siberian Sea

Bering Sea

OCEAN

Laptev Sea

Ambarchik

170°

KHREBET GYDAN

Anadyr'

Nordvik

POLUOSTROV KAMCHATKA

Magadan

Petropavlovsk-Kamchatskiy

Olenek

Lena

GORY PUTORANA

Sea of Okhotsk

160°

Yakutsk

SAKHALIN

Tura

150°

Komsomol'sk-na-Amure

40°

Krasnoyarsk

Amur

HOKKAIDŌ

Lake Baikal

RANGE

Sapporo

Amur

KHINGAN

Irkutsk

Harbin

Vladivostok

Sea of Japan

HONSHŪ

30°

Ulaan Baatar

GREATER

TOKYO

SHENYANG

ALTAI MTS

SEOUL

140°

Ürümqi

GOBI (DESERT)

PEKING

Yellow Sea

30°

Huang-Ho

KYŪSHŪ

SHAN

Zhengzhou

East China Sea

PACIFIC OCEAN

SHANGHAI

120°

130°

90°   100°   110°

| 0 | 100 | 200 | 400 | 600 | 800 Miles |
| 0 | 150 | 300 | 600 | 900 | 1200 Kilometers |

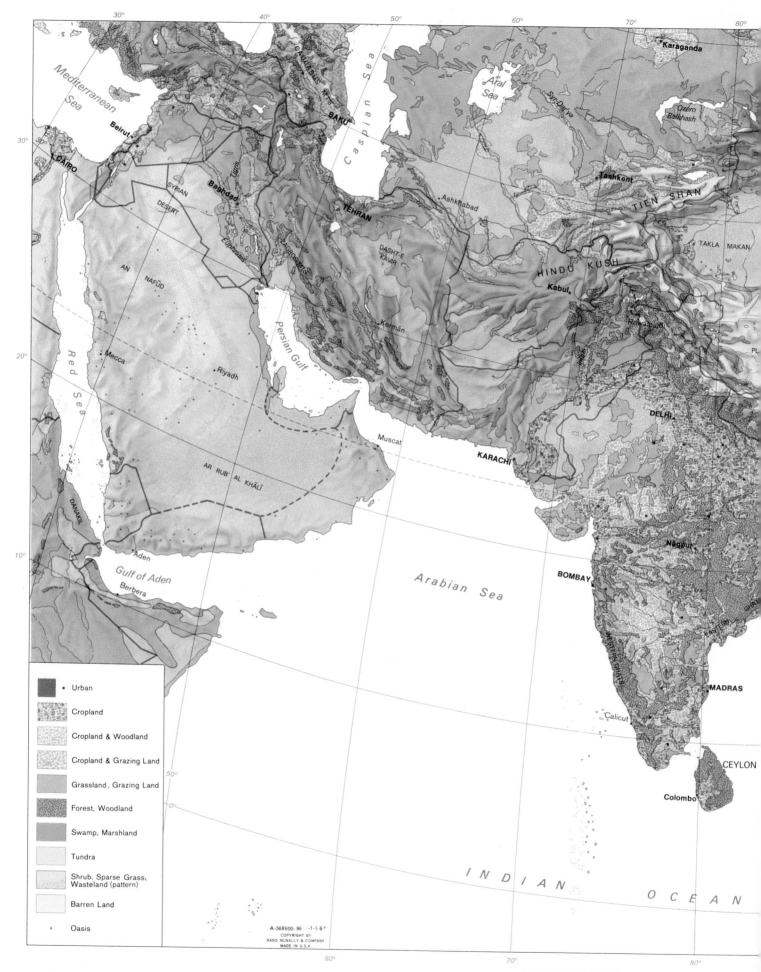

Urban

Cropland

Cropland & Woodland

Cropland & Grazing Land

Grassland, Grazing Land

Forest, Woodland

Swamp, Marshland

Tundra

Shrub, Sparse Grass, Wasteland (pattern)

Barren Land

• Oasis

A-568600-96 -1-1-6 P
COPYRIGHT BY
RAND McNALLY & COMPANY
MADE IN U.S.A.

Scale 1:24,000,000; one inch to 380 miles. Lambert Azimuthal Equal-Area Projection

ALTAI MTS.

Ürümqi

Ulaan Baatar

GOBI (DESERT)

GREATER KHINGAN RA.

Harbin

Vladivostok

Sea
of
Japan

HONSHŪ

TOKYO

SHENYANG

SEOUL

PEKING

Huang He

Yellow
Sea

KYŪSHŪ

PACIFIC

OCEAN

SHAN

Zhengzhou

SHANGHAI

East
China
Sea

TIBET

WUHAN

Mekong

CHONGQING

T'aipei

Tropic of Cancer

FORMOSA

I M A L A Y A S

Brahmaputra

Kunming

CANTON

Philippine

Sea

Ganges

Sea

CALCUTTA

Hanoi

HAINAN DAO

MANILA

Mandalay

Salween

Mekong

China

Cebu

Bay of

South

MINDANAO

Bengal

Rangoon

BANGKOK

Kota Kinabalu

Celebes

Andaman

HO CHI MINH CITY

Sea

Manado

Sea

China

Medan

Kuching

BORNEO

CELEBES

SINGAPORE

S U M A T R A

Ujung Pandang

Equator

Java Sea

JAKARTA

JAVA

0   100   200   400   600   800 Miles

0   150   300   600   900   1200 Kilometers

90°   100°

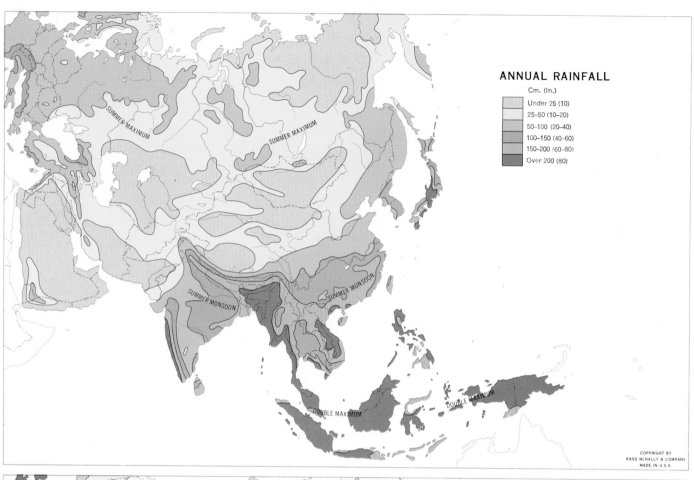

ANNUAL RAINFALL

Cm. (In.)

- Under 25 (10)
- 25–50 (10–20)
- 50–100 (20–40)
- 100–150 (40–60)
- 150–200 (60–80)
- Over 200 (80)

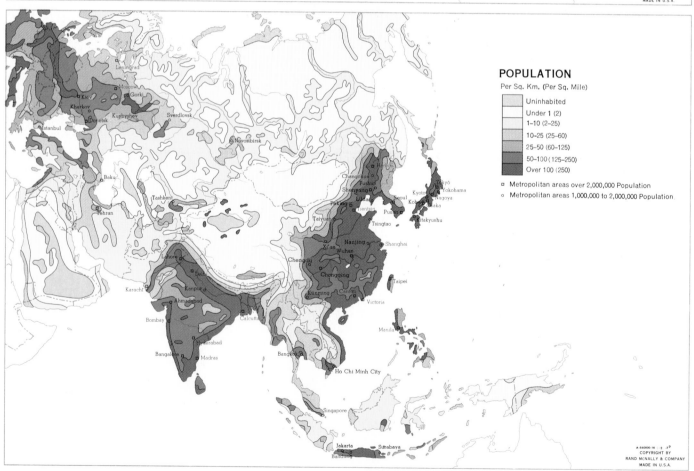

POPULATION

Per Sq. Km. (Per Sq. Mile)

- Uninhabited
- Under 1 (2)
- 1–10 (2–25)
- 10–25 (25–60)
- 25–50 (60–125)
- 50–100 (125–250)
- Over 100 (250)

□ Metropolitan areas over 2,000,000 Population

○ Metropolitan areas 1,000,000 to 2,000,000 Population

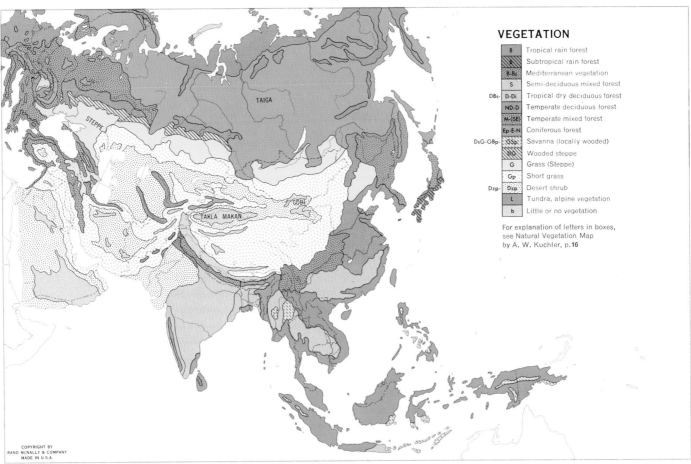

VEGETATION

B		Tropical rain forest
B		Subtropical rain forest
B-Bs		Mediterranean vegetation
S		Semi-deciduous mixed forest
DBs-	D-Di	Tropical dry deciduous forest
	ND-D	Temperate deciduous forest
	M-(SE)	Temperate mixed forest
	Ep-E-N	Coniferous forest
DsG-GBp-	GSp	Savanna (locally wooded)
	DG	Wooded steppe
	G	Grass (Steppe)
	Gp	Short grass
Dzp-	Dzp	Desert shrub
	L	Tundra, alpine vegetation
	b	Little or no vegetation

For explanation of letters in boxes,
see Natural Vegetation Map
by A. W. Kuchler, p.16

TAIGA

STEPPE

GOBI

TAKLA MAKAN

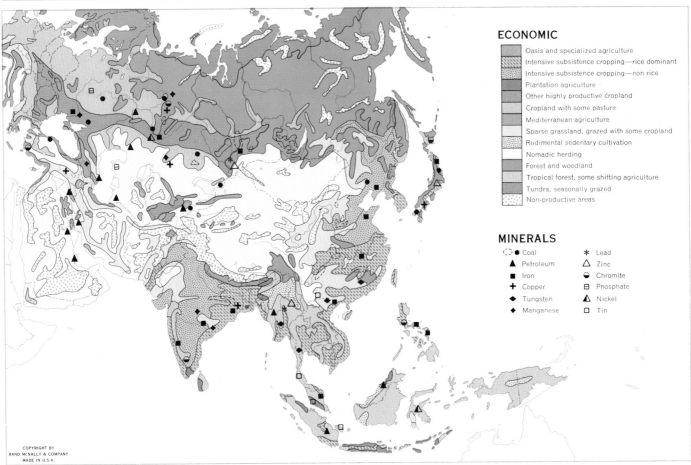

ECONOMIC

	Oasis and specialized agriculture
	Intensive subsistence cropping—rice dominant
	Intensive subsistence cropping—non rice
	Plantation agriculture
	Other highly productive cropland
	Cropland with some pasture
	Mediterranean agriculture
	Sparse grassland, grazed with some cropland
	Rudimental sedentary cultivation
	Nomadic herding
	Forest and woodland
	Tropical forest, some shifting agriculture
	Tundra, seasonally grazed
	Non-productive areas

MINERALS

●	Coal	∗	Lead
▲	Petroleum	△	Zinc
■	Iron	◖	Chromite
✚	Copper	⊟	Phosphate
◆	Tungsten	▲	Nickel
◆	Manganese	□	Tin

Continued on page 209

Relief

Meters	Feet
3050	10 000
1525	5000
610	2000
305	1000
0 Sea Level	Sea Level 0
	Below
152.5	500 Sea Level
1525	5000
3050	10 000
6100	20 000

A-519695-76
COPYRIGHT BY
RAND McNALLY & COMPANY
MADE IN U.S.A.

Scale 1:40 000 000; one inch to 630 miles. Lambert's Azimuthal, Equal Area Projection
Elevations and depressions are given in feet

Areas occupied by Israel since June 1967

Scale 1:4 000 000
JABAL MAZHAFAH
10   20   30   40   50 Miles
20   40   60   80 Kilometers

Scale 1:4 000 000
0   10   20   30   40   50 Miles
0   20   40   60   80 Kilometers

Cities, Towns, and Villages

0 to 25,000 ○	100,000 to 250,000 ⊙	1,000,000 and over ⊙
25,000 to 100,000 •	250,000 to 1,000,000 ◎	Major urbanized area

184

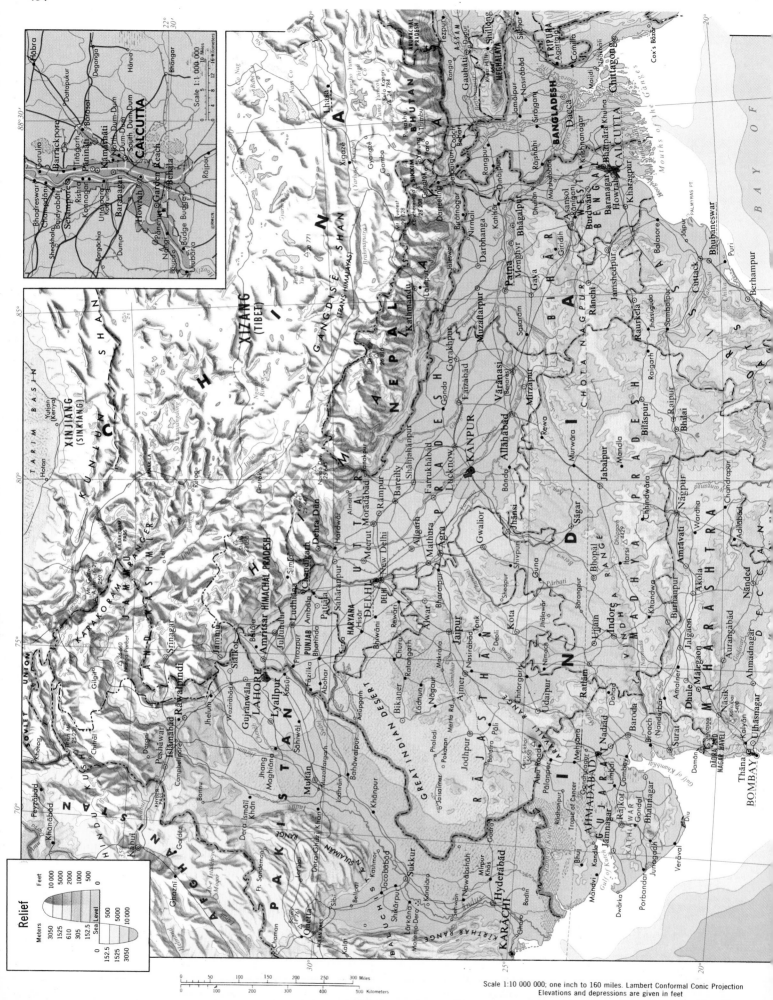

CALCUTTA

Scale 1:1 000 000

Relief

Meters	Feet
3050	10 000
1525	5000
610	2000
305	1000
152.5	500
0	Sea Level 0
152.5	500
1525	5000
3050	10 000

Scale 1:10 000 000; one inch to 160 miles. Lambert Conformal Conic Projection
Elevations and depressions are given in feet

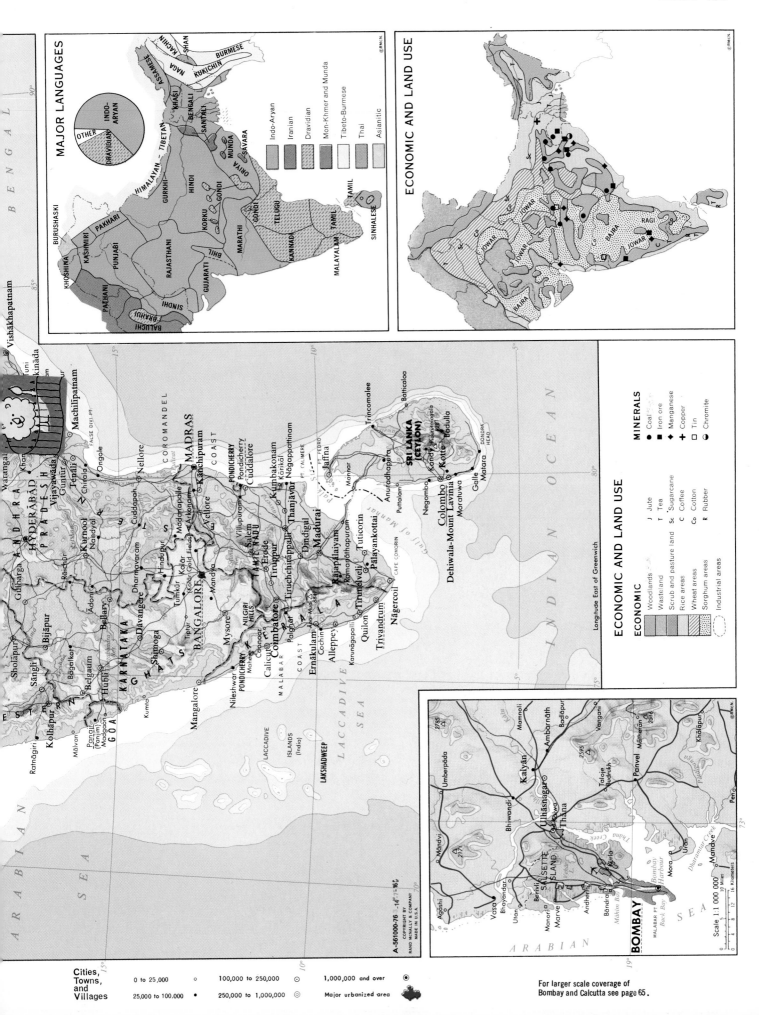

Relief

Meters		Feet
3050		10 000
1525		5000
610		2000
305		1000
152.5		500
0	Sea Level	0
152.5		500	Below
1525		5000	Sea Level
3050		10 000

Continued on pages 210-211

A-569400-76 -11-9-20
COPYRIGHT BY
RAND McNALLY & COMPANY
MADE IN U.S.A.

Scale 1:16 000 000; one inch to 250 miles. Polyconic Projection
Elevations and depressions are given in feet

Longitude East of Greenwich

inued on pages 172–173

S. S. R.

Kzyl-Orda

Ozero Balkhash

PESKI MUYUN-KUM

AFGHANISTAN

PAKISTAN

Dargaí

Jalālābād

Chārsadda

Peshāwar

KHYBER PASS

MORGA RA.

Scale 1:4 000 000

Turkestan · Dzhambul · KIRGIZSKIY KHREBET · Frunze

TASHKENT · Namangan · Dzhalal-Abad

Kokand · Andizhan · Osh

Leninabad · Fergana

Yarkand · TADZHIK S.S.R. · Pik Kommunizma · Garm

Karshi · Dushanbe · Kurgan-Tyube · Khorog

Termez · Feyzabad

Mazār-e Sharif · Balkh

Qandahār · Kābul

Peshāwar · Ghaznī

JAMMU AND KASHMIR

AFGHANISTAN

PAKISTAN

HIMACHAL PRADESH

PUNJAB

HARYANA

UTTAR PRADESH

NEPAL

SIKKIM

BHUTAN

ARUNACHAL PRADESH

ASSAM

NAGALAND

MEGHALAYA

RAJASTHĀN

BIHAR

BANGLADESH

MIZORAM

GUJARAT

MADHYA PRADESH

WEST BENGAL

ORISSA

BURMA

MAHĀRASHTRA

ARABIAN SEA

BAY OF BENGAL

KARNATAKA

ANDHRA PRADESH

KERALA

TAMIL NADU

SRI LANKA (CEYLON)

INDIA · POLITICAL

1-TRIPURA
2-MANIPUR
3-LAKSHADWEEP
4-DELHI
5-DĀDRA AND NAGAR HAVELI
6-PONDICHERRY
7-GOA, DAMĀN, AND DIU

Continued on pages 188–189

Scale 1:40 000 000

Tropic of Cancer

CHINA

XIZAGN (TIBET)

KASHGAR (Kashi)

TAKLA MAKAN

Shache (Yarkand)

XINJIANG (SINKIANG)

Hotan

PAMIRS

Muztagata

Mt. Godwin Austen (K-2)

KARAKORAM RANGE

KARAKORAM PASS

HINDU KUSH

Gilgit

Chitrāl

JAMMU AND KASHMIR

Srīnagar

Islāmābād

Rāwalpindi

H I M A L A Y A

XIZANG (TIBET)

GANGDISÊ SHAN

Lhasa

Kābul

Peshāwar

KHYBER PASS

Ghaznī

Jammu

Siālkot

Amritsar

Gujrānwāla

LAHORE

Lyallpur

Ludhiāna

Jullundur

Simla

Chandīgarh

Dehra Dūn

Hardwār

Kāthmāndu

Mt. Everest

SIKKIM

Gangtok

Thimbu

BHUTAN

ARUNACHAL PRADESH

Tinsukia

Sibsāgar

Jorhāt

PAKISTAN

Qandahār

Ft. Sandeman

Quetta

Chaman

Loralai

BOLAN PASS

Dera Ghāzi Khān

Multān

Bahāwalpur

PUNJAB

Patiāla

Bhatinda

HARYANA

Meerut

DELHI

New Delhi

UTTAR

Rampur

Bareilly

Shāhjahānpur

Morādābād

Alīgarh

Mathura

Bharatpur

PRADESH

Lucknow

Faizābād

Gorakhpur

Darbhanga

Muzaffarpur

NEPAL

Lalitpur

Gānganagar

Cooch Behar

Gauhāti

Shillong

KHASI HILLS

MEGHALAYA

NAGALAND

Kohima

Silchar

MANIPUR

Imphāl

TROPIC OF CANCER

Bhamo

BURMA

Mogok

Mogaung

Myitkyina

Qandahār

Shikārpur

Sukkur

Mohenjo-Daro (Ruins)

KIRTHAR RANGE

SULAIMĀN RANGE

KĀRĀCHI

Hyderābād

Bīkaner

Alwar

Jaipur

Ajmer

Jodhpur

RĀJASTHĀN

GREAT INDIAN DESERT

ARAVALLI RA.

Tonk

Gwalior

Āgra

Farrukhābād

KĀNPUR

Jhānsi

Allāhābād

Vārānasi (Benares)

Patna

Gaya

Monghyr

Bhāgalpur

BIHĀR

Girīdih

Rājshāhi

Sirājganj

BANGLADESH

Dacca

Comilla

Khulna

N0ākhāli

Chittagong

Mt. Victoria 10 018

Paletwa

BURMA

Mandalay

Monywa

Myingyan

Sagaing

Abu Road

Pālanpur

INDIA

Udaipur

Jhālāwār

Kota

Sāgar

Bhopāl

Jabalpur

Murwāra

Rewa

Mirzāpur

Sāsarām

Rānchi

Asansol

Burdwān

Bhātpāra

Howrah

CALCUTTA

Kharagpur

WEST BENGAL

Mouths of the Ganges

Hooghly

Shwebo

Mogē

Yamēthin

AHMADĀBĀD

Bhuj

GUJARAT

KĀTHIĀWĀR PENINSULA

Rājkot

Jāmnagar

Porbandar

Verāval

Junāgadh

Bhāvnagar

Gulf of Kutch

Rann of Kutch

Gulf of Khambāt

Ujjain

Indore

Baroda

Surat

Dāmān

Diu

VINDHYA RA.

Narmada

MADHYA PRADESH

Burhānpur

Bilāspur

Raigarh

Raipur

Jhānsi

Jamshedpur

Rāurkela

Sambalpur

ORISSA

Jājpur

Cuttack

Bhubaneswar

Puri

Balasore

Mahānadi

BAY OF BENGAL

Kyaukpyu

Sittwe

Sandoway

ARAKAN YOMA

PEGU

Magwe

Yenangyaung

Prome

Pyinmana

Nāsik

Dhule

Akola

Amrāvati

Nāgpur

Wardhā

Chandrapur

Aurangābād

DECCAN

Godavari

Indrāvati

Berhampur

Vizianagaram

Henzada

Bassein

Rangoon

PAGODA PT.

Mouths of the Irrawaddy

BOMBAY

MAHĀRASHTRA

Ahmadnagar

Pune

Sholāpur

Nizāmābād

HYDERĀBĀD

Warangal

Vishākhapatnam

Rajahmundry

Kākināda

Yanam

Sāngli

Gulbarga

Kolhāpur

Raichūr

Vijayawāda

Elūru

Machilīpatnam

Guntūr

Hubli

Belgaum

Kurnool

Bellary

Cuddapah

Nellore

GOA

Panaji (Panjim)

KARNATAKA

WESTERN GHĀTS

EASTERN GHĀTS

Krishna

ANDHRA PRADESH

COROMANDEL COAST

Mangalore

BANGALORE

Mysore

Kolār

Vellore

MADRAS

Kānchipuram

Pondicherry

Salem

Cuddalore

Mahē

TAMIL NADU

Calicut

Coimbatore

Kumbakonam

LACCADIVE ISLANDS (India)

Ernākulam

Tiruchchirāppalli

Thanjāvūr

Madurai

KERALA

Sri Lanka (Ceylon) inset:

Tiruchchirāppalli

Ernākulam

KERALA

Alleppey

Quilon

Trivandrum

CAPE COMORIN

Thanjāvūr

TAMIL NADU

Madurai

Tuticorin

Tirunelveli

Nāgappattinam

Jaffna

Mannar

Trincomalee

Anurādhapura

Puttalam

SRI LANKA (CEYLON)

Colombo

Kandy

Galle

Matara

DONDRA HEAD

INDIAN OCEAN

Same scale as main map

0 50 100 200 300 400 500 Miles

0 200 400 600 800 Kilometers

Cities, Towns, and Villages

| 0 to 25,000 | 100,000 to 250,000 | 1,000,000 and over |
| 25,000 to 100,000 | 250,000 to 1,000,000 | Major urbanized area |

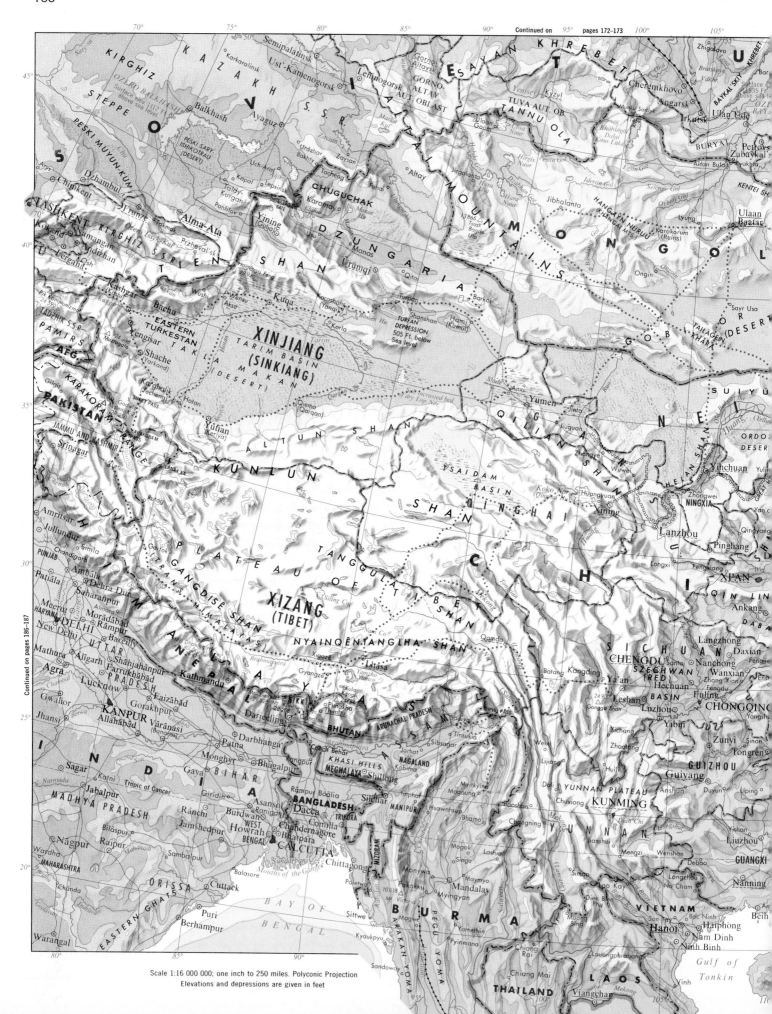

Continued on pages 172–173

Continued on pages 186–187

Scale 1:16 000 000; one inch to 250 miles. Polyconic Projection
Elevations and depressions are given in feet

N
USSR
ABLONOVYY KHREBET
Chita
Aginskoye
Nerchinsk
Sretensk
Skovorodino
Mohe
Qiqian
Mohe
NERCHINSKIY KHREBET
Choybalsan
Kerulen
Öndör Haan
Buir Nur
Manzhouli
Hailar
Hulun Nur
Goukou
Nenjiang
Keshan
Tongbei
Haslun
Suihua
Tsitsihar (Qiqihar)
Halan
HEILONGJIANG
Skovorodino
Svobodnyy
Blagoveshchensk
Zavitinsk
Birobidzhan
Tongjiang
Fujin
Bikin
Khabarovsk
SEA OF OKHOTSK
KURIL ISLANDS (Sov. Union)
SIMUSHIR
URUP
ITURUP
KUNASHIR
Nemuro
Kushiro
HOKKAIDO
Asahikawa
Sapporo
Muroran
Hakodate
Aomori
PACIFIC OCEAN

MONGOLIA
INNER MONGOLIA
Hohhot
Kalgan (Zhangjiakou)
Fengzhen
PEKING (Beijing)
HEBEI
Baoding
Shijiazhuang
TIENTSIN (Tianjin)
Bo Hai
TAIYUAN
SHANXI
Fenyang
Linfen
Anyang
Zhengzhou
HENAN
Nanyang
Kaifeng
Xinyang
HUBEI
Yichang
Hanyang
WUHAN
Wuchang
Shashi
Changsha
HUNAN
Xiangtan
Hengyang
GUANGDONG
CANTON (Guangzhou)
Foshan
Xinhui
Macau
VICTORIA
HONG KONG (Br.)
Zhanjiang
HAINAN DAO
SOUTH CHINA SEA

SHANDONG
Jinan
Weifang
TSINGTAO (Qingdao)
Weihai
Chefoo (Yantai)
Lianyungang
JIANGSU
NANJING
Hefei
ANHUI
SHANGHAI
SHANGHAI SHI
HANGZHOU
ZHEJIANG
Ningbo
Wenzhou
FUJIAN
Fuzhou
Quanzhou
Amoy (Xiamen)
Shantou
TAIWAN (FORMOSA)
TAIPEI
T'aichung
T'ainan
Kaohsiung

YELLOW SEA
EAST CHINA SEA

NORTH KOREA
P'yongyang
SOUTH KOREA
SEOUL (Soul)
Inch'on
Taegu
PUSAN
Mokp'o

SEA OF JAPAN
HONSHU
TOKYO
YOKOHAMA
NAGOYA
KYOTO
OSAKA
KOBE
Hiroshima
KITAKYUSHU
Fukuoka
Nagasaki
KYUSHU
Kagoshima
SHIKOKU
Sendai
Niigata
Nagano
PHILIPPINE SEA
NANSEI SHOTO
Naha

Chinese Provinces, Autonomous Regions (AR) and Municipalities (M)

Conventional Form	Pinyin Form
Anhwei	Anhui
Chekiang	Zhejiang
Fukien	Fujian
Heilungkiang	Heilongjiang
Honan	Henan
Hopeh	Hebei
Hunan	Hunan
Hupeh	Hubei
Inner Mongolia (AR)	Nei Monggol
Kansu	Gansu
Kiangsi	Jiangxi
Kiangsu	Jiangsu
Kirin	Jilin
Kwangsi (AR)	Guangxi
Kwangtung	Guangdong
Kweichow	Guizhou
Liaoning	Liaoning
Ningsia Hui (AR)	Ningxia
Peking (M)	Beijing
Shanghai (M)	Shanghai
Shansi	Shanxi
Shantung	Shandong
Shensi	Shaanxi
Sinkiang (AR)	Xinjiang
Szechwan	Sichuan
Tibet (AR)	Xizang
Tientsin (M)	Tianjin
Tsinghai	Qinghai
Yunnan	Yunnan

Relief

Meters	Feet
3050	10 000
1525	5000
610	2000
305	1000
152.5	500
0	Sea Level
	Below Sea Level
152.5	500
1525	5000
3050	10 000
6100	20 000

A-569700-76 COPYRIGHT BY RAND McNALLY & COMPANY MADE IN U.S.A.

Continued on pages 196-197

Longitude East of Greenwich

0 50 100 200 300 400 500 Miles
0 100 200 400 600 800 Kilometers

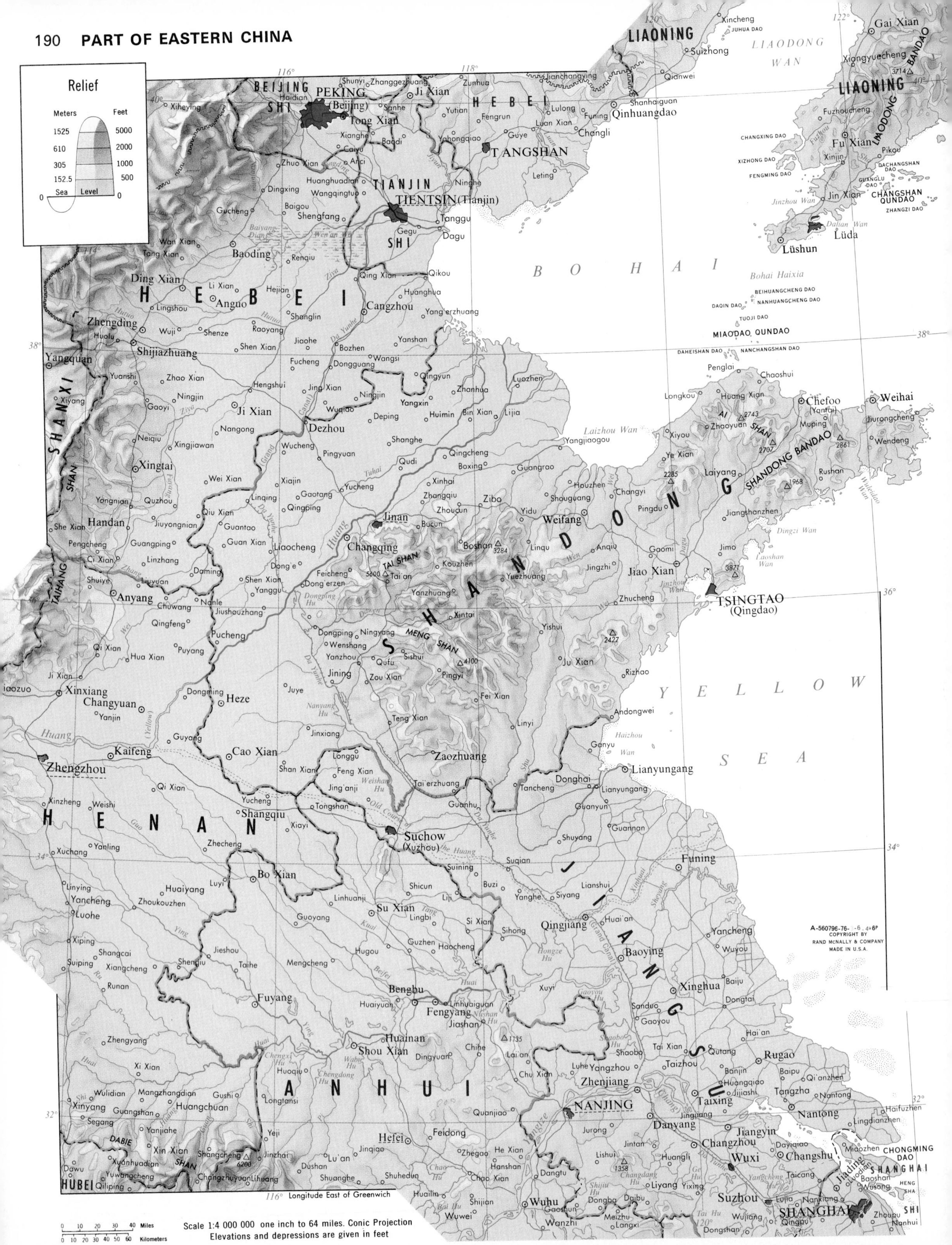

Relief

Meters		Feet
1525		5000
610		2000
305		1000
152.5		500
Sea	Level	0

LIAONING

LIAODONG WAN

LIAONING

Xincheng Juhua Dao Gai Xian CHANGSHAN BANDAO

Xiongyuecheng 3714

Suizhong Qianwei

Fuzhoucheng

CHANGXING DAO Fuxhou

XIZHONG DAO Fu Xian Pikou

FENGMING DAO Xinjin DACHANGSHAN DAO

GUANGLU DAO CHANGSHAN QUNDAO

Jin Xian ZHANGZI DAO

Dalian Wan Lüda

Lüshun

BEIJING SHI PEKING (Beijing)

Haidian Shunyi Zhangggezhuang Ji Xian Zhuha

Xianghe Sanhe HEBEI

Tong Xian Yutian Fengrun

Caiyu Anci Baodi Ningho

TIANJIN TIENTSIN (Tianjin)

Shanghaiguan Qinhuangdao

Lulong Funing

Guye Changli

TANGSHAN Leting

Tanggu Dagu

Gegu

Qikou

BOHAI

Bohai Haixia

BEIHUANGCHENG DAO

DAQIN DAO NANHUANGCHENG DAO

TUOJI DAO

MIAODAO, QUNDAO

DAHEISHAN DAO NANCHANGSHAN DAO

Penglai Chaoshui

Longkou Huang Xian Chefoo (Yantai) Weihai

HEBEI

Xiheying

Zhuo Xian

Dingxing Huanghuadian Wangqingtuo

Baigou Shengfang

Gucheng Baiyang-Dian Wen'an

Wan Xian Renqiu

Tang Xian Baoding Ziya

Ding Xian Li Xian Hejian

Anguo Shanglin

Lingshou Shenze

Zhengding Wuji Raoyang

Huolu Jiaohe Shen Xian Bozhen

Shijiazhuang Hengshui Jing Xian Ningjin

Yuanshi Ningjin Wuqiao

Zhao Xian Gaoyi Fucheng

Yangquan Xiyang

SHANXI SHAN

Xingtai Neiqiu Xingjiawan Wei Xian Xiajin

Yongnian Qiu Xian Linqing

Handan Quzhou Jiuyongnian Qingping

Guangping Guantao Gaotang

Pengcheng Linzhang Daming Liaocheng

Ci Xian Shuiye Liuyuan Shen Xian

Anyang Chuwang Nanle Dong e

Qingfeng Jiushouzhang

Qi Xian Pucheng Dongming

Hua Xian Puyang

Ji Xian Xinxiang Dongming Heze

iaozuo Changyuan Yanjin Guyang

HENAN Cao Xian

Xinzheng Weishi Qi Xian Shan Xian

Zhengzhou Kaifeng

Xuchang Yanling Zhecheng

Linying Luyi Shangqiu Xiayi

Yancheng Huaiyang Guoyang

Luohe Zhoukouzhen

Xiping Shangcai Jieshou Taihe

Suiping Xiangcheng Shenqiu

Runan Mengcheng

Zhengyang Xi Xian

Huoqiu Fuyang

ANHUI

Wulidian Mangzhangdian Gushi Longtansi

Xinyang Guangshan Huangchuan

Dawu Xuanhuadian Jinzhai Dushan

Qiliping Yiwangcheng Changzhuyuanlihuang

HUBEI DABIE SHAN 6200

Segang Yanjiahe Yeji

Xin Xian Shangcheng Jinzhai

Lu'an Shuhetun

Hefei Feidong

Zhegao He Xian

Hanshan

NANJING

Jurong Danyang

Zhenjiang Yangzhou

JIANGSU

Dezhou Wucheng Pingyuan

Shanghe Qudi Qingcheng

Shanghe Boxing Guangrao

SHANDONG

Jinan Changqing

TAI SHAN 5000 Tai an Kouzhen Boshan 3284

Feicheng Yanzhuang

Dong erzen Dongping Hu

Ningyang Xintai

MENG SHAN Sishui 4100

Qufu Pingyi

Jining Zou Xian

Juye Jinxiang Teng Xian Linyi

Nanyang Hu

Longgu Feng Xian Weishan Hu Zaozhuang

Jing'anji Tai erzhuang

Yucheng Tongshan

Suchow (Xuzhou)

Bo Xian Shicun Li Ji

Linhuanji Su Xian Lingbi Si Xian

Guoyang Guzhen Haocheng

Hugou

Bengbu

Huaiyuan Linhuaiguan

Fengyang Jiashan

Huainan Shou Xian Dingyuan

Xi Xian Chengxi Hu Wabu Hu

Quanjiao

Feidong

Zhengding

SHANDONG BANDAO

Zhaoyuan Laiyang 2702 Muping 286

2285 1968 Rushan

Ye Xian Pingdu Jiangshanzhen Wendeng

Xiyou

Yangjiaogou

Changyi Weifang Anqiu Gaomi Jiao Xian Jimo 3871

Houzhen Shouguang Jingzhi Laoshan Wan

Yidu Ziba Zhoucun Zhangqiu Xinhai

Yuezhuang Zhucheng TSINGTAO (Qingdao)

2427

Ju Xian Rizhao

Yishui Andongwei

Linyi Haizhou Wan

Ganyu Lianyungang

Donghai Lianyungang

Tancheng Guanhu Guanyun

Shuyang Guannan

YELLOW SEA

Funing

Suining Buzi Suqian

Yanghe Siyang Lianshui

Qingjiang Huai'an

Baoying Yancheng

Xinghua Baiju Dongtai

Hai an Rugao Baipu Qi'anzhen

Tai Xian Qutang Banjin Tangzha

Taizhou Huangqiao Dijiashi Nantong

Jinguang Haifuzhen Haidianzhen

Danyang Jiangyin CHONGMING DAO

Changzhou Dayukou

Lishui Jintan Wuxi Changshu Jiading

Yixing Hangli SHANGHAI SHI HENG SHA

Wuhu Dangtu 1358 Taihu Suzhou Fujia

Maanshan Liyang Dongba Taicang Nanxiang

Wanzhi Daibu Wujiang Baoshan

Langxi Tai Hu Qingpu Songjiang

Wuwei Meizhou Dongshan SHANGHAI

Yellow River / Huang (Yellow River)

Grand Canal / Da Yunhe

Old Course He Huang

Hongze Hu

Gaoyou Hu

Shaobo Hu

The Huang

Yangtze / Chang

A-560796-76-   -6   4 6P
COPYRIGHT BY
RAND MCNALLY & COMPANY
MADE IN U.S.A.

116° Longitude East of Greenwich

0 10 20 30 40 Miles
0 10 20 30 40 50 60 Kilometers

Scale 1:4 000 000 one inch to 64 miles. Conic Projection
Elevations and depressions are given in feet

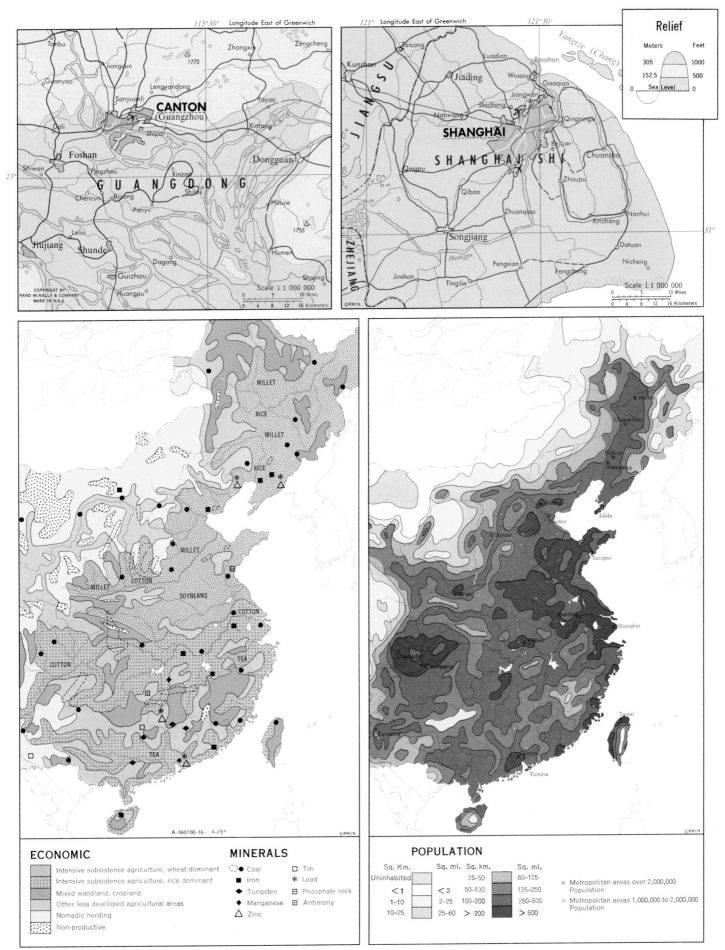

ECONOMIC

- Intensive subsistence agriculture, wheat dominant
- Intensive subsistence agriculture, rice dominant
- Mixed woodland, cropland
- Other less developed agricultural areas
- Nomadic herding
- Non-productive

MINERALS

- Coal
- Iron
- Tungsten
- Manganese
- Zinc
- Tin
- Lead
- Phosphate rock
- Antimony

POPULATION

Sq. Km.	Sq. mi.	Sq. km.	Sq. mi.
Uninhabited		25–50	60–125
<1	<2	50–100	125–250
1–10	2–25	100–200	250–500
10–25	25–60	>200	>500

□ Metropolitan areas over 2,000,000 Population
○ Metropolitan areas 1,000,000 to 2,000,000 Population

Relief

Meters	Feet
305	1000
152.5	500
0 Sea Level	0

For larger scale coverage of Shanghai see page 66.

COPYRIGHT BY
RAND McNALLY & COMPANY
MADE IN U.S.A.

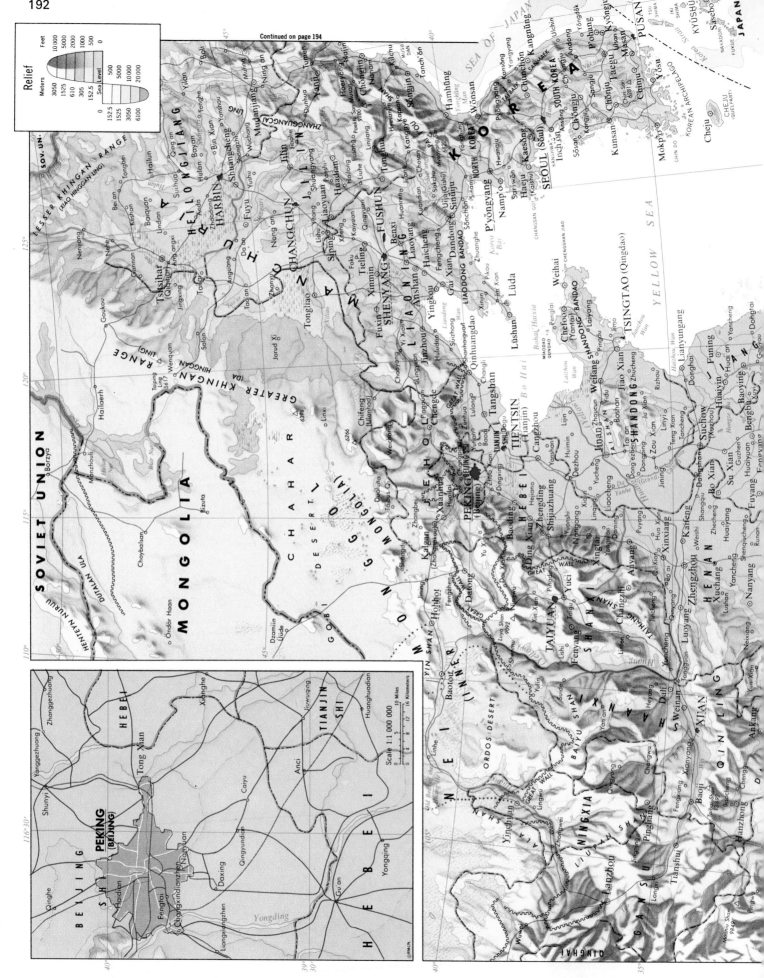

192

Relief

Feet
10000 5000 2000 1000 500 0
Meters
3050 1525 610 305 152.5 0 Sea Level
152.5 500
1525 5000
3050 10000
6100 20000

Continued on page 194

For larger scale coverage
of Peking see page 65.

Scale 1:10 000 000; one inch to 160 miles. Lambert Conformal Conic Projection
Elevations and depressions are given in feet

Scale 1:1 000 000

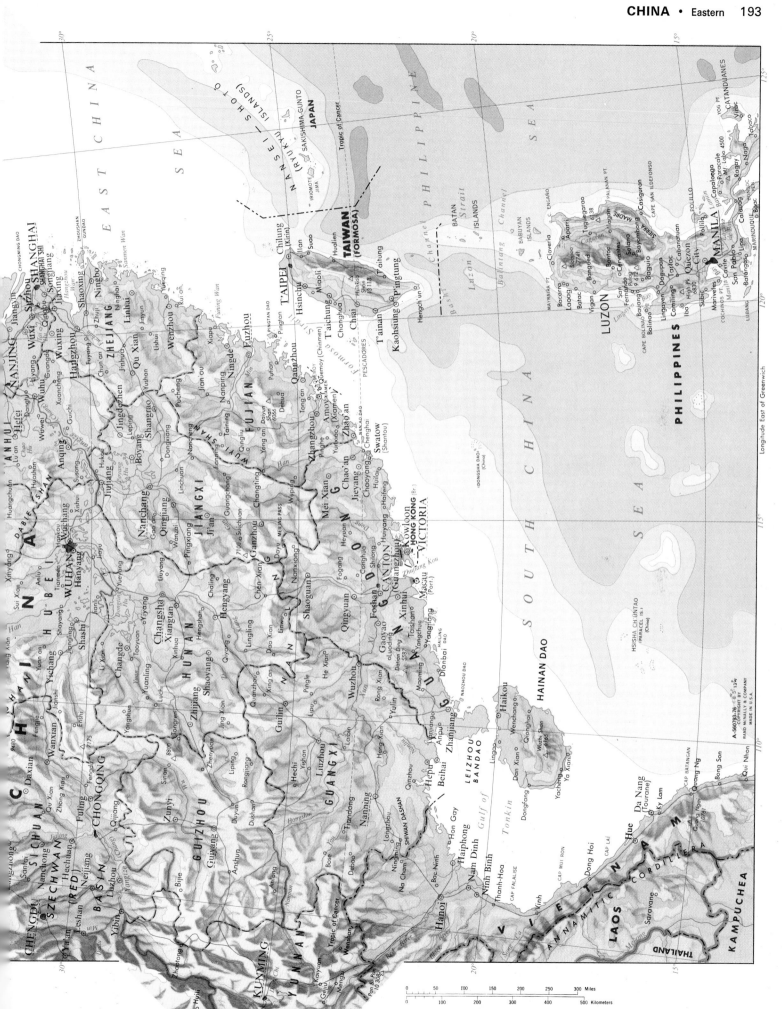

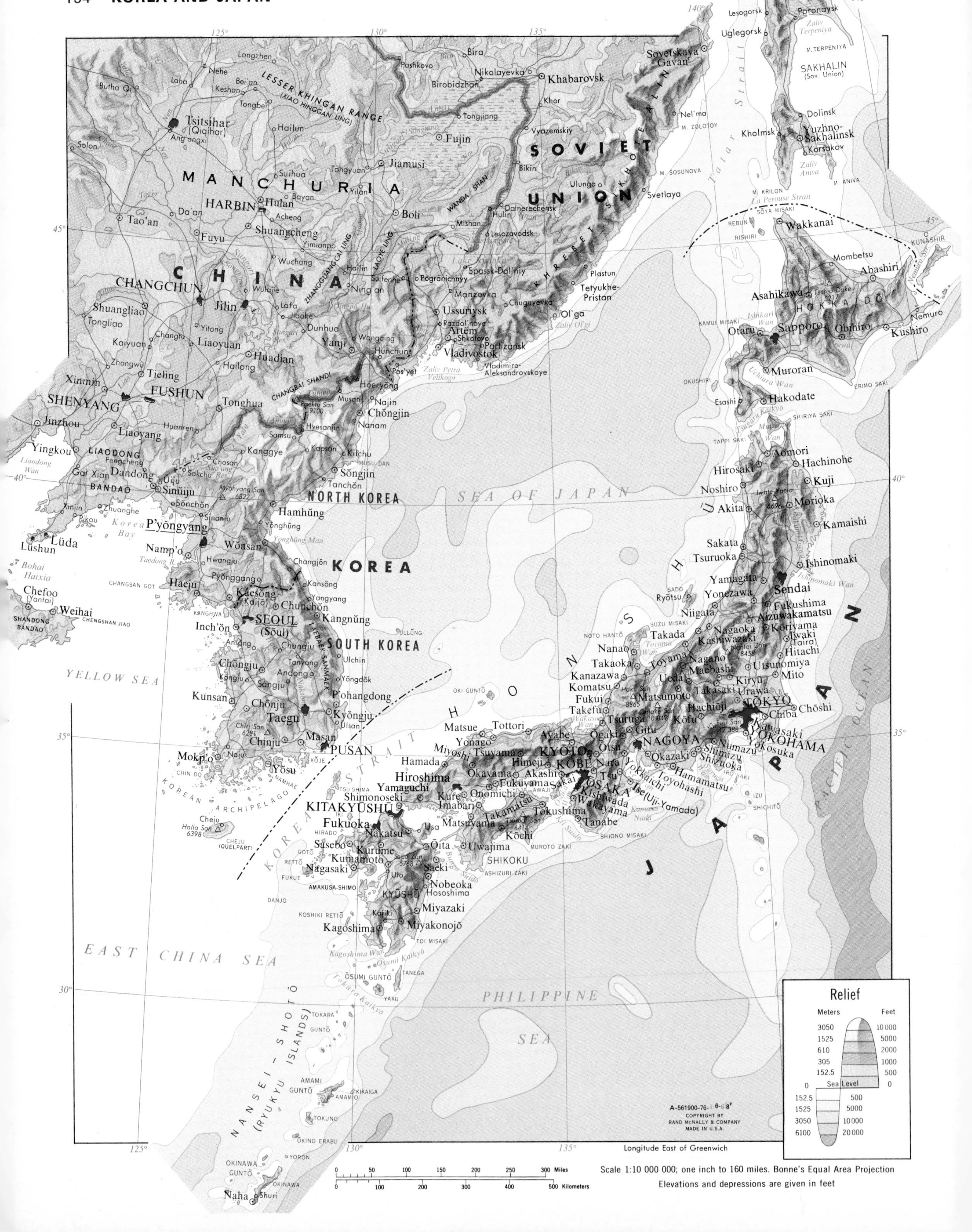

MANCHURIA

CHINA

SOVIET UNION

SAKHALIN (Sov. Union)

NORTH KOREA

KOREA

SOUTH KOREA

JAPAN

HOKKAIDO

HONSHU

SHIKOKU

KYŪSHŪ

YELLOW SEA

SEA OF JAPAN

EAST CHINA SEA

PHILIPPINE SEA

PACIFIC OCEAN

Korea Bay

Bohai Haixia

KOREA STRAIT

KOREAN ARCHIPELAGO

NANSEI SHOTŌ (RYUKYU ISLANDS)

LESSER KHINGAN RANGE (XIAO HINGGAN LING)

Longzhen, Nehe, Laha, Keshan, Butha Qi, Tsitsihar (Qiqihar), Ang'angxi, Solon, Tao'an, Da'an, Fuyu, Tongbei, Hailun, Bei'an, Bayan, Suihua, Yilan, Jiamusi, Fujin, Tongjiang, Bira, Biro, Pashkovo, Nikolayevka, Birobidzhan, Khabarovsk, Khor, Pozharskoye, Bikin, Vyazemskiy, Dalnerechensk, Lesozavodsk, Mishan, Spassk-Dal'niy, Manzovka, Chuguyevka, Svetlaya

Sovetskaya Gavan', M. Terpeniya, Uglegorsk, Lesogorsk, Poronaysk, Zaliv Terpeniya, Dolinsk, Kholmsk, Yuzhno-Sakhalinsk, Korsakov, Zaliv Aniva, M. Aniva

HARBIN, Hulan, Acheng, Shuangcheng, Yimianpo, Wuchang, Lafa, Jiaohe, Dunhua, Jilin, Yitong, Changtu, Kaiyuan, Tieling, Liaoyuan, Liaoyang, FUSHUN, SHENYANG, Xinmin, Jinzhou, Yingkou, Gai Xian, Xinjin, Pikou, Dandong, Fengcheng, Huanren, Tonghua

CHANGCHUN, Shuangliao, Tongliao, Zhangwu, Kaiyuan

Yingkou, LIAODONG, BANDAO, Lüda, Lushun, Bohai Haixia, Chefoo (Yantai), Weihai, SHANDONG BANDAO, CHENGSHAN JIAO

Jilin, Huadian, Hailong, Jiaohe, Wangqing, Yanji, Hunchun, Hoeryong, Musan, Najin, Nanam, Chŏngjin, Hyesanjin, Kilchu, Samsu, Kanggye, Kapsan, Songjin, Tanchon, Kilchu

Ussuriysk, Artëm, Razdol'noye, Shkotovo, Vladivostok, Pos'yet, Zaliv Petra Velikogo, Nakhodka, Vladimiro-Aleksandrovskoye, Ol'ga, Zaliv Ol'gi

Suifenhe, Pogranichnyy, Ning'an

CHANGBAI SHANDI, Paektu San 9100, Chosan, Manp'o, Sinuiju, Sinanju, Anju, Sunch'ŏn, Uiju, Sakchu, Kusong, P'yŏngyang, Namp'o, Taedong R., Hwangju, Kaesong (Kaijō), Haeju, Sariwon, CHANGSAN GOT, KANGHWA, Inch'ŏn, SEOUL (Sŏul), Suwon, Chunch'ŏn, Wŏnsan, Hamhŭng, Yŏnghŭng, Yŏnghŭng Man, Hŭngnam, Hamhŭng

Myohyang San 6822, Hamhŭng, Wŏnsan, Changjŏn, Kansŏng, Yangyang, Kangnŭng, Samch'ŏk, Ulchin, Yŏngdŏk, Pohangdong, Kyŏngju, Ulsan, PUSAN, Masan, Chinju, Chinhae, KŎJE, Taegu, Sangju, Andong, Tanyang, Ch'ungju, Ch'ŏngju, Chŏnju, Kunsan, Kongju, Chiri San 6281, Chŏnju, Naju, Mokp'o, Yŏsu, CHIN DO, Chodo, Cheju (Quelpart), Halla San 6398, CHEJU

TAEBAEK SANMAEK

P'yŏngyang, Pyŏnggang, Ch'ŏrwŏn, P'ungsan

Hiroshima, Yamaguchi, Shimonoseki, KITAKYUSHU, Fukuoka, Nakatsu, Kurume, Saga, Nagasaki, Sasebo, Kumamoto, Uto, AMAKUSA-SHIMO, Minamata, Nobeoka, Hososhima, Miyazaki, Kagoshima, Kojiki, Miyakonojō, Kanoya, Ibusuki, KOSHIKI RETTŌ, DANJO, GOTŌ RETTŌ, FUKUE, Hirado, IKI, TSU SHIMA, ŌSUMI KAIKYŌ, Sata Misaki

Matsue, Yonago, Tottori, Miyoshi, Tsuyama, Okayama, Kurashiki, Fukuyama, Onomichi, Kure, Imabari, Matsuyama, Uwajima, Kōchi, Takamatsu, Tokushima, Tanabe, Wakayama, Sakai, OSAKA, KOBE, KYOTO, Himeji, Akashi, Nara, Tsu, Ōtsu, NAGOYA, Gifu, Ogaki, Toyohashi, Okazaki, Hamamatsu, Shizuoka, Numazu, TOKYO, YOKOHAMA, Kawasaki, Yokosuka, Chiba, Chōshi, Kōfu, Hachiōji, Utsunomiya, Mito, Maebashi, Takasaki, Urawa, Kiryū, Hitachi, Iwaki (Taira), Kōriyama, Aizuwakamatsu, Fukushima, Sendai, Ishinomaki, Yamagata, Yonezawa, Sakata, Tsuruoka, Niigata, Nagaoka, Kashiwazaki, Takada, Nagano, Matsumoto, Toyama, Takaoka, Nanao, Kanazawa, Komatsu, Fukui, Takefu, Tsuruga, Yokkaichi, Ise (Uji-Yamada), Ōmuro, Kuwana, Ōgaki

Aomori, Hirosaki, Hachinohe, Kuji, Morioka, Kamaishi, Akita, Noshiro, Ōdate

Asahikawa, Sapporo, Otaru, Muroran, Hakodate, Esashi, Obihiro, Kushiro, Abashiri, Mombetsu, Wakkanai, Nemuro, RISHIRI, REBUN, KUNASHIR, ISHIKARI WAN, Uchiura Wan, OKUSHIRI, KAMUI MISAKI, ERIMO SAKI, SHIRIYA SAKI, TAPPI SAKI, SOYA MISAKI, La Perouse Strait, SOYA SAKI, Teshio, Abashiri

OKI GUNTŌ, SADO, Ryotsu, NOTO HANTŌ, SUZU MISAKI, Toyama Wan, ULLUNG (Ullŭng)

SHICHITŌ, IZU, SHIMA

MURO TO ZAKI, SHIONO MISAKI, ASHIZURI ZAKI, BUNGO SUIDŌ, KII SUIDŌ, AWAJI, KANMON, Wakasa Wan

AMAMI, AMAMI GUNTŌ, KIKAIGA, TOKUNO, OKINO ERABU, YORON, OKINAWA, OKINAWA GUNTŌ, Naha, Shuri, ŌSUMI GUNTŌ, TANEGA, YAKU, TOKARA GUNTŌ, TANEGA, Kagoshima Wan

A-561900-76- 6-6-8P
COPYRIGHT BY
RAND McNALLY & COMPANY
MADE IN U.S.A.

Longitude East of Greenwich

Relief		
Meters		Feet
3050		10 000
1525		5000
610		2000
305		1000
152.5		500
0	Sea Level	0
152.5		500
1525		5000
3050		10 000
6100		20 000

0 50 100 150 200 250 300 Miles
0 100 200 300 400 500 Kilometers

Scale 1:10 000 000; one inch to 160 miles. Bonne's Equal Area Projection
Elevations and depressions are given in feet

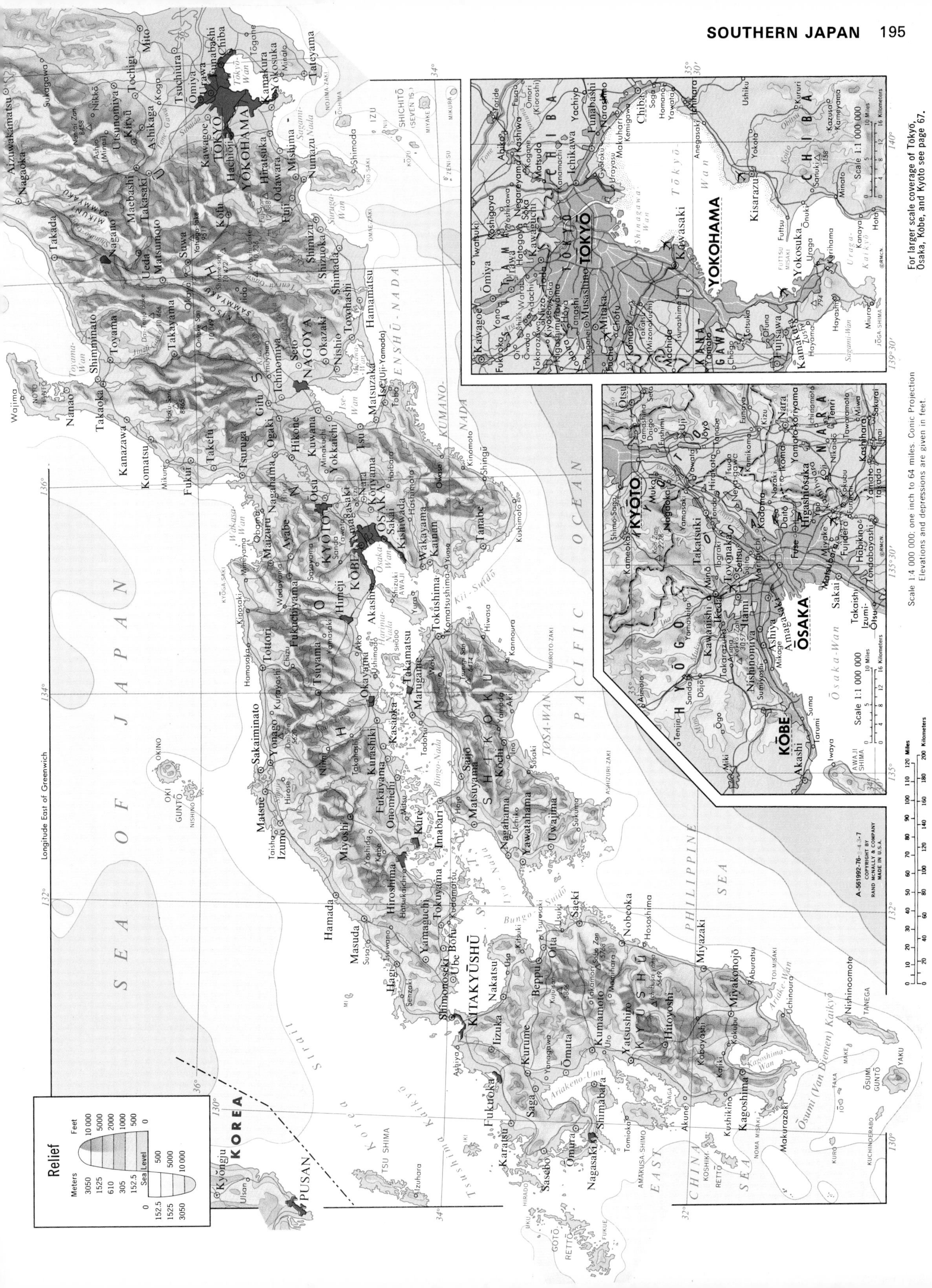

For larger scale coverage of Tōkyō,
Ōsaka, Kōbe, and Kyōto see page 67.

Scale 1:4 000 000; one inch to 64 miles. Conic Projection
Elevations and depressions are given in feet.

TŌKYŌ
YOKOHAMA

C H I B A

K A N A - G A W A

Tōkyō Wan

Scale 1:1 000 000

KYŌTO

ŌSAKA

KŌBE

H Y Ō G O

N A R A

Ōsaka-Wan

Scale 1:1 000 000

Relief

Meters	Feet
3050	10 000
1525	5000
610	2000
305	1000
152.5	500
Sea Level	0
152.5	500
1525	5000
3050	10 000

KOREA

Kyŏngju
Ulsan
PUSAN

S E A   O F   J A P A N

TSU SHIMA

H O N S H Ū

S H I K O K U

K Y Ū S H Ū

KITAKYŪSHŪ

TOKYO
YOKOHAMA
NAGOYA
ŌSAKA
KYOTO
KŌBE

P A C I F I C   O C E A N

PHILIPPINE SEA

EAST CHINA SEA

Aizuwakamatsu
Nagaoka
Takada
Toyama
Shimminato
Takaoka
Kanazawa
Komatsu
Fukui
Nagano
Matsumoto
Ueda
Suwa
Takayama
Gifu
NAGOYA
Okazaki
Toyohashi
Hamamatsu
Shizuoka
Shimizu
Shimada
Fuji
Numazu
Mishima
Odawara
Hiratsuka
Kamakura
Yokosuka
Tateyama
Chiba
Funabashi
Urawa
Omiya
Kawagoe
Utsunomiya
Nikko
Tochigi
Mito
Matsue
Izumo
Hamada
Masuda
Hagi
Yamaguchi
Ube
Shimonoseki
Tokuyama
Hiroshima
Kure
Onomichi
Fukuyama
Kurashiki
Okayama
Tsuyama
Tottori
Yonago
Sakaiminato
Takamatsu
Marugame
Tokushima
Kōchi
Matsuyama
Imabari
Uwajima
Yawatahama
Nagahama
Nobeoka
Miyazaki
Miyakonojō
Kagoshima
Kumamoto
Yatsushiro
Hitoyoshi
Nagasaki
Sasebo
Omura
Saga
Kurume
Omuta
Fukuoka
Iizuka
Nakatsu
Beppu
Ōita
Himeji
Akashi
KŌBE
ŌSAKA
Sakai
Wakayama
Kainan
Tanabe
Tsu
Matsuzaka
Yokkaichi
Kuwana
Hikone
Ōtsu
Nara
Kōriyama

Longitude East of Greenwich

COPYRIGHT BY
RAND MCNALLY & COMPANY
MADE IN U.S.A.
A-561992-76

Miles	Kilometers
0	0
10	16
120	200

Continued on pages 188–189

PHILIPPINE

SOUTH CHINA SEA

PHILIPPINE SEA

LUZON

MANILA
Quezon City
Pasig

ILIPPINES

CATANDUANES ISLAND

azpi

Sorsogon

Catbalogan
SAMAR

Tacloban
LEYTE
PHILIPPINE
DINAGAT ISLAND

Cebu

BOHL

34 578

TRENCH

anao

Butuan
Cagayan

MINDANAO

Davao

ato

9692

Davao Gulf

PULAU MIANGAS

PALAU IS.
(P.I.T.T.)
(U. S.)

SONSOROL ISLANDS

KEPULAUAN TALAUD

PULAU SANGIHE

PULAU SIAU

MOROTAI

nado

Tondano

Ternate

HALMAHERA

KEPULAUAN MAPIA

Laut Maluku
(Molucca Sea)

Laut Halmahera
(Halmahera Sea)

PULAU WAIGEO

Selat Dampier

Manokwari

BIAK

PULAU BACAN

Labuha

SALAWATI

Sorong

PULAU MISOOL

PULAU YAPEN

PULAU NUMFOR

TG. PERKAM

NINIGO GROUP

HERMIT IS.

ADMIRALTY ISLANDS

MUSSAU ISLAND

EMIRA ISLAND

JLAUAN NGGAI

PULAU TALIBU

KEPULAUAN OBI

PULAU MANGOLE

KEPULAUAN SULA

PULAU SANANA

MALUKU
(MOLUCCAS)

JAZIRAH DOBERAI

Teluk Berau

Teluk Cenderawasih

Kaimana

Fakfak

PEGUNUNGAN VAN REES

Jayapura
(Sukarnapura)

Aitape

Wewak

MANUS ISLAND

NEW HANOVER

Kavieng

BISMARCK ARCH.

NEW IRELAND

SERAM

Piru

Bula

PULAU ADI

Namatanai

Rabaul

Kokopo

anui

owoni

BURU

Ambon
PULAU AMBON

KEPULAUAN BANDA

PEGUNUNGAN MAOKE

Puntjak Djaja 16 503
Puntjak Trikora 16 585

Sepik

NEW GUINEA

Ramu

Madang

KARKAR ISLAND

LONG ISLAND

WITU ISLANDS

Talasea

The Father 7546

BISMARCK

S I A

KEPULAUAN TOKANGBESI

KEPULAUAN LUCIPARA

Laut Banda
(BANDA SEA)

KEPULAUAN KAI

KAI KECIL

Dobo

KEPULAUAN ARU

KEPULAUAN KAI

Mt. Gluwe 14 331
Mt. Wilhelm 14 794

Mt. Bangeta 13 521

Lae

NEW BRITAIN

NEW BRITAIN TRENCH

Huon Gulf

PULAU DAMAR

PULAU WETAR

DE ATAURO

AU

Dili

TIMOR

PULAU ALOR

PULAU BABAR

PULAU MOA

PULAU SELARU

YAMDENA

KEPULAUAN TANIMBAR

PULAU TRANGAN

PULAU YOS SUDARSA

TANJUNG VALS

Merauke

ARAFURA SEA

PAPUA NEW GUINEA

Morobe

Mt. Albert Edward 13 091

Buna

TROBRIAND IS.

WOODLARK ISLAND

D'ENTRECASTEAUX IS.

TIMOR SEA

TIMOR

MELVILLE ISLAND

COBOURG PEN.
CROKER ISLAND

BATHURST ISLAND

Van Diemen Gulf

Darwin

WESSEL IS.

Daru

Torres Strait

C. YORK

CAPE YORK PEN.

Port Moresby

Mt. Victoria 13 242

OWEN STANLEY RA.

Samarai

CORAL SEA

GREAT BARRIER REEF

Gulf of Papua

AUSTRALIA

Gulf of Carpentaria

C. ARNHEM

Luzon detail (Scale 1:4 000 000)

Cabugao
Iguig
Tuguegarao

Vigan
Bangued

Narvacan
Lubuagan
Cabagan

Candon
Bontoc
Ilagan
Cauayan

Luna
Cervantes
Mt. Amuyao 8799
Santiago
Echague
Jones

San Fernando
S. Juan
Solano
Bayombong
Bambang

Bauang
Baguio
Dupax
Casiguran

Bolinao
Aringay
Agno
Bani
Alaminos

Burgos
Dagupan
Nicolas
Tayug
S. Quintin

Lingayen
San Carlos
Urdaneta
Rosales
San Jose

Santa Cruz
Infanta
Mangatarem
Bayambang

Candelaria
Camiling
Gerona
Victoria
Cabanatuan

High Pk 6683
Tarlac
Palauig
Iba
Concepcion
Gapan
S. Miguel

Pinatubo 5771
Angeles
Arayat
S. Fernando

S. Narciso
S. Antonio
Guagua
Malolos
Infanta

Olongapo
Orani
Sto. Maria
Polillo

Sampaloc Pt.
Balanga
Malabon
Quezon City

Mariveles
Cavite
Pasig

CORREGIDOR ISLAND
Naic
Laguna de Bay
Sta. Cruz
Calamba Mauban

Silang
Nasugbu
Calamba
Nagcarlan

Lubang
AMBIL ISLAND
Balayan
Lemery
Lipa
Rosario
Lucena
Gumaca

LUBANG IS.
GOLD ISLAND
Batangas
Lobo
Unisan
Catanauan
S. Narciso

CABRA ISLAND
Balavan Bay
MARICABAN
VERDE
Tayabas Bay

CAPE CALAVITE
VERDE I. Passage
Calapan
Boac

Palvan
Mt. Halcon 8471
Naujan
Torrijos
San Pascual

Mamburao
Gasan
MARINDUQUE ISLAND

MINDORO
DUMALI PT.
Pinamalayan

Mt. Baco 8168
BANTON

Sablayan
Jones

DONGON PT.
Knob Pk. 3031
ROMBLON ISLAND
Romblon

S. Jose
ILIN ISLAND
BUSUANGA
TARA
Bolalacao
Odiongan
Looc
TABLAS
SIBUYAN

POLILLO IS.
PATNANONGAN
JOMALIG

CALAGUAS ISLAND

Capalonga
Paracale
Talisay

CABALETE
Labo
Daet

Atimonan
Mt. Labo 5066
Ragay

BALESIN

Lamon Bay

San Miguel Bay

Mt. Isarog 6450
Naga
Pili
Baao
Buhi

Polangui
Ligao
Mayon 8077
Legazpi

Tabaco

TICAO ISLAND
S. Jacinto
Aroroy

Masbate

MASBATE
SIBUYAN SEA

Scale 1:4 000 000

©R.M.C.N.

Equator

0° 10° 15° 16° 20° 14°

120° 122° 125° 130° 135° 140° 145° 150°

0   50   100   200   300   400   500 Miles
0   100   200   400   600   800 Kilometers

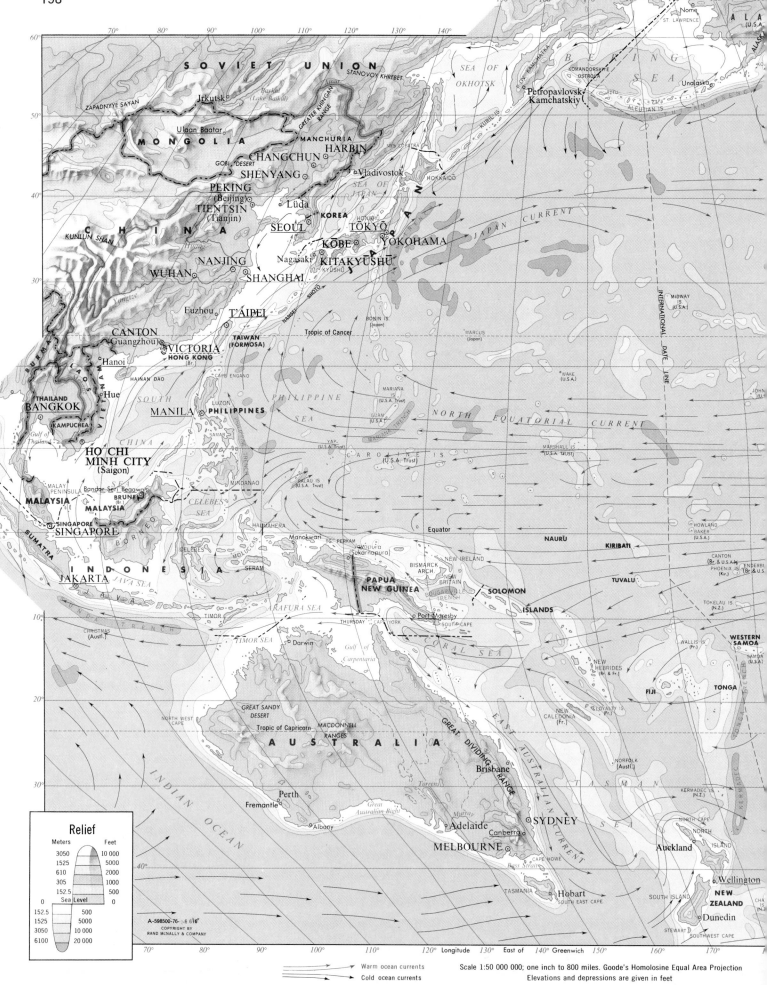

Warm ocean currents

Cold ocean currents

Scale 1:50 000 000; one inch to 800 miles. Goode's Homolosine Equal Area Projection
Elevations and depressions are given in feet

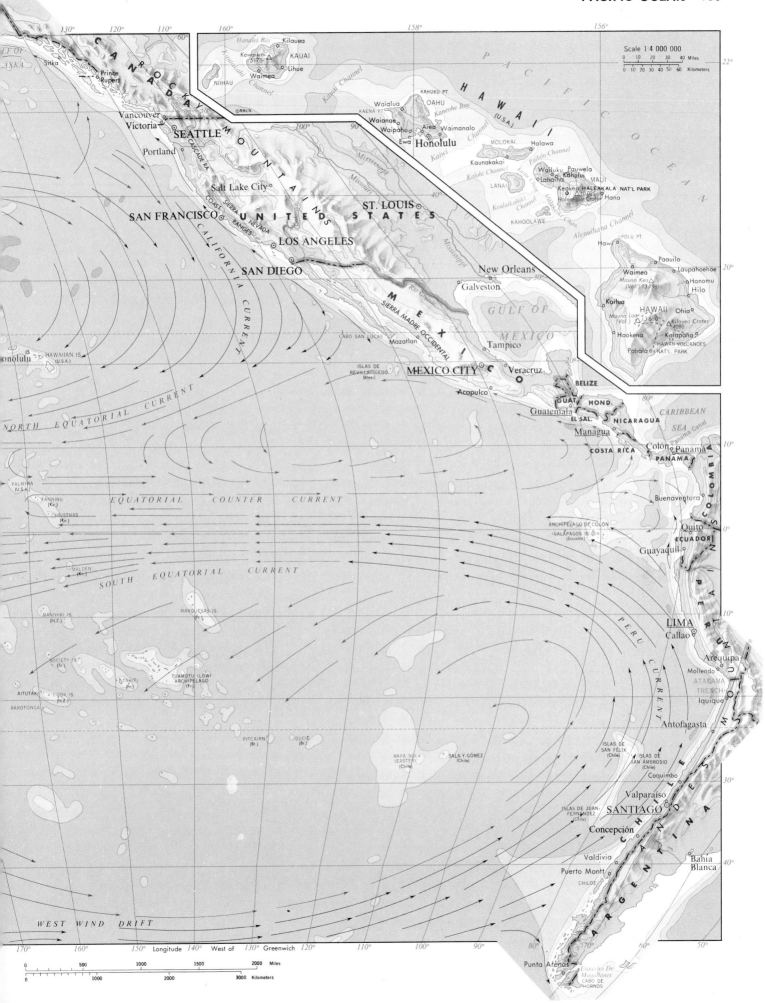

BORNEO

CELEBES

SERAM

Jaya

Palembang

Banjarmasin

Java Sea

Ujung Pandang

SUMATRA

JAKARTA

Surabaya

JAVA

SUMBA

TIMOR

Arafura Sea

Timor Sea

Darwin

Daly

Gulf of

CA

YO

PENIN

Carpentaria

INDIAN OCEAN

KIMBERLEY
PLATEAU

Victoria

Broome

Fitzroy

Mount Isa

GREAT SANDY DESERT

Alice Springs

GREAT
ARTESIAN
BASIN

GIBSON DESERT

SIMPSON
DESERT

Carnarvon

Tropic of Capricorn

GREAT VICTORIA DESERT

*Lake
Eyre*

Kalgoorlie

NULLARBOR PLAIN

*Lake
Gairdner*

FLINDERS RANGES

Broken
Hill

Murray

Perth

DARLING RA.

Great Australian Bight

Adelaide

INDIAN OCEAN

Urban

Cropland

Cropland & Woodland

Cropland & Grazing Land

Grassland, Grazing Land

Forest, Woodland

Swamp, Marshland

Shrub, Sparse Grass,
Wasteland (pattern)

Barren Land

Scale 1:24,000,000; one inch to 380 miles. Lambert Azimuthal Equal-Area Projection

150° 160° 170° 180°

Equator

KIRIBATI

NEW
GUINEA

NEW BRITAIN

SOLOMON ISLANDS

P A C I F I C

O C E A N

Moresby

0°

Coral Sea

Cairns

10°

Townsville

NEW
HEBRIDES

SAMOA ISLANDS

Pago Pago

FIJI
ISLANDS

NEW
CALEDONIA

ÎLES
LOYAUTÉ

Suva

Rockhampton

Nouméa

DIVIDING

RANGE

TONGA ISLANDS

20°

Brisbane

RANGE

DIVIDING

SYDNEY

Canberra

GREAT DIVIDING

Tasman Sea

30°

P A C I F I C

MELBOURNE

Auckland

NORTH ISLAND

O C E A N

TASMANIA

SOUTHERN ALPS

Wellington

Hobart

Christchurch

SOUTH ISLAND

A-590200-96 L-1-6

COPYRIGHT BY
RAND MCNALLY & COMPANY
MADE IN U.S.A.

Dunedin

STEWART
ISLAND

40°

150° 160° 170° 180° 170° 160°

0	100	200	400	600	800 Miles
0	150	300	600	900	1200 Kilometers

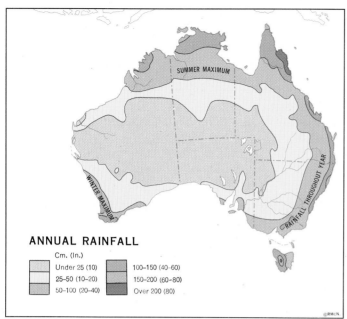

ANNUAL RAINFALL

Cm. (In.)

	Under 25 (10)		100–150 (40–60)
	25–50 (10–20)		150–200 (60–80)
	50–100 (20–40)		Over 200 (80)

©RMcN

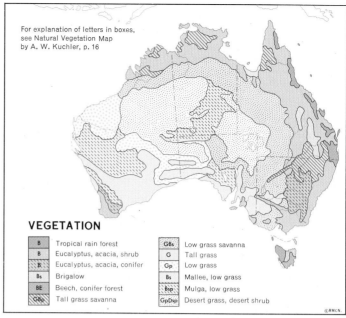

For explanation of letters in boxes,
see Natural Vegetation Map
by A. W. Kuchler, p. 16

VEGETATION

B	Tropical rain forest	GBs	Low grass savanna
B	Eucalyptus, acacia, shrub	G	Tall grass
B	Eucalyptus, acacia, conifer	Gp	Low grass
Bs	Brigalow	Bs	Mallee, low grass
BE	Beech, conifer forest	Bsp	Mulga, low grass
GBp	Tall grass savanna	GpDsp	Desert grass, desert shrub

©RMcN

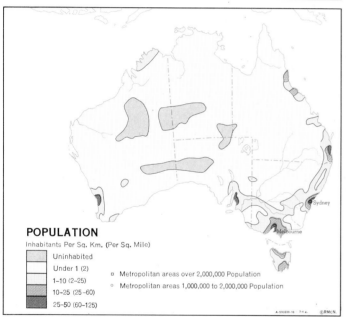

POPULATION

Inhabitants Per Sq. Km. (Per Sq. Mile)

	Uninhabited
	Under 1 (2)
	1–10 (2–25)
	10–25 (25–60)
	25–50 (60–125)

□ Metropolitan areas over 2,000,000 Population

○ Metropolitan areas 1,000,000 to 2,000,000 Population

A-590200-16   3-4-4.   ©RMcN

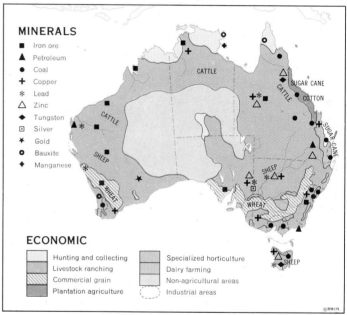

MINERALS

■ Iron ore
▲ Petroleum
● Coal
+ Copper
✳ Lead
△ Zinc
◆ Tungsten
⊡ Silver
✶ Gold
◎ Bauxite
◆ Manganese

ECONOMIC

	Hunting and collecting		Specialized horticulture
	Livestock ranching		Dairy farming
	Commercial grain		Non-agricultural areas
	Plantation agriculture		Industrial areas

©RMcN

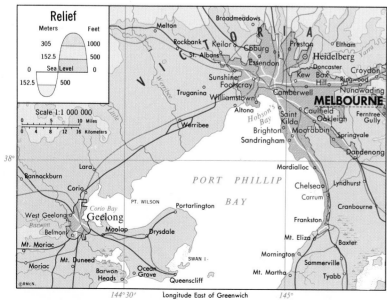

Relief

Meters		Feet
305		1000
152.5		500
0	Sea Level	0
152.5		500

Scale 1:1 000 000

0 1 5 10 Miles
0 4 8 12 16 Kilometers

MELBOURNE

Broadmeadows, Melton, Rockbank, Keilor, Coburg, St. Albans, Essendon, Preston, Eltham, Heidelberg, Doncaster, Croydon, Sunshine, Kew, Box Hill, Ringwood, Footscray, Camberwell, Nunawading, Truganina, Williamstown, Altona, Saint Kilda, Caulfield, Oakleigh, Ferntree Gully, Werribee, Brighton, Moorabbin, Springvale, Sandringham, Mordialloc, Lara, Chelsea, Lyndhurst, Bannockburn, Corio, Carrum, Cranbourne, West Geelong, PT. WILSON, Portarlington, Frankston, Corio Bay, Belmont, Moolap, Drysdale, Mt. Eliza, Mt. Moriac, Geelong, Baxter, Moriac, Mt. Duneed, Ocean Grove, Mornington, Sommerville, Barwon Heads, SWAN I., Mt. Martha, Tyabb, Queenscliff

VICTORIA

Hobson's Bay

PORT PHILLIP BAY

38°

144°30'   Longitude East of Greenwich   145°

©RMcN

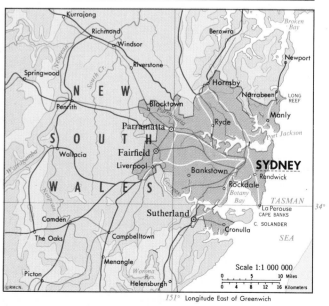

SYDNEY

Kurrajong, Richmond, Windsor, Berowra, Newport, Springwood, Riverstone, Penrith, Hornsby, Narrabeen, LONG REEF, Blacktown, Parramatta, Ryde, Manly, Wallacia, Fairfield, Liverpool, Bankstown, Randwick, Camden, Sutherland, Rockdale, La Perouse, CAPE BANKS, The Oaks, Campbelltown, Cronulla, C. SOLANDER, Menangle, Picton, Helensburgh

NEW SOUTH WALES

Broken Bay

Port Jackson

Botany Bay

TASMAN SEA

151°   Longitude East of Greenwich

Scale 1:1 000 000

0 5 10 Miles
0 4 8 12 16 Kilometers

34°

©RMcN

For larger scale coverage of
Melbourne and Sydney see page 68.

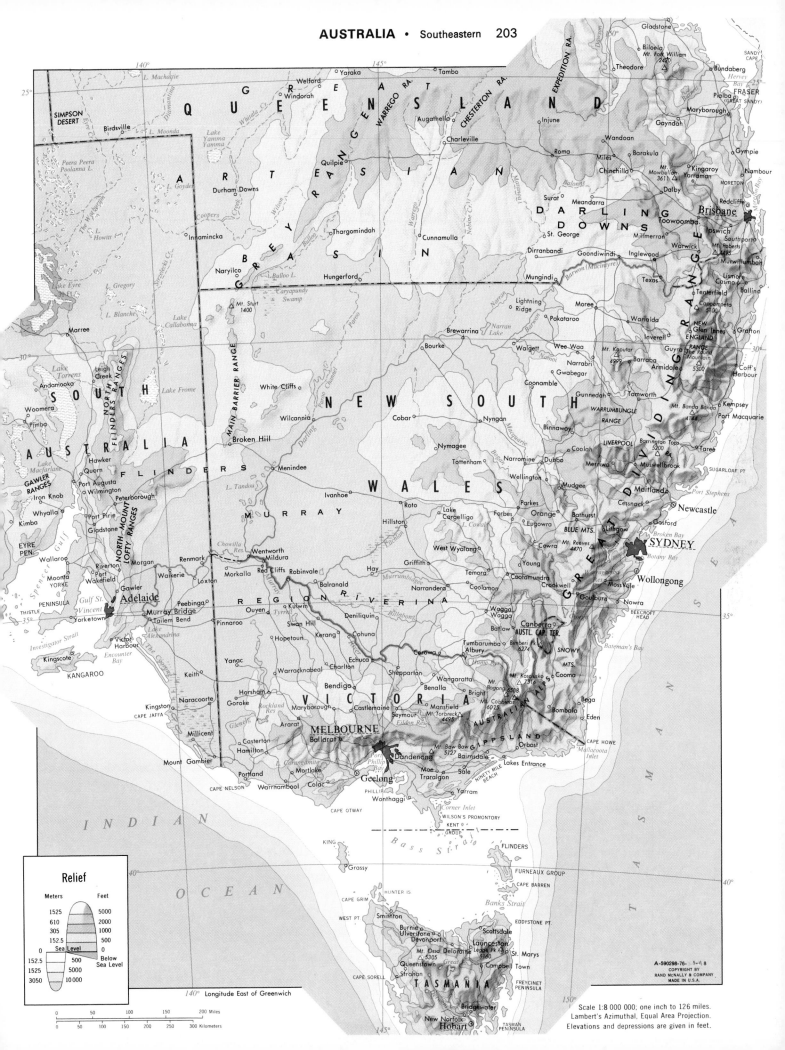

Relief

Meters		Feet
1525		5000
610		2000
305		1000
152.5		500
0	Sea Level	0
152.5	Below	500
1525	Sea Level	5000
3050		10 000

140° Longitude East of Greenwich

0   50   100   150   200 Miles
0   50   100   150   200   250   300 Kilometers

A-590298-76- 5-4 8
COPYRIGHT BY
RAND McNALLY & COMPANY
MADE IN U.S.A.

Scale 1:8 000 000; one inch to 126 miles.
Lambert's Azimuthal, Equal Area Projection.
Elevations and depressions are given in feet.

Continued on pages 196–197

Scale 1:16 000 000; one inch to 250 miles. Lambert's Azimuthal, Equal Area Projection
Elevations and depressions are given in feet

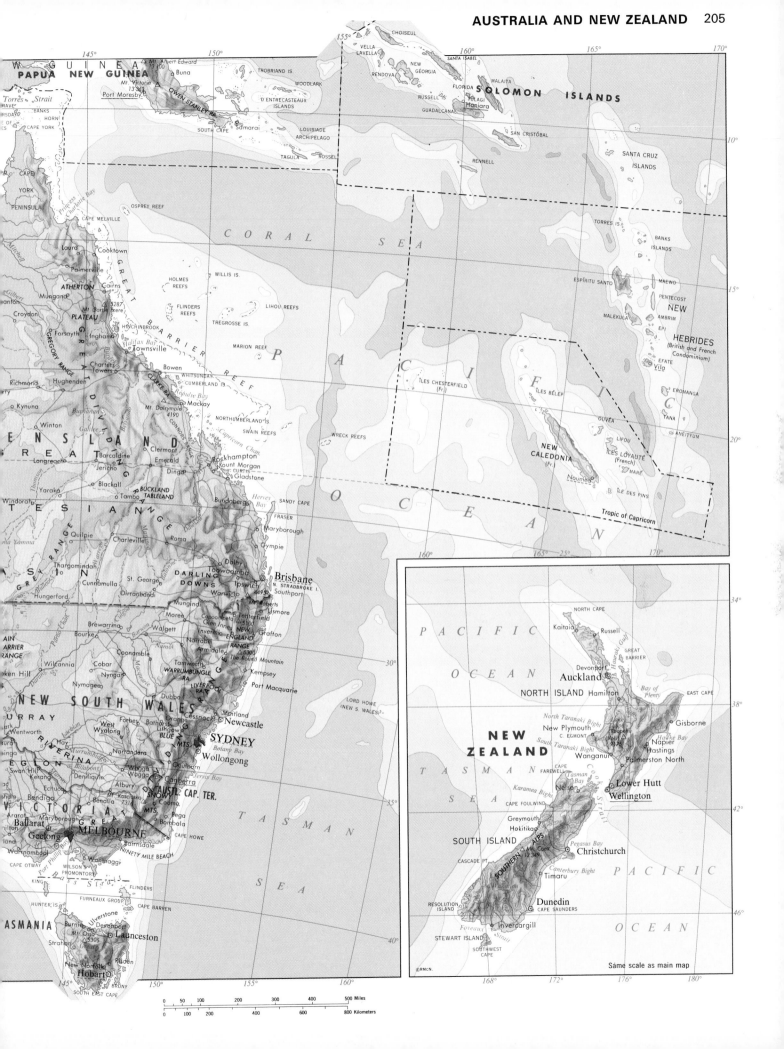

BERLIN

LONDON

PARIS

MADRID

Mediterranean Sea

ALPS

ROME

CORSICA

SARDINIA

SICILY

MALTA

Tunis

Athens

CRETE

Banghazi

Tripoli

Alexandria

CAIRO

Red Sea

ARABIAN DESERT

Nile

LIBYAN   DESERT

Lake Nasser

NUBIAN DESERT

Nile

S   A   H   A   R   A

TIBESTI

ENNEDI

Al-Fas

Algiers

PYRENEES

Casablanca

ATLAS   MOUNTAINS

GRAND ERG OCCIDENTAL

GRAND ERG ORIENTAL

AHAGGAR

Tamanrasset

ADRAR
DES IFORAS

Lake Chad

Ndjamena

Kano

Kaoundo

ATLANTIC

OCEAN

CANARY ISLANDS

Aaiun

EL DJOUF

Tombouctou

Niger

Bamako

Niger

Lagos

Gulf of Guinea

Lake Volta

Abidjan

Tropic of Cancer

Dakar

CAPE VERDE
ISLANDS

Freetown

ATLANTIC

OCEAN

10°   20°   30°   40°   30°

50°   50°   40°   30°   20°   10°   0°

Scale 1:24,000,000; one inch to 380 miles. Lambert Azimuthal Equal-Area Projection

Urban

Cropland

Cropland & Woodland

Cropland & Grazing Land

Grassland, Grazing Land

Forest, Woodland

Swamp, Marshland

Shrub, Sparse Grass,
Wasteland (pattern)

Barren Land

Oasis

INDIAN OCEAN

SEYCHELLES

COMORO ISLANDS

MADAGASCAR

Antananarivo

Mozambique Channel

Gulf of Aden

Aden

Berbera

DANAKIL

Asmera

Blue Nile

Addis Ababa

White Nile

Mountain Nile

Mogadisho

Nairobi

Lake Victoria

Dar-es-Salaam

Lake Tanganyika

Lake Nyasa

Blantyre

Uele

Kisangani

Ubangi

Congo (Zaire)

Kasai

Lubumbashi

Luanda

Kinshasa

Lusaka

Salisbury

Zambezi

Limpopo

Johannesburg

Durban

KALAHARI DESERT

Orange

Windhoek

NAMIB DESERT

Orange

Cape Town

Equator

Tropic of Capricorn

| 0 | 100 | 200 | 400 | 600 | 800 Miles |

| 0 | 150 | 300 | 600 | 900 | 1200 Kilometers |

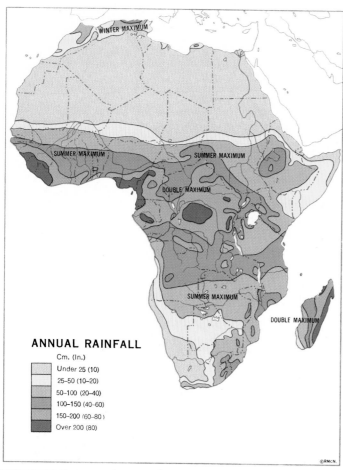

ANNUAL RAINFALL

Cm. (In.)

	Under 25 (10)
	25–50 (10–20)
	50–100 (20–40)
	100–150 (40–60)
	150–200 (60–80)
	Over 200 (80)

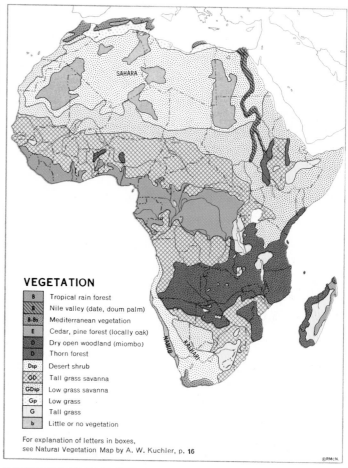

VEGETATION

B	Tropical rain forest
	Nile valley (date, doum palm)
B-Bs	Mediterranean vegetation
E	Cedar, pine forest (locally oak)
D	Dry open woodland (miombo)
D	Thorn forest
Dsp	Desert shrub
GD	Tall grass savanna
GDsp	Low grass savanna
Gp	Low grass
G	Tall grass
b	Little or no vegetation

For explanation of letters in boxes,
see Natural Vegetation Map by A. W. Kuchler, p. 16

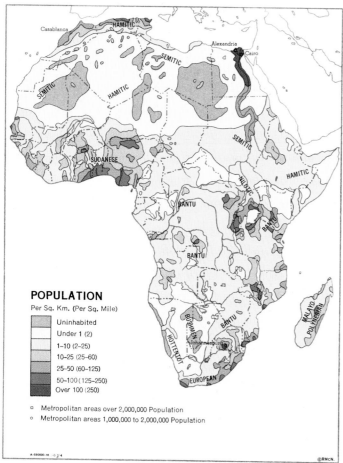

POPULATION

Per Sq. Km. (Per Sq. Mile)

	Uninhabited
	Under 1 (2)
	1–10 (2–25)
	10–25 (25–60)
	25–50 (60–125)
	50–100 (125–250)
	Over 100 (250)

□ Metropolitan areas over 2,000,000 Population

○ Metropolitan areas 1,000,000 to 2,000,000 Population

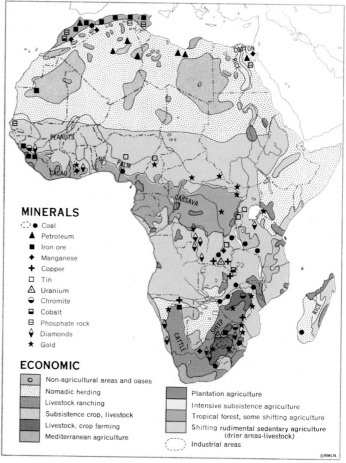

MINERALS

- ● Coal
- ▲ Petroleum
- ■ Iron ore
- ◆ Manganese
- ✚ Copper
- □ Tin
- △ Uranium
- ◖ Chromite
- ▣ Cobalt
- ⊟ Phosphate rock
- ◈ Diamonds
- ★ Gold

ECONOMIC

○	Non-agricultural areas and oases
	Nomadic herding
	Livestock ranching
	Subsistence crop, livestock
	Livestock, crop farming
	Mediterranean agriculture
	Plantation agriculture
	Intensive subsistence agriculture
	Tropical forest, some shifting agriculture
	Shifting rudimental sedentary agriculture (drier areas–livestock)
	Industrial areas

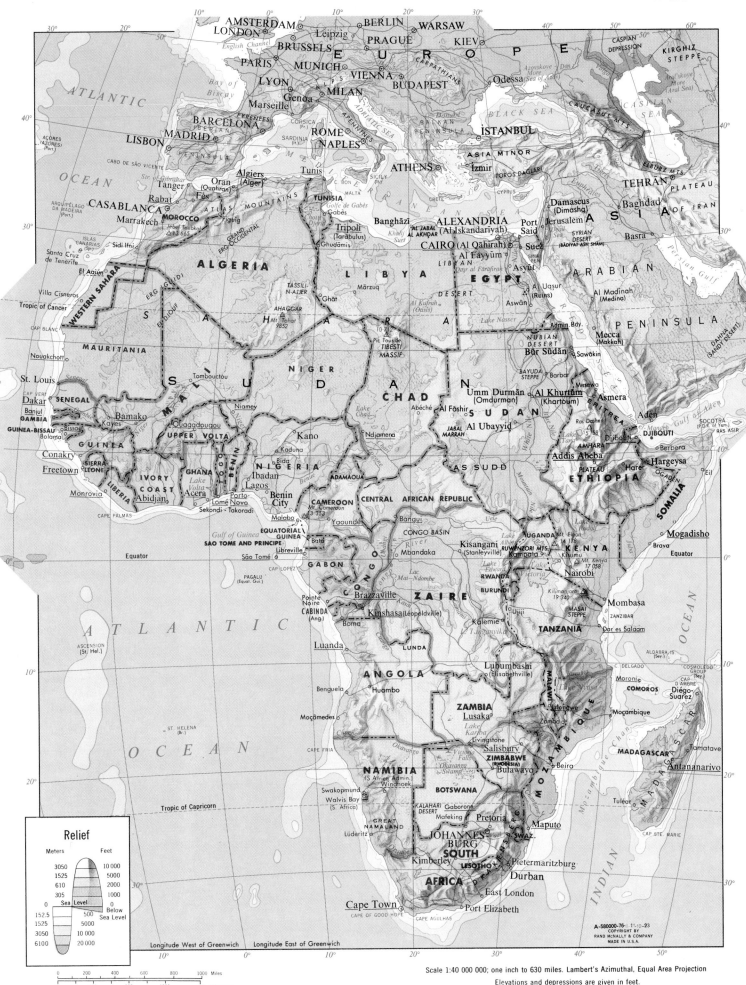

Relief

Meters | Feet
3050 | 10 000
1525 | 5000
610 | 2000
305 | 1000
0 Sea Level | 0 Below Sea Level
152.5 | 500
1525 | 5000
3050 | 10 000
6100 | 20 000

Longitude West of Greenwich | Longitude East of Greenwich

0 200 400 600 800 1000 Miles
0 400 800 1200 1600 Kilometers

A-580000-76- 11-12-23
COPYRIGHT BY
RAND McNALLY & COMPANY
MADE IN U.S.A.

Scale 1:40 000 000; one inch to 630 miles. Lambert's Azimuthal, Equal Area Projection
Elevations and depressions are given in feet.

Insets

AÇORES (AZORES) (Port.)
RMCN.
FAIAL — GRACIOSA — TERCEIRA — SÃO JORGE — PICO — SÃO MIGUEL — Ponta Delgada — STA. MARIA
Same scale as main map

CABO VERDE
SANTO ANTÃO — SÃO VICENTE — SAL — SÃO NICOLAU — BOA VISTA — MAIO — SÃO TIAGO — Praia — FOGO
Same scale as main map

Main Map Labels

S P A I N
Cádiz
Str. of Gibraltar
Gibraltar (U.K.)
Tanger (Tangier)
Larache
Ceuta (Sp.)
Tetouan
Ouezzane
Rabat
Salé
CASABLANCA
Azemmour
El Jadida
Settat
Safi (Asfi)
Kasba-Tadla
Oued-Zem
Meknès
Fès
Taza
MOROCCO
ATLAS MOUNTAINS
Marrakech
Essaouira
Jebel Toubkal 13665
Demnat
Boudenib
Agadir
Taroudant
Figuig
Béchar
ANTI ATLAS
Sidi Ifni
Tiznit
Béni-Abbès
Igli

Algiers (Alger)
Dellys
Cherchell
El Asnam
Mostaganem
Oran
Mascara
Ghazaouet
Sidi-bel Abbès
Saïda
Tlemcen
Oujda
Aïn-Sefra
Laghouat
Ghardaïa
Oued-Zem
Blida
Tizi Ouzou
Médéa
M'sila
Djelfa
Biskra
Bejaïa (Bougie)
Skikda
Annaba (Bône)
Tunis
Constantine
Sétif
Batna
Tébessa
Gafsa
T U N I S
Sfax
El Oued
Touggourt
Ouargla
Hassi Messaoud
El-Goléa
GRAND ERG OCCIDENTAL
GRAND ERG ORIENTAL
A L G E R I A
Timimoun
Adrar
TOUAT
In Salah
PLATEAU DU TADEMAÏT
Zaouia el Kahla
In Aménas
PLATEAU DU TINRHERT
Illizi
TIDIKELT
Chenachane
Ouallene
TASSILI-N-AJJER
Ghat
Djanet
S A H A R A
ERG IGUIDI
ERG CHECH
EL HANK
TANEZROUFT
Mt. Tahat 9852
AHAGGAR
Tamanrasset
T U A R E G
Post Maurice Cortier (Bidon Cinq)
Tamanrasset
ADRAR DES IFORAS
Mt. Gréboun 6562
Iferouâne
Monts Tamgak 5906
AÏR
Monts Bagzane 6300
Agadez

WESTERN SAHARA
El Aaiún
CABO BOJADOR
The Western Sahara is occupied by Morocco.
Tropic of Cancer
EL DJOUF
Taoudenni
Villa Cisneros
Fdérik
OUARANE
EL MREYYÉ
Araouane
Mabrouk
VALLÉE DU TILEMSI
Kidal
Nouadhibou
CAP BLANC
CAP D'ARGUIN
Atar
Chinguetti
Nouamrhar
CAP TIMIRIS
Akjoujt
M A U R I T A N I A
Nouakchott
Tidjikdja
Kiffa
Oualâta
Néma
Tombouctou (Timbuktu)
Bamba
Bourem
Gao
M A L I
Goundam
Niafounké
Nioro du Sahel
Nara

ISLAS CANARIAS (Sp.)
LANZAROTE
LA PALMA
TENERIFE
Sta. Cruz de Tenerife
San Sebastián
GOMERA
HIERRO
GRAN CANARIA
Las Palmas de Gran Canaria
CAP DRÂA
FUERTEVENTURA
C. YUBY

ATLANTIC OCEAN
ARQUIPÉLAGO
ILHA DE PORTO SANTO
Funchal
ILHA DA MADEIRA (Port.)
DA MADEIRA (Port.)

Saint-Louis
Rodor
Dagana
Matam
Kaédi
Mbout
Sélibaby
Louga
Linguère
CAP VERT
Rufisque
Dakar
Thiès
Diourbel
Bakel
S E N E G A L
Kaolack
Kayes
Tambacounda
Bafoulabé
Banjul (Bathurst)
GAMBIA
Ziguinchor
GUINEA-BISSAU
Bissau
Belama
Buba
ARQUIPÉLAGO DOS BIJAGÓS
Boké
Boffao
Kindia
Forécariah
Conakry
FOUTA DJALLON
Labé
Timbo
Mamou
Kouroussa
Kankan
G U I N E A
Kita
Satadougou
Mt. du Tamgué 5046
Siguiri
Bamako
Koulikoro
Ségou
Dédougou
San
Dienné
Mopti
Bandiagara
Goumbou
Sokolo
Ouahigouya
Dori
UPPER VOLTA
Ouagadougou
Koudougou
Tenkodogo
Kaya
Fada Ngourma
Niamey
Tillabéry
Say
Dosso
Tahoua
Madaoua
Tessaoua
Zinder
Gouré
Nguru
Maradi
Sokoto
Katsina
Gumel
Hadejia
Kano
Zaria
Kaduna
Gusau
Kaura Namoda
Birnin Kebbi
Gaya
N I G E R
N I G E R I A
Zungeru
Minna
Jos
Gombe
Bauchi
Kontagora
Tahoua

Kiffa
Bafoulabé
Bougouni
Sikasso
Koutiala
Bobo-Dioulasso
Gaoua
Gambaga
Sansanné-Mango
Natitingou
Malanville
Kandi
Kainji Reservoir
Jebba
SIERRA LEONE
Freetown
Makeni
Kabala
Kissidougou
Faranah
Beyla
Kolahun
Moyamba
Pandembu
Bonthe
Bomi Hills
Robertsport
Monrovia
Buchanan
River Cess
L I B E R I A
Mont Nimba 5748
Odienné
Séguéla
Bouaké
Bouaflé
Korhogo
Boundoukou
KONG
Kong
Dabakala
Bondoukou
IVORY COAST
Gaoua
Bole
Tamale
Yendi
Parakou
TOGO
Sokodé
Atakpame
Savalou
Abomey
GHANA
Kumasi
Koforidua
Accra
Kintampo
Lake Volta
 Abidjan
Port-Bouët
Tarkwa
Grand Lahou
Grand Bassam
Assini
C. THREE POINTS
Sekondi-Takoradi
Cape Coast
Saltpond
Axim
Greenville
CAPE PALMAS
Harper
Tabou

Oyo
Iseyin
Oshogbo
Ogbomosho
Ilesha
Iwo
Ibadan
Ife
Abeokuta
Ijebu Ode
Ilorin
Bida
Baro
Lokoja
Idah
Benin City
Sapele
Warri
Forcados
Lagos
Porto-Novo
Cotonou
Ouidah
Anécho
Lomé
Grand Popo
BIGHT OF BENIN
Enugu
Onitsha
Owerri
Aba
Port Harcourt
Bonny
Brass
Calabar
Katsina Ala
Makurdi
Ibi
Keffi
Mt. Cameroon 13353
Victoria
Douala
Yaoundé
Kribi
Ebolowa
C A M E R
EQUATORIAL GUINEA
Bata
RIO MUNI
MALABO
BIOKO
ILHA DO PRÍNCIPE
SAO TOME AND PRINCIPE
ILHA DE SÃO TOMÉ
São Tomé
Libreville
G A B
BIGHT OF BIAFRA
GULF OF GUINEA
ATLANTIC OCEAN

Scale 1:16 000 000; one inch to 250 miles. Sinusoidal Projection
Elevations and depressions are given in feet

A-589100-76
COPYRIGHT BY
RAND McNALLY & COMPANY
MADE IN U.S.A.

Longitude West of Greenwich
Longitude East of Greenwich

0 50 100 200 300 400 500 Miles
0 100 200 400 600 800 Kilometers

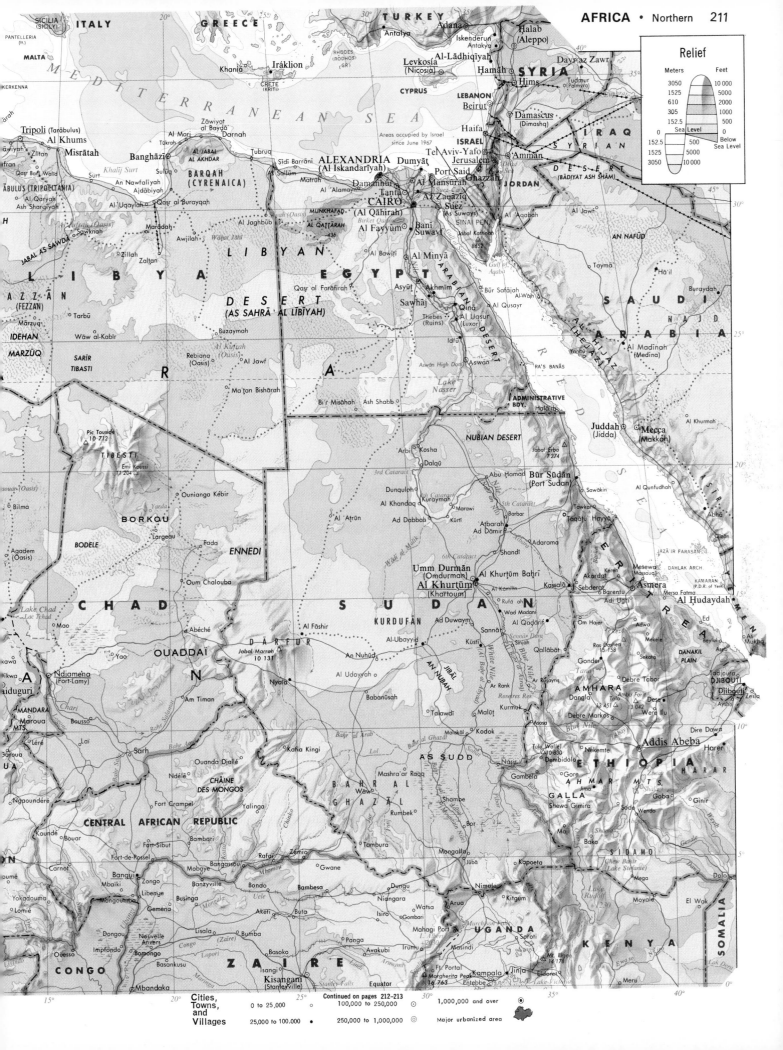

Continued on pages 210-211

Scale 1:16 000 000; one inch to 250 miles. Sinusoidal Projection
Elevations and depressions are given in feet

Equator

SOMALIA
Mt. Kenya 17 058
Ft. Hall
Nairobi
Kismayu
Bur Gavo
Witu
Lamu
Takaungu
Mombasa
Vanga
PEMBA ISLAND
Zanzibar
Bagamoyo
Dar es Salaam
Morogoro
Kisaki
Utete
Kilwa Kivinje
Lindi
Mikindani
CABO DELGADO
Masasi
Mocímboa da Praia
Ibo
Pemba
Lúrio
Memba
Nacala
Moçambique
António Enes
ILHA ANGOCHE
Pebane

INDIAN

MAFIA
ALDABRA IS. (Sey.)
COSMOLEDO GROUP (Sey.)
ÎLES GLORIEUSES (Fr.)
CAP D'AMBRE
Diégo-Suarez
Moroni
COMOROS
GRANDE COMORE
MOHELI
ANJOUAN
Dzaoudzi
MAYOTTE (Fr.)
NOSSI BÉ
Vohémar
Maromokotro 9436
Antalaha
Mandritsara
Maroantsetra
Baie d'Antongil
ÎLE SAINTE-MARIE
Fénérive
Tamatave
CAP SAINT-ANDRÉ
Majunga
MADAGASCAR
Besalampy
Maintirano
ÎLE JUAN DE NOVA (Fr.)
ÎLES BARREN
Tsiafajavona 8671
Antananarivo
Moramanga
Vatomandry
Antsirabe
Mahanoro
Tsiribihina
Morondava
Ambositra
Mananjary
Fianarantsoa
Manakara
Morombe
BASSAS DA INDIA (Fr.)
Manja
EUROPA (Fr.)
Ivohibé
Ihosy
Manambaro
Fort-Dauphin
Farafangana
Betroka
Trafchamby 4417
CAP STE. MARIE
Tuléar
Mahaly

MOZAMBIQUE CHANNEL

Wolhuterskop
Jacksonstuin
Magaliesberg
Kosmos
Hartbeespoort
Skeerpoort
Haribeespoortdam
Magalies
Foothills
Witwatersberg
Olievenhoutpoort
Tarlton
Krugersdorp
Randfontein
5725
JOHANNESBURG
Roodepoort
Discovery
Florida
Maraisburg
Orlando
Scale 1:1 000 000
Pretoria North
Pretoria
Cullinan
Swartspruit
4549
Voortrekkerhoogte
Valhalla
Hennopsrivier
Irene
Tierpoort
Halfway House
Kaalfontein
Modderfontein
Alexandra
Edenvale
Primrose
Boksburg
Germiston
Brakpan
Springs
Benoni
Albertor
Rosettenville
Turffontein
Pimville
WITWATERSRAND
Silverton
Rayton
4426
Bapsfontein
Kempton Park
Putfontein
5557

Arlington
Paul Roux
Senekal
ORANGE FREE STATE
Fouriesburg
Ficksburg
Clocolan
Pitseng
Teyateyaneng
MALOTI MTS.
Butha Buthe
Leribe
Bethlehem
Clarens
ROYAL NATAL NAT'L. PK.
Kestell
Harrismith
Dannhauser
Glencoe
Dundee
Wasbank
Nqutu
Mahlabatini
Babanango
Mt. aux Sources 10 822
Bergville
Winterton
Cathedral Pk. 9856
Ladysmith
Colenso
Pomeroy
Nkandla
Melmoth
Tugela Ferry
Weenen
Greytown
Eshowe
Estcourt
Kranskop
Catkin Pk. 10 438
Mooirivier
Mt. Gilboa 5803
New Hanover
Dalton
Stanger
Mapumulo
Howick
Wartburg
Pietermaritzburg
Mokhotlong
Thabana Ntlenyana
LESOTHO
Mochache 9464
Roma
Nishoni 5851
Impendle
Bulwer
Camperdown
Pinetown
Verulam
Durban
Isipingo
Mohale's Hoek
Orange
The Twins
Swartberg 7619
Underberg
8326
Creighton
Donnybrook
Richmond
Mid Illovo
Zastron
Quthing
9684
Qacha's Nek 9820
Matatiele
Franklin
Umzimkulu
Ixopo
Umkomaas
Scottburgh
Herschel
Winberg 7853
Lady Grey
Rhodes
Ben Macdhui 9846
Mount Fletcher
Gedarville
Mt. Currie 7297
Kokstad
Harding
Umzinto
Sezela
Park Rynie
Jamestown
Rossouw 8430
Elliot
Ugie
Maclear
Mount Frere
Qumbu
Tsolo
Umtata
Mount Ayliff
Bizana
Tabankulu
Flagstaff
Mount Shepstone
Uvongo Beach
Margate
Port Edward
Lasikisiki
Molteno
STORMBERG
Sterkstroom
Dordrecht
Indwe
Lady Frere
Cala
Engcobo
Ngqeleni
Libode
Port St. Johns
RAME HEAD
Waverly
Queenstown
Tarkastad
Cofimvaba
Tsomo
Ndutywa
Mqanduli
Elliotdale
Cradock
Whittlesea
Tylden
CAPE
Carthcart
Ngamakwe
Willowvale
BANKBERG 6606
WINTERBERG 7778
Seymour
Stutterheim
Frankfort
Butterworth
Kentani
SOUTH AFRICA
Pearston
Somerset East
Adelaide
Keiskammahoek
Fort Beaufort
Alice
Komga
Kei Mouth
Morgan's Bay
Bedford
King William Town
Berlin
Brebach
East London
Gonubie
Kidd's Beach
Riebeek-Oos
Peddie
Hamburg
Alicedale
SUURBERGE
Grahamstown
Salem
Kirkwood
Bathurst
Addo
Alexandria
Port Alfred (Kowie)
Uitenhage
SAINT CROIX ISLAND
BIRD ISLAND
Port Elizabeth
KAAP RECIFE

INDIAN OCEAN

NATAL
DRAKENSBERG

Cities, Towns, and Villages
0 to 25,000
25,000 to 100,000
100,000 to 250,000
250,000 to 1,000,000
1,000,000 and over
Major urbanized area

Scale 1:4 000 000
0 10 20 30 40 Miles
0 10 20 30 40 50 60 Kilometers

Relief
Meters		Feet
3050		10 000
1525		5000
610		2000
305		1000
152.5		500
0	Sea Level	
152.5		500
1525		5000
3050		10 000

Relief

Meters	Feet
3050	10 000
1525	5000
610	2000
305	1000
152.5	500
Sea Level	0
0	0
152.5	500
1525	5000
3050	10 000

Copyright by Rand McNally & Co.
Made in U.S.A.
A-589400-76   2ᴹ 6ᵂ

Scale 1:10,000,000; one inch to 160 miles. Lambert Azimuthal Equal Area Projection
Elevations and depressions are given in feet.

WESTERN SAHARA

MAURITANIA

MALI

SENEGAL

GAMBIA

GUINEA-BISSAU

GUINEA

SIERRA LEONE

LIBERIA

IVORY COAST

GHANA

UPPER VOLTA

TOGO

SUDAN

SAHARA

ATLANTIC OCEAN

GULF OF G

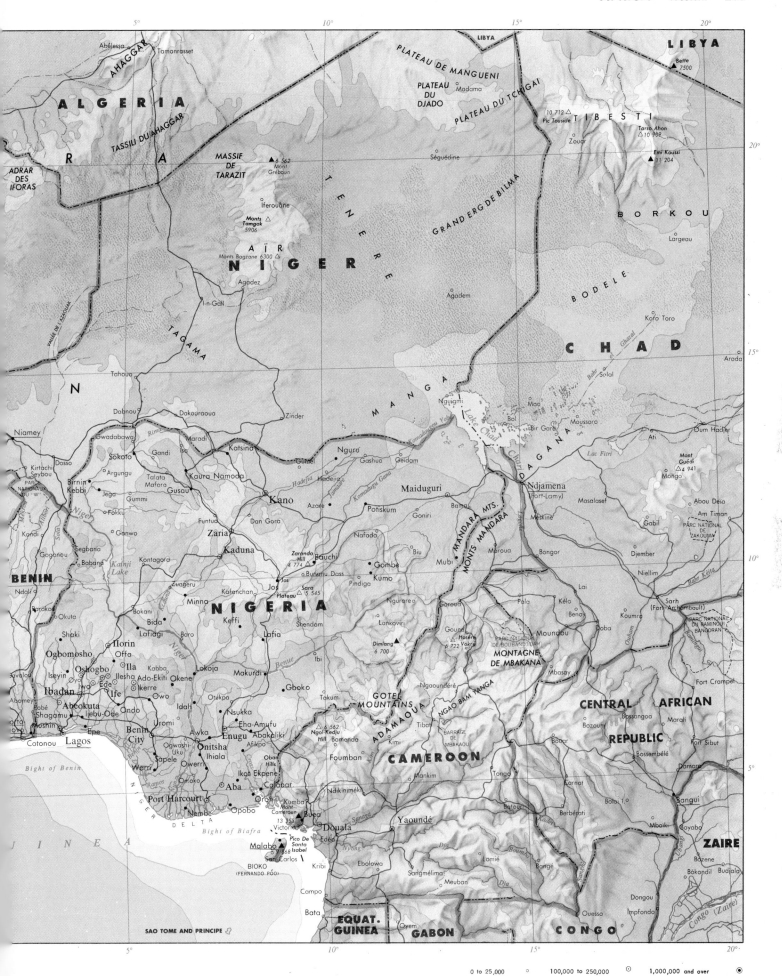

ALGERIA

AHAGGAR
Abélessa Tamanrasset

TASSILI DU AHAGGAR

ADRAR DES IFORAS

R A

LIBYA

PLATEAU DE MANGUENI

PLATEAU DU DJADO

Madama

PLATEAU DU TCH'GAI

LIBYA

Bette 7500 ▲

10 712 △
Pic Toussidé TIBESTI

Tarso Ahon △10 902

Séguédine

Emi Koussi ▲11 204

BORKOU

Largeau

MASSIF DE TARAZIT

6 562 ▲
Mont Grébaun

Iferouâne

Monts Tamgak 5906 △

AÏR

NIGER

Monts Bagzane 6300 △

Agadez

I-n-Gall

TENERE

GRAND ERG DE BILMA

BODELE

Karo Toro

TAGAMA

Tahoua

Dabnou

Dakouraoua

Zinder

MANGA

DAGANA

CHAD

Arada

VALLÉE DE L'AZOUAK

N

Niamey

Gwadabawa

Maradi

Iso

Katsina

Gumel

Nguru

Gashua

Geidam

Nguigmi

Lake Chad

Mao

Bol

Bir Gara

Moussoro

Ati

Oum Hadjer

Bahr

Salal

Chari

Lac Fitri

Dosso

Sokoto

Gandi

Argungu

Talata Mafora

Kaura Namoda

Gusau

Hadejia

Hadejia

Komadugu Gana

Maiduguri

Bama

Ndjamena (Fort-Lamy)

Masalasef

Abou Deia

Am Timan

Gabil

Mont Guédi △4 941

Mongo

Kirtachi Seybou

PARC NATIONAL DU "W"

Birnin Kebbi

Jega

Gummi

Fokku

Dan Gora

Kano

Azare

Goniri

Potiskum

Nafada

Bauchi

Gombe

Kumo

Mubi

MANDARA MTS.

MONTS MANDARA

Maroua

Bongor

Djember

Niellim

Sarh (Fort-Archambault)

PARC NATIONAL DE ZAKOUMA

Kondi

Gogonou

Segbana

Babana

Kainji Lake

Kontagora

Zungeru

Zaria

Kaduna

Zaranda Hill 4 774 △

Jos

Sara △5 545

Plateau

Burumu Dass

Pindiga

Biu

BENIN

Ndali

Karokou

Okuta

Bokani

Bida

Minna

Keffi

NIGERIA

Shendam

Ngurore

Garoua

Pala

Kélo

Benoy

Lai

Koumra

Doba

PARC NATIONAL DU BAMINGUI BANGORAN

Shaki

Lafiagi

Baro

Lafia

Ibi

Lankoviri

Goun

Hosere Yoko 6 722 ▲

Moundou

PARC NATIONAL DE BOUBANDJIDA

Bozoum

Bossangoa

Marali

Fort Crampel

Ogbomosho

Ilorin

Offa

Ila

Kabba

Lokoja

Makurdi

Benue

Dimlang 6 700 ▲

MONTAGNE DE MBAKANA

Mbasay

CENTRAL AFRICAN REPUBLIC

Oshogbo

Iseyin

Oyo

Ilesha

Ede

Ife

Ikerre

Owo

Idah

Gboko

Takum

Ngaoundéré

NGAO BAM YANGA

Bouar

Bossembélé

Fort Sibut

Ibadan

Abeokuta

Ijebu-Ode

Ondo

Otukpa

Nsukka

Ngol Kedju Hill △6 562

GOTEL MOUNTAINS

ADAMAOUA

Tibati

BARRAGE DE MBAKAOU

Bozoum

Bangassou

Iseyin

Shagamu

Epe

Uromi

Awka

Eha-Amufu

Abakaliki

Bamenda

Kimi

Foumban

Mankim

Tongo

Carnot

Bolai 1.

Damara

Bangui

Moshin

Cotonou

Lagos

Benin City

Ogwashi-Uku

Onitsha

Ihiala

Enugu

Afikpo

Oban Hills

Kumba

Mamfe

CAMEROON

Batouri

Berbérati

Mbaiki

Boyaba

ZAIRE

Bight of Benin

Warri

Sapele

Owerri

Omoko

Ikot Ekpene

Calabar

Ndikinimeki

Bazene

Bokondil

Budjala

Port Harcourt

Aba

Oron

Mont Cameroun 13 353 ▲

Buea

Yaoundé

Edéa

Douala

Victoria

Nembe

Opobo

DELTA

Bight of Biafra

Pico De Santa Isabel △ 868

Malabo

San Carlos

BIOKO (FERNANDO POO)

Kribi

Campo

Bata

Eseka

Ebolowa

Sangmélima

Meuban

Dja

Lomié

Bangé

Dja

Boumba

Ouesso

Impfondo

Dongou

Congo (Zaïre)

GUINEA

SAO TOME AND PRINCIPE

EQUAT. GUINEA

Oyem

GABON

Meuban

CONGO

Niger

Sota

Mékrou

Alibori

JINEA

Cross

Sanaga

Nyong

Ntem

0 to 25,000 ○ 100,000 to 250,000 ◉ 1,000,000 and over ◉

25,000 to 100,000 • 250,000 to 1,000,000 ◎ Major urbanized area

Cities, Towns, and Villages

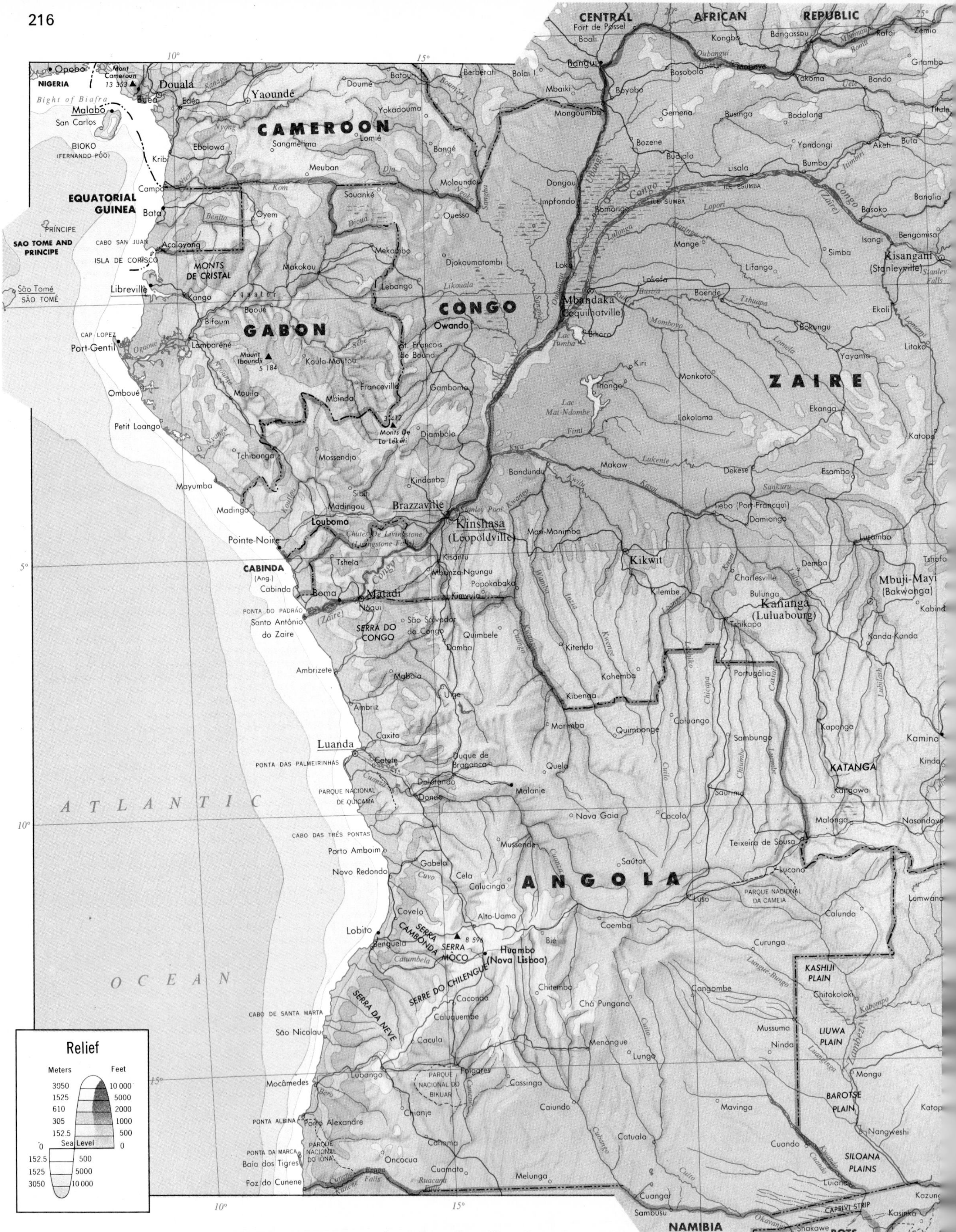

NIGERIA
Opobo
Mont Cameroun 13 353 ▲
Douala
Buea
Malabo
San Carlos
Bight of Biafra
BIOKO (FERNANDO PÓO)
EQUATORIAL GUINEA
Bata
PRÍNCIPE
SAO TOME AND PRINCIPE
CABO SAN JUAN
ISLA DE CORISCO
São Tomé
SÃO TOMÉ
Libreville
Kango

CAMEROON
Edéa
Yaoundé
Ebolowa
Sangmélima
Doumé
Yokadouma
Lomié
Meuban
Bangé
Moloundou
Nyong
Dja
Kom
Campo
Souanké
Oyem
Acalayong
MONTS DE CRISTAL
Makokou
Benito
Djoua
Mekambo
Lebango
Ouesso
Impfondo
Djoumatombi
Likouala

GABON
Booué
Bifoum
Equator
Lambaréné
Mouila
Mount Iboundji 5 184 ▲
Kaula-Moutou
Franceville
Mbinda
3 412
Monts De La Lékéti
Djambala
Gamboma
Owando
St. François de Boundji
Ewo

CONGO
Mbandaka (Coquilhatville)
Lac Tumba
Bokoro
Lac Mai-Ndombe
Kiri
Thonge
Monkoto
Lokolama

ZAIRE
Kisangani (Stanleyville) Stanley Falls
Banalia
Basoko
Bengamisa
Isangi
Simba
Lifanga
Mange
Lakofa
Boende
Tshuapa
Ekoli
Bokungu
Yayama
Litoko
Katopa

CENTRAL AFRICAN REPUBLIC
Fort de Possel
Kongba
Bangassou
Rafaï
Zemio
Boali
Bangui
Boyabo
Bosobolo
Mbaiki
Mongoumba
Bozene
Gemena
Businga
Bodalang
Budjala
Yandongi
Bumba
Akeü
Buta
Lisala
Ubangi
Dongou
Bomongo
ÎLE SUMBA
ÎLE-ESUMBA
Impfondo
Lopori
Busira
Lomami
Momboyo
Lomela
Tshuapa

Ogooué
Port-Gentil
CAP LOPEZ
Omboué
Petit Loango
Tchibanga
Mossendjo
Sibiti
Madingou
Madingo
Mayumba
Nyanga
Loubomo
Chutes De Livingstone (Livingstone Falls)
Pointe-Noire
Tshela
Boma
CABINDA (Ang.)
Cabinda
PONTA DO PADRÃO
Santo António do Zaire
SERRA DO CONGO
Matadi
Nóqui
São Salvador do Congo
Brazzaville
Stanley Pool
Kinshasa (Léopoldville)
Kisantu
Mbanza-Ngungu
Popokabaka
Kimvula
Kwa
Bandundu
Makaw
Dekese
Lukenie
Sankuru
Esambo
Tiebo (Port-Francqui)
Domiongo
Lodja
Kasai
Lubondo

Kindanba
Masi-Manimba
Kikwit
Kilembe
Charlesville
Demba
Bulunga
Kananga (Luluabourg)
Tshikapa
Mbuji-Mayi (Bakwanga)
Kabind
Nanda-Kanda

ATLANTIC
OCEAN

Ambrizete
Maboia
Ambriz
Uige
Marimba
Quimbonge
Kitenda
Kahemba
Kibenga
Kwango
Luanda
PONTA DAS PALMEIRINHAS
Catoté
Cotote
Duque de Bragança
Quela
Sambungo
Kapanga
Kamina
Kinda
Dalatando
Dondo
Malanje
Caxito
PARQUE NACIONAL DE QUICAMA

CABO DAS TRÊS PONTAS
Porto Amboim
Nova Gaia
Cacolo
Saurimo
Malanga
Nasondoye
Teixeira de Sousa
Lucano

Gabela
Mussende
Saútar
Bié
Coemba
PARQUE NACIONAL DA CAMEIA
Lomwan
Novo Redondo
Cuvo
Cela
Calucinga
Luso
Calunda
Covelo
SERRA CAMBONDA
Alto-Uama
Chitembo
Chá Pungana
Cangombe
Curunga

ANGOLA

Lobito
Benguela
Catumbela
SERRA MOCO 8 596 ▲
Huambo (Nova Lisboa)
SERRE DO CHILENGUE
Caconda
Caluquembe
Cacula
SERRA DA NEVE
São Nicolau

KASHIJI PLAIN
Chitokoloki
LIUWA PLAIN
Mussuma
Ninda
BAROTSE PLAIN
Mavinga
Katop
Nangweshi

CABO DE SANTA MARTA
Mocâmedes
Lubango
PARQUE NACIONAL DO BIKUAR
Folgares
Cassinga
Chitembo
Caiundo
Lungo
Mongu
Menongue
SILOANA PLAINS

PONTA ALBINA
Porto Alexandre
Chianje
PARQUE NACIONAL DO IONA
Cahama
Cuamato
Melunga
Catuala
Cuando
Luiana
Kasink
PONTA DA MARCA
Baía dos Tigres
Oncocua
Cuamato
Ruacana Falls
Cunene
Foz do Cunene
Cuangar
Sambusu
NAMIBIA
Okavango
CAPRIVI STRIP
Shakawe
BOTS.
CHOBE NAT'L PARK

Relief

Meters	Feet
3050	10 000
1525	5000
610	2000
305	1000
152.5	500
Sea Level	0
152.5	500
1525	5000
3050	10 000

0   50   100   150   200   250   300 Miles
0   100   200   300   400   500 Kilometers

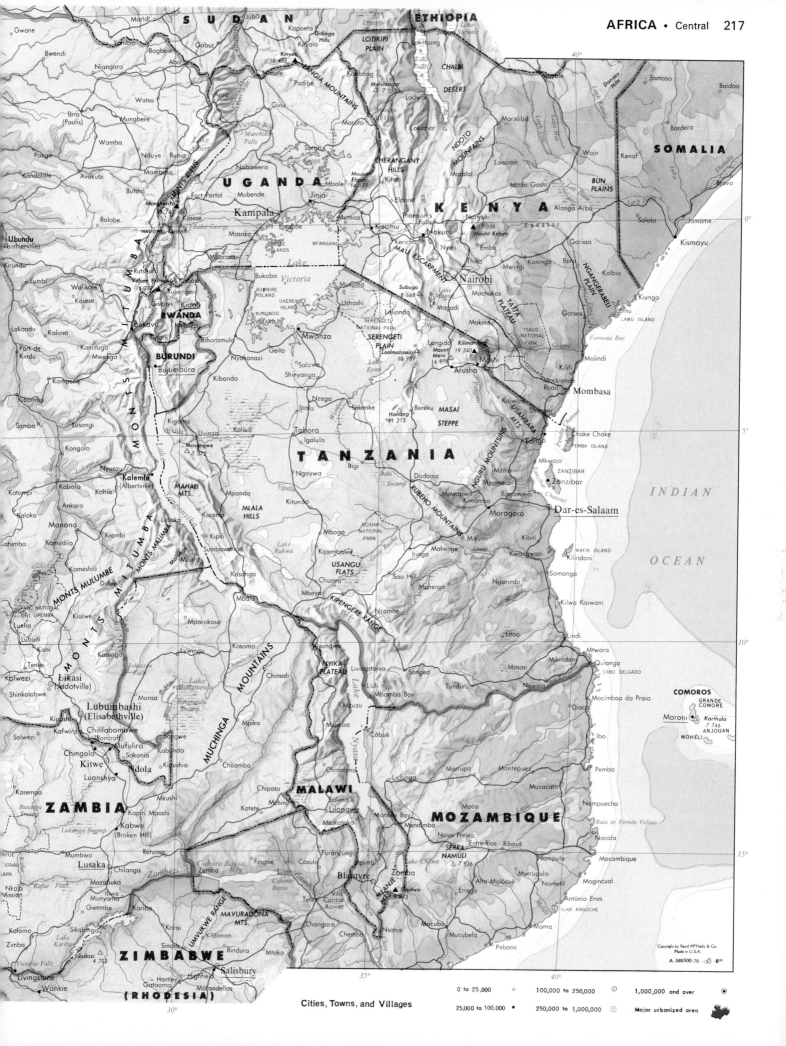

Cities, Towns, and Villages

0 to 25,000   100,000 to 250,000   1,000,000 and over

25,000 to 100,000   250,000 to 1,000,000   Major urbanized area

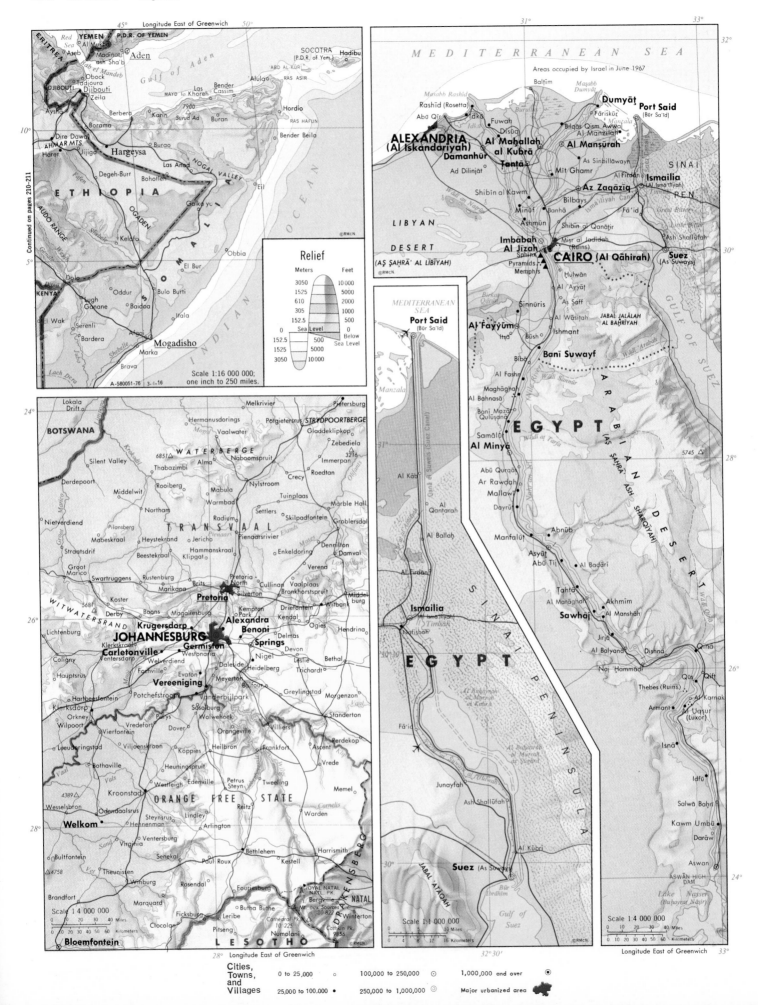

Continued on pages 210–211

Relief

Meters	Feet
3050	10 000
1525	5000
610	2000
305	1000
152.5	500
Sea Level	0
	Below
	Sea Level
152.5	500
1525	5000
3050	10 000

Scale 1:16 000 000;
one inch to 250 miles.

A-580051-76 3-4-16

Areas occupied by Israel in June 1967

Scale 1:4 000 000

Scale 1:4 000 000

Scale 1:4 000 000

Cities, Towns, and Villages

0 to 25,000 ○	100,000 to 250,000 ⊙	1,000,000 and over ◉	
25,000 to 100,000 •	250,000 to 1,000,000 ⊚	Major urbanized area	

Longitude East of Greenwich

Longitude East of Greenwich

Longitude East of Greenwich

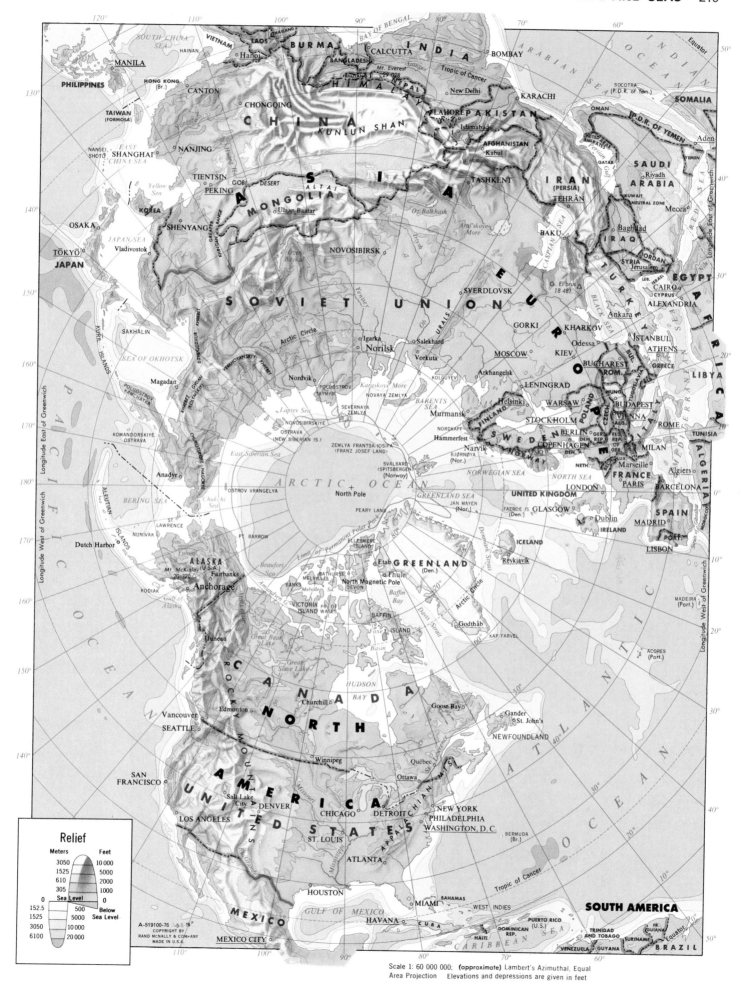

Relief

Meters	Feet
3050	10 000
1525	5000
610	2000
305	1000
Sea Level	0
152.5	500 Below
1525	5000 Sea Level
3050	10 000
6100	20 000

A-519100-76   -5-5-19
COPYRIGHT BY
RAND McNALLY & COMPANY
MADE IN U.S.A.

Scale 1: 60 000 000;   (approximate) Lambert's Azimuthal, Equal
Area Projection   Elevations and depressions are given in feet

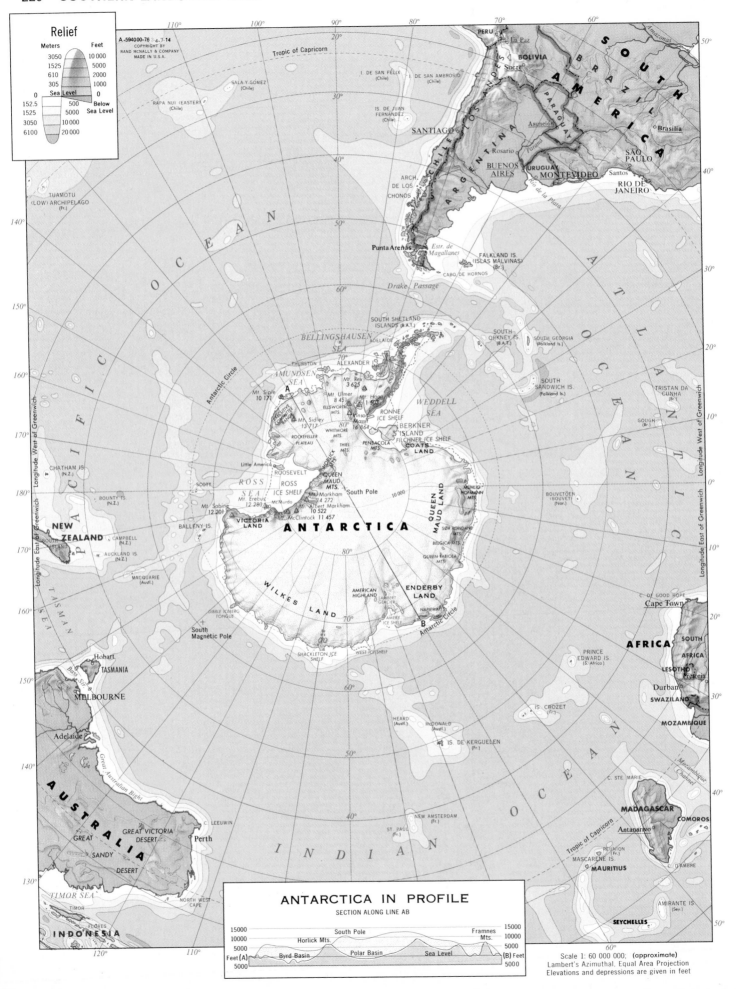

Relief

Meters		Feet
3050		10 000
1525		5000
610		2000
305		1000
Sea Level	0	**0**
	500	Below
152.5		Sea Level
1525	5000	
3050	10 000	
6100	20 000	

A-594000-76 4-7-14
COPYRIGHT BY
RAND MCNALLY & COMPANY
MADE IN U.S.A.

Tropic of Capricorn

SOUTH AMERICA

PERU
La Paz
BOLIVIA
Sucre
BRAZIL
PARAGUAY
Asunción
Brasília
SANTIAGO
CHILE
ARGENTINA
Rosario
BUENOS AIRES
URUGUAY
MONTEVIDEO
SÃO PAULO
Santos
RIO DE JANEIRO

SALA-Y-GÓMEZ (Chile)
I. DE SAN FÉLIX (Chile)
I. DE SAN AMBROSIO (Chile)
RAPA NUI (EASTER) (Chile)
IS. DE JUAN FERNÁNDEZ (Chile)

TUAMOTU (LOW) ARCHIPELAGO (Fr.)

P A C I F I C   O C E A N

ARCH. DE LOS CHONOS
Río de la Plata
FALKLAND IS. (ISLAS MALVINAS) (Br.)

Punta Arenas
Estr. de Magallanes
CABO DE HORNOS

Drake Passage

SOUTH SHETLAND ISLANDS (B.A.T.)
SOUTH ORKNEY IS. (B.A.T.)
SOUTH GEORGIA (Falkland Is.)

A T L A N T I C   O C E A N

BELLINGSHAUSEN SEA
ADELAIDE
THURSTON
ALEXANDER
AMUNDSEN SEA
Mt. Rex 3 625
Mt. Siple 10 171
Mt. Ulmer 8 451
Mt. Hope 1 503
EXECUTIVE COMMITTEE RANGE
ELLSWORTH MTS.
Vinson Massif 16 864
RONNE ICE SHELF
BERKNER ISLAND
WEDDELL SEA
FILCHNER ICE SHELF
COATS LAND
Mt. Sidley 13 717
WHITMORE MTS.
ROCKEFELLER PLATEAU
THIEL MTS.
PENSACOLA MTS.

SOUTH SANDWICH IS. (Falkland Is.)
TRISTAN DA CUNHA (Br.)
GOUGH (Br.)
BOUVETØEN (BOUVET) (Nor.)

Little America
ROOSEVELT ISLAND
ROSS SEA
ROSS ICE SHELF
SCOTT
QUEEN MAUD MTS.
South Pole
QUEEN MAUD LAND
MÜHLIG HOFMANN MTS.
Mt. Markham 14 272
Mt. Albert Markham 10 522
McClintock 11 457
Mt. Erebus 12 280
McMurdo
Mt. Sabine 12 201
VICTORIA LAND
ANTARCTICA
SØR RONDANE MTS.
BELGICA MTS.
QUEEN FABIOLA MTS.

C. OF GOOD HOPE
Cape Town
AFRICA
SOUTH AFRICA
Pretoria
LESOTHO
Durban
SWAZILAND
MOZAMBIQUE

CHATHAM IS. (N.Z.)
BOUNTY IS. (N.Z.)
NEW ZEALAND
SOUTH ISLAND
CAMPBELL IS. (N.Z.)
AUCKLAND IS. (N.Z.)
MACQUARIE (Austl.)
BALLENY IS.

South Magnetic Pole
DIBBLE ICEBERG TONGUE
WILKES LAND
AMERICAN HIGHLAND
LAMBERT GLACIER
ENDERBY LAND
NAPIER MTS.
AMERY ICE SHELF
Antarctic Circle

PRINCE EDWARD IS. (S. Africa)
IS. CROZET (Fr.)

SHACKLETON ICE SHELF
WEST ICE SHELF

TASMAN SEA
Hobart
TASMANIA
MELBOURNE
Adelaide
Bass Str.
Great Australian Bight

HEARD (Austl.)
McDONALD (Austl.)
IS. DE KERGUELEN (Fr.)

I N D I A N   O C E A N

C. STE. MARIE
MADAGASCAR
COMOROS
Antananarivo

AUSTRALIA
GREAT VICTORIA DESERT
GREAT SANDY DESERT
C. LEEUWIN
Perth

NEW AMSTERDAM (Fr.)
ST. PAUL (Fr.)
Tropic of Capricorn
RÉUNION (Fr.)
MASCARENE IS.
MAURITIUS

TIMOR SEA
TIMOR
FLORES
INDONESIA
NORTH WEST CAPE

AMIRANTE IS. (Sey.)
SEYCHELLES

ANTARCTICA IN PROFILE

SECTION ALONG LINE AB

	South Pole		Framnes Mts.	
15000				15000
10000	Horlick Mts.			10000
5000				5000
Feet (A)	Byrd Basin	Polar Basin Sea Level	(B) Feet	
5000				5000

Scale 1: 60 000 000; (approximate)
Lambert's Azimuthal, Equal Area Projection
Elevations and depressions are given in feet

Ocean
Floor
Maps

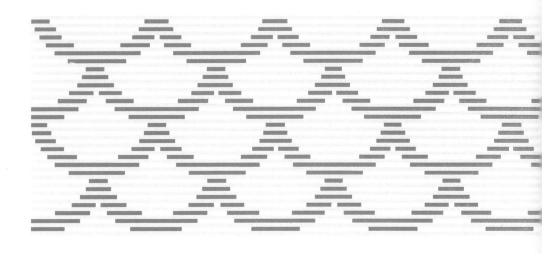

The maps in this section give an artist's view of what the land beneath the surface of the world's oceans looks like. In general, colors used are those which scientists believe may exist on the ocean floor. For continental shelves or shallow inland seas, grayish-green corresponds to sediments washed from the continental areas. Layers of mud, which scientists call *oozes,* cover the ocean bottom. In deeper parts of the oceans, the oozes consist largely of the skeletons of marine life. These appear in white. The fine mud from land is red. In the Atlantic Ocean, materials accumulate relatively rapidly and have a high iron content. These are shown in a brighter red than elsewhere. Slower accumulation in the Pacific and Indian oceans results in more manganese, which results in darker colors. Undersea ridges are shown in black to suggest that they were formed relatively recently from molten rock. Around certain islands white is used to show coral reefs.

The ocean floor has towering mountain ranges, vast canyons, broad plains, and a variety of features that often exceed anything found on the continents. One of the most dramatic features of the ocean floor is the Mid-Atlantic Ridge, a chain of mountains that extends down the middle of the Atlantic Ocean. One distinct characteristic of this ridge is a *trough,* or valley, that runs along the center of the ridge, in effect producing a double line of ridges.

Scientists believe that the ocean ridges mark lines where molten materials from the earth's interior rise to the ocean floor, to form gigantic plates that move slowly apart. This theory, called Continental Drift, suggests that the continents are moving away from each other, having been a single land mass in ancient times. The matching curves of the Atlantic Ocean shorelines of South America and Africa have long been cited as support for this theory.

Where the subsea plates meet certain continental areas or island chains, the ridges plunge downward to form deep trenches. Some of the deepest known trenches are found along the northern and western edges of the Pacific Ocean. These include the Mariana, Tonga, and Kuril trenches.

Deep trenches also parallel the western coasts of Central and South America, the northern coast of Puerto Rico and the Virgin Islands, and other coastal areas. Other identifiable ocean floor features include great submarine canyons that lead from the edges of the continents; seamounts that rise above the ocean floor to form islands; and the continental shelves, which appear to be underwater extensions of the continents.

Scale 1:44,000,000; one inch to 700 miles (approx.)
Modified Cylindrical Projection ▽ Depths in meters.

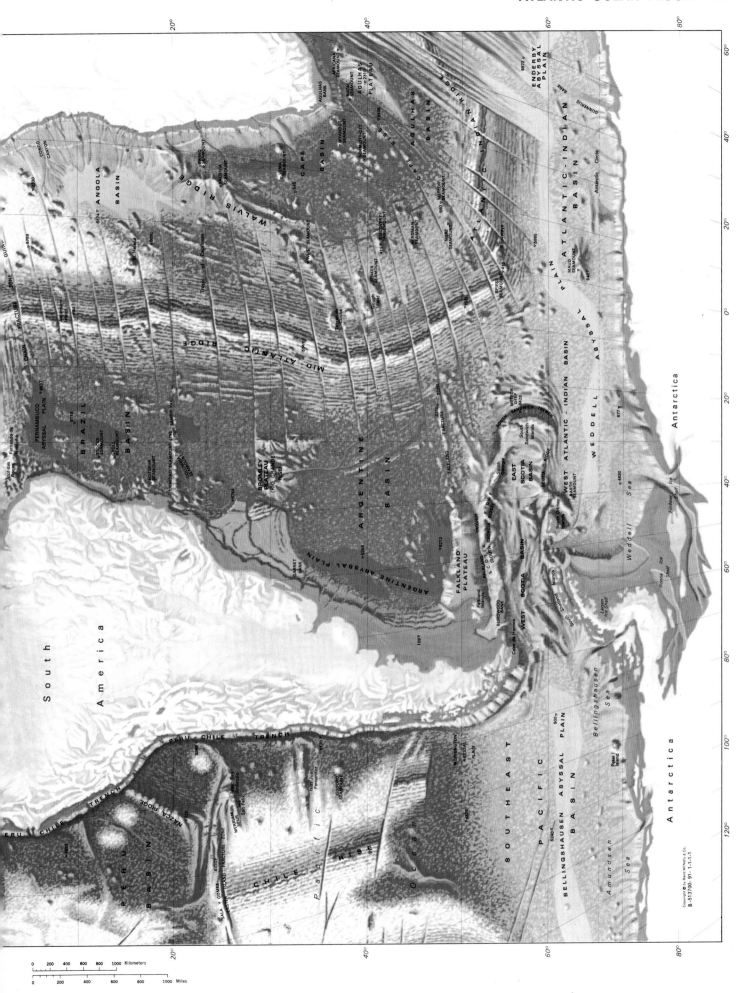

0 200 400 600 800 1000 Kilometers

0 200 400 600 800 1000 Miles

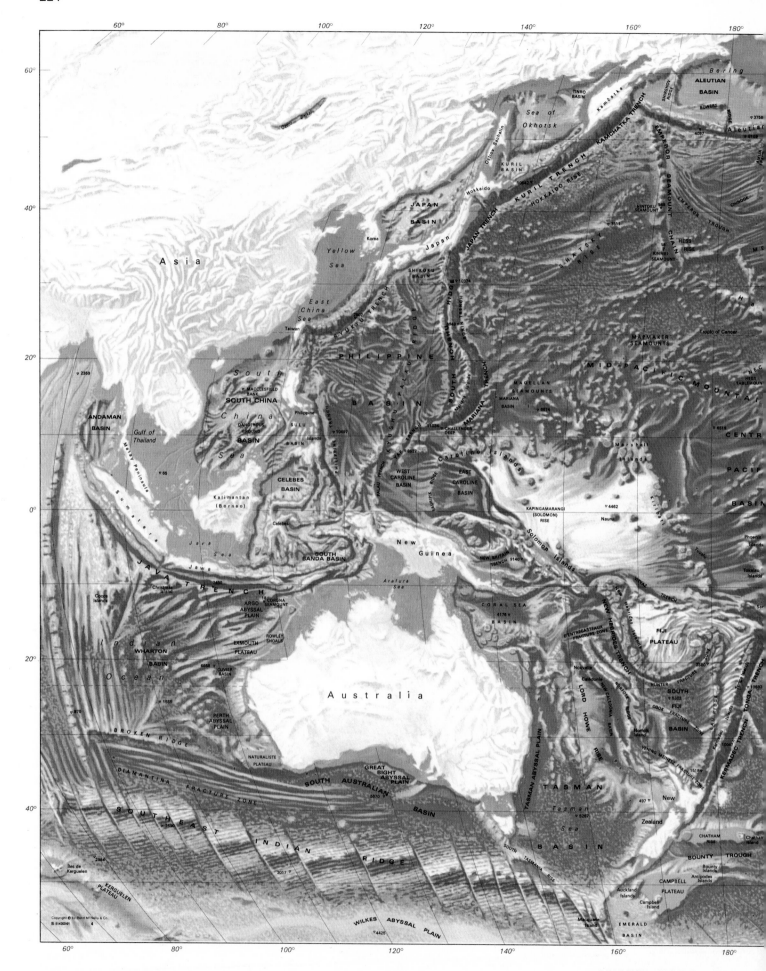

Scale 1:58 000 000; one inch to 900 miles (approx.)
Modified Cylindrical Projection   ▽ Depths in meters.

Scale 1:46 000 000; one inch to 730 miles (approx.)
Modified Cylindrical Projection   ▽ Depths in meters.

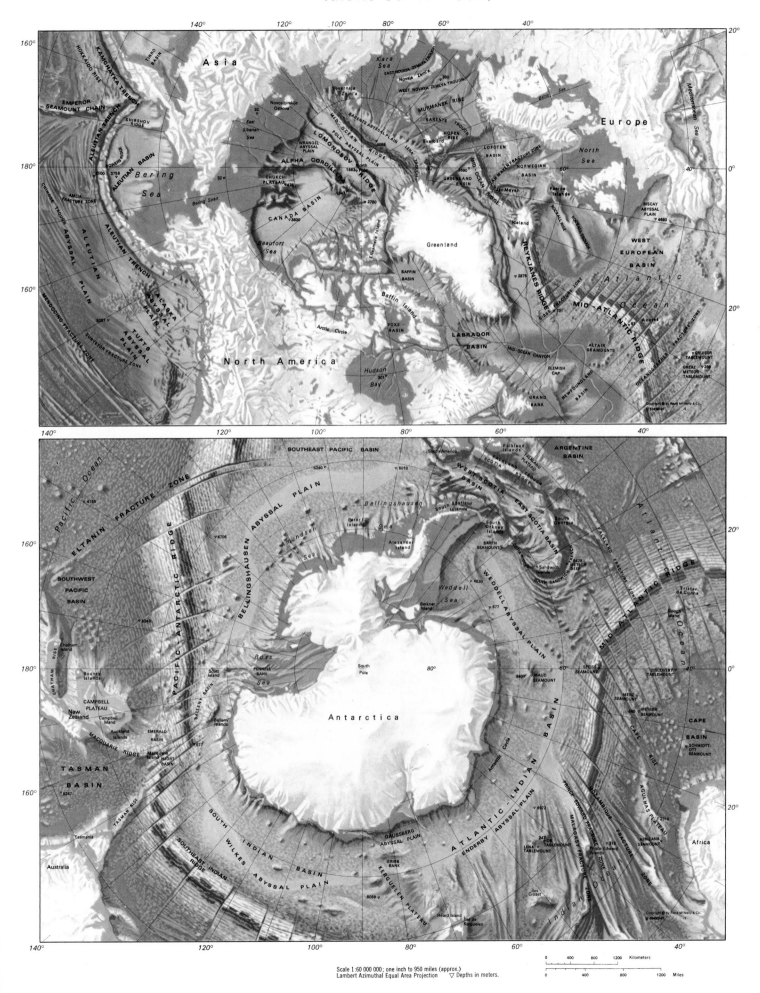

Scale 1:60 000 000; one inch to 950 miles (approx.)
Lambert Azimuthal Equal Area Projection   ▽ Depths in meters.

Index
and
World Facts

The following pages provide a vast store of factual information of geographical interest on the world, the continents, individual countries, and the 50 U.S. states.

Presented in tabular form, this information supplements the maps with data not readily available from the maps themselves. Here are answers to many of the questions raised by those who use the Atlas, particularly questions that ask "How large?" "How many?" and "Where?"

Two indexes are included, one for major cities, and a pronouncing index to the main body of reference maps. The pronouncing index also features latitude and longitude to make it easier for readers to locate places on the maps.

Other aids to the Atlas usage are populations, areas in both square miles and square kilometers, a glossary of foreign terms, and abbreviations.

principal countries and regions of the world

Political Unit	Area in sq. miles	Area in km²	Population*
Afghanistan	250,000	647,497	16,681
Africa	11,714,000	30,339,000	506,000
Alabama (U.S.)	51,609	133,667	3,890
Alaska (U.S.)	589,757	1,527,464	400
Albania	11,100	28,748	2,875
Alberta (Can.)	255,285	661,185	1,838
Algeria	919,595	2,381,741	21,086
American Samoa (U.S.)	76	197	34
Andorra	175	453	34
Angola	481,354	1,246,700	7,402
Antarctica	5,100,000	13,209,000	....
Antigua (incl. Barbuda and Redonda) (U.K.)	171	442	76
Argentina	1,072,163	2,776,889	27,785
Arizona (U.S.)	113,909	295,023	2,718
Arkansas (U.S.)	53,104	137,539	2,286
Asia	17,012,000	44,062,000	2,712,000
Australia	2,966,200	7,682,300	15,032
Austria	32,374	83,849	7,529
Azores Is. (Port.)	905	2,344	273
Bahamas	5,380	13,935	252
Bahrain	240	622	451
Bangladesh	55,598	143,998	93,849
Barbados	166	431	280
Belgium	11,781	30,513	9,909
Belize	8,867	22,965	174
Benin	43,484	112,622	3,757
Bermuda (U.K.)	21	53	63
Bhutan	18,147	47,000	1,374
Bolivia	424,164	1,098,581	5,876
Botswana	231,805	600,372	872
Brazil	3,286,487	8,511,965	128,892
British Columbia (Can.)	366,255	948,596	2,467
Brunei (U.K.)	2,226	5,765	162
Bulgaria	42,823	110,912	8,992
Burma	261,218	676,552	35,133
Burundi	10,747	27,834	4,662
California (U.S.)	158,693	411,013	23,669
Cambodia	69,898	181,035	9,303
Cameroon	183,569	475,442	8,807
Canada	3,831,033	9,922,330	24,554
Canary Is. (Sp.)	2,808	7,273	1,487
Cape Verde	1,557	4,033	339
Cayman Is. (U.K.)	100	259	11
Central African Republic	240,535	622,984	2,565
Central America	201,934	523,009	23,620
Chad	495,755	1,284,000	4,718
Channel Is. (U.K.)	75	195	133
Chile	292,258	756,945	11,486
China (excl. Taiwan)	3,678,470	9,527,200	969,665
Colombia	439,737	1,138,914	28,637
Colorado (U.S.)	104,247	269,998	2,889
Comoros	838	2,171	353
Congo	132,047	342,000	1,615
Connecticut (U.S.)	5,009	12,973	3,108
Cook Is. (N.Z.)	91	236	20
Costa Rica	19,575	50,700	2,372
Cuba	44,218	114,524	10,330
Cyprus	3,572	9,251	623
Czechoslovakia	49,370	127,869	15,569
Delaware (U.S.)	2,057	5,328	595
Denmark	16,629	43,069	5,180
Dist. of Columbia (U.S.)	67	174	638
Djibouti	8,494	22,000	333
Dominica	290	751	87
Dominican Republic	18,816	48,734	5,764
Ecuador	109,484	283,561	8,930
Egypt	386,662	1,001,449	43,876
El Salvador	8,124	21,041	4,877
England (U.K.)	50,362	130,438	46,525
Equatorial Guinea	10,830	28,051	382
Ethiopia	471,778	1,221,900	32,664
Europe	4,063,000	10,524,000	669,000
Faeroe Is. (Den.)	540	1,399	41
Falkland Is. (excl. Deps.) (U.K.)	4,618	11,961	2
Fiji	7,056	18,274	657
Finland	130,120	337,009	4,795
Florida (U.S.)	58,560	151,670	9,740
France	211,208	547,026	54,446
French Guiana (Fr.)	35,135	91,000	67
French Polynesia (Fr.)	1,544	4,000	142
Gabon	103,347	267,667	605
Gambia	4,361	11,295	632
Georgia (U.S.)	58,876	152,488	5,464
German Democratic Republic	41,768	108,178	16,645
Germany, Federal Republic of	96,005	248,651	60,935
Ghana	92,100	238,537	12,394
Gibraltar (U.K.)	2.3	6	33
Greece	50,944	131,944	9,663
Greenland (Den.)	840,004	2,175,600	54
Grenada	133	344	111
Guadeloupe (Fr.)	687	1,779	373
Guam (U.S.)	212	549	111
Guatemala	42,042	108,889	7,423
Guinea	94,926	245,857	5,257
Guinea-Bissau	13,948	36,125	861
Guyana	83,000	214,969	895
Haiti	10,714	27,750	5,174
Hawaii (U.S.)	6,450	16,705	965
Honduras	43,277	112,088	3,939
Hong Kong (U.K.)	1,126	2,916	4,966
Hungary	35,919	93,030	10,839
Iceland	39,769	103,000	235
Idaho (U.S.)	83,557	216,412	944
Illinois (U.S.)	56,400	146,075	11,418
India	1,269,346	3,287,590	692,860
Indiana (U.S.)	36,291	93,993	5,490
Indonesia	788,425	2,042,012	160,210
Iowa (U.S.)	56,290	145,790	2,913
Iran	636,296	1,648,000	40,663
Iraq	167,925	434,924	14,114
Ireland	27,136	70,283	3,519
Isle of Man (U.K.)	227	588	65
Israel	8,019	20,770	4,116
Italy	116,314	301,252	58,159
Ivory Coast	124,504	322,463	8,555
Jamaica	4,244	10,991	2,273
Japan	145,711	377,389	120,448
Jordan	37,738	97,740	3,398
Kansas (U.S.)	82,264	213,063	2,363
Kentucky (U.S.)	40,395	104,623	3,661
Kenya	224,961	582,646	16,840
Kiribati	278	719	51
Korea, North	46,540	120,538	18,918
Korea, South	38,025	98,484	39,556
Kuwait	7,768	20,118	1,519
Laos	91,429	236,800	3,884
Lebanon	4,015	10,400	3,325
Lesotho	11,720	30,355	1,406
Liberia	43,000	111,369	1,984
Libya	679,362	1,759,540	3,227
Liechtenstein	61	157	26
Louisiana (U.S.)	48,523	125,674	4,204
Luxembourg	998	2,586	365
Macao (Port.)	6	16	286
Madagascar	226,658	587,041	9,393
Madeira Is. (Port.)	308	797	263
Maine (U.S.)	33,215	86,026	1,125
Malawi	45,747	118,484	6,283
Malaysia	127,317	329,749	14,798
Maldives	115	298	158
Mali	478,767	1,240,000	7,029
Malta	122	316	370
Manitoba (Can.)	251,000	650,087	1,022
Martinique (Fr.)	425	1,102	381
Maryland (U.S.)	10,577	27,394	4,216
Massachusetts (U.S.)	8,257	21,385	5,737
Mauritania	397,956	1,030,700	1,718
Mauritius	790	2,045	977
Mexico	761,607	1,972,552	76,924
Michigan (U.S.)	58,216	150,779	9,258
Midway Is. (U.S.)	2	5	2
Minnesota (U.S.)	84,068	217,735	4,077
Mississippi (U.S.)	47,716	123,584	2,521
Missouri (U.S.)	69,686	180,486	4,917
Monaco	0.58	1.49	26
Mongolia	604,250	1,565,000	1,767
Montana (U.S.)	147,138	381,086	787
Montserrat (U.K.)	38	98	14
Morocco	172,414	446,550	21,090
Mozambique	309,496	801,590	10,966
Namibia (S. Afr.)	318,261	824,292	1,063
Nauru	8	21	8
Nebraska (U.S.)	77,227	200,017	1,570
Nepal	54,362	140,797	14,595
Netherlands	15,892	41,160	14,467
Neth. Antilles (Neth.)	383	993	256
Nevada (U.S.)	110,540	286,297	799
New Brunswick (Can.)	28,354	73,436	677
New Caledonia (incl. Deps.) (Fr.)	7,335	18,998	148
Newfoundland (Can.)	156,185	404,517	558
New Hampshire (U.S.)	9,304	24,097	921
New Jersey (U.S.)	7,836	20,295	7,364
New Mexico (U.S.)	121,666	315,113	1,300
New York (U.S.)	49,576	128,401	17,557
New Zealand	103,883	269,057	3,156
Nicaragua	50,193	130,000	2,743
Niger	489,191	1,267,000	5,577
Nigeria	356,669	923,768	89,118
Niue (N.Z.)	100	259	5
Norfolk I. (Austl.)	14	36	2
North America	9,400,000	24,345,000	385,000
North Carolina (U.S.)	52,586	136,197	5,874
North Dakota (U.S.)	70,665	183,022	653
Northern Ireland (U.K.)	5,452	14,120	1,541
Northwest Ters. (Can.)	1,304,903	3,379,684	43
Norway	125,182	324,219	4,154
Nova Scotia (Can.)	21,425	55,491	829
Ohio (U.S.)	41,222	106,764	10,797
Oklahoma (U.S.)	69,919	181,089	3,025
Oman	82,030	212,457	948
Ontario (Can.)	412,582	1,068,582	8,264
Oregon (U.S.)	96,981	251,180	2,633
Pac. Is. Tr. Ter. (U.S.)	717	1,857	134
Pakistan	310,404	803,943	87,497
Panama	29,856	77,326	2,092
Papua New Guinea	178,260	461,691	3,306
Paraguay	157,048	406,752	3,239
Pennsylvania (U.S.)	45,333	117,412	11,867
Peru	496,225	1,285,216	18,787
Philippines	115,831	300,000	51,992
Poland	120,725	312,677	36,190
Portugal	35,553	92,082	10,286
Prince Edward I. (Can.)	2,184	5,657	118
Puerto Rico (U.S.)	3,435	8,897	3,188
Qatar	4,247	11,000	181
Quebec (Can.)	594,860	1,540,680	6,234
Reunion (Fr.)	969	2,510	539
Rhode Island (U.S.)	1,214	3,144	947
Romania	91,699	237,500	22,742
Rwanda	10,169	26,338	5,340
St. Helena (incl. Deps.) (U.K.)	162	419	6
St. Kitts-Nevis-Anguilla (U.K.)	138	357	66
St. Lucia	238	616	126
St. Pierre & Miquelon (Fr.)	93	242	5
St. Vincent and the Grenadines	150	388	118
San Marino	24	61	23
São Tomé & Príncipe	372	964	88
Saskatchewan (Can.)	251,700	651,900	921
Saudi Arabia	831,313	2,153,090	8,853
Scotland (U.K.)	30,418	78,781	5,163
Senegal	75,750	196,192	6,033
Seychelles	108	280	67
Sierra Leone	27,699	71,740	3,651
Singapore	238	616	2,471
Solomon Is.	10,983	28,446	245
Somalia	246,201	637,657	3,830
South Africa	471,445	1,221,037	30,815
South America	6,883,000	17,828,000	253,000
South Carolina (U.S.)	31,055	80,432	3,119
South Dakota (U.S.)	77,047	199,551	690
Soviet Union	8,649,500	22,402,000	269,591
Spain	194,885	504,750	38,420
Sri Lanka	25,332	65,610	15,173
Sudan	967,500	2,505,813	19,330
Suriname	63,037	163,265	396
Svalbard (Nor.)	23,958	62,050	...
Swaziland	6,704	17,363	617
Sweden	173,732	449,964	8,369
Switzerland	15,941	41,288	6,291
Syria	71,498	185,180	9,210
Taiwan (Natl. China)	13,885	35,961	18,524
Tanzania	364,900	945,087	19,973
Tennessee (U.S.)	42,244	109,411	4,591
Texas (U.S.)	267,336	692,397	14,228
Thailand	198,457	514,000	49,981
Togo	21,622	56,000	2,670
Tokelau Is. (N.Z.)	4	10	2
Tonga	270	699	93
Trinidad & Tobago	1,981	5,130	1,188
Tunisia	63,170	163,610	6,677
Turkey	301,382	780,576	47,999
Turks & Caicos Is. (U.K.)	166	430	7
Tuvalu	10	26	7
Uganda	91,134	236,036	14,620
United Arab Emirates	32,278	83,600	1,196
United Kingdom	94,251	244,108	56,019
United States	3,618,465	9,371,781	230,086
Upper Volta	105,869	274,200	7,234
Uruguay	68,037	176,215	2,950
Utah (U.S.)	84,916	219,931	1,461
Vanuatu	5,700	14,763	113
Vatican City	0.17	0.44	1
Venezuela	352,145	912,050	14,811
Vermont (U.S.)	9,609	24,887	511
Vietnam	127,242	329,556	54,427
Virginia (U.S.)	40,817	105,716	5,346
Virgin Is. (U.S.-U.K.)	192	497	108
Wales (U.K.)	8,019	20,769	2,790
Washington (U.S.)	68,192	176,616	4,130
Western Sahara	102,703	266,000	165
Western Samoa	1,097	2,842	161
West Virginia (U.S.)	24,181	62,628	1,950
Wisconsin (U.S.)	56,154	145,438	4,705
World	57,626,000	149,251,000	4,551,000
Wyoming (U.S.)	97,914	253,596	471
Yemen	75,290	195,000	6,114
Yemen, People's Dem. Rep. of	128,560	332,968	1,886
Yugoslavia	98,766	255,804	22,709
Yukon (Can.)	186,300	482,515	22
Zaire	905,568	2,345,409	30,438
Zambia	290,586	752,614	6,209
Zimbabwe	150,804	390,580	7,870

*Populations are given in thousands.
Population and area figures are from the 1982 edition of *The World Book Encyclopedia*. They are based on censuses and estimates from official government and United Nations sources.

principal cities of the world

Accra, Ghana (★738,498) ... 636,067
Addis Abeba, Ethiopia ... 1,161,267
Adelaide, Australia ... 857,196
Agra, India (★634,622) ... 591,917
Ahmadābād, India (★1,741,522) ... 1,585,544
Albany, New York (★795,019) ... 101,727
Aleppo (Halab), Syria ... 961,000
Alexandria (Al Iskandarīyah), Egypt ... 2,320,000
Algiers (Alger), Algeria ... 1,503,720
Alma-Ata, Soviet Union ... 910,000
'Ammān, Jordan ... 648,589
Amsterdam, Netherlands (★990,790) ... 757,958
Ankara (Angora), Turkey (★1,794,999) ... 1,701,004
Anshan, China ... 300,000–1,000,000
Antwerp (Antwerpen), Belgium (★662,317) ... 209,200
Asunción, Paraguay ... 392,753
Athens (Athínai), Greece (★2,540,241) ... 867,023
Atlanta, Georgia (★2,029,618) ... 425,022
Auckland, New Zealand ... 742,786

Baghdād, Iraq ... 2,969,000
Baku, Soviet Union (★1,550,000) ... 1,022,000
Baltimore, Maryland (★2,174,023) ... 786,775
Bandung, Indonesia ... 1,282,121
Bangalore, India (★1,653,779) ... 1,540,741
Bangkok (Krung Thep), Thailand ... 4,835,000
Barcelona, Spain ... 1,754,714
Barquisimeto, Venezuela ... 459,000
Barranquilla, Colombia ... 664,533
Beirut, Lebanon ... 702,000
Belém, Brazil (★800,482) ... 771,665
Belfast, No. Ireland ... 363,000
Belgrade (Beograd), Yugoslavia ... 746,105
Belo Horizonte, Brazil (★2,022,846) ... 1,557,464
Berlin, East ... 1,128,983
Berlin, West ... 1,909,706
Bern, Switzerland (★283,600) ... 145,500
Birmingham, Alabama (★847,360) ... 284,413
Birmingham, England (★2,358,980) ... 1,004,030
Bogotá, Colombia (★3,143,200) ... 2,850,000
Bologna, Italy ... 493,639
Bombay, India ... 5,970,575
Bonn, Fed. Rep. of Ger. ... 285,138
Boston, Massachusetts (★2,763,357) ... 562,994
Brasília, Brazil ... 763,254
Bremen, Fed. Rep. of Ger. ... 558,942
Brisbane, Australia ... 892,987
Bristol, England ... 421,800
Brussels (Bruxelles), Belgium (★1,050,787) ... 153,409
Bucharest (Bucureşti), Romania (★1,934,025) ... 1,807,044
Budapest, Hungary ... 2,093,187
Buenos Aires, Argentina (★9,910,000) ... 2,983,000
Buffalo, New York (★1,242,573) ... 357,870

Cairo (Al Qāhirah), Egypt ... 6,133,000
Calcutta, India (★7,031,382) ... 3,148,746
Calgary, Canada ... 469,917
Cali, Colombia (★1,133,500) ... 898,253
Canberra, Australia ... 194,517
Canton (Kuangchou), China ... 1,840,000
Cape Town, South Africa (★1,096,597) ... 691,296
Caracas, Venezuela (★2,755,000) ... 1,279,600
Cardiff, Wales ... 276,880
Casablanca, Morocco ... 1,506,373
Ch'angch'un (Hsinking), China ... 1,000,000
Ch'angsha, China ... 300,000–1,000,000
Chelyabinsk, Soviet Union ... 1,031,000
Chengchou, China ... 300,000–1,000,000
Ch'engtu, China ... 1,107,000
Chicago, Illinois (★7,102,328) ... 3,005,072
Ch'ich'ihaerh (Tsitsihar), China ... 300,000–1,000,000
Chittagong, Bangladesh ... 889,760
Chungking (Ch'ungch'ing), China ... 2,121,000
Cincinnati, Ohio (★1,401,403) ... 385,457
Cleveland, Ohio (★1,898,720) ... 573,822
Cologne (Köln), Fed. Rep. of Ger. ... 976,534
Colombo, Sri Lanka ... 616,000
Columbus, Ohio (★1,093,293) ... 564,871
Copenhagen (København), Denmark (★1,268,426) ... 515,594
Córdoba, Argentina ... 798,663
Curitiba, Brazil (★1,013,279) ... 765,716

Dacca, Bangladesh ... 1,679,572
Dakar, Senegal ... 798,792
Dallas, Texas (★2,974,878) ... 904,078
Damascus (Dimashq), Syria ... 1,200,000
Davao, Philippines (★591,500) ... 484,678
Dayton, Ohio (★830,070) ... 203,588
Delhi, India (★3,647,023) ... 3,287,883
Denver, Colorado (★1,619,921) ... 491,396
Detroit, Michigan (★4,352,762) ... 1,203,339
Dnepropetrovsk, Soviet Union ... 1,066,000
Donetsk (Stalino), Soviet Union ... 1,021,000
Dortmund, Fed. Rep. of Ger. ... 612,769
Dresden, Ger. Dem. Rep. ... 514,508
Dublin (Baile Atha Cliath), Ireland ... 544,586
Durban, South Africa (★843,327) ... 495,458
Düsseldorf, Fed. Rep. of Ger. ... 600,057

Edinburgh, Scotland ... 467,097
El Paso, Texas (★479,899) ... 425,259
Eşfahān, Iran ... 618,000
Essen, Fed. Rep. of Ger. ... 658,358

Florence (Firenze), Italy ... 460,248
Fortaleza, Brazil (★1,317,496) ... 1,109,837
Frankfurt am Main, Fed. Rep. of Ger. ... 631,007
Fuchou (Foochow), China ... 300,000–1,000,000
Fukuoka, Japan ... 1,015,085
Fushun, China ... 300,000–1,000,000

Geneva (Genève), Switzerland (★322,900) ... 150,100
Genoa (Genova), Italy ... 815,708
Giza (Al Jīzah) ... 933,900
Glasgow, Scotland (★1,807,017) ... 856,012
Gorki (Gorkiy), Soviet Union ... 1,344,000
Guadalajara, Mexico (★2,075,773) ... 1,640,902
Guatemala, Guatemala ... 700,504
Guayaquil, Ecuador ... 814,064

Haerhpin (Harbin), China ... 1,552,000
Hamburg, Fed. Rep. of Ger. ... 1,664,305
Hangchou, China ... 300,000–1,000,000
Hannover (Hanover), Fed. Rep. of Ger. ... 538,243
Hanoi, Vietnam ... 1,443,500
Hartford Connecticut (★726,114) ... 136,392
Havana (La Habana), Cuba ... 1,900,240
Helsinki, Finland (★879,149) ... 499,205
Hiroshima, Japan ... 859,244
Ho Chi Minh City (Saigon), Vietnam ... 3,460,500
Honolulu, Hawaii (★762,874) ... 365,048
Houston, Texas (★2,905,350) ... 1,594,086
Hsian (Sian), China ... 1,310,000
Hsüchou (Süchow), China ... 300,000–1,000,000
Hyderābād, India (★1,796,339) ... 1,607,396

Ibadan, Nigeria ... 885,300
Inch'ŏn, Korea (South) ... 800,007
Indianapolis, Indiana (★1,166,929) ... 700,807
Indore, India ... 543,381
Irkutsk, Soviet Union ... 550,000
Istanbul, Turkey (★3,432,234) ... 2,547,364
Izmir, Turkey (★896,062) ... 636,834

Jacksonville, Florida (★737,519) ... 540,898
Jakarta (Batavia), Indonesia ... 5,490,000
Jerusalem, Israel ... 326,400
Johannesburg, South Africa (★1,432,643) ... 654,682

Kābul, Afghanistan ... 749,000
Kānpur, India (★1,275,242) ... 1,154,388
Kansas City, Missouri (★1,327,020) ... 448,159
Kaohsiung, Taiwan ... 828,191
Karāchi, Pakistan ... 3,515,402
Kātmāndu, Nepal ... 150,402
Katowice, Poland ... 349,700
Kawasaki, Japan ... 1,011,543
Kazan', Soviet Union ... 993,000
Khar'kov, Soviet Union ... 1,444,000
Khartoum, Sudan (★784,294) ... 333,906
Kiev, Soviet Union ... 2,144,000
Kingston, Jamaica (★506,200) ... 117,900
Kinshasa, Zaire ... 2,008,352
Kitakyūshū, Japan ... 1,056,983
Kōbe, Japan ... 1,343,375
Kowloon, Hong Kong ... 716,272
Kraków, Poland ... 693,200
Kuala Lumpur, Malaysia ... 1,072,000
K'unming, China ... 300,000–1,000,000
Kuybyshev, Soviet Union ... 1,216,000
Kyōto, Japan ... 1,449,805

Lagos, Nigeria ... 1,149,200
Lahore, Pakistan ... 2,169,742
Lanchou (Lanchow), China ... 300,000–1,000,000
La Paz, Bolivia ... 654,713
La Plata, Argentina ... 506,287
Leeds, England (★1,735,700) ... 500,200
Leipzig, Ger. Dem. Rep. ... 563,980
Leningrad, Soviet Union (★4,588,000) ... 4,073,000
Lille, France (★935,882) ... 172,280
Lima, Peru (★3,254,789) ... 2,941,473
Lisbon (Lisboa), Portugal (★1,635,400) ... 757,700
Liverpool, England (★1,226,310) ... 574,560
Łódź, Poland ... 825,200
London, England ... 7,028,200
Los Angeles, California (★7,477,657) ... 2,966,763
Louisville, Kentucky (★906,240) ... 298,415
Luanda, Angola ... 600,000
Lucknow, India (★813,982) ... 749,239
Lüta (Dairen), China ... 1,508,000
Luxembourg, Luxembourg ... 78,400
L'vov, Soviet Union ... 667,000
Lyallpur, Pakistan ... 823,343
Lyon, France (★1,170,660) ... 456,716

Madras, India (★3,169,930) ... 2,469,449
Madrid, Spain ... 3,201,234
Managua, Nicaragua ... 677,680
Manchester, England (★2,389,260) ... 530,580
Mandalay, Burma ... 472,512
Manila, Philippines (★4,970,006) ... 1,479,116
Mannheim, Fed. Rep. of Ger. ... 302,794
Maracaibo, Venezuela ... 845,000
Marseille, France (★1,070,912) ... 908,600
Mecca (Makkah), Saudi Arabia ... 366,801
Medan, Indonesia ... 700,363
Medellín, Colombia ... 1,064,741
Melbourne, Australia ... 2,479,422
Memphis, Tennessee (★912,887) ... 646,356
Mexico City, Mexico (★13,993,866) ... 8,988,230
Miami, Florida (★1,625,979) ... 346,931
Milan (Milano), Italy ... 1,738,487
Milwaukee, Wisconsin (★1,397,143) ... 636,212
Minneapolis, Minnesota (★2,114,256) ... 370,951
Minsk, Soviet Union (★1,276,000) ... 1,262,000
Mogadisho (Mogadiscio), Somalia ... 444,882
Monterrey, Mexico (★1,725,013) ... 1,090,226
Montevideo, Uruguay ... 1,229,750
Montréal, Canada (★2,802,485) ... 1,080,546
Moscow (Moskva), Soviet Union (★8,011,000) ... 7,831,000
Mukden (Shenyang), China ... 2,411,000
Multān, Pakistan ... 538,949
Munich (München), Fed. Rep. of Ger. ... 1,296,970

Nagoya, Japan ... 2,080,666
Nāgpur, India (★930,459) ... 866,076
Nairobi, Kenya ... 863,000
Nanking, (Nanching), China ... 1,419,000
Naples (Napoli), Italy ... 1,223,659
Newark, New Jersey (★1,965,304) ... 329,248
Newcastle-on-Tyne, England (★788,130) ... 212,430
New Delhi, India ... 301,801
New Orleans, Louisiana (★1,186,725) ... 557,482
New York, New York (★9,119,737) ... 7,071,030
Norfolk, Virginia (★795,602) ... 266,979
Novosibirsk, Soviet Union ... 1,312,000
Nürnberg (Nuremberg, Fed. Rep. of Ger.) ... 485,801

Odessa, Soviet Union ... 1,046,000
Oklahoma City, Oklahoma (★834,088) ... 403,213
Omaha, Nebraska (★570,399) ... 311,681
Omsk, Soviet Union ... 1,014,000
Osaka, Japan ... 2,600,001
Oslo, Norway (★541,190) ... 460,377
Ottawa, Canada (★693,288) ... 304,462

Palembang, Indonesia ... 642,416
Palermo, Italy ... 650,113
Panamá, Panama (★794,300) ... 465,160
Paris, France (★8,549,898) ... 2,299,830
Peking (Peiching), China ... 7,570,000
Perm', Soviet Union ... 999,000
Perth, Australia ... 731,275
Philadelphia, Pennsylvania (★4,716,818) ... 1,688,210
Phoenix, Arizona (★1,508,030) ... 764,911
Pittsburgh, Pennsylvania (★2,263,894) ... 423,938
Port-au-Prince, Haiti (★475,187) ... 386,250
Portland, Oregon (★1,242,187) ... 366,383
Pôrto (Oporto), Portugal (★1,341,000) ... 304,000
Pôrto Alegre, Brazil (★1,836,179) ... 1,043,964
Poznań, Poland ... 536,400
Prague (Praha), Czechoslovakia ... 1,188,573
Pretoria, South Africa (★561,703) ... 543,950
Providence, Rhode Island (★919,216) ... 156,804
Pune, India (★1,135,034) ... 856,105
Pusan, Korea (South) ... 2,450,125
P'yŏngyang, Korea (North) ... 2,500,000

Québec, Canada (★542,158) ... 177,082
Quezon City, Philippines ... 956,864
Quito, Ecuador ... 597,133

Rabat, Morocco ... 367,620
Rangoon, Burma (★2,452,881) ... 1,315,964
Rawalpindi, Pakistan ... 614,809
Recife (Pernambuco), Brazil (★2,153,435) ... 1,249,821
Rīga, Soviet Union ... 835,000
Rio de Janeiro, Brazil (★8,328,784) ... 4,857,716
Riyadh, Saudi Arabia ... 666,840
Rochester, New York (★971,879) ... 241,741
Rome (Roma), Italy ... 2,868,248
Rosario, Argentina ... 810,840
Rostov-na-Donu, Soviet Union ... 934,000
Rotterdam, Netherlands (★1,032,152) ... 620,867

Sacramento, California (★1,014,002) ... 275,741
St. Louis, Missouri (★2,355,276) ... 435,085
St. Paul, Minnesota (★2,114,256) ... 270,230
Salisbury, Zimbabwe ... 557,000
Salt Lake City, Utah (★936,255) ... 163,033
Salvador, Brazil (★1,401,228) ... 1,237,373
San Antonio, Texas (★1,071,954) ... 785,410
San Bernardino, California (★1,557,080) ... 118,057
San Diego, California (★1,861,846) ... 875,504
San Francisco, California (★3,252,721) ... 678,974
San José, Costa Rica (★438,658) ... 215,441
San Juan, Puerto Rico (★1,083,664) ... 422,701
San Salvador, El Salvador ... 397,126
Santiago, Chile ... 3,899,495
Santo Domingo, Dominican Rep. ... 673,470
São Paulo, Brazil (★10,041,132) ... 8,407,500
Sapporo, Japan ... 1,319,007
Saratov, Soviet Union ... 856,000
Seattle, Washington (★1,606,765) ... 493,846
Semarang, Indonesia ... 689,832
Sendai, Japan ... 627,500
Seoul, Korea (South) ... 6,889,502
Sevilla, Spain ... 590,235
Shanghai, China ... 10,820,000
Sheffield, England ... 511,860
Singapore, Singapore ... 2,308,200
Sofia (Sofiya), Bulgaria (★1,064,712) ... 965,729
Soochow (Wuhsien), China ... 300,000–1,000,000
Stockholm, Sweden (★1,374,922) ... 658,435
Stuttgart, Fed. Rep. of Ger. ... 583,700
Surabaya, Indonesia ... 1,660,355
Sverdlovsk, Soviet Union ... 1,211,000
Sydney, Australia ... 2,765,040

Tabrīz, Iran ... 571,000
Taegu, Korea (South) ... 1,310,768
Taipei, Taiwan ... 1,839,640
T'aiyüan (Yangkü), China ... 300,000–1,000,000
Tangshan, China ... 300,000–1,000,000
Tashkent, Soviet Union ... 1,779,000
Tbilisi, Soviet Union ... 1,066,000
Tegucigalpa, Honduras ... 267,754
Tehrān, Iran ... 4,716,000
Tel Aviv-Yafo, Israel (★1,180,700) ... 367,600
The Hague ('s Gravenhage), Netherlands (★678,905) ... 482,879
Tientsin (T'ienching), China ... 4,280,000
Tiranë, Albania ... 192,300
Tōkyō, Japan (★11,683,613) ... 8,219,888
Toronto, Canada (★2,803,101) ... 633,318
Tripoli, (Tarābulus), Libya (★735,083) ... 551,477
Tsinan (Chinan), China ... 1,000,000
Tsingtao (Ch'ingtao), China ... 1,121,000
Tunis, Tunisia (★647,640) ... 1,000,000
Turin (Torino), Italy ... 1,172,476

Ufa, Soviet Union ... 969,000
Ulaan Baatar, Mongolia ... 402,900

Valencia, Spain ... 714,086
Valencia, Venezuela ... 471,000
Vancouver, Canada (★1,166,348) ... 410,188
Vārānāsi (Benares), India (★606,271) ... 583,856
Venice (Venezia), Italy ... 363,540
Viangchan, Laos ... 181,000
Victoria, Hong Kong ... 520,932
Vienna (Wien), Austria ... 1,614,841
Vladivostok, Soviet Union ... 550,000
Volgograd (Stalingrad), Soviet Union ... 929,000

Warsaw (Warszawa), Poland ... 1,552,400
Washington, D.C. (★3,060,240) ... 637,651
Wellington, New Zealand ... 327,414
Winnipeg, Canada (★578,217) ... 560,874
Wrocław (Breslau), Poland ... 597,700
Wuhan, China ... 2,146,000
Wuppertal, Fed. Rep. of Ger. ... 396,125

Yerevan, Soviet Union ... 1,019,000
Yokohama, Japan ... 2,723,940

Zagreb, Yugoslavia ... 566,224
Zaragoza (Saragossa), Spain ... 540,308
Zürich, Switzerland (★707,500) ... 379,600

★Population of metropolitan area, including suburbs.
Population figures are from the 1982 edition of *The World Book Encyclopedia*. They are based on censuses and estimates from official government and United Nations sources.

This index includes the more important cities, towns and other localities that appear on the maps on pages 52–69. For a complete list of abbreviations, see page 246. If a page contains several maps, a lowercase letter identifies the particular map to which the entry is indexed.

A

Page	Name Region	Lat. °′	Long. °′
66h	'abbāsābād	35·44 N	51·25 E
60	Abbey Wood (Neigh.)	51·29 N	0·08 E
60	Abbots Langley	51·43 N	0·25 W
69a	'abd al-Shāhid	29·55 N	31·13 E
66c	Aberdeen (Xianggangzi)	22·15 N	114·09 E
54b	Abington	40·07 N	75·08 W
62c	Ablon-sur-Seine	48·43 N	2·25 E
63d	Abóbada	38·43 N	9·20 W
64b	Abramcevo	55·50 N	37·50 E
60	Abridge	51·39 N	0·07 E
63d	Abrunheira	38·46 N	9·21 W
69a	Abū an-Numrus	29·57 N	31·12 E
69a	Abū Şir Pyramids (P. Int.)	29·54 N	31·12 E
52a	Accord	42·10 N	70·53 W
60	Acton (Neigh.)	51·30 N	0·16 W
67a	Adachi (Neigh.)	35·45 N	139·48 E
60	Addington	51·18 N	0·23 E
60	Addlestone	51·22 N	0·30 W
69a	Ad-Duqqī	30·04 N	31·15 E
54d	Adelphi	39·00 N	76·58 W
64e	Aderklaa	48·17 N	16·32 E
63a	Adlershof (Neigh.)	52·26 N	13·33 E
69d	Agege	6·37 N	3·20 E
52c	Agincourt (Neigh.)	43·48 N	79·17 W
59c	Agostinho Pôrto	22·47 S	43·23 W
58a	Agrícola Oriental	19·24 N	99·05 W
58b	Aguacate	22·59 N	81·49 W
63d	Agualva-Cacém	38·46 N	9·18 W
61	Ahlenberg	51·25 N	7·28 E
63a	Ahrensfelde	52·35 N	13·35 E
52b	Ahuntsic (Neigh.)	45·33 N	73·39 W
62b	Aigburth (Neigh.)	53·22 N	2·55 W
62b	Ainsworth	53·35 N	2·22 W
62b	Aintree	53·29 N	2·56 W
68b	Airport West	37·44 S	144·53 E
64d	Aiyáleo	37·59 N	23·41 E
63d	Ajuda (Neigh.)	38·43 N	9·12 W
66h	Akbarābād	35·41 N	51·21 E
67a	Akishima	35·41 N	139·22 E
64d	Akrópolis (P. Int.)	37·58 N	23·43 E
69d	Alaguntan	6·26 N	3·30 E
56b	Alameda	37·46 N	122·16 W
56b	Albany	37·53 N	122·18 W
56a	Albany Park (Neigh.)	41·58 N	87·43 W
69a	Al-Barājīl	30·04 N	31·09 E
64g	Albertfalva (Neigh.)	47·27 N	19·02 E
69b	Alberton	26·16 S	28·08 E
53	Albertson	40·46 N	73·39 W
69b	Albertville (Neigh.)	26·10 S	27·59 E
68b	Albion	37·47 S	144·49 E
63d	Alcântara (Neigh.)	38·42 N	9·10 W
59d	Aldeia	23·30 S	46·51 W
59d	Aldeia de Carapicuiba	23·35 S	46·48 W
60	Aldenham	51·40 N	0·21 W
61	Aldenrade (Neigh.)	51·31 N	6·44 E
69b	Alexandra	26·06 S	28·05 E
54d	Alexandria	38·48 N	77·03 W
62c	Alfortville	48·49 N	2·25 E
63d	Algés	38·42 N	9·13 W
63d	Alguierão-Mem Martins	38·48 N	9·20 W
57	Alhambra	34·06 N	118·08 W
69a	Al-Ḩawāmidīyah	29·54 N	31·15 E
65a	Alipore (Neigh.)	22·31 N	88·18 E
69a	Al-Jīzah (Giza)	30·01 N	31·13 E
69a	Al-Kunayyisah	29·59 N	31·11 E
55b	Allegheny (R.)	40·27 N	80·00 W
55c	Allen Park	42·15 N	83·13 W
52a	Allerton	42·18 N	70·53 W
62b	Allerton (Neigh.)	53·22 N	2·53 W
55b	Allison Park	40·34 N	79·57 W
69a	Al-lmām (Neigh.)	30·01 N	31·10 E
52a	Allston (Neigh.)	42·22 N	71·08 W
63d	Almada	38·41 N	9·09 W
69a	Al-Manāwāt	29·55 N	31·14 E
69a	Al-Marj (Neigh.)	30·09 N	31·20 E
57	Alondra	33·54 N	118·19 W
53	Alpine	40·56 N	73·56 W
56a	Alsip	41·40 N	87·44 W
57	Altadena	34·12 N	118·08 W
65b	Altar of Heaven (P. Int.)	39·53 N	116·25 E
65b	Altar of the Earth (P. Int.)	39·57 N	116·24 E
65b	Altar of the Moon (P. Int.)	39·55 N	116·20 E
65b	Altar of the Sun (P. Int.)	39·54 N	116·27 E
61	Altenderne Oberbecker (Neigh.)	51·35 N	7·33 E
61	Altenessen (Neigh.)	51·29 N	7·00 E
61	Altenhagen (Neigh.)	51·22 N	7·28 E
61	Altenvoerde	51·18 N	7·22 E
61	Altlünen	51·38 N	7·31 E
64e	Altmannsdorf (Neigh.)	48·10 N	16·20 E
59d	Alto da Mooca (Neigh.)	23·34 S	46·35 W
68b	Altona	37·52 S	144·50 E
68b	Altona B.	37·52 S	144·52 E
68b	Altona North	37·50 S	144·51 E
62b	Altrincham	53·24 N	2·21 W
62b	Alvanley	53·16 N	2·45 W
63d	Amadora	38·45 N	9·14 W
67b	Amagasaki	34·43 N	135·25 E
65c	Ama Keng	1·24 N	103·42 E
64d	Amaroúsion	38·03 N	23·49 E
63d	Ameixoeira (Neigh.)	38·47 N	9·10 W
60	Amersham	51·40 N	0·38 W
55a	Amherst	42·58 N	78·48 W
54d	Anacostia (Neigh.)	38·52 N	76·59 W
57	Anaheim	33·51 N	117·57 W
62c	Andrésy	48·59 N	2·04 E
54d	Andrews Air Force Base (P. Int.)	38·48 N	76·52 W
61	Angerhausen (Neigh.)	51·23 N	6·44 E
61	Angermund	51·20 N	6·47 E
66g	Angono	14·31 N	121·08 E
64g	Angyalföld (Neigh.)	47·33 N	19·05 E
65e	Anik (Neigh.)	19·02 N	72·53 E
52b	Anjou	45·36 N	73·33 W
54d	Annandale	38·50 N	77·12 W
69a	An-Narrānīyah	29·58 N	31·10 E
61	Annen (Neigh.)	51·27 N	7·22 E
62c	Annet-sur-Marne	48·56 N	2·43 E
61	Anschlag	51·10 N	7·29 E
58a	Antiguo Lago de Texcoco, Vaso del (L.)	19·30 N	99·00 W
59a	Antimano (Neigh.)	10·28 N	66·59 W
62c	Antony	48·45 N	2·18 E
69b	Antwerp	26·06 S	28·10 E
69d	Apese (Neigh.)	6·25 N	3·25 E
61	Aplerbeck (Neigh.)	51·29 N	7·33 E
59b	Apoquindo	33·24 S	70·32 W
67a	Ara (R.)	35·39 N	139·51 E
67a	Arakawa (Neigh.)	35·47 N	139·44 E
65d	Arakpur (Neigh.)	28·35 N	77·10 E
63b	Aravaca (Neigh.)	40·28 N	3·46 W
57	Arcadia	34·08 N	118·01 W
62c	Arc de Triomphe (P. Int.)	48·53 N	2·17 E
62c	Arcueil	48·48 N	2·20 E
61	Ardey (Neigh.)	51·26 N	7·23 E
54d	Ardmore, Md.	38·56 N	76·52 W
54b	Ardmore, Pa.	40·01 N	75·18 W
63d	Areeiro	38·39 N	9·12 W
62c	Argenteuil	48·57 N	2·15 E
67b	Arima (Neigh.)	34·48 N	135·15 E
67b	Arino (Neigh.)	34·50 N	135·14 E
52a	Arlington, Ma.	42·25 N	71·09 W
54d	Arlington, Va.	38·52 N	77·05 W
54d	Arlington National Cemetery (P. Int.)	38·53 N	77·04 W
62c	Arnouville-lès-Gonesse	49·00 N	2·25 E
58b	Arroyo Arenas	23·02 N	82·28 W
68a	Artarmon	33·49 S	151·11 E
57	Artesia	33·52 N	118·05 W
59a	Artigas (Neigh.)	10·30 N	66·56 W
54c	Arundel Gardens	39·13 N	76·37 W
54c	Arundel Village	39·13 N	76·36 W
67a	Asaka	35·48 N	139·36 E
65d	Asālafpur (Neigh.)	28·38 N	77·05 E
68a	Ashfield	33·53 S	151·08 E
60	Ashford	51·26 N	0·27 W
67b	Ashiya	34·43 N	135·17 E
62b	Ashley	53·21 N	2·20 W
60	Ashley Green	51·44 N	0·35 W
60	Ashtead	51·19 N	0·18 W
62b	Ashton-under-Lyne	53·29 N	2·06 W
62b	Ashton upon Mersey	53·26 N	2·19 W
62c	Asnières [-sur-Seine]	48·55 N	2·17 E
64e	Aspern (Neigh.)	48·13 N	16·29 E
55b	Aspinwall	40·30 N	79·55 W
61	Asseln (Neigh.)	51·32 N	7·35 E
62b	Astley Bridge	53·36 N	2·26 W
53	Astoria (Neigh.)	40·46 N	73·55 W
64d	Athens (Athínai	37·58 N	23·43 E
62c	Athis-Mons	48·43 N	2·24 E
58a	Atizapán de Zaragoza	19·33 N	99·15 W
53	Atlantic Beach	40·35 N	73·44 W
67a	Atsugi	35·27 N	139·22 E
65d	Atta	28·34 N	77·20 E
69a	Aṭ-Ṭalibiyah	30·00 N	31·11 E
65d	Atzalpur	28·43 N	77·21 E
64e	Atzgersdorf (Neigh.)	48·09 N	16·18 E
62c	Aubervilliers	48·55 N	2·23 E
68a	Auburn	33·51 S	151·02 E
52a	Auburndale	42·21 N	71·22 W
69b	Auckland Park (Neigh.)	26·11 S	28·00 E
62b	Audenshaw	53·28 N	2·08 W
54b	Audubon	40·07 N	75·27 W
61	Auf dem Kreinberge	51·27 N	7·36 E
61	Auf dem Schnee (Neigh.)	51·26 N	7·25 E
62b	Aughton	53·32 N	2·56 W
62b	Aughton Park	53·33 N	2·53 W
62c	Aulnay-sous-Bois	48·57 N	2·31 E
62c	Austerlitz (P. Int.)	48·50 N	2·22 E
56a	Austin (Neigh.)	41·54 N	87·45 W
68a	Austral	33·56 S	150·48 E
55b	Avalon	40·30 N	80·04 W
62b	Avanley	53·16 N	2·45 W
60	Aveley	51·30 N	0·16 E
58d	Avellaneda	34·40 S	58·20 W
53	Avenel	40·35 N	74·17 W
57	Avocado Heights	34·03 N	118·00 W
68b	Avondale Heights	37·46 S	144·51 E
66h	Awīn	35·48 N	51·24 E
69a	Awsīm	30·07 N	31·08 E
67a	Ayase	35·26 N	139·26 E
64d	Ayia Varvára	37·59 N	23·39 E
65d	Azādpur (Neigh.)	28·43 N	77·11 E
58a	Azcapotzalco	19·28 N	99·12 W
57	Azusa	34·08 N	117·55 W
69a	Az-Zamālik (Neigh.)	30·04 N	31·13 E

B

Page	Name Region	Lat. °′	Long. °′
61	Baak	51·25 N	7·10 E
65d	Bābarpur (Neigh.)	28·41 N	77·17 E
63a	Babelsberg (Neigh.)	52·24 N	13·05 E
52a	Babson Park	42·18 N	71·23 W
64b	Babuškin (Neigh.)	55·52 N	37·42 E
52a	Back Bay (Neigh.)	42·21 N	71·05 W
65e	Back B.	18·56 N	72·49 E
69c	Bacongo	4·18 S	15·16 E
63e	Badalona	41·27 N	2·15 E
60	Badger's Mount	51·20 N	0·09 E
65d	Bādli	28·45 N	77·09 E
61	Baerl	51·29 N	6·41 E
62c	Bagneux	48·48 N	2·18 E
62c	Bagnolet	48·52 N	2·25 E
69a	Bahtīm	30·08 N	31·17 E
65a	Baidyabāti	22·47 N	88·20 E
54d	Baileys Crossroads	38·51 N	77·08 W
65a	Bainchipota	22·52 N	88·16 E
65b	Baiyunguan	39·54 N	116·19 E
60	Baker Street	51·30 N	0·21 E
64f	Bakırköy (Neigh.)	40·59 N	28·52 E
54b	Bala-Cynwyd	40·00 N	75·14 W
53	Baldwin, NY.	40·39 N	73·37 W
55b	Baldwin, Pa.	40·23 N	79·58 W
57	Baldwin Park	34·06 N	117·58 W
68a	Balgowlah	33·48 S	151·16 E
65a	Bālihāti	22·44 N	88·19 E
65b	Balizhuang	39·52 N	116·28 E
65a	Ballabhpur	22·44 N	88·21 E
58b	Ballenato, Punta (C.)	23·06 N	82·30 W
65a	Ballygunge (Neigh.)	22·31 N	88·21 E
68a	Balmain	33·51 S	151·11 E
54c	Baltimore	39·17 N	76·37 W
54c	Baltimore Highlands	39·14 N	76·38 W
68b	Balwyn	37·49 S	145·05 E
65b	Banbidian	39·54 N	116·32 E
65a	Bāndel	22·56 N	88·22 E
66k	Bandir C.	6·11 S	106·49 E
65e	Bāndra (Neigh.)	19·03 N	72·49 E
66f	Bang Khun Thian	13·42 N	100·28 E
66f	Bangkok (Krung Thep)	13·45 N	100·31 E
59c	Bangu (Neigh.)	22·52 S	44·27 W
69a	Bani Majdūl	30·02 N	31·07 E
66f	Ban Khlong Samrong	13·39 N	100·36 E
68a	Banks, C.	34·00 S	151·15 E
68a	Banksmeadow	33·58 S	151·13 E
68a	Bankstown	33·55 S	151·02 E
66f	Ban Lat Phrao	13·47 N	100·36 E
65a	Banstala	22·32 N	88·25 E
60	Banstead	51·19 N	0·12 W
66m	Ba-queo	10·48 N	106·38 E
65a	Bara	22·46 N	88·17 E
69b	Baragwanath	26·16 S	27·59 E
63b	Barajas de Madrid (Neigh.)	40·28 N	3·35 E
65a	Baranagar	22·38 N	88·22 E
65a	Bārāsat	22·51 N	88·22 E
63d	Barcarena	38·44 N	9·17 W
63e	Barcelona	41·23 N	2·11 E
63b	Barcelona (Neigh.)	40·22 N	3·34 E
54d	Barcroft, Lake (Res.)	38·51 N	77·09 W
54c	Bare Hills	39·23 N	76·40 W
65a	Bariti Bil (L.)	22·48 N	88·26 E
60	Barking (Neigh.)	51·33 N	0·06 E
60	Barkingside (Neigh.)	51·36 N	0·05 E
61	Barmen (Neigh.)	51·17 N	7·13 E
60	Barnes (Neigh.)	51·28 N	0·15 W
62b	Barnston	53·21 N	3·05 W
53	Barnum Island	40·36 N	73·39 W
58d	Barracas (Neigh.)	34·38 S	58·22 W
65a	Barrackpore	22·46 N	88·21 E
65a	Barrackpore Cantonment	22·46 N	88·22 E
59d	Barra Funda (Neigh.)	23·31 S	46·39 W
59b	Barrancas	33·27 S	70·46 W
58c	Barranco	12·09 S	77·02 W
63d	Barreiro	38·40 N	9·05 W
63e	Barriada Pomar Alto	41·29 N	2·14 E
54b	Barrington	39·52 N	75·04 W
58c	Barrio Obrero Industrial	12·04 S	77·04 W
59a	Baruta	10·26 N	66·53 W
65d	Basai Dārāpur (Neigh.)	28·40 N	77·08 E
69a	Bashtīl	30·05 N	31·11 E
60	Basildon	51·35 N	0·25 E
68a	Bass Hill	33·54 S	151·00 E
65a	Bāsudebpur	22·49 N	88·25 E
61	Batenbrock (Neigh.)	51·31 N	6·57 E
60	Battersea (Neigh.)	51·28 N	0·10 W
61	Bauernschaft	51·34 N	6·33 E
55b	Bauerstown	40·30 N	79·59 W
61	Baukau (Neigh.)	51·33 N	7·12 E
68a	Baulkham Hills	33·46 S	151·00 E
63a	Baumschulenweg (Neigh.)	52·28 N	13·29 E
60	Bayford	51·46 N	0·06 W
53	Bayonne	40·41 N	74·07 W
53	Bay Park	40·38 N	73·40 W
53	Bay Ridge (Neigh.)	40·37 N	74·02 W
52a	Bayside	42·18 N	70·53 W
53	Bayside (Neigh.)	40·46 N	73·46 W
68b	Bayswater	37·51 S	145·16 E
68b	Bayswater North	37·49 S	145·17 E
56b	Bayview (Neigh.)	37·44 N	122·23 W
54a	Bay Village	41·29 N	81·55 W
53	Bayville	40·54 N	73·33 W
54a	Beachwood	41·34 N	81·28 W
68a	Beacon Hill	33·45 S	151·15 E
66c	Beacon H.	22·21 N	114·09 E
52b	Beaconsfield	0·00	0·00
60	Bean	51·25 N	0·17 E
63d	Beato (Neigh.)	38·44 N	9·06 W
64f	Bebek (Neigh.)	41·04 N	29·02 E
62b	Bebington	53·23 N	3·01 W
58d	Beccar (Neigh.)	34·28 S	58·31 W
60	Beckenham (Neigh.)	51·24 N	0·02 W
60	Beddington (Neigh.)	51·22 N	0·08 W
52a	Bedford, Ma.	42·29 N	71·17 W
54a	Bedford, Oh.	41·23 N	81·32 W
54a	Bedford Heights	41·22 N	81·30 W
56a	Bedford Park	41·46 N	87·49 W
53	Bedford Park (Neigh.)	40·52 N	73·53 W
53	Bedford-Stuyvesant (Neigh.)	40·41 N	73·55 W
60	Bedmond	51·43 N	0·25 W
65c	Bedok	1·19 N	103·57 E
55b	Beechview (Neigh.)	40·25 N	80·02 W
61	Beeck (Neigh.)	51·29 N	6·44 E
61	Beeckerwerth (Neigh.)	51·29 N	6·41 E
65a	Behāla (South Suburban)	22·31 N	88·19 E
65b	Beiyuan	40·01 N	116·24 E
54d	Bel Air	38·52 N	77·10 W
57	Bel Air (Neigh.)	34·05 N	118·27 W
63d	Belas	38·47 N	9·16 W
59d	Bela Vista (Neigh.)	23·33 S	46·38 W
63d	Belém (Neigh.)	38·42 N	9·12 W
59d	Belenzinho (Neigh.)	23·32 S	46·35 W
59c	Belford Roxo	22·46 S	43·24 W
58d	Belgrano (Neigh.)	34·34 S	58·28 W
68b	Belgrave	37·55 S	145·21 E
57	Bell	33·58 N	118·11 W
58d	Bella Vista, Arg.	34·32 S	58·40 W
59b	Bellavista, Chile	33·31 S	70·37 W
58c	Bellavista, Peru	12·04 S	77·08 W
54c	Belle Farm Estates	39·23 N	76·45 W
54d	Bellehaven	38·47 N	77·04 W
53	Bellerose	40·44 N	73·43 W
53	Belleville	40·48 N	74·09 W
55b	Bellevue	40·30 N	80·03 W
57	Bellflower	33·53 N	118·07 W
57	Bell Gardens	33·58 N	118·09 W
54b	Bellmawr	39·51 N	75·06 W
53	Bellmore	40·40 N	73·32 W
58b	Bello	23·07 N	82·24 W
56a	Bellwood	41·53 N	87·52 W
56b	Belmont, Ca.	37·31 N	122·17 W
52a	Belmont, Ma.	42·24 N	71·10 W
68a	Belmore	33·55 S	151·05 E
58b	Belot	23·08 N	82·19 W
56b	Belvedere, Ca.	37·52 N	122·28 W
54d	Belvedere, Va.	38·50 N	77·10 W
60	Belvedere (Neigh.)	51·29 N	0·09 E
64e	Belvedere (P. Int.)	48·11 N	16·23 E
55b	Ben Avon	40·31 N	80·05 W
59c	Benfica (Neigh.), Braz.	22·53 S	43·15 W
63d	Benfica (Neigh.), Port.	38·45 N	9·12 W
68b	Bennettswood	37·51 S	145·07 E
61	Benninghofen (Neigh.)	51·29 N	7·31 E
69b	Benoni	26·12 S	28·18 E
69b	Benoni South	26·13 S	28·18 E
61	Benrath (Neigh.)	51·10 N	6·52 E
56a	Bensenville	41·57 N	87·57 W
53	Bensonhurst (Neigh.)	40·35 N	73·59 W
68b	Bentleigh	37·55 S	145·02 E

C

Page	Name Region	Lat. °′	Long. °′
64b	Čer'omuski (Neigh.)	55·41 N	37·35 E
64b	Čertanovo (Neigh.)	55·38 N	37·37 E
63c	Cesano Boscone	45·27 N	9·06 E
59a	Chacao	10·30 N	66·51 W
62b	Chadderton	53·33 N	2·08 W
68b	Chadstone	37·53 S	145·05 E
60	Chadwell Saint Mary	51·29 N	0·22 E
65a	Chakdaha	22·20 N	88·20 E
60	Chaldon	51·17 N	0·07 W
55b	Chalfant	40·25 N	79·52 W
60	Chalfont Common	51·38 N	0·33 W
60	Chalfont Saint Giles	51·38 N	0·34 W
60	Chalfont Saint Peter	51·37 N	0·33 W
60	Chalk	51·26 N	0·25 E
62c	Chambourcy	48·54 N	2·03 E
65a	Champdāni	22·48 N	88·21 E
62c	Champigny-sur-Marne	48·49 N	2·31 E
62c	Champlan	48·43 N	2·16 E
62c	Champs-sur-Marne	48·51 N	2·36 E
65a	Chāmrāil	22·38 N	88·18 E
65a	Chandannagar	22·51 N	88·21 E
60	Chandler's Cross	51·40 N	0·27 W
65b	Changdian	40·01 N	116·32 E
65c	Changi	1·23 N	103·59 E
65b	Changxindianzhen	39·49 N	116·12 E
66m	Chanh-hung	10·43 N	106·41 E
62c	Chanteloup-les-Vignes	48·59 N	2·02 E
66f	Chao Phraya (R.)	13·39 N	100·31 E
54d	Chapel Oaks	38·54 N	76·55 W
62b	Chapeltown	53·38 N	2·24 W
57	Chapman Woods	34·08 N	118·05 W
58a	Chapultepec, Castillo de (P. Int.)	19·25 N	99·11 W
62c	Charenton-le-Pont	48·49 N	2·25 E
52a	Charles (R.)	42·22 N	71·03 W
62c	Charles de Gaulle, Aéroport (Arpt.)	49·00 N	2·34 E
63a	Charlottenburg (Neigh.)	52·31 N	13·16 E
63a	Charlottenburg, Schloss (P. Int.)	52·31 N	13·14 E
60	Charlton (Neigh.)	51·29 N	0·02 E
63d	Charneca (Neigh.)	38·47 N	9·08 W
55b	Charterwood	40·33 N	80·00 W
62c	Châteaufort	48·44 N	2·06 E
62c	Châtenay-Malabry	48·46 N	2·17 E
62c	Châtillon	48·48 N	2·17 E
62c	Chatou	48·54 N	2·09 E
65a	Chatpur (Neigh.)	22·36 N	88·23 E
68a	Chatswood	33·48 S	151·12 E
62c	Chavenay	48·51 N	1·59 E
62c	Chaville	48·48 N	2·10 E
62b	Cheadle	53·24 N	2·13 W
62b	Cheadle Hulme	53·22 N	2·12 W
60	Cheam (Neigh.)	51·21 N	0·13 W
55a	Cheektowaga	42·55 N	78·46 W
62b	Cheetham Hill (Neigh.)	53·31 N	2·15 W
63d	Chelas (Neigh.)	38·45 N	9·07 W
62c	Chelles	48·53 N	2·36 E
60	Chelmsford	51·44 N	0·28 E
52a	Chelsea	42·24 N	71·02 W
68b	Cheltenham, Austl.	37·58 S	145·03 E
65e	Chembūr (Neigh.)	19·04 N	72·54 E
60	Chenies	51·41 N	0·32 W
62c	Chennevières	49·00 N	2·07 E
55b	Cherry City	40·29 N	79·58 W
55b	Cherry Hill	39·55 N	75·01 W
54c	Cherry Hill (Neigh.)	39·15 N	76·38 W
60	Chertsey	51·24 N	0·30 W
60	Chesham	51·43 N	0·38 W
60	Chesham Bois	51·41 N	0·37 W
60	Cheshunt	51·43 N	0·02 W
60	Chessington (Neigh.)	51·21 N	0·18 W
54b	Chester	39·51 N	75·21 W
54d	Chesterbrook	38·55 N	77·09 W
52a	Chestnut Hill, Ma.	42·20 N	71·10 W
54c	Chestnut Hill, Md.	39·17 N	76·47 W
55b	Cheswick	40·32 N	79·47 W
60	Chevening	51·18 N	0·08 E
54d	Cheverly	38·55 N	76·55 W
62c	Chevilly-Larue	48·46 N	2·21 E
62c	Chevreuse	48·42 N	2·03 E
54d	Chevy Chase	38·58 N	77·05 W
54d	Chevy Chase View	39·01 N	77·05 W
65d	Chhalera Bāngar	28·33 N	77·20 E
65a	Chhināmor	22·48 N	88·18 E
56a	Chicago	41·53 N	87·38 W
56a	Chicago, North Branch (R.)	41·53 N	87·38 W
56a	Chicago Lawn (Neigh.)	41·47 N	87·41 W
56a	Chicago-O'Hare International Arpt.	41·59 N	87·54 W
56a	Chicago Ridge	41·42 N	87·47 W
56a	Chicago Sanitary and Ship Canal (Can.)	41·42 N	87·58 W
60	Chignall Saint James	51·46 N	0·25 E
60	Chigwell	51·38 N	0·05 E
60	Chigwell Row	51·37 N	0·07 E
62b	Childer Thornton	53·17 N	2·57 W
54d	Chillum	38·58 N	76·59 W
62c	Chilly-Mazarin	48·42 N	2·19 E
64b	Chimki	55·54 N	37·26 E
64b	Chimki-Chovrino (Neigh.)	55·51 N	37·30 E
56b	Chinatown (Neigh.)	37·48 N	122·26 W
60	Chingford (Neigh.)	51·38 N	0·01 E
66d	Chingmei	24·59 N	121·32 E
60	Chipperfield	51·42 N	0·29 W
60	Chipping Ongar	51·43 N	0·15 E
60	Chipstead, Eng.	51·18 N	0·10 W
60	Chipstead, Eng.	51·17 N	0·09 E
65d	Chirāgh Delhi (Neigh.)	28·32 N	77·14 E
60	Chislehurst (Neigh.)	51·25 N	0·04 E
60	Chiswellgreen	51·44 N	0·22 W
60	Chiswick (Neigh.)	51·29 N	0·16 W
65c	Choa Chu Kang	1·22 N	103·41 E
60	Chobham	51·21 N	0·36 W
67a	Chōfu	35·39 N	139·33 E
62c	Choisel	48·41 N	2·01 E
62c	Choisy-le-Roi	48·46 N	2·25 E
66m	Cho-lon (Neigh.)	10·46 N	106·40 E
66m	Cho Moi	10·51 N	106·38 E
65c	Chong Pang	1·26 N	103·50 E
60	Chorleywood	51·39 N	0·31 W
62b	Chorlton-cum-Hardy (Neigh.)	53·27 N	2·17 W
64b	Chorošovo (Neigh.)	55·47 N	37·28 E
58b	Chorrera de Managua	23·02 N	82·19 W
58c	Chorrillos	12·12 S	77·02 W
66b	Chŭngsanha-ri (Neigh.)	37·35 N	126·54 E
67a	Chūō (Neigh.)	35·40 N	139·47 E
55b	Churchill, Pa.	40·27 N	79·51 W
54d	Churchill, Va.	38·54 N	77·10 W
60	Church Street	51·26 N	0·28 E
56a	Cicero	41·51 N	87·45 W
69b	Cinderella	26·15 S	28·16 E
63c	Cinisello Balsamo	45·33 N	9·13 E
64g	Cinkota (Neigh.)	47·31 N	19·14 E
63c	Cisliano	45·27 N	8·59 E
53	City College of New York (P. Int.)	40·49 N	73·57 W
53	City Island (Neigh.)	40·51 N	73·47 W
54d	City of Baltimore	39·18 N	76·37 W
57	City of Baltimore	33·59 N	118·08 W
57	City of Industry	34·01 N	117·57 W
60	City of London (Neigh.)	51·31 N	0·05 W
60	City of Westminster (Neigh.)	51·30 N	0·09 W
58a	Ciudad de Naucalpan de Juárez	19·28 N	99·14 W
58a	Ciudad Deportiva (P. Int.)	19·24 N	99·06 W
58d	Ciudad General Belgrano	34·44 S	58·32 W
63b	Ciudad Lineal (Neigh.)	40·27 N	3·40 W
63b	Ciudad Universitaria (Neigh.)	40·27 N	3·44 W
55b	Clairton	40·18 N	79·53 W
62c	Clamart	48·48 N	2·16 E
60	Claremont	51·21 N	0·22 W
53	Clark	40·38 N	74·19 W
52c	Clarkson	43·31 N	79·37 W
55c	Clawson	42·32 N	83·09 W
62c	Claye-Souilly	48·57 N	2·42 E
60	Claygate	51·22 N	0·20 W
60	Claygate Cross	51·16 N	0·19 E
56a	Clearing (Neigh.)	41·47 N	87·47 W
54a	Cleveland	41·30 N	81·41 W
54a	Cleveland Heights	41·30 N	81·34 W
54a	Cleveland Museum of Art (P. Int.)	41·31 N	81·37 W
54d	Cleveland Park (Neigh.)	38·56 N	77·04 W
62c	Clichy	48·54 N	2·18 E
62c	Clichy-sous-Bois	48·55 N	2·33 E
53	Cliffside Park	40·49 N	73·59 W
52a	Clifton, Ma.	42·29 N	70·53 W
53	Clifton, NJ.	40·53 N	74·08 W
54b	Clifton Heights	39·56 N	75·18 W
68a	Clontarf	33·48 S	151·16 E
53	Closter	40·59 N	73·58 W
69b	Cloverdene	26·09 S	28·22 E
65b	Coal Hill Park (P. Int.)	39·56 N	116·23 E
60	Cobham	51·23 N	0·24 E
68b	Coburg	37·45 S	144·58 E
60	Cockfosters (Neigh.)	51·39 N	0·09 W
59c	Cocotá (Neigh.)	22·49 S	43·11 W
59c	Coelho da Rocha	22·47 S	43·23 W
58b	Cojimar	23·10 N	82·18 W
69d	Coker	6·29 N	3·20 E
65e	Colāba (Neigh.)	18·54 N	72·48 E
60	Coldblow (Neigh.)	51·26 N	0·10 E
54d	College Park	39·00 N	76·55 W
53	College Point (Neigh.)	40·47 N	73·51 W
60	Collier Row (Neigh.)	51·36 N	0·10 E
54b	Collingdale	39·55 N	75·17 W
54b	Collingswood	39·55 N	75·04 W
68b	Collingwood	37·48 S	145·00 E
60	Colnbrook	51·29 N	0·31 W
60	Colney Heath	51·44 N	0·15 W
60	Colney Street	51·42 N	0·20 W
63c	Cologno Monzese	45·32 N	9·17 E
62c	Colombes	48·55 N	2·15 E
53	Colonia	40·35 N	74·18 W
54b	Colonial Manor	39·51 N	75·09 W
54c	Colonial Park	39·19 N	76·45 W
64c	Colosseo (P. Int.)	41·54 N	12·29 E
54c	Columbia	39·13 N	76·52 W
53	Columbia University (P. Int.)	40·48 N	73·58 W
54b	Colwyn	39·55 N	75·15 W
58c	Comas	11·57 S	77·04 W
68a	Como	34·00 S	151·04 E
62c	Compans	49·00 N	2·40 E
57	Compton	33·54 N	118·13 W
59b	Conchali	33·24 S	70·39 W
68a	Concord, Austl.	33·52 S	151·06 E
52c	Concord, Can.	43·48 N	79·29 W
68a	Concord West	33·51 S	151·05 E
53	Coney Island (Neigh.)	40·34 N	74·00 W
62c	Conflans-Sainte-Honorine	48·59 N	2·06 E
69c	Congo (Zaïre) (R.)	0·00	0·00
54d	Congress Heights (Neigh.)	38·51 N	77·00 W
54b	Connaughton	40·05 N	75·19 W
54b	Conshohocken	40·05 N	75·18 W
59d	Consolação (Neigh.)	23·33 S	46·39 W
69b	Consolidated Main Reef Mines (P. Int.)	26·11 S	27·56 E
58d	Constitución (Neigh.)	34·37 S	58·23 W
68b	Coode Can.	37·49 S	144·55 E
68a	Coogee	33·55 S	151·16 E
68b	Cook, Pt.	37·55 S	144·48 E
60	Cooksmill Green	51·44 N	0·22 E
60	Coopersale Common	51·42 N	0·08 E
59c	Copacabana (Neigh.)	22·58 S	43·11 W
63c	Cormano	45·33 N	9·10 E
62c	Cormeilles-en-Parisis	48·59 N	2·12 E
63e	Cornellà	41·21 N	2·04 E
60	Corringham	51·31 N	0·28 E
63d	Corroios	38·38 N	9·09 W
63c	Corsico	45·26 N	9·07 E
56b	Corte Madera	37·55 N	122·31 W
63b	Cortes (P. Int.)	40·25 N	3·41 W
64c	Corviale (Neigh.)	41·52 N	12·25 E
63d	Costa de Caparica	38·38 N	9·14 W
58d	Costanero, Canal de (Can.)	34·34 S	58·22 W
52b	Côte-Saint-Luc	45·28 N	73·40 W
52b	Côte Visitation (Neigh.)	45·33 N	73·36 W
54d	Cottage City	38·56 N	76·57 W
60	Coulsdon (Neigh.)	51·19 N	0·08 W
62c	Courbevoie	48·54 N	2·15 E
62c	Courcelle	48·42 N	2·06 E
54c	Courtleigh	39·22 N	76·46 W
62c	Courtry	48·55 N	2·36 E
63d	Cova da Piedade	38·40 N	9·10 W
53	Cove Neck	40·53 N	73·31 W
57	Covina	34·05 N	117·53 W
57	Cowan Heights	33·47 N	117·47 W
60	Cowley (Neigh.)	51·32 N	0·29 W
58a	Coyoacán	19·20 N	99·10 W
55b	Crafton	40·26 N	80·04 W
69b	Craighall (Neigh.)	26·07 S	28·02 E
69b	Craighall Park (Neigh.)	26·08 S	28·01 E
53	Cranford	40·39 N	74·19 W
62b	Crank	53·29 N	2·45 W
60	Creekmouth (Neigh.)	51·31 N	0·06 E
54b	Crescentville (Neigh.)	40·02 N	75·05 W
53	Cresskill	40·57 N	73·57 W
54d	Crest Haven	39·02 N	76·59 W
56a	Crestwood	41·39 N	87·44 W
62c	Créteil	48·48 N	2·28 E
59c	Cristo Redentor, Estatua do (P. Int.)	22·57 S	43·13 W
60	Crockenhill	51·23 N	0·10 E
62c	Croissy-Beaubourg	48·50 N	2·40 E
62c	Croissy-sur-Seine	48·53 N	2·09 E
68a	Cromer	33·44 S	151·17 E
61	Cronenberg (Neigh.)	51·12 N	7·08 E
62b	Cronton	53·23 N	2·46 W
62b	Crosby	53·30 N	3·02 W
69b	Crosby (Neigh.)	26·12 S	27·59 E
62c	Crosne	48·43 N	2·28 E
68a	Cross Roads	33·58 S	150·53 E
55b	Crouse Run (R.)	40·35 N	79·58 W
68a	Crows Nest	33·50 S	151·12 E
60	Croxley Green	51·39 N	0·27 W
68b	Croydon, Austl.	37·48 S	145·17 E
60	Croydon (Neigh.)	51·23 N	0·06 W
54b	Crum Lynne	39·52 N	75·20 W
55a	Crystal Beach	42·52 N	79·04 W
64g	Csömör	47·33 N	19·14 E
58b	Cuatro Caminos	22·54 N	82·23 W
58a	Cuautepec el Alto	19·34 N	99·08 W
60	Cudham (Neigh.)	51·19 N	0·05 E
60	Cuffley	51·47 N	0·07 W
65b	Cuigezhuang	40·01 N	116·28 E
54d	Culmore	38·51 N	77·08 W
57	Culver City	34·01 N	118·24 W
60	Culverstone Green	51·20 N	0·21 E
54c	Curtis B.	39·13 N	76·35 W
63c	Cusano Milanino	45·33 N	9·11 E
60	Cuxton	51·22 N	0·27 E
54a	Cuyahoga (R.)	41·30 N	81·42 W
54a	Cuyahoga Heights	41·26 N	81·39 W
57	Cypress	33·50 N	118·01 W
69b	Cyrildene (Neigh.)	26·11 S	28·06 E

D

Page	Name Region	Lat. °′	Long. °′
66a	Dachang	31·18 N	121·25 E
65e	Dadar (Neigh.)	19·01 N	72·50 E
60	Dagenham (Neigh.)	51·32 N	0·10 E
69b	Daggafontein	26·18 S	28·28 E
65d	Dahirpur (Neigh.)	28·43 N	77·12 E
61	Dahl	51·18 N	7·31 E
63a	Dahlem (Neigh.)	52·28 N	13·17 E
61	Dahlerau	51·13 N	7·19 E
63a	Dahlwitz	52·30 N	13·38 E
67b	Daitō	34·42 N	135·38 E
63a	Dallgow	52·32 N	13·05 E
62b	Dalton	53·34 N	2·46 W
56b	Daly City	37·42 N	122·29 W
68b	Dandenong	37·59 S	145·12 E
54c	Daniels	39·26 N	77·03 W
52a	Danvers	42·34 N	70·56 W
66h	Darakeh	35·48 N	51·23 E
69a	Dār as-Salām	29·59 N	31·13 E
66h	Darband	35·49 N	51·26 E
54b	Darby	39·54 N	75·15 W
60	Dartford	51·27 N	0·14 E
60	Datchet	51·29 N	0·34 W
69b	Daveyton Location	26·09 S	28·25 E
62b	Davyhulme	53·27 N	2·22 W
65b	Dawuji	39·51 N	116·30 E
62b	Dean Row	53·20 N	2·11 W
55c	Dearborn	42·18 N	83·10 W
55c	Dearborn Heights	42·19 N	83·14 W
52a	Dedham	42·15 N	71·10 W
68a	Deewhy	33·45 S	151·17 E
54b	Delair	39·59 N	75·03 W
54b	Delaware (R.)	39·50 N	75·23 W
65d	Delhi	28·40 N	77·13 E
65d	Delhi Cantonment	28·36 N	77·08 E
61	Dellwig (Neigh.)	51·29 N	6·56 E
69b	Delmas	26·06 S	28·26 E
54b	Delran	40·02 N	74·58 W
58d	Del Viso	34·26 S	58·46 W
53	Demarest	40·57 N	73·58 W
61	Demmeltrath (Neigh.)	51·11 N	7·03 E
67a	Denenchōfu (Neigh.)	35·35 N	139·41 E
62b	Denshaw	53·35 N	2·02 W
62b	Denton	53·27 N	2·07 W
60	Deptford (Neigh.)	51·28 N	0·02 W
61	Derendorf (Neigh.)	51·15 N	6·48 E
61	Derne (Neigh.)	51·34 N	7·31 E
56a	Des Plaines	42·02 N	87·54 W
56a	Chicago Sanitary and Ship Can.	41·42 N	87·58 W
55c	Detroit	42·20 N	83·03 W
55c	Detroit (R.)	42·06 N	83·08 W
55c	Detroit Metropolitan-Wayne County Arpt.	42·13 N	83·22 W
62c	Deuil-la-Barre	48·59 N	2·20 E
61	Deusen (Neigh.)	51·33 N	7·26 E
52b	Deux-Montagnes	45·23 N	73·53 W
64d	Dhāfni	37·48 N	22·01 E
68b	Diamond Creek	37·41 S	145·09 E
65b	Diancun	39·55 N	116·14 E
62b	Didsbury (Neigh.)	53·25 N	2·14 W
63a	Diepensee	52·22 N	13·31 E
61	Diersfordt	51·42 N	6·33 E
61	Diessem (Neigh.)	51·20 N	6·35 E
62b	Digmoor	53·32 N	2·45 W
65a	Digra	22·50 N	88·20 E
54d	Dillon Park	38·52 N	76·56 W
62b	Dingle (Neigh.)	53·23 N	2·57 W
61	Dinslaken	51·34 N	6·44 E
61	Dinslakener Bruch	51·35 N	6·43 E
69b	Dinwiddie	26·16 S	28·10 E
69b	Discovery	26·10 S	27·54 E
57	Disneyland (P. Int.)	33·48 N	117·55 W
61	Disteln	51·36 N	7·09 E
54d	District Heights	38·51 N	76·53 W
60	Ditton, Eng.	51·18 N	0·27 E
52c	Dixie	43·36 N	79·36 W
64b	Djakovo (Neigh.)	55·39 N	37·40 E
69c	Djelo-Binza	4·23 S	15·16 E
69c	Djoué (R.)	4·19 S	15·14 E
64e	Döbling (Neigh.)	48·15 N	16·22 E
60	Doddinghurst	51·40 N	0·18 E
52b	Dollard-des-Ormeaux	45·29 N	73·49 W
56a	Dolton	41·39 N	87·37 W
57	Dominguez	33·50 N	118·13 W
64c	Domitilla, Catacombe di (P. Int.)	41·52 N	12·31 E
52c	Don (R.)	43·39 N	79·21 W
64e	Donaufeld (Neigh.)	48·15 N	16·25 E
64e	Donaustadt (Neigh.)	48·13 N	16·30 E
64e	Donauturm (P. Int.)	48·14 N	16·25 E
61	Dönberg	51·18 N	7·10 E
58d	Don Bosco (Neigh.)	34·42 S	58·19 W
68b	Doncaster, Austl.	37·47 S	145·08 E
52c	Doncaster, Can.	43·48 N	79·25 W
68b	Doncaster East	37·47 S	145·10 E
65b	Dongba	39·58 N	116·32 E
65b	Dongbahe	39·58 N	116·27 E
65b	Dongshi	39·49 N	116·34 E
58d	Don Torcuato	34·30 S	58·40 W
52a	Dorchester Heights National Historic Site (P. Int.)	42·20 N	71·03 W
55b	Dormont	40·24 N	80·03 W
61	Dornap	51·15 N	7·04 E
55b	Dorseyville	40·35 N	79·53 W
61	Dorstfeld (Neigh.)	51·31 N	7·25 E
61	Dortmund	51·31 N	7·28 E

Page	Name Region	Lat. °′	Long. °′
52b	Dorval	45·27 N	73·44 W
68a	Dover Heights	33·53 S	151·17 E
68b	Doveton	38·00 S	145·14 E
66h	Dowlatābād	35·37 N	51·27 E
57	Downey	33·56 N	118·08 W
62c	Drancy	48·56 N	2·27 E
62c	Draveil	48·41 N	2·25 E
55b	Dravosburg	40·21 N	79·51 W
63a	Drewitz (Neigh.)	52·22 N	13·08 E
54b	Drexel Hill	39·57 N	75·19 W
62b	Droylsden	53·29 N	2·10 W
68a	Drummoyne	33·51 S	151·09 E
64b	Družba	55·53 N	37·45 E
57	Duarte	34·08 N	117·58 W
62c	Dugny	48·57 N	2·25 E
61	Duisburg	51·25 N	6·46 E
61	Duissern (Neigh.)	51·26 N	6·47 E
62b	Dukinfield	53·29 N	2·05 W
60	Dulwich (Neigh.)	51·26 N	0·05 W
65a	Dum-Dum	22·35 N	88·24 E
53	Dumont	40·56 N	74·00 W
61	Dümpten (Neigh.)	51·27 N	6·54 E
54c	Dundalk	39·15 N	76·31 W
68a	Dundas	33·48 S	151·02 E
62b	Dunham Town	53·23 N	2·24 W
68a	Dunheved	33·45 S	150·47 E
54d	Dunn Loring	38·53 N	77·14 W
60	Dunton Green	51·18 N	0·11 E
60	Dunton Wayletts	51·35 N	0·24 E
69b	Dunvegan	26·09 S	28·09 E
63c	Duomo (P. Int.)	45·27 N	9·11 E
59c	Duque de Caxias	22·47 S	43·18 W
55b	Duquesne	40·21 N	79·51 W
69b	Durban Roodepoort Deep Gold Mines (P. Int.)	26·10 S	27·51 E
61	Durchholz	51·23 N	7·17 E
61	Düssel	51·16 N	7·03 E
61	Düsseldorf	51·12 N	6·47 E
64b	Dzeržinskij	55·38 N	37·50 E

E

Page	Name Region	Lat. °′	Long. °′
57	Eagle Rock (Neigh.)	34·09 N	118·12 W
60	Ealing (Neigh.)	51·31 N	0·20 W
53	East (R.)	40·48 N	73·48 W
52a	East Arlington	42·25 N	71·08 W
60	East Barnet (Neigh.)	51·38 N	0·09 W
60	East Bedfont (Neigh.)	51·27 N	0·26 W
52a	East Braintree	42·13 N	70·58 W
68b	East Burwood	37·51 S	145·09 E
60	Eastbury	51·37 N	0·25 W
53	Eastchester	40·57 N	73·49 W
54a	East Cleveland	41·32 N	81·35 W
68b	East Coburg	37·45 S	144·59 E
60	Eastcote (Neigh.)	51·35 N	0·24 W
55c	East Detroit	42·28 N	82·56 W
69b	Eastern Native (Neigh.)	26·13 S	28·05 E
54b	East Falls (Neigh.)	40·01 N	75·11 W
62b	Eastham	53·19 N	2·58 W
60	East Ham (Neigh.)	51·32 N	0·03 E
68a	East Hills, Austl.	33·58 S	150·59 E
53	East Hills, NY.	40·47 N	73·38 W
66c	East Lamma Chan.	22·15 N	114·07 E
54b	East Lansdowne	39·56 N	75·16 W
55b	East Liberty (Neigh.)	40·27 N	79·55 W
68a	East Lindfield	33·46 S	151·11 E
57	East Los Angeles	34·01 N	118·09 W
60	East Malling	51·17 N	0·26 E
53	East Meadow	40·43 N	73·34 W
60	East Molesey	51·24 N	0·21 W
53	East Newark	40·45 N	74·10 W
53	East New York (Neigh.)	40·40 N	73·53 W
53	East Norwich	40·50 N	73·32 W
53	East Orange	40·46 N	74·13 W
55b	East Pittsburgh	40·24 N	79·48 W
56b	East Richmond	37·57 N	122·19 W
53	East Rockaway	40·39 N	73·40 W
60	East Tilbury	51·28 N	0·26 E
57	East Tustin	33·46 N	117·49 W
52a	East Walpole	42·10 N	71·13 W
52a	East Watertown	42·22 N	71·10 W
52a	East Weymouth	42·13 N	70·55 W
54b	Eastwick (Neigh.)	39·55 N	75·14 W
60	East Wickham (Neigh.)	51·28 N	0·07 E
68a	Eastwood	33·48 S	151·05 E
52c	East York	43·41 N	79·20 W
62c	Eaubonne	49·00 N	2·17 E
67a	Ebina	35·26 N	139·25 E
69d	Ebute-ikorodu	6·37 N	3·30 E
62b	Eccles	53·29 N	2·21 W
62b	Eccleston, Eng.	53·27 N	2·47 W
54c	Eccleston, Md.	39·24 N	76·44 W
55c	Ecorse	42·15 N	83·09 W
67a	Eda (Neigh.)	35·34 N	139·34 E
59c	Éden	22·48 S	43·24 W
69b	Edendale	26·09 S	28·09 E
69b	Edenvale	26·08 S	28·09 E
69b	Edenvale Location	26·08 S	28·11 E
62b	Edge Hill (Neigh.)	53·24 N	2·57 W
54c	Edgemere	39·14 N	76·27 W
53	Edgewater, NJ.	40·50 N	73·58 W
55a	Edgewater, NY.	43·03 N	78·55 W
60	Edgware (Neigh.)	51·37 N	0·17 W
62b	Edgworth	53·39 N	2·24 W
56a	Edison Park (Neigh.)	42·01 N	87·49 W
54d	Edmonston	38·57 N	76·56 W
60	Edmonton (Neigh.)	51·37 N	0·04 W
67a	Edo (R.)	35·41 N	139·53 E
67a	Edogawa (Neigh.)	35·42 N	139·52 E
60	Egham	51·26 N	0·34 W
67a	Egota (Neigh.)	35·43 N	139·40 E
61	Ehingen (Neigh.)	51·22 N	6·42 E
61	Ehringhausen	51·11 N	7·33 E
61	Ehringhausen (Neigh.)	51·09 N	7·11 E
63a	Eiche	52·34 N	13·36 E
61	Eichlinghofen (Neigh.)	51·29 N	7·24 E
63a	Eichwalde	52·22 N	13·37 E
61	Eickerend	51·13 N	6·34 E
62c	Eiffel, Tour (P. Int.)	48·51 N	2·18 E
61	Eigen (Neigh.)	51·33 N	6·57 E
61	Eilpe (Neigh.)	51·21 N	7·29 E
65a	Eksāra	22·38 N	88·17 E
59a	El Aguacate	10·28 N	66·59 W
69b	Elandsfontein	26·10 S	28·12 E
61	Elberfeld (Neigh.)	51·16 N	7·08 E
58b	El Calvario (Neigh.)	23·05 N	82·20 W
63b	El Campamento (Neigh.)	40·24 N	3·46 W
59a	El Caribe	10·37 N	66·49 W
56b	El Cerrito	37·55 N	122·18 W
59a	El Cojo	10·37 N	66·53 W
59a	El Corozo	10·35 N	66·58 W
58b	El Cotorro	23·03 N	82·16 W
52c	Elder Mills	43·49 N	79·38 W
59a	El Encantado	10·27 N	66·47 W
65e	Elephanta I. (Ghārpuri)	18·57 N	72·55 E
56b	El Granada	37·30 N	122·28 W
59a	El Guarapo	10·36 N	66·58 W
53	Elizabeth, NJ.	40·40 N	74·11 W
55b	Elizabeth, Pa.	40·16 N	79·53 W
54b	Elkins Park	40·05 N	75·08 W
54c	Elkridge	39·13 N	76·42 W
62b	Ellesmere Park	53·29 N	2·20 W
62b	Ellesmere Port	53·17 N	2·54 W
54c	Ellicott City	39·16 N	76·48 W
59a	El Limoncito	10·29 N	66·47 W
61	Ellinghorst (Neigh.)	51·34 N	6·57 E
56a	Elmhurst	41·53 N	87·56 W
53	Elmhurst (Neigh.)	40·44 N	73·53 W
58a	El Molinito	19·27 N	99·15 W
53	Elmont	40·42 N	73·42 W
54b	Elmwood (Neigh.)	39·56 N	75·14 W
56a	Elmwood Park	41·55 N	87·49 W
59a	El Palmar	10·38 N	66·52 W
59a	El Pedregal (Neigh.)	10·30 N	66·51 W
63b	El Plantío (Neigh.)	40·28 N	3·49 W
59a	El Recreo (Neigh.)	10·30 N	66·53 W
58a	El Reloj	19·18 N	99·08 W
59b	El Rincón de La Florida	33·33 S	70·34 W
69b	Elsburg	26·15 S	28·12 E
57	El Segundo	33·55 N	118·24 W
61	Elsey	51·22 N	7·34 E
60	Elstree	51·39 N	0·16 W
60	Eltham (Neigh.)	51·27 N	0·04 E
62b	Elton	53·16 N	2·49 W
58a	El Toreo (P. Int.)	19·27 N	99·13 W
59a	El Valle (Neigh.)	10·27 N	66·55 W
59a	El Zamural	10·27 N	67·00 W
59a	El Zig-Zag	10·33 N	66·58 W
59d	Embu	23·39 S	46·51 W
62c	Émerainville	48·49 N	2·37 E
53	Emerson	40·58 N	74·02 W
56b	Emeryville	37·50 N	122·17 W
69b	Emmarentia (Neigh.)	26·10 S	28·01 E
61	Emst (Neigh.)	51·21 N	7·30 E
55b	Emsworth	40·30 N	80·04 W
63d	Encarnação (Neigh.)	38·47 N	9·06 W
57	Encino (Neigh.)	34·09 N	118·30 W
68a	Enfield	33·53 S	151·06 E
59c	Engenho de Dentro (Neigh.)	22·54 S	43·18 W
59c	Engenho do Mato	22·52 S	43·01 W
59c	Engenho Nôvo (Neigh.)	22·55 S	43·17 W
62c	Enghien-les-Bains	48·58 N	2·19 E
60	Englefield Green	51·26 N	0·35 W
53	Englewood	40·54 N	73·59 W
56a	Englewood (Neigh.)	41·47 N	87·39 W
53	Englewood Cliffs	40·53 N	73·57 W
61	Ennepetal	51·18 N	7·22 E
62c	Épinay-sous-Sénart	48·42 N	2·31 E
62c	Épinay-sur-Seine	48·57 N	2·19 E
61	Eppendorf (Neigh.)	51·27 N	7·11 E
61	Eppenhausen (Neigh.)	51·21 N	7·31 E
68a	Epping, Austl.	33·46 S	151·05 E
60	Epping, Eng.	51·43 N	0·07 E
60	Epping Green, Eng.	51·44 N	0·05 E
60	Epping Upland	51·43 N	0·06 E
60	Epsom	51·20 N	0·16 W
64f	Erenköy (Neigh.)	40·58 N	29·04 E
61	Ergste	51·25 N	7·34 E
60	Erith (Neigh.)	51·29 N	0·10 E
61	Erkrath	51·13 N	6·55 E
61	Erle (Neigh.)	51·33 N	7·05 E
62c	Ermont	48·59 N	2·16 E
68a	Erskine Park	33·49 S	150·47 E
61	Esborn	51·23 N	7·20 E
58a	Escuadrón 201	19·22 N	99·06 W
60	Esher	51·23 N	0·22 W
63e	Esplugas	41·23 N	2·06 E
61	Essel (Neigh.)	51·37 N	7·15 E
61	Essen	51·28 N	7·01 E
61	Essenberg	51·26 N	6·42 E
68b	Essendon	37·46 S	144·55 E
54c	Essex	39·18 N	76·29 W
53	Essex Fells	40·50 N	74·17 W
54b	Essington	39·52 N	75·18 W
64e	Essling (Neigh.)	48·13 N	16·32 E
58a	Estrella, Cerro de la (Mtn.)	19·21 N	99·05 W
55b	Etna	40·30 N	79·57 W
52c	Etobicoke	43·39 N	79·34 W
60	Eton	51·31 N	0·37 W
56a	Evanston	42·02 N	87·42 W
52a	Everett	42·24 N	71·03 W
56a	Evergreen Park	41·43 N	87·42 W
62b	Everton (Neigh.)	53·25 N	2·58 W
61	Eving (Neigh.)	51·33 N	7·29 E
60	Ewell	51·21 N	0·15 W
69d	Ewu	6·33 N	3·19 E
60	Eynsford	51·22 N	0·13 E
64f	Eyüp (Neigh.)	41·03 N	28·55 E
69a	Ezbekīyah (Neigh.)	30·03 N	31·15 E

F

Page	Name Region	Lat. °′	Long. °′
52b	Fabreville (Neigh.)	45·34 N	73·50 W
63a	Fahrland	52·28 N	13·01 E
62b	Failsworth	53·31 N	2·09 W
68a	Fairfield, Austl.	33·52 S	150·57 E
53	Fairfield, NJ.	40·53 N	74·17 W
68a	Fairfield West	33·52 S	150·55 E
54d	Fairhaven	38·47 N	77·05 W
53	Fair Lawn	40·56 N	74·07 W
54d	Fairlee	38·52 N	77·16 W
54d	Fairmount Heights	38·54 N	76·55 W
60	Fairseat	51·20 N	0·20 E
53	Fairview	40·49 N	74·00 W
54a	Fairview Park	41·27 N	81·51 W
63a	Falkensee	52·33 N	13·04 E
54d	Falls Church	38·53 N	77·11 W
63e	Famadas	41·21 N	2·05 E
66h	Farazād	35·47 N	51·21 E
55c	Farmington	42·28 N	83·22 W
55c	Farmington Hills	42·28 N	83·23 W
60	Farnborough (Neigh.)	51·21 N	0·04 E
60	Farningham	51·23 N	0·13 E
62b	Farnworth	53·33 N	2·24 W
53	Far Rockaway (Neigh.)	40·36 N	73·45 W
64e	Favoriten (Neigh.)	48·11 N	16·23 E
60	Fawkham Green	51·22 N	0·17 E
68b	Fawkner	37·43 S	144·58 E
54d	Fawsett Farms	38·59 N	77·14 W
65b	Fengtai	39·51 N	116·16 E
63a	Ferbitz	52·30 N	13·01 E
64g	Ferencváros (Neigh.)	47·28 N	19·06 E
54c	Ferndale, Md.	39·11 N	76·38 W
55c	Ferndale, Mi.	42·28 N	83·08 W
68b	Ferntree Gully	37·53 S	145·18 E
68b	Ferny Creek	37·53 S	145·21 E
59d	Ferraz de Vasconcelos	23·32 S	46·22 W
62c	Ferrières	48·49 N	2·42 E
55a	Ferry Village	43·58 N	78·57 W
60	Fetcham	51·17 N	0·22 W
63a	Fichtenau	52·27 N	13·42 E
60	Fiddlers Hamlet	51·41 N	0·08 E
64b	Fili (Neigh.)	55·45 N	37·31 E
69b	Finaalspan	26·17 S	28·15 E
60	Finchley (Neigh.)	51·36 N	0·10 W
63a	Finkenkrug	52·34 N	13·03 E
62b	Firgrove	53·37 N	2·08 W
61	Fischeln (Neigh.)	51·18 N	6·35 E
56b	Fisherman's Wharf (P. Int.)	37·48 N	122·25 W
52c	Fisherville	43·47 N	79·28 W
62b	Fishpool	53·35 N	2·17 W
68b	Fitzroy	37·48 S	144·59 E
68a	Five Dock	33·52 S	151·08 E
53	Flatbush (Neigh.)	40·39 N	73·56 W
60	Flaunden	51·42 N	0·32 W
61	Flehe (Neigh.)	51·12 N	6·47 E
61	Fley (Neigh.)	51·23 N	7·30 E
61	Flingern (Neigh.)	51·14 N	6·49 E
53	Floral Park	40·43 N	73·42 W
57	Florence	33·58 N	118·15 W
69b	Florentia	26·16 S	28·08 E
58d	Flores (Neigh.)	34·38 S	58·28 W
58d	Floresta (Neigh.)	34·38 S	58·29 W
69b	Florida	26·11 S	27·55 E
58a	Flotantes, Jardines (P. Int.)	19·16 N	99·06 W
54b	Flourtown	40·07 N	75·13 W
53	Flower Hill	40·49 N	73·41 W
53	Flushing (Neigh.)	40·45 N	73·49 W
54b	Folcroft	39·54 N	75·17 W
54b	Folsom	39·54 N	75·19 W
69b	Fontainebleau	26·07 S	27·59 E
62c	Fontenay-aux-Roses	48·47 N	2·17 E
62c	Fontenay-le-Fleury	48·49 N	2·03 E
62c	Fontenay-sous-Bois	48·51 N	2·29 E
68b	Footscray	37·48 S	144·54 E
59c	Fora, Ponta de (C.)	22·57 S	43·07 W
65b	Forbidden City (P. Int.)	39·55 N	116·23 E
53	Fordham University (P. Int.)	40·51 N	73·53 W
53	Fords	40·32 N	74·19 W
69b	Fordsburg (Neigh.)	26·13 S	28·02 E
60	Forest Gate (Neigh.)	51·33 N	0·02 E
54d	Forest Heights	38·49 N	77·00 W
68b	Forest Hill	37·50 S	145·11 E
52c	Forest Hill (Neigh.)	43·42 N	79·24 W
55b	Forest Hills	40·26 N	79·52 W
53	Forest Hills (Neigh.)	40·42 N	73·51 W
56a	Forest Park	41·53 N	87·50 W
54c	Forest Park (Neigh.)	39·19 N	76·41 W
68a	Forestville, Austl.	33·46 S	151·13 E
54d	Forestville, Md.	38·50 N	76·52 W
62b	Formby	53·34 N	3·05 W
62b	Formby Pt.	53·33 N	3·06 W
65e	Fort (Neigh.)	18·56 N	72·50 E
55a	Fort Erie	42·54 N	78·56 W
54c	Fort Howard	39·12 N	76·27 W
53	Fort Lee	40·51 N	73·58 W
54c	Fort McHenry National Monument (P. Int.)	39·16 N	76·35 W
54d	Fort McNair (P. Int.)	38·52 N	77·04 W
55c	Fort Wayne Military Museum (P. Int.)	42·18 N	83·06 W
65a	Fort William (P. Int.)	22·33 N	88·20 E
56b	Foster City	37·34 N	122·16 W
62c	Fourqueux	48·53 N	2·04 E
55b	Fox Chapel	40·30 N	79·55 W
68a	Fox Valley	33·45 S	151·06 E
62c	Franconville	48·59 N	2·14 E
55b	Frank	40·16 N	79·48 W
62b	Frankby	53·22 N	3·08 W
54b	Frankford (Neigh.)	40·01 N	75·05 W
55c	Franklin	42·31 N	83·18 W
56a	Franklin Park, Il.	41·56 N	87·49 W
55b	Franklin Park, Pa.	40·35 N	80·06 W
54d	Franklin Park, Va.	38·55 N	77·09 W
69b	Franklin Roosevelt Park (Neigh.)	26·09 S	27·59 E
53	Franklin Square	40·43 N	73·40 W
55c	Fraser	42·32 N	82·57 W
63a	Fredersdorf bei Berlin	52·31 N	13·44 E
53	Freeport	40·39 N	73·35 W
61	Freisenbruch (Neigh.)	51·27 N	7·06 E
68a	French's Forest	33·45 S	151·14 E
62b	Freshfield	53·34 N	3·04 W
53	Fresh Meadows (Neigh.)	40·44 N	73·48 W
63a	Friedenau (Neigh.)	52·28 N	13·20 E
61	Friedrichsfeld	51·38 N	6·39 E
63a	Friedrichsfelde (Neigh.)	52·31 N	13·31 E
63a	Friedrichshagen (Neigh.)	52·27 N	13·38 E
63a	Friedrichshain (Neigh.)	52·31 N	13·27 E
61	Friemersheim	51·23 N	6·42 E
65d	Friends Colony (Neigh.)	28·34 N	77·16 E
54c	Friendship International Arpt.	39·11 N	76·40 W
60	Friern Barnet (Neigh.)	51·37 N	0·10 W
61	Frillendorf (Neigh.)	51·28 N	7·05 E
62b	Frodsham	53·18 N	2·44 W
63a	Frohnau (Neigh.)	52·38 N	13·18 E
61	Frohnhausen (Neigh.)	51·27 N	6·58 E
60	Fryerning	51·41 N	0·22 E
67a	Fuchū	35·40 N	139·29 E
63b	Fuencarral (Neigh.)	40·30 N	3·41 W
61	Fuhlenbrock (Neigh.)	51·32 N	6·54 E
67b	Fujiidera	34·34 N	135·36 E
67a	Fukagawa (Neigh.)	35·40 N	139·48 E
67b	Fukiai (Neigh.)	34·42 N	135·12 E
67b	Fukushima (Neigh.)	34·42 N	135·29 E
61	Fulerum (Neigh.)	51·26 N	6·57 E
57	Fullerton	33·52 N	117·55 W
60	Fulmer	51·33 N	0·34 W
67b	Funasaka	34·49 N	135·17 E
59c	Fundão, Ilha do (I.)	22·51 S	43·14 W
65e	Funde	18·54 N	72·58 E
67a	Futatsubashi	35·28 N	139·30 E
60	Fyfield	51·45 N	0·16 E

G

Page	Name Region	Lat. °′	Long. °′
62c	Gagny	48·53 N	2·32 E
61	Gahmen (Neigh.)	51·36 N	7·32 E
64f	Galata (Neigh.)	41·01 N	28·58 E
64f	Galata Köprüsü (P. Int.)	41·00 N	28·57 E
64d	Galátsion	38·01 N	23·45 E
68b	Galvin	37·51 S	144·49 E
65b	Gaobaita	39·53 N	116·30 E
65b	Gaobeidian	39·54 N	116·33 E
63c	Garbagnate Milanese	45·35 N	9·05 E
64c	Garbatella (Neigh.)	41·52 N	12·29 E
62c	Garches	48·51 N	2·11 E
57	Gardena	33·53 N	118·18 W
55c	Garden City, Mi.	42·20 N	83·20 W
53	Garden City, NY.	40·43 N	73·37 W
53	Garden City Park	40·44 N	73·40 W
57	Garden Grove	33·46 N	117·57 W
65a	Garden Reach	22·33 N	88·17 E
61	Garenfeld	51·24 N	7·31 E
53	Garfield	40·53 N	74·07 W
54a	Garfield Heights	41·26 N	81·37 W
62c	Garges-lès-Gonesse	48·58 N	2·25 E
54c	Garland	39·11 N	76·39 W
54c	Garrison	39·24 N	76·45 W
60	Garston	51·41 N	0·23 W
62b	Garston (Neigh.)	53·21 N	2·53 W
61	Gartenstadt (Neigh.)	51·30 N	7·26 E
65a	Garulia	22·49 N	88·22 E
53	Garwood	40·39 N	74·19 W
62b	Gateacre (Neigh.)	53·23 N	2·51 W

Page	Name Region	Lat. °′	Long. °′
65e	Gateway of India (P. Int.)	18·55 N	72·50 E
62b	Gatley	53·23 N	2·14 W
59a	Gato Negro	10·33 N	66·57 W
65e	Gāvanpāda	18·57 N	73·01 E
59c	Gávea (Neigh.)	22·58 S	43·14 W
62b	Gayton	53·19 N	3·06 W
62b	Gee Cross	53·26 N	2·04 W
61	Gellep-Stratum (Neigh.)	51·20 N	6·41 E
68b	Gellibrand, Pt.	37·52 S	144·54 E
61	Gelsenkirchen	51·31 N	7·07 E
58d	General Pacheco	34·28 S	58·40 W
58d	General San Martín	34·35 S	58·30 W
58d	General Sarmiento (San Miguel)	34·33 S	58·43 W
58d	General Urquiza (Neigh.)	34·34 S	58·29 W
61	Gennebreck	51·19 N	7·12 E
62c	Gennevilliers	48·56 N	2·18 E
62c	Gentilly	48·49 N	2·21 E
68a	Georges Hall	33·55 S	150·59 E
54d	Georgetown (Neigh.)	38·54 N	77·03 W
54d	Georgetown University (P. Int.)	38·54 N	77·04 W
69b	Gerdview	26·10 S	28·11 E
58d	Gerli (Neigh.)	34·41 S	58·23 W
54b	Germantown (Neigh.)	40·03 N	75·11 W
69b	Germiston	26·15 S	28·05 E
60	Gerrards Cross	51·35 N	0·34 W
63b	Getafe	40·18 N	3·43 W
55a	Getzville	43·01 N	78·46 W
61	Gevelsberg	51·19 N	7·20 E
61	Geweke (Neigh.)	51·22 N	7·25 E
65e	Ghārāpuri	18·54 N	72·56 E
65e	Ghātkopar (Neigh.)	19·05 N	72·54 E
65d	Ghāzipur (Neigh.)	28·38 N	77·19 E
65d	Ghonda (Neigh.)	28·41 N	77·16 E
65d	Ghondi (Neigh.)	28·42 N	77·16 E
65a	Ghushuri	22·37 N	88·22 E
66m	Gia-dinh	10·48 N	106·42 E
54b	Gibbsboro	39·50 N	74·58 W
52c	Gibraltar Pt.	43·36 N	79·23 W
60	Gidea Park (Neigh.)	51·35 N	0·12 E
62c	Gif-sur-Yvette	48·42 N	2·08 E
67a	Ginza (Neigh.)	35·40 N	139·47 E
65e	Girgaum (Neigh.)	18·57 N	72·48 E
69a	Giza Pyramids (P. Int.)	29·59 N	31·08 E
61	Gladbeck	51·34 N	6·59 E
68a	Gladesville	33·50 S	151·08 E
54b	Gladwyne	40·02 N	75·17 W
61	Glashütte (Neigh.)	51·13 N	6·52 E
54d	Glassmanor	38·49 N	76·59 W
55b	Glassport	40·19 N	79·54 W
61	Glehn	51·10 N	6·35 E
54d	Glenarden	38·56 N	76·52 W
53	Glen Cove	40·52 N	73·37 W
57	Glendale	34·10 N	118·17 W
57	Glendora, Ca.	34·08 N	117·52 W
54b	Glendora, NJ.	39·50 N	75·04 W
54d	Glen Echo	38·58 N	77·08 W
68a	Glenfield	33·58 S	150·54 E
53	Glen Head	40·50 N	73·37 W
68b	Glenhuntly	37·54 S	145·03 E
54c	Glenmore	39·11 N	76·36 W
54b	Glenolden	39·54 N	75·17 W
53	Glen Ridge	40·49 N	74·13 W
53	Glen Rock	40·58 N	74·08 W
68b	Glenroy	37·42 S	144·55 E
55b	Glenshaw	40·31 N	79·57 W
54b	Glenside	40·06 N	75·09 W
56a	Glenview	42·04 N	87·48 W
68b	Glen Waverley	37·53 S	145·10 E
53	Glenwood Landing	40·50 N	73·39 W
63a	Glienicke	52·37 N	13·19 E
54b	Gloucester City	39·54 N	75·07 W
60	Goff's Oak	51·43 N	0·05 W
65a	Golabāri	22·36 N	88·20 E
56b	Golden Gate (Str.)	37·49 N	122·29 W
60	Golders Green (Neigh.)	51·35 N	0·12 W
56a	Golf	42·03 N	87·48 W
56a	Golf Park Terrace	42·03 N	87·51 W
62c	Gonesse	48·59 N	2·27 E
58d	González Catán	34·46 S	58·39 W
68a	Gordon (Ku-ring-gai)	33·45 S	151·08 E
54d	Gordons Corner	38·50 N	76·57 W
68a	Gore Hill	33·49 S	151·11 E
62b	Gorton (Neigh.)	53·27 N	2·10 W
63a	Gosen	52·24 N	13·43 E
67a	Gotanno (Neigh.)	35·46 N	139·49 E
61	Götterswickerhamm	51·35 N	6·40 E
63a	Göttin	52·27 N	12·54 E
62c	Gournay-sur-Marne	48·52 N	2·34 E
62c	Goussainville	49·01 N	2·28 E
66m	Go-vap	10·49 N	106·42 E
59c	Governador, Ilha do (I.)	22·48 S	43·12 W
61	Grafenberg (Neigh.)	51·14 N	6·50 E
58a	Gran Canal del Desagüe (Can.)	19·29 N	99·05 W
55a	Grand Island	43·01 N	78·58 W
55a	Grand I.	43·02 N	78·58 W
55a	Grandyle	43·00 N	78·57 W
60	Grange Hill	51·37 N	0·05 E
54c	Granite	39·21 N	76·51 W
56a	Grant Park (P. Int.)	41·52 N	87·37 W
68a	Granville	33·50 S	151·01 E
62b	Grassendale (Neigh.)	53·21 N	2·54 W
60	Gravesend	51·27 N	0·24 E
60	Grays	51·29 N	0·20 E
62b	Greasby	53·23 N	3·07 W
62b	Great Altcar	53·33 N	3·01 W
60	Great Bookham	51·16 N	0·22 W
60	Great Burstead	51·36 N	0·25 E
62b	Great Crosby	53·29 N	3·01 W
54d	Great Falls	39·00 N	77·17 W
53	Great Kills (Neigh.)	40·33 N	74·10 W
53	Great Neck	40·47 N	73·44 W
60	Great Oxney Green	51·44 N	0·25 E
60	Great Parndon	51·45 N	0·05 E
62b	Great Sutton	53·17 N	2·56 W
60	Great Warley	51·35 N	0·17 E
63c	Greco (Neigh.)	45·30 N	9·13 E
54d	Greenbelt	39·01 N	76·53 W
56b	Greenbrae	37·57 N	122·31 W
52b	Greenfield Park	45·29 N	73·29 W
60	Greenhithe	51·27 N	0·17 E
54d	Green Meadows	38·58 N	76·57 W
62b	Greenmount	53·37 N	2·20 W
68b	Greensborough	37·42 S	145·06 E
69b	Greenside (Neigh.)	26·09 S	28·01 E
60	Greenstead	51·42 N	0·14 E
60	Green Street	51·40 N	0·16 W
60	Green Street Green (Neigh.)	51·21 N	0·04 E
53	Greenvale	40·49 N	73·38 W
68a	Green Valley	33·54 S	150·53 E
68a	Greenwich	33·50 S	151·11 E
60	Greenwich (Neigh.)	51·28 N	0·02 E
60	Greenwich Observatory (P. Int.)	51·28 N	0·00
53	Greenwich Village (Neigh.)	40·44 N	74·00 W
52a	Greenwood	42·29 N	71·04 W
61	Greiffenburg (P. Int.)	51·20 N	6·38 E
61	Grevel (Neigh.)	51·34 N	7·33 E
68a	Greystanes	0·00	0·00
61	Grimlinghausen (Neigh.)	51·10 N	6·44 E
64e	Grinzing (Neigh.)	48·15 N	16·21 E
63a	Grossbeeren	52·21 N	13·18 E
61	Grossenbaum (Neigh.)	51·22 N	6·47 E
64e	Gross-Enzersdorf	48·12 N	16·33 E
55c	Grosse Pointe	42·24 N	82·55 W
55c	Grosse Pointe Farms	42·25 N	82·53 W
55c	Grosse Pointe Park	42·23 N	82·56 W
55c	Grosse Pointe Woods	42·27 N	82·55 W
64e	Grossjedlersdorf (Neigh.)	48·17 N	16·25 E
63a	Gross Ziethen	52·24 N	13·27 E
61	Gruiten	51·14 N	7·01 E
61	Grumme (Neigh.)	51·30 N	7·14 E
63a	Grünau (Neigh.)	52·25 N	13·34 E
61	Grünewald	51·13 N	7·37 E
63a	Grunewald (Neigh.)	52·30 N	13·17 E
58a	Guadalupe, Basílica de (P. Int.)	19·29 N	99·07 W
59d	Guaianazes (Neigh.)	23·33 S	46·25 W
59a	Guaire (R.)	10·25 N	66·46 W
58b	Guanabacoa	23·07 N	82·18 W
59c	Guanabara, Baía de (B.)	22·50 S	43·10 W
65b	Guanyintang	39·52 N	116·31 E
59a	Guaracarumbo	10·34 N	66·59 W
59d	Guarulhos	23·28 S	46·32 W
62c	Guermantes	48·51 N	2·42 E
68a	Guildford	33·51 S	150·59 E
54b	Gulph Mills	40·04 N	75·21 W
58a	Gustavo A. Madero	19·29 N	99·07 W
53	Guttenberg	40·48 N	74·01 W
62c	Guyancourt	48·46 N	2·04 E

H

Page	Name Region	Lat. °′	Long. °′
61	Haan	51·11 N	7·00 E
61	Haar (Neigh.)	51·26 N	7·13 E
68a	Haberfield	33·53 S	151·08 E
67a	Hachiōji	35·39 N	139·20 E
57	Hacienda Heights	33·58 N	117·58 W
53	Hackensack	40·53 N	74·03 W
60	Hacketts	51·45 N	0·05 W
60	Hackney (Neigh.)	51·33 N	0·03 W
54b	Haddonfield	39·54 N	75·02 W
54b	Haddon Heights	39·52 N	75·02 W
64e	Hadersdorf (Neigh.)	48·13 N	16·14 E
68b	Hadfield	37·42 S	144·56 E
66b	Haemgon-ni (Neigh.)	37·35 N	126·49 E
61	Hagen	51·22 N	7·28 E
61	Hahnenberg	51·12 N	7·24 E
65d	Haidārpur (Neigh.)	28·43 N	77·09 E
65b	Haidian	39·59 N	116·18 E
67a	Haijima	35·42 N	139·21 E
60	Hainault (Neigh.)	51·36 N	0·06 E
61	Halden (Neigh.)	51·23 N	7·31 E
62b	Hale, Eng.	53·23 N	2·21 W
62b	Halebarns	53·22 N	2·19 W
53	Haledon	40·56 N	74·11 W
54c	Halethorpe	39·15 N	76·41 W
62b	Halewood	53·22 N	2·49 W
64f	Haliç (B.)	41·02 N	28·58 E
68b	Hallam	38·01 S	145·06 E
60	Halstead	51·20 N	0·08 E
61	Halver	51·11 N	7·30 E
60	Ham (Neigh.)	51·26 N	0·19 W
69b	Hamberg	26·11 S	27·53 E
61	Hamborn (Neigh.)	51·29 N	6·46 E
61	Hamm (Neigh.), F.R.G.	51·12 N	6·44 E
60	Hammersmith (Neigh.)	51·30 N	0·14 W
56a	Hammond	41·36 N	87·30 W
68a	Hammondville	33·57 S	150·57 E
60	Hampstead (Neigh.)	51·33 N	0·11 W
60	Hampstead Heath (P. Int.)	51·34 N	0·10 W
68b	Hampton	37·56 S	145·00 E
60	Hampton (Neigh.)	51·25 N	0·22 W
54c	Hampton National Historic Site (P. Int.)	39·25 N	76·35 W
55c	Hamtramck	42·24 N	83·03 W
62b	Handforth	53·21 N	2·13 W
66b	Han-gang (R.)	37·36 N	126·47 E
66c	Hang Hau Town	22·19 N	114·16 E
54c	Hanover	39·11 N	76·42 W
60	Hanworth (Neigh.)	51·26 N	0·23 W
62b	Hapsford	53·16 N	2·48 W
67a	Haramachida	35·33 N	139·27 E
57	Harbor City (Neigh.)	33·48 N	118·17 W
68a	Harbord	33·45 S	151·26 E
53	Harbor Isle	40·36 N	73·40 W
60	Harefield (Neigh.)	51·36 N	0·29 W
60	Haringey (Neigh.)	51·35 N	0·07 W
54b	Harker Village	39·51 N	75·09 W
53	Harlem (Neigh.)	40·49 N	73·56 W
60	Harlesden (Neigh.)	51·32 N	0·15 W
60	Harlington (Neigh.)	51·29 N	0·26 W
55b	Harmar Heights	40·33 N	79·49 W
55b	Harmarville	40·32 N	79·51 W
65d	Harola	28·36 N	77·19 E
60	Harold Hill (Neigh.)	51·36 N	0·13 E
60	Harold Wood (Neigh.)	51·36 N	0·14 E
61	Harpen (Neigh.)	51·29 N	7·16 E
55c	Harper Woods	42·24 N	82·55 W
62b	Harpurhey (Neigh.)	53·31 N	2·13 W
53	Harrison, NJ.	40·45 N	74·10 W
53	Harrison, NY.	40·58 N	73·43 W
54c	Harrisonville	39·23 N	77·50 W
68a	Harris Park	33·49 S	151·01 E
60	Harrow (Neigh.)	51·35 N	0·21 W
60	Harrow on the Hill (Neigh.)	51·34 N	0·20 W
60	Hartley	51·23 N	0·19 E
60	Harvel	51·21 N	0·22 E
56a	Harvey	41·37 N	87·39 W
55b	Harwick	40·34 N	79·48 W
62b	Harwood, Eng.	53·35 N	2·23 W
54c	Harwood, Md.	38·52 N	76·37 W
56a	Harwood Heights	41·59 N	87·48 W
54c	Harwood Park	39·12 N	76·44 W
66h	Ḥasanābād	35·44 N	51·19 E
53	Hasbrouck Heights	40·52 N	74·04 W
62b	Haskayne	53·34 N	2·58 W
64f	Hasköy (Neigh.)	41·02 N	28·58 E
61	Hasselbeck-Schwarzbach	51·16 N	6·53 E
61	Hassels (Neigh.)	51·10 N	6·53 E
61	Hasslinghausen	51·20 N	7·17 E
61	Hästen (Neigh.), F.R.G.	51·09 N	7·06 E
61	Hasten (Neigh.), F.R.G.	51·12 N	7·09 E
60	Hastingwood	51·45 N	0·09 E
61	Hattingen	51·23 N	7·10 E
60	Hatton (Neigh.)	51·28 N	0·25 W
67b	Hattori	34·46 N	135·27 E
61	Hatzfeld (Neigh.)	51·17 N	7·11 E
62b	Haughton Green	53·27 N	2·06 W
65d	Hauz Rāni (Neigh.)	28·32 N	77·13 E
58b	Havana	23·08 N	82·22 W
63a	Havel-Kanal (Can.)	52·36 N	13·12 E
54b	Haverford	40·01 N	75·18 W
60	Havering (Neigh.)	51·34 N	0·14 E
60	Havering-atte-Bower (Neigh.)	51·37 N	0·11 E
60	Havering's Grove	51·38 N	0·23 E
54b	Havertown	39·59 N	75·18 W
57	Hawaiian Gardens	33·50 N	118·04 W
69a	Ḥawf, Jabal (Hills)	29·55 N	31·21 E
60	Hawley	51·25 N	0·14 E
53	Haworth	40·58 N	73·59 W
68b	Hawthorn	37·49 S	145·02 E
57	Hawthorne, Ca.	33·55 N	118·21 W
53	Hawthorne, NJ.	40·57 N	74·09 W
60	Hayes (Neigh.), Eng.	51·23 N	0·01 E
62b	Hazel Grove	53·23 N	2·08 W
60	Headley	51·17 N	0·16 W
62b	Heald Green	53·22 N	2·14 W
68b	Heathmont	37·49 S	145·15 E
62b	Heaton Moor	53·25 N	2·11 W
60	Heaverham	51·18 N	0·15 E
62b	Heaviley	53·24 N	2·09 W
54c	Hebbville	39·20 N	77·46 W
61	Heerdt (Neigh.)	51·13 N	6·43 E
61	Heide (Neigh.), F.R.G.	51·31 N	6·52 E
68b	Heidelberg, Austl.	37·45 S	145·04 E
55b	Heidelberg, Pa.	40·23 N	80·05 W
61	Heil	51·38 N	7·35 E
61	Heiligenhaus	51·19 N	6·59 E
63a	Heiligensee (Neigh.)	52·36 N	13·13 E
63a	Heinersdorf	52·23 N	13·20 E
63a	Heinersdorf (Neigh.)	52·34 N	13·27 E
61	Heisingen (Neigh.)	51·25 N	7·04 E
69a	Heliopolis, see Miṣr al-Jadīdah (Neigh.)	30·06 N	31·20 E
69a	Heliopolis (P. Int.)	30·08 N	31·17 E
62b	Helsby	53·16 N	2·46 W
60	Hemel Hempstead	51·46 N	0·28 W
53	Hempstead	40·42 N	73·37 W
63a	Hennigsdorf	52·38 N	13·13 E
61	Herbede	51·25 N	7·16 E
61	Herdecke	51·24 N	7·26 E
64e	Hermannskogel (Mtn.)	48·16 N	16·18 E
57	Hermosa Beach	33·52 N	118·24 W
63a	Hermsdorf (Neigh.)	52·37 N	13·18 E
64e	Hernals (Neigh.)	48·13 N	16·20 E
61	Herne	51·32 N	7·13 E
54c	Hernwood Heights	39·22 N	77·50 W
58a	Héroes Chapultepec	19·28 N	99·04 W
58a	Héroes de Churubusco	19·22 N	99·06 W
60	Herongate	51·36 N	0·21 E
60	Heronsgate	51·38 N	0·31 W
60	Hersham	51·22 N	0·23 W
61	Herten	51·35 N	7·07 E
62b	Heswall	53·20 N	3·06 W
64e	Hetzendorf (Neigh.)	48·10 N	16·18 E
61	Heven (Neigh.)	51·26 N	7·17 E
53	Hewlett	40·38 N	73·42 W
53	Hewlett Harbor	40·38 N	73·41 W
60	Hextable	51·25 N	0·11 E
62b	Heywood	53·36 N	2·13 W
56a	Hickory Hills	41·43 N	87·49 W
53	Hicksville	40·46 N	73·32 W
61	Hiddinghausen	51·22 N	7·17 E
61	Hiesfeld	51·33 N	6·46 E
64e	Hietzing (Neigh.)	48·11 N	16·18 E
67b	Higashi (Neigh.)	34·41 N	135·31 E
67a	Higashimurayama	35·46 N	139·29 E
67b	Higashinada (Neigh.)	34·43 N	135·16 E
67a	Higashinakano	35·38 N	139·25 E
67b	Higashinari (Neigh.)	34·40 N	135·33 E
67a	Higashiōizumi (Neigh.)	35·45 N	139·36 E
67b	Higashiōsaka	34·39 N	135·35 E
67b	Higashisumiyoshi (Neigh.)	34·37 N	135·32 E
66e	Higashiyama (Neigh.)	34·52 N	135·48 E
67b	Higashiyodogawa (Neigh.)	34·44 N	135·29 E
60	Higham Upshire	51·26 N	0·28 E
60	High Beach	51·39 N	0·02 E
55b	Highcliff	40·32 N	80·03 W
62b	Higher Broughton (Neigh.)	53·30 N	2·15 W
55b	Highland	40·33 N	80·04 W
54d	Highland Park, Md.	38·54 N	76·54 W
55c	Highland Park, Mi.	42·24 N	83·06 W
69b	Highlands North (Neigh.)	26·09 S	28·05 E
60	High Laver	51·45 N	0·13 E
60	High Ongar	51·43 N	0·16 E
62b	Hightown	53·32 N	3·04 W
61	Hilden	51·10 N	6·56 E
69b	Hillbrow (Neigh.)	26·11 S	28·03 E
54b	Hill Crest	40·05 N	75·11 W
54d	Hillcrest Heights	38·52 N	76·57 W
61	Hillen (Neigh.)	51·37 N	7·13 E
60	Hillingdon (Neigh.)	51·32 N	0·27 W
54d	Hillside	38·52 N	76·55 W
53	Hillside (Neigh.)	40·42 N	73·47 W
54d	Hillwood	38·52 N	77·10 W
61	Hiltrop (Neigh.)	51·30 N	7·15 E
61	Himmelgeist (Neigh.)	51·10 N	6·49 E
52a	Hingham	42·14 N	70·53 W
52a	Hingham	42·17 N	70·55 W
67a	Hino	35·41 N	139·24 E
56a	Hinsdale	41·48 N	87·56 W
61	Hinsel (Neigh.)	51·26 N	7·05 E
67b	Hirota	34·45 N	135·21 E
64e	Hirschstetten (Neigh.)	48·14 N	16·29 E
60	Hither Green (Neigh.)	51·27 N	0·01 W
53	Hoboken	40·45 N	74·03 W
68b	Hobsons B.	37·51 S	144·56 E
61	Hochdahl	51·13 N	6·56 E
61	Hochheide	51·27 N	6·41 E
66m	Ho Chi Minh City (Saigon)	10·45 N	106·40 E
61	Hochlar (Neigh.)	51·36 N	7·10 E
61	Höchsten	51·27 N	7·29 E
56a	Hodgkins	41·46 N	87·51 W
64e	Hofburg (P. Int.)	48·12 N	16·22 E
58a	Hogar y Redención	19·22 N	99·13 W
61	Hohenlimburg	51·21 N	7·35 E
63a	Hohen-Neuendorf	52·40 N	13·16 E
63a	Hohenschönhausen (Neigh.)	52·33 N	13·30 E
61	Hohensyburg (P. Int.)	51·25 N	7·29 E
61	Höhscheid (Neigh.)	51·09 N	7·04 E
61	Hoisten	51·08 N	6·42 E
60	Holborn (Neigh.)	51·31 N	0·07 W
52a	Holbrook	42·09 N	71·01 W
62b	Hollins	53·34 N	2·17 W
53	Hollis (Neigh.)	40·43 N	73·46 W
57	Hollywood (Neigh.)	34·06 N	118·21 W
57	Hollywood Bowl (P. Int.)	34·07 N	118·20 W
54b	Holmes	39·54 N	75·19 W
54d	Holmes Run Acres	38·51 N	77·13 W
68a	Holroyd	33·50 S	150·58 E
61	Holten (Neigh.)	51·31 N	6·48 E
61	Holthausen (Neigh.)	51·34 N	7·26 E
61	Holzen	51·26 N	7·31 E
61	Holzheim	51·09 N	6·39 E
61	Holzwickede	51·30 N	7·36 E
61	Homberg, F.R.G.	51·28 N	6·43 E

Page	Name Region	Lat. ° ′	Long. ° ′
54b	Swarthmore	39·54 N	75·21 W
62b	Swinton	53·31 N	2·20 W
55b	Swissvale	40·25 N	79·53 W
68b	Sydenham	37·42 S	144·46 E
60	Sydenham (Neigh.), Eng.	51·26 N	0·03 W
69b	Sydenham (Neigh.), S. Afr.	26·09 S	28·06 E
68a	Sydney	33·52 S	151·13 E
68a	Sylvania	34·01 S	151·07 E
68a	Sylvania Heights	34·02 S	151·06 E
68b	Syndal	37·53 S	145·09 E
53	Syosset	40·50 N	73·30 W
67b	Syukunosho	34·50 N	135·32 E
59d	Taboão da Serra	23·38 S	46·46 W
67a	Tachikawa	35·42 N	139·25 E
54b	Tacony (Neigh.)	40·02 N	75·03 W
58a	Tacuba (Neigh.)	19·28 N	99·12 W
58a	Tacubaya (Neigh.)	19·25 N	99·12 W
60	Tadworth	51·17 N	0·14 W
66d	T'aipei	25·03 N	121·30 E
66d	Taipei Institute of Technology (P. Int.)	25·02 N	121·32 E
66c	Tai Po Tsai	22·21 N	114·15 E
67a	Taitō (Neigh.)	35·43 N	139·47 E
66d	Taiwan Normal University (P. Int.)	25·02 N	121·31 E
66c	Tai Wan Tau	22·18 N	114·17 E
66c	Tai Wan Tsun	22·19 N	114·12 E
65b	Taiyanggong	39·58 N	116·25 E
64b	Tajninka	55·54 N	37·45 E
66h	Tajrish	35·48 N	51·25 E
67b	Takarazuka	34·49 N	135·21 E
67b	Takatsuki	34·51 N	135·37 E
67a	Takenotsuka (Neigh.)	35·48 N	139·48 E
54d	Takoma Park	38·59 N	77·01 W
68b	Tally Ho	37·52 S	145·09 E
67a	Tama	35·37 N	139·27 E
67a	Tama (R.)	35·32 N	139·47 E
67a	Tamagawa (Neigh.)	35·37 N	139·39 E
67a	Tama-kyūryō (Hills)	35·35 N	139·30 E
67a	Tanashi	35·44 N	139·33 E
66m	Tan-binh	10·48 N	106·40 E
66k	Tanjungpriok (Neigh.)	6·06 S	106·53 E
66m	Tan-qui-dong	10·44 N	106·43 E
66d	Tanshui Ho (R.)	25·08 N	121·27 E
66m	Tan Son Nhut	10·49 N	106·40 E
66m	Tan-thoi-nhut	10·50 N	106·36 E
66m	Tan-thuan-dong	10·45 N	106·44 E
58d	Tapiales	34·44 S	58·30 W
65a	Tapsiā (Neigh.)	22·32 N	88·22 E
59c	Taquara (Neigh.)	22·55 S	43·21 W
66h	Tarasht	35·42 N	51·21 E
62b	Tarbock Green	53·23 N	2·49 W
65e	Taredo (Neigh.)	19·58 N	72·49 E
57	Tarzana (Neigh.)	34·10 N	118·32 W
60	Tate Gallery (P. Int.)	51·29 N	0·08 W
66c	Tathong Chan.	22·15 N	114·15 E
60	Tatsfield	51·18 N	0·02 E
54b	Tavistock	39·53 N	75·02 W
55c	Taylor	42·13 N	83·16 W
64d	Tāyros	37·58 N	23·42 E
66g	Taytay	14·34 N	121·08 E
53	Teaneck	40·53 N	74·01 W
55c	Tecumseh	42·19 N	82·54 W
60	Teddington (Neigh.)	51·25 N	0·20 W
63a	Tegel (Neigh.)	52·35 N	13·17 E
63a	Tegeler See (L.)	52·35 N	13·15 E
65d	Tehar (Neigh.)	28·38 N	77·07 E
66h	Tehrān	35·40 N	51·26 E
64b	Tekstil'ščiki (Neigh.)	55·42 N	37·44 E
65d	Tela	28·44 N	77·20 E
63a	Teltow	52·23 N	13·16 E
63a	Teltower Hochfläche (Plat.)	52·22 N	13·20 E
63a	Tempelhof (Neigh.)	52·28 N	13·23 E
57	Temple City	34·07 N	118·03 W
54d	Temple Hills	38·49 N	76·57 W
65b	Temple of Heaven (P. Int.)	39·53 N	116·25 E
68b	Templestowe	37·45 S	145·07 E
54b	Temple University (P. Int.)	39·59 N	75·09 W
53	Tenafly	40·56 N	73·58 W
67b	Tennōji (Neigh.)	34·39 N	135·31 E
58a	Tepalcates	19·23 N	99·04 W
58a	Tepepan	19·16 N	99·08 W
57	Terminal I.	33·45 N	118·15 W
53	Teterboro	40·52 N	74·03 W
64c	Tevere (Tiber) (R.)	41·49 N	12·25 E
65a	Thākurpukur	22·28 N	88·19 E
60	Thames (R.)	51·30 N	0·29 E
60	Thames Ditton	51·23 N	0·21 W
65e	Thāna Cr.	19·00 N	72·57 E
62b	Thatto Heath	53·26 N	2·45 W
68b	The Basin	37·51 S	145·19 E
54d	The Capital (P. Int.)	38·53 N	77·00 W
53	The Narrows (Str.)	40·37 N	74·03 W
60	The Oval (P. Int.)	51·29 N	0·07 W
68a	The Sound (Str.)	33·49 S	151·17 E
60	Theydon Bois	51·40 N	0·06 E
62c	Thiais	48·46 N	2·23 E
61	Thier	51·05 N	7·22 E
52c	Thistletown (Neigh.)	43·44 N	79·33 W
53	Thomaston	40·47 N	73·43 W
68b	Thomastown	37·41 S	145·01 E
66f	Thon Buri (Neigh.)	13·43 N	100·29 E
60	Thong	51·24 N	0·24 E
65c	Thong Hoe	1·25 N	103·42 E
66m	Thong-tay-hoi	10·50 N	106·39 E
62c	Thorigny-sur-Marne	48·53 N	2·42 E
68b	Thornbury	37·45 S	145·00 E
69b	Thornhill	26·07 S	28·09 E
68a	Thornleigh	33·44 S	151·05 E
62b	Thornton	53·30 N	3·00 W
62b	Thornton Hough	53·19 N	3·03 W
62b	Thornton-le-Moors	53·16 N	2·50 W
60	Thornwood Common	51·43 N	0·08 E
56b	Tiburon	36·04 N	119·19 W
61	Tiefenbroich	51·18 N	6·49 E
63a	Tiergarten (Neigh.)	52·31 N	13·21 E
63a	Tiergarten (P. Int.)	52·31 N	13·21 E
59d	Tietê (R.)	23·29 S	46·51 W
60	Tilbury	51·28 N	0·23 E
54c	Timberview	39·13 N	76·45 W
53	Times Square (P. Int.)	40·45 N	74·00 W
62b	Timperley	53·24 N	2·19 W
66c	Ting Kau	22·23 N	114·04 E
54b	Tioga (Neigh.)	40·00 N	75·10 W
63d	Tires	38·43 N	9·21 W
65a	Titāgarh	22·45 N	88·22 E
66c	Tiu Keng Wan	22·18 N	114·15 E
58a	Tizapán	19·20 N	99·13 W
58a	Tlāhuac	19·16 N	99·00 W
58a	Tlalnepantla	19·33 N	99·12 W
58a	Tlalpan	19·17 N	99·10 W
58a	Tlaltenco	19·17 N	99·01 W
67a	Toda	35·48 N	139·41 E
67a	Tokorozawa	35·47 N	139·28 E
66b	Toksu Palace (P. Int.)	37·35 N	126·58 E
67a	Tōkyō	35·42 N	139·46 E
65a	Tollygunge (Neigh.)	22·30 N	88·21 E
60	Tolworth (Neigh.)	51·23 N	0·17 W
69a	Tombs of the Caliphs (P. Int.)	30·03 N	31·17 E
55a	Tonawanda	43·01 N	78·53 W
55a	Tonawanda, Town of	42·59 N	78·52 W
55a	Tonawanda Cr.	43·02 N	78·53 W
67b	Tonda	34·50 N	135·36 E
61	Tönsholt	51·38 N	6·58 E
68a	Toongabbie	33·47 S	150·57 E
60	Toot Hill	51·42 N	0·12 E
64f	Topkapı (Neigh.)	41·02 N	28·54 E
64f	Topkapı Müzesi (P. Int.)	41·00 N	28·59 E
64b	T'oplyj Stan (Neigh.)	55·37 N	37·30 E
62b	Top of Hebers	53·34 N	2·12 W
62b	Toppings	53·37 N	2·25 W
62c	Torcy	48·51 N	2·39 E
64c	Tor di Quinto (Neigh.)	41·56 N	12·28 E
52c	Toronto	43·39 N	79·23 W
64c	Tor Pignatara (Neigh.)	41·52 N	12·32 E
57	Torrance	33·50 N	118·19 W
63e	Torrellas de Llobregat	41·21 N	1·59 E
64c	Tor Sapienza (Neigh.)	41·54 N	12·35 E
58d	Tortuguitas	34·28 S	58·45 W
67a	Toshima (Neigh.)	35·44 N	139·43 E
53	Totowa	40·54 N	74·13 W
60	Tottenham (Neigh.)	51·35 N	0·04 W
53	Tottenville (Neigh.)	40·31 N	74·15 W
60	Totteridge (Neigh.)	51·38 N	0·12 W
62b	Tottington	53·37 N	2·20 W
62c	Toussus-le-Noble	48·45 N	2·07 E
53	Towaco	40·56 N	74·21 W
60	Tower Hamlets (Neigh.)	51·32 N	0·03 W
60	Tower of London (P. Int.)	51·30 N	0·05 W
65e	Towers of Silence (P. Int.)	18·58 N	72·48 E
65c	Town Reach (Str.)	1·28 N	103·44 E
54c	Towson	39·24 N	76·36 W
67a	Toyoda	35·39 N	139·23 E
67b	Toyonaka	34·47 N	135·28 E
61	Traar (Neigh.)	51·23 N	6·36 E
63d	Trafaria	38·40 N	9·14 W
62b	Trafford Park	53·28 N	2·20 W
62b	Tranmere	53·23 N	3·01 W
62c	Trappes	48·47 N	2·00 E
62c	Tremblay-lès-Gonesse	48·59 N	2·34 E
53	Tremont (Neigh.)	40·51 N	73·55 W
63a	Treptow (Neigh.)	52·29 N	13·29 E
62c	Tressancourt	48·55 N	2·00 E
62c	Triel-sur-Seine	48·59 N	2·00 E
60	Tring	51·48 N	0·40 W
64b	Troice-Lykovo (Neigh.)	55·47 N	37·24 E
65e	Trombay (Neigh.)	19·02 N	72·57 E
64b	Tropar'ovo (Neigh.)	55·39 N	37·29 E
60	Trottiscliffe	51·19 N	0·21 E
69b	Troyville (Neigh.)	26·12 S	28·04 E
66c	Tsing I.	22·21 N	114·05 E
66c	Tsin Shui Wan (B.)	22·13 N	114·10 E
67b	Tsuda	34·49 N	135·43 E
67b	Tsukumono (Neigh.)	34·50 N	135·11 E
67a	Tsunashima (Neigh.)	35·32 N	139·38 E
66c	Tsun Wan (Quanwan)	22·22 N	114·07 E
67a	Tsurumi (R.)	35·29 N	139·41 E
53	Tuckahoe	40·57 N	73·50 W
68b	Tullamarine	37·41 S	144·52 E
69b	Turffontein (Neigh.)	26·15 S	28·02 E
68a	Turramurra	33·44 S	151·08 E
55b	Turtle Creek	40·25 N	79·49 W
57	Tustin	33·45 N	117·49 W
54d	Tuxedo	38·55 N	76·55 W
60	Twickenham (Neigh.)	51·27 N	0·20 W
54d	Tyler Park	38·52 N	77·12 W
54d	Tysons Corner	38·55 N	77·14 W
	U		
61	Ückendorf (Neigh.)	51·30 N	7·07 E
61	Uedesheim (Neigh.)	51·10 N	6·48 E
61	Uerdingen (Neigh.)	51·21 N	6·39 E
66e	Uji	34·53 N	135·48 E
67a	Ukita (Neigh.)	35·40 N	139·52 E
61	Üllendahl (Neigh.)	51·19 N	7·18 E
58a	Unidad Santa Fe	19·23 N	99·15 W
53	Union	40·42 N	74·16 W
53	Union City	40·46 N	74·02 W
53	Uniondale	40·43 N	73·36 W
53	United Nations Headquarters (P. Int.)	40·45 N	73·58 W
54a	University Heights	41·30 N	81·32 W
54d	University Park	38·58 N	76·57 W
64e	Untermauerbach	48·14 N	16·12 E
62b	Upholland	53·33 N	2·44 W
54b	Upland	39·51 N	75·23 W
53	Upper Brookville	40·51 N	73·34 W
54b	Upper Darby	39·58 N	75·16 W
68b	Upper Ferntree Gully	37·54 S	145·19 E
53	Upper New York B.	40·41 N	74·03 W
55b	Upper Saint Clair	40·21 N	80·05 W
60	Upper Tooting (Neigh.)	51·26 N	0·10 W
60	Upton, Eng.	51·30 N	0·35 W
56a	Uptown (Neigh.)	41·58 N	87·40 W
68b	Upwey	37·54 S	145·20 E
67a	Urayasu	35·39 N	139·54 E
62b	Urmston	53·27 N	2·21 W
64f	Üsküdar (Neigh.)	41·01 N	29·03 E
65d	Usmānpur (Neigh.)	28·41 N	77·15 E
61	Utfort	51·28 N	6·38 E
59d	Utinga	23·38 S	46·32 W
65a	Uttarpara-Kotrung	22·40 N	88·21 E
60	Uxbridge (Neigh.)	51·33 N	0·29 W
67b	Uyama	34·50 N	135·41 E
	V		
62c	Vaires-sur-Marne	48·52 N	2·39 E
64c	Valcanuta (Neigh.)	41·53 N	12·25 E
58d	Valentin Alsina (Neigh.)	34·40 S	58·25 W
62c	Valérien, Mont (Hill)	48·53 N	2·13 E
63e	Valldoreix	41·28 N	2·04 E
63b	Vallecas (Neigh.)	40·23 N	3·37 W
57	Valleydale	34·06 N	117·56 W
54c	Valley Mede	39·17 N	76·50 W
54c	Valley Stream, Md.	39·23 N	76·41 W
53	Valley Stream, NY.	40·40 N	73·42 W
64f	Vaniköy (Neigh.)	41·04 N	29·04 E
57	Van Nuys (Neigh.)	34·11 N	118·26 W
62c	Vanves	48·50 N	2·18 E
63c	Vanzago	45·32 N	9·00 E
59c	Vargem Grande (Neigh.)	22·59 S	43·29 W
64g	Várpalota (P. Int.)	47·30 N	19·02 E
64a	Vasiljevskij, Ostrov (I.)	59·56 N	30·15 E
64c	Vatican City (Città del Vaticano)	41·54 N	12·27 E
68a	Vaucluse	33·51 S	151·17 E
52c	Vaughan	43·47 N	79·36 W
62c	Vauhallan	48·44 N	2·12 E
62c	Vaujours	48·56 N	2·35 E
61	Velbert	51·20 N	7·02 E
57	Venice (Neigh.)	34·00 N	118·29 W
61	Vennhausen (Neigh.)	51·13 N	6·51 E
69b	Venterspos Location	26·18 S	27·42 E
61	Verberg (Neigh.)	51·22 N	6·36 E
52c	Verdun	45·27 N	73·34 W
54b	Verga	39·52 N	75·10 W
68b	Vermont	37·50 S	145·12 E
53	Verona, NJ.	40·50 N	74·12 W
55b	Verona, Pa.	40·30 N	79·50 W
62c	Verrières-le-Buisson	48·45 N	2·16 E
62c	Versailles, Fr.	48·48 N	2·08 E
55b	Versailles, Pa.	40·21 N	79·51 W
58d	Versailles (Neigh.)	34·38 S	58·31 W
62c	Versailles, Château de (P. Int.)	48·48 N	2·07 E
60	Verulamium (P. Int.)	51·45 N	0·22 W
64b	Vešn'aki (Neigh.)	55·44 N	37·49 E
63b	Vicálvaro (Neigh.)	40·24 N	3·36 W
58d	Vicente López	34·32 S	58·29 W
66c	Victoria (Xianggang)	22·17 N	114·09 E
58d	Victoria (Neigh.)	34·28 S	58·31 W
69d	Victoria I.	6·26 N	3·26 E
68b	Victoria Lawn Tennis Association Courts (P. Int.)	37·51 S	145·02 E
66c	Victoria Peak (Mtn.)	22·17 N	114·08 E
62b	Victoria Station (P. Int.)	53·29 N	2·15 W
64e	Vienna (Wien), Aus.	48·13 N	16·20 E
54d	Vienna, Va.	38·29 N	75·49 W
61	Vieringhausen (Neigh.)	51·11 N	7·10 E
57	View Park	34·00 N	118·21 W
63c	Vigentino (Neigh.)	45·25 N	9·11 E
59d	Vila Augusta	23·28 S	46·32 W
59d	Vila Boacaya (Neigh.)	23·29 S	46·44 W
59d	Vila Guilherme (Neigh.)	23·30 S	46·36 W
59c	Vila Isabel (Neigh.)	22·55 S	43·15 W
59d	Vila Jaguára (Neigh.)	23·31 S	46·45 W
59d	Vila Madalena (Neigh.)	23·33 S	46·42 W
59d	Vila Mariana (Neigh.)	23·35 S	46·38 W
59c	Vila Progresso	22·55 S	43·03 W
59d	Vila Prudente (Neigh.)	23·35 S	46·33 W
58d	Villa Adelina (Neigh.)	34·31 S	58·32 W
64c	Villa Borghese (P. Int.)	41·55 N	12·29 E
58d	Villa Bosch (Neigh.)	34·36 S	58·34 W
58d	Villa Ciudadela (Neigh.)	34·38 S	58·34 W
58d	Villa de Mayo	34·31 S	58·41 W
58d	Villa Devoto (Neigh.)	34·36 S	58·31 W
58d	Villa Diamante (Neigh.)	34·41 S	58·26 W
58d	Villa Dominico (Neigh.)	34·41 S	58·20 W
58d	Villa José L. Suárez (Neigh.)	34·32 S	58·34 W
58d	Villa Lugano (Neigh.)	34·41 S	58·28 W
58d	Villa Lynch (Neigh.)	34·36 S	58·32 W
58d	Villa Madero	34·41 S	58·30 W
54c	Villa Nova, Md.	39·21 N	76·44 W
54b	Villanova, Pa.	40·02 N	75·21 W
58a	Villa Obregón	19·21 N	99·12 W
58d	Villa Real (Neigh.)	34·37 S	58·31 W
58d	Villa Sáenz Peña (Neigh.)	34·46 S	58·31 W
58d	Villa San Andrés (Neigh.)	34·33 S	58·32 W
58d	Villa Santos Lugares (Neigh.)	34·36 S	58·32 W
58d	Villa Turdera (Neigh.)	34·48 S	58·25 W
63b	Villaverde (Neigh.)	40·21 N	3·42 W
62c	Villebon-sur-Yvette	48·42 N	2·15 E
62c	Villecresnes	48·43 N	2·32 E
62c	Ville-d'Avray	48·50 N	2·11 E
62c	Villejuif	48·48 N	2·22 E
62c	Villemomble	48·53 N	2·31 E
62c	Villeneuve-la-Garenne	48·56 N	2·20 E
62c	Villeneuve-le-Roi	48·44 N	2·25 E
62c	Villeneuve-Saint-Georges	48·44 N	2·27 E
62c	Villeparisis	48·56 N	2·37 E
62c	Villevaudé	48·55 N	2·39 E
62c	Villiers-le-Bâcle	48·44 N	2·08 E
62c	Villiers-le-Bel	49·00 N	2·23 E
62c	Villiers-sur-Marne	48·50 N	2·33 E
62c	Vincennes	48·51 N	2·26 E
62c	Vincennes, Château de (P. Int.)	48·51 N	2·26 E
59b	Virgen del San Cristó bal (P. Int.)	33·26 S	70·39 W
54d	Virginia Hills	38·47 N	77·06 W
60	Virginia Water	51·24 N	0·34 W
62c	Viroflay	48·48 N	2·10 E
64d	Víron	37·57 N	23·45 E
59b	Vitacura	33·24 S	70·36 W
58c	Vitarte	12·02 S	76·54 W
62c	Vitry-sur-Seine	48·48 N	2·24 E
64b	Vladykino (Neigh.)	55·52 N	37·36 E
61	Voerde, F.R.G.	51·35 N	6·41 E
61	Voesch	51·24 N	6·26 E
61	Vogelheim (Neigh.)	51·29 N	6·59 E
61	Vohwinkel (Neigh.)	51·14 N	7·09 E
62c	Voisins-le-Bretonneux	48·45 N	2·03 E
64b	Volchonka-Zil (Neigh.)	55·40 N	37·37 E
61	Vollme	51·10 N	7·36 E
61	Volmarstein	51·22 N	7·23 E
61	Volmerswerth (Neigh.)	51·11 N	6·46 E
61	Vorhalle (Neigh.)	51·23 N	7·28 E
61	Vormholz	51·24 N	7·18 E
	W		
69b	Wadeville	26·16 S	28·11 E
64e	Währing (Neigh.)	48·14 N	16·21 E
68a	Wahroonga	33·43 S	150·07 E
63a	Waidmannslust (Neigh.)	52·36 N	13·20 E
68a	Waitara	33·43 S	150·06 E
52a	Wakefield	42·30 N	71·04 W
61	Waldbauer (Neigh.)	51·18 N	7·28 E
62b	Walkden	53·32 N	2·24 W
61	Wallach	51·35 N	6·34 E
62b	Wallasey	53·26 N	3·03 W
68a	Wallgrove	33·47 S	150·51 E
54b	Wallingford	39·54 N	75·22 W
53	Wallington	40·51 N	74·07 W
60	Wallington (Neigh.)	51·21 N	0·09 W
62b	Walmersley	53·37 N	2·18 W
57	Walnut	34·01 N	117·51 W
57	Walnut Park	33·58 N	118·13 W
52a	Walpole	42·08 N	71·15 W
61	Walsum	51·32 N	6·41 E
54d	Walter Reed Army Medical Center (P. Int.)	38·58 N	77·02 W
63a	Waltersdorf	52·22 N	13·35 E
52a	Waltham	42·23 N	71·14 W
60	Waltham Forest (Neigh.)	51·35 N	0·01 W
60	Walthamstow (Neigh.)	51·35 N	0·01 W
60	Walton	51·24 N	0·25 W
60	Walton on the Hill	51·17 N	0·15 W
61	Waltrop	51·37 N	7·23 E
54b	Walt Whitman Homes	39·52 N	75·11 W
61	Walze	51·16 N	7·31 E
61	Wambel (Neigh.)	51·32 N	7·32 E
61	Wandhofen	51·26 N	7·33 E

glossary of foreign geographical terms

Annam ... Annamese
Arab ... Arabic
Bantu ... Bantu
Bur ... Burmese
Camb ... Cambodian
Celt ... Celtic
Chn ... Chinese
Czech ... Czech
Dan ... Danish
Du ... Dutch
Fin ... Finnish
Fr ... French
Ger ... German
Gr ... Greek
Hung ... Hungarian
Ice ... Icelandic
India ... India
Indian ... American Indian
Indon ... Indonesian
It ... Italian
Jap ... Japanese
Kor ... Korean
Mal ... Malayan
Mong ... Mongolian
Nor ... Norwegian
Per ... Persian
Pol ... Polish
Port ... Portuguese
Rom ... Romanian
Rus ... Russian
Siam ... Siamese
So. Slav ... Southern Slavonic
Sp ... Spanish
Swe ... Swedish
Tib ... Tibetan
Tur ... Turkish
Yugo ... Yugoslav

å, Nor., Swe ... brook, river
aa, Dan., Nor ... brook
aas, Dan., Nor ... ridge
āb, Per ... water, river
abad, India, Per ... town, city
ada, Tur ... island
adrar, Berber ... mountain
air, Indon ... stream
akrotírion, Gr ... cape
älf, Swe ... river
alp, Ger ... mountain
altipiano, It ... plateau
alto, Sp ... height
archipel, Fr ... archipelago
archipiélago, Sp ... archipelago
arquipélago, Port ... archipelago
arroyo, Sp ... brook, stream
ås, Nor., Swe ... ridge
austral, Sp ... southern
baai, Du ... bay
bab, Arab ... gate, port
bach, Ger ... brook, stream
backe, Swe ... hill
bad, Ger ... bath, spa
bahía, Sp ... bay, gulf
bahr, Arab ... river, sea, lake
baia, It ... bay, gulf
baía, Port ... bay
baie, Fr ... bay, gulf
bajo, Sp ... depression
bak, Indon ... stream
bakke, Dan., Nor ... hill
balkan, Tur ... mountain range
bana, Jap ... point, cape
banco, Sp ... bank
bandar, Mal., Per. ... town, port, harbor
bang, Siam ... village
bassin, Fr ... basin
batang, Indon., Mal ... river
ben, Celt ... mountain, summit
bender, Arab ... harbor, port
bereg, Rus ... coast, shore
berg, Du., Ger., Nor., Swe. ... mountain, hill
bir, Arab ... well
birkat, Arab ... lake, pond, pool
bit, Arab ... house
bjaerg, Dan., Nor ... mountain
bocche, It ... mouth
boğazı, Tur ... strait
bois, Fr ... forest, wood
boloto, Rus ... marsh
bolsón, Sp flat-floored desert valley
boreal, Sp ... northern
borg, Dan., Nor., Swe ... castle, town
borgo, It ... town, suburb
bosch, Du ... forest, wood
bouche, Fr ... river mouth
bourg, Fr ... town, borough
bro, Dan., Nor., Swe ... bridge
brücke, Ger ... bridge
bucht, Ger ... bay, bight
bugt, Dan., Nor., Swe ... bay, gulf
bulu, Indon ... mountain
burg, Du., Ger ... castle, town
buri, Siam ... town
burun, burnu, Tur ... cape
by, Dan., Nor., Swe ... village
caatinga, Port. (Brazil) ... open brushland
cabezo, Sp ... summit
cabo, Port., Sp ... cape
campo, It., Port., Sp ... plain, field
campos, Port. (Brazil) ... plains
cañón, Sp ... canyon
cap, Fr ... cape
capo, It ... cape
casa, It., Port., Sp ... house
castello, It., Port ... castle, fort
castillo, Sp ... castle
càte, Fr ... hill
çay, Tur ... stream, river
cayo, Sp ... rock, shoal, islet
cerro, Sp ... mountain, hill
champ, Fr ... field
chang, Chn ... village, middle
château, Fr ... castle
chen, Chn ... market town
chiang, Chn ... river
chott, Arab ... salt lake
chou, Chn capital of district; island
chu, Tib ... water, stream
cidade, Port ... town, city
cima, Sp ... summit, peak
città, It ... town, city
ciudad, Sp ... town, city
cochilha, Port ... ridge
col, Fr ... pass
colina, Sp ... hill
cordillera, Sp ... mountain chain
costa, It., Port., Sp ... coast
côte, Fr ... coast
cuchilla, Sp ... mountain ridge
dağ, Tur ... mountain(s)
dake, Jap ... peak, summit
dal, Dan., Du., Nor., Swe ... valley
dan, Kor ... point, cape
danau, Indon ... lake
dar, Arab ... house, abode, country
darya, Per ... river, sea
dasht, Per ... plain, desert
deniz, Tur ... sea
désert, Fr ... desert
deserto, It ... desert
desierto, Sp ... desert
détroit, Fr ... strait
dijk, Du ... dam, dike
djebel, Arab ... mountain
do, Kor ... island
dorf, Ger ... village
dorp, Du ... village
duin, Du ... dune
dzong, Tib. ... fort, administrative capital
eau, Fr ... water
ecuador, Sp ... equator
eiland, Du ... island
elv, Dan., Nor ... river, stream
embalse, Sp ... reservoir
erg, Arab ... dune, sandy desert
est, Fr., It ... east
estado, Sp ... state
este, Port., Sp ... east
estrecho, Sp ... strait
étang, Fr ... pond, lake
état, Fr ... state
eyjar, Ice ... islands
feld, Ger ... field, plain
festung, Ger ... fortress
fiume, It ... river
fjäll, Swe ... mountain
fjärd, Swe ... bay, inlet
fjeld, Nor ... mountain, hill
fjord, Dan., Nor ... fiord, inlet
fjördur, Ice ... fiord, inlet
fleuve, Fr ... river
flod, Dan., Swe ... river
flói, Ice ... bay, marshland
fluss, Ger ... river
foce, It ... river mouth
fontein, Du ... a spring
forêt, Fr ... forest
fors, Swe ... waterfall
forst, Ger ... forest
fos, Dan., Nor ... waterfall
fu, Chn ... town, residence
fuente, Sp ... spring, fountain
fuerte, Sp ... fort
furt, Ger ... ford
gang, Kor ... stream, river
gangri, Tib ... mountain
gat, Dan., Nor ... channel
gàve, Fr ... stream
gawa, Jap ... river
gebergte, Du ... mountain range
gebiet, Ger ... district, territory
gebirge, Ger ... mountains
ghat, India ... pass, mountain range
gobi, Mong ... desert
gol, Mong ... river
göl, gölü, Tur ... lake
golf, Du., Ger ... gulf, bay
golfe, Fr ... gulf, bay
golfo, It., Port., Sp ... gulf, bay
gomba, gompa, Tib ... monastery
gora, Rus., So. Slav ... mountain
góra, Pol ... mountain
gorod, Rus ... town
grad, Rus., So. Slav ... town
guba, Rus ... bay, gulf
gundung, Indon ... mountain
guntō, Jap ... archipelago
gunung, Mal ... mountain
haf, Swe ... sea, ocean
hafen, Ger ... port, harbor
haff, Ger ... gulf, inland sea
hai, Chn ... sea, lake
hama, Jap ... beach, shore
hamada, Arab ... rocky plateau
hamn, Swe ... harbor
hāmūn, Per ... swampy lake, plain
hantō, Jap ... peninsula
hassi, Arab ... well, spring
haus, Ger ... house
haut, Fr ... summit, top
hav, Dan., Nor ... sea, ocean
havn, Dan., Nor ... harbor, port
havre, Fr ... harbor, port
háza, Hung ... house, dwelling of
heim, Ger ... hamlet, home
hem, Swe ... hamlet, home
higashi, Jap ... east
hisar, Tur ... fortress
hissar, Arab ... fort
ho, Chn ... river
hoek, Du ... cape
hof, Ger ... court, farmhouse
höfn, Ice ... harbor
hoku, Jap ... north
holm, Dan., Nor., Swe ... island
hora, Czech ... mountain
horn, Ger ... peak
hoved, Dan., Nor ... cape
hsien, Chn district, district capital
hu, Chn ... lake
hügel, Ger ... hill
huk, Dan., Swe ... point
hus, Dan., Nor., Swe ... house
île, Fr ... island
ilha, Port ... island
indsö, Dan., Nor ... lake
insel, Ger ... island
insjö, Swe ... lake
irmak, irmagi, Tur ... river
isla, Sp ... island
isola, It ... island
istmo, It., Sp ... isthmus
järvi, jaur, Fin ... lake
jebel, Arab ... mountain
jima, Jap ... island
jökel, Nor ... glacier
joki, Fin ... river
jökull, Ice ... glacier
kaap, Du ... cape
kai, Jap ... bay, gulf, sea
kaikyō, Jap ... channel, strait
kalat, Per ... castle, fortress
kale, Tur ... fort
kali, Mal ... creek, river
kand, Per ... village
kang, Chn mountain ridge; village
kap, Dan., Ger ... cape
kapp, Nor., Swe ... cape
kasr, Arab ... fort, castle
kawa, Jap ... river
kefr, Arab ... village
kei, Jap ... creek, river
ken, Jap ... prefecture
khor, Arab ... bay, inlet
khrebet, Rus ... mountain range
kiang, Chn ... large river
king, Chn ... capital city, town
kita, Jap ... north
ko, Jap ... lake
köbstad, Dan ... market-town
kol, Mong ... lake
kólpos, Gr ... gulf
kong, Chn ... river
kopf, Ger ... head, summit, peak
köpstad, Swe ... market-town
körfezi, Tur ... gulf
kosa, Rus ... spit
kou, Chn ... river mouth
köy, Tur ... village
kraal, Du. (Africa) ... native village
ksar, Arab ... fortified village
kuala, Mal ... bay, river mouth
kuh, Per ... mountain
kum, Tur ... sand
kuppe, Ger ... summit
küste, Ger ... coast
kyo, Jap ... town, capital
la, Tib ... mountain pass
labuan, Mal ... anchorage, port
lac, Fr ... lake
lago, It., Port., Sp ... lake
lagoa, Port ... lake, marsh
laguna, It., Port., Sp ... lagoon, lake
lahti, Fin ... bay, gulf
län, Swe ... county
landsby, Dan., Nor ... village
liehtao, Chn ... archipelago
liman, Tur ... bay, port
ling, Chn ... pass, ridge, mountain
llanos, Sp ... plains
loch, Celt. (Scotland) ... lake, bay
loma, Sp ... long, low hill
lough, Celt. (Ireland) ... lake, bay
machi, Jap ... town
man, Kor ... bay
mar, Port., Sp ... sea
mare, It., Rom ... sea
marisma, Sp ... marsh, swamp
mark, Ger ... boundary, limit
massif, Fr ... block of mountains
mato, Port ... forest, thicket
me, Siam ... river
meer, Du., Ger ... lake, sea
mer, Fr ... sea
mesa, Sp ... flat-topped mountain
meseta, Sp ... plateau
mina, Port., Sp ... mine
minami, Jap ... south
minato, Jap ... harbor, haven
misaki, Jap ... cape, headland
mont, Fr ... mount, mountain
montagna, It ... mountain
montagne, Fr ... mountain
montaña, Sp ... mountain
monte, It., Port., Sp. ... mount, mountain
more, Rus., So. Slav ... sea
morro, Port., Sp ... hill, bluff
mühle, Ger ... mill
mund, Ger ... mouth, opening
mündung, Ger ... river mouth
mura, Jap ... township
myit, Bur ... river
mys, Rus ... cape
nada, Jap ... sea
nadi, India ... river, creek
naes, Dan., Nor ... cape
nafud, Arab ... desert of sand dunes
nagar, India ... town, city
nahr, Arab ... river
nam, Siam ... river, water
nan, Chn., Jap ... south
näs, Nor., Swe ... cape
nez, Fr ... point, cape
nishi, nisi, Jap ... west
njarga, Fin ... peninsula
nong, Siam ... marsh
noord, Du ... north
nor, Mong ... lake
nord, Dan., Fr., Ger., It., Nor., Swe ... north
norte, Port., Sp ... north
nos, Rus ... cape
nyasa, Bantu ... lake
ö, Dan., Nor., Swe ... island
occidental, Sp ... western
ocna, Rom ... salt mine
odde, Dan., Nor ... point, cape
oedjoeng, Mal ... point, cape
oeste, Port., Sp ... west
oka, Jap ... hill
oost, Du ... east
oriental, Sp ... eastern
óros, Gr ... mountain
ost, Ger., Swe ... east
öster, Dan., Nor., Swe ... eastern
ostrov, Rus ... island
oued, Arab ... river, stream
ouest, Fr ... west
ozero, Rus ... lake
pää, Fin ... mountain
padang, Mal ... plain, field
pampas, Sp. (Argentina) ... grassy plains
pará, Indian (Brazil) ... river
pas, Fr ... channel, passage
paso, Sp ... mountain pass, passage
passo, It., Port. ... mountain pass, passage, strait
patam, India ... city, town
pei, Chn ... north
pélagos, Gr ... open sea
pegunungan, Indon ... mountains
peña, Sp ... rock
peresheyek, Rus ... isthmus
pertuis, Fr ... strait
peski, Rus ... desert
pic, Fr ... mountain peak
pico, Port., Sp ... mountain peak
piedra, Sp ... stone, rock
ping, Chn ... plain, flat
planalto, Port ... plateau
planina, Yugo ... mountains
playa, Sp ... shore, beach
pnom, Camb ... mountain
pointe, Fr ... point
polder, Du., Ger ... reclaimed marsh
polje, So. Slav ... plain, field
poluostrov, Rus ... peninsula
pont, Fr ... bridge
ponta, Port ... point, headland
ponte, It., Port ... bridge
pore, India ... city, town
porthmós, Gr ... strait
porto, It., Port ... port, harbor
potamós, Gr ... river
p'ov, Rus ... peninsula
prado, Sp ... field, meadow
presqu'île, Fr ... peninsula
proliv, Rus ... strait
pu, Chn ... commercial village
pueblo, Sp ... town, village
puerto, Sp ... port, harbor
pulau, Mal ... island
punkt, Ger ... point
punt, Du ... point
punta, It., Sp ... point
pur, India ... city, town
puy, Fr ... peak
qal'a, qal'at, Arab ... fort, village
qasr, Arab ... fort, castle
rann, India ... wasteland
ra's, Arab ... cape, head
reka, Rus., So. Slav ... river
reprêsa, Port ... reservoir
rettō, Jap ... island chain
ría, Sp ... estuary
ribeira, Port ... stream
riberão, Port ... river
rio, It., Port ... stream, river
río, Sp ... river
rivière, Fr ... river
roca, Sp ... rock
rt, Yugo ... cape
rūd, Per ... river
saari, Fin ... island
sable, Fr ... sand
sahara, Arab ... desert, plain
saki, Jap ... cape
sal, Sp ... salt
salar, Sp ... salt flat, salt lake
salto, Sp ... waterfall
san, Jap., Kor ... mountain, hill
sat, satul, Rom ... village
schloss, Ger ... castle
sebkha, Arab ... salt marsh
see, Ger ... lake, sea
şehir, Tur ... town, city
selat, Indon ... stream
selvas, Port. (Brazil) ... tropical rain forests
seno, Sp ... bay
serra, Port ... mountain chain
serranía, Sp ... mountain ridge
seto, Jap ... strait
severnaya, Rus ... northern
shahr, Per ... town, city
shan, Chn ... mountain, hill, island
shatt, Arab ... river
shi, Jap ... city
shima, Jap ... island
shōtō, Jap ... archipelago
si, Chn ... west, western
sierra, Sp ... mountain range
sjö, Nor., Swe ... lake, sea
sö, Dan., Nor ... lake, sea
söder, södra, Swe ... south
song, Annam ... river
sopka, Rus ... peak, volcano
source, Fr ... a spring
spitze, Ger ... summit, point
staat, Ger ... state
stad, Dan., Du., Nor., Swe. ... city, town
stadt, Ger ... city, town
stato, It ... state
step', Rus ... treeless plain, steppe
straat, Du ... strait
strand, Dan., Du., Ger., Nor., Swe ... shore, beach
stretto, It ... strait
strom, Ger ... river, stream
ström, Dan., Nor., Swe stream, river
stroom, Du ... stream, river
su, suyu, Tur ... water, river
sud, Fr., Sp ... south
süd, Ger ... south
suidō, Jap ... channel
sul, Port ... south
sund, Dan., Nor., Swe ... sound
sungai, sungei, Indon., Mal ... river
sur, Sp ... south
syd, Dan., Nor., Swe ... south
tafelland, Ger ... plateau
take, Jap ... peak, summit
tal, Ger ... valley
tandjung, tanjong, Mal ... cape
tao, Chn ... island
târg, târgul, Rom ... market, town
tell, Arab ... hill
teluk, Indon ... bay, gulf
terra, It ... land
terre, Fr ... earth, land
thal, Ger ... valley
tierra, Sp ... earth, land
tō, Jap ... east; island
tonle, Camb ... river, lake
top, Du ... peak
torp, Swe ... hamlet, cottage
tsangpo, Tib ... river
tsi, Chn ... village, borough
tso, Tib ... lake
tsu, Jap ... harbor, port
tundra, Rus ... treeless arctic plains
tung, Chn ... east
tuz, Tur ... salt
udde, Swe ... cape
ufer, Ger ... shore, riverbank
umi, Jap ... sea, gulf
ura, Jap ... bay, coast, creek
ust'ye, Rus ... river mouth
valle, It., Port., Sp ... valley
vallée, Fr ... valley
valli, It ... lake
vár, Hung ... fortress
város, Hung ... town
varoš, So. Slav ... town
veld, Du ... open plain, field
verkh, Rus ... top, summit
ves, Czech ... village
vest, Dan., Nor., Swe ... west
vik, Swe ... cove, bay
vila, Port ... town
villa, Sp ... town
villar, Sp ... village, hamlet
ville, Fr ... town, city
vostok, Rus ... east
wad, wādi, Arab. ... intermittent stream
wald, Ger ... forest, woodland
wan, Chn., Jap ... bay, gulf
weiler, Ger ... hamlet, village
westersch, Du ... western
wüste, Ger ... desert
yama, Jap ... mountain
yarimada, Tur ... peninsula
yug, Rus ... south
zaki, Jap ... cape
zaliv, Rus ... bay, gulf
zapad, Rus ... west
zee, Du ... sea
zemlya, Rus ... land
zuid, Du ... south

abbreviations of geographical names and terms

Afg............Afghanistan
Afr...................Africa
Ak....................Alaska
Al...................Alabama
Alb..................Albania
Alg..................Algeria
And.................Andorra
Ang..................Angola
Ant...............Antarctica
Ar.................Arkansas
Arch............Archipelago
Arc. O..........Arctic Ocean
Arg................Argentina
A. S. S. R.
   Autonomous Soviet
   Socialist Republic
Atl. O.........Atlantic Ocean
Aus..................Austria
Austl..............Australia
Aut..............Autonomous
Az..................Arizona

B..............Bay, Bahia
Ba..................Bahamas
B.A.T.......British Antarctic
   Territory
Bngl.............Bangladesh
Barb..............Barbados
Bdy...............Boundary
Bel................Belgium
Bg....................Berg
Bhu..................Bhutan
Bk.....................Bank
Bol..................Bolivia
Bots...............Botswana
Br....................British
Braz..................Brazil
Bru...................Brunei
Bul................Bulgaria
Bur...................Burma

C...........Cerro, Cape
Ca...............California
Cam...............Cameroon
Can........Canal, Canada
Can. Is........Canary Is.
Cen. Afr. Rep.
   Central African Republic
Chan...............Channel
Co......County, Colorado
Col.................Colombia
Con....................Congo
Comm.........Commonwealth
C. R.............Costa Rica
Cr.....................Creek
Ct................Connecticut
C. V..............Cape Verde
Czech..........Czechoslovakia

DC......District of Columbia
De..................Delaware
Den.................Denmark
Dept...............Department
Des...................Desert
D. F.........Distrito Federal
Dist.................District
Div..................Division
Dom. Rep.
   Dominican Republic

E......................East
Ec..................Ecuador
Eng.................England
Equat. Gui..Equatorial Guinea
Eth.................Ethiopia
Eur...................Europe

Faer................Faeroe Is.
Falk. Is........Falkland Is.
Fd.....................Fjord
Fed. Rep. of Ger., F.R.G.
   Federal Republic of Germany
Fin..................Finland
Fk.......................Fork
Fl...................Florida
For...................Forest
Fr.....................France
Fr. Gu.........French Guiana
Ft......................Fort

G.............Golfo, Gulf
Ga..................Georgia
Gam..................Gambia
Ger. Dem. Rep., G.D.R.
   German Democratic Republic
Gib.................Gibraltar
Grc...................Greece
Grnld...............Greenland
Gt......................Great
Gt. Brit.......Great Britain
Guad..............Guadeloupe
Guat...............Guatemala
Gui...................Guinea
Guy..................Guyana

Hai......................Haiti
Har., Hbr....Harbor, Harbour

Hd......................Head
Hi....................Hawaii
Hond...............Honduras
Hts..................Heights
Hung................Hungary

I......................Island
Ia......................Iowa
Ice..................Iceland
Id.....................Idaho
Il...................Illinois
In.........Inset, Indiana
Ind. O.........Indian Ocean
Indon..............Indonesia
Ind. Res...Indian Reservation
Int., Intl.......International
Ire..................Ireland
Is...................Islands
Isr...................Israel
Isth.................Isthmus
It.......................Italy

Jam..................Jamaica
Jap....................Japan
Jc..................Junction

Kamp.............Kampuchea
Ken....................Kenya
Km...Kilometer, Kilometers
Kor....................Korea
Ks...................Kansas
Kuw..................Kuwait
Ky.................Kentucky

L....Lago, Lake, Loch, Lough
La.................Louisiana
Lat..................Latitude
Leb.................Lebanon
Leso................Lesotho
Lib...................Liberia
Liech...........Liechtenstein
Long...............Longitude
Lux..............Luxembourg

M.............Mile, Miles
Ma...........Massachusetts
Mad...............Madagascar
Mad. Is.......Madeira Islands
Mala................Malaysia
Mand................Mandate
Mart..............Martinique
Max.................Maximum
Max. surf. elev.
   Maximum surface
   elevation
Md.................Maryland
Me......................Maine
Medit...........Mediterranean
Mex...................Mexico
Mi.....Mile, Miles, Michigan
Mn..................Minnesota
Mo..................Missouri
Mong................Mongolia
Mor..................Morocco
Moz..............Mozambique
Ms................Mississippi
Mt.........Mount, Montana
Mtn..................Mountain
Mts.................Mountains

N. A...........North America
Natl..................National
Natl. Mon.
   National Monument
Ne.................Nebraska
NC...........North Carolina
N. Cal.........New Caledonia
ND............North Dakota
Neigh.........Neighborhood
Nep....................Nepal
Neth.............Netherlands
New Hebr......New Hebrides
NH...........New Hampshire
Nic................Nicaragua
Nig...................Nigeria
N. Ire.......Northern Ireland
NJ.................New Jersey
NM...............New Mexico
Nor...................Norway
Nv....................Nevada
NY...................New York
N. Z.............New Zealand

O.....................Ocean
Obs..............Observatory
Oh......................Ohio
Ok..................Oklahoma
Om......................Oman
Or....................Oregon
O-va..................Ostrova

P......................Pass
Pa..............Pennsylvania
Pac. O........Pacific Ocean
Pak.................Pakistan

Pan...................Panama
Pap. N. Gui...........Papua
   New Guinea
Par..................Paraguay
Pass.................Passage
P.D.R. of Yem......Yemen,
   People's Democratic
   Republic of
Pen................Peninsula
Phil..............Philippines
P. Int........Point of Interest
Pk...............Peak, Park
Plat..................Plateau
Pln....................Plain
Pol...................Poland
Port................Portugal
P-Ov..............Poluostrov
P. R.............Puerto Rico
Prov................Province
Pt......................Point
Pta....................Punta
Pte...................Pointe

R.........River, Rio, Rivière
Ra...........Range, Ranges
Reg...................Region
Rep..................Republic
Res.....Reservation, Reservoir
Rf........................Reef
RI..............Rhode Island
Rom.................Romania
R. R..................Railroad
R. S. F. S. R...Russian Soviet
   Federated Socialist
   Republic
Rw...................Rwanda
Ry...................Railway
Rys..................Railways

S.........San, Santo, South
Sa.........Serra, Sierra
S. A...........South America
S. Afr...........South Africa
Sal................El Salvador
Sau. Ar.........Saudi Arabia
SC.............South Carolina
Scot................Scotland
SD..............South Dakota
Sd......................Sound
S. L...............Sierra Leone
Sol. Is............Solomon Is.
Som..................Somalia
Sov. Un..........Soviet Union
Sp......................Spain
Spr., Sprs.....Spring, Springs
S. S. R.......Soviet Socialist
   Republic
St......................Saint
Sta....................Santa
Ste...................Sainte
Str.....................Strait
Strm...................Stream
Sud....................Sudan
Sur..................Surinam
Swaz..............Swaziland
Swe....................Sweden
Switz.............Switzerland
Swp....................Swamp
Syr......................Syria

Tan.................Tanzania
Tas.................Tasmania
Ter..................Territory
Thai................Thailand
Tn.................Tennessee
Trin.....Trinidad and Tobago
Tun..................Tunisia
Tur....................Turkey
Tx......................Texas

U.A.E...United Arab Emirates
Ug.....................Uganda
U. K........United Kingdom
   of Gt. Brit. and N. Ire.
Ur...................Uruguay
U. S., U. S. A.
   United States of America
Ut.......................Utah

Va..................Virginia
Val....................Valley
Ven................Venezuela
Viet.................Vietnam
Vir. Is.............Virgin Is.
Vol..................Volcano
Vt...................Vermont

Wa...............Washington
Wi..................Wisconsin
W. Sah......Western Sahara
W. Sam......Western Samoa
WV............West Virginia
Wy..................Wyoming

Yugo..............Yugoslavia

Zimb...............Zimbabwe

pronunciation of geographical names

Key to the Sound Values of Letters and Symbols Used in the Index to Indicate Pronunciation

ă—ăt, căt, băttle
d̆—d̆ppeal, find̆l
ā—rāte, elāte
â—inanimâte, senâte
a̍—a̍sk, ba̍th
a̤—ma̤rine, sofa̤ (short neutral or indeterminate sound)
â—fâre, prepâre
ch—church, choose
dh—as th in other, either
ē—bē, ōve
ê—crêate, êvent
ĕ—bĕt, ĕnd
ê̆—recê̆nt (short neutral or indeterminate sound)
ẽ—cratẽr, cindẽr
g—gō, gāme
gh—guttural g
ĭ—wĭll, bĭt
ĭ—short neutral or indeterminate sound
i—rīde, bīte
κ—guttural k as ch in German ich
ng—sing
ŋ—baŋk, liŋger
N—indicates nasalized preceding vowel
ŏ—nŏd, ŏdd
o̤—co̤mmit, co̤nnect
ō—ōld, bōld
ô—ôbey, hôtel
ô—ôrder, nôrth
oi—boil
ōō—fōōd, rōōt
ŏŏ—fŏŏt, wŏŏd
ou—thou, out
s—as in soft, so, sane
sh—dish, finish
th—thin, thick
ū—pūre, cūre
u̇—u̇nite, u̇surp
û—ûrn, fûr
ŭ—stŭd, ŭp
ū—as in French tu or as "y" in study
ŭ—circŭs, sŭbmit
zh—as z in azure
'—indeterminate vowel sound

In many cases the spelling of foreign geographic names does not even remotely indicate the pronunciation to an American, i. e., Słupsk in Poland is pronounced swōōpsk; Jujuy in Argentina is pronounced hōō-hwē'; La Spezia in Italy is lä-spē'zyä.

This condition is hardly surprising, however, when we consider that in our own language Worcester, Massachusetts, is pronounced wōōs'tẽr; Sioux City, Iowa, sōō sĭ'tĭ; Schuylkill Haven, Pennsylvania, skōōl'kĭl hä-vĕn; Poughkeepsie, New York, pô-kĭp'sĕ.

The indication of pronunciation of geographic names presents several peculiar problems:

(1) Many foreign tongues use sounds that are not present in the English language and which an American cannot normally articulate. Thus, though the nearest English equivalent sound has been indicated, only approximate results are possible.

(2) There are several dialects in each foreign tongue which cause variation in the local pronunciation of names. This also occurs in identical names in the various divisions of a great language group, as the Slavic or the Latin.

(3) Within the United States there are marked differences in pronunciation, not only of local geographic names, but also of common words, indicating that the sound and tone values for letters as well as the placing of the emphasis vary considerably from one part of the country to another.

(4) A number of different letter and diacritical combinations could be used to indicate essentially the same or approximate pronunciations.

Some variation in pronunciation other than that indicated in this index may be encountered, but such a difference does not necessarily indicate that either is in error, and in many cases it is a matter of individual choice as to which is preferred. In fact, an exact indication of pronunciation of many foreign names using English letters and diacritical marks is extremely difficult and sometimes impossible.

a pronouncing index
of over 30,000 geographical names

This universal index includes in a single alphabetical list all important names that appear on the reference maps. Each place name is preceded by the page number of the map on which it appears. Place names are followed by the pronunciation of the name (see facing page for an explanation of the pronunciation system); the location; and the approximate geographic coordinates.

State locations are listed for all places in the United States. All other place name entries show only country locations. When a name is only shown on an inset map the name of the inset on which it appears is listed.

All minor political divisions are followed by a descriptive term (Dist., Reg., Prov., State, etc.) and by the country in which they are located.

The names of physical features and points of interest that are shown on the maps are listed in the index. Each entry is followed by a descriptive term (Bay, Hill, Mtn., Is., Plat., etc.) to indicate its nature.

The system of alphabetizing used in the index is standard. When more than one name with the same spelling is shown, including both political and physical names, the order of precedence is as follows: *first*, place names; *second*, political divisions; and *third*, physical features.

Local official names are used on the maps for nearly all cities and towns, with the exception of about 50 major world cities for which Anglicized conventional names have been preferred. For these exceptions, the index gives a cross-reference to the official local name.

Page	Name Pronunciation Region	Lat. ° '	Long. ° '
161	Aachen (ä′kĕn) .F.R.G. (Ruhr In.)	50·46 N	6·07 E
156	Aakirkeby (ô-kĭr′kĕ-bü) ......Den.	55·04 N	15·00 E
158	Aalen (ä′lĕn) ............F.R.G.	48·49 N	10·08 E
149	Aalsmeer. .Neth. (Amsterdam In.)	52·16 N	4·44 E
149	Aalst........Bel. (Brussels In.)	50·58 N	4·00 E
158	Aarau (är′ou) ....Switz.	47·22 N	8·03 E
149	Aarschot........Bel. (Brussels In.)	50·59 N	4·51 E
215	Aba............Nig.	5·06 N	7·21 E
217	Aba............Zaïre	3·52 N	30·14 E
186	Abādān (ä-bŭ-dän′) ....Iran	30·15 N	48·30 E
135	Abaetetuba (ä′bäĕ-tĕ-tōō′bá) Braz.	1·44 S	48·45 W
115	Abajo Pk. .(á-bä′hŏ) ......Ut.	37·51 N	109·28 W
215	Abakaliki ....Nig.	6·21 N	8·06 E
172	Abakan (ŭ-bá-kän′).....Sov. Un.	53·43 N	91·28 E
172	Abakan (R.) ....Sov. Un.	53·00 N	91·06 E
134	Abancay (ä-bän-kä′ē) ......Peru	13·44 S	72·46 W
124	Abasolo (ä-bä-sō′lô) ....Mex.	24·05 N	98·24 W
118	Abasolo ....Mex.	27·13 N	101·25 W
	Abay (R.), see Blue Nile		
211	Abay (R.), see Blue Nile .....Eth.	6·24 N	38·22 E
218	'Abbāsah, Tur'at al (Can.) Egypt (Suez In.)	30·45 N	32·15 E
120	Abbeville (ăb′ē-vĭl) ....Al.	31·35 N	85·15 W
160	Abbeville (ȧb-vēl′) ....Fr.	50·08 N	1·49 E
120	Abbeville (ăb′ē-vĭl) ....Ga.	31·53 N	83·23 W
119	Abbeville ....La.	29·59 N	92·07 W
121	Abbeville.............SC	34·09 N	82·25 W
164	Abbiategrasso (äb-byä′tä-gräs′sō) It.	45·23 N	8·52 E
148	Abbots Bromley (ăb′ŭts brŭm′lē) Eng.	52·49 N	1·52 W
112	Abbotsford (ăb′ŭts-fērd) Can. (Vancouver In.)	49·03 N	122·17 W
218	Abd Al Kuri (I.) (ăbd-ĕl-kōō′rē) P.D.R. of Yem. (Horn of Afr. In.)	12·12 N	51·00 E
170	Abdulino (äb-dōō-lē′nô) .Sov. Un.	53·40 N	53·45 E
211	Abéché (ä-bĕ-shā′) ....Chad	13·48 N	20·39 E
214	Abengourou ....Ivory Coast	6·44 N	3·29 W
156	Åbenrå (ô′bĕn-rô) ....Den.	55·03 N	9·20 E
215	Abeokuta (ä-bà-ô-kōō′tä) .....Nig.	7·10 N	3·26 E
	Abercorn, see Mbala		
154	Aberdare (ăb-ēr-dâr′) ....Wales	51·45 N	3·35 W
120	Aberdeen (ăb-ēr-dēn′) ......Ms.	33·49 N	88·33 W
154	Aberdeen ....Scot.	57·10 N	2·05 W
108	Aberdeen ....SD	45·28 N	98·29 W
110	Aberdeen ....Wa.	47·00 N	123·48 W
148	Aberford (ăb′ē-fērd) ....Eng.	53·49 N	1·21 W
154	Abergavenny (ăb′ēr-gá-vĕn′ĭ) Wales	51·45 N	3·05 W
110	Abert L. (ā′bērt) ....Or.	42·39 N	120·24 W
154	Aberystwyth (ă-bēr-ĭst′wĭth) Wales	52·25 N	4·04 W
174	Abestovskiy (ä-bĕs′tôv-skĭ) Sov. Un. (Urals In.)	57·46 N	61·23 E
186	Abhā.............Sau. Ar.	17·47 N	42·29 E
214	Abidjan (ä-bĕd-zhän′).Ivory Coast	5·19 N	4·02 W
195	Abiko (ä-bē′kô) .Jap. (Tōkyō In.)	35·53 N	140·01 E
117	Abilene (ăb′ĭ-lēn) ....Ks.	38·54 N	97·12 W
117	Abilene..............Tx.	32·25 N	99·45 W
148	Abingdon......Eng. (London In.)	51·38 N	1·17 W
109	Abingdon (ăb′ĭng-dŭn) ......Il.	40·48 N	90·21 W
105	Abingdon ....Va.	36·42 N	81·57 W
99	Abington (ăb′ĭng-tŭn) ...Ma. (In.)	42·07 N	70·57 W
115	Abiquiu Res.............NM	36·26 N	106·42 W
91	Abitibi (L.) .(ăb-ĭ-tĭb′Ĭ) ......Can.	48·27 N	80·20 W
91	Abitibi (R.) ....Can.	49·30 N	81·10 W
171	Abkhaz A.S.S.R........Sov. Un.	43·10 N	40·45 E
161	Ablis (à-blē′) ....Fr.	48·31 N	1·50 E
218	Abnūb (ăb-nōōb′).Egypt (Nile In.)	27·18 N	31·11 E
	Åbo, see Turku		
184	Abohar...............India	30·12 N	74·13 E
214	Aboisso.............Ivory Coast	5·28 N	3·12 W
215	Abomey (ȧb-ô-mā′) ....Benin	7·11 N	1·59 E
159	Abony (ŏ′bô-ny′) ....Hung.	47·12 N	20·00 E
215	Abou Deïa ....Chad	11·27 N	19·17 E
197	Abra (R.) .(ä′brä) ....Phil (In.)	17·16 N	120·38 E
137	Abraão (ȧbrä-oun′) Braz. (Rio de Janeiro In.)	23·10 S	44·10 W
129	Abraham's B...........Ba.	22·20 N	73·50 W
148	Abram (ā′brăm) ....Eng.	53·31 N	2·36 W
162	Abrantes (ä-brän′tĕs) ......Port.	39·28 N	8·13 W
135	Abrolhos, Arquipélago dos (Arch.) (ä-rôôĕ-pĕ′lä-gô dôs ä-brô′l-yôs) Braz.	17·58 S	38·40 W
157	Abruka (I.) .(á-brōō′kà) ..Sov. Un.	58·09 N	22·30 E
164	Abruzzi E Molise (Reg.) (ä-brōōt′sē, mô′lĕ-zā)........It.	42·10 N	13·55 E
111	Absaroka Ra. (Mts.) (ȧb-sȧ-rō-kȧ)............Wy.	44·50 N	109·47 W
184	Abu Road (á′bōō).........India	24·38 N	72·45 E
186	Abū Arīsh (ä-bōō ȧ-rēsh′) .Sau. Ar.	16·48 N	43·00 E
211	Abu Ḥamad (ä′bōō hä′-mĕd).Sud.	19·37 N	33·21 E
186	Abū Kamāl............Syr.	34·45 N	40·46 E
134	Abunã (R.) .(á-bōō-nä′)..Bol-Braz.	10·25 S	67·00 W
218	Abū Qīr (ä′bōō kēr′) Egypt (Nile In.)	31·18 N	30·06 E
218	Abū Qurqāṣ (ä′bōō kōōr-käs′) Egypt (Nile In.)	27·57 N	30·51 E
183	Abū Qurūn, Ra's (Mtn.) Egypt (Palestine In.)	30·22 N	33·32 E
195	Aburatsu (ä′bōō-rät′sōō) .....Jap.	31·33 N	131·20 E
218	Abū Tīj ....Egypt (Nile In.)	27·03 N	31·19 E
186	Abū Ẓaby ....U. A. E.	24·15 N	54·28 E
183	Abū Ẓanīmah Egypt (Palestine In.)	29·03 N	33·08 E
	Abyad, Al-Bahr al- (R.), see White Nile		
173	Abyy...............Sov. Un.	68·24 N	134·00 E
134	Acacias (à-kä′sēäs) ...Col. (In.)	3·59 N	73·44 W
98	Acadia Natl. Park (ȧ-kä′dĭ-ȧ).Me.	44·19 N	68·01 W
126	Acajutla (ä-kä-hōōt′lä) .....Mex.	13·37 N	89·50 W
125	Acala (ä-kä′lä) ....Mex.	16·38 N	92·49 W
216	Acalayong.........Equat. Gui.	1·05 N	9·40 E
124	Acámbaro (ä-käm′bä-rō) .....Mex.	20·03 N	100·42 W
126	Acancéh (ä-kän-sĕ′)....Mex. (In.)	20·50 N	89·27 W
124	Acapetlahuaya (ä-kä-pĕt′lä-hwä′yä) ......Mex.	18·24 N	100·04 W
124	Acaponeta (ä-kä-pô-nä′tä) ...Mex.	22·31 N	105·25 W
124	Acaponeta (R.) ....Mex.	22·47 N	105·23 W
124	Acapulco (ä-kä-pōōl′kō) .....Mex.	16·49 N	99·57 W
135	Acaraí Mts............Braz.	1·30 N	57·40 W
135	Acaraú (ä-kärhá-ōō′) ......Braz.	2·55 S	40·04 W
134	Acarigua (ä-kä-rē′gwä) ......Ven.	9·29 N	69·11 W
124	Acatlán de Osorio (ä-kät-län′dä ô-sō′rē-ō) .Mex.	18·11 N	98·04 W
125	Acatzingo de Hidalgo (ä-kät-zĭŋ′gō dä ē-dhäl′gō) .Mex.	18·58 N	97·47 W
125	Acayucan (ä-kä-yōō′kän)...Mex.	17·56 N	94·55 W
104	Accoville (ăk′kô-vĭl) ....WV	37·45 N	81·50 W
214	Accra (ä′krà) ....Ghana	5·33 N	0·13 W
148	Accrington (ăk′rĭng-tŭn).....Eng.	53·45 N	2·22 W
163	Acerra (ä-chĕ′r-rä) It. (Naples In.)	40·42 N	14·22 E
134	Achacachi (ä-chä-kä′chĕ).....Bol.	16·11 S	68·32 W
194	Acheng (ä′chĕng′) ....China	45·32 N	126·59 E
154	Achill (ä-chĭl′) ....Ire.	53·55 N	10·05 W
172	Achinsk (à-chĕnsk′) .....Sov. Un.	56·13 N	90·32 E
164	Acireale (ä-chē-rä-ä′lä) ......It.	37·37 N	15·12 E
120	Ackia Battle Ground Natl. Mon. (ä-kyū′).Ms.	34·22 N	89·05 W
129	Acklins (I.) (ăk′lĭns) ....Ba.	22·30 N	73·55 W
129	Acklins, The Bight of (B.) ....Ba.	22·35 N	74·20 W
125	Acolman (ä-kôl-mä′n) .Mex. (In.)	19·38 N	98·56 W
137	Aconcagua (ä-kôn-kä′gwä) (Prov.) Chile (Santiago In.)	32·20 S	71·00 W
137	Aconcagua, Cerro (Mtn.) Arg. (Santiago In.)	32·38 S	70·00 W
137	Aconcagua (R.) Chile (Santiago In.)	32·43 S	70·53 W
210	Açores (Azores) (Is.) (ä-zō′rĕs) (á-zōrz′).Atl. O.	37·44 N	29·25 W
126	Acoyapa (ä-kô-yä′pä) ......Nic.	11·54 N	85·11 W
164	Acqui (äk′kwē) ....It.	44·41 N	8·22 E
134	Acre (State) (ä′krä) ......Braz.	8·40 S	70·45 W
134	Acre (R.) ....Braz.	10·33 S	68·34 W
106	Acton (ăk′tŭn) Al. (Birmingham In.)	33·21 N	86·49 W
89	Acton........Can. (Toronto In.)	43·38 N	80·02 W
99	Acton ....Ma. (In.)	42·29 N	71·26 W
124	Actopan (ȧk-tô-pän′) ......Mex.	20·16 N	98·57 W
125	Actópan (R.) .(äk-tô′pän) ...Mex.	19·25 N	96·31 W
124	Acuitzio del Canje (ä-kwēt′zĕ-ō dĕl kän′hà) .Mex.	19·28 N	101·21 W
129	Acul, Baie de l' (B.) .(ä-kōōl′) Hai.	19·55 N	72·20 W
108	Ada (ā′dŭ)...............Mn.	47·17 N	96·32 W
104	Ada.................Oh.	40·45 N	83·45 W
117	Ada.................Ok.	34·45 N	96·43 W
165	Ada (ä′dä) ....Yugo.	45·48 N	20·06 E
195	Adachi.........Jap. (Tōkyō In.)	35·50 N	39·36 E
101	Adak (ä-däk′) ....Ak.	56·50 N	176·48 W
101	Adak (I.) ....Ak.	51·40 N	176·28 W
101	Adak Str.............Ak.	51·42 N	177·16 W
	Adalia, see Antalya		
215	Adamaoua (Mts.) .....Cam.-Nig.	6·30 N	11·50 E
93	Adams (R.) ....Can.	51·30 N	119·20 W
105	Adams (ăd′ămz) ....Ma.	42·35 N	73·10 W
109	Adams................Wi.	43·55 N	89·48 W
110	Adams, Mt............Wa.	46·15 N	121·19 W
106	Adamsville (ăd′ămz-vĭl) Al. (Birmingham In.)	33·36 N	86·57 W
171	Adana (ä′dä-nä) ....Tur.	37·05 N	35·20 E
171	Adapazari (ä-dä-pä-zä′rĕ) ...Tur.	40·45 N	30·20 E
211	Adarama (ä-dä-rä′mä) .....Sud.	17·11 N	34·56 E
164	Adda (R.) (äd′dä)..........It.	45·43 N	9·31 E
211	Ad Dabbah.............Sud.	18·04 N	30·58 E
186	Ad Dahnā (Des.) ....Sau. Ar.	26·05 N	47·15 E
211	Ad-Dāmir (ad-dä′mĕr) ......Sud.	17·38 N	33·57 E
186	Ad Dammān............Sau. Ar.	26·27 N	49·59 E
183	Ad Dāmūr....Leb. (Palestine In.)	33·44 N	35·27 E
186	Ad Dawhah ....Qatar	25·02 N	51·28 E
186	Ad Dilam ....Sau. Ar.	23·47 N	47·03 E
218	Ad Dilinjāt ....Egypt (Nile In.)	30·48 N	30·32 E
211	Addis Abeba ....Eth.	9·00 N	38·44 E

248 Addison — Alberche

PRONOUNCING INDEX

Page	Name Pronunciation Region	Lat. °′	Long. °′
113	Addison (ă'dĭ-sŭn) Tx. (Dallas, Fort Worth In.)	32·58 N	96·50 W
213	Addo (ădō) S. Afr. (Natal In.)	33·33 S	25·43 E
211	Ad Duwaym (dōō-ām') Sud.	13·56 N	32·22 E
107	Addyston (ăd'ē-stŭn) Oh. (Cincinnati In.)	39·09 N	84·42 W
120	Adel (ā-dĕl') Ga.	31·08 N	83·55 W
203	Adelaide (ăd'ē-lād) Austl.	34·46 S	139·08 E
213	Adelaide (ăd-ĕl'ād) S. Afr. (Natal In.)	32·41 S	26·07 E
220	Adelaide I. Ant.	67·15 S	68·40 W
186	Aden (ä'dĕn) P. D. R. of Yem.	12·48 N	45·00 E
186	Aden, G. of Asia	11·45 N	45·45 E
197	Adi, Pulau (I.) (ä'dē) Indon.	4·25 S	133·52 E
164	Adige, Fiume (R.) (fyōō'mĕ ä'dē-jā) It.	46·38 N	10·43 E
152	Adige R. Aus.-Switz.	46·34 N	10·51 E
184	Adilābād (ŭ-dĭl-ä-bäd') India	19·47 N	78·30 E
105	Adirondack, Mts. (ăd-ĭ-rŏn'dăk) NY	43·45 N	74·40 W
211	Adi Ugri (ä-dē ōō'grē) Eth.	14·54 N	38·52 E
159	Adjud (äd'zhōōd) Rom.	46·05 N	27·12 E
113	Adkins Tx. (San Antonio In.)	29·22 N	98·18 W
101	Admiralty (I.) Ak.	57·50 N	133·50 W
112	Admiralty Inlet (ăd'mĭrăl-tē) Wa. (Seattle In.)	48·10 N	122·45 W
197	Admiralty Is. Pap. N. Gui.	1·40 S	146·45 E
215	Ado-Ekiti Nig.	7·38 N	5·12 E
113	Adolph (ā'dolf) Mn. (Duluth In.)	46·47 N	92·17 W
185	Ādoni India	15·42 N	77·18 E
160	Adour (R.) (à-dōōr') Fr.	43·43 N	0·38 W
162	Adra (ä'drä) Sp.	36·45 N	3·02 W
164	Adrano (ä-drä'nō) It.	37·42 N	14·52 E
164	Adria (ä'drē-ä) It.	45·03 N	12·01 E
104	Adrian (ā'drĭ-ăn) Mi.	41·55 N	84·00 W
108	Adrian Mn.	43·39 N	95·56 W
	Adrianople, see Edirne		
164	Adriatic Sea Eur.	43·30 N	14·27 E
210	Adrir Alg.	27·53 N	0·15 W
211	Adwa Eth.	14·02 N	38·58 E
148	Adwick-le-Street (ăd'wĭk-lē-strēt') Eng.	53·35 N	1·11 W
173	Adycha (R.) (ä'dĭ-chà) Sov. Un.	66·11 N	136·45 E
167	Adzhamka (àd-zhäm'kà) Sov. Un.	48·33 N	32·28 E
214	Adzopé Ivory Coast	6·06 N	3·52 W
170	Adz'va (R.) (ädz'và) Sov. Un.	67·00 N	59·20 E
153	Aegean Sea (ē-jē'ăn) Asia-Eur.	39·04 N	24·56 E
155	Aerø (I.) (âr'ö) Den.	54·52 N	10·22 E
113	Affton Mo. (St. Louis In.)	38·33 N	90·20 W
182	Afghanistan (ăf-găn-ĭ-stăn') Asia	33·00 N	63·00 E
218	Afgoi (äf-gô'ĭ) Som. (Horn of Afr. In.)	2·08 N	45·08 E
215	Afikpo Nig.	5·53 N	7·56 E
210	Aflou (ä-flōō') Alg.	33·59 N	2·04 E
101	Afognak (I.) (ä-fŏg-nák') Ak.	58·28 N	151·35 W
163	Afragola (ä-frà'gō-lä) It. (Naples In.)	40·40 N	14·19 E
209	Africa (ăf'rĭ-kà)		
113	Afton (ăf'tŭn) Mn. (Minneapolis, St. Paul In.)	44·54 N	92·47 W
117	Afton Ok.	36·42 N	94·56 W
111	Afton Wy.	42·42 N	110·52 W
183	'Afula (a-fōō'là) Isr. (Palestine In.)	32·36 N	35·17 E
171	Afyonkarahisar (ä-fē-ōn-kä-rá-hē-sär') Tur.	38·45 N	30·20 E
215	Agadem (ä'gá-dĕm) Niger	16·50 N	13·17 E
215	Agadez (ä'gá-dĕs) Niger	16·58 N	7·59 E
210	Agadir (ä-gá-dēr) Mor.	30·30 N	9·37 W
126	Agalta, Cord. de (Mts.) (kôr-dēl-yĕ'rä-dĕ-ä-gä'l-tä) Hond.	15·15 N	85·42 W
174	Agapovka (ä-gä-pôv'kä) Sov. Un. (Urals In.)	53·18 N	59·10 E
184	Agartala India	23·53 N	91·22 E
185	Agāshi India (In.)	19·28 N	72·46 E
174	Agashkino (ä-gäsh'kĭ-nô) Sov. Un. (Moscow In.)	55·18 N	38·13 E
101	Agattu (I.) (á'gä-tōō) Ak.	52·14 N	173·40 E
167	Agayman (à-gä-ē-män') Sov. Un.	46·39 N	34·20 E
214	Agboville Ivory Coast	5·56 N	4·13 W
171	Agdam (äg'dām) Sov. Un.	40·00 N	47·00 E
160	Agde (ägd) Fr.	43·19 N	3·30 E
160	Agen (à-zhäN') Fr.	44·13 N	0·31 E
173	Aginskoye (ä-hĭn'skô-yĕ) Sov. Un.	51·15 N	113·15 E
197	Agno (äg'nō) Phil. (In.)	16·07 N	119·49 E
197	Agno (R.) Phil. (In.)	15·42 N	120·28 E
164	Agnone (än-yō'nā) It.	41·49 N	14·23 E
214	Agogo Ghana	6·47 N	1·04 W
184	Agra (ä'grä) India	27·18 N	78·00 E
164	Agri (R.) (ä'grē) It.	40·15 N	16·21 E
165	Agrínion (à-grē'nyôn) Grc.	38·38 N	21·06 E
126	Agua (Vol.) (ä'gwä) Guat.	14·28 N	90·43 W
124	Agua Blanca, Río (R.) (rē'ō-ä-gwä-blä'n-kä) Mex.	21·46 N	102·54 W
124	Agua Brava, Laguna de (L.) (lä-gōō'nä-dĕ-ä'gwä-brä'vä) Mex.	22·04 N	105·40 W
114	Agua Caliente Ind. Res. (ä'gwä kal-yĕn'tä) Ca.	33·50 N	116·24 W
128	Aguada (ä-gwä'dá) Cuba	22·25 N	80·50 W
126	Aguada L. Mex. (In.)	18·46 N	89·40 W
134	Aguadas (ä-gwä'-däs) Col. (In.)	5·37 N	75·27 W
123	Aguadilla (ä-gwä-dēl'yä) P. R. (Puerto Rico In.)	18·27 N	67·10 W
127	Aguadulce (ä-gwä-dōōl'sā) Pan.	8·15 N	80·33 W
125	Agua Escondida, Meseta de (Plat.) (mĕ-sĕ'tä-dĕ-ä'gwä-ĕs-kôn-dē'dä) Mex.	16·54 N	91·35 W
115	Agua Fria (R.) (ă'gûă frĭ'ă) Az.	33·43 N	112·22 W
137	Aguai (ägwä-ē') Braz. (Rio de Janeiro In.)	22·04 S	46·57 W
118	Agualeguas (ä-gwä-lā'gwäs) Mex.	26·19 N	99·33 W
118	Aguanaval, R. (à-guä-nä-väl') Mex.	25·12 N	103·28 W
126	Aguán R. (ä-gwà'n) Hond.	15·22 N	87·00 W
99	Aguanus (R.) (à-gwä'nŭs) Can.	50·45 N	62·03 W
124	Aguascalientes (ä'gwäs-käl-yĕn'tās) Mex.	21·52 N	102·17 W
124	Aguascalientes (State) Mex.	22·00 N	102·18 W
162	Agueda (ä-gwā'dá) Port.	40·36 N	8·26 W
162	Agueda (R.) (ä-gĕ-dä) Sp.	40·50 N	6·44 W
214	Aguelhok Mali	19·28 N	0·52 E
116	Aguilar (ä-gē-lär') Co.	37·24 N	104·38 W
162	Aguilar Sp.	37·32 N	4·39 W
162	Aguilas (ä-gē-läs) Sp.	37·26 N	1·35 W
124	Aguililla (ä-gē-lēl-yä) Mex.	18·44 N	102·44 W
124	Aguililla (R.) Mex.	18·30 N	102·48 W
134	Aguja, Pta. (Pt.) (pŭn'tà á-gōō' hä) Peru	6·00 S	81·15 W
212	Agulhas, C. (ä-gōōl'yäs) S. Afr.	34·47 S	20·00 E
197	Agusan (R.) (ä-gōō'sän) Phil.	8·12 N	126·07 E
210	Ahaggar (Mts.) (á-há-gär') Alg.	23·14 N	6·00 E
161	Ahlen (ä'lĕn) F.R.G. (Ruhr In.)	51·45 N	7·52 E
184	Ahmadābād (ŭ-mĕd-ā-bäd') India	23·04 N	72·38 E
184	Ahmadnagar (ä'mûd-nû-gûr) India	19·09 N	74·45 E
218	Ahmar Mts. Eth. (Horn of Afr. In.)	9·22 N	42·00 E
121	Ahoskie (ā-hŏs'kē) NC	36·15 N	77·00 W
149	Ahrensburg (ä'rĕns-bōōrg) F.R.G. (Hamburg In.)	53·40 N	10·14 E
158	Ahrweiler (är'vī-lĕr) F.R.G.	50·34 N	7·05 E
157	Ahtärin-järvi (L.) Fin.	62·46 N	24·25 E
124	Ahuacatlán (ä-wä-kät-län') Mex.	21·05 N	104·28 W
126	Ahuachapan (ä-wä-chä-pän') Sal.	13·57 N	89·53 W
124	Ahualulco (ä-wä-lōōl'kō) Mex.	20·43 N	103·57 W
124	Ahuatempan (ä-wä-tĕm-pän) Mex.	18·11 N	98·02 W
156	Åhus (ô'hōōs) Swe.	55·56 N	14·19 E
186	Ahvāz Iran	31·15 N	48·54 E
157	Ahvenanmaa (Åland Is.) (ä'vĕ-nàn-mô) (ô'lănd) Fin.	60·36 N	19·55 E
199	Aiea Hi. (In.)	21·18 N	157·52 W
121	Aiken (ā'kĕn) SC	33·32 N	81·43 W
135	Aimorés, Serra dos (Mts.) (sĕ'r-rä-dôs-ī-mō-rĕ's) Braz.	17·40 S	42·38 W
195	Aimoto (ī-mô-tō) Jap. (Ōsaka In.)	34·59 N	135·09 E
210	Aïn Beïda (ä'ēn bā-dä') Alg.	35·57 N	7·25 E
161	Aincourt (ăN-kōō'r) Fr. (Paris In.)	49·04 N	1·47 E
163	Aïne Oussera (ĕn ōō-sä-rà) Alg.	35·25 N	2·50 E
210	Aïn Salah Alg.	27·13 N	2·22 E
108	Ainsworth (ānz'wûrth) Ne.	42·32 N	99·51 W
151	Aïn-Temouchent (ä'ēntĕ-mōō-shaN') Alg.	35·20 N	1·23 W
134	Aipe (ī'pĕ) Col. (In.)	3·13 N	75·15 W
215	Aïr (Mts.) Niger	18·00 N	8·30 E
160	Aire (âr) Fr.	43·42 N	0·17 W
148	Aire (R.) Eng.	53·42 N	1·00 W
183	Airhitam, Selat (Str.) Indon. (Singapore In.)	0·58 N	102·38 E
160	Aisne (R.) (ĕn) Fr.	49·28 N	3·32 E
197	Aitape (ä-ē-tá'pā) Pap. N. Gui.	3·00 S	142·10 E
109	Aitkin (āt'kĭn) Mn.	46·32 N	93·43 W
165	Aitolikón (å-tō'lĭ-kôn) Grc.	38·27 N	21·21 E
165	Aitos (ä-ē'tôs) Bul.	42·42 N	27·17 E
199	Aitutaki (I.) (ī-tōō-tä'kē) Cook Is.	19·00 S	162·00 W
159	Aiud (ä'ē-ōōd) Rom.	46·19 N	23·40 E
137	Aiuruoca (äē'ōō-rōōō'-kà) Braz. (Rio de Janeiro In.)	21·57 S	44·36 W
137	Aiuruoca (R.) Braz. (Rio de Janeiro In.)	22·11 S	44·35 W
160	Aix-en-Provence (ĕks-prô-vàNs) Fr. (In.)	43·32 N	5·27 E
161	Aix-les-Bains (ĕks'-lā-baN') Fr.	45·42 N	5·56 E
165	Aíyina Grc.	37·37 N	22·12 E
165	Aíyina (I.) Grc.	37·43 N	23·35 E
165	Aíyion Grc.	38·13 N	22·04 E
157	Aizpute (ä'ēz-pōō-tĕ) Sov. Un.	56·44 N	21·37 E
195	Aizuwakamatsu Jap.	37·27 N	139·51 E
164	Ajaccio (ä-yät'chō) Fr.	41·55 N	8·42 E
125	Ajalpan (ä-häl'pän) Mex.	18·21 N	97·14 W
204	Ajana (āj-ăn'ēr) Austl.	28·00 S	114·45 E
111	Ajax Mt. (ā'jăks) Mt.	45·19 N	113·43 W
211	Ajdābiyah Libya	30·56 N	20·16 E
183	'Ajmah, Jabal al (Mts.) Egypt (Palestine In.)	29·12 N	34·03 E
186	Ajman U. A. E.	25·15 N	54·30 E
184	Ajmer (ŭj-mēr') India	26·26 N	74·42 E
115	Ajo (ä'hō) Az.	32·20 N	112·55 W
124	Ajuchitlán del Progreso (ä-hōō-chet-lån) Mex.	18·11 N	100·32 W
125	Ajusco (ä-hōō's-kō) Mex. (In.)	19·13 N	99·12 W
125	Ajusco, Cerro (Mtn.) (sĕ'r-rô-ä-hōō's-kō) Mex. (In.)	19·12 N	99·16 W
195	Akaishi-dake (Mtn.) (ä-kī-shē dä'kä) Jap.	35·30 N	138·00 E
195	Akashi (ä'kä-shē) Jap. (Ōsaka In.)	34·38 N	134·59 E
216	Aketi (ä-kå-tē) Zaire	2·44 N	23·46 E
171	Akhaltsikhe (äkä'l-tsĭ-kĕ) Sov. Un.	41·40 N	42·50 E
211	Akhdar, Al Jabal al (Mts.) Libya	32·00 N	22·00 E
165	Akhelóös (R.) (ä-hĕ'lô-ōs) Grc.	38·45 N	21·26 E
171	Akhisar (äk-hĭs-sär') Tur.	38·58 N	27·58 E
167	Akhtarskaya, Bukhta (B.) (bōōk'tä àK-tär'skà-yà) Sov. Un.	45·53 N	38·22 E
165	Akhtopol (äK'tô-pōl) Bul.	42·08 N	27·54 E
167	Akhtyrka (äK-tür'kà) Sov. Un.	50·18 N	34·53 E
174	Akhunovo (ä-kû'nô-vô) Sov. Un. (Urals In.)	54·13 N	59·36 E
195	Aki (ä'kê) Jap.	33·31 N	133·51 E
101	Akiak (äk'yàk) Ak.	61·00 N	161·02 W
91	Akimiski (I.) (ä-kĭ-mĭ'skĭ) Can.	52·54 N	80·22 W
194	Akita (ä'kē-tä) Jap.	39·40 N	140·12 E
214	Akjoujt Mauritania	19·45 N	14·23 W
183	'Akko Isr. (Palestine In.)	32·56 N	35·05 E
90	Aklavik (äk'lä-vĭk) Can.	68·28 N	135·26 W
214	'Aklé 'Âouâna (Dunes) Mali-Mauritania	18·07 N	6·00 W
195	Ako (ä'kô) Jap.	34·44 N	134·22 E
184	Akola (à-kō'lä) India	20·47 N	77·00 E
211	Akordat Eth.	15·34 N	37·54 E
91	Akpatok (I.) (ăk'pà-tŏk) Can.	60·30 N	67·10 W
150	Akranes Ice.	64·18 N	21·40 W
165	Akrítas, Akr. (C.) Grc.	37·45 N	22·00 E
116	Akron (ăk'rŭn) Co.	40·09 N	103·14 W
107	Akron Oh. (Cleveland In.)	41·05 N	81·30 W
171	Aksaray (äk-så-rī') Tur.	38·30 N	34·05 E
171	Aksehir (äk'shå-hĕr) Tur.	38·20 N	31·20 E
171	Aksehir (L.) Tur.	38·40 N	31·30 E
173	Aksha (äk'shà) Sov. Un.	50·28 N	113·00 E
188	Aksu (ä-kŭ-sōō) China	41·29 N	80·15 E
171	Aktyubinsk (äk'tyōō-bĕnsk) Sov. Un.	50·20 N	57·00 E
195	Akune (ä'kōō-nå) Jap.	32·03 N	130·16 E
150	Akureyri (ä-kōō-rá'rē) Ice.	65·39 N	18·01 W
101	Akutan (I.) (ä-kōō-tän') Ak. (In.)	53·58 N	169·54 W
214	Akwatia Ghana	6·04 N	0·49 W
103	Alabama (State) (ăl-á-băm'á) U. S.	32·50 N	87·30 W
120	Alabama (R.) Al.	31·20 N	87·39 W
197	Alabat (I.) (ä-lä-bät') Phil. (In.)	14·14 N	122·05 E
171	Alacam (ä-lä-chäm') Tur.	41·30 N	35·40 E
128	Alacranes (ä-lä-krä'nås) Cuba	22·45 N	81·35 W
186	Al Aflaj (Des.) Sau. Ar.	24·00 N	44·47 E
135	Alagôas (State) (ä-lä-gō'äzh) Braz.	9·50 S	36·33 W
135	Alagoinhas (ä-lä-gō-ēn'yäzh) Braz.	12·13 S	38·12 W
162	Alagón (ä-lä-gōn') Sp.	41·46 N	1·07 W
162	Alagón (R.) Sp.	39·53 N	6·42 W
124	Alahuatán (R.) (ä-lä-wä-tà'n) Mex.	18·30 N	100·00 W
127	Alajuela (ä-lä-hwa'lä) C.R.	10·01 N	84·14 W
122	Alajuela, L. Pan. (In.)	9·15 N	79·34 W
172	Alakol (L.) Sov. Un.	45·45 N	81·13 E
199	Alalakeiki Chan. (ä-lä-lä-kā'kē) Hi. (In.)	20·40 N	156·30 W
211	Al 'Alamayn Egypt	30·53 N	28·52 E
112	Alameda (ăl-á-mā'dá) Ca. (San Francisco In.)	37·46 N	122·15 W
112	Alameda (R.) Ca. (San Francisco In.)	37·36 N	122·02 W
197	Alaminos (ä-lä-mē'nôs) Phil. (In.)	16·09 N	119·58 E
153	Al 'Amirīyah Egypt	31·01 N	29·52 E
112	Alamo (ă'lá-mō) Ca. (San Francisco In.)	37·51 N	122·02 W
125	Alamo (ä'lä-mō) Mex.	20·55 N	97·41 W
114	Alamo (ă'lá-mō) Nv.	37·22 N	115·10 W
118	Alamo, R. (ä'lä-mō) Mex.	26·33 N	99·35 W
115	Alamogordo (ăl-á-mō-gôr'dō) NM	32·55 N	106·00 W
113	Alamo Heights (ă'lá-mō) Tx. (San Antonio In.)	29·28 N	98·27 W
118	Alamo Pk. (ă'lá-mō pēk) NM	32·50 N	105·55 W
115	Alamosa (ăl-á-mō'sá) Co.	37·25 N	105·50 W
174	Alandskiy (ä-länt'skĭ) Sov. Un. (Urals In.)	52·14 N	59·48 E
217	Alanga Arba Ken.	0·07 N	40·25 E
171	Alanya Tur.	36·40 N	32·10 E
213	Alaotra (L.) (ä-lä-ō'trá) Mad.	17·15 S	48·17 E
174	Alapayevsk (ä-lä-pä'yĕfsk) Sov. Un. (Urals In.)	57·50 N	61·35 E
183	Al 'Aqabah Jordan (Palestine In.)	29·32 N	35·00 E
124	Alaquines (ā-là-kē'nås) Mex.	22·07 N	99·35 W
183	Al 'Arīsh (a-rēsh') Egypt (Palestine In.)	31·08 N	33·48 E
75	Alaska (State) (á-lăs'ká) U. S.	64·00 N	150·00 W
101	Alaska, G. of Ak.	57·42 N	147·40 W
101	Alaska Hy. Ak.	63·00 N	142·00 W
101	Alaska Pen. Ak.	55·50 N	162·10 W
101	Alaska Ra. Ak.	62·00 N	152·18 W
211	Al-'Aṭrūn Sud.	18·13 N	26·44 E
170	Alatyr' (ä'lä-tür) Sov. Un.	54·55 N	46·30 E
134	Alausí (ä-lou-sē') Ec.	2·15 S	78·45 W
218	Al 'Ayyāţ (ä-ē-yät') Egypt (Nile In.)	29·38 N	31·18 E
164	Alba (äl'bä) It.	44·41 N	8·02 E
162	Albacete (äl-bä-thā'tā) Sp.	39·00 N	1·49 W
161	Albachten (äl-bä'K-tĕn) F.R.G. (Ruhr In.)	51·55 N	7·31 E
218	Al Badārī Egypt (Nile In.)	26·59 N	31·29 E
162	Alba de Tormes (äl-bà dā tôr'mās) Sp.	40·48 N	5·28 W
218	Al Bahnasā Egypt (Nile In.)	28·35 N	30·30 E
159	Alba Iulia (äl-bä yōō'lyà) Rom.	46·05 N	23·32 E
162	Albalate (äl-bä-lä'tā) Sp.	41·07 N	0·34 W
218	Al Ballaḩ (bä'lä) Egypt (Suez In.)	30·46 N	32·20 E
218	Al Balyanā Egypt (Nile In.)	26·12 N	32·00 E
146	Albania (ăl-bā'nĭ-á) Eur.	41·45 N	20·00 E
163	Albano, Lago (L.) (lä'-gō äl-bä'nō) It. (Rome In.)	41·45 N	12·44 E
163	Albano Laziale (äl-bä'nō lät-zē-ä'lä) It. (Rome In.)	41·44 N	12·43 E
204	Albany (ôl'bá-nĭ) Austl.	35·00 S	118·00 E
112	Albany Ca. (San Francisco In.)	37·54 N	122·18 W
120	Albany Ga.	31·35 N	84·10 W
117	Albany Mo.	40·14 N	94·18 W
105	Albany NY	42·40 N	73·50 W
110	Albany Or.	44·38 N	123·06 W
91	Albany (R.) Can.	51·45 N	83·30 W
186	Al Başrah Iraq	30·35 N	47·59 E
183	Al Batrūn (bä-trōōn') Leb. (Palestine In.)	34·16 N	35·39 E
211	Al Bawīţī Egypt	28·19 N	29·00 E
121	Albemarle (ăl'bē-märl) NC	35·24 N	80·36 W
121	Albemarle Sd. NC	36·00 N	76·17 W
164	Albenga (äl-bĕn'gä) It.	44·04 N	8·13 E
162	Alberche (R.) (äl-bĕr'chå) Sp.	40·08 N	4·19 W

ăt; finăl; rāte; senāte; ärm; åsk; sofá; fâre; ch-choose; dh-as th in other; bē; ēvent; bĕt; recĕnt; cratēr; g-go; gh-guttural g; bĭt; ĭ-short neutral; rīde; K-guttural k as ch in German ich;

Page	Name Pronunciation Region	Lat. °′	Long. °′
204	Alberga, The (R.) (äl-bŭr'gȧ) Austl.	27·15 S	135·00 E
162	Albergaria a-Velha (äl-bĕr-gȧ-rē'ȧ-ä-väl'yȧ) . Port.	40·47 N	8·31 W
113	Alberhill (ăl'bĕr-hĭl) Ca. (Los Angeles In.)	33·43 N	117·23 W
160	Albert (ȧl-bâr') . . . . Fr.	50·00 N	2·49 E
217	Albert (L.) (ăl'bĕrt) (äl-bâr') . . Afr.	1·50 N	30·40 E
217	Albert, Parc Natl. (Natl. Pk.) Zaire	0·05 N	29·30 E
90	Alberta (Prov.) (ăl-bûr'tȧ) . . . Can.	54·33 N	117·10 W
93	Alberta, Mt. . . . Can.	52·18 N	117·28 W
197	Albert Edward, Mt. (ăl'bĕrt ĕd'wērd) . Pap. N. Gui.	8·25 S	147·25 E
137	Alberti (äl-bĕ'r-tē) Arg. (Buenos Aires In.)	35·01 S	60·16 W
149	Albert Kanal (Can.) Bel. (Brussels In.)	51·07 N	5·07 E
109	Albert Lea (ăl'bĕrt lē') . . . . Mn.	43·38 N	93·24 W
217	Albert Nile (R.) . . . . Ug.	3·25 N	31·35 E
98	Alberton (ăl'bĕr-tŭn) . . . . Can.	46·49 N	64·04 W
213	Alberton . . . . S. Afr. (Johannesburg & Pretoria In.)	26·16 S	28·08 E
120	Albertville (ăl'bĕrt-vĭl) . . . . Al.	34·15 N	86·10 W
161	Albertville (ȧl-bâr-vēl') . . . . Fr.	45·42 N	6·25 E
	Albertville, see Kalemie		
160	Albi (äl-bē') . . . . Fr.	43·54 N	2·07 E
109	Albia (ăl-bĭ-ȧ) . . . . Ia.	41·01 N	92·44 W
135	Albina (äl-bē'nä) . . . . Sur.	5·30 N	54·33 W
216	Albina, Ponta (Pt.) . . . . Ang.	15·51 S	11·44 E
107	Albino, Pt. (äl-bē'nō) Can. (Buffalo In.)	42·50 N	79·05 W
104	Albion (ăl'bĭ-ŭn) . . . . Mi.	42·15 N	84·50 W
108	Albion . . . . Ne.	41·42 N	98·00 W
105	Albion . . . . NY	43·15 N	78·10 W
162	Alboran, Isla del (I.) (ē's-lä-dĕl-äl-bō-rä'n) . Sp.	35·58 N	3·02 W
162	Alboran Sea . . . . Afr.-Eur.	35·54 N	4·26 W
156	Ålborg (ôl'bôr) . . . . Den.	57·02 N	9·55 E
162	Albox (äl-bōk') . . . . Sp.	37·23 N	2·08 W
218	Al Buḩayrah al Murrah al Kubrā (Great Bitter) (Salt L.) . Egypt (Suez In.)	30·24 N	32·27 E
218	Al Buḩayrah al Murrah aş Şughrā (Little Bitter) (Salt L.) . Egypt (Suez In.)	30·10 N	32·36 E
115	Albuquerque (ăl-bŭ-kûr'kē) . . . NM	35·05 N	106·40 W
127	Albuquerque, Cayus de (I.) (äl-bŭ-kûr'kē) . Col.	12·12 N	81·24 W
186	Al Buraymī . . . . Om.	23·45 N	55·39 E
162	Alburquerque (äl-bōōr-kĕr'kä) . Sp.	39·13 N	6·58 W
203	Albury (ôl'bĕr-ē) . . . . Austl.	36·00 S	147·00 E
163	Alcabideche (äl-kȧ-bē-dā'chā) Port. (Lisbon In.)	38·43 N	9·24 W
162	Alcacer do Sal (äl-kä'sĕr dōō säl') Port.	38·24 N	8·33 W
163	Alcalá de Chivert (äl-kä-lä'dā chē-vĕrt') . Sp.	40·18 N	0·12 E
163	Alcalá de Henares (äl-kä-lä' dā ā-na'räs) Sp. (Madrid In.)	40·29 N	3·22 W
162	Alcalá de los Gazules (äl-kä-lä' dā lōs gä-thōō'lås) . Sp.	36·29 N	5·44 W
162	Alcalá la Real (äl-kä-lä'lä rā-äl') . Sp.	37·27 N	3·57 W
164	Alcamo (äl'kȧ-mō) . . . . It.	37·58 N	13·03 E
163	Alcanadre (R.) (äl-kä-nä'drå) Sp.	41·41 N	0·18 W
163	Alcanar (äl-kä-när') . . . . Sp.	40·35 N	0·27 E
163	Alcañiz (äl-kän-yēth') . . . . Sp.	41·03 N	0·08 W
135	Alcântara (äl-kän'tȧ-rȧ) . . . . Braz.	2·17 S	44·29 W
162	Alcaraz (äl-kä-räth') . . . . Sp.	38·39 N	2·28 W
162	Alcaudete (äl-kou-dhā'tā) . . . . Sp.	37·38 N	4·05 W
162	Alcazar de San Juan (äl-kä'thär dā sän hwän') . Sp.	39·22 N	3·12 W
163	Alcira (ä-thē'rä) . . . . Sp.	39·09 N	0·26 W
120	Alcoa (ăl-kō'ȧ) . . . . Tn.	35·45 N	84·00 W
163	Alcobendas (äl-kō-bĕn'dås) Sp. (Madrid In.)	40·32 N	3·39 W
163	Alcochete (äl-kō-chā'ta) Port. (Lisbon In.)	38·45 N	8·58 W
163	Alcora (äl-kō'rä) . . . . Sp.	40·05 N	0·12 W
163	Alcorisa (äl-kō-rē'sä) . . . . Sp.	40·53 N	0·20 W
163	Alcorón (äl-kō-rō'n) Sp. (Madrid In.)	40·22 N	3·50 W
137	Alcorta (ȧl-kôr'tä) Arg. (Buenos Aires In.)	33·32 S	61·08 W
111	Alcova Res. (ăl-kō'vȧ) . . . . Wy.	42·31 N	106·33 W
89	Alcove (ăl-kōv') Can. (Ottawa In.)	45·41 N	75·55 W
163	Alcoy (äl-koi') . . . . Sp.	38·42 N	0·30 W
163	Alcudia, Bahia de (B.) (bä-ē'ä-dĕ-äl-kōō-dhē'ä) . Sp.	39·48 N	3·20 E
213	Aldabra Is. (äl-dä'brä) . . . . Afr.	9·16 S	46·17 E
124	Aldama (äl-dä'mä) . . . . Mex.	22·54 N	98·04 W
118	Aldama . . . . Mex.	28·50 N	105·54 W
173	Aldan . . . . Sov. Un.	58·46 N	125·19 E
173	Aldan (R.) . . . . Sov. Un.	63·30 N	132·14 E
173	Aldan Plat. . . . . Sov. Un.	57·42 N	130·28 E
173	Aldanskaya . . . . Sov. Un.	61·52 N	135·29 E
161	Aldekerk (äl'dĕ-kĕ'rk) F.R.G. (Ruhr In.)	51·26 N	6·26 E
161	Aldenhoven (äl'dĕn-hō'vĕn) F.R.G. (Ruhr In.)	50·54 N	6·18 E
112	Aldergrove (ôl'dēr-grōv) Can. (Vancouver In.)	49·03 N	122·28 W
160	Alderney (I.) (ôl'dēr-nĭ) . . Guernsey	49·43 N	2·11 W
148	Aldershot (ôl'dēr-shŏt) Eng. (London In.)	51·14 N	0·46 W
104	Alderson (ôl-dēr-sŭn) . . . . WV	37·40 N	80·40 W
112	Alderwood Manor (ôl'dēr-wŏŏd män'ŏr) Wa. (Seattle In.)	47·49 N	122·18 W
148	Aldridge-Brownhills . . . . Eng.	52·38 N	1·55 W
117	Aledo (ȧ-le'dō) . . . . Il.	41·12 N	90·47 W
214	Aleg . . . . Mauritania	17·03 N	13·55 W
137	Alegre (älĕ'grĕ) Braz. (Rio de Janeiro In.)	20·41 S	41·32 W
136	Alegre (R.) Braz. (Rio de Janeiro In.)	22·22 S	43·34 W
136	Alegrete (ä-lā-grā'tā) . . . . Braz.	29·46 S	55·44 W
174	Aleksandrov (ä-lyĕk-sän' drôf) Sov. Un. (Moscow In.)	56·24 N	38·45 E
174	Aleksandrovsk (ä-lyĕk-sän'drôfsk) Sov. Un. (Urals In.)	59·11 N	57·36 E
173	Aleksandrovsk . . . . Sov. Un.	51·02 N	142·21 E
159	Aleksandrow Kujawski (ä-lĕk-säh'drōōv kōō-yav'skē) Pol.	52·54 N	18·45 E
167	Alekseyevka (ä-lyĕk-sā-yĕf'kȧ) Sov. Un.	50·39 N	38·40 E
166	Aleksin (ä-lyĕk-sēn) . . . . Sov. Un.	54·31 N	37·07 E
165	Aleksinac (ȧ-lyĕk-sē-näk') . . . Yugo.	43·33 N	21·42 E
137	Alem Paraíba (ä-lĕ'm-pȧ-räē'bȧ) Braz. (Rio de Janeiro In.)	21·54 S	42·40 W
160	Alençon (ȧ-läN-sôN') . . . . Fr.	48·26 N	0·08 E
135	Alenquer (ä-lĕŋ-kĕr') . . . . Braz.	1·58 S	54·44 W
162	Alenquer . . . . Port.	39·04 N	9·01 W
162	Alentjo (Reg.) (ä-lĕŋ-tä'zhōō) Port.	38·05 N	7·45 W
199	Alenuihaha Chan. (ä'lȧ-nōō-ê-hä'hä) . Hi. (In.)	20·20 N	156·05 W
153	Aleppo (ȧ-lĕp-ō) . . . . Syr.	36·10 N	37·18 E
160	Alès (ä-lĕs') . . . . Fr.	44·07 N	4·06 E
164	Alessandria (ä-lĕs-sän'drê-ä) . . . . It.	44·53 N	8·35 E
	Alessio, see Lesh		
156	Ålesund (ô'lĕ-sōōn') . . . . Nor.	62·28 N	6·14 E
101	Aleutian Is. (ȧ-lu'shăn) . . . . Ak.	52·40 N	177·30 W
101	Aleutian Trench . . . . Ak.	50·40 N	177·10 E
173	Alevina, Mys (C.) . . . . Sov. Un.	58·49 N	151·44 E
101	Alexander Arch. (ăl-ĕg-zăn'dēr) Ak.	57·05 N	138·10 W
120	Alexander City . . . . Al.	32·55 N	85·55 W
89	Alexander Ind. Res. Can. (Edmonton In.)	53·47 N	114·00 W
220	Alexander I . . . . Ant.	71·00 S	71·00 W
213	Alexandra (ăl-ex-än'drȧ) S. Afr. (Johannesburg & Pretoria In.)	26·07 S	28·07 E
204	Alexandria (ăl-ĕg-zăn'drĭ-ȧ) . Austl.	19·00 S	136·56 E
105	Alexandria . . . . Can.	45·50 N	74·35 W
104	Alexandria . . . . In.	40·20 N	85·20 W
119	Alexandria . . . . La.	31·18 N	92·28 W
108	Alexandria . . . . Mn.	45·53 N	95·23 W
165	Alexandria . . . . Rom.	43·55 N	25·21 E
213	Alexandria (ăl-ĕx-än-drĭ-ȧ) S. Afr. (Natal In.)	33·40 S	26·26 E
108	Alexandria . . . . SD	43·39 N	97·45 W
106	Alexandria (ăl-ĕg-zăn'drĭ-ȧ) Va. (Baltimore In.)	38·50 N	77·05 W
	Alexandria, see Al Iskandarīyah		
105	Alexandria Bay . . . . NY	44·20 N	75·55 W
165	Alexandroúpolis (Dedeagats) (ä-lĕk-sän-drōō'pō-lĭs) (de'dĕ-ä-gäts) . Grc.	40·51 N	25·51 E
162	Alfaro (äl-färō) . . . . Sp.	42·08 N	1·43 W
211	Al-Fāshir (fä'shēr) . . . . Sud.	13·38 N	25·21 E
218	Al Fashn . . . . Egypt (Nile In.)	28·47 N	30·53 E
211	Al Fayyūm . . . . Egypt	29·14 N	30·48 E
137	Alfenas (äl-fĕ'nȧs) Braz. (Rio de Janeiro In.)	21·26 S	45·55 W
165	Alfiós (R.) . . . . Grc.	37·33 N	21·50 E
218	Al Firdān (fer-dän') . . Egypt (Nile In.)	30·43 N	32·20 E
137	Alfonso Claudio (äl-fōn'sō-klou'dēō) Braz. (Rio de Janeiro In.)	20·05 S	41·05 W
89	Alfred (ăl'frĕd) . Can. (Ottawa In.)	45·34 N	74·52 W
148	Alfreton (ăl'fēr-tŭn) . . . . Eng.	53·06 N	1·23 W
162	Algarve (Reg.) (äl-gär'vĕ) . . . Port.	37·15 N	8·12 W
162	Algeciras (äl-hā-thē'räs) . . . . Sp.	36·08 N	5·25 W
210	Alger (Algiers) (ȧl-zhā') (ăl-jēr) Alg.	36·51 N	2·56 E
209	Algeria (ăl-gē'rĭ-ȧ) . . . . Afr.	28·45 N	1·00 E
163	Algete (äl-hā'tā) . . Sp. (Madrid In.)	40·36 N	3·30 W
164	Alghero (äl-gâ'rō) . . . . It.	40·32 N	8·22 E
	Algiers, see Alger		
119	Algoa (ăl-gō'ȧ) . . . . Tx. (In.)	29·24 N	95·11 W
213	Algoabaai (B.) (ăl'gôȧ) S. Afr. (Natal In.)	33·51 S	24·50 E
112	Algoma . . . . Wa. (Seattle In.)	47·17 N	122·15 W
109	Algoma . . . . Wi.	44·38 N	87·29 W
109	Algona . . . . Ia.	43·04 N	94·11 W
104	Algonac (ăl'gô-năk) . . . . Mi.	42·35 N	82·30 W
107	Algonquin (ăl-gŏŋ'kwĭn) Il. (Chicago In.)	42·10 N	88·17 W
105	Algonquin Provincial Park . . . Can.	45·50 N	78·20 W
162	Alhama (äl-hä'mä) . . . . Sp.	37·00 N	3·59 W
162	Alhama . . . . Sp.	37·50 N	1·24 W
113	Alhambra (ăl-hăm'brȧ) Ca. (Los Angeles In.)	34·05 N	118·08 W
153	Al Ḩammām . . . . Egypt	30·46 N	29·42 E
163	Alhandra (äl-yän'drȧ) Port. (Lisbon In.)	38·55 N	9·01 W
186	Al Hasā (Plain) . . . . Sau. Ar.	27·00 N	47·48 E
162	Alhaurín el Grande (ä-lou-rēn'ĕl-grä'n-dĕ) . Sp.	36·40 N	4·40 W
186	Al Ḩijāz (Reg.) . . . . Sau. Ar.	23·45 N	39·08 E
183	Al Hirmil . . . . Leb. (Palestine In.)	34·23 N	36·22 E
163	Alhos Vedros (äl'yōs'vä'drōs) Port. (Lisbon In.)	38·39 N	9·02 W
162	Alhucemas, Baie d' (B.) . . . . Mor.	35·18 N	3·50 W
186	Al Ḩudaydah . . . . Yemen	14·43 N	43·03 E
186	Al Hufūf . . . . Sau. Ar.	25·15 N	49·43 E
165	Aliákmon (R.) (äl-ê-äk'mōn) Grc.	40·26 N	22·17 E
215	Alibori (R.) . . . . Benin	11·40 N	2·55 E
163	Alicante (ä-lê-kän'tä) . . . . Sp.	38·20 N	0·30 W
163	Alicante, Bahia de (B.) (bä-ē'ä-dĕ-ä-lê-kän'tā) . Sp.	38·12 N	0·22 W
213	Alice (ăl-ĭs) . . . S. Afr. (Natal In.)	32·47 S	26·51 E
118	Alice (ăl'ĭs) . . . . Tx.	27·45 N	98·04 W
92	Alice Arm . . . . Can.	55·29 N	129·29 W
213	Alicedale (ăl'ĭs-dāl) S. Afr. (Natal In.)	33·18 S	26·04 E
204	Alice Springs (ăl'ĭs) . . . . Austl.	23·38 S	133·56 E
164	Alicudi (I.) (ä-lē-kōō'dē) . . . . It.	38·34 N	14·21 E
174	Alifkulovo (ä-lĭf-kŭ'lô-vô) Sov. Un. (Urals In.)	55·57 N	62·06 E
184	Alīgarh (ä-lê-gŭr') . . . . India	27·58 N	78·08 E
156	Alingsås (ä'lĭŋ-sôs) . . . . Swe.	57·57 N	12·30 E
107	Aliquippa (ăl-ĭ-kwĭp'ȧ) Pa. (Pittsburgh In.)	40·37 N	80·15 W
218	Al Iskandarīyah (Alexandria) Egypt (Nile In.)	31·12 N	29·58 E
	Al Ismā'ī-līyah, see Ismailia		
212	Aliwal North (ä-lê-wäl') . . . . S. Afr.	31.09 S	28·26 E
186	Al-Jabal Al-Akhḑar (Mts.) . . . Om.	23·30 N	56·43 W
183	Al Jafr, Qa'al (L.) Jordan (Palestine In.)	30·15 N	36·24 E
211	Al Jaghbūb . . . . Libya	29·46 N	24·32 E
211	Al Jawf . . . . Libya	24·14 N	23·15 E
186	Al Jawf . . . . Sau. Ar.	29·45 N	39·30 E
162	Aljezur (äl-zhā-zōōr') . . . . Port.	37·18 N	8·52 W
218	Al Jīzah . . . . Egypt (Nile In.)	30·01 N	31·12 E
210	Al Jufrah (Oasis) . . . . Libya	29·30 N	15·16 E
162	Aljustrel (äl-zhōō-strĕl') . . . . Port.	37·44 N	8·23 W
218	Al Kāb . . . . Egypt (Suez In.)	30·56 N	32·19 E
211	Al Kāmilīn (käm-lēn') . . . . Sud.	15·09 N	33·06 E
183	Al Karak (kĕ-räk') Jordan (Palestine In.)	31·11 N	35·42 E
218	Al Karnak (kär'nak) Egypt (Nile In.)	25·42 N	32·43 E
186	Al Khābūrah . . . . Om.	23·45 N	57·30 E
183	Al Khalīl (Hebron) Jordan (Palestine In.)	31·31 N	35·07 E
211	Al Khandaq (kän-däk') . . . . Sud.	18·38 N	30·29 E
211	Al Khums . . . . Libya	32·35 N	14·10 E
186	Al Khurmah . . . . Sau. Ar.	21·37 N	41·44 E
211	Al Khurţūm (Khartoum) (kär-tōōm') . Sud.	15·34 N	32·36 E
211	Al-Khurţūm Baḩrī . . . . Sud.	15·43 N	32·41 E
183	Al Kiswah . . . Syr. (Palestine In.)	33·31 N	36·13 E
155	Alkmaar (älk-mär') . . . . Neth.	52·39 N	4·42 E
218	Al Kūbrī (kōō'brê) Egypt (Suez In.)	30·01 N	32·35 E
211	Al Kufrah (Oasis) . . . . Libya	24·45 N	22·45 E
183	Al Kuntillah . Egypt (Palestine In.)	29·59 N	34·42 E
186	Al Kuwayt (Kuwait) (koō-wit) Kuw.	29·04 N	47·59 E
153	Al Lādhiqīyah (Latakia) . . . . Syr.	35·32 N	35·51 E
98	Allagash (R.) (ăl'ȧ-găsh) . . . . Me.	46·50 N	69·24 W
184	Allāhābād (ŭl-ŭ-hä-bäd') . . . . India	25·32 N	81·53 E
114	All American Can. (âl ȧ-mĕr'ĭ-kăn) Ca.	32·43 N	115·12 W
149	Alland . . . . Aus. (Vienna In.)	48·04 N	16·05 E
162	Allariz (äl-yä-rēth') . . . . Sp.	42·10 N	7·48 W
120	Allatoona (R.) (ăl'ȧ-tōōn'ȧ) . . . Ga.	34·05 N	84·57 W
160	Allauch (ä-lĕ'ōō) . . . . Fr. (In.)	43·21 N	5·30 E
173	Allaykha (ä-lī'kȧ) . . . . Sov. Un.	70·32 N	148·53 E
96	Allegan (ăl'ē-găn) . . . . Mi.	42·30 N	85·55 W
105	Allegany Ind. Res. (ăl-ē-gā'nĭ) NY	42·05 N	78·55 W
105	Allegheny (R.) . . . . Pa.	41·10 N	79·20 W
105	Allegheny Front (Mts.) . . . . U. S.	38·12 N	80·03 W
103	Allegheny Mts. . . . . U. S.	37·35 N	81·55 W
104	Allegheny Plat. . . . . U. S.	39·00 N	81·15 W
105	Allegheny Res. . . . . Pa.	41·50 N	78·55 W
117	Allen (ăl'ĕn) . . . . Ok.	34·51 N	96·26 W
154	Allen, Lough (B.) (lŏk ăl'ĕn) . . Ire.	54·07 N	8·09 W
106	Allendale (ăl'ĕn-dāl) NJ (New York In.)	41·02 N	74·08 W
121	Allendale . . . . SC	33·00 N	81·19 W
125	Allende (äl-yĕn'dä) . . . . Mex.	18·23 N	92·49 W
118	Allende . . . . Mex.	28·20 N	100·50 W
105	Allentown (ăl'en-toun) . . . . Pa.	40·35 N	75·30 W
185	Alleppey (ȧ-lĕp'ē) . . . . India	9·33 N	76·22 E
158	Aller R. (äl'ĕr) . . . . F.R.G.	52·43 N	9·50 E
108	Alliance (ȧ-lī'ăns) . . . . Ne.	42·06 N	102·53 W
104	Alliance . . . . Oh.	40·55 N	81·10 W
186	Al Lidām . . . . Sau. Ar.	20·45 N	44·12 E
160	Allier (R.) (ȧ-lyā') . . . . Fr.	46·43 N	3·03 E
106	Alligator Pt. (al'ĭ-gā-tēr) La. (New Orleans In.)	30·57 N	89·41 W
156	Allinge (äl'ĭŋ-ĕ) . . . . Den.	55·16 N	14·48 E
126	All Pines (ôl pīnz) . . . . Belize (In.)	16·55 N	88·15 W
186	Al Luḩayyah . . . . Yemen	15·58 N	42·48 E
106	Alluvial City La. (New Orleans In.)	29·51 N	89·42 W
112	Allyn (ăl'ĭn) . . . . Wa. (Seattle In.)	47·23 N	122·51 W
98	Alma (ăl'mȧ) . . . . Can.	45·36 N	64·59 W
98	Alma . . . . Can.	48·29 N	71·42 W
121	Alma . . . . Ga.	31·33 N	82·31 W
104	Alma . . . . Mi.	43·25 N	84·40 W
116	Alma . . . . Ne.	40·08 N	99·21 W
218	Alma . . . S. Afr. (Johannesburg & Pretoria In.)	24·30 S	28·05 E
109	Alma . . . . Wi.	44·21 N	91·57 W
172	Alma-Ata (ăl'mȧ ȧ'tȧ) . . . Sov. Un.	43·19 N	77·08 E
183	Al Mabrak (R.) Sau. Ar. (Palestine In.)	29·16 N	35·12 E
163	Almada (äl-mä'dä) Port. (Lisbon In.)	38·40 N	9·09 W
162	Almadén (äl-mȧ-dhän') . . . . Sp.	38·47 N	4·50 W

ng-sing; ŋ-baŋk; N-nasalized n; nŏd; cŏmmit; ōld; ôbey; ôrder; fōōd; fŏŏt; ou-out; s-soft; sh-dish; th-thin; pūre; ûnite; ûrn; stŭd; circŭs; ü-as "y" in study; '-indeterminate vowel.

Page	Name Pronunciation Region	Lat. °′	Long. °′
186	Al Madīnah (Medina)....Sau. Ar.	24·26 N	39·42 E
183	Al Mafraq..Jordan (Palestine In.)	32·21 N	36·13 E
125	Almagre, Laguna (L.) (lä-gōō'nä-äl-mä'grĕ)......Mex.	23·48 N	97·45 W
162	Almagro (äl-mä'grō)..........Sp.	38·52 N	3·41 W
218	Al Maḥallah al Kubrā Egypt (Nile In.)	31·00 N	31·10 E
186	Al Manāmah...........Bahrain	26·01 N	50·33 E
114	Almanor (R.) (ăl-măn'ôr).....Ca.	40·11 N	121·20 W
162	Almansa (äl-män'sä)..........Sp.	38·52 N	1·09 W
218	Al Manshāh.....Egypt (Nile In.)	26·31 N	31·46 E
162	Almansor (R.) (äl-män-sôr)..Port.	38·41 N	8·27 W
218	Al Manṣūrah....Egypt (Nile In.)	31·02 N	31·25 E
218	Al Manzilah (män'za-la) Egypt (Nile In.)	31·09 N	32·05 E
162	Almanzora (R.) (äl-män-thō'rä) Sp.	37·20 N	2·25 W
218	Al Marāghah Egypt (Nile In.)	26·41 N	31·35 E
163	Almargem (äl-mär-zhĕn) Port. (Lisbon In.)	38·51 N	9·16 W
211	Al-Marj..........Libya	32·44 N	21·08 E
186	Al Maṣīrah (I.).........Om.	20·43 N	58·58 E
186	Al Mawsil...........Iraq	36·00 N	42·53 E
162	Almazán (äl-mä-thän').........Sp.	41·30 N	2·33 W
183	Al Mazār...Jordan (Palestine In.)	31·04 N	35·41 E
183	Al Mazra'ah Jordan (Palestine In.)	31·17 N	35·33 E
162	Almeirim (äl-māī-rēn')......Port.	39·13 N	8·31 W
155	Almelo (äl'mē-lō).........Neth.	52·20 N	6·42 E
162	Almendralejo (äl-mān-drä-lā'hō) Sp.	38·43 N	6·24 W
162	Almería (äl-mā-rē'ä)..........Sp.	36·52 N	2·28 W
162	Almeria, Golfo de (G.) (gôl-fô-dĕ-äl-māī-rĕn').Sp.	36·45 N	2·26 W
162	Almería (R.)..........Sp.	37·00 N	2·40 W
156	Älmhult (ĕlm'hōōlt)........Swe.	56·35 N	14·08 E
162	Almina, Pta. (äl-mē'nä).....Mor.	35·58 N	5·17 W
218	Al Minyā........Egypt (Nile In.)	28·04 N	30·45 E
127	Almirante (äl-mē-rän'tā).....Pan.	9·18 N	82·24 W
127	Almirante, Bahia de (B.) (bä-ē'ä-dĕ-äl-mē-rän'tā).Pan.	9·22 N	82·07 W
165	Almirós.........Grc.	39·13 N	22·47 E
162	Almodóvar (äl-mō-dhō'vär)....Sp.	38·43 N	4·10 W
184	Almoi.........India	29·41 N	79·42 E
124	Almoloya (äl-mō-lō'yä)......Mex.	19·32 N	99·44 W
125	Almoloya.........Mex. (In.)	19·11 N	99·28 W
105	Almonte (ăl-mŏn'tē)..........Can.	45·15 N	76·15 W
162	Almonte (äl-mōn'tā)..........Sp.	37·16 N	6·32 W
162	Almonte (R.)..........Sp.	39·35 N	5·50 W
184	Almora.........India	29·20 N	79·40 E
186	Al Mubarraz..........Sau. Ar.	22·31 N	46·27 E
183	Al Mudawwarah Jordan (Palestine In.)	29·20 N	36·01 E
186	Al Mukallā.....P. D. R. of Yem.	14·27 N	49·05 E
186	Al Mukhā..........Yemen	13·43 N	43·27 E
162	Almuñécar (äl-mōōn-yā'kär)...Sp.	36·44 N	3·43 W
156	Alnö (I.).........Swe.	62·20 N	17·39 E
112	Aloha (ä'lô-hā)..Or. (Portland In.)	45·29 N	122·52 W
197	Alor, Pulau (I.) (ä'lôr).....Indon.	8·07 S	125·00 E
162	Álora (ä'lô-rä)..........Sp.	36·49 N	4·42 W
183	Alor Gajah..Mala (Singapore In.)	2·23 N	102·13 E
196	Alor Setar (ä'lôr stär)......Mala.	6·10 N	100·16 E
112	Alouette (R.) (ä-lōō-ĕt') Can. (Vancouver In.)	49·16 N	122·32 W
104	Alpena (ăl-pē'nȧ)..........Mi.	45·05 N	83·30 W
149	Alphen....Neth. (Amsterdam In.)	52·07 N	4·38 E
162	Alpiarca (äl-pyär'sȧ)........Port.	39·38 N	8·37 W
118	Alpine (ăl'pīn)..........Tx.	30·21 N	103·41 W
152	Alps (Mts.) (ălps)..........Eur.	46·18 N	8·42 E
134	Alpujarra (ál-pōō-ĸá'rá) Col. (In.)	3·23 N	74·56 W
162	Alpujarras (Mts.) (äl-pōō-här'räs) Sp.	36·55 N	3·25 W
211	Al Qaḍārif..........Sud.	14·03 N	35·11 E
218	Al Qāhirah (Cairo) Egypt (Nile In.)	30·00 N	31·17 E
218	Al Qanṭarah.....Egypt (Suez In.)	30·51 N	32·20 E
211	Al Qaryah ash Sharqiyah...Libya	30·36 N	13·13 E
186	Al Qaṭīf..........Sau. Ar.	26·30 N	50·00 E
186	Al Qaysūmah..........Sau. Ar.	28·15 N	46·20 E
183	Al Qunaytirah Syr. (Palestine In.)	33·09 N	35·49 E
186	Al Qunfudhah..........Sau. Ar.	19·08 N	41·05 E
183	Al Quṣaymah Egypt (Palestine In.)	30·40 N	34·23 E
211	Al Quṣayr..........Egypt	26·14 N	34·11 E
183	Al Qusayr...Egypt (Palestine In.)	34·32 N	36·33 E
156	Als (I.) (äls)..........Den.	55·06 N	9·40 E
161	Alsace (Reg.) (äl-sá's).........Fr.	48·25 N	7·24 E
190	Al Shan (Mts.) (äl'shän)....China	37·27 N	120·35 E
156	Alsterån (R.)..........Swe.	56·54 N	15·50 E
113	Altadena (ăl-tȧ-dē'nȧ) Ca. (Los Angeles In.)	34·12 N	118·08 W
136	Alta Gracia (äl'tä grä'sē-a)...Arg.	31·41 S	64·19 W
134	Altagracia..........Ven.	10·42 N	71·34 W
135	Altagracia de Orituco (ä'l-tà-grà'sēā-dĕ-ôrē-tōō'kô) Ven. (In.)	9·53 N	66·22 W
188	Altai Mts. (äl'tī')..........Asia	49·11 N	87·15 E
113	Alta Loma (ăl'tȧ lō'mä) Ca. (Los Angeles In.)	34·07 N	117·35 W
119	Alta Loma (ăl'tȧ lō-mȧ)..Tx. (In.)	29·22 N	95·05 W
121	Altamaha (R.) (ôl-tȧ-mȧ-hô')..Ga.	31·50 N	82·00 W
135	Altamira (äl-tä-mē'rä)......Braz.	3·13 S	52·14 W
125	Altamira..........Mex.	22·25 N	97·55 W
136	Altamirano (äl-tä-mē-rä'nō)..Arg.	35·26 S	58·12 W
164	Altamura (äl-tä-mōō'rä).......It.	40·40 N	16·35 E
173	Altan Bulag.........Mong.	50·18 N	106·31 E
121	Altavista (ăl-tä-vĕs'tȧ)........Va.	37·08 N	79·14 W
188	Altay (äl-tä)..........China	47·52 N	86·50 E
150	Alten (R.) (äl'tĕn)..........Nor.	69·40 N	24·09 E
158	Altenburg (äl-tĕn-bōōrgh).G.D.R.	50·59 N	12·27 E
149	Altenmarkt an der Triesting Aus. (Vienna In.)	48·02 N	16·00 E
162	Alter do Chão (äl-tĕr'dōō shäN'ōN).Port.	39·13 N	7·38 W
124	Altiplanicie Mexicana (Plat.) (äl-tē-plä-nē'syē-mĕ-ĸē-kȧ-nä) Mex.	22·38 N	102·33 W
134	Altiplano (Plat.) (äl-tē-plȧ'nō) Bol.	18·38 S	68·20 W
149	Alt Landsberg (ält länts'bĕrgh) G.D.R. (Berlin In.)	52·34 N	13·44 E
119	Alto (ăl'tō)..........La.	32·21 N	91·52 W
134	Alto Marañón, Rio (R.) (rē'ō-ȧl'tô-mä-rän-yŏ'n).Peru	8·18 S	77·13 W
217	Alto Molócuè..........Moz.	15·38 S	37·42 E
149	Altomünster (äl'tō-mün'stĕr) F.R.G. (Munich In.)	48·24 N	11·16 E
89	Alton (ôl'tŭn)..Can. (Toronto In.)	43·52 N	80·05 W
113	Alton.........Il. (St. Louis In.)	38·53 N	90·11 W
202	Altona.....Austl. (Melbourne In.)	37·52 S	144·50 E
95	Altona..........Can.	49·06 N	97·33 W
149	Altona (äl'tō-nȧ) F.R.G. (Hamburg In.)	53·33 N	9·54 E
120	Altoona (ăl-tōō'nȧ)..........Al.	34·01 N	86·15 W
105	Altoona..........Pa.	40·25 N	78·25 W
112	Altoona.......Wa. (Portland In.)	46·16 N	123·39 W
137	Alto Rio Doce (äl'tō-rē'ō-dō'sĕ) Braz. (Rio de Janeiro In.)	21·02 S	43·23 W
129	Alto Songo (äl-fō-sôŋ'gō)....Cuba	20·10 N	75·45 W
125	Altotonga (ál-tō-tôŋ'gä).....Mex.	19·44 N	97·13 W
216	Alto-Uama..........Ang.	12·14 S	15·33 E
129	Alto Velo (I.) (äl-tô-vĕ'lō) Dom. Rep.	17·30 N	71·35 W
148	Altrincham (ôl'trĭng-ăm).....Eng.	53·18 N	2·21 W
149	Alt Ruppin (ält rōō'ppēn) G.D.R. (Berlin In.)	52·56 N	12·50 E
188	Altun Shan (Mts.) (äl-tōōn shän) China	36·58 N	5·09 E
110	Alturas (ăl-tōō'rȧs)..........Ca.	41·29 N	120·33 W
116	Altus (ăl'tŭs)..........Ok.	34·38 N	99·20 W
211	Al-Ubayyiḍ..........Sud.	13·15 N	30·15 E
211	Al-Uḍayyah..........Sud.	12·06 N	28·16 E
211	Al-'Ugaylah..........Libya	30·15 N	19·07 E
166	Alūksne (ä'lōōks-nĕ).....Sov. Un.	57·24 N	27·04 E
218	'Alula (ä-lōō'lä) Som. (Horn of Afr. In.)	11·53 N	50·40 E
105	Alumette I. (á-lü-mĕt')......Can.	45·50 N	77·00 W
112	Alum Rock Ca. (San Francisco In.)	37·23 N	121·50 W
218	Al Uqṣur (Luxor).Egypt (Nile In.)	25·38 N	32·59 E
167	Alushta (ä'lshōō-tȧ).....Sov. Un.	44·39 N	34·23 E
116	Alva (ăl'vȧ)..........Ok.	36·46 N	98·41 W
125	Alvarado (äl-vä-rä'dhō).....Mex.	18·48 N	95·45 W
125	Alvarado, Luguna de (L.) (lä-gōō'nä-dĕ-äl-vä-rá'dô)..Mex.	18·44 N	96·45 W
156	Älvdalen (ĕlv'dä-lĕn)........Swe.	61·14 N	14·04 E
163	Alverca (al-vĕr'kȧ) Port. (Lisbon In.)	38·53 N	9·02 W
156	Alvesta (äl-vĕs'tä).........Swe.	56·55 N	14·29 E
119	Alvin (ăl'vĭn)..........Tx. (In.)	29·25 N	95·14 W
137	Alvinópolis (äl-vēnō'pō-lēs) Braz. (Rio de Janeiro In.)	20·07 S	43·03 W
112	Alviso (ăl-vī'sō) Ca. (San Francisco In.)	37·26 N	121·59 W
186	Al Wajh..........Sau. Ar.	26·15 N	36·32 E
184	Alwar (ŭl'wŭr)..........India	27·39 N	76·39 E
218	Al Wāsiṭah......Egypt (Nile In.)	29·21 N	31·15 E
157	Alytus (ä'lē-tōōs)........Sov. Un.	54·25 N	24·05 E
124	Amacuzac (R.) (ä-mä-kōō-zäk) Mex.	18·00 N	99·03 W
204	Amadeus, (L.) (ăm-ȧ-dē'ŭs).Austl.	24·30 S	131·25 E
91	Amadjuak (L.) (ä-mädj'wäk).Can.	64·50 N	69 20 W
195	Amagasaki (ä'mä-gä-sä'kē) Jap. (Ōsaka In.)	34·43 N	135·25 E
195	Amakusa-Shimo (I.) (ämä-kōō'sä shē-mō).Jap.	32·24 N	129·35 E
156	Åmål (ô'môl)..........Swe.	59·05 N	12·40 E
134	Amalfi (ä'mȧ'l-fē)......Col. (In.)	6·55 N	75·04 W
163	Amalfi (ä-mä'l-fē).It. (Naples In.)	40·23 N	14·36 E
165	Amaliás (á-măl'yás)..........Grc.	37·48 N	21·23 E
184	Amalner..........India	21·07 N	75·06 E
135	Amambai, Serra de (Mts.) Braz.	20·06 S	57·08 W
194	Amami Guntō (Is.) (ä'mä'mē gōōn'tō').Jap.	28·25 N	129·00 E
194	Amamio (I.) (ä-mä'mē-ō).....Jap.	28·10 N	129·55 E
135	Amapá (ä-mä-pá')..........Braz.	2·14 N	50·48 W
135	Amapá (Ter.)..........Braz.	1·15 N	52·15 W
126	Amapala (ä-mä-pä'lä)......Hond.	13·16 N	87·39 W
135	Amarante (ä-mä-rän'tā).....Braz.	6·17 S	42·43 W
114	Amargosa (R.) (á'mär-gō'sȧ)..Ca.	35·55 N	116·45 W
116	Amarillo (ăm-ȧ-rĭl'ō)..........Tx.	35·14 N	101·49 W
164	Amaro, Mt. (ä-mä'rō).........It.	42·07 N	14·07 E
171	Amasya (ä-mä'sē-ȧ)..........Tur.	40·40 N	35·50 E
125	Amatenango (ä-mä-tā-naŋ'gō) Mex.	16·30 N	92·29 W
101	Amatignak (I.) (ä-mȧ'tē-näk)..Ak.	51·12 N	178·30 W
126	Amatique, Bahía de (B.) (bä-ē'ä-dĕ-ä-mä-tē'kä) Belize-Guat.	15·58 N	88·50 W
126	Amatitlán (ä-mä-tē-tlän')...Guat.	14·27 N	90·39 W
124	Amatlán de Cañas (ä-mät-län'dā kän-yäs).Mex.	20·50 N	104·22 W
134	Amazonas (State) (ä-mä-thō'näs).Braz.	4·15 S	64·30 W
135	Amazonas, Rio (R.) (rē'ō-ä-mä-thō'näs).Braz.	2·03 S	53·18 W
184	Ambāla (ŭm-bä'lŭ)..........India	30·31 N	76·48 E
134	Ambalema (äm-bä-lā'mä) Col. (In.)	4·47 N	74·45 W
173	Ambarchik (ŭm-bär'chĭk).Sov. Un.	69·39 N	162·18 E
185	Ambarnāth...India (Bombay In.)	19·12 N	73·10 E
134	Ambato (äm-bä'tō)..........Ec.	1·15 S	78·30 W
213	Ambatondrazaka..........Mad.	17·58 S	48·43 E
158	Amberg (äm'bĕrgh)........F.R.G.	49·26 N	11·51 E
126	Ambergris Cay (I.) (ăm'bĕr-grēs kāz).Belize	18·04 N	87·43 W
129	Ambergris Cays (Is.) Turks & Caicos Is.	21·20 N	71·40 W
161	Ambérieu (äN-bā-rē-u')........Fr.	45·57 N	5·21 E
160	Ambert (äN-bĕr')..........Fr.	45·32 N	3·41 E
197	Ambil I. (äm'bēl)......Phil. (In.)	13·51 N	120·25 E
106	Ambler (ăm'blēr) Pa. (Philadelphia In.)	40·09 N	75·13 W
160	Amboise (äN-bwăz')..........Fr.	47·25 N	0·56 E
197	Ambon..........Indon.	3·45 S	128·17 E
197	Ambon, Pulau (I.)..........Indon.	4·50 S	128·45 E
213	Ambositra (äN-bô-sē'trä)....Mad.	20·31 S	47·28 E
104	Amboy (ăm'boi)..........Il.	41·41 N	89·15 W
112	Amboy.......Wa. (Portland In.)	45·55 N	122·27 W
213	Ambre, Cap d' (C.)..........Mad.	12·06 S	49·15 E
107	Ambridge (ăm'brĭdj) Pa. (Pittsburgh In.)	40·36 N	80·13 W
205	Ambrim (I.)..........New Heb.	16·25 S	168·15 E
216	Ambriz..........Ang.	7·50 S	13·06 E
216	Ambrizete..........Ang.	7·14 S	12·52 E
101	Amchitka P. (ăm-chĭt'kȧ).....Ak.	51·30 N	179·36 W
124	Amealco (ä-mā-äl'kō).......Mex.	20·12 N	100·08 W
124	Ameca (ä-mĕ'kä)..........Mex.	20·34 N	104·02 W
125	Amecameca (ä-mȧ-kä-mä'kä) Mex. (In.)	19·06 N	98·46 W
149	Ameide...Neth. (Amsterdam In.)	51·57 N	4·57 E
155	Ameland (I.)..........Neth.	53·29 N	5·54 E
107	Amelia (ȧ-mēl'yȧ) Oh. (Cincinnati In.)	39·01 N	84·12 W
114	American (R.) (ȧ-mĕr'ĭ-kăn)...Ca.	38·43 N	120·45 W
137	Americana (ä-mĕ-rē-kȧ'nȧ) Braz. (Rio de Janeiro In.)	22·46 S	47·19 W
111	American Falls (ȧ-mĕr-ĭ-kăn)..Id.	42·45 N	112·53 W
111	American Falls Res..........Id.	42·56 N	113·18 W
115	American Fork..........Ut.	40·20 N	111·50 W
220	American Highland..........Ant.	72·00 S	79·00 E
120	Americus (ȧ-mĕr'ĭ-kŭs).......Ga.	32·04 N	84·15 W
149	Amersfoort (ä'mĕrz-fōrt) Neth. (Amsterdam In.)	52·08 N	5·23 E
95	Amery (ā'mēr-ē)..........Can.	56·34 N	94·03 W
109	Amery..........Wi.	45·19 N	92·24 W
109	Ames (āmz)..........Ia.	42·00 N	93·36 W
99	Amesbury (āmz'bēr-ē)...Ma. (In.)	42·51 N	70·56 W
165	Amfissa (ȧm-fĭ'sȧ)..........Grc.	38·32 N	22·26 E
173	Amga (ŭm-gä')..........Sov. Un.	61·08 N	132·09 E
173	Amga (R.)..........Sov. Un.	61·41 N	133·11 E
173	Amgun (R.)..........Sov. Un.	53·33 N	137·57 E
211	Amhara (Prov.) (äm-hä'rä)...Eth.	11·30 N	36·45 E
98	Amherst (ăm'hĕrst)..........Can.	45·49 N	64·14 W
107	Amherst......Oh. (Cleveland In.)	41·24 N	82·13 W
97	Amherst (I.)..........Can.	44·08 N	76·45 W
160	Amiens (ä-myăN')..........Fr.	49·54 N	2·18 E
220	Amirante Is..........Sey.	6·02 S	52·30 E
95	Amisk L..........Can.	54·35 N	102·13 W
118	Amistad Res..........Tx.	29·20 N	101·00 W
119	Amite (ă-mēt')..........La.	30·43 N	90·32 W
119	Amite R..........La.	30·45 N	90·48 W
107	Amity (ăm'ĭ-tĭ).........Pa. (In.)	40·02 N	80·11 W
106	Amityville (ăm'ĭ-tĭ-vĭl) NY (New York In.)	40·41 N	73·24 W
101	Amlia (I.) (ȧ'm-lēä)..........Ak.	52·00 N	173·28 W
183	'Ammān (äm'mȧn) Jordan (Palestine In.)	31·57 N	35·57 E
149	Ammer L. (äm'mĕr) F.R.G. (Munich In.)	48·00 N	11·08 E
113	Amnicon R. (ăm'nē-kŏn) Wi. (Duluth In.)	46·35 N	91·56 W
	Amnok (R.), see Yalu		
165	Amorgós (I.) (ä-môr'gōs).....Grc.	36·47 N	25·47 E
120	Amory (ām'o-rē)..........Ms.	33·58 N	88·27 W
97	Amos (ā'mŭs)..........Can.	48·31 N	78·04 W
156	Amot (Torpen) (ô'mōt) (tôr'pĕn) Nor.	61·08 N	11·17 E
	Amoy, see Xiamen		
137	Amparo (äm-pá'-rô) Braz. (Rio de Janeiro In.)	22·43 S	46·44 W
149	Amper R. (äm'pĕr) F.R.G. (Munich In.)	48·18 N	11·32 E
163	Amposta (äm-pōs'tä).........Sp.	40·42 N	0·34 E
98	Amqui..........Can.	48·28 N	67·28 W
184	Amrāvati..........India	20·58 N	77·47 E
184	Amritsar (ŭm-rĭt'sŭr).......India	31·43 N	74·52 E
149	Amstelveen Neth. (Amsterdam In.)	52·18 N	4·51 E
149	Amsterdam (äm-stēr-däm') Neth. (Amsterdam In.)	52·21 N	4·52 E
105	Amsterdam (ăm'stĕr-dăm)....NY	42·55 N	74·10 W
158	Amstetten (äm'stĕt-ĕn)......Aus.	48·09 N	14·53 E
211	Am Timan (äm'tē-män')....Chad	11·18 N	20·30 E
186	Amu Darya (R.) (ä-mōō-dä'rēä).Asia	40·40 N	62·00 E
101	Amukta P. (ä-mōōk'tȧ).......Ak.	52·30 N	172·00 W
90	Amundsen G. (ä'mŭn-sĕn).....Can.	70·17 N	123·28 W
220	Amundsen Sea..........Ant.	72·00 S	110·00 W
156	Amungen (L.)..........Swe.	61·07 N	16·00 E
174	Amurskiy (ä-mûr'skĭ) Sov. Un. (Urals In.)	52·35 N	59·36 E
194	Amurskiy, Zaliv (B.) (zä'lĭf ä-mōōr'skĭ).Sov. Un.	43·20 N	131·40 E
124	Amusgos (San Pedro) (ä-mōō's-gôs) (sän-pĕ'drō).Mex.	16·39 N	98·09 W
197	Amuyao, Mt. (ä-mōō-yä'ō) Phil. (In.)	17·04 N	121·09 E
165	Amvrakikos Kólpos (G.).....Grc.	39·00 N	21·00 E
183	Amyun......Leb. (Palestine In.)	34·18 N	35·48 E
173	Anabar (R.) (ăn-ȧ-bär') Sov. Un.	71·15 N	113·00 E
135	Anaco (ä-nȧ'kô)........Ven. (In.)	9·29 N	64·27 W
111	Anaconda (ăn-ȧ-kŏn'dȧ)......Mt.	46·07 N	112·55 W

ăt; finăl; rāte; senāte; ärm; ȧsk; sofȧ; fâre; ch-choose; dh-as th in other; bē; ēvent; bĕt; recĕnt; cratẽr; g-go; gh-guttural g; bĭt; ĭ-short neutral; rīde; ĸ-guttural k as ch in German ich;

PRONOUNCING INDEX

Anacortes — Arabi 251

Page	Name Pronunciation Region	Lat. °'	Long. °'
112	Anacortes (ăn-ȧ-kôr'tĕz) Wa. (Seattle In.)	48·30 N	122·37 W
116	Anadarko (ăn-ȧ-där'kō) Ok.	35·05 N	98·14 W
173	Anadyr' (ŭ-nȧ-dĭr') Sov. Un.	64·47 N	177·01 E
173	Anadyr (R.) Sov. Un.	65·30 N	172·45 E
183	Anadyrskiy Zaliv (B.) Sov. Un.	64·10 N	178·00 W
113	Anaheim (ăn'ȧ-hīm) Ca. (Los Angeles In.)	33·50 N	117·55 W
119	Anahuac (ä-nä'wäk) Tx. (In.)	29·46 N	94·41 W
185	Ānai Mudi (Mtn.) India	10·10 N	77·00 E
95	Anama Bay Can.	51·56 N	98·05 W
128	Ana María, Cayos (Is.) (kä'yōs-ä'nȧ mȧ-rē'ȧ) Cuba	21·55 N	78·50 W
196	Anambas, Kepulauan (Is.) (ä-näm-bäs) Indon.	2·41 N	106·38 E
109	Anamosa (ăn-ȧ-mō'sȧ) Ia.	42·06 N	91·18 W
167	Anan'yev (ȧ-nä'nyĕf) Sov. Un.	47·43 N	29·59 E
167	Anapa (ȧ-nä'pä) Sov. Un.	44·54 N	37·19 E
135	Anápolis (ä-nȧ'pō-lēs) Braz.	16·17 S	48·47 W
136	Añatuya (ȧ-nyä-tōō'yȧ) Arg.	28·22 S	62·45 W
160	Ancenis (äɴ-sē-nē') Fr.	47·24 N	1·12 W
136	Anchieta (än-chyĕ'tä) Braz. (Rio de Janeiro In.)	22·49 S	43·24 W
101	Anchitka (I.) (ăn-chē't-kä) Ak.	51·25 N	178·10 E
148	Ancholme (R.) (ăn'chŭm) Eng.	53·28 N	0·27 W
101	Anchorage (ăŋ'kēr-āj) Ak.	61·12 N	149·48 W
107	Anchorage Ky. (Louisville In.)	38·16 N	85·32 W
192	Anci (än-tsū) China (In.)	39·31 N	116·41 E
89	Ancienne-Lorette (äɴ-syĕn' lō-rĕt') Can. (Quebec In.)	46·48 N	71·21 W
122	Ancon (ăŋ-kōn') Pan. (In.)	8·55 N	79·32 W
164	Ancona (än-kō'nä) It.	43·37 N	13·32 E
136	Ancud (äŋ-kōōdh') Chile	41·52 S	73·45 W
136	Ancud, G. de (gôl-fô-dĕ-äŋ-kōōdh') Chile	41·15 S	73·00 W
192	Anda China	46·20 N	125·20 E
136	Andalgalá (ä'n-däl-gȧ-lá') Arg.	27·35 S	66·14 W
162	Andalucia (Reg.) (än-dä-lōō-sē'ä) Sp.	37·35 N	5·40 W
120	Andalusia (ăn-dȧ-lōō'zhĭȧ) Al.	31·19 N	86·19 W
196	Andaman Is. (ăn-dȧ-măn') Andaman & Nicobar Is.	11·38 N	92·17 E
196	Andaman Sea Asia	12·44 N	95·45 E
149	Anderlecht (än'dēr-lĕkt) Bel. (Brussels In.)	50·49 N	4·16 E
158	Andernach (än'dēr-näk) F.R.G.	50·25 N	7·23 E
137	Anderson (ȧ'n-dĕr-sōn) Arg. (Buenos Aires In.)	35·15 S	60·15 W
110	Anderson (ăn'dēr-sŭn) Ca.	40·28 N	122·19 W
104	Anderson In.	40·05 N	85·50 W
121	Anderson SC	34·30 N	82·40 W
90	Anderson (R.) Can.	68·32 N	125·12 W
133	Andes Mts.(ăn'dēz)(än'dās) S. A.	13·00 S	75·00 W
185	Andheri (Neigh.) India (Bombay In.)	19·08 N	72·50 E
185	Andhra Pradesh (State) India	16·00 N	79·00 E
153	Andikíthira (I.) Grc.	35·50 N	23·20 E
172	Andizhan (än-dē-zhän') Sov. Un.	40·51 N	72·39 E
194	Andong (än'dŭng') Kor.	36·31 N	128·42 E
190	Andongwei (än-dôŋ-wā) China	35·08 N	119·19 E
163	Andorra (än-dôr'rä) And.	42·38 N	1·30 E
151	Andorra Eur.	42·30 N	2·00 E
99	Andover (ăn'dō-vēr) Ma. (In.)	42·39 N	71·08 W
106	Andover NJ (New York In.)	40·59 N	74·45 W
150	Andöy (I.) (ănd-ûē) Nor.	69·12 N	14·58 E
163	Andraitx (än-drä-ītsh') Sp.	39·34 N	2·25 E
101	Andreanof Is. (än-drā-ä'nôf) Ak.	51·10 N	177·00 W
137	Andrelândia (än-drĕ-lä'n-dyȧ) Braz. (Rio de Janeiro In.)	21·45 S	44·18 W
120	Andrew Johnson Natl. Mon. (ăn'drōō jŏn'sŭn) Tn.	36·15 N	82·55 W
120	Andrews (ăn'drōōz) NC	35·12 N	83·48 W
121	Andrews SC	33·25 N	79·32 W
167	Andreyevka (än-drä-yĕf'kȧ) Sov. Un.	48·03 N	37·03 E
164	Andria (än'drē-ä) It.	41·17 N	15·55 E
165	Andros (än'dhrōs) Grc.	37·50 N	24·54 E
128	Andros I. (ăn'drŏs) Ba.	24·30 N	78·00 W
165	Andrós (I.) (än'drôs) Grc.	37·59 N	24·55 E
98	Androscoggin (R.) (ăn-drŭs-kŏg'ĭn) Me.	44·25 N	70·45 W
162	Andújar (än-dōō'här) Sp.	38·04 N	4·03 W
214	Anefis i-n-Darane Mali	18·03 N	0·36 E
195	Anegasaki (ä'nȧ-gä-sä'kē) Jap. (Tōkyō In.)	35·29 N	140·02 E
205	Aneityum (I.) (ä-nȧ-ē'tē-ŭm) New Hebr.	20·15 S	169·49 E
108	Aneta (ă-nē'tȧ) ND	47·41 N	97·57 W
124	Angamacutiro (äŋ'gä-mä-kōō-tē'rō) Mex.	20·08 N	101·44 W
124	Angangueo (än-gäŋ'gwȧ-ō) Mex.	19·36 N	100·18 W
192	Ang'angxi (äŋ-äŋ-shyē) China	47·05 N	123·58 E
	Angara (R.), see Verkhnyaya Tunguska		
172	Angarsk Sov. Un.	52·48 N	104·15 E
156	Ange (ông'ā) Swe.	62·31 N	15·39 E
134	Angel, Salto (Falls) (säl'tō-ä'n-hĕl) Ven.	5·44 N	62·27 W
122	Angel De La Guarda (I.) (ä'n-hĕl-dĕ-lä-gwä'r-dä) Mex.	29·30 N	113·00 W
197	Angeles (än'hā-lās) Phil. (In.)	15·09 N	120·35 E
156	Ängelholm (ĕng'ĕl-hôlm) Swe.	56·14 N	12·50 E
119	Angelina R. (ăn-jē lē'nȧ) Tx.	31·30 N	94·53 W
114	Angels Camp (ān'jĕls kămp') Ca.	38·03 N	120·33 W
150	Angermanälven (R.) Swe.	64·02 N	17·15 E
161	Angermund (än'ngĕr-mŭnd) F.R.G. (Ruhr In.)	51·20 N	6·47 E
158	Angermünde (äng'ĕr-mûn-dĕ) G.D.R.	53·02 N	14·00 E
89	Angers (äɴ-zhā') Can. (Ottawa In.)	41·31 N	75·29 W
160	Angers Fr.	47·29 N	0·36 W
196	Angkor (Ruins) (äng'kôr) Camb.	13·52 N	103·50 E
154	Anglesey (I.) (ăŋ'g'l-sē) Wales	53·35 N	4·28 W
119	Angleton (aŋ'g'l-tŭn) Tx. (In.)	29·10 N	95·25 W
75	Angmagssalik (áŋ-mä'sä-lĭk) Grnld.	65·40 N	37·40 W
217	Angoche, Ilha (I.) (ē'lä-ăn-gō'chȧ) Moz.	16·20 S	40·00 E
136	Angol (aŋ-gōl') Chile	37·47 S	72·43 W
104	Angola (ăŋ-gō'lȧ) In.	41·35 N	85·00 W
209	Angola Afr.	14·15 S	16·00 E
	Angora, see Ankara		
160	Angoulême (äŋ'gōō-lâm') Fr.	45·40 N	0·09 E
137	Angra dos Reis (aŋ'grä dōs rā'ēs) Braz. (Rio de Janeiro In.)	23·01 S	44·17 W
163	Angri (ä'n-grē) It. (Naples In.)	40·30 N	14·35 E
192	Anguang (än-gûäŋ) China	45·28 N	123·42 E
128	Anguilla, Cays (Is.) (ăŋ-gwĭl'ȧ) Ba.	23·30 N	79·35 W
127	Anguilla (I.) St. Kitts-Nevis-Anguilla (In.)	18·15 N	62·54 W
99	Anguille, C. (äŋ-gē'yĕ) Can.	47·55 N	59·25 W
190	Anguo (än-gwô) China	38·27 N	115·19 E
156	Anholt (I). (än'hōlt) Den.	56·43 N	11·34 E
189	Anhui (Prov.) (än-hwā) China	31·30 N	117·15 E
101	Aniak (ä-nyä'k) Ak.	61·32 N	159·35 W
115	Animas (R.) (ä'nē-mäs) Co.	37·03 N	107·50 W
165	Anina (ä-nē'nä) Rom.	45·03 N	21·50 E
105	Anita (ȧ-nē'ȧ) Pa.	41·05 N	79·00 W
194	Aniva, Mys (Pt.) (mĭs á-nē'vȧ) Sov. Un.	46·08 N	143·13 E
194	Aniva, Zaliv (B.) (zä'lĭf á-nē'vȧ) Sov. Un.	46·28 N	143·30 E
89	Anjou Can. (Montreal In.)	45·37 N	73·33 W
213	Anjouan (I.) (äɴ-zhwäɴ) Comoros	12·14 S	44·47 E
192	Ankang (än-käŋ) China	32·38 N	109·10 E
171	Ankara (Angora) (än'kȧ-rȧ) (ăn-gō'rȧ) Tur.	39·55 N	32·50 E
158	Anklam (än'kläm) G.D.R.	53·52 N	13·43 E
217	Ankoro (ăŋ-kō'rō) Zaire	6·45 S	26·57 E
214	Anloga Ghana	5·47 N	0·50 E
193	Anlong (än-loŋ) China	25·01 N	105·32 E
193	Anlu (än'lōō') China	31·18 N	113·40 E
105	Ann, C. (ăn) Ma.	42·40 N	70·40 W
117	Anna (ăn'ȧ) Il.	37·28 N	89·15 W
167	Anna (än'ä) Sov. Un.	51·31 N	40·27 E
210	Annaba (Bône) Alg.	36·57 N	7·39 E
158	Annaberg-Bucholz (än'ä-bĕrgh) G.D.R.	50·35 N	13·02 E
186	An Nafūd (Des.) Sau. Ar.	28·30 N	40·30 E
186	An Najaf (än nä-jäf') Iraq	32·00 N	44·25 E
183	An Nakhl Egypt (Palestine In.)	29·55 N	33·45 E
196	Annamese Cordillera (Mts.) (kôr-dĭl-yä'rȧ) Laos-Viet.	17·34 N	105·38 E
106	Annapolis (ă-năp'ō-lĭs) Md. (Baltimore In.)	39·00 N	76·25 W
98	Annapolis Royal Can.	44·45 N	65·31 W
104	Ann Arbor (ăn är'bēr) Mi.	42·15 N	83·45 W
186	An Nāṣirīyah Iraq	31·08 N	46·15 E
211	An Nawfalīyah Libya	30·57 N	17·38 E
161	Annecy (ȧn sē') Fr.	45·54 N	6·07 E
161	Annemasse (än'mäs') Fr.	46·09 N	6·13 E
174	Annenskoye (ä-nĕn'skô-yĕ) Sov. Un. (Urals In.)	53·09 N	60·25 E
92	Annette I. Ak.	55·13 N	131·30 W
196	An-nhon Viet.	13·55 N	109·00 E
99	Annieopsquotch Mts. Can.	48·37 N	57·17 W
120	Anniston (ăn'ĭs-tŭn) Al.	33·39 N	85·47 W
160	Annonay (ȧ-nō-nĕ') Fr.	45·16 N	4·36 E
128	Annotto Bay (än-nō'tō) Jam.	18·15 N	76·45 W
211	An-Nudūd Sud.	12·39 N	28·18 E
113	Anoka (ȧ-nō'kȧ) Mn. (Minneapolis, St. Paul In.)	45·12 N	93·24 W
134	Anori (ä-nō'rē) Col. (In.)	7·01 N	75·09 W
165	Áno Theológos Grc.	40·37 N	24·41 E
164	Áno Viánnos Grc. (In.)	35·02 N	25·26 E
193	Anpu (än-pōō) China	21·28 N	110·00 E
193	Anqing (än-chĭŋ) China	30·32 N	117·00 E
190	Anqiu (än-chyô) China	36·26 N	119·12 E
158	Ansbach (äns'bäk) F.R.G.	49·18 N	10·35 E
129	Anse à Veau (äɴs' ä-vō') Hai.	18·30 N	73·25 W
129	Anse d' Hainault (äɴs'dĕnō) Hai.	18·45 N	74·25 W
134	Anserma (ȧ'n-sĕ'r-mȧ) Col. (In.)	5·13 N	75·47 W
134	Ansermanuevo (ȧ'n-sĕ'r-mȧ-nwĕ'vō) Col. (In.)	4·47 N	75·59 W
192	Anshan China	41·00 N	123·00 E
193	Anshun (än-shōōn') China	26·12 N	105·50 E
118	Anson (ăn'sŭn) Tx.	32·45 N	99·52 W
204	Anson B. Austl.	13·10 S	130·00 E
194	Ansŏng (än'sŭng') Kor.	37·00 N	127·12 E
214	Ansongo Mali	15·40 N	0·30 E
105	Ansonia (ăn-sō'nĭ-ȧ) Ct.	41·20 N	73·05 W
163	Antakya (än-täk'yä) Tur.	36·20 N	36·10 E
171	Antalya (Adalia) (än-tä'lē-ä) (ä-dä'lē-ȧ) Tur.	37·00 N	30·50 E
171	Antalya Körfezi (G.) Tur.	36·40 N	31·20 E
213	Antananarivo Mad.	18·51 S	47·40 E
220	Antarctica	80·15 S	127·00 E
220	Antartic Pen. Ant.	70·00 S	65·00 W
111	Antelope Cr. (ăn'tē-lōp) Wy.	43·29 N	105·42 W
162	Antequera (än-tĕ-kĕ'rä) Sp.	37·01 N	4·34 W
116	Anthony (ăn'thō-nē) Ks.	37·08 N	98·01 W
210	Anti Atlas (Mts.) Mor.	28·45 N	9·30 W
161	Antibes (äɴ-tēb') Fr.	43·36 N	7·12 E
99	Anticosti, Île d' (I.) (ăn-tĭ-kŏs'tē) Can.	49·30 N	62·00 W
109	Antigo (ăn'tĭ-gō) Wi.	45·09 N	89·11 W
99	Antigonish (ăn-tĭ-gō-nēsh') Can.	45·35 N	61·55 W
126	Antigua (än-tē'gwä) Guat.	14·32 N	90·43 W
123	Antigua N. A.	17·15 N	61·15 W
125	Antigua (R.) Mex.	19·16 N	96·36 W
125	Antigua Veracruz (än-tē'gwä vä-rä-krōōz') Mex.	19·18 N	96·17 W
129	Antilla (än-tē'lyä) Cuba	20·50 N	75·50 W
123	Antilles, Greater (Is.) N. A.	20·30 N	79·15 W
123	Antilles, Lesser (Is.) N. A.	12·15 N	65·00 W
112	Antioch (ăn'tĭ-ŏk) Ca. (San Francisco In.)	38·00 N	121·48 W
107	Antioch Il. (Chicago In.)	42·29 N	88·06 W
108	Antioch Ne.	42·05 N	102·36 W
134	Antioquia (än-tē-ō'kēä) Col. (In.)	6·34 N	75·49 W
134	Antioquia (Dept.) Col. (In.)	6·48 N	75·42 W
117	Antlers (ănt'lērz) Ok.	34·14 N	95·38 W
136	Antofagasta (än-tō-fä-gäs'tä) Chile	23·32 S	70·21 W
136	Antofalla, Salar de (Des.) (sȧ-lär'de àn'tō-fä'lä) Arg.	26·00 S	67·52 W
127	Antón (än-tōn') Pan.	8·24 N	80·15 W
213	Antongil, Baie d' (B.) (äɴ-tôɴ-zhēl') Mad.	16·15 S	50·15 E
137	Antônio Carlos (än-tō'nĕōō-kȧ'r-lôs) Braz. (Rio de Janeiro In.)	21·19 S	43·45 W
217	António Enes (ăn-to-nyŏ ĕn'ĕs) Moz.	16·14 S	39·58 E
116	Antonito (ăn-tō-nē'tō) Co.	37·04 N	106·01 W
166	Antonopole (än'tô-nô-pō lyĕ) Sov. Un.	56·19 N	27·11 E
154	Antrim Mts. (ăn'trĭm) N. Ire.	55·00 N	6·10 W
213	Antsirabe (änt-sē-rä'bā) Mad.	19·49 S	47·16 E
166	Antsla (änt'slȧ) Sov. Un.	57·49 N	26·29 E
136	Antuco (Vol.) (än-tōō'kō) Chile	37·30 S	72·30 W
	Antwerp, see Antwerpen		
149	Antwerpen (Antwerp) (ănt'wērpĕn) Bel. (Brussels In.)	51·13 N	4·24 E
184	Anūpgarh (ŭ-nōōp'gŭr) India	29·22 N	73·20 E
185	Anuradhapura (ŭ-nōō'rä-dŭ-pōō'rŭ) Sri Lanka	8·24 N	80·25 E
188	Anxi (än-shyē) China	40·36 N	95·49 E
190	Anyang (än'yäng) China	36·05 N	114·22 E
157	Anykščiai (anĭksh-chä'ē) Sov. Un.	55·34 N	25·04 E
134	Anzá (än-zá') Col. (In.)	6·19 N	75·51 W
172	Anzhero-Sudzhensk (än'zhâ-rō-sōōd'zhĕnsk) Sov. Un.	56·08 N	86·08 E
163	Anzio (änt'zē-ō) It. (Rome In.)	41·28 N	12·39 E
135	Anzoátegui (State) (án-zôä'tĕ-gē) Ven. (In.)	9·38 N	64·45 W
194	Aomori (äô-mō'rē) Jap.	40·45 N	140·52 E
164	Aosta (ä-ôs'tä) It.	45·45 N	7·20 E
211	Aouk, Bahr (R.) (ä-ōōk') Chad-Cen. Afr. Rep.	9·30 N	20·45 E
214	Aoukâr (Pln.) Mauritania	18·00 N	9·40 W
120	Apalachicola (ăp-ȧ-lăch-ĭ-kō'lȧ) Fl.	29·43 N	84·59 W
125	Apan (ä-pá'n) Mex. (In.)	19·43 N	98·27 W
124	Apango (ä-päŋ'gō) Mex.	17·41 N	99·22 W
134	Apaporis (R.) (ä-pä-pô'rĭs) Col.	0·48 N	72·32 W
196	Aparri (ä-pär'rē) Phil.	18·15 N	121·40 E
124	Apasco (ä-pá's-kō) Mex.	20·33 N	100·43 W
165	Apatin (ŏ'pō-tĭn) Yugo.	45·40 N	19·00 E
124	Apatzingán de la Constitución (ä-pät-zĭŋ-gän'dä lä cōn-stĭ-tōō-sē-ōn') Mex.	19·07 N	102·21 W
155	Apeldoorn (ä'pĕl-dōōrn) Neth.	52·14 N	5·55 E
134	Apía (ä-pē'ä) Col. (In.)	5·07 N	75·58 W
124	Apipilulco (ä-pĭ-pĭ-lōōl'kō) Mex.	18·09 N	99·40 W
165	Apíranthos Grc.	37·07 N	25·32 E
116	Apishapa (R.) (ăp-ĭ-shä'pȧ) Co.	37·40 N	104·08 W
124	Apizaco (ä-pē-zä'kō) Mex.	19·18 N	98·11 W
197	Apo (Mtn.) (ä'pō) Phil.	6·56 N	125·05 E
121	Apopka (ä-pŏp'kȧ) Fl. (In.)	28·37 N	81·30 W
121	Apopka (L.) Fl. (In.)	28·38 N	81·50 W
109	Apostle Is. (ă-pŏs'l) Wi.	47·05 N	90·55 W
120	Appalachia (ăpȧ-lăch'ĭ-ȧ) Va.	36·54 N	82·49 W
103	Appalachian Mts. (ăp-ȧ-lăch'ĭ-ȧn) U. S.	37·20 N	82·00 W
120	Appalachicola R. (ăpȧ-lăch'ĭ-cōlȧ) Fl.	30·11 N	85·00 W
156	Äppelbo (ĕp-ĕl-bōō) Swe.	60·30 N	14·02 E
161	Appelhülsen (ä'pĕl-hül'sĕn) F.R.G. (Ruhr In.)	51·55 N	7·26 E
164	Appennino (Mts.) (äp-pĕn-nē'nō) It.	43·48 N	11·06 E
158	Appenzell (äp'ĕn-tsĕl) Switz.	47·19 N	9·22 E
108	Appleton (ăp'l-tŭn) Mn.	45·10 N	96·01 W
109	Appleton Wi.	44·14 N	88·27 W
117	Appleton City Mo.	38·10 N	94·02 W
121	Appomattox (R.) (ăp-ō-măt'ŭks) Va.	37·22 N	78·09 W
163	Aprília (ȧ-prē'lyȧ) It. (Rome In.)	41·36 N	12·40 E
171	Apsheronskiy, P-Ov. (Pen.) Sov. Un.	40·20 N	50·30 E
161	Apt (äpt) Fr.	43·54 N	5·19 E
	Apulia (Reg.), see Puglia		
134	Apure (R.) (ä-pōō'rä) Ven.	8·08 N	68·46 W
134	Apurimac (R.) (ä-pōō-rē-mäk') Peru	11·39 S	73·48 W
153	Aqaba, G. of (ä'kȧ-bȧ) Asia	28·30 N	34·40 E
183	Aqabah, Wādī al (R.) Egypt (Palestine In.)	29·48 N	34·05 E
106	Aquasco (ȧ'gwă'scō) Md. (Baltimore In.)	38·35 N	76·44 W
135	Aquidauana (ä-kē-däwä'nä) Braz.	20·24 S	55·46 W
162	Aquilianos, Montes (Mts.) (mô'n-tĕs-ä-kē-lyä'nôs) Sp.	42·27 N	6·35 W
129	Aquin (ä-kăn') Hai.	18·20 N	73·25 W
195	Ara (R.) (ä-rä) Jap. (Tōkyō In.)	35·40 N	139·52 E
211	Arab, Baḥr al- (R.) Sud.	9·46 N	26·52 E
218	'Arabah, Wādī Egypt (Nile In.)	29·02 N	32·10 E
167	Arabatskaya Strelka (Tongue of Arabat) (Spit) (ä-rä-băt' skȧ-yȧ strĕl'kȧ) (ȧ-rȧ-băt') Sov. Un.	45·50 N	35·05 E
106	Arabi La. (New Orleans In.)	29·58 N	90·01 W

252 Arabian — Ascheberg
PRONOUNCING INDEX

Page	Name Pronunciation Region	Lat. °'	Long. °'
211	Arabian Des. (Aş Şaḩrā ash Sharqīyah) (ȧ-rā'bĭ-ăn) (Nile In.)	27·06 N	32·49 E
209	Arabian Pen. . . . . . Asia	28·00 N	40·00 E
182	Arabian Sea (ȧ-rā'bĭ-ăn) . . . . . Asia	16·00 N	65·15 E
135	Aracaju (ä-rä'kä-zhōō') . . . . . Braz.	11·00 S	37·01 W
135	Aracati (ä-rä'kä-tē') . . . . . Braz.	4·31 S	37·41 W
135	Araçatuba (ä-rä-sȧ-tōō'bä) . . . Braz.	21·14 S	50·19 W
135	Aracruz (ä-rä-krōō's) . . . . . Braz.	19·58 S	40·11 W
135	Araçuaí (ä-rä-sōō-ä-ē') . . . . . Braz.	16·57 S	41·56 W
183	'Arad . . . . . Isr. (Palestine In.)	31·20 N	35·15 E
159	Arad (ŏ'rŏd) . . . . . Rom.	46·10 N	21·18 E
198	Arafura Sea (ä-rä-fōō'rä) . . Oceania	8·40 S	130·00 E
163	Aragon (Reg.) (ä-rä-gōn') . . . . Sp.	40·55 N	0·45 W
162	Aragón (R.) . . . . . Sp.	42·35 N	1·10 W
135	Aragua (State)(ä-rä'gwä) . Ven.(In.)	10·00 N	67·05 W
135	Aragua de Barcelona (ä-rä'gwä dā bär-thå-lō'nä) Ven. (In.)	9·29 N	64·48 W
135	Araguaía (R.) (ä-rä-gwä'yä) . Braz.	8·37 S	49·43 W
135	Araguari (ä-rä-gwä'rē) . . . . . Braz.	18·43 S	48·03 W
135	Araguatins (ä-rä-gwä-tēns) . . Braz.	5·41 S	48·04 W
135	Aragüita (ärä-gwē'tä) . . . Ven. (In.)	10·13 N	66·28 W
153	Araj (Oasis) (ä-räj') . . . . . Egypt	29·05 N	26·51 E
186	Arāk . . . . . Iran	34·08 N	49·57 E
188	Arakan Yoma (Mts.) (ŭ-rŭ-kŭn'yō'mȧ) . Bur.	19·51 N	94·13 E
165	Arakhthos (R.) (är'äk-thôs) . . Grc.	39·10 N	21·05 E
	Aral Sea, see Aral'skoye More		
172	Aral'sk (ȧ-rälsk') . . . . . Sov. Un.	46·47 N	62·00 E
147	Aral'skoye More (Aral Sea) Sov. Un.	45·17 N	60·02 E
171	Aralsor (L.) (ȧ-räl'sôr') . . Sov. Un.	49·00 N	48·20 E
124	Aramberri (ä-räm-bĕr-rē') . . . . Mex.	24·05 N	99·47 W
154	Aran (I.) (ăr'ăn) . . . . . Ire.	54·58 N	8·33 W
162	Aranda de Duero (ä-rän'dä dā dwā'rō) . Sp.	41·43 N	3·45 W
124	Arandas (ä-rän'däs) . . . . . Mex.	20·43 N	102·18 W
154	Aran Is. . . . . . Ire.	53·04 N	9·59 W
162	Aranjuez (ä-rän-hwāth') . . . . . Sp.	40·02 N	3·24 W
119	Aransas Pass (ȧ-răn'sȧs pȧs) . . . Tx.	27·55 N	97·09 W
214	Araouane . . . . . Mali	18·54 N	3·33 W
171	Arapkir (ä-räp-kēr') . . . . . Tur.	39·00 N	38·10 E
135	Araraquara (ä-rä-rä-kwä'rä) . Braz.	21·47 S	48·08 W
137	Araras (ä-rä'räs) Braz. (Rio de Janeiro In.)	22·21 S	47·22 W
135	Araras, Serra das (Mts.) (sĕ'r-rä-däs-ä-rä'räs) . Braz.	18·03 S	53·23 W
136	Araras, Serra das (Mts.) . . . . Braz.	23·30 S	53·00 W
136	Araras, Serra das (Mts.) . Braz.(In.)	22·24 S	43·15 W
203	Ararat (ăr'ȧrăt) . . . . . Austl.	37·17 S	142·56 E
171	Ararat (Mtn.) . . . . . Tur.	39·50 N	44·20 E
135	Arari (L.) (ä-rä'rē) . . . . . Braz.	0·30 S	48·50 W
135	Araripe, Chapada do (Plain) (shä-pä'dä-dô-ä-rä-rē'pĕ) . Braz.	5·55 S	40·42 W
137	Araruama (ä-rä-rōō-ä'mä) Braz. (Rio de Janeiro In.)	22·53 S	42·19 W
137	Araruama, Lagoa de (L.) (lä-gôä-dĕ-ä-rä-rōō-ä'mä) Braz. (Rio de Janeiro In.)	23·00 S	42·15 W
171	Aras (R.) (ȧ-räs) . . . . Iran-Sov. Un.	39·15 N	47·10 E
135	Aratuípe (ä-rä-tōō-ē'pĕ) . . . . Braz.	13·12 S	38·58 W
134	Arauca (ä-rou'kä) . . . . . Col.	6·56 N	70·45 W
134	Arauca (R.) . . . . . Ven.	7·13 N	68·43 W
184	Aravalli Ra. (ä-rä'vŭ-lē) . . . . . India	24·15 N	72·40 E
135	Araxá (ä-rä-shá') . . . . . Braz.	19·41 S	46·46 W
135	Araya, Punta de (Pt.) (pŭn'tä-dĕ-ä-rä'yȧ) . Ven. (In.)	10·40 N	64·15 W
197	Arayat (ä-rä'yät) . . . . . Phil. (In.)	15·10 N	120·44 E
211	'Arbi . . . . . Sud.	20·36 N	29·57 E
156	Arboga (är-bō'gä) . . . . . Swe.	59·26 N	15·50 E
164	Arborea (är-bō-rē'ä) . . . . . It.	39·50 N	8·36 E
154	Arbroath (är-brōth') . . . . . Scot.	56·36 N	2·25 W
160	Arc (R.) (ärk) . . Fr. (Marseille In.)	43·34 N	5·17 E
160	Arcachon (är-kä-shôn') . . . . . Fr.	44·39 N	1·12 W
160	Arcachon, Bassin d' (Basin) (bä-sĕn' där-kä-shôn') . Fr.	44·42 N	1·50 W
113	Arcadia (är-kā'dĭ-ȧ) Ca. (Los Angeles In.)	34·08 N	118·02 W
121	Arcadia . . . . . Fl. (In.)	27·12 N	81·51 W
119	Arcadia . . . . . La.	32·33 N	92·56 W
109	Arcadia . . . . . Wi.	44·15 N	91·30 W
110	Arcata (är-kȧ'tȧ) . . . . . Ca.	40·54 N	124·05 W
114	Arc Dome Mtn. (ärk dōm) . . . . Nv.	38·51 N	117·21 W
124	Arcelia (är-sā'lē-ä) . . . . . Mex.	18·19 N	100·14 W
105	Archbald (ärch'bôld) . . . . . Pa.	41·30 N	75·35 W
115	Arches Natl. Park (är'ches) . . . Ut.	38·45 N	109·35 W
134	Archidona (är-chē-do'nä) . . . . . Ec.	1·01 S	77·49 W
162	Archidona (är-chē-dô'nä) . . . . . Sp.	37·08 N	4·24 W
162	Arcila (är-sē'lä) . . . . . Mor.	35·30 N	6·05 W
160	Arcis-sur-Aube (är-sēs'sûr-ōb') Fr.	48·31 N	4·04 E
111	Arco (är'kô) . . . . . Id.	43·39 N	113·15 W
106	Arcola (är'cōlă) Va. (Baltimore In.)	38·57 N	77·32 W
119	Arcola . . . . . Tx. (In.)	29·30 N	95·28 W
162	Arcos de la Frontera (är'kōs-dĕ-lä-frôn-tĕ'rä) . Sp.	36·44 N	5·48 W
219	Arctic Ocean (ärk'tĭk)		
165	Arda (R.) (är'dä) . . . . . Bul.	41·36 N	25·18 E
186	Aradabīl . . . . . Iran	38·15 N	48·00 E
171	Ardahan (är-dȧ-hän') . . . . . Tur.	41·10 N	42·40 E
156	Ardals Fd. (är-däls) . . . . . Nor.	58·53 N	7·55 E
170	Ardatov (är-dȧ-tôf') . . . . Sov. Un.	54·58 N	46·10 E
155	Ardennes (Mts.) (ȧr-dĕn') . . . . Bel.	50·01 N	5·12 E
162	Ardila (R.) (är-dē'lä) . . . . . Port.	38·10 N	7·15 W
117	Ardmore (ärd'mōr) . . . . . Ok.	34·10 N	97·08 W
106	Ardmore . . . . Pa. (Philadelphia In.)	40·01 N	75·18 W
89	Ardrossan (är-dros'ăn) Can. (Edmonton In.)	53·33 N	113·08 W
148	Ardsley (ärdz'lē) . . . . . Eng.	53·43 N	1·33 W
150	Åre . . . . . Swe.	63·12 N	13·12 E
162	Arecena (ä-rē-sē'nä) . . . . . Sp.	37·53 N	6·34 W
123	Arecibo (ä-rȧ-sē'bō) P. R. (Puerto Rico In.)	18·28 N	66·45 W
135	Areia Branca (ä-rĕ'yä-brä'n-kä) Braz.	4·58 S	37·02 W
114	Arena, Pt. (ä-rā'nȧ) . . . . . Ca.	38·57 N	123·40 W
135	Arenas, Punta (Pt.) (pōō'n'tä-rĕ'näs) . Ven. (In.)	10·57 N	64·24 W
162	Arenas de San Pedro (ä-rā'nȧs dā sän pā'drō) . Sp.	40·12 N	5·04 W
156	Arendal (ä'rĕn-däl) . . . . . Nor.	58·29 N	8·44 E
149	Arendonk . . . . . Bel. (Brussels In.)	51·19 N	5·07 E
134	Arequipa (ä-rā-kē'pä) . . . . . Peru	16·27 S	71·30 W
164	Arezzo (ä-rĕt'sō) . . . . . It.	43·28 N	11·54 E
162	Arga (R.) (är'gä) . . . . . Sp.	42·35 N	1·55 W
163	Arganda (är-gän'dä) Sp. (Madrid In.)	40·18 N	3·27 W
174	Argazi (L.) (är'gä-zĭ) Sov. Un. (Urals In.)	55·24 N	60·37 E
174	Argazi R. . . . . Sov. Un. (Urals In.)	55·33 N	57·30 E
160	Argentan (ȧr-zhäN-täN') . . . . . Fr.	48·45 N	0·01 W
160	Argentat (är-zhäN-tä') . . . . . Fr.	45·07 N	1·57 E
161	Argenteuil (är-zhäN-tû'y') Fr. (Paris In.)	48·56 N	2·15 E
133	Argentina (är-jĕn-tē'nȧ) . . . . . S. A.	35·30 S	67·00 W
136	Argentino (L.) (är-Kĕn-tē'nō) . Arg.	50·15 S	72·45 W
160	Argenton-sur-Creuse (är-zhäN'tôN-sür-krûs) . Fr.	46·34 N	1·28 E
165	Arges (R.) (ȧr'zhĕsh) . . . . . Rom.	44·27 N	25·22 E
165	Argolikos Kólpos (G.) . . . . . Grc.	37·20 N	23·00 E
160	Argonne (Mts.) (ä'r-gôn) . . . . . Fr.	49·21 N	5·54 E
165	Argos (är'gŏs) . . . . . Grc.	37·38 N	22·45 E
165	Argostólion (är-gŏs-tŏ'lē-ŏn) . . Grc.	38·10 N	20·30 E
114	Arguello, Pt. (är-gwāl'yō) . . . . . Ca.	34·35 N	120·40 W
173	Argun R. (ȧr-gōōn') China-Sov. Un.	50·15 N	118·45 E
215	Argungu . . . . . Nig.	12·45 N	4·31 E
89	Argyle (är'gīl) . Can. (Winnipeg In.)	50·11 N	97·27 W
108	Argyle . . . . . Mn.	48·21 N	96·48 W
156	Århus (ôr'hōōs) . . . . . Den.	56·09 N	10·10 E
195	Ariakeno-Umi (Sea) (ä-rē'ä-Kä'nō ōō'nē) . Jap.	33·03 N	130·18 E
195	Ariake-Wan (B.) (ä'rē-ä'kȧ wän) Jap.	31·19 N	131·15 E
164	Ariano (ä-rē-ä'nō) . . . . . It.	41·09 N	15·11 E
134	Ariari (ä-ryä'rē) (R.) . . . Col. (In.)	3·34 N	73·42 W
214	Aribinda . . . . . Upper Volta	14·14 N	0·52 W
134	Arica (ä-rē'kä) . . . . . Chile	18·34 S	70·14 W
99	Arichat (ä-rĭ-shät') . . . . . Can.	45·31 N	61·01 W
160	Ariège (R.) (ȧ-rē-ĕzh') . . . . . Fr.	43·26 N	1·29 E
112	Ariel (ā'rĭ-ĕl) . . Wa. (Portland In.)	45·57 N	122·34 W
159	Arieşul (R.) (ä-rē-ä'shōōl) . . . Rom.	46·25 N	23·15 E
129	Ariguanabo, L. de (lä'gô-dĕ-ä-rē-gwä-nä'bô) Cuba (In.)	22·17 N	82·33 W
183	Arīḩā (Jericho) Jordan (Palestine In.)	31·51 N	35·28 E
116	Arikaree (R.) (ă-rĭ-kȧ-rē') . . . . . Co.	39·51 N	102·18 W
195	Arima (ä'rē-mä') . Jap. (Ōsaka In.)	34·48 N	135·16 E
197	Aringay (ä-rĭŋ-gä'ē) . . . . Phil. (In.)	16·25 N	120·20 E
135	Arinos (R.) (ä-rē'nôzh) . . . . . Braz.	12·09 S	56·49 W
135	Aripuanã (R.) (ä-rē-pwän'yȧ) Braz.	7·06 S	60·29 W
183	'Arīsh, Wādī al (R.) (ȧ-rēsh') Egypt (Palestine In.)	30·36 N	34·07 E
92	Aristazabal I. . . . . . Can.	52·30 N	129·20 W
102	Arizona (State) (ăr-ĭ-zō'nȧ) . . U. S.	34·00 N	113·00 W
162	Arjona (är-hō'nä) . . . . . Sp.	37·58 N	4·03 W
173	Arka (R.) . . . . . Sov. Un.	60·12 N	142·30 E
120	Arkabutla Res. (är-kȧ-bŭt'lā) . . Ms.	34·48 N	90·00 W
117	Arkadelphia (är-kȧ-dĕl'fĭ-ȧ) . . . . Ar.	34·06 N	93·05 W
103	Arkansas (State) (är'kăn-sô) (är-kăn'sȧs) . U. S.	34·50 N	93·40 W
117	Arkansas City . . . . . Ks.	37·04 N	97·02 W
117	Arkansas R. . . . . . Ok.	35·20 N	94·56 W
170	Arkhangelsk (Archangel) (ar-Kän'gĕlsk) . Sov. Un.	64·30 N	40·25 E
174	Arkhangel'skiy (är-kän-gĕl'skĭ) Sov. Un. (Urals In.)	52·52 N	61·53 E
174	Arkhangel'skoye (är-kän-gĕl'skô-yĕ) Sov. Un. (Urals In.)	54·25 N	56·48 E
154	Arklow (ärk'lō) . . . . . Ire.	52·47 N	6·10 W
156	Arkona, C. (är'kō-nä) . . . . . G.D.R.	54·43 N	13·43 E
185	Arkonam (är-kō-năm') . . . . . India	13·05 N	79·43 E
162	Arlanza (R.) (är-län-thä') . . . . . Sp.	42·08 N	3·45 W
162	Arlanzón (R.) (är-län-thōn') . . . . Sp.	42·12 N	3·58 W
158	Arlberg Tun. (ärl'bĕrgh) . . . . . Aus.	47·05 N	10·15 E
160	Arles (ärl) . . . . . Fr.	43·42 N	4·38 E
120	Arlington (är'lĭng-tun') . . . . . Ga.	31·25 N	84·42 W
99	Arlington . . . . . Ma. (In.)	42·26 N	71·13 W
108	Arlington (är'lĕng-tŭn) . . . . . SD	44·23 N	97·09 W
119	Arlington (är'lĭng-tŭn) Tx. (Dallas, Fort Worth In.)	32·44 N	97·07 W
218	Arlington . S. Afr. (Johannesburg & Pretoria In.)	28·02 S	27·52 E
105	Arlington . . . . . Vt.	43·05 N	73·05 W
106	Arlington . . . . . Va. (Baltimore In.)	38·55 N	77·10 W
112	Arlington . . . . . Wa. (Seattle In.)	48·11 N	122·08 W
107	Arlington Heights (är'lĕng-tŭn-hī'ts) Il. (Chicago In.)	42·05 N	87·59 W
156	Arlöv (är'lûf) . . . . . Swe.	55·38 N	13·05 E
204	Arltunga (ärl-tōōŋ'gȧ) . . . . . Austl.	23·19 S	134·45 E
117	Arma (är'mȧ) . . . . . Ks.	37·34 N	94·43 W
89	Armagh (är-mä') (är-mäk') Can. (Quebec In.)	46·45 N	70·36 W
154	Armagh . . . . . N. Ire.	54·21 N	6·25 W
218	Armant (är-mänt') Egypt (Nile In.)	25·37 N	32·32 E
134	Armaro (är-mȧ'rō) . . . . . Col. (In.)	4·58 N	74·54 W
171	Armavir (är-mȧ-vĭr') . . . . . Sov. Un.	45·00 N	41·00 E
134	Armenia (är-mĕ'nêȧ) . . . . Col. (In.)	4·33 N	75·40 W
126	Armenia (är-mā'nē-ä) . . . . . Sal.	13·44 N	89·31 W
168	Armenian, S. S. R. . . . . Sov. Un.	41·00 N	44·39 E
160	Armentières (är-mäN-tyâr') . . . . Fr.	50·43 N	2·53 E
124	Armeria, Rio de (R.) (rē'ō-dĕ-är-mȧ-rē'ä) . Mex.	19·36 N	104·10 W
107	Armherstburg (ärm'hĕrst-bōōrgh) Can. (Detroit In.)	42·06 N	83·06 W
203	Armidale (är'mĭ-dāl) . . . . . Austl.	30·27 S	151·50 E
108	Armour (är'mēr) . . . . . SD	43·18 N	98·21 W
96	Armstrong Station (ärm'strông) . Can.	50·21 N	89·00 W
167	Armyansk (ärm'yȧnsk) . . . Sov. Un.	46·06 N	33·42 E
162	Arnedo (är-nā'dō) . . . . . Sp.	42·12 N	2·03 W
155	Arnhem (ärn'hĕm) . . . . . Neth.	51·58 N	5·56 E
204	Arnhem, C. . . . . . Austl.	12·15 S	137·00 E
204	Arnhem Land, (Reg.) (ärn'hĕm-lănd) . Austl.	13·15 S	133·00 E
164	Arno (R.) (är'nô) . . . . . It.	43·45 N	10·42 E
148	Arnold (är'nŭld) . . . . . Eng.	53·00 N	1·08 W
113	Arnold (är'nŭld) Mn. (Duluth In.)	46·53 N	92·06 W
107	Arnold . . . . . Pa. (Pittsburgh In.)	40·35 N	79·45 W
105	Arnprior (ärn-prī'ēr) . . . . . Can.	45·25 N	76·20 W
155	Arnsberg (ärns'bĕrgh) . . . . . F.R.G.	51·25 N	8·02 E
158	Arnstadt (ärn'shtät) . . . . . G.D.R.	50·51 N	10·57 E
212	Aroab (är'ō-äb) . . . . . Namibia	25·40 S	19·45 E
98	Aroostook (R.) (ȧ-rōōs'tŏŏk) . . Me.	46·44 N	68·15 W
197	Aroroy (ä-rô-rō'ē) . . . . . Phil. (In.)	12·30 N	123·24 E
161	Arpajon (ăr-pă-jŏ'n) Fr. (Paris In.)	48·35 N	2·15 E
136	Arpoador, Ponta do (Pt.) (pô'n-tä-dō-är'pôä-dō'r) Braz. (In.)	22·59 S	43·11 W
162	Arraiolos (är-rī-ō'lōzh) . . . . . Port.	38·47 N	7·59 W
186	Ar Ramādī . . . . . Iraq	33·30 N	43·12 E
154	Arran (I.) (ă'răn) . . . . . Scot.	55·39 N	5·30 W
211	Ar Rank . . . . . Sud.	11·45 N	32·53 E
160	Arras (ȧ-räs') . . . . . Fr.	50·21 N	2·40 E
218	Ar Rawḑah . . . . . Egypt (Nile In.)	27·47 N	30·52 E
137	Arrecifes (är-rȧ-sē'fās) Arg. (Buenos Aires In.)	34·03 S	60·05 W
137	Arrecifes (R.) Arg. (Buenos Aires In.)	34·07 S	59·50 W
160	Arrée, Mts. d' (är-rā') . . . . . Fr.	48·27 N	4·00 W
125	Arriaga (är-rêä'gä) . . . . . Mex.	16·15 N	93·54 W
	Ar Riyāḑ, see Riyadh		
163	Arrone (R.) . . . . . It. (Rome In.)	41·57 N	12·17 E
113	Arrowhead, L. (lăk ăr'ōhĕd) Ca. (Los Angeles In.)	34·17 N	117·13 W
111	Arrow R. (ăr'ō) . . . . . Mt.	47·29 N	109·53 W
110	Arrowrock Res. (ăr'ō-rŏk) . . . . Id.	43·40 N	115·30 W
129	Arroya Arena (är-rô'yä-rĕ'nä) Cuba (In.)	23·01 N	82·30 W
162	Arroyo de la Luz (är-rō'yō-dĕ-lä-lōō'z) . Sp.	39·39 N	6·46 W
124	Arroyo Grande (R.) (är-rô'yō-grä'n-dĕ) . Mex.	23·30 N	98·45 W
124	Arroyo Seco (är-rō'yō sä'kō) . Mex.	21·31 N	99·44 W
186	Ar Rub' Al Khālī (Des.) . . Sau. Ar.	20·30 N	49·15 E
211	Ar-Ruşayriş . . . . . Sud.	11·38 N	34·42 E
173	Arsen'yev . . . . . Sov. Un.	44·13 N	133·32 E
174	Arsinskiy (är-sĭn'skĭ) Sov. Un. (Urals In.)	53·46 N	59·54 E
165	Árta (är'tä) . . . . . Grc.	39·08 N	21·02 E
118	Arteaga (är-tā-ä'gä) . . . . . Mex.	25·28 N	100·50 W
173	Artëm (ȧr-tyôm') . . . . . Sov. Un.	43·28 N	132·29 E
128	Artemisa (är-tā-mē'sä) . . . . . Cuba	22·50 N	82·45 W
167	Artëmovsk (ȧr-tyŏm'ŏfsk) Sov. Un.	48·37 N	38·00 E
116	Artesia (är-tē'sĭ-ȧ) . . . . . NM	32·44 N	104·23 W
203	Artesian Basin, The (är-tē'zhăn) . Austl.	26·45 S	141·40 E
98	Arthabaska . . . . . Can.	46·03 N	71·54 W
129	Arthur's Town . . . . . Ba.	24·40 N	75·40 W
174	Arti (är'tĭ) . . . Sov. Un. (Urals In.)	56·20 N	58·38 E
129	Artibonite (R.) (är-tē-bō-nē'tā) Hai.	19·00 N	72·25 W
197	Aru, Kepulauan (Is.) . . . . . Indon.	6·20 S	133·00 E
217	Arua (ä'rōō-ä) . . . . . Ug.	3·01 N	30·55 E
134	Aruba (ä-rōō'bȧ) (I.) Neth. Antilles	12·29 N	70·00 W
188	Arunachal Pradesh (Union Ter.) India	27·35 N	92·56 E
217	Arusha (ȧ-rōō'shä) . . . . . Tan.	3·22 S	36·41 E
97	Arvida . . . . . Can.	48·26 N	71·11 W
156	Arvika (är-vē'kȧ) . . . . . Swe.	59·41 N	12·35 E
170	Arzamas (är-zä-mäs') . . . . Sov. Un.	55·20 N	43·52 E
163	Arzew (är-zȧ-ōō') . . . . . Alg.	35·50 N	0·20 W
162	Arzua (är-thōō'ä) . . . . . Sp.	42·54 N	8·19 W
158	As (äsh') . . . . . Czech.	50·12 N	12·13 E
195	Asahi-Gawa (Strm.) (ȧ-sä'hē-gä'wä) . Jap.	35·01 N	133·40 E
194	Asahikawa . . . . . Jap.	43·50 N	142·09 E
195	Asaka (ä-sä'kä) . . Jap. (Tōkyō In.)	35·47 N	139·36 E
184	Asansol . . . . . India	23·45 N	86·58 E
174	Asbest (äs-bĕst') Sov. Un. (Urals In.)	57·02 N	61·28 E
98	Asbestos (ăs-bĕs'tōs) . . . . . Can.	45·49 N	71·52 W
106	Asbury Park (ăz'bĕr-ĭ) NJ (New York In.)	40·13 N	74·01 W
126	Ascención, Bahía de la (B.) (bä-ē'ä-dĕ-lä-äs-sĕn-sē-ōn') Mex. (In.)	19·39 N	87·30 W
124	Ascensión (äs-sĕn-sê-ōn') . . . . Mex.	24·21 N	99·54 W
209	Ascension (I.) (ȧ-sĕn'shŭn) . Atl. O.	8·00 S	13·00 W
218	Ascent (ăs-ĕnt') . . . . S. Afr. (Johannesburg & Pretoria In.)	27·14 S	29·06 E
158	Aschaffenburg (ä-shäf'ĕn-bōōrgh) F.R.G.	49·58 N	9·12 E
161	Ascheberg (ä'shĕ-bĕrg) F.R.G. (Ruhr In.)	51·47 N	7·38 E

ăt: finăl; rāte; senâte; ärm; àsk; sofȧ; fâre; ch-choose; dh-as th in other; bē; ēvent; bĕt; recĕnt; cratēr; g-go; gh-guttural g; bĭt; ĭ-short neutral; rīde; K-guttural k as ch in German ich:

PRONOUNCING INDEX Aschersleben — Auvergne 253

Page	Name Pronunciation Region	Lat. °'	Long. °'
158	Aschersleben (äsh'ĕrs-lā-bĕn) G.D.R.	51·46 N	11·28 E
164	Ascoli Piceno (äs'kô-lēpē-chā'nō) It.	42·50 N	13·55 E
218	Aseb Eth. (Horn of Afr. In.)	12·52 N	43·39 E
165	Asenovgrad Bul.	42·00 N	24·49 E
166	Aseri (ȧ'sĕ-rĭ) Sov. Un.	59·26 N	26·58 E
	Asfi, see Safi		
174	Asha (ä'shä) Sov. Un. (Urals In.)	55·01 N	57·17 E
108	Ashabula (L.) (ăsh'ȧ-bū-lă) ND	47·07 N	97·51 W
174	Ashan (ä'shän) Sov. Un. (Urals In.)	57·08 N	56·25 E
148	Ashbourne (ăsh'bŭrn) Eng.	53·01 N	1·44 W
120	Ashburn (ăsh'bŭrn) Ga.	31·42 N	83·42 W
106	Ashburn Va. (Baltimore In.)	39·02 N	77·30 W
204	Ashburton (R.) (ăsh'bûr-tŭn) Austl.	22·30 S	115·30 E
148	Ashby-de-la-Zouch (ăsh'bĭ-dē-lȧ zōōsh') Eng.	52·44 N	1 23 W
183	Ashdod Isr. (Palestine In.)	31·46 N	34·39 E
117	Ashdown (ăsh'doun) Ar.	33·41 N	94·07 W
121	Asheboro (ăsh'bŭr-ô) NC	35·41 N	79·50 W
118	Asherton (ăsh'ĕr-tŭn) Tx.	28·26 N	99·45 W
121	Asheville (ăsh'vĭl) NC	35·35 N	82·35 W
115	Ash Fork Az.	35·13 N	112·29 W
195	Ashikaga (ä'shē-kä'gȧ) Jap.	36·22 N	139·26 E
195	Ashiya (ä'shē-yä') Jap.	33·54 N	130·40 E
195	Ashiya Jap. (Ōsaka In.)	34·44 N	135·18 E
195	Ashizuri-Zaki (Pt.) (ä-shē-zōō-rē zä-kē) Jap.	32·43 N	133·04 E
147	Ashkhabad (ŭsh-kä-bät') Sov. Un.	39·45 N	58·13 E
120	Ashland (ăsh'lănd) Al.	33·15 N	85·50 W
116	Ashland Ks.	37·11 N	99·46 W
104	Ashland Ky.	38·25 N	82·40 W
98	Ashland Me.	46·37 N	68·26 W
99	Ashland Ma. (In.)	42·16 N	71·28 W
108	Ashland Nb.	41·02 N	96·23 W
104	Ashland Oh.	40·50 N	82·15 W
110	Ashland Or.	42·12 N	122·42 W
105	Ashland Pa.	40·45 N	76·20 W
109	Ashland Wi.	46·34 N	90·55 W
108	Ashley (ăsh'lē) ND	46·03 N	99·23 W
105	Ashley Pa.	41·15 N	75·55 W
196	Ashmore Rf. (ăsh'mōr) Indon.	12·08 S	122·45 E
218	Ashmūn (ásh-mōōn') Egypt (Nile In.)	30·19 N	30·57 E
183	Ashqelon (äsh'kĕ-lōn) Isr. (Palestine In.)	31·40 N	34·36 E
211	Ash Shabb (shĕb) Egypt	22·34 N	29·52 E
218	Ash Shallūfah (shäl'lōō-fȧ) Egypt (Suez In.)	30·09 N	32·33 E
186	Ash Shaqrā' Sau. Ar.	25·10 N	45·08 E
183	Ash Shawbak Jordan (Palestine In.)	30·31 N	35·35 E
186	Ash Shihr P.D.R. of Yem.	14·45 N	49·32 E
104	Ashtabula (ăsh-tȧ-bū'lȧ) Oh.	41·55 N	80·50 W
111	Ashton (ăsh'tŭn) Id.	44·04 N	111·28 W
148	Ashton-in-Makerfield (ăsh'tŭn-ĭn-māk'ēr-fēld) Eng.	53·29 N	2·39 W
148	Ashton-under-Lyne (ăsh'tŭn-ŭn-dēr-līn') Eng.	53·29 N	2·04 W
91	Ashuanipi (L.) (ăsh-wȧ-nĭp'ĭ) Can.	52·40 N	67·42 W
174	Ashukino (á-shōō'ki-nô) Sov. Un. (Moscow In.)	56·10 N	37·57 E
182	Asia (ā'zhȧ)		
147	Asia Minor (ā'zhȧ) Asia	38·18 N	31·18 E
124	Asientos (ä-sē-ĕn'tōs) Mex.	22·13 N	102·05 W
164	Asinara, Golfo di (G.) (gôl'fô-dē-ä-sē-nä'rä) It.	40·58 N	8·28 E
164	Asinara (I.) (ä-sē-nä'rä) It.	41·02 N	8·22 E
186	Asīr (Reg.) (ä-sēr') Sau. Ar.	19·30 N	42·00 E
218	Asir, Ras (C.) Som. (Horn of Afr. In.)	11·55 N	51·30 E
174	Askarovo (äs-kä-rô'vô) Sov. Un. (Urals In.)	53·21 N	58·32 E
156	Askersund (äs'kĕr-sōōnd) Swe.	58·43 N	14·53 E
174	Askino (äs'kĭ-nô) Sov. Un. (Urals In.)	56·06 N	56·29 E
211	Asmera (äs-mä'rä) Eth.	15·17 N	38·56 E
161	Asnieres-sur-Seine (ä-nyâr'sür-sĕ'n) Fr. (Paris In.)	48·55 N	2·18 E
211	Asosa Eth.	10·13 N	34·28 E
110	Asotin (ȧ-sō'tĭn) Wa.	46·19 N	117·01 W
115	Aspen (ăs'pĕn) Co.	39·15 N	106·55 W
149	Asperen Neth. (Amsterdam In.)	51·52 N	5·07 E
93	Aspy B. (ăs'pē) Can.	46·55 N	60·25 W
218	Aş Şaff Egypt (Nile In.)	29·33 N	31·23 E
	Aş Şahrā' al Lībīyah, see Libyan Des.		
	Aş Şaḩrā' ash Sharqīyah, see Arabian Des.		
211	As Sallūm Egypt	31·34 N	25·09 E
183	As Salt Jordan (Palestine In.)	32·02 N	35·44 E
184	Assam (State) (äs-säm') India	26·00 N	91·00 E
156	Assens (äs'sĕns) Den.	55·16 N	9·54 E
218	As Sinbillāwayn Egypt (Nile In.)	30·53 N	31·37 E
210	Assini (á-sê-nē') Ivory Coast.	4·52 N	3·16 W
94	Assiniboia Can.	49·38 N	105·59 W
94	Assiniboine (R.) (ă-sĭn'ĭ-boin) Can.	50·03 N	97·57 W
93	Assiniboine, Mt. Can.	50·52 N	115·39 W
135	Assis (ä-sē's) Braz.	22·39 S	50·21 W
164	Assisi It.	43·04 N	12·37 E
211	As-Sudd (Reg.) Sud.	8·45 N	30·45 E
186	As Sulaymānīyah Iraq	35·47 N	45·23 E
186	As Suwaydā' Syr.	32·41 N	36·41 E
218	As Suways (Suez) Egypt (Suez In.)	29·58 N	32·34 E
165	Astakós (äs'tä-kôs) Grc.	38·42 N	21·00 E
171	Astara Sov. Un.	38·30 N	48·50 E
164	Asti (äs'tē) It.	44·54 N	8·12 E
153	Astipálaia (I.) Grc.	36·31 N	26·19 E
162	Astorga (äs-tôr'gä) Sp.	42·28 N	6·03 W
112	Astoria (ăs-tō'rĭ-ȧ) Or. (Portland In.)	46·11 N	123·51 W
171	Astrakhan' (äs-trȧ-kän') Sov. Un.	46·15 N	48·00 E
212	Astrida (äs-trē'dȧ) Rw.	2·37 S	29·48 E
162	Asturias (Reg.) (äs-tōō'ryäs) Sp.	43·21 N	6·00 W
136	Asunción (ä-sōōn-syōn') Par.	25·25 S	57·30 W
	Asunción, see Ixtaltepec		
	Asunción, see Nochixtlán		
126	Asunción Mita (ä-sōōn-syō'n-mē'tä) Guat.	14·19 N	89·43 W
155	Åsunden (L.) (ô'sōōn-dĕn) Swe.	57·46 N	13·16 E
218	Aswān (ä-swän') Egypt (Nile In.)	24·05 N	32·57 E
218	Aswān High Dam Egypt (Nile In.)	23·58 N	32·53 E
218	Asyūţ (ä-syōōt') Egypt (Nile In.)	27·10 N	31·10 E
136	Atacama, Puna de (Reg.) (pōō'nä-dĕ-ȧtä-kȧ'mä) Chile	23·15 S	68·45 W
134	Atacama, Puna de (Plat.) (pōō'nä-dĕ-ä-tä-kȧ'mä) Bol.	21·35 S	66·58 W
133	Atacama, Desierto de (Des.) (dĕ-syĕ'r-tô-dĕ-ä-tä-kȧ'mä) Chile-Peru	23·50 S	69·00 W
136	Atacama, Salar de (L.) (sȧ-lär'dĕ-ȧtä-kȧ'mä) Chile	23·38 S	68·15 W
136	Atacama Trench S.A.	25·00 S	71·30 W
134	Ataco (ä-tȧ'kō) Col. (In.)	3·36 N	75·22 W
214	Atacora, Chaîne de l' (Mts.) Benin	10·15 N	1·15 E
183	Atā 'itah, Jabal al (Mts.) Jordan (Palestine In.)	30·48 N	35·19 E
214	Atakpamé (ä'tȧk-pȧ-mā') Togo	7·32 N	1·08 E
174	Atamanovskiy (ä-tä-mä'nôv-skĭ) Sov. Un. (Urals In.)	52·15 N	60·47 E
218	'Atāqah, Jabal (Mts.) Egypt (Suez In.)	29·59 N	32·20 E
210	Atar (ä-tär') Mauritania	20·45 N	13·16 W
114	Atascadero (ăt-ăs-kȧ-dâ'rō) Ca.	35·29 N	120·40 W
118	Atascosa R. (ăt-ăs-kō'sȧ) Tx.	28·50 N	98·17 W
197	Atauro, Ilha de (I.) (dĕ-ä-tä'ōō-rô) Indon.	8·20 S	126·15 E
211	'Aţbarah (ät'bȧ-rä) Sud.	17·45 N	33·15 E
211	Atbara R. Sud.	17·14 N	34·27 E
172	Atbasar (ät'bä-sär') Sov. Un.	51·42 N	68·28 E
119	Atchafalaya B. (ăch-ȧ-fȧ-lī'ȧ) La.	29·25 N	91·30 W
119	Atchafalaya R. La.	30·53 N	91·51 W
117	Atchison (ăch'ĭ-sŭn) Ks.	39·33 N	95·08 W
106	Atco (ăt'kō) NJ (Philadelphia In.)	39·46 N	74·53 W
125	Atempan (ä-tĕm-pȧ'n) Mex.	19·49 N	97·25 W
124	Atenguillo (R.) (ä-tĕn-gē'l-yō) Mex.	20·18 N	104·35 W
90	Athabasca (ăth-ȧ-băs'kȧ) Can.	54·43 N	113·17 W
90	Athabasca (L.) Can.	59·04 N	109·10 W
93	Athabasca (R.) Can.	56·00 N	112·35 W
120	Athens (ăth'ĕnz) Al.	34·47 N	86·58 W
120	Athens Ga.	33·55 N	83·24 W
104	Athens Oh.	39·20 N	82·10 W
105	Athens Pa.	42·00 N	76·30 W
120	Athens Tn.	35·26 N	84·36 W
119	Athens Tx.	32·13 N	95·51 W
	Athens, see Athinai		
148	Atherstone (ăth'ĕr-stŭn) Eng.	52·34 N	1·33 W
148	Atherton (ăth'ĕr-tŭn) Eng.	53·32 N	2·29 W
205	Atherton Plat. (ădh-ĕr-tŏn) Austl.	17·00 S	144·30 E
217	Athi (R.) (ä'tē) Ken.	2·43 S	38·30 E
165	Athinai (Athens) (ä-thē'nĕ) Grc.	38·00 N	23·38 E
154	Athlone (ăth-lōn') Ire.	53·24 N	7·30 W
165	Athos (Mtn.) (ăth'ŏs) Grc.	40·10 N	24·15 E
183	Ath Thamad Egypt (Palestine In.)	29·41 N	34·17 E
154	Athy (ȧ-thī) Ire.	52·59 N	7·08 W
215	Ati Chad	13·13 N	18·20 E
137	Atibaia (ä-tē-bȧ'yȧ) Braz. (Rio de Janeiro In.)	23·08 S	46·32 W
91	Atikonak (L.) Can.	52·34 N	63·49 W
197	Atimonan (ä-tē-mō'nän) Phil. (In.)	13·59 N	121·56 E
126	Atiquizaya (ä'tē-kē-zä'yä) Sal.	14·00 N	89·42 W
126	Atitlan (Vol.) (ä-tē-tlän') Guat.	14·35 N	91·11 W
126	Atitlan L. (ä-tē-tlän') Guat.	14·38 N	91·23 W
125	Atizapán (ä'tē-zȧ-pän') Mex. (In.)	19·33 N	99·16 W
101	Atka (ăt'kȧ) Ak.	52·18 N	174·18 W
101	Atka (I.) Ak.	51·58 N	174·30 W
171	Atkarsk (ȧt-kärsk') Sov. Un.	51·50 N	45·00 E
108	Atkinson (ăt'kĭn-sŭn) Ne.	42·32 N	98·58 W
106	Atlanta (ăt-lăn'tȧ) Ga. (Atlanta In.)	33·45 N	84·23 W
117	Atlanta Tx.	33·09 N	94·09 W
109	Atlantic (ăt-lăn'tĭk) Ia.	41·23 N	94·58 W
121	Atlantic NC	34·54 N	76·20 W
106	Atlantic Highlands NJ (New York In.)	40·25 N	74·04 W
105	Atlantic City NJ	39·20 N	74·30 W
4	Atlantic O.		
210	Atlas Mts. (ăt'lăs) Alg.-Mor.	31·22 N	4·57 W
124	Atliaca (ät-lē-ä'kä) Mex.	17·38 N	99·24 W
90	Atlin (L.) (ăt'lĭn) Can.	59·34 N	133·20 W
124	Atlixco (ät-lēz'kō) Mex.	18·52 N	98·27 W
156	Atlöy (I.) (ät-lûê) Nor.	61·24 N	4·46 E
120	Atmore (ăt'mōr) Al.	31·01 N	87·31 W
117	Atoka (ȧ-tō'kȧ) Ok.	34·23 N	96·07 W
117	Atoka Res. Ok.	34·30 N	96·05 W
124	Atotonilco el Alto (ä'tô-tô-nēl'kō ĕl äl'tō) Mex.	20·35 N	102·32 W
124	Atotonilco el Grande (ä'tô-tô-nēl-kō ĕl grän'dā) Mex.	20·17 N	98·41 W
210	Atoui R. (ȧ-tōō-ē') Mauritania-W. Sah.	21·00 N	15·32 W
124	Atoyac (ä-tô-yäk') Mex.	20·01 N	103·28 W
125	Atoyac (R.) Mex.	16·27 N	97·28 W
124	Atoyac (R.) Mex.	18·35 N	98·16 W
124	Atoyac de Alvarez (ä-tô-yäk'dā äl'vä-rāz) Mex.	17·13 N	100·29 W
125	Atoyatempan (ä-tō'yȧ-tĕm-pän') Mex.	18·47 N	97·54 W
186	Atrak (R.) Iran	37·45 N	56·30 E
156	Atran (R.) Swe.	57·02 N	12·43 E
134	Atrato, Rio (R.) (rē'ō-ä-trä'tō) Col.	7·15 N	77·18 W
134	Atrato (R.) (ä-trä'tō) Col. (In.)	5·48 N	76·19 W
183	Aţ Ţafīlah (tä-fē'la) Jordan (Palestine In.)	30·50 N	35·36 E
186	Aţ Ţā'if Sau. Ar.	21·03 N	41·00 E
120	Attalla (ȧ-tăl'yȧ) Al.	34·01 N	86·05 W
91	Attawapiskat (R.) (ăt'ȧ-wȧ-pĭs'kăt) Can.	52·31 N	86·22 W
158	Atter See (L.) (Kammer) Aus.	47·57 N	13·25 E
105	Attica (ăt'ĭ-kȧ) NY	42·55 N	78·15 W
106	Attleboro (ăt''l-bŭr-ô) Ma. (Providence In.)	41·56 N	71·15 W
154	Attow, Ben (Mtn.) (bĕn ăt'tō) Scot.	57·15 N	5·25 W
119	Attoyac Bay (ă-toi'yăk) Tx.	31·45 N	94·23 W
101	Attu (I.) (ät-tōō') Ak.	53·08 N	173·18 E
153	Aţ Ţūr Egypt	28·09 N	33·47 E
186	Aţ Ţurayf Sau. Ar.	31·32 N	38·30 E
156	Åtvidaberg (ôt-vē'dȧ-bĕrgh) Swe.	58·12 N	15·55 E
116	Atwood (ăt'wŏŏd) Ks.	39·48 N	101·06 W
125	Atzcapotzalco (ät'zkä-pô-tzäl'kō) Mex. (In.)	19·29 N	99·11 W
149	Atzgersdorf Aus. (Vienna In.)	48·10 N	16·17 E
100	Auau Chan. (ä'ōō-ä'ōō) Hi. (In.)	20·55 N	156·50 W
161	Aubagne (ō-bän'y') Fr.	43·18 N	5·34 E
160	Aube (R.) (ōb) Fr.	48·42 N	3·49 E
160	Aubenas (ōb-nä') Fr.	44·37 N	4·22 E
161	Aubervilliers (ō-bĕr-vē-yā') Fr. (Paris In.)	48·54 N	2·23 E
160	Aubin (ō-băN') Fr.	44·29 N	2·12 E
89	Aubrey (ô-brē') Can. (Montreal In.)	45·08 N	73·47 W
120	Auburn (ô'bŭrn) Al.	32·35 N	85·26 W
114	Auburn Ca.	38·52 N	121·05 W
117	Auburn Il.	39·36 N	89·46 W
104	Auburn In.	41·20 N	85·05 W
98	Auburn Me.	44·04 N	70·24 W
99	Auburn Ma. (In.)	42·11 N	71·51 W
117	Auburn Ne.	40·23 N	95·50 W
105	Auburn NY	42·55 N	76·35 W
112	Auburn Wa. (Seattle In.)	47·18 N	122·14 W
107	Auburn Hts. Mi. (Detroit In.)	42·37 N	83·13 W
160	Aubusson (ō-bü-sôN') Fr.	45·57 N	2·10 E
160	Auch (ōsh) Fr.	43·38 N	0·35 E
120	Aucilla (R.) (ô-sĭl'ȧ) Fl.-Ga.	30·15 N	83·55 W
205	Auckland (ôk'lănd) N. Z. (In.)	36·53 S	174·45 E
220	Auckland Is. N. Z.	50·30 S	166·30 E
160	Aude (R.) (ōd) Fr.	42·55 N	2·08 E
160	Audierne (ō-dyĕrn') Fr.	48·02 N	4·31 W
161	Audincourt (ō-dăN-kōōr') Fr.	47·30 N	6·49 E
148	Audley (ôd'lĭ) Eng.	53·03 N	2·18 W
218	Audo Ra. Eth. (Horn of Afr. In.)	6·58 N	41·18 E
109	Audubon (ô'dōō-bŏn) Ia.	41·43 N	94·57 W
106	Audubon NJ (Philadelphia In.)	39·54 N	75·04 W
158	Aue (ou'ē) G.D.R.	50·35 N	12·44 E
203	Augathella (ôr'gȧ'thĕ-lȧ) Austl.	25·49 S	146·40 E
212	Augrabiesvalle (Falls) S. Afr.	28·30 S	20·00 E
149	Augsburg (ouks'bŏŏrgh) F.R.G. (Munich In.)	48·23 N	10·55 E
117	Augusta (ô-gŭs'tȧ) Ar.	35·16 N	91·21 W
121	Augusta Ga.	33·26 N	82·00 W
117	Augusta Ks.	37·41 N	96·58 W
104	Augusta Ky.	38·45 N	84·00 W
98	Augusta Me.	44·19 N	69·42 W
106	Augusta NJ (New York In.)	41·07 N	74·44 W
109	Augusta Wi.	44·40 N	91·09 W
159	Augustow (ou-gŏŏs'tōōf) Pol.	53·52 N	23·00 E
161	Aulnay-sous-Bois (ō-nĕ'sōō-bwä') Fr. (Paris In.)	48·56 N	2·30 E
160	Aulne (R.) (ōn) Fr.	48·08 N	3·53 W
161	Auneau (ō-nĕü) Fr. (Paris In.)	48·28 N	1·45 E
212	Auob (R.) (ä'wŏb) Namibia	25·00 S	19·00 E
183	Aur (I.) Mala. (Singapore In.)	2·27 N	104·51 E
184	Aurangābād (ou-rŭŋ-gä-bäd') India	19·56 N	75·19 E
160	Auray (ō-rĕ') Fr.	47·42 N	3·00 W
152	Aurès, Massif de l' (Mts.) Alg.	35·16 N	5·53 E
160	Aurillac (ō-rē-yȧk') Fr.	44·57 N	2·27 E
97	Aurora Can.	43·59 N	79·25 W
107	Aurora (ô-rō'rȧ) Il. (Chicago In.)	41·45 N	88·18 W
107	Aurora In. (Cincinnati In.)	39·04 N	84·55 W
109	Aurora Mn.	47·31 N	92·17 W
117	Aurora Mo.	36·58 N	93·42 W
116	Aurora Ne.	40·54 N	98·01 W
156	Aursunden (L.) (äûr-sûndĕn) Nor.	62·42 N	11·10 E
104	Au Sable (R.) (ô-sä'b'l) Mi.	44·40 N	84·25 W
105	Ausable (R.) NY	44·25 N	73·50 W
109	Austin (ôs'tĭn) Mn.	43·40 N	92·58 W
114	Austin Nv.	39·30 N	117·05 W
119	Austin Tx.	30·15 N	97·42 W
204	Austin (L.) Austl.	27·45 S	117·30 E
119	Austin Bayou (ôs'tĭn bī-ōō') Tx. (In.)	29·17 N	95·21 W
204	Australia (ôs-trā'lĭ-ȧ)		
203	Australian Alps (Mts.) Austl.	37·10 S	147·55 E
203	Australian Capital Ter. (ôs-trā'lĭ-ăn) Austl.	35·30 S	148·40 E
146	Austria (ôs'trĭ-ȧ) Eur.	47·15 N	11·53 E
161	Authon-la-Plaine (ō-tō'N-lă-plĕ'n) Fr. (Paris In.)	48·27 N	1·58 E
124	Autlán (ä-ōōt-län') Mex.	19·47 N	104·24 W
160	Autun (ō-tŭN') Fr.	46·58 N	4·14 E
160	Auvergne (Mts.) (ō-vĕrn'y') Fr.	45·12 N	2·31 E

ng-sing; ŋ-baŋk; N-nasalized n; nŏd; cŏmmit; ōld; ôbey; ôrder; fōōd; fŏŏt; ou-out; s-soft; sh-dish; th-thin; pūre; ûnite; ûrn; stŭd; circŭs; ü-as "y" in study; '-indeterminate vowel.

Page	Name Pronunciation	Region	Lat. °′	Long. °′
160	Auxerre (ō-sâr′)	Fr.	47·48 N	3·32 E
117	Ava (ā′vȧ)	Mo.	36·56 N	92·40 W
217	Avakubi (ä-vȧ-ko͞o′bē̇)	Zaire	1·20 N	27·34 E
160	Avallon (ȧ-vȧ-lôɴ′)	Fr.	47·30 N	3·58 E
107	Avalon (ăv′ȧ-lŏn)	Pa. (Pittsburgh In.)	40·31 N	80·05 W
114	Avalon	Ca.	33·21 N	118·22 W
162	Aveiro (ä-vā′ro͝o)	Port.	40·38 N	8·38 W
136	Avelar (ä′vĕ-lȧ′r)	Braz. (Rio de Janeiro In.)	22·20 S	43·25 W
136	Avellaneda (ä-vĕl-yä-nā′dhä)	Arg. (Buenos Aires In.)	34·25 S	58·23 W
163	Avellino (ä-vĕl-lē′nō)	It. (Naples In.)	40·40 N	14·46 E
156	Averöy (I.) (ävĕr-ûē̇)	Nor.	63·40 N	7·16 E
164	Aversa (ä-vĕr′sä)	It.	40·58 N	14·13 E
117	Avery (ā′vēr-ĭ)	Tx.	33·34 N	94·46 W
156	Avesta (ä-vĕs′tä)	Swe.	60·16 N	16·09 E
160	Aveyron (R.) (ä-vâ-rôɴ)	Fr.	44·07 N	1·45 E
164	Avezzano (ä-vȧt-sä′nō)	It.	42·03 N	13·27 E
164	Avigliano (ä-vēl-yä′nō)	It.	40·45 N	15·44 E
160	Avignon (ȧ-vē-nyôɴ′)	Fr.	43·55 N	4·50 E
162	Ávila (ä-vē̇-lä)	Sp.	40·39 N	4·42 W
162	Avilés (ä-vē̇-lās′)	Sp.	43·33 N	5·55 W
117	Avoca (ȧ-vō′kȧ)	Ia.	41·29 N	95·16 W
105	Avon (ā′vŏn)	Ct.	41·40 N	72·50 W
99	Avon (ā′vŏn)	Ma. (In.)	42·08 N	71·03 W
107	Avon	Oh. (Cleveland In.)	41·27 N	82·02 W
154	Avon (R.) (ā′vŭn)	Eng.	52·05 N	1·55 W
106	Avondale	Ga. (Atlanta In.)	33·47 N	84·16 W
107	Avon Lake	Oh. (Cleveland In.)	41·31 N	82·01 W
89	Avonmore (ä′vōɴ-mōr)	Can. (Ottawa In.)	45·11 N	74·58 W
121	Avon Park (ā′vŏn pärk′)	Fl. (In.)	27·35 N	81·29 W
160	Avranches (ȧ-vräɴsh′)	Fr.	48·43 N	1·34 W
195	Awaji-Shima (I.) (ä′wä-jē̇ shē-mä)	Jap. (Osaka In.)	34·32 N	135·02 E
154	Awe, Loch (L.) (lŏĸ ôr)	Scot.	56·22 N	5·04 W
211	Awjilah	Libya	29·07 N	21·21 E
160	Ax-les-Thermes (äks′lā tĕrm′)	Fr.	42·43 N	1·50 E
124	Axochiapan (äks-ō-chyä′pän)	Mex.	18·29 N	98·49 W
160	Ay (ȧ′ē̇)	Fr.	49·05 N	3·58 E
170	Ay (R.)	Sov. Un.	55·55 N	57·55 E
195	Ayabe (ä′yä-bĕ)	Jap.	35·16 N	135·17 E
152	Ayachi, Arin′ (Mtn.)	Mor.	32·29 N	4·57 W
136	Ayacucho (ä-yä-ko͞o′chō)	Arg.	37·05 S	58·30 W
134	Ayacucho	Peru	12·12 S	74·03 W
172	Ayaguz (ä-yȧ-go͞oz′)	Sov. Un.	48·00 N	80·12 E
162	Ayamonte (ä-yä-mō̂′n-tĕ)	Sp.	37·14 N	7·28 W
173	Ayan (ȧ-yän′)	Sov. Un.	56·26 N	138·18 E
134	Ayata (ä-yä′tä)	Bol.	15·17 S	68·43 W
134	Ayaviri (ä-yä-vē′rē)	Peru	14·46 S	70·38 W
167	Aydar (R.) (ī-där′)	Sov. Un.	49·15 N	38·48 E
121	Ayden (ā′dĕn)	NC	35·27 N	77·25 W
171	Aydın (āīy-dĕn)	Tur.	37·40 N	27·40 E
99	Ayer (âr)	Ma. (In.)	42·33 N	71·36 W
183	Ayer Hitam	Mala. (Singapore In.)	1·55 N	103·11 E
165	Ayiá (ā-yē′ȧ)	Grc.	39·42 N	22·47 E
165	Ayiassos	Grc.	39·06 N	26·25 E
165	Áyion Óros (Mount Athos) (Reg.)	Grc.	40·20 N	24·15 E
165	Aýios Evstrátion (I.)	Grc.	39·30 N	24·58 E
148	Aylesbury (ālz′bēr-ĭ)	Eng. (London In.)	51·47 N	0·49 W
90	Aylmer (L.) (āl′mēr)	Can.	64·27 N	108·22 W
93	Aylmer, Mt.	Can.	51·19 N	115·26 W
89	Aylmer East (āl′mēr)	Can. (Ottawa In.)	45·24 N	75·50 W
124	Ayo el Chico (ä′yō̂ el chē′kō)	Mex.	20·31 N	102·21 W
173	Ayon (I.) (ī-ôn′)	Sov. Un.	69·50 N	168·40 E
214	Ayorou	Niger	14·44 N	0·55 E
125	Ayotla (ä-yōt′lä)	Mex. (In.)	19·18 N	98·55 W
214	Ayoun el Atrous	Mauritania	16·40 N	9·37 W
154	Ayr (âr)	Scot.	55·27 N	4·40 W
154	Ayr (L.)	Scot.	55·25 N	4·20 W
218	Aysha	Eth. (Horn of Afr. In.)	10·48 N	42·32 E
126	Ayutla (ȧ-yo͞ot′lä)	Guat.	14·44 N	92·11 W
124	Ayutla	Mex.	16·50 N	99·16 W
124	Ayutla	Mex.	20·09 N	104·20 W
165	Ayvalik (āīy-wă-lĭk)	Tur.	39·19 N	26·40 E
214	Azaouad (Dunes)	Mali	18·00 N	3·20 W
215	Azaouak, Vallée de l′ (Val.)	Mali	15·50 N	3·10 E
215	Azare	Nig.	11·40 N	10·11 E
210	Azemmour (ȧ-zē-mo͞or′)	Mor.	33·20 N	8·21 W
168	Azerbaydzhan (Azerbaijan) (S. S. R.) (ä′zēr-bä-ē̇-jän′)	Sov. Un.	40·38 N	47·25 E
113	Azle (ȧz′lē)	Tx. (Dallas, Fort Worth In.)	35·54 N	97·33 W
134	Azogues (ä-sō′gās)	Ec.	2·47 S	78·45 W
	Azores (Is.), see Açores			
167	Azov (ȧ-zôf′) (ä-zôf)	Sov. Un.	47·07 N	39·19 E
	Azov, Sea of, see Azovskoye More			
167	Azovskoye More (Sea of Azov) (ȧ-zôf′skô-yĕ mô′rĕ)	Sov. Un.	46·00 N	36·20 E
124	Azoyú (ä-zō̂-yo͞o′)	Mex.	16·42 N	98·46 W
	Azraq, Al-Bahr al- (R.), see Blue Nile			
115	Aztec (ăz′tĕk)	NM	36·40 N	108·00 W
115	Aztec Ruins Natl. Mon.	NM	36·50 N	108·00 W
129	Azua (ä′swä)	Dom. Rep.	18·30 N	70·45 W
162	Azuaga (ä-thwä′gä)	Sp.	38·15 N	5·42 W
118	Azucar, Presa de (Res.) (prĕ′sä-dĕ-ä-zo͞o′kär)	Mex.	26·06 N	98·44 W
127	Azuero, Peninsula de (Pen.) (ä-swā′rō)	Pan.	7·30 N	80·34 W
136	Azufre, Cerro (Copiapó) (Vol.) (sĕr′rō ä-so͞o′frā) (kō-pē̇-äpō′)	Chile	26·10 S	69·00 W
137	Azul (ä-so͞ol′)	Arg. (Buenos Aires In.)	36·46 S	59·51 W
124	Azul, Sierra (Mts.) (sē-ĕ′r-rä-zo͞o′l)	Mex.	23·20 N	98·28 W
134	Azul, Cordillera (Mts.) (kô′r-dē-lyĕ′rä-zo͞o′l)	Peru	7·15 S	75·30 W
113	Azusa (ȧ-zo͞o′sȧ)	Ca. (Los Angeles In.)	34·08 N	117·55 W
183	Az Zabdānī	Syr. (Palestine In.)	33·45 N	36·06 E
186	Aẓ Ẓahrān (Dhahran) (dä-rän′)	Sau. Ar.	26·13 N	50·00 E
218	Az Zaqāzīq	Egypt (Nile In.)	30·36 N	31·36 E
183	Az Zarqā′	Jordan (Palestine In.)	32·03 N	36·07 E
211	Az Zawiyah	Libya	32·28 N	11·55 E

B

Page	Name Pronunciation	Region	Lat. °′	Long. °′
161	Baal (bäl)	F.R.G. (Ruhr In.)	51·02 N	6·17 E
197	Baao (bä′ō)	Phil. (In.)	13·27 N	123·22 E
149	Baarle-Hertog	Bel. (Brussels In.)	51·26 N	4·57 E
149	Baarn	Neth. (Amsterdam In.)	52·12 N	5·18 E
165	Babaeski (bä′bä-ĕs′kĭ)	Tur.	41·25 N	27·05 E
134	Babahoyo (bä-bä-ō′yō)	Ec.	1·56 S	79·24 W
215	Babana	Nig.	10·36 N	3·50 E
213	Babanango	S. Afr. (Natal In.)	28·24 S	31·11 E
211	Babanūsah	Sud.	11·30 N	27·55 E
197	Babar, Pulau (I.) (bä′bȧr)	Indon.	7·50 S	129·15 E
218	Bab-el-Mandeb, Str. of (bäb′ĕl män-dĕb′)	Afr.-Asia (Horn of Afr. In.)	13·17 N	42·49 E
118	Babia, Arroyo de la (är-rō′yō dā lä bä′bē̇-ȧ)	Mex.	28·26 N	101·50 W
92	Babine (R.)	Can.	55·10 N	127·00 W
92	Babine L. (băb′ēn)	Can.	54·45 N	126·00 W
186	Bābol	Iran	36·30 N	52·48 E
173	Babushkin (bä′bo͝osh-kĭn)	Sov. Un.	51·47 N	106·08 W
174	Babushkin	Sov. Un. (Moscow In.)	55·52 N	37·42 E
196	Babuyan Is. (bä-bo͞o-yän′)	Phil.	19·30 N	122·38 E
165	Babyak (bäb′zhȧk)	Bul.	41·59 N	23·42 E
106	Babylon (băb′ĭ-lŏn)	NY (New York In.)	40·42 N	73·19 W
186	Babylon (Ruins)	Iraq	32·15 N	45·23 E
126	Bacalar, Laguna de (L.) (lä-go͞o-nä-dĕ-bä-kä-lär′)	Mex. (In.)	18·50 N	88·31 W
197	Bacan, Pulau (I.)	Indon.	0·30 S	127·00 E
193	Bacarra (bä-kär′rä)	Phil.	18·22 N	120·40 E
159	Bacău	Rom.	46·34 N	27·00 E
161	Baccarat (bȧ-kȧ-rȧ′)	Fr.	48·29 N	6·42 E
113	Bacchus (băk′ŭs)	Ut. (Salt Lake City In.)	40·40 N	112·06 W
125	Bachajón (bä-chä-hōn′)	Mex.	17·08 N	92·18 W
188	Bachu (bä-cho͞o)	China	39·50 N	78·23 E
90	Back (R.)	Can.	65·30 N	104·15 W
165	Bǎcka Palanka (bäch′kä pälän-kä)	Yugo.	45·14 N	19·24 E
165	Bačka Topola (bäch′kä tō̂′pō̂-lä′)	Yugo.	45·48 N	19·38 E
185	Back Bay (băk)	India (In.)	18·55 N	72·45 E
204	Backstairs Pass. (băk-stârs′)	Austl.	35·50 S	138·15 E
193	Bac Ninh (bäk′nēn″)	Viet.	21·10 N	106·02 E
197	Baco, Mt. (bä′kō̂)	Phil. (In.)	12·50 N	121·11 E
163	Bacoli (bä-kō-lē′)	It. (Naples In.)	40·33 N	14·05 E
196	Bacolod (bä-kō′lō̂d)	Phil.	10·42 N	123·03 E
159	Bácsalmás (bäch′ôl-mäs)	Hung.	46·07 N	19·18 E
148	Bacup (băk′ŭp)	Eng.	53·42 N	2·12 W
108	Bad (R.) (băd)	SD	44·04 N	100·58 W
162	Badajoz (bȧ-dhä-hōth′)	Sp.	38·52 N	6·56 W
163	Badalona (bä-dhä-lō′nä)	Sp.	41·27 N	2·15 E
186	Badanah	Sau. Ar.	30·49 N	40·45 E
104	Bad Axe (băd′ ăks)	Mi.	43·50 N	82·55 W
149	Bad Bramstedt (bät bräm′shtĕt)	F.R.G. (Hamburg In.)	53·55 N	9·53 E
161	Bad Ems (bät ĕms)	F.R.G.	50·20 N	7·45 E
149	Baden (bä′dĕn)	Aus. (Vienna In.)	48·00 N	16·14 E
158	Baden	Switz.	47·28 N	8·17 E
158	Baden-Baden (bä′dĕn-bä′dĕn)	F.R.G.	48·46 N	8·11 E
158	Baden Württemberg (State) (bä′dĕn vür′tĕm-bĕrgh)	F.R.G.	48·38 N	9·00 E
158	Bad Freienwalde (bät frī′ĕn-văl′dĕ)	G.D.R.	52·47 N	14·00 E
158	Bad Hersfeld (bät hĕrsh′fĕlt)	F.R.G.	50·53 N	9·43 E
155	Bad Homberg (bät hōm′bĕrgh)	F.R.G.	50·14 N	8·35 E
121	Badin (bă′dĭn)	NC	35·23 N	80·08 W
184	Badīn	Pak.	24·47 N	69·51 E
158	Bad Ischl (bät ĭsh″l)	Aus.	47·46 N	13·37 E
158	Bad Kissingen (bät kĭs′ĭng-ĕn)	F.R.G.	50·12 N	10·05 E
158	Bad Kreuznach (bät kroits′näk)	F.R.G.	49·52 N	7·53 E
108	Badlands (Reg.) (băd′ lănds)	ND	46·43 N	103·22 W
108	Badlands (Reg.)	SD	43·43 N	102·36 W
108	Badlands Natl. Mon.	SD	43·56 N	102·37 W
185	Badlāpur	India (In.)	19·12 N	73·12 E
214	Badogo	Mali	11·02 N	8·13 W
158	Bad Oldeslow (bät ôl′dĕs-lōē)	F.R.G.	53·48 N	10·21 E
158	Bad Reichenhall (bät rī′ĸĕn-häl)	F.R.G.	47·43 N	12·53 E
109	Bad River Ind. Res. (băd)	Wi.	46·41 N	90·36 W
149	Bad Segeberg (bät sĕ′gĕ-bo͞orgh)	F.R.G. (Hamburg In.)	53·56 N	10·18 E
158	Bad Tölz (bät tûltz)	F.R.G.	47·46 N	11·35 E
185	Badulla	Sri Lanka	6·55 N	81·07 E
149	Bad Vöslau	Aus. (Vienna In.)	47·58 N	16·13 E
111	Badwater Cr. (băd′wô-tēr)	Wy.	43·13 N	107·55 W
162	Baena (bä-ā′nä)	Sp.	37·38 N	4·20 W
137	Baependi (bä-å-pĕn′dĭ)	Braz. (Rio de Janeiro In.)	21·57 S	44·51 W
75	Baffin B. (băf′ĭn)	Can.	72·00 N	65·00 W
119	Baffin B.	Tx.	27·11 N	97·35 W
75	Baffin I.	Can.	67·20 N	71·00 W
214	Bafoulabé (bä-fo͞o-lä-bā′)	Mali	13·48 N	10·50 W
186	Bāfq (bäfk)	Iran	31·48 N	55·23 E
171	Bafra (bäf′rä)	Tur.	41·30 N	35·50 E
197	Bagabag (bä-gä-bäg′)	Phil. (In.)	16·38 N	121·16 E
185	Bāgalkot	India	16·14 N	75·40 E
217	Bagamoyo (bä-gä-mō′yō)	Tan.	6·26 S	38·54 E
174	Bagaryak (bȧ-gȧr-yäk′)	Sov. Un. (Urals In.)	56·13 N	61·32 E
217	Bagbele	Zaire	4·21 N	29·17 E
136	Bagé (bä-zhā′)	Braz.	31·17 S	54·07 W
186	Baghdād (bȧgh-dȧd′) (băg′dăd)	Iraq	33·14 N	44·22 E
164	Bagheria (bä-gå-rē′ä)	It.	38·03 N	13·32 E
108	Bagley (băg′lē̇)	Mn.	47·31 N	95·24 W
164	Bagnara (bän-yä′rä)	It.	38·17 N	15·52 E
117	Bagnell Dam (băg′nĕl)	Mo.	38·13 N	92·40 W
160	Bagnères-de-Bigorre (băn-yâr′dē-bē̇-gor′)	Fr.	43·40 N	0·70 E
160	Bagnères-de-Luchon (băn-yâr′ dē-lu chôɴ′)	Fr.	42·46 N	0·36 E
160	Bagnols (bä-nyō̂l′)	Fr.	44·09 N	4·37 E
210	Bagoé R. (bȧ-gō′å)	Mali	12·22 N	6·34 W
97	Bagotville (bȧ-gō̂-vēl′)	Can.	48·21 N	70·53 W
197	Baguio (bä-gē̇-ō′)	Phil. (In.)	16·24 N	120·36 E
215	Bagzane, Monts (Mtn.)	Niger	18·40 N	8·40 E
123	Bahamas (bȧ-hā′mȧs)	N. A.	26·15 N	76·00 W
183	Bahau	Mala. (Singapore In.)	2·48 N	102·25 E
184	Bahāwalpur (bŭ-hä′wŭl-po͞or)	Pak.	29·29 N	71·41 E
217	Bahi Swp	Tan.	6·05 S	35·10 E
	Bahia, see Salvador			
135	Bahia (State)	Braz.	11·05 S	43·00 W
122	Bahía, Islas de la (I.) (ē̇′s-läs-dĕ-lä-bä-ē′ä)	Hond.	16·15 N	86·30 W
136	Bahia Blanca (bä-ē′ä bläŋ′kä)	Arg.	38·45 S	62·07 W
134	Bahía de Caráquez (bä-e′ä dā kä-rä′kĕz)	Ec.	0·45 S	80·29 W
135	Bahía Negra (bä-ē′ä nā′grä)	Par.	20·11 S	58·05 W
136	Bahias, Cabo dos (C.) (kȧ′bô-dôs-bä-ē′äs)	Arg.	44·55 S	65·35 W
129	Bahoruco, Sierra de (Mts.) (sē-ĕ′r-rä-dĕ-bä-ō-ro͞o′kô)	Dom. Rep.	18·10 N	71·25 W
186	Bahrain (bä-rān′)	Asia	26·15 N	51·17 E
211	Baḩr al Ghazāl (Prov.) (bär ĕl ghä-zäl′)	Sud.	7·56 N	27·15 E
153	Baḩrīyah (Oasis) (bȧ-hȧ-rē′yä)	Egypt	28·34 N	29·01 E
183	Baḩrīyah, Jabal Jalālah al (Plat.)	Egypt (Palestine In.)	29·15 N	32·20 E
159	Baia de Cris (bä′yä dā krēs′)	Rom.	46·11 N	22·40 E
216	Baía dos Tigres	Ang.	16·36 S	11·43 E
159	Baia-Mare (bä′yä-mä′rā)	Rom.	47·40 N	23·35 E
218	Baidoa	Som. (Horn of Afr. In.)	3·19 N	44·20 E
184	Baidyabāti	India (In.)	22·47 N	88·21 E
98	Baie-Comeau	Can.	49·13 N	68·10 W
113	Baie de Wasai (bā dē wä-sä′ē̇)	Mi. (Sault Ste. Marie In.)	46·27 N	84·15 W
97	Baie-St. Paul (bā′sånt-pôl′)	Can.	47·27 N	70·30 W
190	Baigou (bī-gō)	China	39·08 N	116·02 E
192	Baihe (bī-hŭ)	China	32·30 N	110·15 E
190	Bai Hu (L.) (bī-ho͞o)	China	31·22 N	117·38 E
190	Baiju (bī-jyo͞o)	China	33·04 N	120·17 E
	Baikal Mts., see Baykal′skiy Khrebet			
	Baikal, L., see Baykal, Ozero			
	Baile Atha Cliath, see Dublin			
162	Bailén (bä-ē̇-lān′)	Sp.	38·05 N	3·48 W
165	Băileşti (bă-ĭ-lĕsh′tē̇)	Rom.	44·01 N	23·21 E
120	Bainbridge (bān′brĭj)	Ga.	30·52 N	84·35 W
112	Bainbridge I.	Wa. (Seattle In.)	47·39 N	122·32 W
190	Baipu (bī-po͞o)	China	32·15 N	120·47 E
192	Baiquan (bī-chyuän)	China	47·22 N	126·00 E
118	Baird (bârd)	Tx.	32·22 N	99·28 W
107	Bairdford (bârd′fŏrd)	Pa. (Pittsburgh In.)	40·37 N	79·53 W
101	Baird Mts.	Ak.	67·35 N	160·10 W
203	Bairnsdale (bârnz′dāl)	Austl.	37·50 S	147·39 E
160	Baïse (R.) (bä-ēz′)	Fr.	43·52 N	0·23 E
190	Baiyang Dian (L.) (bī-yäŋ-dĭĕn)	China	39·00 N	115·45 E
192	Baiyu Shan (Mts.) (bī-yo͞o shän)	China	37·02 N	108·30 E
159	Baja (bŏ′yŏ)	Hung.	46·11 N	18·55 E
122	Baja California Norte (State) (bä-hä)	Mex.	30·15 N	117·25 W
122	Baja California Sur (State)	Mex.	26·00 N	113·30 W
174	Bakal (bä′kȧl)	Sov. Un. (Urals In.)	54·57 N	58·50 E
111	Baker (bā′kēr)	Mt.	46·21 N	104·12 W
110	Baker	Or.	44·46 N	117·52 W
198	Baker (I.)	Oceania	1·00 N	176·00 W
90	Baker (L.)	Can.	63·51 N	96·10 W
110	Baker, Mt.	Wa.	48·46 N	121·52 W

ăt; finăl; rāte; senåte; ärm; ȧsk; sofȧ; fâre; ch-choose; dh-as th in other; bē; ē̇vent; bĕt; recĕnt; cratēr; g-go; gh-guttural g; bĭt; ĭ-short neutral; rīde; ĸ-guttural k as ch in German ich;

PRONOUNCING INDEX Baker — Barisan 255

Page	Name Pronunciation Region	Lat. °'	Long. °'
107	Baker Cr. ... Il. (Chicago In.)	41·13 N	87·47 W
114	Bakersfield (bā'kẽrz-fēld) ... Ca.	35·23 N	119·00 W
107	Bakerstown (bā'kerz-toun) Pa. (Pittsburgh In.)	40·39 N	79·56 W
148	Bakewell (bāk'wĕl) ... Eng.	53·12 N	1·40 W
167	Bakhchisaray (bȧk'chê-sȧ-rī') Sov. Un.	44·46 N	33·54 E
167	Bakhmach (bȧk-mäch') .. Sov. Un.	51·09 N	32·47 E
186	Bakhtegan, Daryācheh-ye (L.) Iran	29·29 N	54·31 E
174	Bakhteyevo (bȧk-tyĕ'yĕ-vô) Sov. Un. (Moscow In.)	55·35 N	38·32 E
211	Bako (bä'kö) ... Eth.	5·47 N	36·39 E
159	Bakony-Erdo (Mts.) (bȧ-kōn'y') Hung.	46·57 N	17·30 E
214	Bakoye (R.) (bȧ-kô'ê) ... Mali	12·47 N	9·35 W
174	Bakr Uzyak (bȧkr ōōz'yák) Sov. Un. (Urals In.)	52·59 N	58·43 E
171	Baku (bȧ-kōō') ... Sov. Un.	40·28 N	49·45 E
	Bakwanga, see Mbuji-Mayi		
196	Balabac I. (bä'lä-bäk) ... Phil.	8·00 N	116·28 E
196	Balabac Str. ... Indon.-Phil.	7·23 N	116·30 E
183	Ba'labakk ... Leb. (Palestine In.)	34·00 N	36·13 E
174	Balabanovo (bȧ-lȧ-bä'nô-vô) Sov. Un. (Moscow In.)	56·10 N	37·44 E
172	Balagansk (bä-lä-gänsk') Sov. Un.	53·58 N	103·09 E
163	Balaguer (bä-lä-gĕr') ... Sp.	41·48 N	0·50 E
172	Balakhta (bȧ'lȧk-tȧ') ... Sov. Un.	55·22 N	91·43 E
167	Balakleya (bȧ'lȧ-klā'yȧ) .. Sov. Un.	49·28 N	36·51 E
171	Balakovo (bȧ'lȧ-kô'vô) ... Sov. Un.	52·00 N	47·40 E
125	Balancán (bä-läŋ-kän') ... Mex.	17·47 N	91·32 W
197	Balanga (bä-läŋ'gä) ... Phil. (In.)	14·41 N	120·31 E
174	Balashikha (bȧ-lä'shĭ-kȧ) Sov. Un. (Moscow In.)	55·48 N	37·58 E
171	Balashov (bȧ'lȧ-shôf) ... Sov. Un.	51·30 N	43·00 E
184	Balasore (bä-lȧ-sōr') ... India	21·38 N	86·59 E
159	Balassagyarmat (bô'lôsh-shô-dyôr'môt). Hung.	48·04 N	19·19 E
159	Balaton L. (bô'lô-tôn) ... Hung.	46·47 N	17·55 E
197	Balayan (bä-lä-yän') ... Phil. (In.)	13·56 N	120·44 E
197	Balayan B. ... Phil. (In.)	13·46 N	120·46 E
127	Balboa Heights (bäl-bô'ä) Pan.	8·59 N	79·33 W
122	Balboa Mt. ... Pan. (In.)	9·05 N	79·44 W
136	Balcarce (bäl-kär'sā) ... Arg.	37·49 S	58·17 W
165	Balchik ... Bul.	43·24 N	28·13 E
113	Bald Eagle (bôld ē'g'l) Mn. (Minneapolis, St. Paul In.)	45·06 N	93·01 W
113	Bald Eagle L. Mn. (Minneapolis, St. Paul In.)	45·08 N	93·03 W
95	Baldock L. ... Can.	56·33 N	97·57 W
113	Baldwin Park (bôld'wĭn) Ca. (Los Angeles In.)	34·05 N	117·58 W
105	Baldwinsville (bôld'wĭns-vĭl) NY	43·10 N	76·20 W
95	Baldy Mtn. ... Can.	51·28 N	100·44 W
115	Baldy Pk. (bôl'dê) ... Az.	33·55 N	109·35 W
118	Baldy Pk. (bôl'dê pēk) ... Tx.	30·38 N	104·11 W
163	Baleares, Islas (Balearic Is.) (e's-läs bä-lĕ-ä'rĕs). Sp.	39·25 N	1·28 E
	Balearic Is., see Baleares, Islas		
163	Balearic Sea (băl-ê-ăr'ĭk) ... Eur.	39·40 N	1·05 E
91	Baleine, Grande Rivière de la (R.) Can.	54·45 N	74·20 W
197	Baler (bä-lar') ... Phil. (In.)	15·46 N	121·33 E
197	Baler B. ... Phil. (In.)	15·51 N	121·40 E
197	Balesin (I.) ... Phil. (In.)	14·28 N	122·10 E
173	Baley (bȧl-yā') ... Sov. Un.	51·29 N	116·12 E
126	Balfate (bäl-fä'tē) ... Hond.	15·48 N	86·24 W
218	Balfour (bȧl'fo͝or) . S. Afr. (Johannesburg & Pretoria In.)	26·41 S	28·37 E
196	Bali (I.) (bä'lê) ... Indon.	8·00 S	115·22 E
171	Balikesir (balĭk'ĭysĭr) ... Tur.	39·40 N	27·50 E
196	Balikpapan (bä'lêk-pä'pän) Indon.	1·13 S	116·52 E
196	Balintang Chan. (bä-lĭn-täng') Phil.	19·50 N	121·08 E
	Balkan Mts., see Stara Planina		
187	Balkh (bälk) ... Afg.	36·48 N	66·50 E
172	Balkhash (bȧl-käsh') ... Sov. Un.	46·58 N	75·00 E
172	Balkhash, Ozero (L.) ... Sov. Un.	45·58 N	72·15 E
167	Balki (bäl'kĭ) ... Sov. Un.	47·22 N	34·56 E
161	Ballancourt (bä-äN-ko͞or') Fr. (Paris In.)	48·31 N	2·23 E
203	Ballarat (băl'ȧ-răt) ... Austl.	37·37 S	144·00 E
204	Ballard (L.) (băl'ȧrd) ... Austl.	29·15 S	120·45 E
154	Ballater (băl'ȧ-tẽr) ... Scot.	57·05 N	3·06 W
214	Ballé ... Mali.	15·20 N	8·35 W
220	Balleny Is. (băl'ĕ nê) ... Ant.	67·00 S	164·00 E
203	Ballina (băl-ĭ-nä') ... Austl.	28·50 S	153·35 E
154	Ballina ... Ire.	54·06 N	9·05 W
154	Ballinasloe (băl'ĭ-nȧ-slō') ... Ire.	53·20 N	8·09 W
118	Ballinger (băl'ĭn-jẽr) ... Tx.	31·45 N	99·58 W
105	Ballston Spa (bôls'tŭn spä') .. NY	43·05 N	73·50 W
159	Balmazújváros (bŏl'mŏz-ōō'y'vä'rôsh). Hung.	47·35 N	21·23 E
217	Balobe ... Zaire	0·05 N	28·00 E
203	Balonne (R.) (băl-ōn') ... Austl.	27·00 S	149·10 E
184	Bālotra ... India	25·56 N	72·12 E
203	Balranald (băl'-rȧn-ăld) ... Austl.	34·42 S	143·30 E
165	Balş (bälsh) ... Rom.	44·21 N	24·05 E
105	Balsam (L.) (bôl'sȧm) ... Can.	44·30 N	78·50 W
135	Balsas (bäl'säs) ... Braz.	7·09 S	46·04 W
122	Balsas (R.) ... Mex.	18·00 N	103·00 W
167	Balta (bȧl'tȧ) ... Sov. Un.	47·57 N	29·38 E
150	Baltic Sea (bôl'tĭk) ... Eur.	55·20 N	16·50 E
218	Baltīm (bȧl-tēm'). Egypt (Nile In.)	31·33 N	31·04 E
106	Baltimore (bôl'tĭ-môr) Md. (Baltimore In.)	39·20 N	76·38 W
157	Baltiysk (bäl-tēysk') ... Sov. Un.	54·40 N	19·55 E
124	Baluarte, Río del (rê'ō-dĕl-bä-lo͞o'r-tĕ). Mex.	23·09 N	105·42 W
187	Baluchistān (Reg.) (bȧ-lo͞o-chĭ-stän') ... Pak.	27·30 N	65·30 E
89	Balzac (bôl'zăk). Can. (Calgary In.)	51·10 N	114·01 W
215	Bama ... Nig.	11·30 N	13·41 E
214	Bamako (bä-mȧ-kō') ... Mali	12·39 N	8·00 W
197	Bambang (bäm-bäng') .. Phil. (In.)	16·24 N	121·08 E
211	Bambari (bäm-bȧ-rē) Cen. Afr. Rep.	5·44 N	20·40 E
158	Bamberg (bäm'bĕrgh) ... F.R.G.	49·53 N	10·52 E
121	Bamberg (băm'bûrg) ... SC	33·17 N	81·04 W
137	Bambuí (bä'm-bo͞o-ê) Braz. (Rio de Janeiro In.)	20·01 S	45·59 W
215	Bamenda ... Cam.	5·56 N	10·10 E
215	Bamingui (R.) ... Cen. Afr. Rep.	7·35 N	19·45 E
215	Bamingui Bangoran, Parc Nat'l. du (Natl. Park). Cen. Afr. Rep.	8·05 N	19·35 E
148	Bampton (bămp'tŭn) Eng. (London In.)	51·42 N	1·33 W
186	Bampūr (bŭm-po͞or') ... Iran	27·15 N	60·22 E
215	Bam Yanga, Ngao (Mts.) ... Cam.	8·20 N	14·40 E
197	Banahao, Mt. (bä-nä-hä'ô) Phil. (In.)	14·04 N	121·45 E
216	Banalia ... Zaire	1·33 N	25·20 E
214	Banamba ... Mali	13·33 N	7·27 W
137	Bananal (bä-nä-näl') Braz. (Rio de Janerio In.)	22·42 S	44·17 W
135	Bananal, Ilha do (I.) (ē'lä-dô-bä-nä-näl'). Braz.	12·09 S	50·27 W
184	Banās (R.) (băn-äs') ... India	25·20 N	74·51 E
211	Banās, Ra's (C.) ... Egypt	23·48 N	36·39 E
165	Banat (Reg.) (bä-nät') Rom.-Yugo.	45·35 N	21·05 E
105	Bancroft (băn'krŏft) ... Can.	45·05 N	77·55 W
	Bancroft, see Chililabombwe		
184	Bānda (bän'dă) ... India	25·36 N	80·21 E
197	Banda, Kepulauan (Is.) ... Indon.	4·40 S	129·56 E
196	Banda Aceh ... Indon.	5·10 N	95·10 E
203	Banda Banda, Mt. (băn'dȧ băn'dȧ). Austl.	31·09 S	152·15 E
197	Banda Laut (Banda Sea) .. Indon.	6·05 S	127·28 E
214	Bandama Blanc (R.) (bän-dä'mä) Ivory Coast	6·15 N	5·00 W
186	Bandar 'Abbās (Hbr.) (bän-där' ȧb-bäs'). Iran	27·04 N	56·22 E
186	Bandar-e Lengeh (Hbr.) ... Iran	26·44 N	54·47 E
186	Bandar-e Shāh ... Iran	37·05 N	54·08 E
186	Bandar-e-Shāhpūr (Hbr.) ... Iran	30·27 N	48·45 E
183	Bandar Maharani (bän-där' mä-hä-rä'nê) Mala. (Singapore In.)	2·02 N	102·34 E
196	Bandar Seri Begawan ... Bru.	5·00 N	114·59 E
137	Bandeira, Pico da (Pk.) (pē'ko͞o dā bän-dā'rä) Braz. (Rio de Janeiro In.)	20·27 S	41·47 W
115	Bandelier Natl. Mon. (băn-dĕ-lēr') NM	35·50 N	106·45 W
124	Banderas, Bahía de (B.) (bä-ē'ä dĕ bän-dĕ'räs). Mex.	20·38 N	105·35 W
171	Bandirma (bän-dĭr'mȧ) ... Tur.	40·25 N	27·50 E
110	Bandon (băn'dŭn) ... Or.	43·06 N	124·25 W
185	Bāndra (Neigh) India (Bombay In.)	19·04 N	72·49 E
216	Bandundu ... Zaire	3·18 S	17·20 E
196	Bandung ... Indon.	7·00 S	107·22 E
129	Banes (bä'näs) ... Cuba	21·00 N	75·45 W
93	Banff (bănf) ... Can.	51·10 N	115·34 W
154	Banff ... Scot.	57·39 N	2·37 W
93	Banff Natl. Park ... Can.	51·38 N	116·22 W
136	Bánfield (bȧ'n-fyĕ'ld) Arg. (Buenos Aires In.)	34·44 S	58·24 W
214	Banfora ... Upper Volta	10·38 N	4·46 W
185	Bangalore (băŋ'gȧ'lôr) ... India	13·03 N	77·39 E
211	Bangassou (bäN-gȧ-so͞o') Cen. Afr. Rep.	4·47 N	22·49 E
215	Bangé ... Cam.	3·01 N	15·07 E
197	Bangeta, Mt. ... Pap. N. Gui.	6·20 S	147·00 E
197	Banggai, Kepulauan (Is.) (bäng-gī'). Indon.	1·05 S	123·45 E
196	Banggi, Pulau (I.) ... Mala.	7·12 N	117·10 E
211	Banghāzī (bĕn-gä'zē) ... Libya	32·08 N	20·06 E
196	Bangka (I.) (bäŋ'kȧ) ... Indon.	2·24 S	106·55 E
196	Bangkalan (bäng-kȧ-län') .. Indon.	6·07 S	112·50 E
	Bangkok, see Krung Thep		
187	Bangladesh ... Asia	24·15 N	90·00 E
184	Bangong Co (L.) (bäŋ-gôŋ tswo) China	33·40 N	79·30 E
98	Bangor (băn'gẽr) ... Me.	44·47 N	68·47 W
104	Bangor ... Mi.	42·20 N	86·05 W
105	Bangor ... Pa.	40·55 N	75·10 W
154	Bangor (băŋ'ẽr) (băŋ'ôr) ... Wales	53·13 N	4·05 W
115	Bangs, Mt. (băngs) ... Az.	36·45 N	113·50 W
197	Bangued (bäŋ-gād') ... Phil. (In.)	17·36 N	120·38 E
215	Bangui (bäN-gē') ... Cen. Afr. Rep.	4·22 N	18·35 E
217	Bangweulu, L. (băng-wê-o͞o'lo͞o) Zambia	10·55 S	30·10 E
217	Bangweulu Swp. ... Zambia	11·25 S	30·10 E
218	Banhā ... Egypt (Nile In.)	30·24 N	31·11 E
129	Bani (bä'-nê) ... Dom. Rep.	18·15 N	70·25 W
197	Bani (bä'nē) ... Phil. (In.)	16·11 N	119·51 E
214	Bani (R.) ... Mali	13·07 N	6·15 W
129	Bánica (bä'-nē-kä) ... Dom. Rep.	19·00 N	71·35 W
218	Banī Mazār ... Egypt (Nile In.)	28·29 N	30·48 E
218	Banī Suwayf ... Egypt (Nile In.)	29·05 N	31·06 E
196	Banjak, Kepulauan (I.) ... Indon.	2·08 N	97·15 E
164	Banja Luka (bän-yä-lo͞o'kȧ) Yugo.	44·45 N	17·11 E
196	Banjarmasin (bän-jẽr-mä'sĕn) Indon.	3·18 S	114·32 E
190	Banjin (bän-jyĭn) ... China	32·23 N	120·14 E
214	Banjul (Bathurst) ... Gam.	13·28 N	16·39 W
213	Bankberg (Mts.) (băŋk'bûrg) S. Afr. (Natal In.)	32·18 S	25·15 E
112	Banks (bănks) .. Or. (Portland In.)	45·37 N	123·07 W
205	Banks (Is.) ... Austl.	10·10 S	143·08 E
202	Banks, C. ... Austl. (Sydney In.)	34·01 S	151·17 E
92	Banks I. ... Can.	53·25 N	130·10 W
75	Banks I. ... Can.	73·00 N	123·00 W
205	Banks Is. ... New Hebr.	13·38 S	168·23 E
203	Banks Str. ... Austl.	40·45 S	148·00 E
154	Bann (R.) (băn) ... N. Ire.	54·50 N	6·29 W
113	Banning (băn'ĭng) Ca. (Los Angeles In.)	33·56 N	116·53 W
121	Bannister (R.) (băn'ĭs-tẽr) ... Va.	36·45 N	79·17 W
202	Bannockburn Austl. (Melbourne In.)	38·03 S	144·11 E
184	Bannu ... Pak.	33·03 N	70·39 E
134	Baños (bä'-nyôs) ... Ec.	1·30 S	78·22 W
159	Banská Bystrica (bän'skä bê'strê-tzä). Czech.	48·46 N	19·10 E
165	Bansko (bän'skō) ... Bul.	41·51 N	23·33 E
148	Banstead (băn'stĕd) ... Eng. (In.)	51·18 N	0·09 W
197	Banton (bän-tōn') ... Phil. (In.)	12·54 N	121·55 E
154	Bantry (băn'trĭ) ... Ire.	51·39 N	9·30 W
154	Bantry B. ... Ire.	51·25 N	10·09 W
196	Banyuwangi (bän-jo͞o-wäŋ'gê) Indon.	8·15 S	114·15 E
211	Banzyville (bäN-zê-vēl') ... Zaire	4·14 N	21·11 E
192	Baocheng (bou-chŭŋ) ... China	33·15 N	106·58 E
190	Baodi (bou-dē) ... China	39·44 N	117·19 E
190	Baoding (bou-dĭŋ) ... China	38·52 N	115·31 E
192	Baoji (bou-jyē) ... China	34·10 N	106·58 E
188	Baoshan (bou-shän) ... China	25·14 N	99·03 E
191	Baoshan ... China (Shanghai In.)	31·25 N	121·29 E
192	Baotou (bou-tō) ... China	40·28 N	110·10 E
190	Baoying (bou-yĭŋ) ... China	33·14 N	119·20 E
213	Bapsfontein (băps-fōn-tān') S. Afr. (Johannesburg & Pretoria In.)	26·01 S	28·26 E
134	Baqueroncito (bä-kĕ-rô'n-sē-tô) Col. (In.)	3·18 N	74·40 W
167	Bar (bär) ... Sov. Un.	49·02 N	27·44 E
172	Barabinsk (bȧ'rȧ-bĭnsk) . Sov. Un.	55·18 N	78·00 E
109	Baraboo (bâr'ȧ-bo͞o) ... Wi.	43·29 N	89·44 W
129	Baracoa (bä-rä-kō'ä) ... Cuba	20·20 N	74·25 W
129	Baracoa ... Cuba (In.)	23·03 N	82·34 W
137	Baradeo (bä-rä-dĕ'ō) Arg. (Buenos Aires In.)	33·50 S	59·30 W
129	Baradères, Baie des (B.) (bä-rä-dâr'). Hai.	18·35 N	73·35 W
129	Barahona (bä-rä-ō'nä). Dom. Rep.	18·15 N	71·10 W
163	Barajas de Madrid (bä-rȧ'häs dā mä-drēdh') Sp. (Madrid In.)	40·28 N	3·35 W
184	Baranagar ... India (In.)	22·38 N	88·25 E
126	Baranco (bä-räŋ'kō) ... Belize	16·01 N	88·55 W
101	Baranof (I.) (bä-rä'nôf) ... Ak.	56·48 N	136·08 W
159	Baranovichi (bä'rä-nô-vē'chê) Sov. Un.	53·08 N	25·59 E
183	Baranpauh. Indon. (Singapore In.)	0·40 N	103·28 E
136	Barão de Juperanã (bȧ-rou'N-dĕ-zho͞o-pe-rȧ'nȧ) Braz. (Rio de Janeiro In.)	22·21 S	43·41 W
135	Barão de Melgaço (bä-rouN-dĕ-mĕl-gä'sō). Braz.	16·12 S	55·48 W
184	Bārāsat ... India (In.)	22·42 N	88·29 E
119	Barataria B. ... La.	29·13 N	89·90 W
134	Baraya (bä-rȧ'yä) ... Col. (In.)	3·10 N	75·04 W
137	Barbacena (bär-bä-sā'nȧ) Braz. (Rio de Janeiro In.)	21·15 S	43·46 W
134	Barbacoas (bär-bä-kō'äs) ... Col.	1·39 N	78·12 W
135	Barbacoas (bär-bä-kô'äs) Ven. (In.)	9·30 N	66·58 W
123	Barbados (bär-bā'dōz) ... N. A.	13·30 N	59·00 W
211	Barbar ... Sud.	18·11 N	34·00 E
163	Barbastro (bär-bäs'trō) ... Sp.	42·05 N	0·05 E
113	Barbeau (bȧr-bō') Mi. (Sault Ste. Marie In.)	46·17 N	84·16 W
107	Barberton (bär'bẽr-tŭn) Oh. (Cleveland In.)	41·01 N	81·37 W
212	Barberton ... S. Afr.	25·48 S	31·04 E
160	Barbezieux (bärb'zyû') ... Fr.	45·30 N	0·11 W
120	Barboorville (bär-bẽr-vĭl) ... Ky.	36·52 N	83·58 W
134	Barbosa (bär-bô'-sȧ) ... Col. (In.)	6·26 N	75·19 W
104	Barboursville (bär'bẽrs-vĭl) ... WV	38·20 N	82·20 W
123	Barbuda (I.) (bär-bo͞o'dȧ) Antigua	17·45 N	61·15 W
205	Barcaldine (bär'kôl-dīn) ... Austl.	23·33 S	145·17 E
163	Barcarena (bär-kä-rĕ'-nä) Port. (Lisbon In.)	38·29 N	9·17 W
162	Barcarrota (bär-kä-rō'tä) ... Sp.	38·31 N	6·50 W
164	Barcellona (bär-chĕl-lō'nä) ... It.	38·07 N	15·15 E
163	Barcelona (bär-thȧ-lō'nä) ... Sp.	41·25 N	2·08 E
135	Barcelona (bär-sä-lō'nä). Ven. (In.)	10·09 N	64·41 W
161	Barcelonnette (bär-sĕ-lô-nĕt') .. Fr.	44·24 N	6·42 E
134	Barcelos (bär-sĕ'lôs) ... Braz.	1·04 S	63·00 W
162	Barcélos (bär-thȧ'lōs) ... Port.	41·34 N	8·39 W
186	Bardar-e Pahlavī ... Iran	37·16 N	49·15 E
183	Bardawīl, Sabkhat al (B.) Egypt (Palestine In.)	31·20 N	33·24 E
159	Bardejov (bär'dyĕ-yôf) ... Czech.	49·18 N	21·18 E
218	Bardera (bär-dā'rä) Som. (Horn of Afr. In.)	2·13 N	42·24 E
154	Bardsey (I.) (bärd'sê) ... Wales	52·45 N	4·50 W
104	Bardstown (bärds'toun) ... Ky.	37·50 N	85·30 W
120	Bardwell (bärd'wĕl) ... Ky.	36·51 N	88·57 W
168	Barents Sea (bä'rĕnts) ... Sov. Un.	72·14 N	37·28 E
211	Barentu (bä-rĕn'to͞o) ... Eth.	15·06 N	37·39 E
160	Barfleur, Pte. de (Pt.) (bȧr-flûr'). Fr.	49·43 N	1·17 W
173	Barguzin (bär'go͞o-zĭn) ... Sov. Un.	53·44 N	109·28 E
98	Bar Harbor (bär här'bẽr) ... Me.	44·22 N	68·13 W
164	Bari (bä'rē) ... It.	41·08 N	16·53 E
134	Barinas (bä-rē'näs) ... Ven.	8·36 N	70·14 W
90	Baring, C. (bâr'ĭng) ... Can.	70·07 N	119·48 W
196	Barisan, Pegunungan (Mts.) (bä-rê-sän'). Indon.	2·38 S	101·45 E

ng-sing; ŋ-baŋk; N-nasalized n; nŏd; cŏmmit; ōld; ôbey; ôrder; fo͞od; fo͝ot; ou-out; s-soft; sh-dish; th-thin; pūre; ûnite; ûrn; stŭd; circŭs; ü-as "y" in study; '-indeterminate vowel.

Page	Name Pronunciation Region	Lat. °′	Long. °′
196	Barito (Strm.) (bä-rē'tō) Indon.	2·10 S	114·38 E
211	Barka (R.) Eth.	16·44 N	37·34 E
92	Barkley Sd. Can.	48·53 N	125·20 W
213	Barkly East (bärk'lē ēst) S. Afr. (Natal In.)	30·58 S	27·37 E
204	Barkly Tableland (Plat.) (bär'klē) Austl.	18·15 S	137·05 E
188	Barkol (bär-kûl) China	43·43 N	92·50 E
160	Bar-le-Duc (bär-lē-dük') Fr.	48·47 N	5·05 E
204	Barlee (L.) (bär-lē') Austl.	29·45 S	119·00 E
164	Barletta (bär-lĕt'tä) It.	41·19 N	16·20 E
149	Barmstedt (bärm'shtĕt) F.R.G. (Hamburg In.)	53·47 N	9·46 E
172	Barnaul (bär-nä-ōōl') Sov. Un.	53·18 N	83·23 E
105	Barnesboro (bärnz'bēr-ô) Pa.	40·45 N	78·50 W
120	Barnesville (bärnz'vĭl) Ga.	33·03 N	84·10 W
108	Barnesville Mn.	46·38 N	96·25 W
104	Barnesville Oh.	39·55 N	81·10 W
105	Barnet (bär'nĕt) Vt.	44·20 N	72·00 W
148	Barnetby le Wold (bär'nĕt-bī) Eng.	53·34 N	0·26 W
128	Barnett Hbr. Ba.	25·40 N	79·20 W
117	Barnsdall (bärnz'dôl) Ok.	36·38 N	96·14 W
148	Barnsley (bärnz'lĭ) Eng.	53·33 N	1·29 W
154	Barnstaple (bärn'stā-p'l) Eng.	51·06 N	4·05 W
121	Barnwell (bärn'wĕl) SC	33·14 N	81·23 W
215	Baro (bä'rō) Nig.	8·37 N	6·25 E
211	Bāro (R.) Eth.	7·40 N	34·17 E
184	Baroda (bä-rō'dä) India	22·21 N	73·12 E
216	Barotse Pln. Zambia	15·50 S	22·55 E
211	Barqah (Cyrenaica) (Prov.) Libya	31·09 N	21·45 E
134	Barquisimeto (bär-kē-sē-mā'tō) Ven.	10·04 N	69·16 W
135	Barra (bär'rä) Braz.	11·04 S	43·11 W
203	Barraba Austl.	30·22 S	150·36 E
135	Barra do Corda (bär'rä dŏŏ cōr-dä) Braz.	5·33 S	45·13 W
154	Barra Is. (băr'ră) Scot.	57·00 N	7·30 W
137	Barra Mansa (bär'rä män'sä) Braz. (Rio de Janeiro In.)	22·35 S	44·09 W
134	Barrancabermeja (bär-räŋ'kä-bēr-mā'hä) Col.	7·06 N	73·49 W
134	Barranquilla (bär-rän-kēl'yä) Col.	10·57 N	75·00 W
135	Barras (bá'r-räs) Braz.	4·13 S	42·14 W
105	Barre (băr'ê) Vt.	44·15 N	72·30 W
137	Barre do Piraí (bár'rĕ-dô-pē'rä-ē') Braz. (Rio de Janeiro In.)	22·30 S	43·49 W
135	Barreiras (bär-rā'räs) Braz.	12·13 S	44·59 W
163	Barreiro (bär-rĕ'ê-rōō) Port. (Lisbon In.)	38·39 N	9·05 W
203	Barren, C. (băr'ĕn) Austl.	40·20 S	149·00 E
213	Barren, Îles (Is.) Mad.	18·18 S	43·57 E
120	Barren (R.) Ky.	37·00 N	86·20 W
135	Barretos (bär-rā'tōs) Braz.	20·40 S	48·36 W
93	Barrhead (băr-hĕd) (bär'ĭd) Can.	54·08 N	114·24 W
105	Barrie (băr'ĭ) Can.	44·25 N	79·45 W
89	Barrington (bă-rĕng-tŏn) Can. (Montreal In.)	45·07 N	73·35 W
107	Barrington Il. (Chicago In.)	42·09 N	88·08 W
106	Barrington RI (Providence In.)	41·44 N	71·16 W
203	Barrington Tops (Mtn.) Austl.	32·00 S	151·25 E
113	Bar River (bär) Can. (Sault Ste. Marie In.)	46·27 N	84·02 W
109	Barron (băr'ŭn) Wi.	45·24 N	91·51 W
101	Barrow (băr'ō) Ak.	71·20 N	156·00 W
154	Barrow Eng.	54·10 N	3·15 W
204	Barrow (I.) Austl.	20·50 S	115·00 E
204	Barrow Creek Austl.	21·23 S	133·55 E
101	Barrow Pt. Ak.	71·20 N	156·00 W
154	Barrow R. (bá-rá) Ire.	52·35 N	7·05 W
162	Barruelo de Santullán (bär-rōō-ā-lō dā sän-tōō-lyän') Sp.	42·55 N	4·19 W
114	Barstow (bär'stō) Ca.	34·53 N	117·03 W
106	Barstow Md. (Baltimore In.)	38·32 N	76·37 W
158	Barth (bärt) G.D.R.	54·20 N	12·43 E
117	Bartholomew Bay (bär-thŏl'ô-mū bī-ōō') Ar.	33·53 N	91·45 W
98	Barthurst (băr-thŭrst') Can.	47·38 N	65·40 W
135	Bartica (bär'tĭ-kȧ) Guy.	6·23 N	58·32 W
171	Bartin (bär'tĭn) Tur.	41·35 N	32·12 E
205	Bartle Frere, Mt. (bärt''l frēr') Austl.	17·30 S	145·46 E
117	Bartlesville (bär'tlz-vĭl) Ok.	36·44 N	95·58 W
107	Bartlett (bärt'lĕt) Il. (Chicago In.)	41·59 N	88·11 W
119	Bartlett Tx.	30·48 N	97·25 W
105	Barton (bär'tŭn) Vt.	44·45 N	72·05 W
148	Barton-upon-Humber (bär'tŭn-ŭp'ŏn-hŭm'bēr) Eng.	53·41 N	0·26 W
159	Bartoszyce (bär-tô-shĭ'tsȧ) Pol.	54·15 N	20·50 E
121	Bartow (bär'tō) Fl. (In.)	27·51 N	81·50 W
167	Barvenkovo (bär'vĕn-kô'vô) Sov. Un.	48·55 N	36·59 E
203	Barwon (R.) (bär'wŭn) Austl.	29·45 S	148·25 E
202	Barwon Heads Austl. (Melbourne In.)	38·17 S	144·29 E
158	Barycz R. (bä'rĭch) Pol.	51·30 N	16·38 E
211	Basankusu (bä-sän-kōō'sōō) Zaire	1·14 N	19·45 E
149	Basbeck (bäs'bĕk) F.R.G. (Hamburg In.)	53·40 N	9·11 E
149	Basdahl (bäs'däl) F.R.G. (Hamburg In.)	53·27 N	9·00 E
113	Basehor (bās'hôr) Ks. (Kansas City In.)	39·08 N	94·55 W
158	Basel (bä'z'l) Switz.	47·32 N	7·35 E
213	Bashee (R.) (bă-shē') S. Afr. (Natal In.)	31·47 S	28·25 E
193	Bashi Chan (băsh'ê) Phil.	21·20 N	120·22 E
170	Bashkir (A.S.S.R.) (bȧsh-kēr') Sov. Un.	54·12 N	57·15 E
167	Bashtanka (bȧsh-tän'kȧ) Sov. Un.	47·32 N	32·31 E
196	Basilan I. Phil.	6·37 N	122·07 E
164	Basilicata (Reg.) (bä-zē-lê-kä'tä) It.	40·30 N	15·55 E
111	Basin (bā'sĭn) Wy.	44·22 N	108·02 W
148	Basingstoke (bā'zĭng-stōk) Eng. (London In.)	51·14 N	1·06 W
164	Baška (bäsh'ka) Yugo.	44·58 N	14·44 E
171	Baskale (bäsh-kä'lĕ) Tur.	38·10 N	44·00 E
97	Baskatong Res. Can.	46·50 N	75·50 W
171	Baskunchak (L.) Sov. Un.	48·20 N	46·40 E
211	Basoko (bȧ-sō'kō) Zaire	0·52 N	23·50 E
93	Bassano (bäs-sän'ō) Can.	50·47 N	112·28 W
164	Bassano It.	45·46 N	11·44 E
214	Bassari Togo	9·15 N	0·47 E
213	Bassas da India (I.) (bäs'säs dä ēn'dê-ȧ) Afr.	21·23 S	39·42 E
196	Bassein (bŭ-sēn') Bur.	16·46 N	94·47 E
127	Basse Terre (bás' târ') Guad. (In.)	16·00 N	61·43 W
127	Basseterre St. Kitts-Nevis-Anguilla (In.)	17·20 N	62·42 W
127	Basse Terre I. Guad. (In.)	16·10 N	62·14 W
121	Bassett (băs'sĕt) Va.	36·45 N	81·58 W
104	Bass Is. (băs) Oh.	41·40 N	82·50 W
203	Bass Str. Austl.	39·40 S	145·40 E
109	Basswood (L.) (băs'wŏŏd) Can.-Mn.	48·10 N	91·36 W
156	Båstad (bô'stät) Swe.	56·26 N	12·46 E
164	Bastia (bäs'tē-ä) Fr.	42·43 N	9·27 E
155	Bastogne (bäs-tôn'y') Bel.	50·02 N	5·45 E
119	Bastrop (băs'trŭp) La.	32·47 N	91·55 W
119	Bastrop Tx.	30·08 N	97·18 W
119	Bastrop Bayou Tx. (In.)	29·07 N	95·22 W
216	Bata (bä'tä) Equat. Gui.	1·51 N	9·45 E
128	Batabanó (bä-tä-bä-nō') Cuba	22·45 N	82·20 W
128	Batabano, Golfo, de (G.) (gôl-fô-dĕ-bä-tä-bá'nô) Cuba	22·10 N	83·05 W
184	Batāla India	31·54 N	75·18 E
174	Bataly (bȧ-tä'lĭ) Sov. Un. (Urals In.)	52·51 N	62·03 E
183	Batam I. (bä-täm') Indon. (Singapore In.)	1·03 N	104·00 E
193	Batan Is. (bä-tän') Phil.	20·58 N	122·20 E
188	Batang (bä-täŋ) China	30·08 N	99·00 E
193	Batangan, C. Viet.	15·18 N	109·10 E
197	Batangas (bä-tän'gäs) Phil. (In.)	13·45 N	121·04 E
159	Bátaszék (bä'tȧ-sĕk) Hung.	46·07 N	18·40 E
107	Batavia (bȧ-tā'vĭ-ȧ) Il. (Chicago In.)	41·51 N	88·18 W
105	Batavia NY	43·00 N	78·15 W
107	Batavia Oh. (Cincinnati In.)	39·05 N	84·10 W
167	Bataysk (bȧ-tĭsk') Sov. Un.	47·08 N	39·44 E
196	Bătdâmbâng (bät-tám-bäng') Kamp.	13·14 N	103·15 E
121	Batesburg (bāts'bûrg) SC	33·53 N	81·34 W
117	Batesville (bāts'vĭl) Ar.	35·46 N	91·39 W
104	Batesville In.	39·15 N	85·15 W
120	Batesville Ms.	34·17 N	89·55 W
166	Batetska (bȧ-tĕ'tskȧ) Sov. Un.	58·36 N	30·21 E
98	Bath (bȧth) Can.	46·31 N	67·36 W
154	Bath Eng.	51·24 N	2·20 W
98	Bath Me.	43·54 N	69·50 W
105	Bath NY	42·25 N	77·20 W
107	Bath Oh. (Cleveland In.)	41·11 N	81·38 W
127	Bathsheba Barb. (In.)	13·13 N	60·30 W
205	Bathurst (bȧth'ŭrst) Aust.	33·28 S	149·30 E
213	Bathurst (băt-hûrst) S. Afr. (Natal In.)	33·26 S	26·53 E
	Bathurst, see Banjul		
101	Bathurst, C. (bȧth'ŭrst) Can.	70·33 N	127·55 W
204	Bathurst (I.) Austl.	11·19 S	130·13 E
90	Bathurst Inlet Can.	68·10 N	108·00 W
214	Batia Benin	10·54 N	1·29 E
197	Batian (I.) Indon.	1·07 S	127·52 E
186	Bāţlāq-E Gāvkhūnī (L.) Iran	31·40 N	52·48 E
148	Batley (băt'lĭ) Eng.	53·43 N	1·37 W
210	Batna (bät'nä) Alg.	35·41 N	6·12 E
119	Baton Rouge (băt'ŭn rōōzh') La.	30·28 N	91·10 W
215	Batouri Cam.	4·26 N	14·22 E
185	Batticaloa Sri Lanka	8·40 N	81·10 E
93	Battle (R.) Can.	52·20 N	111·59 W
94	Battle (R.) Can.	53·05 N	109·40 W
104	Battle Creek (băt''l krēk') Mi.	42·20 N	85·15 W
112	Battle Ground (băt''l ground) Wa. (Portland In.)	45·47 N	122·32 W
91	Battle Harbour (băt''l här'bēr) Can.	52·17 N	55·33 W
110	Battle Mountain Nv.	40·40 N	116·56 W
159	Battonya (bät-tô'nyä) Hung.	46·17 N	21·00 E
196	Batu Kepulauan (I.) (bä'tōō) Indon.	0·10 S	99·55 E
171	Batumi (bŭ-tōō'mē) Sov. Un.	41·40 N	41·30 E
183	Batu Pahat Mala. (Singapore In.)	1·51 N	102·56 E
183	Batupanjang Indon. (Singapore In.)	1·42 N	101·35 E
135	Baturité (bä-tōō-rê-tā') Braz.	4·16 S	38·47 W
197	Bauang (bä'wäng) Phil. (In.)	16·31 N	120·19 E
215	Bauchi (bȧ-ōō'chē) Nig.	10·19 N	9·50 E
212	Baudouinville (bō-dwăN-vēl') Zaire	7·12 S	29·39 E
99	Bauld, C. Can.	51·38 N	55·25 W
184	Bāuria India (In.)	22·29 N	88·08 E
135	Bauru (bou-rōō') Braz.	22·21 S	48·57 W
157	Bauska (bou'skȧ) Sov. Un.	56·24 N	24·12 E
129	Bauta (bá'ōō-tä) Cuba (In.)	22·14 N	82·33 W
158	Bautzen (bout'sĕn) G.D.R.	51·11 N	14·27 E
	Bavaria (State), see Bayern		
203	Baw Baw, Mt. (bȧ-bȧ) Austl.	37·50 S	146·17 E
196	Bawean, Pulau (I.) (bá'vē-än) Indon.	5·50 S	112·40 E
148	Bawtry (bô'trĭ) Eng.	53·26 N	1·01 W
121	Baxley (băks'lĭ) Ga.	31·47 N	82·22 W
202	Baxter (băks'tēr) Austl. (Melbourne In.)	38·12 S	145·10 E
117	Baxter Springs (băks'tēr sprĭngs') Ks.	37·01 N	94·44 W
129	Bayaguana (bä-yä-gwä'nä) Dom. Rep.	18·45 N	69·40 W
152	Bay al Kabīr Wadi (R.) Libya	29·52 N	14·28 E
197	Bayambang (bä-yäm-bäng') Phil. (In.)	15·50 N	120·26 E
128	Bayamo (bä-yä'mō) Cuba	20·25 N	76·35 W
123	Bayamón P. R. (Puerto Rico In.)	18·27 N	66·13 W
192	Bayan (bä-yän) China	46·00 N	127·20 E
172	Bayan-Aul (bä'yän-oul') Sov. Un.	50·43 N	75·37 E
108	Bayard (bā'ērd) Ne.	41·45 N	103·20 W
105	Bayard WV	39·15 N	79·20 W
171	Bayburt (bä'ĭ-bŏŏrt) Tur.	40·15 N	40·10 E
104	Bay City (bā) Mi.	43·35 N	83·55 W
119	Bay City Tx.	28·59 N	95·58 W
188	Baydarag Gol (R.) Mong.	46·09 N	98·52 E
170	Baydaratskaya Guba (B.) Sov. Un.	69·20 N	66·10 E
99	Bay de Verde Can.	48·05 N	52·54 W
158	Bayern (Bavaria) (State) (bī'ērn) (bȧ-vâ-rĭ-ȧ) F.R.G.	49·00 N	11·16 E
160	Bayeux (bȧ-yû') Fr.	49·19 N	0·41 W
109	Bayfield (bā'fēld) Wi.	46·48 N	90·51 W
173	Baykal, Ozero (Baikal, L.) (bī'käl') (bī'kôl) Sov. Un.	53·00 N	109·28 E
173	Baykals'kiy Khrebet (Baikal Mts.) Sov. Un.	53·30 N	102·00 E
172	Baykit (bī-kēt') Sov. Un.	61·43 N	96·39 E
172	Baykonur (bī-kô-nōōr') Sov. Un.	47·46 N	66·11 E
174	Baymak (bȧy'mäk) Sov. Un. (Urals In.)	52·35 N	58·21 E
113	Bay Mills (bā mĭlls) Mi. (Sault Ste. Marie In.)	46·27 N	84·36 W
109	Bay Mills Ind. Res. Mi.	46·19 N	85·03 W
120	Bay Minette (bā'mĭn-ĕt') Al.	30·52 N	87·44 W
197	Bayombong (bä-yôm-bŏng') Phil. (In.)	16·28 N	121·09 E
160	Bayonne (bȧ-yŏn') Fr.	43·28 N	1·30 W
106	Bayonne (bā-yōn') NJ (New York In.)	40·40 N	74·07 W
119	Bayou Bodcau Res. (bī'yōō bŏd'kō) La.	32·49 N	93·22 W
113	Bayport (bā'pōrt) Mn. (Minneapolis, St. Paul In.)	45·02 N	92·46 W
165	Bayramic Tur.	39·48 N	26·35 E
158	Bayreuth (bī-roit') F.R.G.	49·56 N	11·35 E
99	Bay Roberts (bā rŏb'ērts) Can.	47·36 N	53·16 W
	Bayrūt, see Beirut		
105	Bays, L. of (bās) Can.	45·15 N	79·00 W
120	Bay St. Louis (bā' sȧnt lōō'ĭs) Ms.	30·19 N	89·20 W
106	Bay Shore (bā' shôr) NY (New York In.)	40·44 N	73·15 W
183	Bayt Lahm (Bethlehem) (bĕth'lê-hĕm) Jordan (Palestine In.)	31·42 N	35·13 E
119	Baytown (bā'town) Tx. (In.)	29·44 N	95·01 W
106	Bayview (bā'vū) Al. (Birmingham In.)	33·34 N	86·59 W
112	Bayview Wa. (Seattle In.)	48·29 N	122·28 W
107	Bay Village (bā) Oh. (Cleveland In.)	41·29 N	81·56 W
162	Baza (bä'thä) Sp.	37·29 N	2·46 W
171	Bazar-Dyuzi (Mt.) (bä'zár-dyōōz'ĭ) Sov. Un.	41·20 N	47·40 E
212	Bazaruto, Ilha do (I.) (bä-zä-rōō'tō) Moz.	21·42 S	36·10 E
162	Baztán (bäth-tän') Sp.	43·12 N	1·30 W
108	Beach (bēch) ND	46·55 N	104·00 W
155	Beachy Head (bēchē hĕd) Eng.	50·40 N	0·25 E
105	Beacon (bē'kŭn) NY	41·30 N	73·55 W
89	Beaconsfield (bē'kŭnz-fēld) Can. (Montreal In.)	45·26 N	73·51 W
106	Beafort Mtn. (bē'fōrt) NJ (New York In.)	41·08 N	74·23 W
118	Beals Cr. (bēls) Tx.	32·10 N	101·14 W
89	Bear Brook (R.) Can. (Ottawa In.)	45·24 N	75·15 W
111	Bear Creek (bâr krēk) Mt.	45·11 N	109·07 W
120	Bear Cr. (bâr) Al.	34·27 N	88·00 W
113	Bear Cr. Tx. (Dallas, Fort Worth In.)	32·56 N	97·09 W
117	Beardstown (bērds'toun) Il.	40·01 N	90·26 W
112	Bearhead Mtn. (bâr'hĕd) Wa. (Seattle In.)	47·01 N	121·49 W
111	Bear (L.) Id.-Ut.	41·56 N	111·10 W
95	Bear L. Can.	55·08 N	96·00 W
111	Bear R. Id.	42·17 N	111·42 W
113	Bear R. Ut. (Salt Lake City In.)	41·28 N	112·10 W
162	Beas de Segura (bā'äs dā sā-gōō'rä) Sp.	38·16 N	2·53 W
129	Beata (I.) (bĕ-ä'tä) Dom. Rep.	17·40 N	71·40 W
129	Beata, Cabo (C.) (ká'bô-bĕ-ä'tä) Dom. Rep.	17·40 N	71·20 W
117	Beatrice (bē'ȧ-trĭs) Ne.	40·16 N	96·45 W
114	Beatty (bēt'ê) Nv.	36·58 N	116·48 W
104	Beattyville (bēt'ê-vĭl) Ky.	37·35 N	83·40 W
160	Beaucaire (bō-kâr') Fr.	43·49 N	4·37 E
161	Beaucourt (bō-kōōr') Fr.	47·30 N	6·54 E
121	Beaufort (bō'fērt) NC	34·43 N	76·40 W
121	Beaufort SC	32·25 N	80·40 W
101	Beaufort Sea Ak.	70·30 N	138·40 W
212	Beaufort West S. Afr.	32·20 S	22·45 E
89	Beauharnois (bō-är-nwä') Can. (Montreal In.)	45·23 N	73·52 W
113	Beaumont (bō'mŏnt) Ca. (Los Angeles In.)	33·57 N	116·57 W
89	Beaumont Can. (Edmonton In.)	53·22 N	113·18 W
89	Beaumont Can. (Quebec In.)	46·50 N	71·01 W
119	Beaumont Tx.	30·05 N	94·06 W
160	Beaune (bōn) Fr.	47·02 N	4·49 E

ăt; finăl; rāte; senâte; ärm; ȧsk; sofȧ; fâre; ch-choose; dh-as th in other; bē; ėvent; bĕt; recĕnt; cratēr; g-go; gh-guttural g; bĭt; ĭ-short neutral; rīde; K-guttural k as ch in German ich;

Page	Name Pronunciation Region	Lat. °'	Long. °'
89	Beauport (bō-pôr') Can. (Quebec In.)	46·52 N	71·11 W
89	Beaupré (bō-prā') Can. (Quebec In.)	47·03 N	70·53 W
95	Beauséjour..........Can.	50·04 N	96·33 W
160	Beauvais (bō-vě')..........Fr.	49·25 N	2·05 E
116	Beaver (bē'vẽr)..........Ok.	36·46 N	100·31 W
107	Beaver.......Pa. (Pittsburgh In.)	40·42 N	80·18 W
115	Beaver..........Ut.	38·15 N	112·40 W
104	Beaver (I.)..........Mi.	45·40 N	85·30 W
94	Beaver (R.)..........Can.	54·20 N	111·10 W
116	Beaver City..........Nb.	40·08 N	99·52 W
116	Beaver Cr..........Co.	39·42 N	103·37 W
116	Beaver Cr..........Ks.	39·44 N	101·05 W
108	Beaver Cr..........Mt.	46·45 N	104·18 W
108	Beaver Cr..........Wy.	43·46 N	104·25 W
109	Beaver Dam..........Wi.	43·29 N	88·50 W
111	Beaverhead Mts. (bē'vẽr-hĕd).Mt.	44·33 N	112·59 W
111	Beaverhead R..........Mt.	45·25 N	112·35 W
104	Beaver Ind. Res..........Mi.	45·40 N	85·30 W
112	Beaverton (bē'vẽr-tŭn) Or. (Portland In.)	45·29 N	122·49 W
134	Bebará' (bĕ-bä-rá')......Col. (In.)	6·07 N	76·39 W
148	Bebington (bē'bĭng-tŭn)......Eng.	53·20 N	2·59 W
165	Bečej (bĕ'chā)..........Yugo.	45·36 N	20·03 E
162	Becerreá (bā-thā'rē-ä)........Sp.	42·49 N	7·12 W
210	Béchar..........Alg.	31·39 N	2·14 W
101	Becharof (L.) (běk-ȧ-rôf)......Ak.	57·58 N	156·58 W
112	Becher B. (bēch'ẽr) Can. (Seattle In.)	48·18 N	123·37 W
104	Beckley (běk'lĭ)..........WV	37·40 N	81·15 W
160	Bédarieux (bā-dȧ-ryû')........Fr.	43·36 N	3·11 E
89	Beddington Cr. (bĕd'ĕng tŭn) Can. (Calgary In.)	51·14 N	114·13 W
105	Bedford (bĕd'fẽrd)..........Can.	45·10 N	73·00 W
154	Bedford..........Eng.	52·10 N	0·25 W
104	Bedford..........In.	38·50 N	86·30 W
109	Bedford..........Ia.	40·40 N	94·41 W
99	Bedford..........Ma. (In.)	42·30 N	71·17 W
106	Bedford......NY (New York In.)	41·12 N	73·38 W
107	Bedford......Oh. (Cleveland In.)	41·23 N	81·32 W
105	Bedford..........Pa.	40·05 N	78·20 W
213	Bedford.......S. Afr. (Natal In.)	32·43 S	26·19 E
121	Bedford..........Va.	37·19 N	79·27 W
106	Bedford Hills NY (New York In.)	41·14 N	73·41 W
148	Bedworth (bĕd'wẽrth)........Eng.	52·29 N	1·28 W
159	Bedzin (băN-jēn')..........Pol.	50·19 N	19·10 E
117	Beebe (bē'bē)..........Ar.	35·04 N	91·54 W
107	Beecher (bē'chŭr).Il. (Chicago In.)	41·20 N	87·38 W
112	Beechey Hd. (bē'chĭ hĕd) Can. (Seattle In.)	48·19 N	123·40 W
107	Beech Grove (bēch grōv) In. (Indianapolis In.)	39·43 N	86·05 W
203	Beecroft Hd. (bē'krŭft).....Austl.	35·03 S	151·15 E
149	Beelitz (bē'lētz) G.D.R. (Berlin In.)	52·14 N	12·59 E
183	Be'er Sheva' (bēr-shē'bȧ) Isr. (Palestine In.)	31·15 N	34·48 E
183	Be'er Sheva' (R.) Isr. (Palestine In.)	31·23 N	34·30 E
218	Beestekraal....S. Afr. (Johannesburg & Pretoria In.)	25·22 S	27·34 E
148	Beeston (bēs't'n)..........Eng.	52·55 N	1·11 W
149	Beetz R. (bětz) G.D.R. (Berlin In.)	52·28 N	12·37 E
119	Beeville (bē'vĭl)..........Tx.	28·24 N	97·44 W
203	Bega (bā'gȧ)..........Austl.	36·50 S	149·49 E
117	Beggs (běgz)..........Ok.	35·46 N	96·06 W
160	Bégles (bě'gl')..........Fr.	44·47 N	0·34 W
214	Begoro..........Ghana	6·23 N	0·23 W
184	Behala.......India (Calcutta In.)	22·31 N	88·19 E
92	Behm Can..........Ak.	55·41 N	131·35 W
191	Bei (R.) (bā)..China (Canton In.)	22·54 N	113·08 E
192	Bei'an (bā-ān)..........China	48·05 N	126·26 E
1	Beicai (bā-tsī) China (Shanghai In.)	31·12 N	121·33 E
190	Beifei (R.) (bā-fā)........China	33·14 N	117·03 E
193	Beihai (bā-hī)..........China	21·30 N	109·10 E
190	Beihuangcheng Dao (I.) (bā-hûāŋ-chŭŋ dou).China	38·23 N	120·55 E
192	Beijing (Peking) (bā-jyĭŋ) China (In.)	39·55 N	116·23 E
190	Beijing Shi (Mun.) (bā-jyĭŋ shr) China	40·07 N	116·00 E
212	Beira (bā'rȧ)..........Moz.	19·46 S	34·58 E
162	Beira (Reg.) (bĕ'y-rä)........Port.	40·38 N	8·00 W
183	Beirut (Bayrūt) (bā-rōōt') Leb. (Palestine In.)	33·53 N	35·30 E
162	Beja (bā'zhä)..........Port.	38·03 N	7·53 W
151	Béja..........Tun.	36·52 N	9·20 E
210	Bejaïa (Bougie)..........Alg.	36·46 N	5·00 E
162	Bejar..........Sp.	40·25 N	5·43 W
186	Bejestān..........Iran	34·30 N	58·22 E
129	Bejucal (bā-hōō-käl')..Cuba (In.)	22·08 N	82·23 W
127	Bejuco (bĕ-KOO'kō)........Pan.	8·37 N	79·54 W
159	Békés (bā'kāsh)..........Hung.	46·45 N	21·08 E
159	Békéscsaba (bā'kāsh-chô'bô) Hung.	46·39 N	21·06 E
189	Beketova (běk'e-to'vȧ)..Sov. Un.	53·23 N	125·21 E
165	Bela Crkva (bě'lä tsěrk'vä).Yugo.	44·53 N	21·25 E
162	Belalcázar (bāl-āl-kä'thär)....Sp.	38·35 N	5·12 W
163	Belas (bě'-läs).Port. (Lisbon In.)	38·47 N	9·16 W
165	Bela-Slatina (byä'la slä'tēnä) Bul.	43·26 N	23·56 E
135	Bela Vista de Goia's........Braz.	16·57 S	48·47 W
196	Belawan (bå-lä'wån)........Indon.	3·43 N	98·43 E
170	Belaya (R.) (byě'lĭ-yȧ).Sov. Un.	52·30 N	56·15 E
167	Belaya Tserkov' (byě'lĭ-yȧ tsěr'kôf).Sov. Un.	49·48 N	30·09 E
91	Belcher Is. (běl'chẽr)........Can.	56·20 N	80·40 W
104	Belding (běl'dĭng)..........Mi.	43·05 N	85·25 W
170	Belebey (byě'lě-bā'ĭ).....Sov. Un.	54·00 N	54·10 E
135	Belém (Pará) (bå-lĕN') (pä-rä') Braz.	1·18 S	48·27 W
115	Belen (bĕ-lån')..........NM	34·40 N	106·45 W
136	Belén (bā-lān')..........Par.	23·30 S	57·09 W
205	Bélep, Îsles (Is.)..........N. Cal.	19·30 S	160·32 E
166	Belëv (byěl'yěf)........Sov. Un.	53·49 N	36·06 E
112	Belfair (běl'far) Wa. (Seattle In.)	47·27 N	122·50 W
98	Belfast (běl'fȧst)..........Me.	44·25 N	69·01 W
154	Belfast..........N. Ire.	54·36 N	5·45 W
154	Belfast, Lough (B.) (lŏk běl'fȧst) Ire.	54·45 N	6·00 W
161	Belfort (bā-fôr')..........Fr.	47·40 N	7·50 E
185	Belgaum..........India	15·57 N	74·32 E
146	Belgium (běl'jĭ-ŭm)........Eur.	51·00 N	2·52 E
167	Belgorod (byěl'gŭ-rŭt)...Sov. Un.	50·36 N	36·32 E
167	Belgorod (Oblast)........Sov. Un.	50·40 N	36·42 E
167	Belgorod Dnestrovskiy (byěl'gŭ-rŭd nyěs-trôf'skê) Sov. Un.	46·09 N	30·19 E
	Belgrade, see Beograd		
121	Belhaven (běl'hā-věn)........NC	35·33 N	76·37 W
105	Belington (běl'ĭng-tŭn)........WV	39·00 N	79·55 W
165	Beli Timok (R.) (bě'lē tē'môk) Yugo.	43·35 N	22·13 E
196	Belitung (I.)..........Indon.	3·30 S	107·30 E
126	Belize (bě-lēz')........Belize (In.)	17·31 N	88·10 W
122	Belize..........N.A.	17·00 N	88·40 W
126	Belize R..........Belize (In.)	17·16 N	88·56 W
174	Bel'kovo (byěl'kô-vô) Sov. Un. (Moscow In.)	56·15 N	38·49 E
173	Bel'kovskiy (I.) (byěl-kôf'skĭ) Sov. Un.	75·52 N	133·00 E
99	Bell (I.) (běl)..........Can.	50·45 N	55·35 W
97	Bell (R.)..........Can.	49·25 N	77·15 W
92	Bella Bella..........Can.	52·10 N	128·07 W
92	Bella Coola..........Can.	52·22 N	126·46 W
104	Bellaire (běl-âr')..........Oh.	40·00 N	80·45 W
119	Bellaire..........Tx. (In.)	29·43 N	95·28 W
185	Bellary (běl-lä'rê)..........India	15·15 N	76·56 E
136	Bella Union (bě'l-yȧ-ōō-nyô'n).Ur.	30·18 S	57·26 W
136	Bella Vista (bā'lyȧ vēs'tȧ)....Arg.	27·07 S	65·14 W
136	Bella Vista..........Arg.	28·35 S	58·53 W
136	Bella Vista..........Arg. (In.)	34·18 S	58·41 W
135	Bella Vista..........Braz.	22·16 S	56·14 W
129	Belle-Anse..........Hai	18·15 N	72·00 W
99	Belle B. (běl)..........Can.	47·35 N	55·15 W
106	Belle Chasse (běl shäs') La. (New Orleans In.)	29·52 N	90·00 W
104	Bellefontaine (běl-fŏn'tăn)....Oh.	40·25 N	83·50 W
113	Bellefontaine Neighbors......Mo. (St. Louis In.)	38·46 N	90·13 W
108	Belle Fourche (běl' fōōrsh')...SD	44·28 N	103·50 W
108	Belle Fourche (R.)..........Wy.	44·29 N	104·40 W
108	Belle Fourche Res..........SD	44·51 N	103·44 W
161	Bellegarde-sur-Valserine (běl-gärd'sür-väl-så-rēn').Fr.	46·06 N	5·50 E
121	Belle Glade (běl glād)....Fl. (In.)	26·39 N	80·37 W
160	Belle Île (I.) (běl ēl')........Fr.	47·15 N	3·30 W
99	Belle Isle, Str. of..........Can.	51·35 N	56·30 W
106	Belle Mead (běl mēd) NJ (New York In.)	40·28 N	74·40 W
99	Belleoram..........Can.	47·31 N	55·25 W
109	Belle Plaine (běl plān')........Ia.	41·52 N	92·19 W
107	Belle Vernon (běl vûr'nŭn) Pa. (Pittsburgh In.)	40·08 N	79·52 W
105	Belleville (běl'vĭl)..........Can.	44·15 N	77·25 W
113	Belleville.......Il. (St. Louis In.)	38·31 N	89·59 W
117	Belleville..........Ks.	39·49 N	97·37 W
107	Belleville..........Mi. (Detroit In.)	42·12 N	83·29 W
106	Belleville.....NJ (New York In.)	40·47 N	74·09 W
109	Bellevue (běl'vū)..........Ia.	42·14 N	90·26 W
107	Bellevue.....Ky. (Cincinnati In.)	39·06 N	84·29 W
104	Bellevue..........Mi.	42·30 N	85·00 W
104	Bellevue..........Oh.	41·15 N	82·45 W
107	Bellevue.....Pa. (Pittsburgh In.)	40·30 N	80·04 W
112	Bellevue........Wa. (Seattle In.)	47·37 N	122·12 W
161	Belley (bě-lě')..........Fr.	45·46 N	5·41 E
113	Bellflower (běl-flou'ẽr) Ca. (Los Angeles In.)	33·53 N	118·08 W
113	Bell Gardens.Ca. (Los Angeles In.)	33·59 N	118·11 W
99	Bellingham (běl'ĭng-hăm) Ma. (In.)	42·05 N	71·28 W
112	Bellingham.Wa. (Vancouver In.)	48·46 N	122·29 W
112	Bellingham B. Wa. (Vancouver In.)	48·44 N	122·34 W
220	Bellingshausen Sea (běl'ĭngz houz'n).Ant.	72·00 S	80·30 W
164	Bellinzona (běl-ĭn-tsō'nä)...Switz.	46·10 N	9·09 E
99	Bell I..........Can.	50·44 N	55·35 W
106	Bellmore (běl-mōr) NY (New York In.)	40·40 N	73·31 W
134	Bello (bě'l-yô)..........Col. (In.)	6·20 N	75·33 W
105	Bellows Falls (běl'ōz fôls).....Vt.	43·10 N	72·30 W
184	Bellpat..........Pak.	29·08 N	68·00 E
91	Bell Pen..........Can.	63·50 N	81·16 W
89	Bells Corners..Can. (Ottawa In.)	45·20 N	75·49 W
112	Bells Mtn. (běls) Wa. (Portland In.)	45·50 N	122·21 W
164	Belluno (běl-lōō'nō)..........It.	46·08 N	12·14 E
136	Bell Ville (běl vēl')..........Arg.	32·33 S	62·36 W
212	Bellville..........S. Afr. (In.)	33·54 S	18·38 E
119	Bellville (běl'vĭl)..........Tx.	29·57 N	96·15 W
162	Bélmez (běl'měth)..........Sp.	38·17 N	5·17 W
109	Belmond (běl'mŏnd)..........Ia.	42·49 N	93·37 W
112	Belmont..Ca. (San Francisco In.)	37·34 N	122·18 W
135	Belmonte (běl-mōn'tȧ)......Braz.	15·58 S	38·47 W
122	Belmopan..........Belize	17·15 N	88·47 W
173	Belogorsk..........Sov. Un.	51·09 N	128·32 E
137	Belo Horizonte (bě'lôre-sô'n-tě) Braz. (Rio de Janeiro In.)	19·54 S	43·56 W
116	Beloit (bê-loit')..........Ks.	39·26 N	98·06 W
109	Beloit..........Wi.	42·31 N	89·04 W
170	Belomorsk (byěl-ô-môrsk') Sov. Un.	64·30 N	34·42 E
167	Belopol'ye (byě'lô-pôl'yě).Sov. Un.	51·10 N	34·19 E
174	Beloretsk (byě'lō-rětsk) Sov. Un. (Urals In.)	53·58 N	58·25 E
168	Belorussian (S. S. R.)....Sov. Un.	53·30 N	25·33 E
167	Belosarayskaya, Kosa (C.) (kô-sä'byě'lô-sä-räy'skä'yä) Sov. Un.	46·43 N	37·18 E
172	Belovo (bvě'lŭ-vû)......Sov. Un.	54·17 N	86·23 E
167	Belovodsk (byě-lŭ-vôdsk') Sov. Un.	49·12 N	39·36 E
170	Beloye (L.)..........Sov. Un.	60·10 N	38·05 E
170	Belozersk (byě-lŭ-zyôrsk').Sov. Un.	60·00 N	38·00 E
148	Belper (běl'pẽr)..........Eng.	53·01 N	1·28 W
111	Belt (bělt)..........Mt.	47·11 N	110·58 W
111	Belt Cr..........Mt.	47·19 N	110·58 W
119	Belton (běl'tŭn)..........Tx.	31·04 N	97·27 W
119	Belton L..........Tx.	31·15 N	97·35 W
106	Beltsville (belts-vĭl) Md. (Baltimore In.)	39·03 N	76·56 W
167	Bel'tsy (běl'tsě)........Sov. Un.	47·47 N	27·57 E
172	Belukha, Gol'tsy (Mtn.).Sov. Un.	49·47 N	86·23 E
109	Belvidere (běl-vě-dēr')........Il.	42·14 N	88·52 W
105	Belvidere..........NJ	40·50 N	75·05 W
205	Belyando (R.) (běl-yän'dō)..Austl.	22·09 S	146·48 E
174	Belyanka (byěl'yán-kȧ) Sov. Un. (Urals In.)	56·04 N	59·16 E
166	Belynichi (byěl-ĭ-nĭ'chĭ)..Sov. Un.	54·02 N	29·42 E
166	Belyy (byě'lē)..........Sov. Un.	55·52 N	32·58 E
172	Belyy (I.)..........Sov. Un.	73·19 N	72·00 E
174	Belyye Stolby (byě'lĭ-ye stôl'bĭ) Sov. Un. (Moscow In.)	55·20 N	37·52 E
149	Belzig (běl'tsēg) G.D.R. (Berlin In.)	52·08 N	12·35 E
120	Belzoni (běl-zō'nê)..........Ms.	33·09 N	90·30 W
212	Bembe (běN'bě)..........Ang.	7·00 S	14·20 E
162	Bembezar (R.) (běm-bā-thär').Sp.	38·00 N	5·18 W
109	Bemidji (bē-mĭj'ĭ)..........Mn.	47·28 N	94·54 W
212	Bena Dibele (běn'á dē-bě'lě).Zaire	4·00 S	22·49 E
203	Benalla (běn-ăl'ȧ)..........Austl.	36·30 S	146·00 E
	Benares, see Vārānasi		
162	Benavente (bā-nä-věn'tā).....Sp.	42·01 N	5·43 W
113	Benbrook (běn'brōōk) Tx. (Dallas, Fort Worth In.)	32·41 N	97·27 W
113	Benbrook Res. Tx. (Dallas, Fort Worth In.)	32·35 N	97·30 W
110	Bend (běnd)..........Or.	44·04 N	121·17 W
101	Bendeleben, Mt. (běn-děl-běn) Ak.	65·18 N	163·45 W
218	Bender Beila Som. (Horn of Afr. In.)	9·40 N	50·45 E
218	Bender Cassim Som. (Horn of Afr. In.)	11·19 N	49·10 E
167	Bendery (běn-dyě're)....Sov. Un.	46·49 N	29·29 E
203	Bendigo (běn'dĭ-gō)........Austl.	36·39 S	144·20 E
106	Benedict (běně'dĭct) Md. (Baltimore In.)	38·31 N	76·41 W
158	Benešov (běn'ě-shôf)........Czech.	49·48 N	14·40 E
164	Benevento (bā-nā-věn'tō)......It.	41·08 N	14·46 E
182	Bengal, B. of (běn-gôl')......Asia	17·30 N	87·00 E
216	Bengamisa..........Zaire	0·57 N	25·10 E
190	Bengbu (bŭŋ-bōō)........China	32·52 N	117·22 E
183	Bengkalis (běng-kä'lĭs) Indon. (Singapore In.)	1·29 N	102·06 E
196	Bengkulu..........Indon.	3·46 S	102·18 E
216	Benguela (běn-gěl'ȧ)........Ang.	12·35 S	13·25 E
154	Ben Hope (Mtn.) (běn hōp)..Scot.	58·25 N	4·25 W
134	Beni (R.) (bā'nê)..........Bol.	13·41 S	67·30 W
210	Beni-Abbès (bā'nê ä-běs')....Alg.	30·11 N	2·13 W
163	Benicarló (bā-nē-kär-lō')......Sp.	40·26 N	0·25 E
112	Benicia (bê-nĭsh'ĭ-ȧ) Ca. (San Francisco In.)	38·03 N	122·09 W
209	Benin..........Afr.	8·00 N	2·00 E
215	Benin (R.) (běn-ēn')........Nig.	5·55 N	5·15 E
215	Benin City..........Nig.	6·19 N	5·41 E
210	Beni Saf (bā'nê säf')........Alg.	35·23 N	1·20 W
216	Benito (R.)........Equat. Gui.	1·35 N	10·45 E
116	Benkelman (běn-kěl-mȧn)....Ne.	40·05 N	101·35 W
164	Benkovac (běn'kō-vȧts)....Yugo.	44·02 N	15·41 E
213	Ben Macdhui (Mtn.) (běn măk-dōō'ê) Leso-S. Afr. (Natal In.)	30·38 S	27·54 E
121	Bennettsville (běn'ěts vĭl).....SC	34·35 N	79·41 W
105	Bennington (běn'ĭng-tŭn)......Vt.	42·55 N	73·15 W
106	Benns Church (běnz' chûrch') Va. (Norfolk In.)	36·47 N	76·35 W
213	Benoni (bě-nō'nĭ)........S. Afr. (Johannesburg & Pretoria In.)	26·11 S	28·19 E
215	Benoy..........Chad	8·59 N	16·19 E
126	Benque Viejo (běn-kě biě'hō) Belize (In.)	17·07 N	89·07 W
107	Bensenville (běn'sěn-vĭl) Il. (Chicago In.)	41·57 N	87·56 W
158	Bensheim (běns-hīm)......F.R.G.	49·42 N	8·38 E
115	Benson (běn-sŭn)..........Az.	32·00 N	110·20 W
108	Benson..........Mn.	45·18 N	95·36 W
107	Bentleyville (bent'lē vĭl) Pa. (Pittsburgh In.)	40·07 N	80·01 W
117	Benton (běn'tŭn)..........Ar.	34·34 N	92·34 W
114	Benton..........Ca.	37·44 N	118·22 W
98	Benton..........Can.	45·59 N	67·36 W
104	Benton..........Il.	38·00 N	88·55 W
104	Benton Harbor (běn'tŭn här'bẽr) Mi.	42·05 N	86·30 W
117	Bentonville (běn'tŭn-vĭl)......Ar.	36·22 N	94·11 W
215	Benue (R.) (bā'nōō-ȧ)........Nig.	7·55 N	8·55 E
183	Benut (R.)..Mala. (Singapore In.)	1·43 N	103·20 E
104	Benwood (běn-wŏŏd)..........WV	39·55 N	80·45 W
192	Benxi (bŭn-shyē)..........China	41·25 N	123·50 E
165	Beograd (Belgrade) (bě-ô'gråd) (běl'grād).Yugo.	44·48 N	20·32 E
195	Beppu (bě'pōō)..........Jap.	33·16 N	131·30 E

ng-sing; ŋ-baŋk; N-nasalized n; nŏd; cŏmmit; ōld; ôbey; ôrder; fōōd; fŏŏt; ou-out; s-soft; sh-dish; th-thin; pūre; ûnite; ûrn; stŭd; circŭs; ü-as "y" in study; '-indeterminate vowel.

258 Bequia — Bimberi PRONOUNCING INDEX

Page	Name Pronunciation Region	Lat. °'	Long. °'
127	Bequia I. (bĕk-ē'ä)....N. A. (In.)	13·00 N	61·08 W
183	Berakit, Tanjung (C.) Indon. (Singapore In.)	1·16 N	104·44 E
165	Berat (bĕ-rät')....Alb.	40·43 N	19·59 E
197	Berau, Teluk (B.)....Indon.	2·22 S	131·40 E
136	Berazategui (bĕ-rä-zá'tĕ-gē) Arg. (Buenos Aires In.)	34·46 S	58·14 W
218	Berbera (bûr'bûr-á) Som. (Horn of Afr. In.)	10·25 N	45·05 E
215	Berbérati....Cen. Afr. Rep.	4·16 N	15·47 E
160	Berck (bĕrk)....Fr.	50·26 N	1·36 E
153	Berd'ansk....Sov. Un.	46·45 N	36·47 E
167	Berdichev (bĕ-dē'chĕf)...Sov. Un.	49·53 N	28·32 E
167	Berdyanskaya, Kosa (C.) (kô-sä' bĕr-dyän'skä-yä).Sov. Un.	46·38 N	36·42 E
174	Berdyaush (bĕr'dyàûsh) Sov. Un. (Urals In.)	55·10 N	59·12 E
120	Berea (bê-rē'á)....Ky.	37·30 N	84·19 W
107	Berea....Oh. (Cleveland In.)	41·22 N	81·51 W
159	Beregovo (bĕ'rĕ-gô-vô)...Sov. Un.	48·13 N	22·40 E
217	Bereku....Tan.	4·27 S	35·44 E
95	Berens (R.) (bĕr'enz)....Can.	52·15 N	96·30 W
95	Berens I....Can.	52·18 N	97·40 W
95	Berens River....Can.	52·22 N	97·02 W
108	Beresford (bĕr'ĕs-fērd)....SD	43·05 N	96·46 W
159	Berettyóújfalu (bĕ'rĕt-tyō-ōō'y'fô-lōō).Hung.	47·14 N	21·33 E
159	Berëza (bĕ-rā'zá)....Sov. Un.	52·29 N	24·59 E
159	Berezhany (bĕr-yĕ'zhá-nê) Sov. Un.	49·25 N	24·58 E
166	Berezina (R.) (bĕr-yĕ'zē-ná) Sov. Un.	53·20 N	29·05 E
166	Berezino (bĕr-yä'zê-nô)...Sov. Un.	53·51 N	28·54 E
167	Berezna (bĕr-yôz'ná)....Sov. Un.	51·32 N	31·47 E
167	Bereznegovata....Sov. Un.	47·19 N	32·58 E
174	Berezniki (bĕr-yôz'nyê-kê) Sov. Un. (Urals In.)	59·25 N	56·46 E
167	Berëzovka (bĕr-yôz'ôf-ká) Sov. Un.	47·12 N	30·56 E
174	Berëzovka...Sov. Un. (Urals In.)	57·35 N	57·19 E
170	Berëzovo (bĭr-yô'zē-vû)..Sov. Un.	64·10 N	65·10 E
174	Berëzovskiy (bĕr-yô'zôf-skĭ) Sov. Un. (Urals In.)	56·54 N	60·47 E
163	Berga (bĕr'gä)....Sp.	42·05 N	1·52 E
171	Bergama (bĕr'gä-mä)....Tur.	39·08 N	27·09 E
164	Bergamo (bĕr'gä-mō)....It.	45·43 N	9·41 E
135	Bergantín (bĕr-gän-tē'n) Ven. (In.)	10·04 N	64·23 W
149	Bergedorf (bĕr'gē-dôrf) F.R.G. (Hamburg In.)	53·29 N	10·12 E
158	Bergen (bĕr'gĕn)....G.D.R.	54·26 N	13·26 E
156	Bergen....Nor.	60·24 N	5·20 E
106	Bergenfield....NJ (New York In.)	40·55 N	73·59 W
149	Bergen op Zoom Neth. (Amsterdam In.)	51·29 N	4·16 E
160	Bergerac (bĕr-zhē-räk')....Fr.	44·49 N	0·28 E
161	Bergisch Gladbach (bĕrg'ĭsh-glät'bäk) F.R.G. (Ruhr In.)	50·59 N	7·08 E
149	Berglern (bĕrgh'lĕrn) F.R.G. (Munich In.)	48·24 N	11·55 E
213	Bergville (bĕrg'vĭl) S. Afr. (Natal In.)	28·46 S	29·22 E
184	Berhampur....India	19·19 N	84·48 E
75	Bering Sea (bē'rĭng)....Asia-N. A.	58·00 N	175·00 W
101	Bering Str....Ak.	64·50 N	169·50 W
167	Berislav (byĕr'ĭ-sláf)....Sov. Un.	46·49 N	33·24 E
162	Berja (bĕr'hä)....Sp.	36·50 N	2·56 W
112	Berkeley (bûrk'lĭ) Ca. (San Francisco In.)	37·52 N	122·17 W
113	Berkeley....Mo. (St. Louis In.)	38·45 N	90·20 W
105	Berkeley Springs (bûrk'lĭ sprĭngz) WV	39·40 N	78·10 W
148	Berkhamsted (bĕrk'hàm'stĕd) Eng. (London In.)	51·44 N	0·34 W
107	Berkley (bûrk'lĭ).Mi. (Detroit In.)	42·30 N	83·10 W
165	Berkovitsa (bĕ-kō'vê-tsá)....Bul.	43·14 N	23·08 E
93	Berland (R.)....Can.	54·00 N	117·10 W
162	Berlengas (Is.) (bĕr-lĕn'gäzh).Port.	39·25 N	9·33 W
149	Berlin, East (bĕr-lēn') G.D.R. (Berlin In.)	52·31 N	13·28 E
149	Berlin, West...F.R.G. (Berlin In.)	52·31 N	13·20 E
105	Berlin (bûr-lĭn)....NH	44·25 N	71·10 W
106	Berlin....NJ (Philadelphia In.)	39·47 N	74·56 W
213	Berlin (bĕr-lĭn).S. Afr. (Natal In.)	32·53 S	27·36 E
109	Berlin (bûr-lĭn')....Wi.	43·58 N	88·58 W
162	Bermeja, Sierra (Mts.) (sē-ĕ'r-rä-bĕr-mĕ'hä).Sp.	36·35 N	5·03 W
136	Bermejo (R.) (bĕr-mä'hō)....Arg.	25·05 S	61·00 W
162	Bermeo (bĕr-mā'yō)....Sp.	43·23 N	2·43 W
123	Bermuda (I.)....N.A.	32·20 N	65·45 W
158	Bern (bĕrn)....Switz.	46·55 N	7·25 E
136	Bernal (bĕr-näl') Arg. (Buenos Aires In.)	34·27 S	58·17 W
115	Bernalillo (bĕr-nä-lē'yō)....NM	35·20 N	106·30 W
105	Bernard (L.) (bēr-närd')....Can.	45·45 N	79·25 W
106	Bernardsville (būr nârds'vĭl) NJ (New York In.)	40·43 N	74·34 W
149	Bernau (bĕr'nou) G.D.R. (Berlin In.)	52·40 N	13·35 E
158	Bernburg (bĕrn'bŏŏrgh)...G.D.R.	51·48 N	11·43 E
158	Berndorf (bĕrn'dôrf)....Aus.	47·57 N	16·05 E
104	Berne (bûrn)....In.	40·40 N	84·55 W
158	Berner Alpen (Mts.)....Switz.	46·29 N	7·30 E
161	Berneustadt (bĕr'noi'shtät) F.R.G. (Ruhr In.)	51·01 N	7·39 E
204	Bernier (I.) (bĕr-nēr')....Austl.	24·58 S	113·15 E
158	Bernina Pizzo (Pk.)....Switz.	46·23 N	9·58 E
216	Bero (R.)....Ang.	15·10 S	12·20 E
158	Beroun (bā'rōn)....Czech.	49·57 N	14·03 E
158	Berounka R. (bĕ-rōn'kà)...Czech.	49·53 N	13·40 E
202	Berowra....Austl. (Sydney In.)	33·36 S	151·10 E
160	Berre, Étang de (L.) (ā-tôɴ' dĕ bâr').Fr. (In.)	43·27 N	5·07 E
160	Berre-l' Étang (bâr'lā-tôɴ) Fr. (In.)	43·28 N	5·11 E
152	Berriane (bĕr-ê-äɴ')....Alg.	32·50 N	3·49 E
125	Berriozabal (bā'rē-ō-zä-bäl') Mex.	16·47 N	93·16 W
93	Berry Creek (R.)....Can.	51·15 N	111·40 W
114	Berryessa (R.) (bĕ'rĭ ĕs'á)....Ca.	38·35 N	122·33 W
128	Berry Is....Ba.	25·40 N	77·50 W
117	Berryville (bĕr'ê-vĭl)....Ar.	36·21 N	93·34 W
167	Bershad' (byĕr'shät)....Sov. Un.	48·22 N	29·31 E
89	Berthier....Can. (Quebec In.)	46·56 N	70·44 W
112	Bertrand (R.) (bûr'trănd) Wa. (Vancouver In.)	48·58 N	122·31 W
105	Berwick (bûr'wĭk)....Pa.	41·05 N	76·10 W
154	Berwick (bûr'ĭk)....Scot.	55·45 N	2·01 W
107	Berwyn (bûr'wĭn) Il. (Chicago In.)	41·49 N	87·47 W
154	Berwyn Ra....Wales	52·45 N	3·41 W
213	Besalampy (bĕz-à-lám-pē') Mad..	16·48 S	40·40 E
161	Besançon (bē-säɴ-sôɴ)....Fr.	47·14 N	6·02 E
183	Besar, Gunong (Mt.) Mala. (Singapore In.)	2·31 N	103·09 E
166	Besed' (R.) (byĕ'syĕt)...Sov. Un.	52·58 N	31·36 E
166	Beshenkovichi (byĕ'shĕn-kōvē'chĭ).Sov. Un.	55·04 N	29·29 E
159	Beskides (Mts.) (bĕs'kēdz') Czech.-Pol.	49·23 N	19·00 E
160	Bessèges (bĕ-sĕzh')....Fr.	44·20 N	4·07 E
106	Bessemer (bĕs'ê-mēr) Al. (Birmingham In.)	33·24 N	86·58 W
109	Bessemer....Mi.	46·29 N	90·04 W
121	Bessemer City....NC	35·16 N	81·17 W
149	Bestensee (bĕs'tĕn-zā) G.D.R. (Berlin In.)	51·15 N	13·39 E
162	Betanzos (bĕ-tän'thōs)....Sp.	43·18 N	8·14 W
115	Betatakin Ruin (bĕt-á-täk'ĭn) . Az.	36·40 N	110·29 W
218	Bethal (bĕth'ăl).S. Afr. (Johannesburg & Pretoria In.)	26·27 S	29·28 E
113	Bethalto (bá-thàl'tō) Il. (St. Louis In.)	38·54 N	90·03 W
212	Bethanien....Namibia	26·20 S	16·10 E
117	Bethany....Mo.	40·15 N	94·04 W
101	Bethel (bĕth'ĕl)....Ak.	60·50 N	161·50 W
106	Bethel....Ct. (New York In.)	41·22 N	73·24 W
105	Bethel....Vt.	43·50 N	72·40 W
107	Bethel Park..Pa. (Pittsburgh In.)	40·19 N	80·02 W
106	Bethesda (bĕ-thĕs'dá) Md. (Baltimore In.)	39·00 N	77·10 W
105	Bethlehem (bĕth'lê-hĕm)....Pa.	40·40 N	75·25 W
218	Bethlehem.S. Afr. (Johannesburg & Pretoria In.)	28·14 S	28·18 E
	Bethlehem, see Bayt Lahm		
160	Béthune (bā-tün')....Fr.	50·32 N	2·37 E
213	Betroka (bĕ-trōk'á)....Mad.	23·13 S	46·17 E
183	Bet She'an....Isr. (Palestine In.)	32·30 N	35·30 E
98	Betsiamites....Can.	48·57 N	68·36 W
98	Betsiamites, (R.)....Can.	49·11 N	69·20 W
213	Betsiboka (R.) (bĕt-sĭ-bō'ká).Mad.	16·47 S	46·45 E
101	Bettles Field (bĕt'tŭls)....Ak.	66·58 N	151·48 W
184	Betwa (R.) (bĕt'wá)....India	25·00 N	77·37 E
161	Betz (bĕ)....Fr. (Paris In.)	49·09 N	2·58 E
161	Betzdorf (bĕtz'dôrf) F.R.G. (Ruhr In.)	50·47 N	7·53 E
149	Beveren....Bel. (Brussels In.)	51·13 N	4·14 E
148	Beverly (bĕv'ēr-lĭ)....Eng.	53·50 N	0·25 W
99	Beverly....Ma. (Boston In.)	42·34 N	70·53 W
106	Beverly....NJ (Philadelphia In.)	40·03 N	74·56 W
113	Beverly Hills.Ca. (Los Angeles In.)	34·05 N	118·24 W
117	Bevier (bê-vēr')....Mo.	39·44 N	92·36 W
148	Bewdley (būd'lĭ)....Eng.	52·22 N	2·19 W
155	Bexhill (bĕks'hĭl)....Eng.	50·49 N	0·25 E
148	Bexley (bĕks'ly) Eng. (London In.)	51·26 N	0·09 E
214	Beyla (bā'là)....Gui.	8·41 N	8·37 W
211	Beylul....Eth.	13·15 N	42·21 E
171	Beypazari (bā-pà-zä'rĭ)....Tur.	40·10 N	31·40 E
171	Beyşehir (bā-shĕ'h'r)....Tur.	38·00 N	31·45 E
171	Beyşehir Gölü (L.)....Tur.	38·00 N	31·30 E
167	Beysugskiy, Liman (B.) (lĭ-män' bĕy-sōōg'skĭ).Sov. Un.	46·07 N	38·35 E
166	Bezhetsk (byĕ-zhĕtsk')...Sov. Un.	57·46 N	36·40 E
166	Bezhitsa (byĕ-zhĭ'tsà)....Sov. Un.	53·19 N	34·18 E
160	Béziers (bā-zyā')....Fr.	43·21 N	3·12 E
184	Bhadreswar....India (In.)	22·49 N	88·22 E
184	Bhāgalpur (bä'găl-pōōr)....India	25·15 N	86·59 E
188	Bhamo (bŭ-mō')....Bur.	24·00 N	96·15 E
184	Bhāngar....India (In.)	22·30 N	88·36 E
184	Bharatpur (bērt'pōōr)....India	27·21 N	77·33 E
184	Bhatinda (bŭ-tĭn-dà)....India	30·19 N	74·56 E
184	Bhaunagar (bäv-nŭg'ŭr)....India	21·45 N	72·58 E
185	Bhayandar....India (In.)	19·20 N	72·50 E
184	Bhilai....India	21·14 N	81·23 E
184	Bhīma (R.) (bē'má)....India	17·15 N	75·55 E
185	Bhiwandi....India (In.)	19·18 N	73·03 E
184	Bhiwāni....India	28·53 N	76·08 E
184	Bhopāl (bō-päl)....India	23·20 N	77·25 E
184	Bhubaneswar (bōō-bû-năsh'vûr) India	20·21 N	85·53 E
184	Bhuj (bōōj)....India	23·22 N	69·39 E
187	Bhutan (bōō-tän')....Asia	27·15 N	90·30 E
216	Biafra, Bight of....Afr.	4·05 N	7·10 E
197	Biak (I.) (bē'āk)....Indon.	1·00 S	136·00 E
159	Biała Podlaska (byä'wä pōd-läs'kä).Pol.	52·01 N	23·08 E
158	Białogard (byä-wō'gärd)....Pol.	54·00 N	16·01 E
159	Białystok (byä-wĭs'tōk)....Pol.	53·08 N	23·12 E
214	Biankouma....Ivory Coast	7·44 N	7·37 W
160	Biarritz (byä-rēts')....Fr.	43·27 N	1·39 W
218	Bibā (bē'bà)....Egypt (Nile In.)	28·54 N	30·59 E
120	Bibb City (bĭb' sĭ'tê)....Ga.	32·31 N	84·56 W
158	Biberach (bē'bĕräk)....F.R.G.	48·06 N	9·49 E
214	Bibiani....Ghana	6·28 N	2·20 W
98	Bic (bĭk)....Can.	48·22 N	68·42 W
104	Bicknell (bĭk'nĕl)....In.	38·45 N	87·20 W
159	Bicske (bĭsh'kĕ)....Hung.	47·29 N	18·38 E
215	Bida (bē'dä)....Nig.	9·05 N	6·01 E
98	Biddeford (bĭd'ê-fērd)....Me.	43·29 N	70·29 W
148	Biddulph (bĭd'ŭlf)....Eng.	53·07 N	2·10 W
	Bidon Cinq, see Post Maurice Cortier		
216	Bié....Ang.	12·22 S	16·56 E
159	Biebrza R. (byĕb'zhà)....Pol.	53·18 N	22·25 E
158	Biel (bēl)....Switz.	47·09 N	7·12 E
158	Bielefeld (bē'lê-fĕlt)....F.R.G.	52·01 N	8·35 E
165	Bieljina (bê-yĕ'lyê-nä)....Yugo.	44·44 N	19·15 E
164	Biella (byĕl'lä)....It.	45·34 N	8·05 E
159	Bielsk Podlaski (byĕlsk pŭd-lä'skĭ) Pol.	52·47 N	23·14 E
196	Bien Hoa....Viet.	10·59 N	106·49 E
91	Bienville, Lac (L.)....Can.	55·32 N	72·45 W
149	Biesenthal (bē'sĕn-täl) G.D.R. (Berlin In.)	52·46 N	13·38 E
164	Biferno (R.) (bē-fĕr'nō)....It.	41·49 N	14·46 E
216	Bifoum....Gabon	0·22 S	10·23 E
112	Big (L.) (bĭg)...Wa. (Seattle In.)	48·23 N	122·14 W
120	Big (R.)....Ar.	35·55 N	90·10 W
165	Biğa (bē'ghà)....Tur.	40·13 N	27·14 E
109	Big Bay de Noc (bĭg bā dê nok') Mi.	45·48 N	86·41 W
117	Big Bayou (bĭg' bī'yōō)....Ar.	33·04 N	91·28 W
113	Big Bear City (bĭg bâr) Ca. (Los Angeles In.)	34·16 N	116·51 W
111	Big Belt Mts. (bĭg bĕlt)....Mt.	46·53 N	111·43 W
108	Big Bend Dam (bĭg bĕnd)....SD	44·11 N	99·33 W
118	Big Bend Natl. Park....Tx.	29·15 N	103·15 W
120	Big Black (R.) (bĭg blăk)....Ms.	32·05 N	90·49 W
117	Big Blue (R.) (bĭg blōō)....Ne.	40·53 N	97·00 W
118	Big Canyon (bĭg kăn'yŭn)....Tx.	30·27 N	102·19 W
121	Big Cypress Swp. (bĭg sī'prĕs) Fl. (In.)	26·02 N	81·20 W
101	Big Delta (bĭg dĕl'tá)....Ak.	64·08 N	145·48 W
109	Big Fork (R.) (bĭg fôrk)....Mn.	48·08 N	93·47 W
94	Biggar....Can.	52·04 N	108·00 W
111	Big Hole (R.) (bĭg 'hōl)....Mt.	45·53 N	113·15 W
111	Big Hole Natl. Battlefield (bĭg hōl băt''l-fēld).Mt.	45·44 N	113·35 W
111	Big Horn Mts. (bĭg hôrn)....Wy.	44·47 N	107·40 W
111	Bighorn R....Mt.	45·50 N	107·15 W
95	Big I....Can.	49·10 N	94·40 W
112	Big Lake (bĭg lāk) Wa. (Seattle In.)	48·24 N	122·14 W
89	Big L....Can. (Edmonton In.)	53·35 N	113·47 W
95	Big Mossy Pt....Can.	53·45 N	97·50 W
104	Big Muddy (R.)....Il.	37·50 N	89·00 W
111	Big Muddy Cr. (bĭg mud'ĭ)...Mt.	48·53 N	105·02 W
214	Bignona....Senegal	12·49 N	16·14 W
94	Big Quill L....Can.	51·55 N	104·22 W
104	Big Rapids (bĭg răp'ĭdz)....Mi.	43·40 N	85·30 W
94	Big River....Can.	53·50 N	107·01 W
115	Big Sandy (R.) (bĭg sănd'ê)...Az.	34·59 N	113·36 W
104	Big Sandy (R.)....Ky.-WV	38·15 N	82·35 W
116	Big Sandy Cr....Co.	39·08 N	103·36 W
111	Big Sandy Cr....Mt.	48·20 N	110·08 W
95	Bigsby I....Can.	49·04 N	94·35 W
108	Big Sioux (R.) (bĭg sōō)....SD	44·34 N	97·00 W
118	Big Spring (bĭg sprĭng)....Tx.	32·15 N	101·28 W
108	Big Stone (L.) (bĭg stōn) Mn.-SD	45·29 N	96·40 W
120	Big Stone Gap....Va.	36·50 N	82·50 W
111	Bigtimber (bĭg'tĭm-bēr)....Mt.	45·50 N	109·57 W
111	Big Wood R. (bĭg wŏŏd)....Id.	43·02 N	114·30 W
164	Bihać (bē'häch)....Yugo.	44·48 N	15·52 E
184	Bihār (State) (bê-här')....India	23·48 N	84·57 E
217	Biharamulo (bê-hä-rä-mōō'lō) Tan.	2·38 S	31·20 E
159	Bihor, Muntii (Mts.) (bē'hôr) Rom.	46·37 N	22·37 E
214	Bijagós, Arquipélago dos (Is.) (är-kē-pā'lä-gō dôs bē-zhä-gôs) Guinea-Bissau	11·20 N	17·10 W
185	Bijāpur....India	16·53 N	75·42 E
165	Bijelo Polje (bê'yĕ-lô pô'lyĕ) Yugo.	43·02 N	19·48 E
191	Bijiang (bē-jyäŋ) China (Canton In.)	22·57 N	113·15 E
193	Bijie (bē-jyĕ)....China	27·20 N	105·18 E
116	Bijou Cr. (bē'zhōō)....Co.	39·41 N	104·13 W
184	Bīkaner (bĭ-kā'nûr)....India	28·07 N	73·19 E
194	Bikin (bê-kēn')....Sov. Un.	46·41 N	134·29 E
194	Bikin (R.)....Sov. Un.	46·37 N	135·55 E
216	Bikoro (bê-kō'rō)....Zaire	0.45 S	18·07 E
216	Bikuar, Parque Nacional do (Natl. Pk.).Ang.	15·07 S	14·40 E
184	Bilāspur (bê-läs'pōōr)....India	22·08 N	82·12 E
196	Bilauktaung (Ra.)....Thai.	14·40 N	98·50 E
162	Bilbao (bĭl-bä'ō)....Sp.	43·12 N	2·48 W
218	Bilbays....Egypt (Nile In.)	30·26 N	31·37 E
165	Bileća (bē'lĕ-chä)....Yugo.	42·52 N	18·26 E
171	Bilecik (bē-lĕd-zhĕk')....Tur.	40·10 N	29·58 E
159	Bilé Karpaty (Mts.)....Czech.	48·53 N	17·35 E
159	Biłgoraj (bēw-gō'rĭ)....Pol.	50·31 N	22·43 E
174	Bilimbay (bē'lĭm-bày) Sov. Un. (Urals In.)	56·59 N	59·53 E
203	Billabong (R.) (bĭl'ă-bŏng)..Austl.	35·15 S	145·20 E
99	Billerica (bĭl'rĭk-á)....Ma. (In.)	42·33 N	71·16 W
148	Billericay....Eng. (London In.)	51·38 N	0·25 E
111	Billings (bĭl'ĭngz)....Mt.	45·47 N	108·29 W
115	Bill Williams (L.) (bĭl-wĭl'yumz) Az.	34·10 N	113·50 W
211	Bilma (bēl'mä)....Niger	18·41 N	13·20 E
120	Biloxi (bĭ-lŏk'sĭ)....Ms.	30·24 N	88·50 W
218	Bilqās Qism Awwal Egypt (Nile In.)	31·14 N	31·25 E
203	Bimberi Pk. (bĭm'bĕrĭ)....Austl.	35·45 S	148·50 E

ăt; finăl; rāte; senâte; ärm; åsk; sofá; fâre; ch-choose; dh-as th in other; bē; êvent; bĕt; recĕnt; cratēr; g-go; gh-guttural g; bĭt; ĭ-short neutral; rīde; ĸ-guttural k as ch in German ich;

Page	Name Pronunciation Region	Lat. °′	Long. °′
197	Binalonan (bē-nä-lō'nän) Phil. (In.)	16·03 N	120·35 E
186	Binalud (Mtn.) Iran	36·32 N	58·34 E
158	Bingen (bĭn'gĕn) F.R.G.	49·57 N	7·54 E
148	Bingham (bĭng'ăm) Eng.	52·57 N	0·57 W
98	Bingham Me.	45·03 N	69·51 W
113	Bingham Canyon Ut. (Salt Lake City In.)	40·33 N	112·09 W
105	Binghamton (bĭng'ăm-tŭn) NY	42·05 N	75·55 W
195	Bingo-Nada (Sea) (bĭn'gō nä-dä) Jap.	34·06 N	133·14 E
196	Binjai Indon.	3·59 N	108·00 E
203	Binnaway (bĭn'ă-wā) Austl.	31·42 S	149·22 E
183	Bintan (I.) (bĭn'tän) Indon. (Singapore In.)	1·09 N	104·43 E
196	Bintulu (bēn'tōō-lōō) Mala.	3·07 N	113·06 E
190	Bin Xian (bĭn-shyän) China	37·27 N	117·58 E
192	Bin Xian China	45·40 N	127·20 E
210	Binzert (Bizerte) (bē-zĕrt') Tun.	37·23 N	9·52 E
214	Bio Gorge (Val.) Ghana	8·30 N	2·05 W
216	Bioko (Fernando Póo) (I.) Equat. Gui.	3·35 N	7·45 E
194	Bira (bē'rà) Sov. Un.	49·00 N	133·18 E
194	Bira (R.) Sov. Un.	48·55 N	132·25 E
184	Birātnagar (bĭ-rät'nŭ-gŭr) Nep.	26·35 N	87·18 E
112	Birch Bay (bûrch) Wa. (Vancouver In.)	48·55 N	122·45 W
112	Birch B. Wa. (Vancouver In.)	48·55 N	122·52 W
95	Birch I. Can.	52·25 N	99·55 W
90	Birch Mts. Can.	57·36 N	113·10 W
112	Birch Pt. Wa. (Vancouver In.)	48·57 N	122·50 W
213	Bird I. (bērd) S. Afr. (Natal In.)	33·51 S	26·21 E
129	Bird Rock (I.) (bûrd) Ba.	22·50 N	74·20 W
89	Birds Hill (bûrds) Can. (Winnipeg In.)	49·58 N	97·00 W
203	Birdsville (bûrdz'vĭl) Austl.	25·50 S	139·31 E
204	Birdum (bûrd'ŭm) Austl.	15·45 S	133·25 E
171	Birecik (bē-rĕd-zhĕk') Tur.	37·10 N	37·50 E
215	Bir Gara Chad	13·11 N	15·58 E
186	Bīrjand (bēr'jänd) Iran	33·07 N	59·16 E
112	Birkenfeld Or. (Portland In.)	45·59 N	123·20 W
148	Birkenhead (bûr'kĕn-hĕd) Eng.	53·23 N	3·02 W
149	Birkenwerder (bēr'kĕn-vĕr-dĕr) G.D.R. (Berlin In.)	52·41 N	13·22 E
159	Bîrlad Rom.	46·15 N	27·43 E
106	Birmingham (bûr'mĭng-häm) Al. (Birmingham In.)	33·31 N	86·49 W
148	Birmingham Eng.	52·29 N	1·53 W
107	Birmingham Mi. (Detroit In.)	42·32 N	83·13 W
113	Birmingham Mo. (Kansas City In.)	39·10 N	94·22 W
148	Birmingham Can. Eng.	53·07 N	2·40 W
211	Bi'r Misāhah Egypt	22·16 N	28·04 E
215	Birnin Kebbi Nig.	12·32 N	4·12 E
173	Birobidzhan (bē'rō-bē-jän') Sov. Un.	48·42 N	133·28 E
170	Birsk (bĭrsk) Sov. Un.	55·25 N	55·30 E
148	Birstall (bûr'stôl) Eng.	53·44 N	1·39 W
167	Biryuchiy (I.) (bĭr-yōō'chĭ) Sov. Un.	46·07 N	35·12 E
174	Biryulëvo (bĕr-yōōl'yô-vô) Sov. Un. (Moscow In.)	55·35 N	37·39 E
172	Biryusa (R.) (bēr-yōō'sä) Sov. Un.	56·43 N	97·30 E
183	Bi'r Za'farānah Egypt (Palestine In.)	29·07 N	32·38 E
157	Biržai (bēr-zhä'ē) Sov. Un.	56·11 N	24·45 E
115	Bisbee (bĭz'bē) Az.	31·30 N	109·55 W
151	Biscay, B. of (bĭs'kā') Eur.	45·19 N	3·51 W
121	Biscayne B. (bĭs-kān') Fl. (In.)	25·22 N	80·15 W
161	Bischeim (bĭsh'hĭm) Fr.	48·40 N	7·48 E
96	Biscotasi L. Can.	47·20 N	81·55 W
174	Biser (bē'sĕr) Sov. Un. (Urals In.)	58·24 N	58·54 E
164	Biševo (Is.) (bē'shĕ-vō) Yugo.	42·58 N	15·50 E
114	Bishop (bĭsh'ŭp) Ca.	37·22 N	118·25 W
119	Bishop Tx.	27·35 N	97·46 W
148	Bishop's Castle (bĭsh'ŏps käs'l) Eng.	52·29 N	2·57 W
121	Bishopville (bĭsh'ŭp-vĭl) SC	34·11 N	80·13 W
210	Biskra (bēs'krà) Alg.	34·52 N	5·39 E
108	Bismarck (bĭz'märk) ND	46·48 N	100·46 W
197	Bismarck Arch. Pap. N. Gui.	3·15 S	150·45 E
197	Bismarck Ra. Pap. N. Gui.	5·15 S	144·15 E
214	Bissau (bē-sä'ōō) Guinea-Bissau	11·51 N	15·35 W
95	Bissett Can.	51·01 N	95·45 W
119	Bistineau (L.) (bĭs-tĭ-nō') La.	32·19 N	93·45 W
159	Bistrita (bĭs-trĭt-sà) Rom.	47·09 N	24·29 E
159	Bistrita R. Rom.	47·08 N	25·47 E
171	Bitlis (bĭt-lēs') Tur.	38·30 N	42·00 E
165	Bitola (Monastir) (bē'tô-lä) (mō'nä-stêr) Yugo.	41·02 N	21·22 E
164	Bitonto (bē-tôn'tō) It.	41·08 N	16·42 E
111	Bitter Cr. (bĭt'ēr) Wy.	41·36 N	108·29 W
158	Bitterfeld (bĭt'ēr-fĕlt) G.D.R.	51·39 N	12·19 E
110	Bitterroot Ra. (bĭt'ēr-ōōt) Mt.	47·15 N	115·13 W
111	Bitterroot R. Mt.	46·28 N	114·10 W
167	Bityug (R.) (bĭt'yōōg) Sov. Un.	51·23 N	40·33 E
215	Biu Nig.	10·35 N	12·13 E
109	Biwabik (bē-wä'bĭk) Mn.	47·32 N	92·24 W
195	Biwa-ko (L.) (bē-wä'kō) Jap. (Ōsaka In.)	35·03 N	135·51 E
172	Biya (R.) (bĭ'yà) Sov. Un.	52·22 N	87·28 E
172	Biysk (bēsk) Sov. Un.	52·32 N	85·28 E
213	Bizana (bĭz-änä) S. Afr. (Natal In.)	30·51 S	29·54 E
	Bizerte, see Binzert		
192	Bizuta Mong.	46·28 N	115·10 E
164	Bjelovar (byĕ-lō'vär) Yugo.	45·54 N	16·53 E
	Björneborg, see Pori		
156	Bjorne Fd. (byûr'nĕ fyôrd) Nor.	60·11 N	5·26 E
214	Bla Mali	12·57 N	5·46 W
104	Black (L.) (blăk) Mi.	45·25 N	84·15 W
105	Black (L.) NY	44·30 N	75·35 W
117	Black (R.) Ar.	35·47 N	91·22 W
96	Black (R.) Can.	49·20 N	81·15 W
105	Black (R.) NY	43·45 N	75·20 W
121	Black (R.) SC	33·55 N	80·10 W
109	Black (R.) Wi.	44·07 N	90·56 W
205	Blackall (blăk'ŭl) Austl.	24·23 S	145·37 E
109	Black B. (blăk) Can.	48·36 N	88·32 W
148	Blackburn (blăk'bûrn) Eng.	53·45 N	2·28 W
101	Blackburn, Mt. Ak.	61·50 N	143·12 W
115	Black Canyon of the Gunnison Natl. Mon. (blăk kăn'yŭn) Co.	38·35 N	107·45 W
112	Black Diamond (dī'mŭnd) Wa. (Seattle In.)	47·19 N	122·00 W
154	Blackdown Hills (blăk'doun) Eng.	50·58 N	3·19 W
109	Blackduck (blăk'dŭk) Mn.	47·41 N	94·33 W
111	Blackfoot (blăk'fŏŏt) Id.	43·11 N	112·23 W
93	Blackfoot Ind. Res. Can.	50·45 N	113·00 W
111	Blackfoot Ind. Res. Mt.	48·49 N	112·53 W
111	Blackfoot R. Mt.	46·53 N	113·33 W
111	Blackfoot River Res. Id.	42·53 N	111·23 W
108	Black Hills SD	44·08 N	103·47 W
95	Black I. Can.	51·10 N	96·30 W
98	Black Lake Can.	46·02 N	71·24 W
115	Black Mesa (blăk măsá) Az.	36·33 N	110·40 W
89	Blackmud Cr. (blăk'mŭd) Can. (Edmonton In.)	53·28 N	113·34 W
148	Blackpool (blăk'pōōl) Eng.	53·49 N	3·02 W
115	Black Ra. NM	33·15 N	107·55 W
128	Black River (blăk') Jam.	18·00 N	77·50 W
193	Black R. Viet.	20·56 N	104·30 E
109	Black River Falls Wi.	44·18 N	90·51 W
110	Black Rock Des. (rŏk) Nv.	40·55 N	119·00 W
121	Blacksburg (blăks'bûrg) SC	35·09 N	81·30 W
147	Black Sea Eur.-Asia	43·01 N	32·16 E
121	Blackshear (blăk'shĭr) Ga.	31·20 N	82·15 W
121	Blackstone (blăk'stôn) Va.	37·04 N	78·00 W
109	Black Sturgeon (R.) (stû'jŭn) Can.	49·12 N	88·41 W
202	Blacktown (blăk'toun) Austl. (Sydney In.)	33·47 S	150·55 E
98	Blackville (blăk'vĭl) Can.	46·44 N	65·50 W
121	Blackville SC	33·21 N	81·19 W
214	Black Volta (Volta Noire) (R.) (vōl'tà) Afr.	8·55 N	2·30 W
120	Black Warrior (R.) (blăk wŏr'ĭ-ēr) Al.	32·37 N	87·42 W
120	Black Warrior (R.), Locust Fk. Al.	34·06 N	86·27 W
120	Black Warrior (R.), Mulberry Fk. Al.	34·06 N	86·32 W
154	Blackwater (R.) (blăk-wô'tēr) Ire.	52·05 N	9·02 W
117	Blackwater (R.) Mo.	38·53 N	93·22 W
121	Blackwater (R.) Va.	37·07 N	77·10 W
117	Blackwell (blăk'wĕl) Ok.	36·47 N	97·19 W
149	Bladel Neth. (Amsterdam In.)	51·22 N	5·15 E
171	Blagodarnoye (blä'gô-där-nō'yĕ) Sov. Un.	45·00 N	43·30 E
165	Blagoevgrad (Gorna Dzhumaya) Bul.	42·01 N	23·06 E
173	Blagoveshchensk (blä'gō-vyĕsh'chĕnsk) Sov. Un.	50·16 N	127·47 E
174	Blagoveshchensk Sov. Un. (Urals In.)	55·03 N	56·00 E
113	Blaine (blān) Mn. (Minneapolis, St. Paul In.)	45·11 N	93·14 W
112	Blaine Wa. (Vancouver In.)	48·59 N	122·49 W
105	Blaine WV	39·25 N	79·10 W
108	Blair (blâr) Ne.	41·33 N	96·09 W
93	Blairmore Can.	49·38 N	114·25 W
105	Blairsville (blârs'vĭl) Pa.	40·30 N	79·40 W
112	Blake (I.) (blāk) Wa. (Seattle In.)	47·37 N	122·28 W
120	Blakely (blāk'lē) Ga.	31·22 N	84·55 W
210	Blanc, Cap (C.) Mauritania	20·39 N	18·08 W
161	Blanc, Mt. (môn blän) Fr.-It.	45·50 N	6·53 E
136	Blanca, Bahia (B.) (bä-ē'ä-blàn'kä) Arg.	39·30 S	61·00 W
116	Blanca Pk. (blăŋ'kà) Co.	37·36 N	105·22 W
203	Blanche, L. (blănch) Austl.	29·20 S	139·12 E
89	Blanche, (R.) Can. (Ottawa In.)	45·34 N	75·38 W
107	Blanchester (blăn'chĕs-tēr) Oh. (Cincinnati In.)	39·18 N	83·58 W
136	Blanco, C. (bläŋ'kô) Arg.	47·08 S	65·47 W
126	Blanco, Cabo (C.) (kà'bô-bläŋ'kō) C. R.	9·29 N	85·15 W
110	Blanco, C. (blăn'kō) Or.	42·53 N	124·38 W
125	Blanco (R.) Mex.	18·42 N	96·03 W
124	Blanco (R.) Mex.	24·05 N	99·21 W
128	Blancos, Cayo (I.) (kä'yō-bläŋ'kōs) Cuba	23·15 N	80·55 W
115	Blanding Ut.	37·40 N	109·31 W
155	Blankenburg (bläŋ'kĕn-bŏŏrgh) G.D.R	51·45 N	10·58 E
149	Blankenfelde (blän'kĕn-fĕl-dĕ) G.D.R. (Berlin In.)	52·20 N	13·24 E
125	Blanquilla, Arrecife (Reef) (är-rĕ-sē'fĕ-blän-kē'l-yä) Mex.	21·32 N	97·14 W
217	Blantyre (blăn-tīyr) Malawi	15·47 S	35·00 E
107	Blasdell (blāz'dĕl) NY (Buffalo In.)	42·48 N	78·51 W
164	Blato (blä'tō) Yugo.	42·55 N	16·47 E
156	Blåvands Huk (Cape) (blô'văns-hōk) Den.	55·36 N	8·05 E
160	Blaye-et-Ste. Luce (blā'ā-sănt-lüs') Fr.	45·08 N	0·40 W
159	Błazowa (bwä-zhō'và) Pol.	49·51 N	22·05 E
217	Bleus, Monts (Mts.) Zaire	1·10 N	30·10 E
210	Blida Alg.	36·33 N	2·45 E
96	Blind River (blīnd) Can.	46·10 N	83·09 W
104	Blissfield (blĭs-fēld) Mi.	41·50 N	83·50 W
148	Blithe (R.) (blĭth) Eng.	52·22 N	1·49 W
214	Blitta Togo	8·19 N	0·59 E
105	Block (I.) (blŏk) RI	41·05 N	71·35 W
92	Bloedel Can.	50·07 N	125·23 W
218	Bloemfontein (blōōm'fŏn-tān) S. Afr. (Johannesburg & Pretoria In.)	29·09 S	26·16 E
160	Blois (blwä) Fr.	47·36 N	1·21 E
93	Blood Ind. Res. Can.	49·30 N	113·10 W
109	Bloomer (blōōm'ēr) Wi.	45·07 N	91·30 W
104	Bloomfield (blōōm'fēld) In.	39·00 N	86·55 W
109	Bloomfield Ia.	40·44 N	92·21 W
117	Bloomfield Mo.	36·54 N	89·55 W
108	Bloomfield Ne.	42·36 N	97·40 W
106	Bloomfield NJ (New York In.)	40·48 N	74·12 W
107	Bloomfield Hills Mi. (Detroit In.)	42·35 N	83·15 W
109	Blooming Prairie (blōōm'ĭng prā'rĭ) Mn.	43·52 N	93·04 W
113	Bloomington (blōōm'ĭng-tŭn) Ca. (Los Angeles In.)	34·04 N	117·24 W
104	Bloomington Il.	40·30 N	89·00 W
104	Bloomington In.	39·10 N	86·35 W
113	Bloomington Mn. (Minneapolis, St. Paul In.)	44·50 N	93·18 W
105	Bloomsburg (blōōmz'bûrg) Pa.	41·00 N	76·25 W
106	Blossburg (blŏs'bûrg) Al. (Birmingham In.)	33·38 N	86·57 W
105	Blossburg Pa.	41·45 N	77·00 W
212	Bloubergstrand S. Afr. (In.)	33·48 S	18·28 E
120	Blountstown (blŭnts'tun) Fl.	30·24 N	85·02 W
158	Bludenz (blōō-dĕnts') Aus.	47·09 N	9·50 E
99	Blue, Mt. Can.	50·28 N	57·11 W
107	Blue Ash (blōō ăsh) Oh. (Cincinnati In.)	39·14 N	84·23 W
109	Blue Earth (blōō ûrth) Mn.	43·38 N	94·05 W
109	Blue Earth (R.) Mn.	43·55 N	94·16 W
121	Bluefield (blōō'fēld) WV	37·15 N	81·11 W
127	Bluefields (blōō'fēldz) Nic.	12·03 N	83·45 W
107	Blue Island Il. (Chicago In.)	41·39 N	87·41 W
115	Blue Mesa Res. Co.	38·25 N	107.00 W
203	Blue Mts. Austl.	33·35 S	149·00 E
128	Blue Mts. Jam.	18·05 N	76·35 W
110	Blue Mts. Or.	45·15 N	118·50 W
204	Blue Mud B. (blōō mŭd) Austl.	13·20 S	136·45 E
211	Blue Nile (Abay) (R.) (à-bä'ē) Eth.	9·45 N	37·23 E
211	Blue Nile (Al-Bahr al-Azraq) (R.) (bärĕlaz-räk') Sud.	12·50 N	34·10 E
117	Blue Rapids (blōō răp'ĭdz) Ks.	39·40 N	96·41 W
103	Blue Ridge (Mts.) (blōō rĭj) U. S.	35·30 N	82·50 W
93	Blue River Can.	52·05 N	119·17 W
113	Blue R. Mo. (Kansas City In.)	38·55 N	94·33 W
115	Bluff Ut.	37·18 N	109·34 W
106	Bluff Park Al. (Birmingham In.)	33·24 N	86·52 W
104	Bluffton (blŭf-tŭn) In.	40·40 N	85·15 W
104	Bluffton Oh.	40·50 N	83·55 W
136	Blumenau (blōō'mĕn-ou) Braz.	26·53 S	48·58 W
183	Blumut, Gunong (Mt.) Mala. (Singapore In.)	2·03 N	103·34 E
154	Blyth (blīth) Eng.	55·03 N	1·34 W
114	Blythe Ca.	33·37 N	114·37 W
117	Blytheville (blīth'vĭl) Ar.	35·55 N	89·51 W
214	Bo S.L.	7·56 N	11·21 W
197	Boac Phil. (In.)	13·26 N	121·50 E
126	Boaco (bô-ä'kō) Nic.	12·24 N	85·41 W
192	Bo'ai (bwo-ī) China	35·10 N	113·08 E
135	Boa Vista do Rio Branco (bō'ä vēsh'tä dōō rē'ōō brän'kōō) Braz.	2·46 N	60·45 W
210	Boa Vista I. (bō-ä-vēsh'tà) C. V. (In.)	16·01 N	23·52 W
159	Bobĕrka (bō'bēr-kà) Sov. Un.	49·36 N	24·18 E
214	Bobo Dioulasso (bō'bô-dyōō-lás-sō') Upper Volta	11·12 N	4·18 W
166	Bobr (bô'b'r) Sov. Un.	54·19 N	29·11 E
158	Bóbr (R.) (bŭ'br) Pol.	51·44 N	15·13 E
167	Bobrinets (bŏ'brē-nyĭts) Sov. Un.	48·04 N	32·10 E
167	Bobrov (bŭb-rôf') Sov. Un.	51·07 N	40·01 E
167	Bobrovitsa (bŭb-rô'vē-tsá) Sov. Un.	50·43 N	31·27 E
166	Bobruysk (bŏ-brōō'ĭsk) Sov. Un.	53·07 N	29·13 E
135	Boca del Pozo (bô-kä-dĕl-pō'zŏ) Ven. (In.)	11·00 N	64·21 W
135	Boca de Uchire (bô-kä-dĕ-ōō-chē'rĕ) Ven. (In.)	10·09 N	65·27 W
137	Bocaina, Serra da (Mtn.) (sĕ'r-rä-dá-bô-kä'ē-nä) Braz. (Rio de Janeiro In.)	22·47 S	44·39 W
124	Bocas (bō'käs) Mex.	22·29 N	101·03 W
127	Bocas del Toro (bō'käs dĕl tō'rō) Pan.	9·24 N	82·15 W
159	Bochnia (bōk'nyä) Pol.	49·58 N	20·28 E
161	Bocholt (bō'kōlt) F.R.G. (Ruhr In.)	51·50 N	6·37 E
161	Bochum (bō'kōōm) F.R.G. (Ruhr In.)	51·29 N	7·13 E
161	Bockum-Hövel (bō'kōōm-hû'fĕl) F.R.G. (Ruhr In.)	51·41 N	7·45 E
216	Bodalang Zaire	3·14 N	22·14 E
173	Bodaybo (bō-dī'bō) Sov. Un.	57·12 N	114·46 E
215	Bodele (Depression) (bō-dà-lā') Chad	16·45 N	17·05 E
150	Boden Swe.	65·51 N	21·29 E
158	Boden See (L.) (bō'dĕn zā) F.R.G.-Switz.	47·48 N	9·22 E
154	Boderg (L.) (bō'dûrg) Ire.	53·51 N	8·06 W
154	Bodmin (bŏd'mĭn) Eng.	50·29 N	4·45 W
154	Bodmin Moor (bŏd'mĭn mŏŏr) Eng.	50·36 N	4·43 W
150	Bodö (bôd'û) Nor.	67·13 N	14·19 E
171	Bodrum Tur.	37·10 N	27·07 E
216	Boende (bô-ĕn'dâ) Zaire	0·13 S	20·52 E
118	Boerne (bō'ērn) Tx.	29·49 N	98·44 W
213	Boesmans (R.) S. Afr. (Natal In.)	33·29 S	26·09 E
119	Boeuf R. (bĕf) La.	32·23 N	91·57 W
214	Boffa (bôf'à) Gui.	10·10 N	14·02 W
195	Bōfu (bō'fōō) Jap.	34·03 N	131·35 E

260 Bogalusa — Boulder PRONOUNCING INDEX

Page	Name Pronunciation Region	Lat. °'	Long. °'
119	Bogalusa (bō-gȧ-lo͞o'sȧ) ... La.	30·48 N	89·52 W
203	Bogan (R.) (bô'gĕn) ... Austl.	32·10 S	147·40 E
156	Bogense (bô'gĕn-sĕ) ... Den.	55·34 N	10·09 E
127	Boggy Pk. (bŏg'ĭ-pēk) Antigua (In.)	17·03 N	61·50 W
167	Bogodukhov (bŏ-gŏ-do͞o'ĸôf) Sov. Un.	50·10 N	35·31 E
203	Bogong, Mt. ... Austl.	36·50 S	147·15 E
196	Bogor ... Indon.	6·45 S	106·45 E
166	Bogoroditsk (bŏ-gŏ'rô-dĭtsk) Sov. Un.	53·48 N	38·06 E
170	Bogorodsk ... Sov. Un.	56·02 N	43·40 E
174	Bogorodskoye (bô-gô-rôd'skô-yĕ) Sov. Un. (Urals In.)	56·43 N	56·53 E
134	Bogotá (bō-gō-tä') ... Col. (In.)	4·38 N	74·06 W
134	Bogotá, Rio (R.) (rē'ō-bō-gō-tä') Col. (In.)	4·27 N	74·38 W
172	Bogotol (bŏ'gô-tŏl) ... Sov. Un.	56 15 N	89·45 E
167	Bogoyavlenskoye (bŏ'gô-yäf'lĕn-skō'yĕ) . Sov. Un.	48·46 N	33·19 E
171	Boguchar (bō'go͞o-chär) . . Sov. Un.	49·40 N	41·00 E
127	Boguete (bô-gĕ'tĕ) ... Pan.	8·54 N	82·29 W
167	Boguslav (bŏ'go͞o-släf) . . . Sov. Un.	49·34 N	30·51 E
192	Bohai Haixia (Str.) (bwo-hī hī-shyä) . China	38·05 N	121·40 E
160	Bohain-en-Vermandois (bô-ăɴ-ŏɴ-vâr-mäɴ-dwä') . Fr.	49·58 N	3·22 E
	Bohemia (Prov.), see České		
158	Bohemian For. (bô-hē'mĭ-ăn) F.R.G.	49·35 N	12·27 E
197	Bohol (I.) (bô-hôl') ... Phil.	9·28 N	124·35 E
125	Bohom (bŏ-ô'm) ... Mex.	16·47 N	92·42 W
218	Bohotleh (bô-hŏt'lĕ) Som. (Horn of Afr. In.)	8·15 N	46·20 E
98	Boiestown (boiz'toun) ... Can.	46·27 N	66·25 W
104	Bois Blanc (I.) (boi' blăɳk) . . Mi.	45·45 N	84·30 W
89	Boischâtel (bwä-shä-tĕl') Can. (Quebec In.)	46·54 N	71·08 W
89	Bois-des-Filion (bo͞o-ä'dĕ-fē-yōɴ') Can. (Montreal In.)	45·40 N	73·46 W
110	Boise (boi'zē) ... Id.	43·38 N	116·12 W
110	Boise (R.) ... Id.	43·43 N	116·30 W
116	Boise City ... Ok.	36·42 N	102·30 W
95	Boissevain (bois'vān) ... Can.	49·14 N	100·03 W
210	Bojador, Cabo (C.) (kȧ'bô-bō-hä-dōr') (bŏj-ȧ-dōr') W. Sah.	26·21 N	16·08 W
186	Bojnūrd ... Iran	37·29 N	57·13 E
215	Bokani ... Nig.	9·26 N	5·13 E
210	Boké (bō-kā') ... Gui.	10·58 N	14·15 W
156	Bokn Fd. (bôk''n fyôrd) ... Nor.	59·12 N	5·37 E
213	Boksburg (bŏĸs'bûrgh) . . . S. Afr. (Johannesburg & Pretoria In.)	26·13 S	28·15 E
216	Bokungu ... Zaire	0·41 S	22·19 E
215	Bol ... Chad	13·28 N	14·43 E
215	Bolai I. ... Cen. Afr. Rep.	4·20 N	17·21 E
210	Bolama (bô-lä'mä) . Guinea-Bissau	11·34 N	15·41 W
184	Bolan (Mt.) (bô-län') ... Pak.	30·13 N	67·09 E
124	Bolaños (bō-län'yôs) ... Mex.	21·40 N	103·48 W
124	Bolaños (R.) ... Mex.	21·26 N	103·54 W
184	Bolan P. ... Pak.	29·50 N	67·10 E
160	Bolbec (bôl-bĕk') ... Fr.	49·37 N	0·26 E
214	Bole (bō'lâ) ... Ghana	9·02 N	2·29 W
158	Boleslawiec (bō-lĕ-slä'vyĕts) Pol.	51·15 N	15·35 E
214	Bolgatanga ... Ghana	10·46 N	0·52 W
167	Bolgrad (bŏl-grät) ... Sov. Un.	45·41 N	28·38 E
192	Boli (bwo-lē) ... China	45·40 N	130·38 E
197	Bolinao (bō-lê-nä'ô) . . . . Phil. (In.)	16·24 N	119·53 E
137	Bolívar (bō-lē'vär) Arg. (Buenos Aires In.)	36·15 S	61·05 W
134	Bolívar ... Col.	1·46 N	76·58 W
117	Bolivar (bŏl'ĭ-vȧr) ... Mo.	37·37 N	93·22 W
120	Bolivar ... Tn.	35·14 N	88·56 W
134	Bolívar (La Columna) (Mtn.) (bô-lē'vär) (lä-kô-lo͞o'm-nä) . Ven.	8·44 N	70·54 W
119	Bolivar Pen. (bŏl'ĭ-vȧr) Tx. (In.)	29·25 N	94·40 W
133	Bolivia (bô-lĭv'ĭ-ȧ) ... S.A.	17·00 S	64·00 W
166	Bolkhov (bŏl-ĸôf') ... Sov. Un.	53·27 N	35·59 E
148	Bollin (R.) (bŏl'ĭn) ... Eng.	53·18 N	2·11 W
148	Bollington (bôl'ĭng-tŭn) ... Eng.	53·18 N	2·06 W
156	Bollnäs (bôl'nĕs) ... Swe.	61·22 N	16·20 E
156	Bolmen (L.) (bôl'mĕn) ... Swe.	56·58 N	13·25 E
212	Bolobo (bō'lō-bō) ... Zaire	2·14 S	16·18 E
164	Bologna (bô-lōn'yä) ... It.	44·30 N	11·18 E
166	Bologoye (bŏ-lŏ-gô'yĕ) . . . Sov. Un.	57·52 N	34·02 E
126	Bolonchenticul (bô-lôn-chĕn-tē-ko͞o'l) . Mex. (In.)	20·03 N	89·47 W
128	Bolondrón (bô-lôn-drōn') ... Cuba	22·45 N	81·25 W
164	Bolseno, Lago di (L.) (lä'gō-dē-bôl-sā'nô) . It.	42·35 N	11·40 E
170	Bol'shaya Kinel' (R.) ... Sov. Un.	53·20 N	52·40 E
167	Bol'shaya Lepetikha (bŏl-shȧ'yȧ'lyĕ'pyĕ-tē'ĸȧ) Sov. Un.	47·11 N	33·58 E
167	Bol'shaya Viska (vĭs-kȧ') . Sov. Un.	48·34 N	31·54 E
167	Bol'shaya Vradiyevka (vrȧ-dyĕf'kȧ) . Sov. Un.	47·51 N	30·38 E
174	Bol'she Ust'ikinskoye (bôl'she o͞os-tyĭ-kēn'skô-yĕ) Sov. Un. (Urals In.)	55·58 N	58·18 E
173	Bolshoy Anyuy (R.) ... Sov. Un.	67·58 N	161·15 E
173	Bol'shoy Begichëv (I.) . . . Sov. Un.	74·30 N	114·40 E
173	Bolshoy Chuva (R.) ... Sov. Un.	58·15 N	111·13 E
174	Bol'shoye Ivonino (ĭ-vô'nĭ-nô) Sov. Un. (Urals In.)	59·41 N	61·12 E
174	Bol'shoy Kuyash (bôl'-shôy ko͞o'yȧsh) Sov. Un. (Urals In.)	55·52 N	61·07 E
167	Bolshoy Tokmak (bŏl-shôy' tôk-mäk') . Sov. Un.	47·17 N	35·48 E
148	Bolsover (bōl'zō-vẽr) ... Eng.	53·14 N	1·17 W
163	Boltana (bôl-tä'nä) ... Sp.	42·28 N	0·03 E
89	Bolton (bōl'tŭn) Can. (Toronto In.)	43·53 N	79·44 W
148	Bolton ... Eng.	53·35 N	2·26 W
148	Bolton-upon-Dearne (bōl'tŭn-ŭp'ŏn-dûrn) . Eng.	53·31 N	1·19 W
171	Bolu (bō'lo͞o) ... Tur.	40·45 N	31·45 E
166	Bolva (R.) (bôl'vä) ... Sov. Un.	53·30 N	34·30 E
171	Bolvadin (bŏl-vä-dēn') ... Tur.	38·50 N	30·50 E
164	Bolzano (bôl-tsä'nō) ... It.	46·31 N	11·22 E
216	Boma (bō'mä) ... Zaire	5·51 S	13·03 E
203	Bombala (bŭm-bä'lă) ... Austl.	36·55 S	149·07 E
185	Bombay (bŏm-bā') . . . . India (In.)	18·58 N	72·50 E
185	Bombay Hbr. ... India (In.)	18·55 N	72·52 E
210	Bomi Hills ... Lib.	7·00 N	11·00 W
137	Bom Jardim (bôn zhär-dēɴ') Braz. (Rio de Janeiro In.)	22·10 S	42·25 W
137	Bom Jesus do Itabapoana (bôɴ-zhĕ-so͞o's-dô-ē-tȧ'bä-pô-ȧ'nä) . Braz. (Rio de Janeiro In.)	21·08 S	41·51 W
156	Bömlo (I.) (bûmlô) ... Nor.	59·47 N	4·57 E
216	Bomongo ... Zaire	1·22 N	18·21 E
137	Bom Sucesso (bôn-so͞o-sĕ'sô) Braz. (Rio de Janeiro In.)	21·02 S	44·44 W
	Bomu (R.), see Mbomou		
151	Bon, C. (bôɴ) ... Tun.	37·04 N	11·13 E
134	Bonaire (I.) (bô-nâr') Neth. Antilles	12·10 N	68·15 W
162	Boñar (bō-nyär') ... Sp.	42·53 N	5·18 W
99	Bonavista (bŏ-nȧ-vĭs'tȧ) ... Can.	48·39 N	53·07 W
99	Bonavista B. ... Can.	48·45 N	53·20 W
116	Bond (bŏnd) ... Co.	39·53 N	106·40 W
216	Bondo (bôn'dô) ... Zaire	3·49 N	23·40 E
197	Bondoc Pen. (bôn-dŏk') Phil. (In.)	13·24 N	122·30 E
214	Bondoukou (bŏn-do͞o'ko͞o) Ivory Coast	8·02 N	2·48 W
128	Bonds Cay (I.) (bŏnds kē) . . . . Ba.	25·30 N	77·45 W
	Bône, see Annaba		
196	Bone, Teluk (G.) ... Indon.	4·09 S	121·00 E
136	Bonete, Cerro (Mt.) (bô'nĕtĕh çĕrrô) . Arg.	27·50 S	68·35 W
137	Bonfim (bôɴ-fē'ɴ) Braz. (Rio de Janeiro In.)	20·20 S	44·15 W
215	Bongor ... Chad	10·17 N	15·22 E
193	Bong Son ... Viet.	14·20 N	109·10 E
117	Bonham (bŏn'ăm) ... Tx.	33·35 N	96·09 W
129	Bonhomme, Pic (Pk.) ... Hai.	19·10 N	72·20 W
164	Bonifacio (bō-nē-fä'chō) ... Fr.	41·23 N	9·10 E
164	Bonifacio, Str. of ... Eur.	41·14 N	9·02 E
120	Bonifay (bŏn-ĭ-fā') ... Fl.	30·46 N	85·40 W
198	Bonin Is. (bō'nĭn) ... Asia	26·30 N	141·00 E
161	Bonn (bôn) . . . . F.R.G. (Ruhr In.)	50·44 N	7·06 E
99	Bonne B. (bŏn) ... Can.	49·33 N	57·55 W
110	Bonners Ferry (bon'ẽrz fĕr'ĭ) . . Id.	48·41 N	116·19 W
113	Bonner Springs (bŏn'ẽr sprĭngz) Ks. (Kansas City In.)	39·04 N	94·52 W
117	Bonne Terre (bŏn târ') ... Mo.	37·55 N	90·32 W
93	Bonnet Pk. (bŏn'ĭt) ... Can.	51·26 N	115·53 W
110	Bonneville Dam (bŏn'ē-vĭl) Or.-Wa.	45·37 N	121·57 W
99	Bonnie B. (bŏn'ē) ... Can.	49·38 N	58·15 W
210	Bonny (bŏn'ē) ... Nig.	4·29 N	7·13 E
112	Bonny Lake (bŏn'ē lăk) Wa. (Seattle In.)	47·11 N	122·11 W
93	Bonnyville (bŏn'ē-vĭl) ... Can.	54·16 N	110·44 W
164	Bonorva (bô-nôr'vä) ... It.	40·26 N	8·46 E
196	Bonthain (bôn-tīn') ... Indon.	5·30 S	119·52 E
214	Bonthe ... S. L.	7·32 N	12·30 W
197	Bontoc (bôn-tŏk') ... Phil. (In.)	17·10 N	121·01 E
128	Booby Rocks (I.) (bo͞o'bĭ rŏks) Ba.	23·55 N	77·00 W
121	Booker T. Washington Natl. Mon. (bo͝ok'ẽr tē wŏsh'ĭng-tŭn) . Va.	37·07 N	79·45 W
149	Boom ... Bel. (Brussels In.)	51·05 N	4·22 E
109	Boone (bo͞on) ... Ia.	42·04 N	93·51 W
117	Booneville (bo͞on'vĭl) ... Ar.	35·09 N	93·54 W
104	Booneville ... Ky.	37·25 N	83·40 W
120	Booneville ... Ms.	34·37 N	88·35 W
218	Boons ... S. Afr. (Johannesburg & Pretoria In.)	25·59 S	27·15 E
106	Boonton (bo͞on'tŭn) NJ (New York In.)	40·54 N	74·24 W
104	Boonville ... In.	38·00 N	87·15 W
117	Boonville ... Mo.	38·57 N	92·44 W
98	Boothbay Harbor (bo͞oth'bā här'bẽr) . Me.	43·51 N	69·39 W
91	Boothia, G. of (bo͞o'thĭ-ȧ) ... Can.	69·04 N	86·04 W
75	Boothia Pen. ... Can.	73·30 N	95·00 W
148	Bootle (bo͞ot''l) ... Eng.	53·29 N	3·02 W
216	Booué ... Gabon	0·06 S	11·56 E
158	Boppard (bôp'ärt) ... F.R.G.	50·14 N	7·35 E
211	Bor (bôr) ... Sud.	6·13 N	31·35 E
171	Bor (bōr) ... Tur.	37·50 N	34·40 E
111	Borah Pk. (bō'rä) ... Id.	44·12 N	113·47 W
218	Borama (bôr-ȧ-mă) Som. (Horn of Afr. In.)	10·05 N	43·08 E
156	Borås (bo͞o'rōs) ... Swe.	57·43 N	12·55 E
186	Borāzjān (bō-räz-jän') ... Iran	29·13 N	51·13 E
135	Borba (bôr'bä) ... Braz.	4·23 S	59·31 W
135	Borborema, Planalto da (Plat.) (plä-näl'tô-dä-bôr-bō-rĕ'mä) Braz.	7·35 S	36·40 W
160	Bordeaux (bôr-dō') ... Fr.	44·50 N	0·37 W
105	Bordentown (bôr'dĕn-toun) ... NJ	40·05 N	74·40 W
151	Bordj-bou-Arréridj (bôrj-bo͞o-ȧ-rā-rēj') . Alg.	36·03 N	4·48 E
157	Borgå (bôr'gō) ... Fin.	60·26 N	25·41 E
150	Borgarnes ... Ice.	64·31 N	21·40 W
116	Borger (bôr'gẽr) ... Tx.	35·40 N	101·23 W
156	Borgholm (bôrg-hôlm') ... Swe.	56·52 N	16·40 E
119	Borgne (L.) (bôrn'y') ... La.	30·03 N	89·36 W
164	Borgomanero (bôr'gō-mä-nâ'rō) It.	45·40 N	8·28 E
163	Borgo Montello (bô'r-zhō-môn-tĕ'lō) It. (Rome In.)	41·31 N	12·48 E
164	Borgo Val di Taro (bô'r-zhō-väl-dē-tä'rō) . It.	44·29 N	9·44 E
112	Boring (bōring) Or. (Portland In.)	45·26 N	122·22 W
159	Borislav (bô'rĭs-lôf) ... Sov. Un.	49·17 N	23·24 E
171	Borisoglebsk (bŏ-rē sŏ-glyĕpsk') Sov. Un.	51·20 N	42·00 E
166	Borisov (bŏ-rē'sôf) ... Sov. Un.	54·16 N	28·33 E
167	Borisovka (bŏ-rē-sôf'kȧ) . . Sov. Un.	50·38 N	36·00 E
167	Borispol' (bo-rĭs'pol) ... Sov. Un.	50·17 N	30·54 E
185	Borivli ... India (In.)	19·15 N	72·48 E
162	Borja (bôr'hä) ... Sp.	41·50 N	1·33 W
163	Borjas Blancas (bô'r-käs-blä'n-käs) . Sp.	41·29 N	0·53 E
161	Borken (bōr'kĕn) F.R.G. (Ruhr In.)	51·50 N	6·51 E
211	Borkou (Reg.) (bôr-ko͞o') ... Chad	18·11 N	18·28 E
158	Borkum I. (bōr'ko͞om) ... F.R.G.	53·31 N	6·50 E
156	Borlänge (bôr-lĕɳ'gĕ) ... Swe.	60·30 N	15·24 E
196	Borneo (I.) (bôr'nē-ō) ... Asia	0·25 N	112·39 E
156	Bornholm (I.) (bôrn-hôlm) . . . Den.	55·16 N	15·15 E
162	Bornos (bôr'nōs) ... Sp.	36·48 N	5·45 W
167	Borodayevka ... Sov. Un.	48·44 N	34·09 E
167	Boromlya (bŏ-rôm''l-yȧ) . . Sov. Un.	50·36 N	34·58 E
214	Boromo ... Upper Volta	11·45 N	2·56 W
165	Borovan (bŏ-rō-vän') ... Bul.	43·24 N	23·47 E
166	Borovichi (bŏ-rô-vē'chê) . . Sov. Un.	58·22 N	33·56 E
166	Borovsk (bô'rŏvsk) ... Sov. Un.	55·13 N	36·26 E
135	Borracha, Isla la (I.) (ē's-lä-lä-bôr-rȧ'chä) . Ven. (In.)	10·18 N	64·44 W
204	Borroloola (bŏr-rō-lo͞o'lȧ) ... Austl.	16·15 S	136·19 E
159	Borshchëv (bôrsh-chyôf') . Sov. Un.	48·47 N	26·04 E
160	Bort-les-Orgues (bôr-lā-zôrg) . . . Fr.	45·26 N	2·26 E
186	Borūjerd ... Iran	33·45 N	48·53 E
167	Borzna (bôrz'nȧ) ... Sov. Un.	51·15 N	32·26 E
173	Borzya (bôrz'yȧ) ... Sov. Un.	50·37 N	116·53 E
164	Bosa (bō'sä) ... It.	40·18 N	8·34 E
164	Bosanska Dubica (bō'sän-skä do͞o'bĭt-sä) . Yugo.	45·10 N	16·49 E
164	Bosanska Gradiška (bō'sän-skä grä-dĭsh'kä) . Yugo.	45·08 N	17·15 E
164	Bosanski Novi (bō's sän-skĭ nō'vē) Yugo.	45·00 N	16·22 E
164	Bosanski Petrovac (bō'sän-skĭ pĕt'rō-väts) . Yugo.	44·33 N	16·23 E
165	Bosanski Šamac (bō'sän-skĭ shä'mȧts) . Yugo.	45·03 N	18·30 E
109	Boscobel (bŏs'kô-bĕl) ... Wi.	43·08 N	90·44 W
193	Bose (bwo-sŭ) ... China	24·00 N	106·38 E
190	Boshan (bwo-shan) ... China	36·32 N	117·51 E
174	Boskol' (bȧs-kôl') Sov. Un. (Urals In.)	53·45 N	61·17 E
149	Boskoop . . . Neth. (Amsterdam In.)	52·04 N	4·39 E
158	Boskovice (bŏs'kō-vē-tsĕ) . . . Czech.	49·26 N	16·37 E
165	Bosna (R.) ... Yugo.	44·19 N	17·54 E
165	Bosnia (Reg.) (bŏs'nĭ-ȧ) ... Yugo.	44·17 N	16·58 E
216	Bosobolo ... Zaire	4·11 N	19·54 E
	Bosporous (Str.), see İstanbul Boğazı		
215	Bossangoa ... Cen. Afr. Rep.	6·29 N	17·27 E
215	Bossembélé ... Cen. Afr. Rep.	5·16 N	17·39 E
119	Bossier City (bŏsh'ẽr) ... La.	32·31 N	93·42 W
188	Bosten Hu (L.) (bwo-stŭn ho͞o) China	42·06 N	88·01 E
120	Boston (bôs'tŭn) ... Ga.	30·47 N	83·47 W
99	Boston ... Ma. (In.)	42·15 N	71·07 W
107	Boston Heights Oh. (Cleveland In.)	41·15 N	81·30 W
117	Boston Mts. ... Ar.	35·46 N	93·32 W
202	Botany B. (bŏt'ȧ-nĭ) Austl. (Sydney In.)	33·58 S	151·11 E
165	Botevgrad ... Bul.	42·54 N	23·41 E
218	Bothaville (bō'tä-vĭl) ... S. Afr. (Johannesburg & Pretoria In.)	27·24 S	26·38 E
112	Bothell (bŏth'ĕl) . Wa. (Seattle In.)	47·46 N	122·12 W
150	Bothnia, G. of (bŏth'nĭ-ȧ) . . . Eur.	63·40 N	21·30 E
159	Botosani (bō-tō-shän'ĭ) ... Rom.	47·46 N	26·40 E
209	Botswana (bŏtswănă) ... Afr.	22·10 S	23·13 E
108	Bottineau (bŏt-ĭ-nō') ... ND	48·48 N	100·28 W
161	Bottrop (bōt'trōp) F.R.G. (Ruhr In.)	51·31 N	6·56 E
135	Botucatú (bô-to͞o-kä-to͞o') . . . Braz.	22·50 S	48·23 W
99	Botwood (bŏt'wo͝od) ... Can.	49·08 N	55·21 W
214	Bouafle (bo͞o-ȧ-flā') . . . Ivory Coast	6·59 N	5·45 W
214	Bouaké (bo͞o-ȧ-kā') . . . Ivory Coast	7·41 N	5·00 W
215	Bouar (bo͞o-är) ... Cen. Afr. Rep.	5·57 N	15·36 E
215	Boubandjidah, Parc Natl. de (Natl. Pk.) . Cam.	8·20 N	14·40 E
89	Boucherville (bo͞o-shä-vĕl') Can. (Montreal In.)	45·37 N	73·27 W
214	Boucle du Baoulé, Parc Natl. de la (Natl. Pk.) . Mali	13·50 N	9·15 W
210	Boudenib (bo͞o-dĕ-nēb') ... Mor.	32·14 N	3·04 W
109	Boudette (bo͞o-dĕt) ... Mn.	48·42 N	94·34 W
151	Bou Dia, C. (bo͞o dē'ȧ)) ... Tun.	35·18 N	11·17 E
163	Boudouaou ... Alg.	36·44 N	3·25 E
163	Boufarik (bo͞o-fȧ-rēk') ... Alg.	36·35 N	2·55 E
198	Bougainville Trench (bo͞o-găɴ-vēl') . Oceania	7·00 S	152·00 E
	Bougie, see Bejaïa		
210	Bougouni (bo͞o-go͞o-nē') ... Mali	11·27 N	7·30 W
152	Bouira (boo-ē'rȧ) ... Alg.	36·25 N	3·55 E
163	Bouira-Sahary (bwē-rȧ sȧ'ȧ-rē) Alg.	35·16 N	3·23 E
214	Bouka (R.) ... Gui.	11·05 N	10·40 W
204	Boulder (bōl'dẽr) ... Austl.	31·00 S	121·40 E
116	Boulder ... Co.	40·02 N	105·19 W

PRONOUNCING INDEX

Boulder — Bristow 261

Page	Name Pronunciation Region	Lat. °′	Long. °′
111	Boulder (R.)....Mt.	46·10 N	112·07 W
114	Boulder City....Nv.	35·57 N	114·50 W
110	Boulder Cr....Id.	42·53 N	116·49 W
111	Boulder Pk....Id.	43·53 N	114·33 W
161	Boulogne-Billancourt (bōō-lôn'y'-bē-yäN-kōōr') Fr. (Paris In.)	48·50 N	2·14 E
160	Boulogne-sur-Mer (bōō-lôn'y-sür-mâr').Fr.	50·44 N	1·37 E
215	Boumba (R.)....Cam.	3·20 N	14·40 E
163	Bou-Mort, Sierra de (Mts.) (sē-ĕ'r-rä-dĕ-bô-ōō-mô'rt).Sp.	42·11 N	1·05 E
214	Bouna (bōō-nä')....Ivory Coast	9·16 N	3·00 W
214	Bouna, Park Natl. de (Natl. Pk.).Ivory Coast	9·20 N	3·35 W
112	Boundary B. (boun'dȧ-rĭ) Can. (Vancouver In.)	49·03 N	122·59 W
114	Boundary Pk....Nv.	37·52 N	118·20 W
106	Bound Brook (bound brŏŏk) NJ (New York In.)	40·34 N	74·32 W
113	Bountiful (boun'tĭ-fōōl) Ut. (Salt Lake City In.)	40·55 N	111·53 W
113	Bountiful Pk. (boun'tĭ-fōōl) Ut. (Salt Lake City In.)	40·58 N	111·49 W
220	Bounty Is....N. Z.	47·42 S	179·05 E
210	Bourem (bōō-rĕm')....Mali	16·43 N	0·15 W
160	Bourg-en-Bresse (bōōr-gĕN-brĕs') Fr.	46·12 N	5·13 E
160	Bourges (bōōrzh)....Fr.	47·06 N	2·22 E
89	Bourget (bōōr-zhĕ') Can. (Ottawa In.)	45·26 N	75·09 W
161	Bourgoin (bōōr-gwăN')....Fr.	45·46 N	5·17 E
203	Bourke (bûrk)....Austl.	30·10 S	146·00 E
148	Bourne (bôrn)....Eng.	52·46 N	0·22 W
154	Bournemouth (bôrn'mŭth)...Eng.	50·44 N	1·55 W
152	Bou Saâda (bōō-sä'dä)....Alg.	35·13 N	4·17 E
211	Bousso (bōō-sô')....Chad	10·33 N	16·45 E
210	Boutilimit (bōō-tē-lē-mē') Mauritania	17·30 N	14·54 W
	Bouvert (I.), see Bouvetöen		
220	Bouvetöen (Bouvert) (I.)..Alt. O.	54·26 S	3·24 E
164	Bovino (bō-vē'nō)....It.	41·14 N	15·21 E
93	Bow (R.) (bō)....Can.	50·35 N	112·15 W
108	Bowbells (bō'bĕls)....ND	48·50 N	102·16 W
108	Bowdle (bōd''l)....SD	45·28 N	99·42 W
205	Bowen (bō'ĕn)....Austl.	20·02 S	148·14 E
106	Bowie (bōō'ĭ) (bō'ē) Md. (Baltimore In.)	38·59 N	76·47 W
116	Bowie....Tx.	33·34 N	97·50 W
120	Bowling Green (bōlĭng grēn)..Ky.	37·00 N	86·26 W
117	Bowling Green....Mo.	39·19 N	91·09 W
104	Bowling Green....Oh.	41·25 N	83·40 W
108	Bowman (bō'măn)....ND	46·11 N	103·23 W
93	Bowron (R.) (bō'rŭn)....Can.	53·20 N	121·10 W
108	Boxelder Cr. (bŏks'ĕl-dēr)....Mt.	45·35 N	104·28 W
111	Boxelder Cr....Mt.	47·17 N	108·37 W
190	Bo Xian (bwo shyĕn)....China	33·52 N	115·47 E
190	Boxing (bwo-shyĭŋ)....China	37·09 N	118·08 E
149	Boxtel...Neth. (Amsterdam In.)	51·40 N	5·21 E
216	Boyabo....Zaire	3·43 N	18·46 E
193	Boyang (bwo-yäŋ)....China	29·00 N	116·42 E
89	Boyer (R.) (boi'ēr) Can. (Quebec In.)	46·26 N	70·56 W
108	Boyer (R.)....Ia.	41·45 N	95·36 W
154	Boyle (boil)....Ire.	53·59 N	8·15 W
104	Boyne City....Mi.	45·15 N	85·05 W
154	Boyne R. (boin)....Ire.	53·40 N	6·40 W
165	Bozcaada (Tenedos) (bōz-cä'dä) (tĕ'nĕ-dŏs).Tur.	39·50 N	26·05 E
165	Bozcaada (I.)....Tur.	39·50 N	26·00 E
111	Bozeman (bōz'măn)....Mt.	45·41 N	111·00 W
216	Bozene....Zaire	2·56 N	19·12 E
190	Bozhen (bwo-jŭn)....China	38·05 N	116·35 E
215	Bozoum....Cen. Afr. Rep.	6·19 N	16·23 E
164	Bra (brä)....It.	44·41 N	7·52 E
164	Brač (I.) (bräch)....Yugo.	43·18 N	16·36 E
4	Bracciano, Lago di (L.) (lä'gō-dē-brä-chä'nō).It.	42·05 N	12·00 E
105	Bracebridge (brās'brĭj)....Can.	45·05 N	79·20 W
107	Braceville (brās'vĭl) Il. (Chicago In.)	41·13 N	88·16 W
156	Bräcke (brĕk'kĕ)....Swe.	62·44 N	15·28 E
107	Brackenridge (brăk'ĕn-rĭj) Pa. (Pittsburgh In.)	40·37 N	79·44 W
118	Brackettville (brăk'ĕt-vĭl)....Tx.	29·19 N	100·24 W
135	Braço Maior (R.)....Braz.	11·00 S	51·00 W
135	Braço Menor (R.) (brä'zō-mĕ-nō'r).Braz.	11·38 S	50·00 W
164	Brádano (R.) (brä-dä'nō)....It.	40·43 N	16·22 E
107	Braddock (brăd'ŭk) Pa. (Pittsburgh In.)	40·24 N	79·52 W
121	Bradenton (brā'dĕn-tŭn) Fl. (In.)	27·28 N	82·35 W
148	Bradfield (brăd-fēld) Eng. (London In.)	51·25 N	1·08 W
148	Bradford (brăd'fērd)....Eng.	53·47 N	1·44 W
104	Bradford....Oh.	40·10 N	84·30 W
105	Bradford....Pa.	42·00 N	78·40 W
107	Bradley (brăd'lĭ) Il. (Chicago In.)	41·09 N	87·52 W
112	Bradner (brăd'nēr) Can. (Vancouver In.)	49·05 N	122·26 W
118	Brady (brā'dĭ)....Tx.	31·09 N	99·21 W
162	Braga (brä'gä)....Port.	41·20 N	8·25 W
137	Bragado (brä-gä'dō) Arg. (Buenos Aires In.)	35·07 S	60·28 W
135	Bragança (brä-gän'sä)....Braz.	1·02 S	46·50 W
162	Bragança....Port.	41·48 N	6·46 W
137	Bragança Paulista (brä-gän'sä-pä'ōō-lē's-tȧ) Braz. (Rio de Janeiro In.)	22·58 S	46·31 W
89	Bragg Creek (brăg) Can. (Calgary In.)	50·57 N	114·35 W
187	Brahmaputra (R.) (brä'mȧ-pōō'trȧ).India	26·45 N	92·45 E
187	Brāhui (Mts.)....Pak.	28·32 N	66·15 E
107	Braidwood (brād'wŏŏd) Il. (Chicago In.)	41·16 N	88·13 W
167	Brăila (brē'ēlȧ)....Rom.	45·15 N	27·58 E
109	Brainerd (brān'ērd)....Mn.	46·20 N	94·09 W
99	Braintree (brān'trē)....Ma. (In.)	42·14 N	71·00 W
106	Braithwaite (brīth'wīt) La. (New Orleans In.)	29·52 N	89·57 W
213	Brakpan (brăk'păn)....S. Afr. (Johannesburg & Pretoria In.)	26·15 S	28·22 E
92	Bralorne (brā'lôrn)....Can.	50·47 N	122·49 W
89	Bramalea....Can. (Toronto In.)	43·48 N	79·41 W
89	Brampton (brămp'tŭn) Can. (Toronto In.)	43·41 N	79·46 W
136	Branca, Pedra (Mtn.) (pĕ'drä-brä'N-kä) Braz. (Rio de Janeiro In.)	22·55 S	43·28 W
106	Branchville (brȧnch'vĭl) NJ (New York In.)	41·09 N	74·44 W
121	Branchville....SC	33·17 N	80·48 W
135	Branco (R.) (bräŋ'kō)....Braz.	2·21 N	60·38 W
212	Brandberg (Mtn.)....Namibia	21·15 S	14·15 E
149	Brandenburg (brän'dĕn-bōōrgh) G.D.R. (Berlin In.)	52·25 N	12·33 E
158	Brandenburg (Reg.)....G.D.R.	52·12 N	13·31 E
218	Brandfort (brăn'd-fôrt)....S. Afr. (Johannesburg & Pretoria In.)	28·42 S	26·29 E
95	Brandon (brăn'dŭn)....Can.	49·50 N	99·57 W
105	Brandon....Vt.	43·45 N	73·05 W
154	Brandon Hill (brăn-dŏn)....Ire.	52·15 N	10·12 W
106	Brandywine (brăndĭ'wīn) Md. (Baltimore In.)	38·42 N	76·51 W
105	Branford (brăn'fērd)....Ct.	41·15 N	72·50 W
159	Braniewo (brä-nyĕ'vō)....Pol.	54·23 N	19·50 E
159	Brańsk (brän' sk)....Pol.	52·44 N	22·51 E
89	Brantford (brănt'fērd) Can. (Toronto In.)	43·09 N	80·17 W
99	Bras d'Or L. (brä-dôr')....Can.	45·52 N	60·50 W
135	Brasília (brä-sē'lvä)....Braz.	15·49 S	47·39 W
135	Brasilia Legal (Fordlândia) (brä-sē'lyä-lĕ-gål) (fô'rd-län-dyä) Braz.	3·45 S	55·46 W
137	Brasópolis (brä-sô'pô-lēs) Braz. (Rio de Janeiro In.)	22·30 S	45·36 W
165	Braşov (Oraşul-Stalin)....Rom.	45·39 N	25·35 E
210	Brass (brăs)....Nig.	4·28 N	6·28 E
89	Bras St. Michel (R.) Can. (Quebec In.)	46·47 N	70·51 W
149	Brasschaat (bräs'кät) Bel. (Brussels In.)	51·19 N	4·30 E
107	Bratenahl (brä'tĕn-ôl) Oh. (Cleveland In.)	41·34 N	81·36 W
149	Bratislava (brä'tĭs-lä-vä) Czech. (Vienna In.)	48·09 N	17·07 E
172	Bratsk (brätsk)....Sov. Un.	56·10 N	102·04 E
172	Bratskoye Vdkhr. (Res.).Sov. Un.	56·10 N	102·05 E
167	Bratslav (brät'slåf)....Sov. Un.	48·48 N	28·59 E
105	Brattleboro (brăt''l-bŭr-ō)....Vt.	42·50 N	72·35 W
158	Braunau (brou'nou)....Aus.	48·15 N	13·05 E
158	Braunschweig (broun'shvīgh) F.R.G.	52·16 N	10·32 E
218	Brava (brä'vä) Som. (Horn of Afr. In.)	1·20 N	44·00 E
156	Bråviken (R.)....Swe.	58·40 N	16·40 E
	Bravo del Norte, Rio (R.), see Grande, Rio		
114	Brawley (brô'lĭ)....Ca.	32·59 N	115·32 W
154	Bray (brā)....Ire.	53·10 N	6·05 W
117	Braymer (brā'mēr)....Mo.	39·34 N	93·47 W
119	Brays Bay. (brās'bī'yōō).Tx. (In.)	29·41 N	95·33 W
93	Brazeau, Mt. (brȧ-zō')....Can.	52·33 N	117·21 W
93	Brazeau (R.)....Can.	52·55 N	116·10 W
104	Brazil (brȧ-zĭl')....In.	39·30 N	87·00 W
133	Brazil....S. A.	9·00 S	53·00 W
133	Brazilian Highlands (Mts.) (brȧ zĭl yȧn hī-lȧndz).Braz.	14·00 S	48·00 W
102	Brazos (R.) (brä'zōs)....U. S.	33·10 N	98·50 W
118	Brazos (R.), Clear Fk....Tx.	32·56 N	99·14 W
116	Brazos (R.), Double Mountain Fk. Tx.	33·23 N	101·21 W
116	Brazos (R.), Salt Fk. (sôlt fôrk) Tx.	33·20 N	100·57 W
216	Brazzaville (brȧ-zȧ-vēl')....Con.	4·16 S	15·17 E
165	Brčko (bērch'kô)....Yugo.	44·54 N	18·46 E
159	Brda R. (bēr-dä')....Pol.	53·18 N	17·55 E
113	Brea (brē'ȧ).Ca. (Los Angeles In.)	33·55 N	117·54 W
89	Breakeyville....Can. (Quebec In.)	46·40 N	71·13 W
108	Breckenridge (brĕk'ĕn-rĭj)....Mn.	46·17 N	96·35 W
118	Breckenridge....Tx.	32·46 N	98·53 W
107	Brecksville (brĕks'vĭl) Oh. (Cleveland In.)	41·19 N	81·38 W
158	Břeclav (brzhĕl'läf)....Czech.	48·46 N	16·54 E
154	Brecon Beacons (brĕk'ŭn bē kŭns) Wales	52·00 N	3·55 W
149	Breda (brā-dä') Neth. (Amsterdam In.)	51·35 N	4·47 E
212	Bredasdorp (brā'das-dôrp)..S. Afr.	34·15 S	20·00 E
174	Bredy (brĕ'dĭ).Sov. Un. (Urals In.)	52·25 N	60·23 E
158	Bregenz (brā'gĕnts)....Aus.	47·30 N	9·46 E
165	Bregovo (brĕ'gō-vō)....Bul.	44·07 N	22·45 E
213	Breidbach (brĕd'băk) S. Afr. (Natal In.)	32·54 S	27·26 E
150	Breidha Fd. (brā'dĭ)....Ice.	65·15 N	22·50 W
161	Breil (brĕ'y')....Fr.	43·57 N	7·36 E
135	Brejo (brå'zhōō)....Braz.	3·33 S	42·46 W
156	Bremangerland (I.) (brĕ-mängĕr-länd).Nor.	61·51 N	4·25 E
158	Bremen (brā-mĕn)....F.R.G.	53·05 N	8·50 E
104	Bremen (brē'mĕn)....In.	41·25 N	86·05 W
158	Bremerhaven (brām-ēr-hä'fĕn) F.R.G.	53·33 N	8·38 E
112	Bremerton (brĕm'ēr-tŭn) Wa. (Seattle In.)	47·34 N	122·38 W
149	Bremervörde (brĕ'mĕr-fûr-dĕ) F.R.G. (Hamburg In.)	53·29 N	9·09 E
89	Bremner (brĕm'nēr) Can. (Edmonton In.)	53·34 N	113·14 W
119	Bremond (brĕm'ŭnd)....Tx.	31·11 N	96·40 W
119	Brenham (brĕn'ăm)....Tx.	30·10 N	96·24 W
158	Brenner P. (brĕn'ēr)....Aus.-It.	47·00 N	11·30 E
148	Brentwood (brĕnt'wŏŏd) Eng. (London In.)	51·37 N	0·18 E
105	Brentwood....Md.	39·00 N	76·55 W
113	Brentwood...Mo. (St. Louis In.)	38·37 N	90·21 W
107	Brentwood...Pa. (Pittsburgh In.)	40·22 N	79·59 W
164	Brescia (brā'shä)....It.	45·33 N	10·15 E
	Breslau, see Wrocław		
164	Bressanone (brĕs-sä-nō'nā)....It.	46·42 N	11·40 E
160	Bressuire (brĕ-swēr')....Fr.	46·49 N	0·14 W
160	Brest (brĕst)....Fr.	48·24 N	4·30 W
159	Brest....Sov. Un.	52·06 N	23·43 E
166	Brest (Oblast)....Sov. Un.	52·30 N	26·50 E
160	Bretagne, Monts de (Mts.) (mŏN-dĕ-brĕ-tän'yĕ).Fr.	48·25 N	3·36 W
160	Breton, Pertvis (Str.) (pår-twĕ'brĕ-tôN').Fr.	46·18 N	1·43 W
120	Breton Sd. (brĕt'ŭn)....La.	29·38 N	89·15 W
149	Breukelen.Neth. (Amsterdam In.)	52·09 N	5·00 E
120	Brevard (brē-värd')....NC	35·14 N	82·45 W
135	Breves (brā'vĕzh)....Braz.	1·32 S	50·13 W
156	Brevik (brĕ'vĕk)....Nor.	59·04 N	9·39 E
203	Brewarrina (brōō-ēr-rē'nȧ)..Austl.	29·54 S	146·50 E
98	Brewer (brōō'ēr)....Me.	44·46 N	68·46 W
214	Brewerville....Lib.	6·26 N	10·47 W
106	Brewster (brōō'stēr) NY (New York In.)	41·23 N	73·38 W
127	Brewster, Cerro (Mtn.) (sĕ'r-rô-brōō'stēr).Pan.	9·19 N	79·15 W
120	Brewton (brōō'tŭn)....Al.	31·06 N	87·04 W
164	Brežice (brĕ'zhē-tsĕ)....Yugo.	45·55 N	15·37 E
165	Breznik (brĕs'nĕk)....Bul.	42·44 N	22·55 E
161	Briancon (brē-äN-sôN')....Fr.	44·54 N	6·39 E
160	Briare (brē-är')....Fr.	47·40 N	2·46 E
112	Bridal Veil (brīd'ăl vāl) Or. (Portland In.)	45·33 N	122·10 W
128	Bridge Pt. (brĭj)....Ba.	25·35 N	76·40 W
120	Bridgeport (brĭj'pôrt)....Al.	34·55 N	85·42 W
106	Bridgeport....Ct. (New York In.)	41·12 N	73·12 W
104	Bridgeport....Il.	38·40 N	87·45 W
108	Bridgeport....Ne.	41·40 N	103·06 W
104	Bridgeport....Oh.	40·00 N	80·45 W
106	Bridgeport..Pa. (Philadelphia In.)	40·06 N	75·21 W
116	Bridgeport....Tx.	33·13 N	97·46 W
106	Bridgeton (brĭj'tŭn) Al. (Birmingham In.)	33·27 N	86·39 W
113	Bridgeton....Mo. (St. Louis In.)	38·45 N	90·23 W
105	Bridgeton....NJ	39·30 N	75·15 W
98	Bridgetown....Can.	44·51 N	65·18 W
127	Bridgetown (brĭj' toun).Barb. (In.)	13·08 N	59·37 W
107	Bridgeville (brĭj'vĭl) Pa. (Pittsburgh In.)	40·22 N	80·07 W
203	Bridgewater (brĭj'wô-tēr)...Austl.	42·50 S	147·28 E
98	Bridgewater....Can.	44·23 N	64·31 W
148	Bridgnorth (brĭj'nôrth)....Eng.	52·32 N	2·25 W
98	Bridgton (brĭj'tŭn)....Me.	44·04 N	70·45 W
154	Bridlington (brĭd'lĭng-tŭn)...Eng.	54·06 N	0·10 W
161	Brie-Comte-Robert (brē-kônt-ĕ-rō-bâr') Fr. (Paris In.)	48·42 N	2·37 E
149	Brielle....Neth. (Amsterdam In.)	51·54 N	4·08 E
120	Brierfield (brī'ēr-fēld)....Al.	33·01 N	86·55 W
148	Brierfield (brī'ēr fēld)....Eng.	53·49 N	2·14 W
98	Brier I. (brī'ēr)....Can.	44·16 N	66·24 W
148	Brierley Hill (brī'ēr-lē hĭl)....Eng.	52·28 N	2·07 W
149	Brieselang (brē'zĕ-läng) G.D.R. (Berlin In.)	52·36 N	12·59 E
161	Briey (brē-ĕ')....Fr.	49·15 N	5·57 E
158	Brig (brēg)....Switz.	46·17 N	7·59 E
148	Brigg (brĭg)....Eng.	53·33 N	0·29 W
113	Brigham City (brĭg'ăm) Ut. (Salt Lake City In.)	41·31 N	112·01 W
148	Brighouse (brĭg'hous)....Eng.	53·42 N	1·47 W
203	Bright (brīt)....Austl.	36·43 S	147·00 E
107	Bright (brīt)..In. (Cincinnati In.)	39·13 N	84·51 W
148	Brightlingsea (brī't-lĭng-sē) Eng. (London In.)	51·50 N	1·00 E
106	Brighton (brīt'ŭn) Al. (Birmingham In.)	33·27 N	86·56 W
116	Brighton....Co.	39·58 N	104·49 W
154	Brighton....Eng.	50·47 N	0·07 W
113	Brighton....Il. (St. Louis In.)	39·03 N	90·08 W
109	Brighton....Ia.	41·11 N	91·47 W
162	Brihuega (brē-wā'gä)....Sp.	40·32 N	2·52 W
113	Brimley (brĭm'lē) Mi. (Sault Ste. Marie In.)	46·24 N	84·34 W
165	Brindisi (brēn'dē-zē)....It.	40·38 N	17·57 E
164	Brinje (brēn'yĕ)....Yugo.	45·00 N	15·08 E
117	Brinkley (brĭŋk'lĭ)....Ar.	34·52 N	91·12 W
112	Brinnon (brĭn'ŭn) Wa. (Seattle In.)	47·41 N	122·54 W
99	Brion (I.) (brē-ôN')....Can.	47·47 N	61·29 W
160	Brioude (brē-ōōd')....Fr.	45·18 N	3·22 E
203	Brisbane (brĭz' bån)....Austl.	27·30 S	153·10 E
105	Bristol (brĭs'tŭl)....Ct.	41·40 N	72·55 W
154	Bristol....Eng.	51·29 N	2·39 W
106	Bristol....Pa. (Philadelphia In.)	40·06 N	74·51 W
106	Bristol....RI (Providence In.)	41·41 N	71·14 W
121	Bristol....Tn.	36·35 N	82·10 W
105	Bristol....Vt.	44·10 N	73·00 W
121	Bristol....Va.	36·36 N	82·00 W
107	Bristol....Wi. (Milwaukee In.)	42·32 N	88·04 W
101	Bristol B....Ak.	58·08 N	158·54 W
154	Bristol Chan....Eng.	51·20 N	3·47 W
117	Bristow (brĭs'tō)....Ok.	35·50 N	96·25 W

ng-sing; ŋ-baŋk; N-nasalized n; nŏd; cŏmmit; ōld; ōbey; ôrder; fōōd; fŏŏt; ou-out; s-soft; sh-dish; th-thin; pūre; ûnite; ûrn; stŭd; circŭs; ü-as "y" in study; '-indeterminate vowel.

262 British Columbia — Burke PRONOUNCING INDEX

Page	Name Pronunciation Region	Lat. °′	Long. °′
90	British Columbia (Prov.) (brĭt'ĭsh kŏl'ŭm-bĭ-á) . Can.	56·00 N	124·53 W
218	Brits ... S. Afr. (Johannesburg & Pretoria In.)	25·39 S	27·47 E
212	Britstown (brĭts'toun) ... S. Afr.	30·30 S	23·40 E
109	Britt (brĭt) ... Ia.	43·05 N	93·47 W
108	Britton (brĭt'ŭn) ... SD	45·47 N	97·44 W
160	Brive-la-Gaillarde (brēv-lä-gī-yärd'ĕ) . Fr.	45·10 N	1·31 E
162	Briviesca (brē-vyās'kä) ... Sp.	42·34 N	3·21 W
158	Brno (b'r'nô) ... Czech.	49·18 N	16·37 E
128	Broa, Ensenada de la (B.) (ĕn-sĕ-nä'dä-dĕ-lä-brō'ä) . Cuba	22·30 N	82·00 W
184	Broach ... India	21·47 N	72·58 E
120	Broad (R.) (brôd) ... Ga.	34·15 N	83·14 W
121	Broad (R.) ... NC	35·38 N	82·40 W
202	Broadmeadows (brôd'mĕd-ōz) Austl. (Melbourne In.)	37·40 S	144·53 E
107	Broadview Heights (brôd'vū) Oh. (Cleveland In.)	41·18 N	81·41 W
105	Brockport (brŏk'pōrt) ... NY	43·15 N	77·55 W
99	Brockton (brŏk'tŭn) ... Ma. (In.)	42·04 N	71·01 W
97	Brockville (brŏk'vĭl) ... Can.	44·35 N	75·40 W
111	Brockway (brŏk'wā) ... Mt.	47·24 N	105·41 W
159	Brodnica (brôd'nĭt-sá) ... Pol.	53·16 N	19·26 E
159	Brody (brô'dĭ) ... Sov. Un.	50·05 N	25·10 E
117	Broken Arrow (brō'kĕn ăr'ō) .. Ok.	36·03 N	95·48 W
202	Broken B. ... Austl. (Sydney In.)	33·34 S	151·20 E
108	Broken Bow (brō'kĕn bō) ... Ne.	41·24 N	99·37 W
117	Broken Bow ... Ok.	34·02 N	94·43 W
203	Broken Hill (brōk'ĕn) ... Austl.	31·55 S	141·35 E
	Broken Hill, see Kabwe		
148	Bromley (brŭm'lĭ) Eng. (London In.)	51·23 N	0·01 E
105	Bromptonville (brŭmp'tŭn-vĭl) Can.	45·30 N	72·00 W
156	Brønderslev (brûn'dĕr-slĕv) .. Den.	57·15 N	9·56 E
218	Bronkhorstspruit ... S. Afr. (Johannesburg & Pretoria In.)	25·50 S	28·48 E
174	Bronnitsy (brô-nyĭ'tsĭ) Sov. Un. (Moscow In.)	55·26 N	38·16 E
104	Bronson (brŏn'sŭn) ... Mi.	41·55 N	85·15 W
89	Bronte Cr. Can. (Toronto In.)	43·25 N	79·53 W
121	Brood (R.) (brōōd) ... SC	34·46 N	81·25 W
107	Brookfield (brŏŏk'fēld) Il. (Chicago In.)	41·49 N	87·51 W
117	Brookfield ... Mo.	39·45 N	93·04 W
106	Brookhaven (brŏŏk'hāv'n) Ga. (Atlanta In.)	33·52 N	84·21 W
120	Brookhaven ... Ms.	31·35 N	90·26 W
110	Brookings (brŏŏk'ĭngs) ... Or.	42·04 N	124·16 W
108	Brookings ... SD	44·18 N	96·47 W
99	Brookline (brŏŏk'līn) ... Ma. (In.)	42·20 N	71·08 W
99	Brookline ... NH (In.)	42·44 N	71·37 W
107	Brooklyn (brŏŏk'lĭn) Oh. (Cleveland In.)	41·26 N	81·44 W
113	Brooklyn Center Mn. (Minneapolis, St. Paul In.)	45·05 N	93·21 W
107	Brook Park (brŏŏk) Oh. (Cleveland In.)	41·24 N	81·50 W
93	Brooks ... Can.	50·35 N	111·53 W
101	Brooks Ra. (brŏŏks) ... Ak.	68·20 N	159·00 W
121	Brooksville (brŏŏks'vĭl) ... Fl. (In.)	28·32 N	82·28 W
104	Brookville (brŏŏk'vĭl) ... In.	39·20 N	85·00 W
105	Brookville ... Pa.	41·10 N	79·00 W
120	Brookwood (brŏŏk'wŏŏd) ... Al.	33·15 N	87·17 W
154	Broom (B.) (brōōm) ... Scot.	57·59 N	5·32 W
204	Broome (brōōm) ... Austl.	18·00 S	122·15 E
89	Brossard Can. (Montreal In.)	45·26 N	73·28 W
128	Brothers (Is.) (brŭd'hērs) ... Ba.	26·05 N	79·00 W
158	Broumov (brōō'môf) ... Czech.	50·33 N	15·55 E
129	Brown Bk. ... Ba.	21·30 N	74·35 W
116	Brownfield (broun'fēld) ... Tx.	33·11 N	102·16 W
111	Browning (broun'ĭng) ... Mt.	48·37 N	113·05 W
107	Brownsboro (brounz'bô-rô) Ky. (Louisville In.)	38·22 N	85·30 W
89	Brownsburg (brouns'bûrg) Can. (Montreal In.)	45·40 N	74·24 W
107	Brownsburg . In. (Indianapolis In.)	39·51 N	86·23 W
112	Brownsmead (brounz'-mēd) Or. (Portland In.)	46·13 N	123·33 W
104	Brownstown (brounz'toun) ... In.	38·50 N	86·00 W
107	Brownsville (brounz'vĭl) Pa. (Pittsburgh In.)	40·01 N	79·53 W
120	Brownsville ... Tn.	35·35 N	89·15 W
119	Brownsville ... Tx.	25·55 N	97·30 W
98	Brownville Junction (broun'vĭl) Me.	45·20 N	69·04 W
118	Brownwood (broun'wŏŏd) ... Tx.	31·44 N	98·58 W
118	Brownwood (L.) ... Tx.	31·55 N	99·15 W
162	Brozas (brō'thäs) ... Sp.	39·37 N	6·44 W
204	Bruce, Mt. (brōōs) ... Austl.	22·35 S	118·15 E
104	Bruce Pen. ... Can.	44·50 N	81·20 W
120	Bruceton (brōōs'tŭn) ... Tn.	36·02 N	88·14 W
158	Bruchsal (brŏŏk'zäl) ... F.R.G.	49·08 N	8·34 E
158	Bruck (brŏŏk) ... Aus.	47·25 N	15·14 E
149	Brück (brük) .. G.D.R. (Berlin In.)	52·12 N	12·45 E
149	Bruck an der Leitha Aus. (Vienna In.)	48·01 N	16·47 E
89	Bruderheim (brōō'dĕr-hīm) Can. (Edmonton In.)	53·47 N	112·56 W
155	Brugge ... Bel.	51·13 N	3·05 E
161	Brühl (brül) ... F.R.G. (Ruhr In.)	50·49 N	6·54 E
110	Bruneau (R.) (brōō-nō') ... Id.	42·47 N	115·43 W
196	Brunei (brōō-nī') ... Asia	4·52 N	113·38 E
161	Brünen (brü'nĕn) F.R.G. (Ruhr In.)	51·43 N	6·41 E
163	Brunete (brōō-nā'tā) Sp. (Madrid In.)	40·24 N	4·00 W
99	Brunette (I.) (brōō-nĕt') ... Can.	47·16 N	55·54 W
149	Brunn am Gebirge (brōōn'äm gĕ-bĭr'gĕ) Aus. (Vienna In.)	48·07 N	16·18 E
149	Brunsbüttekoog (brōōns'büt-tĕl-kōg) F.R.G. (Hamburg In.)	53·58 N	9·10 E
121	Brunswick (brŭnz'wĭk) ... Ga.	31·08 N	81·30 W
98	Brunswick ... Me.	43·54 N	69·57 W
105	Brunswick ... Md.	39·20 N	77·35 W
117	Brunswick ... Mo.	39·25 N	93·07 W
107	Brunswick ... Oh. (Cleveland In.)	41·14 N	81·50 W
136	Brunswick, Pen. de ... Chile	53·25 S	71·15 W
205	Bruny (I.) (brōō'nē) ... Austl.	43·30 S	147·50 E
116	Brush (brŭsh) ... Co.	40·14 N	103·40 W
136	Brusque (brōō's-kōōĕ) ... Braz.	27·15 S	48·45 W
113	Brussels (brŭs'ĕls) Il. (St. Louis In.)	38·57 N	90·36 W
	Brussels, see Bruxelles		
149	Bruxelles (Brussels) (brü-sĕl') (brŭs'ĕls) . Bel. (Brussels In.)	50·51 N	4·21 E
104	Bryan (brī'ăn) ... Oh.	41·25 N	84·30 W
119	Bryan ... Tx.	30·40 N	96·22 W
166	Bryansk (b'r-yänsk') ... Sov. Un.	53·12 N	34·23 E
166	Bryansk (Oblast) ... Sov. Un.	52·43 N	32·25 E
108	Bryant (brī'ănt) ... SD	44·35 N	97·29 W
112	Bryant ... Wa. (Seattle In.)	48·14 N	122·10 W
115	Bryce Canyon Natl. Park (brīs) Ut.	37·35 N	112·15 W
106	Bryn Mawr (brĭn mâr') Pa. (Philadelphia In.)	40·02 N	75·20 W
120	Bryson City (brīs'ŭn) ... NC	35·25 N	83·25 W
167	Bryukhovetskaya (b'ryŭk'ô-vyĕt-skä'yä) . Sov. Un.	45·56 N	38·58 E
183	Buatan ... Indon. (Singapore In.)	0·45 N	101·49 E
210	Buba (bōō'bá) ... Guinea-Bissau	11·39 N	14·58 W
134	Bucaramanga (bōō-kä'rä-mäŋ'gä) Col.	7·12 N	73·14 W
204	Buccaneer Arch. (bŭk-á-nēr') Austl.	16·05 S	122·00 E
159	Buchach (bŏŏ'chäch) ... Sov. Un.	49·04 N	25·25 E
214	Buchanan (bû-kăn'ăn) ... Lib.	5·57 N	10·02 W
104	Buchanan ... Mi.	41·50 N	86·25 W
205	Buchanan (L.) (bû-kân'nŏn) . Austl.	21·40 S	145·00 E
118	Buchanan (L.) (bû-kăn'ăn) ... Tx.	30·55 N	98·40 W
99	Buchans ... Can.	48·49 N	56·52 W
	Bucharest, see Bucureşti		
149	Buchholtz (bōōk'hōltz) F.R.G. (Hamburg In.)	53·19 N	9·53 E
107	Buck Cr. (bŭk) In. (Indianapolis In.)	39·43 N	85·58 W
105	Buckhannon (bŭk-hăn'ŭn) ... WV	39·00 N	80·10 W
154	Buckhaven (bŭk-hā'v'n) ... Scot.	56·10 N	3·10 W
154	Buckie (bŭk'ĭ) ... Scot.	57·40 N	2·50 W
89	Buckingham (bŭk'ĭng-ăm) Can. (Ottawa In.)	45·35 N	75·25 W
184	Buckingham (R.) (bŭk'ĭng-ăm) India	15·18 N	79·50 E
89	Buckland (bŭk'lănd) Can. (Quebec In.)	46·37 N	70·33 W
205	Buckland Tableland (Reg.) .. Austl.	24·31 S	148·00 E
112	Buckley (buk'lē) . Wa. (Seattle In.)	47·10 N	122·02 W
98	Bucksport (bŭks'pôrt) ... Me.	44·35 N	68·47 W
98	Buctouche (bük-tōōsh') ... Can.	46·28 N	64·43 W
190	Bucun (bōō-tsōōn) ... China	36·38 N	117·26 E
165	Bucureşti (Bucharest) (bōō-kōō-rĕsh'tĭ) (bōō-kä-rĕst') . Rom.	44·23 N	26·10 E
104	Bucyrus (bû-sī'rŭs) ... Oh.	40·50 N	82·55 W
159	Budapest (bōō'dá-pĕsht') ... Hung.	47·30 N	19·05 E
161	Büderich (bü'dĕ-rēk) F.R.G. (Ruhr In.)	51·15 N	6·41 E
184	Budge Budge ... India (In.)	22·28 N	88·08 E
216	Budjala ... Zaire	2·39 N	19·42 E
215	Buea ... Cam.	4·09 N	9·14 E
107	Buechel (bĕ-chŭl') Ky. (Louisville In.)	38·12 N	85·38 W
161	Bueil (bwā') ... Fr. (Paris In.)	48·55 N	1·27 E
113	Buena Park (bwā'ná pärk) Ca. (Los Angeles In.)	33·52 N	118·00 W
134	Buenaventura (bwā'nä-vĕn-tōō'rá) Col.	3·46 N	77·09 W
129	Buenaventura ... Cuba (In.)	22·49 N	82·22 W
134	Buenaventura, Bahia de (B.) (bä-ē'ä-dĕ-bwā'nä-vĕn-tōō'rá) Col.	3·45 N	79·23 W
116	Buena Vista (bū'ná vĭs'tá) ... Co.	38·51 N	106·07 W
120	Buena Vista ... Ga.	32·15 N	84·30 W
105	Buena Vista ... Va.	37·45 N	79·20 W
128	Buena Vista, Bahía (B.) (bä-ē'ä-bwĕ-nä-vē's-tä) . Cuba	22·30 N	79·10 W
114	Buena Vista Lake Res. (bū'ná vĭs'tá) . Ca.	35·14 N	119·17 W
162	Buendia (Res.) ... Sp.	40·30 N	2·45 W
136	Buenos Aires (bwā'nōs ī'rās) .. Arg.	34·20 S	58·30 W
134	Buenos Aires ... Col. (In.)	3·01 N	76·34 W
127	Buenos Aires ... C. R.	9·10 N	83·21 W
136	Buenos Aires (Prov.) ... Arg.	36·15 S	61·45 W
136	Buenos Aires (L.) ... Arg.-Chile	46·30 S	72·15 W
161	Buer (bür) ... F.R.G. (Ruhr In.)	51·35 N	7·03 E
109	Buffalo (buf'á lō) ... Mn.	45·10 N	93·50 W
107	Buffalo ... NY (Buffalo In.)	42·54 N	78·51 W
119	Buffalo ... Tx.	31·28 N	96·04 W
111	Buffalo ... Wy.	44·19 N	106·42 W
117	Buffalo (R.) ... Ar.	35·56 N	92·58 W
213	Buffalo (R.) ... S. Afr. (Natal In.)	28·35 S	30·27 E
120	Buffalo (R.) ... Tn.	35·24 N	87·10 W
119	Buffalo Bayou ... Tx. (In.)	29·46 N	95·32 W
109	Buffalo Cr. ... Mn.	44·46 N	94·28 W
90	Buffalo Head Hills ... Can.	57·16 N	116·18 W
89	Buford (bū'fûrd) Can. (Edmonton In.)	53·15 N	113·55 W
120	Buford (bū'fērd) ... Ga.	34·05 N	84·00 W
159	Bug (R.) (bōōg) ... Pol.	52·29 N	21·20 E
167	Bug (R.) (bŏŏk) ... Sov. Un.	48·12 N	30·13 E
134	Buga (bōō'gä) ... Col. (In.)	3·54 N	76·17 W
149	Buggenhout ... Bel. (Brussels In.)	51·01 N	4·10 E
121	Buggs Island L. ... NC-Va.	36·30 N	78·38 W
164	Bugojno (bōō-gō ĭ nô) ... Yugo.	44·03 N	17·28 E
170	Bugul'ma (bōō-gōōl'má) .. Sov. Un.	54·40 N	52·40 E
170	Buguruslan (bōō-gōō-rōōs-lán') Sov. Un.	53·30 N	52·32 E
197	Buhi (bōō'ē) ... Phil. (In.)	13·26 N	123·31 E
110	Buhl (būl) ... Id.	42·36 N	114·45 W
109	Buhl ... Mn.	47·28 N	92·49 W
137	Buin (bōō-ēn') Chile (Santiago In.)	33·44 S	70·44 W
171	Buinaksk (bōō'ē-näksk) .. Sov. Un.	42·40 N	47·20 E
192	Buir Nur (L.) (bōō-ēr nōōr) China-Mong.	47·50 N	117·00 E
162	Bujalance (bōō-hä-län'thā) ... Sp.	37·54 N	4·22 W
217	Bujumbura ... Burundi	3·23 S	29·22 E
212	Bukama (bōō-kä'mä) ... Zaire	9·08 S	26·00 E
217	Bukavu ... Zaire	2·30 S	28·52 E
147	Bukhara (bōō-kä'rä) ... Sov. Un.	39·31 N	64·22 E
183	Bukitbatu .. Indon. (Singapore In.)	1·25 N	101·58 E
196	Bukittingg ... Indon.	0·25 S	100·28 E
217	Bukoba ... Tan.	1·20 S	31·49 E
159	Bukovina (Reg.) (bōō-kō'vĭ-ná) Sov. Un.	48·06 N	25·20 E
197	Bula (bōō'lä) ... Indon.	3·00 S	130·30 E
197	Bulalacao (bōō-lá-lä'kä-ô) Phil. (In.)	12·20 N	121·20 E
212	Bulawayo (bōō-lá-wä'yō) ... Zimb.	20·12 S	28·43 E
101	Buldir (I.) (bŭl dĭr) ... Ak.	52·22 N	175·50 E
146	Bulgaria (bŏŏl-gā'rĭ-ă) ... Eur.	42·12 N	24·13 E
92	Bulkley Ra. (bŭlk'lē) ... Can.	54·30 N	127·30 W
162	Bullaque (R.) (bŏŏ-lä'kâ) ... Sp.	39·15 N	4·13 W
162	Bullas (bōōl'yäs) ... Sp.	38·07 N	1·48 W
115	Bulldog Cr. (bŭl'dŏg') ... Ut.	37·45 N	110·55 W
92	Bull Harbour (hăr'bēr) ... Can.	50·45 N	127·55 W
128	Bull Head (Mtn.) ... Jam.	18·10 N	77·15 W
205	Bulloo (R.) (bŭ-lōō') ... Austl.	25·23 S	143·30 E
112	Bull Run (R.) (bŏŏl) Or. (Portland In.)	45·26 N	122·11 W
112	Bull Run Res. .. Or. (Portland In.)	45·29 N	122·11 W
117	Bull Shoals Res. (bŏŏl shōlz) Ar.-Mo.	36·35 N	92·57 W
218	Bulo Burti (bōō'lō bŏŏr'tĭ) Som. (Horn of Afr. In.)	3·53 N	45·30 E
148	Bulphan (bŏŏl'făn) Eng. (London In.)	51·33 N	0·21 E
218	Bultfontein (bŏŏlt'fŏn-tān') S. Afr. (Johannesburg & Pretoria In.)	28·18 S	26·10 E
173	Bulun (bōō-lōōn') ... Sov. Un.	70·48 N	127·27 E
216	Bulungu (bōō-lōōŋ'gōō) ... Zaire	6·04 S	21·54 E
213	Bulwer (bŏŏl-wēr) S. Afr. (Natal In.)	29·49 S	29·48 E
216	Bumba (bŏŏm'bá) ... Zaire	2·11 N	22·28 E
217	Bumire I. ... Tan.	1·40 S	32·05 E
197	Buna (bōō'ná) ... Pap. N. Gui.	8·58 S	148·38 E
204	Bunbury (bŭn'bŭrĭ) ... Austl.	33·25 S	115·45 E
203	Bundaberg (bŭn'dá-bûrg) ... Austl.	24·45 S	152·18 E
195	Bungo-Suidō (Chan.) (bōōŋ'gō sōō-ē'dō) . Jap.	33·26 N	131·54 E
196	Bunguran Utara, Kepulauan (Is.) Indon.	3·22 N	108·00 E
217	Bunia ... Zaire	1·34 N	30·15 E
113	Bunker Hill (bŭnk'ēr hĭl) Il. (St. Louis In.)	39·03 N	89·57 W
119	Bunkie (bŭŋ'kĭ) ... La.	30·55 N	92·10 W
217	Bun Plns. ... Ken.	0·55 N	40·35 E
215	Bununu Dass ... Nig.	10·00 N	9·31 E
173	Buor-Khaya, Guba (B.) .. Sov. Un.	71·45 N	131·00 E
173	Buor Khaya, Mys (C.) .. Sov. Un.	71·47 N	133·22 E
217	Bura ... Ken.	1·06 S	39·57 E
218	Buran (bûr'ăn) Som. (Horn of Afr. In.)	10·38 N	48·30 E
218	Burao ... Som. (Horn of Afr. In.)	9·20 N	45·45 E
186	Buraydah ... Sau. Ar.	26·23 N	44·14 E
113	Burbank (bûr'bănk) Ca. (Los Angeles In.)	34·11 N	118·19 W
205	Burdekin (R.) (bûr'dē-kĭn) . Austl.	19·22 S	145·07 E
171	Burdur (bŏŏr-dŏŏr') ... Tur.	37·50 N	30·15 E
184	Burdwān (bŏŏrd-wän') ... India	23·29 N	87·53 E
173	Bureinskiy, Khrebet (Mts.) Sov. Un.	51·15 N	133·30 E
173	Bureya (bŏŏrā'á) ... Sov. Un.	49·55 N	130·00 E
173	Bureya (R.) (bŏŏ-rā'yä) .. Sov. Un.	51·00 N	130·14 E
148	Burford (bûr-fērd) Eng. (London In.)	51·46 N	1·38 W
115	Burford (L.) ... NM	36·37 N	107·21 W
165	Burgas (bŏŏr-gäs') ... Bul.	42·29 N	27·30 E
153	Burgas, Gulf of ... Bul.	42·30 N	27·40 E
213	Bur Gavo ... Som.	1·14 S	41·47 E
121	Burgaw (bûr'gô) ... NC	34·31 N	77·56 W
158	Burgdorf (bŏŏrg'dôrf) ... Switz.	47·04 N	7·37 E
149	Burgenland (State) Aus. (Vienna In.)	47·58 N	16·57 E
99	Burgeo ... Can.	47·36 N	57·34 W
105	Burgess ... Va.	37·53 N	76·21 W
118	Burgos (bŏŏr'gōs) ... Mex.	24·57 N	98·47 W
197	Burgos ... Phil. (In.)	16·03 N	119·52 E
162	Burgos (bōō'r-gōs) ... Sp.	42·20 N	3·44 W
156	Burgsvik (bŏŏrgs'vĭk) ... Swe.	57·04 N	18·18 E
184	Burhānpur (bŏŏr'hän-pōōr) . India	21·26 N	76·08 E
197	Burias I. (bōō'rē-äs) ... Phil. (In.)	12·56 N	122·56 E
197	Burias Pass (bōō'rē-äs) . Phil. (In.)	13 04 N	123·11 E
127	Burica, Punta (Pt.) (pōō'n-tä-bōō'rē-kä) . Pan.	8·02 N	83·12 W
112	Burien (bū'rĭ-ĕn) . Wa. (Seattle In.)	47·28 N	122·20 W
99	Burin (bûr'ĭn) ... Can.	47·02 N	55·10 W
99	Burin Pen. ... Can.	47·00 N	55·40 W
116	Burkburnett (bûrk-bûr'nĕt) ... Tx.	34·04 N	98·35 W
105	Burke (bûrk) ... Vt.	44·40 N	72·00 W
92	Burke Chan. ... Can.	52·07 N	127·38 W

ăt; finăl; rāte; senâte; ärm; åsk; sofá; fâre; ch-choose; dh-as th in other; bē; êvent; bĕt; recĕnt; cratẽr; g-go; gh-guttural g; bĭt; ĭ-short neutral; rīde; K-guttural k as ch in German ich;

PRONOUNCING INDEX
Burketown — Calella 263

Page Name Pronunciation Region Lat. °′ Long. °′
204 Burketown (bûrk'toun).....Austl. 17·50 S 139·30 E
111 Burley (bûr'lĭ)..............Id. 42·31 N 113·48 W
112 Burley.........Wa. (Seattle In.) 47·25 N 122·38 W
174 Burli.......Sov. Un. (Urals In.) 53·36 N 61·55 E
112 Burlingame (bûr'lĭn-găm) Ca. (San Francisco In.) 37·35 N 122·22 W
117 Burlingame...............Ks. 38·45 N 95·49 W
89 Burlington (bûr'lĭng-tŭn) Can. (Toronto In.) 43·19 N 79·48 W
116 Burlington.................Co. 39·17 N 102·26 W
109 Burlington..................Ia. 40·48 N 91·05 W
117 Burlington..................Ks. 38·10 N 95·46 W
107 Burlington...Ky. (Cincinnati In.) 39·01 N 84·44 W
99 Burlington...............Ma. (In.) 42·31 N 71·13 W
106 Burlington..NJ (Philadelphia In.) 40·04 N 74·52 W
121 Burlington.................NC 36·05 N 79·26 W
105 Burlington..................Vt. 44·30 N 73·15 W
112 Burlington......Wa. (Seattle In.) 48·28 N 122·20 W
107 Burlington...Wi. (Milwaukee In.) 42·41 N 88·16 W
182 Burma (bûr'mȧ)............Asia 21·00 N 95·15 E
92 Burnaby.................Can. 49·14 N 122·58 W
118 Burnet (bûrn'ĕt)............Tx. 30·46 N 98·14 W
148 Burnham on Crouch (bûrn'ăm-ŏn-krouch) Eng. (London In.) 51·38 N 0·48 E
203 Burnie (bûr'nē)...........Austl. 41·15 S 146·05 E
148 Burnley (bûrn'lē)...........Eng. 53·47 N 2·19 W
110 Burns (bûrnz)...............Or. 43·35 N 119·05 W
120 Burnside (bûrn'sīd).........Ky. 36·57 N 84·33 W
92 Burns Lake (bûrnz lăk)......Can. 54·14 N 125·46 W
98 Burnsville (bûrnz'vĭl)........Can. 47·44 N 65·07 W
110 Burnt R. (bûrnt).............Or. 44·26 N 117·53 W
95 Burntwood (R.)............Can. 55·53 N 97·30 W
112 Burrard Inlet (bûr'ȧrd) Can. (Vancouver In.) 49·19 N 123·15 W
163 Burriana (bo͞or-rē-ä'nä).......Sp. 39·53 N 0·05 W
171 Bursa (bo͞or'sȧ).............Tur. 40·10 N 28·10 E
211 Būr Safājah..............Egypt 26·57 N 33·56 E
218 Būr Sa'īd (Port Said) Egypt (Suez In.) 31·15 N 32·19 E
161 Burscheid (bo͞or'shīd) F.R.G. (Ruhr In.) 51·05 N 7·07 E
211 Būr Sūdān (Port Sudan) (so͞o-dän').Sud. 19·30 N 37·10 E
107 Burt (bŭrt).....NY (Buffalo In.) 43·19 N 78·45 W
104 Burt (L.) (bŭrt).............Mi. 45·25 N 84·45 W
112 Burton (bûr'tŭn).Wa. (Seattle In.) 47·24 N 122·28 W
148 Burton-on-Trent (bûr'tŭn-ŏn-trĕnt).Eng. 52·48 N 1·37 W
120 Burton Res..................Ga. 34·46 N 83·40 W
106 Burtonsville (bûrtŏns-vil) Md. (Baltimore In.) 39·07 N 76·57 W
197 Buru (I.)..................Indon. 3·30 S 126·30 E
218 Burullus (L.).....Egypt (Nile In.) 31·20 N 30·58 E
209 Burundi...................Afr. 3·00 S 29·30 E
108 Burwell (bûr'wĕl)...........Ne. 41·46 N 99·08 W
148 Bury (bĕr'ĭ)................Eng. 53·36 N 2·17 W
173 Buryat A.S.S.R.........Sov. Un. 55·15 N 112·00 E
155 Bury St. Edmunds (bĕr'ĭ-sānt ĕd'mŭndz).Eng. 52·14 N 0·44 E
136 Burzaco (bo͞or-zä'kô) Arg. (Buenos Aires In.) 34·35 S 58·23 W
217 Busanga Swp...........Zambia 14·10 S 25·50 E
218 Būsh (bo͞osh)....Egypt (Nile In.) 29·13 N 31·08 E
186 Būshehr...................Iran 28·48 N 50·53 E
212 Bushmanland (Reg.) (bo͝osh-măn lănd).S. Afr. 29·15 S 18·45 E
117 Bushnell (bo͝osh'nĕl)..........Il. 40·33 N 90·28 W
216 Businga (bo͞o-sĭŋ'gȧ)........Zaire 3·20 N 20·53 E
216 Busira (R.)...............Zaire 0·05 S 19·20 E
159 Busk (bo͞o'sk)...........Sov. Un. 49·58 N 24·39 E
204 Busselton (bŭs'l-tŭn).......Austl. 33·40 S 115·30 E
149 Bussum...Neth. (Amsterdam In.) 52·16 N 5·10 E
118 Bustamante (bo͞os-tȧ-män'tȧ).Mex. 26·34 N 100·30 W
164 Busto Arsizio (bo͞os'tō är-sēd'zē-ō).It 45·47 N 8·51 E
197 Busuanga (I.) (bo͞o-swäŋ'gä) Phil. (In.) 12·20 N 119·43 E
216 Buta (bo͞o'tȧ)...............Zaire 2·48 N 24·44 E
213 Butha Buthe (bo͞o-thȧ-bo͞o'thȧ) Leso. (Natal In.) 28·49 S 28·16 E
194 Butha Qi (bo͞o-thä chē).....China 47·59 N 122·56 E
120 Butler (bŭt'lẽr)..............Al. 32·05 N 88·10 W
104 Butler......................In. 41·25 N 84·50 W
106 Butler......Md. (Baltimore In.) 39·32 N 76·46 W
106 Butler........NJ (New York In.) 41·00 N 74·20 W
105 Butler......................Pa. 40·50 N 79·55 W
174 Butovo (bo͞o-tô'vô) Sov. Un. (Moscow In.) 55·33 N 37·36 E
217 Butsha...................Zaire 0·57 N 29·13 E
120 Buttahatchie (R.) (bŭt-ȧ-hăch'ē) Al.-Ms. 34·02 N 88·05 W
111 Butte (būt)..................Mt. 46·00 N 112·31 W
213 Butterworth (bŭ tẽr'wûrth) S. Afr. (Natal In.) 32·20 S 28·09 E
154 Butt of Lewis (C.) (bŭt ŏv lū'ĭs) Scot. 58·34 N 6·15 W
197 Butuan (bo͞o-to͞o'än).........Phil. 8·40 N 125·33 E
196 Butung (I.)...............Indon. 5·00 S 122·55 E
167 Buturlinovka (bo͞o-to͞o'lē-nôf'ka) Sov. Un. 50·47 N 40·35 E
149 Buxtehude (bo͞oks-tĕ-ho͞o'dĕ) F.R.G. (Hamburg In.) 53·29 N 9·42 E
148 Buxton (bŭks't'n)..........Eng. 53·15 N 1·55 W
112 Buxton.......Or. (Portland In.) 45·41 N 123·11 W
170 Buy (bwē).............Sov. Un. 58·30 N 41·48 E
165 Buzău (bo͞o-zĕ'o͞o)..........Rom. 45·09 N 26·51 E
167 Buzău R...................Rom. 45·17 N 27·22 E
211 Buzaymah.................Libya 25·14 N 22·13 E
190 Buzi (bo͞o-dz).............China 33·48 N 118·13 E
171 Buzuluk (bo͞o-zo͞o-lo͝ok')..Sov. Un. 52·50 N 52·10 E
217 Bwendi...................Zaire 4·01 N 26·41 E
165 Byala......................Bul. 43·26 N 25·44 E
Byblos, see Jubayl
159 Bydgoszcz (bĭd'gôshch).......Pol. 53·07 N 18·00 E
104 Byesville (bīz-vĭl)............Oh. 39·55 N 81·35 W
156 Bygdin (L.) (bügh-dĕn').....Nor. 61·24 N 8·31 E
156 Byglandsfjord (bügh'lănds-fyôr) Nor. 58·40 N 7·49 E
166 Bykhovo (bĭ-kô'vô)......Sov. Un. 53·32 N 30·15 E
174 Bykovo (bĭ-kô'vô) Sov. Un. (Moscow In.) 55·38 N 38·05 E
172 Byrranga, Gory (Mts.)...Sov. Un. 74·15 N 94·28 E
173 Bytantay (R.) (byăn'tăy).Sov. Un. 68·15 N 132·15 E
159 Bytom (bĭ'tŭm)............Pol. 50·21 N 18·55 E
166 Bytosh' (bĭ-tôsh').......Sov. Un. 53·48 N 34·06 E
159 Bytow (bĭ'tŭf).............Pol. 54·10 N 17·30 E

C

136 Caazapá (kä-zä-pä')........Par. 26·14 S 56·18 W
197 Cabagan (kä-bä-gän')...Phil. (In.) 17·27 N 121·50 E
197 Cabalete (I.) (kä-bä-lä'tȧ) Phil. (In.) 14·19 N 122·00 E
128 Caballones, Canal de (Chan.) (kä-nä'l-dĕ-kä-bäl-yô'nĕs).Cuba 20·45 N 79·20 W
115 Caballo Res. (kä-bä-lyō').....NM 33·00 N 107·20 W
162 Cabañaquinta (kä-bän-yä-kē'n-tä) Sp. 43·10 N 5·37 W
197 Cabanatuan (kä-bä-nä-twän') Phil. (In.) 15·30 N 120·56 E
98 Cabano (kä-bä-nō')..........Can. 47·41 N 68·54 W
197 Cabarruyan (I.) (kä-bä-ro͞o'yän) Phil. (In.) 16·21 N 120·10 E
135 Cabedelo (kä-bē-dā'lo͞o).....Braz. 6·58 S 34·49 W
125 Cabeza, Arrecife (Reef) (är-rĕ-sē'fĕ-kä-bĕ-zä).Mex. 19·07 N 95·52 W
162 Cabeza del Buey (kȧ-bā'thä dĕl bwā').Sp. 38·43 N 5·18 W
134 Cabimas (kä-bē'mäs)........Ven. 10·21 N 71·27 W
209 Cabinda (kä-bĭn'dȧ).........Ang. 5·10 S 10·00 E
216 Cabinda...................Ang. 5·33 S 12·12 E
110 Cabinet Mts. (kăb'ĭ-nĕt)......Mt. 48·13 N 115·52 W
137 Cabo Frio (kä'bô-frē'ô) Braz. (Rio de Janeiro In.) 22·53 S 42·02 W
137 Cabo Frio, Ilha do (ē'lä-dô-kä'bô frē'ô).Braz. (Rio de Janeiro In.) 23·01 S 42·00 W
97 Cabonga Res..............Can. 47·25 N 76·35 W
104 Cabot Hd. (kăb'ŭt).........Can. 45·15 N 81·20 W
99 Cabot Str. (kăb'ŭt).........Can. 47·35 N 60·00 W
162 Cabra (käb'rä)...............Sp. 37·28 N 4·29 W
197 Cabra I.............Phil. (In.) 13·55 N 119·55 E
163 Cabrera (I.) (kä-brā'rä).......Sp. 39·08 N 2·57 E
162 Cabriel (R.) (kä-brē-ĕl').......Sp. 39·25 N 1·20 W
114 Cabrillo Natl. Mon. (kä-brēl'yō) Ca. (In.) 32·41 N 117·03 W
135 Cabrobó (kä-brō-bô').......Braz. 8·34 S 39·13 W
136 Cabuçu (R.) (kä-bo͞o'-so͞o) Braz. (Rio de Janeiro In.) 22·57 S 43·36 W
197 Cabugao (kä-bo͞o'gä-ō) Phil. (In.) 17·48 N 120·28 E
165 Čačak (chä'chȧk)..........Yugo. 43·51 N 20·22 E
137 Caçapava (kä'sä-pȧ'vä) Braz. (Rio de Janeiro In.) 23·05 S 45·52 W
135 Cáceres (kȧ'sĕ-rĕs)..........Braz. 16·11 S 57·32 W
162 Cáceres (kȧ'thȧ-rās)..........Sp. 39·28 N 6·20 W
137 Cachapoal (R.) (kä-chä-pô-ä'l) Chile (Santiago In.) 34·23 S 70·19 W
137 Cacharí (kä-chä-rē') Arg. (Buenos Aires In.) 36·23 S 59·29 W
117 Cache (R.) (kăsh)............Ar. 35·24 N 91·12 W
93 Cache Creek...............Can. 50·48 N 121·19 W
114 Cache Cr. (kăsh).............Ca. 38·53 N 122·24 W
116 Cache la Poudre (R.) (kăsh lȧ po͞od'r').Co. 40·43 N 105·39 W
136 Cachi, Nevados de (Pk.) (nĕ-vȧ'dôs-dĕ-kȧ'chē).Arg. 25·05 S 66·40 W
136 Cachinal (kä-chē-näl')........Chile 24·57 S 69·33 W
135 Cachoeira (kä-shô-ā'rä).....Braz. 12·32 S 38·47 W
136 Cachoeirá do Sul (kä-shô-ā'rä-dô-so͞o'l).Braz. 30·02 S 52·49 W
137 Cachoeiras de Macacu (kä-shô-ā'räs-dĕ-mä-kȧ'ko͞o) Braz. (Rio de Janeiro In.) 22·28 S 42·39 W
137 Cachoeiro de Itapemirim (kä-shô-ā'rô-dĕ-ē'tä-pĕmē-rē'N) Braz. (Rio de Janeiro In.) 20·51 S 41·06 W
216 Cacolo.....................Ang. 10·07 S 19·17 E
216 Caconda (kä-kōn'dä)........Ang. 13·43 S 15·06 E
98 Cacouna...................Can. 47·54 N 69·31 W
216 Cacula.....................Ang. 14·29 S 14·10 E
119 Caddo (L.) (kăd'ō).......La.-Tx. 32·37 N 94·15 W
124 Cadereyta (kä-dȧ-rā'tä)......Mex. 20·42 N 99·47 W
118 Cadereyta Jimenez (kä-dä-rā'tä hē-mā'nāz).Mex. 25·36 N 99·59 W
163 Cadi, Sierra de (Mts.) (sē-ĕ'r-rä-dĕ-kä'dē).Sp. 42·17 N 1·34 E
104 Cadillac (kăd'ĭ-lăk)..........Mi. 44·15 N 85·25 W
114 Cadiz (kā'dĭz)................Ca. 34·33 N 115·30 W
104 Cadiz.......................Oh. 40·15 N 81·00 W
162 Cádiz (kȧ'dēz)...............Sp. 36·34 N 6·20 W
162 Cádiz, Golfo de (G.) (gôl-fô-dĕ-kȧ'dēz).Sp. 36·50 N 7·00 W
160 Caen (käN)...................Fr. 49·13 N 0·22 W
154 Caernarfon...............Wales 53·08 N 4·17 W
154 Caernarfon B.............Wales 53·09 N 4·56 W
137 Caeté (kä'ĕ-tĕ').. Braz. (Rio de Janeiro In.) 19·53 S 43·41 W
135 Caetité (kä-ĕ-tē-tā')........Braz. 14·02 S 42·14 W
197 Cagayan (kä-gä-yän').......Phil. 8·13 N 124·30 E
196 Cagayan (R.)..............Phil. 16·45 N 121·55 E
196 Cagayan Is................Phil. 9·40 N 120·30 E
196 Cagayan Sulu (I.) (kä-gä-yän so͞o'lo͞o).Phil. 7·00 N 118·30 E
164 Cagli (käl'yē)................It. 43·35 N 12·40 E
164 Cagliari (käl'yä-rē)...........It. 39·16 N 9·08 E
164 Cagliari, Golfo di (G.) (gôl-fô-dē-käl'yä-rē).It. 39·08 N 9·12 E
161 Cagnes (kän'y')..............Fr. 43·40 N 7·14 E
135 Cagua (kä'-gwä).......Ven. (In.) 10·12 N 67·27 W
123 Caguas (kä'gwäs) P. R. (Puerto Rico In.) 18·12 N 66·01 W
120 Cahaba (R.) (kȧ hä-bä).......Al. 32·50 N 87·15 W
216 Cahama (kä-ȧ'mä)..........Ang. 16·17 S 14·19 E
113 Cahokia (kȧ-hō'kĭ-ȧ) Il. (St. Louis In.) 38·34 N 90·11 W
217 Cahora-Bassa (Gorge).......Moz. 15·40 S 32·50 E
160 Cahors (kȧ-ôr')..............Fr. 44·27 N 1·27 E
125 Cahuacán (kä-wä-kä'n).Mex. (In.) 19·38 N 99·25 W
127 Cahuita, Punta (Pt.) (po͞o'n-tä-kä-wē'tȧ).C. R. 9·47 N 82·41 W
135 Caiapó, Serra do (Mts.) (sĕ'r-rä-dô-kä-yä-pô').Braz. 17·52 S 52·37 W
128 Caibarién (kī-bä-rē-ĕn').....Cuba 22·35 N 79·30 W
134 Caicedonia (kī-sĕ-dô-nēä) Col. (In.) 4·21 N 75·48 W
129 Caicos Bk. (kī'kōs)...........Ba. 21·35 N 72·00 W
129 Caicos Is......Turks & Caicos Is. 21·45 N 71·50 W
129 Caicos Passage (Str.).........Ba. 21·55 N 72·45 W
119 Caillou B. (kȧ-yo͞o')..........La. 29·07 N 91·00 W
129 Caimanera (kī-mä-nā'rä)....Cuba 20·00 N 75·10 W
197 Caiman Pt. (kī'mȧn)...Phil. (In.) 15·56 N 119·33 E
122 Caimito, (R.) (kä-ē-mē'tô) Pan. (In.) 8·50 N 79·45 W
129 Caimito del Guayabal (kä-ē-mē'tō-dĕl-gwä-yä-bä'l) Cuba (In.) 22·42 N 82·36 W
205 Cairns (kârnz)............Austl. 17·02 S 145·49 E
127 Cairo (kī'-rô)..............C. R. 10·06 N 83·47 W
Cairo, see Al Qāhirah
120 Cairo (kā'rō)................Ga. 30·48 N 84·12 W
117 Cairo........................Il. 36·59 N 89·11 W
148 Caistor (kâs'tẽr)............Eng. 53·30 N 0·20 W
216 Caiundo...................Ang. 15·46 S 17·28 E
192 Caiyu (tsī-yo͞o')........China (In.) 39·39 N 116·36 E
134 Cajamarca (kä-kä-mȧ'r-kä) Col. (In.) 4·25 N 75·25 W
134 Cajamarca (kä-hä-mär'kä)...Peru 7·16 S 78·30 W
165 Čajniče (chī'nĭ-chĕ)........Yugo. 43·32 N 19·04 E
113 Cajon (kȧ-hōn') Ca. (Los Angeles In.) 34·18 N 117·28 W
137 Cajuru (kȧ-zho͞o'-ro͞o) Braz. (Rio de Janeiro In.) 21·17 S 47·17 W
164 Čakovec (chȧ'kō-vĕts)......Yugo. 46·23 N 16·27 E
213 Cala (cä-lȧ)....S. Afr. (Natal In.) 31·33 S 27·41 E
215 Calabar (kăl-ȧ-bär')..........Nig. 4·57 N 8·19 E
129 Calabazar (kä-lä-bä-zä'r) Cuba (In.) 23·02 N 82·25 W
134 Calabozo (kä-lä-bō'zō).......Ven. 8·48 N 67·27 W
164 Calabria (Reg.) (kä-lä'brē-ä)...It. 39·26 N 16·23 E
165 Calafat (kȧ-lȧ-fȧt').........Rom. 43·59 N 22·56 E
197 Calaguas Is. (kä-läg'wäs) Phil. (In.) 14·30 N 123·06 E
89 Calahoo (kă-lȧ-ho͞o') Can. (Edmonton In.) 53·42 N 113·58 W
162 Calahorra (kä-lä-ôr'rä)........Sp. 42·18 N 1·58 W
160 Calais (kȧ-lĕ')...............Fr. 50·56 N 1·51 E
98 Calais......................Me. 45·11 N 67·15 W
136 Calama (kä-lä'mä).........Chile 22·17 S 68·58 W
134 Calamar (kä-lä-mär').......Col. 10·24 N 75·00 W
134 Calamar....................Col. 1·55 N 72·33 W
197 Calamba (kä-läm'bä)...Phil. (In.) 14·12 N 121·10 E
196 Calamian Group (Is.) (kä-lä-myän').Phil. 12·14 N 118·38 E
162 Calañas (kä-län'yäs)...........Sp. 37·41 N 6·52 W
197 Calapan (kä-lä-pän')...Phil. (In.) 13·25 N 121·11 E
153 Călăraşi (kŭ-lŭ-räsh'ĭ).......Rom. 44·09 N 27·20 E
162 Calasparra (kä-lä-spär'rä).....Sp. 38·13 N 1·40 W
162 Calatayud (kä-lä-tä-yo͞odh')...Sp. 41·23 N 1·37 W
197 Calauag B...........Phil. (In.) 14·07 N 122·10 E
112 Calaveras Res. (kăl-ȧ-vĕr'ăs) Ca. (San Francisco In.) 37·29 N 121·47 W
197 Calavite, C. (kä-lä-vē'tä) Phil. (In.) 13·29 N 120·00 E
119 Calcasieu (R.) (kăl'kȧ-shū)....La. 30·22 N 93·08 W
119 Calcasieu L.................La. 29·58 N 93·08 W
184 Calcutta (kăl-kŭt'ȧ)...India (In.) 22·32 N 88·22 E
134 Caldas (kä'l-däs).......Col. (In.) 6·06 N 75·38 W
134 Caldas (Dept.)..........Col. (In.) 5·20 N 75·38 W
162 Caldas de Rainha (käl'däs dä rīn'yȧ).Port. 39·25 N 9·08 W
148 Calder (R.) (kôl'dẽr)........Eng. 53·39 N 1·30 W
136 Caldera (käl-dä'rä).........Chile 27·02 S 70·53 W
148 Calder Can.................Eng. 53·48 N 2·25 W
110 Caldwell (kôld'wĕl)...........Id. 43·40 N 116·43 W
117 Caldwell....................Ks. 37·04 N 97·36 W
104 Caldwell....................Oh. 39·40 N 81·30 W
119 Caldwell....................Tx. 30·30 N 96·40 W
89 Caledon (kăl'ē-dŏn) Can. (Toronto In.) 43·52 N 79·59 W
109 Caledonia (kăl-ē-dō'nĭ-ȧ).....Mn. 43·38 N 91·31 W
154 Caledonian Can. (kăl-ē-dō'nĭ-ȧn) Scot. 56·58 N 4·05 W
163 Calella (kä-lĕl'yä)............Sp. 41·37 N 2·39 E

ng-sing; ŋ-baŋk; N-nasalized n; nŏd; cŏmmit; ōld; ôbey; ôrder; fo͞od; fo͝ot; ou-out; s-soft; sh-dish; th-thin; pūre; ûnite; ûrn; stŭd; circŭs; ü-as "y" in study; '-indeterminate vowel.

ăt; finăl; rāte; senăte; ärm; ásk; sofá; fâre; ch-choose; dh-as th in other; bē; ĕvent; bĕt; recĕnt; cratēr; g-go; gh-guttural g; bĭt; ĭ-short neutral; rīde; ĸ-guttural k as ch in German ich;

PRONOUNCING INDEX Capivari — Castle Dale 265

Page	Name Pronunciation Region	Lat. °'	Long. °'
136	Capivari (R.) Braz. (Rio de Janeiro In.)	22·39 S	43·19 W
203	Capoompeta (Mtn.) (kȧ-po͞om-pē'tȧ). Austl.	29·15 S	152·12 E
164	Capraia (I.) (kä-prä'yä) It.	43·02 N	9·51 E
164	Caprara Pt. (kä-prä'rä) It.	41·08 N	8·20 E
96	Capreol Can.	46·43 N	80·56 W
164	Caprera (I.) (kä-prā'rä) It.	41·12 N	9·28 E
163	Capri It. (Naples In.)	40·18 N	14·16 E
163	Capri, I. di (ē'-sō-lä-dē-kä'prē) It. (Naples In.)	40·19 N	14·10 E
205	Capricorn Chan. (kăp'rĭ-kôrn) Austl.	22·27 S	151·24 E
212	Caprivi Strip (Reg.) Namibia	18·00 S	22·00 E
89	Cap-Rouge (kȧp ro͞ozh') Can. (Quebec In.)	46·45 N	71·21 W
89	Cap-St. Ignace (kĭp săN-tē-nyȧs') Can. (Quebec In.)	47·02 N	70·27 W
164	Capua (kä'pwä) It.	41·07 N	14·14 E
124	Capulhuac (kä-po͝ol-hwäk') Mex.	19·33 N	99·43 W
116	Capulin Mountain Natl. Mon. (kȧ-pū'lĭn). NM	36·15 N	103·58 W
125	Capultitlán (kä-po͞o'l-tē-tlä'n) Mex. (In.)	19·15 N	99·40 W
134	Caquetá (R.) (kä-kā-tä') Col.	0·23 S	73·22 W
163	Carabaña (kä-rä-bän'yä) Sp. (Madrid In.)	40·16 N	3·15 W
135	Carabobo (State) (kä-rä-bô'-bô) Ven. (In.)	10·07 N	68·06 W
165	Caracal (kȧ-rȧ-kȧl') Rom.	44·06 N	24·22 E
135	Caracas (kä-rä'käs) Ven. (In.)	10·30 N	66·58 W
124	Carácuaro de Morelos (kä-rä'kwä-rō-dē-mô-rĕ-lôs). Mex.	18·44 N	101·04 W
137	Caraguatatuba (kä-rä-gwä-tȧ-to͞o'bä). Braz. (Rio de Janeiro In.)	23·37 S	45·26 W
135	Carajás, Serra dos (Mts.) (sĕ'r-rä-dôs-kä-rä-zhà's). Braz.	5·58 S	51·45 W
134	Caramanta, Cerro (Mtn.) (sĕ'r-rô-kä-rä-mà'n-tä). Col. (In.)	5·29 N	76·01 W
136	Caramarca (kä-rä-mà'r-kä) Arg.	28·29 S	65·45 W
137	Carandaí (kä-rän-dȧē') Braz. (Rio de Janeiro In.)	20·57 S	43·47 W
137	Carangola (kä-rȧn'gô'lä) Braz. (Rio de Janeiro In.)	20·46 S	42·02 W
165	Caransebes (kä-rȧn-sä'bĕsh). Rom.	45·24 N	22·13 E
98	Caraquet (kă-rȧ-kĕt') Can.	47·48 N	64·57 W
127	Carata, Laguna (L.) (lä-go͞o'nä-kä-rä'tä). Nic.	13·59 N	83·41 W
127	Caratasca, Laguna (L.) (lä-go͞o'nä-kä-rä-täs'kä). Hond.	15·20 N	83·45 W
162	Caravaca (kä-rä-vä'kä) Sp.	38·05 N	1·51 W
135	Caravelas (kȧ-rä-vĕl'äzh) Braz.	17·46 S	39·06 W
135	Carayaca (kȧ-rä-iȧ'kä). Ven. (In.)	10·32 N	67·07 W
136	Caràzinho (kä-rà'zē-nyō) Braz.	28·22 S	52·33 W
162	Carballino (kär-bäl-yē'nō) Sp.	42·26 N	8·04 W
162	Carballo (kär-bäl'yō) Sp.	43·13 N	8·40 W
112	Carbon (R.) (kär'bŏn). Wa. (Seattle In.)	47·06 N	122·08 W
112	Carbonado (kȧr-bō-nā'dō) Wa. (Seattle In.)	47·05 N	122·03 W
164	Carbonara, C. (kär-bō-nä'rä) It.	39·08 N	9·33 E
89	Carbondale (kär'bŏn-dāl) Can. (Edmonton In.)	53·45 N	113·32 W
117	Carbondale Il.	37·42 N	89·12 W
105	Carbondale Pa.	41·35 N	75·30 W
99	Carbonear (kär-bô-nēr') Can.	47·45 N	53·14 W
120	Carbon Hill (kär'bŏn hĭl) Al.	33·53 N	87·34 W
163	Carcagente (kär-kä-hĕn'tā) Sp.	39·09 N	0·29 W
160	Carcans, Étang de (L.) (ā-taN-dĕ-kär-kän). Fr.	45·12 N	1·00 W
160	Carcassonne (kȧr-kȧ-sôn') Fr.	43·12 N	2·23 E
90	Carcross (kär'krôs) Can.	60·18 N	134·54 W
128	Cárdenas (kär'dȧ-näs) Cuba	23·00 N	81·10 W
125	Cárdenas (kȧ'r-dĕ-näs) Mex.	17·59 N	93·23 W
124	Cárdenas Mex.	22·01 N	99·38 W
128	Cardenas, Bahía de (B.) (bä-ē'ä-dĕ-kär'dȧ-näs). Cuba	23·10 N	81·10 W
89	Cardiff (kär'dĭf) Can. (Edmonton In.)	53·46 N	113·36 W
154	Cardiff Wales	51·30 N	3·18 W
154	Cardigan (kär'dĭ-găn) Wales	52·05 N	4·40 W
154	Cardigan B. Wales	52·35 N	4·40 W
93	Cardston (kärds'tŭn) Can.	49·12 N	113·18 W
159	Carei (kä-rĕ') Rom.	47·42 N	22·28 E
160	Carentan (kä-rôN-täN') Fr.	49·19 N	1·14 W
104	Carey (kā'rē) Oh.	40·55 N	83·25 W
204	Carey (L.) (kâr'ē) Aust.	29·20 S	123·35 E
160	Carhaix (kär-ĕ') Fr.	48·17 N	3·37 W
123	Caribbean Sea (kăr-ĭ-bē'ăn) N.A.-S.A.	14·30 N	75·30 W
125	Caribe, Arroyo (R.) (är-ro'i-kä-rē'bĕ). Mex.	18·18 N	90·38 W
93	Cariboo Mts. (kă'rĭ-bo͞o) Can.	53·00 N	121·00 W
98	Caribou Me.	46·51 N	68·01 W
96	Caribou (I.) Can.	47·22 N	85·42 W
113	Caribou L. Mn. (Duluth In.)	46·54 N	92·16 W
90	Caribou Mts. Can.	59·20 N	115·30 W
135	Carinhanha (kä-rĭ-nyän'yä) Braz.	14·14 S	43·44 W
164	Carini (kä-rē'nē) It.	38·09 N	13·10 E
	Carinthia (State), see Kärnten		
97	Carleton Place (kärl'tŭn) Can.	45·15 N	76·10 W
218	Carletonville S. Afr. (Johannesburg & Pretoria In.)	26·20 S	27·23 E
117	Carlinville (kär'lĭn-vĭl) Il.	39·16 N	89·52 W
154	Carlisle (kär-lĭl') Eng.	54·54 N	3·03 W
104	Carlisle Ky.	38·20 N	84·00 W
105	Carlisle Pa.	40·10 N	77·15 W
160	Carlitte, Pic (Pk.) (pēk' kar-lēt') Fr.	42·33 N	1·56 E
164	Carloforte (kär'lō-fôr-tȧ) It.	39·11 N	8·28 E
137	Carlos Casares (kär-lôs-kä-sä'rĕs) Arg. (Buenos Aires In.)	35·38 S	61·17 W
154	Carlow (kär'lō) Ire.	52·50 N	7·00 W
118	Carlsbad (kärlz'băd) NM	32·24 N	104·12 W
118	Carlsbad Caverns Nat'l Park NM	32·08 N	104·30 W
148	Carlton (kärl'tŭn) Eng.	52·58 N	1·05 W
113	Carlton Mn. (Duluth In.)	46·40 N	92·26 W
104	Carlton Center (kärl'tŭn sĕn'tēr) Mi.	42·45 N	85·20 W
117	Carlyle (kärlīl') Il.	38·37 N	89·23 W
164	Carmagnolo (kär-mä-nyô'lä) It.	44·52 N	7·48 E
95	Carman (kär'mȧn) Can.	49·32 N	98·00 W
154	Carmarthen (kär-mär'thĕn) Wales	51·50 N	4·20 W
154	Carmarthen B. (kär-mär'thĕn) Wales	51·33 N	4·50 W
160	Carmaux (kȧr-mō') Fr.	44·05 N	2·09 E
106	Carmel (kär'mĕl) NY (New York In.)	41·25 N	73·42 W
137	Carmelo (kär-mĕ'lo) Ur. (Buenos Aires In.)	33·59 S	58·15 W
125	Carmen, Isla del (I.) (ē's-lä-dĕl-kȧ'r-mĕn). Mex.	18·43 N	91·40 W
125	Carmen, Laguna del (L.) (lä-go͞o'nä-dĕl-kȧ'r-mĕn). Mex.	18·15 N	93·26 W
137	Carmen de Areco (kär'mĕn' dā ä-rā'kô). Arg. (Buenos Aires In.)	34·21 S	59·50 W
136	Carmen de Patagones (kȧ'r-mĕn-dĕ-pä-tä-gô'nĕs). Arg.	41·00 S	63·00 W
104	Carmi (kär'mī) Il.	38·05 N	88·10 W
137	Carmo (kȧ'r-mô) Braz. (Rio de Janeiro In.)	21·57 S	42·06 W
137	Carmo do Rio Clara (kȧ'r-mô-dô-rē'ô-klä'rä) Braz. (Rio de Janeiro In.)	20·57 S	46·04 W
162	Carmona Sp.	37·28 N	5·38 W
204	Carnarvon (kär-när'vŭn) Austl.	24·45 S	113·45 E
212	Carnarvon S. Afr.	31·00 S	22·15 E
112	Carnation (kär-nā'shŭn) Wa. (Seattle In.)	47·39 N	121·55 W
163	Carnaxide (kär-nä-shē'dĕ) Port. (Lisbon In.)	38·44 N	9·15 W
154	Carndonagh (kärn-dō-nä') Ire.	55·15 N	7·15 W
116	Carnegie (kär-nĕg'ĭ) Ok.	35·06 N	98·38 W
107	Carnegie Pa. (Pittsburgh In.)	40·24 N	80·06 W
105	Carneys Point (kär'nês) NJ	39·45 N	75·25 W
158	Carnic Alps (Mts.) Aus.-It.	46·43 N	12·38 E
163	Carnot (kär nō') Alg.	36·15 N	1·40 E
215	Carnot Cen. Afr. Rep.	5·00 N	15·52 E
154	Carnsore Pt. (kärn'sôr) Ire.	52·10 N	6·16 W
104	Caro (kâ'rō) Mi.	43·30 N	83·25 W
135	Carolina (kä-rô-lē'nä) Braz.	7·26 S	47·16 W
212	Carolina (kăr-ô-lī'nȧ) S. Afr.	26·07 S	30·09 E
126	Carolina (L.) (kä-rŏ-lē'nä) Mex. (In.)	18·41 N	89·40 W
198	Caroline Is. (kăr'ô-līn) Pac. Is. Trust Ter.	9·30 N	143·00 E
134	Caroni (R.) (kä-rō'nē) Ven.	5·49 N	62·57 W
134	Carora (kä-rô'rä) Ven.	10·09 N	70·12 W
153	Carpathians (Mts.) (kär-pā'thĭ-ăn). Eur.	49·23 N	20·14 E
165	Carpatii Meridionali (Transylvanian Alps) (Mts.). Rom.	45·30 N	23·30 E
204	Carpentaria, G. of (kär-pĕn-târ'ĭȧ). Austl.	14·45 S	138·50 E
160	Carpentras (kär-päN-träs') Fr.	44·04 N	5·01 E
164	Carpi It.	44·48 N	10·54 E
120	Carabelle (kăr'ȧ-bĕl) Fl.	29·50 N	84·40 W
154	Carrantuohill (kă-răn-to͞o'ĭl) Ire.	52·01 N	9·48 W
164	Carrara (kä-rä'rä) It.	44·05 N	10·05 E
134	Carretas, Punta (Pt.) (po͞o'n-tä-kär-rĕ'tĕ'rȧs) Peru	14·15 S	76·25 W
127	Carriacou (I.) (kăr-ē-ȧ-ko͞o') Grenada (In.)	12·28 N	61·20 W
154	Carrick (kăr'ĭk) Ire.	52·20 N	7·35 W
89	Carrier (kăr'ĭ-ĕr) Can. (Quebec In.)	46·43 N	71·05 W
120	Carriere (kȧ-rēr') Ms.	30·37 N	89·37 W
104	Carriers Mills (kăr'ĭ-ērs) Il.	37·40 N	88·40 W
108	Carrington (kăr'ĭng-tŭn) ND	47·26 N	99·06 W
112	Carr Inlet (kăr ĭn'lĕt) Wa. (Seattle In.)	47·20 N	122·42 W
128	Carrion Crow Hbr. (kăr'ĭŭn krō) Ba.	26·35 N	77·55 W
162	Carrión de los Condes (kär-rē-ōn' dā lōs kōn'dȧs). Sp.	42·20 N	4·35 W
116	Carrizo Cr. (kär-rē'zō) NM	36·22 N	103·39 W
118	Carrizo Springs Tx.	28·32 N	99·51 W
115	Carrizozo (kär-rē-zō'zō) NM	33·40 N	105·55 W
109	Carroll (kăr'ŭl) Ia.	42·03 N	94·51 W
120	Carrollton (kăr-ŭl-tŭn) Ga.	33·35 N	84·05 W
117	Carrollton Il.	39·18 N	90·22 W
104	Carrollton Ky.	38·45 N	85·15 W
104	Carrollton Mi.	43·30 N	83·55 W
117	Carrollton Mo.	39·21 N	93·29 W
104	Carrollton Oh.	40·35 N	81·10 W
113	Carrollton Tx. (Dallas, Fort Worth In.)	32·58 N	96·53 W
112	Carrols (kăr'ŭlz) Wa. (Portland In.)	46·05 N	122·51 W
154	Carron (L.) (kă'rŭn) Scot.	57·25 N	5·25 W
94	Carrot (R.) Can.	53·12 N	103·50 W
160	Carry-le-Rouet (kä-rē'lĕ-ro͞o-ā') Fr. (In.)	43·20 N	5·10 E
171	Carsamba (chär-shäm'bä) Tur.	41·05 N	36·40 E
114	Carson (R.) (kär'sŭn) Nv.	39·15 N	119·25 W
114	Carson City Nv.	39·10 N	119·45 W
114	Carson Sink Nv.	39·51 N	118·25 W
134	Cartagena (kär-tä-hā'nä) Col.	10·30 N	75·40 W
163	Cartagena (kär-tä-ĸĕ'nä) Sp.	37·46 N	1·00 W
134	Cartago (kär-tä'gō) Col. (In.)	4·44 N	75·54 W
127	Cartago C. R.	9·52 N	83·56 W
162	Cartaxo (kär-tä'shō) Port.	39·10 N	8·48 W
106	Carteret (kär'tē-rĕt) NJ (New York In.)	40·35 N	74·13 W
120	Cartersville (kär'tērs-vĭl) Ga.	34·09 N	84·47 W
117	Carthage (kär'thāj) Il.	40·27 N	91·09 W
117	Carthage Mo.	37·10 N	94·18 W
105	Carthage NY	44·00 N	75·45 W
121	Carthage NC	35·22 N	79·25 W
119	Carthage Tx.	32·09 N	94·20 W
210	Carthage Tun.	37·04 N	10·18 E
213	Carthcart (cärth-cȧ't) S. Afr. (Natal In.)	32·18 S	27·11 E
91	Cartwright (kärt'rīt) Can.	53·36 N	57·00 W
135	Caruaru (kä-ro͝o-ȧ-ro͞o') Braz.	8·19 S	35·52 W
134	Carúpano (kä-ro͞o'pä-nō) Ven.	10·45 N	63·21 W
117	Caruthersville (kȧ-rŭdh'ērz-vĭl) Mo.	36·09 N	89·41 W
112	Carver (kärv'ēr). Or. (Portland In.)	45·24 N	122·30 W
162	Carvoeira, Cabo (C.) (kà'bō-kär-vô-ĕ'y-rä). Port.	39·22 N	9·24 W
107	Cary (kā'rē) Il. (Chicago In.)	42·13 N	88·14 W
137	Casablanca (kä-sä-bläŋ'kä) Chile (Santiago In.)	33·19 S	71·24 W
210	Casablanca Mor.	33·32 N	7·41 W
137	Casa Branca (kà'sä-brà'N-kä) Braz. (Rio de Janeiro In.)	21·47 S	47·04 W
115	Casa Grande (kä'sä grän'dā). Az.	32·50 N	111·45 W
115	Casa Grande Natl. Mon. Az.	33·00 N	111·33 W
164	Casale (kä-sä'lā) It.	45·08 N	8·26 E
164	Casalmaggiore (kä-säl-mäd-jō'rā). It.	45·00 N	10·24 E
214	Casamance (R.) (kä-sä-mäNs') Senegal	12·43 N	16·00 W
205	Cascade Pt. (kăs-kād'). N.Z. (In.)	43·59 S	168·23 E
102	Cascade Ra. U. S.	42·50 N	122·20 W
110	Cascade Tun. Wa.	47·41 N	120·53 W
163	Cascais (käs-kȧ-ēzh) Port. (Lisbon In.)	38·42 N	9·25 W
163	Cascais, Bahía de (B.) (bä-ē'ä-dĕ-käs-kĭ's) Port. (Lisbon In.)	38·41 N	9·24 W
112	Case Inlet (kās). Wa. (Seattle In.)	47·22 N	122·47 W
136	Caseros (kä-sā'rôs) Arg. (In.)	34·35 S	58·34 W
164	Caserta (kä-zĕr'tä) It.	41·04 N	14·21 E
104	Casey (kā'sĭ) Il.	39·20 N	88·00 W
110	Cashmere (kăsh'mĭr) Wa.	47·30 N	120·28 W
197	Casiguran (käs-sē-go͞o'rän) Phil. (In.)	16·15 N	122·10 E
197	Casiguran Sd. Phil. (In.)	16·02 N	121·51 E
137	Casilda (kä-sē'l-dä) Arg. (Buenos Aires In.)	33·02 S	61·11 W
128	Casilda Cuba	21·50 N	80·00 W
137	Casimiro de Abreu (kä'sē-mē'ro-dĕ-ȧ-brĕ'o͞o). Braz. (Rio de Janeiro In.)	22·30 S	42·11 W
203	Casino (kȧ-sē'nō) Austl.	28·35 S	153·10 E
134	Casiquiare (R.) (kä-sē-kyä'rā) Ven.	2·11 N	66·15 W
163	Caspe (käs'pȧ) Sp.	41·18 N	0·02 W
111	Casper (kăs'pēr) Wy.	42·51 N	106·18 W
170	Caspian Dep. (kăs'pĭ-ăn). Sov. Un.	47·40 N	52·35 E
168	Caspian Sea Asia	40·00 N	52·00 E
105	Cass (kăs) WV	38·25 N	79·55 W
109	Cass (L.) Mn.	47·23 N	94·28 W
163	Cassá de la Selva (käs-sä'dĕ-lä-sĕl-vä). Sp.	41·52 N	2·52 E
216	Cassai (R.) (kä-sä'ē) Ang.	7·30 S	21·45 E
104	Cass City (kăs) Mi.	43·35 N	83·10 W
89	Casselman (kăs''l-mȧn) Can. (Ottawa In.)	45·18 N	75·05 W
108	Casselton (kăs''l-tŭn) ND	46·53 N	97·14 W
137	Cássia (kà'syä) Braz. (Rio de Janeiro In.)	20·36 S	46·53 W
113	Cassin (kăs'ĭn) Tx. (San Antonio In.)	29·16 N	98·29 W
212	Cassinga (kä-sĭŋ'gä) Ang.	15·05 S	16·15 E
164	Cassino (käs-sē'nō) It.	41·30 N	13·50 E
109	Cass Lake (kăs) Mn.	47·23 N	94·37 W
104	Cassopolis (kăs-ŏ'pô-lĭs) Mi.	41·55 N	86·00 W
117	Cassville (kăs'vĭl) Mo.	36·41 N	93·52 W
162	Castanheira de Pêra (käs-tän-yā'rä-dĕ-pĕ'rä). Port.	40·00 N	8·07 W
160	Casteljaloux (käs-tĕl-zhä-lo͞o'). Fr.	44·20 N	0·04 E
163	Castellammare di Stabia (käs-tĕl-läm-mä'rā-dē-stä'byä) It. (Naples In.)	40·26 N	14·29 E
137	Castelli (kȧs-tĕ'zhē) Arg. (Buenos Aires In.)	36·07 S	57·48 W
163	Castellón de la Plana (käs-tĕl-yō'n-dĕ-lä-plä'nä). Sp.	39·59 N	0·05 W
160	Castelnaudary (kȧs'tĕl-nō-dȧ-rē') Fr.	43·20 N	1·57 E
137	Castelo (käs-tĕ'lô) Braz. (Rio de Janeiro In.)	21·37 S	41·13 W
162	Castelo Branco (käs-tä'lo͞o bräŋ'ko͝o). Port.	39·48 N	7·37 W
162	Castelo de Vide (käs-tä'lo͞o dĭ vē'dĭ). Port.	39·25 N	7·25 W
160	Castelsarrasin (kȧs'tĕl-sȧ-rȧ-zăN') Fr.	44·03 N	1·05 E
164	Castelvetrano (käs'tĕl-vē-trä'nō) It.	37·43 N	12·50 E
134	Castilla (kȧs-tē'l-yä) Peru	5·18 S	80·40 W
162	Castilla La Nueva (Reg.) (käs-tē'lyä lä nwā'vä). Sp.	39·15 N	3·55 W
162	Castilla La Vieja (Reg.) (käs-tē'lyä lä vyā'hä). Sp.	40·48 N	4·24 W
121	Castillo De San Marcos Natl. Mon. (käs-tē'lyä de-sän măr-kōs) Fl.	29·55 N	81·25 W
129	Castle (I.) (kȧs''l) Ba.	22·05 N	74·20 W
154	Castlebar (kȧs''l-bär) Ire.	53·55 N	9·15 W
115	Castle Dale (kȧs'l dāl) Ut.	39·15 N	111·00 W

ng-sing; ŋ-baŋk; N-nasalized n; nŏd; cŏmmit; ōld; ôbey; ôrder; fo͞od; fo͝ot; ou-out; s-soft; sh-dish; th-thin; pūre; ûnite; ûrn; stŭd; circŭs; ü-as "y" in study; '-indeterminate vowel.

266 Castle Donington — Chamberlain PRONOUNCING INDEX

Page	Name Pronunciation Region	Lat. °′	Long. °′
148	Castle Donington (dŏn'ĭng-tŭn) Eng.	52·50 N	1·21 W
148	Castleford (kȧs'l-fērd) Eng.	53·43 N	1·21 W
93	Castlegar (kȧs''l-gär) Can.	49·19 N	117·40 W
203	Castlemaine (käs''l-mān) Austl.	37·05 S	114·10 E
115	Castle Pk. Co.	39·00 N	106·50 W
110	Castlerock (kȧs''l-rŏk) Wa.	46·17 N	122·53 W
109	Castle Rock Flowage (Res.) Wi.	44·03 N	89·48 W
107	Castle Shannon (shăn'ŭn) Pa. (Pittsburgh In.)	40·22 N	80·02 W
107	Castleton (kȧs''l-tŏn) In. (Indianapolis In.)	39·54 N	86·03 W
89	Castor (R.) (kăs'tôr) Can (Ottawa In.)	45·16 N	75·14 W
117	Castor (R.) Mo.	36·59 N	89·53 W
160	Castres (kȧs'tr') Fr.	43·36 N	2·13 E
127	Castries (kȧs-trē') St. Lucia (In.)	14·01 N	61·00 W
136	Castro (käs'trŏŏ) Braz.	24·56 S	50·00 W
136	Castro (käs'tro) Chile	42·27 S	73·48 W
162	Castro Daire (käs'trŏŏ dīr'ĭ) Port.	40·56 N	7·57 W
162	Castro de Río (käs-trô-dĕ-rē'ō) Sp.	37·42 N	4·28 W
161	Castrop Rauxel (käs'trōp rou'ksĕl) F.R.G. (Ruhr In.)	51·33 N	7·19 E
162	Castro Urdiales (käs'trō ŏŏr-dyä'lās) Sp.	43·23 N	3·11 W
112	Castro Valley Ca. (San Francisco In.)	37·42 N	122·05 W
162	Castro Verde (käs-trō vĕr'dĕ) Port.	37·43 N	8·05 W
164	Castrovillari (käs'trō-vēl-lyä'rē) It.	39·48 N	16·11 E
162	Castuera (käs-tŏŏ-ā'rä) Sp.	38·43 N	5·33 W
217	Casula Moz.	15·25 S	33·40 E
129	Cat (I.) Ba.	25·30 N	75·30 W
126	Catacamas (kä-tä-kȧ'mäs) Hond.	14·52 N	85·55 W
137	Cataguases (kä-tä-gwä'sĕs) Braz. (Rio de Janeiro In.)	21·23 S	42·42 W
119	Catahoula (L.) (kăt-ȧ-hŏŏ'lȧ) La.	31·35 N	92·20 W
135	Catalão (kä-tä-loun') Braz.	18·09 S	47·42 W
129	Catalina (I.) (kä-tä-lē'nä) Dom. Rep.	18·20 N	69·00 W
163	Cataluma (Reg.) (kä-tä-lōō'mä) Sp.	41·23 N	0·50 E
136	Catamarca (Prov.) (kä-tä-mär'kä) Arg.	27·15 S	67·15 W
197	Catanduanes I. (kä-tän-dwä'nĕs) Phil.	13·55 N	125·00 E
135	Catanduva (kä-tȧn-dōō'vä) Braz.	21·12 S	48·47 W
164	Catania (kä-tä'nyä) It.	37·30 N	15·09 E
164	Catania, Golfo di (G.) (gôl-fô-dē-kȧ-tä'nyä) It.	37·24 N	15·28 E
197	Catanaun (kä-tä-nä'wän) Phil. (In.)	13·36 N	122·20 E
164	Catanzaro (kä-tän-dzä'rō) It.	38·53 N	16·34 E
163	Catarroja (kä-tär-rō'hä) Sp.	39·24 N	0·25 W
121	Catawba (L.) SC	35·02 N	81·21 W
121	Catawba (R.) (kȧ-tô'bȧ) NC	35·25 N	80·55 W
125	Catazajá, Laguna de (L.) (lä-gōō'nä-dĕ-kä-tä-zä-hȧ') Mex.	17·45 N	92·03 W
197	Catbalogan (kät-bä-lō'gän) Phil.	11·45 N	124·52 E
125	Catemaco (kä-tā-mä'kō) Mex.	18·26 N	95·06 W
125	Catemaco, Lago (L.) (lä'gô-kä-tā-mä'kō) Mex.	18·23 N	95·04 W
148	Caterham (kā'tēr-ŭm) Eng. (London In.)	51·16 N	0·04 W
216	Catete (kä-tĕ'tĕ) Ang.	9·06 S	13·43 E
118	Cathedral Mt. (kȧ-thē'drȧl) Tx.	30·09 N	103·46 W
213	Cathedral Pk. (kȧ-thē'drȧl) S. Afr. (Natal In.)	28·53 S	29·04 E
117	Catherine, L. (kȧ-thēr-ĭn) Ar.	34·26 N	92·47 W
213	Cathkin Pk. (kăth'kĭn) S. Afr. (Natal In.)	29·08 S	29·22 E
112	Cathlamet (kăth-lăm'ĕt) Wa. (Portland In.)	46·12 N	123·22 W
104	Catlettsburg (kăt'lĕts-bûrg) Ky.	38·20 N	82·35 W
122	Catoche, C. (kä-tô'chĕ) Mex.	21·30 N	87·15 W
106	Catonsville (kā'tŭnz-vĭl) Md. (Baltimore In.)	39·16 N	76·45 W
124	Catorce (kä-tôr'sȧ) Mex.	23·41 N	100·51 W
105	Catskill (kăts'kĭl) NY	42·15 N	73·50 W
105	Catskill Mts. NY	42·20 N	74·35 W
105	Cattaraugus Ind. Res. (kăt'tȧ-rȧ-gŭs) NY	42·30 N	79·05 W
135	Catu (kȧ-tōō) Braz.	12·26 S	38·12 W
216	Catuala Ang.	16·29 S	19·03 E
216	Catumbela (R.) (kä'tŏm-bĕl'ȧ) Ang.	12·40 S	14·10 E
197	Cauayan (kou-ä'yän) Phil. (In.)	16·56 N	121·46 E
134	Cauca (R.) (kou'kä) Col.	7·30 N	75·26 W
135	Caucagua (käōō-kȧ'gwä) Ven.(In.)	10·17 N	66·22 W
171	Caucasus Mts. (kô'kȧ-sŭs) Sov. Un.	43·20 N	42·00 E
95	Cauchon L. (kô-shŏn') Can.	55·25 N	96·30 W
160	Cauderan (kō-dā-räN') Fr.	44·50 N	0·40 W
89	Caughnawaga Can. (Montreal In.)	45·24 N	73·41 W
164	Caulonia (kou-lō'nyä) It.	38·24 N	16·22 E
136	Cauquenes (kou-kā'nās) Chile	35·54 S	72·14 W
134	Caura (R.) (kou'rä) Ven.	6·48 N	64·40 W
98	Causapscal Can.	48·22 N	67·14 W
92	Caution, C. (kô'shŭn) Can.	51·10 N	127·47 W
129	Cauto (R.) (kou'tō) Cuba	20·33 N	76·20 W
184	Cauvery (R.) India	11·15 N	78·06 E
136	Cava (kȧ'vä) Braz. (In.)	22·41 S	43·26 W
163	Cava de' Tirreni (kä'vä-dĕ-tēr-rĕ'nē) It. (Naples In.)	40·27 N	14·43 E
162	Cavado (R.) (kä-vä'dō) Port.	41·43 N	8·08 W
135	Cavalcante (kä-väl-kän'tā) Braz.	13·45 S	47·33 W
108	Cavalier (kăv-ȧ-lēr') ND	48·45 N	97·39 W
214	Cavally (R.) Ivory Coast-Lib.	4·40 N	7·30 W
154	Cavan (kăv'ăn) Ire.	54·01 N	7·00 W
164	Cavarzere (kä-vär'dzā-rā) It.	45·08 N	12·06 E
105	Cavendish (kăv'ĕn-dĭsh) Vt.	43·25 N	72·35 W
135	Caviana, Ilha (I.) (kä-vyä'nä) Braz.	0·45 N	49·33 W
197	Cavite (kä-vē'tä) Phil. (In.)	14·30 N	120·54 E
148	Cawood (kā'wŏŏd) Eng.	53·49 N	1·07 W
137	Caxambu (kä-shä'm-bōō) Braz. (Rio de Janeiro In.)	22·00 S	44·45 W
135	Caxias (kä'shē-äzh) Braz.	4·48 S	43·16 W
136	Caxias do Sul (kä'shē-äzh-dô-sōō'l) Braz.	29·13 S	51·03 W
163	Caxine, Cap (C.) (kăp kăk'sēn) Alg.	36·47 N	2·52 E
216	Caxito (kä-shē'tŏŏ) Ang.	8·33 S	13·36 E
134	Cayambe (kȧ-īä'm-bĕ) Ec.	0·03 N	79·09 W
135	Cayenne (kā-ĕn') Fr. Gu.	4·56 N	52·18 W
124	Cayetano Rubio (kä-yĕ-tȧ-nô-rōō'byô) Mex.	20·37 N	100·21 W
123	Cayey P. R. (Puerto Rico In.)	18·05 N	66·12 W
128	Cayman Brac (I.) (kī-män' brȧk) Cayman Is.	19·45 N	79·50 W
128	Cayman Is. N. A.	19·30 N	80·30 W
128	Cay Sal Bk. (kē-săl) Ba.	23·55 N	80·20 W
105	Cayuga (L.) (kā-yōō'gȧ) NY	42·35 N	76·35 W
162	Cazalla de la Sierra (kä-thäl'yä-dĕ-lä-sē-ĕ'r-rä) Sp.	37·55 N	5·48 W
160	Cazaux, Étang de (L.) (ā-täN' dĕ kä-zō') Fr.	44·32 N	0·59 W
105	Cazenovia (kăz-ê-nō'vĭ-ȧ) NY	42·55 N	75·50 W
107	Cazenovia Cr. NY (Buffalo In.)	42·49 N	78·45 W
164	Čazma (chäz'mä) Yugo.	45·44 N	16·39 E
212	Cazombo (kä-zô'm-bŏ) Ang.	12·25 S	22·40 E
125	Cazones (R.) (kä-zô'nĕs) Mex.	20·37 N	97·28 W
128	Cazones, Ensenada de (B.) (ĕn-sĕ-nä-dä-dĕ-kä-zō'nȧs) Cuba	22·05 N	81·30 W
128	Cazones, Golfo de (G.) (gôl-fô-dĕ-kä-zō'nȧs) Cuba	23·55 N	81·15 W
162	Cazorla (kä-thôr'lȧ) Sp.	37·55 N	2·58 W
162	Cea (R.) (thā'ä) Sp.	42·18 N	5·10 W
	Ceará, see Fortaleza		
135	Ceará (State) (sā-ȧ-rä') Braz.	5·13 S	39·43 W
135	Ceará-Mirim (sā-ä-rä'mē-rē'N) Braz.	6·00 S	35·13 W
127	Cebaco, Isla (I.) (ē's-lä-sä-bä'kō) Pan.	7·27 N	81·08 W
115	Cebolla Cr. (sē-bōl'yä) Co.	38·15 N	107·10 W
162	Cebollera, Sierra (Mts.) (sē-ĕ'r-rä-sĕ-bôl-yĕ-rä) Sp.	42·03 N	2·53 W
162	Cebreros (sĕ-brĕ'rōs) Sp.	40·28 N	4·28 W
197	Cebu (sā-bōō') Phil.	10·22 N	123·49 E
107	Cecil (sē'sĭl) Pa. (Pittsburgh In.)	40·20 N	80·10 W
109	Cedar (R.) Ia.	42·23 N	92·07 W
112	Cedar (R.) Wa. (Portland In.)	45·56 N	122·32 W
109	Cedar (R.) West Fk. Ia.	42·49 N	93·10 W
119	Cedar Bayou Tx. (In.)	29·54 N	94·58 W
115	Cedar Breaks Natl. Mon. Ut.	37·35 N	112·55 W
109	Cedarburg (sē'dĕr bûrg) Wi.	43·23 N	88·00 W
115	Cedar City Ut.	37·40 N	113·10 W
108	Cedar Cr. ND	46·05 N	102·10 W
109	Cedar Falls Ia.	42·31 N	92·29 W
120	Cedar Keys Fl.	29·06 N	83·03 W
107	Cedar Lake In. (Chicago In.)	41·22 N	87·27 W
107	Cedar L. In. (Chicago In.)	41·23 N	87·25 W
109	Cedar Rapids Ia.	42·00 N	91·43 W
104	Cedar Springs Mi.	43·15 N	85·40 W
120	Cedartown (sē'dĕr-toun) Ga.	34·00 N	85·15 W
213	Cedarville (cĕdȧr'vĭl) S. Afr. (Natal In.)	30·23 S	29·04 E
124	Cedral (sā-dräl') Mex.	23·47 N	100·42 W
126	Cedros (sā'drōs) Hond.	14·36 N	87·07 W
122	Cedros (I.) Mex.	28·10 N	115·10 W
204	Ceduna (sê-dōō'nȧ) Austl.	32·15 S	133·55 E
164	Cefalù (chā-fä-lōō') It.	38·01 N	14·01 E
162	Cega (R.) (thā'gä) Sp.	41·25 N	4·27 W
159	Cegléd (tsā'glād) Hung.	47·10 N	19·49 E
165	Ceglie (chĕ'lyĕ) It.	40·39 N	17·32 E
162	Cehegín (thā-ȧ-hēn') Sp.	38·05 N	1·48 W
129	Ceiba del Agua (sā'bä-dĕl-ȧ'gwä) Cuba (In.)	22·08 N	82·38 W
210	Cekhira Tun.	34·17 N	10·00 E
216	Cela (sĕ-lȧ) Ang.	11·25 S	15·07 E
124	Celaya (sā-lä'yä) Mex.	20·33 N	100·49 W
196	Celebes (Sulawesi) (I.) Indon.	2·15 S	120·30 E
196	Celebes Sea Indon.	3·45 N	121·52 E
126	Celestún (sĕ-lĕs-tōō'n) Mex. (In.)	20·57 N	90·18 W
104	Celina (sēlī'na) Oh.	40·30 N	84·35 W
164	Celje (tsĕl'yĕ) Yugo.	46·13 N	15·17 E
158	Celle (tsĕl'ē) F.R.G.	52·37 N	10·05 E
116	Cement (sē-mĕnt') Ok.	34·56 N	98·07 W
197	Cenderawasih Teluk (B.) Indon.	2·20 S	135·30 E
135	Ceniza, Pico (Mtn.) (pē'kō-sĕ-nē'zä) Ven. (In.)	10·24 N	67·26 W
160	Cenon (sĕ-nôN') Fr.	44·51 N	0·33 W
119	Center (sĕn'tēr) Tx.	31·50 N	94·10 W
120	Centerhill Res. (sĕn'tēr-hĭl) Tn.	36·02 N	86·00 W
107	Center Line (sĕn'tēr līn) Mi. (Detroit In.)	42·29 N	83·01 W
109	Centerville (sĕn'tēr-vĭl) Ia.	40·44 N	92·48 W
113	Centerville. Mn. (Minneapolis, St. Paul In.)	45·10 N	93·03 W
107	Centerville Pa. (Pittsburgh In.)	40·02 N	79·58 W
108	Centerville SD	43·07 N	96·56 W
113	Centerville Ut. (Salt Lake City In.)	40·55 N	111·53 W
134	Central, Cordillera (Mts.) (kôr-dĕl-yĕ'rä-sĕn-trä'l) Bol.	19·18 S	65·29 W
134	Central, Cordillera (Mts.) Col. (In.)	3·58 N	75·55 W
129	Central, Cordillera (Cibao Mts.) (kôr-dĕl-yä'rȧ sĕn'träl) (sē-bä'ō) Dom. Rep.	19·05 N	71·30 W
197	Central Cordillera (Mts.) (kôr-dĕl-yĕ'rä-sĕn-träl) Phil. (In.)	17·05 N	120·55 E
209	Central African Republic Afr.	7·50 N	21·00 E
122	Central America (ä-mĕr'ĭ-kȧ) N. A.	10·45 N	87·15 W
120	Central City (sĕn'trȧl) Ky.	37·15 N	87·09 W
108	Central City (sĕn'trȧl sĭ'tĭ) Ne.	41·07 N	98·00 W
106	Central Falls (sĕn'trȧl fôlz) RI (Providence In.)	41·54 N	71·23 W
104	Centralia (sĕn-trā'lĭ-ȧ) Il.	38·35 N	89·05 W
117	Centralia Mo.	39·11 N	92·07 W
110	Centralia Wa.	46·42 N	122·58 W
170	Central Plat. Sov. Un.	55·00 N	33·30 E
106	Central Valley NY (New York In.)	41·19 N	74·07 W
113	Centreville (sĕn'tēr-vĭl) Il. (St. Louis In.)	38·33 N	90·06 W
105	Centreville Md.	39·05 N	76·05 W
120	Century (sĕn'tū-rĭ) Fl.	30·57 N	87·15 W
	Cephalonia (I.), see Kefallinéa		
160	Céret (sā-rĕ') Fr.	42·29 N	2·47 E
134	Cereté (sĕ-rĕ-tĕ') Col.	8·56 N	75·58 W
164	Cerignola (chā-rē-nyô'lä) It.	41·16 N	15·55 E
164	Cerknica (tsĕr'knē-tsȧ) Yugo.	45·48 N	14·21 E
118	Cerralvo (sĕr-räl'vō) Mex.	26·05 N	99·37 W
122	Cerralvo (I.) Mex.	24·00 N	109·59 W
134	Cerrito (sĕr-rē'-tô) Col. (In.)	3·41 N	76·17 W
124	Cerritos (sĕr-rē'tôs) Mex.	22·26 N	100·16 W
134	Cerro de Pasco (sĕr'rō dā päs'kō) Peru	10·45 S	76·14 W
118	Cerro Gordo, Arroyo de (är-rô-yô-dĕ-sĕ'r-rô-gôr-dô) Mex.	26·12 N	104·06 W
134	Certegui (sĕr-tĕ'gē) Col. (In.)	5·21 N	76·35 W
197	Cervantes (sĕr-vän'tās) Phil (In.)	16·59 N	120·42 E
162	Cervantes (thĕr-vän'tās) Sp.	42·43 N	7·04 W
162	Cervera del Río Alhama (thĕr-vā'rȧ dĕl rē'ō-äl-ä'mä) Sp.	42·02 N	1·55 W
163	Cerveteri (chĕr-vĕ'tĕ-rē) It. (Rome In.)	42·00 N	12·06 E
164	Cesena (chĕ'sĕ-nä) It.	44·08 N	12·16 E
157	Cēsis (sā'sĭs) Sov. Un.	57·19 N	25·17 E
158	Česká Lípa (chĕs'kä lē'pa) Czech.	50·41 N	14·31 E
158	České (Bohemia) (Prov.) (chĕs'kā) (bô-hē'mĭ-ȧ) Czech.	49·51 N	13·55 E
158	České Budějovice (chĕs'kā bōō'dyĕ-yô-vēt-sĕ) Czech.	49·00 N	14·30 E
158	Českomoravaska Vysočina (Mts.) Czech.	49·21 N	15·40 E
165	Cesme (chĕsh'mĕ) Tur.	38·20 N	26·20 E
203	Cessnock Austl.	32·58 S	151·15 E
214	Cestos (R.) Lib.	5·40 N	9·25 W
165	Cetinje (tsĕt'in-yĕ) Yugo.	42·23 N	18·55 E
210	Ceuta (Sp.) (thā-ōō'tä) Aft.	36·04 N	5·36 W
160	Cévennes (Reg.) (sā-vĕn') Fr.	44·20 N	3·48 E
153	Ceyhan (R.) Tur.	37·19 N	36·06 E
	Ceylon, see Sri Lanka		
112	Chabot (L.) (sha'bŏt) Ca. (San Francisco In.)	37·44 N	122·06 W
137	Chacabuco (chä-kä-bōō'kō) Arg. (Buenos Aires In.)	34·37 S	60·27 W
125	Chacaltianguis (chä-käl-tē-äŋ'gwēs) Mex.	18·18 N	95·50 W
134	Chachapoyas (chä-chä-poi'yäs) Peru	6·16 S	77·48 W
136	Chaco (Prov.) (chä'kō) Arg.	26·00 S	60·45 W
115	Chaco Canyon Natl. Mon. (chä'kô) NM	35·38 N	108·06 W
174	Chad (chăd) Sov. Un. (Urals In.)	56·33 N	57·11 E
209	Chad Afr.	17·48 N	19·00 E
215	Chad, L. Afr.	13·55 N	13·40 E
121	Chadbourn (chăd'bŭrn) NC	34·19 N	78·55 W
108	Chadron (chăd'rŭn) Ne.	42·50 N	103·10 W
162	Chafarinas (C.) Mor.	35·08 N	2·20 W
117	Chaffee (chăf'ē) Mo.	37·10 N	89·39 W
186	Chāgal Hills Afg.-Pak.	29·15 N	63·28 E
166	Chagodoshcha (R.) (chä-gō-dôsh-chä) Sov. Un.	59·08 N	35·13 E
127	Chagres R. (chä'grĕs) Pan.	9·18 N	79·22 W
107	Chagrin R. (shȧ'grĭn) Oh. (Cleveland In.)	41·34 N	81·24 W
107	Chagrin Falls (shȧ'grĭn fôls) Oh. (Cleveland In.)	41·26 N	81·23 W
192	Chahar (Reg.) (chä-här) China	44·25 N	115·00 E
186	Chāh Bahār (chä'h' bä'här) Iran	25·18 N	60·45 E
217	Chake Chake Tan.	5·15 S	39·46 E
126	Chalatenango (chäl-ä-tĕ-näŋ'gō) Sal.	14·04 N	88·54 W
217	Chalbi Des. Ken.	3·40 N	36·50 E
125	Chalcatongo (chäl-kä-tôŋ'gō) Mex.	17·04 N	97·41 W
124	Chalchihuites (chäl-chê-wē'tās) Mex.	23·28 N	103·57 W
126	Chalchuapa (chäl-chwä'pä) Sal.	14·01 N	89·39 W
173	Chalchyn (R.) (chäl-chyn) China-Mong.	48·00 N	118·45 E
125	Chalco (chäl-kō) Mex. (In.)	19·15 N	98·54 W
98	Chaleur B. (shȧ-lûr') Can.	47·58 N	65·33 W
148	Chalgrove (chăl'grôv) (Eng. (London In.)	51·38 N	1·05 W
193	Chaling (chä'lĭng) China	27·00 N	113·31 E
106	Chalmette (shăl-mĕt') La. (New Orleans In.)	29·57 N	89·57 W
160	Châlons-sur-Marne (shä-lôN-sür-märn) Fr.	48·57 N	4·23 E
160	Châlon-sur-Saône Fr.	46·47 N	4·54 E
136	Chaltel, Cerro (Mtn.) (sĕ'r-rô-chäl'tĕl) Arg.-Chile	48·10 S	73·18 W
115	Chama (R.) (chä'mä) NM	36·19 N	106·31 W
126	Chama, Sierra de (Mts.) (sē-ĕ'r-rä-dĕ-chä-mä) Guat.	15·48 N	90·20 W
160	Chamalières (shä-mä-lyâr) Fr.	45·45 N	2·59 E
217	Chamama Malawi	12·55 S	33·43 E
184	Chaman (chŭm-än') Pak.	30·58 N	66·21 E
184	Chambal (R.) (chŭm-bäl') India	26·05 N	76·37 E
108	Chamberlain (chām'bēr-lĭn) SD	43·48 N	99·21 W
98	Chamberlain (L.) Me.	46·15 N	69·10 W

ăt; finăl; rāte; senâte; ärm; ȧsk; sofȧ; fâre; ch-choose; dh-as th in other; bē; êvent; bĕt; recĕnt; cratēr; g-go; gh-guttural g; bĭt; ĭ-short neutral; rīde; K-guttural k as ch in German ich;

PRONOUNCING INDEX

Chambersburg — Chermoz 267

Page	Name / Pronunciation / Region	Lat. °′	Long. °′
105	Chambersburg (chăm'bẽrz-bûrg) Pa.	40·00 N	77·40 W
161	Chambéry (shäm-bā-rē') Fr.	45·35 N	5·54 E
217	Chambeshi (R.) Zambia	10·35 S	31·20 E
106	Chamblee (chăm-blē') Ga. (Atlanta In.)	33·55 N	84·18 W
89	Chambly (shäN-blē') Can. (Montreal In.)	45·27 N	73·17 W
161	Chambly Fr. (Paris In.)	49·11 N	2·14 E
91	Chambord Can.	48·22 N	72·01 W
127	Chame, Punta (Pt.) (pōō'n-tä-chä'mâ) Pan.	8·41 N	79·27 W
126	Chamelecón (R.) (chä-mĕ-lĕ-kô'n) Hond.	15·09 N	88·42 W
161	Chamonix (shȧ-mô-nē') Fr.	45·55 N	6·50 E
160	Champagne (Reg.) (shäm-pän'yē) Fr.	48·53 N	4·48 E
104	Champaign (shăm-pān') Il.	40·10 N	88·15 W
184	Champdāni India (In.)	22·48 N	88·21 E
126	Champerico (chäm-pā-rē'kō) Guat.	14·18 N	91·55 W
109	Champion (chăm'pĭ-ŭn) Mi.	46·30 N	87·59 W
105	Champlain, L. (shăm-plān') NY-Vt.	44·45 N	73·20 W
161	Champlitte (shäN-plēt') Fr.	47·38 N	5·28 E
125	Champotón (chäm-pō-tōn') Mex.	19·21 N	90·43 W
125	Champotón (R.) Mex.	19·19 N	90·15 W
136	Chañaral (chän-yä-räl') Chile	26·20 S	70·46 W
162	Chanca (R.) (chäŋ'kä) Sp.-Port.	37·48 N	7·18 W
120	Chandeleur Is. (shăn-dē-lōōr') La.	29·53 N	88·35 W
120	Chandeleur Sd. La.	29·47 N	89·08 W
184	Chandīgarh India	30·51 N	77·13 E
91	Chandler (chăn'dlẽr) Can.	48·21 N	64·41 W
117	Chandler Ok.	35·42 N	96·52 W
184	Chandrapur India	19·58 N	79·21 E
	Chang (R.), see Yangtze		
212	Changane (R.) Moz.	22·42 S	32·46 E
217	Changara Moz.	16·54 S	33·14 E
192	Changchun (chäŋ-chōōn) China	43·55 N	125·25 E
190	Changdang Hu (L.) (chäŋ-däŋ hōō) China	31·37 N	119·29 E
193	Changde (chäŋ-dŭ) China	29·00 N	111·38 E
193	Changhua (chäng'hwä') Taiwan	24·02 N	120·32 E
194	Changjŏn (chäng'jŭn') Kor.	38·40 N	128·05 E
192	Changli (chäŋ-lē) China	39·46 N	119·10 E
188	Changning (chäŋ-nĭŋ) China	24·34 N	99·49 E
192	Changping (chäŋ-pĭŋ) China	40·12 N	116·10 E
192	Changpei (chäng'pē') China	41·12 N	114·50 E
190	Changqing (chäŋ-chyĭŋ) China	36·33 N	116·42 E
194	Changsan Cot (I.) Kor.	38·06 N	124·50 E
193	Changsha (chäŋ-shä) China	28·20 N	113·00 E
190	Changshan Qundao (Is.) (chäŋ-shän chyōōn-dou) China	39·08 N	122·26 E
190	Changshu (chäŋ-shōō) China	31·40 N	120·45 E
193	Changting China	25·50 N	116·18 E
194	Changtu China	43·00 N	124·02 E
192	Changwu (chäng'wōō') China	35·12 N	107·45 E
192	Changxindianzhen (chäŋ-shyĭn-dĭĕn-jŭn) China (In.)	39·49 N	116·12 E
190	Changxing Dao (I.) (chäŋ-shyĭŋ dou) China	39·38 N	121·10 E
190	Changyi (chäŋ-yē) China	36·51 N	119·23 E
190	Changyuan (chyäŋ-yuän) China	35·10 N	114·41 E
192	Changzhi (chäŋ-jr) China	35·58 N	112·58 E
190	Changzhou (chäŋ-jō) China	31·47 N	119·56 E
190	Changzhuyuan (chäŋ-jōō-yuän) China	31·33 N	115·17 E
113	Chanhassen (shăn'hăs-sĕn) Mn. (Minneapolis, St. Paul In.)	44·52 N	93·32 W
190	Chanhua (jän'hōōä) China	37·42 N	117·49 E
146	Channel Is. (chăn'ĕl) Eur.	49·15 N	3·30 W
91	Channel-Port-aux-Basques Can.	47·35 N	59·11 W
119	Channelview (chăn'elvū) Tx. (In.)	29·46 N	95·07 W
162	Chantada (chän-tä'dä) Sp.	42·38 N	7·36 W
196	Chanthaburi Thai.	12·37 N	102·04 E
161	Chantilly (shäN-tē-yē') Fr. (Paris In.)	49·12 N	2·30 E
106	Chantilly (shăn'tĭlē) Va. (Baltimore In.)	38·53 N	77·26 W
90	Chantrey Inlet (chăn-trē) Can.	67·49 N	95·00 W
117	Chanute (shȧ-nōōt') Ks.	37·41 N	95·27 W
172	Chany (L.) (chä'nê) Sov. Un.	54·15 N	77·31 E
193	Chao'an (chou-än) China	23·48 N	116·35 E
190	Chao Hu (L.) (chou hōō) China	31·31 N	117·28 E
193	Chao Hu (L.) (chou hōō) China	31·45 N	116·59 E
196	Chao Phraya (R.) Thai.	16·13 N	99·33 E
192	Chaor (R.) (chou-r) China	47·20 N	121·40 E
190	Chaoshui (chou-shwā) China	37·43 N	120·56 E
193	Chaot'ung (chä'ō-tōōng) China	27·18 N	103·50 E
190	Chao Xian (chou shyĕn) China	31·37 N	117·50 E
193	Chaoyang (chou-yäŋ) China	23·18 N	116·32 E
192	Chaoyang China	41·32 N	120·20 E
135	Chapada, Serra da (Mts.) (sĕ'r-rä-dä-shä-pä'dä) Braz.	14·57 S	54·34 W
137	Chapadão Serra do (Mtn.) (sĕ'r-rä-dô-shä-pä-dou'N) Braz. (Rio de Janeiro In.)	20·31 S	46·20 W
124	Chapala (chä-pä'lä) Mex.	20·18 N	103·10 W
124	Chapala, Lago de (L.) (lä'gô-dĕ-chä-pä'lä) Mex.	20·14 N	103·02 W
124	Chapalagana (R.) (chä-pä-lä-gȧ'nä) Mex.	22·11 N	104·09 W
134	Chaparral (chä-pär-rà'l) Col. (In.)	3·44 N	75·28 W
171	Chapayevsk (chä-pī'ĕfsk) Sov. Un.	53·00 N	49·30 E
121	Chapel Hill (chăp''l hĭl) NC	35·55 N	79·05 W
112	Chaplain (L.) (chăp'lĭn) Wa. (Seattle In.)	47·58 N	121·50 W
91	Chapleau (chăp-lō') Can.	47·43 N	83·28 W
93	Chapman, Mt. (chăp'măn) Can.	51·50 N	118·20 W
212	Chapman's B. (chăp'măns bä) S. Afr. (In.)	34·06 S	18·17 E
108	Chappell (chă-pĕl') Ne.	41·06 N	102·29 W
125	Chapultenango (chä-pōōl-tē-näŋ'gō) Mex.	17·19 N	93·08 W
216	Chá Pungana Ang.	13·44 S	18·39 E
124	Charcas (chär'käs) Mex.	23·09 N	101·09 W
127	Charco de Azul, Bahía (B.) (bä-ē'ä-chä'r-kô-dĕ-ä-zōō'l) Pan.	8·14 N	82·45 W
147	Chardzhou (chẽr-jô'ōō) Sov. Un.	38·52 N	63·37 E
160	Charente (R.) (shȧ-räNt') Fr.	45·48 N	0·28 W
215	Chari (R.) (shä-rē') Chad	12·45 N	14·55 E
148	Charing (chă'rĭng) Eng. (London In.)	51·13 N	0·49 E
109	Chariton (châr'ĭ-tŭn) Ia.	41·02 N	93·16 W
117	Chariton (R.) Mo.	40·24 N	92·38 W
89	Charlemagne (shärl-mäny') Can. (Montreal In.)	45·43 N	73·29 W
155	Charleroi (shȧr-lē-rwä') Bel.	50·25 N	4·35 E
107	Charleroi (shär'lē-roi) Pa. (Pittsburgh In.)	40·08 N	79·54 W
121	Charles, C. (chärlz) Va.	37·05 N	75·48 W
89	Charlesbourg (shȧrl-bōōr') Can. (Quebec In.)	46·51 N	71·16 W
109	Charles City (chärlz) Ia.	43·03 N	92·40 W
104	Charleston (chärlz'tŭn) Il.	39·30 N	88·10 W
120	Charleston Ms.	34·00 N	90·02 W
117	Charleston Mo.	36·53 N	89·20 W
121	Charleston SC	32·47 N	79·56 W
104	Charleston WV	38·20 N	81·35 W
107	Charlestown (chärlz'toun) In. (Louisville In.)	38·46 N	85·39 W
127	Charlestown St. Kitts-Nevis-Anguilla (In.)	17·10 N	62·32 W
216	Charlesville Zaire	5·27 S	20·58 E
203	Charleville (chär'lē-vĭl) Austl.	26·16 S	146·28 E
160	Charleville Mézières (shärl-vēl') Fr.	49·48 N	4·41 E
104	Charlevoix (shär'lē-voi) Mi.	45·20 N	85·15 W
109	Charlevoix, L. Mi.	45·17 N	85·43 W
104	Charlotte (shär'lŏt) Mi.	42·35 N	84·50 W
121	Charlotte NC	35·15 N	80·50 W
123	Charlotte Amalie (St. Thomas) (shär-lŏt'ĕ ä-mä'lĭ-ȧ) Virgin Is. (U. S. A.) (St. Thomas In.)	18·21 N	64·54 W
92	Charlotte L. Can.	52·07 N	125·30 W
121	Charlotte Hbr. Fl. (In.)	26·49 N	82·00 W
156	Charlottenberg (shär-lŭt'ĕn-bĕrg) Swe.	59·53 N	12·17 E
105	Charlottesville (shär'lŏtz-vĭl) Va.	38·00 N	78·25 W
99	Charlottetown (shär'lŏt-toun) Can.	46·14 N	63·08 W
204	Charlotte Waters (shär'lŏt) Austl.	26·00 S	134·50 E
161	Charmes (shärm) Fr.	48·23 N	6·19 E
148	Charnwood For. (chärn'wŏŏd) Eng.	52·42 N	1·15 W
89	Charny (shär-nē') Can. (Quebec In.)	46·43 N	71·16 W
161	Chars (shär) Fr. (Paris In.)	49·09 N	1·57 E
187	Chārsadda (chŭr-sä'dä) Pak. (Khyber Pass In.)	34·17 N	71·43 E
205	Charters Towers (chär'tẽrz) Austl.	20·03 S	146·20 E
161	Chartres (shärt'r') Fr. (Paris In.)	48·26 N	1·29 E
137	Chascomús (chäs-kō-mōōs') Arg. (Buenos Aires In.)	35·32 S	58·01 W
121	Chase City (chās) Va.	36·45 N	78·27 W
166	Chashniki (chäsh'nyē-kē) Sov. Un.	54·51 N	29·08 E
113	Chaska (chăs'kȧ) Mn. (Minneapolis, St. Paul In.)	44·48 N	93·36 W
160	Châteaubriant (shȧ-tō-brē-äN') Fr.	47·43 N	1·23 W
160	Châteaudun (shä-tō-dăN') Fr.	48·04 N	1·23 E
160	Château-Gontier (chȧ-tō'gôN'tyā') Fr.	47·48 N	0·43 W
89	Châteauguay (chȧ-tō-gā) Can. (Montreal In.)	45·22 N	73·45 W
89	Châteauguay (R.) Can. (Montreal In.)	45·13 N	73·51 W
160	Chateauneuf-les-Martigues (shä-tō-nûf'lā-mär-tēg'ĕ) Fr. (In.)	43·23 N	5·11 E
160	Château-Renault (shȧ-tō-rē-nō') Fr.	47·36 N	0·57 E
89	Château-Richer (shȧ-tō'rē-shā') Can. (Quebec In.)	47·00 N	71·01 W
160	Châteauroux (shȧ-tō-rōō') Fr.	46·47 N	1·39 E
160	Château-Thierry (shȧ-tō'tyĕr-rē') Fr.	49·03 N	3·22 E
160	Châtellerault (shä-tĕl-rō') Fr.	46·48 N	0·31 E
109	Chatfield (chăt'fēld) Mn.	43·50 N	92·10 W
96	Chatham (chăt'ăm) Can.	42·25 N	82·10 W
98	Chatham Can.	47·02 N	65·28 W
148	Chatham (chăt'ŭm) Eng. (London In.)	51·23 N	0·32 E
106	Chatham (chăt'ăm) NJ (New York In.)	40·44 N	74·23 W
107	Chatham Oh. (Cleveland In.)	41·06 N	82·01 W
198	Chatham Is. N. Z.	44·00 S	178·00 W
92	Chatham Sd. Can.	54·32 N	130·35 W
101	Chatham Str. Ak.	57·00 N	134·40 W
113	Chatsworth (chătz'wûrth) Ca. (Los Angeles In.)	34·16 N	118·36 W
113	Chatsworth Res. Ca. (Los Angeles In.)	34·15 N	118·41 W
120	Chattahoochee (chăt-tȧ-hōō' chē) Fl.	30·42 N	84·47 W
120	Chattahoochee (R.) Al.-Ga.	31·17 N	85·10 W
120	Chattanooga (chăt-ȧ-nōō'gȧ) Tn.	35·01 N	85·15 W
120	Chattooga (R.) (chă-tōō'gȧ) Ga.-SC	34·47 N	83·13 W
97	Chaudière (R.) (shō-dyĕr') Can.	46·26 N	71·10 W
160	Chaumont (shō-môN') Fr.	48·08 N	5·07 E
161	Chaumontel (shō-môN-tĕl') Fr. (Paris In.)	49·07 N	2·26 E
173	Chaunskaya Guba (B.) Sov. Un.	69·15 N	170·00 E
160	Chauny (shō-nē') Fr.	49·40 N	3·09 E
196	Chau-phu Kamp.	10·49 N	104·57 E
166	Chausy (chou'sĭ) Sov. Un.	53·57 N	30·58 E
105	Chautauqua (L.) (shȧ-tô'kwȧ) NY	42·10 N	79·25 W
170	Chavaniga Sov. Un.	66·02 N	37·50 E
162	Chaves (chä'vĕzh) Port.	41·44 N	7·30 W
124	Chavinda (chä-vē'n-dä) Mex.	20·01 N	102·27 W
125	Chazumba (chä-zōōm'bä) Mex.	18·11 N	97·41 W
148	Cheadle (chē'd'l) Eng.	52·59 N	1·59 W
105	Cheat (R.) (chēt) WV	39·35 N	79·40 W
158	Cheb (ĸĕb) Czech.	50·05 N	12·23 E
174	Chebarkul (chĕ-bär-kûl') Sov. Un. (Urals In.)	54·59 N	60·22 E
170	Cheboksary (chyĕ-bôk-sä'rê) Sov. Un.	56·00 N	47·20 E
104	Cheboygan (shê-boi'găn) Mi.	45·40 N	84·30 W
210	Chech, Erg (Dune) Alg.	24·45 N	2·07 W
171	Chechen' (I.) (chyĕch'ĕn) Sov. Un.	44·00 N	48·10 E
117	Checotah (chê-kō'tȧ) Ok.	35·27 N	95·32 W
99	Chedabucto B. (chĕd-ȧ-bŭk-tō) Can.	45·23 N	61·10 W
196	Cheduba I. Bur.	18·45 N	93·01 E
94	Cheecham Hills (chēē'hăm) Can.	56·20 N	111·10 W
107	Cheektowaga (chēk-tŏ-wä'gȧ) NY (Buffalo In.)	42·54 N	78·46 W
190	Chefoo (Yantai) (yän-tī) China	37·32 N	121·22 E
110	Chehalis (chê-hā'lĭs) Wa.	46·39 N	122·58 W
110	Chehalis R. Wa.	46·47 N	123·17 W
194	Cheju (chĕ'jōō') Kor.	33·29 N	126·40 E
194	Cheju (Quelpart) (I.) Kor.	33·20 N	126·25 E
166	Chekalin (chĕ-kä'lĭn) Sov. Un.	54·05 N	36·13 E
212	Chela, Serra da (Mts.) (sĕr'rȧ dā shā'lȧ) Ang.	15·30 S	13·30 E
110	Chelan (chê-lăn') Wa.	47·51 N	119·59 W
110	Chelan (L.) Wa.	48·09 N	120·20 W
163	Cheleiros (shĕ-la'rōzh) Port. (Lisbon In.)	38·54 N	9·19 W
151	Chelia (Mtn.) Alg.	35·22 N	6·47 E
163	Chéliff, Oued (R.) (ōō-ĕd shä-lĕf) Alg.	36·17 N	1·22 E
172	Chelkar (chyĕl'kär) Sov. Un.	47·52 N	59·41 E
171	Chelkar (L.) Sov. Un.	50·30 N	51·30 E
172	Chelkar Tengiz (L.) (chyĕl'kär tĕn'yēz) Sov. Un.	47·42 N	61·45 E
159	Chełm (ĸĕlm) Pol.	51·08 N	23·30 E
159	Chełmno (ĸĕlm'nō) Pol.	53·20 N	18·25 E
96	Chelmsford Can.	46·35 N	81·12 W
148	Chelmsford (chĕlm's-fẽrd) Eng. (London In.)	51·44 N	0·28 E
99	Chelmsford Ma. (In.)	42·36 N	71·21 W
106	Chelsea (chĕl'sê) Al. (Birmingham In.)	33·20 N	86·38 W
202	Chelsea Austl. (Melbourne In.)	38·05 S	145·08 E
89	Chelsea Can. (Ottawa In.)	45·30 N	75·46 W
99	Chelsea Ma. (In.)	42·23 N	71·02 W
104	Chelsea Mi.	42·20 N	84·00 W
117	Chelsea Ok.	36·32 N	95·23 W
154	Cheltenham (chĕlt'nŭm) Eng.	51·57 N	2·06 W
106	Cheltenham (chĕltĕn-hăm) Md. (Baltimore In.)	38·45 N	76·50 W
163	Chelva (chĕl'vä) Sp.	39·43 N	1·00 W
174	Chelyabinsk (chĕl-yä-bĕnsk') Sov. Un. (Urals In.)	55·10 N	61·25 E
173	Chelyuskin, Mys (C.) (chĕl-yōōs'-kĭn) Sov. Un.	77·45 N	104·45 E
217	Chemba Moz.	17·08 S	34·52 E
160	Chemillé (shē-mē-yā') Fr.	47·13 N	0·46 W
	Chemnitz, see Karl-Marx-Stadt		
105	Chemung (R.) (shê-mŭng) NY	42·20 N	77·25 W
173	Chĕn, Gora (Mtn.) Sov. Un.	65·13 N	142·12 E
184	Chenāb (R.) (chê-näb) Pak.	31·33 N	72·28 E
210	Chenachane (shē-nȧ-shän') Alg.	26·14 N	4·14 W
191	Chencun (chŭn-tsōōn) China (Canton In.)	22·58 N	113·14 E
110	Cheney (chē'nȧ) Wa.	47·29 N	117·34 W
192	Chengde (chŭŋ-dŭ) China	40·50 N	117·50 E
190	Chengdong Hu (L.) (chŭŋ-dôŋ hōō) China	32·22 N	116·32 E
193	Chengdu (chŭŋ-dōō) China	30·30 N	104·10 E
192	Chenggu (chŭŋ-gōō) China	33·05 N	107·25 E
193	Chenghai (chŭŋ-hī) China	23·22 N	116·40 E
192	Chengshan, Jiao (C.) (chŭŋ-shän jyou) China	37·28 N	122·40 E
190	Chengxi Hu (L.) (chŭŋ-shyē hōō) China	32·31 N	116·04 E
193	Chen Xian (chŭ -shyĕn) China	25·40 N	113·00 E
134	Chepén (chĕ-pĕ'n) Peru	7·17 S	79·24 W
127	Chepo (chā'pō) Pan.	9·12 N	79·06 W
127	Chepo R. Pan.	9·10 N	78·36 W
160	Cher (R.) (shâr) Fr.	47·14 N	1·34 E
124	Cherán (chā-rän') Mex.	19·41 N	101·54 W
217	Cherangany Hills Ken.	1·25 N	35·20 E
121	Cheraw (chē'rô) SC	34·40 N	79·52 W
160	Cherbourg (shär-bōōr') Fr.	49·39 N	1·43 W
210	Cherchell (shĕr-shĕl') Alg.	36·38 N	2·09 E
170	Cherdyn' (chĕr-dyēn') Sov. Un.	60·25 N	56·32 E
172	Cheremkhovo (chĕr'yĕm-kô-vō) Sov. Un.	52·58 N	103·18 E
174	Cherëmukhovo (chĕr-yĕ-mû-kô-vō) Sov. Un. (Urals In.)	60·20 N	60·00 E
172	Cherepanovo (chĕr'yĕ pä-nô'vō) Sov. Un.	54·13 N	83·18 E
166	Cherepovets (chĕr-yĕ-pô'vyĕtz) Sov. Un.	59·08 N	37·59 E
166	Chereya (chĕr-ā'yä) Sov. Un.	54·38 N	29·16 E
152	Chergui, Chott ech (L.) chĕr gē) Alg.	34·12 N	0·10 W
152	Chergui (I.) Tun.	34·50 N	11·40 E
166	Cherikov (chĕ'rē-kôf) Sov. Un.	53·34 N	31·22 E
167	Cherkassy (chĕr-kȧ'sĭ) Sov. Un.	49·26 N	32·03 E
167	Cherkassy (Oblast) Sov. Un.	48·58 N	30·55 E
172	Cherlak (chĭr-läk') Sov. Un.	54·04 N	74·28 E
174	Chermoz (chĕr-môz') Sov. Un. (Urals In.)	58·47 N	56·08 E

ng-sing; ŋ-baŋk; N-nasalized n; nŏd; cŏmmit; ōld; ôbey; ôrder; fōōd; fŏŏt; ou-out; s-soft; sh-dish; th-thin; pūre; ûnite; ûrn; stŭd; circŭs; ü-as "y" in study; '-indeterminate vowel.

ăt; fīnăl; rāte; senāte; ärm; àsk; sofà; fâre; ch-choose; dh-as th in other; bē; ėvent; bĕt; recĕnt; cratēr; g-go; gh-guttural g; bĭt; ï-short neutral; rīde; ᴋ-guttural k as ch in German ich;

PRONOUNCING INDEX

Chornaya — Clinton 269

Page	Name Pronunciation Region	Lat. °′	Long. °′
174	Chornaya..Sov. Un. (Moscow In.)	55·45 N	38·04 E
134	Chorrillos (chôr-rē'l-yōs).....Peru	12·17 S	76·55 W
159	Chortkov (chôrt'kôf)....Sov. Un.	49·01 N	25·48 E
159	Chorzów (kô-zhŏŏf')........Pol.	50·17 N	19·00 E
194	Chosan (chō-sän')...........Kor.	40·44 N	125·48 E
121	Chosen (chō'z'n).........Fl. (In.)	26·41 N	80·41 W
194	Chōshi (chō'shē)............Jap.	35·40 N	140·55 E
158	Choszczno (chôsh'chnô)......Pol.	53·10 N	15·25 E
184	Chota Nagpur (Reg.).......India	23·40 N	82·50 E
111	Choteau (shō'tō)............Mt.	47·51 N	112·10 W
121	Chowan (R.) (chô-wän')......NC	36·13 N	76·46 W
203	Chowilla Res..............Austl.	34·05 S	141·20 E
93	Chown, Mt. (choun)........Can.	53·24 N	119·22 W
192	Choybalsan...............Mong.	47·50 N	114·15 E
205	Christchurch (krīst'chûrch) N. Z. (In.)	43·30 S	172·38 E
104	Christian (I.) (krĭs'chăn).....Can.	44·50 N	80·00 W
121	Christiansburg (krĭs'chănz-bûrg) Va.	37·08 N	80·25 W
123	Christiansted Vir. Is. (U. S. A.) (Puerto Rico In.)	17·45 N	64·44 W
199	Christmas (I.)...........Oceania	2·20 N	157·40 W
196	Christmas I...............Austl.	10·35 S	105·40 E
117	Christopher (krĭs'tô-fẽr)........Il.	37·58 N	89·04 W
158	Chrudim (ĸrōō'dyĕm)......Czech.	49·57 N	15·46 E
159	Chrzanów (ĸzhä'nŏŏf)........Pol.	50·08 N	19·24 E
191	Chuansha (chuän-shä) China (Shanghai In.)	31·12 N	121·41 E
136	Chubut (Prov.) (chōō-bōōt')..Arg.	44·00 S	69·15 W
136	Chubut (chōō-bōōt') (R.)....Arg.	43·05 S	69·00 W
106	Chuckatuck (chŭck à-tŭck) Va. (Norfolk In.)	36·51 N	76·35 W
127	Chucunaque (R.) (chōō-kōō-nä'kå).Pan.	8·36 N	77·48 W
166	Chudovo (chōō'dô-vô)...Sov. Un.	59·03 N	31·56 S
166	Chudskoye Oz. (Peipus, L.) (chŏŏt'skô-yĕ).Sov. Un.	58·43 N	26·45 E
188	Chuguchak (Reg.) (chōō'gōō-chäk').China	46·09 N	83·58 E
167	Chuguyev (chōō'gōō-yĕf).Sov. Un.	49·52 N	36·40 E
194	Chuguyevka (chōō-gōō'yĕf-kå) Sov. Un.	43·58 N	133·49 E
108	Chugwater Cr. (chŭg'wô-tẽr).Wy.	41·43 N	104·54 W
173	Chukot Natl. Okrug (Reg.) Sov. Un.	68·15 N	170·00 E
173	Chukotskiy (Chukot) P-Ov (Pen.) Sov. Un.	66·12 N	175·00 W
173	Chukotskoye Nagor'ye (Mts.) Sov. Un.	66·00 N	166·00 E
114	Chula Vista (chōō'lå vĭs'tå) Ca. (In.)	32·38 N	117·05 W
174	Chulkovo (chōōl-kô vô) Sov. Un. (Moscow In.)	55·33 N	38·04 E
134	Chulucanas (chōō-lōō-kä'näs).Peru	5·13 S	80·13 W
172	Chulum (R.)...........Sov. Un.	57·52 N	84·45 E
173	Chumikan (chōō-mē-kän') Sov. Un.	54·47 N	135·09 E
193	Chun'an (chōōn-än)........China	29·38 N	119·00 E
194	Chunchŏn (chōōn-chŭn')....Kor.	37·51 N	127·46 E
194	Chungju (chŭng'jōō')........Kor.	37·00 N	128·19 E
217	Chunya.....................Tan.	8·32 S	33·25 E
172	Chunya (R.) (chōōn'yä') Sov. Un.	61·45 N	101·28 E
136	Chuquicamata (chōō-kê-kä-mä'tä) Chile	22·08 S	68·57 W
158	Chur (kōōr)...............Switz.	46·51 N	9·32 E
90	Churchill (chûrch'ĭl).........Can.	58·50 N	94·10 W
90	Churchill, C..............Can.	59·07 N	93·50 W
95	Churchill (R.)............Can.	57·20 N	96·30 W
91	Churchill Falls...........Can.	53·35 N	64·27 W
94	Churchill L...............Can.	56·12 N	108·40 W
90	Churchill Pk..............Can.	58·10 N	125·14 W
148	Church Stretton (chûrch strĕt'ŭn).Eng.	52·32 N	2·49 W
106	Churchton...Md. (Baltimore In.)	38·49 N	76·33 W
184	Churu......................India	28·22 N	75·00 E
124	Churumuco (chōō-rōō-mōō'kō) Mex.	18·39 N	101·40 W
115	Chuska Mts. (chŭs-kå)...Az.-NM	36·21 N	109·11 W
174	Chusovaya R. (chōō-sô-vä'yå) Sov. Un. (Urals In.)	58·08 N	58·35 E
174	Chusovoy (chōō-sô-vôy') Sov. Un. (Urals In.)	58·18 N	57·50 E
172	Chust (chŏŏst).........Sov. Un.	41·05 N	71·28 E
170	Chuvash A. S. S. R. (chōō'vásh) Sov. Un.	55·45 N	46·00 E
118	Chuviscar (R.) (chōō-vês-kär') Mex.	28·34 N	105·36 W
190	Chuwang (chōō-wäŋ).......China	36·08 N	114·53 E
190	Chu Xian (chōō shyĕn).....China	32·19 N	118·19 E
188	Chuxiong (chōō-shyôŋ).....China	25·19 N	101·34 E
107	Cicero (sĭs'ẽr-ō)..Il. (Chicago In.)	41·50 N	87·46 W
171	Cide (jē'dĕ)...............Tur.	41·50 N	33·00 E
159	Ciechanów (tsyĕ-kä'nŏŏf).....Pol.	52·52 N	20·39 E
128	Ciego de Avila (syā'gō dā ä'vē-lä) Cuba	21·50 N	78·45 W
128	Ciego de Avila (Prov.)......Cuba	22·00 N	78·40 W
162	Ciempozuelos (thyĕm-pô-thwā'lōs) Sp.	40·09 N	3·36 W
134	Ciénaga (syā'nä-gä).........Col.	11·01 N	74·15 W
128	Cienfuegos (syĕn-fwā'gōs)...Cuba	22·10 N	80·30 W
128	Cienfuegos (Prov.).........Cuba	22·15 N	80·40 W
128	Cienfuegos, Bahía (B.) (bä-ē'ä-syĕn-fwā'gōs).Cuba	22·00 N	80·35 W
127	Ciervo, Isla de la (I.) (ē's-lä-dĕ-lä-syĕ'r-vô).Nic.	11·56 N	83·20 W
159	Cieszyn (tsyĕ'shĕn)..........Pol.	49·47 N	18·45 E
162	Cieza (thyā'thä).............Sp.	38·13 N	1·25 W
124	Cihuatlán (sē-wä-tlà'n)......Mex.	19·13 N	104·36 W
124	Cihuatlán (R.)..............Mex.	19·11 N	104·30 W
162	Cijara (Res.)................Sp.	39·25 N	5·00 W
171	Cilician Gates (P.).........Tur.	37·30 N	35·30 E
154	Cill Mantainn (Wicklow) (kĭl män'tän) (wĭk'lō).Ire.	52·59 N	6·06 W
116	Cimarron (R.), North Fk......Co.	37·13 N	102·30 W
102	Cimarron R. (sĭm-à-rōn')....U. S.	36·26 N	98·47 W
165	Cîmpina...................Rom.	45·08 N	25·47 E
165	Cîmpulung.................Rom.	45·15 N	25·03 E
159	Cîmpulung Moldovenesc....Rom.	47·31 N	25·36 E
163	Cinca (R.) (thēŋ'kä).........Sp.	42·09 N	0·08 E
107	Cincinnati (sĭn-sĭ-nàt'ĭ) Oh. (Cincinnati In.)	39·08 N	84·30 W
128	Cinco Balas, Cayos (Is.) (kä'yōs-thēŋ'kō bä'läs).Cuba	21·05 N	79·25 W
125	Cintalapa (sên-tä-lä'pä).....Mex.	16·41 N	93·44 W
164	Cinto, Mt. (chēn'tō).........Fr.	42·24 N	8·54 E
101	Circle (sûr'k'l)..............Ak.	65·49 N	144·22 W
104	Circleville (sûr'k'lvĭl).......Oh.	39·35 N	83·00 W
196	Cirebon...................Indon.	6·50 S	108·33 E
118	Cisco (sĭs'kō).................Tx.	32·23 N	98·57 W
134	Cisneros (sês-nĕ'rôs)....Col. (In.)	6·33 N	75·05 W
163	Cisterna di Latina (chēs-tĕ'r-nä-dē-lä-tē'nä).(Rome In.)	41·36 N	12·53 E
162	Cistierna (thês-tyĕr'nä).......Sp.	42·48 N	5·08 W
125	Citlaltépetl (Vol.) (sē-tlàl-tĕ'pĕtl) Mex.	19·04 N	97·14 W
120	Citronelle (cĭt-rô'nĕl).........Al.	31·05 N	88·15 W
164	Cittadella (chēt-tä-dĕl'lä)......It.	45·39 N	11·51 E
164	Città di Castello (chēt-tä'dē käs-tĕl'lō).It.	43·27 N	12·17 E
124	Ciudad Altamirano (syōō-dä'd-äl-tä-mē-rä'nô).Mex.	18·24 N	100·38 W
134	Ciudad Bolívar (syōō-dhädh' bô-lē'vär).Ven.	8·07 N	63·41 W
118	Ciudad Camargo (Santa Rosalia) (syōō-dhädh' kä-mär'gō) (sän'tà rō-sä'lēà).Mex.	27·42 N	105·10 W
126	Ciudad Chetumal (Payo Obispo) (syōō-dhädh' chĕt-ōō-mäl) (pä'yō ō-bēs'pō).Mex. (In.)	18·30 N	88·17 W
126	Ciudad Darío (syōō-dhädh'dä'rē-ō).Nic.	12·44 N	86·08 W
128	Ciudad de la Habana (Prov.) Cuba	23·20 N	82·10 W
125	Ciudad de las Casas (syōō-dä'd-dĕ-läs-kà'säs).Mex.	16·44 N	92·39 W
125	Ciudad del Carmen (syōō-dä'd-dĕl-kà'r-mĕn).Mex.	18·39 N	91·49 W
124	Ciudad del Maíz (syōō-dhädh'del mä-ēz').Mex.	22·24 N	99·37 W
124	Ciudad de Valles (syōō-dhädh'dā vä'lyās).Mex.	21·59 N	99·02 W
163	Ciudadela (thyōō-dhä-dhā'lä).Sp.	40·00 N	3·52 E
124	Ciudad Fernández (syōō-dhädh'fĕr-nän'dĕz).Mex.	21·56 N	100·03 W
124	Ciudad García (syōō-dhädh'gär-sē'ä).Mex.	22·39 N	103·02 W
134	Ciudad Guayana............Ven.	8·30 N	62·45 W
124	Ciudad Guzmán (syōō-dhädh'gŏŏz-män).Mex.	19·40 N	103·29 W
124	Ciudad Hidalgo (syōō-dä'd-ê-dä'l-gô).Mex.	19·41 N	100·35 W
118	Ciudad Juárez (syōō-dhädh hwä'rāz).Mex.	31·44 N	106·28 W
125	Ciudad Madero (syōō-dä'd-mä-dĕ'rô).Mex.	22·16 N	97·52 W
124	Ciudad Mante (syōō-dä'd-màn'tĕ).Mex.	22·34 N	98·58 W
124	Ciudad Manuel Doblado (syōō-dä'd-män-wāl' dō-blä'dō) Mex.	20·43 N	101·57 W
122	Ciudad Obregón (syōō-dhädh-ô-brĕ-gô'n).Mex.	27·40 N	109·58 W
162	Ciudad Real (thyōō-dhädh'rā-äl').Sp.	38·59 N	3·55 W
162	Ciudad Rodrigo (thyōō-dhädh'rô-drē'gō).Sp.	40·38 N	6·34 W
125	Ciudad Serdán (syōō-dä'd-sĕr-dà'n).Mex.	18·58 N	97·26 W
124	Ciudad Victoria (syōō-dhädh'vĕk-tō'rē-ä).Mex.	23·43 N	99·09 W
164	Cividale del Friuli (chē-vê-dä'lā-dĕl-frē-ōō'lē).It.	46·06 N	13·24 E
164	Civitavecchia (chē'vê-tä-vĕk'kyä) It.	42·06 N	11·49 E
190	Ci Xian (tsē shyĕn)........China	36·22 N	114·23 E
112	Clackamas (klăc-kà'măs) Or. (Portland In.)	45·25 N	122·34 W
90	Claire (L.) (klâr)...........Can.	58·33 N	113·16 W
110	Clair Engle L.................Ca.	40·51 N	122·41 W
107	Clairton (klârtŭn) Pa. (Pittsburgh In.)	40·17 N	79·53 W
120	Clanton (klăn'tŭn)...........Al.	32·50 N	86·38 W
104	Clare (klâr).................Mi.	43·50 N	84·45 W
154	Clare (I.)....................Ire.	53·46 N	10·00 W
113	Claremont (klâr'mŏnt) Ca. (Los Angeles In.)	34·06 N	117·43 W
105	Claremont (klâr'mŏnt).......NH	43·20 N	72·20 W
104	Claremont...................WV	37·55 N	81·00 W
117	Claremore (klâr'mōr).........Ok.	36·16 N	95·37 W
154	Claremorris (klâr-mŏr'ĭs)......Ire.	53·46 N	9·05 W
92	Clarence Str..................Ak.	55·25 N	132·00 W
204	Clarence Str. (klăr'ĕns)......Austl.	12·15 S	130·05 E
129	Clarence Town...............Ba.	23·05 N	75·00 W
117	Clarendon (klâr'ĕn-dŭn)......Ar.	34·42 N	91·17 W
116	Clarendon....................Tx.	34·55 N	100·52 W
213	Clarens (clâ-rĕns) S. Afr. (Natal In.)	28·34 S	28·26 E
94	Claresholm (klâr'ĕs-hōlm)....Can.	50·02 N	113·35 W
109	Clarinda (klà-rĭn'dà)..........Ia.	40·42 N	95·00 W
135	Clarines (klä-rē'nĕs)....Ven. (In.)	9·57 N	65·10 W
109	Clarion (klăr'ĭ-ŭn)............Ia.	42·43 N	93·45 W
105	Clarion......................Pa.	41·10 N	79·25 W
108	Clark (klärk).................SD	44·52 N	97·45 W
104	Clark, Pt....................Can.	44·05 N	81·50 W
98	Clarke City..................Can.	50·12 N	66·38 W
115	Clarkdale (klärk-dāl).........Az	34·45 N	112·05 W
205	Clarke Ra...................Austl.	20·30 S	148·00 E
111	Clark Fork (R.)..............Mt.	47·50 N	115·35 W
121	Clark Hill Res. (klärk-hĭl).Ga.-SC	33·50 N	82·35 W
105	Clarksburg (klärkz'bûrg)......WV	39·15 N	80·20 W
120	Clarksdale (klärks-dāl).......Ms.	34·10 N	90·31 W
98	Clark's Harbour (klärks).....Can.	43·26 N	65·38 W
106	Clarkston (klärks'tŭn) Ga. (Altanta In.)	33·49 N	84·15 W
110	Clarkston....................Wa.	46·24 N	117·01 W
117	Clarksville (klärks-vĭl)........Ar.	35·28 N	93·26 W
120	Clarksville...................Tn.	36·30 N	87·23 W
117	Clarksville...................Tx.	33·37 N	95·02 W
112	Clatskanie....Or. (Portland In.)	46·04 N	123·11 W
112	Clatskanie (R.) (klăt-skā'nē) Or. (Portland In.)	46·06 N	123·11 W
112	Clatsop Spit (klăt-sŏp) Or. (Portland In.)	46·13 N	124·04 W
137	Cláudio (klou'-dēō) Braz. (Rio de Janeiro In.)	20·26 S	44·44 W
193	Claveria (klä-vå-rē'ä)........Phil.	18·38 N	121·08 E
107	Clawson (klô's'n).Mi. (Detroit In.)	42·32 N	83·09 W
121	Claxton (klăks'tŭn)..........Ga.	32·07 N	81·54 W
120	Clay (klā)....................Ky.	37·28 N	87·50 W
117	Clay Center (klā sĕn'tẽr)......Ks.	39·23 N	97·08 W
104	Clay City (klā sĭ'tĭ)..........Ky.	37·50 N	83·55 W
113	Claycomo (kla-kō'mo) Mo. (Kansas City In.)	39·12 N	94·30 W
148	Clay Cross (klā krŏs)........Eng.	53·10 N	1·25 W
161	Claye-Souilly (klĕ-sōō-yē') Fr. (Paris In.)	48·56 N	2·43 E
106	Claymont (klā-mŏnt) De. (Philadelphia In.)	39·48 N	75·28 W
120	Clayton (klā'tŭn)............Al.	31·52 N	85·25 W
112	Clayton...Ca. (San Francisco In.)	37·56 N	121·56 W
148	Clayton......................Eng.	53·47 N	1·49 W
113	Clayton......Mo. (St. Louis In.)	38·39 N	90·20 W
116	Clayton.......................NM	36·26 N	103·12 W
121	Clayton.......................NC	35·40 N	78·27 W
114	Clear (L.)....................Ca.	39·05 N	122·50 W
154	Clear, C. (klēr).............Ire.	51·24 N	9·15 W
117	Clear Boggy Cr. (klēr bŏg'ĭ krēk) Ok.	34·21 N	96·22 W
115	Clear Cr......................Az.	34·40 N	111·05 W
119	Clear Cr...............Tx. (In.)	29·34 N	95·13 W
111	Clear Cr......................Wy.	44·35 N	106·20 W
105	Clearfield (klēr-fēld)..........Pa.	41·00 N	78·25 W
113	Clearfield.Ut. (Salt Lake City In.)	41·07 N	112·01 W
90	Clear Hills...................Can.	57·11 N	119·20 W
109	Clear Lake....................Ia.	43·09 N	93·23 W
112	Clear Lake....Wa. (Seattle In.)	48·27 N	122·14 W
110	Clear Lake Res................Ca.	41·53 N	121·00 W
121	Clearwater (klēr-wô'tẽr)..Fl. (In.)	27·43 N	82·45 W
93	Clearwater (R.)...............Can.	52·00 N	114·50 W
93	Clearwater (R.)...............Can.	52·00 N	120·10 W
94	Clearwater (R.)...............Can.	56·10 N	110·40 W
110	Clearwater (R.)................Id.	46·27 N	116·33 W
110	Clearwater (R.), Middle Fork..Id.	46·10 N	115·48 W
110	Clearwater (R.), North Fork...Id.	46·34 N	116·08 W
110	Clearwater (R.), South Fork...Id.	45·46 N	115·53 W
110	Clearwater Mts................Id.	45·56 N	115·15 W
117	Clearwater Res................Mo.	37·20 N	91·04 W
119	Cleburne (klē'bŭrn)..........Tx.	32·21 N	97·23 W
148	Clee Hill (klē)...............Eng.	52·24 N	2·37 W
110	Cle Elum (klē ĕl'ŭm)..........Wa.	47·12 N	120·55 W
106	Clementon (klē'mĕn-tŭn) NJ (Philadelphia In.)	39·49 N	75·00 W
148	Cleobury Mortimer (klē'ô-bĕr'ĭ môr'tĭ-mẽr).Eng.	52·22 N	2·29 W
205	Clermont (klẽr'mŏnt)........Austl.	23·02 S	147·46 E
98	Clermont.....................Can.	47·45 N	70·20 W
160	Clermont-Ferrand (klĕr-môN'fĕr-răN').Fr.	45·47 N	3·03 E
160	Clermont l'Hérault (klĕr-mŏN'lā-rō').Fr.	43·38 N	3·22 E
120	Cleveland (klēv'lănd)........Ms.	33·45 N	90·42 W
107	Cleveland....Oh. (Cleveland In.)	41·30 N	81·42 W
117	Cleveland.....................Ok.	36·18 N	96·28 W
120	Cleveland.....................Tn.	35·09 N	84·52 W
119	Cleveland.....................Tx.	30·18 N	95·05 W
107	Cleveland Heights Oh. (Cleveland In.)	41·30 N	81·35 W
92	Cleveland Pen.................Ak.	55·45 N	132·00 W
107	Cleves (klē'vĕs) Oh. (Cincinnati In.)	39·10 N	84·45 W
154	Clew B. (klōō)...............Ire.	53·47 N	9·45 W
121	Clewiston (klē'wĭs-tŭn)...Fl. (In.)	26·44 N	80·55 W
161	Clichy (klē-shē)....Fr. (Paris In.)	48·54 N	2·18 E
154	Clifden (klĭf'dĕn)............Ire.	53·31 N	10·04 W
115	Clifton (klĭf'tŭn)............Az.	33·05 N	109·20 W
106	Clifton......NJ (New York In.)	40·52 N	74·09 W
121	Clifton.......................SC	35·00 N	81·47 W
119	Clifton.......................Tx.	31·45 N	97·31 W
105	Clifton Forge.................Va.	37·50 N	79·50 W
120	Clinch (R.) (klĭnch)......Tn.-Va.	36·30 N	83·19 W
120	Clingmans Dome (Mtn.) (klĭng'măns dōm).NC	35·37 N	83·26 W
93	Clinton (klĭn-'tŭn)...........Can.	51·05 N	121·35 W
104	Clinton.......................Il.	40·10 N	88·55 W
104	Clinton.......................In.	39·40 N	87·25 W
109	Clinton.......................Ia.	41·50 N	90·13 W
120	Clinton.......................Ky.	36·39 N	88·56 W
106	Clinton......Md. (Baltimore In.)	38·46 N	76·54 W
99	Clinton..................Ma. (In.)	42·25 N	71·41 W
117	Clinton.......................Mo.	38·23 N	93·46 W
121	Clinton.......................NC	35·58 N	78·20 W
116	Clinton.......................Ok.	35·31 N	98·56 W
121	Clinton.......................SC	34·27 N	81·53 W
120	Clinton.......................Tn.	36·05 N	84·08 W
112	Clinton.........Wa. (Seattle In.)	47·59 N	122·22 W

ng-sing; ŋ-baŋk; N-nasalized n; nŏd; cŏmmit; ōld; ôbey; ôrder; fōōd; fŏŏt; ou-out; s-soft; sh-dish; th-thin; pūre; ûnite; ûrn; stŭd; circŭs; ü-as "y" in study; '-indeterminate vowel.

270 Clinton-Colden — Comox PRONOUNCING INDEX

Page	Name Pronunciation Region	Lat. °′	Long. °′
90	Clinton-Colden (L.)........Can.	63·58 N	106·34 W
107	Clinton R.......Mi. (Detroit In.)	42·36 N	83·00 W
109	Clintonville (klĭn′tŭn-vĭl).....Wi.	44·37 N	88·46 W
104	Clio (klē′ō)..................Mi.	43·10 N	83·45 W
204	Cloates, Pt. (klōts)........Austl.	22·47 S	113·45 E
218	Clocolan.S. Afr. (Johannesburg & Pretoria In.)	28·56 S	27·35 E
154	Clonakilty B. (klŏn-ȧ-kĭltē)...Ire.	51·30 N	8·50 W
204	Cloncurry (klŏn-kŭr′ē).....Austl.	20·58 S	140·42 E
154	Clonmel (klŏn-mĕl)..........Ire.	52·21 N	7·45 W
113	Cloquet(klô-kā′).Mn.(Duluth In.)	46·42 N	92·28 W
106	Closter (clōs′tēr) NJ (New York In.)	40·58 N	73·57 W
111	Cloud Pk. (kloud)..........Wy.	44·23 N	107·11 W
121	Clover (klō′vēr).............SC	35·08 N	81·08 W
89	Clover Bar (klō′vēr bär) Can. (Edmonton In.)	53·34 N	113·20 W
114	Cloverdale (klō′vēr-dāl).......Ca.	38·47 N	123·03 W
112	Cloverdale..Can. (Vancouver In.)	49·06 N	122·44 W
104	Cloverport (klō′vēr pōrt).....Ky.	37·50 N	86·35 W
116	Clovis (klō′vĭs).............NM	34·24 N	103·11 W
159	Cluj (klo͝ozh)...............Rom.	46·46 N	23·34 E
148	Clun (R.) (klŭn)............Eng.	52·25 N	2·56 W
160	Cluny (klü-nē′)..............Fr.	46·27 N	4·40 E
205	Clutha (R.) (klo͞o′thȧ).N. Z. (In.)	45·26 S	169·15 E
117	Clyde.......................Ks.	39·34 N	97·23 W
104	Clyde.......................Oh.	41·15 N	83·00 W
154	Clyde (R.).................Scot.	55·35 N	3·50 W
154	Clyde, Firth of (fûrth ŏv klīd) Scot.	55·28 N	5·01 W
154	Clydebank.................Scot.	55·56 N	4·20 W
162	Côa (R.) (kô′ä)............Port.	40·28 N	6·55 W
125	Coacalco (kō-ä-käl′kō).Mex. (In.)	19·37 N	99·06 W
114	Coachella, Can. (kō′chĕl-lȧ)...Ca.	33·15 N	115·25 W
124	Coahuayana, Rio de (R.) (rē′ō-dĕ-kō-ä-wä-yä′nä).Mex.	19·00 N	103·33 W
124	Coahuayutla (kō-ä-wē′lȧ.....Mex.	18·19 N	101·44 W
122	Coahuila (State) (kō-ä-wē′lȧ).Mex.	27·30 N	103·00 W
107	Coal City (kōl sĭ′tĭ) Il. (Chicago In.)	41·17 N	88·17 W
124	Coalcomán, Rio de (R.) (rē′ō-dĕ-kō-äl-kō-män′).Mex.	18·45 N	103·15 W
124	Coalcomán, Sierra de (Mts.) (syĕr′rä dā kō-äl-kō-män′).Mex.	18·30 N	102·45 W
124	Coalcomán de Matamoros (kō-äl-kō-män′ dā mä-tä-mō′rôs) Mex.	18·46 N	103·10 W
94	Coaldale (kōl′dāl)..........Can.	49·43 N	112·37 W
114	Coaldale...................Nv.	38·02 N	117·57 W
117	Coalgate (kōl′gāt)...........Ok.	34·33 N	96·13 W
104	Coal Grove (kōl grōv)........Oh.	38·20 N	82·40 W
114	Coalinga (kō-ȧ-lĭŋ′gȧ)........Ca.	36·09 N	120·23 W
148	Coalville (kōl′vĭl)..........Eng.	52·43 N	1·21 W
123	Coamo (kō-ä′mō) P.R. (Puerto Rico In.)	18·05 N	66·21 W
134	Coari (kō-är′ē).............Braz.	4·06 S	63·10 W
92	Coast Mts. (kōst)...........Can.	54·10 N	128·00 W
102	Coast Ranges, (Mts.).......U. S.	41·28 N	123·30 W
124	Coatepec (kō-ä-tā-pĕk)......Mex.	19·23 N	98·44 W
125	Coatepec...................Mex.	19·26 N	96·56 W
125	Coatepec............Mex. (In.)	19·08 N	99·25 W
126	Coatepeque (kō-ä-tā-pā′kå) . Guat.	14·40 N	91·52 W
126	Coatepeque..................Sal.	13·56 N	89·30 W
105	Coatesville (kōts′vĭl).........Pa.	40·00 N	75·50 W
124	Coatetelco (kō-ä-tå-tĕl′kō)...Mex.	18·43 N	99·47 W
105	Coaticook (kō′tĭ-ko͝ok).......Can.	45·10 N	71·55 W
125	Coatlinchán (kō-ä-tlē′n-chä′n) Mex. (In.)	19·26 N	98·52 W
91	Coats (I.) (kōts)...........Can.	62·23 N	82·11 W
220	Coats Land (Reg.)..........Ant.	74·00 S	30·00 W
125	Coatzacoalcos (Puerto México) (kô-ät′zä-kô-äl′kōs) (pwĕ′r-tô-mĕ′-kē-kô).Mex.	18·09 N	94·26 W
125	Coatzacoalcos (R.)..........Mex.	17·40 N	94·41 W
126	Coba (Ruins) (kô′bä)...Mex. (In.)	20·23 N	87·23 W
91	Cobalt (kō′bôlt)............Can.	47·21 N	79·40 W
126	Cobán (kō-bän′)...........Guat.	15·28 N	90·19 W
203	Cobar.....................Austl.	31·28 S	145·50 E
203	Cobberas, Mt. (cŏ-bēr-ăs)..Austl.	36·45 S	148·15 E
98	Cobequid Mts...............Can.	45·35 N	64·10 W
154	Cobh (kôv)..................Ire.	51·52 N	8·09 W
134	Cobija (kô-bē′hä)............Bol.	11·12 S	68·49 W
105	Cobourg (kō′bo͝orgh).........Can.	43·55 N	78·05 W
128	Cobre (R.) (kō′brä).........Jam.	18·05 N	77·00 W
217	Cóbuè......................Moz.	12·04 S	34·50 E
158	Coburg (kō′bo͝org)........F.R.G.	50·16 N	10·57 E
163	Cocentaina (kō-thān-tä-ē′nȧ)..Sp.	38·44 N	0·27 W
134	Cochabamba (kō-chä-bäm′bä).Bol.	17·30 S	66·08 W
161	Cochem (kō′κĕm).........F.R.G.	50·10 N	7·06 E
185	Cochin (kō-chĭn′)...........India	9·58 N	76·19 E
128	Cochinos, Bahia (B.) (bä-ē′ä-kô-chē′nōs).Cuba	22·05 N	81·10 W
129	Cochinos Bks................Ba.	22·20 N	76·15 W
115	Cochita Res.................NM	35·45 N	106·10 W
120	Cochran (kŏk′răn)...........Ga.	32·23 N	83·23 W
91	Cochrane (kŏk′răn)..........Can.	49·01 N	81·06 W
89	Cochrane......Can. (Calgary In.)	51·11 N	114·28 W
104	Cockburn (I.) (kŏk-būrn)....Can.	45·55 N	83·25 W
106	Cockeysville (kŏk′ĭz-vĭl) Md. (Baltimore In.)	39·30 N	76·40 W
113	Cockrell Hill (kŏk′rĕl) Tx. (Dallas, Fort Worth In.)	32·44 N	96·53 W
127	Coco (Segovia) (R.) (kô-kô) (sĕ-gô′vyä)...Hond-Nic.	14·55 N	83·45 W
128	Coco, Cayo (I.) (kä′-yō-kô′kô) Cuba	22·30 N	78·30 W
122	Coco, Isla del (I.) (ē′s-lä-dĕl-kô-kô) C. R.	5·33 N	87·02 W
121	Cocoa (kō′kō)...........Fl. (In.)	28·21 N	80·44 W
121	Cocoa Beach...........Fl. (In.)	28·20 N	80·35 W
122	Cocoli (kŏ-kô′lē).......Pan. (In.)	8·58 N	79·36 W
115	Coconino, Plat. (kō kō nē′nō)..Az.	35·45 N	112·28 W
7	Cocos (Keeling) Is. (kō′kôs) (kē′lĭng).Oceania	11·50 S	90·50 E
122	Coco Solito (kô-kô-sŏ-lē′tŏ) Pan. (In.)	9·21 N	79·53 W
124	Cocula (kō-ko͞o′lä)..........Mex.	20·23 N	103·47 W
124	Cocula (R.).................Mex.	18·17 N	99·11 W
134	Codajás (kō-dä-häzh′)......Braz.	3·44 S	62·09 W
135	Codera, Cabo (C.) (kȧ′bô-kō-dĕ′rä).Ven. (In.)	10·35 N	66·06 W
135	Codó (kō′dō)..............Braz.	4·21 S	43·52 W
164	Codogno (kô-dō′nyō)..........It.	45·08 N	9·43 E
127	Codrington (kŏd′rĭng-tŭn) Antigua (In.)	17·39 N	61·49 W
111	Cody (kō′dĭ)................Wy.	44·31 N	109·02 W
216	Coemba....................Ang.	12·08 S	18·05 E
161	Coesfeld (kûs′fĕld) F.R.G. (Ruhr In.)	51·56 N	7·10 E
110	Coeur d' Alene (kûr dȧ-lān′)...Id.	47·43 N	116·35 W
110	Coeur d' Alene (L.)...........Id.	47·32 N	116·39 W
110	Coeur d' Alene (R.)...........Id.	47·26 N	116·35 W
117	Coffeyville (kŏf′ĭ-vĭl).........Ks.	37·01 N	95·38 W
203	Coff's Harbour.............Austl.	30·20 S	153·10 E
213	Cofimvaba (căfĭm′vä-bȧ) S. Afr. (Natal In.)	32·01 S	27·37 E
164	Coghinas (R.) (kō′gē-nȧs)......It.	40·31 N	9·00 E
160	Cognac (kôn-yak′)............Fr.	45·41 N	0·22 W
99	Cohasset (kô-hăs′ĕt)....Ma. (In.)	42·14 N	70·48 W
105	Cohoes (kô-hōz′)............NY	42·50 N	73·40 W
136	Coig (kô′ēk) (R.)............Arg.	51·15 S	71·00 W
185	Coimbatore (kô-ēm-bȧ-tôr′) India	11·03 N	76·56 E
162	Coimbra (kô-ēm′brä)........Port.	40·14 N	8·23 W
162	Coín (kô-ēn′)................Sp.	36·40 N	4·45 W
163	Coina (kô-ē′nȧ).Port. (Lisbon In.)	38·35 N	9·03 W
163	Coina (R.) (kô′y-nä) Port. (Lisbon In.)	38·35 N	9·02 W
134	Coipasa, Salar de (Salt Flat) (sä-lä′r-dĕ-koi-pä′-sä).Chile	19·12 S	69·13 W
125	Coixtlahuaca (kō-ēks′tlä-wä′kä) Mex.	17·42 N	97·17 W
135	Cojedes (State) (kô-kĕ′dĕs) Ven. (In.)	9·50 N	68·21 W
129	Cojimar (kō-hē-mär′)..Cuba (In.)	23·10 N	82·19 W
126	Cojutepeque (kô-ho͞o-tĕ-pā′kå) Sal.	13·45 N	88·50 W
109	Cokato (kô-kā′tō)...........Mn.	45·03 N	94·11 W
107	Cokeburg (kōk bŭgh) Pa. (Pittsburgh In.)	40·06 N	80·03 W
203	Colac (kŏ′lȧc).............Austl.	38·25 S	143·40 E
163	Colares (kô-lä′rĕs) Port. (Lisbon In.)	38·47 N	9·27 W
135	Colatina (kô-lä-tē′nä).......Braz.	19·33 S	40·42 W
116	Colby (kōl′bĭ)...............Ks.	39·23 N	101·04 W
137	Colchagua (Prov.) (kôl-chȧ′gwä) Chile (Santiago In.)	34·42 S	71·24 W
155	Colchester (kōl′chĕs-tēr).....Eng.	51·52 N	0·50 E
94	Cold L. (kōld)...............Can.	54·33 N	110·05 W
116	Coldwater (kōld′wô-tēr)......Ks.	37·14 N	99·21 W
104	Coldwater...................Mi.	41·55 N	85·00 W
120	Coldwater (R.)...............Ms.	34·25 N	90·12 W
116	Coldwater Cr.................Tx.	36·10 N	101·45 W
118	Coleman (kōl′mȧn)...........Tx.	31·50 N	99·25 W
213	Colenso (kŏ-lĕnz′ô) S. Afr. (Natal In.)	28·48 S	29·49 E
109	Coleraine (kōl-rān′).........Mn.	47·16 N	93·29 W
154	Coleraine................N. Ire.	55·08 N	6·40 W
148	Coleshill (kōlz′hĭl)..........Eng.	52·30 N	1·42 W
109	Colfax (kōl′făks)............Ia.	41·40 N	93·13 W
119	Colfax......................La.	31·31 N	92·42 W
110	Colfax......................Wa.	46·53 N	117·21 W
136	Colhué Huapi (L.) (kôl-wā′o͞oȧ′pē).Arg.	45·30 S	68·45 W
218	Coligny..S. Afr. (Johannesburg) Pretoria In.)	26·20 S	26·18 E
124	Colima (kōlē′mä)...........Mex.	19·13 N	103·45 W
124	Colima (State).............Mex.	19·10 N	104·00 W
124	Colima, Nevado de (nĕ-vä′dô-dĕ-kô-lē′mä) (Mtn.) Mex.	19·30 N	103·38 W
154	Coll (I.) (kōl).............Scot.	56·42 N	6·23 W
101	College.....................Ak.	64·43 N	147·50 W
106	College Park (kŏl′ĕj) Ga. (Atlanta In.)	33·39 N	84·27 W
106	College Park..Md. (Baltimore In.)	38·59 N	76·58 W
106	Collegeville (kŏl′ĕj-vĭl) Pa. (Philadelphia In.)	40·11 N	75·27 W
204	Collie (kŏl′ē)..............Austl.	33·20 S	116·20 E
204	Collier B. (kŏl-yēr)........Austl.	15·30 S	123·30 E
163	Colli Laziali (Mtn.) (kô′lē-lät-zyä′lē).It. (Rome In.)	41·46 N	12·45 E
106	Collingswood (kŏl′ĭngz-wo͝od) NJ (Philadelphia In.)	39·54 N	75·04 W
104	Collingwood.................Can.	44·30 N	80·20 W
120	Collins (kŏl′ĭns)............Ms.	31·40 N	89·34 W
113	Collinsville (kŏl′ĭnz-vĭl) Il. (St. Louis In.)	38·41 N	89·59 W
117	Collinsville.................Ok.	36·21 N	95·50 W
210	Collo (kôl′ō)...............Alg.	37·02 N	6·29 E
161	Colmar (kôl′mär)............Fr.	48·03 N	7·25 E
162	Colmenar de Oreja (kôl-mā-när′dāōrā′hä).Sp.	40·06 N	3·25 W
163	Colmenar Viejo(kôl-mā-när′vyā′hō) Sp. (Madrid In.)	40·40 N	3·46 W
	Cologne, see Köln		
134	Colombia (kô-lôm′bē-ä).Col. (In.)	3·23 N	74·48 W
133	Colombia....................S. A.	3·30 N	72·30 W
185	Colombo (kô-lôm′bō)...Sri Lanka	6·58 N	79·52 E
137	Colón (kō-lōn′) Arg. (Buenos Aires In.)	33·55 S	61·08 W
128	Colón (kô-lô′n).............Cuba	22·45 N	80·55 W
124	Colón (kō-lōn′).............Mex.	20·46 N	100·02 W
122	Colón (kŏ-lô′n)........Pan. (In.)	9·22 N	79·54 W
134	Colon, Arch. de (Galápagos Is.) (är-chē-pyĕ′l-ågō-dĕ-kō-lōn′) (gä-lå′págôs).Ec.	0·10 S	87·45 W
127	Colōn, Montañas de (Mts.) (môn-tä′n-yäs-dĕ-kō-lô′n) Hond.	14·58 N	84·39 W
137	Colonia (kō-lō′nē-ä) Ur. (Buenos Aires In.)	34·27 S	57·50 W
137	Colonia (Dept.) Ur. (Buenos Aires In.)	34·08 S	57·50 W
137	Colonia Suiza (kô-lô′nēä-so͞oē′zä) Ur. (Buenos Aires In.)	34·17 S	57·15 W
163	Colonna(kô-lô′n-nä).It.(Rome In.)	41·50 N	12·48 E
165	Colonne, C. di (kô-lŏ′n-nĕ).....It.	39·02 N	17·15 E
154	Colonsay (I.) (kŏl-ôn-sā′)....Scot.	56·08 N	6·08 W
136	Coloradas, Lomas (Hills) (lô′mäs-kō-lō-rä′däs).Arg.	43·30 S	68·00 W
102	Colorado (State)............U. S.	39·30 N	106·55 W
119	Colorado (R.)...............Tx.	30·08 N	97·33 W
118	Colorado City (kŏl-ô-rä′dō sĭ′tĭ) Tx.	32·24 N	100·50 W
136	Colorado, Rio (R.)..........Arg.	38·30 S	66·00 W
115	Colorado Natl. Mon..........Co.	39·00 N	108·40 W
102	Colorado Plat..............U. S.	36·20 N	109·25 W
102	Colorado R.................U. S.	36·25 N	112·00 W
114	Colorado River Aqueducts....Ca.	33·38 N	115·43 W
115	Colorado River Ind. Res......Az.	34·03 N	114·02 W
128	Colorados, Arch. de los (Is.) (är-chē-pyĕ-lä-gô-dĕ-lôs-kô-lô-rä′dôs) Cuba	22·25 N	84·25 W
116	Colorado Springs (kŏl-ô-rä′dō).Co.	38·49 N	104·48 W
125	Colotepec (R.) (kô-lô′tĕ-pĕk) Mex.	15·56 N	96·57 W
124	Colotlán′ (kô-lô-tlän′).......Mex.	22·06 N	103·14 W
124	Colotlán (R.)...............Mex.	22·09 N	103·17 W
134	Colquechaca (kôl-kä-chä′kä)..Bol.	18·47 S	66·02 W
111	Colstrip (kōl′strĭp)...........Mt.	45·54 N	106·38 W
113	Colton (kōl′tŭn) Ca. (Los Angeles In.)	34·04 N	117·20 W
113	Columbia (kô-lŭm′bĭ-ȧ) Il. (St. Louis In.)	38·26 N	90·12 W
120	Columbia...................Ky.	37·06 N	85·15 W
106	Columbia....Md. (Baltimore In.)	39·15 N	76·51 W
120	Columbia....................Ms.	31·15 N	89·49 W
117	Columbia....................Mo.	38·55 N	92·19 W
105	Columbia....................Pa.	40·00 N	76·25 W
121	Columbia....................SC	34·00 N	81·00 W
120	Columbia....................Tn.	35·36 N	87·02 W
93	Columbia, Mt...............Can.	52·09 N	117·25 W
93	Columbia (R.)...............Can.	51·30 N	119·00 W
90	Columbia (R.).........Can.-U. S.	46·20 N	123·00 W
104	Columbia City................In.	41·10 N	85·30 W
112	Columbia City.Or. (Portland In.)	45·53 N	112·49 W
113	Columbia Heights Mn. (Minneapolis, St. Paul In.)	45·03 N	93·15 W
93	Columbia Icefield...........Can.	52·08 N	117·26 W
93	Columbia Mts...............Can.	51·30 N	118·30 W
120	Columbiana (kô-ŭm-bĭ-ă′nȧ)..Al..	33·10 N	86·35 W
163	Columbretes (I.) (kô-lo͞om-brĕ′tĕs).Sp.	39·54 N	0·54 E
120	Columbus (kô-lŭm′bŭs).......Ga.	32·29 N	84·56 W
104	Columbus....................In.	39·15 N	85·55 W
117	Columbus....................Ks.	37·10 N	94·50 W
120	Columbus....................Ms.	33·30 N	88·25 W
111	Columbus....................Mt.	45·39 N	109·15 W
108	Columbus....................Ne.	41·25 N	97·25 W
115	Columbus....................NM	31·50 N	107·40 W
104	Columbus....................Oh.	40·00 N	83·00 W
119	Columbus....................Tx.	29·44 N	96·34 W
109	Columbus....................Wi.	43·20 N	89·01 W
129	Columbus Bk. (kô-lŭm′büs)...Ba.	22·05 N	75·30 W
104	Columbus Grove..............Oh.	40·55 N	84·05 W
129	Columbus Pt.................Ba.	24·10 N	75·15 W
114	Colusa (kô-lū′sȧ)............Ca.	39·12 N	122·01 W
110	Colville (kŏl′vĭl)............Wa.	48·33 N	117·53 W
101	Colville (R.)................Ak.	69·00 N	156·25 W
110	Colville R..................Wa.	48·25 N	117·58 W
112	Colvos Pass. (kōl′vōs) Wa. (Seattle In.)	47·24 N	122·32 W
112	Colwood (kŏl′wo͝od) Can. (Seattle In.)	48·26 N	123·30 W
164	Comacchio (kô-mäk′kyō).......It.	44·42 N	12·12 E
124	Comala (kō-mä-lä′).........Mex.	19·22 N	103·47 W
126	Comalapa (kō-mä-lä′-pä)....Guat.	14·43 N	90·56 W
125	Comalcalco (kō-mäl-käl′kō)..Mex.	18·16 N	93·13 W
116	Comanche (kô-măn′chē).......Ok.	34·20 N	97·58 W
118	Comanche....................Tx.	31·54 N	98·37 W
118	Comanche Cr.................Tx.	31·02 N	102·47 W
126	Comayagua (kō-mä-yä′gwä).Hond.	14·24 N	87·36 W
121	Combahee (R.) (kŏm-bȧ-hē′) ..SC	32·42 N	80·40 W
120	Comer (kŭm′ēr)..............Ga.	34·02 N	83·07 W
129	Comete, C. (kô-mā′tå) Turks & Caicos	21·45 N	71·25 W
184	Comilla (kô-mĭl′ä)..........Bngl.	23·33 N	91·17 E
164	Comino, C. (kô-mē′nō).........It.	40·30 N	9·48 E
126	Comitán (kô-mē-tän′).......Mex.	16·16 N	92·09 W
112	Commencement B. (kŏ-mĕns′mĕnt bā) Wa. (Seattle In.)	47·17 N	122·21 W
160	Commentry (kô-män-trē′).....Fr.	46·16 N	2·44 E
120	Commerce (kŏm′ērs)..........Ga.	34·10 N	83·27 W
117	Commerce....................Ok.	36·57 N	94·54 W
117	Commerce....................Tx.	33·15 N	95·52 W
164	Como (kō′mō).................It.	45·48 N	9·03 E
164	Como, Lago di (L.) (lä′gō-dē-kō′mō).It.	46·00 N	9·30 E
136	Comodoro Rivadavia (kō′mô-dō′rō rē-vä-dä′vē-ä).Arg.	45·47 S	67·31 W
89	Como-Est....Can. (Montreal In.)	45·27 N	74·08 W
124	Comonfort (kô-mōn-fô′rt)...Mex.	20·43 N	100·47 W
185	Comorin C. (kŏ′mô-rĭn).......In.	8·05 N	78·05 E
209	Comoros......................Afr.	12·30 S	42·45 E
92	Comox (kō′mŏks).............Can.	49·40 N	124·55 W

PRONOUNCING INDEX

Compainala — Costa Mesa 271

Page	Name Pronunciation Region	Lat. °′	Long. °′
125	Compainalá (kôm-pä-ē-nä-lä′) Mex.	17·05 N	93·11 W
137	Companario, Cerro (Mtn.) (sĕ′r-rô-kôm-pä-nä′ryô) Arg.-Chile (Santiago In.)	35·54 S	70·23 W
160	Compiègne (kôN-pyĕn′y′) . . . . . Fr. .	49·25 N	2·49 E
163	Comporta (kôm-pôr′tá) Port. (Lisbon In.)	38·24 N	8·48 W
124	Compostela (kōm-pô-stā′lä) . . Mex.	21·41 N	104·54 W
113	Compton (kŏmp′tŭn) Ca. (Los Angeles In.)	33·54 N	118·14 W
120	Cona (R.) (kô-ná) . . . . Ga.	34·40 N	84·51 W
214	Conakry (kô-ná-krē′) . . . . Gui.	9·31 N	13·43 W
106	Conanicut (I.) (kŏn′á-nĭ-kŭt) RI (Providence In.)	41·34 N	71·20 W
160	Concarneau (kôN-kär-nō′) . . . . . Fr.	47·54 N	3·52 W
135	Concepción (kôn-sĕp′syōn′) . . . Bol.	15·47 S	61·08 W
136	Concepción . . . . Chile	36·51 S	72·59 W
127	Concepción . . . . Pan.	8·31 N	82·38 W
136	Concepción . . . . Par.	23·29 S	57·18 W
197	Concepcion . . . . Phil. (In.)	15·19 N	120·40 E
122	Concepción (R.) . . . . Mex.	30·25 N	112·20 W
126	Concepción (Vol.) . . . . Nic.	11·36 N	85·43 W
126	Concepción del Mar (kôn-sĕp-syōn′ dĕl mär′) . Guat	14·07 N	91·23 W
118	Concepción del Oro (kôn-sĕp-syōn′ dĕl ō′rō) . Mex.	24·39 N	101·24 W
136	Concepción del Uruguay (kôn-sĕp-syô′n-dĕl-ōō-rōō-gwī′) . Arg.	32·31 S	58·10 W
129	Conception (I.) . . . . Ba.	23·50 N	75·05 W
114	Conception, Pt. . . . . Ca.	34·27 N	120·28 W
99	Conception B. (kŏn-sĕp′shŭn) Can.	47·50 N	52·50 W
118	Concho (R.) (kŏn′chō) . . . . Tx.	31·34 N	100·00 W
118	Conchos (R.) (kōn′chōs) . . . . . Mex.	25·03 N	99·00 W
118	Conchos (R.) . . . . Mex.	29·08 N	105·02 W
112	Concord (kŏŋ′kŏrd) Ca. (San Francisco In.)	37·58 N	122·02 W
99	Concord . . . . Ma. (Boston In.)	42·28 N	71·21 W
105	Concord . . . . NH	43·10 N	71·30 W
121	Concord . . . . NC	35·23 N	80·11 W
136	Concordia (kôn-kôr′dĭ-ä) . . . . . Arg.	31·18 S	57·59 W
134	Concordia . . . . Col. (In.)	6·04 N	75·54 W
117	Concordia . . . . Ks.	39·32 N	97·39 W
124	Concordia (kôn-kô′r-dyä) . . . . Mex.	23·17 N	106·06 W
110	Concrete (kŏn′krēt) . . . . Wa.	48·33 N	121·44 W
108	Conde (kŏn-dē′) . . . . SD	45·10 N	98·06 W
126	Condega (kŏn-dĕ′gä) . . . . Nic.	13·20 N	86·27 W
160	Condem (kôN-dĕN) . . . . Fr.	43·58 N	0·22 E
160	Condé-sur-Noireau (kôN-dā′sür-nwä-rō′) . Fr.	48·50 N	0·36 W
135	Condeúba (kōn-dā-ōō′bä) . . . . Braz.	14·47 S	41·44 W
110	Condon (kŏn′dŭn) . . . . Or.	45·14 N	120·10 W
120	Conecun (R.) (kô-nē′kŭ) . . . . . . Al.	31·05 N	86·52 W
164	Conegliano (kō-nål-yä′nō) . . . . . . It.	45·59 N	12·17 E
115	Conejos (R.) (kô-nā′hōs) . . . . . . Co.	37·07 N	106·19 W
105	Conemaugh (kŏn′ê-mô) . . . . Pa.	40·25 N	78·50 W
106	Coney I. (kō′nĭ) NY (New York In.)	40·34 N	73·27 W
160	Confolens (kôN-fä-läN′) . . . . Fr.	46·01 N	0·41 E
121	Congaree (R.) (kŏŋ-gá-rē′) . . . . SC	33·53 N	80·55 W
193	Conghua (tsôŋ-hwä) . . . . China	23·30 N	113·40 E
148	Congleton (kŏŋ′g′l-tŭn) . . . . . . Eng.	53·10 N	2·13 W
209	Congo (kŏn′gō) . . . . Afr.	3·00 S	13·48 E
216	Congo (Zaire) (R.) . . . . Afr.	1·10 N	18·25 E
216	Congo, Serra do (Mts.) . . . . . . Ang.	6·25 S	13·50 E
	Congo, The, see Zaire		
209	Congo Basin . . . . Zaire	2·47 N	20·58 E
148	Conisbrough (kŏn′ĭs-bŭr-ô) . . Eng.	53·29 N	1·13 W
97	Coniston . . . . Can.	46·29 N	80·51 W
93	Conklin (kŏŋk′lĭn) . . . . Can.	55·38 N	111·05 W
106	Conley (kŏn′lĭ) . Ga. (Atlanta In.)	33·38 N	84·19 W
154	Conn, Lough (L.) (lŏk kŏn) . . . Ire.	53·56 N	9·25 W
154	Connacht (Reg.) (cŏn′ât) . . . . . Ire.	53·50 N	8·45 W
104	Conneaut (kŏn-ê-ôt′) . . . . Oh.	41·55 N	80·35 W
103	Connecticut (State) (kŏ-nĕt′ĭ-kŭt) U. S.	41·40 N	73·10 W
105	Connecticut R. . . . . U. S.	43·55 N	72·15 W
105	Connellsville (kŏn′nĕlz-vĭl) . . . . Pa.	40·00 N	79·40 W
154	Connemara, Mts. of (kŏn-nê-má′rá) . Ire.	53·30 N	9·54 W
104	Connersville (kŏn′ĕrz-vĭl) . . . . . . In.	39·35 N	85·10 W
205	Connors Ra. (kŏn′nŏrs) . . . . . . Austl.	22·15 S	149·00 E
111	Conrad (kŏn′răd) . . . . Mt.	48·11 N	111·56 W
89	Conrich (kŏn′rĭch) Can. (Calgary In.)	51·06 N	113·51 W
119	Conroe (kŏn′rō) . . . . Tx.	30·18 N	95·23 W
137	Conselheiro Lafaiete (kôn-sĕ-lā′rô-lá-fā′ĕ-tĕ) Braz. (Rio de Janeiro In.)	20·40 S	43·46 W
106	Conshohocken (kŏn-shô-hŏk′ĕn) Pa. (Philadelphia In.)	40·04 N	75·18 W
128	Consolación del Sur (kōn-sô-lä-syōn′) . Cuba	22·30 N	83·55 W
196	Con Son (Is.) . . . . Viet.	8·30 N	106·28 E
112	Constance, Mt. (kŏn′stăns) Wa. (Seattle In.)	47·46 N	123·08 W
153	Constanța (kōn-stán′tsä) . . . . . Rom.	44·12 N	28·36 E
162	Constantina (kŏn-stän-tē′nä) Sp.	37·52 N	5·39 W
210	Constantine (kôN-stäN′tēn′) . . . Alg.	36·28 N	6·38 E
104	Constantine (kŏn′stán-tēn) . . . . Mi.	41·50 N	85·40 W
136	Constitución (kōn′stĭ-tōō-syōn′) Chile	35·24 S	72·25 W
106	Constitution (kŏn-stĭ-tū′shŭn) Ga. (Atlanta In.)	33·41 N	84·20 W
137	Contagem (kōn-tá′zhĕm) Braz. (Rio de Janerio In.)	19·54 S	44·05 W
124	Contepec (kōn-tĕ-pĕk′) . . . . . . Mex.	20·04 N	100·07 W
125	Contreras (kôn-trĕ′räs) . Mex. (In.)	19·18 N	99·14 W
90	Contwoyto (L.) . . . . Can.	65·42 N	110·50 W
113	Converse (kŏn′vĕrs) Tx. (San Antonio In.)	29·31 N	98·17 W
117	Conway (kŏn′wā) . . . . Ar.	35·06 N	92·27 W
105	Conway . . . . NH	44·00 N	71·10 W
121	Conway . . . . SC	33·49 N	79·01 W
112	Conway . . . . Wa. (Seattle In.)	48·20 N	122·20 W
120	Conyers (kŏn′yŏrz) . . . . Ga.	33·41 N	84·01 W
184	Cooch Behār (kōōch bê-här′) India	26·25 N	89·34 E
92	Cook, C. (kŏŏk) . . . . Can.	50·08 N	127·55 W
205	Cook, Mt. . . . . N. Z. (In.)	43·27 S	170·13 E
120	Cookeville (kŏŏk′vĭl) . . . . Tn.	36·07 N	85·30 W
89	Cooking Lake (kŏŏk′ĭng) Can. (Edmonton In.)	53·10 N	113·08 W
89	Cooking L. . . Can. (Edmonton In.)	53·25 N	113·02 W
101	Cook Inlet . . . . Ak.	60·50 N	151·38 W
199	Cook Is. . . . . Oceania	19·20 S	158·00 W
205	Cook Str. . . . . N. Z. (In.)	40·37 S	174·15 E
205	Cooktown (kŏŏk′toun) . . . . . . Austl.	15·40 S	145·20 E
121	Cooleemee (kōō-lē′mē) . . . . NC	35·50 N	80·32 W
204	Coolgardie (kōōl-gär′dê) . . . . Austl.	31·00 S	121·25 E
203	Cooma (kōō′má) . . . . Austl.	36·22 S	149·10 E
203	Coonamble (kōō-năm′b′l) . . . Austl.	31·00 S	148·30 E
185	Coonoort . . . . India	10·22 N	76·15 E
113	Coon Rapids (kōōn) . Mn. (Minneapolis, St. Paul In.)	45·09 N	93·17 W
117	Cooper (kōōp′ĕr) . . . . Tx.	33·23 N	95·40 W
101	Cooper Center (kōōp′ĕr sĕn′tĕr) Ak.	61·54 N	145·30 W
203	Coopers Cr. (kōō′pĕrz) . . . . . Austl.	27·32 S	141·19 E
105	Cooperstown (kōōp′ĕrs-toun) NY	42·45 N	74·55 W
108	Cooperstown . . . . ND	47·26 N	98·07 W
203	Coorong, The (L.) (kōō′rŏng) Austl.	36·07 S	139·45 E
120	Coosa (kōō′sá) . . . . Al.	32·43 N	86·25 W
120	Coosa (R.) . . . . Al.	34·00 N	86·00 W
120	Coosawattee (R.) (kōō-sá-wôt′ē) Ga.	34·37 N	84·45 W
110	Coos Bay (kōōs) . . . . Or.	43·21 N	124·12 W
110	Coos B. Or.	43·19 N	124·40 W
203	Cootamundra (kōō′tá-mŭnd′rá) Austl.	34·25 S	148·00 E
136	Copacabana (kô′pä-ká-bá′nä) Braz. (Rio de Janeiro In.)	22·57 S	43·11 W
125	Copalita (R.) (kô-pä-lē′tä) . . . Mex.	15·55 N	96·06 W
126	Copán (Ruins) (kō-pän′) . . . . Hond.	14·50 N	89·10 W
119	Copano B. (kō-pän′ō) . . . . Tx.	28·08 N	97·25 W
	Copenhagen, see København		
136	Copiapó (kō-pyä-pō′) . . . . Chile	27·16 S	70·28 W
107	Copley (kŏp′lê) Oh. (Cleveland In.)	41·06 N	81·38 W
164	Copparo (kôp-pä′rō) . . . . It.	44·53 N	11·50 E
113	Coppell (kŏp′pĕl) Tx. (Dallas, Fort Worth In.)	32·57 N	97·00 W
101	Copper (R.) (kŏp′ĕr) . . . . Ak.	62·38 N	145·00 W
96	Copper Cliff . . . . Can.	46·28 N	81·04 W
109	Copper Harbor . . . . Mi.	47·27 N	87·53 W
120	Copperhill (kŏp′ĕr hĭl) . . . . Tn.	35·00 N	84·22 W
90	Coppermine (kŏp′ĕr-mĭn) . . . . Can.	67·46 N	115·19 W
92	Copper Mtn. . . . . Ak.	55·14 N	132·36 W
90	Copperinine (R.) . . . . Can.	66·48 N	114·59 W
113	Copperton (kŏp′ĕr-tŭn) Ut. (Salt Lake City In.)	40·34 N	112·06 W
	Coquilhatville, see Mbandaka		
110	Coquille (kô-kēl′) . . . . Or.	43·11 N	124·11 W
136	Coquimbo (kô-kēm′bō) . . . . . . Chile	29·58 S	71·31 W
137	Coquimbo (Prov.) Chile (Santiago In.)	31·50 S	71·05 W
112	Coquitlam (L.) (kō-kwĭt-lám) Can. (Vancouver In.)	49·23 N	122·44 W
165	Corabia (kô-rä′bĭ-á) . . . . Rom.	43·45 N	24·29 E
134	Coracora (kō′rä-kō′rä) . . . . Peru	15·12 S	73·42 W
121	Coral Gables . . . . Fl. (In.)	25·43 N	80·14 W
96	Coral Rapids (kŏr′ăl) . . . . Can.	50·18 N	81·49 W
198	Coral Sea (kŏr′ăl) . . . . Oceania	13·30 S	150·00 E
109	Coralville Res. . . . . Ia.	41·45 N	91·50 W
203	Corangamite, L. (cŏr-ăŋg′á-mĭt) Austl.	38·05 S	142·55 E
107	Coraopolis (kō-rä-ŏp′ô-lĭs) Pa. (Pittsburgh In.)	40·30 N	80·09 W
164	Corato (kô′rä-tô) . . . . It.	41·08 N	16·28 E
161	Corbeil-Essonnes (kôr-bā′yĕ-sŏn′) Fr. (Paris In.)	48·31 N	2·29 E
112	Corbett (kôr′bĕt) Or. (Portland In.)	45·31 N	122·17 W
160	Corbie (kôr-bē′) . . . . Fr.	49·55 N	2·27 E
120	Corbin (kôr′bĭn) . . . . Ky.	36·55 N	84·06 W
148	Corby (kôr′bĭ) . . . . Eng.	52·29 N	0·38 W
136	Corcovado (Mtn.) (kôr-kô-vä′dōō) Braz. (Rio de Janeiro In.)	22·57 S	43·13 W
136	Corcovado, Golfo (G.) (kôr-kô-vä′dhō) . Chile	43·40 S	75·00 W
137	Cordeiro (kôr-dā′rō) Braz. (Rio de Janeiro In.)	22·03 S	42·22 W
120	Cordele (kôr-dēl′) . . . . Ga.	31·55 N	83·50 W
116	Cordell (kôr-dĕl′) . . . . Ok.	35·19 N	98·58 W
75	Cordilleran Highlands (Reg.) (kōr dĭl′lŭr ăn) . N. A.	55·00 N	125·00 W
136	Córdoba (kôr′dô-vä) . . . . Arg.	30·20 S	64·03 W
125	Córdoba (kô′r-dô-bä) . . . . Mex.	18·53 N	96·54 W
162	Córdoba (kô′r-dô-bä) . . . . Sp.	37·55 N	4·45 W
136	Córdoba (Prov.) (kôr′dô-vä) Arg.	32·00 S	64·00 W
136	Córdoba, Sa. de (Mts.) . . . . Arg.	31·15 S	64·30 W
120	Cordova (kôr′dô-á) . . . . Al.	33·45 N	86·11 W
101	Cordova (kôr′dô-vä) . . . . Ak.	60·34 N	145·38 W
92	Cordova B. . . . . Ak.	54·55 N	132·35 W
162	Corella (kô-rĕl-yä) . . . . Sp.	42·07 N	1·48 W
164	Corigliano (kō-rē-lyä′nō) . . . . . . It.	39·35 N	16·30 E
120	Corinth (kŏr′ĭnth) . . . . Ms.	34·55 N	88·30 W
	Corinth, see Kórinthos		
135	Corinto (kô-rē′n-tō) . . . . Braz.	18·20 S	44·16 W
134	Corinto . . . . Col. (In.)	3·09 N	76·12 W
126	Corinto (kōr-ĭn′tō) . . . . Nic.	12·30 N	87·12 W
202	Corio . . . . . Austl. (Melbourne In.)	38·05 S	144·22 E
202	Corio B. . . . Austl. (Melbourne In.)	38·07 S	144·25 E
216	Corisco, Isal de (I.) . . . Equat. Gui.	0·50 N	8·40 E
154	Cork (kôrk) . . . . Ire.	51·54 N	8·25 W
154	Cork Hbr. . . . . Ire.	51·44 N	8·15 W
164	Corleone (kôr-lå-ō′nā) . . . . It.	37·48 N	13·18 E
95	Cormorant L. . . . . Can.	54·13 N	100·47 W
120	Cornelia (kôr-nē′lyá) . . . . Ga.	34·31 N	83·30 W
218	Cornelis (R.) (kôr-nē′lĭs) . . . S. Afr. (Johannesburg & Pretoria In.)	27·48 S	29·15 E
113	Cornell (kôr-nĕl′) Ca. (Los Angeles In.)	34·06 N	118·46 W
109	Cornell . . . . Wi.	45·10 N	91·10 W
91	Corner Brook (kôr′nĕr) . . . . . . Can.	48·57 N	57·57 W
203	Corner Inlet . . . . Austl.	38·55 S	146·45 E
	Corneto, see Targuinia		
117	Corning (kôr′nĭng) . . . . Ar.	36·26 N	90·35 W
109	Corning . . . . Ia.	40·58 N	94·40 W
105	Corning . . . . NY	42·10 N	77·05 W
164	Corno, Monte (Mtn.) (kôr′nō) . . It.	42·28 N	13·37 E
128	Cornwall . . . . Ba.	25·55 N	77·15 W
105	Cornwall (kôrn′wôl) . . . . Can.	45·05 N	74·35 W
154	Cornwall Pen. (kôrn′wăl) . . . . Eng.	50·25 N	5·04 W
134	Coro (kō′rō) . . . . Ven.	11·22 N	69·43 W
134	Corocoro (kō-rō-kō′rō) . . . . Bol.	17·15 S	68·21 W
185	Coromandel Coast (kŏr-ô-man′dĕl) India	13·30 N	80·30 E
120	Corona (kô-rō′ná) . . . . Al.	33·42 N	87·28 W
113	Corona . . . . . Ca. (Los Angeles In.)	33·52 N	117·34 W
127	Coronada, Bahía de (B.) (bä-ē′ä-dĕ-kô-rô-nä′dō) . C.R.	8·47 N	84·04 W
113	Corona del Mar (kô-rō′ná dĕl măr) Ca. (Los Angeles In.)	33·36 N	117·53 W
114	Coronado (kŏr-ô-nä′dō) . . Ca. (In.)	32·42 N	117·12 W
90	Coronation G. (kŏr-ô-nā′shŭn) Can.	68·07 N	112·50 W
136	Coronel (kō-rô-nĕl′) . . . . Chile	37·00 S	73·10 W
137	Coronel Brandsen (kŏ-rô-nĕl-brá′nd-sĕn) Arg. (Buenos Aires In.)	35·09 S	58·15 W
136	Coronel Dorrego (kŏ-rô-nĕl-dôr-rĕ′gô) . Arg.	38·43 S	61·16 W
136	Coronel Oviedo (kŏ-rô-nĕl-ô-vêĕ′dô) . Par.	25·28 S	56·22 W
136	Coronel Pringles (kŏ-rô-nĕl-prēn′glĕs) . Arg.	37·54 S	61·22 W
136	Coronel Suárez (kŏ-rô-nĕl-swä′rās) . Arg.	37·27 S	61·49 W
203	Corowa (cŏr-ôwă) . . . . Austl.	36·02 S	146·23 E
126	Corozal (cŏr-ŏth-ăl′) Belize (In.)	18·25 N	88·23 W
119	Corpus Christi (kôr′pŭs krĭs′tê) Tx.	27·48 N	97·24 W
119	Corpus Christi B. . . . . Tx.	27·47 N	97·14 W
118	Corpus Christi L. . . . . Tx.	28·08 N	98·20 W
136	Corral (kô-räl′) . . . . Chile	39·57 S	73·15 W
162	Corral de Almaguer (kô-räl′dā äl-mä-gâr′) . Sp.	39·45 N	3·10 W
128	Corralillo (kô-rä-lē-yō) . . . . . . Cuba	23·00 N	80·40 W
197	Corregidor I. (kô-rā-hē-dōr′) Phil. (In.)	14·21 N	120·25 E
135	Correntina (kô-rĕn-tē-ná) . . Braz.	13·18 S	44·33 W
154	Corrib, Lough (L.) (lŏk kŏr′ĭb) Ire.	53·56 N	9·19 W
136	Corrientes (kō-ryĕn′tās) . . . . . . Arg.	27·25 S	58·39 W
136	Corrientes (Prov.) . . . . Arg.	28·45 S	58·00 W
134	Corrientes, Cabo (C.) (ká′bô-kō-ryĕn′tās) . Col.	5·34 N	77·35 W
128	Corrientes, Cabo (C.) (ká′bô-kôr-rē-ĕn′tĕs) . Cuba	21·50 N	84·25 W
124	Corrientes, Cabo (C.) . . . . Mex.	20·25 N	105·41 W
164	Corse, C. (kôrs) . . . . Fr.	42·59 N	9·19 E
164	Corsica (I.) (kô′r-sē-kä) . . . . Fr.	42·10 N	8·55 E
119	Corsicana (kôr-sĭ-kăn′á) . . . . . . Tx.	32·06 N	96·28 W
124	Cortazar (kôr-tä-zär) . . . . Mex.	20·30 N	100·57 W
164	Corte (kôr′tâ) . . . . Fr.	42·18 N	9·10 E
162	Cortegana (kôr-tā-gä′nä) . . . . . . Sp.	37·54 N	6·48 W
162	Cortes (kôr-tās′) . . . . Sp.	36·38 N	5·20 W
128	Cortés, Ensenada de (B.) (ĕn-sĕ-nä-dä-dĕ-kôr-tās′) . Cuba	22·05 N	83·45 W
115	Cortez . . . . Co.	37·21 N	108·35 W
105	Cortland (kôrt′lănd) . . . . NY	42·35 N	76·10 W
164	Cortona (kôr-tō′nä) . . . . It.	43·16 N	12·00 E
214	Corubal (R.) . . . . Guinea-Bissau	11·43 N	14·40 W
162	Coruche (kô-rōō′she) . . . . Port.	38·58 N	8·34 W
171	Coruh (R.) (chō-rōōk′) . . . . Tur.	40·30 N	41·10 E
171	Corum (chô-rōōm′) . . . . Tur.	40·34 N	34·45 E
135	Corumbá (kō-rōōm-bä′) . . . . . Braz.	19·01 S	57·28 W
104	Corunna (kô-rŭn′á) . . . . Mi.	43·00 N	84·05 W
135	Coruripe (kō-rōō-rē′pĭ) . . . . . Braz.	10·09 S	36·13 W
110	Corvallis (kŏr-văl′ĭs) . . . . Or.	44·34 N	123·17 W
148	Corve (R.) (kôr′vê) . . . . Eng.	52·28 N	2·43 W
105	Corry (kŏr′ĭ) . . . . Pa.	41·55 N	79·40 W
104	Corydon (kŏr′ĭ-dŭn) . . . . In.	38·10 N	86·05 W
109	Corydon . . . . Ia.	40·45 N	93·20 W
104	Corydon . . . . Ky.	37·45 N	87·40 W
125	Cosamaloápan (kô-sä-mä-lwä′pän) Mex.	18·21 N	95·48 W
125	Coscomatepec (kôs′kōmä-tĕ-pĕk′) Mex.	19·04 N	97·03 W
148	Coseley (kôs′lē) . . . . Eng.	52·33 N	2·10 W
164	Cosenza (kô-zĕnt′sä) . . . . It.	39·18 N	16·15 E
104	Coshocton (kô-shŏk′tŭn) . . . . . . Oh.	40·15 N	81·55 W
104	Cosigüina (Vol.) . . . . Nic.	12·59 N	83·35 W
213	Cosmoledo Group (Is.) (kŏs-mô-lā′dō) . Afr.	9·42 S	47·45 E
110	Cosmopolis (kŏz-mŏp′ô-lĭs) . . . . Wa.	46·58 N	123·47 W
160	Cosne-sur-Loire (kōn-sür-lwär′) Fr.	47·25 N	2·57 E
125	Cosoleacaque (kō sō lā-ä-kä′kē) Mex.	18·01 N	94·38 W
113	Costa Mesa (kŏs′tá mā′sá) Ca. (Los Angeles In.)	33·39 N	118·54 W

ng-sing; ŋ-baŋk; N-nasalized n; nŏd; cŏmmit; ōld; ôbey; ôrder; fōōd; fŏŏt; ou-out; s-soft; sh-dish; th-thin; pūre; ûnite; ûrn; stŭd; circŭs; ü-as "y" in study; ′-indeterminate vowel.

Page	Name Pronunciation Region	Lat. °′	Long. °′
123	Costa Rica (kŏs'tȧ rē'kȧ) . . . . N. A.	10·30 N	84·30 W
114	Cosumnes (R.) (kŏ-sŭm'nêz) . . Ca.	38·21 N	121·17 W
134	Cotabambas (kō-tä-bȧm'bäs) . Peru	13·49 S	72·17 W
197	Cotabato (kō-tä-bä'tō) . . . . . . Phil.	7·06 N	124·13 E
125	Cotaxtla (kō-täs'tlä) . . . . Mex.	18·49 N	96·22 W
125	Cotaxtla (R.) . . . . Mex.	18·54 N	96·21 W
89	Coteau-du-Lac (cō-tō'dü-läk) Can. (Montreal In.)	45·17 N	74·11 W
89	Coteau-Landing Can. (Montreal In.)	45·15 N	74·13 W
129	Coteaux . . . . Hai.	18·15 N	74·05 W
160	Côte d'Or (hill) (kōr-dŏr') . . . . . Fr.	47·02 N	4·35 E
124	Cotija de la Paz (kō-tē'-kä-dĕ-lä-pȧ'z) . Mex.	19·46 N	102·43 W
215	Cotonou (kô-tô-nōō') . . . . Benin	6·21 N	2·26 E
134	Cotopaxi (Mtn.) (kō-tô-păk'sê) Ec.	0·40 S	78·26 W
129	Cotorro (kô-tôr-rō) . . . . Cuba (In.)	23·03 N	82·17 W
154	Cotswold Hills (kŭtz'wōld) . . . Eng.	51·35 N	2·16 W
113	Cottage Grove (kŏt'āj grōv) Mn. (Minneapolis, St. Paul In.)	44·50 N	92·52 W
110	Cottage Grove . . . . Or.	43·48 N	123·04 W
158	Cottbus (kōtt'bōōs) . . . . . . G.D.R.	51·47 N	14·20 E
161	Cottian Alps (Mts.) (kŏ'tē-ŭn-ălps) . Fr.-It.	44·46 N	7·02 E
108	Cottonwood (R.) (kŏt'ŭn-wŏŏd) Mn.	44·25 N	95·35 W
110	Cottonwood Cr. . . . . Ca.	40·24 N	122·50 W
129	Cotuí (kô-tōō'-ê) . . . . . . Dom. Rep.	19·05 N	70·10 W
118	Cotulla (kŏ-tŭl'lȧ) . . . . Tx.	28·26 N	99·14 W
161	Coubert (kōō-bâr') Fr. (Paris In.)	48·40 N	2·43 E
105	Coudersport (koŭ'dĕrz-port) . . . Pa.	41·45 N	78·00 W
98	Coudres, Île aux (I.) . . . . Can.	47·17 N	70·12 W
160	Couéron (kōō-ā-rôn') . . . . Fr.	47·16 N	1·45 W
161	Coulommiers (kōō-lô-myā') Fr. (Paris In.)	48·49 N	3·05 E
136	Coulto, Serra do (Mts.) (sĕ'r-rä-dô-kô-ōō'tô) Braz. (Rio de Janeiro In.)	22·33 S	43·27 W
108	Council Bluffs (koun'sĭl blŭf) . . . Ia.	41·16 N	95·53 W
117	Council Grove (koun'sĭl grōv) . Ks.	38·39 N	96·30 W
112	Coupeville (kōōp'vĭl) Wa. (Seattle In.)	48·13 N	122·41 W
135	Courantyne (R.) (kôr'ăntĭn) Guy.-Sur.	4·28 N	57·42 W
92	Courtenay (cōōrt-nā') . . . . Can.	49·41 N	125·00 W
119	Coushatta (kou-shăt'ȧ) . . . . La.	32·02 N	93·21 W
160	Coutras (kōō-trȧ') . . . . Fr.	45·02 N	0·07 W
216	Covelo . . . . Ang.	12·06 S	13·55 E
148	Coventry (kŭv'ĕn-trĭ) . . . . Eng.	52·25 N	1·29 W
162	Covilhã (kô-vēl'yăɴ) . . . . Port.	40·18 N	7·29 W
113	Covina (kô-vē'nȧ) Ca. (Los Angeles In.)	34·06 N	117·54 W
120	Covington (kŭv'ĭng-tŭn) . . . . . . Ga.	33·36 N	83·50 W
104	Covington . . . . In.	40·10 N	87·15 W
107	Covington . . . . Ky. (Cincinnati In.)	39·05 N	84·31 W
119	Covington . . . . La.	30·30 N	90·06 W
104	Covington . . . . Oh.	40·10 N	84·20 W
117	Covington . . . . Ok.	36·18 N	97·32 W
120	Covington . . . . Tn.	35·33 N	89·40 W
105	Covington . . . . Va.	37·50 N	80·00 W
203	Cowal, L. (kou'ăl) . . . . Austl.	33·30 S	147·10 E
204	Cowan, (L.) (kou'ȧn) . . . . Austl.	32·00 S	122·30 E
98	Cowansville . . . . Can.	45·13 N	72·47 W
110	Cow Cr. (kou) . . . . Or.	42·45 N	123·35 W
154	Cowes (kouz) . . . . Eng.	50·43 N	1·25 W
92	Cowichan L. . . . . Can.	48·54 N	124·20 W
110	Cowlitz (R.) (kou'lĭts) . . . . Wa.	46·30 N	122·45 W
203	Cowra (kou'rȧ) . . . . Austl.	33·50 S	148·33 E
135	Coxim (kō-shēɴ') . . . . Braz.	18·32 S	54·43 W
125	Coxquihui (kōz-kē-wē') . . . . . . Mex.	20·10 N	97·34 W
184	Cox's Bāzār . . . . Bngl.	21·32 N	92·00 E
134	Coyaima (kô-yȧē'mä) . . . Col. (In.)	3·48 N	75·11 W
118	Coyame (kō-yä'mā) . . . . Mex.	29·26 N	105·05 W
118	Coyanosa Draw (kŏ yȧ-nō'sä) . Tx.	30·55 N	103·07 W
125	Coyoacán (kô-yô-ȧ-kän') Mex. (In.)	19·21 N	99·10 W
112	Coyote (R.) (kī'ōt) Ca. (San Francisco In.)	37·27 N	121·57 W
124	Coyuca de Benítez (kō-yōō'kä dā bā-nē'tāz) . Mex.	17·04 N	100·06 W
124	Coyuca de Catalán (kō-yōō'kä dā kä-tä-län') . Mex.	18·19 N	100·41 W
125	Coyutla (kō-yōō'tlä) . . . . Mex.	20·13 N	97·40 W
116	Cozad (kō'zăd) . . . . Ne.	40·53 N	99·59 W
107	Cozaddale (kō-zăd-dāl) . . Oh. (Cincinnati In.)	39·16 N	84·09 W
124	Cozoyoapan (kō-zō-yô-ä-pȧ'n) Mex.	16·45 N	98·17 W
126	Cozumel (kŏ-zōō-mĕ'l) . Mex. (In.)	20·31 N	86·55 W
126	Cozumel, Isla de (I.) (ē's-lä-dĕ-kŏ-zōō-mĕ'l) Mex. (In.)	20·26 N	87·10 W
110	Crab Cr. (krăb) . . . . Wa.	46·47 N	119·43 W
110	Crab Cr. . . . . Wa.	47·21 N	119·09 W
213	Cradock (krā'dŭk) S. Afr. (Natal In.)	32·12 S	25·38 E
107	Crafton (krăf'tŭn) Pa. (Pittsburgh In.)	40·26 N	80·04 W
111	Craig (krāg) . . . . Co.	40·32 N	107·31 W
165	Craiova (krá-yō'vá) . . . . Rom.	44·18 N	23·50 E
105	Cranberry (L.) (krăn'bĕr-ĭ) . . . NY	44·10 N	74·50 W
202	Cranbourne Austl. (Melbourne In.)	38·07 S	145·16 E
93	Cranbrook (krăn'brŏŏk) . . . . . Can.	49·31 N	115·46 W
106	Cranbury (krăn'bē-rĭ) NJ (New York In.)	40·19 N	74·31 W
109	Crandon (krăn'dŭn) . . . . Wi.	45·35 N	88·55 W
160	Cransac (krän-zȧk') . . . . Fr.	44·28 N	2·19 E
106	Cranston (krăns'tŭn) RI (Providence In.)	41·46 N	71·25 W
110	Crater L. (krā'tĕr) . . . . Or.	43·00 N	122·08 W
110	Crater Lake Natl. Park . . . . Or.	42·58 N	122·40 W
111	Craters of the Moon Natl. Mon. (krā'tĕr) . Id.	43·28 N	113·15 W
135	Crateús (krä-tâ-ōōzh') . . . . . . Braz.	5·09 S	40·35 W
135	Crato (krä'tōō) . . . . Braz.	7·19 S	39·13 W
108	Crawford (krô'fērd) . . . . Ne.	42·41 N	103·25 W
112	Crawford . . . . . . Wa. (Portland In.)	45·49 N	122·24 W
104	Crawfordsville (krô'fērdz-vĭl) . . In.	40·00 N	86·55 W
111	Crazy Mts. (krā'zĭ) . . . . Mt.	46·11 N	110·25 W
111	Crazy Woman Cr. . . . . Wy.	44·08 N	106·40 W
160	Crécy (krā-sē') . . . . Fr.	50·13 N	1·48 E
218	Crecy (krē-sē) S. Afr. (Johannesburg & Pretoria In.)	24·38 S	28·52 E
161	Crecy-en-Brie (krā-sē'-ĕɴ-brē') Fr. (Paris In.)	48·52 N	2·55 E
89	Credit (R.) . . . . Can. (Toronto In.)	43·41 N	79·55 W
90	Cree (L.) (krē) . . . . Can.	57·35 N	107·52 W
108	Creighton (krā'tŭn) . . . . Ne.	42·27 N	97·54 W
213	Creighton (cre-tŏn) S. Afr. (Natal In.)	30·02 S	28·52 E
160	Creil (krĕ'y') . . . . Fr.	49·18 N	2·28 E
164	Crema (krā'mä) . . . . It.	45·21 N	9·53 E
164	Cremona (krā-mō'nä) . . . . It.	45·09 N	10·02 E
161	Crépy-en-Valois (krā-pē'-ĕɴ-vä-lwä') . Fr. (In.)	49·14 N	2·53 E
164	Cres (Tsrĕs) . . . . Yugo.	44·58 N	14·21 E
164	Cres (I.) . . . . Yugo.	44·50 N	14·31 E
121	Crescent (L.) (krĕs'ĕnt) . . . . Fl.	29·33 N	81·30 W
110	Crescent (L.) . . . . Or.	43·25 N	121·58 W
112	Crescent Beach Can. (Vancouver In.)	49·03 N	122·58 W
110	Crescent City (krĕs'ĕnt) . . . . . . Ca.	41·46 N	124·13 W
121	Crescent City . . . . Fl.	29·26 N	81·35 W
109	Cresco (krĕs'kō) . . . . Ia.	43·23 N	92·07 W
115	Crested Butte (krĕst'ĕd būt) . . Co.	38·50 N	107·00 W
113	Crestline (krĕst-līn) Ca. (Los Angeles In.)	34·15 N	117·17 W
104	Crestline . . . . Oh.	40·50 N	82·40 W
113	Crestmore (krĕst'môr) Ca. (Los Angeles In.)	34·02 N	117·23 W
93	Creston (krĕs'tŭn) . . . . Can.	49·06 N	116·31 W
109	Creston . . . . Ia.	41·04 N	94·22 W
107	Creston . . . . Oh. (Cleveland In.)	40·59 N	81·54 W
120	Crestview (krĕst'vū) . . . . Fl.	30·44 N	86·35 W
107	Crestwood (krĕst'wŏŏd) Ky. (Louisville In.)	38·20 N	85·28 W
113	Crestwood . . . . Mo. (St. Louis In.)	38·33 N	90·23 W
107	Crete (krēt) . . . . . . Il. (Chicago In.)	41·26 N	87·38 W
117	Crete . . . . Ne.	40·38 N	96·56 W
164	Crete (I.) . . . . Grc. (In.)	35·15 N	24·30 E
163	Creus, Cabo de (C.) (kā'-bô-dĕ-krĕ-ōōs) . Sp.	42·16 N	3·18 E
160	Creuse (R.) (krûz) . . . . Fr.	46·51 N	0·49 E
113	Creve Coeur (krēv kōōr) Mo. (St. Louis In.)	38·40 N	90·27 W
163	Crevillente (krå-vê-lyĕn'tâ) . . . . Sp.	38·12 N	0·48 W
148	Crewe (krōō) . . . . Eng.	53·06 N	2·27 W
121	Crewe . . . . Va.	37·09 N	78·08 W
	Crimea P-Ov (Pen.), see Krymskiy		
158	Crimmitschau (krĭm'ĭt-shou) G.D.R.	50·49 N	12·22 E
116	Cripple Creek (krĭp''l) . . . . Co.	38·44 N	105·12 W
105	Crisfield (krĭs-fēld) . . . . Md.	38·00 N	75·50 W
216	Cristal, Monts de (Mts.) . . . Gabon	0·50 N	10·30 E
137	Cristina (krēs-tē'-nä) Braz. (Rio de Janeiro In.)	22·13 S	45·15 W
134	Cristobal Colón, Pico (Pk.) (pē'kô-krēs-tô'bäl-kō-lôn') . Col.	11·00 N	74·00 W
159	Crişul Alb (R.) (krē'shōōl ălb) Rom.	46·20 N	22·15 E
165	Črna (R.) (ts'r'nȧ) . . . . Yugo.	41·03 N	21·46 E
165	Črna Gora (Montenegro) (Reg.) (ts'r-nȧ-gō'rȧ) (mōn-tā-nā'grō) (mōn-tē-nē'grō) . Yugo.	42·55 N	18·52 E
164	Črnomelj (ch'r'nō-māl') . . . . . Yugo.	45·35 N	15·11 E
	Croatia (Reg.), see Hrvatska		
112	Crockett (krŏk'ĕt) Ca. (San Francisco In.)	38·03 N	122·14 W
119	Crockett . . . . Tx.	31·19 N	95·28 W
106	Crofton . . . . . . Md. (Baltimore In.)	39·01 N	76·43 W
108	Crofton . . . . Ne.	42·44 N	97·32 W
109	Croix, Lac la (L.) (krōō-ä' läk lä) . Can.-Mn.	48·19 N	91·53 W
204	Croker (I.) (krō'kȧ) . . . . Austl.	10·45 S	132·25 E
202	Cronulla (krō-nŭl'ȧ) Austl. (Sydney In.)	34·03 S	151·09 E
129	Crooked (I.) . . . . Ba.	22·45 N	74·10 W
99	Crooked (L.) . . . . Can.	48·25 N	56·05 W
92	Crooked (R.) . . . . Can.	54·30 N	122·55 W
110	Crooked (R.) . . . . Or.	44·07 N	120·30 W
117	Crooked Cr. (krōōk'ĕd) . . . . Il.	40·21 N	90·49 W
110	Crooked Cr. . . . . Or.	42·23 N	118·14 W
129	Crooked Island Passage (Str.) . Ba.	22·40 N	74·50 W
108	Crookston (krōōks'tŭn) . . . . Mn.	47·44 N	96·35 W
104	Crooksville (krōōks'vĭl) . . . . Oh.	39·45 N	82·05 W
109	Crosby (krôz'bĭ) . . . . Mn.	46·29 N	93·58 W
108	Crosby . . . . ND	48·55 N	103·18 W
119	Crosby . . . . Tx. (In.)	29·55 N	95·04 W
105	Cross (L.) (krŏs) . . . . Can.	44·55 N	76·55 W
119	Cross (L.) . . . . La.	32·33 N	93·58 W
215	Cross (R.) . . . . Nig.	5·35 N	8·05 E
120	Cross City . . . . Fl.	29·55 N	83·25 W
117	Crossett (krôs'ĕt) . . . . Ar.	33·08 N	92·00 W
128	Cross Hbr. . . . . Ba.	25·55 N	77·15 W
95	Cross Lake . . . . Can.	54·37 N	97·47 W
95	Cross L. Can.	54·45 N	97·30 W
106	Cross River Res. (krôs) NY (New York In.)	41·14 N	73·34 W
101	Cross Sd. (krŏs) . . . . Ak.	58·12 N	137·20 W
104	Crosswell (krôz'wĕl) . . . . Mi.	43·15 N	82·35 W
97	Crotch (R.) . . . . Can.	45·02 N	76·55 W
165	Crotone (krō-tô'nĕ) . . . . It.	39·05 N	17·08 E
106	Croton Falls Res. (krōtŭn) NY (New York In.)	41·22 N	73·44 W
106	Croton-on-Hudson (krō'tŭn-ŏn hŭd'sŭn) . NY (New York In.)	41·12 N	73·53 W
109	Crow (L.) . . . . Can.	49·13 N	93·29 W
111	Crow Agency . . . . Mt.	45·36 N	107·27 W
116	Crow Cr. Co.	41·08 N	104·25 W
108	Crow Creek Ind. Res. . . . . SD	44·17 N	99·17 W
111	Crow Ind. Res. (krō) . . . . Mt.	45·26 N	108·12 W
148	Crowle (kroul) . . . . Eng.	53·36 N	0·49 W
119	Crowley (krou'lē) . . . . La.	30·13 N	92·22 W
123	Crown Mtn. Vir. Is. (U. S. A.) (St. Thomas In.)	18·22 N	64·58 W
112	Crown Mtn. (kroun) Can. (Vancouver In.)	49·24 N	123·05 W
107	Crown Point (kroun point') In. (Chicago In.)	41·25 N	87·22 W
105	Crown Point . . . . NY	44·00 N	73·25 W
93	Crowsnest P. . . . . Can.	49·39 N	114·45 W
109	Crow Wing (R.) (krō) . . . . Mn.	44·50 N	94·01 W
109	Crow Wing (R.) . . . . Mn.	46·42 N	94·48 W
109	Crow Wing (R.), North Fork Mn.	45·16 N	94·28 W
109	Crow Wing (R.), South Fork Mn.	44·59 N	94·42 W
205	Croydon (kroi'dŭn) . . . . Austl.	18·15 S	142·15 E
202	Croydon . . . Austl. (Melbourne In.)	37·48 S	145·17 E
148	Croydon . . . . Eng. (London In.)	51·22 N	0·06 W
106	Croydon . . . Pa. (Philadelphia In.)	40·05 N	74·55 W
220	Crozet Is. (krō-zĕ') . . . . Ind. O.	46·20 S	51·30 E
128	Cruces (krōō'sås) . . . . Cuba	22·20 N	80·20 W
118	Cruces, Arroyo de (är-rŏ'yô-dĕ-krōō'sĕs) . Mex.	26·17 N	104·32 W
118	Cruillas (krōō-ēl'yäs) . . . . Mex.	24·45 N	98·31 W
128	Cruz, Cabo (C.) (kȧ'-bô-krōōz) Cuba	19·50 N	77·45 W
128	Cruz, Cayo (I.) (kä'yō-krōōz) Cuba	22·15 N	77·50 W
136	Cruz Alta (krōōz äl'tä) . . . . . . Braz.	28·41 S	54·02 W
136	Cruz del Eje (krōō's-dĕl-ĕ-kĕ) . Arg.	30·46 S	64·45 W
137	Cruzeiro (krōō-zā'rōō) Braz. (Rio de Janeiro In.)	22·36 S	44·57 W
134	Cruzeiro do Sul (krōō-zā'rōō dōō sōōl) . Braz.	7·34 S	72·40 W
89	Crysler . . . . Can. (Ottawa In.)	45·13 N	75·09 W
118	Crystal City (krĭs'tăl sĭ'tĭ) . . . . Tx.	28·40 N	99·90 W
109	Crystal Falls (krĭs'tăl fôls) . . . . Mi.	46·06 N	88·21 W
107	Crystal Lake (krĭs'tăl lăk) Il. (Chicago In.)	42·15 N	88·18 W
120	Crystal Springs (krĭs'tăl sprĭngz) Ms.	31·58 N	90·20 W
112	Crystal Sprs. Ca. (San Francisco In.)	37·31 N	122·26 W
159	Csongrád (chôn'gräd) . . . . . . Hung.	46·42 N	20·09 E
159	Csorna (chôr'nä) . . . . Hung.	47·39 N	17·11 E
135	Cúa (kōō'ä) . . . . Ven. (In.)	10·10 N	66·54 W
125	Cuajimalpa (kwä-hê-mäl'pä Mex. (In.)	19·21 N	99·18 W
124	Cuale, Sierra del (Mts.) (sē-ĕ'r-rä-dĕl-kwä'lĕ) . Mex.	20·20 N	104·58 W
216	Cuamato (kwä-mä'tō) . . . . Ang.	17·05 S	15·09 E
216	Cuando (kwän'dō) . . . . Ang.	16·32 S	22·07 E
216	Cuando (R.) . . . . Ang.	16·50 S	22·40 E
216	Cuangar . . . . Ang.	17·36 S	18·39 E
216	Cuango (Kwango) (R.) (kwäŋ'gō) . Afr.	6·35 S	16·50 E
216	Cuanza (R.) (kwän'zä) . . . . Ang.	9·05 S	13·15 E
136	Cuarto Saladillo (R.) (kwär'tō-sä-lä-dē'l-yô) . Arg.	33·00 S	63·25 W
129	Cuatro Caminos (kwä'trō-kä-mē'nōs) . Cuba (In.)	23·01 N	82·13 W
118	Cuatro Ciénegas (kwä'trō syā'nȧ-gäs) . Mex.	26·59 N	102·03 W
126	Cuauhtemoc (kwä-ōō-tē-mŏk') Mex.	15·43 N	91·57 W
124	Cuautepec (kwä-ōō-tĕ-pĕk) . . Mex.	16·41 N	99·04 W
124	Cuautepec . . . . Mex.	20·01 N	98·19 W
125	Cuautitlán (kwä-ōō-tēt-län') Mex. (In.)	19·40 N	99·12 W
124	Cuautla (kwä-ōō'tlȧ) . . . . Mex.	18·47 N	98·57 W
162	Cuba (kōō'bȧ) . . . . Port.	38·10 N	7·55 W
123	Cuba (kū'bȧ) . . . . N. A.	22·00 N	79·00 W
135	Cubagua, Isla (I.) (ē's-lä-kōō-bä'gwä) . Ven. (In.)	10·48 N	64·10 W
216	Cubango (Okavango) (R.) (kōō-bäŋ'gō) . Ang.-Namibia	17·10 S	18·20 E
94	Cub Hills (kŭb) . . . . Can.	54·20 N	104·30 W
113	Cucamonga (kōō-kȧ-mōŋ'gȧ) Ca. (Los Angeles In.)	34·05 N	117·35 W
212	Cuchi . . . . Ang.	14·40 S	16·50 E
118	Cuchillo Parado (kōō-chē'lyô pä-rä'dō) . Mex.	29·26 N	104·52 W
126	Cuchumatanes, Sierra de los (Mts.) Guat.	15·35 N	91·10 W
134	Cúcuta (kōō'kōō-tä) . . . . Col.	7·56 N	72·30 W
107	Cudahy (kŭd'ȧ-hī) Wi. (Milwaukee In.)	42·57 N	87·52 W
185	Cuddalore (kŭd ȧ-lōr') . . . . . . India	11·49 N	79·46 E
185	Cuddapah (kŭd'ȧ-pä) . . . . . . India	14·31 N	78·52 E
204	Cue (kū) . . . . Austl.	27·30 S	118·10 E
162	Cuellar (kwā'lyär') . . . . Sp.	41·24 N	4·15 W
134	Cuenca (kwĕn'kä) . . . . Ec.	2·52 S	78·54 W
162	Cuenca . . . . Sp.	40·05 N	2·07 W
162	Cuenca, Sierra de (Mts.) (sē-ĕ'r-rä-dĕ-kwĕ'n-kä) . Sp.	40·02 N	1·50 W
118	Cuencame (kwĕn-kä-mā') . . . . Mex.	24·52 N	103·42 W
124	Cuerámaro (kwā-rä'mä-rō) . . . Mex.	20·39 N	101·44 W
125	Cuernavaca (kwĕr-nä-vä'kä) Mex. (In.)	18·55 N	99·15 W
119	Cuero (kwā'rō) . . . . Tx.	29·05 N	97·16 W
124	Cuetzalá del Progreso (kwĕt-zä-lä dĕl prō-grā'sō) . Mex.	18·07 N	99·51 W

PRONOUNCING INDEX Cuetzalan del Progreso — Dar'a 273

Page	Name Pronunciation Region	Lat. °'	Long. °'
125	Cuetzalan del Progreso (kwĕt-zä-län dĕl prō-grā'sō). Mex.	20·02 N	97·33 W
162	Cuevas del Almanzora (kwĕ'väs-dĕl-äl-män-zō-rä)..Sp.	37·19 N	1·54 W
164	Cuglieri (ko͞o-lyā'rē)..........It.	40·11 N	8·37 E
135	Cuiabá (ko͞o-yä-bä')........Braz.	15·33 S	56·03 W
125	Cuicatlán (kwē-kä-tlän')......Mex.	17·46 N	96·57 W
126	Cuilapa (ko͞o-ē-lä'pä).......Guat.	14·16 N	90·20 W
154	Cuillin Sd..................Scot.	57·09 N	6·20 W
216	Cuilo (R.)..................Ang.	9·15 S	19·30 E
216	Cuito (R.) (ko͞o-ē'tō)........Ang.	14·15 S	19·00 E
124	Cuitzeo (kwēt'zā-ō).........Mex.	19·57 N	101·11 W
124	Cuitzeo, Laguna de (L.) (lä-ō͞o'nä-dĕ-kwēt'zā-ō). Mex.	19·58 N	101·05 W
129	Cul de Sac (Val.) (ko͞o'l-dĕ-sä'k) Dom. Rep.-Hai.	18·35 N	72·05 W
123	Culebra (I.) (ko͞o-lā'brä) P. R. (Puerto Rico In.)	18·19 N	65·32 W
149	Culemborg Neth. (Amsterdam In.)	51·57 N	5·14 E
205	Culgoa (R.) (kŭl-gō'ȧ)......Austl.	29·21 S	147·00 E
122	Culiacán (ko͞o-lyä-kä'n)......Mex.	24·45 N	107·30 W
196	Culion (ko͞o-lē-ōn')..........Phil.	11·43 N	119·58 E
162	Cúllar de Baza (ko͞o'l-yär-dĕ-bä'zä).Sp.	37·36 N	2·35 W
163	Cullera (ko͞o-lyā'rä)..........Sp.	39·12 N	0·15 W
213	Cullinan (ko͝o'lĭ-nàn)......S. Afr. (Johannesburg & Pretoria In.)	25·41 S	28·32 E
120	Cullman (kŭl'măn)............Ala.	34·10 N	86·50 W
105	Culpeper (kŭl'pĕp-ēr).........Va.	38·30 N	77·55 W
89	Culross (kŭl'rôs) Can. (Winnipeg In.)	49·43 N	97·54 W
104	Culver (kŭl'vēr)..............In.	41·15 N	86·25 W
113	Culver City Ca. (Los Angeles In.)	34·00 N	118·23 W
135	Cumaná (ko͞o-mä-nä') Ven. (In.)	10·28 N	64·10 W
89	Cumberland (kŭm'bēr-lănd) Can. (Ottawa In.)	45·31 N	75·25 W
105	Cumberland................Md.	39·40 N	78·40 W
112	Cumberland.....Wa. (Seattle In.)	47·17 N	121·55 W
109	Cumberland.................Wi.	45·31 N	92·01 W
120	Cumberland (R.)...........U. S.	36·45 N	85·33 W
120	Cumberland, L..............Ky.	36·55 N	85·20 W
205	Cumberland Is............Austl.	20·29 S	149·46 E
91	Cumberland Pen...........Can.	65·59 N	64·05 W
120	Cumberland Plat...........Tn.	35·25 N	85·30 W
91	Cumberland Sd.............Can.	65·27 N	65·44 W
134	Cundinamarca (Dept.) (ko͞on-dē-nä-mä'r-kä). Col. (In.)	4·57 N	74·27 W
125	Cunduacán (ko͞on-do͞o-ä-kän') Mex.	18·04 N	93·23 W
216	Cunene (Kunene) (R.) Ang.-Namibia	17·05 S	12·35 E
164	Cuneo (ko͞o'nā-ō).............It.	44·24 N	7·31 E
137	Cunha (ko͞o'nyȧ) Braz. (Rio de Janeiro In.)	23·05 S	44·56 W
203	Cunnamulla (kŭn-ȧ-mŭl-ȧ)..Austl.	28·00 S	145·55 E
122	Cupula, Pico (Mtn.) (pē'kō-ko͞o'po͞o-lä). Mex.	24·45 N	111·10 W
124	Cuquío (ko͞o-kē'ō)..........Mex.	20·55 N	103·03 W
134	Curaçao (ko͞o-rä-sä'ō) (I.) Neth. Antilles	12·12 N	68·58 W
136	Curacautín (kä-rä-käo͞o-tē'n). Chile	38·25 S	71·53 W
137	Curacaví (ko͞o-rä-kä-vē') Chile (Santiago In.)	33·23 S	71·09 W
137	Curaumilla, Punta (Pt.) (ko͞o-rou-mē'lyä). Chile (Santiago In.)	33·05 S	71·44 W
137	Curepto (ko͞o-rĕp-tō) Chile (Santiago In.)	35·06 S	72·02 W
137	Curicó (ko͞o-rē-kō') Chile (Santiago In.)	34·57 S	71·14 W
137	Curicó (Prov.). Chile (Santiago In.)	34·55 S	71·15 W
136	Curitiba (ko͞o-rē-tē'bȧ)......Braz.	25·20 S	49·15 W
128	Curly Cut Cays (Is.).........Ba.	23·40 N	77·40 W
135	Currais Novos (ko͞or-rä'ēs nŏ-vōs). Braz.	6·02 S	36·39 W
89	Curran (kü-räN') Can. (Ottawa In.)	45·30 N	74·59 W
128	Current (I.) (kŭ-rĕnt)........Ba.	25·20 N	76·50 W
117	Current (R.) (kûr'ĕnt).......Mo.	37·18 N	91·21 W
213	Currie, Mt. (cŭ-rē) S. Afr. (Natal In.)	30·28 S	29·23 E
121	Currituck Sd. (kûr'ĭ-tŭk).....NC	36·27 N	75·42 W
165	Curtea de Argeş (ko͝or'tĕ-ȧ dĕ är'zhĕsh). Rom.	45·09 N	24·40 E
116	Curtis (kûr'tĭs)..............Ne.	40·36 N	100·29 W
205	Curtis (I.)................Austl.	23·38 S	151·43 E
107	Curtisville (kûr'tĭs-vĭl) Pa. (Pittsburgh In.)	40·38 N	79·50 W
135	Curuá (R.) (ko͞o-ro͞o-ä')......Braz.	6·26 S	54·39 W
165	Čurug (cho͞o'ro͝og).........Yugo.	45·27 N	20·26 E
216	Curunga...................Ang.	12·51 S	21·12 E
134	Curupira, Serra (Mts.) (sĕr'rȧ ko͞o-ro͞o-pē'rȧ) Braz.-Ven.	1·00 N	65·30 W
135	Cururupu (ko͞o-ro͞o-ro͞o-po͞o'). Braz.	1·40 S	44·56 W
136	Curuzú Cuatiá (ko͞o-ro͞o-zo͞o' kwä-tē-ä'). Arg.	29·45 S	57·58 W
135	Curvelo (ko͝or-vĕl'ō)........Braz.	18·47 S	44·14 W
117	Cushing (kŭsh'ĭng)...........Ok.	35·58 N	96·46 W
160	Cusset (kü-sĕ').............Fr.	46·08 N	3·29 E
108	Custer (kŭs'tēr).............SD	43·46 N	103·36 W
112	Custer......Wa. (Vancouver In.)	48·55 N	122·39 W
111	Custer Battlefield Nat'l. Mon. (kŭs'tēr băt''l-fēld). Mt.	45·44 N	107·15 W
111	Cut Bank (kŭt bănk).........Mt.	48·38 N	112·19 W
120	Cuthbert (kŭth'bērt).........Ga.	31·47 N	84·48 W
184	Cuttack (kŭ-tăk')..........India	20·38 N	85·53 E
124	Cutzamala (R.) (ko͞o-tzä-mä-lä') Mex.	18·57 N	100·41 W
124	Cutzamalá de Pinzón (ko͞o-tzä-mä-lä'dĕ-pēn-zō'n). Mex.	18·28 N	100·36 W
216	Cuvo (R.) (ko͞o'vō).........Ang.	10·55 S	14·00 E
158	Cuxhaven (ko͝oks' hä-fĕn)..F.R.G.	53·51 N	8·43 E
107	Cuyahoga Falls Oh. (Cleveland In.)	41·08 N	81·29 W
107	Cuyahoga R. (kī-ȧ-hō'gȧ) Oh. (Cleveland In.)	41·22 N	81·38 W
114	Cuyapaire Ind. Res. (kū-yá-pâr) Ca.	32·46 N	116·20 W
196	Cuyo Is. (ko͞o'yō)...........Phil.	10·54 N	120·08 E
126	Cuyotenango (ko͞o-yō-tĕ-näŋ'gō) Guat.	14·30 N	91·35 W
135	Cuyuni (R.) (ko͞o-yo͞o'nē) Guy.-Ven.	6·40 N	60·44 W
124	Cuyutlán (ko͞o-yo͞o-tlän')....Mex.	18·54 N	104·04 W
134	Cuzco.....................Peru	13·36 S	71·52 W
104	Cynthiana (sĭn-thĭ-ăn'ȧ)......Ky.	38·20 N	84·20 W
113	Cypress (sī'prĕs) Ca. (Los Angeles In.)	33·50 N	118·03 W
94	Cypress Hills..............Can.	49·40 N	110·20 W
94	Cypress L..................Can.	49·28 N	109·43 W
182	Cyprus (sī'prŭs)............Asia	35·00 N	31·00 E
	Cyrenaica (Prov.), see Barqah		
146	Czechoslovakia (chĕk'ō-slō-vä'kĭ-ȧ). Eur.	49·28 N	16·00 E
159	Czersk (chĕrsk).............Pol.	53·47 N	17·58 E
159	Czestochowa (chĕN-stō kô'vȧ). Pol.	50·49 N	19·10 E

D

Page	Name Pronunciation Region	Lat. °'	Long. °'
192	Da'an (dä-än).............China	45·25 N	124·22 E
210	Dabakala (dä-bä-kä'lä) Ivory Coast	8·16 N	4·36 W
192	Daba Shan (Mts.) (dä-bä shän) China	32·25 N	108·20 E
134	Dabeiba (dȧ-bā'bä).....Col. (In.)	7·01 N	76·16 W
193	Dabie Shan (Mts.) (dä-bĭĕ shän) China	31·40 N	114·50 E
215	Dabnou...................Niger	14·09 N	5·22 E
112	Dabob B. (dā'bŏb) Wa. (Seattle In.)	47·50 N	122·50 W
214	Dabola....................Gui.	10·45 N	11·07 W
159	Dabrowa (dŏN-brō'vȧ).......Pol.	53·37 N	23·18 E
184	Dacca (dä'kä) (dăk'ȧ)......Bngl.	23·45 N	90·29 E
191	Dachang (dä-chäŋ) China (Shanghai In.)	31·18 N	121·25 E
190	Dachangshan Dao (I.) (dä-chäŋ-shän dou). China	39·21 N	122·31 E
149	Dachau (dä'кou) F.R.G. (Munich In.)	48·16 N	11·26 E
89	Dacotah (dȧ-kō'tȧ) Can. (Winnipeg In.)	49·52 N	97·38 W
121	Dade City (dād).........Fl. (In.)	28·22 N	82·09 W
120	Dadeville (dād'vĭl)...........Al.	32·48 N	85·44 W
184	Dādra & Nagar Haveli (Union Ter.). India	20·00 N	73·00 E
193	Dadu (R.) (dä-do͞o)........China	29·20 N	103·30 E
197	Daet (Mtn.) (dä'ĕt)....Phil. (In.)	14·07 N	122·59 E
95	Dafoe (R.)................Can.	55·50 N	95·50 W
113	Dafter (dăf'tēr) Mi. (Sault Ste. Marie In.)	46·21 N	84·26 W
214	Dagana (dä-gä'nä)........Senegal	16·31 N	15·30 W
215	Dagana (Reg.)..............Chad.	12·20 N	15·15 E
191	Dagang (dä-gäŋ) China (Canton In.)	22·48 N	113·24 E
166	Dagda (däg'dȧ).........Sov. Un.	56·04 N	27·30 E
148	Dagenham (dăg'ĕn-ăm) Eng. (London In.)	51·32 N	0·09 E
171	Dagestan (Reg.) (dä-gĕs-tän') Sov. Un.	43·40 N	46·10 E
114	Daggett (dăg'ĕt)..............Ca.	34·50 N	116·52 W
190	Dagu (dä-go͞o).............China	39·00 N	117·42 E
190	Dagu (R.)..................China	36·29 N	120·06 E
197	Dagupan (dä-go͞o'pän)..Phil. (In.)	16·02 N	120·20 E
190	Daheishan Dao (I.) (dä-hā-shän dou). China	37·57 N	120·37 E
	Da Hinggan Ling, see Greater Khingan Range		
161	Dahl (däl).....F.R.G. (Ruhr In.)	51·18 N	7·33 E
211	Dahlak Arch. (Is.)..........Eth.	15·45 N	40·30 E
	Dahomey, see Benin		
190	Daibu (dī-bo͞o)............China	31·22 N	119·29 E
195	Daigo (dī-gō)....Jap. (Ōsaka In.)	34·57 N	135·49 E
162	Daimiel Manzanares (dī-myĕl' män-zä-nä'rĕs). Sp.	39·05 N	3·36 W
112	Dairy (R.) (dâr'ĭ) Or. (Portland In.)	45·33 N	123·04 W
112	Dairy (R.) East Fk. Or. (Portland In.)	45·40 N	123·03 W
195	Dai-Sen (Mtn.) (dī'sĕn')......Jap.	35·22 N	133·35 E
195	Dai-Tenjo-dake (Mtn.) (dī-tĕn'jō dä-кä). Jap.	36·21 N	137·38 E
195	Daitō..........Jap. (Ōsaka In.)	34·42 N	135·38 E
193	Daiyun Shan (Mtn.) (dī-yo͞on shän). China	25·40 N	118·08 E
129	Dajabón (dä-кä-bō'n)..Dom. Rep.	19·35 N	71·40 W
204	Dajarra (dȧ-jăr'ȧ)..........Austl.	21·45 S	139·30 E
214	Dakar (dȧ-kär').........Senegal	14·40 N	17·26 W
215	Dakouraoua.................Niger	13·58 N	6·15 E
156	Dalälven (R.)..............Swe.	60·26 N	15·50 E
216	Dalatando.................Ang.	9·18 S	14·54 E
203	Dalby (dôl'bē)............Austl.	27·10 S	151·15 E
106	Dalcour (dăl-kour) La. (New Orleans In.)	29·49 N	89·59 W
156	Dale (dä'lĕ)................Nor.	60·34 N	5·46 E
120	Dale Hollow (L.) (dāl hŏl'ō)..Tn.	36·33 N	85·03 W
89	Dalemead (dä'lĕ-mēd) Can. (Calgary In.)	50·53 N	113·38 W
156	Dalen (dä'lĕn)...............Nor.	59·28 N	8·01 E
218	Daleside (dāl'sīd).........S. Afr. (Johannesburg & Pretoria In.)	26·30 S	28·03 E
89	Dalesville (dālz'vĭl) Can. (Montreal In.)	45·42 N	74·23 W
204	Daley (L.) (dā'lĭ)..........Austl.	14·15 S	131·15 E
204	Daley Waters (dā lē).......Austl.	16·15 S	133·30 E
116	Dalhart (dăl'härt)............Tx.	36·04 N	102·32 W
98	Dalhousie (dăl-ho͞o'zē).......Can.	48·04 N	66·23 W
191	Dali (dä-lē)...China (Canton In.)	23·27 N	113·06 E
188	Dali......................China	26·00 N	100·08 E
188	Dali......................China	35·00 N	109·38 E
190	Dalian Wan (B.) (dä-lĭĕn wän) China	38·55 N	121·50 E
162	Dalías (dä-lē'äs).............Sp.	36·49 N	2·50 W
101	Dall (I.) (dăl)..............Ak.	54·50 N	133·10 W
110	Dallas (dăl'lăs).............Or.	44·55 N	123·20 W
108	Dallas.....................SD	43·13 N	99·34 W
113	Dallas Tx. (Dallas, Fort Worth In.)	32·45 N	96·48 W
110	Dalles Dam.................Or.	45·36 N	121·08 W
92	Dall I......................Ak.	54·50 N	132·55 W
164	Dalmacija (Reg.) (däl-mä'tsē-yä) Yugo.	43·25 N	16·37 E
173	Dalnerechensk..........Sov. Un.	46·07 N	133·21 E
214	Daloa...............Ivory Coast	6·53 N	6·27 W
211	Dalqū (dĕl'gō)..............Sud.	20·07 N	30·41 E
89	Dalroy (dăl'roi). Can. (Calgary In.)	51·07 N	113·39 W
205	Dalrymple, Mt. (dăl'rĭm-p'l) Austl.	21·14 S	148·46 E
120	Dalton (dôl'tŭn).............Ga.	34·46 N	84·58 W
213	Dalton (dŏl'tŏn).S. Afr. (Natal In.)	29·21 S	30·41 E
112	Daly City (dā'lē) Ca. (San Francisco In.)	37·42 N	122·27 W
135	Dam (däm).................Sur.	4·36 N	54·54 W
184	Damān....................India	20·32 N	72·53 E
218	Damanhūr (dä-män-ho͞or') Egypt (Nile In.)	30·59 N	30·31 E
197	Damar, Pulau (I.)..........Indon.	7·15 S	129·15 E
215	Damara...........Cen. Afr. Rep.	4·58 N	18·42 E
212	Damaraland (Reg.) (dă'nȧ-rȧ-lănd). Namibia	22·15 S	16·15 E
128	Damas Cays (Is.) (dä'mäs)..Ba.	23·50 N	79·50 W
	Damascus, see Dimashq		
171	Damavand (Mtn.).........Iran	36·05 N	52·05 E
216	Damba (däm'bä)...........Ang.	6·41 S	15·08 E
129	Dame Marie, Cap (C.) (dām mȧrē'). Hai.	18·35 N	74·50 W
186	Dāmghān (dām-gän')........Iran	35·50 N	54·15 E
190	Daming (dä-mĭŋ)...........China	36·15 N	115·09 E
161	Dammartin-en-Goële (däN-mär-tăN-äN-gō-ĕl'). Fr. (Paris In.)	49·03 N	2·40 E
197	Dampier, Selat (Str.) (dăm'pēr) Indon.	0·40 S	131·15 E
204	Dampier Arch. (däN-pyâr'). Austl.	20·15 S	116·25 E
204	Dampier Land (Penin).....Austl.	17·30 S	122·25 E
121	Dan (R.) (dăn)..............NC	36·26 N	79·40 W
211	Danakil Pln................Eth.	12·45 N	41·01 E
214	Danané............Ivory Coast	7·16 N	8·09 W
193	Da Nang (Tourane)..........Viet.	16·08 N	108·22 E
106	Danbury (dăn'bēr-ĭ) Ct. (New York In.)	41·23 N	73·27 W
148	Danbury......Eng. (London In.)	51·42 N	0·34 E
119	Danbury..............Tx. (In.)	29·14 N	95·22 W
202	Dandenong (dăn'dē-nông) Austl. (Melbourne In.)	37·59 S	145·13 E
192	Dandong (dän-dôŋ)........China	40·10 N	124·30 E
148	Dane (R.) (dān)............Eng.	53·11 N	2·14 W
214	Danea.....................Gui.	11·27 N	13·12 W
98	Danforth..................Me.	45·38 N	67·53 W
211	Dangla....................Eth.	11·17 N	37·00 E
215	Dan Gora...................Nig.	11·30 N	8·09 E
190	Dangtu (däŋ-to͞o)..........China	31·35 N	118·28 E
214	Dani...............Upper Volta	13·43 N	0·10 W
121	Dania (dā'nĭ-ȧ)..........Fl. (In.)	26·01 N	80·10 W
166	Danilov (dä'nē-lôf)......Sov. Un.	58·12 N	40·08 E
165	Danilov Grad (dä'nē-lôf'gräd) Yugo.	42·31 N	19·08 E
217	Danissa Hills...............Ken.	3·20 N	40·55 E
166	Dankov (dän'kôf)........Sov. Un.	53·17 N	39·09 E
126	Danlí (dän'lē).............Hond.	14·02 N	86·35 W
105	Dannemora (dăn-ē-mō'rȧ).....NY	44·45 N	73·45 W
213	Dannhauser (dän'hou-zēr) S. Afr. (Natal In.)	28·07 S	30·04 E
105	Dansville (dănz'vĭl)..........NY	42·30 N	77·40 W
167	Danube, Mouths of the (dăn'ub) Rom.	45·13 N	29·37 E
99	Danvers (dăn'vērz).....Ma. (In.)	42·34 N	70·57 W
112	Danville (dăn'vĭl) Ca. (San Francisco In.)	37·49 N	122·00 W
104	Danville.....................Il.	40·10 N	87·35 W
104	Danville....................In.	39·45 N	86·30 W
104	Danville....................Ky.	37·35 N	84·50 W
105	Danville....................Pa.	41·00 N	76·35 W
121	Danville....................Va.	36·35 N	79·24 W
193	Dan Xian (dän shyĕn).....China	19·30 N	109·38 E
190	Danyang (dän-yäŋ)........China	32·01 N	119·32 E
150	Danzig, G. of (dăn'tsĭk).......Pol.	54·41 N	19·01 E
193	Dao Xian (dou shyĕn)......China	25·35 N	111·27 E
183	Daphnae (Ruins) Egypt (Palestine In.)	30·43 N	32·12 E
214	Dapango...........Upper Volta	10·52 N	0·12 E
190	Daqin Dao (I.) (dä-chyĭn dou) China	38·18 N	120·50 E
183	Dar'ā........Syria (Palestine In.)	32·37 N	36·07 E

ng-sing; ŋ-baŋk; N-nasalized n; nŏd; cŏmmit; ōld; ôbey; ôrder; fo͞od; fo͝ot; ou-out; s-soft; sh-dish; th-thin; pūre; ůnite; ûrn; stŭd; circŭs; ü-as "y" in study; '-indeterminate vowel.

274 Darabani — Derby

PRONOUNCING INDEX

Page	Name Pronunciation Region	Lat. °′	Long. °′
159	Darabani (dă-ră-bän'ĭ)......Rom.	48·13 N	26·38 E
210	Daraj..................Libya	30·12 N	10·14 E
218	Darāw (dȧ-rä'ōō) Egypt (Nile In.)	24·24 N	32·56 E
184	Darbhanga (dŭr-bŭŋ'gä)....India	26·03 N	85·09 E
106	Darby (där'bĭ) Pa. (Philadelphia In.)	39·55 N	75·16 W
129	Darby (I.)..................Ba.	23·50 N	76·20 W
	Dardanelles (Str.), see Çanakkale Boğazı		
217	Dar-es-Salaam (där ĕs sȧ-läm') Tan.	6·48 S	39·17 E
211	Dārfūr (Prov.) (där-fōōr')....Sud.	13·21 N	23·46 E
187	Dargai (dŭr-gä'ē) Pak. (Khyber Pass In.)	34·35 N	72·00 E
210	D'Arguin, Cap (C.)....Mauritania	20·28 N	17·46 W
134	Darien (dā-rĭ-ĕn').......Col. (In.)	3·56 N	76·30 W
106	Darien (dâ-rē-ĕn') Ct. (New York In.)	41·04 N	73·28 W
126	Darién, Cordillera de (Mts.)..Nic.	13·00 N	85·42 W
134	Darién, Golfo del (G.) (gôl-fô-dĕl-dä-rĭ-ĕn').N. A.-S. A.	9·36 N	77·54 W
127	Darien, Serrania del (Ra.) (sĕr-ä-nē'ä dĕl dä-rē-ĕn').Pan.	8·13 N	77·28 W
184	Darjeeling (dŭr-jē'lĭng)......India	27·05 N	88·16 E
108	Darling (L.) (där'lĭng)........ND	48·35 N	101·25 W
203	Darling (R.)..............Austl.	31·50 S	143·20 E
203	Darling Downs (Reg.)......Austl.	27·22 S	150·50 E
204	Darling Ra.................Austl.	30·30 S	115·45 E
154	Darlington (där'lĭng-tŭn)....Eng.	54·32 N	1·35 W
121	Darlington..................SC	34·15 N	79·52 W
109	Darlington..................Wi.	42·41 N	90·06 W
158	Darłowo (där-lô'vô)..........Pol.	54·26 N	16·23 E
158	Darmstadt (därm'shtät)...F.R.G.	49·53 N	8·40 E
211	Darnah.....................Libya	32·44 N	22·41 E
101	Darnley B. (därn'lē).........Ak.	70·00 N	124·00 W
162	Daroca (dä-rō-kä)............Sp.	41·08 N	1·24 W
154	Dartmoor (därt'mōōr).......Eng.	50·35 N	4·05 W
98	Dartmouth (därt'mŭth).....Can.	44·40 N	63·34 W
154	Dartmouth..................Eng.	50·33 N	3·28 W
197	Daru I. (dä-rōō).....Pap. N. Gui.	9·04 S	143·21 E
164	Daruvar (där'rōō-vär)......Yugo.	45·37 N	17·16 E
148	Darwen (där'wĕn)..........Eng.	53·42 N	2·28 W
204	Darwin (där'wĭn)..........Austl.	12·25 S	131·00 E
136	Darwin, Cordillera (Mts.) (kôr-dēl-yĕ'rä-där'wên) Chile-Arg.	54·40 S	69·30 W
186	Daryācheh-ye Rezā'īyeh (L.).Iran	38·07 N	45·17 E
162	Das Alturas, Serra (Mts.) (sĕ'r-rä-däs-äl-tōō'räs).Port.	40·43 N	7·48 W
112	Dash Point (dăsh) Wa. (Seattle In.)	47·19 N	122·25 W
186	Dasht (R.) (dŭsht)..........Pak.	25·30 N	62·30 E
186	Dasht-e Kavīr Des. (dŭsht-ē-ka-vēr').Iran	34·43 N	53·30 E
186	Dasht-e-Lūt (Des.) (dă'sht-ē-lōōt) Iran	31·47 N	58·38 E
197	Dasol B. (dä-sōl')......Phil. (In.)	15·53 N	119·40 E
193	Datian Ding (Mtn.) (dä-tĭĕn dĭŋ) China	22·25 N	111·20 E
192	Datong (dä-tôŋ)............China	40·00 N	113·30 E
184	Dattapukur..........India (In.)	22·45 N	88·32 E
161	Datteln (dät'tĕln) F.R.G. (Ruhr In.)	51·39 N	7·20 E
196	Datu, Tandjung (C.)......Indon.	2·08 N	110·15 E
191	Datuan (dä-tůän) China (Shanghai In.)	30·57 N	121·43 E
157	Daugava (R.)..........Sov. Un.	56·40 N	24·40 E
166	Daugavpils (dä'ōō-gäv-pêls) Sov .Un.	55·52 N	25·32 E
95	Dauphin (dô'fĭn)...........Can.	51·09 N	100·00 W
95	Dauphin L..................Can.	51·17 N	99·48 W
185	Dāvangere................India	14·30 N	75·55 E
197	Davao (dä'vä-ō)..........Phil.	7·05 N	125·30 E
197	Davao G....................Phil.	6·30 N	125·45 E
109	Davenport (dăv'ĕn-pōrt).......Ia.	41·34 N	90·38 W
205	Davenport..........N. Z. (In.)	37·29 S	174·47 E
110	Davenport..................Wa.	47·39 N	118·07 W
127	David (dä-vēdh')...........Pan.	8·27 N	82·27 W
108	David City (dā'vĭd)..........Ne.	41·15 N	97·10 W
159	David-Gorodok (dȧ-vēt' gô-rō'dôk) Sov. Un.	52·02 N	27·14 E
110	Davidson Lake (Res.)........Wa.	46·20 N	122·10 W
117	Davis (dā'vĭs)...............Ok.	34·34 N	97·08 W
105	Davis........................WV	39·15 N	79·25 W
110	Davis L......................Or.	43·38 N	121·43 W
114	Davis Mts....................Tx.	30·45 N	104·17 W
220	Davis Sea...................Ant.	66·00 S	92·00 E
75	Davis Str....................Can.	66·00 N	60·00 W
158	Davos (dä'vōs)............Switz.	46·47 N	9·50 E
211	Dawa (R.)...................Eth.	4·34 N	41·34 E
186	Dawāsir, Wādī ad (R.).Sau. Ar.	20·48 N	44·07 E
190	Dawen (R.) (dä-wŭn)......China	35·58 N	116·53 E
148	Dawley (dô'lĭ)...............Eng.	52·38 N	2·28 W
196	Dawna Ra. (dô'nȧ)..........Bur.	17·02 N	98·01 E
100	Dawson (dô'sŭn)............Can.	64·04 N	139·22 W
120	Dawson......................Ga.	31·45 N	84·29 W
108	Dawson......................Mn.	44·54 N	96·03 W
203	Dawson (R.)...............Austl.	24·20 S	149·45 E
95	Dawson B....................Can.	52·55 N	100·50 W
93	Dawson Creek..............Can.	55·46 N	120·14 W
101	Dawson Ra..................Can.	62·15 N	138·10 W
120	Dawson Springs.............Ky.	37·10 N	87·40 W
190	Dawu (dä-wōō)............China	31·33 N	114·07 E
160	Dax (dȧks)....................Fr.	43·42 N	1·06 W
193	Daxian (dä-shyĕn).........China	31·12 N	107·30 E
192	Daxing (dä-shyĭŋ).....China (In.)	39·44 N	116·19 E
190	Dayiqiao (dä-yē-chyou)....China	31·43 N	120·40 E
186	Dayr az Zawr (dâ-ēr'ez-zōr')..Syr.	35·15 N	40·01 E
218	Dayrūţ.........Egypt (Nile In.)	27·33 N	30·48 E
107	Dayton (dā'tŭn) Ky. (Cincinnati In.)	39·07 N	84·28 W
116	Dayton.......................NM	32·44 N	104·23 W
104	Dayton.......................Oh	39·45 N	84·15 W
120	Dayton.......................Tn.	35·30 N	85·00 W
119	Dayton.......................Tx.	30·03 N	94·53 W
110	Dayton.......................Wa.	46·18 N	117·59 W
121	Daytona Beach (dā-tō'nȧ).....Fl.	29·11 N	81·02 W
193	Dayu (dä-yōō)............China	25·20 N	114·20 E
190	Da Yunhe (Grand Canal) (dä yōōn-hŭ).China	34·23 N	117·57 E
105	Dayville (dā'vĭl)..............Ct.	41·50 N	71·55 W
212	De Aar (dē-är')..........S. Afr.	30·45 S	24·05 E
108	Dead (L.) (dĕd).............Mn.	46·28 N	96·00 W
183	Dead Sea Isr.-Jordan (Palestine In.)	31·30 N	35·30 E
108	Deadwood (dĕd'wōōd)........SD	44·23 N	103·43 W
105	Deal Island (dēl-ī'lănd)......Md.	38·10 N	75·55 W
92	Dean (R.) (dēn).............Can.	52·45 N	126·00 W
92	Dean Chan...................Can.	52·33 N	127·13 W
136	Deán Funes (dĕ-ȧ'n-fōō-nĕs).Arg.	30·26 S	64·12 W
107	Dearborn (dēr'bŭrn) Mi. (Detroit In.)	42·18 N	83·15 W
154	Dearg, Ben (Mtn.) (bĕn dŭrg) Scot.	57·48 N	4·59 W
100	Dease Str. (dēz).............Can.	68·50 N	108·20 W
114	Death Valley............Ca.-Nv.	36·55 N	117·12 W
114	Death Valley Junction.........Ca.	36·18 N	116·26 W
114	Death Valley Natl. Mon.......Ca.	36·34 N	117·00 W
167	Debal'tsevo (dyĕb'ăl-tsyĕ'vô) Sov. Un.	48·23 N	38·29 E
193	Debao (dŭ-bou).............China	23·18 N	106·40 E
165	Debar (Dibra) (dĕ'bär) (dā'brä) Yugo.	41·31 N	20·32 E
159	Deblin (dăɴ'blĭn)............Pol.	51·34 N	21·49 E
159	Debno (dĕb-nô').........Sov. Un.	50·24 N	25·44 E
214	Debo, Lac (L.)..............Mali.	15·15 N	4·40 W
159	Debrecen (dĕ'brĕ-tsĕn)......Hung.	47·32 N	21·40 E
211	Debre Markos..............Eth.	10·15 N	37·45 E
211	Debre Tabor................Eth.	11·57 N	38·09 E
120	Decatur (dē-kā'tŭr)...........Al.	34·35 N	87·00 W
106	Decatur........Ga. (Atlanta In.)	33·47 N	84·18 W
117	Decatur.......................Il.	39·50 N	88·59 W
104	Decatur.......................In.	40·50 N	84·55 W
104	Decatur.......................Mi.	42·10 N	86·00 W
116	Decatur.......................Tx.	33·14 N	97·33 W
160	Decazeville (dē-käz'vēl')......Fr.	44·33 N	2·16 E
184	Deccan (Plat.) (dĕk'ăn).....India	19·05 N	76·40 E
94	Deception L..................Can.	56·33 N	104·15 W
112	Deception P. (dē-sĕp'shŭn) Wa. (Seattle In.)	48·24 N	122·44 W
158	Decin (dyĕ'chēn)..........Czech.	50·47 N	14·14 E
109	Decorah (dē-kō'rȧ)............Ia.	43·18 N	91·48 W
	Dedeagats, see Alexandroúpolis		
174	Dedenevo (dyĕ-dyĕ'nyĕ-vô) Sov. Un. (Moscow In.)	56·14 N	37·31 E
99	Dedham (dĕd'ăm).......Ma. (In.)	42·15 N	71·11 W
136	Dedo do Deus (Mt.) (dĕ-dô-dô-dĕ'ōōs) Braz. (Rio de Janeiro In.)	22·30 S	43·02 W
214	Dédougou (dā-dōō-gōō') Upper Volta	12·38 N	3·28 W
154	Dee (R.)....................Scot.	57·05 N	2·25 W
154	Dee (R.)..................Wales	53·00 N	3·10 W
97	Deep River..................Can.	46·06 N	77·20 W
121	Deep (R.) (dēp)..............NC	35·36 N	79·32 W
117	Deep Fk. (R.)................Ok.	35·35 N	96·42 W
117	Deepwater (dep-wô-tēr).......Mo.	38·15 N	93·46 W
98	Deer........................Me.	44·07 N	68·38 W
107	Deerfield (dēr'fēld) Il. (Chicago In.)	42·10 N	87·51 W
112	Deer Island....Or. (Portland In.)	45·56 N	122·51 W
99	Deer Lake....................Can.	49·10 N	57·25 W
95	Deer L........................Can.	52·40 N	94·30 W
111	Deer Lodge (dēr lŏj)..........Mt.	46·23 N	112·42 W
107	Deer Park....Oh. (Cincinnati In.)	39·12 N	84·24 W
110	Deer Park....................Wa.	47·58 N	117·28 W
109	Deer River...................Mn.	47·20 N	93·49 W
104	Defiance (dē-fī'ăns)..........Oh.	41·15 N	84·20 W
120	DeFuniak Springs (dē fū'nĭ-ăk) Fl.	30·42 N	86·06 W
184	Deganga............India (In.)	22·41 N	88·41 E
218	Degeh-Bur . Eth (Horn of Afr. In.)	8·10 N	43·25 E
158	Deggendorf (dĕ'ghĕn-dôrf).F.R.G.	48·50 N	12·59 E
124	Degollado (dā-gô-lyä'dō)....Mex.	20·27 N	102·11 W
204	DeGrey (R.) (dē grā').......Austl.	20·20 S	119·25 E
174	Degtyarsk (dĕg-ty'arsk) Sov. Un. (Urals In.)	56·42 N	60·05 E
185	Dehiwala-Mount Lavinia Sri Lanka	6·47 N	79·55 E
184	Dehra Dūn (dā'rŭ).........India	30·09 N	78·07 E
193	Dehua (dŭ-hwä)...........China	25·30 N	118·15 E
159	Dej (däzh)...................Rom.	47·09 N	23·53 E
109	De Kalb (dē kălb')..............Il.	41·54 N	88·46 W
216	Dekese......................Zaire	3·27 S	21·24 E
89	Delacour (dĕ-lä-kōōr') Can. (Calgary In.)	51·09 N	113 45 W
116	Delagua (dĕl-ä'gwä)..........Co.	37·19 N	104·42 W
121	De Land (dē lănd')............Fl.	29·00 N	81·19 W
114	Delano (dĕl'ȧ-nō).............Ca.	35·47 N	119·15 W
115	Delano Pk....................Ut.	38·25 N	112·25 W
109	Delavan (dĕl'ȧ-văn)...........Wi.	42·39 N	88·38 W
104	Delaware (dĕl'ȧ-wâr).........Oh.	40·15 N	83·05 W
103	Delaware (State).............U. S.	38·40 N	75·30 W
117	Delaware (R.).................Ks.	39·45 N	95·47 W
105	Delaware (R.)...............U. S.	41·50 N	75·20 W
105	Delaware B...............De.-NJ	39·05 N	75·10 W
104	Delaware Res..................Oh.	40·30 N	83·05 W
162	Del Eje, Sierra (Mts.) (sē-ĕ'r-rä-dĕl-ĕ'kĕ).Sp.	42·15 N	6·45 W
158	Delemont (dē-lā-môn')......Switz.	47·21 N	7·18 E
118	De Leon (dē lē-ŏn')............Tx.	32·06 N	98·33 W
137	Delfínopolis (dĕl-fē'nô-pō-lēs) Braz. (Rio de Janeiro In.)	20·20 S	46·50 W
149	Delft (dĕlft) Neth. (Amsterdam In.)	52·01 N	4·20 E
155	Delfzijl...................Neth.	53·20 N	6·50 E
136	Delgada Pta. (Pt.) (pōō'n-tä-dĕl-gä'dä).Arg.	43·46 S	63·46 W
217	Delgado, Cabo (C.) (kȧ'bô-dĕl-gä'dō).Moz.	10·40 S	40·35 E
113	Delhi (dĕl'hī)...Il. (St. Louis In.)	39·03 N	90·16 W
184	Delhi........................India	28·54 N	77·13 E
119	Delhi.........................La.	32·26 N	91·29 W
184	Delhi (State)...............India	28·30 N	76·50 E
163	Del Hoyo, Sierra (Mtn.) (sē-ĕ'r-rä-dĕl-ô'yô) Sp. (Madrid In.)	40·39 N	3·56 W
158	Delitzsch (dā'lĭch)........G.D.R.	51·32 N	12·18 E
165	Dell Alice, Pt. (dĕl-ä-lē'chĕ)....It.	39·23 N	17·10 E
108	Dell Rapids (dĕl).............SD	43·50 N	96·43 W
113	Dellwood (dĕl'wōōd) Mn. (Minneapolis, St. Paul In.)	45·05 N	92·58 W
210	Dellys (dĕ'lēs')..............Alg.	36·59 N	3·40 E
114	Del Mar (dĕl mär')......Ca. (In.)	32·57 N	117·16 W
218	Delmas (dĕl'mȧs) S. Afr. (Johannesburg & Pretoria In.)	26·08 S	28·43 E
158	Delmenhorst (dĕl'mĕn-hôrst) F.R.G.	53·03 N	8·38 E
115	Del Norte (ldĕ nôrt')..........Co.	37·40 N	106·25 W
173	De-Longa (I.)............Sov. Un.	76·30 N	153·00 E
101	De Long Mts. (dē'lŏng).......Ak.	68·38 N	162·30 W
203	Deloraine (dĕ-lŭ-rān).......Austl.	41·30 S	146·40 E
104	Delphi (dĕl'fī)................In.	40·35 N	86·40 W
104	Delphos (dĕl'fŏs).............Oh.	40·50 N	84·20 W
121	Delray Beach (dĕl-rā')....Fl. (In.)	26·27 N	80·05 W
118	Del Rio (dĕl rē'ō)..............Tx.	29·21 N	100·52 W
89	Delson (dĕl'snŭ) Can. (Montreal In.)	45·24 N	73·32 W
115	Delta.........................Co.	38·45 N	108·05 W
115	Delta..........................Ut.	39·20 N	112·35 W
89	Delta Beach..Can. (Winnipeg In.)	50·10 N	98·20 W
114	Delta Mendota Can...........Ca.	37·10 N	121·02 W
165	Delvine (dĕl'vē-nä)..........Alb.	39·58 N	20·10 E
170	Dëma (R.) (dyĕm'ä)....Sov. Un.	53·40 N	54·30 E
216	Demba......................Zaire	5·30 S	22·16 E
211	Dembidolo....................Eth.	8·46 N	34·46 E
166	Demidov (dzyĕ'mē-dô'f)..Sov. Un.	55·16 N	31·32 E
115	Deming (dĕm'ĭng).............NM	32·15 N	107·45 W
158	Demmin (dĕm'mēn).........G.D.R.	53·54 N	13·04 E
210	Demnat (dĕm-nät)............Mor.	31·58 N	7·03 W
120	Demopolis (dē-mŏp'ō-lĭs)......Al.	32·30 N	87·50 W
107	Demotte (dē'mŏt) In. (Chicago In.)	41·12 N	87·13 W
196	Dempo, Gunung (Vol.) (dĕm'pô) Indon.	4·04 S	103·11 E
172	Dem'yanka (R.) (dyĕm-yän'kä) Sov. Un.	59·07 N	72·58 E
166	Demyansk (dyĕm-yänsk') Sov. Un.	57·39 N	32·26 E
160	Denain (dē-năɴ')...............Fr.	50·23 N	3·21 E
154	Denbigh (dĕn'bĭ)...........Wales	53·15 N	3·25 W
148	Denbigh (Co.)...............Wales	53·01 N	2·59 W
149	Dendermonde..Bel. (Brussels In.)	51·02 N	4·04 E
121	Dendron (dĕn'drŭn)...........Va.	37·02 N	76·53 W
174	Denezhkin Kamen, Gora (Mtn.) (dzyĕ-ŋĕ'zhkĭn kămĭĕŋ) Sov. Un. (Urals In.)	60·26 N	59·35 E
127	D'Enfer, Pointe (Pt.)...Mart.(In.)	14·21 N	60·48 W
128	Denham, Mt..................Jam.	18·20 N	77·30 W
155	Den Helder (dĕn hĕl'dĕr)...Neth.	52·55 N	5·45 E
163	Denia (dā'nyä)..................Sp.	38·48 N	0·06 E
203	Deniliquin (dĕ-nĭl'ĭ-kwĭn)...Austl.	35·20 S	144·52 E
108	Denison (dĕn'ĭ-sŭn)...........Ia.	42·01 N	95·22 W
117	Denison.......................Tx.	33·45 N	97·02 W
174	Denisovka (dĕ-nē'sof-kȧ) Sov. Un. (Urals In.)	52·26 N	61·45 E
171	Denizli (dĕn-ĭz-lē')...........Tur.	37·40 N	29·10 E
161	Denklingen (dĕn'klēn-gĕn) F.R.G. (Ruhr In.)	50·54 N	7·40 E
121	Denmark (dĕn'märk).........SC	33·18 N	81·09 W
146	Denmark.....................Eur.	56·14 N	8·30 E
75	Denmark Str................Grnld.	66·30 N	27·00 W
218	Dennilton (dĕn-ĭl-tŭn) S. Afr. (Johannesburg & Pretoria In.)	25·18 S	29·13 E
104	Dennison (dĕn'ĭ-sŭn)..........Oh.	40·25 N	81·20 W
91	De Nouvelle-France (C.).....Can.	62·03 N	74·00 W
196	Denpasar...................Indon.	8·35 S	115·10 E
148	Denton (dĕn'tŭn)............Eng.	53·27 N	2·07 W
105	Denton........................Md.	38·55 N	75·50 W
117	Denton........................Tx.	33·12 N	97·06 W
204	D'entrecasteaux, Pt. (däɴ-tr'kȧs-tō').Austl.	34·50 S	114·45 E
197	D'Entrecasteaux Is. (däɴ-tr'-kȧs-tō').Pap. N. Gui.	9·45 S	152·00 E
116	Denver (dĕn'vēr)..............Co.	39·44 N	104·59 W
184	Deoli........................India	25·52 N	75·23 E
109	De Pere (dē pēr')..............Wi.	44·25 N	88·04 W
107	Depew (dē-pū')..NY (Buffalo In.)	42·55 N	78·43 W
190	Deping (dŭ-pĭŋ).............China	37·28 N	116·57 E
104	Depue (dē pū)...................Il.	41·15 N	89·55 W
117	De Queen (dē kwēn')...........Ar.	34·02 N	94·21 W
119	De Quincy (dē kwĭn'sĭ)........La.	30·27 N	93·27 W
184	Dera Ghāzi Khān (dā'rū gä-zē' ĸän')......Pak.	30·09 N	70·39 E
184	Dera Ismāīl Khān (dā'rŭ ĭs-mä-ēl' ĸän') Pak.	31·55 N	70·51 E
171	Derbent (dĕr-bĕnt')......Sov. Un.	42·00 N	48·10 E
204	Derby (där'bē) (dûr'bē)....Austl.	17·20 S	123·40 E
105	Derby (dûr'bē)..................Ct.	41·20 N	73·05 W
148	Derby (där'bē)..............Eng.	52·55 N	1·29 W
218	Derby (där'bĭ) S. Afr. (Johannesburg & Pretoria In.)	25·55 S	27·02 E
148	Derby (Co.) där'bē)..........Eng.	53·11 N	1·30 W

ăt; finăl; rāte; senâte; ärm; ȧsk; sofȧ; fâre; ch-choose; dh-as th in other; bē; ēvent; bĕt; recĕnt; cratēr; g-go; gh-guttural g; bĭt; ĭ-short neutral; rīde; ĸ-guttural k as ch in German ich;

PRONOUNCING INDEX

Derdepoort — Dolores 275

Page	Name Pronunciation Region	Lat. °′	Long. °′
218	Derdepoort S. Afr. (Johannesburg & Pretoria In.)	24·39 S	26·21 E
217	Dere, Lak (R.)............Ken.	0.45 N	40·15 E
154	Derg, Lough (B.) (lŏk dĕrg)...Ire.	53·00 N	8·09 W
119	De Ridder (dē rĭd'ẽr).........La.	30·50 N	93·18 W
117	Dermott (dûr'mŏt)...........Ar.	33·32 N	91·24 W
99	Derry (dâr'ĭ)...........NH (In.)	45·52 N	71·22 W
165	Derventa (dĕr'ven-tȧ)......Yugo.	45·58 N	17·58 E
203	Derwent (R.) (dẽr'wĕnt)....Austl.	42·21 S	146·30 E
148	Derwent (R.)..............Eng.	52·54 N	1·24 W
117	Des Arc (dāz ärk')...........Ar.	34·59 N	91·31 W
137	Descalvado (dĕs-käl-vȧ-dô) Braz. (Rio de Janeiro In.)	21·55 S	47·37 W
94	Deschambault L..............Can.	54·40 N	103·35 W
89	Deschênes.....Can. (Ottawa In.)	45·23 N	75·47 W
89	Deschenes, L...Can. (Ottawa In.)	54·25 N	75·53 W
110	Deschutes R. (dā-shōōt')......Or.	44·25 N	121·21 W
118	Desdemona (dĕz-dē-mō'nȧ)....Tx.	32·16 N	98·33 W
211	Dese.......................Eth.	11·00 N	39·51 E
136	Deseado, Rio (R.) (rē-ō-dā-sā-ä'dhō).Arg.	46·50 S	67·45 W
127	Desirade I. (dā-zē-răs') Guad. (In.)	16·21 N	60·51 W
108	De Smet (dē smĕt')...........SD	44·23 N	97·33 W
109	Des Moines (dē moin')........Ia.	41·35 N	93·37 W
116	Des Moines..................NM	36·42 N	103·48 W
112	Des Moines.....Wa. (Seattle In.)	46·24 N	122·20 W
103	Des Moines (R.)............U. S.	43·45 N	94·20 W
167	Desna (R.) (dyĕs-nȧ')...Sov. Un.	51·05 N	31·03 E
136	Desolación (dĕ-sô-lä-syô'n) (I.) Chile	53·05 S	74·00 W
117	De Soto (dē sō'tō)...........Mo.	38·07 N	90·32 W
113	Des Peres (dĕs pĕr'ĕs) Mo. (St. Louis In.)	38·36 N	90·26 W
107	Des Plaines (dĕs plānz') Il. (Chicago In.)	42·02 N	87·54 W
107	Des Plaines R....Il. (Chicago In.)	41·39 N	88·05 W
158	Dessau (dĕs'ou)..........G.D.R.	51·50 N	12·15 E
158	Detmold (dĕt'mōld)......G.D.R.	51·57 N	8·55 E
107	Detroit (dē-troit') Mi. (Detroit In.)	42·22 N	83·10 W
117	Detroit.....................Tx.	33·41 N	95·16 W
108	Detroit Lakes (dē-troit' lăkz).Mn.	46·48 N	95·51 W
107	Detroit R. Can.-U. S. (Detroit In.)	42·08 N	83·07 W
159	Detva (dyĕt'vȧ)..........Czech.	48·32 N	19·21 E
149	Deurne.......Bel. (Brussels In.)	51·13 N	4·27 E
149	Deutsch Wagram Aus. (Vienna In.)	48·19 N	16·34 E
89	Deux-Montagnes (dû mōN-tăny') Can. (Montreal In.)	45·33 N	73·54 W
89	Deux Montagnes, Lac des (L.) Can. (Montreal In.)	45·28 N	74·00 W
165	Deva (dā'vä)...............Rom.	45·52 N	22·52 E
159	Dévaványa (dā'vô-vän-yô).Hung.	47·01 N	20·58 E
171	Develi (dĕ'vȧ-lē)...........Tur.	38·20 N	35·10 E
155	Deventer (dĕv'ĕn-tẽr).......Neth.	52·14 N	6·07 E
108	Devils (L.) (dĕv''lz).........ND	47·57 N	99·04 W
118	Devils (R.).................Tx.	29·55 N	101·10 W
	Devils I., see Diable, Ile du		
102	Devils Lake.................ND	48·10 N	98·55 W
108	Devils Lake Ind. Res.........ND	48·08 N	99·40 W
114	Devils Postpile Natl. Mon......Ca.	37·42 N	119·12 W
111	Devils Tower Natl. Mon.....Wy.	44·38 N	105·07 W
165	Devoll (R.).................Alb.	40·55 N	20·10 E
89	Devon......Can. (Edmonton In.)	53·23 N	113·43 W
218	Devon (dĕv'ŭn) S. Afr. (Johannesburg & Pretoria In.)	26·23 S	28·47 E
203	Devonport (dĕv'ŭn-pôrt....Austl.	41·20 S	146·30 E
113	Devore (dē-vôr') Ca. (Los Angeles In.)	34·13 N	117·24 W
112	Dewatto (dē-wȧt'ô) Wa. (Seattle In.)	47·27 N	123·04 W
117	Dewey (dū'ĭ)...............Ok.	36·48 N	95·55 W
117	De Witt (dē wĭt')............Ar.	34·17 N	91·22 W
109	De Witt.....................Ia.	41·46 N	90·34 W
148	Dewsbury (dūz'bẽr-ĭ)........Eng.	53·42 N	1·39 W
98	Dexter (dĕks'tẽr)............Me.	45·01 N	69·19 W
117	Dexter......................Mo.	36·46 N	89·56 W
121	Dexter (L.).................Fl.	29·07 N	81·24 W
186	Dezfūl......................Iran	32·14 N	48·37 E
183	Dezhnëva, Mys (East Cape) (dyĕzh'nyĭf).Sov. Un.	68·00 N	172·00 W
190	Dezhou (dŭ-jō).............China	37·28 N	116·17 E
	Dhahran, see Az Zahrān		
185	Dharamtar Cr..........India (In.)	18·49 N	72·54 E
185	Dharmavaram...............India	14·32 N	77·43 E
184	Dhaulāgiri (Mtn.) (dou-lȧ-gē'rē) Nep.	28·42 N	83·31 E
165	Dhenoúsa (I.)..............Grc.	37·09 N	25·53 E
183	Dhībān.....Jordan (Palestine In.)	31·30 N	35·46 E
165	Dhidhimótikhon.............Grc.	41·20 N	26·27 E
165	Dhodhekánisos (Dodecanese) (Is.) Grc.	38·00 N	26·10 E
184	Dhule.......................India	20·58 N	74·43 E
164	Dia (I.) (dē'ä)........Grc. (In.)	35·27 N	25·17 E
135	Diable, Ile du (Devils I.)..Fr. Gu.	5·15 N	57·10 W
112	Diablo, Mt. (dyä'blō) Ca. (San Francisco In.)	37·52 N	121·55 W
122	Diablo Heights (dyȧ'blō) Pan. (In.)	8·58 N	79·34 W
112	Diablo Range (Mts.) Ca. (San Francisco In.)	37·47 N	121·50 W
217	Diaca......................Moz.	11·30 S	39·59 E
214	Diaka (R.)..................Mali	14·40 N	5·00 W
135	Diamantina.................Braz.	18·14 S	43·32 W
204	Diamantina (R.) (dī'man-tē'nȧ) Austl.	25·38 S	139·53 E
135	Diamantino (dē-ȧ-män-tē'no) Braz.	14·22 S	56·23 W
110	Diamond Pk..................Or.	43·32 N	122·08 W
129	Diana Bk. (dī'ăn'ȧ)..........Ba.	22·30 N	74·45 W
193	Dianbai (dĭĕn-bī)..........China	21·30 N	111·20 E
193	Dian Chi (L.) (dĭĕn chē)....China	24·58 N	103·18 E
	Dibra, see Debar		
108	Dickinson (dĭk'ĭn-sŭn).......ND	46·52 N	102·49 W
119	Dickinson (dĭk'ĭn-sŭn)...Tx. (In.)	29·28 N	95·02 W
119	Dickinson Bayou........Tx. (In.)	29·26 N	95·08 W
120	Dickson (dĭk'sŭn)...........Tn.	36·03 N	87·24 W
105	Dickson City................Pa.	41·25 N	75·40 W
171	Dicle (R.) (dĭj'lȧ)...........Tur.	37·50 N	40·40 E
148	Didcot (dĭd'cŏt) Eng. (London In.)	51·35 N	1·15 W
214	Didiéni....................Mali	13·53 N	8·06 W
161	Die (dē).....................Fr.	44·45 N	5·22 E
90	Diefenbaker (Res.)..........Can.	51·20 N	108·10 W
94	Diefenbaker L...............Can.	51·00 N	106·55 W
129	Diego de Ocampo, Pico (Pk.) (pē'-kō-dyĕ'gô-dĕ-ō-kä'm-pô) Dom. Rep.	19·40 N	70·45 W
136	Diego Ramirez, Islas (Is.) (dē ā'gō rä-mē'rāz).Chile	56·15 S	70·15 W
213	Diégo-Suarez (dē-ā'gō-swȧ'rāz) Mad.	12·18 S	49·16 E
214	Diéma......................Mali	14·32 N	9·12 W
188	Dien Bien Phu..............Viet.	21·38 N	102·49 E
98	Dieppe (dē-ĕp')..............Can.	46·06 N	64·45 W
160	Dieppe.......................Fr.	49·54 N	1·05 E
117	Dierks (dērks)...............Ar.	34·06 N	94·02 W
149	Diessen (dēs'sĕn) F.R.G. (Munich In.)	47·57 N	11·06 E
149	Diest..........Bel. (Brussels In.)	50·59 N	5·05 E
98	Digby (dĭg'bĭ)...............Can.	44·37 N	65·46 W
106	Dighton (dī-tŭn) Ma.Providence (In.)	41·49 N	71·05 W
161	Digne (dēn'y')...............Fr.	44·07 N	6·16 E
160	Digoin (dē-gwăN')...........Fr.	46·28 N	4·06 E
197	Digul (R.).................Indon.	7·00 S	140·27 E
197	Dijohan Pt. (dē-kô-än) Phil. (In.)	16·24 N	122·25 E
160	Dijon (dē-zhôN')............Fr.	47·21 N	5·02 E
172	Dikson (dĭk'sŏn)........Sov. Un.	73·30 N	80·35 E
211	Dikwa (dē'kwȧ..............Nig.	12·06 N	13·53 E
197	Dili (dĭl'ē)................Indon.	8·35 S	125·35 E
152	Di Linosa I. (dē-lē-nō'sä)......It.	36·01 N	12·43 E
171	Dilizhan...............Sov. Un.	40·45 N	45·00 E
101	Dillingham (dĭl'ĕng-hăm).....Ak.	59·10 N	158·38 W
111	Dillon (dĭl'ŭn)...............Mt.	45·12 N	112·40 W
121	Dillon......................SC	34·24 N	79·28 W
104	Dillon Res...................Oh.	40·05 N	82·05 W
212	Dilolo (dē-lō'lō)............Zaire	10·19 S	22·23 E
186	Dimashq (Damascus) (dȧ-măs'kŭs).Syria	33·31 N	36·18 E
214	Dimbokro...........Ivory Coast	6·39 N	4·42 W
165	Dimbovita (R.)..............Rom.	44·43 N	25·41 E
	Dimitrovo, see Pernik		
215	Dimlang (Mtn.)..............Nig.	8·24 N	11·47 E
183	Dimona.......Isr. (Palestine In.)	31·03 N	35·01 E
197	Dinagate (I.)...............Phil.	10·15 N	126·15 E
184	Dinājpur...................Bngl.	25·38 N	87·39 E
160	Dinan (dē-näN')..............Fr.	48·27 N	2·03 W
155	Dinant (dē-näN')............Bel.	50·17 N	4·50 E
164	Dinara Planina (Mts.) (dē'nä-rä plä'nē-nä).Yugo.	43·50 N	16·15 E
185	Dindigul....................India	10·25 N	78·03 E
197	Dingalan B. (dĭŋ-gä'län) Phil. (In.)	15·19 N	121·33 E
154	Dingle (dĭng''l)..............Ire.	52·10 N	10·13 W
154	Dingle B....................Ire.	52·02 N	10·15 W
205	Dingo (dĭŋ'gō).............Austl.	23·45 S	149·26 E
214	Dinguiraye..................Gui.	11·18 N	10·43 W
154	Dingwall (dĭng'wôl).........Scot.	57·37 N	4·23 W
190	Ding Xian (dĭŋ shyĕn).....China	38·30 N	115·00 E
190	Dingxing (dĭŋ-shyĭŋ)......China	39·18 N	115·50 E
190	Dingyuan (dĭŋ-yûän)........China	32·32 N	117·40 E
190	Dingzi Wan (B.)............China	36·33 N	121·06 E
111	Dinosaur Natl. Mon. (dī'nō-sŏr) Co.-Ut.	40·45 N	109·17 W
161	Dinslaken (dēns'lä-kĕn) F.R.G. (Ruhr In.)	51·33 N	6·44 E
149	Dinteloord Neth. (Amsterdam In.)	51·38 N	4·21 E
114	Dinuba (dĭ-nū'bȧ)...........Ca.	36·33 N	119·29 W
128	Dios, Cayo de (I.) (kä'yō-dĕ-dē-ōs').Cuba	22·05 N	83·05 W
214	Diourbel (dē-ōōr-bĕl')......Senegal	14·40 N	16·15 W
187	Diphu Pass (dĭ-pōō).........China	28·15 N	96·45 E
127	Diquis (R.) (dē-kēs')........C. R.	8·59 N	83·24 W
218	Dire Dawa.Eth. (Horn of Afr. In.)	9·40 N	41·47 E
126	Diriamba (dēr-yäm'bä).......Nic.	11·52 N	86·15 W
204	Dirk Hartog (I.)............Austl.	26·25 S	113·15 E
149	Dirksland Neth. (Amsterdam In.)	51·45 N	4·04 E
203	Dirranbandi (dĭ-rȧ-băn'dē) Austl.	28·24 S	148·29 E
115	Dirty Devil (R.) (dûr'tĭ dĕv''l).Ut.	38·20 N	110·30 W
204	Disappointment (L.).......Austl.	23·20 S	120·20 E
112	Disappointment, C. (dĭs'ȧ-point'ment).Wa. (Portland In.)	46·16 N	124·11 W
163	D'Ischia, I. (dē'sh-kyä) It. (Naples In.)	40·26 N	13·55 E
213	Discovery (dĭs-kŭv'ẽr-ĭ)l...S. Afr. (Johannesburg & Pretoria In.)	26·10 S	27·53 E
112	Discovery Is. (dĭs-kŭv'ẽr-ē) Can. (Seattle In.)	48·25 N	123·13 W
218	Dishnā (dēsh'nȧ).Egypt (Nile In.)	26·08 N	32·27 E
75	Disko (dĭs'kō) (I.).........Grnld.	70·00 N	54·00 W
121	Dismal Swp. (dĭz'mȧl)....NC-Va.	36·35 N	76·34 W
166	Disna (dēs'nȧ).........Sov. Un.	55·34 N	28·15 E
184	Dispur.....................India	26·00 N	91·50 E
98	Disraëli (dĭs-rā'lĭ)..........Can.	45·53 N	71·23 W
103	District of Columbia.........U. S.	38·50 N	77·00 W
135	Distrito Federal (Dist.) (dēs-trē'tô-fĕ-dĕ-rä'l).Braz.	15·49 S	47·39 W
125	Distrito Federal (Dist.).....Mex.	19·14 N	99·08 W
218	Disūq (dē-sōōk').Egypt (Nile In.)	31·07 N	30·41 E
184	Diu (dē'ōō).................India	20·48 N	70·58 E
160	Dives (dēv)...................Fr.	49·18 N	0·05 W
197	Divilacan B. (dē-vē-lä'kän) Phil. (In.)	17·26 N	122·25 E
137	Divinópolis (dē-vē-nô'pō-lēs) Braz. (Rio de Janeiro In.)	20·10 S	44·53 W
214	Divo................Ivory Coast	5·50 N	5·22 W
109	Dixon (dĭks'ŭn)...............Il.	41·50 N	89·30 W
92	Dixon Ent.............Ak.-Can.	54·25 N	132·00 W
171	Diyarbakir (dē-yär-bĕk'ĭr)....Tur.	38·00 N	40·10 E
215	Dja (R.)....................Cam.	3·25 N	13·17 E
197	Djaja, Puntjak (Pk.)......Indon.	4·00 S	137·15 E
165	Djakovica...................Yugo	42·33 N	20·28 E
216	Djambala....................Con.	2·33 S	14·45 E
210	Djanet......................Alg.	24·29 N	9·26 E
214	Djebobo (Mtn.)............Ghana	8·20 N	0·37 E
152	Djedi (R.)...................Alg.	34·18 N	4·39 E
210	Djelfa (jĕl'fä)...............Alg.	34·40 N	3·17 E
215	Djember....................Chad.	10·25 N	17·50 E
152	Djerba, Île de (I.)..........Tun.	33·53 N	11·26 E
210	Djerid, Chott (L.) (jĕr'ĭd)....Tun.	33·15 N	8·29 E
214	Djibasso............Upper Volta	13·07 N	4·10 W
214	Djibo...............Upper Volta	14·06 N	1·38 W
218	Djibouti (jē-bōō-tē') Djibouti (Horn of Afr. In.)	11·34 N	43·00 E
209	Djibouti....................Afr.	11·35 N	48·08 E
151	Djidjelli (jē-jĕ-lē')..........Alg.	36·49 N	5·47 E
216	Djokoumatombi..............Con.	0·47 N	15·22 E
216	Djoua (R.)............Con.-Gabon	1·25 N	13·40 E
156	Djursholm (djōōrs'hōlm).....Swe.	59·26 N	18·01 E
167	Dmitriyevka (d'mē-trē-yĕf'kȧ) Sov. Un.	47·57 N	38·56 E
167	Dmitriyev L'govskiy (d'mē'trĭ-yĕf l'gôf'skĭ).Sov. Un.	52·07 N	35·05 E
174	Dmitrov (d'mē'trôf) Sov. Un. (Moscow In.)	56·21 N	37·32 E
166	Dmitrovsk (d'mē'trôfsk).Sov. In.	52·30 N	35·10 E
167	Dnepr (Dnieper) (R.) (nē'pẽr) Sov. Un.	46·47 N	32·57 E
167	Dneprodzerzhinsk (d'nyĕp'rô-zĕr-shĭnsk).Sov. Un.	48·32 N	34·38 E
168	Dneprodzerzhinskoye Vdkhr (Res.).Sov. Un.	49·00 N	34·10 E
167	Dnepropetrovsk (d'nyĕp'rô-pä-trôfsk).Sov. Un.	48·23 N	34·10 E
167	Dnepropetrovsk (Oblast).Sov. Un.	48·15 N	34·08 E
167	Dnepr Zaliv (B.) (dnyĕp'r zȧ'lĭf).Sov. Un.	46·33 N	31·45 E
167	Dnestr (Dniester) (R.) (nēst'rōōl) (nēs'tẽr).Sov. Un.	48·21 N	28·10 E
167	Dnestrovskiy Líman (B.) Sov. Un.	46·13 N	29·50 E
	Dnieper (R.), see Dnepr		
	Dniester (R.), see Dnestr		
166	Dno (d'nô')............Sov. Un.	57·49 N	29·59 E
214	Do, Lac (L.)................Mali.	15·50 N	2·20 W
215	Doba.......................Chad	8·39 N	16·51 E
106	Dobbs Ferry (dŏbz' fĕ'rē) NY (New York In.)	41·01 N	73·53 W
204	Dobbyn (dôb'ĭn)...........Austl.	19·45 S	140·02 E
157	Dobele (dô'bĕ-lĕ).........Sov. Un.	56·37 N	23·18 E
158	Döbeln (dû'bĕln)...........G.D.R.	51·08 N	13·07 E
197	Doberai Jazirah (Pen.).....Indon.	1·25 S	133·15 E
197	Dobo......................Indon.	6·00 S	134·18 E
165	Doboj (dō'boi)..............Yugo.	44·42 N	18·04 E
174	Dobryanka (dôb-ryän'kȧ) Sov. Un. (Urals In.)	58·27 N	56·26 E
159	Dobšina (dôp'shē-nä)......Czech.	48·48 N	20·25 E
135	Doce (R.) (dō'sȧ)...........Braz.	19·01 S	42·14 W
128	Doce Leguas, Cayos de las (Is.) (kä'yōs-dĕ-läs-dô-sĕ-lĕ'gwäs) Cuba	20·55 N	79·05 W
124	Doctor Arroyo (dŏk-tōr' är-rō'yô) Mex.	23·41 N	100·10 W
135	Dr. Ir. W. J. van Blommestein Meer (Res.).Sur.	4·45 N	55·05 W
148	Doddington (dŏd'dĭng-tŏn) Eng. (London In.)	51·17 N	0·47 E
	Dodecanese (Is.), see Dhodhekánisos		
116	Dodge City (dŏj)............Ks.	37·44 N	100·01 W
105	Dodgeville (dŏj'vĭl)..........NY	43·10 N	74·45 W
109	Dodgeville..................Wi.	42·58 N	90·07 W
217	Dodoma (dō'dô-mȧ).........Tan.	6·11 S	35·45 E
109	Dog (L.) (dŏg).............Can.	48·42 N	89·24 W
155	Dogger Bk. (dŏg'gẽr)........Eur.	55·07 N	2·25 E
171	Dogubayazit.................Tur.	39·35 N	44·00 E
184	Dohad.......................India	22·52 N	74·18 E
165	Doiran (L.).................Grc.	41·10 N	23·00 E
195	Dōjō (dō-jō) Jap. (Ōsaka In.)	34·51 N	135·14 E
166	Dokshitsy (dôk-shĕtsĕ)..Sov. Un.	54·53 N	27·49 E
97	Dolbeau.....................Can.	48·52 N	72·16 W
161	Dôle (dōl)....................Fr.	47·07 N	5·28 E
167	Dolgaya, Kosa (C.) (kô'sȧ dôl-gä'yä).Sov. Un.	46·42 N	37·42 E
170	Dolgiy (I.)............Sov. Un.	69·20 N	59·20 E
174	Dolgoprudnyy Sov. Un. (Moscow In.)	55·57 N	37·33 E
159	Dolina (dô-lyē'nä)........Sov. Un.	48·57 N	24·01 E
194	Dolinsk (dá-lēnsk')......Sov. Un.	47·29 N	142·31 E
128	Dollar Hbr..................Ba.	25·30 N	79·15 W
211	Dolo........................Som.	4·01 N	42·14 E
106	Dolomite (dŏl'ō-mīt) Al. (Birmingham In.)	33·28 N	86·57 W
164	Dolomitiche, Alpi (Mts.) (äl-pē-dô-lô'mē-tē'chĕ).It.	46·16 N	11·43 E
137	Dolores (dô-lō'rĕs) Arg. (Buenos Aires In.)	36·20 S	57·42 W
134	Dolores.............Col. (In.)	3·33 N	74·54 W

ng-sing; ŋ-baŋk; N-nasalized n; nŏd; cŏmmit; ōld; ôbey; ôrder; fōōd; fŏŏt; ou-out; s-soft; sh-dish; th-thin; pūre; ûnite; ûrn; stŭd; circŭs; ü-as "y" in study; '-indeterminate vowel.

Page	Name Pronunciation	Region	Lat. °′	Long. °′
197	Dolores (dô-lô-rĕs)	Phil. (In.)	17·40 N	120·43 E
118	Dolores (dô-lō'rĕs)	Tx.	27·42 N	99·47 W
137	Dolores	Ur. (Buenos Aires In.)	33·32 S	58·15 W
115	Dolores (R.)	Co.-Ut.	38·35 N	108·50 W
124	Dolores Hidalgo (dô-lō'rĕs-ē-däl'gō)	Mex.	21·09 N	100·56 W
90	Dolphin and Union Str. (dŏl'fĭn ūn'yŭn)	Can.	69·22 N	117·10 W
158	Domažlice (dō'mäzh-lē-tsĕ)	Czech.	49·27 N	12·55 E
161	Dombasle (dôN-bäl')	Fr.	48·38 N	6·18 E
159	Dombóvár (dŏm'bō-vär)	Hung.	46·22 N	18·08 E
160	Dôme, Puy de (Pk.) (pwē'dĕ-dôm')	Fr.	45·47 N	2·54 E
134	Domeyko, Cordillera (Mts.) (kôr-dēl-yĕ'rä-dô-mā'kō)	Chile	20·50 S	69·02 W
123	Dominica (dŏ-mĭ-nē'kȧ)	N. A.	15·30 N	60·45 W
127	Dominica Chan.	N. A. (In.)	15·00 N	61·30 W
123	Dominican Republic (dô-mĭn'ĭ-kăn)	N.A.	19·00 N	70·45 W
99	Dominion (dô-mĭn'yŭn)	Can.	46·13 N	60·01 W
216	Domiongo	Zaire	4·37 S	21·15 E
174	Domodedovo (dô-mô-dyĕ'do-vô)	Sov. Un. (Moscow In.)	55·27 N	37·45 E
137	Dom Silvério (doN-sêl-vĕ'ryō)	Braz. (Rio de Janeiro In.)	20·09 S	42·57 W
148	Don (R.) (dŏn)	Eng.	53·27 N	1·34 W
148	Don (R.)	Eng.	53·39 N	0·58 W
154	Don (R.)	Scot.	57·19 N	2·39 W
168	Don (R.)	Sov. Un.	49·50 N	41·30 E
113	Donaldson (dŏn'ăl-sŭn)	Mi. (Sault Ste. Marie In.)	46·19 N	84·22 W
119	Donaldsonville (dŏn'ăld-sŭn-vĭl)	La.	30·05 N	90·58 W
120	Donalsonville	Ga.	31·02 N	84·50 W
158	Donawitz (dō'nȧ-vĭts)	Aus.	47·23 N	15·05 E
162	Don Benito Mérida (dōn' bȧ-nē'tō-mĕ'rē-dä)	Sp.	38·55 N	6·08 W
202	Doncaster (doŋ'kȧs-tēr)	Austl. (Melbourne In.)	37·47 S	145·08 E
148	Doncaster (doŋ'kăs-tēr)	Eng.	53·32 N	1·07 W
216	Dondo (dōn'dō)	Ang.	9·38 S	14·25 E
212	Dondo	Moz.	19·33 S	34·47 E
185	Dondra Hd.	Sri Lanka	5·52 N	80·52 E
154	Donegal (dŏn-ē-gôl')	Ire.	54·44 N	8·05 W
154	Donegal, Mts. of (dŏn-ē-gôl')	Ire.	54·44 N	8·10 W
154	Donegal Bay (dŏn-ē-gôl')	Ire.	54·35 N	8·36 W
167	Donets (R.) (dō-nyĕts')	Sov. Un.	48·48 N	38·42 E
167	Donets Coal Basin (Reg.) (dō-nyĕts')	Sov. Un.	48·15 N	38·50 E
167	Donetsk (Oblast)	Sov. Un.	47·55 N	37·40 E
167	Donetsk (Stalino) (dō-nyĕts'k) (stä'lĭ-nō)	Sov. Un.	48·00 N	37·35 E
189	Dong (R.) (dôŋ)	China	34·13 N	115·08 E
204	Dongara (dôn-gă'rȧ)	Austl.	29·15 S	115·00 E
190	Dongba (dôŋ-bä)	China	31·40 N	119·02 E
190	Dong'e (dôŋ-ŭ)	China	36·21 N	116·14 E
190	Dong'erzen (dôŋ-är-dzŭn)	China	36·11 N	116·16 E
193	Dongfang (dôŋ-fäŋ)	China	19·08 N	108·42 E
196	Donggala (dôn-gä'lä)	Indon.	0·45 S	119·32 E
191	Dongguan (dôŋ-gûän)	China (Canton In.)	23·03 N	113·46 E
190	Dongguang (dôŋ-gûäŋ)	China	37·54 N	116·33 E
190	Donghai (dôŋ-hi)	China	34·35 N	119·05 E
193	Dong Hoi (dông-hô-ē')	Viet.	17·25 N	106·42 E
190	Dongming (dôŋ-mĭŋ)	China	35·16 N	115·06 E
212	Dongo (dôŋ'gō)	Ang.	14·45 S	15·30 E
197	Dongon Pt. (dŏng-ōn')	Phil. (In.)	12·43 N	120·35 E
216	Dongou (dôŋ-gōō')	Con.	2·02 N	18·04 E
190	Dongping (dôŋ-pĭŋ)	China	35·50 N	116·24 E
190	Dongping Hu (L.) (dôŋ-pĭŋ) hōō)	China	36·06 N	116·24 E
190	Dongshan (doŋ-shän)	China	31·05 N	120·24 E
190	Dongtai	China	32·51 N	120·20 E
193	Dongting Hu (L.) (dôŋ-tĭŋ hōō)	China	29·10 N	112·30 E
193	Dongxiang (dôŋ-shyäŋ)	China	28·18 N	116·38 E
117	Doniphan (dŏn'ĭ-făn)	Mo.	36·37 N	90·50 W
164	Donji Vakuf (dōn'yĭ väk'ōōf)	Yugo.	44·08 N	17·25 E
118	Don Martin, Presa de (Res.) (prĕ'sä-dĕ-dôn-mär-tē'n)	Mex.	27·35 N	100·38 W
98	Donnacona	Can.	46·40 N	71·46 W
161	Donnemarie-en-Montois (dôn-mä-rē'ĕN-môN-twä')	Fr. Paris In.)	48·29 N	3·09 E
110	Donner und Blitzen (R.) (dŏn'ēr ōōnt blĭ'tsĕn)	Or.	42·45 N	118·57 W
213	Donnybrook (dŏ-nĭ-brŏŏk)	S. Afr. (Natal In.)	29·56 S	29·54 E
107	Donora (dŏ-nō'rȧ)	Pa. (Pittsburgh In.)	40·10 N	79·51 W
101	Doonerak (dōō'nē-răk)	Ak.	68·00 N	150·34 W
149	Doorn	Neth. (Amsterdam In.)	52·02 N	5·21 E
109	Door Pen. (dōr)	Wi.	44·40 N	87·36 W
164	Dora Baltea (dō'rä bäl'tä-ä)	It.	45·40 N	7·34 E
106	Doraville (dō'rȧ-vĭl)	Ga. (Atlanta In.)	33·54 N	84·17 W
154	Dorchester (dôr'chĕs-tēr)	Eng.	50·45 N	2·34 W
160	Dordogne (R.) (dôr-dôn'yĕ)	Fr.	44·53 N	0·16 E
149	Dordrecht (dôr'drĕKt)	Neth. (Amsterdam In.)	51·48 N	4·39 E
213	Dordrecht (dô'drĕKt)	S. Afr. (Natal In.)	31·24 S	27·06 E
164	Dorgali (dôr'gä-lē)	It.	40·18 N	9·37 E
94	Doré L.	Can.	54·31 N	107·06 W
89	Dorion-Vaudreuil (dôr-yō)	Can. (Montreal In.)	45·23 N	74·01 W
148	Dorking (dôr'kĭng)	Eng. (London In.)	51·12 N	0·20 W
100	D'Orleans, Ile (I.) dōr-lē-äN', yl)	Can. (Quebec In.)	46·56 N	71·00 W
107	Dormont (dôr'mŏnt)	Pa. (Pittsburgh In.)	40·24 N	80·02 W
158	Dornbirn (dôrn'bêrn)	Aus.	47·24 N	9·45 E
154	Dornoch (dôr'nŏK)	Scot.	57·55 N	4·01 W
154	Dornoch Firth (dôr'nŏK fûrth)	Scot.	57·55 N	3·55 W
166	Dorogobuzh (dôrôgô'-bōō'zh)	Sov. Un.	54·57 N	33·18 E
159	Dorohoi (dō-rô-hoi')	Rom.	47·57 N	26·28 E
	Dorpat, see Tartu			
204	Dorre (I.) (dôr)	Austl.	25·19 S	113·10 E
161	Dorsten (dōr'stĕn)	F.R.G. (Ruhr In.)	51·40 N	6·58 E
161	Dortmund (dôrt'mŏŏnt)	F.R.G. (Ruhr In.)	51·31 N	7·28 E
161	Dortmund-Ems Kanal (can.) (dōrt'mōōnd-ĕms' kä-näl')	F.R.G. (Ruhr In.)	51·50 N	7·25 E
171	Dörtyal (dûrt'yôl)	Tur.	36·50 N	36·20 E
89	Dorval (dôr-vál')	Can. (Montreal In.)	45·26 N	73·44 W
135	Dos Caminos (dôs-kä-mē'nôs)	Ven. (In.)	9·38 N	67·17 W
112	Dosewallips (R.) (dō'sē-wäl'lĭps)	Wa. (Seattle In.)	47·45 N	123·04 W
162	Dos Hermanas (dōsĕr-mä'näs)	Sp.	37·17 N	5·56 W
215	Dosso (dôs-ō')	Niger	13·03 N	3·12 E
120	Dothan (dō'thăn)	Al.	31·13 N	85·23 W
160	Douai (dōō-ā')	Fr.	50·23 N	3·04 E
215	Douala (dōō-ä'lä)	Cam.	4·03 N	9·42 E
160	Douarnenez (dōō-är nē-nĕs')	Fr.	48·06 N	4·18 W
119	Double Bayou (dŭb''l bī'yōō)	Tx. (In.)	29·40 N	94·38 W
214	Douentza	Mali	15·00 N	2·57 W
163	Douéra (dōō-ā'rȧ)	Alg.	36·40 N	2·55 E
101	Douglas (dŭg'lȧs)	Ak.	58·18 N	134·35 W
115	Douglas	Ar.	31·20 N	109·30 W
120	Douglas	Ga.	31·30 N	82·53 W
154	Douglas (dŭg'lȧs)	Isle of Man	54·10 N	4·24 W
99	Douglas (dŭg'lȧs)	Ma. (In.)	42·04 N	71·45 W
111	Douglas (dŭg'lȧs)	Wy.	42·45 N	105·21 W
148	Douglas (R.) (dŭg'lȧs)	Eng.	53·38 N	2·48 W
120	Douglas (R.) (dŭg'lȧs)	Tn.	36·00 N	83·35 W
92	Douglas Chan.	Can.	53·30 N	129·12 W
93	Douglas Lake Ind. Res.	Can.	50·10 N	120·49 W
120	Douglasville (dŭg'lȧs-vĭl)	Ga.	33·45 N	84·47 W
211	Doumé (dōō-mā')	Cam.	4·41 N	13·26 E
135	Dourada, Serra (Mts.) (sĕ'r-rä-dôōō-rȧ'dȧ	Braz.	15·11 S	49·57 W
161	Dourdan (dōōr-däN')	Fr. (Paris In.)	48·32 N	2·01 E
162	Douro, Rio (R.) (rē'ō-dô'ōō-rô)	Port.	41·03 N	8·12 W
148	Dove (R.) (dŭv)	Eng.	52·53 N	1·47 W
105	Dover (dō vēr)	De.	39·10 N	75·30 W
155	Dover	Eng.	51·08 N	1·19 E
105	Dover	NH	43·15 N	71·00 W
106	Dover	NJ (New York In.)	40·53 N	74·33 W
104	Dover	Oh.	40·35 N	81·30 W
218	Dover	S. Afr. (Johannesburg & Pretoria In.)	27·05 S	27·44 E
155	Dover, Str. of	Eur.	50·50 N	1·15 W
98	Dover-Foxcroft (dō'vēr fôks'krôft)	Me.	45·10 N	69·15 W
170	Dovlekanovo (dŏv'lyĕk-à-nô-vô)	Sov. Un.	54·15 N	55·05 E
156	Dovre Fjell (Plat.) (dŏv'rĕ fyĕl')	Nor.	62·03 N	8·36 E
113	Dow (dou)	Il. (St. Louis In.)	39·01 N	90·20 W
104	Dowagiac (dô-wô'jăk)	Mi.	42·00 N	86·05 W
107	Downers Grove (dou'nērz grōv)	Il. (Chicago In.)	41·48 N	88·00 W
113	Downey (dou'nĭ)	Ca. (Los Angeles In.)	33·56 N	118·08 W
114	Downieville (dou'nĭ-nĭl)	Ca.	39·35 N	120·48 W
116	Downs (dounz)	Ks.	39·29 N	98·32 W
107	Doylestown (doilz'toun)	Oh. (Cleveland In.)	40·58 N	81·43 W
210	Drâa, C. (drȧ)	Mor.	28·39 N	12·15 W
210	Drâa, Oued (R.)	Mor.	28·00 N	9·31 W
167	Drabov (drä'bôf)	Sov. Un.	49·57 N	32·14 E
161	Drac (R.) (dräk)	Fr.	44·50 N	5·47 E
99	Dracut (drā'kŭt)	Ma. (In.)	42·40 N	71·19 W
165	Draganovo (drä-gä-nō'vô)	Bul.	43·13 N	25·45 E
165	Drăgăsani (drä-gȧ-shän'ĭ)	Rom.	44·39 N	24·18 E
161	Draguignan (drä-gēn-yäN')	Fr.	43·35 N	6·28 E
212	Drakensberg (Mts.) (drä'kĕnz-bĕrgh)	Leso.-S. Afr.	29·15 S	29·07 E
133	Drake Passage (drāk păs'ĭj)	S. A.-Ant.	57·00 S	65·00 W
165	Dráma (drä'mä)	Grc.	41·09 N	24·10 E
156	Drammen (dräm'ĕn)	Nor.	59·45 N	10·15 E
158	Drau (R.) (drou)	Aus.	46·44 N	13·45 E
164	Drava (R.) (Drä'vä)	Yugo.	46·37 N	15·17 E
164	Dravograd (Drä'vô-gräd')	Yugo.	46·37 N	15·01 E
158	Drawsko Pomorskie (dräv'skō pō-mōr'skyĕ	Pol.	53·31 N	15·50 E
112	Drayton Hbr. (drā'tŭn)	Wa. (Vancouver In.)	48·58 N	122·40 W
107	Drayton Plains	Mi. (Detroit In.)	42·41 N	83·23 W
93	Drayton Valley	Can.	53·13 N	114·59 W
161	Drensteinfurt (drĕn'shtīn-fōōrt)	F.R.G. (Ruhr In.)	51·47 N	7·44 E
158	Dresden (drās'dĕn)	G.D.R.	51·05 N	13·45 E
161	Dreux (drû)	Fr. (Paris In.)	48·44 N	1·24 E
218	Driefontein	S. Afr. (Johannesburg & Pretoria In.)	25·53 S	29·10 E
165	Drin (R.) (drēn)	Alb.	42·13 N	20·13 E
165	Drina (R.) (drē'nä)	Yugo.	44·09 N	19·30 E
165	Drinit, Pellg I (Bght.)	Alb.	41·42 N	19·17 E
166	Drissa (drĭs'sä)	Sov. Un.	55·48 N	27·59 E
166	Drissa (R.)	Sov. Un.	55·44 N	28·58 E
106	Driver	Va. (Norfolk In.)	36·50 N	76·30 W
156	Dröbak (drû'bäk)	Nor.	59·40 N	10·35 E
154	Drogheda (drŏ'hē-dȧ)	Ire.	53·43 N	6·15 W
159	Drogichin (drō-gē'chĭn)	Sov. Un.	52·10 N	25·11 E
159	Drogobych (drô-hô'bĭch)	Sov. Un.	49·21 N	23·31 E
160	Drôme (R.) (drōm)	Fr.	44·42 N	4·53 E
148	Dronfield (drŏn'fēld)	Eng.	53·18 N	1·28 W
93	Drumheller (drŭm-hĕl-ēr)	Can.	51·28 N	112·42 W
104	Drummond (I.) (drŭm'ŭnd)	Mi.	46·00 N	83·50 W
98	Drummondville (drŭm'ŭnd-vĭl)	Can.	45·53 N	72·33 W
117	Drumright (drŭm'rīt)	Ok.	35·59 N	96·37 W
149	Drunen	Neth. (Amsterdam In.)	51·41 N	5·10 E
166	Drut' (R.) (drōōt)	Sov. Un.	53·40 N	29·45 E
166	Druya (drōō'yȧ)	Sov. Un.	55·45 N	27·26 E
159	Drweca R. (d'r-văn'tsȧ)	Pol.	53·06 N	19·13 E
91	Dryden (drī-dĕn)	Can.	49·47 N	92·50 W
202	Drysdale	Austl. (Melbourne In.)	38·11 S	144·34 E
121	Dry Tortugas (I.) (tôr-tōō'gäz)	Fl. (In.)	24·37 N	82·45 W
210	Dschang (dshäng)	Cam.	5·34 N	10·09 E
214	Duabo	Lib.	5·40 N	8·05 W
89	Duagh	Can. (Edmonton In.)	53·43 N	113·24 W
123	Duarte, Pico (mtn.) (dŭ'ărtĕh pēcô)	Dom. Rep	19·00 N	71·00 W
137	Duas Barras (dōō'äs-bȧ'r-räs)	Braz. (Rio de Janeiro In.)	22·03 S	42·30 W
90	Dubawnt (L.) (dōō-bônt')	Can.	63·27 N	103·30 W
90	Dubawnt (R.)	Can.	61·30 N	103·49 W
186	Dubayy	U. A. E.	25·18 N	55·26 E
203	Dubbo (dŭb'ō)	Austl.	32·20 S	148·42 E
217	Dubie	Zaire	8·33 S	28·32 E
112	Dublin (dŭb'lĭn)	Ca. (San Francisco In.)	37·42 N	121·56 W
120	Dublin	Ga.	32·33 N	82·55 W
154	Dublin (Baile Atha Cliath) (bŏ'lĕŏ'hŏclē'ŏh)	Ire.	53·20 N	6·15 W
118	Dublin	Tx.	32·05 N	98·20 W
159	Dubno (dōō'b-nô)	Sov. Un.	50·24 N	25·44 E
105	Du Bois (dōō-bois')	Pa.	41·10 N	78·45 W
167	Dubossary (dōō-bŏ-sä'rĭ)	Sov. Un.	47·16 N	29·11 E
171	Dubovka (dōō-bôf'kȧ)	Sov. Un.	49·00 N	44·50 E
174	Dubrovka (dōō-brôf'kȧ)	Sov. Un. (Leningrad In.)	59·51 N	30·56 S
165	Dubrovnik (Ragusa) (dōō'brôv-nêk) (rä-gōō'sȧ)	Yugo.	42·40 N	18·10 E
166	Dubrovno (dōō-brôf'nō)	Sov. Un.	54·39 N	30·54 E
109	Dubuque (dōō-būk')	Ia.	42·30 N	90·43 W
115	Duchesne (dōō-shān')	Ut.	40·12 N	110·23 W
115	Duchesne (R.)	Ut.	40·20 N	110·50 W
204	Duchess (dŭch'ĕs)	Austl.	21·30 S	139·55 E
199	Ducie I. (dü-sē')	Oceania	25·30 S	126·20 W
120	Duck (R.)	Tn.	35·55 N	87·40 W
112	Duckabush (R.) (dŭk'ȧ-bōōsh)	Wa. (Seattle In.)	47·41 N	123·09 W
94	Duck Lake	Can.	52·47 N	106·13 W
95	Duck Mtn.	Can.	51·35 N	101·00 W
120	Ducktown (dŭk'toun)	Tn.	35·03 N	84·20 W
110	Duck Valley Ind. Res.	Id.-Nv.	42·02 N	115·49 W
114	Duckwater Pk. (dŭk-wô-tēr)	Nv.	39·00 N	115·31 W
134	Duda (dōō'dä) (R.)	Col. (In.)	3·25 N	74·23 W
172	Dudinka (dōō-dĭn'kȧ)	Sov. Un.	69·15 N	85·42 E
148	Dudley (dŭd'lĭ)	Eng.	52·31 N	2·04 W
214	Duékoué	Ivory Coast	6·45 N	7·21 W
162	Duero (R.) (dwĕ'rō)	Sp.	41·30 N	5·10 W
104	Dugger (dŭg'ēr)	In.	39·00 N	87·10 W
164	Dugi Otok (I.) (dōō'gē O'tôk)	Yugo.	44·03 N	14·40 E
161	Duisburg (dōō'ĭs-bōōrgh)	F.R.G. (Ruhr In.)	51·26 N	6·46 E
134	Duitama (dōōē-tä'mä)	Col.	5·48 N	73·09 W
92	Duke L (dōōk)	Ak.	54·56 N	131·20 W
166	Dukhovshchina (dōō-Kôfsh'chēnȧ)	Sov. Un.	55·13 N	32·26 E
148	Dukinfield (dŭk'ĭn-fēld)	Eng.	53·28 N	2·05 W
159	Dukla P. (dōō'klä)	Pol.	49·25 N	21·44 E
127	Dulce, Golfo (G.) (gōl'fô dōōl'sā)	C. R.	8·25 N	83·13 W
	Dulcigno, see Ulcinj			
161	Dülken (dül'kĕn)	F.R.G. (Ruhr In.)	51·15 N	6·21 E
161	Dülmen (dül'mĕn)	F.R.G. (Ruhr In.)	51·50 N	7·17 E
113	Duluth (dōō-lōōth')	Mn. (Duluth In.)	46·50 N	92·07 W
183	Dūmā	Syria (Palestine In.)	33·34 N	36·17 E
197	Dumaguete City (dōō-mä-gä'tā)	Phil.	9·14 N	123·15 E
183	Dumai	Indon. (Singapore In.)	1·39 N	101·30 E
197	Dumali Pt. (dōō-mä'lē)	Phil. (In.)	13·07 N	121·42 E
116	Dumas	Tx.	35·52 N	101·58 W
154	Dumbarton (dŭm'bȧr-tŭn)	Scot.	56·00 N	4·35 W
184	Dum-Dum	India (In.)	22·37 N	88·25 E
154	Dumfries (dŭm-frēs')	Scot.	55·05 N	3·40 W
184	Dumjor	India (In.)	22·37 N	88·14 E
106	Dumont (dōō'mŏnt)	NJ (New York In.)	40·56 N	74·00 W
218	Dumyāţ	Egypt (Nile In.)	31·22 N	31·50 E
218	Dumyāţ, Maşabb (Chan.)	Egypt (Nile In.)	31·36 N	31·45 E
159	Duna (R.) (dōō'nä)	Hung.	46·07 N	18·45 E
159	Dunaföldvar (dōō'nô-fûld'vär)	Hung.	46·48 N	18·55 E
159	Dunajec (R.) (dōō-nä'yĕts)	Pol.	49·52 N	20·53 E
159	Dunapataj (doo'nô-pô-toi)	Hung.	46·42 N	19·03 E
159	Dunaujvaros	Hung.	46·57 N	18·55 E
174	Dunay (dōō'nī)	Sov. Un. (Leningrad In.)	59·59 N	30·57 E
167	Dunayevtsy (dōō-nä'yĕf-tsĭ)	Sov. Un.	48·52 N	26·51 E
154	Dunbar (dŭn'bär)	Scot.	56·00 N	2·25 W
94	Dunblane (dŭn-blān')	Can.	51·11 N	106·52 W
104	Dunbar	WV	38·20 N	81·45 W
92	Duncan (dŭŋ'kăn)	Can.	48·47 N	123·42 W

ăt; finăl; rāte; senâte; ärm; ȧsk; sofȧ; fâre; ch-choose; dh-as th in other; bē; ēvent; bĕt; recĕnt; cratēr; g-go; gh-guttural g; bĭt; ĭ-short neutral; rīde; K-guttural k as ch in German ich;

ng-sing; ŋ-baŋk; N-nasalized n; nŏd; cŏmmit; ōld; ŏbey; ôrder; fōŏd; fŏŏt; ou-out; s-soft; sh-dish; th-thin; pūre; ûnite; ûrn; stŭd; circŭs; ü-as "y" in study; '-indeterminate vowel.

278 Edgeley — Emilia-Romagna
PRONOUNCING INDEX

Page	Name Pronunciation Region	Lat. °'	Long. °'
108	Edgeley (ĕj'lĭ) ND	46·24 N	98·43 W
108	Edgemont (ĕj'mŏnt) SD	43·19 N	103·50 W
109	Edgerton (ĕj'ēr-tŭn) Wi.	42·49 N	89·06 W
106	Edgewater (ĕj-wô-tēr) Al. (Birmingham In.)	33·31 N	86·52 W
106	Edgewater....Md. (Baltimore In.)	38·58 N	76·35 W
93	Edgewood (ĕj'wŏŏd) Can.	49·47 N	118·08 W
165	Édhessa Grc.	40·48 N	22·04 E
113	Edina (ê-dī'nȧ) Mn. (Minneapolis, St. Paul In.)	44·55 N	93·20 W
117	Edina Mo.	40·10 N	92·11 W
104	Edinburg (ĕd''n-bûrg) In.	39·20 N	85·55 W
118	Edinburg Tx.	26·18 N	98·08 W
154	Edinburgh (ĕd''n-bŭr-ô) Scot.	55·57 N	3·10 W
165	Edirne (Adrianople) (ĕ-dĭr'nĕ) (ā-drĭ-ăn-ō'p'l) Tur.	41·41 N	26·35 E
121	Edisto, (R.) (ĕd'ĭs-tō) SC	33·10 N	80·50 W
121	Edisto (R.), North Fk. SC	33·42 N	81·24 W
121	Edisto (R.), South Fk. SC	33·43 N	81·35 W
121	Edisto Island SC	32·32 N	80·20 W
117	Edmond (ĕd'mŭnd) Ok.	35·39 N	97·29 W
112	Edmonds (ĕd'mŭndz) Wa. (Seattle In.)	47·49 N	122·23 W
89	Edmonton...Can. (Edmonton In.)	53·33 N	113·28 W
98	Edmundston (ĕd'mŭn-stŭn) Can.	47·22 N	68·20 W
119	Edna (ĕd'nȧ) Tx.	28·59 N	96·39 W
165	Edremit (ĕd-rĕ-mēt') Tur.	39·35 N	27·00 E
165	Edremit Körfezi (G.) Tur.	39·28 N	26·35 E
93	Edson (ĕd'sŭn) Can.	53·35 N	116·26 W
96	Edward (I.) (ĕd'wērd) Can.	48·21 N	88·29 W
217	Edward (L.) Zaire	0·25 S	29·40 E
113	Edwardsville (ĕd'wērdz-vĭl) Il. (St. Louis In.)	38·49 N	89·58 W
107	Edwardsville..In. (Louisville In.)	38·17 N	85·53 W
113	Edwardsville Ks. (Kansas City In.)	39·04 N	94·49 W
110	Eel (R.) (ēl) Ca.	40·39 N	124·15 W
104	Eel (R.) In.	40·50 N	85·55 W
205	Efate (I.) (ā-fä'tā)....New Hebr.	18·02 S	168·29 E
109	Effigy Mounds Natl. Mon. (ĕf'ĭ-jŭ mounds) Ia.	43·04 N	91·15 W
104	Effingham (ĕf'ĭng-hăm) Il.	39·05 N	88·30 W
162	Ega (R.) (ā'gä) Sp.	42·40 N	2·20 W
164	Egadi, Isole (Is.) (ĕ'sō-lĕ-ĕ'gä-dē) It.	38·01 N	12·00 E
162	Egea de los Caballeros (ā-kā'ā dā lōs kä-bäl-yā'rōs) Sp.	42·07 N	1·05 W
101	Egegik (ĕg'ĕ-jĭt) Ak.	58·10 N	157·22 W
159	Eger (ĕ gĕr) Hung.	47·53 N	20·24 E
	Eger (R.), see Ohře		
156	Egersund (ĕ'ghĕr-sŏŏn') Nor.	58·29 N	6·01 E
105	Egg Harbor (ĕg här'bēr) NJ	39·30 N	74·35 W
148	Egham (ĕg'ăm).Eng. (London In.)	51·24 N	0·33 W
188	Egiin Gol (R.) (ā-gēn') ....Mong.	49·41 N	100·40 E
205	Egmont, C. (ĕg'mŏnt)..N. Z. (In.)	39·18 S	173·49 E
171	Egridir Gölü (L.) (ā-rĭ-dĭr')..Tur.	38·10 N	30·00 E
160	Eguilles (ĕ-gwē') Fr. (In.)	43·34 N	5·21 E
209	Egypt (ē'jĭpt) Afr.	26·58 N	27·01 E
215	Eha-Amufu Nig.	6·40 N	7·46 E
162	Eibar (ā'ê-bär) Sp.	43·12 N	2·20 W
158	Eichstätt (īk'shtät) F.R.G.	48·54 N	11·14 E
149	Eichwalde (īk'väl-dĕ) G.D.R. (Berlin In.)	52·22 N	13·37 E
156	Eid (īdh) Nor.	61·54 N	6·01 E
156	Eidsberg (īdhs'bĕrgh) Nor.	59·32 N	11·16 E
156	Eidsvoll (īdhs'vôl) Nor.	60·19 N	11·15 E
158	Eifel (Plat.) (ī'fĕl) F.R.G.	50·08 N	6·30 E
204	Eighty Mile Beach Austl.	20·45 S	121·00 E
218	Eil.......Som. (Horn of Afr. In.)	7·53 N	49·45 E
158	Eilenburg (ī'lĕn-bŏŏrgh)...G.D.R.	51·27 N	12·38 E
213	Elliot.......S. Afr. (Natal In.)	31·19 S	27·52 E
158	Einbeck (īn'bĕk) F.R.G.	51·49 N	9·52 E
155	Eindhoven (īnd'hō-vĕn) Neth.	51·29 N	5·20 E
134	Eirunepé (ā-rōō-nĕ-pĕ') Braz.	6·37 S	69·58 W
158	Eisenach (ī'zĕn-äk) G.D.R.	50·58 N	10·18 E
158	Eisenhüttenstadt G.D.R.	52·08 N	14·40 E
158	Eisleben (īs'lā'bĕn) G.D.R.	51·31 N	11·33 E
156	Ejdfjord (ĕĭd'fyōr) Nor.	60·28 N	7·04 E
214	Ejura Ghana	7·23 N	1·22 W
125	Ejutla de Crespo (ā-hōōt'lä dā krās'pō) Mex.	16·34 N	96·44 W
216	Ekanga Zaire	2·23 S	23·14 E
157	Ekenäs (Tammisaari) (ĕ'kĕ-nâs) (tám'ĭ-sä'rĭ) Fin.	59·59 N	23·25 E
149	Ekeren........Bel. (Brussels In.)	51·17 N	4·27 E
216	Ekoli Zaire	0·23 S	24·16 E
156	Eksjö (ĕk'shû) Swe.	57·41 N	14·55 E
210	El Aaiún W. Sah.	26·45 N	13·15 W
163	El Affroun (ĕl ȧf-froun') Alg	36·28 N	2·38 E
213	Elands (R.)....S. Afr. (Natal In.)	31·48 S	26·09 E
218	Elands (R.) (ē̇lănds) S. Afr. (Johannesburg & Pretoria In.)	25·11 S	28·52 E
162	El Arahal (ĕl ä-rä-äl') Sp.	37·17 N	5·32 W
152	El Asnam (Orléansville) Alg.	36·14 N	1·32 E
183	Elat........Isr. (Palestine In.)	29·34 N	34·57 E
171	Elâzig (ĕl-ä'zĕz) Tur.	38·40 N	39·00 E
120	Elba (ĕl'bȧ) Al.	31·25 N	86·01 W
164	Elba, Isola di (I.) (ĕ-sō lä-dē-ĕl'bȧ) It.	42·42 N	10·25 E
134	El Banco (ĕl băn'cō) Col.	8·58 N	74·01 W
162	El Barco (ĕl bär'kō) Sp.	42·26 N	6·58 W
165	Elbasan (ĕl-bä-sän') Alb.	41·08 N	20·05 E
152	El Bayadh Alg.	33·42 N	1·06 E
	Elbe (R.), see Labe		
158	Elbe (R.) (ĕl'bĕ) G.D.R.	53·47 N	9·20 E
115	Elbert, Mt. (ĕl'bērt) Co.	39·05 N	106·25 W
120	Elberton (ĕl'bēr-tŭn) Ga.	34·05 N	82·53 W
160	Elbeuf (ĕl-bûf') Fr.	49·16 N	0·59 E
171	Elbistan (ĕl-bē-stän') Tur.	38·20 N	37·10 E
159	Elblag (ĕl'blăng) Pol.	54·11 N	19·25 E
162	El Bonillo (ĕl bō-nēl'yō) Sp.	38·56 N	2·31 W
89	Elbow (R.) (ĕl'bō) Can. (Calgary In.)	51·03 N	114·24 W
128	Elbow Cay (I.) Ba.	26·25 N	77·55 W
108	Elbow Lake Mn.	46·00 N	95·59 W
171	El'brus, Gora (Mt.) (ĕl'brōōs') Sov. Un.	43·20 N	42·25 E
218	El Bur....Som. (Horn of Afr. In.)	4·35 N	46·40 E
171	Elburz Mts. (ĕl'bōōrz') Iran	36·30 N	51·00 E
114	El Cajon Ca. (In.)	32·48 N	116·58 W
134	El Cajon (ĕl-kä-kô'n)...Col. (In.)	4·50 N	76·35 W
135	El Cambur (käm-bōōr').Ven. (In.)	10·24 N	68·06 W
119	El Campo (kăm'pō) Tx.	29·13 N	96·17 W
137	El Carmen (kà'r-mĕn) Chile (Santiago In.)	34·14 S	71·23 W
134	El Carmen (kà'r-mĕn) Col.	9·54 N	75·12 W
113	El Casco (kăs'kō) Ca. (Los Angeles In.)	33·59 N	117·08 W
114	El Centro (sĕn'trō) Ca.	32·47 N	115·33 W
112	El Cerrito (sĕr-rē'tō) Ca. (San Francisco In.)	37·55 N	122·19 W
163	Elche (ĕl'chā) Sp.	38·15 N	0·42 W
126	El Cuyo.........Mex. (In.)	21·30 N	87·42 W
163	Elda (ĕl'dä) Sp.	38·28 N	0·44 W
158	Elde (R.) (ĕl'dĕ) G.D.R.	53·11 N	11·30 E
210	El Djouf (Des.) (ĕl djōōf) Mauritania	21·45 N	7·05 W
109	Eldon (ĕl-dŭn) Ia.	40·55 N	92·15 W
115	Eldon Mo.	38·21 N	92·36 W
109	Eldora (ĕl-dō'rȧ) Ia.	42·21 N	93·08 W
117	El Dorado (ĕl dô-rä'dō) Ar.	33·13 N	92·39 W
104	Eldorado Il.	37·50 N	88·30 W
117	El Dorado Ks.	37·49 N	96·51 W
117	Eldorado Springs (sprĭngz)...Mo.	37·51 N	94·02 W
217	Eldoret (ĕl-dô-rĕt') Ken.	0·31 N	35·17 E
124	El Ebano (ā-bä'nō) Mex.	22·13 N	98·26 W
116	Electra (ê-lĕk'trȧ) Tx.	34·02 N	98·54 W
111	Electric Pk. (ê-lĕk'trĭk) Mt.	45·03 N	110·52 W
174	Elektrogorsk (ĕl-yĕk'trô-gôrsk) Sov. Un. (Moscow In.)	55·53 N	38·48 E
174	Elektrostal (ĕl-yĕk'trô-stál) Sov. Un. (Moscow In.)	55·47 N	38·27 E
174	Elektrougli.Sov. Un. (Moscow In.)	55·43 N	38·13 E
115	Elephant Butte Res. (ĕl'ê-fănt būt).NM	33·25 N	107·10 W
163	El Escorial (ĕl-ĕs-kô-ryä'l) Sp. (Madrid In.)	40·38 N	4·08 W
126	El Espino (ĕl-ĕs-pē'nō) Nic.	13·26 N	86·48 W
129	Eleuthera (I.) (ê-lū'thēr-ȧ) Ba.	25·05 N	76·10 W
129	Eleuthera Pt. Ba.	24·35 N	76·05 W
117	Eleven Point (R.) (ê-lĕv'ĕn).Mo.	36·53 N	91·39 W
162	El Ferrol (fā-rōl') Sp.	43·30 N	8·12 W
107	Elgin (ĕl'jĭn).....Il. (Chicago In.)	42·03 N	88·16 W
108	Elgin Ne.	41·58 N	98·04 W
110	Elgin Or.	45·34 N	117·58 W
154	Elgin Scot.	57·40 N	3·30 W
119	Elgin Tx.	30·21 N	97·22 W
112	Elgin.........Wa. (Seattle In.)	47·23 N	122·42 W
210	El Goléa (gô-lā-ä') Alg.	30·39 N	2·52 E
217	Elgon, Mt. (ĕl'gŏn) Ken.	1·00 N	34·25 E
124	El Grullo (grōōl-yō) Mex.	19·46 N	104·10 W
135	El Guapo (gwà'pō).....Ven. (In.)	10·07 N	66·00 W
110	El Hank (Bluffs).Mauritania-Mali	23·44 N	6·45 W
135	El Hatillo (ä-tē'l-yō)...Ven. (In.)	10·08 N	65·13 W
89	Elie (ĕ'lē)........Can. (Winnipeg In.)	49·55 N	97·45 W
217	Elila (R.) (ĕ-lē'lȧ) Zaire	3·00 S	26·50 E
112	Elisa (I.) (ê-lĭ'sȧ) Wa. (Vancouver In.)	48·43 N	122·37 W
	Élisabethville, see Lubumbashi		
157	Elisenvaara (ā-lē'sĕn-vä'rȧ) Sov. Un.	61·25 N	29·46 E
119	Elizabeth (ê-lĭz'ȧ-bĕth) La.	30·50 N	92·47 W
106	Elizabeth.....NJ (New York In.)	40·40 N	74·13 W
107	Elizabeth....Pa. (Pittsburgh In.)	40·16 N	79·53 W
121	Elizabeth City NC	36·15 N	76·15 W
121	Elizabethton (ê-lĭz-ȧ-bĕth'tŭn).Tn.	36·19 N	82·12 W
104	Elizabethtown (ê-lĭz'ȧ-bĕth-toun) Ky.	37·40 N	85·55 W
210	El Jadida Mor.	33·14 N	8·34 W
159	Elk Pol.	53·53 N	22·23 E
93	Elk (R.) Can.	50·00 N	115·00 W
120	Elk (R.) Tn.	35·05 N	86·36 W
104	Elk (R.) WV	38·30 N	81·05 W
210	El Kairouan (kĕr-ōō-än) Tun.	35·46 N	10·04 E
116	Elk City (ĕlk) Ok.	35·23 N	99·23 W
104	Elkhart (ĕlk'härt) In.	41·40 N	86·00 W
116	Elkhart Ks.	37·00 N	101·54 W
119	Elkhart Tx.	31·38 N	95·35 W
109	Elkhorn (ĕlk'hôrn) Wi.	42·39 N	88·32 W
108	Elkhorn (R.) Ne.	42·06 N	97·46 W
121	Elkin (ĕl'kĭn) NC	36·15 N	80·50 W
105	Elkins (ĕl'kĭnz) WV	38·55 N	79·50 W
95	Elk I. Can.	50·45 N	96·32 W
93	Elk Island Natl. Park (ĕlk ī'lănd) Can.	53·37 N	112·45 W
110	Elko (ĕl'kō) Nv.	40·51 N	115·46 W
108	Elk Point SD	42·41 N	96·41 W
104	Elk Rapids (răp'ĭdz) Mi.	44·55 N	85·25 W
110	Elk River (rĭv'ēr) Id.	46·47 N	116·11 W
109	Elk River Mn.	45·17 N	93·33 W
120	Elkton (ĕlk'tŭn) Ky.	36·47 N	87·08 W
105	Elkton Md.	39·35 N	75·50 W
108	Elkton SD	44·15 N	96·28 W
148	Elland (el'ănd) Eng.	53·41 N	1·50 W
115	Ellen, Mt. (ĕl'ĕn) Ut.	38·05 N	110·50 W
108	Ellendale (ĕl'ĕn-dāl) ND	46·01 N	98·33 W
110	Ellensburg (ĕl'ĕnz-bûrg) Wa.	47·00 N	120·31 W
105	Ellenville (ĕl'ĕn-vĭl) NY	41·40 N	74·25 W
89	Ellerslie (ĕl'ērz-lê) Can. (Edmonton In.)	53·25 N	113·30 W
148	Ellesmere (ĕlz'mēr) Eng.	52·55 N	2·54 W
75	Ellesmere I. Can.	81·00 N	80·00 W
148	Ellesmere Port Eng.	53·17 N	2·54 W
	Ellice Is., see Tuvalu		
106	Ellicott City (ĕl'ĭ-kŏt sĭ'tê) Md. (Baltimore In.)	39·16 N	76·48 W
107	Ellicott Cr......NY (Buffalo In.)	43·00 N	78·46 W
213	Elliotdale (ĕl-ĭ-ŏt'dāl) S. Afr. (Natal In.)	31·58 S	28·42 E
96	Elliot Lake Can.	46·23 N	82·39 W
112	Elliot (el'ĭ-ŭt)..Wa. (Seattle In.)	47·28 N	122·08 W
116	Ellis (ĕl'ĭs) Ks.	38·56 N	99·34 W
120	Ellisville (ĕl'ĭs-vĭl) Ms.	31·37 N	89·10 W
113	Ellisville......Mo. (St. Louis In.)	38·35 N	90·35 W
116	Ellsworth (ĕlz'wûrth) Ks.	38·43 N	98·14 W
98	Ellsworth Me.	44·33 N	68·26 W
220	Ellsworth Highland Ant.	77·00 S	90·00 W
158	Ellwangen (ĕl'văn-gĕn).....F.R.G.	48·47 N	10·08 E
149	Elm (ĕlm)..F.R.G. (Hamburg In.)	53·31 N	9·13 E
108	Elm (R.) SD	45·47 N	98·28 W
104	Elm (R.) WV	38·30 N	81·05 W
110	Elma (ĕl'mȧ) Wa.	47·02 N	123·20 W
117	Elm Cr. Tx.	33·34 N	97·25 W
113	Elmendorf (ĕl'mĕn-dôrf) Tx. (San Antonio In.)	29·16 N	98·20 W
113	Elm Fork (ĕlm fôrk) Tx. (Dallas, Fort Worth In.)	32·55 N	96·56 W
107	Elmhurst (ĕlm'hûrst) Il. (Chicago In.)	41·54 N	87·56 W
210	El Milia (mē'ä) Alg.	36·30 N	6·16 E
105	Elmira (ĕl-mī'rȧ) NY	42·05 N	76·50 W
105	Elmira Heights NY	42·10 N	76·50 W
134	El Misti (Vol.) (mē's-tē).....Peru	16·04 S	71·20 W
113	El Modena (mô-dē'nō) Ca. (Los Angeles In.)	33·47 N	117·48 W
113	El Monte (mōn'tȧ) Ca. (Los Angeles In.)	34·04 N	118·02 W
115	El Morro Natl. Mon. NM	35·05 N	108·20 W
214	El Mreyyé (Des.).....Mauritania	19·15 N	7·50 W
149	Elmshorn (ĕlms'hôrn) F.R.G. (Hamburg In.)	53·45 N	9·39 E
107	Elmwood Place (ĕlm'wŏŏd plās) Oh. (Cincinnati In.)	39·11 N	84·30 W
111	Elokomin (R.) (ê-lō'kō-mĭn) Wa. (Portland In.)	46·16 N	123·16 W
124	El Oro (ô-rō) Mex.	19·49 N	100·04 W
210	El Oued (wĕd') Alg.	33·23 N	6·49 E
134	El Pao (ĕl pá'ō) Ven.	8·08 N	62·37 W
126	El Paraíso (pä-rä-ē'sō).....Hond.	13·55 N	86·35 W
163	El Pardo (pär-dô) Sp. (Madrid In.)	40·31 N	3·47 W
118	El Paso (pas'ō) Tx.	31·47 N	106·27 W
135	El Pilar (pē-lä'r).......Ven. (In.)	9·56 N	64·48 W
127	El Porvenir (pôr-vä-nēr')....Pan.	9·34 N	78·55 W
162	El Puerto de Sta. María (pwĕr tō dā sän tä mä-rē'ä).Sp.	36·36 N	6·18 W
127	El Real (rā-äl) Pan.	8·07 N	77·43 W
116	El Reno (rē'nō) Ok.	35·31 N	97·57 W
135	El Roboré (rô-bō-rĕ') Bol.	18·23 S	59·43 W
109	Elroy (ĕl'roi) Wi.	43·44 N	90·17 W
101	Elsa Can.	63·55 N	135·25 W
113	Elsah (ĕl'zȧ).....Il. (St. Louis In.)	38·57 N	90·22 W
124	El Salto (säl'tō) Mex.	22·48 N	105·22 W
122	El Salvador N. A.	14·00 N	89·30 W
126	El Sauce (ĕl-sà'ōō-sĕ) Nic.	13·00 N	86·40 W
117	Elsberry (ĕlz'bĕr-ĭ) Mo.	39·09 N	90·44 W
161	Elsdorf (ĕls'dōrf) F.R.G. (Ruhr In.)	50·56 N	6·35 E
3	El Segundo (sĕgŭn'dō) Ca. (Los Angeles In.)	33·55 N	118·24 W
13	Elsinore (ĕl'sĭ-nôr) Ca. (Los Angeles In.)	33·40 N	117·19 W
113	Elsinore L...Ca. (Los Angeles In.)	33·38 N	117·21 W
149	Elstorf (ĕls'tōrf) F.R.G. (Hamburg In.)	53·25 N	9·48 E
202	Eltham (ĕl'thăm) Austl. (Melbourne In.)	37·43 S	145·08 E
134	El Tigre (tē'grĕ) Ven.	8·49 N	64·15 W
171	El'ton (L.) Sov. Un.	49·10 N	47·00 E
113	El Toro (tō'rō) Ca. (Los Angeles In.)	33·37 N	117·42 W
126	El Triunfo (ĕl-trē-ōō'n-fô)..Hond.	13·06 N	87·00 W
126	El Triunfo Sal.	13·17 N	88·32 W
187	Elūru India	16·44 N	80·09 E
115	El Vado Res. NM	36·37 N	106·30 W
162	Elvas (ĕl'väzh) Port.	38·53 N	7·11 W
156	Elverum (ĕl'vĕ-rŏŏm) Nor.	60·53 N	11·33 E
126	El Viego (ĕl-vyĕ'kŏ) Nic.	12·10 N	87·10 W
126	El Viejo (Vol.) Nic.	12·44 N	87·03 W
117	Elvins (ĕl'vĭnz) Mo.	37·49 N	90·31 W
211	El Wak (wäk') Ken.	3·00 N	41·00 E
107	Elwood (ĕl'wŏŏd).Il. (Chicago In.)	41·24 N	88·07 W
104	Elwood In.	40·15 N	85·50 W
155	Ely (ē'lĭ) Eng.	52·25 N	0·17 E
109	Ely Mn.	47·54 N	91·53 W
114	Ely Nv.	39·16 N	114·53 W
107	Elyria (ê-lĭr'ĭ-ȧ) Oh. (Cleveland In.)	41·22 N	82·07 W
157	Ema (R.) (â'mȧ) Sov. Un.	58·25 N	27·00 E
156	Emån (R.) Swe.	57·15 N	15·46 E
171	Emba (R.) (yĕm'bȧ) Sov. Un.	46·50 N	54·10 E
134	Embalse Guri (L.) Ven.	7·30 N	63·00 W
104	Embarrass (R.) (ĕm-băr'ăs)...Il.	39·15 N	88·05 W
89	Embrun (ĕm'brŭn) Can. (Ottawa In.)	45·16 N	75·17 W
161	Embrun (äN-brûN') Fr.	44·35 N	6·32 E
217	Embu Ken.	0·32 S	37·27 E
158	Emden (ĕm'dĕn) F.R.G.	53·21 N	7·15 E
205	Emerald (ĕm'ēr-ăld) Austl.	28·34 S	148·00 E
95	Emerson (ĕm'ēr-sŭn) Can.	49·00 N	97·12 W
112	Emeryville (ĕm'ēr-ĭ-vĭl) Ca. (San Francisco In.)	37·50 N	122·17 W
215	Emi Koussi, (Mtn.) (ā'mê kōō-sē') Chad	19·50 N	18·30 E
164	Emilia-Romagna (Reg.) (ā-mēl'yä rô-mà'n-yä).It.	44·35 N	10·48 E

ăt; finăl; rāte; senâte; ärm; ȧsk; sofȧ; fâre; ch-choose; dh-as th in other; bē; êvent; bĕt; recĕnt; cratēr; g-go; gh-guttural g; bĭt; ĭ-short neutral; rīde; K-guttural k as ch in German ich;

PRONOUNCING INDEX

Emiliano Zapata — Everard 279

Page	Name Pronunciation Region	Lat. °′	Long. °′
125	Emiliano Zapata (ĕ-mē-lyä'nô-zä-pä'tȧ). Mex.	17·45 N	91·46 W
104	Eminence (ĕm'-ĭ-nĕns) Ky.	38·25 N	85·15 W
197	Emira I. (ā-mē-rä') Pap. N. Gui.	1·40 S	150·28 E
155	Emmen (ĕm'ĕn) Neth.	52·48 N	6·55 E
161	Emmerich (ĕm'ēr-ĭk) F.R.G. (Ruhr In.)	51·51 N	6·16 E
109	Emmetsburg (ĕm'ĕts-bûrg) Ia.	43·07 N	94·41 W
110	Emmett (ĕm'ĕt) Id.	43·53 N	116·30 W
111	Emmons Mt. (ĕm'ŭnz) Ut.	40·43 N	110·20 W
118	Emory Pk. (ĕ'mō-rē pēk) Tx.	29·13 N	103·20 W
164	Empoli (ām'pô-lē) It.	43·43 N	10·55 E
117	Emporia (ĕm-pō'rĭ-ȧ) Ks.	38·24 N	96·11 W
121	Emporia Va.	37·40 N	77·34 W
105	Emporium (ĕm-pō'rĭ-ŭm) Pa.	41·30 N	78·15 W
158	Ems R. (ĕms) F.R.G.	52·52 N	7·16 E
158	Ems-Weser (Can.) (vā'zĕr) F.R.G.	52·23 N	8·11 E
158	Enånger (ĕn-ôŋ'gĕr) Swe.	61·36 N	16·55 E
122	Encantada, Cerro de la (Mtn.) (sĕ'r-rô-dĕ-lä-ĕn-kän-tä'dä). Mex.	31·58 N	115·15 W
197	Encanto, C. (ĕn-kän'tō). Phil. (In.)	15·44 N	121·46 E
136	Encarnación (ĕn-kär-nä-syōn') Par.	27·26 S	55·52 W
124	Encarnación de Diaz (ĕn-kär-nä-syōn dā dē'äz). Mex.	21·34 N	102·15 W
118	Encinal (ĕn'sĭ-nôl) Tx.	28·02 N	99·22 W
134	Encontrados (ĕn-kōn-trä'dōs). Ven.	9·01 N	72·10 W
203	Encounter B. (ĕn-koun'tēr) Austl.	35·50 S	138·45 E
92	Endako (R.) Can.	54·05 N	125·30 W
183	Endau (R.) Mala. (Singapore In.)	2·29 N	103·40 E
198	Enderbury (I.) (ĕn'dēr-bûrĭ) Oceania	2·00 S	107·50 W
220	Enderby Land (Reg.) (ĕn'dĕr bĭĭ) Ant.	72·00 S	52·00 E
108	Enderlin (ĕn'dēr-lĭn) ND	46·38 N	97·37 W
105	Endicott (ĕn'dĭ-kŏt) NY	42·05 N	76·00 W
101	Endicott Mts. Ak.	67·30 N	153·45 W
165	Enez Tur.	40·42 N	26·05 E
105	Enfield (ĕn'fēld) Ct.	41·55 N	72·35 W
148	Enfield Eng. (London In.)	51·38 N	0·06 W
121	Enfield NC	36·10 N	77·41 W
129	Engano, Cabo (C.) (kȧ'-bô-ĕn-gä-nô). Dom. Rep.	18·40 N	68·30 W
213	Engcobo (ĕŋg-cô-bô) S. Afr. (Natal In.)	31·41 S	27·59 E
171	Engel's (ĕn'gĕls) Sov. Un.	51·20 N	45·40 E
161	Engelskirchen (ĕn'gĕls-kēr'kĕn) F.R.G. (Ruhr In.)	50·59 N	7·25 E
116	Engelwood (ĕn'g'l-wŏŏd) Co.	39·39 N	105·00 W
196	Enggano, Pulau (I.) (ĕng-gä'nō) Indon.	5·22 S	102·18 E
117	England (ĭŋ'glȧnd) Ar.	34·33 N	91·58 W
154	England (Reg.) (ĭŋ'glȧnd) U. K.	51·35 N	1·40 W
99	Englee (ĕn-glē) Can.	50·44 N	56·06 W
106	Englewood NJ (New York In.)	40·54 N	73·59 W
104	English (ĭn'glĭsh) In.	38·15 N	86·25 W
91	English (R.) Can.	50·31 N	94·12 W
151	English Chan. Eng.	49·45 N	3·06 W
163	Énguera (ān'gārä) Sp.	38·58 N	0·42 W
116	Enid (ē'nĭd) Ok.	36·25 N	97·52 W
120	Enid Res. Ms.	34·13 N	89·47 W
212	Enkeldoorn (ĕŋ'k'l-dōōrn) Zimb.	19·59 S	30·58 E
218	Enkeldoring (ĕŋ'k'l-dôr-ĭng). S.Afr. (Johannesburg & Pretoria In.)	25·24 S	28·43 E
156	Enköping (ĕn'kû-pĭng) Swe.	59·39 N	17·05 E
211	Ennedi (Plat.) (ĕn-nĕd'ē) Chad	16·45 N	22·45 E
154	Ennis (ĕn'ĭs) Ire.	52·54 N	9·05 W
119	Ennis Tx.	32·20 N	96·38 W
154	Enniscorthy (ĕn-ĭs-kôr'thĭ) Ire.	52·33 N	6·27 W
154	Enniskillen (ĕn-ĭs-kĭl'ĕn) N. Ire.	54·20 N	7·25 W
158	Enns (R.) (ĕns) Aus.	47·37 N	14·35 E
121	Enoree (ē-nō'rē) SC	34·43 N	81·58 W
121	Enoree, (R.) SC	34·35 N	81·55 W
129	Enriquillo (ĕn-rē-kē'l-yō) Dom. Rep.	17·55 N	71·15 W
129	Enriquillo, Lago (L.) (lä'gô-ĕn-rē-kē'l-yô). Dom. Rep.	18·35 N	71·35 W
155	Enschede (ĕns'kȧ-dĕ) Neth.	52·10 N	6·50 E
122	Ensenada (ĕn-sĕ-nä'dä) Mex.	32·00 N	116·30 W
137	Enseñada Arg. (Buenos Aires In.)	34·50 S	57·55 W
193	Enshi (ŭn-shr) China	30·18 N	109·25 E
195	Enshū-Nada (Sea) (ĕn'shōō nä-dä). Jap.	34·25 N	137·14 E
217	Entebbe (ĕn-tĕb'ĕ) Ug.	0·04 N	32·28 E
120	Enterprise (ĕn'tēr-prīz) Al.	31·20 N	85·50 W
110	Enterprise Or.	45·25 N	117·16 W
110	Entiat, L. Wa.	45·43 N	120·11 W
160	Entraygues (ĕN-trĕg') Fr.	44·39 N	2·33 E
217	Entre-Rios (ĕn-trā rē'ōs) Moz.	14·57 S	37·20 E
136	Entre Ríos (Prov.) Arg.	31·30 S	59·00 W
215	Enugu (ē-nōō'gōō) Nig.	6·27 N	7·27 E
112	Enumclaw (ĕn'ŭm-klô) Wa. (Seattle In.)	47·12 N	121·59 W
134	Envigado (ĕn-vē-gä'dŏ) Col. (In.)	6·10 N	75·34 W
164	Eolie, Isole (Is.) (ĕ'sō-lĕ-ĕ-ō'lyĕ). It.	38·43 N	14·43 E
215	Epe Nig.	6·37 N	3·59 E
165	Epeirus (Reg.) Grc.	39·35 N	20·45 E
160	Epernay (ā-pĕr-nĕ') Fr.	49·02 N	3·54 E
161	Épernon (ā-pĕr-nôN') Fr. (Paris In.)	48·36 N	1·41 E
115	Ephraim (ē'frȧ-ĭm) Ut.	39·20 N	111·40 W
110	Ephrata (ē frā'tȧ) Wa.	47·18 N	119·35 W
205	Epi (ā'pē) New Hebr.	16·59 S	168·29 E
162	Épila (ā'pē-lä) Sp.	41·38 N	1·15 W
161	Épinal (ā-pē-nàl') Fr.	48·11 N	6·27 E
183	Episkopi Cyprus (Palestine In.)	34·38 N	32·55 E
148	Epping (ĕp'ĭng). Eng. (London In.)	51·41 N	0·06 E
216	Epupa Falls Ang.	17·00 S	13·05 E
148	Epworth (ĕp'wûrth) Eng.	53·31 N	0·50 W
210	Equatorial Guinea Afr.	2·00 N	7·15 E
160	Equeurdreville (ā-kûr-dr'vēl') Fr.	49·38 N	1·42 W
89	Eramosa (R.) (ĕr-ȧ-mō'sȧ) Can. (Toronto In.)	43·39 N	80·08 W
211	Erba, Jabal (Mtn.) (ĕr'bȧ) Sud.	20·53 N	36·45 E
153	Erciyeş Daği (Mtn.) Tur.	38·30 N	35·36 E
113	Erda (ĕr'dä) Ut. (Salt Lake City In.)	40·41 N	112·17 W
149	Erding (ĕr'dēng) F.R.G. (Munich In.)	48·19 N	11·54 E
136	Erechim (ĕ-rĕ-shē'N) Braz.	27·43 S	52·11 W
171	Ereğli (ĕ-rā'ĭ-le) Tur.	37·40 N	34·00 E
171	Ereğli Tur.	41·15 N	31·25 E
158	Erfurt (ĕr'fŏŏrt) G.D.R.	50·59 N	11·04 E
165	Ergene (R.) (ĕr'gĕ-nĕ) Tur.	41·17 N	26·50 E
162	Erges (R.) (ĕr'-zhĕs) Port.-Sp.	39·45 N	7·01 W
157	Ērgli Sov. Un.	56·54 N	25·38 E
162	Eria (R.) (ā-rē'ä) Sp.	42·10 N	6·08 W
116	Erick (âr'ĭk) Ok.	35·14 N	99·51 W
117	Erie (ē'rĭ) Ks.	37·35 N	95·17 W
105	Erie Pa.	42·05 N	80·05 W
103	Erie, L. U. S.-Can.	42·15 N	81·25 W
194	Erimo Saki (C.) (ā'rē-mō sä-kē) Jap.	41·53 N	143·20 E
89	Erin (ĕ'rĭn) Can. (Toronto In.)	43·46 N	80·04 W
211	Eritrea (Reg.) (ā-rē-trā'ȧ) Eth.	16·15 N	38·30 E
158	Erlangen (ĕr'läng-ĕn) F.R.G.	49·36 N	11·03 E
107	Erlanger (ĕr'lăng-ĕr) Ky. (Cincinnati In.)	39·01 N	84·36 W
	Ermoúpolis, see Síros		
185	Ernākulam India	9·58 N	76·23 E
154	Erne, Upper Lough (L.) (lŏk ûrn). N. Ire.	54·20 N	7·24 W
154	Erne, Lough (L.) N. Ire.	54·30 N	7·40 W
91	Ernest Sound (ûr'nĕst) Ak.	55·52 N	132·10 W
185	Erode India	11·20 N	77·45 E
205	Eromanga (I.) New Hebr.	18·58 S	169·18 E
119	Eros (ē'rōs) La.	32·23 N	92·22 W
217	Errego Moz.	16·02 S	37·14 E
152	Er Ricani Mor.	31·09 N	4·20 W
154	Errigal, (Mt.) (ĕr-ĭ-gôl') Ire.	55·02 N	8·07 W
112	Errol Heights Or. (Portland In.)	45·29 N	122·38 W
161	Erstein (ĕr'shtīn) Fr.	48·27 N	7·40 E
121	Erwin (ûr'wĭn) NC	35·16 N	78·40 W
121	Erwin Tn.	36·07 N	82·25 W
158	Erzgebirge (Ore Mts.) (ĕrts'gĕ-bē'gĕ). G.D.R.	50·29 N	12·40 E
171	Erzincan (ĕr-zĭn-jän') Tur.	39·50 N	39·30 E
171	Erzurum (ĕrz'rōōm') Tur.	39·55 N	41·10 E
216	Esambo Zaire	3·40 S	23·24 E
194	Esashi (ĕs'ä-shē) Jap.	41·50 N	140·10 E
156	Esbjerg (ĕs'byĕrgh) Den.	55·29 N	8·25 E
162	Escairón (ĕs-kī-rō'n) Sp.	42·34 N	7·40 W
115	Escalante (ĕs-kȧ-lăn'tē) Ut.	37·50 N	111·40 W
115	Escalante (R.) Ut.	37·40 N	111·20 W
118	Escalón Mex.	26·45 N	104·20 W
120	Escambia (R.) (ĕs-kăm'bĭ-ȧ) Fl.	30·38 N	87·20 W
109	Escanaba (ĕs-kȧ-nô'bȧ) Mi.	45·44 N	87·05 W
109	Escanaba (R.) Mi.	46·10 N	87·22 W
196	Escarpada Point Phil.	18·40 N	122·45 E
161	Esch-sur-Alzette Lux.	49·32 N	6·21 E
158	Eschwege (ĕsh'vā-gē) F.R.G.	51·11 N	10·02 E
161	Eschweiler (ĕsh'vī-lēr) F.R.G. (Ruhr In.)	50·49 N	6·15 E
129	Escocesá, Bahia (B.) (bä-ē'ä-ĕs-kō-sĕ'sä). Dom. Rep.	19·25 N	69·40 W
114	Escondido (ĕs-kŏn-dē'dō) Ca.	33·07 N	117·00 W
118	Escondido, Rio (R.) (rē'ō-ĕs-kōn-dē'dô). Mex.	28·30 N	100·45 W
127	Escondido R. Nic.	12·04 N	84·09 W
127	Escudo de Veraguas I. (ĕs-kōō'dä dā vā-rä'gwäs). Pan.	9·07 N	81·25 W
124	Escuinapa (ĕs-kwē-nä'pä) Mex.	22·49 N	105·44 W
126	Escuintla (ĕs-kwēn'tlä) Guat.	14·16 N	90·47 W
125	Escuintla Mex.	15·20 N	92·45 W
127	Ese, Cayos de (I.) Col.	12·24 N	81·07 W
186	Esfahān Iran	32·38 N	51·30 E
162	Esgueva (R.) (ĕs-gĕ'vä) Sp.	41·48 N	4·10 W
213	Eshowe (ĕsh'ō-wê) S. Afr. (Natal In.)	28·54 S	31·28 E
214	Esiama Ghana	4·56 N	2·21 W
104	Eskdale (ĕsk'dāl) WV	38·05 N	81·25 W
150	Eskifjördhur (ĕs'kē-fyûr'dōōr). Ice.	65·04 N	14·01 W
156	Eskilstuna (å'shĕl-stü-na) Swe.	59·23 N	16·28 E
90	Eskimo Lakes (L.) (es'kĭ-mō) Can.	69·40 N	130·10 W
171	Eskişehir (ĕs-kê-shĕ'h'r) Tur.	39·40 N	30·20 E
113	Esko (ĕs'kô) Mn. (Duluth In.)	46·27 N	92·22 W
162	Esla (R.) (ĕs-lä) Sp.	41·50 N	5·48 W
156	Eslöv (ĕs'lûv) Swe.	55·50 N	13·17 E
134	Esmeraldas (ĕs-mä-räl'däs) Ec.	0·58 N	79·45 W
129	Espada, Punta (Pt.) (pōō'n-tä-ĕs-pä'dä). Dom. Rep.	18·30 N	68·30 W
96	Espanola (ĕs-pȧ-nō'lȧ) Can.	46·11 N	81·59 W
127	Esparta (ĕs-pär'tä) C. R.	9·59 N	84·40 W
204	Esperance (ĕs'pē-rȧns) Austl.	33·45 S	122·07 E
128	Esperanza (ĕs-pĕ-rä'n-zä) Cuba	22·30 N	80·10 W
163	Espichel, Cabo (C.) (kä'bō-ĕs-pē-shĕl'). Port. (Lisbon In.)	38·25 N	9·13 W
134	Espinal (ĕs-pē-näl') Col. (In.)	4·10 N	74·53 W
135	Espinhaço, Serra do (Mts.) (sĕ'r-rä-dô-ĕs-pē-nä-sô). Braz.	16·06 S	44·56 W
137	Espinillo, Punta (Pt.) (pōō'n-tä-ĕs-pê-nē'l-yō) Ur. (Buenos Aires In.)	34·49 S	56·27 W
135	Espírito Santo (ĕs-pē'rē-tô-sän'tô). Braz.	20·27 S	40·18 W
135	Espírito Santo (State) Braz.	19·57 S	40·58 W
126	Espíritu Santo, Bahia del (B.) (bä-ē'ä-dĕl-ĕs-pē'rē-tōō-sän'tô) Mex. (In.)	19·25 N	87·28 W
205	Espiritu Santo (I.) (ĕs-pē'rê-tōō sän'tō). New Hebr.	15·45 S	166·50 E
126	Espita (ĕs-pē'tä) Mex. (In.)	20·57 N	88·22 W
157	Espoo Fin.	60·13 N	24·41 E
162	Esposende (ĕs-pō-zĕn'dā) Port.	41·33 N	8·45 W
136	Esquel (ĕs-kĕ'l) Arg.	42·47 S	71·22 W
112	Esquimalt (ĕs-kwī'mŏlt) Can. (Seattle In.)	48·26 N	123·24 W
210	Essaouira Mor.	31·34 N	9·44 W
149	Essen Bel. (Brussels In.)	51·28 N	4·27 E
161	Essen (ĕs'sĕn) F.R.G. (Ruhr In.)	51·26 N	6·59 E
135	Essequibo (R.) (ĕs-ā-kē'bō) Guy.	4·26 N	58·17 W
107	Essex Il. (Chicago In.)	41·11 N	88·11 W
106	Essex (Md. (Baltimore In.)	39·19 N	76·29 W
99	Essex Ma. (In.)	42·38 N	70·47 W
105	Essex Vt.	44·30 N	73·05 W
106	Essex Fells (ĕs'ĕks fĕlz) NJ (New York In.)	40·50 N	74·16 W
104	Essexville (ĕs'ĕks-vĭl) Mi.	43·35 N	83·50 W
158	Esslingen (ĕs'slēn-gĕn) F.R.G.	48·45 N	9·19 E
102	Estacado, Llano (Plain) (yȧ-nō ĕs-tȧ-cȧ-dō') U. S.	33·50 N	103·20 W
136	Estados, Isla de los S. A.	55·05 S	63·00 W
135	Estância (ĕs-tän'sĭ-ä) Braz.	11·17 S	37·18 W
162	Estarreja (ĕs-tär-rā'zhä) Port.	40·44 N	8·39 W
210	Estcourt (ĕst-coort) S. Afr. (Natal In.)	29·04 S	29·53 E
164	Este (ĕs'tā) It.	45·13 N	11·40 E
126	Estelí (ĕs-tā-lē') Nic.	13·10 N	86·23 W
162	Estella (ĕs-tāl'yä) Sp.	42·40 N	2·01 W
162	Estepa (ĕs-tā'pä) Sp.	37·18 N	4·54 W
162	Estepona (ĕs-tā-pō'nä) Sp.	36·26 N	5·08 W
95	Esterhazy (ĕs'tēr-hā-zē) Can.	50·40 N	102·08 W
114	Esteros, B. (ĕs-tā'rōs) Ca.	35·22 N	121·04 W
94	Estevan (ĕ-stē'vȧn) Can.	49·07 N	103·05 W
92	Estevan Group (Is.) Can.	53·05 N	129·40 W
109	Estherville (ĕs'tēr-vĭl) Ia.	43·24 N	94·49 W
121	Estill (ĕs'tĭl) SC	32·46 N	81·15 W
94	Eston Can.	51·10 N	108·45 W
168	Estonian S. S. R. (ĕs-tō'nĭ-ä) Sov. Un.	59·10 N	25·00 E
163	Estoril (ĕs-tô-rēl') Port. (Lisbon In.)	38·45 N	9·24 W
136	Estrêla (R.) (ĕs-trĕ'lä) Braz. (Rio de Janeiro In.)	22·39 S	43·16 W
162	Estrêla, Serra da (Mts.) (sĕr'rȧ dä ĕs-trā'lȧ). Port.	40·25 N	7·45 W
162	Estremadura (Reg.) (ĕs-trā-mä-dōō'rȧ). Port.	41·35 N	8·36 W
162	Estremoz (ĕs-trā-mōzh') Port.	38·50 N	7·35 W
135	Estrondo, Serra do (Mts.) (sĕr'rȧ dōō ĕs-trôn'dōō). Braz.	9·52 S	48·56 W
216	Esumba, Île (I.) Zaire	2·00 N	21·12 E
159	Esztergom (ĕs'tēr-gōm) Hung.	47·46 N	18·45 E
75	Etah (ē'tȧ) Grnld.	78·20 N	72·42 W
161	Étampes (ā-täNp') Fr. (Paris In.)	48·26 N	2·09 E
160	Étaples (ā-täp'l') Fr.	50·32 N	1·38 E
89	Etchemin (R.) (ĕch'ĕ-mĭn) Can. (Quebec In.)	46·39 N	71·03 W
209	Ethiopa (ê-thê-ō'pê-ȧ) Afr.	7·53 N	37·55 E
214	Eticoga Guinea-Bissau	11·09 N	16·08 W
113	Etiwanda (ē-tĭ-wän'dȧ) Ca. (Los Angeles In.)	34·07 N	117·31 W
	Etlatongo, see San Mateo		
107	Etna (ĕt'nȧ) Pa. (Pittsburgh In.)	40·30 N	79·55 W
164	Etna, Mt. (Vol.) It.	37·48 N	15·00 E
89	Etobicoke Can. (Toronto In.)	43·39 N	79·34 W
89	Etobicoke Cr. Can. (Toronto In.)	43·44 N	79·48 W
101	Etolin Str. (ĕt ō lĭn) Ak.	60·35 N	165·40 W
212	Etoshapan (L.) (ĕtō'shä). Namibia	19·07 S	15·30 E
120	Etowah (ĕt'ō-wä) Tn.	35·18 N	84·31 W
120	Etowah (R.) Ga.	34·23 N	84·19 W
161	Étréchy (ā-trā-shē'). Fr. (Paris In.)	48·29 N	2·12 E
149	Etten Neth. (Amsterdam In.)	51·34 N	4·38 E
149	Etterbeek (ĕt'ēr-bāk) Bel. (Brussels In.)	50·51 N	4·24 E
124	Etzatlán (ĕt-zä-tlän') Mex.	20·44 N	104·04 W
204	Eucla (ū'klȧ) Austl.	31·45 S	128·50 E
107	Euclid (ū'klĭd). Oh. (Cleveland In.)	41·34 N	81·32 W
117	Eudora (u-dō'rȧ) Ar.	33·07 N	91·16 W
120	Eufaula (û-fô'lȧ) Al.	31·53 N	85·09 W
117	Eufaula Ok.	35·16 N	95·35 W
117	Eufaula Res. Ok.	35·00 N	94·45 W
110	Eugene (û-jēn') Or.	44·02 N	123·06 W
113	Euless (ū'lĕs) Tx. (Dallas, Fort Worth In.)	32·50 N	97·05 W
119	Eunice (ū'nĭs) La.	30·30 N	92·25 W
155	Eupen (oi'pĕn) Bel.	50·39 N	6·05 E
186	Euphrates (R.) (û-frā'tēz) Asia	36·00 N	39·30 E
160	Eure (R.) (ûr) Fr.	49·03 N	1·22 E
110	Eureka (û-rē'kȧ) Ca.	40·45 N	124·10 W
117	Eureka Ks.	37·48 N	96·17 W
110	Eureka Mt.	48·53 N	115·07 W
114	Eureka Nv.	39·33 N	115·58 W
108	Eureka SD	45·46 N	99·38 W
115	Eureka Ut.	39·55 N	112·10 W
117	Eureka Springs Ar.	36·24 N	93·43 W
186	Eurgun (Mtn.) Iran	28·47 N	57·00 E
146	Europe (ū'rŭp)		
121	Eustis (ūs'tĭs) Fl.	28·50 N	81·41 W
120	Eutaw (ū-tȧ) Al.	32·48 N	87·50 W
92	Eutsuk L. (ōōt'sŭk) Can.	53·20 N	126·44 W
156	Evanger (ĕ-väŋ'gĕr) Nor.	60·40 N	6·06 E
107	Evanston (ĕv'ăn-stŭn) Il. (Chicago In.)	42·03 N	87·41 W
111	Evanston Wy.	41·17 N	111·02 W
104	Evansville (ĕv'ănz-vĭl) In.	38·00 N	87·30 W
109	Evansville Wi.	42·46 N	89·19 W
104	Evart (ĕv'ērt) Mi.	43·55 N	85·10 W
218	Evaton (ĕv'ȧ-tŏn) S. Afr. (Johannesburg & Pretoria In.)	26·32 S	27·53 E
109	Eveleth (ĕv'ē-lĕth) Mn.	47·27 N	92·35 W
204	Everard (L.) (ĕv'ēr-ȧrd) Austl.	36·20 S	134·10 E
204	Everard Ra. Austl.	27·15 S	132·00 E

ng-sing; ŋ-baŋk; N-nasalized n; nŏd; cŏmmit; ōld; ôbey; ôrder; fōōd; fŏŏt; ou-out; s-soft; sh-dish; th-thin; pūre; ûnite; ûrn; stŭd; circŭs; ü-as "y" in study; '-indeterminate vowel.

280 Everest — Ferntree Gully

PRONOUNCING INDEX

Page	Name Pronunciation Region	Lat. °′	Long. °′
184	Everest, Mt. (ĕv′ẽr-ĕst) Nep.-China	28·00 N	86·57 E
99	Everett (ĕv′ẽr-ĕt) Ma. (In.)	42·24 N	71·03 W
112	Everett (ĕv′ẽr-ĕt) Wa. (Seattle In.)	47·59 N	122·11 W
91	Everett Mts. Can.	62·34 N	68·00 W
121	Everglades (ĕv′ẽr-glādz)..Fl. (In.)	25·50 N	81·25 W
128	Everglades, The (Swp.) Fl.	25·35 N	80·55 W
121	Everglades Natl. Park....Fl. (In.)	25·39 N	80·57 W
120	Evergreen (ĕv′ẽr-grēn) Al.	31·25 N	87·56 W
107	Evergreen Park..Il. (Chicago In.)	41·44 N	87·42 W
113	Everman (ĕv′ẽr-măn).. Tx. (Dallas, Fort Worth In.)	32·38 N	97·17 W
112	Everson (ĕv′ẽr-sŭn) Wa. (Vancouver In.)	48·55 N	122·21 W
162	Évora (ĕv′ô-rä) Port.	38·35 N	7·54 W
160	Évreux (ā-vrû′) Fr.	49·02 N	1·11 E
165	Evrotas (R.) (ĕv-rō′tăs) Grc.	37·15 N	22·17 E
165	Evvoia (I.) Grc.	38·38 N	23·45 E
100	Ewa Beach (ē′wä) Hi.	21·17 N	158·03 E
211	Ewaso Ng′iro (R.) Ken.	0·59 N	37·47 E
113	Excelsior (ĕk-sel′sĭ-ŏr) Mn. (Minneapolis, St. Paul In.)	44·54 N	93·35 W
117	Excelsior Springs Mo.	39·20 N	94·13 W
154	Exe (R.) (ĕks) Eng.	50·57 N	3·37 W
114	Exeter (ĕk′sē-tẽr) Ca.	36·18 N	119·09 W
154	Exeter Eng.	50·45 N	3·33 W
105	Exeter NH	43·00 N	71·00 W
154	Exmoor (ĕks′mŏŏr) Eng.	51·10 N	3·55 W
154	Exmouth (ĕks′mŭth) Eng.	50·40 N	3·20 W
204	Exmouth, G. Austl.	21·45 S	114·30 E
99	Exploits (R.) (ĕks-ploits′) Can.	48·50 N	56·15 W
124	Extórrax (R.) (ĕx-tŏ′răx) Mex.	21·04 N	99·39 W
137	Extrema (ĕsh-trĕ′mä) Braz. (Rio de Janeiro In.)	22·52 S	46·19 W
162	Extremadura (Reg.) (ĕks-trā-mä-doo′rä) Sp.	38·43 N	6·30 W
129	Exuma Sd. (ĕk-sōō′mä) Ba.	24·20 N	76·20 W
217	Eyasi, L. (â-yä′sê) Tan.	3·25 S	34·55 E
150	Eyja Fd. Ice.	66·21 N	18·20 W
150	Eyrarbakki Ice.	63·51 N	20·52 W
204	Eyre (âr) Austl.	32·15 S	126·20 E
203	Eyre (L.) Austl.	28·43 S	137·50 E
204	Eyre Pen. Austl.	33·30 S	136·00 E
136	Ezeiza (ĕ-zā′zä) Arg. (Buenos Aires In.)	34·36 S	58·31 W
165	Ezine (â′zĭ-nâ) Tur.	39·47 N	26·18 E

F

Page	Name Pronunciation Region	Lat. °′	Long. °′
118	Fabens (fā′bĕnz) Tx.	31·30 N	106·07 W
156	Fåborg (fô′bôrg) Den.	55·06 N	10·19 E
164	Fabriano (fä-brē-ä′nō) It.	43·20 N	12·55 E
134	Facatativá (fä-kä-tä-tê-vá′) Col. (In.)	4·49 N	74·09 W
211	Fada (fä′dä) Chad	17·06 N	21·18 E
214	Fada Ngourma (fä′dä′n gōōr′mä) Upper Volta	12·04 N	0·21 E
173	Faddeya (I.) (fȧd-yā′) Sov. Un.	76·12 N	145·00 E
156	Faemund (L.) (fā′mōōn′) Nor.	62·17 N	11·40 E
164	Faenza (fä-ĕnd′zä) It.	44·16 N	11·53 E
146	Faeroe Is. (fā′rō) Eur.	62·00 N	5·45 W
162	Fafe (fä′fā) Port.	41·30 N	8·10 W
218	Fafen (R.) Eth. (Horn of Afr. In.)	8·15 N	42·40 E
165	Făgăras (fă-gä′răsh) Rom.	45·50 N	24·55 E
156	Fagerness (fä′ghẽr-nĕs) Nor.	61·00 N	9·10 E
136	Fagnano (L.) (fäk-nä′nô) Arg.-Chile	54·35 S	68·20 W
214	Faguibine, Lac (L.) Mali	16·50 N	4·20 W
210	Faial I. (fä-yä′l) Açores (In.)	38·40 N	29·19 W
218	Fa′id (fä-yēd′) Egypt (Suez In.)	30·19 N	32·18 E
154	Fair (I.) (fâr Scot.	59·34 N	1·41 W
101	Fairbanks (fâr′bănks) Ak.	64·50 N	147·48 W
104	Fairbury (fâr′bĕr-ĭ) Il.	40·45 N	88·25 W
117	Fairbury Ne.	40·09 N	97·11 W
89	Fairchild Cr. (fâr′chīld) Can. (Toronto In.)	43·18 N	80·10 W
109	Fairfax (fâr′făks) Mn.	44·29 N	94·44 W
121	Fairfax SC	32·29 N	81·13 W
106	Fairfax Va. (Baltimore In.)	38·51 N	77·20 W
106	Fairfield (fâr′fēld) Al. (Birmingham In.)	33·30 N	86·50 W
202	Fairfield Austl. (Sydney In.)	33·52 S	150·57 E
106	Fairfield Ct. (New York In.)	41·08 N	73·22 W
104	Fairfield Il.	38·25 N	88·20 W
109	Fairfield Ia.	41·00 N	91·59 W
98	Fairfield Me.	44·35 N	69·38 W
105	Fairhaven (fâr-hā′vĕn) Ma.	41·35 N	70·55 W
105	Fair Haven Vt.	43·35 N	73·15 W
109	Fairmont (fâr′mŏnt) Mn.	43·39 N	94·26 W
105	Fairmont WV	39·30 N	80·10 W
113	Fairmont City..Il. (St. Louis In.)	38·39 N	90·05 W
104	Fairmount In.	40·25 N	85·45 W
113	Fairmount..Ks. (Kansas City In.)	39·12 N	95·55 W
106	Fair Oaks (fâr ōks) Ga. (Atlanta In.)	33·56 N	84·33 W
105	Fairport (fâr′pōrt) NY	43·05 N	77·30 W
104	Fairport Harbor Oh.	41·45 N	81·15 W
116	Fairview (fâr′vū) Ok.	36·16 N	98·28 W
112	Fairview Or. (Portland In.)	45·32 N	112·26 W
115	Fairview Ut.	39·35 N	111·30 W
107	Fairview Park.Oh. (Cleveland In.)	41·27 N	81·52 W
101	Fairweather, Mt. (fâr-wĕdh′ẽr) Can.	59·12 N	137·22 W
108	Faith (fāth) SD	45·02 N	120·02 W
184	Faizābād India	26·50 N	82·17 E
123	Fajardo...P. R. (Puerto Rico In.)	18·20 N	65·40 W
197	Fakfak Indon.	2·56 S	132·25 E
192	Faku (fä-kōō) China	42·28 N	123·20 E
193	Falaise, C. Viet.	19·20 N	106·18 E
135	Falcón (State) (fäl-kō′n).Ven. (In.)	11·00 N	68·28 W
105	Falconer (fô′k′n-ẽr) NY	42·10 N	79·10 W
113	Falcon Heights (fô′k′n) Mn. (Minneapolis, St. Paul In.)	44·59 N	93·10 W
118	Falcon Res. (fôk′n) Tx.	26·47 N	99·03 W
214	Falemé (R.) (fá-lā-mā′) Afr.	13·40 N	12·00 W
167	Faleshty (fä-lăsh′tĭ) Sov. Un.	47·33 N	27·46 E
118	Falfurrias (făl′fōō-rē′ás) Tx.	27·15 N	98·08 W
93	Falher (fäl′ẽr) Can.	55·44 N	117·12 W
156	Falkenberg (fäl′kĕn-bĕrgh) Swe.	56·54 N	12·25 E
149	Falkensee (fäl′kĕn-zā) G.D.R. (Berlin In.)	52·34 N	13·05 E
149	Falkenthal (fäl′kĕn-täl) G.D.R. (Berlin In.)	52·54 N	13·18 E
154	Falkirk (fôl′kûrk) Scot.	55·59 N	3·55 W
136	Falkland Is. (fôk′lănd) S. A.	50·45 S	61·00 W
156	Falköping (fäl′chûp-ĭng) Swe.	58·09 N	13·30 E
112	Fall City Wa. (Seattle In.)	47·34 N	121·53 W
107	Fall Cr. (fôl).In. (Indianapolis In.)	39·52 N	86·04 W
114	Fallon (făl′ŭn) Nv.	39·30 N	118·48 W
106	Fall River...Ma. (Providence In.)	41·42 N	71·07 W
106	Falls Church (fălz chûrch) Va. (Baltimore In.)	38·53 N	77·10 W
117	Falls City Ne.	40·04 N	95·37 W
106	Fallston (făls′ton) Md. (Baltimore In.)	39·32 N	76·26 W
154	Falmouth (făl′mŭth) Eng.	50·08 N	3·04 W
128	Falmouth Jam.	18·30 N	77·40 W
104	Falmouth Ky.	38·40 N	84·20 W
	False (B.), see Valsbaai		
183	False Divi Pt. India	15·45 N	80·50 E
129	Falso, Cabo (C.) (kä′bô-fäl-sô) Dom. Rep.	17·45 N	71·55 W
156	Falster (I.) (fäls′tẽr) Den.	54·48 N	11·58 E
159	Fălticeni (fŭl-tê-chān′y′) Rom.	47·27 N	26·17 E
156	Falun (fä-lōōn′) Swe.	60·38 N	15·35 E
153	Famagusta (fä-mä-gōōs′tä) Cyprus	35·08 N	33·59 E
136	Famatina, Sierra de (Mts.) (sē-ĕ′r-rä-dĕ-fä-mä-tē′-nä).Arg.	29·00 S	67·50 W
193	Fang Xian (fäŋ-shyĕn) China	32·05 N	110·45 E
199	Fanning (I.) (făn′ĭng) Oceania	4·20 N	159·00 W
89	Fannystelle (făn′ĭ-stĕl) Can. (Winnipeg In.)	49·45 N	97·46 W
164	Fano (fä′nō) It.	43·49 N	13·01 E
156	Fanø (I.) (fän′û) Den.	55·24 N	8·10 E
213	Farafangana (fä-rä-fäŋ-gä′nä) Mad.	21·18 S	47·59 E
186	Farāh (fä-rä′) Afg.	32·15 N	62·13 E
124	Farallón, Punta (Pt.) (pōō′n-tä-fä-rä-lōn).Mex.	19·21 N	105·03 W
214	Faranah (fä-rä′nä) Gui.	10·02 N	10·44 W
211	Farasān, Jaza′ir (Is.) Eth.	16·45 N	41·08 E
153	Faregh, Wadi al (R.) (wädê ĕl fä-rĕg′).Libya	30·10 N	19·34 E
205	Farewell, C. (fâr-wĕl′)..N. Z. (In.)	40·37 S	171·46 E
108	Fargo (fär′gō) ND	46·53 N	96·48 W
108	Far Hills (fär hĭlz) NJ (New York In.)	40·41 N	74·38 W
109	Faribault (fâ′rĭ-bō) Mn.	44·19 N	93·16 W
162	Farilhoes (Is.) (fä-rê-lyônzh′) Port.	39·28 N	9·32 W
148	Faringdon (fă′rĭng-dŏn) Eng. (London In.)	51·38 N	1·35 W
218	Fāriskūr (fä-rês-kōōr′) Egypt (Nile In.)	31·19 N	31·46 E
211	Farit, Amba (Mt.) Eth.	10·51 N	37·52 E
159	Farkašd (fär′kăsht) Czech.	48·00 N	17·43 E
113	Farley (fär′lē) Mo. (Kansas City In.)	39·16 N	94·49 W
113	Farmers Branch (fär′mẽrz branch) Tx. (Dallas, Fort Worth In.)	32·56 N	96·53 W
104	Farmersburg (fär′mẽrz-bûrg)...In.	39·15 N	87·25 W
117	Farmersville (fär′mẽrz-vĭl) Tx.	33·11 N	96·22 W
106	Farmingdale (färm′ĕng-dāl) NJ (New York In.)	40·11 N	74·10 W
106	Farmingdale..NY (New York In.)	40·44 N	73·26 W
99	Farmingham (färm-ĭng-hăm) Ma. (In.)	42·17 N	71·25 W
117	Farmington (färm-ĭng-tŭn) Il.	40·42 N	90·01 W
98	Farmington Me.	44·40 N	70·10 W
107	Farmington....Mi. (Detroit In.)	42·28 N	83·23 W
117	Farmington Mo.	37·46 N	90·26 W
115	Farmington NM	36·40 N	108·10 W
113	Farmington Ut. (Salt Lake City In.)	40·59 N	111·53 W
121	Farmville (färm-vĭl) NC	35·35 N	77·35 W
121	Farmville Va.	37·15 N	78·23 W
148	Farnborough (färn′bŭr-ô) Eng. (London In.)	51·15 N	0·45 W
154	Farne (I.) (färn) Eng.	55·40 N	1·32 W
105	Farnham (fär′năm) Can.	45·15 N	72·55 W
148	Farningham (fär′nĭng-ŭm)...Eng.	51·22 N	0·14 E
148	Farnworth (färn′wŭrth) Eng.	53·34 N	2·24 W
135	Faro (fä′rōō) Braz.	2·05 S	56·32 W
162	Faro Port.	37·01 N	7·57 W
157	Fåron (I.) Swe.	57·57 N	19·10 E
204	Farquhar, C. (fär′kwȧr) Austl.	23·50 S	112·55 E
104	Farrell (făr′ĕl) Pa.	41·10 N	80·30 W
184	Farrukhābād (fŭ-rōōk-hä-bäd′) India	27·29 N	79·35 E
165	Fársala (Pharsalus) Grc.	39·18 N	22·25 E
156	Farsund (fär′sōōn) Nor.	58·05 N	6·47 E
136	Fartura, Serra da (Mts.) (sĕ′r-rä-dȧ-fär-tōō′rä).Braz.	26·40 S	53·15 W
75	Farvel, Kap (C.) Grnld.	60·00 N	44·00 W
116	Farwell (fär′wĕl) Tx.	34·24 N	103·03 W
165	Fasano (fä-zä′nō) It.	40·50 N	17·22 E
167	Fastov (fäs′tôf) Sov. Un.	50·04 N	29·57 E
167	Fatëzh Sov. Un.	52·06 N	35·51 E
162	Fatima Port.	39·36 N	9·36 E
171	Fatsa (fät′sä) Tur.	40·50 N	37·30 E
161	Faucilles, Monts (Mts.) (môɴ′ fō-sēl′).Fr.	48·07 N	6·13 E
150	Fauske Nor.	67·15 N	15·24 E
93	Faust (foust) Can.	55·19 N	115·38 W
174	Faustovo..Sov. Un. (Moscow In.)	55·27 N	38·29 E
161	Faverolles (fä-vrōl′).Fr. (Paris In.)	48·42 N	1·34 E
148	Faversham (fă′vẽr-sh′m) Eng. (London In.)	51·19 N	0·54 E
150	Faxaflói (B.) Ice.	64·33 N	22·40 W
120	Fayette (fâ-yĕt′) Al.	33·40 N	87·54 W
109	Fayette Ia.	42·49 N	91·49 W
120	Fayette Ms.	31·43 N	91·00 W
117	Fayette Mo.	39·09 N	92·41 W
117	Fayetteville (fâ-yĕt′vĭl) Ar.	36·03 N	94·08 W
121	Fayetteville NC	35·02 N	78·54 W
120	Fayetteville Tn.	35·10 N	86·33 W
214	Fazao, Forêt Classée du (For.) Togo	8·50 N	0·40 E
184	Fazilka India	30·30 N	74·02 E
211	Fazzān (Fezzan) (Prov.)...Libya	26·45 N	13·01 E
210	Fdérik Mauritania	22·45 N	12·38 W
121	Fear, C. (fēr) NC	33·52 N	77·48 W
114	Feather (R.) (fĕth′ẽr) Ca.	38·56 N	121·41 W
114	Feather, Middle Fk. of (R.)...Ca.	39·49 N	121·10 W
114	Feather, North Fk. of (R.)...Ca.	40·00 N	121·20 W
148	Featherstone (fĕdh′ẽr stŭn)...Eng.	53·39 N	1·21 W
160	Fécamp (fā-käɴ′) Fr.	49·45 N	0·20 E
135	Federal, Distrito (Dist.) (dês-trē′tô-fĕ-dĕ-rä′l).Ven. (In.)	10·34 N	66·55 W
112	Federal Way....Wa. (Seattle In.)	47·20 N	122·20 W
174	Fëdorovka (fyô′dō-rôf-kȧ) Sov. Un. (Moscow In.)	56·15 N	37·14 E
158	Fehmarn I. (fā′märn)....F.R.G.	54·28 N	11·15 E
149	Fehrbellin (fĕr′bĕl-lēn) G.D.R. (Berlin In.)	52·49 N	12·46 E
137	Feia, Logoa (L.) (lô-gôä-fĕ′yä) Braz. (Rio de Janeiro In.)	21·54 S	41·45 W
190	Feicheng (fā-chŭŋ) China	36·18 N	116·45 E
190	Feidong (fā-dôŋ) China	31·53 N	117·28 E
135	Feira de Santana (fĕ′ê-rä dā sänt-än′ä).Braz.	12·16 S	38·46 W
190	Fei Xian (fā-shyĕn) China	35·17 N	117·59 E
163	Felanitx (fā-lä-nēch′) Sp.	39·29 N	3·09 E
158	Feldkirch (fĕlt′kĭrk) Aus.	47·15 N	9·36 E
149	Feldkirchen (fĕld′kĕr-ĸĕn) F.R.G. (Munich In.)	48·09 N	11·44 E
126	Felipe Carrillo Puerto (fĕ-lē′pĕ-kär-rē′l-yô-pwĕ′r-tô) Mex. (In.)	19·36 N	88·04 W
164	Feltre (fĕl′trā) It.	46·02 N	11·56 E
213	Fénérive (fĕ-nâ-rēv′) Mad.	17·30 S	49·31 E
192	Fengcheng (fŭŋ-chŭŋ) China	40·28 N	124·03 E
191	Fengcheng...China (Shanghai In.)	30·55 N	121·38 E
193	Fengdu (fŭŋ-dōō) China	29·58 N	107·50 E
193	Fengjie (fŭŋ-jyĕ) China	31·02 N	109·30 E
190	Fengming Dao (I.) (fŭŋ-mĭŋ dou) China	39·19 N	121·15 E
190	Fengrun (fŭŋ rōōn) China	39·51 N	118·06 E
192	Fengtai (fŭŋ tī)......China (In.)	39·51 N	116·19 E
191	Fengxian (fŭŋ shyĕn) China (Shanghai In.)	30·55 N	121·26 E
190	Feng Xian China	34·41 N	116·36 E
192	Fengxiang (fŭŋ shyäŋ) China	34·25 N	107·20 E
190	Fengyang (fŭng′yäng′) China	32·55 N	117·32 E
192	Fengzhen (fŭŋ-jŭn) China	40·28 N	113·20 E
101	Fenimore P. (fĕn-ĭ-mōr) Ak.	51·40 N	175·38 W
104	Fenton (fĕn-tŭn) Mi.	42·50 N	83·40 W
113	Fenton.......Mo. (St. Louis In.)	38·31 N	90·27 W
192	Fenyang China	37·20 N	111·48 E
167	Feodosiya (Kefe) (fĕ-ô-dō′sē′yȧ) (kyĕ′fĕ).Sov. Un.	45·02 N	35·21 E
186	Ferdows Iran	34·00 N	58·13 E
164	Ferentino (fā-rĕn-tē′nō) It.	41·42 N	13·18 E
172	Fergana Sov. Un.	40·16 N	72·07 E
108	Fergus Falls (fûr′gŭs) Mn.	46·17 N	96·03 W
113	Ferguson (fûr-gŭ-sŭn) Mo. (St. Louis In.)	38·45 N	90·18 W
214	Ferkéssédougou......Ivory Coast	9·36 N	5·12 W
164	Fermo (fĕr′mō) It.	43·10 N	13·43 E
162	Fermoselle (fĕr-mō-säl′yȧ) Sp.	41·20 N	6·23 W
154	Fermoy (fûr-moi′) Ire.	52·05 N	8·06 W
121	Fernandina Beach (fûr-năn-dē′nȧ).Fl.	30·38 N	81·29 W
135	Fernando de Noronha, Arquipélago (Arch.) (är-kê-pĕ′lä-gô-fĕr-nän-dō-dĕ-nô-rō′n-yä).Braz.	3·50 S	33·15 W
	Fernando Póo (I.), see Bioko		
162	Fernān-Núñez (fĕr-nän′nōō′nyâth) Sp.	37·42 N	4·43 W
217	Fernão Veloso, Baia de (B.)..Moz.	14·20 S	40·55 E
110	Ferndale (fûrn′dāl) Ca.	40·34 N	124·18 W
107	Ferndale.......Mi. (Detroit In.)	42·27 N	83·08 W
112	Ferndale.....Wa. (Vancouver In.)	48·51 N	122·36 W
93	Fernie (fûr′nĭ) Can.	49·30 N	115·03 W
112	Fern Prairie (fûrn prâr′ĭ) Wa. (Portland In.)	45·38 N	122·25 W
202	Ferntree Gully Austl. (Melbourne In.)	37·53 S	145·18 E

ăt; finăl; rāte; senâte; ärm; åsk; sofȧ; fâre; ch-choose; dh-as th in other; bē; êvent; bĕt; recĕnt; cratẽr; g-go; gh-guttural g; bĭt; ĭ-short neutral; rīde; ĸ-guttural k as ch in German ich;

PRONOUNCING INDEX

Ferrara — Fort Gaines 281

Page	Name Pronunciation Region	Lat. °′	Long. °′
164	Ferrara (fĕr-rä'rä)............It.	44·50 N	11·37 E
163	Ferrat, Cap (C.) (kăp fĕr-rät).Alg.	35·49 N	0·29 W
162	Ferreira do Alentejo (fĕr-rĕ'ê-rä dōō ä-lĕN-tā'zhōō) Port.	38·03 N	8·06 W
162	Ferreira do Zezere (fĕr-rĕ'ê-rä dōō zâ-zā'rĕ).Port.	39·49 N	8·17 W
113	Ferrelview (fĕr'rĕl-vū) Mo. (Kansas City In.)	39·18 N	94·40 W
134	Ferreñafe (fĕr-rĕn-yä'fĕ).....Peru	6·38 S	79·48 W
119	Ferriday (fĕr'ĭ-dā)...........La.	31·38 N	91·33 W
151	Ferryville (fĕr-ê-vēl')........Tun.	37·12 N	9·51 E
174	Fershampenuaz (fĕr-shàm'pĕn-wäz) Sov. Un. (Urals In.)	53·32 N	59·50 E
108	Fertile (fur'tĭl)..............Mn.	47·33 N	96·18 W
210	Fès (fĕs)....................Mor.	34·08 N	5·00 W
108	Fessenden (fĕs'ĕn-dĕn)........ND	47·39 N	99·40 W
154	Festiniog (fĕs-tĭn-ĭ-ŏg)......Wales	52·59 N	3·58 W
117	Festus (fĕst'ŭs)..............Mo.	38·12 N	90·22 W
171	Fethiye (fĕt-hē'yĕ)..........Tur.	36·40 N	29·05 E
91	Feuilles, Rivière aux (R.)....Can.	58·30 N	70·50 W
	Fezzan (Prov.), see Fazzān		
213	Fianarantsoa (fyȧ-nä'rȧn-tsō'ȧ) Mad.	21·21 S	47·15 E
218	Ficksburg (fĭks'bûrg) S. Afr. (Johannesburg & Pretoria In.)	28·53 S	27·53 E
112	Fidalgo I. (fĭ-dăl'gō) Wa. (Seattle In.)	48·28 N	122·39 W
112	Fieldbrook (fēld'brŏŏk).......Ca.	40·59 N	124·02 W
165	Fier (fyĕr)..................Alb.	40·43 N	19·34 E
154	Fife Ness (C.) (fīf'nes').......Scot.	56·15 N	2·19 W
211	Fifth Cataract..............Sud.	18·27 N	33·38 E
162	Figalo, Cap (C.) (kăp fē-gä-lô) Alg.	35·35 N	1·12 W
160	Figeac (fē-zhàk')............Fr.	44·37 N	2·02 E
156	Figeholm (fē-ghĕ-hōlm)......Swe.	57·24 N	16·33 E
162	Figueira da Foz (fê-gwĕy-rä-dä-fô'z).Port.	40·10 N	8·50 W
210	Figuig....................Mor.	32·20 N	1·30 W
198	Fiji (fē'jē)..............Oceania	18·50 S	175·00 E
126	Filadelfia (fĭl-ȧ-dĕl'fĭ-ȧ).....C. R.	10·26 N	85·37 W
174	Filatovskoye (fĭ-lä'tôf-skô-yĕ) Sov. Un. (Urals In.)	56·49 N	62·20 E
121	Filbert (fĭl'bērt)...........WV	37·18 N	81·29 W
220	Filchner Ice Shelf (fĭlk'nēr)..Ant.	80·00 S	35·00 W
165	Filiatrá...................Grc.	37·10 N	21·35 E
164	Filicudi (I.) (fē'le-kōō'dē).....It.	38·34 N	14·39 E
153	Filigas (R.)................Tur.	41·10 N	32·53 E
174	Filippovskoye (fĭ-lĭ-pôf'skô-yĕ) Sov. Un. (Moscow In.)	56·06 N	38·38 E
156	Filipstad (fĭl'ĭps-städh)......Swe.	59·44 N	14·09 E
115	Fillmore (fĭl'môr)...........Ut.	39·00 N	112·20 W
216	Fimi (R.)..................Zaire	2·43 S	17·50 E
89	Finch (fĭnch)...Can. (Ottawa In.)	45·09 N	75·06 W
104	Findlay (fĭnd'lȧ)............Oh.	41·05 N	83·40 W
217	Fingoè....................Moz.	15·12 S	31·50 E
162	Finisterre, Cabo de (C.) (kȧ'bô-dĕ-fĭn-ĭs-târ').Sp.	42·52 N	9·48 W
204	Finke (R.) (fĭŋ'kē)..........Austl.	25·25 S	134·30 E
146	Finland (fĭn'lănd)...........Eur.	62·45 N	26·13 E
157	Finland, G. of (fĭn'lănd).....Eur.	59·35 N	23·35 E
134	Finlandia (fēn-lä'n-dēä).Col. (In.)	4·38 N	75·39 W
90	Finlay (R.) (fĭn'lȧ)........Can.	57·45 N	125·30 W
149	Finow (fē'nōv) G.D.R. (Berlin In.)	52·50 N	13·44 E
149	Finowfurt (fē'nō-fōōrt) G.D.R. (Berlin In.)	52·50 N	13·41 E
158	Finsterwalde (fĭn'stĕr-väl-dĕ) G.D.R.	51·38 N	13·42 E
171	Firat (R.) (fē-rät')..........Tur.	39·40 N	38·30 E
112	Fircrest (fûr'krĕst) Wa. (Seattle In.)	47·14 N	122·31 W
164	Firenze (Florence) (fê-rĕnt'sä)..It.	43·47 N	11·15 E
164	Firenzuola (fē-rĕnt-swô'lä).....It.	44·08 N	11·21 E
184	Fīrozpur..................India	30·58 N	74·39 E
149	Fischa (R.).....Aus. (Vienna In.)	48·04 N	16·33 E
149	Fischamend Markt Aus. (Vienna In.)	48·07 N	16·37 E
212	Fish (R.) (fĭsh).........Namibia	27·30 S	17·45 E
129	Fish Cay (I.)................Ba.	22·30 N	74·20 W
89	Fish Cr. (fĭsh)..Can. (Calgary In.)	50·52 N	114·21 W
119	Fisher (fĭsh'ēr)..............La.	31·28 N	93·30 W
95	Fisher B....................Can.	51·30 N	97·16 W
92	Fisher Chan.................Can.	52·10 N	127·42 W
91	Fisher Str..................Can.	62·43 N	84·28 W
95	Fishing L. (fĭsh'ĭng)..........Can.	52·07 N	95·25 W
99	Fitchburg (fĭch'bûrg)....Ma. (In.)	42·35 N	71·48 W
215	Fitri, Lac (L.)..............Chad	12·50 N	17·28 E
120	Fitzgerald (fĭts-jĕr'ăld).......Ga.	31·42 N	83·17 W
92	Fitz Hugh Sd. (fĭts hū)......Can.	51·40 N	127·57 W
204	Fitzroy (R.) (fĭts-roi')......Austl.	18·00 S	124·05 E
205	Fitzroy (R.)................Austl.	23·45 S	150·02 E
204	Fitzroy Crossing...........Austl.	18·08 S	126·00 E
104	Fitzwilliam (I.) (fĭts-wĭl'yŭm) Can.	45·30 N	81·45 W
	Fiume, see Rijeka		
163	Fiumicino (fyōō-mē-chē'nô) It. (Rome In.)	41·47 N	12·19 E
156	Fjällbacka (fyĕl'bäk-å)......Swe.	58·37 N	11·17 E
156	Flaam (flôm)...............Nor.	60·15 N	7·01 E
115	Flagstaff (flăg'stȧf)..........Az.	35·15 N	111·40 W
213	Flagstaff (flăg'stäf) S. Afr. (Natal In.)	31·06 S	29·31 E
105	Flagstaff (L.) (flăg-stȧf)......Me.	45·05 N	70·30 W
149	Flalow (flä'lōv) G.D.R. (Berlin In.)	52·44 N	12·58 E
109	Flambeau (R.) (flăm-bō').....Wi.	45·32 N	91·05 W
111	Flaming Gorge Res..........Wy.	41·13 N	109·30 W
121	Flamingo (flȧ-mĭŋ'gō).........Fl.	25·10 N	80·55 W
129	Flamingo Cay (I.) (flȧ-mĭŋ'gō) Ba.	22·50 N	75·50 W
123	Flamingo Pt.....Vir. Is. (U. S. A.) (St. Thomas In.)	18·19 N	65·00 W
155	Flanders (Reg.) (flăn'dērz)....Fr.	50·53 N	2·29 E
108	Flandreau (flăn'drō)..........SD	44·02 N	96·35 W
154	Flannan (Is.) (flăn'ăn)......Scot.	58·13 N	8·14 W
93	Flathead (R.)..............Can.	49·30 N	114·30 W
111	Flathead L. (flăt'hĕd)........Mt.	47·57 N	114·20 W
111	Flathead R..................Mt.	48·45 N	114·20 W
111	Flathead R., Middle Fork....Mt.	48·30 N	113·47 W
111	Flathead R., South Fork.....Mt.	48·05 N	113·45 W
107	Flat Rock (flăt rŏk) Mi. (Detroit In.)	42·06 N	83·17 W
110	Flattery C. (flăt'ēr-ĭ)....... Wa.	48·22 N	125·10 W
111	Flat Willow Cr. (flat wĭl'ô)..Mt.	46·45 N	108·47 W
156	Flekkefjord (fläk'kĕ-fyôr)....Nor.	58·19 N	6·38 E
104	Flemingsburg (flĕm'ĭngz-bûrg).Ky.	38·25 N	83·45 W
158	Flensburg (flĕns'bōōrgh)...F.R.G.	54·48 N	9·27 E
160	Flers-del-l'Orne (flĕr-dĕ-lôrn')..Fr.	48·43 N	0·37 W
121	Fletcher....................NC	35·26 N	82·30 W
204	Flinders (Reg.) (flĭn'dērz)...Austl.	32·15 S	138·45 E
203	Flinders (I.)...............Austl.	39·35 S	148·10 E
205	Flinders (R.)...............Austl.	18·48 S	141·07 E
205	Flinders Rfs...............Austl.	17·30 S	149·02 E
104	Flin Flon (flĭn flŏn).........Can.	54·46 N	101·53 W
148	Flint......................Wales	53·15 N	3·07 W
104	Flint.......................Mi.	43·00 N	83·45 W
148	Flint (Co.)................Wales	53·13 N	3·06 W
120	Flint (R.) (flĭnt)............Ga.	31·25 N	84·15 W
156	Flisen (flē'sĕn).............Nor.	60·35 N	12·03 E
104	Flora (flō'rȧ)...............Il.	38·40 N	88·25 W
104	Flora.......................In.	40·25 N	86·30 W
120	Florala (flŏr-ăl'ȧ)...........Al.	31·01 N	86·19 W
106	Floral Park (flôr'ȧl pärk) NY (New York In.)	40·42 N	73·42 W
120	Florence (flŏr'ĕns)...........Al.	34·46 N	87·40 W
115	Florence....................Az.	33·00 N	111·25 W
116	Florence....................Co.	38·23 N	105·08 W
117	Florence....................Ks.	38·14 N	96·56 W
121	Florence....................SC	34·10 N	79·45 W
112	Florence.......Wa. (Seattle In.)	48·13 N	122·21 W
	Florence, see Firenze		
134	Florencia (flō-rĕn'sē-ȧ).......Col.	1·31 N	75·13 W
137	Florencio Sanchez (flō-rĕn-sēō-sá'n-chĕz).Ur. (Buenos Aires In.)	33·52 S	57·24 W
136	Florencio Varela (flō-rĕn'sē-o vä-rā'lä)..Arg. (Buenos Aires In.)	34·34 S	58·16 W
135	Flores (flō'rĕzh)............Braz.	7·57 S	37·48 W
126	Flores...............Guat. (In.)	16·53 N	89·54 W
137	Flores (Dept.) Ur. (Buenos Aires In.)	33·33 S	57·00 W
196	Flores (I.)................Indon.	8·14 S	121·08 E
137	Flores (R.) Arg. (Buenos Aires In.)	36·13 S	60·28 W
196	Flores Laut (Flores Sea)...Indon.	7·09 N	120·30 E
118	Floresville (flō'rĕs-vĭl)........Tx.	29·10 N	98·08 W
135	Floriano (flō-rȧ-ä'nōō)......Braz.	6·17 S	42·58 W
136	Florianópolis (flō-rê-ä-nō'pô-lês) Braz.	27·30 S	48·30 W
134	Florida (flō-rē'dä).......Col. (In.)	3·20 N	76·12 W
128	Florida.....................Cuba	22·10 N	79·50 W
106	Florida (flŏr'ĭ-dȧ) NY (New York In.)	41·20 N	74·21 W
213	Florida...................S. Afr. (Johannesburg & Pretoria In.)	26·11 S	27·56 E
137	Florida (flô-rê-dhä) Ur. (Buenos Aires In.)	34·06 S	56·14 W
103	Florida (State) (flŏr'ĭ-dȧ).....U.S.	30·30 N	84·40 W
137	Florida (Dept.) (flô-rē'dhä) Ur. (Buenos Aires In.)	33·48 S	56·15 W
205	Florida (I.)..............Sol. Is.	8·56 S	159·45 E
128	Florida, Strs. of..........N. A.	24·10 N	81·00 W
121	Florida B. (flŏr'ĭ-dȧ).....Fl. (In.)	24·55 N	80·55 W
121	Florida Keys (Is.).......Fl. (In.)	24·33 N	81·20 W
115	Florida Mts................NM	32·10 N	107·35 W
118	Florido, R. (flō-rē'dō).......Mex.	27·21 N	104·48 W
149	Floridsdorf (flô'rĭds-dôrf) Aus. (Vienna In.)	48·16 N	16·25 E
165	Florina (flô-rē'nä)..........Grc.	40·48 N	21·24 E
113	Florissant (flŏr'ĭ-sănt) Mo. (St. Louis In.)	38·47 N	90·20 W
156	Florö (flô'ü)................Nor.	61·36 N	5·01 E
108	Floyd (R.) (floid).............Ia.	42·38 N	96·15 W
116	Floydada (floi-dā'dȧ).........Tx.	33·59 N	101·19 W
107	Floyds Fk. (R.) (floi-dz) Ky. (Louisville In.)	38·08 N	85·30 W
164	Flumendosa, R. (flōō-mĕn-dô'sä) It.	39·45 N	9·18 E
104	Flushing (flŭsh'ĭng)..........Mi.	43·05 N	83·50 W
197	Fly (R.) (flī)........Pap. N. Gui.	8·00 S	141·45 E
165	Foča (fō'chä)..............Yugo.	43·29 N	18·48 E
218	Fochville (fŏk'vĭl)..........S. Afr. (Johannesburg & Pretoria In.)	26·29 S	27·29 E
159	Focşani (fōk-shä'nē).........Rom.	45·41 N	27·17 E
193	Fogang (fwo-gäŋ)...........China	23·50 N	113·35 E
164	Foggia (fôd'jä)...............It.	41·30 N	15·34 E
97	Fogo (fō'gō)................Can.	49·43 N	54·17 W
97	Fogo I.....................Can.	49·40 N	54·13 W
210	Fogo I.................C. V. (In.)	14·46 N	24·51 W
158	Fohnsdorf (fōns'dôrf)........Aus.	47·13 N	14·40 E
158	Föhr I. (fûr)..............F.R.G.	54·47 N	8·30 E
160	Foix (fwä)..................Fr.	42·58 N	1·34 E
215	Fokku......................Nig.	11·40 N	4·31 E
216	Folgares...................Ang.	14·54 S	15·08 E
164	Foligno (fô-lēn'yō)............It.	42·58 N	12·41 E
155	Folkeston..................Eng.	51·05 N	1·18 E
148	Folkingham (fō'kĭng-ăm)....Eng.	52·53 N	0·24 W
121	Folkston....................Ga.	30·50 N	82·01 W
116	Folsom (fŏl'sŭm).............NM	36·47 N	103·56 W
114	Folsom City..................Ca.	38·40 N	121·10 W
128	Fomento (fō-mĕ'n-tō).......Cuba	21·35 N	78·20 W
134	Fómeque (fô'mĕ-kĕ).....Col. (In.)	4·29 N	73·52 W
109	Fonda (fŏn'dȧ)...............Ia.	42·33 N	94·51 W
109	Fond du Lac (fŏn dū lăk')....Wi.	43·47 N	88·29 W
109	Fond du Lac Ind. Res........Mn.	46·44 N	93·04 W
164	Fondi (fōn'dē)...............It.	41·23 N	13·25 E
162	Fonsagrada (fôn-sä-grä'dhä)...Sp.	43·08 N	7·07 W
126	Fonseca, Golfo de (G.) (gôl-fô-dĕ-fôn-sā'kä).Hond.	13·09 N	87·55 W
161	Fontainebleau (fôN-tĕn-blō') Fr. (Paris In.)	48·24 N	2·42 E
113	Fontana (fŏn-tă'nȧ) Ca. (Los Angeles In.)	34·06 N	117·27 W
134	Fonte Boa (fōn'tȧ bō'ȧ).....Braz.	2·32 S	66·05 W
160	Fontenay-le-Comte (fôNt-nĕ'lē-kôNt').Fr.	46·28 N	0·53 W
161	Fontenay-Trésigny (fôN-te-hā' tra-sēn-yē').Fr. (Paris In.)	48·43 N	2·53 E
111	Fontenelle Res..............Wy.	42·05 N	110·05 W
125	Fontera, Punta (Pt.) (pōō'n-tä-fôn-tĕ'rä).Mex.	18·36 N	92·43 W
134	Fontibón (fōn-tē-bôn')...Col. (In.)	4·42 N	74·09 W
	Foochow, see Fuchou		
213	Foothills (fōōt-hĭls)........S. Afr. (Johannesburg & Pretoria In.)	25·55 S	27·36 E
101	Foraker, Mt. (fôr'ȧ-kēr)......Ak.	62·40 N	152·40 W
161	Forbach (fôr'bäK)...........Fr.	49·12 N	6·54 E
203	Forbes (fôrbz).............Austl.	33·24 S	148·05 E
93	Forbes, Mt..................Can.	51·52 N	116·56 W
158	Forchheim (fôrK'hīm)......F.R.G.	49·43 N	11·05 E
	Fordlândia, see Brasília Legal		
117	Fordyce (fôr'dīs)............Ar.	33·48 N	92·24 W
214	Forecariah (fōr-kȧ-rē'ä')......Gui.	9·26 N	13·06 W
75	Forel, Mt...............Grnld.	65·50 N	37·41 W
120	Forest (fŏr'ĕst)..............Ms.	32·22 N	89·29 W
108	Forest (R.).................ND	48·08 N	97·45 W
109	Forest City.................Ia.	43·14 N	93·40 W
121	Forest City.................NC	35·20 N	81·52 W
105	Forest City.................Pa.	41·35 N	75·30 W
112	Forest Grove (grōv) Or. (Portland In.)	45·31 N	123·07 W
106	Forest Hill...Md. (Baltimore In.)	39·35 N	76·26 W
113	Forest Hill Tx. (Dallas, Fort Worth In.)	32·40 N	97·16 W
98	Forestville (fŏr'ĕst-vĭl).......Can.	48·45 N	69·06 W
106	Forestville.....Md. (Baltimore In.)	38·51 N	76·55 W
160	Forez, Mts. du (môN dü fô-rā').Fr.	44·55 N	3·43 E
154	Forfar (fôr'fȧr).............Scot.	57·10 N	2·55 W
98	Forillon, Parc Natl. (Natl. Pk.) Can.	48·50 N	64·05 W
163	Forio (Mtn.) (fô'ryō) It. (Naples In.)	40·29 N	13·55 E
107	Forked Cr. (fôrk'd) Il. (Chicago In.)	41·16 N	88·01 W
116	Forked Deer (R.)............Tn.	35·53 N	89·29 W
164	Forli (fôr-lē')...............It.	44·13 N	12·03 E
148	Formby (fôrm'bê)..........Eng.	53·34 N	3·04 W
148	Formby Pt.................Eng.	53·33 N	3·06 W
163	Formello (fôr-mĕ'lō) It. (Rome In.)	42·04 N	12·25 E
163	Formentera, Isla de (I.) (ē's-lä-dĕ-fôr-mĕn-tā'rä).Sp.	38·43 N	1·25 E
137	Formiga (fôr-mē'gȧ) Braz. (Rio de Janeiro In.)	20·27 S	45·25 W
129	Formigas Bk. (fōr-mē'gäs)...N. A.	18·30 N	75·40 W
136	Formosa (fôr-mō'sä).........Arg.	27·25 S	58·12 W
135	Formosa....................Braz.	15·32 S	47·10 W
136	Formosa (Prov.)............Arg.	24·30 S	60·45 W
217	Formosa B..................Ken.	2·45 S	40·30 E
	Formosa (I.), see Taiwan		
135	Formosa, Serra (Mts.) (sĕ'r-rä) Braz.	12·59 S	55·11 W
183	Formosa Str. (fŏr-mō'sȧ).....Asia	24·30 N	120·00 E
174	Fornosovo (fôr-nô'sô vô) Sov. Un. (Leningrad In.)	59·35 N	30·34 E
117	Forrest City (for'ĕst sĭ'tĭ).....Ar.	35·00 N	90·46 W
205	Forsayth (fôr-sīth')........Austl.	18·33 S	143·42 E
156	Forshaga (fôrs'hä'gä).......Swe.	59·34 N	13·25 E
158	Forst (fôrst)..............G.D.R.	51·45 N	14·38 E
120	Forsyth (fôr-sīth')...........Ga.	33·02 N	83·56 W
111	Forsyth....................Mt.	46·15 N	106·41 W
91	Fort Albany (fôrt ôl'bȧ nĭ)...Can.	52·20 N	81·20 W
95	Fort Alexander Ind. Res.....Can.	50·27 N	96·15 W
135	Fortaleza (Ceará) (fôr'tä-lā'zȧ) (sä-ä-rä').Braz.	3·35 S	38·31 W
115	Fort Apache Ind. Res. (ȧ-păch'ê) Az.	34·02 N	110·27 W
109	Fort Atkinson (ăt'kĭn-sŭn)....Wi.	42·55 N	88·46 W
213	Fort Beaufort (bō'fôrt) S. Afr. (Natal In.)	32·47 S	26·39 E
113	Fort Bellefontaine (bĕl-fŏn-tān') Mo. (St. Louis In.)	38·50 N	90·15 W
111	Fort Benton (bĕn'tŭn).......Mt.	47·51 N	110·40 W
108	Fort Berthold Ind. Res. (bĕrth'ôld).ND	47·47 N	103·28 W
104	Fort Branch (brănch).........In.	38·15 N	87·35 W
100	Fort Chipewyan..............Can.	58·46 N	111·15 W
116	Fort Cobb Res...............Ok.	35·12 N	98·28 W
116	Fort Collins (kŏl'ĭns).........Co.	40·36 N	105·04 W
215	Fort Crampel (kràm-pĕl') Cen. Afr. Rep.	6·59 N	19·11 E
213	Fort-Dauphin (dō-făN')......Mad.	24·59 S	46·58 E
127	Fort-de-France (dē fräNs) Mart. (In.)	14·37 N	61·06 W
120	Fort Deposit (dê-pŏz'ĭt).......Al.	31·58 N	86·35 W
211	Fort-de-Possel (dē pô-sĕl') Cen. Afr. Rep.	5·03 N	19·11 E
109	Fort Dodge (dŏj)..............Ia.	42·31 N	94·10 W
105	Fort Edward (wērd)..........NY	43·15 N	73·30 W
107	Fort Erie (ē'rĭ)..Can. (Buffalo In.)	42·55 N	78·56 W
204	Fortescue (R.) (fôr'tĕs-kū)..Austl.	21·25 S	116·50 E
98	Fort Fairfield (fâr'fēld).......Me.	46·46 N	67·53 W
100	Fort Fitzgerald (fĭts-jĕr'ăld)..Can.	59·48 N	111·50 W
95	Fort Frances (frăn'sĕs).......Can.	48·36 N	93·24 W
121	Fort Frederica Natl. Mon. (frĕd'ē-rĭ-kȧ).Ga.	31·12 N	85·25 W
120	Fort Gaines (gānz)...........Ga.	31·35 N	85·03 W

ng-sing; ŋ-baŋk; N-nasalized n; nŏd; cŏmmit; ōld; ôbey; ôrder; fōōd; fŏŏt; ou-out; s-soft; sh-dish; th-thin; pūre; ûnite; ûrn; stŭd; circŭs; ü-as "y" in study; '-indeterminate vowel.

282 Fort George — Fucheng
PRONOUNCING INDEX

Page	Name Pronunciation Region	Lat. °'	Long. °'
91	Fort George (jôrj) Can.	53·40 N	78·58 W
117	Fort Gibson (gĭb'sŭn) Ok.	35·50 N	95·13 W
102	Fort Good Hope (go͝od hōp) Can.	66·19 N	128·52 W
154	Forth, Firth of (fûrth ŏv fôrth) Scot.	56·04 N	3·03 W
211	Fort Hall (hôl) Ken.	0·47 S	37·13 E
111	Fort Hall Ind. Res. Id.	43·02 N	112·21 W
115	Fort Huachuca (wä-cho͞o'kä) Az.	31·30 N	110·25 W
89	Fortier (fôr'tyā') Can. (Winnipeg In.)	49·56 N	97·55 W
212	Fort Jameson (jām'sŭn) Zambia	13·35 S	32·43 E
121	Fort Jefferson Natl. Mon. (jĕf'ẽr-sŭn) Fl. (In.)	24·42 N	83·02 W
212	Fort Johnston Malawi	14·16 S	35·14 E
98	Fort Kent (kĕnt) Me.	47·14 N	68·37 W
112	Fort Langley (lăng'lĭ) Can. (Vancouver In.)	49·10 N	122·35 W
121	Fort Lauderdale (lô'dẽr-dāl) Fl. (In.)	26·07 N	80·09 W
106	Fort Lee NJ (New York In.)	40·50 N	73·58 W
90	Fort Liard Can.	60·16 N	123·34 W
129	Fort Liberté (lē-bĕr-tā') Hai.	19·40 N	71·50 W
120	Fort Louden (R.) (fôrt lou'dĕn) Tn.	35·52 N	84·10 W
116	Fort Lupton (lŭp'tŭn) Co.	40·04 N	104·45 W
110	Fort McDermitt Ind. Res. (măk dẽr'mĭt) Or.	42·04 N	118·07 W
93	Fort Macleod (mȧ-kloud') Can.	49·43 N	113·25 W
210	Fort MacMahon (mȧk mȧ-ôN') Alg.	29·55 N	1·49 E
94	Fort McMurray (mȧk-mŭr'ĭ) Can.	56·44 N	111·23 W
90	Fort McPherson (mȧk-fŭr's'n) Can.	67·37 N	134·59 W
109	Fort Madison (măd'ĭ-sŭn) Ia.	40·40 N	91·17 W
121	Fort Matanzas (mä-tän'zäs) Fl.	29·39 N	81·17 W
121	Fort Meade (mēd) Fl. (In.)	27·45 N	81·48 W
121	Fort Mill (mĭl) SC	35·03 N	80·57 W
152	Fort Miribel (mē-rē-bĕl') Alg.	28·50 N	2·51 E
114	Fort Mohave Ind. Res. (mô-hä'vâ) Ca.	34·59 N	115·02 W
116	Fort Morgan (môr'gȧn) Co.	40·14 N	103·49 W
121	Fort Myers (mī'ẽrz) Fl. (In.)	26·36 N	81·45 W
90	Fort Nelson (nĕl'sŭn) Can.	58·57 N	122·30 W
90	Fort Nelson (R.) (nĕl'sŭn) Can.	58·44 N	122·20 W
120	Fort Payne (pān) Al.	34·26 N	85·41 W
111	Fort Peck (pĕk) Mt.	47·58 N	106·30 W
108	Fort Peck Ind. Res. Mt.	48·22 N	105·40 W
111	Fort Peck Res. Mt.	47·52 N	106·59 W
121	Fort Pierce (pērs) Fl. (In.)	27·25 N	80·20 W
217	Fort Portal (pôr'tăl) Ug.	0·40 N	30·16 E
90	Fort Providence (prŏv'ĭ-dĕns) Can.	61·27 N	117·59 W
121	Fort Pulaski Natl. Mon. (pu-lăs'kĭ) Ga.	31·59 N	80·56 W
94	Fort Qu'Appelle Can.	50·46 N	103·55 W
101	Fort Randall (răn'd'l) Ak.	55·12 N	162·38 W
102	Fort Randall Dam U. S.	42·48 N	98·35 W
90	Fort Resolution (rĕz'ō-lū'shŭn) Can.	61·08 N	113·42 W
117	Fort Riley (rī'lĭ) Ks.	39·05 N	96·46 W
92	Fort St. James (fôrt sânt jāmz) Can.	54·26 N	124·15 W
93	Fort St. John (sānt jŏn) Can.	56·15 N	120·51 W
184	Fort Sandeman (săn'da-mŭn) Pak.	31·28 N	69·29 E
89	Fort Saskatchewan (săs-kăt'cho͞o-ân) Can. (Edmonton In.)	53·43 N	113·13 W
117	Fort Scott (skŏt) Ks.	37·50 N	94·43 W
91	Fort Severn (sĕv'ẽrn) Can.	56·58 N	87·50 W
171	Fort Shevchenko (shĕv-chĕn'kō) Sov. Un.	44·30 N	50·18 E
215	Fort Sibut (fôr sē-bü') Cen. Afr. Rep.	5·44 N	19·05 E
116	Fort Sill (fôrt sĭl) Ok.	34·41 N	98·25 W
90	Fort Simpson (sĭmp'sŭn) Can.	61·52 N	121·48 W
117	Fort Smith (smĭth) Ar.	35·23 N	94·24 W
90	Fort Smith Can.	60·09 N	112·08 W
118	Fort Stockton (stŏk'tŭn) Tx.	30·54 N	102·51 W
116	Fort Sumner (sŭm'nẽr) NM	34·30 N	104·17 W
121	Fort Sumter Natl. Mon. (sŭm'tẽr) SC	32·43 N	79·54 W
107	Fort Thomas (tŏm'ăs) Ky. (Cincinnati In.)	39·05 N	84·27 W
110	Fortuna (fŏr-tū'nȧ) Ca.	40·36 N	124·10 W
99	Fortune (fôr'tŭn) Can.	47·04 N	55·51 W
129	Fortune (I.) Ba.	22·35 N	74·20 W
99	Fortune B. Can.	47·25 N	55·25 W
116	Fort Union Natl. Mon. (ūn'yŭn) NM	35·51 N	104·57 W
120	Fort Valley (văl'ĭ) Ga.	32·33 N	83·53 W
90	Fort Vermilion (vẽr-mĭl'yŭn) Can.	58·23 N	115·50 W
212	Fort Victoria Zimb.	20·07 S	30·47 E
104	Fortville (fôrt-vĭl) In.	40·00 N	85·50 W
104	Fort Wayne (wān) In.	41·00 N	85·10 W
154	Fort William (wĭl'yăm) Scot.	56·50 N	3·00 W
203	Fort William, Mt. (wĭ'ĭ-ăm) Austl.	24·45 S	151·15 E
113	Fort Worth (wûrth) Tx. (Dallas, Fort Worth In.)	32·45 N	97·20 W
101	Fort Yukon (yo͞o'kŏn) Ak.	66·30 N	145·00 W
114	Fort Yuma Ind. Res. (yo͞o'mä) Ca.	32·54 N	114·47 W
160	Fos, Golfe de (G.) (gôlf'dĕ-fôs') Fr. (In.)	43·22 N	4·55 E
191	Foshan China (Canton In.)	23·02 N	113·07 E
164	Fossano (fôs-sä'nō) It.	44·34 N	7·42 E
113	Fossil Cr. (fŏs-ĭl) Tx. (Dallas, Fort Worth In.)	32·53 N	97·19 W
164	Fossombrone (fôs-sôm-brō'nā) It.	43·41 N	12·48 E
116	Foss Res. Ok.	35·38 N	99·11 W
108	Fosston (fôs'tŭn) Mn.	47·34 N	95·44 W
113	Fosterburg (fôs'tẽr-bûrg) Il. (St. Louis In.)	38·58 N	90·04 W
104	Fostoria (fŏs-tō'rĭ-ȧ) Oh.	41·10 N	83·20 W
160	Fougéres (fo͞o-zhâr') Fr.	48·23 N	1·14 W
154	Foula (I.) (fou'lȧ) Scot.	60·08 N	2·04 W
205	Foulwind, C. (foul'wĭnd) N. Z. (In.)	41·45 S	171·37 E
215	Foumban (fo͞om-bän') Cam.	5·43 N	10·55 E
116	Fountain Cr. (foun'tĭn) Co.	38·36 N	104·37 W
113	Fountain Valley Ca. (Los Angeles In.)	33·42 N	117·57 W
117	Fourche le Fave (R.) (fo͞orsh lä fåv') Ar.	34·46 N	93·45 W
218	Fouriesburg (fo͞o'rēz-bûrg) S. Afr. (Johannesburg & Pretoria In.)	28·38 S	28·13 E
160	Fourmies (fo͞or-mē') Fr.	50·01 N	4·01 E
101	Four Mts., Is. of the (fōr) Ak.	52·58 N	170·40 W
211	Fourth Cataract Sud.	18·52 N	32·07 E
210	Fouta Djallon (Mts.) (fo͞o'tä jä-lôN) Gui.	11·37 N	12·29 W
205	Foveaux Str. (fô-vō') N. Z. (In.)	46·30 S	167·43 E
116	Fowler (foul'ẽr) Co.	38·04 N	104·02 W
104	Fowler In.	40·35 N	87·20 W
204	Fowler, Pt. Austl.	32·05 S	132·30 E
118	Fowlerton (foul'ẽr-tŭn) Tx.	28·26 N	98·48 W
112	Fox (I.) (fŏks) Wa. (Seattle In.)	47·15 N	122·08 W
109	Fox (R.) Il.	41·35 N	88·43 W
109	Fox (R.) Wi.	44·18 N	88·23 W
99	Foxboro (fŏks'bŭrō) Ma. (In.)	42·04 N	71·15 W
90	Foxe Basin (fŏks) Can.	67·35 N	79·21 W
91	Foxe Chan. Can.	64·30 N	79·23 W
91	Foxe Pen. Can.	64·57 N	77·26 W
101	Fox Is. (fŏks) Ak.	53·04 N	167·30 W
107	Fox Lake (lăk) Il. (Chicago In.)	42·24 N	88·11 W
107	Fox L. Il. (Chicago In.)	42·24 N	88·07 W
107	Fox Point Wi. (Milwaukee In.)	43·10 N	87·54 W
154	Foyle, Lough (B.) (lŏk foil') Ire.	55·07 N	7·08 W
216	Foz do Cunene Ang.	17·16 S	11·50 E
163	Fraga (frä'gä) Sp.	41·31 N	0·20 E
128	Fragoso, Cayo (I.) (kä'yō-frä-gō'sō) Cuba	22·45 N	79·30 W
135	Franca (frä'n-kä) Braz.	20·28 S	47·20 W
165	Francavilla (fräŋ-kä-vēl'lä) It.	40·32 N	17·37 E
146	France (frȧns) Eur.	46·39 N	0·47 E
90	Frances (L.) (frăn'sĭs) Can.	61·27 N	128·28 W
128	Frances, Cabo (C.) (kä'bô-frän-sĕ's) Cuba	21·55 N	84·05 W
128	Frances, Punta (Pt.) (po͞o'n-tä-frän-sĕ's) Cuba	21·45 N	83·10 W
129	Frances Viejo, Cabo (C.) (kȧ'bô-frän'sȧs vyā'hō) Dom. Rep.	19·40 N	69·35 W
216	Franceville (fräNs-vēl') Gabon.	1·38 S	13·35 E
109	Francis Case, L. (frăn'sĭs) SD	43·15 N	99·00 W
137	Francisco Sales (frän-sē's-kô-sà'lĕs) Braz. (Rio de Janeiro In.)	21·42 S	44·26 W
212	Francistown (frăn'sĭs-toun) Bots.	21·17 S	27·28 E
107	Frankfort (frăŋk'fŭrt) Il. (Chicago In.)	41·30 N	87·51 W
104	Frankfort In.	40·15 N	86·30 W
117	Frankfort Ks.	39·42 N	96·27 W
104	Frankfort Ky.	38·10 N	84·55 W
104	Frankfort Mi.	44·40 N	86·15 W
105	Frankfort NY	43·05 N	75·05 W
218	Frankfort S. Afr. (Johannesburg & Pretoria In.)	27·17 S	28·30 E
213	Frankfort (frănk'fŏrt) S. Afr. (Natal In.)	32·43 S	27·28 E
158	Frankfurt (fräŋk'fo͞ort) G.D.R.	52·20 N	14·31 E
149	Frankfurt (Dist.) G.D.R. (Berlin In.)	52·42 N	13·37 E
158	Frankfurt am Main F.R.G.	50·07 N	8·40 E
104	Franklin (frănk'lĭn) In.	39·25 N	86·00 W
120	Franklin Ky.	36·42 N	86·34 W
119	Franklin La.	29·47 N	91·31 W
99	Franklin Ma. (In.)	42·05 N	71·24 W
116	Franklin Ne.	40·06 N	99·01 W
105	Franklin NH	43·25 N	71·40 W
106	Franklin NJ (New York In.)	41·08 N	74·35 W
104	Franklin Oh.	39·30 N	84·20 W
105	Franklin Pa.	41·25 N	79·50 W
120	Franklin Tn.	35·54 N	86·54 W
213	Franklin S. Afr. (Natal In.)	30·19 S	29·28 E
121	Franklin Va.	36·41 N	76·57 W
90	Franklin, Dist. of Can.	70·46 N	105·22 W
114	Franklin (L.) Nv.	40·23 N	115·10 W
110	Franklin D. Roosevelt L. Wa.	48·12 N	118·43 W
90	Franklin Mts. Can.	65·36 N	125·55 W
107	Franklin Park Il. (Chicago In.)	41·56 N	87·53 W
106	Franklin Square NY (New York In.)	40·43 N	73·40 W
119	Franklinton (frăŋk'lĭn-tŭn) La.	30·49 N	90·09 W
202	Frankston Austl. (Melbourne In.)	38·09 S	145·08 E
107	Franksville (frănkz'vĭl) Wi. (Milwaukee In.)	42·46 N	87·55 W
	Franz Josef Land (Is.), see Zemlya Frantsa Iosifa		
163	Frascati (fräs-kä'tē) It. (Rome In.)	41·49 N	12·45 E
107	Fraser (frā'zẽr) Mi. (Detroit In.)	42·32 N	82·57 W
203	Fraser (Great Sandy) (I.) (frā'zẽr) Austl.	25·12 S	153·00 E
92	Fraser (R.) Can.	52·20 N	122·35 W
154	Fraserburgh (frā'zẽr-bûrg) Scot.	57·40 N	2·01 W
92	Fraser Plateau Can.	51·30 N	122·00 W
163	Frattamaggiore (frät-tä-mäg-zhyô'rĕ) It. (Naples In.)	40·41 N	14·16 E
137	Fray Bentos (frī bĕn'tōs) Ur. (Buenos Aires In.)	33·10 S	58·19 W
108	Frazee (frȧ-zē') Mn.	46·42 N	95·43 W
128	Fraziers Hog Cay (I.) Ba.	25·25 N	77·55 W
161	Frechen (frĕ'kĕn) F.R.G. (Ruhr In.)	50·54 N	6·49 E
156	Fredericia (frĕdh-ĕ-rē'tsē-à) Den.	55·35 N	9·45 E
105	Frederick (frĕd'ẽr-ĭk) Md.	39·25 N	77·25 W
116	Frederick Ok.	34·23 N	99·01 W
96	Frederick House (R.) Can.	49·05 N	81·20 W
118	Fredericksburg (frĕd'ẽr-ĭkz-bûrg) Tx.	30·16 N	98·52 W
105	Fredericksburg Va.	38·20 N	77·30 W
117	Fredericktown (frĕd'ẽr-ĭk-toun) Mo.	37·32 N	90·16 W
98	Fredericton (frĕd'ẽr-ĭk-tŭn) Can.	45·48 N	66·39 W
156	Frederikshavn (frĕdh'ĕ-rĕks-houn) Den.	57·27 N	10·31 E
156	Frederikssund (frĕdh'ĕ-rĕks-so͞on) Den.	55·51 N	12·04 E
134	Fredonia (frĕ-dō'nyȧ) Col. (In.)	5·55 N	75·40 W
117	Fredonia (frê-dō'nĭ-ȧ) Ks.	36·31 N	95·50 W
105	Fredonia NY	42·25 N	79·20 W
156	Fredrikstad (frȧdh'rĕks-stȧd) Nor.	59·14 N	10·58 E
113	Freeburg (frē'bûrg) Il. (St. Louis In.)	38·26 N	89·59 W
106	Freehold (frē'hōld) NJ (New York In.)	40·15 N	74·16 W
106	Freeland (frē'lănd) Pa.	41·00 N	75·50 W
110	Freeland Wa. (Seattle In.)	48·01 N	122·32 W
99	Freels, C. (frēlz) Can.	46·37 N	53·45 W
89	Freelton (frēl'tŭn) Can. (Toronto In.)	43·24 N	80·02 W
128	Freeport Ba.	26·30 N	78·45 W
109	Freeport (frē'pōrt) Il.	42·19 N	89·30 W
106	Freeport NY (New York In.)	40·39 N	73·35 W
113	Freeport Tx.	28·56 N	95·21 W
214	Freetown (frē'toun) S. L.	8·30 N	13·15 W
162	Fregenal de la Sierra (frä-hȧ-näl' dā lä syĕr'rä) Sp.	38·09 N	6·40 W
163	Fregene (frĕ-zhĕ'-nĕ) It. (Rome In.)	41·52 N	12·12 E
158	Freiberg (frī'bĕrgh) G.D.R.	50·54 N	13·18 E
158	Freiburg G.D.R.	48·00 N	7·50 E
149	Freienried (frī'ĕn-rēd) F.R.G. (Munich In.)	48·20 N	11·08 E
136	Freirina (frå-ĭ-rē'nä) Chile	28·35 S	71·26 W
149	Freising (frī'zĭng) F.R.G. (Munich In.)	48·25 N	11·45 E
161	Fréjus (frā-zhüs') Fr.	43·28 N	6·46 E
204	Fremantle (frē'măn-t'l) Austl.	32·03 S	116·05 E
112	Fremont (frê-mŏnt') Ca. (San Francisco In.)	37·33 N	122·00 W
104	Fremont Mi.	43·25 N	85·55 W
108	Fremont Ne.	41·26 N	96·30 W
104	Fremont Oh.	41·20 N	83·05 W
115	Fremont (R.) Ut.	38·20 N	111·30 W
111	Fremont Pk. Wy.	43·05 N	109·35 W
120	French Broad (R.) (frĕnch brôd) Tn.-NC	35·59 N	83·01 W
133	French Guiana (gē-ä'nä) S. A.	4·20 N	53·00 W
104	French Lick (frĕnch lĭk) In.	38·35 N	86·35 W
94	Frenchman (R.) Can.	49·25 N	108·30 W
111	Frenchman Cr. (frĕnch-măn) Mt.	48·51 N	107·20 W
116	Frenchman Cr. Ne.	40·24 N	101·50 W
114	Frenchman Flat Nv.	36·55 N	116·11 W
113	French River Mn. (Duluth In.)	46·54 N	91·54 W
93	Freshfield, Mt. (frĕsh'fēld) Can.	51·44 N	116·57 W
124	Fresnillo (frâs-nēl'yō) Mex.	23·10 N	102·52 W
114	Fresno (frĕz'nō) Ca.	36·43 N	119·47 W
134	Fresno (frĕs'-nō) Col. (In.)	5·10 N	75·01 W
114	Fresno (R.) (frĕz'nō) Ca.	37·00 N	120·24 W
114	Fresno Slough Ca.	36·39 N	120·12 W
158	Freudenstadt (froi'den-shtät) F.R.G.	48·28 N	8·26 E
203	Freycinet Pen. (frā-sē-nĕ') Austl.	42·13 S	148·56 E
115	Fria (R.) (frē-ä) Az.	34·03 N	112·12 W
212	Fria, C. (frĭȧ) Namibia	18·15 S	12·10 E
214	Fria Gui.	10·05 N	13·32 W
136	Frias (frē-äs) Arg.	28·43 S	65·03 W
158	Fribourg (frē-bo͞or') Switz.	46·48 N	7·07 E
113	Fridley (frĭd'lĭ) Mn. (Minneapolis, St. Paul In.)	45·05 N	93·16 W
158	Frieburg (frī'bo͞orgh) F.R.G.	47·59 N	7·50 E
149	Friedberg (frēd'bĕrgh) F.R.G. (Munich In.)	48·22 N	11·00 E
158	Friedland (frēt'länt) G.D.R.	53·39 N	13·34 E
158	Friedrichshafen (frē-drĕks-häf'ĕn) F.R.G.	47·39 N	9·28 E
117	Friend (frĕnd) Ne.	40·40 N	97·16 W
119	Friendswood (frĕnds'-wo͝od) Tx. (In.)	29·31 N	95·11 W
121	Fries (frēz) Va.	36·42 N	80·59 W
149	Friesack (frē'säk) G.D.R. (Berlin In.)	52·44 N	12·35 E
135	Frio, Cabo (C.) (kä'bō-frē'ō) Braz.	22·58 S	42·08 W
118	Frio R. Tx.	29·00 N	99·15 W
162	Friol (frē-ōl') Sp.	43·02 N	7·48 W
155	Frisian (Is.) (frē'zhăn) Neth.	53·30 N	5·20 E
164	Friuli-Venezia Giulia (Reg.) It.	46·20 N	13·20 E
94	Frobisher L. (frŏb'ĭsh'ẽr) Can.	56·25 N	108·20 W
91	Frobisher Bay Can.	63·48 N	68·31 W
91	Frobisher B. Can.	62·49 N	66·41 W
148	Frodsham (frŏdz'ăm) Eng.	53·18 N	2·48 W
203	Frome, L. (fro͞om) Austl.	30·40 S	140·13 E
117	Frontenac (frŏn-tē-năk) Ks.	37·27 N	94·41 W
125	Frontera (frôn-tā'rä) Mex.	18·34 N	92·38 W
160	Frontignan (frôN-tē-nyän') Fr.	43·26 N	3·45 E
111	Front Ra. (frŭnt) Wy.	42·17 N	105·53 W
105	Front Royal (frŭnt) Va.	38·55 N	78·10 W
150	Fro Sea (frô) Nor.	63·49 N	9·12 E
164	Frosinone (frō-zē-nō'nå) It.	41·38 N	13·22 E
105	Frostburg (frôst'bûrg) Md.	39·40 N	78·55 W
115	Fruita (fro͞ot-ȧ) Co.	39·10 N	108·45 W
172	Frunze (fro͞on'zĕ) Sov. Un.	42·49 N	74·42 E
174	Fryanovo (f'ryä'nô-vô) Sov. Un. (Moscow In.)	56·08 N	38·28 E
174	Fryanzino (f'ryän'zĭ-nô) Sov. Un. (Moscow In.)	55·58 N	38·05 E
159	Frýdek (frē'dĕk) Czech.	49·43 N	18·22 E
158	Frydlant (frēd'länt) Czech.	50·56 N	15·05 E
190	Fucheng (fo͞o-chŭŋ) China	37·53 N	116·08 E

ăt; finăl; rāte; senâte; ärm; åsk; sofȧ; fâre; ch-choose; dh-as th in other; bē; êvent; bĕt; recĕnt; cratẽr; g-go; gh-guttural g; bĭt; ĭ-short neutral; rīde; K-guttural k as ch in German ich;

Page	Name Pronunciation Region	Lat. °'	Long. °'
195	Fuchu (fōō'chōō). Jap. (Tōkyō In.)	35·41 N	139·29 E
193	Fuchun (R.) (fōō-chōōn) China	29·50 N	120·00 E
126	Fuego (Vol.) (fwā'gō) Guat.	14·29 N	90·52 W
163	Fuencarral (fuān-kär-räl') Sp. (Madrid In.)	40·29 N	3·42 W
162	Fuensalida (fwān-sä-lē'dä) Sp.	40·04 N	4·15 W
118	Fuente (fwĕ'n-tĕ) Mex.	28·39 N	100·34 W
162	Fuente de Cantos (fwĕn'tâ dā kän'tōs). Sp.	38·15 N	6·18 W
163	Fuente el Saz (fwĕn'tâ ĕl säth') Sp. (Madrid In.)	40·39 N	3·30 W
162	Fuente-Ovejuna (fwĕn'tâ-ōvâ-hōō'nä). Sp.	38·15 N	5·30 W
162	Fuentesaúco (fwĕn-tâ-sä-ōō'kō) Sp.	41·18 N	5·25 W
122	Fuerte, Rio del (R.) (rê'ō-dĕl-fōō-ĕ'r-tĕ). Mex.	26·15 N	108·50 W
135	Fuerte Olimpo (fwĕr'tâ ō-lēm-pō) Par.	21·10 S	57·49 W
210	Fuerteventura I. (fwĕr'tâ-vĕn-tōō'rä). Can. Is.	28·24 N	13·21 W
188	Fuhai China	47·01 N	87·07 E
190	Fuhsien (fōō'siăn) China	39·36 N	121·59 E
195	Fuji (fōō'jê) Jap.	35·11 N	138·44 E
195	Fuji (R.) Jap.	35·20 N	138·23 E
189	Fujian (Prov.) (fōō-jyĕn) China	25·40 N	117·30 E
195	Fujidera Jap. (Ōsaka In.)	34·34 N	135·37 E
189	Fujin (fōō-jyĭn) China	47·13 N	132·11 E
195	Fuji-san (Mtn.) (fōō'jê sän) Jap.	35·23 N	138·44 E
195	Fujisawa (fōō'jê-sä'wa) Jap. (Tōkyō In.)	35·20 N	139·29 E
195	Fukuchiyama (fōō'kōō-chê-yä'mä). Jap.	35·18 N	135·07 E
195	Fukue (I.) (fōō-kōō'ä) Jap.	32·40 N	129·02 E
195	Fukui (fōō'kōō-ê) Jap.	36·05 N	136·14 E
195	Fukuoka (fōō'kōō-ō'kà) Jap.	33·35 N	130·23 E
195	Fukuoka Jap. (Tōkyō In.)	31·52 N	139·31 E
194	Fukushima (fōō'kōō-shē'mà) Jap.	37·45 N	140·29 E
195	Fukuyama (fōō'kōō-yä'mà) Jap.	34·31 N	133·21 E
187	Fūlādī, Kūh-e (Mtn.) Afg.	34·38 N	67·55 E
158	Fulda R. (fōōl'dä) F.R.G.	51·05 N	9·40 E
193	Fuling (fōō-lĭŋ) China	29·40 N	107·30 E
113	Fullerton (fōōl'ēr-tŭn) Ca. (Los Angeles In.)	33·53 N	117·56 W
119	Fullerton La.	31·00 N	93·00 W
108	Fullerton Ne.	41·21 N	97·59 W
120	Fulton (fŭl'tŭn) Ky.	36·30 N	88·53 W
117	Fulton Mo.	38·51 N	91·56 W
105	Fulton NY	43·20 N	76·25 W
106	Fultondale (fŭl'tŭn-dāl) Al. (Birmingham In.)	33·37 N	86·48 W
195	Funabashi (fōō'nà-bä'shē) Jap. (Tōkyō In.)	35·43 N	139·59 E
195	Funaya (fōō-nä'yä) Jap. (Osaka In.)	34·45 N	135·52 E
210	Funchal (fōōn-shäl') Mad. Is.	32·41 N	16·15 W
134	Fundación (fōōn-dä-syō'n) Col.	10·43 N	74·13 W
162	Fundão (fōōn-douN') Port.	40·08 N	7·32 W
96	Fundy, B. of (fŭn'dĭ) Can.	45·00 N	66·00 W
96	Fundy Natl. Park Can.	45·38 N	65·00 W
190	Funing (fōō'nĭng') China	39·55 N	119·16 E
190	Funing (fōō-nĭŋ) China	33·55 N	119·54 E
193	Funing Wan (B.) (fōō'nĭng'). China	26·48 N	120·35 E
215	Funtua Nig.	11·31 N	7·17 E
217	Furancungo Moz.	14·55 S	33·35 E
125	Furbero (fōōr-bĕ'rô) Mex.	20·21 N	97·32 W
166	Furmanov (fûr-mä'nôf) Sov. Un.	57·14 N	41·11 E
136	Furnas, Reprêsa de (Res.) Braz. (Rio dê Janeiro In.)	21·00 S	46·00 W
205	Furneaux Group (Is.) (fûr'nō) Austl.	40·15 S	146·27 E
158	Fürstenfeld (für'stĕn-fĕlt) Aus.	47·02 N	16·03 E
149	Fürstenfeldbruck (fur'stĕn-fĕld' brōōk) F.R.G. (Munich In.)	48·11 N	11·16 E
158	Fürstenwalde (für'stĕn-väl-dĕ) G.D.R.	52·21 N	14·04 E
158	Fürth (fürt) F.R.G.	49·28 N	11·03 E
195	Furuichi (fōō'rōō-ē'chê) Jap. (Ōsaka In.)	34·33 N	135·37 E
195	Fusa (fōō'sä) Jap. (Tōkyō In.)	35·52 N	140·08 E
134	Fusagasugá (fōō-sä-gä-sōō-gà') Col. (In.)	4·22 N	74·22 W
195	Fuse Jap. (Ōsaka In.)	34·40 N	135·43 E
	Fushih, see Yenan		
195	Fushimi (fōō'shē-mê) Jap. (Ōsaka In.)	34·57 N	135·47 E
192	Fushun (fōō'shōōn') China	41·50 N	124·00 E
192	Fusong (fōō-soŋ) China	42·12 N	127·12 E
195	Futtsu (fōō'tsōō') Jap. (Tōkyō In.)	35·19 N	139·49 E
195	Futtsu Misaki (C.) (fōōt'tsōō' mê-sä'kē). Jap. (Tōkyō In.)	35·19 N	139·46 E
218	Fuwah (fōō'wà) Egypt (Nile In.)	31·13 N	30·35 E
190	Fu Xian (fōō shyĕn) China	39·36 N	121·59 E
192	Fuxin (fōō-shyĭn) China	42·05 N	121·40 E
193	Fuyang China	30·10 N	119·58 E
190	Fuyang (fōō-yäŋ) China	32·53 N	115·48 E
190	Fuyang (R.) (fōō-yäŋ) China	36·59 N	114·48 E
192	Fuyu (fōō-yōō) China	45·20 N	125·00 E
193	Fuzhou (fōō-jō) China	26·02 N	119·18 E
190	Fuzhou (R.) China	39·38 N	121·43 E
190	Fuzhoucheng (fōō-jō-chŭŋ) China	39·46 N	121·44 E
156	Fyn (I.) (fü'n) Den.	55·24 N	10·33 E
154	Fyne (L.) (fīn) Scot.	56·14 N	5·10 W
156	Fyresdal Vand (L.) (fu'rĕs-däl vän). Nor.	59·04 N	7·55 E

G

Page	Name Pronunciation Region	Lat. °'	Long. °'
216	Gabela Ang.	10·48 S	14·20 E
212	Gaborone Bots.	24·28 S	25·59 E
210	Gabès (gä'bĕs) Tun.	33·51 N	10·04 E
210	Gabès, Golfe de (G.) Tun.	32·22 N	10·59 E
215	Gabil Chad	11·09 N	18·12 E
202	Gabin (gôN'bĕn) Pol.	52·23 N	19·47 E
209	Gabon (gà-bôN') Afr.	0·30 S	10·45 E
119	Gabriel R. (gā'brĭ-ĕl) Tx.	30·38 N	97·15 W
165	Gabrovo (gäb'rô-vō) Bul.	42·52 N	25·19 E
134	Gachetá (gä-chā'tä) Col (In.)	4·50 N	73·36 W
165	Gacko (gäts'kô) Yugo.	43·10 N	18·34 E
120	Gadsden (gădz'dĕn) Al.	34·00 N	86·00 W
167	Gadyach (gäd-yäch') Sov. Un.	50·22 N	33·59 E
165	Gaesti (gä-yĕsh'tê) Rom.	44·43 N	25·21 E
164	Gaeta (gä-å'tä) It.	41·18 N	13·34 E
121	Gaffney (găf'nĭ) SC	35·04 N	81·47 W
210	Gafsa (gäf'sä) Tun.	34·16 N	8·37 E
166	Gagarin Sov. Un.	55·32 N	34·58 E
98	Gagetown (gāj'toun) Can.	45·47 N	66·09 W
214	Gagnoa Ivory Coast	6·08 N	5·56 W
197	Gagrary (I.) (gä-grä-rê). Phil. (In.)	13·23 N	123·58 E
164	Gaïdhouronísi (I.) Grc. (In.)	34·53 N	25·58 E
146	Gaillac-sur-Tarn (gà-yäk'sür-tärn'). Fr.	43·54 N	1·52 E
122	Gaillard Cut (gä-êl-yä'rd) Pan. (In.)	9·03 N	79·42 W
121	Gainesville (gānz'vĭl) Fl.	29·40 N	82·20 W
120	Gainesville Ga.	34·16 N	83·48 W
117	Gainesville Tx.	33·38 N	97·08 W
148	Gainsborough (gānz'bŭr-ô) Eng.	53·23 N	0·46 W
203	Gairdner, L. (gârd'nĕr) Austl.	32·20 S	136·30 E
106	Gaithersburg (gā'thĕrs'bûrg) Md. (Baltimore In.)	39·08 N	77·13 W
190	Gai Xian (gī-shyĕn) China	40·25 N	122·20 E
217	Galana (R.) Ken.	3·00 S	39·30 E
163	Galapagar (gä-lä-pä-gär') Sp. (Madrid In.)	40·36 N	4·00 W
	Galápagos Is., see Colon, Arch. de		
154	Galashiels (găl-à-shēlz) Scot.	55·40 N	2·57 W
167	Galati (gà-lätz'ĭ) Rom.	45·25 N	28·05 E
165	Galatina (gä-lä-tē'nä) It.	40·10 N	18·12 E
165	Galaxidhion Grc.	38·26 N	22·22 E
156	Galdhöpiggen Nor.	61·37 N	8·17 E
118	Galeana (gä-lå-ä'nä) Mex.	24·50 N	100·04 W
109	Galena (gà-lē'nà) Il.	42·26 N	90·27 W
107	Galena In. (Louisville In.)	38·21 N	85·55 W
117	Galena Ks.	37·06 N	94·39 W
119	Galena Pk. Tx. (In.)	29·44 N	95·14 W
122	Galera, Cerro (Mtn.) (sĕ'r-rô-gä-lĕ'rä). Pan. (In.)	8·55 N	79·38 W
163	Galera (R.) (gä-lĕ'rä) It. (Rome In.)	41·58 N	12·21 E
134	Galeras (Vol.) (gä-lĕ'räs) Col.	0·57 N	77·27 W
112	Gales (R.) (gālz). Or. (Portland In.)	45·33 N	123·11 W
117	Galesburg (gālz'bûrg) Il.	40·56 N	90·21 W
109	Galesville (gālz'vĭl) Wi.	44·04 N	91·22 W
105	Galeton (gāl'tŭn) Pa.	41·45 N	77·40 W
165	Galibolu (Gallipoli) (gĕ-lĭb'ô-lōō) (gà-lĭp'ô-lē). Tur.	40·25 N	26·40 E
170	Galich (gäl'ĭch) Sov. Un.	58·20 N	42·38 E
159	Galicia (Reg.) (gà-lĭsh'ĭ-à) Pol.-Sov. Un.	49·48 N	21·05 E
162	Galicia (Reg.) (gä-lē'thyä) Sp.	43·35 N	8·03 W
205	Galilee (L.) (găl'ĭ-lē) Austl.	22·23 S	145·09 E
183	Galilee, Sea of. Isr. (Palestine In.)	32·53 N	35·45 E
128	Galina Pt. (gä-lē'nä) Jam.	18·25 N	76·50 W
123	Galion (găl'ĭ-ŭn) Oh.	40·45 N	82·50 W
117	Galisteo (gä-lĭs-tâ'ō) NM	35·20 N	106·00 W
151	Galite, La I. (gä-lēt) Alg.	37·36 N	8·03 E
218	Galka'yo. Som. (Horn of Afr. In.)	7·00 N	47·30 E
211	Galla (Prov.) (gäl'lä) Eth.	7·22 N	35·28 E
164	Gallarate (gäl-lä-rä'tä) It.	45·37 N	8·48 E
161	Gallardon (gä-lär-dôN') Fr. (Paris In.)	48·31 N	1·40 E
117	Gallatin (găl'à-tĭn) Mo.	39·55 N	93·58 W
120	Gallatin Tn.	36·23 N	86·28 W
111	Gallatin R. Mt.	45·12 N	111·10 W
185	Galle (gäl) Sri Lanka	6·13 N	80·10 E
163	Gállego (R.) (gäl-yā'gō) Sp.	42·27 N	0·37 W
134	Gallinas, Pta. de (Pt.) (gä-lyē'näs) Col.	12·10 N	72·10 W
165	Gallipoli (gäl-lē'pô-lē) It.	40·03 N	17·58 E
	Gallipoli, see Galibolu		
104	Gallipolis (găl-ĭ-pô-lēs) Oh.	38·50 N	82·10 W
150	Gällivare (yĕl-ĭ-vär'ĕ) Swe.	68·06 N	20·29 E
162	Gallo (R.) (gäl'yō) Sp.	40·43 N	1·42 W
117	Gallup (găl'ŭp) NM	35·30 N	108·45 W
211	Galnale Doria R. Eth.	5·35 N	40·26 E
104	Galt Can.	43·22 N	80·19 W
154	Galty Mts. Ire.	52·19 N	8·20 W
117	Galva (găl'và) Il.	41·11 N	90·02 W
119	Galveston (găl'vĕs-tŭn). Tx. (In.)	29·18 N	94·48 W
119	Galveston B. Tx.	29·39 N	94·45 W
119	Galveston I. Tx. (In.)	29·12 N	94·53 W
154	Galway Ire.	53·16 N	9·05 W
154	Galway B. (gôl'wā) Ire.	53·10 N	9·47 W
184	Gamba (gäm-bä) China	28·23 N	89·42 E
214	Gambaga (gäm-bä'gä) Ghana	10·32 N	0·26 W
211	Gambela (găm-bā'là) Eth.	8·15 N	34·33 E
210	Gambia (găm'bê-à) Afr.	13·38 N	19·38 W
214	Gambia (R.) (Gambie) Afr.	13·20 N	15·55 W
214	Gambie (R.) (Gambia) Afr.	13·20 N	15·55 W
216	Gamboma (gäm-bō'mä) Con.	1·53 S	15·51 E
156	Gamleby (gäm'lĕ-bü) Swe.	57·54 N	16·20 E
193	Gan (R.) (gän) China	26·50 N	115·00 E
184	Gandak (R.) India	26·37 N	84·22 E
99	Gander (găn'dĕr) Can.	48·57 N	54·34 W
99	Gander (R.) Can.	49·10 N	54·35 W
99	Gander L. Can.	48·55 N	55·40 W
184	Gandhinagar India	23·30 N	72·47 E
215	Gandi Nig.	12·55 N	5·49 E
163	Gandia (gän-dē'ä) Sp.	38·56 N	0·10 W
188	Gangdisê Shan (Trans Himalayas) (Mts.) (gäŋ-dē-sŭ shän) (trăns-hĭ-mä'là-yàs). China	30·25 N	83·43 E
184	Ganges, Mouths of (găn'jēz). India	21·18 N	88·40 E
184	Ganges (R.) (găn'jēz) India	24·32 N	87·58 E
164	Gangi (gän'jē) It.	37·48 N	14·15 E
188	Gangtok India	27·15 N	88·30 E
192	Gannan (gän-nän) China	47·50 N	123·30 E
111	Gannett Pk. (găn'ĕt) Wy.	43·10 N	109·38 W
107	Gano (g'nō). Oh. (Cincinnati In.)	39·18 N	84·24 W
149	Gänserndorf Aus. (Vienna In.)	48·21 N	16·43 E
188	Gansu (Prov.) (gän-sōō) China	38·50 N	101·10 E
215	Ganwo Nig.	11·13 N	4·42 E
190	Ganyu (gän-yōō) China	34·52 N	119·07 E
193	Ganzhou (gän-jō) China	25·50 N	114·30 E
214	Gao (gä'ō) Mali	16·16 N	0·03 W
193	Gao'an (gou-än) China	28·30 N	115·02 E
190	Gaomi (gou-mē) China	36·23 N	119·46 E
191	Gaoqiao (gou-chyou) China (Shanghai In.)	31·21 N	121·35 E
190	Gaoshun (gou-shōōn) China	31·22 N	118·50 E
190	Gaotang (gou-täŋ) China	36·52 N	116·12 E
193	Gaoyao (gou-you) China	23·08 N	112·25 E
190	Gaoyi (gou-yē) China	37·37 N	114·39 E
190	Gaoyou (gou-yō) China	32·46 N	119·26 E
190	Gaoyou Hu (L.) (gou-yō hōō) China	32·59 N	119·04 E
161	Gap (gàp) Fr.	44·34 N	6·08 E
197	Gapan (gä-pän) Phil. (In.)	15·18 N	120·56 E
127	Garachiné (gä-rä-chē'nå) Pan.	8·02 N	78·22 W
127	Garachiné, Punta (Pt.) (pōō'n-tä-gä-rä-chē'nå). Pan.	8·08 N	78·35 W
135	Garanhuns (gä-rän-yōōNsh'). Braz.	8·49 S	36·28 W
117	Garber (gàr'bĕr) Ok.	36·28 N	97·35 W
149	Garching (gär'kĕng) F.R.G. (Munich In.)	48·15 N	11·39 E
118	Garcia (gär-sē'ä) Mex.	25·90 N	100·37 W
124	Garcia de la Cadena (dĕ-lä-kä-dĕ-nä). Mex.	21·14 N	103·26 W
164	Garda, Lago di (L.) (lä-gō-dē-gär'dä). It.	45·43 N	10·26 E
160	Gardanne (gàr-dàn') Fr. (In.)	43·28 N	5·29 E
158	Gardelegen (gär-dĕ-lå'ghĕn) G.D.R.	52·32 N	11·22 E
104	Garden (I.) (gär'd'n) Mi.	45·50 N	85·50 W
113	Gardena (gär-dē'nå) Ca. (Los Angeles In.)	33·53 N	118·19 W
107	Garden City Mi. (Detroit In.)	42·20 N	83·21 W
116	Garden City Ks.	37·58 N	100·52 W
113	Garden Grove (gär'd'n grōv) Ca. (Los Angeles In.)	33·47 N	117·56 W
184	Garden Reach. India (Calcutta In.)	22·33 N	88·17 E
113	Garden River Can. (Sault Ste. Marie In.)	46·33 N	84·10 W
184	Gardēz Afg.	33·43 N	69·09 E
98	Gardiner (gärd'nĕr) Me.	44·12 N	69·46 W
111	Gardiner Mt.	45·03 N	110·43 W
112	Gardiner Wa. (Seattle In.)	48·03 N	122·55 W
94	Gardiner Dam Can.	51·17 N	106·51 W
105	Gardner Ma.	42·35 N	72·00 W
92	Gardner, Can. Can.	53·28 N	128·15 W
101	Gareloi (I.) (gär-lōō-ä') Ak.	51·40 N	178·48 W
106	Garfield (gär'fēld) NJ (New York In.)	40·53 N	74·06 W
113	Garfield. Ut. (Salt Lake City In.)	40·45 N	112·10 W
107	Garfield Heights Oh. (Cleveland In.)	41·25 N	81·36 W
165	Gargaliánoi (gär-gä-lyä'nē) Grc.	37·07 N	21·50 E
157	Gargždai (gärgzh'dī) Sov. Un.	55·43 N	20·09 E
92	Garibaldi, Mt. (gâr-ĭ-băl'dê). Can.	49·51 N	123·01 W
136	Garin (gä-rē'n) Arg. (Buenos Aires In.)	34·10 S	58·44 W
217	Garissa Ken.	0·28 S	39·38 E
113	Garland (gär'lănd) Tx. (Dallas, Fort Worth In.)	32·55 N	96·39 W
111	Garland Ut.	41·45 N	112·10 W
172	Garm Sov. Un.	39·12 N	70·28 E
158	Garmisch-Partenkirchen (gär' mĕsh pär'tĕn-kĕr'kĕn) F.R.G.	47·38 N	11·10 E
117	Garnett (gär'nĕt) Ks.	38·16 N	95·15 W
160	Garonne Rivière (R.) (gà-rôn). Fr.	44·43 N	0·25 W
215	Garoua (gär'wä) Cam.	9·18 N	13·24 E
104	Garrett (găr'ĕt) In.	41·20 N	85·10 W
106	Garrison (găr'ĭ-sŭn) NY (New York In.)	41·23 N	73·57 W
108	Garrison ND	47·38 N	101·24 W
162	Garrovillas (gä-rô-vēl'yäs) Sp.	39·42 N	6·30 W
90	Garry (L.) (găr'ĭ) Can.	66·16 N	99·23 W
217	Garsen Ken.	2·16 S	40·07 E
98	Garson Can.	46·34 N	80·52 W
149	Garstedt (gär'shtĕt) F.R.G. (Hamburg In.)	53·40 N	9·58 E
184	Gartok (gär-tŏk') China	31·11 N	80·35 E
184	Garulia India (In.)	22·48 N	88·23 E
159	Garwolin (gär-vō'lēn) Pol.	51·54 N	21·40 E
107	Gary (gā'rĭ) In. (Chicago In.)	41·35 N	87·21 W
119	Garza-Little Elm Res. Tx.	33·16 N	96·54 W
134	Garzón (gär-thōn') Col.	2·13 N	75·44 W
197	Gasan (gä-sän') Phil. (In.)	13·19 N	121·52 E
171	Gasan-Kuli Sov. Un.	37·25 N	53·55 E
104	Gas City (găs) In.	40·30 N	85·40 W
160	Gascogne (Reg.) (gäs-kôn'yĕ). Fr.	43·45 N	1·49 W
117	Gasconade (R.) (găs-kô-nād'). Mo.	37·46 N	92·15 W
204	Gascoyne (R.) (găs-koin'). Austl.	25·15 S	117·00 E
113	Gashland (găsh'-lănd) Mo. (Kansas City In.)	39·15 N	94·35 W
215	Gashua Nig.	12·54 N	11·00 E
161	Gasny (gäs-nē') Fr. (Paris In.)	49·05 N	1·36 E

Page	Name Pronunciation Region	Lat. °′	Long. °′
98	Gaspé....................Can.	48·50 N	64·29 W
98	Gaspé, Baie de (B.) (gas′pā) (gȧs-pā′).Can.	48·35 N	63·45 W
98	Gaspé, Cape de (C.).........Can.	48·45 N	63·34 W
98	Gaspé, Péninsule de (Pen.)...Can.	48·23 N	65·42 W
129	Gasper Hernandez (gäs-pär′ ĕr-nän′dāth).Dom. Rep.	19·40 N	70·15 W
104	Gassaway (găs′ȧ-wā).........WV	38·40 N	80·45 W
112	Gaston (găs′tŭn) Or. (Portland In.)	45·26 N	123·08 W
121	Gastonia (găs-tô′nĭ-ȧ)........NC	35·15 N	81·14 W
136	Gastre (gäs-trĕ).............Arg.	42·12 S	68·50 W
162	Gata, Cabo de (C.) (kȧ′bô-dĕ-gä′tä).Sp.	36·42 N	2·00 W
162	Gata, Sierra de (Mts.) (syĕr′rȧ dā gȧ′tä).Sp.	40·12 N	6·39 W
183	Gátes, Akrotírion (C.) Cyprus (Palestine In.)	34·30 N	33·15 E
174	Gatchina (gä-chē′nȧ) Sov. Un. (Leningrad In.)	59·33 N	30·08 E
154	Gateshead (gāts′hĕd)........Eng.	54·56 N	1·38 W
119	Gatesville (gāts′vĭl).........Mex.	31·26 N	97·34 W
89	Gatineau (gȧ′tē-nō) Can. (Ottawa In.)	45·29 N	75·38 W
89	Gatineau (R.)..Can. (Ottawa In.)	45·45 N	75·50 W
89	Gatineau, Parc de la (Natl. Pk.) Can. (Ottawa In.)	45·32 N	75·53 W
217	Gatooma (gȧ-tōō′mä).......Zimb.	18·21 S	29·55 E
149	Gattendorf.....Aus. (Vienna In.)	48·01 N	17·00 E
122	Gatun (gä-tōōn′).......Pan. (In.)	9·16 N	79·25 W
122	Gatún, L.............Pan. (In.)	9·13 N	79·24 W
122	Gatun (R.)...........Pan. (In.)	9·21 N	79·10 W
122	Gatun Locks.........Pan. (In.)	9·16 N	79·27 W
184	Gauhāti..................India	26·09 N	91·51 E
157	Gauja (R.) (gå′ōō-yå)....Sov. Un.	57·10 N	24·30 E
197	Gauttier-Gebergte (Mts.) (gō-tyā′) Indon.	2·30 S	138·45 E
164	Gávdhos (I.) (gäv′dôs)..Grc. (In.)	34·48 N	24·08 E
108	Gavins Point Dam (gă′-vĭns).Ne.	42·47 N	97·47 W
156	Gävle (yĕv′lĕ)..............Swe.	60·40 N	17·07 E
156	Gavle-bukten (B.)..........Swe.	60·45 N	17·30 E
166	Gavrilov Posad (gȧ′vrê-lôf′ka po-sȧt).Sov. Un.	56·34 N	40·09 E
166	Gavrilov-Yam (gȧ′vrê-lôf yäm′) Sov. Un.	57·17 N	39·49 E
203	Gawler (gô′lēr)............Austl.	34·35 S	138·47 E
203	Gawler Ra.................Austl.	32·35 S	136·30 E
184	Gaya (gŭ′yä) (gī′ȧ).........India	24·53 N	85·00 E
210	Gaya (gä′yä)...............Nig.	11·58 N	9·05 E
104	Gaylord (gā′lôrd)............Mi.	45·00 N	84·35 W
203	Gayndah (gān′däh)........Austl.	25·43 S	151·33 E
167	Gaysin................Sov. Un.	48·46 N	29·22 E
	Gaza, see Ghazzah		
171	Gaziantep (gä-zē-än′tĕp).....Tur.	37·10 N	37·30 E
214	Gbarnga...................Lib.	7·00 N	9·29 W
159	Gdańsk (Danzig) (g′dänsk) (dän′tsēg).Pol.	54·20 N	18·40 E
166	Gdov (g′dôf′)...........Sov. Un.	58·44 N	27·51 E
159	Gdynia (g′dēn′yȧ)...........Pol.	54·29 N	18·30 E
116	Geary (gē′rĭ)................Ok.	35·36 N	98·19 W
214	Géba (R.).........Guinea-Bissau	12·25 N	14·35 W
111	Gebo (gĕb′ō).................Wy.	43·49 N	108·13 W
119	Ged (gĕd)...................La.	30·07 N	93·36 W
153	Gediz (R.)..................Tur.	38·44 N	28·45 E
112	Gedney (I.) (gĕd-nē) Wa. (Seattle In.)	48·01 N	122·18 W
158	Gedser....................Den.	54·35 N	12·08 E
149	Geel...........Bel. (Brussels In.)	51·09 N	5·01 E
202	Geelong (jē-lông′) Austl. (Melbourne In.)	38·06 S	144·13 E
197	Geelvink-baai (B.) (gäl′vĭŋk) Indon.	2·20 S	135·30 E
190	Gegu (gŭ-gōō)............China	39·00 N	117·30 E
190	Ge Hu (L.) (gŭ hōō).......China	31·37 N	119·57 E
215	Geidam....................Nig.	12·57 N	11·57 E
204	Geikie Ra. (gē′kē).........Austl.	17·35 S	125·32 E
158	Geislingen (gis′lĭng-ĕn).....F.R.G.	48·37 N	9·52 E
107	Geist Res. (gēst) In. (Indianapolis In.)	39·57 N	85·59 W
217	Geita......................Tan.	2·52 S	32·10 E
193	Gejiu (gŭ-jĭo).............China	23·32 N	102·50 E
149	Geldermalsen Neth. (Amsterdam In.)	51·53 N	5·18 E
161	Geldern (gĕl′dĕrn) F.R.G. (Ruhr In.)	51·31 N	6·20 E
165	Gelibolu, Yarimada (Pen.) (gĕ-lĭb′ô-lōō).Tur.	40·23 N	25·10 E
167	Gel'myazov.............Sov. Un.	49·49 N	31·54 E
161	Gelsenkirchen (gĕl-zĕn-kĭrk-ĕn) F.R.G. (Ruhr In.)	51·31 N	7·05 E
183	Gemas (jĕm′ȧs) Mala. (Singapore In.)	2·35 N	102·37 E
216	Gemena...................Zaire	3·15 N	19·46 E
171	Gemlik (gĕm′lĭk)............Tur.	40·30 N	29·10 E
218	Genale (R.)................Eth.	5·00 N	41·15 E
137	General Alvear (gĕ-nĕ-rȧl′ȧl-vĕ-ȧ′r).Arg. (Buenos Aires In.)	36·04 S	60·02 W
137	General Arenales (ä-rĕ-nä′lĕs) Arg. (Buenos Aires In.)	34·19 S	61·16 W
137	General Belgrano (bĕl-grȧ′nô) Arg. (Buenos Aires In.)	35·45 S	58·32 W
118	General Cepeda (sĕ-pĕ′dä)...Mex.	25·24 N	101·29 W
137	General Conesa (kô-nĕ′sä) Arg. (Buenos Aires In.)	36·30 S	57·19 W
137	General Guido (gē′dô) Arg. (Buenos Aires In.)	36·41 S	57·48 W
137	General Lavalle (lȧ-vȧ′l-yĕ) Arg. (Buenos Aires In.)	36·25 S	56·55 W
136	General Madariaga (män-dȧ-rêä′gä).Arg.	36·59 S	57·14 W
137	General Paz (pȧ′z) Arg. (Buenos Aires In.)	35·30 S	58·20 W
124	General Pedro Antonio Santios (pĕ′drô-än-tô′nyô-sän-tyōs). Mex.	21·37 N	98·58 W
136	General Pico (pē′kô).........Arg.	36·46 S	63·44 W
136	General Roca (rô-kä)........Arg.	39·01 S	67·31 W
136	General San Martín (sän-mȧr-tē′n) Arg. (Buenos Aires In.)	34·19 S	58·32 W
137	General Viamonte (vēȧ′môn-tĕ) Arg. (Buenos Aires In.)	35·01 S	60·59 W
118	General Zuazua (zwä′zwä)..Mex.	25·54 N	100·07 W
105	Genesee (R.) (jĕn-ê-sē′)......NY	42·25 N	78·10 W
104	Geneseo (jē-nĕs′eō)............Il.	41·28 N	90·11 W
120	Geneva (jê-nē′vȧ)............Al.	31·03 N	85·50 W
107	Geneva..........Il. (Chicago In.)	41·53 N	88·18 W
117	Geneva.....................Ne.	40·32 N	97·37 W
105	Geneva.....................NY	42·50 N	77·00 W
104	Geneva.....................Oh.	41·45 N	80·55 W
	Geneva, see Génève		
158	Geneva, L................Switz.	46·28 N	6·30 E
158	Génève (Geneva) (zhē-nĕv′).Switz.	46·14 N	6·04 E
167	Genichesk (gȧnê-chyĕsk′) Sov. Un.	46·11 N	34·47 E
162	Genil (R.) (hȧ-nēl′)...........Sp.	37·15 N	4·05 W
117	Genoa (jen′ô-ȧ).............Ne.	41·26 N	97·43 W
	Genoa, see Genova		
107	Genoa City..Wi. (Milwaukee In.)	42·31 N	88·19 W
164	Genova (Genoa) (jĕn′ō-vä).....It.	44·23 N	9·52 E
164	Genova, Golfo di (G.) (gôl-fô-dē-jĕn′ō-vä).It.	44·10 N	8·45 E
122	Genovesa (I.) (ĕ′s-lä-gĕ-nō-vĕ-sä) Ec.	0·08 N	90·15 W
155	Gent......................Bel.	51·05 N	3·40 E
158	Genthin (gĕn-tēn′).......G.D.R.	52·24 N	12·10 E
163	Genzano di Roma (gzhĕnt-zȧ′-nô-dē-rô′-mä) It. (Rome In.)	41·43 N	12·49 E
204	Geographe B. (jē-ô-grăf′)...Austl.	33·00 S	114·00 E
204	Geographic Chan. (jēô′gră-fĭk) Austl.	24·15 S	112·50 E
171	Geokchay (gĕ-ôk′chī)....Sov. Un.	40·40 N	47·40 E
121	George (L.) (jôr-ĭj)...........Fl.	29·10 N	81·50 W
105	George (L.) (jôrj)............NY	43·40 N	73·30 W
113	George L. (jôrg) Can.-U. S. (Sault Ste. Marie In.)	46·26 N	84·09 W
107	George, L.......In. (Chicago In.)	41·31 N	87·17 W
217	George, L..................Ug.	0·02 N	30·25 E
202	Georges (R.)..Austl. (Sydney In.)	33·57 S	151·00 E
129	George Town................Ba.	23·30 N	75·50 W
135	Georgetown (jôrj′toun)......Guy.	7·45 N	58·04 W
99	Georgetown (jôr-ĭj-toun).....Can.	46·11 N	62·32 W
89	Georgetown (jôrg-toun) Can. (Toronto In.)	43·39 N	79·56 W
106	Georgetown..Ct. (New York In.)	41·15 N	73·25 W
105	Georgetown.................De.	38·40 N	75·20 W
128	Georgetown..........Cayman Is.	19·20 N	81·20 W
104	Georgetown..................Il.	40·00 N	87·40 W
104	Georgetown.................Ky.	38·10 N	84·35 W
105	Georgetown.................Md.	39·25 N	75·55 W
99	Georgetown (jôrg-toun)..Ma. (In.)	42·43 N	71·00 W
121	Georgetown (jôr-ĭj-toun).....S. C.	33·22 N	79·17 W
119	Georgetown (jôrg-toun).......Tx.	30·37 N	97·40 W
105	George Washington Birthplace Natl. Mon. (jôrj wŏsh′ĭng-tŭn) Va.	38·10 N	77·00 W
117	George Washington Carver Natl. Mon. (jôrg wăsh-ĭng-tŭn kär′vēr).Mo.	36·58 N	94·21 W
118	George West................Tx.	28·20 N	98·07 W
103	Georgia (State) (jôr′ji-ă)....U. S.	32·40 N	83·50 W
92	Georgia, Str. of............Can.	49·20 N	124·00 W
112	Georgia, Str. of Wa. (Vancouver In.)	48·56 N	123·06 W
168	Georgian (S. S. R.)......Sov. Un.	42·17 N	43·00 E
96	Georgian B.................Can.	45·15 N	80·50 W
96	Georgian Bay Is. Natl. Pk....Can.	45·20 N	81·40 W
120	Georgiana (jôr-jē-än′ȧ)........Al.	31·39 N	86·44 W
204	Georgina (R.) (jôr-jē′nȧ)...Austl.	22·00 S	138·15 E
171	Georgiyevsk (gyôr-gyĕfsk′) Sov. Un.	44·05 N	43·30 E
158	Gera (gā′rä).............G.D.R.	50·52 N	12·06 E
136	Geral, Serra (Mts.) (sĕr′rȧ zhȧ-räl′).Braz.	28·30 S	51·00 W
153	Geral de Goiás, Serra (Mts.) (zhȧ-räl′-dĕ-gô-yȧ′s).Braz.	14·22 S	45·40 W
204	Geraldton (jĕr′ăld-tŭn).....Austl.	28·40 S	114·35 E
91	Geraldton..................Can.	49·43 N	87·00 W
162	Gérgal (gĕr′gäl).............Sp.	37·08 N	2·29 W
108	Gering (gē′rĭng)..............Ne.	41·49 N	103·41 W
159	Gerlachovka Pk..........Czech.	49·12 N	20·05 E
146	German Democratic Republic Eur.	53·30 N	12·30 E
104	Germantown (jûr′mȧn-toun)..Oh.	39·35 N	84·25 W
146	Germany, Federal Republic of (jûr′mȧ-nĭ).Eur.	51·45 N	8·30 E
213	Germiston (jûr′mĭs-tŭn)...S. Afr. (Johannesburg & Pretoria In.)	26·19 S	28·11 E
197	Gerona (hā-rō′nä).......Phil. (In.)	15·36 N	120·36 E
162	Gerona (hĕ-rô′nä)............Sp.	41·55 N	2·48 E
148	Gerrards Cross (jĕr′ards krŏs) Eng. (London In.)	51·34 N	0·33 W
163	Gers (R.) (zhĕr)...............Fr.	43·25 N	0·30 E
149	Gersthofen (gĕrst-hō′fĕn) F.R.G. (Munich In.)	48·26 N	10·54 E
163	Getafe (hā-tä′fȧ).Sp. (Madrid In.)	40·19 N	3·44 W
105	Gettysburg (gĕt′ĭs-bûrg)......Pa.	39·50 N	77·15 W
108	Gettysburg..................SD	45·01 N	99·59 W
161	Gevelsberg (gĕ-fĕls′bĕrgh) F.R.G. (Ruhr In.)	51·18 N	7·20 E
184	Ghāghra (R.)...............India	27·19 N	81·22 E
209	Ghana (gän′ä)..............Afr.	8·00 N	2·00 W
212	Ghanzi (gän′zē)............Bots.	21·30 S	22·00 E
210	Ghardaïa (gär-dä′ê-ä)........Alg.	32·29 N	3·38 E
184	Gharo......................Pak.	24·50 N	68·35 E
210	Ghāt......................Libya	24·52 N	10·16 E
211	Ghazāl, Bahr al- (R.).........Sud.	9·11 N	29·37 E
215	Ghazal, Bahr el (R.) (bär ĕl ghä-zäl′).Chad.	14·30 N	17·00 E
151	Ghazaouet..................Alg.	35·19 N	1·09 W
184	Ghaznī (gŭz′nē).............Afg.	33·43 N	68·18 E
183	Ghazzah (Gaza) Gaza Strip (Palestine In.)	31·30 N	34·29 E
159	Gheorghieni...............Rom.	46·48 N	25·30 E
159	Gherla (gĕr′lä)..............Rom.	47·01 N	23·55 E
89	Ghost Lake....Can. (Calgary In.)	51·15 N	114·46 W
210	Ghudāmis.................Libya	30·07 N	9·26 E
164	Giannutri, I. di (jän-nōō′trē)...It.	42·15 N	11·06 E
129	Gibara (hē-bä′rä)...........Cuba	21·05 N	76·10 W
212	Gibeon (gĭb′ê-ŭn).......Namibia	24·45 S	16·40 E
162	Gibraleón (hē-brä-lȧ-ōn′).....Sp.	37·24 N	7·00 W
151	Gibraltar (hē-bräl-tä′r)......Eur.	36·08 N	5·22 W
162	Gibraltar, Bay of............Sp.	35·04 N	5·10 W
162	Gibraltar, Str. of.......Afr.-Eur.	35·55 N	5·45 W
104	Gibson City (gĭb′sŭn).........Il.	40·25 N	88·20 W
204	Gibson Des...............Austl.	24·45 S	123·15 E
106	Gibson Island.Md. (Baltimore In.)	39·05 N	76·26 W
117	Gibson Res.................Ok.	36·07 N	95·08 W
119	Giddings (gĭd′ĭngz)...........Tx.	30·11 N	96·55 W
117	Gideon (gĭd′ê-ŭn)............Mo.	36·27 N	89·56 W
160	Gien (zhē-ăN′)...............Fr.	47·43 N	2·37 E
158	Giessen (gēs′sĕn)..........F.R.G.	50·35 N	8·40 E
89	Giffard (zhē-färd′) Can. (Quebec In.)	46·51 N	71·12 W
195	Gifu (gē′fōō)...............Jap.	35·25 N	136·45 E
112	Gig Harbor (gĭg).Wa. (Seattle In.)	47·20 N	122·36 W
164	Giglio, I. di (jēl′yō)...........It.	42·23 N	10·55 E
162	Gigüela (R.) (hê-gā′lä)........Sp.	39·53 N	2·54 W
162	Gijón (hê-hōn′)..............Sp.	43·33 N	5·37 W
115	Gila (R.) (hē′lȧ).............Az.	32·41 N	113·50 W
115	Gila Bend..................Az.	32·59 N	112·41 W
115	Gila Bend Ind. Res...........Az.	33·02 N	112·48 W
115	Gila Cliff Dwellings Natl. Mon. NM	33·15 N	108·20 W
115	Gila River Ind. Res...........Az.	33·11 N	112·38 W
109	Gilbert (gĭl′bērt).............Mn.	47·27 N	92·29 W
205	Gilbert (R.) (gĭl-bĕrt)......Austl.	17·15 S	142·09 E
92	Gilbert, Mt................Can.	50·51 N	124·20 W
213	Gilboa, Mt. (gĭl-bôȧ) S. Afr. (Natal In.)	29·13 S	30·17 E
92	Gilford I. (gĭl′fērd)..........Can.	50·45 N	126·25 W
184	Gilgit (gĭl′gĭt)..............Pak.	35·58 N	73·48 E
92	Gil I. (gĭl)..................Can.	53·13 N	129·15 W
204	Gillen (I.) (jĭl′ĕn)..........Austl.	26·15 S	125·15 E
117	Gillett (jĭ-lĕt′)...............Ar.	34·07 N	91·22 W
111	Gillette....................Wy.	44·17 N	105·30 W
148	Gillingham (gĭl′ĭng ăm) Eng. (London In.)	51·23 N	0·33 E
104	Gilman (gĭl′măn).............Il.	40·45 N	87·55 W
113	Gilman Hot Springs Ca. (Los Angeles In.)	33·49 N	116·57 W
119	Gilmer (gĭl′mēr).............Tx.	32·43 N	94·57 W
106	Gilmore (gĭl′môr).Ga. (Atlanta In.)	33·51 N	84·29 W
114	Gilroy (gĭl-roi′)..............Ca.	37·00 N	121·34 W
197	Giluwe, Mt..........Pap. N. Gui.	6·04 S	144·00 E
95	Gimli (gĭm′lē)..............Can.	50·39 N	97·00 W
160	Gimone (R.) (zhē-mōn′).......Fr.	43·26 N	0·36 E
211	Ginir......................Eth.	7·13 N	40·44 E
164	Ginosa (jê-nō′zä).............It.	40·35 N	16·48 E
162	Ginzo (hēn-thō′).............Sp.	42·03 N	7·43 W
164	Gioia del Colle (jô′yä dĕl kôl′lā).It.	40·48 N	16·55 E
135	Gi-Paraná (R.) (zhē-pä-rä-nȧ′) Braz.	9·33 S	61·35 W
117	Girard (jĭ-rärd′).............Ks.	37·30 N	94·50 W
134	Girardot (hē-rär-dōt′) Col. (In.)	4·19 N	75·47 W
171	Giresun (ghĕr′ĕ-sōōn′).......Tur.	40·55 N	38·20 E
184	Giridih (jē′rê-dê)...........India	24·12 N	81·18 E
160	Gironde (Est.) (zhē-rôNd′).....Fr.	45·31 N	1·00 W
154	Girvan (gûr′văn)...........Scot.	55·15 N	5·01 W
205	Gisborne (gĭz′bŭrn)....N. Z. (In.)	38·40 S	178·08 E
217	Gisenyi....................Rw.	1·43 S	29·15 E
160	Gisors (zhē-zôr′).............Fr.	49·19 N	1·47 E
216	Gitambo...................Zaire	4·21 N	24·45 E
212	Gitega.................Burundi	3·39 S	30·05 E
165	Giurgui (jōōr′jōō)..........Rom.	43·53 N	25·58 E
160	Givet (zhē-vĕ′)...............Fr.	50·80 N	4·47 E
160	Givors (zhē-vôr′).............Fr.	45·35 N	4·46 E
173	Gizhiga (gē′zhi-gȧ)......Sov. Un.	61·59 N	160·46 E
159	Gizycko (gĭ′zhĭ-ko)...........Pol.	54·03 N	21·48 E
165	Gjinokastër.................Alb.	40·04 N	20·10 E
156	Gjövik (gyû′vêk)............Nor.	60·47 N	10·36 E
149	Glabeek-Zuurbemde Bel. (Brussels In.)	50·52 N	4·59 E
99	Glace Bay (glās bā).........Can.	46·12 N	59·57 W
101	Glacier Bay Natl. Mon. (glā′shēr) Ak.	58·40 N	136·50 W
93	Glacier Natl. Park..........Can.	51·45 N	117·35 W
110	Glacier Pk..................Wa.	48·07 N	121·10 W
112	Glacier Pt......Can. (Seattle In.)	48·24 N	123·59 W
161	Gladbeck (gläd′bĕk) F.R.G. (Ruhr In.)	51·35 N	6·59 E
218	Gladdeklipkop............S. Afr. (Johannesburg & Pretoria In.)	24·17 S	29·36 E
203	Gladstone (glăd′stōn).......Austl.	23·45 S	150·00 E
203	Gladstone.................Austl.	33·15 S	138·20 E
102	Gladstone..................Can.	50·15 N	98·50 W
109	Gladstone...................Mi.	45·50 N	87·04 W
106	Gladstone.....NJ (New York In.)	40·43 N	74·39 W
112	Gladstone......Or. (Portland In.)	45·23 N	122·36 W
104	Gladwin (glăd′wĭn)...........Mi.	44·00 N	84·25 W
164	Glamoč (gläm′ôch).........Yugo.	44·03 N	16·51 E
158	Glarus (glä′rōōs)...........Switz.	47·02 N	9·03 E
120	Glasgow....................Ky.	37·00 N	85·55 W
117	Glasgow....................Mo.	39·14 N	92·48 W
111	Glasgow....................Mt.	48·14 N	106·39 W
154	Glasgow (glȧs′gō)...........Scot.	55·54 N	4·25 W

ăt; finăl; rāte; senȧte; ärm; ȧsk; sofȧ; fâre; ch-choose; dh-as th in other; bē; ėvent; bĕt; recĕnt; cratēr; g-go; gh-guttural g; bĭt; ĭ-short neutral; rīde; K-guttural k as ch in German ich;

PRONOUNCING INDEX Glassport — Grand 285

Page	Name Pronunciation Region	Lat. °′	Long. °′
107	Glassport (glȧs′pōrt) Pa. (Pittsburgh In.)	40·19 N	79·53 W
158	Glauchau (glou′κou) G.D.R.	50·51 N	12·28 E
170	Glazov (glä′zôf) Sov. Un.	58·05 N	52·52 E
158	Glda (R.) (g′l′dȧ) Pol.	53·27 N	16·52 E
148	Glen (R.) (glĕn) Eng.	52·44 N	0·18 W
160	Glénans, Iles de (Is.) (ēl-dĕ-glā-näN′). Fr.	47·43 N	4·42 W
106	Glen Burnie (bûr′nē) Md. (Baltimore In.)	39·10 N	76·38 W
115	Glen Canyon Dam (glĕn kăn′yŭn) Az.	36·57 N	111·25 W
113	Glen Carbon (kär′bŏn) Il. (St. Louis In.)	38·45 N	89·59 W
107	Glencoe Il. (Chicago In.)	42·08 N	87·45 W
109	Glencoe (glĕn′kō) Mn.	44·44 N	94·07 W
213	Glencoe (glĕn-cō) S. Afr. (Natal In.)	28·14 S	30·09 E
106	Glen Cove (kōv) NY (New York In.)	40·51 N	73·38 W
115	Glendale (glĕn′dāl) Az.	33·30 N	112·15 W
113	Glendale Ca. (Los Angeles In.)	34·09 N	118·15 W
107	Glendale Oh. (Cincinnati In.)	31·16 N	84·22 W
111	Glendive (glĕn′dīv) Mt.	47·08 N	104·41 W
111	Glendo Wy.	42·32 N	104·54 W
113	Glendora (glĕn-dō′rȧ) Ca. (Los Angeles In.)	34·08 N	117·52 W
203	Glenelg (R.) Austl.	37·20 S	141·30 E
107	Glen Ellyn (glĕn ĕl′-lĕn) Il. (Chicago In.)	41·53 N	88·04 W
203	Glen Innes (ĭn′ĕs) Austl.	29·45 S	152·02 E
119	Glenmora (glĕn-mō′rȧ) La.	30·58 N	92·36 W
110	Glenns Ferry (fĕr′ĭ) Id.	42·58 N	115·21 W
121	Glenville (glĕn′vĭl) Ga.	31·55 N	81·56 W
106	Glen Olden (ōl′d′n) Pa. (Philadelphia In.)	39·54 N	75·17 W
111	Glenrock (glĕn′rŏk) Wy.	42·50 N	105·53 W
105	Glens Falls (glĕnz fôlz) NY	43·20 N	73·40 W
107	Glenshaw (glĕn′shô) Pa. (Pittsburgh In.)	40·33 N	79·57 W
108	Glen Ullin (glĕn′ŭl′ĭn) ND	46·47 N	101·49 W
112	Glen Valley. Can. (Vancouver In.)	49·09 N	122·30 W
107	Glenview (glĕn′vū) Il. (Chicago In.)	42·04 N	87·48 W
108	Glenwood Ia.	41·03 N	95·44 W
108	Glenwood Mn.	45·39 N	95·23 W
115	Glenwood Springs Co.	39·35 N	107·20 W
149	Glienicke (glē′nē-kĕ) G.D.R. (Berlin In.)	52·38 N	13·19 E
149	Glinde (glĕn′dĕ) F.R.G.(Hamburg In.)	53·32 N	10·13 E
156	Glittertinden (Mtn.) Nor.	61·39 N	8·12 E
159	Gliwice (gwĭ-wĭt′sĕ) Pol.	50·18 N	18·40 E
115	Globe (glōb) Az.	33·20 N	110·50 W
167	Globino (glôb′ê-nō) Sov. Un.	49·22 N	33·17 E
158	Głogów (gwō′gōōv) Pol.	51·40 N	16·04 E
156	Glomma (R.) (glômmä) Nor.	61·22 N	11·02 E
156	Glommen (R.) (glôm′ĕn) Nor.	60·03 N	11·15 E
149	Glonn (glônn) F.R.G. (Munich In.)	47·59 N	11·52 E
13	Glorieuses, Îles (Is.) Afr.	11·28 S	47·50 E
148	Glossop (glŏs′ŭp) Eng.	53·26 N	1·57 W
120	Gloster (glŏs′tĕr) Ms.	31·10 N	91·00 W
154	Gloucester (glŏs′tĕr) Eng.	51·54 N	2·11 W
99	Gloucester Ma. (In.)	42·37 N	70·40 W
106	Gloucester City NJ (Philadelphia In.)	39·53 N	75·08 W
104	Glouster (glŏs′tĕr) Oh.	39·35 N	82·05 W
99	Glover I. (glŭv′ĕr) Can.	48·44 N	57·45 W
105	Gloversville (glŭv′ĕrz-vĭl) NY	43·05 N	74·20 W
99	Glovertown (glŭv′ĕr-toun) Can.	48·41 N	54·02 W
166	Glubokoye (glōō-bô-kō′yĕ) Sov. Un.	55·08 N	27·44 E
149	Glückstadt (glük-shtät) F.R.G. (Hamburg In.)	53·47 N	9·25 E
167	Glukhov (glōō′κôf′) Sov. Un.	51·42 N	33·52 E
167	Glushkovo (glōōsh′kô-vō). Sov. Un.	51·21 N	34·43 E
158	Gmünden (g′mōōn′dĕn) Aus.	47·57 N	13·47 E
159	Gniezno (g′nyåz′nô) Pol.	52·32 N	17·34 E
165	Gnjilane (gnyē′lȧ-nĕ) Yugo.	42·28 N	21·27 E
185	Goa (Ter.) (gō′ȧ) India	15·45 N	74·00 E
126	Goascorán (gō-äs′kō-rän′) Hond.	13·37 N	87·43 W
211	Goba (gō′bä) Eth.	7·17 N	39·58 E
212	Gobabis (gō-bä′bĭs) Namibia	22·25 S	18·50 E
188	Gobi or Shamo (Des.) (gō′be) Mong.	43·29 N	103·15 E
112	Goble (gō′b′l) Or. (Portland In.)	46·01 N	122·53 W
161	Goch (gōκ) F.R.G. (Ruhr In.)	51·35 N	6·10 E
184	Godāvari (R.) (gô-dä′vŭ-rê). India	17·42 N	81·15 E
204	Goddards Soak (Swp.) (gŏd′ȧrdz) Austl.	31·20 S	123·30 E
104	Goderich (gŏd′rĭch) Can.	43·45 N	81·45 W
113	Godfrey (gŏd′frê) Il. (St. Louis In.)	38·57 N	90·12 W
75	Godhavn (gōdh′hȧvn) Grnld.	69·15 N	53·30 W
95	Gods (R.) (ğodz) Can.	55·17 N	93·35 W
95	Gods Lake Can.	54·40 N	94·09 W
75	Godthåb (gŏt′hōōb) Grnld.	64·10 N	51·32 W
189	Godwin Austen, Mt. (gŏd wĭn ôs′tĕn). Pak.	36·06 N	76·38 E
97	Goéland, Lac au (L.) Can.	49·47 N	76·41 W
114	Goffs (gôfs) Ca.	34·57 N	115·06 W
109	Gogebic (L.) (gô-gē′bĭk) Mi.	46·24 N	89·25 W
109	Gogebic Ra. Mi.	46·37 N	89·48 W
149	Goggingen (gŭg′gĕn-gĕn) F.R.G. (Munich In.)	48·21 N	10·53 E
157	Gogland (I.) Sov. Un.	60·04 N	26·55 E
215	Gogonou Benin	10·50 N	2·50 E
124	Gogorrón (gō-gô-rōn′) Mex.	21·51 N	100·54 W
135	Goiânia (gô-yä′nyä) Braz.	16·41 S	48·57 W
135	Goiás (gô-yȧ′s) Braz.	15·57 S	50·10 W
135	Goiás (State) Braz.	12·35 S	48·38 W
149	Goirle Neth. (Amsterdam In.)	51·31 N	5·06 E
171	Göksu (R.) (gûk′sōō′) Tur.	36·40 N	33·30 E
156	Göl (gûl) Nor.	60·58 N	8·54 E
121	Golax (gō′lăks) Va.	36·41 N	80·56 W
148	Golcar (gŏl′kȧr) Eng.	53·38 N	1·52 W
117	Golconda (gŏl-kŏn′dȧ) Il.	37·21 N	88·32 W
159	Gołdap (gôl′dăp) Pol.	54·17 N	22·17 E
93	Golden Can.	51·18 N	116·58 W
116	Golden Co.	39·44 N	105·15 W
110	Goldendale (gōl′dĕn-dāl) Wa.	45·49 N	120·48 W
112	Golden Gate (Str.) (gōl′dĕn gāt) Ca. (San Francisco In.)	37·48 N	122·32 W
92	Golden Hinde (hĭnd) Can.	49·40 N	125·45 W
106	Golden's Bridge NY (New York In.)	41·17 N	73·41 W
113	Golden Valley. Mn. (Minneapolis, St. Paul In.)	44·58 N	93·23 W
114	Goldfield (gōld′fēld) Nv.	37·42 N	117·15 W
122	Gold Hill (Mtn.) Pan. (In.)	9·03 N	79·08 W
112	Gold Mtn. (gōld). Wa. (Seattle In.)	47·33 N	122·48 W
121	Goldsboro (gōldz-bûr′ô) NC	35·23 N	77·59 W
118	Goldthwaite (gōld′thwāt) Tx.	31·27 N	98·34 W
158	Goleniów (gô-lĕ-nyŭf′) Pol.	53·33 N	14·51 E
173	Golets-Purpula, Gol′tsy (Mtn.) Sov. Un.	59·08 N	115·22 E
127	Golfito (gôl-fē′tō) C. R.	8·40 N	83·12 W
	Golfo Dulce, see Izabal, L.		
119	Goliad (gō-lĭ-ăd′) Tx.	28·40 N	97·12 W
164	Golo (R.) Fr.	42·28 N	9·18 E
197	Golo I. (gō′lō) Phil. (In.)	13·38 N	120·17 E
167	Golovchino (gō-lôf′chê-nō) Sov. Un.	50·34 N	35·52 E
165	Golyamo Konare (gō′lȧ-mō-kō′nä-rĕ). Bul.	42·16 N	24·33 E
149	Golzow (gōl′tsōv) G.D.R. (Berlin In.)	52·17 N	12·36 E
217	Gombari (gōōm-bä-rê) Zaire	2·45 N	29·00 E
215	Gombe Nig.	10·19 N	11·02 E
166	Gomel′ (go′mĕl′) Sov. Un.	52·20 N	31·03 E
166	Gomel′ (Oblast) Sov. Un.	52·18 N	29·00 E
210	Gomera I. (gô-mā′rä) Can. Is.	28·00 N	18·01 W
118	Gomez Farias (gō′māz fä-rē′ȧs) Mex.	24·59 N	101·02 W
118	Gómez Palacio (pä-lä′syō) Mex.	25·35 N	103·30 W
129	Gonaïves (gō-nȧ-ēv′) Hai.	19·25 N	72·45 W
129	Gonaïves, Golfe des (G.) (gō-nȧ-ēv′). Hai.	19·20 N	73·20 W
129	Gonâve, Ile De La (I.) (gô-nȧv′) Hai.	18·50 N	73·30 W
184	Gonda India	27·13 N	82·00 E
184	Gondal India	22·02 N	70·47 E
211	Gonder Eth.	12·39 N	37·30 E
161	Gonesse (gô-nĕs′) Fr. (Paris In.)	48·59 N	2·28 E
188	Gongga Shan (Mt.) (gôŋ-gä shän) China	29·16 N	101·46 E
215	Goniri Nig.	11·30 N	12·20 E
195	Gonō (R.) (gô′nō) Jap.	35·00 N	132·25 E
89	Gonor (gō′nŏr) Can. (Winnepeg In.)	50·04 N	96·57 W
213	Gonubie (gŏn′ōō-bē) S. Afr. (Natal In.)	32·56 S	28·02 E
124	Gonzales (gôn-zá′lĕs) Mex.	22·47 N	98·26 W
119	Gonzales (gŏn-zä′lĕz) Tx.	29·31 N	97·25 W
136	González Catán (gōn-zá′lĕz-kä-tá′n) Arg. (Buenos Aires In.)	34·31 S	58·39 W
92	Good Hope Mtn. Can.	51·09 N	124·10 W
212	Good Hope, C. of (kāp ov gŏŏd hōp). S. Afr. (In.)	34·21 S	18·29 E
110	Gooding (gŏŏd′ĭng) Id.	42·55 N	114·43 W
104	Goodland (gŏŏd′lănd) In.	40·50 N	87·15 W
116	Goodland Ks.	39·19 N	101·43 W
212	Goodwood (gŏŏd′wŏŏd) S. Afr. (In.)	33·54 S	18·33 E
148	Goole (gōōl) Eng.	53·42 N	0·52 W
108	Goose (R.) ND	47·40 N	97·41 W
91	Goose Bay Can.	53·19 N	60·33 W
111	Gooseberry Cr. (gōōs-bĕr′ĭ) Wy.	44·04 N	108·35 W
111	Goose Cr. (gōōs) Id.	42·07 N	113·53 W
110	Goose L. Ca.	41·56 N	120·35 W
184	Gorakhpur (gō′rŭk-pōōr) India	26·45 N	82·39 E
128	Gorda, Punta (Pt.) (pōō′n-tä-gôr-dä). Cuba	22·25 N	82·10 W
128	Gorda Cay (gôr′dä) Ba.	26·05 N	77·30 W
89	Gordon (gôr′dŭn) Can. (Winnipeg In.)	50·00 N	97·20 W
108	Gordon Ne.	42·47 N	102·14 W
211	Gore (gō′rĕ) Eth.	8·12 N	35·34 E
186	Gorgān Iran	36·44 N	54·30 E
164	Gorgona (I.) (gôr-gō′nä) It.	43·27 N	9·55 E
171	Gori (gō′rê) Sov. Un.	42·00 N	44·08 E
149	Gorinchem (gō′rĭn-κĕm) Neth. (Amsterdam In.)	51·50 N	4·59 E
148	Goring (gôr′ĭng) Eng. (London In.)	51·30 N	1·08 W
164	Gorizia (gô-rê′tsê-yä) It.	44·56 N	13·40 E
170	Gorki (gôr′kē) Sov. Un.	56·15 N	44·05 E
170	Gor'kovskoye Sov. Un.	56·38 N	43·40 E
166	Gor′kovskoye Vdkhr. (Res.) (gôr-kôf-skō-yĕ). Sov. Un.	57·38 N	41·18 E
159	Gorlice (gôr-lē′tsĕ) Pol.	49·38 N	21·11 E
158	Görlitz (gûr′lĭts) G.D.R.	51·10 N	15·01 E
167	Gorlovka (gôr′lôf-kȧ) Sov. Un.	48·17 N	38·03 E
118	Gorman (gôr′mȧn) Tx.	32·13 N	98·40 W
165	Gorna-Oryakhovitsa (gôr′nä-ôr-yĕk′ô-vē-tsȧ). Bul.	43·08 N	25·40 E
165	Gornji Milanovac (gôrn′yē-mē′la-nô-väts). Yugo.	44·02 N	20·29 E
172	Gorno-Altay Aut. Oblast Sov. Un.	51·00 N	86·00 E
172	Gorno-Altaysk (gôr′nŭ-ŭl-tīsk′) Sov. Un.	52·28 N	82·45 E
159	Gorodënka (gō-rô-deŋ′kä) Sov. Un.	48·40 N	25·30 E
170	Gorodets (Res.) Sov. Un.	57·00 N	43·55 E
174	Gorodishche (gô-rô′dĭsh-chĕ) Sov. Un. (Urals In.)	57·57 N	57·03 E
167	Gorodnya (gô-rôd′′nyä) Sov. Un.	51·54 N	31·31 E
159	Gorodok (gô-rô-dôk′) Sov. Un.	49·37 N	23·40 E
166	Gorodok Sov. Un.	55·27 N	29·58 E
172	Gorodok Sov. Un.	50·30 N	103·58 E
196	Gorontalo (gō-rōn-tä′lo) Indon.	0·40 N	123·04 E
159	Goryn′ R. (gō′rĕn′) Sov. Un.	50·55 N	26·07 E
158	Gorzow Wielkopolski (gō-zhōōv′vyĕl-ko-pōl′skē) Pol.	53·44 N	15·15 E
104	Goshen (gō′shĕn) In.	41·35 N	85·50 W
107	Goshen Ky. (Louisville In.)	38·24 N	85·34 W
106	Goshen NY (New York In.)	41·24 N	74·19 W
107	Goshen Oh. (Cincinnati In.)	39·14 N	84·09 W
115	Goshute Ind. Res. (gō-shōōt′) Ut.	39·50 N	114·00 W
158	Goslar (gôs′lär) F.R.G.	51·55 N	10·25 E
135	Gospa (R.) (gôs-pä) Ven. (In.)	9·43 N	64·23 W
164	Gospić (gôs′pĭch) Yugo.	44·31 N	15·03 E
165	Gostivar (gos′tê-vär) Yugo.	41·46 N	20·58 E
159	Gostynin (gôs-tē′nĭn) Pol.	52·24 N	19·30 E
156	Göta alv (R.) (gōĕtä ăĕl′v) Swe.	58·11 N	12·03 E
156	Göta Can. (yû′tȧ) Swe.	58·35 N	15·24 E
156	Göteborg (yû′tĕ-bôrgh) Swe.	57·39 N	11·56 E
215	Gotel Mts. Cam.-Nig.	7·05 N	11·20 E
126	Gotera (gō-tā′rä) Sal.	13·41 N	88·06 W
158	Gotha (gō′tȧ) G.D.R.	50·57 N	10·43 E
116	Gothenburg (gŏth′ĕn-bûrg) Ne.	40·57 N	100·08 W
156	Gotland (I.) Swe.	57·35 N	17·35 E
195	Gotō-Rettō (Is.) (gō′tō rĕt′tō) Jap.	33·06 N	128·54 E
157	Gotska Sandön (I.) Swe.	58·24 N	19·15 E
158	Göttingen (gût′ĭng-ĕn) F.R.G.	51·32 N	9·57 E
149	Gouda (gou′dä) Neth. (Amsterdam In.)	52·00 N	4·42 E
220	Gough (I.) (gŏf) Atl. O.	40·00 S	10·00 W
91	Gouin, Rés. Can.	48·15 N	74·15 W
192	Goukou (gō-kō) China	48·45 N	121·42 E
96	Goulais (R.) Can.	46·45 N	84·10 W
203	Goulburn (gōl′bŭrn) Austl.	34·47 S	149·40 E
214	Goumbati (Mtn.) Senegal	13·08 N	12·06 W
214	Goumbou (gōōm-bōō′) Mali	14·59 N	7·27 W
215	Gouna Cam.	8·32 N	13·34 E
210	Goundam (gōōn-däN′) Mali	16·29 N	3·37 W
210	Gouré (gōō-rā′) Niger	13·53 N	10·44 E
105	Gouverneur (gŭv-ĕr-nōōr′) NY	44·20 N	75·25 W
94	Govenlock (gŭvĕn-lŏk) Can.	49·15 N	109·48 W
136	Governador Ilhado (I.) (gô-vĕr-nä-dō′r-ē-lȧ′dô) Braz. (Rio de Janeiro In.)	22·48 S	43·13 W
136	Governador Portela (pōr-tĕ′lȧ) Braz. (Rio de Janeiro In.)	22·28 S	43·30 W
135	Governador Valadares (vä-lä-dä′rĕs). Braz.	18·47 S	41·45 W
129	Governor's Harbour Ba.	25·15 N	76·15 W
105	Gowanda (gô-wŏn′dȧ) NY	42·30 N	78·55 W
136	Goya (gō′yä) Arg.	29·06 S	59·12 W
148	Goyt (R.) (goit) Eng.	53·19 N	2·03 W
212	Graaff-Reinet (gräf′rī′nĕt) S. Afr.	32·10 S	24·40 E
164	Gracac (grä′chäts) Yugo.	44·16 N	15·50 E
165	Gračanico Yugo.	44·42 N	18·19 E
120	Graceville (grās′vĭl) Fl.	30·57 N	85·30 W
108	Graceville Mn.	45·33 N	96·25 W
126	Gracias (grä′sê-äs) Hond.	14·35 N	88·37 W
127	Gracias a Dios, Cabo (C.) (kȧ′bô-grä-syäs-ä-dyô′s). Hond.	15·00 N	83·13 W
210	Graciosa I. (grä-syô′sä) Açores (In.)	39·07 N	27·30 W
165	Gradačac (gra-dä′chats) Yugo.	44·50 N	18·28 E
162	Gradelos (grä-dĕ-lôs) Sp.	42·38 N	5·15 W
167	Gradizhsk (grä-dēzhsk′) Sov. Un.	49·12 N	33·06 E
162	Grado (grä′dō) Sp.	43·24 N	6·04 W
149	Gräfelfing (grä′fĕl-fēng) F.R.G. (Munich In.)	48·07 N	11·27 E
149	Grafing (grä′fēng) F.R.G. (Munich In.)	48·03 N	11·58 E
203	Grafton (grăf′tŭn) Austl.	29·38 S	153·05 E
113	Grafton Il. (St. Louis In.)	38·58 N	90·26 W
99	Grafton Ma. (In.)	42·13 N	71·41 W
108	Grafton ND	48·24 N	97·25 W
107	Grafton Oh. (Cleveland In.)	41·16 N	82·04 W
105	Grafton WV	39·20 N	80·00 W
163	Gragnano (grän-yä′nō) It. (Naples In.)	40·27 N	14·32 E
121	Graham (grā′ăm) NC	36·03 N	79·23 W
116	Graham Tx.	33·07 N	98·34 W
112	Graham Wa. (Seattle In.)	47·03 N	122·18 W
90	Graham (I.) Can.	53·50 N	132·40 W
213	Grahamstown (grā′ăms′toun) S. Afr. (Natal In.)	33·19 S	26·33 E
161	Graian Alps (Mts.) (grā′yăn) Fr.-It.	45·17 N	6·52 E
135	Grajaú (grȧ-zhȧ-ōō′) Braz.	5·59 S	46·03 W
135	Grajaú (R.) Braz.	4·24 S	46·04 W
159	Grajewo (grä-yä′vo) Pol.	53·38 N	22·28 E
137	Grama, Serra de (Mtn.) (sĕ′r-rä-dĕ-grä′mȧ) Braz. (Rio de Janeiro In.)	23·42 S	42·28 W
165	Gramada (grä′mä-dä) Bul.	43·46 N	22·41 E
149	Gramatneusiedl. Aus. (Vienna In.)	48·02 N	16·29 E
164	Grammichele (gräm-mê-kĕ′lā) It.	37·15 N	14·40 E
154	Grampian Mts. (grăm′pĭ-ăn). Scot.	56·30 N	4·55 W
126	Granada (grä-nä′dhä) Nic.	11·55 N	85·58 W
162	Granada (grä-nä′dä) Sp.	37·13 N	3·37 W
136	Gran Bajo (Pln.) (grán′bä′kō). Arg.	47·35 S	68·45 W
119	Granbury (grăn′bĕr-ĭ) Tx.	32·26 N	97·45 W
105	Granby (grăn′bĭ) Can.	45·30 N	72·40 W
117	Granby Mo.	36·54 N	94·15 W
116	Granby (L.) Co.	40·07 N	105·40 W
210	Gran Canaria I. (grän′kä-nä′rê-ä). Can. Is.	27·39 N	15·39 W
136	Gran Chaco (Reg.) (grän′chä′kô) Arg.-Par.	25·30 S	62·15 W
109	Grand (I.) Mi.	46·37 N	86·38 W
98	Grand (L.) Can.	45·17 N	67·42 W

ng-sing; ŋ-baŋk; N-nasalized n; nŏd; cŏmmit; ōld; ôbey; ôrder; fōōd; fŏŏt; ou-out; s-soft; sh-dish; th-thin; pūre; ûnite; ûrn; stŭd; circŭs; ü-as "y" in study; ′-indeterminate vowel.

ăt; fĭnǎl; rāte; senāte; ärm; ȧsk; sofȧ; fâre; ch-choose; dh-as th in other; bē; ĕvent; bĕt; recĕnt; cratẽr; g-go; gh-guttural g; bĭt; ĭ-short neutral; rīde; ᴋ-guttural k as ch in German ich;

PRONOUNCING INDEX Grevenbroich — Guines 287

Page	Name Pronunciation Region	Lat. °′	Long. °′
161	Grevenbroich (grĕ'fen-broik) F.R.G. (Ruhr In.)	51·05 N	6·36 E
161	Grevenbrück (grĕ'fĕn-brük) F.R.G. (Ruhr In.)	51·08 N	8·01 E
99	Grey (R.) (grā) Can.	47·53 N	57·00 W
112	Grey, Pt. ... Can. (Vancouver In.)	49·22 N	123·16 W
111	Greybull (grā'bo͝ol) Wy.	44·28 N	108·05 W
111	Greybull R. Wy.	44·13 N	108·43 W
218	Greylingstad (grā-lĭng'shtȧt) S. Afr. (Johannesburg & Pretoria In.)	26·40 S	29·13 E
205	Greymouth (grā'mouth) N. Z. (In.)	42·27 S	171·17 E
203	Grey Ra. Austl.	28·40 S	142·05 E
110	Greys Hbr. (grās) Wa.	46·55 N	124·23 W
213	Greytown (grā'toun) S. Afr. (Natal In.)	29·07 S	30·38 E
	Greytown, see San Juan del Norte		
112	Grey Wolf Pk. (grā wo͝olf) Wa. (Seattle In.)	48·53 N	123·12 W
114	Gridley (grĭd'lĭ) Ca.	39·22 N	121·43 W
120	Griffin (grĭf'ĭn) Ga.	33·15 N	84·16 W
203	Griffith (grĭf-ĭth) Austl.	34·16 S	146·10 E
107	Griffith In. (Chicago In.)	41·31 N	87·26 W
167	Grigoriopol' (grĭ'gor-i-ô'pôl) Sov. Un.	47·09 N	29·18 E
125	Grijalva (R.) (grē-häl'vä) Mex.	17·25 N	93·23 W
203	Grim, C. (grĭm) Austl.	40·43 S	144·30 E
158	Grimma (grĭm'ȧ) G.D.R.	51·14 N	12·43 E
89	Grimsby (grĭmz'bĭ) Can. (Toronto In.)	43·11 N	79·33 W
150	Grimsey (I.) (grĭms'ȧ) Ice.	66·30 N	17·50 W
156	Grimstad (grĭm-städh) Nor.	58·21 N	8·30 E
99	Grindstone Island Can.	47·25 N	61·51 W
109	Grinnel (grĭ-nĕl') Ia.	41·44 N	92·44 W
109	Griswold (grĭz'wŭld) Ia.	41·11 N	95·05 W
166	Griva (grē'vȧ) Sov. Un.	55·51 N	26·31 E
99	Groais I. Can.	50·57 N	55·35 W
157	Grobina (grō'bĭŋia) Sov. Un.	56·35 N	21·10 E
218	Groblersdal S. Afr. (Johannesburg & Pretoria In.)	25·11 S	29·25 E
159	Grodno (grôd'nŏ) Sov. Un.	53·40 N	23·49 E
159	Grodzisk Masowieki (grō'jēsk mä-zō-vyĕts'ke). Pol.	52·06 N	20·40 E
158	Grodzisk Wielkopolski (grō'jēsk vyĕl-ko-pōl'skē). Pol.	52·14 N	16·22 E
119	Groesbeck (grōs'bĕk) Tx.	31·32 N	96·31 W
160	Groix, I. de (ēl dē grwä') Fr.	47·39 N	3·28 W
159	Grójec (grō'yĕts) Pol.	51·53 N	20·52 E
158	Gronau (grō'nou) F.R.G.	52·12 N	7·05 E
155	Groningen (grō'nĭng-ĕn) Neth.	53·13 N	6·30 E
204	Groote Eylandt (I.) (grō'tē ī'länt). Austl.	13·50 S	137·30 E
212	Grootfontein (grōt'fōn-tān') Namibia	18·15 S	19·30 E
213	Groot-Kei (kē). S. Afr. (Natal In.)	32·17 S	27·30 E
212	Grootkop (Mtn.) S. Afr. (In.)	34·11 S	18·23 E
218	Groot Marico S. Afr. (Johannesburg & Pretoria In.)	25·36 S	26·23 E
218	Groot R. S. Afr. (Johannesburg & Pretoria In.)	25·13 S	26·20 E
213	Groot-Vis (R.). S. Afr. (Natal In.).	33·04 S	36·08 E
212	Groot Vloer (L.) (grōt' vlo͞or') S. Afr.	30·00 S	20·16 E
99	Gros Morne (Mtn.) (grō môrn') Can.	49·36 N	57·48 W
91	Gros Morne Natl. Pk. Can.	49·40 N	59·15 W
99	Gros Pate (Mtn.) Can.	50·16 N	57·25 W
149	Gross Behnitz (grōss bĕ'nētz) G.D.R. (Berlin In.)	52·35 N	12·45 E
107	Grosse I. (grōs). Mi. (Detroit In.)	42·08 N	83·09 W
89	Grosse Isle (īl') Can. (Winnipeg In.)	50·04 N	97·27 W
158	Grossenhain (grōs'ĕn-hīn). G.D.R.	51·17 N	13·33 E
149	Grossenzersdorf. Aus. (Vienna In.)	48·13 N	16·33 E
107	Grosse Pointe (point') Mi. (Detroit In.)	42·23 N	82·54 W
107	Grosse Pointe Farms (färm) Mi. (Detroit In.)	42·25 N	82·53 W
107	Grosse Pointe Park (pärk) Mi. (Detroit In.)	42·23 N	82·55 W
164	Grosseto (grôs-sā'tō) It.	42·46 N	11·09 E
158	Grossglockner Pk. (glôk'nēr). Aus.	47·06 N	12·45 E
149	Gross Höbach (hû'bäk) F.R.G. (Munich In.)	48·21 N	11·36 E
149	Gross Kreutz (kroitz) G.D.R. (Berlin In.)	52·24 N	12·47 E
161	Gross Reken (rĕ'kĕn) F.R.G. (Ruhr In.)	51·50 N	7·20 E
149	Gross Schönebeck (shō'nĕ-bĕk) G.D.R. (Berlin In.)	52·54 N	13·32 E
111	Gros Ventre R. (grōvĕn't'r) Wy.	43·38 N	110·34 W
105	Groton (grôt'ŭn) Ct.	41·20 N	72·00 W
99	Groton Ma. (In.)	42·37 N	71·34 W
108	Groton SD	45·25 N	98·04 W
165	Grottaglie (grôt-täl'yä) It.	40·32 N	17·26 E
100	Grouard Can.	55·31 N	116·09 W
99	Groveland (grōv'land). Ma. (In.)	42·45 N	71·02 W
105	Groveton (grōv'tŭn) NH	44·35 N	71·30 W
119	Groveton Tx.	31·04 N	95·07 W
171	Groznyy (grôz'nĭ) Sov. Un.	43·20 N	45·40 E
159	Grudziadz (gro͞o'jônts) Pol.	53·30 N	18·48 E
89	Grues, Île aux (I.) (ō grü) Can. (Québec In.)	47·05 N	70·32 W
149	Grumpholds-Kirchen Aus. (Wien In.)	48·03 N	16·17 E
109	Grundy Center (grŭn'dĭ sĕn'tēr) Ia.	42·22 N	92·45 W
124	Gruñidora (gro͞o-nyê-dô'rō). Mex.	24·10 N	101·49 W
149	Grünwald (gro͞on'väld) F.R.G. (Munich In.)	48·04 N	11·34 E
166	Gryazi (gryä'zĭ) Sov. Un.	52·31 N	39·59 E
146	Gryazovets (gryä'zô-vĕts) Sov. Un.	58·52 N	40·14 E
158	Gryfice (grĭ'fĭ-tsĕ) Pol.	53·55 N	15·11 E
158	Gryfino (grĭ'fē-nô) Pol.	53·16 N	14·30 E
127	Guabito (gwä-bē'tô) Pan.	9·30 N	82·33 W
128	Guacanayabo, Golfo de (G.) (gôl-fô-dĕ-gwä-kä-nä-yä'bō). Cuba	20·30 N	77·40 W
135	Guacara (gwȧ'kä-rä). Ven. (In.)	10·16 N	67·48 W
134	Guacarí (gwä-kä-rē'). Col. (In.)	3·45 N	76·20 W
137	Guaçuí (gwä'so͞o-ē') Braz. (Rio de Janeiro In.)	20·47 S	41·40 W
124	Guadalajara (gwä-dhä-lä-hä'rä) Mex.	20·41 N	103·21 W
162	Guadalajara (gwä-dä-lä-kä'rä) Sp.	40·37 N	3·10 W
162	Guadalcanal (gwä-dhäl-kä-näl') Sp.	38·05 N	5·48 W
205	Guadalcanal (I.) Sol. Is.	9·48 S	158·43 E
124	Guadalcázar (gwä-dhäl-kä'zär) Mex.	22·38 N	100·24 W
162	Guadalete (R.) (gwä-dhä-lā'tȧ). Sp.	38·53 N	5·38 W
162	Guadalhorce (R.) (gwä-dhäl-ôr'thā). Sp.	37·05 N	4·50 W
162	Guadalimar (R.) (gwä-dhä-lē-mär'). Sp.	38·29 N	2·53 W
163	Guadalope (R.) (gwä-dä-lô-pĕ). Sp.	40·48 N	0·10 W
162	Guadalquivir, Río (R.) (rê'ō-gwä-dhäl-kê-vēr'). Sp.	5·57 N	6·00 W
118	Guadalupe Mex.	31·23 N	106·06 W
162	Guadalupe, Sierra de (Mts.) (syĕr'rä dā gwä-dhä-lo͞o'pä). Sp.	39·30 N	5·25 W
122	Guadalupe I. Mex.	29·00 N	118·45 W
118	Guadalupe Mts. NM-Tx.	32·00 N	104·55 W
118	Guadalupe Pk. Tx.	31·55 N	104·55 W
118	Guadalupe R. (gwä-dhä-lo͞o'pȧ) Tx.	29·54 N	99·03 W
162	Guadarrama, Sierra de (Mts.) (gwä-dhär-rä'mä). Sp.	41·00 N	3·40 W
163	Guadarrama (R.) (gwä-dhär-rä'mä). Sp. (Madrid In.)	40·34 N	3·58 W
123	Guadeloupe (gwä-dē-lo͞op'). N. A.	16·40 N	61·10 W
127	Guadeloupe Pass N. A. (In.)	16·26 N	62·00 W
128	Guadiana, Bahía de (B.) (bä-ē'ä-dĕ-gwä-dhē-ä'nä). Cuba	22·10 N	84·35 W
162	Guadiana, Río (R.) (rê'ō-gwä-dvä'nä). Port.	37·43 N	7·43 W
162	Guadiana Alto (R.) (äl'tō). Sp.	39·02 N	2·52 W
162	Guadiana Menor (R.) (mā'nôr). Sp.	37·43 N	2·45 W
162	Guadiaro (R.) (gwä-dhê-ä rō). Sp.	37·38 N	5·25 W
163	Guadiato (R.) (gwä-dhê-ä'tō). Sp.	38·10 N	5·05 W
162	Guadiela (R.) (gwä-dhê-ā'lä). Sp.	40·27 N	2·05 W
162	Guadix (gwä-dhēsh') Sp.	37·18 N	3·09 W
135	Guaira (gwä-ē-rä) Braz.	24·03 S	44·02 W
135	Guaire (R.) (gwī'rĕ). Ven. (In.)	10·25 N	66·43 W
128	Guajaba, Cayo (I.) (kä'yō-gwä-hä'bä). Cuba	21·50 N	77·35 W
134	Guajará Mirim (gwä-zhä-rä'mē-rēɴ'). Braz.	10·58 S	65·12 W
134	Guajira, Pen. de (Pen.) (pĕ-nē'ng-so͞o-lä-dĕ-gwä-ᴋē'rä) Col.-Ven.	12·35 N	73·00 W
126	Gualán (gwä-län') Guat.	15·08 N	89·21 W
137	Gualeguay (gwä-lĕ-gwä'y) Arg. (Buenos Aires In.)	33·10 S	59·20 W
137	Gualeguay (R.) Arg. (Buenos Aires In.)	32·49 S	59·05 W
137	Gualeguaychú (gwä-lā-gwī-cho͞o') Arg. (Buenos Aires In.)	33·01 S	58·32 W
137	Gualeguaychú (R.) Arg. (Buenos Aires In.)	32·58 S	58·27 W
136	Gualicho, Salina (F.) (sä-lē'nä-gwä-lē'chō). Arg.	40·20 S	65·15 W
198	Guam (gwäm) Oceania	14·00 N	143·20 E
136	Guaminí (gwä-mê-nē') Arg.	37·02 S	62·21 W
134	Guamo (gwȧ'mŏ) Col. (In.)	4·02 N	74·58 W
192	Gu'an (go͞o-än) China (In.)	39·25 N	116·18 E
190	Guan (R.) (gûän) China	31·56 N	115·19 E
129	Guanabacoa (gwä-nä-bä-kō'ä) Cuba (In.)	23·08 N	82·19 W
136	Guanabara, Baia de (B.) Braz. (Rio de Janeiro In.)	22·44 S	43·09 W
126	Guanacaste Cord. (Mts.) (kôr-dēl-yĕ'rä-gwä-nä-käs'tā) C. R.	10·54 N	85·27 W
122	Guanacevi (gwä-nä-sĕ-vē'). Mex.	25·30 N	105·45 W
128	Guanahacabibes, Pen. de (pĕ-nēn-so͞o-lä-dĕ-gwä-nä hä-kä-bē'bås) Cuba	21·55 N	84·35 W
128	Guanajay (gwä-nä-hī'). Cuba	22·55 N	82·40 W
124	Guanajuato (gwä-nä-hwä'tō). Mex.	21·01 N	101·16 W
122	Guanajuato (State) Mex.	21·00 N	101·00 W
135	Guanape (gwä-nä'pĕ). Ven. (In.)	9·55 N	65·32 W
135	Guanape (R.) Ven. (In.)	9·52 N	65·20 W
134	Guanare (gwä-nä'rȧ) Ven.	8·57 N	69·47 W
136	Guanduçu (R.) (gwä'n-do͞o'so͞o) Braz. (Rio de Janeiro In.)	22·50 S	43·40 W
128	Guane (gwä'nȧ) Cuba	22·10 N	84·05 W
193	Guangchang (gûäŋ-chäŋ). China	25·50 N	116·18 E
193	Guangde (gûäŋ-dŭ) China	30·40 N	119·20 E
189	Guangdong (Prov.) (gûäŋ-dôŋ) China	23·45 N	113·15 E
190	Guanglu Dao (I.) (gûäŋ-lo͞o dou) China	39·13 N	122·21 E
190	Guangping (gûäŋ-pĭŋ) China	36·30 N	114·57 E
190	Guangrao (gûäŋ-rou) China	37·04 N	118·24 E
190	Guangshan (gûäŋ-shän) China	32·02 N	114·53 E
188	Guangxi (Aut. Reg.) (gûäŋ-shyē) China	24·00 N	108·30 E
191	Guangzhou (Canton) (gûäŋ-jō) China (Canton In.)	23·07 N	113·15 E
190	Guanhu (gûän-ho͞o) China	34·26 N	117·59 E
190	Guannan (gûän-nän) China	34·17 N	119·17 E
135	Guanta (gwän'tä) Ven. (In.)	10·15 N	64·35 W
129	Guantanamo (gwän-tä'nä-mô) Cuba	20·10 N	75·10 W
129	Guantánamo (Prov.) Cuba	20·10 N	75·05 W
129	Guantanamo, Bahía de (B.) (bä-ē'ä-dĕ). Cuba	19·35 N	75·35 W
190	Guantao (gûän-tou) China	36·39 N	115·25 E
190	Guan Xian (gûän-shyĕn) China	36·30 N	115·28 E
191	Guanyao (gûän-you) China (Canton In.)	23·13 N	113·04 E
190	Guanyun (gûän-yo͞on) China	34·28 N	119·16 E
137	Guapé (gwä-pĕ) Braz. (Rio de Janeiro In.)	20·45 S	45·55 W
127	Guapiles (gwä-pē-lĕs) C. R.	10·05 N	83·54 W
136	Guapimirim (gwä-pê-mē-rē'ɴ) Braz. (Rio de Janeiro In.)	22·31 S	42·59 W
134	Guaporé (R.) (gwä-pô-rā') Bol.-Braz.	12·11 S	63·47 W
134	Guaqui (guä'kē) Bol.	16·42 S	68·47 W
163	Guara, Sierra de (Mts.) (sē-ĕ'r-rä-dĕ-gwä'rä). Sp.	42·24 N	0·15 W
135	Guarabira (gwä-rä-bē'rȧ) Braz.	6·49 S	35·27 W
134	Guaranda (gwä-rån'dä) Ec.	1·39 S	78·57 W
135	Guarapari (gwä-rä-pä'rē) Braz.	20·34 S	40·31 W
137	Guarapiranga, Represa do (Res.) (r'ĕ-prĕ-sä-dô-gwä'rä-pē-rä'n-gä) Braz. (Rio de Janeiro In.)	23·45 S	46·44 W
136	Guarapuava (gwä-rä-pwä'vȧ) Braz.	25·29 S	51·26 W
137	Guaratinguetá (guä-rä-tĭɴ-gȧ-tä') Braz. (Rio de Janeiro In.)	22·49 S	45·10 W
162	Guarda (gwär'dä) Port.	40·32 N	7·17 W
162	Guarena (gwä-rā'nyä) Sp.	38·52 N	6·08 W
135	Guaribe (R.) (gwä-rê'bĕ) Ven. (In.)	9·48 N	65·17 W
135	Guárico (State) Ven. (In.)	9·42 N	67·25 W
135	Guárico (R.) Ven. (In.)	9·50 N	67·07 W
137	Guarulhos (gwȧ-ro͞o'l-yôs) Braz. (Rio de Janeiro In.)	32·28 S	46·30 W
137	Guarus (gwȧ'ro͞os) Braz. (Rio de Janeiro In.)	21·44 S	41·19 W
134	Guasca (gwäs'kä) Col. (In.)	4·52 N	73·52 W
135	Guasipati (gwä-sê-pä'tē) Ven.	7·26 N	61·57 W
164	Guastalla (gwäs-täl'lä) It.	44·53 N	10·39 E
113	Guasti (gwäs'tĭ) Ca. (Los Angeles In.)	34·04 N	117·35 W
126	Guatemala (guä-tȧ-mä'lä) Guat.	14·37 N	90·32 W
122	Guatemala N. A.	15·45 N	91·45 W
135	Guatire (gwä-tê'rĕ) Ven. (In.)	10·28 N	66·34 W
137	Guaxupé (gwä-sho͞o-pĕ') Braz. (Rio de Janeiro In.)	21·18 S	46·42 W
128	Guayabal (gwä-yä-bä'l) Cuba	20·40 N	77·40 W
124	Guayalejo (R.) (gwä-yä-lĕ'hô) Mex.	23·24 N	99·09 W
123	Guayama (gwä-yä'mä) P. R. (Puerto Rico In.)	18·00 N	66·08 W
129	Guayamouc (R.) Hai.	19·05 N	72·00 W
134	Guayaquil (gwī-ä-kēl') Ec.	2·16 S	79·53 W
134	Guayaquil, Golfo de (G.) (gôl-fô-dĕ). Ec.	3·03 S	82·12 W
134	Guayiare (R.) (gwä-yȧ'rĕ) Col.	3·35 N	69·28 W
122	Guaymas (gwȧ'y-mäs) Mex.	27·49 N	110·58 W
129	Guayubin (gwȧ-yo͞o-bê'n) Dom. Rep.	19·40 N	71·25 W
126	Guazacapán (gwä-zä-kä-pän') Guat.	14·04 N	90·26 W
174	Gubakha (go͞o-bä'kȧ) Sov. Un. (Urals In.)	58·53 N	57·35 E
164	Gubbio (go͞ob'byô) It.	43·23 N	12·36 E
190	Gucheng (go͞o-chŭŋ) China	39·09 N	115·43 E
163	Gudar, Sierra de (Mts.) (syĕr'rä dā go͞o'dhär). Sp.	40·28 N	0·47 W
156	Gudenaa (R.) Den.	56·20 N	9·47 E
156	Gudinge Fjärden (Fd.) Swe.	57·43 N	16·55 E
156	Gudvangen (go͞odh'väŋ-gĕn). Nor.	60·52 N	6·45 E
161	Guebwiller (gĕb-vê-lâr') Fr.	47·53 N	7·10 E
215	Guédi, Mont (Mtn.) Chad	12·14 N	18·58 E
210	Guelma (gwĕl'mä) Alg.	36·32 N	7·17 E
89	Guelph (gwĕlf). Can. (Toronto In.)	43·33 N	80·15 W
135	Güere (gwĕ'rĕ) (R.) Ven. (In.)	9·39 N	65·00 W
160	Guéret (gā-rĕ') Fr.	46·09 N	1·52 E
160	Guernsey (I.) (gûrn'zĭ) Eur.	49·27 N	2·36 W
152	Guerrara (gĕr-rä'rä) Alg.	32·50 N	4·26 E
118	Guerrero (gĕr-rā'rō) Mex.	26·47 N	99·20 W
118	Guerrero Mex.	28·20 N	100·24 W
124	Guerrero (State) Mex.	17·45 N	100·15 W
160	Gueugnon (gû-nyôn') Fr.	46·35 N	4·01 E
119	Gueydan (gā'dăn) La.	30·01 N	92·31 W
136	Guia de Pacobaíba (gwê'ä-dĕ-pä'kō-bī'bä) Braz. (Rio de Janeiro In.)	22·42 S	43·10 W
133	Guiana Highlands (Mts.) Braz.	3·20 N	60·00 W
193	Guichi (gwā-chr) China	30·35 N	117·28 E
125	Guichicovi (San Juan) (gwē-chê-kō'vê). Mex.	16·58 N	95·10 W
163	Guidonia (gwē-dō'nyȧ) It. (Rome In.)	42·00 N	12·45 E
214	Guiglo Ivory Coast	6·33 N	7·29 W
161	Guignes (gēɴ'yĕ). Fr. (Paris In.)	48·38 N	2·48 E
135	Güigüe (gwĕ'gwĕ) Ven. (In.)	10·05 N	67·48 W
126	Guija, L. (gē'hä) Sal.	14·16 N	89·21 W
148	Guildford (gĭl'fērd) Eng. (London In.)	51·13 N	0·34 W
107	Guilford (gĭl'fērd) In. (Cincinnati In.)	39·10 N	84·55 W
193	Guilin (gwā-lĭn) China	25·18 N	110·22 E
162	Guimarães (gē-mä-rȧɴsh'). Port.	41·27 N	8·22 W
209	Guinea (gĭn'ē) Afr.	10·48 N	12·28 W
209	Guinea, G. of Afr.	2·00 N	1·00 E
209	Guinea-Bissau (gĭn'ē) Afr.	12·00 N	20·00 W
128	Güines (gwē'nās) Cuba	22·50 N	82·05 W

288 Guingamp — Hango PRONOUNCING INDEX

Page	Name Pronunciation Region	Lat. °'	Long. °'
160	Guingamp (găɴ-găɴ') Fr.	48·35 N	3·10 W
128	Güira de Melena (gwē'rä dā mȧ-lā'nä) Cuba	22·45 N	82·30 W
134	Güiria (gwê-rē'ä) Ven.	10·43 N	62·16 W
152	Guir (R.) Mor.-Alg.	31·55 N	2·48 W
161	Guise (guēz) Fr.	49·54 N	3·37 E
126	Guisisil (Vol.) (gê-sê-sēl') Nic.	12·40 N	86·11 W
193	Guiyang (gwā-yäŋ) China	26·45 N	107·00 E
191	Guizhou (gwā-jō) China (Canton In.)	22·46 N	113·15 E
188	Guizhou (Prov.) China	27·00 N	106·10 E
184	Gujarat (State) India	22·54 N	79·00 E
184	Gujrānwāla (gŏŏj-rän'va-lȧ) Pak.	32·08 N	74·14 E
156	Gula (R.) (gōō'lȧ) Nor.	62·55 N	10·45 E
185	Gulbarga (gŏŏl-bûr'gȧ) India	17·25 N	76·52 E
166	Gulbene (gŏŏl-bā'nĕ) Sov. Un.	57·09 N	26·49 E
120	Gulfport (gŭlf'pōrt) Ms.	30·24 N	89·05 W
	Gulja, see Yining		
94	Gull Lake Can.	50·10 N	108·25 W
92	Gull L. Can.	52·35 N	114·00 W
217	Gulu Ug.	2·47 N	32·18 E
167	Gulyay Pole Sov. Un.	47·39 N	36·12 E
197	Gumaca (gōō-mä-kä') Phil. (In.)	13·55 N	122·06 E
164	Gumbeyka R. (gōōm-bĕy'kȧ) Sov. Un. (Urals In.)	53·20 N	59·42 E
215	Gumel Nig.	12·39 N	9·22 E
158	Gummersbach (gŏŏm'ĕrs-bäk) F.R.G.	51·02 N	7·34 E
215	Gummi Nig.	12·09 N	5·09 E
149	Gumpoldskirchen Aus.	48·04 N	16·15 E
184	Guna India	24·44 N	77·17 E
95	Gunisao (R.) (gŭn-ĭ-sä'ō) Can.	53·40 N	97·35 W
95	Gunisao L. Can.	53·54 N	97·58 W
203	Gunnedah (gŭ'nē-dä) Austl.	31·00 S	150·10 E
115	Gunnison (gŭn'ĭ-sŭn) Co.	38·33 N	106·56 W
115	Gunnison Ut.	39·10 N	111·50 W
115	Gunnison (R.) Co.	38·30 N	106·40 W
120	Guntersville (gŭn'tērz-vĭl) Al.	34·20 N	86·19 W
120	Guntersville L. Al.	34·30 N	86·20 W
149	Guntramsdorf... Aus. (Vienna In.)	48·04 N	16·19 E
185	Guntūr (gŏŏn'tōōr) India	16·22 N	80·29 E
190	Guo (R.) (gwô) China	33·04 N	117·16 E
190	Guoyang (gwô-yäŋ) China	33·32 N	116·10 E
117	Gurdon (gûr'dŭn) Ar.	33·56 N	93·10 W
135	Gurgucia (R.) (gōōr-gōō'syä) Braz.	8·12 S	43·49 W
107	Gurnee (gûr'nē)... Il. (Chicago In.)	42·22 N	87·55 W
156	Gurskõy (I.) (gōōrskûê) Nor.	62·18 N	5·20 E
135	Gurupá (gōō-rōō-pä') Braz.	1·28 S	51·32 W
135	Gurupi, Serra do (Mts.) (sĕ'r-rä-dô-gōō-rōō-pē') Braz.	5·32 S	47·02 W
135	Gurupí (R.) (gōō-rōō-pē') Braz.	2·37 S	46·45 W
184	Guru Sikhar Mt. India	29·42 N	72·50 E
171	Gur'yev (gōōr'yĕf) Sov. Un.	47·10 N	51·50 E
172	Gur'yevsk (gōōr-yĭfsk') Sov. Un.	54·14 N	86·07 E
215	Gusau (gōō-zä'ōō) Nig.	12·12 N	6·40 E
157	Gusev (gōō'sĕf) Sov. Un.	54·35 N	22·15 E
190	Gushi (gōō-shr) China	32·11 N	115·39 E
214	Gushiago Ghana	9·55 N	0·12 W
165	Gusinje (gōō-sēn'yĕ) Yugo.	42·34 N	19·54 E
166	Gus'-Khrustal'nyy (gōōs-ĸrōō-stäl'ny') Sov. Un.	55·39 N	40·41 E
125	Gustavo A. Madero (gōōs-tä'vô-ä-mä-dĕ'rô) Mex. (In.)	19·29 N	99·07 W
158	Güstrow (güs'trō) G.D.R.	53·48 N	12·12 E
158	Gütersloh (gü'tērs-lō) F.R.G.	51·54 N	8·22 E
117	Guthrie (gŭth'rĭ) Ok.	35·52 N	97·26 W
109	Guthrie Center Ia.	41·41 N	94·33 W
125	Gutiérrez Zamora (gōō-tē-âr'räz zä-mō'rä) Mex.	20·27 N	97·17 W
109	Guttenberg (gŭt'ĕn-bûrg) Ia.	42·48 N	91·09 W
133	Guyana (gŭy'ănă) S. A.	7·45 N	59·00 W
190	Guyang (gōō-yäŋ) China	34·56 N	114·57 E
190	Guye (gōō-yŭ) China	39·46 N	118·23 E
116	Guymon (gī'mŏn) Ok.	36·41 N	101·29 W
99	Guysborough (gīz'bŭr-ô) Can.	45·23 N	61·30 W
190	Guzhen (gōō-jŭn) China	33·20 N	117·18 E
157	Gvardeysk (gvȧr-dĕysk') Sov. Un.	54·39 N	21·11 E
215	Gwadabawa Nig.	13·20 N	5·15 E
186	Gwādar (gwä'dŭr) Pak.	25·15 N	62·29 E
217	Gwane (gwän) Zaire	4·43 N	25·50 E
212	Gwelo (gwä'lō) Zimb.	19·15 S	29·48 E
217	Gwembe Zambia	16·30 S	27·35 E
109	Gwinn (gwĭn) Mi.	46·15 N	87·30 W
188	Gyangzê (gyäŋ-dzŭ) China	29·00 N	89·28 E
184	Gyaring Co (L.) (gyä-rĭŋ) China	30·37 N	88·33 E
173	Gydan, Khrebet (Kolymskiy) (Mts.) Sov. Un.	61·45 N	155·00 E
172	Gydanskiy, P-Ov (Pen) Sov. Un.	70·42 N	76·03 E
203	Gympie (gĭm'pē) Austl.	26·20 S	152·50 E
159	Gyöngyös (dyûn'dyûsh) Hung.	47·47 N	19·55 E
159	Györ (dyûr) Hung.	47·40 N	17·37 E
195	Gyōtoku (gyō'tô-kōō') Jap. (Tōkyō In.)	35·42 N	139·56 E
95	Gypsumville (jĭp'sŭm'vĭl) Can.	51·45 N	98·35 W
159	Gyula (dyŏŏ'lä) Hung.	46·38 N	21·18 E

H

Page	Name Pronunciation Region	Lat. °'	Long. °'
161	Haan (hän) F.R.G. (Ruhr In.)	51·12 N	7·00 E
157	Haapamäki (häp'ä-mĕ-kē) Fin.	62·16 N	24·20 E
157	Haapsalu (häp'sä-lōō) Sov. Un.	58·56 N	23·33 E
149	Haar (här) F.R.G. (Munich In.)	48·06 N	11·44 E
183	Ha 'Arava (Wādī al Jayb) Isr. (Palestine In.)	30·33 N	35·10 E
149	Haarlem (här'lĕm) Neth. (Amsterdam In.)	52·22 N	4·37 E
128	Habana (Prov.) (hä-vä'nä) Cuba	22·45 N	82·25 W
163	Habibas (C.) (hä-bē'bås) Alg.	35·50 N	0·45 W
195	Habikino Jap. (Ōsaka In.)	34·32 N	135·37 E
184	Hābra India (In.)	22·49 N	88·38 E
194	Hachinohe (hä'chē-nō'hå) Jap.	40·29 N	141·40 E
195	Hachiōji (hä'chê-ō'jê) Jap.	35·39 N	139·18 E
106	Hackensack (hăk'ĕn-săk) NJ (New York In.)	40·54 N	74·03 W
186	Hadd, Ra's al (C.) Om.	22·29 N	59·46 E
106	Haddonfield (hăd'ŭn-fēld) NJ (Philadelphia In.)	39·53 N	75·02 W
106	Haddon Heights (hăd'ŭn hīts) NJ (Philadelphia In.)	39·53 N	75·03 W
215	Hadejia (hä-dā'jä) Nig.	12·30 N	9·59 E
215	Hadejia (R.) Nig.	12·15 N	9·40 E
183	Hadera (ĸȧ-dĕ'rȧ) Isr. (Palestine In.)	32·26 N	34·55 E
156	Haderslev (hä'dhĕrs-lĕv) Den.	55·17 N	9·28 E
218	Hadibu P. D. R. of Yem. (Horn of Afr. In.)	12·40 N	53·50 E
112	Hadlock (hăd'lŏk) Wa. (Seattle In.)	48·02 N	122·46 W
186	Ḩaḑramawt (Reg.) P. D. R. of Yem.	15·22 N	48·40 E
186	Hadur Shuayb, Jabal (Mtn.) Yemen	15·45 N	43·45 E
194	Haeju (hä'ĕ-jŭ) Kor.	38·03 N	125·42 E
150	Hafnarfjördhur Ice.	64·02 N	21·32 W
218	Hafun, Ras (C.) (hä-fōōn') Som. (Horn of Afr. In.)	10·15 N	51·35 E
111	Hageland (hăge'lănd) Mt.	48·53 N	108·43 W
161	Hagen (hä'gĕn) F.R.G. (Ruhr In.)	51·21 N	7·29 E
104	Hagerstown (hā'gērz-toun) In.	39·55 N	85·10 W
105	Hagerstown Md.	39·40 N	77·45 W
195	Hagi (hä'gĭ) Jap.	34·25 N	131·25 E
160	Hague, C. de la (dĕ lä ăg') Fr.	49·44 N	1·55 W
	Hague, The, see 's Gravenhage		
161	Haguenau (ăg'nō') Fr.	48·47 N	7·48 E
190	Hai'an (hī-än) China	32·35 N	120·25 E
195	Haibara (hä'ê-bä'rä) Jap.	34·29 N	135·57 E
192	Haicheng (hī-chŭŋ) China	40·58 N	122·45 E
192	Haidian (hī-dĭĕn) China (In.)	39·59 N	116·17 E
183	Haifa (Hefa) (hä'ē-fȧ) Isr. (Palestine In.)	32·48 N	35·00 E
193	Haifeng (hä'ê-fĕng') China	23·00 N	115·20 E
190	Haifuzhen (hī-fōō-jŭn) China	31·57 N	121·48 E
193	Haikou (hī-kō) China	20·00 N	110·20 E
182	Ḩā'il (hāl) Sau. Ar.	27·30 N	41·47 E
192	Hailaerh China	49·10 N	118·40 E
111	Hailey (hā'lĭ) Id.	43·31 N	114·19 W
97	Haileybury Can.	47·27 N	79·38 W
117	Haileyville (hā'lĭ-vĭl) Ok.	34·51 N	95·34 W
194	Hailin (hä'ê-lĕn') China	44·31 N	129·11 E
193	Hailing Dao (I.) (hī-lĭŋ dou) China	21·30 N	112·15 E
193	Hailong (hī-loŋ) China	42·32 N	125·52 E
192	Hailun (hä'ê-lōōn') China	47·18 N	126·50 E
193	Hainan Dao (I.) (hī-nän dou) China	19·00 N	111·10 E
149	Hainburg an der Donau Aus. (Vienna In.)	48·09 N	16·57 E
101	Haines (hānz) Ak.	59·10 N	135·38 W
121	Haines City Fl. (In.)	28·05 N	81·38 W
193	Haiphong (hī'fông') (hä'ēp-hông) Viet.	20·52 N	106·40 E
123	Haiti (hā'tĭ) N. A.	19·00 N	72·15 W
192	Haizhou Wan (B.) China	35·49 N	120·35 E
159	Hajduböszormény (hôl'dōō-bû'sûr-mān') Hung.	47·41 N	21·30 E
159	Hajduhadház (hô'ĭ-dōō-hôd'häz) Hung.	47·32 N	21·32 E
159	Hajdunánás (hô'ĭ-dōō-nä'näsh) Hung.	47·52 N	21·27 E
159	Hajduszoboszló (hô'ĭ-dōō-sô'bôs-lō) Hung.	47·24 N	21·25 E
194	Hakodate (hä-kō-dä't ȧ) Jap.	41·46 N	140·42 E
195	Haku-San (Mtn.) (hä'kōō-sän') Jap.	36·11 N	136·45 E
125	Halachó (ä-lä-chō') Mex.	20·28 N	90·06 W
211	Halā'ib (hä-lä'ĕb) Egypt	22·10 N	36·40 E
183	Halbā Leb. (Palestine In.)	34·33 N	36·03 E
149	Halbe (häl'bĕ) G.D.R. (Berlin In.)	52·07 N	13·43 E
158	Halberstadt (häl'bĕr-shtät) G.D.R.	51·54 N	11·07 E
197	Halcon, Mt. (häl-kōn') Phil. (In.)	13·19 N	120·55 E
156	Halden (häl'dĕn) Nor.	59·10 N	11·21 E
148	Hale (hāl) Eng.	53·22 N	2·20 W
100	Haleakala Crater (hä'lä-ä'kä-lä) Hi.	20·44 N	156·15 W
100	Haleakala Natl. Park Hi.	20·46 N	156·00 W
107	Hales Corners (hālz kŏr'nērz) Wi. (Milwaukee In.)	42·56 N	88·03 W
148	Halesowen (hālz'ô-wĕn) Eng.	52·26 N	2·03 W
106	Halethorpe (hāl-thôrp) Md. (Baltimore In.)	39·15 N	76·40 W
120	Haleyville (hā'lĭ-vĭl) Al.	34·11 N	87·36 W
112	Half Moon Bay (hăf'mōōn). Ca. (San Francisco In.)	37·28 N	122·26 W
213	Halfway House (häf-wā hous) S. Afr. (Johannesburg & Pretoria In.)	26·00 S	28·08 E
149	Halfweg.. Neth. (Amsterdam In.)	52·23 N	4·45 E
98	Halifax (hăl'ĭ-fāks) Can.	44·39 N	63·36 W
148	Halifax Eng.	53·44 N	1·52 W
205	Halifax B. (hăl'ĭ-făx) Austl.	18·56 S	147·07 E
98	Halifax Hbr. Can.	44·35 N	63·31 W
101	Halkett, C. Ak.	70·50 N	151·15 W
93	Hallam Park Can.	52·11 N	118·46 E
194	Halla San (Mt.) (häl'lá-sän) Kor.	33·20 N	126·37 E
149	Halle (häl'lĕ)... Bel. (Brussels In.)	50·45 N	4·13 E
158	Halle G.D.R.	51·30 N	11·59 E
119	Hallettsville (hăl'ĕts-vĭl) Tx.	29·26 N	96·55 W
108	Hallock (hăl'ŭk) Mn.	48·46 N	96·57 W
91	Hall Pen (hôl) Can.	63·14 N	65·40 W
119	Halls Bayou Tx. (In.)	29·55 N	95·23 W
156	Hallsberg (häls'bĕrgh) Swe.	59·04 N	15·04 E
204	Halls Creek (hôlz) Austl.	18·15 S	127·45 E
197	Halmahera (I.) (häl-mä-hä'rä) Indon.	0·45 N	128·45 E
197	Halmahera, Laut (Halmahera Sea) Indon.	1·00 S	129·00 E
156	Halmstad (hälm'städ) Swe.	56·40 N	12·46 E
156	Halse Fd. (häl'sĕ fyôrd) Nor.	63·03 N	8·23 E
117	Halstead (hôl'stĕd) Ks.	38·02 N	97·36 W
161	Haltern (häl'tĕrn) F.R.G. (Ruhr In.)	51·45 N	7·10 E
113	Haltom City (hôl'tŏm) Tx. (Dallas, Fort Worth In.)	32·48 N	97·13 W
149	Halvarenbeek Neth. (Amsterdam In.)	51·29 N	5·10 E
153	Ḩamāh (hä'mä) Syr.	35·08 N	36·53 E
186	Hamadān (hŭ-mŭ-dän') Iran	34·45 N	48·07 E
195	Hamamatsu (hä'mä-mät'sōō) Jap.	34·41 N	137·43 E
156	Hamar (hä'mär) Nor.	60·49 N	11·05 E
191	Hamasaka (hä'mä-sä'kȧ) Jap.	35·57 N	134·27 E
161	Hamborn (häm'bōrn) F.R.G. (Ruhr In.)	51·30 N	6·43 E
117	Hamburg (hăm'bûrg) Ar.	33·15 N	91·49 W
149	Hamburg (häm'bōōrgh) F.R.G. (Hamburg In.)	53·34 N	10·02 E
108	Hamburg Ia.	40·39 N	95·40 W
106	Hamburg NJ (New York In.)	41·09 N	74·35 W
107	Hamburg NY (Buffalo In.)	42·44 N	78·51 W
213	Hamburg (hăm'bûrg) S. Afr. (Natal In.)	33·18 S	27·28 E
105	Hamden (hăm'dĕn) Ct.	41·20 N	72·55 W
157	Hämeenlinna (hĕ'mân-lĭn-nȧ) Fin.	61·00 N	24·29 E
158	Hameln (hä'mĕln) F.R.G.	52·06 N	9·23 E
149	Hamelwörden (hä'mĕl-vûr-dĕn) F.R.G. (Hamburg In.)	53·47 N	9·19 E
204	Hamersley Ra. (hăm'ērz-lē) Austl.	22·15 S	117·50 E
194	Hamhŭng (häm'hōōng') Kor.	39·57 N	127·35 E
188	Hami (Kumul) (hä-mē) (kô-mōōl') China	42·58 N	93·14 E
120	Hamilton Al.	34·09 N	88·01 W
203	Hamilton (hăm'ĭl-tŭn) Austl.	37·50 S	142·10 E
89	Hamilton Can. (Toronto In.)	43·15 N	79·52 W
99	Hamilton Ma. (In.)	42·37 N	70·52 W
117	Hamilton Mo.	39·43 N	93·59 W
111	Hamilton Mt.	46·15 N	114·09 W
205	Hamilton N. Z. (In.)	37·45 S	175·28 E
107	Hamilton Oh. (Cincinnati In.)	39·22 N	84·33 W
118	Hamilton Tx.	31·42 N	98·07 W
117	Hamilton, L. Ar.	34·25 N	93·32 W
89	Hamilton Hbr.. Can. (Toronto In.)	43·17 N	79·50 W
91	Hamilton Inlet Can.	54·20 N	56·57 W
157	Hamina (hä'mê-nȧ) Fin.	60·34 N	27·15 E
121	Hamlet (hăm'lĕt) NC	35·52 N	79·46 W
116	Hamlin (hăm'lĭn) Tx.	32·54 N	100·08 W
161	Hamm (häm).. F.R.G. (Ruhr In.)	51·40 N	7·48 E
218	Hammanskraal (hä-mȧns-kräl') S. Afr. (Johannesburg & Pretoria In.)	25·24 S	28·17 E
149	Hamme Bel. (Brussels In.)	51·06 N	4·07 E
149	Hamme-Oste Kanal (Can.) (hä'mĕ-ōs'tĕ kä-näl) F.R.G. (Hamburg In.)	53·20 N	8·59 E
150	Hammerfest (häm'mĕr-fĕst).. Nor.	70·38 N	23·59 E
107	Hammond (hăm'ŭnd) In. (Chicago In.)	41·37 N	87·31 W
119	Hammond La.	30·30 N	90·28 W
112	Hammond Or. (Portland In.)	46·12 N	123·57 W
105	Hammonton (hăm'ŭn-tŭn) NJ	39·40 N	74·45 W
98	Hampden (hăm'dĕn) Me.	44·44 N	68·51 W
154	Hampshire Downs (hămp'shĭr dounz) Eng.	51·01 N	1·05 W
106	Hampstead... Md. (Baltimore In.)	39·36 N	76·54 W
148	Hampstead Norris (hămp-stĕd nŏ'rĭs) Eng. (London In.)	51·27 N	1·14 W
98	Hampton (hămp'tŭn) Can.	45·32 N	65·51 W
109	Hampton Ia.	42·43 N	93·15 W
106	Hampton Va. (Norfolk In.)	37·02 N	76·21 W
106	Hampton Roads (Inlet) Va. (Norfolk In.)	36·56 N	76·23 W
210	Ḩamrā, al- Ḩammadah al- (Plat.) Libya	29·39 N	10·53 E
156	Hamrånge (häm'rông'ĕ) Swe.	60·56 N	17·00 E
107	Hamtramck (hăm-trăm'ĭk) Mi. (Detroit In.)	42·24 N	83·03 W
186	Hāmūn-i Māshkel (L.) (hä-mōōn'ē māsh-kĕl') Pak.	28·28 N	64·13 E
193	Han (R.) (hän) China	25·00 N	116·35 E
193	Han (R.) China	31·40 N	112·04 E
194	Han (R.) Kor.	37·10 N	127·40 E
100	Hana (hä'nä) Hi.	20·43 N	155·59 W
128	Hanábana (R.) (hä-nä-bä'nä) Cuba	22·30 N	80·55 W
100	Hanalei B. (hä-nä-lā'ê) Hi.	22·15 N	159·40 W
217	Hanang (Mtn.) Tan.	4·26 S	35·24 E
158	Hanau (hä'nou) F.R.G.	50·08 N	8·56 E
109	Hancock (hăn'kŏk) Mi.	47·08 N	88·37 W
93	Haney (hā-nē) Can.	49·13 N	122·36 W
114	Hanford (hăn'fērd) Ca.	36·20 N	119·38 W
188	Hangayn Nuruu (Khangai Mts.) Mong.	48·03 N	99·45 E
193	Hangchou (hăng'chō') China	30·17 N	120·12 E
157	Hango (häŋ'gû) Fin.	59·49 N	22·56 E

ăt; finăl; rāte; senâte; ärm; ȧsk; sofȧ; fâre; ch-choose; dh-as th in other; bē; êvent; bĕt; recĕnt; cratẽr; g-go; gh-guttural g; bĭt; ĭ-short neutral; rīde; ĸ-guttural k as ch in German ich;

PRONOUNCING INDEX

Hangzhou Wan — Helgoland 289

Page	Name Pronunciation Region	Lat. °′	Long. °′
193	Hangzhou Wan (B.) (häŋ-jō wän) China	30·20 N	121·25 E
190	Handan (hän-dän) … China	36·37 N	114·30 E
119	Hankamer (hăn'ká-mẽr) .. Tx. (In.)	29·52 N	94·42 W
108	Hankinson (hăŋ'kĭn-sŭn) … ND	46·04 N	96·54 W
193	Hankou (hän-kō) … China	30·42 N	114·22 E
204	Hann, Mt. (hän) … Austl.	16·05 S	126·07 E
93	Hanna (hăn'á) … Can.	51·38 N	111·54 W
111	Hanna … Wy.	41·51 N	106·34 W
108	Hannah … ND	48·58 N	98·42 W
117	Hannibal (hăn'ĭ băl) … Mo.	39·42 N	91·22 W
158	Hannover (hän-ō'vẽr) … F.R.G.	52·22 N	9·45 E
156	Hanö-bukten (B.) … Swe.	55·54 N	14·55 E
193	Hanoi (hä-noi') … Viet.	21·04 N	105·50 E
104	Hanover (hăn'ô-vẽr) … Can.	44·10 N	81·05 W
99	Hanover … Ma. (In.)	42·07 N	70·49 W
105	Hanover … NH	43·45 N	72·15 W
105	Hanover … Pa.	39·50 N	77·00 W
136	Hanover (I.) … Chile	51·00 S	74·45 W
190	Hanshan (hän'shän') … China	31·43 N	118·06 E
123	Hans Lollick (I.) (häns'lôl'ĭk) Vir. Is. (U. S. A.) (St. Thomas In.)	18·24 N	64·55 W
99	Hanson (hăn'sŭn) … Ma. (In.)	42·04 N	70·53 W
112	Hansville (hăns'-vĭl) Wa. (Seattle In.)	47·55 N	122·33 W
188	Hantengri Feng (Mtn.) (hän-tŭŋ-rē fŭŋ) . China	42·10 N	80·20 E
98	Hantsport (hănts'pōrt) … Can.	45·04 N	64·11 W
193	Hanyang (han'yäng') … China	30·30 N	114·10 E
192	Hanzhong (hän-jôŋ) … China	33·02 N	107·00 E
190	Haocheng (hou-chŭŋ) … China	33·19 N	117·33 E
150	Haparanda (hä-pä-rän'dä) … Swe.	65·54 N	23·57 E
106	Hapeville (hăp'vĭl) Ga. (Atlanta In.)	33·39 N	84·25 W
183	Haql … Sau. Ar. (Palestine In.)	29·15 N	34·57 E
217	Har, Laga (R.) … Ken.	2·15 N	39·30 E
162	Harana Sierra (Mts.) (sē-ĕ'r-rä-rä'nä) . Sp.	37·17 N	3·28 W
188	Hara Nuur (L.) … Mong.	47·47 N	94·01 E
211	Harar (Prov.) … Eth.	8·15 N	41·00 E
188	Hara Usa (L.) … Mong.	48·00 N	92·32 E
192	Harbin … China	45·40 N	126·30 E
104	Harbor Beach (här'bẽr bēch) .. Mi.	43·50 N	82·40 W
104	Harbor Springs … Mi.	45·25 N	85·05 W
99	Harbour Breton (brĕt'ŭn) (brē-tôN') . Can.	47·29 N	55·48 W
99	Harbour Grace (grās) … Can.	47·32 N	53·13 W
149	Harburg (här-bŏŏrgh) F.R.G. (Hamburg In.)	53·28 N	9·58 E
156	Hardanger Fd. (här-däng'ẽr fyôrd) . Nor.	59·58 N	6·30 E
156	Hardanger Fjell (Mts.) (fyĕl') . Nor.	60·15 N	6·56 E
156	Hardanger Jöklen (Mtn.) (yû'kōōl-ĕn) . Nor.	60·33 N	7·23 W
111	Hardin (här'dĭn) … Mt.	45·44 N	107·36 W
213	Harding (här'dĭng) S. Afr. (Natal In.)	30·34 S	29·54 E
120	Harding (L.) … Al.-Ga.	32·43 N	85·00 W
184	Hardwār (hŭr'dvär) … India	29·56 N	78·06 E
114	Hardy (R.) (här'dĭ) … Mex.	32·04 N	115·10 W
97	Hare B. (hâr) … Can.	51·18 N	55·50 W
218	Harer (hå-rär') Eth. (Horn of Afr. In.)	9·43 N	42·10 E
218	Hargeysa (här-gā'ê-så) Som. (Horn of Afr. In.)	9·20 N	43·57 E
159	Harghita, Muntii (Mts.) … Rom.	46·25 N	25·40 E
195	Harima-Nada (Sea) (hä'rê-mä nä-dä) . Jap.	34·34 N	134·37 E
149	Haring Vliet (R.) Neth. Amsterdam In.)	51·49 N	4·03 E
118	Harlan (här'lăn) … Ia.	41·40 N	95·10 W
120	Harlan … Ky.	36·50 N	83·19 W
116	Harlan Co. Res. … Ne.	40·03 N	99·51 W
111	Harlem (hàr'lĕm) … Mt.	48·33 N	108·50 W
155	Harlingen (här'lĭng-ĕn) … Neth.	53·10 N	5·24 E
119	Harlingen … Tx.	26·12 N	97·42 W
148	Harlow (här'lō) . Eng. (London In.)	51·46 N	0·08 E
111	Harlowton (här'lō-tŭn) … Mt.	46·26 N	109·50 W
104	Harmony (här'mô-nĭ) … In.	39·35 N	87·00 W
110	Harney Basin (här'nĭ) … Or.	43·26 N	120·19 W
110	Harney L. … Or.	43·11 N	119·23 W
108	Harney Pk. … SD	43·52 N	103·32 W
156	Härnosand (hĕr-nû-sänd) … Swe.	62·37 N	17·54 E
162	Haro (ä'rō) … Sp.	42·35 N	2·49 W
112	Haro Str. (hă'rō) Can.-U. S. (Seattle In.)	48·27 N	123·11 W
148	Harpenden (här'pĕn-d'n) Eng. (London In.)	51·48 N	0·22 W
116	Harper (här'pẽr) … Ks.	37·17 N	98·02 W
214	Harper … Lib.	4·25 N	7·43 W
112	Harper … Wa. (Seattle In.)	47·31 N	122·32 W
105	Harpers Ferry (här'pẽrz) … WV	39·20 N	77·45 W
97	Harricana (R.) … Can.	50·10 N	78·50 W
120	Harriman (hăr'ĭ-măn) … Tn.	35·55 N	84·34 W
105	Harrington (hăr'ĭng-tŭn) … De.	38·55 N	75·35 W
186	Harri Rud (R.) … Afg.	34·29 N	61·16 E
154	Harris (I.) (hăr'ĭs) … Scot.	57·55 N	6·40 W
121	Harris (L.) … Fl. (In.)	28·43 N	81·40 W
104	Harrisburg (hăr'ĭs-bûrg) … Il.	37·45 N	88·35 W
105	Harrisburg … Pa.	40·15 N	76·50 W
218	Harrismith (hă-rĭs'mĭth) S. Afr. (Johannesburg & Pretoria In.)	28·17 S	29·08 E
117	Harrison (hăr'ĭ-sŭn) … Ar.	36·13 N	93·06 W
107	Harrison … Oh. (Cincinnati In.)	39·16 N	84·45 W
93	Harrison L. … Can.	49·31 N	121·59 W
105	Harrisonburg (hăr'ĭ-sŭn-bûrg) Va.	38·30 N	78·50 W
117	Harrisonville (hăr-ĭ-sŭn-vĭl) … Mo.	38·39 N	94·21 W
113	Harrisville (hăr'ĭs-vĭl) Ut. (Salt Lake City In.)	41·17 N	112·00 W
104	Harrisville … WV	39·10 N	81·05 W
104	Harrodsburg (hăr'ŭdz-bûrg) .. Ky.	37·45 N	84·50 W

Page	Name Pronunciation Region	Lat. °′	Long. °′
107	Harrods Cr. (hăr'ŭdz) Ky. (Louisville In.)	38·24 N	35·33 W
148	Harrow (hăr'ō) . Eng. (London In.)	51·34 N	0·21 W
149	Harsefeld (här'zĕ-fĕld') F.R.G. (Hamburg In.)	53·27 N	9·30 E
150	Harstad (här'städh) … Nor.	68·49 N	16·10 E
104	Hart (härt) … Mi.	43·40 N	86·25 W
218	Hartbeesfontein . S. Afr. (Johannesburg & Pretoria In.)	26·46 S	26·25 E
213	Hartbeespoortdam (L.) . S. Afr. (Johannesburg & Pretoria In.)	25·47 S	27·43 E
213	Hartsbeespoort . S. Afr. (Johannesburg & Pretoria In.)	25·44 S	27·51 E
120	Hartford (härt'fẽrd) … Al.	31·05 N	85·42 W
117	Hartford … Ar.	35·01 N	94·21 W
105	Hartford … Ct.	41·45 N	72·40 W
113	Hartford … Il. (St. Louis In.)	38·50 N	90·06 W
120	Hartford … Ky.	37·25 N	86·50 W
104	Hartford … Mi.	42·15 N	86·15 W
109	Hartford … Wi.	43·19 N	88·25 W
104	Hartford City … In.	40·35 N	85·25 W
148	Hartington (härt'ĭng-tŭn) … Eng.	53·08 N	1·48 W
108	Hartington … Ne.	42·37 N	97·18 W
154	Hartland Pt. … Eng.	51·03 N	4·40 W
154	Hartlepool (här't'l-pōōl) … Eng.	54·40 N	1·12 W
217	Hartley … Zimb.	18·18 S	30·10 E
108	Hartley (härt'lĭ) … Ia.	43·12 N	95·29 W
92	Hartley Bay … Can.	53·25 N	129·15 W
95	Hart Mtn. (härt) … Can.	52·25 N	101·30 W
120	Hartselle (härt'sĕl) … Al.	34·24 N	86·55 W
117	Hartshorne (härts'hôrn) … Ok.	34·49 N	95·34 W
121	Hartsville (härts'vĭl) … SC	34·20 N	80·04 W
120	Hartwell (härt'wĕl) … Ga.	34·21 N	82·56 W
120	Hartwell Res. … Ga.	34·30 N	83·00 W
184	Hārua … India (In.)	22·36 N	88·40 E
109	Harvard (här'vȧrd) … Il.	42·25 N	88·39 W
99	Harvard … Ma (In.)	42·30 N	71·35 W
116	Harvard … Ne.	40·36 N	98·08 W
115	Harvard, Mt. … Co.	38·55 N	106·20 W
98	Harvey … Can.	45·44 N	64·46 W
107	Harvey … Il. (Chicago In.)	41·37 N	87·39 W
106	Harvey … La. (New Orleans In.)	29·54 N	90·05 W
108	Harvey … ND	47·46 N	99·55 W
155	Harwich (här'wĭch) … Eng.	51·53 N	1·13 E
184	Haryana (State) … India	29·00 N	75·45 E
158	Harz Mts. (härts) … G.D.R.	51·42 N	10·50 E
183	Hasā, Wādī al (R.) Jordan (Palestine In.)	30·55 N	35·50 E
195	Hashimoto (hä'shē-mō'tō) … Jap.	34·19 N	135·37 E
117	Haskell (hăs'kĕl) … Ok.	35·49 N	95·41 W
116	Haskell … Tx.	33·09 N	99·43 W
148	Haslingden (hăz'lĭng dĕn) … Eng.	53·43 N	2·19 W
156	Hassela (häs'ĕl-ô) … Swe.	62·05 N	16·46 E
149	Hasselt (häs'ĕlt) Bel. (Brussels In.)	50·56 N	5·23 E
210	Hassi Messaoud … Alg.	31·17 N	6·13 E
156	Hässjö (hĕs'shû) … Swe.	62·36 N	17·33 E
156	Hassleholm (häs'lĕ-hōlm) … Swe.	56·10 N	13·44 E
155	Hastings (hās'tĭngz) … Eng.	50·52 N	0·28 E
104	Hastings … Mi.	42·40 N	85·20 W
113	Hastings Mn. (Minneapolis, St. Paul In)	44·44 N	92·51 W
116	Hastings … Ne.	40·34 N	98·42 W
205	Hastings … N. Z. (In.)	39·33 S	176·53 E
106	Hastings-on-Hudson (ŏn-hŭd'sŭn) NY (New York In.)	40·59 N	75·53 W
120	Hatchie (R.) (hăch'ē) … Tn.	35·28 N	89·14 W
165	Hateg (kät-säg') … Rom.	45·35 N	22·57 E
148	Hatfield Broad Oak (hăt-fēld brôd ōk) . Eng.	51·50 N	0·14 E
195	Hatogaya (hä'tō-gä-yä) Jap. (Tōkyō In.)	35·50 N	139·45 E
195	Hatsukaichi (hät'sōō-kä'ê-chê) Jap.	34·22 N	132·19 E
121	Hatteras, C. (hăt'ẽr-ȧs) … NC	35·15 N	75·24 W
120	Hattiesburg (hăt'ĭz-bûrg) … Ms.	31·20 N	89·18 W
161	Hattingen (hä'tĕn-gĕn) F.R.G. (Ruhr In.)	51·24 N	7·11 E
159	Hatvan (hôt'vôn) … Hung.	47·39 N	19·44 E
156	Haugesund (hou'gĕ-soon') … Nor.	59·26 N	5·20 E
157	Haukivesi (L.) (hou'kê-vĕ'sê) . Fin.	62·02 N	29·02 E
94	Haultain (R.) … Can.	56·15 N	106·35 W
218	Hauptsrus … S. Afr. (Johannesburg & Pretoria In.)	26·35 S	26·16 E
205	Hauraki, G. (hä-ōō-rä'kê) N. Z. (In.)	36·44 S	175·15 E
98	Haut, Isle au (hō) … Me.	44·03 N	68·13 W
152	Haut Atlas (Mts.) … Mor.	32·10 N	5·49 W
98	Hauterive … Can.	49·11 N	68·16 W
100	Hauula … Hi.	21·37 N	157·45 W
117	Havana (hȧ-vă'nȧ) … Il.	40·17 N	90·02 W
	Havana, see La Habana		
115	Havasu L. (hăv'ȧ-sōō) … Az.	34·26 N	114·09 W
158	Havel R. (hä'fĕl) … G.D.R.	53·09 N	13·10 E
99	Haverhill (hā'vẽr-hĭl) … Ma. (In.)	42·46 N	71·05 W
105	Haverhill … NH	44·00 N	72·05 W
106	Haverstraw (hā'vẽr-strô) NY (New York In.)	41·11 N	73·58 W
158	Havlíckuv Brod … Czech.	49·38 N	15·34 E
99	Havre-Bouche Boucher (hăv'rá-bōō-shā') . Can.	45·42 N	61·30 W
111	Havre (hăv'ẽr) … Mt.	48·34 N	109·42 W
105	Havre de Grace (hăv'ẽr dē grăs') Md.	39·35 N	76·05 W
99	Havre-St. Pierre … Can.	50·15 N	63·36 W
121	Haw (R.) (hô) … NC	36·17 N	79·46 W
102	Hawaii (State) … U. S.	20·00 N	157·40 W
100	Hawaii (I.) (hä wī'ē) … Hi.	19·50 N	157·15 W
102	Hawaiian Is. (hä-wī'ăn) … U. S.	22·00 N	158·00 W
108	Hawaii Volcanoes Natl. Pk. … Hi.	19·30 N	155·25 W
108	Hawarden (hā'wár-dĕn) … Ia.	43·00 N	96·28 W
100	Hawi (hä'wē) … Hi.	20·16 N	155·48 W
154	Hawick (hô'ĭk) … Scot.	55·25 N	2·55 W

Page	Name Pronunciation Region	Lat. °′	Long. °′
205	Hawke B. (hôk) … N. Z. (In.)	39·17 S	177·58 E
203	Hawker (hô'kẽr) … Austl.	31·58 S	138·12 E
105	Hawkesbury (hôks'bẽr-ĭ) … Can.	45·35 N	74·35 W
120	Hawkinsville (hô'kĭnz-vĭl) … Ga.	32·15 N	83·30 W
129	Hawks Nest Pt. … Ba.	24·05 N	75·30 W
108	Hawley (hô'lĭ) … Mn.	46·52 N	96·18 W
148	Haworth (hā'wûrth) … Eng.	53·50 N	1·57 W
186	Hawtah … Sau. Ar.	15·58 N	48·26 E
113	Hawthorne (hô'thôrn) Ca. (Los Angeles In.)	33·55 N	118·22 W
114	Hawthorne … Nv.	38·33 N	118·39 W
116	Haxtun (hăks'tŭn) … Co.	40·39 N	102·38 W
204	Hay (R.) (hā) … Austl.	23·00 S	136·45 E
90	Hay (R.) … Can.	60·21 N	117·14 W
195	Hayama (hä-yä'mä) Jap. (Tōkyō In.)	35·16 N	139·35 E
195	Hayashi (hä-yä'shē) Jap. (Tōkyō In.)	35·13 N	139·38 E
115	Hayden (hā'dĕn) … Az.	33·00 N	110·50 W
101	Hayes, Mt. (hāz) … Ak.	63·32 N	146·40 W
105	Hayes (R.) … Can.	55·25 N	93·55 W
119	Haynesville (hānz'vĭl) … La.	32·55 N	93·08 W
165	Hayrabolu … Tur.	41·14 N	27·05 E
100	Hay River … Can.	60·50 N	115·53 W
116	Hays (hāz) … Ks.	38·51 N	99·20 W
183	Ḩaysī, Wādī al (R.) … Egypt	29·24 N	34·32 E
112	Haystack Mtn. (hā-stăk') Wa. (Seattle In.)	48·26 N	122·07 W
112	Hayward (hā'wẽrd) Ca. (San Francisco In.)	37·40 N	122·06 W
109	Hayward … Wi.	46·01 N	91·31 W
120	Hazard (hăz'ȧrd) … Ky.	37·13 N	83·10 W
121	Hazelhurst (hā'z'l-hûrst) … Ga.	31·50 N	82·36 W
107	Hazel Park … Mi. (Detroit In.)	42·28 N	83·06 W
92	Hazelton (hā'z'l-tŭn) … Can.	55·15 N	127·40 W
92	Hazelton Mts. … Can.	55·00 N	128·00 W
120	Hazlehurst … Ms.	31·52 N	90·23 W
105	Hazleton … Pa.	41·00 N	76·00 W
120	Headland (hĕd'lănd) … Al.	31·22 N	85·20 W
114	Healdsburg (hēldz'bûrg) … Ca.	38·37 N	122·52 W
117	Healdton (hēld'tŭn) … Ok.	34·13 N	97·28 W
148	Heanor (hēn'ōr) … Eng.	53·01 N	1·22 W
220	Heard I. (hûrd) … Ind. O.	53·10 S	74·35 E
119	Hearne (hûrn) … Tx.	30·53 N	96·35 W
91	Hearst (hûrst) … Can.	49·36 N	83·40 W
108	Heart (R.) (härt) … ND	46·46 N	102·34 W
93	Heart Lake Ind. Res. … Can.	55·02 N	111·30 W
99	Heart's Content (härts kŏn'tĕnt) Can.	47·52 N	53·22 W
99	Heath Pte. (hēth) … Can.	49·06 N	61·45 W
117	Heavener (hēv'nẽr) … Ok.	34·52 N	94·36 W
118	Hebbronville (hē'brŭn-vĭl) … Tx.	27·18 N	98·40 W
189	Hebei (Prov.) (hŭ-bā) … China	39·15 N	115·40 E
115	Heber (hē'bẽr) … Ut.	40·30 N	111·25 W
117	Heber Springs … Ar.	35·28 N	91·59 W
111	Hebgen Res. (hĕb'gĕn) … Mt.	44·47 N	111·38 W
154	Hebrides, Sea of … Scot.	57·00 N	7·00 W
91	Hebron (hē'brŭn) … Can.	58·11 N	62·56 W
107	Hebron … In. (Chicago In.)	41·19 N	87·13 W
107	Hebron … Ky. (Cincinnati In.)	39·04 N	84·43 W
117	Hebron … Ne.	40·11 N	97·36 W
108	Hebron … ND	46·54 N	102·04 W
	Hebron, see Al Khalīl		
156	Heby (hĭ'bü) … Swe.	59·56 N	16·48 E
92	Hecate Str. (hĕk'ȧ-tē) … Can.	53·00 N	131·00 W
125	Hecelchakán (ā-sĕl-chä-kän') . Mex.	20·10 N	90·09 W
193	Hechi (hŭ-chr) … China	24·50 N	108·18 E
193	Hechuan (hŭ-chyuän) … China	30·00 N	106·20 E
95	Hecla I. … Can.	51·08 N	96·45 W
156	Hedemora (hĭ-dĕ-mō'rä) … Swe.	60·16 N	15·55 E
156	Hedesunda Fd. (hi-de-sōōn'dä) Swe.	60·22 N	16·50 E
148	Hedon (hĕdŭn) … Eng.	53·44 N	0·12 W
149	Heemstede . Neth. (Amsterdam In.)	52·20 N	4·36 E
155	Heerlen … Neth.	50·55 N	5·58 E
	Hefa, see Haifa		
190	Hefei (hŭ-fā) … China	31·51 N	117·15 E
120	Heflin (hĕf'lĭn) … Al.	33·40 N	85·33 W
158	Heide (hī'dē) … F.R.G.	54·13 N	9·06 E
202	Heidelberg (hī'dĕl-bûrg) Austl. (Melbourne In.)	37·45 S	145·04 E
158	Heidelberg (hīdĕl-bĕrgh) … F.R.G.	49·24 N	8·43 E
158	Heidenheim (hī'dĕn-hīm) … F.R.G.	48·41 N	10·09 E
218	Heilbron (hīl'brōn) … S. Afr. (Johannesburg & Pretoria In.)	27·17 S	27·58 E
158	Heilbronn (hīl'brōn) … F.R.G.	49·09 N	9·16 E
161	Heiligenhaus (hī'lē-gĕn-houz) F.R.G. (Ruhr In.)	51·19 N	6·58 E
158	Heiligenstadt (hī'lē-gĕn-shtät) G.D.R.	51·21 N	10·10 E
192	Heilong (R.) (hā-loŋ) China-Sov. Un.	49·38 N	127·25 E
189	Heilongjiang (Prov.) (hā-lôŋ-jyäŋ) . China	46·36 N	128·07 E
157	Heinola (hå-nō'lå) … Fin.	61·13 N	26·03 E
161	Heinsberg (hīnz'bĕrgh) F.R.G. (Ruhr In.)	51·04 N	6·07 E
149	Heist-op-den-Berg Bel. (Brussels In.)	51·05 N	4·14 E
	Hejaz, see Al Ḩijāz		
190	Hejian (hŭ-jyĕn) … China	38·28 N	116·05 E
150	Hekla (Vol.) (hĕk'lȧ) … Ice.	63·53 N	19·37 W
159	Hel (hāl) … Pol.	54·37 N	18·53 E
156	Helagsfjället (Mtn.) … Swe.	62·54 N	12·24 E
188	Helan Shan (Mts.) (hŭ-län shän) China	38·02 N	105·20 E
117	Helena (hē-lē'nȧ) … Ar.	34·33 N	90·35 W
111	Helena (hĕ-lē'nȧ) … Mt.	46·35 N	112·01 W
202	Helensburgh (hĕl'ĕnz-bŭr-ô) Austl. (Sydney In.)	34·11 S	150·59 E
154	Helensburgh … Scot.	56·01 N	4·53 W
156	Helge (R.) (hĕl'gĕ) … Swe.	56·31 N	13·47 E
158	Helgoland I. (hĕl'gō-lănd) .. F.R.G.	54·13 N	7·30 E

ng-sing; ŋ-baŋk; N-nasalized n; nŏd; cŏmmit; ōld; ôbey; ôrder; fōōd; fŏŏt; ou-out; s-soft; sh-dish; th-thin; pūre; ûnite; ûrn; stŭd; circŭs; ü-as "y" in study; '-indeterminate vowel.

290 Hellier — Holdrege PRONOUNCING INDEX

Page	Name Pronunciation Region	Lat. °′	Long. °′
121	Hellier (hĕl'yēr) . . . . Ky.	37·16 N	82·27 W
162	Hellín (ĕl-yēn') . . . . Sp.	38·30 N	1·40 W
186	Helmand (R.) (hĕl'mŭnd) . . . . Afg.	31·00 N	63·48 E
155	Helmond (hĕl'mōnt) (ĕl'môN') Neth.	51·35 N	5·04 E
158	Helmstedt (hĕlm'shtĕt) . . . . F.R.G.	52·14 N	11·03 E
113	Helotes (hē'lōts) Tx. (San Antonio In.)	29·35 N	98·41 W
115	Helper (hĕlp'ēr) . . . . Ut.	39·40 N	110·55 W
156	Helsingborg (hĕl'sĭng-bôrgh) . . Swe.	56·04 N	12·40 E
	Helsingfors, see Helsinki		
156	Helsingør (hĕl-sĭng-ŭr') . . . . . . Den.	56·03 N	12·33 E
157	Helsinki (Helsingfors) (hĕl'sēn-kē) (hĕl'sĭng-fôrs') . Fin.	60·10 N	24·53 E
148	Hemel Hempstead (hĕm'ĕl hĕmp'stĕd) Eng. (London In.)	51·43 N	0·29 W
113	Hemet (hĕm'ĕt) Ca. (Los Angeles In.)	33·45 N	116·57 W
108	Hemingford (hĕm'ĭng-fērd) . . . . Ne.	42·21 N	103·30 W
119	Hemphill (hĕmp'hĭl) . . . . Tx.	31·20 N	93·48 W
107	Hempstead (hĕmp'stĕd) NY (New York In.)	40·42 N	73·37 W
119	Hempstead . . . . Tx.	30·07 N	96·05 W
156	Hemse (hĕm'sē) . . . . Swe.	57·15 N	18·25 E
156	Hemsö (I.) . . . . Swe.	62·43 N	18·22 E
156	Hen (hĭn) . . . . Nor.	60·14 N	10·10 E
189	Henan (Prov.) (hŭ-nän) . . . . China	33·58 N	112·33 E
162	Henares (R.) (å-nä'rås) . . . . . . Sp.	40·50 N	2·55 W
160	Hendaye (äN-dā') . . . . Fr.	43·20 N	1·46 W
104	Henderson (hĕn'dēr-sŭn) . . . . . Ky.	37·50 N	87·30 W
114	Henderson . . . . Nv.	36·09 N	115·04 W
121	Henderson . . . . NC	36·18 N	78·24 W
120	Henderson . . . . Tn.	35·25 N	88·40 W
119	Henderson . . . . Tx.	32·09 N	94·48 W
121	Hendersonville (hĕn'dēr-sŭn-vĭl) NC	35·17 N	82·28 W
148	Hendon (hĕn'dŭn) Eng. (London In.)	51·34 N	0·13 W
218	Hendrina (hĕn-drē'nȧ) . . . . . S. Afr. (Johannesburg & Pretoria In.)	26·10 S	29·44 E
193	Hengch'un (hĕng'chŭn') . . . Taiwan	22·00 N	120·42 E
155	Hengelo (hĕngē-lō) . . . . Neth.	52·20 N	6·45 E
193	Hengshan (hĕng'shän') . . . . . China	27·20 N	112·40 E
190	Hengshui (hĕng'shōō-ē') . . . . China	37·43 N	115·42 E
193	Heng Xian (hŭŋ shyĕn) . . . . China	22·40 N	104·20 E
193	Hengyang . . . . China	26·58 N	112·30 E
148	Henley on Thames (hĕn'lē ŏn tĕmz) . Eng. (London In.)	51·31 N	0·54 W
105	Henlopen, C. (hĕn-lō'pĕn) . . . . . De.	38·45 N	75·05 W
160	Hennebont (ĕn-bôN') . . . . Fr.	47·47 N	3·16 W
218	Hennenman . . . . S. Afr. (Johannesburg & Pretoria In.)	27·59 S	27·03 E
116	Hennessey (hĕn'ĕ-sĭ) . . . . Ok.	36·04 N	97·53 W
149	Hennigsdorf (hĕ'nĕngz-dōrf) G.D.R. (Berlin In.)	52·39 N	13·12 E
213	Hennops (R.) (hĕn'ŏps) . . . . S. Afr. (Johannesburg & Pretoria In.)	25·51 S	27·57 E
213	Hennopsrivier . . . . S. Afr. (Johannesburg & Pretoria In.)	25·50 S	27·59 E
117	Henrietta (hĕn-rĭ-ĕt'ȧ) . . . . Ok.	35·25 N	95·58 W
116	Henrietta (hen-rĭ-ĕ'tȧ) . . . . Tx.	33·47 N	98·11 W
91	Henrietta Maria, C. (hĕn-rĭ-ĕt'ȧ) Can.	55·10 N	82·20 W
115	Henry Mts. (hĕn'rĭ) . . . . Ut.	38·55 N	110·45 W
192	Henteyn Nuruu (Mts.) . . . Sov. Un.	49·40 N	111·00 E
196	Henzada . . . . Bur.	17·38 N	95·28 E
110	Heppner (hĕp'nēr) . . . . Or.	45·21 N	119·33 W
193	Hepu (hŭ-pōō) . . . . China	21·28 N	109·10 E
186	Herāt (hĕ-rät') . . . . Afg.	34·28 N	62·13 E
165	Hercegovina (Reg.) (hĕr-tsĕ-gô'vē-nȧ) . Yugo.	43·23 N	17·52 E
89	Hercules . . . . Can. (Edmonton In.)	53·27 N	113·20 W
161	Herdecke (hĕr'dĕ-kĕ) F.R.G. (Ruhr In.)	51·24 N	7·26 E
127	Heredia (ā-rā'dhē-ä) . . . . C. R.	10·04 N	84·06 W
154	Hereford (hĕrĕ'fērd) . . . . Eng.	52·05 N	2·44 W
148	Hereford (Co.) . . . . Eng.	52·22 N	2·52 W
106	Hereford . . . . . Md. (Baltimore In.)	39·35 N	76·42 W
116	Hereford (hĕr'ĕ-fērd) . . . . Tx.	34·47 N	102·25 W
162	Herencia (ā-rān'thē-ä) . . . . Sp.	39·23 N	3·22 W
149	Herentals . . . . . . Bel. (Brussels In.)	51·10 N	4·51 E
158	Herford (hĕr'fôrt) . . . . F.R.G.	52·06 N	8·42 E
117	Herington (hĕr'ĭng-tŭn) . . . . Ks.	38·41 N	96·57 W
158	Herisau (hā'rē-zou) . . . . Switz.	47·23 N	9·18 E
149	Herk-de-Stad . . Bel. (Brussels In.)	50·56 N	5·13 E
105	Herkimer (hûr'kĭ-mēr) . . . . NY	43·05 N	75·00 W
154	Herma Ness (Prom.) (hûr'mȧ nĕs) Scot.	60·50 N	1·10 W
117	Hermann (hûr'mȧn) . . . . Mo.	38·41 N	91·27 W
104	Hermansville (hûr'mȧns-vĭl) . . . Mi.	45·40 N	87·35 W
113	Hermantown (hēr'mȧn-toun) Mn. (Duluth In.)	46·46 N	92·12 W
218	Hermanusdorings . . . . S. Afr. (Johannesburg & Pretoria In.)	24·08 S	27·46 E
107	Herminie (hûr-mī'nē) Pa. (Pittsburgh In.)	40·16 N	79·45 W
99	Hermitage B. (hûr'mĭ-tĕj) . . . Can.	47·35 N	56·05 W
197	Hermit Is. (hûr'mĭt) . Pap. N. Gui.	1·48 S	144·55 E
113	Hermosa Beach (hēr-mō'sȧ) Ca. (Los Angeles In.)	33·51 N	118·24 W
122	Hermosillo (ĕr-mô-sē'l-yō) . . . Mex.	29·00 N	110·57 W
106	Herndon (hērn'don) Va. (Baltimore In.)	38·58 N	77·22 W
161	Herne (hĕr'nĕ) . . F.R.G. (Ruhr In.)	51·32 N	7·13 E
156	Herning (hĕr'nĭng) . . . . Den.	56·08 N	8·55 E
108	Heron (L.) (hĕr'ŭn) . . . . Mn.	43·42 N	95·23 W
108	Heron Lake . . . . Mn.	43·48 N	95·20 W
126	Herrero, Punta (pt.) (pōō'n-tä-ĕr-rĕ'rô) . Mex.	19·18 N	87·24 W
104	Herrin (hĕr'ĭn) . . . . Il.	37·50 N	89·00 W
213	Herschel (hēr'-shĕl) S. Afr. (Natal In.)	30·37 S	27·12 E
107	Herscher (hēr'shēr) Il. (Chicago In.)	41·03 N	88·06 W
155	Herstal (hĕr'stäl) . . . . Bel.	50·42 N	5·32 E
148	Hertford (hûrt'fērd) . . . . Eng.	51·46 N	0·05 W
121	Hertford . . . . NC	36·10 N	76·30 W
149	Hertzberg (hĕrtz'bĕrgh) G.D.R. (Berlin In.)	52·54 N	12·58 E
183	Herzliyya . . . . . . Isr. (Palestine In.)	32·10 N	34·49 E
160	Hesdin (ē-dăN') . . . . Fr.	50·24 N	1·59 E
158	Hessen (State) (hĕs'ĕn . . . . F.R.G.	50·16 N	8·48 E
114	Hetch Hetchy Aqueduct (hĕtch hĕt'-chĭ ăk'wē-dŭkt) . Ca.	37·27 N	120·54 W
108	Hettinger (hĕt'ĭn-jēr) . . . . ND	45·58 N	102·36 W
218	Heuningspruit . . . . S. Afr. (Johannesburg & Pretoria In.)	27·28 S	27·26 E
193	He Xian (hŭ shyĕn) . . . . China	24·20 N	111·28 E
190	He Xian . . . . China	31·44 N	118·20 E
192	Heyang (hŭ-yäŋ) . . . . China	35·18 N	110·18 E
218	Heystekrand . . . . S. Afr. (Johannesburg & Pretoria In.)	25·16 S	27·14 E
193	Heyuan (hŭ-yūän) . . . . China	23·48 N	114·45 E
148	Heywood (hā'wŏŏd) . . . . Eng.	53·36 N	2·12 W
190	Heze (hŭ-dzŭ) . . . . China	35·13 N	115·28 E
121	Hialeah (hī-ȧ-lē'ăh) . . . . . . Fl. (In.)	25·49 N	80·18 W
117	Hiawatha (hī-ȧ-wô'thȧ) . . . . Ks.	39·50 N	95·33 W
115	Hiawatha . . . . Ut.	39·25 N	111·05 W
109	Hibbing (hĭb'ĭng) . . . . Mn.	47·26 N	92·58 W
120	Hickman (hĭk'mȧn) . . . . Ky.	34·33 N	89·10 W
121	Hickory (hĭk'ô-rĭ) . . . . NC	35·43 N	81·21 W
106	Hicksville (hĭks'vĭl) NY (New York In.)	40·47 N	73·25 W
104	Hicksville . . . . Oh.	41·15 N	84·45 W
118	Hico (hī'kō) . . . . Tx.	32·00 N	98·02 W
114	Hidalgo (ē-dhäl'gō) . . . . Mex.	24·14 N	99·25 W
118	Hidalgo . . . . Mex.	27·49 N	99·53 W
122	Hidalgo (State) . . . . Mex.	20·45 N	99·30 W
118	Hidalgo del Parral (ē-dä'l-gō-dĕl-pär-rȧ'l) . Mex.	26·55 N	105·40 W
125	Hidalgo Yalalag (ē-dhäl'gō-yä-lä-läg) . Mex.	17·12 N	96·11 W
218	Hiedelberg . . . . S. Afr. (Johannesburg & Pretoria In.)	26·32 S	28·22 E
210	Hierro I. (yĕ'r-rô) . . . . Can. Is.	27·37 N	18·29 W
195	Higashimurayama Jap. (Tōkyō In.)	35·46 N	139·28 E
195	Higashiōsaka . . . . . Jap. (Ōsaka In.)	34·40 N	135·44 E
104	Higgins (L.) (hĭg'ĭnz) . . . . Mi.	44·20 N	84·45 W
117	Higginsville (hĭg'ĭnz-vĭl) . . . . . . Mo.	39·05 N	93·44 W
104	High (I.) . . . . Mi.	45·45 N	85·45 W
89	High Bluff . . . Can. (Winnipeg In.)	50·01 N	98·08 W
128	Highborne Cay (hībôrn kē) . . . Ba.	24·45 N	76·50 W
113	Highgrove (hī'grōv) Ca. (Los Angeles In.)	34·01 N	117·20 W
119	High Island . . . . Tx. (In.)	29·34 N	94·24 W
113	Highland (hī'lȧnd) Ca. (Los Angeles In.)	34·08 N	117·13 W
117	Highland . . . . Il.	38·44 N	89·41 W
107	Highland . . . . In. (Chicago In.)	41·33 N	87·28 W
107	Highland . . . . . . Mi. (Detroit In.)	42·38 N	83·37 W
107	Highland Park . . . Il. (Chicago In.)	42·11 N	87·47 W
107	Highland Park . . . Mi. (Detroit In.)	42·24 N	83·06 W
106	Highland Park NJ (New York In.)	40·30 N	74·25 W
113	Highland Park Tx. (Dallas, Fort Worth In.)	32·49 N	96·48 W
106	Highlands (hī-lȧndz) NJ (New York In.)	40·24 N	73·59 W
113	Highlands . . . . Tx. (In.)	29·49 N	95·01 W
108	Highmore (hī'mōr) . . . . SD	44·30 N	99·26 W
148	High Ongar (on'gēr) Eng. (London In.)	51·43 N	0·15 E
197	High Pk . . . . Phil. (In.)	15·38 N	120·05 E
121	High Point . . . . NC	35·55 N	80·00 W
93	High Prairie . . . . Can.	55·26 N	116·29 W
113	High Ridge . . . . Mo. (St. Louis In.)	38·27 N	90·32 W
93	High River . . . . Can.	50·35 N	113·52 W
121	Highrock (R.) (hī'-rŏk) . . . . NC	35·40 N	80·15 W
121	High Springs . . . . Fl.	29·48 N	82·38 W
106	Hightstown (hīts-toun) NJ (New York In.)	40·16 N	74·32 W
148	High Wycombe (wĭ-kŭm) Eng. (London In.)	51·36 N	0·45 W
123	Higuero, Pta. (Pt.) P. R. (Puerto Rico In.)	18·21 N	67·11 W
135	Higuerote (ē-gĕ-rô'-tĕ) . . Ven. (In.)	10·29 N	66·06 W
129	Higüey (ē-gwĕ'y) . . . . . . Dom. Rep.	18·40 N	68·45 W
157	Hiiumaa (D'Ago) (hē'ōōm-ô) . Sov. Un.	58·47 N	22·05 E
195	Hikone (hē'kô-nĕ) . . . . Jap.	35·15 N	136·15 E
158	Hildburghausen (hĭld'bŏŏrg hou-zĕn) . . . G.D.R.	50·26 N	10·45 E
161	Hilden (hēl'dĕn) F.R.G. (Ruhr In.)	51·10 N	6·56 E
158	Hildesheim (hĭl'dĕs-hĭm) . . . F.R.G.	52·08 N	9·56 E
127	Hillaby, Mt. (hĭl'ȧ-bĭ) Barb. (In.)	13·15 N	59·35 W
116	Hill City (hĭl) . . . . Ks.	39·22 N	99·54 W
109	Hill City . . . . Mn.	46·58 N	93·38 W
149	Hillegersberg Neth. (Amsterdam In.)	51·57 N	4·29 E
156	Hillerød (hē'lĕ-rûdh) . . . . Den.	55·56 N	12·17 E
117	Hillsboro (hĭlz'bŭr-ō) . . . . Il.	39·09 N	89·28 W
117	Hillsboro . . . . Ks.	38·22 N	97·11 W
105	Hillsboro . . . . NH	43·05 N	71·55 W
108	Hillsboro . . . . ND	47·23 N	97·05 W
104	Hillsboro . . . . Oh.	39·10 N	83·40 W
110	Hillsboro . . . . Or. (Portland In.)	45·31 N	122·59 W
119	Hillsboro . . . . Tx.	32·01 N	97·06 W
109	Hillsboro . . . . Wi.	43·39 N	90·20 W
89	Hillsburgh (hĭlz'bûrg) Can. (Toronto In.)	43·48 N	80·09 W
110	Hills Creek Res. . . . . Or.	43·41 N	122·26 W
114	Hillsdale (hĭls-dāl) . . . . Mi.	41·55 N	84·35 W
100	Hilo (hē'lō) . . . . Hi.	19·44 N	155·01 W
149	Hilversum (hĭl'vēr-sŭm) Neth. (Amsterdam In.)	52·13 N	5·10 E
184	Himachal Pradesh (State) . . . India	36·03 N	77·41 E
187	Himalaya Mts. (hĭ-mä'lȧ-yȧ) . Asia	29·30 N	85·02 E
195	Himeji (hē'mȧ-jē) . . . . Jap.	34·50 N	134·42 E
149	Himmelpforten (hē'mĕl-pfōr-tĕn) F.R.G. (Hamburg In.)	53·37 N	9·19 E
129	Hinche (hēn'chȧ) (ănsh) . . . . . Hai.	19·10 N	72·05 W
205	Hinchinbrook (I.) (hĭn-chĭn-brōōk) Austl.	18·23 S	146·57 W
148	Hinckley (hĭnk'lĭ) . . . . Eng.	52·32 N	1·21 W
148	Hindley (hĭnd'lĭ) . . . . Eng.	53·32 N	2·35 W
187	Hindu Kush (Mts.) (hĭn'dōō kōōsh') . Asia	35·15 N	68·44 E
185	Hindupur (hĭn'dōō-pōōr) . . . . India	13·52 N	77·34 E
99	Hingham (hĭng'ȧm) . . . . . Ma. (In.)	42·14 N	70·53 W
107	Hinkley (hĭnk'-lĭ) Oh. (Cleveland In.)	41·14 N	81·45 W
162	Hinojosa (ē-nô-kô'sä) . . . . Sp.	38·30 N	5·09 W
107	Hinsdale (hĭnz'dāl) Il. (Chicago In.)	41·48 N	87·56 W
93	Hinton (hĭn'tŭn) . . . . Can.	53·25 N	117·34 W
104	Hinton (hĭn'tŭn) . . . . WV	37·40 N	80·55 W
195	Hirado (I.) (hē'rä-dō) . . . . Jap.	33·19 N	129·18 E
195	Hirakata (hē'rä-kä'tä) Jap. (Ōsaka In.)	34·49 N	135·40 E
195	Hiratsuka (hē-rät-sōō'kȧ) . . . . . Jap.	35·20 N	139·19 E
188	Hirgis Nuur (L.) . . . . Mong.	49·18 N	94·21 E
194	Hirosaki (hē'rô-sä'kē) . . . . Jap.	40·31 N	140·38 E
195	Hirose (hē'rô-sā) . . . . Jap.	35·20 N	133·11 E
195	Hiroshima (hē-rô-shē'mȧ) . . . . Jap.	34·22 N	132·25 E
160	Hirson (ēr-sôN') . . . . Fr.	49·54 N	4·00 E
189	Hisar . . . . India	29·15 N	75·47 E
123	Hispaniola (I.) (hĭ'spăn-ĭ-ō-lȧ) N. A.	17·30 N	73·15 W
194	Hitachi (hē-tä'chē) . . . . Jap.	36·42 N	140·47 E
119	Hitchcock (hĭch'kŏk) . . . . Tx. (In.)	29·21 N	95·01 W
161	Hitdorf (hēt'dōrf) F.R.G. (Ruhr In.)	51·04 N	6·56 E
195	Hitoyoshi (hē'tô-yō'shē) . . . . . . Jap.	32·13 N	130·45 E
150	Hitra (I.) (hĭträ) . . . . Nor.	63·34 N	7·37 E
149	Hittefeld (hē'tĕ-fĕld) F.R.G. (Hamburg In.)	53·23 N	9·59 E
195	Hiwasa (hē'wȧ-sä) . . . . Jap.	33·44 N	134·31 E
120	Hiwassee (R.) (hī-wôs'sē) . . . . . Tn.	35·10 N	84·35 W
156	Hjälmaren (L.) . . . . Swe.	59·07 N	16·05 E
156	Hjo (yō) . . . . Swe.	58·19 N	14·11 E
156	Hjørring (jûr'ĭng) . . . . Den.	57·27 N	9·59 E
159	Hlohovec (hlō'ho-vĕts) . . . . . Czech.	48·24 N	17·49 E
203	Hobart (hō'bȧrt) . . . . Austl.	43·00 S	147·30 E
107	Hobart . . . . In. (Chicago In.)	41·31 N	87·15 W
116	Hobart . . . . Ok.	35·02 N	99·06 W
112	Hobart . . . . Wa. (Seattle In.)	47·25 N	121·58 W
116	Hobbs (hŏbs) . . . . NM	32·41 N	104·04 W
188	Hobdo Gol (R.) . . . . Mong.	49·06 N	91·16 E
149	Hoboken (hō'bō-kĕn) Bel. (Brussels In.)	51·11 N	4·20 E
106	Hoboken . . . . . NJ (New York In.)	40·43 N	74·03 W
156	Hobro (hô-brô') . . . . Den.	56·38 N	9·47 E
106	Hobson (hŏb'sŭn) . Va. (Norfolk In.)	36·54 N	76·31 W
202	Hobson's B. (hŏb'sŭnz) Austl. (Melbourne In.)	37·54 S	144·45 E
196	Ho Chi Minh City (Saigon) . . Viet.	10·46 N	106·34 E
112	Hockinson (hŏk'-ĭn-sŭn) Wa. (Portland In.)	45·44 N	122·29 W
126	Hoctún (ôk-tōō'n) . . . . . Mex. (In.)	20·52 N	89·10 W
104	Hodgenville (hŏj'ĕn-vĭl) . . . . . . Ky.	37·35 N	85·45 W
97	Hodges Hill (Mtn.) (hŏj'ĕz) . . Can.	49·04 N	55·53 W
159	Hódmezövásárhely (hōd'mĕ-zû-vô' shôr-hĕl-y') . Hung.	46·24 N	20·21 E
151	Hodna, Chott el (L.) . . . . Alg.	35·20 N	3·27 E
159	Hodonin (hē'dô-nēn) . . . . Czech.	48·50 N	17·06 E
149	Hoegaarden . . . . Bel. (Brussels In.)	50·46 N	4·55 E
149	Hoek van Holland Neth. (Amsterdam In.)	51·59 N	4·05 E
194	Hoeryŏng (hwĕr'yŭng) . . . . Kor.	42·28 N	129·39 E
161	Hoetmar (hût'mär) F.R.G. (Ruhr In.)	51·52 N	7·54 E
158	Hof (hōf) . . . . F.R.G.	50·19 N	11·55 E
150	Hofsjökull (Gl.) (hôfs'yü'kōōl) . Ice.	64·55 N	18·40 W
104	Hog (I.) . . . . Mi.	45·50 N	85·20 W
120	Hogansville (hō'gȧnz-vĭl) . . . . . Ga.	33·10 N	84·54 W
129	Hog Cay (I.) . . . . Ba.	23·35 N	75·30 W
129	Hogsty Rf . . . . Ba.	21·45 N	73·50 W
149	Hohenbrunn (hō'hĕn-brōōn) F.R.G. (Munich In.)	48·03 N	11·42 E
161	Hohenlimburg (hō'hĕn lēm'bōōrg) F.R.G. (Ruhr In.)	51·20 N	7·35 E
149	Hohen Neuendorf (hō'hĕn noi'ĕn-dōrf) . . . G.D.R. (Berlin In.)	52·40 N	13·22 E
158	Hohe Tauern (Mts.) (hō'ĕ tou'ērn) Aus.	47·11 N	12·12 E
192	Hohhot (hŭ-hōō-tŭ) . . . . China	41·05 N	111·50 E
214	Hohoe . . . . Ghana	7·09 N	0·28 E
106	Hohokus (hō-hō-kŭs) NJ (New York In.)	41·01 N	74·08 W
116	Hoisington (hoi'zĭng-tŭn) . . . . . Ks.	38·30 N	98·46 W
195	Hojo (hō'jō) . . . . Jap.	33·58 N	132·50 E
205	Hokitika (hō-kĭ-tē'kä) . . N. Z. (In.)	42·43 S	171·12 E
194	Hokkaido (I.) (hŏk'kĭ-dō) . . . . Jap.	43·30 N	142·45 E
156	Holbaek (hôl'bĕk) . . . . Den.	55·42 N	11·40 E
126	Holbox (ôl-bŏ'x) . . . . Mex. (In.)	21·33 N	87·19 W
126	Holbox, Isla (I.) (ē's-lä-ôl-bŏ'x) Mex. (In.)	21·40 N	87·21 W
115	Holbrook (hōl'brŏŏk) . . . . Az.	34·55 N	110·15 W
99	Holbrook . . . . Ma. (In.)	42·10 N	71·01 W
99	Holden (hōl'dĕn) . . . . Ma. (In.)	42·21 N	71·51 W
117	Holden . . . . Mo.	38·42 N	94·00 W
104	Holden . . . . WV	37·45 N	82·05 W
117	Holdenville (hōl'dĕn-vĭl) . . . . . . Ok.	35·05 N	96·25 W
116	Holdrege (hōl'drĕj) . . . . Ne.	40·25 N	99·28 W

Page	Name Pronunciation	Region	Lat. °'	Long. °'
156	Hölen (hûl'ĕn)	Nor.	59·34 N	10·40 E
129	Holguín (ôl-gēn')	Cuba	20·55 N	76·15 W
129	Holguín (Prov.)	Cuba	20·40 N	76·15 W
105	Holidaysburg (hŏl'ĭ-dāz-bûrg)	Pa.	40·30 N	78·30 W
158	Hollabrunn	Aus.	48·33 N	16·04 E
104	Holland (hŏl'ănd)	Mi.	42·45 N	86·10 W
149	Hollandsch Diep (Chan.)	Neth. (Amsterdam In.)	51·43 N	4·25 E
149	Hollenstedt (hō'lĕn-shtĕt)	F.R.G. (Hamburg In.)	53·22 N	9·43 E
99	Hollis (hŏl'ĭs)	NH (In.)	42·30 N	71·29 W
116	Hollis	Ok.	34·39 N	99·56 W
114	Hollister (hŏl'ĭs-tẽr)	Ca.	36·50 N	121·25 W
99	Holliston (hŏl'ĭs-tŭn)	Ma. (In.)	42·12 N	71·25 W
104	Holly (hŏl'ĭ)	Mi.	42·45 N	83·30 W
112	Holly	Wa. (Seattle In.)	47·34 N	122·58 W
120	Holly Springs (hŏl'ĭ sprĭngz)	Ms.	34·45 N	89·28 W
113	Hollywood (hŏl'ē-wŏŏd)	Ca. (Los Angeles In.)	34·06 N	118·20 W
121	Hollywood	Fl. (In.)	26·00 N	80·11 W
205	Holmes Rfs. (hōmz)	Austl.	16·33 S	148·43 E
156	Holmestrand (hôl'mĕ-strän)	Nor.	59·29 N	10·17 E
156	Holmsbu (hôlms'bōō)	Nor.	59·36 N	10·26 E
156	Holmsjön (L.)	Swe.	62·23 N	15·43 E
156	Holstebro (hôl'stĕ-brō)	Den.	56·22 N	8·39 E
120	Holston (R.) (hōl'stŭn)	Tn.	36·02 N	83·42 W
148	Holt (hōlt)	Eng.	53·05 N	2·53 W
117	Holton (hōl'tŭn)	Ks.	39·27 N	95·43 W
154	Holy (I.) (hō'lĭ)	Wales	53·45 N	4·45 W
154	Holy (I.)	Eng.	55·43 N	1·48 W
101	Holy Cross (hō'lĭ krôs)	Ak.	62·10 N	159·40 W
154	Holyhead (hŏl'ē-hĕd)	Wales	53·48 N	4·45 W
116	Holyoke (hōl'yōk)	Co.	40·36 N	102·18 W
105	Holyoke	Ma.	42·10 N	72·40 W
195	Homano (hō-mä'nō)	Jap. (Tōkyō In.)	35·33 N	140·08 E
161	Homberg (hōm'bĕrgh)	F.R.G. (Ruhr In.)	51·27 N	6·42 E
214	Hombori	Mali	15·17 N	1·42 W
113	Home Gardens (hōm gär'd'nz)	Ca. (Los Angeles In.)	33·53 N	117·32 W
113	Homeland (hōm'lănd)	Ca. (Los Angeles In.)	33·44 N	117·07 W
101	Homer (hō'mẽr)	Ak.	59·42 N	151·30 W
119	Homer	La.	32·46 N	93·05 W
121	Homestead (hōm'stĕd)	Fl. (In.)	25·27 N	80·28 W
113	Homestead	Mi. (Sault Ste. Marie In.)	46·20 N	84·07 W
107	Homestead	Pa. (Pittsburgh In.)	40·29 N	79·55 W
118	Homestead Natl. Mon. of America	Ne.	40·16 N	96·51 W
106	Homewood (hōm'wŏŏd)	Al. (Birmingham In.)	33·28 N	86·48 W
107	Homewood	Il. (Chicago In.)	41·34 N	87·40 W
118	Hominy (hŏm'ĭ-nĭ)	Ok.	36·25 N	96·24 W
120	Homochiho (R.) (hō-mō-chĭt'ō)	Ms.	31·23 N	91·15 W
153	Homs (hōms)	Syr.	34·42 N	36·52 E
134	Honda (hōn'dà)	Col. (In.)	5·13 N	74·45 W
128	Honda, Bahía (B.) (bä-ē'ä-ô'n-dä)	Cuba	23·10 N	83·20 W
118	Hondo	Tx.	29·20 N	99·08 W
126	Hondo, Rio (R.) (hon-dō')	Belize (In.)	18·16 N	88·32 W
116	Hondo (R.)	NM	33·22 N	105·06 W
122	Honduras (hŏn-dōō'răs)	N. A.	14·30 N	88·00 W
122	Honduras, Gulf of	N. A.	16·30 N	87·30 W
121	Honea Path (hŭn'ĭ păth)	SC	34·25 N	82·16 W
156	Hönefoss (hẽ'nĕ-fôs)	Nor.	60·10 N	10·15 E
105	Honesdale (hōnz'dāl)	Pa.	41·30 N	75·15 W
114	Honey (R.) (hŭn'ĭ)	Ca.	40·11 N	120·34 W
117	Honey Grove (hŭn'ĭ grōv)	Tx.	33·35 N	95·54 W
89	Honfleur (ôɴ-flûr')	Can. (Quebec In.)	46·39 N	70·53 W
160	Honfleur (ôɴ-flûr')	Fr.	49·26 N	0·13 E
193	Hon Gay	Viet.	20·58 N	107·10 E
193	Hongshui (R.) (hôŋ-shwā)	China	25·00 N	107·22 E
98	Honguedo, Détroit d' (Str.)	Can.	49·08 N	63·45 W
190	Hongze Hu (L.) (hôŋ-dzŭ hōō)	China	33·17 N	118·37 E
205	Honiara	Sol. Is.	9·15 S	159·45 E
154	Honiton (hŏn'ĭ-tŏn)	Eng.	50·49 N	3·10 W
189	Hong Kong (hŏng' kŏng')	Asia	21·45 N	115·00 E
100	Honolulu (hŏn-ō-lōō'lōō)	Hi.	21·18 N	157·50 W
100	Honomu (hŏn'ō-mōō)	Hi.	19·50 N	155·04 W
194	Honshū (I.) (hŏn'shōō)	Jap.	36·50 N	135·20 E
110	Hood, Mt.	Or.	45·20 N	121·43 W
112	Hood Can. (hŏŏd)	Wa. (Seattle In.)	47·45 N	122·45 W
110	Hood River	Or.	45·42 N	121·30 W
112	Hoodsport (hŏŏdz'pōrt)	Wa. (Seattle In.)	47·25 N	123·09 W
184	Hoogly (R.) (hōōg'lĭ)	India	21·35 N	87·50 E
149	Hoogstraten	Bel. (Brussels In.)	51·24 N	4·46 E
116	Hooker (hŏŏk'ẽr)	Ok.	36·49 N	101·13 W
126	Hool (ōō'l)	Mex. (In.)	19·32 N	90·22 W
101	Hoonah (hōō'nā)	Ak.	58·05 N	135·25 W
110	Hoopa Valley Ind. Res. (hōō'pà)	Ca.	41·18 N	123·35 W
117	Hooper (hŏŏp'ẽr)	Ne.	41·37 N	96·31 W
113	Hooper	Ut. (Salt Lake City In.)	41·10 N	112·08 W
101	Hooper Bay	Ak.	61·32 N	166·02 W
104	Hoopeston (hōōps'tŭn)	Il.	40·35 N	87·40 W
105	Hoosick Falls (hōō'sĭk)	NY	42·55 N	73·15 W
114	Hoover Dam (hōō'vẽr)	Nv.	36·00 N	115·06 W
106	Hopatcong, L. (hō-păt'kong)	NJ (New York In.)	40·57 N	74·38 W
101	Hope (hōp)	Ak.	60·54 N	149·48 W
117	Hope	Ar.	33·41 N	93·35 W
93	Hope	Can.	49·23 N	121·26 W
108	Hope	ND	47·17 N	97·45 W
91	Hopedale (hōp'dāl)	Can.	55·26 N	60·11 W
99	Hopedale (hōp'dāl)	Ma. (In.)	42·08 N	71·33 W
126	Hopelchén (o-pĕl-chĕ'n)	Mex. (In.)	19·47 N	89·51 W
91	Hopes Advance, C. (hōps ăd-văns')	Can.	61·05 N	69·35 W
204	Hopetoun (hōp'toun)	Austl.	33·50 S	120·15 E
121	Hopewell (hōp'wĕl)	Va.	37·14 N	77·15 W
212	Hopetown (hōp'toun)	S. Afr.	29·35 S	24·10 E
115	Hopi Ind. Res. (hō'pē)	Az.	36·20 N	110·30 W
113	Hopkins (hŏp'-kĭns)	Mn. (Minneapolis, St. Paul In.)	44·55 N	93·24 W
120	Hopkinsville (hŏp'-kĭns-vĭl)	Ky.	36·50 N	87·28 W
99	Hopkinton (hŏp'-kĭn-tŭn)	Ma. (In.)	42·14 N	71·31 W
110	Hoquiam (hō'kwĭ-ăm)	Wa.	47·00 N	123·53 W
156	Horby (hûr'bü)	Swe.	55·50 N	13·41 E
127	Horconcitos (ŏr-kōn-sē'-tōs)	Pan.	8·18 N	82·11 W
218	Hordio	Som. (Horn of Afr. In.)	10·43 N	51·05 E
158	Horgen (hôr'gĕn)	Switz.	47·16 N	8·35 E
109	Horicon (hŏr'ĭ-kŏn)	Wi.	43·26 N	88·40 W
186	Hormuz, Str. of (hôr'mŭz')	Asia	26·30 N	56·30 E
	Horn, C., see Hornos, Cabo de			
205	Horn (Is.) (hôrn)	Austl.	10·30 S	143·30 E
150	Hornavan (L.)	Swe.	65·54 N	16·17 E
149	Horneburg (hōr'nĕ-bŏŏrgh)	F.R.G. (Hamburg In.)	53·30 N	9·35 E
105	Hornell (hôr-nĕl')	NY	42·10 N	77·40 W
90	Horn Mts.	Can.	62·12 N	120·29 W
136	Hornos, C. de (Horn, C.) (kà'-bô-dĕ-ŏ'r-nôs) (kā'p-hŏr'n)	Chile	56·00 S	67·00 W
202	Hornsby (hôrnz'bĭ)	Austl. (Sydney In.)	33·43 S	151·06 E
156	Hornslandet (I.)	Swe.	61·40 N	17·58 E
136	Horqueta (ŏr-kĕ'tä)	Par.	23·20 S	57·00 W
116	Horse Cr. (hôrs)	Co.	38·49 N	103·48 W
108	Horse Cr.	Wy.	41·33 N	104·39 W
99	Horse Is.	Can.	50·11 N	55·45 W
156	Horsens (hôrs'ĕns)	Den.	55·50 N	9·49 E
112	Horseshoe B. (hôrs-shōō)	Can. (Vancouver In.)	49·23 N	123·16 W
148	Horsforth (hôrs'fŭrth)	Eng.	53·50 N	1·38 W
203	Horsham, (hôr'shăm) (hôrs'ăm)	Austl.	36·42 S	142·17 E
149	Horst (hôrst)	F.R.G. (Hamburg In.)	53·49 N	9·37 E
156	Horten (hôr'tĕn)	Nor.	59·26 N	10·27 E
118	Horton (hôr'tŭn)	Ks.	39·38 N	95·32 W
101	Horton (R.) (hôr'tŭn)	Ak.	68·38 N	122·00 W
148	Horwich (hŏr'ĭch)	Eng.	53·36 N	2·33 W
215	Hoséré Vokré (Mtn.)	Cam.	8·20 N	13·15 E
195	Hososhima (hō'sô-shē'mä)	Jap.	32·25 N	131·40 E
136	Hoste (ôs'tā) (I.)	Chile	55·20 S	70·45 W
124	Hostotipaquillo (ôs-tō'tĭ-pä-kēl'yō)	Mex.	21·09 N	104·05 W
195	Hota (hō'tä)	Jap. (Tōkyō In.)	35·08 N	139·50 E
188	Hotan (hwô-tän)	China	37·11 N	79·50 E
188	Hotan (R.)	China	39·09 N	81·08 E
129	Hoto Mayor (ô-tô-mä-yō'r)	Dom. Rep.	18·45 N	69·10 W
101	Hot Springs (hŏt sprĭngs)	Ak.	65·00 N	150·20 W
117	Hot Springs	Ar.	34·29 N	93·02 W
108	Hot Springs	SD	43·28 N	103·32 W
105	Hot Springs	Va.	38·00 N	79·55 W
117	Hot Springs Natl. Park	Ar.	34·30 N	93·00 W
129	Hotte, Massif de la (Mts.)	Hai.	18·25 N	74·00 W
114	Hotville (hŏt'-vĭl)	Ca.	32·50 N	115·24 W
161	Houdan (ōō-dän')	Fr. (Paris In.)	48·47 N	1·36 E
109	Houghton (hŏ'tŭn)	Mi.	47·06 N	88·36 W
104	Houghton (L.)	Mi.	44·20 N	84·45 W
161	Houilles (ōō-yĕs')	Fr. (Paris In.)	48·55 N	2·11 E
191	Houjie (hwô-jyĕ)	China (Canton In.)	22·58 N	113·39 E
98	Houlton (hōl'tŭn)	Me.	46·07 N	67·50 W
119	Houma (hōō'mà)	La.	29·36 N	90·43 W
214	Houndé	Upper Volta	11·30 N	3·31 W
105	Housatonic (R.) (hōō-sà-tŏn'ĭk)	Ct.-Ma.	41·50 N	73·25 W
113	House Springs (hous sprĭngs)	Mo. (St. Louis In.)	38·24 N	90·34 W
120	Houston (hūs'tŭn)	Ms.	33·53 N	89·00 W
119	Houston	Tx. (In.)	29·46 N	95·21 W
119	Houston Ship Chan.	Tx. (In.)	29·38 N	94·57 W
212	Houtbaai	S. Afr. (In.)	34·03 S	18·22 E
204	Houtman Rocks (Is.) (hout'män)	Austl.	28·15 S	112·45 E
190	Houzhen (hwô-jŭn)	China	36·59 N	118·59 E
154	Hove (hōv)	Eng.	50·50 N	0·09 W
115	Hovenweep Natl. Mon. (hō'v'n-wēp)	Co.-Ut.	37·27 N	108·50 W
117	Howard (hou'ărd)	Ks.	37·27 N	96·10 W
108	Howard	SD	44·01 N	97·31 W
148	Howden (hou'dĕn)	Eng.	53·44 N	0·52 W
203	Howe, C. (hou)	Austl.	37·30 S	150·40 E
104	Howell (hou'ĕl)	Mi.	42·40 N	84·00 W
92	Howe Sd.	Can.	49·22 N	123·18 W
89	Howick (hou'ĭk)	Can. (Montreal In.)	45·11 N	73·51 W
213	Howick	S. Afr. (Natal In.)	29·29 S	30·16 E
198	Howland (I.) (hou'lănd)	Oceania	1·00 N	176·00 W
184	Howrah (hou'rä)	India (In.)	22·33 N	88·20 E
93	Howse Pk.	Can.	51·30 N	116·40 W
92	Howson Pk.	Can.	54·25 N	127·45 W
117	Hoxie (kŏh'sĭ)	Ar.	36·03 N	91·00 W
154	Hoy (I.) (hoi)	Scot.	58·53 N	3·10 W
195	Hōya	Jap. (Tōkyō In.)	35·45 N	139·35 E
148	Hoylake (hoi-lāk')	Eng.	53·23 N	3·11 W
158	Hradec Králové (hrà'dĕts krä'lô-vā)	Czech.	50·14 N	15·50 E
159	Hranice (hrän'yĕ-tsĕ)	Czech.	49·33 N	17·45 E
159	Hrinová (hrĕn'yô-vä)	Czech.	48·36 N	19·32 E
159	Hron R.	Czech.	48·22 N	18·42 E
159	Hrubieszów (hrōō-byā'shōōf)	Pol.	50·48 N	23·54 E
164	Hrvatska (Croatia) (Reg.) (hr-väts'kä)	Yugo.	45·24 N	15·18 E
188	Hsawnhsup	Bur.	24·29 N	94·45 E
190	Hsiaoku Ho (R.) (sĭou'gōō hŭ)	China	36·29 N	120·06 E
193	Hsich'ang	China	26·50 N	102·25 E
192	Hsiliao (R.)	China	43·23 N	121·40 E
184	Hsinchiang (Mts.)	China	41·52 N	81·20 E
193	Hsinchu (hsĭn'chōō')	Taiwan	24·48 N	121·00 E
193	Hsinkao Shan (Mtn.)	Taiwan	23·38 N	121·05 E
134	Huacho (wä'chō)	Peru	11·13 S	77·29 W
192	Huadian (hwä-dĭĕn)	China	42·38 N	126·45 E
190	Huai'an (hwī-än)	China	33·31 N	119·11 E
189	Huai (R.) (hwī)	China	32·07 N	114·38 E
192	Huailai	China	40·20 N	115·45 E
190	Huailin (hwī-lĭn)	China	31·27 N	117·36 E
190	Huainan	China	32·38 N	117·02 E
190	Huaiyang (hōōäī'yang)	China	33·45 N	114·54 E
190	Huaiyuan (hwī-yüän)	China	32·53 N	117·13 E
124	Huajicori (wä-jē-kō'rē)	Mex.	22·41 N	105·24 W
125	Huajuapan de León (wäj-wä'päm dā lā-ón')	Mex.	17·46 N	97·45 W
115	Hualapai Ind. Res. (wäl'apĭ)	Az.	35·41 N	113·38 W
115	Hualapai Mts.	Az.	34·53 N	113·54 W
193	Hualien (hwä'lyĕn')	Taiwan	23·58 N	121·58 E
134	Huallaga (R.) (wäl-yä'gä)	Peru	8·12 S	76·34 W
134	Huamachuco (wä-mä-chōō'kō)	Peru	7·52 S	78·11 W
125	Huamantla (wä-män'tlà)	Mex.	19·18 N	97·54 W
216	Huambo (Nova Lisboa)	Ang.	12·44 S	15·47 E
124	Huamuxtitlán (wä-mōōs-tē-tlän')	Mex.	17·49 N	98·38 W
188	Huan (R.) (hûän)	China	36·45 N	106·30 E
134	Huancavelica (wän'kä-vā-lē'kä)	Peru	12·47 S	75·02 W
134	Huancayo (wän-kä'yô)	Peru	12·09 S	75·04 W
134	Huanchaca (wän-chä'kä)	Bol.	20·09 S	66·40 W
189	Huang (Yellow River) (hûäŋ)	China	35·06 N	113·39 E
189	Huang, Old Beds of the (Yellow) (R.)	China	40·28 N	106·34 E
190	Huangchuan (hûäŋ-chûän)	China	32·07 N	115·01 E
190	Huang He, Old Course of the (R.) (hûäŋ-hŭ)	China	34·28 N	116·59 E
190	Huanghua (hûäŋ-hwä)	China	38·28 N	117·18 E
192	Huanghuadian (hûäŋ-hwä-dĭĕn)	China (In.)	39·22 N	116·53 E
190	Huangli (hōōäɴg'lē)	China	31·39 N	119·42 E
191	Huangpu (hûäŋ-pōō)	China (Canton In.)	22·44 N	113·20 E
191	Huangpu (R.)	China (Shanghai In.)	30·56 N	121·16 E
190	Huangqiao (hûän-chyou)	China	32·15 N	120·13 E
190	Huang Xian (hûäŋ shyĕn)	China	37·39 N	120·32 E
188	Huangyuan (hûäŋ-yüän)	China	37·00 N	101·01 E
192	Huanren (hûän-rŭn)	China	41·10 N	125·30 E
134	Huánuco (wä-nōō'kô)	Peru	9·50 S	76·17 W
134	Huánuni (wä-nōō'nē)	Bol.	18·11 S	66·43 W
127	Huapí, Montañas de (Mts.) (môn-tä'n-yäs-dĕ-wà'-pē')	Nic.	12·35 N	84·43 W
124	Huaquechula (wä-kĕ-chōō'-lä)	Mex.	18·44 N	98·37 W
134	Huaral (wä-rä'l)	Peru	11·28 S	77·11 W
134	Huarás (ōōä'rà's)	Peru	9·32 S	77·29 W
134	Huascarán, Nevs. (Pk.) (wäs-kä-rän')	Peru	9·05 S	77·50 W
136	Huasco (wäs'kō)	Chile	28·32 S	71·16 W
125	Huatla de Jiménez (wà'-tlä-dĕ-ĸē-mĕ'-nĕz)	Mex.	18·08 N	96·49 W
125	Huatlatlauch (wä'tlä-tlä-ōō'ch)	Mex.	18·40 N	98·04 W
125	Huatusco (wä-tōōs'kô)	Mex.	19·09 N	96·57 W
124	Huauchinango (wä-ōō-chê-näŋ'gô)	Mex.	20·09 N	98·03 W
127	Huaunta (wä-ōō'n-tä)	Nic.	13·30 N	83·32 W
127	Huaunta, Laguna (L.) (lä-gōō'-nä-wä-ōō'n-tä)	Nic.	13·35 N	83·46 W
124	Huautla (wä-ōō'tlä)	Mex.	21·04 N	98·13 W
190	Hua Xian (hwä shyĕn)	China	35·34 N	114·32 E
124	Huaynamota, Rió de (R.) (rē'ō-dĕ-wäy-nä-mô'tä)	Mex.	22·10 N	104·36 W
125	Huazolotitlán (Santa María) (wäzô-lô-tē-tlän')	Mex.	16·18 N	97·55 W
99	Hubbard (hŭb'ẽrd)	NH (In.)	42·53 N	71·12 W
119	Hubbard	Tx.	31·53 N	96·46 W
104	Hubbard (L.)	Mi.	44·45 N	83·30 W
118	Hubbard Creek Res.	Tx.	32·50 N	98·55 W
189	Hubei (Prov.) (hōō-bā)	China	31·20 N	111·58 E
185	Hubli (hŏŏ'blē)	India	15·25 N	75·09 E
161	Hückeswagen (hü'kĕs-vä'gĕn)	F.R.G. (Ruhr In.)	51·09 N	7·20 E
148	Hucknall (hŭk'năl)	Eng.	53·02 N	1·12 W
148	Huddersfield (hŭd'ẽrz-fēld)	Eng.	53·39 N	1·47 W
156	Hudiksvall (hōō'dĭks-väl)	Swe.	61·44 N	17·05 E
89	Hudson (hŭd'sŭn)	Can. (Montreal In.)	45·26 N	74·08 W
99	Hudson	Ma. (In.)	42·24 N	71·34 W
104	Hudson	Mi.	41·50 N	84·15 W
105	Hudson	NY	42·15 N	73·45 W
107	Hudson	Oh. (Cleveland In.)	41·15 N	81·27 W
113	Hudson	Wi. (Minneapolis, St. Paul In.)	44·59 N	92·45 W
95	Hudson Bay	Can.	52·52 N	102·25 W
91	Hudson B.	Can.	60·15 N	85·30 W
105	Hudson Falls	NY	43·20 N	73·30 W
89	Hudson Heights	Can. (Montreal In.)	45·28 N	74·09 W
104	Hudson R.	NY	41·55 N	73·55 W
91	Hudson Str.	Can.	63·25 N	74·05 W
193	Hue (ü-ā')	Viet.	16·28 N	107·42 E
162	Huebra (R.) (wĕ'brä)	Sp.	40·44 N	6·17 W
126	Huehuetenango (wā-wà-tà-näŋ'gô)	Guat.	15·19 N	91·26 W
124	Huejotzingo (wā-hô-tzĭŋ'gō)	Mex.	19·09 N	98·24 W
124	Huejúcar (wā-hōō'kär)	Mex.	22·26 N	103·12 W

ng-sing; ŋ-baŋk; ɴ-nasalized n; nŏd; cŏmmit; ōld; ôbey; ôrder; fōōd; fŏŏt; ou-out; s-soft; sh-dish; th-thin; pūre; ûnite; ûrn; stŭd; circŭs; ü-as "y" in study; '-indeterminate vowel.

292 Huejuquilla el Alto — Ilukste PRONOUNCING INDEX

Page	Name Pronunciation Region	Lat. °′	Long. °′
124	Huejuquilla el Alto (wā-hōō-kēl'yä ĕl äl'tō). Mex.	22·42 N	102·54 W
124	Huejutla (wā-hōō'tlä). . . . . . . Mex.	21·08 N	98·26 W
162	Huelma (wĕl'mä). . . . . Sp.	37·39 N	3·36 W
162	Huelva (wĕl'vä). . . . . Sp.	37·16 N	6·58 W
162	Huercal-Overa (wĕr-käl' ō-vā'rä) Sp.	37·12 N	1·58 W
116	Huerfano (R.) (wâr'fȧ-nō). . . . . Co.	37·41 N	105·13 W
163	Huésca (wĕs-kä). . . . . Sp.	42·07 N	0·25 W
162	Huéscar (wās'kär). . . . . Sp.	37·50 N	2·34 W
124	Huetamo de Múñez (wå-tä'mō dā-mōōn'yĕz). Mex.	18·34 N	100·53 W
162	Huete (wā'tå). . . . . Sp.	40·09 N	2·42 W
124	Hueycatenango (wĕy-kå-tĕ-nä'n-gô). Mex.	17·31 N	99·10 W
125	Hueytlalpan (wā'ī-tlăl'păn). . Mex.	20·03 N	97·41 W
106	Hueytown. . . Al. (Birmingham In.)	33·28 N	86·59 W
106	Huffman (hŭf'mån) Al. (Birmingham In.)	33·36 N	86·42 W
116	Hugh Butler (L.). . . . . Ne.	40·21 N	100·40 W
205	Hughenden (hū'ĕn-dĕn). . . . . Austl.	20·58 S	144·13 E
204	Hughes (hūz). . . . . Austl.	30·45 S	129·30 E
106	Hughesville. . . Md. (Baltimore In.)	38·32 N	76·48 W
113	Hugo (hū'gō) Mn. (Minneapolis, St. Paul In.)	45·10 N	93·00 W
117	Hugo. . . . . Ok.	34·01 N	95·32 W
116	Hugoton (hū'gō-tǎn). . . . . Ks.	37·10 N	101·28 W
190	Hugou (hōō-gō). . . . . China	33·22 N	117·07 E
124	Huichapan (wē-chä-pän'). . . . Mex.	20·22 N	99·39 W
134	Huila (Dept.) (wē'lä). . . Col. (In.)	3·10 N	75·20 W
134	Huila, Nevado de (Pk.) (nĕ-vä-dô-de-wē'lä). Col. (In.)	2·59 N	76·01 W
193	Huilai. . . . . China	23·02 N	116·18 E
193	Huili. China	26·48 N	102·20 E
125	Huimanguillo (wē-män-gēl'yō) Mex.	17·50 N	93·16 W
190	Huimin (hōōĭ mĭn). . . . . China	37·29 N	117·32 E
125	Huitzilac (ōōē't-zē-lä'k). Mex. (In.)	19·01 N	99·16 W
124	Huitzitzilingo (wē-tzē-tzē-lē'n-go) Mex.	21·11 N	98·42 W
124	Huitzuco (wê-tzōō'kō). . . . . . . Mex.	18·16 N	99·20 W
125	Huixquilucan (ōōē'x-kē-lōō-kä'n) Mex. (In.)	19·21 N	99·22 W
125	Huixtla (wēs'tlä). . . . . Mex.	15·12 N	92·28 W
193	Huiyang. . . . . China	23·05 N	114·25 E
193	Hukou (hōō-kō). . . . . China	29·58 N	116·20 E
192	Hulan (hōō'län'). . . . . China	45·58 N	126·32 E
192	Hulan (R.). . . . . China	42·20 N	126·30 E
194	Hulin (hōō'lĭn'). . . . . China	45·45 N	133·25 E
89	Hull (hŭl). . . . . . Can. (Ottawa In.)	45·26 N	75·43 W
99	Hull. . . . . Ma. (In.)	42·18 N	70·54 W
148	Hull (R.). . . . . Eng.	53·47 N	0·20 W
149	Hulst (hōōlst) Neth. (Amsterdam In.)	51·17 N	4·01 E
192	Huludao (hōō-lōō-dou). . . . . . China	40·40 N	122·55 E
192	Hulun Nur (L.) (hōō-lōōn nōōr) China	48·50 N	116·45 E
218	Ḩulwān (hĕl'wän). Egypt (Nile In.)	29·51 N	31·20 E
123	Humacao (ōō-mä-kä'ō) P. R. (Puerto Rico In.)	18·09 N	65·49 W
124	Humaitá (ōō-mä-ē-tä'). . . . . . Braz.	7·37 S	62·58 W
134	Humaitá. . . . . Par.	27·08 S	58·18 W
212	Humansdorp (hōō'mäns-dôrp) S. Afr.	33·57 S	24·45 E
212	Humbe (hōōm'bâ). . . . . Ang.	16·50 S	14·55 E
154	Humber (L.) (hŭm'bēr). . . . . . Eng.	53·38 N	0·40 W
89	Humber (R.). . Can. (Toronto In.)	43·53 N	79·40 W
99	Humbermouth (hŭm'bēr-mŭth) Can.	48·58 N	57·55 W
119	Humble (hŭm'b'l). . . . . Tx.	29·58 N	95·15 W
94	Humboldt (hŭm'bōlt). . . . . . . Can.	52·12 N	105·07 W
109	Humboldt. . . . . Ia.	42·43 N	94·11 W
117	Humboldt. . . . . Ks.	37·48 N	95·26 W
117	Humboldt. . . . . Ne.	40·10 N	95·57 W
102	Humboldt (R.). . . . . U. S.	40·30 N	116·50 W
110	Humboldt B. . . . . Ca.	40·48 N	124·25 W
110	Humboldt R., East Fork. . . . . Nv.	40·59 N	115·21 W
110	Humboldt R., North Fork. . . . Nv.	41·25 N	115·45 W
120	Humbolt. . . . . Tn.	35·47 N	88·55 W
114	Humbolt Ra. . . . . Nv.	40·12 N	118·16 W
114	Humbolt Salt Marsh. . . . . Nv.	39·49 N	117·41 W
114	Humbolt Sink. . . . . Nv.	39·58 N	118·54 W
191	Humenchai. . China (Canton In.)	22·49 N	113·39 E
115	Humphreys Pk. (hŭm'frĭs). . . . Az.	35·20 N	111·40 W
158	Humpolec (hōōm'pō-lĕts). . Czech.	49·33 N	15·21 E
126	Humuya R. (ōō-mōō'yä). . . . Hond.	14·38 N	87·36 W
150	Hunaflói (B.) (hōō'nä-flō'ĭ). . . . Ice.	65·41 N	20·44 W
189	Hunan (Prov.) (hōō'nän'). . . China	28·08 N	111·25 E
189	Hunchun (hōōn-chûn). . . . . . China	42·53 N	130·34 E
165	Hunedoara (kōō'nĕd-wä'rȧ). Rom.	45·45 N	22·54 E
146	Hungary (hŭŋ'gȧ-rĭ). . . . . Eur.	46·44 N	17·55 E
203	Hungerford (hŭn'gēr-fērd). . Austl.	28·50 S	144·32 E
111	Hungry Horse Res. (hŭŋ'gȧ-rĭ hôrs). Mt.	48·11 N	113·30 W
158	Hunsrück (Mts.) (hōōns'rûk) F.R.G.	49·43 N	7·12 E
158	Hunte R. (hōōn'tē). . . . . . . F.R.G.	52·45 N	8·26 E
205	Hunter Is. (hŭn-tēr). . . . . . . Austl.	40·33 S	143·36 E
104	Huntingburg (hŭnt'ĭng-bûrg). . In.	38·15 N	86·55 W
105	Huntingdon (hŭnt'ĭng-dŭn). . Can.	45·10 N	74·05 W
112	Huntingdon. Can. (Vancouver In.)	49·00 N	122·16 W
120	Huntingdon. . . . . Tn.	36·00 N	88·23 W
148	Huntingdon and Peterborough (Co.). Eng.	52·26 N	0·19 W
104	Huntington. . . . . In.	40·55 N	85·30 W
105	Huntington. . . . . Pa.	40·30 N	78·00 W
104	Huntington. . . . . WV	38·25 N	82·25 W
113	Huntington Beach Ca. (Los Angeles In.)	33·39 N	118·00 W
113	Huntington Park Ca. (Los Angeles In.)	33·59 N	118·14 W
106	Huntington Station NY (New York In.)	40·51 N	73·25 W
111	Huntley. . . . . Mt.	45·54 N	108·01 W
120	Huntsville (hŭnts'-vĭl). . . . . Al.	34·44 N	86·36 W
105	Huntsville. . . . . Can.	45·20 N	79·15 W
117	Huntsville. . . . . Mo.	39·24 N	92·32 W
119	Huntsville. . . . . Tx.	30·44 N	95·34 W
113	Huntsville. Ut. (Salt Lake City In.)	41·16 N	111·46 W
125	Hunucmá (hōō-nōōk-mä'). . . Mex.	21·01 N	89·54 W
190	Huolu (hōōŭ lōō). . . . . China	38·05 N	114·20 E
197	Huon G. . . . . Pap. N. Gui.	7·15 S	147·45 E
190	Huoqiu (hwô-chyô). . . . . China	32·19 N	116·17 E
193	Huoshan (hwô-shän). . . . . . . China	31·30 N	116·25 E
183	Ḩuraydin, Wādī (R.) Egypt (Palestine In.)	30·55 N	34·12 E
104	Hurd, C. (hûrd). . . . . Can.	45·15 N	81·45 W
109	Hurley (hûr'lĭ). . . . . Wi.	46·26 N	90·11 W
136	Hurlingham (ōō'r-lēn-gäm) Arg. (Buenos Aires In.)	34·20 S	58·38 W
104	Huron (hū'rŏn). . . . . Oh.	41·20 N	82·35 W
108	Huron. . . . . SD	44·22 N	98·15 W
103	Huron, L. (hū'rŏn). . . . . U. S.-Can.	45·15 N	82·40 W
109	Huron Mts. (hū'rŏn). . . . . Mi.	46·47 N	87·52 W
107	Huron R. . . . . Mi. (Detroit In.)	42·12 N	83·26 W
101	Hurricane (hŭr'ĭ-kān). . . . . Ak.	63·00 N	149·30 W
115	Hurricane. . . . . Ut.	37·10 N	113·20 W
128	Hurricane Flats (Shoal) (hŭ-rĭ-kăn flăts). Ba.	23·35 N	78·30 W
150	Húsavik. . . . . Ice.	66·00 N	17·10 W
167	Husi (kōōsh'). . . . . Sov. Un.	46·52 N	28·04 E
156	Huskvarna (hōōsk-vär'nȧ). . . Swe.	57·48 N	14·16 E
113	Hurst. Tx. (Dallas, Ft. Worth In.)	32·48 N	97·12 W
158	Husum (hōō'zōōm). . . . . F.R.G.	54·29 N	9·04 E
113	Hutchins (hŭch'ĭnz) Tx. (Dallas, Fort Worth In.)	32·38 N	96·43 W
116	Hutchinson (hŭch'ĭn-sŭn). . . . . Ks.	38·02 N	97·56 W
109	Hutchinson. . . . . Mn.	44·53 N	94·23 W
192	Hut'o Ho (R.) (hōō'tō'hō'). China	38·10 N	114·00 E
155	Huy (û-ē') (hû'ē). . . . . Bel.	50·33 N	5·14 E
150	Hvannadalshnukur (Mtn.). . . . Ice.	64·09 N	16·46 W
164	Hvar (I.) (кhvär). . . . . Yugo.	43·08 N	16·28 E
194	Hwangju (hwäng'jōō'). . . . . . . Kor.	38·39 N	125·49 E
106	Hyattsville (hī'ăt's-vil) Md. (Baltimore In.)	38·57 N	76·58 W
101	Hydaburg (hī-dă'bûrg). . . . . . . Ak.	55·12 N	132·49 W
148	Hyde (hīd). . . . . Eng.	53·27 N	2·05 W
185	Hyderābād (hī-dēr-â-băd'). . India	17·29 N	79·28 E
184	Hyderābād (hī-dēr-â-băd'). . . Pak.	25·29 N	68·28 E
185	Hyderabad (State). . . . . India	23·29 N	76·50 E
161	Hyéres (ē-âr'). . . . . Fr.	43·09 N	6·08 E
161	Hyéres, Iles d' (Is.) (ēl'dyâr'). . Fr.	42·57 N	6·17 E
194	Hyesanjin (hyĕ'sän-jĭn'). . . . . Kor.	41·11 N	128·12 E
104	Hymera (hī-mē'rȧ). . . . . In.	39·10 N	87·20 W
111	Hyndman Pk. (hīnd'mȧn). . . . . Id.	43·38 N	114·04 W
195	Hyōgo (Pref.) (hĭyō'gō) Jap. (Ōsaka In.)	34·54 N	135·15 E
100	Hythe. Can.	55·20 N	119·33 W

I

Page	Name Pronunciation Region	Lat. °′	Long. °′
195	Ia (R.) (ē'ä). . . . . Jap. (Ōsaka In.)	34·54 N	135·34 E
165	Ialomita (R.). . . . . Rom.	44·37 N	26·42 E
159	Iasi (yä'shē). . . . . Rom.	47·10 N	27·40 E
197	Iba (ē'bä). . . . . Phil. (In.)	15·20 N	119·59 E
215	Ibadan (ē-bä'dän). . . . . Nig.	7·17 N	3·30 E
134	Ibagué (ē-bä-gā'). . . . . . . Col. (In.)	4·27 N	75·13 W
165	Ibar (R.) (ē'bär). . . . . Yugo.	43·22 N	20·35 E
195	Ibaraki (ē-bä'rä-gē) Jap. (Ōsaka In.)	34·49 N	135·35 E
134	Ibarra (ē-bär'rä). . . . . Ec.	0·19 N	78·08 W
209	Iberian Pen. . . . . Port.-Sp.	41·00 N	0·07 W
98	Iberville (ē-bår-vēl') (ĭ'bēr-vĭl) Can.	45·14 N	73·01 W
215	Ibi (ē'bē). . . . . Nig.	8·12 N	9·45 E
135	Ibiapaba, Serra da (Mts.) (sĕ'r-rä-dä-ē-byä-pȧ'bä). Braz.	3·30 S	40·55 W
163	Ibiza (ē-bē'thä). . . . . Sp.	38·55 N	1·24 E
163	Ibiza, Isla de (Iviza I.) (ē's-lä-dĕ-ē-bē'zä). Sp.	39·07 N	1·05 E
217	Ibo (ē'bō). . . . . Moz.	12·20 S	40·35 E
216	Iboundji, Mont (Mtn.). . . . Gabon	1·08 S	11·48 E
218	Ibrāhīm, Būr (B.). . . . . Egypt	29·57 N	32·33 E
186	Ibrahim, Jabal (Mtn.). . . . Sau. Ar.	20·31 N	41·17 E
217	Ibwe Munyama. . . . . Zambia	16·09 S	28·34 E
134	Ica (ē'kå). . . . . Peru	14·09 S	75·42 W
134	Icá (R.) (ē-kä'). . . . . Braz.	2·56 S	69·12 W
134	Içana (ē-sä'nä). . . . . Braz.	0·15 N	67·19 W
110	Ice Harbor Dam. . . . . Wa.	46·15 N	118·54 W
146	Iceland (īs'lȧnd). . . . . Eur.	65·12 N	19·45 W
195	Ichibusayama (Mt.) (ē'chē-bōō'sȧ-yä'mä). Jap.	32·19 N	131·08 E
195	Ichihara. . . . . Jap. (Tōkyō In.)	35·31 N	140·05 E
195	Ichikawa (ē'chē-kä'wä) Jap. (Tōkyō In.)	35·44 N	139·54 E
195	Ichinomiya (ē'chē-nō-mē'yȧ). Jap.	35·19 N	136·49 E
195	Ichinomoto (ē-chē'nō-mō-tō) Jap. (Ōsaka In.)	34·37 N	135·50 E
167	Ichnya (ĭch'nyä). . . . . Sov. Un.	50·47 N	32·23 E
135	Icó (ē-kô'). . . . . Braz.	6·25 S	38·43 W
134	Icutú, Cerro (Mtn.) (sĕ'r-rô-ē-kōō-tōō') Ven.	7·07 N	65·30 W
101	Icy C. (ī'sĭ) . . . . Ak.	70·20 N	161·40 W
117	Idabel (ī'dȧ-bĕl). . . . . Ok.	33·52 N	94·47 W
108	Idagrove (ī'dȧ-grōv). . . . . Ia.	42·22 N	95·29 W
215	Idah (ē'dä). . . . . Nig.	7·07 N	6·43 E
102	Idaho (State) (ī'dȧ-hō). . . . . . U. S.	44·00 N	115·10 W
111	Idaho Falls. . . . . Id.	43·30 N	112·01 W
116	Idaho Springs. . . . . Co.	39·43 N	105·32 W
162	Idanha-a-Nova (ē-dän'yȧ-ä-nō'vȧ). Port.	39·58 N	7·13 W
188	Ideriin Gol (R.). . . . . Mong.	48·58 N	98·38 E
218	Idfū (ĕd'fōō). . . . . Egypt (Nile In.)	24·57 N	32·53 E
165	Idhra (I.). . . . . Grc.	37·20 N	23·30 E
196	Idi (ē'dē). . . . . Indon.	4·58 N	97·47 E
218	Idkū (ĕd'kōō). . . . Egypt (Nile In.)	31·18 N	30·20 E
218	Idkū L. . . . . Egypt (Nile In.)	31·13 N	30·22 E
148	Idle (R.) (īd''l). . . . . Eng.	53·22 N	0·56 W
164	Idriaj (ē'drē-ȧ). . . . . Yugo.	46·01 N	14·01 E
213	Idutywa (ē-dōō-tī'wȧ) S. Afr. (Natal In.)	32·06 S	28·18 E
155	Ieper. . . . . Bel.	50·50 N	2·53 E
164	Ierápetra. . . . . Grc. (In.)	35·01 N	25·48 E
164	Iesi (yā'sē). . . . . It.	43·37 N	13·20 E
215	Ife. . . . . Nig.	7·30 N	4·30 E
215	Iferouâne (ēf'rōō-än'). . . . . . . Niger	19·04 N	8·24 E
215	Iforas, Adrar des (Mts.) (ä-drär') Alg.-Mali	19·55 N	2·00 E
217	Igalula. Tan.	5·14 S	33·00 E
172	Igarka (ē-gär'kȧ). . . . . Sov. Un.	67·22 N	86·16 E
165	Ighil Izane. . . . . Alg.	35·43 N	0·43 E
164	Iglesias (ē-lĕ'syôs). . . . . It.	39·20 N	8·34 E
210	Igli (ē-glē'). . . . . Alg.	30·32 N	2·15 W
91	Igloolik. . . . . Can.	69·33 N	81·18 W
112	Ignacio (ĭg-nä'cĭ-ō) Ca. (San Francisco In.)	38·05 N	122·32 W
136	Iguaçu (R.) (ē-gwä-sōō') Braz. (Rio de Janeiro In.)	22·42 S	43·19 W
124	Iguala (ē-gwä'lä). . . . . Mex.	18·18 N	99·34 W
163	Igualada (ē-gwä-lä'dä). . . . . Sp.	41·35 N	1·38 E
136	Iguassu (R.) (ē-gwä-sōō') . . . Braz.	25·45 S	52·30 W
136	Iguassu Falls. . . . . Braz.	25·40 S	54·16 W
137	Iguatama (ē-gwä-tá'mä) Braz. (Rio de Janeiro In.)	20·13 S	45·40 W
135	Iguatu (ē-gwä-tōō'). . . . . Braz.	6·22 S	39·17 W
210	Iguidi, Erg (Dune). . . . . Alg.	26·22 N	6·53 W
197	Iguig (ē-gēg'). . . . . Phil. (In.)	17·46 N	121·44 E
215	Ihiala. . . . . Nig.	5·51 N	6·51 E
195	Iida (ē'ē-dȧ). . . . . Jap.	35·39 N	137·53 E
170	Iijoki (R.) (ē'yō'kĭ). . . . . Fin.	65·28 N	27·00 E
195	Iizuka (ē'ē-zōō-kä). . . . . Jap.	33·39 N	130·39 E
215	Ijebu-Ode (ē-jĕ'bōō ōdȧ). . . . . Nig.	6·50 N	3·56 E
155	IJsselmeer (L.) (ī'sĕl-mār) . . Neth.	52·46 N	5·14 E
157	Ikaalinen (ē'kä-lĭ-nĕn). . . . . . . Fin.	61·47 N	22·55 E
165	Ikaría (I.) (ē-kä'ryȧ). . . . . Grc.	37·43 N	26·07 E
195	Ikeda (ē'kȧ-dä). . . Jap. (Ōsaka In.)	34·49 N	135·26 E
215	Ikerre. . . . . Nig.	7·31 N	5·14 E
165	Ikhtiman (ēk'tē-män). . . . . Bul.	42·26 N	23·49 E
195	Iki (I.) (ē'kē). . . . . Jap.	33·46 N	129·44 E
195	Ikoma. . . . . Jap. (Ōsaka In.)	34·41 N	135·43 E
212	Ikoma (ē-kō'mä). . . . . Tan.	2·08 S	34·47 E
174	Iksha (ĭk'shȧ) Sov. Un. (Moscow In.)	56·10 N	37·30 E
215	Ila. . . . . Nig.	8·01 N	4·55 E
197	Ilagen (ē-lä'gän). . . . . . . Phil. (In.)	17·09 N	121·52 E
193	Ilan (ē'län'). . . . . Taiwan	24·50 N	121·42 E
159	Iława (ē-lä'vȧ). . . . . Pol.	53·35 N	19·36 E
94	Île-á-la-Crosse. . . . . Can.	55·34 N	108·00 W
216	Ilebo (Port-Franqui). . . . . Zaire	4·19 S	20·35 E
171	Ilek (ē'lyĕk). . . . . Sov. Un.	51·30 N	53·10 E
171	Ilek (R.). . . . . Sov. Un.	51·20 N	53·10 E
89	Île-Perrot (yl-pĕ-rōt') Can. (Montreal In.)	45·21 N	73·54 W
215	Ilesha. . . . . Nig.	7·38 N	4·45 E
148	Ilford (ĭl'fērd). . Eng. (London In.)	51·33 N	0·06 E
154	Ilfracombe (ĭl-frȧ-kōōm'). . . . Eng.	51·13 N	4·08 W
137	Ilhabela (ē'lä-bĕ'lä) Braz. (Rio de Janeiro In.)	23·47 S	45·21 W
137	Ilha Grande, Baia de (B.) (ēl'yȧ grän'dĕ) Braz. (Rio de Janeiro In.)	23·17 S	44·25 W
162	Ilhavo (ēl'yȧ-vô) . . . . Port.	40·36 N	8·41 W
135	Ilhéus (ē-lĕ'ōōs). . . . . Braz.	14·52 S	39·00 W
101	Iliamna (ē-lē-ăm'nȧ). . . . . Ak.	59·45 N	155·05 W
101	Iliamna (L.). . . . . Ak.	59·25 N	155·30 W
101	Iliamna (Vol.). . . . . Ak.	60·18 N	153·25 W
172	Ilim (R.) ((ē-lyēm'). . . . . . Sov. Un.	57·28 N	103·00 E
172	Ilimsk (ē-lyêmsk'). . . . . . . Sov. Un.	56·47 N	103·43 E
197	Ilin I. (ē-lyēn'). . . . . Phil. (In.)	12·16 N	120·57 E
167	Il'intsiy. . . . . Sov. Un.	49·07 N	29·13 E
165	Iliodhrómia (I.). . . . . Grc.	39·18 N	23·35 E
105	Ilion (ĭl'ĭ-ŭn). . . . . NY	43·00 N	75·05 W
188	Ili R. (ē'lē). . . . . Sov. Un.	43·46 N	77·41 E
148	Ilkeston (ĭl'kĕs-tŭn). . . . . Eng.	52·58 N	1·19 W
134	Illampu, Nevado (Pk.) (nĕ-vȧ'dô-ēl-yäm-pōō'). Bol.	15·50 S	68·15 W
137	Illapel (ē-zhä-pĕ'l) Chile (Santiago In.)	31·37 S	71·10 W
158	Iller R. (ĭl'er). . . . . F.R.G.	47·52 N	10·06 E
134	Illimani, Nevado (Pk.) (nĕ-vȧ'dô-ēl-yē-mä'nē). Bol.	16·50 S	67·38 W
103	Illinois (State) (ĭl-ĭ-noi') (ĭl-ĭ-noiz') U. S.	40·25 N	90·40 W
117	Illinois (R.). . . . . Il.	40·52 N	89·31 W
210	Illizi. . . . . Alg.	26·35 N	8·24 E
166	Il'men', Ozero (L.) (ô'zĕ-rô el'' men'') (ĭl'mĕn). Sov. Un.	58·18 N	32·00 E
155	Ilmenau (R.) (ēl'mē-nou) . . F.R.G.	53·20 N	10·20 E
134	Ilo. . . . . Peru	17·46 S	71·13 W
126	Ilobasco (ē-lô-bäs'kô). . . . . Sal.	13·57 N	88·46 W
196	Iloilo (ē-lô-ē'lō). . . . . Phil.	10·49 N	112·33 E
126	Ilopango, L. (ē-lô-päŋ'gō). . . . . Sal.	13·48 N	88·50 W
215	Ilorin (ē-lô-rēn'). . . . . Nig.	8·30 N	4·32 E
166	Ilūkste. . . . . Sov. Un.	55·59 N	26·20 E

ăt; finăl; rāte; senâte; ärm; åsk; sofȧ; fâre; ch-choose; dh-as th in other; bē; ēvent; bĕt; recĕnt; cratēr; g-go; gh-guttural g; bĭt; ĭ-short neutral; rīde; κ-guttural k as ch in German ich;

PRONOUNCING INDEX Ilwaco — Itabapoana 293

Page	Name Pronunciation Region	Lat. °′	Long. °′
112	Ilwaco (ĭl-wā′kô) Wa. (Portland In.)	46·19 N	124·02 W
170	Ilych (R.) (ê′l′ĭch) .... Sov. Un.	62·30 N	57·30 E
195	Imabari (ē′mä-bä′rê) .... Jap.	34·05 N	132·58 E
195	Imai (ê-mī′) ..... Jap. (Ōsaka In.)	34·30 N	135·47 E
194	Iman (R.) (ê-män′) ..... Sov. Un.	45·40 N	134·31 E
170	Imandra (L.) (ē-män′drȧ) Sov. Un.	67·40 N	32·30 E
218	Imbābah (ēm-bä′bȧ) Egypt (Nile In.)	30·06 N	31·09 E
136	Imbarié (ēm-bä-ryĕ′) Braz. (Rio de Janeiro In.)	22·38 S	43·13 W
174	Imeni Morozova (ĭm-yĕ′nyĭ mô rô′zô vȧ) Sov. Un. (Leningrad In.)	59·58 N	31·02 E
166	Imeni Moskvy, Kanal (Moscow Can.) (kȧ-näl′ĭm-yă′ nĭ mŏs-kvĭ). Sov. Un.	56·33 N	37·15 E
174	Imeni Tsyurupy .... Sov. Un. (Moscow In.)	55·30 N	38·39 E
174	Imeni Vorovskogo Sov. Un. (Moscow In.)	55·43 N	38·21 E
104	Imlay City (ĭm′lā) .... Mi.	43·00 N	83·15 W
158	Immenstadt (ĭm′ĕn-shtät) .. F.R.G.	47·34 N	10·12 E
218	Immerpan (ĭmĕr-pän) ...... S. Afr. (Johannesburg & Pretoria In.)	24·29 S	29·14 E
164	Imola (ē′mô-lä) .... It.	44·19 N	11·43 E
164	Imotski (ê-môts′kê) .... Yugo.	43·25 N	17·15 E
135	Impameri .... Braz.	17·44 S	48·03 W
213	Impendle (ĭm-pĕnd′lȧ) S. Afr. (Natal In.)	29·38 S	29·54 E
164	Imperia (êm-pā′rê-ä) .... It.	43·52 N	8·00 E
107	Imperial (ĭm-pē′rĭ-ăl) Pa. (Pittsburgh In.)	40·27 N	80·15 W
114	Imperial Beach .... Ca. (In.)	32·34 N	117·08 W
115	Imperial Res. .... Az.	32·57 N	114·19 W
114	Imperial Valley .... Ca.	33·00 N	115·22 W
216	Impfondo (ĭmp-fōn′dô) ...... Con.	1·37 N	18·04 E
187	Imphāl (ĭmp′hŭl) .... India	24·42 N	94·00 E
165	Imroz (I.) (ĭm′rŏz) .... Tur.	40·10 N	25·27 E
195	Ina (R.) (ê-nä′). Jap. (Osaka In.)	34·56 N	135·21 E
114	Inaja Ind. Res. (ê-nä′hä) ...... Ca.	32·56 N	116·37 W
150	Inari (L.) .... Fin.	69·02 N	26·22 E
163	Inca (ēŋ′kä) .... Sp.	39·43 N	2·53 E
171	Ince Burun (C.) (ĭn′jȧ) ...... Tur.	42·00 N	35·00 E
194	Inch′ŏn (ĭn′chŭn) .... Kor.	37·26 N	126·46 E
164	Incudine, Mt. (Mtn.) (ēn-kōō-dē′ nȧ) (ăN-kü-dēn′). Fr.	41·53 N	9·17 E
156	Indalsälven (R.) .... Swe.	62·50 N	16·50 E
118	Indé (ēn′dȧ) .... Mex.	25·53 N	105·15 W
117	Independence (ĭn-dê-pĕn′dĕns). Ks.	37·14 N	95·42 W
113	Independence Mo. (Kansas City In.)	39·06 N	94·26 W
107	Independence. Oh. (Cleveland In.)	41·23 N	81·39 W
110	Independence .... Or.	44·49 N	123·13 W
110	Independence Mts. .... Nv.	41·15 N	116·02 W
171	Inder (L.) .... Sov. Un.	48·20 N	52·10 E
182	India (ĭn′dĭ-ȧ) .... Asia	23·00 N	77·30 E
109	Indian (L.) (ĭn′dĭ-ăn) .... Mi.	46·04 N	86·34 W
105	Indian (R.) .... NY	44·05 N	75·45 W
105	Indiana (ĭn-dĭ-än′ȧ) .... Pa.	40·40 N	79·10 W
103	Indiana (State) .... U. S.	39·50 N	86·45 W
107	Indianapolis (ĭn-dĭ-ăn-ăp′ô-lĭs) In. (Indianapolis In.)	39·45 N	86·08 W
112	Indian Arm (R.) (ĭn′dĭ-ăn ärm) Can. (Vancouver In.)	49·21 N	122·55 W
94	Indian Head .... Can.	50·29 N	103·44 W
96	Indian L. .... Can.	47·00 N	82·00 W
5	Indian O.		
109	Indianola (ĭn-dĭ-ăn-ō′lȧ) .... Ia.	41·22 N	93·33 W
120	Indianola .... Ms.	33·29 N	90·35 W
173	Indigirka (R.) (ên-dê-gēr′kȧ) Sov. Un.	67·45 N	145·45 E
122	Indio (R.) (ē′n-dyô) .... Pan. (In.)	9·13 N	78·28 W
196	Indochina (Reg.) (ĭn-dô-chī′nȧ) Asia	17·22 N	105·18 E
196	Indonesia (ĭn′dô-nê-zhȧ) ..... Asia	4·38 S	118·45 E
184	Indore (ĭn-dōr′) .... India	22·48 N	76·51 E
196	Indragiri (R.) (ĭn-drȧ-jē′rê). Indon.	0·27 S	102·05 E
126	Indrāvati (R.) (ĭn-drŭ-vä′tê) India	19·15 N	80·54 E
160	Indre (R.) (ăN′dr′) .... Fr.	47·13 N	0·29 E
156	Indre Solund (I.) (ĭndrĕ-sô-lûnd) Nor.	61·09 N	4·37 E
89	Indus (ĭn′dŭs). Can. (Calgary In.)	50·55 N	113·45 W
184	Indus (R.) .... Pak.	26·43 N	67·41 E
213	Indwe (ĭnd′wȧ). S. Afr. (Natal In.)	31·30 S	27·21 E
171	Inebolu (ê-nȧ-bō′lōō) .... Tur.	41·50 N	33·40 E
171	Inego (ê′nȧ-gŭ) .... Tur.	40·05 N	29·20 E
197	Infanta (ên-fän′tä) ..... Phil. (In.)	14-44 N	121·39 E
197	Infanta .... Phil. (In.)	15·50 N	119·53 E
162	Infantes (ên-fän′tȧs) .... Sp.	38·44 N	3·00 W
125	Inferror, Laguna (L.) (lä-gōō′nä-ên-fĕr-rôr). Mex.	16·18 N	94·40 W
125	Infiernillo, Presa de (Res.) ... Mex.	18·50 N	101·50 W
162	Infiesto (ēn-fyĕ′s-tô) .... Sp.	43·21 N	5·24 W
215	I-n-Gall .... Niger	16·47 N	6·56 E
104	Ingersoll (ĭn′gēr-sŏl) .... Can.	43·05 N	81·00 W
205	Ingham (ĭng′ăm) .... Austl.	18·45 S	146·14 E
128	Ingles, Cayos (Is.) (kä-yōs-ê′n-glĕ′s). Cuba	21·55 N	82·35 W
113	Inglewood (ĭn′g′l-wŏŏd) Ca. (Los Angeles In.)	33·57 N	118·22 W
89	Inglewood ..... Can. (Toronto In.)	43·48 N	79·56 W
173	Ingoda (R.) (ên-gō′dȧ) ... Sov. Un.	51·29 N	112·32 E
158	Ingolstadt (ĭŋ′gôl-shtät) .... F.R.G.	48·46 N	11·27 E
167	Ingul (R.) (ên-gŏŏl′) ..... Sov. Un.	47·22 N	32·52 E
167	Ingulets (R.) (ên-gōōl′yĕts′) Sov. Un.	47·12 N	33·12 E
171	Ingur (R.) (ên-gŏŏr′) .... Sov. Un.	42·30 N	42·00 E
212	Inhambane (ên-äm-bä′-nĕ) ... Moz.	23·47 S	35·28 E
135	Inhambupe (ên-yäm-bōō′pä). Braz.	11·47 S	38·13 W
212	Inharrime (ên-yär-rē′mä) .... Moz.	24·17 S	35·07 E
136	Inhomirim (ē-nô-mê-rē′N) Braz. (Rio de Janeiro In.)	22·34 S	43·11 W
134	Iniridía (R.) (ē-nê-rē′dä) ..... Col.	2·25 N	70·38 W
203	Injune (ĭn′jŏŏn) .... Austl.	25·52 S	148·30 E
157	Inkeroinem (ĭn′kĕr-oi-nĕn) .... Fin.	60·42 N	26·50 E
107	Inkster (ĭngk′stēr). Mi. (Detroit In.)	42·18 N	83·19 W
203	Innamincka (ĭnn-ȧ′mĭn-kȧ) .. Austl.	27·50 S	140·48 E
123	Inner Brass (I.) (bräs) Vir. Is. (U.S.A.) (St. Thomas In.)	18·23 N	64·58 W
154	Inner Hebrides (Is.) .... Scot.	57·20 N	6·20 W
	Inner Mongolia (Aut. Reg.), see Nei Monggol		
93	Innisfail .... Can.	52·02 N	113·57 W
158	Inn R. (ĭn) .... F.R.G.-Aus.	48·19 N	13·16 E
158	Innsbruck (ĭns′brŏŏk) .... Aus.	47·15 N	11·25 E
195	Ino (ē′nô) .... Jap.	33·34 N	133·23 E
216	Inongo (ê-nôŋ′gō) .... Zaire	1·57 S	18·16 E
159	Inowroctaw (ē-nô-vrŏts′läf) ... Pol.	52·48 N	18·16 E
210	In Salah .... Alg.	27·13 N	2·22 E
115	Inscription House Ruin (ĭn′skrĭp-shŭn hous rōō′ĭn). Az.	36·45 N	110·47 W
124	Inter-American Hy. (ĭn′tēr ȧ-mĕr′ĭ-kăn). Mex.	22·30 N	99·08 W
109	International Falls (ĭn′tēr-năsh′ŭn-ăl fôlz). Mn.	48·34 N	93·26 W
90	Inuvik ... . Can.	68·40 N	134·10 W
195	Inuyama (ē′nōō-yä′mä) ...... Jap.	35·24 N	137·01 E
205	Invercargil (ĭn-vēr-kär′gĭl) N. Z. (In.)	47·18 S	168·27 E
203	Inverel (ĭn-vēr-el′) .... Austl.	29·50 S	151·32 E
113	Invergrove Hts. (ĭn′vēr-grōv) Mn. (Minneapolis, St. Paul In.)	44·51 N	93·01 W
99	Inverness (ĭn-vēr-nĕs′) .... Can.	46·14 N	61·18 W
121	Inverness .... Fl.	28·48 N	82·22 W
154	Inverness .... Scot.	57·30 N	4·07 W
203	Investigator Str. (ĭn-vĕst′ĭ′gā-tôr) Austl.	35·33 S	137·00 E
212	Inyangani, Mt. (ên-yän-gä′nê) Zimb.	18·06 S	32·37 E
114	Inyokern .... Ca.	35·39 N	117·51 W
114	Inyo Mts. (ĭn′yō) .... Ca.	36·55 N	118·04 W
174	Inzer R. (ĭn′zĕr) Sov. Un. (Urals In.)	54·24 N	57·17 E
216	Inzia (R.) .... Zaire	5·55 S	17·50 E
195	Iō (I.) (ē′wō) .... Jap.	30·46 N	130·15 E
165	Ioánnina (Yannina) (yô-ä′nê-nȧ) (yä′nê-nȧ). Grc.	39·39 N	20·52 E
112	Ioco .... Can. (Vancouver In.)	49·18 N	122·53 W
117	Iola (ī-ō′lȧ) .... Ks.	37·55 N	95·23 W
216	Iôna, Parque Nacional do (Natl. Pk.). Ang.	16·35 S	12·00 E
104	Ionia (ī-ō′nĭ-ȧ) .... Mi.	43·00 N	85·10 W
165	Ionian Is. (ī-ō′nĭ-ăn) .... Grc.	39·10 N	20·05 E
153	Ionian Sea .... Eur.	38·59 N	18·48 E
165	Ios (I.) (ĭ′ŏs) .... Grc.	36·48 N	25·25 E
103	Iowa (State) (ī′ô-wȧ) .... U. S.	42·05 N	94·20 W
109	Iowa (R.) .... Ia.	41·55 N	92·20 W
109	Iowa City .... Ia.	41·39 N	91·31 W
109	Iowa Falls .... Ia.	42·32 N	93·16 W
116	Iowa Park .... Tx.	33·57 N	98·39 W
217	Ipala .... Tan.	4·30 S	32·53 E
159	Ipel R. (ê′pĕl) ...... Czech.-Hung.	48·08 N	19·00 E
134	Ipiales (ē-pê-ä′lȧs) .... Col.	0·48 N	77·45 W
196	Ipoh .... Mala.	4·45 N	101·05 E
203	Ipswich (ĭps′wĭch) .... Austl.	27·40 S	152·50 E
155	Ipswich .... Eng.	52·05 N	1·05 E
99	Ipswich .... Ma. (In.)	42·41 N	70·50 W
108	Ipswich .... SD	45·26 N	99·01 W
135	Ipu (ē-pōō) .... Braz.	4·11 S	40·45 W
166	Iput′ (R.) (ê-pŏŏt′) ...... Sov. Un.	52·53 N	31·57 E
134	Iquique (ē-kê′kĕ) .... Chile	20·16 S	70·07 W
134	Iquitos (ê-kē′tōs) .... Peru	3·39 S	73·18 W
164	Iráklion (Candia) .... Grc. (In.)	35·20 N	25·10 E
182	Iran (ē-rän′) .... Asia	31·15 N	53·30 E
186	Iran, Plat. of .... Iran	32·28 N	58·00 E
196	Iran Mts. .... Mala.	2·30 N	114·30 E
124	Irapuato (ē-rä-pwä′tō) ...... Mex.	20·41 N	101·24 W
182	Iraq (ē-räk′) .... Asia	32·00 N	42·30 E
127	Irazu Vol. (ē-rä-zōō′) .... C. R.	9·58 N	83·54 W
183	Irbid (êr-bēd′) Jordan (Palestine In.)	32·33 N	35·51 E
171	Irbil .... Iraq	36·10 N	44·00 E
170	Irbit (êr-bêt′) .... Sov. Un.	57·40 N	63·10 E
212	Irébou (ē-rā′bōō) .... Zaire	0·40 S	17·48 E
146	Ireland (īr-lănd) .... Eur.	53·33 N	13·00 W
174	Iremel′, Gora (Mt.) (gȧ-rä′ ĭ-rĕ′mĕl). Sov. Un. (Urals In.)	54·32 N	58·52 E
213	Irene (ĭ-rē-nē) .... S. Afr. (Johannesburg & Pretoria In.)	25·53 S	28·13 E
172	Irgiz (ĭr-gēz′) .... Sov. Un.	48·30 N	61·17 E
172	Irgiz (R.) .... Sov. Un.	49·30 N	60·32 E
214	Irîgui (Reg.) ..... Mali-Mauritania	16·45 N	5·35 W
170	Iriklinskoye Vdkhr (Res.) Sov. Un.	52·20 N	58·50 E
217	Iringa (ê-rĭŋ′gä) .... Tan.	7·46 S	35·42 E
193	Iriomote Jima (I.) (ērē′-ō-mō-tā) Jap.	24·20 N	123·30 E
126	Iriona (ê-rê-ō′nä) .... Hond.	15·53 N	85·12 W
154	Irish Sea (ī′rĭsh) .... Eur.	53·55 N	5·25 W
172	Irkutsk (ĭr-kŏŏtsk′) ...... Sov. Un.	52·16 N	104·00 E
148	Irlam (ûr′lăm) .... Eng.	53·26 N	2·26 W
129	Irois, Cap des (C.) .... Hai.	18·25 N	74·50 W
106	Irondale (ī′ērn-dăl) Al. (Birmingham In.)	33·32 N	86·43 W
165	Iron Gate (Gorge) .... Yugo.-Rom.	44·43 N	22·32 E
203	Iron Knob (ī-ăn nŏb) .... Austl.	32·47 S	137·10 E
109	Iron Mountain (ī′ērn) .... Mi.	45·49 N	88·04 W
109	Iron River .... Mi.	46·09 N	88·39 W
104	Ironton (ī′ērn-tŭn) .... Oh.	38·30 N	82·45 W
109	Ironwood (ī′ērn-wŏŏd) .... Mi.	46·28 N	90·10 W
104	Iroquois (.R) (ĭr′ô-kwoi) .... Il.-In.	40·55 N	87·20 W
91	Iroquois Falls .... Can.	48·41 N	80·39 W
195	Irō-Saki (C.) (ē′rō sä′kē) ..... Jap.	34·35 N	138·54 E
167	Irpen′ (R.) (ĭr-pĕn′) ..... Sov. Un.	50·13 N	29·55 E
187	Irrawaddy (R.) (ĭr-ȧ-wäd′ê) .. Bur.	23·27 N	96·25 E
172	Irtysh (R.) (ĭr-tĭsh′) ..... Sov. Un.	58·32 N	68·31 E
211	Irumu (ê-rŏŏ′mōō) .... Zaire	1·30 N	29·52 E
162	Irun (ê-rōōn′) .... Sp.	43·20 N	1·47 W
113	Irvine (ûr′vĭn) Ca. (Los Angeles In.)	33·40 N	117·45 W
154	Irvine .... Scot.	55·39 N	4·40 W
104	Irvine .... Ky.	37·40 N	84·00 W
117	Irving (ûr′vēng) Tx. (Dallas, Fort Worth In.)	32·49 N	96·57 W
106	Irvington (ûr′vēng-tŭn) NJ (New York In.)	40·43 N	74·15 W
107	Irwin (ûr′-wĭn) Pa. (Pittsburgh In.)	40·19 N	79·42 W
215	Isa .... Nig.	13·14 N	6·24 E
174	Is (ēs) .... Sov. Un. (Urals In.)	58·48 N	59·44 E
122	Isaacs, Mt. (ē-sä-ȧ′ks) .. Pan. (In.)	9·22 N	79·01 W
124	Isabela (I.) (ê-sä-bĕ′-lä) ..... Mex.	21·56 N	105·53 W
134	Isabela (I.) (ē-sä-bā′lä) .... Ec.	0·47 S	91·35 W
129	Isabela, Cabo (C.) (kȧ′bô-ê-sä-bĕ′lä). Dom. Rep.	20·00 N	71·00 W
126	Isabella, Cord. (Mts.) (kôr-dēl-yĕ′rä-ē-sä-bĕlä). Nic.	13·20 N	85·37 W
104	Isabella Ind. Res. (ĭs-ȧ-bĕl′-lȧ). Mi.	43·35 N	84·55 W
167	Isaccea (ê-säk′chä) .... Rom.	45·16 N	28·26 E
150	Isafjördhur (ēs′ȧ-fyûr-dŏŏr) .. Ice.	66·09 N	22·39 W
216	Isangi (ê-säŋ′gē) .... Zaire	0·46 N	24·15 E
158	Isar R. (ē′zär) .... F.R.G.	48·27 N	12·02 E
164	Isarco (R.) (ê-sär′kō) .... It.	46·37 N	11·25 E
197	Isarog, Mt. (ê-sä-rô-g) .. Phil. (In.)	13·40 N	123·23 E
163	Ischia (ēs′kyä) .... It. (Naples In.)	40·29 N	13·58 E
195	Ise (Uji-Yamada) (ĭs′hĕ) (û′gē-yă′mă′dȧ). Jap.	34·30 N	136·43 E
164	Iseo, Lago di (L.) (lä-′gō-dē-ê-zĕ′ō). It.	45·50 N	9·55 E
161	Isère (R.) (ê-zâr′) .... Fr.	45·24 N	6·04 E
161	Iserlohn (ē′zĕr-lōn) F.R.G. (Ruhr In.)	51·22 N	7·42 E
164	Isernia (ê-zĕr′nyä) .... It.	41·35 N	14·14 E
195	Ise-Wan (B.) (ē′sĕ wän) ...... Jap.	34·49 N	136·44 E
215	Iseyin .... Nig.	7·58 N	3·36 E
194	Ishikari Wan (B.) (ē′shē-kä-rē wän). Jap.	43·30 N	141·05 E
172	Ishim (ĭsh-êm′) .... Sov. Un.	56·07 N	69·13 E
172	Ishim (R.) .... Sov. Un.	53·17 N	67·45 E
174	Ishimbay (ē-shēm-bī′) Sov. Un. (Urals In.)	53·28 N	56·02 E
194	Ishinomaki (ĭsh-nō-mä′kē) .... Jap.	38·22 N	141·22 E
194	Ishinomaki Wan (B.) (ē-shē-nō-mä′kē wän). Jap.	38·10 N	141·40 E
174	Ishly (ĭsh′lĭ). Sov. Un. (Urals In.)	54·13 N	55·55 E
174	Ishlya (ĭsh′lyȧ) Sov. Un. (Urals In.)	53·54 N	57·48 E
165	Ishm .... Alb.	41·32 N	19·35 E
218	Ishmant .... Egypt (Nile In.)	29·17 N	31·15 E
109	Ishpeming (ĭsh′pê-mĭng) ...... Mi.	46·28 N	87·42 W
213	Isipingo (ĭs-ĭ-pĭŋg-gô) S. Afr. (Natal In.)	29·59 S	30·58 E
217	Isiro (Paulis) .... Zaire	2·47 N	27·37 E
171	İskenderun (ĭs-kĕn′dĕr-ōōn) .. Tur.	36·45 N	36·15 E
153	İskenderun Körfezi (G.) ..... Tur.	36·22 N	35·25 E
171	Iskilip (ês′kĭ-lêp′) .... Tur.	40·40 N	34·30 E
165	Iskūr (R.) (ĭs′k′r) .... Bul.	43·05 N	23·37 E
162	Isla-Cristina (ĭs′lä-krê-stē′nä) .. Sp.	37·13 N	7·20 W
187	Islāmābād .... Pak.	33·55 N	73·05 E
126	Isla Mujeres (ê′s-lä-mōō-kĕ′rĕs) Mex. (In.)	21·25 N	86·53 W
95	Island L. .... Can.	53·47 N	94·25 W
99	Islands, B. of (ī′lăndz) .... Can.	49·10 N	58·15 W
154	Islay (I.) (ī′lā) .... Scot.	55·55 N	6·35 W
160	Isle (R.) (ēl) .... Fr.	45·02 N	0·29 E
148	Isle of Axholme (Reg.) (ăks′-hôm) Eng.	53·33 N	0·48 W
154	Isle of Man (măn) .... Eur.	54·26 N	4·21 W
109	Isle Royale Nat′l Park (īl′roi-ăl′) U. S.	47·57 N	88·37 W
115	Isleta (ês-lā′tä) (ī-lē′tȧ) ...... NM	34·55 N	106·45 W
98	Isle Verte (ēl vĕrt′) .... Can.	48·01 N	69·20 W
218	Ismailia (Al Isma′īlīyah) (ēs-mā-ēl′êȧ). Egypt (Suez In.)	30·35 N	32·17 E
218	Ismā′īlīyah Can.. Egypt (Suez In.)	30·25 N	31·45 E
149	Ismaning (ēz′mä-nēng) F.R.G. (Munich In.)	48·14 N	11·41 E
218	Isnā (ês′nȧ) ...... Egypt (Nile In.)	25·17 N	32·33 E
157	Isojärvi (L.) .... Fin.	61·47 N	22·00 E
171	Isparta (ê-spär′tȧ) .... Tur.	37·50 N	30·40 E
186	Israel .... Asia	32·40 N	34·00 E
112	Issaquah (ĭz′să-kwăh) Wa. (Seattle In.)	47·32 N	122·02 W
161	Isselburg (ē′sĕl-bŏŏrg) F.R.G. (Ruhr In.)	51·50 N	6·28 E
160	Issoire (ē-swȧr′) .... Fr.	45·32 N	3·13 E
160	Issoudun (ē-sōō-dăN′) .... Fr.	46·56 N	2·00 E
161	Issum (ē′sōōm). F.R.G. (Ruhr In.)	51·32 N	6·24 E
172	Issyk-Kul, Ozero (L.) .... Sov. Un.	42·13 N	76·12 E
184	Īstādeh-ye Moqor, Ab-e (L.) .. Afg.	32·35 N	68·00 E
171	İstanbul (ê-stän-bōōl′) .... Tur.	41·02 N	29·00 E
171	İstanbul Boğazı (Bosporous) (Str.) Tur.	41·10 N	29·10 E
165	Istiaía (ĭs-tyĭ′yä) .... Grc.	38·58 N	23·11 E
134	Istmina (ēst-mê′nä) .... Col. (In.)	5·10 N	76·40 W
121	Istokpoga (L.) (ĭs-tŏk-pō′gȧ) Fl. (In.)	27·20 N	81·33 W
164	Istra (pen.) (ê-strä) .... Yugo.	45·18 N	13·48 E
165	Istranca Dağ (Mts.) (ĭ-strän′jȧ) Bul.-Turk.	41·50 N	27·25 E
160	Istres (ēs′tr′) .... Fr. (In.)	43·30 N	5·00 E
136	Itá (ê-tȧ′) .... Par.	25·39 S	57·14 W
135	Itabaiana (ē-tä-bä-yȧ-nä) .... Braz.	10·42 S	37·17 W
137	Itabapoana (ē-tä′-bä-pôä′nä) Braz. (Rio de Janeiro In.)	21·19 S	40·58 W

ng-sing; ŋ-baŋk; N-nasalized n; nŏd; cŏmmit; ōld; ôbey; ôrder; fōōd; fŏŏt; ou-out; s-soft; sh-dish; th-thin; pūre; ûnite; ûrn; stŭd; circŭs; ü-as "y" in study; ′-indeterminate vowel.

294 Itabapoana — Jaunjelgava
PRONOUNCING INDEX

Page Name Pronunciation Region Lat. °' Long. °'

137 Itabapoana (R.) Braz. (Rio de Janeiro In.) 21·11 s 41·18 w
137 Itabirito (ē-tä-bê-rē'tô) Braz. (Rio de Janeiro In.) 20·15 s 43·46 w
137 Itaboraí (ē-tä-bō-rä-ē') Braz. (Rio de Janeiro In.) 22·46 s 42·50 w
135 Itabuna (ē-tä-bōō'nà)....... Braz. 14·47 s 39·17 w
137 Itacoara (ē-tä-kô'ä-rä) Braz. (Rio de Janeiro In.) 21·41 s 42·04 w
135 Itacoatiara (ē-tà-kwá-tyä'rà). Braz. 3·03 s 58·18 w
137 Itaguaí (ē-tä-gwä-ē') Braz. (Rio de Janeiro In.) 22·52 s 43·46 w
134 Itagüi (ē-tä'gwê)....... Col. (In.) 6·11 n 75·36 w
136 Itagui (R.) Braz. (Rio de Janeiro In.) 22·53 s 43·43 w
136 Itaipava (ē-tī-pà'-vä) Braz. (Rio de Janeiro In.) 22·23 s 43·09 w
136 Itaipu (ē-tī'pōō) Braz. (Rio de Janiero In.) 22·58 s 43·02 w
135 Itaituba (ē-tä'ī-tōō'bà)...... Braz. 4·12 s 56·00 w
136 Itajái (ē-tä-zhī')........... Braz. 26·52 s 48·39 w
137 Itajubá (ē-tä-zhōō-bà') Braz. (Rio de Janeiro In.) 22·26 s 45·27 w
218 Itala...... Som. (Horn of Afr. In.) 2·45 n 46·15 e
146 Italy (ĭt'á-lê)............... Eur. 43·58 n 11·14 e
119 Italy......................... Tx. 32·11 n 96·51 w
136 Itambi (ē-tä'm-bê) Braz. (Rio de Janeiro In.) 22·44 s 42·57 w
195 Itami (ē'tä'mē').. Jap. (Ōsaka In.) 34·47 n 135·25 e
137 Itapecerica (ē-tä-pě-sě-rē'kà) Braz. (Rio de Janeiro In.) 21·29 s 45·08 w
135 Itapecurú (R.) (ē-tä-pě-kōō-rōō') Braz. 4·05 s 43·49 w
135 Itapēcuru-Mirim (ê-tä-pě'kōō-rōō-mê-rēɴ'). Braz. 3·17 s 44·15 w
137 Itaperuna (ē-tà-pâ-rōō'nä) Braz. (Rio de Janeiro In.) 21·12 s 41·53 w
137 Itapetininga (ē-tä-pě-tê-nē'ɴ-gä) Braz. (Rio de Janeiro In.) 23·37 s 48·03 w
135 Itapira (ē-tà-pē'rà)......... Braz. 20·42 s 51·19 w
137 Itapira. Braz. (Rio de Janeiro In.) 21·27 s 46·47 w
184 Itarsi...................... India 22·43 n 77·45 e
119 Itasca (ī-tăs'ká)............. Tx. 32·09 n 97·08 w
109 Itasca (L.).................. Mn. 47·13 n 95·14 w
137 Itatiaia, Pico da (Pk.) (pē'-kô-dà-ē-tä-tyà'ēä) Braz. (Rio de Janeiro In.) 22·18 s 44·41 w
137 Itatiba (ē-tä-tē'bä) Braz. (Rio de Janeiro In.) 23·01 s 46·48 w
137 Itaúna (ē-tä-ōō'nä) Braz. (Rio de Janeiro In.) 20·05 s 44·35 w
137 Itaverá (ē-tä-vě-rà') Braz. (Rio de Janeiro In.) 22·44 s 44·07 w
104 Ithaca (ĭth'á-ká)............ Mi. 43·20 n 84·35 w
105 Ithaca...................... NY 42·25 n 76·30 w
165 Itháki (I.) (ē'thä-kě)........ Grc. 38·27 n 20·48 e
217 Itigi......................... Tan. 5·42 s 34·29 e
216 Itimbiri (R.)................ Zaire 2·40 n 23·30 e
212 Itoko (ē-tō'kō).............. Zaire 1·13 s 22·07 e
218 Iṭsā (ēt'sá)...... Egypt (Nile In.) 29·13 n 30·47 e
137 Itu (ē-tōō') Braz. (Rio de Janeiro In.) 23·16 s 47·16 w
134 Ituango (ē-twäŋ'gō)..... Col. (In.) 7·07 n 75·44 w
135 Ituiutaba (ē-tōō-ēōō-tä'bä).. Braz. 18·56 s 49·17 w
137 Itumirim (ē-tōō-mê-rē'ɴ) Braz. (Rio de Janeiro In.) 21·20 s 44·51 w
125 Itundujia Santa Cruz (ē-tōōn-dōō-hē'ä sä'n-tä krōō'z). Mex. 16·50 n 97·43 w
126 Iturbide (ē'tōōr-bē'dhā) Mex. (In.) 19·38 n 89·31 w
173 Iturup (I.) (ē-tōō-rōōp').. Sov. Un. 45·35 n 147·15 e
136 Ituzaingo (ē-tōō-zä-ē'n-gō) Arg. (Buenos Aires In.) 34·24 s 58·40 w
149 Itzehoe (ē'tzě-hō) F.R.G. (Hamburg In.) 53·55 n 9·31 e
120 Iuka (ī-ū'ká)................ Ms. 34·47 n 88·10 w
137 Iúna (ē-ōō'-nä) Braz. (Rio de Janeiro In.) 20·22 s 41·32 w
172 Iva (R.).............. Sov. Un. 53·45 n 99·30 e
203 Ivanhoe (ĭv'ăn-hō)......... Austl. 32·53 s 144·10 e
159 Ivano-Frankovsk (ē-vä'nō frän-kôvsk'). Sov. Un. 48·53 n 24·46 e
166 Ivanovo (ê-vä'nô-vō).... Sov. Un. 57·02 n 41·54 e
166 Ivanovo (Oblast)........ Sov. Un. 56·55 n 40·30 e
167 Ivanpol' (ê-vän'pôl)..... Sov. Un. 49·51 n 28·11 e
174 Ivanteyevka (ê-vàn-tyě'yěf-kà) Sov. Un. (Moscow In.) 55·58 n 37·56 e
174 Ivdel' (ĭv'dyěl) Sov. Un. (Urals In.) 60·42 n 60·27 e
Iviza I., see Ibiza, Isla de
213 Ivohibé (ē-vô-hê-bā')....... Mad. 22·28 s 46·59 e
209 Ivory Coast................. Afr. 7·43 n 6·30 w
164 Ivrea (ê-vrě'ä).............. It. 45·25 n 7·54 e
91 Ivujivik................... Can. 62·17 n 77·52 w
194 Iwaki (Taira)............... Jap. 37·03 n 140·57 e
194 Iwate Yama (Mt.) (ē-wä-tě-yä'mä). Jap. 39·50 n 140·56 e
195 Iwatsuki......... Jap. (Tōkyō In.) 35·48 n 139·43 e
195 Iwaya (ē'wä-yà).. Jap. (Ōsaka In.) 34·35 n 135·01 e
215 Iwo......................... Nig. 7·38 n 4·11 e
124 Ixcateopán (ēs-kä-tä-ō-pän'). Mex. 18·29 n 99·49 w
149 Ixelles......... Bel. (Brussels In.) 50·49 n 4·23 e
125 Ixhuatán (San Francisco) (ēs-hwä-tän'). Mex. 16·19 n 94·30 w
124 Ixhautlán (ēs-wàt-län')...... Mex. 20·41 n 98·01 w
124 Ixmiquilpan (ēs-mê-kēl'pän). Mex. 20·30 n 99·12 w
213 Ixopo......... S. Afr. (Natal In.) 30·10 s 30·04 e
125 Ixtacalco (ēs-tä-käl'kō). Mex. (In.) 19·23 n 99·07 w
125 Ixtaltepec (Asunción) (ēs-täl-tě-pěk'). Mex. 16·33 n 95·04 w
125 Ixtapalapa (ēs'tä-pä-lä'pä) Mex. (In.) 19·21 n 99·06 w
125 Ixtapaluca (ēs'tä-pä-lōō'kä) Mex. (In.) 19·18 n 98·53 w
125 Ixtepec (êks-tě'pěk)......... Mex. 16·37 n 95·09 w
125 Ixtlahuaca (ēs-tlä-wä'kä) Mex. (In.) 19·34 n 99·46 w
125 Ixtlán de Juárez (ēs-tlän' dā hwä'râz). Mex. 17·20 n 96·29 w
124 Ixtlán del Río (ēs-tlän'děl rē'ō) Mex. 21·05 n 104·22 w
195 Iyo-Nada (Sea) (ē'yō nä-dä).. Jap. 33·33 n 132·07 e
126 Izabal (ē'zä-bäl')........... Guat. 15·23 n 89·10 w
126 Izabal, L. (Golfo Dulce) (gôl'fō dōōl'så). Guat. 15·30 n 89·04 w
126 Izalco (ē-zäl'kō)............. Sal. 13·50 n 89·40 w
126 Izamal (ē-zä-mä'l)..... Mex. (In.) 20·55 n 89·00 w
170 Izhevsk (ê-zhyěfsk')..... Sov. Un. 56·50 n 53·15 e
170 Izhma (ĭzh'mà).......... Sov. Un. 65·00 n 54·05 e
170 Izhma (R.).............. Sov. Un. 64·00 n 53·00 e
174 Izhora R. (ēz'hô-rà) Sov. Un. (Leningrad In.) 59·36 n 30·20 e
167 Izmail (ēz-mà-ēl')........ Sov. Un. 45·00 n 28·49 e
171 İzmir (ĭz-mēr')............... Tur. 38·25 n 27·05 e
165 Izmir Körfezi (G.)........... Tur. 38·43 n 26·37 e
171 Izmit (ĭz-mêt')............... Tur. 40·45 n 29·45 e
125 Iztaccíhuatl (Mtn.) Mex. (Mexico City In.) 19·10 n 98·38 w
195 Izu (I.) (ē'zōō)............. Jap. 34·32 n 139·25 e
195 Izuhara (ē'zōō-hä'rä)........ Jap. 34·11 n 129·18 e
195 Izumi-Ōtsu (ē'zōō-mōō ō'tsōō) Jap. (Osaka In.) 34·30 n 135·24 e
195 Izumo (ē'zōō-mō)............. Jap. 35·22 n 132·45 e

J

149 Jaachimsthal (yä'ĸēm-stäl) G.D.R. (Berlin In.) 52·58 n 13·45 e
211 Jabal, Baḩr al (R.).......... Sud. 7·02 n 30·45 e
184 Jabalpur.................... India 23·18 n 79·59 e
158 Jablonec (Nad Nisou) (yäb'lô-nyěts). Czech. 50·43 n 15·12 e
159 Jablunkov P. (yäb'lōōn-kôf) Czech. 49·31 n 18·35 e
135 Jaboatão (zhä-bô-à-touɴ).... Braz. 8·14 s 35·08 w
163 Jaca (hä'kä).................. Sp. 42·35 n 0·30 w
124 Jacala (hä-kä'lä)............. Mex. 21·01 n 99·11 w
126 Jacaltenango (hä-käl-tě-nàŋ'gō) Guat. 15·39 n 91·41 w
137 Jacareí (zhä-kà-rě-ē') Braz. (Rio de Janeiro In.) 23·19 s 45·57 w
136 Jacarepaguá (zhä-kä-rā'pä-gwä') Braz. (Rio de Janeiro In.) 22·55 s 43·22 w
135 Jacarézinho (zhä-kä-rě'zê-nyô) Braz. 23·13 s 49·58 w
158 Jachymov (yä'chĭ-môf).... Czech. 50·22 n 12·51 e
119 Jacinto City (hä-sēn'tō) (jà-sĭn'tō) Tx. (In.) 29·45 n 95·14 w
116 Jacksboro (jăks'bŭr-ô)........ Tx. 33·13 n 98·11 w
120 Jackson (jăk'sŭn)............ Al. 31·31 n 87·52 w
114 Jackson...................... Ca. 38·22 n 120·47 w
120 Jackson...................... Ga. 33·19 n 83·55 w
120 Jackson...................... Ky. 37·32 n 83·17 w
119 Jackson...................... La. 30·50 n 91·13 w
104 Jackson...................... Mi. 42·15 n 84·25 w
109 Jackson...................... Mn. 43·37 n 95·00 w
120 Jackson...................... Ms. 32·17 n 90·10 w
117 Jackson...................... Mo. 37·23 n 89·40 w
104 Jackson...................... Oh. 39·00 n 82·40 w
120 Jackson...................... Tn. 35·37 n 88·49 w
202 Jackson, Port.. Austl. (Sydney In.) 33·50 s 151·18 e
111 Jackson L.................... Wy. 43·57 n 110·28 w
120 Jacksonville (jăk'sŭn-vĭl)...... Al. 33·52 n 85·45 w
121 Jacksonville.................. Fl. 30·20 n 81·40 w
117 Jacksonville.................. Il. 39·43 n 90·12 w
119 Jacksonville.................. Tx. 31·58 n 95·18 w
121 Jacksonville Beach........... Fl. 31·18 n 81·25 w
119 Jacmel (zhàk-měl')........... Hai. 18·15 n 72·30 w
118 Jaco, L. (hä'kō).............. Mex. 27·51 n 103·50 w
184 Jacobābad.................... Pak. 28·22 n 68·30 e
135 Jacobina (zhä-kô-bē'ná)..... Braz. 11·13 s 40·30 w
100 Jacques-Cartier (zhàk'kär-tyā) Can. (Montreal In.) 45·30 n 72·39 w
98 Jacques Cartier, Mt........ Can. 48·59 n 66·00 w
89 Jacques-Cartier, (R.) Can. (Quebec In.) 47·04 n 71·28 w
99 Jacques Cartier, Détroit de (Str.) Can. 50·07 n 63·58 w
98 Jacquet River (zhà-kě') (jăk'ĕt) Can. 47·55 n 66·00 w
137 Jacuí (zhä-kōō-ē') Braz. (Rio de Janeiro In.) 21·03 s 46·43 w
137 Jacutinga (zhä-kōō-tēn'gä) Braz. (Rio de Janeiro In.) 21·17 s 46·36 w
158 Jade B. (yä'dě)............. F.R.G. 53·28 n 8·17 e
Jadotville, see Likasi
134 Jaén (ĸä-ě'n)................ Peru 5·38 s 78·49 w
162 Jaen......................... Sp. 37·45 n 3·48 w
203 Jaffa, C. (jăf'ă)............ Austl. 36·58 s 139·29 e
185 Jaffna (jäf'ná).......... Sri Lanka 9·44 n 80·09 e
128 Jagüey Grande (hä'gwā grän'dā) Cuba 22·35 n 81·05 w
183 Jahore Str... Mala. (Singapore In.) 1·22 n 103·37 e
186 Jahrom...................... Iran 28·30 n 53·28 e
119 Jaibo (R.) (hä-ē'bō)......... Cuba 20·10 n 75·20 w
184 Jaipur...................... India 27·00 n 75·50 e
184 Jaisalmer................... India 27·00 n 70·54 e
164 Jajce (yī'tsě)............... Yugo. 44·20 n 17·19 e
184 Jajpur...................... India 20·49 n 86·37 e
196 Jakarta (yä-kär'tä)......... Indon. 6·17 s 106·45 e
150 Jakobstad (yá'kôb-stádh)..... Fin. 63·33 n 22·31 e
125 Jalacingo (hä-lä-sĭŋ'gō)...... Mex. 97·16 n 19·47 w
187 Jalālābād (jŭ-lä-là-bäd) Afg. (Khyber Pass In.) 34·25 n 70·27 e
218 Jalālah al Baḩrīyah, Jabal, (Mts.) Egypt (Nile In.) 29·20 n 32·00 e
126 Jalapa (hä-lä'pà)........... Guat. 14·38 n 89·58 w
125 Jalapa de Diaz (San Felipe) (dā dē-äz') (sän fā-lē'pā). Mex. 18·06 n 96·33 w
125 Jalapa del Marqués (děl mär-kās'). Mex. 16·30 n 95·29 w
125 Jalapa Enríquez (ěn-rē'kāz).. Mex. 19·32 n 96·53 w
184 Jaleswar.................... Nep. 26·50 n 85·55 e
184 Jalgaon..................... India 21·08 n 75·33 e
124 Jalisco (hä-lēs'kō)........... Mex. 21·27 n 104·54 w
122 Jalisco (State)............... Mex. 20·07 n 104·45 w
162 Jalón (R.) (hä-lōn').......... Sp. 41·22 n 1·46 w
124 Jalostotitlán (hä-lōs-tē-tlán'). Mex. 21·09 n 102·30 w
125 Jalpa (häl'pā)................ Mex. 18·12 n 93·06 w
124 Jalpa (häl'pä)................ Mex. 21·40 n 103·04 w
124 Jalpan (häl'pän).............. Mex. 21·13 n 99·31 w
125 Jaltepec (häl-tà-pěk')........ Mex. 17·20 n 95·15 w
125 Jaltipan (häl-tà-pän')........ Mex. 17·59 n 94·42 w
124 Jaltocan (häl-tô-kän')........ Mex. 21·08 n 98·32 w
211 Jālū, Wāhat (Oasis)......... Libya 28·58 n 21·45 e
215 Jamaare (R.)................. Nig. 11·50 n 10·10 e
123 Jamaica..................... N. A. 17·45 n 78·00 w
129 Jamaica Cay (I.)............. Ba. 22·45 n 75·55 w
184 Jamālpur.................... Bngl. 24·56 n 89·58 e
124 Jamay (hä-mī')............... Mex. 20·16 n 103·43 w
196 Jambi (mäm'bê).............. Indon. 1·45 s 103·28 e
165 Jambol (yàm'bôl)............. Bul. 42·28 n 26·31 e
117 James (R.)................... Mo. 36·51 n 93·22 w
121 James (R.)................... NC 36·07 n 81·48 w
102 James (R.)................... U. S. 46·25 n 98·55 w
105 James (R.)................... Va. 37·35 n 77·50 w
91 James B. (jāmz)............. Can. 53·53 n 80·40 w
106 Jamesburg (jāmz'bûrg) NJ (New York In.) 40·21 n 74·26 w
129 James Pt..................... Ba. 25·20 n 76·30 w
204 James Ra.................... Austl. 24·15 s 133·30 e
133 James Ross (I.).............. Ant. 64·20 s 58·20 w
105 Jamestown (jāmz'toun)....... NY 42·05 n 79·15 w
108 Jamestown.................... ND 46·54 n 98·42 w
106 Jamestown... RI (Providence In.) 41·30 n 71·21 w
213 Jamestown..... S. Afr. (Natal In.) 31·07 s 26·49 e
108 Jamestown Res................ ND 47·16 n 98·40 w
125 Jamiltepec (hä-mēl-tà-pěk').. Mex. 16·16 n 97·54 w
156 Jammerbugt (B.).............. Den. 57·20 n 9·28 e
184 Jammu....................... India 32·50 n 74·52 e
184 Jammu and Kashmir (Disputed Reg.) (kàsh-mēr'). India-Pak. 39·10 n 75·05 e
184 Jāmnagar (jäm-nŭ'gŭr)..... India 22·33 n 70·03 e
184 Jamshedpur (jäm'shäd-pōōr). India 22·52 n 86·11 e
134 Jamundí (hä-mōō'n-dē'). Col. (In.) 3·15 n 76·32 w
162 Jándula (R.) (hän'dōō-là)..... Sp. 38·28 n 3·52 w
109 Janesville (jānz'vĭl)........... Wi. 42·41 n 89·03 w
183 Janin...... Jordan (Palestine In.) 32·27 n 35·19 e
150 Jan Mayen (I.) (yän mī'ěn).. Nor. 70·59 n 8·05 w
156 Jannelund (yän'ē-lōōnd)..... Swe. 59·14 n 14·24 e
159 Jánoshalma (yä'nôsh-hôl-mô) Hung. 46·17 n 19·18 e
159 Janów Lubelski (yä'nōōf lŭ-běl'skĭ) Pol. 50·40 n 22·25 e
135 Januária (zhä-nwä'rê-ä)..... Braz. 15·31 s 44·17 w
183 Japan (já-păn')............. Asia 36·30 n 133·30 e
194 Japan, Sea of (já-păn')...... Asia 40·08 n 132·55 e
136 Japeri (zhà-pě'rê) Braz. (Rio de Janeiro In.) 22·38 s 43·40 w
134 Japurá (R.) (zhä-pōō-rä').... Braz. 1·30 s 67·54 w
119 Jarabacoa (ĸä-rä-bä-kô'ä) Dom. Rep. 19·05 n 70·40 w
124 Jaral del Progreso (hä-räl děl prô-grā'sō). Mex. 20·21 n 101·05 w
162 Jarama (R.) (hä-rä'mä)....... Sp. 40·33 n 3·30 w
183 Jarash...... Jordan (Palestine In.) 32·17 n 35·53 e
128 Jardines, Banco (Bk.) (bä'n-kō-här-dē'nâs). Cuba 21·45 n 81·40 w
135 Jari (R.) (zhä-rē)........... Braz. 0·28 n 53·00 w
160 Jarnac (zhár-nák')............ Fr. 45·42 n 0·09 w
159 Jarocin (yä-rō'tsyēn).......... Pol. 51·58 n 17·31 e
159 Jarosław (yä-rôs-wáf)......... Pol. 50·01 n 22·41 e
192 Jarud Xi (jyä-lōō-tŭ shyē).. China 44·35 n 120·40 e
183 Jasin....... Mala. (Singapore In.) 2·19 n 102·26 e
157 Jašiūnai (dzá-shōō-nà'yě). Sov. Un. 54·27 n 25·25 e
186 Jāsk (jäsk).................. Iran 25·46 n 57·48 e
159 Jasło (yäs'wō)................ Pol. 49·44 n 21·28 e
183 Jason B..... Mala. (Singapore In.) 1·53 n 104·14 e
104 Jasonville (jā'sŭn-vĭl)......... In. 39·10 n 87·15 w
120 Jasper (jăs'pēr).............. Al. 33·50 n 87·17 w
93 Jasper...................... Can. 52·53 n 118·05 w
120 Jasper....................... Fl. 30·30 n 82·56 w
104 Jasper....................... In. 38·20 n 86·55 w
108 Jasper....................... Mn. 43·51 n 96·22 w
119 Jasper....................... Tx. 30·55 n 93·59 w
93 Jasper Natl. Park........... Can. 53·09 n 117·45 w
159 Jászapáti (yäs'ô-pä-tē)..... Hung. 47·29 n 20·10 e
125 Jatatė (R.) (hä-tä-tā')....... Mex. 16·30 n 91·29 w
128 Jatibonico (hä-tê-bô-nē'kō).. Cuba 22·00 n 79·15 w
163 Játiva (hä'tê-vä)............. Sp. 38·58 n 0·31 w
136 Jau' (zhà-ōō')............... Braz. 22·16 s 48·31 w
134 Jauja (ĸä-ōō'ĸ).............. Peru 11·43 s 75·32 w
124 Jaumave (hou-mä'vå)......... Mex. 23·23 n 99·24 w
157 Jaunjelgava (youn'yěl'gà-và) Sov. Un. 56·37 n 25·06 e

PRONOUNCING INDEX

Java Trench — Jujuy 295

Page	Name Pronunciation Region	Lat. °′	Long. °′
197	Java Trench .... Indon.	9·45 s	107·30 E
134	Javari (R.) (ká-vä-rē) ... Col.-Peru	4·25 s	72·07 W
163	Jávea (há-vā'ä) .... Sp.	38·45 N	0·07 E
196	Jawa (I.) .... Indon.	8·35 N	111·11 E
196	Jawa, Laut (Java Sea) .... Indon.	5·10 s	110·30 E
158	Jawor (yä'vôr) .... Pol.	51·04 N	16·12 E
159	Jaworzno (yä-vôzh'nô) ...... Pol.	50·11 N	19·18 E
197	Jayapura (Sukarnapura) ... Indon.	2·30 s	140·45 W
	Jayb, Wādī al (R.), see Ha 'Arava		
159	Jászberény (yäs'bě-rān') .... Hung.	47·30 N	19·56 E
183	Jazzīn .... Leb. (Palestine In.)	33·34 N	35·37 E
119	Jeanerette (jěn-ēr-et') (zhän-rět') La.	29·54 N	91·41 W
210	Jebba (jěb'á) .... Nig.	9·07 N	4·46 E
99	Jeddore L. .... Can.	48·07 N	55·35 W
159	Jędrzejów (yăN-dzhā'yŏŏf) .... Pol.	50·38 N	20·18 E
120	Jefferson (jěf'ēr-sŭn) .... Ga.	34·05 N	83·35 W
109	Jefferson .... Ia.	42·10 N	94·22 W
106	Jefferson ... La. (New Orleans In.)	29·57 N	90·04 W
119	Jefferson .... Tx.	32·47 N	94·21 W
109	Jefferson .... Wi.	42·59 N	88·45 W
110	Jefferson, Mt. .... Or.	44·41 N	121·50 W
117	Jefferson City .... Mo.	38·34 N	92·10 W
111	Jefferson R. .... Mt.	45·37 N	112·22 W
107	Jeffersontown (jěf'ēr-sŭn-toun) Ky. (Louisville In.)	38·11 N	85·34 W
107	Jeffersonville (jěf'ēr-sŭn-vĭl) In. (Louisville In.)	38·17 N	85·44 W
215	Jega .... Nig.	12·15 N	4·23 E
189	Jehol (Reg.) (jě-hŏl) ...... China	42·31 N	118·12 E
153	Jeib, Wadi el (R.) ..... Jordan-Isr.	30·30 N	35·20 E
157	Jēkabpils (yěk'áb-pĭls) ... Sov. Un.	56·29 N	25·50 E
158	Jelenia Góra (yě-lěn'yá gōō'rá) Pol.	50·53 N	15·43 E
157	Jelgava (yěl'gá-vá) ...... Sov. Un.	56·39 N	23·40 E
120	Jellico (jěl'ĭ-kō) .... Tn.	36·34 N	84·06 W
151	Jemmapes (zhē-map') .... Alg.	36·43 N	7·21 E
158	Jena (yā'nä) .... G.D.R.	50·55 N	11·37 E
121	Jenkins (jěŋ'kĭnz) .... Ky.	37·09 N	82·38 W
106	Jenkintown (jěŋ'kĭn-toun) Pa. (Philadelphia In.)	40·06 N	75·08 W
119	Jennings (jěn'ĭngz) .... La.	30·14 N	92·40 W
104	Jennings .... Mi.	44·20 N	85·20 W
113	Jennings ...... Mo. (St. Louis In.)	38·43 N	90·16 W
135	Jequié (zhě-kyě') .... Braz.	13·53 s	40·06 W
135	Jequitinhonha (R.) (zhě-kē-têŋ-ŏ'n-yä) . Braz.	16·47 s	41·19 W
129	Jérémie (zhā-rā-mē') .... Hai.	18·40 N	74·10 W
135	Jeremoabo (zhě-rā-mō-ä'bō) . Braz.	10·03 s	38·13 W
125	Jerez, Punta (Pt.) (pōō'n-tä-kě-räz') . Mex.	23·04 N	97·44 W
162	Jerez de la Frontera (kě-rāth' dā lä frôn-tā'rä) . Sp.	36·42 N	6·09 W
162	Jerez de los Caballeros (kě-rath' dā lōs kä-väl-yā'rōs) . Sp.	38·20 N	6·45 W
205	Jericho (jěr'ĭ-kō) .... Austl.	28·38 s	146·24 E
218	Jericho (jěr-ĭkô) .... S. Afr. (Johannesburg & Pretoria In.)	25·16 s	27·47 E
	Jericho, see Arīḥā		
115	Jerome (jē-rōm') .... Az.	34·45 N	112·10 W
111	Jerome .... Id.	42·44 N	114·31 W
160	Jersey (I.) (jûr'zĭ) .... Eur.	49·13 N	2·07 W
106	Jersey City ... NJ (New York In.)	40·43 N	74·05 W
105	Jersey Shore .... Pa.	41·10 N	77·15 W
117	Jerseyville (jěr'zē-vĭl) .... Il.	39·07 N	90·18 W
183	Jerusalem (jē-rōō'sá-lěm) Isr.-Jordan (Palestine In.)	31·46 N	35·14 E
121	Jesup (jěs'ŭp) .... Ga.	31·36 N	81·53 W
125	Jesús Carranza (hě-sōō's-kär-rá'n-zä) . Mex.	17·26 N	95·01 W
108	Jewel Cave Natl. Mon. .... SD	43·44 N	103·52 W
112	Jewel (jū'ěl) .... Or. (Portland In.)	45·56 N	123·30 W
184	Jhālawār .... India	24·29 N	79·09 E
184	Jhang Maghiāna .... Pak.	31·21 N	72·19 E
184	Jhānsi (jän'sē) .... India	25·29 N	78·32 E
184	Jhārsuguda .... India	22·51 N	86·13 E
184	Jhelum (R.) (jā'lŭm) .... Pak.	31·40 N	71·51 E
190	Jiache (jyä-chŭ) .... China	38·03 N	116·18 E
191	Jiading (jyä-dĭŋ) China (Canton In.)	31·23 N	121·15 E
193	Jialing (R.) (jyä-lĭŋ) .... China	30·30 N	106·20 E
193	Ji'an (jyē-än) .... China	27·15 N	115·10 E
192	Ji'an .... China	41·00 N	126·04 E
190	Jianchangying (jyěn-chäŋ-yĭŋ) China	40·09 N	119·47 E
191	Jiangcun (jyäŋ-tsōōn) China (Canton In.)	23·16 N	113·14 E
193	Jiangling (jyäŋ-lĭŋ) .... China	30·30 N	112·10 E
190	Jiangshanzhen (jyäŋ-shän-jŭn) China	36·39 N	120·31 E
189	Jiangsu (Prov.) (jyäŋ-sōō) . China	33·45 N	120·30 E
191	Jiangwan (jyäŋ-wän) China (Shanghai In.)	31·18 N	121·29 E
189	Jiangxi (Prov.) (jyäŋ-shyē) . China	28·15 N	116·00 E
190	Jiangyin (jyäŋ-yĭn) .... China	31·54 N	120·15 E
193	Jianli (jyěn-lē) .... China	29·50 N	112·52 E
193	Jianning (jyěn-nĭŋ) .... China	26·50 N	116·55 E
193	Jian'ou (jyěn-ō) .... China	27·10 N	118·18 E
193	Jianshi (jyěn-shr) .... China	30·40 N	109·45 E
192	Jiaohe (jyou-hŭ) .... China	43·40 N	127·20 E
190	Jiao Xian (jyou shyěn) .... China	36·18 N	120·01 E
190	Jiaozuo (jyou-dzwō) .... China	35·15 N	113·18 E
190	Jiashan (jyä-shän) .... China	32·41 N	118·00 E
193	Jiaxing (jyä-shyĭŋ) .... China	30·45 N	120·50 E
193	Jiayu (jyä-yōō) .... China	33·00 N	114·00 E
190	Jiazhou Wan (B.) (jyä-jō wän) China	36·10 N	119·55 E
188	Jibhalanta .... Mong.	47·49 N	97·00 E
115	Jicarilla Ind. Res. (kē-ká-rēl'yá) NM	36·45 N	107·00 W
127	Jicaron, Isla (I.) (kē-kä-rōn') . Pan.	7·14 N	81·41 W
	Jidda, see Juddah		
190	Jieshou .... China	33·17 N	115·20 E
193	Jieyang (jyě-yäŋ) .... China	23·38 N	116·20 E
159	Jiffa R. .... Rom.	47·35 N	27·02 E
204	Jiggalong (jĭg'á-lông) .... Austl.	23·20 s	120·45 E
129	Jiguani (kē-gwä-nē') .... Cuba	20·20 N	76·30 W
128	Jigüey, Bahía (B.) (bä-ē'ä-kē'gwā) . Cuba	22·15 N	78·10 W
158	Jihlava (yē'hlá-vá) .... Czech.	49·23 N	15·33 E
190	Jijiashi (jyē-jyä-shr) .... China	32·10 N	120·17 E
218	Jijiga ..... Eth. (Horn of Afr. In.)	9·15 N	42·48 E
163	Jijona (kē-hō'nä) .... Sp.	38·31 N	0·29 W
211	Jilf al-Kabīr, Hadabat al (Plat.) . Egypt	24·09 N	25·29 E
192	Jilin (jyē-lĭn) .... China	43·58 N	126·40 E
189	Jilin (Prov.) .... China	44·20 N	124·50 E
162	Jiloca (R.) (kē-lō'kä) .... Sp.	41·13 N	1·30 W
126	Jilotepeque (kē-lô-tě-pě'kě) .. Guat.	14·39 N	89·36 W
211	Jima .... Eth.	7·41 N	36·52 E
165	Jimbolia (zhĭm-bô'lyä) ...... Rom.	45·45 N	20·44 E
124	Jiménez (kē-mā'nâz) .... Mex.	24·12 N	98·29 W
118	Jimenez .... Mex.	27·09 N	104·55 W
118	Jiménez .... Mex.	29·03 N	100·42 W
124	Jiménez del Téul (tě-ōō'l) .... Mex.	21·28 N	103·51 W
190	Jimo (jyē-mwo) .... China	36·22 N	120·28 E
105	Jim Thorpe (jĭm' thôrp') ..... Pa.	40·50 N	75·45 W
190	Jinan (jyē-nän) .... China	36·40 N	117·01 E
192	Jincheng (jyĭn-chŭŋ) .... China	35·30 N	112·50 E
158	Jindřichov Hradec (yēn'd'r-zhĭ-kōōf hrä'děts) . Czech.	49·09 N	15·02 E
192	Jing (R.) (jyĭŋ) .... China	34·40 N	108·20 E
190	Jing'anji (jyĭŋ-än-jē) .... China	34·30 N	116·55 E
193	Jingdezhen (jyĭn-dŭ-jŭn) .... China	29·18 N	117·18 E
190	Jingjiang (jyĭŋ-jyäŋ) .... China	32·02 N	120·15 E
192	Jingning (jyĭŋ-nĭŋ) .... China	35·28 N	105·50 E
192	Jingpo Hu (L.) (jyĭŋ-pwo hōō) China	44·10 N	129·00 E
193	Jing Xian (jyĭŋ shyěn) ..... China	26·32 N	109·45 E
190	Jing Xian .... China	37·43 N	116·17 E
192	Jingxing (jyĭŋ-shyĭŋ) .... China	47·00 N	123·00 E
190	Jingzhi (jyĭŋ-jr) .... China	36·19 N	119·23 E
193	Jinhua (jyĭn-hwä) .... China	29·10 N	119·42 E
190	Jining (jyē-nĭŋ) .... China	35·26 N	116·34 E
192	Jining .... China	41·00 N	113·10 E
217	Jinja (jĭn'jä) .... Ug.	0·26 N	33·12 E
126	Jinotega (kē-nô-tā'gä) .... Nic.	13·07 N	86·00 W
126	Jinotepe (kē-nô-tā'pā) .... Nic.	11·52 N	86·12 W
190	Jinqiao (jyĭn-chyou) .... China	31·46 N	116·46 E
191	Jinshan (jyĭn-shän) China (Shanghai In.)	30·53 N	121·09 E
188	Jinta (jyĭn-tä) .... China	40·11 N	98·45 E
190	Jintan (jyĭn-tän) .... China	31·47 N	119·34 E
190	Jin Xian (jyĭn shyěn) ...... China	39·04 N	121·40 E
190	Jinxiang (jyĭn-shyäŋ) .... China	35·03 N	116·20 E
193	Jinyun (jyĭn-yōōn) .... China	28·40 N	120·08 E
190	Jinzhai (jyĭn-jī) .... China	31·41 N	115·51 E
192	Jinzhou (jyĭn-jō) .... China	41·00 N	121·00 E
190	Jinzhou Wan (B.) (jyĭn-jō wän) China	39·07 N	121·17 E
195	Jinzū-Gawa (Strm.) (jēn'zōō gä'wä) . Jap.	36·26 N	137·18 E
134	Jipijapa (kē-pē-hä'pä) .... Ec.	1·36 s	80·52 W
126	Jiquilisco (kē-kē-lē's-kō) ...... Sal.	13·18 N	88·32 W
124	Jiquilpan de Juarez (kē-kēl'pän dā hwä'räz) . Mex.	20·00 N	102·43 W
125	Jiquipilco (hē-kē-pē'l-kô) Mex. (In.)	19·32 N	99·37 W
188	Jirgalanta .... Mong.	48·08 N	91·40 E
218	Jirjā (jĭr'gá) ..... Egypt (Nile In.)	26·20 N	31·51 E
162	Jistredo, Sierra de (Mts.) (sē-ě'r-rä-dě-kēs-trě'dô) . Sp.	42·50 N	6·15 W
125	Jitotol (kē-tô-tōl') .... Mex.	17·03 N	92·54 W
165	Jiu (R.) .... Rom.	44·45 N	23·17 E
191	Jiujiang (jyô-jyäŋ) China (Canton In.)	22·50 N	113·02 E
193	Jiujiang .... China	29·43 N	116·00 E
188	Jiuquan (jyô-chyän) .... China	39·46 N	98·26 E
190	Jiurongcheng (jyô-rôŋ-chŭŋ) China	37·23 N	122·31 E
190	Jiushouzhang (jyô-shō-jäŋ) .. China	35·59 N	115·52 E
192	Jiuwuqing (jyō-wōō-chyĭŋ) China (In.)	32·39 N	116·51 E
190	Jiuyongnian (jyô-yôŋ-nĭěn) . China	36·41 N	114·46 E
190	Ji Xian (jyē shyěn) .... China	35·25 N	114·03 E
190	Ji Xian .... China	37·37 N	115·33 E
190	Ji Xian .... China	40·03 N	117·25 E
190	Jiyum (R.) (jyē-yōōm) ..... China	39·35 N	117·34 E
212	João Belo (zho'un-bě'lō) .... Moz.	25·00 s	33·45 E
135	João Pessoa (Paraíba) (shô-ouN' pě-sōá') (pä-rä-ē'bá) . Braz.	7·09 s	34·45 W
137	João Ribeiro (zhô-un-rē-bā'rō) Braz. (Rio de Janeiro In.)	20·42 s	44·03 W
128	Jobabo (R.) (hō-bä'bä) ...... Cuba	20·50 N	77·15 W
89	Jock (R.) (jŏk) Can. (Ottawa In.)	45·08 N	75·51 W
124	Jocotepec (hô-kō-tå-pěk') .... Mex.	20·17 N	103·26 W
162	Jodar (hō'där) .... Sp.	37·54 N	3·20 W
184	Jodhpur (jōd'pōōr) .... India	26·23 N	73·00 E
157	Joensuu (yô-ěn'sōō) .... Fin.	62·35 N	29·46 E
93	Joffre, Mt. (jŏ'f'r) .... Can.	50·32 N	115·13 W
195	Jōga-Shima (I.) (jō'gä shē'mä) Jap. (Tōkyō In.)	35·07 N	139·37 E
166	Jōgeva (yû'gě-vá) ...... Sov. Un.	58·45 N	26·23 E
96	Joggins (jŏ'gĭnz) .... Can.	45·42 N	64·27 W
213	Johannesburg (yô-hän'ěs-bōōrgh) S. Afr. (Johannesburg & Pretoria In.)	26·08 s	27·54 E
110	John Day Dam .... Or.	45·40 N	120·15 W
110	John Day R. (jŏn dā) .... Or.	44·46 N	120·15 W
110	John Day R., Middle Fork .... Or.	44·53 N	119·04 W
110	John Day R., North Fork ..... Or.	45·03 N	118·50 W
116	John Martin Res. (jŏn mär'tĭn) Co.	37·57 N	103·04 W
112	Johnson (R.) (jŏn'sŭn) Or. (Portland In.)	45·27 N	122·20 W
105	Johnsonburg (jŏn'sŭn-bûrg) ... Pa.	41·30 N	78·40 W
104	Johnson City (jŏn'sŭn) .... Il.	37·50 N	88·55 W
105	Johnson City .... NY	42·10 N	76·00 W
121	Johnson City .... Tn.	36·17 N	82·23 W
198	Johnston (I.) (jŏn'stŭn) ... Oceania	17·00 N	168·00 W
92	Johnstone St. .... Can.	50·25 N	126·00 W
217	Johnston Falls .... Afr.	10·35 s	28·50 E
105	Johnstown (jonz'toun) .... NY	43·00 N	74·20 W
105	Johnstown .... Pa.	40·20 N	78·50 W
183	Johor (R.) (jŭ-hōr') Mala. (Singapore In.)	1·39 N	103·52 E
183	Johor Bahru (bá-hŭ-rōō') Mala. (Singapore In.)	1·28 N	103·46 E
166	Jōhvi (yû'vĭ) .... Sov. Un.	59·21 N	27·21 E
160	Joigny (zhwán-yē') .... Fr.	47·58 N	3·26 E
136	Joinville (zhwăN-vēl') .... Braz.	26·18 s	48·47 W
160	Joinville .... Fr.	48·28 N	5·05 E
133	Joinville (I.) .... Ant.	63·00 s	53·30 W
124	Jojutla (hō-hōō'tlá) .... Mex.	18·39 N	99·11 W
150	Jōkullsá (R.) (yû'kōōls-ô) ..... Ice.	65·38 N	16·08 W
124	Jola (kō'lä) .... Mex.	21·08 N	104·26 W
107	Joliet (jō-lĭ-ět') ... Il. (Chicago In.)	41·37 N	88·05 W
97	Joliette (zhô-lyět') .... Can.	46·01 N	73·30 W
196	Jolo (hō-lō) .... Phil.	5·59 N	121·05 E
196	Jolo I. .... Phil.	5·55 N	121·15 E
197	Jomalig (I.) (hô-mä'lēg) . Phil. (In.)	14·44 N	122·34 E
124	Jomulco (hô-mōōl'kō) .... Mex.	21·08 N	104·24 W
124	Jonacatepec (hō-nä-kä-tå-pěk') Mex.	18·39 N	98·46 W
157	Jonava (yō-nä'vá) .... Sov. Un.	55·05 N	24·15 E
156	Jondal (yōn'däl) .... Nor.	60·16 N	6·16 E
197	Jones (jōnz) .... Phil. (In.)	13·56 N	122·05 E
197	Jones .... Phil. (In.)	16·35 N	121·39 E
117	Jonesboro (jōnz'bûro) .... Ar.	35·49 N	90·42 W
119	Jonesboro .... La.	32·14 N	92·43 W
119	Jonesville (jōnz'vĭl) .... La.	31·35 N	91·50 W
104	Jonesville .... Mi	42·00 N	84·45 W
214	Jong (R.) .... S. L.	8·10 N	12·10 W
157	Joniškis (yô'nĭsh-kĭs) .... Sov. Un.	56·14 N	23·36 E
156	Jönköping (yûn'chû-pĭng) ... Swe.	57·47 N	14·10 E
97	Jonquiere (zhôN-kyâr') ...... Can.	48·25 N	71·15 W
125	Jonuta (hô-nōō'tä) .... Mex.	18·07 N	92·09 W
160	Jonzac (zhôN-zák') .... Fr.	45·27 N	0·27 W
117	Joplin (jŏp'lĭn) .... Mo.	37·05 N	94·31 W
182	Jordan (jôr'dăn) .... Asia	30·15 N	38·00 E
183	Jordan (R.) . Jordan (Palestine In.)	31·58 N	35·36 E
113	Jordan R.. Ut. (Salt Lake City In.)	40·42 N	111·56 W
187	Jorhāt (jôr-hät') .... India	26·43 N	94·16 E
124	Jorullo, Vol. de (vôl-kä'n-dě-hô-rōōl'yō) . Mex.	18·54 N	101·38 W
215	Jos Plat. (jôs) .... Nig.	9·53 N	9·05 E
204	Joseph Bonaparte, G. (jō'sěf bō'ná-pärt) . Austl.	13·30 s	128·40 E
89	Josephburg. . Can. (Edmonton In.)	53·45 N	113·06 W
89	Joseph L. (jō'sěf lāk) Can. (Edmonton In.)	53·18 N	113·06 W
114	Joshua Tree Natl. Mon. (jō'shū-á trē) . Ca.	34·02 N	115·53 W
215	Jos Plat. .... Nig.	9·53 N	9·05 E
156	Jostedalsbreen (Gl.) (yôstě-däls-brěěn) . Nor.	61·40 N	6·55 E
156	Jotun Fjell (Mts.) (yō'tōōn fyel') Nor.	61·44 N	8·11 E
128	Joulter's Cays (Is.) (jōl'tērz) .. Ba.	25·20 N	78·10 W
161	Jouy-le-Chatel (zhwē-lě-shä-těl') Fr. (Paris In.)	48·40 N	3·07 E
128	Jovellanos (hō-věl-yä'nōs) ... Cuba	22·50 N	81·10 W
195	Jōyō .... Jap. (Ōsaka In.)	34·51 N	135·48 E
120	J. Percy Priest Res. .... Tn.	36·00 N	86·45 W
124	Juan Aldama (kōōá'n-äl-dá'mä) Mex.	24·16 N	103·21 W
110	Juan de Fuca, Str. of (hwän' dā fōō'kä) . Wa.-Can.	48·25 N	124·37 W
213	Juan de Nova, Île (I.) .... Afr.	17·18 s	43·07 E
122	Juan Diaz, (R.) (kōōá'n-dē'-äz) Pan. (In.)	9·05 N	79·30 W
133	Juan Fernández, Islas de (Is.) (ē's-läs-dě-hwän' fěr-nän'dāth) Chile	33·30 s	79·00 W
137	Juan L. Lacaze (hōōá'n-ě'lě-lä-kä'zě) . Ur. (Buenos Aires In.)	34·25 s	57·28 W
128	Juan Luis, Cayos de (Is.) (ka-yōs-dě-hwän lōō-ēs') . Cuba	22·15 N	82·00 W
135	Juàzeiro (zhōōá'zā'rô) .... Braz.	9·27 s	40·28 W
135	Juazeiro do Norte (zhōōá'zā'rô-dô-nôr-tě) . Braz.	7·16 s	38·57 W
136	Juárez (hōōá'rěz) .... Arg.	37·42 s	59·46 W
211	Jūbā .... Sud.	4·58 N	31·37 E
218	Juba R. (jōō'bá) Som. (Horn of Afr. In.)	1·30 N	42·25 E
183	Jubayl (Byblos) (jōō-bīl') Leb. (Palestine In.)	34·07 N	35·38 E
162	Júcar (R.) (hōō'kär) .... Sp.	39·10 N	1·22 W
128	Júcaro (hōō'ká-rô) .... Cuba	21·40 N	78·50 W
124	Juchipila (hōō-chē-pē'lá) .... Mex.	21·26 N	103·09 W
122	Juchitán (hōō-chē-tän') ..... Mex.	16·15 N	95·00 W
125	Juchitán de Zaragoza (hōō-chē-tän' dā thä-rä-gō'thä) . Mex.	16·27 N	95·03 W
124	Juchitlán (hōō-chē-tlän) ..... Mex.	20·05 N	104·07 W
126	Jucuapa (kōō-kwä'pä) .... Sal.	13·30 N	88·24 W
186	Juddah .... Sau. Ar.	21·30 N	39·15 E
158	Judenburg (jōō'děn-bûrg) .... Aus.	47·10 N	14·40 E
111	Judith R. (jōō'dĭth) .... Mt.	47·20 N	109·36 W
190	Juhua Dao (I.) (jyōō-hwä dou) China	40·30 N	120·47 E
126	Juigalpa (hwē-gäl'pä) .... Nic.	12·02 N	85·24 W
161	Juilly (zhwē-yē') ... Fr. (Paris In.)	49·01 N	2·41 E
155	Juist (I.) (yōō'ēst) .... F.R.G.	53·41 N	6·50 E
137	Juiz de Fora (zhōō-ēzh' dā fō'rä) Braz. (Rio de Janeiro In.)	21·47 s	43·20 W
136	Jujuy (hōō-hwē') .... Arg.	24·14 s	65·15 W
136	Jujuy (Prov.) (hōō-hwē') .... Arg.	23·00 s	65·45 W

ng-sing; ŋ-baŋk; N-nasalized n; nŏd; cŏmmit; ōld; ôbey; ôrder; fōōd; fŏŏt; ou-out; s-soft; sh-dish; th-thin; pūre; ûnite; ûrn; stŭd; circŭs; ū-as "y" in study; '-indeterminate vowel.

296 Jukskei — Kaneohe PRONOUNCING INDEX

Page	Name Pronunciation Region	Lat. °'	Long. °'
213	Jukskei (R.) S. Afr. (Johannesburg & Pretoria In.)	25·58 S	27·58 E
116	Julesburg (jōōlz'bûrg) Co.	40·59 N	102·16 W
134	Juliaca (hōō-lē-ä'kä) Peru	15·26 S	70·12 W
75	Julianehåb Grnld.	60·07 N	46·20 W
161	Jülich (yü'lēk) F.R.G. (Ruhr In.)	50·55 N	6·22 E
164	Julijske Alpe (Mts.) (û'lēy-skě' äl'pě) Yugo.	46·05 N	14·05 E
184	Jullundur India	31·29 N	75·39 E
184	Julpaiguri India	26·35 N	88·48 E
129	Jumento Cays (Is.) (hōō-měn'tō) Ba.	23·05 N	75·40 W
155	Jumet (zhü-mě') Bel.	50·28 N	4·30 E
162	Jumilla (hōō-mēl'yä) Sp.	38·28 N	1·20 W
109	Jump (R.) (jŭmp) Wi.	45·18 N	90·53 W
89	Jumpingpound Cr. (jŭmp-ĭng-pound) Can. (Calgary In.)	51·01 N	114·34 W
183	Jumrah Indon. (Singapore In.)	1·48 N	101·04 E
135	Jumundá (R.) (zhōō-mōō'n-dä') Braz.	1·33 S	57·42 W
184	Junagādh (jōō-nä'gŭd) India	21·33 N	70·25 E
218	Junayfah Egypt (Suez In.)	30·11 N	32·26 E
183	Junaynah, Ra's al (Mt.) Egypt (Palestine In.)	29·02 N	33·58 E
118	Junction (jŭŋk'shŭn) Tx.	30·29 N	99·48 W
117	Junction City Ks.	39·01 N	96·49 W
137	Jundiaí (zhōō'n-dyä-ē') Braz. (Rio de Janeiro In.)	23·12 S	46·52 W
101	Juneau (jōō'nō) Ak.	58·25 N	134·30 W
158	Jungfrau Pk. (yŏŏng'frou) Switz.	46·30 N	7·59 E
137	Junín (hōō-nē'n) Arg. (Buenos Aires In.)	34·35 S	60·56 W
134	Junín Col. (In.)	4·47 N	73·39 W
183	Juniyah (jōō-nē'ě) Leb. (Palestine In.)	33·59 N	35·38 E
150	Junkeren (Mtn.) (yŏŏn'kě-rěn) Nor.	66·29 N	14·58 E
112	Jupiter, Mt. Wa. (Seattle In.)	47·42 N	123·04 W
99	Jupiter (R.) Can.	49·40 N	63·20 W
211	Jur (R.) (jŏŏr) Sud.	6·38 N	27·52 E
154	Jura (I.) (jōō'rȧ) Scot.	56·09 N	6·45 W
161	Jura (Mts.) (zhü-rȧ') Switz.	46·55 N	6·49 E
154	Jura, Sd. of (jōō'rȧ) Scot.	55·45 N	5·55 W
157	Jurbarkas (yŏŏr-bär'käs) Sov. Un.	55·06 N	22·50 E
157	Jūrmala Sov. Un.	56·57 N	23·37 E
190	Jurong (jyōō-rôŋ) China	31·58 N	119·12 E
134	Juruá (R.) (zhōō-rōō-ä') Braz.	5·27 S	67·39 W
135	Juruena (R.) (zhōō-rōōě'nä) Braz.	12·22 S	58·34 W
134	Jutaí (R.) (zhōō-tåy) Braz.	4·26 S	68·16 W
126	Jutiapa (hōō-tê-ä'pä) Guat.	14·16 N	89·55 W
126	Juticalpa (hōō-tê-käl'pä) Hond.	14·35 N	86·17 W
124	Juventino Rosas (ĸōō-věn-tē'nô-rô-säs) Mex.	20·38 N	101·02 W
128	Juventud, Isla de la (I.) Cuba	21·40 N	82·45 W
61	Juvisy-sur-Orge (zhü-vē-sē'sür-ôrzh') Fr. (Paris In.)	48·41 N	2·22 E
190	Ju Xian (jyōō shyěn) China	35·35 N	118·50 E
124	Juxtahuaca (hōōs-tlȧ-hwä'kä) Mex.	17·20 N	98·02 W
165	Južna Morava (R.) (û'zhnä mô'rä-vä) Yugo.	42·30 N	22·00 E
190	Juye (jyōō-yů) China	35·25 N	116·05 E
156	Jylland (Reg.) Den.	56·04 N	9·00 E
157	Jyväskylä (yû'věs-kû-lě) Fin.	62·14 N	25·46 E

K

Page	Name Pronunciation Region	Lat. °'	Long. °'
217	Kaabong Ug.	3·31 N	34·08 E
213	Kaalfontein (kärl-fŏn-tān) S. Afr. (Johannesburg & Pretoria In.)	26·02 S	28·16 E
212	Kaappunt (C.) S. Afr. (In.)	34·21 S	18·30 E
196	Kabaena, Pulau (I.) (kä-bȧ-ä'nȧ) Indon.	5·35 S	121·07 E
210	Kabala (kȧ-bȧ'lȧ) S. L.	9·43 N	11·39 W
217	Kabale Ug.	1·15 S	29·59 E
217	Kabalo (kä-bä'lō) Zaire	6·03 S	26·55 E
212	Kabambare (kä-bäm-bä'rȧ) Zaire	4·47 S	27·45 E
215	Kabba Nig.	7·50 N	6·03 E
195	Kabe (kä'bā) Jap.	34·32 N	132·30 E
96	Kabinakagami (R.) Can.	49·00 N	84·15 W
216	Kabinda (kä-bēn'dä) Zaire	6·08 S	24·29 E
216	Kabompo (R.) (kȧ-bôm'pō) Zambia	14·00 S	23·40 E
212	Kabongo (kȧ-bông'ô) Zaire	7·58 S	25·10 E
214	Kabot Gui.	10·48 N	14·57 W
152	Kaboudia, Ra's (C.) Tun.	35·17 N	11·28 E
184	Kābul (kä'bŏŏl) Afg.	34·39 N	69·14 E
187	Kabul (R.) (kä'bŏŏl) Asia	34·44 N	69·43 E
217	Kabunda Zaire	12·25 S	29·22 E
217	Kabwe (Broken Hill) Zambia	14·27 S	28·27 E
173	Kachuga (kȧ-chōō-gȧ) Sov. Un.	54·09 N	105·43 E
215	Kadei (R.) Cam.-Cen. Afr. Rep.	4·00 N	15·10 E
167	Kadiyevka (kȧ-dĭ-yěf'kȧ) Sov. Un.	48·34 N	38·37 E
170	Kadnikov (käd'nê-kôf) Sov. Un.	59·30 N	40·10 E
95	Kadoma Jap. (Ōsaka In.)	34·43 N	135·36 E
15	Kaduna (kä-dōō'nä) Nig.	10·33 N	7·27 E
15	Kaduna (R.) Nig.	9·30 N	6·00 E
14	Kaédi (kä-ā-dē') Mauritania	16·09 N	13·30 W
00	Kaena Pt. (kä'ā-nä) Hi.	21·33 N	158·19 W
194	Kaesŏng (Kaijo) (kä'ě-sŭng) (kī'jō) Kor.	38·00 N	126·35 E
215	Kafanchan Nig.	9·36 N	8·17 E
211	Kafia Kingi (kä'fê-ȧ kĭŋ'gê) Sud.	9·17 N	24·28 E
212	Kafue (kä'fōō) Zambia	15·45 S	28·17 E
217	Kafue (R.) Zambia	15·45 S	26·30 E
217	Kafue Flats (Pln.) Zambia	16·15 S	26·30 E
217	Kafue Natl. Pk. Zambia	15·00 S	25·35 E
217	Kafwira Zaire	12·10 S	27·33 E
167	Kagal'nik (R.) (kä-gäl''nêk) Sov. Un.	46·58 N	39·25 E
217	Kagera (R.) (kä-gā'rȧ) Tan.	1·10 S	31·10 E
195	Kagoshima (kä'gô-shē'mȧ) Jap.	31·35 N	130·31 E
195	Kagoshima-Wan (B.) (kä'gô-shē'mä wän) Jap.	31·24 N	130·39 E
167	Kagul (ka-gōōl') Sov. Un.	45·49 N	28·17 E
196	Kahayan (R.) Indon.	1·45 S	113·40 E
216	Kahemba Zaire	7·17 S	19·00 E
217	Kahia Zaire	6·21 S	28·24 E
117	Kahoka (kȧ-hō'kȧ) Mo.	40·26 N	91·42 W
100	Kahoolawe (I) (kä-hōō-lä'wē) Hi.	20·28 N	156·48 W
214	Kahoué, Mont (Mtn.) Ivory Coast	7·06 N	7·15 W
109	Kahshahpiwi (R.) Can.	48·24 N	90·56 W
100	Kahuku Pt. (kä-hōō'kōō) Hi.	21·50 N	157·50 W
100	Kahului Hi.	20·53 N	156·28 W
197	Kai, Kepulauan (Is.) Indon.	5·35 S	132·45 E
183	Kaiang Mala. (Singapore In.)	3·00 N	101·47 E
96	Kaiashk (R.) Can.	49·40 N	89·30 W
115	Kaibab Ind. Res. (kä'ē-bȧb) Az.	36·55 N	112·45 W
115	Kaibab Plat. Az.	36·30 N	112·10 W
188	Kaidu (R.) (kī-dōō) China	42·35 N	84·04 E
135	Kaieteur Fall (kī-ē-tōōr') Guy.	4·48 N	59·24 W
190	Kaifeng (kī-fŭŋ) China	34·48 N	114·22 E
	Kaijo, see Kaesong		
197	Kai Kecil (I.) Indon.	5·45 S	132·40 E
169	Kaikyō, Sōya (Str.) (sô'yȧ kȧ-ē'kĭ-ô) Sov. Un.	45·45 N	141·20 E
100	Kailua (kä'ē-lōō'ȧ) Hi.	21·18 N	157·43 W
100	Kailua Kona Hi.	19·49 N	155·59 W
197	Kaimana Indon.	3·32 S	133·47 E
195	Kainan (kä'ē-nän') Jap.	34·09 N	135·14 E
215	Kainji L. Nig.	10·25 N	4·50 E
158	Kaiserslautern (kī-zěrs-lou'těrn) F.R.G.	49·26 N	7·46 E
205	Kaitaia (kä-ē-tä'ē-ȧ) N. Z. (In.)	35·30 S	173·28 E
100	Kaiwi Chan (kä'ē-wē) Hi.	21·10 N	157·38 W
193	Kaiyuan (kī-yuän) China	23·42 N	103·20 E
192	Kaiyuan (kī'yōō-än') China	42·30 N	124·00 E
101	Kaiyuh Mts. (kī-yōō') Ak.	64·25 N	157·38 W
150	Kajaani (kä'yȧ-nē) Fin.	64·15 N	27·16 E
183	Kajang, Gunong (Mt.) Mala. (Singapore In.)	2·47 N	104·05 E
195	Kajiki (kä'jē-kê) Jap.	31·44 N	130·41 E
167	Kakhovka (kä-ĸôf'kȧ) Sov. Un.	46·46 N	33·32 E
167	Kakhovskoye (L.) (kȧ-ĸôf'skô-yě) Sov. Un.	47·21 N	33·33 E
187	Kākināda India	16·58 N	82·18 E
101	Kaktovik (kăk-tō'vĭk) Ak.	70·08 N	143·51 W
93	Kakwa (R.) (kăk'wȧ) Can.	54·00 N	118·55 W
171	Kalach (kȧ-lăch') Sov. Un.	50·15 N	40·55 E
188	Kaladan (R.) Bur.	21·07 N	93·04 E
212	Kalahari Des. (kä-lä-hä'rē) Bots.	23·00 S	22·03 E
112	Kalama (kȧ-lăm'ȧ) Wa. (Portland In.)	46·01 N	122·50 W
112	Kalama (R.) Wa. (Portland In.)	46·03 N	122·47 W
165	Kalámai (kä-lä-mī') Grc.	37·04 N	22·08 E
104	Kalamazoo (kăl-ȧ-mȧ-zōō') Mi.	42·20 N	85·40 W
104	Kalamazoo (R.) Mi.	42·35 N	86·00 W
167	Kalanchak (kä-län-chäk') Sov. Un.	46·17 N	33·14 E
100	Kalapana (kä-lä-pȧ'nä) Hi.	19·25 N	155·00 W
186	Kalar (Mtn.) Iran	31·43 N	51·41 E
184	Kalāt (kŭ-lät') Pak.	29·05 N	66·36 E
196	Kalatoa, Pulau (I.) Indon.	7·22 S	122·30 E
161	Kaldenkirchen (käl'děn-kēr-ĸěn) F.R.G. (Ruhr In.)	51·19 N	6·13 E
217	Kalemie (Albertville) Zaire	5·56 S	29·12 E
192	Kalgan (Zhangjiakou) (käl-gän) (jäŋ-jyä-kō) China	40·45 N	114·58 E
204	Kalgoorlie (kăl-gōōr'lē) Austl.	30·45 S	121·35 E
153	Kaliakra, Nos (Pt.) Rom.	43·25 N	28·42 E
217	Kalima Zaire	2·34 S	26·37 E
166	Kalinin (Tver) (kä-lē'nēn) (tvěr) Sov. Un.	56·52 N	35·57 E
166	Kalinin (Oblast) Sov. Un.	56·50 N	33·08 E
157	Kaliningrad (Königsberg) (kä-lē-nēn'grät) (kû'něks-běrgh) Sov. Un.	54·42 N	20·32 E
174	Kaliningrad (kä-lē-nēn'grät) Sov. Un. (Moscow In.)	55·55 N	37·49 E
167	Kalinkovichi (kä-lēn-ko-vē'chē) Sov. Un.	52·07 N	29·19 E
110	Kalispel Ind. Res. (kăl-ĭ-spěl') Wa.	48·25 N	117·30 W
111	Kalispell (kăl'ĭ-spěl) Mt.	48·12 N	114·18 W
159	Kalisz (kä'lēsh) Pol.	51·45 N	18·05 E
217	Kaliua Tan.	5·04 S	31·48 E
150	Kalix (R.) (kä'lēks) Swe.	67·12 N	21·41 E
156	Kalmar (käl'mär) Swe.	56·40 N	16·19 E
156	Kalmar Sund (Sd.) (käl'mär) Swe.	56·30 N	16·17 E
167	Kal'mius (R.) (käl''myōōs) Sov. Un.	47·15 N	37·38 E
149	Kalmthout Bel. (Brussels In.)	51·23 N	4·28 E
171	Kalmyk A. S. S. R. (kȧl'mĭk) Sov. Un.	46·56 N	46·00 E
159	Kalocsa (kä'lô-chä) Hung.	46·32 N	19·00 E
100	Kalohi Chan. (kä-lō'hĭ) Hi.	20·55 N	157·15 W
217	Kaloko Zaire	6·47 S	25·48 E
217	Kalomo (kä-lō'mō) Zambia	17·02 S	26·30 E
184	Kalsubai Mt. India	24·43 N	73·47 E
149	Kaltenkirchen (käl'těn-kēr-ĸěn) F.R.G. (Hamburg In.)	53·50 N	9·57 E
185	Kālu (R.) India (In.)	19·18 N	73·14 E
166	Kaluga (kȧ-lōō'gä) Sov. Un.	54·29 N	36·12 E
166	Kaluga (Oblast) Sov. Un.	54·10 N	34·30 E
156	Kalundborg (kȧ-lōōn''bôr') Den.	55·42 N	11·07 E
159	Kalush (kä'lōōsh) Sov. Un.	49·02 N	24·24 E
157	Kalvarija (käl-vä-rē'yȧ) Sov. Un.	54·24 N	23·17 E
185	Kalwa India (Bombay In.)	19·12 N	72·59 E
174	Kal'ya (käl'yȧ) Sov. Un. (Urals In.)	60·17 N	59·58 E
185	Kalyān India (In.)	19·16 N	73·07 E
166	Kalyazin (käl-yȧ'zēn) Sov. Un.	57·13 N	37·55 E
173	Kalyma (R.) Sov. Un.	66·32 N	152·46 E
170	Kama (L.) Sov. Un.	55·28 N	51·00 E
170	Kama (R.) (kä'mä) Sov. Un.	56·10 N	53·50 E
194	Kamaishi (kä'mä-ē'shê) Jap.	39·16 N	142·03 E
195	Kamakura (kä'mä-kōō'rä) Jap. (Tōkyō In.)	35·19 N	139·33 E
186	Kamarān (I.) P. D. R. of Yem.	15·19 N	41·47 E
184	Kāmārhāti India (In.)	22·41 N	88·23 E
212	Kambove (käm-bō'vě) Zaire	10·58 S	26·43 E
173	Kamchatka, P-Ov (Pen.) Sov. Un.	55·19 N	157·45 E
173	Kamchatka (R.) Sov. Un.	54·15 N	158·38 E
161	Kamen (kä'měn) F.R.G. (Ruhr In.)	51·35 N	7·40 E
167	Kamenets-Podol skiy (kȧ-mă'něts pô-dôl'skĭ) Sov. Un.	48·41 N	26·34 E
164	Kamenjak, Rt (C.) (ĸä'mě-nyäk) Yugo.	44·45 N	13·57 E
167	Kamenka (kä-měŋ'kȧ) Sov. Un.	48·02 N	28·43 E
159	Kamenka Sov. Un.	50·06 N	24·20 E
172	Kamen'-na-Obi (kä-mĭny'nŭ ô'bē) Sov. Un.	53·43 N	81·28 E
167	Kamensk-Shakhtinskiy (kä'měnsk-shäk'tĭn-skĭ) Sov. Un.	48·17 N	40·16 E
174	Kamensk-Ural'skiy (kä'měn-skĭ ōō-räl'skĭ) Sov. Un. (Urals In.)	56·27 N	61·55 E
158	Kamenz (kä'měnts) G.D.R.	51·16 N	14·05 E
195	Kameoka (kä'mā-ōkä) Jap. (Ōsaka In.)	35·01 N	135·35 E
184	Kāmet (Mt.) India	35·50 N	79·42 E
158	Kamień Pomorski Pol.	53·57 N	14·48 E
195	Kamikoma (kä'mê-kō'mä) Jap. (Ōsaka In.)	34·45 N	135·50 E
216	Kamina Zaire	8·44 S	25·00 E
109	Kaministikwia (R.) (kȧ-mĭ-nĭ-stĭk'wĭ-ȧ) Can.	48·40 N	89·41 W
217	Kamituga Zaire	3·04 S	28·11 E
93	Kamloops (kăm'lōōps) Can.	50·40 N	120·20 W
	Kammer, see Atter See		
217	Kampala (käm-pä'lä) Ug.	0·19 N	32·25 E
196	Kampar (R.) (käm'pär) Indon.	0·30 N	101·30 E
216	Kampene Zaire	3·36 S	26·40 E
149	Kampenhout Bel. (Brussels In.)	50·56 N	4·33 E
161	Kamp-Lintfort (kämp-lēnt'fôrt) F.R.G. (Ruhr In.)	51·30 N	6·34 E
196	Kâmpóng Saôm Kamp.	10·40 N	103·50 E
196	Kâmpóng Thum (kŏm'pŏng-tŏm) Kamp.	12·41 N	104·29 E
196	Kâmpôt (käm'pōt) Kamp.	10·41 N	104·07 E
158	Kamp R. (kămp) Aus.	48·30 N	15·45 E
196	Kampuchea Asia	12·15 N	104·00 E
95	Kamsack (kăm'săk) Can.	51·34 N	101·54 W
141	Kamskoye (Res.) Sov. Un.	59·08 N	56·30 E
174	Kamskoye Vdkhr. (Res.) Sov. Un. (Urals In.)	59·03 N	56·48 E
217	Kamudilo Zaire	7·42 S	27·18 E
100	Kamuela Hi.	20·01 N	155·40 W
127	Kamuk, Cerro (Mt.) (sě'r-rô-kä-mōō'k) C. R.	9·18 N	83·02 W
194	Kamu Misaki (C.) (kä'mōō mê-sä'kē) Jap.	43·25 N	139·35 E
167	Kamyshevatskaya (kȧ-mwēsh'ě-vät'skä-yȧ) Sov. Un.	46·24 N	37·58 E
171	Kamyshin (kä-mwēsh'ĭn) Sov. Un.	50·08 N	45·20 E
170	Kamyshlov (kä-mēsh'lôf) Sov. Un.	56·50 N	62·32 E
172	Kan (R.) (kän) Sov. Un.	56·30 N	94·17 E
115	Kanab (kăn'ăb) Ut.	37·00 N	112·30 W
115	Kanab Plat. Az.	36·31 N	112·55 W
174	Kanabeki (kȧ-nä'byě-kĭ) Sov. Un. (Urals In.)	57·48 N	57·16 E
101	Kanaga (I.) (kă-nä'gȧ) Ak.	52·02 N	117·38 W
195	Kanagawa (Pref.) (kä'nä-gä'wä) Jap. (Tōkyō In.)	35·29 N	139·32 E
153	Kanā'is, Ra's al (C.) Egypt	31·14 N	28·08 E
195	Kanamachi (kä-nä-mä'chē) Jap. (Tōkyō In.)	35·46 N	139·52 E
216	Kananga (Luluabourg) (lōō'lōō-a-bōōrg') Zaire	6·14 S	22·17 E
174	Kananikol'skoye (kȧ-nȧ-nĭ-kôl'skô-yě) Sov. Un. (Urals In.)	52·48 N	57·29 E
126	Kanasín (kä-nä-sē'n) Mex. (In.)	20·54 N	89·31 W
101	Kanatak (kă-nä'tŏk) Ak.	57·35 N	155·48 W
103	Kanawha (R.) (kȧ-nô'wȧ) U. S.	37·55 N	81·50 W
195	Kanaya (kä-nä'yä) Jap. (Tōkyō In.)	35·10 N	139·49 E
195	Kanazawa (kä'nȧ-zä'wȧ) Jap.	36·34 N	136·38 E
184	Kānchenjunga (Mtn.) (kĭn-chĭn-jōōn'gȧ) India-Nep.	27·30 N	88·18 E
185	Kānchipuram India	12·55 N	79·43 E
216	Kanda Kanda (kän'dȧ kän'dȧ) Zaire	6·56 S	23·36 E
170	Kandalaksha (kȧn-dȧ-lȧk'shȧ) Sov. Un.	67·10 N	33·05 E
170	Kandalakshskiy Zaliv (B.) Sov. Un.	66·20 N	35·00 E
157	Kandava (kän'dȧ-vȧ) Sov. Un.	57·03 N	22·45 E
215	Kandi (käN-dē') Benin	11·08 N	2·56 E
184	Kandiāro Pak.	27·09 N	68·12 E
184	Kandla (kŭnd'lŭ) India	23·00 N	70·20 E
185	Kandy (kän'dê) Sri Lanka	7·18 N	80·42 E
105	Kane (kān) Pa.	41·40 N	78·50 W
100	Kaneohe (kä-nä-ō'hā) Hi.	21·25 N	157·47 W

ăt; finȧl; rāte; senāte; ärm; ȧsk; sofȧ; fâre; ch-choose; dh-as th in other; bē; ēvent; bět; recěnt; cratẽr; g-go; gh-guttural g; bĭt; ĭ-short neutral; rīde; ĸ-guttural k as ch in German ich;

Page	Name Pronunciation Region	Lat. °′	Long. °′
100	Kaneohe B. Hi.	21·32 N	157·40 W
167	Kanëv (kä-nyôf′) Sov. Un.	49·46 N	31·27 E
167	Kanevskaya (kȧ-nyĕf′skȧ) Sov. Un.	46·07 N	38·58 E
171	Kanevskoye Vdkhr (Res.) Sov. Un.	50·10 N	30·40 E
203	Kangaroo (I.) (kăŋ-gȧ-rōō′). Austl.	36·05 S	137·05 E
186	Kangāvar (kŭn′gä-vär) Iran	34·37 N	46·45 E
188	Kangding (käŋ-dĭŋ) China	30·15 N	101·58 E
196	Kangean, Kepulauan (I.) (käŋ′gē-än). Indon.	6·50 S	116·22 E
194	Kanggye (käng′gyĕ) Kor.	40·55 N	126·40 E
194	Kanghwa (I.) (käng′hwä) Kor.	37·38 N	126·00 E
194	Kangnŭng′nōōng) Kor.	37·42 N	128·50 E
216	Kango (kän-gō) Gabon	0·09 N	10·08 E
216	Kangowa Zaire	9·55 S	22·48 E
170	Kanin, P-Ov. (Pen.) (kȧ-nēn′) Sov. Un.	68·00 N	45·00 E
170	Kanin Nos, Mys (G.) Sov. Un.	68·40 N	44·00 E
217	Kaningo Ken.	0·49 S	38·32 E
165	Kanjiža (kä′nyē-zhä) Yugo.	46·05 N	20·02 E
107	Kankakee (kăŋ-kȧ-kē′) Il. (Chicago In.)	41·07 N	87·53 W
104	Kankakee (R.) Il.	41·15 N	88·15 W
214	Kankan (kän-kän) (kän-kän′). Gui	10·23 N	9·18 W
121	Kannapolis (kăn-ăp′ô-lĭs) NC	35·30 N	80·38 W
195	Kannoura (kä′nō-ōō′rä) Jap.	33·34 N	134·18 E
215	Kano (kä′nō) Nig.	12·00 N	8·30 E
212	Kanonkop (Mtn.) S. Afr. (In.)	33·49 S	18·37 E
116	Kanopolis Res. (kăn-ŏp′ô-lĭs). Ks.	38·44 N	98·01 W
184	Kānpur (kän′pûr) India	26·00 N	82·45 E
102	Kansas (State) (kăn′zȧs) U. S.	38·30 N	99·40 W
117	Kansas (R.) Ks.	39·08 N	95·52 W
113	Kansas City. Ks. (Kansas City In.)	39·06 N	94·39 W
113	Kansas City. Mo. (Kansas City In.)	39·05 N	94·35 W
172	Kansk Sov. Un.	56·14 N	95·43 E
194	Kansŏng Kor.	38·09 N	128·29 E
196	Kantang (kän′täng′) Thai.	7·26 N	99·28 E
214	Kantchari Upper Volta	12·29 N	1·31 E
126	Kantunilkin (kän-tōō-nēl-kē′n) Mex. (In.)	21·07 N	87·30 W
174	Kanzhakovskiy Kamen Gora (kȧn-zhă′kôvs-kēē kămĭen) Sov. Un. (Urals In.)	59·38 N	59·12 E
193	Kaohsiung (kä-ô-syōōng′). Taiwan	22·35 N	120·25 E
214	Kaolack Senegal	14·09 N	16·04 W
211	Kaouar (Oasis) Niger	19·16 N	13·09 E
193	Kaoyu Hu (L.) (kä′ō-yōō′hōō) China	32·42 N	118·40 E
100	Kapaa Hi.	22·06 N	159·20 W
172	Kapal (kȧ-päl′) Sov. Un.	45·13 N	79·08 E
216	Kapanga Zaire	8·21 S	22·35 E
183	Kapchagay Sov. Un.	43·55 N	77·45 E
158	Kapfenberg (kȧp′fĕn-bĕrgh). Aus.	47·27 N	15·16 E
217	Kapiri Mposhi Zambia	13·58 S	28·41 E
211	Kapoeta Sud.	4·45 N	33·35 E
159	Kaposvár (kô′pôsh-vär) Hung.	46·21 N	17·45 E
194	Kapsan (käp′sän′) Kor.	40·59 N	128·22 E
91	Kapuskasing Can.	49·28 N	82·22 W
96	Kapuskasing (R.) Can.	48·55 N	82·55 W
171	Kapustin Yar (kä′pŏŏs-tēn yär′) Sov. Un.	48·30 N	45·40 E
203	Kaputar, Mt. (kă-pû-tăr) Austl.	30·11 S	150·11 E
158	Kapuvár (kô′pōō-vär) Hung.	47·35 N	17·02 E
172	Kara (kärȧ) Sov. Un.	68·42 N	65·30 E
170	Kara (R.) Sov. Un.	68·30 N	65·20 E
174	Karabanovo (kä′rȧ-bä-nō-vō) Sov. Un. (Moscow In.)	56·19 N	38·43 E
174	Karabash (kó-rȧ-bäsh′) Sov. Un. (Urals In.)	55·27 N	60·14 E
171	Kara-Bogaz-Gol, Zaliv (B.) (kȧrä′ bŭ-gäs′). Sov. Un.	41·30 N	53·40 E
166	Karachev (kȧ-rȧ-chôf′) Sov. Un.	53·08 N	34·54 E
184	Karāchi Pak.	24·59 N	68·56 E
172	Karacumy (Des.) Sov. Un.	39·08 N	59·53 E
172	Karaganda (kȧ-rȧ-gän′dä) Sov. Un.	49·42 N	73·18 E
174	Karaidel (kä′rī-dĕl) Sov. Un. (Urals In.)	55·52 N	56·54 E
171	Kara-Khobda (R.) (kä-rȧ kôb′dȧ). Sov. Un.	50·40 N	55·00 E
187	Karakoram Pass India-Pak.	35·35 N	77·45 E
188	Karakoram Ra. (kä′rä kō′rōōm) India-Pak.	35·24 N	76·38 E
188	Karakorum (Ruins) Mong.	47·25 N	102·22 E
171	Karaköse (kä-rä-kŭ′sĕ) Tur.	39·50 N	43·10 E
168	Karakumy (kara-kum) (Des.) Sov. Un.	40·00 N	57·00 E
171	Karaman (kä-rä-män′) Tur.	37·10 N	33·00 E
188	Karamay (kär-äm-ā) China	45·37 N	84·53 E
205	Karamea Bght. (kȧ-rȧ-mē′ȧ bĭt) N. Z. (In.)	41·10 S	170·42 E
	Kara Sea, see Karskoye More		
188	Karashahr (Yanqi) (kä-rä-shä-är) (yän-chyē). China	42·14 N	86·28 E
195	Karatsu (kä′rȧ-tsōō) Jap.	33·28 N	129·59 E
172	Karaul (kä-rä-ōōl′) Sov. Un.	70·13 N	83·46 E
158	Karawanken Mts. Aus.	46·32 N	14·07 E
186	Karbalā′ (kŭr′bȧ-lä) Iraq	32·31 N	43·58 E
159	Karcag (kär′tsäg) Hung.	47·18 N	20·58 E
165	Kardhítsa Grc.	39·23 N	21·57 E
157	Kärdla (kĕrd′lȧ) Sov. Un.	58·59 N	22·44 E
168	Karelian (A. S. S. R.) Sov. Un.	62·30 N	32·35 E
217	Karema Tan.	6·49 S	30·26 E
172	Kargat (kär-gät′) Sov. Un.	55·17 N	80·07 E
188	Karghalik (Yecheng) (kä-är-gä-lē-kŭ) (yŭ-chŭŋ) China	37·30 N	79·26 E
170	Kargopol′ (kär-gō-pōl″). Sov. Un.	61·30 N	38·50 E
165	Kariaí Grc.	40·14 N	24·15 E
217	Kariba, L. Afr.	17·15 S	27·55 E
212	Karibib (kȧr′ȧ-bĭb) Namibia	21·55 S	15·50 E
185	Kārikāl (kä-rē-käl′) India	10·58 N	79·49 E
196	Karimata, Pulau-Pulau (Is.) (kä-rē-mä′tȧ). Indon.	1·08 S	108·10 E
196	Karimata, Selat (Karimata Strait) Indon.	1·00 S	107·10 E
183	Karimun Besar (I.) Indon. (Singapore In.)	1·10 N	103·28 E
196	Karimunjawa, Kepulauan (Is.) (kä′rē-mōōn-yä′vä). Indon.	5·36 S	110·15 E
218	Karin (kȧr′ĭn) Som. (Horn of Afr. In.)	10·43 N	45·50 E
172	Karkaralinsk (kär-kär-ä-lēnsk′) Sov. Un.	49·18 N	75·28 E
197	Karkar I. (kär′kär). Pap. N. Gui.	4·50 S	146·45 E
186	Karkheh (R.) Iran	32·45 N	47·50 E
167	Karkinitskiy Zailv (B.) (kär-kē-net′skĭ-ē zä′lĭf). Sov. Un.	45·50 N	32·45 E
158	Karl-Marx-Stadt (Chemnitz) G.D.R.	50·48 N	12·53 E
185	Karnataka (State) India	14·55 N	75·00 E
164	Karlobag (kär-lō-bäg′) Yugo.	44·30 N	15·03 E
164	Karlovac (kär′lô-vȧts) Yugo.	45·29 N	15·16 E
167	Karlovka (kȧr′lôv-kȧ) Sov. Un.	49·26 N	35·08 E
165	Karlovo (kär′lô-vō) Bul.	42·39 N	24·48 E
158	Karlovy Vary (kär′lô-vē vä′rê) Czech.	50·13 N	12·53 E
156	Karlshamn (kärls′häm) Swe.	56·11 N	14·50 E
156	Karlskrona (kärls′krō-nä) Swe.	56·10 N	15·33 E
158	Karlsruhe (kärls′rōō-ĕ) F.R.G.	49·00 N	8·23 E
156	Karlstad (kärl′städ) Swe.	59·25 N	13·28 E
101	Karluk (kär′lŭk) Ak.	57·30 N	154·22 W
156	Karmöy (I.) (kärm-ûe) Nor.	59·14 N	5·00 E
165	Karnobat (kär-nô′bät) Bul.	42·39 N	26·59 E
158	Kärnten (Carinthia) (State) (kĕrn′tĕn). Aus.	46·55 N	13·42 E
212	Karonga (kȧ-rōŋ′gȧ) Malawi	9·52 S	33·57 E
153	Kárpathos (I.) Grc.	35·34 N	27·26 E
174	Karpinsk (kär′pĭnsk) Sov. Un. (Urals In.)	59·46 N	60·00 E
171	Kars (kärs) Tur.	40·35 N	43·00 E
172	Karsakpay (kär-säk-pī′). Sov. Un.	47·47 N	67·07 E
166	Kārsava (kär′sä-vä) Sov. Un.	56·46 N	27·39 E
186	Karshi (kär′shē) Sov. Un.	38·30 N	66·08 E
172	Karskiye Vorota, Proliv (Str.) Sov. Un.	70·30 N	58·07 E
172	Karskoye More (Kara Sea) Sov. Un.	74·00 N	68·00 E
174	Kartaly (kȧr′tá lê) Sov. Un. (Urals In.)	53·05 N	60·40 E
185	Karunagapalli India	9·09 N	76·34 E
159	Karvina Czech.	49·50 N	18·30 E
92	Kasaan Ak.	55·32 N	132·24 E
216	Kasai (R.) Zaire	3·45 S	19·10 E
217	Kasama (kȧ-sä′mȧ) Zambia	10·13 S	31·12 E
217	Kasanga (kȧ-säŋ′gȧ) Tan.	8·28 S	31·09 E
195	Kasaoka (kä′sȧ-ō′kȧ) Jap.	34·33 N	133·29 E
210	Kasba-Tadla (käs′bȧ-täd′lȧ). Mor.	32·37 N	5·57 W
217	Kasempa (kȧ-sĕm′pȧ) Zambia	13·27 S	25·50 E
217	Kasenga (kȧ-seŋ′gȧ) Zaire	10·22 S	28·38 E
217	Kasese Ug.	0·10 N	30·05 E
217	Kasese Zaire	1·38 S	27·07 E
186	Kāshān (kā-shän′) Iran	33·52 N	51·15 E
188	Kashgar (Kashi) (käsh-gär) (kä-shr). China	39·29 N	76·00 E
	Kashi, see Kashgar		
188	K′ashih (Kashgar) China	39·29 N	76·00 E
195	Kashihara (kä′shê-hä′rä) Jap. (Ōsaka In.)	34·31 N	135·48 E
216	Kashiji Pln. Zambia	13·25 S	22·30 E
166	Kashin (kä-shēn′) Sov. Un.	57·20 N	37·38 E
166	Kashira (kä-shē′rȧ) Sov. Un.	54·49 N	38·11 E
195	Kashiwa (kä′shē-wä) Jap. (Tōkyō In.)	35·51 N	139·58 E
195	Kashiwara Jap. (Ōsaka In.)	34·35 N	135·38 E
170	Kashiwazaki (kä′shē-wä-zä′kê) Jap.	37·06 N	138·17 E
	Kashmir (Disputed Reg.) see Jammu and Kashmir		
184	Kashmor Pak.	28·33 N	69·34 E
174	Kashtak (käsh′täk) Sov. Un. (Urals In.)	55·18 N	61·25 E
166	Kasimov (kȧ-sē′môf) Sov. Un.	54·56 N	41·23 E
101	Kaskanak (kăs-kă′năk) Ak.	60·00 N	158·00 W
104	Kaskaskia (R.) (kăs-kăs′kĭ-ȧ) Il.	39·10 N	88·50 W
95	Kaskattama (R.) (kăs-kă-tä′mȧ). Can.	56·28 N	90·55 W
	Kaskinen, see Kaskö		
157	Kaskö (Kaskinen) (käs′kû) (käs′kē-nĕn). Fin.	62·24 N	21·18 E
174	Kasli (käs′lĭ). Sov. Un. (Urals In.)	55·54 N	60·46 E
212	Kasongo (kä-sôŋ′gō) Zaire	4·31 S	26·42 E
153	Kásos (I.) Grc.	35·20 N	26·55 E
211	Kassalā (kä-sä′lä) Sud.	15·26 N	36·28 E
158	Kassel (käs′ĕl) F.R.G.	51·19 N	9·30 E
109	Kasson (kăs′ŭn) Mn.	44·01 N	92·45 W
171	Kastamonu (kä-stȧ-mō′nōō). Tur.	41·20 N	33·50 E
164	Kastélli Grc. (In.)	35·13 N	24·11 E
165	Kastoría (kȧs-tō′rĭ-ȧ) Grc.	40·28 N	21·17 E
165	Kastron (käs′trôn) Grc.	39·52 N	25·01 E
184	Kasūr Pak.	31·10 N	74·29 E
216	Kataba Zambia	16·05 S	25·10 E
98	Katahdin, Mt. (kȧ-tä′dĭn) Me.	45·56 N	68·57 W
212	Katanga (Reg.) (kȧ-täŋ′gȧ). Zaire	8·30 S	25·00 E
204	Katanning (kȧ-tăn′ĭng) Austl.	33·45 S	117·45 E
174	Katav-Ivanovsk (kä′tăf ĭ-vä′nôfsk). Sov. Un. (Urals In.)	54·46 N	58·13 E
174	Kateninskiy (kȧtyĕ′nĭs-kĭ) Sov. Un. (Urals In.)	53·12 N	61·05 E
165	Kateríni Grc.	40·18 N	22·36 E
217	Katete Zambia	14·05 S	32·07 E
204	Katherine (kăth′ẽr-ĭn) Austl.	14·15 S	132·20 E
184	Kāthiāwār (Pen.) (kä′tyȧ-wär′) India	22·10 N	70·20 E
184	Kathmandu (kāt-mān-dōō′). Nep.	27·49 N	85·21 E
89	Kathryn (kăth′rĭn) Can. (Calgary In.)	51·13 N	113·42 W
113	Kathryn Ca. (Los Angeles In.)	33·42 N	117·45 W
184	Katihār India	25·39 N	87·39 E
214	Katiola Ivory Coast	8·08 N	5·06 W
101	Katmai Natl. Mon. (kăt′mī). Ak.	58·38 N	155·00 W
217	Katompi Zaire	6·11 S	26·20 E
216	Katopa Zaire	2·45 S	25·06 E
159	Katowice Pol.	50·15 N	19·00 E
211	Katrinah, Jabal (Mtn.) Egypt	28·43 N	34·00 E
156	Katrineholm (kȧ-trē′nĕ-hōlm) Swe.	59·01 N	16·10 E
174	Katsbakhskiy (kȧts-bäk′skĭ) Sov. Un. (Urals In.)	52·57 N	59·37 E
215	Katsina (kät′sē-nȧ) Nig.	13·00 N	7·32 E
195	Katsura (R.) (kä′tsōō-rä) Jap. (Ōsaka In.)	34·55 N	135·43 E
172	Katta-Kurgan (kȧ-tȧ-kōōr-gän′) Sov. Un.	39·45 N	66·42 E
156	Kattegat (Str.) (kăt′ĕ-gät). Eur.	56·57 N	11·25 E
217	Katumba Zaire	7·45 S	25·18 E
172	Katun′ (R.) (kȧ-tōōn′). Sov. Un.	51·30 N	86·18 E
149	Katwijkaan Zee Neth. (Amsterdam In.)	52·12 N	4·23 E
100	Kauai (I.) Hi.	22·09 N	159·15 W
100	Kauai Chan. (kä-ōō-ä′ē) Hi.	21·35 N	158·52 W
158	Kaufbeuren (kouf′boi-rĕn). F.R.G.	47·52 N	10·38 E
119	Kaufman (kôf′măn) Tx.	32·36 N	96·18 W
109	Kaukauna (kô-kô′nȧ) Wi.	44·17 N	88·15 W
100	Kaulakahi Chan. (kä′ōō-lȧ-kä′hē) Hi.	22·00 N	159·55 W
100	Kaunakakai (kä′ōō-nȧ-kä′kī). Hi.	21·06 N	156·59·W
157	Kaunas (Kovno) (kou′nȧs) (kôv′nô). Sov. Un.	54·52 N	23·54 E
215	Kaura Namoda Nig.	12·35 N	6·35 E
165	Kavajë (kȧ-vä′yŭ) Alb.	41·11 N	19·36 E
165	Kavála (kȧ-vä′lä) Grc.	40·55 N	24·24 E
165	Kavallas, Kólpos (G.) Grc.	40·45 N	24·20 E
197	Kavieng (kä-vē-ĕng′). Pap. N. Gui.	2·44 S	151·02 E
195	Kawagoe (kä-wă-gō′ā) Jap. (Tōkyō In.)	35·55 N	139·29 E
195	Kawaguchi (kä-wä-gōō-chē) Jap. (Tōkyō In.)	35·48 N	139·44 E
100	Kawaikini (Mtn.) (kä-wä′ē-kĭ-nĭ). Hi.	22·05 N	159·33 W
195	Kawanishi (kä-wä′nē-shē) Jap. (Ōsaka In.)	34·49 N	135·26 E
195	Kawasaki (kä-wä-sä′kê) Jap. (Tōkyō In.)	35·32 N	139·43 E
218	Kawm Umbū Egypt (Nile In.)	24·30 N	32·59 E
188	Kaxgar (R.) China	39·26 N	74·30 E
214	Kaya (kä′yä) Upper Volta	13·05 N	1·05 W
196	Kayan (R.) Indon.	1·45 N	115·38 E
111	Kaycee (kā-sē′) Wy.	43·43 N	106·38 W
214	Kayes (kāz) Mali	14·27 N	11·26 W
171	Kayseri (kī′sĕ-rē) Tur.	38·45 N	35·20 E
113	Kaysville (kāz′vĭl) Ut. (Salt Lake City In.)	41·02 N	111·56 W
173	Kazach′ye Sov. Un.	70·46 N	135·47 E
168	Kazakh S.S.R. (kȧ-zäk′). Sov. Un.	48·45 N	59·00 E
170	Kazan′ (kȧ-zän′) Sov. Un.	55·50 N	49·18 E
167	Kazanka (kȧ-zän′kȧ) Sov. Un.	47·49 N	32·50 E
165	Kazanlŭk (kȧ′zȧn-lêk) Bul.	42·47 N	25·23 E
167	Kazatin Sov. Un.	49·43 N	28·50 E
171	Kazbek, Gora (Mt.) (kȧz-bĕk′) Sov. Un.	42·45 N	44·30 E
186	Kāzerūn Iran	29·37 N	51·44 E
159	Kazincbarcika (kô′zĭnts-bôr-tsĭ-ko). Hung.	48·15 N	20·39 E
217	Kazungula Zambia	17·45 S	25·20 E
195	Kazusa Kameyama (kä-zōō-sä kä-mȧ′yä-mä). Jap. (Tōkyō In.)	35·14 N	140·06 E
172	Kazym (R.) (kä-zēm′) Sov. Un.	63·30 N	67·41 E
165	Kéa (I.) Grc.	37·36 N	24·13 E
100	Kealaikahiki Chan. (kā-ä′lä-ē-kä-hē′kē). Hi.	20·38 N	157·00 W
106	Keansburg (kēnz′bûrg) NJ (New York In.)	40·26 N	74·08 W
116	Kearney (kär′nĭ) Ne.	40·42 N	99·05 W
106	Kearny NJ (New York In.)	40·46 N	74·09 W
112	Keasey (kēz′ĭ) Or. (Portland In.)	45·51 N	123·20 W
171	Keban Gölü (L.) Tur.	38·20 N	39·50 E
150	Kebnekaise Mt. (kĕp′nĕ-kȧ-ēs′ĕ). Swe.	67·53 N	18·10 E
159	Kecskemét (kĕch′kĕ-māt). Hung.	46·52 N	19·42 E
196	Kedah State (kä′dä) Mala.	6·00 N	100·31 E
157	Kédainiai (kē-dī′nĭ-ī) Sov. Un.	55·16 N	23·58 E
98	Kedgwick (kĕdj′wĭk) Can.	47·39 N	67·21 W
113	Keenbrook (kēn′brōōk) Ca. (Los Angeles In.)	34·16 N	117·29 W
105	Keene (kēn) NH	42·55 N	72·15 W
212	Keetmanshoop (kāt′mȧns-hōp) Namibia	26·30 S	18·05 E
115	Keet Seel Ruin (kēt sēl) Az.	36·46 N	110·32 W
109	Keewatin (kē-wä′tĭn) Mn.	47·24 N	93·03 W
100	Keewatin, Dist. of Can.	61·26 N	97·54 W
165	Kefallinía (Cephalonia) (I.). Grc.	38·08 N	20·58 E
	Kefe, see Feodosiya		
215	Keffi (kĕf′ē) Nig.	8·51 N	7·52 E
196	Ke-Ga, Mui (Pt.) Viet.	12·58 N	109·50 E
213	Kei (R.) (kā). S. Afr. (Natal In.)	32·57 S	26·50 E
157	Keila (kā′lȧ) Sov. Un.	59·19 N	24·25 E
213	Kei Mouth S. Afr. (Natal In.)	32·40 S	28·23 E
213	Keiskammahoek (kās′kämä-hōōk′) S. Afr. (Natal In.)	32·42 S	27·11 E
215	Kéita, Bahr (R.) Chad.	9·30 N	19·17 E
157	Keitele (L.) (kā′tĕ-lĕ) Fin.	62·50 N	25·40 E
100	Kekaha Hi.	21·57 N	159·42 W
218	Kelafo Eth. (Horn of Afr. In.)	5·40 N	44·00 E
183	Kelang Mala. (Singapore In.)	3·20 N	101·27 E
183	Kelang (R.) Mala. (Singapore In.)	3·00 N	101·40 E

ng-sing; ŋ-baŋk; ɴ-nasalized n; nŏd; cŏmmit; ōld; ôbey; ôrder; fōōd; fŏŏt; ou-out; s-soft; sh-dish; th-thin; pūre; ûnite; ûrn; stŭd; circŭs; ü-as "y" in study; ′-indeterminate vowel.

298 Kelkit — Kings PRONOUNCING INDEX

Page	Name Pronunciation Region	Lat. °′	Long. °′
153	Kelkit (R.) Tur.	40·38 N	37·03 E
113	Keller (kĕl'ẽr) Tx. (Dallas, Fort Worth In.)	32·56 N	97·15 W
149	Kellinghusen (kĕ'lĕng-hōō-zĕn) F.R.G. (Hamburg In.)	53·57 N	9·43 E
110	Kellogg (kĕl'ŏg) Id.	47·32 N	116·07 W
157	Kelme' (kĕl-mâ) Sov. Un.	55·36 N	22·53 E
215	Kélo Chad	9·19 N	15·48 E
93	Kelowna Can.	49·53 N	119·29 W
92	Kelsey Bay (kĕl'sê) Can.	50·24 N	125·57 W
112	Kelso Wa. (Portland In.)	46·09 N	122·54 W
183	Keluang Mala. (Singapore In.)	2·01 N	103·19 E
170	Kem' (kĕm) Sov. Un.	65·00 N	34·48 E
113	Kemah (kē'mȧ) Tx. (In.)	29·32 N	95·01 W
172	Kemerovo Sov. Un.	55·31 N	86·05 E
150	Kemi (kā'mê) Fin.	65·48 N	24·38 E
150	Kemi (R.) Fin.	67·02 N	27·50 E
195	Kemigawa (kĕ'mê-gä'wä) Jap. (Tōkyō In.)	35·38 N	140·07 E
150	Kemijarvi (kā'mê-yĕr-vĕ) Fin.	66·48 N	27·21 E
150	Kemi-joki (L.) Fin.	66·37 N	28·13 E
111	Kemmerer (kĕm'ẽr-ẽr) Wy.	41·48 N	110·36 W
116	Kemp (L.) (kĕmp) Tx.	33·55 N	99·22 W
161	Kempen (kĕm'pĕn) F.R.G. (Ruhr In.)	51·22 N	6·25 E
203	Kempsey (kĕmp'sê) Austl.	30·59 S	152·50 E
98	Kempt (L.) (kĕmpt) Can.	47·28 N	74·00 W
158	Kempten (kĕmp'tĕn) F.R.G.	47·44 N	10·17 E
213	Kempton Park (kĕmp'tŏn pärk) S. Afr. (Johannesburg & Pretoria In.)	26·07 S	28·29 E
184	Ken (R.) India	25·00 N	79·55 E
101	Kenai (kĕ-nī') Ak.	60·38 N	151·18 W
101	Kenai Mts. Ak.	60·00 N	150·00 W
101	Kenai Pen. Ak.	64·40 N	150·18 W
154	Kendal (kĕn'dȧl) Eng.	54·20 N	1·48 W
218	Kendal...S. Afr. (Johannesburg & Pretoria In.)	26·03 S	28·58 E
104	Kendallville (kĕn'dȧl-vĭl) In.	41·25 N	85·20 W
113	Kenedy (kĕn'ĕ-dĭ) Tx.	28·49 N	97·50 W
214	Kenema SL.	7·52 N	11·12 W
152	Kenitra (Port Lyautey) (kĕ-nē'trȧ) Mor.	34·21 N	6·34 W
108	Kenmare (kĕn-mâr') ND	48·41 N	102·05 W
107	Kenmore (kĕn'mōr) NY (Buffalo In.)	42·58 N	78·53 W
98	Kennebec (R.) (kĕn-ê-bĕk') Me.	44·23 N	69·48 W
98	Kennebunk (kĕn-ê-buŋk') Me.	43·24 N	70·33 W
113	Kennedale (kĕn'-ê-dāl) Tx. (Dallas, Fort Worth In.)	32·38 N	97·13 W
	Kennedy, C., see Canaveral		
101	Kennedy, Mt. Can.	60·25 N	138·50 W
119	Kenner (kĕn'ẽr) La.	29·58 N	90·15 W
117	Kennett (kĕn'ĕt) Mo.	36·14 N	90·01 W
110	Kennewick (kĕn'ê-wĭk) Wa.	46·12 N	119·06 W
92	Kenney Dam Can.	53·37 N	124·58 W
112	Kennydale (kĕn-nê'dāl) Wa. (Seattle In.)	47·31 N	122·12 W
97	Kénogami (kĕn-ŏ'gä-mê) Can.	48·26 N	71·14 W
96	Kenogamissi L. Can.	48·15 N	81·31 W
101	Keno Hill Can.	63·58 N	135·18 W
95	Kenora (kê-nō'rȧ) Can.	49·47 N	94·29 W
107	Kenosha (kĕ-nō'shȧ) Wi. (Milwaukee In.)	42·34 N	87·50 W
104	Kenova (kê-nō'vȧ) WV	38·20 N	82·35 W
106	Kensico Res. (kĕn'sĭ-kō) NY (New York In.)	41·08 N	73·45 W
104	Kent (kĕnt) Oh.	41·05 N	81·20 W
112	Kent Wa. (Seattle In.)	47·23 N	122·14 W
213	Kentani (kĕnt-änĭ') S. Afr. (Natal In.)	32·31 S	28·19 E
188	Kentei Shan (Mts.) (kĕn'tĭ'shän') Mong.	49·25 N	107·51 E
104	Kentland (kĕnt'lȧnd) In.	40·50 N	87·25 W
104	Kenton (kĕn'tŭn) Oh.	40·40 N	83·35 W
90	Kent Pen. Can.	68·28 N	108·10 W
103	Kentucky (State) (kĕn-tŭk'ĭ) U. S.	37·30 N	87·35 W
103	Kentucky (L.) U. S.	36·20 N	88·50 W
103	Kentucky (R.) U. S.	38·15 N	85·01 W
119	Kentwood (kĕnt'wŏŏd) La.	30·56 N	90·31 W
209	Kenya (kēn'yȧ) Afr.	1·00 N	36·53 E
217	Kenya, Mt. Ken.	0·10 S	37·20 E
109	Kenyon (kĕn'yŭn) Mn.	44·15 N	92·58 W
117	Keokuk (kē'ô-kŭk) Ia.	40·24 N	91·34 W
89	Keoma (kē-ō'mȧ) Can. (Calgary In.)	51·13 N	113·39 W
99	Kepenkeck L. Can.	48·13 N	54·45 W
159	Kepno (kăŋ'pnō) Pol.	51·17 N	17·59 E
185	Kerala (State) India	16·38 N	76·00 E
203	Kerang (kê-răng') Austl.	35·32 S	143·58 E
167	Kerch' (kĕrch) Sov. Un.	45·20 N	36·26 E
167	Kerchenskiy Proliv (Str.) (Kerch Str.) (kĕr-chĕn'skĭ prô'lĭf) Sov. Un.	45·08 N	36·35 E
171	Kerempe Burun (C.) Tur.	42·00 N	33·20 E
211	Keren Eth.	15·46 N	38·28 E
220	Kerguelen, Is. de (kĕr'gȧ-lĕn) Ind. O.	49·50 S	69·30 E
217	Kericho Ken.	0·22 S	35·17 E
196	Kerinci, Gunung (Mtn.) Indon.	1·45 S	101·18 E
188	Keriya (R.) (kĕ'rê-yä) China	37·13 N	81·59 E
	Keriya, see Yütian		
211	Kerkenna, Îles (I.) (kĕr'kĕn-nä) Tun.	34·49 N	11·37 E
187	Kerki (kĕr'kê) Sov. Un.	37·52 N	65·15 E
165	Kérkira Grc.	39·36 N	19·56 E
165	Kérkira (I.) Grc.	39·33 N	19·36 E
198	Kermadec Is. (kẽr-măd'ĕk) N. Z.	30·30 S	177·00 E
198	Kermadec Tonga Trench (kẽr-măd'ĕk tŏŋ'gȧ) Oceania	23·00 S	172·30 W
186	Kermān (kĕr-män') Iran	30·23 N	57·08 E
186	Kermānshāh (kĕr-män-shä') Iran	34·01 N	47·00 E
114	Kern (R.) Ca.	35·31 N	118·37 W
114	Kern, South Fork of (R.) Ca.	35·40 N	118·15 W
114	Kern Can. (kûrn) Ca.	36·57 N	119·37 W
214	Kérouané Gui.	9·16 N	9·01 W
161	Kerpen (kĕr'pĕn) F.R.G. (Ruhr In.)	50·52 N	6·42 E
94	Kerrobert Can.	51·53 N	109·13 W
118	Kerrville (kûr'vĭl) Tx.	30·02 N	99·07 W
154	Kerry, Mts. (kĕr'ĭ) Ire.	51·48 N	10·02 W
189	Kerulen (R.) (kĕr'ōō-lĕn) Mong.	47·52 N	113·22 E
97	Kesagami L. Can.	50·23 N	80·15 W
165	Kesan (kĕ'shàn) Tur.	40·50 N	26·37 E
192	Keshan (kŭ-shän) China	48·00 N	126·30 E
152	Kesour, Monts des (Mts.) Alg.	32·51 N	0·30 W
218	Kestell (kĕs'tĕl) S. Afr. (Johannesburg & Pretoria In.)	28·19 N	28·43 E
148	Kesteven (Co.) (kĕs'tê-vĕn) Eng.	52·57 N	0·30 W
159	Keszthely (kĕst'hĕl-lĭ) Hung.	46·46 N	17·12 E
172	Ket' (R.) (kyĕt) Sov. Un.	58·30 N	84·15 E
210	Keta Ghana	6·00 N	1·00 E
183	Ketamputih Indon. (Singapore In.)	1·25 N	102·19 E
196	Ketapang (kê-tȧ-päng') Indon.	2·00 S	109·57 E
92	Ketchikan (kĕch-ĭ-kăn') Ak.	55·21 N	131·35 W
159	Ketrzyn (kăŋ't'r-zĭn) Pol.	54·04 N	21·24 E
148	Kettering (kĕt'ẽr-ĭng) Eng.	52·23 N	0·43 W
104	Kettering Oh.	39·40 N	84·15 W
93	Kettle (R.) Can.	49·40 N	119·00 W
109	Kettle (R.) (kĕt''l) Mn.	46·20 N	92·57 W
161	Kettwig (kĕt'vēg) F.R.G. (Ruhr In.)	51·22 N	6·56 E
159	Kety (kăŋ tĭ) Pol.	49·54 N	19·16 E
149	Ketzin (kĕ'tzēn) G.D.R. (Berlin In.)	52·29 N	12·51 E
105	Keuka (L.) (kê-ū'kȧ) NY	42·30 N	77·10 W
161	Kevelaer (kĕ'fĕ-lăr) F.R.G. (Ruhr In.)	51·35 N	6·15 E
109	Kewanee (kê-wä'nê) Il.	41·15 N	89·55 W
109	Kewaunee (kê-wô'nê) Wi.	44·27 N	87·33 W
109	Keweenaw B. (kē'wê-nô) Mi.	46·59 N	88·15 W
109	Keweenaw Pen. Mi.	47·28 N	88·12 W
108	Keya Paha (R.) (kē-yȧ pä'hä) S.D.	43·11 N	100·10 W
121	Key Largo (I.) Fl. (In.)	25·11 N	80·15 W
106	Keyport (kē'pōrt) NJ (New York In.)	40·26 N	74·12 W
112	Keyport Wa. (Seattle In.)	47·42 N	122·38 W
105	Keyser (kī'sẽr) WV	39·25 N	79·00 W
121	Key West (kē wĕst') Fl. (In.)	24·31 N	81·47 W
159	Kežmarok (kĕzh'mà-rôk) Czech.	49·10 N	20·27 E
172	Khabarovo (kŭ-bȧr-ôvŏ) Sov. Un.	69·31 N	60·41 E
173	Khabarovsk (Kä-bä'rôfsk) Sov. Un.	48·35 N	135·12 E
172	Khakass Aut. Oblast Sov. Un.	52·32 N	89·33 E
185	Khālāpur India (In.)	18·48 N	73·17 E
165	Khalkidhiki Khers (Pen.) Grc.	40·30 N	23·18 E
165	Khalkís (Kȧl'kĭs) Grc.	38·28 N	23·38 E
172	Khal'mer-Yu (kŭl-myĕr'-yōō') Sov. Un.	67·52 N	64·25 E
170	Khalturin (Kȧl'tōō-rēn) Sov. Un.	58·28 N	49·00 E
184	Khambhāt, G. of India	21·20 N	72·27 E
185	Khammam India	17·09 N	80·13 E
184	Khānābād Afg.	36·43 N	69·11 E
184	Khandwa India	21·53 N	76·22 E
	Khangai Mts., see Hangayn Nuruu		
196	Khanh-Hung Viet.	9·45 N	105·50 E
164	Khaniá (Canea) (kä-nĕ'ȧ) (kä-nē'ä) Grc. (In.)	35·29 N	24·04 E
164	Khaniόn, Kólpos (G.) Grc. (In.)	35·35 N	23·55 E
189	Khanka (L.) (Kän'kȧ) Sov. Un.	45·09 N	133·28 E
184	Khānpur Pak.	28·42 N	70·42 E
172	Khanty-Mansiysk (Kŭn-te'mŭn-sēsk') Sov. Un.	61·02 N	69·01 E
183	Khān Yūnus Gaza Strip (Palestine In.)	31·21 N	34·19 E
184	Kharagpur (kŭ-rŭg'pōōr) India	22·26 N	87·21 E
167	Khar'kov (Kär'kôf) Sov. Un.	50·00 N	36·10 E
167	Khar'kov (Oblast) Sov. Un.	49·33 N	35·55 E
170	Kharlovka Sov. Un.	68·47 N	37·20 E
165	Kharmanli (Kȧr-män'lê) Bul.	41·54 N	25·55 E
	Khartoum, see Al Khurṭūm		
186	Khāsh Iran	28·08 N	61·08 E
186	Khāsh (R.) Afg.	32·30 N	64·27 E
184	Khasi Hills India	25·38 N	91·55 E
165	Khaskovo (Kȧs'kô-vô) Bul.	41·56 N	25·32 E
173	Khatanga (Kȧ-tän'gȧ) Sov. Un.	71·48 N	101·47 E
173	Khatangskiy Zaliv (B.) (kä-tăŋ'g-skê) Sov. Un.	73·45 N	108·30 E
151	Khemis Miliana Alg.	36·19 N	1·56 E
167	Kherson (Kĕr-sôn') Sov. Un.	46·38 N	32·34 E
167	Kherson (Oblast) Sov. Un.	46·32 N	32·55 E
184	Khetan (R.) India	10·57 N	78·23 E
157	Khiitola (khē'tō-lȧ) Sov. Un.	61·14 N	29·40 E
174	Khimki (Kēm'kĭ) Sov. Un. (Moscow In.)	55·54 N	37·27 E
165	Khíos (kē'ôs) Grc.	38·23 N	26·09 E
165	Khíos (I.) Grc.	38·20 N	25·45 E
147	Khiva (kē'vȧ) Sov. Un.	41·15 N	60·30 E
167	Khmel'nik Sov. Un.	49·34 N	27·58 E
171	Khmel'nitskiy (kmĭĕ'lnē'ts-kēē) Sov. Un.	49·29 N	26·54 E
167	Khmel'nitskiy (Oblast) (Kmĕl-nĕt'skĭ ôb'làst') Sov. Un.	49·27 N	26·30 E
188	Khöbsögol Dalai (Koso Lake) Mong.	51·11 N	99·11 E
166	Kholm (Kôlm) Sov. Un.	57·09 N	31·07 E
173	Kholmsk (Kŭlmsk) Sov. Un.	47·09 N	142·33 E
171	Khopër (R.) (Kô'pĕr) Sov. Un.	52·00 N	43·00 E
194	Khor (Kôr') Sov. Un.	47·50 N	134·52 E
194	Khor (R.) Sov. Un.	47·23 N	135·20 E
164	Khóra Sfakíon Grc. (In.)	35·12 N	24·10 E
172	Khorog (Kôr'ôg) Sov. Un.	37·30 N	71·47 E
184	Khorog Sov. Un.	37·10 N	71·43 E
167	Khorol (Kô'rôl) Sov. Un.	49·48 N	33·17 E
167	Khorol (R.) Sov. Un.	49·50 N	33·21 E
186	Khorramshahr (kô-ram'shär) Iran	30·36 N	48·15 E
167	Khotin (Kô'tĕn) Sov. Un.	48·29 N	26·32 E
174	Khot'Kovo (Moscow In.) Sov. Un.	56·15 N	38·00 E
186	Khoybār Sau. Ar.	25·45 N	39·28 E
167	Khoyniki Sov. Un.	51·54 N	30·00 E
184	Khulna Bngl.	22·50 N	89·38 E
186	Khūryān Mūryān (Is.) Om.	17·27 N	56·02 E
159	Khust (Kōōst) Sov. Un.	48·10 N	23·18 E
171	Khvalynsk (Kvȧ-lĭnsk') Sov. Un.	52·30 N	48·00 E
186	Khvoy Iran	38·32 N	45·01 E
187	Khyber Pass (kī'bẽr) Pak. (Khyber Pass In.)	34·28 N	71·18 E
217	Kialwe Zaire	9·22 S	27·08 E
217	Kiambi (kyäm'bê) Zaire	7·20 S	28·01 E
117	Kiamichi (R.) (kyȧ-mē'chê) Ok.	34·31 N	95·34 W
170	Kianta (L.) (kyȧn'tȧ) Fin.	65·00 N	28·15 E
216	Kibenga Zaire	7·55 S	17·35 E
217	Kibiti Tan.	7·44 S	38·57 E
217	Kibombo Zaire	3·54 S	25·55 E
217	Kibondo Tan.	3·35 S	30·42 E
165	Kičevo (kē'chĕ-vô) Yugo.	41·30 N	20·59 E
109	Kickapoo (R.) (kĭk'ȧ-pōō) Wi.	43·20 N	90·55 W
93	Kicking Horse P. Can.	51·25 N	116·10 W
210	Kidal (kê-dȧl') Mali	18·33 N	1·00 E
148	Kidderminster (kĭd'ẽr-mĭn-stẽr) Eng.	52·23 N	2·14 W
213	Kidd's Beach (kĭdz) S. Afr. (Natal In.)	33·09 S	27·43 E
148	Kidsgrove (kĭdz'grōv) Eng.	53·05 N	2·30 W
158	Kiel (kēl) F.R.G.	54·19 N	10·08 E
109	Kiel Wi.	43·52 N	88·04 W
158	Kiel B. F.R.G.	54·33 N	10·19 E
	Kiel Can., see Nord-Ostsee Kan.		
159	Kielce (kyĕl'tsĕ) Pol.	50·50 N	20·41 E
149	Kieldrecht (kēl'drĕkt) Bel. (Brussels In.)	51·17 N	4·09 E
	Kiev, see Kiyev		
167	Kiev (Oblast) (kē'yĕf) (ôb'làst') Sov. Un.	50·05 N	30·40 E
171	Kievskoye Vdkhr (Res.) Sov. Un.	51·00 N	30·20 E
214	Kiffa (kēf'ȧ) Mauritania	16·37 N	11·24 W
212	Kigali (kê-gä'lê) Rw.	1·59 S	30·05 E
217	Kigoma (kê-gō'mä) Tan.	4·52 S	29·38 E
195	Kii-Suido (Chan.) (kē sōō-ē'dō) Jap.	33·53 N	134·55 E
194	Kikaiga (I.) Jap.	28·25 N	130·10 E
165	Kikinda (kē'kên-dä) Yugo.	45·49 N	20·30 E
165	Kikladhes (Is.) Grc.	37·30 N	24·45 E
216	Kikwit (kē'kwêt) Zaire	5·02 S	18·49 E
156	Kil (kêl) Swe.	59·30 N	13·15 E
100	Kilauea (kē-lä-ōō-ä'ä) Hi.	22·12 N	159·25 W
100	Kilauea Crater Hi.	19·28 N	155·18 W
101	Kilbuck Mts. (kĭl-bŭk) Ak.	60·05 N	160·00 W
194	Kilchu (kĭl'chōō) Kor.	40·59 N	129·23 E
153	Kildare (kĭl-dār') Ire.	53·09 N	7·05 W
216	Kilembe Zaire	5·42 S	19·55 E
119	Kilgore Tx.	32·23 N	94·53 W
217	Kilifi Ken.	3·38 S	39·51 E
213	Kilimanjaro (Mtn.) (kyl-ê-măn-jä'rô) Tan.	3·09 S	37·19 E
212	Kilimatinde (kĭl-ê-mä-tĭn'dȧ) Tan.	5·48 S	34·58 E
217	Kilindoni Tan.	7·55 S	39·39 E
157	Kilingi-Nōmme (kē'lĭŋ-gê-nôm'mĕ) Sov. Un.	58·08 N	25·03 E
171	Kilis (kē'lês) Tur.	36·50 N	37·20 E
167	Kiliya (kē'lyȧ) Sov. Un.	45·28 N	29·17 E
154	Kilkenny (kĭl-kĕn-ĭ) Ire.	52·40 N	7·30 W
165	Kilkis (kĭl'kĭs) Grc.	40·59 N	22·51 E
154	Killala (kĭ-lä'lȧ) Ire.	54·11 N	9·10 W
154	Killarney Ire.	52·03 N	9·05 W
108	Killdeer (kĭl'dẽr) ND	47·22 N	102·45 W
154	Kilmarnock (kĭl-mär'nŭk) Scot.	55·38 N	4·25 W
154	Kilrush (kĭl'rŭsh) Ire.	52·40 N	9·16 W
217	Kilwa Kisiwani Tan.	8·58 S	39·30 E
213	Kilwa Kivinje Tan.	8·43 S	39·18 E
215	Kim (R.) Cam.	5·40 N	11·17 E
217	Kimamba Tan.	6·47 S	37·08 E
203	Kimba (kĭm'bȧ) Austl.	33·08 S	136·25 E
108	Kimball (kĭm-bȧl) Ne.	41·14 N	103·41 W
108	Kimball SD	43·44 N	98·58 W
93	Kimberley (kĭm'bẽr-lĭ) Can.	49·41 N	115·59 W
212	Kimberley S. Afr.	28·40 S	24·50 E
215	Kimi Cam.	6·05 N	11·30 E
165	Kími Grc.	38·38 N	24·05 E
165	Kímolos (I.) (kē'mô-lôs) Grc.	36·52 N	24·20 E
166	Kimry (kĭm'rê) Sov. Un.	56·53 N	37·24 E
216	Kimvula Zaire	5·44 S	15·58 E
196	Kinabalu, Gunong (Mtn.) Mala.	5·45 N	115·26 E
104	Kincardine (kĭn-kär'dĭn) Can.	44·10 N	81·15 W
216	Kinda Zaire	9·18 S	25·04 E
216	Kindanba Con.	3·44 S	14·31 E
119	Kinder (kĭn'dẽr) La.	30·30 N	92·50 W
94	Kindersley (kĭn'dẽrz-lê) Can.	51·27 N	109·10 W
214	Kindia (kĭn'dê-ȧ) Gui.	10·04 N	12·51 W
170	Kinel'-Cherkassy Sov. Un.	53·32 N	51·32 E
166	Kineshma (kê-nĕsh'mȧ) Sov. Un.	57·27 N	41·02 E
203	King (I.) (kĭng) Austl.	39·35 S	143·40 E
203	Kingaroy (kĭŋ'gă-roi) Austl.	26·37 S	151·50 E
114	King City (kĭng sĭ'tĭ) Ca.	36·12 N	121·08 W
89	King City Can. (Toronto In.)	43·56 N	79·32 W
92	Kingcome Inlet (kĭng'kŭm) Can.	50·50 N	126·10 W
116	Kingfisher (kĭng'fĭsh-ẽr) Ok.	35·51 N	97·55 W
93	King George, Mt. Can.	50·35 N	115·24 W
204	King George Sd. (jôrj) Austl.	35·17 S	118·30 E
166	Kingisepp (kĭŋ-gê-sep') Sov. Un.	59·22 N	28·38 E
204	King Leopold Ranges (lē'ô-pōld) Austl.	16·25 S	125·00 E
115	Kingman (kĭng'măn) Az.	35·10 N	114·05 W
116	Kingman (kĭng'măn) Ks.	37·38 N	98·07 W
114	Kings (R.) Ca.	36·28 N	119·43 W

ă : finȧl; rāte; senâte; ärm; ȧsk; sofȧ; fâre; ch-choose; dh-as th in other; bē; êvent; bĕt; recĕnt; cratẽr; g-go; gh-guttural g; bĭt; ĭ-short neutral; rīde; K-guttural k as ch in German ich;

PRONOUNCING INDEX Kings Canyon Natl. Park — Kom 299

Page	Name Pronunciation Region	Lat. °′	Long. °′
114	Kings Canyon Natl. Park (kăn'yŭn). Ca.	36·52 N	118·53 W
148	Kingsclere (kĭngs-clēr) Eng. (London In.)	51·18 N	1·15 W
203	Kingscote (kĭngz'kŭt) . . . . . . Austl.	35·45 S	137·32 E
155	Kings Lynn (kĭngz lĭn') . . . . . . Eng.	52·45 N	0·20 E
121	Kings Mt. . . . . NC	35·13 N	81·30 W
148	Kings Norton (nôr'tŭn) . . . . . . Eng.	52·25 N	1·54 W
204	King Sd. . . . . Austl.	16·50 S	123·35 E
106	Kings Park (kĭngz pärk) NY (New York In.)	40·53 N	73·16 W
111	Kings Pk. . . . . Ut.	40·46 N	110·20 W
121	Kingsport (kĭngz'pōrt) . . . . Tn.	36·33 N	82·36 W
203	Kingston (kĭngz'tŭn) . . . . Austl.	37·52 S	139·52 E
105	Kingston . . . . Can.	44·15 N	76·30 W
128	Kingston . . . . Jam.	18·00 N	76·45 W
105	Kingston . . . . NY	42·00 N	74·00 W
105	Kingston . . . . Pa.	41·15 N	75·50 W
112	Kingston . . . . Wa. (Seattle In.)	47·04 N	122·29 W
148	Kingston upon Hull . . . . Eng.	53·45 N	0·25 W
127	Kingstown (kĭngz'toun) St. Vincent (In.)	13·10 N	61·14 W
121	Kingstree (kĭngz'trē) . . . . SC	33·30 N	79·50 W
118	Kingsville (kĭngz'vĭl) . . . . Tx.	27·32 N	97·52 W
100	King William I. (kĭng wĭl'yăm) Can.	69·25 N	97·00 W
213	King William's Town (kĭng-wĭl'-yŭmz-toun) . S. Afr. (Natal In.)	32·53 S	27·24 E
213	Kinira (R.) . . . . S. Afr. (Natal In.)	30·37 S	28·52 E
113	Kinloch (kĭn-lŏk) Mo. (St. Louis In.)	38·44 N	90·19 W
93	Kinnaird (kĭn-ärd') . . . . Can.	49·17 N	117·39 W
154	Kinnairds Hd. (kĭn-ârds'hĕd) . Scot.	57·42 N	3·55 W
195	Kinomoto (kē'nō-mōtō) . . . . . . Jap.	33·53 N	136·07 E
195	Kinosaki (kē'nō-sä'kē) . . . . Jap.	35·38 N	134·47 E
154	Kinsale Hbr. (kĭn-sāl') . . . . Ire.	51·35 N	8·17 W
216	Kinshasa (Léopoldville) . . . . . Zaire	4·18 S	15·18 E
116	Kinsley (kĭnz'lĭ) . . . . Ks.	37·55 N	99·24 W
121	Kinston (kĭnz'tŭn) . . . . NC	35·15 N	77·35 W
214	Kintampo (kēn-täm'pō) . . . . Ghana	8·03 N	1·43 W
154	Kintyre Pen. . . . . Scot.	55·50 N	5·40 W
	Kioroshi, see Ōmori		
116	Kiowa (kī'ô-wȧ) . . . . Ks.	37·01 N	98·30 W
117	Kiowa . . . . Ok.	34·42 N	95·53 W
165	Kiparissía . . . . Grc.	37·17 N	21·43 E
165	Kiparissiakós Kólpos (G.) . . . . Grc.	37·28 N	21·15 E
97	Kipawa Lac (L.) . . . . Can.	46·55 N	79·00 W
217	Kipembawe (kê-pĕm-bä'wȧ) . . Tan.	7·39 S	33·24 E
217	Kipengere Ra. . . . . Tan.	9·10 S	34·00 E
217	Kipili . . . . Tan.	7·26 S	30·36 E
217	Kipusha . . . . Zaire	11·46 N	27·14 E
217	Kipushi . . . . Zaire	11·46 N	27·14 E
113	Kirby (kŭr'bĭ) Tx. (San Antonio In.)	29·29 N	98·23 W
119	Kirbyville (kŭr'bĭ-vĭl) . . . . Tx.	30·39 N	93·54 W
173	Kirenga (R.) (kê-rĕŋ'gȧ) . . Sov. Un.	56·30 N	103·18 E
173	Kirensk (kē-rĕnsk') . . . . . . Sov. Un.	57·47 N	108·22 E
168	Kirghiz S. S. R. (kĭr-gēz') . Sov. Un.	41·45 N	74·38 E
168	Kirghiz Steppe (Plain) . . . Sov. Un.	49·28 N	57·07 E
187	Kirgizskiy Khrebet (Kirgiz) (Mts.) . Sov. Un.	37·58 N	72·23 E
216	Kiri . . . . Zaire	1·27 S	19·00 E
198	Kiribati . . . . Oceania	1·30 S	173·00 E
	Kirin, see Chilung		
148	Kirkby-in-Ashfield (kŭrk'bē-ĭn-ăsh'fēld) . Eng.	53·06 N	1·16 W
154	Kirkcaldy (kēr-kô'dĭ) . . . . Scot.	56·06 N	3·15 W
150	Kirkenes . . . . Nor.	69·40 N	30·03 E
148	Kirkham (kûrk'ăm) . . . . Eng.	53·47 N	2·53 W
112	Kirkland (kûrk'lănd) Wa. (Seattle In.)	47·41 N	122·12 W
165	Kirklareli (kĕrk'lär-ĕ'lê) . . . . . . Tur.	41·44 N	27·15 E
117	Kirksville (kŭrks'vĭl) . . . . Mo.	40·12 N	92·35 W
186	Kirkūk (kĭr-kōōk') . . . . Iraq	35·28 N	44·22 E
154	Kirkwall (kûrk'wôl) . . . . Scot.	58·58 N	2·59 W
113	Kirkwood (kûrk'wŏŏd) Mo. (St. Louis In.)	38·35 N	90·24 W
213	Kirkwood . . . . . . S. Afr. (Natal In.)	33·26 S	25·24 E
158	Kirn (kērn) . . . . F.R.G.	49·47 N	7·23 E
166	Kirov . . . . Sov. Un.	54·04 N	34·19 E
170	Kirov . . . . Sov. Un.	58·35 N	49·35 E
171	Kirovabad (kē-rŭ-vŭ-bät') Sov. Un.	40·40 N	46·20 E
174	Kirovgrad (kē'rŭ-vŭ-grad) Sov. Un. (Urals In.)	57·26 N	60·03 E
167	Kirovograd (kē-rŭ-vŭ-grät') Sov. Un.	48·33 N	32·17 E
167	Kirovograd (Oblast) . . . . . Sov. Un.	48·23 N	31·10 E
170	Kirovsk . . . . Sov. Un.	67·40 N	33·58 E
174	Kirovsk (kē-rôfsk') Sov. Un. (Leningrad In.)	59·52 N	30·59 E
171	Kirsanov (kēr-sä'nôf) . . . . Sov. Un.	52·40 N	42·40 E
171	Kırşehir (kĕr-shĕ'hĕr) . . . . Tur.	39·10 N	34·00 E
215	Kirtachi Seybou . . . . Niger	12·48 N	2·29 E
184	Kīrthar Ra. (kĭr-tŭr) . . . . Pak.	27·00 N	67·10 E
148	Kirton (kûr'tŭn) . . . . Eng.	53·29 N	0·35 W
150	Kiruna (kē-rōō'nä) . . . . Swe.	67·49 N	20·08 E
217	Kirundu . . . . Zaire	0·44 S	25·32 E
116	Kirwin Res. (kûr'wĭn) . . . . Ks.	39·34 N	99·04 W
195	Kiryū (kē'rĭ-ōō) . . . . Jap.	36·26 N	139·18 E
166	Kirzhach (kēr-zhàk') . . . . . Sov. Un.	56·08 N	38·53 E
213	Kisaki (kē-sä'kē) . . . . Tan.	7·37 S	37·43 E
164	Kisámou, Kólpos (G) . . . Grc. (In.)	35·40 N	23·37 E
216	Kisangani (Stanleyville) . . . . . Zaire	0·30 S	25·12 E
195	Kisarazu (kē'sä-rä'zōō) Jap. (Tōkyō In.)	35·23 N	139·55 E
172	Kiselëvsk (kē-sĭ-lyôfsk') . . Sov. Un.	54·05 N	86·19 E
167	Kishinëv (ke-shē-nyôf') . . Sov. Un.	47·02 N	28·52 E
195	Kishiwada (kē'shē-wä'dä) . . . . Jap.	34·25 N	135·18 E
174	Kishkino (kēsh'kĭ-nô) Sov. Un. (Moscow In.)	55·15 N	38·04 E
217	Kisiwani . . . . Tan.	4·08 S	37·57 E
101	Kiska (I.) (kĭs'kä) . . . . Ak.	52·08 N	177·10 E
93	Kiskatinaw (R.) . . . . Can.	55·10 N	120·20 W
95	Kiskitto L. (kĭs-kĭ'tō) . . . . Can.	54·16 N	98·34 W
95	Kiskittogisu L. . . . . Can.	54·05 N	99·00 W
159	Kiskunfélegyháza (kĭsh'kōōn-fā'lĕd-y'hä'zô) . Hung.	46·42 N	19·52 E
159	Kiskunhalas (kĭsh'kōōn-hô'lôsh) Hung.	46·24 N	19·26 E
159	Kiskunmajsa (kĭsh'kōōn-mī'shô) Hung.	46·29 N	19·42 E
213	Kismayu . . . . Som.	0·18 S	42·30 E
195	Kiso-Gawa (Strm.) (kē'sō-gä'wä) Jap.	35·29 N	137·12 E
195	Kiso-Sammyaku (Mts.) (kē'sō säm'myȧ-kōō) . Jap.	35·47 N	137·39 E
214	Kissidougou (kē'sē-dōō'gōō) . . Gui.	9·11 N	10·06 W
121	Kissimmee (kĭ-sĭm'ē) . . . . . Fl. (In.)	28·17 N	81·25 W
121	Kissimmee (L.) . . . . Fl. (In.)	27·58 N	81·17 W
121	Kissimmee (R.) . . . . Fl. (In.)	27·45 N	81·07 W
150	Kistrand (kē'stränd) . . . . Nor.	70·29 N	25·01 E
159	Kisujszallás (kĭsh'ōō'y'sä'läsh) Hung.	47·12 N	20·47 E
217	Kisumu (kē'sōō-mōō) . . . . Ken.	0·06 S	34·45 E
214	Kita (kē'tȧ) . . . . Mali	13·03 N	9·29 W
194	Kitakami Gawa (R.) (kē'tȧ-kä'mē gä-wä) . Jap.	39·20 N	141·10 E
195	Kitakyūshū (kē'tȧ-kyōō'shōō') Jap.	34·15 N	130·23 E
217	Kitale . . . . Ken.	1·01 N	35·00 E
116	Kit Carson . . . . Co.	38·46 N	102·48 W
104	Kitchener (kĭch'ĕ-nēr) . . . . Can.	43·25 N	80·35 W
216	Kitenda . . . . Zaire	6·53 S	17·21 E
211	Kitgum (kĭt'gōōm) . . . . Ug.	3·29 N	33·04 E
153	Kíthira (I.) . . . . Grc.	36·15 N	22·56 E
165	Kíthnos (I.) . . . . Grc.	37·24 N	24·10 E
92	Kitimat (kĭ'tĭ-măt) . . . . Can.	54·03 N	128·33 W
92	Kitimat (R.) . . . . Can.	53·50 N	129·00 W
92	Kitimat Ra. . . . . Can.	53·30 N	128·50 W
92	Kitlope (R.) (kĭt'lōp) . . . . Can.	53·00 N	128·00 W
195	Kitsuki (kēt'sōō-kē) . . . . Jap.	33·24 N	131·35 E
105	Kittanning (kĭ-tăn'ĭng) . . . . Pa.	40·50 N	79·30 W
106	Kittatinny Mts. (kĭ-tȧ-tĭ'nē) NJ (New York In.)	41·16 N	74·44 W
98	Kittery (kĭt'ēr-ĭ) . . . . Me.	43·07 N	70·45 W
149	Kittsee . . . . Aus. (Vienna In.)	48·05 N	17·05 E
121	Kitty Hawk (kĭt'tē hôk) . . . . . . NC	36·04 N	75·42 W
217	Kitunda . . . . Tan.	6·48 S	33·13 E
217	Kitwe . . . . Zambia	12·49 S	28·13 E
158	Kitzingen (kĭt'zĭng-ĕn) . . . . . F.R.G.	49·44 N	10·08 E
217	Kiunga . . . . Ken.	1·45 S	41·29 E
217	Kivu, Lac (L.) . . . . Zaire	1·45 S	28·55 E
171	Kiyev (Kiev) (kē'yĕf) . . . . Sov. Un.	50·27 N	30·30 E
195	Kiyose . . . . Jap. (Tōkyō In.)	35·47 N	139·32 E
174	Kizel (kē'zĕl) . . Sov. Un. (Urals In.)	59·05 N	57·42 E
171	Kızıl Irmak (R.) (kĭz'ĭl ĭr-mäk') Tur.	40·15 N	34·00 E
174	Kizil'skoye (kĭz'ĭl-skô-yĕ) Sov. Un. (Urals In.)	52·43 N	58·53 E
171	Kizlyar (kĭz-lyär') . . . . Sov. Un.	44·00 N	46·50 E
195	Kizu (kē'zōō) . . . . Jap. (Ōsaka In.)	34·43 N	135·49 E
147	Kizy-Arvat (kē'zĭl-ŭr-vät') Sov. Un.	38·55 N	56·33 E
213	Klaas Smits (R.) S. Afr. (Natal In.)	31·45 S	26·33 E
149	Klaaswaal . Neth. (Amsterdam In.)	51·46 N	4·25 E
158	Kladno (kläd'nō) . . . . Czech.	50·10 N	14·05 E
158	Klagenfurt (klä'gĕn-fōōrt) . . . . Aus.	46·38 N	14·19 E
157	Klaipéda (Memel) (klī'pȧ-dȧ) (mā'mĕl) . Sov. Un.	55·43 N	21·10 E
110	Klamath Falls . . . . Or.	42·13 N	121·49 W
110	Klamath Mts. . . . . Ca.	42·00 N	123·25 W
110	Klamath R. . . . . Ca.	41·40 N	122·25 W
156	Klarälven (R.) . . . . Swe.	60·40 N	13·00 E
112	Klaskanine (R.) (klăs'kȧ-nīn) Or. (Portland In.)	46·02 N	123·43 W
158	Klatovy (klȧ'tô-vē) . . . . Czech.	49·23 N	13·18 E
101	Klawock (klā'wăk) . . . . Ak.	55·32 N	133·10 W
149	Kleinmachnow (klīn-mäĸ'nō) G.D.R. (Berlin In.)	52·22 N	13·12 E
218	Klerksdorp (klĕrks'dôrp) . . . S. Afr. (Johannesburg & Pretoria In.)	26·52 S	26·40 E
218	Klerksraal (klĕrks'kräl) . . . . S. Afr. (Johannesburg & Pretoria In.)	26·15 N	27·10 E
166	Kletnya (klyĕt'nyȧ) . . . . Sov. Un.	52·19 N	33·14 E
166	Kletsk (klĕtsk) . . . . Sov. Un.	53·04 N	26·43 E
161	Kleve (klĕ'fĕ) . . F.R.G. (Ruhr In.)	51·47 N	6·09 E
110	Klickitat R. . . . . Wa.	46·01 N	121·07 W
166	Klimovichi (klē-mô-vē'chē) Sov. Un.	53·37 N	31·21 E
174	Klimovsk (klĭ'môfsk) Sov. Un. (Moscow In.)	55·21 N	37·32 E
166	Klin (klēn) . . . . Sov. Un.	56·18 N	36·43 E
156	Klintehamn (klēn'tē-häm) . . . Swe.	57·24 N	18·14 E
166	Klintsy (klĭn'tsĭ) . . . . Sov. Un.	52·46 N	32·14 E
218	Klip (R.) (klĭp) . . . . S. Afr. (Johannesburg & Pretoria In.)	27·18 N	29·25 E
218	Klipgat . . . . S. Afr. (Johannesburg & Pretoria In.)	25·26 S	27·57 E
156	Klippan (klyp'pån) . . . . Swe.	56·08 N	13·09 E
164	Ključ (klyōōch) . . . . Yugo.	44·32 N	16·48 E
158	Kłodzko (klôd'skô) . . . . Pol.	50·26 N	16·38 E
101	Klondike Reg. (klŏn'dīk) Ak.-Can.	64·12 N	142·38 W
149	Klosterfelde (klōs'tĕr-fĕl-dĕ) G.D.R. (Berlin In.)	52·47 N	13·29 E
149	Klosterneuburg (klōs-tēr-noi'bōōrgh) . Aus. (Vienna In.)	48·19 N	16·20 E
90	Kluane (L.) . . . . Can.	61·15 N	138·40 W
90	Kluane Natl. Pk. . . . . Can.	60·25 N	137·53 W
159	Kluczbork (klōōch'bŏrk) . . . . . . Pol.	50·59 N	18·15 E
166	Klyaz'ma (R.) (klyäz'mȧ) Sov. Un.	55·49 N	39·19 E
173	Klyuchevskaya (Vol.) (klyōō-chĕfskä'yä) . Sov. Un.	56·13 N	160·00 E
174	Klyuchi (klyōō'chĭ) Sov. Un. (Urals In.)	57·03 N	57·20 E
165	Knezha (knyā'zhȧ) . . . . Bul.	43·27 N	24·03 E
108	Knife (R.) (nīf) . . . . ND	47·06 N	102·33 W
92	Knight Inlet (nīt) . . . . Can.	50·41 N	125·40 W
104	Knightstown (nīts'toun) . . . . In.	39·45 N	85·30 W
164	Knin (knēn) . . . . Yugo.	44·02 N	16·14 E
158	Knittelfeld . . . . Aus.	47·13 N	14·50 E
197	Knob Pk. (nŏb) . . . . Phil. (In.)	12·30 N	121·20 E
154	Knockmealdown Mts. (nŏk-mēl'doun) . Ire.	52·13 N	8·09 W
148	Knottingley (nŏt'ĭng-lĭ) . . . . . . Eng.	53·42 N	1·14 W
104	Knox (nŏks) . . . . In.	41·15 N	86·40 W
92	Knox, C. . . . . Can.	54·12 N	133·20 W
109	Knoxville (nŏks'vĭl) . . . . Ia.	41·19 N	93·05 W
120	Knoxville . . . . Tn.	35·58 N	83·55 W
148	Knutsford (nŭts'fērd) . . . . Eng.	53·18 N	2·22 W
159	Knyszyn (knĭ'shĭn) . . . . Pol.	53·16 N	22·59 E
195	Kobayashi (kō'bȧ-yä'shē) . . . . Jap.	31·58 N	130·59 E
195	Kōbe (kō'bĕ) . . . . Jap. (Ōsaka In.)	34·30 N	135·10 E
167	Kobelyaki (kō-bĕl-yä'kē) . Sov. Un.	49·11 N	34·12 E
156	København (Copenhagen) (kû-b'n-houn') . Den.	55·43 N	12·27 E
158	Koblenz (kō'blĕntz) . . . . F.R.G.	50·18 N	7·36 E
166	Kobozha (R.) (kô-bō'zhȧ) Sov. Un.	58·55 N	35·18 E
159	Kobrin (kō'brēn') . . . . Sov. Un.	52·13 N	24·23 E
174	Kobrinskoye (kô-brĭn'skô-yĕ) Sov. Un. (Leningrad In.)	59·25 N	30·07 E
101	Kobuk (R.) (kō'bŭk) . . . . Ak.	66·58 N	158·48 W
171	Kobuleti (kô-bōō-lyā'tē) . Sov. Un.	41·50 N	41·40 E
165	Kocani (kô'chä-nĕ) . . . . Yugo.	41·54 N	22·25 E
164	Kočevje (kô'chāv-ye) . . . . . . Yugo.	45·38 N	14·51 E
158	Kocher R. (kôĸ'ĕr) . . . . F.R.G.	49·00 N	9·52 E
195	Kōchi (kō'chē) . . . . Jap.	33·35 N	133·32 E
195	Kodaira . . . . Jap. (Tōkyō In.)	35·43 N	139·29 E
101	Kodiak (kō'dyăk) . . . . Ak.	57·50 N	152·30 W
101	Kodiak (I.) . . . . Ak.	57·24 N	153·32 W
211	Kodok (ko'dŏk) . . . . Sud.	9·57 N	32·08 E
214	Koforidua (kō fô-rĭ-dōō'ȧ) . . Ghana	6·03 N	0·17 W
195	Kōfu (kō'fōō') . . . . Jap.	35·41 N	138·34 E
195	Koga (kō'gȧ) . . . . Jap.	36·13 N	139·40 E
214	Kogan (R.) . . . . Gui.	11·30 N	14·05 W
195	Kogane (kō'gä-nȧ) Jap. (Tōkyō In.)	35·50 N	139·56 E
195	Koganei (kō'gä-nā) Jap. (Tōkyō In.)	35·42 N	139·31 E
156	Køge (kû'gĕ) . . . . Den.	55·27 N	12·09 E
156	Køge Bugt (B.) . . . . Den.	55·30 N	12·25 E
167	Kogil'nik (R.) (kô-gêl-nēk') Sov. Un.	46·08 N	29·10 E
214	Kogoni . . . . Mali	14·44 N	6·02 W
184	Koh-i Baba Mt. . . . . Afg.	39·39 N	67·09 E
187	Kohīma (kô-ē'mȧ) . . . . India	25·45 N	94·41 E
195	Koito (R.) (kô'ē-tō) Jap. (Tōkyō In.)	35·19 N	139·58 E
194	Kōje (I.) (kû'jĕ) . . . . Kor.	34·53 N	129·00 E
172	Kokand (kô-känt') . . . . Sov. Un.	40·27 N	71·07 E
172	Kokchetav (kôk'chĕ-tȧf) . Sov. Un.	53·15 N	69·13 E
157	Kokemäen (R.) (kô'kĕ-mȧ'ĕn) . Fin.	61·23 N	22·03 E
166	Kokhma (kôĸ'mȧ) . . . . Sov. Un.	56·57 N	41·08 E
150	Kokkola (kô'kô-lȧ) . . . . Fin.	63·47 N	22·58 E
104	Kokomo (kō'kô-mō) . . . . In.	40·30 N	86·20 W
	Koko Nor (L.), see Ch'ing Hai		
188	Koko Nor (Quinghai Hu) (L.) (kō'kō nor) (chyĭŋ-hī hōō) . China	37·26 N	98·30 E
197	Kokopo (kô-kô'pō) . . . Pap. N. Gui.	4·25 S	152·27 E
91	Koksoak (R.) (kôk'sō-ăk) . . . . Can.	57·42 N	69·50 W
213	Kokstad (kôk'shtät) S. Afr. (Natal In.)	30·33 S	29·27 E
195	Kokubu (kō'kōō-bōō) . . . . Jap.	31·42 N	130·46 E
195	Kokuou (kō'kōō-ō'ōō) Jap. (Ōsaka In.)	34·34 N	135·39 E
	Kola Pen., see Kol'skiy P-Ov.		
185	Kolār (Kolār Gold Fields) (kôl-är') . India	13·39 N	78·33 E
159	Kolárvo (kōl-ároVō) . . . . Czech.	47·54 N	17·59 E
217	Kolbio . . . . Ken.	1·10 S	41·15 E
166	Kol'chugino (kôl-chōō'gē-nō) Sov. Un.	56·19 N	39·29 E
214	Kolda . . . . Sen.	12·53 N	14·57 W
156	Kolding (kŭl'dĭng) . . . . Den.	55·29 N	9·24 E
212	Kole (kō'lȧ) . . . . Zaire	3·19 S	22·46 E
170	Kolguyev (I.) (kôl-gōō'yĕf) Sov. Un.	69·00 N	49·00 E
158	Kolín (kō'lēn) . . . . Czech.	50·01 N	15·11 E
157	Kolkasrags (Pt.) (kôl-käs'rȧgz) Sov. Un.	57·46 N	22·39 E
161	Köln (Cologne) . F.R.G. (Ruhr In.)	50·56 N	6·57 E
159	Kolno (kôw'nô) . . . . Pol.	53·23 N	21·56 E
159	Koło (kô'wô) . . . . Pol.	52·11 N	18·37 E
158	Kołobrzeg (kô-lôb'zhĕk) . . . . . . Pol.	54·10 N	15·35 E
174	Kolomna (kȧl-ôm'nȧ) Sov. Un. (Moscow In.)	55·06 N	38·47 E
159	Kolomyya (kō'lô-mē'yȧ) . Sov. Un.	48·32 N	25·04 E
166	Kolp' (R.) (kôlp) . . . . Sov. Un.	59·29 N	35·32 E
172	Kolpashevo (kŭl pȧ shô'vȧ) Sov. Un.	58·16 N	82·43 E
174	Kolpino (kôl'pē-nô) Sov. Un. (Leningrad In.)	59·45 N	30·37 E
166	Kolpny (kôlp'nyē) . . . . Sov. Un.	52·14 N	36·54 E
170	Kol'skiy P-Ov. (Kola Pen.) Sov. Un.	67·15 N	37·40 E
170	Kolva (R.) . . . . Sov. Un.	61·00 N	57·00 E
217	Kolwezi (kôl-wĕ'zē) . . . . Zaire	10·43 S	25·28 E
174	Kolyberovo (kô-lĭ-byâ'rô-vô) Sov. Un. (Moscow In.)	55·16 N	38·45 E
173	Kolyma (R.) . . . . Sov. Un.	66·30 N	151·45 E
	Kolymskiy (Mts.), see Gydan, Khrebet		
172	Kolyvan' (kôl-ê-vän') . . . . Sov. Un.	55·28 N	82·59 E
216	Kom (R.) . . . . Cam.-Gabon	2·15 N	12·05 E

ng-sing; ŋ-baŋk; ɴ-nasalized n; nŏd; cŏmmit; ōld; ôbey; ôrder; fōōd; fŏŏt; ou-out; s-soft; sh-dish; th-thin; pūre; ûnite; ûrn; stŭd; circŭs; ü-as "y" in study; '-indeterminate vowel.

Page	Name Pronunciation Region	Lat. °′	Long. °′
219	Komadorskie Ostrova (Is.) Sov. Un.	55·40 N	167·13 E
215	Komadougou Yobé (R.) Niger-Nig.	13·20 N	12·45 E
215	Komadugu Gana (R.) Nig.	12·15 N	11·10 E
195	Komae Jap. (Tōkyō In.)	35·37 N	139·35 E
159	Komárno (kô'mär-nô) Czech.	47·46 N	18·08 E
159	Komarno Sov. Un.	49·38 N	23·43 E
159	Komaron (kô'mä-rôm) Hung.	47·45 N	18·06 E
212	Komatipoort (kō-mä'tē-pōrt) S. Afr.	25·21 S	32·00 E
195	Komatsu (kō-mät'sōō) Jap.	36·23 N	136·26 E
195	Komatsushima (kō-mät'sōō-shē'mä) Jap.	34·04 N	134·32 E
217	Komeshia Zaire	8·01 S	27·07 E
213	Komga (kōm'gȧ) S. Afr. (Natal In.)	32·36 S	27·54 E
168	Komi (A. S. S. R.) (kômė) Sov. Un.	61·31 N	53·15 E
212	Kommetjie S. Afr. (In.)	34·09 S	18·19 E
188	Kommunizma, Pik (Pk.) Sov. Un.	39·46 N	71·23 E
214	Komoe (R.) Ivory Coast	5·40 N	3·40 W
165	Komotiní Grc.	41·07 N	25·22 E
167	Komrat (kôm-rät') Sov. Un.	46·17 N	28·38 E
174	Komsomolets (kôm-sô-mô'lĕts) Sov. Un. (Urals In.)	53·45 N	63·04 E
171	Komsomolets Zaliv (B.) Sov. Un.	45·40 N	52·00 E
173	Komsomol'sk-na-Amure (kŭm-sŭ-môlsk'nŭ-ŭ-mōōr'yĭ) Sov. Un.	50·46 N	137·14 E
167	Komsomol'skoye (kôm-sô-môl'skô-yĕ) Sov. Un.	48·42 N	28·44 E
214	Kona Mali	14·57 N	3·53 W
170	Konda (R.) (kôn'dȧ) Sov. Un.	60·50 N	64·00 E
174	Kondas R. (kôn'dȧs) Sov. Un. (Urals In.)	59·30 N	56·28 E
212	Kondoa (kôn-dō'ȧ) Tan.	4·52 S	36·00 E
217	Kondolole Zaire	1·20 N	25·58 E
210	Kong (kông) Ivory Coast	9·05 N	4·41 W
216	Kongbo Cen. Afr. Rep.	4·44 N	21·23 E
217	Kongolo (kôŋ'gō'lō) Zaire	5·23 S	27·00 E
156	Kongsberg (kŭngs'bĕrg) Nor.	59·40 N	9·36 E
156	Kongsvinger (kŭngs'viŋ-gẽr) Nor.	60·12 N	12·00 E
212	Koni (kō'nē) Zaire	10·32 S	27·27 E
	Königsberg, see Kaliningrad		
149	Königsbrunn (kû'nēgs-brōōn) F.R.G. (Munich In.)	48·16 N	10·53 E
149	Königs Wusterhausen (kû'nēgs vōōs'tĕr-hou-zĕn) G.D.R. (Berlin In.)	52·18 N	13·38 E
159	Konin (kô'nyĕn) Pol.	52·11 N	18·17 E
165	Kónitsa (kô'nyē'tsȧ) Grc.	40·03 N	20·46 E
165	Konjic (kôn'yēts) Yugo.	43·38 N	17·59 E
195	Konju Kor.	36·21 N	127·05 E
214	Konkouré (R.) Gui.	10·30 N	13·25 W
184	Konnagar India (In.)	22·41 N	88·22 E
167	Konotop (kô-nô-tôp') Sov. Un.	51·13 N	33·14 E
214	Konpienga (R.) Upper Volta	11·15 N	0·35 E
188	Konqi (R.) (kôn-chyē) China	41·09 N	87·46 E
159	Końskie (koin''skyĕ) Pol.	51·12 N	20·26 E
167	Konstantinovka (kôn-stȧn-tē'nôf-kȧ) Sov. Un.	48·33 N	37·42 E
158	Konstanz (kôn'shtänts) F.R.G.	47·39 N	9·10 E
215	Kontagora (kōn-tȧ-gō'rä) Nig.	10·24 N	5·28 E
171	Konya (kōn'yȧ) Tur.	36·55 N	32·25 E
93	Kootenay (R.) Can.	49·45 N	117·05 W
93	Kootenay L. Can.	49·35 N	116·50 W
90	Kootenay Natl. Park (kōō'tē-nâ) Can.	51·06 N	117·02 W
195	Kōō-zan (Mtn.) (kōō'zän) Jap. (Ōsaka In.)	34·53 N	135·32 E
156	Kopervik (kô'pĕr-vēk) Nor.	59·18 N	5·20 E
174	Kopeysk (kô-pāsk') Sov. Un. (Urals In.)	55·07 N	61·36 E
156	Köping (chû'pĭng) Swe.	59·32 N	15·58 E
156	Kopparberg (kŏp'pȧr-bĕrgh) Swe.	59·53 N	15·00 E
186	Koppeh Dāgh (Mts.) Iran	37·28 N	58·29 E
218	Koppies S. Afr. (Johannesburg & Pretoria In.)	27·15 S	27·35 E
164	Koprivnica (kô'prēv-nē'tsȧ) Yugo.	46·10 N	16·48 E
159	Kopychintsy (kô-pē-chĕn'tsĕ) Sov. Un.	49·06 N	25·55 E
165	Korçë (kôr'chĕ) Alb.	40·37 N	20·48 E
164	Korčula (I.) (kôr'chōō-lȧ) Yugo.	42·50 N	17·05 E
194	Korea B. China-Kor.	39·18 N	123·50 E
183	Korea (kô-rē'ȧ) Asia	38·45 N	130·00 E
194	Korean Arch. Kor.	34·05 N	125·35 E
194	Korea Str. Kor.-Jap.	33·30 N	128·30 E
159	Korets (kô-rĕts') Sov. Un.	50·35 N	27·13 E
214	Korhogo (kôr-hō'gō) Ivory Coast	9·27 N	5·38 W
165	Korinthiakós Kólpos (G.) Grc.	38·15 N	22·33 E
165	Kórinthos (Corinth) (kô-rēn'thôs) (kŏr'ĭnth) Grc.	37·56 N	22·54 E
194	Kōriyama (kō'rē-yä'mä) Jap.	37·18 N	140·25 E
174	Korkino (kôr'kē-nŭ) Sov. Un. (Urals In.)	54·53 N	61·25 E
188	Korla (kōr-lä) China	41·37 N	86·03 E
158	Körmend (kûr'mĕnt) Hung.	47·02 N	16·36 E
164	Kornat (I.) (kôr-nät') Yugo.	43·46 N	15·10 E
149	Korneuburg (kôr'noi-bōōrgh) Aus. (Vienna In.)	48·22 N	16·21 E
214	Koro Mali	14·04 N	3·05 W
167	Korocha (kô-rō'chȧ) Sov. Un.	50·50 N	37·13 E
167	Korop (kō'rôp) Sov. Un.	51·33 N	33·54 E
167	Korosten' (kô'rôs-tĕn) Sov. Un.	50·51 N	28·39 E
167	Korostyshev (kô-rôs'tē-shôf) Sov. Un.	50·19 N	29·05 E
215	Koro Toro Chad	16·05 N	18·30 E
167	Korotoyak (kô'rô-tô-yák') Sov. Un.	51·00 N	39·06 E
173	Korsakov (kôr'sȧ-kôf') Sov. Un.	46·42 N	143·16 E
157	Korsnäs (kôrs'nĕs) Fin.	62·51 N	21·17 E
151	Korsør (kôrs'ûr') Den.	55·19 N	11·08 E
155	Kortrijk Bel.	50·49 N	3·10 E
173	Koryakskiy Khrebet (Mts.) Sov. Un.	62·00 N	168·45 E
167	Koryukovka (kôr-yōō-kôf'kȧ) Sov. Un.	51·44 N	32·24 E
158	Kościan (kŭsh'tsyȧn) Pol.	52·05 N	16·38 E
159	Kościerzyna (kŭsh-tsyĕ-zhĕ'nȧ) Pol.	54·08 N	17·59 E
120	Kosciusko (kŏs-ĭ-ŭs'kō) Ms.	33·04 N	89·35 W
203	Kosciusko, Mt. Austl.	36·26 S	148·20 E
166	Kosel'sk (kô-zĕlsk') Sov. Un.	54·01 N	35·49 E
211	Kosha (kō'shä) Sud.	20·49 N	30·27 E
195	Koshigaya (kō'shē-gä'yä) Jap. (Tōkyō In.)	35·53 N	139·48 E
195	Koshiki-Rettō (Is.) (kō-shē'kē rȧt'tō) Jap.	31·51 N	129·40 E
184	Kosi (R.) (kō'sē) India	26·00 N	86·20 E
159	Košice (kō'shē-tsĕ') Czech.	48·43 N	21·17 E
213	Kosmos (kŏz'mŏs) S. Afr. (Johannesburg & Pretoria In.)	25·45 S	27·51 E
174	Kosobrodskiy (kä-sô'brôd-skĭ) Sov. Un. (Urals In.)	54·14 N	60·53 E
	Koso Lake, see Khöbsögol Dalai		
165	Kosovska Mitrovica (kô'sôv-skä' mē'trô-vē-tsä') Yugo.	42·51 N	20·50 E
164	Kostajnica (kôs'tä-ē-nē'tsȧ) Yugo.	45·14 N	16·32 E
218	Koster S. Afr. (Johannesburg & Pretoria In.)	25·52 S	26·52 E
174	Kostino (kôs'tĭ-nô) Sov. Un. (Moscow In.)	55·54 N	37·51 E
166	Kostroma (kôs-trô-mȧ') Sov. Un.	57·46 N	40·55 E
166	Kostroma (Oblast) Sov. Un.	57·50 N	41·10 E
158	Kostrzyń (kôst'chĕn) Pol.	52·35 N	14·38 E
174	Kos'va R. (kôs'vȧ) Sov. Un. (Urals In.)	58·44 N	57·08 E
158	Koszalin (kô-shä'lĭn) Pol.	54·12 N	16·10 E
158	Köszeg (kû'sĕg) Hung.	47·21 N	16·32 E
184	Kota India	25·17 N	75·49 E
196	Kota Baharu (kō'tä bä'rōō) Mala.	6·15 N	102·23 E
196	Kotabaru Indon.	3·22 S	116·15 E
196	Kota Kinabalu Mala.	5·55 N	116·05 E
212	Kota Kota (kō-tȧ kō-tȧ) Malawi	12·52 S	34·16 E
183	Kota Tinggi Mala. (Singapore In.)	1·43 N	103·54 E
165	Kotel (kô-tĕl') Bul.	42·54 N	26·28 E
170	Kotel'nich (kô-tyĕl'nĕch) Sov. Un.	58·15 N	48·20 E
173	Kotel'nyy (I.) (kô-tyĕl'nē) Sov. Un.	74·51 N	134·09 E
185	Kothapur India	16·48 N	74·15 E
157	Kotka (kŏt'kȧ) Fin.	60·28 N	26·56 E
170	Kotlas (kôt'lȧs) Sov. Un.	61·10 N	46·50 E
174	Kotlin, Ostrov (I.) (ôs-trôf' kôt'lĭn) Sov. Un. (Leningrad In.)	60·02 N	29·49 E
165	Kotor (kō'tôr) Yugo.	42·26 N	18·48 E
166	Kotorosl' (R.) (kô-tô'rôsl) Sov. Un.	57·18 N	39·08 E
164	Kotor Varoš (kō'tôr vä'rôsh) Yugo.	44·37 N	17·23 E
167	Kotovsk (kô-tôfsk') Sov. Un.	47·49 N	29·31 E
185	Kotte Sri Lanka	6·50 N	80·05 E
211	Kotto (R.) Cen. Afr. Rep.	5·17 N	22·04 E
173	Kotuy (R.) (kô-tōō') Sov. Un.	71·00 N	103·15 E
101	Kotzebue (kôt'sē-bōō) Ak.	66·48 N	162·42 W
101	Kotzebue Sd. Ak.	67·00 N	164·28 W
214	Koualé Mali	11·24 N	7·01 W
98	Kouchibouguac Natl. Pk. Can.	46·53 N	65·35 W
214	Koudougou (kōō-dōō'gōō) Upper Volta	12·15 N	2·22 W
216	Kouilou (R.) Con.	4·00 S	12·05 E
216	Koula-Moutou Gabon	1·08 S	12·29 E
214	Koulikoro (kōō-lē-kō'rō) Mali	12·53 N	7·33 W
214	Koulouguidi Mali	13·27 N	11·30 W
215	Koumra Chad	8·55 N	17·33 E
214	Koundara Gui.	12·29 N	13·18 W
211	Koundé (kōōn-dā') Cen. Afr. Rep.	6·08 N	14·32 E
172	Kounradskiy (kŭ-ōōn-rät'skē) Sov. Un.	47·25 N	75·10 E
214	Kouroussa (kōō-rōō'sä) Gui.	10·39 N	9·53 W
210	Koutiala (kōō-tē-ȧ'lä) Mali	12·29 N	5·29 W
157	Kouvola (kō'ŏŏ-vô-lä) Fin.	60·51 N	26·40 E
190	Kouzhen (kō-jŭn) China	36·19 N	117·37 E
170	Kovda (L.) (kôv'dȧ) Sov. Un.	66·45 N	32·00 E
159	Kovel' (kō'vĕl) Sov. Un.	51·13 N	24·45 E
	Kovno, see Kaunas		
166	Kovrov (kôv-rôf') Sov. Un.	56·23 N	41·21 E
	Kowie, see Port Alfred		
193	Kowloon (kō'lōōn') Hong Kong	22·28 N	114·20 E
101	Koyuk (kô-yōōk') Ak.	65·00 N	161·18 W
101	Koyukuk (R.) (kô-yōō'kŏŏk) Ak.	66·25 N	153·50 W
165	Kozáni Grc.	40·16 N	21·51 E
167	Kozelets (kôzĕ-lyĕts) Sov. Un.	50·53 N	31·07 E
159	Kozienice (kō-zyĕ-nē'tsĕ) Pol.	51·34 N	21·35 E
159	Koźle (kôzh'lĕ) Pol.	50·19 N	18·10 E
165	Kozloduy (kŭz'lô-dwē) Bul.	43·45 N	23·42 E
195	Kōzu (I.) (kō'zōō) Jap.	34·16 N	139·03 E
196	Kra, Isth. of Thai.	9·30 S	99·45 E
213	Kraai (R.) (krā'ê) S. Afr. (Natal In.)	30·50 S	27·03 E
149	Krabbendijke Neth. (Amsterdam In.)	51·26 N	4·05 E
196	Krâchéh Kamp.	12·28 N	106·06 E
156	Kragerö (krä'gĕr-û) Nor.	58·53 N	9·21 E
165	Kragujevac (krä'gōō'yĕ-vȧts) Yugo.	44·01 N	20·55 E
159	Kraków (krä'kōōf) Pol.	50·05 N	20·00 E
151	Kraljevo (kräl'ye-vô) Yugo.	43·39 N	20·48 E
167	Kramatorsk (krȧ-mä'tôrsk) Sov. Un.	48·43 N	37·32 E
156	Kramfors (kräm'fôrs) Swe.	62·54 N	17·49 E
164	Kranj (krän') Yugo.	46·16 N	14·23 E
213	Kranskop (kränz'kŏp) S. Afr. (Natal In.)	28·57 S	30·54 E
166	Krāslava (kräs'lä-vä) Sov. Un.	55·53 N	27·12 E
158	Kraslice (kräs'lē-tsĕ) Czech.	50·19 N	12·30 E
174	Kransnaya Gorka (kräs'nȧ-yȧ gôr'kȧ) Sov. Un. (Urals In.)	55·13 N	56·43 E
171	Krasnaya Sloboda Sov. Un.	48·25 N	44·35 E
159	Kraśnik (kräsh'nĭk) Pol.	50·53 N	22·15 E
174	Krasnoarmeysk (kräs'nô-ȧr-maśk') Sov. Un. (Moscow In.)	56·06 N	38·09 E
167	Krasnoarmeyskoye Sov. Un.	48·19 N	37·04 E
167	Krasnodar (kräs'nô-dȧr) Sov. Un.	45·03 N	38·55 E
167	Krasnodarskiy (Oblast) Province (krȧs-nô-där'skĭ ôb'lȧst) Sov. Un.	47·28 N	38·13 E
174	Krasnogorsk Sov. Un. (Moscow In.)	55·49 N	37·20 E
174	Krasnogorskiy (kräs-nô-gôr'skĭ) Sov. Un. (Urals In.)	54·36 N	61·25 E
167	Krasnograd (kräs'nô-grät) Sov. Un.	49·23 N	35·26 E
174	Krasnogvardeyskiy (krȧ'sno-gvȧr-dzyē ĕs-kēē) Sov. Un. (Urals In.)	57·17 N	62·05 E
170	Krasnokamsk (kräs-nô-kämsk') Sov. Un.	58·00 N	55·45 E
167	Krasnokutsk (krȧs-nô-kōōtsk') Sov. Un.	50·03 N	35·05 E
167	Krasnosel'ye (kräs'nô-sĕl'yĕ) Sov. Un.	48·44 N	32·24 E
170	Krasnoslobodsk (kräs'nô-slôbôtsk') Sov. Un.	54·20 N	43·50 E
174	Krasnotur'insk (krŭs-nŭ-tōō-rensk') Sov. Un. (Urals In.)	59·47 N	60·15 E
174	Krasnoufimsk (krŭs-nŭ-ōō-fēmsk') Sov. Un. (Urals In.)	56·38 N	57·46 E
174	Krasnoural'sk (kräs'nô-ōō-rälsk') Sov. Un. (Urals In.)	58·21 N	60·05 E
174	Krasnousol'skiy (kräs-nô-ōō-sôl'skĭ) Sov. Un. (Urals In.)	53·53 N	56·30 E
170	Krasnovishersk (kräs-nô-vēshersk') Sov. Un.	60·22 N	57·20 E
171	Krasnovodsk (krȧs-nô-vôtsk') Sov. Un.	40·00 N	52·50 E
172	Krasnoyarsk (kräs-nô-yärsk') Sov. Un.	56·13 N	93·12 E
174	Krasnoye Selo (kräs'nŭ-yŭ sâ'lō) Sov. Un. (Leningrad In.)	59·44 N	30·06 E
166	Krasny Kholm (kräs'nê kōlm) Sov. Un.	58·03 N	37·11 E
159	Krasnystaw (kräs-nê-stäf') Pol.	50·59 N	23·11 E
174	Krasnyy Bor (kräs'nê bôr) Sov. Un. (Leningrad In.)	59·41 N	30·40 E
174	Krasnyy Klyuch (kräs'nê klyûch') Sov. Un. (Urals In.)	55·24 N	56·43 E
171	Krasnyy Kut (krȧs-nê kōōt') Sov. Un.	50·50 N	47·00 E
174	Kratovo (krä'tô-vô) Sov. Un. (Moscow In.)	55·35 N	38·10 E
165	Kratovo (krä'tô-vô) Yugo.	42·04 N	22·12 E
161	Krefeld (krā'fĕlt) F.R.G. (Ruhr In.)	51·20 N	6·34 E
167	Kremenchug (krĕm'ĕn-chōōgh') Sov. Un.	49·04 N	33·26 E
167	Kremenchugskoye (Res.) (krĕm-ĕn-chōōgh'skô-ye) Sov. Un.	49·20 N	32·45 E
159	Kremenets (krĕ-mĕn-yĕts') Sov. Un.	50·06 N	25·43 E
149	Kremmen (krĕ'mĕn) G.D.R. (Berlin In.)	52·45 N	13·02 E
149	Krempe (krĕm'pĕ) F.R.G. (Hamburg In.)	53·50 N	9·29 E
158	Krems (krĕms) Aus.	48·25 N	15·36 E
157	Krestsy Sov. Un.	58·18 N	32·26 E
166	Kresttsy (krȧst'sė) Sov. Un.	58·16 N	32·25 E
157	Kretinga (krĕ-tĭŋ'gȧ) Sov. Un.	55·55 N	21·17 E
215	Kribi (krē'bė) Cam.	2·57 N	9·55 E
166	Krichëv (krē'chôf) Sov. Un.	53·44 N	31·39 E
194	Krillon, Mys (Pt.) (mĭs krĭl' ôn) Sov. Un.	45·58 N	142·00 E
149	Krimpenald Ijssel Neth. (Amsterdam In.)	51·55 N	4·34 E
187	Krishna (R.) India	16·23 N	75·00 E
184	Krishnanagar India	23·29 N	88·33 E
156	Kristiansand (krĭs-tyȧn-sän'') Nor.	58·09 N	7·59 E
156	Kristianstad (krĭs-tyȧn-städ') Swe.	56·02 N	14·09 E
156	Kristiansund (krĭs-tyȧn-sōōn'') Nor.	63·07 N	7·49 E
156	Kristinehamn (krēs-tē'nĕ-häm') Swe.	59·20 N	14·05 E
157	Kristinestad (krĭs-tē'nĕ-städh) Fin.	62·16 N	21·28 E
165	Kriva-Palanka (krē-vȧ-pȧ-läŋ'kȧ) Yugo.	42·12 N	22·21 E
167	Krivoy Rog (krê-voi' rôgh') Sov. Un.	47·54 N	33·22 E
167	Krivoye Ozero Sov. Un.	47·57 N	30·21 E
164	Križevci (krē'zhĕv-tsĭ) Yugo.	46·02 N	16·30 E
164	Krk (I.) (k'rk) Yugo.	45·06 N	14·33 E
159	Krnov (k'r'nôf) Czech.	50·05 N	17·41 E
156	Kröderen (krû'dĕ-rĕn) Nor.	60·07 N	9·49 E
218	Krokodil (R.) (krŏ'kō-dĭ) S. Afr. (Johannesburg & Pretoria In.)	24·25 S	27·08 E
167	Krolevets (krô-lĕ'vyĕts) Sov. Un.	51·33 N	33·21 E
159	Kroměříž (krô'myĕr-zhēzh) Czech.	49·18 N	17·23 E
166	Kromy (krô'mė) Sov. Un.	52·44 N	35·41 E
169	Kronotskiy, Mys (C.) (krô'nôt'skĭ-ĕ) Sov. Un.	54·58 N	163·15 E
174	Kronshtadt (krōn'shtät) Sov. Un. (Leningrad In.)	59·59 N	29·47 E
218	Kroonstad (krōn'shtät) S. Afr. (Johannesburg & Pretoria In.)	27·40 S	27·15 E
171	Kropotkin (krȧ-pôt'kĭn) Sov. Un.	45·25 N	40·30 E

ăt; finăl; rāte; senâte; ärm; ȧsk; sofȧ; fâre; ch-choose; dh-as th in other; bē; êvent; bĕt; recĕnt; cratẽr; g-go; gh-guttural g; bĭt; ĭ-short neutral; rīde; K-guttural k as ch in German ich;

PRONOUNCING INDEX

Krosno — La Cross 301

Page	Name Pronunciation Region	Lat. °'	Long. °'
159	Krosno (krôs'nô) . . . . Pol.	49·41 N	21·46 E
159	Krotoszyn (krô-tō'shĭn) . . . . . . Pol.	51·41 N	17·25 E
164	Krško (k'rsh'kô) . . . . Yugo.	45·58 N	15·30 E
212	Kruger Natl. Park (krōō'gẽr) (krü'gẽr) . S. Afr.	23·22 S	30·18 E
213	Krugersdorp (krōō'gẽrz-dôrp) S. Afr. (Johannesburg & Pretoria In.)	26·06 S	27·46 E
165	Krujë (krōō'yȧ) . . . . Alb.	41·32 N	19·49 E
196	Krung Thep (Bangkok) . . . . . Thai.	13·50 N	100·29 E
165	Kruševac (krōō'shĕ-vȧts) . . . Yugo.	43·34 N	21·21 E
165	Kruševo . . . . Yugo.	41·20 N	21·15 E
156	Krylbo (krül'bô) . . . . Swe.	60·07 N	16·14 E
167	Krymskaya (krĭm'skȧ-yȧ) Sov. Un.	44·58 N	38·01 E
167	Krymskaya (Oblast) . . . . . Sov. Un.	45·08 N	34·05 E
167	Krymskiy P-Ov (Crimea) (Pen.) (krēm-skĭ pô-lōō-ôs'trôf) Sov. Un.	45·18 N	33·30 E
159	Krynki (krĭn'kê) . . . . Pol.	53·15 N	23·47 E
167	Kryukov (k'r'yōō-kôf') . . . Sov. Un.	49·02 N	33·26 E
163	Ksar Chellala . . . . Alg.	35·12 N	2·20 E
163	Ksar el Boukhari . . . . Alg.	35·50 N	2·48 E
152	Ksar el Kebir . . . . Mor.	35·01 N	5·48 W
152	Ksar-es-Souk . . . . Mor.	31·58 N	4·25 W
190	Kuai (R.) (kōō-ī) . . . . China	33·30 N	116·56 E
183	Kuala Klawang Mala. (Singapore In.)	2·57 N	102·04 E
183	Kuala Lumpur (kwä'lä lōōm-pōōr') Mala. (Singapore In.)	3·08 N	101·42 E
192	Kuandian (kûän-dĭĕn) . . . . . . China	40·40 N	124·50 E
	Kuanghsi, see Kwangsi Chuang		
	Kuantung (Prov.), see Kwangtung		
171	Kuba (kōō'bȧ) . . . . Sov. Un.	41·05 N	48·30 E
167	Kuban' (R.) (kōō-bȧn'') . . Sov. Un.	45·10 N	37·55 E
171	Kuban (R.) . . . . Sov. Un.	45·20 N	40·05 E
153	Kuban R. . . . . Sov. Un.	45·14 N	38·20 E
170	Kubenskoye (L.) . . . . Sov. Un.	59·40 N	39·40 E
	Kucha, see Kuch'e		
196	Kuching (kōō'chĭng) . . . . Mala.	1·30 N	110·26 E
195	Kuchinoerabo (I.) (kōō'chē nō ĕr'ȧ-bō) . Jap.	30·31 N	129·53 E
195	Kudamatsu (kōō'dȧ-mä'tsōō) . Jap.	34·00 N	131·51 E
183	Kudap . . . . Indon. (Singapore In.)	1·14 N	102·30 E
196	Kudat (kōō-dät') . . . . Mala.	6·56 N	116·48 E
157	Kudirkos Naumiestis (kōōdĭr-kôs nä'ōō-mē'stĭs) . Sov. Un.	54·51 N	23·00 E
172	Kudymakar (kōō-dĭm-kär') Sov. Un.	58·43 N	54·52 E
158	Kufstein (kōōf'shtīn) . . . . Aus.	47·34 N	12·11 E
149	Kuhstedt (kōō'shtĕt) F.R.G. (Hamburg In.)	53·23 N	8·58 E
	Kuibyshev, see Kuybyshev		
212	Kuilsrivier . . . . S. Afr. (In.)	33·56 S	18·41 E
195	Kuji . . . . Jap.	33·57 N	131·18 E
195	Kujū-san (Mt.) (kōō'jōō-sän') . Jap.	33·07 N	131·14 E
165	Kukës (kōō'kĕs) . . . . Alb.	42·03 N	20·25 E
165	Kula (kōō'lȧ) . . . . Bul.	43·52 N	23·13 E
171	Kula . . . . Tur.	38·32 N	28·30 E
184	Kula Kangri Mt. . . . . China	33·11 N	90·36 E
173	Kular, Khrebet (Mts.) (kōō-lär') Sov. Un.	69·00 N	131·45 E
157	Kuldīga (kōōl'dē-gȧ) . . . . . Sov. Un.	56·59 N	21·59 E
170	Kulebaki (kōō-lĕ-bäk'ĭ) . . Sov. Un.	55·22 N	42·30 E
158	Kulmbach (klōōlm'bäĸ) . . . . F.R.G.	50·07 N	11·28 E
172	Kulunda (kōō-lōōn'dȧ) . . Sov. Un.	52·38 N	74·00 E
172	Kulundinskoye (L.) . . . . . Sov. Un.	52·45 N	77·18 E
194	Kum (R.) (kōōm) . . . . Kor.	36·50 N	127·30 E
171	Kuma (R.) (kōō'mä) . . . . . Sov. Un.	44·50 N	45·10 E
195	Kumamoto (kōō'mä-mō'tô) . . . Jap.	32·49 N	130·40 E
195	Kumano-Nada (Sea) (kōō-mä'nō nä-dä) . Jap.	34·03 N	136·36 E
165	Kumanovo (kōō-mä'nô-vô) . Yugo.	42·10 N	21·41 E
214	Kumasi (kōō-mä'sê) . . . . Ghana	6·41 N	1·35 W
215	Kumba (kōōm'bȧ) . . . . Cam.	4·38 N	9·25 E
185	Kumbakonam (kōōm'bŭ-kō'nŭm) India	10·59 N	79·25 E
165	Kumkale . . . . Tur.	39·59 N	26·10 E
215	Kumo . . . . Nig.	10·03 N	11·13 E
185	Kumta . . . . India	14·19 N	75·28 E
	Kumul, see Hami		
174	Kunashak (kû-nä'shȧk) Sov. Un. (Urals In.)	55·43 N	61·35 E
194	Kunashir (I.) (kōō-nŭ-shēr') Sov. Un.	44·40 N	145·45 E
166	Kunda (kōō'dȧ) . . . . Sov. Un.	59·30 N	26·28 E
209	Kundelungu, Plateau des (Plat.) Zaire	9·00 S	25·30 E
174	Kundravy (kōōn'drȧ-vĭ) Sov. Un. (Urals In.)	54·50 N	60·14 E
183	Kundur (I.) . Indon .(Singapore In.)	0·49 N	103·20 E
216	Kunene (Cunene) (R.) Ang.-Namibia	17·05 S	12·35 E
156	Kungälv (kŭng'ĕlf) . . . . Swe.	57·53 N	12·01 E
174	Kungur (kōōn-gōōr') Sov. Un. (Urals In.)	57·27 N	56·53 E
147	Kungrad (kōōn-grät') . . . . Sov. Un.	42·59 N	59·00 E
156	Kungsbacka (kŭngs'bä-kȧ) . . . Swe.	57·31 N	12·04 E
188	Kunlun Shan (Mts.) (kōōn-lōōn shän) . China	35·26 N	83·09 E
193	Kunming (kōōn-mĭŋ) . . . . China	25·10 N	102·50 E
193	Kunsan (kōōn'sän') . . . . Kor.	35·54 N	126·46 E
191	Kunshan (kōōn-shän) China (Shanghai In.)	31·23 N	120·57 E
174	Kuntsëvo (kōōn-tsyô'vô) Sov. Un. (Moscow In.)	55·43 N	37·27 E
174	Kun'ya . . . . . . Sov. Un. (Urals In.)	58·42 N	56·47 E
166	Kun'ya (R.) (kōōn'yȧ) . . . Sov. Un.	56·45 N	30·53 E
150	Kuopio (kōō-ô'pē-ŏ) . . . . Fin.	62·48 N	28·30 E
164	Kupa (R.) . . . . Yugo.	45·32 N	14·50 E
197	Kupang . . . . Indon.	10·14 S	123·37 E
174	Kupavna . . Sov. Un. (Moscow In.)	55·49 N	38·11 E
172	Kupino (kōō-pĭ'nô) . . . . . . Sov. Un.	54·00 N	77·47 E
137	Kupiškis (kōō-pĭsh'kĭs) . . . Sov. Un.	55·50 N	24·55 E
167	Kupyansk (kōōp-yänsk') . Sov. Un.	49·44 N	37·38 E
188	Kuqa (kōō-chyä) . . . . China	41·34 N	82·44 E
171	Kura (R.) (kōō'rȧ) . . . . . . Sov. Un.	41·10 N	45·40 E
195	Kurashiki (kōō'rä-shē'kê) . . . . . Jap.	34·37 N	133·44 E
211	Kuraymah . . . . Sud.	18·34 N	31·49 E
195	Kurayoshi (kōō'rȧ-yō'shê) . . . . Jap.	35·25 N	133·49 E
171	Kurdistan (Reg.) (kûrd'ĭ-stăn) Tur.-Iran	37·40 N	43·30 E
211	Kurdufān (Prov.) (kôr-dô-fän') Sud.	14·08 N	28·39 E
165	Kŭrdzhali . . . . Bul.	41·39 N	25·21 E
195	Kure (kōō'rĕ) . . . . Jap.	34·17 N	132·35 E
157	Kuressaare (kōō'rĕ-sä'rĕ) . Sov. Un.	58·15 N	22·26 E
172	Kurgan (kōōr-găn') . . . . . . Sov. Un.	55·28 N	65·14 E
172	Kurgan Tyube (kōōr-gän' tyōō'bĕ) Sov. Un.	38·00 N	68·49 E
195	Kurihama (kōō-rē-hä'mä) Jap. (Tōkyō In.)	35·14 N	139·42 E
173	Kuril Is. (kōō'rĭl) . . . . Sov. Un.	46·20 N	149·30 E
157	Kurisches Haff (Bay) . . . Sov. Un.	55·10 N	21·08 E
185	Kurla (Neigh.) India (Bombay In.)	19·03 N	72·53 E
211	Kurmuk (kōōr'mōōk) . . . . Sud.	10·40 N	34·13 E
185	Kurnool (kōōr-nōōl') . . . . India	16·00 N	78·04 E
195	Kuro (I.) kōō'rô) . . . . Jap.	30·49 N	129·56 E
202	Kurrajong . . . . Austl. (Sydney In.)	33·33 S	150·40 E
147	Kuršenai (kōōr'shȧ-nī) . . . Sov. Un.	56·01 N	22·56 E
157	Kursk (kōōrsk) . . . . Sov. Un.	51·44 N	36·08 E
157	Kursk (Oblast) (kōōrsk) . . Sov. Un.	51·30 N	35·13 E
155	Kuršumlija (kōōr'shōōm'lĭ-yȧ) Yugo.	43·08 N	21·18 E
211	Kūrtī . . . . Sud.	18·08 N	31·39 E
212	Kuruman (kōō-rōō-män') . . . S. Afr.	27·25 S	23·30 E
195	Kurume (kōō'rōō-mĕ) . . . . Jap.	33·10 N	130·30 E
195	Kururi(kōō'rōō-rē) . Jap(Tōkyō In.)	35·17 N	140·05 E
174	Kusa (kōō'sȧ) . Sov. Un. (Urals In.)	55·19 N	59·27 E
167	Kushchëvskaya . . . . Sov. Un.	46·34 N	39·40 E
195	Kushikino (kōō'shĭ-kē'nō) . . . . Jap.	31·44 N	130·19 E
195	Kushimoto (kōō'shĭ-mō'tō) . . . Jap.	33·29 N	135·47 E
194	Kushiro (kōō'shē-rō) . . . . Jap.	43·00 N	144·22 E
172	Kush-Murun (L.) (kōōsh-mōō-rōōn') . Sov. Un.	52·30 N	64·15 E
171	Kushum (R.) (kōō-shōōm') Sov. Un.	50·30 N	50·40 E
174	Kushva (kōōsh'vȧ) Sov. Un. (Urals In.)	58·18 N	59·51 E
101	Kuskokwim (R.) . . . . Ak.	61·32 N	160·36 W
101	Kuskokwim B. (kŭs'kô-kwĭm) . Ak.	59·25 N	163·14 W
101	Kuskokwim Mts. . . . . Ak.	62·08 N	158·00 W
101	Kuskovak (kŭs-kō'văk) . . . . Ak.	60·10 N	162·50 W
172	Kustanay (kōōs-tȧ-nī') . . . Sov. Un.	53·10 N	63·39 E
211	Kūstī . . . . Sud.	13·09 N	32·39 E
171	Kütahya (kû-tä'hyȧ) . . . . Tur.	39·20 N	29·50 E
171	Kutaisi (kōō-tŭ-ē'sē) . . . . . Sov. Un.	42·15 N	42·40 E
196	Kutaradja . . . . Indon.	5·30 N	95·20 E
184	Kutch, Gulf of . . . . India	22·45 N	68·33 E
184	Kutch, Rann of (Swp.) . . . . . India	23·59 N	69·13 E
149	Kutenholz (kōō'tĕn-hōlts) F.R.G. (Hamburg In.)	53·29 N	9·20 E
174	Kutim (kōō'tĭm) Sov. Un. (Urals In.)	60·22 N	58·51 E
164	Kutina (kōō'tē-nȧ) . . . . Yugo.	45·29 N	16·48 E
159	Kutno (kōōt'nô) . . . . Pol.	52·14 N	19·22 E
170	Kutno (L.) . . . . Sov. Un.	65·15 N	31·30 E
171	Kutulik (kōō tōō'lyĭk) . . Sov. Un.	53·12 N	102·51 E
159	Kuty (kōō'tê) . . . . Sov. Un.	48·16 N	25·12 E
150	Kuusamo (kōō'sȧ-mô) . . . . Fin.	65·59 N	29·10 E
166	Kuvshinovo (kōōv-shē'nô-vô) Sov. Un.	57·01 N	34·09 E
	Kuwait, see Al Kuwayt		
182	Kuwait . . . . Asia	29·00 N	48·45 E
195	Kuwana (kōō'wȧ-nȧ) . . . . Jap.	35·02 N	136·40 E
170	Kuybyshev (Kuibyshev) (kōō'ē-bĭ-shĭf) . Sov. Un.	53·10 N	50·05 E
170	Kuybyshevskoye (Res.) . . Sov. Un.	53·40 N	49·00 E
174	Kuzneckovo Sov. Un. (Moscow In.)	55·29 N	38·22 E
171	Kuznetsk (kōōz-nyĕtsk') . Sov. Un.	53·00 N	46·30 E
172	Kuznetsk Basin . . . . Sov. Un.	57·15 N	86·15 E
174	Kuznetsovka (kōōz-nyĕt'sôf-kȧ) Sov. Un. (Urals In.)	54·41 N	56·40 E
166	Kuznetsovo (kōōz-nyĕt-sô'vô) Sov. Un.	56·39 N	36·55 E
174	Kuznetsy . . Sov. Un. (Moscow In.)	55·50 N	38·39 E
164	Kvarnerski Zaliv (B.) (kvär'nĕr-skē' zä'lĕv) . Yugo.	44·41 N	14·05 E
101	Kvichak (vĭc'-hăk) . . . . Ak.	59·00 N	156·48 W
216	Kwa (R.) . . . . Zaire	3·00 S	16·45 E
214	Kwahu Plat. . . . . Ghana	7·00 N	1·35 W
216	Kwando (R.) . . . . Zambia	16·50 S	22·40 E
216	Kwango (Cuango) (R.) (kwäng'ō') . Afr.	6·35 S	16·50 E
217	Kwangwazi . . . . Tan.	7·47 S	38·15 E
216	Kwenge (R.) (kwĕŋ'gĕ) . . . . . Zaire	6·45 S	18·23 E
159	Kwidzyń (kvē'dzĭn) . . . . Pol.	53·45 N	18·56 E
216	Kwilu (R.) (kwē'lōō) . . . . Zaire	3·22 S	17·22 E
173	Kyakhta (kyäĸ'ta) . . . . . . Sov. Un.	51·00 N	107·30 E
184	Kyayisu (R.) . . . . India	38·05 N	74·36 E
188	Kyaukpyu (chouk'pyoo') . . . . . Bur.	19·19 N	93·33 E
157	Kybartai (kē'bär-tī') . . . . Sov. Un.	54·40 N	22·46 E
193	Ky Lam . . . . Viet.	15·48 N	108·30 E
174	Kyn (kĭn') . . . Sov. Un. (Urals In.)	57·52 N	58·42 E
205	Kynuna (kī-nōō'nȧ) . . . . Austl.	21·30 S	142·12 E
217	Kyoga, L. . . . . Ug.	1·30 N	32·45 E
195	Kyōga-Saki (C.) (kyō'gä sa'kê) Jap.	35·46 N	135·14 E
194	Kyŏngju (kyŭng'yōō) . . . . Kor.	35·48 N	129·12 E
195	Kyōto (kyō'tō') . Jap. (Ōsaka In.)	35·00 N	135·46 E
195	Kyōto (Pref.) . . . . Jap. (Ōsaka In.)	34·56 N	135·42 E
172	Kyren (kĭ-rĕn') . . . . Sov. Un.	51·46 N	102·13 E
157	Kyrön (R.) (kû'rô) . . . . Fin.	63·03 N	22·20 E
174	Kyrya (kēr'yȧ) Sov. Un. (Urals In.)	59·18 N	59·03 E
174	Kyshtym (kĭsh-tĭm') Sov. Un. (Urals In.)	55·43 N	60·33 E
174	Kytlym (kĭt'lĭm) Sov. Un. (Urals In.)	59·30 N	59·15 E
195	Kyūshū (I.) (kyōō'shōō') . . . . Jap.	32·27 N	131·03 E
165	Kyustendil (kyōōs-tĕn-dĭl') . . . Bul.	42·16 N	22·39 E
172	Kyzyl (kĭ zĭl) . . . . Sov. Un.	51·37 N	93·38 E
147	Kyzyl Kum, Peski (Des.) (kĭ zĭl kōōm) . Sov. Un.	42·47 N	64·45 E
172	Kzyl-Orda (kzêl-ôr'dȧ) . . . Sov. Un.	44·58 N	65·45 E

L

Page	Name Pronunciation Region	Lat. °'	Long. °'
158	Laa . . . . Aus.	48·42 N	16·23 E
162	La Almunia de Doña Godina (lä'äl-mōōn'yä dā dō nyä gô-dē'nä) . Sp.	41·29 N	1·22 W
134	La Asunción (lä ä-sōōn-syōn') . Ven.	11·02 N	63·57 W
136	La Banda (lä bän'dä) . . . . Arg.	27·48 S	64·12 W
124	La Barca (lä bär'kȧ) . . . . Mex.	20·17 N	102·33 W
214	Labé (lȧ-bā') . . . . Gui.	11·19 N	12·17 W
158	Labe (Elbe) (R.) (lä'bĕ) (ĕl'bĕ) Czech.	50·05 N	15·20 E
90	Laberge (L.) (lȧ-bĕrzh') . . . . . . Can.	61·08 N	136·42 W
128	Laberinto de las Doce Leguas (Is.) (lä-bȧ-rēn tô dā läs dō'sȧ lā'gwäs) . Cuba	20·40 N	78·35 W
171	Labinsk . . . . Sov. Un.	44·30 N	40·40 E
183	Labis (läb'ĭs) Mala. (Singapore In.)	2·23 N	103·01 E
163	La Bisbal (lä bēs-bäl') . . . . Sp.	41·55 N	3·00 E
197	Labo (lä'bô) . . . . Phil. (In.)	14·11 N	122·49 E
197	Labo, Mt. . . . . Phil. (In.)	14·00 N	122·47 E
160	Labouheyre (lȧ-bōō-âr') . . . . Fr.	44·14 N	0·58 W
136	Laboulaye (lä-bô'ōō-lä-yĕ) . . . Arg.	34·01 S	63·10 W
91	Labrador (Reg.) (lăb'rȧ-dôr) . Can.	53·05 N	63·30 W
99	Labrador Sea . . . . Can.	50·38 N	55·00 W
134	Lábrea (lä-brā'ä) . . . . Braz.	7·28 S	64·39 W
196	Labuan, Pulau (I.) (lä-bōō-än') Mala.	5·28 N	115·11 E
197	Labuha . . . . Indon.	0·43 S	127·35 E
89	L'Acadie (lȧ-kȧ-dē') Can. (Montreal In.)	45·18 N	73·22 W
89	L'Acadie (R.) . Can. (Montreal In.)	45·24 N	73·21 W
137	La Calera (lä-kä-lĕ-rä) Chile (Santiago In.)	32·47 S	71·11 W
136	La Calera . . . . Col. (In.)	4·43 N	73·58 W
99	Lac Allard . . . . Can.	50·38 N	63·28 W
151	La Calle (lȧ kȧl') . . . . Alg.	36·52 N	8·23 E
113	La Canada (lä kän-yä'dä) Ca. (Los Angeles In.)	34·13 N	118·12 W
125	Lacantum (R.) (lä-kän-tōō'm) Mex.	16·13 N	90·52 W
162	La Carolina (lä kä-rô-lē'nä) . . . Sp.	38·16 N	3·48 W
125	La Catedral, Cerro (Mtn.) (sĕ'r-rô-lä-kä-tĕ-drȧ'l) . Mex. (In.)	19·32 N	99·31 W
89	Lac-Beauport (läk-bō-pōr') Can. (Quebec In.)	46·58 N	71·17 W
185	Laccadive Is. (lăk'ȧ-dīv) . . . . India	11·00 N	73·02 E
184	Laccadive Sea . . . . Asia	9·10 N	75·17 E
109	Lac Court Oreille Ind. Res. (lăk kôrt-ô-rĕl) (läk kōōr tô-rā'y') . Wi.	46·04 N	91·18 W
109	Lac du Flambeau Ind. Res. . . . Wi.	46·12 N	89·50 W
126	La Ceiba (lȧ sēbä) . . . . Hond.	15·45 N	86·52 W
134	La Ceja (lä-sĕ-kä) . . . . . . Col. (In.)	6·02 N	75·25 W
91	Lac-Frontière . . . . Can.	46·42 N	70·00 W
170	Lacha (L.) (lȧ'chä) . . . . . . Sov. Un.	61·15 N	39·05 E
158	La Chaux de Fonds (lȧ shō dē-fôN') . Switz.	47·07 N	6·47 E
218	Lach Dera (R.) (läk dā'rä) Som. (Horn of Afr. In.)	0·45 N	41·26 E
89	L'Achigan (R.) (lä-shē-gäN) Can. (Montreal In.)	45·49 N	73·48 W
89	Lachine (lȧ-shēn') Can. (Montreal In.)	45·26 N	73·40 W
203	Lachlan (R.) (läk'lăn) . . . . . . Austl.	33·54 S	145·15 E
122	La Chorrera (láchôr-rā'rä) Pan. (In.)	8·54 N	79·47 W
89	Lachute (lȧ-shōōt') Can. (Montreal In.)	45·39 N	74·20 W
161	La Ciotat (lȧ syō-tȧ') . . . . Fr.	43·13 N	5·35 E
107	Lackawanna (lak-ȧ-wŏn'ȧ) NY (Buffalo In.)	42·49 N	78·50 W
93	Lac la Biche . . . . Can.	54·46 N	112·58 W
	La Columna (Mtn.), see Bolivar		
93	Lacombe . . . . Can.	52·28 N	113·44 W
125	La Concordia (lä-kōn-kô'r-dyä) Mex.	16·07 N	92·40 W
105	Laconia (lȧ-kō'nĭ-ȧ) . . . . NH	43·30 N	71·30 W
112	La Conner (lȧ kŏn'ẽr) Wa. (Seattle In.)	48·23 N	122·30 W
162	La Coruña (lȧ kô-rōōn'yä) . . . . Sp.	43·20 N	8·20 W
108	Lacreek (L.) (lă'krēk) . . . . SD	43·04 N	101·46 W
113	La Cresenta (lȧ krĕs'ĕnt-ȧ) Ca. (Los Angeles In.)	34·14 N	118·13 W
116	La Cross (lȧ-krôs') . . . . Ks.	38·30 N	99·20 W

302 La Crosse — Lankoviri PRONOUNCING INDEX

Page	Name Pronunciation Region	Lat. °′	Long. °′
109	La Crosse Wi.	43·48 N	91·14 W
126	La Cruz (lä-kro͞o′z) C. R.	11·05 N	85·37 W
134	La Cruz (lȧ kro͞oz′) Col.	1·37 N	77·00 W
108	Lacs, Riviere des (R.) (rē-vyĕr′ de läk) ND	48·30 N	101·45 W
97	Lac Simard, (L.) Can.	47·38 N	78·40 W
127	La Cuesta (lä-kwĕ′s-tä) C. R.	8·32 N	82·51 W
162	La Culebra, Sierra de (Mts.) (sē-ĕ′r-rä-dĕ-lä-ko͞o-lĕ-brä) Sp.	41·52 N	6·21 W
117	La Cygne (lȧ-sēn′y′) (lȧ-sēn′) Ks.	38·20 N	94·45 W
104	Ladd (lăd) Il.	41·25 N	89·25 W
162	La Demanda, Sierra de (Mts.) (sē-ĕ′rä-dĕ-lä-dĕ-mä′n-dä) Sp.	42·10 N	2·35 W
163	Ladíspoli (lä-dē′s-pô-lē) It. (Rome In.)	41·57 N	12·05 E
112	Ladner (lăd′nēr) Can. (Vancouver In.)	49·05 N	123·05 W
184	Lādnun (läd′no͞on) India	27·45 N	74·20 E
	Ladoga, Lake, see Ladozhskoye Ozero		
134	La Dorado (lä dō-rä′dȧ) Col. (In.)	5·28 N	74·42 W
157	Ladozhskoye Ozero (Ladoga, L.) (lȧ-dôsh′skô-yĕ ô′zĕ-rô) Sov. Un.	60·59 N	31·30 E
89	La Durantaye (lä dü-räN-tā′) Can. (Quebec In.)	46·51 N	70·51 W
213	Lady Frere (lā-dē frâ′r′) S. Afr. (Natal In.)	31·48 S	27·16 E
213	Lady Grey S. Afr. (Natal In.)	30·44 S	27·17 E
92	Ladysmith (lā′dĭ-smĭth) Can.	48·58 N	123·49 W
213	Ladysmith S. Afr. (Natal In.)	28·38 S	29·48 E
109	Ladysmith Wi.	45·27 N	91·07 W
197	Lae (lä′ā) Pap. N. Gui.	6·15 S	146·57 E
156	Laerdal (lâr′däl) Nor.	61·03 N	7·24 E
156	Laerdalsören (lâr′dȧls-û′rĕn) Nor.	61·08 N	7·26 E
156	Laesø (I.) (lâs′û) Den.	57·17 N	10·57 E
126	La Esperanza (lä ĕs-pȧ-rän′zä) Hond.	14·20 N	88·21 W
162	La Estrada (lä ĕs-trä′dä) Sp.	42·42 N	8·29 W
194	Lafa (lä′fä) China	43·49 N	127·19 E
160	La-Fare-les-Oliviers (lä-fär′lā-ō-lē-vyā) Fr. (In.)	43·33 N	5·12 E
120	Lafayette Al.	32·52 N	85·25 W
112	Lafayette Ca. (San Francisco In.)	37·53 N	122·07 W
120	Lafayette (lă-fā-yĕt′) Ga.	34·41 N	85·19 W
104	Lafayette In.	40·25 N	86·55 W
119	Lafayette La.	30·15 N	92·02 W
106	La Fayette RI (Providence In.)	41·34 N	71·29 W
161	La Ferté-Alais (lä-fĕr-tā′-ä-lā′) Fr. (Paris In.)	48·29 N	2·19 E
161	La Ferté-sous-Jouarre (lȧ fĕr-tā′so͞o-zho͞o-är′) Fr. (Paris In.)	48·56 N	3·07 E
215	Lafia Nig.	8·30 N	8·30 E
215	Lafiagi Nig.	8·52 N	5·25 E
160	La Flèche (lȧ flāsh′) Fr.	47·43 N	0·03 W
160	La Flotte (lȧ flôt′) Fr.	46·09 N	1·20 W
120	La Follette (lä-fŏl′ĕt) Tn.	36·23 N	84·07 W
119	Lafourche, Bay. (bȧ-yo͞o′lȧ-fo͞orsh′) La.	29·25 N	90·15 W
135	La Gaiba (lä-gī′bä) Braz.	17·54 S	57·32 W
154	Lagan (lā′gȧn) N. Ire.	54·30 N	6·00 W
156	Lagan (R.) Swe.	56·34 N	13·25 E
150	Laganes (Pt.) Ice.	66·21 N	14·02 W
122	Lagarto, R. (lä-gä′r-tô) Pan. (In.)	9·08 N	80·05 W
126	Lagartos L. (lä-gä′r-tôs) Mex. (In.)	21·32 N	88·15 W
156	Lågan (R.) (lô′ghĕn) Nor.	59·15 N	9·47 E
210	Laghouat (lä-gwät′) Alg.	33·45 N	2·49 E
161	Lagny (län-yē′) Fr. (Paris In.)	48·53 N	2·41 E
137	Lagoa da Prata (lȧ-gô′ä-dȧ-prä′tȧ) Braz. (Rio de Janeiro In.)	20·04 S	45·33 W
137	Lagoa Dourada (lȧ-gô′ä-dō-rä′dä) Braz. (Rio de Janeiro In.)	20·55 S	44·03 W
197	Lagonay Phil. (In.)	13·44 N	123·31 E
197	Lagonoy G. (lä-gô-noi′) Phil. (In.)	13·34 N	123·46 E
215	Lagos (lä′gōs) Nig.	6·27 N	3·24 E
162	Lagos (lä′gôzh) Port.	37·08 N	8·43 W
124	Lagos de Moreno (lä′gōs dā mō-rā′nō) Mex.	21·21 N	101·55 W
160	La Grand′ Combe (lȧ gräN kaNb′) Fr.	44·12 N	4·03 E
110	La Grande (lȧ grănd′) Or.	45·20 N	118·06 W
91	La Grande (R.) Can.	53·55 N	77·30 W
204	La Grange (lȧ grānj) Austl.	18·40 S	122.00 E
120	La Grange (lȧ-grānj′) Ga.	33·01 N	85·00 W
107	La Grange Il. (Chicago In.)	41·49 N	87·53 W
104	Lagrange In.	41·40 N	85·25 W
104	La Grange Ky.	38·20 N	85·25 W
117	La Grange Mo.	40·04 N	91·30 W
107	Lagrange Oh. (Cleveland In.)	41·14 N	82·07 W
119	Lagrange Tx.	29·55 N	96·50 W
134	La Grita (lä grē′tȧ) Ven.	8·02 N	71·59 W
135	La Guaira (lä gwä′ē-rä) Ven. (In.)	10·36 N	66·54 W
162	La Guardia (lä gwär′dē-ȧ) Sp.	41·55 N	8·48 W
136	Laguna (lä-go͞o′nä) Braz.	28·19 S	48·42 W
128	Laguna, Cayos (Is.) (kä′yōs-lä-go͞o′nȧ) Cuba	22·15 N	82·45 W
197	Laguna de Bay (L.) (lä-go͞o′nȧ dȧ bä′ē) Phil. (In.)	14·24 N	121·13 E
115	Laguna Ind. Res. NM	35·00 N	107·30 W
134	Lagunillas (lä-go͞o-nēl′yäs) Bol.	19·42 S	63·38 W
124	Lagunillas (lä-go͞o-nē′l-yäs) Mex.	21·34 N	99·41 W
129	La Habana (Havana) (lä-ä-bȧ′nä) Cuba (In.)	23·08 N	82·23 W
116	La Habra (lȧ hȧb′rȧ) Ca. (Los Angeles In.)	34·56 N	117·57 W
100	Lahaina (lä-hä′ē-nä) Hi.	20·52 N	156·39 W
160	La Haye-Descartes (lȧ ā-dȧ-kärt′) Fr.	46·58 N	0·42 E
158	Lahn R. (län) F.R.G.	50·21 N	7·54 E
156	Laholm (lä′hôlm) Swe.	56·30 N	13·00 E
112	La Honda (lā hŏn′dă) Ca. (San Francisco In.)	37·20 N	122·16 W
184	Lahore (lä-hōr′) Pak.	32·00 N	74·18 E
158	Lahr (lär) F.R.G.	48·19 N	7·52 E
157	Lahti (lä′tē) Fin.	60·59 N	27·39 E
193	Lai, C. Viet.	17·08 N	107·30 E
215	Lai Chad.	9·29 N	16·18 E
190	Lai′an (lī-än) China	32·27 N	118·25 E
193	Laibin (lī-bĭn) China	23·42 N	109·20 E
190	Laichou Wan (B.) (läī′jō wäN) China	37·22 N	119·19 E
160	Laigle (lĕ′gl′) Fr.	48·45 N	0·37 E
217	Laisamis Ken.	1·36 N	37·48 E
190	Laiyang (läī′yäNG) China	36·59 N	120·42 E
190	Laizhou Wan (B.) (lī-jō wän) China	37·22 N	119·19 E
124	Laja, Río de la (R.) (rē′ō-dĕ-lä-lȧ′Kä) Mex.	20·17 N	100·57 W
128	Lajas (lä′häs) Cuba	22·25 N	80·20 W
136	Lajeado (lä-zhĕă′dō) Braz.	29·24 S	51·46 W
136	Lajes (lȧ′-zhĕs) Braz.	27·47 S	50·17 W
137	Lajinha (lä-zhē′nyä) Braz. (Rio de Janeiro In.)	20·08 S	41·36 W
114	La Jolla (lȧ hōl′yȧ) Ca. (In.)	32·51 N	117·16 W
114	La Jolla Ind. Res. Ca.	33·19 N	116·21 W
116	La Junta (lȧ ho͞on′tȧ) Co.	37·59 N	103·35 W
119	Lake Arthur (är′thŭr) La.	30·06 N	92·40 W
120	Lake Barkley (Res.) Tn.	36·45 N	88·00 W
108	Lake Benton (bĕn′tŭn) Mn.	44·15 N	96·17 W
107	Lake Bluff (blŭf) Il. (Chicago In.)	42·17 N	87·50 W
204	Lake Brown (broun) Austl.	31·03 S	118·30 E
119	Lake Charles (chärlz′) La.	30·15 N	93·14 W
121	Lake City Fl.	30·09 N	82·40 W
109	Lake City Ia.	42·14 N	94·43 W
109	Lake City Mn.	44·28 N	92·19 W
121	Lake City SC	33·57 N	79·45 W
92	Lake Cowichan (kou′ĭ-chȧn) Can.	48·50 N	124·03 W
109	Lake Crystal (krĭs′tȧl) Mn.	44·05 N	94·12 W
154	Lake Dist. (lāk) Eng.	54·25 N	3·20 W
116	Lake Elmo (ĕlmō) Mn. (Minneapolis, St. Paul In.)	45·00 N	92·53 W
107	Lake Forest (fŏr′ĕst) Il. (Chicago In.)	42·16 N	87·50 W
115	Lake Fork (R.) Ut.	40·30 N	110·25 W
109	Lake Geneva (jĕ-nē′vȧ) Wi.	42·36 N	88·28 W
91	Lake Harbour (här′bēr) Can.	62·43 N	69·40 W
114	Lake Havasu City Az.	34·27 N	114·22 W
113	Lake June (jo͞on) Tx. (Dallas, Fort Worth In.)	32·43 N	96·45 W
121	Lakeland (lāk′lȧnd) Fl. (In.)	28·02 N	81·58 W
120	Lakeland Ga.	31·02 N	83·02 W
113	Lakeland Mn. (Minneapolis, St. Paul In.)	44·57 N	92·47 W
109	Lake Linden (lĭn′dĕn) Mi.	47·11 N	88·26 W
93	Lake Louise (lo͞o-ēz′) Can.	51·26 N	116·11 W
109	Lake Mills (mĭlz′) Ia.	43·25 N	93·32 W
107	Lakemore (lāk-mōr) Oh. (Cleveland In.)	41·01 N	81·24 W
104	Lake Odessa Mi.	42·50 N	85·15 W
110	Lake Oswego (ŏs-wē′go) Or. (Portland In.)	45·25 N	122·40 W
105	Lake Placid NY	44·17 N	73·59 W
113	Lake Point Ut. (Salt Lake City In.)	40·41 N	112·16 W
114	Lakeport (lāk′pōrt) Ca.	39·03 N	122·54 W
108	Lake Preston (prēs′tŭn) SD	44·21 N	97·23 W
119	Lake Providence (prŏv′ĭ-dĕns) La.	32·48 N	91·12 W
109	Lake Red Rock (Res.) Ia.	41·30 N	93·15 W
108	Lake Sharpe (Res.) SD	44·30 N	100·00 W
114	Lakeside (lāk′sīd) Ca. (In.)	32·52 N	116·55 W
107	Lake Station In. (Chicago In.)	41·34 N	87·15 W
112	Lake Stevens Wa. (Seattle In.)	48·01 N	122·04 W
106	Lake Success (sŭk-sĕs′) NY (New York In.)	40·46 N	73·43 W
113	Lakeview (lāk-vū′) Ca. (Los Angeles In.)	33·50 N	117·07 W
110	Lakeview Or.	42·11 N	120·21 W
117	Lake Village Ar.	33·20 N	91·17 W
121	Lake Wales (wālz′) Fl. (In.)	27·54 N	81·35 W
113	Lakewood (lāk′wo͝od) Ca. (Los Angeles In.)	33·50 N	118·09 W
116	Lakewood Co.	39·44 N	105·06 W
107	Lakewood Oh. (Cleveland In.)	41·29 N	81·48 W
105	Lakewood Pa.	40·05 N	74·10 W
110	Lakewood Wa. (Seattle In.)	48·09 N	122·13 W
112	Lakewood Center Wa. (Seattle In.)	47·10 N	122·31 W
121	Lake Worth (wûrth′) Fl. (In.)	26·37 N	80·04 W
113	Lake Worth Village Tx. (Dallas, Fort Worth In.)	32·49 N	97·26 W
107	Lake Zürich (tsü′rĭk) Il. (Chicago In.)	42·11 N	88·05 W
157	Lakhdenpokh′ya (l′äk-die′npōKyȧ) Sov. Un.	61·33 N	30·10 E
174	Lakhtinskiy (lȧk-tĭn′skĭ) Sov. Un. (Leningrad In.)	59·59 N	30·10 E
108	Lakota (lȧ-kō′tȧ) ND	48·04 N	98·21 W
185	Lakshadweep (State) India	10·10 N	72·50 E
126	La Libertad (lä lē-bĕr-tädh′) Guat.	15·31 N	91·44 W
126	La Libertad Guat. (In.)	16·46 N	90·12 W
126	La Libertad Sal.	13·29 N	89·20 W
137	La Ligua (lä lē′gwä) Chile (Santiago In.)	32·21 S	71·13 W
162	Lalín (lä-lē′n) Sp.	42·40 N	8·05 W
162	La Línea (lä lē′nȧ-ä) Sp.	36·11 N	5·22 W
184	Lalitpur Nep.	27·23 N	85·24 E
155	La Louviere (lȧ lo͞o-vyâr′) Bel.	50·30 N	4·10 E
124	La Luz (lä lo͞oz′) Mex.	21·04 N	101·19 W
160	La Machine (lȧ mȧ-shēn′) Fr.	46·53 N	3·26 E
214	Lama-Kara Togo	9·33 N	1·12 E
97	La Malbaie (lȧ mäl-bā′) Can.	47·39 N	70·10 W
162	La Mancha (Mts.) (lä män′chä) Sp.	38·55 N	4·20 W
116	Lamar (lȧ-mär′) Co.	38·04 N	102·44 W
117	Lamar Mo.	37·28 N	94·15 W
166	La Marmora, Pta. (Mtn.) (lä-mä′r-mô-rä) It.	40·00 N	9·28 E
119	La Marque (lȧ-märk) Tx. (In.)	29·23 N	94·58 W
134	Lamas (lä′mȧs) Peru	6·24 S	76·41 W
160	Lamballe (läN-bäl′) Fr.	48·29 N	2·36 W
216	Lambaréné (läN-bȧ-rā-nā′) Gabon	0·42 S	10·13 E
137	Lambari (läm-bȧ′rē) Braz. (Rio de Janeiro In.)	21·58 S	45·22 W
134	Lambayeque (läm-bä-yā′kȧ) Peru	6·41 S	79·58 W
120	Lambert (lăm′bērt) Ms.	34·10 N	90·16 W
105	Lambertville (lăm′bērt-vĭl) NJ	40·20 N	75·00 W
111	Lame Deer (lām dēr′) Mt.	45·36 N	106·40 W
162	Lamego (lä-mā′gō) Port.	41·07 N	7·47 W
114	La Mesa (lä mā′sä) Ca. (In.)	32·46 N	117·01 W
134	La Mesa Col. (In.)	4·38 N	74·27 W
116	Lamesa Tx.	32·44 N	101·54 W
165	Lamía (lȧ-mē′ȧ) Grc.	38·54 N	22·25 E
197	Lamon B. (lä-mōn′) Phil. (In.)	14·35 N	121·52 E
137	La Mora (lä-mō′rä) Chile (Santiago In.)	32·28 S	70·56 W
108	La Moure (lȧ mo͞or′) ND	46·23 N	98·17 W
137	Lampa (R.) (lä′m-pä) Chile (Santiago In.)	33·15 S	70·55 W
118	Lampasas (lăm-păs′ȧs) Tx.	31·06 N	98·10 W
118	Lampasas R. Tx.	31·18 N	98·08 W
118	Lampazos (läm-pä′zōs) Mex.	27·03 N	100·30 W
151	Lampedusa (I.) (läm-pȧ-do͞o′sä) It.	35·29 N	12·58 E
149	Lamstedt (läm′shtĕt) F.R.G. (Hamburg In.)	53·38 N	9·06 E
217	Lamu (lä′mo͞o) Ken.	2·16 S	40·54 E
217	Lamu I. Ken.	2·25 S	40·50 E
161	La Mure (lȧ mür′) Fr.	44·55 N	5·50 E
166	Lan′ (R.) (lȧn′) Sov. Un.	52·38 N	27·05 E
100	Lanai (I.) (lä-nä′ē) Hi.	20·48 N	157·06 W
100	Lanai City Hi.	20·50 N	156·56 W
184	Lanak La (P.) China	34·40 N	79·50 E
163	La Nao, Cabo de (C.) (kȧ′bô-dĕ-lä-nä′ō) Sp.	38·43 N	0·14 E
154	Lanark (lăn′ȧrk) Scot.	55·40 N	3·50 W
148	Lancashire (Co.) (lăŋ′kȧ-shĭr) Scot.	53·38 N	2·30 W
98	Lancaster (lăŋ′kȧs-tēr) Can.	45·15 N	66·06 W
154	Lancaster Eng.	54·04 N	2·55 W
104	Lancaster Ky.	37·35 N	84·30 W
99	Lancaster Ma. (In.)	42·28 N	71·40 W
105	Lancaster NH	44·25 N	71·30 W
107	Lancaster NY (Buffalo In.)	42·54 N	78·42 W
104	Lancaster Oh.	39·40 N	82·35 W
105	Lancaster Pa.	40·05 N	76·20 W
113	Lancaster Tx. (Dallas, Fort Worth In.)	32·36 N	96·45 W
109	Lancaster Wi.	42·51 N	90·44 W
160	Lançon-Provence (läN-sôN′prô-vĕNs′) Fr. (In.)	43·35 N	5·08 E
212	Lândana (län-dä′nä) Ang.	5·15 S	12·07 E
158	Landau (län′dou) F.R.G.	49·13 N	8·07 E
111	Lander (lăn′dēr) Wy.	42·49 N	108·24 W
160	Landerneau (läN-dĕr-nō′) Fr.	48·28 N	4·14 W
160	Landes (Moorland) (Plain) (läNd) Fr.	44·22 N	0·52 W
149	Landsberg (länds′bo͞orgh) F.R.G. (Munich In.)	48·03 N	10·53 E
154	Lands End Pt. Eng.	50·03 N	5·45 W
158	Landshut (länts′ho͞ot) F.R.G.	48·32 N	12·09 E
156	Landskrona (läns-kro͞o′nȧ) Swe.	55·51 N	12·47 E
120	Lanett (lȧ-nĕt′) Al.	32·52 N	85·13 W
165	Langadhás Grc.	40·44 N	24·10 E
183	Langat (R.) Mala. (Singapore In.)	2·46 N	101·33 E
89	Langdon (lăng′dŭn) Can. (Calgary In.)	50·58 N	113·40 W
113	Langdon Mn. (Minneapolis, St. Paul In.)	44·49 N	92·56 W
89	L′Ange-Gardien (länzh gȧr-dyăN′) Can. (Quebec In.)	46·55 N	71·06 W
156	Langeland (I.) Den.	54·52 N	10·46 E
161	Langenthal Switz.	47·11 N	7·50 E
149	Langenzersdorf Aus. (Vienna In.)	48·30 N	16·22 E
156	Langesund (läng′ĕ-so͞on′) Nor.	58·59 N	9·38 E
156	Lang Fd. (läng′fyôr′) Nor.	62·40 N	7·45 E
106	Langhorne (lăng′hôrn) Pa. (Philadelphia In.)	40·10 N	74·55 W
217	Langia Mts. Ug.	3·35 N	33·35 E
150	Langjökoll (Glacier) (läng-yû′ko͞ol) Ice.	64·40 N	20·31 W
184	Langla Co (L.) (läŋ-lä tswo) China	30·42 N	80·40 E
97	Langlade (I.) St. Pierre & Miquelon	46·50 N	56·20 W
112	Langley (lăng′lĭ) Can. (Vancouver In.)	49·06 N	122·39 W
121	Langley SC	33·32 N	81·52 W
112	Langley Wa. (Seattle In.)	48·02 N	122·25 W
112	Langley Ind. Res. Can. (Vancouver In.)	49·12 N	122·31 W
158	Langnau (läng′nou) Switz.	46·56 N	7·46 E
160	Lagogne (laN-gōn′y′) Fr.	44·43 N	3·50 E
160	Langon (läN-gōN′) Fr.	44·34 N	0·16 W
160	Langres (läN′gr′) Fr.	47·53 N	5·20 E
160	Langres, Plateaux de (Plat.) (plä-tō′dĕ-läN′grĕ) Fr.	47·39 N	5·00 E
196	Langsa (läng′sȧ) Indon.	4·33 N	97·52 E
196	Lang Son (läng′sŏn′) Viet.	21·52 N	106·42 E
117	L′Anguille (R.) (läN-gē′y′) Ar.	35·23 N	90·52 W
190	Langxi (läŋ-shē) China	31·10 N	119·09 E
193	Langzhong (läŋ-jôŋ) China	31·40 N	106·05 E
106	Lanham (lăn′ăm) Md. (Baltimore In.)	38·58 N	76·54 W
94	Lanigan (lăn′ĭ-gȧn) Can.	51·52 N	105·02 W
215	Lankoviri Nig.	9·00 N	11·25 E

ăt; finȧl; rāte; senâte; ärm; ȧsk; sofȧ; fâre; ch-choose; dh-as th in other; bē; ēvent; bĕt; recĕnt; cratēr; g-go; gh-guttural g; bĭt; ĭ-short neutral; rīde; K-guttural k as ch in German ich;

PRONOUNCING INDEX

Lansdale — Leghorn 303

Page	Name Pronunciation Region	Lat. °′	Long. °′
105	Lansdale (lănz'dāl)........Pa.	40·20 N	75·15 W
106	Lansdowne..Pa. (Philadelphia In.)	39·57 N	75·17 W
109	L'Anse (läns)........Mi.	46·43 N	88·28 W
109	L'Anse and Vieux Desert Ind. Res. Mi.	46·41 N	88·12 W
114	Lansford (lănz'fẽrd)........Pa.	40·50 N	75·50 W
107	Lansing........Il. (Chicago In.)	41·34 N	87·33 W
109	Lansing........Ia.	43·22 N	91·16 W
113	Lansing....Ks. (Kansas City In.)	39·15 N	94·53 W
104	Lansing........Mi.	42·45 N	84·35 W
136	Lanús (lä-nōōs')........Arg. (In.)	34·27 S	58·24 W
164	Lanusei (lä-nōō-sĕ'y)........It.	39·51 N	9·34 E
163	Lanúvio (lä-nōō'vyô) It. (Rome In.)	41·41 N	12·42 E
210	Lanzarote I. (län-zȧ-rō'tā).Can. Is.	29·04 N	13·03 W
192	Lanzhou (län-jō)........China	35·55 N	103·55 E
196	Laoag (lä-wäg')........Phil.	18·13 N	120·38 E
189	Lao Ho (R.) (lä'ō hō')......China	43·37 N	120·05 E
160	Laon (läɴ)........Fr.	49·36 N	3·35 E
134	La Oroya (lä-ô-rŏ'yä)........Peru	11·30 S	76·00 W
196	Laos (lā-ōs) (là-ōs')........Asia	20·15 N	102·00 E
190	Laoshan Wan (B.) (lou-shän wän) China	36·21 N	120·48 E
127	La Palma (lä-päl'mä)........Pan.	8·25 N	78·07 W
162	La Palma........Sp.	37·24 N	6·36 W
210	La Palma I........Can. Is.	28·42 N	19·03 W
136	La Pampa (Prov.)........Arg.	37·25 S	67·00 W
136	Lapa Rio Negro (lä-pä-rē'ō-nĕ'grô).Braz.	26·12 S	49·56 W
136	La Paz (lä päz')........Arg.	30·48 S	59·47 W
135	La Paz........Bol.	16·31 S	68·03 W
126	La Paz........Hond.	14·15 N	87·40 W
124	La Paz (lä-pá'z)........Mex.	23·39 N	100·44 W
122	La Paz........Mex.	24·00 N	110·15 W
104	Lapeer (lȧ-pēr')........Mi.	43·05 N	83·15 W
160	La-Penne-sur-Huveaune (la-pĕn'sür-ü-vōn').Fr. (In.)	43·18 N	5·33 E
124	La Piedad Cabadas (lä pyå-dhädh' kä-bä'dhäs).Mex.	20·20 N	102·04 W
150	Lapland (Reg.) (lăp'lȧnd)....Eur.	68·20 N	22·00 E
137	La Plata (lä plä'tä) Arg. (Buenos Aires In.)	34·54 S	57·57 W
117	La Plata (lȧ plā'tȧ)........Mo.	40·03 N	92·28 W
115	La Plata Pk........Co.	39·00 N	106·25 W
163	La Pobla de Lillet (lä-pô'blä-dĕ-lêl-yĕ't).Sp.	42·14 N	1·58 E
98	La Pocatière (lȧ pō-kȧ-tyâr').Can.	47·24 N	70·01 W
99	La Poile B. (lȧ pwäl')........Can.	47·38 N	58·20 W
104	La Porte (lȧ pōrt')........In.	41·35 N	86·45 W
107	Laporte......Oh. (Cleveland In.)	41·19 N	82·05 W
119	La Porte........Tx. (In.)	29·40 N	95·01 W
109	La Porte City........Ia.	42·20 N	92·10 W
157	Lappeenranta (lä'pēn-rän'tä)..Fin.	61·04 N	28·08 E
89	La Prairie (lȧ-prâ-rē') Can. (Montreal In.)	45·24 N	73·30 W
165	Lapseki (läp'sȧ-kē)........Tur.	40·20 N	26·41 E
168	Laptev Sea (läp'tyĭf)....Sov. Un.	75·39 N	120·00 E
162	La Puebla (lä pwā'blä)........Sp.	39·46 N	3·02 E
162	La Puebla de Montalbán (lä pwā'blä dā mōnt-äl-bän').Sp.	39·54 N	4·21 W
113	La Puente (pwĕn'tē) Ca. (Los Angeles In.)	34·01 N	117·57 W
159	Lapusul (R.) (lä'pōō-shōōl)..Rom.	47·29 N	23·46 E
136	La Quiaca (lä kē-ä'kä)........Arg.	22·15 S	65·44 W
164	L'Aquila (lä'kē-lä)........It.	42·22 N	13·24 E
186	Lār (lär)........Iran	27·31 N	54·12 E
202	Lara......Austl. (Melbourne In.)	38·02 S	144·24 E
210	Larache (lä-räsh')........Mor.	35·15 N	6·09 W
102	Laramie (lăr'ȧ-mĭ)........Wy.	41·20 N	105·40 W
116	Laramie (R.)........Co.	40·56 N	105·55 W
163	L'Arba (l'är'bȧ)........Alg.	36·35 N	3·10 E
106	Larchmont (lärch'mŏnt) NY (New York In.)	40·56 N	73·46 W
112	Larch Mtn. (lärch) Or. (Portland In.)	45·32 N	122·06 W
162	Laredo (lȧ-rā'dhō)........Sp.	43·24 N	3·24 W
118	Laredo........Tx.	27·31 N	99·29 W
160	La Réole (lä rȧ-ōl')........Fr.	44·37 N	0·03 W
215	Largeau (lär-zhō')........Chad	17·55 N	19·07 E
128	Largo, Cayo (kä'yō-lär'gō).Cuba	21·40 N	81·30 W
108	Larimore (lăr'ĭ-môr)........ND	47·53 N	97·38 W
164	Larino (lä-rē'nô)........It.	41·48 N	14·54 E
136	La Rioja (lä rē-ōhä)........Arg.	29·18 S	67·42 W
136	La Rioja (Prov.) (lä-rē-ō'-kä).Arg.	28·45 S	68·00 W
165	Lárisa (lä'rē-sȧ)........Grc.	39·38 N	22·25 E
184	Lārkāma........Pak.	27·40 N	68·12 E
183	Lárnakos, Kólpos (B.) Cyprus (Palestine In.)	36·50 N	33·45 E
183	Lárnax.....Cyprus (Palestine In.)	34·55 N	33·37 E
116	Larned (lär'nĕd)........Ks.	38·09 N	99·07 W
162	La Robla (lä rōb'lä)........Sp.	42·48 N	5·36 W
160	La Rochelle (lȧ rô-shĕl')......Fr.	46·10 N	1·09 W
160	La Roche-sur-Yon (lȧ rôsh'sûr-yôɴ').Fr.	46·39 N	1·27 W
162	La Roda (lä rō'dä)........Sp.	39·13 N	2·08 W
129	La Romona (lä-rä-mô'nä) Dom. Rep.	18·25 N	69·00 W
204	Larrey Pt. (lăr'ē)........Austl.	19·15 S	118·15 E
160	Laruns (lȧ-räɴs')........Fr.	42·58 N	0·28 W
156	Larvik (lär'vēk)........Nor.	59·06 N	10·03 E
135	La Sabana (lä-sä-bá'nä).Ven. (In.)	10·38 N	66·24 W
129	La Sabina (lä-sä-bē'nä) Cuba (In.)	22·10 N	82·07 W
162	La Sagra (Mtn.) (lä sä'grä)....Sp.	37·56 N	2·35 E
115	La Sal (lȧ säl')........Ut.	38·10 N	109·20 W
107	La Salle (lȧ sȧl') Can. (Detroit In.)	42·14 N	83·06 W
89	La Salle......Can. (Montreal In.)	45·26 N	73·39 W
89	La Salle......Can. (Winnipeg In.)	49·41 N	97·16 W
104	La Salle........Il.	41·20 N	89·05 W
116	Las Animas (lás ă'nĭ-mȧs)....Co.	38·03 N	103·16 W
218	Las Anod (läs ăn'ŏd) Som. (Horn of Afr. In.)	8·24 N	47·20 E
97	La Sarre........Can.	48·43 N	79·12 W
129	Lascahobas (läs-kä-ō'bȧs)....Hai.	19·00 N	71·55 W
125	Las Cruces (läs-krōō'-sĕs)....Mex.	16·37 N	93·54 W
115	Las Cruces........NM	32·20 N	106·50 W
129	La Selle, Massif De (Mts.) (lä sĕl').Hai.	18·25 N	72·05 W
136	La Serena (lä-sĕ-rĕ'nä)....Chile	29·55 S	71·24 W
161	La Seyne-sur-Mer (lä-sân'sür-mĕr').Fr.	43·07 N	5·52 E
137	Las Flores (läs flo'rĕs) Arg. (Buenos Aires In.)	36·01 S	59·07 W
188	Lashio (lăsh'ē-ō)........Bur.	22·58 N	98·03 E
126	Las Juntas (läs-ĸōō'n-täs)...C. R.	10·15 N	85·00 W
218	Las Khoreh (läs ĸō'rā) Som. (Horn of Afr. In.)	11·13 N	48·19 E
162	Las Maismas (Reg.) (läs-mī's-mäs).Sp.	37·05 N	6·25 W
162	La Solano (lä-sô-lä-nō)........Sp.	38·56 N	3·13 W
210	Las Palmas de Gran Canaria, (läs päl'mäs).Can. Is.	28·07 N	15·28 W
127	Las Palmas........Pan.	8·08 N	81·30 W
164	La Spezia (lä-spĕ'zyä)........It.	44·07 N	9·48 E
137	Las Piedras (läs-pyĕ'dräs) Ur. (Buenos Aires In.)	34·42 S	56·08 W
126	Las Pilas (Vol.) (läs-pē'läs) Nic.	12·32 N	86·43 W
125	Las Rosas (läs rō thäs)......Mex.	16·24 N	92·23 W
163	Las Rozas de Madrid (läs rō'thas dā mä-dhrēdh').Sp. (Madrid In.)	40·29 N	3·53 W
149	Lassee........Aus. (Vienna In.)	48·14 N	16·50 E
110	Lassen Pk. (lăs'ĕn)........Ca.	40·30 N	121·32 W
110	Lassen Volcanic Natl. Park...Ca.	40·43 N	121·35 W
89	L'Assomption (lás-sôm-syôɴ) Can. (Montreal In.)	45·50 N	73·25 W
127	Las Tablas (läs tä'bläs)......Pan.	7·48 N	80·16 W
94	Last Mountain (L.) (låst moun'tĭn).Can.	51·05 N	105·10 W
212	Lastoursville (lȧs-tōōr-vēl').Gabon	1·00 S	12·49 E
122	Las Tres Virgenes, Vol. (vē'r-hĕ-nĕs).Mex.	26·00 N	111·45 W
128	Las Tunas (Prov.)........Cuba	21·05 N	77·00 W
125	Las Vacas (läs-vá'käs)......Mex.	16·24 N	95·48 W
137	Las Vegas (läs-vĕ'gäs) Chile (Santiago In.)	30·50 S	70·59 W
114	Las Vegas (läs vā'gäs)........Nv.	36·12 N	115·10 W
116	Las Vegas........NM.	35·36 N	105·13 W
135	Las Vegas (läs-vĕ'gäs)..Ven. (In.)	10·26 N	64·08 W
124	Las Vigas........Mex.	19·38 N	97·03 W
136	Las Vizcachas, Meseta de (Plat.) (mĕ-sĕ'tä-dĕ-läs-vēz-kä'chàs) Arg.	49·35 S	71·00 W
134	Latacunga (lä-tä-kōōŋ'gä)......Ec.	1·02 S	78·33 W
	Latakia, see Al Lādhiqīah		
160	La Teste-de-Buch (lä-tĕst-dĕ-büsh).Fr.	44·38 N	1·11 W
117	Lathrop (lā'thrŭp)........Mo.	39·32 N	94·21 W
	Latium (Reg.), see Lazio		
161	Latoritsa R. (lȧ-tô'rĭ-tsȧ).Sov. Un.	48·27 N	22·30 E
112	Latourell (lȧ-tou'rĕl) Or. (Portland In.)	45·32 N	122·13 W
160	La Tremblade (lä-trĕɴ-bläd')..Fr.	45·45 N	1·12 W
105	Latrobe (lȧ-trōb')........Pa.	40·25 N	79·15 W
91	La Tuque (lȧ tük')........Can.	47·27 N	72·49 W
185	Lātūr (lä-tōōr')........India	18·20 N	76·35 E
168	Latvian (S. S. R.)......Sov. Un.	57·28 N	24·29 E
203	Launceston (lôn'sĕs-tŭn)....Austl.	41·35 S	147·22 E
154	Launceston (lôrn'stŏn)......Eng.	50·38 N	4·26 W
136	La Unión (lä-ōō-nyô'n)......Chile	40·15 S	73·04 W
124	La Unión (lä ōōn-nyōn')....Mex.	17·59 N	101·48 W
126	La Unión........Sal.	13·18 N	87·51 W
163	La Unión........Sp.	37·38 N	0·50 W
205	Laura (lôrȧ)........Austl.	15·40 S	144·45 E
166	Laura (lou'rȧ)........Sov. Un.	57·36 N	27·29 E
105	Laurel (lô'rĕl)........De.	38·30 N	75·40 W
106	Laurel......Md. (Baltimore In.)	39·06 N	76·51 W
120	Laurel........Ms.	31·42 N	89·07 W
111	Laurel........Mt.	45·41 N	108·45 W
112	Laurel......Wa. (Vancouver In.)	48·52 N	122·29 W
112	Laurelwood (lô'rĕl-wŏŏd) Or. (Portland In.)	45·25 N	123·05 W
121	Laurens (lô'rĕnz)........SC	34·29 N	82·03 W
75	Laurentian Highlands (Reg.) (lô'rĕn-tĭ-ăn).Can.	49·00 N	74·50 W
89	Laurentides (lô'rĕn-tīdz) Can. (Montreal In.)	45·51 N	73·46 W
164	Lauria (lou'rē-ä)........It.	40·03 N	15·02 E
121	Laurinburg (lô'rĭn-bûrg)......NC	34·45 N	79·27 W
109	Laurium (lô'rĭ-ŭm)........Mi.	47·13 N	88·28 W
158	Lausanne (lō-zȧn')........Switz.	46·32 N	6·35 E
196	Laut, Pulau (I.)........Indon.	3·39 S	116·07 E
136	Lautaro (lou-tä'rô)........Chile	38·40 S	72·24 W
196	Laut Kecil, Kepulauan (Is.) Indon.	4·44 S	115·43 E
89	Lauzon (lō-zōɴ').Can. (Quebec In.)	46·50 N	71·10 W
110	Lava Beds Natl. Mon. (lä'vȧ bĕds).Ca.	41·38 N	121·44 W
119	Lavaca R. (lȧ-văk'ȧ)........Tx.	29·05 N	96·50 W
111	Lava Hot Springs........Id.	42·37 N	111·58 W
89	Laval........Can. (Montreal In.)	45·31 N	73·44 W
160	Laval (lä-väl')........Fr.	48·05 N	0·47 W
160	Lavaur (lȧ-vōr')........Fr.	43·41 N	1·48 E
160	Lavaveix-les-Mines (lȧ-vȧ-vĕ'lā-mēn').Fr.	46·05 N	2·05 E
129	La Vega (lä-vĕ'-gä)....Dom. Rep.	19·15 N	70·35 W
205	Lavella (I.)........Sol. Is.	7·50 S	155·45 E
164	Lavello (lä-vĕl'lô)........It.	41·05 N	15·50 E
113	La Verne (lȧ vûrn') Ca. (Los Angeles In.)	34·06 N	117·46 W
204	Laverton (lā'vẽr-tŭn)......Austl.	28·45 S	122·30 E
135	La Victoria (lä vēk-tō'rē-ä) Ven. (In.)	10·14 N	67·20 W
120	Lavonia (lȧ-vō'nĭ-ȧ)........Ga.	34·26 N	83·05 W
119	Lavon Res........Tx.	33·06 N	96·20 W
137	Lavras (lä'vräzh) Braz. (Rio de Janeiro In.)	21·15 S	44·59 W
165	Lávrion (läv'rĭ-ŏn)........Grc.	37·44 N	24·05 E
113	Lawndale (lôn'dāl) Ca. (Los Angeles In.)	33·54 N	118·22 W
214	Lawra........Ghana	10·39 N	2·52 W
107	Lawrence (lô'rĕns) In. (Indianapolis In.)	39·59 N	86·01 W
117	Lawrence........Ks.	38·57 N	95·13 W
99	Lawrence........Ma. (In.)	42·42 N	71·09 W
107	Lawrence.....Pa. (Pittsburgh In.)	40·18 N	80·07 W
107	Lawrenceburg (lô'rĕns-bûrg) In. (Cincinnati In.)	39·06 N	84·47 W
104	Lawrenceburg........Ky.	38·00 N	85·00 W
120	Lawrenceburg........Tn.	35·13 N	87·20 W
120	Lawrenceville (lô-rĕns-vĭl).....Ga.	33·56 N	83·57 W
104	Lawrenceville........Il.	38·45 N	87·45 W
106	Lawrenceville..NJ (New York In.)	40·17 N	74·44 W
121	Lawrenceville........Va.	36·43 N	77·52 W
105	Lawsonia (lô-sō'nĭ-ȧ)........Md.	38·00 N	75·50 W
116	Lawton (lô'tŭn)........Ok.	34·36 N	98·25 W
186	Lawz, Jabal al (Mtn.)....Sau. Ar.	28·46 N	35·37 E
183	Layang Layang (lä-yäng' lä-yäng').Mala. (Singapore In.)	1·49 N	103·28 E
113	Layton (lā'tŭn) Ut. (Salt Lake City In.)	41·04 N	111·58 W
157	Lazdijai (läzh'dē-yī')....Sov. Un.	54·12 N	23·35 E
164	Lazio (Latium) (Reg.) (lä'zyô) (lā't-zēōōm).It.	42·05 N	12·25 E
108	Lead (lēd)........SD	44·22 N	103·47 W
94	Leader........Can.	50·55 N	109·32 W
116	Leadville (lĕd'vĭl)........Co.	39·14 N	106·18 W
120	Leaf (R.) (lēf)........Ms.	31·43 N	89·20 W
119	League City (lēg)......Tx. (In.)	29·31 N	95·05 W
104	Leamington (lĕm'ĭng-tŭn)....Can.	42·05 N	82·35 W
154	Leamington (lē'mĭng-tŭn)....Eng.	52·17 N	1·25 W
148	Leatherhead (lĕdh'ẽr-hĕd') Eng. (London In.)	51·17 N	0·20 W
113	Leavenworth (lĕv'ĕn-wûrth) Ks. (Kansas City In.)	39·19 N	94·54 W
110	Leavenworth........Wa.	47·35 N	120·39 W
113	Leawood (lē'wŏŏd) Ks. (Kansas City In.)	38·58 N	94·37 W
159	Leba (lā'bä)........Pol.	54·45 N	17·34 E
183	Lebam R....Mala. (Singapore In.)	1·35 N	104·09 E
216	Lebango........Con.	0·22 N	14·49 E
113	Lebanon (lĕb'ȧ-nŭn) Il. (St. Louis In.)	38·36 N	89·49 W
104	Lebanon........In.	40·00 N	86·30 W
120	Lebanon........Ky.	37·32 N	85·15 W
117	Lebanon........Mo.	37·40 N	92·43 W
105	Lebanon........NH	43·40 N	72·15 W
104	Lebanon........Oh.	39·25 N	84·10 W
110	Lebanon........Or.	44·31 N	122·53 W
105	Lebanon........Pa.	40·20 N	76·20 W
120	Lebanon........Tn.	36·10 N	86·16 W
186	Lebanon........Asia	34·00 N	34·00 E
153	Lebanon Mts........Leb.	33·30 N	35·32 E
167	Lebedin (lyĕ'bĕ-dēn).....Sov. Un.	48·56 N	31·35 E
167	Lebedin........Sov. Un.	50·34 N	34·27 E
166	Lebedyan' (lyĕ'bĕ-dyän').Sov. Un.	53·03 N	39·08 E
160	Le Blanc (lĕ-bläɴ')........Fr.	46·38 N	0·59 E
129	Le Borgne (lē bōrn'y')........Hai.	19·50 N	72·30 W
159	Lebork (lăɴ-bŏŏrk')........Pol.	54·33 N	17·46 E
160	Le Boucau (lĕ-bōō-kō')........Fr.	43·33 N	1·28 W
160	Le Bouscat (lē bōōs-kȧ)......Fr.	44·53 N	0·38 W
162	Lebrija (lȧ-brē'hä)........Sp.	36·55 N	6·06 W
136	Lebú (lā-bōō')........Chile	37·35 S	73·37 W
165	Lecce (lĕt'chā)........It.	40·22 N	18·11 E
164	Lecco (lĕk'kō)........It.	45·52 N	9·28 E
161	Le Châtelet-en-Brie (lĕ-shä-tĕ-lā' ĕɴ-brē').Fr. (Paris In.)	48·29 N	2·50 E
128	Leche, Laguna de (L.) (lä-gōō'nä-dĕ-lĕ'chĕ).Cuba	22·10 N	78·30 W
118	Leche, Laguna de la (L.)....Mex.	27·16 N	102·45 W
161	Lechenich (lĕ'ĸĕ-nēĸ) F.R.G. (Ruhr In.)	50·47 N	6·46 E
158	Lech R. (lĕk)........F.R.G.	47·41 N	10·52 E
119	Lecompte........La.	31·06 N	92·25 W
160	Le Coteau (lē kō-tō')........Fr.	46·01 N	4·06 E
160	Le Creusot (lēkrû-zô)........Fr.	46·48 N	4·23 E
160	Lectoure (lĕĸ-tōōr)........Fr.	43·56 N	0·38 E
162	Ledesma (lȧ-dĕs'mä)........Sp.	41·05 N	5·59 W
93	Leduc (lĕ-dōōk')........Can.	53·16 N	113·33 W
109	Leech (L.) (lēch)........Mn.	47·06 N	94·16 W
106	Leeds (lēdz)..Al. (Birmingham In.)	33·33 N	86·33 W
148	Leeds........Eng.	53·48 N	1·33 W
108	Leeds........ND	48·18 N	99·24 W
148	Leeds and Liverpool Can. (lĭv'ẽr-pōōl).Eng.	53·36 N	2·38 W
149	Leegebruch (lĕh'gĕn-brōōĸ) G.D.R. (Berlin In.)	52·43 N	13·12 E
148	Leek (lēk)........Eng.	53·06 N	2·01 W
158	Leer (lār)........F.R.G.	53·14 N	7·27 E
154	Lee R. (lē)........Ire.	51·52 N	8·30 W
121	Leesburg (lēz'bûrg)........Fl.	28·49 N	81·53 W
105	Leesburg........Va.	39·10 N	77·30 W
115	Lees Ferry........Az.	36·55 N	111·45 W
113	Lees Summit Mo. (Kansas City In.)	38·55 N	94·23 W
129	Lee Stocking (I.)........Ba.	23·45 N	76·05 W
119	Leesville (lēz'vĭl)........La.	31·09 N	93·17 W
104	Leetonia (lē-tō'nĭ-ȧ)........Oh.	40·50 N	80·45 W
155	Leeuwarden (lā'wär-dĕn)....Neth.	53·12 N	5·50 E
204	Leeuwin, C. (lōō'wĭn)......Austl.	34·15 S	114·30 E
119	Leeward Is. (lē'wẽrd).......N. A.	12·25 N	62·15 W
127	Le Francois........Mart. (In.)	14·37 N	60·55 W
204	Lefroy (L.) (lē-froi')........Austl.	31·30 S	122·00 E
163	Leganés (lā-gä'nás) Sp. (Madrid In.)	40·20 N	3·46 W
197	Legazpi (lā-gäs'pē).....Phil. (In.)	13·09 N	123·44 E
203	Legge Pk. (lĕg)........Austl.	41·33 S	148·10 E
	Leghorn, see Livorno		

ng-sing; ŋ-baŋk; ɴ-nasalized n; nŏd; cŏmmit; ōld; ôbey; ôrder; fōōd; fŏŏt; ou-out; s-soft; sh-dish; th-thin; pūre; ûnite; ûrn; stŭd; circŭs; ü-as "y" in study; '-indeterminate vowel.

ăt; fĭnắl; rāte; senâte; ärm; àsk; sofạ; fâre; ch-choose; dh-as in other; bē; ĕvent; bĕt; recĕnt; cratēr; g-go; gh-guttural g; bĭt; ĭ-short neutral; rīde; к-guttural k as ch in German ich;

ng-sing; ŋ-bank; ɴ-nasalized n; nŏd; cŏmmit; ōld; ŏbey; ôrder; fōōd; fŏŏt; ou-out; s-soft; sh-dish; th-thin; pūre; únite; ûrn; stŭd; circŭs; ü-as "y" in study; '-indeterminate vowel.

306 Lobos — Lowville

PRONOUNCING INDEX

Page	Name Pronunciation Region	Lat. °'	Long. °'
125	Lobos, Isla de (I.) (ĕ's-lä-dĕ-lô'bŏs). Mex.	21·24 N	97·11 W
134	Lobos de Tierra (I.) (lô'bō-dĕ-tyĕ'r-rä). Peru	6·29 S	80·55 W
174	Lobva (lôb'vȧ) Sov. Un. (Urals In.)	59·12 N	60·28 E
174	Lobva R. Sov. Un. (Urals In.)	59·14 N	60·17 E
158	Locarno (lô-kär'nō) Switz.	46·10 N	8·43 E
160	Loches (lôsh) Fr.	47·08 N	0·56 E
121	Lochloosa (L.) (lŏk-lō'sȧ) Fl.	29·33 N	82·07 W
106	Loch Raven Res. Md. (Baltimore In.)	39·28 N	76·38 W
154	Lochy (L.) (lŏk'ĭ) Scot.	56·57 N	4·45 W
121	Lockhart (lŏk'härt) SC	34·47 N	81·30 W
119	Lockhart Tx.	29·54 N	97·40 W
105	Lock Haven (lŏk'hā-vĕn) Pa.	41·05 N	77·30 W
107	Lockland (lŏk'lănd) Oh. (Cincinnati In.)	39·14 N	84·27 W
89	Lockport (lŏk'pōrt) Can. (Winnipeg In.)	50·05 N	96·56 W
96	Lockeport Can.	43·42 N	65·07 W
107	Lockport Il. (Chicago In.)	41·35 N	88·04 W
107	Lockport NY (Buffalo In.)	43·11 N	78·43 W
196	Loc-ninh (lōk'nĭng') Viet.	12·00 N	106·30 E
183	Lod (lôd) Isr. (Palestine In.)	31·57 N	34·55 E
160	Lodève (lô-dĕv') Fr.	43·43 N	3·18 E
157	Lodeynoye Pole (lô-dĕy-nô'yĕ) Sov. Un.	60·43 N	33·24 E
94	Lodge Cr. (lŏj) Can.	49·20 N	110·20 W
111	Lodge Cr. Mt.	48·51 N	109·30 W
108	Lodgepole Cr. (lŏj'pōl) Wy.	41·22 N	104·48 W
184	Lodhran Pak.	29·40 N	71·39 E
114	Lodi (lō'dī) Ca.	38·07 N	121·17 W
164	Lodi (lô'dē) It.	45·18 N	9·30 E
107	Lodi (lō'dī) Oh. (Cleveland In.)	41·02 N	82·01 W
162	Lodosa (lô-dō'sä) Sp.	42·27 N	2·04 W
217	Lodwar Ken.	3·07 N	35·36 E
159	Łódź (wŏŏdzh) Pol.	51·46 N	19·13 E
163	Loeches (lô-āch'ĕs) Sp. (Madrid In.)	40·22 N	3·25 W
214	Loffa (R.) Lib.	7·10 N	10·35 W
150	Lofoten (Is.) (lô'fō-tĕn) Nor.	68·26 N	13·42 E
104	Logan (lō'găn) Oh.	39·35 N	82·25 W
111	Logan Ut.	41·46 N	111·51 W
104	Logan WV	37·50 N	82·00 W
90	Logan, Mt. Can.	60·54 N	140·33 W
104	Logansport (lō'gănz-pōrt) In.	40·45 N	86·25 W
215	Logone (R.) (lō-gō'nä) (lô-gôn') Afr.	11·15 N	15·10 E
162	Logroño (lô-grō'nyō) Sp.	42·28 N	2·25 W
162	Logrosán (lô-grô-sän') Sp.	39·22 N	5·29 W
156	Løgstør (lügh-stûr') Den.	56·56 N	9·15 E
160	Loir (R.) (lwȧr) Fr.	47·40 N	0·07 E
160	Loire (R.) Fr.	47·19 N	1·11 W
134	Loja (lō'hä) Ec.	3·49 S	79·13 W
162	Loja (lô'-kä) Sp.	37·10 N	4·11 W
216	Loka Zaire	0·20 N	17·57 E
218	Lokala Drift (lô'kä-lȧ drĭft). Bots. (Johannesburg & Pretoria In.)	24·00 S	26·38 E
217	Lokandu Zaire	2·31 S	25·47 E
167	Lokhvitsa (lôk-vĕt'sȧ) Sov. Un.	50·21 N	33·16 E
217	Lokichar Ken.	2·23 N	35·39 E
217	Lokitaung Ken.	4·16 N	35·45 E
216	Lokofa-Bokolongo Zaire	0·12 N	19·22 E
215	Lokoja (lô-kō'yä) Nig.	7·47 N	6·45 E
216	Lokolama Zaire	2·34 S	19·53 E
214	Lokosso Upper Volta	10·19 N	3·40 W
211	Lol R. (lōl) Sud.	9·06 N	28·09 E
217	Loliondo Tan.	2·03 S	35·37 E
156	Lolland (lôl'än') Den.	54·41 N	11·00 E
111	Lolo Mt.	46·45 N	114·05 W
165	Lom (lōm) Bul.	43·48 N	23·15 E
113	Loma Linda (lō'mȧ lĭn'dȧ) Ca. (Los Angeles In.)	34·04 N	117·16 W
214	Loma Mansa (Mtn.) S.L.	9·13 N	11·07 W
216	Lomami (R.) Zaire	0·50 S	24·40 E
136	Lomas de Zamora (lō'mäs dā zä-mō'rä). Arg. (Buenos Aires In.)	34·31 S	58·24 W
107	Lombard (lŏm-bärd) Il. (Chicago In.)	41·53 N	88·01 W
164	Lombardia (Reg.) (lôm-bär-dē'ä). It.	45·20 N	9·30 E
197	Lomblen, Pulau (I.) (lŏm-blĕn') Indon.	8·08 S	123·45 E
196	Lombok (I.) (lŏm-bŏk') Indon.	9·15 S	116·15 E
214	Lomé (lō-mā') (lô'mā) Togo.	6·08 N	1·13 E
212	Lomela (lô-mā'lȧ) Zaire	2·19 S	23·33 E
216	Lomela (R.) Zaire	0·35 S	21·20 E
118	Lometa (lō-mē'tȧ) Tx.	31·10 N	98·25 W
215	Lomie (lô-mê-ā') Cam.	3·10 N	13·37 E
113	Lomita (lō-mē'tȧ) Ca. (Los Angeles In.)	33·48 N	118·20 W
149	Lommel Bel. (Brussels In.)	51·14 N	5·21 E
154	Lomond, Loch (L.) (lŏk lō'mŭnd) Scot.	56·15 N	4·40 W
174	Lomonosov (lô-mô'nô-sof) Sov. Un. (Leningrad In.)	59·54 N	29·47 E
114	Lompoc (lŏm-pōk') Ca.	34·39 N	120·30 W
159	Łomża (lôm'zhȧ) Pol.	53·11 N	22·04 E
105	Lonaconing (lō-nȧ-kō'nĭng) Md.	39·35 N	78·55 W
104	London (lŭn'dŭn) Can.	43·00 N	81·20 W
148	London Eng. (London In.)	51·30 N	0·07 W
120	London Ky.	37·07 N	84·06 W
104	London Oh.	39·50 N	83·30 W
98	Londonderry (lŭn'dŭn-dĕr-ĭ). Can.	45·29 N	63·36 W
154	Londonderry N. Ire.	55·00 N	7·19 W
204	Londonderry, C. Austl.	13·30 S	127·00 E
135	Londrina (lôn-drē'nä) Braz.	21·53 S	51·17 W
104	Lonely (I.) (lōn'lĭ) Can.	45·35 N	81·30 W
114	Lone Pine Ca.	36·36 N	118·03 W
127	Lone Star Nic.	13·58 N	84·25 W
129	Long (I.) Ba.	23·25 N	75·10 W
98	Long (I.) Can.	44·21 S	66·25 W
108	Long (L.) ND	46·47 N	100·14 W
112	Long (L.) Wa. (Seattle In.)	47·29 N	122·36 W
216	Longa Ang.	14·42 S	18·32 E
216	Longa (R.) (lôŋ'gȧ) Ang.	10·20 S	13·50 E
121	Long B. SC	33·30 N	78·54 W
113	Long Beach (lông bēch) Ca. (Los Angeles In.)	33·46 N	118·12 W
106	Long Beach. NY (New York In.)	40·35 N	73·38 W
106	Long Branch (lông brȧnch) NJ (New York In.)	40·18 N	73·59 W
108	Longdon (lông'-dŭn) ND	48·45 N	98·23 W
148	Long Eaton (ē'tŭn) Eng.	52·54 N	1·16 W
154	Longford (lông'fērd) Ire.	53·43 N	7·40 W
190	Longgu (lôŋ-gōō) China	34·52 N	116·48 E
113	Longhorn (lông-hôrn) Tx. (San Antonio In.)	29·33 N	98·23 W
217	Longido Tan.	2·44 S	.36·41 E
92	Long I. Ak.	54·54 N	132·45 W
105	Long I. (lông) NY	40·50 N	72·50 W
197	Long I. Pap. N. Gui.	5·10 S	147·30 E
105	Long Island Sd. (lông ī'lănd) Ct.-NY	41·05 N	72·45 W
161	Longjumeau (lôN-zhü-mō') Fr. (Paris In.)	48·42 N	2·17 E
190	Longkou (lôŋ-kō) China	37·39 N	120·21 E
96	Longlac (lông'lăk) Can.	49·41 N	86·28 W
96	Long L. Can.	49·10 N	86·45 W
108	Longlake (lông-lāk) SD	45·52 N	99·06 W
116	Longmont (lông'mŏnt) Co.	40·11 N	105·07 W
161	Longnes (lôN'yĕ) Fr. (Paris In.)	48·56 N	1·37 W
148	Longnor (lông'nôr) Eng.	53·11 N	1·52 W
108	Long Pine (lông pīn) Ne.	42·31 N	99·42 W
105	Long Pt. Can.	42·35 N	80·05 W
99	Long Pt. Can.	48·48 N	58·46 W
95	Long Pt. Can.	53·02 N	98·40 W
105	Long Point B. Can.	42·40 N	80·10 W
109	Long Prairie (lông prâr'ĭ) Mn.	45·58 N	94·49 W
99	Long Range Mts. Can.	48·00 N	58·30 W
205	Longreach (lông'rēch) Austl.	23·32 S	144·17 E
98	Long Reach (R.) Can.	45·26 N	66·05 W
202	Long Rf. Austl. (Sydney In.)	33·45 S	151·22 E
148	Longridge (lông'rĭj) Eng.	53·51 N	2·37 W
116	Longs Pk. (lôngz) Co.	40·17 N	105·37 W
190	Longtansi (lôŋ-tä-sz) China	32·12 N	115·53 E
148	Longton (lông'tŭn) Eng.	52·59 N	2·08 W
89	Longueuil (lôN-gû'y') Can. (Montreal In.)	45·32 N	73·30 W
110	Longview (lông-vū) Or. (Portland In.)	46·06 N	123·02 W
119	Longview Tx.	32·29 N	94·44 W
119	Longville (lông'vĭl) La.	30·36 N	93·14 W
161	Longwy (lôN-wē') Fr.	49·32 N	6·14 E
192	Longxi (lôŋ-shyē) China	35·00 N	104·40 E
196	Long-xuyen (loung' sōō'yĕn) Viet.	10·31 N	105·28 E
173	Longzhen (lôŋ-jŭn) China	48·47 N	126·43 E
193	Longzhou (lôŋ-jō) China	22·20 N	107·02 E
117	Lonoke (lō'nōk) Ar.	34·48 N	91·52 W
161	Lons-le-Saunier (lôN-lē-sō-nyā') Fr.	46·40 N	5·33 E
137	Lontue (lōn-tōōĕ') (R.) Chile (Santiago In.)	35·20 S	70·45 W
197	Looc (lô-ōk') Phil. (In.)	12·16 N	121·59 E
104	Loogootee In.	38·40 N	86·55 W
121	Lookout, C. (lŏŏk'out) NC	34·34 N	76·38 W
110	Lookout Pt. Res. Or.	43·51 N	122·38 W
217	Loolmalasin (Mtn.) Tan.	3·03 S	35·46 E
89	Looma (ōō'mȧ) Can. (Edmonton In.)	53·22 N	113·15 W
154	Loop Head (lōōp) Ire.	52·32 N	9·59 W
120	Loosahatchie (R.) (lōz-ȧ-hă'chē) Tn.	35·20 N	89·45 W
149	Loosdrechtsche Plassen (L.) Neth. (Amsterdam In.)	52·11 N	5·09 E
169	Lopatka, Mys (C.) (lô-pät'kȧ) Sov. Un.	51·00 N	156·52 E
216	Lopez, Cap (C.) Gabon	0·37 S	8·43 E
197	Lopez B. (lō'pāz) Phil. (In.)	14·04 N	122·00 E
112	Lopez I. Wa. (Seattle In.)	48·25 N	122·53 W
216	Lopori (R.) (lō-pō'rē) Zaire	1·35 N	20·43 E
162	Lora (lō'rä) Sp.	37·40 N	5·31 W
107	Lorain (lō-rān') Oh. (Cleveland In.)	41·28 N	82·10 W
184	Loralai (lō-rŭ-lī') Pak.	30·31 N	68·35 E
162	Lorca (lôr'kä) Sp.	37·39 N	1·40 W
205	Lord Howe (I.) (lôrd hou). Austl.	31·44 S	157·56 E
115	Lordsburg (lôrdz'bûrg) NM	32·20 N	108·45 W
137	Lorena (lô-rā'nȧ) Braz. (Rio de Janeiro In.)	22·45 S	45·07 W
135	Loreto (lô-rā'tō) Braz.	7·09 S	45·10 W
89	Loretteville (lô-rĕt-vĕl') Can. (Quebec In.)	46·51 N	71·21 W
134	Lorica (lô-rē'kä) Col.	9·14 N	75·54 W
160	Lorient (lō-rē'äN') Fr.	47·45 N	3·22 W
154	Lorne, Firth of (fûrth ŏv lôrn') Scot.	56·10 N	6·09 W
158	Lörrach (lûr'äk) F.R.G.	47·36 N	7·38 E
113	Los Alamitos (lōs ál-ȧ-mē'tōs) Ca. (Los Angeles In.)	33·48 N	118·04 W
115	Los Alamos (ál-ȧ-môs') NM	35·53 N	106·20 W
112	Los Altos (ál-tōs') Ca. (San Francisco In.)	37·23 N	122·06 W
137	Los Andes (án'dĕs) Chile (Santiago In.)	32·44 S	70·36 W
113	Los Angeles (ăŋ'gĕl-ĕs) (ăn'jĕl-ĕs) (äŋ'hȧ-lȧs). Ca. (Los Angeles In.)	34·00 N	118·15 W
136	Los Angeles (äŋ'hȧ-lās) Chile	37·27 S	72·15 W
114	Los Angeles Aqueduct Ca.	35·12 N	118·02 W
113	Los Angeles R. Ca. (Los Angeles In.)	33·50 N	118·13 W
137	Los Bronces (lōs brō'n-sĕs) Chile (Santiago In.)	33·09 S	70·18 W
110	Loscha R. (lōs'chă) Id.	46·20 N	115·11 W
136	Los Chonos, Archipielago de (är-chē-pyĕ'lä-gô dĕ lōs chô'nŏs) Chile	44·35 N	76·15 W
136	Los Estados, Isla de (I.) (ĕ's-lä dĕ lōs ĕs-tȧ'dōs). Arg.	54·45 S	64·25 W
162	Los Filabres, Sierra de (Mts.) (sē-ĕ'r-rä dĕ lōs fē-lä'brĕs). Sp.	37·19 N	2·48 W
114	Los Gatos (gä'tōs) Ca.	37·13 N	121·59 W
118	Los Herreras (ĕr-rä-räs) Mex.	25·55 N	99·23 W
129	Los Ilanos (lōs ē-lä'nōs). Dom. Rep.	18·35 N	69·30 W
128	Los Indios, Cayos de (Is.) (kä'yōs dĕ lōs ē'n-dyô's). Cuba	21·50 N	83·10 W
164	Lošinj (lô'shēn') Yugo.	44·30 N	14·29 E
164	Lošinj (I.) Yugo.	44·35 N	14·34 E
174	Losino Petrovskiy Sov. Un. (Moscow In.)	55·52 N	38·12 E
163	Los Monegros (Mts.) (mô-nĕ'grōs). Sp.	41·31 N	0·18 W
113	Los Nietos (nyā'tōs) Ca. (Los Angeles In.)	33·57 N	118·05 W
128	Los Palacios Cuba	22·35 N	83·15 W
115	Los Pinos (R.) (pē'nōs) Co.-NM	36·58 N	107·35 W
124	Los Reyes (rā'yĕs) Mex.	19·35 N	102·29 W
125	Los Reyes Mex. (In.)	19·21 N	98·58 W
127	Los Santos (săn'tōs) Pan.	7·57 N	80·24 W
162	Los Santos (sän'tōs) Sp.	38·38 N	6·30 W
135	Los Teques (tĕ'kĕs) Ven. (In.)	10·22 N	67·04 W
111	Lost R. (lôst) Id.	43·56 N	113·38 W
110	Lost R. Or.	42·07 N	121·30 W
111	Lost River Mts. (rĭ'vēr) Id.	44·23 N	113·48 W
137	Los Vilos (vē'lōs) Chile (Santiago In.)	31·56 S	71·29 W
160	Lot (R.) (lôt) Fr.	44·32 N	1·08 E
136	Lota (lō'tä) Chile	37·11 S	73·14 W
106	Lothian (lōth'ĭăn) Md. (Baltimore In.)	38·50 N	76·38 W
217	Lotikipi Pln. Ken.	4·25 N	34·55 E
158	Lötschen Tun. (lŭt'shĕn) Switz.	46·26 N	7·54 E
196	Louangphrabang (lōō-ang'-prä-băng'). Laos	19·47 N	102·15 E
120	Loudon (lou'dŭn) Tn.	35·43 N	84·20 W
104	Loudonville (lou'dŭn-vĭl) Oh.	40·40 N	82·15 W
160	Loudun (lōō-dŭN') Fr.	47·03 N	0·00
214	Louga (lōō'gä) Senegal	15·37 N	16·13 W
148	Loughborough (lŭf'bŭr-ô) Eng.	56·46 N	1·12 W
104	Louisa (lōō'ēz-ȧ) Ky.	38·05 N	82·40 W
205	Louisade Arch. (lōō-ĭs-äd ăr-kĭ-pĕl-ĭ-gō). Pap. N. Gui.	10·44 S	153·58 E
121	Louisberg (lōō'ĭs-bûrg) NC	36·05 N	79·19 W
99	Louisburg (lōō'ĭs-bourg) Can.	45·55 N	59·58 W
98	Louiseville Can.	46·17 N	72·58 W
91	Louis XIV, Pte. Can.	54·35 N	79·51 W
117	Louisiana (lōō-ē-zē-ăn'ȧ) Mo.	39·24 N	91·03 W
103	Louisiana (State) U. S.	30·50 N	92·50 W
212	Louis Trichardt (lōō'ĭs trĭch'art) S. Afr.	22·52 S	29·53 E
116	Louisville (lōō'ĭs-vĭl) (lōō'ē-vĭl) Co.	39·58 N	105·08 W
121	Louisville Ga.	33·00 N	82·25 W
107	Louisville Ky. (Louisville In.)	38·15 N	85·45 W
120	Louisville Ms.	33·07 N	89·02 W
162	Loule (lō-lā') Port.	37·08 N	8·03 W
158	Louny (lō'nĕ) Czech.	50·20 N	13·47 E
108	Loup (R.) (lōōp) Ne.	41·17 N	97·58 W
108	Loup City Ne.	41·15 N	98·59 W
162	Lourdes (lōōrd) Fr.	43·06 N	0·03 W
	Lourenço Marques, see Maputo		
163	Loures (lō'rĕzh). Port. (Lisbon In.)	38·49 N	9·10 W
162	Lousa (lō'zȧ) Port.	40·05 N	8·12 W
154	Louth (louth) Eng.	53·27 N	0·02 W
160	Louviers (lōō-vyā') Fr.	49·13 N	1·11 E
161	Louvres (lōōvr') Fr. (Paris In.)	49·02 N	2·28 E
166	Lovat' (lô-vȧt'y') Sov. Un.	57·23 N	31·18 E
165	Lovech (lō'vĕts) Bul.	43·10 N	24·40 E
116	Loveland (lŭv'lănd) Co.	40·24 N	105·04 W
107	Loveland Oh. (Cincinnati In.)	39·16 N	84·15 W
111	Lovell (lŭv'ĕl) Wy.	44·50 N	108·23 W
114	Lovelock (lŭv'lŏk) Nv.	40·10 N	118·37 W
106	Lovick (lŭ'vĭk) Al. (Birmingham In.)	33·34 N	86·38 W
157	Loviisa (lô'vē-sȧ) Fin.	60·28 N	26·10 E
91	Low, C. (lō) Can.	62·58 N	86·50 W
212	Lowa (lō'wȧ) Zaire	1·30 S	27·18 E
107	Lowell In. (Chicago In.)	41·17 N	87·26 W
99	Lowell Ma. (In.)	42·38 N	71·18 W
104	Lowell Mi.	42·55 N	85·20 W
149	Löwenberg (lû' vĕn-bĕrgh) G.D.R. (Berlin In.)	52·53 N	13·09 E
93	Lower Arrow (L.) (ăr'ō) Can.	49·40 N	118·08 W
	Lower Austria (State), see Niederösterreich		
108	Lower Brule Ind. Res. (brü'lā) SD	44·15 N	100·21 W
205	Lower Hutt (hŭt) N. Z. (In.)	41·08 S	175·00 E
110	Lower Klamath L. (klăm'ȧth) Ca.	41·55 N	121·50 W
110	Lower L. Ca.-Nv.	41·21 N	119·53 W
106	Lower Marlboro (lō'ēr mărl'bōrô) Md. (Baltimore In.)	38·40 N	76·42 W
110	Lower Monumental Res. Wa.	46·45 N	118·50 W
114	Lower Otay Res. (ō'tā). Ca. (San Diego In.)	32·37 N	116·46 W
109	Lower Red (L.) (rĕd) Mn.	47·58 N	94·31 W
	Lower Saxony (State), see Niedersachsen		
155	Lowestoft (lō'stŏft) Eng.	52·31 N	1·45 E
159	Łowicz (lô'vĭch) Pol.	52·06 N	19·57 E
159	Low Tatra Mts. Czech.	48·57 N	19·18 E
105	Lowville (lou'vĭl) NY	43·45 N	75·30 W

Page	Name Pronunciation	Region	Lat. °′	Long. °′
125	Loxicha (Santa Catarina) (lô-zē'chä) (sän-tä kä-tä-rē'nä)	Mex.	16·03 N	96·46 W
203	Loxton (lôks'tŭn)	Austl.	34·25 S	140·38 E
205	Loyauté, Iles	N. Cal.	21·17 S	168·16 E
165	Ložnica (lôz'nē-tsà)	Yugo.	44·31 N	19·16 E
149	Lozorno	Czech. (Vienna In.)	48·21 N	17·03 E
167	Lozova (lô-zô'vá)	Sov. Un.	48·54 N	36·17 E
167	Lozovatka (lô-zô-vät'kä)	Sov. Un.	48·03 N	33·19 E
167	Lozovaya (lô-zo-vä'yä)	Sov. Un.	48·27 N	38·37 E
163	Lozoya, Canal de (kä-nä'l dě lô-thō'yä)	Sp. (Madrid In.)	40·36 N	3·41 W
217	Lualaba (R.) (lōō-ȧ-lä'bä)	Zaire	1·00 S	25·45 E
217	Luama (R.) (lōō'ä-mà)	Zaire	4·17 S	27·45 E
190	Lu'an (lōō-än)	China	31·45 N	116·29 E
192	Luan (R.)	China	41·25 N	117·15 E
216	Luanda (lōō-än'dä)	Ang.	8·48 S	13·14 E
212	Luanguinga (R.) (lōō-än-gĭŋ'gȧ)	Ang.	14·00 S	20·45 E
217	Luangwa (R.) (lōō-äŋ'gwȧ)	Zambia	11·25 S	32·55 E
217	Luanshya	Zambia	13·08 S	28·24 E
190	Luan Xian (luän shyĕn)	China	39·47 N	118·40 E
162	Luarca (lwär'kä)	Sp.	43·33 N	6·30 W
169	Lubaczów (lōō-bä'chōōf)	Pol.	50·08 N	23·10 E
158	Lubán (lōō'bän')	Pol.	51·08 N	15·17 E
157	Lubānas Ezers (L.) (lōō-bä'nàs ā'zĕrs)	Sov. Un.	56·48 N	26·30 E
197	Lubang (lōō-bäng')	Phil. (In.)	13·49 N	120·07 E
197	Lubang (Is.)	Phil. (In.)	13·47 N	119·56 E
216	Lubango	Ang.	14·55 S	13·30 E
197	Lubao (lōō-bä'ō)	Phil. (In.)	14·55 N	120·36 E
159	Lubartow (lōō-bär'tōōf)	Pol.	51·27 N	22·37 E
159	Lubawa (lōō-bä'vä)	Pol.	53·31 N	19·47 E
158	Lübben (lüb'ĕn)	G.D.R.	51·56 N	13·53 E
116	Lubbock (lŭb'ŭk)	Tx.	33·35 N	101·50 W
98	Lubec (lū'bĕk)	Me.	44·49 N	67·01 W
158	Lübeck (lü'bĕk)	F.R.G.	53·53 N	10·42 E
158	Lübecker Bucht (B.) (lü'bĕ-kĕr bōōkt)	G.D.R.	54·10 N	11·20 E
216	Lubilash (R.) (lōō-bē-lȧsh')	Zaire	7·35 S	23·55 E
158	Lubin (lyōō'bĭn)	Pol.	51·24 N	16·14 E
159	Lublin (lyōō'blēn')	Pol.	51·14 N	22·33 E
167	Lubny (lōōb'nē)	Sov. Un.	50·01 N	33·02 E
197	Lubuagan (lōō-bwä-gä'n)	Phil. (In.)	17·24 N	121·11 E
217	Lubudi	Zaire	9·57 S	25·58 E
217	Lubudi (R.) (lōō-bōō'dē)	Zaire	9·20 S	25·20 E
217	Lubumbashi (Élisabethville)	Zaire	11·40 S	27·28 E
217	Lucano	Ang.	11·16 S	21·38 E
164	Lucca (lōōk'kä)	It.	43·51 N	10·29 E
154	Luce B. (lūs)	Scot.	54·45 N	4·45 W
128	Lucea	Jam.	18·25 N	78·10 W
197	Lucena (lōō-sä'nä)	Phil. (In.)	13·55 N	121·36 E
162	Lucena (lōō-thä'nä)	Sp.	37·25 N	4·28 W
163	Lucena del Cid (lōō'thā'nä dā thēdh')	Sp.	40·08 N	0·18 W
159	Lučenec (lōō'chā-nyĕts)	Czech.	48·19 N	19·41 E
164	Lucera (lōō-châ'rä)	It.	41·31 N	15·22 E
193	Luchi	China	28·18 N	110·10 E
111	Lucin (lû-sēn')	Ut.	41·23 N	113·59 W
197	Lucipara, Kepulauan (I.) (lōō-sē-pä'rȧ)	Indon.	5·45 S	128·15 E
149	Luckenwalde (lōōk-ĕn-väl'dĕ)	G.D.R. (Berlin In.)	52·05 N	13·10 E
184	Lucknow (lŭk'nou)	India	26·54 N	80·58 E
160	Luçon (lü-sôN')	Fr.	46·27 N	1·12 W
129	Lucrecia, Cabo (C.) (kȧ'bô-lōō-krā'sē-ȧ)	Cuba	21·05 N	75·30 W
190	Lüda (lü-dä)	China	38·54 N	121·35 E
165	Luda Kamchiya (R.)	Bul.	42·46 N	27·13 E
161	Lüdenscheid (lü'dĕn-shīt)	F.R.G. (Ruhr In.)	51·13 N	7·38 E
212	Lüderitz (lü'dēr-ĭts) (lü'dĕ-rĭts)	Namibia	26·35 S	15·15 E
212	Lüderitz Bucht (B.)	Namibia	26·35 S	14·30 E
184	Ludhiāna	India	31·00 N	75·52 E
161	Lüdinghausen (lü'dēng-hou-zĕn)	F.R.G. (Ruhr In.)	51·46 N	7·27 E
104	Ludington (lŭd'ĭng-tŭn)	Mi.	44·00 N	86·25 W
148	Ludlow (lŭd'lō)	Eng.	52·22 N	2·43 W
107	Ludlow	Ky. (Cincinnati In.)	39·05 N	84·33 W
156	Ludvika (loodh-vē'kä)	Swe.	60·10 N	15·09 E
158	Ludwigsburg (lōōt'vēks-bōōrgh)	F.R.G.	48·53 N	9·14 E
149	Ludwigsfelde (lōōd'vēgs-fĕl-dĕ)	G.D.R. (Berlin In.)	52·18 N	13·16 E
158	Ludwigshafen (lōōt'vēks-hä'fĕn)	F.R.G.	49·29 N	8·26 E
158	Ludwigslust (lōōt'vēks-lōōst)	G.D.R.	53·18 N	11·31 E
166	Ludza (lōōd'zȧ)	Sov. Un.	56·33 N	27·45 E
212	Luebo (lōō-ā'bō)	Zaire	5·15 S	21·22 E
217	Luena	Zaire	9·27 S	25·47 E
212	Lufira (R.) (lōō-fē'rȧ)	Zaire	9·32 S	27·15 E
119	Lufkin (lŭf'kĭn)	Tx.	31·21 N	94·43 W
166	Luga (lōō'gȧ)	Sov. Un.	58·43 N	29·52 E
166	Luga (R.)	Sov. Un.	59·00 N	29·25 E
158	Lugano (lōō-gä'nō)	Switz.	46·01 N	8·52 E
217	Lugenda (R.) (lōō-zhĕn'dä)	Moz.	12·05 S	38·15
218	Lugh Ganane	Som. (Horn of Afr. In.)	3·38 N	42·35 E
154	Lugnaquilla, Mt. (lōōk-nȧ-kwĭ-lȧ)	Ire.	52·56 N	6·30 W
164	Lugo (lōō'gō)	It.	44·28 N	11·57 E
162	Lugo (lōō'gō)	Sp.	43·01 N	7·32 W
165	Lugoj	Rom.	45·51 N	21·56 E
190	Luhe (lōō-hŭ)	China	32·22 N	118·50 E
	Luhe, see Winsen			
216	Luiana	Ang.	17·23 S	23·03 E
212	Luilaka (R.) (lōō-ē-lä'kȧ)	Zaire	2·18 S	21·15 E
154	Luimneach (lĭm'nȧk)	Ire.	52·39 N	8·35 W
124	Luis Moya (lōōē's-mô-yä)	Mex.	22·26 N	102·14 W
137	Luján (lōō'hän')	Arg. (Buenos Aires In.)	34·36 S	59·07 W
137	Luján (R.)	Arg. (Buenos Aires In.)	34·33 S	58·59 W
189	Lujchow Pen.	China	20·40 N	110·30 E
190	Lujia (lōō-jyä)	China	3[illegible]·17 N	120·54 E
217	Lukanga Swp. (lōō-käŋ'gȧ)	Zambia	14·30 S	27·25 E
216	Lukenie (R.) (lōō-kā'nyȧ)	Zaire	3·10 S	19·05 E
212	Lukolela	Zaire	1·03 S	17·01 E
165	Lukovit (lōō'kō-vēt')	Bul.	43·13 N	24·07 E
159	Łuków (wōō'kōōf)	Pol.	51·57 N	22·25 E
217	Lukuga (R.) (lōō-kōō'gȧ)	Zaire	5·50 S	27·35 E
170	Lule (R.)	Swe.	66·20 N	20·25 E
150	Luleå (lōō-lĕ-ō)	Swe.	65·39 N	21·52 E
165	Lüleburgaz (lü'lĕ-bōōr-gäs')	Tur.	41·25 N	27·23 E
119	Luling	Tx.	29·41 N	97·38 W
190	Lulong (lōō-lôŋ)	China	39·54 N	118·53 E
216	Lulonga (R.)	Zaire	1·00 N	18·37 E
112	Lulu (I.) (lū'lōō)	Can. (Vancouver In.)	49·09 N	123·05 W
216	Lulua (R.) (lōō'lōō-ȧ)	Zaire	15·40 S	22·07 E
	Luluabourg, see Kananga			
92	Lulu I.	Ak.	55·28 N	133·30 W
92	Lulu I.	Can.	49·09 N	123·05 W
184	Lumajangdong Co (L.) (lōō-mä-jäŋ-dôŋ tswo)	China	34·00 N	81·47 E
121	Lumber (R.) (lŭm'bĕr)	NC	35·12 N	79·35 W
120	Lumberton (lŭm'bĕr-tŭn)	Ms.	31·00 N	89·25 W
121	Lumberton	NC	34·47 N	79·00 W
137	Luminárias (lōō-mē-nȧ'ryäs)	Braz. (Rio de Janeiro In.)	21·32 S	44·53 W
112	Lummi (I.)	Wa. (Vancouver In.)	48·42 N	122·43 W
112	Lummi B. (lŭm'ĭ)	Wa. (Vancouver In.)	48·47 N	122·44 W
112	Lummi Island	Wa. (Vancouver In.)	48·44 N	122·42 W
216	Lumwana	Zambia	11·50 S	25·10 E
193	Luna (lōō'nȧ)	Phil. (Manila In.)	16·51 N	120·22 E
156	Lund (lŭnd)	Swe.	55·42 N	13·10 E
209	Lunda (Reg.) (lōōn'dȧ)	Ang.	8·53 S	20·00 E
212	Lundi (R.) (lōōn'dē)	Zimb.	21·09 S	30·10 E
154	Lundy (I.) (lŭn'dē)	Eng.	51·12 N	4·50 W
158	Lüneberger Heide (Reg.) (lü'nĕ-bōōr-gĕr hī'dĕ)	F.R.G.	53·08 N	10·00 E
158	Lüneburg (lü'nĕ-bōōrgh)	F.R.G.	53·16 N	10·25 E
160	Lunel (lü-nĕl')	Fr.	43·41 N	4·07 E
161	Lünen (lü'nĕn)	F.R.G. (Ruhr In.)	51·36 N	7·30 E
98	Lunenburg (lōō'nĕn-bûrg)	Can.	44·23 N	64·19 W
99	Lunenburg	Ma. (Boston In.)	42·36 N	71·44 W
161	Lunéville (lü-nȧ-vel')	Fr.	48·37 N	6·29 E
212	Lunga (R.) (lōōŋ'gȧ)	Zambia	12·58 S	26·18 E
216	Lungué-Bungo (R.)	Ang.	13·00 S	21·27 E
184	Lūni (R.)	India	25·20 N	72·00 E
166	Luninets (R.) (lōō-nēn'yets)	Sov. Un.	52·14 N	26·54 E
214	Lunsar	S. L.	8·41 N	12·32 W
191	Luodian (lwô-dĭĕn)	China (Canton In.)	31·25 N	121·20 E
193	Luoding (lwô-dĭŋ)	China	23·42 N	111·35 E
190	Luohe (lwô-hŭ)	China	33·35 N	114·02 E
192	Luoyang (lwô-yäŋ)	China	34·45 N	112·32 E
190	Luozhen (lwô-jŭn)	China	37·45 N	118·29 E
136	Luque (loo'kä)	Par.	25·18 S	57·17 W
184	Lūrah (R.)	Afg.	32·10 N	67·20 E
105	Luray (lū-rā')	Va.	38·40 N	78·25 W
154	Lurgan (lûr'găn)	N. Ire.	54·27 N	6·28 W
213	Lúrio (lōō'rē-ō)	Moz.	13·17 S	40·29 E
217	Lúrio (R.)	Moz.	14·00 S	38·45 E
217	Lusaka	Zaire	7·10 S	29·27 E
217	Lusaka (lōō-sä'kȧ)	Zambia	15·25 S	28·17 E
216	Lusambo (lōō-säm'bō)	Zaire	4·58 S	23·27 E
217	Lusangi	Zaire	4·37 S	27·08 E
184	Lushai Hills	Bur.	28·28 N	92·50 E
192	Lushan	China	33·45 N	113·00 E
216	Lushiko (R.)	Zaire	6·35 S	19·45 E
213	Lushoto (lōō-shō'tō)	Tan.	4·47 S	38·17 E
190	Lüshun (lü-shŭn)	China	38·49 N	121·15 E
213	Lusikisiki (lōō-sē-kē-sē'kē)	S. Afr. (Natal In.)	31·22 S	29·37 E
108	Lusk (lŭsk)	Wy.	42·46 N	104·27 W
216	Luso (lōō'sô)	Ang.	11·45 S	19·55 E
119	Lutcher (lŭch'ĕr)	La.	30·03 N	90·43 W
154	Luton (lū'tŭn)	Eng.	51·55 N	0·28 W
159	Lutsk (lōōtsk)	Sov. Un.	50·45 N	25·20 E
120	Luverne (lū-vûrn')	Al.	31·42 N	86·15 W
108	Luverne (lū-vûrn')	Mn.	43·40 N	96·13 W
217	Luvua (R.) (lōō'vōō-ȧ)	Zaire	7·00 S	27·45 E
217	Luwingu	Zambia	10·15 S	29·55 E
120	Luxapalila Cr. (lŭk-sȧ-pôl'ĭ-lȧ)	Al.	33·36 N	88·08 W
161	Luxembourg (lŭk-sĕm-bûrg) (lük sän-bōōr') (look-sĕm-bōōrgh)	Lux.	49·38 N	6·30 E
146	Luxembourg	Eur.	49·30 N	6·22 E
161	Luxeuil (lük-sû'y')	Fr.	47·49 N	6·19 E
106	Luxomni (lŭx'ôm-nī)	Ga. (Atlanta In.)	33·54 N	84·07 W
	Luxor, see Al Uqșur			
192	Luya Shan (Mtn.)	China	38·50 N	111·40 E
190	Luyi (lōō-yē)	China	33·52 N	115·32 E
170	Luza (R.) (lōō'zä)	Sov. Un.	60·30 N	47·10 E
158	Luzern (lōō-tsĕrn)	Switz.	47·03 N	8·18 E
193	Luzhou (lōō-jō)	China	28·58 N	105·25 E
135	Luziânia (lōō-zyȧ'nēȧ)	Braz.	16·17 S	47·44 W
196	Luzon (I.) (lōō-zŏn')	Phil.	17·10 N	119·45 E
193	Luzon Str.	Phil.	20·40 N	121·00 E
159	L'vov (l'vōōf)	Sov. Un.	49·51 N	24·01 E
173	Lyakhovskiye (Is.) (lya'kô'v-skyê)	Sov. Un.	73·45 N	145·15 E
184	Lyallpur (lī'ǎl-pûr)	Pak.	31·29 N	73·06 E
89	Lyalta	Can. (Calgary In.)	51·07 N	113·36 W
174	Lyalya R. (lyȧ'lyȧ)	Sov. Un. (Urals In.)	58·58 N	60·17 E
165	Lyaskovets	Bul.	43·07 N	25·41 E
212	Lydenburg (lī'dĕn-bûrg)	S. Afr.	25·06 S	30·21 E
114	Lyell, Mt. (lī'ĕl)	Ca.	37·44 N	119·22 W
105	Lykens (lī'kĕnz)	Pa.	40·35 N	76·45 W
159	Lyna R. (lĭn'ȧ)	Pol.	53·56 N	20·30 E
120	Lynch (lĭnch)	Ky.	36·56 N	82·55 W
121	Lynchburg (lĭnch'bûrg)	Va.	37·23 N	79·08 W
112	Lynch Cove (lĭnch)	Wa. (Seattle In.)	47·26 N	122·54 W
89	Lynden (lĭn'dĕn)	Can. (Toronto In.)	43·14 N	80·08 W
112	Lynden	Wa. (Vancouver In.)	48·56 N	122·27 W
202	Lyndhurst	Austl. (Melbourne In.)	38·03 S	145·14 E
107	Lyndon (lĭn'dŭn)	Ky. (Louisville In.)	38·15 N	85·36 W
105	Lyndonville (lĭn'dŭn-vĭl)	Vt.	44·35 N	72·00 W
99	Lynn (lĭn)	Ma. (In.)	42·28 N	70·57 W
95	Lynn Lake (lăk)	Can.	56·51 N	100·30 W
113	Lynwood (lĭn'wōōd)	Ca. (Los Angeles In.)	33·56 N	118·13 W
160	Lyon (lē-ôN')	Fr.	45·44 N	4·52 E
121	Lyons (lī'ŭnz)	Ga.	32·08 N	82·19 W
116	Lyons	Ks.	38·20 N	98·11 W
108	Lyons	Ne.	41·57 N	96·28 W
106	Lyons	NJ (New York In.)	40·41 N	74·33 W
105	Lyons	NY	43·05 N	77·00 W
156	Lyse Fd. (lü'sĕ fyôr')	Nor.	58·59 N	6·35 E
156	Lysekil (lü'sĕ-kēl)	Swe.	58·17 N	11·22 E
174	Lys'va (lĭs'vȧ)	Sov. Un. (Urals In.)	58·07 N	57·47 E
148	Lytham (lĭth'ǎm)	Eng.	53·44 N	2·58 W
174	Lytkarino	Sov. Un. (Moscow In.)	55·25 N	37·55 E
213	Lyttelton (lĭt'l'ton)	S. Afr. (Johannesburg & Pretoria In.)	25·51 S	28·13 E
174	Lyuban' (lyōō'bàn)	Sov. Un. (Leningrad In.)	59·21 N	31·15 E
167	Lyubar (lyōō'bär)	Sov. Un.	49·56 N	27·44 E
174	Lyubertsy (lyōō'bĕr-tsê)	Sov. Un. (Moscow In.)	55·40 N	37·55 E
166	Lyubim (lyōō-bêm')	Sov. Un.	58·24 N	40·39 E
174	Lyublino (lyōōb'lĭ-nô)	Sov. Un. (Moscow In.)	55·41 N	37·45 E
166	Lyudinovo (lū-dē'novō)	Sov. Un.	53·52 N	34·28 E
188	Lyung	Mong.	47·58 N	104·52 E

M

Page	Name Pronunciation	Region	Lat. °′	Long. °′
183	Ma'ān (mä-än')	Jordan (Palestine In.)	30·12 N	35·45 E
156	Maarianhamina (Mariehamn) (mä'rē-ȧn-hä'mē-na) (mȧ-rē'ĕ-häm''n)	Fin.	60·07 N	19·57 E
149	Maartensdijk	Neth. (Amsterdam In.)	52·09 N	5·10 E
161	Maas (R.)	Neth. (Ruhr In.)	51·32 N	6·07 E
155	Maastricht (mäs'trĭkt)	Neth.	50·51 N	5·35 E
211	Maaten (Bishidra (Oasis)	Libya	23·11 N	22·34 E
216	Mabaia	Ang.	7·13 S	14·03 E
112	Mabana (mä-bä-nä)	Wa. (Seattle In.)	48·06 N	122·25 W
119	Mabank (mā'bănk)	Tx.	32·21 N	96·05 W
218	Mabeskraal	S. Afr. (Johannesburg & Pretoria In.)	25·12 S	26·47 E
106	Mableton (mā'b'l-tŭn)	Ga. (Atlanta In.)	33·49 N	84·34 W
210	Mabrouk	Mali	19·27 N	1·16 W
218	Mabula (mȧ'bōō-la)	S. Afr. (Johannesburg & Pretoria In.)	24·49 S	27·59 E
98	McAdam (măk-ăd'ăm)	Can.	45·36 N	67·20 W
137	Macaé (mä-kä-ā')	Braz. (Rio de Janeiro In.)	22·22 S	41·47 W
106	McAfee (mǎk-ȧ'fē)	NJ (New York In.)	41·10 N	74·32 W
135	Macaira (R.) (mä-kī'rä)	Ven. (In.)	9·37 N	66·16 W
197	Macalelon (mä-kä-lā-lōn')	Phil. (In.)	13·46 N	122·09 E
117	McAlester (mǎk ăl'ĕs-tĕr)	Ok.	34·55 N	95·45 W
118	McAllen (măk-ăl'ĕn)	Tx.	26·12 N	98·14 W
135	Macapá (mä-kä-pä')	Braz.	0·08 N	50·02 W
189	Macau (mȧ-kä'ōō)	Asia	22·00 N	113·00 E
135	Macau (mȧ-kà'ōō)	Braz.	5·12 S	36·34 W
129	Macaya, Pico de (Pk.)	Hai.	18·25 N	74·00 W
93	McBride (mǎk-brīd')	Can.	53·18 N	120·10 W
106	McCalla (mǎk-kǎl'lȧ)	Al. (Birmingham In.)	33·20 N	87·00 W
118	McCamey (mǎ-kā'mĭ)	Tx.	31·08 N	102·13 W
163	Maccarese (mäk-kä-rē'zĕ)	It. (Rome In.)	41·53 N	12·13 E
120	McCaysville (mǎ-kāz'vĭl)	Ga.	34·57 N	84·21 W
148	Macclesfield (mǎk''lz-fēld)	Eng.	53·15 N	2·07 W
148	Macclesfield Can. (mǎk''lz-fēld)	Eng.	53·14 N	2·07 W
121	McColl (mǎ-kól')	SC	34·40 N	79·34 W

ng-sing; ŋ-baŋk; N-nasalized n; nŏd; cŏmmit; ōld; ôbey; ôrder; fōōd; fŏŏt; ou-out; s-soft· sh-dish; th-thin; pūre; ûnite; ûrn; stŭd; circŭs; ü-as "y" in study; '-indeterminate vowel.

308 McComb — Makarska PRONOUNCING INDEX

Page	Name Pronunciation Region	Lat. °′	Long. °′
120	McComb (mȧ-kōm′)........Ms.	31·14 N	90·27 W
108	McConaughy, L. (măk kō′nō ĭ′) Ne.	41·24 N	101·40 W
116	McCook (mȧ-kŏŏk′)........Ne.	40·13 N	100·37 W
121	McCormick (mȧ-kôr′mĭk).....SC	33·56 N	82·20 W
154	Macdhui, Ben (Mtn.) (bĕn măk-dōō′ė). Scot.	57·06 N	3·45 W
113	Macdona (măk-dō′nā) Tx. (San Antonio In.)	29·20 N	98·42 W
107	McDonald (măk-dŏn′ăld) Pa. (Pittsburgh In.)	40·22 N	80·13 W
204	Macdonald (I.) (măk-dŏn′ăld) Austl.	23·40 S	127·40 E
220	McDonald I..............Austl.	53·00 S	72·45 E
89	McDonald L. (măk-dŏn-ăld) Can. (Calgary In.)	51·12 N	113·53 W
204	Macdonnell Ra. (măk-dŏn′ĕl) Austl.	23·40 S	131·30 E
95	MacDowell L. (măk-dou ĕl)..Can.	52·15 N	92·45 W
107	Macedonia (măs-ė-dō′nĭ-ȧ) Oh. (Cleveland In.)	41·19 N	81·30 W
165	Macedonia (Reg.) (măs-ė-dō′nĭ-ȧ) Eur.	41·05 N	22·15 E
135	Maceió (mä-sȧ-yō′).........Braz.	9·33 S	35·35 W
164	Macerata (mä-chȧ-rä′tä).......It.	43·18 N	13·28 E
203	Macfarlane, L. (mȧc′făr-lān) Austl.	32·10 S	137·00 E
217	Mackinnon Road..........Ken.	3·44 S	39·03 E
117	McGehee (mȧ-gē′)...........Ar.	33·39 N	91·22 W
114	McGill (mȧ-gĭl′)............Nv.	39·25 N	114·47 W
112	McGowan (măk-gou′ăn) Wa. (Portland In.)	46·15 N	123·55 W
101	McGrath (măk′grȧth)........Ak.	62·58 N	155·20 W
107	McGregor (măk-grĕg′ẽr) Can. (Detroit In.)	42·08 N	82·58 W
109	McGregor..................Ia.	42·58 N	91·12 W
119	McGregor..................Tx.	31·26 N	97·23 W
93	McGregor (R.)..............Can.	54·10 N	121·00 W
89	McGregor L. (măk-grĕg′ẽr) Can. (Ottawa In.)	45·38 N	75·44 W
213	Machache (Mtn.) Leso. (Natal In.)	29·22 S	27·53 E
137	Machado (mä-shȧ-dō) Braz. (Rio de Janeiro In.)	21·42 S	45·55 W
217	Machakos..................Ken.	1·31 S	37·16 E
134	Machala (mä-chȧ′lä).........Ec.	3·18 S	78·54 W
107	McHenry (măk-hĕn′rĭ) Il. (Chicago In.)	42·21 N	88·16 W
113	Machens (măk′ĕns) Mo. (St. Louis In.)	38·54 N	90·20 W
98	Machias (mȧ-chī′ȧs).........Me.	44·22 N	67·29 W
195	Machida (mä-chė′dä) Jap. (Tōkyō In.)	35·32 N	139·28 E
185	Machilīpatnam...............India	16·22 N	81·10 E
134	Machu Picchu (mȧ′chōō-pė′k-chōō). Peru	8·01 S	72·24 W
167	Măcin (mȧ-chēn′)..........Rom.	45·15 N	28·09 E
214	Macina (Depression)........Mali	14·50 N	4·40 W
108	McIntosh (măk′ĭn-tŏsh).......SD	45·54 N	101·22 W
205	Mackay (mȧ-kī′)..........Austl.	21·15 S	149·08 E
111	Mackay (măk-kā′)...........Id.	43·55 N	113·38 W
204	Mackay (I.) (mȧ-kī′).......Austl.	22·30 S	127·45 E
90	MacKay (L.) (măk-kā′).....Can.	64·10 N	112·35 W
94	Mackay (R.)................Can.	56·50 N	112·30 W
112	McKay (R.)..................Or.	45·43 N	123·00 W
107	McKeesport (mȧ-kez′pōrt) Pa. (Pittsburgh In.)	40·21 N	79·51 W
107	McKees Rocks (mȧ-kēz′ rŏks) Pa. (Pittsburgh In.)	40·29 N	80·05 W
120	McKenzie (mȧ-kĕn′zĭ)........Tn.	36·07 N	88·30 W
90	Mackenzie, Dist. of.........Can.	63·48 N	125·25 W
90	Mackenzie (R.)..............Can.	63·28 N	124·23 W
101	Mackenzie B.................Ak.	69·20 N	137·10 W
90	Mackenzie Mts. (mȧ-kĕn′zĭ) Can.	63·41 N	129·27 W
110	McKenzie R..................Or.	44·07 N	122·20 W
104	Mackinac, Str. of (măk′ĭ-nô) (măk′ĭ-năk). Mi.	45·50 N	84·40 W
104	Mackinaw (R.)...............Il.	40·35 N	89·25 W
104	Mackinaw City (măk′ĭ-nô)....Mi.	45·45 N	84·45 W
101	McKinley, Mt. (mȧ-kĭn′lĭ)....Ak.	63·00 N	151·02 W
117	McKinney (mȧ-kĭn′ĭ)........Tx.	33·12 N	96·35 W
108	McLaughlin (măk-lŏf′lĭn).....SD	45·48 N	100·45 W
106	McLean (mȧc′lān) Va. (Baltimore In.)	38·56 N	77·11 W
104	McLeansboro (mȧ-klānz′bŭr-ō). Il.	38·10 N	88·35 W
213	Macleantown (măk-lān′toun) S. Afr. (Natal In.)	32·48 S	27·48 E
213	Maclear (mȧ-klēr′) S. Afr. (Natal In.)	31·06 S	28·23 E
90	McLennan (măk-lĭn′năn)....Can.	55·42 N	116·54 W
92	McLeod Lake...............Can.	54·59 N	123·02 W
93	McLeod (R.)................Can.	53·45 N	115·15 W
110	McLoughlin, Mt. (măk-lŏk′lĭn) Or.	42·27 N	122·20 W
118	McMillan L. (măk-mĭl′ăn)....Tx.	32·40 N	104·09 W
112	McMillin (măk-mĭl′ĭn) Wa. (Seattle In.)	47·08 N	122·14 W
110	McMinnville (măk-mĭn′vĭl)....Or.	45·13 N	123·13 W
120	McMinnville................Tn.	35·41 N	85·47 W
112	McMurray (măk-mŭr′ĭ) Wa. (Seattle In.)	48·19 N	122·15 W
115	McNary (măk-nâr′ė).........Az.	34·10 N	109·55 W
119	McNary.....................La.	30·58 N	92·32 W
110	McNary Dam..........Or.-Wa.	45·57 N	119·15 W
117	Macomb (mȧ-kōōm′)...........Il.	40·27 N	90·40 W
160	Mâcon (mä-kôN)..............Fr.	46·19 N	4·51 E
120	Macon (mā′kŏn)..............Ga.	32·49 N	83·39 W
120	Macon.......................Ms.	32·07 N	88·31 W
117	Macon.......................Mo.	39·42 N	92·29 W
117	McPherson (măk-fŭr′s′n).....Ks.	38·21 N	97·41 W
203	Macquarie (R.)............Austl.	31·43 S	148·04 E
220	Macquarie Is. (mȧ-kwŏr′ė) Austl.	54·36 S	158·45 E
120	McRae (măk-rā′)............Ga.	32·02 N	82·55 W
120	McRoberts (măk-rŏb′ẽrts) Ky.	37·12 N	82·40 W
126	Macuelizo (mä-kwĕ-lē′zō)...Hond.	15·22 N	88·32 W
183	Ma′dabā... Jordan (Palestine In.)	31·43 N	35·47 E
209	Madagascar (măd-ȧ-găs′kȧr) Afr.	18·05 S	43·12 E
99	Madame (I.) (mȧ-dȧm′).....Can.	45·33 N	61·02 W
185	Madanapalle...............India	13·06 N	78·09 E
197	Madang (mä-däng′) Pap. N. Gui.	5·15 S	145·45 E
210	Madaoua (mȧ-dou′ȧ).......Niger	14·04 N	6·03 E
105	Madawaska (R.) (măd-ȧ-wôs′kȧ) Can.	45·20 N	77·25 W
210	Madeira, Ilha da (I.) (mä-dā′rä) Mad. Is.	32·41 N	16·15 W
210	Madeira, Arquipelado da (Is.) (är-kē-pĕ′lä-gō-dä-mä-dĕý-rä) Port.	33·26 N	16·44 W
134	Madeira (R.)..............Braz.	6·48 S	62·43 W
109	Madelia (mȧ-dē′lĭ-ȧ).........Mn.	44·03 N	94·23 W
109	Madeline (I.) (măd′ĕ-lĭn).....Wi.	46·47 N	91·30 W
114	Madera (mȧ-dā′rȧ)...........Ca.	36·57 N	120·04 W
126	Madera (Vol.)..............Nic.	11·27 N	85·30 W
185	Madgaon...................India	15·09 N	73·58 E
184	Madhya Pradesh (State) (mŭd′vŭ prŭ-dāsh′). India	22·04 N	77·48 E
117	Madill (mȧ-dĭl′)............Ok.	34·04 N	96·45 W
186	Madīnat ash Sha′b P. D. R. of Yem.	12·45 N	44·00 E
216	Madingo...................Con.	4·07 S	11·22 E
216	Madingou..................Con.	4·09 S	13·34 E
120	Madison (măd′ĭ-săn).........Fl.	30·28 N	83·25 W
120	Madison...................Ga.	33·34 N	83·29 W
113	Madison........Il. (St. Louis In.)	38·40 N	90·09 W
104	Madison...................In.	38·45 N	85·25 W
117	Madison...................Ks.	38·08 N	96·07 W
98	Madison...................Me.	44·47 N	69·52 W
108	Madison...................Mn.	44·59 N	96·13 W
108	Madison...................Ne.	41·49 N	97·27 W
106	Madison......NJ (New York In.)	40·46 N	74·25 W
121	Madison...................NC	36·22 N	79·59 W
108	Madison...................SD	44·01 N	97·08 W
109	Madison...................Wi.	43·05 N	89·23 W
111	Madison Res...............Mt.	45·25 N	111·28 W
111	Madison R.................Mt.	45·15 N	111·30 W
104	Madisonville (măd′ĭ-săn-vĭl) Ky.	37·20 N	87·30 W
113	Madisonville...............La.	30·22 N	90·10 W
113	Madisonville...............Tx.	30·57 N	95·55 W
214	Madjori............Upper Volta	11·26 N	1·15 E
166	Madona (mȧ′dō′nȧ)....Sov. Un.	56·50 N	26·14 E
186	Madrakah, Ra′s al (C.)......Om.	18·53 N	57·48 E
185	Madras (mȧ-drȧs′) (mŭ-drŭs′) India	13·08 N	80·15 E
113	Madre, Laguna L. (lä-gōō′nä mä′drȧ). Mex.	25·08 N	97·41 W
124	Madre, Sierra (Mts.) (sē-ĕ′r-rä-mȧ′drĕ). Mex.	15·55 N	92·40 W
197	Madre, Sierra (Mts.)...Phil. (In.)	16·40 N	122·10 E
136	Madre de Dios, Arch. (mȧ′drȧ dā dė-ōs′). Chile	50·40 S	76·30 W
134	Madre de Dios, Rio (R.) (rė′ō-mä′drȧ dā dė-ōs′). Bol.	12·07 S	68·20 W
124	Madre del Sur, Sierra (Mts.) (sē-ĕ′r-rä-mä′drȧ dĕlsōōr′). Mex.	17·35 N	100·35 W
109	Madrid (măd′rĭd)............Ia.	41·51 N	93·48 W
163	Madrid (mä-drė′d) Sp. (Madrid In.)	40·26 N	3·42 W
162	Madridejos (mä-dhrė-dhā′hōs..Sp.	39·29 N	3·32 W
110	Mad R. (măd)...............Ca.	40·38 N	123·37 W
217	Mado Gashi.................Ken.	0·44 N	39·10 E
196	Madura (I.) (mȧ-dōō′rä)...Indon.	6·45 S	113·30 E
185	Madurai (mä-dōō′rä).......India	9·57 N	78·04 E
136	Madureira, Serra do (Mtn.) (sĕ′r-rä-dō-mä-dōō-rā′rȧ) Braz. (Rio de Janeiro In.)	22·49 S	43·30 W
195	Maebashi (mä-ė-bä′shė)......Jap.	36·26 N	139·04 E
163	Maella (mä-āl′yä)...........Sp.	41·10 N	0·07 E
128	Maestra, Sierra (Mts.) (sē-ĕ′r-rä-mä-ās′trä). Cuba	20·05 N	77·05 W
205	Maewo (I.)...........New Hebr.	15·17 S	168·16 E
212	Mafeking (măf′ė-kĭng).....S. Afr.	25·46 S	24·45 E
217	Mafia (I.) (mä-fē′ȧ).........Tan.	7·47 S	40·00 E
136	Mafra (mä′frä)..............Braz.	26·21 S	49·59 W
163	Mafra (mäf′rȧ). Port. (Lisbon In.)	38·56 N	9·20 W
173	Magadan (mȧ-gȧ-dän′)...Sov. Un.	59·39 N	150·43 E
173	Magadan Oblast.........Sov. Un.	63·00 N	170·30 E
217	Magadi.....................Ken.	1·54 S	36·17 E
217	Magadi (L.) (mȧ-gä′dė).....Ken.	1·50 S	36·00 E
213	Magalies (R.) (mä-gä′lyĕs).S. Afr. (Johannesburg & Pretoria In.)	25·51 S	27·42 E
213	Magaliesberg (Mts.)........S. Afr. (Johannesburg & Pretoria In.)	25·45 S	27·43 E
218	Magaliesburg............S. Afr. (Johannesburg & Pretoria In.)	26·01 S	27·32 E
197	Magallanes (mä-gäl-yä′nās) Phil. (In.)	12·48 N	123·52 E
136	Magallanes, Estrecho de (Str.) (ĕs-trĕ′chō-dĕ-mä-gäl-yä′nĕs) Arg.-Chile	52·30 S	68·45 W
134	Magangué (mä-gän′gā).......Col.	9·08 N	74·56 W
197	Magat (R.) (mä-gät′)...Phil. (In.)	16·45 N	121·16 E
137	Magdalena (mäg-dä-lā′nä) Arg. (Buenos Aires In.)	35·05 S	57·32 W
134	Magdalena..................Bol.	13·17 S	63·57 W
102	Magdalena..................Mex.	30·34 N	110·50 W
115	Magdalena..................NM	34·10 N	107·45 W
136	Magdalena (I.)..............Chile	44·45 S	73·15 W
122	Magdalena, Bahia (B.) (bä-ē′ä-mäg-dä-lā′nä). Mex.	24·30 N	114·00 W
134	Magdalena, Rio (R.).........Col.	7·45 N	74·04 W
99	Magdalen Is. (măg′dȧ-lĕn)...Can.	47·27 N	61·25 W
158	Magdeburg (mäg′dĕ-bōōrgh) G.D.R.	52·07 N	11·39 E
136	Magé (mä-zhā′) Braz. (Rio de Janeiro In.)	22·39 S	43·02 W
164	Magenta (mȧ-jĕn′tȧ)..........It.	45·26 N	8·53 E
150	Mageröy (I.) (mä′ghĕr-ûė)...Nor.	71·10 N	24·11 E
164	Maggiore, Lago di (L.)........It.	46·03 N	8·25 E
162	Maghnia...................Alg.	35·07 N	2·10 W
218	Maghāghah......Egypt (Nile In.)	28·38 N	30·50 E
152	Maghnia...................Alg.	34·52 N	1·40 W
124	Magiscatzin (mä-kės-kät-zēn′) Mex.	22·48 N	98·42 W
165	Maglaj (mȧ′glä-ė)..........Yugo.	44·34 N	18·12 E
165	Maglić (mäg′lėch)..........Yugo.	43·36 N	20·36 E
165	Maglie (mäl′yā).............It.	40·06 N	18·20 E
113	Magna (măg′nȧ) Ut. (Salt Lake City In.)	40·43 N	112·06 W
174	Magnitogorsk (mäg-nyē′tō-gôrsk) Sov. Un. (Urals In.)	53·26 N	59·05 E
117	Magnolia (măg-nō′lĭ-ȧ)........Ar.	33·16 N	93·13 W
120	Magnolia...................Ms.	31·08 N	90·27 W
161	Magny-en-Vexin (mä-nyē′ĕN-vĕ-sȧN′) Fr. (Paris In.)	49·09 N	1·45 E
105	Magog (mȧ-gŏg′)............Can.	45·15 N	72·10 W
96	Magpie (R.)................Can.	50·40 N	64·30 W
98	Magpie Lac (L.)............Can.	50·55 N	64·39 W
109	Magpie (R.)................Can.	48·13 N	84·50 W
93	Magrath....................Can.	49·25 N	112·52 W
212	Magude (mä-gōō′dȧ)........Moz.	24·58 S	32·39 E
188	Magwe (mŭg-wā′)............Bur.	20·19 N	94·57 E
171	Mahabād....................Iran	36·55 N	45·50 E
211	Mahagi Port (mȧ-hä′gė).....Zaire	2·14 N	31·12 E
196	Mahakam (Strm.)..........Indon.	0·30 S	116·15 E
217	Mahali Mts.................Tan.	6·20 S	30·00 E
213	Mahaly (mȧ-hȧl-ē′)..........Mad.	24·09 S	46·20 E
196	Mahameru, Gunung (Mtn.) .Indon.	8·00 S	112·50 E
184	Mahānadi (R.) (mŭ-hä-nŭd′ė) India	20·50 N	84·27 E
213	Mahanoro (mȧ-hȧ-nō′rō)....Mad.	19·57 S	48·47 E
105	Mahanoy City (mä-hȧ-noi′)...Pa.	40·50 N	76·10 W
184	Mahārāshtra (State)........India	19·06 N	75·00 E
183	Maḩaţţat al Qaţrānah Jordan (Palestine In.)	31·15 N	36·04 E
183	Maḩaţţat ‘Aqabat al Ḩijāzīyah Jordan (Palestine In.)	29·45 N	35·55 E
183	Maḩaţţat ar Ramlah......Jordan	29·31 N	35·57 E
183	Maḩaţţat Jurf ad Darāwīsh Jordan (Palestine In.)	30·41 N	35·51 E
213	Mahavavy (R.) (mä-hä-vä′vė) Mad.	17·42 S	46·06 E
184	Mahaweli (R.)..............India	7·47 N	80·43 E
151	Mahdia (mä-dē′ȧ) (mä′dė-ȧ) Tun.	35·30 N	11·09 E
185	Mahe (mä-ā′)...............India	11·42 N	75·39 E
217	Mahenge (mä-hĕŋ′gȧ).......Tan.	7·38 S	36·16 E
184	Mahi (R.)..................India	23·16 N	73·20 E
185	Māhīm Bay...........India (In.)	19·03 N	72·45 E
213	Mahlabatini (mä′lȧ-bȧ-tē′nė) S. Afr. (Natal In.)	28·15 S	31·29 E
149	Mahlow (mä′lōv) G.D.R. (Berlin In.)	52·23 N	13·24 E
108	Mahnomen (mô-nō′mĕn).....Mn.	47·18 N	95·58 W
163	Mahón (mä-ōn′)..............Sp.	39·52 N	4·15 E
98	Mahone Bay (mȧ-hōn′)......Can.	44·27 N	64·23 W
98	Mahone B...................Can.	44·30 N	64·15 W
106	Mahopac, L. (mā-hō′păk) NY (New York In.)	41·24 N	73·45 W
106	Mahwah (mȧ-wă′) NJ (New York In.)	41·05 N	74·09 W
148	Maidenhead (măd′ĕn-hĕd) Eng. (London In.)	51·30 N	0·44 W
148	Maidstone.....Eng. (London In.)	51·17 N	0·32 E
215	Maiduguri (mä′ē-dȧ-gōō′rė)...Nig.	11·51 N	13·10 E
134	Maigualida Sierra (Mts.) (sē-ĕ′r-rȧ-mī-gwä′lē-dĕ). Ven.	6·30 N	65·50 W
184	Maijdi......................Bngl.	22·59 N	91·08 E
	Maikop, see Maykop		
203	Main Barrier Ra. (băr′ĕr).Austl.	31·25 S	141·40 E
212	Mai-Ndombe, Lac (Leopold II, L.) Zaire	2·16 S	19·00 E
103	Maine (State) (mān).........U. S.	45·25 N	69·50 W
154	Mainland (I.) (mān-lănd) Scot. (In.)	60·19 N	2·40 W
158	Main (R.) (mīn)............F.R.G.	49·49 N	9·20 E
161	Maintenon (mäN-tĕ-nôN′) Fr. (Paris In.)	48·35 N	1·35 E
213	Maintirano (mä′ēn-tė-rä′nō).Mad.	18·05 S	44·08 E
158	Mainz (mīnts)..............F.R.G.	49·59 N	8·16 E
210	Maio I. (mä′yo).......C. V. (In.)	15·15 N	22·50 W
137	Maipo (mī′pō) (R.) Chile (Santiago In.)	33·45 S	71·08 W
136	Maipo (Vol.)...............Arg.	34·08 S	69·51 W
137	Maipú (mī′pōō′) Arg. (Buenos Aires In.)	36·51 S	57·54 W
135	Maiquetía (mī-kĕ-tė′ä)..Ven. (In.)	10·37 N	66·56 W
129	Maisí, Punta (Pt.) (pōōn′n-tä-mī-sē′). Cuba	20·10 N	74·00 W
161	Maison-Rouge (mȧ-zôN-rōōzh′) Fr. (Paris In.)	48·34 N	3·09 E
203	Maitland (māt′lănd).......Austl.	32·45 S	151·40 E
195	Maizuru (mä-ĭ′zōō-rōō)......Jap.	35·26 N	135·15 E
196	Majene....................Indon.	3·34 S	119·00 E
211	Maji.......................Eth.	6·14 N	35·34 E
	Majorca I., see Mallorca, Isle de		
213	Majunga (mȧ-jŭŋ′gä)........Mad.	15·12 S	46·26 E
110	Makah Ind. Res. (mȧ kī′)....Wa.	48·17 N	124·52 W
213	Makanya (mä-kän′yä).......Tan.	4·15 S	37·49 E
164	Makarska (mȧ′kär-skȧ).....Yugo.	43·17 N	17·05 E

ăt; finăl; rāte; senȧte; ärm; ȧsk; sofȧ; fâre; ch-choose; dh-as th in other; bē; ėvent; bĕt; recĕnt; cratẽr; g-go; gh-guttural g; bĭt; ĭ-short neutral; rīde; K-guttural k as ch in German ich;

PRONOUNCING INDEX
Makar'yev — Manteo 309

Page	Name Pronunciation Region	Lat. °'	Long. °'
170	Makar'yev Sov. Un.	57·50 N	43·48 E
	Makasar, see Ujung Pandang		
196	Makasar, Selat (Makassar Strait) Indon.	2·00 S	118·07 E
216	Makaw Zaire	3·29 S	18·19 E
195	Make (I.) (mä'kȧ) Jap.	30·43 N	130·49 E
214	Makeni S. L.	8·53 N	12·03 W
167	Makeyevka (mŭk-yā'ŭf-kȧ) Sov. Un.	48·03 N	38·00 E
218	Makgadikgadi Pans (L.) Bots.	20·38 S	21·31 E
171	Makhachkala (mäᴋ'äch-kä'lä) Sov. Un.	43·00 N	47·40 E
213	Makhaleng (R.) Leso. (Natal In.)	29·53 S	27·33 E
165	Makhlata (mäᴋ'lä-tä) Bul.	43·27 N	24·16 E
217	Makindu Ken.	2·17 S	37·49 E
186	Makkah (Mecca) (mĕk'ȧ) Sau. Ar.	21·27 N	39·45 E
91	Makkovik Can.	55·01 N	59·10 W
159	Makó (mô'kō) Hung.	46·13 N	20·30 E
216	Makokou (mȧ-kô-ko͞o') Gabon	0·34 N	12·52 E
159	Maków Mazowiecki (mä'kōov mä-zō-vyĕts'kē) Pol.	52·51 N	21·07 E
195	Makuhari (mä-ko͞o-hä'rē) Jap. (Tōkyō In.)	35·39 N	140·04 E
195	Makurazaki (mä'ko͞o-rä-zä'kê) Jap.	31·16 N	130·18 E
215	Makurdi Nig.	7·45 N	8·32 E
101	Makushin (mȧ-ko͞o'shĭn) Ak.	53·57 N	166·28 W
172	Makushino (mȧ-ko͞o-shēn'ō) Sov. Un.	55·03 N	67·43 E
185	Malabar Coast (măl'ȧ-bär) India	11·19 N	75·33 E
216	Malabo Equat. Gui.	3·45 N	8·47 E
197	Malabon Phil. (In.)	14·39 N	120·57 E
196	Malacca, Str. of (mȧ-lăk'ȧ) Asia	4·15 N	99·44 E
111	Malad (mȧ-läd') Id.	42·11 N	112·15 W
163	Maladetta (Mts.) (mä-lä-dĕt'tä) Sp.	42·30 N	0·38 E
163	Malafede (R.) (mä-lä-fĕ'dĕ) It. (Rome In.)	41·43 N	12·28 E
134	Málaga (mȧ'lä-gȧ) Col.	6·41 N	72·46 W
162	Málaga Sp.	36·45 N	4·25 W
162	Málaga, Bahía de (B.) (bä-ē'ä-dĕ-mȧ'lä-gä) Sp.	36·35 N	4·10 W
162	Malagón (mä-lä-gōn') Sp.	39·12 N	3·52 W
205	Malaita (I.) (mȧ-lä'ê-tȧ) Sol. Is.	8·38 S	161·15 E
211	Malakāl (mȧ-lȧ-käl') Sud.	9·46 N	31·54 E
174	Malakhovka (mȧ-läk'ôf-kȧ) Sov. Un. (Moscow In.)	55·38 N	38·01 E
196	Malang Indon.	8·06 S	112·50 E
216	Malanje (mȧ-läŋ-gȧ) Ang.	9·32 S	16·20 E
210	Malanville Benin	12·04 N	3·09 E
98	Malapedia (R.) Can.	48·11 N	67·08 W
127	Mala Punta (Pt.) (po͞o'n-tä-mä'lä) Pan.	7·32 N	79·44 W
156	Mälaren (L.) Swe.	59·38 N	16·55 E
91	Malartic Can.	48·07 N	78·11 W
92	Malaspina Str. (măl-ȧ-spē'nȧ) Can.	49·44 N	124·20 W
171	Malatya (mȧ-lä'tyȧ) Tur.	38·30 N	38·15 E
209	Malawi Afr.	11·15 S	33·45 E
	Malawi, L., see Nyasa, L.		
196	Malaya (Reg.) (mȧ-lā'yȧ) Mala.	3·35 N	101·30 E
166	Malaya Vishera (vē-shä'rä) Sov. Un.	58·51 N	32·13 E
196	Malay Pen. (mȧ-lā') (mā'lā) Asia	7·46 N	101·06 E
196	Malaysia (mȧ-lā'zhȧ) Asia	4·10 N	101·22 E
154	Mal B. (măl) Ire.	52·51 N	9·45 W
204	Malbon (măl'bŭn) Austl.	21·15 S	140·30 E
159	Malbork (mäl'bôrk) Pol.	54·02 N	19·04 E
163	Malcabran (R.) (mäl-kä-brän') Port. (Lisbon In.)	38·47 N	8·46 W
99	Malden (môl'dĕn) Ma. (In.)	42·26 N	71·04 W
117	Malden Mo.	36·32 N	89·56 W
199	Malden (I.) Oceania	4·20 S	154·30 W
182	Maldives Asia	4·30 N	71·30 E
148	Maldon (môrl'dŏn) Eng. (London In.)	51·44 N	0·39 E
136	Maldonado (mäl-dŏ-nä'dō) Ur.	34·54 S	54·57 W
124	Maldonado, Punta (Pt.) (po͞o'n-tä) Mex.	16·18 N	98·34 W
165	Maléa, Akr. (C.) Grc.	37·31 N	23·13 E
184	Mālegaon India	20·35 N	74·30 E
159	Male Karpaty (Mts.) Czech.	48·31 N	17·15 E
205	Malekula (I.) (mä-lä-ko͞o'lä) New Hebr.	16·44 S	167·45 E
162	Malhão da Estrêla (Mtn.) (mäl-you'ɴ-dä-ĕs-trĕ'lä) Sp.	40·20 N	7·38 W
110	Malheur L. (mȧ-lo͞or') Or.	43·16 N	118·37 W
110	Malheur R. (mȧ-lo͞or') Or.	43·45 N	117·41 W
209	Mali Afr.	15·45 N	0·15 W
113	Malibu (mă'lĭ-bo͞o) Ca. (Los Angeles In.)	34·03 N	118·38 W
217	Malimba, Monts (Mts.) Zaire	7·45 S	29·15 E
167	Malin (mȧ-lēn') Sov. Un.	50·44 N	29·15 E
124	Malinalco (mä-lē-näl'kō) Mex.	18·54 N	99·31 W
124	Malinaltepec (mä-lē-näl-tȧ-pĕk') Mex.	17·01 N	98·41 W
213	Malindi (mä-lēn'dê) Ken.	3·14 S	40·04 E
159	Málinec (mä'lē-nyets') Czech.	48·31 N	19·40 E
154	Malin Hd. N. Ire.	55·23 N	7·24 W
217	Malindi Ken.	3·13 S	40·07 E
154	Malinmore Hd. (mă'lĭn-mōr) Ire.	54·45 N	8·30 W
174	Malino (mä'lĭ-nô) Sov. Un. (Moscow In.)	55·07 N	38·12 E
167	Malinovka (mȧ-lē-nôf'kȧ) Sov. Un.	49·50 N	36·43 E
165	Malkara (mäl'ᴋȧ-rȧ) Tur.	40·51 N	26·52 E
165	Malko Tŭrnovo (mäl'kō-t'r'nô-vȧ) Bul.	41·59 N	27·28 E
154	Mallaig Scot.	56·59 N	5·55 W
218	Mallawī (mȧ-lä'wê) Egypt (Nile In.)	27·43 N	30·49 E
107	Mallet Creek (măl'ĕt) Oh. (Cleveland In.)	41·10 N	81·55 W
163	Mallorca, Isla de (Majorca I.) (ē's-lä-dĕ-mäl-yō'r-kä) Sp.	39·18 N	2·22 E
154	Mallow (măl'ō) Ire.	52·07 N	9·04 W
155	Malmédy (mȧl-mā-dē') Bel.	50·25 N	6·01 E
212	Malmesbury (mämz'bĕr-ĭ) S. Afr.	33·30 S	18·35 E
156	Malmköping (mälm'chû'pĭng) Swe.	59·09 N	16·39 E
156	Malmö (mälm'û) Swe.	55·36 N	12·58 E
173	Malmyzh (mȧl-mēzh') Sov. Un.	49·58 N	137·07 E
170	Malmyzh Sov. Un.	56·30 N	50·48 E
166	Maloarkhangelsk (mä'lô-är-ᴋäŋ'gĕlsk) Sov. Un.	52·26 N	36·29 E
197	Malolos (mä-lô'lôs) Phil. (In.)	14·51 N	120·49 E
174	Malomal'sk (mȧ-lô-mälsk'') Sov. Un. (Urals In.)	58·47 N	59·55 E
105	Malone (mȧ-lōn') NY	44·50 N	74·20 W
216	Malonga Zaire	10·24 S	23·10 E
213	Maloti Mts. Leso (Natal In.)	29·00 S	28·29 E
166	Maloyaroslavets (mä'lô-yä-rô-slä-vyĕts) Sov. Un.	55·01 N	36·25 E
170	Malozemel'skaya Tundra (Plains) Sov. Un.	67·30 N	50·00 E
136	Malpas (măl'pȧz) Eng.	53·01 N	2·46 W
134	Malpelo, Isla de (I.) (mäl-pā'lō) Col.	3·55 N	81·30 W
98	Malpeque B. (môl-pĕk') Can.	46·30 N	63·47 W
111	Malta (môl'tȧ) Mt.	48·20 N	107·50 W
146	Malta Eur.	35·52 N	13·30 E
212	Maltahöhe (mäl'tä-hō'ĕ) Namibia	24·45 S	16·45 E
125	Maltrata (mäl-trä'tä) Mex.	18·48 N	97·16 W
197	Maluku (Moluccas) (Is.) Indon.	2·22 S	128·25 E
197	Maluku, Laut (Molucca) (Sea) Indon.	0·15 N	125·41 E
211	Malūt Sud.	10·30 N	32·17 E
185	Mālvan India	16·08 N	73·32 E
117	Malvern (măl'vĕrn) Ar.	34·21 N	92·47 W
173	Malyy Anyuy (R.) Sov. Un.	67·52 N	164·30 E
173	Malyy Lyakhovskiye (I.) Sov. Un.	74·15 N	142·30 E
173	Malyy Tamir (I.) Sov. Un.	78·10 N	107·30 E
125	Mamantel (mä-mȧn-tĕl') Mex.	18·36 N	91·06 W
106	Mamaroneck (măm'ȧ-rō-nĕk) NY (New York In.)	40·57 N	73·44 W
210	Mamau Gui.	10·26 N	12·07 W
217	Mambasa Zaire	1·21 N	29·03 E
197	Mamberamo (R.) (mäm-bȧ-rä'mō) Indon.	2·30 S	138·00 E
197	Mamburao (mäm-bo͞o'rä-ō) Phil. (In.)	13·14 N	120·35 E
162	Mamede, Serra de (Mts.) (sĕ'r-rä-dĕ-mä-mĕ'dĕ) Port.	39·29 N	7·11 W
210	Mamfe (mäm'fĕ) Cam.	5·46 N	9·17 E
195	Mamihara (mä'mê-hä-rä) Jap.	32·41 N	131·12 E
120	Mammoth Cave (măm'ŏth) Ky.	37·10 N	86·04 W
120	Mammoth Cave Natl. Park Ky.	37·20 N	86·21 W
111	Mammoth Hot Springs (măm'ŭth hôt sprĭngz) Wy.	44·55 N	110·50 W
185	Mamnoli India (In.)	19·17 N	73·15 E
134	Mamoré (R.) (mä-mô-rā') Bol.	13·19 S	65·27 W
214	Mampong Ghana	7·04 N	1·24 W
159	Mamry L. (mäm'rĭ) Pol.	54·10 N	21·28 E
214	Man Ivory Coast	7·24 N	7·33 W
163	Manacor (mä-nä-kôr') Sp.	39·35 N	3·15 E
197	Manado Indon.	1·29 N	124·50 E
129	Managua (mä-nä'gwä) Cuba (In.)	22·14 N	82·17 W
126	Managua Nic.	12·10 N	86·16 W
126	Managua, Lago de (L.) (lȧ'gô-dĕ) Nic.	12·28 N	86·10 W
213	Manakara (mä-nä-kä'rŭ) Mad.	22·17 S	48·06 E
213	Mananara (R.) (mä-nä-nä'rŭ) Mad.	23·15 S	48·15 E
213	Mananjary (mä-nän-zhä'rê) Mad.	20·16 S	48·13 E
	Manáos, see Manaus		
188	Manas (mä-nä-sz) China	44·30 N	86·00 E
188	Manas (R.) China	45·00 N	85·45 E
188	Manas Hu (L.) (mä-nä-sŭ ho͞o) China	45·49 N	86·08 E
105	Manassas (mȧ-năs'ȧs) Va.	38·45 N	77·30 W
135	Manaus (Manáos) (mä-nä'o͞ozh) Braz.	3·01 S	60·00 W
104	Mancelona (măn-sê-lō'nȧ) Mi.	44·50 N	85·05 W
162	Mancha Real (män'chä rā-äl') Sp.	37·48 N	3·37 W
174	Manchazh (män'chȧsh) Sov. Un. (Urals In.)	56·30 N	58·10 E
105	Manchester (măn'chĕs-tēr) Ct.	41·45 N	72·30 W
148	Manchester Eng.	53·28 N	2·14 W
120	Manchester Ga.	32·50 N	84·37 W
109	Manchester Ia.	42·30 N	91·30 W
99	Manchester Ma. (In.)	42·35 N	70·47 W
113	Manchester Mo. (St. Louis In.)	38·36 N	90·31 W
105	Manchester NH	43·00 N	71·30 W
104	Manchester Oh.	38·40 N	83·35 W
148	Manchester Ship Canal Eng.	53·20 N	2·40 W
189	Manchuria (Reg.) (măn-cho͞o'rē-ȧ) China	48·00 N	124·58 E
186	Mand (R.) Iran	28·20 N	52·30 E
156	Mandal (män'däl) Nor.	58·03 N	7·28 E
188	Mandalay (măn'dȧ-lā) Bur.	22·00 N	96·08 E
156	Mandalselv (R.) (män'dälsĕlv) Nor.	58·25 N	7·30 E
108	Mandan (măn'dăn) ND	46·49 N	100·54 W
215	Mandara Mts. (män-dä'rä) Cam.-Nig.	10·15 N	13·23 E
183	Mandau Siak (R.) Indon. (Singapore In.)	1·03 N	101·25 E
217	Mandimba Moz.	14·21 S	35·39 E
127	Mandinga (män-dĭŋ'gä) Pan.	9·32 N	79·04 W
184	Mandla India	22·43 N	80·23 E
165	Mándra (män'drä) Grc.	38·06 N	23·32 E
213	Mandritsara (mȧn-drēt-sä'rȧ) Mad.	15·49 S	48·47 E
165	Manduria (män-do͞o'rê-ä) It.	40·23 N	17·41 E
185	Mandve India (In.)	18·47 N	72·52 E
185	Māndvi (mŭnd'vē) India (In.)	19·29 N	72·53 E
184	Māndvi (mŭnd'vē) India	22·54 N	69·23 E
185	Mandya India	12·40 N	77·00 E
218	Manfalūţ (män-fȧ-loot') Egypt (Nile In.)	27·18 N	30·59 E
164	Manfredonia (män-frȧ-dô'nyä) It.	41·39 N	15·55 E
164	Manfredónia, Golfo di (G.) (gôl-fô-dē) It.	41·34 N	16·05 E
135	Mangabeiras, Chap. das (Plains) (shä-pä'däs-däs-mäŋ-gä-bē'ê-räzh) Braz.	8·05 S	47·32 W
215	Manga (Reg.) Niger	14·00 N	11·50 E
185	Mangalore (mŭŋ-gŭ-lōr') India	12·53 N	74·52 E
137	Mangaratiba (män-gä-rä-tē'bȧ) Braz. (Rio de Janeiro In).	22·56 S	44·03 W
197	Mangatarem (män'gȧ-tä'rĕm) Phil. (In.)	15·48 N	120·18 E
216	Mange Zaire	0·54 N	20·30 E
196	Mangkalihat, Tandjoeng (C.) (mäng'kȧ-lē-hät') Indon.	1·25 N	119·55 E
128	Mangles, Islas de (ê's-läs-dĕ-mäŋ'glās) (măn'g'lz) Cuba	22·05 N	83·50 W
213	Mangoky (R.) (män-gō'kē) Mad.	22·02 S	44·11 E
197	Mangole, Pulau (I.) Indon.	1·35 S	126·22 E
162	Mangualde (män-gwäl'dĕ) Port.	40·38 N	7·44 W
136	Mangueira, L. da (L.) (män-gā'ê-rȧ) Braz.	33·15 S	52·45 W
116	Mangum (măŋ'gŭm) Ok.	34·52 N	99·31 W
171	Mangyshlak, P.-ov. (Pen.) Sov. Un.	44·30 N	50·40 E
190	Mangzhangdian (mäŋ-jäŋ-dĭĕn) China	32·07 N	114·44 E
107	Manhattan Il. (Chicago In.)	41·25 N	87·29 W
117	Manhattan (măn-hăt'ăn) Ks.	39·11 N	96·34 W
113	Manhattan Beach Ca. (Los Angeles In.)	33·53 N	118·24 W
137	Manhuaçu (män-o͞oȧ'so͞o) Braz. (Rio de Janeiro In.)	20·17 S	42·01 W
137	Manhumirim (män-o͞o-mê-rē'ɴ) Braz. (Rio de Janeiro In.)	20·22 S	41·57 W
213	Mania (R.) (män'yä) Mad.	19·52 S	46·02 E
135	Manicoré (mä-nê-kō-rā') Braz.	5·53 S	61·13 W
91	Manicouagane (R.) Can.	50·00 N	68·35 W
91	Manicouagane, Lac (L.) Can.	51·30 N	68·19 W
135	Manicuare (mä-nē-kwä'rĕ) Ven. (In.)	10·35 N	64·10 W
96	Manikuagen, Rivière (R.) Can.	49·30 N	68·30 W
199	Manihiki Is. (mä'nē-hē'kê) Oceania	9·40 S	158·00 W
197	Manila (mȧ-nĭl'ȧ) Phil. (In.)	14·37 N	121·00 E
197	Manila B. Phil. (In.)	14·38 N	120·46 E
188	Manipur (State) India	25·00 N	94·00 E
171	Manisa (mä'nê-sȧ) Tur.	38·40 N	27·30 E
104	Manistee (măn-ĭs-tē') Mi.	44·15 N	86·20 W
104	Manistee (R.) Mi.	44·25 N	85·45 W
109	Manistique (măn-ĭs-tēk') Mi.	45·58 N	86·16 W
109	Manistique (L.) Mi.	46·14 N	85·30 W
109	Manistique (R.) Mi.	46·05 N	86·09 W
90	Manitoba (Prov.) (măn-ĭ-tō'bȧ) Can.	55·12 N	97·29 W
95	Manitoba (L.) Can.	51·00 N	98·45 W
94	Manito L. (măn'ĭ-tō) Can.	52·45 N	109·45 W
109	Manitou (I.) (măn'ĭ-to͞o) Mi.	47·21 N	87·33 W
109	Manitou (L.) Can.	49·21 N	93·01 W
104	Manitou Is. Mi.	45·05 N	86·00 W
104	Manitoulin I. (măn-ĭ-to͞o'lĭn) Can.	45·45 N	81·30 W
116	Manitou Springs Co.	38·51 N	104·58 W
109	Manitowoc (măn-ĭ-tô-wŏk') Wi.	44·05 N	87·42 W
97	Maniwaki Can.	46·23 N	76·00 W
134	Manizales (mä-nê-zä'lȧs) Col. (In.)	5·05 N	75·31 W
212	Manjacaze (man'yä-kä'zĕ) Moz.	24·37 S	33·49 E
184	Mānjra (R.) India	18·18 N	77·00 E
116	Mankato (măn-kā'tō) Ks.	39·45 N	98·12 W
109	Mankato Mn.	44·10 N	93·59 W
215	Mankim Cam.	5·01 N	12·00 E
163	Manlleu (män-lyā'o͞o) Sp.	42·00 N	2·16 E
185	Mannar (mȧ-när') Sri Lanka	9·48 N	80·03 E
184	Mannar, G. of India	8·47 N	78·33 E
149	Mannersdorf am Leithagebirge Aus. (Vienna In.)	47·58 N	16·36 E
158	Mannheim (män'hīm) F.R.G.	49·30 N	8·31 E
109	Manning (măn'ĭng) Ia.	41·53 N	95·04 W
121	Manning SC	33·41 N	80·12 W
104	Mannington (măn'ĭng-tŭn) WV	39·30 N	80·55 W
164	Mannu (R.) (mä'n-no͞o) It.	39·32 N	9·03 E
214	Mano (R.) Lib.	7·00 N	11·25 W
119	Man of War B. Ba.	21·05 N	74·05 W
119	Man of War Chan. Ba.	22·45 N	76·10 W
197	Manokwari (mȧ-nŏk-wä'rê) Indon.	0·56 S	134·10 E
217	Manono Zaire	7·18 S	27·25 E
95	Manor (măn'ēr) Can.	49·36 N	102·05 W
112	Manor Wa. (Portland In.)	45·45 N	122·36 W
185	Manori (Neigh.) India (Bombay In.)	19·13 N	72·43 E
161	Manosque (mȧ-nôsh') Fr.	43·51 N	5·48 E
89	Manotick Can. (Ottawa In.)	45·13 N	75·41 W
163	Manresa (män-rā'sä) Sp.	41·44 N	1·52 E
217	Mansa Zambia	11·12 S	28·53 E
214	Mansabá Guinea-Bissau	12·18 N	15·15 W
91	Mansel (I.) (măn'sĕl) Can.	61·56 N	81·10 W
134	Manseriche, Pongo de (Water Gap) (pŏ'n-gô-dĕ-män-sĕ-rē'chĕ) Peru	4·15 S	77·45 W
148	Mansfield (mănz'fēld) Eng.	53·08 N	1·12 W
119	Mansfield La.	32·02 N	93·43 W
104	Mansfield Oh.	40·45 N	82·30 W
110	Mansfield Wa.	47·48 N	119·39 W
105	Mansfield, Mt. Vt.	44·30 N	72·45 W
148	Mansfield Woodhouse (wo͝od-hous) Eng.	53·08 N	1·12 W
135	Manso (R.) Braz.	13·30 S	51·45 W
134	Manta (män'tä) Ec.	1·03 S	80·16 W
91	Manteno (măn-tē-nō) Il. (Chicago In.)	41·15 N	87·50 W
121	Manteo NC	35·55 N	75·40 W

ng-sing; ŋ-baŋk; ɴ-nasalized n; nŏd; cŏmmit; ōld; ôbey; ôrder; fo͞od; fo͝ot; ou-out; s-soft; sh-dish; th-thin; pūre; ûnite; ûrn; stŭd; circŭs; ü-as "y" in study; '-indeterminate vowel.

310 Mantes-la-Jolie — Marshall PRONOUNCING INDEX

Page	Name Pronunciation Region	Lat. °'	Long. °'
161	Mantes-la-Jolie (mäɴt-ĕ-lä-zhŏ-lē') Fr. (Paris In.)	48·59 N	1·42 E
115	Manti (măn'tī) Ut.	39·15 N	111·40 W
137	Manitqueira, Serra da (Mts.) (sĕr'rä dä män-tê-kā'ê-rȧ) Braz. (Rio de Janeiro In.)	22·40 S	45·12 W
164	Mantova (Mantua) (män'tô-vä) (măn'tû-ȧ). It.	45·09 N	10·47 E
128	Mantua (män-tōō'ä) Cuba	22·20 N	84·15 W
113	Mantua (măn'tû-ȧ) Ut. (Salt Lake City In.)	41·30 N	111·57 W
	Mantua, see Mantova		
98	Manuan (L.) (mä-nōō'ȧn) Can.	50·36 N	70·50 W
98	Manuan (R.) Can.	50·15 N	70·30 W
197	Manui, Pulau (Is.) (mä-nōō'ē) Indon.	3·35 S	123·38 E
197	Manus I. (mä'nōōs) Pap. N. Gui.	22·2 S	146·22 E
119	Manvel (măn'vel) Tx. (In.)	29·28 N	95·22 W
106	Manville (măn'vĭl) NJ (New York In.)	40·33 N	74·36 W
106	Manville RI (Providence In.)	41·57 N	71·27 W
171	Manych (R.) (mä-nĭch') Sov. Un.	47·00 N	41·10 E
147	Manych Dep. Sov. Un.	46·32 N	42·44 E
171	Manych-Gudilo (Lake) Sov. Un.	46·40 N	42·50 E
218	Manzala L. Egypt (Nile In.)	31·14 N	32·04 E
134	Manzanares (män-sä-nä'rĕs) Col. (In.)	5·15 N	75·09 W
163	Manzanares (R.) (mänz-nä'rĕs) Sp. (Madrid In.)	40·36 N	3·48 W
163	Manzanares, Canal de (kä-nä'l-dĕ-män-thä-nä'rĕs) Sp. (Madrid In.)	40·20 N	3·38 W
128	Manzanillo (män'zä-nēl'yō) Cuba	20·20 N	77·05 W
124	Manzanillo Mex.	19·02 N	104·21 W
129	Manzanillo, Bahía de (B.) Hai.	19·55 N	71·50 W
124	Manzanillo, Bahía de (B.) (bä-ē'ä-dĕ-män-zä-nē'l-yō) Mex.	19·00 N	104·38 W
127	Manzanillo, Punta (Pt.) Pan.	9·40 N	79·33 W
192	Manzhouli (män-jō-lē) China	49·25 N	117·15 E
194	Manzovka (mán-zhô'f-kȧ) Sov. Un.	44·16 N	132·13 E
215	Mao (mä'ô) Chad	14·07 N	15·19 E
129	Mao Dom. Rep.	19·35 N	71·10 W
197	Maoke, Pegunungan (Mtn.) Indon.	4·00 S	138·00 E
193	Maoming China	21·55 N	110·40 E
192	Maoniu Shan (Mtn.) (mou-nĭô shän) China	32·45 N	104·09 E
125	Mapastepec (ma-päs-tâ-pĕk') Mex.	15·24 N	92·52 W
197	Mapia, Kepulauan (I.) (mä'pē-ȧ) Indon.	0·57 N	134·22 E
118	Mapimi (mä-pê-mē') Mex.	25·50 N	103·50 W
118	Mapimi, Bolsón de (Des.) (bôl-sŏ'n-dĕ-mä-pē'mē) Mex.	27·27 N	103·20 W
94	Maple Creek (mā'p'l) (crēk) Can.	49·55 N	109·27 W
89	Maple Grove (grōv) Can. (Montreal In.)	45·19 N	73·51 W
107	Maple Heights Oh. (Cleveland In.)	41·25 N	81·34 W
106	Maple Shade (shād) NJ (Philadelphia In.)	39·57 N	75·01 W
112	Maple Valley (văl'ē) Wa. (Seattle In.)	47·24 N	122·02 W
113	Maplewood (wŏŏd) Mn. (Minneapolis, St. Paul In.)	45·00 N	93·03 W
113	Maplewood Mo. (St. Louis In.)	38·37 N	90·20 W
213	Mapumulo (mä-pä-mōō'lō) S. Afr. (Natal In.)	29·12 S	31·05 E
212	Maputo (Lourenço Marques) Moz.	26·50 S	32·30 E
197	Maqueda Chan. (mä-kā'dä) Phil. (In.)	13·40 N	123·52 E
212	Maquela do Zombo (mȧ-kā'lȧ dōō zôm'bōō) Ang.	6·08 S	15·15 E
109	Maquoketa (mȧ-kō-kê-tȧ) Ia.	42·04 N	90·42 W
109	Maquoketa (R.) Ia.	42·08 N	90·40 W
136	Mar, Serra do (Mts.) (sĕr'rȧ dōō mär') Braz.	26·30 S	49·15 W
134	Maracaibo (mä-rä-kī'bō) Ven.	10·38 N	71·45 W
134	Maracaibo, Lago de (L.) (lä'gô-dĕ-mä-rä-kī'bō) Ven.	9·55 N	72·13 W
135	Maracay (mä-rä-käy') Ven. (In.)	10·15 N	67·35 W
211	Marādah Libya	29·10 N	19·07 E
215	Maradi (mȧ-rȧ-dē') Niger	13·29 N	7·06 E
171	Marāgheh Iran	37·20 N	46·10 E
213	Maraisburg S. Afr. (Johannesburg & Pretoria In.)	26·12 S	27·57 E
117	Marais des Cygnes (R.) Ks.	38·30 N	95·30 W
135	Marajó, Ilha de (I.) (mä-rä-zhō') Braz.	0·30 S	50·00 W
217	Maralal Ken.	1·06 N	36·42 E
215	Marali Cen. Afr. Rep.	6·01 N	18·24 E
217	Marandelles (mä-rȧn-dāl'ȧs) Zimb.	18·10 S	31·36 E
135	Maranguape (mä-räŋ-gwä'pĕ) Braz.	3·48 S	38·38 W
	Maranhão, see São Luis		
135	Maranhão (State) (mä-rän-youɴ) Braz.	5·15 S	45·52 W
203	Maranoa (R.) (mä-rä-nō'ä) Austl.	27·01 S	148·03 E
163	Marano di Napoli (mä-rä'nô-dē-nä'pô-lē) It. (Naples In.)	40·39 N	14·12 E
134	Marañón, Rio (R.) (rê'ō-mä-rä-nyōn') Peru	4·26 S	75·08 W
135	Marapanim (mä-rä-pä-nē'ɴ) Braz.	0·45 S	47·42 W
171	Maras (mä-räsh') Tur.	37·40 N	36·50 W
96	Marathon Can.	48·50 N	86·10 W
121	Marathon (măr'ȧ-thŏn) Fl. (In.)	24·41 N	81·06 W
107	Marathon Oh. (Cincinnati In.)	39·09 N	83·59 W
124	Maravatio (mä-rȧ-vä'tê-ō) Mex.	19·54 N	100·25 W
211	Marawi Sud.	18·07 N	31·57 E
204	Marble Bar (märb''l bär) Austl.	21·15 S	119·15 E
115	Marble Can. (mär'b'l) Az.	36·21 N	111·48 W
218	Marble Hall (hâll) S. Afr. (Johannesburg & Pretoria In.)	24·59 S	29·19 E
99	Marblehead (mär'b'l-hĕd) Ma. (In.)	42·30 N	70·51 W
158	Marburg (mär'bŏŏrgh) F.R.G.	50·49 N	8·46 E
216	Marca, Ponta da (Pt.) Ang.	16·31 S	11·42 E
126	Marcala (mär-kä-lä) Hond.	14·08 N	88·01 W
166	Marche (Reg.) (mär'kā) It.	43·35 N	12·33 E
149	Marchegg Aus. (Vienna In.)	48·18 N	16·55 E
144	Marchena (mär-chā'nä) Sp.	37·20 N	5·25 W
134	Marchena (I.) (ê's-lä-mär-chĕ'nä) Ec.	0·29 N	90·31 W
149	Marchfeld (Reg.) Aus. (Vienna In.)	48·14 N	16·37 E
117	Marceline (mär-sê-lēn') Mo.	39·42 N	92·56 W
137	Marcos Paz (mär-kōs' päz) Arg. (Buenos Aires In.)	34·49 S	58·51 W
198	Marcus (I.) (mär'kŭs) Asia	24·00 N	155·00 E
106	Marcus Hook (mär'kŭs hŏŏk) Pa. (Phildelphia In.)	39·49 N	75·25 W
105	Marcy, Mt. (mär'sē) NY	44·10 N	73·55 W
137	Mar de Espanha (mär-dĕ-ĕs-pȧ'nyȧ) Braz. (Rio de Janeiro In.)	21·53 S	43·00 W
136	Mar del Plata (mär dĕl plä'ta) Arg.	37·59 S	57·35 W
171	Mardin (mär-dēn') Tur.	37·25 N	40·40 E
205	Mare (I.) (mȧ-rā') N. Cal.	21·53 S	168·30 E
154	Maree (L.) (mä-rē') Scot.	57·40 N	5·44 W
109	Marengo (mȧ-rĕŋ'gō) Ia.	41·47 N	92·04 W
160	Marennes (mȧ-rĕn') Fr.	45·49 N	1·08 W
161	Mareuil-sur-Ourcq (mä-rû'yĕ-sür-ōōrk') Fr. (Paris In.)	49·08 N	2·04 E
118	Marfa (mär'fȧ) Tx.	30·19 N	104·01 W
167	Marganets Sov. Un.	47·41 N	34·33 E
122	Margarita (mär-gōō-rē'tä) Pan. (In.)	9·20 N	79·55 W
135	Margarita, Isla de (I.) (mär-gȧ-rē'tȧ) Ven. (In.)	11·00 N	64·15 W
154	Margate (mär'gāt) Eng.	51·21 N	1·17 E
213	Margate (mär-gāt') S. Afr. (Natal In.)	30·52 S	30·21 E
217	Margherita Pk. Afr.	0·22 N	29·51 E
98	Marguerite (R.) Can.	50·39 N	66·42 W
170	Mari (A. S. S. R.) (mä'rê) Sov. Un.	56·20 N	48·00 E
98	Maria (mȧ-rē'ȧ) Can.	48·10 N	66·04 W
162	Maria, Sierra de (Mts.) (sē-ĕ'r-rä-dĕ-mä-ryä) Sp.	37·42 N	2·25 W
124	María Cleofas (I.) (mä-rē'ä klā'ô-fäs) Mex.	21·17 N	106·14 W
156	Mariager (mä-rê-ägh'ĕr) Den.	56·38 N	10·00 E
156	Mariager Fd. Den.	56·44 N	10·32 E
124	María Magdalena (I.) (mä rē'ä mäg-dä-lā'nä) Mex.	21·25 N	106·23 W
137	Mariana (mä-ryȧ'nä) Braz. (Rio de Janeiro In.)	20·23 S	43·24 W
198	Mariana Is. (mä-rê-ä'nȧ) Oceania	17·20 N	145·00 E
198	Mariana Trench Oceania	12·00 N	144·00 E
129	Marianao (mä-rê-ä-nä'ō) Cuba (In.)	23·05 N	82·26 W
117	Marianna (mā-rĭ-ăn'ȧ) Ar.	34·45 N	90·45 W
120	Marianna Fl.	30·46 N	85·14 W
107	Marianna Pa. (Pittsburgh In.)	40·01 N	80·05 W
136	Mariano Acosta (mä-rêä'nô-á-kŏs'tä) Arg. (Buenos Aires In.)	34·28 S	58·48 W
148	Mariánské Lázně (mär'yȧn-skĕ'läz'nyĕ) Czech.	49·58 N	12·42 E
122	Marias, Islas (Is.) (mä-rē'äs) Mex.	21·30 N	106·40 W
111	Marias R. (mȧ-rī'ȧz) Mt.	48·15 N	110·50 W
127	Mariato, Punta (Pt.) Pan.	7·17 N	81·09 W
156	Maribo (mä'rê-bô) Den.	54·46 N	11·29 E
164	Maribor (mä're-bôr) Yugo.	46·33 N	15·37 E
137	Maricá (mä-rē-kä') Braz. (Rio de Janeiro In.)	22·55 S	42·49 W
197	Maricaban (I.) (mä-rê-kä-bän') Phil. (In.)	13·40 N	120·44 E
218	Marico R. (mä'rĭ-cô) S. Afr. (Johannesburg & Pretoria In.)	24·53 S	26·22 E
220	Marie Byrd Land (mȧ rē' bûrd') Ant.	78·00 S	130·00 W
156	Mariefred (mä-rē'ĕ-frĭd) Swe.	59·17 N	17·09 E
127	Marie Galante I. (mȧ-rē' gȧ-läɴt') Guad. (In.)	15·58 N	61·05 W
	Mariehamn, see Maarianhamina		
156	Mariestad (mä-rē'ĕ-städ') Swe.	58·43 N	13·45 E
106	Marietta (mā-rĭ-ĕt'ȧ) Ga. (Atlanta In.)	33·57 N	84·33 W
104	Marietta Oh.	39·25 N	81·30 W
117	Marietta Ok.	33·53 N	97·07 W
112	Marietta Wa. (Vancouver In.)	48·48 N	122·35 W
172	Mariinsk (mȧ-re'ĭnsk) Sov. Un.	56·15 N	87·28 E
157	Marijampole (mä-rê-yäm-pô'lĕ) Sov. Un.	54·33 N	23·26 E
218	Marikana (mă'-rĭ-kä-nă) S. Afr. (Johannesburg & Pretoria In.)	25·40 S	27·28 E
135	Marília (mä-rē'lyȧ) Braz.	22·02 S	49·48 W
216	Marimba Ang.	8·28 S	17·08 E
197	Marinduque I. (mä-rên-dōō'kā) Phil. (In.)	13·14 N	121·45 E
113	Marine (mȧ-rēn') Il. (St. Louis In.)	38·48 N	89·47 W
104	Marine City Mi.	42·45 N	82·30 W
113	Marine L. Mn. (Minneapolis, St. Paul In.)	45·13 N	92·55 W
113	Marine on St. Croix (ăɴ sɛɴ krōō-ä) Mn. (Minneapolis, St. Paul In.)	45·11 N	92·47 W
109	Marinette (măr-ĭ-nĕt') Wi.	45·05 N	87·40 W
216	Maringa (R.) (mä-riŋ'gä) Zaire	1·15 N	20·05 E
162	Marinha Grande (mä-rēn'yȧ grän'dĕ) Port.	39·49 N	8·53 W
120	Marion (măr'ĭ-ŭn) Al.	32·36 N	87·19 W
104	Marion Il.	37·40 N	88·55 W
104	Marion In.	40·35 N	85·45 W
109	Marion Ia.	42·01 N	91·39 W
117	Marion Ks.	38·21 N	97·02 W
120	Marion Ky.	37·19 N	88·05 W
121	Marion NC	35·40 N	82·00 W
108	Marion ND	46·37 N	98·20 W
104	Marion Oh.	40·35 N	83·10 W
121	Marion SC	34·08 N	79·23 W
121	Marion Va.	36·48 N	81·33 W
121	Marion (R.) SC	33·25 N	80·35 W
205	Marion Rf. Austl.	18·57 S	151·31 E
137	Mariposa (mä-rê-pô'sä) Chile (Santiago In.)	35·33 S	71·21 W
114	Mariposa Cr. Ca.	37·14 N	120·30 W
134	Mariquita (mä-rē-kē'tä) Col. (In.)	5·13 N	74·52 W
135	Mariscal Estigarribia (mä-rēs-käl'ĕs-tē-gär-rē'byä) Par.	22·03 S	60·28 W
136	Marisco, Ponta do (Pt.) (pô'n-tä-dô-mä-rē's-kō) Braz. (Rio de Janeiro In.)	23·01 S	43·17 W
161	Maritime Alps (Mts.) (mȧ'rĭ-tīm ălps) Fr.-It.	44·20 N	7·02 E
165	Maritsa (R.) (mä'rê-tsȧ) Grc.-Tur.	40·43 N	26·19 E
197	Mariveles Phil. (In.)	14·27 N	120·29 E
183	Marj Uyan Leb. (Palestine In.)	33·21 N	35·36 E
218	Marka Som. (Horn of Afr. In.)	1·45 N	44·47 E
188	Marka Kul' (L.) Sov. Un.	49·15 N	85·48 E
156	Markaryd (mär'kä-rüd) Swe.	56·30 N	13·34 E
117	Marked Tree (märkt trē) Ar.	35·31 N	90·26 W
149	Marken, I. Neth. (Amsterdam In.)	52·26 N	5·08 E
148	Market Bosworth (bŏz'wûrth) Eng.	52·37 N	1·23 W
148	Market Deeping (dēp'ĭng) Eng.	52·40 N	0·19 W
148	Market Drayton (drā'tŭn) Eng.	52·54 N	2·29 W
148	Market Harborough (här'bŭr-ô) Eng.	52·28 N	0·55 W
148	Market Rasen (rā'zĕn) Eng.	53·23 N	0·21 W
89	Markham (märk'ȧm) Can. (Toronto In.)	43·53 N	79·15 W
220	Markham, Mt. Ant.	82·59 S	159·30 E
167	Markovka (mär-kôf'kȧ) Sov. Un.	49·32 N	39·34 E
173	Markovo (mär'kô-vô) Sov. Un.	64·46 N	170·48 E
184	Markrāna India	27·08 N	74·43 E
171	Marks Sov. Un.	51·40 N	46·40 E
119	Marksville (märks'vĭl) La.	31·09 N	92·05 W
149	Markt Indersdorf (märkt ēn'dĕrs-dōrf) F.R.G. (Munich In.)	48·22 N	11·23 E
158	Marktredwitz (märk-rĕd'vēts) F.R.G.	50·02 N	12·05 E
149	Markt Schwaben (märkt shvä'bĕn) F.R.G. (Munich In.)	48·12 N	11·52 E
161	Marl (märl) F.R.G. (Ruhr In.)	51·40 N	7·05 E
106	Marlboro NJ (New York In.)	40·18 N	74·15 W
99	Marlborough Ma. (In.)	42·21 N	71·33 W
104	Marlette (mär-lĕt') Mi.	43·25 N	83·05 W
119	Marlin (mär'lĭn) Tx.	31·18 N	96·52 W
105	Marlinton (mär'lĭn-tŭn) WV	38·15 N	80·10 W
148	Marlow (mär'lō) Eng. (London In.)	51·33 N	0·46 W
116	Marlow Ok.	34·38 N	97·56 W
128	Marls, The (Shoals) (märls) Ba.	26·30 N	77·15 W
160	Marmande (mȧr-mäɴd') Fr.	44·30 N	0·10 E
165	Marmara (I.) (mär'mȧ-rȧ) Tur.	40·38 N	27·35 E
171	Marmara Denizi (Sea) Tur.	40·40 N	28·00 E
108	Marmarth (mär'mȧrth) ND	46·19 N	103·57 W
125	Mar Muerto (L.) (mär-mōōĕ'r-tô) Mex.	16·13 N	94·22 W
149	Marne (mär'nĕ) F.R.G. (Hamburg In.)	53·57 N	9·01 E
160	Marne (R.) (märn) Fr.	49·08 N	3·39 E
134	Maroa (mä-rō'ä) Ven.	2·43 N	67·37 W
213	Maroantsetra (mȧ-rō-äŋ-tsā'trȧ) Mad.	15·18 S	49·48 E
134	Maro Jarapeto (Mtn.) (mä-rô-hä-rä-pĕ'tô) Col. (In.)	6·29 N	76·39 W
213	Maromokotro (Mtn.) Mad.	14·00 S	49·11 E
135	Maroni (R.) (mȧ-rō'nê) Fr. Gu.-Sur.	3·02 N	53·54 W
215	Maroua (mär'wä) Cam.	10·36 N	14·20 E
149	Marple (mär'p'l) Eng.	53·24 N	2·04 W
218	Marquard S. Afr. (Johannesburg & Pretoria In.)	28·41 S	27·26 E
199	Marquesas Is. (mär-kĕ'säs) Fr. Polynesia	8·50 S	141·00 W
121	Marquesas Keys (Is.) (mȧr-kē'zȧs) Fl. (In.)	24·37 N	82·15 W
137	Marquês de Valença (mȧr-kĕ's-dĕ-vä-lĕ'n-sȧ) Braz. (Rio de Janeiro In.)	22·16 S	43·42 W
89	Marquette (mär-kĕt') Can. (Winnipeg In.)	50·04 N	97·43 W
109	Marquette Mi.	46·32 N	87·25 W
119	Marquez (mär-kāz') Tx.	31·14 N	96·15 W
211	Marra, Jabal (Mt.) (jĕb'ĕl mär'ä) Sud.	13·00 N	23·47 E
210	Marrakech (mȧr-rä'kĕsh) Mor.	31·38 N	8·00 W
203	Marree (măr'rē) Austl.	29·38 S	137·55 E
106	Marrero La. (New Orleans In.)	29·55 N	90·06 W
162	Marroqui, Pta. (mä-rō-kē') Sp.	36·03 N	5·36 W
217	Marrupa Moz.	13·08 S	37·30 E
107	Mars (märz) Pa. (Pittsburgh In.)	40·42 N	80·01 W
217	Marsabit Ken.	2·20 N	37·59 E
164	Marsala (mär-sä'lä) It.	37·48 N	12·28 E
148	Marsden (märz'dĕn) Eng.	53·36 N	1·55 W
160	Marseille (mȧr-sâ'y') Fr. (In.)	43·18 N	5·25 E
160	Marseille, Canal de (mȧr-sâ-yaɴ') Fr. (In.)	43·34 N	5·16 E
104	Marseilles (mär-sĕlz') Il.	41·20 N	88·40 W
104	Marshall (mär'shăl) Il.	39·20 N	87·40 W
104	Marshall Mi.	42·20 N	84·55 W
108	Marshall Mn.	44·28 N	95·49 W
117	Marshall Mo.	39·07 N	93·12 W
119	Marshall Tx.	32·33 N	94·22 W
198	Marshall Is. Pac. Is. Trust Ter.	10·00 N	165·00 E

ăt; finăl; rāte; senâte; ärm; àsk; sofȧ; fâre; ch-choose; dh-as th in other; bē; êvent; bĕt; recĕnt; cratẽr; g-go; gh-guttural g; bĭt; ĭ-short neutral; rīde; ĸ-guttural k as ch in German ich;

PRONOUNCING INDEX

Marshalltown — Mechanicsburg 311

Page	Name Pronunciation Region	Lat. °'	Long. °'
109	Marshalltown (mär'shȧl-toun) .. Ia.	42·02 N	92·55 W
120	Marshallville (mär'shȧl-vĭl) ... Ga.	32·29 N	83·55 W
99	Marshfield (märsh'fēld) .. Ma. (In.)	42·06 N	70·43 W
117	Marshfield ... Mo.	37·20 N	92·53 W
109	Marshfield ... Wi.	44·40 N	90·10 W
128	Marsh Harbour ... Ba.	26·30 N	77·00 W
107	Mars Hill (märz' hĭl') In. (Indianapolis In.)	39·43 N	86·15 W
98	Mars Hill ... Me.	46·34 N	67·54 W
156	Marstrand (mär'stränd) ... Swe.	57·54 N	11·33 E
174	Marsyaty (märs'yȧ-tĭ) Sov. Un. (Urals In.)	60·03 N	60·28 E
119	Mart (märt) ... Tx.	31·32 N	96·49 W
196	Martaban, G. of (mär-tŭ-bän') Bur.	16·34 N	96·58 E
196	Martapura ... Indon.	3·19 S	114·45 E
105	Marthas Vineyard (I.) (mär'thȧz vĭn'yȧrd) . Ma.	41·25 N	70·35 W
128	Martí (mär-tē') ... Cuba	23·00 N	80·55 W
158	Martigny-Bourg (mȧr-tē-nyē') Switz.	46·06 N	7·00 E
160	Martigues (mȧr-tēg') ... Fr. (In.)	43·24 N	5·05 E
120	Martin (mär'tĭn) ... Tn.	36·20 N	88·45 W
120	Martin (R.) ... Al.	32·40 N	86·05 W
165	Martina Franca (mär-tē'nä fräŋ'kä) . It.	40·43 N	17·21 E
112	Martinez (mär-tē'nĕz) Ca. (San Francisco In.)	38·01 N	122·08 W
113	Martinez ... Tx. (San Antonio In.)	29·25 N	98·20 W
123	Martinique (mȧr-tē-nēk') ... N. A.	14·50 N	60·40 W
101	Martin Pt. ... Ak.	70·10 N	142·00 W
105	Martinsburg (mär'tĭnz-bûrg) .. WV	39·30 N	78·00 W
104	Martins Ferry (mär'tĭnz) ... Oh.	40·05 N	80·45 W
104	Martinsville (mär'tĭnz-vĭl) ... In.	39·25 N	86·25 W
121	Martinsville ... Va.	36·40 N	79·53 W
162	Martos (mär'tōs) ... Sp.	37·43 N	3·58 W
90	Martre, Lac la (L.) (läk la märtr) . Can.	63·24 N	119·58 W
195	Marugame (mä'rōō-gä'mā) ... Jap.	34·19 N	133·48 E
217	Marungu (Mts.) ... Tan.	7·50 S	29·50 E
156	Mårvatn (L.) (môr-vät'n) ... Nor.	60·10 N	8·28 E
185	Marve (Neigh.) India (Bombay In.)	19·12 N	72·43 E
162	Marvín (mär-vē'n) ... Sp.	42·24 N	8·40 W
141	Mary (mä'rē) ... Sov. Un.	37·45 N	61·47 E
167	Mar'yanskaya (mȧr-yän'skȧ-yȧ) Sov. Un.	45·04 N	38·39 E
203	Maryborough (mā'rĭ-bŭr-ō) . Austl.	25·35 S	152·40 E
203	Maryborough ... Austl.	37·00 S	143·50 E
103	Maryland (State) (mĕr'ĭ-lȧnd) U. S.	39·10 N	76·25 W
110	Mary's R. (mā'rĭz) ... Nv.	41·25 N	115·10 W
99	Marystown (mâr'ĭz-toun) ... Can.	47·11 N	55·10 W
98	Marysville ... Can.	45·59 N	66·35 W
114	Marysville ... Ca.	39·09 N	121·37 W
117	Marysville ... Ks.	39·49 N	96·38 W
104	Marysville ... Oh.	40·15 N	83·25 W
112	Marysville ... Wa. (Seattle In.)	48·03 N	122·11 W
218	Maryūţ (L.) ... Egypt (Nile In.)	31·09 N	30·10 E
113	Maryville (mā'rĭ-vĭl) Il. (St. Louis In.)	38·44 N	89·57 W
117	Maryville ... Mo.	40·21 N	94·51 W
120	Maryville ... Tn.	35·44 N	83·59 W
211	Mārzuq ... Libya	26·00 N	14·09 E
211	Marzūq, Idehan (Dunes) ... Libya	24·30 N	13·00 E
217	Masai Steppe (Plat.) ... Tan.	4·30 S	36·40 E
217	Masaka ... Ug.	0·20 S	31·44 E
215	Masalasef ... Chad	11·43 N	17·08 E
196	Masalembo-Besar (I.) ... Indon.	5·40 S	114·28 E
194	Masan (mä-sän') ... Kor.	35·10 N	128·31 E
217	Masangwe ... Tan.	5·28 S	30·05 E
217	Masasi (mä-sä'sē) ... Tan.	10·43 S	38·48 E
126	Masatepe (mä-sä-tě'pě) ... Nic.	11·57 N	86·10 W
126	Masaya (mä-sä'yä) ... Nic.	11·58 N	86·05 W
197	Masbate (mäs-bä'tä) ... Phil. (In.)	12·21 N	123·38 E
197	Masbate (I.) ... Phil. (In.)	12·19 N	123·03 E
210	Mascara (mäs'kä-rä) (mȧs-kȧ-rȧ') Alg.	35·25 N	0·08 E
220	Mascarene Is. ... Mauritius	20·20 S	56·40 E
120	Mascot (măs'kŏt) ... Tn.	36·04 N	83·45 W
124	Mascota (mäs-kō'tä) ... Mex.	20·33 N	104·45 W
124	Mascota (R.) ... Mex.	20·33 N	104·52 W
89	Mascouche (mȧs-kōōsh') Can. (Montreal In.)	45·45 N	73·36 W
89	Mascouche (R.) Can. (Montreal In.)	45·44 N	73·45 W
113	Mascoutah (măs-kū'tä) Il. (St. Louis In.)	38·29 N	89·48 W
212	Maseru (măz'ēr-ōō) ... Leso.	29·09 S	27·11 E
186	Mashhad ... Iran	36·17 N	59·30 E
211	Mashra'ar-Ragg ... Sud.	8·28 N	29·15 E
216	Masi-Manimba ... Zaire	4·46 S	17·55 E
211	Masindi (mä-sēn'dē) ... Ug.	1·44 N	31·43 E
186	Masjed Soleymān ... Iran	31·45 N	49·17 E
154	Mask, Lough (B.) (lŏk mȧsk) .. Ire.	53·35 N	9·23 W
174	Maslovo (mäs'lô-vô) Sov. Un. (Urals In.)	60·08 N	60·28 E
104	Mason (mā'sŭn) ... Mi.	42·35 N	84·25 W
107	Mason ... Oh. (Cincinnati In.)	39·22 N	84·18 W
118	Mason ... Tx.	30·46 N	99·14 W
109	Mason City ... Ia.	43·08 N	93·14 W
99	Masquaro (L.) ... Can.	50·34 N	60·40 W
164	Massa (mäs'sä) ... It.	44·02 N	10·08 E
103	Massachusetts (State) (măs-ȧ-chōō'sĕts) . U. S.	42·20 N	72·30 W
98	Massachusetts B. ... Ma.	42·26 N	70·20 W
164	Massafra (mäs-sä'frä) ... It.	40·35 N	17·05 E
164	Massa Marittima ... It.	43·03 N	10·55 E
106	Massapequa .. NY (New York In.)	40·41 N	73·28 W
	Massaua, see Mesewa		
105	Massena (mă-sē'nȧ) ... NY	44·55 N	74·55 W
90	Masset (măs'ĕt) ... Can.	54·02 N	132·09 W
92	Masset Inlet ... Can.	53·42 N	132·20 W
160	Massif Central (Plat.) (mȧ-sēf' säN-trȧl') . Fr.	45·12 N	3·02 E
104	Massillon (măs'ĭ-lŏn) ... Oh.	40·50 N	81·35 W
212	Massinga (mä-sĭn'gä) ... Moz.	23·18 S	35·18 E
115	Massive, Mt. (mȧs'ĭv) ... Co.	39·05 N	106·30 W
89	Masson (măs-sŭn) Can. (Ottawa In.)	45·33 N	75·25 W
195	Masuda (mä-sōō'dȧ) ... Jap.	34·42 N	131·53 E
159	Masuria (Reg.) ... Pol.	53·40 N	21·10 E
216	Matadi (mȧ-tä'dē) ... Zaire	5·49 S	13·27 E
126	Matagalpa (mä-tä-gäl'pä) ... Nic.	12·52 N	85·57 W
91	Matagami (L.) (mȧ-tä-gä'mē) Can.	50·10 N	78·28 W
119	Matagorda B. (măt-ȧ-gôr'dȧ) .. Tx.	28·32 N	96·13 W
119	Matagorda I. ... Tx.	28·13 N	96·27 W
214	Matam (mä-täm') ... Senegal	15·40 N	13·15 W
118	Matamoros (mä-tä-mō'rōs) .. Mex.	25·32 N	103·13 W
119	Matamoros ... Mex.	25·52 N	97·30 W
217	Matandu (R.) ... Tan.	8·55 S	38·35 E
98	Matane (mȧ-tȧn') ... Can.	48·51 N	67·32 W
128	Matanzas (mä-tän'zäs) ... Cuba	23·05 N	81·35 W
128	Matanzas (Prov.) ... Cuba	22·45 N	81·20 W
128	Matanzas, Bahía (B.) (bä-ē'ä) Cuba	23·10 N	81·30 W
127	Matapalo, Cabo (C.) (kȧ'bô-mä-tä-pä'lō) . C. R.	8·22 N	83·25 W
98	Matapédia (mă-tȧ-pā'dē-ȧ) ... Can.	47·58 N	66·56 W
98	Matapédia, (L.) ... Can.	48·33 N	67·32 W
98	Matapédia (R.) ... Can.	48·10 N	67·10 W
137	Mataquito (R.) (mä-tä-kē'tô) Chile (Santiago In.)	35·08 S	71·35 W
185	Matara (mä-tä'rä) ... Sri Lanka	5·59 N	80·35 E
196	Mataram ... Indon.	8·45 S	116·15 E
163	Mataró (mä-tä-rō') ... Sp.	41·33 N	2·27 E
213	Matatiele (mä-tä-tyā'lā) S. Afr. (Natal In.)	30·21 S	28·49 E
106	Matawan ... NJ (New York In.)	40·24 N	74·13 W
98	Matawin (R.) (măt ȧ-wĭn) ... Can.	46·46 N	73·25 W
124	Matehuala (mä-tȧ-wä'lä) ... Mex.	23·38 N	100·39 W
164	Matera (mä-tâ'rä) ... It.	40·42 N	16·37 E
151	Mateur (mȧ-tûr') ... Tun.	37·09 N	9·43 E
185	Mātherān ... India (In.)	18·58 N	73·16 E
97	Matheson ... Can.	48·35 N	80·33 W
113	Mathews, L. (măth'ūz) Ca. (Los Angeles In.)	33·50	117·24 W
184	Mathura (mu-tōō'rŭ) ... India	27·39 N	77·39 E
137	Matias Barbosa (mä-tē'äs-bȧr-bô-sä) Braz. (Rio de Janeiro In.)	21·53 S	43·19 W
125	Matillas, Laguna (L.) (lä-gōō'nä-mä-tē'l-yäs) . Mex.	18·02 N	92·36 W
127	Matina (mä-tē'nä) ... C. R.	10·06 N	83·20 W
157	Matiši (mä'tē-sē) ... Sov. Un.	57·43 N	25·09 E
124	Matlalcueyetl, Cerra (sě'r-rä-mä-tläl-kwě'yětl) . Mex.	19·13 N	98·02 W
148	Matlock (măt'lŏk) ... Eng.	53·08 N	1·33 W
148	Matlock Bath (măt'lŏk bäth) . Eng.	53·06 N	1·34 W
172	Matochkin Shar (mä'tŏch-kĭn) Sov. Un.	73·57 N	56·16 E
135	Mato Grosso (mät'ōō grōs'ōō) Braz.	15·04 S	59·58 W
135	Mato Grosso (State) ... Braz.	14·38 S	55·36 W
135	Mato Grosso, Chapada de (Plain) (shä-pä'dä-dě) . Braz.	13·39 S	55·42 W
162	Matozinhos (Leixoes) (mȧ-tô-zēn'yōzh) (lě'y-shô'-ĕs) Port.	41·10 N	8·48 W
186	Matrah (mȧ-trä') ... Om.	23·36 N	58·27 E
211	Matrūh ... Egypt	31·19 N	27·14 E
195	Matsubara ... Jap. (Ōsaka In.)	34·34 N	135·34 E
195	Matsudo (mät'sōō-dō) Jap. (Tōkyō In.)	35·48 N	139·55 E
195	Matsue (mät'sōō-ĕ) ... Jap.	35·29 N	133·04 E
195	Matsumoto (mät'sōō-mō'tō) .. Jap.	36·15 N	137·59 E
195	Matsuyama (mät'sōō-yä'mä) .. Jap.	33·48 N	132·45 E
195	Matsuzaka (mät'sōō-zä'kä) ... Jap.	34·35 N	136·34 E
121	Mattamuskeet (R.) (măt-tȧ-mŭs'kĕt) . NC	35·34 N	76·03 W
105	Mattaponi (R.) (măt'ȧ-ponī') .. Va.	37·45 N	77·00 W
97	Mattawa (măt'ȧ-wȧ) ... Can.	46·15 N	78·49 W
158	Matterhorn Mt. (mät'ēr-hôrn) Switz.	45·57 N	7·36 E
107	Matteson (măt't'ē-sŭn) Il. (Chicago In.)	41·30 N	87·42 W
129	Matthew Town (măth'ū toun) . Ba.	21·00 N	73·40 W
104	Mattoon (mă-tōōn') ... Il.	39·30 N	88·20 W
134	Maturín (mä-tōō-rēn') ... Ven.	9·48 N	63·16 W
217	Maúa ... Moz.	13·51 S	37·10 E
197	Mauban (mä'ōō-bän') .. Phil. (In.)	14·11 N	121·44 E
160	Maubeuge (mô-bûzh') ... Fr.	50·18 N	3·57 E
107	Maud (môd) .. Oh. (Cincinnati In.)	39·21 N	84·23 W
149	Mauer (mou'ēr) . Aus. (Vienna In.)	48·09 N	16·16 E
135	Maués (mȧ-wě's) ... Braz.	3·34 S	57·30 W
217	Mau Escarpment (Cliff) ... Ken.	0·45 S	35·50 E
100	Maui (I.) (mä'ōō-ē) ... Hi.	20·52 N	156·02 W
137	Maule (R.) (mà'ōō-lě) Chile (Santiago In.)	35·45 S	70·50 W
104	Maumee (mô-mē') ... Oh.	41·30 N	83·40 W
104	Maumee (R.) ... In.-Oh.	41·10 N	84·50 W
104	Maumee B. ... Oh.	41·50 N	83·20 W
212	Maun (mä-ōōn') ... Bots.	19·52 S	23·40 E
100	Mauna Kea (Vol.) (mä'ōō-nä-kā'ä) Hi.	19·52 N	155·30 W
100	Mauna Loa (Vol.) (mä'ōō-nä-lō'ä) Hi.	19·28 N	155·38 W
196	Maung Nakhon Sawan ... Thai.	16·00 N	99·52 E
119	Maurepas L. (mō-rē-pä') ... La.	30·18 N	90·40 W
98	Mauricie, Parc Natl. de la (Natl. Pk.) . Can.	46·46 N	73·00 W
209	Mauritania (mô-rē-tā'nĭ-ȧ) ... Afr.	19·38 N	13·30 W
220	Mauritius (mô-rĭsh'ĭ-ŭs) ... Afr.	20·18 S	57·36 E
112	Maury (mô'rĭ) ... Wa. (Seattle In.)	47·22 N	122·23 W
109	Mauston (môs'tŭn) ... Wi.	43·46 N	90·05 W
115	Maverick ,(R.) (mā-vûr'ĭk) ... Az.	33·40 N	109·30 W
216	Mavinga ... Ang.	15·50 S	20·21 E
125	Maxcanú (mäs-kä-nōō') ... Mex.	20·35 N	89·59 W
89	Maxville (măks'vĭl) Can. (Ottawa In.)	45·17 N	74·52 W
113	Maxville ... Mo. (St. Louis In.)	38·26 N	90·24 W
173	Maya (R.) (mä'yä) ... Sov. Un.	58·00 N	135·45 E
129	Mayaguana (I.) ... Ba.	22·25 N	73·00 W
129	Mayaguana Passage (Str.) ... Ba.	22·20 N	73·25 W
123	Mayagüez (mä-yä-gwāz') P. R. (Puerto Rico In.)	18·12 N	67·10 W
119	Mayarí (mä-yä-rē') ... Cuba	20·45 N	75·40 W
119	Mayari (R.) ... Cuba	20·25 N	75·35 W
126	Mayas, Montañas (Mts.) (mōntäŋ'äs mā'äs) . Belize (In.)	16·43 N	89·00 W
218	Mayd (I.) . Som. (Horn of Afr. In.)	11·24 N	46·38 E
158	Mayen (mī'ĕn) ... F.R.G.	50·19 N	7·14 E
160	Mayenne (mä-yěn') ... Fr.	48·19 N	0·35 W
160	Mayenne (R.) ... Fr.	48·14 N	0·45 W
120	Mayfield (mā'fēld) ... Ky.	36·44 N	88·19 W
121	Mayfield Cr. ... Ky.	36·54 N	88·47 W
107	Mayfield Heights Oh. (Cleveland In.)	41·31 N	81·26 W
110	Mayfield Res. ... Wa.	46·31 N	122·34 W
171	Maykop (Maikop) (mī-kôp') Sov. Un.	44·35 N	40·10 E
174	Maykor (mī-kôr') Sov. Un. (Urals In.)	59·01 N	55·52 E
188	Maymyo (mī'myō) ... Bur.	22·14 N	96·32 E
99	Maynard (mā'nȧrd) ... Ma. (In.)	42·25 N	71·27 W
112	Mayne (mān) Can. (Vancouver In.)	48·51 N	123·18 W
112	Mayne (I.) .. Can. (Vancouver In.)	48·52 N	123·14 W
90	Mayo (mā-yō') ... Can.	63·40 N	135·51 W
120	Mayo ... Fl.	30·02 N	83·08 W
106	Mayo ... Md. (Baltimore In.)	38·54 N	76·31 W
154	Mayo, Mts. of ... Ire.	54·01 N	9·01 W
121	Mayodan (mā-yō'dȧn) ... NC	36·25 N	79·59 W
197	Mayon (Vol.) (mä-yōn') . Phil. (In.)	13·21 N	123·43 E
213	Mayotte (I.) (mȧ-yôt') ... France	13·07 S	45·32 E
128	May Pen ... Jam.	18·00 N	77·25 W
193	Mayraira Pt. ... Phil.	18·40 N	120·45 E
118	Mayran, Laguna de (L.) (lä-ōō'nä-dě-mī-rän') . Mex.	25·40 N	102·35 W
104	Maysville (māz'vĭl) ... Ky.	38·35 N	83·45 W
216	Mayumba ... Gabon	3·25 S	10·39 E
105	Mayville (mā'vĭl) ... NY	42·15 N	79·30 W
108	Mayville ... ND	47·30 N	97·20 W
109	Mayville ... Wi.	43·30 N	88·45 W
113	Maywood (mā'wŏŏd) Ca. (Los Angeles In.)	33·59 N	118·11 W
107	Maywood ... Il. (Chicago In.)	41·53 N	87·51 W
217	Mazabuka (mä-zä-bōō'kä) . Zambia	15·51 S	27·46 E
135	Mazagão (mä-zä-gou'N) ... Braz.	0·05 S	51·27 W
118	Mazapil (mä-zä-pēl') ... Mex.	24·40 N	101·30 W
184	Mazār-i-Sharīf (mȧ-zär'-ē-shȧ-rēf') . Afg.	36·48 N	67·12 E
162	Mazarrón (mä-zär-rô'n) ... Sp.	36·37 N	1·29 W
135	Mazaruni (R.) (mä-zä-rōō'nē) Guy.	5·58 N	59·37 W
126	Mazatenango (mä-zä-tȧ-näŋ'gō) Guat.	14·30 N	91·30 W
125	Mazatla ... Mex. (In.)	19·30 N	99·24 W
125	Mazatlán (San Juan) (mä-zä-tlän') (sän hwän') . Mex.	17·05 N	95·26 W
124	Mazatlán ... Mex.	23·14 N	106·27 W
157	Mažeikiai (mȧ-zhā'kē-ī) .. Sov. Un.	56·19 N	22·24 E
183	Mazḩafah, Jabal (Mts.) Sau. Ar. (Palestine In.)	28·56 N	35·05 E
217	Mazoe (R.) ... Moz.	16·40 S	32·50 E
164	Mazzara del Vallo (mät-sä'rä dĕl väl'lō) . It.	37·40 N	12·37 E
164	Mazzarino (mät-sä-rē'nō) ... It.	37·16 N	14·15 E
212	Mbabane (m'bä-bä'nĕ) ... Swaz.	26·18 S	31·14 E
215	Mbaiki (m'bȧ-ē'kē) . Cen. Afr. Rep.	3·53 N	18·00 E
215	Mbakana, Montagne de (Mts.) Cam.	7·55 N	14·40 E
215	Mbakaou, Barrage de ... Cam.	6·10 N	12·55 E
217	Mbala (Abercorn) ... Zambia	8·50 S	31·22 E
217	Mbale ... Ug.	1·05 N	34·10 E
217	Mbamba Bay ... Tan.	11·17 S	34·46 E
216	Mbandaka (Coquilhatville) .. Zaire	0·04 N	18·16 E
216	Mbanza-Ngungu ... Zaire	5·20 S	10·55 E
217	Mbarara ... Ug.	0·37 S	30·39 E
215	Mbasay ... Chad	7·39 N	15·40 E
217	Mbeya ... Tan.	8·54 S	33·27 E
212	Mbigou (m-bē-gōō') ... Gabon	2·07 S	11·30 E
216	Mbinda ... Con.	2·00 S	12·55 E
217	Mbogo ... Tan.	7·26 S	33·26 E
216	Mbomou (Bomu) (R.) (m'bō'mōō) Cen. Afr. Rep.-Zaire	4·50 N	23·35 E
216	Mbuji-Mayi (Bakwanga) ... Zaire	6·09 S	23·28 E
210	Mbout (m'bōō') ... Mauritania	16·03 N	12·31 W
217	Mchinji ... Malawi	13·42 S	32·50 E
115	Mead, L. ... Az.-Nv.	36·20 N	114·14 W
116	Meade (mēd) ... Ks.	37·17 N	100·21 W
111	Meade Pk. ... Id.	42·19 N	111·16 W
94	Meadow Lake (mĕd'ō lāk) ... Can.	54·08 N	108·26 W
89	Meadows (mĕd'ōz) Can. (Winnipeg In.)	50·02 N	97·35 W
105	Meadville (mēd'vĭl) ... Pa.	41·40 N	80·10 W
104	Meaford (mē'fērd) ... Can.	44·35 N	80·40 W
91	Mealy Mts. (mē'lē) ... Can.	53·32 N	57·58 W
203	Meandarra (mē-ăn-dä'rȧ) ... Austl.	27·47 S	149·40 E
161	Meaux (mō) ... Fr. (Paris In.)	48·58 N	2·53 E
125	Mecapalapa (mă-kä-pä-lä'pä) Mex.	20·32 N	97·52 W
99	Mecatina (I.) (mā-kȧ-tē'nȧ) .. Can.	50·50 N	58·33 W
99	Mecatina (R.) (mā-kȧ-tē'nȧ) . Can.	50·50 N	59·45 W
	Mecca, see Makkah		
98	Mechanic Falls (mē-kăn'ĭk) ... Me.	44·05 N	70·23 W
105	Mechanicsburg (mē-kăn'ĭks-bŭrg) . Pa.	40·15 N	77·00 W

312 Mechanicsville — Metchosin PRONOUNCING INDEX

Page	Name Pronunciation Region	Lat. °′	Long. °′
106	Mechanicsville (mê-kăn'ĭks-vĭl) Md. (Baltimore In.)	38·27 N	76·45 W
105	Mechanicville (mê-kăn'ĭk-vĭl) NY	42·55 N	73·45 W
149	Mechelen Bel. (Brussels In.)	51·01 N	4·28 E
152	Méchéria Mor.	33·30 N	0·13 W
158	Mecklenburg (Reg.) (měk'lĕn-bo͝orgh) G.D.R.	53·34 N	12·18 E
196	Medan (mȧ-dän') Indon.	3·35 N	98·35 E
136	Medanosa, Punta (Pt.) (po͞o'n-tä-mĕ-dä-nô'sä) Arg.	47·50 S	65·53 W
148	Medden (R.) (mĕd'ĕn) Eng.	53·14 N	1·05 W
163	Médéa (mā-dā'ä) Alg.	36·18 N	2·40 E
134	Medellín (mȧ-dhĕl-yēn') Col. (In.)	6·15 N	75·34 W
125	Medellín (mĕ-dĕl-yē'n) Mex.	19·03 N	96·08 W
152	Médenine (mā-dĕ-nēn') Tun.	33·22 N	10·33 E
99	Medfield (mĕd'fēld) Ma. (In.)	42·11 N	71·19 W
99	Medford (mĕd'fērd) Ma. (In.)	42·25 N	71·07 W
106	Medford NJ (Philadelphia In.)	39·54 N	74·50 W
116	Medford Ok.	36·47 N	97·44 W
110	Medford Or.	42·19 N	122·52 W
109	Medford Wi.	45·09 N	90·22 W
106	Media (mē'dĭ-ȧ) Pa. (Philadelphia In.)	39·55 N	75·24 W
159	Medias (mĕd-yäsh') Rom.	46·09 N	24·21 E
110	Medical Lake (mĕd'ĭ-kăl) Wa.	47·34 N	117·40 W
116	Medicine Bow Ra. (mĕd'ĭ-sĭn bō) Co.-Wy.	40·55 N	106·02 W
111	Medicine Bow R. Wy.	41·58 N	106·30 W
94	Medicine Hat (mĕd'ĭ-sĭn hăt) Can.	50·03 N	110·40 W
111	Medicine L. (mĕd'ĭ-sĭn) Mt.	48·24 N	104·15 W
116	Medicine Lodge Ks.	37·17 N	98·37 W
116	Medicine Lodge (R.) Ks.	37·20 N	98·57 W
105	Medina (mê-dī'nȧ) NY	43·15 N	78·20 W
107	Medina Oh. (Cleveland In.)	41·08 N	81·52 W
	Medina, see Al Madīnah		
162	Medina del Campo (mȧ-dē'nä dĕl käm'pō) Sp.	41·18 N	4·54 W
162	Medina de Rioseco (mȧ-dē'nä dā rē-ō-sā'kō) Sp.	41·53 N	5·05 W
214	Médina Gonassé Sen.	13·08 N	13·45 W
118	Medina L. Tx.	29·36 N	98·47 W
118	Medina R. Tx.	29·45 N	99·13 W
162	Medina Sidonia (sē-dō'nyä) Sp.	36·28 N	5·58 W
137	Medio (mĕ'dyô) (R.) Arg. (Buenos Aires In.)	33·40 S	60·30 W
152	Mediterranean Sea (mĕd-ĭ-tēr-ā'nē-ăn) Afr.-Asia-Eur.	36·22 N	13·25 E
151	Medjerda, Oued (R.) (wĕd mĕ-jĕr'dȧ) Tun.	36·43 N	9·54 E
172	Mednogorsk Sov. Un.	51·27 N	57·22 E
171	Medvedista (R.) (mĕd-vyĕ'dê tsȧ) Sov. Un.	50·10 N	43·40 E
170	Medvezhegorsk (mĕd-vyĕzh'yĕ-gôrsk') Sov. Un.	63·00 N	34·20 E
173	Medvezh'y (Is.) Sov. Un.	71·00 N	161·25 E
99	Medway (mĕd'wā) Ma. (In.)	42·08 N	71·23 W
166	Medyn' (mĕ-dēn') Sov. Un.	54·58 N	35·53 E
167	Medzhibozh (mĕd-zhê-bōzh') Sov. Un.	49·23 N	27·29 E
204	Meekatharra (mē-kȧ-thăr'ȧ) Austl.	26·30 S	118·38 E
115	Meeker (mēk'ēr) Co.	40·00 N	107·55 W
99	Meelpaeg L. (mēl'pȧ-ĕg) Can.	48·22 N	56·52 W
158	Meerane (mā-rä'nē) G.D.R.	50·51 N	12·27 E
184	Meerut (mē'ro͞ot) India	28·59 N	77·43 E
165	Megalópolis (mĕg-ȧ lŏ'pō-lĭs) Grc.	37·22 N	22·08 E
167	Meganom, M. (C.) (mĭs mĕ-gȧ-nôm') Sov. Un.	44·48 N	35·17 E
165	Mégara (mĕg'ȧ-rȧ) Grc.	37·59 N	23·21 E
121	Megget (mĕg'ĕt) SC	32·44 N	80·15 W
188	Meghalaya (State) India	25·30 N	91·30 E
112	Megler (mĕg'lēr) Wa. (Portland In.)	46·15 N	123·52 W
166	Meglino (L.) (mȧ-glē'nô) Sov. Un.	58·32 N	35·27 E
121	Meherrin (R.) (mê-hĕr'ĭn) Va.	36·40 N	77·49 W
113	Mehlville Mo. (St. Louis In.)	38·30 N	90·19 W
184	Mehsāna India	23·42 N	72·23 E
160	Mehun-sur-Yèvre (mē-ŭɴ-sür-yĕvr') Fr.	47·11 N	2·14 E
193	Meiling Pass (mā'lĭng') China	25·22 N	115·00 E
161	Meinerzhagen (mī'nĕrts-hä-gĕn) F.R.G. (Ruhr In.)	51·06 N	7·39 E
158	Meiningen (mī'nĭng-ĕn) G.D.R.	50·35 N	10·25 E
158	Meiringen Switz.	46·45 N	8·11 E
158	Meissen G.D.R.	51·11 N	13·28 E
193	Mei Xian (mā shyĕn) China	24·20 N	116·10 E
190	Meizhu (mā-jo͞o) China	31·17 N	119·12 E
136	Mejillones (mȧ-kê-lyō'nȧs) Chile	23·07 S	70·31 W
216	Mekambo Gabon	1·01 N	13·56 E
211	Mekele Eth.	13·31 N	39·19 E
210	Meknès (mĕk'nĕs) (mĕk-nĕs') Mor.	33·56 N	5·44 W
188	Mekong (Lancang) (R.) (län-tsäŋ) China	24·45 N	100·31 E
196	Mekong R. Thai.-Laos	17·53 N	103·57 E
215	Mékrou (R.) Afr.	11·35 N	2·25 E
183	Melaka (Malacca) Mala. (Singapore In.)	2·11 N	102·15 E
183	Melaka (State) Mala. (Singapore In.)	2·19 N	102·09 E
202	Melbourne (mĕl'bŭrn) Austl. (Melbourne In.)	37·52 S	145·08 E
121	Melbourne Fl. (In.)	28·05 N	80·37 W
148	Melbourne Eng.	52·49 N	1·26 W
107	Melbourne Ky. (Cincinnati In.)	39·02 N	84·22 W
109	Melcher (mĕl'chēr) Ia.	41·13 N	93·11 W
170	Melekess (mĕl-yĕk ĕs) Sov. Un.	54·20 N	49·30 E
166	Melenki (mĕ-lyĕŋ'kê) Sov. Un.	55·25 N	41·34 E
94	Melfort (mĕl'fôrt) Can.	52·52 N	104·36 W
211	Melik, Wadi el (R.) Sud.	16·48 N	29·30 E
210	Melilla (Sp.) (mȧ-lēl'yä) Afr.	35·24 N	3·30 W
137	Melipilla (mȧ-lê-pē'lyä) Chile (Santiago In.)	33·40 S	71·12 W
95	Melita Can.	49·11 N	101·09 W
167	Melitopol' (mā-lê-tô'pôl-y') Sov. Un.	46·49 N	35·19 E
218	Melkrivier S. Afr. (Johannesburg & Pretoria In.)	24·01 S	28·23 E
109	Mellen (mĕl'ĕn) Wi.	46·20 N	90·40 W
156	Mellerud (mål'ĕ-ro͞odh) Swe.	58·43 N	12·25 E
213	Melmoth S. Afr. (Natal In.)	28·38 S	31·26 E
136	Melo (mā'lō) Ur.	32·18 S	54·07 W
89	Melocheville (mĕ-lôsh-vēl') Can. (Montreal In.)	45·24 N	73·56 W
174	Melozha R. (myĕ'lô-zhȧ) Sov. Un. (Moscow In.)	56·06 N	38·34 E
210	Melrhir Chott (L.) (mĕl'rēr) Alg.	33·52 N	5·22 E
99	Melrose (mĕl'rōz) Ma. (In.)	42·29 N	71·06 W
109	Melrose Mn.	45·39 N	94·49 W
107	Melrose Park Il. (Chicago In.)	41·54 N	87·52 W
212	Melsetter (mĕl-sĕt'ēr) Zimb.	19·44 S	32·51 E
148	Meltham (mĕl'thăm) Eng.	53·35 N	1·51 W
202	Melton (mĕl'tŭn) Austl. (Melbourne In.)	37·41 S	144·35 E
148	Melton Mowbray (mō'brȧ) Eng.	52·45 N	0·52 W
217	Melúli (R.) Moz.	16·10 S	39·30 E
161	Melun (mē-lŭɴ') Fr. (In.)	48·32 N	2·40 E
216	Melunga Ang.	17·16 S	16·24 E
94	Melville (mĕl'vĭl) Can.	50·55 N	102·48 W
113	Melville La.	30·39 N	91·45 W
205	Melville, C. Austl.	14·15 S	145·50 E
204	Melville (I.) Austl.	11·30 S	131·12 E
91	Melville (R.) Can.	53·46 N	59·31 W
90	Melville Hills Can.	69·18 N	124·57 W
91	Melville Pen. Can.	67·44 N	84·09 W
107	Melvindale (mĕl'vĭn-dāl) Mi. (Detroit In.)	42·17 N	83·11 W
159	Mélykút (mā'l'ko͞ot) Hung.	46·14 N	19·21 E
213	Memba (mĕm'bȧ) Moz.	14·12 S	40·35 E
	Memel, see Klaipéda		
218	Memel (mĕ'mĕl) S. Afr. (Johannesburg & Pretoria In.)	27·42 S	29·35 E
158	Memmingen (mĕm'ĭng-ĕn) F.R.G.	47·59 N	10·10 E
135	Memo (R.) (mĕ'mō) Ven. (In.)	9·32 N	66·30 W
117	Memphis (mĕm'fĭs) Mo.	40·27 N	92·11 W
120	Memphis (mĕm'fĭs) Tn.	35·07 N	90·03 W
116	Memphis Tx.	34·42 N	100·33 W
218	Memphis (Ruins) Egypt (Nile In.)	29·50 N	31·12 E
105	Memphremagog (L.) (mĕm'frê-mā'gŏg) Can.	45·05 N	72·10 W
117	Mena (mē'nȧ) Ar.	34·35 N	94·09 W
167	Mena (mē-nȧ') Sov. Un.	51·31 N	32·14 E
202	Menangle Austl. (Sydney In.)	34·08 S	150·48 E
118	Menard (mê-närd') Tx.	30·56 N	99·48 W
109	Menasha (mê-năsh'ȧ) Wi.	44·12 N	88·29 W
160	Mende (mäɴd) Fr.	44·31 N	3·30 E
161	Menden (mĕn'dĕn) F.R.G. (Ruhr In.)	51·26 N	7·47 E
171	Menderes (R.) (mĕn'dĕr-ĕs) Tur.	37·50 N	28·20 E
136	Mendes (mĕn'-dĕs) Braz. (In.)	22·32 S	43·44 W
110	Mendocino, C. (mĕn'dô-sē'nō) Ca.	40·25 N	124·22 W
109	Mendota (mĕn-dō'tȧ) Il.	41·34 N	89·06 W
109	Mendota (L.) Wi.	43·09 N	89·41 W
136	Mendoza (mĕn-dō'sä) Arg.	32·48 S	68·45 W
136	Mendoza (Prov.) Arg.	35·10 S	69·00 W
190	Mengcheng (mŭŋ-chŭŋ) China	33·15 N	116·34 E
190	Meng Shan (Mts.) (mŭŋ shän) China	35·47 N	117·23 E
188	Mengzi China	23·22 N	103·20 E
203	Menindee (mĕ-nĭn-dē) Austl.	32·23 S	142·30 E
112	Menlo Park (mĕn'lō pärk) Ca. (San Francisco In.)	37·27 N	122·11 W
108	Menno (mĕn'ô) SD	43·14 N	97·34 W
109	Menominee (mê-nŏm'ĭ-nē) Mi.	45·08 N	87·40 W
109	Menominee (R.) Mi.-Wi.	45·37 N	87·54 W
107	Menomonee Falls (fôls) Wi. (Milwaukee In.)	43·11 N	88·06 W
109	Menominee Ra. Mi.	46·07 N	88·53 W
107	Menomonee R. Wi. (Milwaukee In.)	43·09 N	88·06 W
109	Menomonie Wi.	44·53 N	91·55 W
216	Menongue Ang.	14·36 S	17·48 E
163	Menorca, Isla de (Minorca) (I.) (ē's-lä-dĕ-mĕ-nō'r-kä) Sp.	40·05 N	3·58 E
163	Mentana (mĕn-tȧ'nä) It. (Rome In.)	42·02 N	12·40 E
196	Mentawai, Kepulauan (Is.) (mĕn-tä-vī') Indon.	1·08 S	98·10 E
161	Menton (mäɴ-tôɴ') Fr.	43·46 N	7·37 E
113	Mentone (mĕn'tōne) Ca. (Los Angeles In.)	34·05 N	117·08 W
213	Mentz (R.) (mĕnts) S. Afr. (Natal In.)	33·13 S	25·15 E
170	Menzelinsk (mĕn'zyĕ-lĕnsk') Sov. Un.	55·40 N	53·15 E
204	Menzies (mĕn'zēz) Austl.	29·45 S	122·15 E
118	Meoqui (mȧ-ō'gē) Mex.	28·17 N	105·28 W
155	Meppel (mĕp'ĕl) Neth.	52·41 N	6·08 E
158	Meppen (mĕp'ĕn) F.R.G.	52·40 N	7·18 E
163	Mequinenza Res. Sp.	41·15 N	0·35 W
164	Merabéllou, Kólpos (G.) Grc. (In.)	35·16 N	25·55 E
117	Meramec (R.) (mĕr'ȧ-mĕk) Mo.	38·06 N	91·06 W
164	Merano (mȧ-rä'nō) It.	46·39 N	11·10 E
99	Merasheen (I.) (mē'rȧ-shēn) Can.	47·30 N	54·15 W
197	Merauke (mȧ-rou'kä) Indon.	8·32 S	140·17 E
106	Meraux (mē-ro') La. (New Orleans In.)	29·56 N	89·56 W
163	Mercato San Severino (mĕr-kä'tō sän sĕ-vĕ-rē'nō) It. (Naples In.)	40·34 N	14·38 E
114	Merced (mĕr-sĕd') Ca.	37·17 N	120·30 W
114	Merced (R.) Ca.	37·25 N	120·31 W
137	Mercedario, Cerro (Mtn.) (mĕr-sȧ-dhä'rê-ō) Chile (Santiago In.)	31·58 S	70·07 W
136	Mercedes (mĕr-sā'dhās) Arg.	29·04 S	58·01 W
137	Mercedes Arg. (Buenos Aires In.)	34·41 S	59·26 W
118	Mercedes Tx.	26·09 N	97·55 W
137	Mercedes Ur. (Buenos Aires In.)	33·17 S	58·04 W
137	Mercedita (mĕr-sĕ-dê'tä) Chile (Santiago In.)	33·51 S	71·10 W
112	Mercer Island (mûr'sēr) Wa. (Seattle In.)	47·35 N	122·15 W
137	Mercês (mĕr-sĕ's) Braz. (Rio de Janeiro In.)	21·13 S	43·20 N
183	Merchong (R.) Mala. (Singapore In.)	3·08 N	103·13 E
149	Merchtem Bel. (Brussels In.)	50·57 N	4·13 E
89	Mercier Can. (Montreal In.)	45·19 N	73·45 W
163	Mercier-Lacombe (mĕr-syā' lȧ-kôɴb) Alg.	35·18 N	0·11 W
91	Mercy, C. Can.	64·48 N	63·22 W
105	Meredith (mĕr'ê-dĭth) NH	43·35 N	71·35 W
167	Merefa (mȧ-rĕf'ȧ) Sov. Un.	49·49 N	36·04 E
126	Merendón, Serranía de (Mts.) (sĕr-rä-nē'ä-dä mȧ-rĕn-dōn') Hond.	15·01 N	89·05 W
148	Mereworth (mĕ-rĕ'wûrth) Eng. (London In.)	51·15 N	0·23 E
196	Mergui (mĕr-gē') Bur.	12·29 N	98·39 E
196	Mergui Arch. Asia	12·04 N	97·02 E
126	Mérida Mex. (Yucatan In.)	20·58 N	89·37 W
134	Mérida Ven.	8·30 N	71·15 W
134	Mérida, Cordillera de (Mts.) (mĕ'rê-dhä) Ven.	8·30 N	70·45 W
105	Meriden (mĕr'ĭ-dĕn) Ct.	41·30 N	72·50 W
120	Meridian (mê-rĭd-ĭ-ăn) Ms.	32·21 N	88·41 W
119	Meridian Tx.	31·56 N	97·37 W
157	Merikarvia (mā'rē-kàr'vê-ȧ) Fin.	61·51 N	21·30 E
149	Mering (mĕ'rĕng) F.R.G. (Munich In.)	48·16 N	11·00 E
120	Meriwether Lewis Natl. Mon. (mĕr'ĭ-wĕth-ēr lo͞o'ĭs) Tn.	35·25 N	87·25 W
118	Merkel (mûr'kĕl) Tx.	32·26 N	100·02 W
157	Merkinė (mĕr'kĭ-nê) Sov. Un.	54·09 N	24·10 E
149	Merksem Bel. (Brussels In.)	51·15 N	4·27 E
159	Merkys R. (màr'kĭs) Sov. Un.	54·23 N	25·00 E
136	Merlo (mĕr-lô) Arg. (In.)	34·25 S	58·44 W
113	Merriam (mĕr-rĭ-yàm) Ks. (Kansas City In.)	39·01 N	94·42 W
113	Merriam Mn. (Minneapolis, St. Paul In.)	44·44 N	93·36 W
106	Merrick (mĕr'ĭk) NY (New York In.)	40·40 N	73·33 W
106	Merrifield (mĕr'ĭ-fēld) Va. (Baltimore In.)	38·50 N	77·12 W
109	Merrill (mĕr'ĭl) Wi.	45·11 N	89·42 W
99	Merrimac (mĕr'ĭ-măk) Ma. (In.)	42·50 N	71·00 W
99	Merrimack NH (In.)	42·51 N	71·25 W
105	Merrimack (R.) (mĕr'ĭ-măk) Ma.-NH	43·10 N	71·30 W
99	Merrimack R. Ma. (In.)	42·49 N	70·44 W
93	Merritt (mĕr'ĭt) Can.	50·07 N	120·47 W
119	Merryville (mĕr'ĭ-vĭl) La.	30·46 N	93·34 W
211	Mersa Fatma Eth.	14·54 N	40·14 E
158	Merseburg (mĕr'zĕ-bo͞orgh) G.D.R.	51·21 N	11·59 E
148	Mersey (R.) (mûr'zê) Eng.	52·52 N	2·04 W
154	Mersey (R.) Eng.	53·15 N	2·51 W
171	Mersin (mĕr-sēn') Tur.	37·00 N	34·40 E
183	Mersing Mala. (Singapore In.)	2·25 N	103·51 E
184	Merta Road (mār'tŭ rōd) India	26·50 N	73·54 E
154	Merthyr Tydfil (mûr'thēr tĭd'vĭl) Wales	51·46 N	3·30 W
162	Mértola Almodóvar (mĕr-tô-lȧ-äl-mô-dô'vär) Port.	37·39 N	8·04 W
161	Méru (mā-rü') Fr. (In.)	49·14 N	2·08 E
211	Meru (mā'ro͞o) Ken.	0·01 N	37·45 E
217	Meru, Mt. Tan.	3·15 S	36·43 E
135	Merume Mts. (mĕr-ü'mĕ) Guy.	5·45 N	60·15 W
149	Merwerde, Kanal (Can.) Neth. (Amsterdam In.)	52·15 N	5·01 E
112	Merwin (L.) (mĕr'wĭn) Wa. (Portland In.)	45·58 N	122·27 W
171	Merzifon (mĕr'ze-fōn) Tur.	40·50 N	35·30 E
161	Merzig (mĕr'tsēg) F.R.G.	49·27 N	6·54 E
115	Mesa (mā'sȧ) Az.	33·25 N	111·50 W
109	Mesabi Ra. (mā-sŏb'bē) Mn.	47·17 N	93·04 W
165	Mesagne (mā-sän'yȧ) It.	40·34 N	17·51 E
115	Mesa Verde Natl. Park. (vĕr'dē) Co.	37·22 N	108·27 W
115	Mescalero Ind. Res. (mĕs-kä-lā'rō) NM	33·10 N	105·45 W
211	Mesewa (Massaua) Eth.	15·40 N	39·19 E
166	Meshchovsk (myĕsh'chĕfsk) Sov. Un.	54·17 N	35·19 E
115	Mesilla (mȧ-sē'yä) NM	32·15 N	106·45 W
215	Meskine Chad	11·25 N	15·21 E
165	Mesolóngion (mĕ-sô-lôŋ'gê-ôn) Grc.	38·23 N	21·28 E
164	Messina (mĕ-sē'nȧ) It.	38·11 N	15·34 E
212	Messina S. Afr.	22·17 S	30·13 E
164	Messina, Stretto di (Str.) (strĕ't-tô dē) It.	38·10 N	15·34 E
165	Messíni Grc.	37·05 N	22·00 E
165	Messiniakós Kólpos (G.) Grc.	36·59 N	22·00 E
165	Mesta (R.) (mĕ-stä') Bul.	41·42 N	23·40 E
164	Mestre (mĕs'trā) It.	45·29 N	12·15 E
134	Meta (Dept.) (mĕ'tä) Col. (In.)	3·28 N	74·07 W
134	Meta (R.) Col.	4·33 N	72·09 W
98	Métabetchouane (R.) (mĕ-tȧ-bĕt-cho͞o-än') Can.	47·45 N	72·00 W
119	Metairie La.	30·00 N	90·11 W
136	Metán (mĕ-tà'n) Arg.	25·32 S	64·51 W
212	Metangula Moz.	12·42 S	34·48 E
126	Metapán (mā-tä-pän') Sal.	14·21 N	89·26 W
89	Metcalfe (mĕt-käf) Can. (Ottawa In.)	45·14 N	75·27 W
112	Metchosin Can. (Seattle In.)	48·22 N	123·33 W

ăt; finăl; rāte; senāte; ärm; àsk; sofȧ; fâre; ch-choose; dh-as th in other; bē; ēvent; bĕt; recĕnt; cratēr; g-go; gh-guttural g; bĭt; ĭ-short neutral; rīde; ĸ-guttural k as ch in German ich;

Page	Name Pronunciation Region	Lat. °′	Long. °′
124	Metepec (mâ-tĕ-pĕk′)........Mex.	18·56 N	98·31 W
125	Metepec.............Mex. (In.)	19·15 N	99·36 W
110	Methow R. (mĕt′hou) (mĕt hou′) Wa.	48·26 N	120·15 W
99	Methuen (mê-thū′ĕn)... Ma. (In.)	42·44 N	71·11 W
165	Metkovic′ (mĕt′kō-vĭch)....Yugo.	43·02 N	17·40 E
101	Metlakatla (mĕt-lȧ-kăt′lȧ).....Ak.	55·08 N	131·35 W
117	Metropolis (mê-trŏp′ô-lĭs)......Il.	37·09 N	88·46 W
121	Metter (mĕt′ẽr)..............Ga.	32·21 N	82·05 W
161	Mettmann (mĕt′män) F.R.G. (Ruhr In.)	51·15 N	6·58 E
106	Metuchen (mĕ-tŭ′chĕn) NJ (New York In.)	40·32 N	74·21 W
161	Metz (mĕtz)..................Fr.	49·08 N	6·10 E
124	Metztitlán (mĕtz-têt-län′)...Mex.	20·36 N	98·45 W
215	Meuban.....................Cam.	2·27 N	12·41 E
160	Meuse (R.) (mûz) (müz)......Eur.	50·32 N	5·22 E
148	Mexborough (mĕks′bŭr-ô)...Eng.	53·30 N	1·17 W
119	Mexia (mȧ-hē′ä)..............Tx.	31·32 N	96·29 W
125	Mexicalcingo (mĕ-kē-käl-sēn′go) Mex. (In.)	19·13 N	99·34 W
114	Mexicali (mâk-sê-kä′lê)......Mex.	32·28 N	115·29 W
115	Mexican Hat (mĕk′sĭ-kăn hăt).Ut.	37·10 N	109·55 W
98	Mexico (mĕk′sĭ-kō)..........Me.	44·34 N	70·33 W
117	Mexico......................Mo.	39·09 N	91·51 W
122	Mexico (State) (mâk′sê-kō)..Mex.	19·50 N	99·50 W
75	Mexico.....................N. A.	23·45 N	104·00 W
122	Mexico, G. of...............N. A.	25·15 N	93·45 W
125	Mexico City (mĕk′sĭ-kō) Mex. (In.)	19·28 N	99·09 W
124	Mexticacán (mĕs′tê-kä-kän′).Mex.	21·12 N	102·43 W
92	Meyers Chuck.................Ak.	55·44 N	132·15 W
105	Meyersdale (mī′ẽrz-dāl)........Pa.	39·55 N	79·00 W
218	Meyerton (mī′ẽr-tŭn)......S. Afr. (Johannesburg & Pretoria In.)	26·35 S	28·01 E
186	Meymaneh...................Afg.	35·53 N	64·38 E
170	Mezen′.................Sov. Un.	65·50 N	44·05 E
170	Mezen′ (R.)...........Sov. Un.	65·20 N	44·45 E
160	Mézenc, Mt. (mĕɴ-mä-zĕɴ′)...Fr.	44·55 N	4·12 E
166	Mezha (R.) (myä′zhȧ)...Sov. Un.	55·53 N	31·44 E
161	Mézières-sur-Seine (mā-zyâr′sür-sân′).Fr. (In.)	48·58 N	1·49 E
159	Mezőkövesd (mĕ′zû-kû′vĕsht) Hung.	47·49 N	20·36 E
159	Mezötúr (mĕ′zû-tōōr).......Hung.	47·00 N	20·36 E
124	Mezquital (mâz-kê-täl′)......Mex.	23·30 N	104·20 W
124	Mezquital (R.)...............Mex.	23·07 N	104·52 W
124	Mezquitic (mâz-kê-tēk′)......Mex.	22·25 N	103·43 W
124	Mezquitic (R.)...............Mex.	22·25 N	103·45 W
217	Mfangano I..................Ken.	0·28 S	33·35 E
174	Mga (m′gȧ) Sov. Un. (Leningrad In.)	59·45 N	31·04 E
213	Mgeni (R.).....S. Afr. (Natal In.)	29·38 S	30·53 E
166	Mglin (m′glēn′).........Sov. Un.	53·03 N	32·52 E
124	Miacatlán (mê′ä-kä-tlän′)...Mex.	18·42 N	99·17 W
125	Miahuatlán (mê′ä-wä-tlän′)..Mex.	16·20 N	96·38 W
162	Miajadas (mê-ä-hä′däs).......Sp.	39·10 N	5·53 W
115	Miami........................Az.	33·20 N	110·55 W
121	Miami..................Fl. (In.)	25·45 N	80·11 W
117	Miami........................Ok.	36·51 N	94·51 W
116	Miami........................Tx.	35·41 N	100·39 W
104	Miami (R.)....................Oh.	39·20 N	84·45 W
121	Miami Beach............Fl. (In.)	25·47 N	80·07 W
128	Miami Drainage Can..........Fl.	26·25 N	80·50 W
104	Miamisburg (mī-ăm′iz-bûrg)..Oh.	39·40 N	84·20 W
107	Miamitown (mī-ăm′ĭ-toun) Oh. (Cincinnati In.)	39·13 N	84·43 W
186	Mīāneh.......................Iran	37·15 N	47·13 E
197	Miangas, Pulau (I.) (myä′n-gäs) Phil.	5·30 N	127·00 E
190	Miaodao Qundao (Is.) (mĭou-dou chyōōn-dou).China	38·06 N	120·35 E
193	Miaoli (mê-ou′lĭ).........Tiawan	24·30 N	120·48 E
190	Miaozhen (mĭou-jŭn).........China	31·44 N	121·28 E
174	Miass (mī-äs′).Sov. Un. (Urals In.)	55·00 N	60·03 E
158	Miastko (myäst′kô)...........Pol.	54·01 N	17·00 E
159	Michalovce (mē′κä-lôf′tsĕ).Czech.	48·44 N	21·56 E
92	Michel Pk....................Can.	53·35 N	126·26 W
101	Michelson, Mt. (mĭch′ĕl-sŭn)..Ak.	69·11 N	144·12 W
149	Michendorf (mē′κĕn-dōrf) F.R.G. (Berlin In.)	52·19 N	13·02 E
129	Miches (mē′chĕs).....Dom. Rep.	19·00 N	69·05 W
103	Michigan (State) (mĭsh′ĭ-găn) U. S.	45·55 N	87·00 W
103	Michigan, L.................U. S.	43·20 N	87·10 W
104	Michigan City.................In.	41·40 N	86·55 W
91	Michikamau (L.).............Can.	54·11 N	63·21 W
109	Michipicoten (I.) (mĕ-shĭ-pĭ-kō′tĕn).Can.	47·49 N	85·50 W
109	Michipicoten (R.)............Can.	47·56 N	84·42 W
109	Michipicoten Harbour........Can.	47·58 N	84·58 W
124	Michoacán (State)...........Mex.	19·15 N	101·30 W
166	Michurinsk (mĭ-chōō-rĭnsk′) Sov. Un.	52·53 N	40·32 E
127	Mico, Punta (Pt.) (pōō′n-tä-mē′kô).Nic.	11·38 N	83·24 W
110	Midas (mī′dȧs)...............Nv.	41·15 N	116·50 W
212	Middleburg (mĭd′ĕl-bûrg)..S. Afr.	31·30 S	25·00 E
218	Middleburg................S. Afr. (Johannesburg & Pretoria In.)	25·47 S	29·30 E
218	Middlewit (mĭd′l′wĭt)......S. Afr. (Johannesburg & Pretoria In.)	24·50 S	27·00 E
92	Middle (R.)..................Can.	55·00 N	125·50 W
196	Middle Andaman I. (ăn-dȧ-măn′) Andaman & Nicobar Is.	12·44 N	93·21 E
119	Middle Bayou..........Tx. (In.)	29·38 N	95·06 W
128	Middle Bight (B.) (bīt)........Ba.	24·20 N	77·35 W
105	Middlebury (mĭd′l-bĕr-ĭ)......Vt.	44·00 N	73·10 W
118	Middle Concho (kŏn′chō)......Tx.	31·21 N	100·50 W
156	Middlefart (mĕd′′l-färt)......Den.	55·30 N	9·45 E
108	Middle Loup (R.) (lōōp)......Ne.	41·49 N	100·20 W
104	Middleport (mĭd′′l-pōrt).......Oh.	39·00 N	82·05 W
106	Middle River.Md. (Baltimore In.)	39·20 N	76·27 W
120	Middlesboro (mĭd′′lz-bŭr-ô)...Ky.	36·36 N	83·42 W
154	Middlesbrough (Teesside) (mĭd′′lz-brŭ).Eng.	54·35 N	1·18 W
106	Middlesex (mĭd′′l-sĕks) NJ (New York In.)	40·34 N	74·30 W
98	Middleton (mĭd′′l-tŭn)......Can.	44·57 N	65·04 W
148	Middleton...................Eng.	53·04 N	2·12 W
101	Middleton (I.)................Ak.	59·35 N	146·35 W
105	Middletown....................Ct.	41·35 N	72·40 W
105	Middletown....................De.	39·30 N	75·40 W
99	Middletown...........Ma. (In.)	42·35 N	71·01 W
106	Middletown..NY (New York In.)	41·26 N	74·25 W
104	Middletown....................Oh.	39·30 N	84·25 W
148	Middlewich (mĭd′′l-wĭch)....Eng.	53·11 N	2·27 W
106	Midfield....Al. (Birmingham In.)	33·28 N	86·54 W
163	Midi, Canal du (kä-näl-dü-mê-dê′) Fr.	43·22 N	1·35 E
213	Mid Illovo (mĭd ĭl′ô-vō) S. Afr. (Natal In.)	29·59 S	30·32 E
105	Midland (mĭd′lănd)..........Can.	44·45 N	79·50 W
104	Midland.......................Mi.	43·40 N	84·20 W
118	Midland.......................Tx.	32·05 N	102·05 W
113	Midvale (mĭd′vāl) Ut. (Salt Lake City In.)	40·37 N	111·54 W
120	Midway (mĭd′wā)..............Al.	32·03 N	85·30 W
198	Midway Is................Pac. O.	28·00 N	179·00 W
111	Midwest (mĭd-wĕst′).........Wy.	43·25 N	106·15 W
171	Midye (mēd′yĕ)...............Tur.	41·35 N	28·10 E
158	Miedzyrzecz (myăn-dzû′zhĕch) Pol.	52·26 N	15·35 E
159	Mielec (myĕ′lĕts).............Pol.	50·17 N	21·27 E
118	Mier (myâr)..................Mex.	26·26 N	99·08 W
162	Mieres (myā′rās)..............Sp.	43·14 N	5·45 W
124	Mier y Noriega (myâr′ê nô-rê-ā′gä).Mex.	22·28 N	100·08 W
167	Migorod................Sov. Un.	49·56 N	33·36 E
124	Miguel Auza (mē-gĕ′l-ä-ōō′zä) Mex.	24·17 N	103·27 W
136	Miguel Pereira (pĕ-rā′rä) Braz. (In.)	22·27 S	43·28 W
163	Mijares (R.) (mē-hä′râs).......Sp.	40·05 N	0·42 W
195	Mikage (mē′kȧ-gȧ) Jap. (Ōsaka In.)	34·42 N	135·15 E
195	Mikawa-Wan (B.) (mē′kä-wä wän).Jap.	34·43 N	137·09 E
166	Mikhaylov (mē-κäy′lôf)..Sov. Un.	54·14 N	39·03 E
167	Mikhaylovka............Sov. Un.	47·16 N	35·12 E
171	Mikhaylovka............Sov. Un.	50·05 N	43·10 E
174	Mikhaylovka (mê-kä′ê-lôf-kȧ) Sov. Un. (Urals In.)	55·35 N	57·57 E
174	Mikhaylovka Sov. Un. (Leningrad In.)	59·20 N	30·21 E
174	Mikhnëvo (mĭk-nyô′vô) Sov. Un. (Moscow In.)	55·08 N	37·57 E
195	Miki (mē′kê).....Jap. (Osaka In.)	34·47 N	134·59 E
217	Mikindani (mē-kên-dä′nê)...Tan.	10·17 S	40·07 E
157	Mikkeli (mĭk′ĕ-lĭ)............Fin.	61·42 N	27·14 E
165	Míkonos (I.)..................Grc.	37·26 N	25·30 E
158	Mikulov (mĭ′kōō-lôf)......Czech.	48·47 N	16·39 E
217	Mikumi.......................Tan.	7·24 S	36·59 E
195	Mikuni (mē′kōō-nê)..........Jap.	36·09 N	136·14 E
195	Mikuni-Sammyaku (Mts.) (säm′myä-kōō).Jap.	36·51 N	138·38 E
195	Mikura (I.) (mē′kōō-rä)......Jap.	33·53 N	139·26 E
109	Milaca (mê-lăk′ȧ).............Mn.	45·45 N	93·41 W
104	Milan (mĭ′lăn).................Mi.	42·05 N	83·40 W
117	Milan.........................Mo.	40·13 N	93·07 W
120	Milan.........................Tn.	35·54 N	88·47 W
	Milan, see Milano		
164	Milano (Milan) (mê-lä′nō).....It.	45·29 N	9·12 E
171	Milâs (mē′läs)................Tur.	37·10 N	27·25 E
164	Milazzo (mê-lät′sō)............It.	38·13 N	15·17 E
108	Milbank (mĭl′băŋk)............SD	45·13 N	96·38 W
203	Mildura (mĭl-dū′rȧ)........Austl.	34·10 S	142·18 E
111	Miles City (mīlz)..............Mt.	46·24 N	105·50 W
105	Milford (mĭl′fẽrd)..............Ct.	41·15 N	73·05 W
105	Milford........................De.	38·55 N	75·25 W
99	Milford..............Ma. (In.)	42·09 N	71·31 W
107	Milford.........Mi. (Detroit In.)	42·35 N	83·36 W
105	Milford........................NH	42·50 N	71·40 W
107	Milford......Oh. (Cincinnati In.)	39·11 N	84·18 W
115	Milford........................Ut.	38·20 N	113·05 W
154	Milford Haven (hăv′n).....Wales	51·40 N	5·10 W
204	Miling (mĭl′′ng)............Austl.	30·30 S	116·25 E
112	Milipitas (mĭl-ĭ-pĭ′tăs) Ca. (San Francisco In.)	37·26 N	121·54 W
93	Milk River (mĭlk)............Can.	49·09 N	112·05 W
111	Milk R...............Can.-U.S.	48·25 N	108·45 W
114	Mill Cr........................Ca.	40·07 N	121·55 W
89	Mill Cr. (mĭl).Can. (Edmonton In.)	53·13 N	113·25 W
160	Millau (mē-yō′)................Fr.	44·06 N	3·04 E
112	Millbrae (mĭl′brā) Ca. (San Francisco In.)	37·36 N	122·23 W
99	Millbury (mĭl′bĕr-ĭ).....Ma. (In.)	42·12 N	71·46 W
120	Milledgeville (mĭl′ĕj-vĭl)......Ga.	33·05 N	83·15 W
89	Mille Îles, R. des (rê-vyâr′ dā mĭl′ĭl′) Can. (Montreal In.)	45·41 N	73·40 W
109	Mille Lac Ind. Res. (mĭl lăk′)..Mn.	46·14 N	94·13 W
109	Mille Lacs (L.)...............Mn.	46·25 N	93·22 W
109	Mille Lacs, Lac des (L.) (läk dĕ mēl läks).Can.	48·52 N	90·53 W
121	Millen (mĭl′ĕn)................Ga.	32·47 N	81·55 W
108	Miller (mĭl′ẽr)................SD	44·31 N	99·00 W
167	Millerovo (mĭl′ĕ-rô-vô)...Sov. Un.	48·58 N	40·27 E
97	Millersburg (mĭl′ẽrz-bûrg)....Ky.	38·15 N	84·10 W
97	Millersburg...................Oh.	40·35 N	81·55 W
105	Millersburg...................Pa.	40·35 N	76·55 W
120	Millers Ferry Lake (Res.).....Al.	32·10 N	87·15 W
98	Millerton (mĭl′ẽr-tŭn).......Can.	46·56 N	65·40 W
99	Millertown (mĭl′ẽr-toun).....Can.	48·49 N	56·32 W
203	Millicent (mĭl-ĭ-sĕnt).......Austl.	37·30 S	140·20 E
98	Millinocket (mĭl-ĭ-nŏk′ĕt).....Me.	45·40 N	68·44 W
99	Millis (mĭl-ĭs)..........Ma. (In.)	42·10 N	71·22 W
113	Millstadt (mĭl′stăt) Il. (St. Louis In.)	38·27 N	90·06 W
106	Millstone (R.) (mĭl′stōn) NJ (New York In.)	40·27 N	74·38 W
204	Millstream (mĭl′strēm).....Austl.	21·45 S	117·10 E
98	Milltown (mĭl′toun).........Can.	45·13 N	67·19 W
107	Milvale (mĭl′vāl) Pa. (Pittsburgh In.)	40·29 N	79·58 W
112	Mill Valley (mĭl) Ca. (San Francisco In.)	37·54 N	122·32 W
105	Milville (mĭl′vĭl)..............NJ	39·25 N	75·00 W
117	Millwood Res..................Ar.	33·00 N	94·00 W
161	Milly-la-Forêt (mē-yē′-la-fō-rĕ′) Fr. (Paris In.)	48·24 N	2·28 E
212	Milnerton (mĭl′nẽr-tŭn) S. Afr. (In.)	33·52 S	18·30 E
108	Milnor (mĭl′nẽr).............ND	46·17 N	97·29 W
98	Milo.........................Me.	44·16 N	69·01 W
	Milo (I.), see Mílos		
165	Mílos (Milo) (I.) (mē′lŏs)....Grc.	36·45 N	24·35 E
125	Mílpa Alta (mē′l-pä-ȧ′l-tä) Mex. (In.)	19·11 N	99·01 W
89	Milton........Can. (Toronto In.)	43·31 N	79·53 W
120	Milton (mĭl′tŭn)...............Fl.	30·37 N	87·02 W
99	Milton................Ma. (In.)	42·16 N	71·03 W
105	Milton........................Pa.	41·00 N	76·50 W
113	Milton...Ut. (Salt Lake City In.)	41·04 N	111·44 W
112	Milton.............Wa. (Seattle In.)	47·15 N	122·20 W
109	Milton........................Wi.	42·45 N	89·00 W
110	Milton-Freewater.............Or.	45·57 N	118·25 W
107	Milwaukee...Wi. (Milwaukee In.)	43·03 N	87·55 W
107	Milwaukee R..Wi. (Milwaukee In.)	43·10 N	87·56 W
112	Milwaukee (mĭl-wô′kê) Or. (Portland In.)	45·27 N	122·38 W
125	Mimiapan (mē-myä-pàn′) Mex. (In.)	19·26 N	99·28 W
137	Mimoso do Sul (mē-mô′sō-dô-sōō′l) Braz. (Rio de Janeiro In.)	21·03 S	41·21 W
193	Min (R.) (mēn)..............China	26·30 N	118·30 E
193	Min (R.)....................China	29·30 N	104·00 E
163	Mina (R.) (mē′nȧ).............Alg.	35·24 N	0·51 E
95	Minago (R.) (mĭ-nä′gō)......Can.	54·25 N	98·45 W
195	Minakuchi (mē′nȧ-kōō′chê)...Jap.	34·59 N	136·06 E
128	Minas (mē′näs)...............Cuba	21·03 N	77·35 W
183	Minas.....Indon. (Singapore In.)	0·52 N	101·29 E
136	Minas (mē′näs)................Ur.	34·18 S	55·12 W
126	Minas, Sierra de las (Mts.) (syĕr′rȧ dā läs mē′näs).Guat.	15·08 N	90·25 W
98	Minas Basin (mĭ′nȧs)........Can.	45·20 N	64·00 W
98	Minas Chan...................Can.	45·15 N	64·45 W
126	Minas de Oro (mê′-näs-dĕ-ō-rō) Hond.	14·52 N	87·19 W
162	Minas de Ríontinto (mē′näs dā rē-ô-tēn′tō).Sp.	37·43 N	6·35 W
135	Minas Gerais (State) (mē′näzh-zhĕ-rȧ′ēs).Braz.	17·45 S	43·50 W
135	Minas Nova (mē′näzh nō′väzh) Braz.	17·20 S	42·19 W
108	Minatare (L.) (mĭn′ȧ-târ).....Ne.	41·56 N	103·07 W
125	Minatitlan (mê-nä-tê-tlän′)..Mex.	17·59 N	94·33 W
124	Minatitlan...................Mex.	19·21 N	104·02 W
195	Minato (mē′nȧ-tô) Jap. (Tōkyō In.)	35·13 N	139·52 E
154	Minch, The (Chan.)..........Scot.	58·04 N	6·04 W
154	Minch, The Little (Chan.) (mĭnch).Scot.	57·35 N	6·45 W
197	Mindanao (I.) (mĭn-dä-nou′).Phil.	7·30 N	125·10 E
197	Mindanao Sea.................Phil.	8·55 N	124·00 E
210	Mindelo............C. V. Is. (In.)	16·53 N	25·00 W
158	Minden (mĭn′dĕn)...........F.R.G.	52·17 N	8·58 E
119	Minden........................La.	32·36 N	93·19 W
116	Minden........................Ne.	40·30 N	98·54 W
197	Mindoro (I.) (mĭn-dô′rō) Phil. (In.)	13·04 N	121·06 E
197	Mindoro Str...........Phil. (In.)	12·28 N	120·33 E
174	Mindyak (mēn′dyȧk) Sov. Un. (Urals In.)	54·01 N	58·48 E
106	Mineola (mĭn-ê-ō′lȧ) NY (New York In.)	40·43 N	73·38 W
119	Mineola.......................Tx.	32·39 N	95·31 W
124	Mineral del Chico (mê-nȧ-räl′dĕl chē′kō).Mex.	20·13 N	98·46 W
124	Mineral del Monte (mê-nȧ-räl dĕl mōn′tȧ).Mex.	20·18 N	98·39 W
171	Mineral′nyye Vody.......Sov. Un.	44·10 N	43·15 E
109	Mineral Point (mĭn′ẽr-ăl).....Wi.	42·50 N	90·10 W
118	Minerál Wells (mĭn′ẽr-ăl wĕlz) Tx.	32·48 N	98·06 W
104	Minerva (mĭ-nur′vȧ)..........Oh.	40·45 N	81·10 W
164	Minervino (mē-nĕr-vē′nō)......It.	41·07 N	16·05 E
195	Mineyama (mē-nĕ-yä′mä)....Jap.	35·38 N	135·05 E
98	Mingan.......................Can.	50·18 N	64·02 W
171	Mingechaur (R.)........Sov. Un.	41·00 N	47·20 E
204	Mingenew (mĭn′gĕ-nû).....Austl.	29·15 S	115·45 E
104	Mingo Junction (mĭŋ′gō)......Oh.	40·15 N	80·40 W
162	Minho (Reg.) (mēn yō̄o)......Port.	41·32 N	8·13 W
128	Minho (R.)..................Jam.	17·55 N	77·20 W
162	Minho, Rio (R.) (rē′ō-mē′n-yô) Port.	41·28 N	9·05 W
89	Ministik L. (mĭ-nĭs′tĭk) Can. (Edmonton In.)	53·23 N	113·05 W
215	Minna (mĭn′ȧ).................Nig.	9·37 N	6·33 E
117	Minneapoli (mĭn-ê-ăp′ô-lĭ)....Ks.	39·07 N	97·41 W
113	Minneapolis (mĭn-ê-ăp′ô-lĭs) Mn. (Minneapolis, St. Paul In.)	44·58 N	93·15 W
95	Minnedosa (mĭn-ê-dō′sȧ).....Can.	50·14 N	99·51 W
108	Minneota (mĭn-ê-ō′tȧ).........Mn.	44·34 N	95·59 W
103	Minnesota (State) (mĭn-ê-sō′tȧ) U. S.	46·10 N	90·20 W
108	Minnesota (R.)...............Mn.	45·04 N	96·03 W

ng-sing; ŋ-baŋk; ɴ-nasalized n; nŏd; cŏmmit; ōld; ôbey; ôrder; fōōd; fŏŏt; ou-out; s-soft; sh-dish; th-thin; pūre; ûnite; ûrn; stŭd; circŭs; ü-as "y" in study; ′-indeterminate vowel.

314 Minnetonka — Monchengladbach PRONOUNCING INDEX

Page Name Pronunciation Region Lat. °' Long. °'

109 Minnetonka (L.) (mĭn-ê-tôŋ'kȧ) Mn. 44·52 N 93·34 W
115 Minnie Maud Cr. (mĭn'ĭmôd') . Ut. 39·50 N 110·30 W
95 Minnitaki L. (mĭ'nĭ-tä'kê) . . . Can. 49·58 N 92·00 W
195 Minō (mē'nō) . . . . Jap. (Ōsaka In.) 34·49 N 135·28 E
195 Mino (R.) . . . . Jap. (Ōsaka In.) 34·56 N 135·06 E
162 Miño (R.) (mē'nyō) . . . . Sp. 42·28 N 7·48 W
104 Minonk (mī'nŏnk) . . . . Il. 40·55 N 89·00 W
107 Minooka (mĭ-nōō'kȧ) Il. (Chicago In.) 41·27 N 88·15 W
Minorca (I.), see Menorca, Isla de
108 Minot (mī'nŏt) . . . . ND 48·13 N 101·16 W
166 Minsk (mênsk) . . . . Sov. Un. 53·54 N 27·35 E
166 Minsk (Oblast) . . . . Sov. Un. 53·50 N 27·43 E
159 Mińsk Mazowiecki (mēn'sk mä-zô-vyĕt'skĭ) . Pol. 52·10 N 21·35 E
148 Minsterley (mĭnstēr-lē) . . . . . . Eng. 52·38 N 2·55 W
98 Minto . . . . Can. 46·05 N 66·05 W
91 Minto (L.) . . . . Can. 57·18 N 75·50 W
164 Minturno (mēn-tōōr'nō) . . . . It. 41·17 N 13·44 E
218 Minūf (mê-nōōf') . Egypt (Nile In.) 30·26 N 30·55 E
172 Minusinsk (mē-nōō-sênsk') Sov. Un. 53·47 N 91·45 E
174 Min'yar (mēn'yȧr) Sov. Un. (Urals In.) 55·06 N 57·33 E
99 Miquelon (I.) (mĭk-ē-lôn') St. Pierre & Miquelon 47·00 N 56·40 W
89 Miquelon L. (mĭ'kē-lôn) Can. (Edmonton In.) 53·16 N 112·55 W
124 Miquihuana (mê-kê-wä'nä) . . Mex. 23·36 N 99·45 W
159 Mir (mēr) . . . . Sov. Un. 53·27 N 26·25 E
162 Mira (R.) (mē'rȧ) . . . . Port. 37·29 N 8·15 W
137 Miracema (mē-rä-sĕ'mä) Braz. (Rio de Janeiro In.) 21·24 S 42·10 W
135 Mirador (mê-rȧ-dōr') . . . . . . Braz. 6·19 S 44·12 W
134 Miraflores (mē-rä-flō'räs) . . . . . Col. 5·10 N 73·13 W
134 Miraflores . . . . Peru 16·19 S 71·20 W
122 Miraflores Locks . . . . Pan. (In.) 9·00 N 79·35 W
129 Miragoâne (mê-rȧ-gwän') . . . . Hai. 18·25 N 73·05 W
137 Miraí (mē-rȧ-ē') Braz. (Rio de Janeiro In.) 21·13 S 42·36 W
113 Mira Loma (mĭ'rȧ lō'mȧ) Ca. (Los Angeles In.) 34·01 N 117·32 W
114 Miramar (mĭr'ȧ-mär) . . . . Ca. (In.) 32·53 N 117·08 W
160 Miramas . . . . Fr. (In.) 43·35 N 5·00 E
98 Miramichi B. (mĭr'ȧ-mē'shē) . . Can. 47·08 N 65·08 W
134 Miranda (mē-rä'n-dä) . . . Col. (In.) 3·14 N 76·11 W
135 Miranda . . . . Ven. (In.) 10·09 N 68·24 W
135 Miranda (State) . . . . Ven. (In.) 10·17 N 66·41 W
162 Miranda de Ebro (mē-rä'n-dä-dĕ-ĕ'l-brō) . Sp. 42·42 N 2·59 W
162 Miranda de Ebro (mê-rän'dä dōō-dwĕ'rō) . Port. 41·30 N 6·17 W
162 Mirandela (mê-rän-dā'lȧ) . . . . Port. 41·28 N 7·10 W
118 Mirando City (mĭr-ȧn'dō) . . . . . Tx. 27·25 N 99·03 W
129 Mira Por Vos Islets (Is.) (mē'rä pôr vōs) . Ba. 22·05 N 74·30 W
129 Mira Por Vos Pass (Str.) . . . . . . Ba. 22·10 N 74·35 W
186 Mirbāt . . . . Om. 16·58 N 54·42 E
129 Mirebalais (mēr-bȧ-lĕ') . . . . Hai. 18·50 N 72·05 W
161 Mirecourt (mēr-kōōr') . . . . Fr. 48·20 N 6·08 E
160 Mirepoix (mēr-pwä') . . . . Fr. 43·06 N 1·52 E
148 Mirfield (mûr'fēld) . . . . Eng. 53·41 N 1·42 W
196 Miri (mē'rē) . . . . Mala. 4·13 N 113·56 E
136 Mirim, L. (mê-rēɴ') . . . . . . Braz.-Ur. 33·00 S 53·15 W
167 Miropol'ye (mē-rō-pôl'yĕ) Sov. Un. 51·02 N 35·13 E
184 Mīrpur Khās (mēr'pōōr ĸäs) . . Pak. 25·36 N 69·10 E
184 Mirzāpur (mēr'zä-pōōr) . . . . . India 25·12 N 82·38 E
125 Misantla (mê-sän'tlä) . . . . Mex. 19·55 N 96·49 W
98 Miscou (I.) (mĭs'kō) . . . . Can. 47·58 N 64·35 W
98 Miscou Pt. . . . . Can. 48·04 N 64·32 W
163 Miseno, C. (mê-zĕ'nō) It. (Naples In.) 40·33 N 14·12 E
127 Misery, Mt. (mĭz'rē-ĭ) St. Kitts-Nevis-Anguilla (In.) 17·28 N 62·47 W
194 Mishan (mĭ'shäɴ) . . . . China 45·32 N 132·19 E
104 Mishawaka (mĭsh-ȧ-wôk'ȧ) . . . . In. 41·45 N 86·15 W
195 Mishina (mê'shē-mä) . . . . Jap. 35·09 N 138·56 E
136 Misiones (Prov.) (mê-syō'näs) Arg. 27·00 S 54·30 W
127 Miskito, Cayos (Is.) . . . . Nic. 14·34 N 82·30 W
159 Miskolc (mĭsh'kôlts) . . . . Hung. 48·07 N 20·50 E
197 Misool, Pulau (I.) (mê-sōōl') Indon. 2·00 S 130·05 E
109 Misquah Hills (mĭs-kwä' hĭlz) . Mn. 47·50 N 90·30 W
218 Miṣr al Jadīdah (Ruins) Egypt (Nile In.) 30·06 N 31·35 E
211 Misrātah . . . . Libya 32·23 N 14·58 E
91 Missinaibi (R.) (mĭs'ĭn-ä'ē-bē) Can. 50·27 N 83·01 W
96 Missinaibi L. . . . . Can. 48·23 N 83·40 W
113 Mission (mĭsh'ŭn) Ks. (Kansas City In.) 39·02 N 94·39 W
118 Mission . . . . Tx. 26·14 N 98·19 W
100 Mission City (sĭ'tĭ) Can. (Vancouver In.) 49·08 N 122·18 W
96 Mississagi (R.) . . . . Can. 46·35 N 83·30 W
89 Mississauga . . . . Can. (Toronto In.) 43·34 N 79·37 W
104 Mississinewa (R.) (mĭs-ĭ-sĭn'ê-wä) In. 40·30 N 85·45 W
103 Mississippi (State) (mĭs-ĭ-sĭp'ê) U. S. 32·30 N 89·45 W
105 Mississippi (L.) . . . . Can. 45·05 N 76·15 W
103 Mississippi (R.) . . . . U. S. 31·50 N 91·30 W
120 Mississippi Sd. . . . . Ms. 34·16 N 89·10 W
111 Missoula (mĭ-zōō'lȧ) . . . . Mt. 46·52 N 114·00 W
103 Missouri (State) (mĭ-sōō'rê) . . U. S. 38·00 N 93·40 W
103 Missouri (R.) . . . . U. S. 40·40 N 96·00 W
119 Missouri City . . . . Tx. (In.) 29·37 N 95·32 W
102 Missouri Coteau, (Plat.) . . . . . U. S. 47·30 N 101·00 W
108 Missouri Valley . . . . Ia. 41·35 N 95·53 W
112 Mist (mĭst) . . . . . Or. (Portland In.) 46·00 N 123·15 W
98 Mistassibi (R.) (mĭs-tȧ-sĭ'bē) . Can. 49·44 N 69·58 W
98 Mistassini (mĭs-tȧ-sĭ'nē) . . . . . Can. 48·56 N 71·55 W
91 Mistassini (L.) (mĭs-tȧ-sĭ'nē) . Can. 50·48 N 73·30 W
98 Mistassini (R.) . . . . Can. 50·02 N 72·38 W
158 Mistelbach (mĭs'tĕl-bäk) . . . . . Aus. 48·34 N 16·33 E
126 Misteriosa, L. (mēs-tĕ-ryô'sä) Mex. (In.) 18·05 N 90·15 W
164 Mistretta (mê-strĕt'tä) . . . . It. 37·54 N 14·22 E
124 Mita, Punta de (Pt.) (pōō'n-tä-dĕ-mē'tä) . Mex. 20·44 N 105·34 W
195 Mitaka (mê'tä-kä) Jap. (Tōkyō In.) 35·42 N 139·34 E
113 Mitchell (mĭch'ĕl) . Il (St. Louis In.) 38·46 N 90·05 W
104 Mitchell . . . . In. 38·45 N 86·25 W
108 Mitchell . . . . Ne. 41·56 N 103·49 W
108 Mitchell . . . . SD 43·42 N 98·01 W
205 Mitchell (R.) . . . . Austl. 15·30 S 142·15 E
121 Mitchell, Mt. . . . . NC 35·47 N 82·15 W
218 Mīt Ghamr . . . . . . Egypt (Nile In.) 30·43 N 31·20 E
165 Mitilíni . . . . Grc. 39·09 N 26·35 E
183 Mitla P. . . . . Egypt (Palestine In.) 30·03 N 32·40 E
195 Mito (mē'tō) . . . . Jap. 36·20 N 140·23 E
195 Mitsu (mēt'sōō) . . . . Jap. 34·21 N 132·49 E
158 Mittelland (can.) (mĭt'ĕl-länd) G.D.R. 52·18 N 10·42 E
149 Mittenwalde (mē'tĕn-väl-dĕ) G.D.R. (Berlin In.) 52·16 N 13·33 E
158 Mittweida (mĭt-vī'dä) . . . . . G.D.R. 50·59 N 12·58 E
217 Mitumba, Monts (Mts.) . . . . . Zaire 10·50 S 27·00 E
174 Mityayevo (mĭt-yä'yĕ-vô) Sov. Un. (Urals In.) 60·17 N 61·02 E
195 Miura . . . . Jap. (Tōkyō In.) 35·08 N 139·37 E
167 Mius (R.) (mê-ōōs') . . . . . Sov. Un. 47·30 N 38·48 E
195 Miwa (mê'wä) . . . Jap. (Osaka In.) 34·32 N 135·51 E
126 Mixico (mēs'kō) . . . . Guat. 14·37 N 90·37 W
124 Mixquiahuala (mēs-kê-wä'lä) . Mex. 20·12 N 99·13 W
124 Mixteco (R.) (mês-tā'kō) . . . . Mex. 17·45 N 98·10 W
195 Miyake (mê'yä-kå) Jap. (Ōsaka In.) 34·35 N 135·34 E
195 Miyake (I.) (mē'yä-kå) . . . . . . Jap. 34·06 N 139·21 E
195 Miyakonojō (mē'yä-kô'nô-jô) . Jap. 31·42 N 131·03 E
195 Miyazaki (mē'yä-zä'kê) . . . . . . Jap. 31·55 N 131·27 E
195 Miyoshi (mê-yō'shē') . . . . Jap. 34·48 N 132·49 E
152 Mizdah (mēz'dä) . . . . Libya 31·29 N 13·09 E
165 Mizil (mē'zêl) . . . . Rom. 45·01 N 26·30 E
Mizonokuchi, see Takatsu
184 Mizoram (Union Ter.) . . . . . . India 23·25 N 92·45 E
156 Mjölby (myûl'bü) . . . . Swe. 58·20 N 15·09 E
156 Mjörn (L.) . . . . Swe. 57·55 N 12·22 E
156 Mjösa (myûsä) . . . . Nor. 60·41 N 11·25 E
156 Mjösvatn (myûs-vät'n) . . . . . . Nor. 59·55 N 7·50 E
212 Mkalama . . . . Tan. 4·07 S 34·38 E
215 Mkomazi (R.) . . S. Afr. (Natal In.) 30·10 S 3·30 E
217 Mkushi . . . . Zambia 13·40 S 29·20 E
217 Mkwaja . . . . Tan. 5·47 S 38·51 E
158 Mladá Boleslav (mlä'dä bô'lĕ-slåf) Czech. 50·26 N 14·52 E
217 Mlala Hills . . . . Tan. 6·47 S 31·45 E
217 Mlanje Mts. . . . . Malawi 15·55 S 35·30 E
159 Mława (mwä'vå) . . . . Pol. 53·07 N 20·25 E
213 Mlazi (R.) . . . . S. Afr. (Natal In.) 29·52 S 30·42 E
165 Mljet (I.) (mlyĕt) . . . . Yugo. 42·40 N 17·45 E
214 Mo (R.) . . . . Togo 9·05 N 0·55 E
197 Moa, Pulau (I.) . . . . Indon. 8·30 S 128·30 E
214 Moa (R.) . . . . S. L. 7·40 N 11·15 W
115 Moab (mō'ăb) . . . . Ut. 38·35 N 109·35 W
212 Moanda . . . . Gabon 1·37 S 13·09 E
114 Moapa River Ind. Res. (mō-ăp'ȧ) Nv. 36·44 N 115·01 W
95 Moar L. (môr) . . . . Can. 52·00 N 95·09 W
216 Mobaye (mô-bä'y') . Cen. Afr. Emp. 4·19 N 21·11 E
117 Moberly (mō'bēr-lĭ) . . . . Mo. 39·24 N 92·25 W
93 Moberly (R.) . . . . Can. 55·40 N 121·15 W
120 Mobile (mô-bēl') . . . . Al. 30·42 N 88·03 W
120 Mobile (R.) . . . . Al. 31·15 N 88·00 W
120 Mobile B. Al. 30·26 N 87·56 W
108 Mobridge (mō'brĭj) . . . . SD 45·32 N 100·26 W
129 Moca (mô'kä) . . . . Dom. Rep. 19·25 N 70·35 W
217 Moçambique (mō-säɴ-bē'kĕ) . Moz. 15·03 S 40·42 E
216 Moçâmedes (mō-zȧ-mĕ-dĕs) . . Ang. 15·10 S 12·09 E
212 Moçâmedes (Reg.) . . . . Ang. 16·00 S 12·15 E
186 Mocha (mō'kä) . . . . Yemen 13·11 N 43·20 E
124 Mochitlán (mō-chê-tlän') . . . . Mex. 17·10 N 99·19 W
212 Mochudi (mō-chōō'dê) . . . . . . Bots. 24·13 S 26·07 E
217 Mocímboa da Praia (mō-sē'ĕm-bô-ȧ dȧ prä'ēȧ) . Moz. 11·20 S 40·21 E
110 Moclips . . . . Wa. 47·14 N 124·13 W
216 Môco, Serra (Mts.) . . . . Arg. 12·25 S 15·10 E
137 Mococa (mô-kô'kȧ) Braz. (Rio de Janeiro In.) 21·29 S 46·58 W
124 Moctezuma (môk'tȧ-zōō'mä) . Mex. 22·44 N 101·06 W
217 Mocuba . . . . Moz. 16·50 S 36·59 E
213 Modderfontein . . . . S. Afr. (Johannesburg & Pretoria In.) 26·06 S 28·10 E
164 Modena (mô'dĕ-nä) . . . . It. 44·38 N 10·54 E
114 Modesto (mô-dĕs'tō) . . . . Ca. 37·39 N 121·00 W
164 Modica (mô'dê-kä) . . . . It. 36·50 N 14·43 E
149 Mödling (mûd'lĭng) Aus. (Vienna In.) 48·06 N 16·17 E
135 Moengo . . . . Sur. 5·43 N 54·19 W
115 Moenkopi . . . . Az. 36·07 N 111·13 W
161 Moers (mûrs) . . F.R.G. (Ruhr In.) 51·27 N 6·38 E
116 Moffat Tun. (môf'ăt) . . . . Co. 39·52 N 106·20 W
218 Mogadisho (mô-gȧ-dē'shō) Som. (Horn of Afr. In.) 2·08 N 45·22 E
107 Mogadore (mŏg-ȧ-dōr') Oh. (Cleveland In.) 41·04 N 81·23 W
188 Mogaung (mô-gä'ōōng) . . . . . . Bur. 25·30 N 96·52 E
137 Mogi das Cruzes (mô-gê-däs-krōō'sĕs) Braz. (Rio de Janeiro In.) 23·33 S 46·10 W
137 Mogi-Guaçu (R.) (mô-gê-gwȧ'sōō) Braz. (Rio de Janeiro In.) 22·06 S 47·12 W
166 Mogilëv (mô-gê-lyôf') . . . . Sov. Un. 53·53 N 30·22 E
166 Mogilëv (Oblast) (mô-gê-lyôf') Sov. Un. 53·28 N 30·15 E
167 Mogilëv-Podol'skiy (mô-gê-lyôf) (pô-dôl'skĭ) Sov. Un. 48·27 N 27·51 E
159 Mogilno (mô-gēl'nô) . . . . Pol. 52·38 N 17·58 E
137 Mogi-Mirim (mô-gê-mē-rē'ɴ) Braz. (Rio de Janeiro In.) 22·26 S 46·57 W
217 Mogincual . . . . Moz. 15·35 S 40·25 E
188 Mogok (mô-gôk') . . . . Bur. 23·14 N 96·38 E
115 Mogollon (mō-gô-yōn') . . . . NM 33·25 N 108·45 W
115 Mogollon, Plat. (mō-gô-yōn') . Az. 34·26 N 111·17 W
218 Mogol R. (mô-gŏl) . . . . S. Afr. (Johannesburg & Pretoria In.) 24·12 S 27·55 E
162 Moguer (mô-gĕr') . . . . Sp. 37·15 N 6·50 W
159 Mohács (mô'häch) . . . . Hung. 45·59 N 18·38 E
213 Mohale's Hoek . . Leso. (Natal In.) 30·09 S 27·28 E
108 Mohall (mō'hôl) . . . . ND 48·46 N 101·29 W
163 Mohammadia . . . . Alg. 35·35 N 0·05 E
114 Mohave (L.) (mô-hä'vä) . . . . . . Nv. 35·23 N 114·40 W
105 Mohawk (R.) (mō'hôk) . . . . NY 43·15 N 75·20 W
189 Mohe (mwo-hŭ) . . . . China 53·33 N 122·30 E
213 Moheli (I.) (mô-ā-lē') (mô-hā'lē) Comoros 12·23 S 43·38 E
184 Mohenjo-Dero (Ruins) . . . . . . Pak. 27·20 N 68·10 E
150 Mo-i-Rana . . . . Nor. 65·54 N 13·15 E
157 Mõisaküla (mĕē'sȧ-kü'lä) . Sov. Un. 58·07 N 25·12 E
99 Moisie (R.) (mwȧ-zē') . . . . Can. 50·35 N 66·25 W
160 Moissac (mwä-säk') . . . . Fr. 44·07 N 1·05 E
163 Moita (mô-ē'tȧ) . Port. (Lisbon In.) 38·39 N 9·00 W
114 Mojave . . . . Ca. 35·06 N 118·09 W
114 Mojave (R.) (mô-hä'vä) . . . . . . Ca. 34·46 N 117·24 W
114 Mojave Desert . . . . Ca. 35·05 N 117·30 W
114 Mokelumne (R.) (mō-kē-lŭm'nē) Ca. 38·30 N 120·17 W
213 Mokhotlong . . . . Leso. (Natal In.) 29·18 S 29·06 E
194 Mokp'o (mōk'pō') . . . . Kor. 34·50 N 126·30 E
170 Moksha (R.) (môk-shä') . Sov. Un. 54·50 N 43·20 E
149 Mol . . . . Bel. (Brussels In.) 51·21 N 5·09 E
164 Molat (I.) (mô'lät) . . . . Yugo. 44·15 N 14·40 E
159 Moldavia (Reg.) . . . . Rom. 47·20 N 27·12 E
168 Moldavian S. S. R. . . . . . . Sov. Un. 48·00 N 28·00 E
156 Molde (môl'dĕ) . . . . Nor. 62·44 N 7·15 E
156 Molde Fd. (môl'dĕ fyôrd) . . . . Nor. 62·40 N 7·05 E
159 Moldova R. . . . . Rom. 47·17 N 26·27 E
212 Molepolole (mō-lå-pô-lō'lå) . . Bots. 24·15 S 25·33 E
164 Molfetta (môl-fĕt'tä) . . . . It. 41·11 N 16·38 E
137 Molina (mō-lē'nä) Chile (Santiago In.) 35·07 S 71·17 W
162 Molina de Aragón (mô-lē'nä dĕ ä-rä-gô'n) . Sp. 41·40 N 1·54 W
162 Molína de Segura (mô-lē'nä dĕ sĕ-gōō'rä) . Sp. 38·03 N 1·07 W
109 Moline (mô-lēn') . . . . Il. 41·31 N 90·34 W
217 Moliro . . . . Zaire 8·13 S 30·34 E
164 Moliterno (mōl-ē-tĕr'nō) . . . . . . It. 40·13 N 15·54 E
134 Mollendo (mô-lyĕn'dō) . . . . Peru 17·02 S 71·59 W
101 Moller, Port (pōrt mōl'ēr) . . . . . Ak. 56·18 N 161·30 W
156 Mölndal (mûln'däl) . . . . Swe. 57·39 N 12·01 E
167 Molochnaya (R.) (mô-lôch'nȧ-yȧ) (rĕ-kä') Sov. Un. 47·05 N 35·22 E
167 Molochnoye, Ozero (L.) (ô'zĕ-rô mô-lôch'nô-yĕ) . Sov. Un. 46·35 N 35·32 E
166 Molodechno (mô-lô-dĕch'nô) Sov. Un. 54·18 N 26·57 E
166 Molodechno (Oblast) . . . . Sov. Un. 54·27 N 27·38 E
174 Molody Tud (mō-lō-dô'ê tōō'd) Sov. Un. (Moscow In.) 55·17 N 37·31 E
166 Mologa (R.) (mô-lô'gȧ) . . Sov. Un. 58·05 N 35·43 E
100 Molokai (I.) (mō-lô kä'ē) . . . . . . Hi. 21·15 N 157·05 E
174 Molokcha R. (mô'lôk-chä) Sov. Un. (Moscow In.) 56·15 N 38·29 E
212 Molopo (R.) (mō-lō-pô) . . . . S. Afr. 27·45 S 20·45 E
95 Molson L. (mōl'sŭn) . . . . Can. 54·12 N 96·45 W
213 Molteno (môl-tā'nô) S. Afr. (Natal In.) 31·24 S 26·23 E
217 Moma . . . . Moz. 16·44 S 39·14 E
217 Mombasa (mōm-bä'sȧ) . . . . Ken. 4·03 S 39·40 E
194 Mombetsu (môm'bĕt-sōō') . . . . Jap. 44·21 N 142·48 E
216 Momboyo (R.) . . . . Zaire 0·20 S 19·20 E
107 Momence (mō-mĕns') Il. (Chicago In.) 41·09 N 87·40 W
126 Momostenango (mô-môs-tā-näŋ'gô) . Guat. 15·02 N 91·25 W
126 Momotombo . . . . Nic. 12·25 N 86·43 W
197 Mompog Pass (mōm-pŏg') Phil. (In.) 13·35 N 122·09 E
134 Mompos (mōm-pōs') . . . . Col. 8·05 N 74·30 W
156 Møn (I.) (mûn) . . . . Den. 54·54 N 12·30 E
107 Monaca (mŏ-nȧ'kō) Pa. (Pittsburgh In.) 40·41 N 80·17 W
151 Monaco (mŏn'ȧ-kō) . . . . Eur. 43·43 N 7·47 E
154 Monaghan (mŏn'ȧ-găn) . . . . Ire. 54·16 N 7·20 W
123 Mona Pass. (mō'nä) . . . . N. A. 18·00 N 68·10 W
92 Monarch Mtn. (mŏn'ērk) . . . . Can. 51·54 N 125·53 W
93 Monashee Mts. (mŏ-nă'shē) . . Can. 50·30 N 118·30 W
151 Monastir (mōn-ȧs-tēr') . . . . . . Tun. 35·49 N 10·56 E
Monastir, see Bitola
167 Monastyrishche (mô-nȧs-tē-rēsh'chȧ) . Sov. Un. 48·57 N 29·53 E
166 Monastyrshchina (mô-nȧs-tērsh'chĭ-nȧ) . Sov. Un. 54·19 N 31·49 E
135 Monçao (mon-souɴ') . . . . Braz. 3·39 S 45·23 W
162 Moncayo (Mtn.) (môn-kä'yō) . Sp. 41·44 N 1·48 W
170 Monchegorsk (mŏn'chĕ-gôrsk) Sov. Un. 69·00 N 33·35 E
161 Mönchengladbach (mûn'ĸĕn gläd'bäĸ) F.R.G. (Ruhr In.) 51·12 N 6·28 E

Page	Name Pronunciation Region	Lat. °′	Long. °′
162	Moncique, Serra de (Mts.)		
	(sĕr′rä dä môn-chē′kĕ).Port.	37·22 N	8·37 W
118	Monclovra (môn-klō′vä).....Mex.	26·53 N	101·25 W
98	Moncton (mŭŋk′tŭn)........Can.	46·06 N	64·47 W
162	Mondego, Cabo (C.)		
	(kä′bō môn-dā′gŏō).Port.	40·12 N	8·55 W
162	Mondêgo (R.) (môn-dĕ′gō)..Port.	40·10 N	8·36 W
212	Mondombe (môn-dôm′bä)...Zaire	0·45 S	23·06 E
162	Mondoñedo (môn-dô-nyä′dō)..Sp.	43·35 N	7·18 W
164	Mondoví (môn-dô′vē′)........It.	44·23 N	7·53 E
109	Mondovi (môn-dō′vĭ)........Wi.	44·35 N	91·42 W
107	Monee (mō-nī)...Il. (Chicago In.)	41·25 N	87·45 W
107	Monessen (mŏ′nĕs′sen)		
	Pa. (Pittsburgh In.)	40·09 N	79·53 W
117	Monett (mŏ-nĕt′)............Mo.	36·55 N	93·55 W
162	Monforte de Lemos		
	(môn-fôr′tä dĕ lĕ′mōs).Sp.	42·30 N	7·30 W
215	Monga................Chad.	4·12 N	22·49 E
211	Mongala R. (môn-gäl′ä)....Zaire	3·20 N	21·30 E
211	Mongalla................Sud.	5·11 N	31·46 E
184	Monghyr (môn-gēr′)......India	25·23 N	86·34 E
214	Mongo (R.)..............S. L.	9·50 N	11·50 W
182	Mongolia (môŋ-gō′lĭ- á)......Asia	46·00 N	100·00 E
211	Mongos, Chaîne des (Mts.)		
	Cen. Afr. Rep.	8·04 N	21·59 E
216	Mongoumba (môŋ-gŏōm′bä)		
	Cen. Afr. Emp.	3·38 N	18·36 E
216	Mongu (môŋ-gŏō′)......Zambia	15·15 S	23·09 E
174	Monino....Sov. Un. (Moscow In.)	55·50 N	38·13 E
217	Monkey Bay............Malawi	14·05 S	34·55 E
126	Monkey River (mŭŋ′kĭ)		
	Belize (In.)	16·22 N	88·33 W
89	Monkland (mŭngk-lănd)		
	Can. (Ottawa In.)	45·12 N	74·52 W
216	Monkoto (môn-kō′tō)........Zaire	1·38 S	20·39 E
117	Monmouth		
	(môn′mŭth) (môn′mouth).Il.	40·54 N	90·38 W
106	Monmouth Junction		
	(môn′mouth jŭngk′shŭn)		
	NJ (New York In.)	40·23 N	74·33 W
92	Monmouth Mtn. (môn′mŭth).Can.	51·00 N	123·47 W
114	Mono (L.) (mō′nō).........Ca.	38·04 N	119·00 W
214	Mono (R.)............Togo	7·20 N	1·25 E
104	Monon (mō′nŏn)..........In.	40·55 N	86·55 W
105	Monongah (mô-nŏn′gä)....WV	39·25 N	80·10 W
107	Monongahela (mô-nŏn-gä-hē′lä)		
	Pa. (Pittsburgh In.)	40·11 N	79·55 W
105	Monongahela (R.).........WV	39·30 N	80·10 W
165	Monopoli (mô-nô′pô-lē).....It.	40·55 N	17·17 E
163	Monovar (mô-nô′vär)........Sp.	38·26 N	0·50 W
164	Monreale (môn-rä′ä′lä)......It.	38·04 N	13·15 E
120	Monroe (mŭn-rō′).........Ga.	33·47 N	83·43 W
119	Monroe................La.	32·30 N	92·06 W
104	Monroe................Mi.	41·55 N	83·25 W
106	Monroe.....NY (New York In.)	41·19 N	74·11 W
121	Monroe................NC	34·58 N	80·34 W
115	Monroe................Ut.	38·35 N	112·10 W
112	Monroe......Wa. (Seattle In.)	47·52 N	121·58 W
109	Monroe................Wi.	42·35 N	89·40 W
121	Monroe (L.).............Fl.	28·50 N	81·15 W
120	Monroeville (mŭn-rō′vĭl).....Al.	31·33 N	87·19 W
117	Monroe City............Mo.	39·38 N	91·41 W
113	Monrovia (môn-rō′vĭ-á)		
	Ca. (Los Angeles In.)	34·09 N	118·00 W
214	Monrovia................Lib.	6·18 N	10·47 W
155	Mons (môn′)............Bel.	50·29 N	3·55 E
98	Monson (môn′sŭn).........Me.	45·17 N	69·28 W
156	Mönsterås (mŭn′stĕr-ôs)....Swe.	57·04 N	16·24 E
188	Montagh Ata (Mt.)........China	38·26 N	75·23 E
103	Montagne Tremblante Prov. Pk.		
	Can.	46·30 N	75·51 W
99	Montague (môn′tá-gū)......Can.	46·10 N	62·39 W
104	Montague..............Mi.	43·30 N	86·25 W
101	Montague (I.)...........Ak.	60·10 N	147·00 W
135	Montalbán........Ven. (In.)	10·14 N	68·19 W
164	Montalcone (môn-täl-kō′nĕ)...It.	43·48 N	13·30 E
162	Montalegre (môn-tä-lā′grĕ).Port.	41·49 N	7·48 W
102	Montana (State) (môn-tăn′á).U.S.	47·10 N	111·50 W
162	Montánchez (môn-tän′chäth)..Sp.	39·18 N	6·09 W
160	Montargis (môn-tár-zhē′)....Fr.	47·59 N	2·42 E
161	Montataire (môn-tä-tär′)		
	Fr. (Paris In.)	49·15 N	2·26 E
160	Montauban (môn-tô-bän′)....Fr.	44·01 N	1·22 E
105	Montauk................NY	41·03 N	71·57 W
105	Montauk Pt. (môn-tôk′)......NY	41·05 N	71·55 W
160	Montbanch (môn-bän′ch)....Sp.	41·20 N	1·08 E
160	Montbard (môn-bár′).......Fr.	47·40 N	4·19 E
161	Montbéliard (môn-bä-lyär′)..Fr.	47·32 N	6·45 E
119	Mont Belvieu (mônt bĕl′vū)		
	Tx. (In.)	29·51 N	94·53 W
161	Mont Blanc Tunnel (môn blän)		
	Fr.-It.	45·53 N	6·53 E
160	Montbrison (môn-brē-zôn′)...Fr.	45·38 N	4·06 E
160	Montcalm, Pic de (Pk.)		
	(pēk dĕ môn-kám′).Fr.	42·43 N	1·13 E
160	Montceau-les-Mines		
	(môn-sō′lä-mēn′).Fr.	46·39 N	4·22 E
106	Montclair (mônt-klâr′)		
	NJ (New York In.)	40·49 N	74·13 W
160	Mont-de-Marsan		
	(môn-dĕ-már-sän′).Fr.	43·54 N	0·32 W
160	Montdidier (môn-dē-dyä′)....Fr.	49·42 N	2·33 E
137	Monte (mô′n-tĕ)		
	Arg. (Buenos Aires In.)	35·25 S	58·49 W
134	Monteagudo (môn′tä-ä-gŏō′dhō)		
	Bol.	19·49 S	63·48 W
113	Montebello (môn-tĕ-bĕl′ō)		
	Ca. (Los Angeles In.)	34·01 N	118·06 W
89	Montebello.....Can. (Ottawa In.)	45·40 N	74·56 W
204	Monte Bello (Is.).........Austl.	20·30 S	114·10 E
136	Monte Caseros		
	(mô′n-tĕ-kä-sĕ′rôs).Arg.	30·16 S	57·39 W

Page	Name Pronunciation Region	Lat. °′	Long. °′
126	Mont Ecillos, Cord. de (Mts.)		
	(kôr-dēl-yĕ′rä dĕ mô′nt		
	ĕ-sē′l-yōs).Hond.	14·19 N	87·52 W
129	Monte Cristi (mô′n-tĕ-krē′stē)		
	Dom. Rep.	19·50 N	71·40 W
164	Montecristo (I.)		
	(môn′tä-krēs′tō).It.	42·20 N	10·19 E
124	Monte Escobedo		
	(môn′tä ĕs-kô-bä′dhō).Mex.	22·18 N	103·34 W
163	Monteforte Irpino		
	(môn-tĕ-fô′r-tĕ ē′r-pĕ′nō)		
	It. (Naples In.)	40·39 N	14·42 E
162	Montefrío (môn-tä-frē′ō)......Sp.	37·20 N	4·02 W
128	Montego Bay (môn-tē′gō)...Jam.	18·30 N	77·55 W
136	Monte Grande (mô′n-tĕ grän′dĕ)		
	Arg. (Buenos Aires In.)	34·34 S	58·28 W
163	Montelavar (môn-tĕ-lá-vär′)		
	Port. (Lisbon In.)	38·51 N	9·20 W
160	Montélimar (môn-tä-lē-mär′)..Fr.	44·33 N	4·47 E
162	Montellano (môn-tä-lyä′nō)...Sp.	37·00 N	5·34 W
109	Montello (môn-tĕl′ō).........Wi.	43·47 N	89·20 W
118	Montemorelos (môn′tä-mô-rä′lōs)		
	Mex.	25·14 N	99·50 W
162	Montemor-o-Novo		
	(môn-tĕ-môr′ŏō-nō′vŏō).Port.	38·39 N	8·11 W
	Montenegro (Reg.), see Crna Gora		
217	Montepuez................Moz.	13·07 S	39·00 E
164	Montepulciano		
	(môn′tä-pŏōl-chä′nō).It.	43·05 N	11·48 E
160	Montereau-faut-Yonne		
	(môn-t′rō′fō-yôn′).Fr.	48·24 N	2·57 E
114	Monterey (môn-tĕ-rā′).......Ca.	36·36 N	121·53 W
120	Monterey................Tn.	36·06 N	85·15 W
114	Monterey B...............Ca.	36·48 N	122·01 W
113	Monterey Park		
	Ca. (Los Angeles In.)	34·04 N	118·08 W
134	Montería (môn-tä-rä′ä)......Col.	8·47 N	75·57 W
136	Monteros (môn-tĕ′rôs)......Arg.	27·14 S	65·29 W
163	Monterotondo (môn-tĕ-rô-tô′n-dō)		
	It. (Rome In.)	42·03 N	12·39 E
118	Monterrey (môn-tĕ-rā′).....Mex.	25·43 N	100·19 W
164	Monte Sant′ Angelo		
	(mô′n-tĕ sän ä′n-gzhĕ-lô).It.	41·43 N	15·59 E
110	Montesano (môn-tĕ-sä′nō)....Wa.	46·59 N	123·35 W
135	Montes Claros (môn-tĕs-klä′rôs)		
	Braz.	16·44 S	43·41 W
120	Montevallo (môn-tĕ-väl′ō)....Al.	33·05 N	86·49 W
164	Montevarchi (môn-tä-vär′kē)..It.	43·30 N	11·45 E
137	Montevideo (môn-tĕ-vē-dhä′ō)		
	Ur. (Buenos Aires In.)	34·50 S	56·10 W
115	Monte Vista (môn′tĕ vĭs′tá)..Co.	37·35 N	106·10 W
120	Montezuma (môn-tĕ-zŏō′má)..Ga.	32·17 N	84·00 W
115	Montezuma Castle Natl. Mon..Az.	34·38 N	111·50 W
149	Montfoort..Neth. (Amsterdam In.)	52·02 N	4·56 E
161	Montfort l′Amaury		
	(môN-fôr′lä-mō-rē′)		
	Fr. (Paris In.)	48·47 N	1·49 E
160	Montfort-sur-Meu		
	(môn-fôr-sür-mú′).Fr.	48·09 N	1·58 W
120	Montgomery (mônt-gŭm′ĕr-i).Al.	32·23 N	86·17 W
104	Montgomery..............WV	38·10 N	81·25 W
117	Montgomery City.........Mo.	38·58 N	91·29 W
117	Monticello (môn-tĭ-sĕl′ō)....Ar.	33·38 N	91·47 W
120	Monticello..............Fl.	30·32 N	83·53 W
120	Monticello..............Ga.	33·00 N	83·11 W
104	Monticello..............Il.	40·05 N	88·35 W
104	Monticello..............In.	40·40 N	86·50 W
109	Monticello..............Ia.	42·14 N	91·13 W
120	Monticello..............Ky.	36·47 N	84·50 W
98	Monticello..............Me.	46·19 N	67·53 W
109	Monticello..............Mn.	45·18 N	93·48 W
105	Monticello..............NY	41·35 N	74·40 W
115	Monticello..............Ut.	37·55 N	109·25 W
161	Montigny-lès-Metz		
	(môn-tēn-yē′lä-mĕts′).Fr.	49·06 N	6·07 E
163	Montijo (môn-tē′zhō)		
	Port. (Lisbon In.)	38·42 N	8·58 W
162	Montijo (môn-tē′hō)........Sp.	38·55 N	6·35 W
127	Montijo, Bahia (B.)		
	(bä-ē′ä môn-tē′hō).Pan.	7·36 N	81·11 W
98	Mont-Joli (môn zhô-lē′).....Can.	48·35 N	68·11 W
160	Montluçon (môn-lü-sôn′)....Fr.	46·20 N	2·35 E
89	Montmagny (môn-män-yē′)		
	Can. (Quebec In.)	46·59 N	70·33 W
89	Montmorency (mônt-mô-rĕn′sĭ)		
	Can. (Quebec In.)	46·53 S	71·09 W
161	Montmorency (môn′mō-rän-sē′)		
	Fr. (Paris In.)	48·59 N	2·19 E
89	Montmorency (R.)		
	(mônt-mô-rĕn′sĭ)		
	Can. (Quebec In.)	47·30 N	71·10 W
160	Montmorillon (môn′mō-rē-yôn′)		
	Fr.	46·26 N	0·50 E
164	Montone (R.) (môn-tô′nĕ)....It.	44·03 N	11·45 E
162	Montoro (môn-tô′rō)........Sp.	38·01 N	4·22 W
104	Montpelier (mônt-pēl′yer)....In.	40·35 N	85·20 W
111	Montpelier..............Id.	42·19 N	111·19 W
104	Montpelier..............Oh.	41·35 N	84·35 W
105	Montpelier..............Vt.	44·20 N	72·35 W
160	Montpellier (môn-pĕ-lyä′)....Fr.	43·38 N	3·53 E
89	Montréal (môn-trē-ôl′)		
	Can. (Montréal In.)	45·30 N	73·35 W
94	Montreal L...............Can.	54·20 N	105·40 W
96	Montreal (R.)............Can.	47·15 N	84·20 W
97	Montreal (R.)............Can.	47·50 N	80·30 W
89	Montréal-Nord		
	Can. (Montréal In.)	45·36 N	73·38 W
158	Montreux (môn-trü′)......Switz.	46·26 N	6·52 E
113	Montrose (môn-trōz′)		
	Ca. (Los Angeles In.)	34·13 N	118·13 W
115	Montrose (môn-trōz′).......Co.	38·30 N	107·55 W
107	Montrose.....Oh. (Cleveland In.)	41·08 N	81·38 W

Page	Name Pronunciation Region	Lat. °′	Long. °′
105	Montrose (mônt-rōz′)........Pa.	41·50 N	75·50 W
154	Montrose................Scot.	56·45 N	2·25 W
89	Mont-Royal..Can. (Montreal In.)	47·31 N	73·39 W
98	Monts, Pointe des (Pt.)		
	(pwănt′ dä môn′).Can.	49·19 N	67·22 W
161	Mont St. Martin		
	(môn sän′ mär-tăn′).Fr.	49·34 N	6·13 E
123	Montserrat (mônt-sĕ-rät′)...N. A.	16·48 N	63·15 W
106	Montvale (mônt-vāl′)		
	NJ (New York In.)	41·02 N	74·01 W
196	Monywa (mŏn′yŏō-wä)......Bur.	22·02 N	95·16 E
164	Monza (môn′tsä)............It.	45·34 N	9·17 E
163	Monzón (môn-thôn′).........Sp.	41·54 N	1·09 E
119	Moody (mŏŏ′dĭ)...........Tx.	31·18 N	97·20 W
218	Mooi (R.) (mŏŏ′ĭ)........S. Afr.		
	(Johannesburg & Pretoria In.)	26·34 S	27·03 E
213	Mooi (R.)...S. Afr. (Natal In.)	29·00 S	30·15 E
213	Mooirivier...S. Afr. (Natal In.)	29·14 S	29·59 E
202	Moolap....Austl. (Melbourne In.)	38·11 S	144·26 E
203	Moonta (mŏŏn′tä)........Austl.	34·05 S	137·42 E
204	Moora (mŏŏ′rá).........Austl.	30·35 S	116·12 E
111	Moorcroft (mŏr′krôft)......Wy.	44·17 N	104·59 W
204	Moore (L.) (mŏr).........Austl.	29·50 S	128·12 E
149	Moorenweis (mō′rĕn-viz)		
	F.R.G. (Munich In.)	48·10 N	11·05 E
105	Moore Res.............Vt.-NH	44·20 N	72·10 W
106	Moorestown (morz′toun)		
	NJ (Philadelphia In.)	39·58 N	74·56 W
107	Mooresville (mŏrz′vĭl)		
	In. (Indianapolis In.)	39·30 N	86·22 W
121	Mooresville (mŏrz′vĭl).....NC	35·34 N	80·48 W
108	Moorhead (mŏr′hĕd)........Mn.	46·52 N	96·44 W
120	Moorhead................Ms.	33·25 N	90·30 W
	Moorland (Plain), see Landes		
90	Moose (L.) (mŏŏs).........Can.	54·14 N	99·28 W
91	Moose (R.).............Can.	51·01 N	80·42 W
89	Moose Creek...Can. (Ottawa In.)	45·16 N	74·58 W
98	Moosehead (mŏŏs′hĕd).....Me.	45·37 N	69·15 W
95	Moose I................Can.	51·50 N	97·09 W
94	Moose Jaw (mŏŏs jô).....Can.	50·23 N	105·32 W
94	Moose Jaw (Cr.).........Can.	50·34 N	105·17 W
95	Moose Lake............Can.	53·40 N	100·28 W
95	Moose Mtn.............Can.	49·45 N	102·37 W
94	Moose Mtn. Cr..........Can.	49·12 N	102·10 W
105	Moosilauke (Mtn.)		
	(mŏŏ-sĭ-lá′kē).NH	44·00 N	71·50 W
149	Moosinning (mō′zĕ-nēng)		
	F.R.G. (Munich In.)	48·17 N	11·51 E
95	Moosomin (mŏŏ′sô-mĭn)....Can.	50·07 N	101·40 W
91	Moosonee (mŏŏ′sô-nē)......Can.	51·20 N	80·44 W
214	Mopti (mŏp′tĕ)..........Mali	14·30 N	4·12 W
134	Moquegua (mô-kä′gwä)....Peru	17·15 S	70·54 W
159	Mór (mōr)..............Hung.	47·51 N	18·14 E
185	Mora................India	18·54 N	72·56 E
109	Mora (mō′rá)............Mn.	45·52 N	93·18 W
116	Mora..................NM	35·58 N	105·17 W
162	Mora (mô-rä)............Sp.	39·42 N	3·45 W
163	Mora..................Sp.	41·06 N	0·25 E
184	Morādābād (mô-rä-dä-bäd′).India	28·57 N	78·48 E
126	Morales (mô-rä′lĕs)......Guat.	15·29 N	88·46 W
213	Moramanga (mô-rä-män′gä).Mad.	18·48 S	48·09 E
129	Morant Pt. (mô-ränt′).....Jam.	17·55 N	76·10 W
156	Morastrand (mô-rä-stränd)..Swe.	61·00 N	14·29 E
163	Morata de Tajuña		
	(mô-rä′tä dä tä-hŏō′nyä)		
	Sp. (Madrid In.)	40·14 N	3·27 W
185	Moratuwa (mô-rä′tŏō-wä)..Sri Lanka	6·35 N	79·59 E
159	Morava (Moravia) (Prov.)		
	(mô′rä-vä) (mô-rä′vĭ-á).Czech.	49·21 N	16·57 E
158	Morava R..............Czech.	49·53 N	16·53 E
	Moravia, see Morava		
135	Morawhanna (mô-rä-hwä′ná).Guy.	8·12 N	59·33 W
154	Moray Firth (mŭr′á).......Eng.	57·41 N	3·55 W
156	Mörbylånga (mŭr′bü-lôn′gä).Swe.	56·32 N	16·23 E
95	Morden (mōr′dĕn)........Can.	49·11 N	98·05 W
202	Mordialloc (môr-dĭ-ăl′ôk)		
	Austl. (Melbourne In.)	38·00 S	145·05 E
170	Mordvin (A.S.S.R.)....Sov. Un.	54·18 N	43·50 E
154	More, Ben (Mtn.) (bĕn môr).Scot.	58·09 N	5·01 W
108	Moreau (mô-rō′)..........SD	45·13 N	102·22 W
154	Morecambe B. (môr′kăm)...Eng.	53·55 N	3·25 W
203	Moree (mô′rē)...........Austl.	29·20 S	149·50 E
104	Morehead (mô′rē).........Ky.	38·10 N	83·25 W
121	Morehead City (môr′hĕd)....NC	34·43 N	76·43 W
117	Morehouse (môr′hous).....Mo.	36·49 N	89·41 W
124	Morelia (mô-rā′lyä).......Mex.	19·43 N	101·12 W
163	Morella (mô-rāl′yä).........Sp.	40·38 N	0·07 W
124	Morelos (mô-rä′lōs).......Mex.	22·46 N	102·36 W
118	Morelos................Mex.	28·24 N	100·51 W
125	Morelos..........Mex. (In.)	19·41 N	99·29 W
118	Morelos, R.............Mex.	25·27 N	99·35 W
112	Morena, Sierra (Mt.)		
	(syĕr′rä mô-rä′nä)		
	Ca. (San Francisco In.)	37·24 N	122·19 W
162	Morena, Sierra (Mts.)		
	(syĕr′rä mô-rä′nä).Sp.	38·15 N	5·45 W
115	Morenci (mô-rĕn′sĭ)........Az.	33·05 N	109·25 W
104	Morenci................Mi.	41·50 N	84·50 W
136	Moreno (mô-rĕ′nō).......Arg.	34·25 S	58·47 W
113	Moreno....Ca. (Los Angeles In.)	33·55 N	117·09 W
128	Mores (I.) (mōrz)..........Ba.	26·20 N	77·35 W
112	Moresby (I.) (mōrz′bĭ)		
	Can. (Vancouver In.)	48·43 N	123·15 W
90	Moresby I.............Can.	52·50 N	131·55 W
203	Moreton (I.) (môr′tŭn)....Austl.	26·53 S	152·42 E
203	Moreton B. (môr′tŭn)....Austl.	27·12 S	153·10 E
89	Morewood (mōr′wŏŏd)		
	Can. (Ottawa In.)	45·11 N	75·17 W
111	Morgan (môr′găn).........Mt.	48·55 N	107·56 W
111	Morgan................Ut.	41·04 N	111·42 W
119	Morgan City...........La.	29·41 N	91·11 W
104	Morganfield (môr′găn-fēld)..Ky.	37·40 N	87·55 W
213	Morgan's Bay..S. Afr. (Natal In.)	32·42 S	28·19 E

ng-sing; ŋ-baŋk; N-nasalized n; nŏd; cŏmmit; ōld; ôbey; ôrder; fŏŏd; fŏŏt; ou-out; s-soft; sh-dish; th-thin; pūre; ûnite; ûrn; stŭd; circŭs; ü-as "y" in study; ′-indeterminate vowel.

316 Morganton — Muling

PRONOUNCING INDEX

Page	Name Pronunciation Region	Lat. °'	Long. °'
121	Morganton (môr′găn-tŭn) . . . . . NC	35·44 N	81·42 W
105	Morgantown (môr′găn-toun) . . WV	39·40 N	79·55 W
187	Morga Ra. . Afg. (Khyber Pass In.)	34·02 N	70·38 E
218	Morgenzon (môr′gănt-sŏn) . . S. Afr. (Johannesburg & Pretoria In.)	26·44 S	29·39 E
202	Moriac. . . . Austl. (Melbourne In.)	38·15 S	144·12 E
92	Morice L. . . . . Can.	54·00 N	127·37 W
195	Moriguchi (mō′rē-gōō′chē) Jap. (Ōsaka In.)	34·44 N	135·34 E
89	Morinville (mō′rĭn-vĭl) Can. (Edmonton In.)	53·48 N	113·39 W
194	Morioka (mō′rē-ō′kȧ) . . . . Jap.	39·40 N	141·21 E
173	Morkoka (R.) (môr-kô′kȧ) Sov. Un.	65·35 N	111·00 E
160	Morlaix (mŏr-lĕ′) . . . . Fr.	48·36 N	3·48 W
89	Morley (mŏr′lē) . Can. (Calgary In.)	51·10 N	114·51 W
161	Mormant. . . . . Fr. (Paris In.)	48·35 N	2·54 E
127	Morne Diablotin, Mt. (môrn dē-ȧ-blō-tăN′) Dominica (In.)	15·31 N	61·24 W
127	Morne Gimie, Mt. (môrn′ zhē-mē′) . St. Lucia (In.)	13·53 N	61·03 W
202	Mornington Austl. (Melbourne In.)	38·13 S	145·02 E
197	Morobe . . . . Pap. N. Gui.	8·03 S	147·45 E
209	Morocco (mô-rŏk′ō) . . . . Afr.	32·00 N	7·00 W
217	Morogoro (mō-rô-gō′rō) . . . . . . Tan.	6·49 S	37·40 E
124	Moroleón (mô-rō-lā-ōn′) . . . . . Mex.	20·07 N	101·15 W
213	Morombe (mōō-rōōm′bā) . . . . Mad.	21·39 S	43·34 E
136	Morón (mō-rŏ′n) Arg. (Buenos Aires In.)	34·24 S	58·37 W
128	Morón (mô-rōn′) . . . . Cuba	22·05 N	78·35 W
135	Morón (mô-rŏ′n) . . . . Ven. (In.)	10·29 N	68·11 W
213	Morondava (mô-rōn-dȧ′vȧ) . . Mad.	20·17 S	44·18 E
162	Morón de la Frontera (mô-rōn′dā läf rôn-tā′rä) . Sp.	37·08 N	5·20 W
114	Morongo Ind. Res. (mō-rôŋ′gō) Ca.	33·54 N	116·47 W
212	Moroni . . . . Comoros	11·41 S	43·16 E
115	Moroni (mô-rō′nĭ) . . . . Ut.	39·30 N	111·40 W
197	Morotai (I.) (mō-rô-tä′ē) . . . Indon.	2·12 N	128·30 E
217	Moroto . . . . Ug.	2·32 N	34·39 E
171	Morozovsk . . . . Sov. Un.	48·20 N	41·50 E
108	Morrill (mŏr′ĭl) . . . . Ne.	41·59 N	103·54 W
117	Morrilton (mŏr′ĭl-tŭn) . . . . Ar.	35·09 N	92·42 W
135	Morrinhos (mô-rēn′yōzh) . . . . Braz.	17·45 S	48·56 W
95	Morris (mŏr′ĭs) . . . . Can.	49·21 N	97·22 W
104	Morris . . . . Il.	41·20 N	88·25 W
108	Morris . . . . Mn.	45·35 N	95·53 W
95	Morris (R.) . . . . Can.	49·30 N	97·30 W
109	Morrison (mŏr′ĭ-sŭn) . . . . Il.	41·48 N	89·58 W
106	Morris Plains (mŏr′ĭs pláns) NJ (New York In.)	40·49 N	74·29 W
113	Morris Res. . . Ca. (Los Angeles In.)	34·11 N	117·49 W
106	Morristown (mŏr′rĭs-toun) NJ (New York In.)	40·48 N	74·29 W
120	Morristown . . . . Tn.	36·10 N	83·18 W
106	Morrisville (mŏr′ĭs-vĭl) Pa. (Philadelphia In.)	40·12 N	74·46 W
135	Morro do Chapéu (môr-ōō dōō-shä-pĕ′ōō) . Braz.	11·34 S	41·03 W
107	Morrow (mŏr′ō) Oh. (Cincinnati In.)	39·21 N	84·07 W
171	Morshansk (môr-shȧnsk′) Sov. Un.	53·25 N	41·35 E
156	Mofs (I.) . . . . Den.	56·46 N	8·38 E
164	Mortara (môr-tä′rä) . . . . It.	45·13 N	8·47 E
136	Morteros (môr-tĕ′rôs) . . . . Arg.	30·47 S	62·00 W
137	Mortes, Rio das (R.) (rē′-o-däs-mô′r-tĕs) Braz. (Rio de Janeiro In.)	21·04 S	44·29 W
109	Morton Ind. Res. (mŏr′tŭn) . . Mn.	44·35 N	94·48 W
149	Mortsel (môr-sĕl′) Bel. (Brussels In.)	51·10 N	4·28 E
160	Morvan, Mts. du (môr-väN′) . . Fr.	46·45 N	4·00 E
170	Morzhovets (I.) (môr′zhô-vyĕts′) Sov. Un.	66·40 N	42·30 E
166	Mosal'sk (mō-zȧlsk′) . . . . . Sov. Un.	54·27 N	34·57 E
110	Moscow (mŏs′kō) . . . . Id.	46·44 N	116·57 W
	Moscow, see Moskva		
	Moscow Can., see Imeni Moskvy, Kanal		
158	Mosel R. (mō′sĕl) (mô-zĕl) . F.R.G.	49·49 N	7·00 E
110	Moses Lake . . . . Wa.	47·08 N	119·15 W
110	Moses L. (mō′zĕz) . . . . Wa.	47·09 N	119·30 W
218	Moses R. . . . . S. Afr. (Johannesburg & Pretoria In.)	25·17 S	29·04 E
157	Moshchnyy (Is.) (môsh′chnĭ) Sov. Un.	59·56 N	28·07 E
217	Moshi (mō′shē) . . . . Tan.	3·21 S	37·20 E
150	Mosjøen . . . . Nor.	65·50 N	13·10 E
174	Moskva (Moscow) (mŏs-kvä′) Sov. Un. (Moscow In.)	55·45 N	37·37 E
166	Moskva (Oblast) . . . . Sov. Un.	55·38 N	36·48 E
166	Moskva (R.) . . . . Sov. Un.	55·50 N	37·05 E
159	Mosonmagyaróvár . . . . Hung.	47·51 N	17·16 E
127	Mosquitos, Costa de (kôs-tä-dĕ-mŏs-kē′tō) . Nic.	12·05 N	83·49 W
127	Mosquitos, Gulfo de los (G.) (gōō′l-fô-dĕ-lôs-mŏs-kē′tōs) . Pan.	9·17 N	80·59 W
156	Moss (môs) . . . . Nor.	59·29 N	10·39 E
112	Moss Beach (môs bēch) Ca. (San Francisco In.)	37·32 N	122·31 W
212	Mosselbaai (mô′sul bā) . . . . S. Afr.	34·06 S	22·23 E
216	Mossendjo . . . . Con.	2·57 S	12·44 E
148	Mossley (môs′lĭ) . . . . Eng.	53·31 N	2·02 W
135	Mossoró (mō-sô-rōō′) . . . . Braz.	5·13 S	37·14 W
120	Moss Point (môs) . . . . Ms.	30·25 N	88·32 W
158	Most (môst) . . . . Czech.	50·32 N	13·37 E
210	Mostaganem (mŏs′tä-gȧ-nĕm′) Alg.	36·04 N	0·11 E
165	Mostar (môs′tär) . . . . Yugo.	43·20 N	17·51 E
163	Móstoles (môs-tō′lās) Sp. (Madrid In.)	40·19 N	3·52 W
94	Mostoos Hills (mŏs′tōōs) . . . . . Can.	54·50 N	108·45 W
126	Motagua R. (mô-tä′gwä) . . . Guat.	15·29 N	88·39 W
156	Motala (mô-tô′lä) . . . . Swe.	58·34 N	15·00 E
154	Motherwell (mŭdh′ēr-wĕl) . . . Scot.	55·45 N	4·05 W
162	Motril (mô-trēl′) . . . . Sp.	36·44 N	3·32 W
126	Motul (mō-tōō′l) . . . . . . Mex. (In.)	21·07 N	89·14 W
129	Mouchoir Bk. (mōō-shwȧr′) . . . Ba.	21·35 N	70·40 W
129	Mouchoir Passage (Str.) . . . . . . Ba.	21·05 N	71·05 W
161	Moudon . . . . Switz.	46·40 N	6·47 E
214	Moudjéria . . . . Mauritania	17·53 N	12·20 W
216	Mouila . . . . Gabon	1·52 S	11·01 E
212	Mouille Pt. . . . . S. Afr. (In.)	33·54 S	18·19 E
160	Moulins (mōō-lăN′) . . . . Fr.	46·34 N	3·19 E
196	Moulmein (mōl-mān′) . . . . Bur.	16·30 N	97·39 E
152	Moulouya, Oued (R.) (mōō-lōō′yȧ) Mor.	34·07 N	3·27 W
120	Moultrie (mōl′trĭ) . . . . Ga.	31·10 N	83·48 W
121	Moultrie (Dam) . . . . SC	33·12 N	80·00 W
117	Mound City (mound) . . . . Il.	37·06 N	89·13 W
117	Mound City . . . . Mo.	40·08 N	95·13 W
104	Mound City Group Natl. Mon. Oh.	39·25 N	83·00 W
215	Moundon . . . . Chad	8·34 N	16·05 E
104	Moundsville (moundz′vĭl) . . . . WV	39·50 N	80·50 W
161	Mounier, Mt. (mōō-nyā′) . . . . . . Fr.	44·10 N	6·59 E
214	Mount, C. . . . . Lib.	6·47 N	11·20 W
106	Mountain Brook (moun′tĭn brŏŏk) Al. (Birmingham In.)	33·30 N	86·45 W
113	Mountain Creek L. Tx. (Dallas, Fort Worth In.)	32·43 N	97·03 W
117	Mountain Grove (grōv) . . . . . . Mo.	37·07 N	92·16 W
110	Mountain Home (hōm) . . . . Id.	43·08 N	115·43 W
93	Mountain Park (pärk) . . . . Can.	52·55 N	117·14 W
112	Mountain View (moun′tĭn vū) Ca. (San Francisco In.)	37·25 N	122·07 W
117	Mountain View . . . . Mo.	36·59 N	91·46 W
121	Mount Airy (âr′ĭ) . . . . NC	36·28 N	80·37 W
	Mount Athos (Reg.), see Áyion Óros		
213	Mount Ayliff (ā′lĭf) S. Afr. (Natal In.)	30·48 S	29·24 E
109	Mount Ayr (âr) . . . . Ia.	40·43 N	94·06 W
104	Mount Carmel (kär′mĕl) . . . . Il.	38·25 N	87·45 W
105	Mount Carmel . . . . Pa.	40·50 N	76·25 W
109	Mount Carroll . . . . Il.	42·05 N	89·55 W
107	Mount Clemens (klĕm′ĕnz) Mi. (Detroit In.)	42·36 N	82·52 W
98	Mount Desert (I.) (dē-zûrt′) . . Me.	44·15 N	68·08 W
121	Mount Dora (dō′rȧ) . . . . . . Fl. (In.)	28·45 N	81·38 W
202	Mount Duneed Austl. (Melbourne In.)	38·15 S	144·20 E
202	Mount Eliza Austl. (Melbourne In.)	38·11 S	145·05 E
108	Mountevideo (mōn′tȧ-vē-dhā′ō) Mn.	44·56 N	95·42 W
213	Mount Fletcher (flĕ′chēr) S. Afr. (Natal In.)	30·42 S	28·32 E
104	Mount Forest (fŏr′ĕst) . . . . Can.	44·00 N	80·45 W
213	Mount Frere (frâr′) S. Afr. (Natal In.)	30·54 S	29·02 E
203	Mount Gambier (găm′bēr) . . Austl.	37·30 S	140·53 E
104	Mount Gilead (gĭl′ēăd) . . . . Oh.	40·30 N	82·50 W
107	Mount Healthy (hĕlth′ē) Oh. (Cincinnati In.)	39·14 N	84·32 W
106	Mount Holly (hŏl′ĭ) NJ (Philadelphia In.)	39·59 N	74·47 W
89	Mount Hope . . Can. (Toronto In.)	43·09 N	79·55 W
106	Mount Hope (hōp) NJ (New York In.)	40·55 N	74·32 W
104	Mount Hope . . . . WV	37·55 N	81·10 W
204	Mount Isa (ī′zȧ) . . . . Austl.	21·00 S	139·45 E
106	Mount Kisco (kĭs′ko) NY (New York In.)	41·12 N	73·44 W
112	Mountlake Terrace (mount lāk tĕr′ĭs) Wa. (Seattle In.)	47·48 N	122·19 W
107	Mount Lebanon (lĕb′ȧ-nŭn) Pa. (Pittsburgh In.)	40·22 N	80·03 W
101	Mount McKinley Natl. Park (mȧ-kĭn′lĭ) . Ak.	63·48 N	153·02 W
204	Mount Magnet (măg-nĕt) . . Austl.	28·00 S	118·00 E
202	Mount Martha Austl. (Melbourne In.)	38·17 S	145·01 E
205	Mount Morgan (môr-găn) . . Austl.	23·42 S	150·45 E
202	Mount Moriac Austl. (Melbourne In.)	38·13 S	144·12 E
104	Mount Morris (mŏr′ĭs) . . . . Mi.	43·10 N	83·45 W
105	Mount Morris . . . . NY	42·45 N	77·50 W
214	Mt. Nimba Natl. Pk. Gui.-Ivory Coast	7·35 N	8·10 W
121	Mount Olive (ŏl′ĭv) . . . . NC	35·11 N	78·05 W
115	Mount Peale . . . . Ut.	38·26 N	109·16 W
109	Mount Pleasant (plĕz′ănt) . . . . . Ia.	40·59 N	91·34 W
104	Mount Pleasant . . . . Mi.	43·35 N	84·45 W
121	Mount Pleasant . . . . SC	32·46 N	79·51 W
120	Mount Pleasant . . . . Tn.	35·31 N	87·12 W
117	Mount Pleasant . . . . Tx.	33·10 N	94·56 W
115	Mount Pleasant . . . . Ut.	39·35 N	111·20 W
107	Mount Prospect (prŏs′pĕkt) Il. (Chicago In.)	42·03 N	87·56 W
110	Mount Rainier Natl. Park (rȧ-nēr′) . Wa.	46·47 N	121·17 W
90	Mount Revelstoke Natl. Park. (rĕv′ĕl-stōk) . Can.	51·22 N	120·15 W
105	Mount Savage (săv′âj) . . . . Md.	39·45 N	78·55 W
110	Mount Shasta (shăs′tȧ) . . . . Ca.	41·18 N	122·17 W
117	Mount Sterling (stûr′lĭng) . . . . . Ill.	39·59 N	90·44 W
104	Mount Sterling . . . . Ky.	38·05 N	84·00 W
109	Mount Stewart (stū′ărt) . . . . . Can.	46·22 N	62·52 W
105	Mount Union (ūn′yŭn) . . . . Pa.	40·25 N	77·50 W
104	Mount Vernon (vûr′nŭn) . . . . . . Il.	38·20 N	88·50 W
104	Mount Vernon . . . . In.	37·55 N	87·50 W
117	Mount Vernon . . . . Mo.	37·09 N	93·48 W
106	Mount Vernon NY (New York In.)	40·55 N	73·51 W
104	Mount Vernon . . . . Oh.	40·25 N	82·30 W
106	Mount Vernon Va. (Baltimore In.)	38·43 N	77·06 W
112	Mount Vernon . . . Wa. (Seattle In.)	48·25 N	122·20 W
135	Moura (mō′rȧ) . . . . Braz.	1·33 S	61·38 W
162	Moura . . . . Port.	38·08 N	7·28 W
160	Mourenx (mōō-rän) . . . . Fr.	43·24 N	0·40 W
154	Mourne, Mts. (môrn) . . . . . . N. Ire.	54·10 N	6·09 W
215	Moussoro . . . . Chad	13·39 N	16·29 E
161	Moûtiers (mōō-tyâr′) . . . . Fr.	45·31 N	6·34 E
203	Mowbullan, Mt. (mō′bōō-lăn) Austl.	26·50 S	151·34 E
124	Moyahua (mô-yä′wä) . . . . Mex.	21·16 N	103·10 W
211	Moyale (mô-yä′lä) . . . . Ken.	3·28 N	39·04 E
214	Moyamba (mô-yäm′bä) . . . . . S. L.	8·10 N	12·26 W
152	Moyen Atlas (Mts.) . . . . Mor.	32·49 N	5·28 W
161	Moyeuvre Grande . . . . Fr.	49·15 N	6·26 E
110	Moyie R. (moi′yē) . . . . Id.	48·50 N	116·10 W
134	Moyobamba (mō-yô-bäm′bä) Peru	6·12 S	76·56 W
126	Moyuta (mô-ē-ōō′tä) . . . . Guat.	14·01 N	90·05 W
173	Moyyero (R.) . . . . Sov. Un.	67·15 N	104·10 E
209	Mozambique (mō-zăm-bēk′) . . Afr.	20·15 S	33·53 E
213	Mozambique Chan. (mō-zăm-bek′) Afr.	24·00 S	38·00 E
171	Mozdok (môz-dôk′) . . . . . . Sov. Un.	43·45 N	44·35 E
166	Mozhaysh (mô-zhäysh′) . Sov. Un.	55·31 N	36·02 E
174	Mozhayskiy (mô-zhȧy′skĭ) Sov. Un. (Leningrad In.)	59·42 N	30·08 E
167	Mozyr' (mô-zür′) . . . . Sov. Un.	52·03 N	29·14 E
217	Mpanda . . . . Tan.	6·22 S	31·02 E
217	Mpika . . . . Zambia	11·54 S	31·26 E
217	Mpimbe . . . . Malawi	15·18 S	35·04 E
217	Mporokoso ('m-pō-rô-kō′sō) Zambia	9·23 S	30·05 E
217	Mpwapwa ('m-pwä′pwä) . . . . . Tan.	6·21 S	36·29 E
213	Mqanduli ('m-kän′dōō-lē) S. Afr. (Natal In.)	31·50 S	28·42 E
159	Mragowo (mräŋ′gô-vô) . . . . Pol.	53·52 N	21·18 E
210	M'sila (m′sē′lȧ) . . . . Alg.	35·47 N	4·34 E
166	Msta (R.) (m′stȧ′) . . . . . . Sov. Un.	58·33 N	32·08 E
166	Mstislavl' (m′stē-slävl′) . . Sov. Un.	54·01 N	31·42 E
217	Mtakataka . . . . Malawi	14·12 S	34·32 E
213	Mtamvuna (R.) . S. Afr. (Natal In.)	30·43 S	29·53 E
213	Mtata (R.) . . S. Afr. (Natal In.)	31·48 S	29·03 E
166	Mtsensk (m′tsĕnsk) . . . . . . Sov. Un.	53·17 N	36·33 E
217	Mtwara . . . . Tan.	10·16 S	40·11 E
196	Muang Khon Kaen . . . . Thai.	16·37 N	102·41 E
196	Muang Lamphum . . . . Thai.	18·40 N	98·59 E
183	Muar (R.) . . Mala. (Singapore In.)	2·18 N	102·43 E
217	Mubende . . . . Ug.	0·35 N	31·23 E
215	Mubi . . . . Nig.	10·18 N	13·20 E
217	Mucacata . . . . Moz.	13·20 S	39·59 E
161	Much (mōōK) . . F.R.G. (Ruhr In.)	50·54 N	7·24 E
217	Muchinga Mts. . . . . Zambia	12·40 S	30·50 E
148	Much Wenlock (mŭch wĕn′lŏk) Eng.	52·35 N	2·33 W
120	Muckalee Cr. (mŭk′ă lē) . . . . . . Ga.	31·55 N	84·10 W
112	Muckleshoot Ind. Res. (mŭck′′l-shōōt) . Wa. (Seattle In.)	47·21 N	122·04 W
217	Mucubela . . . . Moz.	16·55 S	37·52 E
135	Mucugê (mōō-kōō-zhĕ′) . . . . . Braz.	13·02 S	41·19 W
109	Mud (L.) (mŭd) . . . . Mi.	46·12 N	84·32 W
114	Mud (L.) . . . . Nv.	40·28 N	119·11 W
192	Mudan (R.) (mōō-dän) . . . . . China	45·30 N	129·40 E
192	Mudanjiang (mōō-dän-jyäŋ) China	44·28 N	129·38 E
114	Muddy (R.) (mŭd′ĭ) . . . . Nv.	36·56 N	114·42 W
117	Muddy Boggy Cr. (mud′ĭ bôg′ĭ) Ok.	34·42 N	96·11 W
115	Muddy Cr. (mŭd′ĭ) . . . . Ut.	38·45 N	111·10 W
203	Mudgee (mŭ-jē) . . . . Austl.	32·47 S	149·10 E
94	Mudjatik (R.) . . . . Can.	56·23 N	107·40 W
217	Mufulira . . . . Zambia	12·33 S	28·14 E
162	Mugía (mōō-kē′ä) . . . . Sp.	43·05 N	9·14 W
171	Muğla (mōōg′lä) . . . . Tur.	37·10 N	28·20 E
158	Mühldorf (mül-dôrf) . . . . F.R.G.	48·15 N	12·33 E
158	Mühlhausen (mül′hou-zĕn) G.D.R.	51·13 N	10·25 E
157	Muhu (I.) (mōō′hōō) . . . . Sov. Un.	58·41 N	22·55 E
193	Mui Ron, C. . . . . Viet.	18·05 N	106·45 E
114	Muir Woods Natl. Mon (mūr) . Ca.	37·54 N	123·22 W
212	Muizenberg (mwĭz-ĕn-bûrg′) S. Afr. (In.)	34·07 S	18·28 E
159	Mukachëvo (mŏŏ-kȧ-chyô′vô) Sov. Un.	48·25 N	22·43 E
173	Mukhtuya (mŏŏk-tōō′yȧ) Sov. Un.	61·00 N	113·00 E
112	Mukilteo (mū-kĭl-tā′ō) Wa. (Seattle In.)	47·57 N	122·18 W
195	Muko (mōō′kô) . Jap. (Ōsaka In.)	34·57 N	135·43 E
195	Muko (R.) (mōō′kô) Jap. (Ōsaka In.)	34·52 N	135·17 E
95	Mukutawa (R.) . . . . Can.	53·10 N	97·28 W
107	Mukwonago (mū-kwō-nȧ′gō) Wi. (Milwaukee In.)	42·52 N	88·19 W
162	Mula (mōō′lä) . . . . Sp.	38·05 N	1·12 W
158	Mulde R. (mŏŏl′dĕ) . . . . . . G.D.R.	50·30 N	12·30 E
124	Muleros (mōō-lā′rōs) . . . . Mex.	23·44 N	104·00 W
116	Muleshoe . . . . Tx.	34·13 N	102·43 W
106	Mulga (mŭl′gȧ) Al. (Birmingham In.)	33·33 N	86·59 W
99	Mulgrave (mŭl′grāv) . . . . Can.	45·37 N	61·23 W
205	Mulgrave (I.) . . . . Austl.	10·08 S	142·14 E
162	Mulhacén (Mtn.) . . . . Sp.	37·04 N	3·18 W
161	Mülheim (mül′hīm) F.R.G. (Ruhr In.)	51·25 N	6·53 E
161	Mulhouse (mü-lōōz′) . . . . Fr.	47·46 N	7·20 E
192	Muling (mōō-lĭŋ) . . . . China	44·32 N	130·18 E

ăt; finăl; rāte; senâte; ärm; ȧsk; sofȧ; fâre; ch-choose; dh-as th in other; bē; êvent; bĕt; recĕnt; cratēr; g-go; gh-guttural g; bĭt; ĭ-short neutral; rīde; K-guttural k as ch in German ich;

PRONOUNCING INDEX Muling — Namp'o 317

Page	Name Pronunciation	Region	Lat. °′	Long. °′
192	Muling (R.)	China	44·40 N	130·30 E
154	Mull (I.) (mŭl)	Scot.	56·40 N	6·19 W
110	Mullan (mŭl'ăn)	Id.	47·26 N	115·50 W
196	Müller, Pegunungan (Mts.) (mül'ĕr)	Indon.	0·22 N	113·05 E
154	Mullet Pen.	Ire.	54·15 N	10·12 W
154	Mullinger (mŭl-ĭn-gär)	Ire.	53·31 N	7·26 W
121	Mullins (mŭl'ĭnz)	SC	34·11 N	79·13 W
126	Mullins River	Belize (In.)	17·08 N	88·18 W
184	Multān (mōō-tän')	Pak.	30·17 N	71·13 E
112	Multnomah Chan. (mŭl nō mȧ)	Or. (Portland In.)	45·41 N	122·53 W
217	Mulumbe, Monts (Mts.)	Zaire	8·47 S	27·20 E
117	Mulvane (mŭl-vān')	Ks.	37·30 N	97·13 W
217	Mumbwa (mōōm'bwä)	Zambia	14·59 S	27·04 E
217	Mumias	Ken.	0·20 N	34·29 E
126	Muna (mōō'nȧ)	Mex. (In.)	20·28 N	89·42 W
149	München (Munich) (mün'kĕn)	F.R.G. (Munich In.)	48·08 N	11·35 E
104	Muncie (mŭn'sĭ)	In.	40·10 N	85·30 W
107	Mundelein (mŭn-dē-lĭn')	Il. (Chicago In.)	42·16 N	88·00 W
134	Mundonueva, Pico de (Pk.) (pē'kô-dĕ-mōō'n-dô-nwĕ'vä)	Col. (In.)	4·18 N	74·12 W
125	Muneco, Cerro (Mtn.) (sĕ'r-rô-mōō-nĕ'kô)	Mex. (In.)	19·13 N	99·20 W
205	Mungana (mŭn-găn'ȧ)	Austl.	17·15 S	144·18 E
217	Mungbere	Zaire	2·38 N	28·30 E
113	Munger (mŭn'gĕr)	Mn. (Duluth In.)	46·48 N	92·20 W
203	Mungindi (mŭn-gĭn'dē)	Austl.	32·00 S	148·45 E
107	Munhall (mŭn'hôl)	Pa. (Pittsburgh In.)	40·24 N	79·53 W
212	Munhango (mōōn-häŋ'gȧ)	Ang.	12·15 S	18·55 E
	Munich, see München			
109	Munising (mū'nĭ-sĭng)	Mi.	46·24 N	86·41 W
172	Munku Sardyk (Mtn.) (mōōn'kōō sär-dĭk')	Sov. Un.-Mong.	51·45 N	100·30 E
197	Muñoz (mōōn-nyōth')	Phil. (In.)	15·44 N	120·53 E
161	Münster (mün'stĕr)	F.R.G. (Ruhr In.)	51·57 N	7·38 E
107	Munster (mŭn'stĕr)	In. (Chicago In.)	41·34 N	87·31 W
154	Munster (mŭn-stĕr)	Ire.	52·30 N	9·24 W
196	Muntok (mōōn-tŏk')	Indon.	2·05 S	105·11 E
137	Munzi Freire (mōō-nē'z-frā'rĕ)	Braz. (Rio de Janeiro In.)	20·29 S	41·25 W
196	Muong Sing (mōō'ông-sĭng')	Laos	21·06 N	101·17 E
150	Muonio (R.)	Fin.-Swe.	68·15 N	23·00 E
190	Muping (mōō-pĭŋ)	China	37·23 N	121·36 E
137	Muqui (mōō-kōōē)	Braz. (Rio de Janeiro In.)	20·56 S	41·20 W
171	Muradiye (mōō-rä'dē-yĕ)	Tur.	39·00 N	43·40 E
160	Murat (mü-rä')	Fr.	45·05 N	2·56 E
171	Murat (R.) (mōō-rät')	Tur.	38·50 N	40·40 E
204	Murchison (R.) (mûr'chĭ-sŭn)	Austl.	26·45 S	116·15 E
217	Murchison Falls (mûr'chĭ-sŭn)	Ug.	2·15 N	31·41 E
162	Murcia (mōōr'thyä)	Sp.	38·00 N	1·10 W
162	Murcia (Reg.)	Sp.	38·35 N	1·51 W
108	Murdo (mûr'dô)	SD	43·53 N	100·42 W
159	Mureşul R. (mōō'rĕsh-ōōl)	Rom.	46·02 N	21·50 E
160	Muret (mü-rĕ')	Fr.	43·28 N	1·17 E
120	Murfreesboro (mûr'frēz-bŭr-ô)	Tn.	35·50 N	86·19 W
141	Murgab (R.) (mōōr-gäb')	Sov. Un.	37·07 N	62·32 E
137	Muriaé (mōō-ryȧ-ĕ')	Braz. (Rio de Janeiro In.)	21·10 S	42·21 W
137	Muriaé (R.)	Braz. (Rio de Janeiro In.)	21·20 S	41·40 W
174	Murino (mōō'rĭ-nō)	Sov. Un. (Leningrad In.)	60·03 N	30·28 E
158	Müritz See (L.) (mür'ĭts)	G.D.R.	53·20 N	12·33 E
188	Murku Sardyk (Pk.)	Sov. Un.-Mong.	51·56 N	100·21 E
170	Murmansk (mōōr-mänsk')	Sov. Un.	69·00 N	33·20 E
170	Murom (mōō'rôm)	Sov. Un.	55·30 N	42·00 E
194	Muroran (mōō'rô-rän)	Jap.	42·21 N	141·05 E
162	Muros (mōō'rōs)	Sp.	42·48 N	9·00 W
195	Muroto-Zaki (Pt.) (mōō'rô-tō zä'kē)	Jap.	33·14 N	134·12 E
113	Murphy (mŭr'fĭ)	Mo. (St. Louis In.)	38·29 N	90·29 W
120	Murphy	NC	35·05 N	84·00 W
117	Murphysboro (mŭr'fĭz-bŭr-ô)	Il.	37·46 N	89·21 W
120	Murray (mŭr'ĭ)	Ky.	36·39 N	88·17 W
113	Murray	Ut. (Salt Lake City In.)	40·40 N	111·53 W
93	Murray (R.)	Can.	55·00 N	121·00 W
121	Murray (R.) (mŭr'ĭ)	SC	34·07 N	81·18 W
203	Murray Bridge	Austl.	35·10 S	139·35 E
98	Murray Harbour	Can.	46·00 N	62·31 W
205	Murray Reg. (mŭ'rē)	Austl.	33·20 S	142·30 E
203	Murray R.	Austl.	34·20 S	142·21 W
158	Mur R. (mōōr)	Aus.	47·10 N	14·08 E
203	Murrumbidgee (R.) (mŭr-ŭm-bĭd'jē)	Austl.	34·30 S	145·20 E
217	Murrupula	Moz.	15·27 S	38·47 E
184	Murshidābād (mōōr'shē-dä-bäd')	India	24·08 N	87·11 E
164	Murska Sobota (mōōr'skä sô'bô-tä)	Yugo.	46·40 N	16·14 E
217	Muruasigar (Mtn.)	Ken.	3·08 N	35·02 E
184	Murwāra	India	23·54 N	80·23 E
203	Murwillumbah (mŭr-wĭl'lŭm-bŭ)	Austl.	28·15 S	153·30 E
158	Mürz R. (mürts)	Aus.	47·30 N	15·21 E
158	Murzzuschlag (mürts'tsōō-shlägh)	Aus.	47·37 N	15·41 E
171	Mus (mōōsh)	Tur.	38·55 N	41·30 E
165	Musala (Mtn.)	Bul.	42·05 N	23·24 E
194	Musan (mōō'sän)	Kor.	41·11 N	129·10 E
195	Musashino (mōō-sä'shē-nō)	Jap. (Tōkyō In.)	35·43 N	139·35 E
186	Muscat (mŭs-kăt')	Om.	23·23 N	58·30 E
	Muscat & Oman, see Oman			
109	Muscatine (mŭs-kȧ-tēn')	Ia.	41·26 N	91·00 W
120	Muscle Shoals (mŭs''l shōlz)	Al.	34·44 N	87·38 W
204	Musgrave Ra. (mŭs'grāv)	Austl.	26·15 S	131·15 E
212	Mushie (mŭsh'ē)	Zaire	3·04 S	16·50 E
215	Mushin	Nig.	6·32 N	3·22 E
196	Musi (Strm.) (mōō'sē)	Indon.	2·40 S	103·42 E
134	Musinga, Alto (Ht.) (ȧ'l-tô-mōō-sē'n-gä)	Col. (In.)	6·40 N	76·13 W
107	Muskego L. (mŭs-kē'gō)	Wi. (Milwaukee In.)	42·53 N	88·10 W
104	Muskegon (mŭs-kē'gŭn)	Mi.	43·15 N	86·20 W
104	Muskegon (R.)	Mi.	43·20 N	85·55 W
104	Muskegon Heights	Mi.	43·10 N	86·20 W
104	Muskingum (R.) (mŭs-kĭŋ'gŭm)	Oh.	39·45 N	81·55 W
117	Muskogee (mŭs-kō'gē)	Ok.	35·44 N	95·21 W
105	Muskoka (L.) (mŭs-kō'kȧ)	Can.	45·00 N	79·30 W
217	Musoma	Tan.	1·30 S	33·48 E
197	Mussau I. (mōō-sä'ōō)	Pap. N. Gui.	1·30 S	149·32 E
154	Musselburgh (mŭs''l-bŭr-ô)	Scot.	55·55 N	3·08 W
111	Musselshell R. (mŭs''l-shĕl)	Mt.	46·25 N	108·20 W
216	Mussende	Ang.	10·32 S	16·05 E
216	Mussuma	Ang.	14·14 S	21·59 E
171	Mustafakemalpasa	Tur.	40·05 N	28·30 E
119	Mustang Bayou	Tx. (In.)	29·22 N	95·12 W
116	Mustang Cr. (mŭs'tăng)	Tx.	36·22 N	102·46 W
119	Mustang I.	Tx.	27·43 N	97·00 W
127	Mustique I. (müs-tēk')	St. Vincent (In.)	12·53 N	61·03 W
166	Mustvee (mōōst'vĕ-ĕ)	Sov. Un.	58·50 N	26·54 E
189	Musu Dan (C.) (mōō'sōō dän)	Kor.	40·51 N	130·00 E
194	Musu Dan (Pt.) (mōō'sōō dän)	Kor.	40·48 N	129·50 E
203	Muswellbrook (mŭs'wŭl-brōōk)	Austl.	32·15 S	150·50 E
212	Mutombo Mukulu (mōō-tôm'bō mōō-kōō'lōō)	Zaire	8·12 S	23·56 E
194	Mutsu Wan (B.) (mōōt'sōō wän)	Jap.	41·20 N	140·55 E
99	Mutton Bay (mŭt''n)	Can.	50·48 N	59·02 W
137	Mutum (mōō-tōō'm)	Braz. (Rio de Janeiro In.)	19·48 S	41·24 W
172	Muyun-Kum, Peski (Des.) (mōō-yōōn' kōōm')	Sov. Un.	44·30 N	70·00 E
184	Muzaffargarh	Pak.	30·09 N	71·15 E
184	Muzaffarpur	India	26·13 N	85·20 E
92	Muzon, C.	Ak.	54·41 N	132·44 W
118	Muzquiz (mōōz'kēz)	Mex.	27·53 N	101·31 W
188	Muztagata (Mtn.)	China	38·20 N	75·28 E
217	Mvomero	Tan.	6·20 S	37·25 E
213	Mvoti (R.)	S. Afr. (Natal In.)	29·18 S	30·52 E
217	Mwanza (mwän'zä)	Tan.	2·31 S	32·54 E
217	Mwaya (mwä'yä)	Tan.	9·19 S	33·51 E
217	Mwenga	Zaire	3·02 S	28·26 E
217	Mweru (L.)	Zaire-Zambia	8·50 S	28·50 E
217	Mwingi	Ken.	0·56 S	38·04 E
152	Mya R. (myä')	Alg.	29·26 N	3·15 E
188	Myingyan (myĭng-yŭn')	Bur.	21·37 N	95·26 E
188	Myitkyina (myĭ'chē-nȧ)	Bur.	25·33 N	97·25 E
159	Myjava (mûĕ'yȧ-vä)	Czech.	48·45 N	17·33 E
194	Myohyang San (Mtn.) (myō'hyang)	Kor.	40·00 N	126·12 E
150	Mýrdalsjökull (Gl.) (mür'däls-yû'kōōl)	Ice.	63·34 N	18·04 W
121	Myrtle Beach (mûr't'l)	SC	33·42 N	78·53 W
110	Myrtle Point	Or.	43·04 N	124·08 W
166	Myshkino (mêsh'kē-nô)	Sov. Un.	57·48 N	38·21 E
185	Mysore (mī-sōr')	India	12·31 N	76·42 E
157	Mysovka (mē' sôf-kȧ)	Sov. Un.	55·11 N	21·17 E
109	Mystic (mĭs'tĭk)	Ia.	40·47 N	92·54 W
174	Mytishchi (mê-tēsh'chi)	Sov. Un. (Moscow In.)	55·55 N	37·46 E
217	Mziha	Tan.	5·54 S	37·47 E
217	Mzimba ('m-zĭm'bä)	Malawi	11·52 S	33·34 E
213	Mzimkulu (R.)	S. Afr. (Natal In.)	30·12 S	29·57 E
213	Mzimvubu (R.)	S. Afr. (Natal In.)	31·22 S	29·20 E
217	Mzuzu	Malawi	11·30 S	34·10 E

N

Page	Name Pronunciation	Region	Lat. °′	Long. °′
158	Naab R. (näp)	F.R.G.	49·38 N	12·15 E
149	Naaldwijk	Neth. (Amsterdam In.)	52·00 N	4·11 E
100	Naalehu	Hi.	19·00 N	155·35 W
157	Naantali (nän'tȧ-lē)	Fin.	60·29 N	22·03 E
204	Nabberu (L.) (năb'ĕr-ōō)	Austl.	26·05 S	120·35 E
210	Nabeul (nā-bûl')	Tun.	36·34 N	10·45 E
217	Nabiswera	Ug.	1·28 N	32·16 E
218	Naboomspruit (Johannesburg & Pretoria In.)	S. Afr.	24·32 S	28·43 E
183	Nābulus	Jordan (Palestine In.)	32·13 N	35·16 E
217	Nacala (nă-kȧ'lȧ)	Moz.	14·34 S	40·41 E
126	Nacaome (nä-kä-ō'mȧ)	Hond.	13·32 N	87·28 W
152	Naceur, Bou Mt.	Mor.	33·50 N	3·55 W
193	Na Cham (nä chäm')	Viet.	22·02 N	106·30 E
110	Naches R. (năch'ĕz)	Wa.	46·51 N	121·03 W
158	Náchod (näk'ôt)	Czech.	50·25 N	16·08 E
114	Nacimiento (R.) (nȧ-sĭ-myĕn'tô)	Ca.	35·50 N	121·00 W
119	Nacogdoches (năk'ô-dō'chĕz)	Tx.	31·36 N	94·40 W
118	Nadadores (nä-dä-dō'rās)	Mex.	27·04 N	101·36 W
184	Nadiād	India	22·45 N	72·51 E
123	Nadir	Vir. Is. (U. S. A.) (St. Thomas In.)	18·19 N	64·53 W
165	Nădlac	Rom.	46·09 N	20·52 E
	Nad Nisou, see Jablonec			
	Nad Váhom, see Nové Mesto			
159	Nadvornaya (näd-vōōr'nȧ-yȧ)	Sov. Un.	48·37 N	24·35 E
172	Nadym (R.) (nȧ'dĭm)	Sov. Un.	64·30 N	72·48 E
156	Naestved (nĕst'vĭdh)	Den.	55·14 N	11·46 E
215	Nafada	Nig.	11·08 N	11·20 E
218	Nafishah	Egypt (Suez In.)	30·34 N	32·15 E
187	Nafūd ad Daḩy (Des.)	Sau. Ar.	22·15 N	44·15 E
184	Nag, Co (L.)	China	31·38 N	91·18 E
197	Naga (nä'gä)	Phil. (In.)	13·37 N	123·12 E
195	Naga (I.)	Jap.	32·09 N	130·16 E
195	Nagahama (nä'gä-hä'mä)	Jap.	33·32 N	132·29 E
195	Nagahama	Jap.	35·23 N	136·16 E
188	Nagaland (State)	India	25·47 N	94·15 E
195	Nagano (nä'gä-nô)	Jap.	36·42 N	138·12 E
195	Nagaoka (nä'gȧ-ō'kȧ)	Jap.	37·22 N	138·49 E
195	Nagaoka	Jap. (Ōsaka In.)	34·54 N	135·42 E
185	Nāgappattinam	India	10·48 N	79·51 E
126	Nagarote (nä-gä-rô'tĕ)	Nic.	12·17 N	86·35 W
195	Nagasaki (nä'gȧ-sä'kē)	Jap.	32·48 N	129·53 E
184	Nāgaur	India	27·19 N	73·41 E
174	Nagaybakskiy (nȧ-gȧy-bäk'skĭ)	Sov. Un. (Urals In.)	53·33 N	59·33 E
197	Nagcarlan (näg-kär-län')	Phil. (In.)	14·07 N	121·24 E
185	Nāgercoil	India	8·15 N	77·29 E
171	Nagornokarabakh (Reg.) (nu-gôr'nŭ-kŭ-rŭ-bäk')	Sov. Un.	40·10 N	46·50 E
195	Nagoya (nä'gō'yȧ)	Jap.	35·09 N	136·53 E
184	Nāgpur (näg'pōōr)	India	21·12 N	79·09 E
129	Nagua (nȧ'gwä)	Dom. Rep.	19·20 N	69·40 W
158	Nagykanizsa (nôd'y'kô'nē-shô)	Hung.	46·27 N	17·00 E
159	Nagykōrōs (nôd'y'kŭ-rŭsh)	Hung.	47·02 N	19·46 E
189	Naha (nä'hä)	Jap.	26·02 N	127·43 E
90	Nahanni Natl. Pk.	Can.	62·10 N	125·15 W
99	Nahant (nȧ-hănt)	Ma. (In.)	42·26 N	70·55 W
183	Nahariyya	Isr. (Palestine In.)	33·01 N	35·06 E
171	Nahr al Khābur (R.)	Syr.	35·50 N	41·00 E
163	Nahr-Ouassel (R.) (när-wä-sĕl')	Alg.	35·30 N	1·55 E
136	Nahuel Huapi (L.) (nä'wâl wä'pē)	Arg.	41·00 S	71·30 W
126	Nahuizalco (nä-wē-zäl'kō)	Sal.	13·50 N	89·43 W
197	Naic (nä-ēk)	Phil. (In.)	14·20 N	120·46 E
118	Naica (nä-ē'kä)	Mex.	27·53 N	105·30 W
135	Naiguatá (nī-gwä-tȧ')	Ven. (In.)	10·37 N	66·44 W
135	Naiguata, Pico (Mtn.) (pē'kô)	Ven. (In.)	10·32 N	66·44 W
184	Naihāti	India (In.)	22·54 N	88·25 E
91	Nain (nīn)	Can.	56·29 N	61·52 W
154	Nairn (nârn)	Scot.	57·35 N	3·54 W
217	Nairobi (nī-rō'bē)	Ken.	1·17 S	36·49 E
213	Naivasha (nī-vä'shȧ)	Ken.	0·47 S	36·29 E
186	Najd (Des.)	Sau. Ar.	25·18 N	42·38 E
218	Naj 'Ḩammādī (näg'hä-mä'dē)	Egypt (Nile In.)	26·02 N	32·12 E
194	Najin (nä'jĭn)	Kor.	42·04 N	130·35 E
186	Najran (Des.) (nŭj-rän')	Sau. Ar.	17·29 N	45·30 E
194	Naju (nä'jōō')	Kor.	35·02 N	126·42 E
128	Najusa (R.) (nä-hōō'sä)	Cuba	21·55 N	77·55 W
192	Nakadorishima (I.) (nä'kä'dô'rē-shē'mä)	Jap.	33·00 N	128·20 E
195	Nakatsu (nä'käts-ōō)	Jap.	33·34 N	131·10 E
171	Nakhichevan (nȧ-ĸē-chĕ-vȧn')	Sov. Un.	39·10 N	45·30 E
173	Nakhodka (nŭ-ĸôt'kŭ)	Sov. Un.	43·03 N	133·08 E
196	Nakhon Ratchasima	Thai.	14·56 N	102·14 E
196	Nakhon Sawan	Thai.	15·42 N	100·06 E
196	Nakhon Si Thammarat	Thai.	8·27 N	99·58 E
156	Nakskov (näk'skou)	Den.	54·51 N	11·06 E
159	Nakto nad Notecia (näk'wō näd nō-tĕ'chōɴ)	Pol.	53·10 N	17·35 E
194	Naktong (R.) (näk'tŭng)	Kor.	36·10 N	128·30 E
171	Nal'chik (nȧl-chĕk')	Sov. Un.	43·30 N	43·35 E
162	Nalón (R.) (nä-lōn')	Sp.	43·15 N	5·38 W
210	Nālūt (nä-lōōt')	Libya	31·51 N	10·49 E
186	Namak, Daryacheh-ye (L.)	Iran	34·58 N	51·33 E
109	Namakan (L.) (nă'mȧ-kăn)	Mn.	48·20 N	92·43 W
186	Namakzār-e Shāhdād (L.) (nŭ-mŭk-zär')	Iran	31·00 N	58·30 E
172	Namangan (nȧ-mȧn-gän')	Sov. Un.	41·08 N	71·59 E
89	Namao	Can. (Edmonton In.)	53·43 N	113·30 W
197	Namatanai (nä'mä-tä-nä'ē)	Pap. N. Gui.	3·43 S	152·26 E
115	Nambe Pueblo Ind. Res. (näm'bā pwĕb'lō)	NM	35·52 N	105·39 W
203	Nambour (năm'bōōr)	Austl.	26·48 S	153·00 E
184	Nam Co (L.) (näm tswo)	China	30·30 N	91·10 E
196	Nam-Dinh (näm dēnĸ')	Viet.	20·30 N	106·10 E
217	Nametil	Moz.	15·43 S	39·21 E
194	Namhae (I.) (näm'hī')	Kor.	34·23 N	128·05 E
212	Namib Des. (nä-mēb')	Namibia	18·45 S	12·45 E
209	Namibia	Afr.	19·30 S	16·13 E
203	Namoi (R.) (năm'oi)	Austl.	30·10 S	148·43 E
152	Namous, Oued en (R.) (nȧ-mōōs')	Alg.	31·48 N	00·19 W
110	Nampa (năm'pȧ)	Id.	43·35 N	116·35 W
192	Namp'o	Kor.	38·47 N	125·28 E

ng-sing; ŋ-baŋk; ɴ-nasalized n; nŏd; cŏmmit; ōld; ôbey; ôrder; fōōd; fŏŏt; ou-out; s-soft; sh-dish; th-thin; pūre; ûnite; ûrn; stŭd; circŭs; ü-as "y" in study; '-indeterminate vowel.

318 Nampuecha — Nelson
PRONOUNCING INDEX

Page	Name Pronunciation Region	Lat. °′	Long. °′
217	Nampuecha ... Moz.	13·59 S	40·18 E
217	Nampula ... Moz.	15·07 S	39·15 E
150	Namsos (näm'sôs) ... Nor.	64·28 N	11·14 E
92	Namu ... Can.	51·03 N	127·50 W
217	Namuli, Serra (Mts.) ... Moz.	15·05 S	37·05 E
155	Namur (nà-mür') ... Bel.	50·29 N	4·55 E
212	Namutoni (nä-mōō-tō'nē) Namibia	18·45 S	17·00 E
196	Nan (R.) ... Thai.	18·11 N	100·29 E
125	Nanacamilpa (nä-nä-kä-mē'l-pä) Mex. (In.)	19·30 N	98·33 W
92	Nanaimo (nà-nī'mō) ... Can.	49·10 N	123·56 W
194	Nanam (nä'nän') ... Kor.	41·38 N	129·37 E
195	Nanao (nä'nä-ō) ... Jap.	37·03 N	136·59 E
193	Nan'ao Dao (I.) (nän-ou dou) China	23·30 N	117·30 E
193	Nanchang (nän-chäŋ) ... China	28·38 N	115·48 E
190	Nanchangshan Dao (I.) (nän-chäŋ-shän dou) . China	37·56 N	120·42 E
193	Nancheng ... China	26·50 N	116·40 E
193	Nanchong (nän-chôŋ) ... China	30·45 N	106·05 E
161	Nancy (näN-sē') ... Fr.	48·42 N	6·11 E
106	Nancy Cr. (năn'cē) Ga. (Atlanta In.)	33·51 N	84·25 W
184	Nanda Devi (Mt.) (nän'dä dā'vē) India	30·30 N	80·25 E
184	Nānded ... India	19·13 N	77·21 E
184	Nandurbār ... India	21·29 N	74·13 E
185	Nandyāl ... India	15·54 N	78·09 E
184	Nanga Parbat ... Pak.	35·20 N	74·35 E
184	Nangi ... India (In.)	22·30 N	88·14 E
161	Nangis (näN-zhē') .. Fr. (Paris In.)	48·33 N	3·01 E
190	Nangong (nän-gôŋ) ... China	37·22 N	115·22 E
216	Nangweshi ... Zambia	16·26 S	23·17 E
190	Nanhuangcheng Dao (I.) (nän-hûäŋ-chŭŋ dou) . China	38·22 N	120·54 E
191	Nanhui ..... China (Shanghai In.)	31·03 N	121·45 E
193	Nani Dinh ... Viet.	20·25 N	106·08 E
190	Nani Hu (L.) (nän'yi' hōō) . China	31·12 N	119·05 E
190	Nanjing (nän-jyĭŋ) ... China	32·04 N	118·46 E
190	Nanjuma (R.) (nän-jyōō-mä) China	39·37 N	115·45 E
190	Nanle (nän-lŭ) ... China	36·03 N	115·13 E
193	Nanliu (R.) (nän-lĭō) ... China	22·00 N	109·18 E
193	Nan Ling (Mts.) ... China	25·15 N	111·40 E
204	Nannine (nă-nēn') ... Austl.	26·50 S	118·30 E
193	Nanning (nän'nĭng') ... China	22·56 N	108·10 E
193	Nanpan (R.) (nän-pän) ... China	24·50 N	105·30 E
193	Nanping (nän-pĭŋ) ... China	26·40 N	118·05 E
189	Nansei-shotō (Ryukyu Islands) Jap.	27·30 N	127·00 E
106	Nansemond (năn'sē-mŭnd) Va. (Norfolk In.)	36·46 N	76·32 W
106	Nansemond R. .. Va. (Norfolk In.)	36·50 N	76·34 W
195	Nantai Zan (Mtn.) (nän-täē zän) Jap.	36·47 N	139·28 E
160	Nantes (nänt') ... Fr.	47·13 N	1·37 W
161	Nanteuil-le-Haudouin (näN-tû-lĕ-ō-dwăN') . Fr. (Paris In.)	49·08 N	2·49 E
105	Nanticoke (năn'tĭ-kōk) ... Pa.	41·10 N	76·00 W
190	Nantong (nän-tôŋ) ... China	32·02 N	120·51 E
190	Nantong ... China	32·08 N	121·06 E
105	Nantucket (I.) (năn-tŭk'ĕt) ... Ma.	41·15 N	70·05 W
148	Nantwich (nănt'wĭch) ... Eng.	53·04 N	2·31 W
191	Nanxiang (nän-shyäŋ) China (Shanghai In.)	31·17 N	121·17 E
193	Nanxiong (nän-shôŋ) ... China	25·10 N	114·20 E
192	Nanyang ... China	33·00 N	112·42 E
190	Nanyang Hu (L.) (nän-yäŋ hōō) China	35·14 N	116·24 E
192	Nanyuan (nän-yûän) .. China (In.)	39·48 N	116·24 E
125	Naolinco (nä-o-lēŋ'kō) ... Mex.	19·39 N	96·50 W
165	Náousa (nä'ōō-sà) ... Grc.	40·38 N	22·05 E
193	Naozhou Dao (I.) (nou-jō dou) China	20·58 N	110·58 E
114	Napa (năp'à) ... Ca.	38·20 N	122·17 W
105	Napanee (năp'à-nē) ... Can.	44·15 N	77·00 W
107	Naperville (nā'pēr-vĭl) Il. (Chicago In.)	41·46 N	88·09 W
205	Napier (nā'pĭ-ēr) ... N. Z. (In.)	39·30 S	177·00 E
89	Napierville (nā'pī-ēr-vĭl) Can. (Montreal In.)	45·11 N	73·24 W
121	Naples (nă'p'lz) ... Fl. (In.)	26·07 N	81·46 W
	Naples, see Napoli		
134	Napo (R.) (nä'pō) ... Peru	1·49 S	74·20 W
104	Napoleon (nā-pō'lē-ŭn) ... Oh.	41·20 N	84·10 W
119	Napoleonville (nā-pō'lē-ŭn-vĭl) . La.	29·56 N	91·03 W
163	Napoli (Naples) (nä'pô-lē) It. (Naples In.)	40·37 N	14·12 E
163	Napoli, Golfo di (G.) (gôl-fô-dē) . It. (Naples In.)	40·29 N	14·08 E
104	Nappanee (năp'à-nē) ... In.	41·30 N	86·00 W
195	Nara (nä'rä) ..... Jap. (Ōsaka In.)	34·41 N	135·50 E
210	Nara ... Mali	15·09 N	7·27 W
195	Nara (Pref.) ..... Jap. (Ōsaka In.)	34·36 N	135·49 E
166	Nara (R.) ... Sov. Un.	55·05 N	37·16 E
203	Naracoorte (nà-rà-kōōn'tē) .. Austl.	36·50 S	140·50 E
185	Narasapur ... India	16·32 N	81·43 E
195	Narashino ..... Jap. (Tōkyō In.)	35·41 N	140·01 E
106	Narberth (när'bûrth) Pa. (Philadelphia In.)	40·01 N	75·17 W
160	Narbonne (nàr-bôn') ... Fr.	43·12 N	3·00 E
165	Nardò (när-dô') ... It.	40·11 N	18·02 E
134	Nare (nä'rĕ) ... Col. (In.)	6·12 N	74·37 W
159	Narew R. (nä'rĕf) ... Pol.	52·43 N	21·19 E
184	Narmada (R.) ... India	22·17 N	74·45 E
166	Naroch' (L.) (nä'rôch) ... Sov. Un.	54·51 N	27·00 E
170	Narodnaya, Gora (Mtn.) (nà-rôd'nà-yà) . Sov. Un.	65·10 N	60·10 E
166	Naro Fominsk (nä'rô-fô-mēnsk') Sov. Un.	55·23 N	36·43 E
157	Närpeså (R.) ... Fin.	62·35 N	21·24 E
202	Narrabeen (năr-à-bĭn) Austl. (Sydney In.)	33·44 S	151·18 E
106	Narragansett (năr-ă-găn'sĕt) RI (Providence In.)	41·26 N	71·27 W
105	Narragansett B. ... RI	41·20 N	71·15 W
203	Narrandera (nà-rän-dē'rà) ... Austl.	34·40 S	146·40 E
204	Narrogin (năr'ô-gĭn) ... Austl.	33·00 S	117·15 E
166	Narva (nàr'và) ... Sov. Un.	59·24 N	28·12 E
197	Narvacan (när-vä-kän') . Phil. (In.)	17·27 N	120·29 E
166	Narva Jõesuu (nàr'và ōō-ô-ā'sōō-ōō) . Sov. Un.	59·26 N	28·02 E
150	Narvik (när'vêk) ... Nor.	68·21 N	17·18 E
157	Narvskiy Zaliv (B.) (nàr'vskĭ zä'lĭf) . Sov. Un.	59·35 N	27·25 E
170	Nar'yan-Mar (när'yàn mär') Sov. Un.	67·42 N	53·30 E
203	Naryilco (năr-ĭl'kô) ... Austl.	28·40 S	141·50 E
172	Narym (nä-rēm') ... Sov. Un.	58·47 N	82·05 E
187	Naryn (R.) (nŭ-rĭn') ..... Sov. Un.	41·46 N	73·00 E
148	Naseby (nāz'bĭ) ... Eng.	52·23 N	0·59 W
113	Nashua (năsh'ŭ-à) Mo. (Kansas City In.)	39·18 N	94·34 W
99	Nashua ... NH (In.)	42·47 N	71·23 W
117	Nashville (năsh'vĭl) ... Ar.	33·56 N	93·50 W
120	Nashville ... Ga.	31·12 N	83·15 W
117	Nashville ... Il.	38·21 N	89·42 W
104	Nashville ... Mi.	42·35 N	85·05 W
120	Nashville ... Tn.	36·10 N	86·48 W
109	Nashwauk (năsh'wôk) ... Mn.	47·21 N	93·12 W
165	Našice (nä'shē-tsĕ) ... Yugo.	45·29 N	18·06 E
159	Nasielsk (nä'syĕlsk) ... Pol.	52·35 N	20·50 E
170	Näsijärvi (L.) (nĕ'sē-yĕr'vē) .. Fin.	61·42 N	24·05 E
184	Nāsik (nä'sĭk) ... India	20·02 N	73·49 E
211	Nāşir (nä-zēr') ... Sud.	8·30 N	33·06 E
	Nāşir, Buhayrat, see Nasser, L.		
184	Nasirābād ... Bngl.	24·48 N	90·28 E
184	Nasirabād ... India	26·13 N	74·48 E
91	Naskaupi (R.) (näs'kô-pĭ) ... Can.	53·59 N	61·10 W
216	'Nasondoye ... Zaire	10·22 S	25·06 E
92	Nass (R.) (năs) ... Can.	55·00 N	129·30 W
128	Nassau (năs'ô) ... Ba.	25·05 N	77·20 W
149	Nassenheide (nä'sĕn-hī-dĕ) G.D.R. (Berlin In.)	52·49 N	13·13 E
218	Nasser, L. (Nāşir, Buḩayrat) Egypt (Nile In.)	23·50 N	32·50 E
156	Nässjö (nĕs'shû) ... Swe.	57·39 N	14·39 E
197	Nasugbu (nà-sōōg-bōō') . Phil. (In.)	14·05 N	120·37 E
118	Nasworthy L. (năz'wûr-thē) ... Tx.	31·17 N	100·30 W
127	Natá (nä-tà') ... Pan.	8·20 N	80·30 W
134	Natagaima (nä-tä-gī'mä) . Col. (In.)	3·38 N	75·07 W
135	Natal (nä-täl') ... Braz.	6·00 S	35·13 W
212	Natal (Prov.) (nà-täl') ..... S. Afr.	28·50 S	30·07 E
99	Natashquan (nä-täsh'kwän) .. Can.	50·11 N	61·49 W
99	Natashquan (R.) ... Can.	50·35 N	61·35 W
120	Natchez (năch'ĕz) ... Ms.	1·35 N	91·20 W
119	Natchitoches (năk'ĭ-tŏsh) (nàch-ĭ-tōsh') . La.	31·46 N	93·06 W
99	Natick (nā'tĭk) ... Ma. (In.)	42·17 N	71·21 W
173	National Area (Reg.) .... Sov. Un.	66·30 N	170·30 E
111	National Bison Ra. (Mts.) (năsh'ŭn-ăl bī's'n) . Mt.	47·18 N	113·58 W
114	National City ... Ca. (In.)	32·38 N	117·01 W
214	Natitingou ... Benin	10·19 N	1·22 E
135	Natividade (nä-tē-vē-dä'dĕ) .. Braz.	11·43 S	47·34 W
217	Natron, L. (nā'trŏn) ... Tan.	2·17 S	36·10 E
107	Natrona Hts. (nā'trō nā) Pa. (Pittsburgh In.)	40·38 N	79·43 W
218	Naţrūn, Wādī an. Egypt (Nile In.)	30·33 N	30·12 E
196	Natuna Besar (I.) ... Indon.	4·00 N	106·50 E
115	Natural Bridges Natl. Mon. (năt'û-răl brĭj'ĕs) . Ut.	37·20 N	110·20 W
204	Naturaliste, C. (năt-û-rà-lĭst') Austl.	33·30 S	115·10 E
125	Naucalpan (nä'ōō-käl-pà'n) Mex. (In.)	19·28 N	99·14 W
125	Nauchampatepetl (Mtn.) (näōō-chäm-pä-tĕ'pĕtl) . Mex.	19·32 N	97·09 W
149	Nauen (nou'ĕn) G.D.R. (Berlin In.)	52·36 N	12·53 E
105	Naugatuck (nô'gà-tŭk) ... Ct.	41·25 N	73·05 W
197	Naujan (nä-ōō-hän') .... Phil. (In.)	13·19 N	121·17 E
158	Naumburg (noum'bōōrgh) . G.D.R.	51·10 N	11·50 E
198	Nauru ... Oceania	0·30 S	167·00 E
125	Nautla (nä-ōōt'lä) ... Mex.	20·14 N	96·44 W
118	Nava (nä'vä) ... Mex.	28·25 N	100·44 W
162	Nava, L. de la ... Sp.	42·05 N	4·42 W
162	Nava del Rey (nä-vä dĕl rā'ē) .. Sp.	41·22 N	5·04 W
162	Navahermosa (nä-vä-ĕr-mō'sä) . Sp.	39·39 N	4·28 W
128	Navajas (nä-vä-häs') ... Cuba	22·40 N	81·20 W
115	Navajo Ind. Res. (năv'à-hō) Az.-NM	36·31 N	109·24 W
115	Navajo Natl. Mon. ... Az.	36·43 N	110·39 W
115	Navajo Res. ... NM	36·57 N	107·26 W
163	Navalcarnero (nä-väl'kär-nā'rō) Sp. (Madrid In.)	40·17 N	4·05 W
162	Navalmoral de la Mata (nä-väl'mōräl' dā lä mä'tä) . Sp.	39·53 N	5·32 W
89	Navan (nă'vàn) . Can. (Ottawa In.)	45·25 N	75·26 W
136	Navarino (nà-vä-rē'nô) (I.) .. Chile	55·30 S	68·15 W
162	Navarra (Reg.) (nä-vär'rä) ... Sp.	42·40 N	1·35 W
137	Navarro (nä-và'r-rō) Arg. (Buenos Aires In.)	35·00 S	59·16 W
119	Navasota (năv-à-sō'tà) ... Tx.	30·24 N	96·05 W
119	Navasota R. ... Tx.	31·03 N	96·11 W
129	Navassa (I.) (nä-vàs'à) ... N. A.	18·25 N	75·15 W
162	Navia (R.) (nä-vē'ä) ... Sp.	43·10 N	6·45 W
137	Navidad (nä-vē-dä'd) Chile (Santiago In.)	34·57 S	71·51 W
129	Navidad Bk. (nä-vē-dädh') .... Ba.	20·05 N	69·00 W
137	Navidade do Carangola (nä-vē-dä'dĕ-dô-kà-rän-gô'la) Braz. (Rio de Janeiro In.)	21·04 S	41·58 W
122	Navojoa (nä-vô-kô'ä) ... Mex.	27·00 N	109·40 W
165	Návplion ... Grc.	37·33 N	22·46 E
184	Nawābshāh (nà-wäb'shä) ... Pak.	26·20 N	68·30 E
165	Náxos (I.) (nák'sôs) ... Grc.	37·15 N	25·20 E
122	Nayarit (State) (nä-yä-rēt') .. Mex.	22·00 N	105·15 W
124	Nayarit, Sierra de (Mts.) (sē-ĕ'r-rä-dĕ) . Mex.	23·20 N	105·07 W
214	Naye ... Senegal	14·25 N	12·12 W
108	Naylor (nā'lŏr) Md. (Baltimore In.)	38·43 N	76·46 W
135	Nazaré (nä-zä-rĕ') ... Braz.	13·04 S	38·49 W
162	Nazaré (nä-zä-rā') ... Port.	39·38 N	9·04 W
135	Nazaré da Mata (dä-mä-tä) .. Braz.	7·46 S	35·13 W
118	Nazas (nä'zäs) ... Mex.	25·14 N	104·08 W
118	Nazas, R. ... Mex.	25·08 N	104·20 W
183	Nazerat ... Isr. (Palestine In.)	32·43 N	35·19 E
171	Nazilli (nà-zĭ-lē') ... Tur.	37·40 N	28·10 E
174	Naziya R. (nà-zē'yà) Sov. Un. (Leningrad In.)	59·48 N	31·18 E
92	Nazko (R.) ... Can.	52·35 N	123·10 W
215	Ndali ... Benin	9·51 N	2·43 E
211	Ndélé (n'dā-lā') .... Cen. Afr. Rep.	8·21 N	20·43 E
215	Ndikiniméki ... Cam.	4·46 N	10·50 E
215	Ndjamena (Fort-Lamy) (là-mē') Chad	12·07 N	15·03 E
212	Ndjolé (n'dzhô-lā') ... Gabon	0·15 S	10·45 E
217	Ndola (n'dō'lä) ... Zambia	12·58 S	28·38 E
217	Ndoto Mts. ... Ken.	1·55 N	37·05 E
214	Ndrhamcha, Sebkha de (L.) Mauritania	18·50 N	15·15 W
217	Nduye ... Zaire	1·50 N	29·01 E
154	Neagh Lough (L.) (lŏk nā) .. N. Ire.	54·40 N	6·47 W
183	Néa Páfos. . Cyprus (Palestine In.)	34·46 N	32·27 E
202	Neapean (R.) .. Austl. (Sydney In.)	33·40 S	150·39 E
165	Neápolis (nā-ŏp' ô-lĭs) ... Grc.	36·35 N	23·08 E
164	Neápolis ... Grc. (In.)	35·17 N	25·37 E
101	Near Is. (nēr) ... Ak.	52·20 N	172·40 E
154	Neath (nēth) ... Wales	51·41 N	3·50 W
203	Nebine Cr. (nĕ-bēne') ... Austl.	27·50 S	147·00 E
171	Nebit-Dag (nyĕ-bēt'däg') . Sov. Un.	39·30 N	54·20 E
102	Nebraska (State) (nē-brăs'kà) U. S.	41·45 N	101·30 W
117	Nebraska City ... Ne.	40·40 N	95·50 W
92	Nechako Plat. (nĭ-chă'kō) ... Can.	54·00 N	124·30 W
92	Nechako Ra. ... Can.	53·20 N	124·30 W
92	Nechako Res. ... Can.	53·25 N	125·10 W
92	Nechako (R.) ... Can.	52·45 N	124·55 W
119	Neches R. (nĕch'ĕz) ... Tx.	31·03 N	94·40 W
158	Neckar R. (nĕk'är) ... F.R.G.	49·16 N	9·06 E
136	Necochea (nā-kō-chā'ä) ... Arg.	38·30 S	58·45 W
167	Nedrigaylov (nĕ-drĭ-gī'lôf) . Sov. Un.	50·49 N	33·52 E
99	Needham (nēd'ăm) ..... Ma. (In.)	42·17 N	71·14 W
114	Needles (nē'd'lz) ... Ca.	34·51 N	114·39 W
109	Neenah (nē'nà) ... Wi.	44·10 N	88·30 W
95	Neepawa ... Can.	50·13 N	99·29 W
116	Nee Res. (nēē) ... Co.	38·26 N	102·56 W
155	Neetze (R.) (nē'tzē) ... F.R.G.	53·04 N	11·00 E
195	Negareyama (nă'gä-rà-yä'mä) Jap. (Tōkyō In.)	35·52 N	139·54 E
109	Negaunee (nē-gô'nē) ... Mi.	46·30 N	87·37 W
183	Negeri Sembilan (State) (nā'grē-sĕm-bē-län') Mala. (Singapore In.)	2·46 N	101·54 E
183	Negev (Des.) (nĕ'gĕv) Isr. (Palestine In.)	30·34 N	34·43 E
165	Negoi (Mtn.) (nā-goi') ... Rom.	45·33 N	24·38 E
185	Negombo ... Sri Lanka	7·39 N	79·49 E
165	Negotin (nĕ'gô-tēn) ... Yugo.	44·13 N	22·33 E
136	Negro (R.) ... Arg.	39·50 S	65·00 W
134	Negro, Rio (R.) (rē'ō nā'grōō) Braz.	0·18 S	63·21 W
162	Negro, C. (na'grô) ... Mor.	35·25 N	4·51 W
127	Negro, Cerro (Mt.) (sĕ'r-rô-nā'grô) . Pan.	8·44 N	80·37 W
137	Negro (R.) .. Ur. (Buenos Aires In.)	33·17 S	58·18 W
126	Negro R. ... Nic.	13·01 N	87·10 W
196	Negros (I.) (nā'grôs) ... Phil.	9·50 N	121·45 E
134	Neguá (nā-gwà') ... Col. (In.)	5·51 N	76·36 W
110	Nehalem R. (nē-hăl'ĕm) ... Or.	45·52 N	123·37 W
192	Nehe (nŭ-hŭ) ... China	48·23 N	124·58 E
161	Neheim-Hüsten (nĕ'hīm) F.R.G. (Ruhr In.)	51·28 N	7·58 E
129	Neiba (nâ-ē'bä) ... Dom. Rep.	18·30 N	71·20 W
129	Neiba, Bahai de (B.) (bä-ä'ē-dĕ) Dom. Rep.	18·10 N	71·00 W
129	Neiba, Sierra de (Mts.) (sē-ĕr'rä-dĕ) . Dom. Rep.	18·40 N	71·40 W
111	Neihart (nī'härt) ... Mt.	46·54 N	110·39 W
193	Neijiang (nā-jyäŋ) ... China	29·38 N	105·01 E
109	Neillsville (nēlz'vĭl) ... Wi.	44·35 N	90·37 W
188	Nei Monggol (Inner Mongolia) (Aut. Reg.) (nā-mŭŋ-gol) . China	40·15 N	105·00 E
190	Neiqiu (nā-chyō) ... China	37·17 N	114·32 E
134	Neira (nā'rä) ... Col. (In.)	5·10 N	75·32 W
158	Neisse (R.) (nēs) ... Pol.	51·30 N	15·00 E
134	Neiva (nâ-ē'vä) (nā'vä) .. Col. (In.)	2·55 N	75·16 W
192	Neixiang (nā-shyäŋ) ... China	33·00 N	111·38 E
211	Nekemte ... Eth.	9·09 N	36·29 E
109	Nekoosa (nē-kōō'sà) ... Wi.	44·19 N	89·54 W
156	Neksø (nĕk'sû) ... Den.	55·05 N	15·05 E
108	Neligh (nē'lĭg) ... Ne.	42·06 N	98·02 W
173	Nel'kan (nĕl-kän') ... Sov. Un.	57·45 N	136·36 E
185	Nellore (nĕl-lōr') ... India	14·28 N	79·59 E
194	Nel'ma (nĕl-mä') ... Sov. Un.	47·34 N	139·05 E
93	Nelson (nĕl'sŭn) ... Can.	49·29 N	117·17 W
148	Nelson ... Eng.	53·50 N	2·13 W
205	Nelson ... N. Z. (In.)	41·15 S	173·22 E
101	Nelson (I.) ... Ak.	60·38 N	164·42 W
203	Nelson, C. ... Austl.	38·29 S	141·20 E

ăt; finăl; rāte; senâte; ärm; àsk; sofà; fâre; ch-choose; dh-as th in other; bē; ēvent; bĕt; recĕnt; cratēr; g-go; gh-guttural g; bĭt; ĭ-short neutral; rīde; K-guttural k as ch in German ich;

PRONOUNCING INDEX Nelson — Ngangla Ringco 319

Page	Name Pronunciation Region	Lat. °′	Long. °′
95	Nelson (R.) Can.	56·50 N	93·40 W
114	Nelson Cr. Nv.	40·22 N	114·43 W
104	Nelsonville (nĕl'sŭn-vĭl) Oh.	39·30 N	82·15 W
214	Néma (nā'mä) Mauritania	16·37 N	7·15 W
113	Nemadji R. (nĕ-măd'jē) Wi. (Duluth In.)	46·33 N	92·16 W
157	Neman (ŋĕ'-màn) Sov. Un.	55·02 N	22·01 E
159	Neman R. Sov. Un.	53·28 N	24·45 E
215	Nembe Nig.	4·35 N	6·26 E
94	Nemeiban L. (nĕ-mē'bán) Can.	55·20 N	105·20 W
167	Nemirov (nyå-mē'rôf) Sov. Un.	48·56 N	28·51 E
160	Nemours Fr.	48·16 N	2·41 E
194	Nemuro (nä'mo͞o-rō) Jap.	43·13 N	145·10 E
194	Nemuro Str. Jap.	43·07 N	145·10 E
189	Nen (R.) (nŭn) China	47·07 N	123·28 E
148	Nen (R.) (nĕn) Eng.	52·32 N	0·19 W
154	Nenagh (nē'ná) Ire.	52·50 N	8·05 W
101	Nenana (nå-nä'ná) Ak.	64·28 N	149·18 W
174	Nenikyul' (nĕ-nyē'kyûl) Sov. Un. (Leningrad In.)	59·26 N	30·40 E
192	Nenjiang (nŭn-jyäŋ) China	49·02 N	125·15 E
117	Neodesha (nē-ô-dĕ-shô') Ks.	37·24 N	95·41 W
117	Neosho Mo.	36·51 N	94·22 W
117	Neosho (R.) (nē-ō'shō) Ks.	38·07 N	95·40 W
182	Nepal (nĕ-pôl') Asia	28·45 N	83·00 E
115	Nephi (nē'fī) Ut.	39·40 N	111·50 W
98	Nepisiguit (R.) (nĭ-pĭ'sĭ-kwĭt) Can.	47·25 N	66·28 W
137	Nepomuceno (nĕ-pô-mo͞o-sĕ'no) Braz. (Rio de Janeiro In.)	21·15 S	45·13 W
164	Nera (R.) (nā'rä) It.	42·45 N	12·54 E
160	Nérac (nā-rák') Fr.	44·08 N	0·19 E
173	Nerchinsk (nyĕr' chĕnsk) Sov. Un.	51·47 N	116·17 E
173	Nerchinskiy Khrebet (Mts.) Sov. Un.	50·30 N	118·30 E
173	Nerchinskiy Zavod (nyĕr'chĕn-skĭzå-vôt') Sov. Un.	51·35 N	119·46 E
166	Nerekhta (nyĕ-rĕĸ'tå) Sov. Un.	57·29 N	40·34 E
165	Neretva (R.) (nĕ'rĕt-vå) Yugo.	43·08 N	17·50 E
162	Nerja (nĕr'hä) Sp.	36·45 N	3·53 W
166	Nerl' (R.) (nyĕrl) Sov. Un.	56·59 N	37·57 E
174	Nerskaya R. (nyĕr'skå-yå) Sov. Un. (Moscow In.)	55·31 N	38·46 E
166	Nerussa (R.) (nyå-ro͞o'så) Sov. Un.	52·24 N	34·20 E
154	Ness, Loch (L.) (lŏĸ nĕs) Scot.	57·23 N	4·20 W
116	Ness City (nĕs) Ks.	38·27 N	99·55 W
159	Nesterov (ŋĕs'-tzhyé-rôf) Sov. Un.	50·03 N	23·58 E
157	Nesterov (nyĕs-tă'rôf) Sov. Un.	54·39 N	22·38 E
165	Néstos (R.) (näs'tôs) Grc.	41·25 N	24·12 E
166	Nesvizh (nyĕs'vēsh) Sov. Un.	53·13 N	26·44 E
183	Netanya Isr. (Palestine In.)	32·19 N	34·52 E
106	Netcong (nĕt'cŏnj) NJ (New York In.)	40·54 N	74·42 W
146	Netherlands (nĕdh'ĕr-lăndz) Eur.	53·01 N	3·57 E
	Netherlands Guiana, see Surinam		
91	Nettilling (L.) Can.	66·30 N	70·40 W
109	Nett Lake Ind. Res. (nĕt lāk) Mn.	48·23 N	93·19 W
163	Nettuno (nĕt-to͞o'nô) It. (Rome In.)	41·28 N	12·40 E
161	Neubeckum (noi'bĕ-ko͞om) F.R.G. (Ruhr In.)	51·48 N	8·01 E
158	Neubrandenburg (noi-brän'dĕn-bo͝orgh) G.D.R.	53·33 N	13·16 E
158	Neuburg (noi'bo͝orgh) F.R.G.	48·43 N	11·12 E
158	Neuchâtel (nû-shá-tĕl') Switz.	47·00 N	6·52 E
158	Neuchatel, Lac de (L.) Switz.	46·48 N	6·53 E
149	Neuenhagen (noi'ĕn-hä-gĕn) G.D.R. (Berlin In.)	52·31 N	13·41 E
161	Neuenrade (noi'ĕn-rä-dĕ) F.R.G. (Ruhr In.)	51·17 N	7·47 E
160	Neufchâtel-en-Bray (nû-shä-tĕl'ĕɴ-brā') Fr.	49·43 N	1·25 E
158	Neuhaldensleben (noi-häl'dĕns-lā'bĕn) G.D.R.	52·18 N	11·23 E
149	Neuhaus (Oste) (noi'houz) (ŏz'tĕ) F.R.G. (Hamburg In.)	53·48 N	9·02 E
149	Neulengbach Aus. (Vienna In.)	48·13 N	15·55 E
158	Neumarkt (noi'märkt) F.R.G.	49·17 N	11·30 E
158	Neumünster (noi'münstĕr) F.R.G.	54·04 N	10·00 E
158	Neunkirchen (noin'kĭrĸ-ĕn) Aus.	47·43 N	16·05 E
161	Neunkirchen F.R.G.	49·21 N	7·20 E
136	Neuquén (nĕ-o͞o-kān') Arg.	38·52 S	68·12 W
136	Neuquen (Prov.) Arg.	39·40 S	70·45 W
136	Neuquén (R.) Arg.	38·45 S	69·00 W
149	Neuruppin (noi'ro͞o-pēn) G.D.R. (Berlin In.)	52·55 N	12·48 E
121	Neuse (R.) (nūz) NC	36·12 N	78·50 W
158	Neusiedler See (L.) (noi-zēd'lēr) Aus.	47·54 N	16·31 E
161	Neuss (nois) F.R.G. (Ruhr In.)	51·12 N	6·41 E
158	Neustadt (noi'shtät) F.R.G.	49·21 N	8·08 E
158	Neustadt F.R.G.	54·06 N	10·50 E
158	Neustadt bei Coburg (bī kō'bo͝orgh) F.R.G.	50·20 N	11·09 E
158	Neustrelitz (noi-strā'lĭts) G.D.R.	53·21 N	13·05 E
94	Neutral Hills (nū'trăl) Can.	52·10 N	110·50 W
158	Neu Ulm (noi o͞o lm') F.R.G.	48·23 N	10·01 E
89	Neuville (nū'vĭl) Can. (Quebec In.)	46·39 N	71·35 W
158	Neuwied (noi'vēdt) F.R.G.	50·26 N	7·28 E
174	Neva (R.) (nyĕ-vä') Sov. Un. (Leningrad In.)	59·49 N	30·54 E
109	Nevada (nê-vä'dá) Ia.	42·01 N	93·27 W
117	Nevada Mo.	37·49 N	94·21 W
102	Nevada (State) U. S.	39·30 N	117·00 W
162	Nevada, Sierra (Mts.) (syĕr'rä nā-vä'dhä) Sp.	37·01 N	3·28 W
102	Nevada, Sierra (Mts.) (sē-ĕ'r-rä nĕ-vä'dá) U. S.	39·20 N	120·25 W
114	Nevada City Ca.	39·16 N	120·01 W
134	Nevado, Cerro el (Mtn.) (sĕ'r-rō-ĕl-nĕ-vä'dō) Col. (In.)	4·02 N	74·08 W
124	Nevado de Colima (Mtn.) (nå-vä'dhō dä kô-lē'mä) Mex.	19·34 N	103·39 W
154	Neva Stantsiya (nyĕ-vä' stän'tsĭ-yå) Sov. Un. (Leningrad In.)	59·53 N	30·30 E
216	Neve, Serra da (Mts.) Ang.	13·40 S	13·20 E
166	Nevel' (nyĕ'vĕl) Sov. Un.	56·03 N	29·57 E
135	Neveri (nĕ-vĕ-rē) (R.) Ven. (In.)	10·13 N	64·18 W
160	Nevers (nē-vâr') Fr.	46·59 N	3·10 E
165	Nevesinje (nĕ-vĕ'sĕn-yĕ) Yugo.	43·15 N	18·08 E
154	Nevis, Ben (Mtn.) (bĕn) Scot.	56·47 N	5·00 W
127	Nevis I. (nē'vĭs) St. Kitts-Nevis-Anguilla (In.)	17·05 N	62·38 W
127	Nevis Pk. St. Kitts-Nevis-Anguilla (In.)	17·11 N	62·33 W
165	Nevrokop (nĕv'rō-kôp') Bul.	41·35 N	23·46 E
171	Nevşehir (nĕv-shĕ'hĕr) Tur.	38·40 N	34·35 E
174	Nev'yansk (nĕv-yänsk') Sov. Un. (Urals In.)	57·29 N	60·14 E
121	New (R.) (nū) Va.	37·20 N	80·35 W
217	Newala Tan.	10·56 S	39·18 E
107	New Albany (nū ôl'bá-nĭ) In. (Louisville In.)	38·17 N	85·49 W
120	New Albany Ms.	34·28 N	39·00 W
135	New Amsterdam (ăm'stĕr-dăm) Guy.	6·14 N	57·30 W
220	New Amsterdam (I.) Ind. O.	37·52 S	77·32 E
112	Newark (nū'ērk) Ca. (San Francisco In.)	37·32 N	122·02 W
105	Newark (no͞o'ärk) De.	39·40 N	75·45 W
148	Newark (nū'ērk) Eng.	53·04 N	0·49 W
106	Newark (no͞o'ûrk) NJ (New York In.)	40·44 N	74·10 W
105	Newark (nū'ērk) NY	43·05 N	77·10 W
104	Newark Oh.	40·05 N	82·25 W
104	Newaygo (nū'wā-go) Mi.	43·25 N	85·50 W
105	New Bedford (bĕd'fērd) Ma.	41·35 N	70·55 W
104	Newberg (nū'bûrg) Or.	45·17 N	122·58 W
121	New Bern (bûrn) NC	35·05 N	77·05 W
120	Newbern Tn.	36·05 N	89·12 W
109	Newberry (nū'bĕr-ĭ) Mi.	46·22 N	85·31 W
121	Newberry SC	34·15 N	81·40 W
107	New Boston (bôs'tŭn) Mi. (Detroit In.)	42·10 N	83·24 W
104	New Boston Oh.	38·45 N	82·55 W
118	New Braunfels (nū broun'fĕls) Tx.	29·43 N	98·07 W
113	New Brighton (brī'tŭn) Mn. (Minneapolis, St. Paul In.)	45·04 N	93·12 W
107	New Brighton Pa. (Pittsburgh In.)	40·34 N	80·18 W
105	New Britain (brĭt''n) Ct.	41·40 N	72·45 W
197	New Britain (I.) Pap. N. Gui.	6·45 S	149·38 E
106	New Brunswick (brŭnz'wĭk) NJ (New York In.)	40·29 N	74·27 W
91	New Brunswick (Prov.) Can.	47·14 N	66·30 W
104	Newburg In.	38·00 N	87·25 W
117	Newburg Mo.	37·54 N	91·53 W
105	Newburgh NY	41·30 N	74·00 W
107	Newburgh Heights Oh. (Cleveland In.)	41·27 N	81·40 W
154	Newbury (nū'bĕr-ĭ) Eng.	51·24 N	1·26 W
99	Newbury Ma. (In.)	42·48 N	70·52 W
99	Newburyport (nū'bĕr-ĭ-pōrt) Ma. (In.)	42·48 N	70·53 W
205	New Caledonia Oceania	21·28 S	164·40 E
106	New Canaan (kā-nán) Ct. (New York In.)	41·06 N	73·30 W
98	New Carlisle (kär-līl') Can.	48·01 N	65·20 W
203	Newcastle (nū-kás''l) Austl.	33·00 S	151·55 E
98	Newcastle Can.	47·00 N	65·34 W
105	New Castle De.	39·40 N	75·35 W
148	Newcastle (nú-kás''l) (nû-käs''l) Eng.	53·01 N	2·14 W
154	Newcastle Eng.	55·00 N	1·45 W
104	New Castle In.	39·55 N	82·25 W
104	New Castle Oh.	40·20 N	82·10 W
104	New Castle Pa.	41·00 N	80·25 W
116	Newcastle Tx.	33·13 N	98·44 W
108	Newcastle Wy.	43·51 N	104·11 W
204	Newcastle Waters (wô'tērz) Austl.	17·10 S	133·25 E
104	Newcomerstown (nū'kŭm-ērz-toun) Oh.	40·15 N	81·40 W
106	New Croton Res. (krŏ'tôn) NY (New York In.)	41·15 N	73·47 W
184	New Delhi (dĕl'hī) India	28·43 N	77·18 E
108	Newell (nū'ĕl) SD	44·43 N	103·26 W
205	New England Ra. (nû ĭŋ'glănd) Austl.	29·32 S	152·30 E
101	Newenham, C. (nū-ĕn-hăm) Ak.	58·40 N	162·32 W
107	Newfane (nū-fān) NY (Buffalo In.)	43·17 N	78·44 W
91	Newfoundland (Prov.) (nū-fŭn-lănd') (nū'fŭnd-lănd) (nû'found-lănd') Can. (Newfoundland In.)	48·15 N	56·53 W
93	Newgate (nū'gāt) Can.	49·01 N	115·10 W
205	New Georgia (I.) (jôr'jĭ-á) Sol. Is.	8·08 S	158·00 E
109	New Glasgow (glás'gō) Can.	45·35 N	62·36 W
197	New Guinea (I.) (gĭne) Asia	5·45 S	140·00 E
110	Newhalem (nū hă'lŭm) Wa.	48·44 N	121·11 W
103	New Hampshire (State) (hămp'shĭr) U. S.	43·55 N	71·40 W
109	New Hampton (hămp'tŭn) Ia.	43·03 N	92·20 W
213	New Hanover (hăn'ôvēr) S. Afr. (Natal In.)	29·23 S	30·32 E
197	New Hanover (I.) Pap. N. Gui.	2·37 S	150·15 E
104	New Harmony (nū här'mô-nĭ) In.	38·10 N	87·55 W
105	New Haven (hā'vĕn) Ct.	41·20 N	72·55 W
155	Newhaven Eng.	50·45 N	0·10 E
104	New Haven (nū hăv''n) In.	41·05 N	85·00 W
205	New Hebrides (hĕb'rĭ-dēz) Oceania	16·02 S	169·15 E
148	New Holland (hŏl'ănd) Eng.	53·42 N	0·21 W
121	New Holland NC	35·27 N	76·14 W
106	New Hope Mtn. (hōp) Al. (Birmingham In.)	33·23 N	86·45 W
107	New Hudson (hŭd'sŭn) Mi. (Detroit In.)	42·30 N	83·36 W
119	New Iberia (ī-bē'rĭ-á) La.	30·00 N	91·50 W
89	Newington (nū'ēŋ-tŏn) Can. (Ottawa In.)	45·07 N	75·00 W
197	New Ireland (I.) (īr'lănd) Pap. N. Gui.	3·15 S	152·30 E
103	New Jersey (State) (jûr'zĭ) U. S.	40·30 N	74·50 W
	New Kensington (kĕn'zĭng-tŭn) Pa. (Pittsburgh In.)	40·34 N	79·35 W
117	Newkirk (nū'kûrk) Ok.	36·52 N	97·03 W
107	New Lenox (lĕn'ŭk) Il. (Chicago In.)	41·31 N	87·58 W
104	New Lexington (lĕk'sĭng-tŭn) Oh.	39·40 N	82·10 W
109	New Lisbon (lĭz'bŭn) Wi.	43·52 N	90·11 W
97	New Liskeard Can.	47·30 N	79·40 W
105	New London (lŭn'dŭn) Ct.	41·20 N	72·05 W
109	New London Wi.	44·24 N	88·45 W
117	New Madrid (măd'rĭd) Mo.	36·34 N	89·31 W
121	Newman (L.) Fl.	29·41 N	82·13 W
108	Newman's Grove (nū'măn grōv) Ne.	41·46 N	97·44 W
105	Newmarket (nū'mär-kĕt) Can.	44·00 N	79·30 W
104	New Martinsville (mär'tĭnz-vĭl) WV	39·35 N	80·50 W
110	New Meadows Id.	44·58 N	116·20 W
102	New Mexico (State) (mĕk'sĭ-kō) U. S.	34·30 N	107·10 W
148	New Mills (mĭlz) Eng.	53·22 N	2·00 W
107	New Munster (mŭn'stēr) Wi. (Milwaukee In.)	42·35 N	88·13 W
120	Newnan (nū'năn) Ga.	33·22 N	84·47 W
203	New Norfolk (nôr'fŏk) Austl.	42·50 S	147·17 E
106	New Orleans (ôr'lē-ănz) La. (New Orleans In.)	30·00 N	90·05 W
104	New Philadelphia (fĭl-á-dĕl'fĭ-á) Oh.	40·30 N	81·30 W
205	New Plymouth (plĭm'ŭth) N. Z. (In.)	39·04 S	174·13 E
117	Newport (nū'pōrt) Ar.	35·35 N	91·16 W
202	Newport Austl. (Sydney In.)	33·39 S	151·19 E
154	Newport (nū-pôrt) Eng.	50·41 N	1·25 W
154	Newport Wales	51·36 N	3·05 W
148	Newport Eng.	52·46 N	2·22 W
107	Newport Ky. (Cincinnati In.)	39·05 N	84·30 W
98	Newport Me.	44·49 N	69·20 W
113	Newport Mn. (Minneapolis, St. Paul In.)	44·52 N	92·59 W
105	Newport NH	43·20 N	72·10 W
110	Newport Or.	44·39 N	124·02 W
106	Newport RI (Providence In.)	41·29 N	71·16 W
120	Newport Tn.	35·55 N	83·12 W
105	Newport Vt.	44·55 N	72·15 W
110	Newport Wa.	48·12 N	117·01 W
113	Newport Beach (bēch) Ca. (Los Angeles In.)	33·36 N	117·55 W
106	Newport News Va. (Norfolk In.)	36·59 N	76·24 W
109	New Prague (nū prāg) Mn.	44·33 N	93·35 W
128	New Providence (I.) (prŏv'ĭ-dĕns) Ba.	25·00 N	77·25 W
104	New Richmond (rĭch'mŭnd) Oh.	38·55 N	84·15 W
109	New Richmond Wi.	45·07 N	92·34 W
119	New Roads (rōds) La.	30·42 N	91·26 W
106	New Rochelle (rū-shĕl') NY (New York In.)	40·55 N	73·47 W
108	New Rockford (rŏk'fērd) ND	47·40 N	99·08 W
158	New Ross (rôs) Ire.	52·25 N	6·55 W
89	New Sarepta Can. (Edmonton In.)	53·17 N	113·09 W
	New Siberian Is., see Novosibirskiye O-va		
121	New Smyrna Beach (smûr'ná) Fl.	29·00 N	80·57 W
205	New South Wales (State) (wālz) Austl.	32·45 S	146·14 E
89	Newton (nū'tŭn) Can. (Winnipeg In.)	49·56 N	98·04 W
148	Newton Eng.	53·27 N	2·37 W
104	Newton Il.	39·00 N	88·10 W
109	Newton Ia.	41·42 N	93·04 W
117	Newton Ks.	38·03 N	97·22 W
99	Newton Ma. (In.)	42·21 N	71·13 W
120	Newton Ms.	32·18 N	89·10 W
106	Newton NJ (New York In.)	41·03 N	74·45 W
121	Newton NC	35·40 N	81·19 W
119	Newton Tx.	30·47 N	93·45 W
107	Newtonsville (nū'tŭnz-vĭl) Oh. (Cincinnati In.)	39·11 N	84·04 W
108	Newtown (nū'toun) ND	47·57 N	102·25 W
107	Newtown Oh. (Cincinnati In.)	39·08 N	84·22 W
106	Newtown Pa. (Philadelphia In.)	40·13 N	74·56 W
154	Newtownards (nu-t'n-ardz') Ire.	54·35 N	5·39 W
109	New Ulm (ŭlm) Mn.	44·18 N	94·27 W
99	New Waterford (wô'tēr-fērd) Can.	46·15 N	60·05 W
112	New Westminster (wĕst'mĭn-stēr) Can. (Vancouver In.)	49·12 N	122·55 W
106	New York (yôrk) NY (New York In.)	40·40 N	73·58 W
103	New York (State) U. S.	42·45 N	78·05 W
205	New Zealand (zē'lănd) Oceania	39·14 S	169·30 E
124	Nexapa (R.) (nĕks-ä'pä) Mex.	18·32 N	98·29 W
195	Neya-gawa (nā'yä gä'wä) Jap. (Ōsaka In.)	34·47 N	135·38 E
186	Neyshābūr Iran	36·06 N	58·45 E
174	Neyva R. (nēy'vá) Sov. Un. (Urals In.)	57·39 N	60·37 E
167	Nezhin (nyĕzh'ēn) Sov. Un.	50·03 N	31·52 E
110	Nez Perce (nĕz' pûrs') Id.	46·16 N	116·15 W
212	Ngami (R.) (n'gä'mē) Bots.	20·56 S	22·31 E
217	Ngangerabeli Pln. Ken.	1·20 S	40·10 E
184	Ngangla Ringco (L.) (ŋäŋ-là rĭŋ-tswo) China	31·42 N	82·53 E

ng-sing; ŋ-baŋk; ɴ-nasalized n; nŏd; cŏmmit; ōld; ôbey; ôrder; fo͞od; fo͝ot; ou-out; s-soft; sh-dish; th-thin; pūre; ûnite; ûrn; stŭd; circŭs; ü-as "y" in study; '-indeterminate vowel.

320 Ngaoundere — Norra Dellen PRONOUNCING INDEX

Page	Name Pronunciation Region	Lat. °′	Long. °′
215	Ngaoundéré (n'gōn-dâ-rā') ... Cam.	7·19 N	13·35 E
217	Ngarimbi ... Tan.	8·28 S	38·36 E
216	Ngoko (R.) ... Afr.	1·55 N	15·53 E
215	Ngol-Kedju Hill ... Cam.	6·20 N	9·45 E
213	Ngong ('n-gông) ... Ken.	1·27 S	36·39 E
216	Ngounié (R.) ... Gabon	1·15 S	10·43 E
217	Ngoywa ... Tan.	5·56 S	32·48 E
213	Ngqeleni ('ng-kĕ-lā'nē) S. Afr. (Natal In.)	31·41 S	29·04 E
215	Nguigmi ('n-gēg'mê) ... Niger	14·15 N	13·07 E
215	Ngurore ... Nig.	9·18 N	12·14 E
210	Nguru ('n-gōō'rōō) ... Nig.	12·53 N	10·26 E
217	Nguru Mts. ... Tan.	6·10 S	37·35 E
196	Nha-trang (nyä-träng') ... Viet.	12·08 N	108·56 E
210	Niafounke ... Mali	16·03 N	4·17 W
109	Niagara (nī-ăg'á-rá) ... Wi.	45·45 N	88·05 W
107	Niagara Falls ... Can. (Buffalo In.)	43·05 N	79·05 W
107	Niagara Falls ... NY (Buffalo In.)	43·06 N	79·02 W
89	Niagara-on-the-Lake Can. (Toronto In.)	43·16 N	79·05 W
107	Niagara R. U. S.-Can. (Buffalo In.)	43·12 N	79·03 W
214	Niakaramandougou ... Ivory Coast	8·40 N	5·17 W
215	Niamey (nē-ä-mâ') ... Niger	13·31 N	2·07 E
214	Niamtougou ... Togo	9·46 N	1·06 E
217	Niangara (nē-äŋ-gá'rà) ... Zaire	3·42 N	27·52 E
117	Niangua (R.) (nī-ăŋ'gwà) ... Mo.	37·30 N	93·05 W
196	Nias, Pulau (I.) (nē'ás') ... Indon.	0·58 N	97·43 E
156	Nibe (nē'bĕ) ... Den.	56·57 N	9·36 E
122	Nicaragua (nĭk-á-rä'gwá) ... N. A.	12·45 N	86·15 W
126	Nicaragua, Lago de (L.) (lä'gô dĕ) Nic.	11·45 N	85·28 W
164	Nicastro (nê-käs'trō) ... It.	38·39 N	16·15 E
126	Nicchehabin, Punta (Pt.) (pōō'n-tä-nĕk-chĕ-ä-bē'n) Mex. (In.)	19·50 N	87·20 W
161	Nice (nēs) ... Fr.	43·42 N	7·21 E
191	Nicheng (nē-chŭŋ) China (Shanghai In.)	30·54 N	121·48 E
91	Nichicun (L.) (nĭch'ĭ-kŭn) ... Can.	53·07 N	72·10 W
128	Nicholas Chan. (nĭk'ô-lás) ... Ba.	23·30 N	80·20 W
104	Nicholasville (nĭk'ô-lás-vĭl) ... Ky.	37·55 N	84·35 W
196	Nicobar Is. (nĭk-ô-bär') Andaman & Nicobar Is.	8·28 N	94·04 E
112	Nicolai Mtn. (nē-cō lī') Or. (Portland In.)	46·05 N	123·27 W
125	Nicolás Romero (nē-kô-lá's rô-mĕ'rô). Mex. (In.)	19·38 N	99·20 W
113	Nicolet, L. (nĭ'kŏ-lĕt) Mi. (Sault Ste. Marie In.)	46·22 N	84·14 W
128	Nicolls Town ... Ba.	25·10 N	78·00 W
113	Nicols (nĭk'ĕls) Mn. (Minneapolis, St. Paul In.)	44·50 N	93·12 W
112	Nicomeki (R.) Can. (Vancouver In.)	49·04 N	122·47 W
153	Nicosia (nē-kô-sē'á) ... Cyprus	35·10 N	33·22 E
126	Nicoya (nē-kō'yä) ... C. R.	10·08 N	85·27 W
126	Nicoya, Golfo de (G.) (gôl-fô-dĕ). C. R.	10·03 N	85·04 W
126	Nicoya, Pen. de ... C. R.	10·05 N	86·00 W
	Nidaros, see Trondheim		
159	Nidzica (nê-jēt'sà) ... Pol.	53·21 N	20·30 E
158	Niedere Tauern (Mts.) ... Aus.	47·15 N	13·41 E
161	Niederkrüchten (nē'dĕr-krük-tĕn) F.R.G. (Ruhr In.)	51·12 N	6·14 E
149	Niederösterreich (Lower Austria) (State). Aus. (Vienna In.)	48·24 N	16·20 E
158	Niedersachsen (Lower Saxony) (State) (nē'dĕr-zäκ-sĕn). F.R.G.	52·52 N	8·27 E
214	Niélé ... Ivory Coast	10·12 N	5·38 W
215	Niellim ... Chad	9·42 N	17·49 E
158	Nienburg (nē'ĕn-bōōrgh) ... F.R.G.	52·40 N	9·15 E
214	Niénokoué, Mont (Mtn.) Ivory Coast	5·26 N	7·10 W
218	Nietverdiend ... S. Afr. (Johannesburg & Pretoria In.)	25·02 S	26·10 E
135	Nieuw Nickerie (nê-nē'kĕ-rē') Sur.	5·51 N	57·00 W
124	Nieves (nyā'vås) ... Mex.	24·00 N	102·57 W
171	Niğde (nĭg'dĕ) ... Tur.	37·55 N	34·40 E
218	Nigel (nī'jĕl) ... S. Afr. (Johannesburg & Pretoria In.)	26·26 S	28·27 E
209	Niger (nī'jēr) ... Afr.	18·02 N	8·30 E
215	Niger (R.) ... Afr.	5·33 N	6·33 E
215	Niger Delta ... Nig.	4·45 N	5·20 E
209	Nigeria (nī-jē'rĭ-á) ... Afr.	8·57 N	6·30 E
195	Nii (I.) (nē) ... Jap.	34·26 N	139·23 E
194	Niigata (nē'ê-gä'tà) ... Jap.	37·47 N	139·04 E
100	Niihau (I.) (nē'ê-hä'ōō) ... Hi.	21·50 N	160·05 E
195	Niimi (nē'mê) ... Jap.	34·59 N	133·28 E
195	Niiza ... Jap. (Tōkyō In.)	35·48 N	139·34 E
155	Nijmegen (nī'mā-gĕn) ... Neth.	51·50 N	5·52 E
195	Nikaidō (nē'ki-dō) Jap. (Ōsaka In.)	34·36 N	135·48 E
166	Nikitinka (nê-kĭ'tĭn-kà) .. Sov. Un.	55·33 N	33·19 E
195	Nikkō (nēk'kō) ... Jap.	36·44 N	139·35 E
167	Nikolayev (nē-kô-lä'yĕf) .. Sov. Un.	46·58 N	32·02 E
167	Nikolayev (Oblast) (ôb'låst) Sov. Un.	47·27 N	31·25 E
194	Nikolayevka ... Sov. Un.	48·37 N	134·49 E
174	Nikolayevka (nē-kô-lä'yĕf-ká) Sov. Un. (Leningrad In.)	59·29 N	29·48 E
171	Nikolayevskiy ... Sov. Un.	50·00 N	45·30 E
173	Nikolayevsk-na-Amure ... Sov. Un.	53·18 N	140·49 E
170	Nikol'sk (nê-kôlsk') ... Sov. Un.	59·30 N	45·40 E
174	Nikol'skoye (nê-kôl'skô-yĕ) Sov. Un. (Leningrad In.)	59·27 N	30·00 E
165	Nikopol (nē'kô-pŏl') ... Bul.	43·41 N	24·52 E
167	Nikopol' ... Sov. Un.	47·36 N	34·24 E
165	Nikšić (nēk'shēch) ... Yugo.	42·45 N	18·57 E
	Nīl, Nahr an-, see Nile (R.)		
137	Nilahue (R.) (nē-lá'wĕ) Chile (Santiago In.)	36·36 S	71·50 W
211	Nile (R.) (nīl) ... Afr.	19·15 N	32·30 E
104	Niles (nīlz) ... Mi.	41·50 N	86·15 W
104	Niles ... Oh.	41·15 N	80·45 W
185	Nileshwar ... India	12·08 N	74·14 E
185	Nilgiri Hills ... India	17·05 N	76·22 E
136	Nilópolis (nē-lô'pō-lēs) Braz. (Rio de Janeiro In.)	22·48 S	43·25 W
184	Nīmach ... India	24·32 N	74·51 E
210	Nimba, Mont (Mtn.) (nĭm'bà) Ivory Coast	7·40 N	8·33 W
214	Nimba Mts ... Gui.-Ivory Coast	7·30 N	8·35 W
160	Nîmes (nēm) ... Fr.	43·49 N	4·22 E
117	Nimrod Res. (nĭm'rŏd) ... Ar.	34·58 N	93·46 W
211	Nimule (nê-mōō'lå) ... Sud.	3·38 N	32·12 E
216	Ninda ... Ang.	14·47 S	21·24 E
203	Ninety Mile Bch. ... Austl.	38·20 S	147·30 E
171	Nineveh (Ruins) (nĭn'ê-và) ... Iraq	36·30 N	43·10 E
192	Ning'an (nĭŋ-än) ... China	44·20 N	129·20 E
193	Ningbo (nĭŋ-bwo) ... China	29·56 N	121·30 E
193	Ningde (nĭŋ-dŭ) ... China	26·38 N	119·33 E
193	Ninghai (nĭng'hī') ... China	29·20 N	121·20 E
190	Ninghe (nĭŋ-hŭ) ... China	39·20 N	117·50 E
190	Ningjin (nĭŋ-jyĭn) ... China	37·39 N	116·47 E
190	Ningjin ... China	37·37 N	114·55 E
193	Ningming ... China	22·22 N	107·06 E
192	Ningwu (nĭng'wōō') ... China	39·00 N	112·12 E
188	Ningxia (Aut. Reg.) (nĭŋ-shyä) China	37·10 N	106·00 E
190	Ningyang (nĭng'yäng') ... China	35·46 N	116·48 E
193	Ninh Binh (nēn bēnk') ... Viet.	20·22 N	106·00 E
197	Ninigo Group (Is.) ... Pap. N. Gui.	1·15 S	143·30 E
116	Ninnescah (R.) (nĭn'ĕs-kä) ... Ks.	37·37 N	98·31 W
135	Nioaque (nēō-á'-kĕ) ... Braz.	21·14 S	55·41 W
108	Niobrara (R.) (nī-ô-brâr'á) ... Ne.	42·46 N	98·46 W
214	Niokolo Koba, Parc Natl. du (Natl. Pk.). Senegal	13·05 N	13·00 W
214	Nioro du Sahel (nê-ô'rō) ... Mali	15·15 N	9·35 W
160	Niort (nē-ôr') ... Fr.	46·17 N	0·28 W
94	Nipawin ... Can.	53·22 N	104·00 W
129	Nipe, Bahía de (B.) (bä-ē'ä-dĕ-nē'pā). Cuba	20·50 N	75·30 W
129	Nipe, Sierra de (Mts.) (sē-ĕ'r-rä-dĕ). Cuba	20·20 N	75·50 W
104	Nipigon (nĭp'ĭ-gŏn) ... Can.	48·58 N	88·17 W
96	Nipigon (L.) ... Can.	49·37 N	89·55 W
109	Nipigon B. ... Can.	48·56 N	88·00 W
98	Nipisiguit (R.) (nĭ-pĭ'sĭ-kwĭt). Can.	47·26 N	66·15 W
97	Nipissing (L.) (nĭp'ĭ-sĭng) ... Can.	45·59 N	80·19 W
128	Niquero (nē-kā'rō) ... Cuba	20·00 N	77·35 W
184	Nirmali ... India	26·30 N	86·43 E
165	Niš (nêsh) ... Yugo.	43·18 N	21·55 E
162	Nisa (nē'sá) ... Port.	39·32 N	7·41 W
165	Nišava (R.) (nē'shá-vá) ... Yugo.	43·17 N	22·17 E
195	Nishino (I.) (nēsh'ê-nô) ... Jap.	36·06 N	132·49 E
195	Nishinomiya (nēsh'ê-nô-mē'yà) Jap. (Ōsaka In.)	34·44 N	135·21 E
195	Nishinoomote (nēsh'ê-nô-mō'tō) Jap.	30·44 N	130·59 E
195	Nishio (nēsh'ê-ô) ... Jap.	34·50 N	137·01 E
94	Niska L. (nĭs'ká) ... Can.	55·35 N	108·38 W
159	Nisko (nēs'kô) ... Pol.	50·30 N	22·07 E
89	Nisku (nĭs-kū') Can. (Edmonton In.)	53·21 N	113·33 W
110	Nisqually R. (nĭs-kwôl'ĭ) ... Wa.	46·51 N	122·33 W
156	Nissan (R.) ... Swe.	57·06 N	13·22 E
156	Nisser Vand (L.) (nĭs'ĕr vän) .. Nor.	59·14 N	8·35 E
156	Nissum Fd. ... Den.	56·24 N	7·35 E
136	Niterói (nē-tĕ-rô'ĭ) Braz. (Rio de Janeiro In.)	22·53 S	43·07 W
154	Nith (R.) (nĭth) ... Scot.	55·13 N	3·55 W
159	Nitra (nē'trà) ... Czech.	48·18 N	18·04 E
159	Nitra R. ... Czech.	48·13 N	18·14 E
104	Nitro (nī'trô) ... WV	38·25 N	81·50 W
199	Niue (nĭ'ōō) ... Oceania	19·50 S	167·00 W
155	Nivelles (nē'vĕl') ... Bel.	50·33 N	4·17 E
160	Nivernais, Côtes de (Hills) (nē-vĕr-nĕ'). Fr.	47·40 N	3·09 E
119	Nixon (nĭk'sŭn) ... Tx.	29·16 N	97·48 W
184	Nizāmābād ... India	18·48 N	78·07 E
173	Nizhne-Angarsk (nyēzh'nyĭ-ŭngärsk'). Sov. Un.	55·49 N	108·46 E
171	Nizhne-Chirskaya (nyĭ-ŭn-gärsk') Sov. Un.	48·20 N	42·50 E
173	Nizhne-Kolymsk (kô-lêmsk') Sov. Un.	68·32 N	160·56 E
172	Nizhneudinsk (nêzh'nyĭ-ōōdēnsk') Sov. Un.	54·58 N	99·15 E
174	Nizhniye Sergi (nyēzh' [nyĕ] sĕr'gē) Sov. Un. (Urals In.)	56·41 N	59·19 E
167	Nizhniye Serogozy (nyēzh'nyĭ sĕ-rô-gô'zĭ). Sov. Un.	46·51 N	34·25 E
174	Nizhniy Tagil (tŭgēl') Sov. Un. (Urals In.)	57·54 N	59·59 E
174	Nizhnyaya Kur'ya (nyĕ'zhnyá-yá kōōr'yá) Sov. Un. (Urals In.)	58·01 N	56·00 E
174	Nizhnyaya Salda (nyĕ'zh[nya'ya] säl'da') Sov. Un. (Urals In.)	58·05 N	60·43 E
172	Nizhnyaya Taymyra (R.). Sov. Un.	72·30 N	95·18 E
172	Nizhnyaya (Lower) Tunguska (R.) (tōōn-gōōs'kå). Sov. Un.	64·13 N	91·30 E
174	Nizhnyaya Tura (tōō'rà) Sov. Un. (Urals In.)	58·38 N	59·50 E
174	Nizhnyaya Us'va (ōō'vá) Sov. Un. (Urals In.)	59·05 N	58·53 E
217	Njombe ... Tan.	9·20 S	34·46 E
156	Njurunda (nyōō-rōōn'dá) ... Swe.	62·15 N	17·24 E
217	Nkala Mission ... Zambia	15·55 S	26·00 E
213	Nkandla ('n-känd'lä) S. Afr. (Natal In.)	28·40 S	31·06 E
214	Nkawkaw ... Ghana	6·33 N	0·47 W
184	Noākhāli ... Bngl.	22·52 N	91·08 E
101	Noatak (nô-á'ták) ... Ak.	67·22 N	163·28 W
101	Noatak (R.) ... Ak.	67·58 N	162·15 W
195	Nobeoka (nō-bà-ō'kà) ... Jap.	32·36 N	131·41 E
104	Noblesville (nō'bl'z-vĭl) ... In.	40·00 N	86·00 W
89	Nobleton (nō'bl'tŭn) Can. (Toronto In.)	43·54 N	79·39 W
163	Nocero Inferiore (nô-chĕ'rô-ēn-fĕ-ryô'rĕ) It. (Naples In.)	40·30 N	14·38 E
124	Nochistlán (nô-chēs-tlän') ... Mex.	21·23 N	102·52 W
125	Nochixtlón (Asunción) (ä-sōōn-syōn'). Mex.	17·28 N	97·12 W
115	Nogales (nô-gä'lĕs) ... Az.	31·20 N	110·55 W
125	Nogales (nô-gä'lĕs) ... Mex.	18·49 N	97·09 W
122	Nogales ... Mex.	31·15 N	111·00 W
218	Nogal Val. (nó'gäl) Som. (Horn of Afr. In.)	8·30 N	47·50 E
167	Nogaysk (nô-gīsk') ... Sov. Un.	46·43 N	36·21 E
161	Nogent-le-Roi (nŏ-zhŏN-lĕ-rwä') Fr. (Paris In.)	48·39 N	1·32 E
160	Nogent-le-Rotrou (rŏ-trōō') ... Fr.	48·22 N	0·47 E
174	Noginsk (nô-gēnsk') Sov. Un. (Moscow In.)	55·52 N	38·28 E
162	Nogueira (nô-gā'rä) ... Sp.	42·25 N	7·43 W
163	Nogueira Pallaresa (R.) (nô-gĕ'y-rä-päl-yä-rĕ-sä). Sp.	42·18 N	1·03 E
160	Noires, Mts. (nwår) ... Fr.	48·07 N	3·42 W
160	Noirmoutier, Île de (I.) (nwår-mōō-tyā'). Fr.	47·03 N	3·08 W
195	Nojimä-Zaki (Pt.) (nō'jê-mä zä-kê). Jap.	35·54 N	139·48 E
104	Nokomis (nô-kō'mĭs) ... Il.	39·15 N	89·10 W
163	Nola (nô'lä) ... It. (Naples In.)	40·41 N	14·32 E
170	Nolinsk (nô-lēnsk') ... Sov. Un.	57·32 N	49·50 E
195	Noma Misaki (C.) (nô'mä mê'sä-kē). Jap.	31·25 N	130·09 E
124	Nombre de Dios (nôm-brĕ-dĕ-dyô's). Mex.	23·50 N	104·14 W
127	Nombre de Dios (nô'm-brĕ).. Pan.	9·34 N	79·28 W
101	Nome (nōm) ... Ak.	64·30 N	165·20 W
90	Nonacho (L.) ... Can.	61·48 N	111·20 W
192	Nong'an (nôŋ-än) ... China	44·25 N	125·10 E
212	Nongoma (nŏn-gō'má) ... S. Afr.	27·48 S	31·45 E
102	Nooksack (nōōk'săk) Wa. (Vancouver In.)	48·55 N	122·19 W
112	Nooksack (R.) Wa. (Vancouver In.)	48·54 N	122·31 W
149	Noorden .. Neth. (Amsterdam In.)	52·09 N	4·49 E
149	Noordwijk aan Zee Neth. (Amsterdam In.)	52·14 N	4·25 E
149	Noordzee, Kanal, (Can.) Neth. (Amsterdam In.)	52·27 N	4·42 E
90	Nootka (I.) (nōōt'ká) ... Can.	49·32 N	126·42 W
92	Nootka Sd. ... Can.	49·33 N	126·38 W
216	Nóqui (nô-kē') ... Ang.	5·51 S	13·25 E
194	Nor (R.) (nou') ... China	46·55 N	132·45 E
107	Nora (nō'rä). In. (Indianapolis In.)	39·54 N	86·08 W
156	Nora ... Swe.	59·32 N	14·56 E
97	Noranda ... Can.	48·15 N	79·01 W
106	Norbeck (nŏr'bĕk) Md. (Baltimore In.)	39·06 N	77·05 W
117	Norborne (nôr'bôrn) ... Mo.	39·17 N	93·39 W
113	Norco (nôr'kô) Ca. (Los Angeles In.)	33·57 N	117·33 W
106	Norcross (nôr'krôs) Ga. (Atlanta In.)	33·56 N	84·13 W
89	Nord, Riviere du (rēv-yĕr' dü nōr) Can. (Montreal In.)	45·45 N	74·02 W
93	Nordegg (nûr'dĕg) ... Can.	52·28 N	116·04 W
158	Norden (nôr'dĕn) ... F.R.G.	53·35 N	7·14 E
158	Norderney I. (nōr'dĕr-nĕy). F.R.G.	53·45 N	6·58 E
156	Nord Fd. (nô'fyôr) ... Nor.	61·50 N	5·35 E
158	Nordhausen (nôrt'hau-zĕn) G.D.R.	51·30 N	10·48 E
158	Nordhorn (nôrt'hôrn) ... F.R.G.	52·26 N	7·05 E
150	Nord Kapp (C.) (nôr-kapp).. Nor.	71·07 N	25·57 E
112	Nordland (nôrd'lànd) Wa. (Seattle In.)	48·03 N	122·41 W
158	Nördlingen (nûrt'lĭng-ĕn) .. F.R.G.	48·51 N	10·30 E
158	Nord-Ostsee Kan. (Kiel) Can. (nōrd-ōzt-zā) (kēl) ... F.R.G.	54·03 N	9·23 E
158	Nordrhein-Westfalen (North Rhine-Westphalia) (State) (nŏrd'hīn-vĕst-fä-lĕn) ... F.R.G.	50·50 N	6·53 E
173	Nordvik (nôrd'vĕk) ... Sov. Un.	73·57 N	111·15 E
154	Nore R. (nōr) ... Ire.	52·34 N	7·15 W
120	Norfield (nôr'fēld) ... Ms.	31·24 N	90·25 W
99	Norfolk (nôr'fŏk) ... Ma. (In.)	42·07 N	71·19 W
108	Norfolk ... Ne.	42·10 N	97·25 W
106	Norfolk ... Va. (Norfolk In.)	36·55 N	76·15 W
198	Norfolk ... Oceania	27·10 S	166·50 E
117	Norfork, L. ... Ar.	36·25 N	92·09 W
124	Noria (nō'rē-á) ... Mex.	23·04 N	106·20 W
172	Noril'sk (nô rēlsk') ... Sov. Un.	69·00 N	87·11 E
104	Normal (nôr'măl) ... Il.	40·35 N	89·00 W
117	Norman (nôr'măn) ... Ok.	35·13 N	97·25 W
221	Norman, L. ... NC	35·30 N	80·53 W
105	Norman (R.) ... Austl.	18·27 S	141·29 E
160	Normandie (Reg.) (nŏr-mäN-dē') Fr.	49·02 N	0·17 E
160	Normandie, Collines de (Hills) (kŏ-lēn'dĕ-nŏr-män-dē'). Fr.	48·35 N	0·30 W
205	Normanton (nôr'măn-tŭn) .. Austl.	17·45 S	141·10 E
148	Normanton ... Eng.	53·40 N	1·21 W
90	Norman Wells ... Can.	65·26 N	127·00 W
204	Nornalup (nôr-năl'ŭp) ... Austl.	35·00 S	117·00 E
156	Norra Dellen (L.) ... Swe.	61·57 N	16·25 E

ăt; finăl; rāte; senâte; ärm; åsk; sofá; fâre; ch-choose; dh-as th in other; bē; êvent; bĕt; recĕnt; cratẽr; g-go; gh-guttural g; bĭt; ĭ-short neutral; rīde; κ-guttural k as ch in German ich;

PRONOUNCING INDEX

Norre Sundby — Novotatishchevskiy 321

Page	Name Pronunciation Region	Lat. °′	Long. °′
156	Norre Sundby (nû-rĕ-sŏŏn'bü) Den.	57·04 N	9·55 E
120	Norris (nŏr'ĭs) . . . Tn.	36·09 N	84·05 W
120	Norris (R.) . . . Tn.	36·17 N	84·10 W
106	Norristown (nŏr'ĭs-town) Pa. (Philadelphia In.)	40·07 N	75·21 W
156	Norrköping (nôr'chûp'ĭng) . . . Swe.	58·37 N	16·10 E
156	Norrtälje (nôr-tĕl'yĕ) . . . Swe.	59·47 N	18·39 E
204	Norseman (nôrs'măn) . . . Austl.	32·15 S	122·00 E
137	Norte, Punta (Pt.) (pōō'n-tä-nŏr'tĕ) Arg. (Buenos Aires In.)	36·17 S	56·46 W
135	Norte, Serra do (Mts.) (sĕ'r-rä-dô-nôr'te) . Braz.	12·04 S	59·08 W
99	North, C. . . . Can.	47·02 N	60·25 W
205	North, C. . . . N. Z. (In.)	34·31 S	173·02 E
114	North, I. . . . Ca. (San Diego In.)	32·39 N	117·14 W
205	North, I. . . . N. Z. (In.)	37·34 S	171·12 E
105	North Adams (ăd'ămz) . . . Ma.	42·40 N	73·05 W
204	Northam (nôr-dhăm) . . . Austl.	31·50 S	116·45 E
218	Northam (nôr'thăm) . . . S. Afr. (Johannesburg & Pretoria In.)	24·52 S	27·16 E
75	North America (à-mĕr'ĭ-kà)		
123	North American Basin (à-mĕr'ĭ-kăn) . Atl. O.	23·45 N	62·45 W
204	Northampton (nôr-thămp'tŭn) Austl.	28·22 S	114·45 E
154	Northampton (nôrth-ămp'tŭn) Eng.	52·14 N	0·56 W
105	Northampton . . . Ma.	42·20 N	72·45 W
105	Northampton . . . Pa.	40·45 N	75·30 W
148	Northampton (Co.) . . . Eng.	52·25 N	0·47 W
196	North Andaman I. (ăn-dà-măn') Andaman & Nicobar Is.	13·15 N	93·30 E
99	North Andover (ăn'dô-vēr) Ma. (In.)	42·42 N	71·07 W
112	North Arm (ärm) Can. (Vancouver In.)	49·13 N	123·01 W
106	North Atlanta (ăt-lăn'tà) Ga. (Atlanta In.)	33·52 N	84·20 W
106	North Attleboro (ăt''l-bŭr-ô) Ma. (Providence In.)	41·59 N	71·18 W
104	North Baltimore (bôl'tĭ-môr) . . Oh.	41·10 N	83·40 W
118	North Basque (băsk) . . . Tx.	31·56 N	98·01 W
94	North Battleford (băt''l-fērd) . Can.	52·47 N	108·17 W
97	North Bay . . . Can.	46·13 N	79·26 W
110	North Bend (bĕnd) . . . Or.	43·23 N	124·13 W
98	North Berwick (bûr'wĭk) . . . Me.	43·18 N	70·46 W
128	North Bght. (bĭt) . . . Ba.	24·30 N	77·40 W
128	North Bimini (I). (bĭ'mĭ-nē) . . Ba.	25·45 N	79·20 W
	North Borneo (Reg.), see Sabah		
99	Northborough (nôrth'bûr-ô) Ma. (In.)	42·19 N	71·39 W
99	Northbridge (nôrth'brĭj) Ma. (In.)	42·09 N	71·39 W
129	North Caicos (I.) (kī'kôs) . Turks & Caicos	21·55 N	72·00 W
103	North Carolina (State) (kăr-ô-lī'nà) . U. S.	35·40 N	81·30 W
93	North Cascades Natl. Pk. . . . Wa.	48·50 N	120·50 W
128	North Cat Cay (I.) . . . Ba.	25·35 N	79·20 W
104	North Chan (B.) (chăn) . . . Can.	46·10 N	83·20 W
154	North Chan. . . . N. Ire.-Scot.	55·15 N	7·56 W
121	North Charleston (chärlz'tŭn) SC	32·49 N	79·57 W
107	North Chicago (shĭ-kô'gō) Il. (Chicago In.)	42·19 N	87·51 W
107	North College Hill (kŏl'ĕj hĭl) Oh. (Cincinnati In.)	39·13 N	84·33 W
118	North Concho (kŏn'chō) . . . Tx.	31·40 N	100·48 W
89	North Cooking Lake (kŏŏk'ĭng lāk) Can. (Edmonton In.)	53·28 N	112·57 W
102	North Dakota (State) (dà-kō'tà) U. S.	47·20 N	101·55 W
154	North Downs (dounz) . . . Eng.	51·11 N	0·01 W
184	North Dum-Dum . . . India (In.)	22·38 N	88·23 E
101	Northeast C. (nôrth-ēst) . . . Ak.	63·15 N	169·04 W
129	Northeast Pt. . . . Ba.	21·25 N	73·00 W
129	Northeast Pt. . . . Ba.	22·45 N	73·50 W
128	Northeast Providence Chan. (prŏv'ĭ-dĕns) . Ba.	25·45 N	77·00 W
158	Northeim (nôrt'hīm) . . . F.R.G.	51·42 N	9·59 E
128	North Elbow Cays (Is.) . . . Ba.	23·55 N	80·30 W
111	Northern Cheyenne Ind. Res. . Mt.	45·32 N	106·43 W
	Northern Dvina (R.), see Severnaya Dvina		
154	Northern Ireland (īr'lănd) . . U. K.	54·48 N	7·00 W
	Northern Land (Is.), see Severnaya Zemlya		
204	Northern Territory . . . Austl.	18·15 S	133·00 E
109	Northfield (nôrth'fēld) . . . Mn.	44·28 N	93·11 W
203	North Flinders, Ra. (flĭn'dērz) Austl.	31·55 S	138·45 E
155	North Foreland (fōr'lànd) . . . Eng.	51·20 N	1·30 E
118	North Franklin Mt. (frăŋ'klĭn) . Tx.	31·55 N	106·30 W
156	North Frisian Is. . . . Den.	55·16 N	8·15 E
122	North Gamboa (gäm-bô'ä) Pan. (In.)	9·07 N	79·40 W
89	North Gower (gŏw'ēr) Can. (Ottawa In.)	45·08 N	75·43 W
113	North Hollywood (hŏl'ē-wŏŏd) Ca. (Los Angeles In.)	34·10 N	118·23 W
104	North Judson (jŭd'sŭn) . . . In.	41·15 N	86·50 W
93	North Kamloops (kăm'lōōps) . Can.	50·41 N	120·22 W
113	North Kansas City (kăn'zàs) Mo. (Kansas City In.)	39·08 N	94·34 W
106	North Kingstown RI (Providence In.)	41·34 N	71·26 W
117	North Little Rock (lĭt''l rŏk) . . . Ar.	34·46 N	92·13 W
108	North Loup (R.) (lōōp) . . . Ne.	42·05 N	100·10 W
104	North Manchester (măn'chĕs-tēr) In.	41·00 N	85·45 W
113	Northmoor (nôrth'mŏŏr) Mo. (Kansas City In.)	39·10 N	94·37 W
95	North Moose L. . . . Can.	54·09 N	100·20 W
203	North Mount Lofty Ranges . Austl.	33·50 S	138·30 E
113	North Ogden (ŏg'dĕn) Ut. (Salt Lake City In.)	41·18 N	111·58 W
113	North Ogden Pk. Ut. (Salt Lake City. In.)	41·23 N	111·59 W
107	North Olmsted (ōlm-stĕd) Oh. (Cleveland In.)	41·25 N	81·55 W
116	North Pease (R.) (pēz) . . . Tx.	34·19 N	100·58 W
112	North Pender (I.) (pĕn'dēr) Can. (Vancouver In.)	48·48 N	123·16 W
112	North Plains (plānz) Or. (Portland In.)	45·36 N	123·00 W
108	North Platte (plăt) . . . Ne.	41·08 N	100·45 W
102	North Platte, (R.) . . . U. S.	41·20 N	102·40 W
104	North Pt. . . . Mi.	45·00 N	83·20 W
127	North Pt. . . . Barb. (In.)	13·22 N	59·36 W
120	Northport (nôrth'pōrt) . . . Al.	33·12 N	87·35 W
106	Northport . . . NY (New York In.)	40·53 N	73·20 W
110	Northport . . . Wa.	48·53 N	117·47 W
99	North Reading (rĕd'ĭng) . Ma. (In.)	42·34 N	71·04 W
	North Rhine-Westphalia (State), see Nordrhein-Westfalen		
113	North Richland Hills Tx. (Dallas, Ft. Worth In.)	32·50 N	97·13 W
113	Northridge (nôrth'ridj) Ca. (Los Angeles In.)	34·14 N	118·32 W
107	North Ridgeville (rĭj-vĭl) Oh. (Cleveland In.)	41·23 N	82·01 W
107	North Royalton (roi'ăl-tŭn) Oh. (Cleveland In.)	41·19 N	81·44 W
113	North St. Paul (sânt pôl') . . . Mn. (Minneapolis, St. Paul In.)	45·01 N	92·59 W
94	North Saskatchewan (R.) (săn-kăch'ē-wän) . Can.	52·40 N	106·45 W
150	North Sea . . . Eur.	56·09 N	3·16 E
109	North Skunk (R.) (skŭnk) . . . Ia.	41·39 N	92·46 W
205	North Stradbroke I. (străd'brōk) Austl.	27·45 S	154·18 E
99	North Sydney (sĭd'nē) . . . Can.	46·13 N	60·15 W
205	North Taranaki Bght. (tà-rà-nä'kĭ bĭt) . N. Z. (In.)	38·23 S	172·03 E
106	North Tarrytown (tăr'ĭ-toun) NY (New York In.)	41·05 N	73·52 W
93	North Thompson (R.) . . . Can.	50·50 N	120·10 W
107	North Tonawanda (tŏn-à-wŏn'dà) NY (Buffalo In.)	43·02 N	78·53 W
115	North Truchas Pks. (Mts.) (trōō'chäs) . NM	35·58 N	105·37 W
99	North Twillingate (I.) (twĭl'ĭn-gāt) Can.	49·47 N	54·37 W
154	North Uist (I.) (û'ĭst) . . . Scot.	57·37 N	7·22 W
98	Northumberland Str. (nôr thŭm'bēr-lànd) . Can.	46·25 N	64·20 W
105	Northumberland . . . NH	44·30 N	71·30 W
205	Northumberland, Is. . . . Austl.	21·42 S	151·30 E
110	North Umpqua R. (ŭmp'kwà) . . Or.	43·20 N	122·50 W
112	North Vancouver (văn-kōō'vēr) Can. (Vancouver In.)	49·19 N	123·04 W
104	North Vernon (vûr'nŭn) . . . In.	39·05 N	85·45 W
107	Northville (nôrth-vĭl) Mi. (Detroit In.)	42·26 N	83·28 W
106	North Wales (wālz) Pa. (Philadelphia In.)	40·12 N	75·16 W
204	North West C. (nôrth'wĕst) . Austl.	21·50 S	112·25 E
121	Northwest Cape Fear, (R.) (cāp fēr) . NC	34·34 N	79·46 W
99	North West Gander (R.) (găn'dēr) Can.	48·40 N	55·15 W
154	Northwest Highlands . . . Scot.	56·50 N	5·20 W
128	Northwest Providence Chan. (prŏv'ĭ-dĕns) . Ba.	26·15 N	78·45 W
90	Northwest Territories (tĕr'ĭ-tō'rĭs) . Can.	64·42 N	119·09 W
155	Northwich (nôrth'wĭch) . . . Eng.	53·15 N	2·31 W
121	North Wilkesboro (wĭlks'bûrô) . NC	36·08 N	81·10 W
109	Northwood (nôrth'wŏŏd) . . . Ia.	43·26 N	93·13 W
108	Northwood . . . ND	47·44 N	97·36 W
111	North Wood Cr. . . . Wy.	44·02 N	107·37 W
112	North Yamhill (R.) (yăm' hĭl) Or. (Portland In.)	45·22 N	123·21 W
154	North York Moors (yôrk mŏŏrz') Eng.	54·20 N	0·40 W
89	North York . . . Can. (Toronto In.)	43·47 N	79·25 W
116	Norton (nôr'tŭn) . . . Ks.	39·40 N	99·54 W
106	Norton . . . Ma. (Providence In.)	41·58 N	71·08 W
121	Norton . . . Va.	36·54 N	82·36 W
101	Norton B. . . . Ak.	64·22 N	162·18 W
106	Norton Res. . Ma. (Providence In.)	42·01 N	71·07 W
101	Norton Sd. . . . Ak.	63·48 N	164·50 W
89	Norval (nôr'vål) Can. (Toronto In.)	43·39 N	79·52 W
113	Norwalk (nôr'wôk) Ca. (Los Angeles In.)	33·54 N	118·05 W
106	Norwalk . . . Ct. (New York In.)	41·06 N	73·25 W
104	Norwalk . . . Oh.	41·15 N	82·35 W
146	Norway (nôr'wā) . . . Eur.	63·48 N	11·17 E
98	Norway . . . Me.	44·11 N	70·35 W
109	Norway . . . Mi.	45·47 N	87·55 W
95	Norway House . . . Can.	53·59 N	97·50 W
150	Norwegian Sea (nôr-wē'jăn) . . Eur.	66·54 N	1·43 E
99	Norwell (nôr'wĕl) . . . Ma. (In.)	42·10 N	70·47 W
105	Norwich (nôr'wĭch) . . . Ct.	41·20 N	72·00 W
155	Norwich . . . Eng.	52·40 N	1·15 E
105	Norwich . . . NY	42·35 N	75·30 W
99	Norwood (nôr'wŏŏd) . . . Ma. (In.)	42·11 N	71·13 W
121	Norwood . . . NC	35·15 N	80·08 W
107	Norwood . . . Oh. (Cincinnati In.)	39·10 N	84·27 W
89	Nose Cr. (nōz) . Can. (Calgary In.)	51·09 N	114·02 W
194	Noshiro (nō'shē-rô) . . . Jap.	40·09 N	140·02 E
167	Nosovka (nô'sôf-kà) . . . Sov. Un.	50·54 N	31·35 E
213	Nossi Bé (B.) (nōō'sē bā) . . Mad.	13·14 S	47·28 E
212	Nossob (R.) (nô'sŏb) . . . Namibia	24·15 S	19·10 E
158	Noteć R. (nô'tĕcn) . . . Pol.	52·50 N	16·19 E
151	Noto (nô'tô) . . . It.	36·49 N	15·08 E
156	Notodden (nōt'ôd'n) . . . Nor.	59·35 N	9·15 E
195	Noto-Hantō (Pen.) (nô'tō hän'tō) Jap.	37·18 N	137·03 E
98	Notre Dame, Monts (Mts.) . Can.	46·35 N	70·35 W
99	Notre Dame B. (nō't'r dàm') . Can.	49·45 N	55·15 W
100	Notre-Dame-des-Laurentides (dĕ-lō-räɴ-tēd') . Can. (Quebec In.)	46·55 N	71·20 W
98	Notre-Dame-du-Lac . . . Can.	47·37 N	68·51 W
104	Nottawasaga B. (nŏt'à-wa-sä'gà) Can.	44·45 N	80·35 W
91	Nottaway (R.) (nôt'à-wā) . . . Can.	50·58 N	78·02 W
148	Nottingham (nŏt'ĭng-ăm) . . . Eng.	52·58 N	1·09 W
148	Nottingham (Co.) . . . Eng.	53·03 N	1·05 W
91	Nottingham I. . . . Can.	62·58 N	78·53 W
121	Nottoway, (R.) (nôt'à-wā) . . . Va.	36·53 N	77·47 W
94	Notukeu Cr. . . . Can.	49·55 N	106·30 W
210	Nouadhibou . . . Mauritania	21·02 N	17·09 W
214	Nouakchott . . . Mauritania	18·06 N	15·57 W
214	Nouamrhar . . . Mauritania	19·22 N	16·31 W
205	Noumea (nōō-mā'ä) . . . N. Cal.	22·18 S	166·48 E
98	Nouvelle (nōō-vĕl') . . . Can.	48·09 N	66·22 W
211	Nouvelle Anvers (äɴ-vâr') . . . Zaire	1·42 N	19·08 E
160	Nouzonville (nōō-zôɴ-vēl') . . . Fr.	49·51 N	4·43 E
135	Nova Cruz (nō'vá-krōō'z) . . . Braz.	6·22 S	35·20 W
217	Nova Freixo . . . Moz.	14·49 S	36·33 E
137	Nova Friburgo (frê-bōōr'gōō) Braz. (Rio de Janeiro In.)	22·18 S	42·31 W
216	Nova Gaia . . . Ang.	10·09 S	17·31 E
136	Nova Iguaçu (nō'vä-ē-gwä-sōō') Braz. (Rio de Janeiro In.)	22·45 S	43·27 W
137	Nova Lima (lē'mä) Braz. (Rio de Janeiro In.)	19·59 S	43·51 W
	Nova Lisboa, see Huambo		
212	Nova Mambone (nō'vá-mäm-bŏ'nĕ.) Moz.	21·04 S	35·13 E
164	Novara (nô-vä'rä) . . . It.	45·24 N	8·38 E
137	Nova Resende Braz. (Rio de Janeiro In.)	21·12 S	46·25 W
91	Nova Scotia (Prov.) (skō'shà) . Can.	44·28 N	65·00 W
165	Nova Varoš (nô'vá vä'rôsh) . Yugo.	43·24 N	19·53 E
157	Novaya Ladoga (nô'vá-yà là-dô-gô) . Sov. Un.	60·06 N	32·16 E
174	Novaya Lyalya (lyà'lyà) Sov. Un. (Urals In.)	59·03 N	60·36 E
167	Novaya Odessa (ô-dĕs'ä) . Sov. Un.	47·18 N	31·48 E
167	Novaya Praga (prä'gà) . . Sov. Un.	48·34 N	32·54 E
173	Novaya Sibir (I.) (sê-bēr') Sov. Un.	75·42 N	150·00 E
167	Novaya Vodolaga (vô-dôl'à-gà) Sov. Un.	49·43 N	35·51 E
172	Novaya Zemlya (I.) (zĕm-lyà') Sov. Un.	72·00 N	54·46 E
165	Nova Zagora (zä'gô-rá) . . . Bul.	42·30 N	26·01 E
163	Novelda (nō-vĕl'dä) . . . Sp.	38·22 N	0·46 W
159	Nové Mesto (Nad Váhom) (nô'vĕ myĕs'tō) . Czech.	48·44 N	17·47 E
159	Nové Zámky (zäm'kĕ) . . . Czech.	47·58 N	18·10 E
166	Novgorod (nôv'gô-rŏt) . . . Sov. Un.	58·32 N	31·16 E
166	Novgorod (Oblast) . . . Sov. Un.	58·27 N	31·55 E
164	Novi (nô'vē) . . . It.	44·43 N	8·48 W
107	Novi (nō'vĭ) . . . Mi. (Detroit In.)	42·29 N	83·28 W
164	Novi Grad (gràd) . . . Yugo.	44·09 N	15·34 E
117	Novinger (nŏv'ĭn-jēr) . . . Mo.	40·14 N	92·43 W
165	Novi-Pazar (pà-zär') . . . Bul.	43·22 N	27·26 E
165	Novi Pazar (pà-zär') . . . Yugo.	43·08 N	20·30 E
165	Novi Sad (säd') . . . Yugo.	45·15 N	19·53 E
174	Novoasbest (nô-vô-ä-bĕst') Sov. Un. (Urals In.)	57·43 N	60·14 E
167	Novoaydar (nô'vô-ī-där') . Sov. Un.	48·57 N	39·01 E
167	Novocherkassk (nô'vô-chĕr-kásk') Sov. Un.	47·25 N	40·04 E
167	Novogorod-Severskiy . . . Sov. Un.	52·01 N	33·14 E
159	Novogrudok (nô-vô-grōō'dôk) Sov. Un.	53·35 N	25·51 E
141	Novo-Kazalinsk (nô-vŭ-kŭ-zà-lyĕnsk') . Sov. Un.	45·47 N	62·00 E
172	Novokuznetsk (Stalinsk) (nō'vô-kōō'z-nyĕ'tsk) (stà'lênsk) . Sov. Un.	53·43 N	86·59 E
174	Novoladozhskiy Kanal (Can.) (nô-vô-lä'dôzh-skĭ kà-näl') Sov. Un. (Leningrad In.)	59·54 N	31·19 E
164	Novo Mesto (nôvô mās'tô) . Yugo.	45·48 N	15·13 E
167	Novomirgorod (nô'vô-mēr'gô-rôt) Sov. Un.	48·46 N	31·44 E
166	Novomoskossk . . . Sov. Un.	54·06 N	38·08 E
167	Novomoskovsk (nô'vô-môs-kôfsk') Sov. Un.	48·37 N	35·12 E
174	Novonikol'skiy (nô'vô-nyĭ-kôl'skĭ) Sov. Un. (Urals In.)	52·28 N	57·12 E
216	Novo Redondo (nô'vōō rà-dôn'dōō) . Ang.	11·13 S	13·50 E
167	Novorossiysk (nô'vô-rô-sēsk') Sov. Un.	44·43 N	37·48 E
166	Novorzhev (nô'vô-rzhêv') Sov. Un.	57·01 N	29·17 E
165	Novo-Selo (nô'vô-sĕ'lô) . . . Bul.	44·09 N	22·46 E
172	Novosibirsk (nô'vô-sê-bērsk') Sov. Un.	55·09 N	82·58 E
173	Novosibirskiye O-va (New Siberian Is.) (no'vŭ-sĭ-bĭr'skē-ĕ) . Sov. Un.	76·45 N	140·30 E
166	Novosil' (nô'vô-sĭl) . . . Sov. Un.	52·58 N	37·03 E
166	Novosokol'niki (nô'vô-sô-kôl'nē-kē) . Sov. Un.	56·18 N	30·07 E
174	Novotatishchevskiy (nô'vô-tà-tyĭsh'chĕv-skĭ) Sov. Un. (Urals In.)	53·22 N	60·24 E

ng-sing; ŋ-baŋk; ɴ-nasalized n; nŏd; cŏmmit; ōld; ôbey; ôrder; fōōd; fŏŏt; ou-out; s-soft; sh-dish; th-thin; pūre; ûnite; ûrn; stŭd; circŭs; ü-as "y" in study; '-indeterminate vowel.

322 Novoukrainka — Odintsovo PRONOUNCING INDEX

Page	Name Pronunciation Region	Lat. °'	Long. °'
167	Novoukrainka (nōvō-ōō'krȧ) Sov. Un.	48·18 N	31·33 E
171	Novouzensk (nô-vô-ōō-zĕnsk') Sov. Un.	50·40 N	48·08 E
166	Novozybkov (nô'vô-zēp'kôf) Sov. Un.	52·31 N	31·54 E
159	Nový Jičín (nô'vē yē'chēn). Czech.	49·36 N	18·02 E
167	Novyy Bug (bōōk) Sov. Un.	47·43 N	32·33 E
167	Novyy Oskol (ôs-kôl') Sov. Un.	50·46 N	37·53 E
172	Novyy Port (nô'vē) Sov. Un.	67·19 N	72·28 E
159	Nowa Huta (nō'vä hōō'tä) Pol.	50·04 N	20·20 E
158	Nowa Sól (nô'vȧ sŭl') Pol.	51·49 N	15·41 E
117	Nowata (nô-wä'tȧ) Ok.	36·42 N	95·38 W
203	Nowra (nou'rȧ) Austl.	34·55 S	150·45 E
159	Nowy Dwór Mazowiecki (nō'vĭ dvōōr mä-zo-vyĕts'ke). Pol.	52·26 N	20·46 E
159	Nowy Sącz (nô'vē sônch') Pol.	49·36 N	20·42 E
159	Nowy Targ (tärk') Pol.	49·29 N	20·02 E
110	Noxon Res. Mt.	47·50 N	115·40 W
120	Noxubee (R.) (nŏks'ū-bē) Ms.	33·20 N	88·55 W
162	Noya (nō'yä) Sp.	42·46 N	8·50 W
92	Noyes I. (noiz) Ak.	55·30 N	133·40 W
195	Nozaki (nō'zä-kē). Jap. (Ōsaka In.)	34·43 N	135·39 E
213	Nqamakwe ('n-gä-mä'kwä) S. Afr. (Natal In.)	32·13 S	27·57 E
213	Nqutu ('n-kōō'tōō) S. Afr. (Natal In.)	28·17 S	30·41 E
214	Nsawam Ghana	5·50 N	0·20 W
215	Nsukka Nig.	6·52 N	7·24 E
213	Ntshoni (Mtn.). S. Afr. (Natal In.)	29·34 S	30·03 E
212	Ntwetwe Pan (Salt Flat) Bots.	20·00 S	24·18 E
188	Nu (Salween) (R.) (nōō) China	30·08 N	96·38 E
211	Nubah, Jibāl an-(Mts.) Sud.	12·22 N	30·39 E
211	Nubian Des. (nōō'bĭ-ăn) Sud.	21·13 N	33·09 E
134	Nudo Coropuna (Mt.) (nōō'dô kō-rō-pōō'nä). Peru	15·53 S	72·04 W
134	Nudo de Pasco (Mt.) (dĕ päs'kô) Peru	10·34 S	76·12 W
118	Nueces R. (nû-ā'sȧs) Tx.	28·20 N	98·08 W
90	Nueltin (L.) (nwĕl'tin) Can.	60·14 N	101·00 W
126	Nueva Armenia (nwā'vä är-mā'nē-ȧ). Hond.	15·47 N	86·32 W
135	Nueva Esparta (State) (nwĕ'vä ĕs-pä'r-tä). Ven. (In.)	10·50 N	64·35 W
128	Nueva Gerona (kĕ-rô'nä) Cuba	21·55 N	82·45 W
137	Nueva Palmira (päl-mē'rä) Ur. (Buenos Aires In.)	33·53 S	58·23 W
102	Nueva Rosita (nōōĕ'vä rô-sē'tä) Mex.	27·55 N	101·10 W
126	Nueva San Salvador (Santa Tecla) (sän' säl-vȧ-dōr) (sän'tä tĕ'klä) Sal.	13·41 N	89·16 W
137	Nueve de Julio (nwā'vȧ dā hōō'lyō) Arg. (Buenos Aires In.)	35·26 S	60·51 W
128	Nuevitas (nwā-vē'täs) Cuba	21·35 N	77·15 W
128	Nuevitas, Bahía de (bä-ē'ä dĕ nwā-vē'täs). Cuba	21·30 N	77·05 W
113	Nuevo (nwā'vō) Ca. (Los Angeles In.)	33·48 N	117·09 W
118	Nuevo Laredo (lä-rā'dhō) Mex.	27·29 N	99·30 W
122	Nuevo Leon (State) (lā-ōn') Mex.	26·00 N	100·00 W
122	Nuevo San Juan (nwĕ'vô sän kōō-ä'n). Pan. (In.)	9·14 N	79·43 W
174	Nugumanovo (nû-gû-mä'nô-vô) Sov. Un. (Urals In.)	55·28 N	61·50 E
101	Nulato (nōō-lä'tō) Ak.	64·40 N	158·18 W
204	Nullagine (nŭ-lă'jēn) Austl.	22·00 S	120·07 E
204	Nullarbor Plain (Reg.) (nŭ-lär'bôr). Austl.	31·45 S	126·30 E
94	Numabin B. (nōō-mä'bĭn) Can.	56·30 N	103·08 W
149	Numansdorp Neth. (Amsterdam In.)	51·43 N	4·25 E
195	Numazu (nōō'mä-zōō) Jap.	35·06 N	138·55 E
137	No 1, Canal Arg. (Buenos Aires In.)	36·43 S	58·14 W
137	No. 9, Canal Arg. (Buenos Aires In.)	36·22 S	58·19 W
137	No. 12, Canal Arg. (Buenos Aires In.)	36·47 S	57·20 W
197	Numfoor, Pulau (I.) Indon.	1·20 S	134·48 E
215	Nun (R.) Nig.	5·05 N	6·10 E
148	Nuneaton (nŭn'ē-tŭn) Eng.	52·31 N	1·28 W
101	Nunivak (I.) (nōō'nĭ-văk) Ak.	60·25 N	167·42 W
126	Nunkiní (nōōn-kē-nē'). Mex. (In.)	20·19 N	90·14 W
101	Nunyama (nûn-yä'mȧ). Sov. Un.	65·49 N	170·32 W
164	Nuoro (nwô'rō) It.	40·29 N	9·20 E
172	Nura (R.) (nōō'rä) Sov. Un.	49·48 N	73·54 E
172	Nurata (nōōr'ät'ȧ) Sov. Un.	40·33 N	65·28 E
158	Nürnberg (nürn'bĕrgh) F.R.G.	49·28 N	11·07 E
129	Nurse Cay (I.) Ba.	22·30 N	75·50 W
171	Nusabyin (nōō'sī-bēn) Tur.	37·05 N	41·10 E
101	Nushagak (R.) (nū-shä-găk'). Ak.	59·28 N	157·40 W
190	Nushan Hu (L.) (nü'shän hōō) China	32·50 N	117·59 E
187	Nushki (nŭsh'kē) Pak.	29·30 N	66·02 E
149	Nuthe R. (nōō'tĕ) G.D.R (Berlin In.)	52·15 N	13·11 E
106	Nutley (nŭt'lē). NJ (New York In.)	40·49 N	74·09 W
105	Nutter Fort (nŭt'ēr fôrt) WV	39·15 N	80·15 W
113	Nutwood (nŭt'wōōd) Il. (St. Louis In.)	39·05 N	90·34 W
183	Nuwaybi 'al Muzayyinah Egypt (Palestine In.)	28·59 N	34·40 E
212	Nuweland S. Afr. (In.)	33·58 S	18·28 E
106	Nyack (nī'ăk). NY (New York In.)	41·05 N	73·55 W
188	Nyaiqêntanglha Shan (Mts.) (nyä-ĭn-chyŭn-täŋ-lä shän). China	29·55 N	88·08 E
217	Nyakanazi Tan.	3·00 S	31·15 E
211	Nyala Sud.	12·00 N	24·52 E
216	Nyanga (R.) Gabon	2·45 S	10·30 E
217	Nyanza Rw.	2·21 S	29·45 E
217	Nyasa, L. (Malaw , L.) (nyä'sä) Afr.	10·45 S	34·30 E
174	Nyazepetrovsk (nyä'zĕ-pĕ-trôvsk') Sov. Un. (Urals In.)	56·04 N	59·38 E
156	Nyborg (nü'bôr') Den.	55·20 N	10·45 E
156	Nybro (nü'brô) Swe.	56·44 N	15·56 E
217	Nyeri Ken.	0·25 S	36·57 E
156	Nyhem (nü'hĕm) Swe.	56·39 N	12·50 E
217	Nyika Plat. Malawi	10·30 S	35·50 E
159	Nyíregyháza (nyē'rĕd-y'hä'zä) Hung.	47·58 N	21·45 E
156	Nykøbing (nü'kû-bĭng) Den.	56·46 N	8·47 E
156	Nykøbing Falster Den.	54·45 N	11·54 E
156	Nykøbing Sjaelland Den.	55·55 N	11·37 E
156	Nyköping (nü'chû-pĭng) Swe.	58·46 N	16·58 E
218	Nylstroom (nĭl'strōm) S. Afr. (Johannesburg & Pretoria In.)	24·42 S	28·25 E
203	Nymagee (nī-mȧ-gē') Austl.	32·17 S	146·18 E
158	Nymburk (nêm'bōōrk) Czech.	50·12 N	15·03 E
154	Nymphe Bk. (nĭmpf) Ire.	51·36 N	7·35 W
156	Nynäshamn (nü-nĕs-häm'n). Swe.	58·53 N	17·55 E
203	Nyngan (nĭŋ'găn) Austl.	31·31 S	147·25 E
215	Nyong (R.) (nyông) Cam.	3·40 N	10·25 E
214	Nyou Upper Volta	12·46 N	1·56 W
158	Nyrány (nêr-zhä'nê) Czech.	49·43 N	13·13 E
159	Nysa (nē'sȧ) Pol.	50·29 N	17·20 E
	Nystad, see Uusikaupunki		
170	Nytva Sov. Un.	58·00 N	55·10 E
217	Nyungwe Malawi	10·16 S	34·07 E
217	Nyunzu Zaire	5·57 S	28·01 E
173	Nyuya (R.) (nyōō'yȧ) Sov. Un.	60·30 N	111·45 E
217	Nzega Tan.	4·13 S	33·11 E
214	Nzérékoré Gui.	7·45 N	8·49 W
214	Nzi (R.) Ivory Coast	7·00 N	4·27 W

O

Page	Name Pronunciation Region	Lat. °'	Long. °'
108	Oahe Dam (ō-ȧ-hē) SD	44·28 N	100·34 W
108	Oahe Res. SD	45·20 N	100·00 W
100	Oahu (I.) (ō-ä'hōō) (ō-ä'hü) Hi.	21·38 N	157·48 W
92	Oak Bay Can.	48·27 N	123·18 W
89	Oak Bluff (ōk blŭf) Can. (Winnipeg In.)	49·47 N	97·21 W
111	Oak Creek (ōk krēk') Co.	40·20 N	106·50 W
114	Oakdale (ōk'dāl) Ca.	37·45 N	120·52 W
104	Oakdale Ky.	38·15 N	85·50 W
119	Oakdale La.	30·49 N	92·40 W
107	Oakdale Pa. (Pittsburgh In.)	40·24 N	80·11 W
148	Oakengates (ōk'ĕn-gāts) Eng.	52·41 N	2·27 W
108	Oakes (ōks) ND	46·10 N	98·50 W
98	Oakfield (ōk'fēld) Me.	46·08 N	68·10 W
106	Oakford (ōk'fōrd) Pa. (Philadelphia In.)	40·08 N	74·58 W
112	Oak Grove (grōv) Or. (Portland In.)	45·25 N	122·38 W
148	Oakham (ōk'ăm) Eng.	52·40 N	0·38 W
104	Oakharbor (ōk'här'bēr) Oh.	41·30 N	83·05 W
112	Oak Harbor Wa. (Seattle In.)	48·18 N	122·39 W
112	Oakland (ōk'lănd) Ca. (San Francisco In.)	37·48 N	122·16 W
108	Oakland Ne.	41·50 N	96·28 W
104	Oakland City In.	38·20 N	87·20 W
107	Oaklawn (ōk'lôn). Il. (Chicago In.)	41·43 N	87·45 W
202	Oakleigh (ōk'lȧ) Austl. (Melbourne In.)	37·54 S	145·05 E
111	Oakley (ōk'lĭ) Id.	42·15 N	135·53 W
116	Oakley Ks.	39·08 N	100·49 W
120	Oakman (ōk'măn) Al.	33·42 N	87·20 W
107	Oakmont (ōk'mōnt) Pa. (Pittsburgh In.)	40·31 N	79·50 W
106	Oak Mtn. Al. (Birmingham In.)	33·22 N	86·42 W
107	Oak Park (pärk). Il. (Chicago In.)	41·53 N	87·48 W
112	Oak Point Wa. (Portland In.)	46·11 N	123·11 W
120	Oak Ridge (rĭj) Tn.	36·01 N	84·15 W
89	Oakville (ōk'vĭl) Can. (Toronto In.)	43·27 N	79·40 W
89	Oakville Can. (Winnipeg In.)	49·56 N	97·58 W
113	Oakville Mo. (St. Louis In.)	38·27 N	90·18 W
89	Oakville Cr. Can. (Toronto In.)	43·34 N	79·54 W
119	Oakwood (ōk'wōōd) Tx.	31·36 N	95·48 W
115	Oatman (ōt'măn) Az.	34·00 N	114·25 W
122	Oaxaca (State) (wä-hä'kä) Mex.	16·45 N	97·00 W
125	Oaxaca, Sierra de (Mts.) (sē-ĕ'r-rä dĕ). Mex.	16·15 N	97·25 W
125	Oaxaca de Juárez (kōōä'rĕz). Mex.	17·03 N	96·42 W
172	Ob' (R.) Sov. Un.	62·15 N	67·00 E
96	Oba (ō'bȧ) Can.	48·58 N	84·09 W
195	Obama (ō'bȧ-mä) Jap.	35·29 N	135·44 E
154	Oban (ō'băn) Scot.	56·25 N	5·35 W
215	Oban Hills Nig.	5·35 N	8·30 E
107	O'Bannon (ō-băn'nŏn) Ky. (Louisville In.)	38·17 N	85·30 W
97	Obatogamau (L.) (ō-bȧ-tō'găm-ô). Can.	49·38 N	74·10 W
218	Obbia (ôb'byä) Som. (Horn of Afr. In.)	5·24 N	48·28 E
161	Oberhausen (ō'bĕr-hou'zĕn) F.R.G. (Ruhr In.)	51·27 N	6·51 E
116	Oberlin (o'bēr-lĭn) Ks.	39·49 N	100·30 W
104	Oberlin Oh.	41·15 N	82·15 W
158	Oberösterreich (Prov.) Aus.	48·05 N	13·15 E
149	Oberroth (ō'bĕr-rōt) F.R.G. (Munich In.)	48·19 N	11·20 E
149	Ober-Schleisshiem (ō'bĕr-shlīs-hēm) F.R.G.(Munich In.)	48·15 N	11·34 E
197	Obi, Kepulauan (Is.) (ō'bē). Indon.	1·25 S	128·15 E
197	Obi, Pulau (I.) Indon.	1·30 S	127·45 E
135	Óbidos (ō'bē-dōōzh) Braz.	1·57 S	55·32 W
194	Obihiro (ō'bē-hē'rō) Jap.	42·55 N	142·50 E
120	Obion (R.) Tn.	36·10 N	89·25 W
120	Obion (R.), North Fk. (ō-bī'ŏn) Tn.	35·49 N	89·06 W
167	Obitochnaya, Kosa (C.) (kō-sä' ō-bē-tôch'nȧ-yȧ) Sov. Un.	46·32 N	36·07 E
195	Obitsu (R.) (ō'bēt'sōō) Jap. (Tōkyō In.)	35·19 N	140·03 E
218	Obock (ō-bŏk') Djibouti (Horn of Afr. In.)	11·55 N	43·15 E
166	Obol' (R.) (ô-bŏl') Sov. Un.	55·24 N	29·24 E
167	Oboyan' (ô-bô-yän') Sov. Un.	51·14 N	36·16 E
172	Obskaya Guba (B.) Sov. Un.	67·13 N	73·45 E
214	Obuasi Ghana	6·14 N	1·39 W
167	Obukhov (ō'bōō-kôf) Sov. Un.	50·07 N	30·36 E
174	Obukhovo. Sov. Un. (Moscow In.)	55·50 N	38·17 E
121	Ocala (ô-kä'lȧ) Fl.	29·11 N	82·09 W
124	Ocampo (ô-käm'pō) Mex.	22·49 N	99·23 W
134	Ocaña (ô-kän'yä) Col.	8·15 N	73·37 W
162	Ocaña (ô-kä'n-yä) Sp.	39·58 N	3·31 W
210	Occidental, Grand Erg (Dunes) Alg.	29·30 N	00·45 W
134	Occidental, Cordillera (Mts.) (kôr-dēl-yĕ'rä ôk-sē-dĕn-täl') Col. (In.)	5·05 N	76·04 W
134	Occidental, Cordillera (Mts.) Peru	10·12 S	76·58 W
122	Occidental, Sierra Madre (Mts.) (sē-ĕ'r-rä-mä'drĕ-ôk-sē-dĕn-tä'l) Mex	29·30 N	107·30 W
114	Ocean Beach (ō'shăn bēch) Ca. (In.)	32·44 N	117·14 W
119	Ocean Bight (B.) Ba.	21·15 N	73·15 W
105	Ocean City Md.	38·20 N	75·10 W
105	Ocean City NJ	39·15 N	74·35 W
92	Ocean Falls (Fôls) Can.	52·21 N	127·40 W
202	Ocean Grove Austl. (Melbourne In.)	38·16 S	144·32 E
105	Ocean Grove (grōv) NJ	40·10 N	74·00 W
114	Oceanside (ō'shăn-sīd) Ca.	33·11 N	117·22 W
106	Oceanside NY (New York In.)	40·38 N	73·39 W
120	Ocean Springs (sprĭngs) Ms.	30·25 N	88·49 W
165	Ocenele Mari Rom.	45·05 N	24·17 E
167	Ochakov (ô-chä'kôf) Sov. Un.	46·38 N	31·33 E
120	Ochlockonee R. (ŏk-lō-kō'nē) Fl.-Ga.	30·10 N	84·38 W
120	Ocilla (ô-sĭl'ȧ) Ga.	31·36 N	83·15 W
156	Ockelbo (ôk'ĕl-bō) Swe.	60·54 N	16·35 E
121	Ocmulgee (R.) Ga.	32·35 N	83·30 W
120	Ocmulgee Natl. Mon. (ôk-mŭl'gē) Ga.	32·45 N	83·28 W
165	Ocna-Sibiului (ōk'nȧ-sē-byōō-lōō-ē) Rom.	45·52 N	24·04 E
129	Ocoa, Bahai de (B.) (bä-ä'ē-ô-kō'ȧ) Dom. Rep.	18·20 N	70·40 W
125	Ococingo (ô-kô-sē'n-gō) Mex.	17·03 N	92·18 W
126	Ocom, L. (ô-kō'm) Mex. (In.)	19·26 N	88·18 W
120	Oconee, (R.) (ô-kō'nē) Ga.	32·45 N	83·00 W
109	Oconomowoc (ô-kŏn'ô-mô-wŏk') Wi.	43·06 N	88·24 W
109	Oconto (ô-kŏn'tō) Wi.	44·54 N	87·55 W
109	Oconto (R.) Wi.	45·08 N	88·24 W
109	Oconto Falls Wi.	44·53 N	88·11 W
126	Ocós (ô-kōs') Guat.	14·31 N	92·12 W
126	Ocotal (ô-kô-täl') Nic.	13·36 N	86·31 W
126	Ocotepeque (ô-kô-tā-pā'kȧ). Hond.	14·25 N	89·13 W
124	Ocotlán (ō-kō-tlän') Mex.	20·19 N	102·44 W
125	Ocotlán de Morelos (dā mô-rā'lōs) Mex.	16·46 N	96·41 W
125	Ocozocoautla (ô-kō'zō-kwä-ōō'tlä) Mex.	16·44 N	93·22 W
135	Ocumare del Tuy (ō-kōō-mä'rā del twē') Ven. (In.)	10·07 N	66·47 W
214	Oda Ghana	5·55 N	0·59 W
195	Odawara (ō'dȧ-wä'rä) Jap.	35·15 N	139·10 E
156	Odda (ôdh-ȧ) Nor.	60·04 N	6·30 E
218	Oddur Som. (Horn of Afr. In.)	3·55 N	43·45 E
108	Odebolt (ō'dē-bōlt) Ia.	42·20 N	95·14 W
162	Odemira (ō-dȧ-mē'rȧ) Port.	37·35 N	8·40 W
171	Ödemis (û'dĕ-mēsh) Tur.	38·12 N	28·00 E
218	Odendaalsrus (ō'dĕn-däls-rûs') S. Afr. (Johannesburg & Pretoria In.)	27·52 S	26·41 E
156	Odense (ō'dhĕn-sĕ) Den.	55·24 N	10·20 E
106	Odenton (ō'dĕn-tŭn) Md. (Baltimore In.)	39·05 N	76·43 W
158	Odenwald (For.) (ō'dĕn-väld) F.R.G.	49·39 N	8·55 E
158	Oder R. (ō'dēr) G.D.R.	52·40 N	14·19 E
167	Odessa (ô-dĕs'sä) Sov. Un.	46·28 N	30·44 E
118	Odessa (ô-dĕs'ȧ) Tx.	31·52 N	120·21 W
110	Odessa Wa.	47·20 N	118·42 W
167	Odessa (Oblast) Sov. Un.	46·05 N	29·48 E
162	Odiel (R.) (ō-dē-ĕl') Sp.	37·47 N	6·42 W
214	Odienné (ō-dē-ĕn-nā') Ivory Coast	9·30 N	7·34 W
148	Odiham (ŏd'ē-ăm) Eng. (London In.)	51·14 N	0·56 W
174	Odintsovo (ô dĕn'tsô-vô) Sov. Un. (Moscow In.)	55·40 N	37·16 E

ăt; finăl; rāte; senâte; ärm; ȧsk; sofȧ; fâre; ch-choose; dh-as th in other; bē; ēvent; bĕt; recĕnt; cratēr; g-go; gh-guttural g; bĭt; ĭ-short neutral; rīde; K-guttural k as ch in German ich;

PRONOUNCING INDEX Odiongan — Orange 323

Page Name Pronunciation Region Lat. °' Long. °'

197 Odiongan (ō-dê-ôŋ'gän). Phil. (In.) 12·24 N 121·59 E
163 Odivelas (ō-dê-vä'lyäs) Port. (Lisbon In.) 38·47 N 9·11 W
159 Odobesti (ō-dô-běsh't') Rom. 45·46 N 27·08 E
116 O'Donnell (ō-dŏn'ĕl) Tx. 32·59 N 101·51 W
159 Odorhei (ō-dôr-hā') Rom. 46·18 N 25·17 E
159 Odra R. (ô'drä) Pol. 50·28 N 17·55 E
135 Oeiras (wå-ê-räzh') Braz. 7·05 S 42·01 W
163 Oeirás (ô-ĕ'y-rà's) Port. (Lisbon In.) 38·42 N 9·18 W
109 Oelwein (ōl'wīn) Ia. 42·40 N 91·56 W
116 O'Fallon (ō-făl'ŭn) Il. (St. Louis In.) 38·36 N 89·55 W
111 O'Fallon Cr. Mt. 46·25 N 104·47 W
164 Ofanto (R.) (ô-fän'tō) It. 41·08 N 15·33 E
215 Offa Nig. 8·09 N 4·44 E
158 Offenbach (ôf'ĕn-bäk) F.R.G. 50·06 N 8·50 E
158 Offenburg (ôf'ĕn-bŏŏrgh) F.R.G. 48·28 N 7·57 E
195 Ofuna (ō'fōō-nä). Jap (Tōkyō In.) 35·21 N 139·32 E
211 Ogaden Plat. Eth. (Horn of Afr. In.) 6·45 N 44·53 E
195 Ogaki Jap. 35·21 N 136·36 E
108 Ogallala (ō-gä-lä'lä) Ne. 41·08 N 101·44 W
215 Ogbomosho (ŏg-bô-mō'shō) Nig. 8·08 N 4·15 E
109 Ogden (ŏg'dĕn) Ia. 42·10 N 94·20 W
113 Ogden. Ut. (Salt Lake City In.) 41·14 N 111·58 W
113 Ogden Pk. Ut. (Salt Lake City In.) 41·11 N 111·51 W
113 Ogden R. Ut. (Salt Lake City In.) 41·16 N 111·54 W
106 Ogdensburg (ŏg'dĕnz-bûrg) NJ (New York In.) 41·05 N 74·36 W
105 Ogdensburg NY 44·40 N 75·30 W
121 Ogeechee, (R.) (ō-gē'chê) Ga. 32·35 N 81·50 W
218 Ogies S. Afr. (Johannesburg & Pretoria In.) 26·03 S 29·04 E
90 Ogilvie Mts. (ō'g'l-vĭ) Can. 64·45 N 138·10 W
104 Oglesby (ō'g'lz-bĭ) Il. 41·20 N 89·00 W
164 Oglio (R.) (ōl'yō) It. 45·15 N 10·19 E
195 Ōgo (ō'gô) Jap. (Ōsaka In.) 34·49 N 135·06 E
216 Ogooué (R.) Gabon 0·50 S 9·20 E
214 Ogou (R.) Togo 8·05 N 1·30 E
174 Ogudnëvo (ôg-ŏŏg-nyô'vô) Sov. Un. (Moscow In.) 56·04 N 38·17 E
164 Ogulin (ō-gōō-lēn') Yugo. 45·17 N 15·11 E
215 Ogwashi-Uku Nig. 6·10 N 6·31 E
137 O'Higgins (Prov.) (ô-kê'gēns) Chile (Santiago In.) 34·17 S 70·52 W
103 Ohio, (State) (ō'hī'ō) U. S. 40·30 N 83·15 W
104 Ohio R. U. S. 37·25 N 88·05 W
121 Ohoopee (R.) (ō-hōō'pē) Ga. 32·32 N 82·38 W
158 Ohře (Eger) R. (ŏr'zhě) (ā'gĕr) Czech. 50·08 N 12·45 E
165 Ohrid (ō'krēd) Yugo. 41·08 N 20·46 E
165 Ohrid (L.) Alb.-Yugo. 40·58 N 20·35 E
195 Ōi (oi') Jap. (Tōkyō In.) 35·51 N 139·31 E
156 Oieren (L.) (ûĕĕrĕn) Nor. 59·50 N 11·25 E
195 Oi-Gawa (Strm.) (ō'ê-gä'wä) Jap. 35·09 N 138·05 E
105 Oil City (oil sĭ'tĭ) Pa. 41·25 N 79·40 W
149 Oirschot. Neth. (Amsterdam In.) 51·30 N 5·20 E
160 Oise (R.) (wäz) Fr. 49·30 N 2·56 E
149 Oisterwijk. Neth. (Amsterdam In.) 51·34 N 5·13 E
195 Oita (ō'ê-tä) Jap. 33·14 N 131·38 E
195 Oji (ō'jê) Jap. (Ōsaka In.) 34·36 N 135·43 E
118 Ojinaga (ō-Kê-nä'gä) Mex. 29·34 N 104·26 W
125 Ojitlán (San Lucas) (ōkê-tlän') (sän-lōō'käs) Mex. 18·04 N 96·23 W
124 Ojo Caliente (ōkō käl-yěn'tā) Mex. 21·50 N 100·43 W
124 Ojocaliente (ô-kô-kä-lyě'n-tě) Mex. 22·39 N 102·15 W
128 Ojo del Toro, Pico (Pk.) (pē'kô-ô-kō-děl-tô'rô) Cuba 19·55 N 77·25 W
89 Oka (ō-kä) Can. (Montreal In.) 45·28 N 74·05 W
171 Oka (R.) (ô-kä') Sov. Un. 52·10 N 35·20 E
172 Oka (R.) (ō-kä') Sov. Un. 53·28 N 101·09 E
170 Oka (R.) (ô-kà') Sov. Un. 55·10 N 42·10 E
212 Okahandja Namibia 21·50 S 16·45 E
93 Okanagan (R.) (ō'kȧ-näg'ăn) Can. 49·06 N 119·43 W
93 Okanagan L. Can. 50·00 N 119·28 W
210 Okano (R.) (ô'kä'nō) Gabon 0·15 N 11·08 E
110 Okanogan Wa. 48·20 N 119·34 W
110 Okanogan R. Wa. 48·36 N 119·33 W
120 Okatibbee (R.) (ō'kä-tĭb'ē) Ms. 32·37 N 88·54 W
120 Okatoma Cr. (ô-kà-tō'mă) Ms. 31·43 N 89·34 W
216 Okavango (Cubango) (R.) Ang.-S. W. Afr. 17·10 S 18·20 E
212 Okavango Swp. Bots. 19·30 S 23·02 E
195 Okaya (ō'kà-yà) Jap. 36·04 N 138·01 E
195 Okayama (ō'kà-yä'mà) Jap. 34·39 N 133·54 E
195 Okazaki (ō'kà-zä'kê) Jap. 34·58 N 137·09 E
121 Okeechobee (ō-kê-chō'bē) Fl. 27·15 N 80·50 W
121 Okeechobee, L. Fl. (In.) 27·00 N 80·49 W
116 Okeene (ō-kēn') Ok. 36·06 N 98·19 W
121 Okefenokee Swp. (ō'kê-fê-nō'kê) Ga. 30·54 N 82·20 W
117 Okemah (ô-kē'mä) Ok. 35·26 N 96·18 W
215 Okene Nig. 7·33 N 6·15 E
155 Oker (R.) (ō'kĕr) F.R.G. 52·23 N 10·00 E
173 Okha (ŭ-kä') Sov. Un. 53·44 N 143·12 E
174 Okhotino (ô-kô'tĭ-nô) Sov. Un. (Moscow In.) 56·14 N 38·24 E
173 Okhotsk (ô-kôtsk') Sov. Un. 59·28 N 143·32 E
183 Okhotsk, Sea of (ô-kôtsk') Asia 56·45 N 146·00 E
195 Oki Guntō (Arch.) (ō'kê gōōn'tō) Jap. 36·17 N 133·05 E
194 Okinawa (I.) (ō'kê-nä'wà) Jap. 26·30 N 128·30 E
194 Okinawa Guntō (Is.) (gōōn'tō') Jap. 26·50 N 127·25 E
195 Okino (I.) (ō'kê-nô) Jap. 36·22 N 133·27 E
194 Ōkino Erabu (I.) (ō-kē'nô-â-rä'bōō) Jap. 27·18 N 129·00 E
102 Oklahoma (State) (ô-klà-hō'mà) U. S. 36·00 N 98·20 W
117 Oklahoma City Ok. 35·27 N 97·32 W
121 Oklawaha (R.) (ŏk-lȧ-wô'hô) Fl. 29·13 N 82·00 W
117 Okmulgee (ŏk-mŭl'gē) Ok. 35·37 N 95·58 W
107 Okolona (ō-kô-lō'nȧ) Ky. (Louisville In.) 38·08 N 85·41 W
120 Okolona Ms. 33·59 N 88·43 W
194 Okushiri (I.) (ō'koo-shē'rē) Jap. 42·12 N 139·30 E
215 Okuta Nig. 9·14 N 3·15 E
112 Olalla (ō-lä'lä) Wa. (Seattle In.) 47·26 N 122·33 W
126 Olanchito (ō'län-chē'tô) Hond. 15·28 N 86·35 W
156 Öland (I.) (û-länd') Swe. 57·03 N 17·15 E
113 Olathe (ō-lā'thê) Ks. (Kansas City In.) 38·53 N 94·49 W
136 Olavarría (ō-lä-vär-rē'ä) Arg. 36·49 N 60·15 W
159 Oława (ô-lä'và) Pol. 50·57 N 17·18 E
137 Olazcoago (ô-läz-kôä'gô) Arg. (Buenos Aires In.) 35·14 S 60·37 W
164 Olbia (ô'l-byä) It. 40·55 N 9·28 E
149 Olching (ōl'kēng) F.R.G. (Munich In.) 48·13 N 11·21 E
128 Old Bahama Chan. (bȧ-hā'mȧ) N. A. 22·45 N 78·30 W
129 Old Bight Ba. 24·15 N 75·20 W
106 Old Bridge (brĭj) NJ (New York In.) 40·24 N 74·22 W
90 Old Crow (crō) Can. 67·51 N 139·58 W
158 Oldenburg (ôl'dĕn-bŏŏrgh) F.R.G. 53·09 N 8·13 E
105 Old Forge (fôrj) Pa. 41·20 N 75·50 W
148 Oldham (ōld'ȧm) Eng. 53·32 N 2·07 W
101 Old Harbor (här'bĕr) Ak. 57·18 N 153·20 W
154 Old Head of Kinsale (ōld hĕd ŏv kĭn-sāl) Ire. 51·35 N 8·35 W
119 Old R. Tx. (In.) 29·54 N 94·52 W
93 Olds (ōldz) Can. 51·47 N 114·06 W
212 Old Tate Bots. 21·18 S 27·43 E
98 Old Town (toun) Me. 44·55 N 68·42 W
94 Old Wives L. (wīvz) Can. 50·56 N 106·00 W
105 Olean (ō-lê-ăn') NY 42·05 N 78·25 W
159 Olecko (ô-lĕt'skô) Pol. 54·02 N 22·29 E
173 Olekma (R.) (ô-lyĕk-mà') Sov. Un. 55·41 N 120·33 E
173 Olëkminsk (ô-lyĕk-mĕnsk') Sov. Un. 60·39 N 120·40 E
173 Olenëk (R.) (ô-lyĕ-nyôk') Sov. Un. 70·18 N 121·15 E
160 Oléron Île, d' (I.) (ēl' dō lā-rôN') Fr. 45·52 N 1·58 W
159 Oleśnica (ô-lĕsh-nĭ'tsà) Pol. 51·13 N 17·24 E
161 Olfen (ōl'fĕn) F.R.G. (Ruhr In.) 51·43 N 7·22 E
173 Ol'ga (ôl'gà) Sov. Un. 43·48 N 135·44 E
194 Ol'gi, Zaliv (B.) (zä'lĭf ôl'gĭ) Sov. Un. 43·43 N 135·25 E
167 Ol'gopol (ôl-gô-pôl'y') Sov. Un. 48·11 N 29·28 E
162 Olhão (ôl-youN') Port. 37·02 N 7·54 W
213 Olievenhoutpoort S. Afr. (Johannesburg & Pretoria In.) 25·58 S 27·55 E
212 Olifants (R.) (ŏl'ĭ-fănts) S. Afr. 23·58 S 31·00 E
165 Ólimbos Grc. 40·03 N 22·22 E
183 Ólimbos (Mtn.) Cyprus (Palestine In.) 34·56 N 32·52 E
124 Olinalá (ô-lê-nä-lä') Mex. 17·47 N 98·51 W
135 Olinda (ô-lē'n-dä) Braz. 8·00 S 34·58 W
163 Oliva (ô-lē'vä) Sp. 38·54 N 0·07 W
162 Oliva de Jerez (ô-lē'vä dā hā'rĕth) Sp. 38·33 N 6·55 W
163 Olivais (ô-lê-vá'ys) Port. (Lisbon In.) 38·46 N 9·06 W
104 Olive Hill (ŏl'ĭv) Ky. 38·15 N 83·10 W
137 Oliveira (ô-lē-vā'rä) Braz. (Rio de Janeiro In.) 20·42 S 44·49 W
162 Olivenza (ō-lê-věn'thä) Sp. 38·42 N 7·06 W
93 Oliver (ŏ'lĭ-vĕr) Can. 49·11 N 119·33 W
89 Oliver Can. (Edmonton In.) 53·38 N 113·21 W
113 Oliver (ŏ'lĭvĕr) Wi. (Duluth In.) 46·39 N 92·12 W
89 Oliver L. Can. (Edmonton In.) 53·19 N 113·00 W
100 Olivia (ō-lĭv'ê-ȧ) Mn. 44·46 N 95·00 W
136 Olivos (ōlē'vōs) Arg. (Buenos Aires In.) 34·15 S 58·29 W
158 Olkusz (ôl'kōōsh) Pol. 50·16 N 19·41 E
134 Ollagüe (ô-lyä'gâ) Chile 21·17 S 68·17 W
148 Ollerton (ŏl'ĕr-tŭn) Eng. 53·12 N 1·02 W
113 Olmos Park (ŏl'mŭs pärk') Tx. (San Antonio In.) 29·27 N 98·32 W
104 Olney (ŏl'nĭ) Il. 38·45 N 88·05 W
112 Olney (ŏl'nē) Or. (Portland In.) 46·06 N 123·45 W
116 Olney Tx. 33·24 N 98·43 W
99 Olomane (R.) (ō'lô mä'nē) Can. 51·05 N 60·50 W
159 Olomouc (ô'lô-mōts) Czech. 49·37 N 17·15 E
157 Olonets (ô-lô'nĕts) Sov. Un. 60·58 N 32·54 E
197 Olongapo Phil. (In.) 14·49 S 120·17 E
160 Oloron, Gave d' (Strm.) (gäv-dō-lō-rôN') Fr. 43·21 N 0·44 W
160 Oloron-Ste. Marie (ō-lō-rôNt'sănt mȧ-rē') Fr. 43·11 N 1·37 W
163 Olot (ô-lōt') Sp. 42·09 N 2·30 E
161 Olpe (ōl'pē) F.R.G. (Ruhr In.) 51·02 N 7·51 E
167 Ol'shanka (ôl'shäŋ-kä) Sov. Un. 48·14 N 30·52 E
167 Ol'shany (ôl'shän-ê) Sov. Un. 50·02 N 35·54 E
158 Olsnitz (ōlz'nētz) G.D.R. 50·25 N 12·11 E
159 Olsztyn (ôl'shtĕn) Pol. 53·47 N 20·28 E
158 Olten (ôl'tĕn) Switz. 47·20 N 7·53 E
165 Oltenita (ôl-tā'nĭ-tsȧ) Rom. 44·05 N 26·39 E
153 Oltul (R.) Rom. 44·09 N 24·40 E
162 Olvera (ôl-vĕ'rä) Sp. 36·55 N 7·16 W
110 Olympia (ô-lĭm'pĭ-ȧ) Wa. 47·02 N 122·52 W
110 Olympic Mts. Wa. 47·54 N 123·58 W
110 Olympic Natl. Park (ô-lĭm'pĭk) Wa. 47·54 N 123·00 W
110 Olympus Mt. (ô-lĭm'pŭs) Wa. 47·43 N 123·30 W
105 Olyphant (ŏl'ĭ-fănt) Pa. 41·30 N 75·40 W
173 Olyutorskiy, Mys (C.) (ŭl-yōō'tŏr-skê) Sov. Un. 59·49 N 167·16 E
195 Omae-Zaki (Pt.) (ō'mä-â zä'kê) Jap. 34·37 N 138·15 E
154 Omagh (ō'mä) N. Ire. 54·35 N 7·25 W
108 Omaha (ō'mȧ-hä) Ne. 41·18 N 95·57 W
108 Omaha Ind. Res. Ne. 42·09 N 96·08 W
182 Oman Asia 20·00 N 57·45 E
186 Oman, G. of Asia 24·24 N 58·58 E
12 Omaruru (ō-mä-rōō'rōō) Namibia 21·25 S 16·50 E
216 Omboué Gabon 1·34 S 9·15 E
164 Ombrone (R.) (ôm-brō'nä) It. 42·48 N 11·18 E
Omdurman, see UmmDurmān
125 Omealca (ōmȧ-äl'kō) Mex. 18·44 N 96·45 W
124 Ometepec (ô-mā-tâ-pĕk') Mex. 16·41 N 98·27 W
211 Om Hajer Eth. 14·06 N 36·46 E
92 Omineca (R.) (ô-mĭ-nĕk'ȧ) Can. 55·10 N 125·45 W
92 Omineca Mts. Can. 56·00 N 125·00 W
195 Ōmiya (ō'mê-yȧ). Jap. (Tōkyō In.) 35·54 S 139·38 E
126 Omoa (ô-mō'rä) Hond. 15·43 N 88·03 W
173 Omolon (R.) (ō'mō) Sov. Un. 67·43 N 159·15 E
195 Ōmori (Kioroshi) (ō'mô-rê) (kē'ō-rō'shē) Jap. (Tōkyō In.) 35·50 N 140·09 E
211 Omo R. (ō'mō) Eth. 5·54 N 36·09 E
215 Omoko Nig. 5·20 N 6·39 E
126 Omotepe, Isla de (I.) (ē's-lä-dĕ-ō-mô-tā'pâ) Nic. 11·32 N 85·30 W
109 Omro (ŏm'rō) Wi. 44·01 N 89·46 W
172 Omsk (ômsk) Sov. Un. 55·12 N 73·19 E
195 Ōmura (ō'mōō-rȧ) Jap. 32·56 N 129·57 E
195 Ōmuta (ō-mōō-tȧ) Jap. 33·02 N 130·28 E
170 Omutninsk (ō'mōō-tēnsk) Sov. Un. 58·38 N 52·10 E
108 Onawa (ŏn-ȧ-wȧ) Ia. 42·02 N 96·05 W
104 Onaway Mi. 45·25 N 84·10 W
216 Oncócua Ang. 16·34 S 13·28 E
163 Onda (ōn'dä) Sp. 39·58 N 0·13 W
159 Ondava (R.) (ōn'dȧ-vȧ) Czech. 48·51 N 21·40 E
215 Ondo Nig. 7·04 N 4·47 E
192 Öndör Haan Mong. 47·20 N 110·40 E
170 Onega (ô-nyĕ'gȧ) Sov. Un. 63·50 N 38·08 E
170 Onega (.R) Sov. Un. 63·20 N 39·20 E
Onega, L., see Onezhskoye Ozero
105 Oneida (ō-nī'dȧ) NY 43·05 N 75·40 W
105 Oneida (L.) NY 43·10 N 76·00 W
108 O'Neill (ō-nēl') Ne. 42·28 N 98·38 W
173 Onekotan (I.) (ŭ-nyĕ-kŭ-tän') Sov. Un. 49·45 N 153·45 E
105 Oneonta (ō-nê-ŏn'tȧ) NY 42·25 N 75·05 W
170 Onezhskaja Guba (B.) Sov. Un. 64·30 N 36·00 E
170 Onezhskiy, P-Ov. (Pen.) Sov. Un. 64·30 N 37·40 E
170 Onezhskoye Ozero (Onega, L.) (ô-năsh'skô-yĕ ô'zĕ-rô) Sov. Un. 62·02 N 34·35 E
188 Ongin (ŏn'gĭn') Mong. 46·00 N 102·46 E
185 Ongole India 15·36 N 80·03 E
213 Onilahy (R.) Mad. 23·41 S 45·00 E
215 Onitsha (ô-nĭt'shȧ) Nig. 6·09 N 6·47 W
195 Onomichi (ō'nō-mē'chê) Jap. 34·27 N 133·12 E
173 Onon (R.) (ô'nôn) Sov. Un. 50·33 N 114·18 E
173 Onon Gol (R.) (ô'nôn) Sov. Un. 48·30 N 110·38 E
135 Onoto (ô-nŏ'tō) Ven. (In.) 9·38 N 65·03 W
204 Onslow (ŏnz'lō) Austl. 21·53 S 115·00 E
121 Onslow B. (ŏnz'lō) NC 34·22 N 77·35 W
195 Ontake San (Mtn.) (ôn'tä-kȧ sän) Jap. 35·55 N 137·29 E
113 Ontario (ŏn-tā'rĭ-ō) Ca. (Los Angeles In.) 34·04 N 117·39 W
110 Ontario Or. 44·02 N 116·57 W
91 Ontario (Prov.) Can. 50·47 N 88·50 W
103 Ontario, L. U. S.-Can. 43·35 N 79·05 W
163 Onteniente (ōn-tȧ-nyĕn'tā) Sp. 38·48 N 0·35 W
109 Ontonagon (ŏn-tô-năg'ŏn) Mi. 46·50 N 89·20 W
195 Ōnuki (ō'nōō-kê). Jap. (Tōkyō In.) 35·17 N 139·51 E
204 Oodnadatta (ōōd'nȧ-dȧ'tȧ) Austl. 27·38 S 135·40 E
204 Ooldea Station (ōōl-dā'ȧ) Austl. 30·35 S 132·08 E
117 Oologah Res. Ok. 36·43 N 95·32 W
149 Ooltgensplaat Neth. (Amsterdam In.) 51·41 N 4·19 E
120 Oostanaula (R.) (ōō-stȧ-nô'lȧ) Ga. 34·25 N 85·10 W
155 Oostende (ōst-ĕn'dē) Bel. 51·14 N 2·55 E
149 Oosterhout. Neth. (Amsterdam In.) 51·38 N 4·52 E
155 Ooster Schelde (R.) Neth. 51·40 N 3·40 E
92 Ootsa L. Can. 53·49 N 126·18 W
126 Opalaca, Sierra de (Mts.) (sē-ĕ'r-rä-dĕ-ō-pä-lä'kä) Hond. 14·30 N 88·29 W
95 Opasquia (ō-păs'kwê-ȧ) Can. 53·16 N 93·53 W
159 Opatow (ô-pä'tōōf) Pol. 50·47 N 21·25 E
159 Opava (ō'pä-vä) Czech. 49·56 N 17·52 E
156 Opdal (ôp'däl) Nor. 62·37 N 9·41 E
120 Opelika (ŏp-ê-lĭ'kȧ) Al. 32·39 N 85·23 W
119 Opelousas (ŏp-ē-lōō'sȧs) La. 30·33 N 92·04 W
105 Opeongo (L.) (ŏp-ê-ôŋ'gō) Can. 45·40 N 78·20 W
111 Opheim (ô-fīm') Mt. 48·51 N 106·19 W
101 Ophir (ō'fĕr) Ak. 63·10 N 156·28 W
183 Ophir, Mt. Mala. (Singapore In.) 2·22 N 102·37 E
126 Opico (ô-pē'kō) Sal. 13·50 N 89·23 W
91 Opinaca (R.) (ŏp-ĭ-nä'kȧ) Can. 52·28 N 77·40 W
161 Opladen (ōp'lä-dĕn) F.R.G. (Ruhr In.) 51·04 N 7·00 E
215 Opobo Nig. 4·34 N 7·27 E
166 Opochka (ō-pôch'kȧ) Sov. Un. 56·43 N 28·39 E
159 Opoczno (ō-pôch'nō) Pol. 51·22 N 20·18 E
159 Opole (ô-pôl'ȧ) Pol. 50·42 N 17·55 E
159 Opole Lubelskie (ô-pō'lă lōō-bĕl'skyĕ) Pol. 51·09 N 21·58 E
Oporto, see Pôrto
110 Opportunity (ŏp-ŏr tū'nĭ tĭ) Wa. 47·37 N 117·20 W
167 Oposhnya (ô-pôsh'nyȧ) Sov. Un. 49·57 N 34·34 E
120 Opp (ŏp) Al. 31·18 N 86·15 W
113 Oquirrh Mts. (ō'kwĕr) Ut. (Salt Lake City In.) 40·38 N 112·11 W
159 Oradea (ô-räd'yä) Rom. 47·02 N 21·55 E
152 Oran (Ouahran) (ō-rän) (ô-räN') Alg. 35·46 N 0·45 W
136 Orán (ô-rȧ'n) Arg. 23·13 S 64·17 W
117 Oran (ŏr'ȧn) Mo. 37·05 N 89·39 W
203 Orange (ŏr'ĕnj) Austl. 33·15 S 149·08 E

ng-sing; ŋ-baŋk; N-nasalized n; nŏd; cŏmmit; ōld; ôbey; ôrder; fōōd; fŏŏt; ou-out; s-soft; sh-dish; th-thin; pūre; ûnite; ûrn; stŭd; circŭs; ü-as "y" in study; '-indeterminate vowel.

324 Orange — Ouezzane PRONOUNCING INDEX

Page	Name Pronunciation Region	Lat. °′	Long. °′
113	Orange.....Ca. (Los Angeles In.)	33·48 N	117·51 W
105	Orange.....Ct.	41·15 N	73·00 W
160	Orange (ô-ranzh')..........Fr.	44·08 N	4·48 E
106	Orange.......NJ (New York In.)	40·46 N	74·14 W
116	Orange..........Tx.	30·07 N	93·44 W
135	Orange, Cabo (C.) (kä-bô-rà'n-zhě).Braz.	4·25 N	51·30 W
121	Orange (L.)..........Fl.	29·30 N	82·12 W
212	Orange (R.)......Namibia-S. Afr.	29·15 S	17·30 E
121	Orangeburg (ŏr'ĕnj-bûrg)......SC	33·30 N	80·50 W
128	Orange Cay (I.) (ŏr-ĕnj kē)...Ba.	24·55 N	79·05 W
108	Orange City..........Ia.	43·01 N	96·06 W
212	Orange Free State (Prov.)..S. Afr.	28·15 S	26·00 E
89	Orangeville (ŏr'ĕnj-vĭl) Can. (Toronto In.)	43·55 N	80·06 W
218	Orangeville..........S. Afr. (Johannesburg & Pretoria In.)	27·05 S	28·13 E
126	Orange Walk (wôl''k)..Belize (In.)	18·09 N	88·32 W
197	Orani (ō-rä'nē).........Phil. (In.)	14·47 N	120·32 E
149	Oranienburg (ō-rä'nē-ĕn-bŏŏrgh) G.D.R. (Berlin In.)	52·45 N	13·14 E
212	Oranjemund..........Namibia	28·33 S	16·20 E
165	Orastie (ô-rûsh'tyå)........Rom.	45·50 N	23·14 E
	Oraşul-Stalin, see Braşov		
164	Orbetello (ôr-bå-těl'lō).........It.	42·27 N	11·15 E
162	Orbigo (R.) (ôr-bē'gō)........Sp.	42·30 N	5·55 W
203	Orbost (ôr'bŭst)..........Austl.	37·43 S	148·20 E
112	Orcas (I.) (ôr'kås) Wa. (Vancouver In.)	48·43 N	122·52 W
113	Orchard Farm (ôr'chērd färm) Mo. (St. Louis In.)	38·53 N	90·27 W
107	Orchard Park....NY (Buffalo In.)	42·46 N	78·46 W
112	Orchards (ôr'chēdz) Wa. (Portland In.)	45·40 N	122·33 W
134	Orchilla (ôr-kĭl-ȧ)..........Ven.	11·47 N	66·34 W
108	Ord (ôrd)..........Ne.	41·35 N	98·57 W
204	Ord (R.)..........Austl.	17·30 S	128·40 E
174	Orda (ôr'dà) Sov. Un. (Urals In.)	56·50 N	57·12 E
162	Ōrdenes (ōr'då-nās)..........Sp.	43·46 N	8·24 W
192	Ordos Des..........China	39·12 N	108·10 E
115	Ord Pk..........Az.	33·55 N	109·40 W
171	Ordu (ôr'dŏŏ)..........Tur.	41·00 N	37·50 E
162	Orduña (ôr-dōō'nyä)..........Sp.	42·59 N	3·01 W
116	Ordway (ôrd'wā)..........Co.	38·11 N	103·46 W
171	Ordzhonikidze (ora ghō nĭ kĭd ze) Sov. Un.	43·05 N	44·35 E
156	Örebro (û'rē-brō)..........Swe.	59·16 N	15·11 E
174	Oredezh R. (ô'rě-dězh) Sov. Un. (Leningrad In.)	59·23 N	30·21 E
109	Oregon..........Il.	42·01 N	89·21 W
102	Oregon (State)..........U. S.	43·40 N	121·50 W
110	Oregon Caves Natl. Mon. (cāvz) Or.	42·05 N	123·13 W
112	Oregon City....Or. (Portland In.)	45·21 N	122·36 W
156	Öregrund (û-rĕ-grŏŏnd)......Swe.	60·20 N	18·26 E
167	Orekhov (ôr-yě'kôf).....Sov. Un.	47·34 N	35·51 E
166	Orekhovo-Zuyevo (ôr-yě'kô-vô zōō'yě-vô).Sov. Un.	55·46 N	39·00 E
166	Orël (ôr-yôl')..........Sov. Un.	52·54 N	36·03 E
166	Orël (Oblast)..........Sov. Un.	52·35 N	36·08 E
167	Orel' (R.)..........Sov. Un.	49·08 N	34·55 E
115	Orem (ŏ'rěm)..........Ut.	40·15 N	111·50 W
	Ore Mts., see Erzgebirge		
171	Orenburg (ô'rěn-bŏŏrg)..Sov. Un.	51·50 N	55·05 E
162	Orense (ô-rěn'sā)..........Sp.	42·20 N	7·52 W
128	Organos, Sierra de los (Mts.) (sē-ě'r-rä-dě-lôs-ŏ'r-gä-nôs).Cuba	22·20 N	84·10 W
115	Organ Pipe Cactus Natl. Mon (ôr'găn pīp kăk'tŭs).Az.	32·14 N	113·05 W
137	Orgãos, Serra das (Mtn.) (sě'r-rä-däs-ôr-gouN's) Braz. (Rio de Janeiro In.)	22·30 S	43·01 W
167	Orgeyev (ôr-gyě'yěf).....Sov. Un.	47·27 N	28·49 E
188	Orhon Gol (R.)..........Mong.	48·33 N	103·07 E
134	Oriental, Cordillera (Mts.) (kôr-dēl-yě'rä ō-rē-ĕn-täl').Bol.	14·00 S	68·33 W
134	Oriental, Cordillera (Mts.) (kôr-dēl-yě'rä).Col. (In.)	3·30 N	74·27 W
129	Oriental, Cordillera (Mts.) (kôr-dēl-yě'rä-ô-ryě'n-täl) Dom. Rep.	18·55 N	69·40 W
122	Oriental, Sierra Madre, (Mts.) (sē-ě'r-rä-mä'drě-ô-ryě'n-täl') Mex.	25·30 N	100·45 W
163	Orihuela (ō'rê-wā'lä)........Sp.	38·04 N	0·55 W
105	Orillia (ô-rĭl'ĭ-ȧ)..........Can.	44·35 N	79·25 W
111	Orin..........Wy.	42·40 N	105·10 W
112	Orinda....Ca. (San Francisco In.)	37·53 N	122·11 W
134	Orinoco, Rio (R.) (rē'ō-ô-rĭ-nō'kô).Ven.	8·32 N	63·13 W
197	Orion (ō-rē-ōn')........Phil. (In.)	14·37 N	120·34 E
184	Orissa (State) (ô-rĭs'ȧ)......India	25·09 N	83·50 E
164	Oristano (ô-rēs-tä'nō)..........It.	39·53 N	8·38 E
164	Oristano, Golfo di (G.) (gôl-fô-dē-ô-rēs-tä'nō).It.	39·53 N	8·12 E
135	Orituco (R.) (ô-rē-tōō'kō) Ven. (In.)	9·37 N	66·25 W
135	Oriuco (ô-rēōō'kō) (R.).Ven. (In.)	9·36 N	66·25 W
157	Orivesi (L.)..........Fin.	62·15 N	29·55 E
125	Orizaba (ô-rē-zä'bä)........Mex.	18·52 N	97·05 E
156	Orkdal (ôr'k-däl)..........Nor.	63·19 N	9·54 W
150	Örkedalen (ûr'kě-dä-lěn).....Nor.	63·13 N	9·53 E
156	Örken (L.) (ûr'kěn).........Swe.	57·11 N	14·45 E
156	Orkla (R.) (ôr'klå)..........Nor.	62·55 N	9·50 E
218	Orkney (ôrk'nĭ)..........S. Afr. (Johannesburg & Pretoria In.)	26·58 S	26·39 E
154	Orkney (Is.)..........Scot.	59·01 N	2·08 W
121	Orlando (ôr-lăn'dō)......Fl. (In.)	28·32 N	81·22 W
213	Orlando (ôr-län-dô).......S. Afr. (Johannesburg & Pretoria In.)	26·15 S	27·56 E
107	Orland Park (ôr-lănd') Il. (Chicago In.)	41·38 N	87·52 W
89	Orleans (ôr-lå-äN') Can. (Ottawa In.)	45·28 N	75·31 W
160	Orléans (ôr-lā-äN')..........Fr.	47·55 N	1·56 E
104	Orleans (ôr-lēnz')..........In.	38·40 N	86·25 W
89	Orléans, Île d' (I.) Can. (Quebec In.)	46·56 N	70·57 W
	Orléansville, see El Asnam		
121	Ormond Beach (ôr'mŏnd)......Fl.	29·15 N	81·05 W
148	Ormskirk (ôrms'kērk).......Eng.	53·34 N	2·53 W
89	Ormstown (ôrms'toun) Can. (Montreal In.)	45·07 N	74·00 W
160	Orne (R.) (ôrn')..........Fr.	49·05 N	0·32 W
159	Orneta (ôr-nyě'tä)..........Pol.	54·07 N	20·10 E
156	Ornö (I.)..........Swe.	59·02 N	18·35 E
150	Örnsköldsvik (ûrn'skôlts-vēk).Swe.	63·10 N	18·32 E
124	Oro, Rio del (R.) (rē'ō děl ō'rō) Mex.	18·04 N	100·59 W
108	Oro, Rio del (R.)..........Mex.	26·04 N	105·40 W
164	Orobie, Alpi (Mts.) (äl'pē-ô-rŏ'byě).It.	46·05 N	9·47 E
134	Orocué (ô-rô-kwā')..........Col.	4·48 N	71·26 W
215	Oron..........Nig.	4·48 N	8·14 E
154	Oronsay, Pass .of (ō'rŏn-så)..Scot.	55·55 N	6·25 W
164	Orosei, Golfo di (G.) (gôl-fô-dē-ō-rô-sā'ē).It.	40·12 N	9·45 E
159	Orosháza (ô-rôsh-hä'sô)....Hung.	46·33 N	20·31 E
126	Orosi Vol. (ō-rō'sē)........C. R.	11·00 N	85·30 W
114	Oroville (ōr'ō-vĭl)..........Ca.	39·29 N	121·34 W
110	Oroville..........Wa.	48·55 N	119·25 W
104	Orrville (ôr'vĭl)..........Oh.	40·45 N	81·50 W
156	Orsa (ōr'sä)..........Swe.	61·08 N	14·35 E
89	Orsainville.....Can. (Quebec In.)	46·23 N	71·17 W
156	Örsdals Vand (L.) (ûrs-däls vän) Nor.	58·39 N	6·06 E
166	Orsha (ôr'shå)..........Sov. Un.	54·29 N	30·28 E
171	Orsk (ôrsk)..........Sov. Un.	51·15 N	58·50 E
165	Orsova (ôr'shô-vä)..........Rom.	44·43 N	22·26 E
134	Ortega (ôr-tě'gä).......Col. (In.)	3·56 N	75·12 W
162	Ortegal, Cabo (C.) (kå'bô-ôr-tå-gäl').Sp.	43·46 N	8·15 W
149	Orth..........Aus. (Vienna In.)	48·09 N	16·42 E
163	Orthez (ôr-těz')..........Fr.	43·29 N	0·43 W
162	Ortigueira (ôr-tê-gā'ê-rä)......Sp.	43·40 N	7·50 W
112	Orting (ôrt'ĭng).Wa. (Seattle In.)	47·06 N	122·12 W
164	Ortona (ôr-tō'nä)..........It.	42·22 N	14·22 E
108	Ortonville (ôr-tŭn-vĭl).......Mn.	45·18 N	96·26 W
134	Oruro (ô-rōō'rō)..........Bol.	17·57 S	66·59 W
164	Orvieto (ôr-vyå'tō)..........It.	42·43 N	12·08 E
165	Oryakhovo..........Bul.	43·43 N	23·59 E
156	Os (ôs)..........Nor.	60·24 N	5·22 E
170	Osa (ô'så)..........Sov. Un.	57·18 N	55·25 E
127	Osa, Pen. de (ō'sä)..........C. R.	8·30 N	83·25 W
109	Osage (ō'sāj)..........Ia.	43·16 N	92·49 W
117	Osage (R.)..........Mo.	38·10 N	93·12 W
117	Osage City (ō'sāj sĭ'tĭ)........Ks.	38·28 N	95·53 W
195	Ōsaka (ō'sä-kä)..Jap. (Ōsaka In.)	34·40 N	135·27 E
195	Ōsaka (Pref.)....Jap. (Ōsaka In.)	34·45 N	135·36 E
195	Ōsaka-Wan (B.) (wän).......Jap.	34·34 N	135·16 E
109	Osakis (ô-sā'kĭs)..........Mn.	45·51 N	95·09 W
109	Osakis (L.)..........Mn.	45·55 N	94·55 W
117	Osawatomie (ŏs-ȧ-wăt'ô-mē)..Ks.	38·29 N	94·57 W
116	Osborne (ŏz'bŭrn)..........Ks.	39·25 N	98·42 W
117	Osceola (ŏs-ē-ō'lå)..........Ar.	35·42 N	89·58 W
109	Osceola..........Ia.	41·04 N	93·45 W
117	Osceola..........Mo.	38·02 N	93·41 W
108	Osceola..........Ne.	41·11 N	97·34 W
117	Osceola..........Tn.	35·42 N	89·58 W
104	Oscoda (ŏs-kō'dȧ)..........Mi.	44·25 N	83·20 W
166	Osëtr (R.) (ô'sět'r).......Sov. Un.	54·27 N	38·15 E
104	Osgood (ŏz'gŏŏd)..........In.	39·10 N	85·20 W
89	Osgoode.......Can. (Ottawa In.)	45·09 N	75·37 W
172	Osh (ôsh)..........Sov. Un.	40·28 N	72·47 E
105	Oshawa (ŏsh'ȧ-wȧ)..........Can.	43·50 N	78·50 W
195	Ōshima (I.) (ō'shē'mä).......Jap.	34·47 N	139·35 E
108	Oshkosh (ŏsh'kŏsh)..........Ne.	41·24 N	102·22 W
109	Oshkosh..........Wi.	44·01 N	88·35 W
157	Oshmyany (ôsh-myä'nĭ)..Sov. Un.	54·27 N	25·55 E
215	Oshogbo..........Nig.	7·47 N	4·34 E
165	Osijek (ôs'ĭ-yěk)..........Yugo.	45·33 N	18·48 E
172	Osinniki (ŭ-sē'nyĭ-kē)....Sov. Un.	53·29 N	85·19 E
109	Oskaloosa (ŏs-kȧ-lōō'sȧ)......Ia.	41·16 N	92·40 W
156	Oskarshamm (ôs'kärs-häm'n) Swe.	57·16 N	16·24 E
156	Oskarström (ôs'kärs-strûm) Swe.	56·48 N	12·55 E
167	Oskol (R.) (ôs-kôl')......Sov. Un.	51·00 N	37·41 E
156	Oslo (ôs'lō)..........Nor.	59·56 N	10·41 E
156	Oslo Fd (fyôrd)..........Nor.	59·03 N	10·35 E
162	Osma (ōs'mä)..........Sp.	41·35 N	3·02 W
171	Osmaniye..........Tur.	37·10 N	36·30 E
158	Osnabrück (ôs-nä-brük')...F.R.G.	52·16 N	8·05 E
136	Osorno (ō-sō'r-nō)..........Chile	40·42 S	73·13 W
205	Osprey Reef (I.) (ŏs'prå)....Austl.	14·00 S	146·45 E
203	Ossa, Mt. (ŏsȧ)..........Austl.	41·45 S	146·05 E
113	Osseo (ŏs'sē-ō)..........Mn. (Minneapolis, St. Paul In.)	45·07 N	93·24 W
106	Ossining (ŏs'ĭ-nĭng) NY (New York In.)	41·09 N	73·51 W
98	Ossipee (ŏs'ĭ-pē)..........NH	43·42 N	71·08 W
156	Ossjöen (L.) (ôs-syûěn).....Nor.	61·20 N	12·00 E
166	Ostashkov (ôs-täsh'kôf)..Sov. Un.	57·07 N	33·04 E
155	Oste (R.) (ŏz'tě)..........F.R.G.	53·20 N	9·19 E
167	Oster (ōs'těr)..........Sov. Un.	50·55 N	30·52 E
167	Oster-daläven (R.)..........Swe.	61·40 N	13·00 E
167	Oster Fd. (ûs'těr fyôr')......Nor.	60·40 N	5·25 E
167	Östersund (ûs'tēr-sŏŏnd).....Swe.	63·09 N	14·49 E
167	Östhammar (ûst'häm'är).....Swe.	60·16 N	18·21 E
163	Ostia Antica (ô's-tyä-än-tē'kä) It. (Rome In.)	41·46 N	12·24 E
	Ostia Lido, see Lido di Roma		
159	Ostrava..........Czech.	49·51 N	18·18 E
159	Ostróda (ôs'trŏŏt-å)..........Pol.	53·41 N	19·58 E
167	Ostróg (ôs-trôk')........Sov. Un.	50·21 N	26·40 E
167	Ostrogozhsk (ôs-trô-gôzhk') Sov. Un.	50·53 N	39·03 E
159	Ostrołeka (ôs-trô-woN'kå).....Pol.	53·04 N	21·35 E
167	Ostropol' (ôs-trô-pôl')....Sov. Un.	49·48 N	27·32 E
166	Ostrov (ôs-trôf')........Sov. Un.	57·21 N	28·22 E
159	Ostrowiec Świętokrzyski (ōs-trō'vyěts shvyěN-tō-kzhĭ'ske) Pol.	50·55 N	21·24 E
159	Ostrów Lubelski (ôs'trŏŏf lōō'běl-skĭ).Pol.	51·32 N	22·49 E
159	Ostrów Mazowiecka (mä-zō-vyět'skä).Pol.	52·47 N	21·54 E
159	Ostrów Wielkopolski (ôs'trŏŏv vyěl-kō-pōl'skē).Pol.	51·38 N	17·49 E
159	Ostrzeszów (ôs-tzhä'shŏŏf)....Pol.	51·26 N	17·56 E
165	Ostuni (ôs-tōō'nē)..........It.	40·44 N	17·35 E
165	Osum (R.) (ō'sŏŏm).........Alb.	40·37 N	20·00 E
195	Ōsumi-Guntō (Arch.) (ō'sōō-mē gŏŏn'tō).Jap	30·34 N	130·30 E
195	Ōsumi Kaikyō (Van Diemen) (Str.) (käê'kyô) (văn dē'měn) Jap.	31·02 N	130·10 E
162	Osuna (ô-sōō'nä)..........Sp.	37·18 N	5·05 W
166	Osveya (ôs'vě-yȧ).......Sov. Un.	56·00 N	28·08 E
148	Oswaldtwistle (ŏz-wăld-twĭs''l) Eng.	53·44 N	2·23 W
105	Oswegatchie (R.) (ŏs-wê-găch'ĭ) NY	44·15 N	75·20 W
117	Oswego (ŏs-wē'gō)..........Ks.	37·10 N	95·08 W
105	Oswego..........NY	43·25 N	76·30 E
159	Oswiecim (ôsh-vyăN'tsyĭm)...Pol.	50·02 N	19·17 E
194	Otaru (ō'tȧ-rōō)..........Jap.	43·07 N	141·00 W
134	Otavalo (ōtä-vä'lō)..........Ec.	0·14 N	78·16 W
212	Otavi (ô-tä'vē)..........Namibia	19·35 S	17·20 E
114	Otay (ō'tā)..........Ca. (In.)	32·36 N	117·04 W
166	Otepää (ō'tě-pâ)........Sov. Un.	58·03 N	26·31 E
165	Othonoí (I.)..........Grc.	39·51 N	19·26 E
165	Óthris, Óros (Mts.)..........Grc.	39·00 N	22·15 E
214	Oti (R.)..........Ghana	9·00 N	0·10 E
91	Otish, Mts. (ô-tĭsh')..........Can.	52·15 N	70·20 W
212	Otjiwarongo (ŏt-jē-wȧ-rôn'gō) Namibia	20·20 S	16·25 E
164	Otočac (ō'tô-chȧts).........Yugo.	44·53 N	15·15 E
174	Otradnoye (ô-trå'd-nôyě) Sov. Un. (Leningrad In.)	59·46 N	30·50 E
165	Otranto (ô'trän-tô) (ô-trän'tō).It.	40·07 N	18·30 E
165	Otranto, C. di..........It.	40·06 N	18·32 E
165	Otranto, Strait of.........It.-Alb.	40·30 N	18·45 E
174	Otra R. (ôt'rå) Sov. Un. (Moscow In.)	55·22 N	38·20 E
104	Otsego (ŏt-sē'gō)..........Mi.	42·25 N	85·45 W
195	Otsu (ō'tsŏŏ).....Jap. (Ōsaka In.)	35·00 N	135·54 E
156	Ottavand (L.) (ôt'tȧ-vän)....Nor.	61·53 N	8·40 E
89	Ottawa (ŏt'ȧ-wȧ) Can. (Ottawa In.)	45·25 N	75·43 W
104	Ottawa..........Il.	41·20 N	88·50 W
117	Ottawa..........Ks.	38·37 N	95·16 W
104	Ottawa..........Oh.	41·00 N	84·00 W
91	Ottawa (R.)..........Can.	46·05 N	77·20 W
91	Ottawa Is..........Can.	59·50 N	81·00 W
156	Otteråen (ôt'ěr-ôěn).........Nor.	59·13 N	7·20 E
115	Otter Cr. (ŏt'ēr)..........Ut.	38·20 N	111·55 W
105	Otter Cr..........Vt.	44·05 N	73·15 W
112	Otter Pt........Can. (Seattle In.)	48·21 N	123·50 W
108	Otter Tail (L.)..........Mn.	46·21 N	95·52 W
113	Otterville (ŏt'ēr-vĭl) Il. (St. Louis In.)	39·03 N	90·24 W
212	Ottery (ŏt'ēr-ĭ).......S. Afr. (In.)	34·02 S	18·31 E
109	Ottumwa (ô-tŭm'wȧ)..........Ia.	41·00 N	92·26 W
215	Otukpa..........Nig.	7·09 N	7·41 E
125	Otumba (ô-tŭm'bä)....Mex. (In.)	19·41 N	98·46 W
203	Otway, C. (ŏt'wā)..........Austl.	38·55 S	153·40 E
136	Otway, Seno (B.) (sě'nō-ô't-wä'y) Chile	53·00 S	73·00 W
159	Otwock (ôt'vôtsk)..........Pol.	52·05 N	21·18 E
103	Ouachita, (R.)..........U. S.	33·25 N	92·30 W
117	Ouachita Mts. (wŏsh'ĭ-tô).....Ok.	34·29 N	95·01 W
211	Ouaddaï (Reg.) (wä-dī').....Chad	13·04 N	20·00 E
214	Ouagadougou (wä'gȧ-dōō'gōō) Upper Volta	12·22 N	1·31 W
214	Ouahigouya (wä-ê-gōō'yä) Upper Volta	13·35 N	2·25 W
	Ouahran, see Oran		
210	Oualâta (wä-lä'tä).....Mauritania	17·11 N	6·50 W
210	Ouallene (wäl-lân')..........Alg.	24·43 N	1·15 E
129	Ouanaminthe..........Hai.	19·35 N	71·45 W
211	Ouanda Djallé (wän'dȧ jä'lā') Cen. Afr. Rep.	8·56 N	22·46 E
210	Ouarane (Dunes).......Mauritania	20·44 N	10·27 W
210	Ouargla (wär'glä)..........Alg.	32·00 N	5·18 E
214	Ouarkoye..........Upper Volta	12·05 N	3·40 W
216	Oubangui (Ubangi) (R.) (ōō-bäŋ'gê) Afr.	4·30 N	20·35 E
149	Oude Rijn (R.) Neth. (Amsterdam In.)	52·09 N	4·33 E
149	Oudewater.Neth. (Amsterdam In.)	52·01 N	4·52 E
149	Oud-Gastel.Neth. (Amsterdam In.)	51·35 N	4·27 E
212	Oudtshoorn (outs'hōrn)....S. Afr.	33·33 S	23·36 E
163	Oued Rhiou..........Alg.	35·55 N	0·57 E
163	Oued Tiélat..........Alg.	35·33 N	0·28 W
210	Oued-Zem (wěd-zěm')........Mor.	33·05 N	5·49 W
214	Ouellé..........Ivory Coast	7·18 N	4·01 W
160	Ouessant, I. d' (ēl-dwě-säN')...Fr.	48·28 N	5·00 W
216	Ouesso..........Con.	1·37 N	16·04 E
129	Ouest, Pt..........Hai.	19·00 N	73·25 W
210	Ouezzane (wě-zan')..........Mor.	34·48 N	5·40 W

PRONOUNCING INDEX Oughter — Pandu 325

Page	Name Pronunciation Region	Lat. °′	Long. °′
154	Oughter (L.) (lôk ok′tĕr)..... Ire.	54·02 N	7·40 W
215	Ouham (R.).. Cen. Afr. Rep.-Chad	8·30 N	17·50 E
210	Ouidah (wē-dä′)........... Benin	6·25 N	2·05 E
210	Oujda..................... Mor.	34·41 N	1·45 W
152	Ouled-Naïl, Monts des (Mts.). Alg.	34·43 N	2·44 E
161	Oulins (ōō-lăN′).... Fr. (Paris In.)	48·52 N	1·27 E
160	Oullins (ōō-lăN′)............. Fr.	45·44 N	4·46 E
150	Oulu (ō′lōō)................ Fin.	64·58 N	25·43 E
150	Oulu-jarvi (L.)............. Fin.	64·20 N	25·48 E
211	Oum Chalouba (ōōm shä-lōō′bä) Chad	15·48 N	20·30 E
215	Oum Hadjer................ Chad	13·18 N	19·41 E
150	Ounas (R.) (ō′nȧs)........... Fin.	67·46 N	24·40 E
148	Oundle (ôn′d'l)............. Eng.	52·28 N	0·28 W
211	Ounianga Kébir (ōō-nê-äŋ′gȧ kē-bēr′). Chad	19·04 N	20·22 E
117	Ouray (ōō-rā′)............... Co.	38·00 N	107·40 W
135	Ourinhos (ôōō-rē′nyôs)...... Braz.	23·04 S	49·45 W
162	Ourique (ō-rē′kĕ)........... Port.	37·39 N	8·10 W
137	Ouro Fino (ōŭ-rô-fē′nō) Braz. (Rio de Janeiro In.)	22·18 S	46·21 W
137	Ouro Prêto (ō′rōō prā′tōō) Braz. (Rio de Janeiro In.)	20·24 S	43·30 W
154	Ouse (R.).................. Eng.	53·45 N	1·09 W
99	Outardes, Rivière aux (R.)... Can.	50·53 N	68·50 W
109	Outer (I.) (out′ēr)........... Wi.	47·03 N	90·20 W
123	Outer Brass (I.) (bräs).... Vir. Is. (U. S. A.) (St. Thomas In.)	18·24 N	64·58 W
154	Outer Hebrides (Is.)......... Scot.	57·20 N	7·50 W
94	Outlook.................... Can.	51·31 N	107·05 W
212	Outjo (ōt′yō)........... Namibia	20·05 S	17·10 E
89	Outremont (ōō-trē-môN′) Can. (Montreal In.)	45·31 N	73·36 W
203	Ouyen (ōō-ĕn)............. Austl.	35·05 S	142·10 E
136	Ovalle (ō-väl′yā)........... Chile	30·43 S	71·16 W
212	Ovamboland (Reg.).... S. W. Afr.	18·10 S	15·00 E
129	Ovando, Bahía de (B.) (bä-ē′ä-dĕ-ô-vä′n-dō). Cuba	20·10 N	74·05 W
162	Ovar (ô-vär′)............... Port.	40·52 N	8·38 W
149	Overijsche..... Bel. (Brussels In.)	50·46 N	4·32 E
113	Overland (ō-vēr-lănd) Mo. (St. Louis In.)	38·42 N	90·22 W
113	Overland Park Ks. (Kansas City In.)	38·59 N	94·40 W
106	Overlea (ō′vēr-lā) (ō′vēr-lē) Md. (Baltimore In.)	39·21 N	76·31 W
150	Övertornea................. Swe.	66·19 N	23·31 E
167	Ovidiopol′ (ô-vê-dê-ô′pôl′) Sov. Un.	46·15 N	03·28 E
129	Oviedo (ô-vyĕ′dō)..... Dom. Rep.	17·50 N	71·25 W
162	Oviedo (ō-vê-ā′dhō).......... Sp.	43·22 N	5·50 W
167	Ovruch (ôv′rōōch)....... Sov. Un.	51·19 N	28·51 E
195	Owada (ō′wä-dȧ). Jap. (Tōkyō In.)	35·49 N	139·33 E
216	Owando.................... Con.	0·29 S	15·55 E
105	Owasco (L.) (ō-wăs′kō)....... NY	42·50 N	76·30 W
195	Owase (ō′wä-shê)............ Jap.	34·03 N	136·12 E
105	Owego (ō-wē′gō)............. NY	42·05 N	76·15 W
109	Owen (ō′ĕn)................. Wi.	44·56 N	90·35 W
114	Owens (L.) (ō′ĕnz)........... Ca.	36·27 N	117·45 W
114	Owens (R.).................. Ca.	37·13 N	118·20 W
104	Owensboro (ō′ĕnz-bŭr-ô)...... Ky.	37·45 N	87·05 W
104	Owen Sound (ō′ĕn).......... Can.	44·30 N	80·55 W
197	Owen Stanley Ra. (stăn′lê) Pap. N. Gui.	9·00 S	147·30 E
104	Owensville (ō′ĕnz-vĭl)......... In.	38·15 N	87·40 W
117	Owensville.................. Mo.	38·20 N	91·29 W
107	Owensville.... Oh. (Cincinnati In.)	39·08 N	84·07 W
104	Owenton (ō′ĕn-tŭn)........... Ky.	38·35 N	84·55 W
210	Owerri (ô-wĕr′ê)............ Nig.	5·26 N	7·04 E
106	Owings Mill (ōwĭngz mĭl) Md. (Baltimore In.)	39·25 N	76·50 W
111	Owl Cr. (oul)............... Wy.	43·45 N	108·46 W
215	Owo...................... Nig.	7·15 N	5·37 E
104	Owosso (ô-wŏs′ō)............ Mi.	43·00 N	84·15 W
110	Owyhee Mts. (ô-wī′hê)........ Id.	43·15 N	116·48 W
110	Owyhee Res................. Or.	43·27 N	117·30 W
110	Owyhee R................... Or.	43·04 N	117·45 W
110	Owyhee R., South Fork........ Id.	42·07 N	116·43 W
95	Oxbow.................... Can.	49·12 N	102·11 W
125	Oxchuc (ôs-chōōk′).......... Mex.	16·47 N	92·24 W
120	Oxford (ŏks′fērd)............. Al.	33·38 N	80·46 W
97	Oxford (ŏks′fērd)........... Can.	45·44 N	63·52 W
148	Oxford........ Eng. (London In.)	51·43 N	1·16 W
99	Oxford............... Ma. (In.)	42·07 N	71·52 W
104	Oxford..................... Mi.	42·50 N	83·15 W
120	Oxford..................... Ms.	34·22 N	89·30 W
121	Oxford..................... NC	36·17 N	78·35 W
104	Oxford..................... Oh.	39·30 N	84·45 W
95	Oxford L.................. Can.	54·51 N	95·37 W
126	Oxkutzcab (ôx-kōō′tz-käb) Mex. (In.)	20·18 N	89·22 W
106	Oxmoor (ŏks′mōōr) Al. (Birmingham In.)	33·25 N	86·52 W
154	Ox Mts. (ŏks)............... Ire.	54·05 N	9·05 W
114	Oxnard (ŏks′närd)............ Ca.	34·08 N	119·12 W
106	Oxon Hill (ōks′ōn hĭl) Md. (Baltimore In.)	38·48 N	77·00 W
125	Oxtotepec (ôx-tô-tĕ′pĕk) Mex. (In.)	19·10 N	99·04 W
135	Oyapock (R.) (ō-yȧ-pŏk′) Braz.-Fr. Gu.	2·45 N	52·15 W
216	Oyem (ô-yĕm) (ô-yăN′).... Gabon	1·37 N	11·35 E
173	Oymyakon (oi-myŭ-kôn′). Sov. Un.	63·14 N	142·58 E
215	Oyo (ō′yō)................. Nig.	7·51 N	3·56 E
161	Oyonnax (ô-yô-nȧks′).......... Fr.	46·16 N	5·40 E
106	Oyster Bay.. NY (New York In.)	40·52 N	73·32 W
119	Oyster Bayou.......... Tx. (In.)	29·41 N	94·33 W
119	Oyster Cr. (ois′tēr)...... Tx. (In.)	29·13 N	95·29 W
129	Ozama (R.) (ô-zä′mä).. Dom. Rep.	18·45 N	69·55 W
197	Ozamiz (ô-zä′mêz)........... Phil.	8·06 N	123·43 E
120	Ozark (ō′zärk)............... Al.	31·28 N	85·28 W
117	Ozark...................... Ar.	35·29 N	93·49 W
117	Ozarks, L. of the (ō′zärkz).... Mo.	38·06 N	93·26 W
117	Ozark Plat.................. Mo.	36·37 N	93·56 W
166	Ozëry (ô-zyô′rê).......... Sov. Un.	54·53 N	38·31 E
164	Ozieri...................... It.	40·38 N	8·53 E
159	Ozorków (ô-zôr′kōōf).......... Pol.	51·58 N	19·20 E
125	Ozuluama (ō′zōō-lōō-ä′mä)... Mex.	21·34 N	97·52 W
125	Ozumba (ô-zōō′m-bä).. Mex. (In.)	19·02 N	98·48 W

P

Page	Name Pronunciation Region	Lat. °′	Long. °′
212	Paarl (pärl).............. S. Afr.	33·45 S	18·55 E
100	Paauilo (pä-ä-ōō′ê-lō).......... Hi.	20·03 N	155·25 W
159	Pabianice (pä-byȧ-nē′tsĕ)..... Pol.	51·40 N	19·29 E
134	Pacaás Novos, Massiço de (Mts.) (mä-sē′sô-dĕ-pä-kȧ′s-nô′vōs) Braz.	11·03 S	64·02 W
134	Pacaraima, Serra (Mts.) (sĕr′rȧ pä-kä-rä-ē′mȧ) Braz.-Ven.	3·45 N	62·30 W
134	Pacasmayo (pä-käs-mä′yō)... Peru	7·24 S	79·30 W
125	Pachuca (pä-chōō′kä)........ Mex.	20·07 N	98·43 W
112	Pacific (pȧ-sĭf′ĭk). Wa. (Seattle In.)	47·16 N	122·15 W
112	Pacifica (pȧ-sĭf′ĭ-kä) Ca. (San Francisco In.)	37·38 N	122·29 W
114	Pacific Beach........... Ca. (In.)	32·47 N	117·22 W
114	Pacific Grove................ Ca.	36·37 N	121·54 W
4	Pacific O.		
92	Pacific Ra.................. Can.	51·00 N	125·30 W
92	Pacific Rim Natl. Pk......... Can.	49·00 N	126·00 W
121	Pacolet (R.) (pā′cō-lēt)........ SC	34·55 N	81·49 W
161	Pacy-sur-Eure (pä-sē-sür-ûr′) Fr. (Paris In.)	49·01 N	1·24 E
196	Padang (pä-däng′)......... Indon.	1·01 S	100·28 E
183	Padang, Palau (I.) Indon. (Singapore In.)	1·12 N	102·21 E
183	Padang Endau Mala. (Singapore In.)	2·39 N	103·38 E
104	Paden City (pā′dĕn).......... WV	39·30 N	80·55 W
158	Paderborn (pä-dĕr-bôrn′).. F.R.G.	51·43 N	8·46 E
217	Padibe..................... Ug.	3·28 N	32·50 E
148	Padiham (păd′ĭ-hăm)........ Eng.	53·48 N	2·19 W
124	Padilla (pä-dēl′yä).......... Mex.	24·00 N	98·45 W
112	Padilla B. (pä-dĕl′lȧ) Wa. (Seattle In.)	48·31 N	122·34 W
164	Padova (Padua) (pä′dô-vä) (păd′û-ȧ). It.	45·24 N	11·53 E
119	Padre I. (pä′drā)............. Tx.	27·09 N	97·15 W
	Padua, see Padova		
120	Paducah (pȧ-dū′kȧ).......... Ky.	37·05 N	88·36 W
116	Paducah.................... Tx.	34·01 N	100·18 W
194	Paektu San (Mt.) (pâk′tōō-sän′) China-Kor.	42·00 N	128·03 E
164	Pag (I.) (päg).............. Yugo.	44·30 N	14·48 E
196	Pagai Selatan, Pulau (I.)... Indon.	2·48 S	100·22 E
196	Pagai Utara, Pulau (I.).... Indon.	2·45 S	100·02 E
209	Pagalu (I.).......... Equat. Gui.	2·00 S	3·30 E
165	Pagasitikós Kólpos (G.)...... Grc.	39·15 N	23·00 E
117	Page....................... Az.	36·57 N	111·27 W
117	Pagosa Springs (pȧ-gō′sȧ)..... Co.	37·15 N	107·05 W
100	Pahala (pä-hä′lä)............ Hi.	19·11 N	155·28 W
183	Pahang (State) Mala. (Singapore In.)	3·02 N	102·57 E
196	Pahang R................. Mala.	3·39 N	102·41 E
121	Pahokee (pȧ-hō′kē)...... Fl. (In.)	26·45 N	80·40 W
157	Paide (pī′dĕ)........... Sov. Un.	58·54 N	25·30 E
157	Päijänna (L.) (pĕ′ē-yĕn-nĕ)... Fin.	61·38 N	25·05 E
100	Pailolo Chan. (pä-ê-lō′lō)...... Hi.	21·05 N	156·41 W
137	Paine (pī′nĕ).. Chile (Santiago In.)	33·49 S	70·44 W
104	Painesville (pānz′vĭl)......... Oh.	41·40 N	81·15 W
117	Painted Des. (pānt′ēd)........ Az.	36·15 N	111·35 W
117	Painted Rock Res............ Az.	33·00 N	113·05 W
104	Paintsville (pānts′vĭl)........ Ky.	37·50 N	82·50 W
154	Paisley (pāz′lĭ)............. Scot.	55·50 N	4·30 W
134	Paita (pä-ē′tä).............. Peru	5·11 S	81·12 W
192	Pai T'ou Shan (Mts.)....... Korea	40·30 N	127·20 E
117	Paiute Ind. Res.............. Ut.	38·17 N	113·50 W
125	Pajápan (pä-hä′pän)........ Mex.	18·16 N	94·41 W
196	Pakanbaru............... Indon.	0·43 N	101·15 E
174	Pakhra R. (päk′rá) Sov. Un. (Moscow In.)	55·29 N	37·51 E
182	Pakistan.................. Asia	28·00 N	67·30 E
	Pakistan East, see Bangladesh		
196	Pakokku (pȧ-kŏk′kōō)....... Bur.	21·29 N	95·00 E
164	Pakrac (pä′krȧts).......... Yugo.	45·25 N	17·13 E
159	Paks (pôksh)............. Hung.	46·38 N	18·53 E
215	Pala..................... Chad	9·22 N	14·54 E
119	Palacios (pä-lä′syōs).......... Tx.	28·42 N	96·12 W
163	Palafrogell (pä-lä-frô-gĕl)...... Sp.	41·55 N	3·09 E
164	Palagruža (Is.) (pä′lä-grōō′zhä) Yugo.	42·20 N	16·23 E
161	Palaiseau (pȧ-lĕ-zō′). Fr. (Paris In.)	48·44 N	2·16 E
173	Palana.............. Sov. Un.	59·07 N	159·58 E
197	Palanan B. (pä-lä′nän). Phil. (In.)	17·14 N	122·35 E
197	Palanan Pt............ Phil. (In.)	17·12 N	122·40 E
184	Pālanpur (pä′lŭn-pōōr)...... India	24·08 N	73·29 E
212	Palapye (pȧ-läp′yĕ)......... Bots.	22·34 S	27·28 E
107	Palatine (păl′ȧ-tīn) Il. (Chicago In.)	42·07 N	88·03 W
121	Palatka (pȧ-lăt′kȧ)........... Fl.	29·39 N	81·40 W
197	Palau Is. (pä-lä′ōō) Pac. Is. Trust. Ter.	7·15 N	134·30 E
197	Palauig (pȧ-lou′ēg)..... Phil. (In.)	15·27 N	119·54 E
196	Palawan (I.) (pä-lä′wȧn)..... Phil.	9·50 N	117·38 E
185	Pālayankottai.............. India	8·50 N	77·50 E
157	Paldiski (päl′dĭ-skĭ)...... Sov. Un.	59·22 N	24·04 E
196	Palembang (pä-lĕm-bäng′). Indon.	2·57 S	104·40 E
126	Palencia (pä-lĕn′sê-ȧ)....... Guat.	14·40 N	90·22 W
162	Palencia (pä-lĕ′n-syä).......... Sp.	42·02 N	4·32 W
125	Palenque (pä-lĕŋ′kȧ)........ Mex.	17·34 N	91·58 W
129	Palenque, Punta (Pt.) (pōō′n-tä) Dom. Rep.	18·10 N	70·10 W
134	Palermo (pä-lĕr′mô)..... Col. (In.)	2·53 N	75·26 W
164	Palermo..................... It.	38·08 N	13·24 E
119	Palestine................... Tx.	31·46 N	95·38 W
183	Palestine (Reg.) (păl′ĕs-tīn) Asia (Palestine In.)	31·33 N	35·00 E
188	Paletwa (pŭ-lĕt′wä)......... Bur.	21·19 N	92·52 E
185	Palghāt................... India	10·49 N	76·40 E
184	Pāli...................... India	25·53 N	73·18 E
214	Palimé.................... Togo	6·54 N	0·38 E
126	Palín (pä-lēn′)............. Guat.	14·42 N	90·42 W
110	Palisade (păl-ĭ-sād′).......... Nv.	40·39 N	116·11 W
125	Palizada (pä-lê-zä′dä)....... Mex.	18·17 N	92·04 W
184	Palk Str. (pôk)............. India	10·00 N	79·23 E
137	Palma (päl′mä) Braz. (Rio de Janeiro In.)	21·23 S	42·18 W
163	Palma, Ba. de (B.) (bä-ē′ä-dĕ). Sp.	39·24 N	2·37 E
162	Palma del Rio (dĕl rē′ō)...... Sp.	37·43 N	5·19 W
163	Palma de Mallorca (dĕ-mäl-yô′r-kä). Sp.	39·35 N	2·38 E
135	Palmares (päl-mȧ′rĕs)....... Braz.	8·46 S	35·28 W
136	Palmas (päl′mäs)........... Braz.	26·20 S	51·56 W
214	Palmas, C.................. Lib.	4·22 N	7·44 W
129	Palma Soriano (sô-ré-ä′nō).. Cuba	20·15 N	76·00 W
121	Palm Beach (päm bēch′).. Fl. (In.)	26·43 N	80·03 W
135	Palmeira dos Índios (päl-mā′rä-dôs-ē′n-dyôs). Braz.	9·26 S	36·33 W
216	Palmeirinhas, Ponta das (Pt.). Arg.	9·05 S	13·00 E
163	Palmela (päl-mā′lä) Port. (Lisbon In.)	38·34 N	8·54 W
101	Palmer (päm′ēr).............. Ak.	61·38 N	149·15 W
112	Palmer......... Wa. (Seattle In.)	47·19 N	121·53 W
205	Palmerston North (päm′ēr-stŭn) N. Z. (In.)	40·21 S	175·43 E
205	Palmerville (päm′ēr-vĭl).... Austl.	16·08 S	144·15 E
121	Palmetto (pȧl-mĕt′ô)..... Fl. (In.)	27·32 N	82·34 W
129	Palmetto Pt................. Ba.	21·15 N	73·25 W
164	Palmi (päl′mē)............... It.	38·21 N	15·54 E
134	Palmira (päl-mē′rä)..... Col. (In.)	3·33 N	76·17 W
128	Palmira................... Cuba	22·15 N	80·25 W
117	Palmyra (păl-mī′rȧ).......... Mo.	39·45 N	91·32 W
106	Palmyra.... NJ (Philadelphia In.)	40·01 N	75·00 W
199	Palmyra (I.)............ Oceania	6·00 N	162·20 W
186	Palmyra (Ruins)............ Syr.	34·25 N	38·28 E
184	Palmyras Pt............... India	20·42 N	87·45 E
147	Palmyre.................... Syr.	30·35 N	37·58 E
112	Palo Alto (pä′lō äl′tō) Ca. (San Francisco In.)	37·27 N	122·09 W
116	Paloduro Cr. (pā-lô-dōō′rô).... Tx.	36·16 N	101·12 W
183	Paloh...... Mala. (Singapore In.)	2·11 N	103·12 E
118	Paloma, L. (pä-lō′mä)....... Mex.	26·53 N	104·02 W
137	Palomo, Cerro el (Mtn.) (sĕ′r-rô-ĕl-pä-lô′mô) Chile (Santiago In.)	34·36 S	70·20 W
163	Palos, Cabo de (C.) (kȧ′bô-dĕ-pä′lôs). Sp.	39·38 N	0·43 W
113	Palos Verdes Estates (pă′lŭs vûr′dĭs) Ca. (Los Angeles In.)	33·48 N	118·24 W
110	Palouse (pȧ-lōōz′)........... Wa.	46·54 N	117·04 W
110	Palouse Hills............... Wa.	46·48 N	117·47 W
110	Palouse R.................. Wa.	47·02 N	117·35 W
171	Palu (pä-loo′).............. Tur.	38·55 N	40·10 E
197	Paluan (pä-lōō′än)..... Phil. (In.)	13·25 N	120·29 E
173	Pamamushir (I.)......... Sov. Un.	50·42 N	153·45 E
160	Pamiers (pȧ-myā′)............ Fr.	43·07 N	1·34 E
187	Pamirs (Plat.).......... Sov. Un.	38·14 N	72·27 E
121	Pamlico R. (păm′lĭ-kō)....... NC	35·25 N	76·59 W
121	Pamlico Sd.................. NC	35·10 N	76·10 W
116	Pampa (păm′pȧ).............. Tx.	35·32 N	100·56 W
136	Pampa de Castillo (Plat.) (pä′m-pä-dĕ-käs-tê′l-yô). Arg.	45·30 S	67·30 W
214	Pampana (R.).............. S. L.	8·35 N	11·55 W
197	Pampanga (R.) (päm-päŋ′gä) Phil. (In.)	15·20 N	120·48 E
136	Pampas (Reg.) (päm′päs).... Arg.	37·00 S	64·30 W
162	Pampilhosa do Botão (päm-pê-lyō′sȧ-dô-bō-to′uN) Port.	40·21 N	8·32 W
134	Pamplona (päm-plō′nä)...... Col.	7·19 N	72·41 W
162	Pamplona (päm-plô′nä)........ Sp.	42·49 N	1·39 W
105	Pamunkey (R.) (pȧ-mŭŋ′kĭ)... Va.	37·40 N	77·20 W
104	Pana (pā′nȧ)................. Il.	39·25 N	89·05 W
126	Panabá (pä-nä-bȧ′).... Mex. (In.)	21·18 N	88·15 W
165	Panagyurishte (pȧ-nȧ-gyōō′rêsh-tĕ). Bul.	42·30 N	24·11 E
185	Panaji (Panjim)............ India	15·33 N	73·52 E
123	Panamá (păn-ȧ-mä′)......... N.A.	8·35 N	81·08 W
127	Panamá, B. de............. Pan.	8·50 N	79·08 W
123	Panamá, G. de............. Pan.	7·45 N	79·20 W
123	Panamá, Istmo de.......... Pan.	9·00 N	81·00 W
120	Panama City (păn-ȧ mä′ sĭ′tĭ). Fl.	30·08 N	85·39 W
114	Panamint Ra. (păn-ȧ-mĭnt′).. Ca.	36·40 N	117·30 W
164	Panaria (Is.) (pä-nä′rê-a)...... It.	38·37 N	15·05 E
164	Panaro (R.) (pä-nä′rô)......... It.	44·47 N	11·06 E
196	Panay (I.) (pä-nī′).......... Phil.	11·15 N	121·38 E
165	Pančevo (pȧn′chĕ-vô)....... Yugo.	44·52 N	20·42 E
183	Panchor.... Mala. (Singapore In.)	2·10 N	102·43 E
184	Pānchur............ India (In.)	22·31 N	88·17 E
212	Panda (pän′dä′)............ Zaire	10·59 S	27·24 E
171	Pandar-e Pahlavī.......... Iran	37·30 N	49·30 E
128	Pan de Guajaibon (Mtn.) (pän dā gwä-jȧ-bōn′). Cuba	22·50 N	83·20 W
216	Pandu.................... Zaire	5·00 N	19·15 E

ng-sing; ŋ-baŋk; N-nasalized n; nŏd; cŏmmit; ōld; ôbey; ôrder; fōōd; fōōt; ou-out; s-soft; sh-dish; th-thin; pūre; ûnite; ûrn; stŭd; circŭs; ū-as "y" in study; ′-indeterminate vowel.

326 Panevezys — Pavlo'f PRONOUNCING INDEX

Page	Name Pronunciation Region	Lat. °'	Long. °'
157	Panevėžys (pä'nyĕ-vāzh'ēs) Sov. Un.	55·44 N	24·21 E
172	Panfilov (pŭn-fē'lŏf) Sov. Un.	44·12 N	79·58 E
217	Panga (päŋ'gä) Zaire	1·51 N	26·25 E
213	Pangani (pän-gä'nē) Tan.	5·28 S	38·58 E
217	Pangani (R.) Tan.	4·40 S	37·45 E
196	Pangkalpinang (päng-käl'pē-näng') Indon.	2·11 S	106·04 E
91	Pangnirtung Can.	66·08 N	65·26 W
117	Panguitch (päŋ'gwĭch) Ut.	37·50 N	112·30 W
184	Pānihāti India (Calcutta In.)	22·42 N	88·23 E
137	Panimávida (pä-nē-mä'vē-dä) Chile (Santiago In.)	36·44 S	71·26 W
	Panjim, see Panaji		
192	Panshi (pän-shē) China	42·50 N	126·48 E
193	Pan Si Pan (Mtn.) Viet.	22·25 N	103·50 E
197	Pantar, Pulau (I.) (pän'tär) Indon.	8 40 S	123·45 E
151	Pantelleria (I.) (pän-tĕl-lå-rē'ä) It.	36·43 N	11·59 E
125	Pantepec (pän-tå-pĕk') Mex.	17·11 N	93·04 W
124	Panuco (pä'nōō-kô) Mex.	22·04 N	98·11 W
124	Pánuco (pä'nōō-kô) Mex.	29·47 N	105·55 W
124	Panuco (R.) Mex.	21·59 N	98·20 W
118	Pánuco de Coronado (pä'nōō-kô dā kō-rô-nä'dhō) Mex.	24·33 N	104·20 W
185	Panvel India (In.)	18·59 N	73·06 E
191	Panyu (pän-yōō) China (Canton In.)	22·56 N	113·22 E
126	Panzós (pän-zós') Guat.	15·26 N	89·40 W
135	Pao (pá'ō) (R.) Ven. (In.)	9·52 N	67·57 W
117	Paola (pā-ō'lȧ) Ks.	38·34 N	94·51 W
104	Paoli (pā-ō'lī) In.	38·35 N	86·30 W
106	Paoli Pa. (Philadelphia In.)	40·03 N	75·29 W
115	Paonia (pā-ō'nyȧ) Co.	38·50 N	107·40 W
192	Paoting China	42·04 N	125·00 E
159	Pápa (pä'pô) Hung.	47·18 N	17·27 E
126	Papagayo, Golfo del (G.) (gôl-fô-dĕl-pä-pä-gä'yō) C. R.	10·44 N	85·56 W
124	Papagayo, Laguna (L.) (lä-ōō-nä) Mex.	16·44 N	99·44 W
124	Papagayo (R.) (pä-pä-gä'yō) Mex.	16·52 N	99·41 W
115	Papago Ind. Res. (pä'pä'gō) Az.	32·33 N	112·12 W
122	Papantla de Olarte (pä-pän'tlä dā-ō-lä'r-tĕ) Mex.	20·30 N	97·15 W
125	Papatoapan (R.) (pä-pä-tô-ä-pä'n) Mex.	18·00 N	96·22 W
158	Papenburg (päp'ĕn-bōōrgh) F.R.G.	53·05 N	7·23 E
137	Papinas (pä-pē'näs) Arg. (Buenos Aires In.)	35·30 S	57·19 W
89	Papineauville (pä-pē-nō'vēl) Can. (Ottawa In.)	45·38 N	75·01 W
197	Papua, Gulf of (păp-ōō-ȧ) Pap. N. Gui.	8·20 S	144·45 E
197	Papua New Guinea (păp-ōō-ȧ) (gĭne) Oceania	7·00 S	142·15 E
137	Papudo (pä-pōō'dô) Chile (Santiago In.)	32·30 S	71·25 W
136	Paquequer Pequeno (pä-kĕ-kĕ'r-pĕ-kĕ'nô) Braz. (Rio de Janeiro In.)	22·19 S	43·02 W
	Pará, see Belém		
135	Pará (State) (pä-rä') Braz.	4·45 S	53·30 W
137	Pará (pä-rä') (R.) Braz. (Rio de Janeiro In.)	20·21 S	44·38 W
135	Pará, Rio do (R.) (rē'ō-dô-pä-rä') Braz.	1·09 S	48·48 W
166	Para (R.) Sov. Un.	53·45 N	40·58 E
197	Paracale (pä-rä-kä'lå) Phil. (In.)	14·17 N	122·47 E
136	Paracambi (pä-rä-kà'm-bē) Braz. (Rio de Janeiro In.)	22·36 S	43·43 W
135	Paracatu (pä-rä-kä-tōō') Braz.	17·17 S	46·43 W
196	Parcel Islands China	16·40 N	113·00 E
165	Paraćin (pá'rä-chēn) Yugo.	43·51 N	21·26 E
137	Para de Minas (pä-rä-dĕ-mē'näs) Braz. (Rio de Janeiro In.)	19·52 S	44·37 W
128	Paradise (I.) Ba.	25·05 N	77·20 W
110	Paradise Valley (păr'ȧ-dīs) Nv.	41·28 N	117·32 W
134	Parados, Cerro de los (Mtn.) (sĕ'r-rô-dĕ-lôs-pä-rä'dōs) Col. (In.)	5·44 N	75·13 W
117	Paragould (păr'ȧ-gōōld) Ar.	36·03 N	90·29 W
135	Paraguaçu (R.) (pä-rä-gwä-zōō') Braz.	12·25 S	39·46 W
134	Paraguaná, Pen. de (Pen.) (pĕ-nē'ng-sōō-lä-dĕ-pä-rä-gwä-nä') Ven.	12·00 N	69·55 W
133	Paraguay (păr'ȧ-gwā) S. A.	24·00 S	57·00 W
135	Paraguay, Rio (R.) (rē'ō-pä-rä-gwä'y) S. A.	21·12 S	57·31 W
	Paraíba, see João Pessoa		
135	Paraíba (State) (pä-rä-ē'bä) Braz.	7·11 S	37·05 W
137	Paraíba (R.) Braz. (Rio de Janeiro In.)	23·02 S	45·43 W
137	Paraíba do Sul (dô-sōō'l) Braz. (Rio de Janeiro In.)	22·10 S	43·18 W
137	Paraibuna (pä-rä-ē-bōō'nä) Braz. (Rio de Janeiro In.)	23·23 S	45·38 W
122	Paraiso (pä-rä-ē'sō) Pan. (In.)	9·02 N	79·38 W
127	Paraíso C. R.	9·50 N	83·53 W
125	Paraíso Mex.	18·24 N	93·11 W
137	Paraisópolis (pä-rä-ē-sô'pō-lēs) Braz. (Rio de Janeiro In.)	22·35 S	45·45 W
137	Paraitinga (pä-rä-ē-tē'n-gä) (R.) Braz. (Rio de Janeiro In.)	23·15 S	45·24 W
215	Parakou (pȧ-rȧ-kōō') Benin	9·21 N	2·37 E
135	Paramaribo (pȧ-rȧ-mä'rē-bō) Sur.	5·50 N	55·15 W
202	Paramatta (păr-ȧ-măt'ȧ) Austl. (Sydney In.)	33·49 S	150·59 E
160	Paramé (pȧ-rȧ-mā') Fr.	48·40 N	1·58 W
134	Paramillo (Mtn.) (pä-rä-mē'l-yō) Col. (In.)	7·06 N	75·55 W
106	Paramus NJ (New York In.)	40·56 N	74·04 W
173	Paramushir (I.) Sov. Un.	50·45 N	154·00 E
183	Paran (R.) Isr. (Palestine In.)	30·05 N	34·50 E
136	Paraná (pä-rä-nä') Arg.	31·44 S	60·29 W
136	Paraná (State) Braz.	24·25 S	52·00 W
136	Paraná, Rio (R.) Arg.	32·15 S	60·55 W
135	Paraná (R.) Braz.	13·05 S	47·11 W
135	Paranaguá (pä-rä'nä-gwá') Braz.	25·39 S	48·42 W
135	Paranaíba (pä-rä-nȧ-ē'bȧ) Braz.	19·43 S	51·13 W
135	Paranaíba (R.) Braz.	18·58 S	50·44 W
137	Parana Ibicuy (R.) (ē-bē-kōō'ē) Arg. (Buenos Aires In.)	33·27 S	59·26 W
135	Paranam Sur.	5·39 N	55·13 W
136	Paranápanema (R.) (pä-rä'nȧ'pä-nĕ-mä) Braz.	22·28 S	52·15 W
137	Paraopeda (R.) (pä-rä-o-pĕ'dä) Braz. (Rio de Janeiro In.)	20·09 S	44·14 W
135	Parapara (pä-rä-pä-rä) Ven. (In.)	9·44 N	67·17 W
137	Parati (pä-rätē) Braz. (Rio de Janeiro In.)	23·14 S	44·43 W
160	Paray-le-Monial (pȧ-rĕ'lē-mô-nyȧl') Fr.	46·27 N	4·14 E
184	Pārbati (R.) India	24·50 N	76·44 E
158	Parchim (par'kĭm) G.D.R.	53·25 N	11·52 E
159	Parczew (pär'chĕf) Pol.	51·38 N	22·53 E
135	Pardo (R.) (pär'dō) Braz.	15·25 S	39·40 W
137	Pardo (R.) Braz. (Rio de Janeiro In.)	21·32 S	46·40 W
158	Pardubice (pär'dōō-bĭt-sĕ) Czech.	50·02 N	15·47 E
135	Parecis, Serra dos Hills (sĕr'rȧ dōs pä-rȧ-sēzh') Braz.	13·45 S	59·28 W
162	Paredes de Nava (pä-rā'dȧs dā nä'vä) Sp.	42·10 N	4·41 W
118	Paredón Mex.	25·56 N	100·58 W
97	Parent Can.	47·59 N	74·30 W
97	Parent, Lac (L.) Can.	48·40 N	77·00 W
196	Pare Pare Indon.	4·01 S	119·38 E
174	Pargolovo (pȧr-gô'lô vô) Sov. Un. (Leningrad In.)	60·04 N	30·18 E
134	Paria, Golfo de (G.) (gôl-fô-dĕ-pä-rē-ä) Ven.	10·33 N	62·14 W
115	Paria (R.) Az.-Ut.	37·07 N	111·51 W
124	Paricutín, Vol. (pä-rē-kōō-tē'n) Mex.	19·27 N	102·14 W
118	Parida, Rio de la (R.) (rē'ō-dĕ-lä-pä-rē'dä) Mex.	26·23 N	104·40 W
134	Parima, Serra (Mts.) (sĕr'rȧ pä-rē'mä) Braz.-Ven.	3·45 N	64·00 W
134	Pariñas, Punta (Pt.) (pōō'n-tä-pä-rē'n-yäs) Peru	4·30 S	81·23 W
135	Parintins (pä-rĭn-tĭNzh') Braz.	2·34 S	56·30 W
113	Paris (păr'ĭs) Ar.	35·17 N	93·43 W
104	Paris Can.	43·15 N	80·23 W
161	Paris (pȧ-rē') Fr. (Paris In.)	48·51 N	2·20 E
104	Paris Il.	39·35 N	87·40 W
104	Paris Ky.	38·15 N	84·15 W
117	Paris Mo.	39·27 N	91·59 W
120	Paris Tn.	36·16 N	88·20 W
117	Paris Tx.	33·39 N	95·33 W
127	Parita, Golfo de (G.) (gôl-fô-dĕ-pä-rē'tä) Pan.	8·06 N	80·10 W
111	Park City Ut.	40·39 N	111·33 W
108	Parker (pär'kēr) SD	43·24 N	97·10 W
117	Parker Dam Az.-Ca.	34·20 N	114·00 W
104	Parkersburg (pär'kērz-bûrg) WV	39·15 N	81·35 W
203	Parkes (pärks) Austl.	33·10 S	148·10 E
109	Park Falls (pärk) Wi.	45·55 N	90·29 W
107	Park Forest Il. (Chicago In.)	41·29 N	87·41 W
112	Parkland (pärk'lănd) Wa. (Seattle In.)	47·09 N	122·26 W
111	Park Ra. Co.	40·54 N	106·40 W
109	Park Rapids Mn.	46·53 N	95·05 W
107	Park Ridge Il. (Chicago In.)	42·00 N	87·50 W
108	Park River ND	48·22 N	97·43 W
112	Parkrose (pärk'rōz) Or. (Portland In.)	45·33 N	122·33 W
213	Park Rynie S. Afr. (Natal In.)	30·22 S	30·43 E
108	Parkston (pärks'tŭn) SD	43·22 N	97·59 W
115	Park View (vū) NM	36·45 N	106·30 W
106	Parkville Md. (Baltimore In.)	39·22 N	76·32 W
113	Parkville Mo. (Kansas City In.)	39·12 N	94·41 W
163	Parla (pär'lä) Sp. (Madrid In.)	40·14 N	3·46 W
164	Parma (pär'mä) It.	44·48 N	10·20 E
107	Parma Oh. (Cleveland In.)	41·23 N	81·44 W
107	Parma Heights Oh. (Cleveland In.)	41·23 N	81·36 W
135	Parnaguá (pär-nä-gwá') Braz.	9·52 S	44·27 W
135	Parnaíba (pär-nä-ē'bä) Braz.	3·00 S	41·42 W
135	Parnaiba (R.) Braz.	3·57 S	42·30 W
165	Parnassós (Mtn.) Grc.	38·36 N	22·35 E
149	Parndorf Aus. (Vienna In.)	48·00 N	16·52 E
157	Pärnu (pĕr'nōō) Sov. Un.	58·24 N	24·29 E
157	Pärnu (R.) Sov. Un.	58·40 N	25·05 E
157	Pärnu Laht (B.) (läkt) Sov. Un.	58·15 N	24·17 E
184	Paro (pä'rô) Bhu.	27·30 N	89·30 E
203	Paroo (R.) (pä'rōō) Austl.	29·40 S	144·24 E
186	Paropamisus (Mts.) Afg.	34·45 N	63·58 E
165	Páros (pä'rôs) (pā'rŏs) Grc.	37·05 N	25·14 E
165	Páros (I.) Grc.	37·11 N	25·00 E
212	Parow (pă'rô) S. Afr. (In.)	33·54 S	18·36 E
115	Parowan (păr'ô-wăn) Ut.	37·50 N	112·50 W
136	Parral (pär-rä'l) Chile	36·07 S	71·47 W
118	Parral, R. Mex.	27·25 N	105·08 W
202	Parramatta (R.) (păr-ȧ-măt'ȧ) Aust. (Sydney In.)	33·42 S	150·58 E
118	Parras (pär-räs') Mex.	25·28 N	102·08 W
127	Parrita (pär-rē'tä) C. R.	9·32 N	84·17 W
98	Parrsboro (pärz'bŭr-ô) Can.	45·24 N	64·20 W
104	Parry (I.) (păr'ĭ) Can.	45·15 N	80·00 W
92	Parry, Mt. Can.	52·53 N	128·45 W
75	Parry Is. Can.	75·30 N	110·00 W
105	Parry Sound Can.	45·20 N	80·00 W
92	Parsnip (R.) (pärs'nĭp) Can.	54·45 N	122·20 W
117	Parsons (pär's'nz) Ks.	37·20 N	95·16 W
105	Parsons WV	39·05 N	79·40 W
160	Parthenay (pȧr-t'nĕ') Fr.	46·39 N	0·16 W
164	Partinico (pär-tē'nē-kô) It.	38·02 N	13·11 E
194	Partizansk Sov. Un.	43·15 N	133·19 E
218	Parys (pȧ-rīs') S. Afr. (Johannesburg & Pretoria In.)	26·53 S	27·28 E
113	Pasadena (păs-ȧ-dē'nȧ) Ca. (Los Angeles In.)	34·09 N	118·09 W
106	Pasadena Md. (Baltimore In.)	39·06 N	76·35 W
119	Pasadena Tx. (In.)	29·43 N	95·13 W
120	Pascagoula (păs-kȧ-gōō'lȧ) Ms.	30·22 N	88·33 W
120	Pascagoula (R.) Ms.	30·52 N	88·48 W
159	Paşcani (päsh-kän'') Rom.	47·46 N	26·42 E
110	Pasco (păs'kō) Wa.	46·13 N	119·04 W
158	Pasewalk (pä'zĕ-välk) G.D.R.	53·31 N	14·01 E
174	Pashiya (pä'shĭ-yȧ) Sov. Un. (Urals In.)	58·27 N	58·17 E
194	Pashkovo (pȧsh-kô'vō) Sov. Un.	48·52 N	131·09 E
167	Pashkovskaya (pȧsh-kôf'skȧ-yȧ) Sov. Un.	45·29 N	39·04 E
197	Pasig Phil. (In.)	14·34 N	121·05 E
126	Pasión, Rio de la (R.) (rē'ō-dĕ-lä-pä-syōn') Guat. (In.)	16·31 N	90·11 W
136	Paso de los Libres (pä-sô-dĕ-lôs-lē'brĕs) Arg.	29·33 S	57·05 W
137	Paso de los Toros (tŏ'rôs) Ur. (Buenos Aires In.)	32·43 S	56·33 W
114	Paso Robles (pă'sō rō'blĕs Ca.	35·38 N	120·44 W
96	Pasquia Hills (păs'kwē-ȧ) Can.	53·13 N	102·37 W
106	Passaic (pă-sā'ĭk) NJ (New York In.)	40·52 N	74·08 W
106	Passaic R. NJ (New York In.)	40·42 N	74·26 W
98	Passamaquoddy B. (păs'ȧ-mȧ-kwŏd'ĭ) Can.	45·06 N	66·59 W
137	Passa Tempo (pä's-sä-tĕ'm-pô) Braz. (Rio de Janeiro In.)	21·40 S	44·29 W
158	Passua (päs'ou) F.R.G.	48·34 N	13·27 E
120	Pass Christian (pȧs krĭs'tyĕn) Ms.	30·20 N	89·15 W
151	Passero, C. ((päs-sĕ'rō) It.	36·34 N	15·13 E
136	Passo Fundo (pä'sŏ fōō'n'dōō) Braz.	28·16 S	52·13 W
137	Passos (pä's-sōs) Braz. (Rio de Janeiro In.)	20·45 S	46·37 W
134	Pastaza (R.) (päs-tä'zä) Peru	3·05 S	76·18 W
134	Pasto (päs'tô) Col.	1·15 N	77·19 W
124	Pastora (päs-tô-rä) Mex.	22·08 N	100·04 W
196	Pasuruan Indon.	7·45 S	112·50 E
157	Pasvalys (päs-vä-lēs') Sov. Un.	56·04 N	24·23 E
136	Patagonia (Reg.) (păt-ȧ-gō'nĭ-ȧ) Arg.	46·45 S	69·30 W
185	Pātālganga (R.) India (In.)	18·52 N	73·08 E
106	Patapsco R. (pȧ-tăps'kō) Md. (Baltimore In.)	39·12 N	76·30 W
164	Paternò (pä-tĕr-nô') It.	37·25 N	14·58 E
106	Paterson (păt'ēr-sŭn) NJ (New York In.)	40·55 N	74·10 W
111	Pathfinder Res. (păth'fīn-dĕr) Wy.	42·22 N	107·10 W
184	Patiāla (pŭt-ē-ä'lŭ) India	30·25 N	76·28 E
136	Pati do Alferes (pä-tē-dô-äl-fē'rĕs) Braz. (Buenos Aires In.)	22·25 S	43·25 W
184	Patna (pŭt'nŭ) India	25·33 N	85·18 E
197	Patnanongan (pät-nä-nôŋ'gän) Phil. (In.)	14·50 N	122·25 E
104	Patoka (R.) (pȧ-tō'kȧ) Ind.	38·25 N	87·25 W
173	Patom Plat. Sov. Un.	59·30 N	115·00 E
135	Patos (pä'tōzh) Braz.	7·03 S	37·14 W
112	Patos (pä'tōs) Wa. (Vancouver In.)	48·47 N	122·57 W
136	Patos, Lago dos (L.) (lä'gō-ä dozh pä'tōzh) Braz.	31·15 S	51·30 W
135	Patos de Minas (dĕ-mē'näzh) Braz.	18·39 S	46·31 W
165	Pátrai (Patras) (pä-trī') (pä-träs') Grc.	38·15 N	21·48 E
165	Patraïkós Kólpos (G.) Grc.	38·16 N	21·19 E
	Patras, see Pátrai		
135	Patrocínio (pä-trō-sē'nē-ōō) Braz.	18·48 S	46·47 W
196	Pattani (pät'ȧ-nē) Thai.	6·56 N	101·13 E
98	Patten (păt''n) Me.	45·59 N	68·27 W
119	Patterson (păt'ēr-sŭn) La.	29·41 N	91·20 W
105	Patton Pa.	40·40 N	78·45 W
127	Patuca, Punta (Pt.) (pōō'n-tä-pä-tōō'kä) Hond.	15·23 N	84·05 W
127	Patuca R. Hond.	15·22 N	84·31 W
105	Patuxent (R.) (pȧ-tŭk'sĕnt) Md.	39·10 N	77·10 W
124	Pátzcuaro (päts'kwä-rô) Mex.	19·30 N	101·36 W
124	Pátzcuaro, Lago de (L.) (lä'gô-dĕ) Mex.	19·36 N	101·38 W
126	Patzicia (pät-zē'syä) Guat.	14·36 N	90·57 W
126	Patzún (pät-zōōn') Guat.	14·40 N	91·00 W
160	Pau (pō) Fr.	43·18 N	0·23 W
160	Pau, Gave de (strm.) (gäv-dĕ) Fr.	43·33 N	0·51 W
160	Pauillac (pō-yäk') Fr.	45·12 N	0·46 W
104	Paulding (pôl'dĭng) Oh.	41·05 N	84·35 W
149	Paulinenaue (pou'lē-nĕ-nou-ĕ) G.D.R. (Berlin In.)	52·40 N	12·43 E
	Paulis. see Isiro		
135	Paulistana (pou-lēs-tȧ-nä) Braz.	8·13 S	41·06 W
135	Paulo Afonso, Salto (falls) (säl-tô-pou'lōō äf-fôn'sōō) Braz.	9·33 S	38·32 W
218	Paul Roux (pôrl rōō) S. Afr. (Johannesburg & Pretoria In.)	28·18 S	27·57 E
106	Paulsboro (pôlz'bē-rô) NJ (Philadelphia In.)	39·50 N	75·16 W
117	Pauls Valley (pôlz văl'ē) Ok.	34·43 N	97·13 W
134	Pavarandocito (pä-vä-rän-dô-sē'tô) Col. (In.)	7·18 N	76·32 W
174	Pavda (päv'da) Sov. Un. (Urals In.)	59·16 N	59·32 E
164	Pavia (pä-vē'ä) It.	45·12 N	9·11 E
172	Pavlodar (páv-lô-dár') Sov. Un.	52·17 N	77·23 E
101	Pavlo'f B. (păv-lôf) Ak.	55·20 N	161·20 W

ăt; finăl; rāte; senåte; ärm; ȧsk; sofȧ; fâre; ch-choose; dh-as th in other; bē; ėvent; bĕt; recĕnt; cratēr; g-go; gh-guttural g; bĭt; ĭ-short neutral; rīde; K-guttural k as ch in German ich;

PRONOUNCING INDEX Pavlograd — Pescia 327

Page	Name Pronunciation Region	Lat. °′	Long. °′
167	Pavlograd (pàv-lô-gràt')..Sov. Un.	48·32 N	35·52 E
167	Pavlovsk (pàv-lôfsk')....Sov. Un.	50·28 N	40·05 E
174	Pavlovsk.Sov. Un. (Leningrad In.)	59·41 N	30·27 E
174	Pavlovskiy Posad (pàv-lôf'skĭ pô-sàt') Sov. Un. (Moscow In.)	55·47 N	38·39 E
136	Pavuna (pä-vōō'nȧ) Braz. (Rio de Janeiro In.)	22·48 S	43·21 W
149	Päwesin (pǎ'vě-zēn) G.D.R. (Berlin In.)	52·31 N	12·44 E
117	Pawhuska (pô-hŭs'kȧ) Ok.	36·41 N	96·20 W
117	Pawnee (pô-nē') Ok.	36·20 N	96·47 W
116	Pawnee (R.) Ks.	38·18 N	99·42 W
117	Pawnee City Ne.	40·08 N	96·09 W
104	Paw Paw (pô'pô) Mi.	42·15 N	85·55 W
109	Paw Paw (R.) Mi.	42·14 N	86·21 W
106	Pawtucket (pô-tŭk'ět) RI (Providence In.)	41·53 N	71·23 W
165	Paxoi (I.) Grc.	39·14 N	20·15 E
104	Paxton (păks'tŭn) Il.	40·35 N	88·00 W
110	Payette (pȧ-ĕt') Id.	44·05 N	116·55 W
110	Payette R. Id.	43·57 N	116·26 W
110	Payette R., North Fork Id.	44·35 N	116·10 W
110	Payette R., South Fork Id.	44·07 N	115·43 W
170	Pay-Khoy, Khrebet (Mts.) Sov. Un.	68·08 N	63·04 E
91	Payne (L.) (pān) Can.	59·22 N	73·16 W
109	Paynesville (pānz'vĭl) Mn.	45·23 N	94·43 W
	Payo Obispo, see Cuidad Chetumal		
136	Paysandú (pī-sän-dōō') Ur.	32·16 S	57·55 W
115	Payson (pā's'n) Ut.	40·05 N	111·45 W
165	Pazardzhik (pä-zár-dzhek') Bul.	42·10 N	24·22 E
164	Pazin (pä'zēn) Yugo.	45·14 N	13·57 E
117	Peabody (pē'bŏd-ĭ) Ks.	38·09 N	97·09 W
99	Peabody Ma. (In.)	42·32 N	70·56 W
93	Peace (R.) Can.	55·40 N	118·30 W
121	Peace Cr. (pēs) Fl. (In.)	27·16 N	81·53 W
106	Peace Dale (dāl) RI (Providence In.)	41·27 N	71·30 W
93	Peace River (rĭv'ẽr) Can.	56·14 N	117·17 W
90	Peacock Hills (pē-kŏk' hĭlz) Can.	66·08 N	109·55 W
148	Peak, The (Mt.) (pēk) Eng.	53·23 N	1·52 W
204	Peak Hill Austl.	25·38 S	118·50 E
120	Pearl (R.) (pûrl) La.-Ms.	31·06 N	89·44 W
119	Pearland (pûrl'ănd) Tx. (In.)	29·34 N	95·17 W
100	Pearl Harbor Hi.	21·20 N	157·53 W
118	Pearsall (pēr'sôl) Tx.	28·53 N	99·06 W
92	Pearse I. (pērs) Can.	54·51 N	130·21 W
213	Pearston (pē'ērstŏn) S. Afr. (Natal In.)	32·36 S	25·09 E
219	Peary Land (Reg.) (pēr'ĭ) Grnld.	82·00 N	40·00 W
116	Pease (R.) (pēz) Tx.	34·07 N	99·53 W
119	Peason (pēz''n) La.	31·25 N	93·19 W
217	Pebane (pě-bà'nē) Moz.	17·10 S	38·08 E
165	Peć (pěch) Yugo.	42·39 N	20·18 E
118	Pecan Bay (pê-kăn') Tx.	32·04 N	99·15 W
135	Peçanha (pā-kän'yȧ) Braz.	18·37 S	42·26 W
109	Pecatonica (R.) (pěk-ȧ-tŏn-ĭ-kȧ) Il.	42·21 N	89·28 W
170	Pechenga (pyě'chěŋ-gà) Sov. Un.	69·30 N	31·10 E
170	Pechora (R.) Sov. Un.	66·00 N	52·30 E
172	Pechora Basin (pyě-chô'rà) Sov. Un.	67·55 N	58·37 E
170	Pechorskaya Guba (B.) Sov. Un.	68·40 N	55·00 E
115	Pecos (pā'kôs) NM	35·29 N	105·41 W
118	Pecos Tx.	31·26 N	103·30 W
102	Pecos (R.) U. S.	31·10 N	103·10 W
159	Pécs (pāch) Hung.	46·04 N	18·15 E
213	Peddie S. Afr. (Natal In.)	33·13 S	27·09 E
166	Pededze (R.) (pā'dĕd-zĕ) Sov. Un.	57·18 N	27·13 E
113	Pedley (pĕd'lē) Ca. (Los Angeles In.)	33·59 N	117·29 W
135	Pedra Azul (pā'drä-zōō'l) Braz.	16·03 S	41·13 W
135	Pedreiras (pě-drā'räs) Braz.	4·30 S	44·31 W
185	Pedro, Pt. (pē'drô) Sri Lanka	9·50 N	80·14 E
126	Pedro Antonio Santos (Sta. Cruz Chico) (pā'drô än-tō'nê-ô sän'tōs) (sän'tä krōōz' chē'kô) Mex. (In.)	18·55 N	88·13 W
128	Pedro Betancourt (bā-täŋ-kōrt') Cuba	22·40 N	81·15 W
136	Pedro de Valdivia (pě'drô-dě-väl-dē'vê-ä) Chile	22·32 S	69·55 W
136	Pedro do Rio (dô-rē'ô) Braz. (Rio de Janeiro In.)	22·20 S	43·09 W
135	Pedro Juan Caballero (hōōá'n-kä-bäl-yě'rō) Par.	22·40 S	55·42 W
122	Pedro Miguel (mê-gāl') Pan. (In.)	9·01 N	79·36 W
122	Pedro Miguel Locks (mê-gāl') Pan. (In.)	9·01 N	79·36 W
135	Pedro II (pā'drōō sȧ-gōōn'dōō) Braz.	4·20 S	41·27 W
203	Peebinga (pê-bĭng'ȧ) Austl.	34·43 S	140·55 E
154	Peebles (pē'b'lz) Scot.	55·40 N	3·15 W
121	Pee Dee (R.) (pē-dē') NC-SC	34·01 N	79·26 W
106	Peekskill (pēks'kĭl) NY (New York In.)	41·17 N	73·55 W
205	Pegasus B. (pěg'ȧ-sŭs) N. Z.	43·18 S	173·37 E
158	Pegnitz R. (pěgh-nēts) F.R.G.	49·38 N	11·40 E
163	Pego (pā'gō) Sp.	38·50 N	0·09 W
196	Pegu (pě-gōō') Bur.	17·17 N	96·29 E
95	Peguis Ind. Res. Can.	51·20 N	97·35 W
188	Pegu Yoma (Mts.) (pě-gōō'yō'mä) Bur.	19·16 N	95·59 E
165	Pehčevo (pěk'chě-vô) Yugo.	41·42 N	22·57 E
93	Peigan Ind. Res. Can.	49·35 N	113·40 W
	Peipus, L., see Chudskoye Ozero		
104	Pekin (pē'kĭn) Il.	40·35 N	89·30 W
	Peking, see Beijing		
152	Pelagie, Isole I. It.	35·46 N	12·32 E
165	Pélagos (I.) Grc.	39·17 N	24·05 E

Page	Name Pronunciation Region	Lat. °′	Long. °′
120	Pelahatchee (pěl-à-hăch'ē) Ms.	32·17 N	89·48 W
161	Pelat, Mt. (pē-lá') Fr.	44·16 N	6·43 E
173	Peleduy (pyěl-yĭ-dōō'ē) Sov. Un.	59·50 N	112·47 E
127	Pelee, Mt. (Vol.) (pē-lā') Mart. (In.)	14·49 N	61·10 W
104	Pelee, Pt. Can.	41·55 N	82·30 W
104	Pelee I. (pē'lê) Can.	41·45 N	82·30 W
137	Pelequén (pě-lě-kě'n) Chile (Santiago In.)	34·26 S	71·52 W
	Pelew (I.), see Palau		
120	Pelham (pěl'hăm) Ga.	31·07 N	84·10 W
99	Pelham NH (In.)	42·43 N	71·22 W
109	Pelican (L.) Mn.	46·36 N	94·00 W
95	Pelican B. Can.	52·45 N	100·20 W
128	Pelican Hbr. (pěl'ĭ-kăn) Ba.	26·20 N	76·45 W
108	Pelican Rapids (pěl'ĭ-kăn) Mn.	46·34 N	96·05 W
109	Pella (pěl'ȧ) Ia.	41·25 N	92·50 W
158	Pell-Worm I. (pěl'vôrm) F.R.G.	54·33 N	8·25 E
90	Pelly (L.) Can.	66·08 N	102·57 W
90	Pelly (R.) Can.	62·20 N	113·26 W
90	Pelly B. (pěl'ĭ) Can.	68·57 N	91·05 W
101	Pelly Crossing Can.	62·50 N	136·50 W
90	Pelly Mts. Can.	61·50 N	133·05 W
115	Peloncillo Mts. (pěl-ôn-sĭl'lō) Az.	32·40 N	109·20 W
165	Peloponnisos (Reg.) Grc.	37·28 N	22·14 E
136	Pelotas (pâ-lō'tăzh) Braz.	31·45 S	52·18 W
107	Pelton (pěl'tŭn) Can. (Detroit In.)	42·15 N	82·57 W
161	Pelvoux, Mt. (pěl-vōō') Fr.	44·56 N	6·24 E
170	Pelym (R.) Sov. Un.	60·20 N	63·05 E
121	Pelzer (pěl'zēr) SC	34·38 N	82·30 W
183	Pemanggil (I.) Mala. (Singapore In.)	2·37 N	104·41 E
196	Pematangsiantar Indon.	2·58 N	99·03 E
217	Pemba (pěm'bȧ) Moz.	12·58 S	40·30 E
212	Pemba Zambia	15·29 S	27·22 E
217	Pemba (I.) Tan.	5·20 S	39·57 E
217	Pemba Chan. Afr.	5·10 S	39·30 E
108	Pembina (pěm'bĭ-nȧ) ND	48·58 N	97·15 W
93	Pembina (R.) Can.	53·05 N	114·30 W
95	Pembina (R.) Can.	49·08 N	98·20 W
105	Pembroke (pěm' brōk) Can.	45·50 N	77·00 W
99	Pembroke (pěm'brōk) Ma. (In.)	42·05 N	70·49 W
154	Pembroke Wales	51·40 N	5·00 W
185	Pen India (In.)	18·44 N	73·06 E
162	Penafiél (pā-nȧ-fyěl') Port.	41·12 N	8·19 W
162	Peñafiel (pā-nyȧ-fyěl') Sp.	41·38 N	4·08 W
162	Peñalara (Mtn.) (pā-nyä-lä'rä) Sp.	40·52 N	3·57 W
124	Pena Nevada, Cerro Mex.	23·47 N	99·52 W
162	Peñaranda de Bracamonte (pā-nyä-rän'dä dā brä-kä-mōn'tå) Sp.	40·54 N	5·11 W
163	Peña Roya (Mtn.) (pä'nyä rō'yä) Sp.	40·18 N	0·42 W
162	Peñarroya-Peublonuevo (pěn-yär-rô'yä-pwě'blô-nwě'vô) Sp.	38·18 N	5·18 W
162	Peñas, Cabo de (C.) (kà'bô-dě-pā'nyäs) Sp.	43·42 N	6·12 W
136	Penas, Golfo de (gôl-fô-dě-pě'n-äs) Chile	47·15 S	77·30 W
118	Penasco R. (pā-nȧs'kō) Tx.	32·50 N	104·45 W
214	Pendembu (pěn-děm'bōō) S. L.	8·06 N	10·42 W
108	Pender (pěn'dẽr) Ne.	42·08 N	96·43 W
134	Penderisco (R.) (pěn-dě-rē's-kô) Col. (In.)	6·30 N	76·21 W
214	Pendjari, Parc Natl. de la (Natl. Pk.) Dahomey	11·25 N	1·30 E
110	Pendleton (pěn'd'l-tŭn) Or.	45·41 N	118·47 W
110	Pend Oreille L. (pŏn-dô-rā') (pěn-dô-rěl') Id.	48·09 N	116·38 W
110	Pend Oreille R. Wa.	48·44 N	117·20 W
135	Penedo (pâ-nā'dōō) Braz.	10·17 S	36·28 W
105	Penetanguishene (pěn'ê-tăŋ-gĭ-shēn') Can.	44·45 N	79·55 W
190	Pengcheng (pŭŋ-chŭŋ) China	36·24 N	114·11 E
190	Penglai (pŭŋ-lī) China	37·49 N	120·45 E
162	Peniche (pě-nē'chȧ) Port.	39·22 N	9·24 W
107	Peninsula (pěn-ĭn'sū-lȧ) Oh. (Cleveland In.)	41·14 N	81·32 W
148	Penistone (pěn'ĭ-stŭn) Eng.	53·31 N	1·38 W
124	Penjamillo (pěn-hä-mēl'yō) Mex.	20·06 N	101·56 W
124	Penjamo (pān'hä-mō) Mex.	20·27 N	101·43 W
148	Penk (R.) (pěnk) Eng.	52·41 N	2·10 W
148	Penkridge (pěnk'rĭj) Eng.	52·43 N	2·07 W
164	Penne (pěn'nā) It.	42·28 N	13·57 E
184	Penner (R.) (pěn'ẽr) India	14·43 N	79·09 E
158	Pennine Alpi (Mts.) Switz.	46·02 N	7·07 E
154	Pennine Chain (Mts.) (pěn-īn') Eng.	53·44 N	1·59 W
104	Pennsboro (pěnz'bŭr-ô) WV	39·10 N	81·00 W
106	Penns Grove (pěnz grōv) NJ (Philadelpahia In.)	39·44 N	75·28 W
103	Pennsylvania (State) (pěn-sĭl-vā'nĭ-ȧ) U. S.	41·00 N	78·10 W
105	Penn Yan (pěn yăn') NY	42·40 N	77·00 W
95	Pennycutaway (R.) Can.	56·10 N	93·25 W
166	Peno (L.) (pā'nô) Sov. Un.	56·55 N	32·28 E
98	Penobscot (R.) Me.	45·00 N	68·36 W
98	Penobscot B. (pê-nŏb'skŏt) Me.	44·20 N	69·00 W
204	Penong (pê-nông') Austl.	32·00 S	133·00 E
127	Penonomé (pā-nō-nō-mā') Pan.	8·32 N	80·21 W
202	Penrith Austl. (Sydney In.)	33·45 S	150·42 E
120	Pensacola (pěn-sȧ-kō'lȧ) Fl.	30·25 N	87·13 W
117	Pensacola Dam Ok.	36·27 N	95·02 W
124	Pensilvania (pěn-sěl-vá'nyä) Col. (In.)	5·31 N	75·05 W
205	Pentecost (I.) (pěn'tê-kōst) New Hebr.	16·05 S	168·28 E
93	Penticton Can.	49·30 N	119·35 W
154	Pentland Firth (pěnt'lănd) Scot.	58·44 N	3·25 W
171	Penza (pěn'zȧ) Sov. Un.	53·10 N	45·00 E

Page	Name Pronunciation Region	Lat. °′	Long. °′
154	Penzance (pěn-zăns') Eng.	50·07 N	5·40 W
158	Penzberg (pěnts'běrgh) F.R.G.	47·43 N	11·21 E
173	Penzhina (R.) (pyĭn-zē-nŭ) Sov. Un.	62·15 N	166·30 E
173	Penzhino Sov. Un.	63·42 N	168·00 E
173	Penzhinskay'a Guba (B.) Sov. Un.	60·30 N	161·30 E
104	Peoria (pē-ō'rĭ-ȧ) Il.	40·45 N	89·35 W
124	Peotillos (pā-ō-tel'yōs) Mex.	22·30 N	100·39 W
107	Peotone (pē'ō-tôn) Il. (Chicago In.)	41·20 N	87·47 W
105	Pepacton Res. (pěp-ȧc'tŭn) NY	42·05 N	74·40 W
128	Pepe, Cabo (kä'bô-pě'pě) (C.) Cuba	21·30 N	83·10 W
99	Pepperell (pěp'ẽr-ěl) Ma. (In.)	42·40 N	71·36 W
165	Peqin (pě-kēn') Alb.	41·03 N	19·48 E
163	Perales (R.) (pā-rä'lās) Sp.	40·24 N	4·07 W
163	Perales de Tajuña (dā tä-hōō'nyä) Sp. (Madrid In.)	40·14 N	3·22 W
98	Percé (pěr'sā') Can.	48·31 N	64·13 W
149	Perchtoldsdorf (pěrk'tôlts-dôrf) Aus. (Vienna In.)	48·07 N	16·17 E
218	Perdekop S. Afr. (Johannesburg & Pretoria In.)	27·11 S	29·38 E
163	Perdido, Mt. (pěr-dē'dō) Sp.	42·40 N	0·00
120	Perdido (R.) (pěr-dī'dō) Al.-Fl.	30·45 N	87·38 W
137	Perdões (pěr-dô'ěs) Braz. (Rio de Janeiro In.)	21·05 S	45·05 W
134	Pereira (pā-rā'rä) Col. (In.)	4·49 N	75·42 W
167	Perekop (pěr-â-kôp') Sov. Un.	46·08 N	33·39 E
104	Pere Marquette Mi.	43·55 N	86·10 W
167	Pereshchepino (pâ'râsh-chě'pê-nô) Sov. Un.	49·02 N	35·19 E
166	Pereslavl'-Zalesskiy (pâ-râ-slàv''l zà-lyěs'kĭ) Sov. Un.	56·43 N	38·52 E
167	Pereyaslav (pě-râ-yäs'läv) Sov. Un.	50·05 N	31·25 E
137	Pergamino (pěr-gä-mē'nō) Arg. (Buenos Aires In.)	33·53 S	60·36 W
108	Perham (pěr'hăm) Mn.	46·37 N	95·35 W
97	Peribonca (R.) (pěr-ĭ-bŏŋ'kȧ) Can.	49·10 N	71·20 W
160	Périgueux (pā-rê-gû') Fr.	45·12 N	0·43 E
134	Perija, Sierra de (Mts.) (sē-ě'r-rà-dě-pě-rē'Kä) Col.	9·25 N	73·30 W
197	Perkam, Tandjung (C.) Indon.	1·20 S	138·45 E
89	Perkins (pěr'kěns) Can. (Ottawa In.)	45·37 N	75·37 W
	Perlas, Arch. de Las (är-chē-pyě'lä-gô-dě-läs-pěr'läs) Pan.	8·29 N	79·15 W
127	Perlas, Laguna las (L.) (lä-gōō'nä-dě-läs) Nic.	12·34 N	83·19 W
158	Perleberg (pěr'lē-běrg) G.D.R.	53·06 N	11·51 E
174	Perm' (pěrm) Sov. Un. (Urals In.)	58·00 N	56·15 E
	Pernambuco, see Recife		
135	Pernambuco (State) (pěr-näm-bōō'kō) Braz.	8·08 S	38·54 W
165	Pernik (pěr-nēk') Bul.	42·36 N	23·04 E
160	Peronne (pā-rôn') Fr.	49·57 N	2·49 E
125	Perote (pě-rô'tě) Mex.	19·33 N	97·13 W
194	Perouse Str. Jap.-Sov. Un.	45·45 N	141·38 E
174	Perovo (pâ'rô-vô) Sov. Un. (Moscow In.)	55·43 N	37·47 E
160	Perpignan (pěr-pē-nyäN') Fr.	42·42 N	2·48 E
113	Perris (pěr'ĭs) Ca. (Los Angeles In.)	33·46 N	117·14 W
128	Perros, Bahía (B.) (bä-ē'ä-pā'rōs) Cuba	22·25 N	78·35 W
89	Perrot Île (I.) (pěr'ŭt) Can. (Montreal In.)	45·23 N	73·57 W
120	Perry (pěr'ĭ) Fl.	30·06 N	83·35 W
120	Perry Ga.	32·27 N	83·44 W
109	Perry Ia.	41·49 N	94·40 W
105	Perry NY	42·45 N	78·00 W
117	Perry Ok.	36·17 N	97·18 W
113	Perry Ut. (Salt Lake City In.)	41·27 N	112·02 W
106	Perry Hall Md. (Baltimore In.)	39·24 N	76·29 W
107	Perryopolis (pě-rê-ŏ'pô-lĭs) Pa. (Pittsburgh In.)	40·05 N	79·45 W
104	Perrysburg (pěr' ĭz-bûrg) Oh.	41·35 N	83·35 W
116	Perryton (pěr'ĭ-tŭn) Tx.	36·23 N	100·48 W
101	Perryville (pěr-ĭ-vĭl) Ak.	55·58 N	159·28 W
117	Perryville Mo.	37·41 N	89·52 W
161	Persan (pěr-säN') Fr. (In.)	49·09 N	2·15 E
141	Persepolis (Ruins) (pēr-sěp'o-lĭs) Iran	30·15 N	53·08 E
	Persia, see Iran		
186	Persian G. (pûr'zhȧn) Asia	27·38 N	50·30 E
204	Perth (pûrth) Austl.	31·50 S	116·10 E
105	Perth Can.	44·40 N	76·15 W
154	Perth Scot.	56·24 N	3·25 W
106	Perth Amboy (ăm'boi) NJ (New York In.)	40·31 N	74·16 W
161	Pertuis (pěr-tüē') Fr.	43·43 N	5·29 E
104	Peru (pē-rōō') Il.	41·20 N	89·10 W
104	Peru In.	40·45 N	86·00 W
133	Peru S. A.	10·00 S	75·00 W
164	Perugia (pā-rōō'jä) It.	43·08 N	12·24 E
113	Peruque (pě rō'kě) Mo. (St. Louis In.)	38·52 N	90·36 W
167	Pervomaysk (pěr-vô-mīsk') Sov. Un.	48·04 N	30·52 E
174	Pervoural'sk (pěr-vô-ōō-rálsk') Sov. Un. (Urals In.)	56·54 N	59·58 E
173	Pervyy Kuril'skiy Proliv (Str.) Sov. Un.	51·43 N	154·32 E
164	Pesaro (pā'zä-rō) It.	43·54 N	12·55 E
135	Pescado (pěs-kä'dō) (R.) Ven. (In.)	9·33 N	65·32 W
164	Pescara (päs-kä'rä) It.	42·26 N	14·15 E
164	Pescara (R.) It.	42·18 N	13·22 E
171	Peschanyy, Mys (C.) Sov. Un.	43·10 N	51·20 E
164	Pescia (pä'shä) It.	43·53 N	11·42 E

ng-sing; ŋ-baŋk; N-nasalized n; nŏd; cŏmmit; ōld; ôbey; ôrder; fōōd; fŏŏt; ou-out; s-soft; sh-dish; th-thin; pūre; ûnite; ûrn; stŭd; circŭs; ü-as "y" in study; '-indeterminate vowel.

Page	Name Pronunciation Region	Lat. °′	Long. °′
187	Peshāwar (pĕ-shä'wŭr) Pak. (Khyber Pass In.)	34·01 N	71·34 E
165	Peshtera Bul.	42·03 N	24·19 E
109	Peshtigo (pĕsh'tē-gō) Wi.	45·03 N	87·46 W
109	Peshtigo (R.) Wi.	45·15 N	88·14 W
141	Peski Sov. Un.	39·46 N	59·47 E
141	Peski Sov. Un.	44·07 N	63·17 E
174	Peski (pyâs'kĭ) Sov. Un. (Moscow In.)	55·13 N	38·48 E
162	Pêso da Régua (pā-sōō-dä-rā'gwä) Port.	41·09 N	7·47 W
126	Pespire (pås-pē'rå) Hond.	13·35 N	87·20 W
118	Pesqueria, R. (pås-kå-rē'ä) Mex.	25·55 N	100·25 W
124	Petacalco, Bahía de (B.) (bä-ē'ä-dĕ-pĕ-tä-kål'kō) Mex.	17·55 N	102·00 W
183	Petah Tiqwa Isr. (Palestine In.)	32·05 N	34·53 E
114	Petaluma (pét-à-lōō'mà) Ca.	38·15 N	122·38 W
135	Petare (pĕ-tä'rĕ) Ven. (In.)	10·28 N	66·48 W
124	Petatlán (pā-tä-tlän') Mex.	17·31 N	101·17 W
97	Petawawa Can.	45·54 N	77·17 W
126	Petén, Laguna de (L.) (lä-gōō'nä-dĕ-på-tān') Guat. (In.)	17·05 N	89·54 W
109	Petenwell Res. Wi.	44·10 N	89·55 W
105	Peterborough (pē'tēr-bŭr-ō) Can.	44·20 N	78·20 W
203	Peterborough Austl.	32·53 S	138·58 E
148	Peterborough Eng.	52·35 N	0·14 W
154	Peterhead (pē-tēr-hĕd') Scot.	57·36 N	3·47 W
105	Peter Pt. Can.	43·50 N	77·00 W
94	Peter Pond L. (pŏnd) Can.	55·55 N	108·44 W
101	Petersburg (pē'tērz-bûrg) Ak.	56·52 N	133·10 W
117	Petersburg Il.	40·01 N	89·51 W
104	Petersburg In.	38·30 N	87·15 W
107	Petersburg Ky. (Cincinnati In.)	39·04 N	84·52 W
121	Petersburg Va.	37·12 N	77·30 W
149	Petershagen (pĕ'tĕrs-hä-gĕn) G.D.R. (Berlin In.)	52·32 N	13·46 E
149	Petershausen (pĕ'tĕrs-hou-zĕn) F.R.G. (Munich In.)	48·25 N	11·29 E
129	Pétionville Hai.	18·30 N	72·20 W
98	Petitcodiac (pē-tē-kô-dyàk') Can.	45·56 N	65·10 W
127	Petite Terre I. (pē-tēt'târ') Guad. (In.)	16·12 N	61·00 W
129	Petit Goâve (pē-tē' gô-äv') Hai.	18·25 N	72·50 W
117	Petit Jean Cr. (pē-tē'zhäN') Ar.	35·05 N	93·55 W
216	Petit Loango Gabon	2·16 S	9·35 E
125	Petlalcingo (pĕ-tläl-sĕŋ'gō) Mex.	18·05 N	97·53 W
126	Peto (pĕ'tô) Mex. (In.)	20·07 N	88·49 W
125	Petorca (pā-tōr'kä) Chile (Santiago In.)	32·14 S	70·55 W
104	Petoskey (pê-tŏs'kĭ) Mi.	45·25 N	84·55 W
183	Petra Jordan (Palestine In.)	30·21 N	35·25 E
194	Petra Velikogo, Zaliv (B.) (zä'lĭf pĕt-rä' vĕ-lĭ'kô-vô) Sov. Un.	42·40 N	131·50 E
165	Petrich (pā'trĭch) Bul.	41·24 N	23·13 E
115	Petrified Forest Natl. Park (pĕt'rĭ-fīd fôr'ĕst) Az.	34·58 N	109·35 W
167	Petrikovka (pyĕ'trê-kôf-kä) Sov. Un.	48·43 N	34·29 E
167	Petrikov (pyĕ'trê-kô-v) Sov. Un.	52·09 N	28·30 E
164	Petrinja (pā'trēn-yà) Yugo.	45·25 N	16·17 E
174	Petrodvorets (pyĕ-trô-dvô-ryĕts') Sov. Un. (Leningrad In.)	59·53 N	29·55 E
174	Petrokrepost' (pyĕ'trô-krĕ-pôst) Sov. Un. (Leningrad In.)	59·56 N	31·03 E
104	Petrolia (pē-trō'lĭ-à) Can.	42·50 N	82·10 W
135	Petrolina (pĕ-trō-lē'nà) Braz.	9·18 S	40·28 W
149	Petronell Aus. (Vienna In.)	48·07 N	16·52 E
167	Petropavlovka (pyĕ'trô-päv'lôf-kȧ) Sov. Un.	48·24 N	36·23 E
174	Petropavlovka. Sov. Un. (Urals In.)	54·10 N	59·50 E
172	Petropavlovsk (pyĕ-trô-päv'lôfsk) Sov. Un.	54·44 N	69·07 E
173	Petropavlovsk-Kamchatskiy (käm-chät'skĭ) Sov. Un.	53·13 N	158·56 E
136	Petrópolis (på-trô-pô-lēzh') Braz. (Rio de Janeiro In.)	22·31 S	43·10 W
165	Petroseni Rom.	45·24 N	23·24 E
171	Petrovsk (pyĕ-trôfsk') Sov. Un.	52·20 N	45·15 E
167	Petrovskaya (pyĕ-trôf'skà-yà) Sov. Un.	45·25 N	37·50 E
171	Petrovskoye Sov. Un.	45·20 N	43·00 E
173	Petrovsk-Zabaykal'skiy (pyĕ-trôfskzä-bī-käl'skĭ) Sov. Un.	51·13 N	109·08 E
157	Petrozavodsk (pyā'trô-zà-vôtsk') Sov. Un.	61·46 N	34·25 E
218	Petrus Steyn (pā'trōōs stān') S. Afr. (Johannesburg & Pretoria In.)	27·40 S	28·09 E
166	Petseri (pĕt'sĕ-rê) Sov. Un.	57·48 N	27·33 E
107	Pewaukee (pĭ-wô'kē) Wi. (Milwaukee In.)	43·05 N	88·15 W
107	Pewaukee L. Wi. (Milwaukee In.)	43·03 N	88·18 W
107	Pewee Valley (pe wē) Ky. (Louisville In.)	38·19 N	85·29 W
170	Peza (R.) (pyâ'zà) Sov. Un.	65·35 N	46·50 E
160	Pézenas (pā-zē-nä') Fr.	43·26 N	3·24 E
158	Pforzheim (pfôrts'hīm) F.R.G.	48·52 N	8·43 E
184	Phalodi India	27·13 N	72·22 E
196	Phan-thiet Viet.	11·30 N	108·43 E
	Pharsalus, see Fársala		
120	Phenix City (fē'nĭks) Al.	32·29 N	85·00 W
106	Philadelphia (fĭl-à-dĕl'phĭ-à) Ms.	32·45 N	89·07 W
106	Philadelphia Pa. (Philadelphia In.)	40·00 N	75·13 W
108	Philip (fĭl'ĭp) SD	44·03 N	101·35 W
	Philippeville, see Skikda		
183	Philippines (fĭl'ĭ-pēnz) Asia	14·25 N	125·00 E
198	Philippine Sea (fĭl'ĭ-pēn) Asia	16·00 N	133·00 E
197	Philippine Trench Phil.	10·30 N	127·15 E
	Philippopolis, see Plovdiv		
105	Philipsburg (fĭl'lĭps-bērg) Pa.	40·55 N	78·10 W
111	Philipsburg Wy.	46·19 N	113·19 W
203	Phillip (I.) (fĭl'ĭp) Austl.	38·32 S	145·10 E
183	Phillip Chan. Indon. (Singapore In.)	1·04 N	103·40 E
105	Phillipi (fĭ-lĭp'ĭ) WV	39·10 N	80·00 W
109	Phillips (fĭl'ĭps) Wi.	45·41 N	90·24 W
116	Phillipsburg (fĭl'lĭps-bērg) Ks.	39·44 N	99·19 W
105	Phillipsburg NJ	40·45 N	75·10 W
196	Phitsanulok Thai.	16·51 N	100·15 E
196	Phnum Pénh (nŏm'pĕn') Kamp.	11·39 N	104·53 E
115	Phoenix (fē'nĭks) Az.	33·30 N	112·00 W
106	Phoenix Md. (Baltimore In.)	39·31 N	76·40 W
198	Phoenix Is. Oceania	4·00 S	174·00 W
106	Phoenixville (fē'nĭks-vĭl) Pa. (Philadelphia In.)	40·08 N	75·31 W
196	Phra Nakhon Si Ayutthaya Thai.	14·16 N	100·37 E
196	Phu Bia (Pk.) Laos	19·36 N	103·00 E
196	Phu-Quoc, Dao (I.) Camb.	10·13 N	104·00 E
196	Phuket Thai.	7·57 N	98·19 E
190	Pi (R.) (bē) China	32·06 N	116·31 E
164	Piacenza (pyä-chĕnt'sä) It.	45·02 N	9·42 E
164	Pianosa (I.) (pyä-nō'sä) It.	42·13 N	15·45 E
159	Piatra-Neamt (pyä'trà-nä-ämts') Rom.	46·54 N	26·24 E
135	Piauí (State) (pyou'ē) Braz.	7·40 S	42·25 W
135	Piauí, Serra do (Mts.) (sĕr'rà dōō pyou'ē) Braz.	10·45 S	44·36 W
164	Piave (R.) (pyä'vā) It.	45·45 N	12·15 E
164	Piazza Armerina (pyät'sä är-må-rē'nä) It.	37·23 N	14·26 E
211	Pibor R. (pē'bôr) Sud.	7·21 N	32·54 E
109	Pic (R.) (pēk) Can.	48·48 N	86·28 W
123	Picara Pt. (pē-kä'rä) Vir. Is. (U. S. A.) (St. Thomas In.)	18·23 N	64·57 W
120	Picayune (pĭk'à yōōn) Ms.	30·32 N	89·41 W
164	Piccole Alpi Dolomitiche (Mts.) (pē'k-kô-le-âl'pē-dô-lô'mē-tē'chĕ) It.	46·05 N	12·17 E
163	Pic du Midi d'Ossau (Mtn.) (pēk dü mê-dē' dôs-sō') Fr.	42·51 N	0·25 W
117	Picher (pĭch'ēr) Ok.	36·58 N	94·49 W
137	Pichilemu (pē-chē-lĕ'mōō) Chile (Santiago In.)	34·22 S	72·01 W
125	Pichucalco (pē-chōō-käl'kô) Mex.	17·34 N	93·06 W
125	Pichucalco (R.) Mex.	17·40 N	93·02 W
109	Pickerel (L.) (pĭk'ēr-ĕl) Can.	48·35 N	91·10 W
120	Pickwick (R.) (pĭk'wĭck) Tn.	35·04 N	88·05 W
113	Pico (pē'kō) Ca. (Los Angeles In.)	34·01 N	118·05 W
163	Pico de Aneto (Mtn.) (pē'kō-dĕ-ä-nĕ'tô) Sp.	42·35 N	0·38 E
210	Pico I. (pē'kōō) Açores (In.)	38·16 N	28·49 W
135	Picos (pē'kōzh) Braz.	7·13 S	41·23 W
113	Pico Rivera Ca. (Los Angeles In.)	34·01 N	118·05 W
202	Picton (pĭk'tŭn) Austl. (Sydney In.)	34·11 S	150·37 E
98	Pictou (pĭk-tōō') Can.	45·41 N	62·43 W
183	Pidálion, Akrotírion (C.) Cyprus (Palestine In.)	34·50 N	34·05 E
185	Pidurutalagala Mt. (pē'dōō-rōō-tä'lȧ-gä'lȧ) Sri Lanka	12·27 N	80·45 E
109	Pie (I.) (pī) Can.	48·10 N	89·07 W
137	Piedade (pyā-dä'dĕ) Braz. (Rio de Janeiro In.)	23·42 S	47·25 W
120	Piedmont (pēd'mŏnt) Al.	33·54 N	85·36 W
112	Piedmont Ca. (San Francisco In.)	37·50 N	122·14 W
117	Piedmont Mo.	37·09 N	90·42 W
121	Piedmont SC	34·40 N	82·27 W
105	Piedmont WV	39·30 N	79·05 W
162	Piedrabuena (pyā-drä-bwā'nä) Sp.	39·01 N	4·10 W
137	Piedras, Punta (Pt.) (pōō'n-tä-pyĕ'dräs) Arg. (Buenos Aires In.)	35·25 S	57·10 W
118	Piedras Negras (pyā'dräs nā'gräs) Mex.	28·41 N	100·33 W
157	Pieksämäki (pyĕk'sĕ-mĕ-kē) Fin.	62·18 N	27·14 E
162	Piélagos (pyā'lä-gōs) Sp.	43·23 N	3·55 W
164	Piemonte (Reg.) (pyĕ-mô'n-tĕ) It.	44·30 N	7·42 E
218	Pienaars R. S. Afr. (Johannesburg & Pretoria In.)	25·13 S	28·05 E
218	Pienaarsrivier S. Afr. (Johannesburg & Pretoria In.)	25·12 S	28·18 E
108	Pierce (pērs) Ne.	42·11 N	97·33 W
105	Pierce WV	39·15 N	79·30 W
106	Piermont (pēr'mŏnt) NY (New York In.)	41·03 N	73·55 W
108	Pierre (pēr) SD	44·22 N	100·20 W
89	Pierrefonds Can. (Montreal In.)	45·29 N	73·52 W
159	Piešťany (pyĕsh'tyà-nûĭ) Czech.	48·36 N	17·48 E
213	Pietermaritzburg (pê-tēr-mà-rĭts-bûrg) S. Afr. (Natal In.)	29·36 S	30·23 E
218	Pietersburg (pē'tērz-bûrg) S. Afr. (Johannesburg & Pretoria In.)	23·56 S	29·30 E
97	Pieton Can.	44·00 N	77·15 W
212	Piet Retief (pēt rĕ-tēf') S. Afr.	27·00 S	30·58 E
159	Pietrosul Pk. Rom.	47·35 N	24·49 E
164	Pieve di Cadore (pyā'vå dē kä-dō'rå) It.	46·26 N	12·22 E
109	Pigeon (R.) (pĭj'ŭn) Can.-Mn.	48·05 N	90·13 W
93	Pigeon L. Can.	53·00 N	114·00 W
89	Pigeon Lake Can. (Winnipeg In.)	49·57 N	97·36 W
117	Piggott (pĭg-ŭt) Ar.	36·22 N	90·10 W
125	Pijijiapan (pēkē-kê-ä'pän) Mex.	15·40 N	93·12 W
149	Pijnacker Neth. (Amsterdam In.)	52·01 N	4·25 E
116	Pikes Pk. (pīks) Co.	38·49 N	105·03 W
121	Pikeville (pīk'vĭl) Ky.	37·28 N	82·31 W
190	Pikou (pē-kō) China	39·25 N	122·19 E
95	Pikwitonei (pĭk'wĭ-tōn) Can.	55·35 N	97·09 W
158	Piła (pē'là) Pol.	53·09 N	16·44 E
218	Pilansberg (pĭ'ăns'bûrg) S. Afr. (Johannesburg & Pretoria In.)	25·08 S	26·55 E
137	Pilar (pē'lär) Arg. (Buenos Aires In.)	34·27 S	58·55 W
136	Pilar Par.	27·00 S	58·15 W
135	Pilar de Goiás (dĕ-gô'yà's) Braz.	14·47 S	49·33 W
112	Pilchuck (R.) Wa. (Seattle In.)	48·03 N	121·58 W
112	Pilchuck Cr. (pĭl'chŭck) Wa. (Seattle In.)	48·19 N	122·11 W
112	Pilchuck Mtn. Wa. (Seattle In.)	48·03 N	121·48 W
136	Pilcomayo (R.) (pēl-cō-mī'ô) Par.	24·45 S	69·15 W
197	Pili (pē'lē) Phil. (In.)	13·34 N	123·17 E
159	Pilica R. (pê-lēt'sä) Pol.	51·00 N	19·48 E
112	Pillar Pt. (pĭl'ár) Can. (Seattle In.)	48·14 N	124·06 W
112	Pillar Rock Wa. (Portland In.)	46·16 N	123·35 W
124	Pilón (R.) (pê-lōn') Mex.	24·13 N	99·03 W
117	Pilot Point (pī'lŭt) Tx.	33·24 N	97·00 W
	Pilsen, see Plzeň		
157	Piltene (pĭl'tĕ-nĕ) Sov. Un.	57·17 N	21·40 E
124	Pimal, Cerra (Mtn.) (sĕ'r-rä-pē-mäl') Mex.	22·58 N	104·19 W
204	Pimba (pĭm'bà) Austl.	31·15 S	146·50 E
213	Pimville (pĭm'vĭl) (Neigh.) S. Afr. (Johannesburg & Pretoria In.)	26·17 S	27·54 E
122	Pinacate, Cerro (Mtn.) (sĕ'r-rô-pē-nä-kä'tĕ) Mex.	31·45 N	113·30 W
197	Pinamalayan (pē-nä-mä-lä'yän) Phil. (In.)	13·04 N	121·31 E
196	Pinang Mala.	5·21 N	100·09 E
171	Pinarbaşi (pē'när-bä'shĭ) Tur.	38·50 N	36·10 E
128	Pinar del Río (pē-när' dĕl rē'ô) Cuba	22·25 N	83·35 W
128	Pinar del Río (Prov.) Cuba	22·45 N	83·25 W
197	Pinatubo (Mtn.) (pē-nä-tōō'bô) Phil. (In.)	15·09 N	120·19 E
93	Pincher Creek (pĭn'chēr krēk) Can.	49·29 N	113·57 W
117	Pinckneyville (pĭnk'nĭ-vĭl) Il.	38·06 N	89·22 W
159	Pińczów (pēn''chōōf) Pol.	50·32 N	20·33 E
137	Pindamonhangaba (pĕ'n-dä-mōnyà'n-gä-bä) Braz. (Rio de Janeiro In.)	22·56 S	45·26 W
128	Pinder Pt. Ba.	26·35 N	78·35 W
165	Píndhos Oros (Mts.) Grc.	39·48 N	21·19 E
215	Pindiga Nig.	9·59 N	10·54 E
92	Pine (R.) (pīn) Can.	55·30 N	122·20 W
109	Pine (R.) Wi.	45·50 N	88·37 W
117	Pine Bluff (pīn blŭf) Ar.	34·13 N	92·01 W
109	Pine City (pīn) Mn.	45·50 N	93·01 W
204	Pine Creek Austl.	13·45 S	132·00 E
114	Pine Cr. Nv.	40·15 N	116·17 W
95	Pine Falls Can.	50·35 N	96·15 W
110	Pine Forest Ra. Nv.	41·35 N	118·45 W
170	Pinega (pê-nyĕ'gà) Sov. Un.	64·40 N	43·30 E
170	Pinega (R.) Sov. Un.	64·10 N	42·30 E
106	Pine Hill (pīn hĭl) NJ (Philadelphia In.)	39·47 N	74·59 W
121	Pine Is. Fl. (In.)	24·48 N	81·32 W
121	Pine Island Sd. Fl. (In.)	26·32 N	82·30 W
106	Pine Lake Estates (lāk ĕs-tāts') Ga. (Atlanta In.)	33·47 N	84·13 W
212	Pinelands (pĭn'lănds) S. Afr. (In.)	33·57 S	18·30 E
113	Pine Lawn (lôn) Mo. (St. Louis In.)	38·42 N	90·17 W
92	Pine Pass Can.	55·22 N	122·40 W
108	Pine Ridge Ind. Res. (rĭj) SD	43·33 N	102·13 W
164	Pinerolo (pē-nå-rô'lō) It.	44·47 N	7·18 E
119	Pines, Lake o' the Tx.	32·50 N	94·40 W
213	Pinetown (pīn'toun) S. Afr. (Natal In.)	29·47 S	30·52 E
113	Pine View Res. (vū) Ut. (Salt Lake City In.)	41·17 N	111·54 W
120	Pineville (pīn'vĭl) Ky.	36·48 N	83·43 W
119	Pineville La.	31·20 N	92·25 W
196	Ping (R.) Thai.	17·54 N	98·29 E
192	Pingding (pĭŋ-dĭŋ) China	37·50 N	113·30 E
190	Pingdu (pĭŋ-dōō) China	36·46 N	119·57 E
183	Pinggir Indon. (Singapore In.)	1·05 N	101·12 E
193	Pingh (pĭŋ-hŭ) China	24·30 N	117·02 E
193	Pingle (pĭŋ-lŭ) China	24·30 N	110·22 E
192	Pingliang (pĭŋ'lyäŋ') China	35·12 N	106·50 E
192	Pingquan (pĭŋ-chyŭän) China	40·58 N	118·40 E
193	Pingtan (pĭŋ-tän) China	25·30 N	119·45 E
193	Pingtan Dao (I.) (pĭŋ-tän dou) China	25·40 N	119·45 E
193	P'ingtung Taiwan	22·40 N	120·35 E
192	Pingwu (pĭŋ-wōō) China	32·20 N	104·40 E
193	Pingxiang (pĭŋ-shyäŋ) China	27·40 N	113·50 E
190	Pingyi (pĭŋ-yē) China	35·30 N	117·38 E
190	Pingyuan (pĭŋ-yŭän) China	37·11 N	116·26 E
191	Pingzhou (pĭŋ-jō) China (Canton In.)	23·01 N	113·11 E
137	Pinhal (pē-nyà'l) Braz. (Rio de Janeiro In.)	22·11 S	46·43 W
163	Pinhal Novo (nô vōō) Port. (Lisbon In.)	38·38 N	8·54 W
162	Pinhel (pēn-yĕl') Port.	40·45 N	7·03 W
196	Pini, Pulau (I.) Indon.	0·07 S	98·38 E
165	Piniós (R.) Grc.	40·33 N	21·40 E
114	Pinnacles Natl. Mon. (pĭn'à-k'lz) Ca.	36·30 N	121·00 W
149	Pinneberg (pĭn'ĕ-bĕrg) F.R.G. (Hamburg In.)	53·40 N	9·48 E
112	Pinole (pĭ-nō'lē) Ca. (San Francisco In.)	38·01 N	122·17 W
162	Pinos-Puente (pwān'tå) Sp.	37·15 N	3·43 W
124	Pinotepa Nacional (pē-nō-tà'pä nä-syō-näl') Mex.	16·21 N	98·04 W
205	Pins, Ile des N. Cal.	22·44 S	167·44 E
159	Pinsk (pēn'sk) Sov. Un.	52·07 N	26·05 E
134	Pinta (I.) Ec.	0·41 N	90·47 W
89	Pintendre (pĕN-täNdr') Can. (Quebec In.)	46·45 N	71·07 W
163	Pinto (pēn'tō) Sp. (Madrid In.)	40·14 N	3·42 W

ăt; finăl; rāte; senâte; ärm; àsk; sofà; fâre; ch-choose; dh-as th in other; bē; êvent; bĕt; recĕnt; cratēr; g-go; gh-guttural g; bĭt; ĭ-short neutral; rīde; K-guttural k as ch in German ich;

PRONOUNCING INDEX

Pinto Butte — Ponta Delgada 329

Page	Name Pronunciation Region	Lat. °'	Long. °'
94	Pinto Butte (pĭn'tō) Can.	49·22 N	107·25 W
115	Pioche (pī-ō'chē) Nv.	37·56 N	114·28 W
164	Piombino (pyôm-bē'nō) It.	42·56 N	10·33 E
111	Pioneer Mts. (pī'ō-nēr') Mt.	45·23 N	112·51 W
159	Piotrków Trybunalski (pyōtr'kōōv trĭ-bōō-nal'skē) Pol.	51·23 N	19·44 E
120	Piper (pī'pēr) Al.	33·04 N	87·00 W
113	Piper Ks. (Kansas City In.)	39·09 N	94·51 W
165	Pipéri (I.) (pē'per-ê) Grc.	39·19 N	24·20 E
115	Pipe Spring Natl. Mon. (pīp spring) Az.	36·50 N	112·45 W
108	Pipestone (pīp'stōn) Mn.	44·00 N	96·19 W
108	Pipestone Natl. Mon. Mn.	44·03 N	96·24 W
98	Pipmaucan, Rés. (pĭp-mä-kän') Can.	49·45 N	70·00 W
104	Piqua (pĭk'wȧ) Oh.	40·10 N	84·15 W
137	Piracaia (pē-rä-kä'yä) Braz. (Rio de Janeiro In.)	23·04 S	46·20 W
137	Piracicaba (pê-rä-sê-kä'bä) Braz. (Rio de Janeiro In.)	22·43 S	47·39 W
137	Piraí (pē-rä-ē') Braz. (Rio de Janeiro In.)	22·38 S	43·54 W
137	Piraíba (R.) (pä-rä-ē'bȧ) Braz. (Rio de Janeiro In.)	21·38 S	41·29 W
172	Piramida, Gol'tsy (Mtn.) Sov. Un.	54·00 N	96·00 E
164	Piran (pē-rȧ'n) Yugo.	45·31 N	13·34 E
137	Piranga (pē-rä'n-gä) Braz. (Rio de Janeiro In.)	20·41 S	43·17 W
137	Pirapetinga (pē-rä-pě-tē'n-gä) Braz. (Rio de Janeiro In.)	21·40 S	42·20 W
135	Pirapora (pê-rä-pō'rȧ) Braz.	17·39 S	44·54 W
137	Pirassununga (pē-rä-sōō-nōō'n-gä) Braz. (Rio de Janeiro In.)	22·00 S	47·24 W
135	Pirenópolis (pē-rě-nô'pō-lês) Braz.	15·56 S	48·49 W
165	Pírgos Grc.	37·51 N	21·28 E
135	Piritu, Laguna de (L.) (lä-gōō'nä-dě-pē-rē'tōō) Ven. (In.)	10·00 N	64·57 W
158	Pirmasens (pĭr-mä-zěns') F.R.G.	49·12 N	7·34 E
158	Pirna (pĭr'nä) G.D.R.	50·57 N	13·56 E
165	Pirot (pē'rōt) Yugo.	43·09 N	22·35 E
115	Pirtleville (pûr't'l-vĭl) Az.	31·25 N	109·35 W
197	Piru (pê-rōō') Indon.	3·15 S	128·25 E
167	Piryatin (pēr-yä-tēn') Sov. Un.	50·13 N	32·31 E
164	Pisa (pē'sä) It.	43·52 N	10·24 E
134	Pisagua (pē-sä'gwä) Chile	18·43 S	70·12 W
106	Piscataway (pĭs-kă-tă-wā) Md. (Baltimore In.)	38·42 N	76·59 W
106	Piscataway NJ (New York In.)	40·35 N	74·27 W
134	Pisco (pēs'kō) Peru	13·43 S	76·07 W
134	Pisco, Bahia de (B.) (bä-ē'ä-dě) Peru	13·43 S	77·48 W
105	Piseco (L.) (pĭ-sā'kô) NY	43·25 N	74·35 W
158	Pisek (pē'sěk) Czech.	49·18 N	14·08 E
164	Pisticci (pês-tē'chē) It.	40·24 N	16·34 E
164	Pistoia (pês-tô'yä) It.	43·57 N	11·54 E
162	Pisuerga (R.) (pê-swěr'gä) Sp.	41·48 N	4·28 W
134	Pitalito (pē-tä-lē'tō) Col.	1·45 N	75·09 W
107	Pitcairn (pĭt'kârn) Pa. (Pittsburgh In.)	40·29 N	79·47 W
199	Pitcairn Oceania	24·30 S	133·00 W
150	Pite (R.) (pē'tě) Swe.	66·08 N	18·51 E
150	Piteå (pē'tě-ô') Swe.	65·21 N	21·10 E
165	Pitesti (pê-těsht'') Rom.	44·51 N	24·51 E
204	Pithara (pĭt'ărȧ) Austl.	30·27 S	116·45 E
160	Pithiviers (pē-tē-vyā') Fr.	48·12 N	2·14 E
106	Pitman (pĭt'măn) NJ (Philadelphia In.)	39·44 N	75·08 W
127	Pitons du Carbet, Mt. Mart. (In.)	14·40 N	61·05 W
110	Pit R. (pĭt) Ca.	40·58 N	121·42 W
213	Pitseng Leso. (Natal In.)	29·03 S	28·13 E
112	Pitt (R.) Can. (Vancouver In.)	49·19 N	122·39 W
92	Pitt I. Can.	53·35 N	129·45 W
112	Pittsburg (pĭts'bûrg) Ca. (San Francisco In.)	38·01 N	121·52 W
117	Pittsburg Ks.	37·25 N	94·43 W
117	Pittsburg Tx.	32·00 N	94·57 W
107	Pittsburgh Pa. (Pittsburgh In.)	40·26 N	80·01 W
117	Pittsfield (pĭts'fēld) Il.	39·37 N	90·47 W
98	Pittsfield Me.	44·45 N	69·44 W
105	Pittsfield Ma.	42·25 N	73·15 W
105	Pittston (pĭts'tŭn) Pa.	41·20 N	75·50 W
137	Piũi (pē-ōō'ē) Braz. (Rio de Janeiro In.)	20·27 S	45·57 W
134	Piura (pê-ōō'rä) Peru	5·13 S	80·46 W
174	Piya (pē'yȧ) Sov. Un. (Urals In.)	58·34 N	61·12 E
113	Placentia (plă-sěn'shĭ-ȧ) Ca. (Los Angeles In.)	33·52 N	117·50 W
99	Placentia Can.	47·15 N	53·58 W
99	Placentia B. Can.	47·14 N	54·30 W
114	Placerville (plăs'ēr-vĭl) Ca.	38·43 N	120·47 W
128	Placetas (plä-thā'täs) Cuba	22·10 N	79·40 W
105	Placid (L.) (plăs'ĭd) NY	44·20 N	74·00 W
113	Plain City (plān) Ut. (Salt Lake City In.)	41·18 N	112·06 W
107	Plainfield (plān'fēld) Il. (Chicago In.)	41·37 N	88·12 W
107	Plainfield In. (Indianapolis In.)	39·42 N	86·23 W
106	Plainfield NJ (New York In.)	40·38 N	74·25 W
117	Plainview (plān'vū) Ar.	34·59 N	93·15 W
109	Plainview Mn.	44·09 N	92·12 W
108	Plainview Ne.	42·20 N	97·47 W
106	Plainview NY (New York In.)	40·47 N	73·28 W
116	Plainview Tx.	34·11 N	101·42 W
104	Plainwell (plan'wĕl) Mi.	42·25 N	85·40 W
89	Plaisance (plě-zäns') Can. (Ottawa In.)	45·37 N	75·07 W
129	Plana or Flat Cays (Is.) (plä'nä) Ba.	22·35 N	73·35 W
160	Plan-de-Cuques (plä-dě-kük') Fr. (In.)	43·22 N	5·29 E
149	Planegg (plä'něg) F.R.G. (Munich In.)	48·06 N	11·27 E
117	Plano (plā'nō) Tx.	33·01 N	96·42 W
89	Plantagenet (plän-tăzh-nē') Can. (Ottawa In.)	45·33 N	75·00 W
121	Plant City (plȧnt sĭ'tĭ) Fl. (In.)	28·00 N	82·07 W
119	Plaquemine (plăk'mēn') La.	30·17 N	91·14 W
162	Plasencia (plä-sěn'thê-ä) Sp.	40·02 N	6·07 W
174	Plast (plȧst) Sov. Un. (Urals In.)	54·22 N	60·48 E
98	Plaster Rock (plȧs'tēr rŏk) Can.	46·54 N	67·24 W
194	Plastun (plȧs-tōōn') Sov. Un.	44·41 N	136·08 E
136	Plata, R. de la (R.) (dālä plä'tä) Arg.-Ur.	34·35 S	58·15 W
164	Platani (R.) (plä-tä'nē) It.	37·26 N	13·28 E
129	Plateforme, Pte. Hai.	19·35 N	73·50 W
101	Platinum (plăt'ĭ-nŭm) Ak.	59·00 N	161·27 W
134	Plato (plä'tō) Col.	9·49 N	74·48 W
124	Platón Sánchéz (plä-tōn' sän'chěz) Mex.	21·14 N	98·20 W
108	Platte (plăt) SD	43·22 N	98·51 W
117	Platte (R.) Mo.	40·09 N	94·40 W
102	Platte (R.) U. S.	40·50 N	100·40 W
109	Platteville (plăt'vĭl) Wi.	42·44 N	90·31 W
117	Plattsburg (plăts'bûrg) Mo.	39·33 N	94·26 W
105	Plattsburgh NY	44·40 N	73·30 W
108	Plattsmouth (plăts'mŭth) Ne.	41·00 N	95·53 W
158	Plauen (plou'ěn) G.D.R.	50·30 N	12·08 E
129	Playa de Guanabo (plä-yä-dě-gwä-nä'bô) Cuba (In.)	23·10 N	82·07 W
129	Playa de Santa Fe (sä'n-tä-fě') Cuba (In.)	23·05 N	82·31 W
115	Playas (L.) (plä'yȧs) NM	31·50 N	108·30 W
125	Playa Vicente (vē-sěn'tā) Mex.	17·49 N	95·49 W
125	Playa Vicente (R.) Mex.	17·36 N	96·13 W
95	Playgreen L. (plā'grēn) Can.	54·00 N	98·10 W
105	Pleasant (L.) (plěz'ănt) NY	43·25 N	74·25 W
106	Pleasant Grove Al. (Birmingham In.)	33·29 N	86·57 W
112	Pleasant Hill Ca. (San Francisco In.)	37·57 N	122·04 W
117	Pleasant Hill Mo.	38·46 N	94·18 W
112	Pleasanton (plěz'ăn-tŭn) Ca. (San Francisco In.)	37·40 N	121·53 W
117	Pleasanton Ks.	38·10 N	94·41 W
118	Pleasanton Tx.	28·58 N	98·30 W
107	Pleasant Plain (plěz'ănt) Oh. (Cincinnati In.)	39·17 N	84·06 W
107	Pleasant Ridge Mi. (Detroit In.)	42·28 N	83·09 W
107	Pleasure Ridge Park (plězh'ēr rĭj) Ky (Louisville In.)	38·09 N	85·49 W
113	Pleasant View (plěz'ănt vū) Ut. (Salt Lake City In.)	41·20 N	112·02 W
106	Pleasantville (plěz'ănt-vĭl) NY (New York In.)	41·08 N	73·47 W
205	Plenty, B. of (plěn'tê) N. Z. (In.)	37·23 S	177·10 E
111	Plentywood (plěn'tē-wŏŏd) Mt.	48·47 N	104·38 W
166	Ples (plyěs) Sov. Un.	57·26 N	41·29 E
166	Pleshcheyevo (L.) (plěsh-chă'yě-vô) Sov. Un.	56·50 N	38·22 E
98	Plessisville (plě-sē'vēl') Can.	46·12 N	71·47 W
159	Pleszew (plě'zhěf) Pol.	51·54 N	17·48 E
161	Plettenberg (plě'těn-běrgh) F.R.G. (Ruhr In.)	51·13 N	7·53 E
165	Pleven (plě'věn) Bul.	43·24 N	24·26 E
165	Pljevlja (plěv'lyä) Yugo.	43·20 N	19·21 E
159	Płock (pwôtsk) Pol.	52·32 N	19·44 E
160	Ploërmel (plô-ěr-mêl') Fr.	47·56 N	2·25 W
165	Ploeşti (plô-yěsht'') Rom.	44·56 N	26·01 E
165	Plomárion (plô-mä'rĭ-ŏn) Grc.	38·51 N	26·24 E
160	Plomb du Cantal (Mt.) (plôN'dükän-täl') Fr.	45·30 N	2·49 E
94	Plonge, Lac la (L.) (plōnzh) Can.	55·08 N	107·25 W
165	Plovdiv (Philippopolis) (plôv'dĭf) (fĭl-ĭp-ŏp'ô-lĭs) Bul.	42·09 N	24·43 E
125	Pluma Hidalgo (plōō'mä ē-däl'gō) Mex.	15·54 N	96·23 W
157	Plunge (plōōn'gä) Sov. Un.	55·56 N	21·45 E
154	Plymouth (plĭm'ŭth) Eng.	50·25 N	4·14 W
104	Plymouth In.	41·20 N	86·20 W
105	Plymouth Ma.	42·00 N	70·45 W
107	Plymouth Mi. (Detroit In.)	42·23 N	83·27 W
105	Plymouth NH	43·50 N	71·40 W
121	Plymouth NC	35·50 N	76·44 W
105	Plymouth Pa.	41·15 N	75·55 W
127	Plymouth Montserrat (In.)	16·43 N	62·12 W
109	Plymouth Wi.	43·45 N	87·59 W
166	Plyussa (R.) (plyōō'sȧ) Sov. Un.	58·33 N	28·30 E
158	Plzeň (Pilsen) Czech.	49·46 N	13·25 E
214	Pô Upper Volta	11·10 N	1·09 W
164	Po, Bocche del (Mouth) (bô'chě-děl-pô') It.	44·57 N	12·38 E
164	Po, Fiume (R.) (fyōō'mě-pō) It.	45·00 N	11·23 E
215	Pobé (pô-bā') Benin	6·58 N	2·41 E
117	Pocahontas (pō-kȧ-hŏn'tȧs) Ar.	36·15 N	91·01 W
109	Pocahontas Ia.	42·43 N	94·41 W
111	Pocatello (pō-kȧ-těl'ō) Id.	42·54 N	112·30 W
166	Pochëp (pô-chěp') Sov. Un.	52·56 N	32·27 E
166	Pochinok (pô-chē'nôk) Sov. Un.	54·14 N	32·27 E
170	Pochinski Sov. Un.	54·40 N	44·50 E
124	Pochotitán (pô-chō-tē-tä'n) Mex.	21·37 N	104·33 W
125	Pochutla (San Pedro) (pō-chōō'tlä) (sän pā'drō) Mex.	15·46 N	96·28 W
105	Pocomoke City (pō-kō-mōk') Md.	38·05 N	75·35 W
105	Pocono Mts. (pō-cō'nō) Pa.	41·10 N	75·05 W
137	Poços de Caldas (pō-sôs-dě-käl'dȧs) Braz. (Rio de Janeiro In.)	21·48 S	46·34 W
210	Poder (pō-dōr') Senegal	16·35 N	15·04 W
172	Podkamennaya (Stony) Tunguska (R.) Sov. Un.	61·43 N	93·45 E
174	Podol'sk (pô-dôl''sk) Sov. Un. (Moscow In.)	55·26 N	37·33 E
167	Podvolochisk Sov. Un.	49·32 N	26·16 E
164	Poggibonsi (pôd-jē-bôn'sē) It.	43·27 N	11·12 E
166	Pogodino (pô-gô'dê-nô) Sov. Un.	54·17 N	31·00 E
194	P'ohang Kor.	35·57 N	129·23 E
127	Pointe-à-Pitre (pwănt' ȧ pē-tr') Guad. (In.)	16·15 N	61·32 W
89	Pointe-aux-Trembles (pōō-änt' ō-tränbl) Can. (Montreal In.)	45·39 N	73·30 W
89	Pointe Claire (pōō-änt' klěr) Can. (Montreal In.)	45·27 N	73·48 W
89	Pointe-des-Cascades (kăs-kādz') Can. (Montreal In.)	45·19 N	73·58 W
89	Pointe Fortune (fôr'tün) Can. (Montreal In.)	45·34 N	74·23 W
89	Pointe-Gatineau (pōō-änt'gä-tē-nō') Can. (Ottawa In.)	45·28 N	75·42 W
216	Pointe Noire Con.	4·48 S	11·51 E
101	Point Hope (hōp) Ak.	68·18 N	166·38 W
104	Point Pleasant (plěz'ănt) WV	38·50 N	82·10 W
112	Point Roberts (rŏb'ērts) Wa. (Vancouver In.)	48·59 N	123·04 W
161	Poissy (pwȧ-sē') Fr. (Paris In.)	48·55 N	2·02 E
160	Poitiers (pwȧ-tyā') Fr.	46·35 N	0·18 E
184	Pokaran (pō'kŭr-ŭn) India	27·00 N	72·05 E
166	Pokrov (pô-krôf) Sov. Un.	55·56 N	39·09 E
167	Pokrovskoye (pô-krôf'skô-yě) Sov. Un.	47·27 N	38·54 E
166	Pola (R.) (pō'lä) Sov. Un.	56·44 N	31·53 E
162	Pola de Allade (dě-äl-yä'dě) Sp.	43·18 N	6·35 W
162	Pola de Laviana (dě-lä-vyä'nä) Sp.	43·15 N	5·29 W
146	Poland (pō'lănd) Eur.	52·37 N	17·01 E
197	Polangui (pô-län'gē) Phil. (In.)	13·18 N	123·29 E
174	Polazna (pô'lȧz-nȧ) Sov. Un. (Urals In.)	58·18 N	56·25 E
157	Polessk (pô'lěsk) Sov. Un.	54·50 N	21·14 E
171	Poles'ye (Pripyat Marshes) Sov. Un.	52·10 N	27·30 E
174	Polevskoy (pô-lě'vs-kô'ê) Sov. Un. (Urals In.)	56·28 N	60·14 E
159	Polgár (pôl'gär) Hung.	47·54 N	21·10 E
164	Policastro, Golfo di (G.) It.	41·00 N	13·23 E
161	Poligny (pō-lē-nyē') Fr.	46·48 N	5·42 E
165	Políkhnitos Grc.	39·05 N	26·11 E
197	Polillo (pō-lēl'yō) Phil. (In.)	14·42 N	121·56 E
197	Polillo Is. Phil. (In.)	15·05 N	122·15 E
197	Polillo Str. Phil. (In.)	15·02 N	121·40 E
166	Polist' (R.) (pô'lĭst) Sov. Un.	57·42 N	31·02 E
164	Polistena (pō-lēs-tä'nä) It.	40·25 N	16·05 E
165	Políyiros Grc.	40·23 N	23·27 E
172	Polkan, Gol'tsy (Mtn.) Sov. Un.	60·18 N	92·08 E
163	Pollensa (pōl-yěn'sä) Sp.	39·50 N	3·00 E
126	Polochic R. (pō-lō-chēk') Guat.	15·19 N	89·45 W
167	Polonnoye (pô'lô-nô-yě) Sov. Un.	50·07 N	27·31 E
166	Polotsk (pô'lôtsk) Sov. Un.	55·30 N	28·48 E
137	Polpaico (pôl-pà'y-kô) Chile (Santiago In.)	33·10 S	70·53 W
111	Polson (pōl'sŭn) Mt.	47·40 N	114·10 W
167	Poltava (pôl-tä'vä) Sov. Un.	49·35 N	34·33 E
167	Poltava (Oblast) Sov. Un.	49·53 N	32·58 E
166	Põltsamaa (pŏlt'sȧ-mä) Sov. Un.	58·39 N	26·00 E
166	Põltsamaa (R.) Sov. Un.	58·35 N	25·55 E
174	Polunochnoye (pô-lōō-nô'ch-nô'yě) Sov. Un. (Urals In.)	60·52 N	60·27 E
172	Poluy (R.) (pôl'wê) Sov. Un.	65·45 N	68·15 E
174	Polyakovka (pŭl-yȧ'kôv-kȧ) Sov. Un. (Urals In.)	54·38 N	59·42 E
170	Polyarnyy (pŭl-yär'nē) Sov. Un.	69·10 N	33·30 E
137	Pomba (pô'm-bȧ) (R.) Braz. (Rio de Janeiro In.)	21·28 S	42·28 W
158	Pomerania (Reg.) (pŏm-ê-rā'nĭ-ȧ) Pol.	53·50 N	15·20 E
156	Pomeranian B. (pō'mě-rä-ny-än) G.D.R.	54·10 N	14·20 E
213	Pomeroy (pŏm'ēr-roi) S. Afr. (Natal In.)	28·36 S	30·26 E
110	Pomeroy (pŏm'ēr-oi) Wa.	46·28 N	117·35 W
163	Pomezia (pô-mě't-zyä) It. (Rome In.)	41·41 N	12·31 E
163	Pomigliano d'Arco (pô-mē-lyȧ'nō-d-ä'r-kô) It. (Naples In.)	40·39 N	14·23 E
108	Pomme de Terre (pôm dē těr') Mn.	45·22 N	95·52 W
113	Pomona (pô-mō'nȧ) Ca. (Los Angeles In.)	34·04 N	117·45 W
165	Pomorie Bul.	42·24 N	27·41 E
121	Pompano Beach (pŏm'pȧ-nô) Fl. (In.)	26·12 N	80·07 W
163	Pompeii Ruins It. (Naples In.)	40·31 N	14·29 E
106	Pompton Lakes (pŏmp'tŏn) NJ (New York In.)	41·01 N	74·16 W
126	Pomuch (pô-mōō'ch) Mex. (In.)	20·12 N	90·10 W
108	Ponca (pŏn'kȧ) Ne.	42·34 N	96·43 W
117	Ponca City Ok.	36·42 N	97·07 W
100	Ponce (pōn'sā) P. R. (Puerto Rico In.)	18·01 N	66·43 W
185	Pondicherry (pôn-dĭ-shěr'ē') (pŏn-dĭ-shěr'ē) India	11·58 N	79·48 E
185	Pondicherry (State) India	11·50 N	74·50 E
162	Ponferrada (pôn-fěr-rä'dhä) Sp.	42·33 N	6·38 W
93	Ponoka (pŏ-nō'kȧ) Can.	52·42 N	113·35 W
170	Ponoy Sov. Un.	66·58 N	41·00 E
170	Ponoy (R.) Sov. Un.	65·50 N	38·40 E
210	Ponta Delgada (pôn'tȧ děl-gä'dȧ) Açores (In.)	37·40 N	25·45 W

ng-sing; ŋ-baŋk; N-nasalized n; nŏd; cŏmmit; ōld; ôbey; ôrder; fōōd; fŏŏt; ou-out; s-soft; sh-dish; th-thin; pūre; ûnite; ûrn; stŭd; circŭs; ü-as "y" in study; '-indeterminate vowel.

330 Ponta Grossa— Potsdam PRONOUNCING INDEX

Page	Name Pronunciation Region	Lat. °'	Long. °'
136	Ponta Grossa (grō′sȧ)....... Braz.	25·09 S	50·05 W
161	Pont-à-Mousson (pôN′tȧ-mōōsôN′) Fr.	48·55 N	6·02 E
135	Ponta Porã................ Braz.	22·30 S	55·31 W
161	Pontarlier (pôN′tȧr-lyā′)....... Fr.	46·53 N	6·22 E
160	Pont-Audemer (pôN′tōd′mâr′).. Fr.	49·23 N	0·28 E
161	Pontcarré (pôN-kȧ-rā′) Fr. (Paris In.)	48·48 N	2·42 E
119	Pontchartrain L. (pôN-shȧr-trăn′) La.	30·10 N	90·10 W
164	Pontedera (pōn-tȧ-dā′rä)...... It.	43·37 N	10·37 E
162	Ponte de Sor (pōŋ′tĕ dȧ sōr′). Port.	39·14 N	8·03 W
148	Pontefract (pŏn′tē-frăkt).... Eng.	53·41 N	1·18 W
137	Ponte Nova (pô′n-tĕ-nô′vȧ) Braz. (Rio de Janeiro In.)	20·26 S	42·52 W
162	Pontevedra (pôn-tĕ-vĕ-drä)... Sp.	42·28 N	8·38 W
	Ponthierville, see Ubundi		
104	Pontiac (pŏn′tĭ-ăk)............. Il.	40·55 N	88·35 W
107	Pontiac......... Mi. (Detroit In.)	42·37 N	83·17 W
196	Pontianak (pôn-tē-ä′nȧk)... Indon.	0·04 S	109·20 E
183	Pontian Kechil Mala. (Singapore In.)	1·29 N	103·24 E
171	Pontic Mts................ Turk.	41·20 N	34·30 E
160	Pontivy (pôN-tē-vē′).......... Fr.	48·05 N	2·57 W
160	Pont-l'Abbe (pôN-lȧ-bā′)...... Fr.	47·53 N	4·12 W
161	Pontoise (pôN-twȧz′) Fr. (Paris In.)	49·03 N	2·05 E
174	Pontonnyy (pôn′tôn-nyĭ) Sov. Un. (Leningrad In.)	59·47 N	30·39 E
120	Pontotoc (pŏn-tō-tŏk′)....... Ms.	34·11 N	88·59 W
164	Pontremoli (pôn-trĕm′ô-lē)..... It.	44·21 N	9·50 E
164	Ponza, Isole di (I.) (ē′sō-lĕ-dē-pōn′tsä). It.	40·55 N	12·58 E
154	Poole (pōōl)................ Eng.	50·43 N	2·00 W
106	Poolesville (poolĕs-vĭl) Md. (Baltimore In.)	39·08 N	77·26 W
92	Pooley I. (pōō′lē)........... Can.	52·44 N	128·16 W
134	Poopó, Lago de (L.) (lä′gô-dĕ-pō-ô-pô′). Bol.	18·16 S	67·57 W
134	Popayán (pō-pä-yän′)........ Col.	2·21 N	76·43 W
111	Poplar (pŏp′lēr)............. Mt.	48·08 N	105·10 W
117	Poplar Bluff (blŭf)........... Mo.	36·43 N	90·22 W
104	Poplar Plains (plāns)......... Ky.	38·20 N	83·40 W
89	Poplar Point.. Can. (Winnipeg In.)	50·04 N	97·57 W
111	Poplar R.................... Mt.	48·34 N	105·20 W
111	Poplar R., West Fork........ Mt.	48·59 N	106·06 W
120	Poplarville (pŏp′lēr-vĭl)....... Ms.	30·50 N	89·33 W
125	Popocatépetl Volcán (Vol.) (pô-pô-kä-tā′pĕt′l). Mex. (In.)	19·01 N	98·38 W
216	Popokabaka (pō′pô-kȧ-bä′kȧ) Zaire	5·42 S	16·35 E
167	Popovka (pô′pôf-kȧ)..... Sov. Un.	50·03 N	33·41 E
167	Popovka.............. Sov. Un.	51·13 N	33·08 E
165	Popovo (pô′pô-vō)........... Bul.	43·23 N	26·17 E
184	Porbandar (pōr-bŭn′dŭr).... India	21·44 N	69·40 E
134	Porce (pôr-sĕ) (R.)...... Col. (In.)	7·11 N	74·55 W
92	Porcher I. (pôr′kēr)......... Can.	53·57 N	130·30 W
162	Porcuna (pôr-kōō′nä)......... Sp.	37·54 N	4·10 W
101	Porcupine (R.).............. Ak.	67·00 N	143·25 W
90	Porcupine (R.).............. Can.	67·38 N	140·07 W
111	Porcupine Cr. (pôr′kū-pīn).... Mt.	46·38 N	107·04 W
111	Porcupine Cr................ Mt.	48·27 N	106·24 W
95	Porcupine Hills.............. Can.	52·30 N	101·45 W
164	Pordenone (pōr-dȧ-nō′nȧ)...... It.	45·58 N	12·38 E
164	Poreč (pô′rĕch)............ Yugo.	45·13 N	13·37 E
157	Pori (Björneborg) (pô′rē) (byûr′nē-bôrgh). Fin.	61·29 N	21·45 E
137	Poriúncula (po-rēōō′n-kōō-lä) Braz. (Rio de Janeiro In.)	20·58 S	42·02 W
150	Porjus (pôr′yōōs)........... Swe.	66·54 N	19·40 E
166	Porkhov (pôr′κôf)....... Sov. Un.	57·46 N	29·33 E
134	Porlamar (pôr-lä-mär′)...... Ven.	11·00 N	63·55 W
160	Pornic (pôr-nēk′)............ Fr.	47·08 N	2·07 W
173	Poronaysk (pô′rô-nīsk)... Sov. Un.	49·21 N	143·23 E
158	Porrentruy (pô-räN-trūē′)... Switz.	47·25 N	7·02 E
156	Porsgrunn (pôrs′grōōn′)...... Nor.	59·09 N	9·36 E
134	Portachuelo (pôrt-ä-chwā′lō).. Bol.	17·20 S	63·12 W
105	Portage (pôr′tâj)............. Pa.	40·25 N	78·35 W
109	Portage.................... Wi.	43·33 N	89·29 W
113	Portage Des Sioux (dē sōō) Mo. (St. Louis In.)	38·56 N	90·21 W
89	Portage-la-Prairie (lä-prā′rĭ) Can. (Winnipeg In.)	49·57 N	98·25 W
92	Port Alberni (pōr äl-bĕr-nē′).. Can.	49·14 N	124·48 W
162	Portalegre (pôr-tä-lā′grĕ).... Port.	39·18 N	7·26 W
116	Portales (pôr-tä′lĕs)......... NM	34·10 N	103·11 W
97	Port-Alfred (ăl′frĕd)......... Can.	48·20 N	70·53 W
213	Port Alfred (Kowie) (kou′ĭ) S. Afr. (Natal In.)	33·36 S	26·55 E
92	Port Alice (ăl′ĭs)............ Can.	50·23 N	127·27 W
105	Port Allegany (ăl-ē-gā′nĭ)..... Pa.	41·50 N	78·10 W
110	Port Angeles (ăn′jē-lĕs)...... Wa.	48·07 N	123·26 W
129	Port Antonio............... Jam.	18·10 N	76·25 W
202	Portarlington Austl. (Melbourne In.)	38·07 S	144·39 E
119	Port Arthur................. Tx.	29·52 N	93·59 W
203	Port Augusta (ô-gŭs′tȧ).... Austl.	32·28 S	137·50 E
99	Port au Port B. (pôr′tō pōr′).. Can.	48·41 N	58·45 W
129	Port-au-Prince (prăNs′)...... Hai.	18·35 N	72·20 W
104	Port Austin (ôs′tĭn).......... Mi.	44·00 N	83·00 W
99	Port aux Basques........... Can.	47·36 N	59·09 W
196	Port Blair (blâr) Andaman & Nicobar Is.	12·07 N	92·45 E
119	Port Bolivar (bŏl′ĭ-vȧr).. Tx. (In.)	29·22 N	94·46 W
98	Port Borden (bôr′dĕn)....... Can.	46·15 N	63·42 W
210	Port-Bouët.......... Ivory Coast	5·24 N	3·56 W
98	Port-Cartier................ Can.	50·01 N	66·53 W
106	Port Chester (chĕs′tēr) NY (New York In.)	40·59 N	73·40 W
112	Port Chicago (shĭ-kô′gō) Ca. (San Francisco In.)	38·03 N	122·01 W
104	Port Clinton (klĭn′tŭn)....... Oh.	41·30 N	83·00 W
97	Port Colborne.............. Can.	42·53 N	79·13 W
112	Port Coquitlam (kô-kwĭt′lȧm) Can. (Vancouver In.)	49·16 N	122·46 W
89	Port Credit (krĕd′ĭt) Can. (Toronto In.)	43·33 N	79·35 W
160	Port-de-Bouc (pôr-dē-bōōk′) Fr. (In.)	43·24 N	5·00 E
217	Port de Kindu............. Zaire	2·57 S	25·56 E
129	Port de Paix (pĕ)........... Hai.	19·55 N	72·50 W
183	Port Dickson (dĭk′sŭn) Mala. (Singapore In.)	2·33 N	101·49 E
112	Port Discovery (B.) (dĭs-kŭv′ēr-ĭ) Wa. (Seattle In.)	48·05 N	122·55 W
213	Port Edward (ĕd′wērd) S. Afr. (Natal In.)	31·04 S	30·14 E
98	Port Elgin (ĕl′jĭn).......... Can.	46·03 N	64·05 W
213	Port Elizabeth (ē-lĭz′ȧ-bĕth) S. Afr. (Natal In.)	33·57 S	25·37 E
120	Porterdale (pōr′tēr-dāl)....... Ga.	33·34 N	83·53 W
114	Porterville (pōr′tēr-vĭl)....... Ca.	36·03 N	119·05 W
136	Portezuelo de Tupungato (Vol.) (pôr-tĕ-zwĕ-lō-dĕ-tōō-pōō′n-gä-tô) Arg.-Chile	33·30 S	69·52 W
	Port Francqui, see Ilebo		
112	Port Gamble (găm′bŭl) Wa. (Seattle In.)	47·52 N	122·36 W
112	Port Gamble Ind. Res. Wa. (Seattle In.)	47·54 N	122·33 W
216	Port-Gentil (zhäN-tē′)...... Gabon	0·43 S	8·47 E
120	Port Gibson (gĭb′sŭn)........ Ms.	31·56 N	90·57 W
215	Port Harcourt (här′kŭrt)..... Nig.	4·43 N	7·05 E
92	Port Hardy (här′dĭ).......... Can.	50·43 N	127·29 W
99	Port Hawkesbury............ Can.	45·37 N	61·21 W
204	Port Hedland (hĕd′lănd).... Austl.	20·30 S	118·30 E
110	Porthill..................... Id.	49·00 N	116·30 W
99	Port Hood (hŏŏd)............ Can.	46·01 N	61·32 W
105	Port Hope (hōp)............ Can.	43·55 N	78·10 W
104	Port Huron (hū′rŏn).......... Mi.	43·00 N	82·30 W
163	Portici (pôr′tē-chē). It. (Naples In.)	40·34 N	14·20 E
137	Portillo (pôr-tē′l-yô) Chile (Santiago In.)	32·51 S	70·09 W
162	Portimão (pôr-tē-mo′uN).... Port.	37·09 N	8·34 W
106	Port Jervis (jûr′vĭs) NY (New York In.)	41·22 N	74·41 W
183	Port Kelang. Mala. (Singapore In.)	3·00 N	101·25 E
203	Portland (pōrt′lănd)....... Austl.	38·20 S	142·40 E
104	Portland.................... In.	40·25 N	85·00 W
98	Portland.................... Me.	43·40 N	70·16 W
104	Portland.................... Mi.	42·50 N	85·00 W
112	Portland....... Or. (Portland In.)	45·31 N	123·41 W
119	Portland.................... Tx.	27·53 N	97·20 W
128	Portland Bight (B.).......... Jam.	17·45 N	77·05 W
92	Portland Can................ Ak.	55·10 N	130·08 W
92	Portland Inlet.............. Can.	54·50 N	130·15 W
128	Portland Pt................ Jam.	17·40 N	77·20 W
119	Port Lavaca (lȧ-vä′kȧ)....... Tx.	28·36 N	96·38 W
203	Port Lincoln (lĭŋ′kŭn)...... Austl.	34·39 S	135·50 E
112	Port Ludlow (lŭd′lō) Wa. (Seattle In.)	47·26 N	122·41 W
	Port Lyautey, see Kenitra		
203	Port Macquarie (mȧ-kwŏ′rĭ). Austl.	31·25 S	152·45 E
112	Port Madison Ind. Res. (măd′ĭ-sŭn). Wa. (Seattle In.)	47·46 N	122·38 W
128	Port Maria (mȧ-rī′ȧ)........ Jam.	18·20 N	76·55 W
98	Port-Menier (mē-nyā′)...... Can.	49·49 N	64·20 W
112	Port Moody (mōōd′ĭ) Can. (Vancouver In.)	49·17 N	122·51 W
197	Port Moresby (mōrz′bē) Pap. N. Gui.	9·34 S	147·20 E
119	Port Neches (nĕch′ĕz)........ Tx.	29·59 N	93·57 W
95	Port Nelson (nĕl′sŭn)........ Can.	57·03 N	92·36 W
98	Portneuf-Sur-Mer (pôr-nûf′sür mĕr). Can.	48·36 N	69·06 W
212	Port Nolloth (nŏl′ŏth)..... S. Afr.	29·10 S	17·00 E
162	Pôrto (Oporto) (pōr′tōō).... Port.	41·10 N	8·38 W
134	Pôrto Acre (ä′krĕ).......... Braz.	9·38 S	67·34 W
136	Pôrto Alegre (ä-lā′grĕ)...... Braz.	29·58 S	51·11 W
216	Porto Alexandre (ȧ-lĕ-zhän′drĕ) Ang.	15·49 S	11·53 E
216	Porto Amboim............. Ang.	11·01 S	13·45 E
127	Portobelo (pôr′tō-bā′lō)..... Pan.	9·32 N	79·40 W
135	Pôrto de Pedras (pā′dräzh).. Braz.	9·09 S	35·20 W
137	Pôrto Feliz (fĕ-lē′s) Braz. (Rio de Janeiro In.)	23·12 S	47·30 W
164	Portoferraio (pōr′tō-fĕr-rä′yō).. It.	42·47 N	10·20 E
135	Port of Spain (spān)........ Trin.	10·44 N	61·24 W
164	Portogruaro (pōr′tô-grōō-ä′rō).. It.	45·48 N	12·49 E
114	Portola (pôr′tō-lȧ)........... Ca.	39·47 N	120·29 W
135	Pôrto Mendes (mĕ′n-dĕs).... Braz.	24·41 S	54·13 W
135	Pôrto Murtinho (mōōr-tēn′yōō) Braz.	21·43 S	57·43 W
135	Pôrto Nacional (nȧ-syô-näl′). Braz.	10·43 S	48·14 W
215	Porto Novo (pōr′tô-nō′vō) Benin	6·29 N	2·37 E
112	Port Orchard (ôr′chērd) Wa. (Seattle In.)	47·32 N	122·38 W
112	Port Orchard (B.). Wa. (Seattle In.)	47·40 N	122·39 W
210	Porto Santo, Ilha de (I.) (sȧN′tōō). Mad. Is.	32·41 N	16·15 W
135	Pôrto Seguro (sā-gōō′rōō)... Braz.	16·26 S	38·59 W
164	Porto Torres (tôr′rĕs)......... It.	40·49 N	8·25 E
164	Porto-Vecchio (vĕk′ē-ô)....... Fr.	41·36 N	9·17 E
134	Pôrto Velho (väl′yōō)....... Braz.	8·45 S	63·43 W
134	Portoviejo (pôr-tō-vyā′hō).... Ec.	1·11 S	80·28 W
203	Port Phillip B. (fĭl′ĭp)...... Austl.	37·57 S	144·50 E
203	Port Pirie (pĭ′rē)........... Austl.	33·10 S	138·00 E
90	Port Radium (rā′dē-ŭm)..... Can.	66·06 N	118·03 W
128	Port Royal (B.) (roi′ăl)...... Jam.	17·50 N	76·45 W
	Port Said, see Būr Sa'īd		
213	Port St. Johns (sânt jŏnz) S. Afr. (Natal In.)	31·37 S	29·32 E
213	Port Shepstone (shĕps′tŭn) S. Afr. (Natal In.)	30·45 S	30·23 E
154	Portsmouth (pôrts′mŭth).... Eng.	50·45 N	1·03 W
105	Portsmouth................. NH	43·05 N	70·50 W
104	Portsmouth................. Oh.	38·45 N	83·00 W
106	Portsmouth..... Va. (Norfolk In.)	36·50 N	76·19 W
127	Portsmouth....... Dominica (In.)	15·33 N	61·28 W
	Port Sudan, see Būr Sūdān		
120	Port Sulphur (sŭl′fēr)......... La.	29·28 N	89·41 W
112	Port Susan (B.) (sū-zăn′) Wa. (Seattle In.)	48·11 N	122·25 W
121	Port Tampa (tăm′pȧ).... Fl. (In.)	27·50 N	82·30 W
112	Port Townsend (tounz′ĕnd) Wa. (Seattle In.)	48·07 N	122·46 W
112	Port Townsend (B.) Wa. (Seattle In.)	48·05 N	122·47 W
146	Portugal (pōr′tu-găl)........ Eur.	38·15 N	8·08 W
162	Portugalete (pōr-tōō-gä-lā′tä) Sp.	43·18 N	3·05 W
216	Portugália................. Ang.	7·20 S	20·47 E
	Portuguese East Africa, see Mozambique		
	Portuguese India, see Gôa, Daman & Diu		
	Portuguese West Africa, see Angola		
160	Port Vendres (pôr väN′dr′).... Fr.	42·32 N	3·07 E
203	Port Wakefield (wāk′fēld).. Austl.	34·12 S	138·10 E
106	Port Washington (wôsh′ĭng-tŭn) NY (New York In.)	40·49 N	73·42 W
109	Port Washington........... Wi.	43·24 N	87·52 W
136	Posadas (pō-sä′dhäs)........ Arg.	27·32 S	55·56 W
162	Posadas (pô-sä-däs)......... Sp.	37·48 N	5·09 W
166	Poshekhon 'ye Volodarsk (pô-shyĕ′κôn-yĕ vôl′ô-dȧrsk) Sov. Un.	58·31 N	39·07 E
196	Poso, Danau (L.) (pō′sō)... Indon.	2·00 S	119·40 E
174	Pospelkova (pôs-pyĕl′kô-vȧ) Sov. Un. (Urals In.)	59·25 N	60·50 E
112	Possession Sd. (pŏ-zĕsh′ŭn) Wa. (Seattle In.)	47·59 N	122·17 W
118	Possum Kingdom Res. (pŏs′ŭm kĭng′dŭm). Tx.	32·58 N	98·12 W
116	Post (pōst).................. Tx.	33·12 N	101·21 W
210	Post Maurice Cortier (Bidon Cing). Alg.	22·22 N	0·33 E
164	Postojna (pōs-tōynȧ)....... Yugo.	45·45 N	14·13 E
194	Pos'yet (pos-yĕt′)....... Sov. Un.	42·27 N	130·47 E
117	Potawatomi Ind. Res. (pŏt-ȧ-wā′tō mē). Ks.	39·30 N	96·11 W
218	Potchefstroom (pŏch′ĕf-strōm) S. Afr. (Johannesburg & Pretoria In.)	26·42 S	27·06 E
117	Poteau (pô-tō′).............. Ok.	35·03 N	94·37 W
118	Poteet (pô-tēt).............. Tx.	29·05 N	98·35 W
164	Potenza (pô-tĕnt′sä).......... It.	40·39 N	15·49 E
164	Potenza (R.)................. It.	43·09 N	13·00 E
218	Potgietersrus (pôt-κē′tērs-rûs) S. Afr. (Johannesburg & Pretoria In.)	24·09 S	29·04 E
110	Potholes Res................ Wa.	47·00 N	119·20 W
171	Poti (pô′tē)............ Sov. Un.	42·10 N	41·40 E
215	Potiskum................... Nig.	11·43 N	11·05 E
106	Potomac (pô-tō′măk) Md. (Baltimore In.)	39·01 N	77·13 W
105	Potomac (R.) (pô-tō′măk).... Va.	38·15 N	76·55 W
134	Potosí (pō-tō-sē′)........... Bol.	19·42 S	65·42 W
117	Potosi (pô-tō′sĭ)............ Mo.	37·56 N	90·46 W
118	Potosí, R. (pô-tô-sē′)....... Mex.	25·04 N	99·36 W
126	Potrerillos (pō-trȧ-rēl′yôs).. Hond.	15·13 N	87·58 W
149	Potsdam (pôts′däm) G.D.R. (Berlin In.)	52·24 N	13·04 E
105	Potsdam (pŏts′dăm).......... NY	44·40 N	75·00 W
149	Potsdam (Dist.) (pôts′dăm) G.D.R. (Berlin In.)	52·31 N	12·45 E

ăt; finăl; rāte; senâte; ärm; ȧsk; sofȧ; fâre; ch-choose; dh-as th in other; bē; ēvent; bĕt; recĕnt; cratēr; g-go; gh-guttural g; bĭt; ĭ-short neutral; rīde; κ-guttural k as ch in German ich;

ng-sing; ŋ-baŋk; N-nasalized n; nŏd; cŏmmit; ōld; ôbey; ôrder; fōōd; fŏot; ou-out; s-soft; sh-dish; th-thin; pūre; ūnite; ûrn; stŭd; circŭs; ü-as "y" in study; '-indeterminate vowel.

332 Puerto Casado — Queen Charlotte PRONOUNCING INDEX

Page	Name	Region	Lat. °'	Long. °'
136	Puerto Casado (pwĕ'r-tō kä-sä'dō)	Par.	22·16 s	57·57 w
126	Puerto Castilla (pwĕ'r-tô käs-tēl'yō)	Hond.	16·01 N	86·01 w
134	Puerto Chicama (pwĕ'r-tô chē-kä'mä)	Peru	7·46 s	79·18 w
134	Puerto Columbia (pwĕr'tô kô-lôm'bê-ä)	Col.	11·08 N	75·09 w
127	Puerto Cortés (pwĕ'r-tô kôr-tās')	C. R.	9·00 N	83·37 w
126	Puerto Cortés (pwĕ'r-tô kôr-tās')	Hond.	15·48 N	87·57 w
134	Puerto Cumarebo (pwĕ'r-tō kōō-mä-rĕ'bô)	Ven.	11·25 N	69·17 w
163	Puerto de Beceite (Mts.) (pwĕ'r-tō dĕ bĕ-sĕ'y-tĕ)	Sp.	40·43 N	0·05 w
116	Puerto de Luna (pwĕr'tô dā lōō'nä)	NM	34·49 N	104·36 w
134	Puerto de Nutrias (pwĕ'r-tō dĕ nōō-trê-äs')	Ven.	8·02 N	69·19 w
136	Puerto Deseado (pwĕ'r-tō dā-sā-ä'dhō)	Arg.	47·38 s	66·00 w
134	Puerto Eten (pwĕ'r-tō ĕ-tĕ'n)	Peru	6·59 s	79·51 w
127	Puerto Jimenez (pwĕ'r-tô κê-mĕ'nĕz)	C. R.	8·35 N	83·23 w
137	Puerto La Cruz (pwĕ'r-tō lä krōō'z)	Ven. (In.)	10·14 N	64·38 w
162	Puertollano (pwĕr-tôl-yä'nō)	Sp.	38·41 N	4·05 w
136	Puerto Madryn (pwĕ'r-tō mä-drēn')	Arg.	42·45 s	65·01 w
134	Puerto Maldonado (pwĕ'r-tō mäl-dō-nä'dô)	Peru	12·43 s	69·01 w
	Puerto Mexico, see Coatzacoalcos			
124	Puerto Miniso (pwĕ'r-tō mē-nē'sô)	Mex.	16·06 N	98·02 w
136	Puerto Montt (pwĕ'r-tō mô'nt)	Chile	41·29 s	73·00 w
136	Puerto Natales (pwĕ'r-tō nä-tá'lĕs)	Chile	51·48 s	72·01 w
134	Puerto Niño (pwĕ'r-tō nê'n-yô)	Col. (In.)	5·57 N	74·36 w
128	Puerto Padre (pwĕ'r-tō pä'drā)	Cuba	21·10 N	76·40 w
122	Puerto Peñasco (pwĕ'r-tō pĕn-yä's-kô)	Mex.	31·39 N	113·15 w
136	Puerto Pinasco (pwĕ'r-tō pē-nà's-kô)	Par.	22·31 s	57·50 w
135	Puerto Píritu (pwĕ'r-tō pē'rē-tōō)	Ven. (In.)	10·05 N	65·04 w
129	Puerto Plata (pwĕ'r-tô plä'tä)	Dom. Rep.	19·50 N	70·40 w
196	Puerto Princesa (pwĕr-tô prên-sä'sä)	Phil.	9·45 N	118·41 E
123	Puerto Rico (pwĕr'tô rē'kō)	N. A.	18·16 N	66·50 w
123	Puerto Rico Trench	N. A.	19·45 N	66·30 w
134	Puerto Salgar (pwĕ'r-tō säl-gär')	Col. (In.)	5·30 N	74·39 w
136	Puerto Santa Cruz (pwĕ'r-tō sän'tä krōōz')	Arg.	50·04 s	68·32 w
135	Puerto Suárez (pwĕ'r-tō swä'râz)	Bol.	18·55 s	57·39 w
134	Puerto Tejada (pwĕ'r-tō tĕ-κä'dä)	Col. (In.)	3·13 N	76·23 w
124	Puerto Vallarta (pwĕ'r-tō väl-yär'tä)	Mex.	20·36 N	105·13 w
136	Puerto Varas (pwĕ'r-tō vä'räs)	Chile	41·16 s	73·03 w
134	Puerto Wilches (pwĕ'r-tō vēl'c-hĕs)	Col.	7·19 N	73·54 w
171	Pugachëv (pōō'gà-chyôf)	Sov. Un.	52·00 N	48·40 E
112	Puget (pū'jĕt)	Wa. (Portland In.)	46·10 N	123·23 w
110	Puget Sd.	Wa.	47·49 N	122·26 w
164	Puglia (Apulia) (Reg.) (pōō'lyä) (ä-pōō'lyä)	It.	41·13 N	16·10 E
96	Pukaskwa Natl. Pk.	Can.	48·22 N	85·55 w
93	Pukeashun Mtn.	Can.	51·12 N	119·14 w
183	Pukin (R.)	Mala. (Singapore In.)	2·53 N	102·54 E
164	Pula (pōō'lä)	Yugo.	44·52 N	13·55 E
134	Pulacayo (pōō-lä-kä'yō)	Bol.	20·12 s	66·33 w
120	Pulaski (pû-lăs'kĭ)	Tn.	35·11 N	87·03 w
121	Pulaski	Va.	37·00 N	81·45 w
159	Pulawy (pōō-wä'vê)	Pol.	51·24 N	21·59 E
184	Pulizat (R.)	India	13·58 N	79·52 E
110	Pullman (pōōl'măn)	Wa.	46·44 N	117·10 w
197	Pulog (Mtn.) (pōō'lôg)	Phil. (In.)	16·38 N	120·53 E
150	Pultusk (pōōl'tōōsk)	Pol.	52·40 N	21·09 E
184	Puma Yumco (L.) (pōō-mä yōōm-tswo)	China	28·30 N	90·10 E
111	Pumpkin Cr. (pŭmp'kĭn)	Mt.	45·47 N	105·35 w
184	Punakha (pōō-nŭk'ŭ)	Bhu.	27·45 N	89·59 E
134	Punata (pōō-nä'tä)	Bol.	17·43 s	65·43 w
184	Pune	India	18·38 N	73·53 E
184	Punjab (State) (pŭn'jäb')	India	31·00 N	75·30 E
134	Puno (pōō'nô)	Peru	15·58 s	7·02 w
136	Punta Arenas (pōō'n-tä-rĕ'näs)	Chile	53·09 s	70·48 w
135	Punta de Piedras (pōō'n-tä dĕ pyĕ'dräs)	Ven. (In.)	10·54 N	64·06 w
126	Punta Gorda (pōōn'tä gôr'dä)	Belize	16·07 N	88·50 w
121	Punta Gorda (pŭn'tá gôr'dá)	Fl. (In.)	26·55 N	82·02 w
127	Punta Gorda, Rio (R.) (pōō'n-tä gô'r-dä)	Nic.	11·34 N	84·13 w
137	Punta Indio, Can. (pōō'n-tä ê'n-dyô)	Arg. (Buenos Aires In.)	34·56 s	57·20 w
127	Puntarenas (pōōnt-ä-rā'näs)	C. R.	9·59 N	84·49 w
134	Punto Fijo (pōō'n-tô fē'κô)	Ven.	11·48 N	70·14 w
105	Punxsutawney (pŭnk-sŭ-tô'nê)	Pa.	40·55 N	79·00 w
134	Puquio (pōō'kyô)	Peru	14·43 s	74·02 w
172	Pur (R.)	Sov. Un.	65·30 N	77·30 E
117	Purcell (pûr-sĕl')	Ok.	35·01 N	97·22 w
93	Purcell Mts. (pûr-sĕl')	Can.	50·00 N	116·30 w
112	Purdy (pûr'dē)	Wa. (Seattle In.)	47·23 N	122·37 w
124	Purépero (pōō-rā'pâ-rō)	Mex.	19·56 N	102·02 w
116	Purgatoire (R.) (pûr-gà-twär')	Colo.	37·25 N	103·53 w
184	Puri (pōō'rê)	India	19·52 N	85·51 E
129	Purial, Sierra de (Mts.) (sē-ĕ'r-rà-dĕ-pōō-rê-äl')	Cuba	20·15 N	74·40 w
134	Purificacion (pōō-rê-fê-kä-syōn')	Col. (In.)	3·52 N	74·54 w
124	Purificación (pōō-rē-fê-kä-syô'n)	Mex.	19·44 N	104·38 w
124	Purificación (R.)	Mex.	19·30 N	104·54 w
149	Purkersdorf	Aus. (Vienna In.)	48·13 N	16·11 E
124	Puruandiro (pōō-rōō-än'dê-rō)	Mex.	20·04 N	101·33 w
134	Purús (R.) (pōō-rōō's)	Braz.	6·45 s	64·34 w
194	Pusan	Kor.	35·08 N	129·05 E
174	Pushkin (pōōsh'kĭn)	Sov. Un. (Leningrad In.)	59·43 N	30·25 E
174	Pushkino (pōōsh'kê-nô)	Sov. Un. (Moscow In.)	56·01 N	37·51 E
166	Pustoshka (pûs-tôsh'kà)	Sov. Un.	56·20 N	29·33 E
125	Pustunich (pōōs-tōō'nēch)	Mex.	19·10 N	90·29 w
137	Putaendo (pōō-tä-ĕn-dô)	Chile (Santiago In.)	32·37 s	70·42 w
161	Puteaux (pü-tō')	Fr. (Paris In.)	48·52 N	2·12 E
213	Putfontein (pōōt'fŏn-tān)	S. Afr. (Johannesburg & Pretoria In.)	26·08 s	28·24 E
193	Putian (pōō-tĭĕn)	China	25·40 N	119·02 E
167	Putivl' (pōō-tēv'l')	Sov. Un.	51·22 N	33·24 E
125	Putla de Guerrero (pōō'tlä-dĕ-gĕr-rĕ'rō)	Mex.	17·03 N	97·55 w
105	Putnam (pŭt'năm)	Ct.	41·55 N	71·55 w
172	Putorana, Gory (Mts.)	Sov. Un.	68·45 N	93·15 E
185	Puttalam	Sri Lanka	8·02 N	79·44 E
134	Putumayo (R.) (pōō-tōō-mä'yō)	Col.-Peru	1·02 s	73·50 w
196	Putung, Tandjung (C.)	Indon.	3·35 s	111·50 E
157	Puulavesi (L.)	Fin.	61·49 N	27·10 E
112	Puyallup (pū-ăl'ŭp)	Wa. (Seattle In.)	47·12 N	122·18 w
190	Puyang (pōō-yäŋ)	China	35·42 N	114·58 E
212	Pweto (pwā'tō)	Zaire	8·29 s	28·58 E
172	Pyasina (R.) (pyä-sē'nà)	Sov. Un.	72·45 N	87·37 E
171	Pyatigorsk (pyà-tê-gôrsk')	Sov. Un.	44·00 N	43·00 E
	Pye, see Prome			
157	Pyhäjärvi (L.)	Fin.	60·57 N	21·50 E
188	Pyinmana (pyĕn-mä'nŭ)	Bur.	19·47 N	96·15 E
104	Pymatuning Res. (pī-mà-tûn'ĭng)	Pa.	41·40 N	80·30 w
194	Pyŏnggang (pyŭng'gäng')	Kor.	38·21 N	127·18 E
194	P'yŏngyang	Kor.	39·03 N	125·48 E
114	Pyramid (L.) (pĭ'rà-mĭd)	Nv.	40·02 N	119·50 w
114	Pyramid Lake Ind. Res.	Nv.	40·17 N	119·52 w
218	Pyramids	Egypt (Nile In.)	29·53 N	31·10 E
163	Pyrenees (Mts.) (pĭr-e-nēz')	Fr.-Sp.	43·00 N	0·05 E
158	Pyrzyce (pĕzhĭ'tsĕ)	Pol.	53·09 N	14·53 E

Q

Page	Name	Region	Lat. °'	Long. °'
186	Qal'at Bīshah	Sau. Ar.	20·01 N	42·30 E
211	Qallābāt	Sud.	12·55 N	36·12 E
188	Qamdo (chyäm-dwō)	China	31·06 N	96·30 E
218	Qana el Suweis (Suez Can.)	Egypt (Suez In.)	30·53 N	32·21 E
187	Qandahār	Afg.	31·43 N	65·58 E
153	Qārah (Oasis)	Egypt	29·28 N	26·29 E
171	Qareh Sū (R.)	Iran	38·50 N	47·10 E
188	Qarqan (R.)	China	38·55 N	87·15 E
	Qarqan, see Qiemo			
218	Qārūn, Birket (L.)	Egypt (Nile In.)	29·34 N	30·34 E
211	Qasr al-Burayqah	Libya	30·25 N	19·20 E
211	Qasr al-Farāfirah	Egypt	27·04 N	28·13 E
211	Qaṣr Banī Walīd	Libya	31·45 N	14·04 E
182	Qatar (kä'tàr)	Asia	25·00 N	52·45 E
211	Qaṭṭārah, Munkhafaḍ (Dep.)	Egypt	30·07 N	27·30 E
186	Qāyen	Iran	33·45 N	59·08 E
186	Qeshm	Iran	26·51 N	56·10 E
186	Qeshm (I.)	Iran	26·52 N	56·15 E
186	Qezel Owzan	Iran	37·00 N	48·23 E
171	Qezel Owzan (R.)	Iran	37·00 N	47·35 E
183	Qeẓi'ot	Egypt-Isr. (Palestine In.)	30·53 N	34·28 E
190	Qianwei (chyĕn-wā)	China	40·11 N	120·05 E
190	Qi'anzhen (chyē-än-jŭn)	China	32·16 N	120·59 E
191	Qibao (chyē-bou)	China (Shanghai In.)	31·06 N	121·16 E
183	Qiblīyah, Jabal al Jalālat al (Plat.)	Egypt (Palestine In.)	28·49 N	32·21 E
188	Qiemo (Qarqan) (chyär-chyän)	China	38·02 N	85·16 E
218	Qifṭ (kêft)	Egypt (Nile In.)	25·58 N	32·52 E
193	Qijiang (chyē-jyäŋ)	China	29·05 N	106·40 E
190	Qikou (chyē-kō)	China	38·37 N	117·33 E
188	Qilian Shan (Mts.) (chyē-lĭĕn shän)	China	38·43 N	98·00 E
190	Qiliping (chyē-lē-pĭŋ)	China	31·28 N	114·41 E
218	Qinā (kä'nà)	Egypt (Nile In.)	26·10 N	32·48 E
218	Qinā, Wādī	Egypt (Nile In.)	26·38 N	32·53 E
190	Qindao (Tsingtao) (chyĭn-dou)	China	36·05 N	120·10 E
192	Qing'an (chyĭŋ-än)	China	46·50 N	127·30 E
190	Qingcheng (chyĭŋ-chŭŋ)	China	37·12 N	117·43 E
190	Qingfeng (chyĭŋ-fŭŋ)	China	35·52 N	115·05 E
188	Qinghai (Prov.) (chyĭŋ-hī)	China	36·14 N	95·30 E
	Qinghai Hu (L.), see Koko Nor			
192	Qinghe (chyĭŋ-hŭ)	China (In.)	40·08 N	116·16 E
193	Qingjiang (chyĭŋ-jyäŋ)	China	28·00 N	115·30 E
190	Qingjiang	China	33·34 N	118·58 E
193	Qingliu (chyĭŋ-lĭô)	China	26·15 N	116·50 E
191	Qingningsi (chyĭŋ-nĭŋ-sz)	China (Shanghai In.)	31·16 N	121·33 E
190	Qingping (chyĭŋ-pĭŋ)	China	36·46 N	116·03 E
191	Qingpu (chyĭŋ-pōō)	China (Shanghai In.)	31·08 N	121·06 E
190	Qing Xian (chyĭŋ shyĕn)	China	38·37 N	116·48 E
192	Qingyang (chyĭŋ-yäŋ)	China	36·02 N	107·42 E
193	Qingyuan (chyĭŋ-yôän)	China	23·43 N	113·10 E
192	Qingyuan	China	42·05 N	125·00 E
190	Qingyun (chyĭŋ-yōōn)	China	37·52 N	117·26 E
192	Qingyundian (chĭŋ-yōōn-dĭĕn)	China (In.)	39·41 N	116·31 E
190	Qinhuangdao (chyĭn-huaŋ-dou)	China	39·57 N	119·34 E
183	Qin Ling (Mts.) (chyĭn lĭŋ)	China	33·25 N	108·58 E
192	Qin Ling (Mts.)	China	33·35 N	108·25 E
192	Qinyang (chyĭn-yäŋ)	China	35·00 N	112·55 E
193	Qinzhou (chyĭn-jō)	China	22·00 N	108·35 E
193	Qionghai (chyôŋ-hī)	China	19·10 N	110·28 E
189	Qiqian (chyē-chyĕn)	China	52·23 N	121·04 E
	Qiqihar, see Tsitsihar			
183	Qiryat Gat	Isr. (Palestine In.)	31·38 N	34·36 E
183	Qiryat Shemona	Isr. (Palestine In.)	33·12 N	35·34 E
188	Qitai (chyē-tī)	China	44·07 N	89·04 E
190	Qiu Xian (chyô shyĕn)	China	36·43 N	115·13 E
190	Qi Xian (chyē-shyĕn)	China	34·33 N	114·47 E
190	Qi Xian	China	35·36 N	114·13 E
193	Qiyang (chyē-yäŋ)	China	26·40 N	112·00 E
186	Qom	Iran	34·28 N	50·53 E
105	Quabbin Res. (kwā'bĭn)	Ma.	42·20 N	72·10 w
117	Quachita, L. (kwä shĭ'tô)	Ar.	34·47 N	93·37 w
92	Quadra, Boca de, Str. (bŏk'ǎ dē kwŏd'rá)	Ak.	55·08 N	130·50 w
92	Quadra I.	Can.	50·08 N	125·16 w
105	Quakertown (kwā'kēr-toun)	Pa.	40·30 N	75·20 w
116	Quanah (kwä'nà)	Tx.	34·19 N	99·43 w
193	Quang Ngai (kwäng n'gä'ê)	Viet.	15·05 N	108·58 E
193	Quang Ngai (Mtn.)	Viet.	15·10 N	108·20 E
190	Quanjiao (chyuän-jyou)	China	32·06 N	118·17 E
193	Quanzhou (chyuän-jō)	China	24·58 N	118·40 E
193	Quanzhou	China	25·58 N	111·02 E
94	Qu'Appelle Dam	Can.	51·00 N	106·25 w
94	Qu'Appelle (R.)	Can.	50·35 N	103·25 w
164	Quartu Sant' Elena (kwär-tōō' sänt a'lâ-nä)	It.	39·16 N	9·12 E
115	Quartzsite	Az.	33·40 N	114·13 w
92	Quatsino Sd (kwŏt-sē'nō)	Can.	50·25 N	128·10 w
190	Qudi	China	37·06 N	117·15 E
89	Québec (kwê-bĕk') (kå-bĕk')	Can. (Québec In.)	46·49 N	71·13 w
91	Quebec (Prov.)	Can.	51·07 N	70·25 w
158	Quedlinburg (kvĕd'lĕn-bōōrgh)	G.D.R.	51·49 N	11·10 E
92	Queen Bess, Mt.	Can.	51·16 N	124·34 w
92	Queen Charlotte Is. (kwēn shär'lŏt)	Can.	53·30 N	132·25 w

ăt; finăl; rāte; senâte; ärm; åsk; sofá; fâre; ch-choose; dh-as th in other; bē; êvent; bĕt; recĕnt; cratēr; g-go; gh-guttural g; bĭt; ĭ-short neutral; rīde; κ-guttural k as ch in German ich;

PRONOUNCING INDEX

Queen Charlotte — Ra's an Naqb 333

Page	Name Pronunciation Region	Lat. °′	Long. °′
92	Queen Charlotte Ra. . . . . Can.	53·00 N	132·00 W
92	Queen Charlotte Sd. . . . . Can.	51·30 N	129·30 W
92	Queen Charlotte Str. (strāt) . . Can.	50·40 N	127·25 W
75	Queen Elizabeth Is. (ê-lĭz′ȧ-bĕth) Can.	78·20 N	110·00 W
90	Queen Maud G. (mäd) . . . . . . Can.	68·27 N	102·55 W
220	Queen Maud Land . . . . Ant.	75·00 S	10·00 E
220	Queen Maud Mts. . . . . Ant.	85·00 S	179·00 W
204	Queens Chan. (kwēnz) . . . . . . Austl.	14·25 S	129·10 E
202	Queenscliff. Austl. (Melbourne In.)	38·16 S	144·39 E
205	Queensland (State) (kwēnz′lănd) Austl.	22·45 S	141·01 E
203	Queenstown (kwēnz′toun) . . . Austl.	42·00 S	145·40 E
213	Queenstown . . . . S. Afr. (Natal In.)	31·54 S	26·53 E
162	Queija, Sierra de (Mts.) (sē-ĕ′r-rä-dĕ-kĕ′y-kä). Sp.	42·08 N	7·23 W
136	Queimados (kā-mȧ′dôs) Braz. (Rio de Janeiro In.)	22·42 S	43·34 W
216	Quela . . . . Ang.	9·16 S	17·02 E
212	Quelimane (kā-lê-mä′nĕ) . . . . . Moz.	17·48 S	37·05 E
	Quelpart (I.), see Cheju		
128	Quemado de Güines (kā-mä′dhä-dĕ-gwē′nĕs) . Cuba	22·45 N	80·20 W
193	Quemoy (Chinmen) . . . . Taiwan	24·30 N	118·20 E
193	Quemoy (I.) . . . . Taiwan	24·35 N	118·45 E
127	Quepos (kā′pôs) . . . . C. R.	9·26 N	84·10 W
127	Quepos, Punta (Pt.) (pōō′n-tä) . C. R.	9·23 N	84·20 W
212	Que Que (kwĕ′kwĕ) . . . . Zimb.	18·49 S	29·45 E
124	Querétaro (kå-rā′tä-rō) . . . . . . Mex.	20·37 N	100·25 W
124	Querétaro (State) . . . . Mex.	21·00 N	100·00 W
162	Quesada (kå-sä′dhä) . . . . Sp.	37·51 N	3·04 W
92	Quesnel (kā-nĕl′) . . . . Can.	52·59 N	122·30 W
93	Quesnel L. . . . . Can.	52·32 N	121·05 W
92	Quesnel (R.) . . . . Can.	52·15 N	122·00 W
134	Quetame (kĕ-tä′mĕ) . . . . . Col. (In.)	4·20 N	73·50 W
184	Quetta (kwĕt′ä) . . . . Pak.	30·19 N	67·01 E
126	Quezaltenango (kå-zäl′tå-näŋ′gō) Guat.	14·50 N	91·30 W
126	Quezaltepeque (kå-zäl′tå-pā′kå) Guat.	14·39 N	89·26 W
126	Quezaltepeque (kĕ-zäl′tĕ′pĕ-kĕ) Sal.	13·50 N	89·17 W
197	Quezon City (kā-zōn) . . . Phil. (In.)	14·40 N	121·02 E
190	Qufu (chyōō-fōō) . . . . China	35·37 N	116·54 E
134	Quibdo (kēb′dō) . . . . Col. (In.)	5·42 N	76·41 W
160	Quiberon (kê-bē-rôN′) . . . . Fr.	47·29 N	3·08 W
216	Quiçama, Parque Nacional de (Natl. Pk.) . Ang.	10·00 S	13·25 E
126	Quiché (kē-shā′) . . . . Guat.	15·05 N	91·08 W
149	Quicksborn (kvēks′bōrn) F.R.G. (Hamburg In.)	53·44 N	9·54 E
112	Quilcene (kwĭl-sēn′) Wa. (Seattle In.)	47·50 N	122·53 W
137	Quilimari (kē-lē-mä′rē) Chile (Santiago In.)	32·06 S	71·28 W
160	Quillan (kê-yäN′) . . . . Fr.	43·53 N	2·13 E
137	Quillota (kêl-yō′tä) Chile (Santiago In.)	32·52 S	71·14 W
136	Quilmes (kēl′mās) Arg. (Buenos Aires In.)	34·28 S	58·16 W
185	Quilon (kwê-lōn′) . . . . India	8·58 N	76·16 E
203	Quilpie (kwĭl′pê) . . . . Austl.	26·34 S	149·20 E
137	Quilpué (kēl-pōō ĕ′) Chile (Santiago In.)	33·03 S	71·22 W
134	Quimbaya (kēm-bä′yä) . . Col. (In.)	4·38 N	75·46 W
216	Quimbele . . . . Ang.	6·28 S	16·13 E
216	Quimbonge . . . . Ang.	8·36 S	18·30 E
160	Quimper (kăN-pĕr′) . . . . Fr.	47·59 N	4·04 W
110	Quinalt R. . . . . Wa.	47·23 N	124·10 W
110	Quinault Ind. Res. . . . . Wa.	47·27 N	124·34 W
120	Quincy (kwĭn′sê) . . . . Fl.	30·35 N	84·35 W
117	Quincy . . . . Il.	39·55 N	91·23 W
99	Quincy . . . . Ma. (In.)	42·15 N	71·00 W
104	Quincy . . . . Mi.	42·00 N	84·50 W
112	Quincy . . . . Or. (Portland In.)	46·08 N	123·10 W
196	Qui-nhon (kwĭnyôn) . . . . Viet.	13·51 N	109·03 E
110	Quinn R. (kwĭn) . . . . Nv.	41·42 N	117·45 W
162	Quintana de la Serena (kēn-tä′nä dā lä så-rā′nä) . Sp.	38·45 N	5·39 W
162	Quintanar (kēn-tä-när′) . . . . Sp.	39·36 N	3·02 W
126	Quintana Roo (State) (rô′ô) Mex. (In.)	19·30 N	88·30 W
137	Quintero (kēn-tĕ′rô) Chile (Santiago In.)	32·48 S	71·30 W
217	Quionga . . . . Moz.	10·37 S	40·30 E
124	Quiroga (kē-rô′gä) . . . . Mex.	19·39 N	101·30 W
162	Quiroga (kē-rô′gä) . . . . Sp.	42·28 N	7·18 W
120	Quitman (kwĭt′măn) . . . . Ga.	30·46 N	83·35 W
120	Quitman . . . . Ms.	33·02 N	88·43 W
134	Quito (kē′tō) . . . . Ec.	0·17 S	78·32 W
135	Quixadá (kê-shä-dä′) . . . . Braz.	4·58 S	38·58 W
218	Qulūşanā (kōō-lōōs′nä) Egypt (Nile In.)	28·22 N	30·44 E
213	Qumbu (kōōm′bōō) S. Afr. (Natal In.)	31·10 S	28·48 E
203	Quorn (kwôrn) . . . . Austl.	32·20 S	138·00 E
183	Qurayyah, Wādī (R.) Egypt (Palestine In.)	30·08 N	34·27 E
218	Qūş (kōōs) . . . . Egypt (Nile In.)	25·53 N	32·48 E
190	Qutang (chyōō-täŋ) . . . . China	32·33 N	120·07 E
213	Quthing . . . . Leso. (Natal In.)	30·35 S	27·42 E
205	Quvea (I.) . . . . N. Cal.	20·43 S	166·48 E
193	Qu Xian (chyōō-shyĕn) . . . . . China	28·58 N	118·58 E
193	Qu Xian . . . . China	30·40 N	106·48 E
190	Quzhou (chyōō-jō) . . . . China	36·47 N	114·58 E
186	Quzvīn . . . . Iran	36·10 N	49·59 E

R

Page	Name Pronunciation Region	Lat. °′	Long. °′
158	Raab R. (räp) . . . . Aus.	46·55 N	15·55 E
150	Raahe (rä′ĕ) . . . . Fin.	64·39 N	24·22 E
164	Rab (I.) (räb) . . . . Yugo.	44·45 N	14·40 E
196	Raba . . . . Indon.	8·32 S	118·49 E
159	Raba R. . . . . Hung.	47·28 N	17·12 E
210	Rabat (rȧ-bät′) . . . . Mor.	33·59 N	6·47 W
197	Rabaul (rä′boul) . . . . . Pap. N. Gui.	4·15 S	152·19 E
109	Raccoon (R.) (ră-kōōn′) . . . . Ia.	42·07 N	94·45 W
129	Raccoon Cay (I.) . . . . Ba.	22·25 N	75·50 W
99	Race, C. (rās) . . . . Can.	46·40 N	53·10 W
183	Rachado, C. . Mala. (Singapore In.)	2·26 N	101·29 E
159	Racibórz (rä-chē′bōōzh) . . . . . . Pol.	50·06 N	18·14 E
107	Racine (rȧ-sēn′) Wi. (Milwaukee In.)	42·43 N	87·49 W
113	Raco (rȧ cō) Mi. (Sault Ste. Marie In.)	46·22 N	84·43 W
159	Rădăuti (rû-dû-ōōts″) . . . . Rom.	47·53 N	25·55 E
148	Radcliffe (răd′klĭf) . . . . Eng.	53·34 N	2·20 W
161	Radevormwald (rä′dĕ-fōrm-väld) F.R.G. (Ruhr In.)	51·12 N	7·22 E
121	Radford (răd′fērd) . . . . Va.	37·06 N	81·33 W
184	Rādhanpur . . . . India	23·57 N	71·38 E
218	Radium (rā′dĭ-ŭm) . . . . S. Afr. (Johannesburg & Pretoria In.)	25·06 S	28·18 E
159	Radom (rä′dôm) . . . . Pol.	51·24 N	21·11 E
165	Radomir (rä′dô-mêr) . . . . Bul.	42·33 N	22·58 E
159	Radomsko (rä-dôm′skô) . . . . . . Pol.	51·04 N	19·27 E
167	Radomyshl (rä-dô-mēsh″l) Sov. Un.	50·30 N	29·13 E
165	Radoviš (rä-dô-vêsh) . . . . Yugo.	41·39 N	22·28 E
167	Radul′ (rȧ′dōōl) . . . . Sov. Un.	51·52 N	30·46 E
157	Radviliškis (rȧd′vê-lēsh′kês) Sov. Un.	55·49 N	23·31 E
186	Radwah, Jabal (Mtn.) . . . . Sau. Ar.	24·44 N	38·14 E
159	Radzyń Podlaski (räd′zên-y′ pŭd-lä′skĭ) . Pol.	51·49 N	22·40 E
121	Raeford (rā′fērd) . . . . NC	34·57 N	79·15 W
161	Raesfeld (răz′fĕld) F.R.G. (Ruhr In.)	51·46 N	6·50 E
204	Raeside (rā′sīd) . . . . Austl.	29·20 S	122·30 E
90	Rae Str. (rā) . . . . Can.	68·40 N	95·03 W
136	Rafaela (rä-fä-â′lä) . . . . Arg.	31·15 S	61·21 W
183	Rafah (rä′fä) Egypt (Palestine In.)	31·14 N	34·12 E
211	Rafaï (rä-fī′) . . . . . . Cen. Afr. Rep.	4·59 N	23·58 E
186	Rafḩā . . . . Sau. Ar.	29·43 N	43·13 E
186	Rafsanjān . . . . Iran	30·45 N	56·30 E
111	Raft R. (răft) . . . . Id.	42·20 N	113·17 W
197	Ragay (rä-gī′) . . . . Phil. (In.)	13·49 N	122·45 E
197	Ragay G. . . . . Phil. (In.)	13·44 N	122·38 E
171	Ragga . . . . Egypt	36·00 N	39·00 E
156	Ragunda (rä-gōōn′dä) . . . . Swe.	63·07 N	16·24 E
151	Ragusa (rä-gōō′sä) . . . . It.	36·58 N	14·41 E
	Ragusa, see Dubrovnik		
106	Rahway (rô′wā) NJ (New York In.)	40·37 N	74·16 W
185	Rāichūr (rä′ê-chōōr′) . . . . India	16·23 N	77·18 E
184	Raigarh (rī′gŭr) . . . . India	21·57 N	83·32 E
115	Rainbow Bridge Natl. Mon. (rān′bō) . Ut.	37·05 N	111·00 W
122	Rainbow City . . . . Pan. (In.)	9·20 N	79·23 W
112	Rainier . . . . Or. (Portland In.)	46·05 N	122·56 W
110	Rainier, Mt. (rā-nēr′) . . . . Wa.	46·52 N	121·46 W
95	Rainy (L.) (rān′ê) . . . . . . Can.-Mn.	48·43 N	94·29 W
95	Rainy (R.) . . . . Can.-Mn.	48·50 N	94·41 W
95	Rainy River . . . . Can.	48·43 N	94·29 W
184	Raipur (rä′jŭ-bōō-rê′) . . . . India	21·25 N	81·37 E
104	Raisin (R.) (rā′zĭn) . . . . Mi.	42·00 N	83·35 W
106	Raitan (rā-tăn) NJ (New York In.)	40·34 N	74·40 W
185	Rājahmundry (räj-ŭ-mŭn′drê) India	17·03 N	81·51 E
196	Rajang (Strm.) . . . . Mala.	2·10 N	113·30 E
184	Rājapālaiyam . . . . India	9·30 N	77·33 E
184	Rājasthān (State) (rä′jŭs-tän) India	31·20 N	72·00 E
184	Rājkot (räj′kôt) . . . . India	22·20 N	70·48 E
184	Rājpur . . . . India (In.)	22·24 N	88·25 E
184	Rājshāhi . . . . Bngl.	24·26 S	88·39 E
159	Rakhov (rä′κôf) . . . . Sov. Un.	48·02 N	24·13 E
174	Rakh′ya (räk′yȧ) Sov. Un. (Leningrad In.)	60·06 N	30·50 E
167	Rakitnoye (rȧ-kēt′nô-yĕ) Sov. Un.	50·51 N	35·53 E
158	Rakovnik (rä′kôv-nyêk) . . . . Czech.	50·07 N	13·45 E
166	Rakvere (rȧk′vĕ-rĕ) . . . . . . Sov. Un.	59·22 N	26·14 E
121	Raleigh . . . . NC	35·45 N	78·39 W
121	Raleigh, B. . . . . NC	34·50 N	76·15 W
93	Ram (R.) . . . . Can.	52·10 N	115·05 W
127	Rama (rä′mä) . . . . Nic.	12·11 N	84·14 W
137	Ramallo (rä-mä′l-yô) Arg. (Buenos Aires In.)	33·28 S	60·02 W
185	Ramanāthapuram . . . . India	9·13 N	78·52 E
161	Rambouillet (räN-bōō-yĕ′) Fr. (Paris In.)	48·39 N	1·49 E
213	Rame Hd. . . . . . S. Afr. (Natal In.)	31·48 S	29·22 E
174	Ramenskoye (rȧ′mĕn-skô-yĕ) Sov. Un. (Moscow In.)	55·34 N	38·15 E
186	Ramlat as Sab′atayn (Reg.) Sau. Ar.	16·08 N	45·15 E
183	Ramm, Jabal (Mts.) Jordan (Palestine In.)	29·37 N	35·32 E
124	Ramos (rä′mōs) . . . . Mex.	22·46 N	101·52 W
215	Ramos (R.) . . . . Nig.	5·10 N	5·40 E
118	Ramos Arizpe (ä-rēz′pâ) . . . . . Mex.	25·33 N	100·57 W
101	Rampart (răm′pȧrt) . . . . Ak.	65·28 N	150·18 W
106	Rampo Mts. (răm′pō) NJ-NY (New York In.)	41·06 N	72·12 W
184	Rāmpur (räm′pōōr) . . . . India	28·53 N	79·03 E
196	Ramree I. (räm′rē′) . . . . Bur.	19·01 N	93·23 E
89	Ramsayville (răm′zê vĭl) Can. (Ottawa In.)	45·23 N	75·34 W
148	Ramsbottom (rămz′bŏt-ŭm) . . Eng.	53·39 N	2·20 W
154	Ramsey (răm′zê) . . . . . Isle of Man	54·20 N	4·25 W
106	Ramsey . . . . . . NJ (New York In.)	41·03 N	74·09 W
96	Ramsey L. . . . . Can.	47·15 N	82·16 W
155	Ramsgate (rămz″gāt) . . . . Eng.	51·19 N	1·20 E
156	Ramsjö (räm′shû) . . . . Swe.	62·11 N	15·44 E
197	Ramu (R.) (rä′mōō) . Pap. N. Gui.	5·35 S	145·16 E
137	Rancagua (rän-kä′gwä) Chile (Santiago In.)	34·10 S	70·43 W
160	Rance (R.) (räNs) . . . . Fr.	48·17 N	2·30 W
184	Rānchī (rän′chē) . . . . India	23·24 N	85·18 E
129	Rancho Boyeros (rä′n-chô-bô-yĕ′rôs) . Cuba (In.)	23·00 N	82·23 W
106	Randallstown (răn′dȧlz-toun) Md. (Baltimore In.)	39·22 N	76·48 W
156	Randers (rän′ĕrs) . . . . Den.	56·28 N	10·03 E
213	Randfontein (rănt′fŏn-tān) . S. Afr. (Johannesburg & Pretoria In.)	26·10 S	27·42 E
121	Randleman (răn′d′l-măn) . . . . . NC	35·49 N	79·50 W
99	Randolph (răn′dôlf) . . . . . Ma. (In.)	42·10 N	71·03 W
108	Randolph . . . . Ne.	42·22 N	97·22 W
105	Randolph . . . . Vt.	43·55 N	72·40 W
99	Random I. (răn′dŭm) . . . . Can.	48·12 N	53·25 W
156	Rands Fd. (räns′ fyôr) . . . . Nor.	60·35 N	10·10 E
214	Ranérou . . . . Senegal	15·18 N	13·58 W
98	Rangeley (ränj′lê) . . . . Me.	44·56 N	70·38 W
98	Rangeley (L.) . . . . Me.	45·00 N	70·25 W
118	Ranger (rān′jēr) . . . . Tx.	32·26 N	98·41 W
184	Rangia . . . . India	26·32 N	91·39 E
196	Rangoon (rȧŋ-gōōn′) . . . . Bur.	16·46 N	96·09 E
184	Rangpur (rŭng′pōōr) . . . . Bngl.	25·48 N	89·19 E
183	Rangsang (I.) (räng′säng′) Indon. (Singapore In.)	0·53 N	103·05 E
149	Rangsdorf (rängs′dōrf) G.D.R. (Berlin In.)	52·17 N	13·25 E
184	Rānīganj (rä-nē-gŭnj′) . . . . . . India	23·40 N	87·08 E
90	Rankin Inlet (răŋ′kĕn) . . . . . . Can.	62·45 N	94·27 W
166	Ranova (R.) (rä′nô-vȧ) . . Sov. Un.	53·55 N	40·03 E
107	Ransomville (răn′sum-vĭl) NY (Buffalo In.)	43·15 N	78·54 W
183	Rantau . . . . . Mala. (Singapore In.)	2·35 N	101·58 E
196	Rantelkomboa, Bulu (Mtn.) Indon.	3·22 S	119·50 E
104	Rantoul (răn-tōōl′) . . . . Il.	40·25 N	88·05 W
190	Raoyang (rou-yäŋ) . . . . China	38·16 N	115·45 E
164	Rapallo (rä-päl′lô) . . . . It.	44·21 N	9·14 E
199	Rapa Nui (Easter) (I.) (rä′pä nōō′ê) (ēs′tēr) . Chile	26·50 S	109·00 W
137	Rapel (rä-pål′) (R.) Chile (Santiago In.)	34·05 S	71·30 W
109	Rapid (R.) (răp′ĭd) . . . . Mn.	48·21 N	94·50 W
108	Rapid City . . . . SD	44·06 N	103·14 W
157	Rapla (räp′lȧ) . . . . Sov. Un.	59·02 N	24·46 E
105	Rappahannock (R.) (răp′ȧ-hăn′ŭk) . Va.	38·20 N	75·25 W
105	Raquette (L.) (răk′ĕt) . . . . NY	43·50 N	74·35 W
159	Rara Mazowiecka (rä′rä mä-zō-vyĕts′kä) . Pol.	51·46 N	20·17 E
106	Raritan R. (răr′ĭ-tăn) NJ (New York In.)	40·32 N	74·27 W
199	Rarotonga (rä′rô-tŏŋ′gȧ) . . Cook Is.	20·40 S	163·00 W
183	Ra's an Naqb Jordan (Palestine In.)	30·00 N	35·29 E

ng-sing; ŋ-baŋk; N-nasalized n; nŏd; cŏmmit; ōld; ôbey; ôrder; fōōd; fŏŏt; ou-out; s-soft; sh-dish; th-thin; pūre; ûnite; ûrn; stŭd; circŭs; ü-as "y" in study; ′-indeterminate vowel.

334 Ras Dashen — Reutov PRONOUNCING INDEX

Page	Name Pronunciation Region	Lat. °'	Long. °'
211	Ras Dashen (Mtn.) (räs dä-shän') Eth.	12·49 N	38·14 E
157	Raseiniai (rä-syā'nyī)....Sov. Un.	55·23 N	23·04 E
186	Ra's Fartak (C.)..P. D. R. of Yem.	15·43 N	52·17 E
183	Rashayya.....Leb. (Palestine In.)	33·30 N	35·50 E
218	Rashīd (Rosetta) (rå-shēd') (rô-zĕt'ȧ) Egypt (Nile In.)	31·22 N	30·25 E
218	Rashîd, Masabb (R. Mth.) Egypt (Nile In.)	31·30 N	29·58 E
174	Rashkina (råsh'kĭ-nå) Sov. Un. (Urals In.)	59·57 N	61·30 E
167	Rashkov (räsh'kôf)......Sov. Un.	47·55 N	28·51 E
186	Rasht......................Iran	37·13 N	49·45 E
165	Raška (räsh'kå)...........Yugo.	43·16 N	20·40 E
184	Ras Kuh Mt..................Pak.	34·03 N	65·10 E
171	Rasskazovo (räs-kä'sô-vô) Sov. Un.	52·40 N	41·40 E
158	Rastatt (rä-shtät).........F.R.G.	48·51 N	8·12 E
174	Rastes (rås'tĕs) Sov. Un. (Urals In.)	59·24 N	58·49 E
174	Rastunovo (rås-tōō'nô-vô) Sov. Un. (Moscow In.)	55·15 N	37·50 E
162	Ras Uarc (C.)..............Mor.	35·28 N	2·58 W
184	Ratangarh (rŭ-tŭn'gŭr).....India	28·10 N	74·30 E
119	Ratcliff (răt'klĭf)..............Tx.	31·22 N	95·09 W
158	Rathenow (rä'tĕ-nō)......G.D.R.	52·36 N	12·20 E
154	Rathlin (I.) (răth-lĭn)........Ire.	55·18 N	6·13 W
161	Ratingen (rä'tēn-gĕn) F.R.G. (Ruhr In.)	51·18 N	6·51 E
101	Rat Is. (răt)................Ak.	51·35 N	176·48 E
184	Ratlām...................India	23·19 N	75·05 E
185	Ratnāgiri.................India	17·04 N	73·24 E
116	Raton (rȧ-tōn')..............NM	36·52 N	104·26 W
110	Rattlesnake Cr. (răt''l snāk)...Or.	42·38 N	117·39 W
156	Rättvik (rĕt'vēk)..........Swe.	60·54 N	15·07 E
158	Ratzeburger See (L.) (rä'tzĕ-bōōr-gĕr-zā)....G.D.R.	53·48 N	11·02 E
137	Rauch (rȧ'ōōch) Arg. (Buenos Aires In.)	36·47 S	59·05 W
156	Raufoss (rou'fôs)............Nor.	60·44 N	10·30 E
137	Raúl Soares (rä-ōō'l-sôä'rĕs) Braz. (Rio de Janeiro In.)	20·05 S	42·28 W
157	Rauma (rä'ōō-mȧ)...........Fin.	61·07 N	21·31 E
157	Rauna (râū'nå).........Sov. Un.	57·21 N	25·31 E
184	Raurkela.................India	22·15 N	84·53 E
157	Rautalampi (rä'ōō-tê-läm'pô).Fin.	62·39 N	26·25 E
159	Rava-Russkaya (rä'vå rōōs'kä-yȧ) Sov. Un.	50·14 N	23·40 E
164	Ravenna (rä-vĕn'nä)..........It.	44·27 N	12·13 E
108	Ravenna (rȧ-vĕn'ȧ)..........Ne.	41·20 N	98·50 W
104	Ravenna...................Oh.	41·10 N	81·20 W
158	Ravensburg (rä'vĕns-bōōrgh) F.R.G.	47·48 N	9·35 E
112	Ravensdale (rā'vĕnz-dāl) Wa. (Seattle In.)	47·22 N	121·58 W
204	Ravensthorpe (rā'vĕns-thôrp) Austl.	33·30 S	120·20 E
104	Ravenswood (rā'vĕnz-wŏŏd)...WV	38·55 N	81·50 W
184	Rāwalpindi (rä-wŭl-pēn'dê)...Pak.	33·40 N	73·10 E
186	Rawāndūz.................Iraq	36·37 N	44·30 E
158	Rawicz (rä'vēch)............Pol.	51·36 N	16·51 E
204	Rawlina (rôr-lēnȧ)........Austl.	31·13 S	125·45 E
111	Rawlins (rô'lĭnz)............Wy.	41·46 N	107·15 W
136	Rawson (rô'sŭn)............Arg.	43·16 S	65·09 W
137	Rawson...Arg. (Buenos Aires In.)	34·36 S	60·03 W
148	Rawtenstall (rô'tĕn-stôl).....Eng.	53·42 N	2·17 W
99	Ray, C. (rā)...............Can.	47·40 N	59·18 W
196	Raya, Bukit (Mtn.).......Indon.	0·45 S	112·11 E
173	Raychikinsk (rī'chĭ-kĕnsk) Sov. Un.	49·52 N	129·17 E
148	Rayleigh (rā'lê).Eng. (London In.)	51·35 N	0·36 E
93	Raymond (rā'mŭnd) ....Can.	49·27 N	112·39 W
110	Raymond..................Wa.	46·41 N	123·42 W
116	Raymondville (rā'mŭnd-vĭl)...Tx.	26·30 N	97·46 W
100	Ray Mts...................Ak.	65·40 N	151·45 W
119	Rayne (rān)................La.	30·12 N	92·15 W
124	Rayón (rä-yōn')............Mex.	21·49 N	99·39 W
213	Rayton (rā'tŭn)..........S. Afr. (Johannesburg & Pretoria In.)	25·45 S	28·33 E
113	Raytown (rā'toun) Mo. (Kansas City In.)	39·01 N	94·48 W
119	Rayville (rā-vĭl).............La.	32·28 N	91·46 W
160	Raz, Pte. du (Pt.) (pwănt dü rä).Fr.	48·02 N	4·43 W
167	Razdel'naya (räz-dĕl'nä-yȧ) Sov. Un.	46·47 N	30·08 E
194	Razdol'noye (räz-dôl'nô-yĕ) Sov. Un.	43·38 N	131·58 E
165	Razgrad...................Bul.	43·32 N	26·32 E
165	Razlog (räz'lôk).............Bul.	41·54 N	23·32 E
92	Razorback Mtn. (rā'zēr-băk).Can.	51·35 N	124·42 W
160	Ré, Île de (I.) (ēl dē rā') ......Fr.	46·10 N	1·53 W
148	Rea (R.) (rē)...............Eng.	52·25 N	2·31 W
89	Reaburn (rā'bûrn) Can. (Winnipeg In.)	50·06 N	97·53 W
148	Reading (rĕd'ĭng) Eng. (London In.)	51·25 N	0·58 W
99	Reading...............Ma (In.)	42·32 N	71·07 W
104	Reading....................Mi.	41·45 N	84·45 W
107	Reading......Oh. (Cincinnati In.)	39·14 N	84·26 W
105	Reading....................Pa.	40·20 N	75·55 W
136	Realengo (rĕ-ä-län-gô) Braz. (Rio de Janeiro In.)	23·50 S	43·25 W
211	Rebiana (Oasis)...........Libya	24·10 N	22·03 E
194	Rebun (I.) (rē'bōōn).........Jap.	45·25 N	140·54 E
164	Recanati (rā-kä-nä'tê).........It.	43·25 N	13·35 E
204	Recherche, Arch. of the (rē-shârsh').Austl.	34·17 S	122·30 E
166	Rechitsa (ryĕ'chêt-sȧ)....Sov. Un.	52·22 N	30·24 E
135	Recife (Pernambuco) (rå-sē'fĕ) (pĕr-näm-bōō'kô).Braz.	8·09 S	34·59 W
213	Recife, Kapp (C.) (rå-sē'fĕ) S. Afr. (Natal In.)	34·03 S	25·43 E
136	Reconquista (rā-kôn-kēs'tä)..Arg.	29·01 S	59·41 W
117	Rector (rĕk'tēr)..............Ar.	36·16 N	90·21 W
95	Red (R.) (rĕd)........Can.-U. S.	49·11 N	97·18 W
120	Red (R.)...................Tn.	36·35 N	86·55 W
116	Red (R.), North Fk..........Tx.	35·20 N	100·08 W
103	Red (R.).................U. S.	31·40 N	92·55 W
196	Red (R.)..................Viet.	22·25 N	103·50 E
	Red (Basin), see Szechwan		
110	Redan (rê-dăn') (rĕd'ăn) Ga. (Atlanta In.)	33·44 N	84·09 W
110	Red Bank (băngk) NJ (New York In.)	40·21 N	74·06 W
112	Red Bluff (blŭf).............Ca.	40·10 N	122·14 W
118	Red Bluff Res...............Tx.	32·03 N	103·52 W
109	Redby (rĕd'bê)..............Mn.	47·52 N	94·55 W
109	Red Cedar (R.) (sē'dēr)......Wi.	45·03 N	91·48 W
94	Redcliff (rĕd'clĭf)...........Can.	50·05 N	110·47 W
109	Red Cliff Ind. Res............Wi.	46·48 N	91·22 W
197	Redcliffe (rĕd'clĭf).........Austl.	27·20 S	153·12 E
116	Red Cloud (kloud)............Ne.	40·06 N	98·32 W
93	Red Deer (dēr)..............Can.	52·16 N	113·48 W
93	Red Deer (R.)..............Can.	52·05 N	113·00 W
94	Red Deer (R.)..............Can.	52·55 N	102·10 W
95	Red Deer L.................Can.	52·58 N	101·28 W
111	Reddick (rĕd'dĭk).Il. (Chicago In.)	41·06 N	88·16 W
110	Redding (rĕd'ĭng)............Ca.	40·36 N	122·25 W
137	Redenção da Serra (rĕ-dĕn-souN-dä-sĕ'r-rä) Braz. (Rio de Janeiro In.)	23·17 S	45·31 W
108	Redfield (rĕd'fēld)............SD	44·53 N	98·30 W
119	Red Fish Bar...........Tx. (In.)	29·29 N	94·53 W
99	Red Indian L. (ĭn'dĭ-ăn).....Can.	48·40 N	56·50 W
161	Redklinghausen (rĕk'lĭng-hou-zĕn) F.R.G. (Ruhr In.)	51·36 N	7·13 E
95	Red Lake (lāk)..............Can.	51·03 N	93·49 W
108	Red Lake (R.)..............Mn.	48·02 N	96·04 W
108	Red Lake Falls (lāk fôls).....Mn.	47·52 N	96·17 W
108	Red Lake Ind. Res...........Mn.	48·09 N	95·55 W
113	Redlands (rĕd'lăndz) Ca. (Los Angeles In.)	34·04 N	117·11 W
105	Red Lion (lī'ŭn).............Pa.	39·55 N	76·30 W
111	Red Lodge..................Mt.	45·13 N	107·16 W
112	Redmond (rĕd'mŭnd) Wa. (Seattle In.)	47·40 N	122·07 W
158	Rednitz R. (rĕd'nētz)......F.R.G.	49·10 N	11·00 E
108	Red Oak (ōk)................Ia.	41·00 N	95·12 W
160	Redon (rē-dôN')...............Fr.	47·42 N	2·03 W
136	Redonda, Isla (ē's-lä-rĕ-dô'n-dä) Braz. (Rio de Janeiro In.)	23·05 S	43·11 W
127	Redonda I. (rĕ-dŏn'dȧ) Antigua (In.)	16·55 N	62·28 W
162	Redondela (rā-dhôn-dā'lä).....Sp.	42·16 N	8·34 W
162	Redondo (rå-dôn'dōō).......Port.	38·40 N	7·32 W
112	Redondo (rê-dŏn'dō) Wa. (Seattle In.)	47·21 N	122·19 W
113	Redondo Beach Ca. (Los Angeles In.)	33·50 N	118·23 W
93	Red Pass (pȧs)..............Can.	52·59 N	118·59 W
116	Red R., Prairie Dog Town Fk. (prā'rĭ).Tx.	34·54 N	101·31 W
116	Red R., Salt Fk..............Tx.	35·04 N	100·31 W
111	Red Rock Cr.................Mt.	44·54 N	112·44 W
211	Red Sea...............Afr.-Asia	23·15 N	37·00 E
92	Redstone (rĕd'stōn).........Can.	52·08 N	123·42 W
95	Red Sucker L. (sŭk'ēr).......Can.	54·09 N	93·40 W
111	Redwater Cr..................Mt.	47·37 N	105·25 W
116	Red Willow Cr................Ne.	40·34 N	100·48 W
109	Red Wing...................Mn.	44·34 N	92·35 W
112	Redwood City (rĕd' wŏŏd) Ca. (San Francisco In.)	37·29 N	122·13 W
109	Redwood Falls...............Mn.	44·32 N	95·06 W
154	Ree, Lough (B.) (lŏK'rē')......Ire.	53·30 N	7·45 W
104	Reed City (rēd)...............Mi.	43·50 N	85·35 W
95	Reed L......................Can.	54·37 N	100·30 W
114	Reedley (rēd'lê)..............Ca.	36·37 N	119·27 W
109	Reedsburg (rēdz'bûrg).........Wi.	43·32 N	90·01 W
110	Reedsport (rēdz'pôrt)..........Or.	43·42 N	124·08 W
120	Reelfoot (R.) (rēl'fŏŏt).......Tn.	36·18 N	89·20 W
161	Rees (rĕz)......F.R.G. (Ruhr In.)	51·46 N	6·25 E
203	Reeves, Mt. (rēv's)........Austl.	33·50 S	149·56 E
120	Reform (rê-fôrm')..............Al.	33·23 N	88·00 W
119	Refugio (rå-fōō'hyô) (rĕ-fū'jō).Tx.	28·18 N	97·15 W
158	Rega (R.) (rĕ-gä)............Pol.	53·48 N	15·30 E
158	Regen R. (rā'ghĕn)........F.R.G.	49·09 N	12·21 E
158	Regensburg (rā'ghĕns-bŏŏrgh) F.R.G.	49·02 N	12·06 E
210	Reggane....................Alg.	27·08 N	0·06 E
164	Reggio (rĕ'jô)................It.	44·43 N	10·34 E
106	Reggio (rĕg'jĭ-ō) La. (New Orleans In.)	29·50 N	89·46 W
164	Reggio di Calabria (rĕ'jô dē kä-lä'brê-ä).It.	38·07 N	15·42 E
159	Reghin (rå-gēn')...........Rom.	46·47 N	24·44 E
94	Regina (rê-jī'nȧ)............Can.	50·25 N	104·39 W
119	Regla (rĕg'lä).........Cuba (In.)	23·08 N	82·20 W
158	Regnitz (R.) (rĕg'nētz).....F.R.G.	49·50 N	10·55 E
162	Reguengos de Monsaraz (rå-gĕŋ'gōzh dā mōn-sä-räzh') Port.	38·26 N	7·30 W
212	Rehoboth..............Namibia	23·10 S	17·15 E
183	Rehovot.......Isr. (Palestine In.)	31·53 N	34·49 E
158	Reichenbach (rī'Kĕn-bäK)..G.D.R.	50·36 N	12·18 E
121	Reidsville (rēdz'vĭl)..........NC	36·20 N	79·37 W
148	Reigate (rī'gāt).Eng. (London In.)	51·12 N	0·12 W
160	Reims (răNs)................Fr.	49·16 N	4·00 E
136	Reina Adelaida, Arch. (är-chê'-pyĕ'lȧ-gô-rā'nä-ä-dĕ-lī'dä) Chile	52·00 S	74·15 W
109	Reinbeck (rīn'bĕk)............Ia.	42·22 N	92·34 W
90	Reindeer (L.) (rān'dēr)......Can.	57·36 N	101·23 W
94	Reindeer (R.)...............Can.	55·45 N	103·30 W
95	Reindeer I..................Can.	52·25 N	98·00 W
95	Reindeer L..................Can.	57·15 N	102·40 W
162	Reinosa (rå-ê-nō'sä)..........Sp.	43·01 N	4·08 W
106	Reistertown (rēs'tēr-toun) Md. (Baltimore In.)	39·28 N	76·50 W
218	Reitz.....................S. Afr. (Johannesburg & Pretoria In.)	27·48 S	28·25 E
186	Rema, Jabal (Mtn.).......Yemen	14·13 N	44·38 E
183	Rembau....Mala. (Singapore In.)	2·36 N	102·06 E
134	Remedios (rĕ-mĕ'dyōs)...Col. (In.)	7·03 N	74·42 W
128	Remedios (rā-mā'dhê-ōs)....Cuba	22·30 N	79·35 W
127	Remedios (rĕ-mĕ'dyōs)......Pan.	8·14 N	81·46 W
161	Remiremont (rē-mēr-môN').....Fr.	48·01 N	6·35 E
183	Rempang I..Indon. (Singapore In.)	0·51 N	104·04 E
161	Remscheid (rĕm'shīt) F.R.G. (Ruhr In.)	51·10 N	7·11 E
205	Rendova (I.) (rĕn'dô-vȧ)...Sol. Is.	8·38 S	156·26 E
158	Rendsburg (rĕnts'bŏŏrgh)..F.R.G.	54·19 N	9·39 E
105	Renfrew (rĕn'frōō)..........Can.	45·30 N	76·30 W
183	Rengam (rĕn'gäm') Mala. (Singapore In.)	1·53 N	103·24 E
137	Rengo (rĕn'gō).Chile (Santiago In.)	34·22 S	70·50 W
167	Reni (ran')............Sov. Un.	45·26 N	28·18 E
203	Renmark (rĕn'märk).......Austl.	34·10 S	140·50 E
205	Rennel (I.) (rĕn-nĕl')......Sol. Is.	11·50 S	160·38 E
160	Rennes (rĕn).................Fr.	48·07 N	1·02 W
105	Rensselaer (rĕn'sē-lâr).........NY	42·40 N	73·45 W
114	Reno (rē'nō)................Nv.	39·32 N	119·49 W
164	Reno (R.) (rā'nô)..............It.	44·10 N	10·55 E
105	Renovo (rê-nō'vō).............Pa.	41·20 N	77·50 W
190	Renqiu (rŭn-chyō)..........China	38·44 N	116·05 E
104	Rensselaer (rĕn'sē-lâr)..........In.	41·00 N	87·10 W
113	Rentchler (rĕnt'chlēr) Il. (St. Louis In.)	38·30 N	89·52 W
112	Renton (rĕn'tŭn).Wa. (Seattle In.)	47·29 N	122·13 W
109	Renville (rĕn'vĭl).............Mn.	44·44 N	95·13 W
89	Repentigny...Can. (Montreal In.)	45·47 N	73·26 W
106	Republic (rê-pŭb'lĭk) Al. (Birmingham In.)	33·37 N	86·54 W
110	Republic....................Wa.	48·38 N	118·44 W
116	Republican (R.), South Fk. (rê-pŭb'lĭ-kăn).Co.	39·35 N	102·28 W
117	Republican (R.)..............Ks.	39·40 N	97·40 W
205	Repulse B. (rê-pŭls')........Austl.	20·56 S	149·22 E
162	Requena (rå-kā'nä)...........Sp.	39·29 N	1·03 W
137	Resende (rĕ-sĕ'n-dĕ) Braz. (Rio de Janeiro In.)	22·30 S	44·26 W
137	Resende Costa (kôs-tä) Braz. (Rio de Janeiro In.)	20·55 S	44·12 W
167	Reshetilovka (ryĕ' shĕ-tê-lôf-kȧ) Sov. Un.	49·34 N	34·04 E
136	Resistencia (rā-sês-tĕn'syä)...Arg.	27·24 S	58·54 W
165	Reşita (rå'shê-tȧ)...........Rom.	45·18 N	21·56 E
75	Resolute (rĕz-ô-lūt').........Can.	74·41 N	95·00 W
91	Resolution (I.) (rĕz-ô-lū'shŭn) Can.	61·30 N	63·58 W
205	Resolution (I.) (rĕz-ŏl-ûshûn) N. Z. (In.)	45·43 S	166·00 E
98	Restigouche (R.) (rĕs-tê-gōōsh') Can.	47·35 N	67·35 W
134	Restrepo (rĕs-trĕ'pô)....Col. (In.)	3·49 N	76·31 W
134	Restrepo..............Col. (In.)	4·16 N	73·32 W
126	Retalhuleu (rā-täl-ōō-lān')...Guat.	14·31 N	91·41 W
160	Rethel (r-tĕl')................Fr.	49·34 N	4·20 E
164	Réthimnon..............Grc. (In.)	35·21 N	24·30 E
149	Retie.........Bel. (Brussels In.)	51·16 N	5·08 E
112	Retsil (rĕt'sĭl)....Wa. (Seattle In.)	47·33 N	122·37 W
220	Reunion (rā-ü-nyôn')..........Afr.	21·06 S	55·36 E
163	Reus (rā'ōōs).................Sp.	41·08 N	1·05 E
158	Reutlingen (roit'lĭng-ĕn)...F.R.G.	48·29 N	9·14 E
174	Reutov (rĕ-ōōt'ôf) Sov. Un. (Moscow In.)	55·45 N	37·52 E

ăt; finăl; rāte; senâte; ärm; åsk; sofȧ; fâre; ch-choose; dh-as th in other; bē; êvent; bĕt; recĕnt; cratēr; g-go; gh-guttural g; bĭt; ĭ-short neutral; rīde; K-guttural k as ch in German ich;

Page	Name Pronunciation Region	Lat. °′	Long. °′
	Reval, see Tallinn		
174	Revda (ryâv'dá) Sov. Un. (Urals In.)	56·48 N	59·57 E
93	Revelstoke (rěv'ěl-stōk) Can.	51·59 N	118·12 W
127	Reventazon, R. (rå-věn-tä-zōn') C. R.	10·10 N	83·30 W
99	Revere (rê-vēr') Ma. (In.)	42·24 N	71·01 W
92	Revillagigedo Chan (rě-vĭl'á-gĭ-gē'dō). Ak.	55·10 N	131·13 W
92	Revillagigedo I. Ak.	55·35 N	131·23 W
122	Revillagigedo, Islas (I.) (ē's-läs-rě-věl-yä-hě'gě-dô). Mex.	18·45 N	111·00 W
160	Revin (rē-văN) Fr.	49·56 N	4·34 E
184	Rewa (rā'wä) India	24·41 N	81·11 E
184	Rewāri India	28·19 N	76·39 E
111	Rexburg (rěks'bûrg) Id.	43·50 N	111·48 W
118	Rey, L. (rā) Mex.	27·00 N	103·33 W
127	Rey, Isla del (I.) (ē's-lä-děl-rā'ē). Pan.	8·20 N	78·40 W
134	Reyes (rā'yěs) Bol.	14·19 S	67·16 W
114	Reyes, Pt. Ca.	38·00 N	123·00 W
146	Reykjanes (C.) (rā'kyà-něs) Ice.	63·37 N	24·33 W
150	Reykjavik (rā'kyà-vēk) Ice.	64·09 N	21·39 W
118	Reynosa (rā-ē-nō'sä) Mex.	26·05 N	98·21 W
186	Rezā'īyeh (rě-zī'â) Iran	37·30 N	45·15 E
166	Rēzekne (rå'zěk-ně) Sov. Un.	56·31 N	27·19 E
174	Rezh (rězh') Sov. Un. (Urals In.)	57·22 N	61·23 E
167	Rezina (ryězh'ě-nĭ) Sov. Un.	47·44 N	28·56 E
164	Rhaetien Alps (Mts.) It.	46·22 N	10·33 E
155	Rheden (rā'děn) Neth.	52·02 N	6·02 E
161	Rheinberg (rīn'běrgh) F.R.G. (Ruhr In.)	51·33 N	6·37 E
158	Rheine (rī'ně) F.R.G.	52·16 N	7·26 E
158	Rheinland-Pfalz (Rhineland-Palatinate) (State) F.R.G.	50·05 N	6·40 E
158	Rhein R. (rīn) F.R.G.	50·34 N	7·21 E
161	Rheydt (rě'yt) F.R.G. (Ruhr In.)	51·10 N	6·28 E
140	Rhine (R.) Eur.	50·34 N	7·21 E
109	Rhinelander (rīn'lăn-dēr) Wi.	45·39 N	89·25 W
149	Rhin Kanal (Can.) (rēn kä-näl') G.D.R. (Berlin In.)	52·47 N	12·40 E
149	Rhin R. (rēn) G.D.R. (Berlin In.)	52·52 N	12·49 E
106	Rhode I. RI (Providence In.)	41·31 N	71·14 W
103	Rhode Island (State) (rōd ī'lănd) U. S.	41·35 N	71·40 W
213	Rhodes (rôdz) S. Afr. (Natal In.)	30·48 S	27·56 E
165	Rhodope Mts. (rô'dô-pě) Bul.	42·00 N	24·08 E
154	Rhondda (rŏn'dhà) Wales	51·40 N	3·40 W
160	Rhône (R.) (rōn) Fr.	45·14 N	4·53 E
149	Rhoon Neth. (Amsterdam In.)	51·52 N	4·24 E
154	Rhum (I.) (rŭm) Scot.	57·00 N	6·20 W
135	Riachão (rē-ä-chouN') Braz.	7·15 S	46·30 W
113	Rialto (rē-ăl'tō) Ca. (In.)	34·06 N	117·23 W
183	Riau (Prov.) Indon. (Singapore In.)	0·56 N	101·25 E
196	Riau, Kepulauan (I.) Indon.	0·30 N	104·55 E
183	Riau, Selat (Str.) Indon. (Singapore In.)	0·40 N	104·27 E
162	Riaza (R.) (rê-ä'thä) Sp.	41·25 N	3·25 W
162	Ribadavia (rē-bä-dhä'vē-ä) Sp.	42·18 N	8·06 W
162	Ribadeo (rē-bä-dhā'ō) Sp.	37·32 N	7·05 W
162	Ribadesella (rē'bä-dā-sāl'yä) Sp.	43·30 N	5·02 W
217	Ribauè Moz.	14·57 S	38·17 E
154	Ribble, R. (rĭb''l) Eng.	53·10 N	3·15 W
156	Ribe (rē'bě) Den.	55·20 N	8·45 E
137	Ribeirão Prêto (rē-bä-rouN-prě'tō) Braz. (Rio de Janeiro In.)	21·11 S	47·47 W
116	Ribera (rē-bě'rä) NM	35·23 N	105·27 W
134	Riberalta (rē-bà-räl'tä) Bol.	11·06 S	66·02 W
109	Rib Lake (rĭb lāk) Wi.	45·20 N	90·11 W
114	Rice (rīs) Ca.	34·05 N	114·50 W
105	Rice (L.) Can.	44·05 N	78·10 W
113	Rice L. Mn. (Minneapolis, St. Paul In.)	45·10 N	93·09 W
109	Rice Lake Wi.	45·30 N	91·44 W
101	Richards I. (rĭch'ērds) Can.	69·45 N	135·30 W
113	Richards Landing (lănd'ĭng) Can. (Sault Ste. Marie In.)	46·18 N	84·02 W
113	Richardson (rĭch'ērd-sŭn) Tx. (Dallas, Fort Worth In.)	32·56 N	96·44 W
112	Richardson Wa. (Seattle In.)	48·27 N	122·54 W
90	Richardson Mts. Can.	66·58 N	136·19 W
105	Richardson Park (pärk) De.	39·45 N	75·35 W
105	Richelieu (R.) (rēsh'lyû') Can.	45·05 N	73·25 W
113	Richfield (rĭch-fēld) Mn. (Minneapolis, St. Paul In.)	44·53 N	93·17 W
107	Richfield Oh. (Cleveland In.)	41·14 N	81·38 W
115	Richfield Ut.	38·45 N	112·05 W
105	Richford (rĭch'fērd) Vt.	45·00 N	72·35 W
117	Rich Hill (rĭch hĭl) Mo.	38·05 N	94·21 W
98	Richibucto (rĭ-chĭ-bŭk'tō) Can.	46·41 N	64·52 W
120	Richland (rĭch'lănd) Ga.	32·05 N	84·40 W
110	Richland Wa.	46·17 N	119·19 W
109	Richland Center (sěn'tēr) Wi.	43·20 N	90·25 W
205	Richmond (rĭch'mŭnd) Austl.	20·47 S	143·14 E
202	Richmond Austl. (Sydney In.)	33·36 S	150·45 E
112	Richmond Ca. (San Francisco In.)	37·56 N	122·21 W
98	Richmond Can.	45·40 N	72·07 W
89	Richmond Can. (Ottawa In.)	45·12 N	75·49 W
107	Richmond Il. (Chicago In.)	42·29 N	88·18 W
104	Richmond In.	39·50 N	85·00 W
104	Richmond Ky.	37·45 N	84·20 W
117	Richmond Mo.	39·16 N	93·58 W
119	Richmond Tx.	29·35 N	95·45 W
213	Richmond S. Afr. (Natal In.)	29·52 S	30·17 E
111	Richmond Ut.	41·55 N	111·50 W
105	Richmond Va.	37·35 N	77·30 W
112	Richmond Beach Wa. (Seattle In.)	47·47 N	122·23 W
113	Richmond Heights Mo. (St. Louis In.)	38·38 N	90·20 W
112	Richmond Highlands Wa. (Seattle In.)	47·46 N	122·22 W
89	Richmond Hill (hĭl) Can. (Toronto In.)	43·53 N	79·26 W
120	Richton (rĭch'tŭn) Ms.	31·20 N	89·54 W
104	Richwood (rĭch'wŏŏd) WV	38·10 N	80·30 W
149	Ridderkerk Neth. (Amsterdam In.)	51·52 N	4·35 E
89	Rideau (R.) Can. (Ottawa In.)	45·17 N	75·41 W
105	Rideau L. (rē-dō') Can.	44·40 N	76·20 W
106	Ridgefield (rĭj'fēld) Ct. (New York In.)	41·16 N	73·30 W
112	Ridgefield Wa. (Portland In.)	45·49 N	122·40 W
105	Rigeley (rĭj'lē) WV	39·40 N	78·45 W
107	Ridgeway (rĭj'wā) Can. (Buffalo In.)	42·53 N	79·02 W
106	Ridgewood (ridj'wŏŏd) NJ (New York In.)	40·59 N	74·08 W
105	Ridgway Pa.	41·25 N	78·40 W
95	Riding Mtn. (rīd'ĭng) Can.	50·37 N	99·37 W
90	Riding Mountain Natl. Park (rīd'ĭng). Can.	50·59 N	99·19 W
128	Riding Rocks (Is.) Ba.	25·20 N	79·10 W
213	Riebeek-Oos S. Afr. (Natal In.)	33·14 S	26·09 E
158	Ried (rēd) Aus.	48·13 N	13·30 E
158	Riesa (rē'zà) G.D.R.	51·17 N	13·17 E
164	Rieti (rê-â'tē) It.	42·25 N	12·51 E
213	Rievleidam (L.) S. Afr. (Johannesburg & Pretoria In.)	25·52 S	28·18 E
115	Rifle (rī'f'l) Co.	39·35 N	107·50 W
157	Rīga (rē'gà) Sov. Un.	56·55 N	24·05 E
157	Rīga, G. of Sov. Un.	57·56 N	23·05 E
186	Rīgān Iran	28·45 N	58·55 E
89	Rigaud (rê-gō') Can. (Montreal In.)	45·29 N	74·18 W
111	Rigby (rĭg'bê) Id.	43·40 N	111·55 W
186	Rīgestān (Reg.) Afr.	30·53 N	64·42 E
91	Rigolet (rĭg-ō-lā') Can.	54·10 N	58·40 W
157	Riihimäki Fin.	60·44 N	24·44 E
164	Rijeka (Fiume) (rĭ-yě'kä) Yugo.	45·22 N	14·24 E
149	Rijkevorsel Bel. (Brussels In.)	51·21 N	4·46 E
149	Rijswijk Neth. (Amsterdam In.)	52·03 N	4·19 E
159	Rika R. (rê'kà) Sov. Un.	48·21 N	23·37 E
160	Rille (R.) (rēl) Fr.	49·12 N	0·43 E
215	Rima (R.) Nig.	13·30 N	5·50 E
159	Rimavska Sobota (rē'màf-skä sô'bô-tà). Czech.	48·25 N	20·01 E
156	Rimbo (rēm'bŏŏ) Swe.	59·45 N	18·22 E
164	Rimini (rē'mē-nē) It.	44·03 N	12·33 E
165	Rîmnicu Sărat Rom.	45·24 N	27·06 E
165	Rîmnicu-Vîlcea Rom.	45·07 N	24·22 E
98	Rimouski (rē-mōōs'kē) Can.	48·27 N	68·32 W
124	Rinc n de Romos (rēn-kōn dā rô-mōs'). Mex.	22·13 N	102·21 W
156	Ringkøbing (rĭng'kûb-ĭng) Den.	56·06 N	8·14 E
156	Ringkøbing Fd. Den.	55·55 N	8·04 E
156	Ringsaker (rĭngs'äk-ēr) Nor.	60·55 N	10·40 E
156	Ringsted (rĭng'stědh) Den.	55·27 N	11·49 E
150	Ringvassöy (I.) (rĭng'väs-ûē). Nor.	69·58 N	16·43 E
202	Ringwood Austl. (Melbourne In.)	37·49 S	145·14 E
196	Rinjani, Gunung (Mtn.) Indon.	8·39 S	116·22 E
122	Rio Abajo (rē'ō-ä-bä'кô) Pan. (In.)	9·01 N	78·30 W
124	Rio Balsas (rê'ō-bäl-säs) Mex.	17·59 N	99·45 W
134	Riobamba (rē'ō-bäm-bä) Ec.	1·45 S	78·37 W
137	Rio Bonito (rē'ŏŏ bō-nē'tŏŏ) Braz. (Rio de Janeiro In.)	22·44 S	42·38 W
134	Rio Branco (rē'ŏŏ bräŋ'kŏŏ) Braz.	9·57 S	67·50 W
136	Río Branco (rĭô blăncô) Ur.	32·33 S	53·29 W
135	Rio Branco (Ter.) Braz.	2·35 N	61·25 W
137	Rio Casca (rē'ō-kà's-kä) Braz. (Rio de Janeiro In.)	20·15 S	42·39 W
135	Rio Chico (rê'ō chē'kŏ) Ven. (In.)	10·20 N	65·58 W
137	Rio Claro (rē'ŏŏ klä'rŏŏ) Braz. (Rio de Janeiro In.)	21·25 S	47·33 W
136	Río Cuarto (rē'ō kwär'tō) Arg.	33·05 S	64·15 W
137	Rio das Flores (rē'ō-däs-flô-rěs) Braz. (Rio de Janeiro In.)	22·10 S	43·35 W
136	Rio de Janeiro (rē'ŏŏ dā zhä-nâ'ē-rŏŏ) Braz. (Rio de Janeiro In.)	22·50 S	43·20 W
135	Rio de Janeiro (State) Braz.	22·27 S	42·43 W
127	Río de Jesús (rē'ō-dě-кě-sōō's) Pan.	7·54 N	80·59 W
136	Río Dercero (rê'ō děr-sě'rô) Arg.	32·12 S	63·59 W
125	Rio Frío (rē'ō-frē'ô) Mex. (In.)	19·21 N	98·40 W
136	Río Gallegos (rē'ō gä-lā'gōs) Arg.	51·43 S	69·15 W
136	Rio Grande (rē'ŏŏ grän'dě) Braz.	31·04 S	52·14 W
124	Rio Grande (rē'ō grän'dā) Mex.	23·51 N	102·59 W
118	Riogrande (rē'ō grăn-dā) Tx.	26·23 N	98·48 W
115	Rio Grande (R.) (rē'ŏŏ grän'dě) Co.	37·44 N	106·51 W
135	Rio Grande do Norte (State) (rē'ŏŏ grän'dě dōō nôr'tě). Braz.	5·26 S	37·20 W
136	Rio Grande do Sul (State) (rē'ŏŏ grän'dě-dô-sōō'l). Braz.	29·00 S	54·00 W
134	Ríohacha (rē'ō-ä'chä) Col.	11·30 N	72·54 W
127	Río Hato (rē'ō-ä'tō) Pan.	8·19 N	80·11 W
160	Riom (rê-ôN') Fr.	45·54 N	3·08 E
209	Rio Muni (Prov.) (rē'ō mōō'nē) Equat. Gui.	1·47 N	8·33 E
134	Ríonegro (rê'ō-ně'grō) Col. (In.)	6·09 N	75·22 W
136	Río Negro (Prov.) (rē'ō nā'grō) Arg.	40·15 S	68·15 W
137	Río Negro (Dept.) (rê'ō-ně'grō) Ur. (Buenos Aires In.)	32·48 S	57·45 W
136	Rio Negro, Embalse del (Res.) (ěm-bä'l-sě-děl-rě'ō-ně'grō). Ur.	32·45 S	55·50 W
164	Rionero (rē-ō-nâ'rô) It.	40·55 N	15·42 E
137	Rio Novo (rē'ō-nô'vô) Braz. (Rio de Janeiro In.)	21·30 S	43·08 W
135	Rio Pardo de Minas (rē'ō pär'dō-dě-mē'näs). Braz.	15·43 S	42·24 W
137	Rio Pombo (rē'ō pôm'bä) Braz. (Rio de Janeiro In.)	21·17 S	43·09 W
137	Rio Sorocaba, Represado (Res.) (rě-prě-sä-dô-rē'ō-sô-rô-kä'bä) Braz. (Rio de Janeiro In.)	23·37 S	47·19 W
134	Ríosucio (rē'ō-sōō'syô) Col. (In.)	5·25 N	75·41 W
163	Riou, Oued (R.) (ōō-ěd rĭ-ōō) Alg.	35·45 N	1·18 E
196	Riouw, Pulau-Pulau (Is.) Indon.	0·30 N	104·55 E
135	Rio Verde (věr'dě) Braz.	17·47 S	50·49 W
124	Ríoverde (rē'ō-věr'då) Mex.	21·54 N	99·59 W
148	Ripley (rĭp'lē) Eng.	53·03 N	1·24 W
120	Ripley Ms.	34·44 N	88·55 W
120	Ripley Tn.	35·44 N	89·34 W
163	Ripoll (rê-pōl'') Sp.	42·10 N	2·10 E
109	Ripon (rĭp'ŏn) Wi.	43·49 N	88·50 W
204	Ripon (I.) Austl.	20·05 S	118·10 E
211	Ripon Falls Ug.	0·38 N	33·02 E
134	Risaralda (Dept.) Col. (In.)	6·45 S	76·00 W
205	Risdon (rĭz'dŭn) Austl.	42·37 S	147·32 E
194	Rishiri (I.) (rē-shē'rē) Jap.	45·10 N	141·08 E
183	Rishon le Ziyyon Isr. (Palestine In.)	31·57 N	34·48 E
184	Rishra India (In.)	22·42 N	88·22 E
104	Rising Sun (rīz'ĭng sŭn) In.	38·55 N	84·55 W
156	Risor (rēs'ûr) Nor.	58·44 N	9·10 E
134	Ritacuva, Alto (Mtn.) (ä'l-tô-rē-tä-kōō'vä). Col.	6·22 N	72·13 W
107	Rittman (rĭt'năn) Oh. (Cleveland In.)	40·58 N	81·47 W
110	Ritzville (rĭts'vĭl) Wa.	47·08 N	118·23 W
156	Riuvenfjell (Mts.) (rĭu-věn-fyěl') Nor.	59·20 N	6·55 E
129	Riva (rē'vä) Dom. Rep.	19·10 N	69·55 W
164	Riva (rê'vä) It.	45·54 N	10·49 E
106	Riva (rĭ'vă) Md. (Baltimore In.)	38·57 N	76·36 W
126	Rivas (rē'väs) Nic.	11·25 N	85·51 W
160	Rive-de-Gier (rēv-dě-zhē-ā') Fr.	45·32 N	4·37 E
136	Rivera (rê-vā'rä) Ur.	30·52 S	55·32 W
210	River Cess (rĭv'ěr sěs) Lib.	5·46 N	9·52 W
107	Riverdale (rĭv'ēr dāl) Il. (Chicago In.)	41·38 N	87·36 W
113	Riverdale Ut. (Salt Lake City In.)	41·11 N	112·00 W
120	River Falls Al.	31·20 N	86·25 W
109	River Falls Wi.	44·48 N	92·38 W
105	Riverhead (rĭv'ēr hěd) NY	40·55 N	72·40 W
203	Riverina (Reg.) (rĭv-ēr-ē'nä). Austl.	34·55 S	144·30 E
92	River Jordan (jôr'dăn) Can. (Seattle In.)	48·25 N	124·03 W
113	River Oaks (ōkz) Tx. (Dallas, Fort Worth In.)	32·47 N	97·24 W
107	River Rouge (rōōzh) Mi. (Detroit In.)	42·16 N	83·09 W
95	Rivers Can.	50·01 N	100·15 W
113	Riverside (rĭv'ēr-sīd) Ca. (Los Angeles In.)	33·59 N	117·21 W
106	Riverside NJ (Philadelphia In.)	40·02 N	74·58 W
92	Rivers Inlet Can.	51·45 N	127·15 W
202	Riverstone Austl. (Sydney In.)	33·41 S	150·52 E
105	Riverton Va.	39·00 N	78·15 W
111	Riverton Wy.	43·02 N	108·24 W
160	Rivesaltes (rēv'zält') Fr.	42·48 N	2·48 E
121	Riviera Beach (rĭv-ĭ-ěr'à bēch) Fl. (In.)	26·46 N	80·04 W
106	Riviera Beach Md. (Baltimore In.)	39·10 N	76·32 W
89	Rivie're Beaudette (bō-dět') Can. (Montreal In.)	45·14 N	74·20 W
98	Rivière-du-Loup (rē-vyâr' dü lōō') Can.	47·50 N	69·32 W
89	Rivière Que Barre (rēv-yěr' kē-bär) Can. (Edmonton In.)	53·47 N	113·51 W
98	Rivière-Trois-Pistoles (trwä'pěs-tôl'). Can.	48·07 N	69·10 W
186	Riyadh (Ar Riyāḍ) Sau. Ar.	24·31 N	46·47 E

ng-sing; ŋ-baŋk; N-nasalized n; nŏd; cŏmmit; ōld; ôbey; ôrder; fōōd; fŏŏt; ou-out; s-soft; sh-dish; th-thin; pūre; ûnite; ûrn; stŭd; circŭs ü-as "y" in study; '-indeterminate vowel.

Page	Name Pronunciation	Region	Lat. °'	Long. °'
171	Rize (rē'zĕ)	Tur.	41·00 N	40·30 E
190	Rizhao (rē-jou)	China	35·27 N	119·28 E
165	Rizzuto, C. (rēt-sōō'tô)	It.	38·53 N	17·05 E
156	Rjukan (ryōō'kän)	Nor.	59·53 N	8·30 E
160	Roanne (rō-än')	Fr.	46·02 N	4·04 E
120	Roanoke (rō'á-nōk)	Al.	33·08 N	85·21 W
121	Roanoke	Va.	37·16 N	79·55 W
121	Roanoke (R.)	NC-Va.	36·17 N	77·22 W
121	Roanoke (Staunton) (R.)	Va.	37·05 N	79·20 W
121	Roanoke Rapids	NC	36·25 N	77·40 W
121	Roanoke Rapids, L.	NC	36·28 N	77·37 W
115	Roan Plat. (rōn)	Co.	39·25 N	108·50 W
126	Roatan (rō-ä-tän')	Hond.	16·18 N	86·33 W
126	Roatan I.	Hond.	16·19 N	86·46 W
212	Robbeneiland (I.)	S. Afr. (In.)	33·48 S	18·22 E
107	Robbins (rŏb'ĭnz)	Il. (Chicago In.)	41·39 N	87·42 W
113	Robbinsdale (rŏb'ĭnz-dāl)	Mn. (Minneapolis, St. Paul In.)	45·03 N	93·22 W
112	Robe (rōb)	Wa. (Seattle In.)	48·06 N	121·50 W
205	Roberts, Mt. (rŏb'ērts)	Austl.	32·05 S	152·30 E
110	Roberts, Pt. (rŏb'ērts)	Wa. (Vancouver In.)	48·58 N	123·05 W
99	Robertson, Lac (L.)	Can.	51·00 N	59·10 W
214	Robertsport (rŏb'ērts-pōrt)	Lib.	6·45 N	11·22 W
91	Roberval (rŏb'ēr-văl) (rô-bĕr-vál')	Can.	48·32 N	72·15 W
104	Robinson (rŏb'ĭn-sŭn)	Il.	39·00 N	87·45 W
99	Robinson's	Can.	48·16 N	58·50 W
203	Robinvale (rŏb-ĭn'vāl)	Austl.	34·45 S	142·45 E
95	Roblin	Can.	51·15 N	101·25 W
93	Robson, Mt. (rŏb'sŭn)	Can.	53·07 N	119·09 W
119	Robstown (rŏbz'toun)	Tx.	27·46 N	97·41 W
163	Roca, Cabo da (C.) (kå'bō-dä-rô'kă)	Port. (Lisbon In.)	38·47 N	9·30 W
212	Roçadas (rô-kä'däs)	Ang.	16·50 S	15·05 E
135	Rocas, Atol das (Atoll) (ä-tôl-däs-rō'kås)	Braz.	3·50 S	33·46 W
133	Rocedos São Pedro E São Paulo (I.) (rô-zĕ'dôs-souN-pĕ'drô-ĕ-souN-päōō-lô)	Braz.	1·50 N	30·00 W
136	Rocha (rō'chås)	Ur.	34·26 S	54·14 W
148	Rochdale (rŏch'dāl)	Eng.	53·37 N	2·09 W
129	Roche à Bateau (rôsh à bá-tō')	Hai.	18·10 N	74·00 W
160	Rochefort (rôsh-fŏr')	Fr.	45·55 N	0·57 W
109	Rochelle (rô-shĕl')	Il.	41·53 N	89·06 W
104	Rochester (rŏch'ĕs-tēr)	In.	41·05 N	86·20 W
107	Rochester	Mi. (Detroit In.)	42·41 N	83·09 W
109	Rochester	Mn.	44·01 N	92·30 W
105	Rochester	NH	43·20 N	71·00 W
105	Rochester	NY	43·15 N	77·35 W
107	Rochester	Pa. (Pittsburgh In.)	40·42 N	80·16 W
109	Rock (R.)	Il.	41·40 N	89·52 W
108	Rock (R.)	Ia.	43·17 N	96·13 W
112	Rock (R.)	Or. (Portland In.)	45·34 N	122·52 W
112	Rock (R.)	Or. (Portland In.)	45·52 N	123·14 W
106	Rockaway (rŏck'å-wā)	NJ (New York In.)	40·54 N	74·30 W
202	Rockbank	Austl. (Melbourne In.)	37·44 S	144·40 E
89	Rockcliffe Park (rok'klĭf pärk)	Can. (Ottawa In.)	45·27 N	75·40 W
94	Rock Cr. (rŏk)	Can.	49·01 N	107·00 W
107	Rock Cr.	Il. (Chicago In.)	41·16 N	87·54 W
111	Rock Cr.	Mt.	46·25 N	113·40 W
110	Rock Cr.	Or.	45·30 N	120·06 W
110	Rock Cr.	Wa.	47·09 N	117·50 W
106	Rockdale	Md. (Baltimore In.)	39·22 N	76·49 W
119	Rockdale (rŏk'dāl)	Tx.	30·39 N	97·00 W
109	Rock Falls (rŏk fôlz)	Il.	41·45 N	89·42 W
109	Rockford (rŏk'fērd)	Il.	42·16 N	89·07 W
205	Rockhampton (rŏk-hămp'tŭn)	Austl.	23·26 S	150·29 E
121	Rockhill (rŏk'hĭl)	SC	34·55 N	81·01 W
121	Rockingham (rŏk'ĭng-hăm)	NC	34·54 N	79·45 W
148	Rockingham For. (rok'ĭng-hăm)	Eng.	52·29 N	0·43 W
109	Rock Island	Il.	41·31 N	90·37 W
110	Rock Island Dam (ī lănd)	Wa.	47·17 N	120·33 W
89	Rockland (rŏk'lănd)	Can. (Ottawa In.)	45·33 N	75·17 W
98	Rockland	Me.	44·06 N	69·09 W
99	Rockland	Ma. (In.)	42·07 N	70·55 W
203	Rockland Res.	Austl.	36·55 S	142·20 E
120	Rockmart (rŏk'märt)	Ga.	33·58 N	85·00 W
113	Rockmont (rŏk'mŏnt)	Wi. (Duluth In.)	46·34 N	91·54 W
104	Rockport (rŏk'pōrt)	In.	38·20 N	87·00 W
99	Rockport	Ma. (In.)	42·39 N	70·37 W
117	Rockport	Mo.	40·25 N	95·30 W
119	Rockport	Tx.	28·03 N	97·03 W
108	Rock Rapids (răp'ĭdz)	Ia.	43·26 N	96·10 W
129	Rock Sd.	Ba.	24·50 N	76·05 W
118	Rocksprings (rŏk sprĭngs)	Tx.	30·02 N	100·12 W
111	Rock Springs	Wy.	41·35 N	109·13 W
135	Rockstone (rŏk'stôn)	Guy.	5·55 N	57·27 W
108	Rock Valley (văl'ĭ)	Ia.	43·13 N	96·17 W
104	Rockville (rŏk'vĭl)	In.	39·45 N	87·15 W
106	Rockville	Md. (Baltimore In.)	39·05 N	77·11 W
106	Rockville Centre (sĕn'tēr)	NY (New York In.)	40·39 N	73·39 W
117	Rockwall (rŏk'wôl)	Tx.	32·55 N	96·23 W
109	Rockwell City (rŏk'wĕl)	Ia.	42·22 N	94·37 W
89	Rockwood (rŏk-wŏŏd)	Can. (Toronto In.)	43·37 N	80·08 W
98	Rockwood	Me.	45·39 N	69·45 W
120	Rockwood	Tn.	35·51 N	84·41 W
111	Rocky Boys Ind. Res.	Mt.	48·08 N	109·34 W
116	Rocky Ford	Co.	38·02 N	103·43 W
106	Rocky Hill (hĭl)	NJ (New York In.)	40·24 N	74·38 W
96	Rocky Island L.	Can.	46·56 N	83·04 W
121	Rocky Mount	NC	35·55 N	77·47 W
93	Rocky Mountain House	Can.	52·22 N	114·55 W
116	Rocky Mountain Natl. Park	Co.	40·29 N	106·06 W
75	Rocky Mts.	N. A.	50·00 N	114·00 W
107	Rocky River	Oh. (Cleveland In.)	41·29 N	81·51 W
107	Rocky R., East Br.	Oh. (Cleveland In.)	41·13 N	81·43 W
107	Rocky R., West Br.	Oh. (Cleveland In.)	41·17 N	81·54 W
129	Rodas (rō'dhås)	Cuba	22·20 N	80·35 W
148	Roden (R.) (rō'dĕn)	Eng.	52·49 N	2·38 W
112	Rodeo (rō'dēō)	Ca. (San Francisco In.)	38·02 N	122·16 W
118	Rodeo (rô-dā'ō)	Mex.	25·12 N	104·34 W
92	Roderick I. (rŏd'ē-rĭk)	Can.	52·40 N	128·22 W
160	Rodez (rō-dĕz')	Fr.	44·22 N	2·34 E
153	Rōdhos	Grc.	36·24 N	28·15 E
153	Ródhos (I.)	Grc.	36·00 N	28·29 E
159	Rodnei, Muntii (Mts.) (rôd'nĕ-ê)	Rom.	47·41 N	24·05 E
166	Rodniki (rôd'nê-kê)	Sov. Un.	57·08 N	41·48 E
165	Rodonit, Kep I (C.)	Alb.	41·38 N	19·01 E
	Rodosto, see Tekirdağ			
106	Roebling (rōb'lĭng)	NJ (Philadelphia In.)	40·07 N	74·48 W
204	Roebourne (rō'bŭrn)	Austl.	20·50 S	117·15 E
204	Roebuck, B. (rō'bŭck)	Austl.	18·15 S	121·10 E
218	Roedtan	S. Afr. (Johannesburg & Pretoria In.)	24·37 S	29·08 E
155	Roermond (rōōr'mônt)	Neth.	51·11 N	6·00 E
155	Roeselare	Bel.	50·55 N	3·05 E
112	Roesiger (L.) (rōz'ĭ-gēr)	Wa. (Seattle In.)	47·59 N	121·56 W
91	Roes Welcome Sd. (rōz)	Can.	64·10 N	87·23 W
166	Rogachëv (rôg'á-chyôf)	Sov. Un.	53·07 N	30·04 E
165	Rogatica (rô-gä'tê-tsä)	Yugo.	43·46 N	19·00 E
159	Rogatin (rô-gä'tĭn)	Sov. Un.	49·22 N	24·37 E
117	Rogers (rŏj-ērz)	Ar.	36·19 N	94·07 W
104	Rogers City	Mi.	45·30 N	83·50 W
120	Rogersville	Tn.	36·21 N	83·00 W
160	Rognac (rŏn-yäk')	Fr. (In.)	43·29 N	5·15 E
134	Rogoaguado (L.) (rō'gō-ä-gwä-dō)	Bol.	12·42 S	66·46 W
167	Rogovskaya (rô-gôf'ská-yá)	Sov. Un.	45·43 N	38·42 E
158	Rogózno (rô'gôzh-nô)	Pol.	52·44 N	16·53 E
110	Rogue R. (rōg)	Or.	42·32 N	124·13 W
156	Röikenviken (rûē'kĕn-vêk-ĕn)	Nor.	60·27 N	10·26 E
137	Rojas (rō'häs)	Arg. (Buenos Aires In.)	34·11 S	60·42 W
125	Rojo, Cabo (C.) (rō'hō)	Mex.	21·35 N	97·16 W
123	Rojo, Cabo (C.) (rō'hō)	P. R. (Puerto Rico In.)	17·55 N	67·14 W
214	Rokel (R.)	S. L.	9·00 N	11·55 W
195	Rokkō-Zan (Mtn.) (rôk'kō zän)	Jap. (Osaka In.)	34·46 N	135·16 E
158	Rokycany (rô'kĭ'tsá-nĭ)	Czech.	49·44 N	13·37 E
134	Roldanillo (rôl-dä-nē'l-yō)	Col. (In.)	4·24 N	76·09 W
117	Rolla	Mo.	37·56 N	91·45 W
108	Rolla	ND	48·52 N	99·32 W
156	Rollag (rōō'lägh)	Nor.	59·55 N	8·48 E
129	Rolleville	Ba.	23·40 N	76·00 W
203	Roma (rō'må)	Austl.	26·30 S	148·48 E
213	Roma	Leso. (Natal In.)	29·28 S	27·43 E
163	Roma (Rome) (rō'mä) (rōm)	It. (Rome In.)	41·52 N	12·37 E
99	Romaine (R.) (rô-mĕn')	Can.	51·22 N	63·23 W
159	Roman (rō'män)	Rom.	46·56 N	26·57 E
146	Romania (rō-mā'nē-à)	Eur.	46·18 N	22·53 E
121	Romano, C. (rō-mā'nō)	Fl. (In.)	25·48 N	82·00 W
128	Romano, Cayo (I.) (kä'yō-rô-mä'nô)	Cuba	22·15 N	78·00 W
174	Romanovo (rô-mä'nô-vô)	Sov. Un. (Urals In.)	59·09 N	61·24 E
160	Romans-sur-Isère (rô-mäN'-sür-ē-sĕr')	Fr.	45·04 N	4·49 E
197	Romblon (rōm-blōn')	Phil. (In.)	12·34 N	122·16 E
197	Romblon I.	Phil. (In.)	12·33 N	122·17 E
120	Rome (rōm)	Ga.	34·14 N	85·10 W
105	Rome	NY	43·15 N	75·25 W
	Rome, see Roma			
104	Romeo (rō'mê-ō)	Mi.	42·50 N	83·00 W
148	Romford (rŭm'fērd)	Eng. (London In.)	51·35 N	0·11 E
160	Romilly-sur-Seine (rô-mê-yē'sür-sān')	Fr.	48·32 N	3·41 E
124	Romita (rō-mē'tä)	Mex.	20·53 N	101·32 W
167	Romny (rôm'nĭ)	Sov. Un.	50·46 N	33·31 E
156	Rømø (I.) (rûm'û)	Den.	55·08 N	8·17 E
113	Romoland (rō'mō'lănd)	Ca. (Los Angeles In.)	33·44 N	117·11 W
160	Romorantin (rô-mô-räN-tăN')	Fr.	47·24 N	1·46 E
183	Rompin	Mala. (Singapore In.)	2·42 N	102·30 E
183	Rompin (R.)	Mala. (Singapore In.)	2·54 N	103·10 E
107	Romulus (rom'ū lŭs)	Mi. (Detroit In.)	42·14 N	83·24 W
154	Ronaldsay, North (I.)	Scot.	59·21 N	2·23 W
154	Ronaldsay, South (I.) (rŏn'ăld-s'ā)	Scot.	59·48 N	2·55 W
111	Ronan (rō'nán)	Mt.	47·28 N	114·03 W
135	Roncador, Serra do (Mts.) (sĕr'rá dōō rôn-kä-dôr')	Braz.	12·44 S	52·19 W
162	Roncesvalles (rôn-sĕs-vä'l-yĕs)	Sp.	43·00 N	1·17 W
104	Ronceverte (rŏn'sê-vûrt)	WV	37·45 N	80·30 W
162	Ronda (rōn'dä)	Sp.	37·45 N	5·10 W
134	Rondônia (Ter.)	Braz.	10·15 S	63·07 W
94	Ronge, Lac la (L.) (rŏnzh)	Can.	55·10 N	105·00 W
193	Rongjiang (rôŋ-jyäŋ)	China	25·52 N	108·45 E
193	Rong Xian	China	22·50 N	110·32 E
156	Rønne (rûn'ĕ)	Den.	55·08 N	14·46 E
156	Ronneby (rōn'ĕ-bü)	Swe.	56·13 N	15·17 E
220	Ronne Ice Shelf	Ant.	77·30 S	38·00 W
116	Ront Ra. (Mts.) (rŏnt)	Co.	40·59 N	105·29 W
213	Roodepoort (rō'dĕ-pōrt)	S. Afr. (Johannesburg & Pretoria In.)	26·10 S	27·52 E
117	Roodhouse (rōōd'hous)	Il.	39·29 N	90·21 W
218	Rooiberg	S. Afr. (Johannesburg & Pretoria In.)	24·46 S	27·42 E
149	Roosendaal (rō'zĕn-däl)	Neth. (Amsterdam In.)	51·32 N	4·27 E
115	Roosevelt (rōz''vĕlt)	Ut.	40·20 N	110·00 W
115	Roosevelt (R.)	Az.	33·45 N	111·00 W
135	Roosevelt (R.) (rô'sĕ-vĕlt)	Braz.	9·22 S	60·28 W
220	Roosevelt I.	Ant.	79·30 S	168·00 W
107	Root R.	Wi. (Milwaukee In.)	42·49 N	87·54 W
204	Roper (R.) (rōp'ēr)	Austl.	14·50 S	134·00 E
174	Ropsha (rôp'shà)	Sov. Un. (Leningrad In.)	59·44 N	29·53 E
160	Roquefort	Fr.	43·59 N	3·00 E
134	Roques, Islas los (Is.)	Ven.	21·25 N	67·40 W
137	Roque Pérez (rô'kĕ-pĕ'rĕz)	Arg. (Buenos Aires In.)	35·23 S	59·22 W
163	Roquetas (rô-kā'täs)	Sp.	40·50 N	0·32 E
134	Roraima (Ter.) (rô'rīy-mă)	Braz.	2·00 N	62·15 W
135	Roraima, Mtn. (rô-rä-ē'mä)	Ven.-Guy.	5·12 N	60·52 W
156	Röros (rûr'ôs)	Nor.	62·36 N	11·25 E
158	Rorschach (rōr'shäk)	Switz.	47·27 N	9·28 E
167	Ros' (R.) (rôs)	Sov. Un.	49·40 N	30·22 E
158	Rosa, Monte (Mt.) (mōn'tā rō'zä)	It.	45·56 N	7·51 E
118	Rosales (rō-zä'lās)	Mex.	28·15 N	100·43 W
197	Rosales (rô-sä'lĕs)	Phil. (In.)	15·54 N	120·38 E
124	Rosamorada (rō'zä-mō-rä'dhä)	Mex.	22·06 N	105·16 W
125	Rosaria, Laguna (L.) (lä-gōō'nä-rō-sá'ryä)	Mex.	17·50 N	93·51 W
137	Rosario (rô-zä'rê-ō)	Arg. (Buenos Aires In.)	32·58 S	60·42 W
135	Rosario (rô-zä'rê-ōō)	Braz.	2·49 S	44·15 W
124	Rosario	Mex.	22·58 N	105·54 W
118	Rosario	Mex.	26·31 N	105·40 W
197	Rosario	Phil. (In.)	13·49 N	121·13 W
137	Rosario	Ur. (Buenos Aires In.)	34·19 S	57·24 E
128	Rosario, Cayo (I.) (kä'yō-rô-sä'ryō)	Cuba	21·40 N	81·55 W
136	Rosário do Sul (rô-zä'rê-ōō-dô-sōō'l)	Braz.	30·17 S	54·52 W
135	Rosário Oeste (ō'ĕst'ĕ)	Braz.	14·47 S	56·20 W
112	Rosario Str.	Wa. (Seattle In.)	48·27 N	122·45 W
163	Rosas, Golfo de (G.) (gôl-fô-dĕ-rō'zäs)	Sp.	42·10 N	3·20 E
161	Rosbach (rōz'bäk)	F.R.G. (Ruhr In.)	50·47 N	7·38 E
118	Roscoe (rôs'kō)	Tx.	32·26 N	100·38 W
108	Roseau (rô-zō')	Mn.	48·52 N	95·47 W
127	Roseau	Dominica (In.)	15·17 N	61·23 W
108	Roseau (R.)	Mn.	48·52 N	96·11 W
110	Roseberg (rōz'bûrg)	Or.	43·13 N	123·30 W
93	Rosebud (R.) (rōz'bŭd)	Can.	51·20 N	112·20 W
111	Rosebud Cr.	Mt.	45·48 N	106·34 W
108	Rosebud Ind. Res.	SD	43·13 N	100·42 W
120	Rosedale	Ms.	33·49 N	90·56 W
112	Rosedale	Wa. (Seattle In.)	47·20 N	122·39 W
210	Roseires Res.	Sud.	11·15 N	34·45 E
107	Roselle (rō-zĕl')	Il. (Chicago In.)	41·59 N	88·05 W
89	Rosemere (rōz'mēr)	Can. (Montreal In.)	45·38 N	73·48 W
113	Rosemount (rōz'mount)	Mn. (Minneapolis, St. Paul In.)	44·44 N	93·08 W
218	Rosendal (rô-sĕn'täl)	S. Afr. (Johannesburg & Pretoria In.)	28·32 S	27·56 E
158	Rosenheim (rō'zĕn-hīm)	F.R.G.	47·52 N	12·06 E
94	Rosetown (rōz'toun)	Can.	51·33 N	108·00 W
	Rosetta, see Rashīd			

PRONOUNCING INDEX

Rosettenville — Sabine 337

Page	Name Pronunciation Region	Lat. °'	Long. °'
213	Rosettenville (Neigh.) S. Afr. (Johannesburg & Pretoria In.)	26·15 S	28·04 E
114	Roseville (rōz'vĭl) Ca.	38·44 N	121·19 W
107	Roseville Mi. (Detroit In.)	42·30 N	82·55 W
113	Roseville Mn. (Minneapolis, St. Paul In.)	45·01 N	93·10 W
104	Rosiclare (rōz'ĭ-klâr) Il.	37·30 N	88·15 W
135	Rosignol (rŏs-ĭg-nŏl) Guy.	6·16 N	57·37 W
165	Rosiorii de Vede (rō-shôr'ê dĕ vĕ-dĕ) Rom.	44·06 N	25·00 E
156	Roskilde (rôs'kêl-dĕ) Den.	55·39 N	12·04 E
166	Roslavl' (rôs'läv'l) Sov. Un.	53·56 N	32·52 E
110	Roslyn (rŏz'lĭn) Wa.	47·14 N	121·00 W
167	Rosovka Sov. Un.	47·14 N	36·35 E
161	Rösrath (rûz'rät) F.R.G. (Ruhr In.)	50·53 N	7·11 E
107	Ross (rôs) Oh. (Cincinnati In.)	39·19 N	84·39 W
164	Rossano (rô-sä'nō) It.	39·34 N	16·38 E
89	Ross Cr. Can. (Edmonton In.)	53·50 N	113·08 W
110	Ross Dam Wa.	48·40 N	121·07 W
97	Rosseau (L.) (rôs-sō') Can.	45·15 N	79·30 W
205	Rossel (I.) (rô-sĕl') Pap. N. Gui.	11·31 S	154·00 E
89	Rosser (rôs'sẽr) Can. (Winnipeg In.)	49·59 N	97·27 W
98	Rossignol, L. Can.	44·10 N	65·10 W
95	Ross I. Can.	54·14 N	97·45 W
93	Rossland (rôs'lănd) Can.	49·05 N	118·48 W
214	Rosso Mauritania	16·30 N	15·49 W
167	Rossosh' (rôs'sŭsh) Sov. Un.	50·12 N	39·32 E
213	Rossouw S. Afr. (Natal In.)	31·12 S	27·18 E
220	Ross Sea Ant.	76·00 S	178·00 W
220	Ross Shelf Ice Ant.	81·30 S	175·00 W
120	Rossville (rôs'vĭl) Ga.	34·57 N	85·22 W
94	Rosthern Can.	52·41 N	106·25 W
158	Rostock (rôs'tŭk) G.D.R.	54·04 N	12·06 E
166	Rostov Sov. Un.	57·13 N	39·23 E
167	Rostov (Oblast) Sov. Un.	47·38 N	39·15 E
171	Rostov-na-Donu (rôstôv-nȧ-dô-nōō) Sov. Un.	47·16 N	39·47 E
150	Rösvatn (L.) (rûs-vät'n) Nor.	65·36 N	13·08 E
120	Roswell (rŏz'wĕl) Ga.	34·02 N	84·21 W
116	Roswell NM	33·23 N	104·32 W
116	Rotan (rô-tăn') Tx.	32·51 N	100·27 W
158	Rothenburg F.R.G.	49·20 N	10·10 E
148	Rotherham (rŏdh'ẽr-ăm) Eng.	53·26 N	1·21 W
98	Rothesay (rôth'sâ) Can.	45·23 N	66·00 W
154	Rothesay Scot.	55·50 N	3·14 W
148	Rothwell Eng.	53·44 N	1·30 W
196	Roti, Pulau (I.) (rō'tē) Indon.	10·30 S	122·52 E
203	Roto (rō'tô) Austl.	33·07 S	145·30 E
149	Rotterdam (rôt'ẽr-däm') Neth. (Amsterdam In.)	51·55 N	4·27 E
158	Rottweil (rōt'vīl) F.R.G.	48·10 N	8·36 E
160	Roubaix (rōō-bĕ') Fr.	50·42 N	3·10 E
160	Rouen (rōō-äN') Fr.	49·25 N	1·05 E
107	Rouge, R. Mi. (Detroit In.)	42·30 N	83·15 W
97	Rouge (R.) Can.	46·40 N	74·50 W
89	Rouge (R.) (rōōzh) Can. (Toronto In.)	43·53 N	79·21 W
104	Rough River Res. Ky.	37·45 N	86·10 W
107	Round Lake Il. (Chicago In.)	42·21 N	88·05 W
99	Round Pd. Can.	48·15 N	55·57 W
119	Round Rock Tx.	30·31 N	97·41 W
112	Round Top (Mtn.) (tŏp) Or. (Portland In.)	45·41 N	123·22 W
111	Roundup (round'ŭp) Mt.	46·25 N	108·35 W
154	Rousay (I.) (rōō'zȧ) Scot.	59·10 N	3·04 W
91	Rouyn (rōōn) Can.	48·22 N	79·03 W
150	Rovaniemi (rô'vȧ-nyĕ'mĭ) Fin.	66·29 N	25·45 E
164	Rovato (rô-vä'tō) It.	45·33 N	10·00 E
167	Roven'ki (rô-vĕn'kĭ') Sov. Un.	48·06 N	39·44 E
167	Roven'ki Sov. Un.	49·54 N	38·54 E
164	Rovereto (rō-vå-rā'tô) It.	45·53 N	11·05 E
164	Rovigo (rô-vē'gô) It.	45·05 N	11·48 E
164	Rovinj (rô'vēn') Yugo.	45·05 N	13·40 E
134	Rovira (rô-vē'rä) Col. (In.)	4·14 N	75·13 W
159	Rovno (rôv'nô) Sov. Un.	50·37 N	26·17 E
167	Rovno (Oblast) Sov. Un.	50·55 N	27·00 E
167	Rovnoye (rôv'nô-yĕ) Sov. Un.	48·11 N	31·46 E
217	Rovuma (Ruvuma) (R.) Moz.-Tan.	10·50 S	39·50 E
99	Rowley (rou'lē) Ma. (In.)	42·43 N	70·53 W
113	Roxana (rŏks'ăn-nȧ) Il. (St. Louis In.)	38·51 N	90·05 W
196	Roxas (rô-xäs) Phil.	11·30 N	122·47 E
121	Roxboro (rŏks' bŭr-ô) NC	36·22 N	78·58 W
214	Roxo, Cap (C.) Senegal	12·20 N	16·43 W
116	Roy (roi) NM	35·54 N	104·09 W
113	Roy Ut. (Salt Lake City In.)	41·10 N	112·02 W
128	Royal (I.) Ba.	25·30 N	76·50 W
154	Royal Can. (roi-ăl) Ire.	53·28 N	6·45 W
213	Royal Natal Natl. Pk. (roi'ăl) S. Afr. (Natal In.)	28·35 S	28·54 E
112	Royal Oak (roi'ăl ōk) Can. (Seattle In.)	48·30 N	123·24 W
107	Royal Oak Mi. (Detroit In.)	42·29 N	83·09 W
104	Royalton (roi'ăl-tŭn) Mi.	42·00 N	86·25 W
160	Royan (rwä-yäN') Fr.	45·40 N	1·02 W
160	Roye (rwä) Fr.	49·43 N	2·40 E
106	Royersford (rô' yẽrz-fẽrd) Pa. (Philadelphia In.)	40·11 N	75·32 W
120	Royston (roiz'tŭn) Ga.	34·15 N	83·06 W
148	Royton (roi'tŭn) Eng.	53·34 N	2·07 W
161	Rozay-en-Brie (rô-zā-ĕN-brē') Fr. (Paris In.)	48·41 N	2·57 E
174	Rozhaya R. (rô'zhȧ-yȧ) Sov. Un. (Moscow In.)	55·20 N	37·37 E
159	Rožňava (rôzh'nyȧ-vȧ) Czech.	48·39 N	20·32 E
171	Rtishchevo ('r-tĭsh'chĕ-vô) Sov. Un.	52·15 N	43·40 E
190	Ru (R.) (rōō) China	33·07 N	114·18 E
212	Ruacana Falls Ang.-Namibia	17·15 S	14·45 E
217	Ruaha Natl. Pk. Tan.	7·15 S	34·50 E
205	Ruapehu (Mtn.) (rōō-ȧ-pā'hōō) N. Z. (In.)	39·15 S	175·37 E
217	Rubeho Mts. Tan.	6·45 S	36·15 E
113	Rubidoux Ca. (Los Angeles In.)	33·59 N	117·24 W
217	Rubondo I. Tan.	2·10 S	31·55 E
172	Rubtsovsk Sov. Un.	51·31 N	81·17 E
101	Ruby (rōō'bê) Ak.	64·38 N	155·22 W
114	Ruby (L.) Nv.	40·11 N	115·20 W
114	Ruby Mts. Nv.	40·11 N	115·36 W
111	Ruby R. Mt.	45·06 N	112·10 W
156	Rudkøbing (rōōdh'kûb-ĭng) Den.	54·56 N	10·44 E
149	Rüdnitz (rüd'nētz) G.D.R. (Berlin In.)	52·44 N	13·38 E
217	Rudolf, L. (rōō'dŏlf) Ken.-Eth.	3·30 N	36·05 E
155	Rudolstadt (rōō'dôl-shtät) G.D.R.	50·46 N	13·30 E
211	Rufā'ah (rōō-fä'ä) Sud.	14·52 N	33·30 E
160	Ruffec (rü-fĕk') Fr.	46·03 N	0·11 E
217	Rufiji (R.) (rōō-fē'jê) Tan.	8·00 S	39·20 E
214	Rufisque (rü-fēsk') Senegal	14·43 N	17·17 W
217	Rufunsa Zambia	15·05 S	29·40 E
110	Rufus Woods Wa.	48·02 N	119·33 W
190	Rugao (rōō-gou) China	32·24 N	120·33 E
148	Rugby (rŭg'bê) Eng.	52·22 N	1·15 W
108	Rugby ND	48·22 N	100·00 W
148	Rugeley (rōōj'lē) Eng.	52·46 N	1·56 W
158	Rügen (Pen.) (rü'ghĕn) G.D.R.	54·28 N	13·47 E
157	Ruhnu-Saar (I.) (rōōnŏŏ-sȧ'ȧr) Sov. Un.	57·46 N	23·15 E
158	Ruhr R. (rōōr) F.R.G.	51·18 N	8·17 E
193	Rui'an (rwā-än) China	27·48 N	120·40 E
124	Ruiz (rōōē'z) Mex.	21·55 N	105·09 W
134	Ruiz, Nevado del (Pk.) (nĕ-vá'dô-dĕl-rōōē'z) Col. (In.)	4·52 N	75·20 W
157	Rūjiena (rōō'yĭ-ă-nȧ) Sov. Un.	57·54 N	25·19 E
216	Ruki (R.) Zaire	0·05 S	18·55 E
217	Rukwa, L. (rōōk-wä') Tan.	8·00 S	32·25 E
109	Rum (R.) (rŭm) Mn.	45·52 N	93·45 W
165	Ruma (rōō'mȧ) Yugo.	45·00 N	19·53 E
211	Rumbek (rŭm'bĕk) Sud.	6·52 N	29·43 E
129	Rum Cay (I.) Ba.	23·40 N	74·50 W
98	Rumford (rŭm'fẽrd) Me.	44·32 N	70·35 W
186	Rummah, Wādī ar (R.) Sau. Ar.	26·17 N	41·45 E
183	Rummānah Egypt (Palestine In.)	31·01 N	32·39 E
190	Runan (rōō-nän) China	32·59 N	114·22 E
148	Runcorn (rŭŋ'kôrn) Eng.	53·20 N	2·44 W
188	Ruo (R.) (rwô) China	41·15 N	100·46 E
183	Rupat, Palau (I.) (rōō'pät) Indon. (Singapore In.)	1·55 N	101·35 E
183	Rupat, Selat (Str.) Indon. (Singapore In.)	1·55 N	101·17 E
111	Rupert (rōō'pẽrt) Id.	42·36 N	113·41 W
91	Rupert, Rivière de (R.) Can.	51·35 N	76·30 W
165	Ruse (Russe) (rōō'sĕ) (rōō'sĕ) Bul.	43·50 N	25·59 E
190	Rushan (rōō-shän) China	36·54 N	121·31 E
109	Rush City Mn.	45·40 N	92·59 W
117	Rushville (rŭsh'vĭl) Il.	40·08 N	90·34 W
104	Rushville In.	39·35 N	85·30 W
108	Rushville Ne.	42·43 N	102·27 W
217	Rusizi (R.) Zaire	3·00 S	29·05 E
119	Rusk (rŭsk) Tx.	31·49 N	95·09 W
112	Ruskin (rŭs'kĭn) Can. (Vancouver In.)	49·10 N	122·25 W
149	Russ (R.) Aus. (Vienna In.)	48·12 N	16·55 E
135	Russas (rōō's-säs) Braz.	4·48 S	37·50 W
	Russe, see Ruse		
112	Russell Ca. (San Francisco In.)	37·39 N	122·08 W
95	Russell (rŭs'ĕl) Can.	50·47 N	101·15 W
89	Russell Can. (Ottawa In.)	45·15 N	75·22 W
116	Russell Ks.	38·51 N	98·51 W
104	Russell Ky.	38·30 N	82·45 W
205	Russell N. Z. (In.)	35·38 S	174·13 E
205	Russell Is. Sol. Is.	9·16 S	158·30 E
95	Russel L. Can.	56·15 N	101·30 W
120	Russellville (rŭs'ĕl-vĭl) Al.	34·29 N	87·44 W
117	Russellville Ar.	35·16 N	93·08 W
120	Russelville Ky.	36·48 N	86·51 W
114	Russian (R.) (rŭsh'ăn) Ca.	38·59 N	123·10 W
168	Russian S. F. S. R. Sov. Un.	61·00 N	60·00 E
218	Rustenburg (rŭs'tĕn-bûrg) S. Afr. (Johannesburg & Pretoria In.)	25·40 S	26·15 E
119	Ruston (rŭs'tŭn) La.	32·32 N	92·39 W
112	Ruston Wa. (Seattle In.)	47·18 N	122·30 W
167	Rutchenkovo (rōō-chĕn'kô-vô) Sov. Un.	47·54 N	37·36 E
162	Rute (rōō'tā) Sp.	37·20 N	4·34 W
114	Ruth (rōōth) Nv.	39·17 N	115·00 W
159	Ruthenia (Reg.) Sov. Un.	48·25 N	23·00 E
121	Rutherfordton (rŭdh'ẽr-fẽrd-tŭn) NC	35·23 N	81·58 W
105	Rutland Vt.	43·35 N	72·55 W
148	Rutland (Co.) Eng.	52·40 N	0·37 W
106	Rutledge (rŭt'lĕdj) Md. (Baltimore In.)	39·34 N	76·33 W
184	Rutog (rōō-tô-gŭ) China	33·42 N	79·56 E
217	Rutshuru (rōōt-shōō'rōō) Zaire	1·11 S	29·27 E
164	Ruvo (rōō'vô) It.	41·07 N	16·32 E
217	Ruvuma (Rovuma) (R.) Moz.-Tan.	10·50 S	39·50 E
211	Ruwenzori Mts. (rōō-wĕn-zō'rê) Afr.	0·53 N	30·00 E
166	Ruza (rōō'zȧ) Sov. Un.	55·42 N	36·12 E
159	Ruzhany (rōō-zhän'ĭ) Sov. Un.	52·49 N	24·54 E
209	Rwanda Afr.	2·10 S	29·37 E
174	Ryabovo (ryä'bô-vô) Sov. Un. (Leningrad In.)	59·24 N	31·08 E
166	Ryazan' (ryä-zän'') Sov. Un.	54·37 N	39·43 E
166	Ryazan' (Oblast) Sov. Un.	54·10 N	39·37 E
166	Ryazhsk (ryäzh'sk') Sov. Un.	53·43 N	40·04 E
170	Rybachiy, P-Ov. (Pen.) Sov. Un.	69·50 N	33·20 E
174	Rybatskoye (rĭ-bät'skô-yĕ) Sov. Un. (Leningrad In.)	59·50 N	30·31 E
166	Rybinsk (ry-bĭ'nsk) Sov. Un.	58·02 N	38·52 E
166	Rybinskoye Vdkhr. (Res.) Sov. Un.	58·23 N	38·15 E
159	Rybnik (rĭb'nêk) Pol.	50·06 N	18·37 E
167	Rybnitsa (rĭb'nêt-sȧ) Sov. Un.	47·45 N	29·02 E
154	Ryde (rīd) Eng.	50·43 N	1·16 W
106	Rye (rī) NY (New York In.)	40·58 N	73·42 W
167	Ryl'sk (rêl''sk) Sov. Un.	51·33 N	34·42 E
194	Ryōtsu (ryōt'sōō) Jap.	38·02 N	138·23 E
159	Rypin (rĭ'pên) Pol.	53·04 N	19·25 E
	Ryukyu, see Nansei-shotō		
159	Rzeszów (zhȧ-shōōf) Pol.	50·02 N	22·00 E
166	Rzhev ('r-zhĕf) Sov. Un.	56·16 N	34·17 E
167	Rzhishchëv ('r-zhĭsh'chĕf) Sov. Un.	49·58 N	31·05 E

S

Page	Name Pronunciation Region	Lat. °'	Long. °'
158	Saale R. (sä-lĕ) G.D.R.	51·14 N	11·52 E
158	Saalfeld (säl'fĕlt) G.D.R.	50·38 N	11·20 E
158	Saar (State) (zär) F.R.G.	49·25 N	6·50 E
158	Saarbrücken (zähr'brü-kĕn) F.R.G.	49·15 N	7·01 E
157	Saaremaa (Ezel) (I.) (sä'rĕ-mä) Sov. Un.	58·28 N	21·30 E
136	Saavedra (sä-ä-vā'drä) Arg.	37·45 S	62·23 W
165	Šabac (shä'bȧts) Yugo.	44·45 N	19·49 E
163	Sabadell (sä-bä-dhål') Sp.	41·32 N	2·07 E
196	Sabah (Reg.) Mala.	5·10 N	116·25 E
127	Saba I. (sä'bä) Neth. Antilles (In.)	17·39 N	63·20 W
128	Sabana, Arch. de (är-chē-pyĕ'lä-gô dĕ sä-bä'nä) Cuba	23·05 N	80·00 W
127	Sabana, R. (sä-bä'nä) Pan.	8·40 N	78·02 W
129	Sabana de la Mar (sä-bä'nä dā lä mär') Dom. Rep.	19·05 N	69·30 W
135	Sabana de Uchire (sä-bȧ'nä dĕ ōō-chē'rĕ) Ven. (In.)	10·02 N	65·32 W
126	Sabanagrande (sä-bä'nä-grä'n-dĕ) Hond.	13·47 N	87·16 W
134	Sabanalarga (sä-bȧ'nä-lär'gä) Col.	10·38 N	75·02 W
134	Sabanas Páramo (Mtn.) (sä-bȧ'näs pȧ'rä-mô) Col. (In.)	6·28 N	76·08 W
125	Sabancuy (sä-bäŋ-kwē') Mex.	18·58 N	91·09 W
196	Sabang (sä'bäng) Indon.	5·52 N	95·26 E
166	Sabaudia (sȧ-bou'dê-ä) It.	41·19 N	13·00 E
117	Sabetha (sȧ-bĕth'ȧ) Ks.	39·54 N	95·49 W
212	Sabi (R.) (sä'bê) Zimb.	20·18 S	32·07 E
157	Sabile (sȧ'bê-lĕ) Sov. Un.	57·03 N	22·34 E
118	Sabinal (sȧ-bī'năl) Tx.	29·19 N	99·27 W
128	Sabinal, Cayo (I.) (kä'yō sä-bē-näl') Cuba	21·40 N	77·20 W
122	Sabinas Mex.	28·05 N	102·30 W
118	Sabinas, R. (sä-bē'näs) Mex.	26·37 N	99·52 W
118	Sabinas, Rio (R.) (rē'ō sä-bē'näs) Mex.	27·25 N	100·33 W
118	Sabinas Hidalgo (ê-däl'gô) Mex.	26·30 N	100·10 W
119	Sabine (sȧ-bēn') Tx.	29·44 N	93·54 W
220	Sabine, Mt. Ant.	72·05 S	169·10 E
103	Sabine (R.) U. S.	31·35 N	94·00 W
119	Sabine L. La.-Tx.	29·53 N	93·41 W

338 Sablayan — St. Jean PRONOUNCING INDEX

Page	Name Pronunciation Region	Lat. °'	Long. °'
197	Sablayan (säb-lä-yän') Phil. (In.)	12·49 N	120·47 E
98	Sable, C. (sā'b'l) Can.	43·25 N	65·24 W
121	Sable, C. Fl. (In.)	25·12 N	81·10 W
97	Sables, Rivière aux (R.) Can.	49·00 N	70·20 W
160	Sablé-sur-Sarthe (säb-lā-sür-särt') Fr.	47·50 N	0·17 W
170	Sablya, Gora (Mtn.) Sov. Un.	64·50 N	59·00 E
162	Sàbor (R.) (sä-bōr') Port.	41·18 N	6·54 W
117	Sac (R.) (sôk) Mo.	38·11 N	93·45 W
105	Sacandaga Res. (să-kăn-dâ'gȧ) NY	43·10 N	74·15 W
163	Sacavém (sä-kä-věɴ') Port. (Lisbon In.)	38·47 N	9·06 W
163	Sacavem (R.) Port. (Lisbon In.)	38·52 N	9·06 W
109	Sac City (sŏk) Ia.	42·25 N	95·00 W
95	Sachigo L. (săch'ĭ-gō) Can.	53·49 N	92·08 W
158	Sachsen (Reg.) (zäᴋ'sĕn) G.D.R.	50·45 N	12·17 E
105	Sacketts Harbor (săk'ĕts) NY	43·55 N	76·05 W
98	Sackville (săk'vĭl) Can.	45·54 N	64·22 W
98	Saco (sô'kô) Me.	43·30 N	70·28 W
136	Saco (R.) (sä'kô) Braz. (Rio de Janeiro In.)	22·20 S	43·26 W
98	Saco (R.) Me.	43·53 N	70·46 W
136	Sacra Famalia do Tinguá (sä-krä fä-mä'lyä dô tēn-gwȧ') Braz. (Rio de Janeiro In.)	22·29 S	43·36 W
114	Sacramento (săk-rȧ-mĕn'tō) Ca.	38·35 N	121·30 W
118	Scaramento Mex.	25·45 N	103·22 W
118	Sacramento Mex.	27·05 N	101·45 W
114	Sacramento (R.) Ca.	40·20 N	122·07 W
186	Şa'dah Yemen	16·50 N	43·45 E
93	Saddle Lake Ind. Res. Can.	54·00 N	111·40 W
112	Saddle Mtn. (săd''l) Or. (Portland In.)	45·58 N	123·40 W
187	Sadiya (sŭ-dē'yä) India	27·53 N	95·35 E
194	Sado (I.) (sä'dō) Jap.	38·05 N	138·26 E
162	Sado (R.) (sä'dōō) Port.	38·15 N	8·20 W
156	Saeby (sě'bü) Den.	57·21 N	10·29 E
195	Saeki (sä'ȧ-kê) Jap.	32·56 N	131·51 E
115	Safford (săf'fērd) Az.	32·50 N	109·45 W
210	Safi (Asfi) (sä'fê) (äs'fê) Mor.	32·24 N	9·09 W
171	Safid Rud (R.) Iran	36·50 N	49·40 E
195	Saga (sä'gä) Jap.	33·15 N	130·18 E
195	Sagami-Nada (Sea) (sä'gä'mê nä-dä) Jap.	35·06 N	139·24 E
107	Sagamore Hills (săg'ȧ-môr hĭlz) Oh. (Cleveland In.)	41·19 N	81·34 W
109	Saganaga (L.) (să-gȧ-nä'gȧ) Can.-Mn.	48·13 N	91·17 W
184	Sāgar India	23·55 N	78·45 E
104	Saginaw (săg'ĭ-nô) Mi.	43·25 N	84·00 W
113	Saginaw Mn. (Duluth In.)	46·51 N	92·26 W
113	Saginaw Tx. (Dallas, Fort Worth In.)	32·52 N	97·22 W
104	Saginaw B. Mi.	43·50 N	83·40 W
171	Sagiz (R.) (sä'gēz) Sov. Un.	48·30 N	56·10 E
105	Saguache (sȧ-wăch') (sȧ-gwä'chê) Co.	38·05 N	106·10 W
105	Sagauche Cr. Co.	38·05 N	106·40 W
129	Sagua de Tánamo (sä-gwä dĕ tȧ'nä-mō) Cuba	20·40 N	75·15 W
128	Sagua la Grande (sä-gwä lä grä'n-dĕ) Cuba	22·45 N	80·05 W
115	Saguaro Natl. Mon. (säg-wä'rō) Az.	32·12 N	110·40 W
96	Saguenay (R.) (săg-ē-nā') Can.	48·20 N	70·15 W
163	Sagunto (sä-gōōn'tō) Sp.	39·40 N	0·17 W
209	Sahara Des. (sȧ-hä'rȧ) Afr.	23·44 N	1·40 W
152	Saharan Atlas (Mts.) Mor.-Alg.	32·51 N	1·02 W
184	Sahāranpur (sŭ-hä'rŭn-pōōr') India	29·58 N	77·41 E
113	Sahara Village (sȧ-hä'rȧ) Ut. (Salt Lake City In.)	41·06 N	111·58 W
184	Sāhiwāl Pak.	30·43 N	73·04 E
124	Sahuayo de Dias Mex.	20·03 N	102·43 W
210	Saïda (sä'ê-dä) Alg.	34·51 N	00·07 E
	Saigon, see Ho Chi Minh City		
195	Saijō (sä'ê-jō) Jap.	33·55 N	133·13 E
157	Saimaa (sä'ĭ-mä) Fin.	61·24 N	28·45 E
124	Sain Alto (sä-ēn' äl'tō) Mex.	23·35 N	103·13 W
89	St. Adolphe (sânt a'dŏlf) (săɴ' tȧ-dôlf') Can. (Winnipeg In.)	49·40 N	97·07 W
160	St. Affrique (săɴ' tȧ-frēk') Fr.	43·58 N	2·52 E
202	St. Albans (sânt ôl'bănz) Austl. (Melbourne In.)	37·44 S	144·47 E
148	St. Albans Eng. (London In.)	51·44 N	0·20 W
105	St. Albans Vt.	44·50 N	73·05 W
104	St. Albans WV	38·20 N	81·50 W
154	St. Albans Hd. Eng.	50·34 N	2·00 W
89	St. Albert (sânt ăl'bērt) Can. (Edmonton In.)	53·38 N	113·38 W
160	St. Amand Montrond (săɴ't ȧ-mäɴ' môɴ-rôɴ') Fr.	46·44 N	2·28 E
213	St. André, Cap (C.) Mad.	16·15 S	44·31 E
89	St. André-Est Can. (Montreal In.)	45·33 N	74·19 W
120	St. Andrew, B. Fl.	30·20 N	85·45 W
98	St. Andrews Can.	45·05 N	67·03 W
154	St. Andrews Scot.	56·20 N	2·40 W
99	St. Andrew's Chan. (ăn'drōōz) Can.	46·06 N	60·28 W
89	St. Anicet (sěɴt ä-nē-sě') Can. (Montreal In.)	45·07 N	74·23 W
113	St. Ann (sânt ăn') Mo. (St. Louis In.)	38·44 N	90·23 W
98	Ste. Anne (săɴt' ȧn') (sânt ăn') Can.	46·55 N	71·46 W
107	St. Anne Il. (Chicago In.)	41·01 N	87·44 W
127	Ste. Anne Guad. (In.)	16·15 N	61·23 W
89	Ste.-Anne (R.) Can. (Quebec In.)	47·07 N	70·50 W
89	Ste. Anne-de-Beaupré (dē bō-prā') Can. (Quebec In.)	47·02 N	70·56 W
89	Ste. Anne-des-Plaines (dā plĕɴ) Can. (Montreal In.)	45·46 N	73·49 W
99	St. Anns B. (ănz) Can.	46·20 N	60·30 W
128	St. Ann's Bay Jam.	18·25 N	77·15 W
89	St. Anselme (săɴ' täɴ-sělm') Can. (Quebec In.)	46·37 N	70·58 W
99	St. Anthony (săɴ ăn'thô-nê) Can.	51·24 N	55·35 W
111	St. Anthony (sânt ăn'thô-nê) Id.	43·59 N	111·42 W
89	St. Antoine-de-Tilly Can. (Quebec In.)	46·00 N	71·31 W
89	St. Apollinaire (săɴ' tȧ-pôl-ê-nâr') Can. (Quebec In.)	46·36 N	71·30 W
161	St. Arnoult-en-Yvelines (săɴ-tär-nōō'ĕɴ-nēv-lēn') Fr. (Paris In.)	48·33 N	1·55 E
89	St. Augustin-de-Québec (sĕn tō-güs-tēn') Can. (Quebec In.)	46·45 N	71·27 W
89	St. Augustin-Deux-Montagnes Can. (Montreal In.)	45·38 N	73·59 W
121	St. Augustine (sânt ô'gŭs-tēn) Fl.	29·53 N	81·21 W
89	Ste. Barbe (sânt bärb') Can. (Montreal In.)	45·14 N	74·12 W
127	St. Barthelemy I. Guad. (In.)	17·55 N	62·32 W
154	St. Bees Hd. (sânt bēz' hĕd) Eng.	54·30 N	3·40 W
89	St. Benoit (sĕɴ bĕ-nōō-ä') Can. (Montreal In.)	45·34 N	74·05 W
106	St. Bernard (bēr-närd') La. (New Orleans In.)	29·52 N	89·52 W
107	St. Bernard Oh. (Cincinnati In.)	39·10 N	84·30 W
93	St. Bride Mt. (sânt brīd) Can.	51·30 N	115·57 W
154	St. Brides B. (sânt brīdz') Wales	51·17 N	4·45 W
160	St. Brieuc (săɴ' brēs') Fr.	48·32 N	2·47 W
89	St. Bruno (brū'nō) Can. (Montreal In.)	45·31 N	73·40 W
89	St. Canut (săɴ' kȧ-nū') Can. (Montreal In.)	45·43 N	74·04 W
98	St. Casimir (kȧ-zê-mēr') Can.	46·45 N	72·34 W
89	St. Catharines (kăth'ȧ-rĭnz) Can. (Toronto In.)	43·10 N	79·14 W
127	St. Catherine, Mt. Grenada (In.)	12·10 N	62·42 W
160	St. Chamas (săɴ-shä-mä') Fr. (In.)	43·32 N	5·03 E
160	St. Chamond (săɴ' shȧ-môɴ') Fr.	45·30 N	4·17 E
89	St. Charles (săɴ' shärlz') Can. (Quebec In.)	46·47 N	70·57 W
107	St. Charles (sânt chärlz') Il. (Chicago In.)	41·55 N	88·19 W
104	St. Charles Mi.	43·20 N	84·10 W
109	St. Charles Mn.	43·56 N	92·05 W
113	St. Charles Mo. (St. Louis In.)	38·47 N	90·29 W
89	St. Charles, Lac (L.) Can. (Quebec In.)	46·56 N	71·21 W
104	St. Clair (sânt klâr) Mi.	42·55 N	82·30 W
104	St. Clair (L.) Can.-Mi.	42·25 N	82·30 W
104	St. Clair (R.) Can.-Mi.	42·45 N	82·25 W
89	Ste. Claire Can. (Quebec In.)	46·36 N	70·52 W
107	St. Clair Shores Mi. (Detroit In.)	42·30 N	82·54 W
161	St. Claude (săɴ' klōd') Fr.	46·24 N	5·53 E
89	St. Clet (săɴt' klā') Can. (Montreal In.)	45·22 N	74·21 W
121	St. Cloud (sânt kloud') Fl. (In.)	28·13 N	81·17 W
109	St. Cloud Mn.	45·33 N	94·08 W
89	St. Constant (kŏn'stănt) Can. (Montreal In.)	45·23 N	73·34 W
213	St. Croix I. (săɴ krwä) S. Afr. (Natal In.)	33·48 S	25·45 E
123	Saint Croix (I.) (sânt kroi') Vir. Is. (U. S. A.) (Puerto Rico In.)	17·40 N	64·43 W
98	St. Croix (R.) (kroi') Can.-Me.	45·28 N	67·32 W
109	St. Croix Ind. Res. Wi.	45·40 N	92·21 W
109	St. Croix R. (sânt kroi') Mn.-Wi.	45·00 N	92·44 W
89	St. Damien-de-Buckland (sânt dā'mê-ĕn) Can. (Quebec In.)	46·37 N	70·39 W
89	St. David (dā'vĭd) Can. (Quebec In.)	46·47 N	71·11 W
154	St. David's Hd. Wales	51·54 N	5·25 W
161	St.-Denis (săɴ'dē-nē') Fr. (Paris In.)	48·26 N	2·22 E
161	St. Dié (dê-ā') Fr.	48·18 N	6·55 E
160	St. Dizier (dê-zyā') Fr.	48·49 N	4·55 E
89	St. Dominique (sĕɴ dō-mē-nēk') Can. (Montreal In.)	45·19 N	74·09 W
89	St. Edouard-de-Napierville (sĕɴ-tē-dōō-är') Can. (Montreal In.)	45·14 N	73·31 W
101	St. Elias, Mt. (sânt ê-lī'ăs) Can.	60·25 N	141·00 W
160	St. Étienne Fr.	45·26 N	4·22 E
89	St. Etienne-de-Lauzon (săɴ' tā-tyĕn') Can. (Quebec In.)	46·39 N	71·19 W
89	Ste. Euphémie (sĕɴt û-fē-mē') Can. (Quebec In.)	46·47 N	70·27 W
89	St. Eustache (săɴ' tû-stȧsh') Can. (Montreal In.)	45·34 N	73·54 W
89	St. Eustache Can. (Winnipeg In.)	49·58 N	97·47 W
127	St. Eustatius I. (sânt u-stā'shŭs) Neth. Antilles (In.)	17·32 N	62·45 W
89	Ste. Famille (săɴ't fȧ-mē'y') Can. (Quebec In.)	46·58 N	70·58 W
99	St. Félicíen (săɴ fā-lê-syăɴ') Can.	48·39 N	72·28 W
98	Ste. Felicite Can.	48·54 N	67·20 W
89	St. Féréol (fa-rā-ôl') Can. (Quebec In.)	47·07 N	70·52 W
164	St. Florent, Golfe de (G.) Fr.	42·55 N	9·08 E
160	St. Florent-sur-Cher (săɴ' flô-räɴ'sür-shâr') Fr.	46·58 N	2·15 E
160	St. Flour (săɴ flōōr') Fr.	45·02 N	3·09 E
89	Ste. Foy (săɴt fwä) Can. (Quebec In.)	46·47 N	71·18 W
117	St. Francis (R.) Ar.	35·56 N	90·27 W
105	St. Francis L. (săɴ frăn'sĭs) Can.	45·00 N	74·20 W
89	St. François (săɴ'fräɴ-swä') Can. (Quebec In.)	47·01 N	70·49 W
218	St. François de Boundji Con.	1·03 S	15·22 E
89	St. Francois Xavier Can. (Winnepeg In.)	49·55 N	97·32 W
160	St. Gaudens (gō-dăɴs') Fr.	43·07 N	0·43 E
117	Ste. Genevieve (sânt jĕn'ĕ-vēv) Mo.	37·58 N	90·02 W
203	St. George (sânt jôrj') Austl.	28·02 S	148·40 E
98	St. George (săɴ jôrj') Can.	45·08 N	66·49 W
89	St. George (săɴ'zhôrzh') Can. (Toronto In.)	43·14 N	80·15 W
121	St. George (sânt jôrj') SC	33·11 N	80·35 W
115	St. George Ut.	37·05 N	113·40 W
101	St. George (I.) Ak.	56·30 N	169·40 W
99	St. George, C. Can.	48·28 N	59·15 W
120	St. George, C. Fl.	29·30 N	85·20 W
99	St. George's (jôrj'ĕs) Can.	48·26 N	58·29 W
135	St. Georges Fr. Gu.	3·48 N	51·47 W
127	St. Georges Grenada (In.)	12·02 N	61·57 W
99	St. Georges B. Can.	45·49 N	61·45 W
99	St. George's B. Can.	48·20 N	59·00 W
154	St. George's Chan. (jôr-jĕz) Eng.-Ire.	51·45 N	6·30 W
161	St. Germain-en-Laye (săɴ' zhĕr-măɴ-äɴ-lā') Fr. (Paris In.)	48·53 N	2·05 E
89	St. Gervais (zhĕr-vĕ') Can. (Quebec In.)	46·43 N	70·53 W
160	St. Girons (zhē-rôɴ') Fr.	42·58 N	1·08 E
158	St. Gotthard Tun. (sânt gôthȧrd) (săɴ gô-tȧr') Switz.	46·38 N	8·55 E
99	St. Gregory, Mt. (sânt grĕg'ēr-ê) Can.	49·19 N	58·13 W
209	St. Helena Atl. O.	16·01 S	5·16 W
212	St. Helenabaai (B.) Afr.	32·25 S	17·15 E
148	St. Helens (sânt hĕl'ĕnz) Eng.	53·27 N	2·44 W
112	St. Helens (hĕl'ĕnz) Or. (Portland In.)	45·52 N	122·49 W
110	St. Helens, Mt. Wa.	46·13 N	122·10 W
160	St. Helier (hyĕl'yēr) Jersey	49·12 N	2·06 W
89	St. Henri (săɴ' hĕn'rê) Can. (Quebec In.)	46·41 N	71·04 W
89	St. Hubert Can. (Montreal In.)	45·29 N	73·24 W
105	St. Hyacinthe (săɴ' tê-ä-săɴt') (sânt hī'ȧ-sĭnth) Can.	45·35 N	72·55 W
98	St.-Ignace Can.	46·42 N	70·30 W
109	St. Ignace (sânt ĭg'nȧs) Mi.	45·51 N	84·39 W
109	St. Ignace (I.) (săɴ' ĭg'nȧs) Can.	48·47 N	88·14 W
98	St. Irenee (săɴ' tē-rā-nā') Can.	47·34 N	70·15 W
89	St. Isidore-de-Laprairie (saɴ' tē-zê-dôr') (sânt ĭz'ĭ-dôr) Can. (Montreal In.)	45·18 N	73·41 W
89	St. Isidore-de-Prescott (săɴ' ĭz'ĭ-dôr-prĕs-kŏt) Can. (Ottawa In.)	45·23 N	74·54 W
89	St. Isidore-Dorchester (dŏr-chĕs'tēr) Can. (Quebec In.)	46·35 N	71·05 W
113	St. Jacob (jā-kŏb) Il. (St. Louis In.)	38·43 N	89·46 W
109	St. James (sânt jămz') Mn.	43·58 N	94·37 W
107	St. James Mo.	37·59 N	91·37 W
92	St. James, C. Can.	51·58 N	131·00 W
89	St. Janvier (săɴ' zhän-vyā') Can. (Montreal In.)	45·43 N	73·56 W
105	St. Jean (săɴ' zhäɴ') Can.	45·20 N	73·15 W
89	St. Jean Can. (Quebec In.)	46·55 N	70·54 W
97	St. Jean, Lac (L.) Can.	48·35 N	72·00 W

PRONOUNCING INDEX

St. Jean-Chrysostome — Salawati 339

Page	Name Pronunciation Region	Lat. °′	Long. °′
89	St. Jean-Chrysostome (krĭ-zōs-tōm′). Can. (Quebec (In.)	46·43 N	71·12 W
160	St. Jean-d'Angely (däN-zhä-lē′) Fr.	45·56 N	0·33 W
160	St. Jean de Luz (dē lüz′) Fr.	43·23 N	1·40 W
89	St. Jérôme (sânt jĕ-rōm′) (săN zhā-rōm′) Can. (Montreal In.)	45·47 N	74·00 W
89	St. Joachim-de-Montmorency (sânt jō′ȧ-kĭm) Can. (Quebec In.)	47·04 N	70·51 W
98	St. John (sânt jŏn) Can.	45·16 N	66·03 W
107	St. John In. (Chicago In.)	41·27 N	87·29 W
116	St. John Ks.	37·59 N	98·44 W
108	St. John ND	48·57 N	99·42 W
98	St. John (R.) Can.	46·39 N	67·40 W
99	St. John B. Can.	50·54 N	57·08 W
99	St. John, C. Can.	50·00 N	55·32 W
99	St. John I. Can.	50·49 N	57·14 W
123	St. John (I.) Vir. Is. (U. S. A.) (Puerto Rico In.)	18·16 N	64·48 W
91	St. John (R.) N.A.	45·15 N	67·40 W
99	St. John's (jŏns) Can.	47·34 N	52·43 W
115	St. Johns (jŏnz) Az.	34·30 N	109·25 W
104	St. Johns Mi.	43·05 N	84·35 W
127	St. Johns Antigua (In.)	17·07 N	61·50 W
121	St. Johns (R.) Fl.	29·54 N	81·32 W
105	St. Johnsbury (jŏnz′bĕr-ē) Vt.	44·25 N	72·00 W
98	St. Joseph (jō′zhûf) Can.	46·17 N	70·52 W
104	St. Joseph Mi.	42·05 N	86·30 W
117	St. Joseph (sânt jō-sĕf) Mo.	39·44 N	94·49 W
127	St. Joseph Dominica (In.)	15·25 N	61·26 W
104	St. Joseph (I.) Can.	46·15 N	83·55 W
91	St. Joseph (L.) (jō′zhûf) Can.	51·31 N	90·40 W
104	St. Joseph (R.) (sânt jō′sĕf) Mi.	41·45 N	85·50 W
120	St. Joseph, B. (jō′zhûf) Fl.	29·48 N	85·26 W
97	St. Joseph-de-Beauce (sĕN zhō-zĕf′dĕ bōs). Can.	46·18 N	70·52 W
89	St. Joseph-du-Lac (sĕN zhō-zĕf′ dü läk) Can. (Montreal In.)	45·32 N	74·00 W
119	St. Joseph I. (sânt jō-sĕf) Tx.	27·58 N	96·50 W
160	St. Junien (săN′zhü-nyăN′) Fr.	45·53 N	0·54 E
89	Ste. Justine-de-Newton (sânt jŭs-tēn′) Can. (Montreal In.)	45·22 N	74·22 W
154	St. Kilda (I.) (kĭl′dȧ) Scot.	57·10 N	8·32 W
123	St. Kitts (I.) (sânt kĭtts) St. Kitts-Nevis-Anguilla	17·24 N	63·30 W
89	St. Lambert (săN′ läN-bĕr′) (sânt lăm′bērt) Can. (Montreal In.)	45·29 N	73·29 W
89	St. Lambert-de-Lévis Can. (Quebec In.)	46·35 N	71·12 W
89	St. Laurent (săN′lō-rän) Can. (Montreal In.)	45·31 N	73·41 W
135	St. Laurent Fr. Gu.	5·27 N	53·56 W
89	St. Laurent-d'Orleans Can. (Quebec In.)	46·52 N	71·00 W
99	St. Lawrence (sânt lô′rĕns) Can.	46·55 N	55·23 W
101	St. Lawrence (I.) (sânt lô′rĕns). Ak.	63·10 N	172·12 W
99	St. Lawrence, Gulf of Can.	48·00 N	62·00 W
91	St. Lawrence R. (Fleuve St.-Laurent). Can.-U. S.	48·24 N	69·30 W
89	St. Lazare (săN′lȧ-zär′) Can. (Quebec In.)	46·39 N	70·48 W
89	St. Lazare-de-Vaudreuil Can. (Montreal In.)	45·24 N	74·08 W
161	St. Léger-en-Yvelines (sàN-lā-zhĕ′ĕN-nēv-lēn′) Fr. (Paris In.)	48·43 N	1·45 E
98	St. Leonard (sânt lĕn′ārd) Can.	47·10 N	67·56 W
89	St. Léonard Can. (Montreal In.)	45·36 N	73·35 W
106	St. Leonard Md. (Baltimore In.)	38·29 N	76·31 W
160	St. Léonard-de-Noblat (săN′ lā-ô-nȧr′dĕ-nô-blȧ′). Fr.	45·51 N	1·30 E
160	St.-Lô (săN′lō′) Fr.	49·08 N	1·07 W
104	St. Louis (sânt lōō′ĭs) Mi.	43·25 N	84·35 W
113	St. Louis (sânt lōō′ĭs) (lōō′ē) Mo. (St. Louis In.)	38·39 N	90·15 W
214	St.-Louis Senegal	16·02 N	16·30 W
89	St. Louis, Lac (L.) (săN′ lōō-ē′) Can. (Montreal In.)	45·24 N	73·51 W
109	St. Louis (R.) (sânt lōō′ĭs) Mn.	46·57 N	92·58 W
89	St. Louis-de-Gonzague (săN′ lōō ē′) Can. (Montreal In.)	45·13 N	74·00 W
113	St. Louis Park Mn. (Minneapolis, St. Paul In.)	44·56 N	93·21 W
123	Saint Lucia N. A.	13·54 N	60·40 W
127	St. Lucia Chan. (lū′shĭ-ȧ) N. A. (In.)	14·15 N	61·00 W
121	St. Lucie Can. (lū′sē) Fl. (In.)	26·57 N	80·25 W
154	St. Magnus B. (măg′nŭs) Scot.	60·25 N	2·09 W
160	St. Maixent (săN′ mĕk-săN′) Fr.	46·25 N	0·12 W
160	St. Malo (săN′ mȧ-lō′) Fr.	48·40 N	2·02 W
160	St. Malo, Golfe de (G.) (gôlf-dĕ-sàN-mä-lō′). Fr.	48·50 N	2·49 W
129	St. Marc (săN′ mȧrk′) Hai.	19·10 N	72·40 W
129	St.-Marc, Canal de (Chan.) Hai.	19·05 N	73·15 W
161	St. Marcellin (mär-sĕ-lăN′) Fr.	45·08 N	5·15 E
213	Ste.-Marie, Île (I.) Mad.	16·58 S	50·15 E
213	Ste. Marie, Cap (C.) Mad.	25·31 S	45·00 E
161	Ste. Marie aux Mines (sàN′tĕ-mä-rē′ō-mēn′). Fr.	48·14 N	7·08 E
98	Ste. Marie-Beauce (săNt′mȧ-rē′) Can.	46·27 N	71·03 W
110	St. Maries (sânt mā′rēs) Id.	47·18 N	116·34 W
106	St. Margarets. Md. (Baltimore In.)	39·02 N	76·30 W
89	Ste. Martine Can. (Montreal In.)	45·14 N	73·37 W
127	St. Martin I. (mär′tĭn) Guad.-Neth-Antilles (In.)	18·06 N	62·54 W
98	St. Martins (mär′tĭnz) Can.	45·21 N	65·32 W
119	St. Martinville (mär′tĭn-vĭl) La.	30·08 N	91·50 W
93	St. Mary (R.) (mā′rē) Can.	49·25 N	113·00 W
93	St. Mary (Res.) Can.	49·30 N	113·00 W
214	St. Mary, C. Gam.	13·28 N	16·40 W
203	St. Marys (mā′rēz) Austl.	41·40 S	148·10 E
104	St. Marys Can.	43·15 N	81·10 W
121	St. Marys Ga.	30·43 N	81·35 W
117	St. Mary's Ks.	39·12 N	96·03 W
104	St. Mary's Oh.	40·30 N	84·25 W
105	St. Marys Pa.	41·25 N	78·30 W
104	St. Marys WV	39·20 N	81·15 W
121	St. Marys (R.) Ga.-Fl.	30·37 N	82·05 W
98	St. Mary's B. Can.	44·20 N	66·10 W
99	St. Mary's B. Can.	46·50 N	53·47 W
99	St. Marys Is. Can.	50·19 N	59·17 W
113	St. Marys R. Can.-U. S. (Sault Ste. Marie In.)	46·27 N	84·33 W
121	St. Mathew (măth′ū) SC	33·40 N	80·46 W
101	St. Matthew (I.) Ak.	60·25 N	172·10 W
107	St. Matthews (măth′ūz) Ky. (Louisville In.)	38·15 N	85·39 W
161	St. Maur-des-Fossés. Fr. (Paris In.)	48·48 N	2·29 E
98	St. Maurice (R.) (săN′ mô-rēs′) (sânt mô′rĭs). Can.	47·20 N	72·55 W
101	St. Michael (sânt mī′kĕl) Ak.	63·22 N	162·20 W
89	St. Michel (săN′mē-shĕl′) Can. (Quebec In.)	46·52 N	70·54 W
129	St. Michel-de-l'Atalaye Hai.	19·25 N	72·20 W
89	St. Michel-de-Napierville Can. (Montreal In.)	45·14 N	73·34 W
161	St. Mihiel (săN′ mē-yĕl′) Fr.	48·53 N	5·30 E
160	St. Mitre (sàN mēt-rĕ′) Fr. (In.)	43·27 N	5·02 E
158	St. Moritz (sânt mō′rĭts) (zäŋkt mō′rēts) Switz.	46·31 N	9·50 E
160	St. Nazaire (săN′nȧ-zâr′) Fr.	47·18 N	2·13 W
89	St. Nérée (nā-rā′) Can. (Quebec In.)	46·43 N	70·43 W
89	St. Nicolas (ne-kô-lä′) Can. (Quebec In.)	46·42 N	71·32 W
129	St. Nicolas, Cap (C.) Hai.	19·45 N	73·35 W
160	St. Omer (săN′tô-mâr′) Fr.	50·44 N	2·16 E
98	St. Pascal (săN pä-skăl′) Can.	47·32 N	69·48 W
93	St. Paul (sânt pôl′) Can.	53·59 N	111·17 W
113	St. Paul Mn. (Minneapolis, St. Paul In.)	44·57 N	93·05 W
108	St. Paul Ne.	41·13 N	98·28 W
101	St. Paul (I.) Ak.	57·10 N	170·20 W
214	St. Paul (R.) Lib.	7·10 N	10·00 W
99	St. Paul I. Can.	47·15 N	60·10 W
220	St. Paul I. Ind. O.	38·43 S	77·31 E
113	St. Paul Park (pärk) Mn. (Minneapolis, St. Paul In.)	44·51 N	93·00 W
121	St. Pauls (pôls) NC	34·47 N	78·57 W
109	St. Peter (pē tēr) Mn.	44·20 N	93·56 W
160	St. Peter Port Guernsey	49·27 N	2·35 W
121	St. Petersburg (pē′tērz-bûrg) Fl. (In.)	27·47 N	82·38 W
89	Ste. Pétronille (sĕNt pĕt-rō-nēl′) Can. (Quebec In.)	46·51 N	71·08 W
89	St. Philémon (sĕN fēl-mōN′) Can. (Quebec In.)	46·41 N	70·28 W
89	St. Philippe-d'Argenteuil (săn′fe-lēp′) Can. (Montreal In.)	45·20 N	73·28 W
89	St. Philippe-de-Lapairie Can. (Montreal In.)	45·38 N	74·25 W
127	St. Pierre (săn′pyâr′) Mart. (In.)	14·45 N	61·12 W
99	St. Pierre (I.) St. Pierre & Miquelon	46·47 N	56·11 W
98	St. Pierre, Lac (L.) Can.	46·07 N	72·45 W
99	St. Pierre & Miquelon N. A.	46·53 N	56·40 W
89	St. Pierre-d'Orléans Can. (Quebec In.)	46·53 N	71·04 W
89	St. Pierre-Montmagny Can. (Quebec In.)	46·55 N	70·37 W
89	St. Placide (plăs′ĭd) Can. (Montreal In.)	45·32 N	74·11 W
160	St. Pol-de-Léon (săN-pô′dĕ-lā-ôN′) Fr.	48·41 N	4·00 W
158	St. Pölten (zäŋkt-pûl′tĕn) Aus.	48·12 N	15·38 E
160	St. Quentin (săN′kăN-tăN′) Fr.	49·52 N	3·16 E
89	St. Raphaël (rä-fȧ-ĕl′) Can. (Quebec In.)	46·48 N	70·46 W
98	St. Raymond (săN′ rā-môN′) (sânt rā′mŭnd) Can.	46·50 N	71·51 W
89	St. Rédempteur (săN rā-dăNp-tûr′) Can. (Quebec In.)	46·42 N	71·18 W
89	St. Rémi (sĕN rĕ-mē′) Can. (Montreal In.)	45·15 N	73·36 W
89	St. Romuald-d'Etchemin (sĕN rŏ′mōō-äl) Can. (Quebec In.)	46·45 N	71·14 W
127	Ste. Rose Guad. (In.)	16·19 N	61·45 W
160	Saintes Fr.	45·44 N	0·41 W
89	Ste. Scholastique (skô-lȧs-tēk′) Can. (Montreal In.)	45·39 N	74·05 W
160	St. Servan-sur-Mer (sĕr-väN′) Fr.	48·37 N	1·59 W
98	St. Siméon Can.	47·51 N	69·55 W
89	St. Stanislas-de-Kostka (sĕN stä-nēs-läz′ de kōst′kä) Can. (Montreal In.)	45·11 N	74·08 W
98	St. Stephen (stē′vĕn) Can.	45·12 N	66·17 W
89	St. Sulpice Can. (Montreal In.)	45·50 N	73·21 W
89	St. Thérèse-de-Blainville (tĕ-rĕz′ dĕ blĕN-vēl′) Can. (Montreal In.)	45·38 N	73·51 W
104	St. Thomas (tŏm′ȧs) Can.	42·45 N	81·15 W
	St. Thomas, see Charlotte Amalie		
123	St. Thomas (I.) Vir. Is. (U. S. A.) (St. Thomas In.)	18·22 N	64·57 W
123	St. Thomas Hbr. (tŏm′ȧs) Vir. Is. (U. S. A.) (St. Thomas In.)	18·19 N	64·56 W
89	St. Timothée (tē-mô-tā′) Can. (Montreal In.)	45·17 N	74·03 W
161	St. Tropez (trô-pĕ′) Fr.	43·15 N	6·42 E
89	St. Valentin (väl-ĕn-tīn) Can. (Montreal In.)	45·07 N	73·19 W
160	St. Valéry (vȧ-lā-rē′) Fr.	50·10 N	1·39 E
89	St. Vallier (väl-yā′) Can. (Quebec In.)	46·54 N	70·49 W
158	St. Veit (zäŋkt vīt′) Aus.	46·46 N	14·20 E
98	St. Victor (vĭk′tēr) Can.	46·09 N	70·56 W
123	St. Vincent N. A.	13·20 N	60·50 W
203	St. Vincent, G. (vĭn′sĕnt) Austl.	34·55 S	138·00 E
127	St. Vincent Pass N. A. (In.)	13·35 N	61·10 W
94	St. Walburg Can.	53·39 N	109·12 W
160	St. Yrieix (ē-rē-ĕ′) Fr.	45·30 N	1·08 E
195	Saitama (Pref.) (sī′tä-mä) Jap. (Tōkyō In.)	35·52 N	139·40 E
174	Saitbaba (sá-ĕt′bá-bȧ) Sov. Un. (Urals In.)	54·06 N	56·42 E
134	Sajama, Nevada (Pk.) (nĕ-vȧ′dä-sä-hȧ′mä). Bol.	18·13 S	68·53 W
195	Sakai (sä′kä-ē) Jap. (Ōsaka In.)	34·34 N	135·28 E
195	Sakaiminato Jap.	35·33 N	133·15 E
186	Sakākah Sau. Ar.	29·58 N	40·03 E
108	Sakakawea, Lake ND	47·49 N	101·58 W
217	Sakania (sȧ-kä′nĭ-ȧ) Zaire	12·45 S	28·34 E
171	Sakarya (R.) (sȧ-kär′yȧ) Tur.	40·10 N	31·00 E
194	Sakata (sä′kä-tä) Jap.	38·56 N	139·57 E
194	Sakchu (säk′chōō) Kor.	40·29 N	125·09 E
173	Sakhalin (I.) (sȧ-kȧ-lēn′) Sov. Un.	51·52 N	144·15 E
157	Šakiai (shä′kĭ-ī) Sov. Un.	54·59 N	23·05 E
193	Sakishima-Gunto (Is.) (sä′kē-shē′ma gŏŏn′tō′). Jap.	24·25 N	125·00 E
171	Sakmara (R.) Sov. Un.	52·00 N	56·10 E
106	Sakomet R. (sȧ-kō′mĕt) RI (Providence In.)	41·32 N	71·11 W
195	Sakurai Jap. (Ōsaka In.)	34·31 N	135·51 E
95	Sakwaso L. (sȧ-kwȧ′sō) Can.	53·01 N	91·55 W
128	Sal, Cay (I.) (kē săl) Ba.	23·45 N	80·25 W
171	Sal (R.) (sȧl) Sov. Un.	47·20 N	42·10 E
156	Sala (sô′lä) Swe.	59·56 N	16·34 E
164	Sala Consilina (sä′lä kôn-sē-lē′nä) It.	40·24 N	15·38 E
114	Salada, Laguna (L.) (lä-gōō′nä-sä-lä′dä). Mex.	32·34 N	115·45 W
137	Saladillo (sä-lä-dēl′yō) Arg. (Buenos Aires In.)	35·38 S	59·48 W
126	Salado (sä-lä′dhō) Hong.	15·44 N	87·03 W
136	Salado (sä-lä′dō) (R.) Arg.	26·05 S	63·35 W
137	Salado (R.) Arg. (Buenos Aires In.)	35·53 S	58·12 W
125	Salado (R.) (sä-lä′dō) Mex.	18·30 N	97·29 W
118	Salado, Rio (R.) (rē′ō) Mex.	26·55 N	99·36 W
113	Salado Cr. Tx. (San Antonio In.)	29·23 N	98·25 W
118	Salado de los Nadadores Rio (R.) (dĕ-lōs-nä-dä-dō′rĕs). Mex.	27·26 N	101·35 W
215	Salal Chad.	14·51 N	17·13 E
126	Salamá (sä-lä′mä) Guat.	15·06 N	90·19 W
126	Salamá (sä-lä-mȧ′) Hond.	14·43 N	86·30 W
137	Salamanca (sä-lä-mä′n-kä) Chile (Santiago In.)	31·48 S	70·57 W
124	Salamanca Mex.	20·36 N	101·10 W
105	Salamanca (săl-ȧ-măŋ′kȧ) NY	42·10 N	78·45 W
162	Salamanca (sä-lä-mä′n-kȧ) Sp.	40·54 N	5·42 W
211	Salamat, Bahr (R.) (bär sä-lä-mät′). Chad.	10·06 N	19·16 E
134	Salamina (sä-lä-mē′-nä) Col. (In.)	5·25 N	75·29 W
165	Salamis (săl′ȧ-mĭs) Grc.	37·58 N	23·30 E
134	Salaverry (sä-lä-vā′rē) Peru	8·16 S	78·54 W
197	Salawati (I.) (sä-lä-wä′tē) Indon.	1·22 N	130·15 E

ng-sing; ŋ-baŋk; N-nasalized n; nŏd; cŏmmit; ōld; ôbey; ôrder; fōōd; fŏŏt; ou-out; s-soft; sh-dish; th-thin; pūre; ůnite; ûrn; stŭd; circŭs; ü-as "y" in study; ′-indeterminate vowel.

340 Salawe — Sancti Spiritus PRONOUNCING INDEX

Page	Name Pronunciation Region	Lat. °′	Long. °′
217	Salawe Tan.	3·19 S	32·52 E
199	Sala-y-Gómez (I.) Chile	26·50 S	105·50 W
129	Salcedo (säl-sā'dō) Dom. Rep.	19·25 N	70·30 W
134	Saldaña (R.) (säl-dä'n-yä) Col. (In.)	3·42 N	75·16 W
212	Saldanha S. Afr.	32·55 S	18·05 E
157	Saldus (sål'dŏŏs) Sov. Un.	56·39 N	22·30 E
203	Sale (sāl) Austl.	38·10 S	147·07 E
148	Sale Eng.	53·24 N	2·20 W
210	Salé (sȧ-lā') Mor.	34·09 N	6·42 W
89	Sale (R.) (sȧl'rê-vyâr') Can. (Winnipeg In.)	49·44 N	97·11 W
170	Salekhard (sŭ-lyĭ-kärt) Sov. Un.	66·35 N	66·50 E
104	Salem (sā'lĕm) Il.	38·40 N	89·00 W
185	Salem India	11·39 N	78·11 E
104	Salem In.	38·35 N	86·00 W
99	Salem Ma. (In.)	42·31 N	70·54 W
117	Salem Mo.	37·36 N	91·33 W
99	Salem NH (In.)	42·46 N	71·16 W
105	Salem NJ	39·35 N	75·30 W
104	Salem Oh.	40·55 N	80·50 W
110	Salem Or.	44·55 N	123·03 W
108	Salem SD	43·43 N	97·23 W
213	Salem S. Afr. (Natal In.)	33·29 S	26·30 E
121	Salem Va.	37·16 N	80·05 W
104	Salem WV	39·15 N	80·35 W
164	Salemi (sä-lå'mē) It.	37·49 N	12·48 E
163	Salerno (sä-lĕr'nô). It. (Naples In.)	40·27 N	14·46 E
164	Salerno, Golfo di (G.) (gôl-fô-dē) It.	40·30 N	14·40 E
148	Salford (săl'fērd) Eng.	53·26 N	2·19 W
167	Salgir (R.) (sål'gēr) Sov. Un.	45·25 N	34·22 E
159	Salgótarján (shôl'gô-tôr-yän) Hung.	48·06 N	19·50 E
116	Salida (sȧ-lī'dȧ) Co.	38·31 N	106·01 W
160	Salies (sȧ-lēs') Fr.	43·27 N	0·58 W
217	Salima Malawi	13·47 S	34·26 E
117	Salina (sȧ-lī'nȧ) Ks.	38·50 N	97·37 W
115	Salina Ut.	39·00 N	111·55 W
164	Salina (I.) (sä-lē'nä) It.	38·35 N	14·48 E
129	Salina Pt. Ba.	22·10 N	74·20 W
125	Salina Cruz (sä-lē'nä krōōz'). Mex.	16·10 N	95·12 W
114	Salinas (sȧ-lē'nȧs) Ca.	36·41 N	121·40 W
124	Salinas Mex.	22·38 N	101·42 W
123	Salinas P. R. (Puerto Rico In.)	17·58 N	66·16 W
114	Salinas (R.) Ca.	36·33 N	121·29 W
125	Salinas (R.) (sä-lē'näs) Mex.	16·15 N	90·31 W
126	Salinas, Bahia de (B.) (bä-ē'ä-dĕ-sȧ-lē'nȧs). Nic.-C. R.	11·05 N	85·55 W
163	Salinas, Cape (sä-lēnäs) Sp.	39·14 N	1·02 E
118	Salinas Victoria (sä-lē'näs vêk-tō'rē-ä). Mex.	25·59 N	100·19 W
117	Saline (R.) (sȧ-lēn') Ak.	34·06 N	92·30 W
116	Saline (R.) Ks.	39·05 N	99·43 W
161	Salins-les-Bains (sȧ-lăN'-lā-băN') Fr.	46·55 N	5·54 E
98	Salisbury Can.	46·03 N	65·05 W
154	Salisbury (sôlz'bē-rê) Eng.	50·35 N	1·51 W
105	Salisbury Md.	38·20 N	75·40 W
117	Salisbury Mo.	39·24 N	92·47 W
121	Salisbury NC	35·40 N	80·29 W
217	Salisbury Zimb.	17·50 S	31·03 E
91	Salisbury (I.) Can.	63·36 N	76·20 W
154	Salisbury Plain Eng.	51·15 N	1·52 W
210	Sal. I. (säal) C. V. Is. (In.)	16·45 N	22·39 W
121	Salkehatchie (R.) (sô-kê-hăch'ê) SC	33·09 N	81·10 W
117	Sallisaw (săl'ĭ-sô) Ok.	35·27 N	94·48 W
111	Salmon (săm'ŭn) Id.	45·11 N	113·54 W
92	Salmon (R.) Can.	54·00 N	123·50 W
98	Salmon (R.) Can.	46·19 N	65·36 W
110	Salmon (R.) Id.	45·30 N	115·45 W
105	Salmon (R.) NY	44·35 N	74·15 W
112	Salmon (R.) Wa. (Portland In.)	45·44 N	122·36 W
110	Salmon (R.), Middle Fork Id.	44·54 N	114·50 W
110	Salmon (R.), South Fork Id.	44·51 N	115·47 W
93	Salmon Arm Can.	50·42 N	119·16 W
110	Salmon Falls (R.) Id.	42·22 N	114·53 W
204	Salmon Gums (gŭmz) Austl.	33·00 S	122·00 E
110	Salmon River Mts. Id.	44·15 N	115·44 W
161	Salon-de-Provence (sȧ-lôN-dē-prô-văNs'). Fr.	43·48 N	5·09 E
159	Salonta (sä-lôn'tä) Rom.	46·46 N	21·38 E
214	Saloum (R.) Senegal	14·10 N	15·45 W
185	Salsette I. India (Bombay In.)	19·12 N	72·52 E
171	Sal'sk (sälsk) Sov. Un.	46·30 N	41·20 E
115	Salt, (R.) (sôlt) Az.	33·28 N	111·35 W
117	Salt (R.) Mo.	39·54 N	92·11 W
136	Salta (säl'tä) Arg.	24·50 S	65·16 W
136	Salta (Prov.) Arg.	25·15 S	65·00 W
113	Saltair (sôlt'âr) Ut. (Salt Lake City In.)	40·46 N	112·09 W
129	Salt Cay (I.) Turks & Caicos Is.	21·20 N	71·15 W
107	Salt Cr. (sôlt) Il. (Chicago In.)	42·01 N	88·01 W
118	Saltillo (säl-tēl'yō) Mex.	25·24 N	100·59 W
113	Salt Lake City (sôlt lāk sĭ'tĭ) Ut. (Salt Lake City In.)	40·45 N	111·52 W
137	Salto (säl'tō) Arg. (Buenos Aires In.)	34·17 S	60·15 W
136	Salto Ur.	31·18 S	57·45 W
137	Salto, Serra do (Mtn.) (sĕ'r-rä-dô) Braz. (Rio de Janeiro In.)	20·26 S	43·28 W
124	Salto (R.) Mex.	22·16 N	99·18 W
135	Salto Grande (grän'dā) Braz.	22·57 S	49·58 W
114	Salton Sea (sôlt'ŭn) Ca.	33·28 N	115·43 W
210	Saltpond Ghana	5·16 N	1·07 W
115	Salt River Ind. Res. (sôlt rĭv'ēr) Az.	33·40 N	112·01 W
156	Saltsjöbaden (sält'shû-bäd'ĕn) Swe.	59·15 N	18·20 E
92	Saltspring I (sält'sprĭng) Can.	48·47 N	123·30 W
121	Saltville (sôlt'vĭl) Va.	36·50 N	81·45 W
174	Saltykovka (sål-tē'kôf-kå) Sov. Un. (Moscow In.)	55·45 N	37·56 E
122	Salud, Mt. (sä-lōō'th) Pan. (Panama Canal In.)	9·14 N	79·42 W
121	Saluda (sȧ-lōō'dȧ) SC	34·02 N	81·46 W
121	Saluda (R.) SC	34·07 N	81·48 W
164	Saluzzo (sä-lōōt'sō) It.	44·39 N	7·31 E
135	Salvador (Bahia) (säl-vä-dōr') (bä-ē'ä). Braz.	12·59 S	38·27 W
119	Salvador L. La.	29·45 N	90·20 W
128	Salvador Pt. Ba.	24·30 N	77·45 W
124	Salvatierra (säl-vä-tyĕr'rä) Mex.	20·13 N	100·52 W
218	Salwā Baḥrī Egypt (Nile In.)	24·43 N	32·58 E
188	Salween R. (săl-wēn') Bur.	26·46 N	98·19 E
171	Sal'yany Sov. Un.	39·40 N	49·10 E
158	Salzburg (sälts'bŏŏrgh) Aus.	47·48 N	13·04 E
158	Salzburg (State) Aus.	47·30 N	13·18 E
158	Salzwedel (sälts-vā'dĕl) G.D.R.	52·51 N	11·10 E
218	Samālūt (sä-mä-lōōt') Egypt (Nile In.)	28·17 N	30·43 E
129	Samaná (sä-mä-nä') Dom. Rep.	19·15 N	69·25 W
129	Samana Cabo (C.) (kȧ'bô) Dom. Rep.	19·20 N	69·00 W
129	Samana or Atwood Cay (I.) Ba.	23·05 N	73·45 W
197	Samar (I.) (sä'mär) Phil.	11·30 N	126·07 E
171	Samara (R.) Sov. Un.	52·50 N	50·35 E
167	Samara (R.) (sȧ-mä'rȧ) Sov. Un.	48·47 N	35·30 E
197	Samarai (sä-mä-rä'ê). Pap. N. Gui.	10·45 S	150·49 E
172	Samarkand (sȧ-mȧr-känt') Sov. Un.	39·42 N	67·00 E
217	Samba Zaire	4·38 S	26·22 E
184	Sambalpur (sŭm'bŭl-pŏŏr) India	21·30 N	84·05 E
184	Sāmbhar (R.) India	27·00 N	74·58 E
159	Sambor (säm'bôr) Sov. Un.	49·31 N	23·12 E
137	Samborombón, Bahia (B.) (bä-ē'ä-säm-bô-rôm-bô'n) Arg. (Buenos Aires In.)	35·57 S	57·05 W
137	Samborombón (R.) Arg. (Buenos Aires In.)	35·20 S	57·52 W
155	Sambre (R.) (säNbr') Bel.	50·20 N	4·15 E
216	Sambungo Ang.	8·39 S	20·43 E
112	Sammamish, L. (sȧ-măm'ĭsh) Wa. (Seattle In.)	47·35 N	122·02 W
112	Sammamish (R.). Wa. (Seattle In.)	47·43 N	122·08 W
165	Samokov (sä'mô-kôf) Bul.	42·20 N	23·33 E
163	Samora Correia (sä-mô'rä-kôr-rĕ'yä) Port. (Lisbon In.)	38·55 N	8·52 W
172	Samorovo (sȧ-mȧ-rô'vô). Sov. Un.	60·47 N	69·13 E
165	Sámos (I.) (să'mŏs) Grc.	37·53 N	26·35 E
165	Samothráki (I.) Grc.	40·23 N	25·10 E
197	Sampaloc Pt. (säm-pä'lôk) Phil. (In.)	14·43 N	119·56 E
119	Sam Rayburn Res. Tx.	31·10 N	94·15 W
156	Samsø (I.) (säm'sû) Den.	55·49 N	10·47 E
120	Samson (săm'sŭn) Al.	31·06 N	86·02 W
194	Samsu (säm'sōō') Kor.	41·12 N	128·00 E
171	Samsun (sȧm'sōōn') Tur.	41·20 N	36·05 E
171	Samtredia (sȧm'trĕ-dê) Sov. Un.	42·18 N	42·25 E
112	Samuel (I.) (săm'ū-ĕl) Can. (Vancouver In.)	48·50 N	123·10 W
171	Samur (R.) (sä-mōōr') Sov. Un.	41·40 N	47·20 E
214	San (sän) Mali	13·18 N	4·54 W
186	Ṣan'ā' (sän'ä) Yemen	15·17 N	44·05 E
215	Sanaga (R.) (sä-nä'gä) Cam.	4·10 N	10·40 E
133	San Ambrosio, Isla de (I.) (ē's-lä-dĕ-sän äm-brō'zê-ō). Chile	26·40 S	80·00 W
197	Sanana, Pulau (I.) Indon.	2·15 S	126·38 E
186	Sanandaj Iran	36·44 N	46·43 E
114	San Andreas (săn ăn'drê-ȧs) Ca.	38·10 N	120·42 W
102	San Andreas (L.) Ca. (San Francisco In.)	37·36 N	122·26 W
134	San Andrés (sän-än-drĕ's) Col. (In.)	6·57 N	75·41 W
125	San Andrés (sän än-drās') Mex. (In.)	19·15 N	99·10 W
125	San Andres, Laguna de (L.). Mex.	22·40 N	97·50 W
102	San Andres, Mts. (săn ăn'drê-ȧs) U. S.	33·00 N	106·40 W
	San Andrés (L.), see Petén, Laguna de		
137	San Andrés de Giles (sän-än-drĕ's-dĕ-gē'lĕs) Arg. (Buenos Aires In.)	34·26 S	59·28 W
127	San Andres I. Col.	12·32 N	81·34 W
115	San Andres Mts. NM	33·45 N	106·40 W
125	San Andrés Tuxtla (sän-än-drā's-tōōs'tlä). Mex.	18·27 N	95·12 W
118	San Angelo (săn ăn-jĕ-lō) Tx.	31·28 N	100·22 W
164	San Antioco, I. di (ē'sō-lä-dē-sän-än-tyō'kô). It.	39·00 N	8·25 E
137	San Antonio (sän-ån-tô'nyō) Chile (Santiago In.)	33·34 S	71·36 W
134	San Antonio Col. (In.)	2·57 N	75·06 W
134	San Antonio Col. (In.)	3·55 N	75·38 W
197	San Antonio Phil. (In.)	14·57 N	120·05 E
113	San Antonio (săn ăn-tō'nê-ô) Tx. (San Antonio In.)	29·25 N	98·30 W
114	San Antonio (R.) Ca.	36·00 N	121·13 W
128	San Antonio, Cabo (C.) (kȧ'bô-sän-än-tô'nyô). Cuba	21·55 N	84·55 W
163	San Antonio Abad (sän än-tō'nyô ä-bädh'). Sp.	38·59 N	1·17 E
119	San Antonio B. Tx.	28·20 N	97·08 W
137	San Antonio de Areco (dā ä-rā'kô) Arg. (Buenos Aires In.)	34·16 S	59·30 W
129	San Antonio de las Vegas (sän än-tô'nyô-dĕ-läs-vĕ'gäs) Cuba (In.)	22·07 N	82·16 W
129	San Antonio de los Baños (dâ lōs bän'yōs). Cuba (In.)	22·08 N	82·30 W
136	San Antonio de los Cobres (dâ lōs kō'brâs). Arg.	24·15 S	66·29 W
137	San Antônio de Pádua (dĕ-pá'dwä) Braz. (Rio de Janeiro In.)	21·32 S	42·09 W
135	San Antonio de Tamanaco (sän-ån-tô-nyō-dĕ-tá-mä-nȧ'kô) Ven. (In.)	9·42 N	66·03 W
136	San Antonio Oeste (sän-nä-tō'nyô ô-ĕs'tâ). Arg.	40·49 S	64·56 W
113	San Antonio Pk. (săn ăn-tō'nĭ-ō) Ca. (Los Angeles In.)	34·17 N	117·39 W
118	San Antonio R. Tx.	29·00 N	97·58 W
126	Sanarate (sä-nä-rä'tĕ) Guat.	14·47 N	90·12 W
119	San Augustine (săn ô'gŭs-tēn). Tx.	31·33 N	94·08 W
118	San Bartolo Mex.	24·43 N	103·12 W
125	San Bartolo (sän bär-tō'lô) Mex. (In.)	19·36 N	99·43 W
164	San Bartolomeo (bär-tô-lô-mā'ô) It.	41·25 N	15·04 E
164	San Benedetto del Tronto (bā'nâ-dĕt'tô dĕl trōn'tô). It.	42·58 N	13·54 E
119	San Benito (săn bĕ-nē'tô) Tx.	26·07 N	97·37 W
114	San Benito (R.) Ca.	36·40 N	121·20 W
113	San Bernardino (bûr-när-dē'nô) Ca. (Los Angeles In.)	34·07 N	117·19 W
114	San Bernardino Mts. Ca.	34·05 N	116·23 W
137	San Bernardo (sän bĕr-när'dô) Chile (Santiago In.)	33·35 S	70·42 W
124	San Blas (sän bläs') Mex.	21·33 N	105·19 W
120	San Blas, C. Fl.	29·38 N	85·38 W
127	San Blas, Cord. de (Mts.) (kôr-dēl-yĕ'rä-dĕ). Pan.	9·17 N	78·20 W
127	San Blas, Golfo de (G.) Pan.	9·33 N	78·42 W
127	San Blas, Punta (Pt.) Pan.	9·35 N	78·55 W
112	San Bruno (săn brū-nô) Ca. (San Francisco In.)	37·38 N	122·25 W
118	San Buenaventura (bwā'nȧ-vĕn-tōō'rȧ). Mex.	27·07 N	101·30 W
112	San Carlos (săn kär'lōs) Ca. (San Francisco In.)	37·30 N	122·15 W
136	San Carlos (sän-kȧ'r-lōs) Chile	36·23 S	71·58 W
134	San Carlos Col. (In.)	6·11 N	74·58 W
216	San Carlos Equat. Gui.	3·27 N	8·33 E
125	San Carlos (sän kär'lōs) Mex.	17·49 N	92·33 W
118	San Carlos Mex.	24·36 N	98·52 W
127	San Carlos (sän-kä'r-lōs) Nic.	11·08 N	84·48 W
197	San Carlos Phil. (In.)	15·56 N	120·20 E
134	San Carlos Ven.	9·36 N	68·35 W
136	San Carlos de Bariloche (sän-kä'r lōs-dĕ-bä-rē'lô'chĕ) Arg.	41·15 S	71·26 W
115	San Carlos Ind. Res. (sän kär'lōs) Az.	33·27 N	110·15 W
115	San Carlos Res. Az.	33·05 N	110·29 W
127	San Carlos R. C. R.	10·36 N	84·18 W
135	San Casimiro (kä-sē-mê'rô) Ven. (In.)	10·01 N	67·02 W
164	San Cataldo (kä-täl'dō) It.	37·30 N	13·59 E
129	Sánchez (sän'chĕz) Dom. Rep.	19·15 N	69·40 W
124	Sanchez, Río de los (R.) (rē'ō-dĕ-lôs). Mex.	20·31 N	102·29 W
124	Sánchez Román (Tlaltenango) (rô-mȧ'n) (tlä'l-tĕ-nän-gô). Mex.	21·48 N	103·20 W
162	San Clemente (sän klå-mĕn'tâ). Sp.	39·25 N	2·24 W
114	San Clemente (I.) Ca.	33·02 N	118·36 W
129	San Cristobal (krēs-tô'bäl) Dom. Rep.	18·25 N	70·05 W
126	San Cristóbal Guat.	15·22 N	90·26 W
134	San Cristóbal Ven.	7·43 N	72·15 W
134	San Cristobal (I.) Ec.	1·05 S	89·15 W
205	San Cristobal (I.) Sol. Is.	10·47 S	162·17 E
164	San Croce, C. (krô'chā) It.	37·15 N	15·18 E
128	Sancti Spíritus (säŋk'tê spē'rê-tōōs). Cuba	21·55 N	79·25 W

Page	Name	Pronunciation	Region	Lat. or	Long. or

128 Sancti Spiritus (Prov.)......Cuba 22·05 N 79·20 W
160 Sancy, Puy de (Pk.)
(pwē-dĕ-sáN-sē').Fr. 45·30 N 2·53 E
122 Sand (I.) (sănd).Or. (Portland In.) 46·16 N 124·01 W
109 Sand (I.)................Wi. 46·03 N 91·09 W
218 Sand (R.)................S. Afr.
(Johannesburg & Pretoria In.) 28·09 S 26·46 E
213 Sand (I.)..S. Afr. (Natal In.) 28·30 S 29·30 E
195 Sanda (sän'dä)...Jap. (Ōsaka In.) 34·53 N 135·14 E
196 Sandakan (sản-dä'kản).....Mala. 5·51 N 118·03 E
154 Sanday (I.) (sănd'ā).......Scot. 59·17 N 2·25 W
148 Sandbach (sănd'băch).....Scot. 53·08 N 2·22 W
156 Sandefjord (sän'dĕ-fyồr').....Nor. 59·09 N 10·14 E
112 San de Fuca (de-fōō-cä)
Wa. (Seattle In.) 48·14 N 122·44 W
115 Sanders................Az. 35·13 N 109·20 W
118 Sanderson (săn'dẽr-săn)....Tx. 30·09 N 102·24 W
120 Sandersville (săn'dẽrz-vĭl)....Ga. 32·57 N 82·50 W
156 Sandhammar, C.
(sănt'häm-màr).Swe. 55·24 N 14·37 E
108 Sand Hills (Reg.) (sănd)......Ne. 41·57 N 101·29 W
106 Sand Hook (sănd hōŏk)
NJ (New York In.) 40·29 N 74·05 W
148 Sandhurst (sănd'hûrst)
Eng. (London In.) 51·20 N 0·48 W
114 San Diego (săn dĕ-ā'gồ)..Ca. (In.) 32·43 N 117·10 W
116 San Diego................Tx. 27·47 N 98·13 W
114 San Diego (R.)............Ca. 32·53 N 116·57 W
124 San Diego de la Unión
(sän dĕ-â-gồ dä lä ōō-nyōn')
Mex. 21·27 N 100·52 W
119 Sandies Cr. (sănd'ēz)......Tx. 29·13 N 97·34 W
113 San Dimas (săn dĕ-màs)
Ca. (Los Angeles In.) 34·07 N 117·49 W
116 San Dimas (dĕ-mäs').....Mex. 24·08 N 105·57 W
156 Sandnes (sänd'nĕs).........Nor. 58·52 N 5·44 E
212 Sandoa (săn-dō'ä).........Zaire 9·39 S 23·00 E
159 Sandomierz (sän-dō'myĕzh)...Pol. 50·39 N 21·45 E
164 San Donà di Piave
(sän dồ nä' dĕ pyä'vĕ).It. 45·38 N 12·34 E
188 Sandoway (sän-dồ-wī').....Bur. 18·24 N 94·28 E
110 Sandpoint (sănd point)........Id. 48·17 N 116·34 W
202 Sandringham
Austl. (Melbourne In.) 37·57 S 145·01 E
164 Sandrio (sä'n-dryồ)..........It. 46·11 N 9·53 E
117 Sand Springs (sănd sprĭnz)....Ok. 36·08 N 96·06 W
204 Sandstone (sănd'stōn)......Austl. 28·00 S 119·25 E
107 Sandstone................Mn. 46·08 N 92·53 W
190 Sanduo (săn-dwồ)........China 32·49 N 119·39 E
106 Sandusky (săn-dŭs'kē)
Al. (Birmingham In.) 33·32 N 86·50 W
104 Sandusky................Mi. 43·25 N 82·50 W
104 Sandusky................Oh. 41·25 N 82·45 W
104 Sandusky (R.)..........Oh. 41·10 N 83·20 W
104 Sandwich (săn'wĭch)......Il. 42·35 N 88·53 W
112 Sandy (sănd'ē)..Or. (Portland In.) 45·24 N 122·16 W
113 Sandy....Ut. (Salt Lake City In.) 40·36 N 111·53 W
112 Sandy (R.)....Or. (Portland In.) 45·28 N 122·17 W
203 Sandy C.............Austl. 24·25 S 153·10 E
111 Sandy Cr.............Wy. 42·08 N 109·35 W
106 Sandy Hook (hōŏk)
Ct. (New York In.) 41·25 N 73·17 W
89 Sandy L.....Can. (Edmonton In.) 53·46 N 113·58 W
99 Sandy L.................Can. 49·16 N 57·00 W
95 Sandy L.................Can. 53·00 N 93·07 W
119 Sandy Point...........Tx. (In.) 29·22 N 95·27 W
102 Sandy Pt....Wa. (Vancouver In.) 48·48 N 122·42 W
106 Sandy Springs (springz)
Ga. (Atlanta In.) 33·55 N 84·23 W
137 San Enrique (sän-ĕn-rē'kĕ)
Arg. (Buenos Aires In.) 35·47 S 60·22 W
136 San Estanislao (ĕs-tä-nēs-lá'ồ).Par. 24·38 S 56·20 W
126 San Esteban (ĕs-tĕ'bän)....Hond. 15·13 N 85·53 W
197 San Fabian (fä-byä'n)..Phil. (In.) 16·14 N 120·28 E
137 San Felipe (fâ-lē'pĕ)
Chile (Santiago In.) 32·45 S 70·43 W
124 San Felipe (fĕ-lē'pĕ).......Mex. 21·29 N 101·13 W
124 San Felipe................Mex. 22·21 N 105·26 W
134 San Felipe (fĕ-lē'pĕ).......Ven. 10·13 N 68·45 W
114 San Felipe, Cr. (sän fê-lēp'á)..Ca. 33·10 N 116·03 W
128 San Felipe, Cayos de (Is.)
(kä'yōs-dĕ-sän-fĕ-lē'pĕ).Cuba 22·00 N 83·30 W
163 San Felíu de Guixols
(sän fâ-lē'ồ dä gê-hôls).Sp. 41·45 N 3·01 E
133 San Felix, Isla de (I.)
(ē's-lä-dĕ-sän fâ-lēks').Chile 26·20 S 80·10 W
162 San Fernanda (fẽr-nä'n-dä).Sp. 36·28 N 6·13 W
136 San Fernando (fẽr-nä'n-dồ)
Arg. (Buenos Aires In.) 34·11 S 58·34 W
113 San Fernando (fẽr-nä'n'dồ)
Ca. (Los Angeles In.) 34·17 N 118·27 W
137 San Fernando.Chile (Santiago In.) 36·36 S 70·58 W
118 San Fernando (fẽr-nän'dồ)..Mex. 24·52 N 98·10 W
197 San Fernando (sän fẽr-nä'n-dồ)
Phil. (In.) 16·38 N 120·19 E
134 San Fernando de Apure
(sän-fẽr-nä'n-dồ-dĕ-ä-pōō'rä)
Ven. 7·46 N 67·29 W
134 San Fernando de Atabapo
(dĕ-ä-tä-bä'pồ).Ven. 3·58 N 67·41 W

163 San Fernando de Henares
(dĕ-ä-nä'räs).Sp. (Madrid In.) 40·23 N 3·31 W
118 San Fernando R.
(sän fẽr-nän'dồ).Mex. 25·07 N 98·25 W
156 Sånfjället (Mtn.)............Swe. 62·19 N 13·30 E
89 Sanford (săn'fẽrd)
Can. (Winnipeg In.) 49·41 N 97·27 W
121 Sanford (săn'fồrd)......Fl. (In.) 28·46 N 80·18 W
98 Sanford (săn'fẽrd)........Me. 43·26 N 70·47 W
121 Sanford................NC 35·26 N 79·10 W
136 San Francisco (săn frăn'sĭs'kồ)
Arg. 31·23 S 62·09 W
112 San Francisco
Ca. (San Francisco In.) 37·45 N 122·26 W
126 San Francisco............Sal. 13·48 N 88·11 W
San Francisco, see Ixhuatán
115 San Francisco (R.)........NM 33·35 N 108·55 W
112 San Francisco B. (săn frăn'sĭs'kồ)
Ca. (San Francisco In.) 37·45 N 122·21 W
122 San Francisco del Oro (dĕl ồ'rồ)
Mex 27·00 N 106·37 W
124 San Francisco del Rincón
(dĕl rĕn-kōn').Mex. 21·01 N 101·51 W
135 San Francisco de Macaira
(dĕ-mä-kī'rä).Ven. (In.) 9·58 N 66·17 W
129 San Francisco de Macoris
(dä-mä-kō'rĕs).Dom. Rep. 19·20 N 70·15 W
129 San Francisco de Paula
dä pou'lä).Cuba (In.) 23·04 N 82·18 W
113 San Gabriel
(săn gä-brĕ-ĕl').(gä'brĕ-ĕl)
Ca. (Los Angeles In.) 34·06 N 118·06 W
124 San Gabriel Chilac
(sän-gä-brĕ-ĕl-chê-läk').Mex. 18·19 N 97·22 W
113 San Gabriel Mts.
Ca. (Los Angeles In.) 34·17 N 118·03 W
113 San Gabriel Res.
Ca. (Los Angeles In.) 34·14 N 117·48 W
113 San Gabriel R.
Ca. (Los Angeles In.) 33·47 N 118·06 W
117 Sangamon (R.) (săn'gà-mйn)...Il. 40·08 N 90·08 W
114 Sanger (săng'ẽr)............Ca. 36·42 N 119·33 W
158 Sangerhausen (säng'ẽr-hou-zĕn)
G.D.R. 51·28 N 11·17 E
215 Sangha (R.)................Afr. 2·40 N 16·10 E
197 Sangihe, Pulau (I.) (säŋ'gê-ē)
Indon. 3·30 N 125·30 E
134 San Gil (sän-κĕ'l)..........Col. 6·32 N 73·13 W
164 San Giovanni in Fiore
(sän jồ-vän'nê ēn fyồ'rä).It. 39·15 N 16·40 E
163 San Giuseppe Vesuviano
(sän-zhĕōō-sĕ'p-pĕ-vĕ-sōō-vyä'nồ)
It. (Naples In.) 40·36 N 14·31 E
194 Sangju (säng'jōō').........Kor. 36·20 N 128·07 E
185 Sāngli................India 16·56 N 74·38 E
215 Sangmélima................Cam. 2·56 N 11·59 E
162 Sangonera (R.) (säŋ-gồ-nā'rä)..Sp. 37·43 N 1·58 W
113 San Gorgonio Mt. (sän gồr-gồ'nĭ-ồ)
Ca. (Los Angeles In.) 34·06 N 116·50 W
100 Sangre De Cristo, Range
(săng'ẽr-de-krēs-tồ).U. S. 37·45 N 105·50 W
112 San Gregoria (sän grĕ-gồr'ä)
Ca. (San Francisco In.) 37·20 N 122·23 W
164 Sangro (R.) (säŋ'grồ)........It. 41·38 N 13·56 E
162 Sangüesa (sän-gwĕ'sä)........Sp. 42·36 N 1·15 W
190 Sanhe (sän-hŭ)............China 39·59 N 117·06 E
121 Sanibel I. (săn'ĭ-bĕl)....Fl. (In.) 26·26 N 82·15 W
126 San Ignacio............Belize (In.) 17·11 N 89·04 W
San Ildefonso, see Villa Alta
197 San Ildefonso, C.
(sän-ĕl-dĕ-fồn-sồ).Phil. (In.) 16·03 N 122·10 E
162 San Ildefonso o la Granja
(ồ lä grän'khä).Sp. 40·54 N 4·02 W
136 San Isidro (ē-sĕ'drồ)
Arg. (Buenos Aires In.) 34·13 S 58·31 W
127 San Isidro..............C. R. 9·24 N 83·43 W
113 San Jacinto (săn já-sĭn'tồ)
Ca. (Los Angeles In.) 33·47 N 116·57 W
197 San Jacinto (sän hä-sēn'tồ)
Phil. (In.) 12·33 N 123·43 E
119 San Jacinto (R.), West Fork...Tx. 30·35 N 95·37 W
113 San Jacinto R. (săn já-sĭn'tồ)
Ca. (Los Angeles In.) 33·44 N 117·14 W
119 San Jacinto R...........Tx. 30·25 N 95·05 W
137 San Javier (sän-hä-vē'ẽr)
Chile (Santiago In.) 35·35 S 71·43 W
125 San Jerónimo..........Mex. (In.) 19·31 N 98·46 W
124 San Jerónimo de Juárez
(hâ-rō'nê-mồ dä hwä'râz).Mex. 17·08 N 100·30 W
135 San Joaquin (hồ-ä-kê'n).Ven. (In.) 10·16 N 67·47 W
114 San Joaquin (R.) (săn hwä-kēn')
Ca. 37·10 N 120·51 W
114 San Joaquin Valley..........Ca. 36·45 N 120·30 W
136 San Jorge, Golfo (G.)
(gồl-fồ-sän-κồ'r-κĕ).Arg. 46·15 S 66·45 W
135 San José (sän hồ-sā')......Bol. 17·54 S 60·42 W
112 San Jose (sän hồ-zā')
Ca. (San Francisco In.) 37·20 N 121·54 W
127 San Jose (sän hồ-sā')....C. R. 9·57 N 84·05 W
126 San José................Guat. 13·56 N 90·49 W

197 San Jose..............Phil. (In.) 12·22 N 121·04 E
197 San Jose..............Phil. (In.) 15·49 N 120·57 E
137 San José (hồ-sĕ')
Ur. (Buenos Aires In.) 34·20 S 56·43 W
137 San José (Dept.)
Ur. (Buenos Aires In.) 34·17 S 56·23 W
122 San José (I.) (κồ-sĕ')......Mex. 25·00 N 110·35 W
115 San José (R.) (sän hồ-zā')...NM 35·15 N 108·10 W
137 San José (R.) (sän-hồ-sĕ')
Ur. (Buenos Aires In.) 34·05 S 56·47 W
127 San Jose, Isla de (I.)
(ē's-lä-dĕ-sän hồ-sā').Pan. 8·17 N 79·20 W
136 San José de Feliciano
(dä lä ĕs-kē'nä).Arg. 30·26 S 58·44 W
135 San José de Gauribe
(sän-hồ-sĕ'dĕ-gáōō-rĕ'bĕ)
Ven. (In.) 9·51 N 65·49 W
129 San Jose de las Lajas
(sän-κồ-sĕ'dĕ-läs-lá'käs)
Cuba (In.) 22·13 N 82·10 W
124 San José Iturbide
(ē-tōōr-bē'dĕ).Mex. 21·00 N 100·24 W
136 San Juan (hwän')..........Arg. 31·36 S 68·29 W
134 San Juan (hōŏá'n).....Col. (In.) 3·23 N 73·48 W
129 San Juan (sän hwän').Dom. Rep. 18·50 N 71·15 W
197 San Juan..............Phil. (In.) 16·41 N 120·20 E
123 San Juan (sän hwän')
P. R. (Puerto Rico In.) 18·30 N 66·10 W
San Juan, see Guichicovi
San Juan, see Mazatlán
136 San Juan (Prov.)..........Arg. 31·00 S 69·30 W
123 San Juan, Cabezas de (C.)
P. R. (Puerto Rico In.) 18·29 N 65·30 W
216 San Juan, Cabo (C.)..Equat. Gui. 1·08 N 9·23 E
128 San Juan, Pico (Pk.)
(pĕ'κồ-sän-κōŏá'n).Cuba 21·55 N 80·00 W
125 San Juan (R.) (sän-hōō-än').Mex. 18·10 N 95·23 W
118 San Juan, Rio (R.)
(rē'ồ-sän-hwän).Mex. 25·35 N 99·15 W
115 San Juan (R.)..............Ut. 37·10 N 110·30 W
136 San Juan Bautista
(sän hwän' bou-tēs'tä).Par. 26·48 S 57·09 W
124 San Juan Capistrano
(sän-hōō-än' kä-pês-trä'nồ)
Mex. 22·41 N 104·07 W
114 San Juan Cr. (săn hwän')....Ca. 35·24 N 120·12 W
118 San Juan de Guadalupe
(sän hwan dä gwä-dhä-lōō'pä)
Mex. 24·37 N 102·43 W
127 San Juan del Norte (Greytown)
(dĕl nôr-tĕ) (grā'toun).Nic. 10·55 N 83·44 W
127 San Juan del Norte Bahia de (B.)
(bä-ē'ä-dĕ-sän hwän dĕl nôr'tä)
Nic. 11·12 N 83·40 W
124 San Juan de los Lagos
(sän-hōō-än'dä los lä'gồs).Mex. 21·15 N 102·18 W
124 San Juan de los Lagos (R.)
(dä lōs lä'gồs).Mex. 21·13 N 102·12 W
135 San Juan de los Morros
(dĕ-lồs-mồ'r-rồs).Ven. (In.) 9·54 N 67·22 W
124 San Juan del Rio (dĕl rē'ồ)...Mex. 20·21 N 99·59 W
118 San Juan del Rio
(sän hwän del rē'ồ).Mex. 24·47 N 104·29 W
126 San Juan del Sur (dĕl sōōr)...Nic. 11·15 N 85·53 W
118 San Juan de Sabinas
(dĕ-sä-bē'näs).Mex. 27·56 N 101·23 W
125 San Juan Evangelista
(sän-hōō-ä'n-â-vän-kä-lēs'ta')
Mex. 17·57 N 95·08 W
112 San Juan I......Wa. (Seattle In.) 48·28 N 123·08 W
112 San Juan Is. (sän hwän)
Can. (Vancouver In.) 48·49 N 123·14 W
125 San Juan Ixtenco (ēx-tĕ'n-kồ)
Mex. 19·14 N 97·52 W
128 San Juan Martinez
(sän κōō ä'n-mär-tĕ'nĕz).Cuba 22·15 N 83·50 W
115 San Juan Mts. (san hwän')....Co. 37·50 N 107·30 W
127 San Juan R..............Nic. 10·58 N 84·18 W
136 San Julián (sän hōō-lyä'n)....Arg. 49·17 S 68·02 W
136 San Justo
Arg. (Buenos Aires In.) 34·25 S 58·33 W
214 Sankanbiriwa (Mtn.).......S. L. 8·56 N 10·48 W
214 Sankarani R. (sän'kä-rä'nĕ)
Gui.-Mali 11·10 N 8·35 W
158 Sankt Gallen............Switz. 47·25 N 9·22 E
216 Sankuru (R.) (sän-kōō'rōō)..Zaire 4·00 S 22·35 E
122 San Lazaro, C. (sän-lá'zä-rồ).Mex. 24·58 N 113·30 W
112 San Leandro (sän lê-än'drồ)
Ca. (San Francisco In.) 37·43 N 122·10 W
137 San Lorenzo (sän lồ-rĕn'zồ)
Arg. (Buenos Aires In.) 32·46 S 60·44 W
112 San Lorenzo
Ca. (San Francisco In.) 37·41 N 122·08 W
126 San Lorenzo (sän lồ-rĕn'zồ).Hond. 13·24 N 87·24 W
163 San Lorenzo de El Escorial
(sän lồ-rĕn'tho dĕl ĕs-kồ-rê-äl')
Sp. (Madrid In.) 40·36 N 4·04 W
162 Sanlúcar (sän-lōō'kär)........Sp. 36·46 N 6·21 W
134 San Lucas (lōō'käs)........Bol. 20·12 N 65·06 W

Page	Name Pronunciation	Region	Lat. °'	Long. °'
	Santa Maria, see Huazolotitlán			
124	Santa Maria (R.) (sän'tȧ mä-rē'ȧ)	Mex.	21·33 N	100·17 W
129	Santa Maria, C.	Ba.	23·45 N	75·30 W
162	Santa Maria, Cabo de (C.) (kȧ'bō-dě-sän-tä-mä-rē'ä)	Port.	36·58 N	7·54 W
128	Santa Maria, Cayo (I.) (kä'yō-sän'tȧ mȧ-rē'ȧ)	Cuba	22·40 N	79·00 W
124	Santa María del Oro (sän'tä-mä-rē'ä-děl-ô-rô)	Mex.	21·21 N	104·35 W
124	Santa Maria de los Angeles (dě-lôs-ȧ'n-hě-lěs)	Mex.	22·10 N	103·34 W
124	Santa María del Rio (sän'tȧ mä-rē'ȧ děl rē'ō)	Mex.	21·46 N	100·43 W
124	Santa Maria de Ocotán (sän'tä-mä-rē'ä-dě-ô-kô-tä'n)	Mex.	22·56 N	104·30 W
210	Santa Maria I. (sän-tä-mä-rē'ä)	Açores (In.)	37·09 N	26·02 W
137	Santa Maria Madalena (sän-tä-mä-rē'ä-mȧ-dȧ-lě-nä)	Braz. (Rio de Janeiro In.)	22·00 S	42·00 W
134	Santa Marta (sän'tȧ mär'tȧ)	Col.	11·15 N	74·13 W
216	Santa Marta, Cabo de (C.)	Ang.	13·52 S	12·25 E
113	Santa Monica (săn'tȧ mŏn'ĭ-kȧ)	Ca. (Los Angeles In.)	34·01 N	118·29 W
113	Santa Monica Mts.	Ca. (Los Angeles In.)	34·08 N	118·38 W
136	Santana (R.) (sän-tä'nä)	Braz. (Rio de Janeiro In.)	22·33 S	43·37 W
134	Santander (sän-tän-děr')	Col. (In.)	3·00 N	76·25 W
162	Santander (sän-tän-dâr')	Sp.	43·27 N	3·50 W
163	Sant'Angelo Romano (sän-tä'n-gzhě-lô-rô-mä'nô)	It. (Rome In.)	42·02 N	12·45 E
163	Sant' Antimo	It. (Naples In.)	40·40 N	14·11 E
163	Santañy (sän-tän'yē)	Sp.	39·21 N	3·08 E
114	Santa Paula (săn'tȧ pô'lȧ)	Ca.	34·24 N	119·05 W
135	Santarém (sän-tä-rěN')	Braz.	2·28 S	54·37 W
162	Santarém	Port.	39·18 N	8·48 W
128	Santaren Chan. (sän-tȧ-rěn')	Ba.	24·15 N	79·30 W
115	Santa Rita (săn'tȧ rē'tȧ)	NM	32·45 N	108·05 W
137	Santa Rita do Passo Quatro (sän-tä-rē'tȧ-dô-pä'sô-kwȧ'trô)	Braz. (Rio de Janeiro In.)	21·43 S	47·27 W
137	Santa Rita do Sapucai (sä-pōō-kȧ'ē)	Braz. (Rio de Janeiro In.)	22·15 S	45·41 W
136	Santa Rosa (sän-tä-rô-sä)	Arg.	36·45 S	64·10 W
114	Santa Rosa (săn'tȧ rō'zȧ)	Ca.	38·27 N	122·42 W
134	Santa Rosa (sän-tä-rô-sä)	Col. (In.)	6·38 N	75·26 W
134	Santa Rosa	Ec.	3·29 S	78·55 W
126	Santa Rosa (sän'tȧ rō'sȧ)	Guat.	14·21 N	90·16 W
126	Santa Rosa	Hond.	14·45 N	88·51 W
116	Santa Rosa (săn'tȧ rō'sȧ)	NM	34·55 N	104·41 W
135	Santa Rosa (sän-tä-rô-sä)	Ven. (In.)	9·37 N	64·10 W
134	Santa Rosa de Cabal (sän-tä-rô-sä-dě-kä-bä'l)	Col. (In.)	4·53 N	75·38 W
137	Santa Rosa de Viterbo (sän-tä-rô-sȧ-dě-vē-těr'-bô)	Braz. (Rio de Janeiro In.)	21·30 S	47·21 W
114	Santa Rosa Ind. Res. (săn'tȧ rō'zȧ')	Ca.	33·28 N	116·50 W
122	Santa Rosalía (sän'tȧ rô-zä'lē-ȧ)	Mex.	27·13 N	112·15 W
	Santa Rosalia, see Ciudad Camargo			
110	Santa Rosa Mts. (săn'tȧ rō'zȧ)	Nv.	41·33 N	117·50 W
113	Santa Susana (săn'tȧ sōō-zä'nȧ)	Ca. (Los Angeles In.)	34·16 N	118·42 W
	Santa Tecla, see Nueva San Salvador			
137	Santa Teresa (sän-tä-tě-rě'sä)	Arg. (Buenos Aires In.)	33·27 S	60·47 W
135	Santa Teresa	Ven. (In.)	10·14 N	66·40 W
136	Santa Vitória do Palmar (sän-tä-vē-tô'ryä-dô-päl-mȧr)	Braz.	33·30 S	53·16 W
114	Santa Ynez (R.) (săn'tȧ ē-něz')	Ca.	34·40 N	120·20 W
114	Santa Ysabel Ind. Res. (săn-tȧ ĭ-zȧ-běl')	Ca.	33·05 N	116·46 W
114	Santee (săn tē')	Ca. (In.)	32·50 N	116·58 W
121	Santee (R.)	SC	33·27 N	80·02 W
136	Santiago (sän-tyȧ'gô)	Braz.	29·05 S	54·46 W
137	Santiago (sän-tě-ä'gô)	Chile (Santiago In.)	33·26 S	70·40 W
127	Santiago	Pan.	8·07 N	80·58 W
197	Santiago (sän-tyä'gô)	Phil. (In.)	16·42 N	121·33 E
162	Santiago	Sp.	42·52 N	8·32 W
	Santiago, see Zacatepec			
137	Santiago (Prov.) (sän-tyȧ'gō)	Chile (Santiago In.)	33·28 S	70·55 W
124	Santiago, Rio Grande de (R.) (rē'o-grä'n-dě-dě-sän-tyȧ'gô)	Mex.	21·15 N	104·05 W
197	Santiago (I.)	Phil. (In.)	16·29 N	120·03 E
129	Santiago de los Cabelleros (sän-tyȧ'gô-dȧ lōs kȧ-bä-yā'rôs)	Dom. Rep.	19·30 N	70·45 W
129	Santiago de Cuba (sän-tyȧ'gô-dā kōō'bȧ)	Cuba	20·00 N	75·50 W
129	Santiago de Cuba (Prov.)	Cuba	20·20 N	76·05 W
129	Santiago de las Vegas (sän-tyȧ'gô-dě-läs-vě'gäs)	Cuba (In.)	22·13 N	82·23 W
136	Santiago del Estero (sän-tē-ȧ'gō-děl ěs-tā'rō)	Arg.	27·50 S	64·14 W
136	Santiago del Estero (Prov.) (sän-tē-ȧ'gō-děl ěs-tā'rô)	Arg.	27·15 S	63·30 W
118	Santiago Mts. (sän-tē-ä'gô)	Tx.	30·00 N	103·30 W
113	Santiago Res.	Ca. (Los Angeles In.)	33·47 N	117·42 W
129	Santiago Rodriguez (sän-tyȧ'gô-rô-drē'gěz)	Dom. Rep.	19·30 N	71·25 W
125	Santiago Tuxtla (sän-tyȧ'gô-tōō'x-tlä)	Mex.	18·28 N	95·18 W
118	Santiaguillo, Laguna de (L.) (lä-ōō'nä-dě-sän-tê-a-gēl'yō)	Mex.	24·51 N	104·43 W
110	Santiam R. (săn'tyăm)	Or.	44·42 N	122·26 W
162	Santisteban del Puerto (sän'tē stȧ-bän'děl pwěr'tô)	Sp.	38·15 N	3·12 W
135	Santo Amaro (sän'tōō ä-mä'rōō)	Braz.	12·32 S	38·33 W
137	Santo Amaro de Campos (sän-tô-ä-mä'rô-dě-kȧm'pôs)	Braz. (Rio de Janeiro In.)	22·01 S	41·05 W
137	Santo André (sän-tô-än-drě')	Braz. (Rio de Janeiro In.)	23·40 S	46·31 W
136	Santo Angelo (sän-tô-ȧ'n-zhě-lô)	Braz.	28·16 S	53·59 W
137	Santo Antônio do Monte (sän-tô-än-tô'nyô-dô-môn'tě)	Braz. (Rio de Janeiro In.)	20·06 S	45·18 W
216	Santo Antonio do Zaire (sän'tōō än-tō'nē-ōō)	Ang.	6·10 S	12·25 E
128	Santo Domingo (sän'tô-dōmĭŋ'gô)	Cuba	22·35 N	80·20 W
126	Santo Domingo (sän-tô-dô-mē'n-gō)	Nic.	12·15 N	84·56 W
129	Santo Domingo (sän'tô dô-mĭn'gô)	Dom. Rep.	18·30 N	69·55 W
	Santo Domingo, see Zanatepec			
162	Santo Domingo de la Caizada (dā lä käl-thä'dä)	Sp.	42·27 N	2·55 W
162	Santoña (sän-tō'nyä)	Sp.	43·25 N	3·27 W
137	Santos (sän'tozh)	Braz. (Rio de Janeiro In.)	23·58 S	46·20 W
137	Santos Dumont (sän'tôs-dōō-mô'nt)	Braz. (Rio de Janeiro In.)	21·28 S	43·33 W
136	Santo Tomé (sän-tô-tô-mě')	Arg.	28·32 S	56·04 W
195	Sanuki (sä'nōō-kē)	Jap. (Tōkyō In.)	35·16 N	139·53 E
137	San Urbano (sän-ōōr-bä'nô)	Arg. (Buenos Aires In.)	33·39 S	61·28 W
136	San Valentin, M. (Mtn.) (sän-vä-lěn-tē'n)	Chile	46·41 S	73·30 W
160	Sanvic (säN-vēk')	Fr.	49·34 N	0·08 E
137	San Vicente (sän-vē-sěn'tě)	Arg. (Buenos Aires In.)	35·00 S	58·26 W
137	San Vicente	Chile (Santiago In.)	34·25 S	71·06 W
126	San Vicente (sän vē-sěn'tȧ)	Sal.	13·41 N	88·43 W
162	San Vincente de Alcántara (sän vē-thěn'tȧ dȧ äl-kän'tä-rä)	Sp.	39·24 N	7·08 W
164	San Vito (sän vē'tô)	It.	45·53 N	12·52 E
115	San Xavier Ind. Res. (x-ā'vĭēr)	Az.	32·07 N	111·12 W
191	Sanyuanli (sän-yüän-lē)	China (Canton In.)	23·11 N	113·16 E
114	San Ysidro (săn yĭ-drō')	Ca. (In.)	32·33 N	117·02 W
137	São Bernardo do Campo (souN-běr-nȧr'dô-dô-kȧ'm-pô)	Braz. (Rio de Janeiro In.)	23·44 S	46·33 W
136	São Borja (souN-bôr-zhä)	Braz.	28·44 S	55·59 W
137	São Carlos (souN kär'lōzh)	Braz. (Rio de Janeiro In.)	22·02 S	47·54 W
135	São Cristovão (souN-krěs-tō-vouN)	Braz.	11·04 S	37·11 W
137	São Fidélis (souN-fē-dě'lēs)	Braz. (Rio de Janeiro In.)	21·41 S	41·45 W
135	São Francisco (souN fräN-sěsh'kōō)	Braz.	15·59 S	44·42 W
135	São Francisco, Rio (R.) (rē'ō-sän-frän-sē's-kō)	Braz.	8·56 S	40·20 W
136	São Francisco do Sul (souN fräN-sěsh'kōō-dô-sōō'l)	Braz.	26·15 S	48·42 W
136	São Gabriel (souN'gä-brē-ěl')	Braz.	30·28 S	54·11 W
137	São Geraldo (souN-zhě-rä'l-dô)	Braz. (Rio de Janeiro In.)	21·01 S	42·49 W
136	São Gonçalo (souN'gōŋ-sä'lōō)	Braz. (Rio de Janeiro In.)	22·55 S	43·04 W
137	São Gonçalo do Sapucaí (souN-gôn-sä'lō-dô-sä-pōō-kī')	Braz. (Rio de Janeiro In.)	21·55 S	45·34 W
217	São Hill	Tan.	8·20 S	35·12 E
214	Sao Joao	Guinea-Bissau	11·32 N	15·26 W
136	São João da Barra (souN-zhôuN-dä-bȧ'rä)	Braz. (Rio de Janeiro In.)	21·40 S	41·03 W
137	São João da Boa Vista (souN-zhôuN-dä-bôä-vē's-tä)	Braz. (Rio de Janeiro In.)	21·58 S	46·45 W
137	São João del Rei (souN zhô-ouN'děl-rā)	Braz. (Rio de Janeiro In.)	21·08 S	44·14 W
136	São João de Meriti (souN-zhôuN-dě-mě-rē-tê)	Braz. (Rio de Janeiro In.)	22·47 S	43·22 W
137	São João do Araguaia (souN zhô-ouN'dô-ä-rä-gwä'yä)	Braz.	5·29 S	48·44 W
163	São João dos Lampas (souN' zhô-ouN' dōzh län-päzh')	Port (Lisbon In.)	38·52 N	9·24 W
137	São João Nepomuceno (souN-zhôuN-ně-pô-mōō-sě-nō)	Braz. (Rio de Janeiro In.)	21·33 S	43·00 W
210	São Jorge I. (souN zhôr' zhě)	Açores (In.)	38·28 N	27·34 W
137	São José do Rio Pardo (souN-zhô-sě'dô-rē'ō-pȧ'r-dō)	Braz. (Rio de Janeiro In.)	21·36 S	46·50 W
135	São José do Rio Prêto (souN zhô-zě'dô-rē'ō-prě-tō)	Braz.	20·57 S	49·12 W
137	São José dos Campos (souN zhô-zā'dōzh käN pōzh')	Braz. (Rio de Janeiro In.)	23·12 S	45·53 W
136	São Leopoldo (souN-lě-ô-pôl'dô)	Braz.	29·46 S	51·09 W
135	São Luis (Maranhão) (souN-lōōē's-mä-rän-youN')	Braz.	2·31 S	43·14 W
137	São Luis do Paraitinga (souN-lōōē's-dô-pä-rä-ē-tē'n-gä)	Braz. (Rio de Janeiro In.)	23·15 S	44·18 W
135	São Mateus (souN mä-tā'ōōzh)	Braz.	18·44 S	39·45 W
137	São Miguel Arcanjo (souN-mē-gě'l-ȧr-kän-zhō)	Braz. (Rio de Janeiro In.)	23·54 S	47·59 W
210	São Miguel I.	Açores (In.)	37·59 N	26·38 W
129	Saona (I.) (sä-ō'nä)	Dom. Rep.	18·10 N	68·55 W
160	Saône (R.) (sōn)	Fr.	46·27 N	4·58 E
216	São Nicolau	Ang.	14·15 S	12·21 E
210	São Nicolau (souN' nē-kô-louN')	C. V. (In.)	16·19 N	25·19 W
137	São Paulo (souN' pou'lōō)	Braz. (Rio de Janeiro In.)	23·34 S	46·38 W
135	São Paulo (State) (souN pou'lōō)	Braz.	21·45 S	50·47 W
134	São Paulo de Olivença (souN'pou'lōōdȧ ô-lê-věn'sȧ)	Braz.	3·32 S	68·46 W
137	São Pedro (souN-pě'drô)	Braz. (Rio de Janeiro In.)	22·34 S	47·54 W
137	São Pedro de Aldeia (souN-pě'drô-dě-äl-dě'yä)	Braz. (Rio de Janeiro In.)	22·50 S	42·04 W
135	São Raimundo Nonato (souN' rī-mōō'n-do nô-nä'tōō)	Braz.	9·09 S	42·32 W
137	São Roque (souN' rō'kě)	Braz. (Rio de Janeiro In.)	23·32 S	47·08 W
135	São Roque, Cabo de (C.) (kä'bo-dě-souN' rō'kě)	Braz.	5·06 S	35·11 W
216	São Salvador do Congo (souN säl-vȧ-dôr)	Ang	6·30 S	14·10 E
137	São Sebastião (souN sȧ-bäs-tê-ouN')	Braz. (Rio de Janeiro In.)	23·48 S	45·25 W
137	São Sebastião, Ilha de (I.) (ēl'yȧ dȧ souN' sȧ-bäs-tê-ouN')	Braz. (Rio de Janeiro In.)	23·52 S	45·22 W
137	São Sebastião do Paraíso (souN-sě-bäs-tē-ouN-dô-pä-rä-ē'sō)	Braz. (Rio de Janeiro In.)	20·54 S	46·58 W
137	São Simão (souN-sē-mouN)	Braz. (Rio de Janeiro In.)	21·30 S	47·33 W
210	São Tiago I. (souN tê-ä'gōō)	C. V. (In.)	15·09 N	24·45 W
216	São Tomé (souN tô-mä')	São Tomé & Príncipe	0·20 N	6·44 E
216	São Tomé (I.)	São Tomé & Príncipe	0·20 N	7·00 E
137	São Tomé, Cabo de (C.) (kä'bō-dě-souN-tô-mě')	Braz. (Rio de Janeiro In.)	22·00 S	40·00 W
209	Sao Tome & Principe (prēn'sē-pě)	Afr.	1·00 N	6·00 E
152	Saoura, Oued (R.)	Alg.	29·39 N	1·42 W

ng-sing; ŋ-baŋk; N-nasalized n; nŏd; cŏmmit; ōld; ôbey; ôrder; fōōd; fŏŏt; ou-out; s-soft; sh-dish; th-thin; pūre; ûnite; ûrn; stŭd; circŭs; ü-as "y" in study; '-indeterminate vowel.

344 Sao Vicente — Scottdale PRONOUNCING INDEX

Page	Name Pronunciation Region	Lat. °'	Long. °'
137	São Vicente (souN ve-se'n-tĕ) Braz. (Rio de Janeiro In.)	23·57 s	46·25 w
210	Sao Vincente I. (souN vê-sĕn'tȧ) C. V. (In.)	16·51 N	24·35 w
162	São Vinente, Cabo de (C.) (kȧ'bō-dĕ-sän-vê-sĕ'n-tĕ). Port.	37·03 N	9·31 w
215	Sapele (sä-pā'lā) Nig.	5·54 N	5·41 E
217	Sapitwa (Mtn.) Malawi	15·58 s	35·38 E
166	Sapozhok (sä-pô-zhôk') Sov. Un.	53·58 N	40·44 E
194	Sapporo (säp-pô'rō) Jap.	43·02 N	141·29 E
174	Sapronovo (sȧp-rô'nô-vô) Sov. Un. (Moscow In.)	55·13 N	38·25 E
137	Sapucaí (R.) (sä-pōō-kȧ-ē') Braz. (Rio de Janeiro In.)	21·07 s	45·53 w
137	Sapucaia (sä-pōō-kä'yȧ) Braz. (Rio de Janeiro In.)	22·01 s	42·54 w
137	Sapucaí Mirim (R.) (sä-pōō-kȧ-ē'mē-rēN) Braz. (Rio de Janeiro In.)	21·06 s	47·03 w
117	Sapulpa (sȧ-pŭl'pȧ) Ok.	36·01 N	96·05 w
137	Saquarema (sä-kwä-rĕ-mä) Braz. (Rio de Janeiro In.)	22·56 s	42·32 w
112	Sara (sä'rä) Wa. (Portland In.)	45·45 N	122·42 w
211	Sara, Bahr (R.) (bär) Chad-Cen. Afr. Rep.	8·19 N	17·44 E
165	Sarajevo (sä-rȧ-yĕv'ô) (sȧ-rä'ya-vô). Yugo.	43·15 N	18·26 E
174	Sarana (sá-rä'ná) Sov. Un. (Urals In.)	56·31 N	57·44 E
105	Saranac Lake NY	44·20 N	74·05 w
105	Saranac L. (săr'á-năk) NY	44·15 N	74·20 w
136	Sarandi (sä-rän'dē) Arg. (Buenos Aires In.)	34·26 s	58·21 w
137	Sarandi Grande (sä-rän'dē-grän'dĕ) Ur. (Buenos Aires In.)	33·42 s	56·21 w
184	Sārangpur India	23·39 N	76·32 E
170	Saransk (sá-ränsk') Sov. Un.	54·10 N	45·10 E
174	Sarany (sȧ-rá'nĭ) Sov. Un. (Urals In.)	58·33 N	58·48 E
215	Sara Pk. Nig.	9·37 N	9·25 E
170	Sarapul (sä-rä-pōōl') Sov. Un.	56·28 N	53·50 E
121	Sarasota (săr-ȧ-sōtȧ) Fl. (In.)	27·27 N	82·30 w
119	Saratoga (săr-ȧ-tō'gȧ) Tx.	30·17 N	94·31 w
112	Saratoga Wa. (Seattle In.)	48·04 N	122·29 w
112	Saratoga Pass Wa. (Seattle In.)	48·09 N	122·33 w
105	Saratoga Springs (springz) NY	43·05 N	74·50 w
171	Saratov (sȧ rä'tôf) Sov. Un.	51·30 N	45·30 E
193	Saravane Laos	15·48 N	106·40 E
196	Sarawak (Reg.) (sȧ-rä'wäk) Mala.	2·30 N	112·45 E
159	Sárbogárd (shär'bô-gärd) Hung.	46·53 N	18·38 E
89	Sarcee Ind. Res. (sär'sē) Can. (Calgary In.)	50·58 N	114·23 w
210	Sardalas Libya	25·59 N	10·33 E
164	Sardinia (I.) (sär-dĭn'ĭȧ) It.	40·08 N	9·05 E
120	Sardis (sär'dĭs) Ms.	34·26 N	89·55 w
108	Sargent (sär'jĕnt) Ne.	41·40 N	99·38 w
215	Sarh (Fort-Archambault) (är-chaN-bô') Chad	9·09 N	18·23 E
171	Sarikamis Tur.	40·30 N	42·40 E
163	Sariñena (sä-rēn-yĕ'nä) Sp.	41·46 N	0·11 w
192	Sariwŏn (sä'rē-wŭn') Korea	38·40 N	125·45 E
160	Sark (I.) (särk) Guernsey	49·28 N	2·22 w
165	Şarkoy (shär'kû-ê) Tur.	40·39 N	27·07 E
160	Sarlat (sär-lä') Fr.	44·52 N	1·13 E
136	Sarmiento, Monte (Mt.) (mô'n-tĕ-sär-myĕn'tō) Chile	54·28 s	70·40 w
104	Sarnia (sär'nē-ȧ) Can.	43·00 N	82·25 w
163	Sarno (sä'r-nô) It. (Naples In.)	40·35 N	14·38 E
159	Sarny (sär'nê) Sov. Un.	51·17 N	26·39 E
165	Saronikós Kólpos (G.) Grc.	37·51 N	23·30 E
165	Saros Körfezi (G.) (sä'rôs) Tur.	40·30 N	26·20 E
159	Sárospatak (shä'rôsh-pô'tôk) Hung.	48·19 N	21·35 E
165	Šar Planina (Mts.) (shär plä'nê-na). Yugo.	42·07 N	21·54 E
156	Sarpsborg (särps'bôrg) Nor.	59·17 N	11·07 E
161	Sarrebourg (sär-bōōr') Fr.	48·44 N	7·02 E
161	Sarreguemines (sär-gē-mēn') Fr.	49·06 N	7·05 E
162	Sarria (sär'ê-ä) Sp.	42·14 N	7·17 w
126	Sarstun R. (särs-tōō'n) Guat.	15·50 N	89·26 w
164	Sartène (sär-tĕn') Fr.	41·36 N	8·59 E
160	Sarthe (R.) (särt) Fr.	47·44 N	0·32 w
158	Sárvár (shär'vär) Hung.	47·14 N	16·55 E
171	Sarych, Mys (C.) (mĭs sȧ-rēch') Sov. Un.	44·25 N	33·00 E
172	Sary-Ishikotrau, Peski (des.) (sä'rē ē' shĕk-ô'trou). Sov. Un.	46·12 N	75·30 E
172	Sarysu (R.) (sä'rê-sōō) Sov. Un.	47·47 N	69·14 E
184	Sasarām (sŭs-ŭ-räm') India	25·00 N	84·00 E
195	Sasayama (sä'sä-yä'mä) Jap.	35·05 N	135·14 E
195	Sasebo (sä'sȧ-bô) Jap.	33·12 N	129·43 E
	Saseno (I.), see Sazan		
158	Sašice Czech.	49·14 N	13·31 E
90	Saskatchewan (Prov.) Can.	54·46 N	107·40 w
94	Saskatchewan (R.) (săs-kăch'ê-wän). Can.	53·45 N	103·20 w
94	Saskatoon (săs-kȧ-tōōn') Can.	52·07 N	106·38 w
218	Sasolburg S. Afr. (Johannesburg & Pretoria In.)	26·52 s	27·47 E
170	Sasovo (sȧs'ô-vô) Sov. Un.	54·20 N	42·00 E
113	Saspamco (săs-păm'cō) Tx. (San Antonio In.)	29·13 N	98·18 w
214	Sassandra Ivory Coast	4·58 N	6·05 w
214	Sassandra (R.) (sȧs-sän'drȧ) Ivory Coast	5·35 N	6·25 w
164	Sassari (säs'sä-rê) It.	40·44 N	8·33 E
158	Sassnitz (säs'nêts) G.D.R.	54·31 N	13·37 E
214	Satadougou (sä-tá-dōō-gōō') Mali	12·21 N	10·07 w
156	Säter (sĕ'tēr) Swe.	60·21 N	15·50 E
121	Satilla (R.) (sȧ-tĭl'ȧ) Ga.	31·15 N	82·13 w
174	Satka (sät'kȧ). Sov. Un. (Urals In.)	55·03 N	59·02 E
159	Sátoraljaujhely (shä'tô-rô-lyô-ōō'yĕl'). Hung.	48·24 N	21·40 E
159	Satu-Mare (sá'tōō-má'rĕ) Rom.	47·50 N	22·53 E
112	Saturna (să-tûr'nȧ) Can. (Vancouver In.)	48·48 N	123·12 w
112	Saturna (I.). Can. (Vancouver In.)	48·47 N	123·03 w
156	Saude (sou'dĕ) Nor.	59·40 N	6·21 E
150	Sáudharkrókur Ice.	65·41 N	19·38 w
182	Saudi Arabia (sȧ-ōō'dĭ ȧ-rä'bĭ-ȧ) Asia	22·40 N	46·00 E
149	Sauerlach (zou'ĕr-läK) F.R.G. (Munich In.)	47·58 N	11·39 E
104	Saugatuck (sô'gȧ-tŭk) Mi.	42·40 N	86·10 w
104	Saugeer (R.) (sô'gēr) Can.	44·20 N	81·20 w
105	Saugerties (sô'gēr-tēz) NY	42·05 N	73·55 w
99	Saugus (sô'gŭs) Ma. (In.)	42·28 N	71·01 w
109	Sauk (R.) (sôk) Mn.	45·30 N	94·45 w
109	Sauk Centre Mn.	45·43 N	94·58 w
109	Sauk City Wi.	43·16 N	89·45 w
109	Sauk Rapids (răp'ĭd) Mn.	45·35 N	94·08 w
96	Sault Ste. Marie Can.	46·31 N	84·20 w
113	Sault Ste. Marie (sōō sānt má-rē') Mi. (Sault Ste. Marie In.)	46·29 N	84·21 w
129	Saumatre, Etang (L.) Hai.	18·40 N	72·10 w
205	Saunders, C. (sôrn'dērs). N. Z. (In.)	45·55 s	170·50 E
89	Saunders L. (sän'dērs) Can. (Edmonton In.)	53·18 N	113·25 w
216	Saurimo Ang.	9·39 s	20·24 E
112	Sausalito (sô-sȧ-lē'tô) Ca. (San Francisco In.)	37·51 N	122·29 w
160	Sausset-les-Pins (sō-sĕ'lā-pàN') Fr. (In.)	43·20 N	5·08 E
216	Saútar Ang.	11·06 s	18·27 E
112	Sauvie I. (sô'vē). Or. (Portland In.)	45·43 N	123·49 w
165	Sava (R.) (sä'vä) Yugo.	44·50 N	17·00 E
106	Savage (săv'ĕj) Md. (Baltimore In.)	39·07 N	76·49 w
113	Savage Mn. (Minneapolis, St. Paul In)	44·47 N	93·20 w
171	Savalan (Mtn.) Iran	38·20 N	48·00 E
215	Savalou Benin	7·56 N	1·58 E
109	Savanna (sȧ-văn'ȧ) Il.	42·05 N	90·09 w
121	Savannah (sȧ-văn'ȧ) Ga.	32·04 N	81·07 w
109	Savannah Mo.	39·58 N	94·49 w
120	Savannah Tn.	35·13 N	88·14 w
121	Savannah (R.) Ga.-SC	33·11 N	81·51 w
196	Savannakhét Indo China	16·33 N	104·45 E
128	Savanna la Mar (sȧ-vän'ȧ lȧ mär') Jam.	18·10 N	78·10 w
158	Sávava R. Czech.	49·36 N	15·24 E
210	Savé (sȧ-vā') Benin	8·09 N	2·03 E
160	Save (R.) Fr.	43·32 N	0·50 E
212	Save, Rio (R.) (rē'ō-sä'vĕ) Moz.	21·28 s	34·14 E
161	Saverne (sȧ-vĕrn') Fr.	48·40 N	7·22 E
164	Savigliano (sä-vêl-yä'nô) It.	44·38 N	7·42 E
164	Savona (sä-nō'nä) It.	44·19 N	8·28 E
157	Savonlinna (sȧ'vôn-lên'nȧ) Fin.	61·53 N	28·49 E
167	Savran' (säv-rän') Sov. Un.	48·07 N	30·09 E
196	Sawahlunto Indon.	0·37 s	100·50 E
211	Sawākin Sud.	19·02 N	37·19 E
211	Sawda, Jabal as (Mts.) Libya	28·14 N	13·46 E
152	Sawfjjin, Wadi (R.) Libya	31·18 N	13·16 E
218	Sawhāj Egypt (Nile In.)	26·34 N	31·40 E
211	Sawknah Libya	29·04 N	15·53 E
196	Sawu, Laut (Savu Sea) Indon.	9·15 s	122·15 E
196	Sawu, Pulau (I.) Indon.	10·15 s	122·00 E
112	Sawyer (L.) (sô'yēr) Wa. (Seattle In.)	47·20 N	122·02 w
210	Say (sä'ê) Niger	13·09 N	2·16 E
172	Sayan Khrebet (Mts.) (sŭ-yän') Sov. Un.	51·30 N	90·00 E
183	Şaydā (Sidon) (sä'ê-dä) (sī'dŏn) Leb. (Palestine In.)	33·34 N	35·23 E
186	Sayḩūt P. D. R. of Yem.	15·23 N	51·28 E
116	Sayre (sā'ēr) Ok.	35·19 N	99·40 w
105	Sayre Pa.	41·55 N	76·30 w
106	Sayreton (sā'ēr-tŭn) Al. (Birmingham In.)	33·34 N	86·51 w
106	Sayreville (sâr'vĭl) NJ (New York In.)	40·28 N	74·21 w
188	Sayr Usa Mong.	44·51 N	107·00 E
125	Sayula (sä-yōō'lä) Mex.	17·51 N	94·56 w
124	Sayula Mex.	19·50 N	101·33 w
124	Sayula, Luguna de (L.) (lä-gōō'nä-dĕ). Mex.	20·00 N	103·33 w
186	Say'un P.D.R. of Yem.	16·00 N	48·59 E
105	Sayville (sā'vĭl) NY	40·45 N	73·10 w
165	Sazan (Saseno) (I.) Alb.	40·30 N	19·17 E
174	Sazhino (sȧz-hē'nô) Sov. Un. (Urals In.)	56·20 N	58·15 E
156	Scäffle Swe.	59·10 N	12·55 E
182	Scandinavian Pen. Eur.	62·00 N	14·00 E
113	Scanlon (skăn'lôn) Mn. (Duluth In.)	46·27 N	92·26 w
112	Scappoose (skă-pōōs') Or. (Portland In.)	45·46 N	122·53 w
112	Scappoose (R.). Or. (Portland In.)	45·47 N	122·57 w
89	Scarborough (skär'bēr-ô) Can. (Toronto In.)	43·45 N	79·12 w
154	Scarborough (skär'bŭr-ô) Eng.	54·16 N	0·19 w
106	Scarsdale (skärz'dāl) NY (New York In.)	41·01 N	73·47 w
97	Scatari I (skăt'ȧ-rē) Can.	46·00 N	59·44 w
149	Schaerbeek (skär'bāk) Bel. (Brussels In.)	50·53 N	4·23 E
158	Schaffhausen (shäf'hou-zĕn). Switz.	47·42 N	8·38 E
91	Schefferville Can.	54·52 N	67·01 w
155	Schelde, R. Bel.	51·04 N	3·55 E
105	Schenectady (skĕ-nĕk'tȧ-dê). NY.	42·50 N	73·55 w
149	Scheveningen Neth. (Amsterdam In.)	52·06 N	4·15 E
149	Schiedam. Neth. (Amsterdam In.)	51·55 N	4·23 E
161	Schiltigheim (shêl'tegh-hīm) Fr.	48·48 N	7·47 E
164	Schio (skē'ô) It.	45·43 N	11·23 E
158	Schleswig (shlĕs'vêgh) F.R.G.	54·32 N	9·32 E
158	Schleswig-Holstein (State) (shlĕs'vêgh-hōl'shtīn) F.R.G.	54·40 N	9·10 E
158	Schmalkalden (shmäl'käl-dĕn) G.D.R.	50·41 N	10·25 E
107	Schneider (schnīd'ēr) In. (Chicago In.)	41·12 N	87·26 w
109	Schofield (skō'fêld) Wi.	44·52 N	89·37 w
158	Schönebeck (shû'nĕ-bergh). G.D.R.	52·01 N	11·44 E
149	Schoonhoven Neth. (Amsterdam In.)	51·56 N	4·51 E
158	Schramberg (shräm'bĕrgh). F.R.G.	48·14 N	8·24 E
96	Schreiber Can.	48·50 N	87·10 w
105	Schroon (L.) (skrōōn) NY	43·50 N	73·50 w
149	Schultzendorf (shōōl'tzĕn-dōrf) G.D.R. (Berlin In.)	52·21 N	13·35 E
96	Schumacher Can.	48·30 N	81·30 w
108	Schuyler (slī'ler) Ne.	41·28 N	97·05 w
106	Schuylkill (R.) (skōōl'kĭl) Pa.	40·10 N	75·31 w
105	Schuylkill-Haven (hā-vĕn) Pa.	40·35 N	76·10 w
158	Schwabach (shvä'bäk) F.R.G.	49·19 N	11·02 E
158	Schwäbische Alb (Mts.) (shvă'bē-shĕ älb) F.R.G.	48·11 N	9·09 E
158	Schwäbisch Gmünd (shvă'bēsh gmünd) F.R.G.	48·47 N	9·49 E
158	Schwäbisch Hall (häl) F.RG.	49·08 N	9·44 E
158	Schwandorf (shvän'dôrf) F.R.G.	49·19 N	12·08 E
196	Schwaner, Pegunungan Mts. (sKvän'ēr). Indon.	1·05 s	112·30 E
158	Schwarzwald (For.) (shvärts' väld) F.R.G.	47·54 N	7·57 E
158	Schwaz Aus.	47·20 N	11·45 E
149	Schwechat (shvĕk'ät) Aus. (Vienna In.)	48·09 N	16·29 E
158	Schwedt (shvĕt) G.D.R.	53·04 N	14·17 E
158	Schweinfurt (shvīn'fōōrt). F.R.G.	50·03 N	10·14 E
161	Schwelm (shvĕlm) F.R.G. (Ruhr In.)	51·17 N	7·18 E
158	Schwenningen (shvĕn'ĭng-ĕn) F.R.G.	48·04 N	8·33 E
158	Schwerin (shvĕ-rēn') G.D.R.	53·36 N	11·25 E
158	Schweriner See (L.) (shvĕ'rē-nĕr zā) G.D.R.	53·40 N	11·06 E
161	Schwerte (shvĕr'tĕ) F.R.G. (Ruhr In.)	51·26 N	7·34 E
149	Schwielow L. (shvē'lōv) G.D.R. (Berlin In.)	52.20 N	12·52 E
158	Schwyz (schēts) Switz.	47·01 N	8·38 E
164	Sciacca (shê-äk'kä) It.	37·30 N	13·09 E
154	Scilly (Is.) (sĭl'ê) Eng.	49·56 N	6·50 w
104	Scioto (R.) (sī-ō'tō) Oh.	39·10 N	82·55 w
99	Scituate (sĭt'ū-āt) Ma. (In.)	42·12 N	70·45 w
111	Scobey (skō'bê) Mt.	48·48 N	105·29 w
112	Scoggin (skō'gĭn) Or. (Portland In.)	45·28 N	123·14 w
89	Scotch (R.) (skŏch) Can. (Ottawa In.)	45·21 N	74·56 w
110	Scotia (skō'shȧ) Ca.	40·29 N	124·06 w
154	Scotland (skŏt'lȧnd) U. K.	57·05 N	5·10 w
108	Scotland SD	43·08 N	97·43 w
121	Scotland Neck (nĕk) NC	36·06 N	77·25 w
105	Scotstown (skŏts'toun) Can.	45·35 N	71·15 w
90	Scott, C. (skŏt) Can.	50·47 N	128·26 w
110	Scott, Mt. Or.	42·55 N	122·00 w
112	Scott, Mt. Or. (Portland In.)	45·27 N	122·33 w
113	Scott Air Force Base Il. (St. Louis In.)	38·33 N	89·52 w
213	Scottburgh (skŏt'bŭr-ô) S. Afr. (Natal In.)	30·18 s	30·42 E
116	Scott City Ks.	38·28 N	100·54 w
106	Scottdale (skŏt' dāl) Ga. (Atlanta In.)	33·47 N	84·16 w

ăt; finăl; rāte; senâte; ärm; ȧsk; sofȧ; fâre; ch-choose; dh-as th in other; bē; êvent; bĕt; recĕnt; cratēr; g-go; gh-guttural g; bĭt; ĭ-short neutral; rīde; K-guttural k as ch in German ich

Page	Name Pronunciation Region	Lat. °′	Long. °′
220	Scott Is. . . . . Ant.	67·00 S	178·00 E
220	Scott Ra. . . . . Ant.	68·00 S	55·00 E
108	Scottsbluff (skŏts′blŭf) . . . . Ne.	41·52 N	103·40 W
108	Scotts Bluff Natl. Mon. . . . . . . Ne.	41·45 N	103·47 W
95	Scottsboro (skŏts′bŭro) . . . . Al.	34·40 N	86·03 W
104	Scottsburg (skŏts′ bûrg) . . . . In.	38·40 N	85·50 W
203	Scottsdale (skŏts′dāl) . . . . Austl.	41·12 S	147·37 E
95	Scottsville (skŏts′vĭl) . . . . Ky.	36·45 N	86·10 W
104	Scottville . . . . Mi.	44·00 N	86·20 W
105	Scranton (skrăn′tŭn) . . . . Pa.	41·45 N	75·45 W
105	Scugog (L.) (skū′gôg) . . . . Can.	44·05 N	78·55 W
148	Scunthorpe (skŭn′thôrp) . . . . . Eng.	53·36 N	0·38 W
	Scutari, see Shkodër		
165	Scutari (R.) (sko͞o′tä-rê) . . . . . . Alb.	42·14 N	19·33 E
121	Sea, Is. (sē) . . . . Ga.-SC	31·21 N	81·05 W
112	Seabeck (sē′bĕck) . Wa. (Seattle In.)	47·38 N	122·50 W
106	Sea Bright (sē brīt) NJ (New York In.)	40·22 N	73·58 W
119	Seabrook (sē′bro͝ok) . . . . Tx.	29·34 N	95·01 W
105	Seaford (sē′fērd) . . . . De.	38·35 N	75·40 W
116	Seagraves (sē′grāvs) . . . . Tx.	32·51 N	102·38 W
90	Seal (R.) . . . . Can.	59·08 N	96·37 W
113	Seal Beach . . Ca. (Los Angeles In.)	33·44 N	118·06 W
129	Seal Cays (Is.) . Turks & Caicos Is.	21·10 N	71·45 W
129	Seal Cays (Is.) . . . . Ba.	22·40 N	75·55 W
212	Seal I. (sēl) . . . . S. Afr. (In.)	34·07 S	18·36 E
119	Sealy (sē′lê) . . . . Tx.	29·46 N	96·10 W
117	Searcy (sûr′sê) . . . . Ar.	35·13 N	91·43 W
114	Searles (L.) (sûrl′s) . . . . Ca.	35·44 N	117·22 W
98	Searsport (sērz′pōrt) . . . . Me.	44·28 N	68·55 W
110	Seaside (sē′sīd) . . . . Or.	45·59 N	123·55 W
112	Seattle (sê-ăt′′l) . Wa. (Seattle In.)	47·36 N	122·20 W
126	Sebaco (sĕ-bä′kô) . . . . Nic.	12·50 N	86·03 W
98	Sebago (sê-bā′gō) . . . . Me.	43·52 N	70·20 W
122	Sebastion Vizcaino, Bahia (B.) (bä-ê′ä-sĕ-bäs-tyô′n-vês-kä-ê′nô) Mex.	28·45 N	115·15 W
114	Sebastopol (sê-bȧs′tô-pôl) . . . . . Ca.	38·27 N	122·50 W
211	Sebderat . . . . Eth.	15·30 N	36·45 E
216	Sébé (R.) . . . . Gabon	0·45 S	13·30 E
165	Sebes . . . . Rom.	45·58 N	23·34 E
104	Sebewaing (se′bê-wăng) . . . . Mi.	43·45 N	83·25 W
166	Sebezh (syĕ′bĕzh) . . . . Sov. Un.	56·16 N	28·29 E
171	Sebinkarahisar . . . . Tur.	40·15 N	38·10 E
162	Sebkha bou Areg (Marsh) . . . Mor.	35·09 N	3·02 W
163	Sebkhan d′Oran (L.) . . . . Alg.	35·28 N	0·28 W
158	Sebnitz (zĕb′nêts) . . . . G.D.R.	51·01 N	14·16 E
163	Seborbe (sĕ-bôr-dĕ) . . . . Sp.	39·50 N	0·30 W
152	Sebou, Oued R. . . . . Mor.	34·23 N	5·18 W
104	Sebree (sê-brē′) . . . . Ky.	37·35 N	87·30 W
121	Sebring (sē′brĭng) . . . . Fl. (In.)	27·30 N	81·26 W
104	Sebring . . . . Oh.	40·55 N	81·05 W
164	Secchia (R.) (sĕ′kyä) . . . . It.	44·25 N	10·25 E
125	Seco (R.) (sĕ′kô) . . . . Mex.	18·11 N	93·18 W
117	Sedalia . . . . Mo.	38·42 N	93·12 W
160	Sedan (sē-däN) . . . . Fr.	49·49 N	4·55 E
117	Sedan (sê-dăn′) . . . . Ks.	37·07 N	96·08 W
183	Sedom . . . . Isr. (Palestine In.)	31·04 N	35·24 E
112	Sedro Woolley (sē′drô-wo͝ol′ê) Wa. (Seattle In.)	48·30 N	122·14 W
157	Seduva (shĕ′do͝o-vȧ) . . . . Sov. Un.	55·46 N	23·45 E
212	Seekoevlei (L.) (zā′ko͝of-lī) S. Afr. (In.)	34·04 S	18·33 E
149	Seestall (zā′shtäl) F.R.G. (Munich In.)	47·58 N	10·52 E
152	Sefrou (sē-fro͞o′) . . . . Mor.	33·49 N	4·46 W
170	Seg (L.) (syĕgh) . . . . Sov. Un.	64·00 N	33·30 E
183	Segamat (sā′gȧ-mȧt) Mala. (Singapore In.)	2·30 N	102·49 E
190	Segang (sŭ-gäŋ) . . . . China	31·59 N	114·13 E
215	Segbana . . . . Benin	10·56 N	3·42 E
214	Ségou (sā-go͞o′) . . . . Mali	13·27 N	6·16 W
134	Segovia (sĕ-gô′vēä) . . . . . Col. (In.)	7·08 N	74·42 W
162	Segovia (sȧ-gō′vê-ä) . . . . Sp.	40·58 N	4·05 W
	Segovia (R.), see Coco		
163	Segre (R.) (sȧ′grā) . . . . Sp.	41·54 N	1·10 E
101	Seguam (I.) (sē′gwäm) . . . . Ak.	52·16 N	172·10 W
101	Seguam P. . . . . Ak.	52·20 N	173·00 W
215	Séguédine . . . . Niger	20·12 N	12·59 E
214	Séguéla (sā-gā-lä′) . . . . Ivory Coast	7·57 N	6·40 W
118	Seguin (sĕ-gēn′) . . . . Tx.	29·35 N	97·58 W
101	Segula (I.) (sē-gū′lȧ) . . . . Ak.	52·08 N	178·35 E
163	Segura (R.) (sȧ-go͞o′rä) . . . . Sp.	38·07 N	0·33 W
162	Segura, Sierra de (Mts.) (sē-ĕ′r-rä-dĕ) . Sp.	38·05 N	2·45 W
162	Segura (R.) . . . . Sp.	38·24 N	2·12 W
184	Sehwān . . . . Pak.	26·33 N	67·51 E
129	Seibo (sĕ′y-bō) . . . . Dom. Rep.	18·45 N	69·05 W
116	Seiling . . . . Ok.	36·09 N	98·56 W
157	Seinäjoki (sȧ′ê-nĕ-yô′kê) . . . . . . Fin.	62·47 N	22·50 E
160	Seine, Baie de la (B.) (bī dĕ lä sȧn) . Fr.	49·37 N	0·53 W
96	Seine (R.) (sân) . . . . Can.	49·04 N	91·00 W
89	Seine (R.) (sân) Can. (Winnipeg In.)	49·48 N	96·30 W
160	Seine, Rivière (R.) (rēv-yâr′) . . Fr.	49·21 N	1·17 E
136	Seio do Venus (Mtn.) (sĕ-yô-dô-vĕ′no͞os) Braz. (Rio de Janeiro In.)	22·28 S	43·12 W
163	Seixal (sȧ-ê-shäl′) Port. (Lisbon In.)	38·38 N	9·06 W
217	Sekenke . . . . Tan.	4·16 S	34·10 E
214	Sekondi-Takoradi (sĕ-kôn′dê tä-kô-rä′dê) . Ghana	4·59 N	1·43 W
211	Sekota . . . . Eth.	12·47 N	38·59 E
183	Selangor (State) (sȧ-län′gōr) Mala. (Singapore In.)	2·53 N	101·29 E
165	Selanoutsi (sȧl′á-nôv-tsĭ) . . . . . Bul.	43·42 N	24·05 E
197	Selaru I. . . . . Indon.	8·30 S	130·30 E
196	Selatan, Tandjung (C.) (sȧ-lä′tän) Indon.	4·09 S	114·40 E
101	Selawik (sē-lȧ-wĭk) . . . . Ak.	66·30 N	160·09 W
196	Selayar (I.) . . . . Indon.	6·15 S	121·15 E
156	Selbusjøen (L.) . . . . Nor.	63·18 N	11·55 E
148	Selby (sĕl′bê) . . . . Eng.	53·47 N	1·03 W
101	Seldovia (sĕl-dō′vê-ȧ) . . . . Ak.	59·26 N	151·42 W
173	Selemdzha (R.) (sâ-lĕmt-zhä′) Sov. Un.	52·28 N	131·50 E
173	Selenga (R.) (sĕ lĕŋ gä′) . . . Sov. Un.	51·00 N	106·40 E
188	Selenge Gol. (R.) . . . . Mong.	49·04 N	102·23 E
173	Selennyakh (R.) (sĕl-yĭn-yäk) Sov. Un.	67·42 N	141·45 E
161	Sélestat (sē-lē-stä′) . . . . Fr.	48·16 N	7·27 E
210	Selibaby (sȧ-lê-bȧ-bē′) . Mauritania	15·21 N	12·11 W
166	Seliger (L.) (sĕl′lê-gĕr) . . Sov. Un.	57·14 N	33·18 E
166	Selizharovo (sȧ′lê-zhä′rô-vô) Sov. Un.	56·51 N	33·28 E
95	Selkirk (sêl′kûrk) . . . . Can.	50·09 N	96·52 W
90	Selkirk Mts. . . . . Can.	51·00 N	117·40 W
112	Selleck (sĕl′ĕck) . . Wa. (Seattle In.)	47·22 N	121·52 W
107	Sellersburg (sĕl′ĕrs-bûrg) In. (Louisville In.)	38·25 N	85·45 W
173	Sellya Khskaya, Guba (B.) (sĕl-yäk′skȧ-yȧ) . Sov. Un.	72·30 N	136·00 E
120	Selma (sĕl′mȧ) . . . . Al.	32·25 N	87·00 W
114	Selma . . . . Ca.	36·34 N	119·37 W
121	Selma . . . . NC	35·33 N	78·16 W
113	Selma . . . . . . Tx. (San Antonio In.)	29·33 N	98·19 W
120	Selmer . . . . Tn.	35·11 N	88·36 W
149	Selsingen (zĕl′zēn-gĕn) F.R.G. (Hamburg In.)	53·22 N	9·13 E
212	Selukwe (sê-lŭk′wê) . . . . Zimb.	19·34 S	30·03 E
110	Selway R. (sĕl′wȧ) . . . . Id.	46·07 N	115·12 W
90	Selwyn (L.) (sĕl′wĭn) . . . . Can.	59·41 N	104·30 W
165	Seman (R.) . . . . Alb.	40·48 N	19·53 E
196	Semarang (sĕ-mä′räng) . . . . . Indon.	7·03 S	110·27 E
196	Semarinda . . . . Indon.	0·30 S	117·10 E
	Semendria, see Smederevo		
167	Semënovka (sĕ-myôn′ôf-kȧ) Sov. Un.	52·10 N	32·34 E
196	Semeru, Gunung (Mtn.) . . . Indon.	8·06 S	112·55 E
112	Semiahmoo Ind. Res. Can. (Vancouver In.)	49·01 N	122·43 W
112	Semiahmoo Spit (sĕm′ĭ-ȧ-mo͞o) Wa. (Vancouver In.)	48·59 N	122·52 W
101	Semichi Is. (sē-mē′chī) . . . . Ak.	52·40 N	174·50 W
111	Seminoe Res. (sĕm′ĭ nô) . . . . . . Wy.	42·08 N	107·10 W
117	Seminole (sĕm′ĭ-nōl) . . . . Ok.	35·13 N	96·41 W
118	Seminole . . . . Tx.	32·43 N	102·39 W
121	Seminole Ind. Res. . . . . Fl. (In.)	26·19 N	81·11 W
121	Seminole Ind. Res. . . . . Fl. (In.)	27·05 N	81·25 W
120	Seminole, L. . . . . Fl.-Ga.	30·57 N	84·46 W
172	Semipalatinsk (sĕ′mê-pȧ-lȧ-tyēnsk′) . Sov. Un.	50·28 N	80·29 E
101	Semisopochnoi (I.) (sĕ-mē-sȧ-pōsh′ noi) . Ak.	51·45 N	179·25 W
172	Semiyarskoye (sĕ′mê-yär′skô-yĕ) Sov. Un.	51·03 N	78·28 E
211	Semliki R. (sĕm′lê-kē) . . . Ug.-Zaire	0·45 N	29·36 E
	Semlin, see Zemun		
158	Semmering P. (sĕm′ĕr-ĭng) . . . Aus.	47·39 N	15·50 E
171	Semnān . . . . Iran	35·30 N	53·30 E
135	Senador Pompeu (sĕ-nä-dōr-pôm-pĕ′o͞o) . Braz.	5·34 S	39·18 W
120	Senatobia (sĕ-nȧ-tō′bê-ȧ) . . . . . Ms.	34·36 N	89·56 W
194	Sendai (sĕn-dī′) . . . . Jap.	38·18 N	141·02 E
117	Seneca (sĕn′ĕ-kȧ) . . . . Ks.	39·49 N	96·03 W
120	Seneca . . . . SC	34·40 N	82·58 W
106	Seneca . . . . Md. (Baltimore In.)	39·04 N	77·20 W
105	Seneca (L.) . . . . NY	42·30 N	76·55 W
105	Seneca Falls . . . . NY	42·55 N	76·55 W
209	Senegal (sĕn-ĕ-gôl′) . . . . Afr.	14·53 N	14·58 W
214	Sénégal (R.) . . . . Afr.	16·00 N	14·00 W
218	Senekal (sĕn′ê-kȧl) . . . . S. Afr. (Johannesburg & Pretoria In.)	28·20 S	27·37 E
158	Senftenberg (zĕnf′tĕn-bĕrgh) G.D.R.	51·32 N	14·00 E
213	Sengunyane (R.) . . Leso (Natal In.)	29·35 S	28·08 E
135	Senhor do Bonfim (sĕn-yôr dô bôN-fē′N) . Braz.	5·21 S	40·09 W
164	Senigallia (sâ-nê-gäl′lyä) . . . . It.	43·42 N	13·16 E
164	Senj (sĕn′) . . . . Yugo.	44·58 N	14·55 E
150	Senja (I.) (sĕnyä) . . . . Nor.	69·28 N	16·10 E
161	Senlis (säN-lēs′) . . . . Fr. (Paris In.)	49·13 N	2·35 E
211	Sennar Dam . . . . Sud.	13·38 N	33·38 E
91	Senneterre . . . . Can.	48·20 N	77·22 W
166	Senno (syĕ′nô) . . . . Sov. Un.	54·48 N	29·43 E
160	Sens (säNs) . . . . Fr.	48·05 N	3·18 E
126	Sensuntepeque (sĕn-so͞on-tȧ-pā′kȧ) . Sal.	13·53 N	88·34 W
165	Senta (sĕn′tä) . . . . Yugo.	45·54 N	20·05 E
195	Senzaki (sĕn′zä-kē) . . . . Jap.	34·22 N	131·09 E
	Seoul, see Sŏul		
183	Sepang . . . . . Mala. (Singapore In.)	2·43 N	101·45 E
136	Sepetiba, Baia de (B.) (bäē′ä dĕ sȧ-pȧ-tē′bȧ) Braz. (Rio de Janeiro In.)	23·01 S	43·42 W
197	Sepik (R.) (sĕp-ēk′) . . Pap. N. Gui.	4·07 S	142·40 E
160	Septèmes-les-Vallons (sĕ-tȧm′la-vä-ôN′) Fr. (Marseille In.)	43·25 N	5·23 E
129	Septentrional, Cordillera (Mts.) (kôr-dēl-yĕ′rä sĕp-tĕn-tryô-nä′l) Dom. Rep.	19·50 N	71·15 W
161	Septeuil (sĕ-tû′) . . . . Fr. (Paris In.)	48·53 N	1·40 E
98	Sept-Îles (sĕ-tēl′) . . . . Can.	50·12 N	66·23 W
120	Sequatchie (R.) (sê-kwăch′ê) . . Tn.	35·33 N	85·14 W
112	Sequim (sē′kwĭm) Wa. (Seattle In.)	48·05 N	123·07 W
112	Sequim B. . . . . . . Wa. (Seattle In.)	48·04 N	122·58 W
114	Sequoia Natl. Park (sê-kwoi′ȧ) . Ca.	36·34 N	118·37 W
155	Seraing (sē-răN′) . . . . Bel.	50·38 N	5·28 E
197	Seram (I.) . . . . Indon.	2·45 S	129·30 E
184	Serāmpore . . . . India (Calcutta In.)	22·44 N	88·21 E
196	Serang (sȧ-räng′) . . . . Indon.	6·13 S	106·10 E
183	Seranggung . Indon. (Singapore In.)	0·49 N	104·11 E
	Serbia (Reg.), see Srbija		
171	Serdobsk (sĕr-dôpsk′) . . . . Sov. Un.	52·30 N	44·20 E
159	Sered . . . . Czech.	48·17 N	17·43 E
167	Seredina-Buda (sĕ-rȧ-dē′nȧ-bo͞o′dȧ) . Sov. Un.	52·11 N	34·03 E
183	Seremban (sĕr-ĕm-bän′) Mala. (Singapore In.)	2·44 N	101·57 E
217	Serengeti Natl. Pk. . . . . Tan.	2·20 S	34·50 E
217	Serengeti Pln. . . . . Tan.	2·40 S	34·55 E
212	Serenje (sē-rĕn′yê) . . . . Zambia	13·12 S	30·49 E
218	Serenli (sȧ-rĕn′lê) Som. (Horn of Afr. In.)	2·28 N	42·15 E
	Seres, see Sérrai		
159	Seret . . . . Czech.	48·17 N	17·43 E
159	Seret . . . . Rom.	47·58 N	26·01 E
159	Seret R. (sĕr′ĕt) . . . . Sov. Un.	49·45 N	25·30 E
172	Sergeya Kirova (I.) (sēr-gyē′yȧ kê′rô-vȧ) . Sov. Un.	77·30 N	86·10 E
135	Sergipe (State) (sĕr-zhē′pĕ) Braz.	10·27 S	37·04 W
170	Sergiyevsk . . . . Sov. Un.	53·58 N	51·00 E
165	Sérifos . . . . Grc.	37·10 N	24·32 E
165	Sérifos (I.) . . . . Grc.	37·42 N	24·17 E
137	Serodino (sĕ-rô-dê′nō) Arg. (Buenos Aires In.)	32·36 S	60·56 W
136	Seropédica (sĕ-rô-pĕ′dē-kä) Braz. (Rio de Janeiro In.)	22·44 S	43·43 W
174	Serov (syĕ-rôf′) Sov. Un. (Urals In.)	59·36 N	60·30 E
212	Serowe (sĕ-rō′wĕ) . . . . Bots.	22·18 S	26·39 E
162	Serpa (sĕr-pä) . . . . Port.	37·56 N	7·38 W
166	Serpukhov (syĕr′po͝o-kôf) . Sov. Un.	54·53 N	37·27 E
165	Sérrai (Seres) (sĕr′rĕ) (sĕr′ĕs) . . Grc.	41·06 N	23·36 E
118	Serranias Del Burro (sĕr-rä-nê′äs dĕl bo͞o′r-rô) . Mex.	29·39 N	102·07 W
135	Serrinha (sĕr-rēn′yȧ) . . . . Braz.	11·43 S	38·49 W
162	Serta (sĕr′tȧ) . . . . Port.	39·48 N	8·01 W
135	Sertânia (sĕr-tȧ′nyä) . . . . Braz.	8·28 S	37·13 W
137	Sertãozinho (sĕr-touN-zê′n-yô) Braz. (Rio de Janeiro In.)	21·10 S	47·58 W
183	Serting (R.) . Mala. (Singapore In.)	3·01 N	102·32 E
136	Seruí (sĕ-ro͝o-ē′) Braz. (Rio de Janeiro In.)	22·40 S	43·08 W
217	Sese Is. . . . . Ug.	0·30 S	32·30 E
164	Sesia (R.) (sȧz′yä) . . . . It.	45·33 N	8·25 E
163	Sesimbra (sĕ-sê′m-brä) Port. (Lisbon In.)	38·27 N	9·06 W
213	Sesmyl (R.) . . . . S. Afr. (Johannesburg & Pretoria In.)	25·51 S	28·06 E
164	Sestri Levante (sĕs′trê lȧ-vän′tȧ) It.	44·15 N	9·24 E
174	Sestroretsk (sĕs-trô-rĕtsk) Sov. Un. (Leningrad In.)	60·06 N	29·58 E
174	Sestroretskiy Razliv, Ozero (L.) (ô′zĕ-rô sĕs-trô′ rĕts-kĭ-räz′lĭf) Sov. Un. (Leningrad In.)	60·05 N	30·07 E
195	Seta (sĕ′tä) . . . . . . Jap. (Osaka In.)	34·58 N	135·56 W
160	Sète (sĕt) . . . . Fr.	43·24 N	3·42 E
135	Sete Lagoas (sĕ-tĕ lä-gô′äs) . . Braz.	19·23 S	43·58 W
210	Setif (sȧ-tēf′) . . . . Alg.	36·18 N	5·21 E
195	Seto (sē′tō) . . . . Jap.	35·11 N	137·07 E
195	Seto-Naikai (Sea) (sĕ′tô nī′kī) . Jap.	33·50 N	132·25 E
210	Settat (sĕt-ät′) (sē-tȧ′) . . . . . . Mor.	33·02 N	7·30 W
212	Sette-Cama (sĕ-tĕ-kä-mä′) . Gabon.	2·29 S	9·40 E
128	Settlement Pt. (sĕt′l-mĕnt) . . . . Ba.	26·40 N	79·00 W
218	Settlers (sĕt′lērs) . . . . S. Afr. (Johannesburg & Pretoria In.)	24·57 S	28·33 E
195	Settsu . . . . Jap. (Osaka In.)	34·46 N	135·33 E
163	Setúbal (sȧ-to͞o′bäl) Port. (Lisbon In.)	30·32 N	8·54 W

ng-sing; ŋ-baŋk; N-nasalized n; nŏd; cŏmmit; ōld; ôbey; ôrder; fo͞od; fo͝ot; ou-out; s-soft; sh-dish; th-thin; pūre; ûnite; ûrn; stŭd; circŭs; ü-as "y" in study; ′-indeterminate vowel.

Page	Name Pronunciation Region	Lat. °'	Long. °'
162	Setúbal, B. de (bä-ē'ä) Port.	38·27 N	9·08 W
95	Seul, Lac (L.) (lȧk sûl) Can.	50·20 N	92·30 W
156	Sevalen (L.) (sĕ'vä-lĕn) Nor.	62·19 N	10·15 E
171	Sevan (L.) (syĭ-vän') Sov. Un.	40·10 N	45·20 E
167	Sevastopol' (Akhiar) (syĕ-vȧs-tô'pôl'') (äĸ'yȧr) Sov. Un.	44·34 N	33·34 E
	Seven Is., see Shichitō		
148	Sevenoaks (sĕ-vĕn-ôks') Eng. (London In.)	51·16 N	0·12 E
174	Severka R. (sâ'vĕr-kȧ) Sov. Un. (Moscow In.)	55·11 N	38·41 E
91	Severn (R.) (sĕv'ērn) Can.	55·21 N	88·42 W
154	Severn (R.) Eng.	51·42 N	2·25 W
106	Severna Park (sĕv'ērn-ȧ) Md. (Baltimore In.)	39·04 N	76·33 W
170	Severnaya Dvina (Northern Dvina (R.) Sov. Un.	63·00 N	42·40 E
169	Severnaya Zemlya (Northern Land) (Is.) (sĕ-vyĭr-nī'u zĭ-m'lyä') Sov. Un.	79·33 N	101·15 E
174	Severoural'sk (sĕ-vyĭ-rŭ-ōō-rälsk') Sov. Un. (Urals In.)	60·08 N	59·53 E
115	Sevier (L.) (sê-vēr') Ut.	38·55 N	113·10 W
115	Sevier R. Ut.	39·25 N	112·20 W
115	Sevier R., East Fork Ut.	37·45 N	112·10 W
134	Sevilla (sĕ-vê'l-yä) Col. (In.)	4·16 N	75·56 W
162	Sevilla (sâ-vēl'yä) Sp.	37·29 N	5·58 W
107	Seville (sĕ'vĭl) Oh. (Cleveland In.)	41·01 N	81·45 W
165	Sevlievo (sĕv'lyĕ-vô) Bul.	41·02 N	25·05 E
160	Sèvre Nantaise (R.) (sâ'vrĕ nän-tȧz') Fr.	47·00 N	1·02 W
160	Sèvre Niortaise (R.) (sâ'vr' nyôr-tâz') Fr.	46·23 N	1·05 W
166	Sevsk (syĕfsk) Sov. Un.	52·08 N	34·28 E
101	Seward (sū'ȧrd) Ak.	60·18 N	149·28 W
117	Seward Ne.	40·55 N	97·06 W
101	Seward Pen. Ak.	65·40 N	164·00 W
136	Sewell (sĕ'ōō-ĕl) Chile	34·01 S	70·18 W
107	Sewickley (sê-wĭk'lê) Pa. (Pittsburgh In.)	40·33 N	80·11 W
125	Seybaplaya (sā-ê-bä-plä'yä) Mex.	19·38 N	90·40 W
20	Seychelles (sā-shĕl') Afr.	5·20 S	55·10 E
150	Seydhisfjördhur (sā'dês-fyûr-dōōr) Ice.	65·21 N	14·08 W
126	Seyé (sĕ-yĕ') Mex. (In.)	20·51 N	89·22 W
153	Seyhan (R.) Tur.	37·28 N	35·40 E
167	Seym (R.) (sĕym) Sov. Un.	51·23 N	33·22 E
97	Seymour (sē'mōr) In.	38·55 N	85·55 W
109	Seymour Ia.	40·41 N	93·03 W
116	Seymour Tx.	33·35 N	99·16 W
213	Seymour (sē'môr) S. Afr. (Natal In.)	32·33 S	26·48 E
213	Sezela S. Afr. (Natal In.)	30·33 S	30·37 E
164	Sezze (sĕt'sâ) It.	41·32 N	13·30 E
210	Sfaz (sfäks) Tun.	34·51 N	10·45 E
165	Sfîntu-Gheorghe Rom.	45·53 N	25·49 E
149	's Gravenhage (The Hague) ('s Krä'vĕn-hä'ĸĕ) (hāg) Neth. (Amsterdam In.)	52·05 N	4·16 E
189	Sha (R.) (shä) China	33·33 N	114·30 E
188	Shaanxi (Prov.) (shän-shyē) China	35·30 N	109·10 E
212	Shabani Zimb.	20·15 S	30·28 E
174	Shablykino (sháb-lē'kĭ-nô) Sov. Un. (Moscow In.)	56·22 N	38·37 E
188	Shache (Yarkand) (shä-chŭ) China	38·15 N	77·15 E
220	Shackleton Shelf Ice (shăk''l-tŭn) Ant.	65·00 S	100·00 E
106	Shades Cr. (shādz) Al. (Birmingham In.)	33·20 N	86·55 W
106	Shades Mtn. Al. (Birmingham In.)	33·22 N	86·51 W
215	Shagamu Nig.	6·51 N	3·39 E
184	Shāhjahānpur (shä-jŭ-hän'pōōr) India	27·58 N	79·58 E
186	Shahrezā (shä-rā'zā) Iran	31·47 N	51·47 E
171	Shahsavār Iran	36·40 N	51·00 E
191	Shajing (shä-jyĭŋ) China (Canton In.)	22·44 N	113·48 E
107	Shaker Hts. (shā'kēr) Oh. (Cleveland In.)	41·28 N	81·34 W
167	Shakhty (shäĸ'tê) Sov. Un.	47·41 N	40·11 E
215	Shaki Nig.	8·39 N	3·25 E
113	Shakopee (shăk'ô-pe) Mn. (Minneapolis, St. Paul In.)	44·48 N	93·31 W
211	Shala L. (shä'lȧ) Eth.	7·34 N	39·00 E
186	Shām, Jabal ash (Mtn.) Om.	23·01 N	57·45 E
211	Shambe (shäm'bā) Sud.	7·08 N	30·46 E
186	Shammar, Jabal (Mts.) (jĕb'ĕl shŭm'ȧr) Sau. Ar.	27·13 N	40·16 E
211	Shamo (L.) Eth.	5·58 N	37·00 E
105	Shamokin (shȧ-mō'kĭn) Pa.	40·45 N	76·30 W
116	Shamrock (shăm'rŏk) Tx.	35·14 N	100·12 W
212	Shamva (shäm'vȧ) Zimb.	17·18 S	31·35 E
211	Shandī Sud.	16·44 N	33·29 E
107	Shandon (shăn-dŭn) Oh. (Cincinnati In.)	39·20 N	84·13 W
189	Shandong (Prov.) (shän-dôŋ) China	36·03 N	117·09 E
192	Shandong, Bandao (Pen.) (shän-dôŋ bän-dou) China	37·00 N	120·10 E
190	Shangcai (shäŋ-tsī) China	33·16 N	114·16 E
190	Shangcheng (shäŋ-chŭŋ) China	31·47 N	115·22 E
192	Shangdu (shäŋ-dōō) China	41·38 N	113·22 E
191	Shanghai (shäng'hī') China (Shanghai In.)	31·14 N	121·27 E
189	Shanghai-Shi (Mun.) (shäŋ-hī shr) China	31·30 N	121·45 E
190	Shanghe (shäŋ-hŭ) China	37·18 N	117·10 E
190	Shanglin (shäŋ-lĭn) China	38·20 N	116·05 E
190	Shangqiu (shäŋ-chyô) China	34·24 N	115·39 E
193	Shangrao (Shäŋ-rou) China	28·25 N	117·58 E
192	Shangzhi (shäŋ-jr) China	45·18 N	127·52 E
190	Shanhaiguan China	40·01 N	119·45 E
106	Shannon (shăn'ŭn) Al. (Birmingham In.)	33·23 N	86·52 W
154	Shannon R. (shăn'ŏn) Ire.	52·30 N	9·58 W
188	Shanshan (shän'shän') China	42·51 N	89·53 E
173	Shantar (I.) (shän'tär) Sov. Un.	55·13 N	138·42 E
193	Shantou (Swatow) (shän-tō) China	23·20 N	116·40 E
189	Shanxi (Prov.) (shän-shyē) China	37·30 N	112·00 E
190	Shan Xian (shän shyĕn) China	34·47 N	116·04 E
190	Shaobo (shou-bwo) China	32·33 N	119·30 E
190	Shaobo Hu (L.) (shou-bwo hōō) China	32·07 N	119·13 E
193	Shaoguan (shou-gûän) China	24·58 N	113·42 E
193	Shaoxing (shou-shyĭŋ) China	30·00 N	120·40 E
174	Shapki (shäp'kĭ) Sov. Un. (Leningrad In.)	59·36 N	31·11 E
204	Shark B. (shärk) Austl.	25·30 S	113·00 E
99	Sharon (shăr'ŏn) Ma. (In.)	42·07 N	71·11 W
104	Sharon Pa.	41·15 N	80·30 W
116	Sharon Springs Ks.	38·51 N	101·45 W
107	Sharonville (shăr'ŏn vĭl) Oh. (Cincinnati In.)	39·16 N	84·24 W
107	Sharpsburg (shărps'bûrg) Pa. (Pittsburgh In.)	40·30 N	79·54 W
186	Sharr, Jabal (Mtn.) Sau. Ar.	28·00 N	36·07 E
193	Shashi (shä-shē) China	30·20 N	112·18 E
110	Shasta, Mt. Ca.	41·35 N	122·12 W
110	Shasta L. (shăs'tȧ) Ca.	40·51 N	122·32 W
170	Shatsk (shȧtsk) Sov. Un.	54·00 N	41·40 E
116	Shattuck (shăt'ŭk) Ok.	36·16 N	99·53 W
94	Shaunavon Can.	49·40 N	108·25 W
120	Shaw (shô) Ms.	33·36 N	90·44 W
109	Shawano (shȧ-wô'nô) Wi.	44·41 N	88·13 W
91	Shawinigan Can.	46·32 N	72·46 W
113	Shawnee (shô-nē') Ks. (Kansas City In.)	39·01 N	94·43 W
117	Shawnee Ok.	35·20 N	96·54 W
104	Shawneetown (shô'nē-toun) Il.	37·40 N	88·05 W
193	Shayang China	31·00 N	112·38 E
159	Shchara (R.) (sh-chä'rȧ) Sov. Un.	53·17 N	25·12 E
174	Shchëlkovo (shchĕl'kô-vô) Sov. Un. (Moscow In.)	55·55 N	38·00 E
167	Shchëtovo (shchĕ'tô-vô) Sov. Un.	48·11 N	39·13 E
167	Shchigry (shchē'grê) Sov. Un.	51·52 N	36·54 E
167	Shchors (shchôrs) Sov. Un.	51·38 N	31·58 E
174	Shchuch'ye Ozero (shchōōch'yĕ ô'zĕ-rō) Sov. Un. (Urals In.)	56·31 N	56·35 E
184	Sheakhala India (In.)	22·47 N	88·10 E
218	Shebele R. (shā'bâ-lē) Eth. (Horn of Afr. In.)	6·07 N	43·10 E
218	Shebelle (R.) Som. (Horn of Afr. In.)	1·38 N	43·50 E
109	Sheboygan (shê-boi'gȧn) Wi.	43·45 N	87·44 W
109	Sheboygan Falls Wi.	43·43 N	87·51 W
183	Shechem (Ruins) Jordan (Palestine In.)	32·15 N	35·22 E
92	Shedin Pk. (shĕd'ĭn) Can.	55·55 N	127·32 W
98	Shediac (shĕ'dê-ăk) Can.	46·13 N	64·32 W
154	Sheelin (L.) (shēlĭn) Ire.	53·46 N	7·34 W
148	Sheerness (shēr'nĕs) Eng. (London In.)	51·26 N	0·46 E
120	Sheffield (shĕf'fēld) Al.	35·42 N	87·42 W
89	Sheffield Can. (Toronto In.)	43·20 N	80·13 W
148	Sheffield Eng.	53·23 N	1·28 W
107	Sheffield Oh. (Cleveland In.)	41·26 N	82·05 W
107	Sheffield Lake Oh. (Cleveland In.)	41·30 N	82·03 W
154	Shehy, Mts. Ire.	51·46 N	9·45 W
170	Sheksna (R.) (shĕks'nȧ) Sov. Un.	59·50 N	38·40 E
173	Shelagskiy, Mys (C.) (shĭ-läg'skē) Sov. Un.	70·08 N	170·52 E
117	Shelbina (shĕl-bī'nȧ) Ar.	39·41 N	92·03 W
104	Shelburn (shĕl'bŭrn) In.	39·10 N	87·30 W
98	Shelburne Can.	43·46 N	65·19 W
105	Shelburne Can.	44·04 N	80·12 W
107	Shelby (shĕl'bê) In. (Chicago In.)	41·12 N	87·21 W
104	Shelby Mi.	43·35 N	86·20 W
120	Shelby Ms.	33·56 N	90·44 W
111	Shelby Mt.	48·35 N	111·55 W
121	Shelby NC	35·16 N	81·35 W
104	Shelby Oh.	40·50 N	82·40 W
104	Shelbyville (shĕl'bê-vĭl) Il.	39·20 N	88·45 W
104	Shelbyville In.	39·30 N	85·45 W
104	Shelbyville Ky.	38·10 N	85·15 W
120	Shelbyville Tn.	35·30 N	86·28 W
186	Shelbyville Res. Il.	39·30 N	88·45 W
108	Sheldon (shĕl'dŭn) Ia.	43·10 N	95·50 W
119	Sheldon Tx. (In.)	29·52 N	95·07 W
173	Shelekhova, Zaliv (B.) Sov. Un.	60·00 N	156·00 E
101	Shelikof Str. (shĕ'lê-kôf) Ak.	57·56 N	154·20 W
94	Shellbrook Can.	53·15 N	106·22 W
111	Shelley (shĕl'lê) Id.	43·24 N	112·06 W
109	Shellrock (R.) (shĕl'rŏk) Ia.	43·25 N	93·19 W
166	Shelon' (R.) (shȧ'lôn) Sov. Un.	57·50 N	29·40 E
105	Shelton (shĕl'tŭn) Ct.	41·15 N	73·05 W
116	Shelton Ne.	40·46 N	98·41 W
110	Shelton Wa.	47·14 N	123·05 W
174	Shemakha (shĕ-mȧ-kä') Sov. Un. (Urals In.)	56·16 N	59·19 E
171	Shemakha Sov. Un.	40·35 N	48·40 E
117	Shenandoah (shĕn-ăn-dō'ȧ) Ia.	40·46 N	95·23 W
105	Shenandoah Pa.	40·50 N	76·15 W
105	Shenandoah Va.	38·30 N	78·30 W
105	Shenandoah Natl. Park Va.	38·35 N	78·25 W
105	Shenandoah (R.) Va.	38·55 N	78·05 W
215	Shendam Nig.	8·53 N	9·32 E
190	Shengfang (shengfäng) China	39·05 N	116·40 E
174	Shenkursk (shĕn-kōōrsk') Sov. Un.	62·10 N	43·08 E
192	Shenmu China	38·55 N	110·35 E
190	Shenqiu China	33·11 N	115·06 E
190	Shen Xian (shŭn shyĕn) China	36·14 N	115·38 E
190	Shen Xian (shŭn shyän) China	38·02 N	115·33 E
192	Shenyang (shŭn-yäŋ) China	41·45 N	123·22 E
190	Shenze (shŭn-dzŭ) China	38·12 N	115·12 E
184	Sheopur India	25·37 N	78·10 E
89	Shepard (shĕ'pärd) Can. (Calgary In.)	50·57 N	113·55 W
167	Shepetovka (shĕ-pĕ-tôf'kȧ) Sov. Un.	50·10 N	27·01 E
203	Shepparton (shĕp'ăr-tŭn) Austl.	36·15 S	145·25 E
99	Sherborn (shûr'bŭrn) Ma. (In.)	42·15 N	71·22 W
214	Sherbro I. S. L.	7·30 N	12·55 W
105	Sherbrooke Can.	45·24 N	71·54 W
148	Sherburn (shûr'bŭrn) Eng.	53·47 N	1·15 W
159	Shereshevo (shĕ-rĕ-shê-vô) Sov. Un.	52·31 N	24·08 E
117	Sheridan (shĕr'ĭ-dăn) Ar.	34·19 N	92·21 W
110	Sheridan Or.	45·06 N	123·22 W
111	Sheridan Wy.	44·48 N	106·56 W
117	Sherman (shĕr'măn) Tx.	33·39 N	96·37 W
174	Sherna R. (shĕr'nȧ) Sov. Un. (Moscow In.)	56·08 N	38·45 E
95	Sherridon Can.	55·10 N	101·10 W
149	's Hertogenbosch (sĕr-tō'ghĕn-bôs) Neth. (Amsterdam In.)	51·41 N	5·19 E
112	Sherwood Or. (Portland In.)	45·21 N	122·50 W
148	Sherwood For. Eng.	53·11 N	1·07 W
93	Sherwood Park Can.	53·31 N	113·19 W
154	Shetland (Is.) (shĕt'lănd) Scot.	60·35 N	2·10 W
186	Shevchenko Sov. Un.	44·00 N	51·10 E
211	Shewa Gimira Eth.	7·13 N	35·49 E
190	She Xian (shŭ shyĕn) China	36·34 N	113·42 E
190	Sheyang (R.) (she-yäŋ) China	33·42 N	119·40 E
108	Sheyenne (R.) (shī-ĕn') ND	46·42 N	97·52 W
190	Shi (R.) (shr) China	31·58 N	115·50 E
190	Shi (R.) China	32·09 N	114·11 E
104	Shiawassee (R.) (shī-ȧ-wôs'ê) Mi.	43·15 N	84·05 W
186	Shibām (shē'bäm) P. D. R. of Yem.	16·02 N	48·40 E
218	Shibīn al Kawn (shê-bēn'ĕl kōm') Egypt (Nile In.)	30·31 N	31·01 E
218	Shibīn al Qanāṭir (kȧ-nä'têr) Egypt (Nile In.)	30·18 N	31·21 E
195	Shichitō (Seven Is.) (shē'chê-tō) Jap.	34·18 N	139·28 E
190	Shicun (shr-tsōōn) China	33·47 N	117·18 E
111	Shields R. (shēldz) Mt.	45·54 N	110·40 W
148	Shifnal (shĭf'năl) Eng.	52·40 N	2·22 W
190	Shijian (shr-jyĕn) China	31·27 N	117·51 E
190	Shijiazhuang (shr-jyä-jûäŋ) China	38·04 N	114·31 E
190	Shijiu Hu (L.) (shr-jyô hōō) China	31·29 N	119·07 E
184	Shikārpur Pak.	27·51 N	68·52 E
195	Shiki (shē'kê) Jap. (Tōkyō In.)	35·50 N	139·35 E
195	Shikoku (I.) (shē'kō'kōō) Jap.	33·43 N	133·33 E
173	Shilka (R.) (shĭl'kȧ) Sov. Un.	53·00 N	118·45 E
184	Shilla (Mt.) India	37·18 N	78·17 E
184	Shillong (shêl-lông') India	25·39 N	91·58 E
113	Shiloh (shī'lō) Il. (St. Louis In.)	38·34 N	89·54 W
193	Shilong (shr-lôŋ) China	23·05 N	113·58 E
191	Shilou China (Canton In.)	22·58 N	113·29 E
195	Shimabara (shē'mä-bä'rä) Jap.	32·46 N	130·22 E
195	Shimada (shē'mä-dä) Jap.	34·49 N	138·13 E
195	Shimizu (shē'mê-zōō) Jap.	35·00 N	138·29 E
195	Shimminato (shêm'mê'nä-tô) Jap.	36·47 N	137·05 E
195	Shimoda (shē'mô-dä) Jap.	34·41 N	138·58 E
185	Shimoga India	13·59 N	75·38 E
217	Shimoni Ken.	4·39 S	39·23 E

ăt; finăl; rāte; senâte; ärm; ȧsk; sofȧ; fâre; ch-choose; dh-as th in other; bē; ėvent; bĕt; recĕnt; cratēr; g-go; gh-guttural g; bĭt; ĭ-short neutral; rīde; ĸ-guttural k as ch in German ich;

PRONOUNCING INDEX Shimonoseki — Sincelejo 347

Page	Name Pronunciation Region	Lat. °′	Long. °′
195	Shimonoseki (shē'mô-nō-sĕ'kê) (shê-mô-nô'sĕ-kĭ). Jap.	33·58 N	130·55 E
195	Shimo-Saga (shê'mô sä'gä) Jap. (Ōsaka In.)	35·01 N	135·41 E
154	Shin, Loch (L.) (lŏk shĭn)... Scot.	58·08 N	4·02 W
195	Shinagawa-Wan (B.) (shê'nä-gä'wä wän) Jap. (Tōkyō In.)	35·37 N	139·49 E
195	Shinano-Gawa (Strm). (shê-nä'nô gä'wä). Jap.	36·43 N	138·22 E
195	Shingū (shĭn'gōō)........... Jap.	33·43 N	135·59 E
195	Shinji (L.) (shĭn'jê).......... Jap.	35·23 N	133·05 E
217	Shinkolobwe.............. Zaire	11·02 S	26·35 E
211	Shinyanga (shĭn-yäŋ'gä)..... Tan.	3·40 S	33·26 E
194	Shiono Misaki (C.) (shê-ô'nô mē'sä-kê). Jap.	33·20 N	136·10 E
191	Shipai (shr-pī). China (Canton In.)	23·07 N	113·23 E
128	Ship Channel Cay (I.) (shĭp chă-nĕl kē). Ba.	24·50 N	76·50 W
148	Shipley (shĭp'lê)........... Eng.	53·50 N	1·47 W
98	Shippegan (shĭ'pê-găn)...... Can.	47·45 N	64·42 W
98	Shippegan I................ Can.	47·50 N	64·38 W
105	Shippenburg (shĭp'ĕn bûrg).... Pa.	40·00 N	77·30 W
98	Shipshaw (R.) (shĭp'shô)..... Can.	48·50 N	71·03 W
183	Shiqma (R.)... Isr. (Palestine In.)	31·31 N	34·40 E
195	Shirane-san (Mtn.) (shē'rä'nâ-sän'). Jap.	35·44 N	138·14 E
194	Shira Saki (C.) (shê'rä sä'kê).. Jap.	41·25 N	142·10 E
212	Shirati (shê-rä'tē).......... Tan.	1·15 S	34·02 E
186	Shīrāz (shē-räz')........... Iran	29·32 N	52·27 E
217	Shire (R.) (shē'râ)........ Malawi	16·20 S	35·05 E
167	Shirokoye (shē'rô-kô-yĕ).. Sov. Un.	47·40 N	33·18 E
101	Shishaldin Vol. (shī-shăl'dĭn).. Ak.	54·48 N	164·00 W
107	Shively (shīv'lê) Ky. (Louisville In.)	38·11 N	85·47 W
184	Shivpuri................. India	25·31 N	77·46 E
183	Shivta, Horvot (Ruins) Isr. (Palestine In.)	30·54 N	34·36 E
115	Shivwits (Shebit) Ind. Res. (shĭv'wĭts) (shĕ'bĭt). Ut.	37·10 N	113·50 W
115	Shivwits Plat............... Az.	36·13 N	113·42 W
99	Shirley (shûr'lê)........ Ma. (In.)	42·33 N	71·39 W
191	Shiwan (shr-wän) China (Canton In.)	23·01 N	113·04 E
193	Shiwan Dashan (Mts.) (shr-wän dä-shän). China	22·10 N	107·30 E
195	Shizuki (shĭ'zōō-kê)........ Jap.	34·29 N	134·51 E
195	Shizuoka (shē'zōō'ōkä)....... Jap.	34·58 N	138·24 E
166	Shklov (shklôf)......... Sov. Un.	54·11 N	30·23 E
165	Shkodër (Scutari) (shkô'dûr) (skōō'târē). Alb.	42·04 N	19·30 E
194	Shkotovo (shkô'tô-vô)... Sov. Un.	43·15 N	132·21 E
117	Shoal Cr. (shōl)............... Il.	38·37 N	89·25 W
95	Shoal L................... Can.	49·32 N	95·00 W
104	Shoals (shōlz)............... In.	38·40 N	86·45 W
195	Shōdo (I.) (shō'dō).......... Jap.	34·27 N	134·27 E
185	Sholāpur (shō'lä-pōōr)...... India	17·42 N	75·51 E
107	Shorewood (shōr'wŏŏd) Wi. (Milwaukee In.)	43·05 N	87·54 W
111	Shoshone (shô-shōn'ê)......... Id.	42·56 N	114·24 W
111	Shoshone L................. Wy.	44·17 N	110·50 W
111	Shoshone R................. Wy.	44·20 N	109·28 W
111	Shoshoni.................... Wy.	43·14 N	108·05 W
167	Shostka (shôst'kå)....... Sov. Un.	51·51 N	33·31 E
190	Shougouang (shō-gůäŋ)..... China	36·53 N	118·45 E
190	Shou Xian (shō shyĕn)...... China	32·36 N	116·45 E
167	Shpola (shpô'lå)......... Sov. Un.	49·01 N	31·36 E
119	Shreveport (shrēv'pôrt)....... La.	32·30 N	93·46 W
148	Shrewsbury (shrōōz'bĕr-ĭ).... Eng.	52·43 N	2·44 W
99	Shrewsbury........... Ma. (In.)	42·18 N	71·43 W
148	Shropshire (Co.) (shrŏp'shĕr). Eng.	52·36 N	2·45 W
128	Shroud Cay (I.) (shroud)..... Ba.	24·20 N	76·40 W
190	Shu (R.) (shōō).............. China	34·47 N	118·27 E
192	Shuangcheng (shůäŋ-chŭŋ).. China	45·18 N	126·18 E
190	Shuanghe (shůäŋ-hŭ)....... China	31·33 N	116·48 E
189	Shuangliao............... China	43·37 N	123·30 E
192	Shuangyang............... China	43·28 N	125·45 E
190	Shuhedun (shōō-hŭ-dōōn)... China	31·33 N	117·01 E
190	Shuiye (shwā-yŭ)......... China	36·08 N	114·07 E
188	Shule (R.) (shōō-lŭ)........ China	40·53 N	94·55 E
109	Shullsburg (shŭlz'bûrg)...... Wi.	42·35 N	90·16 W
101	Shumagin (Is.) (shōō'må-gĕn).. Ak.	55·22 N	159·20 W
165	Shumen................... Bul.	43·15 N	26·54 E
191	Shunde (shōōn-dŭ) China (Canton In.)	22·50 N	113·15 E
101	Shungnak (shŭng'nåk)........ Ak.	66·55 N	157·20 W
174	Shunut, 'Gora (Mt.) (gá-rä shōō'nŏŏt) Sov. Un. (Urals In.)	56·33 N	59·45 E
192	Shunyi (Shōōn-yē).... China (In.)	40·09 N	116·38 E
186	Shuqrah........ P. D. R. of Yem.	13·32 N	46·02 E
186	Shūrāb (R.) (shōō räb)....... Iran	31·08 N	55·30 E
194	Shuri (shōō'rê).............. Jap.	26·10 N	127·48 E
171	Shur R. (shōōr)............. Iran	35·40 N	50·10 E
186	Shūshtar (shōōsh'tŭr)....... Iran	31·50 N	48·46 E
93	Shuswap L. (shōōs'wŏp)..... Can.	50·57 N	119·15 W
166	Shuya (shōō'yå)......... Sov. Un.	56·52 N	41·23 E
190	Shuyang (shōō yäng)....... China	34·09 N	118·47 E
193	Shweba..................... Bur.	22·23 N	96·13 E
	Shyaulyay, see Šiauliai		
183	Siak Ketjil (R.) Indon. (Singapore In.)	1·01 N	101·45 E
183	Siaksriinderapura (sê-äks'rĭ ēn'drá-pōō'rä) Indon. (Singapore In.)	0·48 N	102·05 E
184	Siālkot (sê-äl'kōt)........... Pak.	32·39 N	74·30 E
165	Siátista (syä'tĭs-ta)......... Grc.	40·15 N	21·32 E
197	Siau, Pulau (I.)........... Indon.	2·40 N	126·00 E
157	Šiauliai (Shyaulyay) (shê-ou'lê-ī) Sov. Un.	55·57 N	23·19 E
174	Sibay (sē'báy). Sov. Un. (Urals In.)	52·41 N	58·40 E
164	Šibenik (shê-bā'nēk)....... Yugo.	43·44 N	15·55 E
182	Siberia (Reg.)............... Asia	57·00 N	97·00 E
196	Siberut, Pulau (I.) (sē-bå-rōōt) Indon.	1·22 S	99·45 E
184	Sibī........................ Pak.	29·41 N	67·52 E
216	Sibiti (sê-bê-tē')............ Con.	3·41 S	13·21 E
165	Sibiu (sê-bĭ-ōō')........... Rom.	45·47 N	24·09 E
108	Sibley (sĭb'lê)................ Ia.	43·24 N	95·33 W
196	Sibolga (sê-bō'gä)......... Indon.	1·45 N	98·45 E
187	Sibsāgar (sêb-sŭ'gŭr)........ India	26·47 N	94·45 E
196	Sibutu I.................... Phil.	4·40 N	119·30 E
197	Sibuyan (I.) (sē-bōō-yän') Phil. (In.)	12·19 N	122·25 E
196	Sibuyan Sea................. Phil.	12·43 N	122·38 E
188	Sichuan (Prov.) (sz-chůän). China	31·20 N	103·00 E
151	Sicily (I.) (sĭs'ĭ-lê)............ It.	37·38 N	13·30 E
126	Sico R. (sê-kô)........... Hond.	15·32 N	85·42 W
134	Sicuaní (sê-kwä'nē).......... Peru	14·12 S	71·12 W
218	Sidamo (Prov.) (sē-dä'mô)... Eth.	5·08 N	37·45 E
164	Siderno Marina (sê-dĕr'nô mä-rē'nä). It.	38·18 N	16·19 E
164	Sídheros, Akr. (C.)..... Grc. (In.)	35·19 N	26·20 E
165	Sidhiró Kastron............ Grc.	41·13 N	23·27 E
163	Sidi-Aïsa................... Alg.	35·53 N	3·44 E
211	Sīdī Barrānī............. Egypt	31·41 N	26·09 E
210	Sidi bel Abbès (sē'dē-bĕl á-bĕs') Alg.	35·15 N	0·43 W
210	Sidi Ifni (ēf'nê)........... Mor.	29·22 N	10·15 W
220	Sidley, Mt. (sĭd'lê).......... Ant.	77·25 S	129·00 W
92	Sidney..................... Can.	48·39 N	123·24 W
111	Sidney (sĭd'nê).............. Mt.	47·43 N	104·07 W
108	Sidney...................... Ne.	41·10 N	103·00 W
104	Sidney...................... Oh.	40·20 N	84·10 W
120	Sidney Lanier, L. (lăn'yĕr).... Ga.	34·27 N	83·56 W
214	Sido....................... Mali	11·40 N	7·36 W
	Sidon, see Şaydā		
183	Sidr, Wādī (R.) Egypt (Palestine In.)	29·43 N	32·58 E
159	Siedlce (syĕd''l-tsĕ).......... Pol.	52·09 N	22·20 E
161	Siegburg (zēg'bōōrgh) F.R.G. (Ruhr In.)	50·48 N	7·13 E
161	Siegen (zē'ghĕn) F.R.G. (Ruhr In.)	50·52 N	8·01 E
149	Sieghartskirchen. Aus. (Vienna In.)	48·16 N	16·00 E
158	Sieg R. (zēg)............ F.R.G.	50·51 N	7·53 E
159	Siemiatycze (syĕm'yä'tĕ-chĕ).. Pol.	52·26 N	22·52 E
159	Siemionówka (sêĕ-mēō'nôf-kä) Pol.	52·53 N	23·50 E
196	Siem Reap (syĕm'rä'áp)... Kamp.	13·32 N	103·54 E
164	Siena (sê-ĕn'ä)................ It.	43·19 N	11·21 E
159	Sieradz (syĕ'rädz)........... Pol.	51·35 N	18·45 E
162	Siero (syā'rō)................ Sp.	43·24 N	5·39 W
159	Sierpc (syĕrpts).............. Pol.	52·51 N	19·42 E
118	Sierra Blanca (sē-ĕ'rá blaŋ-kä). Tx.	31·10 N	105·20 W
115	Sierra Blanca Pk. (blăn'ká)... NM	33·25 N	105·50 W
209	Sierra Leone (sê-ĕr'rä lå-ō'nå). Afr.	8·48 N	12·30 W
113	Sierra Madre (mă'drē) Ca. (Los Angeles In.)	34·10 N	118·03 W
118	Sierra Mojada (sē-ĕ'r-rä-mô-ĸä'dä). Mex.	27·22 N	103·42 W
165	Sífnos (I.)................... Grc.	36·58 N	24·30 E
156	Sigdal (sēgh'däl)............ Nor.	60·01 N	9·35 E
160	Sigean (sē-zhōɴ')............ Fr.	43·02 N	2·56 E
109	Sigeurney (sē-gûr-nĭ).......... Ia.	41·16 N	92·10 W
159	Sighet (sê-gât')............. Rom.	47·57 N	23·55 E
159	Sighisoara (sē-gê-shwä'rá)... Rom.	46·11 N	24·48 E
150	Siglufjördhur................ Ice.	66·06 N	18·45 W
171	Signakhi............... Sov. Un.	41·45 N	45·50 E
113	Signal Hill (sĭg'năl hĭl) Ca. (Los Angeles In.)	33·48 N	118·11 W
134	Sigsig (sêg-sēg')............. Ec.	3·05 S	78·44 W
156	Sigtuna (sēgh-tōō'nå)....... Swe.	59·40 N	17·39 E
128	Siguanea, Ensenada de la (B.) (ĕn-sĕ-nä-dä-dĕ-lä-sê-gwä-nā'ä) Cuba	21·45 N	83·15 W
126	Siguatepeque (sē-gwá'tĕ-pĕ-kĕ) Hond.	14·33 N	87·51 W
162	Sigüenza (sē-gwĕ'n-zä)........ Sp.	41·03 N	2·38 W
214	Siguiri (sê-gê-rē')........... Gui.	11·25 N	9·10 W
190	Sihong (sz-hôŋ)............. China	33·25 N	118·13 E
184	Siling Co (L.).............. China	32·05 N	89·10 E
188	Simao (sz-mou)............. China	22·56 N	101·07 E
171	Siirt (sĭ-ērt')............... Tur.	38·00 N	42·00 E
217	Sikalongo.................. Zambia	16·46 S	27·07 E
214	Sikasso (sê-käs'sō).......... Mali	11·19 N	5·40 W
117	Sikeston (sīks'tŭn)........... Mo.	36·50 N	89·35 W
173	Sikhote Alin', Khrebet (Mts.) (se-ĸô'ta a-lēn'). Sov. Un.	45·00 N	135·45 E
165	Sikinos (I.) (sĭ'kĭ-nōs)........ Grc.	36·45 N	24·55 E
184	Sikkim (State)............. India	27·42 N	88·25 E
159	Siklós (sĭ'klōsh)........... Hong.	45·51 N	18·18 E
162	Sil (R.) (sê'l)................ Sp.	42·20 N	7·13 W
197	Silang (sê-läng')........ Phil. (In.)	14·14 N	120·58 E
124	Silao (sê-lä'ō).............. Mex.	20·56 N	101·25 W
184	Silchar (sĭl-chär')........... India	24·52 N	92·50 E
218	Silent Valley (sī'lĕnt vă'lē). S. Afr. (Johannesburg & Pretoria In.)	24·32 S	26·40 E
121	Siler City (sī'lĕr)............ NC	35·45 N	79·29 W
159	Silesia (Reg.) (sĭ-lē'shå)...... Pol.	50·58 N	16·53 E
171	Silifke...................... Tur.	36·20 N	34·00 E
153	Silistra (sê-lēs'trå)........... Bul.	44·01 N	27·13 E
156	Siljan (R.) (sêl'yän)......... Swe.	60·48 N	14·28 E
156	Silkeborg (sĭl'kĕ-bôr')....... Den.	56·10 N	9·33 E
89	Sillery (sĕl'-re'). Can. (Quebec In.)	46·46 N	71·15 W
117	Siloam Springs (sĭ-lōm)....... Ar.	36·10 N	94·32 W
216	Siloana Plns............... Zambia	16·55 S	23·10 E
124	Silocayoápan (sē-lô-kä-yô-á'pän) Mex.	17·29 N	98·09 W
119	Silsbee (sĭlz' bê)............. Tx.	30·19 N	94·09 W
157	Šilutė (shĭ-lōō'tå)....... Sov. Un.	55·23 N	21·26 E
137	Silva Jardim (sê'l-vä-zhär-dêɴ) Braz. (Rio de Janeiro In.)	22·40 S	42·24 W
112	Silvana (sĭl-vän'á) Wa. (Seattle In.)	48·12 N	122·16 W
135	Silvânia (sēl-vá'nyä)........ Braz.	16·43 S	48·33 W
184	Silvassa.................... India	20·10 N	73·00 E
117	Silver (L.).................. Mo.	39·38 N	93·12 W
112	Silverado (sĭl-vĕr-ä'dō) Ca. (Los Angeles In.)	33·45 N	117·40 W
129	Silver Bk.................... Ba.	20·40 N	69·40 W
129	Silver Bank Passage (Str.).... Ba.	20·40 N	70·20 W
109	Silver Bay.................. Mn.	47·24 N	91·07 W
115	Silver City (sĭl'vĕr sĭ'tĭ)...... NM	32·45 N	108·20 W
127	Silver City................. Pan.	9·20 N	79·54 W
105	Silver Creek (crēk)........... NY	42·35 N	79·10 W
115	Silver Cr.................... Az.	34·30 N	110·05 W
107	Silver Cr....... In. (Louisville In.)	38·20 N	85·45 W
107	Silver Cr., Muddy Fk. In. (Louisville In.)	38·26 N	85·52 W
112	Silverdale (sĭl'vĕr-dāl) Wa. (Seattle In.)	49·39 N	122·42 W
107	Silver Lake (lāk) Wi. (Milwaukee In.)	42·33 N	88·10 W
107	Silver L...... Wi. (Milwaukee In.)	42·35 N	88·08 W
106	Silver Spring (spring) Md. (Baltimore In.)	39·00 N	77·00 W
112	Silver Star Mtn. Wa. (Portland In.)	45·45 N	122·15 W
92	Silverthrone Mtn. (sĭl'vĕr-thrōn). Can.	51·31 N	126·06 W
115	Silverton (sĭl'vĕr-tŭn)........ Co.	37·50 N	107·40 W
107	Silverton..... Oh. (Cincinnati In.)	39·12 N	84·24 W
110	Silverton.................... Or.	45·02 N	122·46 W
213	Silverton................ S. Afr. (Johannesburg & Pretoria In.)	25·45 S	28·13 E
162	Silves (sēl'vĕzh)........... Port.	37·15 N	8·24 W
110	Silvies R. (sĭl'vēz).......... Or.	43·44 N	119·15 W
174	Sim (sĭm).... Sov. Un. (Urals In.)	55·00 N	57·42 E
216	Simba..................... Zaire	0·36 N	22·55 E
105	Simcoe (sĭm'kō)............. Can.	42·50 N	80·20 W
105	Simcoe (L.)................ Can.	44·30 N	79·20 W
196	Simeulue, Pulau (I.)....... Indon.	2·27 N	95·30 E
167	Simferopol' (Akmechet) (sêm-fĕ-rô'pôl') (ák-mĕch'ĕt) Sov. Un.	44·58 N	34·04 E
153	Simi (I.)................... Grc.	36·27 N	27·41 E
112	Similk Beach (sē'mĭlk) Wa. (Seattle In.)	48·27 N	122·35 W
184	Simla (sĭm'lå).............. India	31·09 N	77·15 E
159	Simleul-Silvaniei (shêm-lā'ōōl-sêl-vä'nyĕ-ê). Rom.	47·14 N	22·46 E
128	Simms Pt.................... Ba.	25·00 N	77·40 W
125	Simojovel (sê-mō-hô-vĕl').... Mex.	17·12 N	92·43 W
157	Simola (sē'mô-lå)............ Fin.	60·55 N	28·06 E
137	Simonésia (sē-mô-nĕ'syä) Braz. (Rio de Janeiro In.)	20·04 S	41·53 W
93	Simonette (R.) (sī-mŏn-ĕt')... Can.	54·15 N	118·00 W
212	Simonstad........... S. Afr. (In.)	34·11 S	18·25 E
92	Simood Sound............... Can.	50·45 N	126·25 W
158	Simplon P. (sĭm'plŏn) (săɴ-plôɴ') Switz.	46·13 N	7·53 E
158	Simplon Tun........... It.-Switz.	46·16 N	8·20 E
109	Simpson (I.)................ Can.	48·43 N	87·44 W
204	Simpson Des. (sĭmp-sŭn)... Austl.	24·40 S	136·40 E
156	Simrishamn (sēm'rês-häm'n). Swe.	55·35 N	14·19 E
174	Sim R........ Sov. Un. (Urals In.)	55·00 N	57·42 E
119	Sims Bayou (sĭmz bī-yōō') Tx. (In.)	29·37 N	95·23 W
189	Simushir (I.) (se-mōō'shĕr) Sov. Un.	47·15 N	150·47 E
165	Sinaia (sĭ-nä'yå)........... Rom.	45·20 N	25·30 E
211	Sinai Pen. (sī'nī)........... Egypt	29·24 N	33·29 E
122	Sinaloa (State) (sē-nä-lô-ä)... Mex.	25·15 N	107·45 W
193	Sinan (sz-nän).............. China	27·50 N	108·30 E
194	Sinanju (sĭ'nän-jōō')........ Kor.	39·39 N	125·41 E
171	Sinap...................... Tur.	42·00 N	35·05 E
134	Sincé (sēn'sâ)............... Col.	9·15 N	75·14 W
134	Sincelejo (sēn-sâ-lā'hō)....... Col.	9·12 N	75·30 W

ng-sing; ŋ-baŋk; ɴ-nasalized n; nŏd; cŏmmit; ōld; ôbey; ôrder; fōōd; fŏŏt; ou-out; s-soft; sh-dish; th-thin; pūre; ůnite; ûrn; stŭd; circŭs; ü-as "y" in study; '-indeterminate vowel.

ăt; fĭnăl; rāte; senăte; ârm; àsk; sofá; fâre; ch-choose; dh-as th in other; bē; ĕvent; bĕt; recĕnt; cratēr; g-go; gh-guttural g; bĭt; ĭ-short neutral; rīde; к-guttural k as ch in German ich;

PRONOUNCING INDEX Socotra — South Sandwich 349

Page	Name Pronunciation Region	Lat. °′	Long. °′
218	Socotra I. (sô-kō'trȧ) P. D. R. of Yem. (Horn of Afr. In.)	13·00 N	52·30 E
162	Socuellamos (sô-kōō-äl'yä-mōs) Sp.	39·18 N	2·48 W
114	Soda (L.) (sō'dȧ)....Ca.	35·12 N	116·25 W
112	Soda Pk.....Wa. (Portland In.)	45·53 N	122·04 W
111	Soda Springs (sprĭngz)....Id.	42·39 N	111·37 W
156	Söderhamn (sû-dĕr-häm''n)...Swe.	61·20 N	17·00 E
156	Söderköping....Swe.	58·30 N	16·14 E
156	Södertälje (sû-dĕr-tĕl'yĕ)....Swe.	59·12 N	17·35 E
211	Sodo....Eth.	7·03 N	37·46 E
156	Södra Dellen (L.)....Swe.	61·45 N	16·30 E
158	Soest (zōst)....F.R.G.	51·35 N	8·05 E
	Sofia, see Sofiya		
165	Sofiya (Sofia) (sô'fê-yȧ) (sô'fê-ȧ) Bul.	42·43 N	23·20 E
167	Sofiyevka (sô-fē'yĕf-kȧ)...Sov. Un.	48·03 N	33·53 E
195	Soga (sō'gä)....Jap (Tōkyō In.)	35·35 N	140·08 E
134	Sogamoso (sô-gä-mô'sō)....Col.	5·42 N	72·51 W
156	Sogndal (sôghn'dȧl)....Nor.	58·20 N	6·17 E
156	Sogndal....Nor.	61·14 N	7·04 E
156	Sogne Fd. (sôgn'ĕ fyôrd)....Nor.	61·09 N	5·30 E
166	Sogozha (R.) (sô'gô-zhȧ)..Sov. Un.	58·35 N	39·08 E
160	Soissons (swä-sôɴ')....Fr.	49·23 N	3·17 E
195	Sōka (sō'kä)....Jap. (Tōkyō In.)	35·50 N	139·49 E
159	Sokal (sô'käl')....Sov. Un.	50·28 N	24·20 E
171	Soke (sû'kĕ)....Tur.	37·40 N	27·10 E
214	Sokodé (sô-kô-dā')....Togo	8·59 N	1·08 E
159	Sokolka (sô-kōōl'kȧ)....Pol.	53·23 N	23·30 E
210	Sokolo (sô-kô-lō')....Mali	14·51 N	6·09 W
214	Sokone....Senegal	13·53 N	16·22 W
215	Sokoto (sō'kô-tō)....Nig.	13·04 N	5·16 E
159	Sokotów Podlaski (sô-kô-wōōf' pŭd-lä'skĭ).Pol.	52·24 N	22·15 E
125	Sola de Vega (San Miguel) (sō'lä dā vā'gä) (sän mê-gāl') Mex.	16·31 N	96·58 W
202	Solander, C....Austl. (Sydney In.)	34·03 S	151·16 E
197	Solano (sō-lä'nō)....Phil. (In.)	16·31 N	121·11 E
134	Soledad (sŏ-lĕ-dä'd)....Col.	10·47 N	75·00 W
124	Soledad Díez Gutierrez (sô-lâ-dhädh'dē'äz gōō-tyā'rĕz) Mex.	22·19 N	100·54 W
110	Soleduck R. (sōl'dŭk)....Wa.	47·59 N	124·28 W
126	Solentiname, Islas de (Is.) (ē's-läs-dĕ-sô-lĕn-tê-nä'mȧ).Nic.	11·15 N	85·16 W
148	Solihull (sō'lĭ-hŭl)....Eng.	52·25 N	1·46 W
174	Solikamsk (sô-lē-kȧmsk') Sov. Un. (Urals In.)	59·38 N	56·48 E
134	Solimões, Rio (R.) (rē'ō-sô-lē-mô'ĕs).Braz.	2·45 S	67·44 W
161	Solingen (zō'lĭng-ĕn) F.R.G. (Ruhr In.)	51·10 N	7·05 E
156	Sollefteå (sôl-lĕf'tĕ-ô)....Swe.	63·06 N	17·17 E
163	Sóller (sō'lyĕr)....Sp.	39·45 N	2·40 E
171	Sol'-Iletsk....Sov. Un.	51·10 N	55·05 E
160	Sologne (Reg.) (sō-lōn'yĕ)....Fr.	47·36 N	1·53 E
126	Solola (sō-lō'lä)....Guat.	14·45 N	91·12 W
198	Solomon Is. (sŏ'lō-mŭn)...Oceania	7·00 S	148·00 E
116	Solomon R....Ks.	39·24 N	98·19 W
116	Solomon R. North Fk....Ks.	39·34 N	99·52 W
116	Solomon R., South Fk....Ks.	39·19 N	99·52 W
192	Solon (swo-lōōn)....China	47·32 N	121·18 E
107	Solon (sō'lŭn)..Oh. (Cleveland In.)	41·23 N	81·26 W
158	Solothurn (zō'lō-thōōrn)....Switz.	47·13 N	7·30 E
170	Solov'etskiy (I.)....Sov. Un.	65·10 N	35·40 E
164	Šolta (I.) (shōl'tä)....Yugo.	43·20 N	16·15 E
158	Soltau (sôl'tou)....F.R.G.	53·00 N	9·50 E
166	Sol'tsy (sôl'tsĕ)....Sov. Un.	58·04 N	30·13 E
105	Solvay (sŏl'vā)....NY	43·05 N	76·10 W
156	Sölvesborg (sûl'vĕs-bôrg)....Swe.	56·04 N	14·35 E
170	Sol'vychegodsk (sôl'vê-chĕ-gôtsk') Sov. Un.	61·18 N	46·58 E
154	Solway Firth (sŏl'wā fûrth') Eng.-Scot.	54·42 N	3·55 W
217	Solwezi....Zambia	12·11 S	26·25 E
209	Somalia (sō-ma'lē-ă)....Afr.	3·28 N	44·47 E
217	Somanga....Tan.	8·24 S	39·17 E
165	Sombor (sôm'bôr)....Yugo.	45·45 N	19·10 E
124	Sombrerete (sōm-brå-rā'tȧ)..Mex.	23·38 N	103·37 W
135	Sombrero, Cayo (C.) (kä-yô-sôm-brĕ'rô).Ven. (In.)	10·52 N	68·12 W
120	Somerset (sŭm'ēr-sĕt)....Ky.	37·05 N	84·35 W
106	Somerset....Ma. (Providence In.)	41·46 N	71·05 W
105	Somerset....Pa.	40·00 N	79·05 W
113	Somerset...Tx. (San Antonio In.)	29·13 N	98·39 W
213	Somerset East..S. Afr. (Natal In.)	32·44 S	25·36 E
98	Somersworth (sŭm'ērz-wûrth).NH	43·16 N	70·53 W
114	Somerton (sŭm'ēr-tŭn)....Az.	32·36 N	114·43 W
99	Somerville (sŭm'ēr-vĭl)..Ma. (In.)	42·23 N	71·06 W
106	Somerville....NJ (New York In.)	40·34 N	74·37 W
120	Somerville....Tn.	35·14 N	89·21 W
119	Somerville....Tx.	30·21 N	96·31 W
159	Somesul R. (sô-mȧ'shōōl)....Rom.	47·43 N	23·09 E
163	Somma Vesuviana (sôm'mä vā-zōō-vê-ä'nä) It. (Naples In.)	40·38 N	14·27 E
160	Somme (R.) (sŏm)....Fr.	50·02 N	2·04 E
149	Sommerfeld (zō'mĕr-fĕld) G.D.R. (Berlin In.)	52·48 N	13·02 E
202	Sommerville Austl. (Melbourne In.)	38·14 S	145·10 E
126	Somoto (sô-mō'tō)....Nic.	13·28 N	86·37 W
136	Somuncurá, Meseta de (Plat.) (mĕ-sĕ'tä-dĕ-sô-mōō'n-kōō-rá') Arg.	41·15 S	68·00 W
184	Son (R.) (sōn)....India	24·40 N	82·35 E
127	Soná (sō'nä)....Pan.	8·00 N	81·19 W
194	Sŏnchŏn (sŭn'shŭn)....Kor.	39·49 N	124·56 E
213	Sondags (R.)...S. Afr. (Natal In.)	33·17 S	25·14 E
156	Sønderborg (sûn''er-bôrgh)...Den.	54·55 N	9·47 E
158	Sondershausen (zôn'dērz-hou'zĕn) G.D.R.	51·17 N	10·45 E
193	Song Ca (R.)....Viet.	19·15 N	105·00 E
217	Songea (sôn-gā'ȧ)....Tan.	10·41 S	35·39 E
	Songhua (R.), see Sungari		
191	Songjiang (sôŋ-jyäŋ) China (Shanghai In.)	31·01 N	121·14 E
194	Sŏngjin (sŭng'jĭn')....Kor.	40·38 N	129·10 E
196	Songkhla (sông'klä')....Thai.	7·09 N	100·34 E
217	Songwe....Zaire	12·25 S	29·40 E
158	Sonneberg (sôn'ē-bĕrgh)...G.D.R.	50·20 N	11·14 E
114	Sonora (sô-nō'rȧ)....Ca.	37·58 N	120·22 W
118	Sonora....Tx.	30·33 N	100·38 W
122	Sonora (State)....Mex.	29·45 N	111·15 W
122	Sonora (R.)....Mex.	28·45 N	111·35 W
114	Sonora Pk....Ca.	38·22 N	119·39 W
162	Sonseca (sôn-sā'kä)....Sp.	39·41 N	3·56 W
134	Sonsón (sôn-sôn')....Col. (In.)	5·42 N	75·28 W
126	Sonsonate (sōn-sô-nä'tȧ)....Sal.	13·46 N	89·43 W
197	Sonsorol Is. (sŏn-sô-rōl') Pas. Is. Trust Ter.	5·03 N	132·33 E
112	Sooke Basin (sōōk) Can. (Seattle In.)	48·21 N	123·47 W
113	Soo Locks (sōō lŏks)...Can.-U. S.	46·30 N	84·30 W
134	Sopetrán (sô-pĕ-trä'n)...Col. (In.)	6·30 N	75·44 W
156	Sopot (sô'pôt)....Pol.	54·26 N	18·25 E
158	Sopron (shŏp'rôn)....Hung.	47·41 N	16·36 E
164	Sora (sô'rä)....It.	41·43 N	13·37 E
156	Sör Aurdal (sŭr äūr-däl)....Nor.	60·54 N	9·24 E
162	Sorbas (sôr'bäs)....Sp.	37·05 N	2·07 W
125	Sordo (R.) (sô'r-dō)....Mex.	16·39 N	97·33 W
97	Sorel (sô-rĕl')....Can.	46·01 N	73·07 W
203	Sorell, C....Austl.	42·10 S	144·50 E
164	Soresina (sō-rå-zē'nä)....It.	45·17 N	9·51 E
162	Soria (sō'rê-ä)....Sp.	41·46 N	2·28 W
137	Soriano (sŏ-rêä'nô) (Dept.) Ur. (Buenos Aires In.)	33·25 S	58·00 W
137	Sorocaba (sô-rô-kä'bȧ) Braz. (Rio de Janeiro In.)	23·29 S	47·27 W
167	Soroki (sō-rō'kĕ)....Sov. Un.	48·09 N	28·17 E
197	Sorong (sō-rông')....Indon.	1·00 S	131·20 E
166	Sorot' (R.) (sō-rō'tzh)....Sov. Un.	57·08 N	29·23 E
217	Soroti (sō-rō'tê)....Ug.	1·43 N	33·37 E
150	Söröy (I.) (sûr'ûê)....Nor.	70·37 N	20·58 E
162	Sorraia (R.) (sôr-rī'ȧ)....Port.	38·55 N	8·42 W
163	Sorrento (sôr-rĕn'tō) It. (Naples In.)	40·23 N	14·23 E
197	Sorsogon (sôr-sôgōn')....Phil.	12·51 N	124·02 E
157	Sortavala (sôr'tä-vä-lä)...Sov. Un.	61·43 N	30·40 E
192	Sŏsan (sŭ'sän)....Korea	36·40 N	126·25 E
167	Sosna (R.) (sôs'nȧ)....Sov. Un.	50·33 N	38·15 E
167	Sosnitsa (sôs-nē'tsȧ)....Sov. Un.	51·30 N	32·29 E
172	Sosnogorsk....Sov. Un.	63·13 N	54·09 E
159	Sosnowiec (sôs-nô'vyĕts)....Pol.	50·17 N	19·10 E
194	Sosunova, Mys (Pt.) (mĭs sô'sōō-nôf'ȧ).Sov. Un.	46·28 N	138·06 E
174	Sos'va R. (sôs'vȧ) Sov. Un. (Urals In.)	59·55 N	60·40 E
170	Sos'va (R.) (sôs'vȧ)....Sov. Un.	63·10 N	63·30 E
215	Sota (R.)....Benin	11·10 N	3·20 E
124	Sota la Marina (sô-tä-lä-mä-rē'nä) Mex.	22·45 N	98·11 W
125	Soteapan (sō-tȧ-ä'pän)....Mex.	18·14 N	94·51 W
124	Soto la Marina, Rio (R.) (rē'ō-sō'tō lä mä-rē'nä).Mex.	23·55 N	98·30 W
126	Sotuta (sō-tōō'tä)....Mex. (In.)	20·35 N	89·00 W
216	Souanké....Con.	2·05 N	14·03 E
135	Soublette (sŏ-ōō-blĕ'tĕ)..Ven. (In.)	9·55 N	66·06 W
164	Soúdhas, Kolpós (G.)...Grc. (In.)	35·33 N	24·22 E
165	Souflion....Grc.	41·12 N	26·17 E
127	Soufriere (sōō-frê-âr') St. Lucia (In.)	13·50 N	61·03 W
127	Soufriere, Mt....St. Vincent (In.)	13·19 N	61·12 W
127	Soufrière (Vol.)...Montserrat (In.)	16·43 N	62·10 W
151	Souk-Ahras (sōōk-ä-räs')....Alg.	36·18 N	8·19 E
194	Sŏul (Seoul)....Kor.	37·35 N	127·03 E
94	Sounding Cr. (soun'dĭng)....Can.	51·35 N	111·00 W
218	Sources, Mt. aux (môɴ'tō sōōrs') Leso.-S. Afr. (Natal In.)	28·47 S	29·04 E
162	Soure (sōr-ĕ)....Port.	40·04 N	8·37 W
99	Souris (sōō'rē')....Can.	46·20 N	62·17 W
95	Souris....Can.	49·38 N	100·15 W
95	Souris (R.)....Can.	49·10 N	102·00 W
119	Sourlake (sour'lāk)....Tx.	30·09 N	94·24 W
210	Sousse (sōōs)....Tun.	36·00 N	10·39 E
160	Soustons (sōōs-tôɴ')....Fr.	43·46 N	1·22 W
121	South (R.)....NC	34·49 N	78·33 W
209	South Africa....Afr.	28·00 S	24·50 E
106	South Amboy (south'ăm'boi) NJ (New York In.)	40·28 N	74·17 W
133	South America		
154	Southampton (south-ămp'tŭn) Eng.	50·54 N	1·30 W
105	Southampton....NY	40·53 N	72·24 W
91	Southampton I....Can.	64·38 N	84·00 W
196	South Andaman I. (ăn-dȧ-măn') Andaman & Nicobar Is.	11·57 N	93·24 E
204	South Australia (State) (ôs-trā'lĭ-ȧ).Austl.	29·45 S	132·00 E
129	South B....Ba.	20·55 N	73·35 W
104	South Bend (bĕnd)....In.	41·40 N	86·20 W
110	South Bend (bĕnd)....Wa.	46·39 N	123·48 W
128	South Bight (B.)....Ba.	24·20 N	77·35 W
128	South Bimini (I.) (bē'mê-nê)..Ba.	25·40 N	79·20 W
99	Southborough (south'bŭr-ô) Ma. (In.)	42·18 N	71·33 W
121	South Boston (bôs'tŭn)....Va.	36·41 N	78·55 W
105	Southbridge (south'brĭj)....Ma.	42·05 N	72·00 W
129	South Caicos (I.) (kī'kōs) Turks & Caicos	21·30 N	71·35 W
103	South Carolina (State) (kăr-ô-lī'nȧ).U. S.	34·15 N	81·10 W
148	South Cave (cāv)....Eng.	53·45 N	0·35 W
104	South Charleston (south chärlz'tŭn).WV	38·20 N	81·40 W
196	South China Sea (chī'nȧ)....Asia	15·23 N	114·12 E
202	South Cr.....Austl. (Sydney In.)	33·43 S	167·00 E
102	South Dakota (State) (dȧ-kō'tȧ) U. S.	44·20 N	101·55 W
154	South Downs (dounz)....Eng.	50·55 N	1·13 W
184	South Dum-Dum....India (In.)	22·36 N	88·25 E
205	Southeast, C....Austl.	43·47 S	146·03 E
148	Southend-on-Sea (south-ĕnd') Eng. (London In.)	51·33 N	0·41 E
205	Southern Alps (Mts.) (sŭ-thûrn ălps).N. Z. (In.)	44·08 S	169·18 E
204	Southern Cross....Austl.	31·13 S	119·30 E
93	Southern Indian (L.) (sŭth'ērn ĭn'dĭ-ăn).Can.	56·46 N	98·57 W
121	Southern Pines (sŭth'ērn pīnz).NC	35·10 N	79·23 W
154	Southern Uplands (ŭp'lȧndz).Scot.	55·15 N	4·28 W
115	Southern Ute Ind. Res. (ūt)...Co.	37·05 N	108·23 W
	Southern Yemen, see Yemen, People's Democratic Republic of		
107	South Euclid (ū'klĭd) Oh. (Cleveland In.)	41·30 N	81·34 W
104	South Fox (I.) (fŏks)....Mi.	45·25 N	85·55 W
113	South Gate (gāt) Ca. (Los Angeles In.)	33·57 N	118·13 W
133	South Georgia (I.) (jôr'jȧ).Falk Is.	54·00 S	37·00 W
104	South Haven (hāv''n)....Mi.	42·25 N	86·15 W
121	South Hill....Va.	36·44 N	78·08 W
95	South Indian Lake....Can.	56·50 N	99·00 W
105	Southington (sŭdh'ĭng-tŭn)....Ct.	41·35 N	72·55 W
205	South I....N. Z. (In.)	43·15 S	167·00 E
108	South Loup (R.) (lōōp)....Ne.	41·21 N	100·08 W
99	South Merrimack (mĕr'ĭ-măk) NH (In.)	42·47 N	71·36 W
107	South Milwaukee (mĭl-wô'kê) Wi. (Milwaukee In.)	42·55 N	87·52 W
95	South Moose L....Can.	53·51 N	100·20 W
89	South Nation (R.) (nā'shŭn) Can. (Ottawa In.)	45·12 N	75·07 W
128	South Negril Pt. (nȧ-grēl')...Jam.	18·15 N	78·25 W
113	South Ogden (ŏg'dĕn) Ut. (Salt Lake City In.)	41·12 N	111·58 W
98	South Paris (păr'ĭs)....Me.	44·13 N	70·32 W
107	South Park (pärk) Ky. (Louisville In.)	38·06 N	85·43 W
113	South Pasadena (păs-ȧ-dē'nȧ) Ca. (Los Angeles In.)	34·06 N	118·08 W
115	South Pease (R.) (pēz)....Tx.	33·54 N	100·45 W
112	South Pender (I.) (pĕn'dēr) Can. (Vancouver In.)	48·45 N	123·09 W
120	South Pittsburgh (pĭts'bûrg)..Tn.	35·00 N	85·42 W
102	South Platte (R.) (plăt)....U. S.	40·40 N	102·40 W
96	South Porcupine....Can.	48·28 N	81·13 W
104	South Pt....Mi.	44·50 N	83·20 W
127	South Pt....Barb. (In.)	13·00 N	59·43 W
203	Southport (south'pōrt)....Austl.	27·57 S	153·27 E
121	Southport....NC	35·55 N	78·02 W
148	Southport (south'pôrt)....Eng.	53·38 N	3·00 W
107	Southport...In. (Indianapolis In.)	39·40 N	86·07 W
98	South Portland (pōrt-lănd)...Me.	43·37 N	70·15 W
112	South Prairie (prā'rĭ) Wa. (Seattle In.)	47·08 N	122·06 W
113	South Range (rānj) Wi. (Duluth In.)	46·37 N	91·59 W
106	South River (rĭv'ēr) NJ (New York In.)	40·27 N	74·23 W
106	South R.....Ga. (Atlanta In.)	33·40 N	84·15 W
113	South St. Paul....Mn. (Minneapolis, St. Paul In.)	44·54 N	93·02 W
113	South Salt Lake (sôlt lāk) Ut. (Salt Lake City In.)	40·44 N	111·53 W
133	South Sandwich Is. (sănd'wĭch) Falk. Is.	58·00 S	27·00 W

350 South Sandwich — Stawno PRONOUNCING INDEX

Page	Name Pronunciation Region	Lat. °′	Long. °′
133	South Sandwich Trench S. A.-Ant.	55·00 S	27·00 W
112	South San Francisco (săn frăn-sĭs'kô) Ca. (San Francisco In.)	37·39 N	122·24 W
94	South Saskatchewan (R.) (sȧs-kach'ĕ-wän) . Can.	53·15 N	105·05 W
154	South Shields (shēldz) . . . . Eng.	55·00 N	1·22 W
154	South Shropshire Hills (shrŏp'shĭr) . Eng.	52·30 N	3·02 W
108	South Sioux City (sōō sĭt'ê) . . . Ne.	42·28 N	96·26 W
205	South Taranaki Bight (tä-rä-nä'kê) . N. Z. (In.)	39·27 S	171·44 E
93	South Thompson (R.) (tŏmp'sŭn) . Can.	50·41 N	120·21 W
113	Southton (south'tŭn) Tx. (San Antonio In.)	29·18 N	98·26 W
154	South Uist (I.) (û'ĭst) . . . . Scot.	57·15 N	7·24 W
110	South Umpqua R. (ŭmp'kwȧ) . Or.	43·00 N	122·54 W
148	Southwell (south'wĕl) . . . . Eng.	53·04 N	0·56 W
	South West Africa, see Namibia		
205	Southwest C. . . . . N. Z. (In.)	47·17 S	167·12 E
98	Southwest Miramichi (R.) (mĭr ȧ-mê'shē) . Can.	46·35 N	66·17 W
129	Southwest Pt. . . . . Ba.	23·55 N	74·30 W
128	Southwest Pt. . . . . Ba.	25·50 N	77·10 W
157	Sovetsk (Tilsit) (sô-vyĕtsk') Sov. Un.	55·04 N	21·54 E
173	Sovetskaya Gavan' (sŭ-vyĕt'skī-u gä'vŭn') . Sov. Un.	48·59 N	140·14 E
182	Soviet Union (sō-vĭ-ĕt') . . Eur.-Asia	60·30 N	64·00 E
148	Sow (R.) (sou) . . . . Eng.	52·45 N	2·12 W
194	Sōya Misaki (C.) (sō'yȧ mê'sä-kē) Jap.	45·35 N	141·25 E
166	Sozh (R.) (sôzh) . . . . Sov. Un.	52·17 N	31·00 E
165	Sozopol (sôz'ô-pôl') . . . . Bul.	42·18 N	27·50 E
155	Spa (spä) . . . . Bel.	50·30 N	5·50 E
146	Spain (spān) . . . . Eur.	40·15 N	4·30 W
108	Spalding (spôl'dĭng) . . . . Ne.	41·43 N	98·23 W
112	Spanaway (spăn'ȧ-wā) Wa. (Seattle In.)	47·06 N	122·26 W
105	Spangler (spăng'lēr) . . . . Pa.	40·40 N	78·50 W
115	Spanish Fork (spăn'ĭsh fôrk) Ut.	40·10 N	111·40 W
128	Spanish Town . . . . Jam.	18·00 N	76·55 W
114	Sparks (spärks) . . . . Nv.	39·34 N	119·45 W
106	Sparrows Point (spăr'ōz) Md. (Baltimore In.)	39·13 N	76·29 W
120	Sparta (spär'tȧ) . . . . Ga.	33·16 N	82·59 W
117	Sparta . . . . Il.	38·07 N	89·42 W
104	Sparta . . . . Mi.	43·10 N	85·45 W
120	Sparta . . . . Tn.	35·54 N	85·26 W
109	Sparta . . . . Wi.	43·56 N	90·50 W
	Sparta, see Spárti		
106	Sparta Mts. . . NJ (New York In.)	41·00 N	74·38 W
121	Spartanburg (spär'tăn-bûrg) . . SC	34·57 N	82·13 W
162	Spartel (C.) (spär-tĕl') . . . . . . Mor.	35·48 N	5·50 W
165	Spárti (Sparta) . . . . Grc.	37·07 N	22·28 E
164	Spartivento, C. (spär-tê-vĕn'tô) . It.	37·55 N	16·09 E
164	Spartivento, C. . . . . It.	38·54 N	8·52 E
166	Spas-Demensk (spȧs dyĕ-mĕnsk') Sov. Un.	54·24 N	34·02 E
166	Spas-Klepiki (spȧs klĕp'ê-kê) Sov. Un.	55·09 N	40·11 E
173	Spassk-Dal'niy (spŭsk'däl'nyē) Sov. Un.	44·30 N	133·00 E
166	Spassk-Ryazanskiy (ryä-zän'skĭ) Sov. Un.	54·24 N	40·21 E
164	Spátha, Akr. (C.) . . . . Grc. (In.)	35·42 N	24·45 E
106	Spaulding (spôl'dĭng) Al. (Birmingham In.)	33·27 N	86·50 W
99	Spear, C. (spēr) . . . . Can.	47·32 N	52·32 W
108	Spearfish (spēr'fĭsh) . . . . SD	44·28 N	103·52 W
107	Speed (spēd) . . . In. (Louisville In.)	38·25 N	85·45 W
107	Speedway (spēd'wā) In. (Indianapolis In.)	39·47 N	86·14 W
149	Speicher L. (shpī'kĕr) F.R.G. (Munich In.)	48·12 N	11·47 E
104	Spencer (spĕn'sēr) . . . . In.	39·15 N	86·45 W
109	Spencer . . . . Ia.	43·09 N	95·08 W
121	Spencer . . . . NC	35·43 N	80·25 W
104	Spencer . . . . WV	38·55 N	81·20 W
203	Spencer G. (spĕn'sēr) . . . . . . Austl.	34·20 S	136·55 E
149	Sperenberg (shpĕ'rĕn-bĕrgh) G.D.R. (Berlin In.)	52·09 N	13·22 E
165	Sperkhiós (R.) . . . . Grc.	38·54 N	22·02 E
154	Sperrin Mts. (spĕr'ĭn) . . . . . N. Ire.	54·55 N	6·45 E
158	Spessart (Mts.) (shpĕ'särt) . F.R.G.	50·07 N	9·32 E
154	Spey (L.) (spā) . . . . Scot.	57·25 N	3·29 W
158	Speyer (shpī'ēr) . . . . F.R.G.	49·18 N	8·26 E
218	Sphinx (Pyramid) (sfĭnks) Egypt (Nile In.)	29·57 N	31·08 E
149	Spijkenisse Neth. (Amsterdam In.)	51·51 N	4·18 E
164	Spinazzola (spê-nät'zô-lä) . . . . . . It.	40·58 N	16·05 E
110	Spirit Lake (spĭr'ĭt) . . . . Id.	47·58 N	116·51 W
109	Spirit Lake (lāk) . . . . Ia.	43·25 N	95·08 W
159	Spišská Nová Ves (spēsh'skä nō'vä vĕs) . Czech.	48·56 N	20·35 E
	Spitsbergen (Is.), see Svalbard		
158	Spittal (shpê-täl') . . . . Aus.	46·48 N	13·28 E
164	Split (splêt) . . . . Yugo.	43·30 N	16·28 E
95	Split L. . . . . Can.	56·08 N	96·15 W
110	Spokane (spō-kăn') . . . . Wa.	47·39 N	117·25 W
110	Spokane R. . . . . Wa.	47·47 N	118·00 W
164	Spoleto (spô-lā'tō) . . . . It.	42·44 N	12·44 E
117	Spoon (R.) (spōōn) . . . . Il.	40·36 N	90·22 W
109	Spooner (spōōn'ēr) . . . . Wi.	45·50 N	91·53 W
165	Sporádhes (Is.) . . . . Grc.	38·55 N	24·05 E
106	Spotswood (spŏtz'wŏŏd) NJ (New York In.)	40·23 N	74·22 W
110	Sprague R. (sprāg) . . . . Or.	42·30 N	121·42 W
196	Spratly (I.) (sprăt'lê) . . . . China	8·38 N	11·54 E
121	Spray (sprā) . . . . NC	36·30 N	79·44 W
158	Spree R. (shprā) . . . . G.D.R.	51·53 N	14·08 E
158	Spremberg (shprĕm'bĕrgh) . G.D.R.	51·35 N	14·23 E
117	Spring (R.) . . . . Ar.	36·25 N	91·35 W
212	Springbok (sprĭng'bŏk) . . . . . S. Afr.	29·35 S	17·55 E
114	Spring, Cr. (sprĭng) . . . . Nv.	40·18 N	117·45 W
119	Spring Cr. . . . . Tx.	30·03 N	95·43 W
118	Spring Cr. . . . . Tx.	31·08 N	100·50 W
99	Springdale . . . . Can.	49·30 N	56·05 W
117	Springdale (sprĭng'dāl) . . . . Ar.	36·10 N	94·07 W
107	Springdale . . . Pa. (Pittsburgh In.)	40·33 N	79·46 W
116	Springer (sprĭng'ēr) . . . . NM	36·21 N	104·37 W
115	Springerville . . . . Az.	34·08 N	109·17 W
116	Springfield (sprĭng'fēld) . . . . Co.	37·24 N	102·04 W
109	Springfield . . . . Mn.	44·14 N	94·59 W
110	Springfield . . . . Or.	44·01 N	123·02 W
117	Springfield . . . . Il.	39·46 N	89·37 W
104	Springfield . . . . Ky.	37·35 N	85·10 W
105	Springfield . . . . Ma.	42·05 N	72·35 W
117	Springfield . . . . Mo.	37·13 N	93·17 W
104	Springfield . . . . Oh.	39·55 N	83·50 W
120	Springfield . . . . Tn.	36·30 N	86·53 W
105	Springfield . . . . Vt.	43·20 N	72·35 W
212	Springfontein (sprĭng'fôn-tīn) S. Afr.	30·16 S	25·45 E
99	Springhill (sprĭng-hĭl') . . . . Can.	45·39 N	64·03 W
114	Spring Mts. . . . . Nv.	36·18 N	115·49 W
213	Springs (sprĭngs) . . . . S. Afr. (Johannesburg & Pretoria In.)	26·16 S	28·27 E
89	Springstein (sprĭng'stīn) Can. (Winnipeg In.)	49·49 N	97·29 W
106	Springton Res. (sprĭng-tŭn) Pa. (Philadelphia In.)	39·57 N	75·26 W
202	Springvale . Austl. (Melbourne In.)	37·57 N	145·09 E
114	Spring Valley . . . . Ca. (In.)	32·46 N	117·01 W
104	Springvalley (sprĭng-văl'ĭ) . . . . . . Il.	41·20 N	89·15 W
109	Spring Valley . . . . Mn.	43·41 N	92·26 W
106	Spring Valley . NY (New York In.)	41·07 N	74·03 W
115	Springville (sprĭng-vĭl) . . . . Ut.	40·10 N	111·40 W
202	Springwood . . . Austl. (Sydney In.)	33·42 S	150·34 E
89	Spruce Grove (sprōōs grōv) Can. (Edmonton In.)	53·32 N	113·55 W
116	Spur (spûr) . . . . Tx.	33·29 N	100·51 W
105	Squam (L.) (skwôm) . . . . NH	43·45 N	71·30 W
92	Squamish (skwŏ'mĭsh) . . . . Can.	49·42 N	123·09 W
92	Squamish (R.) . . . . Can.	50·10 N	124·30 W
164	Squillace, Gulfo di (G.) (gōō'l-fô-dē skwēl-lä'châ) . . . . . It.	38·44 N	16·47 E
165	Srbija (Serbia) (Reg.) (sr bê-yä) (sĕr'bê-ä) . Yugo.	44·05 N	20·35 E
165	Srbobran (s'r'bô-brän') . . . . . Yugo.	45·32 N	19·50 E
173	Sredne-Kolymsk (s'rĕd'nyê kô-lêmsk') . Sov. Un.	67·49 N	154·55 E
174	Sredne Rogartka (s'red'nȧ-ya) (rô gär'tkȧ) Sov. Un. (Leningrad In.)	59·49 N	30·20 E
174	Sredniy Ik (R.) (srĕd'nĭ ĭk) Sov. Un. (Urals In.)	55·46 N	58·50 E
174	Sredniy Ural (Mts.) (ŏŏ'răl) Sov. Un. (Urals In.)	57·47 N	59·00 E
159	Śrem (shrĕm) . . . . Pol.	52·06 N	17·01 E
165	Sremska Karlovci (srĕm'skê kär'lov-tsê) . Yugo.	45·10 N	19·57 E
165	Sremska Mitrovica (srĕm'skä mē'trô-vê-tsä') . Yugo.	44·59 N	19·39 E
173	Sretensk (s'rĕ'tĕnsk) . . . . . Sov. Un.	52·13 N	117·39 E
182	Sri Lanka (Ceylon) . . . . Asia	8·45 N	82·30 E
184	Srīnagar (srē-nŭg'ŭr) . . . . India	34·11 N	74·49 E
159	Sroda (shrô'dȧ) . . . . Pol.	52·14 N	17·17 E
149	Stabroek . . . . . . Bel. (Brussels In.)	51·20 N	4·21 E
149	Stade (shtä'dĕ) F.R.G. (Hamburg In.)	53·36 N	9·28 E
150	Stadhur . . . . Ice.	65·08 N	20·56 W
156	Städjan (Mtn.) (stĕd'yän) . . . Swe.	61·53 N	12·50 E
148	Stafford (stăf'fērd) . . . . Eng.	52·48 N	2·06 W
116	Stafford . . . . Ks.	37·58 N	98·37 W
148	Stafford (Co.) . . . . Eng.	52·45 N	2·00 W
149	Stahnsdorf (shtäns'dôrf) G.D.R. (Berlin In.)	52·22 N	13·10 E
	Stalin, see Varna		
	Stalinabad, see Dushanbe		
	Stalingrad, see Volgograd		
	Stalino, see Donetsk		
167	Stalino (Oblast) (stä'lĭ-nô) (ôb'lȧst) . Sov. Un.	47·54 N	37·13 E
172	Stalino, Pik (Mtn.) . . . . . . Sov. Un.	39·00 N	72·15 E
	Stalinsk, see Novokuznetsk		
148	Stalybridge (stā'lê-brĭj) . . . . . . Eng.	53·29 N	2·03 W
109	Stambaugh (stăm'bô) . . . . Mi.	46·03 N	88·38 W
106	Stamford (stăm'fērd) Ct. (New York In.)	41·03 N	73·32 W
148	Stamford . . . . Eng.	52·39 N	0·28 W
116	Stamford . . . . Tx.	32·57 N	99·48 W
149	Stammersdorf (shtäm'ērs-dôrf) Aus. (Vienna In.)	48·19 N	16·25 E
117	Stamps (stămps) . . . . Ar.	33·22 N	93·31 W
117	Stanberry (stan'bĕr-ê) . . . . Mo.	40·12 N	94·34 W
218	Standerton (stăn'dēr-tŭn) . . S. Afr. (Johannesburg & Pretoria In.)	26·57 S	29·17 E
108	Standing Rock Ind. Res. (stănd'ĭng rŏk) . ND	47·07 N	101·05 W
148	Standish (stăn'dĭsh) . . . . Eng.	53·36 N	2·39 W
120	Stanford (stăn'fērd) . . . . Ky.	37·29 N	84·40 W
213	Stanger (stăŋ-ger) S. Afr. (Natal In.)	29·22 S	31·18 E
156	Stangvik Fd. (stang'vêk fyôrd) Nor.	62·54 N	8·55 E
128	Staniard Creek . . . . Ba.	24·50 N	77·55 W
114	Stanislaus (R.) (stăn'ĭs-lô) . . . . Ca.	38·10 N	120·16 W
98	Stanley (stăn'lê) . . . . Can.	46·17 N	66·44 W
136	Stanley . . . . Falk. Is.	51·46 S	57·59 W
108	Stanley . . . . ND	48·20 N	102·25 W
109	Stanley . . . . Wi.	44·56 N	90·56 W
216	Stanley Falls . . . . Zaire	0·30 N	25·12 E
215	Stanley Pool (L.) . . . . Zaire	4·07 S	15·40 E
184	Stanley Res. (stăn'lê) . . . . India	12·07 N	77·27 E
	Stanleyville, see Kisangani		
126	Stann Creek (stăn krēk) Belize (In.)	17·01 N	88·14 W
173	Stanovoy Khrebet (Mts.) (stŭn-ȧ-voi') . Sov. Un.	56·12 N	127·12 E
113	Stanton (stăn'tŭn) Ca. (Los Angeles In.)	33·48 N	118·00 W
108	Stanton . . . . Ne.	41·57 N	97·15 W
118	Stanton . . . . Tx.	32·08 N	101·46 W
112	Stanwood (stăn'wŏŏd) Wa. (Seattle In.)	48·14 N	122·23 W
109	Staples (stā'p'lz) . . . . Mn.	46·21 N	94·48 W
120	Stapleton . . . . Al.	30·45 N	87·48 W
146	Stara Planina (Balkan Mts.) Bul.	42·50 N	24·45 E
174	Staraya Kupavna (stä'rȧ-yȧ kû-päf'nȧ) Sov. Un. (Moscow In.)	55·48 N	38·10 E
166	Staraya Russa (stä'rȧ-yȧ rōōsȧ) Sov. Un.	57·58 N	31·21 E
165	Stara Zagora (zä'gô-rȧ) . . . . . . Bul.	42·26 N	25·37 E
89	Starbuck (stär'bŭk) Can. (Winnipeg In.)	49·46 N	97·36 W
158	Stargard Szczeciński (shtär'gärt shchĕ-chyn'skē) . Pol.	53·19 N	15·03 E
166	Staritsa (stä'rê-tsȧ) . . . . . . Sov. Un.	56·29 N	34·58 E
121	Starke (stärk) . . . . Fl.	29·55 N	82·07 W
116	Starkville (stärk'vĭl) . . . . Co.	37·06 N	104·34 W
120	Starkville . . . . Ms.	33·27 N	88·47 W
149	Starnberg (shtärn-bĕrgh) F.R.G. (Munich In.)	47·59 N	11·20 E
167	Starobel'sk (stä-rô-byĕlsk') Sov. Un.	49·19 N	38·57 E
166	Starodub (stä-rô-drŏŏp') . Sov. Un.	52·25 N	32·49 E
159	Starogard Gdański (stä'rō-grad gdĕn'skē) . . . . Pol.	53·58 N	18·33 E
167	Staro-Konstantinov (stä'rô kŏn-stȧn-tē'nôf) Sov. Un.	49·45 N	27·12 E
167	Staro-Minskaya (stä'rô mĭn'skȧ-yȧ) . Sov. Un.	46·19 N	38·51 E
167	Staro-Shcherbinovskaya . Sov. Un.	46·38 N	38·38 E
174	Staro-Subkhangulovo (stȧro-sōōb-kan-gōō'lōvō) Sov. Un. (Urals In.)	53·08 N	57·24 E
174	Staroutkinsk (stȧ-rô-ōōt'kĭnsk) Sov. Un. (Urals In.)	57·14 N	59·21 E
167	Staroverovka . . . . Sov. Un.	49·31 N	35·48 E
154	Start Pt. (stärt) . . . . Eng.	50·14 N	3·34 W
159	Stary Sacz (stä-rē sôɲch') . . . . . Pol.	49·32 N	20·36 E
167	Staryy Oskol (stä'rê ôs-kôl') Sov. Un.	51·18 N	37·51 E
158	Stassfurt (shtäs'fōōrt) . . . . . G.D.R.	51·52 N	11·35 E
159	Staszów (stä'shŏŏf) . . . . Pol.	50·32 N	21·13 E
105	State College (stāt kŏl'ĕj) . . . . . Pa.	40·50 N	77·55 W
113	State Line (līn) . . Mn. (Duluth In.)	46·36 N	92·18 W
106	Staten I. (stăt'ĕn) NY (New York In.)	40·35 N	74·10 W
121	Statesboro (stāts'bŭr-ô) . . . . Ga.	32·26 N	81·47 W
121	Statesville (stāts'vĭl) . . . . NC	34·45 N	80·54 W
113	Staunton (stôn'tŭn) Il. (St. Louis In.)	39·01 N	89·47 W
105	Staunton . . . . Va.	38·10 N	79·05 W
156	Stavanger (stä'väng'ēr) . . . . . . Nor.	58·59 N	5·44 E
112	Stave (R.) (stāv) Can. (Vancouver In.)	49·12 N	122·24 W
148	Staveley (stāv'lê) . . . . Eng.	53·17 N	1·21 W
149	Stavenisse . Neth. (Amsterdam In.)	51·35 N	3·59 E
171	Stavropol' . . . . Sov. Un.	45·05 N	41·50 E
158	Stawno (swav'nō) . . . . Pol.	54·21 N	16·38 E

ăt; finȧl; rāte; senâte; ärm; ȧsk; sofȧ; fâre; ch-choose; dh-as th in other; bē; ēvent; bĕt; recĕnt; cratēr; g-go; gh-guttural g; bĭt; ĭ-short neutral; rīde; ĸ-guttural k as ch in German ich;

PRONOUNCING INDEX Steamboat Springs — Suita 351

Page	Name Pronunciation Region	Lat. °'	Long. °'
116	Steamboat Springs (stēm'bōt').Co.	40·30 N	106·48 W
167	Steblëv (styĕp'lyôf)......Sov. Un.	49·23 N	31·03 E
109	Steel (R.) (stēl)............Can.	49·08 N	86·55 W
105	Steelton (stĕl'tŭn)............Pa.	40·15 N	76·45 W
149	Steenbergen Neth. (Amsterdam In.)	51·35 N	4·18 E
110	Steens Mts. (stēnz)...........Or.	42·15 N	118·52 W
204	Steep Pt. (stēp)...........Austl.	26·15 N	112·05 E
	Stefaniee, L., see Chew Bahir		
107	Steger (stē'gēr)..Il. (Chicago In.)	41·28 N	87·38 W
158	Steiermark (Styria) (State) (shtī'ēr-märk).Aus.	47·22 N	14·40 E
90	Steinbach..................Can.	49·32 N	96·41 W
150	Steinkjer (stēïn-kyĕr)........Nor.	64·00 N	11·19 E
112	Stella (stĕl'á)..Wa. (Portland In.)	46·11 N	123·12 W
98	Stellarton (stĕl'ár-tŭn).......Can.	45·34 N	62·40 W
158	Stendal (shtĕn'däl).......G.D.R.	52·37 N	11·51 E
171	Stepanakert (styĕ'pän-à-kĕrt) Sov. Un.	39·50 N	46·40 E
203	Stephens, Port (stē'fĕns)....Austl.	32·43 N	152·55 E
99	Stephenville (stē'vĕn-vĭl).....Can.	48·33 N	58·35 W
172	Stepnyak (styĭp-nyäk')..Sov. Un.	52·37 N	70·43 E
161	Sterkrade (shtĕr'krädĕ) F.R.G. (Ruhr In.)	51·31 N	6·51 E
213	Sterkstroom...S. Afr. (Natal In.)	31·33 S	26·36 E
116	Sterling (stûr'lĭng)...........Co.	40·38 N	103·14 W
109	Sterling......................Il.	41·48 N	89·42 W
116	Sterling.....................Ks.	38·11 N	98·11 W
99	Sterling..............Ma. (In.)	42·26 N	71·41 W
118	Sterling.....................Tx.	31·53 N	100·58 W
174	Sterlitamak (styĕr'lĭ-ta-mäk') Sov. Un. (Urals In.)	53·38 N	55·56 E
159	Šternberk (shtĕrn'bĕrk)....Czech.	49·44 N	17·18 E
	Stettin, see Szczecin		
158	Stettiner Haff (L.) (shtĕ'tē-nēr häf)....G.D.R.	53·47 N	14·02 E
93	Stettler.....................Can.	52·19 N	112·43 W
104	Steubenville (stū'bĕn-vĭl).....Oh.	40·20 N	80·40 W
112	Stevens (L.) (stē'vĕnz) Wa. (Seattle In.)	47·59 N	122·06 W
109	Stevens Point...............Wi.	44·30 N	89·35 W
111	Stevensville (stē'vĕnz-vĭl).....Mt.	46·31 N	114·03 W
90	Stewart (R.) (stū'ērt).......Can.	63·27 N	138·48 W
205	Stewart I............N. Z. (In.)	46·50 S	168·06 E
98	Stewiacke (stū'wē-ăk).......Can.	45·08 N	63·21 W
218	Steynsrus (stīns'rōōs)......S. Afr. (Johannesburg & Pretoria In.)	27·58 S	27·33 E
158	Steyr (shtīr)................Aus.	48·03 N	14·24 E
90	Stikine (R.) (stĭ-kēn').......Can.	58·17 N	130·10 W
90	Stikine Ranges.............Can.	59·05 N	130·00 W
112	Stillaguamish (R.) Wa. (Seattle In.)	48·11 N	122·18 W
112	Stillaguamish (R.), South Fk. (stĭl-á-gwä'mĭsh).Wa. (Seattle In.)	48·05 N	121·59 W
113	Stillwater (stĭl'wô-tēr) Mn. (Minneapolis, St. Paul In.)	45·04 N	92·48 W
111	Stillwater...................Mt.	45·23 N	109·45 W
117	Stillwater...................Ok.	36·06 N	97·03 W
114	Stillwater Ra................Nv.	39·43 N	118·11 W
110	Stillwater R.................Mt.	48·47 N	114·40 W
165	Štip (shtĭp)...............Yugo.	41·43 N	22·07 E
154	Stirling (stûr'lĭng)..........Scot.	56·05 N	3·59 W
89	Stittsville (stĭts'vĭl) Can. (Ottawa In.)	45·15 N	75·54 W
156	Stjördalshalsen (styûr-däls-hälsĕn).Nor.	63·26 N	11·00 E
109	Stockbridge Munsee Ind. Res. (stŏk'brĭdj mŭn-sē).Wi.	44·49 N	89·00 W
149	Stockerau (shtô'kĕ-rou) Aus. (Vienna In.)	48·24 N	16·13 E
98	Stockholm (stŏk'hōlm).......Me.	47·05 N	68·08 W
156	Stockholm (stôk'hôlm')......Swe.	59·23 N	18·00 E
148	Stockport (stŏk'pôrt).......Eng.	53·24 N	2·09 W
114	Stockton (stŏk'tŭn)..........Ca.	37·56 N	121·16 W
154	Stockton...................Eng.	54·35 N	1·25 W
116	Stockton....................Ks.	39·26 N	99·16 W
109	Stockton (I.)................Wi.	46·56 N	90·25 W
118	Stockton Plat................Tx.	30·34 N	102·35 W
117	Stockton Res................Mo.	37·40 N	93·45 W
156	Stöde (stû'dĕ).............Swe.	62·26 N	16·35 E
148	Stoke-on-Trent (stōk-ŏn-trĕnt) Eng.	53·01 N	2·12 W
159	Stokhod (R.) (stō-kōd)..Sov. Un.	51·24 N	25·20 E
165	Stolac (stō'làts)...........Yugo.	43·03 N	17·59 E
173	Stolbovoy (Is.) (stôl-bô-voi') Sov. Un.	73·43 N	133·05 E
159	Stolin (stô'lēn)..........Sov. Un.	51·54 N	26·52 E
161	Stommeln (shtō'mĕln) F.R.G. (Ruhr In.)	51·01 N	6·46 E
156	Stömstad..................Swe.	58·58 N	11·09 E
148	Stone......................Eng.	52·54 N	2·09 W
89	Stoneham (stōn'ám) Can. (Quebec In.)	46·59 N	71·22 W
99	Stoneham.......Ma. (Boston In.)	42·30 N	71·05 W
154	Stonehaven (stōn'hā-v'n)....Scot.	56·57 N	2·09 W
106	Stone Mountain (stōn) Ga. (Atlanta In.)	33·49 N	84·10 W
89	Stonewall (stōn'wôl) Can. (Winnipeg In.)	50·09 N	97·21 W
120	Stonewall...................Ms.	32·08 N	88·44 W
89	Stoney Creek (stō'nē) Can. (Toronto In.)	43·13 N	79·45 W
105	Stonington (stōn'ĭng-tŭn).....Ct.	41·20 N	71·55 W
114	Stony Cr. (stō'nē)...........Ca.	39·28 N	122·35 W
89	Stony Indian Res. Can. (Calgary In.)	51·10 N	114·45 W
89	Stony Mountain Can. (Winnipeg In.)	50·05 N	97·13 W
89	Stony Plain (stō'nē plān) Can. (Edmonton In.)	53·02 N	114·00 W
89	Stony Plain Ind. Res. Can. (Edmonton In.)	53·29 N	113·48 W
106	Stony Point..NY (New York In.)	41·13 N	73·58 W
156	Storå (R.)..................Den.	56·22 N	8·35 E
170	Stora Lule (R.) (stōō'rä lōō'lĕ) Swe.	67·00 N	19·30 E
156	Stord (I.) (stôrd)...........Nor.	59·54 N	5·15 E
156	Store Baelt (Str.)...........Den.	55·25 N	10·50 E
150	Stören (stûrĕn).............Nor.	62·58 N	10·21 E
156	Store Sotra (Sartor) (stô-rĕ-sô'-trà) (sär'tôr).Nor.	60·24 N	4·35 E
156	Stor Fd. (stôr fyôrd)........Nor.	62·17 N	6·19 E
213	Stormberg (Mts.) (stôrm'bûrg) S. Afr. (Natal In.)	31·28 S	26·35 E
109	Storm Lake..................Ia.	42·39 N	95·12 W
123	Stormy Pt. (stôrm'ē) Vir. Is. (U. S. A.) (St. Thomas In.)	18·22 N	65·01 W
154	Stornoway (stôr'nô-wā)......Scot.	58·13 N	6·21 W
159	Storozhinets (stô-rô'zhēn-yĕts) Sov. Un.	48·10 N	25·44 E
156	Störsjo (stôr'shû)...........Swe.	62·49 N	13·08 E
156	Störsjoen (L.) (stôr-syûĕn)...Nor.	61·32 N	11·30 E
156	Störsjon (L.)...............Swe.	63·06 N	14·00 E
156	Storvik (stôr'vêk)...........Swe.	60·37 N	16·31 E
99	Stoughton (stō'tŭn).....Ma. (In.)	42·07 N	71·06 W
109	Stoughton..................Wi.	42·54 N	89·15 W
155	Stour (R.) (stour)...........Eng.	52·09 N	0·29 E
148	Stourbridge (stour'brĭj)......Eng.	52·27 N	2·08 W
99	Stow (stō).............Ma. (In.)	42·56 N	71·31 W
107	Stow.........Oh. (Cleveland In.)	41·09 N	81·26 W
218	Straatsdrif...............S. Afr. (Johannesburg & Pretoria In.)	25·19 S	26·22 E
154	Strabane (stră-băn') N. Ire.	54·59 N	7·27 W
161	Straelen (shtră'lĕn) F.R.G. (Ruhr In.)	51·26 N	6·16 E
205	Strahan (strā'ăn)..........Austl.	42·08 S	145·28 E
158	Strakonice (strä'kô-nyĕ-tsĕ) Czech.	49·18 N	13·52 E
165	Straldzha (sträl'dzhà)........Bul.	42·37 N	26·44 E
158	Stralsund (shräl'sōōnt)....G.D.R.	54·18 N	13·04 E
156	Strand (stränd).............Nor.	59·05 N	5·59 E
154	Strangford, Lough (B.) (lŏk străng'fērd).Ire.	54·30 N	5·34 W
156	Strängnas (strĕng'nĕs).......Swe.	59·23 N	16·59 E
154	Stranraer (străn-rär')........Scot.	54·55 N	5·05 W
161	Strasbourg (stràs-bōōr').......Fr.	48·36 N	7·49 E
104	Stratford (străt'fērd)........Can.	43·20 N	81·05 W
105	Stratford....................Ct.	41·10 N	73·05 W
154	Stratford...................Eng.	52·13 N	1·41 W
109	Stratford...................Wi.	44·16 N	90·02 W
92	Strathcona Prov. Pk.........Can.	49·40 N	125·50 W
158	Straubing (strou'bĭng).....F.R.G.	48·52 N	12·36 E
158	Strausberg (strous'bĕrgh)..G.D.R.	52·35 N	13·50 E
115	Strawberry (R.)..............Ut.	40·05 N	110·55 W
110	Strawberry Mts. (strô'bĕr'ĭ)..Or.	44·19 N	119·20 W
118	Strawn (strôn)...............Tx.	32·38 N	98·28 W
104	Streator (strē'tēr)............Il.	41·05 N	88·50 W
108	Streeter....................ND	46·40 N	99·22 W
89	Streetsville (strētz'vĭl) Can. (Toronto In.)	43·34 N	79·43 W
165	Strehaia (strĕ-ĸä'yà)........Rom.	44·37 N	23·13 E
174	Strel'na (strĕl'nà) Sov. Un. (Leningrad In.)	59·52 N	30·01 E
148	Stretford (strĕt'fērd)........Eng.	53·25 N	2·19 W
197	Strickland (R.) (strĭk'lănd) Pap. N. Gui.	6·15 S	142·00 E
149	Strijen....Neth. (Amsterdam In.)	51·44 N	4·32 E
165	Strimonikós Kólpos (G.)......Grc.	40·40 N	23·55 E
164	Strómboli (Vol.) (strôm'bô-lē)..It.	38·46 N	15·16 E
174	Stromyn (strô'mĭn) Sov. Un. (Moscow In.)	56·02 N	38·29 E
120	Strong (R.) (strông).........Ms.	32·03 N	89·42 W
107	Strongsville (strôŋgz'vĭl) Oh. (Cleveland In.)	41·19 N	81·50 W
154	Stronsay (I.) (strŏn'sā)......Scot.	59·09 N	2·35 W
105	Stroudsburg (stroudz'bûrg)....Pa.	41·00 N	75·15 W
156	Struer......................Den.	56·29 N	8·34 E
166	Strugi Krasnyye (strōō'gĭ krä's-ny'yĕ).Sov. Un.	58·14 N	29·10 E
165	Struma (R.) (strōō'mà)......Bul.	41·55 N	23·05 E
165	Strumica (strōō'mĭ-tsà).....Yugo.	41·26 N	22·38 E
174	Strunino...Sov. Un. (Moscow In.)	56·23 N	38·34 E
104	Struthers (strŭdh'ērz)........Oh.	41·00 N	80·35 W
149	Struvenhütten (shtrōō'vĕn-hü-tĕn) F.R.G. (Hamburg In.)	53·52 N	10·04 E
218	Strydpoortberge (Mts.)....S. Afr. (Johannesburg & Pretoria In.)	24·08 N	29·18 E
159	Stryy (strē')...........Sov. Un.	49·16 N	3·521 E
159	Strzelce Opolskie (stzhĕl'tsĕ o-pŏl'skyĕ).Pol.	50·31 N	18·20 E
159	Strzelin (stzhĕ-lĭn)...........Pol.	50·48 N	17·06 E
159	Strzelno (stzhål'nô)..........Pol.	52·37 N	18·10 E
121	Stuart (stū'ērt).........Fl. (In.)	27·10 N	80·14 W
109	Stuart.......................Ia.	41·31 N	94·20 W
101	Stuart (I.)...................Ak.	63·25 N	162·45 W
112	Stuart (I.)...Wa. (Vancouver In.)	48·42 N	123·10 W
92	Stuart L....................Can.	54·32 N	124·35 W
204	Stuart Ra..................Austl.	29·00 S	134·30 E
196	Stung Treng (stōōng'trĕng') Kamp.	13·36 N	106·00 E
149	Stupava......Czech. (Vienna In.)	48·17 N	17·02 E
159	Stupsk (swōōpsk)............Pol.	54·28 N	17·02 E
89	Sturgeon (R.) Can. (Edmonton In.)	53·41 N	113·46 W
109	Sturgeon (R.)................Mi.	46·43 N	88·43 W
109	Sturgeon Bay.................Wi.	44·50 N	87·22 W
95	Sturgeon B..................Can.	52·00 N	98·00 W
91	Sturgeon Falls..............Can.	46·19 N	79·49 W
104	Sturgis......................Ky.	37·35 N	88·00 W
104	Sturgis......................Mi.	41·45 N	85·25 W
108	Sturgis......................SD	44·25 N	103·31 W
204	Sturt Cr...................Austl.	19·40 S	127·40 E
107	Sturtevant (stŭr'tĕ-vănt) Wi. (Milwaukee In.)	42·42 N	87·54 W
213	Stutterheim (stŭrt'ēr-hīm) S. Afr. (Natal In.)	32·34 S	27·27 E
117	Stuttgart (stŭt'gärt)..........Ar.	34·30 N	91·33 W
158	Stuttgart (shtōōt'gärt).....F.R.G.	48·48 N	9·15 E
150	Stykkisholmur...............Ice.	65·00 N	21·48 W
159	Styr' R. (stēr).........Sov. Un.	51·44 N	26·07 E
	Styria, see Steiermark		
193	Suao (sōō'ou)............Taiwan	24·35 N	121·45 E
184	Subarnarakha (R.).........India	22·38 N	86·26 E
157	Subata (sōō'bà-tà).......Sov. Un.	56·02 N	25·54 E
197	Subic (sōō'bĭk).........Phil. (In.)	14·52 N	120·15 E
197	Subic B...............Phil. (In.)	14·41 N	120·11 E
165	Subotica (sōō'bô'tē-tsä)....Yugo.	46·06 N	19·41 E
217	Subugo (Mtn.).............Ken.	1·40 S	35·49 E
106	Succasunna (sŭk'kà-sŭn'nà) NJ (New York In.)	40·52 N	74·37 W
159	Suceava (sōō-châ-ä'và)......Rom.	47·39 N	26·17 E
159	Suceava R.................Rom.	47·45 N	26·10 E
159	Sucha (sōō'ĸä)..............Pol.	49·44 N	19·40 E
125	Suchiapa (sōō-chê-ä'pä).....Mex.	16·38 N	93·08 W
125	Suchiapa (R.)..............Mex.	16·27 N	93·26 W
126	Suchitoto (sōō-chê-tō'tō)......Sal.	13·58 N	89·03 W
190	Suchow (Xuzhou) (shōō-jō).China	34·17 N	117·10 E
112	Sucia Is. (sōō'sê-á) Wa. (Vancouver In.)	48·46 N	122·54 W
134	Sucio (R.) (sōō'syô)....Co. (In.)	6·55 N	76·15 W
154	Suck (sŭk)..................Ire.	53·34 N	8·16 W
134	Sucre (sōō'krā)..............Bol.	19·06 S	65·16 W
135	Sucre (State) (sōō'krĕ)..Ven. (In.)	10·18 N	64·12 W
129	Sud, Canal du (Chan.).......Hai.	18·40 N	73·15 W
89	Sud, Rivière du (rê-vyâr'dü süd') Can. (Québec In.)	46·56 N	70·35 W
174	Suda (sōō'dá).Sov. Un. (Urals In.)	56·58 N	56·45 E
166	Suda (R.) (sōō'dà).......Sov. Un.	59·24 N	36·40 E
186	Sudair (sŭ-dä'ēr).........Sau. Ar.	25·48 N	46·28 E
209	Sudan......................Afr.	14·00 N	28·00 E
215	Sudan (Reg.) (sōō-dän').......Afr.	15·00 N	7·00 E
91	Sudbury (sŭd'bēr-ê).........Can.	46·28 N	81·00 W
99	Sudbury..............Ma. (In.)	42·23 N	71·25 W
158	Sudetes (Mts.)............Czech.	50·41 N	15·37 E
166	Sudogda (sōō'dôk-dà)....Sov. Un.	55·57 N	40·29 E
166	Sudost' (R.) (sōō-dôst')..Sov. Un.	52·43 N	33·13 E
167	Sudzha (sōōd'zhà).......Sov. Un.	51·14 N	35·11 E
163	Sueca (swā'kä)...............Sp.	39·12 N	0·18 W
92	Suemez I....................Ak.	55·17 N	133·21 W
	Suez, see As Suways		
218	Suez, G. of (sōō-ĕz') Egypt (Suez In.)	29·53 N	32·33 E
	Suez Can., see Qana el Suweis		
106	Suffern (sŭf'fērn) NY (New York In.)	41·07 N	74·09 W
106	Suffolk (sŭf'ŭk)..Va. (Norfolk In.)	36·43 N	76·35 W
104	Sugar (Cr.)..................In.	39·55 N	87·10 W
116	Sugar City..................Co.	38·12 N	103·42 W
113	Sugar Creek Mo. (Kansas City In.)	39·07 N	94·27 W
117	Sugar Cr. (shōōg'ēr)...........Il.	40·14 N	89·28 W
113	Sugar I..Mi. (Sault Ste. Marie In.)	46·31 N	84·12 W
203	Sugarloaf Pt. (sōōgēr'lôf)...Austl.	32·19 S	153·04 E
95	Suggi L.....................Can.	54·22 N	102·47 W
183	Suhaymī, Wādī as (R.) Egypt (Palestine In.)	29·48 N	33·12 E
158	Suhl (zōōl).................G.D.R.	50·37 N	10·41 E
193	Suichuan (Mtn.)............China	26·25 N	114·10 E
192	Suide (swā-dŭ)..............China	37·32 N	110·12 E
173	Suifenhe (swā-fŭn-hŭ)........China	44·47 N	131·13 E
192	Siuhua.....................China	46·38 N	126·50 E
190	Suining (sōō'ê-nĭng').......China	33·54 N	117·57 E
137	Suipacha (swê-pä'chä) Arg. (Buenos Aires In.)	34·45 S	59·43 W
190	Suiping (swā-pĭŋ)..........China	33·09 N	113·58 E
154	Suir R. (sūr)................Ire.	52·20 N	7·32 W
112	Suisun B. (sōō-ê-sōōn') Ca. (San Francisco In.)	38·07 N	122·02 W
195	Suita (sōō'ê-tä)..Jap. (Ōsaka In.)	34·45 N	135·32 E

ng-sing; ŋ-baŋk; ĸ-nasalized n; nŏd; cŏmmit; ōld; ôbey; ôrder; fōōd; fŏŏt; ou-out; s-soft; sh-dish; th-thin; pūre; ûnite; ûrn; stŭd; circŭs; ü-as "y" in study; '-indeterminate vowel.

352 Suitland — Syktyvkar PRONOUNCING INDEX

Page	Name Pronunciation Region	Lat. °′	Long. °′
106	Suitland (sōōt'lănd) Md. (Baltimore In.)	38·51 N	76·57 W
193	Sui Xian (swā shyĕn) China	31·42 N	113·20 E
188	Suiyüan (Reg.) (swā-yüĕn) China	41·31 N	107·04 E
190	Suizhong (swā-jôŋ) China	40·22 N	120·20 E
196	Sukabumi Indon.	6·52 S	106·56 E
196	Sukadana Indon.	1·15 S	110·30 E
195	Sukagawa (sōō'kä-gä'wä) Jap.	37·08 N	140·07 E
	Sukarnapura, see Jayapura		
166	Sukhinichi (sōō'kē'nē-chē) Sov. Un.	54·07 N	35·18 E
170	Sukhona (R.) (sŏŏ-kô'nȧ) Sov. Un.	59·30 N	42·20 E
174	Sukhoy Log (sōō'kôy lôg) Sov. Un. (Urals In.)	56·55 N	62·03 E
171	Sukhumi (sŏŏ-kŏŏm') Sov. Un.	43·00 N	41·00 E
184	Sukkur (sŭk'ŭr) Pak.	27·49 N	68·50 E
92	Sukkwan I. Ak.	55·05 N	132·45 W
174	Suksun (sŏŏk'sŏŏn) Sov. Un. (Urals In.)	57·08 N	57·22 E
195	Sukumo (sōō'kŏŏ-mô) Jap.	32·58 N	132·45 E
93	Sukunka (R.) Can.	55·00 N	121·50 W
197	Sula, Kepulauan (I.) Indon.	2·20 S	125·20 E
167	Sula (R.) (sōō-lȧ') Sov. Un.	50·36 N	33·13 E
126	Sulaco R. (sōō-lä'kō) Hond.	14·55 N	87·31 W
184	Sulaimān Ra. (sōō-lä-ē-män') Pak.	29·47 N	69·10 E
171	Sulak (R.) (sōō-lȧk') Sov. Un.	43·30 N	47·00 E
	Sulawesi (I.), see Celebes		
156	Suldals Vand (L.) (sŭl-däls vän) Nor.	59·35 N	6·59 E
174	Suleya (sŏŏ-lĕ'ya) Sov. Un. (Urals In.)	55·12 N	58·52 E
149	Sulfeld (zōōl'fĕld) F.R.G. (Hamburg In.)	53·48 N	10·13 E
167	Sulina (sōō-lē'nȧ) Rom.	45·08 N	29·38 E
150	Sulitelma (Mtn.) (sōō-lē-tyĕl'mȧ) Nor.-Swe.	67·03 N	16·09 E
134	Sullana (sōō-lyä'nä) Peru	4·57 N	80·47 W
120	Sulligent (sŭl'ĭ-jĕnt) Al.	33·52 N	88·06 W
104	Sullivan (sŭl'ĭ-văn) Il.	41·35 N	88·35 W
104	Sullivan In.	39·05 N	87·20 W
117	Sullivan Mo.	38·13 N	91·09 W
164	Sulmona (sōōl-mō'nä) It.	42·02 N	13·58 E
117	Sulphur (sŭl'fŭr) Ok.	34·31 N	96·58 W
117	Sulphur (R.) Tx.	33·26 N	95·06 W
117	Sulphur Springs (springz) Tx.	33·09 N	95·36 W
112	Sultan (sŭl'tăn) Wa. (Seattle In.)	47·52 N	121·49 W
112	Sultan (R.) Wa. (Seattle In.)	47·55 N	121·49 W
124	Sultepec (sōōl-tȧ-pĕk') Mex.	18·50 N	99·51 W
196	Sulu Arch. (sōō'lōō) Phil.	5·52 N	122·00 E
153	Suluntah Libya	32·39 N	21·49 E
196	Sulu Sea Phil.	8·25 N	119·00 E
195	Suma (sōō'mä) Jap. (Ōsaka In.)	34·39 N	135·08 E
112	Sumas (sū'mȧs) Wa. (Vancouver In.)	49·00 N	122·16 W
	Sumatera (I.), see Sumatra		
196	Sumatra (Sumatera) (I.) (sŏŏ-mä'trȧ) Indon.	2·06 N	99·40 E
196	Sumba (I.) (sŭm'bȧ) Indon.	9·52 S	119·00 E
216	Sumba, Île (I.) Zaire	1·44 N	19·32 E
196	Sumbawa (I.) (sŏŏm-bä'wä) Indon.	9·00 S	118·18 E
196	Sumbawa-Besar Indon	8·32 S	117·20 E
217	Sumbawanga Tan.	7·58 S	31·37 E
159	Sümeg (shü'mĕg) Hung.	46·59 N	17·19 E
195	Sumida (R.) (sōō'mē-dä) Jap.	36·01 N	139·24 E
137	Sumidouro (sōō-mē-dō'rōō) Braz. (Rio de Janeiro In.)	22·04 S	42·41 W
195	Sumiyoshi (sōō'mē-yō'shē) Jap. (Ōsaka In.)	34·43 N	135·16 E
110	Summer L. (sŭm'ẽr) Or.	42·50 N	120·35 W
93	Summerland (sŭ'mẽr-lănd) Can.	49·39 N	117·33 W
98	Summerside (sŭm'ẽr-sīd) Can.	46·25 N	63·47 W
121	Summerton (sŭm'ẽr-tŭn) SC	33·37 N	80·22 W
121	Summerville (sŭm'ẽr-vĭl) SC	33·00 N	80·10 W
107	Summit (sŭm'mĭt) Il. (Chicago In.)	41·47 N	87·48 W
106	Summit N.J. (New York In.)	40·43 N	74·21 W
110	Summit Lake Ind. Res. Nv.	41·35 N	119·30 W
115	Summit Pk. Co.	37·20 N	106·40 W
112	Sumner (sŭm'nẽr) Wa. (Seattle In.)	47·12 N	122·14 W
158	Šumperk (shŏŏm'pĕrk) Czech.	49·57 N	17·02 E
120	Sumrall (sŭm'rôl) Ms.	31·25 N	89·34 W
121	Sumter (sŭm'tẽr) SC	33·55 N	80·21 W
167	Sumy (sōō'mĭ) Sov. Un.	50·54 N	34·47 E
167	Sumy (Oblast) Sov. Un.	51·02 N	34·05 E
111	Sunburst Mt.	48·53 N	111·55 W
105	Sunbury (sŭn'bẽr-ē) Pa.	40·50 N	76·45 W
111	Sundance (sŭn'dăns) Wy.	44·24 N	104·27 W
184	Sundarbans (Swp.) (sŏŏn'dẽr-bŭns) Bngl.-India	21·50 N	89·00 E
196	Sunda Selat (Str.) Indon.	5·45 S	106·15 E
204	Sunday Str. (sŭn'dā) Austl.	15·50 S	122·45 E
156	Sundbyberg (sŏŏn'bü-bĕrgh) Swe.	59·24 N	17·56 E
154	Sunderland (sŭn'dẽr-lănd) Eng.	54·55 N	1·25 W
106	Sunderland Md. (Baltimore In.)	38·41 N	76·36 W
156	Sundsvall (sŏŏnds'väl) Swe.	62·24 N	19·19 E
120	Sunflower, (R.) (sŭn-flou'ẽr) Ms.	32·57 N	90·40 W
189	Sungari (Songhua) (R.) (sŏŋ-hwä) China	46·09 N	127·53 E
192	Sungari Res. China	42·55 N	127·50 E
171	Sungurlu (sōōn'gŏŏr-lōō') Tur.	40·08 N	34·20 E
184	Sun Kosi (R.) Nep.	27·13 N	85·52 E
113	Sunland (sŭn-lănd) Ca. (Los Angeles In.)	34·16 N	118·18 W
156	Sunne (sōōn'ĕ) Swe.	59·51 N	13·07 E
148	Sunninghill (sŭnĭng'hĭl) Eng. (London In.)	51·23 N	0·40 W
113	Sunnymead (sŭn'ĭ-mēd) Ca. (Los Angeles In.)	33·56 N	117·15 W
115	Sunnyside Ut.	39·35 N	110·20 W
110	Sunnyside Wa.	46·19 N	120·00 W
112	Sunnyvale (sŭn-nē-vāl) Ca. (San Francisco In.)	37·23 N	122·02 W
112	Sunol (sōō'nŭl) Ca. (San Francisco In.)	37·36 N	122·53 W
111	Sun R. (sŭn) Mt.	47·34 N	111·53 W
113	Sunset (sŭn-sĕt) Ut. (Salt Lake City In.)	41·08 N	112·02 W
115	Sunset Crater Natl. Mon. (krā'tẽr) Az.	35·20 N	111·30 W
202	Sunshine Austl. (Melbourne In.)	37·47 S	144·50 E
173	Suntar (sŏŏn-tȧr') Sov. Un.	62·14 N	117·49 E
214	Sunyani Ghana	7·20 N	2·20 W
157	Suoyarvi (sōō'ô-yĕr'vē) Sov. Un.	62·12 N	32·29 E
115	Superior (su-pē'rĭ-ẽr) Az.	33·15 N	111·10 W
116	Superior Ne.	40·04 N	98·05 W
113	Superior Wi. (Duluth In.)	46·44 N	92·06 W
111	Superior Wy.	41·45 N	108·57 W
125	Superior, Laguna (L.) (lä-gōō'nȧ sōō-pā-rē-ōr') Mex.	16·20 N	94·55 W
91	Superior, L. Can.-U. S.	47·38 N	89·20 W
113	Superior Village Wi. (Duluth In.)	46·38 N	92·07 W
194	Sup'ung Res. (sōō'pōōng) Kor.-China	40·35 N	126·00 E
190	Suqian (sōō-chyĕn) China	33·57 N	118·17 E
112	Suquamish (sōō-gwä'mĭsh) Wa. (Seattle In.)	47·44 N	122·34 W
183	Şūr (Tyre) (sōōr) (tīr) Leb. (Palestine In.)	33·16 N	35·13 E
186	Sūr Om.	22·23 N	59·28 E
196	Surabaya Indon.	7·23 S	112·45 E
196	Surakarta Indon.	7·35 S	110·45 E
159	Šurany (shōō'rȧ-nû') Czech.	48·05 N	18·11 E
203	Surat (sū-rät) Austl.	27·18 S	149·00 E
184	Surat (sōō'rŭt) India	21·08 N	73·22 E
196	Surat Thani Thai.	8·59 N	99·14 E
166	Surazh (sōō-rȧzh') Sov. Un.	53·02 N	32·27 E
166	Surazh Sov. Un.	55·24 N	30·46 E
160	Surgères (sür-zhâr') Fr.	46·06 N	0·51 W
172	Surgut (sŏŏr-gōōt') Sov. Un.	61·18 N	73·38 E
133	Suriname (sōō-rē-năm') S.A.	4·00 N	56·00 W
218	Surud Ad (Mtn.) Som. (Horn of Afr. In.)	10·40 N	47·23 E
195	Suruga-Wan (B.) (sōō'rōō-gä wän) Jap.	34·52 N	138·36 E
211	Surt Libya	31·14 N	16·37 E
153	Surt, Khalij (G.) Afr.	31·30 N	18·28 E
164	Susa (sōō'sä) It.	45·01 N	7·09 E
195	Susa Jap.	34·40 N	131·39 E
164	Sušac (sōō'shäts) Yugo.	44·31 N	14·15 E
164	Sušak (sōō'shȧk) Yugo.	45·20 N	14·24 E
164	Sušak (I.) Yugo.	42·45 N	16·30 E
195	Susaki (sōō'sä-kē) Jap.	33·23 N	133·16 E
101	Susitna (sōō-sĭt'nȧ) Ak.	61·28 N	150·28 W
101	Susitna (R.) Ak.	62·00 N	150·28 W
193	Susong (sōō-sôŋ) China	30·18 N	116·08 E
105	Susquehanna (sŭs'kwē-hăn'ȧ) Pa.	41·55 N	73·35 W
105	Susquehanna (R.) Pa.	39·50 N	76·20 W
107	Sussex Wi. (Milwaukee In.)	43·08 N	88·12 W
98	Sussex (sŭs'ĕks) Can.	45·43 N	65·31 W
106	Sussex NJ (New York In.)	41·12 N	74·36 W
202	Sutherland (sŭdh'ẽr-lănd) Austl. (Sydney In.)	34·02 S	151·04 E
212	Sutherland (sŭ'thẽr-lănd) S. Afr.	32·25 S	20·40 E
184	Sutlej (R.) (sŭt'lĕj) Pak.-India	30·15 N	72·25 E
148	Sutton (sut''n) Eng. (London In.)	51·21 N	0·12 W
99	Sutton Ma. (In.)	42·09 N	71·46 W
148	Sutton Coldfield (kōld'fēld) Eng.	52·34 N	1·49 W
148	Sutton-in-Ashfield (ĭn-ăsh'fēld) Eng.	53·07 N	1·15 W
213	Suurberge (Mts.) S. Afr. (Natal In.)	33·15 S	25·32 E
195	Suwa (sōō'wä) Jap.	36·03 N	138·08 E
95	Suwannee L. Can.	56·08 N	100·10 W
159	Suwatki (sŏŏ-vou'kē) Pol.	54·05 N	22·58 E
120	Suwannee (R.) (sōō-wô'nē) Fl.-Ga.	29·42 N	83·00 W
218	Suways al Ḩulwah, Tur'at as (Can.) Egypt (In.)	30·15 N	32·20 E
190	Su Xian (sōō shyĕn) China	33·37 N	117·51 E
166	Suzdal' (sōōz'dȧl) Sov. Un.	56·26 N	40·29 E
190	Suzhou (sōō-jō) China	31·19 N	120·37 E
194	Suzu Misaki (C.) (sōō'zōō mē'sä-kē) Jap.	37·30 N	137·35 E
168	Svalbard (Spitsbergen) (Is.) (säl'bärt) (spĭts'bûr-gĕn) Eur.	77·00 N	20·00 E
156	Svaneke (svä'nĕ-kĕ) Den.	55·08 N	15·07 E
167	Svatovo (svä'tô-vô) Sov. Un.	49·23 N	38·10 E
156	Svedala (svĕ'dä-lä) Swe.	55·29 N	13·11 E
156	Sveg Swe.	62·03 N	14·22 E
156	Svelvik (svĕl'vĕk) Nor.	59·37 N	10·18 E
157	Švenčionys Sov. Un.	55·09 N	26·09 E
156	Svendborg (svĕn-bôrgh) Den.	55·05 N	10·35 E
112	Svensen (svĕn'sĕn) Or. (Portland In.)	46·10 N	123·39 W
174	Sverdlovsk (svĕrd-lôfsk') Sov. Un. (Urals In.)	56·50 N	61·10 E
194	Svetlaya (svyĕt'lȧ-yȧ) Sov. Un.	46·09 N	137·53 E
165	Svilajnac (svē'lȧ-ē-nȧts) Yugo.	44·12 N	21·14 E
165	Svilengrad (svĕl'ĕn-grȧt) Bul.	41·44 N	26·11 E
170	Svir' (R.) Sov. Un.	60·55 N	33·40 E
157	Svir Kanal (can.) (kȧ-näl') Sov. Un.	60·10 N	32·40 E
165	Svishtov (svēsh'tôf) Bul.	43·36 N	25·21 E
166	Svisloch' (svēs'lôk) Sov. Un.	53·38 N	28·10 E
158	Svitavy Czech.	49·46 N	16·28 E
159	Svitsa (R.) (svĭ-tsȧ) Sov. Un.	49·09 N	24·10 E
173	Svobodnyy (svô-bôd'nĭ) Sov. Un.	51·28 N	128·28 E
150	Svolvaer (svôl'vĕr) Nor.	68·15 N	14·29 E
173	Svyatoy Nos, Mys (C.) (svyŭ'toi nôs) Sov. Un.	72·18 N	139·28 E
148	Swadlincote (swŏd'lĭn-kôt) Eng.	52·46 N	1·33 W
205	Swain Rfs. (swän) Austl.	22·12 S	152·08 E
121	Swainsboro (swānz'bŭr-ô) Ga.	32·37 N	82·21 W
212	Swakopmund (svä'kôp-mŏŏnt) (swä'kôp-mōōnd) Namibia	22·40 S	14·30 E
154	Swale (R.) (swāl) Eng.	54·12 N	1·30 W
148	Swallowfield (swŏl'ô-fēld) Eng. (London In.)	51·21 N	0·58 W
99	Swampscott (swômp'skŏt) Ma. (In.)	42·28 N	70·55 W
202	Swan, I. (swŏn) Austl. (Melbourne In.)	38·15 S	144·41 E
204	Swan (R.) Austl.	31·30 S	126·30 E
95	Swan (R.) Can.	51·58 N	101·45 W
203	Swan Hill Austl.	35·20 S	143·30 E
93	Swan Hills (hĭlz) Can.	54·52 N	115·45 W
95	Swan L. Can.	52·30 N	100·45 W
204	Swanland (Reg.) (swŏn'lănd) Austl.	31·45 S	119·15 E
111	Swan Ra. Mt.	47·50 N	113·40 W
95	Swan River (swŏn rĭv'ẽr) Can.	52·06 N	101·16 W
111	Swan R. Mt.	47·50 N	113·40 W
154	Swansea Wales	51·37 N	3·59 W
113	Swansea (swŏn'sē) Il. (St. Louis In.)	38·32 N	89·59 W
106	Swansea Ma. (Providence In.)	41·45 N	71·09 W
154	Swansea B. Wales	51·25 N	4·12 W
116	Swanson Res. (swŏn'sŭn) Ne.	40·13 N	101·30 W
213	Swartberg (Mtn.) S. Afr. (Natal In.)	30·08 S	29·34 E
212	Swartkop (Mtn.) S. Afr. (In.)	34·13 S	18·27 E
218	Swartruggens S. Afr. (Johannesburg & Pretoria In.)	25·59 S	26·40 E
213	Swartspruit S. Afr. (Johannesburg & Pretoria In.)	25·44 S	28·01 E
	Swatow, see Shantou		
212	Swaziland (Swä'zē-lănd) Afr.	26·45 S	31·30 E
146	Sweden (swē'dĕn) Eur.	60·10 N	14·10 E
106	Swedesboro (swēdz'bē-rô) NJ (Philadelphia In.)	39·45 N	75·22 W
120	Sweetwater (swēt'wô-tẽr) Tn.	35·36 N	84·29 W
118	Sweetwater Tx.	32·28 N	100·25 W
108	Sweetwater (L.) ND	48·15 N	98·35 W
114	Sweetwater Res. Ca. (San Diego In.)	32·42 N	116·54 W
111	Sweetwater R. Wy.	42·19 N	108·35 W
158	Świdnica (shvĭd-nē'tsä) Pol.	50·50 N	16·30 E
158	Świdwin (shvĭd'vĭn) Pol.	53·46 N	15·48 E
158	Świebodziec (shvyĕn-bo' jĕts) Pol.	52·16 N	15·36 E
158	Świebodzin (shvyăn-bôd'jĕn) Pol.	50·51 N	16·17 E
159	Swiecie (shvyăn'tsyĕ) Pol.	53·23 N	18·26 E
159	Swietokrzyskie Góry (Mts.) (shvyĕn-tō-kzhĭ'skyĕ gōō'rĭ) Pol.	50·57 N	21·02 E
148	Swift (R.) Eng.	52·26 N	1·08 W
98	Swift (R.) (swĭft) Me.	44·42 N	70·40 W
94	Swift Current (swĭft kûr'ĕnt) Can.	50·17 N	107·50 W
110	Swift Res. Wa.	46·03 N	122·10 W
154	Swilly, Lough (B.) (lŏk swĭ-lē) Ire.	55·10 N	7·38 W
92	Swindle I. Can.	52·32 N	128·35 W
154	Swindon (swĭn'dŭn) Eng.	51·35 N	1·55 W
112	Swinomish Ind. Res. (swĭ-nō'mĭsh) Wa. (Seattle In.)	48·25 N	122·27 W
158	Świnoujście (shvĭ-nĭ-ô-wēsh'chyĕ) Pol.	53·56 N	14·14 E
148	Swinton (swĭn'tŭn) Eng.	53·30 N	1·19 W
107	Swissvale (swĭs'vāl) Pa. (Pittsburgh In.)	40·25 N	79·53 W
146	Switzerland (swĭt'zẽr-lănd) Eur.	46·30 N	7·43 E
166	Syas' (R.) (syäs) Sov. Un.	59·28 N	33·24 E
109	Sycamore (sĭk'ȧ-mōr) Il.	42·00 N	88·42 W
166	Sychëvka (sē-chôf'kȧ) Sov. Un.	55·52 N	34·18 E
202	Sydney (sĭd'nē) Austl. (Sydney In.)	33·55 S	151·17 E
97	Sydney Can.	46·09 N	60·11 W
97	Sydney Mines Can.	46·14 N	60·14 W
170	Syktyvkar (sük-tüf'kär) Sov. Un.	61·35 N	50·40 E

ăt; finăl; rāte; senâte; ärm; àsk; sofȧ; fâre; ch-choose; dh-as th in other; bē; êvent; bĕt; recĕnt; cratẽr; g-go; gh-guttural g; bĭt; ĭ-short neutral; rīde; K-guttural k as ch in German ich;

Page	Name	Pronunciation	Region	Lat. °′	Long. °′
120	Sylacauga	(sĭl-á-kô′gá)	Al.	33·10 N	86·15 W
156	Sylfjällen (Mtn.)	(sül′fyĕl-ĕn)	Swe.	63·00 N	12·10 E
156	Sylling	(sül′lĭng)	Nor.	59·52 N	10·12 E
158	Sylt I.	(sĭlt)	F.R.G.	54·55 N	8·30 E
121	Sylvania	(sĭl-vā′nĭ-á)	Ga.	32·44 N	81·40 W
120	Sylvester	(sĭl-vĕs′tēr)	Ga.	31·32 N	83·50 W
116	Syracuse	(sĭr′á-kūs)	Ks.	37·59 N	101·44 W
105	Syracuse		NY	43·05 N	76·10 W
113	Syracuse		Ut. (Salt Lake City In.)	41·06 N	112·04 W
153	Syra I.		Grc.	37·19 N	25·10 E
141	Syr-Dar′ya (R.)		Sov. Un.	44·15 N	65·45 E
182	Syria	(sĭr′ĭ-á)	Asia	35·00 N	37·15 E
186	Syrian Des. (Bādiyat ash Shām)	(sĭr′ĭ-án)	Asia	32·03 N	39·30 E
174	Sysert'	(sĕ′sĕrt)	Sov. Un. (Urals In.)	56·30 N	60·48 E
170	Syso'la (R.)		Sov. Un.	60·50 N	50·40 E
171	Syzran'	(sĕz-rän′)	Sov. Un.	53·10 N	48·10 E
159	Szabadszallas	(sô′bôd-sä′läsh)	Hung.	46·52 N	19·15 E
158	Szamotuty	(shá-mô-tōō′wĕ)	Pol.	52·36 N	16·34 E
159	Szarvas	(sôr′vôsh)	Hung.	46·51 N	20·36 E
159	Szczebrzeszyn	(shchĕ-bzhā′shĕn)	Pol.	50·41 N	22·58 E
158	Szczecin (Stettin)	(shchĕ′tsĭn) (shtĕ-tēn′)	Pol.	53·25 N	14·35 E
158	Szczecinek	(shchĕ′tsĭ-nĕk)	Pol.	53·42 N	16·42 E
159	Szczuczyn	(shchōō′chĕn)	Pol.	53·32 N	22·17 E
159	Szczytno	(shchĭt′nô)	Pol.	53·33 N	21·00 E
188	Szechwan Basin (Red)		China	30·45 N	104·40 E
159	Szeged	(sĕ′gĕd)	Hung.	46·15 N	20·12 E
159	Székesfehérvár	(sā′kĕsh-fĕ′hār-vär)	Hung.	47·12 N	18·26 E
159	Szekszárd	(sĕk′särd)	Hung.	46·19 N	18·42 E
159	Szentendre	(sĕnt′ĕn-drĕ)	Hung.	47·40 N	19·07 E
159	Szentes	(sĕn′tĕsh)	Hung.	46·38 N	20·18 E
159	Szigetvar	(sĕ′gĕt-vär)	Hung.	46·05 N	17·50 E
159	Szolnok	(sôl′nôk)	Hung.	47·11 N	20·12 E
158	Szombathely	(sôm′bôt-hĕl′)	Hung.	47·14 N	16·35 E
158	Szprotawa	(shprô-tä′vä)	Pol.	51·34 N	15·29 E
159	Szydłowiec	(shid-wô′vyets)	Pol.	51·13 N	20·53 E

T

Page	Name	Pronunciation	Region	Lat. °′	Long. °′
197	Taal (L.)	(tä-äl′)	Phil. (In.)	13·58 N	121·06 E
197	Tabaco	(tä-bä′kô)	Phil. (In.)	13·27 N	123·40 E
213	Tabankulu	(tä-bän-kōō′la)	S. Afr. (Natal In.)	30·56 S	29·19 E
127	Tabasara, Serrania de (Ra.)	(sĕr-rä-nē′ä dä tä-bä-sä′rä)	Pan.	8·29 N	81·22 W
124	Tabasco	(tä-bäs′kô)	Mex.	21·47 N	103·04 W
125	Tabasco (State)		Mex.	18·10 N	83·00 W
93	Taber		Can.	49·47 N	112·08 W
197	Tablas (I.)	(tä′bläs)	Phil. (In.)	12·26 N	112·15 E
197	Tablas Str.		Phil. (In.)	12·17 N	121·41 E
212	Table B.	(tä′b′l)	S. Afr. (In.)	33·41 S	18·27 E
212	Table Mt.		S. Afr. (In.)	33·58 S	18·26 E
117	Table Rock Lake		Mo.	36·37 N	93·29 W
214	Tabligbo		Togo	6·35 N	1·30 E
122	Taboga (I.)	(tä-bō′gä)	Pan. (In.)	8·48 N	79·35 W
122	Taboguilla (I.)	(tä-bô-gē′l-yä)	Pan. (In.)	8·48 N	79·31 W
135	Taboleiro (Plat.)	(tä-bô-lā′rô)	Braz.	9·34 S	39·22 W
158	Tábor	(tä′bôr)	Czech.	49·25 N	14·40 E
217	Tabora	(tä-bō′rä)	Tan.	5·01 S	32·48 E
214	Tabou	(tä-bōō′)	Ivory Coast	4·25 N	7·21 W
186	Tabrīz	(tá-brēz′)	Iran	38·00 N	46·13 E
124	Tacámbaro (R.)	(tä-käm′bä-rô)	Mex.	18·55 N	101·25 W
124	Tacambaro de Codallos	(dä kô-däl′yôs)	Mex.	19·12 N	101·28 W
126	Tacaná (Vol.)	(tä-kä-nä′)	Mex.-Guat.	15·09 N	92·07 W
135	Tacarigua, Laguna de la (L.)	(lä-gōō′nä-dĕ-lä-tä-kä-rē′gwä)	Ven. (In.)	10·18 N	65·43 W
188	Tacheng	(tä-chŭŋ)	China	46·50 N	83·24 E
92	Tachie	(tä-chē)	Can.	54·30 N	125·00 W
197	Tacloban	(tä-klō′bän)	Phil.	11·06 N	124·58 E
134	Tacna	(täk′nä)	Peru	18·34 S	70·16 W
112	Tacoma	(tá-kō′má)	Wa. (Seattle In.)	47·14 N	122·27 W
105	Taconic Ra.	(tä-kŏn′ĭk)	NY	41·55 N	73·40 W
125	Tacotalpa	(tä-kô-täl′pä)	Mex.	17·37 N	92·51 W
125	Tacotalpa (R.)		Mex.	17·24 N	92·38 W
136	Tacuarembó	(tä-kwä-rĕm′bô)	Ur.	31·44 S	55·56 W

Page	Name	Pronunciation	Region	Lat. °′	Long. °′
210	Tademaït, Plat. du	(tä-dĕ-mä′ĕt)	Alg.	28·00 N	2·15 E
214	Tadio, Lagune (Lagoon)		Ivory Coast	5·20 N	5·25 W
218	Tadjoura	(tád-zhōō′rà)	Djibouti (Horn of Afr. In.)	11·48 N	42·54 E
148	Tadley	(tăd′lĕ)	Eng. (London In.)	51·19 N	1·08 W
134	Tadó	(tä-dô′)	Col. (In.)	5·15 N	76·30 W
195	Tadotsu	(tä′dô-tsōō)	Jap.	34·14 N	133·43 E
97	Tadoussac	(tá-dōō-säk′)	Can.	48·09 N	69·43 W
168	Tadzhik (S. S. R.)	(tát′zhĕk)	Sov. Un.	39·22 N	69·30 E
194	Taebaek Sanmaek (Mts.)	(tī-bĭk′ sän-mĭk′)	Kor.	37·20 N	128·50 E
194	Taedong R.	(tī-dŏŋ)	Kor.	38·38 N	124·32 E
194	Taegu	(tī′gōō)	Kor.	35·49 N	128·41 E
162	Tafalla	(tä-fäl′yä)	Sp.	42·30 N	1·42 W
163	Tafna (R.)	(täf′nä)	Alg.	35·28 N	1·00 W
114	Taft	(täft)	Ca.	35·09 N	119·27 W
215	Tagama (Reg.)		Niger	15·50 N	6·30 E
167	Taganrog	(tá-gán-rôk′)	Sov. Un.	47·13 N	38·44 E
167	Taganrogskiy Zaliv (B.)	(tá-gán-rôk′skī zä′lĭf)	Sov. Un.	46·55 N	38·17 E
164	Tagliamento (R.)	(täl-yä-mĕn′tô)	It.	46·11 N	12·53 E
205	Tagula (I.)	(tä′gōō-lä)	Pap. N. Gui.	11·45 S	153·46 E
	Tagus (R.), see Tajo, Río				
196	Tahan, Gunong (Pk.)		Mala.	4·33 N	101·52 E
210	Tahat, Mt.	(tä-hät′)	Alg.	23·22 N	5·21 E
199	Tahiti (I.)	(tä-hē′tē) (tä′ē-tē′)	Fr. Polynesia	17·30 S	149·30 W
157	Tahkuna Nina	(täh-kōō′nä nē′nä)	Sov. Un.	59·08 N	22·03 E
117	Tahlequah	(tä-lĕ-kwä′)	Ok.	35·54 N	94·58 W
114	Tahoe (L.)	(tä′hō)	Ca.-Nv.	39·09 N	120·18 W
215	Tahoua	(tä′ōō-ä)	Niger	14·54 N	5·16 E
218	Ṭaḥṭā	(tä′tä)	Egypt (Nile In.)	26·48 N	31·29 E
92	Tahtsa (L.)	(tät′-sä-pēk)	Can.	53·33 N	127·47 W
112	Tahuya	(tá-hū-yä′)	Wa. (Seattle In.)	47·23 N	123·03 W
112	Tahuya (R.)		Wa. (Seattle In.)	47·28 N	122·55 W
190	Tai'an	(tī-än)	China	36·13 N	117·08 E
192	Taibai Shan (Mtn.)	(tī-bī shän)	China	33·42 N	107·25 E
192	Taibus Qi	(tī-bōō-sz chyē)	China	41·52 N	115·25 E
191	Taicang	(tī-tsäŋ)	China (Shanghai In.)	31·26 N	121·06 E
193	T'aichung	(tī′chŏŋg)	Taiwan	24·10 N	120·42 E
190	Tai'erzhuang	(tī-är-júaŋ)	China	34·34 N	117·44 E
	Taigones (C.), see Taygonos				
192	Taigu	(tī-gōō)	China	37·25 N	112·35 E
192	Taihang Shan (Mts.)	(tī-häŋ shän)	China	35·45 N	112·00 E
190	Taihe	(tī-hŭ)	China	33·10 N	115·38 E
190	Tai Hu (L.)	(tī hōō)	China	31·13 N	120·00 E
188	Tailagein Khara (Reg.)	(tī′lá-gän′ kä′rä)	Mong.	43·39 N	105·54 E
192	Tailai	(tī-lī)	China	46·20 N	123·10 E
203	Tailem Bend	(tā-lĕm)	Austl.	35·15 S	139·30 E
	Taimyr, P-Ov (Pen.),see Taymyr				
193	T'ainan	(tī′nan′)	Taiwan	23·08 N	120·18 E
153	Tainaron, Akra (C.)		Grc.	36·20 N	21·20 E
193	Taining	(tī′nĭŋ′)	China	26·58 N	117·15 E
193	T'aipei	(tī′pá′)	Taiwan	25·02 N	121·38 E
196	Taiping		Mala.	4·56 N	100·39 E
192	Taiping, Ling (Mtn.)	(lĭŋ tī-pĭŋ)	China	47·30 N	120·30 E
	Taira, see Iwaki				
195	Taisha	(tī′shä)	Jap.	35·23 N	132·40 E
193	Taishan	(tī-shän)	China	22·15 N	112·50 E
190	Tai Shan (Mtn.)	(tī shän)	China	36·16 N	117·05 E
	Taishet, see Tayshet				
136	Taitao, Peninsula de	(pĕ-nĕ′ng-sōō-lä-dĕ-tä-ē-tä′ō)	Chile	46·20 S	77·15 W
193	T'aitung	(tī′tōōng′)	Taiwan	22·45 N	121·02 E
183	Taiwan (Formosa)	(tī-wän) (fôr-mō′sá)	Asia	23·30 N	122·20 E
190	Tai Xian	(tī shyĕn)	China	32·31 N	119·54 E
190	Taixing	(tī-shyĭŋ)	China	32·12 N	119·58 E
192	Taiyuan	(tī-yúän)	China	37·32 N	112·38 E
190	Taizhou	(tī-jō)	China	32·23 N	119·41 E
137	Tajano de Morais	(tĕ-zhä′nô-dĕ-mô-rä′ēs)	Braz. (Rio de Janeiro In.)	22·05 S	42·04 W
162	Tajo, Río (Tagus) (R.)	(tä′hō-tä′hô) (tä′gŭs)	Sp.	39·40 N	5·07 W
126	Tajumulco (Vol.)	(tä-hōō-mōōl′kô)	Guat.	15·03 N	91·53 W
162	Tajuña (R.)	(tä-hōō′n-yä)	Sp.	40·23 N	2·36 W
152	Tājūrā′		Libya	32·56 N	13·24 E
196	Tak		Thai.	16·57 N	99·12 E
195	Taka (I.)	(tä′kä)	Jap.	30·47 N	130·23 E
195	Takada	(tä′kä-dä)	Jap.	37·08 N	138·30 E
195	Takahashi	(tä′kä′hä-shǐ′)	Jap.	34·47 N	133·35 E
195	Takaishi		Jap. (Osaka In.)	34·32 N	135·27 E
195	Takamatsu	(tä′kä′mä-tsōō′)	Jap.	34·20 N	134·02 E
195	Takamori	(tä′kä′mô-rē′)	Jap.	32·50 N	131·08 E

Page	Name	Pronunciation	Region	Lat. °′	Long. °′
195	Takaoka	(ta′kä′ô-kä)	Jap.	36·45 N	136·59 E
195	Takarazuka	(tä′kä-rä-zōō′kä)	Jap. (Ōsaka In.)	34·48 N	135·22 E
195	Takasaki	(tä′kät′sōō-kē′)	Jap.	36·20 N	139·00 E
195	Takatsu (Mizonokuchi)	(tä-kät′sōō) (mē′zô-nô-kōō′chĕ)	Jap. (Tōkyō In.)	35·36 N	139·37 E
195	Takatsuki	(tä′kät′sōō-kē′)	Jap. (Ōsaka In.)	34·51 N	135·38 E
185	Takaungu	(tä′kä′ōôŋ-gōō′)	Ken.	3·41 S	39·48 E
195	Takayama	(tä′kä′yä′mä)	Jap.	36·11 N	137·16 E
195	Takefu	(tä′kĕ-fōō)	Jap.	35·57 N	136·09 E
92	Takla L.		Can.	55·25 N	125·53 W
188	Takla Makan (Des.)	(mä-kän′)	China	39·22 N	82·34 E
106	Takoma Park	(tä′kōmă părk)	Md. (Baltimore In.)	38·59 N	77·00 W
215	Takum		Nig.	7·17 N	9·59 E
124	Tala	(tä′lä)	Mex.	20·39 N	103·42 W
137	Talagante	(tä-lä-gä′n-tĕ)	Chile (Santiago In.)	33·39 S	70·54 W
126	Talanga	(tä-lä′n-gä)	Hond.	14·21 N	87·09 W
134	Talara	(tä-lä′rä)	Peru	4·32 N	81·17 W
197	Talasea	(tä-lä-sä′ä)	Pap. N. Gui.	5·20 S	150·00 E
215	Talata Mafara		Nig.	12·35 N	6·04 E
197	Talaud, Kepulauan (Is.)	(tä-lout′)	Indon.	4·17 N	127·30 E
162	Talavera de la Reina	(tä-lä-vā′rä dä lä rå-ē′nä)	Sp.	39·58 N	4·51 W
211	Talawdī		Sud.	10·41 N	30·21 E
137	Talca	(täl′kä)	Chile (Santiago In.)	35·25 S	71·39 W
137	Talca (Prov.)		Chile (Santiago In.)	35·23 S	71·15 W
137	Talca, Punta (Pt.)	(pōō′n-tä-täl′kä)	Chile (Santiago In.)	33·25 S	71·42 W
136	Talcahuano	(täl-kä-wä′nô)	Chile	36·41 S	73·05 W
166	Taldom	(täl-dôm)	Sov. Un.	56·44 N	37·33 E
172	Taldy-Kurgan	(täl′dĭ-kōōr-gän′)	Sov. Un.	45·03 N	77·18 E
125	Talea de Castro (San Miguel)	(tä′lä-ä dä käs′trô)	Mex.	17·22 N	96·14 W
197	Talibu, Pulau (I.)		Indon.	1·30 S	125·00 E
197	Talim (I.)	(tä-lēm′)	Phil. (In.)	14·21 N	121·14 E
197	Talisay	(tä-lē′sī)	Phil. (In.)	14·08 N	122·56 E
101	Talkeetna	(tăl-kēt′ná)	Ak.	62·18 N	150·02 W
171	Talkheh Rūd (R.)		Iran	38·00 N	46·50 E
120	Talladega	(tăl-á-dē′gá)	Al.	33·25 N	86·06 W
120	Tallahassee	(tăl-á-hăs′ē)	Fl.	30·25 N	84·17 W
120	Tallahatchie (R.)	(tal-á hăch′ē)	Ms.	34·21 N	90·03 W
120	Tallapoosa	(tăl-á-pōō′sá)	Ga.	33·44 N	85·15 W
120	Tallapoosa (R.)		Al.	32·22 N	86·08 W
120	Tallassee	(tăl′á-sè)	Al.	32·30 N	85·54 W
157	Tallinn (Reval)	(tăl′lĕn) (rä′väl)	Sov. Un.	59·26 N	24·44 E
107	Tallmadge	(tăl′mĭj)	Oh. (Cleveland In.)	41·06 N	81·26 W
119	Tallulah	(tä-lōō′lá)	La.	32·25 N	91·13 W
127	Talmanca, Cord. de (Mts.)	(kôr-dĕl-yĕ′rä-dĕ-täl-mä′n-kä)	C. R.	9·37 N	83·55 W
167	Tal'noye	(tál′nô-yĕ)	Sov. Un.	48·52 N	30·43 E
211	Talo (Mt.)		Eth.	10·45 N	37·55 E
185	Taloje Budrukh		India (In.)	19·05 N	73·05 E
124	Talpa de Allende	(täl′pä dä äl-yĕn′dä)	Mex.	20·25 N	104·48 W
157	Talsi	(tal′sĭ)	Sov. Un.	57·16 N	22·35 E
136	Taltal	(täl-täl′)	Chile	25·26 S	70·32 W
167	Taly	(täl′ĭ)	Sov. Un.	49·51 N	40·07 E
109	Tama	(tä′mä)	Ia.	41·57 N	92·36 W
195	Tama (R.)		Jap. (Tōkyō In.)	35·38 N	139·35 E
214	Tamale	(tä-mä′là)	Ghana	9·25 N	0·50 W
167	Taman'	(tä-män′)	Sov. Un.	45·13 N	36·46 E
134	Tamaná, Cerro (Mtn.)	(sĕ′r-rô-tä-mä-nä′)	Col. (In.)	5·06 N	76·10 W
135	Tamanaco (tä-mä-nä′kō) (R.)		Ven. (In.)	9·32 N	66·00 W
210	Tamanrasset (R.)	(tä-män-räs′set)	Alg.	22·15 N	2·51 E
210	Tamanrasset		Alg.	22·34 N	5·34 E
105	Tamaqua	(tá-mô′kwá)	Pa.	40·45 N	75·50 W
154	Tamar (R.)	(tä′mär)	Eng.	50·35 N	4·15 W
163	Tamarite	(tä-mä-rē′tä)	Sp.	41·52 N	0·24 E
213	Tamatave	(tä-mä-täv′)	Mad.	18·14 S	49·25 E
124	Tamaulipas (State)	(tä-mä-ōō-lē′päs)	Mex.	23·45 N	98·30 W
124	Tamazula de Gordiano	(tä-mä-zōō′lä dä gôr-dē-ä′nô)	Mex.	19·44 N	103·09 W
125	Tamazulapan del Progreso	(tä-mä-zōō-lä′päm-dĕl-prô-grĕ-sō)	Mex.	17·41 N	97·34 W
124	Tamazunchale	(tä-mä-zōōn-chä′lä)	Mex.	21·16 N	98·46 W
214	Tambacounda	(täm-bä-kōōn′dä)	Senegal	13·47 N	13·40 W
135	Tambador, Serra do (Mts.)	(sĕr-rä-dô-täm′bä-dôr)	Braz.	10·33 S	41·16 W
196	Tambelan, Kepulauan (Is.)	(täm-bä-län′)	Indon.	0·38 N	107·38 E

354 Tambo — Tecalitlan

PRONOUNCING INDEX

Page	Name Pronunciation Region	Lat. °′	Long. °′
203	Tambo (tăm'bō) Austl.	24·50 s	146·15 E
171	Tambov (tȧm-bôf') Sov. Un.	52·45 N	41·10 E
166	Tambov (Oblast) Sov. Un.	52·50 N	40·42 E
162	Tambre (R.) (täm'brā) Sp.	42·59 N	8·33 W
211	Tambura (täm-bōō'rä) Sud.	5·34 N	27·30 E
148	Tame (R.) (tām) Eng.	52·41 N	1·42 W
162	Tamega (R.) (tȧ-mā'gȧ) Port.	41·30 N	7·45 W
124	Tamesí (R.) (tä-mĕ-sē') Mex.	22·36 N	98·32 W
215	Tamgak, Monts (Mtn.) (tam-gäk') Niger	18·40 N	8·40 E
214	Tamgue, Massif du (Mtn.) Gui.	12·15 N	12·35 W
125	Tamiahua (tä-myä-wä) Mex.	21·17 N	97·26 W
125	Tamiahua, Laguna (L.) (lä-gōō'nä-tä-myä-wä) Mex.	21·38 N	97·33 W
121	Tamiami, Can. (tă-mī-ăm'ĭ) Fl. (In.)	25·52 N	80·08 W
185	Tamil Nadu (State) India	11·30 N	78·00 E
157	Tammela (tȧm'ĕ-lȧ) Fin.	60·49 N	23·45 E
	Tammisaari, see Ekenäs		
121	Tampa (tăm'pȧ) Fl. (In.)	27·57 N	82·25 W
121	Tampa B. Fl. (In.)	27·35 N	82·38 W
150	Tampere (tȧm'pĕ-rĕ) Fin.	61·21 N	23·39 E
125	Tampico (täm-pē'kō) Mex.	22·14 N	97·51 W
125	Tampico Alto (täm-pē'kō äl'tō) Mex.	22·07 N	97·48 W
183	Tampin Mala. (Singapore In.)	2·28 N	102·15 E
124	Tamuín (tä-mōō-ē'n) Mex.	22·04 N	98·47 W
203	Tamworth (tăm'wûrth) Austl.	31·01 S	151·00 E
148	Tamworth Eng.	52·58 N	1·41 W
217	Tana (R.) (tä'nä) Ken.	2·00 S	40·15 E
205	Tana (I.) New Hebr.	19·32 S	169·27 E
150	Tana (R.) Nor.-Fin.	69·20 N	24·54 E
195	Tanabe (tä-nä'bā) Jap.	33·45 N	135·21 E
195	Tanabe Jap. (Ōsaka In.)	34·49 N	135·46 E
101	Tanacross (tă'nȧ-crōs) Ak.	63·20 N	143·30 W
101	Tanaga (I.) (tä-nä'gä) Ak.	51·28 N	178·10 W
196	Tanahbala, Pulau (I.) (tȧ-nä-bä'lä) Indon.	0·30 S	98·22 E
196	Tanahmasa, Pulau (I.) (tȧ-nä-mä'sä) Indon.	0·03 S	97·30 E
184	Tanakpur (tǎn'ăk-pōōr) India	29·10 N	80·07 E
211	Tana L. Eth.	12·09 N	36·41 E
204	Tanami (tȧ-nä'mē) Austl.	19·45 S	129·50 E
101	Tanana (tă'nȧ-nô) Ak.	65·18 N	152·20 W
101	Tanana (R.) Ak.	64·26 N	148·40 W
164	Tanaro (R.) (tä-nä'rô) It.	44·45 N	8·02 E
195	Tanashi Jap. (Tōkyō In.)	35·44 N	139·34 E
191	Tanbu (tän-bōō) China (Canton In.)	23·20 N	113·06 E
190	Tancheng (tän-chŭŋ) China	34·37 N	118·22 E
194	Tanchŏn (tän'chŭn) Kor.	40·29 N	128·50 E
124	Tancítaro (tän-sē'tä-rō) Mex.	19·16 N	102·24 W
124	Tancítaro, Cerro de (sĕ'r-rô-dĕ) Mex.	19·24 N	102·19 W
125	Tancoco (tän-kō'kō) Mex.	21·16 N	99·45 W
126	Tandil (tän-dēl') Arg.	36·16 S	59·01 W
126	Tandil, Sierra del (Mts.) Arg.	38·40 S	59·40 W
195	Tanega (I.) (tä'nȧ-gä') Jap.	30·36 N	131·11 E
210	Tanezrouft (Reg.) (tä'nĕz-rōōft) Alg.	24·17 N	0·30 W
190	Tang (R.) (täŋ) China	33·38 N	117·29 E
190	Tang (R.) China	39·13 N	14·45 E
217	Tanga (täŋ'gȧ) Tan.	5·04 S	39·06 E
124	Tangancícuaro (täŋ-gän-sē'kwä rô) Mex.	19·52 N	102·13 W
217	Tanganyika, L. Afr.	5·15 S	29·40 E
210	Tanger (Tangier) (tăn-jēr') Mor.	35·52 N	5·55 W
158	Tangermünde (täŋ'ĕr-mün'de) G.D.R.	52·33 N	11·58 E
190	Tanggu (täŋ-gōō) China	39·04 N	117·41 E
188	Tanggula Shan (Mts.) (täŋ-gōō-lä shän) China	33·15 N	89·07 E
192	Tangho China	32·40 N	112·50 E
	Tangier, see Tanger		
119	Tangipahoa R. (tăn'jē-pȧ-hō'ȧ) La.	30·48 N	90·28 W
184	Tangra Tsho (L.) China	30·38 N	85·40 E
190	T'angshan China	39·38 N	118·11 E
190	Tang Xian (täŋ shyĕn) China	38·09 N	115·00 E
190	Tangzha (täŋ-jä) China	32·06 N	120·48 E
197	Tanimbar, Kepulauan (Is.) Indon.	8·00 S	132·00 E
183	Tanjong (C.) Mala. (Singapore In.)	1·53 N	102·29 E
183	Tanjong Piai (I.) Mala. (Singapore In.)	1·16 N	103·11 E
183	Tanjong Ramunia (C.) Mala. (Singapore In.)	1·27 N	104·44 E
183	Tanjungbalai (tän'jông-bä'lȧ) Indon. (Singapore In.)	1·00 N	103·26 E
196	Tanjungkarang Indon.	5·16 S	105·06 E
196	Tanjungpandan Indon.	2·47 S	107·51 E
183	Tanjungpinang (tän'jông-pē'näng) Indon. (Singapore In.)	0·55 N	104·29 E
169	Tannu-Ola (Mts.) Sov. Un.	51·00 N	94·00 E
186	Tannūrah, Ra's al (C.) Sau. Ar.	26·45 N	49·59 E
214	Tano (R.) Ghana	5·40 N	2·30 W
125	Tanquijo, Arrecife (Reef) (är-rĕ-sē'fē-tän-kē'kô) Mex.	21·07 N	97·16 W
218	Ţanţā (tän'tä) Egypt (Nile In.)	30·50 N	31·00 E
124	Tantoyuca (tän-tō-yōō'kä) Mex.	21·22 N	98·13 W
194	Tanyang Kor.	36·53 N	128·20 E
209	Tanzania Afr.	6·48 S	33·58 E
192	Tao'an (tou-än) China	45·15 N	122·45 E
192	Tao'er (R.) (tou-är) China	45·40 N	122·00 E
192	Tao (R.) (tou) China	35·30 N	103·40 E
164	Taormina (tä-ôr-mē'nä) It.	37·53 N	15·18 E
115	Taos (tä'ôs) NM	36·25 N	105·35 W
210	Taoudenni (tä'ōō-dĕ-nē') Mali	22·57 N	3·37 W
214	Taoussa Mali	16·55 N	0·35 W
193	Taoyuan (tou-yüän) China	29·00 N	111·15 E
157	Tapa (tȧ'pȧ) Sov. Un.	59·16 N	25·56 E
126	Tapachula Mex.	14·55 N	92·20 W
135	Tapajós (R.) (tä-pä-zhō's) Braz.	3·27 S	55·33 W
137	Tapalque (tä-päl-kĕ') Arg. (Buenos Aires In.)	36·22 S	60·05 W
125	Tapanatepec (tä-pä-nä-tĕ-pĕk) Mex.	16·22 N	94·19 W
184	Tāpi (R.) India	21·33 N	74·30 E
194	Tappi Saki (C.) (täp'pē sä'kē) Jap.	41·05 N	139·40 E
112	Tapps (L.) (tăpz) Wa. (Seattle In.)	47·20 N	122·12 W
211	Taqātu' Hayyā Sud.	18·10 N	36·17 E
135	Taquara, Serra de (Mts.) (sĕ'r-rä-dĕ-tä-kwä'rä) Braz.	15·28 S	54·33 W
135	Taquari (R.) (tä-kwä'rĭ) Braz.	18·35 S	56·50 W
121	Tar (R.) (tär) NC	35·58 N	78·06 W
172	Tara (tä'rȧ) Sov. Un.	56·58 N	74·13 E
197	Tara (I.) (tä'rä) Phil. (In.)	12·18 N	120·28 E
172	Tara (R.) (tä'rȧ) Sov. Un.	56·32 N	76·13 E
183	Ţarābulus (Tripoli) (tȧ-rä'bōō-lōōs) Leb. (Palestine In.)	34·25 N	35·50 E
211	Tarābulus (Tripoli) Libya	32·50 N	13·13 E
211	Tarābulus (Tripolitania) (Prov.) Libya	31·00 N	12·26 E
196	Tarakan Indon.	3·17 N	118·04 E
162	Tarancón (tä-rän-kōn') Sp.	40·01 N	3·00 W
164	Taranto (tä'rän-tô) It.	40·30 N	17·15 E
164	Taranto, Golfo di (G.) (gôl-fô-dē tä'rän-tô) It.	40·03 N	17·10 E
134	Tarapoto (tä-rä-pô'tō) Peru	6·29 S	76·26 W
160	Tarare (tȧ-rär') Fr.	45·55 N	4·23 E
160	Tarascon (tȧ-rȧs-kôN') Fr.	42·53 N	1·35 E
160	Tarascon-sur-Rhône (tȧ-räs-kôN-sür-rōn') Fr.	43·47 N	4·41 E
167	Tarashcha (tä'rȧsh-chȧ) Sov. Un.	49·34 N	30·52 E
134	Tarata (tä-rä'tä) Bol.	17·43 S	66·00 W
164	Taravo (R.) Fr.	41·54 N	8·58 E
215	Tarazit, Massif de (Mts.) Niger	20·05 N	7·35 E
162	Tarazona (tä-rä-thō'nä) Sp.	41·54 N	1·45 W
162	Tarazona de la Mancha (tä-rä-zô'nä-dĕ-lä-mä'n-chä) Sp.	39·13 N	1·50 W
154	Tarbat Ness (Hd.) (tȧr'bȧt) Scot.	57·51 N	3·50 W
160	Tarbes (tȧrb) Fr.	43·04 N	0·05 E
121	Tarboro (tär'bŭr-ô) NC	35·53 N	77·34 W
211	Tarbū Libya	26·07 N	15·49 E
203	Taree (tȧ-rē') Austl.	31·52 S	152·21 E
107	Tarentum (tȧ-rĕn'tŭm) Pa. (Pittsburgh In.)	40·36 N	79·44 W
218	Tarfa, Wādī at Egypt (Nile In.)	28·14 N	31·00 E
210	Tarfaya Mor.	27·58 N	12·55 W
162	Tarifa (tä-rē'fä) Sp.	36·02 N	5·35 W
134	Tarija (tär-rē'hä) Bol.	21·42 S	64·52 W
186	Tarīm (tȧ-rīm') P. D. R. of Yem.	16·13 N	49·08 E
188	Tarim (R.) (tȧ-rīm') China	40·45 N	85·39 E
188	Tarim Basin (tȧ-rīm') China	39·52 N	82·34 E
213	Tarka (R.) (tä'kȧ) S. Afr. (Natal In.)	32·15 S	26·00 E
213	Tarkastad S. Afr. (Natal In.)	32·01 S	26·18 E
167	Tarkhankut, Mys (C.) (mĭs tȧr-Kän'kŏŏt) Sov. Un.	45·18 N	32·08 E
117	Tarkio (tär'kĭ-ō) Mo.	40·27 N	95·22 W
214	Tarkwa (tärk'wä) Ghana	5·19 N	1·59 W
197	Tarlac (tär'läk) Phil. (In.)	15·29 N	120·36 E
213	Tarlton (tärl'tŭn) S. Afr. (Johannesburg & Pretoria In.)	26·05 S	27·38 E
134	Tarma (tär'mä) Peru	11·26 S	75·40 W
160	Tarn (R.) (tärn) Fr.	44·03 N	2·41 E
161	Târnava Mica R. (tĕr-nä'vȧ mē'kŏ) Rom.	46·17 N	24·20 E
161	Tarnów (tär'nŏŏf) Pol.	50·02 N	21·00 E
164	Taro (R.) (tä'rō) It.	44·41 N	10·03 E
210	Taroudant (tȧ-rōō-dänt') Mor.	30·39 N	8·52 W
121	Tarpon Springs (tär'pŏn) Fl. (In.)	28·07 N	82·44 W
148	Tarporley (tär'pĕr-lē) Eng.	53·09 N	2·40 W
129	Tarpum B. (tär'pŭm) Ba.	25·05 N	76·20 W
164	Tarquinia (Corneto) (tär-kwē'nē-ä) (kôr-nā'tô) It.	42·16 N	11·46 E
163	Tarragona (tär-rä-gō'nä) Sp.	41·05 N	1·15 E
106	Tarrant (tăr'ănt) Al. (Birmingham In.)	33·35 N	86·46 W
163	Tarrasa (tär-rä'sä) Sp.	41·34 N	2·01 E
163	Tárrega (tä rȧ-gä) Sp.	41·40 N	1·09 E
163	Tarrejón de Ardoz (tär-rĕ-Kô'n-dĕ-är-dôz) Sp. (Madrid In.)	40·28 N	3·29 W
106	Tarrytown (tăr'ĭ-toun) NY (New York In.)	41·04 N	73·52 W
171	Tarsus (tȧr'sŏŏs) (tär'sŭs) Tur.	37·00 N	34·50 E
136	Tartagal (tär-tä-gä'l) Arg.	23·31 S	63·47 W
166	Tartu (Dorpat) (tär'tōō) (dôr'pät) Sov. Un.	58·23 N	26·44 E
153	Ţarţūs Egypt	34·54 N	35·59 E
195	Tarumi (tä'rōō-mē) Jap. (Ōsaka In.)	34·38 N	135·04 E
166	Tarusa (tä-rōōs'ȧ) Sov. Un.	54·43 N	37·11 E
113	Tarzana (tär-ză'ȧ) Ca. (Los Angeles In.)	34·10 N	118·32 W
147	Tashauz (tŭ-shŭ-ōōs') Sov. Un.	41·50 N	59·45 E
172	Tashkent (tȧsh'kĕnt) Sov. Un.	41·23 N	69·04 E
205	Tasman B. (tăz'măn) N. Z. (In.)	39·11 S	173·22 E
203	Tasmania (State) (tăz-mā'nĭ-ȧ) Austl.	38·20 S	146·30 E
205	Tasmania (I.) Austl.	41·28 S	142·30 E
203	Tasman Pen. Austl.	43·00 S	148·30 E
198	Tasman Sea Oceania	29·30 S	155·00 E
124	Tasquillo (täs-kē'lyō) Mex.	20·34 N	99·21 W
210	Tassili-n-Ajjer (Plat.) (tȧs'ē-lē ä'jĕr) Alg.	25·40 N	6·57 E
170	Tatar (A. S. S. R.) (tȧ-tär') Sov. Un.	55·30 N	51·00 E
172	Tatarsk (tȧ-tärsk') Sov. Un.	55·15 N	75·00 E
173	Tatar Str. Sov. Un.	51·00 N	141·45 E
112	Tater Hill (Mtn.) (tāt'ēr hĭl) Or. (Portland In.)	45·47 N	123·02 W
195	Tateyama (tä'tē-yä'mä) Jap.	35·04 N	139·52 E
92	Tatlow, Mt. Can.	51·23 N	123·52 W
137	Tatuí (tä-tōō-ē') Braz. (Rio de Janeiro In.)	23·21 S	47·49 W
137	Taubaté (tou-bȧ-tā') Braz. (Rio de Janeiro In.)	23·03 S	45·32 W
158	Tauern Tun. Aus.	47·12 N	13·17 E
212	Taung (tä'ŏŏng) S. Afr.	27·25 S	24·47 E
106	Taunton (tän'tŭn) Ma. (Providence In.)	41·54 N	71·03 W
106	Taunton R. RI (Providence In.)	41·50 N	71·02 W
155	Taunus (Mts.) (tou'nŏŏz) F.R.G.	50·15 N	8·33 E
205	Taupo, L. (tä'ōō-pō) N. Z. (In.)	38·38 S	175·27 E
157	Taurage (tou'rȧ-gä) Sov. Un.	55·15 N	22·18 E
	Taurus Mts., see Toros Dağlari		
162	Tauste (tä-ōōs'tȧ) Sp.	41·55 N	1·15 W
172	Tavda (tȧv-dȧ') Sov. Un.	58·00 N	64·44 E
170	Tavda (R.) Sov. Un.	59·20 N	63·28 E
161	Taverny (tȧ-vĕr-nē') Fr. (Paris In.)	49·02 N	2·13 E
125	Taviche (tä-vē'chĕ) Mex.	16·43 N	96·35 W
162	Tavira (tä-vē'rȧ) Port.	37·09 N	7·42 W
196	Tavoy Bur.	14·04 N	98·19 E
171	Tavşanli (tȧv'shän-lĭ) Tur.	39·30 N	29·30 E
119	Tawakoni (L.) Tx.	32·51 N	95·59 W
195	Tawaramoto (tä'wä-rä-mô-tô) Jap. (Ōsaka In.)	34·33 N	135·48 E
104	Tawas City Mi.	44·15 N	83·30 W
104	Tawas Pt. (tô'wȧs) Mi.	44·15 N	83·25 W
196	Tawitawi Group (Is.) (tä'wē-tä'wē) Phil.	4·52 N	120·35 E
211	Tawkar Sud.	18·28 N	37·46 E
124	Taxco de Alarcón (täs'kō dĕ ä-lär-kô'n) Mex.	18·34 N	99·37 W
154	Tay, Firth of (fûrth ŏv tā) Scot.	56·26 N	2·45 W
154	Tay (L.) Scot.	56·25 N	5·07 W
154	Tay (R.) Scot.	56·35 N	3·37 W
197	Tayabas B. (tä-yä'bäs) Phil. (In.)	13·44 N	121·40 E
172	Tayga (tī'gä) Sov. Un.	56·12 N	85·47 E
173	Taygonos, Mys (Taigonos) (C.) Sov. Un.	60·37 N	160·17 E
119	Taylor Tx.	30·35 N	97·25 W
115	Taylor, Mt. NM	35·20 N	107·40 W
104	Taylorville (tā'lēr-vĭl) Il.	39·30 N	89·20 W
186	Taymā Sau. Ar.	27·45 N	38·55 E
173	Taymyr (Taimyr) (L.) (tī-mĭr') Sov. Un.	74·13 N	100 45 E
172	Taymyr, P-Ov (Taimyr) (Pen.) Sov. Un.	75·15 N	95·00 E
172	Tayshet (Taishet) (tī-shĕt') Sov. Un.	56·09 N	97·49 E
172	Taytay (tī-tī) Phil.	10·37 N	119·10 E
197	Tayung (tā-yōōng') Phil. (In.)	16·01 N	120·45 E
172	Taz (R.) (tȧz) Sov. Un.	67·15 N	80·45 E
210	Taza (tä'zä) Mor.	34·08 N	4·00 W
172	Tazovskoye Sov. Un.	66·58 N	78·28 E
171	Tbilisi ('tbĭl-yē'sē) Sov. Un.	41·40 N	44·45 E
216	Tchibanga (chē-bäŋ'gä) Gabon	2·51 S	11·02 E
214	Tchien Lib.	6·04 N	8·08 W
215	Tchigai, Plat. du (Plat.) Chad-Niger	21·20 N	14·50 E
159	Tczew (t'chĕf') Pol.	54·06 N	18·48 E
126	Teabo (tĕ-ä'bô) Mex. (In.)	20·25 N	89·14 W
119	Teague (tēg) Tx.	31·39 N	96·16 W
125	Teapa (tā-ä'pä) Mex.	17·35 N	92·56 W
210	Tébessa (tā'bĕs'ä) Alg.	35·27 N	8·13 E
183	Tebing Tinggi (I.) (teb'ĭng-tĭng'gä) Indon. (Singapore In.)	0·54 N	102·39 E
196	Tebukbetung Indon.	5·30 S	105·04 E
124	Tecalitlán (tā-kä-lē-tlän') Mex.	19·28 N	103·17 W

ăt; finăl; rāte; senâte; ärm; ȧsk; sofȧ; fâre; ch-choose; dh-as th in other; bē; ēvent; bĕt; recĕnt; cratēr; g-go; gh-guttural g; bĭt; ĭ-short neutral; rīde; K-guttural k as ch in German ich;

356 Texistepec — Tirgu-Jiu PRONOUNCING INDEX

Page	Name Pronunciation Region	Lat. °′	Long. °′
125	Texistepec (tĕk-sēs-tā-pĕk')..Mex.	17·51 N	94·46 W
125	Texmelucan (tās-mâ-lōō'kän) Mex. (In.)	19·17 N	98·26 W
117	Texoma, L. (tĕk'ō-mă).......Ok.	34·03 N	96·28 W
213	Teyateyaneng...Leso. (Natal In.)	29·11 S	27·43 E
166	Teykovo (tĕy-kô-vô).....Sov. Un.	56·52 N	40·34 E
125	Teziutlán (tâ-zê-ōō-tlän')....Mex.	19·48 N	97·21 W
124	Tezontepec (tâ-zōn-tâ-pĕk')..Mex.	19·52 N	98·48 W
124	Tezontepec de Aldama (dā äl-dä'mä).Mex.	20·19 N	99·19 W
184	Tezpur..................India	26·42 N	92·52 E
90	Tha-anne (R.)...............Can.	60·50 N	96·56 W
213	Thabana Ntlenyana (Mtn.) Leso. (Natal In.)	29·28 S	29·17 E
218	Thabazimbi.............S. Afr. (Johannesburg & Pretoria In.)	24·36 S	27·22 E
182	Thailand..................Asia	16·30 N	101·00 E
196	Thailand, G. of.............Asia	11·37 N	100·46 E
196	Thale Luang (L.)...........Thai.	7·51 N	99·39 E
148	Thame (tām)...Eng. (London In.)	51·43 N	0·59 W
104	Thames (R.) (tĕmz).........Can.	42·40 N	81·45 W
155	Thames (R.)...............Eng.	51·26 N	0·54 E
153	Thāmit, Wadi (R.).........Libya	30·39 N	16·23 E
185	Thāna (thä'nŭ)........India (In.)	19·13 N	72·58 E
185	Thāna Cr............India (In.)	19·03 N	72·58 E
193	Thanh-Hoa (tän'hō'ä).......Viet.	19·46 N	105·42 E
185	Thanjāvūr.................India	10·51 N	79·11 E
161	Thann (tän)................Fr.	47·49 N	7·05 E
161	Thaon-les-Vosges (tä-ôN-lā-vōzh') Fr.	48·16 N	6·24 E
203	Thargomindah (thàr'gō-mĭn'dà) Austl.	27·58 S	143·57 E
165	Thásos (I.) (thă'sôs).........Grc.	40·41 N	24·53 E
123	Thatch Cay (I.) (thăch) Vir. Is. (U. S. A.) (St. Thomas In.)	18·22 N	64·53 W
158	Thaya R. (tä'yà).....Aus.-Czech.	48·48 N	15·40 E
117	Thayer (thâ'ēr).............Mo.	36·30 N	91·34 W
	Thebes, see Thivai		
218	Thebes (Ruins) (thēbz) Egypt (Nile In.)	25·47 N	32·39 E
112	The Brothers (Mtn.) (brŭth'ērs) Wa. (Seattle In.)	47·39 N	123·08 W
94	The Coteau (Hills).........Can.	51·10 N	107·30 W
110	The Dalles (dălz)............Or.	45·36 N	121·10 W
197	The Father (Mtn.)...Pap. N. Gui.	5·05 S	151·30 E
	The Hague, see 's Gravenhage		
184	Thelum...................Pak.	32·59 N	73·43 E
202	The Oaks.....Austl. (Sydney In.)	34·04 S	150·36 E
203	Theodore (thēō'dôr)........Austl.	24·51 S	150·09 E
115	Theodore Roosevelt Dam (thê-ô-dōr rōō-sa-vĕlt).Az.	33·46 N	111·25 W
108	Theodore Roosevelt Natl. Mem. Park.ND	47·20 N	103·42 W
95	The Pas (pä)..............Can.	53·50 N	101·15 W
93	The Rajah (Mtn.)............Can.	53·15 N	118·31 W
111	Thermopolis (thēr-mŏp'ō-lĭs)..Wy.	43·38 N	108·11 W
203	The Round Mtn...........Austl.	30·17 S	152·19 E
165	Thessalía (Reg.)............Grc.	39·50 N	22·09 E
91	Thessalon.................Can.	46·11 N	83·37 W
165	Thessaloníki (thĕs-sà-lô-nē'kê) Grc.	40·38 N	22·59 E
98	Thetford Mines (thĕt'fērd mīns) Can.	46·05 N	71·20 W
213	The Twins (Mtn.) (twĭnz) Leso.-S. Afr. (Natal In.)	30·09 S	28·29 E
218	Theunissen..............S. Afr. (Johannesburg & Pretoria In.)	28·25 S	26·44 E
95	Thibaudeau (tĭ'bō-dō')......Can.	57·05 N	94·08 W
119	Thibodaux (tê-bô-dō')........La.	29·48 N	90·48 W
108	Thief (L.) (thēf)............Mn.	48·32 N	95·46 W
108	Thief (R.).................Mn.	48·18 N	96·07 W
108	Thief River Falls (thēf rĭv'ēr fôlz).Mn.	48·07 N	96·11 W
160	Thiers (tyâr)...............Fr.	45·51 N	3·32 E
214	Thiès (tê-ĕs')............Senegal	14·48 N	16·56 W
217	Thika.....................Ken.	1·03 S	37·05 E
184	Thimbu...................Bhu.	27·33 N	89·42 E
150	Thingvallavatn (L.)..........Ice.	64·12 N	20·22 W
161	Thionville (tyôN-vēl')........Fr.	49·23 N	6·31 E
211	Third Cataract.............Sud.	19·53 N	30·11 E
156	Thisted (tēs'tĕdh)..........Den.	56·57 N	8·38 E
150	Thisti Fd. (tēs'tēl)..........Ice.	66·29 N	14·59 W
203	Thistle (I.) (thĭs''l)........Austl.	34·55 S	136·11 E
165	Thivai (Thebes).............Grc.	38·20 N	23·18 E
150	Thjórsá (R.) (tyûr'sà)........Ice.	64·23 N	19·18 W
149	Tholen....Neth. (Amsterdam In.)	51·32 N	4·11 E
116	Thomas (tŏm'ăs)............Ok.	35·44 N	98·43 W
105	Thomas....................WV	39·15 N	79·30 W
120	Thomaston (tŏm'ăs-tŭn)......Ga.	32·51 N	84·17 W
120	Thomasville (tŏm'ăs-vĭl)......Al.	31·55 N	87·43 W
121	Thomasville................NC	35·52 N	80·05 W
92	Thomlinson, Mt............Can.	55·33 N	127·29 W
95	Thompson.................Can.	55·48 N	97·59 W
93	Thompson (R.)..............Can.	50·15 N	121·20 W
117	Thompson (R.)..............Mo.	40·32 N	93·49 W
110	Thompson Falls.............Mt.	47·35 N	115·20 W
121	Thomson (tŏm'sŭn)..........Ga.	33·28 N	82·29 W
205	Thomson (R.) (tŏm-sŏn)....Austl.	29·30 S	143·07 E
217	Thomson's Falls............Ken.	0·02 N	36·22 E
161	Thonon-les-Bains (tô-nôN'lā-băN') Fr.	46·22 N	6·27 E
150	Thórisvatn (L.).............Ice.	64·02 N	19·09 W
148	Thorne (thôrn)..............Eng.	53·37 N	0·58 W
104	Thorntown (thôrn'tŭn)........In.	40·05 N	86·35 W
89	Thorold (thō'rōld) Can. (Toronto In.)	43·13 N	79·12 W
160	Thouars (tōō-är')............Fr.	47·00 N	0·17 W
105	Thousand Is. (thou'zănd) NY-Can.	44·15 N	76·10 W
165	Thrace (Reg.) (thrās)...Grc.-Tur.	41·20 N	26·07 E
148	Thrapston (thrăp'stŭn)......Eng.	52·23 N	0·32 W
111	Three Forks (thrē fôrks)......Mt.	45·56 N	111·35 W
104	Three Oaks (thrē ōks)........Mi.	41·50 N	86·40 W
214	Three Points, C...........Ghana	4·45 N	2·06 W
104	Three Rivers................Mi.	42·00 N	83·40 W
75	Thule....................Grnld.	76·34 N	68·47 W
158	Thun (tōōn)..............Switz.	46·46 N	7·34 E
96	Thunder Bay...............Can.	48·28 N	89·12 W
109	Thunder B. (thŭn'dēr).......Can.	48·29 N	88·52 W
94	Thunder Hills..............Can.	54·30 N	106·00 W
158	Thuner See (L.)...........Switz.	46·40 N	7·30 E
118	Thurber (thûr'bēr)...........Tx.	32·30 N	98·23 W
158	Thüringen (Thuringia) (former state or region) (tü'rĭng-ĕn).G.D.R.	51·07 N	10·45 E
154	Thurles (thûrlz).............Ire.	52·44 N	7·45 W
148	Thurrock (thŭ'rŏk) Eng. (London In.)	51·28 N	0·19 E
205	Thursday (I.) (thûrz-dā)....Austl.	10·17 S	142·23 E
89	Thurso (thŭr'sô) Can. (Ottawa In.)	45·36 N	75·15 W
154	Thurso...................Scot.	58·35 N	3·40 W
220	Thurston Pen. (thûrs'tŭn)....Ant.	71·20 S	98·00 W
212	Thysville (tês-vēl')..........Zaire	5·08 S	14·58 E
193	Tiandong (tĭĕn-dôŋ)........China	23·32 N	107·10 E
	Tianjin, see T'ienching		
190	Tianjin Shi (Mun.) (tĭĕn-jyĭn shr) China	39·30 N	117·13 E
193	Tianmen (tĭĕn-mŭn).......China	30·40 N	113·10 E
192	Tianshui (tĭĕn-shwā).......China	34·25 N	105·40 E
210	Tiaret......................Alg.	35·28 N	1·15 E
136	Tibagi (tē'bà-zhē)..........Braz.	24·40 S	50·35 W
211	Tibasti, Sarir (Des.)........Chad	24·00 N	16·30 E
215	Tibati....................Cam.	6·27 N	12·38 E
	Tiber (R.), see Tévere		
211	Tibesti Massif (Mts.).......Chad	20·40 N	17·48 E
188	Tibet, Plat. of (tĭ-bĕt').....China	32·22 N	83·30 E
	Tibet (Aut. Reg.), see Xizang		
183	Tibnīn.......Leb. (Palestine In.)	33·12 N	35·23 E
112	Tiburon (tē-bōō-rōn') Ca. (San Francisco In.)	37·53 N	122·27 W
129	Tiburon...................Hai.	18·35 N	74·25 W
122	Tiburón (I.)...............Mex.	28·45 N	113·10 W
127	Tiburon, Cabo (C.) (kà'bô)...Pan.	8·42 N	77·19 W
112	Tiburon I..Ca. (San Francisco In.)	37·52 N	122·26 W
197	Ticaco Pass (tê-kä-kô)..Phil. (In.)	12·38 N	123·50 E
197	Ticao I. (tê-kä'ō).......Phil. (In.)	12·40 N	123·30 E
148	Tickhill (tĭk'ĭl).............Eng.	53·26 N	1·06 W
105	Ticonderoga (tī-kŏn-dēr-ō'ga).NY	43·50 N	73·30 W
126	Ticul (tē-kōō'l)........Mex. (In.)	20·22 N	89·32 W
156	Tidaholm (tē'dà-hōlm).......Swe.	58·11 N	13·53 E
148	Tideswell (tīdz'wĕl).........Eng.	53·17 N	1·47 W
210	Tidikelt (Reg.) (tē-dê-kĕlt')...Alg.	25·53 N	2·11 E
214	Tidjikdja (tê-jĭk'jä)...Mauritania	18·33 N	11·25 W
192	Tieling (tĭĕ-lĭŋ)............China	42·18 N	123·50 E
163	Tielmes (tyâl-màs') Sp. (Madrid In.)	40·15 N	3·20 W
190	T'ienching (Tianjin) (tĭĕn-chĭŋ) (tĭĕn-jyĭn).China	39·08 N	117·14 E
149	Tienen.........Bel. (Brussels In.)	50·49 N	4·58 E
188	Tien Shan (Mts.)..Sov. Un.-China	42·00 N	78·46 E
190	Tienshan Hu (L.) (dĭän'shän'hōō) China	31·08 N	120·30 E
156	Tierp (tyĕrp)...............Swe.	60·21 N	17·28 E
213	Tierpoort...............S. Afr. (Johannesburg & Pretoria In.)	25·53 S	28·26 E
125	Tierra Blanca (tyĕ'r-rä-blä'n-kä) Mex.	18·28 N	96·19 W
136	Tierra del Fuego (Reg.) (tyĕr'rä dĕl fwā'gô).Chile-Arg.	53·50 S	68·45 W
162	Tiétar (R.) (tê-ā'tär).........Sp.	39·56 N	5·44 W
137	Tietê (tyā-tā') Braz. (Rio de Janeiro In.)	23·08 S	47·42 W
135	Tieté (R.)................Braz.	20·46 S	50·46 W
104	Tiffin (tĭf'ĭn)...............Oh.	41·10 N	83·15 W
120	Tifton (tĭf'tŭn).............Ga.	31·25 N	83·34 W
112	Tigard (tī'gärd).Or. (Portland In.)	45·25 N	122·46 W
98	Tignish (tĭg'nĭsh)..........Can.	46·57 N	64·02 W
174	Tigoda R. (tē'gô-dà) Sov. Un. (Leningrad In.)	59·29 N	31·15 E
136	Tigre (tê'grĕ)...........Arg. (In.)	34·09 S	58·35 W
134	Tigre (R.).................Peru	2·20 S	75·41 W
212	Tigres, Península dos (Pen.) (pĕ-nê'ŋ-sōō-lä-dôs-tĕ'grĕs).Ang.	16·30 S	11·45 E
186	Tigris (R.)................Asia	34·45 N	44·10 E
183	Tīh, Jabal at (Mts.) Egypt (Palestine In.)	29·23 N	34·05 E
125	Tihuatlán (tê-wä-tlän')......Mex.	20·43 N	97·34 W
114	Tijuana (tê-hwä'nä)....Mex. (In.)	32·32 N	117·02 W
136	Tijuca, Pico da (Mtn.) (pē'kō-dä-tê-zhōō'kà) Braz. (Rio de Janeiro In.)	22·56 S	43·17 W
126	Tikal (Ruins) (tê-käl').Guat. (In.)	17·16 N	89·49 W
171	Tikhoretsk (tê-Kôr-yĕtsk') Sov. Un.	45·55 N	40·05 E
166	Tikhvin (têK-vēn')......Sov. Un.	59·36 N	33·38 E
186	Tikrīt.....................Iraq	34·36 N	43·31 E
173	Tiksi (têk-sē')..........Sov. Un.	71·42 N	128·32 E
149	Tilburg (tĭl'bûrg) Neth. (Amsterdam In.)	51·33 N	5·05 E
214	Tilemsi, Vallée du (Val.).....Mali	17·50 N	0·25 E
173	Tilichiki (tyĭ-le-chĭ-kê)...Sov. Un.	60·49 N	166·14 E
167	Tiligul (R.) (tē'lĭ-gûl)....Sov. Un.	47·25 N	30·27 E
210	Tillabéry (tē-yà-bā-rē').....Niger	14·14 N	1·30 E
110	Tillamook (tĭl'a-mŏŏk)........Or.	45·27 N	123·50 W
110	Tillamook B.................Or.	45·32 N	124·26 W
156	Tillberga (tēl-bĕr'ghà).......Swe.	59·40 N	16·34 E
97	Tillsonburg (tĭl'sŭn-bûrg)....Can.	42·50 N	80·50 W
	Tilsit, see Sovetsk		
167	Tim (têm)..............Sov. Un.	51·39 N	37·07 E
205	Timaru (tĭm'ā-rōō)....N. Z. (In.)	44·26 S	171·17 E
167	Timashevskaya (tēmă-shĕfs-kă'yă).....Sov. Un.	45·47 N	38·57 E
119	Timbalier B. (tĭm'bà-lēr)......La.	28·55 N	90·14 W
112	Timber (tĭm'bēr) Or. (Portland In.)	45·43 N	123·17 W
210	Timbo (tĭm'bō).............Gui.	10·41 N	11·51 W
	Timbuktu, see Tombouctou		
156	Time (tē'mĕ)...............Nor.	58·45 N	5·39 E
214	Timétrine Monts (Mts.).....Mali.	19·50 N	0·30 W
210	Timimoun (tē-mê-mōōn')....Alg.	29·14 N	0·22 E
214	Timiris, Cap (C.).....Mauritania	19·23 N	16·32 W
165	Timis (R.)................Rom.	45·28 N	21·06 E
91	Timiskaming Station (tê-mĭs'ka-mĭng).Can.	46·41 N	79·01 W
91	Timmins (tĭm'ĭnz)..........Can.	48·25 N	81·22 W
121	Timmonsville (tĭm'ŭnz-vĭl)....SC	34·09 N	79·55 W
197	Timor (I.) (tê-mōr').......Indon.	10·08 S	125·00 E
198	Timor Sea..................Asia	12·40 S	125·00 E
165	Timoşoara................Rom.	45·44 N	21·21 E
115	Timpanogos Cave Natl. Mon. (tĭ-măn'ō-gŏz).Ut.	40·25 N	111·45 W
119	Timpson (tĭmp'sŭn)..........Tx.	31·55 N	94·24 W
173	Timpton (R.) (têmp'tôn).Sov. Un.	57·15 N	126·35 E
218	Timsāh (L.) (tĭm'sä) Egypt (Suez In.)	30·34 N	32·22 E
129	Tina, Monte (Mtn.) (mô'n-tĕ-tē'nà).Dom. Rep.	18·50 N	70·40 W
213	Tina (R.) (tē'nă) S. Afr. (Natal In.)	30·50 S	28·44 E
135	Tinaguillo (tê-nä-gē'l-yô) Ven. (In.)	9·55 N	68·18 W
183	Tīnah, Khalīj at (G.) Egypt (Palestine In.)	31·06 N	32·42 E
210	Tindouf (tên-dōōf')..........Alg.	27·43 N	7·44 W
183	Tinggi, Palau (I.) Mala. (Singapore In.)	2·16 N	104·16 E
214	Tingi Mts.................S. L.	9·00 N	10·50 W
191	Tinglin.....China (Shanghai In.)	30·53 N	121·18 E
134	Tingo María (tē'ngô-mä-rē'ä).Peru	9·15 S	76·04 W
214	Tingréla............Ivory Coast	10·29 N	6·24 W
156	Tingsryd (tĭngs'rüd).........Swe.	56·32 N	14·58 E
190	Tingtzu Wan (B.) (dĭng'tze wän) China	36·33 N	121·06 E
124	Tinguindio Paracho (tēn'kē'n-dyō-pärä-chô).Mex.	19·38 N	102·02 W
137	Tinguiririca (R.) (tē'n-gē-rē-rē'kä) Chile (Santiago In.)	36·48 S	70·45 W
107	Tinley Park (tĭn'lê) Il. (Chicago In.)	41·34 N	87·47 W
156	Tinnosset (tên'nôs'sĕt).......Nor.	59·44 N	9·00 E
156	Tinnsjö (tĭnnsyû)...........Nor.	59·55 N	8·49 E
136	Tinogasta (tē-nô-gäs'tä)......Arg.	28·07 S	67·30 W
165	Tínos (I.)..................Grc.	37·45 N	25·12 E
210	Tinrhert, Plat. du...........Alg.	27·30 N	7·30 E
187	Tinsukia (tin-sōō'kĭ-à)......India	27·18 N	95·29 E
115	Tintic (tĭn'tĭk)...............Ut.	39·55 N	112·15 W
214	Tio, Pic de (Pk.).............Gui.	8·55 N	8·55 W
183	Tioman (I.) Mala. (Singapore In.)	2·25 N	104·30 E
126	Tipitapa (tē-pê-tä'pä)........Nic.	12·14 N	86·05 W
126	Tipitapa R..................Nic.	12·13 N	85·57 W
120	Tippah Cr., (R.) (tĭp'pa).....Ms.	34·43 N	88·15 W
104	Tippecanoe (R.) (tĭp-ê-ka-nōō') In.	40·55 N	86·45 W
154	Tipperary (tĭ-pē-râ'rê)........Ire.	52·28 N	8·13 W
117	Tippo Bay. (tĭp'ō bīōō')......Ms.	33·35 N	90·06 W
104	Tipton......................In.	40·15 N	86·00 W
109	Tipton......................Ia.	41·46 N	91·10 W
165	Tirane (tê-rä'nä)............Alb.	41·18 N	19·50 E
164	Tirano (tê-rä'nō).............It.	46·12 N	10·09 E
167	Tiraspol' (tē-räs'pôl')....Sov. Un.	46·52 N	29·38 E
171	Tire (tē'rĕ)..................Tur.	38·05 N	27·48 E
154	Tiree (I.) (tī-rē')...........Scot.	56·34 N	6·30 W
165	Tîrgovişte.................Rom.	44·54 N	25·29 E
165	Tîrgu-Jiu..................Rom.	45·02 N	23·17 E

ăt; finăl; rāte; senâte; ärm; àsk; sofa; fâre; ch-choose; dh-as th in other; bē; êvent; bĕt; recĕnt; cratēr; g-go; gh-guttural g; bĭt; ĭ-short neutral; rīde; K-guttural k as ch in German ich;

Page	Name Pronunciation Region	Lat. °′	Long. °′
159	Tîrgu-Mureş . . . . . Rom.	46·33 N	24·35 E
159	Tîrgu Neamt . . . . . Rom.	47·14 N	26·23 E
159	Tîrgu-Ocna . . . . . Rom.	46·18 N	26·38 E
159	Tîrgu Săcuesc . . . . . Rom.	46·04 N	26·06 E
184	Tirich Mir (Mt.) . . . . . Pak.	36·50 N	71·48 E
174	Tirlyanskiy (tĭr-lyän'skĭ) Sov. Un. (Urals In.)	54·13 N	58·37 E
165	Tírnavos . . . . . Grc.	39·50 N	22·14 E
159	Tîrnăveni . . . . . Rom.	46·19 N	24·18 E
158	Tirol (State) (tē-rōl') . . . . . Aus.	47·13 N	11·10 E
164	Tirso (R.) (tēr'sô) . . . . . It.	40·15 N	9·03 E
185	Tiruchchirāppalli (tĭr'ōō-chĭ-rä'pá-lĭ) . India	10·49 N	78·48 E
185	Tirunelveli . . . . . India	8·53 N	77·43 E
185	Tiruppur . . . . . India	11·11 N	77·08 E
94	Tisdale (tĭz'dāl) . . . . . Can.	52·51 N	104·04 W
184	Tista (R.) . . . . . India	26·03 N	88·52 E
165	Tisza (R.) (tē'sä) . . . . . Yugo.	45·50 N	20·13 E
159	Tisza R. (tē'sä) . . . . . Hung.	46·30 N	20·08 E
184	Titāgarh . . . . . India (In.)	22·44 N	88·23 E
134	Titicaca, Lago (L.) (lä'gô-tē-tē-kä'kä) . Bol.-Peru	16·12 S	70·33 W
134	Titiribi (tē-tē-rē-bē') . . . . Col. (In.)	6·05 N	75·47 W
217	Tito, Lagh (R.) . . . . . Ken.	2·25 N	39·05 E
165	Titograd . . . . . Yugo.	42·25 N	20·42 E
165	Titovo Užice (tē'tô-vô ōō'zhē-tsĕ) Yugo.	43·51 N	19·53 E
165	Titov Veles (tē'tôv vĕ'lĕs) . . Yugo.	41·42 N	21·50 E
216	Titule . . . . . Zaire	3·17 N	25·32 E
121	Titusville (tĭ'tŭs-vĭl) . . . . . Fl. (In.)	28·37 N	80·44 W
105	Titusville . . . . . Pa.	40·40 N	79·40 W
161	Titz (tētz) . . . . . F.R.G. (Ruhr In.)	51·00 N	6·26 E
106	Tiverton (tĭv'ēr-tŭn) RI (Providence In.)	41·38 N	71·11 W
163	Tívoli (tē'vô-lē) . . . . It. (Rome In.)	41·58 N	12·48 E
126	Tixkokob (tēx-kō-kō'b) . Mex. (In.)	21·01 N	89·23 W
124	Tixtla de Guerrero (tē'x-tlä-dĕ-gĕr-rĕ'rô) . Mex.	17·36 N	99·24 W
196	Tizard Bk. and Rf. (tĭz'árd) . China	10·51 N	113·20 E
126	Tizimín (tē-zē-mē'n) . . . Mex. (In.)	21·08 N	88·10 W
210	Tizi-Ouzou (tē'zē-ōō-zōō') . . . . Alg.	36·44 N	4·04 E
135	Tiznados (R.) (tēz-nä'dôs) Ven. (In.)	9·53 N	67·49 W
210	Tiznit (tēz-nēt) . . . . . Mor.	29·52 N	9·39 W
125	Tlacolula de Matamoros (tlä-kô-lōō'lä dā mätä-mō'rôs) Mex.	16·56 N	96·29 W
125	Tlacotálpan (tlä-kô-täl'pän) Mex.	18·39 N	95·40 W
124	Talcotepec (tlä-kô-tâ-pĕ'k) . . Mex.	17·46 N	99·57 W
125	Tlacotepec . . . . . Mex.	18·41 N	97·40 W
124	Tlacotepec . . . . . Mex.	19·11 N	99·41 W
125	Tláhuac (tlä-wäk') . . . . . Mex. (In.)	19·16 N	99·00 W
124	Tlajomulco de Zúñiga (tlä-hô-mōō'l-ko-dĕ-zōō'n-yē-gä) Mex.	20·30 N	103·27 W
124	Tlalchapa (tläl-chä'pä) . . . . . Mex.	18·26 N	100·29 W
125	Tlalixcoyan (tlä-lēs'kō-yän') . Mex.	18·53 N	96·04 W
125	Tlalmanalco (tläl-mä-nä'l-kô) Mex. (In.)	19·12 N	98·48 W
125	Tlalnepantia (tläl-nĕ-pà'n-tyä) Mex. (In.)	19·32 N	99·13 W
125	Tlalnepantla (tläl-nâ-pàn'tlä) Mex. (In.)	18·59 N	99·01 W
125	Tlalpan (tläl-pä'n) . . . . . Mex. (In.)	19·17 N	99·10 W
124	Tlalpujahua (tläl-pōō-кä'wä) . Mex.	19·50 N	100·10 W
	Tlaltenango, see Sánchez Román		
124	Tlapa (tlä'pä) . . . . . Mex.	17·30 N	98·09 W
125	Tlapacoyan (tlä-pä-kō-yá'n) . Mex.	19·57 N	97·11 W
124	Tlapaneco (R.) (tlä-pä-nĕ'kô) Mex.	17·59 N	98·44 W
124	Tlapehuala (tlä-pâ-wä'lä) . . . . Mex.	18·17 N	100·30 W
124	Tlaquepaque (tlä-kĕ-pä'kĕ) . . Mex.	20·39 N	103·17 W
124	Tlatlaya (tlä-tlä'yä) . . . . . Mex.	18·36 N	100·14 W
124	Tlaxcala (tläs-kä'lä) . . . . . Mex.	19·16 N	98·14 W
124	Tlaxcala (State) . . . . . Mex.	19·30 N	98·15 W
124	Tlaxco (tläs'kō) . . . . . Mex.	19·37 N	98·06 W
125	Tlaxiaco Sta. Maria Asunción (tläk-sē-ä'kō sän'tä mä-rē'ä ä-sōōn-syōn') . Mex.	17·16 N	95·41 W
125	Tlayacapan (tlä-yä-kä-pá'n) Mex. (In.)	18·57 N	99·00 W
210	Tlemcen (tlĕm-sĕn') . . . . . Alg.	34·53 N	1·21 W
92	Tlevak Str. . . . . . Ak.	55·03 N	132·58 W
159	Tlumach (t'lû-mäch') . . . . Sov. Un.	48·47 N	25·00 E
129	Toa (R.) (tō'ä) . . . . . Cuba	20·25 N	74·35 W
111	Toana Ra. (Mts.) (tō-á-nō') . . . Nv.	40·45 N	114·11 W
129	Toar, Cuchillas de (Mtn.) (kōō-chē'l-lyäs-dĕ-tō-ä'r) . Cuba	18·20 N	74·50 W
123	Tobago (I.) (tô-bā'gō) . . . . . N. A.	11·15 N	60·30 W
92	Toba Inlet . . . . . Can.	50·20 N	124·50 W
162	Tobarra (tô-bär'rä) . . . . . Sp.	38·37 N	1·42 W
172	Tobol (R.) (tô-bôl') . . . . . Sov. Un.	56·02 N	65·30 E
172	Tobol'sk (tô-bôlsk') . . . . . Sov. Un.	58·09 N	68·28 E
134	Tocaima (tô-kä'y-mä) . . . Col. (In.)	4·28 N	74·38 W
135	Tocantinópolis (tō-kän-tē-nŏ'pō-lēs) . Braz.	6·27 S	47·18 W
135	Tocantins (R.) (tō-kän-tēɴs') . Braz.	3·28 S	49·22 W
120	Toccoa (tŏk'ō-á) . . . . . Ga.	34·35 N	83·20 W
120	Toccoa (R.) . . . . . Ga.	34·53 N	84·24 W
195	Tochigi (tō'chē-gĭ) . . . . . Jap.	36·25 N	139·45 E
126	Tocoa (tō-kō'ä) . . . . . Hond.	15·37 N	86·01 W
136	Tocopilla (tō-kô-pēl'yä) . . . . . Chile	22·03 S	70·08 W
135	Tocuyo de la Costa (tô-kōō'yō-dĕ-lä-kôs'tä) Ven. (In.)	11·03 N	68·24 W
195	Toda . . . . . Jap. (Tōkyō In.)	35·48 N	139·42 E
148	Todmorden (tŏd'môr-dĕn) . . . Eng.	53·43 N	2·05 W
214	Tóecé . . . . . Upper Volta	11·50 N	1·16 W
92	Tofino (tō-fē'nō) . . . . . Can.	49·09 N	125·54 W
156	Töfsingdalens (Natl. Park) . . . Swe.	62·09 N	13·05 E
195	Tōgane (tō'gä-nā) . . . . . Jap.	35·29 N	140·16 E
196	Togian, Kepulauan (Is.) . . . Indon.	0·20 S	122·00 E
209	Togo (tō'gō) . . . . . Afr.	8·00 N	0·52 E
174	Toguzak R. (tô'gōō-zák) Sov. Un. (Urals In.)	53·40 N	61·42 E
121	Tohopekaliga (L.) (tō'hô-pē'kà-lĭ'gá) . Fl. (In.)	28·16 N	81·09 W
157	Toijala (toi'yá-là) . . . . . Fin.	61·11 N	21·46 E
195	Toi-Misaki (C.) (toi mē'sä-kē) . Jap.	31·20 N	131·20 E
114	Toiyabe Ra. (toi'yă-bē) . . . . . Nv.	38·59 N	117·22 W
194	Tokachi Gawa (R.) (tō-kä'chē gä'wä) . Jap.	43·10 N	142·30 E
159	Tokaj (tô'kô-ē) . . . . . Hung.	48·06 N	21·24 E
194	Tokara Guntō (Is.) (tō-kä'rä gōōn'tō') . Jap.	29·45 N	129·15 E
194	Tokara Kaikyo (Str.) (tô'kä-rä kī'kyô) . Jap.	30·20 N	129·50 E
171	Tokat (tô-кät') . . . . . Tur.	40·20 N	36·30 E
198	Tokelau Is. (tō-kē-lä'ōō) . . Oceania	8·00 S	176·00 W
172	Tokmak (tôk'mák) . . . . . Sov. Un.	42·44 N	75·41 E
195	Tokorozawa (tô'kô-rô-zä'wä) Jap. (Tōkyō In.)	35·47 N	139·29 E
194	Tokuno (I.) (tô-kōō'nō) . . . . . Jap.	27·42 N	129·25 E
195	Tokushima (tō'kōō'shē-mä) . . . Jap.	34·06 N	134·31 E
195	Tokuyama (tō'kōō'yä-mä) . . . . Jap.	34·04 N	131·49 E
195	Tōkyō (tō'kē-ō) . . Jap. (Tōkyō In.)	35·41 N	139·44 E
195	Tōkyō (Pref.) . . . . Jap. (Tōkyō In.)	35·42 N	139·40 E
195	Tōkyō-Wan (B.) (tō'kyō wän) Jap. (Tōkyō In.)	35·32 N	139·56 E
165	Tolbukhin . . . . . Bul.	43·33 N	27·52 E
124	Tolcayuca (tôl-kä-yōō'kä) . . . Mex.	19·55 N	98·54 W
109	Toledo (tô-lē'dō) . . . . . Ia.	41·59 N	92·35 W
104	Toledo . . . . . Oh.	41·40 N	83·35 W
110	Toledo . . . . . Or.	44·37 N	123·58 W
162	Toledo (tô-lĕ'dô) . . . . . Sp.	39·53 N	4·02 W
162	Toledo, Montes de (Mts.) (mô'n-tĕs-dĕ-tô-lĕ'dô) . Sp.	39·33 N	4·40 W
103	Toledo Bend Res. . . . . . La.-Tx.	31·30 N	93·30 W
134	Tolima (Dept.) (tô-lē'mä) Col. (In.)	4·07 N	75·20 W
134	Tolima, Nevado del (Pk.) (nĕ-vä-dô-dĕl-tô-lē'mä) . Col. (In.)	4·40 N	75·20 W
124	Tolimán (tô-lē-män') . . . . . Mex.	20·54 N	99·54 W
148	Tollesbury (tōl'z-bĕrĭ) Eng. (London In.)	51·46 N	0·49 E
164	Tolmezzo (tôl-mĕt'zô) . . . . . It.	46·25 N	13·03 E
164	Tolmin (tôl'mēn) . . . . . Yugo.	46·12 N	13·45 E
159	Tolna (tôl'nô) . . . . . Hung.	46·25 N	18·47 E
196	Tolo, Teluk (B.) (tō'lō) . . . . Indon.	2·00 S	122·06 E
162	Tolosa (tô-lō'sä) . . . . . Sp.	43·10 N	2·05 W
112	Tolt (R.) (tōlt) . . Wa. (Seattle In.)	47·13 N	121·49 W
104	Toluca (tô-lōō'ká) . . . . . Il.	41·00 N	89·10 W
125	Toluca (tô-lōō'kà) . . . . Mex. (In.)	19·17 N	99·40 W
125	Toluca, Nevado de (Mtn.) (nĕ-vä-dô-dĕ-tô-lōō'kä) Mex. (In.)	19·09 N	99·42 W
170	Tolyatti . . . . . Sov. Un.	53·30 N	49·10 E
172	Tom' (R.) . . . . . Sov. Un.	55·33 N	85·00 E
109	Tomah (tō'má) . . . . . Wi.	43·58 N	90·31 W
109	Tomahawk (tŏm'á-hôk) . . . . . Wi.	45·27 N	89·44 W
167	Tomakovka (tô-mä'kôf-kà) Sov. Un.	47·49 N	34·43 E
162	Tomar (tō-mär') . . . . . Port.	39·36 N	8·26 W
159	Tomashevka (tô-má'shĕf-kà) Sov. Un.	51·34 N	23·37 E
159	Tomaszow Lubelski (tô-mä'shōōf lōō-bĕl'skĭ) . Pol.	50·20 N	23·27 E
159	Tomaszów Mazowiecki (tô-mä'shōōf mä-zô'vyĕt-skĭ) Pol.	51·33 N	20·00 E
124	Tomatlán (tô-mä-tlà'n) . . . . . Mex.	19·54 N	105·14 W
124	Tomatlán (R.) . . . . . Mex.	19·56 N	105·14 W
214	Tombadonkéa . . . . . Gui.	11·00 N	14·23 W
135	Tombador, Serra do (Mts.) (sĕr'rá dōō tôm-bä-dôr') . Braz.	11·31 S	57·33 W
120	Tombigbee (R.) (tŏm-bĭg'bē) . . . Al.	31·45 N	88·02 W
137	Tombos (tô'm-bōs) Braz. (Rio de Janeiro In.)	20·53 S	42·00 W
214	Tombouctou (Timbuktu) (tôm-bōōk-tōō') . Mali	16·46 N	3·01 W
115	Tombstone (tōōm'stōn) . . . . . Az.	31·40 N	110·00 W
156	Tomelilla (tô'mĕ-lēl-lä) . . . . . Swe.	55·34 N	13·55 E
162	Tomelloso (tō-mâl-lyō'sō) . . . . Sp.	39·09 N	3·02 W
196	Tomini, Teluk (B.) (tô-mē'nē) Indon.	0·10 N	121·00 E
173	Tommot (tŏm-mŏt') . . . . . Sov. Un.	59·13 N	126·22 E
172	Tomsk (tŏmsk) . . . . . Sov. Un.	56·29 N	84·57 E
125	Tonalá (tō-nä-lä') . . . . . Mex.	16·05 N	93·45 W
124	Tonala . . . . . Mex.	20·38 N	103·14 W
125	Tonalá (R.) . . . . . Mex.	18·05 N	94·08 W
107	Tonawanda (tôn-á-wŏn'dá) NY (Buffalo In.)	43·01 N	78·53 W
107	Tonawanda Cr. . . NY (Buffalo In.)	43·05 N	78·43 W
192	Tonbei (tôŋ-bā) . . . . . China	48·00 N	126·48 E
148	Tonbridge (tŭn-brij) Eng. (London In.)	51·11 N	0·17 E
195	Tonda (tôn'dä) . . . Jap. (Ōsaka In.)	34·51 N	135·38 E
195	Tondabayashi (tôn-dä-bä'yä-shē) Jap. (Ōsaka In.)	34·29 N	135·36 E
197	Tondano (tôn-dä'nō) . . . . . Indon.	1·15 N	124·50 E
156	Tønder (tûn'nĕr) . . . . . Den.	54·47 N	8·49 E
125	Tondlá . . . . . Mex.	16·04 N	93·57 W
195	Tone (R.) (tō'nē) . Jap. (Tōkyō In.)	35·55 N	139·57 E
195	Tone-Gawa (Strm.) (tô'nĕ gä'wa) Jap.	36·12 N	139·19 E
198	Tonga (tŏŋ'gá) . . . . . Oceania	18·50 S	175·20 W
193	Tong'an (tôŋ-än) . . . . . China	24·48 N	118·02 E
192	Tongguan (tôŋ-gūän) . . . . . China	34·48 N	110·25 E
192	Tonghe (tôŋ-hŭ) . . . . . China	45·58 N	128·40 E
192	Tonghua (tôŋ-hwä) . . . . . China	41·43 N	125·50 E
189	Tongjiang (tôŋ-jyäŋ) . . . . . China	47·38 N	132·54 E
192	Tongliao (tôŋ-lĭou) . . . . . China	43·30 N	122·15 E
215	Tongo . . . . . Cam.	5·11 N	14·00 E
136	Tongoy (tōn-goi') . . . . . Chile	30·16 S	71·29 W
193	Tongren (tôŋ-rŭn) . . . . . China	27·45 N	109·12 E
190	Tongshan (tôŋ-shän) . . . . . China	34·27 N	116·27 E
188	Tongtian (R.) (tôŋ-tĭĕn) . . . . China	34·11 N	96·08 E
	Tongue of Arabat (Spit), see Arabatskaya Strelka		
128	Tongue of the Ocean (Chan.) (tŭng ŏv thē ōshăn) . Ba.	24·05 N	77·20 W
111	Tongue R. (tŭng) . . . . . Mt.	45·08 N	106·40 W
192	Tong Xian (tôŋ shyĕn) . . . . . China	39·55 N	116·40 E
211	Tonj R. (tônj) . . . . . Sud.	6·18 N	28·33 E
184	Tonk (Tŏŋk) . . . . . India	26·13 N	75·45 E
117	Tonkawa (tŏŋ'ká-wô) . . . . . Ok.	36·42 N	97·19 W
193	Tonkin, Gulf of (tôn-kăn') . . . Viet.	20·30 N	108·10 E
196	Tonle Sap (L.) (tôn'lā säp') . Camb.	13·03 N	102·49 E
160	Tonneins (tô-năɴ') . . . . . Fr.	44·24 N	0·18 E
158	Tönning (tû'nĕng) . . . . . F.R.G.	54·20 N	8·55 E
114	Tonopah (tō-nô-pä') . . . . . Nv.	38·04 N	117·15 W
156	Tönsberg (tûns'bĕrgh) . . . . . Nor.	59·19 N	10·25 E
125	Tonto (R.) (tōn'tō) . . . . . Mex.	18·15 N	96·13 W
115	Tonto Cr. . . . . . Az.	34·05 N	111·15 W
115	Tonto Natl. Mon. (tôn'tô) . . . . Az.	33·33 N	111·08 W
113	Tooele (tōō-ĕl'ē) Ut. (Salt Lake City In.)	40·33 N	112·17 W
193	Toohsien . . . . . China	25·30 N	111·32 E
203	Toowoomba (tōō wōōm'bá) . Aust.	27·32 S	152·10 E
113	Topanga (tō'păn-gà) Ca. (Los Angeles In.)	34·05 N	118·36 W
117	Topeka (tô-pē'ká) . . . . . Ks.	39·02 N	95·41 W
125	Topilejo (tô-pē-lĕ'hô) . . Mex. (In.)	19·12 N	99·09 W
115	Topock . . . . . Az.	34·40 N	114·20 W
159	Topol'čany (tô-pôl'chä-nü) . Czech.	48·38 N	18·10 E
122	Topolobampo (tō-pō-lô-bä'm-pô) Mex.	25·45 N	109·00 W
165	Topolovgrad . . . . . Bul.	42·05 N	26·19 E
110	Toppenish (tôp'ĕn-ĭsh) . . . . . Wa.	46·22 N	120·00 W
214	Tora, Île (I.) . . . . . Mauritania	19·50 N	16·45 W
99	Torbay (tôr-bā') . . . . . Can.	47·40 N	52·43 W
	Torbay, see Torquay		
203	Torbreck, Mt. (tôr-brĕk) . . . Austl.	37·05 S	146·55 E
104	Torch (L.) (tôrch) . . . . . Mi.	45·00 N	85·30 W
156	Töreboda (tû'rĕ-bō'dä) . . . . . Swe.	58·44 N	14·04 E
155	Torhout . . . . . Bel.	51·01 N	3·04 E
134	Toribío (tô-rē-bē'ô) . . . . Col. (In.)	2·58 N	76·14 W
195	Toride (tô'rē-dā) . Jap. (Tōkyō In.)	35·54 N	104·04 E
164	Torino (Turin) (tô-rē'no) (tū'rĭn) It.	45·05 N	7·44 E
150	Torino (R.) (tôr'nĭ-ô) . . . Fin.-Swe.	67·00 N	23·50 E
162	Tormes (R.) (tōr'mās) . . . . . Sp.	41·12 N	6·15 W
150	Torne (R.) (tôr'nĕ) . . . . . Swe.	67·29 N	21·44 E
150	Torne Träsk (L.) (tôr'nĕ trĕsk) Swe.	68·10 N	20·36 E
91	Torngat Mts. . . . . . Can.	59·18 N	64·35 W
150	Tornio (tôr'nĭ-ô) . . . . . Fin.	65·55 N	24·09 E
98	Toro, Lac (L.) . . . . . Can.	46·53 N	73·46 W
165	Toronaíos Kólpos (G.) . . . . . Grc.	40·10 N	23·35 E
89	Toronto (tô-rŏn'tō) Can. (Toronto In.)	43·40 N	79·23 W
104	Toronto . . . . . Oh.	40·30 N	80·35 W
118	Toronto, L. (lä'gô-tô-rô'n-tō) . Mex.	27·35 N	105·37 W
166	Toropets (tô'rô-pyĕts) . . . Sov. Un.	56·31 N	31·37 E
171	Toros Dağlari (Taurus Mts.) (tô'rŭs) . Tur.	37·00 N	32·40 E
163	Torote (R.) (tô-rō'tā) Sp. (Madrid In.)	40·36 N	3·24 W
156	Torp (tôrp) . . . . . Swe.	62·30 N	16·04 E
	Torpen, see Åmot		
154	Torquay (Torbay) (tôr-kē') . . Eng.	50·30 N	3·26 W
134	Torra, Cerro (Mtn.) (sĕ'r-rô-tô'r-rä) . Col. (In.)	4·41 N	76·22 W
113	Torrance (tŏr'rănc) Ca. (Los Angeles In.)	33·50 N	118·20 W

ng-sing; ŋ-baŋk; ɴ-nasalized n; nŏd; cŏmmit; ōld; ôbey; ôrder; fōōd; fŏŏt; ou-out; s-soft; sh-dish; th-thin; pūre; ûnite; ûrn; stŭd; circŭs; ü-as "y" in study; '-indeterminate vowel.

358 Torre Annunziata — Troy PRONOUNCING INDEX

Page	Name Pronunciation Region	Lat. °'	Long. °'
163	Torre Annunziata (tôr'rā ä-nōōn-tsê-ä'tä) It. (Naples In.)	40·31 N	14·27 E
162	Torre de Cerredo (Mtn.) (tôr'rå dā thå-rā'dhō).Sp.	43·10 N	4·47 W
163	Torre del Greco (tôr'rå děl grā'kô) It. (Naples In.)	40·32 N	14·23 E
162	Torrejoncillo (tôr'rā-hōn-thē'lyō) Sp.	39·54 N	6·26 W
162	Torrelavega (tôr-rā'lä-vä'gä)..Sp.	43·22 N	4·02 W
164	Torre Maggiore (tôr'rā mäd-jō'rā) It.	40·41 N	15·18 E
203	Torrens, L. (tŏr-ĕns)........Austl.	30·07 S	137·40 E
163	Torrente (tôr-rĕn'tā)..........Sp.	39·25 N	0·28 W
118	Torreon (tôr-rå-ōn')..........Mex.	25·32 N	103·26 W
163	Torre-Pacheco (tôr-rĕ-pä-chĕ'kô) Sp.	37·44 N	0·58 W
205	Torres Is. (tôr'rĕs) (tŏr'ĕz) New Hebr.	13·18 N	165·59 E
114	Torres Martinez Ind. Res. (tôr'ĕz mär-tē'nĕz).Ca.	33·33 N	116·21 W
162	Tôrres Novas (tôr'rĕzh nō'väzh) Port.	39·28 N	8·37 W
197	Torres Str. (tôr'rĕs)........Austl.	10·30 S	141·30 E
162	Tôrres Vedras (tôr'rĕzh vā'dräzh) Port.	39·08 N	9·18 W
163	Torrevieja (tôr-rā-vyā'hä).....Sp.	37·58 N	0·40 W
187	Torrijos (tôr-rē'hōs)....Phil. (In.)	13·19 N	122·06 E
105	Torrington (tŏr'ĭng-tŭn).......Ct.	41·50 N	73·10 W
108	Torrington.................Wy.	42·04 N	104·11 W
162	Torro (tô'r-rō)..............Sp.	41·27 N	5·23 W
156	Torsby (tôrs'bü)............Swe.	60·07 N	12·56 E
156	Torshälla (tôrs'hĕl-ä)........Swe.	59·26 N	16·21 E
150	Tórshavn (tôrs-houn').......Faer.	62·00 N	6·55 W
123	Tortola (I.) (tôr-tō'lä) Vir. Is. (Br.) (Puerto Rico In.)	18·34 N	64·40 W
164	Tortona (tôr-tō'nä)...........It.	44·52 N	8·52 W
163	Tortosa (tôr-tō'sä)...........Sp.	40·59 N	0·33 E
163	Tortosa, Cabo de (C.) (kå'bô-dĕ-tôr-tō-sä).Sp.	40·42 N	0·55 E
129	Tortue, Canal de la (Chan.) (tôr-tü').Hai.	20·05 N	73·20 W
129	Tortue, Ile de la (I.).........Hai.	20·10 N	73·00 W
89	Tortue, Rivière de la (R.) (lä tōr-tü').Can. (Montreal In.)	45·12 N	73·32 W
135	Tortuga, Isla la (I.) (ē's-lä-lä-tôr-tōō'gä).Ven. (In.)	10·55 N	65·18 W
159	Toruń (tō'rōōn')............Pol.	53·01 N	18·37 E
166	Tõrva (t'r'vå)..........Sov. Un.	58·02 N	25·56 E
154	Tory (I.) (tō'rê).............Ire.	55·17 N	8·10 W
166	Torzhok (tôr'zhôk).......Sov. Un.	57·03 N	34·53 E
195	Tosa-Wan (B.) (tô'sä wän)...Jap.	33·14 N	133·39 E
164	Toscana (Reg.) (tôs-kä'nä).....It.	43·23 N	11·08 E
174	Tosna R. Sov. Un..(Leningrad In.)	59·38 N	30·52 E
174	Tosno (tôs'nô) Sov. Un. (Leningrad In.)	59·32 N	30·52 E
136	Tostado (tôs-tä'dô)..........Arg.	29·10 S	61·43 W
171	Tosya (tôz'yå)..............Tur.	41·00 N	34·00 E
162	Totana (tô-tä-nä)............Sp.	37·45 N	1·28 W
170	Tot'ma (tôt'må).........Sov. Un.	60·00 N	42·20 E
135	Totness....................Sur.	5·51 N	56·17 W
126	Totonicapán (tô-tō-nê-kä'pän) Guat.	14·55 N	91·20 W
137	Totoras (tô-tô'räs) Arg. (Buenos Aires In.)	32·33 S	61·13 W
195	Totsuka (tōt'sōō-kä).........Jap.	35·24 N	139·32 E
148	Tottenham (tŏt'ĕn-ăm) Eng. (London In.)	51·35 N	0·06 W
195	Tottori (tô'tô-rê)............Jap.	35·30 N	134·15 E
210	Touat (Oases) (tōō'ät).......Alg.	27·22 N	0·38 W
214	Touba.............Ivory Coast	8·17 N	7·41 W
214	Touba...................Senegal	14·51 N	15·53 W
210	Toubkal Jebel (Mtn.).......Mor.	31·15 N	7·46 W
214	Tougan...............Upper Volta	13·04 N	3·04 W
210	Touggourt (tōō-gōōrt') (tōō-gōōr') Alg.	33·09 N	6·07 E
152	Touil R. (tōō-ēl')............Alg.	34·42 N	2·16 E
161	Toul (tōōl)...................Fr.	48·39 N	5·51 E
98	Toulnustouc (R.)...........Can.	50·23 N	67·55 W
161	Toulon (tōō-lôn')............Fr.	43·09 N	5·54 E
160	Toulouse (tōō-lōōz')..........Fr.	43·37 N	1·27 E
196	Toungoo (tŏ-ōōŋ-gōō').......Bur.	19·00 N	96·29 E
	Tourane, see Da Nang		
160	Tourcoing (tōōr-kwăN').......Fr.	50·44 N	3·06 E
161	Tournan-en-Brie (tōōr-näN-ĕN-brē') Fr. (Paris In.)	48·45 N	2·47 E
160	Tours (tōōr)..................Fr.	47·23 N	0·39 E
211	Touside, Pic (Pk.) (tōō-sē-dā') Chad	21·10 N	16·30 E
156	Tovdalselv (R.) (tôv-däls-ĕlv) Nor.	58·23 N	8·16 E
105	Towanda (tô-wän'dȧ).........Pa.	41·45 N	76·30 W
119	Town Bluff L...............Tx.	30·52 N	94·30 W
108	Towner (tou'nĕr)............ND	48·21 N	100·24 W
99	Townsend (toun'zĕnd)..Ma. (In.)	42·41 N	71·42 W
111	Townsend...................Mt.	46·19 N	111·35 W
112	Townsend, Mt...Wa. (Seattle In.)	47·52 N	123·03 W
135	Townsville (tounz'vĭl)......Austl.	19·18 S	146·50 E
106	Towson (tou'sŭn) Md. (Baltimore In.)	39·24 N	76·36 W
196	Towuti, Danau (L.) (tô-wōō'tê) Indon.	3·00 S	121·45 E
188	Toxkan (R.).............China	40·34 N	77·15 E
118	Toyah (tô'yȧ)...............Tx.	31·19 N	103·46 W
195	Toyama (tō'yä-mä)..........Jap.	36·42 N	137·14 E
195	Toyama-Wan (B.)...........Jap.	36·58 N	137·16 E
195	Toyohashi (tō'yô-hä'shê).....Jap.	34·44 N	137·21 E
195	Toyonaka (tō'yô-nä'kå) Jap. (Ōsaka In.)	34·47 N	135·28 E
152	Tozeur (tô-zûr')............Tun.	33·59 N	8·11 E
162	Trabancos (R.) (trä-băŋ'kōs)..Sp.	41·15 N	5·13 W
171	Trabzon (tråb'zôn)..........Tur.	41·00 N	39·45 E
114	Tracy (trā'sê)...............Ca.	37·45 N	121·27 W
98	Tracy......................Can.	46·00 N	73·13 W
108	Tracy.......................Mn.	44·13 N	95·37 W
120	Tracy City..................Tn.	35·15 N	85·44 W
162	Trafalgar, Cabo de (C.) (kå'bô-dĕ-trä-fäl-gä'r).Sp.	36·10 N	6·02 W
213	Trafonomby (Mtn.)........Mad.	24·32 S	46·35 E
93	Trail (trāl).................Can.	49·06 N	117·42 W
149	Traisen (R.)....Aus. (Vienna In.)	48·15 N	15·55 E
149	Traiskirchen....Aus. (Vienna In.)	48·01 N	16·18 E
157	Trakai (trå-kåy).........Sov. Un.	54·38 N	24·59 E
159	Trakiszki (trå-kē'-sh-kê)......Pol.	54·16 N	23·07 E
154	Tralee (trȧ-lē')..............Ire.	52·16 N	9·20 W
156	Tranas (trän'ôs)............Swe.	58·03 N	14·56 E
162	Trancoso (träŋ-kō'sōō)......Port.	40·46 N	7·23 W
197	Trangan, Pulau (I.) (träŋ'gän) Indon.	6·52 S	133·30 E
164	Trani (trä'nē)................It.	41·15 N	16·25 E
141	Transcaucasia (Reg.)....Sov. Un.	41·17 N	44·30 E
	Trans Himalayas (Mts.), see Gangdisê Shan		
212	Transvaal (Prov.) (träns-väl') S. Afr.	24·21 S	28·18 E
159	Transylvania (Reg.) (trăn-sĭl-vā'nĭ-ȧ).Rom.	46·30 N	22·35 E
	Transylvanian Alps (Mts.), see Carpatii Meridionali		
164	Trapani (trä'pä-nê)...........It.	38·02 N	12·34 E
161	Trappes (tråp).....Fr. (Paris In.)	48·47 N	2·01 E
203	Traralgon (tră'răl-gŏn).....Austl.	38·15 S	146·33 E
214	Trarza (Reg.)........Mauritania	17·35 N	15·15 W
164	Trasimeno, Lago (L.) (lä'gō trä-sê-mā'nō).Ir.	43·00 N	12·12 E
162	Tras os Montes (Mts.) (träzh'ōzh môn'tāzh).Port.	41·33 N	7·13 W
162	Trasparga (träs-pär-gä).......Sp.	43·13 N	7·50 W
158	Traun R. (troun)...........Aus.	48·10 N	14·15 E
158	Traunstein (troun'stīn)....F.R.G.	47·52 N	12·38 E
108	Traverse, L. (trăv'ērs)..Mn.-SD	45·46 N	96·53 W
104	Traverse City...............Mi.	44·45 N	85·40 W
164	Travnik (träv'nēk).........Yugo.	44·13 N	17·43 E
112	Treasure I. (trĕzh'ēr) Ca. (San Francisco In.)	37·49 N	122·22 W
149	Trebbin (trĕ'bēn) G.D.R. (Berlin In.)	52·13 N	13·13 E
158	Třebič (t'rzhĕ'bēch).......Czech.	49·13 N	15·53 E
165	Trebinje (trå'bēn-yĕ).......Yugo.	42·43 N	18·21 E
159	Trebisov (trĕ'bê-shôf).......Czech.	48·36 N	21·32 E
158	Třeboň (t'rzhĕ'bôn').........Czech.	49·00 N	14·48 E
205	Tregrosse Is. (trê-grōs').....Austl.	18·08 S	150·53 E
136	Treinta y Tres (trå-ēn'tä ē träs') Ur.	33·14 S	54·17 W
160	Trélazé (trā-lå-zā')...........Fr.	47·27 N	0·32 W
136	Trelew (trē'lū)..............Arg.	43·15 S	65·25 W
156	Trelleborg..................Swe.	55·24 N	13·07 E
154	Tremadoc B. (trĕ-mă'dŏk)..Wales	52·43 N	4·27 W
164	Tremiti, Isole di (Is.) (ē'sō-lĕ dētrā-mē'tē).It.	42·07 N	16·33 E
159	Trenčín (trĕn'chēn)........Czech.	48·52 N	18·02 E
136	Trenque Lauquén (trĕn'kĕ-lå'ōō-kĕ'n).Arg.	35·50 S	62·44 W
97	Trent (R.) (trĕnt)..........Can.	44·15 N	77·55 W
154	Trent (R.)..................Eng.	53·05 N	1·00 W
148	Trent and Mersey Can. (trĕnt) (mûr zē).Eng.	53·11 N	2·24 W
164	Trento (trĕn'tô)..............It.	46·04 N	11·07 E
164	Trento (Reg.)................It.	46·16 N	10·47 E
91	Trenton (trĕn'tŭn)..........Can.	44·05 N	77·35 W
99	Trenton....................Can.	45·37 N	62·38 W
107	Trenton........Mi. (Detroit In.)	42·08 N	83·12 W
117	Trenton.....................Mo.	40·05 N	93·36 W
106	Trenton......NJ (New York In.)	40·13 N	74·46 W
120	Trenton.....................Tn.	35·57 N	88·55 W
99	Trepassey (trê-păs'ê)........Can.	46·44 N	53·22 W
99	Trepassey B................Can.	46·40 N	53·20 W
136	Tres Arroyos (trās'är-rō'yōs).Arg.	38·18 S	60·16 W
137	Três Coracoes (trĕ's kō-rä-zô'ĕs) Braz. (Rio de Janeiro In.)	21·41 S	45·14 W
125	Tres Cumbres (trĕ's kōō'm-brĕs) Mex. (In.)	19·03 N	99·14 W
135	Três Lagoas (trĕ's lä-gô'ås)..Braz.	20·48 S	51·42 W
135	Três Marias, Reprêsa (Res.) (rĕ-prā'sä trĕs' mä-rē'äs).Braz.	18·15 S	45·30 W
134	Tres Morros, Alto de (Mtn.) (á'l-tō dĕ trĕ's mô'r-rôs) Col. (In.)	7·08 N	76·10 W
137	Três Pontas (trĕ's pô'n-täs) Braz. (Rio de Janeiro In.)	21·22 S	45·30 W
216	Três Pontas, Cabo das (C.)..Ang.	10·23 S	13·32 E
137	Três Rios (trĕ's rê'ōs) Braz. (Rio de Janeiro In.)	22·07 S	43·13 W
89	Très-St. Rédempteur (săN rā-dăNp-tûr') Can. (Montreal In.)	45·26 N	74·23 W
149	Treuenbrietzen (troi'ĕn-brē-tzĕn) G.D.R. (Berlin In.)	52·06 N	12·52 E
164	Treviglio (trā-vē'lyô).........It.	45·30 N	9·34 E
164	Treviso (trĕ-vē'sō)............It.	45·39 N	12·15 E
188	Triangle, The (Reg.)........Asia	26·00 N	98·00 E
218	Trichardt (trĭ-кärt').......S. Afr.	26·32 N	29·16 E
164	Trieste (trê-ĕs'tä)............It.	45·39 N	13·48 E
164	Trieste, G. of................It.	45·38 N	13·40 E
162	Trigueros (trê-gā'rōs).........Sp.	37·23 N	6·50 W
165	Tríkkala...................Grc.	39·33 N	21·49 E
197	Trikora, Puntjak (Pk.).....Indon.	4·15 S	138·45 E
107	Trim Cr. (trĭm) Il. (Chicago In.)	41·19 N	87·39 W
185	Trincomalee (trĭŋ-kô-mȧ-lē') Sri Lanka	8·39 N	81·12 E
148	Tring (trĭng)...Eng. (London In.)	51·46 N	0·40 W
134	Trinidad (trē-nê-dhädh').....Bol.	14·48 S	64·43 W
116	Trinidad (trĭn'ĭdăd)..........Co.	37·11 N	104·31 W
128	Trinidad (trē-nê-dhädh')....Cuba	21·50 N	80·00 W
137	Trinidad...Ur. (Buenos Aires In.)	33·29 S	56·55 W
128	Trinidad, Sierra de (Mts.) (sē-ĕ'r-rå dĕ trê-nê-dä'd).Cuba	21·50 N	79·55 W
135	Trinidad (I.) (trĭn'ĭ-dăd)....Trin.	10·00 N	61·00 W
123	Trinidad and Tobago (trĭn'ĭ-dăd) (tô-bā'gō).N. A.	11·00 N	61·00 W
133	Trinidade, Ilha da (I.) (ē'lä dä trê-nē-dä-dĕ).Braz.	21·00 S	32·00 W
122	Trinidad R............Pan. (In.)	8·55 N	80·01 W
125	Trinitaria (trē-nē-tä'ryä)....Mex.	16·09 N	92·04 W
127	Trinité............Mart. (In.)	14·47 N	61·00 W
99	Trinity (trĭn'ĭ-tê)..........Can.	48·59 N	53·55 W
119	Trinity.....................Tx.	30·52 N	95·27 W
101	Trinity (Is.)................Ak.	56·25 N	153·15 W
116	Trinity (R.), East Fk. ....Tx.	33·24 N	96·42 W
117	Trinity (R.), West Fk. ....Tx.	33·22 N	98·26 W
99	Trinity B...................Can.	48·00 N	53·40 W
110	Trinity R...................Ca.	40·50 N	123·20 W
119	Trinity R...................Tx.	30·50 N	95·09 W
164	Trino (trē'nô)................It.	45·11 N	8·16 E
120	Trion (trī'ŏn)...............Ga.	34·32 N	85·18 W
	Tripoli, see Ţarābulus		
	Tripoli, see Ţarābulus		
165	Tripolis (trĭ'pô-lĭs).........Grc.	37·32 N	22·32 E
	Tripolitania (Prov.), see Ţarābulus		
108	Tripp (trĭp)................SD	43·13 N	97·58 W
184	Tripura (State)............India	24·00 N	92·00 E
220	Tristan da Cunha Is. (três-tän'dä kōōn'yå).Alt. O.	35·30 S	12·15 W
135	Triste, Golfo (G.) (gôl-fô trē's-tĕ) Ven. (In.)	10·40 N	68·05 W
106	Triticus Res. (trī tĭ-cŭs) NY (New York In.)	41·20 N	73·36 W
185	Trivandrum (trê-vŭn'drŭm).India	8·34 N	76·58 E
159	Trnava (t'r'nà-vå)..........Czech.	48·22 N	17·34 E
197	Trobriand Is. (trō-brê-ănd') Pap. N. Gui.	8·25 S	151·45 E
164	Trogir (trô'gēr)...........Yugo.	43·32 N	16·17 E
91	Trois-Rivières (trwä'rê-vyâr') Can.	46·21 N	72·35 W
174	Troitsk (trô'êtsk) Sov. Un. (Urals In.)	54·06 N	61·34 E
172	Troitsko-Pechorsk (trô'ĭtsk-ô-pyĕ-chôrsk').Sov. Un.	62·18 N	56·07 E
167	Troitskoye...............Sov. Un.	47·39 N	30·16 E
156	Trollhättan (trôl'hĕt-ĕn).....Swe.	58·17 N	12·17 E
156	Trollheim (Mts.) (trôll-hĕĭm).Nor.	62·48 N	9·05 E
150	Tromsö (trôm'sû)...........Nor.	69·38 N	19·12 E
114	Trona (trō'nȧ) ....Ca.	35·49 N	117·20 W
136	Tronador, Cerro (Mtn.) (sĕ'r-rō trō-nä'dôr).Arg.	41·17 S	71·56 W
124	Troncoso (trôn-kô'sō).......Mex.	22·43 N	102·22 W
156	Trondheim (Nidaros) (trôn'hâm) (nē'dhä-rôs).Nor.	63·25 N	11·35 E
156	Trosa (trō'sä)...............Swe.	58·54 N	17·25 E
91	Trout (L.)..................Can.	51·16 N	92·46 W
90	Trout (L.)..................Can.	61·10 N	121·30 W
110	Trout Cr....................Or.	42·18 N	118·31 W
112	Troutdale (trout'dāl) Or. (Portland In.)	45·32 N	122·23 W
109	Trout Lake..................Mi.	46·20 N	85·02 W
95	Trout L....................Can.	51·13 N	93·20 W
160	Trouville (trōō-vēl')..........Fr.	49·23 N	0·05 E
120	Troy (troi)..................Al.	31·47 N	85·46 W
113	Troy..........Il. (St. Louis In.)	38·44 N	89·53 W
117	Troy........................Ks.	39·46 N	95·07 W
117	Troy.......................Mo.	38·56 N	99·57 W
110	Troy........................Mt.	48·28 N	115·56 W

ăt; finăl; rāte; senâte; ärm; ȧsk; sofȧ; fâre; ch-choose; dh-as th in other; bē; êvent; bĕt; recĕnt; cratēr; g-go; gh-guttural g; bĭt; ĭ-short neutral; rīde; к-guttural k as ch in German ich;

PRONOUNCING INDEX Troy — Tuxtepec 359

Page	Name Pronunciation Region	Lat. °′	Long. °′
105	Troy NY	42·45 N	73·45 N
121	Troy NC	35·21 N	79·58 W
104	Troy Oh.	40·00 N	84·10 W
165	Troy (Ruins) Tur.	39·59 N	26·14 E
160	Troyes (trwä) Fr.	48·18 N	4·03 E
	Trst, see Trieste		
165	Trstenik (t'r'stě-nêk) Yugo.	43·36 N	20·00 E
166	Trubchëvsk (trōōp'chĕfsk) Sov. Un.	52·36 N	32·46 E
	Trucial States, see United Arab Emirates		
114	Truckee (trŭk'ė) Ca.	39·20 N	120·12 W
114	Truckee (R.) Ca.-Nv.	39·25 N	120·07 W
202	Truganina. Austl. (Melbourne In.)	37·49 N	144·44 E
134	Trujillo (trōō-kĕ'l-yō) Col. (In.)	4·10 N	76·20 W
126	Trujillo (trōō-kĕl'yō) Hond.	15·55 N	85·58 W
134	Trujillo Peru	8·08 S	79·00 W
162	Trujillo (trōō-kĕ'l-yô) Sp.	39·27 N	5·50 W
134	Trujillo Ven.	9·15 N	70·28 W
124	Trujillo (R.) Mex.	23·12 N	103·10 W
129	Trujin, L. (trōō-kēn') Dom. Rep.	17·45 N	71·25 W
117	Trumann (trōō'măn) Ar.	35·41 N	90·31 W
165	Trŭn (trŭn) Bul.	42·49 N	22·39 E
98	Truro (trōō'rō) Can.	45·22 N	63·16 W
154	Truro Eng.	50·17 N	5·05 W
106	Trussville (trŭs'vĭl) Al. (Birmingham In.)	33·37 N	86·37 W
115	Truth or Consequences (trōōth ŏr kŏn'sė-kwĕn-sĭs) NM	33·10 N	107·20 W
158	Trutnov (trōōt'nôf) Czech.	50·36 N	15·36 E
158	Trzcianka (tchyän'kȧ) Pol.	53·02 N	16·27 E
158	Trzebiatow (tchĕ-byä'tōō-v) Pol.	54·03 N	15·16 E
188	Tsaidam Basin (tsī-däm) China	37·19 N	94·08 E
121	Tsala Apopka (R.) (tsä'lȧ ă-pŏp'kȧ) Fl.	28·57 N	82·11 W
188	Tsast Bogda Ula (Mt.) Mong.	46·44 N	92·34 E
217	Tsavo Natl. Pk. Ken.	2·35 S	38·45 E
112	Tsawwassen Ind. Res. Can. (Vancouver In.)	49·03 N	123·11 W
172	Tselinograd (tsĕ'lē-nô-grä'd) Sov. Un.	51·10 N	71·43 E
174	Tsentral'nyy-Kospashskiy (tsĕn-träl'nyĭ-kôs-pȧsh'skĭ) Sov. Un. (Urals In.)	59·03 N	57·48 E
216	Tshela (tshā'lȧ) Zaire	4·59 S	12·56 E
216	Tshikapa (tshê-kä'pä) Zaire	6·25 S	20·48 E
216	Tshofa Zaire	5·14 S	25·15 E
216	Tshuapa (R.) Zaire	10·15 S	21·25 E
213	Tsiafajovona (Mtn.) Mad.	19·17 S	47·27 E
171	Tsimlyanskiy (Res.) (tsym-lyă'ns-kēė) Sov. Un.	47·50 N	43·40 E
213	Tsiribihina (R.) (tsē'rê-bē-hê-nä') Mad.	19·45 S	43·30 E
213	Tsitsa (R.) (tsê'tsȧ) S. Afr. (Natal In.)	31·28 S	28·53 E
192	Tsitsihar (Qiqihar) (chyē-chyē-har) China	47·18 N	124·00 E
213	Tsolo (tsō'lō) S. Afr. (Natal In.)	31·19 S	28·47 E
213	Tsomo S. Afr. (Natal In.)	32·03 S	27·49 E
213	Tsomo (R.) S. Afr. (Natal In.)	31·53 S	27·48 E
195	Tsu (tsōō) Jap.	34·42 N	136·31 E
195	Tsuchiura (tsōō'chê-ōō-rä) Jap.	36·04 N	140·09 E
195	Tsuda (tsōō'dä) Jap. (Ōsaka In.)	34·48 N	135·43 E
194	Tsugaru Kaikyō (str.) (tsōō'gä-rōō kī'kyō) Jap.	41·25 N	140·20 E
212	Tsumeb (tsōō'mĕb) Namibia	19·10 S	17·45 E
195	Tsunashima (tsōō'nä-shê'mä) Jap. (Tōkyō In.)	35·32 N	139·37 E
195	Tsuruga (tsōō'rōō-gä) Jap.	35·39 N	136·04 E
195	Tsurugi San (Mtn.) (tsōō'rōō-gê sän) Jap.	33·52 N	134·07 E
194	Tsuruoka (tsōō'rōō-ō'kä) Jap.	38·43 N	139·51 E
195	Tsurusaki (tsōō'rōō-sä'kê) Jap.	33·15 N	131·42 E
195	Tsu Shima (I.) (tsōō shê'mä) Jap.	34·28 N	129·30 E
195	Tsushima Kaikyō (Str.) (tsōō'shê-mä kī'kyō) Asia	33·52 N	129·30 E
195	Tsuwano (tsōō'wȧ-nō') Jap.	34·28 N	131·47 E
195	Tsuyama (tsōō'yä-mä') Jap.	35·05 N	134·00 E
162	Tua (R.) (tōō'ä) Port.	41·23 N	7·18 W
112	Tualatin (R.) (tōō'ȧ-lā-tĭn) Or. (Portland In.)	45·25 N	122·54 W
199	Tuamotu (Low), Arch. (tōō-ä-mō'tōō) Fr. Polynesia	19·00 S	141·20 W
171	Tuapse (tōō'äp-sĕ) Sov. Un.	44·00 N	39·10 E
210	Tuareg (Reg.) Alg.	21·26 N	2·51 E
136	Tubarão (tōō-bä-rouN') Braz.	28·23 S	48·56 W
158	Tübingen (tü'bĭng-ĕn) F.R.G.	48·33 N	9·05 E
174	Tubinskiy (tû bĭn'skĭ) Sov. Un. (Urals In.)	52·53 N	58·15 E
211	Tubruq Libya	32·03 N	24·04 E
135	Tucacas (tōō-kä'käs) Ven. (In.)	10·48 N	68·20 W
106	Tucker (tŭk'ẽr) Ga. (Atlanta In.)	33·51 N	84·13 W
115	Tucson (tōō-sŏn') Az.	32·15 N	111·00 W
136	Tucumán (tōō-kōō-män') Arg.	26·52 S	65·08 W
136	Tucumán (Prov.) Arg.	26·30 S	65·30 W
116	Tucumcari (tōō'kŭm-kâr-ė) NM	35·11 N	103·43 W
134	Tucupita (tōō-kōō-pê'tä) Ven.	9·00 N	62·09 W
135	Tucuruí (tōō-kōō-tōō-ē') Braz.	3·34 S	49·44 W
162	Tudela (tōō-dhā'lä) Sp.	42·03 N	1·37 W
120	Tugaloo (R.) (tŭg'ȧ-lōō) Ga.-SC	34·35 N	83·05 W
213	Tugela (R.) (tōō-gel'ȧ) S. Afr. (Natal In.)	28·50 S	30·52 E
213	Tugela Ferry S. Afr. (Natal In.)	28·44 S	30·27 E
104	Tug Fork (R.) (tŭg) WV	37·50 N	82·30 W
197	Tuguegarao (tōō-gā-gȧ-rä'ō) Phil. (In.)	17·37 N	121·44 E
190	Tuhai (R.) (tōō-hī) China	37·05 N	116·56 E
218	Tuinplaas S. Afr. (Johannesburg & Pretoria In.)	24·54 S	28·46 E
113	Tujunga (tōō-jŭŋ'gȧ) Ca. (Los Angeles In.)	34·15 N	118·16 W
174	Tukan (tōō'kȧn) Sov. Un. (Urals In.)	53·52 N	57·25 E
197	Tukangbesi, Kepulauan (Is.) Indon.	6·00 S	124·15 E
211	Tūkrah Libya	32·34 N	20·47 E
90	Tuktoyaktuk (tōōk-tō-yäk'tōōk) Can.	69·32 N	132·37 W
170	Tukum (tōō'kōōm) Sov. Un.	57·00 N	22·50 E
157	Tukums (tōō'kōōms) Sov. Un.	56·57 N	23·09 E
212	Tukuyu (tōō-kōō'yȧ) Tan.	9·13 S	33·43 E
112	Tukwila (tŭk'wĭ-lȧ) Wa. (Seattle In.)	47·28 N	122·16 W
124	Tula (tōō'lä) Mex.	20·04 N	99·22 W
166	Tula (tōō'lȧ) Sov. Un.	54·12 N	37·37 E
166	Tula (Oblast) Sov. Un.	53·45 N	37·19 E
124	Tula (R.) (tōō'lä) Mex.	20·40 N	99·27 W
205	Tulagi (I.) (tōō-lä'gē) Sol. Is.	9·15 S	160·17 E
112	Tulalip (tū-lă'lĭp) Wa. (Seattle In.)	48·04 N	122·18 W
112	Tulalip Ind. Res. Wa. (Seattle In.)	48·06 N	122·16 W
124	Tulancingo (tōō-län-sĭŋ'gō) Mex.	20·04 N	98·24 W
196	Tulangbawang (R.) Indon.	4·17 S	105·00 E
114	Tulare (tōō-lä'rȧ) (tul-âr') Ca.	36·12 N	119·22 W
114	Tulare Basin Ca.	35·57 N	120·18 W
115	Tularosa (tōō-lȧ-rō'zȧ) NM	33·05 N	106·05 W
134	Tulcán (tōōl-kän') Ec.	0·44 N	77·52 W
167	Tulcea (tōōl'chȧ) Rom.	45·10 N	28·47 E
167	Tul'chin (tōōl'chĕn) Sov. Un.	48·42 N	28·53 E
124	Tulcingo (tōōl-sĭŋ'gō) Mex.	18·03 N	98·27 W
114	Tule (R.) (tōō'lä) Ca.	36·08 N	118·50 W
213	Tuléar (tōō-lā-är') Mad.	20·16 S	43·44 E
114	Tule River Ind. Res. (tōō'lȧ) Ca.	36·05 N	118·35 W
212	Tuli (tōō'lê) Zimb.	20·58 S	29·12 E
116	Tulia (tōō'lĭ-ȧ) Tx.	34·32 N	101·46 W
125	Tulijá (R.) (tōō-lē-Kä') Mex.	17·28 N	92·11 W
101	Tulik Vol. (tōō'lĭk) Ak.	53·28 N	168·10 W
183	Tūlkarm (tōōl kärm) Jordan (Palestine In.)	32·19 N	35·02 E
120	Tullahoma (tŭl-ȧ-hō'mȧ) Tn.	35·21 N	86·12 W
154	Tullamore (tŭl-ȧ-mōr') Ire.	53·15 N	7·29 W
160	Tulle (tül) Fr.	45·15 N	1·45 E
149	Tulln (tōōln) Aus. (Vienna In.)	48·21 N	16·04 E
149	Tullner Feld (Reg.) Aus. (Vienna In.)	48·20 N	15·59 E
125	Tulpetlac (tōōl-pȧ-tläk') Mex. (Mexico City In.)	19·33 N	99·04 W
117	Tulsa (tŭl'sȧ) Ok.	36·08 N	95·58 W
134	Tuluá (tōō-lōō-ȧ') Col. (In.)	4·06 N	76·12 W
126	Tulum (tōō-lōō'm) Mex. (In.)	20·17 N	87·26 W
172	Tulun (tōō-lōōn') Sov. Un.	54·29 N	100·43 E
115	Tumacacori Natl. Mon. (tōō-mä-kä'kȧ-rē) Az.	31·36 N	110·20 W
134	Tumaco (tōō-mä'kô) Col.	1·41 N	78·44 W
126	Tuma R. (tōō'mä) Nic.	13·07 N	85·32 W
216	Tumba, Lac (L.) (tōōm'bä) Zaire	0·50 S	17·45 E
134	Tumbes (tōō'm-bĕs) Peru	3·39 S	80·27 W
124	Tumbiscatío (tōōm-bê-skȧ-tē'ō) Mex.	18·32 N	102·23 W
112	Tumbo (I.) Can. (Vancouver In.)	48·49 N	123·04 W
192	Tumen (tōō-mŭn) China	43·00 N	129·50 E
194	Tumen (R.) China	42·08 N	128·40 E
135	Tumeremo (tōō-mȧ-rā'mō) Ven.	7·15 N	61·28 W
185	Tumkūr India	13·22 N	77·05 E
135	Tumuc-Humac Mts. (tōō-mōōk'ōō-mäk') S. A.	2·15 N	54·50 W
128	Tunas de Zaza (tōō'näs dā zä'zä) Cuba	21·40 N	79·35 W
154	Tunbridge Wells (tŭn'brĭj welz') Eng.	51·05 N	0·09 E
172	Tundra (Reg.) Sov. Un.	70·45 N	84·00 E
217	Tunduru Tan.	11·07 S	37·21 E
184	Tungabhadra Res. India	15·26 N	75·57 E
190	Tungpa (tōōng-bä) China	35·56 N	116·19 E
185	Tuni India	17·29 N	82·38 E
120	Tunica (tū'nĭ-kȧ) Ms.	34·41 N	90·23 W
210	Tunis (tū'nĭs) Tun.	36·59 N	10·06 E
151	Tunis, Golfe de (G.) Tun.	37·06 N	10·43 E
209	Tunisia (tu-nĭzh'ê-ȧ) Afr.	35·00 N	10·11 E
134	Tunja (tōō'n-hȧ) Col.	5·32 N	73·19 W
105	Tunkhannock (tŭnk-hăn'ŭk) Pa.	41·35 N	75·55 W
112	Tunnel (R.) (tŭn'ĕl) Wa. (Seattle In.)	47·48 N	123·04 W
190	Tuoji Dao (I.) (twô-jyē dou) China	38·11 N	120·45 E
114	Tuolumne (R.) (twô-lŭm'nê) Ca.	37·35 N	120·37 W
173	Tuostakh (R.) Sov. Un.	67·09 N	137·30 E
135	Tupã (tōō-pȧ) Braz.	21·47 S	50·33 W
120	Tupelo (tū'pê-lō) Ms.	34·14 N	88·43 W
135	Tupinambaranas, Ilha (I.) (ē'lä-tōō-pē-näN-bä-rä'näs) Braz.	3·04 S	58·09 W
134	Tupiza (tōō-pē'zä) Bol.	21·26 S	65·43 W
105	Tupper Lake (tŭp'ẽr) NY	44·15 N	74·25 W
134	Tuquerres (tōō-kĕ'r-rĕs) Col.	1·12 N	77·44 W
172	Tura (tōōr'ȧ) Sov. Un.	64·08 N	99·58 E
141	Tura (R.) Sov. Un.	57·15 N	64·23 E
124	Turbio (R.) (tōōr-byô) Mex.	20·28 N	101·40 W
134	Turbo (tōō'bō) Col.	8·02 N	76·43 W
159	Turciansky Sväty Martin (tōōr'chyȧn-skû'svă'tû' mär'tyĕn) Czech.	49·02 N	18·48 E
159	Turda (tōōr'dȧ) Rom.	46·35 N	23·47 E
	Turfan, see T'ulufan		
188	Turfan Depression China	42·16 N	90·00 E
213	Turffontein (Neigh.) S. Afr. (Johannesburg & Pretoria In.)	26·15 S	28·03 E
172	Turgay (tōōr'gī) Sov. Un.	49·42 N	63·39 E
147	Turgayka (R.) (tōōr-gī'kă) Sov. Un.	49·44 N	66·15 E
165	Tŭrgovishte Bul.	43·14 N	26·36 E
171	Turgutlu Tur.	38·30 N	27·20 E
157	Türi (tü'rĭ) Sov. Un.	58.49 N	25·29 E
162	Turia (R.) (tōō'ryä) Sp.	40·12 N	1·18 W
124	Turicato (tōō-rê-kä'tō) Mex.	19·03 N	101·24 W
128	Turiguano (I.) (tōō-rê-gwä'nō) Cuba	22·20 N	78·35 W
	Turin, see Torino		
159	Turka (tōōr'kȧ) Sov. Un.	49·10 N	23·02 E
172	Turkestan (tûr-kĕ-stăn') (tōōr-kĕ-stan') Sov. Un.	42·40 N	65·00 E
168	Turkestan (Reg.) Sov. Un.	43·27 N	62·14 E
182	Turkey Eur.-Asia	38·45 N	32·00 E
109	Turkey (R.) (tûrk'ė) Ia.	43·20 N	92·16 W
168	Turkmen (S. S. R.) (tōōrk-mĕn') Sov. Un.	40·46 N	56·01 E
129	Turks I. Pass. Turks & Caicos Is.	21·15 N	71·25 W
123	Turks (Is.) (tûrks) Turks & Caicos Is.	21·40 N	71·45 W
157	Turku (Åbo) (tōōr'kōō) (ô'bô) Fin.	60·28 N	22·12 E
114	Turlock (tûr'lŏk) Ca.	37·30 N	120·51 W
126	Turneffe (I.) (tûr-nĕf'fê) Belize (In.)	17·25 N	87·43 W
113	Turner (tûr'nẽr) Ks. (Kansas City In.)	39·05 N	94·42 W
128	Turner Sd. Ba.	24·20 N	78·05 W
214	Turners Pen. S.L.	7·20 N	12·40 W
149	Turnhout (tŭrn-hout') Bel. (Brussels In.)	51·19 N	4·58 E
158	Turnov (tōōr'nôf) Czech.	50·36 N	15·12 E
165	Turnu Măgurele (tōōr'nōō mŭ-gōō-rĕ'ly') Rom.	43·54 N	24·49 E
165	Turnu-Severin (sĕ-vĕ-rēn') Rom.	44·37 N	22·38 E
188	Turpan (tōō-är-pän) China	43·06 N	88·41 E
128	Turquino, Pico de (Pk.) (pē'kō dā tōōr-kē'nō) Cuba	20·00 N	76·50 W
127	Turrialba (tōōr-ryä'l-bä) C. R.	9·54 N	83·41 W
165	Turski Trstenik Bul.	43·26 N	24·50 E
147	Turtkul' (tōōrt-kōōl') Sov. Un.	41·28 N	61·02 E
95	Turtle (R.) Can.	49·20 N	92·30 W
119	Turtle B. Tx. (In.)	29·48 N	94·38 W
108	Turtle Cr. SD	44·40 N	98·53 W
108	Turtle Mountain Ind. Res. ND	48·45 N	99·57 W
108	Turtle Mts. ND	48·57 N	100·11 W
172	Turukhansk (tōō-rōō-känsk') Sov. Un.	66·03 N	88·39 E
159	Turya R. (tōōr'yȧ) Sov. Un.	51·18 N	24·55 E
120	Tuscaloosa (tŭs-kȧ-lōō'sȧ) Al.	33·10 N	87·35 W
110	Tuscarora (tŭs-kȧ-rō'rȧ) Nv.	41·18 N	116·15 W
107	Tuscarora Ind. Res. NY (Buffalo In.)	43·10 N	78·51 W
104	Tuscola (tŭs-kō-lȧ) Il.	39·50 N	88·20 W
120	Tuscumbia (tŭs-kŭm'bĭ-ȧ) Al.	34·41 N	87·42 W
174	Tushino (tōō'shĭ-nô) Sov. Un. (Moscow In.)	55·51 N	37·24 E
120	Tuskegee (tŭs-kē'gē) Al.	32·25 N	85·40 W
113	Tustin (tŭs'tĭn) Ca. (Los Angeles In.)	33·44 N	117·49 W
166	Tutayev (tōō-tȧ-yĕf') Sov. Un.	57·53 N	39·34 E
148	Tutbury (tŭt'bẽr-ė) Eng.	52·52 N	1·51 W
185	Tuticorin (tōō-tê-kô-rĭn') India	8·51 N	78·09 E
125	Tutitlan (tōō-tē-tlä'n) Mex. (In.)	19·38 N	99·10 W
135	Tutóia (tōō-tō'yȧ) Braz.	2·42 S	42·21 W
165	Tutrakan Bul.	44·02 N	26·36 E
117	Tuttle Creek Res. Ks.	39·30 N	96·38 W
158	Tuttlingen (tōōt'lĭng-ĕn) F.R.G.	47·58 N	8·50 E
120	Tutwiler (tŭt'wĭ-lẽr) Ms.	34·01 N	90·25 W
172	Tuva Aut. Oblast Sov. Un.	51·15 N	90·45 E
198	Tuvalu Oceania	5·20 S	174·00 E
186	Tuwayq, Jabal (Mts.) Sau. Ar.	20·45 N	46·30 E
106	Tuxedo Park (tŭk-sē'dō pärk) NY (New York In.)	41·11 N	74·11 W
148	Tuxford (tŭks'fẽrd) Eng.	53·14 N	0·54 W
124	Tuxpan (tōōs'pän) Mex.	19·34 N	103·22 W
125	Túxpan Mex.	20·57 N	97·26 W
125	Túxpan (R.) (tōōs'pän) Mex.	20·55 N	97·52 W
125	Túxpan, Arrecife (Rf.) (är-rē-sē'fē-tōō'x-pä'n) Mex.	21·01 N	97·12 W
125	Tuxtepec (tōōs-tȧ-pĕk') Mex.	18·06 N	96·09 W

Page	Name Pronunciation Region	Lat. °′	Long. °′
125	Tuxtla Gutiérrez (tōōs'tlä gōō-tyâr'rĕs) . Mex.	16·44 N	93·08 W
150	Tuy . Sp.	42·07 N	8·49 W
135	Tuy (tōō'ē) (R.) . Ven. (In.)	10·15 N	66·03 W
127	Tuyra R. (tōō-ē'rȧ) . Pan.	7·55 N	77·37 W
171	Tuz Gölü (L.) . Tur.	39·00 N	33·30 E
115	Tuzigoot Natl. Mon. . Az.	34·40 N	111·52 W
165	Tuzla (tōōz'lȧ) . Yugo.	44·33 N	18·46 E
156	Tvedestrand (tvĭ'dhĕ-stränd) . Nor.	58·39 N	8·54 E
156	Tveitsund (tvāt'sōōnd) . Nor.	59·03 N	8·29 E
	Tver, see Kalinin		
146	Tvertsa (L.) (tvĕr'tsȧ) . Sov. Un.	56·58 N	35·22 E
154	Tweed (R.) (twēd) . Scot.	55·32 N	2·35 W
218	Tweeling (twē'lĭng) . S. Afr. (Johannesburg & Pretoria In.)	27·34 S	28·31 E
107	Twelvemile Cr. (twĕlv'mīl) NY (Buffalo In.)	43·13 N	78·58 W
89	Twenty Mile Cr. (twĕn'tĭ mīl) Can. (Toronto In.)	43·09 N	79·49 W
148	Twickenham (twĭk''n-ǎm) Eng. (London In.)	51·26 N	0·20 W
99	Twillingate (twĭl'ĭn-gāt) . Can.	49·39 N	54·46 W
111	Twin Bridges (twĭn brĭ-jĕz) . Mt.	45·34 N	112·17 W
111	Twin Falls (fôls) . Id.	42·33 N	114·29 W
107	Twinsburg (twĭnz'bŭrg) Oh. (Cleveland In.)	41·19 N	81·26 W
114	Twitchell Res. . Ca.	34·50 N	120·10 W
116	Two Butte Cr. (tōō būt) . Co.	37·39 N	102·45 W
109	Two Harbors . Mn.	47·00 N	91·42 W
117	Two Prairie Bay (prā'rĭ bī ōō') . Ar.	34·48 N	92·07 W
109	Two Rivers (rĭv'ērz) . Wi.	44·09 N	87·36 W
202	Tyabb . Austl. (Melbourne In.)	38·16 S	145·11 E
159	Tyachev (tyä'chĕf) . Sov. Un.	48·01 N	23·42 E
167	Tyasmin (R.) (tyȧs-mĭn') . Sov. Un.	49·14 N	32·23 E
213	Tylden (tĭl-dĕn) S. Afr. (Natal In.)	32·08 S	27·06 E
148	Tyldesley (tĭldz'lē) . Eng.	53·32 N	2·28 W
108	Tyler (tī'lēr) . Mn.	44·18 N	96·08 W
119	Tyler . Tx.	32·21 N	95·19 W
120	Tylertown (tī'lēr-toun) . Ms.	31·08 N	90·06 W
108	Tyndall (tĭn'dȧl) . SD	42·58 N	97·52 W
173	Tyndinskiy . Sov. Un.	55·22 N	124·45 E
154	Tyne (R.) (tīn) . Eng.	54·59 N	1·56 W
154	Tynemouth (tīn'mŭth) . Eng.	55·04 N	1·39 W
156	Tynest (tün'sĕt) . Nor.	62·17 N	10·45 E
99	Tyngsboro (tĭnj-bûr'ō) . Ma. (In.)	42·40 N	71·27 W
	Tyre, see Şūr		
156	Tyri Fd. (tü'rē) . Nor.	60·03 N	10·25 E
115	Tyrone (tī'rōn) . NM	32·40 N	108·20 W
105	Tyrone . Pa.	40·40 N	78·15 W
203	Tyrrell, L. (tĭr'ĕll) . Austl.	35·12 S	143·00 E
151	Tyrrhenian Sea (tĭr-rē'nĭ-ǎn) . It.	40·10 N	12·15 E
157	Tyrvää (tür'vȧ) . Fin.	61·19 N	22·51 E
171	Tyub-Karagan, Mys (C.) . Sov. Un.	44·30 N	50·10 E
172	Tyukalinsk (tyōō-kȧ-lĭnsk') Sov. Un.	56·03 N	71·43 E
173	Tyukyan (R.) (tyōōk'yȧn) Sov. Un.	65·42 N	116·09 E
171	Tyuleniy (I.) . Sov. Un.	44·30 N	48·00 E
172	Tyumen' (tyōō-mĕn') . Sov. Un.	57·02 N	65·28 E
172	Tyura-Tam . Sov. Un.	46·00 N	63·15 E
126	Tzucacab (tzōō-kä-kä'b) Mex. (In.)	20·06 N	89·03 W

U

Page	Name Pronunciation Region	Lat. °′	Long. °′
152	Uarc, Ras (C.) . Mor.	35·31 N	2·45 W
134	Uaupés (wä-ōō'pās) . Braz.	0·02 S	67·03 W
137	Ubá (ōō-bȧ') Braz. (Rio de Janeiro In.)	21·08 S	42·55 W
216	Ubangi (Oubangui) (R.) (ōō-bäŋ'gē) . Afr.	4·30 N	20·35 E
137	Ubatuba (ōō-bȧ-tōō'bȧ) Braz. (Rio de Janeiro In.)	23·25 S	45·06 W
162	Ubeda (ōō'bȧ-dä) . Sp.	38·01 N	3·23 W
135	Uberaba (ōō-bȧ-rä'bȧ) . Braz.	19·47 S	47·47 W
135	Uberlândia (ōō-bĕr-lȧ'n-dyä) Braz.	18·54 S	48·11 W
212	Ubombo (ōō-bôm'bô) . S. Afr.	27·33 S	32·13 E
196	Ubon Ratchathani (ōō'bŭn rä'chätá-nē) . Thai.	15·15 N	104·52 E
167	Ubort' (R.) (ōō-bôrt') . Sov. Un.	51·18 N	27·43 E
162	Ubrique (ōō-brē'kȧ) . Sp.	36·43 N	5·36 W
188	Ubsa Nuur (L.) . Mong.	50·29 N	93·32 E
217	Ubundi (Ponthierville) . Zaire	00·21 S	25·29 E
134	Ucayali (R.) (ōō'kä-yä'lē) . Peru	8·58 S	74·13 W
149	Uccle (ü'kl') . Bel. (Brussels In.)	50·48 N	4·17 E
174	Uchaly (û-chä'lĭ) Sov. Un. (Urals In.)	54·22 N	59·28 E
172	Uch-Aral (ōōch'ȧ-ral') . Sov. Un.	46·14 N	80·58 E
195	Uchiko (ōō'chê-kō) . Jap.	33·30 N	132·39 E
195	Uchinoura (ōō'chê-nô-ōō'rȧ) Jap.	31·16 N	131·03 E
174	Uchinskoye Vodokhranilishche L. (ōōch-ēn'skô-yĕ vô-dô-ᴋrȧ-nĭ'lĭ-shchĕ) Sov. Un. (Moscow In.)	56·08 N	37·44 E
194	Uchiura-Wan (B.) (ōō'chê-ōō'rä wän) . Jap.	42·20 N	140·44 E
173	Uchur (R.) (ōō-chōōr') . Sov. Un.	58·27 N	131·34 E
173	Uda (R.) (ōō'dȧ) . Sov. Un.	52·28 N	110·51 E
173	Uda (R.) . Sov. Un.	53·54 N	131·29 E
184	Udaipur (ōō-dŭ'ē-pōōr) . India	24·41 N	73·41 E
167	Uday (R.) (ōō-dī') . Sov. Un.	50·45 N	32·13 E
156	Uddevalla (ōōd'dĕ-väl-ȧ) . Swe.	58·21 N	11·55 E
164	Udine (ōō'dē-nȧ) . It.	46·05 N	13·14 E
172	Udmurt (A. S. S. R.) . Sov. Un.	57·00 N	53·00 E
196	Udon Thani . Thai.	17·31 N	102·51 E
135	Udskaya Guba (B.) . Sov. Un.	55·00 N	136·30 E
195	Ueda (wä'dä) . Jap.	36·26 N	138·16 E
158	Uekermünde (ü'kĕr-mün-dĕ) G.D.R.	53·43 N	14·01 E
216	Uele R. (wā'lȧ) . Zaire	3·55 N	23·30 E
174	Ufa (ōō'fa) . Sov. Un. (Urals In.)	54·45 N	55·57 E
170	Ufa (R.) . Sov. Un.	56·00 N	57·05 E
212	Ugab (R.) (ōō'gäb) . Namibia	21·10 S	14·00 E
217	Ugalla (R.) (ōō-gä'lä) . Tan.	6·15 S	32·30 E
209	Uganda (ōō-gän'dä) (û-găn'dȧ) . Afr.	2·00 N	32·28 E
101	Ugashik L. (ōō'gȧ-shêk) . Ak.	57·36 N	157·10 W
213	Ugie (ōō'jē) . S. Afr. (Natal In.)	31·13 S	28·14 E
173	Uglegorsk (ōō-glĕ-gôrsk) . Sov. Un.	49·00 N	142·31 E
174	Ugleural'sk (ōōg-lĕ-ōō-rálsk') Sov. Un. (Urals In.)	58·58 N	57·35 E
166	Uglich (ōōg-lêch') . Sov. Un.	57·33 N	38·19 E
174	Uglitskiy (ōōg-lĭt'skĭ) Sov. Un. (Urals In.)	53·50 N	60·18 E
166	Uglovka (ōōg-lôf'kȧ) . Sov. Un.	58·14 N	33·24 E
166	Ugra (R.) (ōōg'rȧ) . Sov. Un.	54·43 N	34·20 E
165	Ugŭrchin . Bul.	43·06 N	24·23 E
104	Uhrichsville (ū'rĭks-vĭl) . Oh.	40·25 N	81·20 W
216	Uíge . Ang.	7·37 S	15·03 E
194	Uiju (ōō'êjōō) . Kor.	40·09 N	124·33 E
171	Uil (R.) (ōō-ēl') . Sov. Un.	49·30 N	55·10 E
115	Uinkaret Plat. (û-ĭn'kâr-ēt) . Az.	36·43 N	113·15 W
174	Uinskoye (ōō-ĭn'skô-yĕ) Sov. Un. (Urals In.)	56·53 N	56·25 E
115	Uinta (R.) (û-ĭn'tȧ) . Ut.	40·25 N	109·55 W
113	Uintah (û-ĭn'tȧ) Ut. (Salt Lake City In.)	41·09 N	111·56 W
115	Uintah and Ouray Ind. Res. . Ut.	39·55 N	109·20 W
218	Uitenhage . S. Afr. (Natal In.)	33·46 S	25·26 E
149	Uithoorn . Neth. (Amsterdam In.)	52·13 N	4·49 E
195	Uji (ōō'jē) . Jap. (Osaka In.)	34·53 N	135·49 E
217	Ujiji (ōō-jē'jē) . Tan.	4·55 S	29·41 E
184	Ujjain (ōō-jŭēn) . India	23·18 N	75·37 E
196	Ujung Pandang (Makasar) . Indon.	5·08 S	119·28 E
217	Ukerewe I. . Tan.	2·00 S	32·40 E
172	Ukhta . Sov. Un.	63·08 N	53·42 E
170	Ukhta (ōōk'tȧ) . Sov. Un.	65·22 N	31·30 E
114	Ukiah (ū-kī'ȧ) . Ca.	35·09 N	122·12 W
157	Ukmergė (ōōk'mĕr-ghâ) . Sov. Un.	55·16 N	24·45 E
168	Ukrainian (S. S. R.) (ū'krān) Sov. Un.	49·15 N	30·15 E
195	Uku (I.) (ōōk'ōō) . Jap.	33·18 N	129·02 E
188	Ulaan Baatar . Mong.	47·56 N	107·00 E
188	Ulaan Goom . Mong.	50·23 N	92·14 E
	Ulanhad, see Chifeng		
173	Ulan-Ude (ōō'län ōō'dȧ) . Sov. Un.	51·59 N	107·41 E
194	Ulchin (ōōl'chĕn') . Kor.	36·57 N	129·26 E
165	Ulcinj (Dulcigno) (ōōl'tsēn') Yugo.	41·56 N	19·15 E
185	Ulhās (R.) . India (In.)	19·13 N	73·03 E
185	Ulhāsnagar . India (Bombay In.)	19·10 N	73·07 E
216	Ulindi (R.) (ōō-lĭn'dē) . Zaire	1·55 S	26·17 E
166	Ulla (ōōl'ȧ) . Sov. Un.	55·14 N	29·15 E
166	Ulla (R.) . Sov. Un.	54·58 N	29·03 E
162	Ulla (R.) (ōō'lä) . Sp.	42·45 N	8·33 W
194	Ullŭng (I.) (ōōl'lōōng') . Kor.	37·29 N	130·50 E
158	Ulm (ōōlm) . F.R.G.	48·24 N	9·59 E
220	Ulmer, Mt. (ŭl'mûr') . Ant.	77·30 S	86·00 W
156	Ulricehamn (ōōl-rē'sĕ-häm) . Swe.	57·49 N	13·23 E
194	Ulsan (ōōl'sän') . Kor.	35·35 N	129·22 E
154	Ulster (Reg.) (ŭl'stēr) . Ire.-N. Ire.	54·41 N	7·10 W
126	Ulua R. (ōō-lōō'ȧ) . Hond.	15·49 N	87·45 W
184	Ulubāria . India (In.)	22·27 N	88·09 E
217	Uluguru Mts. . Tan.	7·15 S	37·30 E
171	Ulukışla (ōō-lōō-kēsh'lȧ) . Tur.	36·40 N	34·30 E
194	Ulunga (ōō-lōōn'gȧ) . Sov. Un.	46·16 N	136·29 E
188	Ulungur (R.) (ōō-lōōn-gûr) . China	46·31 N	149·00 E
174	Ulu-Telyak (ōō lōō'tĕlyǎk) Sov. Un. (Urals In.)	54·54 N	57·01 E
203	Ulverstone (ŭl'vēr-stǔn) . Austl.	41·20 S	146·22 E
156	Ulvik (ōōl'vêk) . Nor.	60·35 N	6·53 E
174	Ul'yanovka (ōō-lyä'nôf-kȧ) Sov. Un. (Leningrad In.)	59·38 N	30·47 E
170	Ul'yanovsk (ōō-lyä'nôfsk) Sov. Un.	54·20 N	48·05 E
116	Ulysses (ū-lĭs'ēz) . Ks.	37·34 N	101·25 W
158	Ülzen (ült'sĕn) . F.R.G.	52·58 N	10·34 E
125	Umán (ōō-män'') . Mex.	20·52 N	89·44 W
167	Uman' (ōō-mȧn') . Sov. Un.	48·44 N	30·13 E
110	Umatilla Ind. Res. (ū-mȧ-tĭl'ȧ) . Or.	45·38 N	118·35 W
185	Umberpāda . India (In.)	19·28 N	73·04 E
164	Umbria (Reg.) (ŭm'brĭ-ǎ) . It.	42·53 N	12·22 E
150	Ume (R.) (ōō'mĕ) . Swe.	64·57 N	18·51 E
150	Umeå (ōō'mĕ-ô) . Swe.	63·48 N	20·29 E
213	Umhlatuzi (R.) (ōōm'hlȧ-tōō'zĭ) S. Afr. (Natal In.)	28·47 S	31·17 E
101	Umiat (ōō'mĭ-ǎt) . Ak.	69·20 N	152·28 W
213	Umkomaas (ōōm-kō'mäs) S. Afr. (Natal In.)	30·12 S	30·48 E
211	Umm Durmān (Omdurman) (ŏm-dōōr-män') . Sud.	15·45 N	32·30 E
101	Umnak (I.) (ōōm'nȧk) . Ak.	53·10 N	169·08 W
101	Umnak P. . Ak.	53·10 N	168·04 W
212	Umniati (R.) . Zimb.	17·08 S	29·11 E
110	Umpqua R. (ŭmp'kwȧ) . Or.	43·42 N	123·50 W
212	Umtali (ōōm-tä'lē) . Zimb.	18·49 S	32·39 E
213	Umtata (ōōm-tä'tä) S. Afr. (Natal In.)	31·36 S	28·47 E
213	Umtentweni . S. Afr. (Natal In.)	30·41 S	30·29 E
213	Umzimkulu (ōōm-zēm-kōō'lōō) S. Afr. (Natal In.)	30·12 S	29·53 E
213	Umzinto (ōōm-zĭn'tô) S. Afr. (Natal In.)	30·19 S	30·41 E
164	Una (R.) (ōō'nȧ) . Yugo.	44·38 N	16·10 E
101	Unalakleet (ū-nȧ-lȧk'lēt) . Ak.	63·50 N	160·42 W
101	Unalaska (ū-nȧ-lȧs'kȧ) . Ak.	53·30 N	166·20 W
135	Unare (R.) . Ven. (In.)	9·45 N	65·12 W
135	Unare, Laguna de (L.) (lä-gōō'nä-de-ōō-nä'rĕ) Ven. (In.)	10·07 N	65·23 W
186	Unayzah . Sau. Ar.	25·50 N	44·02 E
89	Uncas (ŭŋ'kǎs) Can. (Edmonton In.)	53·30 N	113·02 W
134	Uncía (ōōn'sē-ä) . Bol.	18·28 S	66·32 W
115	Uncompahgre (R.) . Co.	38·20 N	107·45 W
115	Uncompahgre Pk. (ŭn-kŭm-pä'grē) . Co.	38·00 N	107·30 W
115	Uncompahgre Plat. . Co.	38·40 N	108·40 W
218	Underberg (ŭn'dēr-bûrg) S. Afr. (Natal In.)	29·51 S	29·32 E
211	Undo . Eth.	6·37 N	38·29 E
166	Unecha (ōō-nĕ'chȧ) . Sov. Un.	52·51 N	32·44 E
91	Ungava B. (ŭŋ-gȧ'vȧ) . Can.	59·46 N	67·18 W
91	Ungava, Péninsule d' (Pen.) . Can.	59·55 N	74·00 W
136	União da Vitória (ōō-nē-oun' dä vē-tō'ryä) . Braz.	26·17 S	51·13 W
164	Unije (I.) (ōō'nē-yĕ) . Yugo.	44·39 N	14·10 E
101	Unimak (I.) (ōō-nē-mȧk') . Ak.	54·30 N	163·35 W
101	Unimak P. . Ak.	54·22 N	165·22 W
120	Union (ūn'yŭn) . Ms.	32·35 N	89·07 W
117	Union . Mo.	38·28 N	90·59 W
121	Union . NC	34·42 N	81·40 W
110	Union . Or.	45·13 N	117·52 W
111	Union City . Ca. (San Francisco In.)	37·36 N	122·01 W
104	Union City . In.	40·10 N	85·00 W
104	Union City . Mi.	42·00 N	85·10 W
105	Union City . Pa.	41·50 N	79·50 W
120	Union City . Tn.	36·25 N	89·04 W
128	Union de Reves (ōō-nyō'n-dĕ-rĕ-vĕ's) . Cuba	22·45 N	81·30 W
124	Union de San Antonio (sän än-tō'nyō) . Mex.	21·07 N	101·56 W
124	Union de Tula (tōō'lä) . Mex.	19·57 N	104·14 W
107	Union Grove (ūn-yǔn grōv) Wi. (Milwaukee In.)	42·41 N	88·03 W
125	Unión Hidalgo (ê-dä'lgô) . Mex.	16·29 N	94·51 W
120	Union Point . Ga.	33·37 N	83·08 W
120	Union Springs (sprĭngz) . Al.	32·08 N	85·43 W
120	Uniontown (ūn'yǔn-toun) . Al.	32·26 N	87·30 W
107	Uniontown . Oh. (Cleveland In.)	40·58 N	81·25 W
105	Uniontown . Pa.	39·55 N	79·45 W
117	Unionville (ūn'yǔn-vĭl) . Mo.	40·28 N	92·58 W
197	Unisan (ōō-nē'sän) . Phil. (In.)	13·50 N	121·59 E
102	Unitas, Mts. (ū-nĭ'tǎs) . U. S.	40·35 N	111·00 W
182	United Arab Emirates . Asia	24·00 N	54·00 E
	United Arab Republic, see Egypt		
150	United Kingdom . Eur.	56·30 N	1·40 W
115	United Pueblo Ind. Res. (u-nĭt'ĕd pōō-ĕb'lō) (pwā'blō) NM	35·30 N	107·00 W
75	United States . N. A.	38·00 N	110·00 W
94	Unity . Can.	52·27 N	109·10 W
104	Universal (ū-nĭ-vûr'sǎl) . In.	39·35 N	87·30 W
162	Universales, Montes (Mts.) (mōn'tȧs ōō-nē-vĕr-sä'lȧs) . Sp.	40·21 N	1·43 W
113	University City (ū'nĭ-vûr'sĭ-tĭ) Mo. (St. Louis In.)	38·40 N	90·19 W
113	University Park Tx. (Dallas, Fort Worth In.)	32·51 N	96·48 W
161	Unna (ōō'nȧ) . F.R.G. (Ruhr In.)	51·32 N	7·41 E
154	Unst (I.) (ōōnst) . Scot.	60·50 N	1·24 W
149	Unterhaching (ōōn'tĕr-hä-ᴋĕng) F.R.G. (Munich In.)	48·03 N	11·38 E

ăt; finǎl; rāte; senāte; ärm; ȧsk; sofǎ; fâre; ch-choose; dh-as th in other; bē; ēvent; bĕt; recĕnt; cratēr; g-go; gh-guttural g; bĭt; ĭ-short neutral; rīde; ᴋ-guttural k as ch in German ich;

PRONOUNCING INDEX Unye — Vallenar 361

Page Name Pronunciation Region Lat. °' Long. °'

171 Unye (ün'yĕ)....Tur. 41·00 N 37·10 E
170 Unzha (R.) (ōōn'zhȧ)....Sov. Un. 57·45 N 44·10 E
166 Upa (R.) (ōō'pȧ)....Sov. Un. 53·54 N 36·48 E
209 Upanda, Sierra do (Mts.) (sē-ĕ'r-rä-dô-ōō-pä'n-dä).Ang. 13·15 S 14·15 E
134 Upata (ōō-pä'tä)....Ven. 7·58 N 62·27 W
217 Upemba, Parc Natl. de l' (Natl. Pk.).Zaire 9·10 S 26·15 E
212 Upington (ŭp'ĭng-tŭn)....S. Afr. 28·25 S 21·15 E
113 Upland (ŭp'lănd) Ca. (Los Angeles In.) 34·06 N 117·38 W
100 Upolu Pt. (ōō-pô'lōō)....Hi. 20·15 N 155·48 W
93 Upper Arrow L. (ăr'ō)....Can. 50·30 N 117·55 W
106 Upper Darby (där'bĭ) Pa. (Philadelphia In.) 39·58 N 75·16 W
108 Upper de Lacs (R.) (dē läk)...ND 48·58 N 101·55 W
196 Upper Kapuas Mts....Mala. 1·45 N 112·06 E
110 Upper L. (ŭp'ēr)....Nv. 41·42 N 119·59 W
106 Upper Marlboro (ûpēr mărl'bōrô) Md. (Baltimore In.) 38·49 N 76·46 W
112 Upper Mill (mĭl).Wa. (Seattle In.) 47·11 N 121·55 W
109 Upper Red L. (rĕd)....Mn. 48·14 N 94·53 W
104 Upper Sandusky (săn-dŭs'kē)..Oh. 40·50 N 83·20 W
112 Upper San Leandro Res. ŭp'ēr săn lē-ăn'drô) Ca. (San Francisco In.) 37·47 N 122·04 W
209 Upper Volta (vôl'tȧ)....Afr. 11·46 N 3·18 E
148 Uppingham (ŭp'ĭng-ăm)....Eng. 52·35 N 0·43 W
156 Uppsala (ōōp'sȧ-lä)....Swe. 59·53 N 17·39 E
99 Uptown (ŭp'toun)....Ma. (In.) 42·10 N 71·36 W
195 Uraga (ōō'rȧ-gȧ').Jap. (Tōkyō In.) 35·15 N 139·43 E
195 Uraga-Kaikyō (Str.) (ōō'rä-gä kī'kyō) Jap. (Tōkyō In.) 35·11 N 139·44 E
171 Ural (R.) (ŏŏ-räl'') (ū-rôl).Sov. Un. 49·50 N 51·30 E
168 Urals (Mts.)....Sov. Un. 56·28 N 58·13 E
171 Ural'sk (ōō-rȧlsk')....Sov. Un. 51·15 N 51·10 E
185 Uran (ōō-rän')....India (In.) 18·53 N 72·46 E
90 Uranium City....Can. 59·34 N 108·59 W
195 Urawa (ōō'rä-wä') Jap. (Tōkyō In.) 35·52 N 139·39 E
195 Urayasu (ōō'rä-yä'sōō) Jap. (Tōkyō In.) 35·40 N 139·54 W
167 Urazovo (ŏŏ-rȧ'zô-vô)....Sov. Un. 50·08 N 38·03 E
104 Urbana (ûr-băn'ȧ)....Il. 40·10 N 88·15 W
104 Urbana....Oh. 40·05 N 83·50 W
164 Urbino (ōōr-bē'nō)....It. 43·43 N 12·37 E
171 Urda (ōōr'dȧ)....Sov. Un. 48·50 N 47·30 E
197 Urdaneta (ōōr-dä-nā'tä).Phil. (In.) 15·59 N 120·34 E
137 Urdinarrain (ōōr-dē-när-rȧē'n) Arg. (Buenos Aires In.) 32·43 S 58·53 W
172 Urdzhar (ŏŏrd-zhär')....Sov. Un. 47·28 N 82·00 E
171 Urfa (ōōr'fȧ)....Tur. 37·20 N 38·45 E
147 Urgench (ŏŏr-gĕnch')....Sov. Un. 41·32 N 60·33 E
174 Uritsk (ōō'rĭtsk) Sov. Un. (Leningrad In.) 59·50 N 30·11 E
165 Urla (ōōr'lȧ)....Tur. 38·20 N 26·44 E
174 Urman (ōōr'mán) Sov. Un. (Urals In.) 54·53 N 56·52 E
194 Urmi (R.) (ŏŏr'mē)....Sov. Un. 48·50 N 134·00 E
215 Uromi....Nig. 6·44 N 6·18 E
134 Urrao (ōōr-rä'ô)....Col. (In.) 6·19 N 76·11 W
166 Urshel'skiy (ōōr-shĕl'skēē) Sov. Un. 55·50 N 40·11 E
134 Urubamba (R.) (ōō-rōō-bäm'bä) Peru 11·48 S 72·34 W
136 Uruguaiana (ōō-rōō-gwī-ä'nȧ) Braz. 29·45 S 57·00 W
133 Uruguay (ōō-rōō-gwī') (ū'rōō-gwā) S. A. 32·45 S 56·00 W
136 Uruguay, Rio (R.) (rē'ō-ŏŏ-rōō-gwī).Braz. 27·05 S 55·15 W
188 Ürümqi (ū-rûm-chyē)....China 43·49 N 87·43 E
173 Urup (I.) (ōō'rŏŏp')....Sov. Un. 46·08 N 149·00 E
171 Uryupinsk (ŏŏr'yŏŏ-pēn-sk') Sov. Un. 50·50 N 42·00 E
165 Urziceni (ŏŏ-zē-chĕn'')....Rom. 44·45 N 26·42 E
194 Usa....Jap. 33·31 N 131·22 E
170 Usa (R.) (ōō'sȧ)....Sov. Un. 66·00 N 58·20 E
171 Uşak (ōō'shȧk)....Tur. 39·50 N 29·15 E
212 Usakos (ōō-sä'kōs)....Namibia 22·00 S 15·40 E
174 Ushaki (ōō'shá-kĭ) Sov. Un. (Leningrad In.) 59·28 N 31·00 E
174 Ushakovskoye (ŏŏ-shá-kôv'skô-yĕ) Sov. Un. (Urals In.) 56·18 N 62·23 E
217 Usambara Mts....Tan. 4·40 S 38·25 E
217 Usangu Flats (Pln.)....Tan. 8·10 S 34·00 E
217 Ushashi....Tan. 2·00 S 33·57 E
195 Ushiku (ōō'shē-kōō) Jap. (Tōkyō In.) 35·24 N 140·09 E
195 Ushimado (ōō'shē-mä'dō)....Jap. 34·37 N 134·09 E
136 Ushuaia (ōō-shōō-ī'ä)....Arg. 54·46 S 68·24 W
171 Üsküdar....Tur. 40·55 N 29·00 E
166 Usman' (ōōs-mán')....Sov. Un. 52·03 N 39·40 E
174 Usol'ye (ŏŏ-sô'lyĕ) Sov. Un. (Urals In.) 59·24 N 56·40 E
172 Usol'ye-Sibirskoye (ŏŏ-sô'lyĕsĭ' bēr'skô-yĕ).Sov. Un. 52·44 N 103·46 E
136 Uspallata P. (ōōs-pä-lyä'tä) Arg.-Chile 32·47 S 70·08 W
125 Uspanapa (R.) (ōōs-pä-nä'pä) Mex. 17·43 N 94·14 W
160 Ussel (üs'ĕl)....Fr. 45·33 N 2·17 E
189 Ussuri (R.) (ōō-sōō'rē)....China 46·30 N 133·56 E
173 Ussuriysk....Sov. Un. 43·48 N 132·09 E
173 Ust'-Bol'sheretsk....Sov. Un. 52·41 N 157·00 E
164 Ustica, I. di (ē'sō-lä-dē-ōōs'tē-kä) It. 38·43 N 12·11 E
158 Ústí nad Labem (ōōs'tē)...Czech. 50·39 N 14·02 E
167 Ustinovka (ŏŏs-tē'nôf-kä).Sov. Un. 47·59 N 32·31 E
174 Ust'-Izhora (ŏŏst-ēz'hô-rȧ) Sov. Un. (Leningrad In.) 59·49 N 30·35 E
158 Ustka (ōōst'kȧ)....Pol. 54·34 N 16·52 E
173 Ust'-Kamchatsk....Sov. Un. 56·13 N 162·18 E
172 Ust'-Kamenogorsk....Sov. Un. 49·58 N 80·43 E
174 Ust'-Katav (ŏŏst kȧ'tȧf) Sov. Un. (Urals In.) 54·55 N 58·12 E
174 Ust'-Kishert' (ŏŏst kē'shĕrt) Sov. Un. (Urals In.) 57·21 N 57·13 E
170 Ust'-Kulom (kŏŏ'lŭn)....Sov. Un. 61·38 N 54·00 E
173 Ust'-Maya (mä'yȧ)....Sov. Un. 60·33 N 134·43 E
173 Ust' Olenëk....Sov. Un. 72·52 N 120·15 E
173 Ust-Ordynskiy (ŏŏst-ôr-dyĕnsk'ĭ) Sov. Un. 52·47 N 104·39 E
173 Ust' Penzhimo....Sov. Un. 63·00 N 165·10 E
172 Ust' Port (ŏŏst'pôrt')....Sov. Un. 69·20 N 83·41 E
170 Ust'-Tsil'ma (tsĭl'mȧ)....Sov. Un. 65·25 N 52·10 E
173 Ust'-Tyrma (tor'mȧ)....Sov. Un. 50·27 N 131·17 E
174 Ust'Uls (ŏŏls).Sov. Un. (Urals In.) 60·35 N 58·32 E
168 Ust'-Urt, Plato (Plat.) (ōōrt) Sov. Un. 44·03 N 54·58 E
166 Ustyuzhna (yōōzh'nȧ)...Sov. Un. 58·49 N 36·19 E
188 Usu (ū-sōō)....China 44·28 N 84·07 E
195 Usuki (ōō'sōō-kē')....Jap. 33·06 N 131·47 E
126 Usulutan (ōō-sōō-lä-tän')....Sal. 13·22 N 88·25 W
125 Usumacinta (R.) (ōō'sōō-mä-sēn'tō).Mex. 18·24 N 92·30 W
174 Us'va (ōōs'vȧ) Sov. Un. (Urals In.) 58·41 N 57·38 E
102 Utah (State) (ū'tô)....U. S. 39·25 N 112·40 W
115 Utah (L.)....Ut. 40·10 N 111·55 W
185 Utan....India (In.) 19·27 N 72·43 E
115 Ute Mtn. Ind. Res....NM 36·57 N 108·34 W
157 Utena (ōō'tā-nä)....Sov. Un. 55·32 N 25·40 E
213 Utete (ōō-tā'tȧ)....Tan. 8·05 S 38·47 E
107 Utica (ū'tĭ-kȧ)..In. (Louisville In.) 38·20 N 85·39 W
105 Utica....NY 43·05 N 75·10 W
162 Utiel (ōō-tyȧl')....Sp. 39·34 N 1·13 W
107 Utika (ū'tĭ-kȧ)...Mi. (Detroit In.) 42·37 N 83·02 W
95 Utik L....Can. 55·16 N 96·00 W
94 Utikuma L....Can. 55·50 N 115·25 W
126 Utila I. (ōō-tē'lä)....Hond. 16·07 N 87·05 W
195 Uto (ōō'tō')....Jap. 32·43 N 130·39 E
149 Utrecht (ü'trĕKt) (ū'trĕkt) Neth. (Amsterdam In.) 52·05 N 5·06 E
162 Utrera (ōō-trā'rä)....Sp. 37·12 N 5·48 W
156 Utsira (I.) (ütsĭrä)....Nor. 59·21 N 4·50 E
195 Utsunomiya (ōōt'sŏŏ-nô-mē-yȧ') Jap. 36·35 N 139·52 E
196 Uttaradit....Thai. 17·47 N 100·10 E
184 Uttarpara-Kotrung India (Calcutta In.) 22·40 N 88·21 E
184 Uttar Pradesh (State) (ŏŏt-tär-prä-dĕsh).India 27·00 N 80·00 E
148 Uttoxeter (ŭt-tôk'sē-tēr)....Eng. 52·54 N 1·52 W
123 Utuado (ōō-tōō-ä'dhō) P. R. (Puerto Rico In.) 18·16 N 66·40 W
157 Uusikaupunki (Nystad) (ōō'sĭ-kou'pŏŏŋ-kĭ) (nü'städh) Fin. 60·48 N 21·24 E
118 Uvalde (ū-văl'dē)....Tx. 29·14 N 99·47 W
174 Uvel'skiy (ŏŏ-vyĕl'skĭ) Sov. Un. (Urals In.) 54·27 N 60·22 E
217 Uvinza....Tan. 5·06 S 30·22 E
12 Uvira (ōō-vē'rä)....Zaire 3·28 S 29·03 E
166 Uvod' (R.) (ŏŏ-vôd')....Sov. Un. 56·52 N 41·03 E
213 Uvongo Beach..S. Afr. (Natal In.) 30·49 S 30·23 E
195 Uwajima (ōō-wä'jē-mä)....Jap. 33·12 N 132·35 E
99 Uxbridge (ŭks'brĭj)....Ma. (In.) 42·05 N 71·38 W
126 Uxmal (Ruins) (ōō'x-mä'l) Mex. (In.) 20·22 N 89·44 W
174 Uy R. (ōōy)..Sov. Un. (Urals In.) 54·05 N 62·11 E
174 Uyskoye (ûy'skô-yĕ) Sov. Un. (Urals In.) 54·22 N 60·01 E
134 Uyuni (ōō-yōō'nē)....Bol. 20·28 S 66·45 W
134 Uyuni, Salar de (Salt Flat) (sä-lär-dĕ).Bol. 20·58 S 67·09 W
168 Uzbek S. S. R. (ŏŏz-bĕk').Sov. Un. 42·42 N 60·00 E
171 Uzen, Bol'shoy (R.)....Sov. Un. 49·50 N 49·35 E
167 Uzh (R.) (ŏŏzh)....Sov. Un. 51·07 N 29·05 E
159 Uzhgorod (ōōzh'gō-rôt)..Sov. Un. 48·38 N 22·18 E
165 Uzunköpru (ōō'zōōn'kû-prü)..Tur. 41·17 N 26·42 E

V

212 Vaal (R.) (väl)....S. Afr. 28·15 S 24·30 E
218 Vaaldam (L.)....S. Afr. (Johannesburg & Pretoria In.) 26·58 S 28·37 E
218 Vaalplaas....S. Afr. (Johannesburg & Pretoria In.) 25·39 S 28·56 E
218 Vaalwater....S. Afr. (Johannesburg & Pretoria In.) 24·17 S 28·08 E
157 Vaasa (vä'sȧ)....Fin. 63·06 N 21·39 E
159 Vác (väts)....Hung. 47·46 N 19·10 E
129 Vache, Ila À (I.) (väsh)....Hai. 18·05 N 73·40 W
150 Vadsö (vädh'sû)....Nor. 70·08 N 29·52 E
156 Vadstena (väd'stĭ'nȧ)....Swe. 58·27 N 14·53 E
158 Vaduz (vä'dŏŏts)....Liech. 47·10 N 9·32 E
170 Vaga (R.) (va'gȧ)....Sov. Un. 61·55 N 42·30 E
156 Vågsöy (I.)....Nor. 61·58 N 4·44 E
159 Vah R. (väK)....Czech. 48·07 N 17·52 E
184 Vaigai (R.)....India 10·20 N 78·13 E
172 Vakh (R.) (vȧK)....Sov. Un. 61·30 N 81·33 E
165 Valachia (Reg.)....Rom. 44·45 N 24·17 E
89 Valcartier-Village (väl-kärt-yĕ' vē-läzh') Can. (Quebec In.) 46·56 N 71·28 W
166 Valdai Hills (vȧl-dī' gô'rĭ) Sov. Un. 57·50 N 32·35 E
166 Valday (Valdai) (vȧl-dī').Sov. Un. 57·58 N 33·13 E
162 Valdecañas Res....Sp. 39·15 N 5·30 W
157 Valdemārpils....Sov. Un. 57·22 N 22·34 E
163 Valdemorillo (väl-dā-mô-rēl'yō) Sp. (Madrid In.) 40·30 N 4·04 W
162 Valdepeñas (väl-dâ-pān'yäs)...Sp. 38·46 N 3·22 W
162 Valderaduey (R.) (väl-dĕ-rä-dwĕ'y).Sp. 41·39 N 5·35 W
136 Valdés, Pen. (vȧl-dĕ's)....Arg. 42·15 S 63·15 W
101 Valdez (văl'dĕz)....Ak. 61·10 N 146·18 W
163 Valdilecha (väl-dē-lā'chä) Sp. (Madrid In.) 40·17 N 3·19 W
136 Valdivia (väl-dē'vä)....Chile 39·47 S 73·13 W
134 Valdivia (väl-dē'vēä)....Col. (In.) 7·10 N 75·26 W
97 Val-d' Or....Can. 48·03 N 77·50 W
120 Valdosta (văl-dŏs'tȧ)....Ga. 30·50 N 83·18 W
162 Valdovino (väl-dô-vē'nō)....Sp. 43·36 N 8·05 W
110 Vale (vāl)....Or. 43·59 N 117·14 W
135 Valença (vä-lĕN'sȧ)....Braz. 13·43 S 38·58 W
160 Valence-sur-Rhône (vä-lĕNs-sür-rōn').Fr. 44·56 N 4·54 E
162 Valencia (vä-lĕ'n-syä)....Port. 42·03 N 8·36 W
163 Valencia (vä-lĕn'thē-ä)....Sp. 39·26 N 0·23 W
162 Valencia....Sp. 39·34 N 7·13 W
135 Valencia (vä-lĕn'syä)...Ven. (In.) 10·11 N 68·00 W
163 Valencia (Reg.) (vä-lĕn'thē-ä)..Sp. 39·08 N 0·43 W
154 Valencia (I.) (vȧ-lĕn'shȧ)....Ire. 51·55 N 10·26 W
135 Valencia, Lago de (L.)..Ven. (In.) 10·11 N 67·45 W
160 Valenciennes (vȧ-läN-syĕn')....Fr. 50·24 N 3·36 E
108 Valentine (vȧ lăn-tē-nyē')....Ne. 42·52 N 100·34 W
134 Valera (vä-lĕ'rä)....Ven. 9·12 N 70·45 W
174 Valerianovsk (vȧ-lĕ-rĭ-ä'nôvsk) Sov. Un. (Urals In.) 58·47 N 59·34 E
213 Valhalla (văl-hăl-ȧ)....S. Afr. (Johannesburg & Pretoria In.) 25·49 S 28·09 E
111 Valier (vă-lēr')....Mt. 48·17 N 112·14 W
165 Valjevo (väl'yȧ-vô)....Yugo. 44·17 N 19·57 E
166 Valka (väl'gȧ)....Sov. Un. 57·47 N 26·03 E
167 Valki (väl'kē)....Sov. Un. 49·49 N 35·40 E
126 Valladolid (väl-yä-dhô-lēdh') Mex. (In.) 20·39 N 88·13 W
162 Valladolid (väl-yä-dhô-lēdh')...Sp. 41·41 N 4·41 W
163 Vall de Uxo' (väl-dĕ-ōōx-ô')....Sp. 39·50 N 0·15 W
134 Valle (Dept.) (vä'l-yĕ)...Col. (In.) 4·03 N 76·13 W
114 Valle, Arroyo del (ä-rō'yō dĕl väl'yȧ).Ca. 37·36 N 121·43 W
163 Vallecas (väl-yā'käs) Sp. (Madrid In.) 40·23 N 3·37 W
118 Valle de Allende (väl'yā dā äl-yĕn'dȧ).Mex. 26·55 N 105·25 W
124 Valle de Bravo (brä'vô)....Mex. 19·12 N 100·07 W
135 Valle de Guanape (vä'l-yĕ-dĕ-gwä-nä'pĕ) Ven. (In.) 9·54 N 65·41 W
134 Valle de la Pascua (lä-pä's-kōōä) Ven. 9·12 N 65·08 W
124 Valle de Santiago (sän-tē-ä'gô) Mex. 20·23 N 101·11 W
134 Valledupar (dōō-pär')....Col. 10·13 N 73·39 W
134 Valle Grande (grän'dā)....Bol. 18·27 S 64·03 W
112 Vallejo (vä-yä'hō) (vă-lā'hō) Ca. (San Francisco In.) 38·06 N 122·15 W
124 Vallejo, Sierra de (Mts.) (sē-ĕ'r-rä-dĕ-väl-yĕ'Kō).Mex. 21·00 N 105·10 W
136 Vallenar (väl-yȧ-när')....Chile 28·39 S 70·52 W

ng-sing; ŋ-baŋk; N-nasalized n; nŏd; cŏmmit; ōld; ôbey; ôrder; fōōd; fŏŏt; ou-out; s-soft; sh-dish; th-thin; pūre; ûnite; ûrn; stŭd; circŭs; ü-as "y" in study; '-indeterminate vowel.

362 Vallerano — Veakhniy Ufaley PRONOUNCING INDEX

Page Name Pronunciation Region Lat. °' Long. °'

163 Vallerano (R.) (vä-lĕ-rä'nô) It. (Rome In.) 41·46 N 12·29 E
152 Valletta (väl-lĕt'ä) Malta 35·50 N 14·29 E
113 Valle Vista (văl'yȧ vĭs'tȧ) Ca. (Los Angeles In.) 33·45 N 116·53 W
108 Valley City ND 46·55 N 97·59 W
107 Valley City (văl'ĭ) Oh. (Cleveland In.) 41·14 N 81·56 W
117 Valley Falls Ks. 39·25 N 95·26 W
89 Valleyfield (văl'ē-fēld) Can. (Montréal In.) 45·16 N 74·09 W
91 Valleyfield Can. 45·05 N 74·00 W
113 Valley Park (văl'ē pärk) Mo. (St. Louis In.) 38·33 N 90·30 W
106 Valley Stream (văl'ĭ strēm) NY (New York In.) 40·39 N 73·42 W
164 Valli di Comácchio (L.) (vä'lē-dē-kô-mȧ'chyô) It. 44·38 N 12·15 E
129 Vallière (väl-yâr') Hai. 19·30 N 71·55 W
137 Vallimanca (R.) (väl-yē-mä'n-kä) Arg. (Buenos Aires In.) 36·21 S 60·55 W
163 Valls (väls) Sp. 41·15 N 1·15 E
157 Valmiera (vȧl'myĕ-rȧ) Sov. Un. 57·34 N 25·54 E
160 Valognes (vȧ-lôn'y') Fr. 49·32 N 1·30 W
Valona, see Vlorë
137 Valparaíso (väl'pä-rä-ē'sô) Chile (Santiago In.) 33·02 S 71·32 W
104 Valparaiso (văl-pȧ-rā'zô) In. 41·25 N 87·05 W
124 Valparaiso Mex. 22·49 N 103·33 W
137 Valpariso (Prov.) Chile (Santiago In.) 32·58 S 71·23 W
160 Valréas (vȧl-rȧ-ä') Fr. 45·25 N 4·56 E
218 Vals (R.) S. Afr. (Johannesburg & Pretoria In.) 27·32 S 26·51 E
197 Vals, Tandjung (C.) Indon. 8·30 S 137·15 E
212 Valsbaai (False Bay) S. Afr. (In.) 34·14 S 18·35 E
174 Valuyevo (vȧ-lōō'yĕ-vô) Sov. Un. (Moscow In.) 55·34 N 37·21 E
167 Valuyki (vȧ-lŏŏ-ē'kê) Sov. Un. 50·14 N 38·04 E
162 Valverde del Camino (väl-vĕr-dĕ-dĕl-kä-mē'nō) Sp. 37·34 N 6·44 W
184 Vambanād (R.) India 10·00 N 76·03 E
171 Van (vän) Tur. 38·04 N 43·10 E
117 Van Buren (văn bū'rĕn) At. 35·26 N 94·20 W
98 Van Buren Me. 47·09 N 67·58 W
104 Vanceburg (văns'bûrg) Ky. 38·35 N 83·20 W
112 Vancouver (văn-kōō'vẽr) Can. (Vancouver In.) 49·16 N 123·06 W
112 Vancouver Wa. (Portland In.) 45·37 N 122·40 W
92 Vancouver I. Can. 49·50 N 125·05 W
92 Vancouver Island Ra. Can. 49·25 N 125·25 W
104 Vandalia (văn-dā'lĭ-ȧ) Il. 39·00 N 89·00 W
117 Vandalia Mo. 39·19 N 91·30 W
218 Vanderbijlpark S. Afr. (Johannesburg & Pretoria In.) 26·43 S 27·50 E
92 Vanderhoof Can. 54·01 N 124·01 W
Van Diemen (Str.), see Ōsumi Kaikyō
204 Van Diemen, C. (văndē'mĕn) Austl. 11·05 S 130·15 E
204 Van Diemen G. Austl. 11·50 S 131·30 E
124 Vanegas (vä-nĕ'gäs) Mex. 23·54 N 100·54 W
156 Vänern (L.) Swe. 58·52 N 13·17 E
156 Vänersborg (vĕ'nĕrs-bôr') Swe. 58·24 N 12·15 E
213 Vanga (väŋ'gä) Ken. 4·38 S 39·10 E
185 Vangani India (In.) 19·07 N 73·15 E
171 Van Gölü (L.) Tur. 38·45 N 43·00 E
118 Van Horn Tx. 31·03 N 104·50 W
89 Vanier Can. (Ottawa In.) 45·27 N 75·39 W
104 Van Lear (văn lēr') Ky. 37·45 N 82·50 W
160 Vannes (vȧn) Fr. 47·42 N 2·46 W
113 Van Nuys (văn nīz') Ca. (Los Angeles In.) 34·11 N 118·27 W
197 Van Rees, Pegunungan (Mtn.) Indon. 2·30 S 138·45 E
157 Vantaan (R.) Fin. 60·25 N 24·43 E
104 Van Wert (văn wûrt') Oh. 40·50 N 84·35 W
156 Vara (vä'rä) Swe. 58·17 N 12·55 E
164 Varakļāni Sov. Un. 56·38 N 26·46 E
164 Varallo (vä-räl'lô) It. 45·44 N 8·14 E
184 Vārānasi (Benares) India 25·25 N 83·00 E
150 Varanger Fd. (vä-räng'gẽr) Nor. 70·05 N 30·53 E
164 Varano, Lago di (L.) (lä'gō-dē-vä-rä'nô) It. 41·52 N 15·55 E
164 Varaždin (vä'räzh'dēn) Yugo. 46·17 N 16·20 E
164 Varazze (vä-rät'sā) It. 44·23 N 8·34 E
156 Varberg (vär'bĕrg) Swe. 57·06 N 12·16 E
165 Vardar (R.) (vär'där) Yugo. 41·40 N 21·50 E
156 Varde (vär'dĕ) Den. 55·39 N 8·28 E
150 Vardö (värd'û) Nor. 70·23 N 30·43 E
157 Varėna (vä-rā'nȧ) Sov. Un. 54·16 N 24·35 E
89 Varennes (vȧ-rĕn') Can. (Montréal In.) 45·41 N 73·27 W
165 Vareš (vä'rĕsh) Yugo. 44·10 N 18·20 E
164 Varese (vä-rā'sā) It. 45·45 N 8·49 E
137 Varginha (vär-zhē'n-yä) Braz. (Rio de Janeiro In.) 21·33 S 45·25 W
157 Varkaus (vär'kous) Fin. 62·19 N 27·51 E
174 Varlamovo (vár-lá'mô-vô) Sov. Un. (Urals In.) 54·37 N 60·41 E
165 Varna (Stalin) (vär'nȧ) (stä'lĭn) Bul. 43·14 N 27·58 E
174 Varna Sov. Un. (Urals In.) 53·22 N 60·59 E
156 Värnamo (vĕr'nȧ-mô) Swe. 57·11 N 13·45 E
158 Varnsdorf (värns'dôrf) Czech. 50·54 N 14·36 E
121 Varnville (värn'vĭl) SC 32·49 N 81·05 W
89 Vars (värz) Can. (Ottawa In.) 45·21 N 75·21 W
167 Varvaropolye (vár'vár'ô-pô-lyĕ) Sov. Un. 48·38 N 38·37 E
185 Vasa India (In.) 19·20 N 72·47 E
162 Vascongadas (Reg.) (väs-kôn-gä'däs) Sp. 42·35 N 2·46 W
170 Vashka (R.) Sov. Un. 63·20 N 47·50 E
112 Vashon (văsh'ŭn) Wa. (Seattle In.) 47·27 N 122·28 W
112 Vashon Heights (hītz) Wa. (Seattle In.) 47·30 N 122·28 W
112 Vashon I. Wa. (Seattle In.) 47·27 N 122·27 W
167 Vasil'kov (vȧ-sēl'-kôf') Sov. Un. 50·10 N 30·22 E
159 Vaslui (vȧs-lōō'ē) Rom. 46·39 N 27·49 E
104 Vassar (văs'ẽr) Mi. 43·25 N 83·35 W
136 Vassouras (väs-sō'räzh) Braz. (Rio de Janeiro In.) 22·25 S 43·40 W
156 Västanfors (vĕst'ȧn-fôrs) Swe. 59·59 N 15·49 E
156 Västerås (vĕs'tĕr-ôs) Swe. 59·39 N 16·30 E
156 Väster-dalälven (R.) Swe. 61·06 N 13·10 E
156 Västervik (vĕs'tĕr-vēk) Swe. 57·45 N 16·35 E
164 Vasto (väs'tô) It. 42·06 N 12·42 E
172 Vasyugan (R.) (vȧs-yōō-gȧn') Sov. Un. 58·52 N 77·30 E
163 Vatican City (Cittádel Vaticano) (văt'ĭ-kăn sĭt'ē) (chē-tȧ'del vä-tē-kä'nô) Eur. (Rome In.) 41·54 N 12·22 E
164 Vaticano, C. (vä-tē-kä'nô) It. 38·38 N 15·52 E
150 Vatnajökull (Gl.) (vät'nȧ-yû-kōōl) Ice. 64·34 N 16·41 W
213 Vatomandry (vä-tōō-män'drē) Mad. 18·53 S 48·13 E
159 Vatra Dornei (vät'rȧ dôr'nā') Rom. 47·22 N 25·20 E
156 Vättern (L.) Swe. 58·15 N 14·24 E
89 Vaudreuil (vô-drû'y') Can. (Montreal In.) 45·24 N 74·02 W
112 Vaugh (vôn) Wa. (Seattle In.) 47·21 N 122·47 W
89 Vaughan Can. (Toronto In.) 43·47 N 79·36 W
116 Vaughn NM 34·37 N 105·13 W
134 Vaupés (R.) (vȧ'ōō-pĕ's) Col. 1·18 N 71·14 W
156 Vaxholm (väks'hôlm) Swe. 59·26 N 18·19 E
156 Växjo (vĕks'shû) Swe. 56·53 N 14·46 E
170 Vaygach (I.) (vī-gàch') Sov. Un. 70·00 N 59·00 E
135 Veadeiros, Chapadas dos (Mts.) (shä-pä'däs-dôs-vĕ-ȧ-dā'rōs) Braz. 15·20 S 48·43 W
156 Veblungsnares (vib'lōōngs-nĕs) Nor. 62·33 N 7·46 E
165 Vedea (R.) (vȧ'dyȧ) Rom. 44·25 N 24·45 E
137 Vedia (vĕ'dyä) Arg. (Buenos Aires In.) 34·29 S 61·30 W
104 Veedersburg (vē'dẽrz-bûrg) In. 40·05 N 87·15 W
125 Vega de Alatorre (vā'gä dā ä-lä-tōr'rȧ) Mex. 20·02 N 96·39 W
129 Vega Real (Mts.) (vĕ'gä-rĕ-ä'l) Dom. Rep. 19·30 N 71·05 W
150 Vegen (I.) (vĕ'ghĕn) Nor. 65·38 N 10·51 E
94 Vegreville Can. 53·30 N 112·03 W
185 Vehār L. India (In.) 19·11 N 72·52 E
137 Veinticinco de Mayo (vȧ-ēn'tē-sēn'kō dā mä'yō) Arg. (Buenos Aires In.) 35·26 S 60·09 W
162 Vejer (vā-kĕr') Sp. 36·15 N 5·58 W
156 Vejle (vī'lĕ) Den. 55·41 N 9·29 E
161 Velbert (fĕl'bĕrt) F.R.G. (Ruhr In.) 51·20 N 7·03 E
164 Velebit (Mts.) (vā'lĕ-bēt) Yugo. 44·25 N 15·23 E
161 Velen (fĕ'lĕn) F.R.G. (Ruhr In.) 51·54 N 7·00 E
162 Vélez-Málaga (vā'lāth-mä'lä-gä) Sp. 36·48 N 4·05 W
162 Vélez Rubio (rōō'bē-ô) Sp. 37·38 N 2·05 W
164 Velika Kapela (Mts.) (vĕ'lê-kä kä-pĕ'lä) Yugo. 45·03 N 15·20 E
165 Velika Morava (R.) (mô'rä-vä) Yugo. 44·20 N 21·10 E
165 Velika Tŭrnovo Bul. 43·06 N 25·38 E
166 Velikaya (R.) (vȧ-lē'kȧ-yȧ) Sov. Un. 57·25 N 28·07 E
159 Velikiy Bychkov (vĕ-lē'kē bōōch-kôf') Sov. Un. 47·59 N 24·01 E
166 Velikiye Luki (vyē-lē'-kyē lōō'ke) Sov. Un. 56·19 N 30·32 E
170 Velikiy Ustyug (vȧ-lē'kĭ ōōs-tyōōg') Sov. Un. 60·45 N 46·38 E
166 Velikoye (vȧ-lē'kô-yĕ) Sov. Un. 57·21 N 39·45 E
166 Velikoye (L.) Sov. Un. 57·00 N 36·53 E
166 Velizh (vā'lēzh) Sov. Un. 55·37 N 31·11 E
158 Velke Meziříčí (vĕl'kā mĕzh''r-zhĭ-chĭ) Czech. 49·21 N 16·01 E
205 Vella (I.) (väl'yä) Sol. Is. 8·00 S 156·42 E
163 Velletri (vĕl-lā'trē) It. (Rome In.) 41·42 N 12·48 E
185 Vellore (vĕl-lōr') India 12·57 N 79·09 E
174 Vels (vĕls) Sov. Un. (Urals In.) 60·35 N 58·47 E
170 Vel'sk (vĕlsk) Sov. Un. 61·00 N 42·18 E
149 Velten (fel'tĕn) G.D.R. (Berlin In.) 52·41 N 13·11 E
174 Velya R. (vĕl'yȧ) Sov. Un. (Moscow In.) 56·23 N 37·54 E
134 Venadillo (vĕ-nä-dē'l-yō) Col. (In.) 4·43 N 74·55 W
124 Venado (vȧ-nä'dō) Mex. 22·54 N 101·07 W
136 Venado Tuerto (vĕ-nä'dô-tōōĕ'r-tô) Arg. 33·28 S 61·47 W
160 Vendée, Collines de (hills) (kō-lēn' dĕ vĕn-dā') Fr. 46·44 N 0·17 W
160 Vendôme (väN-dōm') Fr. 47·46 N 1·05 E
164 Veneto (Reg.) (vĕ-nĕ'tô) It. 45·58 N 11·24 E
166 Venëv (vĕn-ĕf') Sov. Un. 54·19 N 38·14 E
164 Venezia (Venice) (vā-nāt'sē-ä) It. 45·25 N 12·18 E
164 Venezia, Golfo di (G.) (gôl-fô-dē-vā-nāt'sē-ä) It. 45·23 N 13·00 E
133 Venezuela (vĕn-ē-zwē'lȧ) S. A. 8·00 N 65·00 W
134 Venezuela, Golfo de (G.) (gôl-fô-dĕ) Ven. 11·34 N 71·02 W
101 Veniaminof, Mt. Ak. 56·12 N 159·20 W
113 Venice (vĕn'ĭs) Ca. (Los Angeles In.) 33·59 N 118·28 W
113 Venice Il. (St. Louis In.) 38·40 N 90·10 W
Venice, see Venezia
161 Venlo Neth. (Ruhr In.) 51·22 N 6·11 E
157 Venta (R.) (vĕn'tȧ) Sov. Un. 57·05 N 21·45 E
136 Ventana, Sierra de la (Mts.) (sē-ĕ'r-rȧ-dĕ-lä-vĕn-tȧ'nä) Arg. 38·00 S 63·00 W
218 Ventersburg (vĕn-tērs'bûrg) S. Afr. (Johannesburg & Pretoria In.) 28·06 S 27·10 E
218 Ventersdorp (vĕn-tērs'dôrp) S. Afr. (Johannesburg & Pretoria In.) 26·20 S 26·48 E
164 Ventimiglia (vĕn-tê-mēl'yä) It. 43·46 N 7·37 E
105 Ventnor (vĕnt'nẽr) NJ 39·20 N 74·25 W
157 Ventspils (vĕnt'spēls) Sov. Un. 57·24 N 21·41 E
134 Ventuari (R.) (vĕn-tōōȧ'rē) Ven. 4·47 N 65·56 W
114 Ventura (vĕn-tōō'rȧ) Ca. 34·18 N 119·18 W
174 Venukovsky (vĕ-nōō'kôv-skĭ) Sov. Un. (Moscow In.) 55·10 N 37·26 E
124 Venustiano Carranza (vĕ-nōōs-tyä'nō-kär-rä'n-zä) Mex. 19·44 N 103·48 W
125 Venustiano Carranzo (kär-rä'n-zô) Mex. 16·21 N 92·36 W
136 Vera (vĕ-rä) Arg. 29·22 S 60·09 W
162 Vera (vā'rä) Sp. 37·18 N 1·53 W
122 Vera Cruz (State) (vā-rä-krōōz') Mex. 20·30 N 97·15 W
125 Veracruz Mex. 19·13 N 96·07 W
184 Verāval (vĕr'ŭ-väl) India 20·59 N 70·49 E
164 Vercelli (vĕr-chĕl'lē) It. 45·18 N 8·27 E
89 Verchères (vĕr-shâr') Can. (Montréal In.) 45·46 N 73·21 W
115 Verde (R.) (vûrd) Az. 34·04 N 111·40 W
129 Verde, Cap (C.) Ba. 22·50 N 75·00 W
129 Verde, Cay (I.) Ba. 22·00 N 75·05 W
125 Verde (R.) Mex. 16·05 N 97·44 W
124 Verde (R.) Mex. 20·50 N 103·00 W
124 Verde (R.) Mex. 21·48 N 99·50 W
197 Verde (I.) (vĕr'dā) Phil. (In.) 13·34 N 121·11 E
197 Verde Island Pass. (vĕr'dē) Phil. (In.) 13·36 N 120·39 E
113 Verdemont (vûr'dê-mŏnt) Ca. (Los Angeles In.) 34·12 N 117·22 W
158 Verden (fĕr'dĕn) F.R.G. 52·55 N 9·15 E
117 Verdigris (R.) (vûr'dê-grēs) Ok. 36·50 N 95·29 W
89 Verdun (vĕr'dŭN') Can. (Montréal In.) 45·27 N 73·34 W
160 Verdun (vâr-dûN') Fr. 49·09 N 5·21 E
218 Vereeniging (vĕ-rā'nĭ-gĭng) S. Afr. (Johannesburg & Pretoria In.) 26·40 S 27·56 E
218 Verena (vĕr-ĕn ȧ) S. Afr. (Johannesburg & Pretoria In.) 25·30 S 29·02 E
166 Vereya (vĕ-rā'yȧ) Sov. Un. 55·21 N 36·08 E
162 Vergara (vĕr-gä'rä) Sp. 43·08 N 2·23 W
162 Verin (vå-rēn') Sp. 41·56 N 7·26 W
174 Verkhne Chusovskiye Gorodki (vyĕrk'nyĕ chōō-sôv'skĭ-ye gȧ-rôd'ki) Sov. Un. (Urals In.) 58·13 N 75·06 E
173 Verkhne-Kamchatsk (vyĕrk'nyĕ kȧm-chatsk') Sov. Un. 54·42 N 158·41 E
174 Verkhne Neyvinskiy (nā-vĭn'skĭ) Sov. Un. (Urals In.) 57·17 N 60·10 E
174 Verkhne Ural'sk (ōō-ralsk') Sov. Un. (Urals In.) 53·53 N 59·15 E
167 Verkhneye (vyĕrK'nĕ-yĕ) Sov. Un. 48·53 N 38·29 E
174 Verkhniy Avzyan (vyĕrk'nyĕ ȧv-zyȧn') Sov. Un. (Urals In.) 53·32 N 57·30 E
174 Verkhniye Kigi (vyĕrk'nĭ-yĕ kĭ'gĭ) Sov. Un. (Urals In.) 55·23 N 58·37 E
174 Verkhniy Ufaley (ōō-fá'lā) Sov. Un. (Urals In.) 56·04 N 60·15 E

ăt; finăl; rāte; senāte; ärm; ȧsk; sofȧ; fâre; ch-choose; dh-as th in other; bē; ēvent; bĕt; recĕnt; cratẽr; g-go; gh-guttural g; bĭt; ĭ-short neutral; rīde; K-guttural k as ch in German ich;

PRONOUNCING INDEX Verkhnyaya Pyshma — Villa Ocampo 363

Page	Name Pronunciation Region	Lat. °′	Long. °′
174	Verkhnyaya Pyshma (vyĕrk'nyä-yä pōōsh'nȧ) Sov. Un. (Urals In.)	56·57 N	60·37 E
174	Verkhnyaya Salda (säl'dȧ) Sov. Un. (Urals In.)	58·03 N	60·33 E
172	Verkhnyaya Tunguska (Angara) (R.) (tŏŏn-gōōs'kȧ). Sov. Un.	58·13 N	97·00 E
174	Verkhnyaya Tura (tōō'rȧ) Sov. Un. (Urals. In.)	58·22 N	59·51 E
174	Verkhnyaya Yayva (yäy'vȧ) Sov. Un. (Urals In.)	59·28 N	59·38 E
174	Verkhotur'ye (vyĕr-kô-tōōr'yĕ) Sov. Un. (Urals In.)	58·52 N	60·47 E
173	Verkhoyansk (vyĕr-kô-yänsk') Sov. Un.	67·43 N	133·33 E
173	Verkhoyanskiy Khrebet (Mts.) (vyĕr-kô-yänsk'). Sov. Un.	67·45 N	128·00 E
93	Vermilion (vẽr-mĭl'yŭn) Can.	53·22 N	110·51 W
109	Vermilion (L.) Mn.	47·49 N	92·35 W
93	Vermilion (R.) Can.	53·30 N	111·00 W
98	Vermilion (R.) Can.	47·30 N	73·15 W
104	Vermilion (R.) Il.	41·05 N	89·00 W
109	Vermilion (R.) Mn.	48·09 N	92·31 W
94	Vermilion Hills Can.	50·43 N	106·50 W
109	Vermilion Ra. Mn.	47·55 N	91·59 W
108	Vermillion SD	42·46 N	96·56 W
108	Vermillion (R.) SD	43·54 N	97·14 W
119	Vermillion B. La.	29·47 N	92·00 W
103	Vermont (State) (vẽr-mŏnt'). U. S.	43·50 N	72·50 W
111	Vernal (vûr'nȧl) Ut.	40·29 N	109·40 W
212	Verneuk Pan (L.) (vĕr-nŭk') S. Afr.	30·10 S	21·46 E
113	Vernon (vûr'nŭn) Ca. (Los Angeles In.)	34·01 N	118·12 W
93	Vernon (vẽr-nôN') Can.	50·18 N	119·15 W
89	Vernon Can. (Ottawa In.)	45·10 N	75·27 W
104	Vernon (vûr'nŭn) In.	39·00 N	85·40 W
106	Vernon NJ (New York In.)	41·12 N	74·29 W
116	Vernon Tx.	34·09 N	99·16 W
121	Vero Beach (vē'rō) Fl. (In.)	27·36 N	80·25 W
165	Véroia Grc.	40·30 N	22·13 E
164	Verona (vā-rō'nä) It.	45·28 N	11·02 E
112	Vernonia (vûr-nō'nyȧ) Or. (Portland In.)	45·52 N	123·12 W
161	Versailles (vĕr-sī'y'). Fr. (Paris In.)	48·48 N	2·07 E
104	Versailles (vẽr-sālz') Ky.	38·05 N	84·45 W
117	Versailles Mo.	38·27 N	92·52 W
214	Vert, Cap (C.) Senegal	14·43 N	17·30 W
213	Verulam (vĕ-rōō-lăm) S. Afr. (Natal In.)	29·39 S	31·08 E
155	Verviers (vĕr-vyā') Bel.	50·35 N	5·57 E
167	Vesëloye (vĕ-syô'lô-yĕ) Sov. Un.	46·59 N	34·56 E
157	Vesijärvi (L.) Fin.	61·09 N	25·10 E
161	Vesoul (vē-sōōl') Fr.	47·38 N	6·11 E
106	Vestavia Hills Al. (Birmingham In.)	33·26 N	86·46 W
150	Vester Aalen (Is.) (vĕs'tĕr ô'lĕn) Nor.	68·54 N	14·03 E
150	Vestfjord Nor.	67·33 N	12·59 E
150	Vestmannaeyjar (vĕst'män-ä-ā'yär). Ice.	63·12 N	20·17 W
163	Vesuvio (vesuvius) (Mtn.) (vĕ-sōō'vyä). It. (Naples In.)	40·35 N	14·26 E
166	Ves'yegonsk (vĕ-syĕ-gônsk') Sov. Un.	58·42 N	37·09 E
159	Veszprem (vĕs'prām) Hung.	47·05 N	17·53 E
159	Vesztö (vĕs'tû) Hung.	46·55 N	21·18 E
166	Vetka (vyĕt'kȧ) Sov. Un.	52·36 N	31·05 E
156	Vetlanda (vĕt-län'dä) Swe.	57·26 N	15·05 E
170	Vetluga (vyĕt-lōō'gȧ) Sov. Un.	57·50 N	45·42 E
170	Vetluga (R.) Sov. Un.	56·50 N	45·50 E
165	Vetovo (vā'tô-vô) Bul.	43·42 N	26·18 E
165	Vetren (vĕt'rĕn') Bul.	42·16 N	24·04 E
218	Vet R. (vĕt) S. Afr. (Johannesburg & Pretoria In.)	28·25 S	26·37 E
104	Vevay (vē'vā) In.	38·45 N	85·05 W
161	Veynes (vān'') Fr.	44·31 N	5·47 E
160	Vézère (R.) (vā-zer') Fr.	45·01 N	1·00 E
134	Viacha (vēä'chȧ) Bol.	16·43 S	68·16 W
164	Viadana (vê-ä-dä'nä) It.	44·55 N	10·30 E
117	Vian (vī'ăn) Ok.	35·30 N	95·00 W
135	Viana (vē-ä'nä) Braz.	3·09 S	44·44 W
162	Viana del Bollo (vê-ä'nä dĕl bôl'yô). Sp.	42·10 N	7·07 W
162	Viana do Alentejo (vê-ä'nȧ dōō ä-lĕN-tä'hōō). Port.	38·20 N	8·02 W
162	Viana do Castélo (dōō käs-tā'lōō) Port.	41·41 N	8·45 W
196	Viangchan Laos	18·07 N	102·33 E
162	Viar (R.) (vê-ä'rä) Sp.	38·15 N	6·08 W
164	Viareggio (vê-ä-rĕd'jô) It.	43·52 N	10·14 E
156	Viborg (vē'bôr) Den.	56·27 N	9·22 E
164	Vibo Valentia (vē'bô-vä-lĕ'n-tyä) It.	38·47 N	16·06 E
163	Vicálvero (vē-kä'l-vĕ-rō) Sp. (Madrid In.)	40·25 N	3·37 W
136	Vicente López (vē-sĕ'n-tĕ-lō'pĕz) Arg. (Buenos Aires In.)	34·15 S	58·29 W
164	Vicenza (vê-chĕnt'sä) It.	45·33 N	11·33 E
163	Vich (vēch) Sp.	41·55 N	2·14 E
166	Vichuga (vē-chōō'gȧ) Sov. Un.	57·13 N	41·58 E
160	Vichy (vê-shē') Fr.	46·06 N	3·28 E
104	Vicksburg (vĭks'bûrg) Mi.	42·10 N	85·30 W
120	Vicksburg Ms.	32·20 N	90·50 W
137	Viçosa (vē-sô'sä) Braz. (Rio de Janeiro In.)	23·46 S	42·51 W
137	Victoria (vēk-tô'rēä) Arg. (Buenos Aires In.)	32·36 S	60·09 W
92	Victoria (vĭk-tō'rĭ-ȧ) Can.	48·26 N	123·23 W
136	Victoria (vēk-tô-rēä) Chile	38·15 S	72·16 W
193	Victoria (vĭk-tō'rĭ-ȧ) Hong Kong	22·10 N	114·18 E
134	Victoria (vēk-tô'rēä) Col. (In.)	5·19 N	74·54 W
215	Victoria (vĭk-tō'rĭ-ȧ) Cam.	4·01 N	9·12 E
197	Victoria (vêk-tô-ryä) Phil. (In.)	15·34 N	120·41 E
119	Victoria (vĭk-tō'rĭ-ȧ) Tx.	28·48 N	97·00 W
121	Victoria Va.	36·57 N	78·13 W
205	Victoria (State) Austl.	36·46 S	143·15 E
217	Victoria (L.) Afr.	0·50 S	32·50 E
204	Victoria (R.) Austl.	17·25 S	130·50 E
188	Victoria, Mt Bur.	21·26 N	93·59 E
197	Victoria, Mt Pap. N. Gui.	9·35 S	147·45 E
128	Victoria de las Tunas (vêk-tō'rē-ä dā läs tōō'näs) Cuba	20·55 N	77·05 W
217	Victoria Falls Rh.	17·55 S	25·51 E
217	Victoria Falls Zambia	17·56 S	25·50 E
90	Victoria I. Can.	70·13 N	107·45 W
99	Victoria L. Can.	48·20 N	57·40 W
220	Victoria Land Ant.	75·00 S	160·00 E
217	Victoria Nile (R.) Ug.	2·20 N	31·35 E
126	Victoria Pk. (vêk-tōrĭ'ȧ) Belize (In.)	16·47 N	88·40 W
92	Victoria Pk. Can.	50·03 N	126·06 W
204	Victoria River Downs (vĭc-tôr'ĭȧ) Austl.	16·30 S	131·10 E
90	Victoria Str. (vĭk-tō'rĭ-ȧ) Can.	69·10 N	100·58 W
97	Victoriaville (vĭk-tō'rĭ-ȧ-vĭl) Can.	46·04 N	71·59 W
212	Victoria West (wĕst) S. Afr.	31·25 S	23·10 E
121	Vidalia (vĭ-dā'lĭ-ȧ) Ga.	32·10 N	82·26 W
119	Vidalia La.	31·33 N	91·28 W
165	Vidin (vĭ'dên) Bul.	44·00 N	22·53 E
174	Vidnoye Sov. Un. (Moscow In.)	55·33 N	37·41 E
166	Vidzy (vê'dzĭ) Sov. Un.	55·23 N	26·46 E
136	Viedma (vyād'mä) Arg.	40·55 S	63·03 W
136	Viedma (L.) Arg.	49·40 S	72·35 W
126	Viejo R. (vyā'hō) Nic.	12·45 N	86·19 W
120	Vienna (vê-ĕn'ȧ) Ga.	32·03 N	83·50 W
117	Vienna Il.	37·24 N	88·50 W
106	Vienna Va. (Baltimore In.)	38·54 N	77·16 W
	Vienna, see Wien		
160	Vienne (vyĕn') Fr.	45·31 N	4·54 E
160	Vienne (R.) Fr.	47·06 N	0·20 E
123	Vieques (vyā'kâs) P. R. (Puerto Rico In.)	18·09 N	65·27 W
123	Vieques (I.) (vyā'kâs) P. R. (Puerto Rico In.)	18·05 N	65·28 W
218	Vierfontien (vēr'fôn-tān) S. Afr. (Johannesburg & Pretoria In.)	27·06 S	26·45 E
161	Viersen (fēr'zĕn) F.R.G. (Ruhr In.)	51·15 N	6·24 E
158	Vierwaldstätter See (L.) Switz	46·54 N	8·36 E
160	Vierzon (vyâr-zôN') Fr.	47·14 N	2·04 E
118	Viesca (vē-ās'kä) Mex.	25·21 N	102·47 W
118	Viesca, Laguna de (L.) (lä-ōō'nä-dĕ). Mex.	25·30 N	102·40 W
164	Vieste (vyĕs'tā) It.	41·52 N	16·10 E
196	Vietnam (vyĕt'näm') Asia	18·00 N	107·00 E
197	Vigan (vēgän) Phil. (In.)	17·36 N	120·22 E
164	Vigevano (vē-jā-vä'nô) It.	45·18 N	8·52 E
161	Vigny (vēn-y'ē') Fr. (Paris In.)	49·05 N	1·54 E
162	Vigo (vē'gō) Sp.	42·18 N	8·42 W
157	Vihti (vē'tĭ) Fin.	60·27 N	24·18 E
	Viipuri, see Vyborg		
185	Vijayawāda India	16·31 N	80·37 E
165	Vijosë (R.) Alb.	40·15 N	20·30 E
150	Vik Ice.	63·22 N	18·58 W
156	Vik (vĭk) Nor.	61·06 N	6·35 E
205	Vila New Hebr.	18·00 S	168·30 E
217	Vila Caldas Xavier Moz.	15·59 S	34·12 E
212	Vila de Manica (vē'lä dā mä-nē'kȧ). Moz.	18·48 S	32·49 E
162	Vila de Rei (vē'lȧ dā rā'ĭ) Port.	39·42 N	8·03 W
162	Vila do Conde (vē'lȧ dōō kôn'dĕ) Port.	41·21 N	8·44 W
162	Vila Franca de Xira (fräŋ'kȧ dā shē'rȧ). Port.	38·58 N	8·59 W
160	Vilaine (R.) (vē-lân') Fr.	47·34 N	0·20 W
212	Vilanculos (vê-län-kōō'lôs) Moz.	22·03 S	35·13 E
166	Vilāni (vē'lȧ-nĭ) Sov. Un.	56·31 N	27·00 E
162	Vila Nova de Fozcoa (nō'vȧ dā fôz-kō'ȧ). Port.	41·08 N	7·11 W
162	Vila Nova de Gaia (vē'lȧ nō'vȧ dā gä'yä). Port.	41·08 N	8·40 W
162	Vila Nova de Milfontes (nō'vȧ dā mêl-fôn'tāzh). Port.	37·44 N	8·48 W
162	Vila Real (rā-äl') Port.	41·18 N	7·48 W
162	Vila Real de Santo Antonio (vē'lä-rĕ-ä'l-dĕ-sän-tô-än-tô'nyô) Port.	37·14 N	7·25 W
162	Vila Vicosa (vê-sō'zȧ) Port.	38·47 N	7·24 W
166	Vileyka (vê-lā'ê-kȧ) Sov. Un.	54·19 N	26·58 E
150	Vilhelmina Swe.	64·37 N	16·30 E
157	Viljandi (vēl'yän-dê) Sov. Un.	58·24 N	25·34 E
218	Viljoenskroon S. Afr. (Johannesburg & Pretoria In.)	27·13 S	26·58 E
157	Vilkaviškis (vêl-kȧ-vēsh'kês) Sov. Un.	54·40 N	23·08 E
157	Vilkija (vêl-kē'ēȧ) Sov. Un.	55·04 N	23·30 E
172	Vil'kitskogo (I.) (vyl-kēts-kōgō) Sov. Un.	73·25 N	76·00 E
171	Vilkovo (vĭl-kô-vô) Sov. Un.	45·24 N	29·36 E
118	Villa Acuña (vêl'yä-kōō'n-yä) Mex.	29·20 N	100·56 W
118	Villa Ahumada (ä-ōō-mä'dä). Mex.	30·43 N	106·30 W
125	Villa Alta (San Ildefonso) (äl'tä) (sän ēl-dâ-fōn'sō). Mex.	17·20 N	96·08 W
136	Villa Angela (vē'l-yä á'n-kĕ-lä) Arg.	27·31 S	60·42 W
162	Villaba (vēl-yä'bä) Sp.	43·18 N	7·43 W
136	Villa Ballester (vê'l-yä-bál-yĕs-tĕr) Arg. (Buenos Aires In.)	34·18 S	58·33 W
134	Villa Bella (bĕ'l-yä) Bol.	10·25 S	65·22 W
162	Villablino (vêl-yä-blē'nô) Sp.	42·58 N	6·18 W
162	Villacañas (vêl-yä-kän'yäs) Sp.	39·39 N	3·20 W
162	Villacarrillo (vêl-yä-kä-rēl'yô) Sp.	38·09 N	3·07 W
158	Villach (fē'läk) Aus.	46·38 N	13·50 E
164	Villacidro (vē-lä-chē'drô) It.	39·28 N	8·41 E
210	Villa Cisneros (vēl'yä thês-nā'rôs) W. Sah.	23·45 N	16·04 W
128	Villa Clara (Prov.) Cuba	22·40 N	80·10 W
137	Villa Constitución (kōn-stê-tōō-syōn') Arg. (Buenos Aires In.)	33·15 S	60·19 W
118	Villa Coronado (kō-rō-nä'dhō) Mex.	26·45 N	105·10 W
125	Villa Cuauhtémoc (vêl'yä-kōō-äōō-tĕ'mŏk). Mex.	22·11 N	97·50 W
118	Villa de Allende (vēl'yä dā äl-yĕn'dâ). Mex.	25·18 N	100·01 W
124	Villa de Alvarez (vêl'yä-dĕ-ä'l-vä-rĕz). Mex.	19·17 N	103·44 W
135	Villa de Cura (dĕ-kōō'rä) Ven. (In.)	10·03 N	67·29 W
124	Villa de Guadalupe (dĕ-gwä-dhä-lōō'pâ). Mex.	23·22 N	100·44 W
136	Villa Dolores (vēl'yä dô-lō'rās) Arg.	31·50 S	65·05 W
124	Villa Escalante (vêl'yä-ĕs-kä-lán'tĕ). Mex.	19·24 N	101·36 W
163	Villafamés (vēl'yä-fä-mās') Sp.	40·07 N	0·05 W
125	Villa Flores (vêl'yä-flō'rās) Mex.	16·13 N	93·17 W
164	Villafranca (vēl-lä-fräŋ'kä) It.	45·22 N	10·53 E
162	Villafranca del Bierzo (vēl'yä-fräŋ'kä dĕl byĕr'thō). Sp.	42·37 N	6·49 W
162	Villafranca de los Barros (vēl-yä-fräŋ'kä dā lōs bär'rōs) Sp.	38·34 N	6·22 W
163	Villafranca del Panadés (vēl-yäfrän'kä dĕl pä-nä-dās') Sp.	41·20 N	1·40 E
124	Villa García (gär-sē'ä) Mex.	22·07 N	101·55 W
162	Villagarcia (vēl'yä-gär-thē'ä) Sp.	42·38 N	8·43 W
118	Villagram (vēl-yä-gräm') Mex.	24·28 N	99·30 W
104	Villa Grove (vĭl'ȧ grōv') Il.	39·55 N	88·15 W
136	Villaguay (vē'l-yä-gwī) Arg.	31·47 S	58·53 W
136	Villa Hayes (vēl'yä äyâs) (hāz) Par.	25·07 S	57·31 W
125	Villahermosa (vēl'yä-ĕr-mō'sä) Mex.	17·59 N	92·56 W
124	Villa Hidalgo (vēl'yäē-däl'gō) Mex.	21·39 N	102·41 W
163	Villajoyosa (vēl'yä-hô-yō'sä) Sp.	38·30 N	0·14 W
118	Villaldama (vēl-yäl-dä'mä) Mex.	26·30 N	100·26 W
118	Villa Lopez (vēl'yä lō'pĕz) Mex.	27·00 N	105·02 W
162	Villalpando (vēl-yäl-pän'dō) Sp.	41·54 N	5·24 W
136	Villa María (vĕ'l-yä-mä-rē'ä) Arg.	32·17 S	63·08 W
162	Villamatín (vēl-yä-mä-tē'n) Sp.	36·50 N	5·38 W
136	Villa Mercedes (mĕr-sā'dâs) Arg.	33·38 S	65·16 W
134	Villa Montes (vē'l-yä-mô'n-tĕs) Bol.	21·13 S	63·26 W
124	Villa Morelos (mô-rĕ'lōs) Mex.	20·01 N	101·24 W
134	Villanueva (vĕ'l-yä-nōōĕ'vä) Col.	10·44 N	73·08 W
126	Villanueva (vēl'yä-nwä'vä). Hond.	15·19 N	88·02 W
124	Villanueva (vêl'yä-nōōĕ'vä) Mex.	22·25 N	102·53 W
162	Villanueva de Córdoba (vêl-yä-nwĕ'vä-dā kôr'dô-bä) Sp.	38·18 N	4·38 W
162	Villanueva de la Serena (lä sā-rā'nä). Sp.	38·59 N	5·56 W
163	Villanueva y Geltrú (ēkĕl-trōō') Sp.	41·13 N	1·44 E
125	Villa Obregón (vē'l-yä-ô-brĕ-gô'n) Mex. (In.)	19·21 N	99·11 W
118	Villa Ocampo (ô-käm'pō) Mex.	26·26 N	105·30 W

ng-sing; ŋ-baŋk; N-nasalized n; nŏd; cŏmmit; ōld; ôbey; ôrder; fōōd; fŏŏt; ou-out; s-soft; sh-dish; th-thin; pūre; ûnite; ûrn; stŭd; circŭs; ü-as "y" in study; '-indeterminate vowel.

364 Villa Pedro Montoya — Vychegda PRONOUNCING INDEX

Page	Name Pronunciation Region	Lat. °'	Long. °'
124	Villa Pedro Montoya (vēl'yä-pě'drō-môn-tō'yȧ). Mex.	21·38 N	99·51 W
161	Villard-Bonnot (vēl-yär'bôn-nō') Fr.	45·15 N	5·53 E
163	Villarreal (vêl-yär-rĕ-äl) Sp.	39·55 N	0·07 W
136	Villarrica (vēl-yä-rē'kä) Par.	25·55 S	56·23 W
162	Villarrobledo (vēl-yär-rô-blā'dhō) Sp.	39·15 N	2·37 W
162	Villa Sanjurjo (vêl-yä-sän-kōō'r-kô). Sp.	35·15 N	3·55 W
124	Villa Union (vêl'yä-ōō-nyōn') Mex.	23·10 N	106·14 W
134	Villavicencio (vē'l-yä-vē-sĕ'n-syō) Col. (In.)	4·09 N	73·38 W
163	Villaviciosa de Odón (vēl'yä-vē-thē-ō'sä dā ō-dōn') Sp. (Madrid In.)	40·22 N	3·54 W
134	Villavieja (vē'l-yä-vē-ĕ'kä) Col. (In.)	3·13 N	75·13 W
136	Villazón (vē'l-yä-zô'n) Bol.	22·02 S	65·42 W
160	Villafranche-de-Lauragais (vēl-fränsh'dĕ-lō-rä-gā'). Fr.	43·25 N	1·41 E
160	Villafranche-de-Rouergue (dĕ-rōō-ĕrg'). Fr.	44·21 N	2·02 E
160	Villafranche sur-Saône (sür-sä-ōn'). Fr.	45·59 N	4·43 E
161	Villejuif (vēl'zhüst'). Fr. (Paris In.)	48·48 N	2·22 E
97	Ville-Marie Can.	47·18 N	79·22 W
163	Villena (vē-lyā'nȧ) Sp.	38·37 N	0·52 W
89	Villeneuve (vēl'nûv') Can. (Edmonton In.)	53·40 N	113·49 W
161	Villeneuve-St. Georges (săn-zhôrzh'). Fr. (Paris In.)	48·43 N	2·27 E
160	Villeneuve-sur-Lot (sür-lō') Fr.	44·25 N	0·41 E
119	Ville Platte (vēl plȧt') La.	30·41 N	92·17 W
160	Villers Cotterêts (vē-âr'kô-trā') Fr. (In.)	49·15 N	3·05 E
161	Villerupt (vēl'rüp') Fr.	49·28 N	6·16 E
96	Ville-St.-Georges (vĭl-sĕn-zhôrzh') Can.	46·07 N	70·40 W
134	Villeta (vē'l-yĕ'tä) Col. (In.)	5·02 N	74·29 W
160	Villeurbanne (vēl-ûr-bän') Fr.	45·43 N	4·55 E
218	Villiers (vĭl'ĭ-ērs) S. Afr. (Johannesburg & Pretoria In.)	27·03 S	28·38 E
158	Villingen (fĭl'ĭng-ĕn) F.R.G.	48·04 N	8·28 E
109	Villisca (vĭ'lĭs'kȧ) Ia.	40·56 N	94·56 W
185	Villupuram India	11·59 N	79·33 E
157	Vilnius (Wilno) (vĭl'nē-ōōs) Sov. Un.	54·40 N	25·26 E
157	Vilppula (vĭl'pŭ-lȧ) Fin.	62·01 N	24·24 E
149	Vilvoorde Bel. (Brussels In.)	50·56 N	4·25 E
173	Vilyuy (R.) (vēl'yȧ) Sov. Un.	65·22 N	108·45 E
173	Vilyuysk (vê-lyōō'ĭsk') Sov. Un.	63·41 N	121·47 E
156	Vimmerby (vĭm'ĕr-bü) Swe.	57·41 N	15·51 E
158	Vimperk (vĭm-pěrk') Czech.	49·04 N	13·41 E
137	Viña del Mar (vē'nyä děl mär') Chile (Santiago In.)	33·00 S	71·33 W
98	Vinalhaven (vī-năl-hā'věn) Me.	44·03 N	68·49 W
163	Vinaroz (vē-nä'rōth) Sp.	40·29 N	0·27 E
161	Vincennes (văn-sĕn') Fr. (Paris In.)	48·51 N	2·27 E
104	Vincennes (vĭn-zĕnz') In.	38·40 N	87·30 W
120	Vincent (vĭn'sĕnt) Al.	33·21 N	86·25 W
150	Vindelälven (R.) Swe.	65·02 N	18·30 E
150	Vindeln (vĭn'dĕln) Swe.	64·10 N	19·52 E
184	Vindhya Ra. (vĭnd'yä) India	22·30 N	75·50 E
105	Vineland (vīn'lănd) NJ	39·30 N	75·00 W
193	Vinh (vên'y') Viet.	18·38 N	105·42 E
162	Vinhais (vên-yä'ēzh) Port.	41·51 N	7·00 W
106	Vinings (vī'nĭngz) Ga. (Atlanta In.)	33·52 N	84·28 W
117	Vinita (vĭ-nē'tȧ) Ok.	36·38 N	95·09 W
165	Vinkovci (vēn'kôv-tsē) Yugo.	45·17 N	18·47 E
167	Vinnitsa (vē'nēt-sȧ) Sov. Un.	49·13 N	28·31 E
167	Vinnitsa (Oblast) Sov. Un.	48·45 N	28·01 E
174	Vinogradovo (vĭ-nô-grä'do-vô) Sov. Un. (Moscow In.)	55·25 N	38·33 E
220	Vinson Massif (Mtn.) Ant.	77·40 S	87·00 W
109	Vinton (vĭn'tŭn) Ia.	42·08 N	92·01 W
119	Vinton La.	30·12 N	93·35 W
106	Violet (vī'ô-lĕt) La. (New Orleans In.)	29·54 N	89·54 W
193	Virac (vê-räk') Phil.	13·38 N	124·20 E
157	Virbalis (vêr'bȧ-lēs) Sov. Un.	54·38 N	22·55 E
90	Virden (vûr'dĕn) Can.	49·51 N	101·55 W
117	Virden Il.	39·28 N	89·46 W
115	Virgin (R.) U. S.	36·51 N	113·50 W
109	Virginia (vēr-jĭn'yȧ) Mn.	47·32 N	92·36 W
218	Virginia S. Afr. (Johannesburg & Pretoria In.)	28·07 S	26·54 E
103	Virginia (State) U. S.	37·00 N	80·45 W
106	Virginia Beach. Va. (Norfolk In.)	36·50 N	75·58 W
114	Virginia City Nv.	39·18 N	119·40 W
123	Virgin Is. (vûr'jĭn) N. A.	18·15 N	64·00 W
157	Virmo (vĭr'mô) Fin.	60·41 N	21·58 E
109	Viroqua (vĭ-rō'kwȧ) Wi.	43·33 N	90·54 W
164	Virovitica (vê-rô-vē'tē-tsȧ) Yugo.	45·50 N	17·24 E
165	Virpazar (vêr'pä-zär') Yugo.	42·16 N	19·06 E
157	Virrat (vĭr'ät) Fin.	62·15 N	23·45 E
156	Virserum (vĭr'sĕ-rōōm) Swe.	57·22 N	15·35 E
164	Vis (vēs) Yugo.	43·03 N	16·11 E
164	Vis (I.) Yugo.	43·00 N	16·10 E
164	Visa, Mt. (Mtn.) (vē'sä) It.	45·42 N	7·08 E
114	Visalia (vĭ-sā'lĭ-ȧ) Ca.	36·20 N	119·18 W
156	Visby (vĭs'bü) Swe.	57·39 N	18·19 E
75	Viscount Mellville Sound Can.	74·80 N	110·00 W
165	Višegrad (vē'shĕ-gräd) Yugo.	43·45 N	19·19 E
185	Vishākhapatnam India	17·48 N	83·21 E
174	Vishera R. (vĭ'shĕ-rȧ) Sov. Un. (Urals In.)	60·40 N	58·46 E
174	Vishnyakovo Sov. Un. (Moscow In.)	55·44 N	38·10 E
212	Vishoek S. Afr. (In.)	34·13 S	18·26 E
174	Visim (vē'sĭm) Sov. Un. (Urals In.)	57·38 N	59·32 E
156	Viskan (R.) Swe.	57·20 N	12·25 E
166	Viški (vēs'kĭ) Sov. Un.	56·02 N	26·47 E
165	Visoko (vē'sô-kô) Yugo.	43·59 N	18·10 E
165	Vistonís (L.) (vēs'tô-nĭs) Grc.	40·58 N	25·12 E
	Vistula (R.), see Wisla		
165	Vitanovac (vē'tä'nô-vȧts) Yugo.	43·44 N	20·50 E
166	Vitebsk (vē'tyĕpsk) Sov. Un.	55·12 N	30·16 E
166	Vitebsk (Oblast) Sov. Un.	55·05 N	29·18 E
164	Viterbo (vē-tĕr'bō) It.	42·24 N	12·08 E
173	Vitim (vē'têm) Sov. Un.	59·22 N	112·43 E
173	Vitim (R.) (vē'têm) Sov. Un.	56·12 N	115·30 E
174	Vitino (vē'tĭ-nô) Sov. Un. (Leningrad In.)	59·40 N	29·51 E
135	Vitória (vē-tō'rē-ä) Braz.	20·09 S	40·17 W
162	Vitoria (vē-tō-ryä) Sp.	42·43 N	2·43 W
135	Vitória de Conquista (-dä-kōn-kwē's-tä). Braz.	14·51 S	40·44 W
160	Vitré (vē-trā') Fr.	48·09 N	1·15 W
160	Vitrolles (vē-trōl') Fr. (In.)	43·27 N	5·15 E
160	Vitry-le-François (vē-trē'lĕ-frän-swȧ'). Fr.	48·44 N	4·34 E
151	Vittoria (vē-tô'rē-ô) It.	37·01 N	14·31 E
164	Vittorio (vē-tô'rē-ô) It.	45·59 N	12·17 E
162	Vivero (vē-vā'rō) Sp.	43·39 N	7·37 W
119	Vivian (vĭv'ĭ-ȧn) La.	32·51 N	93·59 W
165	Vize (vē'zĕ) Tur.	41·34 N	27·46 E
185	Vizianagaram India	18·10 N	83·29 E
149	Vlaardingen (vlär'dĭng-ĕn) Neth. (Amsterdam In.)	51·54 N	4·20 E
166	Vladimir (vlȧ-dyē'mēr) Sov. Un.	56·08 N	40·24 E
166	Vladimir (Oblast) (vlä-dyē'mēr) Sov. Un.	56·08 N	39·53 E
194	Vladimiro-Aleksandrovskoye (vlȧ-dyē'mē-rô ȧ-lĕk-sän'drôf-skô-yĕ). Sov. Un.	42·50 N	133·00 E
159	Vladimir-Volynskiy (vlȧ-dyē'mēr vô-lēn'skĭ) Sov. Un.	50·50 N	24·20 E
173	Vladivostok (vlȧ-dē-vôs-tŏk') Sov. Un.	43·06 N	131·47 E
165	Vlasenica (vlä'sĕ-nēt'sȧ) Yugo.	44·11 N	18·58 E
165	Vlasotinci (vlä'sô-tēn-tsĕ) Yugo.	42·58 N	22·08 E
155	Vlieland (I.) (vlē'länt) Neth.	53·19 N	4·55 E
155	Vlissingen (vlĭs'sĭng-ĕn) Neth.	51·30 N	3·34 E
165	Vlorë (Valona) (vlō'rŭ) Alb.	40·28 N	19·31 E
158	Vltana R. Czech.	49·24 N	14·18 E
170	Vodl (L.) (vôd''l) Sov. Un.	62·20 N	37·20 E
212	Voël (R.) S. Afr.	32·52 S	25·12 E
164	Voghera (vô-gā'rä) It.	44·58 N	9·02 E
213	Vohémar (vô-ā-mär') Mad.	13·35 S	50·05 E
112	Voight (R.) Wa. (Seattle In.)	47·03 N	122·08 W
214	Voinjama Lib.	8·25 N	9·45 W
163	Voiron (vwȧ-rôn') Fr.	45·23 N	5·48 E
94	Voisin, Lac (L.) (vwŏ'-zĭn) Can.	54·13 N	107·15 W
165	Voïviïs (L.) Grc.	39·34 N	22·50 E
167	Volchansk (vôl-chänsk') Sov. Un.	50·18 N	36·56 E
167	Volch'ya (R.) (vôl-chyä') Sov. Un.	49·42 N	34·39 E
134	Volcán Misti (Vol.) Peru	16·04 S	71·20 W
171	Volga (R.) (vôl'gä) Sov. Un.	47·30 N	46·20 E
171	Volga, Mouths of the Sov. Un.	46·00 N	49·10 E
171	Volgograd (Stalingrad) (vŏl-gō-grä't) (stȧ'lēn-grat) Sov. Un.	48·40 N	42·20 E
171	Volgogradskoye (Res.) (vôl-gô-grad'skô-yĕ). Sov. Un.	51·10 N	45·10 E
166	Volkhov (vôl'kôf) Sov. Un.	59·54 N	32·21 E
166	Volkhov (R.) Sov. Un.	58·45 N	31·40 E
159	Volkovysk (vôl-kô-vêsk') Sov. Un.	53·11 N	24·29 E
174	Volodarskiy (vô-lô-där'skĭ) Sov. Un. (Leningrad In.)	59·49 N	30·06 E
166	Vologda (vô'lôg-dȧ) Sov. Un.	59·12 N	39·52 E
166	Vologda (Oblast) Sov. Un.	59·00 N	37·26 E
167	Volokonovka (vô-lô-kô'nôf-kȧ) Sov. Un.	50·28 N	37·52 E
166	Volokolamsk (vô-lô-kôlȧmsk) Sov. Un.	56·02 N	35·58 E
165	Vólos (vô'lôs) Grc.	39·23 N	22·56 E
166	Volozhin (vô'lô-shên) Sov. Un.	54·04 N	26·38 E
171	Vol'sk (vôl'sk) Sov. Un.	52·10 N	47·00 E
214	Volta, L. (vôl'tȧ) Ghana	7·10 N	0·30 W
214	Volta (R.) Ghana	6·05 N	0·30 E
214	Volta Blanche (R.) Upper Volta	11·30 N	0·40 W
214	Volta Noire (Black Volta) (R.) Afr.	10·30 N	2·55 W
137	Volta Redonda (vōl'tä-rā-dôn'dä) Braz. (Rio de Janeiro In.)	22·32 S	44·05 W
164	Volterra (vôl-tĕr'rä) It.	43·22 N	10·51 E
164	Voltri (vōl'trē) It.	44·25 N	8·45 E
164	Volturno (R.) (vôl-tōōr'nô) It.	41·12 N	14·20 E
166	Volzhskoye (L.) (vôl'sh-skô-yĕ) Sov. Un.	56·43 N	36·18 E
113	Von Ormy (vŏn ôr'mē) Tx. (San Antonio In.)	29·18 N	98·36 W
166	Võõpsu (vōōp'-sōō) Sov. Un.	58·06 N	27·30 E
149	Voorberg Neth. (Amsterdam In.)	52·04 N	4·21 E
213	Voortrekkerhoogte S. Afr. (Johannesburg & Pretoria In.)	25·48 S	28·10 E
166	Vop' (R.) (vôp) Sov. Un.	55·20 N	32·40 E
150	Vopnafjördhur Ice.	65·43 N	14·58 W
158	Vorarlberg (Prov.) Aus.	47·20 N	9·55 E
156	Vordingborg (vôr'dĭng-bôr) Den.	55·10 N	11·55 E
165	Voríai (Is.) Grc.	39·12 N	24·03 E
165	Vorios Evvïkós Kólpos (G.) Grc.	38·48 N	23·02 E
170	Vorkuta (vôr-kōō'tȧ) Sov. Un.	67·28 N	63·40 E
157	Vormsi (I.) (vôrm'sĭ) Sov. Un.	59·06 N	23·05 E
171	Vorona (R.) (vô-rô'na) Sov. Un.	51·50 N	42·00 E
170	Voron'ya (R.) (vô-rô'nyȧ) Sov. Un.	68·20 N	35·20 E
167	Voronezh (vô-rô'nyĕzh) Sov. Un.	51·39 N	39·11 E
167	Voronezh (Oblast) Sov. Un.	51·10 N	39·13 E
166	Voronezh (R.) Sov. Un.	52·17 N	39·32 E
159	Voronovo (vô'rô-nô-vô) Sov. Un.	54·07 N	25·16 E
174	Vorontsovka (vô-rônt'sôv-kȧ) Sov. Un. (Urals In.)	59·40 N	60·14 E
171	Voroshilovgrad Sov. Un.	48·34 N	39·18 E
167	Voroshilovgrad (Oblast) Sov. Un.	49·08 N	38·37 E
166	Võrts-Järv (L.) (vôrts yärv) Sov. Un.	58·15 N	26·12 E
166	Võru (vô'rû) Sov. Un.	57·50 N	26·58 E
174	Vorya R. (vôr'yȧ) Sov. Un. (Moscow In.)	55·55 N	38·15 E
161	Vosges (Mts.) (vōzh) Fr.	48·09 N	6·57 E
174	Voskresensk (vôs-krĕ-sĕnsk') Sov. Un. (Moscow In.)	55·20 N	38·42 E
156	Voss (vôs) Nor.	60·40 N	6·24 E
174	Vostryakovo Sov. Un. (Moscow In.)	55·23 N	37·49 E
170	Votkinsk (vôt-kēnsk') Sov. Un.	57·00 N	54·00 E
170	Votkinskoye Vdkhr (Res.) Sov. Un.	57·30 N	55·00 E
162	Vouga (R.) (vō'gȧ) Port.	40·43 N	7·51 W
160	Vouziers (vōō-zyā') Fr.	49·25 N	4·40 E
156	Voxna älv (R.) Swe.	61·30 N	15·24 E
109	Voyageurs Natl. Park Mn.	48·30 N	92·40 W
170	Vozhe (L.) (vôzh'yĕ) Sov. Un.	60·40 N	39·00 E
167	Voznesensk (vôz-nyĕ-sĕnsk') Sov. Un.	47·34 N	31·22 E
168	Vrangelya (Wrangel) (I.) Sov. Un.	71·25 N	173·38 E
165	Vranje (vrän'yĕ) Yugo.	42·33 N	21·55 E
165	Vratsa (vrät'tsȧ) Bul.	43·12 N	23·31 E
165	Vrbas (v'r'bäs) Yugo.	45·34 N	19·43 E
164	Vrbas (R.) Yugo.	44·25 N	17·17 E
160	Vrchlabi (v'r'chlä-bē) Czech.	50·32 N	15·51 E
218	Vrede (vrĭ'dĕ) (vrēd) S. Afr. (Johannesburg & Pretoria In.)	27·25 S	29·11 E
218	Vredefort (vrĭ'dĕ-fôrt) (vrēd'fôrt) S. Afr. (Johannesburg & Pretoria In.)	27·00 S	27·21 E
149	Vreeswijk. Neth. (Amsterdam In.)	52·00 N	5·06 E
165	Vršac (v'r'shȧts) Yugo.	45·08 N	21·18 E
159	Vrutky (vrōōt'kē) Czech.	49·09 N	18·55 E
212	Vryburg (vrī'bûrg) S. Afr.	26·55 S	29·45 E
212	Vryheid (vrī'hīt) S. Afr.	27·43 S	30·58 E
159	Vsetín (fsĕt'yēn) Czech.	49·21 N	18·01 E
174	Vsevolozhskiy (vsyĕ'vôlô'zh-skēē) Sov. Un. (Leningrad In.)	60·01 N	30·41 E
128	Vuelta Abajo (Mts.) (vwĕl'tä ä-bä'hō). Cuba	22·20 N	83·45 W
149	Vught Neth. (Amsterdam In.)	51·38 N	5·18 E
165	Vukovar (vōō'kô-vär) Yugo.	45·20 N	19·00 E
104	Vulcan (vŭl'kăn) Mi.	45·45 N	87·50 W
164	Vulcano (I.) (vōōl-kä'nô) It.	38·23 N	15·00 E
165	Vülchedrŭm Bul.	43·43 N	23·29 E
157	Vyartsilya (vyȧr-tsē'lyȧ). Sov. Un.	62·10 N	30·40 E
170	Vyatka (R.) (vyȧt'kȧ) Sov. Un.	58·25 N	51·25 E
194	Vyazemskiy (vyȧ-zĕm'skĭ) Sov. Un.	47·29 N	134·39 E
166	Vyaz'ma (vyȧz'mȧ) Sov. Un.	55·12 N	34·17 E
170	Vyazniki (vyȧz'nê-kē) Sov. Un.	56·10 N	42·10 E
157	Vyborg (Viipuri) (vwē'bôrk) Sov. Un.	60·43 N	28·46 E
170	Vychegda (R.) (vē'chĕg-dȧ) Sov. Un.	61·40 N	48·00 E

ăt; finăl; rāte; senâte; ärm; ȧsk; sofȧ; fâre; ch-choose; dh-as th in other; bē; ēvent; bĕt; recĕnt; cratēr; g-go; gh-guttural g; bĭt; ĭ-short neutral; rīde; κ-guttural k as ch in German ich;

366 Wasatch — West Cape Howe PRONOUNCING INDEX

Page	Name Pronunciation Region	Lat. °′	Long. °′
102	Wasatch Ra. . . . . U. S.	39·10 N	111·30 W
213	Wasbank. . . . . . S. Afr. (Natal In.)	28·27 S	30·09 E
110	Wasco (wäs'kō). . . . . Or.	45·36 N	120·42 W
109	Waseca (wô-sē'kȧ). . . . . Mn.	44·04 N	93·31 W
155	Wash, The (Est.) (wŏsh). . . . Eng.	53·00 N	0·20 E
98	Washburn (wŏsh'bŭrn). . . . . . . Me.	46·46 N	68·10 W
109	Washburn. . . . . Wi.	46·41 N	90·55 W
111	Washburn, Mt. . . . . Wy.	44·55 N	110·10 W
106	Washington (wŏsh'ĭng-tŭn) DC (Washington DC In.)	38·50 N	77·00 W
120	Washington. . . . . Ga.	33·43 N	82·46 W
104	Washington. . . . . In.	38·40 N	87·10 W
109	Washington. . . . . Ia.	41·17 N	91·42 W
117	Washington. . . . . Ks.	39·48 N	97·04 W
117	Washington. . . . . Mo.	38·33 N	91·00 W
121	Washington. . . . . NC	35·32 N	77·01 W
107	Washington. . Pa. (Pittsburgh In.)	40·10 N	80·14 W
102	Washington (State). . . . . U. S.	47·30 N	121·10 W
105	Washington, Mt. . . . . NH	44·15 N	71·15 W
112	Washington, L. . Wa. (Seattle In.)	47·34 N	122·12 W
109	Washington (I.). . . . . Wi.	45·18 N	86·42 W
104	Washington Court House. . . . . Oh.	39·30 N	83·25 W
113	Washington Park. Il. (St. Louis In.)	38·38 N	90·06 W
116	Washita (R.) (wŏsh'ĭ-tô). . . . . . Ok.	35·33 N	99·16 W
112	Washougal (wŏ-shōō'gȧl) Wa. (Portland In.)	45·35 N	122·21 W
112	Washougal (R.) Wa. (Portland In.)	45·38 N	122·17 W
159	Wasilkow (vȧ-sēl'kōōf). . . . . . . Pol.	53·12 N	23·13 E
95	Waskaiowaka L. (wŏ'skă-yō'wō-kă). Can.	56·30 N	96·20 W
95	Wass L. (wŏs). . . . . Can.	53·40 N	95·25 W
161	Wassenberg (vä'sĕn-bĕrgh) F.R.G. (Ruhr In.)	51·06 N	6·07 E
114	Wassuk Ra. (wȧs'sŭk). . . . . Nv.	38·58 N	119·00 W
97	Waswanipi, Lac (L.). . . . . Can.	49·35 N	76·15 W
123	Water (I.) (wô'tēr) Vir. Is. (U. S. A.) (St. Thomas In.)	18·20 N	64·57 W
218	Waterberge (Mts.) (wôrtēr'bûrg). S. Afr. (Johannesburg & Pretoria In.)	24·25 S	27·53 E
121	Waterboro (wô'tēr-bûr-ō). . . . . . SC	32·50 N	80·40 W
105	Waterbury (wô'tēr-bĕr-ê). . . . . . Ct.	41·30 N	73·00 W
129	Water Cay (I.). . . . . Ba.	22·55 N	75·50 W
89	Waterdown (wô'tēr-doun) Can. (Toronto In.)	43·20 N	79·54 W
121	Wateree (R.) (wô'tēr-ē). . . . . . . SC	34·40 N	80·48 W
154	Waterford (wô'tēr-fērd). . . . . . . Ire.	52·20 N	7·03 W
107	Waterford. . . Wi. (Milwaukee In.)	42·46 N	88·13 W
149	Waterloo. . . . . . . Bel. (Brussels In.)	50·44 N	4·24 E
97	Waterloo (wô-tēr-lōō'). . . . . . . Can.	43·30 N	80·40 W
97	Waterloo. . . . . Can.	45·25 N	72·30 W
117	Waterloo. . . . . Il.	38·19 N	90·08 W
107	Waterloo. . . . . Ia.	42·30 N	92·22 W
106	Waterloo. . . . . Md. (Baltimore In.)	39·11 N	76·50 W
105	Waterloo. . . . . NY	42·55 N	76·50 W
90	Waterton-Glacier Intl. Peace Park (wô'ter-tŭn-glā'shûr). Mt.-Can.	48·55 N	114·10 W
93	Waterton Lakes Nat. Pk. . . . . Can.	49·05 N	113·50 W
99	Watertown (wô'tēr-toun) Ma. (In.)	42·22 N	71·11 W
105	Watertown. . . . . NY	44·00 N	75·55 W
108	Watertown. . . . . SD	44·53 N	97·07 W
107	Watertown. . . . . Wi.	43·13 N	88·40 W
120	Water Valley (văl'ê). . . . . Ms.	34·08 N	89·38 W
98	Waterville. . . . . Me.	44·34 N	69·37 W
107	Waterville. . . . . Mn.	44·10 N	93·35 W
110	Waterville. . . . . Wa.	47·38 N	120·04 W
105	Watervliet (wô'tēr-vlēt'). . . . . . NY	42·45 N	73·54 W
148	Watford (wŏt'fŏrd) Eng. (London In.)	51·38 N	0·24 W
94	Wathaman L. . . . . Can.	56·55 N	103·43 W
	Watling (I.), see San Salvador		
148	Watlington (wŏt'lĭng-tŭn) Eng. (London In.)	51·37 N	1·01 W
116	Watonga (wŏ-tôŋ'gȧ). . . . . Ok.	35·50 N	98·26 W
217	Watsa (wät'sä). . . . . Zaire	3·03 N	29·32 E
104	Watseka (wŏt-sē'kȧ). . . . . Il.	40·45 N	87·45 W
107	Watson (wŏt'sŭn) In. (Louisville In.)	38·21 N	85·42 W
90	Watson Lake. . . . . Can.	60·18 N	128·50 W
114	Watsonville (wŏt'sŭn-vĭl). . . . . Ca.	36·55 N	121·46 W
161	Wattenscheid (vä'tĕn-shīd) F.R.G. (Ruhr In.)	51·30 N	7·07 E
113	Watts (wŏts). Ca. (Los Angeles In.)	33·56 N	118·15 W
120	Watts Bar (R.) (bär). . . . . Tn.	35·45 N	84·49 W
108	Waubay (wô'bā). . . . . SD	45·19 N	97·18 W
121	Wauchula (wô-chōō'lȧ). . . Fl. (In.)	27·32 N	81·48 W
107	Wauconda (wô-kŏn'dȧ) Il. (Chicago In.)	42·15 N	88·08 W
107	Waukegan (wŏ-kē'gȧn) Il. (Chicago In.)	42·22 N	87·51 W
107	Waukesha (wô'kê-shô) Wi. (Milwaukee In.)	43·01 N	88·13 W
109	Waukon (wô kŏn). . . . . Ia.	43·15 N	91·30 W
109	Waupaca (wô-păk'ȧ). . . . . Wi.	44·22 N	89·06 W
109	Waupun (wô-pŭn'). . . . . Wi.	43·37 N	88·45 W
116	Waurika (wô-rē'kȧ). . . . . Ok.	34·09 N	97·59 W
109	Wausau (wô'sô). . . . . Wi.	44·58 N	89·40 W
109	Wausaukee (wô-sô'kê). . . . . . . Wi.	45·22 N	87·58 W
104	Wauseon (wô'sê-ŏn). . . . . Oh.	41·30 N	84·10 W
109	Wautoma (wô-tō'mȧ). . . . . Wi.	44·04 N	89·11 W
107	Wauwatosa (wô-wȧ-t'ō'sȧ) Wi. (Milwaukee In.)	43·03 N	88·00 W
155	Waveney (R.) (wāv'nê). . . . . Eng.	52·27 N	1·17 E
109	Waverly (wā'vēr-lê). . . . . Ia.	42·43 N	92·29 W
213	Waverly. . . . . . . S. Afr. (Natal In.)	31·54 S	26·29 E
120	Waverly. . . . . Tn.	36·04 N	87·46 W
211	Wāw. Sud.	7·41 N	28·00 E
96	Wawa. . . . . Can.	47·59 N	84·47 W
211	Wāw al-Kabir. . . . . Libya	25·23 N	16·52 E
95	Wawanesa (wŏ'wŏ-nē'să). . . . Can.	49·36 N	99·41 W
104	Wawasee (L.) (wô-wô-sē'). . . . . In.	41·25 N	85·45 W
119	Waxahachie (wăk-sȧ-hăch'ê). . Tx.	32·23 N	96·50 W
121	Waycross (wā'krôs). . . . . Ga.	31·11 N	82·24 W
120	Wayland (wā'lănd). . . . . Ky.	37·25 N	82·47 W
99	Wayland. . . . . Ma. (In.)	42·23 N	71·22 W
107	Wayne. . . . . Mi. (Detroit In.)	42·17 N	83·23 W
108	Wayne. . . . . Ne.	42·13 N	97·03 W
106	Wayne. . . . . . . NJ (New York In.)	40·56 N	74·16 W
106	Wayne. . . . . Pa. (Philadelphia In.)	40·03 N	75·22 W
121	Waynesboro (wānz'bŭr-ô). . . . . Ga.	33·05 N	82·02 W
105	Waynesboro. . . . . Pa.	39·45 N	77·35 W
105	Waynesboro. . . . . Va.	38·05 N	78·50 W
105	Waynesburg (wānz'bûrg). . . . . . Pa.	39·55 N	80·10 W
120	Waynesville (wānz'vĭl). . . . . . . NC	35·28 N	82·58 W
116	Waynoka (wā-nō'kȧ). . . . . Ok.	36·34 N	98·52 W
113	Wayzata (wā-zä-tȧ). . . . . Mn. (Minneapolis, St. Paul In.)	44·58 N	93·31 W
184	Wazīrbad. . . . . Pak.	32·39 N	74·11 E
95	Weagamow L. (wē'ăg-ă-mou) Can.	52·53 N	91·22 W
154	Weald, The (Reg.) (wēld). . . . Eng.	50·58 N	0·15 W
116	Weatherford (wĕ-dhēr-fērd). . . Ok.	35·32 N	98·41 W
119	Weatherford. . . . . Tx.	32·45 N	97·46 W
148	Weaver (R.) (wē'vēr). . . . . Eng.	53·09 N	2·31 W
110	Weaverville (wē'vēr-vĭl). . . . . . Ca.	40·44 N	122·55 W
117	Webb City. . . . . Mo.	37·10 N	94·26 W
113	Weber R. . Ut. (Salt Lake City In.)	41·13 N	112·07 W
99	Webster. . . . . Ma. (In.)	42·04 N	71·52 W
108	Webster. . . . . SD	45·19 N	97·30 W
109	Webster City. . . . . Ia.	42·28 N	93·49 W
113	Webster Groves (grōvz) Mo. (St. Louis In.)	38·36 N	90·22 W
105	Webster Springs (sprĭngz). . . . WV	38·30 N	80·20 W
220	Weddell Sea (wĕd'ĕl). . . . . Ant.	73·00 S	45·00 W
149	Wedel (vā'dĕl) F.R.G. (Hamburg In.)	53·35 N	9·42 E
92	Wedge Mtn. (wĕj). . . . . Can.	50·10 N	122·50 W
98	Wedgeport (wĕj'pōrt). . . . . . . Can.	43·44 N	65·59 W
148	Wednesfield (wĕd''nz-fēld). . . Eng.	52·36 N	2·04 W
110	Weed (wēd). . . . . Ca.	41·35 N	122·21 W
213	Weenen (vā'nĕn) S. Afr. (Natal In.)	28·52 S	30·05 E
155	Weert. . . . . Neth.	51·16 N	5·39 E
149	Weesp. . . . Neth. (Amsterdam In.)	52·18 N	5·01 E
159	Wegorzewo (vôŋ-gō'zhĕ-vô). . . Pol.	54·14 N	21·46 E
159	Wegrow (vôŋ'grōōf). . . . . Pol.	52·23 N	22·02 E
190	Wei (R.) (wā). . . . . China	35·47 N	114·27 E
192	Wei (R.) (wā). . . . . China	34·00 N	108·10 E
192	Weichang (wā-chäŋ). . . . . . . China	41·50 N	118·00 E
190	Weifang. . . . . China	36·43 N	119·08 E
190	Weihai (wa'hăī'). . . . . China	37·30 N	122·05 E
158	Weilheim (vīl'hīm'). . . . . F.R.G.	47·50 N	11·06 E
158	Weimar (vī'mär). . . . . G.D.R.	50·59 N	11·20 E
192	Weinan. . . . . China	34·32 N	109·40 E
205	Weipa. . . . . Austl.	12·25 S	141·54 E
95	Weir River (wēr-rĭv-ēr). . . . . . Can.	56·49 N	94·04 W
104	Weirton (wēr'tŭn). . . . . WV	40·25 N	80·35 W
110	Weiser (wē'zēr). . . . . Id.	44·15 N	116·58 W
110	Weiser R. . . . . Id.	44·26 N	116·40 W
190	Weishi (wā-shr). . . . . China	34·23 N	114·12 E
158	Weissenburg (vī'sĕn-bōōrgh) F.R.G.	49·04 N	11·20 E
158	Weissenfels (vī'sĕn-fĕlz). . . G.D.R.	51·13 N	11·58 E
189	Weixi (wā-shyē). . . . . China	27·27 N	99·30 E
190	Wei Xian (wā shyĕn). . . . . China	36·59 N	115·17 E
159	Wejherowo (vā-hĕ-rô'vô). . . . . Pol.	54·36 N	18·15 E
121	Welch (wĕlch). . . . . WV	37·24 N	81·28 W
121	Weldon (wĕl'dŭn). . . . . NC	36·24 N	77·36 W
117	Weldon (R.). . . . . Mo.	40·22 N	93·39 W
117	Weleetka (wê-lēt'kȧ). . . . . Ok.	35·19 N	96·08 W
203	Welford (wĕl'fērd). . . . . Austl.	25·08 S	144·43 E
218	Welkom (wĕl'kŏm). . . . . S. Afr. (Johannesburg & Pretoria In.)	27·57 S	26·45 E
107	Welland (wĕl'ănd) Can. (Buffalo In.)	42·59 N	79·13 W
154	Welland (R.). . . . . Eng.	52·38 N	0·40 W
99	Wellesley (wĕlz'lê). . . . . . Ma. (In.)	42·18 N	71·17 W
204	Wellesley Is. . . . . Austl.	16·15 S	139·25 E
203	Wellington (wĕl'lĭng-tŭn). . . Austl.	32·40 S	148·50 E
148	Wellington. . . . . Eng.	52·42 N	2·30 W
117	Wellington. . . . . Ks.	37·16 N	97·24 W
205	Wellington. . . . . N. Z. (In.)	41·15 S	174·45 E
104	Wellington. . . . . Oh.	41·10 N	82·10 W
116	Wellington. . . . . Tx.	34·51 N	100·12 W
136	Wellington (I.) (ŏŏĕ'lĕng-tŏn) Chile	49·30 S	76·30 W
204	Wells (wĕlz). . . . . Austl.	26·35 S	123·40 E
93	Wells. Can.	53·06 N	121·34 W
104	Wells. Mi.	45·50 N	87·00 W
109	Wells. Mn.	43·44 N	93·43 W
110	Wells. Nv.	41·07 N	115·04 W
105	Wellsboro (wĕlz'bŭ-rô). . . . . . . Pa.	41·45 N	77·15 W
104	Wellsburg (wĕlz'bûrg). . . . . . . WV	40·10 N	80·40 W
110	Wells Res. . . . . Wa.	48·05 N	119·45 W
104	Wellston (wĕlz'tŭn). . . . . Oh.	39·05 N	82·30 W
117	Wellsville (wĕlz'vĭl). . . . . Mo.	39·04 N	91·33 W
105	Wellsville. . . . . NY	42·10 N	78·00 W
104	Wellsville. . . . . Oh.	40·35 N	80·40 W
111	Wellsville. . . . . Ut.	41·38 N	111·57 W
158	Wels (vĕls). . . . . Aus.	48·10 N	14·01 E
154	Welshpool (wĕlsh'pōōl). . . . . Wales	52·44 N	3·10 W
218	Welverdiend (vĕl-vēr-dēnd'). S. Afr. (Johannesburg & Pretoria In.)	26·23 S	27·16 E
148	Welwyn Garden City (wĕl'ĭn) Eng. (London In.)	51·46 N	0·17 W
148	Wem (wĕm). . . . . Eng.	52·51 N	2·44 W
217	Wembere (R.). . . . . Tan.	4·35 S	33·55 E
190	Wen (R.) (wŭn). . . . . China	36·24 N	119·00 E
190	Wenan Wa (Swp.) (wĕn'än' wä) China	38·56 N	116·29 E
110	Wenatchee (wê-năch'ê). . . . . . . Wa.	47·24 N	120·18 W
110	Wenatchee Mts. . . . . Wa.	47·28 N	121·10 W
193	Wenchang (wŭn-chäŋ). . . . . . China	19·32 N	110·42 E
214	Wenchi. . . . . Ghana	7·42 N	2·07 W
190	Wendeng (wŭn-dŭŋ). . . . . China	37·14 N	112·03 E
211	Wendo. . . . . Eth.	6·37 N	38·29 E
111	Wendorer. . . . . Ut.	40·47 N	114·01 W
89	Wendover (wĕn-dōv'ēr) Can. (Ottawa In.)	45·34 N	75·07 W
148	Wendover. . . . . Eng. (London In.)	51·44 N	0·45 W
99	Wenham (wĕn'ăm). . . . . . Ma. (In.)	42·36 N	70·53 W
106	Wenonah (wĕn'ō-nă) NJ (Philadelphia In.)	39·48 N	75·08 W
192	Wenquan (wŭn-chyûän). . . . China	47·10 N	120·00 E
193	Wenshan. . . . . China	23·20 N	104·15 E
190	Wenshang (wĕn'shäng). . . . . China	35·43 N	116·31 E
188	Wensu (wĕn-sōō). . . . . China	41·45 N	80·30 E
155	Wensum (R.) (wĕn'sŭm). . . . . Eng.	52·45 N	1·08 E
203	Wentworth (wĕnt'wûrth). . . Austl.	24·03 S	141·53 E
193	Wenzhou (wŭn-jō). . . . . China	28·00 N	120·40 E
212	Wepener (wē'pĕn-ēr) (vā'pĕn-ēr) S. Afr.	29·43 S	27·04 E
149	Werder (vĕr'dĕr) G.D.R. (Berlin In.)	52·23 N	12·56 E
211	Were Ilu. . . . . Eth.	10·39 N	39·21 E
161	Werl (vĕrl). . . . . F.R.G. (Ruhr In.)	51·33 N	7·55 E
161	Werne (vĕr'nĕ). F.R.G. (Ruhr In.)	51·39 N	7·38 E
149	Werneuchen (vĕr'hoi-ĸĕn) G.D.R. (Berlin In.)	52·38 N	13·44 E
158	Werra R. (vĕr'ä). . . . . F.R.G.	51·16 N	9·54 E
202	Werribee. . Austl. (Melbourne In.)	37·54 S	144·40 E
202	Werribee (R.) Austl. (Melbourne In.)	37·40 S	144·37 E
158	Wertach R. (vĕr'täk). . . . . . F.R.G.	48·12 N	10·40 E
161	Weseke (vĕ'zĕ-kĕ) F.R.G. (Ruhr In.)	51·54 N	6·51 E
161	Wesel (vā'zĕl). . F.R.G. (Ruhr In.)	51·39 N	6·37 E
158	Weser R. (vā'zĕr). . . . . F.R.G.	53·08 N	8·35 E
118	Weslaco (wĕs-lā'kō). . . . . Tx.	26·10 N	97·59 W
97	Weslemkoon (L.). . . . . Can.	45·02 N	77·25 W
99	Wesleyville (wĕs'lē-vĭl). . . . . . Can.	49·09 N	53·34 W
204	Wessel (Is.) (wĕs'ĕl). . . . . Austl.	11·45 S	136·25 E
218	Wesselsbron (wĕs'ĕl-brŏn). . S. Afr. (Johannesburg & Pretoria In.)	27·51 S	26·22 E
108	Wessington Springs (wĕs'ĭng-tŭn). SD	44·06 N	98·35 W
122	West, Mt. . . . . Pan. (In.)	9·10 N	79·52 W
107	West Allis (wĕst-ăl'ĭs) Wi. (Milwaukee In.)	43·01 N	88·01 W
113	West Alton (ôl'tŭn) Mo. (St. Louis In.)	38·52 N	90·13 W
119	West B. . . . . Tx. (In.)	29·11 N	95·03 W
109	West Bend (wĕst bĕnd). . . . . . . Wi.	43·25 N	88·13 W
184	West Bengal (State) (bĕn-gôl') India	23·30 N	87·30 E
149	West Berlin (bĕr-lēn') F.R.G. (Berlin In.)	52·31 N	13·20 E
120	West Blocton (blŏk'tŭn). . . . . . . Al.	33·05 N	87·05 W
99	Westborough (wĕst'bŭr-ô) Ma. (In.)	42·17 N	71·37 W
99	West Boylston (boil'stŭn) Ma. (In.)	42·22 N	71·46 W
104	West Branch (wĕst brȧnch). . . Mi.	44·15 N	84·10 W
148	West Bridgford (brĭj'fērd). . . . Eng.	52·55 N	1·08 W
148	West Bromwich (wĕst brŭm'ĭj) Eng.	52·32 N	1·59 W
98	Westbrook (wĕst'brŏŏk). . . . . . Me.	43·41 N	70·23 W
109	Westby (wĕst'bê). . . . . Wi.	43·40 N	90·52 W
129	West Caicos (I.) (käē'kō) (kī'kōs) Turks & Caicos	21·40 N	72·30 W
204	West Cape Howe (C.). . . . . . Austl.	35·15 S	117·30 E

ăt; finăl; rāte; senâte; ärm; ȧsk; sofȧ; fâre; ch-choose; dh-as th in other; bē; ėvent; bĕt; recĕnt; cratēr; g-go; gh-guttural g; bĭt; ĭ-short neutral; rīde; ĸ-guttural k as ch in German ich;

PRONOUNCING INDEX

West Chester — Wilber 367

Page	Name Pronunciation Region	Lat. °′	Long. °′
107	West Chester (chĕs'tẽr) Oh. (Cincinnati In.)	39·20 N	84·24 W
106	West Chester Pa. (Philadelphia In.)	39·57 N	75·36 W
107	West Chicago (chĭ-kȧ'gō) Il. (Chicago In.)	41·53 N	88·12 W
121	West Columbia (cŏl'ŭm-bē-ȧ) SC	33·58 N	81·05 W
119	West Columbia Tx.	29·08 N	95·39 W
119	West Cote Blanche B. (kōt blănch) La.	29·30 N	92·17 W
113	West Covina (wĕst kô-vē'nȧ) Ca. (Los Angeles In.)	34·04 N	117·55 W
109	West Des Moines (dē moin') Ia.	41·35 N	93·42 W
109	West Des Moines (R.) Ia.	42·52 N	94·32 W
128	West End Ba.	26·40 N	78·55 W
148	Westerham (wĕ'stẽr'ŭm) Eng. (London In.)	51·15 N	0·05 E
149	Westerhorn (vĕs'tĕr-hōrn) F.R.G. (Hamburg In.)	53·52 N	9·41 E
149	Westerlo Bel. (Brussels In.)	51·05 N	4·57 E
105	Westerly (wĕs'tẽr-lê) RI	41·25 N	71·50 W
158	Western Alps (Mts.) Switz.-Fr.	46·19 N	7·03 E
204	Western Australia (State) (ôs-trā'lĭ-ȧ) Austl.	24·15 S	121·30 E
154	Western Downs Eng.	50·50 N	2·25 W
185	Western Ghāts (Mts.) India	17·35 N	74·00 E
105	Western Port (wĕs'tẽrn pōrt) Md.	39·30 N	79·00 W
209	Western Sahara (sȧ-hä'rȧ) Afr.	23·05 N	15·33 W
198	Western Samoa Oceania	14·30 S	172·00 W
168	Western Siberian Lowland Sov. Un.	63·37 N	72·45 E
104	Westerville (wĕs'tẽr-vĭl) Oh.	40·10 N	83·00 W
158	Westerwald (For.) (vĕs'tĕr-väld) F.R.G.	50·35 N	7·45 E
105	Westfield (wĕst'fēld) Ma.	42·05 N	72·45 W
106	Westfield NJ (New York In.)	40·39 N	74·21 W
106	Westfield (wĕst'fēld) NY	42·20 N	79·40 W
99	Westford (wĕst'fẽrd) Ma. (In.)	42·35 N	71·26 W
106	West Frankfort (frăŋk'fŭrt) Il.	37·55 N	88·55 W
148	West Ham Eng. (London In.)	51·30 N	0·00
105	West Hartford (härt'fẽrd) Ct.	41·45 N	72·45 W
117	West Helena (hĕl'ĕn-ȧ) Ar.	34·32 N	90·39 W
123	West Indies (Reg.) (ĭn'dēz) N. A.	19·00 N	78·30 W
113	West Jordan (jôr'dăn) Ut. (Salt Lake City In.)	40·37 N	111·56 W
148	West Kirby (kûr'bê) Eng.	53·22 N	3·11 W
104	West Lafayette (lä-fâ-yĕt') In.	40·25 N	86·55 W
107	Westlake Oh. (Cleveland In.)	41·27 N	81·55 W
218	Westleigh (wĕst-lē) S. Afr. (Johannesburg & Pretoria In.)	27·39 S	27·18 E
109	West Liberty (wĕst lĭb'ẽr-tĭ) Ia.	41·34 N	91·15 W
112	West Linn (lĭn) Or. (Portland In.)	45·22 N	122·37 W
93	Westlock (wĕst'lŏk) Can.	54·09 N	113·52 W
117	West Memphis Ar.	35·08 N	90·11 W
113	Westminster (wĕst'mĭn-stẽr) Ca. (Los Angeles In.)	33·45 N	117·59 W
105	Westminster Md.	39·40 N	76·55 W
120	Westminster SC	34·38 N	83·10 W
89	Westmount (wĕst'mount) Can. (Montréal In.)	45·29 N	73·36 W
99	West Newbury (nū'bẽr-ê) Ma. (In.)	42·47 N	70·57 W
107	West Newton (nū'tŭn) Pa. (Pittsburgh In.)	40·12 N	79·45 W
106	West New York (nů yŏrk) NJ (New York In.)	40·47 N	74·01 W
117	West Nishnabotna (R.) (nĭsh-nȧ-bŏt'nȧ) Ia.	40·56 N	95·37 W
99	Weston (wĕs'tŭn) Ma. (In.)	42·22 N	71·18 W
104	Weston WV	39·00 N	80·30 W
218	Westonaria S. Afr. (Johannesburg & Pretoria In.)	26·19 S	27·38 E
154	Weston-super-Mare (wĕs'tŭn sū'pẽr-mā'rê) Eng.	51·23 N	3·00 W
106	West Orange (wĕst ŏr'ĕnj) NJ (New York In.)	40·46 N	74·14 W
121	West Palm Beach (päm bēch) Fl. (In.)	26·44 N	80·04 W
120	West Pensacola (pĕn-sȧ-kō'lȧ) Fl.	30·24 N	87·18 W
112	West Pittsburg (pĭts'bûrg) Ca. (San Francisco In.)	38·02 N	121·56 W
117	Westplains (wĕst-plānz') Mo.	36·42 N	91·51 W
120	West Point Ga.	32·52 N	85·10 W
120	West Point Ms.	33·36 N	88·39 W
108	Westpoint Ne.	41·50 N	96·00 W
106	West Point NY (New York In.)	41·23 N	73·58 W
113	West Point Ut. (Salt Lake City In.)	41·07 N	112·05 W
105	West Point Va.	37·25 N	76·50 W
106	Westport (wĕst'pōrt) Ct. (New York In.)	41·07 N	73·22 W
154	Westport Ire.	53·44 N	9·36 W
112	Westport (wĕst'pôrt) Or. (Portland In.)	46·08 N	123·22 W
154	Westray (I.) (wĕs'trā) Scot.	59·19 N	3·05 W
92	West Road (R.) (rōd) Can.	53·00 N	124·00 W
113	West St. Paul (sȧnt pôl') Mn. (Minneapolis, St. Paul In.)	44·55 N	93·05 W
129	West Sand Spit (I.) Ba.	21·25 N	72·10 W
155	West Schelde (R.) Neth.	51·25 N	3·30 E
112	West Slope Or. (Portland In.)	45·30 N	122·46 W
115	West Tavaputs Plat. (wĕst tăv'ȧ-po͞ots) Ut.	39·45 N	110·35 W
104	West Terre Haute (tĕr-ê hōt') In.	39·30 N	87·30 W
109	West Union (ūn'yŭn) Ia.	42·58 N	91·48 W
119	West University Place Tx. (In.)	29·43 N	95·26 W
107	Westview (wĕst'vů) Oh. (Cleveland In.)	41·21 N	81·54 W
107	West View Pa. (Pittsburgh In.)	40·31 N	80·02 W
99	Westville (wĕst'vĭl) Can.	45·34 N	62·43 W
104	Westville Il.	40·00 N	87·40 W
103	West Virginia (State) (wĕst vẽr-jĭn'ĭ-ȧ) U. S.	39·00 N	80·50 W
114	West Walker (R.) (wôk'ẽr) Ca.	38·25 N	119·25 W
106	West Warwick (wŏr'ĭk) RI (Providence In.)	41·42 N	71·31 W
106	Westwego (wĕst-wē'gō) La. (New Orleans In.)	29·55 N	90·09 W
114	Westwood (wĕst'wo͝od) Ca.	40·18 N	121·00 W
113	Westwood Ks. (Kansas City In.)	39·03 N	94·37 W
99	Westwood Ma. (In.)	42·13 N	71·14 W
106	Westwood NJ (New York In.)	40·59 N	74·02 W
203	West Wyalong (wī'alông) Austl.	34·00 S	147·20 E
197	Wetar, Pulau (I.) (wĕt'ár) Indon.	7·34 S	126·00 E
93	Wetaskiwin (wĕ-tăs'kê-wŏn) Can.	52·58 N	113·22 W
113	Wetmore (wĕt'mōr) Tx. (San Antonio In.)	29·34 N	98·25 W
161	Wettin (vĕ'tēn) F.R.G. (Ruhr In.)	51·23 N	7·23 E
120	Wetumpka (wê-tŭmp'kȧ) Al.	32·33 N	86·12 W
161	Wetzlar (vets'lär) F.R.G.	50·35 N	8·30 E
197	Wewak (wȧ-wäk') Pap. N. Gui.	3·19 S	143·30 E
117	Wewoka (wê-wō'kȧ) Ok.	35·09 N	96·30 W
154	Wexford (wĕks'fẽrd) Ire.	52·20 N	6·30 W
148	Weybridge (wā'brĭj) Eng. (London In.)	51·20 N	0·26 W
94	Weyburn (wā'-bûrn) Can.	49·41 N	103·52 W
211	Weyib (R.) Eth.	6·25 N	41·21 E
154	Weymouth (wā'mŭth) Eng.	50·37 N	2·34 W
99	Weymouth Ma. (In.)	42·44 N	70·57 W
107	Weymouth Oh. (Cleveland In.)	41·11 N	81·48 W
128	Whale Cay (I.) Ba.	24·50 N	77·45 W
128	Whale Cay Chans. Ba.	26·45 N	77·10 W
154	Wharfe (R.) (hwôr'fê) Eng.	54·01 N	1·53 W
106	Wharton (hwôr'tŭn) NJ (New York In.)	40·54 N	74·35 W
119	Wharton Tx.	29·19 N	96·06 W
109	What Cheer (hwŏt chēr) Ia.	41·23 N	92·24 W
112	Whatcom, L. (hwät'kŭm) Wa. (Portland In.)	48·44 N	123·34 W
93	Whatshan L. (wŏt'-shăn) Can.	50·00 N	118·03 W
111	Wheatland (hwēt'lănd) Wy.	42·04 N	104·52 W
107	Wheaton (hwē'tŭn) Il. (Chicago In.)	41·52 N	88·06 W
106	Wheaton Md. (Baltimore In.)	39·05 N	77·05 W
108	Wheaton Mn.	45·48 N	96·29 W
115	Wheeler Pk. Nv.	38·58 N	114·15 W
107	Wheeling (hwēl'ĭng) Il. (Chicago In.)	42·08 N	87·54 W
104	Wheeling WV	40·05 N	80·45 W
137	Wheelwright (o͞oē'l-rē'gt) Arg. (Buenos Aires In.)	33·46 S	61·14 W
112	Whidbey I. (hwĭd'bê) Wa. (Seattle In.)	48·13 N	122·50 W
106	Whippany (hwĭp'á-nē) NJ (New York In.)	40·49 N	74·25 W
120	Whistler (hwĭs'lẽr) Al.	30·46 N	88·07 W
97	Whitby (hwĭt'bê) Can.	43·50 N	79·00 W
148	Whitchurch (hwĭt'chûrch) Eng.	52·58 N	2·49 W
97	White (L.) Can.	45·15 N	76·35 W
96	White (L.) Can.	48·47 N	85·50 W
96	White (R.) Can.	48·34 N	85·46 W
117	White (R.) Ar.	34·32 N	91·11 W
115	White (R.) Co.	40·10 N	108·55 W
104	White (R.) In.	39·15 N	86·45 W
108	White (R.) SD	43·41 N	99·48 W
108	White (R.), South Fork SD	43·13 N	101·04 W
116	White (R.) Tx.	36·25 N	102·20 W
105	White (R.) Vt.	43·45 N	72·35 W
114	White, Mt. Ca.	37·38 N	118·13 W
99	White B. Can.	50·00 N	56·30 W
113	White Bear Lake Mn. (Minneapolis, St. Paul In.)	45·05 N	93·01 W
113	White Bear L. Mn. (Minneapolis, St. Paul In.)	45·04 N	92·58 W
95	White Bear Ind. Res. Can.	49·15 N	102·15 W
119	White Castle La.	30·10 N	91·09 W
112	White Center Wa. (Seattle In.)	47·31 N	122·21 W
104	White Cloud Mi.	43·35 N	85·45 W
93	Whitecourt (wīt'-côrt) Can.	54·09 N	115·41 W
108	White Earth (R.) ND	48·30 N	102·44 W
108	White Earth Ind. Res. Mn.	47·18 N	95·42 W
109	Whiteface (R.) (whīt'fās) Mn.	47·12 N	92·13 W
105	Whitefield (hwīt'fēld) NH	44·20 N	71·35 W
111	Whitefish (hwīt'fĭsh) Mt.	48·24 N	114·25 W
109	Whitefish (B.) Mi.	46·36 N	84·50 W
109	Whitefish (R.) Mi.	46·12 N	86·56 W
95	Whitefish B. Can.	49·26 N	94·14 W
107	Whitefish Bay Wi. (Milwaukee In.)	43·07 N	77·54 W
117	White Hall Il.	39·26 N	90·23 W
104	Whitehall (hwīt'hôl) Mi.	43·20 N	86·20 W
105	Whitehall NY	43·30 N	73·25 W
154	Whitehaven (hwīt'hā-vĕn) Eng.	54·35 N	3·30 W
112	Whitehorn, Pt. (hwīt'hôrn) Wa. (Vancouver In.)	48·54 N	122·48 W
90	Whitehorse (whīt'hôrs) Can.	60·39 N	135·01 W
119	White L. La.	29·40 N	92·35 W
98	White Mts. Me.	44·22 N	71·15 W
105	White Mts. NH	42·20 N	71·05 W
108	Whitemouth (L.) Can.	49·14 N	95·40 W
211	White Nile (Abyad, Al-Bahr al-) (R.) Sud.	14·00 N	32·35 E
109	White Otter (L.) Can.	49·15 N	91·48 W
90	White P. Ak.-Can.	59·35 N	135·03 W
106	White Plains NY (New York In.)	41·02 N	73·47 W
96	White River Can.	48·38 N	85·23 W
104	White R., East Fork In.	38·45 N	86·20 W
110	White R. Wa.	47·07 N	121·48 W
115	White River Plat. Co.	39·45 N	107·50 W
112	White Rock Can. (Vancouver In.)	49·01 N	122·49 W
113	Whiterock Res. (hwīt'rŏk) Tx. (Dallas, Fort Worth In.)	32·51 N	96·40 W
92	Whitesail L. (whīt'-sāl) Can.	53·30 N	127·00 W
115	White Sands Natl. Mon. NM	32·50 N	106·20 W
170	White Sea Sov. Un.	66·00 N	40·00 E
113	White Settlement Tx. (Dallas, Fort Worth In.)	32·45 N	97·28 W
111	White Sulphur Springs Mt.	46·32 N	110·49 W
213	White Umfolzi (R.) (ŭm-fô-lō'zē) S. Afr. (Natal In.)	28·12 S	30·55 E
121	Whiteville (hwīt'vĭl) NC	34·18 N	78·45 W
214	White Volta (R.) Ghana	9·40 N	1·10 W
109	Whitewater (whīt-wŏt'ẽr) Wi.	42·49 N	88·40 W
108	Whitewater (L.) Can.	49·14 N	100·39 W
121	Whitewater B. Fl. (In.)	25·16 N	80·21 W
111	Whitewater Cr. Mt.	48·50 N	107·50 W
95	Whitewater L. Can.	49·15 N	100·20 W
107	Whitewater R. In. (Cincinnati In.)	39·19 N	84·55 W
120	Whitewell (hwīt'wĕl) Tn.	35·11 N	85·31 W
117	Whitewright (hwīt'rīt) Tx.	33·33 N	96·25 W
154	Whitham (R.) (wĭth'ŭm) Eng.	53·08 N	0·15 W
107	Whiting (hwīt'ĭng) In. (Chicago In.)	41·41 N	87·30 W
99	Whitinsville (hwīt'ĕns-vĭl) Ma. (In.)	42·06 N	71·40 W
99	Whitman (hwĭt'mȧn) Ma. (In.)	42·05 N	70·57 W
121	Whitmire (hwĭt'mīr) SC	34·30 N	81·40 W
114	Whitney, Mt. Ca.	36·34 N	118·18 W
119	Whitney L. (hwĭt'nê) Tx.	32·02 N	97·36 W
148	Whitstable (wĭt'stȧb'l) Eng. (London In.)	51·22 N	1·03 E
205	Whitsunday (I.) (hwĭt's'n-dā) Austl.	20·16 S	149·00 E
113	Whittier (hwĭt'ĭ-ẽr) Ca. (Los Angeles In.)	33·58 N	118·02 W
213	Whittlesea (wĭt'l'sē) S. Afr. (Natal In.)	32·11 S	26·51 E
148	Whitworth (hwĭt'wŭrth) Eng.	53·40 N	2·10 W
203	Whyalla (hwī-ăl'ȧ) Austl.	33·00 S	137·32 E
92	Whymper, Mt. (wĭm'-pẽr) Can.	48·57 N	124·10 W
96	Wiarton (wī'ăr-tŭn) Can.	44·45 N	80·45 W
117	Wichita (wĭch'ĭ-tô) Ks.	37·42 N	97·21 W
116	Wichita (R.) Tx.	33·50 N	99·38 W
116	Wichita Falls (fôls) Tx.	33·54 N	98·29 W
154	Wichita Mts. Ok.	34·48 N	98·43 W
154	Wick (wĭk) Scot.	58·25 N	3·05 W
106	Wickatunk (wĭk'á-tŭnk) NJ (New York In.)	40·21 N	74·15 W
115	Wickenburg Az.	33·58 N	112·44 W
107	Wickliffe (wĭk'klĭf) Oh. (Cleveland In.)	41·37 N	81·29 W
	Wicklow, see Cill Mantainn		
154	Wicklow Mts. (wĭk'lō) Ire.	52·49 N	6·20 W
112	Wickup Mtn. (wĭk'ŭp) Or. (Portland In.)	46·06 N	123·35 W
105	Wiconisco (wĭ-kŏn'ĭs-kō) Pa.	43·35 N	76·45 W
104	Widen (wī'dĕn) WV	38·25 N	80·55 W
148	Widnes (wĭd'nĕs) Eng.	53·21 N	2·44 W
158	Wieden (vē'dĕn) F.R.G.	49·41 N	12·09 E
159	Wieliczka (vyĕ-lēch'kȧ) Pol.	49·58 N	20·06 E
159	Wieluń (vyĕ'lo͞on') Pol.	51·13 N	18·33 E
149	Wien (Vienna (vēn) (vê-ĕn'ä) Aus. (Vienna In.)	48·13 N	16·22 E
149	Wien (State) Aus. (Vienna In.)	48·11 N	16·23 E
158	Wiener Neustadt (vē'nĕr noi'shtät) Aus.	47·48 N	16·15 E
149	Wiener Wald (For.) Aus. (Vienna In.)	48·09 N	16·05 E
159	Wieprz, R. (vyĕpzh) Pol.	51·25 N	22·45 E
119	Wiergate (wẽr'găt) Tx.	31·00 N	93·42 W
158	Wiesbaden (vēs'bä-dĕn) F.R.G.	50·05 N	8·15 E
148	Wigan (wĭg'ăn) Eng.	53·33 N	2·37 W
120	Wiggins (wĭg'ĭnz) Ms.	30·51 N	89·05 W
145	Wight, Isle of (I.) (wīt) Eng.	50·44 N	1·17 W
117	Wilber (wĭl'bẽr) Ne.	40·29 N	96·57 W

ng-sing; ŋ-baŋk; N-nasalized n; nŏd; cŏmmit; ōld; ôbey; ôrder; fo͞od; fo͝ot; ou-out; s-soft; sh-dish; th-thin; pūre; ůnite; ûrn; stŭd; circŭs; ü-as "y" in study; '-indeterminate vowel.

368 Wilburton — Wollaston PRONOUNCING INDEX

Page	Name Pronunciation Region	Lat. °′	Long. °′
117	Wilburton (wĭl'bẽr-tŭn) Ok.	34·54 N	95·18 W
203	Wilcannia (wĭl-căn-ĭȧ) Austl.	31·30 S	143·30 E
149	Wildau (vēl'dou) G.D.R. (Berlin In.)	52·20 N	13·39 E
149	Wildberg (vēl'bĕrgh) G.D.R.(Berlin In.)	52·52 N	12·39 E
94	Wildcat Hill (wīld'kăt) Can.	53·17 N	102·30 W
93	Wildhay (R.) (wīld'-hā) Can.	53·15 N	117·20 W
113	Wildomar (wĭl'dô-mär) Ca. (Los Angeles In.)	33·35 N	117·17 W
108	Wild Rice (R.) Mn.	47·10 N	96·40 W
108	Wild Rice (R.) ND	46·10 N	97·12 W
113	Wild Rice L. Mn. (Duluth In.)	46·54 N	92·10 W
158	Wild Spitze Pk. Aus.	46·49 N	10·50 E
105	Wildwood NJ	39·00 N	74·50 W
116	Wiley (wī'lê) Co.	38·08 N	102·41 W
218	Wilge R. (wĭl'jê) S. Afr. (Johannesburg & Pretoria In.)	25·38 S	29·09 E
218	Wilge R. S. Afr. (Johannesburg & Pretoria In.)	27·27 S	28·46 E
205	Wilhelm, Mt. Pap. N. Gui.	5·58 S	144·58 E
135	Wilhelmina Gebergte (Mts.) Sur.	4·30 N	57·00 W
158	Wilhelmshaven (vêl-hĕlms-hä'fĕn) F.R.G.	53·30 N	8·10 E
149	Wilhemina, Kanal (can.) Neth. (Amsterdam In.)	51·37 N	4·55 E
105	Wilkes-Barre (wĭlks'băr-ê) Pa.	41·15 N	75·50 W
220	Wilkes Land Ant.	71·00 S	126·00 E
112	Wilkeson (wĭl-kē'sŭn) Wa. (Seattle In.)	47·06 N	122·03 W
94	Wilkie (wĭlk'ē) Can.	52·25 N	108·43 W
107	Wilkinsburg (wĭl'kĭnz-bûrg) Pa. Pittsburgh In.)	40·26 N	79·53 W
110	Willamette R. Or.	44·15 N	123·13 W
104	Willard (wĭl'ȧrd) Oh.	41·00 N	82·50 W
113	Willard Ut. (Salt Lake City In.)	41·24 N	112·02 W
115	Willcox (wĭl'kŏks) Az.	32·15 N	109·50 W
134	Willemstad Neth. Antilles	12·12 N	68·58 W
148	Willesden (wĭlz'dĕn) Eng. (London In.)	51·31 N	0·17 W
93	W. A. C. Bennett Dam Can.	56·01 N	122·10 W
204	William Creek (wĭl'yăm) Austl.	28·45 S	136·20 E
115	Williams (wĭl'yămz) Az.	35·15 N	112·15 W
128	Williams (I.) Ba.	25·30 N	78·30 W
120	Williamsburg (wĭl'yămz-bûrg) Ky.	36·42 N	84·09 W
107	Williamsburg Oh. (Cincinnati In.)	39·04 N	84·02 W
121	Williamsburg Va.	37·15 N	76·41 W
93	Williams Lake Can.	52·08 N	122·09 W
104	Williamson (wĭl'yăm-sŭn) WV	37·40 N	82·15 W
105	Williamsport Md.	39·35 N	77·45 W
105	Williamsport Pa.	41·15 N	77·05 W
121	Williamston (wĭl'yămz-tŭn) NC	35·50 N	77·04 W
121	Williamston SC	34·36 N	82·30 W
104	Williamstown (wĭl'yămz-toun) WV	39·20 N	81·30 W
107	Williamsville (wĭl'yăm-vĭl) NY (Buffalo In.)	42·58 N	78·46 W
105	Willimantic (wĭl-ĭ-măn'tĭk) Ct.	41·40 N	72·10 W
119	Willis (wĭl'ĭs) Tx.	30·24 N	95·29 W
205	Willis Is. Austl.	16·15 S	150·30 E
108	Williston (wĭl'ĭs-tŭn) ND	48·08 N	103·38 W
92	Williston, L. Can.	55·40 N	123·40 W
93	Willmar (wĭl'mär) Mn.	45·07 N	95·05 W
107	Willoughby (wĭl'ô-bê) Oh. (Cleveland In.)	41·39 N	81·25 W
111	Willow Cr. (wĭl'ô) Mt.	48·45 N	111·34 W
110	Willow Cr. Or.	44·21 N	117·34 W
106	Willow Grove Pa. (Philadelphia In.)	40·07 N	75·07 W
107	Willowick (wĭl'ô-wĭk) Oh. (Cleveland In.)	41·39 N	81·28 W
212	Willowmore (wĭl'ô-môr) S. Afr.	33·15 S	23·37 E
107	Willow Run (wĭl'ô rŭn) Mi. (Detroit In.)	42·16 N	83·34 W
114	Willows (wĭl'ōz) Ca.	39·32 N	122·11 W
117	Willow Springs (sprĭngz) Mo.	36·59 N	91·56 W
213	Willowvale (wĭ-lô'văl) S. Afr. (Natal In.)	32·17 S	28·32 E
119	Wills Point (wĭlz point) Tx.	32·42 N	96·02 W
113	Wilmer (wĭl'mẽr) Tx. (Dallas, Fort Worth In.)	32·35 N	96·40 W
107	Wilmette (wĭl-mĕt') Il. (Chicago In.)	42·04 N	87·42 W
203	Wilmington Austl.	32·39 S	138·07 E
113	Wilmington (wĭl'mĭng-tŭn) Ca. (Los Angeles In.)	33·46 N	118·16 W
106	Wilmington De. (Philadelphia In.)	39·45 N	75·33 W
107	Wilmington Il. (Chicago In.)	41·19 N	88·09 W
99	Wilmington Ma. (In.)	42·34 N	71·10 W
121	Wilmington NC	34·12 N	77·56 W
104	Wilmington Oh.	39·20 N	83·50 W
104	Wilmore (wĭl'mōr) Ky.	37·50 N	84·35 W
148	Wilmslow (wĭlmz' lō) Eng.	53·19 N	2·14 W
	Wilno, see Vilnius		
218	Wilpoort S. Afr. (Johannesburg & Pretoria In.)	26·57 S	26·17 E
117	Wilson (wĭl'sŭn) Ar.	35·35 N	90·02 W
121	Wilson NC	35·42 N	77·55 W
117	Wilson Ok.	34·09 N	97·27 W
120	Wilson, L. Al.	34·45 N	86·58 W
120	Wilson (R.) Al.	34·53 N	87·28 W
202	Wilson, Pt. Austl. (Melbourne In.)	38·05 S	144·31 E
113	Wilson, Mt. Ca. (Los Angeles In.)	34·15 N	118·06 W
111	Wilson Pk. Ut.	40·46 N	110·27 W
203	Wilson's Prom. (wĭl'sŭnz) Austl.	39·05 S	146·50 E
113	Wilsonville (wĭl'sŭn-vĭl) Il. (St. Louis In.)	39·04 N	89·52 W
149	Wilstedt (vēl'shtĕt) F.R.G. (Hamburg In.)	53·45 N	10·04 E
149	Wilster (vēl'stẽr) F.R.G. (Hamburg In.)	53·55 N	9·23 E
106	Wilton (wĭl'tŭn) Ct. (New York In.)	41·11 N	73·25 W
108	Wilton ND	47·09 N	100·47 W
204	Wiluna (wĭ-lōō'nȧ) Austl.	26·35 S	120·25 E
104	Winamac (wĭn'ȧ măk) In.	41·05 N	86·40 W
218	Winburg (wĭm-bûrg) S. Afr. (Johannesburg & Pretoria In.)	28·31 S	27·02 E
113	Winchester (wĭn'chĕs-tẽr) Ca. (Los Angeles In.)	33·41 N	117·06 W
154	Winchester Eng.	51·04 N	1·20 W
110	Winchester Id.	46·14 N	116·39 W
104	Winchester In.	40·10 N	84·50 W
104	Winchester Ky.	38·00 N	84·15 W
99	Winchester Ma. (Boston In.)	42·28 N	71·09 W
105	Winchester NH	42·45 N	72·25 W
115	Winchester Tn.	35·11 N	86·06 W
105	Winchester Va.	39·10 N	78·10 W
105	Windber (wĭnd'bẽr) Pa.	40·15 N	78·45 W
108	Wind Cave Natl. Park SD	43·36 N	103·53 W
115	Winder (wīn'dẽr) Ga.	33·58 N	83·43 W
154	Windermere (wĭn'dẽr-mẽr) Eng.	54·25 N	2·59 W
93	Windfall (wĭnd'fôl) Can.	54·11 N	116·15 W
105	Windham (wĭnd'ăm) Ct.	41·45 N	72·05 W
99	Windham NH (Boston In.)	42·49 N	71·21 W
212	Windhoek (vĭnt'hŏŏk) Namibia	22·05 S	17·10 E
107	Wind L. Wi. (Milwaukee In.)	42·49 N	88·06 W
118	Wind Mtn. NM	32·02 N	105·30 W
109	Windom (wĭn'dŭm) Mn.	43·50 N	95·04 W
203	Windora (wĭn-dō'rȧ) Austl.	25·15 S	142·50 E
111	Wind R. Wy.	43·17 N	109·02 W
111	Wind River Ind. Res. Wy.	43·07 N	109·08 W
111	Wind River Ra. Wy.	43·19 N	109·47 W
202	Windsor (wĭn'zẽr) Austl. (Sydney In.)	33·37 S	150·49 E
107	Windsor Can. (Detroit In.)	42·19 N	83·00 W
98	Windsor Can.	44·59 N	64·08 W
99	Windsor Can.	48·57 N	55·40 W
116	Windsor Co.	40·27 N	104·51 W
148	Windsor Eng. (London In.)	51·27 N	0·37 W
117	Windsor Mo.	38·32 N	93·31 W
98	Windsor Vt.	43·30 N	72·25 W
121	Windsor NC	35·58 N	76·57 W
123	Windward Is. (wind'wẽrd) N. A.	12·45 N	61·40 W
129	Windward Pass N. A.	19·30 N	74·20 W
94	Winefred L. Can.	55·30 N	110·35 W
117	Winfield Ks.	37·14 N	97·00 W
111	Winifred (wĭn ĭ frĕd) Mt.	47·35 N	109·20 W
91	Winisk (R.) Can.	54·30 N	86·30 W
118	Wink (wĭŋk) Tx.	31·48 N	103·06 W
95	Winkler (wĭnk'lẽr) Can.	49·11 N	97·56 W
214	Winneba (wĭn'ê-bȧ) Ghana	5·25 N	0·36 W
109	Winnebago (wĭn'ê-bā'gō) Mn.	43·45 N	94·08 W
109	Winnebago, L. Wi.	44·09 N	88·10 W
108	Winnebago Ind. Res. Ne.	42·15 N	96·06 W
110	Winnemucca (wĭn-ê-mŭk'ȧ) Nv.	40·59 N	117·43 W
114	Winnemucca (L.) Nv.	40·06 N	119·07 W
108	Winner (wĭn'ẽr) SD	43·22 N	99·50 W
107	Winnetka (wĭ-nĕt'kȧ) Il. (Chicago In.)	42·07 N	87·44 W
111	Winnett (wĭn'ĕt) Mt.	47·01 N	108·20 W
119	Winnfield (wĭn'fēld) La.	31·56 N	92·39 W
109	Winnibigoshish (L.) (wĭn'ĭ-bĭ-gō'shĭsh) Mn.	47·30 N	93·45 W
89	Winnipeg (wĭn'ĭ-pĕg) Can. (Winnipeg In.)	49·53 N	97·09 W
95	Winnipeg, L. Can.	52·00 N	97·00 W
90	Winnipeg (R.) Can.	52·20 N	95·54 W
95	Winnipeg Beach Can.	50·31 N	96·58 W
95	Winnipegosis (wĭn'ĭ-pê-gō'sĭs) Can.	51·39 N	99·56 W
95	Winnipegosis (L.) Can.	52·30 N	100·00 W
105	Winnipesaukee (L.) (wĭn'ê-pê-sô'kê) NH	43·40 N	71·20 W
119	Winnsboro (wĭnz'bŭr'ô) La.	32·09 N	91·42 W
121	Winnsboro SC	34·29 N	81·05 W
117	Winnsboro Tx.	32·56 N	95·15 W
89	Winona (wĭ-nō'nȧ) Can. (Toronto In.)	43·13 N	79·39 W
109	Winona Mn.	44·03 N	91·40 W
120	Winona Ms.	33·29 N	89·43 W
105	Winooski (wĭ'nōōs-kê) Vt.	44·30 N	73·10 W
149	Winsen (Luhe) (vēn'zĕn) (lōō'hĕ) F.R.G. (Hamburg In.)	53·22 N	10·13 E
148	Winsford (wĭnz'fẽrd) Eng.	53·11 N	2·30 W
115	Winslow (wĭnz'lō) Az.	35·00 N	110·45 W
112	Winslow Wa. (Seattle In.)	47·38 N	122·31 W
105	Winsted (wĭn'stĕd) Ct.	41·55 N	73·05 W
148	Winster (wĭn'stẽr) Eng.	53·08 N	1·38 W
121	Winston-Salem (wĭn stŭn-sā'lĕm) NC	36·05 N	80·15 W
213	Winterberge (Mts.) S. Afr. (Natal In.)	32·18 S	26·25 E
121	Winter Garden (wĭn'tẽr gär'd'n) Fl. (In.)	28·32 N	81·35 W
92	Winter Harbour Can.	50·31 N	128·02 W
121	Winter Haven (hā'vĕn) Fl. (In.)	28·01 N	81·38 W
95	Wintering L. (wĭn'tẽr-ĭng) Can.	55·24 N	97·42 W
121	Winter Park (pärk) Fl. (In.)	28·35 N	81·21 W
118	Winters (wĭn'tẽrz) Tx.	31·59 N	99·58 W
109	Winterset (wĭn'tẽr-sĕt) Ia.	41·19 N	94·03 W
161	Winterswijk Neth. (Ruhr In.)	51·58 N	6·44 E
158	Winterthur (vĭn'tẽr-tōōr) Switz.	47·30 N	8·32 E
213	Winterton S. Afr. (Natal In.)	28·51 S	29·33 E
98	Winthrop (wĭn'thrŭp) Me.	44·19 N	70·00 W
99	Winthrop Ma. (In.)	42·23 N	70·59 W
109	Winthrop Mn.	44·31 N	94·20 W
205	Winton (wĭn-tŭn) Austl.	22·17 S	143·08 E
161	Wipperfürth (vĕ'pĕr-fürt) F.R.G. (Ruhr In.)	51·07 N	7·23 E
148	Wirksworth (wûrks'wûrth) Eng.	53·05 N	1·35 W
103	Wisconsin (State) (wĭs-kŏn'sĭn) U. S.	44·30 N	91·00 W
109	Wisconsin (R.) Wi.	43·14 N	90·34 W
109	Wisconsin Dells Wi.	43·38 N	89·46 W
109	Wisconsin Rapids Wi.	44·24 N	89·50 W
108	Wishek (wĭsh'ĕk) ND	46·15 N	99·34 W
159	Wisla (Vistula) R. (vēs'wȧ) (vĭs'tû-lȧ) Pol.	52·48 N	19·02 E
159	Wisloka R. (vês-wô'kȧ) Pol.	49·55 N	21·26 E
135	Wismar (wĭs'mȧr) Guy.	5·58 N	58·15 W
158	Wismar (vĭs'mär) G.D.R.	53·53 N	11·28 E
108	Wisner (wĭz'nẽr) Ne.	42·00 N	96·55 W
161	Wissembourg (vē-säN-bōōr') Fr.	49·03 N	7·58 E
117	Wister, L. (vĭs'tẽr) Ok.	35·02 N	94·52 W
218	Witbank (wĭt-băŋk) S. Afr. (Johannesburg & Pretoria In.)	25·53 S	29·14 E
213	Witberg (Mtn.) S. Afr. (Natal In.)	30·32 S	27·18 E
148	Witham (wĭdh'ăm) Eng. (London In.)	51·48 N	0·37 E
148	Witham (R.) Eng.	53·11 N	0·20 W
107	Withamsville (wĭdh'ămz-vĭl) Oh. (Cincinnati In.)	39·04 N	84·16 W
121	Withlacoochee (R.) (wĭth-lȧ-kōō'chê) Fl. (In.)	28·58 N	82·30 W
120	Withlacoochee (R.) Ga.	31·15 N	83·30 W
113	Withrow (wĭdh'rō) Mn. (Minneapolis, St. Paul In.)	45·08 N	92·54 W
148	Witney (wĭt'nê) Eng. (London In.)	51·45 N	1·30 W
104	Witt (vĭt) Il.	39·10 N	89·15 W
161	Witten (vē'tĕn) F.R.G. (Ruhr In.)	51·26 N	7·19 E
158	Wittenberg (vē'tĕn-bĕrgh) G.D.R.	51·53 N	12·40 E
158	Wittenberge (vĭt-ĕn-bĕr'gē) G.D.R.	52·59 N	11·45 E
158	Wittlich (vĭt'lĭk) F.R.G.	49·58 N	6·54 E
213	Witu (wē'tōō) Ken.	2·18 S	40·28 E
197	Witu Is. Pap. N. Gui.	4·45 S	149·50 E
213	Witwatersberg (Mts.) (wĭt-wôr-tẽrz-bûrg) S. Afr. (Johannesburg & Pretotia In.)	25·58 S	27·53 E
218	Witwatersrand (Ridge) (wĭt-wôr'tẽrs-rănd) S. Afr. (Johannesburg & Pretoria In.)	25·55 S	26·27 E
159	Wkra R. (f'krȧ) Pol.	52·40 N	20·35 E
159	Wloclawek (vwô-tswä'vĕk) Pol.	52·38 N	19·08 E
159	Wlodawa (vwô-dä'vä) Pol.	51·33 N	23·33 E
159	Wloszczowa (vwôsh-chô'vä) Pol.	50·51 N	19·58 E
99	Woburn (wōō'bŭrn) (wō'bŭrn) Ma. (In.)	42·29 N	71·10 W
149	Woerden Neth. (Amsterdam In.)	52·05 N	4·52 E
148	Woking Eng. (London In.)	51·18 N	0·33 W
148	Wokingham (wô'kĭng-hăm) Eng. (London In.)	51·23 N	0·50 W
113	Wolcott (wōl'kŏt) Ks. (Kansas City In.)	39·12 N	94·47 W
105	Wolf (I.) (wŏŏlf) Can.	44·10 N	76·25 W
120	Wolf (R.) Ms.	30·45 N	89·36 W
109	Wolf (R.) Wi.	45·14 N	88·45 W
158	Wolfenbüttel (vôl'fĕn-büt-ĕl) F.R.G.	52·10 N	10·32 E
107	Wolf L. Il. (Chicago In.)	41·39 N	87·33 W
111	Wolf Point (wŏŏlf point) Mt.	48·07 N	105·40 W
149	Wolfratshausen (vôlf'räts-hou-zĕn) F.R.G. (Munich In.)	47·55 N	11·25 E
158	Wolfsburg (vôlfs'bŏŏrgh) F.R.G.	52·30 N	10·37 E
98	Wolfville (wŏŏlf'vĭl) Can.	45·05 N	64·22 W
158	Wolgast (vôl'gäst) G.D.R.	54·04 N	13·46 E
213	Wolhuterskop S. Afr. (Johannesburg & Pretoria In.)	25·41 S	27·40 E
149	Wolkersdorf Aus. (Vienna In.)	48·24 N	16·31 E
90	Wollaston (L.) (wŏŏl'ȧs-tŭn) Can.	58·15 N	103·20 W

ăt; finȧl; rāte; senâte; ärm; ȧsk; sofȧ; fâre; ch-choose; dh-as th in other; bē; êvent; bĕt; recĕnt; cratẽr; g-go; gh-guttural g; bĭt; ĭ-short neutral; rīde; K-guttural k as ch in German ich;

PRONOUNCING INDEX

Wollaston — Yahongqiao 369

Page	Name Pronunciation Region	Lat. °′	Long. °′
90	Wollaston Pen. Can.	70·00 N	115·00 W
203	Wollongong (wo͝ol'ŭn-gŏng). Austl.	34·26 S	151·05 E
159	Wolomin (vô-wō'mên) Pol.	52·19 N	21·17 E
94	Wolseley Can.	50·25 N	103·15 W
148	Wolstanton (wo͝ol-stăn'tŭn) Eng.	53·02 N	2·13 W
149	Woltersdorf (vōl'tĕrs-dōrf) G.D.R. (Berlin In.)	52·07 N	13·13 E
148	Wolverhampton (wo͝ol'vēr-hămp-tŭn). Eng.	52·35 N	2·07 W
218	Wolwehoek S. Afr. (Johannesburg & Pretoria In.)	26·55 S	27·50 E
194	Wŏnsan (wŭn'săn') Kor.	39·08 N	127·24 E
203	Wonthaggi (wônt-hăg'ē) Austl.	38·45 S	145·42 E
108	Wood (wo͝od) SD	43·26 N	100·25 W
108	Woodbine (wo͝od'bīn) Ia.	41·44 N	95·42 W
106	Woodbridge (wo͝od'brĭj') NJ (New York In.)	40·33 N	74·18 W
90	Wood Buffalo Natl. Park Can.	59·50 N	118·53 W
113	Woodburn (wo͝od'bûrn) Il. (St. Louis In.)	39·03 N	90·01 W
110	Woodburn Or.	45·10 N	122·51 W
106	Woodbury (wo͝od'bĕr-ê) NJ (Philadelpahi In.)	39·50 N	75·14 W
113	Woodcrest (wo͝od'krĕst) Ca. (Los Angeles In.)	33·53 N	117·18 W
112	Woodinville (wo͝od'ĭn-vĭl) Wa. (Seattle In.)	47·46 N	122·09 W
114	Woodland (wo͝od'lănd) Ca.	38·41 N	121·47 W
112	Woodland Wa. (Portland In.)	45·54 N	122·45 W
113	Woodland Hills Ca. (Los Angeles In.)	34·10 N	118·36 W
197	Woodlark I. (wo͝od'lark) Pap. N. Gui.	9·07 S	152·00 E
107	Woodlawn Beach (wo͝od'lôn bēch) NY (Buffalo In.)	42·48 N	78·51 W
94	Wood Mountain Can.	49·14 N	106·20 W
113	Wood River Il. (St. Louis In.)	38·52 N	90·06 W
204	Woodroffe, Mt. (wo͝od'rŭf) Austl.	26·05 S	132·00 E
121	Woodruff (wo͝od'rŭf) SC	34·43 N	82·03 W
204	Woods (L.) (wo͝odz) Austl.	18·00 S	133·18 E
103	Woods, L. of the Can.-Mn.	49·25 N	93·25 W
113	Woods Cross (krôs) Ut. (Salt Lake City In.)	40·53 N	111·54 W
104	Woodsfield (wo͝odz-fēld) Oh.	39·45 N	81·10 W
112	Woodson (wo͝odsŭn) Or. (Portland In.)	46·07 N	123·20 W
98	Woodstock (wo͝od'stŏk) Can.	43·10 N	80·50 W
98	Woodstock Can.	46·09 N	67·34 W
148	Woodstock Eng. (London In.)	51·48 N	1·22 W
109	Woodstock Il.	42·20 N	88·29 W
105	Woodstock Va.	38·55 N	78·25 W
105	Woodsville (wo͝odz'vĭl) NH	44·10 N	72·00 W
120	Woodville (wo͝od'vĭl) Ms.	31·06 N	91·11 W
119	Woodville Tx.	30·48 N	94·25 W
116	Woodward (wo͝od'wôrd) Ok.	36·25 N	99·24 W
148	Woolwich (wo͝ol'ĭj) Eng. (London In.)	51·28 N	0·05 E
203	Woomera (wo͞om'ērȧ) Austl.	31·15 S	136·43 E
106	Woonsocket (wo͞on-sŏk'ĕt) RI (Providence In.)	42·00 N	71·30 W
108	Woonsocket SD	44·03 N	98·17 W
104	Wooster (wo͝os'tēr) Oh.	40·50 N	81·55 W
154	Worcester (wo͝o'stēr) Eng.	52·09 N	2·14 W
99	Worcester Ma. (In.)	42·16 N	71·49 W
212	Worcester (wo͝os'tēr) S. Afr.	33·35 S	19·31 E
148	Worcester (Co.) (wo͝o'stēr) Eng.	52·24 N	2·15 W
113	Worden (wôr'dĕn) Il. (St. Louis In.)	38·56 N	89·50 W
154	Workington (wûr'kĭng-tŭn) Eng.	54·40 N	3·30 W
148	Worksop (wûrk'sŏp) (wûr'sŭp) Eng.	53·18 N	1·07 W
111	Worland (wûr'lănd) Wy.	44·02 N	107·56 W
158	Worms (vōrms) F.R.G.	49·37 N	8·22 E
202	Worona Res. Austl. (Sydney In.)	34·12 S	150·55 E
107	Worth (wûrth) Il. (Chicago In.)	41·42 N	87·47 W
117	Worth L. Tx. (Dallas, Fort Worth In.)	32·48 N	97·32 W
119	Wortham (wûr'dhăm) Tx.	31·46 N	96·22 W
154	Worthing (wûr'dhĭng) Eng.	50·48 N	0·29 W
104	Worthington (wûr'dhĭng-tŭn) In.	39·05 N	87·00 W
108	Worthington Mn.	43·38 N	95·36 W
197	Wowoni, Pulau (I.) (wō-wō'nê) Indon.	4·05 S	123·45 E
148	Wragby (răg'bê) Eng.	53·17 N	0·19 W
101	Wrangell (rănōgĕl) Ak.	56·28 N	132·25 W
101	Wrangell, Mt. Ak.	61·58 N	143·50 W
101	Wrangell Mts. Ak.-Can.	62·28 N	142·40 W
154	Wrath, C. (răth) Scot.	58·34 N	5·01 W
116	Wray (rā) Co.	40·06 N	102·14 W
137	Wreak (R.) (rēk) Eng.	52·45 N	0·59 W
205	Wreck Rfs. (rĕk) Austl.	22·00 S	155·52 E
148	Wrekin, The (Mt. (rĕk'ĭn) Eng.	54·20 N	2·33 W
121	Wrens (rĕnz) Ga.	33·15 N	82·25 W
99	Wrentham Ma. (Boston In.)	42·04 N	71·20 W
148	Wrexham (rĕk'săm) Wales	53·03 N	3·00 W
107	Wrights Corners (rīts kôr'nērz) NY (Buffalo In.)	43·14 N	78·42 W
121	Wrightsville (rīts'vĭl) Ga.	32·44 N	82·44 W
159	Wroclaw (Breslau) (vrôtsläv) (brĕs'lou). Pol.	51·07 N	17·10 E
148	Wrotham (ro͞ot'ŭm) Eng. (London In.)	51·18 N	0·19 E
159	Wrzesnia (vzhäsh'nyȧ) Pol.	52·19 N	17·33 E
193	Wuchang (wo͞o-chäŋ) China	30·32 N	114·25 E
192	Wuchang China	44·59 N	127·00 E
190	Wucheng (wo͞o-chŭŋ) China	37·14 N	116·03 E
193	Wuhan China	30·30 N	114·15 E
190	Wuhu (wo͞o'ho͞o') China	31·22 N	118·22 E
193	Wui Shan (Mts.) China	26·38 N	116·35 E
190	Wuji (wo͞o-jyĭ) China	38·12 N	114·57 E
190	Wujiang (wo͞o-jyäŋ) China	31·10 N	120·38 E
194	Wulajie (wo͞o-lä-jyĕ) China	44·08 N	126·25 E
190	Wuleidao Wan (C.) (wo͞o-lā-dou wän). China	36·55 N	122·00 E
196	Wu Liang Shan (Mts.) China	23·07 N	100·45 E
190	Wulidian (wo͞o-lē-dĭĕn) China	32·09 N	114·17 E
149	Wünsdorf (vüns'dorf) G.D.R. (Berlin In.)	52·10 N	13·29 E
115	Wupatki Nat'l Mon. Ariz.	35·35 N	111·45 W
193	Wuping (wo͞o-pĭŋ) China	25·05 N	116·01 E
161	Wuppertal (vo͝op'ēr-täl) F.R.G. (Ruhr In.)	51·16 N	7·14 E
190	Wuqiao (wo͞o-chyou) China	37·37 N	116·29 E
193	Wu R. (wo͞o') China	27·30 N	108·00 E
158	Würm See (L.) (vürm zā) F.R.G.	47·58 N	11·30 E
161	Würselen (vür'zĕ-lĕn) F.R.G. (Ruhr In.)	50·49 N	6·09 E
158	Würzburg (vürts'bo͝orgh) F.R.G.	49·48 N	9·57 E
158	Wurzen (vo͝ort'sĕn) G.D.R.	51·22 N	12·45 E
188	Wushi (wo͞o-shr) China	41·13 N	79·08 E
191	Wusong (wo͞o-sôŋ) China (Shanghai In.)	31·23 N	121·29 E
149	Wustermark (vo͞os'tĕr-märk) G.D.R. (Berlin In.)	52·33 N	12·57 E
149	Wustrau (vōost'rou) G.D.R. (Berlin In.)	52·51 N	12·51 E
149	Wuustwezel Bel. (Brussels In.)	51·23 N	4·36 E
190	Wuwei (wo͞o'wā') China	31·19 N	117·53 E
190	Wuxi (wo͞o-shyē) China	31·36 N	120·17 E
193	Wuxing (wo͞o-shyĭŋ) China	30·38 N	120·10 E
193	Wuyi Shan (Mts.) (wo͞o-yē shän) China	26·38 N	116·35 E
190	Wuyou (wo͞o-yō) China	33·18 N	120·15 E
193	Wuzhi Shan (Mtn.) (wo͞o-jr shän). China	18·48 N	109·30 E
193	Wuzhou (wo͞o-jō) China	23·32 N	111·25 E
107	Wyandotte (wī'ăn-dŏt) Mi. (Detroit In.)	42·12 N	83·10 W
148	Wye (wī) Eng. (London In.)	51·12 N	0·57 E
148	Wye (R.) Eng.	53·14 N	1·46 W
117	Wymore (wī'mōr) Ne.	40·09 N	96·41 W
212	Wynberg (wĭn'bĕrg) S. Afr. (In.)	34·00 S	18·28 E
204	Wyndham (wĭnd'ăm) Austl.	15·30 S	128·15 E
117	Wynne (wĭn) Ar.	35·12 N	90·46 W
117	Wynnewood (wĭn'wo͝od) Ok.	34·39 N	97·10 W
117	Wynona (wī-nō'nȧ) Ok.	36·33 N	96·19 W
94	Wynyard (wĭn'yērd) Can.	51·47 N	104·10 W
107	Wyoming (wī-ō'mĭng) Oh. (Cincinnati In.)	39·14 N	84·28 W
102	Wyoming (State) U. S.	42·50 N	108·30 W
111	Wyoming Ra. Wy.	42·43 N	110·35 W
148	Wyre For. (wīr) Eng.	52·24 N	2·24 W
158	Wysokie Mazowieckie (vê-sô'kyĕ mä-zô-vyĕts'kyĕ). Pol.	52·55 N	22·42 E
158	Wyszkow (vêsh'ko͝of) Pol.	52·35 N	21·29 E
121	Wytheville (wĭth'vĭl) Va.	36·55 N	81·06 W

X

Page	Name Pronunciation Region	Lat. °′	Long. °′
128	Xagua, Banco (Bk.) (bä'n-kō-sä'gwä). Cuba	21·35 N	80·50 W
161	Xanten (ksän'tĕn) F.R.G. (Ruhr In.)	51·40 N	6·28 E
165	Xanthi Grc.	41·08 N	24·53 E
212	Xau, L. Bots.	21·15 S	24·38 E
126	Xcalak (sä-lä'k) Mex. (In.)	18·15 N	87·50 W
104	Xenia (zē'nĭ-ȧ) Oh.	39·40 N	83·55 W
193	Xi (R.) (shyē) China	23·15 N	112·10 E
190	Xiajin (shyä-jyĭn) China	36·58 N	115·59 E
193	Xiamen (I.) (shyä-mŭn) China	24·28 N	118·20 E
193	Xiamen (Amoy) China	24·30 N	118·10 E
192	Xi'an (shyē-ān) China	34·20 N	109·00 E
193	Xiang (R.) (shyäŋ) China	26·18 N	112·25 E
190	Xiangcheng (shyäŋ-chŭŋ) China	33·52 N	113·31 E
192	Xianghe (shyäŋ-hŭ) China (In.)	39·46 N	116·59 E
193	Xiangtan (shyäŋ-tän) China	27·55 N	112·45 E
192	Xianyang (shyĕn-yäŋ) China	34·20 N	108·40 E
	Xiao Hinggan Ling (Ra.), see Lesser Khingan		
194	Xiaoxingkai Hu (L.) (shyou-shyĭŋ-kī ho͞o). China	42·25 N	132·45 E
193	Xiapu (shyä-po͞o) China	27·00 N	120·00 E
190	Xiayi (shyä-yē) China	34·15 N	116·07 E
124	Xicotencatl (sē-kô-tĕn-kät''l). Mex.	32·00 N	98·58 W
192	Xifeng (shyē-fŭŋ) China	42·40 N	124·40 E
184	Xigazê (shyē-gä-dzŭ) China	29·22 N	88·57 E
190	Xiheying (shyē-hŭ-yĭŋ) China	39·58 N	114·50 E
192	Xiliao (R.) (shyē-lĭou) China	41·40 N	122·40 E
124	Xilitla (sē-lē'tlä) Mex.	21·24 N	98·59 W
191	Xinchang (shyĭn-chäŋ) China (Shanghai In.)	31·02 N	121·38 E
193	Xing'an (shyĭŋ-än) China	25·44 N	110·32 E
190	Xingcheng (shyĭŋ-chŭŋ) China	40·38 N	120·41 E
190	Xinghua (shyĭŋ-hwä) China	32·58 N	119·48 E
190	Xingjiawan (shyĭŋ-jyä-wän) China	37·16 N	114·54 E
190	Xingtai (shyĭŋ-tī) China	37·04 N	114·33 E
135	Xingú (R.) (zhêŋ-go͞o') Braz.	6·20 S	52·34 W
190	Xinhai (shyĭn-hī) China	36·59 N	117·33 E
193	Xinhua (shyĭn-hwä) China	27·45 N	111·20 E
190	Xinhuai (R.) (shyĭn-hwī) China	33·48 N	119·30 E
193	Xinhui (shyn-hwā) China	22·40 N	113·08 E
188	Xining (shyē-nĭŋ) China	36·52 N	101·36 E
188	Xinjiang (Sinkiang) (Aut. Reg.) (shyĭn-jyäŋ). China	40·15 N	82·15 E
190	Xinjin (shyĭn-jyĭn) China	39·23 N	121·57 E
192	Xinmin (shyĭn-mĭn) China	42·00 N	122·42 E
190	Xintai (shyĭn-tī) China	35·55 N	117·44 E
191	Xintang (shyĭn-täŋ) China (Canton In.)	23·08 N	113·36 E
190	Xin Xian (shyĭn shyĕn) China	31·47 N	114·50 E
192	Xin Xian China	38·20 N	112·45 E
190	Xinxiang (shyĭn-shyäŋ) China	35·17 N	113·49 E
190	Xinyang (shyĭn-yäŋ) China	32·08 N	114·04 E
192	Xinye (shyĭn-yŭ) China	32·40 N	112·20 E
191	Xinzao (shyĭn-dzou) China (Canton In.)	23·01 N	113·25 E
190	Xinzheng (shyĭn-jŭŋ) China	34·24 N	113·43 E
190	Xiongyuecheng (shyôŋ-yůĕ-chŭŋ) China	40·10 N	112·08 E
190	Xiping (shyē-pĭŋ) China	33·21 N	114·01 E
193	Xishui (shyē-shwā) China	30·30 N	115·10 E
190	Xi Xian (shyē shyĕn) China	32·20 N	114·42 E
190	Xiyang (shyē-yäŋ) China	37·37 N	113·42 E
190	Xiying (shyē-yĭŋ) China	31·26 N	119·57 E
190	Xiyou (shyē-yō) China	37·21 N	119·59 E
188	Xizang (Tibet) (Aut. Reg.) (shyē-dzäŋ) China	31·15 N	87·30 E
190	Xizhong Dao (I.) (shyē-jôŋ dou) China	39·27 N	121·06 E
124	Xochihuehuetlan (sô-chē-wĕ-wĕ-tlä'n). Mex.	17·53 N	98·29 W
125	Xochimilco (sō-chê-mēl'kô) Mex. (In.)	19·05 N	99·06 W
193	Xuancheng (shyůän-chŭŋ) China	30·52 N	118·48 E
192	Xuanhua (shyůän-hwä) China	40·35 N	115·05 E
190	Xuanhuadian (shyůän-hwä-dĭĕn) China	31·42 N	114·29 E
190	Xuchang (shyo͞o-chäŋ) China	34·02 N	113·49 E
193	Xun (R.) (shyo͞on) China	23·28 N	110·30 E
190	Xuyi (shyo͞o-yē) China	31·02 N	113·49 E
	Xuzhou, see Suchow		

Y

Page	Name Pronunciation Region	Lat. °′	Long. °′
193	Ya'an (yä-än) China	30·00 N	103·20 E
159	Yablonitskiy Pereval (P.) (yȧb-lô'nĭt-skĭ pĕ-rĕ-väl'). Sov. Un.	48·20 N	24·25 E
173	Yablonovyy Khrebet (Mts.) (yȧ-blô-nô-vē'). Sov. Un.	51·15 N	111·30 E
193	Yacheng (yä-chŭŋ) China	18·20 N	109·10 E
195	Yachiyo Jap. (Tōkyō In.)	35·43 N	140·07 E
112	Yacolt (yă'kôlt) Wa. (Portland In.)	45·52 N	122·24 W
112	Yacolt (Mt.) Wa. (Portland In.)	45·52 N	122·27 W
120	Yacona (R.) (yȧ'cō nȧ) Ms.	34·13 N	89·30 W
136	Yacuiba (yȧ-ko͞o-ē'bȧ) Arg.	22·02 S	63·44 W
121	Yadkin (R.) (yăd'kĭn) NC	36·12 N	80·40 W
211	Yafran Libya	31·57 N	12·04 E
167	Yagotin (yä'gô-tên) Sov. Un.	50·18 N	31·46 E
128	Yaguajay (yä-guä-hä'ē) Cuba	22·20 N	79·20 W
195	Yahagi-Gawa (Strm.) (yä'hä-gê gä'wä). Jap.	35·16 N	137·22 E
190	Yahongqiao (yä-hôŋ-chyou). China	39·45 N	117·52 E

ng-sing; ŋ-baŋk; N-nasalized n; nŏd; cŏmmit; ōld; ôbey; ôrder; fo͞od; fo͝ot; ou-out; s-soft; sh-dish; th-thin; pūre; ůnite; ûrn; stŭd; circŭs; ü-as "y" in study; '-indeterminate vowel.

370 Yahualica — Yosonotu PRONOUNCING INDEX

Page	Name Pronunciation Region	Lat. °′	Long. °′
124	Yahualica (yä-wä-lē′kä) . . . . . Mex.	21·08 N	102·53 W
125	Yajalon (yä-hä-lōn′) . . . . Mex.	17·16 N	92·20 W
174	Yakhroma (yäk′rô-ma) Sov. Un. (Moscow In.)	56·17 N	37·30 E
174	Yakhroma R. Sov. Un. (Moscow In.)	56·15 N	37·38 E
110	Yakima (yăk′ĭmȧ) . . . . Wa.	46·35 N	120·30 W
110	Yakima R. (tăk′ĭ-mȧ) . . . . Wa.	46·48 N	120·22 W
216	Yakoma . . . . Zaire	4·05 N	22·27 E
195	Yaku (I.) (yä′ko͞o) . . . . Jap.	30·15 N	130·41 E
173	Yakut A.S.S.R. . . . . Sov. Un.	65·21 N	117·13 E
101	Yakutat (yăk′o͝o-tăt) . . . . Ak.	59·32 N	139·35 W
173	Yakutsk (yȧ-ko͝otsk′) . . . . Sov. Un.	62·13 N	129·49 E
104	Yale . . . . Mi.	43·05 N	82·45 W
117	Yale . . . . Ok.	36·07 N	96·42 W
110	Yale Res. . . . . Wa.	46·00 N	122·20 W
211	Yalinga (yȧ-lĭŋ′gȧ) . Cen. Afr. Rep.	6·56 N	23·22 E
120	Yalobusha (R.) (yȧ-lô-bo͝osh′ȧ) Ms.	33·48 N	90·02 W
188	Yalong (R.) (yä-lôŋ) . . . . China	32·29 N	98·41 E
171	Yalta (yäl′tȧ) . . . . Sov. Un.	44·29 N	34·12 E
194	Yalu (R.) (yä-lo͞o) . . . . China	48·20 N	122·35 E
194	Yalu (Amnok) (R.) . . . . China-Kor.	41·20 N	126·35 E
172	Yalutorovsk (yä-lo͞o-tô′rôfsk) Sov. Un.	56·42 N	66·32 E
195	Yamada (yä′mȧ-dȧ) . . . . Jap.	33·37 N	133·39 E
194	Yamagata (yä-mȧ′gä-tȧ) . . . . . Jap.	38·12 N	140·24 E
195	Yamaguchi (yä-mȧ′go͞o-chê) . . Jap.	34·10 N	131·30 E
172	Yamal, P-ov (Pen.) (yä-mäl′) Sov. Un.	71·15 N	70·00 E
174	Yamantau, Gora (Mt.) (gȧ-rä′ yä′ man-tȧw) Sov. Un. (Urals In.)	54·16 N	58·08 E
129	Yamasá (yä-mä′sä) . . . . Dom. Rep.	18·50 N	70·00 W
195	Yamasaki (yä′mä′sä-kê) . . . . . . Jap.	35·01 N	134·33 E
195	Yamasaki . . . . Jap. (Osaka In.)	34·53 N	135·41 E
195	Yamashina (yä′mä-shê′nä) Jap. (Osaka In.)	34·59 N	135·50 E
195	Yamashita (yä′mä-shê′tä) Jap. (Osaka In.)	34·53 N	135·25 E
195	Yamato . . . . Jap. (Tōkyō In.)	35·28 N	139·28 E
195	Yamato-Kōriyama Jap. (Osaka In.)	34·39 N	135·48 E
195	Yamato-takada (yä′mä-tô tä′kä-dä) . Jap. (Osaka In.)	34·31 N	135·45 E
134	Yambi, Mesa de (mĕ′sä-dĕ-yȧ′m-bē) . Col.	1·55 N	71·45 W
197	Yamdena (I.) . . . . Indon.	7·23 S	130·30 E
188	Yamethin (yŭ-mē′thên) . . . . . . Bur.	20·14 N	96·27 E
112	Yamhill (yăm′hĭl) Or. (Portland In.)	45·20 N	123·11 W
174	Yamkino (yäm′kĭ-nô) Sov. Un. (Moscow In.)	55·56 N	38·25 E
203	Yamma Yamma, L. (yăm′ȧ yăm′ȧ) . Austl.	26·15 S	141·30 E
173	Yamsk (yämsk) . . . . Sov. Un.	59·41 N	154·09 E
184	Yamuna (R.) . . . . India	26·50 N	80·10 E
188	Yamzho Yumco (L.) (yäm-jwo yo͞om-tswo) . China	29 11 N	91·26 E
173	Yana (R.) (yä′nȧ) . . . . Sov. Un.	69·42 N	135·45 E
203	Yanac (yăn′ăk) . . . . Austl.	36·10 S	141·30 E
195	Yanagawa (yä-nä′gä-wä) . . . . . Jap.	33·11 N	130·24 E
184	Yanam (yŭnŭm′) . . . . India	16·48 N	82·15 E
188	Yan′an (yän-än) . . . . China	36·46 N	109·15 E
192	Yan′an . . . . China	36·35 N	109·32 E
186	Yanbu′ . . . . Sau. Ar.	23·57 N	38·02 E
190	Yancheng (yän-chŭŋ) . . . . . . China	33·23 N	120·11 E
190	Yancheng . . . . China	33·38 N	113·59 E
216	Yandongi . . . . Zaire	2·51 N	22·16 E
190	Yangcheng Hu (L.) (yäŋ-chŭŋ ho͞o) . China	31·30 N	120·31 E
193	Yangchun (yäŋ-cho͝on) . . . . . China	22·08 N	111·48 E
190	Yang′erzhuang (yäŋ-är-jûäŋ) China	38·18 N	117·31 E
192	Yanggezhuang (yäŋ-gŭ-jûäŋ) China (Peking In.)	40·10 N	116·48 E
190	Yanggu (yäŋ-go͞o) . . . . China	36·06 N	115·46 E
190	Yanghe (yäŋ-hŭ) . . . . China	33·48 N	118·23 E
193	Yangjiang (yäŋ-jyäŋ) . . . . . . China	21·52 N	111·58 E
190	Yangjiaogou (yäŋ-jyou-gō) . . China	36·17 N	118·53 E
190	Yangquan (yäŋ-chyûän) . . . . China	37·52 N	113·36 E
189	Yangtze Chang (R.) (yängtse) (chäŋ) . China	30·30 N	117·25 E
190	Yangxin (yäŋ-shyĭn) . . . . China	37·39 N	117·34 E
194	Yangyang (yäng′yäng′) . . . . . . Kor.	38·02 N	128·38 E
189	Yangzhou (yäŋ-jō) . . . . China	32·24 N	119·24 E
192	Yanji (yän-jyē) . . . . China	42·55 N	129·35 E
190	Yanjiahe (yän-jyä-hŭ) . . . . . . China	31·55 N	114·47 E
190	Yanjin (yän-jyĭn) . . . . China	35·09 N	114·13 E
108	Yankton (yănk′tŭn) . . . . SD	42·51 N	97·24 W
190	Yanling (yän-lĭŋ) . . . . China	34·07 N	114·12 E
	Yannina, see Ioánnina		
	Yanqi, see Karashahr		
190	Yanshan (yän-shän) . . . . China	38·05 N	117·15 E
192	Yanshou (yän-shō) . . . . China	45·25 N	128·43 E
	Yantai, see Chefoo		
174	Yanychi (yä′nĭ-chĭ) Sov. Un. (Urals In.)	57·42 N	56·24 E
190	Yanzhou (yäŋ-jō) . . . . China	35·35 N	116·50 E
190	Yanzhuang (yän-jûäŋ) . . . . . China	36·08 N	117·47 E
211	Yao (yä′ō) . . . . Chad	13·00 N	17·38 E
195	Yao . . . . Jap. (Osaka In.)	34·37 N	135·76 E
215	Yaoundé (yȧ-o͞on-dā′) . . . . Cam.	3·52 N	11·31 E
197	Yapen, Pulau (I.) . . . . Indon.	1·30 S	136·15 E
198	Yap (yăp) (I) . . Pac. Is. Trust Ter.	11·00 N	138·00 E
129	Yaque del Norte (R.) (yä′kȧ dĕl nôr′tȧ) . Dom. Rep.	19·40 N	71·25 W
129	Yaque del Sur (R.) (yä-kĕ-dĕl-so͞o′r) . Dom. Rep.	18·35 N	71·05 W
122	Yaqui (R.) (yä′kē) . . . . Mex.	28·15 N	109·40 W
135	Yaracuy (State) (yä-rä-ko͞o′ē) Ven. (In.)	10·10 N	68·31 W
203	Yaraka (yȧ-răk′ȧ) . . . . Austl.	24·50 S	144·08 E
170	Yaransk (yä-ränsk′) . . . . . Sov. Un.	57·18 N	48·05 E
211	Yarda (Well) (yär′dȧ) . . . . . . Chad	18·29 N	19·13 E
	Yarkand, see Shache		
184	Yarkand (R.) (yär-känt′) . . . . India	36·11 N	76·10 E
	Yarlung Zangbo (R.), see Brahmaputra		
98	Yarmouth (yär′mŭth) . . . . Can.	43·50 N	66·07 W
174	Yaroslavka (yȧ-rô-släv′kȧ) Sov. Un. (Urals In.)	55·52 N	57·59 E
166	Yaroslavl′ (yȧ-rô-släv′′l) . . Sov. Un.	57·57 N	39·54 E
166	Yaroslavl′ (Oblast) . . . . . . Sov. Un.	58·05 N	38·05 E
170	Yarra-to (L.) (yȧ′rô-tô′) . . Sov. Un.	68·30 N	71·30 E
166	Yartsevo (yär′tsyĕ-vô) . . . Sov. Un.	55·04 N	32·38 E
172	Yartsevo . . . . Sov. Un.	60·13 N	89·52 E
134	Yarumal (yä-ro͞o-mäl′) . . Col. (In.)	6·57 N	75·24 W
159	Yasel′da R. (yä-syŭl′dȧ) . . Sov. Un.	53·13 N	25·53 E
159	Yasinya . . . . Sov. Un.	48·17 N	24·21 E
129	Yateras (yä-tā′räs) . . . . Cuba	20·00 N	75·00 W
117	Yates Center (yāts) . . . . Ks.	37·53 N	95·44 W
90	Yathkyed (L.) (yȧth-kī-ĕd′) . . Can.	62·41 N	98·00 W
195	Yatsuga-take (Mtn.) (yät′so͞o-gä dä′kā) . Jap.	36·01 N	138·21 W
195	Yatsushiro (yät′so͞o′shē-rô) . . . Jap.	32·30 N	130·35 E
217	Yatta Plat. . . . . Ken.	1·55 S	38·10 E
124	Yautepec (yä-o͞o-tȧ-pĕk′) . . . . Mex.	18·53 N	99·04 W
159	Yavorvo (yä′vō-rō′yê) . . . Sov. Un.	49·56 N	23·24 E
195	Yawata (yä′wä-tä) Jap. (Osaka In.)	34·52 N	135·43 E
195	Yawatahama (yä′wä′tä′hä-mä) Jap.	33·24 N	132·25 E
193	Ya Xian (yä shyĕn) . . . . China	18·10 N	109·32 E
216	Yayama . . . . Zaire	1·16 S	23·07 E
191	Yayao (yä-you) China (Canton In.)	23·10 N	113·40 E
186	Yazd . . . . Iran	31·59 N	54·03 E
120	Yazoo (R.) (yă′zo͞o) . . . . Ms.	32·32 N	90·40 W
120	Yazoo City . . . . Ms.	32·50 N	90·18 W
196	Ye (yā) . . . . Bur.	15·13 N	97·52 E
106	Yeadon (yē′dŭn) Pa. (Philadelphia In.)	39·56 N	75·16 W
	Yecheng, see Karghalik		
162	Yecla (yā′klä) . . . . Sp.	38·35 N	1·09 W
166	Yefremov (yĕ-frä′môf) . . . Sov. Un.	53·08 N	38·04 E
166	Yegor′yevsk (yĕ-gôr′yĕfsk) Sov. Un.	55·23 N	38·59 E
190	Yeji (yŭ-jyē) . . . . China	31·52 N	115·57 E
170	Yelabuga (yĕ-lä′bo͝o-gȧ) . . Sov. Un.	55·50 N	52·18 E
171	Yelan . . . . Sov. Un.	50·50 N	44·00 E
166	Yelets (yĕ-lyĕts′) . . . . Sov. Un.	52·35 N	38·28 E
174	Yelizavetpol′skiy (yĕ′lĭ-za-vĕt-pôl-skĭ) . Sov. Un. (Urals In.)	52·51 N	60·38 E
173	Yelizavety, Mys (C.) (yĕ-lyĕ-sȧ-vyĕ′tȧ) . Sov. Un.	54·28 N	142·59 E
154	Yell (I.) (yĕl) . . . . Scot.	60·35 N	1·27 W
120	Yellow (R.) (yĕl′ō) . . . . Fl.	30·33 N	86·53 W
93	Yellowhead Pass (yĕl′ô-hĕd) . . Can.	52·52 N	118·35 W
90	Yellowknife (yĕl′ô-nīf) . . . . . . Can.	62·29 N	114·38 W
	Yellow R., see Huang		
192	Yellow Sea . . . . Asia	35·20 N	122·15 E
111	Yellowstone L. . . . . Wy.	44·27 N	110·03 W
111	Yellowstone Natl. Park (yĕl′ô-stōn) . Wy.	44·45 N	110·35 W
111	Yellowstone R. . . . . Mt.	46·28 N	105·39 W
111	Yellowstone R., Clark Fk. . . . . Wy.	44·55 N	109·05 W
111	Yellowtail Res. . . . . Mt.-Wy.	45·00 N	108·10 W
166	Yel′nya (yĕl′nyȧ) . . . . Sov. Un.	54·34 N	33·12 E
174	Yemanzhelinsk (yĕ-mȧn-zhâ′lĭnsk) Sov. Un. (Urals In.)	54·47 N	61·24 E
182	Yemen (yĕm′ĕn) . . . . Asia	15·45 N	44·30 E
182	Yemen, People′s Democratic Republic of . Asia	14·45 N	46·45 E
170	Yemetsk . . . . Sov. Un.	63·28 N	41·28 E
167	Yenakiyevo (yĕ-nä′kĭ-yĕ-vô) Sov. Un.	48·14 N	38·12 E
187	Yenangyaung (yā′nän-d oung) Bur.	20·27 N	94·59 E
214	Yendi (yĕn′dê) . . . . Ghana	9·26 N	0·01 W
188	Yengisar (yŭn-gē-sär) . . . . . . China	39·01 N	75·29 E
171	Yenice (R.) . . . . Tur.	41·10 N	33·00 E
172	Yenisey (R.) (yĕ-nê-sĕ′ê) . Sov. Un.	67·48 N	87·15 E
172	Yeniseysk (yĕ-nĭĕsā′ĭsk) Sov. Un.	58·27 N	90·28 E
204	Yeo (I.) (yō) . . . . Austl.	28·15 S	124·00 E
171	Yerevan (yĕ-rĕ-vän′) . . . . . Sov. Un.	40·10 N	44·30 E
154	Yerington (yê′rĭng-tŭn) . . . . Nv.	38·59 N	119·10 W
170	Yermak (I.) . . . . Sov. Un.	66·30 N	71·30 E
162	Yeste (yĕs′tȧ) . . . . Sp.	38·23 N	2·19 W
160	Yeu, Île d′ (I.) (ēl dyû) . . . . Fr.	46·43 N	2·45 W
167	Yevpatoriya (yĕf-pä′tô-rĭ-yȧ) Sov. Un.	45·13 N	33·22 E
190	Ye Xian (yŭ-shyĕn) . . . . China	37·09 N	119·57 E
167	Yeya (R.) (yă′yȧ) . . . . Sov. Un.	46·25 N	39·17 E
173	Yevrey Aut. Oblast . . . . . . Sov. Un.	48·45 N	132·00 E
167	Yeysk (yĕysk) . . . . Sov. Un.	46·41 N	38·13 E
	Yg (R.), see Yug		
165	Yiannitsá . . . . Grc.	40·47 N	22·26 E
193	Yibin (yē-bĭn) . . . . China	28·50 N	104·40 E
193	Yichang (yē-chäŋ) . . . . China	30·38 N	111·22 E
190	Yidu (yē-do͞o) . . . . China	36·42 N	118·30 E
190	Yi He (R.) (yē hŭ) . . . . China	34·38 N	118·07 E
192	Yilan (yē-län) . . . . China	46·10 N	129·40 E
194	Yimianpo (yē-mĭĕn-pwo) . . . China	44·59 N	127·56 E
192	Yinchuan (yĭn-chûän) . . . . . . China	38·22 N	106·22 E
192	Yingkou (yĭŋ-kō) . . . . China	40·35 N	122·10 E
188	Yining (Gulja) (yē-nĭŋ) . . . . . China	43·58 N	80·40 E
192	Yin Shan (Mtn.) (yĭng′shän′) China	40·50 N	110·30 E
165	Yioúra (I.) . . . . Grc.	37·52 N	24·42 E
193	Yishan (yē-shän) . . . . China	24·32 N	108·42 E
190	Yishui (yē-shwā) . . . . China	35·49 N	118·40 E
165	Yíthion . . . . Grc.	36·50 N	22·37 E
194	Yitong (yē-tôŋ) . . . . China	43·15 N	125·10 E
192	Yi Xian (yē-shyĕn) . . . . China	41·30 N	121·15 E
193	Yiyang (yē-yäŋ) . . . . China	28·52 N	112·12 E
93	Ymir (wī′-mēr) . . . . Can.	49·17 N	117·13 W
119	Yoakum (yō′kŭm) . . . . Tx.	29·18 N	97·09 W
120	Yockanookany, (R.) (yŏk′ȧ-no͞o-kă-nĭ) . Ms.	32·47 N	89·38 W
195	Yodo-Gawa (Str.) (yō′dō′gä-wä) Jap. (Osaka In.)	34·46 N	135·35 E
193	Yog Pt. (yōg) . . . . Phil.	14·00 N	124·30 E
196	Yogyakarta (yŏg-yȧ-kär′tȧ) Indon.	7·50 S	110·20 E
93	Yoho Natl. Park (yō′hō) . . . . . Can.	51·26 N	116·30 W
126	Yojoa, Lago de (L.) (lä′gô dĕ yô-hō′ä) . Hond.	14·49 N	87·53 W
195	Yokkaichi (yô′kä′ê-chê) . . . . . . Jap.	34·58 N	136·35 E
195	Yokohama (yō′kô-hä′mȧ) Jap. (Tōkyō In.)	35·37 N	139·40 E
195	Yokosuka (yô-kō′so͞o-kä) Jap. (Tōkyō In.)	35·17 N	139·40 E
195	Yokota (yô-kō′tä) Jap. (Tōkyō In.)	35·23 N	140·02 E
210	Yola (yō′lä) . . . . Nig.	9·13 N	12·27 E
127	Yolaina, Cord. de (Mts.) (kôr-dĕl-yĕ′rä dĕ yō-lä-ē′nä) . Nic.	11·34 N	84·34 W
134	Yolombó (yô-lôm-bŏ′) . . . Col. (In.)	6·37 N	74·59 W
214	Yomon . . . . Gui.	7·34 N	9·16 W
195	Yonago (yō′nä-gō) . . . . Jap.	35·27 N	133·19 E
194	Yonezawa (yō′nĕ′zȧ-wä) . . . . . . Jap.	37·50 N	140·07 E
193	Yong′an (yôŋ-än) . . . . China	26·00 N	117·22 E
192	Yongding (R.) (yôŋ-dĭŋ) . . . China	40·25 N	115·00 E
194	Yŏngdŏk (yŭng′dŭk′) . . . . Kor.	36·28 N	129·25 E
194	Yŏnghŭng (yŭng′ho͝ong′) . . . . Kor.	39·31 N	127·11 E
194	Yonghŭng Man (B.) . . . . Kor.	39·10 N	128·00 E
190	Yongnian (yôŋ-nĭĕn) . . . . China	36·47 N	114·32 E
192	Yongqing (yôŋ-chyĭŋ) . China (In.)	39·18 N	116·27 E
193	Yongshun (yôŋ-sho͝on) . . . . . China	29·05 N	109·58 E
106	Yonkers (yŏŋ′kērz) NY (New York In.)	40·57 N	73·54 W
160	Yonne (R.) (yôn) . . . . Fr.	48·18 N	3·15 E
195	Yono (yō′nō) . . . . Jap. (Tōkyō In.)	35·53 N	139·36 E
113	Yorba Linda (yôr′bă lĭn′dȧ) Ca. (Los Angeles In.)	33·55 N	117·51 W
120	York (yôrk) . . . . Al.	32·33 N	88·16 W
204	York . . . . Austl.	32·00 S	117·00 E
89	York . . . . Can. (Toronto In.)	43·41 N	79·29 W
154	York . . . . Eng.	53·58 N	1·10 W
117	York . . . . Ne.	40·52 N	97·36 W
105	York . . . . Pa.	40·00 N	76·40 W
121	York . . . . SC	34·59 N	81·14 W
205	York, C. . . . . Austl.	10·45 S	142·35 E
75	York, Kap (C.) . . . . Grnld.	75·30 N	73·00 W
203	Yorketown . . . . Austl.	35·00 S	137·28 E
95	York Factory . . . . Can.	57·05 N	92·18 W
203	York Pen. . . . . Austl.	34·24 S	137·20 E
154	Yorkshire Wolds (Hills) (yôrk′shĭr) . Eng.	54·00 N	0·35 W
94	Yorkton (yôrk′tŭn) . . . . Can.	51·13 N	102·28 W
119	Yorktown (yôrk′toun) . . . . Tx.	28·57 N	97·30 W
121	Yorktown . . . . Va.	37·12 N	76·31 W
126	Yoro (yō′rô) . . . . Hond.	15·09 N	87·05 W
198	Yoron (I.) . . . . Jap.	26·48 N	128·40 E
114	Yosemite Natl. Park (yô-sĕm′ĭ-tê) . Ca.	38·03 N	119·36 W
195	Yoshida (yō′shê-dȧ) . . . . Jap.	34·39 N	132·41 E
195	Yoshikawa (yō-shê′kä′wä′) Jap. (Tōkyō In.)	35·53 N	139·51 E
195	Yoshino (R.) (yō′shē-nō) . . . . . Jap.	34·04 N	133·57 E
170	Yoshkar-Ola (yôsh-kär′ô-lä′) Sov. Un.	56·35 N	48·05 E
125	Yosonotú (Santa Catarina) (yô-sō-nô-to͞o′) (sän′tä kä-tä-rē′nä) . Mex.	16·51 N	97·37 W

ăt; finăl; rāte; senâte; ärm; ȧsk; sofȧ; fâre; ch-choose; dh-as th in other; bē; êvent; bĕt; recĕnt; cratẽr; g-go; gh-guttural g; bĭt; ĭ-short neutral; rīde; ĸ-guttural k as ch in German ich;

PRONOUNCING INDEX

Yos Sudarsa — Zhanggezhuang 371

Page	Name Pronunciation Region	Lat. °′	Long. °′
197	Yos Sudarsa, Pulau (I.) . . . . Indon.	7·20 S	138·30 E
194	Yŏsu (yŭ'sōō') . . . . Kor.	34·42 N	127·42 E
193	You (R.) (yō) . . . . China	23·55 N	106·50 E
154	Youghal B. (yōō'ôl) (yôl) . . . . Ire.	51·52 N	7·46 W
154	Youhal . . . . Ire.	51·58 N	7·57 W
203	Young (yŭng) . . . . Austl.	34·15 S	148·18 E
137	Young (yô-ōō'ng) Ur. (Buenos Aires In.)	32·42 S	57·38 W
112	Youngs (L.) (yŭngz) Wa. (Seattle In.)	47·25 N	122·08 W
107	Youngstown . . . . NY (Buffalo In.)	43·15 N	79·02 W
104	Youngstown . . . . Oh.	41·05 N	80·40 W
171	Yozgat (yôz'gȧd) . . . . Tur.	39·50 N	34·50 E
107	Ypsilanti (ĭp-sĭ-lăn'tĭ) Mi. (Detroit In.)	42·15 N	83·37 W
110	Yreka (wī-rē'kȧ) . . . . Ca.	41·43 N	122·36 W
118	Ysleta (ēz-lĕ'tȧ) . . . . Tx.	31·42 N	106·18 W
160	Yssingeaux (ē-săN-zhō') . . . . Fr.	45·09 N	4·08 E
156	Ystad (ü'städ) . . . . Swe.	55·29 N	13·28 E
156	Ytre Solund (I.) (ü'trĕ sōō'lĕn) Nor.	61·01 N	4·25 E
183	Yu'alliq, Jabal (Mts.) Egypt (Palestine In.)	30·12 N	33·42 E
193	Yuan (R.) (yûän) . . . . China	28·50 N	110·50 E
193	Yuan'an (yûän-än) . . . . China	31·08 N	111·28 E
193	Yuanling (yûän-lĭŋ) . . . . China	28·30 N	110·18 E
190	Yuanshi (yûän-shr) . . . . China	37·45 N	114·32 E
195	Yuasa . . . . Jap.	34·02 N	135·10 E
114	Yuba City (yōō'bȧ) . . . . Ca.	39·08 N	121·38 W
210	Yuby, C. (yōō'bē) . . . . Mor.	28·01 N	13·21 W
113	Yucaipa (yŭ-kȧ-ĕ'pȧ) Ca. (Los Angeles In.)	34·02 N	117·02 W
122	Yucatan (State) (yōō-kä-tän') Mex.	20·45 N	89·00 W
122	Yucatán Chan . . . . Mex.	22·30 N	87·00 W
190	Yucheng (yōō-chŭŋ) . . . . China	34·31 N	115·54 E
190	Yucheng . . . . China	36·55 N	116·39 E
192	Yuci (yōō-tsz) . . . . China	37·32 N	112·40 E
173	Yudoma (R.) (yōō-dō'mȧ) Sov. Un.	59·13 N	137·00 E
193	Yueyang (yûĕ-yäŋ) . . . . China	92·25 N	113·05 E
193	Yueqing (yûĕ-chyĭŋ) . . . . China	28·02 N	120·40 E
190	Yuezhuang (yûĕ-jûäŋ) . . . . China	36·13 N	118·17 E
170	Yug (R.) (yōōg) . . . . Sov. Un.	59·50 N	45·55 E
146	Yugoslavia (yōō-gô-slä-vĭ-ȧ) Eur.	44·48 N	17·29 E
166	Yukhnov (yŏŏk'-nof) . . . . Sov. Un.	54·44 N	35·15 E
90	Yukon (Ter.) (yōō'kŏn) . . . . Can.	63·16 N	135·30 W
102	Yukon R. . . . . Ak.-Can.	62·10 N	143·00 W
101	Yukutat B. (yōō-kū tăt') . . . . Ak.	59·34 N	140·50 W
174	Yuldybayevo (yŏŏld'-bä'yĕ-vô) Sov. Un. (Urals In.)	52·20 N	57·52 E
193	Yulin (yōō-lĭn) . . . . China	22·38 N	110·10 E
192	Yulin . . . . China	38·18 N	109·45 E
115	Yuma (yōō'mä) . . . . Az.	32·40 N	114·40 W
116	Yuma . . . . Co.	40·08 N	102·50 W
129	Yuma, Bahia de (B.) (bä-ē'ä-dĕ-yōō'mä) . Dom. Rep.	18·20 N	68·05 W
129	Yuma (R.) . . . . Dom. Rep.	19·05 N	70·05 W
217	Yumbi . . . . Zaire	1·14 S	26·14 E
188	Yumen (yōō-mŭn) . . . . China	40·14 N	96·56 E
192	Yuncheng (yŏŏn-chŭŋ) . . . . China	35·00 N	110·40 E
188	Yunnan (Prov.) (yun'nän') . . China	24·23 N	101·03 E
188	Yunnan Plat. (yŏŏ-nän) . . . . China	26·03 N	101·26 E
192	Yun Xian (yŏŏ shyĕn) . . . . China	32·50 N	110·55 E
193	Yunxiao (yŏŏn-shyou) . . . . China	24·00 N	117·20 E
195	Yura (yōō'rä) . . . . Jap.	34·18 N	134·54 E
124	Yurécuaro (yōō-rā'kwä-rô) . . . Mex.	20·21 N	102·16 W
134	Yurimaguas (yōō-rê-mä'gwäs) Peru	5·59 S	76·12 W
124	Yuriria (yōō'rê-rē'ä) . . . . Mex.	20·11 N	101·08 W
174	Yurovo Sov. Un. (Moscow In.)	55·30 N	38·24 E
170	Yur'yevets . . . . Sov. Un.	57·15 N	43·08 E
174	Yuryuzan' (yŏŏr-yŏŏ-zän') Sov. Un. (Urals In.)	54·47 N	58·45 E
126	Yuscarán (yōōs-kä-rän') . . . . Hond.	13·57 N	86·48 W
193	Yushan (yōō-shän) . . . . China	28·42 N	118·20 E
192	Yushu (yōō-shōō) . . . . China	44·58 N	126·32 E
190	Yutian (yōō-tĭĕn) . . . . China	39·54 N	117·45 E
188	Yutian (Keriya) (yōō-tĭĕn) (kŭ-r-yä) . China	36·55 N	81·39 E
136	Yuty (yōō-tē') . . . . Par.	26·45 S	56·13 W
190	Yuwangcheng (yü'wäng'chĕng) China	31·32 N	114·26 E
192	Yu Xian (yōō shyĕn) . . . . China	39·40 N	114·38 E
170	Yuzha (yōō'zhȧ) . . . . Sov. Un.	56·38 N	42·20 E
174	Yuzhnny Ural (Mts.) (yōō'zhnĭ ōō-räl') . Sov. Un. (Urals In.)	52·51 N	57·48 E
173	Yuzhno-Sakhalinsk (yōōzh'nô-sä-κä-lĭnsk') . Sov. Un.	47·11 N	143·04 E
174	Yuzhnoural'skiy (yōōzh-nô-ōō-räl'skĭ) . Sov. Un. (Urals In.)	54·26 N	61·17 E
158	Yverdon (ē-vĕr-dôn) . . . . Switz.	46·46 N	6·35 E
160	Yvetot (ēv-tō') . . . . Fr.	49·39 N	0·45 E

Z

Page	Name Pronunciation Region	Lat. °′	Long. °′
152	Za R. . . . . Mor.	34·19 N	2·23 W
125	Zaachila (sä-ä-chē'lä) . . . . Mex.	16·56 N	96·45 W
149	Zaandam (zän'dȧm) Neth. (Amsterdam In.)	52·25 N	4·49 E
158	Zabkowice (zaNb'kô-vē'tsĕ) . . . Pol.	50·35 N	16·48 E
159	Zabrze (zäb'zhĕ) . . . . Pol.	50·18 N	18·48 E
126	Zacapa (sä-kä'pä) . . . . Guat.	14·56 N	89·30 W
125	Zacapoaxtla (sä-kä-pō-äs'tlä) Mex.	19·51 N	97·34 W
124	Zacatecas (sä-kä-tā'käs) . . . . Mex.	22·44 N	102·32 W
122	Zacatecas (State) . . . . Mex.	24·00 N	102·45 W
126	Zacatecoluca (sä-kä-tå-kô-lōō'kä) Sal.	13·31 N	88·50 W
124	Zacateko (zä-kä-tĕ'kō) . . . . Mex.	19·12 N	98·12 W
125	Zacatepec (Santiago) (sä-kä-tå-pĕk') (sän-tê-ä'gô) . Mex.	17·10 N	95·53 W
125	Zacatlán (sä-kä-tlän') . . . . Mex.	19·55 N	97·57 W
124	Zacoalco de Torres (sä-kô-äl'kô dā tōr'rĕs) . Mex.	20·12 N	103·33 W
124	Zacualpan (sä-kōō-äl-pän') . . . Mex.	18·43 N	99·46 W
124	Zacualtipan (sȧ-kōō-äl-tē-pän') Mex.	20·38 N	98·39 W
164	Zadar (zä'där) . . . . Yugo.	44·08 N	15·16 E
166	Zadonsk (zä-dônsk') . . . . Sov. Un.	52·22 N	38·55 E
158	Zagan (zhä'gan') . . . . Pol.	51·34 N	15·32 E
163	Zagarolo (tzä-gä-rô'lô) It. (Rome In.)	41·51 N	12·53 E
157	Žagare (zhȧgȧrĕ) . . . . Sov. Un.	56·21 N	23·14 E
210	Zaghouan (zȧ-gwäN') . . . . Tun.	36·30 N	10·04 E
165	Zagorá (zä'gô-rȧ) . . . . Grc.	39·29 N	23·04 E
174	Zagorsk (zä-gôrsk') Sov. Un. (Moscow In.)	56·18 N	38·08 E
164	Zagreb (zä'grĕb) . . . . Yugo.	45·50 N	15·58 E
186	Zagro Mts. . . . . Iran	33·30 N	46·30 E
186	Zāhedān (zä'hȧ-dän) . . . . Iran	29·37 N	60·31 E
183	Zahlah (zä'lā') Leb. (Palestine In.)	33·50 N	35·54 E
149	Zahorska-Ves. Czech. (Vienna In.)	48·24 N	16·51 E
163	Zahrez Chergui (L.) . . . . Alg.	35·10 N	2·17 E
209	Zaire . . . . Afr.	1·00 S	22·15 E
216	Zaire (Congo) (R.) (kŏn'gō) . . . Afr.	1·10 N	18·25 E
165	Zaječar (zä'yĕ-chär') . . . . Yugo.	43·54 N	22·16 E
165	Zákinthos . . . . Grc.	37·48 N	20·55 E
165	Zákinthos (Zante) (I.) . . . . Grc.	37·45 N	20·32 E
159	Zakopane (zȧ-kô-pä'nĕ) . . . . Pol.	49·18 N	19·57 E
215	Zakouma, Parc Natl. de (Natl. Pk.) . Chad	10·50 N	19·20 E
158	Zalaegerszeg (zŏ'lô-ĕ'gĕr-sĕg) Hung.	46·50 N	16·50 E
159	Zalău (zȧ-lŭ'ŏŏ) . . . . Rom.	47·11 N	23·06 E
159	Zalew Wiślany (B.) (zä'lĕf vĭsh-lä'nĭ) . Pol.	54·22 N	19·39 E
211	Zalţan . . . . Libya	28·20 N	19·40 E
149	Zaltbommel Neth. (Amsterdam In.)	51·48 N	5·15 E
217	Zambezi (R.) (zȧm-bā'zē) . . . . Afr.	15·45 S	33·15 E
209	Zambia (zăm'bē-ȧ) . . . . Afr.	14·23 S	24·15 E
196	Zamboanga (säm-bô-aŋ'gä) . . . Phil.	6·58 N	122·02 E
159	Zambrów (zäm'brōōf) . . . . Pol.	52·59 N	22·17 E
124	Zamora (sä-mō'rä) . . . . Mex.	19·59 N	102·16 W
162	Zamora (thä-mō'rä) . . . . Sp.	41·32 N	5·43 W
159	Zamość (zä'môshch) . . . . Pol.	50·42 N	23·17 E
125	Zanatepec (Santo Domingo) (sä-nä-tå-pek') (sän-tô dō-miŋ'gô) . Mex.	16·30 N	94·22 W
149	Zandvoort. Neth. (Amsterdam In.)	52·22 N	4·30 E
104	Zanesville (zānz'vĭl) . . . . Oh.	39·55 N	82·00 W
214	Zangasso . . . . Mali	12·09 N	5·37 W
186	Zanjān . . . . Iran	36·26 N	48·24 E
217	Zansibar (zăn'zĭ-bär) . . . . Tan.	6·10 S	39·11 E
217	Zanzibar Chan. . . . . Tan.	6·05 S	39·00 E
217	Zanzibar (I.) . . . . Tan.	6·20 S	39·37 E
210	Zaouia el Kahla . . . . Alg.	28·06 N	6·34 E
190	Zaozhuang (dzou-jûäŋ) . . . . China	34·51 N	117·34 E
166	Zapadnaya Dvina (R.) (zä'pȧd-nȧ-yȧ dvē'nȧ) . Sov. Un.	55·30 N	28·27 E
136	Zapala (zä-pä'lä) . . . . Arg.	38·53 S	70·02 W
118	Zapata (sä-pä'tä) . . . . Tx.	26·52 N	99·18 W
128	Zapata, Ciénaga de (Swp.) (syĕ'nä-gä-dĕ-zä-pȧ'tä) . Cuba	22·30 N	81·20 W
128	Zapata, Península de (pĕ-nē'n-sōō-lä-dĕ-zä-pȧ'tä) . Cuba	22·20 N	81·30 W
126	Zapatera, Isla (I.) (ē's-lä-sä-pä-tā'rō) . Nic.	11·45 N	85·45 W
124	Zapopan (sä-pō'pän) . . . . Mex.	20·42 N	102·23 W
157	Zaporoshskoye (zȧ-pô-rôsh'skô-yĕ) . Sov. Un.	60·36 N	30·31 E
167	Zaporozh'ye (zä-pô-rôzh'yĕ) Sov. Un.	47·53 N	35·25 E
167	Zaporozh'ye (Oblast) (zä-pô-rôzh'yĕ ôb'ȧst) . Sov. Un.	47·20 N	35·05 E
124	Zapotiltic (sä-pô-tēl-tēk') . . . . Mex.	19·37 N	103·25 W
124	Zapotitlán (sä-pô-tē-tlän') . . . Mex.	17·13 N	98·58 W
125	Zapotitlán, Punta (Pt.) . . . . Mex.	18·34 N	94·48 W
124	Zapotlanejo (sä-pô-tlä-nā'hô) Mex.	20·38 N	103·05 W
124	Zaragoza (sä-rä-gō'sä) . . . . Mex.	23·59 N	99·45 W
124	Zaragoza . . . . Mex.	22·02 N	100·45 W
163	Zaragoza (thä-rä-gō'thä) . . . . Sp.	41·39 N	0·53 W
215	Zaranda Hill . . . . Nig.	10·15 N	9·35 E
159	Zărandului, Muntii (Mts.) . . . Rom.	46·07 N	22·21 E
157	Zarasai (zä-rä-sī') . . . . Sov. Un.	55·45 N	26·18 E
137	Zárate (zä-rä'tä) Arg. (Buenos Aires In.)	34·05 S	59·05 W
166	Zaraysk (zä-rä'ēsk) . . . . Sov. Un.	54·46 N	38·53 E
215	Zaria (zä'rē-ä) . . . . Nig.	11·07 N	7·44 E
171	Zarineh, Rūd-é (R.) . . . . Iran	36·40 N	46·35 E
183	Zarga (R.) . . Jordan (Palestine In.)	32·13 N	35·43 E
158	Zary (zhä'rē) . . . . Pol.	51·38 N	15·08 E
134	Zarzal (zär-zä'l) . . . . Col. (In.)	4·23 N	76·04 W
173	Zashiversk (zȧ'shĭ-vĕrsk') . Sov. Un.	67·08 N	144·02 E
159	Zastavna (zȧs-täf'nȧ) . . . . Sov. Un.	48·32 N	25·50 E
213	Zastron (zȧs'trŭn) S. Afr. (Natal In.)	30·19 S	27·07 E
158	Žatec (zhä'tĕts) . . . . Czech.	50·19 N	13·32 E
174	Zavitinsk . . . . Sov. Un.	50·12 N	129·44 E
159	Zawiercie (zȧ-vyĕr'tsyĕ) . . . . Pol.	50·28 N	19·25 E
211	Zāwiyat al-Baydā' . . . . Libya	32·49 N	21·46 E
186	Zāyandeh (R.) . . . . Iran	32·15 N	51·00 E
172	Zaysan (zī'sȧn) . . . . Sov. Un.	47·43 N	84·44 E
172	Zaysan (L.) . . . . Sov. Un.	48·16 N	84·05 E
128	Zaza (R.) (zȧ'zȧ) . . . . Cuba	21·40 N	79·25 W
159	Zbarazh (zbä-räzh') . . . . Sov. Un.	49·39 N	25·48 E
159	Zbruch R. (zbrōōch) . . . . Sov. Un.	48·56 N	26·18 E
159	Zdolbunov (zdôl-bōō'nôôf) Sov. Un.	50·31 N	26·17 E
159	Zdunska Wola (zdōōn''skä vō'lä) Pol.	51·36 N	18·27 E
218	Zebediela . . . . S. Afr. (Johannesburg & Pretoria In.)	24·19 S	29·21 E
155	Zeebrugge (zā'brŏŏg'gĕ) . . . . Bel.	51·20 N	3·12 W
104	Zeeland (zē'lănd) . . . . Mi.	42·50 N	86·00 W
183	Zefat . . . . Isr. (Palestine In.)	32·58 N	35·30 E
149	Zehdenick (tsā'dĕ-nēk) G.D.R. (Berlin In.)	52·59 N	13·20 E
149	Zehlendorf (tsā'lĕn-dôrf) G.D.R. (Berlin In.)	52·47 N	13·23 E
218	Zeila (zā'lä) Som. (Horn of Afr. In.)	11·19 N	43·20 E
149	Zeist . . . . Neth. (Amsterdam In.)	52·05 N	5·14 E
159	Zelechów (zhĕ-lĕ'kōōf) . . . . Pol.	51·48 N	21·55 E
157	Zelenogorsk (zĕ-lă'nô-gôrsk) Sov. Un.	60·13 N	29·39 E
158	Zella-Mehlis (tsâl'ȧ-mā'lēs) G.D.R.	50·40 N	10·38 E
211	Zémio (za-myō') . . . Cen. Afr. Rep.	5·03 N	25·11 E
168	Zemlya Frantsa Iosifa (Franz Josef Land) (Is.) . Sov. Un.	81·32 N	40·00 E
125	Zempoala, Punta (Pt.) (pōō'n-tä-sĕm-pô-ä'lä) . Mex.	19·30 N	96·18 W
125	Zempoatlépetl (Mtn.) (sĕm-pô-ä-tlā'pĕt'l) . . . Mex.	17·13 N	95·59 W
165	Zemun (Semlin) (zĕ'mōōn) (sĕm'lĭn) . Yugo.	44·50 N	20·25 E
191	Zengcheng (dzŭŋ-chŭŋ) China (Canton In.)	23·18 N	113·49 E
165	Zenica (zĕ'nēt-sä) . . . . Yugo.	44·10 N	17·54 E
195	Zeni-Su (Is.) (zĕ'nē sōō) . . . . Jap.	33·55 N	138·55 E
167	Zen'kov (zĕn-kof') . . . . Sov. Un.	50·13 N	34·23 E
167	Žepče (zhĕp'chĕ) . . . . Yugo.	44·26 N	18·01 E
149	Zepernick (tsĕ'pĕr-nēk) G.D.R. (Berlin In.)	52·39 N	13·32 E
141	Zeravshan (R.) (zȧ-räf-shän') Sov. Un.	40·00 N	65·42 E
158	Zerbst (tsĕrbst) . . . . G.D.R.	51·58 N	12·03 E
149	Zerpenschleuse (tsĕr'pĕn-shloi-zĕ) G.D.R. (Berlin In.)	52·51 N	13·30 E
149	Zeuthen (tsoi'tĕn) G.D.R. (Berlin In.)	52·21 N	13·38 E
161	Zevenaar . . . . Neth. (Ruhr In.)	51·56 N	6·06 E
149	Zevenbergen Neth. (Amsterdam In.)	51·38 N	4·36 E
173	Zeya (zâ'yȧ) . . . . Sov. Un.	53·43 N	127·29 E
173	Zeya (R.) . . . . Sov. Un.	52·31 N	128·30 E
171	Zeytun (zā-tōōn') . . . . Tur.	38·00 N	36·40 E
162	Zezere (R.) (zĕ'zȧ-rĕ) . . . . Port.	39·54 N	8·12 W
183	Zghartā . . . . Leb. (Palestine In.)	34·24 N	35·53 E
159	Zgierz (zgyĕzh) . . . . Pol.	51·51 N	19·26 E
167	Zgurovka (zgōō'rôf-kä) . . . Sov. Un.	50·31 N	31·43 E
190	Zhang (R.) (jäŋ) . . . . China	36·17 N	114·31 E
192	Zhangbei (jäŋ-bā) . . . . China	41·12 N	114·50 E
192	Zhang Guangcai Ling (Mts.) (jäŋ-gûäŋ-tsī lĭŋ) . China	43·50 N	127·55 E
192	Zhanggezhuang (jäŋ-gŭ-jûäŋ) China (In.)	40·09 N	116·56 E

ng-sing; ŋ-baŋk; N-nasalized n; nŏd; cŏmmit; ōld; ôbey; ôrder; fōōd; fŏŏt; ou-out; s-soft; sh-dish; th-thin; pūre; ûnite; ûrn; stŭd; circŭs; ü-as "y" in study; '-indeterminate vowel.

Page	Name	Pronunciation	Region	Lat. or	Long. or

Zhangjiakou, see Kalgan
190 Zhangqiu (jän-chyŏ) . . . . . . China 36·50 N 117·29 E
194 Zhangwu (jän-wōō) . . . . China 42·21 N 123·00 E
188 Zhangye (jän-yu) . . . . China 38·46 N 101·00 E
193 Zhangzhou (jän-jō) . . . . China 24·35 N 117·45 E
190 Zhangzi Dao (I.) (jän-dz dou)
 China 39·02 N 122·44 E
190 Zhanhua (jän-hwä) . . . . China 37·42 N 117·49 E
193 Zhanjiang (jän-jyän) . . . . . . China 21·20 N 110·28 E
192 Zhanyu (jän-yōō) . . . . China 44·30 N 122·30 E
193 Zhao'an (jou-än) . . . . China 23·48 N 117·10 E
192 Zhaodong (jou-dŏŋ) . . . . . . China 45·58 N 126·00 E
193 Zhaotong (jou-tŏŋ) . . . . China 27·18 N 103·50 E
190 Zhao Xian (jou shyěn) . . . . China 37·46 N 114·48 E
190 Zhaoyuan (jou-yuän) . . . . . China 37·22 N 120·23 E
167 Zhdanov (zhdä'nôf) . . . . . Sov. Un. 47·07 N 37·32 E
190 Zhecheng (jü-chǔŋ) . . . . . . China 34·05 N 115·19 E
190 Zhegao (jǔ-gou) . . . . China 31·47 N 117·44 E
189 Zhejiang (Prov.) (jü-jyän) . . China 29·30 N 120·00 E
172 Zhelaniya, Mys (C.) (zhě'lä-nǐ-yà)
 Sov. Un. 75·43 N 69·10 E
190 Zhengding (jǔŋ-dǐŋ) . . . . . . China 38·10 N 114·35 E
190 Zhengyang (jǔŋ-yän) . . . . . China 32·34 N 114·22 E
190 Zhengzhou (jǔŋ-jō) . . . . China 34·46 N 113·42 E
190 Zhenjiang (jǔn-jyän) . . . . . China 32·13 N 119·24 E
193 Zhenyuan (jǔn-yüän) . . . . . China 27·08 N 108·30 E
173 Zhigalovo (zhě-gä'lô-vô) . . Sov. Un. 54·52 N 105·05 E
173 Zhigansk (zhě-gänsk') . . . . Sov. Un. 66·45 N 123·20 E
193 Zhijiang (jr-jyän) . . . . China 27·25 N 109·45 E
167 Zhitomir (zhě'tô'měr) . . . . Sov. Un. 50·15 N 28·40 E
167 Zhitomir (Oblast) . . . . Sov. Un. 50·40 N 28·07 E
166 Zhizdra (zhěz'drà) . . . . Sov. Un. 53·47 N 34·41 E
166 Zhizhitskoye (R.)
 (zhě-zhět'skô-yě) . Sov. Un. 56·08 N 31·34 E
167 Zhmerinka (zhmyě'rěŋ-kà)
 Sov. Un. 49·02 N 28·09 E
192 Zhongwei (jŏŋ-wä) . . . . . . China 37·32 N 105·10 E
193 Zhong Xian (jŏŋ shyěn) . . . . China 30·20 N 108·00 E
191 Zhongxin (jŏŋ-shyǐn)
 China (Canton In.) 23·16 N 113·38 E
190 Zhoucun (jō-tsōōn) . . . . China 36·49 N 117·52 E
190 Zhoukouzhen (jō-kō-jǔn) . . . China 33·39 N 114·40 E
191 Zhoupu (jō-pōō)
 China (Shanghai In.) 31·07 N 121·33 E
193 Zhoushan Qundao (Is.)
 (jō-shän-chyŏŏn-dou), China 30·00 N 123·00 E
190 Zhou Xian (jō shyěn) . . . . . China 39·30 N 115·59 E
191 Zhu (R.) (jōō)
 China (Canton In.) 23·48 N 113·36 E
192 Zhuanghe (jǔäŋ-hǔ) . . . . . . China 39·40 N 123·00 E
191 Zhuanqiao (jǔän-chyou)
 China (Shanghai In.) 31·20 N 121·30 E
190 Zhucheng (jōō-chǔŋ) . . . . . China 36·01 N 119·24 E
193 Zhuji (jōō-jyē) . . . . China 29·58 N 120·10 E

193 Zhujiang Kou (Can.)
 (jōō-jyän kō) . China 22·00 N 114·00 E
174 Zhukovskiy (zhōō-kôf'skǐ)
 Sov. Un. (Moscow In.) 55·33 N 38·09 E
193 Zi (R.) (dzē) . . . . China 26·50 N 111·00 E
190 Zibo (dzē-bwo) . . . . China 36·48 N 118·04 E
204 Ziel, Mt. (zēl) . . . . Austl. 23·15 S 132·45 E
158 Zielona Góra (zhyě-lô'nä gōō'rä)
 Pol. 51·56 N 15·30 E
174 Zigazinskiy (zǐ-gazinskēē)
 Sov. Un. (Urals In.) 53·50 N 57·18 E
151 Zighouf Youcef . . . . Alg. 36·34 N 6·51 E
214 Ziguinchor . . . . Senegal 12·35 N 16·16 W
174 Zilair (zē'lä-ǐr)
 Sov. Un. (Urals In.) 52·12 N 57·23 E
171 Zile (zē-lě') . . . . Tur. 40·20 N 35·50 E
159 Žilina (zhě'lǐ-nä) . . . . Czech. 49·14 N 18·45 E
211 Zillah . . . . Libya 28·26 N 17·52 E
172 Zima (zē'mä) . . . . Sov. Un. 53·58 N 102·08 E
124 Zimapan (sē-mä'pän) . . . . . Mex. 20·43 N 99·23 W
125 Zimatlán de Alvarez
 (sē-mä-tlän' dä äl'vä-räz) . Mex. 16·52 N 96·47 W
217 Zimba . . . . Zambia 17·19 S 26·13 E
209 Zimbabwe (Rhodesia)
 (rô-dē'zhǐ-à) . Afr. 17·50 S 29·30 E
165 Zimnicea (zêm-nē'chä) . . . . Rom. 43·39 N 25·22 E
183 Zin (R.) . . . . Isr. (Palestine In.) 30·50 N 35·12 E
125 Zinacatepec (zē-nä-kä-tě'pěk)
 Mex. 18·19 N 97·15 W
124 Zinapécuaro (sē-nä-pä'kwä-rô)
 Mex. 19·50 N 100·49 W
215 Zinder (zǐn'děr) . . . . Niger 13·48 N 8·59 E
107 Zion (zī'ŭn) . . . . Il. (Chicago In.) 42·27 N 87·50 W
115 Zion Natl. Park . . . . Ut. 37·20 N 113·00 W
107 Zionsville (zīŭnz-vǐl)
 In. (Indianapolis In.) 39·57 N 86·15 W
95 Zionz L. (zī'ŏnz) . . . . Can. 51·25 N 91·52 W
134 Zipaquirá (sē-pä-kē-rä') . Col. (In.) 5·01 N 74·01 W
124 Zirandaro (sē-rän-dä'rō) . . . . Mex. 18·28 N 101·02 W
124 Zitacuaro (sē-tà-kwä'rō) . . . . Mex. 19·25 N 100·22 W
124 Zitlala (sè-tlä'lä) . . . . Mex. 17·38 N 99·09 W
158 Zittau (tsē'tou) . . . . G.D.R. 50·55 N 14·48 E
211 Ziway (L.) . . . . Eth. 8·08 N 39·11 E
190 Ziya (R.) (dzē-yä) . . . . China 38·38 N 116·31 E
165 Zlatograd . . . . Bul. 41·24 N 25·05 E
174 Zlatoust (zlä-tô-ŏŏst')
 Sov. Un. (Urals In.) 55·13 N 59·39 E
211 Zlītan . . . . Libya 32·27 N 14·33 E
159 Zloczew (zwô'chěf) . . . . Pol. 51·23 N 18·34 E
166 Zlynka (zlěŋ'kà) . . . . Sov. Un. 52·28 N 31·39 E
167 Znamenka (znä'měn-kä) . Sov. Un. 48·43 N 32·35 E
157 Znamensk (znä'měnsk) . . Sov. Un. 54·39 N 21·49 E
158 Znojmo (znoi'mô) . . . . Czech. 48·52 N 16·03 E
149 Zoetermeer . Neth. (Amsterdam In.) 52·03 N 4·29 E

149 Zoeterwoude
 Neth. (Amsterdam In.) 52·03 N 4·29 E
149 Zohor . . . . Czech. (Vienna In.) 48·20 N 17·00 E
151 Zolocheěv (zô'lô-chěf) . . . . Sov. Un. 49·48 N 24·55 E
167 Zolotonosha (zô'lô-tô-nô'shá)
 Sov. Un. 49·41 N 32·03 E
194 Zolotoy, Mys (Pt.)
 (mǐs zô-lô-tôy') . Sov. Un. 47·24 N 139·10 E
217 Zomba (zôm'bá) . . . . Malawi 15·23 S 35·18 E
211 Zongo (zôŋ'gô) . . . . Zaire 4·19 N 18·36 E
171 Zonguldak (zôŋ'gōōl'dàk) . . Tur. 41·25 N 31·50 E
149 Zonhoven . . . . . . Bel. (Brussels In.) 50·59 N 5·24 E
125 Zoquitlán (sô-kēt-län') . . . . . Mex. 18·09 N 97·02 W
162 Zorita (thô-rē'tä) . . . . Sp. 39·18 N 5·41 W
149 Zossen (tsô'sěn)
 G.D.R. (Berlin In.) 52·13 N 13·27 E
190 Zou Xian (dzō shyěn) . . . . . China 35·24 N 116·54 E
166 Zubtsov (zōōp-tsôf') . . . . Sov. Un. 56·13 N 34·34 E
163 Zuera (thwä'rä) . . . . Sp. 41·40 N 0·48 W
158 Zuger See (L.) (tsōōg) . . . . Switz. 47·10 N 8·40 E
158 Zugspitze Pk. . . . . Aus.-F.R.G. 47·25 N 11·00 E
162 Zújar (R.) (zōō'kär) . . . . Sp. 38·55 N 5·05 W
128 Zulueta (zōō-lōō-ě'tä) . . . . Cuba 22·20 N 79·35 W
212 Zululand (Reg.) (zōō'lōō-länd)
 S. Afr. 27·45 S 31·29 E
217 Zumbo (zōōm'bôô) . . . . Moz. 15·36 S 30·25 E
109 Zumbro (R.) (zǔm'brō) . . . . Mn. 44·18 N 92·14 W
109 Zumbrota (zǔm-brō'tá) . . . . Mn. 44·16 N 92·39 W
124 Zumpango (sōōm-päŋ-gō) . . Mex. 19·48 N 99·06 W
149 Zundert . . . Neth. (Amsterdam In.) 51·28 N 4·39 E
215 Zungeru (zōōŋ-gä'rōō) . . . . Nig. 9·48 N 6·09 E
190 Zunhua (dzōōn-hwä) . . . . . China 40·12 N 117·55 E
115 Zuni (R.) . . . . Az.-NM 34·40 N 109·30 W
115 Zuni Ind. Res. (zōō'nē) . . . . NM 35·10 N 108·40 W
115 Zuni Mts. . . . . NM 35·10 N 108·10 W
188 Zunyi . . . . China 27·58 N 106·40 E
158 Zürich (tsü'rǐk) . . . . Switz. 47·22 N 8·32 E
158 Zürich See (L.) . . . . Switz. 47·18 N 8·47 E
195 Zushi (zōō'shē) . . Jap. (Tōkyō In.) 35·17 N 139·35 E
211 Zuwārah . . . . Libya 32·33 N 12·07 E
183 Zuwayzā . . . Jordan (Palestine In.) 31·42 N 35·58 E
166 Zvenigorod (zvä-nē'gô-rôt)
 Sov. Un. 55·46 N 36·54 E
167 Zvenigorodka (zvä-nē'gô-rôt'kä)
 Sov. Un. 49·07 N 30·59 E
159 Zvolen (zvô'lěn) . . . . Czech. 48·35 N 19·10 E
165 Zvornik (zvôr'něk) . . . . Yugo. 44·24 N 19·08 E
158 Zweibrücken (tsvī-brük'ěn)
 F.R.G. 49·16 N 7·20 E
158 Zwickau (tsvĭk'ou) . . . . G.D.R. 50·43 N 12·30 E
155 Zwolle (zvôl'ě) . . . . Neth. 52·33 N 6·05 E
159 Zyradow (zhě-rär'dōōf) . . . . Pol. 52·04 N 20·28 E
173 Zyryanka (zē-ryän'kà) . . . Sov. Un. 65·45 N 151·15 E
172 Zyryanovsk (zē-ryä'nôfsk)
 Sov. Un. 49·43 N 83·52 E
159 Zywiec (zhǐ'vyěts) . . . . Pol. 49·42 N 19·14 E

conversion tables

Length

1 inch	=	2.54	centimeters
1 foot	=	.305	meter
1 yard	=	.914	meter
1 mile	=	1.609	kilometers
1 nautical mile	=	1.151	statute miles
1 nautical mile	=	1.852	kilometers
1 meter	=	1.094	yards
1 kilometer	=	.621	mile

Area

1 square inch	=	6.452	square centimeters
1 square foot	=	.093	square meter
1 square yard	=	.836	square meter
1 acre	=	.405	hectare
1 square mile	=	2.59	square kilometers
1 square kilometer	=	.386	square mile
1 hectare	=	2.471	acres
1 square meter	=	1.196	square yards

Volume

1 cubic inch	=	16.387	cubic centimeters
1 cubic foot	=	.028	cubic meter
1 cubic yard	=	.765	cubic meter
1 cubic meter	=	1.308	cubic yards

Mass

1 ounce	=	28.35	grams
1 pound	=	.454	kilogram
1 long ton	=	1.016	metric tons
1 gram	=	.035	ounce
1 kilogram	=	2.2	pounds

Capacity

1 U.S. fluid ounce	=	2.957	centiliters
1 U.S. liquid pint	=	.473	liter
1 U.S. liquid quart	=	.946	liter
1 U.S. gallon	=	3.785	liters
1 U.S. gallon	=	.833	British gallon
1 liter	=	1.057	U.S. liquid quarts

ăt; fĭnăl; rāte; senàte; ärm; àsk; sofá; fâre; ch-choose; dh-as th in other; bē; ĕvent; bĕt; recĕnt; cratēr; g-go; gh-guttural g; bĭt; ɨ-short neutral; rĭde; ᴋ-guttural k as ch in German ich;